THE NEW
SCHAFF-HERZOG
ENCYCLOPEDIA

OF

RELIGIOUS KNOWLEDGE

Editor-in-Chief

SAMUEL MACAULEY JACKSON, D.D., LL.D.

Editor-in-Chief
of
Supplementary Volumes

LEFFERTS A. LOETSCHER, Ph.D., D.D.
ASSOCIATE PROFESSOR OF CHURCH HISTORY
PRINCETON THEOLOGICAL SEMINARY

BAKER BOOK HOUSE
GRAND RAPIDS, MICHIGAN

THE NEW

SCHAFF-HERZOG ENCYCLOPEDIA

OF

RELIGIOUS KNOWLEDGE

EDITED BY

SAMUEL MACAULEY JACKSON, D.D., LL.D.

(Editor-in-Chief)

WITH THE SOLE ASSISTANCE, AFTER VOLUME VI., OF

GEORGE WILLIAM GILMORE, M.A.

(Associate Editor)

AND THE FOLLOWING DEPARTMENT EDITORS

CLARENCE AUGUSTINE BECKWITH, D.D.
(Department of Systematic Theology)

JAMES FREDERIC McCURDY, PH.D., LL.D.
(Department of the Old Testament)

HENRY KING CARROLL, LL.D.
(Department of Minor Denominations)

HENRY SYLVESTER NASH, D.D.
(Department of the New Testament)

JAMES FRANCIS DRISCOLL, D.D.
(Department of Liturgics and Religious Orders)

ALBERT HENRY NEWMAN, D.D., LL.D.
(Department of Church History)

FRANK HORACE VIZETELLY, LL.D., F.S.A.
(Department of Pronunciation and Typography)

VOLUME XII
TRENCH — ZWINGLI
APPENDIX

BAKER BOOK HOUSE
GRAND RAPIDS, MICHIGAN
1964

First Printing, October 1950
Second Printing, January 1954
Third Printing, January 1957
Fourth Printing, January 1960
Fifth Printing, July 1964

PHOTOLITHOPRINTED BY CUSHING - MALLOY, INC.
ANN ARBOR, MICHIGAN, UNITED STATES OF AMERICA
1964

PREFACE

It is now eight years and a half since this encyclopedia was begun. Unbroken harmony has characterized my relations with the members of the staff, and I take this opportunity to return my heartfelt thanks for their devotion and interest, which have made each day's work a pleasure.

The following persons whose names are not elsewhere mentioned have contributed for longer or shorter periods their services as translators: EDWIN B. CHILTON, WILLIAM LLOYD BEVAN, Ph.D., ABRAM LIPSKY, the REV CHARLES ADAM MOHR, B.A., DANIEL LONGS PEACOCK, MRS. L. DE QUESADA, and SIMEON STRUNSKY, B.A.; and as assistant office editors: HUBERT EVANS, Ph.D., FREDERICK W. HUMPHREY, and CHARLES JOSEPH GILLEN.

Two persons have greatly helped us to correct errors into which, notwithstanding our care, we have fallen: BERNHARD PICK, Ph.D., D.D., for vols. i. and ii., and REV. MALBORNE W. GRAHAM, of Williams, Ohio, for all the volumes. The mistakes which these and others have pointed out have been frankly acknowledged in the succeeding volumes and corrected. It is to be hoped that other publishers of encyclopedias will pursue this plan, thus enabling the purchasers of the first editions of their works to be at least in part on a footing of equality with the purchasers of later editions.

In this connection I thank MR. ISIDOR FURST, proof-reader for the Publishers Printing Company, whose skill and watchfulness have united to give the public the typographical accuracy which I believe these volumes can boast. Thanks are also due to PROFESSOR E. A. A. O. A. VON DOBSCHUETZ, of the University of Breslau, for his contributions to the accuracy and completeness with which the sketches of contemporary German theologians are furnished.

But my closing word must concern the REV. GEORGE WILLAM GILMORE, the associate editor from the beginning to the end and the managing editor of the last six volumes. He brought to the work wide knowledge, especially in the two little-cultivated fields of comparative religion and bibliography. He has shared, however, in all the other departments of this encyclopedia as translator and collaborator. It is only truth to say that it is due largely to his devotion and remarkable intelligence and learning that the work is so worthy the confidence of the public.

SAMUEL MACAULEY JACKSON,
Editor-in-Chief.

FEBRUARY 14th, 1912.

EDITORS

AMY GASTON CHARLES AUGUSTE BONET-MAURY, D.D., LL.D.,
Professor of Church History, Independent School of Divinity, Paris.

GOTTLIEB NATHANAEL BONWETSCH, Th.D.,
Professor of Church History, University of Göttingen.

GUSTAV BOSSERT, Ph.D., Th.D.,
Retired Pastor, Stuttgart.

CHARLES AUGUSTUS BRIGGS, D.D., Litt.D.,
Professor of Theological Encyclopedia and Symbolics, Union Theological Seminary, New York.

FRANTS PEDER WILLIAM BUHL, Ph.D., Th.D.,
Professor of Semitic Languages, University of Copenhagen.

KARL RITTER VON BURGER (†), Th.D.,
Late Supreme Consistorial Councilor, Munich.

CARL CAMENISCH, Ph.D.,
Professor at the Oberrealschule, Basel.

HENRY KING CARROLL, LL.D.,
Secretary of the Executive Committee of the Western Section for the Fourth Ecumenical Methodist Conference.

JACQUES EUGENE CHOISY, Th.D.,
Professor of Church History, University of Geneva.

PAUL CHRIST (†), Th.D.,
Late Professor of Systematic and Practical Theology, University of Zurich.

FRANCIS ALBERT CHRISTIE, D.D.,
Professor of Church History, Meadville Theological School, Meadville, Pa.

FRANCIS EDWARD CLARK, D.D., LL.D.,
Founder of the United Society of Christian Endeavor, Boston.

JOSEPH BOURNE CLARK, D.D.,
Editorial Secretary of the Congregational Home Missionary Society, New York.

OTTO CONSTANTIN CLEMEN, Ph.D., Th.Lic.,
Gymnasial Professor at Zwickau.

ALBERTO CLOT, D.D.,
Professor of French Literature in the State University of Palermo, Italy.

FERDINAND EDUARD THEODOR COHRS, Th.D.,
Consistorial Councilor, Ilfeld, Germany.

ALEXIS IRÉNÉE DU PONT COLEMAN, M.A.,
Instructor in English, College of the City of New York.

HENRY COWAN, D.D., D.C.L.,
Professor of Church History, University of Aberdeen, Scotland.

EUGENE RICHARD COX,
Member of Christian Science Committee on Publication.

THOMAS WITTON DAVIES, Ph.D., D.D.,
Professor of Semitic Languages, University College of North Wales, Bangor.

SAMUEL MARTIN DEUTSCH (†), Th.D.,
Late Professor of Church History, University of Berlin.

LUDWIG DIESTEL (†), Ph.D.,
Late Professor of Theology, University of Tübingen.

PAUL GOTTFRIED DREWS, Th.D.,
Professor of Practical Theology, University of Halle.

JAMES FRANCIS DRISCOLL, D.D.,
Pastor of St. Gabriel's, New Rochelle, N. Y.

SAMUEL AUGUSTUS WILLOUGHBY DUFFIELD (†),
Late Presbyterian Minister, Bloomfield, N. J.

THEODOR ELZE (†), Th.D.,
Late Pastor in Venice.

JOHN OLUF EVJEN, Ph.D.,
Professor of Theology, Augsburg Seminary, Minneapolis, Minn.

CHRISTIAN THEODOR FICKER, Ph.D.,
Pastor Emeritus, Leipsic.

GERHARD PAUL FICKER, Ph.D., Th.D.,
Professor of Church History, University of Kiel.

JOHANNES FICKER, Ph.D., Th.D.,
Professor of Church History, Evangelical Theological Faculty, University of Strasburg.

GUSTAV WILHELM FRANK (†), Th.D.,
Late Professor of Dogmatics, Symbolics, and Christian Ethics, University of Vienna.

ALBERT FREYBE (†), Ph.D., Th.D.,
Late Gymnasial Professor, Parchim, Mecklenburg.

EMIL ALBERT FRIEDBERG (†), Th.D., Dr.Jur.,
Late Professor of Ecclesiastical, Public, and German Law, University of Leipsic.

GEORGE WILLIAM GILMORE, M.A.,
Former Professor of Biblical History and Lecturer on Comparative Religion, Bangor Theological Seminary, Bangor, Me.

FRANZ GOERRES, Ph.D.,
Assistant Librarian, University of Bonn.

WILHELM GUSTAV GOETERS,
Privat-docent in Church History, University of Halle.

WILHELM GOETZ (†), Ph.D.,
Late Honorary Professor of Geography, Technical High School, and Professor, Military Academy, Munich.

RICHARD JAMES HORATIO GOTTHEIL, Ph.D.,
Professor of Semitic Languages, Columbia University, New York.

GEORG GRUETZMACHER, Ph.D., Th.Lic.,
Extraordinary Professor of Historical Theology and of New-Testament Exegesis, University of Heidelberg.

RICHARD HEINRICH GRUETZMACHER, Th.D.,
Professor of Systematic Theology, University of Rostock.

EDWARD GUEDER (†), Th.D.,
Late Pastor, Canton of Bern, Switzerland.

RUDOLF GUENTHER, Th.Lic.,
Privat-docent in Practical Theology, University of Marburg.

HERMANN GUTHE, Ph.D., Th.D.,
Extraordinary Professor of Old-Testament Exegesis, University of Leipsic.

WILHELM HADORN, Th.Lic.,
Pastor in Bern and Lecturer on New-Testament Exegesis, University of Bern.

EDWARD EVERETT HALE (†), S.T.D., LL.D.,
Late Author and Minister of the South Congregational (Unitarian) Church, Boston.

FRANCIS JOSEPH HALL, D.D.,
Professor of Dogmatic Theology, Western Theological Seminary, Chicago, Ill.

JOHN TAYLOR HAMILTON, D.D.,
Missionary Bishop, Unity of the Brethren, Herrnhut, Saxony.

ALBERT HAUCK, Ph.D., Th.D., Dr.Jur.,
Professor of Church History, University of Leipsic, Editor-in-chief of the Hauck-Herzog *Realencyklopädie*.

JOHANNES HAUSSLEITER, Ph.D., Th.D.,
Professor of the New Testament, University of Greifswald.

WILLIAM FRANKLIN HEIL,
Bishop of the United Evangelical Church, Highland Park, Ill.

CARL FRIEDRICH GEORG HEINRICI, Ph.D., Th.D.,
Professor of New-Testament Exegesis, University of Leipsic.

HEINRICH HERMELINK, Ph.D., Th.Lic.,
Privat-docent in Church History, University of Leipsic.

ROBERT W. HILL,
Of Universalist Young People's Union.

PAUL HINSCHIUS (†), Th.D., Dr.Jur.,
Late Professor of Ecclesiastical Law, University of Berlin.

GUSTAV HOENNICKE, Ph.D., Th.D.,
Extraordinary Professor of New-Testament Exegesis, University of Breslau.

HEINRICH FRIEDRICH MAX HOFFMANN, Ph.D., Th.Lic.,
Privat-docent in Church History, University of Leipsic.

OSWALD HOLDER-EGGER (†), Ph.D.,
Late Professor at Berlin and Director for the Publication of the *Monumenta Germaniæ historica*, Berlin.

HEINRICH JULIUS HOLTZMANN (†), Ph.D., Th.D.,
Late Professor of New-Testament Exegesis, Evangelical Theological Faculty, University of Strasburg.

EWALD HORN, Ph.D.,
Director of the Information Bureau for Higher Education, Berlin.

LOUISE SEYMOUR HOUGHTON,
Author and Translator.

AUGUST WILHELM REINHARD EMIL HUNZINGER, Ph.D., Th.D.,
Professor of Dogmatics, Apologetics, and Theological Encyclopedia, University of Erlangen.

HEINRICH FRIEDRICH JACOBSON (†), Th.D.,
Late Professor of Law, University of Königsberg.

HARRY JEFFS,
Editor of *The Christian World Pulpit*, London.

ARTHUR NEWTON JOHNSON, M.A.,
Home Secretary of the London Missionary Society.

GUSTAV ADOLF JUELICHER, Ph.D., Th.D.,
Professor of Church History and New-Testament Exegesis, University of Marburg.

MARTIN KAEHLER, Th.D.,
Professor of Dogmatics and New-Testament Exegesis, University of Halle.

DEMETRIUS KALOPOTHAKES, Ph.D.,
Athens, Greece.

ADOLF HERMANN HEINRICH KAMPHAUSEN (†), Th.D.,
Late Professor of Old-Testament Exegesis, University of Bonn.

EMIL FRIEDRICH KAUTZSCH (†), Ph.D., Th.D.,
Late Professor of Old-Testament Exegesis, University of Halle.

PETER GUSTAV KAWERAU, Ph.D., Th.D.,
Supreme Consistorial Councilor, Provost of St. Peter's, Berlin, and Honorary Professor, University of Berlin.

DIETRICH KERLER (†), Ph.D.,
Late Head Librarian, Würzburg.

OTTO KIRN (†), Ph.D., Th.D.,
Late Professor of Dogmatics, University of Leipsic.

RUDOLF KITTEL, Ph.D., Th.D.,
Professor of Old-Testament Exegesis, University of Leipsic.

GEORGE THOMSON KNIGHT (†), D.D.,
Late Professor of Christian Theology, Tufts College, Mass.

KARL THEODOR RUDOLF BERNHARD KOCH,
Pastor in Rehweiler, Bavaria.

JUSTUS ADOLF KOEBERLE (†), Th.D.,
Late Professor of the Old Testament, University of Rostock.

THEODOR FRIEDRICH HERMANN KOLDE, Ph.D., Th.D.,
Professor of Church History, University of Erlangen.

HERMANN GUSTAV EDUARD KRUEGER, Ph.D., Th.D.,
Professor of Church History, University of Giessen.

LUTHER M. KUHNS,
General Secretary, Luther League of America.

EUGEN LACHENMANN,
City Pastor in Leonberg, Württemberg.

JOSIAH PENNABECKER LANDIS, Ph.D., LL.D.,
President of Bonebrake Theological Seminary, Dayton, O.

GEORG RITTER VON LAUBMANN (†), Ph.D.,
Late Director of the Royal Library, Munich.

GOTTHARD VICTOR LECHLER (†), Ph.D., Th.D.,
Late Professor of Theology, University of Leipsic.

WILLIAM LEE (†), D.D.,
Late Professor of Church History, University of Glasgow.

WILHELM JOHANNES LEIPOLDT, Ph.D., Th.D.,
Professor of New-Testament Exegesis, University of Kiel.

LUDWIG LEMME, Th.D.,
Professor of Systematic Theology, University of Heidelberg.

C. H. D'E. LEPPINGTON,
Fellow of the Royal Economic Society, England.

ALBERT LIENHARD,
Pastor in Wickersheim, Lower Alsace.

GEORG KARL DAVID LOESCHE, Ph.D., Th.D.,
Professor of Church History, Evangelical Theological Faculty, University of Vienna.

JOHANN LOSERTH, Ph.D.,
Professor of History, University of Graz.

WILHELM PHILIPP FRIEDRICH FERDINAND LOTZ, Ph.D., Th.D.,
Professor of Old-Testament Exegesis, University of Erlangen.

ERNEST CHRISTIAN MARGRANDER, D.C.,
Chancellor to the Orthodox Catholic Archbishop of America.

PAUL MEHLHORN, Ph.D., Th.D.,
Pastor of the Reformed Church, Leipsic.

PHILIPP MEYER, Th.D.,
Supreme Consistorial Councilor, Hanover.

CARL THEODOR MIRBT, Th.D.,
Professor of Church History, University of Marburg.

JACOB ISIDOR MOMBERT, D.D.,
Author, Paterson, N. J.

JOHN HENRY MOORE,
Elder and Bishop of the Dunker Church, Editor of *The Gospel Messenger*, Elgin, Ill.

RICHARD CARY MORSE, M.A.,
General Secretary of the International Committee of the Young Men's Christian Association, New York.

ERNST FRIEDRICH KARL MUELLER, Th.D.,
Professor of Reformed Theology, University of Erlangen.

GEORG MUELLER, Ph.D., Th.D.,
Inspector of Schools, Leipsic.

JOSEPH THEODOR MUELLER, Th.D.,
Keeper of the Archives of the Unity of the Brethren, Herrnhut.

CHRISTOF EBERHARD NESTLE, Ph.D., Th.D.,
Professor in the Theological Seminary, Maulbronn, Württemberg.

KARL JOHANNES NEUMANN, Ph.D.,
Professor of Ancient History, University of Strasburg.

ALBERT HENRY NEWMAN, D.D., LL.D.,
Professor of Church History, Southwestern Baptist Theological Seminary, Fort Worth, Texas.

THEODOR JULIUS NEY, Th.D.,
Supreme Consistorial Councilor, Speyer, Bavaria.

CHRISTIAN VON PALMER (†), Th.D.,
Late Professor of Theology, Tübingen.

CARL PESTALOZZI (†), Ph.D.,
Late Pastor in Zurich.

CARL PFENDER,
Pastor of St. Paul's Evangelical Lutheran Church, Paris.

ERWIN FRIEDRICH WILHELM FERDINAND PREUSCHEN, Ph.D., Th.D.,
Pastor at Hirschhorn-on-the-Neckar, Germany.

PAUL MARTIN RADE, Th.D.,
Extraordinary Professor of Systematic Theology, University of Marburg.

HERMANN RAHLENBECK,
Pastor in Cologne.

EDWIN MORTIMER RANDALL, D.D.,
General Secretary, Epworth League.

MATTHEW BROWN RIDDLE, D.D., LL.D.,
Professor of New-Testament Exegesis, Western Theological Seminary, Pittsburg, Pa.

CHRISTIAN GEORG RIETSCHEL, Th.D.,
Professor of Practical Theology and University Preacher, University of Leipsic.

SIEGFRIED RIETSCHEL, Dr.Jur.,
Professor of German Law, University of Tübingen.

ALBRECHT BENJAMIN RITSCHL (†), Ph.D., Dr. Jur.,
Late Professor of Theology, University of Göttingen.

ARNOLD RUEEGG (†),
Late Pastor at Birmensdorf and Lecturer at the University of Zurich, Switzerland.

GEORG WILHELM RUNZE, Ph.D., Th.D.,
Extraordinary Professor of the Philosophy of Religion and Systematic Theology, University of Berlin.

CARL VICTOR RYSSEL (†), Ph.D., Th.D.,
Late Professor of Theology, University of Zurich.

ERNST SCHAEFER, Ph.D.,
Editor of *Der alte Glaube*, Leipsic.

PHILIPP HEINRICH WILHELM THEODOR SCHAEFER, Th.D.,
Head of the Deaconess Institute, Altona, Prussia.

DAVID SCHLEY SCHAFF, D.D.,
Professor of Church History, Western Theological Seminary, Pittsburg, Pennsylvania.

PHILIP SCHAFF (†), D.D., LL.D.,
Late Professor of Church History, Union Theological Seminary, New York.

OTTO YEOUAN SCHMID,
New York City.

REINHOLD SCHMID, Th.Lic.,
Pastor at Oberholzheim, Württemberg.

ARTHUR BENNO SCHMIDT, Dr.Jur.,
Professor of German and Ecclesiastical Law, University of Giessen.

CARL WILHELM ADOLF SCHMIDT (†), Th.D.,
Late Professor of Theology, University of Strasburg.

CHARLES SCHNETZLER,
Pastor at Cormoret, Canton of Bern.

KARL SCHOTTENLOHER, Ph.D.,
Assistant at the Royal Library, Munich.

MAXIMILIAN VICTOR SCHULTZE, Th.D.,
Professor of Church History and Christian Archeology, University of Greifswald.

LUDWIG THEODOR SCHULZE, Ph.D., Th.D.,
Retired Professor of Dogmatics and Ethics, University of Rostock.

EDMUND ALEXANDER DE SCHWEINITZ (†), D.D.,
Late Bishop of the Unity of the Brethren, Bethlehem, Pa.

REINHOLD SEEBERG, Ph.D., Th.D.,
Professor of Systematic Theology, University of Berlin.

EMIL SEHLING, Dr.Jur.,
Professor of Ecclesiastical and Commercial Law, University of Erlangen.

ERNST SELLIN, Ph.D., Th.D.,
Professor of the Old Testament, University of Rostock.

ISAAC SHARPLESS, B.S., LL.D., L.H.D.,
President of Haverford College, Haverford, Pa.

HENRY FOX SHUPE, D.D.,
Editor of *The Watchword*, Dayton, O.

FRIEDRICH ANTON EMIL SIEFFERT (†), Ph.D., Th.D.,
Late Professor of New-Testament Exegesis, University of Bonn.

AGNES G. SMITH,
Of The Volunteers of America.

NEWMAN SMYTH, D.D.,
Pastor Emeritus of the First Congregational Church, New Haven, Conn.

PHILIPP FRIEDRICH ADOLPH THEODOR SPAETH (†), **D.D., LL.D.,**

Late Professor in the Lutheran Theological Seminary, Mount Airy, Philadelphia.

EMIL ELIAS STEINMEYER, Ph.D.,

Professor of the German Language and Literature, University of Erlangen.

HORST STEPHAN, Th.Lic.,

Privat-docent in Systematic Theology and Church History, University of Marburg.

HERMANN LEBERECHT STRACK, Ph.D., Th.D.,

Honorary Professor of Old-Testament Exegesis and Semitic Languages, University of Berlin.

P. M. TZSCHIRNER (†), **Ph.D.,**

Late of Leipsic, Germany.

FRIEDRICH UHLHORN,

Pastor at Hameln, Prussia.

HENRY VAN ARSDALE,

Santa Barbara, Cal.

SIETSE DOUWES VAN VEEN, Th.D.,

Professor of Church History and Christian Archeology, University of Utrecht.

EBERHARD VISCHER, Th.D.,

Professor of Church History, University of Basel.

FRIEDRICH VOGTHERR, Dr.Jur.,

Assistant Circuit Judge, Weissenburg, Bavaria.

GUSTAV WARNECK (†), **Ph.D., Th.D.,**

Late Honorary Professor of Missions, University of Halle.

GEORGE WASHBURN, D.D., LL.D.,

Lecturer, Lowell Institute, Boston, and former President of Robert College, Constantinople.

GEORGE THOMAS WEBB,

Editor, American Baptist Publication Society.

JOHANNES WEISS, Th.D.,

Professor of New-Testament Exegesis, University of Heidelberg.

EDWARD ELIHU WHITFIELD, M.A.,

Retired Public Schoolmaster, London.

ERNST WITTICH, Ph.D., Th.D.,

Retired General Superintendent, Stuttgart.

RUDOLF ZEHNPFUND, Ph.D.,

Pastor in Oranienbaum, Germany.

OTTO ZOECKLER (†), **Ph.D., Th.D.,**

Late Professor of Church History and Apologetics, University of Greifswald.

BIBLIOGRAPHICAL APPENDIX—VOLS. I—XII

The following list of books is supplementary to the bibliographies given at the end of the articles contained in vols. I.–XII., and brings the literature down to December 31, 1911. In this list each title entry is printed in capital letters. It is to be noted that, throughout the work, in the articles as a rule only first editions are given. In the bibliographies the aim is to give either the best or the latest edition, and in case the book is published both in America and in some other country, the American place of issue is usually given the preference.

AFRICA: J. Du Plessis, *A History of Christian Missions in South Africa*, London, 1911.

D. Fraser, *The Future of Africa*, London, 1911.

J. Z. Gibson, *The Story of the Zulus*, New York, 1911.

E. Gilliat, *Heroes of Modern Africa. True Stories of the Intrepid Bravery and Stirring Adventures of the Pioneers, Explorers and Founders of Modern Africa*, London, 1911.

Dora S. Y. Mills, *What we do in Nyasaland*, London, 1911.

J. Roscoe, *The Baganda: an Account of their Native Customs and Beliefs*, London, 1911.

H. S. Smith, *" Yakusu," the Very Heart of Africa. Being some Account of the Protestant Mission at Stanley Falls, Upper Congo*, London, 1911.

J. Spieth, *Die Religion der Eweer in Süd-Togo*, Leipsic, 1911.

ALBERTUS MAGNUS: H. Lauer, *Die Moraltheologie Alberts des Grossen mit besonderer Berücksichtigung ihrer Beziehungen zur Lehre des heiligen Thomas*, Freiburg, 1911.

ANDREÄ, J. V.: W. Begemann, *Die Fruchtbringende Gesellschaft und Johann Valentin Andreä. Entgegnung auf Ludwig Kellers Ausführungen im Maiheft der Comenius-Gesellschaft*, Berlin, 1911.

ANSELM, SAINT, OF CANTERBURY: J. Fischer, *Die Erkenntnislehre Anselms von Canterbury*, Münster, 1911.

ANTHONY, SAINT, OF PADUA: C. M. Antony, *Saint Antony of Padua, the Miracle-Worker (1195–1231)*, New York, 1911.

APOLOGETICS: C. D. Burns, *Old Creeds and the New Faith*, London, 1911.

C. Coignet, *De Kant à Bergson. Reconciliation de la religion et de la science dans un spiritualisme nouveau*, Paris, 1911.

C. Douais, *L'Apologétique*, Paris, 1911.

W. Elert, *Prolegomena der Geschichtsphilosophie. Studie zur Grundlegung der Apologetik*, Leipsic, 1911.

H. Felder, *Jesus Christus. Apologie seiner Messianität und Gottheit gegenüber der neuesten ungläubigen Jesus-Forschung*, vol. i., *Das Bewusstsein Jesu*, Paderborn, 1911.

APOLOGETICS: F. X. Kiefl, *Der geschichtliche Christus und die moderne Philosophie. Eine genetische Darlegung der philosophischen Voraussetzungen im Streit um die Christusmythe*, Mainz, 1911.

J. B. Koehne, *A Challenge to Modern Skepticism*, Philadelphia, 1911.

D. A. Murray, *Christian Faith and the New Psychology: Evolution and Recent Science as Aids to Faith*, London, 1911.

A. Seitz, *Cyprian und der römische Primat oder urchristliche Primatsentwicklung und Hugo Kochs modernistisches Kirchenrecht. Eine dogmengeschichtliche Apologie nach kritischer Methode*, Regensburg, 1911.

F. Wilke, *Das Alte Testament und der christliche Glaube*, Leipsic, 1911.

ARABIA: S. M. and A. E. Zwemer, *Zigzag Journeys in the Camel Country: Arabia in Picture and Story*, London, 1911.

ARCHEOLOGY, BIBLICAL: E. Goblet d'Alviella, *Croyances, rites, institutions*, vol. i., *Archéologie et histoire religieuse, Hiérographie*, vol. ii., *Questions de méthode et d'origines, Hiérologie*, vol. iii., *Problèmes du temps présent, Hiérosophie*, Paris, 1911.

ARMENIA: M. Ormanian, *L'Église arménienne, son histoire, sa doctrine, son régime, sa discipline, sa liturgie, sa littérature, son présent*, Paris, 1910.

ART AND CHURCH: C. Diehl, *Manuel d'art byzantin*, Paris, 1910.

ASSYRIA: E. Klauber, *Assyrisches Beamtentum nach Briefen aus der Sargonidenzeit*, Leipsic, 1910.

ATONEMENT: C. F. Creighton, *Law and the Cross. The Legal Aspects of the Atonement viewed in the Light of the Common Sense of Mankind*, Cincinnati, 1911.

G. C. Workman, *Atonement of Reconciliation with God*, New York, 1911.

AUGUSTINE, SAINT, OF HIPPO: O. Schilling, *Die Staats- und Soziallehre des heiligen Augustinus*, Freiburg, 1910.

T. Allin, *The Augustinian Revolution in Theology*, London, 1911.

H. Scholz, *Glaube und Unglaube in der Weltgeschichte. Ein Kommentar zu Augustins De Civitate Dei*, Leipsic, 1911.

AUGUSTINE, SAINT, OF HIPPO: B. Seidel, *Die Lehre des heiligen Augustinus vom Staate*, Breslau, 1911.

BABISM: *Kitáb-i Nuqtatu'l-Káf. Being the Earliest History of the Bábís compiled by Ḥájji Mírzá Jáni of Káshán between the Years A.D. 1850 and 1852*, edited from the unique Paris MS. Suppl. Persan 1071 by E. G. Browne, London, 1911.

BABYLONIA: C. Frank, *Studien zur babylonischen Religion*, vol. i., Strasburg, 1911.

W. J. Hinke, *Selected Babylonian Kudurra Inscriptions*, no. xiv. of *Semitic Study Series*, ed. R. Gottheil and M. Jastrow, Leyden, 1911.

H. Radau, *Sumerian Hymns and Prayers to God Ninib from the Temple Library of Nippur*, in *The Babylonian Expedition of the University of Pennsylvania*, xxix., pt. 1, Philadelphia, 1911.

BAMPTON LECTURES: J. H. Skrine, *Creed and the Creeds: their Function in Religion. Being the Bampton Lectures of 1911*, London, 1911.

BANKS, L. A.: *The Great Themes of the Bible*, New York, 1911; idem, *The Sunday-Night Evangel: A Series of Sunday Evening Discourses delivered in Independence Avenue Methodist Episcopal Church, Kansas City, Missouri*, New York, 1911.

BAPTISTS: C. T. Byford, *Peasants and Prophets*, London, 1911.

J. N. Prestridge, *Modern Baptist Heroes and Martyrs*, Louisville, 1911.

A. L. Vail, *Baptists Mobilized for Missions*, Philadelphia, 1911.

BATIFFOL, P. H.: *Primitive Catholicism*, New York, 1911.

BELLARMINE: X.-M. Le Bachelet, *Bellarmin*, Paris, 1911.

BENEDICT XII.: K. Jacob, *Studien über Papst Benedikt XII.*, Berlin, 1910.

BERNARDIN OF SIENNA: P. T. Dangin, *The Life of S. Bernardino of Siena*, London, 1911.

BIBLE TEXT: *Codex Sinaiticus Petropolitanus. The New Testament, the Epistle of Barnabas and the Shepherd of Hermas. Preserved in the Imperial Library of St. Petersburg. Now reproduced in Facsimile with a Description and Introduction to the History of the Codex by Kirsopp Lake*, London, 1911.

E. S. Buchanan, *The Records Unrolled. The Story of the Most Ancient MSS. of the New Testament*, London, 1911.

J. Hänel, *Die aussermasorethischen Uebereinstimmungen zwischen der Septuaginta und der Peschittha in der Genesis*, Giessen, 1911.

Sir H. Thompson, *A Coptic Palimpsest, containing Joshua, Judges, Ruth, Judith and Esther*, London, 1911.

Der Cambridger Psalter, zum ersten Male herausgegeben mit besonderer Berücksichtigung des lateinischen Textes von Karl Wildhagen. I. Text mit Erklärungen. Hamburg, 1910.

BIBLE VERSIONS: C. Heller, *Untersuchungen über die Peschîttâ zur gesamten hebräischen Bibel*, part 1, Berlin, 1911.

BIBLE VERSIONS: J. I. Munro, *The Samaritan Pentateuch and Modern Criticism*, London, 1911.

BIBLICAL CRITICISM: C. W. Emmet, *The Eschatological Question in the Gospels, and other Studies in recent New Testament Criticism*, London, 1911.

A. Harnack, *Kritik des Neuen Testaments von einem griechischen Philosophen des 3. Jahrhunderts*, Leipsic, 1911.

W. St. Clair Tisdall, *Why I am not a Higher Critic*, London, 1911.

The Higher Criticism and the New Theology, Unscientific, Unscriptural, and Unwholesome, ed. R. A. Torrey, Montrose, Pa., 1911.

BIBLICAL INTRODUCTION: T. Engert, *Das Alte Testament im Lichte modernistisch-katholischer Wissenschaft*, Munich, 1910.

H. Anz, *Literaturgeschichte des Alten Testaments im Abriss*, Berlin, 1911.

F. V. N. Painter, *Introduction to Bible Study: The Old Testament*, Boston, 1911.

J. Warschauer, *What is the Bible? A Modern Survey*, London, 1911.

BIBLICAL THEOLOGY: H. J. Holtzmann, *Lehrbuch der neutestamentlichen Theologie*, 2 vols., 2d ed., Tübingen, 1911.

H. Weinel, *Biblische Theologie des Neuen Testaments. Die Religion Jesu und des Urchristentums*, Tübingen, 1911.

BOEHME, J.: *The Forty Questions and The Clavis*, ed. Mrs. D. S. Hehner, London, 1911.

BONIFACE VIII.: Count L. Tosti, *History of Pope Boniface VIII. and his Times*, New York, 1911.

BRAHMANISM: M. N. Rory, *A Commentary on the Sankhya Philosophy of Kapila*, London, 1911.

BUDDHISM: A. David, *Le Modernisme bouddhiste et le bouddhisme de Bouddha*, Paris, 1911.

CALVIN, J.: A reprint of the first ed. of his *Institutes* was issued in 2 vols., Paris, 1911.

CAMPBELL, J. M.: *The Presence*, New York, 1911.

CAPISTRANO, G. DI: F. V. Fitzgerald, *Saint John Capistran*, London and New York, 1911.

CARPENTER, W. B.: *Some Pages of my Life*, New York, 1911.

CATHERINE, SAINT, OF SIENNA: H. Riesch, *Die heilige Katharina von Sienna. Ein Zeitbild aus dem italienischen Mittelalter*, Freiburg, 1911.

CELTIC CHURCH: G. Gougaud, *Les Chrétientés celtiques*, Paris, 1911.

CEMETERIES: H. T. Oberman, *De oud-christelijke sarkophagen en hun godsdienstige beteekenis*, The Hague, 1911.

CHAPMAN, J. W.: *Revival Sermons*, New York, 1911.

CHINA: Chen Huan-Chang, *The Economic Principles of Confucius and his School*, 2 vols., New York, 1911.

W. E. Geil, *Eighteen Capitals of China*, Philadelphia, 1911.

H. D. Porter, *William Scott Ament, Missionary of the American Board to China*, New York, 1911.

CHRISTOLOGY: E. S. Ames, *The Divinity of Christ*, Chicago, 1911.

E. H. Gifford, *The Incarnation: a Study of Philippians II., 5–11 and a University Sermon on Psalm CX.*, new ed., London, 1911.

CHURCH: J. M. Frost, *The School of the Church, its Pre-eminent Place and Purpose*, London, 1911.

J. J. Lanier, *The Church Universal: a Restatement of Christianity in Terms of Modern Thought*, New York, 1911.

J. Oman, *The Church and the Divine Order*, London, 1911.

CHURCH HISTORY: H. Appel, *Kirchengeschichte des Mittelalters*, vol. ii. of *Kurzgefasste Kirchengeschichte für Studierende*, Leipsic, 1911.

The Cambridge Medieval History, ed. H. M. Gwatkin and J. P. Whitney, vol. i., *The Christian Roman Empire and the Foundation of the Teutonic Kingdoms*, New York, 1911.

K. Heussi, *Kompendium der Kirchengeschichte*, Tübingen, 1911.

H. Jordan, *Geschichte der altchristlichen Literatur*, Leipsic, 1911.

A. Schmidtke, *Neue Fragmente und Untersuchungen zu den judenchristlichen Evangelien. Ein Beitrag zur Literatur und Geschichte der Judenchristen*, Leipsic, 1911.

H. Wace and W. C. Piercy, *Dictionary of Christian Biography and Literature*, London, 1911.

COMPARATIVE RELIGION: W. W. G. Baudissin, *Adonis und Esmun. Eine Untersuchung zur Geschichte des Glaubens an Auferstehungsgötter und an Heilgötter*, Leipsic, 1911.

W. H. I. Bleek and L. C. Lloyd, *Specimens of Bushman Folklore*, London, 1911.

F. Boas, *The Mind of Primitive Man*, New York, 1911.

F. V. M. Cumont, *Oriental Religions in Roman Paganism*, Chicago, 1911.

S. Endle, *The Kacharis*, New York, 1911.

J. G. Frazer, *Taboo and the Perils of the Soul*, London, 1911 (a part of the 3d ed. of the *Golden Bough*).

Sir J. Lubbock, *Marriage, Totemism and Religion: an Answer to Critics*, New York, 1911.

J. A. MacCulloch, *The Religion of the Ancient Celts*, London, 1911.

M. P. Nilsson, *Primitive-religion*, Stockholm, 1911.

J. Réville, *Les Phases successives de l'histoire des religions*, Paris, 1911.

J. Roscoe, *The Baganda: an Account of their Native Customs and Beliefs*, New York, 1911.

W. von Unwerth, *Untersuchungen über Totenkult und Odinverehrung bei Nordgermanen und Lappen mit Exkursen zur altnordischen Literaturgeschichte*, Breslau, 1911.

H. Visscher, *Religion und soziales Leben bei den Naturvölkern*, vol. i., *Prolegomena*, Bonn, 1911.

Warren, William Fairfield, *The Religions of the World and the World-Religion*, New York, 1911.

CONFUCIUS: W. E. Soothill, *The Analecta of Confucius*, London, 1911.

CONSCIENCE: J. Triollet, *Examen de conscience*, Paris, 1911.

CREATION: F. M. Parker, *Religious Essays, including a Scientific Exposition of the Mosaic Story of Creation and the Fall of Man*, Louisville, Ky., 1911.

DEMON, DEMONISM: A. Jirku, *Die Dämonen und ihre Abwehr im Alten Testament*, Leipsic, 1911.

DENNEY, J.: *The Way Everlasting: Sermons*, London, 1911.

DESCARTES, R.: Elizabeth S. Haldane and G. R. T. Ross, *The Philosophical Works of Descartes*, vol. i., Cambridge, 1911.

DIDACHE: A. Schlatter, *Die Lehre der Apostel*, Calw and Stuttgart, 1910.

DOCTRINE, HISTORY OF: F. Haase, *Begriff und Ausgabe der Dogmengeschichte*, Breslau, 1911.

DOGMA, DOGMATICS: D. S. Adam, *Cardinal Elements of the Christian Faith*, London, 1911.

K. Heim, *Das Gewissheitsproblem in der systematischen Theologie bis zu Schleiermacher*, Leipsic, 1911.

P. A. Lobstein, *Introduction to Protestant Dogmatics*, London, 1911.

A. Schlatter, *Das christliche Dogma*, Calw and Stuttgart, 1911.

H. B. Workman, *Christian Thought to the Reformation*, New York, 1911.

DOMINIC, SAINT, AND THE DOMINICAN ORDER: B. Altauer, *Venturino von Bergamo, O. Pr. 1304–1346. Zugleich ein Beitrag zur Geschichte des Dominikanerordens im 14. Jahrhundert*, Breslau, 1911.

EGYPT: E. A. W. Budge, *Osiris and the Egyptian Resurrection*, 2 vols., New York, 1911.

G. E. Smith, *The Ancient Egyptians and Their Influence upon the Civilization of Europe*, New York, 1911.

A. E. P. Weigall, *The Life and Times of Akhnaton, Pharao of Egypt*, London, 1911; idem, *The Treasury of Ancient Egypt. Miscellaneous Chapters on Ancient History and Archeology*, London, 1911.

EGYPT EXPLORATION FUND: W. F. Nash, *Egypt Exploration Fund: General Index to the Archæological Reports*, vols. 1–8, London, 1911.

ELAGABALUS: K. Hönn, *Quellenuntersuchungen zu den Viten des Heliogabalus und des Severus Alexander*, in *Scriptores Historiæ Augustæ*, Leipsic, 1911.

ELLINWOOD, F. F.: Mary G. Ellinwood, *Frank Field Ellinwood: his Life and Work*, New York, 1911.

ENGLAND, CHURCH OF: Gertrude Hollis, *What the Church did for England: Being the Story of the Church of England from A. D. 690 to 1215*, London, 1911.

A. H. Thompson, *The Historical Growth of the English Parish Church*, New York, 1911.

J. D. Thompson, *Central Churchmanship: or, The Position, Principles and Policy of Evangelical Churchmen in Relation to Modern Thought and Work*, London, 1911.

ENGLAND AND WALES: H. W. Clark, *History of English Non-Conformity, from Wiclif to the Close of the 19th Century*, vol. i., *From Wiclif to the Restoration*, London, 1911.

ENGLAND AND WALES: G. R. Wynne, *The Church in Greater Britain*, 3d ed., London, 1911.

ESCHATOLOGY: H. B. Pratt, *The Buried Nations of the Infant Dead: a Study in Eschatology*, Hackensack, N. J., 1911.

ETHICS: G. F. Barbour, *A Philosophical Study of Christian Ethics*, London, 1911.

E. Dürr, *Das Gute und das Sittliche. Grundprobleme der Ethik*, Heidelberg, 1911.

G. T. Ladd, *The Teacher's Practical Philosophy. A Treatise of Education as a Species of Conduct*, New York, 1911.

EUCHARIST: N. Dimock, *On the Doctrine of the Church of England, concerning the Eucharistic Presence*, London, 1911.

EUSEBIUS OF CÆSAREA: *Die Chronik des Eusebius. Aus dem Armenischen übersetzt*, ed. J. Karst, Leipsic, 1911.

EXEGESIS: H. Foston, *The Beatitudes and the Contrasts: a Study in Methodic Interpretation*, London, 1911.

FAITH: W. W. Gueth, *The Assurance of Faith*, Cincinnati, 1911.

FEASTS AND FESTIVALS: V. Staley, *The Seasons, Fasts and Festivals of the Christian Year*, London, 1911.

FORSYTH, P. T.: *Christ on Parnassus. Lectures on Art, Ethic and Theology*, London, 1911.

FRANCE: L. Gougaud, *Les Chrétientés celtiques*, Paris, 1911.

A. Mathiez, *Rome et le clergé français sous la constituante. La constitution civile du clergé. L'affaire d'Avignon*, Paris, 1911.

FRANCIS, SAINT, OF ASSISI: G. Lafenestre, *Saint François d'Assise et Savonarole, inspirateurs de l'art italien*, Paris, 1911.

FREEMASONS: L. Keller, *Die geistigen Grundlagen der Freimaurerei und das öffentliche Leben*, Jena, 1911.

FRENCH REVOLUTION: T. Bitterauf, *Geschichte der französischen Revolution*, Leipsic, 1911.

FRIENDS, SOCIETY OF: R. M. Jones, *The Quakers in the American Colonies*, New York, 1911.

FUNDAMENTAL DOCTRINES OF CHRISTIANITY: S. F. Halfvard, *Fundamentals of the Christian Religion*, Cincinnati, 1911.

GASQUET, F. A.: *Leaves from my Diary, 1894–96*, St. Louis, 1911 (deals with the works of the Roman Catholic Commission on the validity of Anglican orders).

GIBBONS, J.: A. S. Will, *Life of James Cardinal Gibbons*, Baltimore, 1911.

GIFFORD LECTURES: J. Ward, *The Realm of Ends: or, Pluralism and Theism, Gifford Lectures, 1907–10*, Cambridge, 1911.

GNOSTICISM: *Iamblichos, Theurgia; or, the Egyptian Mysteries: Reply of Abammon, the Teacher, to the Letter of Porphyry to Anebo. Together with Solutions of the Questions therein contained;* transl. from the Greek by A. Wilder, New York, 1911.

GOD: J. Gurnhill, *Some Thoughts on God and His Methods of Manifestation in Nature and Revelation*, New York, 1911.

GOSPEL AND GOSPELS: F. K. Feigel, *Der Einfluss des Weissagungsbeweises und anderer Motive auf die Leidensgeschichte. Ein Beitrag zur Evangelienkritik*, Tübingen, 1910.

G. Friedlander, *The Jewish Sources of the Sermon on the Mount*, New York, 1911.

A. Harnack, *The Date of the Acts and the Synoptic Gospels*, London, 1911.

F. R. M. Hitchcock, *A Fresh Study of the Fourth Gospel*, London, 1911.

O. Moe, *Paulus und die evangelische Geschichte. Zugleich ein Beitrag zur Vorgeschichte der Evangelien*, Leipsic, 1911.

GRAVES, A. R.: *The Farmer Boy who became a Bishop. The Autobiography of the Rt. Rev. Anson Rogers Graves*, Akron, 1911.

GREGORY I.: *The Dialogues of St. Gregory Surnamed the Great, Pope of Rome, and the First of that Name.* Transl. by P. W. ⸻. Re-edited with Introduction and Notes by Edmund G. Gardner, London, 1911.

HAMMURABI: H. Fehr, *Hammurapi und das salische Recht. Eine Rechtsvergleichung*, Bonn, 1910.

HARNACK, G. A.: *New Testament Studies*, vol. iv., *The Date of the Acts and of the Synoptic Gospels*, New York, 1911.

HARTMANN, K. R. E. VON: R. E. Pohorilles, *Entwicklung und Kritik der Erkenntnistheorie Eduard von Hartmanns*, Vienna, 1911.

HEAVEN: E. P. Berg, *Where is Heaven? Musings on the Life Eternal*, London, 1911.

HEBREWS, EPISTLE TO THE: Sir R. Anderson, *The Hebrew Epistle in the Light of the Types*, London, 1911.

HELENA, SAINT: R. Couzard, *Sainte Hélène*, Paris, 1911.

HELLENISM: G. Plaumann, *Ptolemais in Oberägypten. Ein Beitrag zur Geschichte des Hellenismus in Aegypten*, Leipsic, 1910.

HESSE: K. Eger and J. Frederich, *Kirchenrecht der evangelischen Kirche im Grossherzogtum Hessen*, vol. ii., Darmstadt, 1911.

HEXATEUCH: A. T. Chapman, *An Introduction to the Pentateuch*, Cambridge, 1911.

The Book of Exodus in the Revised Version. With Introduction and Notes by the Rev. S. R. Driver, Cambridge, 1911.

The Book of Numbers in the Revised Version. With Introduction and Notes by A. H. McNeile, Cambridge, 1911.

J. Sinclair, *Bible Beginnings. A Plain Commentary on the First Eleven Chapters of Genesis*, London, 1911.

HINDUISM: J. C. Oman, *Cults, Customs and Superstitions of India*, reissue, London, 1911.

HITTITES: A. Gleye, *Hettitische Studien*, Leipsic, 1910.

HOLLAND: W. G. Goeters, *Die Vorbereitung des Pietismus in der reformierten Kirche der Niederlande. I. Die Entwicklung der kirchlichen Reformtendenzen (1619 bis 1666). II. Die Labadistische Krisis (1666 bis 1670)*, London, 1911.

HOLLAND: L. Knappert, *Geschiedenis der Nederlandsche Hervormde Kerk gedurende de 16e en 17e eeuw*, Amsterdam, 1911.

J. H. Mackay, *Religious Thought in Holland during the Nineteenth Century*, London, 1911.

HUMANISM: *Das Zeitalter der Renaissance. Ausgewählte Quellen zur Geschichte der italienischen Kultur. Hgb. von Marie Herzfeld*, 1st series, vol. i–ii., Jena, 1910.

HUME, D.: A. Thomsen, *David Hume, hans liv og hans filosofi*, vol. i., Copenhagen, 1911.

HUTTON, W. H.: *A Disciple's Religion: Sermons*, London, 1911.

HYMNOLOGY: W. Bäumker, *Das katholische deutsche Kirchenlied in seinen Singweisen*, vol. iv., Freiburg, 1911.

C. S. Nutter and W. F. Tillett, *The Hymns and Hymn Writers of the Church: an Annotated Edition of the Methodist Hymnal*, New York, 1911.

Carl F. Price, *The Music and Hymnody of the Methodist Hymnal*, New York, 1911.

IMMORTALITY: H. Carrington and J. R. Meader, *Death, its Causes and Phenomena, with special Reference to Immortality*, London, 1911.

J. Denney, *Factors of Faith in Immortality*, London, 1911.

INDIA: R. A. Hume, *An Interpretation of India's Religious History*, New York and Chicago, 1911.

W. C. B. Purser, *Christian Missions in Burma*, London, 1911.

INQUISITION: See below, PIUS V.

INTERMEDIATE STATE: E. Hicks, *The Life Hereafter: Thoughts on the Intermediate State*, London, 1911.

ISAIAH: G. W. Wade, *The Book of the Prophet Isaiah*, London, 1911.

ISRAEL, HISTORY OF: F. Böhl, *Kanaanäer und Hebräer. Untersuchungen zur Vorgeschichte des Volkstums und der Religion Israels auf dem Boden Kanaans. Inhalt: I. Kanaanäer. II. Hethiter. III. Amoriter. IV. Völker Kanaans und Hebräer. V. Synkretismus und Mosaismus*, Leipsic, 1911.

A. Geiger, *Judaism and its History*, 2 parts, New York, 1911.

C. F. Lehmann-Haupt, *Israel. Seine Entwicklung im Rahmen der Weltgeschichte*, Tübingen, 1911.

W. M. F. Petrie, *Egypt and Israel*, New York, 1911.

E. Sachau, *Aramäische Papyrus und Ostraka aus Elephantine. Altorientalische Sprachdenkmäler aus einer jüdischen Militär-Kolonie des 5. Jahrhunderts vor Chr.*, Leipsic, 1911.

JAMES, W.: K. A. Busch, *William James als Religionsphilosoph*, Göttingen, 1911.

JANSEN, CORNELIUS, AND JANSENISM: J. Hild, *Honoré Tournely und seine Stellung zum Jansenismus, mit besonderer Berücksichtigung der Stellung der Sorbonne zum Jansenismus*, Freiburg, 1911.

JAPAN: A. Lloyd, *The Creed of Half Japan: Historical Sketches of Japanese Buddhism*, London, 1911.

JAPAN: E. Schiller, *Shinto, die Volksreligion Japans*, Berlin, 1911.

JERUSALEM: *Underground Jerusalem. Discoveries on the Hill of Ophel, 1909*, London, 1911.

JESUITS: Count Paul von Hoensbroech, *Fourteen Years a Jesuit: a Record of Personal Experiences and a Criticism*, 2 vols., New York, 1911.

H. Stoeckius, *Forschungen zur Lebensdornung der Gesellschaft Jesu im 16. Jahrhundert. II., Das gesellschaftliche Leben im Ordenshause*, Munich, 1911.

JESUS CHRIST: J. E. Carpenter, *The Historical Jesus and the Theological Christ*, London, 1911.

W. N. Clarke, *The Ideal of Jesus*, London, 1911.

J. Denney, *The Death of Christ. Revised and Enlarged Ed., including The Atonement and the Modern Mind*, London, 1911.

W. W. Holdsworth, *The Christ of the Gospels*, New York, 1911.

G. Jahn, *Ueber die Person Jesu und über die Entstehung des Christentums und den Wert desselben für modern Gebildete, mit einer Kritik der neuesten Schriften über Jesu*, Leyden, 1911.

F. B. Macnutt, *The Inevitable Christ*, London, 1911.

JEWS, HISTORY OF: E. Dujardin, *The Source of the Christian Tradition. Critical History of Ancient Judaism*, rev. ed., London, 1911.

C. F. Kent, *The Makers and Teachers of Judaism from the Fall of Jerusalem to the Death of Herod the Great*, New York, 1911.

JEWS, MISSIONS TO THE: T. C. Gilbert, *From Judaism to Christianity and Gospel Work among the Hebrews*, Concord, 1911.

JOB, BOOK OF: S. Landersdorfer, *Eine babylonische Quelle für das Buch Job?* Freiburg, 1911.

JOHN THE APOSTLE: F. Overbeck, *Das Johannesevangelium. Studien zur Kritik seiner Erforschung*, Tübingen, 1911.

JOHN THE BAPTIST: A. Konrad, *Johannes der Täufer*, Graz, 1911.

A. Pottgiesser, *Johannes der Täufer und Jesus Christus*, Cologne, 1911.

JUSTIN MARTYR: A. Béry, *Saint Justin: sa vie et sa doctrine*, Paris, 1911.

KANT, I.: *Kant's Critique of Aesthetic Judgement. Translated with Seven Introductory Essays, Notes and Analytical Index*, by James Creed Meredith, London, 1911.

KINGS, BOOKS OF: A. Sanda, *Die Bücher der Könige*, Münster, 1911.

KOREA: M. C. Fenwick, *The Church of Christ in Corea*, London, 1911.

J. H. Longford, *The Story of Korea*, London, 1911.

LAMAISM: G. Schulemann, *Die Geschichte der Dalailamas*, Heidelberg, 1911.

LAYING ON OF HANDS: J. Behm, *Die Handauflegung im Urchristentum nach Verwendung, Herkunft und Bedeutung, in religionsgeschichtlichem Zusammenhang untersucht*, Leipsic, 1911.

LIBERTY, RELIGIOUS: H. F. R. Smith, *The Theory of Religious Liberty in the Reigns of Charles II. and James II.*, Cambridge, 1911.

LITURGICS: G. Semeria, *The Eucharistic Liturgy in the Roman Rite: its History and Symbolism* adapted from the Italian by Rev. E. S. Berry, New York, 1911.

LORD'S SUPPER: F. Dibelius, *Das Abendmahl. Eine Untersuchung über die Anfänge der christlichen Religion*, Leipsic, 1911.

K. Kircher, *Die sakrale Bedeutung des Weines im Altertum*, Giessen, 1911.

LUTHER, MARTIN: P. Drews, *Beiträge zu Luthers liturgischen Reformen. 1. Lateinische und deutsche Litanei von 1529. 2. Luthers deutsche Versikel und Kollekten*, Tübingen, 1910.

H. Grisar, *Luther*, vol. ii., *Auf der Höhe des Lebens*, Freiburg, 1911.

A. C. McGiffert, *Martin Luther: the Man and his Work*, New York, 1911.

O. Scheel, *Dokumente zu Luthers Entwicklung (bis 1519)*, Tübingen, 1911.

P. Smith, *The Life and Letters of Martin Luther*, Boston, 1911.

LUTHERANS: A. H. Smith, *The Lutheran Church and Child Nurture*, Philadelphia, 1911.

MACLAGAN, W. D.: F. D. How, *Archbishop Maclagan. Being a Memoir of William Dalrymple Maclagan, D.D., Archbishop of York and Primate of England*, London, 1911.

MARGARET, SAINT: *St. Margaret, Queen of Scotland*, London, 1911.

MARPRELATE TRACTS: *The Marprelate Tracts 1588, 1589. Edited with Notes Historical and Explanatory by William Pierce*, London, 1911.

MATHER, COTTON: *Diary of Cotton Mather*, part 1, Boston, 1911.

METHODISTS: W. McKinley, *A Story of Minnesota Methodism*, Cincinnati, 1911.

MILLENNIAL DAWN: E. L. Eaton, *The Millennial Dawn Heresy. An Examination of Pastor Charles T. Russell's Teaching concerning the Purpose of the Second Advent and the Millennium, as set forth in his Published Books and Papers—" The Divine Plan of the Ages," and others of similar Import*, Cincinnati, 1911.

MILLER, J. R.: *The Beauty of Self-Control*, New York, 1911.

MISSIONS TO THE HEATHEN: *World Atlas of Christian Missions, containing a Directory of Missionary Societies, a Classified Summary of Statistics, an Index of Mission Stations, and Maps showing the Location of Mission Stations throughout the World*, ed. J. S. Dennis, H. P. Beach, C. H. Fahs, with maps by J. G. Bartholomew, New York, 1911.

Georgiana M. Forde, *Missionary Adventures. A Simple History of the S. P. G.* With a Preface by Edward Talbot, London, 1911.

John F. Goucher, *Growth of the Missionary Concept. The Nathan Graves Foundation Lectures delivered before Syracuse University*, New York, 1911.

E. T. Reed, *A World Book of Foreign Missions: What They Are, What They Prove, and How To Help*, London, 1911.

T. Walker, *Missionary Ideals. Missionary Studies in the Acts of the Apostles*, London, 1911.

MODERNISM: B. Baur, *Klarheit und Wahrheit. Eine Erklärung des Modernisteneides*, Freiburg, 1911.

MOHAMMED, MOHAMMEDANISM: I. Goldziher, *Vorlesungen über den Islam*, Heidelberg, 1910.

M. Horten, *Die philosophischen Probleme der spekulativen Theologie im Islam*, Bonn, 1910.

D. S. Margoliouth, *Mohammedanism*, London, 1911.

E. Montet, *De l'état présent et de l'avenir de l'Islam*, Paris, 1911.

R. A. Nicholson, *The Kashf al-Mahjúb. The Oldest Persian Treatise on Súfism by 'Ali b. 'Uthmán al-Jullábi al-Hujwiri. Translated from the Text of the Lahore Edition, compared with MSS. in the India Office and British Museum*, London, 1911.

P. Ponafidine, *Life in the Moslem East*, New York, 1911.

H. Stubbe, *An Account of the Rise and Progress of Mahometanism with the Life of Mahomet and a Vindication of Him and His Religion from the Calumnies of the Christians*, London, 1911.

MOHAMMEDANS, MISSIONS TO: *Daylight in the Harem. A New Era for Moslem Women*, ed. Annie Van Sommer and S. M. Zwemer, London, 1911.

S. M. Zwemer and others, *Islam and Missions*, New York, 1911.

MORE, HENRY: R. Ward, *The Life of the Learned and Pious Dr. Henry More. Edited with Introduction and Notes by M. F. Howard*, London, 1911 [original ed., 1710].

MYSTICISM: R. Steiner, *Mystics of the Renaissance and their Relation to Modern Thought. Including Meister Eckhart, Tauler, Paracelsus, Jacob Boehme, Giordano Bruno, and others*, New York, 1911.

NEGRO EDUCATION AND EVANGELIZATION: R. A. Patterson, *The Negro and his Needs*. With a Foreword by W. H. Taft, New York, 1911.

NEW THOUGHT: J. B. Anderson, *New Thought: its Lights and Shadows. An Appreciation and a Criticism*, Boston, 1911.

NEW YEAR'S CELEBRATION: F. Bünger, *Geschichte der Neujahrsfeier in der Kirche*, Göttingen, 1911.

NIETZSCHE, F. W.: E. S. Hamblen, *Friedrich Nietzsche and his New Gospel*, Boston, 1911.

ORIGEN: *The Philocalia of Origen: a Compilation of Selected Passages from Origen's Works made by St. Gregory of Nazianzus and St. Basil of Cæsarea. Translated into English by the Rev. G. Lewis*, New York, 1911.

PAINTING: Baroness Freda de Knoop, " All Hail ": *Simple Teachings on the Bible Illustrations from the Old Masters*, London, 1911.

PALESTINE: *Conférences de Saint-Étienne*, Paris, 1911 (a composite work dealing with recent Palestinian excavation and discussion).

J. E. Dinsmore and G. Dalman, *Die Pflanzen Palæstinas*, Leipsic, 1911.

PASCAL, B.: H. Petitot, *Pascal*, Paris, 1911.

PASTORAL THEOLOGY: S. C. Black, *Building a Working Church*, New York, 1911.

PASTORAL THEOLOGY: C. E. Blakeway, *The Claims of Modern Thought upon the Clergy, or The Present Task and Opportunity of the Pastorate*, Lichfield, 1911.

Non-Church Going: its Reasons and Remedies. A Symposium, ed. W. F. Gray, New York, 1911.

J. G. Haller, *The Redemption of the Prayer-Meeting*, Cincinnati, O., 1911.

A. T. Robertson, *The Glory of the Ministry*, New York, 1911.

W. H. G. Thomas, *The Work of the Ministry*, London, 1911.

PATRICK, SAINT: *St. Patrick, Apostle of Ireland*, London, 1911.

PAUL THE APOSTLE: A. Deissmann, *Paulus. Eine kultur- und religionsgeschichtliche Skizze*, Tübingen, 1911.

M. Dibelius, *Die Briefe des Apostels Paulus. II. An die Thessalonicher. III. An die Philipper*, Tübingen, 1911.

P. Gardner, *The Religious Experience of Saint Paul*, London, 1911.

A. E. Garvie, *Studies of Paul and his Gospel*, London, 1911.

H. L. Goude, *The Mind of St. Paul as Illustrated by his Second Epistle to the Corinthians*, London, 1911.

H. Holtzmann, *Praktische Erklärung des I. Thessalonicherbriefes*, Tübingen, 1911.

K. Lake, *The Earlier Epistles of St. Paul: their Motive and Origin*, London, 1911.

J. E. McFadyen, *The Epistles to the Corinthians, with Notes and Comments*, London, 1911.

C. Wise, *The New Life of St. Paul*, London, 1911.

PERFECTION: J. Mudge, *The Perfect Life in Experience and Doctrine*, Cincinnati, 1911.

PERU: P. F. Martin, *Peru of the Twentieth Century*, New York, 1911.

PETER LOMBARD: W. Benham, *The Letters of Peter Lombard*, ed. Ellen D. Baxter, London, 1911.

PFLEIDERER, O.: *Primitive Christianity, its Writings and Teachings in their Historical Connections*, London, 1911.

PHILIP OF HESSE: P. Wappler, *Die Stellung Kursachsens und des Landgrafen Philipp von Hessen zur Täuferbewegung*, Münster, 1910.

PHOTIUS: E. Martini, *Textgeschichte der Bibliotheke des Patriarchen Photios von Konstantinopel*, part 1, *Die Handschriften, Ausgaben und Uebertragungen*, Leipsic, 1911.

PIERSON, A. T.: *Dr. Pierson and His Message. A Sketch of the Life and Work of a Great Preacher, together with a Varied Selection from His Unpublished Manuscripts. Edited by J. Kennedy Maclean*, London, 1911.

PIETISM: W. Goeters, *Die Vorbereitung des Pietismus in der reformierten Kirche der Niederlande bis zur labadistischen Krisis 1670*, Leipsic, 1911.

PILGRIMAGES: S. Heath, *Pilgrim Life in the Middle Ages*, London, 1911.

PIUS V.: C. M. Antony, *Saint Pius V., Pope of the Holy Rosary* (the preface by Mgr. R. H. Benson contains a defense of the Inquisition), London and New York, 1911.

P. Deslandres, *Saint Pie V.*, Paris, 1911.

PLATONISM: J. Adam, *The Vitality of Platonism and Other Essays*, Cambridge, 1911.

PRACTICAL THEOLOGY: Norman E. Richardson (ed.), *The Religion of Modern Manhood*, New York, 1911.

PRAGMATISM: A. v. C. P. Huizinga, *The American Philosophy, Pragmatism, critically Considered in Relation to Present-Day Theology*, Boston, 1911.

F. H. Johnson, *God in Evolution: a Pragmatic Study of Theology*, New York, 1911 (tentative application of the pragmatic method to religious thought).

PRISON REFORM: J. Friedrich, *Die Bestrafung der Motive und die Motive der Bestrafung. Rechtsphilosophische und kriminalpsychologische Studien*, Berlin, 1910.

PROPHECY: G. C. Aalders, *De valsche profetie in Israël*, Wageningen, 1911.

W. P. Aylsworth, *The Growing Miracle: a Practical Study of Hebrew Prophecy*, Bethany, Neb., 1911.

PROTESTANT EPISCOPALIANS: C. C. Grafton, *The Lineage from Apostolic Times of the American Catholic Church, commonly called the Episcopal Church*, Milwaukee, 1911.

PROTESTANTISM: N. Paulus, *Protestantismus und Toleranz im 16. Jahrh.*, Freiburg, 1911.

PROVIDENCE: H. Siebeck, *Ueber Freiheit, Entwicklung und Vorsehung*, Tübingen, 1911.

RAMABAI, S.: H. S. Dyer, *Pandita Ramabai: the Story of her Life*, New York, 1911.

RAMSAY, SIR W. M.: *The First Christian Century. Notes on Dr. Moffatt's Introduction to the Literature of the New Testament*, London, 1911.

REFORMATION: H. Wace, *Principles of the Reformation, Practical and Historical*, New York, 1911.

H. B. Workman, *Christian Thought to the Reformation*, London, 1911.

REFORMED (DUTCH) CHURCH: J. I. Good, *History of the Reformed Church in the U. S., in the Nineteenth Century*, New York, 1911.

RELIGION, PHILOSOPHY OF: E. Boutroux, *Science and Religion in Contemporary Philosophy*, New York, 1911.

P. Deussen, *Allgemeine Geschichte der Philosophie mit besonderer Berücksichtigung der Religionen*, vol. ii., part 1, *Die Philosophie der Griechen*, Leipsic, 1911.

H. Ehrenberg, *Die Parteiung der Philosophie. Studien wider Hegel und die Kantianer*, Leipsic, 1911.

J. H. Randall, *A New Philosophy of Life*, New York, 1911.

R. Richter, *Dialoge über Religionsphilosophie*, Leipsic, 1911.

RELIGIOUS DRAMAS: M. Blondel, *La Psychologie dramatique du mystère de la passion à Oberammergau*, Paris, 1911.

RELIGIOUS DRAMAS: Netta Syrett, *The Old Miracle Plays of England*, London, 1911.

REVELATION: C. H. Scharling, *Offenbarung und heilige Schrift*, Leipsic, 1911.

REVIVALS: T. B. Kilpatrick, *New Testament Evangelism*, London and Toronto, 1911.

J. S. Simon, *The Revival of Religion in England in the 18th Century*, London, 1911.

ROMAN CATHOLICS: T. J. Campbell, *Pioneer Priests of North America*, vol. iii., *Among the Algonquins*, New York, 1911.

RUFINUS, TYRANNIUS: *The Works of Rufinus of Aquileia*, in vol. xlvi. of *CSEL*.

SACRED MUSIC: W. A. Barrett, *English Church Composers*, new ed., New York, 1911.

C. F. Price, *The Music and Hymnody of the Methodist Hymnal*, New York, 1911.

SAILER, J. M. VON: R. Stölzle, *Johann Michael Sailer, seine Massregelung an der Akademie zu Dillingen und seine Berufung nach Ingolstadt*, Kempten, 1911.

SALVATION ARMY: A. M. Nicol, *General Booth and the Salvation Army*, London, 1911.

SARPI, P.: K. Benrath, *Neue Briefe von Paolo Sarpi (1608–16). Nach den im fürstlichen Dohna'schen Archiv aufgefundenen Originalen*, Leipsic, 1909.

A. Robertson, *Fra Paolo Sarpi, the Greatest of the Venetians*, London, 1911.

SAVONAROLA: See above, FRANCIS, SAINT, OF ASSISI.

SCHLEIERMACHER, F. D. E.: G. Cross, *The Theology of Schleiermacher*, Cambridge, 1911.

H. Süsskind, *Christentum und Geschichte bei Schleiermacher*, part 1, *Die Absolutheit des Christentums und die Religionsphilosophie*, Tübingen, 1911.

H. Westerburg, *Schleiermacher als Mann der Wissenschaft, als Christ und Patriot*, Göttingen, 1911.

SCHOLASTICISM: M. Grabmann, *Die Geschichte der scholastischen Methode. Nach den gedruckten und ungedruckten Quellen*, 2 vols., Freiburg, 1911.

J. M. Verweyen, *Philosophie und Theologie im Mittelalter. Die historischen Voraussetzungen des Anti-Modernismus*, Bonn, 1911.

SCHOPENHAUER, A.: T. Ruyssen, *Schopenhauer*, Paris, 1911.

SEMITIC LANGUAGES: E. Sachau, *Aramäische Papyrus und Ostraka aus einer jüdischen Militärkolonie zu Elephantine*, Leipsic, 1911.

SMYTH, JOHN: W. H. Burgess, *John Smith the Se-Baptist. Thomas Evans and the First Baptist Church in England, with Fresh Light upon the Pilgrim Fathers' Church*, London, 1911.

SOCIAL SERVICE OF THE CHURCH: S. Z. Batten, *The Social Task of Christianity*, New York, 1911.

A. T. Devine, *The Spirit of Social Work*, New York, 1911.

Mary L. Goss, *Welfare Work by Corporations*, Philadelphia, 1911.

R. A. Woods and A. J. Kennedy, *Handbook of Settlements*, New York, 1911.

SOLOMON, ODES OF: *Les Odes de Salomon*, ed. J. Labourt and P. Batiffol, Paris, 1911.

G. Diettrich, *Die Oden Salomos unter Berücksichtigung der überlieferten Stichengliederung. Aus dem Syrischen ins Deutsche übersetzt und mit einem Kommentar versehen*, Berlin, 1911.

H. Grimme, *Die Oden Salomos. Syrisch, hebräisch, deutsch. Ein kritischer Versuch*, Heidelberg, 1911.

SON OF MAN: E. Hertlein, *Die Menschensohnfrage im letzten Stadium. Ein Versuch zur Einsicht in das Wesen altchristlichen Schrifttums*, Stuttgart, 1911.

SPAIN: W. W. Collins, *Cathedral Cities of Spain*, new ed., New York, 1911.

STRAUSS, D. F.: A. Lévy, *David-Frédéric Strauss. La Vie et l'œuvre*, Paris, 1910.

SUFFERING: J. Hinton, *The Mystery of Pain*, London, 1911.

SUNDAY-SCHOOLS: R. C. Harker, *The Work of the Sunday School: a Manual for Teachers*, New York and Chicago, 1911.

SYMBOLICS: M. A. Curtis, *History of Creeds and Confessions of Faith in Christendom and Beyond. With Historical Tables*, New York and London, 1911.

SYRIAC LITERATURE: *CSCO: Scriptores Syri*, series III., vol. vii.–viii., *Eliæ metropolitæ Nisibeni Opus chronologicum*, ed. . . . E. W. Brooks and I.-B. Chabot, series II., vol. ci., *Dionysius bar Salībī in Apocalypsim actus et epistolas catholicas*, ed. . . . I. Sedlacek; *Scriptores Æthiopici*, series II., vol. xxiv., *Vitæ sanctorum indigenarum*, I. *Acta S. Abakerazun*, II. *Acta S. Takla Hawaryat*, ed. . . . K. Conti Rossini, Leipsic, 1911.

TALMUD: *The Mishna on Idolatry, "Aboda Zara." Edited with translation, vocabulary and notes by W. A. L. Elmslie*, Cambridge, 1911.

THEISM: See above, GIFFORD LECTURES.

THEOLOGICAL LIBRARIES: W. H. Allison, *Inventory of Unpublished Material for American Religious History in Protestant Church Archives and Other Repositories*, Washington, 1910.

THEOLOGY AS A SCIENCE: H. W. Robinson, *The Christian Doctrine of Man*, London, 1911.

H. C. Sheldon, *Theological Encyclopædia: A Brief Account of the Organism and Literature of Theology*, Cincinnati, 1911.

THEOSOPHY: Mrs. A. W. Besant, *Popular Lectures on Theosophy*, Chicago, 1910.

O. Hashnu Hara, *Practical Theosophy. A Plain Statement of its Tenets*, London, 1911.

THOMAS AQUINAS: F. Wagner, *Das natürliche Sittengesetz nach der Lehre des heiligen Thomas von Aquin*, Freiburg, 1911.

THOMASSIN, L.: J. Martin, *Thomassin*, Paris, 1911.

TIME: F. Westberg, *Zur neutestamentlichen Chronologie und Golgathas Ortslage*, Leipsic, 1911.

TITHES: A. F. Marr, *God's Stewards: or, Proportionate Almsgiving*, London, 1911.

TOLSTOY, COUNT LEO: P. Birukoff, *The Life of Tolstoy*, New York, 1911.

TRIBAL AND CULTIC MYSTERIES: J. Burel, *Isis et les isiaques sous l'empire romain*, Paris, 1911.

TRINITY: L. Berthé, *La Sainte Trinité*, Paris, 1911.

TURKEY: N. Jorga, *Geschichte des osmanischen Reiches*, vol. iv., Gotha, 1911.

TYLER, M. C.: *Moses Coit Tyler, 1835–1900. Selections from his Letters and Diaries made and edited by Jessica Tyler Austen*, Garden City, 1911.

ULTRAMONTANISM: J. P. Cannegieter, *Het ultramontanisme en de christenen van Nederland sinds 1853*, Utrecht, 1911.

J. Leute, *Der Ultramontanismus in Theorie und Praxis*, Berlin, 1911.

UNION OF THE CHURCHES: T. Christian, *Other Sheep I have. The Proceedings of the Celestial Commission on Church Unity*, New York, 1911.

VATICAN: *Ye Solace of Pilgrimes: a Description of Rome, circa A. D. 1450 by John Capgrave, an Austin Friar of King's Lynn. Edited by C. A. Mills*, London, 1911.

VOLTAIRE: R. Koser and H. Droysen, *Briefwechsel Friedrichs des Grossen mit Voltaire*, part 3, *Briefwechsel König Friedrichs 1753–78*, Leipsic, 1911.

WESLEY, JOHN: E. B. Chappell, *Studies in the Life of John Wesley*, Nashville, Tenn., 1911.

N. Curnock, *Wesley's Journal*, vol. ii., London, 1911.

WHITGIFT, J.: H. J. Clayton, *Archbishop Whitgift and His Times*, London, 1911.

WITCHCRAFT: Grässe, *Bibliotheca magica et pneumatica*, Leipsic, 1843.

Kernot, *Bibliotheca diabolica*, New York, 1874.

Yve-Plessis, *Bibliographie française de la sorcellerie*, Paris, 1900.

WILL: F. Ballard, *Determinism: False and True. A Contribution to Modern Philosophy and Ethics*, London, 1911.

BIOGRAPHICAL ADDENDA

ALEXANDER, WILLIAM (1): d. in Dublin Sept. 12, 1911.

ARNOLD, C. F.: Became consistorial councilor in 1911.

CARPENTER, W. B.: Resigned bishopric of Ripon, 1911.

CLARKE, W. N.: d. at De Land, Fla., Jan. 14, 1912.

FLICKINGER, D. K.: d. at Columbus, O., Aug. 29, 1911.

HARRIS, G.: Resigned presidency of Amherst College to take effect 1912.

JOHNSON, F. F.: Translated to become bishop coadjutor of the diocese of Missouri.

KENDRICK, J. M.: d. at Los Angeles, Cal., Dec. 16, 1911.

MACARTHUR, R. S.: Retired from pastorate of Calvary Baptist Church, New York, 1911.

McCOOK, H. C.: d. at Devon, near Philadelphia, Oct. 31, 1911.

McGARVEY, J. W.: d. at Lexington, Ky., Oct. 6, 1911.

MACKAY-SMITH, A.: d. in Philadelphia Oct. 16, 1911.

MADSEN, P.: d. at Copenhagen Aug. 7, 1911.

MOFFATT, J.: Became Yates professor of N. T. exegesis at Mansfield College, Oxford, England.

OETTLI, S.: d. at Greifswald Sept. 23, 1911.

PATTERSON, R. M.: d. at Philadelphia, Pa., Apr. 5, 1911.

SEWALL, J. S.: d. at Bangor, Me., Oct. 10, 1911.

ADDENDA ET CORRIGENDA

Vol. i., p. 89, col. 1, line 28: Read "Edward VI." for "Edward I."; p. 492, col. 1, line 7 from bottom: Read "*Heralds*" for "*Perils.*"

Vol. iii., p. 350, col. 1, line 29: Read "Evil-Merodach" for "Eril-Merodach"; p. 401, col. 1, bibliography, line 4 from bottom: Read "Nevius" for "Nevins."

Vol. v., p. 32, col. 1: In signature read "Hollenberg" for "Hallenberg"; p. 127, col. 1, line 27: Remove "(q.v.)"; p. 151, col. 1: In signature read "A" for "R"; p. 351, col. 1: In signature read "Herrmann" for "Hermann"; p. 351, col. 2, line 13 from bottom: Read "Cranmer" for "Franmer"; p. 358, col. 1: Remove † from signature.

Vol. viii., p. 102, col. 2, line 8 from bottom: After "Pa." insert "with a total wealth of nearly a million dollars."

Vol. ix., p. 131, col. 1, line 29: Read "Felix" for "Filix"; p. 132, col. 1, line 5 from bottom: Read "1523–34" for "1534–32"; p. 188, col. 1, line 22: Read "M. Bristol" for "T. Bristol"; p. 302, col. 1, line 19 from bottom: Read "Balmes" for "Balme"; p. 365, col. 1, bibliography: Remove the entry under T. Wright; p. 370, col. 1, line 21 from bottom: Read "1887–88" for "1899"; p. 401, col. 2, line 16: Read "W. R. Greg" for "R. W. Gregg"; p. 402, col. 1, line 28 from bottom: Read "New York" for "London."

Vol. x., p. 19, col. 2, signature: Read "G. E." for "D."; p. 130, col. 2, line 17 from bottom: Read "*mosaische*" for "*mosäische*"; p. 251, col. 2, line 26 from bottom: Read "Decorah" for "Decoran"; p. 454, col. 1, line 22 from bottom: Read "*Ancient*" for "*Early*"; p. 499, col. 2, line 7 from bottom: Read "Life" for "Christology."

Vol. xi., p. 4, col. 1, line 39: Read "T. L. Kingsbury" for "F. C. Cook"; p. 31, col. 1, Signature: Read "Ernst" for "Theodor"; p. 32, col. 1, line 30 from bottom: Read "(1887)" for "(1877)"; p. 39, col. 2, line 30 from bottom: Read "Eliot" for "Elliott," and line 28 from bottom: Read "(1889)" for "(1899)"; p. 52, col. 2, lines 24–23 from bottom: Read "F. W. H. Myers" for "F. W. Meyers"; p. 56, col. 2, line 18 from bottom: Read "1906" for "1896"; p. 75, col. 1, line 17 from bottom: Delete "Maximilian" (a mistake from "M" meaning "magister"); p. 105, col. 2, line 9 from bottom: Read "Agamemnon" for "Agememnon"; p. 165, col. 1, line 18 from bottom: Read "Lawrance" for "Lawrence"; p. 166, col. 2, line 23 from bottom: Read "It ran" for "I ran"; p. 204, col. 1, line 29: Read "Abel" for "Cain" and line 31 read "Cain" for "Abel"; p. 247, col. 2, line 25 from bottom: Read "Casluhim" for "Gasluhim," and last line: Read "on both sides" for "beyond"; p. 248, col. 1, line 19, etc., from bottom: For "If Cush . . . from" read "He refers Cush (verses 8–12) to Babel and separates it from the Arabian stocks (verses 26–29), perhaps because he knew of"; col. 2, line 17: Read "700" for "709"; line 23 from bottom: Read "and means the people of the Mediterranean Sea (cf. verse 4)"; p. 249, col. 1, line 29 from bottom: Read "(xviii." for "(xix.," and line 23 from bottom: Read "Napata" for "Meravi"; col. 2, line 2; Read "*Awalites*" for "*Ayalites*," also line 22: Read "Jokshan" for "Joktan," and line 47: Read "south" for "north"; p. 250, col. 1, line 8: Read "*rpk*" for "*rpd*"; col. 2, line 2: Read "required" for "forbidden"; p. 342, col. 2, line 18 from bottom: Read "W. De" for "T. De"; p. 346, col. 1, line 43: Signature should read "P. W. Crannell"; p. 364, col. 1, lines 17–18: Read "Foecht" for "Foehh," "C. W." for "C. M.", and "Yutzy" for "Zutzy"; p. 430, col. 1, lines 30 and 29 from bottom: Read "in Bavarian Franconia, between Erfurt and Würzburg," for "circuit of Nagold"; p. 434, col. 1, line 21: Insert before "Romanists" the words "Arguments of"; p. 467, col. 2, line 19 from bottom: Read "*How to*" for "*How I*"; p. 472, col. 2, line 32 from bottom: Read "Cutten" for "Culten."

LIST OF ABBREVIATIONS

Abbreviations in common use or self-evident are not included here. For additional information concerning the works listed, see vol. i., pp. viii.–xx., and the appropriate articles in the body of the work.

ADB	*Allgemeine deutsche Biographie*, Leipsic, 1875 sqq., vol. 53, 1907
Adv	*adversus*, "against"
AJP	*American Journal of Philology*, Baltimore, 1880 sqq.
AJT	*American Journal of Theology*, Chicago, 1897 sqq.
AKR	*Archiv für katholisches Kirchenrecht*, Innsbruck, 1857–61, Mainz, 1872 sqq.
ALKG	*Archiv für Litteratur- und Kirchengeschichte des Mittelalters*, Freiburg, 1885 sqq.
Am.	American
AMA	*Abhandlungen der Münchener Akademie*, Munich, 1763 sqq.
ANF	*Ante-Nicene Fathers*, American edition by A. Cleveland Coxe, 8 vols. and index, Buffalo, 1887; vol. ix., ed. Allan Menzies, New York, 1897
Apoc.	Apocrypha, apocryphal
Apol	*Apologia, Apology*
Arab.	Arabic
Aram	Aramaic
art.	article
Art. Schmal	Schmalkald Articles
ASB	*Acta sanctorum*, ed. J. Bolland and others, Antwerp, 1643 sqq.
ASM	*Acta sanctorum ordinis S. Benedicti*, ed. J. Mabillon, 9 vols., Paris, 1668–1701
Assyr	Assyrian
A. T.	*Altes Testament*, "Old Testament"
Augs. Con.	Augsburg Confession
A. V.	Authorized Version (of the English Bible)
Baldwin, *Dictionary*	J. M. Baldwin, *Dictionary of Philosophy and Psychology*, 3 vols. in 4, New York, 1901–05
Bardenhewer, *Geschichte*....	O. Bardenhewer, *Geschichte der altkirchlichen Litteratur*, 2 vols., Freiburg, 1902
Bardenhewer, *Patrologie*....	O. Bardenhewer, *Patrologie*, 2d ed., Freiburg, 1901
Bayle, *Dictionary*....	*The Dictionary Historical and Critical of Mr. Peter Bayle*, 2d ed., 5 vols., London, 1734–38
Benzinger, *Archäologie*...	I. Benzinger, *Hebräische Archäologie*, 2d ed., Freiburg, 1907
Bingham, *Origines*....	J. Bingham, *Origines ecclesiasticæ*, 10 vols., London, 1708–22; new ed., Oxford, 1855
Bouquet, *Recueil*	M. Bouquet, *Recueil des historiens des Gaules et de la France*, continued by various hands, 23 vols., Paris, 1738–76
Bower, *Popes*...	Archibald Bower, *History of the Popes . . . to 1758*, continued by S. H. Cox, 3 vols., Philadelphia, 1845–47
BQR	*Baptist Quarterly Review*, Philadelphia, 1867 sqq.
BRG	See Jaffé
Cant.	Canticles, Song of Solomon
cap	*caput*, "chapter"
Ceillier, *Auteurs sacrés*.	R. Ceillier, *Histoire des auteurs sacrés et ecclésiastiques*, 16 vols. in 17, Paris, 1858–69
Chron	*Chronicon*, "Chronicle"
I Chron.	I Chronicles
II Chron	II Chronicles
CIG	*Corpus inscriptionum Græcarum*, Berlin, 1825 sqq.
CIL	*Corpus inscriptionum Latinarum*, Berlin, 1863 sqq.
CIS	*Corpus inscriptionum Semiticarum*, Paris, 1881 sqq.
cod.	codex
cod. Theod	*codex Theodosianus*
Col.	Epistle to the Colossians
col., cols.	column, columns
Conf	*Confessions*, "Confessions"
I Cor.	First Epistle to the Corinthians
II Cor.	Second Epistle to the Corinthians
COT	See Schrader
CQR	*The Church Quarterly Review*, London, 1875 sqq.
CR.	*Corpus reformatorum*, begun at Halle, 1834, vol. lxxxix., Berlin and Leipsic, 1905 sqq.
Creighton, *Papacy*	M. Creighton, *A History of the Papacy from the Great Schism to the Sack of Rome*, new ed., 6 vols., New York and London, 1897
CSCO	*Corpus scriptorum Christianorum orientalium*, ed. J. B. Chabot, I. Guidi, and others, Paris and Leipsic, 1903 sqq.
CSEL	*Corpus scriptorum ecclesiasticorum Latinorum*, Vienna, 1867 sqq.
CSHB	*Corpus scriptorum historiæ Byzantinæ*, 49 vols., Bonn, 1828–78
Currier, *Religious Orders*.......	C. W. Currier, *History of Religious Orders*, New York, 1896
D.	Deuteronomist
Dan.	Daniel
DB.	J. Hastings, *Dictionary of the Bible*, 4 vols. and extra vol., Edinburgh and New York, 1898–1904
DCA	W. Smith and S. Cheetham, *Dictionary of Christian Antiquities*, 2 vols., London, 1875–80
DCB	W. Smith and H. Wace, *Dictionary of Christian Biography*, 4 vols., Boston, 1877–87
DCG	J. Hastings, J. A. Selbie, and J. C. Lambert, *A Dictionary of Christ and the Gospels*, 2 vols., Edinburgh and New York, 1906–1908
Deut.	Deuteronomy
De vir. ill.	*De viris illustribus*
DGQ	See Wattenbach
DNB	L. Stephen and S. Lee, *Dictionary of National Biography*, 63 vols. and supplement 3 vols., London, 1885–1901
Driver, *Introduction*	S. R. Driver, *Introduction to the Literature of the Old Testament*, 10th ed., New York, 1910
E.	Elohist
EB.	T. K. Cheyne and J. S. Black, *Encyclopædia Biblica*, 4 vols., London and New York, 1899–1903
Eccl.	*Ecclesia*, "Church"; *ecclesiasticus*, "ecclesiastical"
Eccles.	Ecclesiastes
Ecclus	Ecclesiasticus
ed.	*edidit*, "edited by"
Eph	Epistle to the Ephesians
Epist	*Epistola, Epistolæ*, "Epistle," "Epistles"
Ersch and Gruber, *Encyklopädie*.	J. S. Ersch and J. G. Gruber, *Allgemeine Encyklopädie der Wissenschaften und Künste*, Leipsic, 1818 sqq.
E. V.	English versions (of the Bible)
Ex.	Exodus
Ezek.	Ezekiel
fasc	fasciculus
Fr	French
Friedrich, *KD* . .	J. Friedrich, *Kirchengeschichte Deutschlands*, 2 vols., Bamberg, 1867–69
Gal	Epistle to the Galatians
Gams, *Series episcoporum* . .	P. B. Gams, *Series episcoporum ecclesiæ Catholicæ*, Regensburg, 1873, and supplement, 1886
Gee and Hardy, *Documents* ...	H. Gee and W. J. Hardy, *Documents Illustrative of English Church History*, London, 1896
Germ	German
GGA	*Göttingische Gelehrte Anzeigen*, Göttingen, 1824 sqq.
Gibbon, *Decline and Fall*....	E. Gibbon, *History of the Decline and Fall of the Roman Empire*, ed. J. B. Bury, 7 vols., London, 1896–1900
Gk.	Greek
Gross, *Sources*..	C. Gross, *The Sources and Literature of English History . . . to 1485*, London, 1900
Hab.	Habakkuk
Haddan and Stubbs, *Councils*	A. W. Haddan and W. Stubbs, *Councils and Ecclesiastical Documents Relating to Great Britain and Ireland*, 3 vols., Oxford, 1869–78

Hær..........	Refers to patristic works on heresies or heretics, Tertullian's *De præscriptione*, the *Pros haireseis* of Irenæus, the *Panarion* of Epiphanius, etc.
Hag..........	Haggai
Harduin, *Concilia*..	J. Harduin, *Conciliorum collectio regia maxima*, 12 vols., Paris, 1715
Harnack, *Dogma*	A. Harnack, *History of Dogma . . . from the 3d German edition*, 7 vols., Boston, 1895–1900
Harnack, *Litteratur*.......	A. Harnack, *Geschichte der altchristlichen Litteratur bis Eusebius*, 2 vols. in 3, Leipsic, 1893–1904
Hauck, *KD* ...	A. Hauck, *Kirchengeschichte Deutschlands*, vol. i., Leipsic, 1904; vol. ii., 1900; vol. iii., 1906; vol. iv., 1903
Hauck-Herzog, *RE*..........	*Realencyklopädie für protestantische Theologie und Kirche*, founded by J. J. Herzog, 3d ed. by A. Hauck, Leipsic, 1896–1909
Heb..........	Epistle to the Hebrews
Hebr.........	Hebrew
Hefele,*Conciliengeschichte*.....	C. J. von Hefele, *Conciliengeschichte*, continued by J. Hergenröther, vols. i.–vi., viii.–ix., Freiburg, 1883–93
Heimbucher, *Orden und Kongregationen*...	M. Heimbucher, *Die Orden und Kongregationen der katholischen Kirche*, 2d ed. 3 vols., Paderborn, 1907
Helyot, *Ordres monastiques*...	P. Helyot, *Histoire des ordres monastiques, religieux et militaires*, 8 vols., Paris, 1714–19; new ed., 1839–42
Henderson, *Documents*	E. F. Henderson, *Select Historical Documents of the Middle Ages*, London, 1892
Hist............	History, *histoire, historia*
Hist. eccl......	*Historia ecclesiastica, ecclesiæ*, "Church History"
Hom...........	*Homilia, homiliai*, "homily, homilies"
Hos...........	Hosea
Isa............	Isaiah
Ital...........	Italian
J.............	Jahvist (Yahwist)
JA............	*Journal Asiatique*, Paris, 1822 sqq.
Jacobus, *Dictionary*....	*A Standard Bible Dictionary*, ed. M. W. Jacobus, ... E. E. Nourse, ... and A. C. Zenos, New York and London, 1909
Jaffé, *BRG*....	P. Jaffé, *Bibliotheca rerum Germanicarum*, 6 vols., Berlin, 1864–73
Jaffé, *Regesta*...	P. Jaffé, *Regesta pontificum Romanorum . . . ad annum 1198*, Berlin, 1851; 2d ed., Leipsic, 1881–88
JAOS.........	*Journal of the American Oriental Society*, New Haven, 1849 sqq.
JBL...........	*Journal of Biblical Literature and Exegesis*, first appeared as *Journal of the Society of Biblical Literature and Exegesis*, Middletown, 1882–88, then Boston, 1890 sqq.
JE............	*The Jewish Encyclopedia*, 12 vols., New York, 1901–06
JE............	The combined narrative of the Jahvist (Yahwist) and Elohist
Jer...........	Jeremiah
Josephus, *Ant* ..	Flavius Josephus, "Antiquities of the Jews"
Josephus, *Apion*..	Flavius Josephus, "Against Apion"
Josephus, *Life*..	Life of Flavius Josephus
Josephus, *War*..	Flavius Josephus, "The Jewish War"
Josh..........	Joshua
JPT	*Jahrbücher für protestantische Theologie*, Leipsic, 1875 sqq.
JQR	*The Jewish Quarterly Review*, London, 1888 sqq.
JRAS.........	*Journal of the Royal Asiatic Society*, London, 1834 sqq.
JTS	*Journal of Theological Studies*, London, 1899 sqq.
Julian, *Hymnology*	J. Julian, *A Dictionary of Hymnology*, revised edition, London, 1907
KAT	See Schrader
KB............	See Schrader
KD	See Friedrich, Hauck, Rettberg
KL............	*Wetzer und Welte's Kirchenlexikon*, 2d ed., by J. Hergenröther and F. Kaulen, 12 vols., Freiburg, 1882–1903
Krüger, *History*	G. Krüger, *History of Early Christian Literature in the First Three Centuries*, New York, 1897
Krumbacher, *Geschichte*....	K. Krumbacher, *Geschichte der byzantinischen Litteratur*, 2d ed., Munich, 1897
Labbe, *Concilia*	P. Labbe, *Sacrorum conciliorum nova et amplissima collectio*, 31 vols., Florence and Venice, 1759–98
Lam	Lamentations
Lanigan, *Eccl. Hist*	J. Lanigan, *Ecclesiastical History of Ireland to the 13th Century*, 4 vols., Dublin, 1829
Lat...........	Latin, Latinized

Leg	*Leges, Legum*
Lev	Leviticus
Lichtenberger, *ESR*	F. Lichtenberger, *Encyclopédie des sciences religieuses*, 13 vols., Paris, 1877–1882
Lorenz, *DGQ* ..	O. Lorenz. *Deutschlands Geschichtsquellen im Mittelalter*, 3d ed., Berlin, 1887
LXX..........	The Septuagint
I Macc	I Maccabees
II Macc	II Maccabees
Mai, *Nova collectio*	A. Mai, *Scriptorum veterum nova collectio*, 10 vols., Rome, 1825–38
Mal...........	Malachi
Mann, *Popes* ...	R. C. Mann, *Lives of the Popes in the Early Middle Ages*, London, 1902 sqq.
Mansi, *Concilia*.	G. D. Mansi, *Sanctorum conciliorum collectio nova*, 31 vols., Florence and Venice, 1728
Matt..........	Matthew
MGH	*Monumenta Germaniæ historica*, ed. G. H. Pertz and others, Hanover and Berlin, 1826 sqq. The following abbreviations are used for the sections and subsections of this work: *Ant., Antiquitates*, "Antiquities"; *Auct. ant., Auctores antiquissimi*, "Oldest Writers"; *Chron. min., Chronica minora*, "Lesser Chronicles"; *Dip., Diplomata*, "Diplomas, Documents"; *Epist., Epistolæ*, "Letters"; *Gest. pont. Rom., Gesta pontificum Romanorum*, "Deeds of the Popes of Rome"; *Leg., Leges*, "Laws"; *Lib. de lite, Libelli de lite inter regnum et sacerdotium sæculorum xi. et xii. conscripti*, "Books concerning the Strife between the Civil and Ecclesiastical Authorities in the Eleventh and Twelfth Centuries"; *Nec., Necrologia Germaniæ*, "Necrology of Germany"; *Poet. Lat. ævi Car., Poetæ Latini ævi Carolini*, "Latin Poets of the Caroline Time"; *Poet. Lat. med. ævi, Poetæ Latini medii ævi*, "Latin Poets of the Middle Ages"; *Script., Scriptores*, "Writers"; *Script. rer. Germ., Scriptores rerum Germanicarum*, "Writers on German Subjects"; *Script. rer. Langob., Scriptores rerum Langobardicarum et Italicarum*, "Writers on Lombard and Italian Subjects"; *Script. rer. Merov., Scriptores rerum Merovingicarum*, "Writers on Merovingian Subjects"
Mic...........	Micah
Milman, *Latin Christianity*..	H. H. Milman, *History of Latin Christianity, Including that of the Popes to . . . Nicholas V.*, 8 vols., London, 1860–61
Mirbt, *Quellen*..	C. Mirbt, *Quellen zur Geschichte des Papsttums und des römischen Katholicismus*, Tübingen, 1901
MPG..........	J. P. Migne, *Patrologiæ cursus completus, series Græca*, 162 vols., Paris, 1857–66
MPL..........	J. P. Migne, *Patrologiæ cursus completus, series Latinæ*, 221 vols., Paris, 1844–64
MS., MSS......	Manuscript, Manuscripts
Muratori, *Scriptores*.........	L. A. Muratori, *Rerum Italicarum scriptores*, 28 vols., **1723–51**
NA	*Neues Archiv der Gesellschaft für ältere deutsche Geschichtskunde*, Hanover, 1876 sqq.
Nah	Nahum
n.d.	no date of publication
Neander, *Christian Church*..	A. Neander, *General History of the Christian Religion and Church*, **6 vols.**, and index, Boston, 1872–81
Neh	Nehemiah
Niceron, *Mémoires*........	R. P. Niceron, *Mémoires pour servir à l'histoire des hommes illustrés* . . . , 43 vols., Paris, 1729–45
Nielsen, *Papacy*.	F. K. Nielsen, *History of the Papacy in the Nineteenth Century*, 2 vols., New York, 1906
Nippold, *Papacy*.	F. Nippold, *The Papacy in the Nineteenth Century*, New York, 1900
NKZ	*Neue kirchliche Zeitschrift*, Leipsic, 1890 sqq.
Nowack, *Archäologie*........	W. Nowack, *Lehrbuch der hebräischen Archäologie*, 2 vols., Freiburg, 1894
n.p.	no place of publication
NPNF.........	*The Nicene and Post-Nicene Fathers*, 1st series, 14 vols., New York, 1887–92; 2d series, 14 vols., New York, 1890–1900
N. T..........	New Testament, *Novum Testamentum, Nouveau Testament, Neues Testament*
Num..........	Numbers
Ob............	Obadiah

O. S. B........ *Ordo sancti Benedicti,* "Order of St. Benedict"

O. T........... Old Testament

OTJC......... See Smith

P............. Priestly document

Pastor, *Popes*... L. Pastor, *The History of the Popes from the Close of the Middle Ages,* 8 vols., London, 1891–1908

PEA.......... *Patres ecclesiæ Anglicanæ,* ed. J. A. Giles, 34 vols., London, 1838–46

PEF........... Palestine Exploration Fund

I Pet.......... First Epistle of Peter

II Pet......... Second Epistle of Peter

Platina, *Popes*.. B. Platina, *Lives of the Popes from . . . Gregory VII. to . . . Paul II.,* 2 vols., London, n.d.

Pliny, *Hist. nat.*...Pliny, *Historia naturalis*

Potthast, *Weg-weiser*...... A. Potthast, *Bibliotheca historica medii ævi. Wegweiser durch die Geschichtswerke,* Berlin, 1896

Prov.......... Proverbs

Ps............ Psalms

PSBA......... *Proceedings of the Society of Biblical Archeology,* London, 1880 sqq.

q.v., qq.v....... *quod (quæ) vide,* "which see"

Ranke, *Popes*... L. von Ranke, *History of the Popes,* 3 vols., London, 1906

RDM......... *Revue des deux mondes,* Paris, 1831 sqq.

RE............ See Hauck-Herzog

Reich, *Documents*......... E. Reich, *Select Documents Illustrating Mediæval and Modern History,* London, 1905

REJ.......... *Revue des études juives,* Paris, 1880 sqq.

Rettberg, *KD*... F. W. Rettberg, *Kirchengeschichte Deutschlands,* 2 vols., Göttingen, 1846–48

Rev........... Book of Revelation

RHR......... *Revue de l'histoire des religions,* Paris, 1880 sqq.

Richardson, *Encyclopaedia*... E. C. Richardson, *Alphabetical Subject Index and Index Encyclopaedia to Periodical Articles on Religion, 1890–99,* New York, 1907

Richter, *Kirchenrecht*........ A. L. Richter, *Lehrbuch des katholischen und evangelischen Kirchenrechts,* 8th ed. by W. Kahl, Leipsic, 1886

Robinson, *Researches,* and *Later Researches*... E. Robinson, *Biblical Researches in Palestine,* Boston, 1841, and *Later Biblical Researches in Palestine,* 3d ed. of the whole, 3 vols., 1867

Robinson, *European History*.. J. H. Robinson, *Readings in European History,* 2 vols., Boston, 1904–06

Robinson and Beard, *Modern Europe*... J. H. Robinson and C. A. Beard, *Development of Modern Europe,* 2 vols., Boston, 1907

Rom.......... Epistle to the Romans

RTP.......... *Revue de théologie et de philosophie,* Lausanne, 1873

R. V.......... Revised Version (of the English Bible)

sæc.......... *sæculum,* "century"

I Sam......... I Samuel

II Sam........ II Samuel

SBA......... *Sitzungsberichte der Berliner Akademie,* Berlin, 1882 sqq.

SBE......... F. Max Müller and others, *The Sacred Books of the East,* Oxford, 1879 sqq., vol. xlviii., 1904

SBOT......... *Sacred Books of the Old Testament* ("Rainbow Bible"), Leipsic, London, and Baltimore, 1894 sqq.

Schaff, *Christian Church*...... P. Schaff, *History of the Christian Church,* vols. i.–iv., vi., vii., New York, 1882–92, vol. v., 2 parts, by D. S. Schaff, 1907–10

Schaff, *Creeds*.. P. Schaff, *The Creeds of Christendom,* 3 vols., New York, 1877–84

Schrader, *COT*.. E. Schrader, *Cuneiform Inscriptions and the Old Testament,* 2 vols., London, 1885–88

Schrader, *KAT*.. E. Schrader, *Die Keilinschriften und das Alte Testament,* 2 vols., Berlin, 1902–03

Schrader, *KB*... E. Schrader, *Keilinschriftliche Bibliothek,* 6 vols., Berlin, 1889–1901

Schürer, *Geschichte*..... E. Schürer, *Geschichte des jüdischen Volkes im Zeitalter Jesu Christi,* 4th ed., 3 vols., Leipsic, 1902 sqq.; Eng. transl., 5 vols., New York, 1891

Script........ *Scriptores,* "writers"

Scrivener, *Introduction*.. F. H. A. Scrivener, *Introduction to New Testament Criticism,* 4th ed., London, 1894

Sent.......... *Sententiæ,* "Sentences"

S. J.......... *Societas Jesu,* "Society of Jesus"

SMA......... *Sitzungsberichte der Münchener Akademie,* Munich, 1860 sqq.

Smith, *Kinship*.. W. R. Smith, *Kinship and Marriage in Early Arabia,* London, 1903

Smith, *OTJC*... W. R. Smith, *The Old Testament in the Jewish Church,* London, 1892

Smith, *Prophets*.. W. R. Smith, *Prophets of Israel . . . to the Eighth Century,* London, 1895

Smith, *Rel. of Sem*.......... W. R. Smith, *Religion of the Semites,* London, 1894

S. P. C. K..... Society for the Promotion of Christian Knowledge

S. P. G....... Society for the Propagation of the Gospel in Foreign Parts

sqq........... and following

Strom......... *Stromata,* "Miscellanies"

s.v........... *sub voce,* or *sub verbo*

Swete, *Introduction*......... H. B. Swete, *Introduction to the Old Testament in Greek,* London, 1900

Syr........... Syriac

Thatcher and McNeal, *Source Book*......... O. J. Thatcher and E. H. McNeal, *A Source Book for Mediæval History,* New York, 1905

I Thess........ First Epistle to the Thessalonians

II Thess....... Second Epistle to the Thessalonians

ThT.......... *Theologische Tijdschrift,* Amsterdam and Leyden, 1867 sqq.

Tillemont, *Mémoires*........ L. S. le Nain de Tillemont, *Mémoires . . . ecclésiastiques des six premiers siècles,* 16 vols., Paris, 1693–1712

I Tim......... First Epistle to Timothy

II Tim........ Second Epistle to Timothy

TJB.......... *Theologischer Jahresbericht,* Leipsic, 1882–1887, Freiburg, 1888, Brunswick, 1889–1897, Berlin, 1898 sqq.

Tob........... Tobit

TQ........... *Theologische Quartalschrift,* Tübingen, 1819 sqq.

TS........... J. A. Robinson, *Texts and Studies,* Cambridge, 1891 sqq.

TSBA......... *Transactions of the Society of Biblical Archæology,* London, 1872 sqq.

TSK.......... *Theologische Studien und Kritiken,* Hamburg, 1826 sqq.

TU........... *Texte und Untersuchungen zur Geschichte der altchristlichen Litteratur,* ed. O. von Gebhardt and A. Harnack, Leipsic, 1882 sqq.

Ugolini, *Thesaurus*.......... B. Ugolinus, *Thesaurus antiquitatum sacrarum,* 34 vols., Venice. 1744–69

V. T.......... *Vetus Testamentum, Vieux Testament,* "Old Testament"

Wattenbach, *DGQ*......... W. Wattenbach, *Deutschlands Geschichtsquellen,* 5th ed., 2 vols., Berlin, 1885; 6th ed., 1893–94; 7th ed., 1904 sqq.

Wellhausen, *Heidentum*.... J. Wellhausen, *Reste arabischen Heidentums,* Berlin, 1887

Wellhausen, *Prolegomena*... J. Wellhausen, *Prolegomena zur Geschichte Israels,* 5th ed., Berlin, 1905, Eng. transl.. Edinburgh, 1885

ZA........... *Zeitschrift für Assyriologie,* Leipsic, 1886–88, Berlin, 1889 sqq.

Zahn, *Einleitung*......... T. Zahn, *Einleitung in das Neue Testament,* 3d ed., Leipsic, 1907; Eng. transl., *Introduction to the New Testament,* 3 vols., Edinburgh, 1909

Zahn, *Kanon*... T. Zahn, *Geschichte des neutestamentlichen Kanons,* 2 vols., Leipsic, 1888–92

ZATW......... *Zeitschrift für die alttestamentliche Wissenschaft,* Giessen, 1881 sqq.

ZDAL......... *Zeitschrift für deutsches Alterthum und deutsche Literatur,* Berlin, 1876 sqq.

ZDMG........ *Zeitschrift der deutschen morgenländischen Gesellschaft,* Leipsic, 1847 sqq.

ZDP......... *Zeitschrift für deutsche Philologie,* Halle, 1869 sqq.

ZDPV........ *Zeitschrift des deutschen Palästina-Vereins,* Leipsic, 1878 sqq.

Zech.......... Zechariah

Zeph.......... Zephaniah

ZHT.......... *Zeitschrift für die historische Theologie,* published successively at Leipsic, Hamburg, and Gotha, 1832–75

ZKG......... *Zeitschrift für Kirchengeschichte,* Gotha, 1876 sqq.

ZKR......... *Zeitschrift für Kirchenrecht,* Berlin, Tübingen, Freiburg, 1861 sqq.

ZKT......... *Zeitschrift für katholische Theologie,* Innsbruck, 1877 sqq.

ZKW......... *Zeitschrift für kirchliche Wissenschaft und kirchliches Leben,* Leipsic, 1880–89

ZNTW........ *Zeitschrift für die neutestamentliche Wissenschaft,* Giessen, 1900 sqq.

ZPK.......... *Zeitschrift für Protestantismus und Kirche,* Erlangen, 1838–76

ZWT......... *Zeitschrift für wissenschaftliche Theologie,* Jena, 1858–60, Halle, 1861–67, Leipsic, 1868 sqq.

SYSTEM OF TRANSLITERATION

The following system of transliteration has been used for Hebrew:

א = ' or omitted at the beginning of a word.	ז = z	ע = '
	ח = ḥ	פ = p
ב = b	ט = ṭ	פ = ph or p
ב = bh or b	י = y	צ = ẓ
ג = g	כ = k	ק = ḳ
ג = gh or g	כ = kh or k	ר = r
ד = d	ל = l	שׂ = s
ד = dh or d	מ = m	שׁ = sh
ה = h	נ = n	ת = ṯ
ו = w	ס = s	ת = th or ṯ

The vowels are transcribed by a, e, i, o, u, without attempt to indicate quantity or quality. Arabic and other Semitic languages are transliterated according to the same system as Hebrew. Greek is written with Roman characters, the common equivalents being used.

KEY TO PRONUNCIATION

When the pronunciation is self-evident the titles are not respelled; when by mere division and accentuation it can be shown sufficiently clearly the titles have been divided into syllables, and the accented syllables indicated.

ɑ	as in sof*a*	ɵ	as in n*o*t	iu	as in d*u*ration
ā	" " *arm*	ō	" " n*or*	c = k	" " *c*at
a	" " *at*	u	" " f*u*ll[2]	ch	" " chur*ch*
ā	" " *fare*	ū	" " r*u*le	cw = qu	as in *qu*een
e	" " p*e*n[1]	ʊ	" " b*u*t	dh (*th*)	" " *the*
ê	" " f*a*te	ʊ̄	" " b*ur*n	f	" " *f*ancy
i	" " t*i*n	ɑi	" " p*i*ne	g (hard)	" " *g*o
î	" " ma*chi*ne	ɑu	" " *ou*t	н	" " lo*ch* (Scotch)
o	" " *o*bey	ei	" " *oi*l	hw (*wh*)	" " *wh*y
ō	" " n*o*	iū	" " f*ew*	j	" " *j*aw

[1] In accented syllables only; in unaccented syllables it approximates the sound of e in over. The letter n, with a dot beneath it, indicates the sound of n as in ink. Nasal n (as in French words) is rendered n.
[2] In German and French names ü approximates the sound of u in dune.

THE NEW SCHAFF-HERZOG

ENCYCLOPEDIA OF RELIGIOUS KNOWLEDGE

TRENCH, RICHARD CHENEVIX: Archbishop of Dublin, Church of Ireland; b. in Dublin, Ireland, Sept. 5 (9?), 1807; d. in London Mar. 28, 1886. He studied at the schools of Twyford and Harrow, and at Trinity College, Cambridge (B.A., 1829; M.A., 1833; B.D., 1850); traveled in Spain, 1830; was ordained deacon, 1832; became curate to H. J. Rose at Hadleigh, Suffolk, 1833; at Colchester, 1834, then going to Italy; returning, he was ordained priest, 1835; became curate of Curdridge, Hampshire, 1835; and of Alverstoke, 1841; became rector of Itchinstoke, Hants, 1844; examining chaplain to Bishop Wilberforce of Oxford, 1845; was Hulsean lecturer at Cambridge, 1845–46; professor of divinity at King's College, 1846–54; professor of exegesis of the New Testament, 1854–58; dean of Westminster, 1856–64; and archbishop of Dublin, 1864–84. He was a devout and conservative High-churchman of the best type, but his theological writings were free from sectional bias. He threw the weight of his influence against disestablishment. As a writer, he showed choice Biblical, patristic, and modern Anglo-German learning, original thought, and a reverential and truly Christian spirit. His repute in philology equaled that in Biblical criticism. Outside of numerous individual and collected sermons, he was the author of *Notes on the Parables of our Lord* (London, 1841, and often); *Genoveva; a Poem* (1842); *Exposition of the Sermon on the Mount . . . from . . . St. Augustine* (1844); *The Fitness of Holy Scripture for Unfolding the Spiritual Life of Men* (Hulsean Lectures for 1845; Cambridge, 1845); *Christ the Desire of all Nations, or the Unconscious Prophecies of Heathendom* (Hulsean Lectures for 1846; 1846); *Notes on the Miracles of our Lord* (London, 1846 and often); *Sacred Latin Poetry* (1849); *On the Study of Words* (Five Lectures; 1851, and often); *On the Lessons in Proverbs* (Five Lectures; 1853, and often); *Synonyms of the New Testament* (Cambridge, 1854, and often); *Commentary on the Epistles to the Seven Churches in Asia. Revelation i.–iii.* (London, 1861); *Studies in the Gospels* (1867); *Plutarch; his Life, Lives, and Morals* (1873); *Lectures on Mediæval Church History* (1877); *Poems* (new ed., 2 vols., 1885); and edited a *Household Book of English Poetry* (1868).

BIBLIOGRAPHY: *Letters and Memorials of Archbishop Trench*, 2 vols., London, 1888; J. Silvester, *Archbishop Trench . . . a Sketch of his Life and Character*, ib. 1891; *DNB*, lvii. 191–194.

XII.—1

TRENKLE, FRANZ SALES: German Roman Catholic; b. at Waldkirch (9 m. n.n.e. of Freiburg) Jan. 26, 1860. He was educated at the universities of Freiburg (1879–82) and Heidelberg (1884–85; D.D., Freiburg, 1886); became privat-docent at Freiburg for New-Testament exegesis, 1868; and associate professor of the same subject, 1894. He has written a novel, *Willa von Waldkirch* (under the pseudonym of Fritz Frei; Heidelberg, 1900); a commentary on James (Freiburg, 1894); and *Einleitung in das Neue Testament* (1897).

TRENT, COUNCIL OF.

Occasion, Sessions, and Attendance (§ 1).
Objects and General Results (§ 2).
The Canons and Decrees (§ 3).
Publication of Documents (§ 4).

The Council of Trent, the nineteenth (or, according to another reckoning, the eighteenth) of the ecumenical councils recognized by the Roman Catholic Church, takes its name from the place where it was held, a city in the southern and Italian part of the Tyrol (73 m. n.w. of Venice), and lasted, with interruptions, from Dec. 13, 1545, to Dec. 4, 1563. From a doctrinal and disciplinary point of view, it was the most important council in the history of the Roman church, fixing her distinctive faith and practise in relation to the Protestant Evangelical churches. Its decrees were supplemented by the Vatican Council of 1870 (q.v.).

In reply to the bull *Exsurge Domine* of Leo X. (1520) Luther had burned the document and appealed to a general council. From 1522 German diets joined in the appeal, and Charles V. seconded and pressed it as a means of settling the controversy started by the Reformation and of reunifying the Church. After the deliverances of Pius II. in his bull *Execrabilis* (1460) and his reply to the University of Cologne (1463), setting aside the theory of the supremacy of general councils laid down by the Council of Constance (see CONSTANCE, COUNCIL OF), it was the papal policy to avoid councils and the free discussions they developed. Unable, however, to resist the urgency of Charles V., Paul III. (q.v.), after proposing Mantua as the place of meeting, convened the council as exclusively Roman at Trent (at that time a free city of the Holy Roman Empire under a prince-bishop), on Dec. 13, 1545; it was transferred to Bologna in Mar., 1547 from fear

1. Occasion, Sessions, and Attendance.

of the plague; indefinitely prorogued, Sept. 17, 1549; reopened at Trent, May 1, 1551, by Pope Julius III.; broken up by the sudden victory of Elector Maurice of Saxony over the Emperor Charles V., and his march into Tyrol, Apr. 28, 1552; and recalled by Pius IV. for the last time, Jan. 18, 1562, when it continued to its final adjournment, Dec. 4, 1563. It closed with "Anathema to all heretics, anathema, anathema." The history of the council is divided into three distinct periods; from 1545 to 1549, from 1551 to 1552, and from 1562 to 1563. The last was the most important. The number of attending members in the three periods varied considerably. It increased toward the close, but never reached the number of the first ecumenical council at Nicæa (which had 318 members), nor of the last of the Vatican (which numbered 764). The decrees were signed by 255 members, including four papal legates, two cardinals, three patriarchs, twenty-five archbishops, 168 bishops, two-thirds of them being Italians. Lists of the signers are added to the best editions of the decrees. England was represented by Cardinal Reginald Pole, Richard Pate, bishop of Worcester, and after 1562 by Thomas Goldwell, bishop of St. Asaph; Ireland by three bishops, and Germany at no time by more than eight. The Italian and Spanish prelates were vastly preponderant in power and numbers. At the passage of the most important decrees not more than sixty prelates were present.

The object of the council was twofold: (1) to condemn the principles and doctrines of Protestantism, and to define the doctrines of the Roman Catholic Church on all disputed points. It is true the emperor intended it to be a strictly general or truly ecumenical council, at which the Protestants should have a fair hearing. He secured, during the council's second period, 1551–52, an invitation, twice given, to the Protestants to be present, and the council issued a letter of safe-conduct (thirteenth session) and offered them the right of discussion, but denied them a vote. Melanchthon and Johann Brenz (qq.v.), with some other German Lutherans, actually started in 1552 on the journey to Trent. Brenz offered a confession, and Melanchthon, who got no farther than Nuremberg, took with him the irenic statement known as the *Confessio Saxonica*. But the refusal to give to the Protestants the right to vote and the consternation produced by the success of Maurice in his campaign against Charles V. in 1552 effectually put an end to Protestant cooperation. (2) To effect a reformation in discipline or administration. This object had been one of the causes calling forth the reformatory councils, and had been lightly touched upon by the Fifth Lateran under Julius II. and Leo X. The corrupt administration of the Church was one of the secondary causes of the Reformation. Twenty-five public sessions were held, but nearly half of them were spent in solemn formalities. The chief work was done in committees or congregations. The entire management was in the hands of the papal legates. The court of Rome, by diplomacy and intrigue, outwitted all the liberal

2. Objects and General Results.

elements. The council abolished some crying abuses, and introduced or recommended disciplinary reforms affecting the sale of indulgences, the morals of convents, the education of the clergy, the non-residence of bishops, and the careless fulmination of censures, and forbade the duel. These deliverances had a salutary influence on the church. But in regard to the department of doctrine, although liberal evangelical sentiments were uttered by some of the ablest members in favor of the supreme authority of the Scriptures, and justification by faith, no concession whatever was made to Protestantism. The doctrinal decisions of the council are divided into decrees (*decreta*), which contain the positive statement of the Roman dogmas, and into short canons (*canones*), which condemn the dissenting Protestant views with the concluding "*anathema sit.*" They are stated with great clearness, precision, and wisdom. The decree on justification betrays special ability and theological circumspection. The Protestant doctrines, however, are almost always exhibited in an exaggerated form, and mixed up with real heresies, which Protestants condemn as emphatically as the Church of Rome.

The doctrinal acts are as follows: after reaffirming the Niceno-Constantinopolitan Creed (third session), the decree was passed (fourth session) placing the Apocrypha on a par with the other books of the canon and coordinating church tradition with the Scriptures as a rule of faith. The Vulgate translation was affirmed to be authoritative for the text of Scripture. Justification (sixth session) was declared to be offered upon the basis of faith and good works as opposed to the Protestant doctrine of faith alone, and faith was treated as a progressive work. The sacramental character of the seven sacraments was affirmed and the eucharist pronounced a veritable propitiatory sacrifice as well as a sacrament, in which the bread and wine were converted into the body and blood of Christ (thirteenth and twenty-second sessions). It is to be offered for dead and living alike and in giving to the apostles the command "do this in remembrance of me," Christ conferred upon them a sacerdotal power. The practise of withholding the cup from the laity was confirmed (twenty-first session) as one which the Church had commanded from of old for good and sufficient reasons; yet in certain cases the pope was made the supreme arbiter as to whether the rule should be strictly maintained. Ordination (twenty-third session) was given an indelible character. The priesthood of the New Testament takes the place of the Levitical priesthood. To the performance of its functions, the consent of the people is not necessary. In the decrees on marriage (twenty-fourth session) the excellence of the celibate state was reaffirmed, concubinage condemned, and the validity of marriage made dependent upon its being performed before a priest and two witnesses. In the case of a divorce the right of the innocent party to marry again is denied so long as the guilty party is alive, even though the other have committed adultery. In the twenty-fifth and last session,

3. The Canons and Decrees.

the doctrines of purgatory, the invocation of saints, and the worship of relics are reaffirmed, as also the efficacy of indulgences as dispensed by the Church according to the power given her, but with some cautionary recommendations. The council appointed, 1562 (eighteenth session), a commission to prepare a list of forbidden books (*Index librorum prohibitorum*), but it later left the matter to the action of the pope. The preparation of a catechism and revised editions of the Breviary and Missal were also left to the pope.

On adjourning, the synod begged the supreme pontiff to ratify all its decrees and definitions. This petition was complied with by Pius IV., Jan. 26, 1564, in a bull which enjoins strict obedience upon all Roman Catholics, and forbids, under pain of excommunication, all unauthorized interpretation, reserving this to the pope alone, and threatening the disobedient with " the indignation of Almighty God and of his blessed apostles, Peter and Paul." Pius appointed a commission of cardinals to assist him in interpreting and enforcing the decrees. The *Index librorum prohibitorum* was announced 1564, and the following books were issued with the papal imprimatur: the Profession of the Tridentine Faith and the Tridentine Catechism (1566), the Breviary (1568), the Missal (1570), and the Vulgate (1590, and then 1592). The decrees of the council were acknowledged in Italy, Portugal, Poland, and by the Roman Catholic princes of Germany at the diet of 1566. Philip II. accepted them for Spain, Netherland, and Sicily so far as they did not infringe on the royal prerogative. In France they were officially recognized by the king only in their doctrinal parts. The disciplinary sections received official recognition at provincial synods and were enforced by the bishops. No attempt was made to introduce it into England. Pius IV. sent the decrees to Mary, queen of Scots, with a letter dated June 13, 1564, requesting her to publish them in Scotland; but she dared not do it in the face of John Knox and the Reformation.

The canons and decrees of the council have been published very often and in many languages (for a large list consult *British Museum Catalogue*, under " Trent, Council of "). The first issue **4. Publica-** was by P. Manutius (Rome, 1564). **tion of** The best Latin editions are by J. Le **Documents.** Plat (Antwerp, 1779), and by F. Schulte and A. L. Richter (Leipsic, 1853). Other good editions are in vol. vii. of the *Acta et decreta conciliorum recentiorum. Collectio Lacensis* (7 vols., Freiburg, 1870–90), reissued as an independent volume (1892); *Concilium Tridentinum: Diariorum, actorum, epistularum, . . . collectio*, ed. S. Merkle (4 vols., Freiburg, 1901 sqq.; only vols. i.–iv. have as yet appeared); not to overlook Mansi, *Concilia*, xxxv. 345 sqq. Note also Mirbt, *Quellen*, 2d ed, pp. 202–255. The best English edition is by J. Waterworth (London, 1848; *With Essays on the External and Internal History of the Council*). The original acts and debates of the council, as prepared by its general secretary, Bishop Angelo Massarelli, in six large folio volumes, are deposited in the Vatican library, and remained there unpublished for more than 300 years, and

were brought to light, though only in part, by Augustin Theiner, priest of the oratory (d. 1874), in *Acta genuina sancti et œcumenici Concilii Tridentini nunc primum integre edita* (2 vols., Leipsic, 1874). Most of the official documents and private reports, however, which bear upon the council, were made known in the sixteenth century and since. The most complete collection of them is that of J. Le Plat, *Monumentorum ad historiam Concilii Tridentini collectio* (7 vols., Louvain, 1781–87). New materials were brought to light by J. Mendham, *Memoirs of the Council of Trent* (London, 1834–36), from the manuscript history of Cardinal Paleotto; more recently by T. Sickel, *Actenstücke aus österreichischen Archiven* (Vienna, 1872); by J. J. I. von Döllinger (*Ungedruckte Berichte und Tagebücher zur Geschichte des Concilii von Trient* (2 parts, Nördlingen, 1876); and A. von Druffel, *Monumenta Tridentina* (Munich, 1884–97). See also TRIDENTINE PROFESSION OF FAITH.

(P. SCHAFF†.) D. S. SCHAFF.

BIBLIOGRAPHY: Fundamental for the history of the council are the accounts by two Roman Catholics of very different spirit: (1) that of the liberal Fra Paolo [Pietro] Sarpi of Venice, *Istoria del Concilio Tridentino*, London, 1619, often republished, e.g., 4 vols., Florence, 1858, best ed. by P. F. Le Courayer, 3 vols., Amsterdam, 1751, in French, 2 vols., London, 1736, Eng. transl. of the original by Sir N. Brent, London, 1619, and another, 1676, Germ. working over of the matter by D. J. T. L. Danz, Jena, 1846; (2) that of Cardinal Sforza Pallavicino, *Istoria del Concilio di Trento*, 2 vols., Rome, 1656–57, issued also Rome, 1665, Milan, 1717, Lat. transl. by J. B. Giattino, 3 parts, Antwerp, 1670, Fr. transl., 3 vols., Montrouge, 1844–45 (for criticism of these cf. Ranke, *Popes*, iii. 46–79; and J. N. Brischar, *Beurtheilung der Controversen Sarpi's und Pallavicini's in der Geschichte des Trienter Concils*, Tübingen, 1844). Further accounts or discussions are: C. A. Salig, *Hist. des tridentinischen Conciliums*, 3 vols., Halle, 1741–45 (Protestant); I. H. Wessenberg, *Die grossen Kirchenversammlung des 15. und 16. Jahrhunderten*, Constance, 1840 (Roman Catholic); I. F. Bungener, *Hist. du concile de Trente*, 2 vols., Paris, 1847, Eng. transl., 2d ed., Edinburgh, 1853, New York, 1855 (Protestant); T. A. Buckley, *Hist. of the Council of Trent*, London, 1852; idem, *The Canons and Decrees of the Council of Trent, with a Supplement, containing the Condemnation of the Early Reformers, and other Matters*, ib. 1851 (Protestant); W. C. Brownlee, *Doctrinal Decrees and Canons of the Council of Trent, with Preface and Notes*, New York, 1857 (Roman Catholic); E. B. Pusey, *Eirenicon*, Oxford, 1865 (Protestant); W. Arthur, *The Pope, the Kings, and the People*, 2 vols., London, 1877 (one of the best); J. C. L. Gieseler, *Text-Book of Church History*, ed. H. B. Smith, v. 21–58, New York, 1880 (excellent sketch); C. Dejob, *De l'influence du concile de Trente sur la littérature et les beaux-arts*, Paris, 1884; D. Lainez, *Disputationes Tridentinæ*, 2 vols., Innsbruck, 1886 (Roman Catholic); T. R. Evans, *Council of Trent*, London, 1888 (Protestant polemic); R. F. Littledale, *Hist. of the Council of Trent*, London, 1888 (Protestant); J. A. Froude, *Lectures on the Council of Trent*, London, 1896 (posthumous; Protestant, brilliant but partisan, and as issued in unrevised shape unreliable); G. Wolf, *Deutsche Geschichte im Zeitalter der Gegenreformation*, Berlin, 1899; A. R. Pennington, *Counter-Reformation in Europe*, London, 1901; J. G. Mayer, *Das Konzil von Trent und die Gegenreformation im der Schweiz*, 2 vols., Stans, 1900–01; J. Susta, *Die römische Curie und das Concil von Trient*, Vienna, 1904; *Cambridge Modern History*, vol. iii. passim, New York, 1905; R. Mumm, *Die Polemik des Martin Chemnitz gegen das Konzil von Trient*, Leipsic, 1905; J. Hergenröther, *Handbuch der allgemeinen Kirchengeschichte*, ed. J. P. Kirsch, Freiburg, 1909 (Roman Catholic); J. Hesner, *Die Entstehungsgeschichte des Trienter Rechtfertigungsdekretes*, Paderborn, 1909; L. Carcereri, *Il Concilio di Trento*, Bologna, 1910; *Die römische Kurie und das Konzil von Trient unter Pius IV.*, Vienna, 1911;

Ranke, *Popes*, i. 100–267; Schaff, *Creeds*, i. 90–100, ii. 77–210. Discussions are to be found also in the works on the history of doctrine by Harnack, vols. iv.–vii. passim; F. Loofs, pp. 664–676, Halle, 1908; R. Seeberg, ii. 422–440, Leipsic, 1895–98; and J. Schwane, Freiburg, 1890.

TRESPASS OFFERING. See SACRIFICE.

TRESSLER, VICTOR GEORGE AUGUSTINE: Lutheran; b. Somerfield, Pa., Apr. 10, 1866. He was educated at Pennsylvania College, Gettysburg, Pa. (B.A., 1886), McCormick Theological Seminary (1891), and the University of Leipsic (Ph.D., 1900). He was ordained to the Lutheran ministry in 1892, and was pastor of Grace Lutheran Church, San José, Cal., from 1891 to 1898, besides being lecturer in history in San José Academy in 1896–98 and president of the Lutheran Synod of California in 1896–97. He was dean and professor of philosophy in Ansgar College, Hutchinson, Minn., in 1901–02, and professor of Greek in Wittenberg College, Springfield, O., in 1903–05, and since 1905 has been professor of New-Testament philology and criticism in Hamma Divinity School, Springfield. He is the author of *The Political Revolution under Elizabeth* (1901).

TREVES, ARCHBISHOPRIC OF: Probably the oldest German diocese. Christianity seems to have been established in the ancient Gallic city of the same name as early as the second century, though it was not until the reign of Constantine that the faith made rapid progress. [Tradition reports, however, that Eucharius, Valerius, and Maternus were sent by Peter the Apostle to preach in the valley of the Rhine, and that Eucharius was the first bishop of Treves, occupying the episcopal chair for twenty-five years.] In the fifth century the Roman hall of justice at Treves was transformed into the church now preserved in the cathedral, though it was not until the end of the Roman period, late in the fifth century, that the city became predominantly Christian. The origin of the diocese is lost in obscurity, for the reputed disciples of Peter, namely, Eucharius, Valerius, and Maternus, are creations of legend. The first certain bishop was

Agroetius, who attended the Synod of Arles in 314. His successors, Maximinus and Paulinus, aided Athanasius against the Arians, though it is uncertain whether they were metropolitans. The capture of Treves by the Franks, who soon became Christianized, made no interruption in the episcopal line, for at the very time of the struggle Bishop Jamblichus (c. 457) is mentioned, and his successors, Nicetius (after 527), Magnericus (570–596), and others were of metropolitan rank. This dignity, however, was lost during the confusion toward the close of the Merovingian period, but was restored by Charlemagne before 811, and retained until the early part of the nineteenth century. The diocese comprised the territory on both sides of the Mosel, from the present boundary with Prussia and Lorraine to the entrance of the river into the Rhine, and, across the Rhine, a small strip of land on both banks of the Lahn to a point above Wetzlar. Metz, Toul, and Verdun were suffragan bishoprics.

(A. HAUCK.)

BIBLIOGRAPHY: Sources are: J. N. von Hontheim, *Historia Trevirensium diplomatum*, 3 vols., Augsburg, 1750; idem, *Prodromus historiæ Trevirensis*, 2 vols., ib. 1757; *Codex diplomaticus Rheno-Mosellanus*, ed. W. Günther, 5 vols., Coblenz, 1822–26; *Urkundenbuch zur Geschichte der . . . mittelrheinischen Territorien*, ed. H. Beyer and others, 3 vols., ib. 1860–74; *MGH, Dip.*, i (1872); *Diplomata regum et imperatorum Germaniæ*, 3 vols., Hanover, 1879–1903; F. X. Kraus, *Die christlichen Inschriften der Rheinlande*, 2 parts, nos. 75–255, Freiburg, 1890; *Gesta Trevirorum*, in *MGH, Script.*, viii (1848), 111 sqq., xxiv (1879), 368 sqq., and *Series archiepiscoporum Treverensium*, in the same, xiii (1881), 296 sqq.; A. Görz, *Regesten der Erzbischöfen von Trier*, 2 vols., Treves, 1859–61. Consult further: J. Marx, *Geschichte des Erzstifts Trier*, 5 vols., Treves, 1858–64; J. Wegler, *Richard von Greiffenclau, Erzbischof und Kurfürst von Trier, 1511-31*, ib. 1881; F. Ferdinand, *Cuno von Falkenstein als Erzbischof von Trier, 1377*, Paderborn, 1886; S. Beissel, *Geschichte der Trierer Kirchen*, Treves, 1887; P. de Lorenzi, *Beiträge zur Geschichte der Pfarreien der Diözese Trier*, 2 vols., ib. 1887; K. Schorn, *Eiflia sacra*, 2 vols., Bonn, 1887–88; H. V. Sauerland, *Trierer Geschichtsquellen des XI. Jahrhunderts*, Treves, 1889; J. Mohr, *Die Heiligen der Diözese Trier*, ib. 1892; K. Vogt, *Die Reichspolitik des Erzbischofs Balduin von Trier in den Jahren 1328-34*, Gotha, 1901; and the *KD* of Rettberg, Friedrich, and Hauck.

TREVES, HOLY COAT OF. See HOLY COAT.

TRIBAL AND CULTIC MYSTERIES.

I. Tribal Mysteries: A mystery is defined by Miss Jane Ellen Harrison (*Prolegomena to the Study of Greek Religion*, p. 151, 2d ed., Cambridge, 1908) as " a rite in which certain *sacra* are exhibited which can not be safely seen by the worshiper till he has undergone certain purifications." This holds true both for tribal and cultic mysteries. Primitive peoples restrain non-initiates from sight of *sacra* for the reasons that such sight is a breach

1. Definitions.

of taboo which (they suppose) would bring evil on the tribe, and punish such breach in order to expurgate the crime and relieve the tribe of the onus of guilt and the evil consequences supposed to result from the transgression. By tribal mysteries are meant those rites of initiation of boys (and in some regions of girls) at the time of reaching manhood (or womanhood) into the rights of adultship as conceived by the tribe, together with the later developments, coming with advance in civilization, into tribal and magical fraternities. By cultic mysteries are meant the more advanced organizations which found place, e.g., in Greece and the Roman Empire and are best exemplified by the Eleusinian, Dionysiac (Bacchic), and Orphic celebrations. The reason for treating these together will be found from the discussion which follows to rest upon an actual genetic relationship and upon a real resemblance in aim, allowance being made for the difference in the grade of culture reached. The reason for discussing the subject at all is its fundamental importance not only in religion but in society, these institutions having had much to do with molding the social, ethical, and religious life of the peoples among which they have existed.

The two bases in nature of the institution here called tribal mysteries are (1) the ineffaceable distinction of sex, the female being almost universally regarded in primitive society as the **2. Basal** inferior and therefore limited in nat-**Factors.** tural privileges; and (2) the distinction, effaceable by age, of the boy from the man, the former being classed in society with the women. Initiation marks the formal separation of the boy from social classification with women and from tutelage by them, together with release from the disabilities which that classification imposes and the assumption of the rights and duties of manhood, or, at any rate, the taking of the first steps toward that assumption. But among primitive peoples in probably most cases the distinction between man and boy not being regarded as erased by age alone, ceremonial must come to the aid of nature. An unitiated male, even though aged, is classed with the women and rests under their tribal disabilities (A. W. Howitt, *Native Tribes of South-Eastern Australia*, p. 530, London, 1904). It is quite in accordance with primitive logic that the ceremonial should have the two characteristics of secrecy and an ordeal. The change from boyhood to manhood involves the power to procreate, and before the mystery of new life the savage stands in awe. It is in his mind related with the power of spirits, therefore within the realm of religion; the favor of these spirits and the successful use of the powers of manhood depend upon a certain correctness of procedure, hence it comes within the domain also of primitive magic. In both of these regions there rule the ideas which under the Romans came to be expressed as *sacra* and *profana*, involving the participation in certain rites by definite classes and the exclusion from them of other classes. Because of the assumed inferiority of the women, on account of their natural disabilities as conceived by primitive logic, they and all who were classed with them could not participate in or even witness the ceremonial which began the transformation of the boy into the man. The adult males alone were possessed of knowledge of the means by which aspirants to adult male rights could attain those rights, or, to express the idea in other words, could become members of the tribe in full standing, sharing by favor of the spirits in its government and in such duties as fell to the men. Hence it was the initiated adult males and the candidates alone who might be present either to participate in or to witness the initiation, and in many cases only the elders, those retired from such services as fighting and the like, conducted the ceremonies. Further, because the initiation marked the admission of the candidate to manhood with its responsibilities, the rites most often assumed the character of an ordeal which aimed to test his qualifications for the rank to which he aspired. Once more, because the successful passing of the ordeal involved ultimate eligibility to marriage, rites were performed looking to the married state, such as Circumcision (q.v.) and sometimes subincision.

It follows directly from the foregoing that the tribe divides into two broad sections, the initiated (males) and the women and non-initi-**3. Develop-** ates. The former constitute what is **ments of** to all intents and purposes a secret **Tribal** society. Secrecy is enforced by a **Societies.** series of taboos, the breach of which involves severe penalties. Thus over a wide area including Australia the sight of a bull-roarer * by a woman subjects her to death. The matter which is kept secret varies with the tribe, but may be described in general terms as the rites of initiation and the methods of performing them, including the masks, disguises of the performers, the dances, and the songs which constitute part of the ceremonies, as well as the traditional significance of them all. The broad division of tribal members into two classes gives place as social order advances into a more complex system which works out in three ways: (1) It may split up into societies in which there are various degrees with admission from one to another and rising in importance and prestige. The basal distinction here is age; but the number of degrees or other distinguishing characteristics varies with the tribe or people. The influence of the individual in the tribe generally depends upon his advancement through and status in the various grades. (2) On the other hand, the society may become intertribal, like the totem gens, and the occasion of initiation, often becoming stated, is an affair not of a single tribe alone, but of the initiates and candidates of the several tribes thus affiliated. The effect of this in the direction of social development will be seen at once. It is wholly natural that at such assemblages intertribal matters be discussed, occasions of dispute be talked over, and that causes that might lead to war, to say nothing of individual differences, may be so considered as to lead to complete pacification. At such times an intertribal peace prevails under penalty of death for its breach. The immediate consequences are a decided advance in social structure and ethical well-being. (3) The third method of development is into what may be described as the magical fraternity, the total re-

---

* A bull-roarer is a piece of wood carved in the shape of an elongated rhomboid or modification of that form, attached by one end to a string, and swung rapidly around the head by the string, producing a peculiar and very penetrating sound. It was used by the Greeks and by them called a rhombos. The sound made by this instrument is often the signal that puberty rites are being or are about to be celebrated and that the profane are to remain at a distance and out of sight. The exhibition of the instrument is usually an invitation or a command to attend the ceremonies.

sults of which are often the reverse of good in their effects upon the social organization.

The initiations being of moment to the tribe, they are celebrated as occasions of festivity which appeal to every initiated member. The materials for the festivities are provided in part by the 4. Social fathers of the candidates, in part by Character. the tribe at large. As culture advances, the number of the initiated comes to be less than all the males of the tribe. In the case where centralization of power in the hands of the chief has not developed, where the government is rather by elders, the ideal fostered by the mysteries is strongly that of fidelity to the tribe as represented by the elders, who conduct the ceremonies in the presence of the initiates. Where centralization has occurred, a less democratic organization may arise, various secret societies may form, more or less limited in membership and with different demands for qualification on the part of aspirants to membership. In these cases the ceremonies may grow in complexity and impressiveness, and the religious element is often more stressed, so that these become largely the guardian of religion. In such a situation puberty ceremonies become more curtailed and do not carry with them membership in the societies. These more aristocratic organizations involve not universal obligation, as do the most primitive type, but special privilege, the obtaining of which requires not only the suffrage of members, but also no slight expenditure, which in turn secures such a degree of consideration in the tribe as seems quite commensurate with the difficulty and expense attendant. The performance of the rites still required at puberty devolves upon the higher grades in the societies, each of which grades has its own ceremony of initiation possibly performed at considerable intervals. Entrance into these, therefore, becomes a desideratum to the ambitious. Where this stage of civilization is reached, the separation of the boy from his parents may take place at as early an age as five years, and the course of instruction and service to the tribe may last till he is forty or till his father dies and he enters upon his inheritance. In the tribal societies the simplicity and naïveté of primitive faith dies, and self-seeking enters in with an almost inevitable duplicity and deceit, advancing to extortion and governing by oppression and even murder, as in the interior of Africa. In cases not a few the tribal society becomes a means of perpetuating the power of the elders and of securing for them an easy support in their old age. Necessarily, the conditions described in the preceding paragraphs tend to die out with progress in culture, the mysteries may come to be no secret, and the proscribed classes may obtain admission at any rate as witnesses. Among the North American Indians, who are in this stage, the institution of initiation has as its central feature the lonely puberty watch of the candidate, who under the stress of fasting and mental effort dreams of an animal or spirit which thus becomes his guardian genius. Still, the fraternities which are associated with this stage evidently often perpetuate the principal religious beliefs and ceremonies of earlier conditions.

With the belief in the virtue of magic invariable among primitive peoples, it is not strange that magical fraternities should form about 5. Magical the rites of initiation, and that the Fraternities. ceremonies should not seldom come to have association with the purpose of securing success in hunting and agriculture. One of the fundamental ideas of initiation is correctness of one's status with respect to marriage (and therefore the obtaining of progeny). In primitive logic the step from this end to consideration of the means of living is a short one. Mimetic magic is resorted to for success in various undertakings, as in the buffalo dance of the Indians (G. Catlin, *Report of Smithsonian Institution for 1885*, ii. 309–311, Washington, 1886). And as deceased ancestors are supposed to have power for good or ill in the directions of increase of progeny and of the fruits of the chase and of toil, it is not strange that societies form around the cult of ancestors. In many societies the dead are regarded as members still active though unseen. Such organizations, in this way bound to the past yet actively interested in present welfare, become repositories of tradition, creators of secret ritual, and protectors of such rude poetic art as exists under such conditions. On the other hand, they may and do degenerate and become the centers of orgies and practises too horrible to describe, especially in Africa, where the worst results of this species of domination are found. In short, the phenomena attending the initiation into the mysteries among primitives illustrate both the noblest and the meanest qualities of humanity. They have contributed both to the uplift and to the degeneration of peoples, and exhibit the lofty and worthy aspirations of man as well as his most lamentable failings.

In the most primitive conditions and when tribes are migratory, no exact location other than some place apart from the tribal camp is 6. The fixed for the ceremonies. In these "Men's circumstances it is usual for the bache-House." lors and boys to camp apart from the place where the families are settled for the time being. The rites are in a still more retired location, guarded from intrusion by the noise of the bull-roarer or other instrument, the sound of which indicates that the ceremonies are in progress. Where settled habitations are the rule, the separation of the sexes already referred to has brought about in many communities the establishment of the "men's house." This is usually the most conspicuous structure in the place, and admission to it is denied to the non-initiates, or at least to those not eligible to initiation. There the unmarried males may live, or at the most sleep, their separation from the women necessitating nonparticipation in family life. This house becomes the center and locus of the mysteries, and as development proceeds, societies and fraternities make it their home. With the multiplication of fraternities, there may be several of these houses in a community. This house serves the purpose also of council house, may answer the uses of the modern club, or may even become the center of defense in case of attack. Celebrations take place in or before it, and to it news is brought which is of importance to the tribe. The area where the " men's house " is known to have existed within the modern period is essentially conterminous with the regions inhabited by primitive peoples in Asia, Oceanica, the New World, and rarely in Australia.

Inasmuch as the reason for the existence of the mysteries is in general the induction of the pubescent youth into the rights and proper manner of performing the duties of manhood, **7. Methods** there is involved preparation for mar-**of** riage in certain ways deemed neces-**Initiation.** sary by peoples in that stage of civilization. The particular methods depend upon the traditions, usages, and ideas of the tribe, group of tribes, or people. The practises that prevail imply two salient ideas: (1) the ordeal, involving much of severe pain, physical and mental, and suffering that may and sometimes does terminate fatally, while successful passing of the trial establishes the right of the candidate to admission to the ranks of warriors, or at least to such instruction as will fit him for that status; (2) instruction in the manner of performing the duties, religious and social, which the new position involves. Very often the ordeal involves mutilations which are permanent, and supposedly may serve the triple purpose of marks that prove the fact of initiation and the right to manhood's privileges, of testing the aspirant's courage and power to endure pain without complaint and even with indifference, and in the most common rite (that of circumcision) of fitting the candidate for the duties of marriage. At the time of initiation the boys are taken from the women and girls, occasionally assuming a particular garb indicative of their candidateship. They are conducted to the men's encampment or men's house (see above, § 6); in some cases the surrender of the boys by the women is the occasion of ceremonies that are dramatic and impressive, and emphasize the new status to which the boys aspire. After their separation the boys are instructed by precept and often by ceremonial, are told that they have passed from childhood and its ways, and that their place is henceforth with the men, from whom they are to receive the lessons in war or hunting or other duties which are to make them worthy members of society. The novice after initiation is supposed to be a new being. Quite generally his death and resurrection are dramatically represented. In the light of more developed institutions it is evident that this ceremonial is a crude way of expressing purification; the fundamental notion is not altogether foreign to the Pauline idea " dead to sin " (Rom. vi. 2). It is not impossible that under hypnotic influence the candidate actually believes that he has died and come again to life. The women either hold this belief or feign it. The candidates are daubed with filth, mud, powder, or gypsum, and the removal of this is symbolic of the casting off of that which had separated them from the full measure of manhood. Sometimes they are believed to pass away and to be reborn. Indeed, it is often startling to find the very arcana of Christianity anticipated in the rites and beliefs and even the words of Australian or primitive American savages. The

period of seclusion varies from a few days to a year, often on scanty, even repulsive, rations. The fact of the new birth or resurrection is signalized by the reception of a new and (it may be) secret name (this feature continues in the cultic mysteries; cf. also Rev. ii. 17 and often, for that book lays great emphasis upon the new name), and even by acquiring a new and mystic language. The initiates may pretend that they have lost all their former stock of knowledge. Over a large area, besides the mutilations already named, depilation, tattooing, painting, boring of nose, lip, or ear, loss of one or more teeth (generally incisors), scorching by fire, drinking of blood, or heavy floggings may serve as accompaniments. Especially is much made of the exhibition of certain paraphernalia, such as the instruments of noise and certain symbolic articles which vary in different surroundings, but may not be spoken of in mixed company.

The instruction during the period of seclusion is in general, even among the rudest tribes, of a character which must astonish by its salutariness those who suppose that with a high grade of civilization alone are developed the moralities, especially those concerning sex and property. Alto-**8. Educa-** gether outside of what pertains to **tional** every-day necessities (which in this **Value.** type of society include besides the ways of obtaining food by hunting and fishing, as well as its preparation, also the art and methods of war), there is the education of the boys in conduct toward women which is not a whit lower than is involved by standards of sexual morality in " enlightened " lands. By inculcation of sheer self-control a restraint upon indulgence is achieved which more pretentious grades of culture accomplish only through the seclusion of women. And the task of self-control is made the more difficult because of the system of taboo and the restrictions imposed by the rules which complicate the ideas of relationship and prevent intermarriage between certain classes within the tribe. So the candidate receives instruction regarding the choice of a wife which may legally be made, and is charged to keep strictly within those lines. He is cautioned against promiscuity and unchastity (though in a few regions the period of initiation is followed by a sort of orgy). He is taught the necessity of obedience to the elders, of fidelity to tribal obligations, is instructed in the geography of the tribal possessions and the necessity in the public interest of remaining within the tribal boundaries. The qualities of truthfulness, justness, honesty, generosity, kindness to the weak, filial regard, courage, good judgment are enjoined, while even the principle of eugenics from the viewpoint of tribal advantage is emphasized. Fidelity to the tribe is urged through the impartation of its history and its relations with other tribes, and the native games, songs, and dances (having religious purport); the secrets and obligations of the system of totems and taboos are also communicated. Through the advice coming from the elders around the camp-fire after the daily labors are ended, the admiration and regard of the youth are won, the feeling of brotherhood is fostered, and a sobering effect is produced. So pronounced are these effects that taken together they almost warrant the fiction of a new birth. This course of instruction may continue over a considerable period—among the Masai of Africa until the age of forty. And the ceremonial has further value in that it requires legitimate membership in the tribe, the children of illegitimate intercourse not being eligible. It involves also a degree of economical forethought in that the parent must have sufficient property to contribute to the feast customary at the mysteries. Those who are barred by disabilities are placed in so inferior a position that the effects can hardly be appreciated by more advanced peoples. Loyalty to the elders and fellow tribesmen and self-interest combine to the perpetuation of the mysteries and the preservation of their secrets, while a useful tribal solidarity is not the least of the benefits. Qualities of real service in the way of character, amid much that is superstitious and harmful, even base, are fostered by this institution.   ..

Impartial study of tribal mysteries, the merest outlines of which are sketched in the preceding paragraphs, makes clear that the entire
9. Influence social, religious, and political economy
on Social of primitive life centers in them. They
Develop- are responsible for the formation of
ment. character in youth; the ideas then instilled control the domestic, social, and religious life of the adult. They are a strongly conservative force, based on a crude, empiric, yet often correct utilitarianism, which in many of its aspects is highly ethical. Individual and social morality are in the main their products. All this is true of even the crudest forms. The secret and magical fraternities into which the primary mysteries develop influence no less profoundly the three departments of human life and are potent in the evolution of the social organism. So that from a historical standpoint alone the subject is worthy of serious attention. When it comes to be seen that the Eleusinian, Orphic, and other mysteries which dominated so large a portion of Greek life, but elaborated and philosophized upon the central ideas of the primitive variety, the historical importance of these primitive forms becomes still more evident.

II. Cultic Mysteries.—1. The Eleusinia: The typical mysteries of this sort are Greek. For a thorough appreciation of their importance and relations a prerequisite is knowledge of at least the
1. Greek barest outlines of Greek religious his-
Religious tory as the study of the last decade
Back- has revealed it. The knowledge of
ground. Greek religion common since the dominance of Christianity is founded upon the pantheon of Homer and the mythology systematized by Hesiod. These were reflected in the writings known as the Greek classics and are the substance on which the official cults were founded. The Homeric deities are Aphrodite, Apollo, Ares, Artemis, Athene, Hephæstos, Hera, Poseidon, and Zeus, " king and ruler of gods and men." But there are constant reminders, in the mention of other deities, even in the classics, that these Homeric gods were not all in whom the Greeks believed. Recent investigation has made it clear that in the folk religion, which had not the prestige of the state cults, these other deities had a large part. It is proved now that the members of the Homeric pantheon were invaders, not indigenous among the dark-haired pre-Homeric Greeks, and that they were the objects of worship of the " fair-haired " hosts that beleaguered Troy. Before them there had come in other cults which had in some cases persisted, and there were indigenous nature deities whose worship and sacrifices the invaders adopted or appropriated, these latter taking over the cults and the shrines of the older gods, even though the sacrifices and the mode of worship were sometimes incongruous and even inappropriate according to common Greek ideas (as when Zeus, a heaven god, in two cases received the sacrifice of a pig, which was appropriate only to a chthonic or earth-god). These earlier deities were for the most part chthonic, their concern was the produce of the earth, and to the worship of these peasants and country folk clung with a persistency that even the gorgeous temples, stately worship, and high art inspired by the new gods could not shake. As in India after the decline of Buddhism the native faiths forced a compromise with the philosophic faith of Brahmanism that resulted in Hinduism, so in Greece the control over the religious mind held by Cybele or Rhea, by Demeter, Persephone, or Ge, by Dionysus and Leto and Selene not only held firm, but in some cases forced recognition by the State. It was in connection with this group of deities, to whom must be added the prophet Orpheus, that the cultic mysteries were observed. And that the mysteries in which these deities were the foci of attention existed practically throughout the Greek world is susceptible of proof. During several centuries immediately preceding the Christian era they were syncretized or diluted or adulterated by ruder elements brought in from Asia Minor or Crete or Thrace, in all of which regions orgiastic and primitive ceremonies seem to have been cultivated with an abandon that removed them but little if at all from savage rites. But the distinction between the Greek cultic mystery and the tribal celebration is, in large, that the former crystallize about personal deities, and these deities are chthonic or concerned with the fruits of the earth (Lenormant, in *Contemporary Review*, 1880, i. 848–849). The deities that stand out in this relation are the " Great Mother " of Asia Minor, who takes form in Greece in, e.g., Demeter and Kore, and, among male gods, Dionysus, " lord of the grape and its blood-red juice."

It may be taken as proved, however, that the Greek mysteries of the historical period are to be
2. Origin traced to clan celebrations probably
of the of the same character as those de-
Eleusinia. scribed in the first part of this discussion. That the clan organization, if not upon a totemic basis at least with totemic accompaniments, existed in Greece in the prehistoric period and that it left observances which survived in the historic period are axiomatic for comparative religionists. And this clan organization implies the mystic initiation. The association of the clan mysteries with definite deities presents no difficulties. The development of ghosts into demi-

gods and of spirits into great deities are well-known phenomena; the centers of crystallization were furnished by foreign gods brought in with the earlier migrations. In such cases as the Eleusinian mysteries (which will be taken as the typical example here), the focusing upon Demeter and Kore is explained by the elements of the myth itself—in the narrative of a period of unfruitfulness followed by a return of harvest attributed to the goddess. The adoption is precisely parallel to the acclaim of Yahweh by Israel after the passage of the Red Sea and the defeat of the Amalekites. The early local character of the mysteries celebrated at Eleusis (12 m. n.w. of Athens) is attested by a large number of facts, the most prominent of which is the performance of the principal rites (" greater mysteries ") at Eleusis while only the preliminary rites (" lesser mysteries ") were performed at Athens. Moreover, this latter celebration was instituted almost certainly after the subjection of Eleusis to Athens in the seventh century B.C., and was clearly a political move to afford the suzerain city a share in the popular observances and to foster local pride. Almost as decisive a proof is the hereditary transmission of the principal functions in the mysteries and the restriction of knowledge of the higher secrets to certain families of Eleusis, the Eumolpidæ, Triptolemidæ, and Diocletidæ, and to these were given a heroic or semi-divine ancestry. Other indications of derivation from primitive puberty rites are the requirements of adultship in the candidates, as well as (in early times) of local citizenship, and (in all times) of legitimacy of birth; here also are to be placed the retention among the *sacra* of implements originally magical (so far as the reports of the *sacra* are to be trusted), the early meaning of which was lost while a palpably secondary and more philosophical symbolism was read into them.

The facts adduced, and a number of others, warrant selection of the Eleusinia as illustrative and typical of this type of rites. Significant are not only the evident ancestry, and a tendency to syncretism, but also the esteem in which

3. Estimates of the Eleusinia. they were held, their duration throughout a millennium of history, and the abiding secrecy which veiled the proceedings. How highly they were regarded is witnessed by a series of testimonies. Thus Pausanias says (V., x. 1): " There is nothing on which the blessing of God rests in so full measure as the rites of Eleusis and the Olympic games "; Pindar (ed. C. J. T. Mommsen, p. 470, Berlin, 1864) declares: " O happy one, who goes beneath the hollow earth having witnessed these (mysteries)! he indeed knows the issues of life "; Sophocles remarks (as cited by Plutarch, *Quomodo adolescens*, iii.): " Thrice blessed the mortals who, having contemplated these mysteries, have descended to Hades; for those only will there be a future life [of happiness], the others will find there nothing but suffering "; and the Homeric Hymn to Demeter reads: " Happy he among mortal men who hath beheld these things! he that is uninitiate, and hath no lot in them, hath never equal lot in death beneath the murky gloom " (Andrew Lang, *Homeric Hymns*, p. 210, London, 1899). The history can be traced from Pindar and

the Homeric Hymns in the seventh century B.C. to 396 A.D.; the mysteries survived the edicts of the Christian emperors, but the monks who accompanied Alaric to Attica in 396 secured the destruction of the temples and buildings at Eleusis in which the mystic drama had its home. For the continuance of the secrecy there are in evidence not only the still dense ignorance respecting the ritual and the fact that what little is known is the result of patient gleaning from every available source covering a millennium of Greek and Roman literature (best gathered in C. A. Lobeck, *Aglaophamus*, Regensburg, 1829), but also the explicit testimony of Gregory Nazianzen: " Eleusis knows as well as the witnesses the secret of this spectacle (the drama), which is with reason kept so profound " (" Oration XXXIX. On the Holy Lights," in *NPNF*, 2 ser., vii., 353).

The myth which lay at the base of the Eleusinia as celebrated in the historical period was that Kore,

4. The Kore Myth. daughter of Demeter, was seized while gathering flowers and carried away by Hades, king of the lower world, Zeus conniving at the deed. Demeter wandered disconsolate over the earth seeking knowledge of her daughter, and at last was told by Helios, who alone had seen the rape, what had been done; after nine days' wandering she arrived at Eleusis in the guise of an old woman, where she seated herself by the sacred spring. She was kindly received by Celeus, king of the place, but declined refreshment in the shape of wine, directing, however, preparation of the *kykeon*—a compound of meal and water flavored with crushed mint, with which she broke her long fast. She became nurse to the infant son of Celeus, whom by daily anointing with ambrosial ointment and nightly baths of fire she intended to make immortal. But the mother was suspicious, spied on the goddess, was terrified at sight of the flames, and, crying out, foiled the purpose of Demeter. The latter then revealed herself, directed a temple to be built in her honor, and in this took up her dwelling; she then inaugurated the mysteries, the conduct of which she taught to the families of Eumolpus, Triptolemus, and Diocles, directing them ever to keep secret the knowledge imparted in the ceremonies from all but initiates (Arnobius, " Against the Heathen," v. 25, *ANF*, vi. 499; A. Lang, ut sup., pp. 209–210). Still she mourned her daughter, and in sympathy the earth refused its fruits, till the extinction of the race of men and discontinuation of offerings to the gods were threatened. Zeus then sent Hermes to the lower world to release Kore and have her brought back to earth. Hades had, however, prevailed upon the maiden to eat a pomegranate seed, and, having eaten, she was bound to return thither, though a season of dwelling upon earth was permitted. So maid and mother were reunited at Eleusis, and the earth once more became fruitful (for a parallel to this myth see TAMMUZ-ADONIS, § 4; for the *descensus ad inferos* see SUN AND SUN WORSHIP, II., § 7). Eumolpus was accredited with the actual establishment of the ceremonies, and in his family remained the chief places in the conduct of the mysteries. The natural objects in Eleusis made sacred by the visit of Demeter were the hill where the shrine was erected, and the spring Callichoros shaded by the olive-tree under which Demeter rested. Into the myth as related above there were gradually woven Dionysiac and Orphic elements, which yet never obscured, as they did elsewhere, the local motif.

The myth is evidently etiological; a dearth may have been the occasion of the introduction of the Demeter and Kore elements that covered the more primitive rationale of the earlier clan rites. What seems to have escaped the attention of observers is the discord between myth and ceremonial. The former relates the reunion in the autumn of maid and mother—the season of harvest and of sowing of winter grain. The disappearance of Kore is by common consent the sowing of the seed corn, and this reappears (comes from the underworld) in its green sprouts in the spring, and spring, according to all analogy, should be the time of reunion of mother and daughter. Moreover, harvest offerings were, according to epigraphic evidence, a part of the involved ritual at Eleusis. The myth was, therefore, forced into connection with the Eleusinia, was superimposed upon the old clan ceremonies, just as the Dionysiac-Iacchic-Orphic elements later came in upon the whole.

As already indicated, the Eleusinia consisted of the " lesser " and the " greater " mysteries. The former were celebrated at Athens and served as the
5. Lesser preliminary degree or preparation for
Mysteries. the greater or real initiation; they were sacred to Kore and Dionysus, while the greater were sacred to Demeter and Kore. The time of the lesser is in doubt, being either in the month Anthesterion (February-March), or in Elaphebolion (March-April); the days were the twentieth to the twenty-first. The place was Agra or Agri, a suburb of Athens, near the spring Callirhoe, where was a temple to Demeter and Persephone (Kore). The memory of the purely supplementary origin of the lesser mysteries is preserved in the legend that they were instituted in honor of Herakles, who wished to be initiated, but could not as his visit to Athens did not coincide with the season of the observance; besides, one not a citizen could not take the greater initiation, and foreigners were allowed to take the lesser degree. The observance then became preliminary to the final ceremonies. Little is known of the rites, though it is certain that the central thought, as of the greater, was purification, there being several marks of that proceeding, fasting (abstention from fowl, certain kinds of fish, beans, pomegranates, and apples), continence, and lustration on the banks of the Ilyssos River (cf. Eusebius, *Præparatio Evangelica*, III., i., Eng. transl., i. 91, Oxford, 1903). The candidates received instruction from the mystagogue (preceptor for the occasion) in the needful matters; this possibly included the Eleusinian version of the myth concerning the principal deities, and may have embraced the Iacchic-Dionysiac corruptions. Certainly the methods of purification were taught, also the dietary restrictions and taboos and the kind and order of sacrifices.

The greater mysteries were divided between Athens and Eleusis, which places were connected by the " sacred way " along which processions passed, with shrines at frequent intervals which had
6. Greater significance for the celebration. The
Mysteries: time was the month Boedromion, the
Initial season of harvest for late fruits, but
Ceremonies. concerning the exact dates and the order of the rites there are considerable differences among the authorities. For three of the dates there is epigraphic evidence which fixes the days for certain ceremonies. The actual opening of the celebration was preceded perhaps two months earlier by the proclamation of the sacred heralds announcing the solemn truce between warring states, in order that would-be participants might travel in safety. The dates fixed by inscriptions (*Corpus inscriptionum Atticarum*, III., 5) are the thirteenth, on which Athenian epheboi proceeded to Eleusis to escort the *sacra*, which in procession were brought by priestesses to Athens on the fourteenth, and on the nineteenth were returned to Eleusis, where they were kept till the next year. The order of events was probably the following. On the fifteenth came the gathering (*agyrmos*) of the mystæ (those who had taken the lesser mysteries) at the Stoa Poikile in Athens, and the address (*prorrhēsis*) by the hierophant (the principal actor in the mysteries), while the herald warned away the defiled and profane, murderers, traitors, and the like, as well as non-Greeks (cf. the parody in Aristophanes' " Frogs," 354). On the sixteenth was the essential and great purification known technically as *halade mystæ*, " to the sea, ye mystai," when the candidates proceeded to the seashore, each carrying the pig which was his sacrifice (the one usual to chthonic gods), and this with himself he purified by bathing. The seventeenth seems to have been the day when the archon-basileus offered at Athens the great *soteria* sacrifice to Demeter and Kore; the eighteenth was apparently devoted to private sacrifices, these two constituting the *Epidauria*, an accretion of the fifth century. On the nineteenth the *sacra* were returned to Eleusis. On the night of the nineteenth or early on the morning of the twentieth took place the great procession of the purified mystæ, wearing myrtle crowns and carrying torches (the torch is usually a symbol of underworld deities such as Kore had become), and the entire day was consumed and far into the night in traversing the sacred way, stops being made for sacrifice and worship at the numerous shrines. This procession escorted also the myrtle-crowned image of the young Iacchus (the Bacchus of the Eleusinia, son of Zeus and Demeter, identified also with Dionysus) attended by two priestesses who bore the liknon (fan, cradle) and playthings, all to the accompaniment of the joyous cry *Iacche* (" O Iacchus "), songs, clashing of cymbals, blowing of trumpets, and dancing. This day had distinction as the real beginning of the mysteries—another of the many facts which mark the performances at Athens as secondary and additional.

The twentieth (or twenty-first; from this point the dates are in uncertainty) was possibly the day of the offering of first-fruits to Demeter (C. F. W. Dittenberger, *Sylloge inscriptionum Græcarum*,

p. 13, Leipsic, 1883), as well as of sacrifices to other deities, demigods, and the Charites. The two nights

7. The Mysteries Proper. following were almost certainly the nights of initiation and of the presentation of the mystic drama, when the mystæ shared the mourning of Demeter and her subsequent joy, visited the spots consecrated, according to the story, by the experiences of the goddess, and then, like her, broke their fast by drinking the kykeon (see above, II., 1, § 4), the chief sacrament of the festival. The two nights of the drama seem to represent two degrees of initiation, the second possibly taken after a year's interval, full initiates being known as *epoptæ*, the term indicating evidently that they had seen and (according to the formula given by Clement of Alexandria) handled the *sacra*. The day following seems to have been a day of games, at which the prize was a measure of new barley, the firstfruits from the sacred field of Demeter near by. The Eleusinia closed with the return of the mystæ to Athens in procession bearing the statue of Iacchus, two final events marking the entry. The first was the passing of the bridge of the Kephissos, the mystæ and the spectators bandying jests, sometimes ribald and perhaps obscene (an addition probably after the admission of Dionysus to a share in the honors; certainly not original); and the pouring of two libations of water at the gate of Athens, most likely one to the East (the place of sunrise and the heavenly gods) and the other to the West (the place of sunset and of the entrance to the underworld). On the next day, the ceremonies being closed, the Athenian senate met to hear the report of the officials concerning the celebration and to try offenders who had offered profanation. There are very clear indications that the celebration was in the latest period prolonged for two or three days, thus deferring by that period the day of assembling of the senate.

The matters given in the preceding paragraphs constitute in the main the externals only, and except for the purifications and sacrifices do not deal with the concerns which gave to the mysteries

8. Essentials and Sacra. their significance and their value. These externals were not closed to any citizens as spectators, women as well as men attending the processions and other rites. The secrecy began with the performances which followed the arrival of Iacchus at Eleusis. The essentials there consisted of four series of acts: *katharsis* or purification, *sustasis* or rites and sacrifices preliminary to initiation (both these open to the public as spectators); *teleutē* or initiation, and *epopteia* or sight of the sacred objects (these only for candidates and initiates). In the *epopteia* are doubtless included the viewing of the sacred drama and the sight and handling of the *sacra*. Scattered cryptic references indicate that the drama included startling transformations effected by sudden transitions from darkness to intense light, while the actors reproduced the scenes of the myth, especially the reappearance of Kore from the underworld and the actions of the other divinities in the myth. The keynotes of all the proceedings were

purification, consecration, and hope for the future both in this life and the next. Concerning the secret rites only a few details are known from incidental allusions in literature and from the excavations at Eleusis, the latter clearing up much concerning the possibilities of the *telesterion* or hall of initiation. It is a Christian Father, Clement of Alexandria (" Exhortation to the Heathen," chap. ii., in *ANF*, ii. 175–177; cf. Harrison, *Prolegomena*, ut sup., pp. 155, 158), who gives the " token " (symbol) by which the initiate proved his adeptship: " I fasted, I drank the kykeon, I took from the chest, I put into the basket and back from the basket into the chest "; or " I ate from the timbrel, I drank from the cymbal, I carried the kernos, I passed beneath the pastos." The meaning of the first two clauses in the first of these formulas is clear; the cryptic character of the rest is evident. But one can not doubt that certain articles were taken out of a chest, and for the time placed in a basket until all had been handled and then returned to the chest. Doubtless the mystagogue explained during the process the symbolical significance of the articles; but what these were is practically unknown. For while certain articles used in the mysteries are spoken of in the classics, in Clement of Alexandria, and in the earlier treatises on antiquities (such as Athenæus, " Banquet," xi. 52–56) and dictionaries, in each case there is doubt whether they belonged to the Eleusinia or to some of the numerous mysteries of the Greek world. With the utmost probability one of the articles was an ear of barley. Another, the kernos, is nearly as certain, and while it has been explained as a winnowing fan, it is now known from excavations to have designated a composite cup (Harrison, *Prolegomena*, ut sup., pp. 158–160)—a platter with a number of little cups attached which held cereals, perhaps honey, and other materials, symbolic of the gifts of Demeter. Clement (ut sup.) tabulates the articles taken from the chest as " sesame, cakes, pyramidal cakes, globular and flat cakes embossed all over, lumps of salt, and a serpent, . . . pomegranates, branches, rods, ivy leaves, . . . poppy seeds, . . . the unmentionable symbols of Themis, marjoram, a lamp, a sword, a woman's comb, which is a euphemism and mystic expression for the *muliebra*." But Clement may have confused these articles with things that were employed in the mysteries of the great mother of Asia Minor.

The sacerdotal functionaries who conducted or took part were the *hierophantes* of the Eumolpis

9. Officials. family, who conducted the initiations and uttered the sacred sayings in which the revelations were made. They were assisted by the *daduchoi*, who seem also to have been Eumolpidæ. These grades seem to have included both sexes. Other officers were the *Iacchogos*, *kourotrophos* (nurse) and *dairites*, who officiated in the Iacchic procession. The *liknophoros* bore the *liknon* (winnowing fan? or was it another name for the kernos?), explained by some as the article used as the cradle of the infant Iacchos. *Hydranoi* purified with water the candidates, *pyrophoroi* maintained the sacred fires, *hieraules* were sacred flutists who trained the chorus of *hymnodoi* or *hymne-treiœ*, *neokoroi* attended to the sacred furniture, and *plaidryntai* cared for the divine statues. There were also *panageis* (office unknown), "initiated of the altar"—children chosen by lot at Eleusis to perform expiatory or avertive rites, *hieropoioi* offered the sacrifices, and the *archon-basileus* supervised the whole. The sacerdotal families had in their hands the many affairs pertaining to the regulation of the mysteries, and controlled the civil status of members of the Eleusinian families. The rules of observance were probably written and kept for reference; this is known to have been the case at Pheneus (Pausanias, VIII., xv. 1), where a stone crypt preserved them. While at Eleusis the mysteries were official and yearly, others said to be identical with these were observed elsewhere at greater intervals, e. g., at Celeæ every third year (Pausanias, II., xiv. 1), and at Pheneus every second year (ib., VIII., xv. 1).

Of the great influence of the Eleusinia over the Greeks for a millennium there can be no doubt. The basis of this influence, in the face of the secrecy which covers the teaching, of which almost nothing is known, can only be inferred. Greeks were in temperament undogmatic. The "formula of confession," as some have called Clement's "token" (ut sup.), is not a statement of belief, but an affirmation that certain actions have been performed. The essentials, apart from the purifications and sacrifices done in public, were symbolical; they consisted in certain articles, probably insignificant in themselves, and in such actions as taking these things from a chest and putting them back. So far as one can learn, there was no teaching of dogma. But the total impression left by the Eleusinia is that of solemnity. The implications of lewdness suggested by Clement are not confirmed by archeology. Demeter herself is an impressive figure—a tender mother, sorrowing for a daughter snatched from her by powers whom she could reach only indirectly. In her sorrow the earth shared, as later it partook of her joy when her daughter was for a season restored to her. No finer or more chaste statue exists, and none more pathetic, than the seated mourning Demeter. And when in the myth Kore is given back to her, there is no hint of orgies, only the grateful joy which spends itself in the renewal of the bountiful soil's gifts to man. That in the later and other forms of mysteries, which Clement confused in his polemic, there were shameful features is true. But nothing that is known of the Eleusinia proper carries such a suggestion. Instead, the one expression of teaching that peeps out through the veil of obscurity is the hope so needed in Greek religion—that the future life was to be made happier because of participation in the mysteries. "Demeter . . . bestowed on us two priceless gifts: the cultivation of the fruits of the earth . . . and the ceremony which brings to the initiated the sweetest consolation at death and the hope of eternity" (Isocrates, "Panegyrics," cited by Philios, *Eleusis*, pp. 41–42, London, 1906). Cicero and others might be quoted to the same effect. Granting the truth of this, one great reason

10. Significance.

for reverence for the Eleusinia is evident. Moreover, much as Christian pilgrims sought and believed they found the favor of God by visiting the Holy Land and traveling the roads trodden by the Savior's feet, so the mystæ thought to secure the goddess's favor by visiting the scenes where she sorrowed and then found joy. Add to these the sense of moral and religious relief brought by the purifications of fasting and lustration, and little more of explanation is needed to justify, from the standpoint of the old religions, the high estimation in which the Eleusinia were held throughout the Greek world and in the Roman.

2. Dionysiac-Orphic Mysteries: Of a very different type from the Eleusinia were the Dionysiac-Orphic mysteries, which from the fifth century B.C. on invaded and pervaded popular Greek religion. The character of the god and of the man from whom these derived their names furnish clues to the character of the observances. Dionysus (Bacchus) was not in the Homeric pantheon, but by the beginning of the sixth century he had scaled Olympus. He was of Thracian origin, in all probability the deity of the Satræ (who gave their name to satyrs—Harrison, ut sup., p. 379) or the Bessi, a mountain tribe which had the reputation of being the worst of brigands, living on Mt. Hæmus (Strabo, vii. 318, and Fragment 25), which yielded in religion or politics to no conqueror till Nicetas of Remesiana (q.v.) at the end of the fourth century won them for Christianity (Paulinus of Nola, *Carmen*, xxx.). The traditional origin of Dionysus from Thebes (as in the *Tyrannus* of Sophocles) is an attempt to give this foreign god, who had been received into the pantheon, a native origin. His late arrival in Greece is avouched in the prologue to the *Bacchœ* of Euripides: "Now I come to Hellas, having taught all the world else my dances and my rite of mysteries" (Harrison, ut sup., p. 371). This statement involves the fact, which could be abundantly attested, that the Dionysiac ceremonies had spread widely, partly in consequence of northern (Thracian) migration in two streams, one via Macedonia to the Greek peninsula, and the other into Asia Minor and thence east and south, having meanwhile assimilated much from the mysteries of the Great Mother for which Asia Minor was celebrated. The names and epithets by which this god was known encyst the facts of his origin, his wanderings, and his nature. "Sabazios" bespeaks Thrace and Phrygia, and contains in itself the idea of sleep brought on by *sabaium*, a fermented drink made of grain. "Bromios" has a Theban ring which expresses confused sounds, as the rumbling of thunder, or of the mob, or of orgiastic music—the noise of the rout. And this fits in with and is used in connection with the myth that Dionysus came untimely to birth when his mother Semele (an earth deity) was smitten with the lightning of Zeus. He was also "Dendrites," the "tree-god," and then specialized as deity of the grape and of wine. Similarly as "Dithyrambos" he suggests the heady mead made of honey. Many other titles might be cited to the same purport were these not sufficient to reveal his

1. Character of Dionysiac Celebration.

nature. All along the line the evidences are those of a deity of the cup; among ruder tribes the drink is a ruder and more primitive ferment—of grain or honey or roots, while among the more civilized it is the juice of the grape. From this the character of his mysteries might be guessed, but other evidence is at hand. For in art and poetry his companions are the satyrs, half man, half horse, " idle, disreputable, and vicious," who " sport and play and harry women," and Mænads, wild women, who, being *entheoi* (" god-possessed "), work strange deeds, rage and rave and play with serpents, whose worship was the ecstatic dance leading to physical exhaustion, and their festivals disorder and excess. Hence it is that with probable justice the more boisterous elements of the later Eleusinia, such as the tilt of ribald jests at the bridge, are traced to the influence of Dionysus, who stands always for intoxication, orgy, and religious frenzy. Yet it should in justice be noted that these are not in themselves the objects, but rather the means by which his worshipers become possessed (" inspired " would be the theological term) by the god. There is the same end here as is connoted by the word " Ecstasy " (q.v.).

Orpheus, also of Thracian origin, never attained to godship, he always remained human. Diodorus (iii. 65) brings him into connection with Dionysus in a twofold manner: explicitly as the grandson of Charops, to whom, in return for a favor, Dionysus taught his rites; and implicitly in that Oiagros, son of Charops and father of Orpheus, handed those rites on to his son, who (and this is important) " made many changes in them." The usual conception of Orpheus stops with his fame as a musician. This has importance, indeed, even for the mysteries; but it is as a religious reformer that Orpheus has most interest in this connection. This fact is brought out in the story of his death, which relates that he honored Helios above Dionysus, and the latter sent his Bassarids (Thracian bacchanals) against him, and they tore him in pieces and scattered the remnants (Eratosthenes, *Katasterismoi,* xxiv.). The Muses gathered these together and buried them, but the head, entombed at Lesbos, continued to sing and to utter oracles. The historic kernel here is doubtless the martyrdom of Orpheus at the hands of Dionysiac mystics because as a reformer of the mysteries he did Dionysus too little honor. It is also deducible from the story and is supported by other data that Orpheus was a prophet and religious teacher; Pausanias (IX., xxx. 12) says that he was credited with discovering rites of the gods, purifications for unholy acts, remedies for sicknesses, and means of turning away the divine wrath (cf. Aristophanes, " Frogs," 1032; Augustine, " City of God," xviii. 14, in *NPNF,* 1 ser., ii. 368). The significant facts in all this are (1) that the wild orgiastic rites of Dionysus, celebrated especially in wooded gorges on the mountains by choruses of ecstatic women, were revised by Orpheus; (2) that this revision took the forms of (a) a sobering down of the orgiastic—the muse of Orpheus is never pictured as stirring and exciting,

2. Significance of Orpheus.

but as entrancing and quieting,* and (b) of engrafting upon the rites a loftier spiritual meaning.

Three particulars in Orphism are noteworthy: (1) it introduced more thoroughly into Greek religion the principle of asceticism (in the shape of abstinence, opposing thereby incidentally the drunken cups of Dionysus) than was otherwise done—the idea was that of good works, a holy life; (2) it either borrowed from Egypt (or India?) or independently evolved the conception of the *samsara* or cycle of births, reincarnation, and release therefrom by abstinence, plus purification in the mysteries and the holy life; (3) it either (more probably) adopted the Egyptian idea of identification of the soul after death with a deity, or itself independently created it. But the foundation-thought in this was the attainment of purity. So Euripides makes Theseus, the hater of the self-righteous and of mystics, taunt the Orphic adept: " Boast, now! Thou so holy that no flesh where life hath been feeds thee who hast Orpheus for thy king " (*Hippolytus,* 952–953). Similarly in the confession of the mystic quoted from Euripides by Porphyry (*De abstinentia,* iv. 19; cf. the passage in Harrison, ut sup., p. 479) the adept is " set free and named by name a Bacchus of the mailed priests, robed in pure white, clean from man's birth and coffined clay (i.e., from the pollutions both of birth and death), while from his lips is ever banished touch of meat where life hath been." It is quite certain that Orphism involved also the habit of self-examination, probably after the pattern of the Pythagoreans: " What that is wrong have I done? What good deed is mine? And what that I should have I not accomplished? " (Diogenes Laertius, " Life of Pythagoras," xix.).

3. Orphic Teachings.

In spite of Orphic attempts to eliminate the extravagant from the rites, the testimonies are too many and too explicit to hide the fact that in the background of the system lurked rites that were disgusting and repellent. Among these were the sacrificial eating of raw, even of living, flesh of bull or goat (cf. COMPARATIVE RELIGION, VI., 1, d. § 1), and with great probability a rite that recalled the earlier eating of the flesh of a child (cf. *Journal of Hellenic Studies,* 1890, p. 343; and for the orgiastic ritual and indications of this feast of raw flesh cf. Plutarch, *De oraculorum defectu,* xiv.; Clement of Alexandria, " Exhortation,"ii., in ANF, ii. 175–176; Arnobius, " Against the Heathen," v. 19–23, in *ANF,* vi. 497–498; Firmicus Maternus, *De errore profanarum religionum,* vi.). How far these survived in the historic period is doubtful. That they were mimicked if not actually carried out is beyond question. And that in more retired regions the mysteries concealed not merely crudities (Plato, *Republic,* 364 B; Heraclitus, Fragment 130) but savageries is true. Still, even in the recrudescence of primitive rites in the Greco-Roman world that took place, having their starting-point in Asia Minor, 200 B.C.–200 A.D.,

4. Summary.

---

* The inscription found at the Iobaccheion at Athens gives as a direction for the performance: " No one is to make a noise, or clap his hands, or sing, but each is to do his part in all quietness and order " (text and translation conveniently given in Harrison, ut sup., pp. 474–475).

there was evidence of a dissatisfaction with the state religion, a waking of the soul to life and of a desire for nobler things, which was in a manner met by the acceptance and symbolic interpretation of primitive performances. In this movement the mysteries described above had the leading part. But other secret cults in considerable numbers had their vogue, some merely local, others (like those of the Great Mother) pervasive, and still others the invention of mountebanks, intent upon using the trend of things in the religious world to their own advantage. Of the first and second, part were associated with the deities already named. Others, like the Pythagorean and Isiac, were on a different basis. But together the effect upon religion was profound, and was by no means unfelt in Christianity (cf. G. Anrich, *Das antike Mysterienwesen in seinem Einfluss auf das Christentum*, Göttingen, 1894; E. H. Hatch, *Influence of Greek Ideas and Usages upon the Christian Church*, London, 1890). Greek tragedians and philosophers were hardly less under the spell of these performances and ideas. So that the mysteries, tribal and cultic, are among the forces the vast effects of which are only now beginning to be appreciated.   GEO. W. GILMORE.

BIBLIOGRAPHY: For tribal mysteries incomparably the best works for the student are those which deal with the life of savages in different lands, compiled by competent observers. Among the best and indispensable works of this kind are: L. Fison and A. W. Howitt, *Kamilaroi and Kurnai*, Melbourne, 1880; R. H. Codrington, *Melanesian Studies*, London, 1891; A. Hamilton, *Maori Art*, Wellington, 1896; B. Spencer and F. J. Gillen; *Native Tribes of Central Australia*, London, 1899; idem, *Northern Tribes of Central Australia*, ib. 1904; F. H. Cushing, *Zuni Folk Tales*, New York, 1902; W. H. Furness, *Borneo Head Hunters*, London, 1902; A. W. Howitt, *Native Tribes of South-East Australia*, ib. 1904; Mrs. K. L. Parker, *Euahlayi Tribe*, ib. 1905; and the *Reports* and *Bulletins* of the Smithsonian Institution, Washington, D. C. The material has been brought together in two books of the highest value: H. Schurtz, *Altersklassen und Männerbunde*, Berlin, 1902; and H. Webster, *Primitive Secret Societies, a Study in Early Politics and Religion*, New York, 1908 (an excellent handbook on the subject). Consult further: E. B. Tylor, in *Journal of Anthropological Studies*, xxviii (1898), 145 sqq.; idem, *Primitive Culture*, new ed., London, 1903; J. G. Frazer, *Golden Bough*, iii. 422–445, ib. 1900; E. Crawley, *Mystic Rose*, pp. 215–223, 270–314, New York, 1902; G. S. Hall, *Adolescence*, ii. 232–260, ib. 1904.

On Greek Mysteries the work of Miss Harrison cited so frequently in the text is of prime importance, adducing evidence which is frequently unique. Consult further: C. A. Lobeck, *Aglaophamus*, Regensburg, 1829 (indispensable for the collection of materials from the classics); L. Preller, *Demeter und Persephone*, Hamburg, 1837; idem, *Griechische Mythologie*, ed. C. Robert, Berlin, 1894; F. Lenormant, *Monographie de la voie sacrée eleusinienne*, Paris, 1864; idem, in *Contemporary Review*, 1880, i. 847 sqq., ii. 119 sqq., 412 sqq.; A. Mommsen, *Heortologie*, Leipsic, 1864; C. Strube, *Ueber den Bilderkreis von Eleusis*, Leipsic, 1870; C. S. Wake, *Evolution of Morality*, ii., chap. vi., London, 1878; W. Mannhardt, *Mythologische Forschungen*, Strasburg, 1884; H. Junker, *Die Studenwachen in den Osirismysterien nach den Inschriften von Dendera, Edfu, und Philæ*, Vienna, 1890; L. Dyer, *Gods in Greece*, pp. 174–218, London, 1891; P. Gardner, *New Chapters in Greek Hist.*, ib. 1892; H. Rubensohn, *Die Mysterienheiligtümer in Eleusis und Samothrace*, Berlin, 1892; A. Dieterich, *Nekyia*, Leipsic, 1893 (important); P. Foucart, *Recherches sur l'origine et la nature des mystères d'Eleusis*, Paris, 1895 (of very considerable value); E. Maass, *Orpheus*, Munich, 1895; D. Philios, *Eleusis, ses mystères, ses ruines, et son musée*, Athens, 1896, Eng. transl., *Eleusis, her Mysteries, Ruins, and Museum*, London, 1906 (the treatment of the mysteries is rather superficial); T. Mommsen, *Die Feste der Stadt Athen*, Leipsic, 1898; A. Lang, *Myth, Ritual, and Religion*, i. 270 sqq., ii. 286 sqq., London, 1899; idem, *Homeric Hymns*, pp. 55–100, 183–210, ib. 1899; G. D'Alviella, in *RHR*, xlvi (1902), nos. 2 and 3, xlvii (1903), nos. 1 and 2; idem, *Eleusinia*, Paris, 1903; E. Rohde, *Psyche*, 3d ed., Tübingen, 1902 (indispensable); O. Gruppe, *Griechische Mythologie und Religionsgeschichte*, Munich, 1906; R. Reitzenstein, *Die hellenistischen Mysterienreligion, ihre Grundgedanken und Wirkungen*, Leipsic, 1910; F. Cumont, *Oriental Religions in Roman Paganism*, Chicago, 1911; Ersch and Gruber, *Encyklopädie*, I., xxxiii. 268–296, lxxxii. 219–380.

TRIBES, HEBREW. See ISRAEL, HISTORY OF, I.

TRIBUR, SYNOD OF: A synod held early in May, 895, at Tribur (12 m. w.n.w. of Darmstadt) in the presence of King Arnulf, and attended by the archbishops of Cologne, Mainz, and Treves, and twenty-six or twenty-seven bishops. It is chiefly noteworthy as marking a closer relation between Arnulf and the higher clergy; for, while a large number of its enactments referred to the restoration of ecclesiastical discipline, a series of important canons bound the king to make sweeping concessions to the higher clergy. The synod was also important as further strengthening the judicial powers of the Curia, to which it enjoined subjection and obedience, even though the yoke should prove heavy. Almost two centuries later (Oct., 1076) a second assembly met at Tribur, at which the secular princes combined with a great portion of the clergy and the Curia against the emperor, subjecting Henry IV. to Gregory VII., and requiring him to appear at Augsburg on Feb. 2, 1077, to receive the verdict of the pope, with the threat that, if he did not purge himself of the ban within a year from the pronouncement of excommunication, he should irrevocably forfeit the empire. The result was Canossa (see GREGORY VII.).   (D. KERLER†.)

BIBLIOGRAPHY: For the *Acta* consult *NA*, xiv. 49–82, 281–326, xv. 411–427, xviii. 365–409. xx. 289–352; *MGH, Cap.*, ii. 196–249. Consult also: E. L. Dümmler, *Geschichte des ostfränkischen Reichs*, iii. 395–404; Hefele, *Conciliengeschichte*, iv. 552–561.

TRIDENTINE PROFESSION OF FAITH (CREED OF PIUS IV.): For practical purposes the most important creed-statement of the Roman Catholic Church. The original name was *Forma professionis fidei Catholicæ*, or *orthodoxæ fidei*. It was preceded by three other professions of faith issued by Pius IV.: that of 1556 in thirty-six articles; that of 1560, intended for prelates; and that of 1563. The decrees of the Council of Trent (q.v.) contain no profession, but in the twenty-fourth session such a form was suggested. This was prepared by a commission of cardinals under the direction of Pius IV. in 1564. It must be subscribed or sworn to by all priests and public teachers of that church, and also by Protestant converts (hence called the " Profession of converts "). It was solemnly affirmed during the Vatican Council of 1870 at its second session. It is a very clear and precise summary of the specific doctrines of the Roman Church as settled by the Council of Trent, put in the form of a binding oath of obedience to the pope, as the successor of the prince of the apostles, and the vicar of Christ. It consists of twelve articles of which the first runs as follows:

" I,——, with a firm faith believe and profess all and every one of the things contained in that creed which the holy Roman Church makes use of, viz.:
" I believe in one God, the Father Almighty," etc. (Here follows the Nicene Creed.)

In the following ten articles the candidate accepts (1) all the conditions and ordinances of the Roman Catholic Church; (2) the interpretation put upon the Scriptures by that church and no other; (3) the seven sacraments and the mode of their administration taught by the church; (4) every article and statement made by the Council of Trent concerning original sin and justification; (5) the doctrine of transubstantiation and the sacrificial nature of the mass; (6) the bread and the wine as each containing the whole Christ; (7) the invocation of saints, the worship of relics, and the doctrine of purgatory, and that the suffrages of the living avail for the souls there confined; (8) the worship of images and the virtue of indulgences; (9) the supremacy of the Roman Church and the authority of the bishop of Rome as the successor of St. Peter and the vicar of Jesus Christ; and (10) the condemnation, rejection, and anathematization of everything contrary to the decrees of the general councils as well as all heresies rejected by the church. The last article contains a most solemn adjuration, and runs as follows:

" I do, at this present, freely profess and truly hold this true Catholic faith, without which no one can be saved; and I promise most constantly to retain and confess the same entire and inviolate, with God's assistance, to the end of my life. And I will take care, as far as in me lies, that it shall be held, taught, and preached by my subjects, or by those the care of whom shall appertain to me in my office. This I, ——, promise, vow, and swear, so help me God, and these holy Gospels of God."

Since that time the Roman Catholic Church has added two articles which enter into the profession, one on the sinlessness of the Virgin Mary. and one on the infallibility of the pope, in the following words:

" (1) That ' the blessed Virgin Mary, by a singular grace and privilege of Almighty God, in view of the merits of Christ Jesus the Savior of mankind, has been preserved free from all stain of original sin.'
" (2) That ' the Roman pontiff, when he speaks *ex cathedrâ*—that is, in discharge of the office of pastor, and doctor of all Christians, by virtue of his supreme apostolic authority, he defines a doctrine regarding faith or morals—is possessed of that infallibility with which the divine Redeemer willed that his Church should be endowed; and that therefore such definitions of the Roman pontiff are irreformable of themselves, and not from the consent of the Church."

P. SCHAFF†. D. S. SCHAFF.

BIBLIOGRAPHY: The papal bulls of Nov. 13 (*Injunctum nobis*) and Dec. 9 (*In sacrosancta*), 1564, are in the *Bullarium magnum Romanum*, 19 vols., Luxemburg, 1727–1758, the former also in Mirbt, *Quellen*, pp. 256–258. The text of the profession is in F. G. Streitwolf and R. E. Klener, *Libri symbolici ecclesiæ catholicæ*, ii. 315–321, cf. i. pp. xlv.–li., 98–100, Göttingen, 1838, and in Schaff, *Creeds*, ii. 207–210, cf. i. 96–99. Consult besides the above: G. C. F. Mohnike, *Urkundliche Geschichte der sogenannten Professei fidei Tridentinæ und . . . andern römisch-catholischen Glaubensbekenntnisse*, Greifswald, 1822; E. Köllner, *Symbolik der römisch-katholischen Kirche*, p. 141, Hamburg, 1844; H. J. D. Denzinger, *Enchiridion symbolorum et definitionum*, pp. 233–235, Würzburg, 1900; *KL*, v. 682–685.

TRIEBS, FRANZ: German Roman Catholic; b. at Gross-Glogau (58 m. n.w. of Breslau) Nov. 7, 1864. He was educated at the universities of Bres-

lau and Münster (1883–87; D.D., Münster, 1888), and after being a parish priest in Waldenburg (Silesia), Merzdorf, Schönau, Schwedt, and Miltisch, 1888–95, resumed his studies at Bonn (1895–1897; Ph.D., 1897), and at Berlin (1897–1900), being at the same time engaged in parochial work in the latter city. In 1902 he became privat-docent for canon law in the University of Breslau, where he was appointed to his present position of extraordinary professor of the same subject in 1905, being made consistorial councilor in 1908. He has written *Veteris Testamenti de Cherubim doctrina* (Münster, 1888) and *Studien zur Lex Dei, i. ii.* (Freiburg, 1905–1907), besides editing Ṣalih ibn al-Ḥusain's *Liber decem quæstionum contra Christianos* (Bonn, 1897).

TRIGLAND, JACOBUS: Dutch Reformed; b. at Vianen (7 m. s.s.w. of Utrecht) July 22, 1583; d. at Leyden Apr. 5, 1654. Of Roman Catholic parentage, he was brought up by relatives at Gouda, and sent, in 1597, to some priests at Amsterdam to study theology. Toward the end of 1598 he removed to Louvain, where doubts arose in his mind which ultimately led him to break with the ancient faith. He was entrusted with a mission to Haarlem by the head of the collegium pontificium, and never returned to Louvain. After a few weeks at Gouda, where his foster relations rejected him, he sought refuge in the house of his parents, where he studied Reformed tenets, meanwhile seeking occupation to gain his livelihood. In 1602 he was made rector of the school at Vianen, and in the following year entered the Reformed Church. Having prepared privately for the ministry, he was ordained pastor at Stolwijk in 1607; and was pastor at Amsterdam, 1610–34. Here, in 1614, he began a noteworthy activity in affairs of Church and State which ended only with his death. In 1617 he received leave of absence to the Reformed church at The Hague, and was a deputy of the provincial synod of North Holland to the Synod of Dort, which appointed him a member of the committee to draw up the Canons of Dort. Trigland was professor of theology at Leyden, 1634–54, lecturing on the exegesis of the Old Testament, on the *loci communes*, 1639–50, and later on " cases of conscience." He was also pastor of the Reformed church at Leyden (1637–45).

The writings of Trigland, which are dogmatic and polemic, reveal him as a man of intense convictions, rigid dogmatism, and great learning in Scripture and the Reformed theology, but also as passionate, intolerant, and haughty, traits which caused him bitter enemies. Yet his hostility, manifested particularly against the Remonstrants, did not come from love of strife, but from sincere feeling that their teachings were pernicious and not to be allowed. This is most plainly shown in his *Den rechtghematichden Christen* (Amsterdam, 1615). In his *Verdedigingh van de Leere end' Eere der Ghereformeerde Kerken ende Leeraren* (1616) he defends the Reformed dogmatics. He sturdily opposed civil intervention in ecclesiastical affairs in his *Antwoordt op drij vraghen dienende tot advys in de huydendagsche kerklijke swarigheden* (1615), and his *Christelijcke ende nootwendighe verclaringhe* (1615). After the Synod of Dort, 1618–19, he continued to work against the Remonstrants, producing, *Christelijcke ende vriendelijcke vermaninge* (2 parts, 1623); *De kracht der godtsaligheydt* (1631); and three treatises resulting from the discussions aroused by the latter book: *Trina Dei gratia, nimirum, electionis, sanctificationis, conservationis applicata, confirmata et indicata* (1636); *Disputatio theologica de civili et ecclesiastica potestate* (1642); and the posthumous *Antapologia, sive examen atque refutatio totius apologiæ Remonstrantium* (Harderwijk, 1664). The Roman Catholics he attacked with his *Valschen Roem des pausdoms* (1631), *Los gebouw des pausdoms* (1633), and *Bodemlooze pausdom* (1638), all against the papacy. He was best known, however, for his *Kerkelijcke geschiedenissen* (Leyden, 1650), in which, while giving a long-desired history of the growth of Protestantism in Holland, he attacked the Remonstrants with his accustomed bitterness, especially the anonymous apology, *Kerkelijcke historie* of J. Uytenbogaert (Rotterdam, 1646). The work was joyfully received by the Reformed Church, but the states-general of Holland declined to accept the dedication, and at Amsterdam its sale was forbidden. All the writings of Trigland previous to 1640 were published in chronological order under the title, *Opuscula Jacobi Triglandi* (3 vols., Amsterdam, 1640). (S. D. van Veen.)

BIBLIOGRAPHY: The funeral oration by J. Cocceius, in the latter's *Opera*, iv. 48 sqq., Amsterdam, 1701; H. W. Ter Haar, *Jacobus Trigland*, The Hague, 1891.

TRINE IMMERSION: A threefold immersion, consisting in the dipping of the candidate in the water three times—first, in the name of the Father, second, in the name of the Son, and, third, in the name of the Holy Spirit. It is the Historical practise observed by the Greek, Armenian, and other oriental churches, as well as by the Brethren (Dunkers) and some other religious bodies of America, and is more extensively employed than many have been led to suppose. Of the 165,000,000 Christians now living who have been immersed, fully nine-tenths have been baptized by trine immersion. Of the 290,000,000 persons who have received sprinkling or pouring at their baptism, not less than 200,000,000 had the water applied three times, showing that a very large per cent of the Christian world holds to the triple action in baptism. The advocates of trine immersion believe that it was the apostolic method of administering the rite, and for their authority they appeal to the formula of baptism as given by Christ in Matt. xxviii. 19: " Baptizing them into the name of the Father, and of the Son, and of the Holy Spirit." It is held that as there are three persons in the Trinity, so are there three actions in baptism, therefore the three actions symbolize the three persons of the Godhead. However, these three actions constitute the " one baptism," referred to by Paul in Eph. iv. 5, they being regarded as one in the sense that the Father, Son, and Holy Spirit are one.

Speaking of this formula of baptism, Chrysostom (fifth century) says: " Christ delivered to his disciples one baptism in three immersions of the body, when he said to them, ' Go teach all nations, baptizing them in the name of the Father and of the

Son and of the Holy Ghost ' " (Bingham, *Origines*, XI., xi., § 7). Jerome (fifth century), commenting on Eph. iv. 5, presents the same view Patristic regarding the three actions constituTestimony. ting one baptism, for he says: " We are thrice dipped in the water, that the mystery of the Trinity may appear to be but one: . . . though we be thrice put under water to represent the mystery of the Trinity—yet it is reputed but one baptism " (Bingham, ut sup., XI., xi., § 6). Tertullian (third century) also believed that the Lord taught trine immersion, for, speaking of the baptismal formula, he says: " He commands them to baptize into the Father and the Son and the Holy Ghost, not into a unipersonal God. And indeed it is not once only, but three times, that we are immersed into three persons, at each several mention of their names " (*Adv. Prax.*, xxvi.; Eng. transl., *ANF*, iii. 623). The Didache, or Teaching of the Twelve Apostles, written according to Schaff between 90 and 100 A.D. (Schaff's ed. of Didache, p. 122, New York, 1890), is wholly on the side of the triple action in baptism. The rite was to be administered (chap. vii.) " into the name of the Father and of the Son and of the Holy Ghost, in living water," or, if that could not be had, in other water, cold or warm. If there was not sufficient to immerse, then " pour water thrice upon the head into the name of the Father and of the Son and of the Holy Ghost." " Three times " applies to the immersion as well as to the pouring. Pouring plenty of water on the head " three times " was the nearest practicable substitute of total trine immersion (cf. Philip Schaff's extended comments in his edition of the Didache, pp. 29–35, New York, 1890). The early Fathers, without a voice to the contrary, believed that triple baptism was the New-Testament form. In his address at the Council of Carthage, 256 A.D., Munnulus or Monulus, bishop of Girba, said: " The truth of our Mother the Catholic Church, brethren, hath always remained and still remains with us, and even especially in the trinity of baptism, as our Lord says, ' Go ye and baptize the nations, in the name of the Father, of the Son, and of the Holy Spirit ' " (Cyprian, " Concerning the Baptism of Heretics," *ANF*, v. 567). Not one of the eighty-seven bishops present challenged the statement. The fiftieth of the Apostolic Canons shows the views on baptism held by the Church of the second, third, and fourth centuries. It reads thus: " If any bishop or presbyter does not perform the three immersions of the one admission, but one immersion which is given into the death of Christ, let him be deprived; for the Lord did not say, ' Baptize into my death '; but, ' Go ye and make disciples of all nations, baptizing them into the name of the Father and of the Son and of the Holy Ghost ' " (*ANF*, vii. 503).

John Wesley thought triple immersion was the apostolic practise (H. Moore's *Life of Wesley*, i. 425, New York, 1824). Trine immersion was the only form of baptism in general use among the early churches. William Wall says: " The way of trine immersion, or plunging the head of the person three times into the water, was the general practise of all antiquity " (*Infant Baptism*, i. 592, Oxford, 1862). Robert Robinson (*History of Baptism*, p. 148, London, 1790) makes this statement: "It

More Modern Opinions.

is not true that dipping was exchanged for sprinkling by choice before the Reformation, for, till after that period, the ordinary baptism was trine immersion." Wharton Booth Marriott, in *DCA*, i. 161, says: "Triple immersion, that is, thrice dipping the head while standing in the water, was all but the universal rule of the church in early times." Trine immersion is supported by the testimony of Basil, 370; Cyril of Jerusalem, 380; Ambrose, 390; Augustine, 420; Theodoret, 450; Alcuin, 775, and others of the Fathers. The churches in the East, where Christianity was first established, still retain the trine form in baptism. Rev. Dr. George Washburn, former president of Robert College, in Constantinople, says (Didache, ed. Schaff, ut sup., p. 43): "As to the baptism question, the orthodox authorities here declare that no oriental church not under Roman Catholic or Protestant influence knows any other baptism than trine immersion." On the same page, foot-note, concerning the practise of the Russian Church, it is stated, "Baptism is always administered by dipping the infant or adult three times into the water." The whole Greek Church, numbering nearly one hundred millions, administers the sacrament of baptism only by trine immersion. This is also the practise of the Armenian church, numbering several millions. Schaff says, "Trine immersion and emersion of the whole body was the general practise of the ancient Church, Greek and Latin, and continues to this day in all Eastern churches and sects, and in the orthodox State Church of Russia" (Didache, ut sup., p. 54).   J. H. MOORE.

BIBLIOGRAPHY: J. Chrystal, *Hist. of the Modes of Baptism*, Philadelphia, 1861; R. Robinson, *Ecclesiastical Researches*, chap. on the Greek Church, Cambridge, 1792; A. Campbell, *Christian Baptism*, Bethany, Va., 1853; G. H. Orchard, *Hist. of Foreign Baptists*, 2 vols., St. Louis, 1855; *Quinter and McConnell Debate*, Cincinnati, 1868; J. H. Moore, *Trine Immersion Traced to the Apostles*, Elgin, Ill., 1874; R. H. Miller, *Doctrine of the Brethren Defended*, ib. 1876; W. Cathcart, *The Baptism of the Ages*, Philadelphia, 1878; J. Quinter, *Trine Immersion*, Elgin, 1886; *Miller and Sommer Debate*, Mount Morris, Ill., 1889; C. F. Yoder, *God's Means of Grace*, Elgin, 1908; J. B. Wampler, *Biblical and Historical Researches*, Grove City, Pa., 1908; the literature cited in the text, and under BAPTISM.

TRINIDAD. See WEST INDIES.

TRINITARIANS: A Roman Catholic order (*Ordo sanctissimæ Trinitatis redemptionis captivorum;* also called *Ordo asinorum*, the members being at first permitted to ride only on asses; and in France, Maturines, from their chapel of St. Mathurin or St. Mathelin at Paris), founded, according to tradition, in 1198 by Jean de Matha (b. at Faucon, near Barcelonette, 31 m. n.w. of Nice, June 23, 1160; d. at Rome Dec. 17, 1213) and Félix de Valois (b. 1127; d. at Paris Jan. 20, 1212). The legendary account of their origin is not wholly sustained by the earliest known document. This is a *privilegium* of Innocent III. of May, 1198, approving the reception of property at Cerfroid, specially the house given by Countess Margaret of Burgundy, and implying the existence of the order

before the legendary journey to Rome, 1198. It is questionable whether the original idea of working for the ransom of the captives was Jean's or Margaret's, but, from the words of this document, more probably the latter's. A second document of Dec., 1198, from Innocent, shows that the pope had sent back Jean for recommendations from the bishop of Paris and the abbot of St. Victor. On Jean's return with these and a copy of the rule, the pope confirmed the order. A new *privilegium* of protection was granted by Innocent, June 18, 1209. The rule of the Trinitarians requires the brothers to live in obedience to the "minister" of their house, and in celibacy and poverty. Each single house is to be occupied by three clerical and three lay brothers, controlled by a "minister," the latter a priest chosen by the brothers and required to hold a chapter each Sunday. At the head of the entire order is the minister superior, who convenes the annual chapter on the octave of Whitsunday and directs the discipline over the ministers inferior. A third of the income of the order is set apart for the liberation of prisoners. The first minister superior was Jean de Matha, who received from Innocent III. the church and hospital of San Tommaso in Formis, on the Celian Hill. A few years after the establishment of the Trinitarians, a female branch was founded in Spain, though it did not receive a definite constitution until 1236. In 1199 the first mission was sent to Tunis and 186 redeemed captives were brought back in triumph to Cerfroid. The order, which had increased chiefly in the Latin countries, was extended to England, Scotland, Ireland, and the East, and was reconfirmed by Honorius III. (1217); Clement IV. permitted certain relaxations of its rule (1267); and Clement VII. sanctioned mendicancy (1574). The Trinitarians did not escape degeneration, and efforts at reform led to divisions. Of the branches the most important is that of the Discalced Trinitarians, established in Spain and recognized as a distinct congregation by Clement VIII. in 1599, and extended to France and Italy. In 1609 Paul V. declared them a mendicant order, but until 1636 they were under the general of the main order.

The internal history of the Trinitarians is obscure. A. König maintained that at the height of their prosperity, in the fifteenth century, they had some 880 monasteries, while Pierre Helyot states for his time, the first half of the eighteenth century, that they still possessed about 250 in eleven provinces. According to O. Braunsberger (*Stimmen aus Maria Laach*, supplement No. 79, 1901) in 1835 forty-seven of the eighty-seven Spanish monasteries of the order were suppressed, a like fate having befallen the six Austrian houses in 1782–90. P. Deslandres shows 102 houses for France and the Netherlands, of which at the end of the eighteenth century there survived ninety-three, besides eleven in England, one in Ireland, and seven in Scotland. The calced Trinitarians became extinct in 1894, while the discalced branch has maintained itself till the present time by four settlements at Rome (1905), including the parish churches of Santa Maria della Fornaci and San Grisogono, besides other settlements in Spain, Austria, America, and elsewhere.

The order devotes itself, for the time being, to the ransom and education of negro children and numbers 450. The female order never flourished, having only ten cloisters in their chief seat, Spain, toward the close of the eighteenth century. P. Dan (*Histoire de Barbarie*, Paris, 1649) gave the number of rescue expeditions as 363, the number of released captives as 30,720. The correct figures, if they could be produced, would undoubtedly be much higher.   (A. Hauck.)

Bibliography: The " Rule " was printed at Paris, 1635, 1652; the " Statutes " at Douai, 1586; cf. L. Holstenius, *Codex regularum*, ed. M. Brockie, ii. 38 sqq., Augsburg, 1759. Consult: M. Gmelin, *Die Litteratur zur Geschichte des Ordens St. Trinitatis*, Carlsruhe, 1870; idem, *Die Trinitarier oder Weissspanier in Oesterreich*, Vienna, 1871; Helyot, *Ordres monastiques*, ii. 310 sqq.; Heimbucher, *Orden und Kongregationen*, ii. 69–78; *Gallia Christiana*, viii. 1731 sqq., 16 vols., Paris, 1715 sqq.; G. Uhlhorn, *Die Liebesthätigkeit im Mittelalter*, pp. 285 sqq., 496 sqq., Stuttgart, 1884; P. Deslandres, *L'Ordre des trinitaires*, 2 vols., Toulouse, 1903; *KL*, xii. 84–91.

TRINITY, DOCTRINE OF THE.

I. The Biblical Doctrine.
  Old Testament (§ 1).
  New Testament (§ 2).
II. The Ontological Doctrine.
  The Eastern Church (§ 1).
  The Western Church (§ 2).
  Protestantism (§ 3).
  Comparison of the Biblical and Ontological Forms (§ 4).
  Various Conceptions (§ 5).
  A Concluding View (§ 6).

The doctrine of the divine Trinity is the summarized statement of the historical revelation of redemption for the Christian consciousness of God. It affirms that God is not only the ruler of the universe, but the Father of Christ, in whom he is perfectly revealed, and the source of a holy and blessed life which transforms nature and is realized in the Church. It constitutes the distinctive characteristic of Christianity as contrasted with Judaism and paganism and is a modification of Christian monotheism. In this, religious thinking may stop with a mere distinction of modes of divine revelation (economic Trinity); or proceed to the assumption of three divine essences (ontological or immanent Trinity). Since the Church has completed this advance from the economic to the immanent concept, the confession of the latter is alone recognized as adequate to a full Christian belief.

I. The Biblical Doctrine: Early dogmaticians were of the opinion that so essential a doctrine as that of the Trinity could not have been unknown to the men of the Old Testament. However, no modern theologian who clearly distinguishes between the degrees of revelation in the Old and New Testaments can longer maintain such a view. Only an inaccurate exegesis which overlooks the more immediate grounds of interpretation can see references to the Trinity in the plural form of the divine name Elohim, the use of the plural in Gen. i. 26, or such liturgical phrases of three members as the Aaronic blessing of Num. vi. 24–26 and the Trisagion (q.v.) of Isa. vi. 3. On the other hand, the development of Christology and, later, of the doctrine of the Trinity has undoubtedly been influenced by certain passages of the Old Testament

1. Old Testament.

which refer to permanent forms and media of divine revelation, as the Word of the Lord in Gen. i.; Ps. xxxiii. 6; Wisdom xvi. 12, xviii. 14–15; Ecclus. xliii. 25; wisdom in Prov. viii. 22 sqq.; and the angel of the Lord in Gen. xxii. 11–12; Ex. iii. 2, 4, 6; and Mal. iii. 1.

Even in the New Testament the doctrine of the Trinity is not enunciated, though it is deduced from a collocation of passages and from the logic of their premises. The chief New-Testament bases for the doctrine of the Trinity so far as the person of Christ is concerned briefly follow; for the rest see Christology. The primitive Christian view of the messiahship of Jesus presupposed that he was close to, and, in some sense, belonged to, God, as the instrument for the realization of the divine theocracy. Even Jewish theology had regarded the Messiah as ideally preexistent, or, more realistically, as reserved for the millennium, though without inquiring whether he was a creature or not. The early Church, in like manner, held Christ to be sent from heaven to earth (Gal. iv. 4). The messianic title of Son of God received the deeper meaning of intimate communion and love between Father and Son (according to the self-witness of Jesus, Matt. xi. 27), which was manifest on earth (John x. 30), but based on premundane existence (Rom. viii. 32; II Cor. viii. 9; Phil. ii. 5 sqq.). Christ can, therefore, act in the name of God since " in him dwelleth all the fulness of the Godhead bodily " (Col. ii. 9), and since he is the image of God (II Cor. iv. 4), and " the brightness of his glory, and the express image of his person " (Heb. i. 3). The Logos is bearer of the original self-revelation of God and is God (John i. 1, 14, 18); the risen and ascended Christ is called God (John xx. 28; I John v. 20; possibly also Rom. ix. 5; Titus ii. 13); prayer is made to the risen Christ (Acts ix. 14; Rom. x. 12 sqq.; I Cor. i. 2); practically Christ is included with God even to identification, though subordinated to the Father wherever a distinction occurs (I Cor. xi. 3, xv. 28). Even with reference to the Johannine Logos there is no thought of an immanent process of divine life, the Logos being simply the mediator of God's revelation to the world (John i. 4, iii. 16, xx. 31); and God, in relation to Christ, may be termed either " God " (John xvii. 3, xx. 17) or " Father " (I Cor. viii. 6). Of the Holy Ghost the New Testament says that he spoke through the prophets (II Pet. i. 21), and that he rested in his plenitude on Jesus, empowering him for his messianic work (Mark i. 10; John iii. 34); at his departure, the latter promised " another comforter " (John xiv. 16–17), who should uphold and perfect the communion between the disciples and their head (John xiv. 26, xvi. 13–14). A similar view is expressed by Paul (Rom. viii. 16; Gal. iv. 6); the Spirit is termed both the " Spirit of God " and the " Spirit of Christ " (Rom. viii. 9). Through this asscciation with the person of Christ the Spirit arrives at a certain proportion of definite content and function (I Cor. xii. 3; Jas. ii.); the risen Christ seems to be identified with the Holy Ghost (II Cor. iii. 17). The Holy Ghost is divine in origin and essentially one with God (I Cor. ii. 10), being the self-consciousness of God and re-

2. New Testament.

vealing the deep things in him, not, however, in a speculative sense. The Spirit internalizes the self-revelation of God revealed in Christ, imparting the new life of divine communion expressed again in moral fruits (Gal. v. 22–23). These operations of the Spirit are regarded as personal (Rom. viii. 16; Gal. iv. 6), and the Spirit himself is considered to be a person, who may be grieved by sinful acts (Eph. iv. 30). A similar concept underlies the Johannine terms " teaching," " reproving," and " declaring," as applied to the personal Paraclete (John xiv. 26, xvi. 8, 13). Nevertheless, to interpret these passages as implying a person distinct from God and Christ, whose Spirit he is called, is not warranted. Of the more directly Trinitarian references, the Apostolic benediction (II Cor. xiii. 13) points to the threefold causality of the redemptive life, in which the unity of the purpose of salvation comes to view, historically brought about by the sending of the Son and the imparting of the Spirit (cf. Gal. iv. 4, 6). The distribution of gifts, administrations, and operations (I Cor. xii. 4–6) refers back again to one Spirit, one Lord, and one God. The baptismal command (Matt. xxviii. 19) distinctly points, beyond doubt, to the faith of the Christian community concerning God, revealed threefold as Father, Son, and Holy Ghost. The dogmatic assertion, however, that the singular " name " signifies the unitary divine being transcendent to revelation, and that the collocation of Father, Son, and Holy Ghost represents their complete coordination, is not permissible. The creed elaborated from this formula mentions neither unity nor coordination, and the New Testament does not go further than a trinity of revelation. The essential emphasis in this connection is on the middle position of the Son; this is also substantiated by the circumstance that Acts and the epistles of Paul recognize baptism in Christ as the widely prevalent custom (Acts ii. 38, viii. 16, x. 48, xix. 5; I Cor. i. 13; Rom. vi. 3; Gal. iii. 27).

II. The Ontological Doctrine: There is no reason to seek for sources or types of the doctrine of the Trinity outside of Christianity or of the Bible, though in the eighteenth century efforts were made to derive the Christian dogma from Plato, and later from Brahmanism and Parseeism, or, later still, from a Babylonian triad. Even were the resemblance between the Christian Trinity and the pagan triads far greater than it is, there could be no serious question of borrowing. The development of the Christian doctrine of the Trinity is historically clear, and its motives are equally well known, being almost exclusively due to Christological speculation. The formulation of the dogma was ruled by the necessity of establishing the absolute character of the Christian revelation, a process which required the closest association of the historic Christ with the life and essence of God. At the same time, Christian faith could tolerate neither any menace to monotheism nor any lowering of the person of the Redeemer to a mere function or transitory phenomenon of the Godhead. The Apostolic Fathers did not feel the relation of the Father and the Son to be a problem, since they either con-

1. The Eastern Church.

sidered the Son simply as an instrument of the Father, or identified him with the Father and the Holy Ghost. The apologetes, on the other hand, who adopted for their basis the concept of the Logos for the interpretation of the person of Jesus, were indeed able to assign the Logos to a place within the revealing activity of God without impairing their monotheism, but could not make sure the concentration of revelation in Christ or his specific relation to the Father. Tertullian, who first formulated the concept *trinitas*, conceived of a self-disclosing of the Father in the Son and the Holy Ghost for the purpose of revelation preceding revelation itself. Origen completed this phase of development by postulating the eternal independence of the Logos with God. While, however, Origen considers the generation of the Son (of the universe as well) an eternal act, thus making him a partaker of the same essence with the Father, he has no clear idea of the nature of the Holy Ghost. He has an idea that the spheres of the persons of the Trinity are concentric; the Father ruling the universe, the Son rational creatures, and the Holy Ghost the saints. The modalistic type of Monarchianism (q.v.) identified the persons of the Father and the Son; while Sabellius (q.v.) held Father, Son, and Holy Ghost to be successive forms of revelation, or " persons " (*prosōpa*) of the Godhead, to which correspond three cosmic periods; namely, of creation and law, redemption, and communion. The advantage of this view was the coordination of the Son with the Father; its disadvantage, the contraction of the religious interest in the permanent mediatorship of Christ, which forced the idea of the hypostasis. As Arius intensified the distinction between the Father and the Son into an antithesis between creator and created, and disputed the eternity of the Son, it became necessary to connect with the eternal personal independence of the Son the assertion of his perfect divinity in the sense of identity of substance with the Father (*homoousios*). The result was its authoritative statement in the Nicene Creed (see Constantinopolitan Creed) and its argument in the theology of Athanasius (q.v.), the essential of which is soteriological, to conserve the essential mediatorship of Christ. Even Athanasius did not unconditionally rank the Father and the Son equal; nor does he have a technical term for the persons of the Trinity. On the other hand, he prepared the way for the *homoousion* of the Holy Spirit; for the Spirit, who imparts to man fellowship in the divine nature, must himself share in that nature. The doctrine of the Holy Ghost as thus developed needed only the opposition of the Pneumatomachi (see Macedonius and the Macedonian Sect) to be crystallized into the teaching of the Church at the Council of Constantinople in 381. By their distinction between " substance," or " essence," and " hypostasis," related to each other as " common " and " peculiar," the Cappadocians created a means of expressing the relation of the Trinity of persons to the unity of essence. According to Gregory Nazianzen (q.v.), the peculiar properties of the three persons were, respectively, " the state of being not begotten," " of being begotten," and " procession," though the Father still remained the primal divine person, the " source of Godhead." In the interest of this unity the final dogmatician of the Eastern Church, John of Damascus, taught the interpenetration and mutual immanence of the three hypostases (*perichōresis*); though he clung to the superiority of the Father, from whom the Holy Ghost proceeded through the Son.

Augustine (*De trinitate;* Eng. transl., *NPNF*, 1st ser., iii.), unlike the Greeks, taught that the unity was neither in Father, Son, nor Spirit; but in the divine being in which all three in like manner participate. Each person is the undivided deity, and the three persons are together the one God. This is conceivable only as the idea of person is sublimated somewhat like a relation of the deity with itself. Augustine's interest in reducing the prominence of personality in favor of simplicity or unity was his Neoplatonism. This view diverges from the older modalism in that it rests not upon a theory of succession but of eternal coexistence and of mutual immanence, as shown by his choice of illustrations. These were the analogies of memory, intelligence, and will, resolving themselves in self-consciousness; or, again, of the lover, the loved, and love. It follows from the equality of persons that the Holy Ghost is to be regarded as proceeding from the Son as well as the Father. Thus became possible such formulations as the Athanasian Creed (q.v.). The doctrine of the immanent Trinity, which with Athanasius was most intimately connected with the doctrine of salvation, had now become fully independent of historical revelation, a subject best suited to a mystical contemplative piety. During the Middle Ages the Augustinian formulas prevailed either for mystical absorption or dialectic refinements, without inherent change. The charge of tritheism (Roscellinus) or countercharge of Sabellianism (Abelard) lay in the nature of the inherited problem, which demanded a delicate poise between unity and difference. Richard of St. Victor (q.v.) endeavored to develop Augustine's speculations, deducing the necessity of a divine self-differentiation from the concept of love. Perfect love requires an object, and in the case of God that object can be only a person equal to himself in eternity, power, and wisdom. But since there can not be two divine substances, the two divine persons must be one and the same substance. The highest love, however, can not be limited to these two, but must rise to *condilectio*, through the wish that a third be loved as they love each other. Thus perfect love necessarily leads to the Trinity; and since God is absolute power, he can correspond fully to this requirement of the concept. Thomas Aquinas (q.v.), likewise seeking to remain in harmony with Augustine, deduced the generation of the Son from the immanent process of divine thought, and the procession of the Holy Ghost from the loving will, without reaching real personal distinctions. Duns Scotus (q.v.), though interested primarily in the latter side of the problem, dared give only a very reserved expression to his tendency.

The Reformers stood upon the ground of the

2. The Western Church.

Church catholic. Protestant dogmatics, placing monotheism first, considers God a single divine being in whom three subjects, Father, Son, and Holy Ghost, share equally, each of the three being termed a person. These persons must not be considered either real parts of the Godhead or individuals of a class, since the divine nature exists entire and undivided in each, so that to each one of them must be ascribed all divine qualities. Each person, however, has a distinctive hypostatic character, which has two features: one as regards its mode of being; and the other as regards its mode of revelation. The internal differences rest upon an immanent activity of the deity, and they refer not to the common action of the Godhead, but to the distinctive activities of the persons—the generation of the Son by the Father and the inspiration of the Holy Ghost by the Father and the Son. This generation differs from the creation of the world in that by the latter is established an essentially different existence from the creator himself, whereas generation implies a person like the Father in essence. In view of these *opera ad intra* the three persons have distinct properties: the Father, " paternity "; the Son, " filiation "; and the Holy Ghost, " procession." While this would seem to imply priority of the Son over the Holy Ghost, and of the Father over both, as a matter of fact the three persons are absolutely equal in virtue of the identity of their divine essence, and mutually condition each other. The priority of the Father relates only to " order of subsistence " not to being; it is merely logical, not real. The Father could not be the Father without the Son, nor could they both be the eternal principles of spirit and life without the procession of the Holy Ghost. In so far as the three persons can be conceived as possessing real distinctions and individualities, the inter-divine life must be regarded as a continuous circle, issuing from the Father, and returning to him through the Son and the Holy Ghost. As regards their mode of revelation; each of the three persons of the Trinity has specific activities: the Father, creation, preservation, and governance; the Son, redemption; and the Holy Ghost, sanctification. Unlike the *opera ad intra*, these functions (*opera ad extra*) are undivided activities of the deity and thus common to all three persons; for though a given function is held to be especially appropriate to the hypostatic character of a given person, the possession of the function in question is not denied the other persons. In this sense it may be said that power is especially characteristic of the Father, love of the Son, and wisdom of the Holy Ghost. It must be borne in mind, however, that dogmatic theology does not offer these explanations as a rational perception of the matter, but it holds the Trinity rather to be a mystery. These statements must, therefore, be considered rather as negative, preventing non-Christian views, than as positive elucidations.

3. Protestantism.

Turning from these ecclesiastical formulations to their Biblical basis, the essential differences are manifest: (1) The New Testament speaks of the essential unity of the Son with the Father, and regards the Holy Ghost as the indwelling of God in the faithful. This religious idea of the presence of God in Son and Spirit is replaced in dogmatics by the identity of the essence of the Son and the Holy Ghost with the Father, with an essentially new element of postulating eternally differentiated subjects as contrasted with the Father. (2) The New Testament contains no reference to an unconditional coordination of the Son with the Father. The Son, at least in his redemptive work, is dependent upon, and obedient to, the Father (cf. John xiv. 28; I Cor. xv. 28). The absence of similar statements concerning the Spirit is due to the representation of him as the medium of divine activity in the world and not as an independent person. While dependence of the Son upon the Father is not inconsistent with essential unity, equality and subordination are incompatible. (3) Dogma employs concepts for the construction of the immanent life in God that in Biblical terminology pertain to the record of revelation. " Son of God " is the name of the historic Christ, while where the preexisting mediator of revelation is referred to " Logos " is used. Thus the doctrine of eternal generation as a basis for the preexistence lacks support in the Bible (" only begotten " of John i. 14, iii. 16 expresses the close relation between Father and Son in regard to its stability, not its origin; and " the firstborn of every creature " of Col. i. 15 alludes to the preeminence of the author of salvation over creation, not to his origin). Particularly is there no reference in the New Testament to the procession of the Holy Spirit, in the sense of his immanent origin, but always as being sent into the world. (4) While conceiving the eternal relation of the Son and the Spirit to the Father as pretemporal and not as supertemporal, dogma does not make any further affirmations beyond what appears in the history of revelation. It converts the circuit of historical redemption into a bare counterpart of an immanent divine movement, wholly inconceivable until referred back to its historical original.

Individual voices against the doctrine of the Trinity during the Reformation (Hans Denk, J. Campanus, M. Servetus; qq.v.) were followed by Socinianism (see SOCINUS, FAUSTUS, SOCINIANISM), which rejected the doctrine as opposed to Scripture and reason, from the standpoint of abstract Unitarian conception and a moral view of religion. Arminianism (see ARMINIUS, JACOBUS, AND ARMINIANISM) comes into contact with Socinianism only as it regards the coordination unpermissible. Rationalism renewed the Socinian contention, and supernaturalism enforced the Arminian weakening of the dogma. Pietism either treated the rationalistic speculations with respectful silence or reduced them critically. The doctrine of the Trinity seemed to find more attention from philosophers than from theologians, especially through the theosophy of Jakob Boehme (q.v.) on speculative thought. But Schelling and Hegel (qq.v.) succeeded only in divorcing the dogma from its original basis, and in confining it merely to

4. Comparison of the Biblical and Ontological Forms.

5. Various Conceptions.

problems of cosmology. Schleiermacher (q.v.) demanded a reconstruction of the doctrine according to the Sabellian rather than the Athanasian point of view, while himself persisting in the presumption of an eternal and original division in the divine being. German theology was scarcely impressed with the negative Unitarianism of England and America, and presents various modern types. (1) The economic Trinity is exclusively adhered to by A. Schweizer, K. A. Hase, and R. A. Lipsius (qq.v.), while O. Pfleiderer (q.v.) assumes an ontological basis for the triad of revelation expressed in the divine qualities of power, wisdom, and love. (2) There is a return to the immanent Trinity, not by way of revelation or experience, but of speculation. Of the two types one holds that the divine self-consciousness needs for its fulfilment a distinction between the thinking subject, the object thought of, and their resolution in unity (A. Twesten; q.v.). F. H. R. Frank (q.v.) modifies this by deducing from personality subject, predicate, and their unity, referred as hypostases in God, and from the Christian experience of God conditioning sense of guilt, guiltlessness, and transference into the state of guiltlessness. The second tendency argues, from God as love upon an adequate subject necessarily distinct from the world and of identical essence with God, the mutuality of this love coming to rest in a third person (E. Sartorius and J. Müller; qq.v.). K. T. A. Liebner (q.v.) combines these two types; and kindred theories on the scheme of love are worked out by I. A. Dorner and W. Beyschlag (qq.v.). In these speculative theories, however, neither the identity of the divine subject and object, nor the mutuality of their love, gives a third independent factor which can be construed as a hypostasis. The same criticism applies to the theory of Frank. (3) More definite meaning is gained when that from which God is held to separate himself is regarded not as a being identical in essence with himself, but as the world (Neo-Hegelians, C. H. Weisse and A. E. Biedermann; q.v.); yet it is obvious that such a theory is antagonistic to the scheme of Christian salvation. (4) Other theologians seek to return to subordinationism, as K. F. A. Kahnis (q.v.), who defines the Son and the Holy Ghost as " God in the second and third sense of the word," and, more cautiously, Christian Thomasius (q.v.). (5) R. Rothe (q.v.) came nearest a real revision of the dogma, not so much by distinguishing in God absolute being, absolute spiritual nature, and absolute personality, as by his concepts of the head of the created world of spirits and of the Holy Ghost as the unity of thought and existence, a theory which contains elements of a system which would connect the conditions of religious and moral life with the eternal being of God. (6) J. C. K. Hofmann (q.v.) has attempted to combine the economic and the immanent Trinity, holding that the relation of the Father and the Son is intra-divine, though comprehensible to man only in its historical self-evidence on the basis of the Bible. Avoiding any attempt to penetrate into the premundane existence of God, he claims to apprehend the historic relation of God to man in redemptive revelation at the same time *sub specie æternitatis*. A somewhat similar position is taken by M. Kähler, (q.v.) who, while inferring from the threefold activity of God a corresponding ontological condition of divine being, urges that this be not employed in constructing intra-divine relations. The idea of the immanent Trinity is to serve only to impress the richness, sufficiency, and activity of the divine life. While A. Ritschl (q.v.), though not employing the word Trinity, had designated Christ and the Church as the eternal contents of God's thought and loving will, H. Schultz (q.v.) saw, further, the eternal indwelling of God in Christ and the Church based upon the eternal unfolding of his being in Word and spirit. Julius Kaftan (q.v.), finally, emphasizes that Trinitarian statements are matters of faith only in so far as they are based on the historic Christ and the historic communication of the Holy Spirit. Moreover, the economic and the immanent Trinity differ only in form, but in content they are congruent.

If it is the nature of faith to conceive the mundane in the supermundane, the historical in the eternal, then the religious realization of the history of redemption is only practicable as the eternal self-revelation and self-communica-

6. A Con- tion of God are perceived in the person
cluding   of the Redeemer and the possession of
View.   the Holy Spirit by the Church. The
           same Christ who, as the founder of a
new religious life, belongs to mankind and to history, belongs at the same time to the eternal life of God, of whom he is the full revelation. The Spirit by whom man calls God Father and is transformed into the likeness of Christ, belongs both to the temporal life of the Christian and to the self-manifestation of God, who desires to fill his personal creatures with his presence. If in the historic revelation of salvation the eternal activity of God be recognized, every other self-revelation of God must be connected with the historic Redeemer, and every other self-communication of God with the Holy Spirit. In all the leadings of mankind in preparation for redemption culminating in Christ, as well as in creation, this divine manifestation is patent. The Biblical term for this universality of revelation is Logos, implying not merely an explanation of revelation, but the expression of the immanent divine activity. All religious prophecy is an effect of the same Spirit who in his fulness dwells in the Christian society. Without this self-evidencing of God, no spiritual existence is conceivable to be complete. In this not only is the thought resumed which Origen associated with the idea of the eternal generation of the Son, but the idea of Paul (Col. i. 15 sqq.) is applied anew to the present world-conception. What, however, stands out clearly in a temporal process in the course of which the religious, moral, personal life takes shape, is, when considered as divine act, not a becoming but an eternal presence, the expression of his unchangeable being. In this sense, Son and Spirit are to be assumed as eternally existent in God. This is the final statement possible for thought. But the how of the immanent Trinity is inscrutable for want of categories of temporal thought to conceive the eternal or for want of analogies in human experience.

To speak of three persons in one Godhead is to use an inadequate symbol. The ancient conception of person was elastic enough to admit a recoalescence after the distinction, but the modern idea of personality as a distinctly self-conscious, self-determining psychical unity would yield only a collective unity as well as extinguish the human self-consciousness of Christ or ascribe to him a double personality. Better is it to speak of three elements, or a threefold eternal determination of the divine being. No theory must impair the personality of the exalted Christ for Christian piety. In him divine grace takes human shape in history, and in unison with the Father he remains the head of the Church. Likewise, God's holiness, transforming the earthly, obtains its historical form in the community of redemption, which joined in the Spirit with God through Christ participates in eternal life. To avoid empty schemata and the barren field of mystical contemplation, in the interest of vital reality, the immanent Trinity must never be isolated from the revealed. The religious value of the doctrine of the Trinity consists alone in expounding the history of revelation as the self-disclosure of the eternal God. The doctrine is a safeguard against false deistic representations of divine transcendence only when God's wisdom and love are viewed, not in an inscrutable self-evolution beyond, but as a world-immanent redeeming revelation. Against pantheism the surest weapon is the strictly personal, ethical conception of God's loving will, of necessity reverting to the historical revelation. Thus the order ever remains from the triad of revelation to unity and not *vice versa*, and the doctrine of the immanent Trinity can be no more than a limiting concept.   (O. Kirn†.)

BIBLIOGRAPHY: The question is treated historically in the works on the history of doctrine and on Biblical theology, and dogmatically in those on systematic theology (see in and under DOGMA, DOGMATICS). Consult also the works cited under ARIANISM; CHRISTOLOGY; GOD; HOLY SPIRIT, etc. The special literature is extensive. On the historical side consult: T. Maurice, *Dissertation on the Oriental Trinities*, London, 1800; E. Burton, *Testimonies of the Ante-Nicene Fathers to the Doctrine of the Trinity and of the Divinity of the Holy Ghost*, Oxford, 1831; G. S. Faber, *The Apostolicity of Trinitarianism*, 2 vols., London, 1832; F. C. Baur, *Die christliche Lehre von der Dreieinigkeit und Menschwerdung Gottes in ihrer geschichtlichen Entwicklung*, 3 parts, Tübingen, 1841–43; G. A. Meier, *Die Lehre von der Trinität in ihrer historischen Entwicklung*, Hamburg, 1844; J. R. Beard, *Historical and Artistic Illustrations of the Trinity*, London, 1846; C. Morgan, *The Trinity of Plato and Philo-Judæus*, ib. 1853; C. P. Caspari, *Der Glaube an die Trinität Gottes in der Kirche des 1. christlichen Jahrhunderts*, Leipsic, 1894; L. L. Paine, *Critical Hist. of the Evolution of Trinitarianism*, Boston, 1900; idem, *Ethnic Trinities and their Relation to the Christian Trinity*, ib. 1901; A. Beck, *Die Trinitätslehre des heiligen Hilarius von Poitiers*, Mainz, 1903; A. Dupin, *Le Dogme de la Trinité dans les trois premiers siècles de l'église*, Paris, 1907; W. S. Bishop, *The Development of Trinitarian Doctrine in the Nicene and Athanasian Creeds, A Study in Theological Definition*, London and New York, 1910; J. Lebreton, *Les Origines du dogme de la Trinité*, Paris, 1910.

For the doctrinal and apologetic side consult: J. Kidd, *An Essay on the Doctrine of the Trinity: attempting to prove it by Reason and Demonstration founded upon Duration and Space*, London, 1815; F. Schleiermacher, in his *Werke*, part I., vol. ii.; R. W. Landis, *A Plea for the Catholic Doctrine of the Trinity*, Philadelphia, 1832; J. Zukrigl, *Wissenschaftliche Rechtfertigung der christlichen Trinitätslehre*, Vienna, 1846; J. Wilson, *Unitarian Prin-*

ciples Confirmed by Trinitarian Testimonies; being Selections from the Works of eminent Theologians belonging to orthodox Churches, Boston, 1855; E. H. Bickersteth, *The Rock of Ages; or, Scripture Testimony to the One Eternal Godhead of the Father, and of the Son, and of the Holy Ghost*, London, 1860, New York, 1861; I. A. Dorner, *Die Lehre von der Person Christi*, 4 vols., Stuttgart, 1846–56, Eng. transl., 5 vols., Edinburgh, 1861–63; C. W. H. Pauli, *Great Mystery; or, How can Three be One?* London, 1863; F. H. Burries, *The Trinity*, Chicago, 1874; C. Braun, *Der Begriff " Person " in seiner Anwendung auf die Lehre von der Trinität und Inkarnation*, Mainz, 1876; A. Norton, *A Statement of Reasons for not Believing the Doctrines of Trinitarians Concerning the Nature of God and the Person of Christ*, 10th ed., Boston, 1877; J. Edwards, *Observations Concerning the Scripture Economy of the Trinity and Covenant of Redemption*, New York, 1880; H. Schultz, *Die Lehre von der Gottheit Christi*, Gotha, 1881; Abelard, *Tractatus de Unitate et Trinitate Divina*, ed., R. Stölzle, Freiburg, 1891; P. H. Steenstra, *The Being of God as Unity and Trinity*, New York, 1891; R. N. Davies, *Doctrine of the Trinity, the Biblical Evidence*, Cincinnati, 1891; R. Rocholl, *Der christliche Gottesbegriff*, Göttingen, 1900; R. F. Horton, *The Trinity*, London, 1901; T. Weber, *Trinität und Weltschöpfung*, Gotha, 1904; G. Krüger, *Das Dogma von der Dreieinigkeit und Gottmenschheit*, Tübingen, 1905; S. B. G. McKinney, *Revelation of the Trinity*, London, 1906; J. R. Illingworth, *Doctrine of Trinity apologetically Considered*, London and New York, 1907; A. F. W. Ingram, *The Love of the Trinity*, New York, 1908; Novatian, *De Trinitate*, ed. W. Y. Fausset, ib., London, 1909; L. Berthé, *La Sainte Trinité*, Paris, 1911.

TRINITY, FESTIVAL OF THE. See TRINITY SUNDAY.

TRINITY SUNDAY: The first Sunday after Pentecost. It was introduced into the calendar by Benedict XI. in 1305, and in the West concludes the festival part of the church year. In the Anglican church the Sundays from Whitsuntide to Advent are counted as the first, second, etc., till the twenty-sixth, Sunday after Trinity. The universal use in the Western Church of this festival of Trinity Sunday dates from Pope John XXII. (1334).

TRIPOLIS. See PHENICIA, PHENICIANS, I., § 8.

TRISAGION: The term applied in liturgics to the *Sanctus* or *Ter sanctus* of Isa. vi. 3 (" Holy, holy, holy, is the Lord of hosts: the whole earth is full of his glory "), and also to a Greek formula, " Holy God; holy, mighty; holy, immortal; have mercy upon us! " The trisagion of Isa. vi. 3 stands, more or less modified and amplified, in all liturgies of both East and West, usually in the preface to the mass, after praising God for the creation and before thanking him for redemption. In the Eastern liturgies, besides the universal insertion of " heaven " (or " heavens ") to supplement " earth," and the omission of " whole," three groups may be distinguished: those retaining " Lord " in the nominative in the first line and " his " in the second; those retaining " Lord " in the nominative but replacing " his " by " thy "; and those changing the nominative " Lord " to the vocative (cf. Rev. iv. 8). To the first group belong the Clementine liturgy (Apostolic Constitutions, viii. 12), the Antiochian liturgy preserved by Chrysostom, the older Egyptian, and the Ethiopic. The second group includes the eucharistic prayer of Serapion, and the liturgies of St. Mark, Asia Minor, and the Coptic Jacobites. In the third group are comprised the Syriac and Greek Jacobite liturgies. The form of the trisagion

given in Rev. iv. 8 occurs only in a fragment on a Coptic ostracum.

In the West the Sacramentary of Gelasius shows Syrian influence, having the form, " Holy, holy, holy, Lord God of Sabaoth: heavens and earth are full of thy glory; hosanna in the highest; blessed is he that cometh in the name of the Lord; hosanna in the highest." Though the Roman liturgy had the *Ter sanctus* as early as the time of Clement (I Clem. xxxiv. 6), the *Liber pontificalis* states that it was introduced into the mass by Sixtus I. (119–128?). Other Western liturgies are profoundly influenced by that of Rome, though the Mozarabic shows particularly strong Syrian influence. While in the East the trisagion and the *Benedictus* were given by the congregation, and while Sixtus had the *Ter sanctus* sung by the priest and the people, the Roman Church early placed it in the mouth of the subdeacon, and since the twelfth century it has been sung by the choir. From the Roman liturgy the trisagion was adopted by Lutheranism. In the *Formula missæ* (1523) Luther placed it after the words of institution, only to drop it in the *Deutsche Messe* of 1526. Subsequent usage varied between the two precedents set by Luther, but the modern Lutheran liturgies have almost without exception restored the trisagion, which they connect with the Hosanna and Benedictus and append to the prayer of the preface. Reformed liturgies, on the other hand, do not recognize it.

The age and the origin of the Greek trisagion are obscure, though legend tells that in the patriarchate of Proclus (434–446), after four months of earthquake, the people, crying to God for mercy, saw a young man raised into the air, where he heard a divine voice bidding him tell the bishop and people to repeat their litany with the words, " Holy God; holy, mighty; holy, immortal; have mercy upon us! " When this was done, the earthquake ceased. At all events, the formula is older than the fifth century, and is certainly not Jewish in origin. It is found in all Oriental liturgies. The fact that it does not occur in the Clementine liturgy may be due either to age or to the circumstance that this liturgy is only for the consecration of bishops, and consequently is abbreviated in its earlier portions. The hymn became so popular that it is sung in the daily offices. Its regular place in the mass is before the lessons, though the Coptic and Abyssinian Jacobite liturgies put it immediately before the Gospel, while it is sung by the Syrian Jacobites between the first and second lessons. The Greek trisagion owes its interest partly to the fact that it became the subject of a dogmatic controversy. While it was originally addressed to God, Petrus Fullo, patriarch of Antioch (about 470), added a phrase which made it an invocation of Christ, the result being deemed by certain circles compatible neither with orthodox trinitarianism nor with orthodox Christology (see THEOPASCHITES). The Concilium quinisextum of 692 rejected the addition of Fullo, but it continued to be used, even with amplifications, in Monophysite liturgies. The Greek trisagion was transplanted to the West, finding a place in the Gallican mass, and still being sung in the Mozarabic rite. It is likewise sung in the

Roman rite in the " Adoration of the Cross " on Good Friday, forming an antiphon of which one choir sings the Greek form, the other responding with the Latin version.   (P. Drews.)

Bibliography: Bingham, *Origines*, XIV., ii. 3, XV., iii: 10 (here the early testimonies are given at length in the original form); E. Martène, *De antiquis ecclesiæ ritibus*, IV., xxiii., 4 vols., Antwerp, 1736–38; E. Renaudot, *Liturgiarum orientalium collectio*, i. 207 sqq., ii. 69, 594, Frankfort, 1847; V. Thalhofer, *Handbuch der katholischen Liturgik*, ii. 183 sqq., Freiburg, 1890; G. Rietschel, *Lehrbuch der Liturgik*, i. 379 sqq., Berlin, 1900; A. Baumstark, *Die Messe im Morgenland*, pp. 133 sqq., 170 sqq., Kempten, 1906; Julian, *Hymnology*, pp. 459–460; *DCA*, ii. 1997; *KL*, xii. 91–92.

TRISTRAM, HENRY BAKER: Church of England; b. at Eglingham (35 m. n. of Newcastle), Northumberland, May 11, 1822; d. at Durham Mar. 8, 1906. He was educated at Lincoln College, Oxford (B.A., 1844). He was successively curate of Morchard Bishop in 1845–46, lecturer of Pembroke, Bermuda, and acting chaplain of the Bermuda dockyard, 1847–49, rector of Castle-Eden, Durham, 1849–60, and master of Greatham Hospital and vicar of Greatham, Durham, 1860–73. From 1873 until his death he was canon of Durham, of which he had been honorary canon, 1870–73. He was also proctor for the archdeaconry of Durham in 1874, 1880, and 1885, rural dean of Stockton, 1872–76, and of Chester-le-Street (west division) from 1876–80, and rector of Sandhutton, Yorkshire, in 1891; rural dean of Durham after 1880, proctor for the dean and chapter of Durham after 1899, and chaplain to the bishop of Durham after 1901. He was also an extensive traveler and an authority in the natural history of Palestine and the East. He wrote *The Great Sahara* (London, 1860); *The Land of Israel: A Journal of Travels with Reference to its Physical History* (1865); *Natural History of the Bible* (1867); *Ornithology of Palestine* (1867); *Scenes in the East* (1870); *The Seven Golden Candlesticks* (1872); *Bible Places: or, the Topography of the Holy Land* (1872); *The Land of Moab* (1873); *Pathways of Palestine* (2 vols., 1882); *Fauna and Flora of Palestine* (1884); *Eastern Customs in Bible Lands* (1894); and *Rambles in Japan* (1895).

TRITHEISM. See Tritheistic Controversy.

TRITHEISTIC CONTROVERSY: A controversy of the sixth century which so emphasized the three persons of the Trinity as to lose sight of the unity. Its history is closely connected with that of Aristotelianism in the Church, and consequently with that of Scholasticism (q.v.). The apologists of the second century in their naive impressions of the early faith were not conscious of the inner inconsistency of the doctrine. Again, they were dependent essentially upon Stoicism and Platonism, both of which are speculative and not rigidly logical. The first to recognize the contradiction between monotheism and the Trinity were the Monarchians (see Monarchianism), the modalistic school proceeding from the Stoic logic, and the dynamistic from Aristotelian dialectics. In the succeeding centuries the problem of the reconciliation of trinitarianism and monotheism sank into the background both because of the fact that the Trinity

was held to be a mystery, to be revered with silence and only to be analyzed so far as necessary to refute heretics; and because of a diminished interest in monotheism in the fourth century (perhaps on account of the entrance of certain pagan conceptions into the Church). Men like Athanasius and Basil the Great openly stated that the Christian doctrine of the Trinity was the correct mean between the extremes of the monotheism of the Jews (and the Sabellians) and the polytheism of the pagans. Thus it is clear that not even the suspected followers of the dynamistic Monarchists, the Arians (also Aristotelian), adhered to strict monotheism. To them Jesus was a man exalted by God, a hero or demigod. The mystical obscurity that veiled the doctrine began to lift with the spread of the rigid Aristotelian logic in the sixth century. Scythian monks, chiefly Leontius of Byzantium (q.v.), attempted to reconcile, with the aid of Aristotelian logic, the Alexandrine view of the acts of Chalcedon with the Western. At that time the Aristotelian philosophy led to the tritheistic controversy under Justinian I. (527–565), and Justin (565–578). The application of the Aristotelian logic might lead either to monarchianism or to tritheism, according to the subjective presupposition taken. Characteristic of the age of Justinian is the preference for the second alternative.

The origins of tritheism lie wholly in obscurity. Abulfaraj (q.v.) designates as the first tritheist a certain Johannes Askusnages (q.v.). Greek sources, on the other hand, point to Johannes Philoponos (q.v.) as the tritheistic heresiarch. At all events, tritheism arose and developed within monophysitism (see Monophysites). Johannes set forth his doctrine of the Trinity chiefly in his " Umpire; or On Unity," expressly confessing his Aristotelian basis, and identifying *hypostasis* and the peripatetic *átomon*. According to him, there are many men each with his own " essence," but " through their common form all men are one," so that in this sense they all have the same " essence." In similar fashion he conceived the relation of the three persons of the Trinity, thus introducing an entirely new theory, and to a certain extent identifying " essence " [" nature "] and " hypostasis " by assuming that each " hypostasis " must have a " nature " of its own, and *vice versa*. Hence, the absurdity of diophysitism was concluded, since if Jesus had two " natures " he must also have two " hypostases." Factions soon arose among the tritheists, chiefly because of the teaching of Johannes that the earthly body is not raised an incorruptible one, but that another is received in its stead. Those of the tritheists who opposed this doctrine were led by Conon of Tarsus (q.v.). No less torn into factions were the antagonists of the tritheists. Among them were the Petriani, who contended that the hypostasis connoted the " properties without the essence "; the Condobauditæ; the Agnoitæ; the Paulianistæ; the Angelitæ, and the Damianitæ (followers of Damianus of Alexandria, q.v.), who taught that neither Father, Son, nor Spirit was God in his own nature, but only in so far as they shared inseparably in the common inherent Godhead, which, common to the three " hypostases," was God in essence and nature (hence called Tetraditæ); and the Niobitæ who held that after the union of the natures in Christ there was no further difference. The tritheistic controversy may be assumed to have been terminated by the invasions of the Persians and Arabs into Egypt, the land which seems to have been its center.

The penetration of Aristotelianism into the West and the rise of scholasticism led to another tritheistic controversy though more restricted. The nominalist Roscelinus (q.v.; see also SCHOLASTICISM) declared that either the Father, Son, and Holy Ghost were *tres res*, or that the Father and the Holy Ghost had become incarnate with the Son, the former being the more probable. In 1092 Roscelinus was compelled, by a synod held at Soissons, to recant; and when he repeated his views, Anselm of Canterbury refuted him in his *De fide trinitatis et de incarnatione verbi contra blasphemias Rucelini.* In more recent times the Cartesian philosophy led some to tritheistic views, such as those of William Sherlock (q.v.) and Pierre Faydit of Paris (d. 1709). Heinrich Nicolai of Danzig (d. 1660), the rationalist Anton Oehmbs (d. 1809), and the Roman Catholic Anton Günther (d. 1863) were charged with teaching tritheism.

(J. LEIPOLDT.)

BIBLIOGRAPHY: The works of Johannes Philoponos (q.v.); Photius, *Bibliotheca*, xxiv., in *MPG*, ciii. 60 sqq.; Leontius of Byzantium, in *MPG*, lxxxvi. 1232D–1233B; Timothy of Constantinople, in *MPG*, lxxxvi. 1, pp. 44 sqq.; Sophronius of Jerusalem, in *MPG*, lxxxvii.; George the Pisidian, in *MPG*, xcii.; John of Damascus, *Hær.*, lxxxiii., in *MPG*, xciv. 744 sqq.; Nicephorus, *Hist. eccl.*, xviii. 47, 49; Abulfaraj (for his works see the article), in Assemani, *Bibliotheca orientalis*, ii.; J. L. von Mosheim, *Institutes of Ecclesiastical Hist.*, i. 431–432, London, 1863; Harnack, *Dogma*, iii. 90, 93–94, 101–102, iv. 124, 235, 240, vi. 182; and part of the historical literature under TRINITY.

TRITHEMIUS, trit-ê'mî-ūs, **JOHANNES:** German Benedictine; b. at Trittenheim (12 m. n.n.e. of Treves) Feb. 1, 1462; d. at Würzburg Dec. 13, 1516. After a youth of severest privation, he was enabled to begin his theological and humanistic education at Heidelberg, but in 1482 a sudden storm which caused him to return to the Benedictine monastery of Sponheim, near Kreuznach, where he had been hospitably received, led him to think himself divinely called to the monastic life. He was gladly accepted, and through his learning, piety, and diligence so won the esteem of the monks that within a year he was chosen abbot. He could now live the scholar's life; he speedily made the monastery library one of the most important in Germany, and was a friend of the leading humanists of the period. At the same time, he improved the tone of monastery life, both morally and intellectually, and greatly bettered its financial and architectural status. Despite all this, Trithemius was ill adapted to rule a monastery. He made repeated mistakes in choosing his priors, and his administration was marked by vacillation. More than this, he was absent from Sponheim more than was advisable, and his authority slipped from his hands before he was aware. Unwilling to fight for his position, he accepted the invitation of the learned Lawrence of Bibra, bishop of Würzburg,

who, in 1506, made him head of the small abbey of the Irish monastery of St. James in the see city. Here, in retirement and study, Trithemius passed the remainder of his life.

Comparatively few of the numerous writings of Trithemius, which were devoted to theology, history, and occultism (his studies in the latter gaining him the reputation of a magician), were published during his lifetime. To the latter category belong his *Steganographia, sive de ratione occulte scribendi* (written in 1500; Frankfort, 1606 [see J. E. Bailey, *John Dee and the "Steganographia" of Trithemius*, London, 1879]); and *Polygraphiæ libri quatuor* (written in 1507; Oppenheim, 1518 [French transl., *Polygraphie, et universelle escriture cabalistique*, Paris, 1561]). Of his theological writings the most important is the *Sermones et exhortationes ad monachos* (written in 1486; Strasburg, 1516). As a historian Trithemius gained wide fame during his lifetime, but he wrote from a partizan point of view, and even invented sources, as " Hunibald's " *Libri octodecim historiarum*, which he cited as an authority for the period from 440 to the reign of Chlodowech, or the Fulda chronicler " Meginfrid." These histories have no value except when treating of their author's own times. His theological writings were collected under the title *Johannis Trithemii Opera pia et spiritualia quotquot reperiri potuerunt* (ed. J. Busæus, Mainz, 1604) and in J. Busæus' *Paralipomena opusculorum Petri Blesensis, Johannis Trithemii, et Hincmari* (1605); his historical writings appeared as *Johannis Trithemii, . . . Opera historica* (ed. M. Freher, 2 parts, Frankfort, 1601), while J. G. Schlegel edited the *Annales Hirsaugienses* (St. Gall, 1690); and his letters formed the volume entitled *Johannis Trithemii, abbatis Sponheimensis, epistolarum familiarium libri duo* (Hagenau, 1536). (A. HAUCK.)

BIBLIOGRAPHY: H. A. Erhard, *Geschichte des Wiederaufblühens wissenschaftlicher Bildung*, iii. 379 sqq., Magdeburg, 1832; Paul, *De fontibus a Trithemio . . .*, Halle, 1867; J. Silbernagl, *J. Trithemius*, Landshut, 1868; K. E. H. Müller, *Quellen welche der Abt Tritheim . . . benutzt hat*, Leipsic, 1871; W. Schneegans, *Abt J. Trithemius und Kloster Sponheim*, Kreuznach, 1882; G. Mentz, *Ist es beweisen, dass Trithemius ein Fälscher war?* Jena, 1892; *ADB*, xxxviii. 626 sqq.; *KL*, vi. 1770 sqq.

TRIUMPHUS, trai'umf-us, **AUGUSTINUS (AUGUSTINO TRIONFO):** Italian Augustinian; b. at Ancona in 1243; d. at Naples Apr. 2, 1328. At the age of eighteen he entered the Augustinian order, and studied at Paris under Thomas Aquinas and Bonaventura, later himself delivering lectures. In 1274 he was summoned by Gregory X. to the Council of Lyons, and three years later became chaplain of Prince Francesco Carrara at Padua. Later he was again at Ancona, whence he was called to Naples by Charles II., where until his death he was royal tutor, counselor, and envoy. A steadfast adherent of papal sovereignty, he wrote, in 1308, his treatise *Contra articulos inventos ad diffamandum sanctissimum patrem . . . Bonifacium papam*, which, while advocating obedience to the French Pope Clement V., urged that the papal throne be filled by Italians. Other writings of this period are *Super facto templariorum* and *De potestate collegii mortuo papa*, the first declaring that the pope alone has power to judge heretics, and accordingly disapproving the royal proceeding in the case of the Knights Templars (see TEMPLARS), and the second opposing the oligarchic tendency of the college of cardinals, an attitude still further emphasized in his *Contra divinatores et somniatores*. These thoughts are summed up in his *Summa de potestate ecclesiastica*, written about 1322 (Augsburg, 1473, etc.; last ed., Rome, 1584), in which the doctrine of papal supremacy over emperor and princes is carried to its utmost extreme.

(R. SCHMID.)

BIBLIOGRAPHY: F. C. Curtius, *Virorum ex ordine erimitarum . . . elogia*, Antwerp, 1636; E. Friedberg, in *ZKR*, 1869; Scholz, in Stutz's *Kirchenrechtliche Abhandlungen*, 1903, parts 6–8; J. Haller, *Papsttum und Kirchenreform*, i. 82, Berlin, 1903.

TROAS. See ASIA MINOR, IV.

TROELTSCH, trȫltsh, ERNST PETER WILHELM: German Protestant; b. at Haunstetten (2 m. s. of Augsburg) Feb. 17, 1865. He was educated at the universities of Erlangen, Berlin, and Göttingen from 1883 to 1888 (lic. theol., Göttingen, 1891); was vicar at Munich in 1890; became privat-docent at Göttingen, 1891; associate professor at Bonn, 1892; professor of systematic theology at Heidelberg, 1904; and succeeded Pfleiderer at Berlin in 1908. He has written *Vernunft und Offenbarung bei Johann Gerhard und Melanchthon* (Göttingen, 1891); *Richard Rothe* (Freiburg, 1899); *Die wissenschaftliche Lage und ihre Anforderungen an die Theologie* (Tübingen, 1900); *Die Absolutheit des Christentums und der Religionsgeschichte* (1902); *Politische Ethik und Christentum* (Göttingen, 1904); *Das Historische in Kants Religionsphilosophie* (Berlin, 1904); *Psychologie und Erkenntnistheorie in der Religionswissenschaft* (Tübingen, 1905); *Die Bedeutung des Protestantismus für die Entstehung der modernen Welt* (Munich, 1906); *Die Trennung von Staat und Kirche* (Tübingen, 1907); and contributed to *Geschichte der christlichen Religion*, in *Kultur der Gegenwart*, I., iv. (Leipsic, 1909); also *Schleiermacher, der Philosoph des Glaubens* to *Moderne Philosophie* (Berlin, 1910).

TRONCHIN, tron-shān, LOUIS: Son of Theodore Tronchin (q.v.); b. at Geneva Dec. 4, 1629; d. there Sept. 8, 1705. He studied at the Protestant academy of Saumur under Moïse Amyraut (q.v.), whose " hypothetical universalism " had been vehemently contested by Tronchin the elder; he became pastor of the congregation of Lyons, 1656; and professor of theology at Geneva, 1661, in which position he represented the liberal trend and advocated tolerance. In 1669 he demanded the abolition of the oath that was imposed on all candidates [in theology], not to attempt any innovations in the Calvinist doctrine. His works were: *Disputatio de providentia Dei* (Geneva, 1670); *De auctoritate Scripturæ Sacræ* (1677).   G. BONET-MAURY.

BIBLIOGRAPHY: E. and É. Haag, *La France protestante*, vol. ix., 2d ed., Paris, 1877 sqq.; J. Gaberel, *Hist. de l'église de Genève*, vol. iii., Geneva, 1862; C. Borgeaud, *L'Académie de Calvin*, ib. 1900; Lichtenberger, *ESR*, xii. 234–236.

TRONCHIN, THEODORE: Orientalist, theologian, and controversialist; b. at Geneva Apr. 17,

1582; d. there Nov. 19, 1657. He studied theology at Geneva, Basel, Heidelberg, Franeker, and Leyden; became professor of oriental languages at the academy of Geneva, 1606; preacher there in 1608; and professor of theology in 1618. In 1618 he was sent with his colleague Giovanni Diodati to the Synod of Dort, as delegate of the venerable company of Genevan ministers; and he there vindicated Calvin's theology against the Arminians. In 1632 he was army chaplain under Duke Henri de Rohan, during his final campaign in Valtellina. His works are: *Cotton plagiaire ou la vérité de Dieu et la fidélité de Genève, maintenues contre les accusations du P. Cotton, jésuite, contre la Bible de Genève* (Geneva, 1620); *De bonis operibus* (1628); *Oratio funebris de Henrico duce Rohani* (1638); *De peccato originali* (1658).   G. BONET-MAURY.

BIBLIOGRAPHY: The same as for the preceding article.

TRONDHJEM, trȫnd'yem: Ancient town and seat of the first bishopric in Norway. The town was founded by Olaf Trygveson in 997; the first bishop was probably Sigurd (1032–50). Originally Norway belonged to the archiepiscopal diocese of Hamburg-Bremen (see BREMEN, BISHOPRIC OF; HAMBURG, BISHOPRIC OF), after 1104 to that of Lund, but in 1148 obtained its own metropolitan, who resided in the city. The cathedral, which contained the shrine of St. Olaf (q.v.), was one of the largest and most magnificent in Scandinavia, though it was never fully completed. It was repeatedly injured by fire. In the time of the Reformation the shrine was removed to Copenhagen. The structure has since 1869 been undergoing careful and complete restoration.

BIBLIOGRAPHY: H. M. Schirmer, *Kristkirken i Nidaros*, Christiania, 1885; *Guide to Trondhjem*, Trondhjem, 1890; H. Mathieson, *Det gamle Throndhjem. Byens Historie 997–1152*, Christiania, 1896; H. G. Heggtveit, *Throndhjem i Fortid og Nutid, 997–1897*, Horten, 1897; *Trondhjems 900 Aars Jubilæum*, Trondhjem, 1897; *Trontheim*, in *Tronhjemske Samlinger*, ib. 1901.

TRUBER, PRIMUS: Reformer in Carniola (in southern Austria); b. at Raschiza, near Auersperg (3 m. n.e. of Triest) in 1508; d. at Derendingen (1 m. s.w. of Tübingen) June 29, 1586. His poverty was such that he was unable to obtain a university education, but in Peter Bonomo, the bishop of Triest, a humanist inclined toward an Evangelical reformation within the Roman Catholic Church, he found a patron who enabled him to enter the priesthood. He became chaplain at Cilli, before 1530, where he began to preach against the abuses in the Church. This led him to Laibach in 1531, where he preached against celibacy, the communion in one species, and for justification by faith alone. Here as early as 1527 a circle of men of an Evangelical cast of mind had collected about Matthias Klombner, which led King Ferdinand I. to forbid their doctrines. In 1536 Truber was joined by the Laibach canon Paul Wiener, who later became the first Protestant bishop of Transylvania, but in 1540 he was obliged to retire as parish priest to Lack, near Ratschoch, and in 1541 the parish of Tüpper was added. He became canon at Laibach in 1542; German and Wendish preacher in the cathedral in 1544; and parish priest of St. Bartholomäenfeld in Lower Carniola in 1546. But in 1547 the storm broke over the Evangelicals, and Truber escaped imprisonment only by flight, losing all his benefices and his library. Returning to his home in 1548, he was again forced to flee, and, reaching Nuremberg, an appointment as morning preacher at Rothenburg on the Tauber was secured for him by Veit Dietrich. Here he began to prepare Evangelical writings in the Wendish language and published, under the pesudonym Philopatridus Illyricus, *Catechismus* (Tübingen, 1550), and "Abecedarium and the Shorter Catechism" (same year). He became pastor at Kempten in 1552, and published the New Testament (Tübingen, 1557–77; 2d ed., 1582); *Articoli oli deili* (1562), a compendium of the Augsburg, Württemberg, and Saxon Confessions; *Ordninga cerkovna*, a church order (1564); *Ta celi Psalter* (1566); *Ta celi catechismus*, a hymn-book (1567; 4th ed., Laibach, 1579); and *Catechismus s dueima islagama* (Tübingen, 1575). At the same time many of these works, including the New Testament, were translated into Croatian. In the mean time Carniola had become so thoroughly Protestantized that in 1560 Truber was recalled. In 1562 he removed to Laibach, but in December he and other Evangelicals were tried before the bishop, who, however, was himself confronted by a formal charge of immorality, which, for the time being, halted the proceedings against Truber. The latter's work of organization now went on unhindered. But when, on Apr. 28, 1564, the archduke, visiting Laibach, attended mass at the cathedral, the nobles of the estates attended him to the door, but, turning, went to the Church of St. Elizæbeth, where Truber was preaching. This gave opportunity to his adversaries not only to secure the prohibition of the church-order which he was attempting to introduce, but also his perpetual banishment from Carniola. Truber now became pastor at Laufen on the Neckar in Württemberg, 1565–66; and then at Derendingen until his death. For the progress of the Reformation and the Counter-Reformation in Carniola see INNER AUSTRIA, THE REFORMATION IN; also FERDINAND II. AND THE COUNTER-REFORMATION IN AUSTRIA, § 5.

(THEODOR ELZE†.)

BIBLIOGRAPHY: Truber's *Briefe*, ed. T. Elze, were issued at Tübingen, 1898; and the funeral sermon by Jakob Andreä at the same place, 1586. Consult further: H. C. W. Sillem, *Primus Truber*, Erlangen, 1861; T. Elze, *Die Superintendenten der evangelischen Kirche in Krain während des 16. Jahrhunderts*, Vienna, 1863; idem, *Die Universität Tübingen und die Studenten aus Krain*, Tübingen, 1877; idem, *Paul Wiener*, Vienna, 1882; J. Loserth, *Die Reformation und Gegenreformation in den innerösterreichischen Ländern*, Stuttgart, 1898.

TRUCE OF GOD: An institution which originated in France from efforts of the Church to mitigate the evils accruing especially to the lower classes of the people from the quarrels of the feudal nobles. The preliminary measures are more properly designated the "peace of God." Agreements of peace were discussed and settled in synods first in 990 at three assemblies in different regions of South and Middle France—in Narbonne, Puy en Velay, and Charroux near Poitiers. In course of time assemblages for this purpose became more frequent, until they reached their culminating point in 1034. The lay population, sometimes only the feudal nobility, was bound by oath to observe the restrictions agreed upon. Church buildings and their surroundings, also special classes of people like clergy and monks, at times also pilgrims, merchants, and women, but especially peasants working in the fields, were protected by statute against attacks arising from feuds.

This older movement for peace was followed by the "truce of God" in the proper sense. Its characteristic, in contrast with the older movements, was the fact that on definite days and at definite periods (the so-called binding days or periods), every feud was prohibited; the armistice, thus introduced, was traced back to the will of God. About 1040 the new institution began to take root in the whole of France. It pervaded also Burgundy, Flanders, southern Italy, Spain, and Germany, but did not attain popularity in England. While the peace of older times was dependent upon the number of people who had sworn to it, it became now, under the influence of the papacy, a general church law. The "binding periods" were originally from Saturday evening to Monday morning; but after 1040 they extended from Wednesday evening to Monday morning. It soon became customary to select not only special days of the week, but longer periods for times of peace; as, for instance, Lent and the period from Easter to Trinity Sunday; also the time from Advent to Epiphany. The punishment of violation was usually ecclesiastical, but sometimes secular. After 1100 the practise waned, other restraints having been introduced; in the canons of the Fourth Lateran Council (1215) no mention is made of it. (SIEGFRIED RIETSCHEL.)

BIBLIOGRAPHY: A. Kluckhohn, *Geschichte des Gottesfrieden*, Leipsic, 1857; E. Semichon, *La Paix et la trève de Dieu*, Paris, 1857; J. Fehr, *Der Gottesfriede, und die katholische Kirche des Mittelalters*, Augsburg, 1861; Hefele, *Conciliengeschichte*, iv. 688 sqq., R. C. Trench, *Mediæval Church History*, pp. 424 sqq., London, 1877; W. E. H. Lecky, *European Morals*, ii. 254, New York, 1894; P. Hinschius, *Kirchenrecht*, v. 305 sqq., Berlin, 1893; E. Sachur, *Die Cluniacenser*, ii. 213, Halle, 1894; E. Mayer, *Deutsche und französiche Verfassungsgeschichte*, i. 161 sqq., Leipsic, 1899; Neander, *Christian Church*, iii. 407. Original documents are accessible in Huberti, ut sup.: in *MGH, Leg.*, Sectio IV., *Constitutiones*, i (1893), 596 sqq.; Reich, *Documents*, pp. 151–152; Henderson, *Documents*, pp. 208–211; Thatcher and McNeal, *Source Book*, pp. 412–419; Robinson, *European History*, i. 187–191; D. C. Munro and G. C. Sellery, *Medieval Civilization*, pp. 183–184, New York, 1904.

On the separate countries, consult for France: C. Pfister, *Étude sur la règne de Robert le Pieux*, pp. 161 sqq., Paris, 1885; L. Huberti, *Studien zur Rechtsgeschichte der Gottesfrieden*, vol. i., Anspach, 1892 (contains all that is really essential). For Germany: E. Steindorff, *Jahrbücher des deutschen Reichs unter Heinrich III.*, i. 337, 448 sqq., Leipsic, 1874; Nitzsch, in *Forschungen zur deutschen Geschichte*, xxi (1881), 269 sqq.; Herzberg-Fränkel, ib., xxiii (1883), 117 sqq.; G. Waitz, *Verfassungsgeschichte*, ed. G. Seeliger, vi. 537, Berlin, 1896. For Italy: Bollati, in *Miscellanea di storia Italiana*, xviii. 373 sqq.; Duc, ib., xxiv. 366 sqq. For England: F. Liebermann, *Ueber die Leges Edwardi Confessoris*, pp. 59 sqq., Halle, 1896.

TRUDBERT, trŭt′bert **(TRUTPERT):** Martyr and founder about 600 of a famous monastery 20 m. s. of Freiburg in the Breisgau; b., possibly in Ireland, in the sixth century; d., according to some, in 607. Legend makes him the brother of Rupert, the apostle to the Bavarians, and states that he made a pilgrimage to Italy. His day is Apr. 26. His remains were disinterred in 816, and his basilica was rebuilt. His legendary life is preserved in three recensions: one of the early ninth century (ed. F. J. Mone, *Quellensammlung der badischen Landesgeschichte*, i. 19–21, Carlsruhe, 1845; *MGH, Script. rer. Merov.*, iv. 352 sqq.), a second by Abbot Erchenbald early in the tenth century (ed. Mone, ut sup., pp. 22–26), and a third written in 1279 or 1280 (ed. *ASB*, Apr., iii. 424 sqq.).

(D. KERLER†.)

BIBLIOGRAPHY: Rettberg, *KD*, ii. 48–50; Friedrich, *KD*, ii. 1, pp. 607–613; Hauck, *KD*, i. 340–341. A number of early sources of greater or lesser value are collected in F. J. Mone, *Quellensammlung der badischen Landesgeschichte*, i. 19–26, Carlsruhe, 1848; and in *ASB*, April, iii. 426–440. Consult further: A. Baur, in *Freiburger Diöcesan-Archiv*, xi (1877), 249–252; also J. G. Meusel, *Neueste Literatur der Geschichtskunde*, p. 355, Erfurt, 1780; Rieder, *Zeitschrift der Gesellschaft für Beförderung der Geschichts-Kunde vom Freiburg*, xiii (1897), 79–104; *KL*, xii. 120.

TRUE REFORMED CHURCH. See REFORMED (DUTCH) CHURCH, II., § 7.

TRUEBLOOD, BENJAMIN FRANKLIN: Friend; b. near Salem, Ind., Nov. 25, 1847. He was educated at Earlham College, Richmond, Ind. (B.A., 1869), and was principal of Raisin Valley Seminary, Adrian, Mich. (1869–71), professor of English literature in Earlham College (1871–73) and of classics in Penn College, Ia. (1873–74), and president of Wilmington College, O. (1874–79), and of Penn College (1879–90). In 1890–91 he studied military conditions in Europe, and since 1892 has been general secretary of the American Peace Society, and editor of *The Advocate of Peace*. He has attended nearly all the international peace conferences and has been a vice-president of several of them. He took part in the National Arbitration conferences at Washington in 1896 and 1904, and in the National Peace Conference at New York in 1907. Theologically he describes himself as " orthodox in a large, general sense," and as accepting the historical method of the study of the Bible, although not acquiescing in some of the extreme conclusions of higher criticism. He has written *The Federation of the World* (Boston, 1899); and *International Arbitration at the Opening of the 20th Century* (1910).

TRULLAN SYNODS: Two synods held in 680 and 692 in the council chamber of the imperial palace at Constantinople, which had an oval vaulted roof (hence the name, Gk.-Lat., *troullos, troulla,* " bowl "). The first of these, the sixth ecumenical council, was convened by the Emperor Constantinus Pogonatus, and in eighteen sessions endeavored to allay the controversies aroused by the Monothelites (q.v.). The second Trullan synod was convened by Justinian II. to complete, and form one council with, the two ecumenical councils of 553 and 680. It issued 102 canons, some of which excited the antagonism of the Western Church. It also ignored almost entirely Western synods, thus disregarding all enactments of the popes. The thirteenth canon sanctioned the marriage of the clergy. The thirty-sixth canon, though ranking the patriarch of Constantinople after the pope, made him equal in power and privileges.

The fifty-fifth canon repeated the Eastern prohibition of fasting on the Saturdays in Lent; the sixty-seventh forbade the eating of blood or of suffocated animals; and the eighty-second prohibited the use of certain pictures of Christ as the Lamb of God, particularly those in which John the Baptist was also represented. Though the legates of Pope Sergius I. signed the canons of the synod, when Justinian demanded the signature of Sergius I., the latter refused and absolutely rejected the canons of the synod, because the authority of Rome was lessened. Yet a definite pronouncement of the church was never delivered. Hadrian I., in 785, spoke as if he approved them, but John VIII. (872–882), while not specifically rejecting any canons, declined to approve any which were contrary to former canons, to papal decrees, or to good morals. The Greek Church, on the other hand, has always recognized the Trullan canons as the valid measures of an ecumenical council. (A. HAUCK.)

BIBLIOGRAPHY: W. Beveridge, *Synodicon, sine pandectæ canonum*, i. 152–283, Oxford, 1672; F. Walch, *Historie der Kirchensammlungen*, pp. 432 sqq., 441 sqq., Leipsic, 1759; idem, *Historie der Ketzereien*, ix. 317 sqq., 387 sqq., 443 sqq., ib. 1780; J. S. Assemani, *Bibliotheca juris orientalis*, i. 120, 408 sqq., v. 55–348, Rome, 1766; J. C. W. Augusti, *Denkwürdigkeiten aus der christlichen Archäologie*, iii. 124 sqq., 12 vols., Leipsic, 1817–31; A. Pichler, *Geschichte der kirchlichen Trennung zwischen Orient und Occident*, i. 87 sqq., Munich, 1864; Hergenröther, *Conciliengeschichte*, iii. 314–347, Eng. transl., v. 206–241, Fr. transl., iii. 1, pp. 539–581; idem, *Photius*, i. 210 sqq., 216 sqq., Regensburg, 1867; Schaff, *Christian Church*, iv. 507–510; Mansi, *Concilia*, xi. 189 sqq., 921 sqq.; *KL*, xii. 120–121.

TRUMBULL, HENRY CLAY: Congregationalist; b. at Stonington, Conn., June 8, 1830; d. in West Philadelphia, Pa., Dec. 8, 1903. His education was chiefly private. He was in business from 1849 till 1858, when he became state missionary of the American Sunday School Union for Connecticut. On Sept. 10, 1862, he was ordained as a Congregational clergyman in order to go as chaplain to the Tenth Regiment Connecticut Volunteers, and was in the army service till Aug. 25, 1865 (prisoner of war in South Carolina and Virginia, 1863). From 1865 till 1871 he was secretary for the New England department of the American Sunday School Union; was normal secretary of the society till 1875, when he came to his final position, the editorship of *The Sunday School Times*, published in Philadelphia, of which he subsequently became owner and which he brought to the front rank of Sunday-school journalism. In consequence of his excessive labors he broke down in the winter of 1880 and in Jan., 1881, went for rest and recreation to Egypt and Palestine. He had no linguistic fitness for oriental or Biblical research, but he devoted much attention to archeology and wrote two volumes which display wide reading and have been well received. The first, *Kadesh Barnea* (New York, 1884), describes, justifies, and puts in its proper setting what has been accepted as the discovery of the true site of Kadesh Barnea, at Ḳadees, visited on Mar. 30, 1881. The second was *The Blood Covenant* (1885). The last was supplemented by *The Threshold Covenant* (1896) and *The Covenant of Salt* (1899), both valuable. Considering how busy his life was, his authorship in the way of books was large, for, in addition to those mentioned, he wrote five biographies, Henry Ward Camp (*The Knightly Soldier*, Boston, 1865); Elliot Beecher Preston (Hartford, 1866); John Wait Barton (*Falling in Harness*, Philadelphia, 1867); Henry Hatch Manning (*The Captured Scout of the Army of the James*, Boston, 1869); and Henry Philemon Haven (*The Model Superintendent*, New York, 1880), and several books on his specialty of Sunday-school instruction, *The Sunday-school Concert* (Boston, 1861); *Teaching and Teachers* (Philadelphia, 1885); *The Sunday-school, its Origin, Mission, Methods and Auxiliaries* (Yale lectures, 1888); and *Principles and Practice* (1889).

BIBLIOGRAPHY: P. E. Howard, *The Life Story of Henry Clay Trumbull*, Philadelphia, 1905.

TRUTH, TRUTHFULNESS.

I. Theory of Religious Knowledge.
    Aristotelian Logic (§ 1).
    Critique of Kant (§ 2).
    Theory of Historical Truth (§ 3).
    Religion and History (§ 4).
    The Value-judgment (§ 5).
    Summary (§ 6).
II. Truthfulness.
    Historical (§ 1).
    Candor and Orthodoxy (§ 2).
    Essentials of Truthfulness (§ 3).

In a treatment consistent with the modern scientific position, truth and truthfulness or reality can no more be separated than " faith which is believed " and " faith which believes." Truthfulness presupposes a " will for truth." Such truth has become a possession that discloses itself to the entire man only as he fulfils certain conditions.

I. Theory of Religious Knowledge: For the naive consciousness human knowledge is the inner picture of outer reality. This postulate lies at the basis of all systems of identity of thought and being. The view prevailed until the time of Kant, and, though not wholly overcome, yet since his day scientific knowledge has come to be contrasted from the naive as critical. Kant opened his critique upon experience, the classified knowledge of experience, or the mathematical scientific knowledge of nature, a sphere in which the identity of thought and being seemed precisely self-evident. All logic (the science of knowledge till Kant) until then was Aristotelian and the logic of the cognition of nature. There was scarcely the inception of a logic of history. Of the Greeks Socrates turned from nature and founded ethics, and Plato's ethics came more and more to be religion. Medieval logic, however, stood upon Aristotle; and how seriously it claimed to deal with experience is best shown in the fundamental contentions over the universal and the particular, a problem occupying anew the inquiry of the theory of knowledge to-day. But upon the point that truth was simply a picture of the real experientially there was no disagreement; and historical, ethical, and religious knowledge was logically conceived in forms derived from the cognition of nature. To the truth thus attained by the natural reason was added, in Christian dogmatics, that given by supernatural revelation alone; and yet positively as revelation was preferred, it did not alter the con-

1. Aristotelian Logic.

ception of truth as such. There has never been a more unitary universal philosophy than Scholasticism (q.v.), and yet this was but the scientific projection of naive knowing and popular faith. Even the peculiar products of the original knowledge of the mystics, derived by contemplation and ecstasy, were not too remote to be incorporated in the general world-view, under the ruling impression that truth was the image of reality and fundamentally one. The first to waver were the nominalists. William of Occam taught that the most important dogmas contained elements inconsistent with the principle of reason. His pupil, Robert Halcot, was the first to teach the " twofold sense," which the Lateran Council (1515) condemned, namely, that the same thing may be theologically false and philosophically true and *vice versa*. Luther was a nominalist, repudiated the Aristotelian logic in theology, adhered to the twofold sense, mysticism, and the Bible; he deserved to be recognized as the first theologian of experience, who from his own inner life and conduct arrived at a new conception of truth. Through Melanchthon, reinspired by a new philological, critical edition of Aristotle, the medieval view again gained central place in Protestantism. Meanwhile, philosophy was diverted from dogmatism to become empiricism, sensationalism, or skepticism.

The mathematical physical science of Sir Isaac Newton had attained a degree of certainty, until recently unanticipated and almost unsurpassable. At this point, Kant sought the fundamentals of this drift, and found them by a critical analysis of human experience. He discovered that the *a priori* forms of time and space and the categories of the intellect were the tools whereby the reason reaches into and legislates upon the undefined raw materials of sense, thus first making scientific sense-experience possible. Reason, together with what it contributes, alone enforces itself upon sense phenomena, producing knowledge, to which it imparts strict conformity with law, necessity, and universality. In drawing attention to the universal relations that make knowledge possible, Kant removed knowledge from the things in themselves, which recede to an inaccessible remoteness, into the inner sanctum of the active human spirit itself. He did not surrender it to the empirical individual; but, by logical critical deduction, he set forth pure reason as an inner structure of the human spirit-life, transcending every form of individuality and all empirical psychology, and possessing its own cohesive laws as well as universal validity. Neither has pure subjectivism any claim here; on the contrary thus is mathematical physical knowledge made possible. The old naive conception of truth with the indulgence of extravagant suppositions on the part of speculative philosophy had to be destroyed, in order, as he professed, to save faith; for to apply the instruments of pure reason to that which is not subject of experience (sense) would lead to unbelief. The truth of the subjects outside of that experience must be approached by another way, that of faith. This way is by the course of the *a priori* moral law,

2. Critique of Kant.

Founded upon the experience of the practical reason, the knowledge of freedom, immortality, and God (on the three postulates, see RELIGION, PHILOSOPHY OF, I., 3, § 4) is more secure than if derived from the complex of outer experience. This meant the reenthronement of the will in philosophy, which in the Aristotelian metaphysics had become a mere attendant of the intellect (cf. Thomas Aquinas, in SCHOLASTICISM, III., 2, § 1). In this realm of the practical reason, ethical truth obtained an impregnable security, and here Kant laid the basis. The doctrine of the twofold sense had become firmly established in principle and method, and notwithstanding recurring attack, it prevails to this day in theology and philosophy.

Certainly there is only one truth; but it does not lend itself so readily to the convenient scheme of reality there and thought here. On the contrary, in different ways, by means of differ-
3. Theory ent powers, and in pursuit of differing
of Historical interests, the human spirit avails itself
Truth. of that accessible to it which proves to be truth. According to the ways pursued, truth is realized as knowledge of nature, of morality, of religion, or of art. A precipitated generalization, like the popular German " monism " of the day, affords no more than an abridgment of the kingdom of realization allotted to man. Thus, by this specialized interest, one side of the truth has come to light only recently, the truth of history. Just as the preparation of the materials of physical knowledge by Newton and his colleagues was necessary to render the critical analysis of Kant possible, so the theory of history, neglected from the time of Aristotle, had to await the preparatory historical research and grouping of material by Leopold von Ranke and his colaborers. Now, the distinction between the processes of knowledge of natural science and scientific history is seriously undertaken as well as an inquiry as to their limits. The human spirit operates under the voluntary impulse toward historical research differently from its method toward the knowledge of natural science. In the latter the process is from the individual as a mere example of the many to the concept of multiplicity, and further to law amidst manifold phenomena. Starting out from the particular, yet essentially indifferent to particularity, the reason ascends by ever repeated and rarer abstractions to the ultimate universal and necessary. But in respect of historical research, the interest attaches to the individual as regards its particularity, singularity, and unity. To invade the mystery of the individual is the specific undertaking of history. This does not mean its isolation; for the experimenter in natural science isolates the individual in order to master its phenomena, but, for the historical investigator, the single indivisible possesses its unity only in its relations, as a social individual. The term individual is not used here to refer only to the single human being, the individual exchange medium, but also to the collective unities, such as the State, the people, or the Church. The correctness of the process with reference to natural science is shown by the applied technical results. While this test is want-

ing in the other, yet in the sum total of scientific knowledge, historical science presents a conception of history which is equally fundamental to a comprehensive world-view with natural science. Natural science aims to grasp the rational in the universe; historical science, the irrational in the particular and singular in the world: both are essential to a knowledge of the whole.

This examination is of the utmost importance to theology as the science of religion; because at the present hour, the question of the verity of religion resolves itself into an inquiry into the truth of historical religion. In fact, religion and
4. Religion history at present constitute the
and ground themes of theology whereby
History. it is to create its master-work. Two reasons may be ascribed for the unrest manifested on this account in certain theological and lay circles: (1) the historical critical theology (from J. S. Semler down) has done its earnest work in advance of a clear theory of the relation of history and religion; but the problems of historical theology lie momentarily more in the order of historical theory than in research; (2) the naive or traditional Christianity of many has not yet adapted itself to that advantage which devolves, with respect to the historical material, upon the subjective factor of appropriation by faith or personal conviction independently achieved. No longer is the truth that system of supernatural cognitions and opinions handed down by the theologians from generation to generation. Nor is it simply search for truth without rest or aim (Lessing). Just as for natural science there is in order a " will for natural science," so for religious truth there is requisite a " will for religious truth." The latter is undoubtedly at hand as idea, in general; but as reality it is present only in that receptive subject in which it has become reality. Religious truth is also the common historical property of the religious society, but only so far as experienced and adapted anew in the experience of the individuals. The absoluteness of Christianity no longer rests upon Aristotelian logic and Platonic mysticism, or syllogistic abstractions and the via negativa; but upon the fact that from the time of Jesus Christ there have been men continually who attributed absolute worth to Christianity and gave their life for it. There is no absoluteness on earth but that of personal estimation and conviction. Religion demands no more than that men affirm: thou art true. God requires no more than that men shall fear, love, and trust him in all things. Christ asks no more than that men accept him as the way, the truth, and the life. The relativity of the history of religion can be overcome only practically, each man working for himself and not by proxy in any other way. The only triumphant answer to the relativity of universal religious history is its mission to the world, which is also its necessary complement for the theory of religious truth.

Under these circumstances error has won a different position in the religious system. There is not only tolerable, but also, on the average, necessary, dissonance in the harmony. Not every error is meant, but that of the sincerely seeking man, who doubts in the interest of his own purity and honesty. Also poetry, myth, legend—every activity and endowment of man may serve as a vessel of truth; whether it is so is in each case a question of fact, which must find its answer partly in the interest of reason and partly in the free personal judgment of the moral person. In this connection the value-judgment (see RITSCHL, ALBRECHT) has become of great importance. This does not imply its substitution for the ontological judgment, but it signifies that man as a religious ethical person, together with those of his kind, discovers himself in the midst of a world of values, without the estimation and possession of which he can not live, and the assent to which affords him grasp and support. Man amidst these value-relations is the man of history, the subject of historical conduct and the object of historical science; therefore preeminently the man of religion. In contrast with morality, which is not to be based on the concepts of values and properties (although belonging in this kingdom of values and value-relations) religion, as to its basis and certainty, refers primarily to values and value-relations. Value and truth are its synonyms. Here also absoluteness is to be predicated. In his personal valuations man continuously fulfils absolute estimations. Whoever would permit himself to be deterred from this privilege, through the relativity of comparative rational criticism, would no longer be a spiritually sound person. To the Christian who is really such, Christianity remains the true religion. This conception of religious truth approves itself also in Scripture, although the problem of truth then appeared differently. The Hebrew *'emeth*, "truth," expresses "firmness," "faithfulness." The Greek *alētheia* denotes that which is manifest. Universally in the New Testament, truth is the revelation of salvation and happiness, a possession rescuing to life. Hence it is no instruction of the intellect but a worth to be conceived through its appropriation on the part of every religious ethical person. Although from the point of view of purely human observation this appears as the moral act of the one who seeks, yet the peculiar religious judgment is to the effect that the religious man always accepts the knowledge of religious truth as simply a gift or act of God, or a divine revelation; namely, as a finding or being found without merit on the part of the finder.

If, after what precedes, truth is not a mental picture of reality to which mind is passive, but comes to realization under conditions arising out of the structure of the human soul, then truth can be conceived only from conditions under which the human spirit produces and possesses truth. Always in speaking of truth it is customary to have in mind something without, independent of self, an outer reality; this even in reflecting on the ego; but truth results only as this apparent reality (connoting phenomena with things) is investigated and resolved. Truth comes to light in receiving the effects of the objects of one's interest. How or under what conditions this takes place is for the

5. The Value-judgment.

6. Summary.

inquiry of the criticism of knowledge. This—according to the manifoldness of inquiring interest—may be criticism of scientific, esthetic, moral, or religious truth. Religious truth is the internal grasp of the objects of the religious interest (" the will for religious truth "), so far as this is manifest to one who is religiously truthful; i.e., has become a factor of his spiritual possession under the conditions peculiar to religious cognition. See also REVELATION; and RELIGION.

II. Truthfulness: As duty and virtue, truthfulness has been recognized in the ethics of all nations at all times. Falsehood from selfish motive points, on the other hand, to radical evil in man. Truthfulness is demanded in Scripture expressly and unconditionally (Matt. v. 37; James v. 12). The lax construction in the East of the injunction of the New Testament is illustrated in the work of Chrysostom, " On the Priesthood." Guilty of leading by deception a friend into the priesthood, which then he himself evaded, he greatly exults over the "advantage of deceit." The end justifies the means. Otherwise testifies Augustine in *De mendacio* (395), and in *Contra mendacium* (420). In the latter, on a special case, he takes the positive ground of repudiating the lie of pretense for pious objects. This precedent unfortunately was not followed in the mendacious casuistry which reached its worst phases in Probabilism (q.v.) and mental reservation (see RESERVATION, MENTAL). Also on Protestant soil a vigorous construction (Kant, Fichte) was in conflict with a laxer theory (Rothe). In practise a decided improvement has made itself apparent: specially in scientific research and representation, the sense for truth and the will to be truthful have manifestly increased. It is a reproach to the Church that this victory had to be won in combating ecclesiastical antagonism. Moral responsibility for the mistaking of historical fact can first with safety be referred to individuals with the rise of Humanism and the printing of books. The passion for controversy and the interest of partizan conviction on the part of the Reformers also misled some into doing violence to historical truth. The psychology of autobiographies presents a chapter full of interesting riddles. The most admirable enthusiasm for truth can under the circumstances pass over into immoral fanaticism. No longer surprising, then, is the hypocritical pretense of H. S. Reimarus (q.v.), in offering his religion of reason for the security of the religion of revelation (1754), when at least ten years previous he had volunteered a new religion and violently assailed the Christian pretending to defend it. The truthful Lessing afterward had to taste the bitterness of this falsehood, as well as that of the customary anonymous authorship, with which, then as always, was invariably covered something untruthful.

1. Historical.

The pathetic complaint of Reimarus was the necessity of double-facedness all his lifetime, and this was the lot of all liberal-minded men under the imminence of orthodox coercion. The situation for science and life has been much relieved; yet the accomplishment of truthfulness in theology and Church is a vital question. The difficulty is due to the Church's acting as guardian of the heritage of its members, while it will not grant its officers and representatives of learn-

2. Candor and Orthodoxy. ing the free use of new knowledge before it has been compromised or reconciled with the old. It is then a matter for individuals or parties to choose between a conservative, a radical, or a mediating position. Mediating tendencies are usually alleged by their opponents to be "counterfeit." This implies the demand that to the words and formulas of tradition must ever be given only their original meaning, while new views must employ new words and new formulas. Such a thing is impossible; for the store of words is limited, and the life of the language must perpetuate itself naturally only through a continuous change of the inherent sense. Even the most rigorous conservative observance of the import of words and formulas can not prevent some shifting of the meaning; for men change, and likewise their relation to tradition. There are no verbal instruments at the disposal of truthfulness other than those offered by a continuously changing language medium. Again, several systematists have drawn attention by placing the problems of truth and truthfulness in the center; namely, in religion W. Herrmann, and in ethics, among others, W. Koppelmann.

Every definition of truthfulness as duty and virtue that exhausts itself simply in the agreement of speech and thought on the part of the professor is both trivial and unsatisfying. It is

3. Essentials of Truthfulness. apt to be wrecked presently on the shoals of casuistry. Truthfulness is to be conceived as no less than that duty and virtue which constitute the ethical person himself and which permeate life uniformly in all its relations to the person. The truthful person is truthful though he be silent or even carries on untrue speech. He is such not only for himself, but disseminates an atmosphere of truthfulness about him. While the regard for the true import and degree of verity of a statement is of great pedagogical interest and solicits frequently the moral verdict upon itself, yet when it comes to the establishment of truthfulness in character and conduct, it all depends on whether men are truthful persons. That means men who do not belie themselves and who prove their uprightness with themselves in their relation with other men and with facts; men who do not deceive God, and hence not themselves or their fellow men; men who from an inner necessity and choice accept things as they are and represent themselves as being what they are. Religion is truthfulness toward God, and morality, if this be granted, is nothing but applied religion. (Martin Rade.)

Bibliography: The subject is of course treated in the works on Ethics (q.v.) such as R. Rothe's, iii. 537–602, Wittenberg, 1848; and W. Herrmann's, 3d ed., Tübingen, 1904. Three important books are: H. Rickert, *Die Grenzen der naturwissenschaftlichen Begriffsbildung*, 2 vols., Leipsic, 1896–1902; G. Simmel, *Die Probleme der Geschichtsphilosophie*, 2d ed., ib. 1905; and S. Eck, *Religion und Geschichte*, Tübingen, 1907. Consult further: A. A. Cournot, *Essai sur les fondements de nos connaissances*, 2 vols., Paris, 1851; J. F. Ferrier, *Institutes of Metaphysics: the Theory of Knowing and Being*, Edinburgh, 1854; W. Windelband, *Ueber die Gewissheit der Erkenntniss*, Berlin, 1873; J. Witte, *Zur Erkenntnisstheorie und Ethik*, ib. 1877; H. P. Biddle, *Elements of Knowledge*, Cincinnati, 1881; J. Rehmke, *Die Welt als Wahrnehmung und Begriff*, Berlin, 1881; H. de Cossoles, *La Certitude philosophique*, Paris, 1883; E. de Pressense, *Les Origines. Le Probleme de la connaissance*, ib. 1883, Eng. transl., *A Study of Origins*, London, 1883; G. Ellinger, *Das Verhältnis der öffentlichen Meinung zu Wahrheit und Lüge im 10.–12. Jahrhundert*, Berlin, 1884; E. Burnouf, *La Vie et la pensée*, Paris, 1886; F. Grung, *Das Problem der Gewissheit*, Heidelberg, 1886; E. L. Fischer, *Die Grundfragen der Erkenntnisstheorie*, Mainz, 1887; B. Lasch, *Das Erwachen und die Entwicklung der historischen Kritik im Mittelalter*, Breslau, 1887; W. Poessnecker, *Die Welt als unsere Erscheinungswelt und unsere Gedankwelt*, Berlin, 1887; H. Bergson, *Essai sur les données immédiates de la conscience*, Paris, 1890, Eng. transl., *Time and Free Will; An Essay on the Immediate Data of Consciousness*, London, 1910; A. Schmid, *Erkenntnisslehre*, 2 vols., Freiburg, 1890; J. Gardair, *La Connaissance*, Paris, 1895; J. Koestlin, *Der Glaube und seine Bedeutung für Erkenntnis*, *Leben und Kirche*, Berlin, 1895; H. Gomperz, *Die Psychologie der logischen Grundthatsachen*, Vienna, 1896; G. Gory, *L'Immanence de la raison dans la connaisance sensible*, Paris, 1896; D. L. Jordan, *The Stability of Truth*, in *Popular Science Monthly*, i (1897), pp. 642–654, 749–757; S. H. Hodgson, *The Metaphysics of Experience*, 4 vols., London and New York, 1898; St. G. Mivart, *The Groundwork of Science*, New York and London, 1898; J. W. Powell, *Truth and Error; or, The Science of Intellection*, Chicago, 1898; F. S. Turner, *Knowledge, Belief and Certitude*, London, 1900; J. Mausbach, *Die katholische Moral*, Cologne, 1901; W. Herrmann, *Römische und evangelische Sittlichkeit*, 3d ed., Marburg, 1903; W. Koppelmann, *Kritik des sittlichen Bewusstseins*, Berlin, 1904; idem, *Die Ethik Kants*, ib. 1907.

TRUXILLO, tru-híl'yō **(TRUJILLO), ORDER OF:** An order of knights under the Cistercian rule, founded in the thirteenth century, and taking its name from the town of Truxillo (130 m. s.w. of Madrid). The times were not favorable to the maintenance of so many separate orders as were then in existence, and after a brief struggle, the order of Truxillo was united with the orders of Alcantara and Calatrava (qq.v.).

TRYGOPHORUS, trai"gof'o-rus, **JOHANNES:** German Reformer; b. at Fritzlar (105 m. e. of Cologne) in 1497; d. at Wildungen (8 m. w. of Fritzlar) June 3, 1542. Born of pious parents named Hefenträger (from which the name he assumed was Grecized), he was early destined for clerical life, and two of his sisters were Benedictine nuns. At Erfurt he became bachelor in philosophy in 1517, was ordained priest in 1521, taking the position of confessor to the Augustinian nuns of his native town. The news of Luther's movement early reached the town, and Trygophorus accepted the new Gospel, which he preached, and married a nun, with the result that he had to leave the town. Meantime the Reformation had begun to work in Waldeck, either through literary connections or because of influences from Hesse and Westphalia. The youthful but far-sighted and energetic Count Philip IV., who ruled in the southern portion of the county, returned from the diet at Worms a confirmed adherent of Luther. Philip III., who controlled the northern part, seems to have been led to Lutheranism by his second wife, Anne of Cleves. Conditions were favorable to a complete introduction of the Reformation when the right man appeared. At this juncture Trygophorus was called by Philip IV. to the little city of Waldeck, and his operations were soon successful. In 1531 he was called to Wildungen, the residence of Philip IV., and there began a work of real significance in establishing the church of the Reformation in Waldeck. He was the leader and initiator of the various steps, introducing catechetical instruction and producing an antiphonary for the church service.

Trygophorus was a man of marked genius and practical bent, was recognized in the region as an authority in religious matters second only to Luther and Melanchthon, and did no little service by his gifts for liturgics. He was a man of great earnestness and strong will, resolute in his fidelity to strict Lutheranism and in opposition to Roman Catholic or sectarian tendencies, so that the Waldeck church possessed always the character of a strictly Lutheran body.　　　　　　　(VICTOR SCHULTZE.)

BIBLIOGRAPHY: V. Schultze, Waldeckische Reformationsgeschichte, Leipsic, 1903, cf. ZKG, 1907, pp. 60 sqq.

TSCHACKERT, tchak′ert, **PAUL MORITZ ROBERT:** German Protestant; b. at Freystadt (22 m. n.w. of Glogau), Lower Silesia, Jan. 10, 1848; d. at Göttingen July 7, 1911. He studied at the universities of Breslau, Halle, and Göttingen, 1868–74 (lic.theol., Breslau, 1875; Ph.D., Leipsic, 1875), and in 1875 became privat-docent for historical theology at Breslau; associate professor of church history at Halle, 1877; full professor of the same subject at Königsberg, 1884; and after 1889 was professor of church history at Göttingen. In theology he belonged to the school of Tholuck and Julius Müller. Besides his work as associate editor of the Zeitschrift der Gesellschaft für niedersächsische Kirchengeschichte and of the thirteenth and fourteenth editions of J. H. Kurtz's Lehrbuch der Kirchengeschichte (in collaboration with G. N. Bonwetsch; Leipsic, 1899, 1906), and of Die unveränderte Augsburger Konfession (1901), he wrote or edited Anna Maria von Schurmann (Gotha, 1876); Peter von Ailli (1877); Die Päpste der Renaissance (Heidelberg, 1879); Evangelische Polemik gegen die römische Kirche (Gotha, 1885); Vorteile und Gefahren, welche der Mission aus der Kolonialpolitik erwachsen (Leipsic, 1886); Johannes Briessmanns Flosculi (Gotha, 1887); Georg von Polenz, Bischof von Samland (Leipsic, 1888); Unbekannte handschriftliche Predigten und Scholien Martin Luthers (1888); Urkundenbuch zur Reformationsgeschichte des Herzogtums Preussen (3 vols., 1890); Paul Speratus von Rötlin (Halle, 1891); Herzog Albrecht von Preussen (Halle, 1894); Ungedruckte Briefe zur allgemeinen Reformationsgeschichte (Göttingen, 1894); Magister Johannes Sutel (Brunswick, 1897); Herzogin Elisabeth von Münden (Leipsic, 1899); Antonius Corvinus' Leben und Schriften (Hanover, 1900); Briefwechsel des Antonius Corvinus (1900); Staat und Kirche im Königreich Preussen (Göttingen, 1901); Modus vivendi. Grundlinien für das Zusammenleben der Konfessionen im deutschen Reich (Munich, 1908); Herzog Albrecht von Preussen als angeblich bedeutender geistlicher Liederdichter der Reformationszeit (Königsberg, 1909); and Die Entstehung der lutherischen und reformierten Kirchenlehre samt ihren innerprotestantischen Gegensätzen (Göttingen, 1910).

TUBAL. See GOG AND MAGOG; and TABLE OF THE NATIONS, § 4.

XII.—3

TUCH, tuн, **FRIEDRICH:** German Lutheran; b. at Quedlinburg Dec. 17, 1806; d. at Leipsic Apr. 12, 1867. He was educated at the University of Halle (1825–29), where he became privat-docent in 1830 in the philosophical faculty, lecturing at first on Hebrew and other Semitic languages, and later on all subjects pertaining to the Old Testament. After being associate professor at Halle for a time, he was called, in 1841, to Leipsic in a similar capacity, becoming full professor two years later; in 1853 he became also canon of Zeitz.

The chief work of Tuch was his Kommentar über die Genesis (Halle, 1838), a book distinguished for its grammatical acumen, wealth of information on the topography, flora, fauna, and customs of Palestine, and recognition of the historical kernel in the primitive records of Israel. The major portion of his writings, however, were brief programs and the like. These fall into two groups: linguistic and geographical. Among the former mention should be made of his De Æthiopicæ linguæ sonorum proprietatibus quibusdam (Leipsic, 1854); De Æthiopicæ linguæ sonorum sibilantium natura et usu (1854); as well as of his Einundzwanzig sinaitische Inschriften (1849), though his attempt to prove these Sinaitic inscriptions pure Arabic is now known to be erroneous. In the second category his most noteworthy contributions were: De Nino urbe (1845), proving that Nineveh could have been situated only on the east bank of the Tigris; Reise des Sheikh Ibrahim el-Krijari el-Medeni durch einen Teil Palästinas (1850), and Antoninus Martyr, seine Zeit und seine Pilgerfahrt nach dem Morgenlande (1864), the first treating of a Mohammedan traveler of the seventeenth century and the second of an Italian pilgrim of the late sixth century; and Masada, die herodianische Felsenfeste (1863), identifying Masada with the heap of ruins at the modern Sabbah. Allusion should also be made to his Die Himmelfahrt Jesu, eine topographische Frage (1857), in which he sought to prove that Bethany was the place of the ascension; as well as to his Commentatio de Maisaloth en Arbelois 1 Mak. 9, 2 (1853), and his Quæstiones de Flavii Josephi libris historicis (1859).

　　　　　　　　　　　　　　　　(VICTOR RYSSEL†.)

BIBLIOGRAPHY: V. Ryssel, in ZKW, 1886, pp. 169 sqq.; ADB, xxxviii. 754 sqq.

TUCKER, BEVERLY DANDRIDGE: Protestant Episcopal assistant bishop of southern Virginia; b. at Richmond, Va., Nov. 9, 1847. During the Civil War he served, despite his youth, on the Confederate side, and after the close of hostilities resumed his studies, being graduated from the Virginia Theological Seminary in 1873. He was ordered deacon in the same year and advanced to the priesthood in 1875, and from 1873 to 1882 was minister and rector in North Farnham Parish, Va. He was then rector of St. Paul's, Norfolk, Va., until 1906, when he was consecrated assistant bishop of southern Virginia.

TUCKER, FREDERICK ST. GEORGE DE LATOUR. See BOOTH TUCKER.

TUCKER, WILLIAM JEWETT: Congregationalist; b. at Griswold, Conn., July 13, 1839. He was educated at Dartmouth (A.B., 1861), and, after being a teacher for two years, entered Andover Theological Seminary (graduated 1866). He was pastor of Franklin Street Congregational Church, Manchester, N. H. (1866–75); pastor of Madison Square Presbyterian Church, New York (1875–79); professor of sacred rhetoric in Andover Theological Seminary (1879–93); and in 1893 was elected president of Dartmouth College, which position he resigned in 1908. At Boston he founded the social settlement called Andover House, and, in addition to assisting in editing *The Andover Review*, has written *The new Movement in Humanity: From Liberty to Unity* (Boston, 1892), and *Making and Unmaking of the Preacher* (Lyman Beecher lectures at Yale; 1899).

TUCKERMAN, JOSEPH: American Unitarian philanthropist; b. in Boston Jan. 18, 1778; d. at Havana Apr. 20, 1840. He was graduated from Harvard College, 1798; was pastor at Chelsea, Mass., 1801–26; in 1812 founded at Boston the first American society for the religious and moral improvement of seamen; in 1826 took charge of the " Ministry at Large," a city mission organized by the Benevolent Fraternity of Churches in Boston; visited Europe to promote similar organizations, and on his return, in 1838, published *Principles and Results of the Ministry at Large*. He has a permanent place in the front rank of those who have promoted reform in philanthropic effort. His principal writings were collected under the title *The Elevation of the Poor* (Boston, 1874).

BIBLIOGRAPHY: His life was written by W. E. Channing, Boston, 1841, and by Mary Carpenter, London, 1849.

TUCKNEY, ANTHONY: b. at Kirton, Lincolnshire, Eng., Sept., 1559; d. Feb., 1670. He was educated at Emmanuel College, Cambridge, and took his master's degree in 1622, his B.D. in 1627. He became domestic chaplain to the earl of Lincoln, but, after he was chosen fellow of his college, returned and was a very successful teacher. He then became assistant to John Cotton at Boston, and, after Cotton's departure to New England, his successor. In 1643 he was appointed member of the Westminster Assembly of Divines for the county of Lincoln, and was one of the most active and influential members. After the death of Herbert Palmer, he was made chairman of the committee on the catechisms. He had a chief hand in the questions relating to the divine law in the Larger Catechism, and in the construction of the entire Shorter Catechism.

While at London, he was minister of St. Michael le Querne until 1648. He was made master of Emmanuel College, Cambridge, in 1645, vice-chancellor of the university in 1648, master of St. John's College in 1653, and regius professor of divinity of the university. He was one of the commissioners at the Savoy, but failed to attend. He was silenced for non-conformity. His controversy with Benjamin Whichcote is important as showing the break of a new era in Whichcote, his pupil, out of the old era in Tuckney, the teacher. These eight letters discuss the use of reason in religion, as well as differences among Christians, in a calm, dignified, and charitable spirit. They are models of Christian

controversy. Tuckney's *Parliament Sermons* and other occasional pieces were published during his lifetime; but his principal works are posthumous: *Forty Sermons upon Several Occasions* (London, 1676); *Prælectiones theologicæ* (Amsterdam, 1679).

C. A. BRIGGS.

BIBLIOGRAPHY: *DNB*, lvii. 286–288 (gives references to scattering notices.

TUDELA, BENJAMIN OF. See BENJAMIN OF TUDELA.

TUDESCHIS, NICOLAUS DE. See PANORMITANUS.

TUEBINGEN BIBLE. See BIBLES, ANNOTATED; PFAFF, CHRISTOPH MATTHÆUS.

TUEBINGEN SCHOOL, NEW. See BAUR, F. C.

TUEBINGEN, tü′bin-gen, SCHOOL, THE OLDER.

Gottlob Christian Storr (§ 1).
Doctrine of Storr (§ 2).
Criticism of Storr's Doctrine; Works (§ 3).
The School of Storr; J. F. Flatt (§ 4).
F. G. Süskind; K. C. Flatt (§ 5).
Critical Review of the School (§ 6).
E. G. Bengel (§ 7).

The older Tübingen school of theology, important in the Protestant theology of the eighteenth and nineteenth centuries through its concept of " Biblical supranaturalism," owed its rise to Gottlob Christian Storr (b. at Stuttgart Sept. 10, 1746; d. there Jan. 17, 1805). He was educated at Tübingen (1763–68), where he long devoted himself exclusively to the study of the New Testament, and in 1769–71 made a tour of Germany, Holland, England, and France, studying and pursuing researches in the libraries of Leyden, Oxford, and Paris. Returning to Tübingen, he embodied his results in his *Observationes super Novi Testamenti versionibus Syriacis* (1772) and *Dissertatio de evangeliis Arabicis* (1775), the latter his inaugural address as associate professor of philosophy. He was transferred to the theological faculty, 1777; became fourth professor of theology, special superintendent, and city pastor, 1780; and full professor, second superintendent of the theological seminary, and third morning preacher, 1786; and he was consistorial councilor and chief court chaplain at Stuttgart, 1797–1805. Characterized by unusual acumen, power of combination, and unwearying energy, though lacking in imagination and speculative talent, he acquired a comprehensive education and profound learning. This was supported by a personality distinguished for upright piety and moral earnestness, tempered with a winsome gentleness and humanity, commanding the esteem of friend and adversary alike. Notwithstanding, his sermons (3 vols., Stuttgart, 1806–10) lack warmth and depth of feeling, being dry, prosaic, didactic, and almost wholly constructed of Bible passages. The attention which they commanded can be explained only by the reflection of his venerable and sincere personality.

The accession of Storr to the faculty marked the beginning of a new epoch in the history of the theology of Tübingen. The Lutheran orthodoxy established there late in the sixteenth century had

retained unbroken sway. The Church of Württemberg had remained true to its Biblical trend,
its essentially irenic position, and its
2. **Doctrine** desire to unite theological theory with
of Storr. practical religion, traits which it owed
specially to the influence of Johann
Brenz (q.v.). In the controversies of the sixteenth
and seventeenth centuries the theologians of Tübingen had stood by the Formula of Concord, without relinquishing their Biblical-practical point of
view. Early in the eighteenth century the chancellor of the university, J. W. Jäger (1702–20), in
dependence on the method of Johannes Cocceius
(q.v.), sought to introduce a system of greater vitality, and his efforts were carried still further by
C .M. Pfaff (q.v.) and C. E. Weismann (q.v.), Pfaff
tending toward the school of Georg Calixtus (q.v.),
and Weismann toward that of Spener and J. A.
Bengel (qq.v.). Nevertheless, neither the Bengel school nor the Wolffian philosophy could introduce a new phase of theology at Tübingen, though
the former imparted its quiet Biblical stimulus.
Meanwhile, in the second half of the eighteenth
century, the Enlightenment (q.v.) began to assail
all positive Christianity. It thus became necessary
to gain a point of view which should retain the inalienable elements of the old truths while changing
their forms in adjustment with the new normative
influences. Such was the task which Storr desired
and sought to accomplish. Abandoning the orthodox substructure, he deemed it possible to lay a
sure foundation for scientific theology and dogmatics on the sole authority of divine revelation as
contained in the Bible, and attempted to derive
the Christian truth from these sources through
grammatical and historical exegesis and through
systematic logic. He aimed first to prove the
authenticity and integrity of the New-Testament
writings from historical evidences, and the credibility of the authors from their relation to the
events reported, from their characteristic points of
view to be identified in the writings, and from the
inevitable controlling influence of partizans and
opponents. These authenticated Scriptures afford
as a result that upon Christ devolves, in the highest sense, the authority of a divine ambassador,
which was substantiated by his perfect ethical
thought and conduct, but particularly the divine
miracles. From this authority follow in order, the
truth of his doctrine, the authority of the apostles
and the truth of their teaching, the inspiration of
the apostolic writings, and, finally, the recognition
and inspiration of the Old Testament, so far as the
latter is attested by divinely accredited men. This
position of Storr was distinguished from orthodoxy
by his substitution of the authority of Jesus and
his apostles for the inspiration of the Scriptures,
by making the Scripture the sole source, even the
text-book, of Christian teaching, and by his derivation of not only " human faith " but indirectly also
" divine faith " from empirical historical deduction,
while in doubt about attributing the virtue of proof
to the " testimony of the Holy Spirit." From the
Enlightenment he differs sharply by the manner in
which he employed historical and logical proofs in
the service of the principle of authority. After the

establishment of the authority of Christ and the
Bible, he needed no further internal proof of Christian truth from reason or experience. Claiming to
deal also reasonably in receiving implicitly upon
the attested authority of Scripture what reason is
unable of itself to establish out of the nature of the
case, Storr thus professes a merely formal principle
of authority, the supernaturalism of the Christian
truth, and a purely instrumental use of reason.
This system was admirably carried out in his *Annotationes theologicæ ad philosophicam Kantii de religione doctrinam* (Tübingen, 1793; Germ. transl.,
1794), in which he maintained that he who refused
to credit authorities that had shared the advantage
of receiving special experiences, merely because
their teachings could not be deduced from the principles of unaided reason, deserted the point of view
of true criticism. Such testimonies, on the contrary,
should be seriously considered, just so soon as their
moral efficacy was firmly established. With respect to the latter, the Christian historical faith in-
dubitably surpassed the pallid, blank belief of pure
reason. Storr also employed Kant's postulate of a
necessary harmony between virtue and happiness
to justify the New-Testament union of religion and
morality.

For Storr there can be no occasion for the material influence of any philosophy whatsoever on the
content of Christian doctrine. According to him,
dogmatics and ethics had simply to combine the
results of exegesis, but this was to result largely, as
F. C. Baur pointed out, in an artificial congeries of
passages from all parts of the Old and New Testaments, without regard to the genetic evolution of
Biblical truth. For him there are no writings of the
canon but only passages without discrimination of
value, which is due to the fact that the principle
of unity is not organic but formal authority. With
reference to the doctrine of sin and grace, the result of his work seems to be a Semipelagian simplification and moderating of the dogma, satisfying
neither deep religious nor scientific in-
3. **Criticism** terest. Thus he debased faith from
of Storr's divinely prepared receptivity for re-
Doctrine; generating grace to an autonomous
Works. human moral relation, and regarded
the Holy Ghost as a mere factor to aid
and complete human activity. On the atonement
he based the remission of punishment only on the
passive obedience of Christ, accepting unquestion-
ingly the formal equivalence of the passion of Christ
with the sins of the world, and deducing from the
active obedience of the Savior (to which he was
also bound for himself) only the positive results
of his exaltation and the beatification of his brethren. In his Christology, Storr, professing to be
in accord with orthodoxy on the deity of Christ,
but avoiding the *Communicatio idiomatum* (q.v.),
and thus losing hold of the true incarnation of
the Logos, perhaps unconsciously approximated a
Socinian view of the person of Christ (see MONAR-
CHIANISM; also SOCINUS, FAUSTUS, SOCINIANS).
The dogmatic system of Storr is set forth especially
in his last important work, *Doctrinæ Christianæ pars
theoreticae sacris litteris repetita* (1793; Germ. transl.
enlarged by K. C. Flatt, Stuttgart, 1803), which

long enjoyed official recognition in Württemberg. In exegesis he combated the accommodation hypothesis represented by J. S. Semler and A. Teller. His principal critical exegetical works are *Neue Apologie der Offenbarung Johannis* (Tübingen, 1783); *Zweck der evangelischen Geschichte und der Briefe Johannis* (1786), a keen and far-sighted study in relation with the Synoptic Gospels, by which, according to Baur, the critical study of the Fourth Gospel was much advanced; and *Erläuterung an die Hebräer* (1789), containing a treatment of the purpose of the death of Jesus.

The school of Storr, in the narrower sense, was composed of J. F. Flatt, F. S. Süskind, and K. C. Flatt, all his immediate pupils and successors, and in part his colleagues in the theological faculty. Johann Friedrich Flatt (b. at Tübingen Feb. 20, 1759; d. there Nov. 24, 1821), educated at Tübingen, and appointed professor of philosophy in 1785, was an enthusiastic Kantian. Transferred to the theological faculty in 1792, he lectured principally on Christian ethics, and, besides, on New-Testament exegesis, apologetics, and practical theology, and, for a brief period, 1798, on dogmatics. From 1796 he edited the *Magazin für Dogmatik und Moral*. The *Vorlesungen über Christliche Moral* was published (Tübingen, 1823), as were his lectures on the Pauline Epistles (1820 sqq.). Theological contributions were, *De deitate Christi* (Göttingen, 1788), a prize treatise assigned by the University of Göttingen, at the direction of George II. of England; and *Beiträge zur christlichen Dogmatik und Moral* (Tübingen, 1792).

Friedrich Gottlieb Süskind (b. at Neustadt-on-the-Linde Feb. 17, 1767; d. at Stuttgart Nov. 12, 1829), educated at Tübingen (1783–88), succeeded Storr as professor of dogmatics (1798); and in 1805 as chief court chaplain and consistorial councilor at Stuttgart, where he was appointed director of the council for higher education in 1814. As a theologian he was enlisted in the solution of the basal problems of apologetics and dogmatics, by the application of philosophy and exegesis. He sharply opposed the contemporary philosophy of religion set forth by Kant, Fichte, and Schelling; and finally came somewhat into accord with the theology of Schleiermacher. He was preeminently the dialectician of the older Tübingen school, but entirely lacking in the speculative power to grasp the organic unity from the point of view of a supreme idea. In his later official position his " categorical and dictatorial " resoluteness often caused offense, especially as redactor of the unpopular Württemberg liturgy of 1809, yet he was a man of the most rigid integrity, and far more stern to himself than to others. He was editor of Flatt's *Magazin* (1803–12), in which many of his apologetic and polemic articles appeared. Karl Christian Flatt (b. at Stuttgart Aug. 18, 1772; d. Nov. 20, 1843), the younger brother of Johann Friedrich, was educated at Tübingen, after which he traveled extensively in Germany, residing for some time at Göttingen. During this period he devoted himself to the Kantian philosophy, the results being set forth in his *Philosophisch-exegetische Untersuchungen über die Lehre von der Versöhnung des Menschen mit Gott* (2 parts, Göttingen and Stuttgart, 1797–98), in which he endeavored to show that the doctrine of the atonement resulting from Kant's system, whereby the forgiveness of sins is determined by the degree of moral improvement, is not only the sole reasonable one, but the only one based on the New Testament. This view he retracted on becoming professor of theology at Tübingen in 1804, apparently on Storr's demand. In his lectures and in his publications later he became in all respects a pliant adherent of the tendency represented by his brother and by Storr. His views appeared in timely articles in Flatt's *Magazin*. With his call to Stuttgart as collegiate preacher and supreme consistorial councilor in 1812, and with his appointment as director of higher education in 1829 (this carrying with it the general superintendency of Ulm), his literary activity ceased.

These three theologians, following in the steps of Storr, endeavored to wrench from the philosophy of the period concessions in behalf of their own theory of revelation. For the conceivableness of revelation, which they held to be the communication of higher truths, they appealed to the limits of human reason, justifying faith in revelation by alleging its value for the furtherance of morality. This apologetic was inadequate to reveal to view the entire depth of the prevailing chasm, or to render justice to the set weight and independent peculiarity of Christian conviction. Their well-meant and not seldom acute defense was hampered in advance by their unvitalized conception of God, and, as a consequence, the externality of their theory of revelation. Another impediment was the absorbent relationship of their own method of demonstration with the leading motive of the very rationalistic mode of thought that they were assailing. Only one result could follow: the rationalizing of their own dogma with increasing measure. The Biblical criticism and exegesis of Storr's school, in like manner, was essentially that of their master, a struggle against the accommodation hypothesis, against the derivation of fundamental Christian truths from contemporary ideas, and against the attacks on the authenticity of the Gospels.

Less intimately connected with this school was Ernst Gottlieb Bengel (b. at Zavelstein, 23 m. w.s.w. of Stuttgart Nov. 3, 1769; d. at Tübingen Mar. 28, 1826), grandson of the famous Johann Albrecht Bengel (q.v.). He became professor of theology at Tübingen, 1806; and prelate, 1820; and chiefly represented historical theology. Even more than the rest of the school, Bengel approximated Socinianism, a result due to the inner relationship of the dogmatic point of view, specially since the supernaturalistic apologetic, too, laid essential stress on the credibility of the Biblical authors and on the purely supernatural character of the revelation imparted through them. The practical rationalism of Socinianism he sought to deepen and complement with the Kantian philosophy, the ethical basis of which he had adopted more fully than the others of the school. Bengel's dogmatic system is therefore to be characterized by the so-called rational supernaturalism (see RATIONALISM AND SUPERNATURALISM, II., § 6), recognizing in revelation a supernatural corroboration and representation in fact of rational truth as also a certain amplification. All this is best represented in the ten dissertations on the development of belief in immortality and the relation of revelation to it (cf. *Opuscula academica*, Hamburg, 1834; also *Reden über Religion und Offenbarung*, Tübingen, 1831). Characteristic also was his Pelagianism which held the divergency between Protestantism and Roman Catholicism regarding justification to be a mere logomachy, while the concept of faith was transposed to that of moral improvement and change of disposition (*Archiv für die Theologie*, I., ii. 469, the journal succeeding Flatt's *Magazin* in 1816; published by Bengel, 1816–26; and renamed *Neues Archiv*, 1822). Obdurate in his position, Bengel stood at bay to every regenerating philosophical influence, taking notice of Schleiermacher only by reproaching him with " mysticism and pantheism " and suppressing the deviation of his junior colleague, G. F. Bockshammer (1784–1822). This dominating preeminence he was able to maintain by the formal device of satisfying the rationalistic party, by disguising, under the obvious attack upon rationalism, a virtual material compromise with it, and, on the other hand, the Biblical positive view was conciliated by the overtowering supernaturalism. To this his imposing personality in the lecture-room and his commanding power at the head of the university added weight, so that upon his sudden death his loss was deemed irreparable. Other theologians of Tübingen and Württemberg, principally J. C. F. Steudel (d. 1837), C. F. Schmid (d. 1852), and C. B. Klaiber (d. 1836), while clearly representing the influence of the older Tübingen school, yet manifest such a diversification of the original views, specially as affected by the theology of Schleiermacher, that they can scarcely be rated with that school. After its disappearance, the school was again revived and continued, in a certain sense, by the independent Biblical theologian J. T. Beck (q.v.) and his followers. For the later Tübingen School see BAUR, FERDINAND CHRISTIAN, AND THE LATER TÜBINGEN SCHOOL.   (O. KIRN†.)

BIBLIOGRAPHY: Consult the works on church history (*Kirchengeschichte*) issued by the Calwer Verlagsverein, pp. 449 sqq., 566 sqq., Stuttgart, 1893; and F. C. Baur, p. 98, Leipsic, 1862; and those on history of doctrine or theology by F. C. Baur, iii. 308 sqq., Leipsic, 1867; W. Gass, iv. 141, 503 sqq., Berlin, 1867; M. A. Landerer, pp. 156 sqq., Altenburg, 1881; and G. Frank, iii. 383, Leipsic, 1905. Also, C. Weizsäcker, *Lehrer und Unterricht a* der *evangelisch-theologischen Fakultät der Universität Tübingen*, pp. 131 sqq., Tübingen, 1877.

TULLOCH, tul'oc, **JOHN:** Church of Scotland, divine and educator; b. at Dron, near Tibbermuir (5 m. w. of Perth), June 1, 1823; d. at Torquay, England, Feb. 13, 1886. He was educated at St. Andrew's and Edinburgh; became parish minister at Dundee 1845, and at Kettins, Forfarshire, 1849, principal and primarius professor of divinity in St. Mary's College, St. Andrew's University, 1854; and senior principal of the university, 1860. His theological standpoint was thus defined by himself: " Broad evangelical. The aim is to see all Christian truth first in its pure historical form—the mind of Christ, the thought of St. Paul, the teaching of St. James; then its living relation to the Christian consciousness—what man needs, what God gives. The historic method, rightly applied, is the primary key to all Christian truth; and the renovation of theology is through this method bringing all Christian ideas freshly into the light of consciousness." He studied theology in Germany in 1847–48 and 1863–64. He was " especially attracted by Neander, and much interested by the problems raised by the Tübingen school and the writings of F. C. Baur, and greatly attracted in late years by Dean Stanley's historical writings and Bishop Lightfoot's critico-historical essays." He was an ardent student of literature and philosophy, and his writings are highly prized. He first came into notice when in Dundee, by his frequent contributions in the *Dundee Advertiser;* but later by his elaborate articles in *The North-British Review, The British Quarterly*, and *Kitto's Journal of Sacred Literature*. Two of his articles—one on *Carlyle's Life of Sterling* (*North-British Review*, vol. iv., 1845), the other on *Bunsen's Hippolytus* (the same, vol. xix., 1853)—attracted wide attention; and the latter so pleased Baron Bunsen that he successfully exerted his influence to press Tulloch's claim to the principalship in St. Mary's College. His appointment when barely thirty years old to this position, one of the most dignified and responsible connected with the Established Church of Scotland, was naturally a great surprise and occasion of unfavorable remark. But he soon proved his fitness for the office. In 1856 he was appointed one of the examiners of the Dick bequest, and so continued until his death. In 1858 he was deputed by the General Assembly of the Church to open the Scotch Presbyterian Church in Paris, and preached there during the summer. In 1859 he was appointed one of her Majesty's chaplains for Scotland, and often preached before the queen at Crathie. In 1862 he became deputy clerk of the General Assembly, in 1875 clerk, and in 1878 was elected moderator. As university head, preacher, essayist, historian, theologian, and in private life he was highly esteemed, his death was sincerely mourned, and his memory is still cherished. Principal Tulloch's chief contributions to literature were: *Theism; the Witness of Reason and Nature to an all-wise and beneficent Creator* (Edinburgh, 1855), second Burnett prize essay; *Leaders of the Reformation, Luther, Calvin, Latimer, Knox* (1859; enlarged ed., *Luther and Other Leaders of the Reformation*, 1888); *English Puritanism and its Leaders, Cromwell, Milton, Baxter, Bunyan* (1861); *The Christ of the Gospels and the Christ of Modern Criticism* (1864), on Renan's *Vie de Jésus; Rational Theology and Christian Philosophy in England in the Seventeenth Century* (2 vols., 1872); *Pascal* (1876); *The Christian Doctrine of Sin* (1877); *Modern Theories in Philosophy and Religion* (1884); *Movements of Religious Thought in Britain during the Nineteenth Century* (1885); *National Religion in Theory and Fact* (1886), two volumes of sermons—*Some Facts of Religion and*

Life (1877), and *Sundays at Balmoral* (1887), as well as occasional sermons, addresses, and the like.

BIBLIOGRAPHY: Mrs. M. O. Oliphant, *Memoir of the Life of John Tulloch*, Edinburgh, 1888; W. Knight, *Principal Shairp and his Friends*, London, 1888; A. K. H. Boyd, *Twenty-five Years of St. Andrews*, 2 vols., ib. 1892–93; *DNB*, lvii. 307–310.

TUNICLE or DALMATIC. See VESTMENTS AND INSIGNIA, ECCLESIASTICAL.

TUNKERS. See DUNKERS.

TUOTILO. See SAINT GALL, § 2.

TURGOT, tür″gō′ **(JOHANNES TURGOTUS):** Bishop of St. Andrews; d. at Durham Aug. 31, 1115. He was born in Lincolnshire of good Saxon family, fled to Norway after the Norman conquest, and prospered there. After a time he undertook to return to England, lost his property by shipwreck, and entered the monastery at Jarrow in 1074. He became prior of Durham in 1087, archdeacon about 1093, in which year he assisted in laying the foundation of the new cathedral. He was confessor, friend, and confidential adviser of Queen Margaret of Scotland (d. 1093; see MARGARET, SAINT), and in 1107 was appointed bishop of St. Andrews by her son Alexander, but, owing to a dispute as to the authority of the archbishop of York over the Scottish Church, was not consecrated till Aug. 1, 1109; the controversy continued to trouble him till his death. He is the probable author of a life of St. Margaret (printed in *ASB*, June, ii. 320–340, where it is ascribed to an otherwise unknown Theodoricus; Eng. transl. by W. Forbes Leith, 3d ed., Edinburgh, 1896); also of *Historia ecclesiæ et episcoporum Dunelmensium*, published in H. Wharton's *Anglia sacra*, i. 705–717, London, 1691.

BIBLIOGRAPHY: T. Wright, *Biographia Britannica literaria*, ii. 70–73, London, 1846; *ASB*, June, ii. 320–322; J. L. Low, *Durham*, London, 1881; W. F. Skene, *Celtic Scotland*, 2d ed., 3 vols., Edinburgh, 1886–90; *DNB*, lvii. 326–327.

TURKEY.

I. Statistical and Political.
   The Empire; the Governing Race (§ 1).
   Constitution; Ecclesiastical Control (§ 2).

II. Protestant Missions.
   General (§ 1).
   American Board (§ 2).

Other Missions (§ 3).
Bible Societies (§ 4).
Results (§ 5).
III. Roman Catholic Missions.

I. Statistical and Political: [Turkey is a composite empire, since 1908 a constitutional monarchy, having possessions or dependencies in three continents —Europe, Asia, and Africa. Its principal boundaries are: on the north Austria, Servia, Bulgaria, and the Black Sea; on the northeast

1. The Empire; the Govern-ing Race. and east Russia, Persia, and the Persian Gulf; on the south the Indian Ocean, the Libyan Desert, and the Sahara; and on the west, in Europe, the Ionian Sea and Adriatic. Its possessions are in Africa, Egypt, Tunis, and Tripoli until 1911, when Italy annexed it. Its area was estimated (1909) at 1,565,000 square miles, and its population, principally Mohammedan, at 35,400,000. For the distribution of the population among the faiths professed only estimates are available. Thus for the Ægean Islands the numbers given (1909) are 296,800 Christians, 27,200 Mohammedans; for Asia Minor, 7,179,900 Mohammedans, 576,200 Armenians, 972,300 other Christians, 184,600 Jews and others; for Armenia, 1,795,800 Mohammedans, 480,700 Armenians, 165,200 other Christians, 30,700 Jews and others. The number of mosques in the empire are 2,120; of Mohammedan clergy, 11,600, of whom the Sheik-ul-Islam is chief.] The Ottoman Turks who founded the Turkish Empire first appeared in Asia Minor in the thirteenth century— a small tribe of 400 families—coming from Central Asia. As conquerors and as rulers over conquered races they have never been surpassed. At the beginning of the fourteenth century they had established a kingdom under Othman, and this dynasty has ruled in an unbroken succession for more than 600 years. In 1326 they captured Brusa and made it their capital. Before the end of the century they had extended their empire to the Danube in Europe and in 1453 they captured Constantinople. In 1529 they were besieging Vienna. Before this, in 1517, they had made themselves masters of Syria, Arabia, and Egypt, and Sultan Selim had won for his house the califate of Islam. The Ottoman Turks were already converted to Mohammedanism when they entered upon their career of conquest, and for 400 years the constitution of the government has been strictly Mohammedan. Since the time of Selim the claim of the sultans to be the califs of the Mohammedan world has been generally recognized on account of their ability to maintain it and their possession of the holy cities, in spite of the fact that the prophet himself declared that the calif must be an Arab of the tribe of Koreish. The sultans have always been absolute autocrats, and the law of the empire has been the *Shériat*, which is based upon the Koran, the traditions, and the decisions of the distinguished doctors of the law. Under pressure from the powers of Europe a body of civil law based upon the *Code Napoléon* was added to the *Shériat* some fifty years ago and courts established to administer it—but the results have been very unsatisfactory and the government has never been more arbitrary and tyrannical than during the past thirty years—and never more fanatically Mohammedan.

July, 1908, seemed to mark the dawn of a new era in Turkey. The Ottoman Turks had seen the power of their empire declining and its extent diminishing for 200 years, while the power and influence of Christian Europe dominated the world. The palace camarilla which ruled in

2. Constitu-tion; Ecclesiastical Control. the name of Sultan Abd-ul-Hamid had not only oppressed and massacred Christian subjects of the empire, but had crushed the spirit of the Turks. Some 50,000 of the more intelligent and enlightened of them had been put to death or exiled. Many had fled to Europe. There they organized a revolution which is expected to transform Turkey into a free, constitutional empire—with equal rights for all. The watchwords of the new régime are liberty, equality, fraternity, and justice. The sultan was not at first deposed, but was made to accept the constitution—which recognizes the sovereignty of the dynasty of Othman, Mohammedanism as the religion of the State, and the sultan as calif of Islam, but promises religious liberty, freedom of the press, freedom of speech, equal rights, and equal duties for all races and religions—secured by a parliament where all are equally represented and by a reformed judiciary. In 1909 an attempt was made to subvert the constitution, but Abd-ul-Hamid was shown to have been concerned in the attempt and was deposed, and his brother, Mohammed V., was raised to the throne. This revolution is the work of the same Ottoman Turks as have ruled the empire for 600 years. They constitute about one-fifth of the population of the empire and hope that a strong and regenerated Turkey will restore their influence in the Mohammedan world. It remains to be seen how far it is possible to graft these Christian principles upon Mohammedanism and how far the Christian nationalities in the empire will consent to give up the special privileges which have been assured to them ever since the capture of Constantinople, and have served to protect their national churches from destruction. The Arabs, Albanians, Kurds, and other Mohammedan races have never loved the Turks, while the Christian races have always hoped and prayed for the decay and disappearance of the Turkish rule. In 1909 in Constantinople, officially recognized by the Porte, there were patriarchs of the Armenian, Armenian Catholic, Latin and Orthodox (Greek) churches, the exarch of the Bulgarian church, the vekil of the Protestants, and the Haham Bashi of the Jews. They are appointed by the sultan and have considerable civil as well as ecclesiastical authority over their flocks. In these organizations political interests have often taken the place of the concerns of religion, and, except the Protestants and Catholics, none of these religious bodies have done anything since the Turkish conquest to propagate their faith. As these communities are protected by European powers it will be impossible for the Turks to deprive them of these privileges by force, and their political interests and aspirations will lead them to cling as far as possible to these separate organizations.

II. Protestant Missions: The Protestant Reformation in Europe was not without influence in Turkey, and some of the highest ecclesiastics of the Orthodox church were more or less in sympathy with it. But the people were too ignorant and too isolated to be reached by any movement from without; and Protestantism was practically

1. General. unknown to them until the establishment of Protestant missions in Turkey, early in the present century. These missions have been confined almost exclusively to the Jews and the Oriental Christians. Thirty-one societies are engaged, including the Church Missionary Society, the Society for the Propagation of the Gospel, the London Jews Society, the Established Church of Scotland, the United Free Church of Scotland, the Irish Presbyterian Mission, the Palestine Church Missionary Society, the British Syrian School Society, the

Lebanon Schools Committee, the Society for Promoting Female Education in the East. All of these are British organizations; and in addition to these there are several independent enterprises, mostly schools, conducted by the English. The American societies are the American Board of Commissioners for Foreign Missions, the Presbyterian Board of Missions, the Reformed Presbyterian Mission, the Christian (Campbellite) Mission, the Society of Friends (American and English). There are also a number of publication societies, both English and American, which have agents in Turkey or work through the missionaries. The most important are the British and Foreign Bible Society, the American Bible Society, the American Tract Society, the London Religious Tract Society. The German missions are the Kaiserswerth Deaconesses, the Krishona Missions, and the Jerusalem Verein. These societies employ about 450 missionaries and assistant missionaries, and about 1,800 native assistants. The whole number of Protestants in Turkey is estimated at 100,000, of whom about 25,000 are communicants.

First of these organizations stands the American Board of Commissioners for Foreign Missions, which originally represented the Presbyterian, Reformed (Dutch), and Congregational churches of America, but since 1870 only the last. The work of this board in Turkey was commenced in 1819, when

2. American two missionaries, Messrs. Fisk and
Board. Parsons, were sent out to begin work at Jerusalem. This mission was never fairly established, but in 1823 the Syrian mission was commenced at Beirut. The Armenian mission was founded at Constantinople in 1831, and the Jewish mission in 1832, the Assyrian mission in 1849, and the Bulgarian in 1858. Several missionaries have at times been appointed to work among the Mohammedans, but without any permanent result. There was a time, after the Crimean war, when the government tolerated work for the Mohammedans and there were a few converts. But in 1865 this toleration ceased, and for the last thirty years it has been impossible for a Moslem to abjure his faith and remain in the country. It remains to be seen how far the religious liberty now promised will be extended to Mohammedans. The board has now four distinct missions in Turkey—the European, Western, Central, and Eastern Turkey missions; and its work is chiefly among the Armenians, Bulgarians, and Greeks. The missionaries at first had no intention of establishing an independent Protestant church in Turkey, but sought rather to reform the existing Christian churches. The peculiar constitution of the Turkish empire, which not only gave civil power to the patriarchs, but treated as an outlaw every person not belonging to some established church, together with the violent animosity of the ecclesiastics against Evangelical teaching, finally forced the missionaries to found a Protestant church, or, more properly, a Protestant civil community, which was recognized by the Porte in 1850, through the influence of England. In 1910 the American Board had in Turkey 354 male and female missionaries. They also supported, wholly or in part, 1,355 native pastors, preachers, teachers,

etc. They have 353 stations and sub-stations, with 16,031 communicants. They have 411 schools of all grades, with about 20,000 pupils in all. They have printed and circulated, since the establishment of the missions, over 3,000,000 books. There are seven colleges connected with the missions of the board—at Aintab, Kharpoot, Marsovan, Marash, Tarsus, Smyrna, and Constantinople— with 1,461 students. The colleges at Constantinople and Marash are for girls.

The mission to Syria was transferred by the American Board in 1870 to the Presbyterian Church, and reports the following statistics for 1910: missionaries, 38; native laborers, 194; churches, 29; communicants, 2,819; theological and high schools, 9; high schools for girls, 3; common schools, 91; printed from beginning, 23,395,410

3. Other Missions. books. The Reformed (Dutch) Church in America in 1894 adopted a mission which had been started as an independent work in Arabia, about the Persian Gulf. There are thirteen missionaries, and their object is to reach the Mohammedans with the Gospel of our Lord Jesus Christ. The missions to the Jews in Turkey are conducted by the London Jews Society, which has 5 stations, 7 missionaries, 2 medical missionaries, 6 helpers, and 6 schools; the church of Scotland, which has 5 stations, 5 missionaries, 1 medical missionary, 6 helpers, and 6 schools; the Free Church of Scotland, which has 2 stations, 2 missionaries, 2 helpers, and 3 schools. In all there are four organized churches. It is supposed that the wives of the missionaries are not included in these statistics, as they are in those which precede them.

The British and Foreign Bible Society has eleven depots and depositories in Turkey, with a central agency at Constantinople. It now employs thirty-three colporteurs. It commenced work

4. Bible Societies. in Turkey about 1806. It has circulated the Bible in thirty-five languages, to the number of about 2,500,000 volumes. The American Bible Society has a central agency at Constantinople. Its most important branch is at Beirut; but it operates through all the stations of the American missions. It now employs 50 colporteurs. It circulates the Bible in 26 languages, and the total number of volumes circulated since 1858 is about 750,000. Both of these societies have worked in such close connection with the missionary societies, and have so generally depended upon the missionaries for their translations and for the work of publication, that it is impossible to say exactly how large a proportion of the volumes reported above is included in the statistics already given in connection with the missions. Up to 1858 the missionaries acted as agents of the American Bible Society. Robert College, founded 1863, at Constantinople, and the Syrian Protestant College at Beirut, are independent, endowed institutions, not connected with any missionary society; but they are the fruit of missionary work. Robert College has 45 professors and instructors, and 450 students. Its course of instruction is similar to that of the best American colleges. The Syrian Protestant College has a medical department and a commercial school in addition to its college course, and was founded in 1866. It has 60 professors and instructors, and 700 students. These colleges are both American institutions, and in both the language of instruction is English. Their students represent almost all the languages, religions, and nationalities of the East.

Of late years most of the missions in Turkey have given prominence to medical work, and a number of hospitals have been established at

5. Results. the mission stations. The most important connected with American missions are at Beirut, Aintab, Cæsarea, Marsovan, Van, and Bâhrein, and there are dispensaries for medical aid at most of the stations. This work reaches all races and religions, and its influence is constantly increasing. The real influence of Protestant missions in Turkey can not be measured by any such statistics as those given above. It has been not only religious, but intellectual, social, and political. It has modified the character of the Oriental churches, and to some extent reformed them. It has carried Western ideas and Christian civilization into the darkest corners of the empire. Many English statesmen familiar with Turkish affairs have declared that American missionaries have accomplished more for the regeneration of the East than all other influences combined. Lord Stratford de Redcliffe and Lord Shaftesbury may be mentioned, among others, as having expressed this opinion.

III. Roman Catholic Missions: Neither the Roman Catholic authorities nor the French embassy at Constantinople are ready to furnish the statistics of Roman Catholic missions in Turkey; although an offer was made to publish what they might furnish, without note or comment. Without such statistics, only general statements can be made. All Roman Catholic missions in Turkey were, until recently, political agencies of the French Government, and as such received pecuniary aid and diplomatic support. In return for this they were expected to propagate and sustain French influence under all circumstances. The principal Roman Catholic organizations in Turkey are the Lazarists, Mechitarists, Franciscans, Dominicans, Capuchins, Carmelites, Jesuits, and various organizations of Sisters of Charity. For many years past they have made but little apparent progress in winning converts from other Christian churches, and they have not attempted to convert Mohammedans. For a time the Bulgarians, after their conversion to Christianity, inclined toward Rome; but they finally united with the Eastern Church; and only a small body of Paulicians are now Roman Catholics. Since the commencement of the conflict between the Bulgarians and the Greek Patriarch, great efforts have been made to win the Bulgarians over to Rome; and, since the expulsion of the religious orders from France, this mission has been largely reenforced, and French protection has been offered to converts, especially in Macedonia. The results have thus far been small. In Albania there is a strong Catholic element. Among the Greeks no progress has been made for fifty years. There is a rich and influential Armenian Catholic Church in Turkey, which during the eighteenth century suffered terrible persecution; but this church has during the past few years been distracted by dissensions, growing out of an effort, on the part of Rome, to Latinize it. Several thousand families have gone back to the old Armenian church.

Among the Arabic-speaking races, the Roman Catholics have won over many of the Jacobites, control the Maronites of Syria, have some influence among the Greeks and Copts, and of course maintain establishments in Tripoli and Tunis. In addition to the native Roman Catholics, there is all through the empire a large foreign population, which is generally Roman Catholic and contributes to the support of the missions. In fact, much of the influence of this faith in Turkey has always come from the diplomatic, consular, and commercial establishments maintained here by Roman Catholic countries. The native Christians have always been taught to feel, that, in becoming Roman Catholics, they became in some sense Europeans, and shared in some degree the honor and immunities of foreigners. In addition to these social and political advantages afforded to converts, the Roman Catholic missions have founded churches, schools, hospitals, and orphanages, monasteries, convents, and seminaries. Their schools have always been of a low order; but they have taught the French language, and such accomplishments as took the fancy of the people. Until the establishment of Protestant missions, they were, no doubt, the best schools in the country. Of late years, whatever progress has been made has been due chiefly to the work of the Sisters of Charity in hospitals, orphanages, schools, and house-to-house visitation. They are to be found everywhere; and, although generally ignorant and bigoted, they are indefatigable workers, well trained to obedience, self-sacrificing, and wholly devoted to these works of Christian charity.

The number of Roman Catholic missionaries in the empire, native and foreign, male and female, including the ecclesiastics of the native Roman Catholic churches, can not be less than 3,000. There is no means of estimating the annual expenditure, but the Roman Catholic missions have certainly been more successful than the Protestant in " living on the country." They depend much less, in proportion to their numbers, upon foreign aid.

It is not easy for a Protestant to form an estimate of the success of Roman Catholic missions. They have no doubt planted the church so firmly in this empire that it can stand by itself without foreign aid; but they have done nothing toward converting the Mohammedans, and have made no progress in winning over the oriental churches to a union with Rome. They have not essentially weakened these churches, nor have they made converts enough to enter into any rivalry with them.

GEORGE WASHBURN.

BIBLIOGRAPHY: Besides the literature under ARMENIA; SYRIA; and SYRIAN CHURCH, consult on the history and life: J. W. Zinkeisen, *Geschichte des osmanischen Reiches in Europa*, 7 vols., Hamburg, 1840–63; J. L. Farley, *Modern Turkey*, London, 1872; idem, *Turks and Christians*, ib. 1876; J. Baker, *Turkey in Europe*, ib. 1877; T. Milner, *The Turkish Empire; Sultan, Territory and People*, ib. 1877; E. L. Clark, *The Races of European Turkey*, Edinburgh, 1878; idem, *Turkey*, New York, 1883; E. J. Davies, *Life in Asiatic Turkey*, London, 1879; J.

Creagh, *Armenians, Koords, and Turks*, 2 vols., ib. 1880; H. F. Tozer, *Turkish Armenia and Eastern Asia Minor*, ib. 1881; J. M. N. Brodhead, *Slav and Moslem, Historical Sketches*, Aiken, 1894; S. L. Poole, *The Mohammedan Dynasties*, Westminster, 1894; R. Davey, *The Sultan and his Subjects*, New York, 1897; Mrs. W. M. Ramsay, *Everyday Life in Turkey*, London, 1903; L. M. Garnett, *Turkish Life in Town and Country*, London and New York, 1904; idem, *Turkey of the Ottomans*, ib. 1911; M. Sykes, *Dar-ul-Islam: a Record of a Journey through ten of the Asiatic Provinces of Turkey*, New York, 1904; W. S. Monroe, *Turkey and the Turks. An Account of the Lands, Peoples and Institutions of the Ottoman Empire*, Boston, 1907, London, 1908; G. F. Abbot, *Turkey in Transition*, New York, 1909; L. Collas, *Histoire de l'empire ottoman jusqu'à la révolution de 1909*, Paris, 1910. And on missions and churches: *The Star in the East; Quarterly Record of the Progress of Christian Missions within the Turkish Empire*, London, 1883; Hilaire, *La France catholique en orient durant les trois derniers siècles*, Paris, 1902; E. von Mülinen, *Die lateinische Kirche im türkischen Reiche*, 2d ed., Berlin, 1903; W. A. Essery, *The Ascending Cross. Some Results of Missions in Bible Lands*, London, 1905; J. E. H., *One Hundred Syrian Pictures, Illustrating the Work of the Syrian Mission*, ib. 1903; C. Lagier, *Byzance et Stamboul: nos droits français et nos missions en orient*, Paris, 1905; N. Jorga, *Geschichte des osmanischen Reiches*, 3 vols., Gotha, 1907–10; J. L. Barton, *Daybreak in Turkey*, Boston, 1909.

TURLUPINS: A medieval sect akin to the Beghards (q.v.), like whom they called themselves " the fellowship of poverty." The origin and meaning of the derisive epithet " Turlupins " are obscure. They seem to have been especially numerous in Paris and the province of Isle-de-France during the reign of Charles V. (1364–80), while in 1460–65 they were in the vicinity of Lille. According to their tenets, which are known only from their opponents, " inward prayer " was the sole religious duty. They carried their endeavor to imitate apostolic poverty to such an extreme that they went almost naked. In their gatherings, which were secret, they are said to have laid aside all their garments to symbolize paradise, and it is also said that they held that those who had reached a certain stage of perfection could no longer sin, and might indulge sensual impulses without hesitation. The Inquisition proceded unsparingly against the Turlupins, and Gregory XI. praised the king for his zeal against them, but they did not entirely disappear from France until the second half of the fifteenth century.

(EUGEN LACHENMANN.)

BIBLIOGRAPHY: J. Gerson, *Opera*, ed. Du Pin, Antwerp, 1706; J. Hermant, *Hist. des hérésies*, iv. 374, Rouen, 1726; P. Fredericq, *Corpus documentorum inquisitionis . . . Neerlandicæ*, i. 409–412, The Hague, 1889; H. C. Lea, *History of the Inquisition of the Middle Ages*, ii. 126, 158, New York, 1906; *KL*, xii. 147–148.

TURNER, ARTHUR BERESFORD: Church of England bishop of Korea; b. at Farley (4 m. e. of Salisbury), Wiltshire, Aug. 24, 1862. He was educated at Keble College, Oxford (B.A., 1885), and was ordained to the priesthood in 1888. After being curate of Watlington, Oxfordshire (1887–89), Downton, Salisbury (1889–92), and St. Nicholas Cathedral, Newcastle-on-Tyne (1892–96), he was a missionary in Korea (q.v.) from 1896 till 1905, when he was consecrated bishop of that country.

TURNER, FRANCIS: Church of England bishop; b. probably at Fecham, Surrey, c. 1638; d. in London Nov. 2, 1700. He was educated at Winchester and at New College, Oxford (B.A., 1659; M.A,

1663; B.D. and D.D., 1669); became rector of Therfield, Hertfordshire, 1664; fellow of St. John's College, Cambridge, 1666; prebend for Sneating at St. Paul's, London, 1669; master of St. John's College, Cambridge, 1670, and vice-chancellor, 1678; rector of Great Hasely, Oxfordshire, 1683; dean of Windsor and bishop of Rochester, 1683; was translated to Ely, 1684; preached the sermon at the coronation of James II., Apr. 23, 1685; joined in the protest of the seven bishops against the king's declaration for liberty of conscience, 1688; refused the oath of allegiance to William and Mary and was suspended, 1689, and deprived, 1690; was arrested but discharged, 1696. He was a controversialist, and evoked a sharp retort from Andrew Marvell. Besides letters and occasional sermons, he wrote *Brief Memoirs of Nicholas Ferrar* (2d ed., London, 1837).

BIBLIOGRAPHY: A. à Wood, *Athenæ Oxonienses*, ed. P. Bliss, iv. 545, 619, and *Fasti*, vol. ii. passim, London, 1813–20; T. Lathbury, *Hist. of the Nonjurors*, ib. 1862; W. H. Hutton, *The English Church (1625–1714)*, pp. 228, 240, ib. 1903; *DNB*, lvii. 336–337.

TURNER, HENRY McNEAL: African Methodist Episcopal bishop; b. at Newberry Court House, S. C., Feb. 1, 1834. In his boyhood he lived in the cotton fields of his native state and learned to read and write by his own exertions, while as a servant in the Abbeville Court House, and later in a medical college at Baltimore, he widened his knowledge. In 1853 he was licensed as a preacher in the Methodist Episcopal Church South and traveled extensively in the southern states. In 1858 he became a member of the African Methodist Episcopal Church and soon joined the Missouri conference, in which he became an itinerant minister. In the fall of the same year he was transferred to the Baltimore Conference, where he remained four years, during which he completed his education at Trinity College. In 1862–63 he was pastor of Israel Church, Washington, D. C., and during the Civil War was chaplain of the First Regiment of United States Colored Troops. At the close of the war, he was commissioned chaplain in the regular army and was detailed to the Freedmen's Bureau in Georgia. He returned to the ministry in 1866 and was active also in educational and political affairs. He was elected a member of the Georgia constitutional convention in 1867 and in the following year entered the legislature of the same state, where he remained two terms (1868–72). He was then appointed successively postmaster of Macon, Ga., in 1870, inspector of customs in 1874, and United States secret detective in 1875. In 1876 the general conference of his denomination elected him general manager of its publications, with his residence at Philadelphia, and in 1880 he was chosen bishop. He is an ardent advocate of the return of the negroes to Africa, where he holds that they should build up a nation of their own, and he has organized four annual conferences in Africa at Sierra Leone, Liberia, Transvaal, and South Africa. He has written *African Methodist Episcopal Hymnal* (Philadelphia, 1876); *African Methodist Episcopal Catechism* (1877); and *Methodist Polity* (1889).

TURNER, SAMUEL HULBEART: Protestant Episcopal; b. in Philadelphia Jan. 23, 1790; d. in New York Dec. 21, 1861. He was graduated from the University of Pennsylvania, 1807; settled as pastor at Chestertown, Md., 1812; became professor of historic theology in the General Theological Seminary, New York, 1818, and from 1821 till his death was professor of Biblical learning. He was a sound and able commentator. He translated, with Bishop Whittingham, Jahn's *Introduction to the Old Testament* (New York, 1827), and Planck's *Introduction to Sacred Philology and Interpretation* (1834); wrote commentaries upon the Greek text of *Hebrews* (1852), *Romans* (1853), *Ephesians* (1856), *Galatians* (1856); prepared *Companion to the Book of Genesis* (1841); *Biographical Notices of some of the most Distinguished Jewish Rabbies, and Translations of Portions of their Commentaries and Other Works* (1847); *Thoughts on the Origin, Character, and Interpretation of Scripture Prophecy* (1852); *Teachings of the Master* (1858); *Spiritual Things compared with Spiritual, or Gospels and Acts illustrated by Parallel References* (1859); *The Gospels according to the Ammonian Sections and the Tables of Eusebius* (1861).

BIBLIOGRAPHY: *Autobiography of Samuel H. Turner*, New York, 1863.

TURNOW, tur'nev, PETER: Waldensian with Taboritic tendencies; b. at Tolkemit (50 m. s.w. of Königsberg), probably about 1390; executed at Speyer probably in Apr., 1426. Of his early life nothing is known, but about 1415 he was in Prague. Henceforth his fortunes were closely connected with those of Johannes Drändorf (q.v.), and somewhat later he apparently visited Greece. A few years before his death he was rector of a school in Speyer, where, together with Drändorf, he began a series of attacks on the clergy of the city. He sought in vain to keep his friend from his own negotiations with Weinsberg, Heilbronn, and Wimpfen, and the pair were involved in common ruin. Besides his attacks on the secular power of the clergy, Turnow is said to have held that general councils could err, that the Eucharist must be administered under both kinds, the priest teaching or acting to the contrary being doomed to eternal punishment at the last day.   (FERDINAND COHRS.)

BIBLIOGRAPHY: M. Flacius, *Catalogus testium veritatis*, Frankfort, 1666; C. D. d'Argentre, *Collectio judiciorum de novis erroribus*, vol. ii., Paris, 1728; J. E. Kapp, *Nachlese Einiger . . . zur Erläuterung der Reformations-Geschichte nützlicher Urkunden*, part iii., Leipsic, 1730; H. Haupt, *Die religiösen Sekten in Franken vor der Reformation*, Würzburg, 1882; idem, in *Historisches Taschenbuch*, VI., vii. 233 sqq.; idem, *Waldensertum und Inquisition im südöstlichen Deutschland*, Freiburg, 1890; L. Keller, *Die Reformation und die älteren Reformparteien*, Leipsic, 1885.

TURRECREMATA, JOHANNES DE. See TORQUEMADA, JUAN DE.

TURRETTINI, tur''rê-tî'nî (TURRETIN): A family of Geneva theologians, whose founder, Francesco Turrettini, left his native Lucca in 1574 and settled in Geneva in 1592.

1. Benedict: Son of Francesco; b. in Zurich 1588; d. at Geneva Mar. 4, 1631. He became pastor and professor of theology at Geneva in 1612. In 1620 he was a delegate to the national synod of Alais, which introduced the results of the Synod of Dort into France. In the following year he was sent on a successful mission to ask the Dutch States General and the Hanseatic cities for aid to put Geneva into a state of defense. Among his numerous writings the most important was his *Défense de la fidelité des traductions de la S. Bible faites à Genève* (3 vols., Geneva, 1618–20), written in answer to the *Genève plagiaire* of the Jesuit Pierre Cotton (Paris, 1618).

2. François: Son of the preceding; b. at Geneva Oct. 17, 1623; d. there Sept. 28, 1687. He was educated at Geneva, Leyden, Utrecht, Paris, Saumur, Montauban, and Nîmes. Returning to his native city, he was made pastor of the Italian church there in 1648, and professor of theology in 1653. He is especially known as a zealous opponent of the theology of Saumur (see AMYRAUT, MOÏSE), as an earnest defender of the orthodoxy represented by the Synod of Dort, and as one of the authors of the Helvetic Consensus (q.v.). Among his writings, which are chiefly dogmatic in character, special mention should be made of his *Institutio theologiæ elencticæ* (3 parts, Geneva, 1679–85). A complete new edition of his works with his life by B. Pictet was issued at Edinburgh (4 vols., 1847–48).

3. Jean Alphonse: Son of the preceding, and the most important member of the family; b. at Geneva Aug. 24, 1671; d. there May 1, 1737. He was educated at Geneva and at Leyden. Destined to depart from his father's defense of rigid Calvinism, and to seek to reunite all Protestants on the basis of a few fundamental doctrines, freeing the church of Geneva from the domination of the Synod of Dort, he began his activity as an author with his *Pyrrhonismus pontificius sive theses theologico-historicæ de variationibus pontificiorum circa ecclesiæ infallibilitatem* (Leyden, 1692) which was practically a refutation of Bossuet's *Variations des églises protestantes* (2 vols., Paris, 1688). From Leyden he went to England and France, and on his return to his native city in 1693 was made a member of the Vénérable compagnie des pasteurs. In 1697 he was appointed professor of church history, and from 1701 to 1711 was rector of the academy of Geneva, his rectorial addresses being later collected under the title of *Orationes academicæ* (Geneva, 1737).

Turrettini was especially important for his part in the abolition in 1725 of the Helvetic Consensus, of which his father had been one of the chief authors, but which was felt to be a burden in Geneva, as well as in other parts of Switzerland. The struggle over this commenced in 1706, over the promise of a young clergyman named Vial to refrain from teaching contrary to the Consensus, a promise not agreeable to the strict minority which had the council of state cancel Vial's inclusion in the Compagnie. The matter was further considered by the latter and recommendations made to the council of state, the general result of which was that the Compagnie, in its session of June 15, resolved to drop the formula of 1706, and to retain only the requirements of belief in the teaching of the prophets and apostles as contained in the Old and New Testaments and as summarized in the catechism. Thus not only the Helvetic Consensus, but the canons of Dort and even the Second Helvetic Confession were

deprived of their binding force upon the clergy, while a sort of symbolic authority was accorded only to Calvin's catechism. The government was evidently in sympathy with the results, though, in accord with eighteenth-century usage, it desired the affair to be kept as quiet as possible. Turrettini, however, was not content with the abolition of the Consensus in Geneva, but desired that it be abrogated throughout Switzerland. To this end he communicated with Archbishop Wake of Canterbury, whereupon the primate, later followed by the king of England, wrote the Swiss cantons urging them to dispense with the Helvetic Consensus.

The abolition of this Consensus was closely connected with another interest which assumed an important place in Turrettini's life—the union between the Lutherans and the Reformed. In 1707 he learned, through a Prussian deputy at Neuchâtel, that Frederick I., who was deeply interested in the union, desired to know the opinion of the church and academy of Geneva on the matter. On Apr. 22, 1707, the Compagnie gave the king the desired information in a letter prepared by Turrettini, in which the utmost readiness for interdenominational comity was expressed. Frederick showed his deep pleasure in a reply read by the Compagnie on July 1, in which he urged the Genevan Church to enter into negotiations with his clergy and theologians in the cause of union. Turrettini himself was rewarded with a gold medal from the king and appointment to membership in the royal academy of Berlin.

The chief source for a knowledge of the theological tendency of Turrettini is his *Nubes testium pro moderato et pacifico de rebus theologicis judicio et instituenda inter Protestantes concordia* (Geneva, 1719; Eng. transl., *A Discourse concerning Fundamental Articles in Religion*, London, 1720), a work inspired by the letter of Archbishop Wake already mentioned. From the preface it appears that Turrettini had corresponded with Leibnitz concerning Protestant union as early as 1707. The work includes a treatise on the fundamental articles of faith, prepared at the request of two Lutheran nobles and first printed before the appearance of the *Nubes*. Here the author maintains that only those are fundamental articles "whose knowledge and faith are necessary for obtaining the grace and salvation of God." Of these there are but few, only those which have been believed by all Christians at all times. He even asserts that the sole doctrines in question are obedience to the commands of God and faith in the promises of the Gospel; though he admits that the Apostles' Creed is the "criterion and standard of fundamentals." His final conclusion is that God alone knows what beliefs are necessary to salvation, and he closes by declaring that union is impossible where there is lack of agreement concerning the basal truths of the Gospel, as between Protestants and Roman Catholics, but that such union should be effected where the divergencies concern mere accessories, as between Lutherans and Reformed.

Another work of importance for Turrettini's theology was his *Cogitationes et dissertationes theologicæ*

(2 vols., 1711–37), setting forth a modified orthodoxy, and maintaining that many subjects of theological debate were really of minor importance. The work contains much material that entitles Turrettini to an honorable place among Christian apologists. His apologetic views, however, were more and more distorted and diluted with rationalism by the free " translations " of his work by J. Vernet, professor of history and belles lettres at Geneva, under the title *Traité de la vérité de la religion chrétienne, tiré du latin de Mr. J. A. Turrettini* (3 vols., Geneva, 1730–40), these liberties being carried still further in the second edition of the French version (1748–51; Eng. transl., *An Argument concerning the Christian Religion*, London, 1800).

In Geneva Turrettini gradually became an ecclesiastical primate, and as such, for example, he introduced the custom of public confirmation. He received repeated requests from abroad for opinions and interventions, but the closing years of his life were deeply troubled by the disturbances in Geneva in 1734. After his death appeared his *Commentarius theoretico-practicus in epistolam Sancti Pauli ad Thessalonicos* (Basel, 1739); his lectures on Rom. xi. (Geneva, 1741); and his treatise on Biblical exegesis (Berlin, 1766). His *Opera omnia* appeared at Leuwarden (3 vols., 1774–76).

(E. CHOISY.)

BIBLIOGRAPHY: F. Turrettini, *Notice biographique sur Bénédict Turrettini*, Geneva, 1871; E. de Budé, *Vie de François Turrettini*, Geneva, 1871; idem, *Vie de J. Alphonse Turrettini*, 2 vols., ib. 1880; G. Keizer, *François Turrettini*, Paris, 1900; J. Senebier, *Hist. littéraire de Genève*, 3 vols., Geneva, 1706; F. Schaller, *Essai sur J. A. Turrettini*, Colmar, 1861; J. Gaberel, *Hist. de l'église de Genève*, vol. iii., Geneva, 1862; H. von der Goltz, *Die reformierte Kirche Genfs im 19. Jahrhundert*, Basel, 1862; H. Heyer, *Catalogue des thèses soutenues à l'académie de Genève*, Geneva, 1898; C. Borgeaud, *L'Académie de Calvin, 1559–1798*, Geneva, 1900; T. Heyer, in *Mémoires de la société d'hist. et archéologie de Genève*, vol. xiii.; Lichtenberger, *ESR*, xii. 249–251.

TUTTLE, DANIEL SYLVESTER: Protestant Episcopal bishop; b. at Windham, N. Y., Jan. 26, 1837. He was educated at Columbia College (B.A., 1857); was a private tutor (1857–59); studied at General Theological Seminary, New York City (1859–62); was ordered deacon in 1862 and ordained priest in 1863; was minister (1862–63), and rector (1863–67) of Zion Church, Morris, N. Y.; was consecrated missionary bishop of Montana, Idaho, and Utah (1867) and took charge of the new diocese of Utah and Idaho (1880), changing in 1886 to the diocese of Missouri; over which he has since presided. In virtue of his age he has been presiding bishop of the Protestant Episcopal Church in the United States since 1903. In theology he terms himself " a Prayer Book Churchman along the historic lines advocated by Bishop Seabury and Bishop Hobart," and has written *Reminiscences of a Missionary Bishop* (New York, 1906).

BIBLIOGRAPHY: W. S. Perry, *The Episcopate in America*, p. 181, New York, 1895.

TUTTLE, HUDSON: Author and lecturer in the interest of spiritualism; b. at Berlin Heights, Ohio, Oct. 4, 1836; d. at Berlin Heights, Ohio, Dec. 14, 1910. He was self-educated, and was connected with the propaganda and journalism of spiritualism throughout his life. Among his works are *Arcana of Nature* (Boston, 1859; 2d ed., 2 vols., 1864; new ed., 1908); *Origin and Antiquity of Physical Man* (1865); *Career of the Christ Idea in History* (1870); *Year-Book of Spiritualism: Record of its Facts, Science, and Philosophy* (1871; in collaboration with J. M. Peebles); *Studies in the Outlying Fields of Psychic Science* (New York, 1889); *Religion of Man and Ethics of Science* (1890); *Life in Two Spheres* (1892); *Evolution of the God and Christ Ideas* (Berlin Heights, O., 1907); and *Studies from beyond the Borderland* (1910).

TWELVE APOSTLES, TEACHING OF THE. See DIDACHE.

TWELVE PATRIARCHS, TESTAMENT OF. See PSEUDEPIGRAPHA, OLD TESTAMENT, III., 23.

TWESTEN, Tves'ten, AUGUST DETLEV CHRISTIAN: German Lutheran; b. at Glückstadt (27 m. n.w. of Hamburg) Apr. 11, 1789; d. at Berlin Jan. 8, 1876. He was educated at the universities of Kiel (1808–10) and Berlin (1810–11), coming under the special influence of Schleiermacher. After teaching for a time at the Werdersches Gymnasium in Berlin, Twesten was appointed, in 1814, associate professor of philosophy and theology at Kiel, where, within a year, he assisted in establishing the *Kieler Blätter*. His lectures dealt with philosophy, systematic theology, and New Testament exegesis. In systematic theology he devoted himself first to philosophic theology, as well as to the theory of the Church and symbolics, later turning to theological encyclopedia, dogmatics, and ethics. His exegetical lectures covered the entire New Testament, while he also edited for his students *Die drei ökumenischen Symbole, die Augsburgische Konfession und die repetitio confessionis Augustanæ* (Kiel, 1816). He likewise wrote as textbooks *Die Logik, insbesondere die Analytik* (Sleswick, 1825), and *Grundriss der analytischen Logik* (Kiel, 1834). More important theologically was his *Vorlesungen über die Dogmatik der evangelisch-lutherischen Kirche nach dem Kompendium des . . . W. M. de Wette* (2 vols., Hamburg, 1826–37), designed in part to supplement the *Glaubenslehre* of Schleiermacher, but never completed. The point of view is essentially that of a middle way between the extremes of mere return to old principles and the rationalism of the period, the possibility of divergent interpretations being at the same time admitted. The sense of uncertainty which pervades the *Vorlesungen* did not, however, extend to his determination to establish his church on a firm foundation and to justify her independence, his views on these matters being expressed in his irenic rectorial address of Mar. 5, 1830, in celebration of the three-hundredth anniversary of the Augsburg Confession.

Twesten's influence was greatly enhanced at Kiel after the call of Klaus Harms in 1816; for the two men supplemented each other, so that it was well said that Twesten converted his hearers and Harms baptized them. When Twesten was asked to become the successor of Schleiermacher at Berlin, he modestly declined, and it was only the insistence of Neander and Johannes Schulze that overcame his modest reluctance, and in 1835 he became professor of dogmatics and New-Testament exegesis there. Here his task was to preserve the middle way between the Hegelianism of Marheineke and the neo-orthodox legalism of Hengstenberg, both of whom found a bond of union in opposition to an undesired colleague. Having points both of sympathy and of antagonism with both Marheineke and Hengstenberg, he yet remained essentially aloof from the trend of either, contenting himself with a clear presentation of his own convictions that recognized all that was good in his opponents, withdrawing approval only where there was evident lack of truthfulness or open denial of Evangelical principles. His ecclesiastical aims found noteworthy expression in the general synod of Berlin in 1846. Here, in the search for a basis for the Evangelical Church of Prussia which should meet the requirements of the time, it became necessary to establish a confession. Opposing the attempt to make a new formulation of the doctrines common to the Evangelical creeds, Twesten urged the retention of the old standards, though without erecting these classical documents of the Reformation into a judicial system. His principles were further exemplified in his attitude toward union, whose antitheses, he held, would lead neither to schism nor to heresy. The end of all efforts for union should be, according to him, the association, for mutual edification, of all Christians living in one place at the same time, a sharp distinction being drawn between the practical and the merely academic. This attitude of mediation was maintained by Twesten in his practical administration of ecclesiastical affairs.

In addition to the works already mentioned, Twesten edited F. Schleiermacher's *Grundriss der philosophischen Ethik* (Berlin, 1841) and L. Hutter's *Compendium locorum theologicorum* (1855), and wrote *Commentatio critica de Hesiodi carmine quod inscribitur opera et dies* (Kiel, 1815); *Matthias Flacius Illyricus* (Berlin, 1844); and *Zur Erinnerung an Friedrich Daniel Ernst Schleiermacher* (1868).
(G. Heinrici.)

Bibliography: The one biography is C. F. G. Heinrici, *August Twesten nach Tagebüchern und Briefen*, Berlin, 1889. Consult further: C. E. Carstens, *Geschichte der Kieler theologischen Fakultät*, Kiel, 1875; P. Kleinert and E. Curtius, *Worte der Erinnerung an Dr. A. Twesten*, Berlin, 1889; E. Hitzig, *Ernst Constantin Ranke*, pp. 151–152, Leipsic, 1906.

TWICHELL, JOSEPH HOPKINS: Congregationalist; b. at Southington, Conn., May 27, 1838. He was educated at Yale (A.B., 1859) and studied at Union Theological Seminary (1859–61) and Andover Theological Seminary (1864–65). He was a chaplain in the Union Army during the Civil War, and since 1865 has been pastor of Asylum Hill Congregational Church, Hartford, Conn. He has written *John Winthrop* (New York, 1891) and has edited *Some Old Puritan Love Letters* (correspondence of John and Margaret Winthrop; 1893).

TWIN (DWIN, DVIN, DEVIN): The early capital and Christian center of Armenia (120 m. s. of Tiflis, Russia). Its significance for church history lies in the facts that seven synods were held there,

and that it became the seat of the catholicos (c. 452) as a result of Persian attacks on Armenian Christians, who were driven from Echmiadzin, the earlier and the prese　seat. Contemporary sources for Armenian history during the sixth century are inadequate and in some cases contradictory. The consequence is that many dates even of the most important events can not be accurately determined. The most probable date for the first synod of Twin is 524, under King Kavadh (d. 531). Among the most eminent of the prelates present were Peter, bishop of Siunik, and Nersapuh, bishop of Taron. Besides authorizing Twin as the seat of the catholicos, the synod determined upon complete separation from the Greeks, involving rejection of the Chalcedonian symbol with its diophysitism and a reassertion of monophysitism; the celebration of the birth and baptism (spiritual birth) on the same day; and the addition of the clause in the Trisagion (q.v.), "Thou wast crucified for us," to the liturgy. The second synod of Twin (Dec. 14, 552) regulated the Armenian calendar and adopted July 11, 552, as the beginning of the Armenian era and the New Year's day of the new era. See Armenia; Nerses.
A. H. Newman.

Bibliography: The literature under Armenia; and W. F. Adeney, *The Greek and Eastern Churches*, pp. 539 sqq., New York, 1908.

TWISSE, WILLIAM: Puritan divine; b. at Speenham-Land, near Newbury (16 m. w.s.w. of Reading), England, c. 1578; d. in London July 20, 1646. He received his education at New College, Oxford (fellow, 1598; B.A., 1600; M.A., 1604; B.D., 1612; D.D., 1614); became chaplain to Elizabeth, eldest daughter of James I., on her marriage in 1613 to Elector-Palatine Frederick V., but was recalled after two months and made vicar of Newton, and in 1620 of Newbury, where he remained, although he received the offer of several preferments in the Church of England and of a professorship of divinity at Franeker, Friesland. He was a Calvinist of the supralapsarian school, learned and of a speculative genius. He was a member of the Westminster Assembly of which he was unanimously elected prolocutor—a post for which he was temperamentally unfitted. He was buried in Westminster Abbey, but by royal mandate his remains were dug up Sept. 14, 1661, and thrown with those of several other persons into a pit in St. Margaret's churchyard, which immediately adjoins the abbey. He distinguished himself by his writings against Arminianism, and his *Opera* appeared at Amsterdam (2 vols., 1652).

Bibliography: The principal source is G. Kendall's *Tuissii vita et victoria*, appended to Kendall's *Fur pro tribunali*, London, 1657. Consult further *DNB*, lvii. 397–399, and the short notices to which reference is there given.

TYANA, APOLLONIUS OF. See Apollonius of Tyana.

TYCHONIUS. See Tichonius.

TYCHSEN, tiH′zen **(TUKA), OLUF GERHARD:** German orientalist; b. at Tondern (106 m. n.w. of Hamburg) Dec. 14, 1734; d. at Rostock Dec. 30, 1815. He was educated at Altona; studied theology and oriental languages at Halle; became in

1759 a member of the Kallenberg missionary institution for the conversion of Jews and Mohammedans, but proved very unsuccessful in his practical attempts; and was in 1760 appointed professor of oriental languages at Bützow, whence in 1789 he was removed to Rostock. He was an authority on Jewish learning and Semitic numismatics, but lacked practical wisdom, as appears from his controversies with Kennicott (*Tentamen de variis codicum Hebr. Veteris Test. MSS. generibus*, Rostock, 1772), and with Bayer (*Die Unechtheit der jüdischen Münzen mit hebräischen und samaritanischen Buchstaben*, Rostock, 1779). The best he wrote is found in his *Bützowsche Nebenstunden* (6 vols., 1766–69), and *Introductio in rem numariam Muhamedanorum* (1794).

BIBLIOGRAPHY: A. T. Hartmann, *Oluf Gerhard Tychsen*, 2 vols., Bremen, 1818–20.

TYERMAN, LUKE: Wesleyan; b. at Osmotherley, Yorkshire, Feb. 26, 1820; d. in London Mar. 21, 1889. He was educated at the Didsbury Wesleyan Methodist Theological Institution, near Manchester, 1842–45, and devoted himself to the ministry. His significance comes from his standard historical works dealing with the origins of Methodism, viz., *Life and Times of Rev. Samuel Wesley* (London, 1866); *Life and Times of Rev. John Wesley* (3 vols., 1870–71); *The Oxford Methodist* (1873); *Life of Rev. George Whitefield* (2 vols., 1876); *Wesley's Designated Successor: the Life, Letters, and Literary Labours of Rev. John W. Fletcher, Vicar of Madeley* (1882).

TYLER, BENJAMIN BUSHROD: Disciple; b. at Decatur, Ill., Apr. 9, 1840. He was educated at Eureka College, Eureka, Ill., and held pastorates in his denomination at Charleston, Ill. (1864–69), Terre Haute, Ind. (1869–73), Frankfort, Ky. (1873–1876), Louisville, Ky. (1876–83), and New York City (1883–1900). Since 1900 he has been pastor of the South Broadway Christian Church, Denver, Col. Since 1893 he has been a member of the editorial board of the St. Louis *Christian Evangelist*. He was also a member of the International Sunday School Lesson Committee in 1890–1908, and while in New York was a member of the committee on versions of the American Bible Society. He has written *History of the Disciples of Christ* (New York, 1894).

TYLER, BENNET: Congregational theologian; b. in Middlebury (then a part of Woodbury), Conn., July 10, 1783; d. at East Windsor, Conn., May 14, 1858. He was graduated at Yale College in 1804; spent a year as teacher in Weston, Conn.; studied theology with the Rev. Asahel Hooker at Goshen, Conn.; was licensed in 1806; began to preach in 1807 at South Britain, where he was ordained in 1808; became president of Dartmouth College in 1822; succeeded Dr. Payson as pastor of Second Congregational Church, Portland, Me., in 1828; was elected president of the Theological Institute of Connecticut, now Hartford Theological Seminary, in 1833 and inagurated May 13, 1834, when the corner-stone of the new edifice was laid in East Windsor, Conn.; resigned this position July 16, 1857, and died suddenly at the house of his daughter. In

all these positions Dr. Tyler was successful; and though much of his public life was spent in theological controversy, his Christian character was recognized even by his opponents, while his friends testify as to his genial temper, unaffected candor, genuine humility, and cheerful piety.

Dr. Tyler's name was conspicuous in connection with a theological controversy among the Congregationalists of Connecticut, which was occasioned by a discourse of Nathaniel William Taylor (q.v.; *Concio ad clerum*, General Association, 1828), professor in the divinity school of Yale College. On a visit to Connecticut in 1829 (he was then pastor at Portland), Dr. Tyler began a correspondence with Dr. Taylor (who had been a classmate at Yale), which passed into a public discussion, continuing for years, and finding its practical issue in the formation of the Pastoral Union of Connecticut (Sept. 10, 1833), and the establishment of the Theological Institute.

The germ of the controversy was the position, attributed to Dr. Taylor, " that no human being can become depraved but by his own act, and that the sinfulness of the race does not pertain to man's nature." In connection with this, regeneration was regarded as the act of man's own will or heart; and the primary cause of this right choice was found in self-love, or a desire for the greatest happiness. (Some of these positions have been disclaimed by Dr. Taylor and his friends.) He claimed to be in accord with the New England Calvinism, represented by the two Edwardses, Bellamy, Hopkins, and Dwight. His position on the doctrine of original sin was not Augustinian: over against Dr. Taylor he asserted depravity of nature and the federal headship of Adam, but did not accept immediate imputation. He denied the self-determining power of the will, or the power of a contrary choice, and would not limit the definition of sin to voluntary transgression of known law. He accepted the distinction of Edwards between natural and moral ability, and denied most resolutely the " happiness theory." By discriminating between an unlimited atonement and limited redemption, he sought to preserve the doctrine of individual election. Regeneration he regarded as " effected, not by moral suasion, or by the efficiency of any means whatever, but by the direct agency of the Holy Spirit, changing the moral disposition, and imparting a new spiritual life to the soul." The controversy, as was usual at that time, was carried on with speculative and dogmatic weapons, though both parties appealed to Scripture.

In later times Dr. Tyler became engaged in discussion with Dr. Bushnell, and his own orthodoxy was called in question before the Pastoral Union in 1856. From this charge he was almost unanimously exonerated.

Dr. Tyler contributed largely to the theological controversy above named; published many sermons and addresses, and contributed many articles to the religious periodicals of the day. Mention may be made of his *Hist. of the New Haven Theology* (Hartford, 1837); *Memoir of Rev. Asahel Nettleton* (1844); *Treatise on the Sufferings of Christ* (New York, 1845); *Treatise on New England Revivals*

(1846); *Letters to Dr. Horace Bushnell* (1847–48), and the posthumous *Lectures on Theology*, with *Memoir* by N. Gale (Boston, 1859). His style is forcible and clear, and his matter always manifests the old Puritan faith in a personal God of holiness.

M. B. RIDDLE.

BIBLIOGRAPHY: See NEW ENGLAND THEOLOGY, v., § 1, and consult: the *Memoir* by N. Gale, ut sup.; E. A. Lawrence, in *New Englander*, 1859; A. H. Quint, in *Congregational Quarterly*, 1860; A. E. Dunning, *Congregationalists in America*, pp. 312, 388, New York, 1894; W. Walker, in *American Church History Series*, iii. 358–361, 366, New York, 1894; idem, *New England Leaders*, pp. 400–436, New York, 1901; F. H. Foster, *New England Theology*, pp. 386–393, Chicago, 1907.

TYMMS, THOMAS VINCENT: English Baptist; b. at Westminster, London, Jan. 5, 1842. He was educated at Regent's Park College, London. He held Baptist pastorates at Berwick-on-Tweed (1865–1868), Accrington (1868–69), and Downs Chapel, Clapton, London (1869–91). From 1891 until his retirement from active life in 1904 he was president and professor of theology in Rawdon College, Leeds. He was Angus lecturer in Regent's Park College in 1903, and has written *The Mystery of God* (London, 1885), the essay on " Christian Theism " in *The Ancient Faith in Modern Light* (Edinburgh, 1897); *The Christian Idea of Atonement* (London, 1904); and *The Private Relationships of Christ*(1907).

TYNDALE, tin'dal, WILLIAM: Biblical translator and martyr; b. most probably at North Nibley (15 m. s.s.w. of Gloucester), England, in 1484; d. at Vilvoorden (6 m. n.e. of Brussels), Belgium, Oct. 6, 1536. He was descended from an ancient Northumbrian family, went to school at Oxford, and afterward to Magdalen Hall and Cambridge, and about 1520 became tutor in the family of Sir John Walsh, at Little Sodbury in Gloucestershire. He was in orders; but the record of his ordination has not yet been verified. Having become attached to the doctrines of the Reformation, and devoted himself to the study of the Scriptures, the open avowal of his sentiments in the house of Walsh, his disputes with Roman Catholic dignitaries there, and especially his preaching, excited much opposition, and led to his removal to London (about Oct., 1523), where he began to preach, and made many friends among the laity, but none among ecclesiastics. He was hospitably entertained at the house of Sir Humphrey Monmouth, and also pecuniarily aided by him and others in the accomplishment of his purpose to translate the Scriptures into the vernacular. Unable to do so in England, he set out for the continent (about May, 1524), and appears to have visited Hamburg and Wittenberg; but the place where he translated the New Testament, although conjectured to have been Wittenberg, can not be named with certainty. It is, however, certain that the printing of the New Testament in quarto was begun at Cologne in the summer of 1525, and completed at Worms, and that there was likewise printed an octavo edition, both before the end of that year. From an entry in Spalatin's Diary, Aug. 11, 1526, it seems that he remained at Worms about a year; but the notices of his connection with Hermann von dem Busche and the University of Marburg are utterly unwarranted conjectures; and,

it being now an established fact that Hans Luft never had a printing-press at Marburg, the colophon to Tyndale's translation of Genesis, and the title pages of several pamphlets purporting to have been printed by Luft at Marburg, only deepen the seemingly impenetrable mystery which overhangs the life of Tyndale during the interval between his departure from Worms and his final settlement at Antwerp. His literary activity during that interval was extraordinary. When he left England, his knowledge of Hebrew, if he had any, was of the most rudimentary nature; and yet he mastered that difficult tongue so as to produce from the original an admirable translation of the entire Pentateuch,* the Books of Joshua, Judges, Ruth, First and Second Samuel, First and Second Kings, First Chronicles, contained in Matthew's Bible of 1537, and of the Book of Jonah, so excellent, indeed, that to this day his work is not only the basis of those portions of the Authorized Version, but constitutes nine-tenths of that translation, and very largely that of the Revised Version. His Biblical translations appeared in the following order: New Testament, 1525–26; Pentateuch, 1530; Jonah, 1531. There is no general title of the Pentateuch; each book has its own title.

In addition to these he produced the following works. His first original composition, *A Pathway into the Holy Scripture*, is really a reprint, slightly altered, of his *Prologue* to the quarto edition of his New Testament, and had appeared in separate form before 1532; *The Parable of the Wicked Mammon* (1527); and *The Obedience of a Christian Man* (1527–28). These several works drew out in 1529 Sir Thomas More's *Dialogue*, etc. In 1530 appeared Tyndale's *Practyse of Prelates*, and in 1531 his *Answer*, etc., to the *Dialogue*, his *Exposition of the First Epistle of St. John*, and the famous *Prologue* to Jonah; in 1532, *An Exposition upon the V. VI. VII. Chapters of Matthew*; and in 1536, *A Brief Declaration of the Sacraments*, etc., which seems to be a posthumous publication. Joshua–Second Chronicles also was published after his death. All these works were written during those mysterious years, in places of concealment so secure and well chosen, that neither the ecclesiastical nor diplomatic emissaries of Wolsey and Henry VIII., charged to track, hunt down, and seize the fugitive, were able to reach them, and they are even yet unknown. Impressed with the idea that the progress of the Reformation in England rendered it safe for him to leave his concealment, he settled at Antwerp in 1534, and combined the work of an evangelist with that of a translator of the Bible. Mainly through the instrumentality of one Philips, the agent either of Henry or of English ecclesiastics, or possibly of both, he was arrested, imprisoned in the castle of Vilvoorden, tried, either for heresy or treason, or both, and convicted; was first strangled,

---

* The only perfect copy is in the Grenville Library of the British Museum; one in the Public Library, New York, is defective, folios XLIV. and XLV., as well as two of the eleven woodcuts of the volume, are wanting; the missing woodcuts have been supplied in facsimile by H. Another copy there lacks Genesis. The copy in the Baptist College, Bristol, England, contains Genesis, edition of 1534, the other four books are of the edition of 1530.

and then burnt in the prison yard, Oct. 6, 1536. His last words were, "Lord, open the king of England's eyes." Excepting the narrative of Foxe, which is very unsatisfactory, and the opportune discovery of a letter written by Tyndale in prison, showing that he was shamefully neglected, and that he continued his literary labors to the last, no official records of his betrayal, arrest, trial, and martyrdom, have as yet been discovered. Indeed, less is known of Tyndale than of almost any of his contemporaries, and his history remains to be written. If the unknown and the mysterious excite and sustain interest, no theme can excel that attached to Tyndale. His life must have abounded in incident, variety, and adventure; and it culminated in tragedy. That his precious life might have been saved can not be doubted; and, although neither Cromwell nor Henry has been convicted of planning and conniving at his death, it is impossible to exonerate them from criminal indifference and culpable neglect.

Tyndale's place in history has not yet been sufficiently recognized as a translator of the Scriptures, as an apostle of liberty, and as a chief promoter of the Reformation in England. In all these respects his influence has been singularly undervalued. The sweeping statement found in almost all histories, that Tyndale translated from the Vulgate and Luther, is most damaging to the reputation of the writers who make it; for, as a matter of fact, it is contrary to truth, since his translations are made directly from the originals.

Correspondence with Prof. Julius Cæsar of Marburg (*Hand-book*, pp. 110 sqq.) proves that Hans Luft never had a printing-house in that town and that Tyndale had no connection with its university. The Prolegomena in Mombert's *William Tyndale's Five Books of Moses* show conclusively that Tyndale's Pentateuch is a translation of the Hebrew original. The full titles of these works are given in the footnote.* As an apostle of liberty, he stands foremost among the writers of the period, whose heroic fortitude and invincible love of the truth were heard with a force superior to royal and ecclesiastical injunctions; and the very flames to which fanaticism and tyranny consigned his writings burnt them into the very hearts of the people, and made them powerful instruments in attaching and converting multitudes to the principles of the Reformation. It is not exaggeration to say that the noble sentiments of William Tyndale, uttered in pure, strong Saxon English, and steeped in the doctrines of the Gospel, gave shape to the views of the more conspicuous promoters of that grand movement, who, like himself, sealed their convictions with their blood.

A monument commemorating the life and work of Tyndale has been erected on the Thames Embankment, London.   J. I. MOMBERT.

---

* J. I. Mombert, *William Tyndale's Five Books of Moses called the Pentateuch, being a literal Reprint of the Edition of 1530, compared with Tyndale's Genesis of 1534, and the Pentateuch in the Vulgate, Luther, and Matthew's Bible with various Collations and Prolegomena* (New York, 1884; this book is out of print); idem, *English Versions of the Bible, a Handbook with copious Examples illustrating the Ancestry and Relationship of the several Versions and Comparative Tables* (London, 1907).

BIBLIOGRAPHY: Besides the treatises on the history of the English Bible given in ii. 141 of this work, consult: R. Demaus, *William Tyndale*, 2d ed., London, 1886; John Fox, *Acts and Monuments*, ed. G. Townsend, vols. i.–v. passim, London, 1843–49 (consult Index); C. Wordsworth, *Ecclesiastical Biography*, i. 187 sqq., London, 1810; J. Strype, *Ecclesiastical Memorials*, i. 2, pp. 363–367, London, 1822; J. Stoughton, *The Pen, the Palm, and the Pulpit*, London, 1858; H. Morley, *English Writers*, pp. 226–229, London, 1864; W. H. D. Adams, *Great English Churchmen*, London, 1879; F. L. Clarke, *The Life of W. Tyndale*, London, 1883; C. E. Heisch, *William Tyndale*, London, 1884; G. B. Smith, *W. Tyndale and his Translation of the English Bible*, London, 1896; C. Tyler, *The Story of William Tyndale*, London, 1898; I. M. Price, *The Ancestry of our English Bible*, chap. xxi., Philadelphia, 1907; *DNB*, lvii. 424–430.

TYNG, STEPHEN HIGGINSON: Protestant Episcopal; b. at Newburyport, Mass., Mar. 1, 1800; d. at Irvington on the Hudson Sept. 4, 1885. He graduated at Harvard College, Cambridge, Mass., 1817; was in business, 1817–19; studied theology, 1819–21; was rector at Georgetown, D. C., 1821–1823; in Queen Anne Parish, Prince George's County, Md., 1823–29; of St. Paul's, Philadelphia, 1829–1833; of the Church of the Epiphany, in the same city, 1833–45; of St. George's, New York City, 1845–78, when he retired as pastor emeritus. He was for years one of the leaders of the Low-church party in his denomination, and was famous for eloquence and Christian zeal. He was prominent in the organization of the American Church Missionary Society and the Evangelical Education Society, and was a ready and polished platform-speaker, much in demand. He edited for several years *The Episcopal Recorder* and *The Protestant Churchman*, and was the author of *Lectures on the Law and the Gospel* (Philadelphia, 1832); *Memoir of Rev. G. T. Bedell* (1835); *Recollections of England* (New York, 1847); *A Lamb from the Flock* (1852); *Christian Titles, a Series of Practical Meditations* (1853); *Fellowship with Christ* (1854); *The Rich Kinsman, or the History of Ruth* (1855); *Mémoir of Rev. E. P. J. Messenger* (1857); *The Captive Orphan, Esther, Queen of Persia* (1859); *Forty Years' Experience in Sunday Schools* (1860); *The Prayer-Book illustrated by Scripture* (8 vols., 1865–67); *The Child of Prayer: a Father's Memorial of D. A. Tyng* (1866); *The Reward of Meekness* (1867); *The Feast Enjoyed* (1868); *The Spencers* (1870); *The Office and Duty of a Christian Pastor* (1874); and several volumes of sermons.

BIBLIOGRAPHY: C. R. Tyng, *Record of the Life and Work of Stephen H. Tyng, and History of St. George's Church, N. Y., to the Close of his Rectorship*, New York, 1890.

TYRE. See PHENICIA, PHENICIANS, I., §§ 2–3.

TYRRELL, tir'el, **GEORGE HENRY:** English Roman Catholic; b. at Dublin Feb. 6, 1861; d. in London July 15, 1909. He matriculated at Trinity College, Dublin, in 1878, but in the following year left the Anglican Church for the Roman Catholic, and in 1880 entered the Society of Jesus. He then studied philosophy at Stonyhurst (1882–85) and theology at St. Beuno's, Wales (1888–92), and speedily became known as one of the ablest Roman Catholic writers in England. From an ultramontane and scholastic position he gradually advanced to an attitude of distinct Modernism (q.v.); but though admonished for his views on hell in 1900, he did not come into serious conflict with his communion until 1906, when in his *Much-Abused Letter* (generally supposed to be to the late St. George Mivart) he denied that Roman Catholic theology is perfect and inerrant, and held that the visible Church is but a mutable organism subject to development and modification, he incurred the extreme displeasure of the ecclesiastical authorities. He had sought release from his obligations as a religious on the condemnation of the works of Loisy in 1904, and now, on his refusal to retract the above teachings, he was expelled from the Jesuit order in Feb., 1906. He was also forbidden to officiate in the archdiocese of Westminster, and declined the proffered right to exercise priestly functions in the archdiocese of Mecheln on condition that he submit any future writings to the censor. When, finally, he sharply criticized the encyclical *Pascendi* in 1907, he incurred the minor excommunication. Theologically he described himself as a " liberal Roman Catholic." His works, some of which have gone through repeated editions and been translated into German and French, are as follows: *Nova et Vetera* (London, 1897); *Hard Sayings* (1898); *External Religion* (1899) ; *Faith of the Millions* (2 vols., 1901); *Lex Orandi* (1903); *Lex Credendi* (1906); *Oil and Wine* (1907); *Through Scylla and Charybdis* (1907); *A Much-Abused Letter* (1907); *Medievalism* (1908); and *Christianity at the Cross Roads* (1909).

TZSCHIRNER, tshîr′ner, **HEINRICH GOTT-LIEB:** German Lutheran; b. at Mittweida (10 m. n.n.e. of Chemnitz), Saxony, Nov. 14, 1778; d. at Leipsic Feb. 17, 1828. He was educated at the University of Leipsic (1796–99), and in 1800 became privat-docent at Wittenberg, where he was soon appointed adjunct of the philosophical faculty. Before long, however, the death of his father led him to exchange his academic position for that of deacon of his native town, where he found leisure, despite his parochial duties, for writing, *Leben und Ende merkwürdiger Selbstmörder* (Weissenfels, 1805); *Ueber den moralischen Indifferentismus* (Leipsic, 1805), and began a *Geschichte der Apologetik* (1805). Largely because of the latter work, he was recalled to Wittenberg in 1805 as professor of theology, thus having occasion to prepare his *De dignitate hominis per religionem Christianam adserta et declarata* (Wittenberg, 1805) and *De virtutum et vitiorum inter se cognatione* (1805), the latter touching upon a theme more fully developed in his *Ueber die Verwandtschaft der Tugenden und Laster* (Leipsic, 1809). In his *De sacris publicis ab ecclesia vetere studiose cultis* (Wittenberg, 1808), moreover, he issued a prelude to his intended history of Christian worship, which his academic duties forced him to relinquish. He lectured on natural theology, dogmatics, and homiletics, as well as on church history after 1806.

In 1809 Tzschirner was called to Leipsic as fourth professor of theology. His ability as a church historian was evinced by his preparation of the ninth and tenth volumes of J. M. Schröckh's great *Christliche Kirchengeschichte seit der Reformation* (Leipsic, 1810–12); while as a dogmatic and homiletic scholar he wrote *Beurteilende Darstellung der dogmatischen Systeme, welche in der protestantischen Kirche gefun-*

den werden (in *Memorabilien,* i., 1810–11), and *Briefe veranlasst durch Reinhards Geständnisse* (1811), in which he sought to prove that the only middle way between rationalism and supernaturalism was an ethical and critical rationalism which held the rational concept of morality to be the supreme principle of Christianity, and criticized the Scriptures on the basis of this concept, retaining all connected with moral requirements, and rejecting all temporal elements derived from the later Jewish theology.

In 1813 Tzschirner was for a short time chaplain in the Saxon army, after which he wrote *Ueber den Krieg, ein philosophischer Versuch* (1815). In the autumn of 1814 he was appointed archdeacon of Thomaskirche, Leipsic, and shortly afterward was made pastor of the same church and superintendent of the diocese of Leipsic (1815). In 1818 he was promoted to be second professor and canon of Meissen. Meanwhile the conditions of his country and his church had changed, and he was now obliged to combat not only unbelief and indifference, but the recrudescence of Roman Catholicism and Roman Catholic tendencies arising within the Protestant Church, and especially Pietism. While he planned a work on *Der Fall des Heidentums*, his interest in contemporary history led him to write *Die Sache der Griechen die Sache Europas* (1821). But the aims of the Roman Catholic hierarchy engaged his special attention, and he defended the Protestant cause in *Protestantismus und Katholicismus aus dem Standpunkte der Politik betrachtet* (1822); *Die Rückkehr katholischer Christen im Grossherzogtum Baden zum evangelischen Christentume* (1823); *Die Gefahr einer deutschen Revolution* (1823); and *Zwei Briefe durch die jüngst zu Dresden erschienene Schrift: Die reine katholische Lehre, veranlasst* (1826). He also wrote four treatises on the relation of the Church to marriage, urging a revision of marriage law, but rejecting civil marriage; while in his *Gutachten über die Annahme der Preussischen Agende* (1824) he advised the rejection of this unsatisfactory liturgy, unless its adoption was expressly recommended, at the same time urging a thorough reform of public worship. Besides two collections of sermons (1812–1816), Tzschirner wrote *Græci et Romani scriptores cur rerum Christianarum raro meminerint* (1824–25); *De perpetua inter Catholicam et Evangelicam Ecclesiam dissentione* (1824); *De causis impeditæ in Francogallia sacrorum publicorum emendationis* (1827); and *De religionis Christianæ per philosophiam Græcam propagatione* (1827). After his death a number of his writings were edited by his friends: a selection of his sermons from 1817 to 1828 (3 vols., Leipsic, 1828); the first part of the uncompleted *Fall des Heidentums* (1829); the *Vorlesungen über die christliche Glaubenslehre* (1829); the academic programs under the title *Tzschirneri opuscula academica* (1829); and the unfinished *Briefe eines Deutschen an die Herren Chateaubriand, de la Mennais und Montlosier über Gegenstände der Religion und Politik* (1828). (P. M. Tzschirner†.)

BIBLIOGRAPHY: H. G. Tzschirner, Skizze seines Lebens, Leipsic, 1828; J. D. Goldhorn, Mittheilungen aus . . . H. G. Tzschirners . . . Amts- und Lebensjahren, ib. 1828; K. H. L. Pölitz, H. G. Tzschirner. Abriss seines Lebens und Wirkens, ib. 1828; J. A. H. Tittmann, Memoria H. G. Tzschirner, ib. 1828; ADB, xxxix. 62 sqq.

U

UBBONITES, ʋb'-bo-naitz: A term applied to a party of Anabaptists in a certain phase of their development. Ubbo Philipps (Ubbe or Obbe Philipzoon), b. at Leeuwarden (70 m. n. e. of Amsterdam) near the beginning of the sixteenth century, had become a Roman Catholic priest some time before Melchior Hoffmann (q.v.) began his propagandism in the Netherlands (1529). With multitudes of others he was persuaded that Hoffmann was a divinely inspired prophet (c. 1531), and was ready to follow him blindly in his exposition of the Old-Testament prophets and the Apocalypse and to expect speedy deliverance from the trials and persecutions that were being inflicted by Catholics and Protestants on true believers. His faith in Hoffmann was considerably shaken by his failure to go forth from his Strasburg prison in 1533, as he predicted he would, at the head of 144,000 enthusiastic believers who would set up Christ's kingdom on earth, and by his failure to keep his vow to live on bread and water until his liberation. When Jan Mathys, weary of waiting for the fulfilment of Hoffmann's promises, proclaimed himself the Elias that should usher in the messianic kingdom and ordered the resumption of baptism which Hoffmann had suspended for two years, Ubbo, who, with many others, had been awaiting Hoffmann's orders, received baptism. With his brother Dirk and Jan David Joris (q.v.), he soon came to distrust Mathys with his sanguinary program and urged the infatuated people to desist from their plan of setting up the kingdom of Christ by violence in Münster. In this he had the cooperation of Menno Simons (q.v.), who did not definitely become an Anabaptist until 1536. When Ubbo, Dirk, and others, after the fall of Münster (1535), saw multitudes that had been under the influence of Hoffmann and Mathys disillusioned and anxious to follow wise Evangelical counsel, they persuaded Menno to assume the leadership, and Ubbo ordained him, his brother Dirk, and David Joris, who had not yet manifested his pantheistic tendencies. During the short period from 1534 to 1536 the quiet, non-resisting Anabaptists that repudiated Mathys and the Münster kingdom might properly be called Ubbonites. After Menno's leadership became established, the name Mennonites (q.v.) is more applicable to the same people. Ubbo afterward deeply regretted the part he had taken in the organization of the Mennonite movement. When Menno came into recognized leadership, his intolerance of opposition in matters of doctrine and discipline, his violent denunciation of other Christian parties, and the strife that occurred among the churches of the connection proved distasteful to Ubbo, and he felt constrained to sever his relations with the Mennonites. Shortly before his death (1568) he wrote an interesting account of his life among the Anabaptists and of the circumstances that led him to break with the party. Whether he united with the Reformed when he left the Mennonites does not clearly appear from his narrative.

His *Bekentniss und Aussage* is published in full in J. C. Jehring's *Grundliche Historie von denen Begebenheiten, Streitigkeiten und Trennungen, so unter den Tauffgesinneten, oder Mennonisten von ihren Ursprung an bis aufs Jahr 1615 vorgegangen* (Jena, 1720; contains lists of the writings of Dirk and Ubbo Philipps).   A. H. NEWMAN.

BIBLIOGRAPHY: H. C. Bergmann, *De Ubbone Philippi et Ubbonitis*, Rostock, 1733; A. H. Newman, *Hist. of Anti-Pedobaptism*, pp. 301, 304 sqq., Philadelphia, 1897.

UBERTINO, ʋ''bār-tî'nō, **OF CASALE:** Italian Franciscan; b. at Casale-Monferrato (32 m. w. of Turin) 1259; d. about 1350. He entered the Franciscan order in 1273, and taught at various places in Italy, later in Paris (1289–98). After 1298 he devoted himself chiefly to propagating the views of Pierre Olivi, whose pupil he had been in the house of Santa Croce. After the death of Olivi Ubertino was recognized as the leader of the " spirituals," the strict party among the Franciscans which insisted upon the rigid rule of poverty (see OLIVI, PIERRE). On Oct. 1, 1317, he received permission from John XXII. to enter the Benedictine monastery of Gembloux, though it is doubtful whether he availed himself of this permission, as he was certainly living at Avignon during 1320–25. In 1325 he fled from Avignon to escape arrest in connection with the condemnation of the works of Olivi, and later he is said to have joined the Carthusians. Besides some minor works (in *ALKG*, iii.) and a defense of Olivi (*ALKG*, ii. 377 sqq.) he wrote *Arbor vitæ crucifixæ* (Venice, 1485), a defense of Olivi's doctrine in the style of the mysticism of Bonaventura and the apocalyptics of Joachim of Fiore. See FRANCIS, SAINT, OF ASSISI, III., §§ 4–5.

BIBLIOGRAPHY: J. C. Huck, *Ubertin von Casale und dessen Ideenkreis*, Freiburg, 1903; J. J. I. von Döllinger, *Sektengeschichte des Mittelalters*, ii. 508–526, Munich, 1890; Ehrle, in *ALKG*, ii. 377–416, iii. 48 sqq.; *KL*, xii. 168–172; F. X. Kraus, *Dante*, pp. 479, 738 sqq., Berlin, 1897.

UBIQUITY.

Preliminary History (§ 1).
Luther's Doctrine (§ 2).
The Reformed Doctrines; Brenz (§ 3).
Chemnitz (§ 4).
Formula of Concord (§ 5).
The Two Schools (§ 6).

Ubiquity is the term applied to the non-spatial (" repletive ") omnipresence of the body of Christ set forth by Luther in the eucharistic controversy. All statements of the Eastern Church which apparently involve the question of ubiquity from Origen to John of Damascus affirm, on the unity of the natures, the logical, not the real, transfer of the qualities of one nature to the other, thus teaching an " exchange," or " community," of names, not an exchange of attributes. Augustine, with his local concept of the " right hand of God " as contrasted with the non-local view of John of Damascus, gained favor in the Middle Ages, and later

1. Preliminary History.

with the Reformed and with Melanchthon. He nowhere clearly expresses the realistic concept of the presence of Christ in the Eucharist, but confines the omnipresence to the divine nature of Christ. Scholasticism gained increasing interest in the question of omnipresence in proportion as the doctrine of the real presence gained the recognition of the Church and obtained its theory in the dogma of Transubstantiation (q.v.). Here Augustine remained the prime authority, and Hugo of St. Victor (q.v.) held that " Christ is humanly in heaven, divinely everywhere." Peter Lombard and Thomas Aquinas (qq.v.) followed John of Damascus (q.v.), in distinguishing between Christ as *totus* and *totum*, Christ being omnipresent in the former case in virtue of the unity of his person, but not in the latter as conception of both natures. Thus the omnipresence of the body was rejected. According to the *anhypostasis* of Leontius (q.v.) the Logos is essentially the person of Christ; deity follows humanity everywhere, but not *vice versa*. Radbertus (q.v.) taught that in each case the body was created anew from the bread by a special miracle. Arno of Reichersberg (q.v.) taught " a special power of Christ of being bodily present wherever he wished," not exercised until after death; and in like manner Peter Lombard taught the presence in one place of the exalted body of Christ, omnipresence of his divinity, and multipresence of his sacramental body. This remained, in all essentials, the teaching of scholasticism. The difficult problem now arose of explaining how the circumscribed celestial body of Christ, with its attributes of quantity and dimension, could replace the bread in the host. Albert the Great (see ALBERTUS MAGNUS), distinguishing between a natural and a spiritual body, held that "the glorious body " of Christ was present in the host " in the fashion of the spiritual body." This, however, combined with the subintration theory (see TRANSUBSTANTIATION, II., § 4), rendered uncertain not only the spatiality but also the actuality of the body of Christ in the host. Bonaventura (q.v.) and Thomas Aquinas accordingly sought to prove " the dimensive quantity of Christ's body " in the host, and to unite their teaching with the theory later taught by William of Occam (q.v.) as " definitive existence," namely, " whenever anything is in place so that the whole is in the whole and in any part whatsoever." The theory of Bonaventura and Thomas Aquinas, however, was self-contradictory in that the portion present in the host was conceived as at once quantitative and non-quantitative. Occam resolved this realistic doctrine of space and quantity critically. To him quantity was something substantial involving " circumscribed existence." " Definitive existence " (ut sup.) pertains only to non-quantitative things. The body of Christ in the host must, therefore, be conceived as non-quantitative, thus returning to the original position of scholasticism, except that the theory of subintration was replaced by a sort of condensation hypothesis, whereby, through divine omnipotence, a substance might be reduced to the mathematical non-extensibility of a point. But Occam proceeded still further, dialectically postulating, at least, the possibility of the " repletive existence " (and thus of the

ubiquity) of the body of Christ. He accordingly taught, (1) the actual " repletive existence " of God; (2) the local presence of the body of Christ in heaven; (3) the non-quantitative, definitive presence in many places of the body of Christ in the host; and (4) the possibility of the ubiquity of this body in the universe.

On this dialectic straining of the doctrine of the ubiquity of the body of Christ Luther based his doctrine. Luther's original eucharistic theory was based entirely on opposition to the Roman Catholic

      opus operatum. The essential part of
2. Luther's the Eucharist was held to be the word,
Doctrine. faith being the right disposition. Luther affirmed his belief in the real presence and transubstantiation in 1519, but within a year he had replaced the latter by the teaching of the consubstantiation (of Occam), postulating, without any attempt at explanation, the substantial coexistence of the bread and the body of Christ in the Eucharist. When, however, Johann Carlstadt and Zwingli denied the real presence, Luther proceeded further than Occam; and in *Wider die himmlischen Propheten von den Bildern und Sakramenten*, in reply to Carlstadt, he set forth the initial statement of the synecdochical theory of the real presence, and the first intimations of the doctrine of ubiquity. Luther maintained that the " this " of the words of institution implied the presence of the body already in the unbroken bread. When Christ says, " This is my body," he takes the " whole " (bread and body) " for the part " (body); this is the synecdoche of Luther, later modified by Melanchthon. Luther introduced his teaching on ubiquity in his *Sermon vom Sakrament des Leibes* (Wittenberg, 1526), and developed it in his polemics against Zwingli and Œcolampadius. *Dass diese Worte (das ist mein Leib) noch feststehen* (1527), and *Bekenntnis vom Abendmahl* (1528). Maintaining the real presence as an immutable article of faith established by the Scriptures, Luther sought with equal zeal to defend the doctrine of the true reality of the body as well as to dispel all gross notions. He teaches that the body of Christ is exceptional and supernatural, different from ordinary human flesh and blood; that his flesh is born of the spirit, of a spiritual nature, and fit for spiritual food; and that the attributes of magnitude and extension do not apply to his body. Two deductions were then drawn: all things being present and permeable to Christ, he can enter and pass through them, being as energy without matter (as proved by the sealed tomb and the closed door), and the entire body of Christ may be in the smallest atom, though not circumscribed by it. This mode of " definitive existence " explains, however, only how it is possible for a corporeal being to be present in material substances without changing itself or them. For an answer to the further problem, how the body of Christ can be present simultaneously in heaven and in the host in countless celebrations of the Lord's Supper, recourse becomes necessary to the omnipotence of God, and Luther returns to the doctrine of the presence in an indefinite number of localities according to his will (Arno) taught by scholasticism. He continually emphasizes the ne-

cessity of the belief that with God all things are possible, and that, therefore, the heavenly body of Christ is miraculously present in the host. Such is wrought by the creative word and the command of God. Although satisfied that " definitive existence " and presence in as many places as Christ willed to be were sufficient to faith in view of the omnipotence of God, he brought still higher arguments to bear against his opponents, developing the one into " repletive existence," and the other into omnipresence. This was done by the symbolic interpretation of the " right hand of God " and by the logical consequences of the *Communicatio idiomatum*. Definitive existence and multipresence pertain, through divine omnipotence, also to angels and demons. The body of Christ, however, possesses a far higher supernatural character, especially as he was at once God and man. Luther then affirmed that " the right hand of God " everywhere followed the divine omnipotence, and he deduced that Christ's body was at the same time at the right hand of God, and in the Eucharist by his syllogism: The body of Christ is at the right hand of God; the right hand of God is everywhere; therefore the body of Christ is in the bread. The same conclusion he reaches also by his Christology, as is fully set forth in his larger *Bekenntnis*. Accordingly, the two natures of Christ in one person demand the participation of the exalted humanity of Christ in the omnipresence of God. Luther now sought to complete his demonstration of ubiquity by developing the *communicatio idiomatum* from the premise of personal union. That the real presence in the host naturally follows repletive existence is self-evident, but proved too much; for it imperiled the unique sacramental presence, making it superfluous. To avert this Luther asserted that the sacramental, distinct from the ubiquitous, presence was such only by the word of God, whereby he binds himself to the bread for the reception of the communicant. This was a recourse to a particular act of the divine will or a retreat to a multiple presence subject to Christ's will. Luther's doctrine of ubiquity remains important only for Christology. There are, then, according to Luther, three demonstrable ways in which the humanity of Christ may anywhere be present: " circumscriptive or local existence," as it was on earth; " definitive existence," as it was during the resurrection through the sealed tombstone, and afterward through the closed door, and as it is also in the host; and " repletive existence," as the humanity is, in virtue of its personal union with God and exaltation to his right hand, everywhere and nowhere, also in the communion substances, yet in itself inapprehensible and inactive (*wirkungslos*). Luther did not restrict the body of Christ or the omnipotence of God to these three modes of being, but merely emphasized the ways human thought can and must establish the doctrine in accordance with faith and the Bible. Though transcending reason, if not contrary to it, yet here is primarily a matter of faith in the miracles of God in nature and grace.

Zwingli, on the grounds of humanistic and rationalistic criticism, denied ubiquity and the real presence, and opposed the *communicatio idiomatum*

with the disparity of the mode of existence of the two natures, maintaining the presence of Christ to be circumscriptive and local in heaven.

3. The Reformed Doctrines; Brenz. Calvin advanced to the doctrine that the predicates of redemptive activity apply also really to the human nature of Christ, but recoiled from the doctrine of ubiquity. He held that the redemptive powers of the passion and resurrection of Christ are really imparted through the symbols of bread and wine. The believer receives, not the substance, but " the communion of the body of Christ " (I Cor. x. 16), mediated by the Holy Ghost. Melanchthon at first adhered to Luther's concept of the real presence, but always remained skeptical regarding the doctrine of ubiquity. The real presence he desired to see established on mandatory, not magical, grounds. His loyalty to the doctrine is shown by his stanch defense at the Marburg Conference (1529), as well as in art. 10 of the Augsburg Confession (1530–31). But after his dialogue with Œcolampadius he inclined more and more to restrict this presence to Christ as God. As early as 1535, in a letter to Johann Brenz, he adopted the figurative exegesis of the " is " in the words of institution, and he finally came absolutely to deny the doctrine of ubiquity, coming to prefer the " communion of the body of Christ " as the membership of the faithful in the body of Christ, later emphasized by Calvin. His increasing hostility to ubiquity led to the local view of " the right hand of God "; and the eucharistic presence of Christ was to him his " power in the believing." Melanchthon thus stood much closer to Calvin than to Luther. However favorable the prospects for Protestantism, they were definitely destroyed by the Stuttgart Synod (q.v.) in 1559, when the confession drawn up by Brenz, and adopted, fastened the tenet of ubiquity as a symbol upon the church in Württemberg. The result was that in the bitter polemics with Heinrich Bullinger and Pietro Martire Vermigli (qq.v.), Brenz in a series of writings erected on the basis of Luther's arguments an imposing Christological system. In his *De majestate Domini nostri* (1562) he reaffirms the two natures in one person upon the broader basis of the incarnation of the Son of God, and consequently the deification of the Son of man. This afforded a double point of departure for the demonstration of ubiquity: " the personal union," and the " deification." The first, which is indissoluble and effected by divine omnipotence, does not involve a mutation of humanity into deity nor a duplication of persons; it is the immediate ground of the *communicatio idiomatum*, which is not an interchange of specific properties in name only but in fact. To save the human nature from total elimination Brenz drew a distinction between essential and separable, accidental qualities. Deity being without accidental properties, humanity is composite with a constant substance but with such accidents as suffering, mortality, and locality, which may be discarded and replaced by hyperphysical qualities, as accidental accessories, however. Brenz's weakness consisted in reducing local existence to an accident or negligible quantity, when it was the brunt of his contention. As to the second basis, the exaltation, Brenz argues the "assumption of humanity into deity," and the infinite domination of the latter. The incarnation is really deification, which transpired *in utero;* then was Christ raised to the right hand of God and to full divine majesty, as Lord of all creatures. The human nature is only passively endowed with this power through the grace of the hypostatic union. There is, therefore, a threefold ascension: at the instant of the incarnation, immediately after the resurrection, and, finally, a merely spectacular one. In the state of exinanition Christ lived, during his earthly period, a twofold existence; a divine-human in heaven dominated by his deity, and a human-divine on earth, dominated by his humanity. The "repletive existence," by virtue of the exaltation at the incarnation, is the real state also of his humanity, only temporarily interrupted or rather attended by the "circumscriptive existence." The "inanition," therefore, postulates only a figurative mode of existence of the man Christ; there was only a "concealment," not a real "kenosis of the function" of the divine properties. Nevertheless, deity was, in an indefinable manner, involved in the process by the *communicatio idiomatum.* God, although impassible, so appropriated the suffering and death of Christ, or was affected by the same, through the hypostatical union, as though he himself suffered and died. But to take part in suffering and mortality and be impassible at once is a contradiction; so is also an indissoluble union in one person of deity and humanity, both dwelling in bliss and reigning over all the world, and at the same time suffering, dying, and rising again on earth; or, that the man Christ was at once alive and dead. The *communicatio* proved incapable of logical conclusion. On the other hand, the humanity was imperiled, inasmuch as the man Jesus, invisible by his exaltation, i.e., incarnation, was only *in loco* subject to his condescension. With the proof of ubiquity, the real presence was also established for Brenz. The Maulbronn Conference (q.v.) of 1564 served to reveal the weakness of the Christology of Brenz, yet more enfeebled by Jakob Andreä (q.v.). The doctrine prevailed in Württemberg for the remainder of the century.

Martin Chemnitz (q.v.) sought vainly to mediate between the Swabian followers of Brenz and the Philippists of Wittenberg, who rejected ubiquity and the "scholastic disputations" over the real presence. His teachings, however, re-

4. Chem- mained a mass of disparate elements
nitz. of both factions (*De duabus naturis in Christo,* 1571). Like Melanchthon, following Aristotle's dictum, "properties do not pass out of their subjects," he held properties to be essential, not accidental; and locality was, therefore, an essential, not accidental, property of human nature. The *genus majestaticum* (see CHRISTOLOGY, VIII., 1) thus negated was by degrees regained. Although conceding that human nature can appropriate divine properties only according to the finite human capacity, in the manner of a reenforcement, yet he argued that in Christ this capacity was so augmented by the "personal union" that the humanity possessed the divine attributes not in substance but efficient power. The humanity was

the automatic organ dynamically of the Logos; the humanity is permeated with deity, after the analogy of heat in the iron, by a process which he termed *perichōresis.* In the humiliation, the Logos, though never wholly quiescent, retreated to a "concealment of function," and even to its "kenosis." Thus, at the same time, a compensation was rendered for the doctrine of inherent ubiquity, which as an intrinsic possession of the humanity was positively declined, and then regained as a sort of potential ubiquitous presence. This was in conflict with his other assertion of the hypostatic union according to which the humanity embracing all creatures is ever present in the Logos. Chemnitz loses himself, therefore, in distraction between an *a priori* ubiquity and an *a posteriori* potential multipresence, and in conflict with his Aristotelian dictum as premise. The logical result of his theories was that the humanity of Jesus was at once essentially circumscribed and potentially omnipresent.

The Formula of Concord (q.v.) presented a loose and incongruous combination of the views of Luther and Brenz and those of Chemnitz. Directly, it may be said, the potential ubiquitous presence is taught by the admission of the views of Chemnitz just mentioned *seriatim.* While the full possession of the divine majesty is ascribed to the human-

5. Formula ity, omnipresence is never mentioned
of Concord. as one of its attributes, being assumed as implied in omnipotence; and the "repletive existence" is never expressly asserted of the humanity. Indirectly is taught the essential ubiquity of the body of Christ, by the adoption of large citations from Luther's eucharistic writings, not excluding the statements on ubiquity and the "repletive existence," particularly by falling back on Luther's idea of the "right hand of God" for a figure of the divine majesty. Moreover, the realistic *communicatio idiomatum,* as the basis of all Christology, was so carried through with strong emphasis on the integrity of the natures and their properties, the non-receptivity of the divine nature for human properties, and the separation of the two states, that the moderated views of Brenz as promulgated by Andreä and the advanced Melanchthonism of Chemnitz could both accept it.

The inconclusiveness of the Formula proved itself in the reservation entered by Chemnitz with his signature, and the mutual efforts to advance the doctrine of ubiquity to the front on the part of the

6. The Two two Swabians, Leonhard Hutter (q.v.),
Schools. who essentially reproduced the views of Brenz; and Ægidius Hunnius (q.v.), who, following Chemnitz (and perhaps even Luther), maintained an immanent universal presence of the humanity in the Logos, or a passive omnipresence. At the same time, he advanced beyond Chemnitz by raising the "internal presence," latent during Christ's humiliation, to an "external omnipresence" through his exaltation, alongside of which, however, was maintained the continuous spatial presence of the body of Christ in heaven, thus making permanent the dualism of the human existence of Christ which Luther and Brenz had restricted to his humiliation. Thus the doctrine of ubiquity had attained to recognition, and only its

closer definition was left to theology. Henceforth, the doctrine was a factor in the kenotic controversies (see KENOSIS; CHRISTOLOGY). Like Chemnitz and Hunnius, the Giessen theologians taught, beside potential possession, the " kenosis of the use " of the divine properties on the part of the humanity and the " immanent presence," in Christ's humiliation, thus reserving the omnipresence of his humanity for his exaltation. The Tübingen theologians, on the other hand, logically maintaining the *communicatio idiomatum* even during the humiliation, granted merely a " concealment of the use " of the divine properties, asserting also for the humanity in the state of humiliation an omnipresence merely dissimulated. A " kenosis of function " is conceded only of the high-priestly functions of Jesus with reference to omnipotence. Thus, however, the humanity of Christ was imperiled. These two types continued to exist side by side, in modified forms, for Lutheran theology, with the former generally in the ascendancy. The rise of Pietism and rationalism retired Christological speculation to the background, and the Lutheran theology of the nineteenth century had scant interest in ubiquity.

A. W. HUNZINGER.

BIBLIOGRAPHY: The subject is to be pursued in the histories of doctrine, such as Harnack, *Dogma*, vi. 239, vii. 243, 262 sqq.; F. A. Loofs, Halle, 1908; and R. Seeberg, 2d ed., Leipsic, 1908; in the works on the history of Protestant theology, such as W. Gass, 4 vols., Berlin, 1854–1867; and G. W. Frank, 4 vols., Leipsic, 1862–1905; in the works on systematic theology, e.g., C. Hodge, ii. 408 sqq., iii. 670 sqq., 3 vols., New York, 1871–72; and W. G. T. Shedd, ii. 323–327, New York, 1889; and in those on Christology, e.g., I. A. Dorner, *Person Christi*, vol. ii., Berlin, 1854, Eng. transl., vol. iv., 5 vols., Edinburgh, 1861–63. Recourse should be had also to the articles mentioned in the text and the literature under them, such as CHRISTOLOGY; EUCHARIST; TRANSUBSTANTIATION; and the like; under LORD'S SUPPER to the works by J. H. A. Ebrard, Frankfort, 1845–46; K. F. A. Kahnis, Leipsic, 1851; A. W. Dieckhoff, Göttingen, 1854; and H. Schmid, Leipsic, 1868. Consult further: F. C. Baur, *Die Lehre von der Dreieinigkeit und Menschwerdung Gottes*, vol. iii., Tübingen, 1843; M. Schneckenburger, *Zur kirchlichen Christologie*, Pforzheim, 1848; idem, *Darstellung des lutherischen und reformirten Lehrbegriffs*, Stuttgart, 1855; H. Heppe, *Geschichte der deutschen Protestanten . . . 1555–81*, 4 vols., Marburg, 1855–59; A. Schweizer, *Die protestantischen Centraldogmen in ihrer Entwickelung in der reformirten Kirche*, 2 vols., Zurich, 1854–56; F. H. R. Frank, *Theologie der Concordienformel*, 4 parts, Erlangen, 1858–64; G. Plitt, *Einleitung in die Augustana*, 2 parts, Erlangen, 1867–68; R. D. Hitchcock, in *Journal of Christian Philosophy*, ii (1883), 381 sqq.; K. G. Götz, *Die Abendmahlsfrage in ihrer geschichtlichen Entwickelung*, Leipsic, 1904; J. Köstlin, *Luthers Theologie*, 2d ed., 2 vols., Stuttgart, 1902; T. M. Lindsay, *Hist. of the Reformation*, pp. 4, 7, 57, 412–413, New York, 1907; Schaff, *Christian Church*, vi. 625–626, 628.

UDALL (UVEDALE), JOHN: Puritan; b. about 1560; d. in London toward the end of 1592. He studied at Christ's and Trinity Colleges, Cambridge (B.A., 1581; M.A., 1584); was presented to the living of Kingston-on-Thames before 1584, of which he was deprived in 1588 for bold and offensive preaching of Puritan doctrine, and issued three volumes of sermons, *Amendment of Life, Obedience to the Gospell*, and *Peter's Fall* (Kingston, 1584). A fourth volume, *The True Remedie against Famine and Warres*, appeared 1586. He was a friend of John Penry (q.v.) and gave him certain information which was used in the first Marprelate tract. Inde-

pendently he wrote *The State of the Church of Englande Laide Open in a Conference* (generally known as " The Dialogue " from its form) and *A Demonstration of the Trueth of that Discipline which Christ hath Prescribed . . . for the Government of his Church*, both printed by Penry's printer, Robert Waldegrave, in 1588 (reprinted by Edward Arber, *The English Scholar's Library*, nos. 5 and 9, London, 1879, 1880). He was suspected of complicity in the Marprelate tracts (q.v.) and summoned to London for examination, Dec., 1589; in July, 1590, he was brought to trial, charged with publishing " a wicked, scandalous, and seditious libel " (the *Demonstration*); was found guilty, and sentenced to death, but no desire was manifested to execute the sentence; in June, 1592, on the intercession of influential friends, he was pardoned by Queen Elizabeth. He was a good Hebrew scholar and translated from Latin into English the Hebrew grammar of Peter Martinius (Paris, 1567), adding exercises and a dictionary (*The Key of the Holy Tongue*, Leyden, 1593), and wrote a commentary on Lamentations (London, 1595).

BIBLIOGRAPHY: *A New Discovery of Old Pontifical Practises for the Maintenance of the Prelates Authority and Hierarchy . . .* , London, 1643; W. Maskell, *Hist. of the Marprelate Controversy*, London, 1845; C. H. and T. Cooper, *Athenæ Cantabrigienses*, ii. 148–150, London, 1861; E. Arber, *An Introductory Sketch to the Martin Marprelate Controversy*, London, 1879; *DNB*, lviii. 4–6; and the introductions to the reprints named in the text.

UGOLINI, ū″gō-lī′nî, **BIAGIO (BLASIUS UGOLINUS):** Italian Roman Catholic Christian antiquarian; flourished in the eighteenth century. Of his life nothing is known, but there is little doubt that he was a Jew by birth. In an open letter to C. B. Michaelis (Venice, 1748) he mentions the fact that he frequently associated at Venice with J. E. I. Walch (b. 1725) and his brother, C. W. F. Walch (b. 1726), and likewise requests Michaelis to give his greetings to the Halle professor, Sigismund Baumgarten (d. 1757).

Ugolini's fame rests upon his *Thesaurus antiquitatum sacrarum*, in thirty-four enormous folios (Venice, 1744–69). This contains first a reprint of numerous treatises on Biblical archeology by various authors, and then a series of studies by Ugolini himself: *Altare exterius, de mensa et panibus propositionis* (x.); *Altare interius: De candelabro* (xi.); *De sacerdote castrensi* [Deut. xx. 2 sqq.], (xii.); *Sacerdotium Hebraicum* (xiii.); *De ritibus in cœna Domini ex antiquitatibus paschalibus illustratis* (xvii.); *De phylacteriis Hebræorum* (xxi.); *Trihæresium* [Pharisees, Sadducees, and Essenes] (xxii.); *De re rustica veterum Hebræorum* (xxix.); *Uxor Hebræa* (xxx.); and *De veterum Hebræorum et reliquarum gentium, præsertim Græcorum et Romanorum, funere et præficis* (xxxiii.). All these treatises show a thorough knowledge of Jewish literature, as well as much other learning. A third portion of the *Thesaurus* consists of the text and Latin translation of ancient Jewish writings: thirty-one tractates of the Tosephthah (collection of pronouncements on matters of the law), twenty tractates of the Palestinian Talmud, three tractates of the Babylonian Talmud, four old Midrashim, and a number of tractates from the great Yad Hazakah of Maimonides.   (H. L. STRACK.)

UHLHORN, ül′horn, **JOHANN GERHARD WIL-
HELM:** German Lutheran; b. at Osnabrück (74 m.
w.s.w. of Hanover) Feb. 17, 1826; d. at Hanover Dec.
15, 1901. He studied at the University of Göttingen,
where he changed his early pietistic views for those
of the mediating type of theology and opposition
to the Tübingen school. He became lecturer at
Göttingen in 1849 and privat-docent three years
later. In the controversy which arose in the
church of Hanover between the High-church neo-
Lutheran orthodoxy represented by Petri and the
faculty of Göttingen, who were charged with desert-
ing their creed and tending toward union, Uhlhorn took the side of his university and edited the
Göttingen *Monatsschrift für Theologie und Kirche.*
Within this controversy was another concerning
home missions, which were welcomed by the mediating theologians, but bitterly opposed by Petri.
To counteract the latter's influence, Uhlhorn was
called, in 1855, to Hanover as assistant preacher
at the castle church and assistant in the consistory.
Here he rose rapidly, becoming second court chaplain in 1857, and first court chaplain and consistorial councilor in 1861. With his practical work
in Hanover, however, his theological and ecclesiastical views underwent a change, and he became
more inclined to orthodoxy and an opponent of
union. He thus became a mediator between the
clergy and the faculty, and was one of the chief
factors in easing the tension between the two. As
court chaplain he restored the old forms of Lutheran
worship and introduced liturgical vespers, while
the castle church with its choir became a model
for the liturgy. His affection for home missions,
awakened at Göttingen, found expression in an
association for the young, and still more in the
foundation of the Henriettenstift, an institute for
deaconesses.

A new problem in the development of the Hanoverian Church was inaugurated by the catechism
controversy of 1862. The old rationalistic catechism of 1790 was replaced, at the command of
the king, by an orthodox catechism drawn up by
Lührs and approved by the faculty of Göttingen.
This act raised a storm, fostered by political liberals,
which led to riots that endangered the lives of consistorial councilor Niemann and of Uhlhorn, who
were regarded as the leaders of ecclesiastical reaction. The affair brought the orthodox party and
the faculty together, and the question of a synodal
organization was again raised. As a result came
the system of vestries and synods which is still
in force, and when Hanover became a Prussian
province in 1866, the independence of its church
was recognized by King William. On Apr. 17 of
the same year it received its own national consistory, of which Uhlhorn remained a member until
his death. In this capacity he used his powers to
make the vestries and synods living and effective
organizations, and took part unceasingly in the
district synods, seeking and gaining the confidence
of pastors and church officers.

For a considerable period Uhlhorn was also general superintendent of Hoya-Diepholz, and both
here, in the national consistory, and elsewhere he
labored to secure the practical freedom of synods
and individual churches from all interference, so
long as the religious bodies concerned remained
true to the principles of Lutheranism. He likewise
advocated the independence of the national consistory from the government, but earnestly opposed
union, which he feared would be harmful to true
Lutheranism. As superintendent of Hanover, Uhlhorn labored in harmony with all under his control
for the extension of churches both in the capital and
in other centers of industry, in the colonies in the
moors of East Frisia, and on the Lüneburger Heide.
He was equally energetic in the cause of home missions. In the district synods he expressed his alarm
at the rising power of Roman Catholicism, and
urged his coreligionists to make every effort to
avert its influence. From the first Uhlhorn opposed
the Kulturkampf, which, he held, was bound to
result in the defeat of the State and to the prejudice
of Lutheranism. The struggle of the liberals against
Rome he regarded as really a war on the Church as
a whole and on all positive Christianity.

The religious decline in the eighth decade of the
nineteenth century, complicated by the rise of social democracy, led Uhlhorn to redouble his efforts
to avert the increasing estrangement of the masses
from Church and religion. He seriously mistrusted
the use of city missions, fearing that they would be
harmful to organized pastoral activity, preferring
to augment the number of theological chairs,
pastoral positions, and churches.

He refused several calls to universities, but in
1878 became abbot of Loccum, a dignity which
carried with it the presidency of the district of
Kalenberg-Grubenhagen, and by his zeal made the
preachers' seminary connected with the ancient
abbey a model institution. He likewise founded
another seminary on the Erichsburg, and Loccum
formed the pattern for seminaries in other Prussian provinces. At first an elected member of the
Hanoverian national synod, Uhlhorn was made a
perpetual member in 1878, and in this body he took
an active part in the creation of laws important for
the development of the national church. He took
a lively interest in the home for fallen women at
Hanover, the women's home at Hildesheim, the
workmen's colony at Kästorf, and the institution
for epileptics at Rotenburg, also seeking to inspire
the national and the district synods with equal zeal
for home missions. No less earnest and successful
were his efforts in behalf of Sunday rest, especially
in 1885, and when the government introduced Sunday laws, Uhlhorn endeavored to promote a better
observance of the day. He also devoted special
attention to the cause of the Lutheran seamen's
mission (see SEAMEN, MISSIONS TO), as well as to
German Lutherans in foreign countries, particularly
in South Africa. To social problems Uhlhorn also
turned his thoughts, discussing them in several lectures in which he reached the conclusion that the
social question is economic, not religious, and does
not, therefore, fall within the province of the Church,
whose sole duty is to preach the word of God, which
contains no revelation on matters of economics.
While Uhlhorn's ideal was the independence of
Church and State, he felt that the time was not
yet ripe for such conditions, and accordingly op-

posed all efforts in that direction. He was likewise distressed by theological developments, for though he advocated freedom of research both in universities and in seminaries, and deprecated any direct influence of the Church in the selection of professors for the theological faculties, he felt that the new movements could work only destruction to the ancient faith and to the Lutheran confession. In 1894 and 1896 he defended the building of motherhouses for deaconesses, and elucidated the difference between Roman Catholic sisterhoods and Lutheran deaconesses. His last weeks were devoted to the preparation of a Lutheran liturgy for Hanover which was unanimously accepted by the national synod, thus completing the organization of an independent Hanoverian church with the exception of a catechism which is still a desideratum.

(F. UHLHORN.)

BIBLIOGRAPHY: Uhlhorn's literary activity was constant, some of his works, however, were ephemeral, dealing with questions of his times. Of the more permanent works mention may be made of: *Die Homilien und Recognitionen des Clemens Romanus*, Göttingen, 1854; *Das Basilidianische System*, 1855; *Urbanus Rhegius*, Elberfeld, 1861; *Die modernen Darstellungen des Lebens Jesu*, Hanover, 1866, Eng. transl., *Modern Representations of the Life of Jesus*, Boston, 1868; *Das römische Concil*, 1870; *Der Kampf des Christenthums mit dem Heidenthum*, Stuttgart, 1874, Eng. transl., *Conflict of Christianity with Heathenism*, New York, 1879; *Die christliche Liebesthätigkeit*, 3 vols., vol. i., *In der alten Kirche*, 1882, Eng. transl., *Christian Charity in the Ancient Church*, Edinburgh, 1883, vol. ii., *Im Mittelalter*, 1884, vol. iii., *Seit der Reformation*, 1890; and also his edition of *Ein Sendbrief von Antonius Corvinus an den Adel von Göttingen*, 1853.

For his life consult F. Uhlhorn, *Gerhard Uhlhorn, Abt zu Loccum*, Stuttgart, 1903; F. Düsterdieck, *Zum Andenken an G. Uhlhorn*, Hanover, 1902.

UHLICH, LEBERECHT. See FREE CONGREGATIONS IN GERMANY, § 1.

ULFILAS, ul'fi-las (**ULPHILAS**).

Origin and Youth (§ 1).
Prominence; Missionary Activities (§ 2).
Later Years (§ 3).
Theology (§ 4).
Works; Bible Translation (§ 5).

Ulfilas, bishop of the Visigoths and the author of practically the sole remnants of the Gothic language, was born in the region of the lower Danube about 310, and died at Constantinople in 383. His name is variously given as Vulfila by Jordanes, Gulfila or Gilfila by Isidore, Vulphilas **1. Origin** by Cassiodorus, Ulfila by Auxentius **and Youth.** and Maximinus, Oulphilas by Socrates, Sozomen, and Theodoret, and Ourphilas by Philostorgius and Photius, all these representing the Gothic Wulfila, " Little Wolf." His grandparents came from the village of Sadagolthina, near Parnassus (probably situated on the River Halys) in western Cappadocia, and were among the Christians taken captive by the Goths when, in 264, they ravaged Cappadocia, Galatia, and Bithynia. In their pagan surroundings these Christian captives not only remained true to the faith, but also converted many of their captors and formed communities with at least some degree of organization. Ulfilas himself seems to have been born of a Gothic father and a woman of Asia Minor, was a serf by origin, but a Christian from his very youth. According to Auxentius, he became bishop

at the age of thirty, and then officiated seven years in the land of the barbarians and thirty-three in " Romania." He was well acquainted with Greek, since he was made a " reader," in which capacity he had not only to read the Scriptures during the services but in all probability also to translate and explain them to the Goths among his hearers. When about thirty years of age, he was chosen to accompany a Gothic embassy to the imperial court, where he became acquainted with Eusebius of Nicomedia, who, with other bishops there assembled, consecrated him to the episcopate apparently at Antioch during the synod of May 22–Sept. 1, 341.

But Ulfilas could labor only a brief time as " bishop of the Christians in the land of the Goths," for about seven years later the " irreligious and sacrilegious judge of the Goths " (apparently Athanarich, who termed himself almost exclusively " judge ") inaugurated a persecution **2. Promi-** so severe that the survivors were forced **nence;** to seek refuge in Roman territory. At **Missionary** the request of Ulfilas, Constantius **Activities.** gave them shelter in the mountains near Nicopolis in lower Moesia, not far from the modern Plevna, and appointed Ulfilas their " judge." It would seem that Ulfilas now ranked only as a Chorepiscopus (q.v.), and he is known to have been present only at the synod held at Constantinople in Jan., 360, so that it would appear that the importance ascribed to him by Auxentius is exaggerated. Whether, in addition to his duties in the vicinity of Plevna, he found time to carry on missionary work among the Goths north of the Danube is uncertain. According to Socrates, during the reign of Valens, but before the persecution of 370–372, war broke out between the Gothic chieftains, Frithigern and Athanarich. The former, defeated, fled to Roman territory, and, aided by the emperor, returned and proved victorious. In gratitude he adopted the faith of Valens, and constrained his subjects to do likewise, while Ulfilas labored among the people of both Frithigern and Athanarich. But the latter would not tolerate the Christians, and in 370–372 persecuted them bitterly. After peace between Frithigern and Athanarich, Ulfilas may well have carried on missionary work, though it would appear that he made no extensive journeys, but rather supported the cause from his mountains near Plevna. He seems to have remained associated with Frithigern, and when, in 376, the greater part of the Visigoths sought a home on Roman soil, Ulfilas is said by Sozomen (*Hist. eccl.*, vi. 37) to have accompanied their embassy to the court and there to have advocated their cause. Whether he maintained these friendly relations with the newcomers when they became involved in strife with the Romans is uncertain, but there is little doubt that, half-Roman by birth, and entirely Roman in religion and education, he took sides against the Goths.

Before Rome had concluded peace with the Goths (Oct. 3, 382), however, Ulfilas himself, through no fault of his own, had become involved in war with the land he had, in all probability, served in a political as well as in an ecclesiastical capacity, with whose bishops and churches he had been on the most friendly terms for more than a generation; and before the issue was decided, he had passed away. The cause and progress of these events

3. Later Years. were wrapped in obscurity. From the letter of Auxentius, the sole document dealing with the death of Ulfilas, it would appear that, shortly after the council of Aquileia, Ulfilas and other bishops went to the imperial court, where, at their request, Theodosius promised to convene another synod for the settlement of the Arian controversy. This journey apparently took place in the autumn of 381 or the winter of 381–382, and somewhat later Ulfilas was summoned by the emperor to return to Constantinople to take part in a disputation on the problems at issue, or, in other words, to attend the synod convened at Constantinople by Theodosius in June, 383. Bishops of every shade of doctrine had already assembled when Nectarius, patriarch of Constantinople, succeeded in preventing the open debate promised by the emperor, who, instead, required each of the theological factions to present its own creed. This done, Theodosius gave his approval to the Nicene formula, tore up the others, and sent the bishops to their homes. It would accordingly seem that Ulfilas had reached the capital in June, 383, had fallen ill shortly afterward, and, though able to take part in the deliberations of his faction concerning the formulation of their creed, so that he himself drew up one for this purpose, had died before the imperial decision was received.

According to Socrates (*Hist. eccl.*, ii. 41), Ulfilas, as a pupil of the Crimgothic bishop Theophilus,

4. Theology. was primarily an adherent of the Nicene Creed, becoming an Arian only at the synod held at Constantinople early in 360. This account is followed in the main by Sozomen (*Hist. eccl.*, vi. 37), while Theodoret (*Hist. eccl.*, iv. 37) makes the Arianism of Ulfilas date from 376. The *Acta Nicetæ*, on the other hand, represent him as a true Catholic throughout his life, and as the founder of none but orthodox communities among the Goths. The creed drawn up by Ulfilas himself runs thus: " I, Ulfilas, bishop and confessor, have ever thus believed, and in this sole true faith I pass unto the Lord: I believe that there is one only God, unbegotten and invisible; and in his only begotten Son, our Lord and God, creator and maker of every creature, not having his like. Therefore, God is one, who is also God of our God. And in one Holy Ghost, virtue illuminating and sanctifying . . . neither God nor Lord, but the [faithful] minister of Christ, not equal, but subject and obedient in all things to the Son; and the Son subject and obedient in all things to God the Father." Of the following lines of this creed only the words " through Christ " and " by the Holy Ghost," as well as a few letters, have survived. It is clear, however, that Ulfilas was unconscious of ever having changed his theological position, and the statements of Socrates, Sozomen, Theodoret, and the *Acta Nicetæ* must, therefore, be rejected. On the other hand, the creed seems to contain no clue as to the anti-Nicene group in which Ulfilas is to be reckoned. But the very fact that Ulfilas avoids all reference to the essence shows that he was a ho-

moian. This is borne out by a number of other facts: Auxentius testifies that he " said the Son was like the Father . . . according to the divine Scriptures and traditions "; he was one of the forty-six bishops who condemned and deposed Ætius at Constantinople early in 360; his pupil Auxentius, his partizans Palladius of Ratiaria, Secundianus, Demophilus of Berea, and Maximinus, and his successor Selinas were all homoians, as was the entire Gothic church. It is true that the homoians first appeared as a distinct faction at a synod held at Sirmium in 357; but the rapidity with which they became dominant along the lower Danube shows that their views had there long met favor, so that they were speedily adopted officially by the majority of the bishops. The homoian rejection of every dogma that could not be proved from the Bible won the hearty support of such a conservative and traditionalist as Ulfilas, who, as Auxentius tells, regarded the Nicene Creed as a " devilish innovation," sided with the anti-Nicene party at Antioch in 341, and, when the Ætians and homoousians began to draw apart, joined the homoians, whose watchword was " according to the Scriptures." Herein he could follow not merely his own inclination, but the example of almost all the bishops and churches of the Danube regions, where Arianism of this sort was so firmly intrenched that orthodoxy was forced to struggle with it until late in the fifth century.

Auxentius reports that Ulfilas " proved by sermons and treatises that there is a difference between the divinity of the Father and of the Son. He preached continually in the one and only Church of Christ in the Greek, Latin, and Gothic tongues, and he also left behind him a number

5. Works; Bible Translation. of treatises and many interpretations in these same three languages." None of these productions has survived under the name of Ulfilas, although it is not impossible that fragments may be included among the numerous remnants of Arian (or, rather, homoian) literature that are still extant. A number of works—the fragments of a homoian commentary on Luke (ed. A. Mai, *Nova collectio*, iii. 2, pp. 191–207, 10 vols., Rome, 1825–38) and of the *Opus imperfectum in Matthæum*, and the Gothic *Skeireins aiwaggeljons thairh Johannen* (" Interpretation of the Gospel according to John ")—have indeed been ascribed to him, but on insufficient basis. The sole fragment of Ulfilas now extant is his incomplete confession of 383, and even this was probably written in Greek, not in Latin, as it now stands. The fame of Ulfilas is chiefly due, however, to two facts: his creation of a Gothic alphabet from modifications and adaptations of the Greek, Latin, and runic alphabets; and his Gothic translation of the Bible. Philostorgius and Socrates exaggerate his services when they ascribe to him the absolute invention of this new script; but there is little doubt that he formed it expressly to commit to writing his version of the Bible. This was intended primarily for the liturgy, not for private devotion; and as there were then no lectionaries, he was obliged to translate the entire Bible. How far he was able to execute this plan is unknown. Philostorgius states that he intentionally omitted I, II Samuel and I, II Kings because their warlike contents rendered them too stimulating for so martial a people as the Goths; but this is improbable, and simply means that those four books were still missing from the Gothic Bible in the second quarter of the fifth century. Only the extant fragments of the Gospels can be referred with any certainty to the hand of Ulfilas; for these would naturally have been the first for him to undertake, while their uniformity of style points to a single author. In method he adhered strictly to his Greek original, sacrificing clarity to accuracy, and adopting a literary Gothic which disregarded the vernacular and admitted Hellenisms without scruple. The fragments are utterly devoid of poetic inspiration, and in their rigid form reveal the habits to which Ulfilas had become accustomed by his long years as an interpreting reader in the services. His work can not be compared with that of Jerome in the Vulgate; if any parallel be sought, it must be with the old Slavic version, which is of the same type and character. See BIBLE VERSIONS, A, X.

The praises heaped on Ulfilas by Auxentius, Maximinus, and Philostorgius are essentially partizan in spirit; and even the exclamation of Constantius (recorded only by Philostorgius), that Ulfilas was " the Moses of our time," alludes only to his leading the confessors from Gothic territory during the persecution of 348–349. The best evidence of his importance is the endeavor of historians of the fifth century to claim him for orthodoxy, though it is difficult to say whether the motive here is because he was a bishop and a primate, or a confessor. Equally exaggerated are the modern assertions that his translation of the Bible enabled the Germans to be at once Christians and Teutons, that he created a school of Gothic Arian church-leaders, and that the Arian creed of the Gothic church and all her Teutonic offshoots were due to him. The time has not yet come for final decision on the importance of Ulfilas in history. (H. Böhmer.)

BIBLIOGRAPHY: The works named under BIBLE VERSIONS, A, X., usually contain introductions on the life of Ulfilas, and for his work are important. Sources are: (1) Arian authors: Auxentius, Epistula de fide, vita et obitu Ulfilæ, included in G. Waitz, Ueber das Leben und die Lehre des Ulfila, Hanover, 1840, and in F. Kauffmann, Aus der Schule des Wulfila, Strasburg, 1899; and Philostorgius, Hist. eccl., ii. 5 (for editions see under PHILOSTORGIUS); (2) Orthodox authors: Socrates, Hist. eccl., ii. 41, iv. 24; Sozomen, Hist. eccl., iv. 24, vi. 37; Theodoret, Hist. eccl., iv. 37 (all these are in Eng. transl. in NPNF, 2 ser., vols. ii.–iii.); Jordanis, Getica, li. 267, in MGH, Auct. ant., v. 1 (1882), 127; and Isidore of Seville, Chronicon, cccl., in MGH, Auct. ant., xi (1894), 469, cf. pp. 270–271 (from the Historia Gotorum). Consult further: the work of G. Waitz, ut sup.; W. Krafft, Die Anfänge des Christentums bei den germanischen Völkern, Berlin, 1854; W. Bessell, Ueber das Leben des Ulfilas und die Bekehrung der Goten zum Christentum, Göttingen, 1860; W. L. Krafft, De fontibus Ulfilæ Arianismi, Bonn, 1860; E. Bernhardt, Wulfila oder die gotische Bibel, Halle, 1875; C. P. V. Kirchner, Die Abstammung des Ulfilas, Chemnitz, 1879; P. Schaff, Companion to the Greek Testament, pp. 160–163, New York, 1883; C. A. A. Scott, Ulfilas, Apostle of the Goths, London, 1885; W. Streitberg, Gotisches Elementarbuch, pp. 9 sqq., Heidelberg, 1906; Stamm, Ulfilas, 11th ed. by F. Wrede, pp. xvii. sqq., 281 sqq., Paderborn, 1908; Cambridge Medieval History, i. 212–213, New York, 1911; ADB, xliv. 270 sqq.

ULLMANN, ūl'-mān, **KARL:** German Protestant; b. at Epfenbach, near Heidelberg, Mar. 15, 1796; d. at Carlsruhe Jan. 12, 1865. He was educated at the universities of Heidelberg (1812–13) and Tübingen (1813–16). After a year as vicar at Kirchheim, near Heidelberg, he resumed his studies at Heidelberg in 1817, where he became privat-docent of theology 1819, associate professor 1821, and full professor 1825. In this period, besides studies on II Peter, the so-called III Corinthians, the cycle of the Christian feasts, and the Hypsistarians, Ullman published Gregor von Nazianz (Darmstadt, 1825; Eng. transl., London, 1851). In collaboration with F. W. K. Umbreit (q.v.), he founded, in 1828, the Theologische Studien und Kritiken for the defense of modern orthodox theology. In 1829 Ullmann was called to Halle, where he lectured primarily on church history, teaching also introduction, symbolics, and dogmatics, and seeking to counteract the rationalism still prevailing in the university. At the same time, in his Theologisches Bedenken (Halle, 1830), he defended unrestricted theological and ecclesiastical development. Of his other writings during this period, special mention may be made of his De Beryllo Bostreno ejusque doctrina (Hamburg, 1835). In 1836 Ullmann was recalled to Heidelberg, where he lectured on the same subjects as at Halle. Meanwhile his activity as author was transferred from church history to apologetics by Strauss' Leben Jesu, which gave rise to his Historisch oder mythisch (Hamburg, 1838); Ueber den Kultus des Genius (1840; Eng. transl., The Worship of Genius, London, 1840); Die Sündlosigkeit Jesu (1842; Eng. transl., The Sinlessness of Jesus, from the 7th ed., new issue Edinburgh, 1902); and Das Wesen des Christenthums (1845; Eng. transl., The Essence of Christianity, London, 1846). But his chief work was his Reformatoren vor der Reformation (2 vols., 1841–42; Eng. transl., Reformers before the Reformation, 2 vols., Edinburgh, 1874–77), in which he blended the biographies of Johann Wessel, Johann von Goch, and Johann von Wesel into a presentation of the theological preparation for the German Reformation. But with these works Ullmann's literary activity virtually came to a close, being replaced by his interest in the practical problems then confronting the Church, so that in the fifth decade of the century there was scarcely a question of the day which he did not discuss exhaustively in the Theologische Studien und Kritiken.

In conformity with the conditions and needs following the German revolution, Ullmann devoted himself mainly to the interests of the national church of Baden, which it became the task of modern orthodox theology to strengthen by sound reforms and to increase its influence on the life of the people and of the State. Ullmann turned the perilous crisis then confronting his communion into good. This he did, in the first place, by convening in semi-annual conferences those who were at once friends of the national church and also disposed toward reform. These " Durlach conferences " first brought Baden pietism and mediating theology into friendly relations, preparing the way for the solution of the problems confronting the national church of the day. The change of rulers in Baden in 1852 increased the prospects of actual reform, and when, in the following year, the Evangelical prelature became vacant, it was but natural that Ullmann should be called to fill it. In 1853, accordingly, Ullmann became prelate, or the representative of the Evangelical church in the upper chamber. His actual administrative power, however, was but slight, and his activity was hampered, rather than aided, when he was appointed director in 1856. The chief exertions of the new prelate were directed to the execution of the reforms proposed in the Durlach conferences, and, accordingly, in 1855 the general synod was convened for the first time since 1843. Its subjects for consideration were a new formulation of the confessional status, a new national catechism, a new liturgy, and a new Biblical history. The catechism, prepared by Ullmann himself from Luther's smaller catechism and that of Heidelberg, found wide favor, so that, within a few years, it was adopted as the union catechism, with slight modifications, in the Rheno-Prussian Church. The new Biblical history was also adopted, as well as the liturgy, and even the new creed, though much debated, was finally accepted. From attacks, urgent and persistent, caused by these measures, Ullmann was, by his position, protected for a time and against involuntary retirement; and he determined to remain at his post as long as he honorably could. At last, however, in 1861, after continued lack of sympathy with his views, he requested leave to resign. Consent was reluctantly given, and Ullmann retired from active life. In the long struggle his health had been seriously impaired, and his eager hopes for a resumption of literary work were frustrated. Henceforth until his death the major portion of his time and strength was devoted to the *Theologische Studien und Kritiken*. During these last years he prepared a memoir of his church administration, but the work was never completed. His principal writings are collected in Perthes' *Theologische Bibliothek* (5 vols., Gotha, 1863–67).

(W. BEYSCHLAG†.)

BIBLIOGRAPHY: W. Beyschlag, *Karl Ullmann, eine biographische Skizze*, Gotha, 1866; A. Hausrath, *Kleine Schriften religionsgeschichtliches Inhalts*, pp. 438–460, Leipsic, 1883; G. Frank, *Die Theologie des 19. Jahrhunderts*, p. 270, ib. 1904.

ULRICH, ūl′riH, **SAINT:** Bishop of Augsburg; b. at Augsburg 890; d. there July 4, 973. He was of noble birth and received his education at the monastery of St. Gall, returning to his native city a short time before the death of Adalbero of Augsburg (Apr. 28, 909). There the bishop appointed him chamberlain, but on the death of his patron Ulrich left Augsburg. When Hiltin died, however, Ulrich was consecrated bishop of Augsburg in his stead (Dec. 28, 923). As a spiritual lord he fortified his see city, and remained loyal to Henry I. and Otto I. In 955, when the Magyars ravaged the land, Ulrich succeeded in holding Augsburg against them until Otto could arrive with his army, and by his victory on the Lechfeld (Aug. 10, 955) annihilate the Magyar peril forever. He was now able to repair the ravages of war in his domains and to establish civil and religious order among his people. His bounty was equaled only by the devoutness of his private life and by the magnificence of his liturgy, while his desire to obtain relics led him on long journeys, from which he brought back to Augsburg dubious remains of the soldiers of the Theban Legion (q.v.) from St. Maurice in Valais and the head of St. Abundus from Rome. He thrice made pilgrimage to Rome (910, 954, 971) and showed much favor to monasticism, restoring monasteries and founding the nunnery of St. Stephen in Augsburg.

The grave of Ulrich gained a reputation as the scene of miracles, and his constant companion in his later years, Gerhard, composed a *Vita Sancti Oudalrici* (ed. Waitz, in *MGH, Script.*, iv., 1841, 377–425) to which he was already able to add many signs and wonders. This biography was taken to Rome by Bishop Liutulf of Augsburg when he went there to gain for his predecessor the reverence of all Christendom; and in Feb., 993, John XV. issued a bull to the bishops and abbots of Gaul and Germany canonizing Ulrich.

The name of Ulrich is attached to a short polemic against celibacy entitled *Rescriptio beati Udelrici epistolæ in qua papæ Nicolao de continentia clericorum non juste sed impie, non canonice sed indiscrete tractanti ita respondit*. This pseudonymous composition was condemned by Gregory VII. in 1079, and seems to have been occasioned by the requirement of celibacy by the Roman synod of 1074. The use of the name Ulrich was certainly intended to imply the bishop of Augsburg, though between 1059 (when the third canon of the Lateran Synod discussed the problem of the celibacy of the clergy) and 1074 there were three Italian bishops named Ulrich: Ulrich of Imola, of Benevento, and of Fermo. To Ulrich of Augsburg is also ascribed a *Sermo synodalis parochianis presbyteris in synodis enuntiandus* (cf. *MPL*, cxxxv. 1069). This sermon is, however, merely a slight revision of the common *Commonitorium cujusque episcopi*.

(A. HAUCK.)

BIBLIOGRAPHY: The sources: *Vita* by the monk Berno; other *Vitæ, miracula, officium, translatio*, etc., are to be found in *ASM*, v. 419–476; *ASB*, July, iv. 73–135; *MGH, Script.*, iv (1841), 375–428; *MPL*, cxxxv. 1001–09, 1059–1080, cxlii. 1183–1204. Consult: P. Braun, *Geschichte von dem Leben und den Wunderwerken des . . . heiligen Ulrichs*, Augsburg, 1796; T. Nelk, *Lebensgeschichte des heiligen Bischofs Ulrich*, Augsburg, 1831; O. Rommel, in *Forschungen zur deutschen Geschichte*, iv. 121–158, Göttingen, 1864; K. Raffler, *Der heilige Ulrich Bischof von Augsburg*, 2d ed., Munich, 1870; J. Koch, *Geschichte und Cult des heiligen Ulrich, Bischofs von Augsburg*, Halle, 1875; J. N. Stützle, *Leben des heiligen Ulrich*, 2d ed., Augsburg, 1880; B. Meyr, *S. Ulrich und Afra; 222 Daten aus der Geschichte ihres Lebens und ihrer Kirche*, ib. 1888; C. Bruckner, *Studien zur Geschichte der sächsischen Kaiser*, Basel, 1889.

ULRICH VON HUTTEN. See HUTTEN, ULRICH VON.

ULRICH OF WUERTTEMBERG. See BLAURER, AMBROSIUS; BRENZ, JOHANN; CHRISTOPHER, DUKE OF WUERTTEMBERG; GRETER, KASPAR; GRYNÆUS, SIMON; MARBURG, CONFERENCE OF; PEASANTS' WAR, II, § 1; SCHNEPFF, ERHARD; TOUSSAIN, PIERRE; WUERTTEMBERG.

ULTRAMONTANISM.

Definition and Use of the Term (§ 1).
Early Foundations (§ 2).
Results Outside and Inside the Church (§ 3).
Effects on Research and Theology (§ 4).
Effects upon the People (§ 5).

A noteworthy definition of Ultramontanism by F. X. Kraus (q.v.) runs as follows: " The distinctive marks of the ultramontane system **1. Defini-** are comprised in five points: (1) he is **tion and** an ultramontanist who sets the con- **Use of the** cept of the Church above that of re- **Term.** ligion; (2) who conceives pope and Church interchangeably; (3) who believes the kingdom of God is of this world, and that the power of the keys, as curialism affirmed it in the Middle Ages, also includes temporal jurisdiction over princes and peoples; (4) who supposes that religious conviction can be coerced through material power, or who may be reduced to submission by such process; (5) who finds himself always ready to sacrifice a clear command of his own conscience to the claim of an alien authority " (by F. X. Kraus, reproduced in E. Hauviller's biography of Kraus, p. 100, Colmar, 1904). The term *Ultramontani*, at Italian seats of learning during the later Middle Ages, was a term applied to students " from over the mountains," e.g., to Germans. And the same designation was used in Rome of the French cardinals, when sharp opposition had developed in connection with the election of Clement V. But the same expression was current in Germany during the time of Henry IV. with reference to the followers of Gregory VII. because they served interests " beyond the mountains "; while in France the name occurs with reference to those with curial, not Gallican, aims. In the nineteenth century, the name became quite prevalent, at first in Munich as applied to the party of the elder Görres; afterward in North Germany on occasion of the church strife at Cologne. The controversial question is inevitable, whether the ultramontanists give the adequate expression to the essence of Roman Catholicism which they profess to do. This question can be clearly resolved only through detailed historical examination.

A preliminary question arises as to how far into the past Ultramontanism may be carried. As early as at the Council of Trent (q.v.) some genuine ultramontane aims were set up in the form of papal assumptions; and if Ultramontanism **2. Early** did not, as yet, carry the victory along **Founda-** all the line, still it achieved important **tions.** results, especially in the canons of the sixth, fourteenth, and twenty-fifth sessions. It was not accidental that these results were won by a Jesuit, since this is the sequel to the transformation of Roman Catholicism from what it had been down to the middle of the sixteenth century, through the genius and activity of the Jesuit order. To be sure this new " Roman type " of Catholicism furnishes nothing absolutely new; and, on another side, even without the direct cooperation of the Jesuits, a phase of papalism was espoused about the middle of the sixteenth century which can not be distinguished from Ultramontanism as defined by Kraus. For instance, in the bull

Cum ex apostolatus officio, promulgated by Paul IV., 1559, where " out of the fulness of apostolic authority" it is stated that " the pope, who is vice-gerent of God and of Christ on earth, and has the supreme power over kingdoms and peoples, and judges all, can be judged by no one. . . . All hierarchs and all sovereigns and princes even to the emperor, the moment they fall into heresy or schism, are by that very fact, and without need of a particular judicial procedure, throughout and for ever forfeit of their position and its honors and revenues, also thenceforth and for ever unfit to be vested therewith " . . . (cf. Mirbt, *Quellen*, under no. 288). If this bull be combined with the bull *In cœna Domini* (q.v.), there is a nearly integral configuration of the ultramontane papal principle. And far back of this it exists in fact in the bull *Unam sanctam* (q.v.) of the year 1302. What lies at loose ends in the *Dictatus* of Gregory VII. stands here compact, and papalism spans its highest arch on a religious foundation: " We declare all human creatures to be subject to the Roman pontiff. . . . Such is the indispensable condition of salvation." In such terms Ultramontanism is set up for a ruling principle alike in regard to the pope's political status, and in regard to the religious relationship of believing Roman Catholics toward the pope. True, J. Hergenröther, in *Anti-Janus* (Freiburg, 1870; cf. J. F. v. Schulte, *Altkatholizismus*, pp. 331 sqq., Giessen, 1887), has contended that this bull should not be regarded as infallible; and in *Kirchenstaat*, pp. 300 sqq., 751 sqq. (Freiburg, 1860), he has brought forward every available argument to the end of annulling its importance in respect to this question. But this was all in vain; the third of the distinctive marks of Ultramontanism enunciated by Kraus has its foundation in the bull of 1302; and thereon rests even in modern times the tendency not to separate the two jurisdictions, but to treat temporal matters constantly according to the synchronous interests of the Church.

The practical operation of the ultramontane tendency during the progress of time has been twofold, outside and inside the ecclesiastical system. On the **3. Results** former side, illustration is furnished **Outside** by the conflict between empire and **and Inside** papacy. By degrees the ultramontane **the Church.** idea as to the superiority of the papacy was introduced into the sphere of secular affairs, and became part of the belief of the faithful, priests and laymen. So that Innocent III. could say without encountering opposition, " The Lord committed not only the Church but the entire secular era to Peter's administration." In answer to the question whether this idea belongs exclusively to the Middle Ages or is of present application, the answer must be that it is only in exceptional cases that such assumptions can still find actual enforcement. Yet even in more modern times the popes have often declared civil laws invalid, as in the case of the Austrian statute law of 1867, and the Prussian " Falk laws " or " May laws " of 1872–75,* although those laws neither hindered

* These laws, which were carried through the Prussian diet by Dr. Falk, minister of public instruction in Prussia, transferred oversight of the schools from the Church to the State,

individual piety nor had anything to do with dogmas of the Church. Where, then, is the limit of "ecclesiastical interests"? The claim of power to release civil subjects from obedience to the civil government, for the sake of those interests, was still essentially maintained in 1805 by Pius VII. On the other side, the reaction of Ultramontanism upon affairs within the Church came still earlier to light. The triumph of Gregorian ideas eliminated the ancient episcopal trend; and, together with the freedom of the bishops, they abolished what independent arrangements there still existed in the national churches. The pope came to be not only supreme, but sole lawgiver; he bears, as Boniface VIII. expresses it, "all rights in the shrine of his breast" (book vi., cap. 1, *De Const.* I., 2). It was only transiently, under stress of the times, that a sort of new episcopal régime took shape during the schism through the great reforming synods; this novelty, however, was condemned and terminated by the Fifth Lateran Council. The Council of Trent still found existent potent expressions of the episcopal drift, but the Vatican Council stopped them once for all. Similarly the Gallican policy, and everything like "Josephinism" or philosophic paternalism (see JOSEPH II.), was ended forever. The sole reaction against such despotism within the Church is nowadays found among the Old Catholics (q.v.).

As concerning the suppression set afoot by Ultramontanism against freedom in scientific theology, the most important example is afforded by the history of German Roman Catholic theology. In Döllinger's address of Sept. 28, 1863, before the Roman Catholic academic assembly in Munich (see DOELLINGER, JOHANN JOSEF IGNAZ VON, § 6), the points were brought forward that the sixteenth century indicates a flourishing period for Roman Catholic theology, whereas with the seventeenth century in Spain, and with the eighteenth in France, decay set in; and that although still high tasks were incumbent upon Germany's theology, these could not be even approached if her freedom of movement were denied. When Döllinger said this, he did not surmise how soon this refusal was to come, that even in the following year, by terms of the *Syllabus errorum*, again in 1870 through the definition of papal infallibility, all freedom was to be taken away from the theologians. Even before that definition was pronounced, on July 19, 1870, Döllinger had discerned what in effect became the fate of Roman Catholic theology in consequence of the dogma. "So then," he says at the close of his *Pope and the Council* (London, 1869), "the newly coined article of faith must plant and settle itself as foundation and cornerstone of the whole Roman Catholic doctrinal structure; the activity of the theologians must reduce itself to the secondary task of finding whether a papal utterance for a given doctrine is extant or not. . . . To what purpose any further toilsome delving in the Bible, to what end the labored study of tradition,

4. Effects on Research and Theology.

prohibited members of religious orders from teaching in the public schools, limited the episcopal powers over the clergy and clerical powers over the laity, changing, in fact, the ecclesiastical law of the land.

if a single utterance of the infallible pope has power to demolish the conscientious theological work of a generation?" As regards the more modern Roman Catholic Biblical research, nobody will call attention, by way of refuting Döllinger, to the "Commission in behalf of advancing Biblical Studies," organized by command of Pope Pius X., as though this were an instrument for advancing such studies. For that this is merely an instrument for shackling them appears from the *Motu proprio* "*Præstantia*" of Sept. 18, 1907 (cf. *Osservatore Romano* of Nov. 21, 1907), as is elsewhere patent from "decisions" hitherto announced in relation to weighty matters of Biblical introduction (Mosaic composition of the Pentateuch [1905]; historic integrity of John's Gospel [1907]; authorship of the Book of Isaiah [1908]); [verbal agreement of the extant Greek text of Matthew with the lost Aramaic original (1911)]. But still far more comprehensive is the curb that was applied to more liberal, theologically technical verifications of results by the two pronouncements against the "Modernists" (see MODERNISM), namely, the decree of the Congregation of Inquisition, *Lamentabili*, of July, 1907; and the papal encyclical, *Pascendi Dominici gregis* (Eng. transl. in *Programme of Modernism*, pp. 149 sqq., New York and London, 1908), of Sept. 8, 1907. That the matters involved do not turn on theoretical exercises of the Curia's rhetoric appears from the extremely sharp measures devised against all "Modernists." For it was principally against Roman Catholic scientific "palpitations" in those countries that the entire procedure was directed, although the first man to use his pen against these decrees was an English scholar, George Henry Tyrrell (q.v.; he wrote in the London *Times*, Sept. 30, Oct. 1, 1907). He was then followed by individual Italian sympathizers in the *Programma dei Modernisti* (Rome, 1907; Eng. transl., *Programme of Modernism*, New York and London, 1908), and in *Rinnovamento* (Milan, since 1907); but the main focus of the cause is to be sought in France. In Germany, where, during the spring of 1908, the *Internationale Wochenschrift* published a series of articles elucidating the importance of the foregoing decrees, the number of deliberate and steadfast modernists among the Roman Catholic theologians is exceedingly small.

If Ultramontanism, therefore, has shackled the motions or aspirations of scientific freedom, the question still remains as to its effects upon the mass of Roman Catholics. In this connection, the scope of this examination embraces that materializing and artificialism of religion which inheres in Roman Catholicism, in so far as the devotional methods which for centuries past have been customary are employed to the end of increasingly extended propagation and fostering of the ultramontane spirit. Some of these devotional methods and devices were set forth by Reusch, both old and newly invented ones, in his *Die deutschen Bischöfe und der Aberglaube* (Bonn, 1879). These and countless others are utilized by Ultramontanism for the sake of advancing its political aims by exciting confessional passion. An advantageous vehicle for the fostering of the ultramontane spirit

5. Effects upon the People.

in that country has been conspicuous for sixty years past in the regularly recurring Roman Catholic conventions, employing a comprehensive daily press, a calculated and apposite pamphlet press, and the literature of art and culture. The fraternizing cause has been developed on the largest scale through all kinds of industrial and professional associations, so that the " Chinese wall " that barricades Roman Catholicism against Protestantism becomes ever higher and higher. But that Roman Catholicism shall stand forth as an outward power along ultramontane lines is carefully provided for by imposing church feasts and processions. The attitude of modern Jesuitical Roman Catholicism (i.e., of Ultramontanism) toward modern culture is negatively comprehended in the *Syllabus errorum* of 1864 (text and Eng. transl. in Schaff, *Creeds*, ii. 213–233), to which the decree *Lamentabili*, together with the encyclical *Pascendi*, forms a complement. In sum, the spirit out of which the reäction against Modernism has proceeded in the broadest sense is to be sought in the Spanish type of Roman Catholic " religiosity " that was embodied in Ignatius Loyola, then organized and systematized, until eventually it became instilled into the veins of Roman Catholicism at large and complete.   K. BENRATH.

BIBLIOGRAPHY: J. J. I. von Döllinger, *Kirche und Kirchen, Papstthum und Kirchenstaat*, Munich, 1861, Eng. transl., *The Church and the Churches, or the Papacy and the Temporal Power*, London, 1862; idem, *Das Papsttum*, Munich, 1869, 2d ed., 1892; idem, *Kleinere Schriften*, ed. Reusch, ib. 1890; Schrader, *Der Papst und die modernen Ideen*, Vienna, 1867; J. F. von Schulte, *Die Macht der römischen Kürie*, Prague, 1871; O. Mejer, *Zur Geschichte der römisch-deutschen Frage*, 3 vols., Rostock, 1871–74; T. Weber, *Staat und Kirche nach . . . den Absichten des Ultramontanismus*, Breslau, 1872; G. R. Badenoch, *Ultramontanism*, London, 1874; J. Fessler, *True and False Infallibility of the Popes*, New York, 1875; E. Michaud, *L'État actuel de l'église catholique en France*, Paris, 1876; J. Friedrich, *Geschichte des vatikanischen Konzils*, 3 vols., Bonn, 1877–82; idem, *Ignaz von Döllinger*, 3 vols., Munich, 1899–1901; G. Droysen, *Geschichte der Gegenreformation*, pp. 149 sqq., Berlin, 1893; P. von Hoensbroech, *Der Ultramontanismus, sein Wesen und seine Bekämpfung*, 2d ed., Berlin, 1898; idem, *Der Ultramontanismus in Deutschland*, Leipsic, 1896; idem, *Das Papsttum in seiner sozialen . . . Wirksamkeit*, 2 vols., ib. 1900–02; F. W. F. Nippold, *The Papacy in the 19th Century* (transl.), New York, 1900; E. G. Man, *Papal Aims and Papal Claims*, London, 1902; Majunke, *Geschichte des Kulturkampfs*, 2d ed., Paderborn, 1902; J. Mausbach, *Die ultramontane Moral nach Graf von Hoensbroech*, Berlin, 1902; C. Mirbt, *Der Ultramontanismus im 19. Jahrhundert*, Leipsic, 1902; J. Oman, *Vision and Authority; or, the Throne of St. Peter*, London, 1902; L. K. Götz, *Der Ultramontanismus als Weltanschauung*, Bonn, 1905; F. Heiner, *Der Syllabus in ultramontaner und antiultramontaner Beleuchtung*, Mainz, 1905; C. Latreille, *Joseph de Maistre et le papauté*, Paris, 1906; G. Anrich, *Der moderne Ultramontanismus in seiner Entstehung und Entwicklung*, Tübingen, 1909; G. B. Thompson, *The Kulturkampf*, Toronto, 1909; the literature under PIUS IX. and PIUS X.; also under INFALLIBILITY; KEYS, POWER OF THE; POPE, PAPACY, PAPAL SYSTEM; and VATICAN COUNCIL.

UMBREIT, ûm' brait, **FRIEDRICH WILHELM CARL:** German theologian; b. at Sonneborn (3 m. n. of Gotha) Apr. 11, 1795; d. at Heidelberg Apr. 26, 1860. He was educated at the gymnasium at Gotha and at the University of Göttingen, in the latter institution coming under the influence of Eichhorn, who stirred in him an enthusiasm for oriental studies which never left him. Herder also affected him in the same direction, and so to study orientalia was henceforth his life-work. He became privat-docent at Göttingen in 1818, extraordinary professor at Heidelberg in 1820, and ordinary professor in the philosophical faculty in 1823, and held this position along with the ordinary professorship of theology after 1829.

From Eichhorn he declared in 1852 that he had learned these three things: (1) that the Scriptures are a free field of investigation for Protestants; (2) this investigation must be pursued largely, if not exclusively, in the spirit of the orient; (3) benevolence and piety should be a part of religion, especially of the true German spirit. He agreed with DeWette that there were legendary recitals or myths in the Old Testament. But Delitzsch has borne witness to him as continuing the work of Herder in bringing out the human side of the Old Testament, without failing to recognize its divine element.

With Carl Ullmann he edited for many years the *Theologische Studien und Kritiken*. His separate publications were mostly on the Old Testament, but the New Testament had a share in his study. He defended the unity of Canticles (1820) against Herder, and thereby won Goethe's approval. His commentary on Job (1824) passed into a second edition in 1828 (Eng. transl., 2 vols., London, 1836–1837); and he issued commentaries on Proverbs (1826) and on the Prophets, except Daniel and Jonah (4 vols., 1841–46). But critical acumen was not among his gifts, emotion sometimes took the place of cool judgment.   (A. KAMPHAUSEN†.)

BIBLIOGRAPHY: Schenkel, in *Allgemeine kirchliche Zeitschrift*, 1860, part 6, pp. 11 sqq.; Mühlhäuser, in *Neue evangelische Kirchenzeitung*, 1860, no. 23; Zittel, in *Allgemeine Kirchenzeitung*, 1860, no. 54; *Zwei Reden gehalten am Grabe* [*Umbreits*], Heidelberg, 1860; J. Holtzmann, R. Rothe, and C. Ullmann, in *TSK*, 1862, part 3.

UNAM SANCTAM: The name of the bull of Boniface VIII. (q.v.) issued in 1302 containing the classic medieval expression of the papal claims to universal temporal sovereignty. The occasion of the bull was the contest of Boniface with Philip IV. (q.v.), in which the underlying question was whether the papacy should control the temporal affairs of European states. The claim had already been made for Rome by Gregory VII. (q.v.) in his struggle with Henry IV. of Germany, being expressed in the letter of that pope to Henry (text in M. Döberl, *Monumenta Germaniæ selecta*, iii. 18–22, Munich, 1889; Eng. transl. in Thatcher and McNeal, *Source Book*, pp. 147–150). But while in Germany the Curia had won decided victories, in France its demands had been resisted and national consciousness had been aroused. The occasion of the struggle between Boniface and Philip which led to the bull was the levy by the latter of taxes upon the clergy of France, to which the Roman reply was the bull *Clericis laicos*, forbidding laymen (including of course rulers of states) to levy subsidies from the clergy and prohibiting clergy from paying them without permission from Rome. Philip retorted by prohibiting export of money, plate, and the like from the realm, thus cutting off papal revenues derived from France. The immediate occasion of the bull *Unam sanctam* was the imprisonment in 1301 of the papal legate to France, Bernard Saisset, bishop of Pamiers, who had violently assailed the king and was charged with treason. Boniface called a synod to regulate affairs in France, claimed papal supremacy in temporal affairs in the bull *Ausculta Fili* (1301), and renewed the bull *Clericis laicos* for France. Philip gained popular support for his measures and his policy in the first meeting of a States General, with pledges of the same in his resistance to papal aggression. Then was issued the *Unam sanctam*.

The contents may be expressed under five heads. (1) There is but one Church, outside of which there is no salvation—one body of Christ with one head; (2) that head is Christ or his representative the pope, and refusal of the pastoral care of this head is *ipso facto* self-exclusion from the flock of Christ; (3) there are two swords, the spiritual and the temporal, one borne by the Church, the other for it, the first by the priest, the second by the king under the direction of the priest; (4) coordination of members of the body involves the elevation of the spiritual power above the temporal and instruction of the latter by the former, and whoever resists this highest power ordained of God resists God; (5) the bull closes with the words: " We, moreover, proclaim, declare, and pronounce that it is altogether necessary to salvation for every human being to be subject to the Roman pontiff."

The following steps were an assembly of French ecclesiastics and nobles held in 1303 under Philip's guidance which charged Boniface with heresy and misconduct and demanded a general council to pass upon the charges. Boniface decided to issue a bull of excommunication and deposition against the king, but before its issue William Nogaret, whom Philip had sent to Rome in behalf of the project of the council, led troops against Boniface at Anagni and captured him. The populace arose, however, after three days and drove out the French, and the pope returned to Rome; but his death in the following October left Philip the virtual victor.

BIBLIOGRAPHY: The text is given in Reich, *Documents*, pp. 191–193; translations are to be found in Thatcher and McNeal, *Source Book*, pp. 314–317; Robinson, *European History*, i. 346–348; F. A. Ogg, *Source Book of Mediæval History*, pp. 385–388, New York, 1908; and Henderson, *Documents*, pp. 435–437. Consult the literature under BONIFACE VIII.; PHILIP IV.; and POPE, PAPACY, PAPAL SYSTEM; the comments in the source books named above; L. Tosti, *Pope Boniface VIII. and his Times*, New York, 1911; and Hefele, *Conciliengeschichte*, vi. 347–351.

UNBELIEF. See AGNOSTICISM; ATHEISM; PANTHEISM; RATIONALISM AND SUPERNATURALISM.

UNCIAL AND CURSIVE MANUSCRIPTS. See BIBLE TEXT, II.

UNCLEANNESS. See DEFILEMENT AND PURIFICATION, CEREMONIAL.

UNCTION. See EXTREME UNCTION.

UNDER-EYCK, ŭn′der-aik′ **(UNDE REYCK, UNTE REYCK, ONDEREICK), THEODOR:** Early German pietist; b. at Duisburg (15 m. n. of Düsseldorf) June 15, 1635; d. at Bremen Jan. 1, 1693. He was educated at Utrecht (1654–57), where he received the Puritanical and pietistic impressions which characterized his entire life, and later resided for some time with Cocceius at Leyden. He then

made a tour of England and France, and also visited Geneva, and on his return in 1660 was appointed pastor at Mülheim-on-the-Ruhr, a name which he made proverbial for the Pietism of the Lower Rhine, completely transforming its distinctly Reformed character. Here his pastoral visits and his insistence on family prayers resulted in popular assemblies for the cultivation of piety, and the people flocked to sermons and conferences. In 1668, however, Under-Eyck, after declining a number of flattering calls, accepted the post of chaplain to the Landgravine Hedwig Sophia at Cassel. Here he enjoyed high favor and established Pietism. Lacking, however, as court chaplain, pastoral activity, and accordingly declining an invitation to become chaplain to Queen Charlotte Amelia of Denmark, he accepted a call to become head pastor of St. Martin's, Bremen, in 1670, where he was to spend the remainder of his life.

At Bremen Under-Eyck became the head of a party opposed to the official clergy of the city. In repeated attacks he was charged with Labadism, mutilation of the liturgy, Quakerism, and the like. The entire city was in an uproar, for no one could remain indifferent concerning him. The sternness of his preaching was terrifying, and sudden conversions of his declared enemies occurred. In 1680 he held daily three hours of private conferences and an hour and a half of catechizing, which on Sunday afternoons gathered the men about him to discuss Scripture. His wife, the daughter of the French Reformed pastor Hulsius of Wesel, was, if possible, still more active, holding repeated meetings daily with the women and children. The other clergy were bitterly hostile, but Under-Eyck could count on the support of the civic authorities, among whom he had warm friends; yet he was frequently careless of the Church's point of view, and neglected the meetings of the clerical conference, although he was alternating president of that body. In addition, he sought to find positions in Bremen for his partizans, succeeding in the case of no less than eleven. Sweeping measures were planned against the established church, the chief requirements being a disciplinary presbytery, the restriction of the Lord's Supper to believers, and the denial of baptism, except in special cases, to the children of unbelieving parents. Though these projects failed, Under-Eyck was successful in his exertions to promote catechization, and his ministry at Bremen was marked by an ever-increasing prestige.

Under-Eyck was to the Reformed Church of Germany what Spener was to the Lutherans. Receiving his inspiration from Holland, he preserved his individuality, and systematically avoided all problems which did not bear on his one interest of personal salvation, the deepening and revival of personal faith, and the revelation of God in the sinner through devoted and carefully regulated obedience. With his zeal he united a wise restraint, and his teachings show no traces of a tendency toward separatism. His influence was far-reaching, establishing piety in the household and rendering the conventicle truly popular. He was apparently a hymn-writer as well, though here little is certain, and he seems to have inspired J(ohannes) D(eusing) to translate three of the writings of Willem Teelinck (q.v.), which appeared at Cassel in 1693. The Thursday meetings at Mülheim, begun probably in 1661, lasted until 1740, making a deep impression on Tersteegen (q.v.), who helped revive them in 1750, after which they long continued, receiving fresh inspiration from Stursberg about 1840. In Bremen De Hase and F. A. Lampe carried Under-Eyck's ideals to victory. He likewise maintained lasting relations with the Hessian court.

The works of Under-Eyck are: *Christi Braut unter den Töchtern zu Laodicœa* (3 parts, Hanau, 1670), an attempt to supply a system of casuistics; *Halleluja, das ist, Gott in den Sünden verkläret* (part i., Bremen, 1678; never completed), a detailed scheme of the plan of salvation in the form of question and answer; *Wegweiser der Einfältigen zu den ersten Buchstaben des wahren Christentums* (Bremen, 1676), one of his two catechisms; *Der einfältige Christ durch wahren Glauben mit Christo vereinigt* (Eschwege, 1700), his second catechism; and *Der närrische Atheist entdeckt und von seiner Thorheit überzeugt* (2 parts, Bremen, 1689), an attempt to solve intellectual doubts. (W. G. Goeters.)

Bibliography: G. Arnold, *Leben der Gläubigen*, pp. 933–945, Halle, 1732; M. Goebel, *Geschichte des christlichen Lebens*, ii. 300 sqq., 3 vols., Coblenz, 1849–60; H. Heppe, *Geschichte des Pietismus*, i. 371 sqq., Leyden, 1879; A. Ritschl, *Geschichte des Pietismus*, i. 371 sqq., Bonn, 1880; J. F. Iken, *Joachim Neander*, pp. 61–76, 272–279, Bremen, 1880; *ADB*, xxxix. 279–280.

UNDERWOOD, HORACE GRANT: Presbyterian; b. in London July 19, 1859. He was educated at New York University (B.A., 1881) and at New Brunswick Theological Seminary. Since 1885 he has been a missionary in Korea under the auspices of the Presbyterian Board of Foreign Missions, and since 1909 has been principal of the John D. Wells Training School and president of the Korean Religious Tract Society (both at Seoul), as well as chairman of the board of Bible translators at Seoul since 1889. He has likewise been professor of homiletics, church government and discipline, etc., in the Presbyterian theological seminary at Pyeng Yang, Korea, and in 1907 was Deems philosophical lecturer at New York University. His theological position is conservative, and he has written *English-Korean and Korean-English Dictionary* (Yokohama, 1889), *Korean Grammar* (1889), *Call of Korea* (New York, 1908), and *Religions of Eastern Asia* (1910).

UNGODLINESS, UNGODLY: Words used in the English Bible versions and equivalent to the Gk. *asebeia, asebēs* (cf. *asebein*, " to live ungodly ": II Pet. ii. 6; Jude 15), less frequently *amartōlos*, and yet more seldom *anomos*, which in turn are the translations in the Septuagint for the Hebrew *rashaʿ*. The Hebrew word denotes in the first place only the impious and unrighteous in the moral sense. Every thing, however, morally evil, according to the Old-Testament conception as early as the Yahwistic narrative of the garden of Eden, is, in the final analysis, renunciation of God and disobedience to his will. And thus all impiety in Israel is continually represented as proceeding from ungodliness. The contrast between righteousness and ungodliness, moreover, becomes ever more marked in Israelitic and Jewish history until two classes of men are set op-

posite each other, of which the ungodly are described, particularly in the Psalms, from the point of view of the upright (i.e., the strict observers of the law), as originators of trespass and violence toward men; and, in relation to God, as despising his word and rebelling against him. The word *asebeia* also occurs frequently in the Old-Testament apocrypha, especially in the Book of Sirach; but in the New Testament it and kindred terms are relatively infrequent, because here unbelief comes more to the front religiously as the root and form of sin. Where they are used, they mean, for the most part, ungodliness, in the Old-Testament sense synonymous with sin in opposition to righteousness (Rom. i. 18, iv. 5, v. 6, xi. 26; I Tim. i. 9; Titus ii. 12; II Pet. ii. 5–6, iii. 7). In a sense somewhat modified by Christianity they refer to those who remain persistently impervious to the Gospel (I Pet. iv. 18); or to teachers of error (II Tim. ii. 16; Jude 4, 15). On the theoretical side ungodliness issues into Atheism (q.v.). F. Sieffert.

Bibliography: H. Cremer, *Biblisch-theologisch Wörterbuch der neutestamentlichen Gräcität*, Gotha, 1889, Eng. transl., 3d ed., Edinburgh and New York, 1886; H. Schultz, *Alttestamentliche Theologie*, pp. 616 sqq., Göttingen, 1885, Eng. transl., London, 1892; R. Smend, *Alttestamentliche Religionsgeschichte*, 387 sqq., 477 sqq., Freiburg, 1893; C. Clemen, *Die christliche Lehre von der Sünde*, i. 68 sqq., Göttingen, 1897.

UNIATES. See Roman Catholics, II.

UNIFORMITY, ACTS OF: The name of several acts of Parliament establishing the worship and ritual of the Church of England. The first, passed Jan. 21, 1549, set forth the penalties for the neglect to use the Prayer Book of Edward VI., which were, for the first offense, loss of the income of a benefice for a year, and imprisonment for six months; for the second, loss of all benefices, and imprisonment for one year; for the third, imprisonment for life. The second act was passed Apr. 6, 1552, and established the second Prayer Book. These acts were repealed under Queen Mary, in Oct., 1553. The third act, under Queen Elizabeth (passed, after a strong opposition, Apr. 28, 1559), established the new Prayer Book under penalties similar to those of Edward VI., subjected all who were absent from church without excuse to a fine of one shilling, and gave to the sovereign liberty to " ordain and publish such further ceremonies and rites as may be most for the advancement of the church," etc. A fourth act, part of the systematic repression of the Puritans known as the Clarendon Code, was passed May 19, 1662, and prescribed episcopal ordination for all ministers, and enforced the new revision of the Prayer Book. It required all ministers to give their unfeigned assent and consent to everything in the book, to read the Prayer Book service on some Sunday before the feast of St. Bartholomew (Aug. 24), and to swear " that it is not lawful, on any pretense whatsoever, to take up arms against the king." About 2,000 clergymen, some of them the most distinguished in England, unable to conform, were deprived of their livings. This act, the most far-reaching of all in its consequences, also formally disavowed the validity of all but episcopal ordinations, and marked the close of the efforts which had been going on ever since Elizabeth's accession to bring the

Church of England into closer connection with the Reformed communions of the continent. The Act of Uniformity was made practically inoperative, though not formally repealed, by the Act of Toleration (see TOLERATION, ACT OF) under William and Mary, May 24, 1689.

BIBLIOGRAPHY: The text is given in Gee and Hardy, *Documents*, pp. 358 sqq., 369 sqq., 458 sqq., in part also in Robinson, *European History*, ii. 256–259. Consult: H. N. Birt, *The Elizabethan Religious Settlement*, pp. 56, 86–206, London, 1907; S. R. Gardiner, *Students' Hist. of England*, pp. 429, 585, new ed., London and New York, 1895; J. H Overton, *The Church in England*, 2 vols., London, 1897; J. Gairdner, *The English Church in the 16th Century*, pp. 262, 267, 302–303, 324, ib. 1903; W. H. Hutton, *The English Church (1625–1714)*, p. 191, ib. 1903.

UNIGENITUS: A constitution issued Sept. 8, 1713, by Clement XI., condemning 101 propositions advanced by Pasquier Quesnel (q.v.) in his *Réflexions morales sur le Nouveau Testament*. The bull was an important step in the successful struggle with Jansenism (see JANSEN, CORNELIUS), and marked a distinct victory of the Jesuits over the Augustinian tendencies of their opponents. The constitution was confirmed by Clement in the bull *Pastoralis officii* (Aug. 28, 1718), by a decree of Innocent XIII. (Jan. 8, 1722), by Benedict XIII. and the Roman synod of 1725, and by Benedict XIV. In the encyclical *Ex omnibus Christiani orbis regionibus* (Oct. 16, 1756). The reason for the condemnation of some of the propositions was simply the rigid Augustinian sense in which they were interpreted by the Jansenists, with denial of any possibility of the cooperation of free will, such as is taught by Semipelagianism. It is only when this is borne in mind that repudiation of many of the propositions becomes clear. It should also be noted that there was yet another side to the question— Jansenism was really one side of Gallicanism (q.v.), so that there was a political as well as a doctrinal reason for its suppression.

In addition to the citations from the constitution cited in JANSEN, CORNELIUS, § 5, the following condemned propositions may be quoted as indicative of the doctrines henceforth forbidden with the Roman Catholic communion:

When God does not soften the heart by the inner unction of his grace, exhortations and external graces avail only to harden it the more (5).

Grace is the operation of the hand of almighty God, which nothing can hinder or retard (10).

When God wishes to save a soul, and touches it with the inner hand of his grace, no human will resists it (13).

The grace of Jesus Christ is a strong, potent, supreme, invincible grace, seeing that it is the operation of almighty will, the sequence and the initiation of the working of God incarnating and revivifying his Son (21).

Faith is the primal grace, and the source of all others (27).

The first grace which God grants the sinner is forgiveness of sins (28).

All whom God wills to save through Christ are saved infallibly (30).

Jesus Christ gave himself to death to liberate forever those first born through his blood, that is, the elect, from the hand of the destroying angel (32).

The grace of Adam produced only human merits (34).

The sinner is not free except to evil without the grace of the Savior (38).

The will which grace does not anticipate has no light except for erring, no ardor except for hurling itself headlong, no strength except for wounding itself, is capable of all evil, and incapable of any good (39).

No knowledge of God, even natural, even among pagan

XII.—5

philosophers, can come except from God; and without grace it produces only presumption, vanity, and opposition to God himself instead of the feelings of adoration, gratitude, and love (41).

The first effect of baptismal grace is to make us die to sin, so that the spirit, heart, and senses have no more life for sin than a dead man has for the things of the world (43).

Charity is the only thing that talks with God; that alone does God hear (54).

The prayer of the impious is a fresh sin; and what God grants them is a fresh judgment against them (59).

The baptized is still under the law like a Jew if he does not fulfil the law, or fulfils it from fear alone (63).

God never afflicts the innocent; and afflictions always serve either to punish sin or to purify the sinner (70).

The mark of the Christian Church is that it is catholic, comprehending both all the angels of heaven and all the elect and just of the earth and of all the ages (72).

The Church, or the whole Christ, has the incarnate Word as its head, and all the saints as its members (74).

He who does not lead a life worthy of the Son of God and a member of Christ ceases to have within God as his Father and Christ as his head (77).

It is useful and necessary at every time, in every place, and for every class of persons to study and to know the spirit, piety, and mysteries of sacred Scripture (79).

The reading of sacred Scripture is for all (80).

The sacred obscurity of the word of God is no reason for the laity to dispense themselves from its reading (81).

The Lord's Day ought to be sanctified by Christians by readings of piety, and above all of the sacred Scriptures; it is wrong to wish to restrain the Christian from this reading (82).

The fear of unjust excommunication ought never to hinder us from fulfilling our duty; we never go forth from the Church, even when, by the wickedness of men, we seem to be expelled from it, when we are afflicted because of love for God, Jesus Christ, and the Church herself (91).

The state of persecution and punishment which any one bears as a heretic, wicked, and impious man is often the final test and most meritorious, since it makes man more in conformity unto Jesus Christ (98).

Many of these propositions, and many others not cited here, will seem to the Protestant unobjectionable, and even praiseworthy; but fair judgment must not forget that the underlying spirit was antagonistic to the teaching of the Roman Church; and the attitude of rebellion which dictated the whole series would very likely, had the *Unigenitus* not served (though only after stubborn resistance) to check it, have proceeded to extremes which even the Jansenists little anticipated.

BIBLIOGRAPHY: H. Denzinger, *Enchiridion symbolorum, definitionum et declarationum de rebus fidei et morum*, pp. 371–379, 10th ed., Freiburg, 1908; Reich, *Documents*, pp. 386–389; A. Schill, *Die Constitution Unigenitus*, Freiburg, 1876; V. Thuillier, *Fragment de l'hist. de la constitution Unigenitus*, Paris, 1901; G. H. Putnam, *Censorship of the Church of Rome*, i. 360 sqq., New York, 1906.

UNION AMERICAN METHODIST EPISCOPAL CHURCH. See METHODISTS, IV., 9.

UNION, CHRISTIAN SOCIAL: A society founded in 1889 within the Church of England with the object of directing the best thought among churchmen toward the study of social problems and of bringing the influence of that church, as a corporate body, to bear upon the usages and practise of the world of commerce and industry. The impetus in this direction had first been given forty years previously by F. D. Maurice, Charles Kingsley (qq.v.), and several other men of deeply religious convictions, who banded themselves together under the title of "Christian Socialists," this name being adopted because, as Maurice wrote, "It is the only title which will define our object and will commit us at once to the conflict we must engage in sooner or later with the unsocial Christians and the unchristian Socialists."

The leaders of the earlier movement were chiefly Broad-churchmen, but the men who resuscitated it in the eighties were among the most practical and broad-minded of the newer High-church school, such as Brooke Foss Westcott, late bishop of Durham, Charles Gore, the present bishop of Oxford, and Henry Scott Holland (qq.v.). One of its main principles is that the personal responsibility of an individual Christian can never be put out of commission. It is not to be evaded, for example, by membership in a commercial company, either as a director or as a shareholder. One of its most characteristic objects is " to study in common how to apply the moral truths and principles of Christianity to the social and economic difficulties of the present time."

The union comprised at the end of 1910 sixty branches, situated in fifty-three towns and having 5,895 members. Its affairs are managed by an executive comprising several clerical dignitaries and ladies, with the bishop of Oxford (Dr. Gore) as its president. The executive submits from time to time such social problems as the questions of unemployment, of children's labor, or the poor-law system for the study and consideration of the branches. These, again, report upon the facts which they ascertain, and the conclusions which they reach, to a meeting of delegates of the whole union held annually. In studying these subjects, the local bodies investigate the conditions actually obtaining in their own towns. The union seeks to promote its views not so much by direct corporate action as by influencing local authorities and institutions through members of its own who serve on those bodies, and by raising the tone of public opinion generally. It directly promotes, however, the practise of exclusive dealing with firms known to accord reasonable pay and conditions of employment to their staff, and it has published a " white list " of tailors for both sexes in London and elsewhere. In this it discharges the functions of the Consumers' Leagues in the United States. Several branches have made tentative beginnings in the provision of suitable housing for the wage-earning classes. The union maintains a library and a central bureau of information for the use of its members. From time to time it issues reports and pamphlets on such various topics as commercial morality, tradeunionism, illicit commissions, investments, and practicable socialism, besides others of a more directly religious character. Lastly, it brings out a quarterly periodical entitled *The Economic Review*, in which articles of considerable value, written by well-known authorities upon the subjects dealt with, frequently appear.   C. H. D'E. LEPPINGTON.

UNION OF THE CHURCHES.*

I. Anglican Position.
1. Historical Survey.
New-Testament Period (§ 1).
Patristic Period (§ 2).
Medieval Period (§ 3).
Modern Period Through the Sixteenth Century (§ 4).
Since the Sixteenth Century (§ 5).
2. Anglican Platform.
General Attitude (§ 1).
In the American Episcopal Church(§2)
The Lambeth Conference (§ 3).
Episcopal and Presbyterian Negotiations (§ 4).
The Commission for a World Conference (§ 5).
3. Principles of Unity.
Organic Union in Faith and Order (§ 1).

External Uniformity and Parity of Ministries (§ 2).
4. How Unity is to be Achieved.
Trust in God and Christian Love (§ 1).
Broad Investigation, Patience, and Prayer (§ 2).
5. Anglo-Swedish Negotiations.
II. Orthodox Catholic Position.
Recent Decline of Denominationalism (§ 1).
The Four Fundamental Principles (§ 2).
Development of Order in the Primitive Church (§ 3).
Development of Doctrine to 787 (§ 4).

Growing Differentiation Between East and West (§ 5).
The Final Schism (§ 6).
Present Positions of Greek and Latin Churches (§ 7).
Orthodox Catholic Church as a Solution (§ 8).
III. Protestant Position.
Efforts for Reunion with Roman Catholicism (§ 1).
Attempts at Anglican and Protestant Union (§ 2).
Present Protestant Situation (§ 3).
IV. Roman Catholic Position.
Unity of Faith, Government, and Worship Requisite (§ 1).
Position Regarding Non-Roman Communions (§ 2).
V. Supplement.

I. Anglican Position. — 1. Historical Survey: During the New-Testament period the union of Christians was insisted upon by our Lord and his apostles, and in terms and connections which make Christian union and Church unity mutually equivalent. " The Church " stands for the totality of Christians in their organic unity. Our Lord speaks of it in the singular number (Matt. xvi. 18), and nowhere do New-Testament writers speak of " churches " except as referring to local assemblies within one Church, having full communion with each other. Its ministers are given universal and permanent mission to make disciples of all who should believe and be baptized (Matt. xxviii. 19–20), and those who refuse to hear the Church are not to be regarded as faithful Christians (Matt. xviii. 17–18). Christians were to become one flock, under one Shepherd (John x. 16), in a unity

1. New-Testament Period. which is described under the organic figure of the vine and its branches (John xv. 1–6). That his followers might be one was a subject-matter of prayer by Christ on the eve of his crucifixion (John xvii. 20–23); and only an organic unity can satisfy the terms of his prayer. The same conception of unity is found in apostolic teaching, particularly in St. Paul's epistles. All baptized Christians are members of one body, the Church (I Cor. xii. 13; cf. Eph. iv. 5), which is the body of Christ (Eph. i. 23; Col. i. 24). This body is one and possesses one Spirit, one Lord, one faith, one baptism, and one God and Father of all (Eph. iv. 4–6). To

* An article from the Greco-Russian standpoint was arranged for but indefinitely delayed. It may appear later. EDS.

this body God supplies ministers for the perfecting of the saints, the banishment of confusion in doctrine, and the organic increase of the body in love (Eph. iv. 11–16; cf. Rom. xii. 4–5; I Cor. x. 17, xii. 12–31). Nevertheless the schismatic spirit soon began to show itself, especially between Jewish and Gentile Christians, and between local factions at Corinth. The dissensions at Corinth led St. Paul sternly to condemn the division of Christians under rival leaderships (I Cor. i. 10–17, iii. 3–9), and to emphasize the necessity of a common speech and mind, and of charity (I Cor. i. 10, xiii.). The quarrel between Jewish and Gentile Christians threatened to cause a lasting schism, and this led to a conference of apostles, elders, and missionaries at Jerusalem, the result being a clear mutual understanding among the leaders of the Church, and a determination to insist only upon essential things, and not to require uniformity in non-essentials (Acts xv. 1–33). Thus was established an apostolic precedent for dealing with ruptures of Christian unity.

The schismatic spirit soon revived, however, at Corinth, and became the occasion of the "Epistle of Clement," written in behalf of the Roman Church about 95 A.D. (see CLEMENT OF ROME, §§ 3–4), in which it is declared that the ministry of the Church was arranged by the apostles with foreknowledge of the contentions that were to arise concerning the office of oversight (xliv.); and the rise of dissident faction is described as "detestable and unholy sedition" (i.). This teaching is echoed by
2. Patristic Period. Ignatius of Antioch (q.v.), about 110 A.D., in his well-known "Epistles." The imperative need of unity is the chief burden of his letters, and it is made to depend upon loyalty to the bishop with his presbyters and deacons, who together constitute the marks of a real *ekklesia* (e.g., *Ad Trallianos*, iii.). He says in one representative passage, "If any man followeth one that maketh a schism, he doth not inherit the kingdom of God" (*Ad Ephesios*, iv.; cf. *Ad Philadelphenos*, iii.). The rise of Montanistic and Gnostic sectarianism caused the obligation of Church unity to be emphasized by various writers (e.g., Irenæus, *Hær.*, IV., xxxiii. 1, 7; Clement of Alexandria, *Strom.*, VII., xvii. 107; Dionysius of Alexandria, in Eusebius, *Hist. eccl.*, vi. 45). Cyprian of Carthage (q.v.) wrote a treatise, *De unitate ecclesiæ*, in which he makes the episcopate the center of unity. The general sentiment of the ancients was registered in the Constantinopolitan Creed, "I believe . . . in one, holy, catholic, and apostolic Church." Various schisms arose, but the sentiment that schism is sinful prevailed throughout this period, and the main body of Christians, both East and West, with a few brief interruptions, succeeded in maintaining intercommunion and visible unity. Each local bishop was recognized as the center of unity within his jurisdiction, while the unity of the episcopate at large was secured by the development of provinces, each having its metropolitan, and of five patriarchates, severally centering in Rome, Constantinople, Alexandria, Antioch, and Jerusalem. Political circumstances gave to Rome the foremost place, and to Constantinople, as new Rome, the second place.

Serious controversies were usually dealt with, however, by councils of bishops—provincial or general, according to necessity (see COUNCILS AND SYNODS, §§ 1–3).

The claims which began to be made by the Roman see in the patristic period became in the Middle Ages a chief cause of permanent schism between the East and West; although other causes also were operative. The division of the Roman Empire, coupled with the decline of civilization, caused mutual isolation, accentuated racial differences, and
3. Medieval Period. gave fictitious importance to every mutual divergence in practise and terminology. Frequent quarrels took place between Rome and Constantinople, and matters reached a climax in 1054 A.D., when a permanent schism began. The more prominent issues between the two Churches were (1) the claims of the papal see; (2) the insertion by the West of the *Filioque* clause in the Nicene Creed (see FILIOQUE CONTROVERSY); and the use by the Westerns of unleavened bread in the Eucharist. Attempts at reunion were made at the councils of Lyons (1274) and Florence (1439), which grew out of the need which the Eastern Empire felt of assistance in its struggle with the Turks. The motive was worldly, and although at each council important concordats were adopted by representatives of both churches, the fanaticism of the Eastern monastic clergy and populace made them abortive. The schism remains unhealed.

The sixteenth century saw the Protestant revolt, out of which has grown the multiplicity of religious bodies which now divide Christian allegiance in the Western world. Its well-known causes need not be described, but it took two forms—the Lutherans and Reformed (Calvinists and Zwinglians) developed presbyterial and congregational ministries; while the Anglicans retained the threefold ministry, although rejecting papal jurisdiction over themselves; and the Swedes retained an episcopate, but abandoned the diaconate. All of the revolting bodies except the Anglicans rejected the sacerdotal conception of the ministry, and with vary-
4. Modern Period Through the Sixteenth Century. ing completeness abandoned the sacramental doctrines of the medieval Church, in order to remove what they regarded as barriers between individual souls and the pardoning grace of God. This revolt had an inevitable tendency to deaden —in some directions to destroy—belief in the visible Church as the mystical body of Christ, and as intended by Christ to be united forever in a visible intercommunion by a common faith and ministry. Accordingly, the spirit of dissent grew mightily; and in spite of efforts to stay the process, Western Christendom has become broken up into several hundred rival bodies.

Numerous attempts at reunion have since been made, but the world-wide aspects of the problem have not often been faced. Among these attempts the following are of chief historical importance: (1) The Conference of Marburg, 1529 (see MARBURG, CONFERENCE OF), between Lutheran and Zwinglian theologians; an attempt to harmonize sacramental views, but defeated by the rigid position of Luther.

(2) The Wittenberg Concord (see WITTENBERG, CONCORD OF), 1536, really Lutheran, but accepted with explanations by the Swiss; soon rendered abortive through the same cause. (3) The *Thirteen Articles*, 1538, adopted by a conference of Anglican and Lutheran theologians in England but nullified in the following year by the reactionary *Six Articles* of Henry VIII. (see SIX ARTICLES, ACT OF THE). (4) The Conference of Regensburg, 1541 (see REGENSBURG, CONFERENCE OF), agreeing that salvation is through the merits of Christ, but blocked by Luther's refusal to compromise, and rejected by the Diet of Regensburg in 1546. (5) The Interims of Augsburg and Leipsic in 1548 (see INTERIM), Charles V. making concessions to the Protestants in the former, and Melanchthon conceding much Roman Catholic ritual, polity, and doctrine as *adiaphora* in the latter; but neither was adopted, and from the Leipsic Interim developed the adiaphoristic and synergistic controversies (1550–55, 1550–70; see ADIAPHORA, AND THE ADIAPHORISTIC CONTROVERSIES; SYNERGISM). (6) The Philippist movement (see PHILIPPISTS) to unite Lutherans and Calvinists, resulting in the crypto-Calvinistic controversy (1552–74) and leading to the crystallization of Lutheranism in the Formula of Concord (q.v.) of 1577. (7) Negotiations with the East were undertaken in 1575 by certain Protestant theologians of Tübingen, who approached Jeremiah II. (q.v.), patriarch of Constantinople; but both sides were soon convinced that the doctrinal and ecclesiastical cleavage between the two bodies was too great to permit union. Cyril Lucar (q.v.), patriarch successively of Alexandria and Constantinople, came in touch with Reformed theologians in 1612, and drew up a confession in the interests of closer relations, which was published in 1629; but the only effect was to bring persecution upon him, and an orthodox creed of Petrus Mogilas (q.v.) of Kief, adopted by all Eastern patriarchs in 1643, accentuated the failure of Cyril's efforts. (8) Georg Calixtus (q.v.), professor at Helmstädt after 1614, founded a Lutheran school which minimized the divergences of Lutheranism from papal doctrine, and advocated union on a basis of return to the symbols and conciliar decisions of the first five centuries. An abortive conference held at Thorn in 1645, arranged by Wladislaus, king of Poland (see THORN, CONFERENCE OF), produced the syncretistic controversies (see SYNCRETISM) between the Calixtines and the conservative Lutherans. Secret travels of Cristoval Rojas de Spinola (q.v.), who sought to win Lutherans to the papal obedience (1676), were followed by negotiations for union (1691–94), in which Gerhard Molanus and Gottfried Wilhelm Leibnitz (qq.v.) represented the Protestants, and Spinola and Jacques Bénigne Bossuet (q.v.) the Roman Catholics, while further correspondence occurred between Bossuet and Leibnitz (1699–1701) but without result. (9) A correspondence between Archbishop William Wake (q.v.) of Canterbury and certain Gallican theologians (from 1716) was prompted by a desire of the Gallicans to enlist the support of the English Church, through its return to the Roman

5. Since the Sixteenth Century.

obedience, in their defense of national liberties; but Wake refused to entertain the idea of such return. (10) The English non-jurors' negotiations with the East (1716–25), given with some fulness in T. Lathbury's *History of the Non-Jurors*, London, 1862, ch. viii., came to no result; but the correspondence throws light on the conditions to be reckoned with in negotiations with Eastern Churches. (11) The Evangelical United Church of Prussia was constituted in 1817 by Frederick William III. through union of the Lutherans and Calvinists in one state Church (see UNION, ECCLESIASTICAL), but the union was only partially successful, and an old Lutheran reaction occurred, the dissidents in time obtaining recognition. (12) In America the Presbyterians, after suffering some disintegration, have achieved partial reunions. The Old School and New School Presbyterians were united in 1869, and the Presbyterian Church in the U.S.A. united with the Cumberland Presbyterian Church in 1906. The Council of Reformed Churches in the U.S. holding the Presbyterian System was constituted in 1907, while the Canadian Presbyterians were united in 1875 into the Presbyterian Church in Canada (see PRESBYTERIANS, VIII., 3a, § 4, 12, § 3). A union of Methodists in Canada in 1874 and 1883 constituted the Methodist Church of Canada (see METHODISTS, IV., 10, § 3), and a large proportion of the Lutherans in the United States are more or less closely affiliated with a General Council (see LUTHERANS, III., § 8). (13) The Bonn Reunion Conferences, held in 1874 and 1875, were attended by theologians of the Old Catholic Eastern Orthodox, Anglican, Lutheran, and Reformed communions, and several propositions were agreed to, especially with regard to the *Filioque* controversy. (14) The Pan-Anglican Movement for unity, initiated by the American House of Bishops in 1886, will be considered in the next part of this article. It may also be well to refer to several movements which, although not reunion movements in the strict sense of the phrase, throw light upon the problem. The Uniate Movements (see ROMAN CATHOLICS, II.) represent various submissions of Eastern Christians to the papal see, the Uniates being given certain concessions, including marriage of the clergy. Members of various Protestant communions have formed alliances and federations, which leave these communions in possession of their denominational independence. They are not church unions, but are designed to reduce the evil effects of disunion, and to secure interdenominational cooperation on certain lines. Notable examples are the Evangelical Alliance (q.v.), founded in 1845, the Alliance of the Reformed Churches throughout the world holding the Presbyterian System, founded in 1875 (see ALLIANCE OF THE REFORMED CHURCHES), and the Federal Council of the Churches of Christ in America, organized in 1906, and including members of thirty-four denominations. [A movement for the union of Canadian Methodists, Presbyterians, and Congregationalists is at present in an advanced stage of progress. Mention should also be made of the efforts of Old Catholics to secure union with the Anglican and Oriental churches. A. H. N.]

2. Anglican Platform: The Anglican communion possesses important points of contact and sympathy with all types of Christianity, whether they are called Catholic or Protestant. Its position is really unique in this regard; and the work of mediating and of laboring for Christian reunion seems to be providentially assigned to the Anglican churches. Accordingly, the problem of unity has loomed large in Anglican thought and effort. The Anglican realizes than an adequate movement for reunion must be world-wide in its scope—embracing both Catholics and Protestants within its ultimate reference; but he also perceives that positive elements of truth are included in the contentions of the different communions, elements which are vital to Christianity, and which may not be surrendered or driven into neglect even in the interests of unity. A union obtained by compromise in such matters can not, he believes, be either permanent or blessed. Love must be paramount, but a love which encourages men to act contrary to their deeper convictions is surely unchristian.

The American Protestant Episcopal Church inherits the Anglican position and the advantages described above in relation to the problem of unity. Moreover, two circumstances have tended to accentuate these advantages: exemption from the hindrances to free action which connection with the State involves, and the fact that immigration has brought almost every communion of Christendom into its immediate neighborhood. Accordingly, the problem of unity has assumed peculiar and increasing importance among the members of that church, and in the deliberations of its general conventions. Since 1853 various joint committees have been appointed and continued on church unity, and on ecclesiastical relations with various churches, and these committees have engaged in much fraternal negotiation, and have helped to remove certain mutual misunderstandings. In response to a memorial, the House of Bishops issued in 1886 its well-known *Declaration on Unity,* to which was appended an expression of " our desire and readiness . . . to enter into brotherly conference with all or any Christian Bodies seeking the restoration of the organic unity of the Church, with a view to the earnest study of the conditions under which so priceless a blessing might happily be brought to pass " (*Journal of the General Convention of 1886,* pp. 79–80). This declaration mentions four particulars—the so-called Quadrilateral (text in FUNDAMENTAL DOCTRINES OF CHRISTIANITY, § 4) —which have been widely understood to represent formal terms of unity, an acceptance of which would suffice to secure union with the Episcopal Church, although, as a matter of fact, these particulars were given as leading instances of what the bishops declared to be " inherent parts " of " the substantial deposit of Christian Faith and Order committed by Christ and his Apostles to the Church unto the end of the world, and therefore incapable of compromise or surrender." The document was expository. The bishops neither did nor could (except with the concurrence of the House of Deputies) offer formal terms of union; they simply declared what they believed to be fundamental principles, and left the discussion of terms to the future.

In 1888 the Lambeth Conference (q.v.) of the bishops in communion with the see of Canterbury adopted a resolution in which the American " Quadrilateral " was embodied, as follows: " That in the opinion of this conference, the following Articles supply a basis on which approach may be by God's blessing made toward Home Reunion: (A) The Holy Scriptures of the Old and New Testaments, as containing all things necessary to salvation, and as being the rule and ultimate standard of faith. (B) The Apostles' Creed, as the Baptismal Symbol; and the Nicene Creed, as the sufficient statement of the Christian Faith. (C) The two sacraments ordained by Christ himself—Baptism and the Supper of the Lord—ministered with unfailing use of Christ's words of Institution, and of the elements ordained by him. (D) The Historic Episcopate, locally adapted in the methods of its administration to the varying needs of the nations and peoples called of God into the unity of his Church." The conference recommended brotherly conferences " in order to consider what steps can be taken either toward corporate reunion, or toward such relations as may prepare the way for fuller organic unity hereafter." Thus the whole Anglican episcopate adopted the American platform (*Lambeth Conferences of 1867, 1878, and 1888,* ed. R. T. Davidson, London, 1889, pp. 280–281). The claim that the historic episcopate was " committed by Christ and his Apostles to the Church unto the end of the world " has been much debated. Modern scholars consider that the episcopate originated by organic development rather than by formal appointment *ab initio;* but the manner of its origin is immaterial, if its development was determined in result by the Holy Spirit, and if the continuance of the episcopate is by Christ's will. The conviction that it is his will can alone justify making acceptance of the episcopate an essential condition of unity, and until non-episcopal bodies reach this conviction, they can not be expected to acknowledge that the historic episcopate is essential. In brief, an important difference of conviction must be removed before the " Quadrilateral " can become a generally accepted basis for the discussion of terms of unity.

The negotiations which followed between committees appointed by the Episcopal and Presbyterian Churches (1887–96) represent in their lack of results what was inevitable. The Presbyterian committee took the ground that no negotiations for union could be pursued by it except on equal terms with regard to the ministry, and the Northern General Assembly of 1896 in courteous terms suspended correspondence with the Episcopal commission until it might " be reopened by the acceptance by that [the Episcopal] Church of the doctrine of ' mutual recognition and reciprocity.' " This negative result accentuates the undeniable fact that, so long as certain existing differences touching faith and order continue, formal negotiations for unity between the bodies thus differing

[margin: 1. General Attitude.]

[margin: 2. In the American Episcopal Church.]

[margin: 3. The Lambeth Conference.]

[margin: 4. Episcopal and Presbyterian Negotiations.]

will be abortive. Sincere Christians will not unite at the cost of convictions which they deem (whether rightly or not) to be vital. The problem of unity is inseparable from the problem of securing sufficient agreement concerning questions of faith and order for Christian communions to unite without sacrificing anything which they deem to be vital, and without sanctioning anything which they consider to be subversive of Christian principles. And yet the cause of unity is too vital, and too directly commended to our efforts by Christ, to be abandoned because formal negotiations for union are not yet practicable. The essentials of Christianity are too well attested, and too mighty in their practical and persuasive power, to be permanently obscured by the controversial issues and prejudices of our time. The work for unity must go on. Christ prayed for it, and declared that his followers should constitute one flock. God wills it; and what God wills he helps us to bring to pass by his Holy Spirit. Recent defeats mean simply that there must be further preparation; and formal schemes of unity must be deferred until efforts have been made to secure a better mutual understanding, and foster common growth into the larger mind of Christ. The only external procedure for promoting union which appears to be available consists of candid and loving conferences between leaders of different communions for the discussion of difference in faith and order.

The appointment of a joint commission for a world conference on faith and order by the General Convention of the Episcopal Church at Cincinnati Oct. 19, 1910, was dictated by these considerations, and its significance can best be defined in the terms of the report and resolution which that convention accepted and unanimously adopted: ". . . We believe that the time has now arrived when representatives of the whole family of Christ, led by the Holy Spirit, may be willing to come together for the consideration of questions of Faith and Order. . . . We would heed this call of the Spirit of God. . . . We would place ourselves by the side of our fellow Christians, . . . convinced that our one hope of mutual understanding is in taking personal counsel together in the spirit of love and forbearance. It is our conviction that such a conference for the purpose of study and discussion, without power to legislate or to adopt resolutions, is the next step toward unity. With grief for our aloofness in the past, and for other faults of pride and self-sufficiency, which make for schism; with loyalty to the truth as we see it, and with respect for the convictions of those who differ from us; holding the belief that the beginnings of unity are to be found in the clear statement and full consideration of those things in which we differ, as well as of those things in which we are at one, we respectfully submit the following resolution: Whereas, There is to-day among all Christian people a growing desire for the fulfilment of our Lord's Prayer that all his disciples may be one; that the world may believe that God has sent him: Resolved, . . . That a Joint Commission be appointed to bring about a conference for the consideration of questions

5. The Commission for a World Conference.

touching Faith and Order, and that all Christian Communions throughout the world which confess our Lord Jesus Christ as God and Savior be asked to unite with us in arranging for and conducting such a conference." Seven bishops, seven presbyters, and seven laymen were duly appointed to constitute this commission, and several members have since been added. The commission organized at once, and appointed a committee on plan and scope to which the executive business is largely given. The Rt. Rev. Charles P. Anderson, bishop of Chicago, is president of the commission; the Rev. William T. Manning, rector of Trinity Church, New York, is chairman of the committee on plan and scope; Mr. R. H. Gardiner, 11 Pemberton Square, Boston, Mass., is secretary; and Mr. George Zabriskie is treasurer. It is to be noticed that the commission is not authorized to retain in its hands the preparation for, and management of, the proposed conference, for this is left to the representatives in general of the commissions which consent to participate, and all are equally to share in the business. While the Cincinnati convention was sitting, the American Congregationalists and the Disciples were constituting similar commissions, and these are in cordial touch with the Episcopal commission. The Presbyterians have also welcomed the movement, and representatives of other bodies, including the Roman Catholic and Eastern Orthodox Churches, have shown interest. The undertaking will necessarily require several years for its achievement, but the signs are encouraging.

3. Principles of Unity: These can be briefly stated. Unity is inseparable from some form of corporate or organic union. Whatever passing expedients may be adopted to reduce the evils of sectarian division, real union is vital to the fulfilment of our Lord's prayer, and of New-Testament teaching—a union that will restore full intercommunion between Christian believers; that will eliminate rivalry between Christian ministries in their internal, religious, and sacramental functions, as well as in those external activities which existing federations seek to harmonize; and that will foster such world-wide harmony of working conditions as is needful for the growth of Christians in one mind and one faith. The New Testament, as has been stated, treats the Church not only as having one Lord, but as constituting one body, which upbuilds itself in love. Corporate union should, therefore, be consciously kept in view as the ultimate aim of all efforts for Christian unity. This is not generally realized; and to bring Christians to see that it is so is an important part of present labor for unity. Nor can this unity be secured except on the basis of a common faith and order—that is, substantial agreement concerning matters which are deemed essential to Christianity and to the fulfilment of Christ's will. This agreement can only be obtained, as the bishops of the Protestant Episcopal Church say in their declaration of 1886, " by the return of all Christian Communions to the principles of unity exemplified by the undivided Catholic Church during the first ages of its existence." If any principles can constitute a common faith and order, they must

1. Organic Union in Faith and Order.

be these; and these surely constitute, as the bishops declared, " the substantial deposit of Christian Faith and Order committed by Christ and his Apostles to the Church unto the end of the world, and therefore incapable of compromise or surrender by those who have been ordained to be its stewards and trustees for the common and equal benefit of all men." The Anglican Church consistently adheres to this standpoint. The whole meaning of its initiation of the movement for a world conference on faith and order is to help to bring about the mutual understanding, and the friendly cooperation in study, which is necessary for the growth of all Christians into one mind concerning what has been received from Christ.

The impossibility of securing external uniformity in non-essentials, and the necessity that a truly Catholic religion should be practically adapted to every race, condition, and tempera-

2. External Uniformity and Parity of Ministries. ment, should be clearly realized. Yet there is an obvious limitation to this principle. True unity requires decency and order, even in things not intrinsically vital. There must be visible harmony even in things of human ordering; so that Christians can feel at home in the Church wherever they go; and so that the divergencies of use that remain shall not appear to represent a conflict of principles and ideals. The Supper of the Lord is the sacramental and working center of unity; and its general method should be at least as uniform, broadly speaking, as is consistent with the edification of diverse peoples and temperaments. The elasticity of the Church's devotional life is most fully to be attained in the devotions and usages which supplement and fill out this central service. The thorny question of parity of ministries ought not to be forced to the front until it is more ripe for settlement. In particular, mutual reciprocity in ministerial functions can not be pressed without imperiling the earlier stages of growth toward unity. For Christians of different bodies to confer successfully is possible only by treating ministerial claims as a subject for discussion and study, rather than as a mutually accepted platform; and to treat the subject in this mutually non-committal way is entirely consistent with faithfulness to conviction on the part of all.

4. How Unity is to be Achieved: This is certainly not by mere human effort and wisdom, nor on lines which can with certainty be described beforehand; but by the working of the Holy Spirit, in manners known only to God, and in God's own time. The certainty that Christian unity, and

1. Trust in God and Christian Love. therefore union, is God's will, and the assurance that the Holy Spirit is the real cause of the growing demand for unity, show clearly that Christians ought to labor for the union of Christendom, and that such labor will not, in the long run, prove abortive. The most powerful human factor is love—love which is strong enough to bridge the gulfs that divide the Christian world, to overcome denominational pride, to fortify patient courtesy and persistent study in the face of polemical war-cries, and to enlighten our minds to distinguish

what is essential truth, and incapable of compromise, from what is not.

Another important human factor would appear to be modern cosmopolitanism in religious investigation. In our day the results of Christian research in every land rapidly become common property. No doubt these results are often obscured

2. Broad Investigation, Patience, and Prayer. and given perverted explication from rationalistic standpoints, but the power of truth to accredit itself, and to prevail against caricature, is to be counted on. Above all, the Holy Spirit can be reckoned upon, 'whose enlightening grace will enable sincere truth-seekers everywhere to profit by cosmopolitan scholarship, and to utilize it from a truly Christian standpoint for the attainment of increasing unity of faith. To doubt it is to doubt Providence. Time also is a vital factor. Reunion may indeed become possible sooner and more suddenly than was dreamed, but in any case it will come as precipitating and revealing results of much hidden growth, of workings that have gone on for generations. The point requiring emphasis is that unity can not be forced before God's moment; and until that moment arrives, efforts to formulate the precise conditions and terms of unity must serve as a hindrance rather than a help to the cause of unity. Prayer—unceasing and habitual prayer for unity, and for the Christian graces and illumination which make for it—is absolutely indispensable. Prayer is necessary to afford the human conditions of the Spirit's work, to develop love, and to enable us all to grow in one. The following prayer is widely used in certain communions, and might well be used by all Christians: " O Lord Jesus Christ, who saidst unto Thine Apostles, Peace I leave with you, My peace I give unto you; regard not our sins, but the Faith of Thy Church; and grant her that peace and unity which is agreeable to Thy will: Who livest and reignest God for ever and ever. Amen."

FRANCIS J. HALL.

5. Anglo-Swedish Negotiations: [After some preliminary unofficial negotiations in 1888 and 1897 between the Anglican and Swedish Churches, the archbishop of Canterbury, at the request of the Lambeth Conference in 1908, appointed a committee to inquire into the possibility of closer relations between the two communions, the initial basis being the fact that the Swedish Church, alone of Lutheran communions, has preserved an episcopate. The report of this commission has declared that " the succession of bishops has been maintained unbroken by the Church of Sweden, and that it has a true conception of the episcopal office. . . . That the office of priest is also rightly conceived as a divinely instituted instrument for the ministry of the Word and Sacraments, and that it has been in intention handed on throughout the whole history of the Church of Sweden." It is, accordingly, recommended that at the next Lambeth Conference (or at a meeting of English bishops) a resolution be adopted which, like that regarding the Old Catholics of Germany, Austria, and Switzerland (adopted in 1888), will permit " members of the National Church of Sweden, otherwise qualified to receive the Sacrament in their own Church," to be admitted to Holy

Communion in the Anglican Church. It is also recommended that, in case Swedish churches are not available, the use of Anglican churches be permitted, with the consent of the diocesan, for marriages, burials, etc.; while Swedish ecclesiastics might profitably be permitted to give addresses occasionally in Anglican pulpits. It is the hope of the commission that there may ultimately be intercommunion between the two churches. On the other hand, it must not be forgotten that there are grave barriers still, even after Anglican acknowledgment of the validity of Swedish orders. Thus in Sweden the diaconate has been lost since the seventeenth century, and confirmation is administered (when administered at all) by the second order of the ministry, as in non-episcopal Lutheran bodies; while reference to the " holy Catholic Church " has been expunged from the Creeds. Though one may waive, as more than counterbalanced by other passages in the liturgy, the substitution in the ordinal, from 1809 to 1894, of " preaching office " (*prediko-embet*) for " priestly offices " (*prestembet*) (but see Bishop G. M. Williams, in *The Living Church*, xliii. 18–19), there can be little doubt that, as has been semiofficially declared by Swedish Lutherans, the Swedish communion regards the episcopate as " a good external order which ought to be retained, but which is not essential to the life of the Church," while the Swedish Church itself is classed as one of several " Lutheran Churches " (the alleged point of contact between the Anglican and Swedish Churches that both are Protestant may be due to the fact that *katolsk* in Swedish means only " Roman Catholic ").

In the United States this movement has encountered bitter opposition on the part of the various Lutheran bodies, especially in the Augustana Synod, an intensely antiepiscopal body (see Bishop Williams, in *The Living Church*, xliv. 165, 173, 201), to which the majority of Swedish immigrants naturally first turn.

The outcome of the efforts for Anglo-Swedish intercommunion it would be premature to forecast.]

II. Orthodox Catholic Position: One of the most promising signs of the times, in the present divided state of Christianity in Europe and America, is that this generation is witnessing the waning of active sectarian antagonism. The former constant strife of partizan polemics inseparable from denominational dissension, which has silenced again and again irenic writers pleading for Christian charity, and urging the mutual approach, recognition, and ultimate union of the several reformed communions in the West, is ending slowly but surely; and even the newer dissenting divisions of those same older communions, each of which, whether large or small, was organized as an evident consequence of minor doctrinal differences, magnified or overstated by implacable theological partizans during the continuation of the successive reforming movements since the sixteenth century, are striving to find in their common ecclesiastical descent, and in their similar statements of belief, an effective basis for cooperation and for union. Until the last decade of the nineteenth century, de-

1. Recent Decline of Denominationalism.

cided and uncompromising denominationalism was the common characteristic of American Christianity; but during this period a movement as significant as it was spontaneous, the gradual restoration of ritual, became evident, and has resulted everywhere in the more and more general observance of the chief festivals and commemorations of the Western church year. That even various praiseworthy leaders in the several reformed communions, whose Puritan forefathers had rejected and repudiated those same Christian symbols and sacred historic ceremonies, should strive so successfully to regain more and more of their ecclesiastical inheritance gives promise of the coming of a second great spiritual renaissance. This revival of ritual, with the restoration of the church year to its former vitalizing function in the parochial life of the people, could not fail to direct the attention of many earnest denominational scholars to the renewed study of the faith, government, and worship of the primitive Catholic Church; while the reexamination of these seemingly separate yet clearly connected subjects which were debated so defiantly in the past by the sectarian scholars of the sixteenth and seventeenth centuries has been facilitated during the present period by searching studies of recently discovered documents that both simplify and at times solve successfully many perplexing ecclesiastical problems. One of the most reassuring results of this recent reaction from post-Reformation prejudices and preferences is seen in the increasing consciousness of the defects and dangers of denominationalism, and there is also a general willingness on the part of these same separated communions to discuss fraternally, and to define irenically, the doctrinal differences which divide them, not only from each other, but also from their common mother, the Western or Latin Church, and from its elder sister, the Eastern or Greek Church.

The well-known " Quadrilateral " of the Protestant Episcopal bishops of America, afterward affirmed in 1888 without change by the Lambeth Conference (q.v.; see also above, I., 2, § 3), called forth many essays discussing, from various denominational positions, the desirability or the necessity of Christian union. This joint Anglican proposal has been thus far seemingly unsuccessful, but it has certainly aided in directing the attention of the clergy and the laity, in both England and America, to the necessity for Christian cooperation and eventual corporate union. In no other way can the Church of Christ even regain, during the present period, much less increase in the future, its all but impotent spiritual influence over modern materialism, that significant symbol and dangerous defect of our complicated Western civilization. At the end of the first decade of the twentieth century, the memorable Edinburgh World Missionary Conference (1910) is evidence of the increasing interest in the searching historic study of the four ecclesiastical fundamentals of the " Quadrilateral," since summarized under the connected titles of " Faith and Order." Faith has always been defined to be generically the authoritative traditional teaching of Christ the Incarnate Logos,

2. The Four Fundamental Principles.

later recorded by the inspired writers of the four canonical Gospels. But this fundamental Christian faith includes necessarily also the inspired teaching contained in the canonical writings of the chosen apostles, which was later expanded logically, and developed consistently into the orthodox doctrinal declarations of the undivided Catholic Church, deduced cautiously as they were, word by word, from these same sacred Scriptures, and defined authoritatively in the accepted conciliar creeds and ecumenically binding dogmatic decrees, and also witnessed continually by the orthodox hierarchical successors of the apostles in the traditional eucharistic liturgies used by the faithful throughout the then known world. The searching analytical study of the apostolic age will reveal clearly how these four historic fundamentals of the primitive Church emerged one by one, and were slowly but consistently coordinated by the inevitable strifes and schisms of that formative missionary period into energizing divine principles for maintaining unity in the faith, sacraments, and order of the expanding Christian Church. Nor was their divinely imparted influence less evident during the succeeding post-apostolic period, when their pervasive spiritual power, both of restraining doctrinal dissension and of controlling destructive division, continued to stimulate and strengthen both the clergy and the faithful to resist resolutely all adverse attacks both from within and from without, until the separate parochial units of the primitive Christian Church, each with its presiding bishop and college of presbyters, became compact and confederated through their participation in, and support of, the successive councils of the undivided Catholic Church.

When the apostles began their appointed work of proclaiming the Gospel of the risen and ascended Christ, by baptizing all nations and teaching them to observe all his commandments (Matt. xxviii. 19), there is already evident the latent presence of these four divine fundamentals: the unwritten, traditional Gospel, the Confession of Faith, " thou art the Christ, the Son of the living God " (Matt. xvi. 16; cf. Acts viii. 37)—soon expanded into fuller and more definite creedal forms—the sacraments of the Church—baptism, the eucharist, and remission of sins, and the unorganized hierarchy contained complete in the apostolate (John xx. 19–

3. Development of Order in the Primitive Church. 23)—this necessarily including the apostolic authority of declaring and defining, from time to time, all parts of that divinely revealed faith, implied in the plenary power to teach, to bind, and to loose, conferred on them by Christ himself. Thus the apostolic Christian Church is seen to be constituted with every essential principle, element, and power needed day by day for its continuous growth and consistent divine development before even the first line of the New Testament had been written, and before the first public proclamation of the Gospel by the twelve chosen witnesses of the resurrection of the ascended Christ. But soon the various needs of the increasing number of believers required the appointment of the first deacons to assist the apostles in the care of converts (Acts vi. 3–6). Here is evidently, by divine direction, both the institution of the diaconate, the lowest of the three orders in the primitive hierarchy, and the addition of ordination, conferred by the proper ordaining prayers with the imposition of hands on the clergy, to the apostolic sacraments of the Christian Church. Although the service of the deacons was at first restricted to the charitable work of the expanding Church, one of them, Philip, was impelled to preach the Gospel to the people of Samaria, whereupon the apostles in Jerusalem, hearing that the people of Samaria had accepted the Gospel, sent Peter and John to lay their hands on them that they might also receive the gift of the Holy Ghost (Acts viii. 5–17), thereby adding confirmation to the primitive sacraments of the Church; while in the general epistle of James (v. 14) is recorded the apostolic rite or sacrament of unction of the sick. The recognition of the converted Paul, the divinely designated apostle to the Gentiles, who had already completed the three orders of the hierarchy by the ordination of elders or presbyters in every church (Acts xiv. 23), occurred at the first council of the Church in Jerusalem, in which the apostolic power of the keys was used in the conflict of the Judaizing missionaries with Paul, whose authoritative teaching was confirmed unto all the churches (Acts xv. 1–29) by the assembled college of the apostles. This simple but divinely inspired decree was thenceforth to transform slowly and silently the expanding Judeo-Gentile Church into that homogeneous Christian Church which was later to carry the Gospel to the farthest boundaries of the known world.

In these historic accounts in the Acts and in the pastoral epistles of Paul are seen continually the energizing effects of the apostolic use of the four fundamentals of the undivided Church, the forming Scriptures of the New Testament, the expanding Creed, the constant administration of the primitive Sacraments, and the presence everywhere of the organized hierarchy of three distinct orders, the itinerant apostles, the settled bishops or presbyters (Acts xx. 17, 28), and the local deacons, who cared for the spiritual and temporal needs of the faithful in the several cities. Since, however, the preaching of that divinely revealed faith evoked from time to time the counter claims of sectarians seeking by their errors to attach followers to themselves, the apostolic witnesses were continually inspired to define more and more clearly the traditional teaching of Christ, until the simple creedal statement of Matt. xvi. 16 and Acts viii. 37 was already amplified in I Cor. viii. 6 and I Tim. iii. 16 (cf. also Heb. vi. 1–2). Its expansion continues by tradition from teacher to teacher in the Christian hierarchy, as is evident from the writings of the post-apostolic witnesses Ignatius (*Ad Trallianos*, ix.), Irenæus (*Hær.*, I., x. 1), Tertullian (*Adv. Praxean*, ii.), Origen of Alexandria (*De principiis*), Gregory Thaumaturgus, Lucian the Martyr, and Eusebius of Cæsarea (qq.v.), until in 325 the orthodox Christian faith was formally defined in the first Nicene creed, which was later enlarged, and officially accepted, through its individual bishops as the hierarchical successors of the

4. Development of Doctrine to 787.

apostles, by the Catholic Church everywhere. From this time onward, the ecumenical councils of the undivided Church assembled again and again to declare and reaffirm the orthodox Christian creed, to define heresy and denounce error, to decide disputes relating to the hierarchy, ritual, and discipline, and to enact canons and decrees for the general government of the Church throughout the Roman Empire. Preceding this conciliar period from 325 A.D. to 787 A.D., and continuing concurrently with it, the two historic complementing halves of the expanding Christian Church, the Church of the East and the Church of the West, were already acquiring unconsciously their later fixed characteristic forms. Both are originally Greek in language, and possess and use in common the same four apostolic fundamentals for the propagation of the Gospel, and for the pastoral care of the faithful.

The Eastern Church, influenced by an environment permeated with Alexandrian mysticism, and also by the philosophical problems of the Greeks, especially the origin of the material world, the existence and nature of the invisible creating Deity, and the hidden source of evil, concentrated more and

5. Growing Differentiation Between East and West.
more consistently its theological teaching on the elucidation of the second question, and thereby eventually completed for the entire Church of all ages the first part of the orthodox Catholic dogma of the ecumenical Christian faith, Christology, by developing cautiously and defining concisely the connected doctrines of the incarnation, the person of Christ, and the Trinity. The Western Church was destined to become more and more different from its elder sister in the East through the influence of its own daughter, the Latin Church of North Africa, whose three illustrious teachers, Tertullian, Cyprian, and Augustine (qq.v.), influenced irresistibly by the legalism of Latin life and civilization, developed successively those distinguishing Latin doctrines of soteriology and the constitution of the Catholic Church which were to transform slowly and steadily the Greek Church of the West into the theocratic Latin Church ruled by the popes of Rome during the coming centuries of strife and struggle. To these directing ecclesiastical influences must be added that potent political factor which has had such far-reaching consequences through the centuries to the present day. When the Roman Emperor Constantine the Great (q.v.) became the victorious ruler of the West, and also the undisputed ruler of the entire East, his powerful personality as the historic convener of the Nicene Concil in 325, and the builder of the new capital of Constantinople in 326, could not fail to affect the ultimate destinies of both the eastern and western branches of that undivided Catholic Church which he now protected personally. While the existence of the successive bishops of Rome was obscured by the presence of the resident emperors, the ruler of the Roman Church was only one of the coequal heads of the confederated Christian communities constituting the Church of the West; and as long as Rome remained the imperial residence, the pope's ecclesias-

tical authority was historically subordinate to the prevailing secular power of the Roman emperors. Constantine's transfer of the center of all political authority from the old Rome of the Cæsars to the new Rome of Constantinople, on the other hand, could not fail to result in the slow but steady increase of the ecclesiastical authority of the bishop of Rome, that spiritual ruler now no longer obscured by, and subordinate to, the departed emperor of the East and the West. From this time onward, the rapid rise of the bishop of Rome from the primacy over the city and over the suburbican bishops to the primacy first over the other bishops of Italy, and then successively over all rival primates of the federated but independent Churches constituting the collective Church of the West is historical. The persistent influence of ancient imperial Rome, its traditions, its customs, and its laws all tended to impress, through the power of the bishops of Rome, the subordinate ecclesiastical relation to him of the primates of the several national churches in the West, in marked contrast with the coordinate apostolic equality of all the primates of the confederated national churches in the East. During the period of the councils, this papal authority of the bishops of Rome became more and more evident, for not only did the invasions of the barbarians from the north, and other favoring events of those troubled times, tend irresistibly toward the accomplishing of the ambitions of these successive rulers of the Roman Church, but their increasing ecclesiastical influence inspired the confident assertion of their primacy over the East as well.

From this time onward, the eventual separation of the two historic, complementing halves of the one "Holy Catholic and Apostolic Church" was foreshadowed; and it actually occurred when Photius (q.v.), patriarch of Constantinople, issued, in 866, the famous encyclical declaring the Latin Church to be heretical, and in the following year, with the concurrence of an assembled synod of Eastern bishops, formally excommunicated

6. The Final Schism.
Pope Nicholas I. (q.v.). Although the two churches were later seemingly reconciled, the controversy was revived under the Patriarch Michael Cærularius (q.v.), 1054 A.D., and became final through the conquest of Constantinople in 1204 by the Venetians, followed, as it was, by the intrusion of Latin bishops into the historic sees of the Eastern Church by Innocent III. (q.v.). All later attempts to reconcile the two historic halves of the one Catholic Church, as at the Council of Lyons (1274) and Council of Ferrara-Florence (1438–39), have finally failed; and Greek antagonism toward the Latin Church is more uncompromising than ever since the theory of the papal primacy has been expanded into its fullest possible form through the definite Vatican declarations in 1870, imposing on the entire Roman Church the doctrines of the universal episcopate of the pope, and his official infallibility when he declares *ex cathedra* any question of faith or morals.

The Eastern Church, in the course of its doctrinal development of the conciliar orthodox Christology, suffered the loss of several dissenting parts, most of which, excepting that first Arian schism, have continued to exist unchanged century after century to the present time. The Syrian, the Coptic (including the Abyssinian), and the Armenian Churches, historically the national churches of those ancient countries, although they reject, under a misconception of meaning, the Chalcedonian canons (see CHRISTOLOGY, IV.), can not be conclusively charged with the error of monophysitism (see MONOPHYSITES).

7. Present Positions of Greek and Latin Churches.

All these primitive parts of the Christian Church in the East are in communion with each other, and the Syrian Church, which is now represented in the hierarchy of the Western patriarchate, has lately officially denied the imputation of this Christological error. The Greco-Russian Church, now numbering nearly 100,000,000 members, both by reason of its peculiar geographical position in Europe, and its rapid extension throughout the North American continent, seems destined to become more and more the mediating influence between the non-Roman divisions of the Western Church and the federated Orthodox Greek Churches of the East; just as the Syrian Church of Antioch already occupies a similar position toward those other primitive national churches which mutually recognize each other. The Russian Church deserves great praise, not only for its sturdy stand on the subject of the validity of Western sacraments, especially baptism by affusion, in opposition to those Eastern prelates who doubt or deny their spiritual efficacy, but even more for its earnest efforts to aid, in every way consistent with its traditional orthodox teaching, the future recognition of the non-Roman communions of the West, and their eventual coordinate confederation with the churches of the East, in which it is deservedly the dominating division. The Roman Church, by accepting the dogmatic decrees of the Vatican Council of 1870, compelled its many ultramontane controversialists to prove the asserted apostolic origin of the papal power, and the historical orthodoxy of this modern addition to its preceding contradictory definitions of the papal primacy and irreconcilable interpretations of the traditional apostolic teaching of the undivided Catholic Church.

All these are, however, denounced as erroneous doctrines no less uncompromisingly by the several Orthodox Greek Synods than by the Old Catholic theologians of Europe and by the scholars of the Reformed Western communions. Furthermore, as a direct result of the Vatican decrees

8. Orthodox Catholic Church as a Solution.

of 1870, there are to-day in almost every country of Europe, and also in America, Catholic bishops independent of the Roman Church in both the Latin and the Syrian successions, presiding over nascent autonomous national Catholic Churches, thus offering equally valid sacraments and orders to all Christians of the Latin rite who can not consistently accept these and previous dogmatic Roman rulings which they regard as additions to the orthodox Catholic faith. The proposed theses of the union conference at Bonn, in 1874, presided over by the great opponent of infallibility, J. J. I. von Döllinger (q.v.), and attended by the Old Cath-

olic leaders and theologians and by clerical and theological representatives from both the Russian and the Greek Churches, besides clergy from the Anglican communions and other reformed communions of the West, offering, as they do, an orthodox synopsis of the traditional Catholic teaching of the undivided Church, and also a definite basis of doctrinal union in theological essentials of dogma, with consistent freedom in all related non-essentials, are a determining force in aiding the coming recognition and future coordinate confederation of all non-Roman communions of the West, both with each other, and with the national Orthodox Greek, Syrian, Coptic, and Armenian Churches of the East. These theses, moreover, as an orthodox summary of the fundamental Christian faith of the undivided Catholic Church, can not fail to serve a double purpose. On the one hand, they indicate by contrast in which particular dogmatic declarations the differing reformed confessions of faith are deficient in over or under statement, or are in essential error in their respective interpretations of the traditional apostolic teaching of the primitive Christian Church. On the other hand, they indicate, with more or less certainty, the elements of a common future creed which will ultimately be developed, defined, and accepted, through a coming ecumenical council of the entire Catholic Church, by all Christian communions both in the East and in the West. The restoration, by the reformed non-episcopal communions, of that primitive apostolic hierarchy of bishops, presbyters, and deacons, rejected and repudiated too hastily by their Puritan forefathers, is necessarily a *sine qua non* of ecclesiastical recognition, not only by the several Orthodox Catholic bishops independent of the Roman Church in the western patriarchate, but also by the entire eastern episcopate, the Orthodox Russian and Greek churches, the Syrian, the Coptic, and the Armenian. The unexpected events of the present period foreshadow unmistakably the trend of the times. The continued disestablishment of the Roman Church in the Latin nations of Europe, aided by Modernism (q.v.), may result eventually either in fundamental reforms of its distinctive doctrines, especially the theory of the papacy; of ritual, especially the perversions of the sacraments and the cult of the saints; and in polity, especially the enforced celibacy of the clergy and the suppression of the diaconate; or it may, through the increasing loss of its political power, become eventually resolved into its former components, which were in the past separate and subordinate churches in the several divisions of the Western Empire, but which will be in the future independent and confederated national churches of the historic Western patriarchate, now including the American continent, in communion both with each other and with the confederated national churches of the Eastern patriarchates.

ERNEST C. MARGRANDER.

III. Protestant Position: Since the Protestant Reformation repeated attempts have been made to bring about the reunion of the churches. The Reformers were not at first willingly separatists from the Roman Church; and in England the Nonconformists left the Established Church only after the failure of their appeals for reform and a larger measure of liberty. Notwithstanding conflicting intolerances and denominational divisions, the instinct of church unity has always been hidden in the heart of the Protestant churches. In the latter part of the seventeenth century an influential though quiet attempt was made to reconcile the Protestant churches of Germany with the Roman Catholic Church, when a Roman Catholic bishop of moderate spirit, Cristoval Rojas de Spinola (q.v.) was commissioned by the Emperor Leopold to make all practical efforts for the peace of the Church in the empire, and this was sanctioned by Pope Innocent XI. This endeavor was carried on through his ceaseless efforts and through a protracted correspondence between the philosopher Gottfried Wilhelm Leibnitz (q.v.) and some Protestant theologians and Jacques Bénigne Bossuet (q.v.), the famous French orator, and others, until, after some thirty years, it came to nothing. The political conditions of Europe, as well as theological differences, foredoomed it to failure, and since then no real effort to reconcile Roman Catholicism and Protestantism has been possible, even though the ideal of the one Church includes both.

In the sixteenth century the separation between the English Church and the Reformed churches on the continent was not so pronounced as it has since become, presbyters from the Reformed churches passing over to England being in several instances received without reordination and occasional intercommunion among the churches being also recognized. Two early archbishops licensed certain Scotch presbyters to officiate as priests, without raising the question of the regularity of their previous ordination. But in the seventeenth century the line of division was sharply drawn in an age of civil and religious strife. Two counter-claims were set up, the presbyterial and the episcopal, each at that time claiming that its polity had explicit authority and existed by a certain divine right; and other separations have multiplied since. But in that age there were not wanting also men of more moderate views, such as John Hales (q.v.) of Eton, Lord Falkland, and a succession of scholars known as the Cambridge Platonists (q.v.), who believed in toleration and comprehension of diversities within the Church; and who supported the episcopal order not because they regarded it as possessed of superior authority by divine right, but because of its antiquity and approved utility. Richard Baxter (q.v.), likewise, and other Presbyterian divines at the time of the Restoration pleaded for reforms and liberty within the Church, and only when their petition had been set aside were they compelled in good conscience by the Act of Conformity (1662) to become Nonconformists. Many individual instances also might be adduced of ideas and projects for church unity, such as Archbishop James Ussher's (q.v.) plan for synodical episcopacy, or the incessant labors of John Durie (q.v.) and his fertile schemes for the reunion of all the churches of the continent and England.

1. Efforts for Reunion with Roman Catholicism.

2. Attempts at Anglican and Protestant Union.

These all have failed, for the times were not ready for them, but they have not been in vain, and they remain for this twentieth century to bring to fruition. The times are favorable now as never before, and this field, where so many have gone forth to sow, is already ripe for the harvest. The idea of church unity has taken strong hold of all the churches, and it is to be the future business of the Church to realize it. The Christian civilization of the world demands it; political alliances of Church and State no longer perpetuate strife, at least in the United States. Modern historical and Biblical criticism has set aside the claims of any church polity to exclusive divine authority, and has left the historic episcopate to justify itself not only by its undoubtedly natural and early development in the primitive Church, but also by its fitness for administrative use and efficiency in possible adaptations to other church polities. A movement has already been started of far-reaching scope and much promise for some real church unity. The General Convention of the Protestant Episcopal Church, which was held in Cincinnati in Oct., 1910, appointed a commission to arrange for a world convention of all other Christian communions of evangelical faith upon questions of faith and order, to consider their differences as well as their agreements as a first step toward unity (see above, A, 2, § 5). At the same time the National Council of the Congregational Churches, in session in Boston, appointed a committee to consider any overtures of this kind from the Protestant Episcopal Church. This movement is receiving assent and support from other denominations, and after several years of preparation and conferences, which must necessarily intervene, the proposed world conference will be held. It will assume no powers of legislation, but the work aims at ultimate results of unity. The ideal of unity has been briefly but nobly set forth in this utterance of the Anglican Convention: " We must fix our eyes on the Church of the future, which is to be adorned with all the precious things, both theirs and ours. We must constantly desire not compromise, but comprehension, not uniformity, but unity." This ideal involves something more than external union or federation in some good work—a union outside the churches rather than unity of the churches. It aims at a comprehensive unity, in which denominational and temperamental diversities may be recognized; an administrative unity, by which wasteful competitions may be avoided; and a dynamic unity, through which the force of the whole Christian Church may be brought to bear wherever its light and power are needed in the world. Such unity will be organic in the sense of the Lord's words when he compared the relation of the disciples to himself and to one another to that of the branches and the vine; and according to the conception of the great missionary apostle when he described the Church as one body having many members.

NEWMAN SMYTH.

3. Present Protestant Situation.

IV. Roman Catholic Position: Church unity as understood by Roman Catholics postulates not merely an internal or spiritual union of Christian believers, but also an external or visible unity under one visible head. It is reducible to three points: unity of faith, government, and worship. The faithful are subject to one teaching and ruling authority, and partake of the same sacraments and forms of worship. Roman Catholics maintain that the Founder of Christianity wished the members of his Church to be united in the one faith or belief delivered in first instance to the apostles whom he sent to teach all nations. It was, furthermore, his intention that this doctrinal unity should be maintained in the Church through all subsequent generations by the authority of the " Ecclesia docens," authority which is vested in the bishops who are successors of the apostles, and particularly in the bishop of Rome, who is the center of all unity, and who, as the successor of Peter, inherits, in his official capacity, the prerogatives implied in the metaphor of the foundation rock (Matt. xvi. 18) and in other familiar passages of the New Testament. To this supreme and infallible teaching authority, which secures unity of belief, is united also, according to the will of the Founder, and vested likewise in the bishops and pope, supreme authority to rule the faithful in all things pertaining to salvation, whence results unity of direction or government, and also unity of worship, since the latter flows logically from the other two. This cultural unity refers chiefly to the sacrifice of the mass and the use of the sacramental system. The faithful are united in the use of the same sacraments because they all accept the Church's teaching relative to their divine institution and efficacy. That the Roman Catholic Church possesses this threefold unity in a far greater degree than any other body of Christian believers can hardly be disputed, and it is scarcely less evident that it is due to the traditional recognition by Roman Catholics that the see of Rome is the one center of unity in the Christian world. Church union, therefore, from the Roman Catholic standpoint entails necessarily this unqualified recognition as one of the fundamental doctrinal principles concerning which no compromise is possible. Without acknowledgment of the supreme authority of the Roman see no unification with dissident Christian communions can be seriously entertained. Historically, this principle was formulated as early as the second century by St. Irenæus, who, though of Asiatic origin, asserts plainly the primatial rights of the Roman see " with which, because of its preeminence, all other churches must agree " (*Hær.*, III., iii. 2).

Consistently with this principle, rejection of the teaching authority of the Roman see in doctrinal matters is ultimately construed as heresy, while revolt against her ruling authority constitutes ecclesiastical schism. The traditional concept of the Church from the beginning is that of a great visible organization destined to be universal—a vast body of which Christ is the head. But a visible Church should have also a visible head, and, according to Roman Catholic belief, the prerogatives that this implies were bestowed by the Founder on Peter and his successors. In the controversies incidental to the heresies and schisms that marked the early cen-

1. Unity of Faith, Government, and Worship Requisite.

turies of Christianity the dissenting bishops and their followers were constantly blamed by the orthodox Fathers for disrupting the unity of the Church, and when they definitely withdrew or were cast out, they were looked upon as branches lopped off from the parent tree and deprived of its life-giving power. Such, indeed, has been the constant attitude of the Roman Catholic Church in all subsequent ages toward seceding sects or nations. She sincerely deplores the fact that Christendom is so hopelessly divided against itself, and in her liturgy she prays constantly for unity, continuing the prayer of her divine Founder that all his followers be one in him. But at the same time, this much-desired unity must be such as Christ himself would have it—a unity the conditions of which must be submitted to her as judge, since she believes herself to be the divinely appointed custodian of his doctrine, the authentic interpreter of his will. If she shows herself rigid and uncompromising, it is because she feels the heavy responsibility of her divine mission. She longs to gather the scattered elements of Christendom under her wings, but however precious and desirable church unity may be, she does not deem herself free to accept it under conditions which in her esteem entail a sacrifice of principle or betrayal of her sacred trust. In matters pertaining to ecclesiastical discipline outside the domain of faith and morals, she is willing to make all reasonable concessions to dissident communions desiring to reenter the fold, but as regards the essential principles above stated she considers compromise to be impossible. That the efforts made in the past, notably in the ecumenical councils of Lyons (1274) and Florence (1438–45), to restore union with the Greek Church were not permanently successful is to be deplored, but Roman Catholics are confident that the impartial historian of these epochs will not make the Church of Rome responsible for the failure. The earnest desire and hope of the Church for Christian unity, as also the conditions under which she considers it possible of realization, are ably and fully set forth by the late Pope Leo XIII. in his encyclical letters " Præclara Gratulationis Publicæ " on the Reunion of Christendom (June 20, 1894) and " Satis Cognitum " on Church Unity (June 20, 1896). JAMES F. DRISCOLL.

2. Position Regarding Non-Roman Communions.

V. Supplement: The question of the union of churches involves three points: (1) union of those churches which acknowledge the historic episcopacy, as the Greek, Roman, Anglican and Protestant Episcopal, and Orthodox Catholic; (2) union of those churches which do not base the validity of ordination on the historic episcopacy; (3) ultimate union of these two great classes in one.

In the first class, union is conditioned, first, by an adjustment between the Greek and the Roman churches by differences centering on the procession of the Holy Spirit from the Father and the Son, on the infallibility of the bishop of Rome, and on the immaculate conception of the Virgin Mary. The question concerning the procession of the Holy Spirit may be solved either by the Roman Church returning to the earlier ecumenical position which does not teach the double procession, but which arose in the West in the ninth century, or by a restatement of the procession of the Holy Spirit from the Father through the Son instead of from the Father and the Son, or the Greek and Roman churches may agree on a double mission of the Spirit from the Father and the Son, leaving the inner-trinitarian process undefined as in the Nicene Creed. The Greek Church would also have to come to an understanding with the Nestorians, Armenians, Jacobites, and Copts. Secondly, the Anglican Church and its daughters, and the Old (Orthodox) Catholic bodies as well as the Greek will have to reconcile themselves to the supremacy of the pope and the dogma of the Immaculate Conception of Mary, unless, indeed, in both of these instances the Roman Church recedes from her unique position on these questions.

In churches of the second class, union is actually in process of realization. Since the great majority of these churches accept the first three positions of the " Quadrilateral," there is no fundamental impediment to their ultimately coming together. A union is therefore possible either by voluntary association for the prosecution of particular interests, as Bible and Tract Societies, Young Men's and Young Women's Christian Associations, and worldwide missionary conferences, in which even the first class may heartily cooperate. There may also be federated union (which is indeed taking place) first among churches having the same general source and name, as Baptist, Methodist, Presbyterian, where the branches become reunited to the parent stock, or where the religious sympathies are closest and the common spirit and aims are more nearly identical. In case, however, the doctrinal differences prevent the sort of union contemplated in the " Quadrilateral," the basis would have to be broadened so as to include Jewish congregations, Unitarians, Universalists, and Independents, and this might be defined by the general religious aim and the conduct of life. To many persons the actual difficulties confronting this class of religious communions seem not unsurmountable. This would require not necessarily uniformity of external organization, or abolition of denominations, but comprehension, each emphasizing the distinctive content of its faith. The problem presented by vested interests, as missionary societies, publishing-houses, and denominational colleges, is susceptible of satisfactory adjustment.

The union of the first and third classes offers a different problem. From the Anglican side a solution appeared in sight about 300 years ago. At that time:

"The Church of England recognized in various ways, directly or indirectly, the validity of Presbyterian ordination, and held communion with Lutheran and Calvinistic Churches on the Continent from the Reformation down to the Restoration in 1662, when the Ordinal was introduced in its present form.

"Archbishop Cranmer, the greatest Anglical liturgist, called Martin Butzer, a mediator between the Lutheran and the Swiss Reformers, from Strasburg to the chair of systematic theology in Cambridge, and Peter Martyr, a strict Calvinist, in the same capacity, to the University of Oxford, and consulted them freely in the preparation of the Articles of Religion and the Book of Common Prayer. The Elizabethan bishops, who, during their exile under Queen Mary. had sought refuge in Zurich, Basel, and Geneva, wrote letters overflowing with gratitude for the hospitality and kindness received from the Swiss Reformers and preachers, and addressed them as spiritual fathers and brethren. Bullinger's *Decades* and Calvin's *Institutes* were the highest authorities in the universities of England, and the influence of Beza's editions of the Greek Testament, his text and notes, is manifest in the Authorized Version of King James. The ' judicious ' Hooker, the standard writer on Church polity, expressed profound veneration for Calvin as ' the wisest man that ever the French Church did enjoy ' (Preface to his *Ecclesiastical Polity*); and he expressly admitted an ' extraordinary kind of vocation where the Church must needs have some ordained and neither hath nor can have possibly a bishop to ordain; in case of such necessity, the ordinary institution of God hath given oftentimes, and may give, place. And therefore we are not simply without exception to urge a lineal descent of power from the Apostles by continued succession of bishops in every effectual ordination ' (*Ecclesiastical Polity*, book vii. 14). Even James I., who hated the Presbyterians, sent five delegates, including three bishops (George Carleton, John Davenant, and Joseph Hall), to the Calvinistic Synod of Dort, who raised no question about the necessity of the episcopate for the being or the well-being of the Church " (Philip Schaff, *The Reunion of Christendom*, pp. 21–23, New York, 1893).

The open door indicated in the above citation being now closed, the situation involves a radical contention all along the line. The problem presented is that of those who affirm and those who deny the exclusive divine legitimacy of particular organization and orders of the ministry. On the one hand, the double claim is advanced, that those only are validly ordained ministers whose ordination rests on the basis of the historic episcopacy, and that such a succession can be traced historically to its authentic source in the apostolic college. On the other hand, it is maintained that valid ordination consists in the immediate and orderly setting apart of suitable persons to the Christian ministry in a manner agreeable to the spirit and aim of particular churches. If, then, union between these two opposed camps is to take place, it can be effected only by coming to an understanding on this vital issue; either the episcopally ordained will have to revise their position as to the historic basis of episcopacy, or broaden their interpretation of ordination to include those of non-episcopal communions who are consecrated according to the usage of their denomination, or else the non-episcopal ministers and churches will have to confess that their ordinations are invalid, and so seek from episcopal sources " authentic " ordination. So far as these two views embody ultimate convictions, expectation that either party will surrender to the other appears to be utopian. The question of the existing parity of ministers is fundamental; it can not be postponed with the view of arriving at a different conclusion as result of further historical inquiry. At the same time one can not even imagine conditions in which non-episcopally ordained ministers will discredit and therefore nullify their ordination. Moreover, one does not see how a discussion is even conceivable between the two parties except on the basis of the equality of episcopal and non-episcopal orders; and this signifies that while there is something to adjust, there is nothing to adjudicate.

C. A. BECKWITH.

BIBLIOGRAPHY: F. W. Newman, *Catholic Union*, London, 1854; W. White, *Principles of Christian Union as laid down in the Word of God*, ib. 1863; E. S. Foulkes, *Christendom's Divisions*, 2 vols., ib. 1865–67; G. Williams, *The*

Orthodox Church of the East in the 18th Century: a Correspondence between the Eastern Patriarchs and the Nonjuring Bishops. With an Introduction on Various Projects of the Reunion, ib. 1868; E. B. Pusey, *Eirenicon,* part III., ib. 1870; H. Bannerman, *Essays on Christian Unity,* ib. 1871; J. J. I. von Döllinger, *Lectures on the Reunion of the Churches,* ib. 1872; H. P. Liddon, *Report of . . . Reunion Conference . . . at Bonn,* 2 vols., ib. 1875–76; T. H. Vail, *The Comprehensive Church; or, Christian Unity and Ecclesiastical Union in the Protestant Episcopal Church,* New York, 1879; W. J. E. Bennett, *Foreign Churches in Relation to the Anglican,* London, 1882; F. Myers, *Catholic Thoughts on the Church,* ib. 1883; B. Franklin, *The Church and the Era,* New York, 1884; J. Tulloch, *Unity of Christendom,* London, 1884; R. I. Woodhouse, *What is the Church?* ib. 1886; J. Justus, *Freie Gedanken zur Beurtheilung der Kirche,* Stuttgart, 1884; P. Schaff, *Christ and Christianity,* New York, 1885; D. G. Bannerman, *Scripture Doctrine of the Church,* Edinburgh, 1887; J. H., *Christianity versus Ecclesiasticism,* London, 1887; C. Wordsworth, *Public Appeals on Behalf of Christian Unity,* Edinburgh, 1887; H. Forrester, *Christian Unity and the Historic Episcopate,* New York, 1889; R. Govett, *What is the Church?* Norwich, 1889; C. Gore, *The Mission of the Church,* London, 1891; idem, *Orders and Unity,* ib. 1910; T. S. Hamlin, *Denominationalism versus Christian Union,* New York, 1891; M. Watson, *Christianity and the Church,* London, 1891; W. J. Dawson, *The Church of Tomorrow,* ib. 1892; E. Naville, *Le Témoignage du Christ et l'unité du monde chrétien,* Geneva, 1893; T. Rohleder, *Politischreligiöse Grundlage für das einige Christentum,* Esslingen, 1893; A. H. Bradford, *The Question of Unity,* New York, 1894; J. Hammond, *The Christian Church,* Oxford, 1894; W. B. Carpenter, *Some Thoughts on Christian Reunion,* London, 1895; D. Dorchester, *The Problem of Religious Progress,* New York, 1895; Eastern Church Association, *Russia and the English Church during the Last Fifty Years,* London, 1895; C. W. Shields, *The United Church of the United States,* New York, 1895; W. Earle, *The Reunion of Christianity made Practicable,* London, 1896; H. H. Jeaffreson, *The Church of the Living God,* ib. 1896; A. J. Mason, *The Principles of Ecclesiastical Unity,* ib. 1896; T. Richey, *Five Lectures upon the Church,* New Haven, Conn., 1896; V. Staley, *Plain Words on the Holy Catholic Church,* London, 1896; V. Charbonnel, *Le Congrès des religions et le Suisse,* Geneva, 1897; T. Fallot, *Qu'est-ce qu'une église?* Paris, 1897; F. J. A. Hort, *The Christian Ecclesia,* London, 1897; E. Montero Ríos, *Restablecimiento de la unidad religiosa en los pueblos cristianos,* Madrid, 1897; E. A. Litton, *The Church of Christ,* London, 1898; W. R. Huntington, *A National Church,* New York, 1891; C. Bigg, *Unity in Diversity,* London, 1899; P. F. Jalaquier, *De l'église,* Paris, 1899; J. B. Nichols, *Evangelical Belief. Essay on the Conflict between Evangelicalism and Sacerdotalism,* London, 1899; R. Palmer, *The Catholic and Apostolic Church,* ib. 1899; H. Symonds, *Lectures on Christian Unity,* Toronto, 1899; J. Boehm, *Die Wiedervereinigung der christlichen Confessionen,* Mainz, 1900; E. T. Green, *The Church of Christ,* in J. H. Burn, *The Churchman's Library,* London, 1900; E. H. A. Scherer, *What is Catholicism?* ib. 1900; N. Dimock, *Christian Unity,* ib. 1902, new ed., New York, 1910; A. J. Harvey, *The Coming Unity. The Problem of the Churches,* London, 1902; H. H. Henson, *Godly Union and Concord,* ib. 1902; idem, *Anglicanism and Reunion. Sermon Preached in Westminster Abbey on Trinity Sunday, June 14, 1908,* ib. 1908; idem, *The Road to Unity,* ib. 1911; S. J. Jones, *England and the Holy See,* ib. 1902; A. T. Turberville, *Steps toward Christian Unity,* ib. 1902; *The Encyclical Letters of Pope Leo XIII.,* New York, 1903; B. W. Archer, *The Question of Reunion with Rome,* London, 1903; W. R. Carson, *Reunion Essays,* ib. 1903; C. Harris, *Christian Reunion from the Nonconformist and Church Point of View,* etc., ib. 1903; J. Hunkey, *A Plea for Christian Unity,* Atchison, Kan., 1903; F. X. Kiefl, *Der Friedensplan des Leibniz zur Wiedervereinigung der getrennten christlichen Kirchen,* Paderborn, 1903; Earl Nelson, *Home Reunion,* London, 1905; A. Campbell, *The Christian System in Reference to the Union of Christians,* Birmingham, 1905; Father Paul James Francis and S. Jones, *The Prince of the Apostles,* Garrison, N. Y., 1907; A. Tanquerey, *Synopsis theologicæ dogmaticæ fundamentalis,* Tournai, 1907; N. Smyth, *Passing Protestantism and Coming Catholicism,* New York, 1908; F. Spence,

Christian Re-union. A Plea for the Restoration of the "Ecclesia of God," London, 1908; C. A. Briggs, *Church Unity: Studies of its most important Problems,* New York, 1909; W. M. Brown, *The Level Plan for Church Union. With an Introduction on the Origin and Development of the Historic Episcopate by G. W. Smith, and an Appendix on the Chief Barrier to Christian Unity, by "Anglican Presbyter,"* New York, 1910; F. J. Firth, *Christian Unity in Effort: Something about the religious Faiths, Creeds, and Deeds of the People of the United States and Churches in their Relation to Christian Unity in Effort,* Philadelphia, 1910; R. de Bary, *A New Rome. A Study of Visible Unity among Non-Papal Christians,* London, 1911; *Church Unity: A Criticism and a Correspondence,* ib. 1911; A. C. A. Hall, *The Sevenfold Unity of the Christian Church,* New York, 1911; Lord Kinnaird (editor), *The Problem of Unity,* London, 1911; W. Sanday, in *Contemporary Review,* 1911; *Report of the Commission appointed by the Archbishop of Canterbury . . . on the Relation of the Anglican Communion to the Church of Sweden,* London, 1911; G. M. Williams, *The Church of Sweden and the Anglican Communion,* Milwaukee, 1911; J. Wordsworth, *The National Church of Sweden,* London, 1911; for a general popular survey from the Swedish point of view see N. Söderblom, "Canterbury och Upsala," in *Det nya Sverige,* vol. iii.

UNION, ECCLESIASTICAL, IN GERMANY.

Ecclesiastical Situation Before Union (§ 1).
Literary Advocacy of Union (§ 2).
Beginnings in Nassau, Prussia, and Elsewhere (§ 3)
Development in Prussia (§ 4).
Present Situation (§ 5).

By ecclesiastical union is meant the uniting of churches of diverse creeds into a single communion without change of denominational peculiarities, such union being distinctively Protestant, and in this discussion especially German. For such movements in England and America see CHURCH FEDERATION. The attempts to unite the Roman Catholic Church and other religions are not, strictly speaking, unionistic, since the Roman Church insists upon acknowledgment of the supremacy of the pope, which itself involves change of doctrine and loss of denominational characteristics.

The Reformation resulted in two confessions distinct in doctrine, organization, and worship, as opposed to each other as both were to the Roman

1. Ecclesiastical Situation Before Union.

Church. In Switzerland, Holland, Scotland, and France the Reformed became supreme; in the Scandinavian lands Lutheranism was triumphant; in Germany alone did the two exist side by side. Here the Lutherans were more opposed to union than were the Reformed, the divergency being essentially doctrinal and eucharistic. Orthodoxy forbade all union during the sixteenth and seventeenth centuries, but when orthodoxy's supremacy was shaken by Pietism and broken by rationalism, thoughts of union, hitherto confined to individuals, gained wide currency. Pietism, laying all its stress on intensity of piety, personal experience, and Christian life, saw too clearly the virtues of other denominations and the faults of its own to have sympathy with denominational distinctions. Rationalism, as opposed both to orthodoxy and to Pietism, which were at one in their adherence to revelation, denied that religion was specifically Christian and was, therefore, indifferent to sectarianism. At the same time, the rationalists, when they advocated union, aimed at the furtherance of toleration and the consequent development of Christianity into a universal religion. Here began the revival of Biblical Christianity in the early nineteenth century. This new piety, however, had no sectarian bias, Lutherans, Reformed, and Roman Catholics feeling themselves essentially one. The two Protestant bodies considered themselves as belonging to the same church, external differences were felt to be undesirable, and the denominational spirit that, a century earlier, had been maintained for truth's sake, was now held blameworthy, again for truth's sake.

This was manifest in the domain of literature. In 1703 Winkler [inspector at Halle], by his *Arcanum regium* [a plan of union which he suggested to Friedrich I., according to which no one could be installed as pastor who had not studied at Halle!], had roused a storm of protest; in 1803 such a work as G. J. Planck's *Ueber die Trennung und Wiedervereinigung der getrennten christlichen Hauptparteien* (Tübingen, 1803) found general ap-

2. Literary Advocacy of Union. proval when it advocated the cautious introduction of union into at least a limited area. Schleiermacher, in his *Zwei unvorgreifliche Gutachten in Sachen des protestantischen Kirchenwesens, zunächst in Beziehung auf den preussischen Staat* (Berlin, 1804), urged the abandonment of sectarian antagonisms, though not of denominational distinctions. Such union, however, he deemed advisable only where its necessity was distinctly and generally felt, as in Prussia; and he maintained that it was to be effected without interference with doctrine or liturgy and should come about under the mandate of the State. Some years later appeared the *Ueber die Vereinigung der beiden protestantischen Kirchengemeinden in der preussischen Monarchie* of F. S. G. Sack (Berlin, 1812), who had, in 1798, proposed a joint liturgy for Lutherans and Reformed in Prussia. Unlike Schleiermacher, Sack held that a creed was necessary for the united church, the Apostles' Creed and the Augsburg Confession being suggested for this purpose; and he likewise substituted for State authority the consent of the clergy of the two churches and the approval of the great majority of their members.

Plans for union received an important impulse through the tricentennial of the Reformation in 1817. The beginning was made in Nassau, where, at the suggestion of the government,

3. Beginnings in Nassau, Prussia, and Elsewhere. a synod of thirty-eight clergy delegated by the State convened at Ildstein and determined that the most fitting celebration of the event commemorated would be the union of both Protestant bodies in the duchy under the name of the Evangelical Christian Church. Their proposal was welcomed both by the synod and by the people, nor was it until later that a number of Lutherans separated from the national church and formed a distinct Lutheran church at Steeden. In Prussia the introduction of union was connected with the same event as in Nassau, though here there was a long preliminary development. Since early in the sixteenth century Lutherans and Reformed had enjoyed equal privileges in the electorate of Brandenburg; and the desire of reconciling the religious differences of their subjects and of uniting the Protestants in their domains had made the Hohenzol-

lerns advocates of union. Frederick William III. was, therefore, only true to the traditions of his house when, in his proclamation of Sept. 27, 1817, he urged the union of Lutherans and Reformed in one new Evangelical Christian Church. The royal appeal was gladly followed, especially in the western portions of Prussia, encountering only sporadic opposition, even outside the kingdom. A series of smaller German states followed the example of Prussia. The first general synod of the Rhenish Palatinate at Kaiserslautern in 1818 resolved upon union; from 1817 to 1822 union was realized in a great portion of the grand duchy of Hesse, and in 1818 in Hanau and Fulda, exclaves of the electorate of Hesse; in Baden and Waldeck union was decreed in 1821; and of the Anhalt principalities Bernburg accepted union in 1820, Dessau in 1827, and Köthen in 1880, though in all these states the organization of the union and its relation to the doctrinal standards of the denominations varied.

In Prussia, meanwhile, efforts were being made, after 1814, to reorganize the church, and in 1817 and the following years a synodo-presbyterian system was actually introduced, but soon proved impracticable. The king was, according-

4. Development in Prussia. ly, obliged to take matters into his own hands in greater measure than he had originally planned. Under the conditions then prevailing, the realization of union was almost entirely restricted to the liturgy, especially as, from the very first, the acceptance of a common communion service was held to imply the acceptance of union. Hitherto, during the rationalistic period, caprice had been dominant in the liturgy, but Frederick William, filled with affection for time-honored usages and realizing the advantages of orderly worship, now urged the necessity of a new liturgy for the Prussian church. Himself a fervent admirer of Luther, the liturgy was modeled essentially on Lutheran lines; and the king felt that, though unable and unwilling to force union, he could yet, in virtue of his ecclesiastical power, command the acceptance of a new liturgy. But the results were most unsatisfactory —too Lutheran for the Reformed, and suspiciously non-Lutheran for the Lutherans. Even Reformed presbyteries eager for union refused this liturgy; and opposition to the ritual led to opposition to union itself, and then to separation of a portion of the Prussian Lutherans from the united national church. Such a spirit of resistance to the new liturgy would not have arisen had there not been a momentous change in religious convictions. The power of rationalism, with its religious indifference, had been broken, and a return to the teachings of the Church was everywhere perceptible. As a consequence, various tendencies arose which construed the nature and purpose of union in very different ways. Some valued union as abrogating sectarianism; others, as representing the common elements of Protestant teachings; others still, as denying neither the validity of Lutheran doctrines in churches historically Lutheran, nor of Reformed teachings in analogous Reformed bodies. The change here indicated is reflected in official utterances respecting union. In 1817 union meant the establishment of a new Evangelical Christian Church by the amalgamation of two sundered Protestant bodies. In the cabinet order of Feb. 28, 1834, union abrogated nothing, and implied only a spirit of toleration which was unwilling to allow individual points of doctrine to form a barrier to external religious unity. Denominational tendencies within the union reached their climax in the cabinet order of Mar. 6, 1852, enacting that the supreme Protestant ecclesiastical council was empowered to represent the Evangelical national church as a whole, and to maintain and protect the rights of the different confessions and the institutions based on these confessions, adding that, in matters which could be determined only on the basis of one of the two confessions, decisions should be rendered not according to the votes of all members, but only of those belonging to the denomination concerned. The development of the organization of the national church in Prussia since 1873 has exercised no direct influence on union, since it was explicitly declared that this organization did not concern union or denominational position. Indirectly, however, it has doubtless strengthened union.

The men who proposed and the churches that accepted union committed no wrong, injustice first beginning when those of different convictions were prevented from acting accordingly.

5. Present Situation. But the problem becomes more difficult when the right or wrong of Protestant union is considered. This has been a moot question for over three centuries, and it is more than probable that it will never definitely be answered, for its solution depends not on objective facts, but on judgment concerning the value of unity and definiteness of the Church's teaching and on the uniformity of ecclesiastical ordinances. This judgment necessarily varies according to the individual, and absolute uniformity of thought and conduct is impossible, however great the general consensus of opinion may be. Both the advocates and the opponents of union had a certain degree of justification, and the fact that the opponents of the movement prevailed in the sixteenth and seventeenth centuries was due to the conditions of the time. Though at the present there is little likelihood that union in Germany will extend beyond its present limits, the advocates of union seem to be in the ascendency. No national church denominationally Lutheran can maintain a hostile attitude toward the Reformed, and in almost every church the Reformed are admitted to the Lord's Supper as guests, the few exceptions being due to the objections of the pastors rather than of the congregations. Extended association with members of other denominations has tended to lessen sectarian distinctions by revealing the many points of mutual belief, and progress in theological thought has led to a complete transformation of the sectarian spirit prevailing in the sixteenth century. In proportion, therefore, as the points of agreement between the Lutherans and the Reformed have gained general recognition, decreasing stress has been laid on the points of divergency. Nevertheless, the distinctive tenets of the two bodies, which are more than eucharistic divergencies, still remain. Union

has obviously failed to remove them, and, in the present condition of affairs, they seem destined to remain permanently.   (A. Hauck.)

Bibliography: K. I. Nitzsch, *Urkundenbuch der evangelischen Union,* Bonn, 1853; J. G. Scheibel, *Aktenmässige Geschichte der neuesten Unternehmung einer Union,* Leipsic, 1834; idem, *Mitteilungen über die neueste Geschichte der lutherischen Kirche,* ib. 1835–36; K. W. Hering, *Geschichte der kirchlichen Unionsversuche,* 2 parts, ib. 1836–1838; A. G. Rudelbach, *Reformation, Lutherthum und Union,* ib. 1839; R. F. Eylert, *Charakterzüge aus dem Leben Friedrich Wilhelm III.,* part iii., Magdeburg, 1846; J. Müller, *Die evangelische Union, ihr Wesen und göttliches Recht,* Berlin, 1854; F. J. Stahl, *Die lutherische Kirche und die Union,* ib. 1859; T. Wangemann, *Sieben Bücher preussischen Kirchengeschichte,* ib. 1859–60; idem, *Die preussische Union in ihrem Verhältnis zur Una sancta,* ib. 1884; idem, *Die kirchliche Kabinetspolitik Friedrich Wilhelms III.,* ib. 1884; K. H. Sack, *Die evangelische Kirche und die Union,* Bremen, 1861; F. Brandes, *Geschichte der kirchlichen Politik des Hauses Brandenburg,* Gotha, 1872; C. O. Firnhaber, *Die evangelische kirchliche Union in Nassau,* Wiesbaden, 1895; E. Förster, *Die Entstehung der preussischen Landeskirche,* 2 vols., Tübingen, 1905–07.

UNION, HYPOSTATIC. See Christology, VI., § 1; Trinity, II.

UNITARIANS.

Constituting an undogmatic religious fellowship, Unitarians have no formal creed. Freedom in church as in university is their fundamental principle. Their ideal is the cultivation of spiritual life in a free fellowship under the authority of reason and conscience. Their churches are constituted by a covenant of common purpose, the form of covenant recommended by the national conference in the United States being: "in the love of truth and the spirit of Jesus Christ we unite for the worship of God and the service of man." Without the constraint of creed Unitarians agree in affirmations of faith. Having abandoned the doctrine of man's total depravity and moral inability, they assert the dignity, worth, and spiritual capacity of human nature. Affirming the pure humanity of Jesus they cherish an enthusiastic veneration for him as a supreme instance of man's religious experience of God and as an inspiring prophet of a free and spiritual religion of love to God and man. Having early declared sound reason and historical interpretation to be the standards for the use of Scripture, Unitarians have fully adopted the methods and conclusions of Biblical criticism and value the Bible thus studied as a classic record of man's religious experience. Having discarded the Calvinist limitation of divine grace, Unitarians reaffirmed the Gospel faith in the universal loving fatherhood of God and have related that faith to their view of human nature. Man is seen as bound to God by kinship of being, impelled by his own nature to seek communion with God and destined to enjoy God's constant indwelling presence with a consciousness like that of Christ. Salvation means the attainment of this divinely intended character of sonship to God in a perfect likeness to the divine

1. Modern Doctrinal Position.

character of love, and it is sought by growth through the exercise of the soul's highest powers, in which God communicates himself to man. Denying all dogmatic limitations of the Church, Unitarians seek to realize as the chief end of human activity and the purpose of God's universal fatherhood a perfect brotherhood of good will. They devote themselves, therefore, to philanthropic activities and cherish faith in the progressive development of all man's higher possibilities. This faith in the possibility of a perfect humanity engages their energy in the promotion of culture and of higher social living as requisite for the fullest nurture of the religious spirit. Unitarians see in the life after death the further unfolding of the eternal life now experienced in obedience to the divine will revealed in the holiest human ideals.

In the early church Unitarian conceptions of God took the two forms of Sabellianism (see Monarchianism) and Adoptionism (q.v.). Only the latter has analogies to modern Unitarianism.

2. Early and Medieval Unitarianism. It conceived Jesus as a man invested with the spirit of God and exalted through death and resurrection to divine authority over the conscience of men. The believer was to be baptized as Christ was baptized, and to be adopted as he was adopted into sonship to God. The ascendency of the Logos Christology after 270 A.D. meant the defeat of Adoptionism in the Greek churches, but it had a continued life among the Paulicians (q.v.) of Armenia, and through their colonization of the Danube country (eighth and tenth centuries) found connection with the anti-ecclesiastical Evangelical movements of the West from the eleventh century onward. In the West also the early Adoptionism had some continuity of life in spite of the establishment of Nicene orthodoxy. Augustine was reared in this view and never lost the influence of it. There are traces of it in early British Christianity, and it was wide-spread in Spain even after ecclesiastics had attempted to reconcile it with the Nicene theology. The condemnation of Felix of Urgel by the Frankish Church (799 A.D.) and the later complete assimilation of the Spanish Church to Roman standards prevented the further development.

In the Reformation era reaction against the trinitarian dogma had sporadic manifestations, but in Poland, partly under Italian influence (e.g., Georgius Blandrata, q.v.), it was one element in a concerted movement to revise dogma by reason. After 1565 this rational Biblicism was the theology of a strong group of Polish churches, and in 1575 obtained the leadership of Faustus Socinus and the impress of his theological scholarship (see Socinus, Faustus, Socinians). Under Sigismund I. and II. Poland enjoyed religious toleration, and the Polish Unitarian church (college at Racow after 1600) developed great activity. Jesuit aggression culminated in the suppression of the college and churches (1638), and finally (1658) in a decree for the expulsion of Socinians from the realm. The exiles were eventually absorbed in the churches of Germany, Holland, and Transylvania. Unitarianism found advocates in Hungary through the influence of the Italian Stancarus (1553) and the Hungarian Aran (1558), and its progress was promoted by the accession to the throne of John Sigismund (1558) after years of exile spent at the Polish court and by the arrival of Blandrata from Poland as court physician. The chief leader of the movement was Franciscus Davidis (q.v.), who in 1556 had become head of the Lutheran church and college of the Magyar capital of Koloszvár, and ten years later, when royal chaplain, adopted Unitarian doctrines. In 1568 Davidis was made bishop of the avowed Unitarian churches which by act of the diet at Torda in that year obtained freedom of worship in common with Lutherans, Calvinists, and Catholics. Court favor ended with the advent to the throne of Stephen Báthory, a Roman Catholic, and the diets of 1576 and 1577 restricted Unitarian synods to Koloszvár and Torda. Unitarian strength was indicated by the Synod of Torda in Mar., 1578, which comprised 322 clergymen.

Since 1571 Davidis had opposed prayer to Christ as an object of worship, but now, in 1578, met resistance from Blandrata, who had begun to retreat from Unitarian views. In 1579 the Roman Catholic viceroy Christopher Báthory placed Davidis under the surveillance of the magistrates and then, at the instance of Blandrata, condemned him to imprisonment for life as an innovator and blasphemer. Davidis' death (Nov. 15, 1579) in the dungeon of Déva established him as a heroic martyr in the sympathies of the Hungarian churches. Though they still had legal existence, the Unitarians suffered hardship. Under Austrian rule, in 1716, their publications were forbidden, their churches confiscated, and all public office denied to them. Since the statute of 1791, which recognized the liberty of the four religions of Transylvania, they have grown moderately in numbers, and are in close fellowship with their coreligionists in England and America. The college at Kaloszvár has 4 professors and 25 students of theology. The number of congregations is 116.

Some of the English martyrs of the sixteenth century suffered for Arian views, but the first noteworthy expression of the spirit and method of Unitarianism was *The Religion of Protestants a Safe Way to Salvation* (London, 1638), by William Chillingworth (q.v.), and the first conspicuous application of this method with express Unitarian results was made by John Biddle (q.v.), who under the Commonwealth gathered a society in London and published his views. In 1662 he was imprisoned for the third time, and soon died of prison disease. His writings were collected and published by his disciple Thomas Firmin in 1691 (*The Faith of One God*). Although Unitarianism was excluded from the operation of the Toleration Act of 1689 (q.v.), while its advocates were threatened by the act of 1698 with loss of civil rights and imprisonment, Socinian and Arian views of the person of Christ found increasing favor in the course of the eighteenth century both in the Church of England and among dissenters. Noted instances of this tendency are Samuel Clarke (see Clarke, Samuel, 4), Nathanael Lard-

3. In Poland and Hungary.

4. British Unitarianism.

ner, Isaac Watts, and Philip Doddridge (qq.v.). The first chapel with the Unitarian name was founded in Essex Street, London, in 1778 by Theophilus Lindsey (q.v.), who on the refusal of parliament (1772) to receive a petition for the relaxation of subscription to the Thirty-nine Articles (q.v.) had resigned his living in Catterick, Yorkshire. In his London Chapel he used Clarke's revision of the English liturgy. Lindsey was aided by the sympathy of Presbyterians, who had made their chapels built since 1688 free from dogmatic restrictions, and, seeking conformity with the Bible alone, had relinquished Calvinistic views and the doctrine of the Trinity. The decisive influence in this change was exercised by the eminent scientist, publicist, and theologian, Joseph Priestley (q.v.). As an avowed Socinian Priestley ministered to congregations in Leeds (1768–80) and Birmingham (1780–91). His expression of favor for the French Republic led to an attack by a Birmingham mob in 1791, who burned his chapel and destroyed his house, books, and scientific instruments. In 1794 he removed to Northumberland, Penn., where he organized a Unitarian church and where he died in 1804. His prolific authorship gave an impetus to the Unitarian cause. The successor of Priestley in Birmingham and of Lindsey in London (1795) was Thomas Belsham (q.v.), who sought to make " the simple and proper humanity of Christ " the acknowledged Unitarian view. Another notable leader was Lant Carpenter (q.v.), preacher in Bristol. In 1813 the legal disabilities of Unitarians were removed and in 1825 the British and Foreign Unitarian Association was formed by a union of Presbyterian and Baptist churches to which were later joined small Methodist groups like the " Christian Brethren." By the Dissenters' Chapels Act of 1844 the possession of ancient endowments and chapels was secured. The national conference, a purely deliberative body, was founded in 1881. In 1911 there were 378 ministers, and 374 churches, of which 295 are in England. Theological instruction is given in Manchester College, Oxford, and the Home Missionary College at Manchester. The Hibbert Fund, instituted by Robert Hibbert, a Jamaica planter (died 1849), has promoted scholarship and established relations with the theological liberalism of the continent. To this foundation are due the famous Hibbert lectures (q.v.) and the *Hibbert Journal* (since Oct., 1902). Welsh Unitarianism began with the Arminian revolt from Calvinism of Jenkin Jones in Llwynrhydowen in 1726. His successors adopted Arian views. There are thirty-four churches in South Wales and a college at Carmarthen. Irish Unitarianism began in 1726, when the presbytery of Antrim separated from the general synod in order to establish worship without subscription to creed. In 1830 the Remonstrant Synod of Ulster was formed on similar principles, and in 1835 an Association of Irish Non-Subscribing Presbyterians united these free churches. There are thirty-eight churches, chiefly in the counties of Antrim and Down. In Scotland there are seven churches, the oldest (Edinburgh) dating from 1776.

In America the avowal of Unitarian views began in 1785, when, at the persuasion of its pastor, James

Freeman (q.v.), King's Chapel, the oldest Episcopal church in Boston, omitted from the Book of Common Prayer all reference to the Trinity and to the deity of Christ. The chief origin of American Unitarianism, however, was in the Congregational parishes of Eastern Massachusetts, where Arminian tendencies began before the middle of the eighteenth century. Aversion to creedal control and a strict adherence to Biblical teaching differentiated these churches from those responsive to the new Calvinism of the school of Jonathan Edwards (q.v.). While individuals criticized the doctrine of the Trinity, the topic was not debated in sermons and publications, and the growing liberalism directed itself mainly against the Calvinist view of human nature. The division of Congregationalism came to pass through the efforts of Jedidiah Morse and others to organize the independent congregations into a denomination with a prescribed creed and a polity admitting close relations to the Presbyterian general assembly. This aggressive element founded the Andover Theological School (1808), secured the election of orthodox pastors in and near Boston, and began to refuse the fellowship of pulpit exchanges with the liberals. Its literary organ was *The Panoplist* (1805–20). Liberalism controlled Harvard University, had eloquent preachers in Joseph Stevens Buckminster and William Ellery Channing (qq.v.) and literary organs in the *Monthly Anthology* (1803 sqq.) and the *Christian Disciple* (1813 sqq.). While Morse's plan to Presbyterianize the church polity was rejected by his associates (1815), he provoked a crisis by a sensational exposure of the progress of Unitarian views and by summoning the orthodox to separate from the liberals (1815). As spokesman of the latter group Channing made a sharp protest against the " system of exclusion and denunciation," but orthodox secession from liberal parishes began (about 80 divisions 1815–35) and new churches were founded with the avowal of Unitarianism. Recognizing the breach as inevitable, Channing boldly challenged his opponents by his Baltimore sermon on " Unitarian Christianity" (1819) and his *Moral Argument against Calvinism* (1820). In 1820 the first step to the association of liberals was taken by the beginning of the Berry Street conference of ministers in Boston. The American Unitarian Association was formed in 1825 for the work of church extension, but for a long time was feebly supported, as the free congregations were averse to the building of a denomination. During the Civil War the experience of Unitarians with the concerted task of organizing and conducting the Sanitary Commission gave new vigor and enthusiasm to the work of the Unitarian Association and led to the first representative convention of the churches in New York, 1865, with the formation there of the National Conference of Unitarian and other Christian Churches. Suggestions of a creed were rejected, but many were dissatisfied with what they regarded as an implied creed in the name of the conference and the preamble of its constitution. This discontent became a distinction of eastern and western views. A Western Unitarian Conference had been founded in 1852 with very conservative utterances respecting the office of Jesus and the significance of miracles, but it had broadened its basis, and in 1875 welcomed " all who desire to work with it in advancing the kingdom of God." These differences were harmonized by the action of the national conference at Saratoga in 1894, which made its preamble declare: " these churches accept the religion of Jesus, holding, in accordance with his teaching, that practical religion is summed up in love to God and love to man."

In 1910 there were 504 societies in the United States and Canada, and the ministers enlisted in the fellowship were 538. There are theological schools at Meadville, Penn. (founded 1844) and Berkeley, Cal. (founded 1904). Students are also trained in the Harvard Divinity School, founded in 1817 and maintained as a Unitarian institution to 1878, when it became the undenominational theological school of Harvard University.

The latest phase of the Unitarian movement is the effort to increase cooperation among those in all lands " who are striving to unite pure religion and perfect liberty." The International Council organized for this purpose in Boston in 1900 has held congresses in London (1901), Amsterdam (1903), Geneva (1905), Boston (1907), and Berlin (1910).

Unitarian religious thought has had successive phases. It began as a method of inquiry, the method of Socinians and Arminians. No truth **6. Genius** was allowed prior validity to the Bible, **of Uni-** the Bible was interpreted by reason **tarianism.** and conscience, and the results obtained from the Bible by this method were held as historic revelation. The pioneer in a movement beyond this position was Channing. Refusing to characterize man by the sin which deprived him of his true being as man, he found the essence of human nature in the moral principle of disinterested justice and benevolence, which is sovereign over the whole self. Religion and virtue are the mind itself, are human nature, and nothing else. Therefore, " we must start in religion from our own souls. In these is the fountain of all divine truth. An outward revelation is possible and intelligible only on the ground of conceptions and principles previously furnished by the soul." " We have faculties for the spiritual as truly as for the outward world." A further development of this view with a polemic against dependence on miracle and mere Biblicism enabled Theodore Parker (q.v.) to inaugurate the freer critical historical valuation of the Bible and to rescue the movement from the rationalism of Locke's school, while the more poetic and romantic transcendentalism of Emerson operated as a powerful stimulus to independent spiritual intuition and emancipation from convention and formula. All these leaders infused into the movement an ardor of mystical communion with God, without ecstasy or loss of self, and at the same time an active passion for all philanthropic reforms. Others, among whom James Freeman Clarke (q.v.) was of greatest eminence, united the insistence on inner personal grounds for faith with more historic feeling for the Christian past. The most eminent philosopher of the Unitarian school was James Martineau (q.v.),

who, with splendor of diction, speculative profundity, and intense ethical interest, elaborated a view of experience in which idealistic rationalism was blended with a refined spiritual mysticism. The most complete exposition of Unitarian theology in a form related to the traditional dogmatics is found in James Drummond's *Studies in Christian Doctrine* (London, 1908).   FRANCIS A. CHRISTIE.

BIBLIOGRAPHY: On Unitarian history consult: W. Turner, Jr., *Lives of Eminent Unitarians, with a Notice of Dissenting Academies*, 2 vols., London, 1840–43; O. Fock, *Socinianismus*, i. 263–287, Kiel, 1847; R. Wallace, *Anti-Trinitarian Biography*, London, 1850; J. Ferenc, *Kleiner Unitarierspiegel*, Vienna, 1879; G. Bonet-Maury, *Les Origines du christianisme unitaire chez les Anglais*, Paris, 1881, Eng. transl., *Early Sources of English Unitarian Christianity*, London, 1884; J. Stoughton, *Religion in England, 1800–50*, i. 23, 211 sqq., ib. 1884; G. d'Alviella, *Religious Thought in England, America, and India*, ib. 1885; A. H. Drysdale, *Hist. of the Presbyterians in England*, i. 522 sqq., 622 sqq., ib. 1889; A. S. Dyer, *Sketches of English Nonconformity*, ib. 1893; J. H. Allen, in *American Church History Series*, vol. x., New York, 1894; A. Gordon, *Heads of English Unitarian Hist.*, London, 1895; W. J. van Douwen, *Socinianen en Doopsgezinden, 1559–1626*, Leyden, 1898; G. E. Evans, *Midland Churches; a Hist. of the Congregations on the Roll of the Midland Christian Union*, Dudley, 1899; W. Lloyd, *The Story of Protestant Dissent and English Unitarianism*, London, 1899; W. C. Bowie, *Liberal Religious Thought at the Beginning of the 20th Century*, ib. 1901; G. W. Cooke, *Unitarianism in America*, Boston, 1903; W. G. Tarrant, *The Story and Significance of the Unitarian Movement*, ib. 1910; W. C. Bowie, *Unitarian Churches in Great Britain and Ireland*, London, 1905; *Memorable Unitarians*, ib. 1906; F. B. Mott, *Short Hist. of Unitarianism*, ib. 1906; H. Triepel, *Unitarismus und Föderalismus im deutschen Reiche*, Tübingen, 1907; A. Rasmussen, *Unitarismen, dens Historie og Theologi*, Copenhagen, 1907; S. A. Eliot, *Heralds of a Liberal Faith*, 3 vols., Boston, 1909; *The Fifth World Congress of Free Christians and Other Religious Liberals at Berlin . . . 1910*, Boston, 1910; Lichtenberger, *ESR*, xii. 263–271.

For the doctrines consult: The writings of Joseph Priestley, W. E. Channing, J. Martineau, and M. J. Savage (qq.v.) and the literature under the articles on them; J. Wilson, *Concessions of Trinitarians*, Manchester, 1842; J. R. Beard, *Unitarianism, Exhibited in its Actual Condition*, London, 1846; J. F. Clarke, *Orthodoxy, its Truths and Errors*, Boston, 1870; R. B. Drummond, *Free Thought and Christian Faith*, Edinburgh, 1890; R. Bartram, *Religion and Life*, London, 1891; J. Wright, *Denials and Beliefs of Unitarians*, ib. 1901; T. R. Slicer, *One World at a Time*, New York, 1902; W. G. Tarrant, *Unitarianism Restated*, London, 1904; J. E. Manning, *The Religion and Theology of Unitarians*, ib. 1906; R. T. Herford, *Unitarian Affirmations*, 2d ed., ib. 1909; J. P. Hoff, *The Unitarians' Justification*, ib. 1910; E. Emerton, *Unitarian Thought*, New York, 1911.

UNITED AMERICAN FREEWILL BAPTISTS, COLORED. See MISCELLANEOUS RELIGIOUS BODIES, 19.

UNITED BAPTISTS. See BAPTISTS, II., 4 (g).

UNITED BRETHREN IN CHRIST.

I. United Brethren in Christ (New Constitution).
    Origin (§ 1).
    Organization and Work (§ 2).
II. United Brethren in Christ, Old Constitution.

I. United Brethren in Christ (New Constitution): A denomination of Evangelical Christians, Arminian in doctrine, founded by Philip William Otterbein (q.v.) in the latter part of the eighteenth century. Otterbein came to America in 1752 as a missionary of the German Reformed Church. His first charge was at Lancaster, Penn., where he experienced what he regarded as his first real change of heart, and his ministry thenceforward assumed a deeply spiritual character. He began to hold frequent evangelistic services and instituted special prayer and experience meetings. In pursuing his evan-

1. **Origin.** gelistic labors, he made numerous visits to places near and remote, often conducted largely attended open-air meetings, and invited to a hearty cooperation all spiritually-minded persons of whatever name or church. His labors resulted in the organization of numerous societies of converts, who, because of their warmer and more earnest spiritual life, frequently found it difficult to remain in harmonious connection with their parent churches. To supply these people with the ministration of the word, Otterbein appointed or approved for them teachers, who visited them at irregular intervals, expounded to them the Gospel, and encouraged them to continue faithful in their religious life. As the work extended, it became necessary to devise a regular system of supply; and conferences of ministers, chiefly for this purpose, began to be held. Finally, in 1800, at one of these conferences, these scattered societies were organized into one body; and the name " United Brethren in Christ " was adopted as the official title of the denomination thus formed. Otterbein and Martin Boehm, a Mennonite, were chosen bishops. The people thus organized spoke at that time almost exclusively the German language; at the present time that language is used by less than four per cent. of the congregations.

The government of the church is vested primarily in a general conference, holding quadrennial sessions. The power of the church is in its laity. • The delegates are ministers and laymen in equal proportions, women being eligible since 1893, all chosen by popular vote. There are also annual conferences, whose powers are chiefly

2. **Organi-** executive, in which each pastoral **zation and** charge is entitled to one lay represent- **Work.** ative. The bishops are elected by the general conference quadrennially, as are also the editors, publishing-house manager, and the several general boards with their executive officers. Ministers are appointed to their charges by a stationing committee for one year, appointments being renewable indefinitely. Presiding elders, elected by their respective conferences, have general supervision over districts or subdivisions of the annual conferences. A home, frontier, and foreign missionary society was organized in 1853; a woman's missionary board in 1875. The general conference of 1905 separated the home and foreign work, creating a board for each. The foreign missions of the church, begun in western Africa in 1855, have since extended to China, Japan, Porto Rico, and the Philippines. The number of missionaries in 1911 was 61, with 141 native preachers and teachers, with 55 in training for Christian work; communicants, 4,335; catechumens and adherents, 11,607. The aggregate funds contributed for the foreign work are something over $1,250,000; for the home work, $1,800,000. A general Sunday-school board was organized by the general conference in 1865, and a church-erection society and a general education board in 1869. On questions of reform, such as tem-

perance and slavery, the historical attitude of the church has been that of strong radicalism, its position concerning slavery having prevented any considerable extension in the southern states before the war.

The denomination has ten colleges and one theological seminary (at Dayton, O.) with over 3,500 students, 65 of whom are in the theological seminary. The total membership in 1911 was 290,516; there were 2,030 itinerant ministers and 475 local ministers; the number enrolled in Sunday-schools was over 360,000. The denomination is found chiefly in Pennsylvania, Maryland, northern Virginia, western New York, Ohio, Indiana, Illinois, Iowa, and Kansas, but extends westward in nearly parallel lines to the Pacific coast and in recent years has entered a number of the southern states. The publishing-house at Dayton, O., issues twenty-six weekly, monthly, semimonthly, and quarterly periodicals, with an aggregate average circulation for the year ending Apr. 1, 1911, of 525,250 copies.

II. United Brethren in Christ, Old Constitution: The general conference of the United Brethren in Christ in 1885 took measures for revising the confession of faith and amending the constitution of the church. A commission consisting of the six bishops and twenty-seven ministers and laymen was appointed to formulate the proposed changes and additions and submit them to popular vote. The result was overwhelmingly in favor of the several measures, and at the next general conference in 1889 this result was declared by the presiding bishops, with the announcement that thenceforth the conference would transact business under the amended constitution and the revised confession of faith. Fourteen delegates, with one bishop, then withdrew from the conference, and proceeded to hold the " General Conference of and for the United Brethren in Christ," elsewhere in the same city, electing general officers and boards, and transacting such other business as would pertain to a general conference. Under the claim that they with their followers were the true church of the United Brethren in Christ, they held that the rightful ownership of the property of the denomination belonged to them. Years of litigation followed, resulting finally in defeat in the courts. This organization had at its beginning a following of between 15,000 and 20,000. Its year-book shows a membership of 18,317, with 304 itinerant and 75 local ministers. The Sunday-school enrolment is 19,386 scholars. The church has three collegiate institutions, a home and foreign missionary society, and a woman's missionary board, with missions in West Africa. Its publishing-house is located at Huntington, Ind., and it issues a church weekly, a missionary monthly, Sunday-school literature, and other publications. The doctrinal standards and the general polity are essentially the same as those of the United Brethren in Christ.   D. BERGER.

BIBLIOGRAPHY: A good list of literature is prefixed to D. Berger. *Hist. of the United Brethren in Christ,* in *American Church History Series,* xii. 310–314, New York, 1897, cf. Berger's work with same title, Dayton, Ohio, 1897. Consult besides the above: H. G. Spayth, *Hist. o he Church of the United Brethren,* Circleville, Ohio, 1851; J. Lawrence,

Hist. of the United Brethren in Christ, Dayton, 1890–93; E. L. Shuey, *Handbook of the United Brethren in Christ*, ib. 1893; the *Year Book*, an annual. Special phases are treated in: C. Newcomer, *Life and Journal*, Hagerstown, Md., 1834; L. Davis, *Life of Bishop David Edwards*, Dayton, 1883; A. W. Drury, *Life of Rev. Philip William Otterbein*, ib. 1884; idem, *Life of Bishop J. J. Glossbrenner*, ib. 1889.

UNITED EVANGELICAL CHURCH: A religious body organized in Naperville, Ill., Nov. 30, 1894, with 55,000 members. Its constituency had been a part of the Evangelical Association (q.v.) and its separate organization was due to a " division brought about by an unwarranted assumption of power exercised by those in official position, in that they refused to submit to the findings of duly constituted trial conferences, assumed to expel ministers and members without trial, and refused to arbitrate the differences existing between the parties in the controversy." Its doctrine is similar to that of the Methodist Episcopal Church. Its conferences are general, annual, and quarterly. The annual conferences are the seat of authority. The general conference has only such powers as are conferred upon it by the discipline. Bishops and presiding elders are eligible for two consecutive terms of four years. Laymen are fully represented in all the conferences. No member can be deprived of his rights without due process. Local church property is held for the benefit of the congregation.

The church embraces 10 annual conferences, 997 organized congregations, 737 ministers, 69,066 members, 911 Sunday-schools with an enrolment of 106,934. Its property has a value of about $3,600,-000. Its annual income is now over $700,000. Three educational institutions are maintained: Albright College at Myerstown, Penn., Western Union, at Le Mars, La., and Dallas, at Dallas, Ore. The publishing-house, located at Harrisburg, Penn., issues fourteen separate periodicals with a combined circulation of 147,632. Missionary operations are under the direction of the board of home and foreign missions. Auxiliary to the general board is the woman missionary society, with a membership of 6,685, and receipts amounting to $13,714.36 in 1905. The receipts of the general board in 1905 were $98,110.74, and its expenditures $96,323.69. It maintains three mission stations in Hunan, China, located at Changsha, Siangtan, and Liling.

W. F. HEIL.

BIBLIOGRAPHY: Consult the works mentioned in EVANGELICAL ASSOCIATION, especially A. Stapleton's *Annals*, and the *Evangelical*, the *Zeitschrift*, and other periodicals of the denomination.

UNITED FREE CHURCH OF SCOTLAND. See PRESBYTERIANS, I., 2.

UNITED FREE CHURCHES. See METHODISTS, I., 7.

UNITED NORWEGIAN LUTHERAN CHURCH. See LUTHERANS, III., 6, § 2.

UNITED ORIGINAL SECESSION CHURCH OF SCOTLAND. See PRESBYTERIANS, I., 6.

UNITED PRESBYTERIAN CHURCH OF NORTH AMERICA. See PRESBYTERIANS, VIII., 6.

UNITED SOCIETIES IN SCOTLAND. See PURVES, JAMES.

UNITED STATES OF AMERICA, RELIGIOUS HISTORY OF.

I. Historical Review.
  The Period of Settlement (§ 1).
  Development Since 1776 (§ 2).
  The Problem of Immigration (§ 3).
II. Separation of Church and State.
  The General Government and the Church (§ 1).
  Effects upon Religious Life (§ 2).
  Attitude of Some States (§ 3).
III. Voluntary System of Church Support.
IV. Leading Denominations.
V. Theological Education.
VI. Development.
VII. Statistics.

I. Historical Review: The religious history of North America opens with the landing of Columbus (1492), whose first act was to raise the banner of the cross and dedicate the new world to Christ and the Church. For more than 300 years, under the devoted lead of Spanish and French monks, the effort to convert the native Indians to the Roman Catholic faith continued, often with brilliant success, though frequently marred by religious intolerance and cruelty peculiar to the spirit of the age (see INDIANS OF NORTH AMERICA, MISSIONS TO THE; HOME MISSIONS; and ROMAN CATHOLICS). The Protestant era in America begins with the settlement of Virginia in 1607, followed in 1620 by the landing of the Pilgrims in Massachusetts Bay. From then on, America was, on an immensely larger scale, what Geneva was under Calvin, a refuge for persecuted Protestants of all lands. Puritans, Presbyterians, Quakers, Baptists, Huguenots, Salzburg Lutherans, Moravians, Lutherans, and Reformed refugees from the Palatinate, Mennonites, and others, emigrated thither in order to find a quiet place to practise their religion, and showed in their new home predominantly a religious earnestness and a tolerance which sprang not from indifferentism, but from bitter experience of unrighteous persecution. English Roman Catholics, also, who then were subjected to severe penalties in England, found in Maryland an asylum. These were joined by the Dutch Reformed in New York, and the English Episcopalians in Virginia, the two Carolinas, and Georgia, who, however, had not come for conscience' sake. Thus the American colonies were made up of almost all branches of European Christianity, mostly Protestants, with a small number of Roman Catholics. Of course these churches were all weak; but they were strong enough to produce a people able to defend themselves against the demands of Great Britain, and under the leadership of George Washington, by the aid of France, to carry on a successful war of seven years' duration, which issued in their complete independence of the British crown.

With the peace of 1783, or even with the declaration of independence in 1776, the colonial period of the country closed. The nation was then composed of thirteen colonies, loosely bound together, and numbering scarcely three million inhabitants. The representatives of the free people, assembled in Philadelphia in 1787, drew up a constitution, modeled, indeed, upon that of England, but further developed upon its principles. A sharp line was drawn between Church and State. Upon this constitution they stood united as a compact nation, with a sovereign national government. At their head was a president, elected every four years. The happy issue of the war of independence compelled such churches as the Episcopal and the Methodist, which had formerly been united with the English bodies, to form separate organizations, on the basis of universal civil and religious liberty. Favored by the uncommon fertility of the soil, the exhaustless mineral wealth, numberless avenues of trade, and free institutions which afforded the fullest play to individual enterprise, and at the same time guaranteed complete security to person and property, the United States has ever since, but particularly during the last fifty years, advanced in a way unparalleled in history. The number of inhabitants has grown since 1800, when it was 5,000,-000, until, according to the official census of 1910, it was 91,972,267, exclusive of Porto Rico and the Philippines. The number of states in the same period has increased [mostly by the organization of the Northwest Territory (1787), the Louisiana Purchase (1803), Florida (1820), and California and New Mexico (1848)], from thirteen to forty-eight; and besides these there is Alaska, as well as the District of Columbia (the seat of the national government).

Up to 1840 the total immigration, from all sources, had not exceeded half a million. Then began the flood. During the next 25

3. The Problem of Immigration. years, the United States received 6,000,000 foreigners, mostly from Ireland and Germany. Between 1865 and 1885 more than 7,000,000 were added to the foreign population. Their quality had not improved. The Irish and German tides were ebbing, while those of southern and eastern Europe were both increasing and threatening. One hundred and sixty American cities, each with a population of more than 25,000 and an aggregate population of 20,000,000, show 53.7 per cent, or more than one-half, foreign-born or of foreign parentage. In this sense it is true, as sometimes declared, that American cities are more foreign than American; all of which constitutes a serious religious problem. Yet hand in hand with the increase in the number of states and inhabitants go industry, wealth, and general culture. The United States has not had to struggle through 2,000 years, out of barbarism to civilization, as the countries of the old world have done. It fell heir to their progress, but with it have come the old world's evils. And the new world has also its troubles, arising from haste after wealth, from reckless speculation, and those misunderstandings between capital and labor which issue sometimes in blood. It is almost incredible how quickly the chaotic confusion of so many different peoples thrown together under one general government is reduced to order, how thoroughly the new dwellers are assimilated in the body politic. Thus it has come about that the type of American civilization is Anglo-Saxon, and the speech English.

The enormous increase of population adds proportionally to the field of labor and to the membership of the different churches. America is the land of church erection, of formation of congregations, and of every conceivable ecclesiastical and religious experiment, in which there are not missing the elements of fanaticism, hypocrisy, and humbug. It is the seed-plot of almost all branches of the Christian Church, and there is no check put upon their fullest development.

The religious life in the United States is in general like that of other lands; but it presents some peculiar features, which are stated in the following paragraphs.

II. Separation of Church and State: A distinction must be made between the general government and the individual states. The general government has been from the beginning limited to po-

1. The General Government and the Church. litical affairs, and has nothing to do with the internal arrangements of the several states, and especially with anything relating to religion. The constitution, adopted under Washington in 1787, provides, " No religious tests shall ever be required as a qualification to any office or public trust under the United States" (Art. vi. § 3). And even more emphatically speaks the first amendment, made by the first congress, 1789: " Congress shall make no law respecting an establishment of religion, or prohibiting the free exercise thereof, or abridging the freedom of speech or of the press, or of the rights of the people peaceably to assemble, and to petition the government for a redress of grievances." In this way there was secured, on the one hand, the separation of the Church from the government, and, on the other, the free, unhindered exercise of religion in every way which does not endanger the State or public morals. The above-quoted articles are not only a declaration of independence of federal control, they are also a declaration of the independence of the Church from the civil power. They did not originate in indifference to religion, but, on the contrary, in so great a respect that their framers would separate religion permanently from the defiling influence of politics, and guarantee to the whole people in a solemn manner religious along with civil liberty. The two institutions, Church and State, were not set opposite each other as foes, but side by side as the two different spheres of the social life, in the conviction that each should restrict its jurisdiction to its own immediate concerns, because the attempt of one to rule the other was sure to issue disastrously. The power of the State is consequently, in the United States, reduced to narrower limits than in Europe, where it has control over the Church. The American status of the Church differs from the hierarchical patronage of the State by the Church, from the imperial and papal patronage of the Church by the State, and also from the pre-Constantinian separation and persecution of the Church by the heathen State: hence the United States presents a new phase in the history of the relation of the two powers.

This separation between Church and State is not to be understood as a separation of the nation from Christianity; for the State represents, in America, only the temporal interests of the people. The independent churches care for the religious and moral interests; and the people are religious and Christian as no other, and express their sentiments in different ways—by the voluntary support of their very numerous churches and sects; by benevolent organizations of every kind; by attendance upon church, and regard for the ministry (who are second to none in dignity and influence); by a respect for the Sabbath which is not equaled elsewhere, except in Scotland (see SUNDAY, OBSERVANCE OF); by constant zeal for home and foreign missions; by reverence for the Bible; by a steady stream of edifying books, tracts, and periodicals; and by public morals. Congress nominates chaplains, of different confessions naturally, and opens every sitting with prayer. The President appoints chaplains for the army and navy. Fast-days have been frequently observed in particular emergencies (see FAST DAY): thus in 1849, during the cholera; in 1865, on the assassination of President Lincoln; and in 1881, on the death of President Garfield. Thanksgiving Day (q.v.) is yearly celebrated in November in all the states, on the proclamation of the president and the concurrent action of the different governors. Indeed, religion has all the more hold upon the American character because it is free from political control. No one is forced to make a religious profession; that is a matter of personal conviction and voluntary action.

2. Effects upon Religious Life.

As far as the individual states are concerned, Church and State are now separated; but this has not been the case from the beginning. Nor is the separation the consequence of independence of England. In some colonies it existed long prior to that event; so it was (at first) in Maryland, founded in 1634 by the Roman Catholic Lord Baltimore; in Rhode Island, settled in 1636 by Baptists under Roger Williams (q.v.), and in Pennsylvania, which William Penn (q.v.) acquired in 1680 from the English crown in payment of a debt, making the region an asylum for his persecuted Quaker coreligionists and all other Christian brethren. Each of these three representatives of Christian toleration adopted it, not in consequence of vague philosophical theories, still less out of religious indifferentism, but because of bitter experience of intolerance and of practical necessity. And this toleration was limited to the different confessions of the Christian faith, and did not apply to infidels or blasphemers, who were excluded from civil rights. In the other and older colonies, Church and State were from the beginning closely connected. In Massachusetts and the other New England colonies, except Rhode Island, the Congregational form of Puritanism was the state religion; and civil rights, in imitation of Jewish theocratic principles, were dependent upon a certain religious adherence. Not only was the Roman Church excluded, but, until the close of the seventeenth century, all Protestants who could not accept the established creed were dealt with as strictly as the Pilgrim fathers had themselves been by the bishops of Old England. Massachusetts banished the Baptist Roger Williams and other Baptists, and the followers of the Antinomian Anne

3. Attitude of Some States.

Hutchinson (see ANTINOMIANISM AND ANTINOMIAN CONTROVERSIES, II., 2); the Quakers were tried, and condemned to public scourging, ear-slitting, nose-boring, and even (by a vote of twelve to eleven in the Boston Legislature) to the gallows (see FRIENDS, SOCIETY OF, I., § 3). It should be remarked, however, that the Quakers in New England between 1658 and 1660 had acted fanatically. They had publicly denounced, in the churches and upon the streets, the civil and spiritual authorities. They thus provoked persecution and martyrdom by their impetuous zeal. Four such fanatics (one a woman), who had already been banished as Antinomians, obstinately rushed into martyrdom, and were hanged in 1660. But the people were opposed even then to such treatment; and the authorities were obliged to defend their action in a published statement, in which they justified themselves by quotations from the Old Testament and by the English laws against the Roman Catholic Church. The Quakers, thus driven out, found a retreat in Rhode Island until the establishment of Pennsylvania. Gradually the bond between Church and State was in New England relaxed; but in Connecticut it was first broken in 1816, while in Massachusetts the last traces remained until 1833. In Virginia and other southern colonies the Church of England was the State Church, and all other denominations felt the pressure of the English laws against dissenters. Nevertheless, the latter increased, especially the Baptists, Presbyterians, Quakers, and, later, the Methodists; and it was from them that the first impulse in Virginia proceeded to separate Church and State. Even before the declaration of independence, the Presbyterians and Baptists presented petitions to the colonial legislature to that intent. The measure found a defender in Thomas Jefferson, who in the interest of free-thinking, not out of any sympathy with the dissenters or out of love for Christianity, favored putting faith and unfaith upon the same political level. Through the exertions of the dissenters, the liberal Episcopalians, and the unbelieving Jefferson, the principle of separation between Church and State was, in Dec., 1776, and, more completely, in 1779, 1785, and the following decade, carried through the Virginia legislature. See LIBERTY, RELIGIOUS.

Soon after the close of the War of Independence (1783), and the adoption of the national constitution by the several states, the connection between Church and State in Maryland, New York, and South Carolina, and the other colonies where the English Episcopal Church was the predominant State Church, was broken, and complete religious freedom proclaimed. Last of all, and only very gradually, did the New England states, where Puritanism was deeply rooted in the mass of the people, adopt the new order of things. Now the principle of entire separation is universally operative. Only among the Mormons (q.v.) in Utah are Church and State combined. But the Mormons are powerless to prevent other sects coming among them; more than 150 churches other than Mormon are found in the state, twenty-five of them in Salt Lake City.

III. Voluntary System of Church Support: There is in the United States no obligatory baptism or confirmation. There are, on the contrary, thousands of grown persons who have not been baptized; but there are comparatively few who hold themselves entirely aloof from all church attendance and from all contributions for religious purposes. And the churches independent of State control are more particular as to the conduct and beliefs of their members than State churches are; so that the churches of America are more faithful to their avowed principles than the mother churches in Europe. The different churches are, almost without exception, dependent entirely upon voluntary subscriptions and contributions. The most prominent exceptions are Trinity Church (Episcopalian) and the Collegiate Church (Reformed Dutch), both in New York City, which have inherited property from the colonial period. But, speaking generally, the churches look to their membership for the means to carry on their work and for support of their ministers. The theological seminaries are the foundations of churches or individuals. The minister's salary is paid by the pew-rents or collections. Voluntary payments support Bible, tract, and other societies, and send out colporteurs and missionaries in city and country. It is considered a general duty and privilege to support religion as a necessary and useful element of society. The average salary of ministers in the United States is about $800; of theological professors, $1,500. A few ministers in large cities receive from $5,000 to $15,000. The voluntary system has its drawbacks, especially in the new congregations formed of immigrants who are accustomed to the European system of State support. But, on the other hand, it promotes liberality and individual enterprise; and the result is a yearly increase in churches, ministers, and ecclesiastical organizations of all sorts, while the old are maintained with vigor. On the average, it is said, each minister serves a thousand souls; but, of course, there is great disproportion. This free, self-regulated, and self-supported Christianity and church existence is one of the most characteristic features, and one of the greatest glories, of the United States, and constitutes a new leaf in church history; but it has its antecedents in the first three centuries and in the history of dissenters and free churches in Europe.

IV. Leading Denominations: For denominational history and statistics see the articles on the denominations in this work. Almost all American denominations are of European origin; but those which in Europe are divided by geographical and political boundaries are in the United States found thrown together. In England there are as many sects as in the United States; but all Christians outside the Church of England are classed together as dissenters. In America, there being no State Church, there can be no dissenters. Churches of many denominations are found in all the large cities. Thus in the city of New York, which has a population of 4,766,883, there are 1,600 congregations, of different nationalities and creeds, each of which has its church or regular place of meeting. This is one church to 2,090 of the population. Twenty-five years ago the ratio was one church to 2,413.

The American denominations may be divided into three groups: (1) the Evangelical churches; i.e., those which stand upon the principles of the Reformation theology, and accept the Bible as the sole guide of faith and life, and the confessions of the sixteenth or seventeenth centuries as a rule of public teaching. They embrace the great majority of the Christian population, and exert the strongest influence upon society. The Protestant Episcopal Church is the oldest, dating from 1607, the year of the settlement of Virginia; next come the Congregationalists, from the landing of the Pilgrims (1620); then the Reformed (Dutch), from 1628, the year of the formation of the first congregation in New York City. The first prominent Baptist in America was Roger Williams (q.v.), the founder of Rhode Island, 1636. The Quakers date from 1680; and the Methodists, from 1766. The German churches, in their organized state, date from the middle of the last century. Among them the Lutheran Church is by far the largest and most influential; then come the German Reformed, the Evangelical United, and the Moravians. A considerable number of Germans belong to the different branches of the Methodist Church, which also sends missionaries to Germany. (2) The Roman Catholic Church was a century ago inconsiderable, but, through the enormous immigration, now outnumbers any other single denomination. Yet it does not keep pace with the Roman Catholic migration, which is reported to form more than one-half of the total immigration to the United States. The emigration from Ireland is predominantly, that from Germany largely, and that from southern Europe almost exclusively Roman Catholic. (3) A third class consists of those denominations which reject the doctrines of the ecumenical creeds and the confessions of the Reformation churches, and strike out in new paths. Among these are the Unitarians, whose headquarters are in Boston and Cambridge, who are distinguished by high literary and social culture and active philanthropy; the Universalists, who teach as one of the three articles of their creed the ultimate restoration of all men to holiness and happiness; and the Swedenborgians, who believe in the divine mission of the great Swedish seer, and accept his revelations of the spirit-world.

V. Theological Education: This differs with the different denominations. It is carried on in Theological Seminaries (q.v.), endowed and supported by free gifts. Each denomination of importance has one or more, and in all there are 150. The faculties number from one to seventeen professors, and the number of students ranges from four to more than 300. The libraries (see THEOLOGICAL LIBRARIES) comprise from a few hundred to over 100,000 volumes. The course of instruction lasts three or four years. Greater stress is laid upon practical gifts and moral and religious character than upon the ministerial training-schools of State churches.

VI. Development: Something of the growth of American religious sentiment under the voluntary system may be seen in the fact that, while in the year 1800 Evangelical church-membership embraced one in fourteen of the population, in the year 1909 it included one in four. Evangelical communicants increased three and one-half times faster than the population in 100 years (1800–1900), and this in spite of the foreign flood. These figures take no note of the millions outside church-membership, old and young, especially the latter, who are brought under the healthful influence of religion in their home lives. An eminent authority estimates that fully 60,000,000 out of a population of 90,000,000 are either directly controlled or indirectly influenced in their daily lives by the churches of the land. The past twenty-five years especially have been marked, not only by large growth and wide diffusion of religious sentiment among the people, but by a significant change of emphasis in the claims of religion itself. The time has been when theology and the creeds formulated therefrom were the sole, or at least the predominant, standard of religious faith and practise. Under the change referred to, theological standards have by no means been abandoned; but they have, so to speak, been supplemented by practical forms of religious effort, to which has been given the significant term " Applied Christianity." This new point of view, or change of emphasis, is seen in the founding of chairs of social ethics in theological seminaries; in the widespread increase of institutional and mission churches which add to the preaching of the Gospel a practical sympathy and care for the neglected and the unprivileged; in the opening of social settlements in the lower wards of the great cities, where consecrated men and women, living on the ground, by personal ministry seek to alleviate distress and elevate the social and spiritual condition of the masses; in the multiplication of Young Men's and Young Women's Christian Associations, ministering to the physical, intellectual, social, and spiritual needs of their members and furnishing a refuge from the temptation of city and town; in the multiplied temperance societies and anti-saloon leagues, waging continuous, and of late most successful war in many states against intemperance and vice; and in institutes of social service, which seek to train the religious sentiment of the people into forms of religious service for the general betterment of society. All these forms of effort are the legitimate development of the religious life of the people, and they enjoy the cordial sympathy of the churches. If they are more numerous and active than they were fifty years ago it is because the need of them has grown with the growth of the population, and, especially, because the massing of foreign elements in great cities has awakened in the churches a lively sense of peril.

One of the most significant developments of applied Christianity is seen in the disposition of the churches to ally themselves with the struggles of the working classes against the tyranny of capital. For many years, and unconsciously on their part, the churches had allowed barriers to grow up between themselves and the laboring masses. Not that sympathy was wanting, but that it seemed to lack the means of adequate expression. It is to-day one of the most hopeful signs of the times that the leading ecclesiastical bodies of the United States, under a quickened sense of Christian brotherhood, not only pass resolutions of sympathy with the working classes, but invite the leaders of labor to plead their cause before the great national councils and conferences of these bodies, and in several instances employ secretaries of labor to cooperate with their working brethren for the betterment of their condition. (PHILIP SCHAFF†.) J. B. CLARK.

VII. Statistics: The figures in the following tables have been compiled chiefly from the year-book

CHURCH STATISTICS IN THE UNITED STATES.

Denominations.	Ministers.	Churches.	Members.
Adventists (7 bodies)	1,198	2,676	94,441
Armenian Church	73	73	19,889
Bahais	....	24	1,280
Baptists (14 bodies)	41,390	56,750	5,620,498
Brethren (Dunkers, 4 bodies) ...	3,477	1,155	120,597
Brethren (Plymouth, 4 bodies)	....	403	10,566
Brethren (River, 3 bodies).....	216	111	4,569
Buddhists (2 bodies)	15	74	3,165
Catholic Apostolic (2 bodies)...	33	24	4,927
Christadelphians...............	....	70	1,412
Christian Catholic Church in Zion—Dowie...	35	17	5,865
Christian Israelite Church	....	5	78
Christian Union...............	295	217	13,905
Christians (Christian Connection).....................	1,011	1,379	110,117
Church of Christ Scientist	2,208	1,104	114,089
Church of God and Saints of Christ (colored)	75	48	1,823
Churches of God, General Eldership......................	509	595	41,475
Churches of the Living God (colored) (3 bodies).........	101	68	4,276
Church of the New Jerusalem (2 bodies)...................	132	152	9,314
Communistic Societies (2 bodies).	....	22	2,272
Congregationalists.............	6,033	6,033	735,563
Disciples of Christ (2 bodies)..	8,163	12,590	1,417,462
Eastern Orthodox Churches (Greek, Russian, Servian, Syrian, Rumanian, Bulgarian, 6 bodies)...................	116	419	132,006
Evangelical Bodies (2)	1,751	2,803	213,121
Evangelistic Associations (14 bodies)...................	356	182	10,842
Free Christian Zion Church of Christ (colored)	20	15	1,835
Friends (4 bodies)	1,479	1,147	113,772
German Evangelical Protestant (2 bodies)...................	59	66	34,704
German Evangelical Synod	1,024	1,314	236,615
Independent Churches	....	874	47,673
International Apostolic Holiness Union......................	178	74	2,774
Jewish Congregations	1,084	1,769	....
Latter Day Saints (2 bodies)....	1,774	1,184	256,647
Lutherans (23 bodies and independent churches)	8,738	13,936	2,273,691
Mennonites (14 bodies)	1,006	604	54,798
Methodists (15 bodies)........	40,187	61,038	6,114,780
Moravians (2 bodies)...........	128	132	17,926
Non-sectarian Churches of Bible Faith	50	204	6,396
Pentecostal Church of the Nazarene...................	545	470	20,501
Polish National Church........	24	24	15,473
Presbyterians (12 bodies).......	13,492	16,570	1,940,835
Protestant Episcopal Church...	5,174	7,897	928,202
Reformed Bodies (4)...........	2,106	2,654	451,282
Reformed Catholic Church.....	10	5	1,250
Reformed Episcopal Church ...	84	81	9,682
Roman Catholic Church.......	17,194	13,461	12,425,946
Salvationists (3 bodies)........	3,391	785	25,538
Schwenkfelders................	5	8	725
Social Brethren...............	15	17	1,262
Society of Ethical Culture	....	5	2,040
Spiritualists..................	185	455	35,056
Swedish Evangelical (2 bodies)..	495	408	27,712
Temple Society................	3	3	376
Theosophical Societies (4 bodies).	....	85	2,336
Unitarians....................	540	503	70,542
United Brethren (2 bodies)....	2,500	4,478	310,815
Universalists..................	673	882	52,751
Vedanta Society...............	....	4	340
Totals....................	169,350	218,146	34,177,827

EDWIN M. BLISS.

and other denominational authorities for 1911, and from the *United States Census Report on Religious Bodies*, 1906. It will be noted that no figures are given for members of Jewish congregations. The *Census Report* gave 101,457 heads of families, but that represented less than two-thirds of the synagogues, 35 per cent of the 1,769 organizations failing to give any such figures at all; and there is no substantial basis even for an estimate. For the membership of the Roman Catholic Church, the figures for population given in the *Official Directory* were taken and 15 per cent deducted to allow for children under nine years of age according to an agreement between the United States Census Bureau and the Church authorities.

It should be remembered that the total of membership represents solely the registered membership of the various religious organizations. It makes no account of Protestant children under about fifteen years of age, of Mormon children under eight years of age, of Roman Catholic children under nine years of age. It is exclusive of the entire Jewish

population and of the great number of persons identified with Protestant churches, as attendants on their services and contributing to their support, but who are not enrolled in their membership.

BIBLIOGRAPHY: The articles in this work on the various denominations and religious agencies, and the literature under them; *The American Church History Series*, 13 vols., New York, 1893–97, especially vols. i. and xiii.; *The Stories of the Churches*, ib. 1904 sqq.; *United States Census: Special Reports, Religious Bodies*, 2 vols., Washington, D. C., 1910; R. Baird, *Religion in the United States of America*, Glasgow, 1844; L. F. Bittinger, *German Religious Life in Colonial Times*, Philadelphia, 1907; N. U. Wallington, *Historic Churches of America*, New York, 1907; M. I. J. Griffin, *Catholics and the American Revolution*, vol. i., Ridley Park, Pa., 1907; W. H. Allison, *Inventory of Unpublished Material for American Religious History in Protestant Church Archives and Other Repositories*, Washington, D. C., 1910; F. J. Zwierlein, *Religion in New Netherland . . . 1623–1664*, New York, 1910; Susan A. Ranlett, *Some Memory Days of the Church in America*, Milwaukee, 1911.

UNITED ZION'S CHILDREN. See RIVER BRETHREN.

UNITY OF THE BRETHREN (UNITAS FRATRUM).

"Unity of the Brethren" (*Unitas fratrum*) is the proper designation of what is generally called the Moravian Church.

I. History: This church, which must not be confounded with the United Brethren in Christ (q.v.), is a resuscitation, in a new form, of the Bohemian Brethren (q.v.). At the beginning of Luther's Reformation, the Brethren numbered about 400 parishes and 200,000 members, were using their own hymnal and catechism, and employing two printing-presses for the spread of Evangelical literature. In spite of frequent persecutions on the part of the Roman Catholics and Utraquists, they increased in number and grew in influence, until they obtained legal recognition (1609). One of the ends for which they labored was a closer fellowship among Protestants. They succeeded in effecting an alliance, based on the *Consensus Sendomiriensis*, among those of Poland (1570). This alliance, however, bore no abiding fruits. The Counter-Reformation, inaugurated by Ferdinand II., overthrew the Brethren as a visible organization in Bohemia and Moravia (1627); but they continued in Poland and Hungary to the end of the seventeenth century. At the same time there was preserved in their original seats a "hidden seed," which kept up, as far as possible, the tenets and usages of the fathers, held religious services in secret, and prayed for a resuscitation of the church. Such prayers were heard.

In 1722 two families named Neisser, led by Christian David, "the servant of the Lord," fled from Moravia, and, by invitation of Count Zinzendorf (q.v.), settled on his domain of Berthelsdorf in Saxony. About 300 Brethren, in the course of the next seven years, emigrated from Moravia and Bo-

hemia to the same place. They built a town called Herrnhut (q.v.), and were joined by a number of other Protestants from various parts of Germany. This settlement became the center of the renewed Brethren's church. In addition to the fact that its nucleus consisted of decendants of the Bohemian Brethren, such a renewal was brought about by the adoption of the leading features of their constitution; by the introduction of their discipline, as set forth in the *Ratio Disciplinæ* of Amos Comenius, and of much of their liturgy as found in their German hymnals; by appropriating their doctrinal tendency in so far as to hold fast to essentials, but not to bind the conscience with regard to non-essentials; and, finally, by the transfer of their episcopate, which had been carefully continued in the hope of a resuscitation. On Mar. 13, 1735, David Nitschmann was consecrated the first bishop of the Moravian Church by Bishop Daniel Ernst Jablonsky, with the concurrence of Christian Sitkovius, these two being the survivors of the old succession. The resuscitation of the Brethren's Church was, however, not accomplished in accordance with a prearranged plan; nor was Herrnhut built with such an end in view. The renewal was the work of God, who gradually led both the Moravian refugees and Zinzendorf to recognize his divine will. When Zinzendorf permitted the Brethren to settle on his estate, he knew little or nothing of the church of their fathers; and the projects which he had formed for the extension of God's kingdom looked in a different direction. It was only after these projects had failed, that he was made to see that Herrnhut, to use his own words, constituted "the parish to which he had from all eternity been ordained." By that time, however, there was gathered a body of Christians, not exclusively descended from the Bohemian fathers, but representing a union of survivors of the almost extinct church of the Bohemian-Moravian Brethren with representatives of German Pietism.

In the very nature of the case, therefore, a new and different development began. It was shaped by Zinzendorf. He had, indeed, declared that he would do all in his power to fulfil those hopes of a renewal of the Brethren's church which filled the heart of its aged Bishop Comenius; but at the same time he was by conviction a Lutheran, and had adopted Spener's idea in its deepest import, of establishing *ecclesiolæ in ecclesia*. This idea he carried out to extremes of which its originator had never thought. On the one hand, the Brethren were to constitute an independent church; and yet, on the other, they were not to interfere with the State Church, but to set forth within the same a union of believers representing the old Brethren, the Lutheran, and the Reformed elements, in one *Unitas Fratrum*. They were to serve as salt within the various confessional ecclesiastical bodies, but were to refrain from seeking to make proselytes for their church. Inner fellowship with the Brethren should neither involve nor demand separation from any existing Evangelical body. Accordingly, he did not allow the Brethren to expand as they had expanded in their original seats; but exclusive Moravian towns were founded, where no one but a member owned real estate, and the church controlled, not only their spiritual concerns, but also their industrial pursuits. In such towns a high type of piety was developed. A missionary spirit was fostered, which sent messengers of the Gospel to all parts of the heathen world, and found fields at home, through the so-called "Diaspora," on the continent of Europe, and, through domestic missions, in Great Britain and America. In their boarding-schools thousands of young people not connected with the Moravian Church received an excellent Christian education; and, during the long and dreary period of rationalism, vital faith in the essentials of the Gospel was cherished in such a manner that positive influences went forth from these centers wholly out of proportion to the paucity of the numbers of those identified with these settlements in the narrowest sense. At the same time there occasionally appeared a self-satisfied spirit, which, on the one hand, looked upon the Moravians as " a peculiar people " in a manner unjustifiable and beyond the warrant of holy writ, and on the other took acceptance with God for granted, as belonging of necessity to all the members of a church in which the Savior was preeminently the central figure of theology and of practical religion, and his name literally constituted a household word. For a brief period (1745–49), known as " the time of sifting," and in a few of the settlements, a far greater evil manifested itself. Fanaticism broke out among ministers and people. It did not lead them into gross sins, but gave rise to the most extravagant conceptions, especially as regarded the atonement in general, and Christ's wounded side in

3. Organization under Zinzendorf.

particular; to sensuous, puerile, and objectionable phraseology and hymns; and to religious services of reprehensible character. For such fanaticism Zinzendorf unwittingly furnished occasion by the fanciful and unwarranted ways in which, from his inclination to hyperbole and paradox, he expressed the believer's joy and the love which the pardoned sinner bears to the Savior. But, when he and his coadjutors began to realize the magnitude of the evil, they earnestly labored to bring back the erring ones to the sober faith and reverent love taught by the Scriptures. Such efforts were crowned with success, and the entire restoration of the church to spiritual health formed the best answer to the many attacks made upon it at that time and for a long period afterward, in part by earnest theologians, who taught the very same things as those the Brethren were aiming to promote, and in part by scurrilous enemies.

Zinzendorf was consecrated a bishop in 1737, and during his lifetime practically stood at the head of the church, although he had many assistants; and synods, in which his influence was all-powerful, were often held. After his death, the synods assumed their proper position, and the executive administration was vested in elective boards. The polity which he had introduced kept the Unitas Fratrum numerically small; but it was gradually established in Saxony, Prussia, Holland, Denmark, Baden, Switzerland, and Russia. In all these countries, except Switzerland, the exclusive system was introduced; on the part of their governments liberal concessions were granted. In the course of time the exclusive system was abolished, even on the continent of Europe, where it had originally been rendered necessary by the operation of ecclesiastical laws—at least in part. There are now twenty-four congregations on the continent of Europe. In Great Britain, the Moravians established themselves in 1738, chiefly through the efforts of Peter Boehler, who became God's instrument in leading John Wesley to a knowledge of the truth. In 1749 they were acknowledged by an act of parliament as " an ancient Episcopal Church." Four exclusive settlements were originally founded; but the rest of their churches, forty in number, never introduced the German polity. Here, too, the peculiarities of the old system have been practically abolished in the former settlements. Georgia was the colony in which the Moravians began their work in North America (1735); but they soon relinquished that field, and came to Pennsylvania (1740), where they built Bethlehem, Nazareth, and Lititz, in which three towns the exclusive system was introduced. Subsequently, they established, on the same plan, Hope in New Jersey (which enterprise proved a failure), and Salem in North Carolina. Their other churches were free from the trammels of this polity, which was totally relinquished in 1844. During the century in which it continued, it necessarily kept the church small in the United States of America also; since its relinquishment, the Moravians have increased rapidly, and during the last twenty years have doubled their membership. The number of their churches is ninety-one,

4. Development Elsewhere.

besides seven congregations in Alberta, Canada, commenced in 1895 as a result of migrations from Russia.

II. German Moravian Towns: Although the exclusive system on the continent of Europe has been abolished, certain features of the former arrangements have been maintained. The membership, " according to difference of age, sex, and station in life," is divided into classes, called " choirs " (from *choros*). At the head of each choir stands an elder, or, in the case of a female class, a deaconess, charged with its spiritual interests. Special religious services are held, and an annual day of covenanting and praise is observed. Such classes, or choirs, are maintained in other Moravian churches also. Every settlement has a brethren's, a sisters', and a widows' house, which provide at moderate charges a modest home for the inmates, who are bound by no vows and are free to come and go at will. A sisters' house is inhabited by unmarried women who maintain themselves by work suited to their sex; and a brethren's house by unmarried men who carry on various trades. There are two superintendents for each house, one looking after the religious concerns of the inmates, the other managing the temporal affairs. Religious services for all the inhabitants are held every evening in the church.

III. Constitution, Ministry, Ritual, and Usages: (1) In 1857 and again in 1899 the entire constitution of the Unitas Fratrum was remodeled. It embraces four provinces, the German, the British, and two American. They are administratively independent, but together constitute one organic whole in regard to doctrine, fundamental principles of discipline and ritual, and foreign missionary work. There is a general and a provincial government. A general synod meets statedly at Herrnhut, and is constituted of delegates from all provinces, as also from the foreign mission-field. Each province has also its provincial synod, which elects its executive board, known as a provincial elders' conference. These four executive boards together with the mission-board jointly constitute the so-called directing board of the unity, a court of appeal and of supreme reference and counsel during the intervals between sessions of the general synod. The mission-board is elected by the general synod, to which it is responsible, and consists of five members, three of whom must be elected by and as such represent the chief nationalities entering into the membership of the Moravian Church, viz., the German, the British, and the American branches. (2) The ministry consists of bishops, presbyters, and deacons. Unordained assistants, whether men or women, are formally constituted acolytes. The Moravian episcopacy is not diocesan, but represents the entire Unitas Fratrum. In the bishops is vested exclusively the power of ordaining. They constitute a body whose duty it is to look to the welfare, and maintain the integrity, of the Unitas Fratrum in all its parts, and especially to bear it on their hearts in unceasing prayer before God; and, although they are not *ex officio* connected with the government, they are, as a rule, elected to the governing boards. (3) The ritual is liturgical in character. A litany is used every Sunday morning. Special services,

at which offices of worship are used, distinguish the festivals of the ecclesiastical year, certain " memorial days " in the history of the Moravian Church, and the annual days of covenanting of the choirs. The hymnology is rich, and church music very fully developed. Some of the best-known Moravian hymnologists are Zinzendorf, Countess Zinzendorf, Spangenberg, Louise von Hayn, Gregor, James Montgomery (q.v.), F. W. Foster, John Cennick (q.v.), Ludolf Schlicht, Benjamin La Trobe, John Swertner, Garve, and Albertini. Love feasts, in imitation of the *agapæ* of apostolic times, are celebrated. The *pedilavium*, or foot-washing, was formerly practised within limited circles, but was abrogated in 1818. At one time the lot was employed in the appointment of all ministers, and marriages were contracted in the same way. Its use has been abolished; its employment with regard to the marriages of members was done away with in 1818.

IV. Doctrine: The Moravian Church does not set forth its doctrines in a formal confession of faith, as was done by its Bohemian fathers; but the cardinal points are found in its catechism, in its Easter Morning Litany (Schaff, *Creeds*, iii. 799), and in its " Synodical Results," or code of statutes drawn up by the general synod. The Holy Scriptures of the Old and New Testament, venerated as God's Word, containing all the truths that declare the will of God for man's salvation, are held to be the only rule of faith and practise. The following truths are held to be clearly attested by Holy Scripture, and as such essential: the doctrine of the total depravity of human nature, the love of God the Father, the real Godhead and real humanity of Jesus Christ, our reconciliation to God and our justification by faith through the sacrifice of Jesus Christ, the Holy Ghost and his operations, good works as the fruit of the Spirit, the fellowship of believers, the second coming of the Lord, and the resurrection of the dead unto life or unto condemnation. On the other hand, Moravians hold that " it is not our business to determine what Scripture has left undetermined, or to contend about mysteries impenetrable to human reason " (A. G. Spangenberg, *Exposition of Christian Doctrine*, London, 1784; H. Plitt, *Glaubenslehre*, Gotha, 1863; idem, *Zinzendorfs Theologie*, 3 vols., Gotha, 1869–74).

V. Enterprises of the Church: There are in the four provinces 28 boarding-schools for young people not connected with the Moravian Church, at which schools about 2,000 pupils of both sexes are annually educated. In 24 day-schools between 2,500 and 3,000 scholars are also under the influence of the church. Besides these are three colleges and theological seminaries.

1. Schools.

Although three Protestant missions existed prior to the Moravian missionary work, such enterprises were all undertaken in connection with the planting of colonies. The Moravians were the first Protestants who went among the heathen with no other purpose in view than that of saving souls. In 1732 Leonard Dober and David Nitschmann (q.v.) inaugurated on the island of St. Thomas that work to which the

2. Missions.

church still chiefly devotes itself, which God has wonderfully blessed. At various times missions— in the service of which large amounts of money were spent and many lives sacrificed, but which eventually proved unsuccessful—were undertaken in the following countries: Lapland (1734–36), shores of the Arctic Ocean (1737–38), Ceylon (1738–41), Algiers (1740), Guinea (1737–41 and 1767–70), Persia (1747–50), Egypt (1752–83), East Indies (1759–96), and the Calmuck territory (1768–1823). In 1900 the mission among the Eskimos of Greenland, commenced in 1733, was transferred to the care of the State Church of Denmark, there being no more professed heathen in this region. The field at the present day embraces the following mission provinces: Labrador (1771), Alaska (1885), Indians of North America (1734), St. Thomas and St. John (1732), St. Croix (1732), Jamaica (1754), Antigua (1756), St. Kitts (1775), Barbados (1765), Tobago (1790, renewed 1827), Trinidad (1890), Sańto Domingo (1907), Demerara (1835, renewed 1878), Nicaragua (1848), Surinam (1735), South African Western Province (1736, renewed 1792), South African Eastern Province (1828), German East Africa (1891), Australia (1849), and West Himalaya (1853). The annual cost of this extensive work is about $500,000. This amount is made up by the contributions of the members of the church, by gifts from friends of the cause, by grants from missionary societies in the home provinces, by the interest of funded legacies, and by the missions themselves through the voluntary donations and the profits of trade. The London Association in aid of the Missions of the United Brethren, founded in 1817, is composed of members of various churches, not of Moravians, and contributes about $80,000 a year. The Brethren's Society for the Furtherance of the Gospel among the Heathen, founded in England in 1741, works for the support of the mission in Labrador and owns a missionary vessel, which has now been annually sailing to that uncharted coast for 141 years without ever wholly failing in its mission. A similar society in Bethlehem, Penn., the Society for the Propagation of the Gospel among the Heathen, founded in 1787, undertakes the support of the mission among the Eskimos of Alaska and of that among the Indians of Southern California. The converts are divided into four classes—new people (or applicants for religious instruction), candidates for baptism, baptized adults, and communicants. According to the latest statistics, the missions comprise 309 stations and 1,213 preaching-places. There are two theological seminaries for the training of native ministers in the field itself; 5 normal schools with about 90 scholars, 347 day-schools with 30,504 pupils, 578 teachers, and 235 monitors; 142 Sunday-schools with 24,357 pupils and 1,354 teachers; 407 missionaries, male and female; 102 native ministers and wives of ministers; 2,134 native assistants, and 102,643 converts, in the care of the mission.

The Bohemian mission work was begun in 1870. At first it advanced very slowly, on account of the restrictions imposed by the Austrian laws. In 1880 these restrictions were removed, and the Unitas Fratrum was legally acknowledged by that same government at whose hands it received its death-

blow in the Counter-Reformation. This mission embraces 5 chief stations, with about 25 filials. Three orphanages are conducted, 12 missionaries are engaged, and the membership numbers 1,178. In 1881 the Moravians took charge, in Jerusalem, of a hospital previously established for lepers. This institution is supported by contributions from the three provinces and the gifts of friends. The inmates number between 50 and 60. The Diaspora (from *diaspora*, in I Pet. i. 1) work is carried on by the German province, and has for its object the evangelization of the state churches on the continent of Europe, without depriving them of their members. Evangelists itinerate through the various countries of Germany, Switzerland, France, Denmark, Norway, and Sweden, and through Poland, Livonia, Esthonia, and other parts of Russia, visiting, preaching, and organizing " societies." This mission embraces 54 central stations, 61 laborers, and about 75,000 " society members."

3. Other Agencies.

VI. Statistics: The home provinces report 411 bishops, presbyters, deacons, and unordained assistants, male and female, in various departments of church work, not counting teachers; 42,791 souls. Foreign and Bohemian missions report 198 bishops, presbyters, and deacons; 60 unordained assistants; 234 female assistants; 2,134 native assistants; 103,-810 souls. The Unitas Fratrum, therefore, numbers in all 888 bishops, presbyters and deacons, and other appointed workers; or, with native assistants, 3,037 workers, and 146,601 souls, and has, besides, about 75,000 souls in its Diaspora societies.

(E. DE SCHWEINITZ†.) J. TAYLOR HAMILTON.

BIBLIOGRAPHY: D. Cranz, *Alte und neue Brüderhistorie*, Barby, 1772, Eng. transl., *Ancient and Modern Hist. of the Brethren*, London, 1780, the German continued by Hegner, 3 parts, Barby and Gnadau, 1791–1816; J. Risler, *Select Narratives from the Hist. of the . . . Unitas Fratrum*, ib. 1806; J. B. Holmes, *Hist. of the Protestant Church of the United Brethren*, 2 vols., ib. 1825, Bethlehem, Pa., 1830; E. H. Reichel, *Historical Sketch of the Church and Missions of the United Brethren*, Bethlehem, 1848; J. Latrobe, *Historical Sketch of the Church of the United Brethren*, Bath, 1850; L. C. Schrautenbach, *Zinzendorf und die Brüder-Gemeinde*, Gnadau, 1851; E. W. Cröger, *Geschichte der alten und erneuerten Brüder-Kirche*, 5 vols., ib. 1851–65; L. T. Reichel, *Hist. of the Moravians in North Carolina*, Bethlehem, 1857; J. Henry, *Sketches of Moravian Life and Character*, Philadelphia, 1859; A. Bost, *Hist. of the Bohemian and Moravian Brethren*, new ed., London, 1863; W. C. Reichel, *Memorials of the Moravian Church*, Philadelphia, 1870; J. M. Martin, *Historical Sketch of Bethlehem and the Moravians*, Bethlehem, 1873; E. de Schweinitz, *Hist. of the Church Known as the Unitas Fratrum*, ib. 1885; idem, *Moravian Manual*, 3d ed., by J. T. Hamilton, ib. 1901; Schultze, *Die Missionsfelder der erneuerten Brüder-Kirche*, ib. 1890; J. T. Hamilton, *Hist. of the Moravian Church during the 18th and 19th Centuries*, ib. 1900; idem, *Hist. of the Moravian Missions*, ib. 1901; idem, *Twenty Years of Pioneer Missionary Enterprise in Nyasa-Land*, Bethlehem, Pa., 1911; J. H. Clewell, *Hist. of Wachovia in N. C.; the Unitas Fratrum or Moravian Church 1572–1902*, New York, 1902; J. M. Levering, *Hist. of Bethlehem, Pa., 1741–1892*, Bethlehem, 1903; A. L. Fries, *Moravians in Georgia, 1735–40*, Winston Salem, 1905; G. Burkhardt, *Die Brüdergemeine*, 2 parts, Gnadau, 1905; O. Steinecke, *Die Diaspora der Brüdergemeine in Deutschland*, Halle, 1905; H. Garst, *Otterbein University, 1847–1907*, Dayton, O., 1908; J. G. E. Heckwelder, *A Narrative of the Mission of the United Brethren among the Delaware and Mohegan Indians from its Commencement in 1740 to the Close of the Year 1808*, Cleveland, 1907; *Missionsatlas der Brüdergemeinde*, Herrnhut, 1908.

UNIVERSALIST DISSENTERS: See PURVES, JAMES.

UNIVERSALISTS.

I. Doctrine and Organiza-   II. History.
     tion.   Universalism in the East
     Doctrine (§ 1).   (§ 1).
     Standards; Conditions of   In the West (§ 2).
       Fellowship (§ 2).   In America (§ 3).
     Polity (§ 3).   Present and Future of
                         the Church (§ 4).

I. Doctrine and Organization: Universalism is the characteristic doctrine of those who believe that all souls will some time be induced to repent and turn from their sins, and that so all will be saved. Advocates of this doctrine are found in nearly all denominations of religion, Christian **1. Doctrine.** and heathen. Some of these advocates differ from their parent religion or sect only in holding that the benefits of salvation will finally be enjoyed by all men. Even among those organized as a Christian church and called Universalists nearly every variety of doctrine is represented except as to the distinctive and confident hope of universal salvation. Yet a large majority of them hold a definite system of doctrine which may be indicated as follows: the Bible contains a revelation from God mingled with elements entirely human and fallible, and has authority such as experts have in their special line of activity. Other good books have the same kind of authority, but in a lower degree. God is a person of infinite excellencies. His nature is best expressed in the one word love, at least the other attributes are entirely consistent with this one. As to the nature of Christ the Universalists are divided. The younger clergy commonly regard him as a man born of Joseph or some other human father and Mary. The older Universalists have commonly regarded him as a being ranking, so to speak, half-way between God and man, born of God and Mary, according to a literal understanding of the Gospels of Matthew and Luke. The Holy Spirit is either God the Father himself or is impersonal. Miracles are the constant or occasional action of God in (human or other) nature for its betterment. Providence is therefore both general and special. Salvation is from sin and its sequences and from all other forms of evil and unto righteousness, holiness, and a perfected humanity, and is constantly going on under the impulse of God and other good spirits and agencies. This is the so-called moral salvation, and contains no element of substitutional satisfaction or transfer of guilt or merit. Punishment is a sequence of sin, is divinely appointed as a remedy therefor, and is consequently one of the agencies of salvation both in this world and in the next. The clergy have no apostolic succession, but are merely the special agents of God in the salvation of men. The Church universal is the great body of all professing Christians, of which body a humble member is the Universalist Church. Religion is right relations with God, and therefore includes right thoughts about him, right feelings toward him, and right acts in the service of him and his children. Hence the Universalists have always been zealous for doctrine for the honor of God and for social reforms and charities. The sacraments (baptism and the Lord's Supper) are chiefly sacred symbols and distinguishing marks of the Christian life and of membership in the Christian Church. Future life is substantially a continuation of the present life, but without the present body of the flesh. There will be no resurrection of this body, and no general judgment, no annihilation of the wicked, no endless punishment in the usual sense of the term, and no second coming of Christ, except in the improvement of souls and of the usual means thereof in this life and in that to come.

The Winchester Profession of Belief has been commonly regarded as the creed of the Universalist church, but in fact it has not been at any time adopted and used as a creed by more than a small fraction of the local churches. In **2. Stand-** order to have the law of the church **ards; Con-** conform to the consent and practise **ditions of** of the people, the general convention **Fellowship.** in 1899 thought best to adopt the following statement:

1. The profession of belief adopted at the session at Winchester, N. H., 1803, is as follows:

Article I. We believe that the Holy Scriptures of the Old and New Testaments contain a revelation of the character of God and of the duty, interest, and final destination of mankind.

Article II. We believe that there is one God, whose nature is Love, revealed in one Lord Jesus Christ, by one Holy Spirit of Grace, who will finally restore the whole family of mankind to holiness and happiness.

Article III. We believe that holiness and true happiness are inseparably connected, and that believers ought to be careful to maintain order and practise good works; for these things are good and profitable unto men.

2. The conditions of fellowship shall be as follows:

A. The acceptance of the essential principles of the Universalist Faith, to wit: 1. The universal fatherhood of God; 2. the spiritual authority and leadership of his son, Jesus Christ; 3. the trustworthiness of the Bible as containing a revelation from God; 4. the certainty of just retribution for sin; 5. the final harmony of all souls with God.

The Winchester profession is commended as containing these principles, but neither this nor any other precise form of words is required as a condition of fellowship, provided always that the principles above stated be professed.

B. The acknowledgment of the authority of the general convention and assent to its laws.

The polity of the Universalist Church may be described as a composite of the Congregational, Presbyterian, and Episcopal systems. Primarily it is democratic, and is modeled somewhat after the constitution of the United States. In each state of **3. Polity.** the union there is a convention, meeting yearly and made up of the ministers in fellowship and residing in the state, and lay representatives chosen by the parishes. Each of these conventions has jurisdiction within the borders of the state, in matters of fellowship, ordination, and local missions. Over all is the general convention of Universalists, which meets biennially, and is composed of delegates, clerical and lay, in definite proportions, chosen by the state conventions. This body has a national charter and a permanent board of trustees who have charge of general interests during the interim of the conventions. For the further administration of affairs and for the quickening of spirit a system of superintendency has lately been adopted. First (in time), the several states appointed each a secretary or superintendent of churches as its servant in the promotion of religious life. Then the general convention appointed a general superintendent of all the churches in its communion. These officials correspond respectively to bishop and archbishop, especially in the original meanings of the words, and without formal authority except to counsel, advise, and encourage. Thus, on the whole, it will be seen that the Universalists are nearly related to the liberal Congregationalists. In popular estimate they are often associated with the Unitarians, but they differ from them in assigning more value to the Bible and to religious life, and in laying emphasis on the personality of God and the endless life of every soul, whereas the Unitarians (q.v.) include many who teach that God is impersonal and that the wicked will be annihilated, and some who doubt the future life altogether. More effectively, perhaps, the Universalists are separated from the Unitarians in having different traditions and in belonging mostly to a different social class, the middle class.

II. History: Pantheists of all times have held a form of universalism, but with an important difference from the modern meaning of the word; they have taught that all souls will be absorbed into the Infinite, and

1. Universalism in the East. will lose their personal identity. Christian Universalists believe that every soul will live forever as an individual and will attain a proper development and final salvation. For this reason orthodox Hindus and Buddhists and many of the speculative philosophers, even some that are called Christian, can hardly be included in this account. The earliest Universalists, more strictly so called, were Zoroaster (whose date is variously estimated from 1500 to 500 B.C.) and his followers the Parsees, who remain in this faith unto the present day (see ZOROASTER, ZOROASTRIANISM). Next in order of time were Jews, some of whom since shortly before the days of Christ were Universalists. Among Christians and those associated with the Church the first advocates of universalism were some Gnostics (the Valentinians, Carpocratians, and Basilidians, about 130 A.D.; see GNOSTICISM; BASILIDES AND THE BASILIDIANS; CARPOCRATES AND THE CARPOCRATIANS; VALENTINUS, VALENTINIANS) although their doctrine as to individualism is not entirely clear. At the same time, or later, certain orthodox Christians who were the authors of the forged Sibylline Oracles (q.v.) were undoubtedly Universalists. The earliest system of Universalistic theology was by Clement of Alexandria (q.v.), who was the head of the theological school in that city until 202 A.D. His successor in the school was the great Origen (q.v.), the most distinguished advocate of this doctrine in all time. His mind had something of the largeness of Plato combined with Christian piety, and his influence was felt for many centuries throughout the East and to some extent in the West. The next great philosophical theologian in the East was Gregory of Nyssa (q.v.). Then came Theodore of Mopsuestia (q.v.), distinguished as the promulgator of the grammatico-historical exegesis (see EXEGESIS OR HERMENEUTICS, III., § 3; and ANTIOCH, SCHOOL OF), and of a Biblical scientific theology containing a portion of the theory of evolution applied to the history of mankind. His influence for some centuries was more extensive than that of Augustine. Johannes Cassianus (q.v.) should also be mentioned. He was the author of Semipelagianism (q.v.). Under the instruction of these great teachers many other theologians believed in universal salvation; and indeed the whole Eastern Church (q.v.) until after 500 A.D. was inclined to it.

In the West this doctrine had fewer adherents and was never accepted by the Church at large. In the first five or six centuries of Christianity there were six

2. In the West. known theological schools, of which four (Alexandria [see ALEXANDRIA, SCHOOL OF], Antioch, Cæsarea, and Edessa or Nisibis) were Universalist, one (Ephesus) accepted conditional immortality; one (Carthage or Rome) taught endless pun-

ishment of the wicked. Other theological schools are mentioned as founded by Universalists, but their actual doctrine on this subject is unknown. Doederlein says that "In proportion as any man was eminent in learning in Christian antiquity, the more did he cherish and defend the hope of the termination of future torments." In the dark ages Universalism almost disappeared, but in the ninth century it had one great representative, John Scotus Erigena (see SCOTUS ERIGENA, JOHANNES), who was the chief Christian luminary of his time. In the Middle Ages, some of the lesser mystics and probably Johann Tauler and Jan van Ruysbroeck (qq.v.), and one leading scholastic, Albertus Magnus (q.v.), were Universalists. In the times of the Reformation Universalists were found among Anabaptists, Lollards, and Protestant mystics; and later there were increasing numbers of individual believers in this doctrine in all northern European countries, including such men as Kant, Schleiermacher, Ritschl and many of his followers, Archbishop Tillotson, Tennyson, the Brownings, Wordsworth, and Coleridge. [The ascription of universalism to many of the ancient, medieval, and modern theologians and institutions would be disapproved by many scholars of the present, probably by a majority. In many cases the expression of the "larger hope" or of doubt as to the endlessness of future punishment is all that can fairly be claimed. A. H. N.]

In America before the time of organized Universalism there were many representatives of this faith: Sir Henry Vane, Jr., and other mystics; the German Baptists commonly called Dunkers;

3. In America. some of the Moravians; several Episcopalians, especially William Smith, founder of the University of Pennsylvania, and for many years president of the general convention of the Protestant Episcopal Church; several leading Congregationalists, including Charles Chauncy and Jonathan Mayhew (qq.v.). The high character and distinguished abilities of these men go far toward extending to modern times also the words of Doederlein above quoted. The Universalist Church in America has not greatly prospered. First, its main idea was so popular in the early period of the United States that the proposal to organize a church in its behalf frightened the other churches and aroused sectarian jealousy. Secondly, the Universalists by removing the fear of hell were supposed to reduce seriously the supports of morality. And finally the church was started among the lower classes of people, and therefore the whole power of social or caste distinction was turned against it. In those days the force of sectarianism was so great and the ministers had so much influence that when nearly all parties united to lay the new church under a ban and to declare a boycott on everything Universalist, they were able almost to destroy the movement. That the conspiracy was partly unconscious did not make it less effective, though time has reduced its power. Of organized Universalism in America the chief representatives in order of time have been John Murray, Elhanan Winchester, the two Hosea Ballous, A. A. Miner (qq.v.), T. J. Sawyer, and Orello Cone (q.v.), not to mention those still living. The Restorationist Controversy arose early in the nineteenth century on occasion of a dispute over future punishment. A few of those who believed in future punishment of the wicked seceded from the main body and called themselves "The Massachusetts Association of Universal Restorationists." This association maintained a feeble existence from 1831 to 1841 and then formally dissolved. There was really no occasion for the secession, for the main body contained many who believed in future punishment but who were not willing to leave the parent organization. Moreover, the opposing idea of immediate and miraculous salvation of all at death was being given up as Universalists progressed in their separation from " orthodox " antecedents. This doctrine was called the " death and glory " theory, and was the usual orthodox Calvinistic theory of the salvation of the elect by irresistible grace, applied by the Calvinistic Universalists to all mankind because all are elect. When the Universalists gave up Calvinism they came to believe in a gradual salvation (by persuasion) here and hereafter, and therefore taught future punishment of limited duration. The death and glory theory was formally renounced (for the purpose of public information) by a local convention in Boston in 1878.

Statistics give 42 state conventions (or their equivalent), 673 ministers, 882 parishes, 52,751 church-members, 644 Sunday-schools with 39,523 members, 743 church edifices with parish property amounting to $12,775,996, and a very active Young People's Christian Union having a membership of 8,000. The Universalists support in the United States 4 colleges, 3 theological schools, and, in connection therewith, 4 fitting-schools or academies. These institutions employ 309 professors and teachers, are attended by 2,627 students, and are supported by funds amounting to $4,750,000. Its foreign mission in Japan was begun by the general convention in 1890, and at present employs three missionaries from the United States and four ordained Japanese clergymen, and publishes a monthly magazine in the Japanese language. It also sustains an important charity, the Blackmer Home for girls in Tokyo, Japan. For further statistics consult *The Universalist Register*. That the course of this church as a separate body is nearly run is a not uncommon opinion. Already on the continent of Europe the doctrines against which the Universalists protested have mostly disappeared except among Roman Catholics, and faith in universal salvation is openly and frequently professed. Great Britain is somewhat more conservative, and the United States still more so. But in the northern states of the union the doctrine is rapidly growing in favor on all sides. Christian Scientists (see EDDY, MARY BAKER GLOVER; SCIENCE, CHRISTIAN) are all Universalists; it is estimated that more than half of the Unitarians, about one-third of the Episcopalians, many of the Congregationalists, and individuals in other sects are of this faith. Already there are more Universalists outside the denomination than inside, and henceforth the work for which the sect was formed will mostly be done by the larger organizations; and there will be less and less occasion

4. Present and Future of the Church.

for a sect specially advocating the triumphant love of God.   GEORGE T. KNIGHT†.

BIBLIOGRAPHY: The literature of Universalism is extensive, especially periodicals, of which the chief now current (all, except the second, published by the Universalist Publishing House of Boston and Chicago) are: *The Universalist Leader* (weekly), *The Universalist Herald* (weekly, published by J. M. Bowers, Canon, Ga.), *The Sunday School Helper* (monthly), *The Universalist Register* (yearly), and *Onward* (weekly), the organ of the young people's associations.

For history consult: Hosea Ballou, 2d, *Ancient History of Universalism*, Boston, 1829, annotated ed., 1872 (learned and cautious); T. Whittemore, *The Modern History of Universalism*, vol. i. (all published), ib. 1860; J. W. Hanson, *A Cloud of Witnesses*, Boston, 1883 (a collection of quotations from many authors more or less favoring Universalism); and above all, for learning and accuracy, R. Eddy, in *The American Church History Series*, x. 255–506, New York, 1894; idem, *The History of Universalism in America*, 2 vols., Boston, 1884–86. These are all published by the Universalist Publishing House, except the volume in *The American Church History Series*.

The most adequate modern systematic statements of this doctrine are: J. S. Dodge, *The Purpose of God*, Boston, 1894, and O. Cone, *What is Universalism?* Boston, n.d. Consult further: The writings of Thomas Erskine of Linlathen (abound with statements of Universalism well correlated with his general thought; consult the article for a list of the writings); T. T. Munger, *Freedom of Faith*, Boston, 1883; idem, *Appeal to Life*, ib. 1887; R. J. Campbell, *The New Theology*, and *The New Theology Sermons*, London and New York, 1907 (presenting a type of Universalism).

Controversial writings: No statement of modern Universalism would be adequate without reference to the controversies which have been so large a part of the life of the denomination. Some of the latest writings of this order are: T. J. Sawyer, *Endless Punishment in the Very Words of its Advocates*, Boston, 1880 (learned and in Addisonian style); G. T. Knight, *The Goodness of God*, ib. 1904 (containing the case for pessimism and the case for optimism, in a critical philosophical manner). Doctrinal defenses of Universalism so far as based on the Bible are to be found in L. R. Paige, *A Commentary on the New Testament*, 6 vols., ib. 1844–70 (now somewhat antiquated); S. Cox, *Salvator Mundi*, New York, 1878; T. B. Thayer, *The Theology of Universalism*, Boston, 1862 (limited to eschatology, and antiquated). Writers who are agnostic as to universal salvation (though decidedly opposed to endless punishment) are: F. W. Farrar, in *Eternal Hope*, London and New York, 1878 (five sermons and other discussions exegetical and historical); idem, in *Mercy and Judgment*, ib. 1881; Edward Beecher, in *Doctrine of Scriptural Retribution*, New York, 1878; and F. N. Oxenham, in *What is the Truth as to Everlasting Punishment?* 1881 (an Anglican reply to Pusey; see below). The most vigorous attacks on Universalism are: W. G. T. Shedd, *Doctrine of Endless Punishment*, New York, 1886 (leaves nothing to be desired in behalf of its subject); H. Johnston, *Beyond Death*, New York, 1903; W. E. Gladstone, in *The North American Review*, Apr., 1896, pp. 453 sqq.; E. B. Pusey, *What is Faith as to Everlasting Punishment?* 2d ed., Oxford, 1880 (making an attempt to restore the traditional doctrine to its position in Scripture and history, from which Farrar's *Eternal Hope* had displaced it; cf. F. N. Oxenham, ut sup., for indications of the success of Pusey's attempt); and R. W. Dale, *Christian Doctrine*, pp. 237–248, New York, 1895. A. H. Strong, *Systematic Theology*, pp. 587–600, Rochester, N. Y., 1886; and S. D. F. Salmond, *Christian Doctrine of Immortality*, 4th ed., Edinburgh, 1901, are perhaps the most fair-minded writers among the opponents of Universalism.

UNIVERSITIES.

Universities are a product of the spiritual life of the Middle Ages, when they were at once ecclesiastical and secular institutions. In origin they date from the twelfth and thirteenth centuries, when they were called " general schools," as at Paris and Bologna, in contradistinction from other institutions termed " special " or " particular " schools. Their characteristics were three: they were institutions for every one who wished to study; their teaching was designed to be for the advantage of all Christendom; and those who completed the course of study considered typical and necessary were declared worthy, on examination, to propagate and teach the learning they had acquired.

1. Basal Ideas.

But the university was something more than the " general school "—it was a juristic corporation. Such organizations of teachers and students arose toward the end of the twelfth century, remolding the schools and securing important privileges. Within these corporate bodies, or *universitates magistrorum et scholarium*, were " faculties " of teachers and " nations " of students. In the course of time the designation of the corporate body was transferred to the corps of teachers, and in Germany *studium generale* and *universitas* were synonyms from the first. The archetype of the university was found in Paris and Bologna in the early twelfth century, the former devoted to theology and the latter to law, but both employing the same new method. This was the dialectic consideration of theology and law respectively, the set task being the dialectic removal of discrepancies between Church Fathers or glossators, the weighing of the pros and cons, and the final conclusion, or *sententia*. In harmony with the medieval doctrine of the universal monarchy and the universal Church, theology and jurisprudence stood in the foreground of interest. The universities were favored with special privileges, the first being the *Authentica habita* of the Emperor Frederick I. (1158) giving imperial protection to those journeying to distant places for the sake of study, exempting them from local jurisdiction, and placing them under the control of teacher or bishop. A similar course was followed by Philip Augustus for the University of Paris in 1200, and the popes later bestowed the right of conferring degrees and the so-called right of residence.

Toward the close of the twelfth century the University of Paris was formed by the union of the teachers of the four subjects of theology, law, medicine, and arts. By degrees the teachers of the same subjects formed still closer associations (caused primarily by the need of regulation of the conferring of degrees), which took place 1310–20. About this same time the term " faculty " was employed to denote first the subject and then the body of those

2. University of Paris; Organization.

teaching it. Among the faculties that of arts was the lowest, serving as introductory to the other three. It taught the traditional seven liberal arts and especially Aristotelian philosophy, while in its study of dialectics it prepared the way for theology. The faculty of law, in like manner, was devoted to canon law. In these same decades the scholars were divided, for administration and discipline, into four " nations," each headed by its chosen " procurator," and all four united under a " rector."

The students of the faculty of arts soon gained the ascendency in the university, especially as their masters were at the same time scholars in the higher faculties, and about 1274 the rector of the nations, which included the entire university except the teachers of the higher faculties, became the head of the faculty of arts. About the same time each of the other faculties seems to have given itself a " dean " as its chief officer, but by 1341 the rector had become supreme over the deans of medicine and law, and even of theology, so that he was now the ruler of the whole university, a development completed shortly before the foundation of the first German university (Prague, 1348).

While in France education had been connected, since the time of Charlemagne, with monasteries and churches, so that both teachers and scholars were clergy; in Italy the laity had also taught from Roman days, and the development of the Bolognese type accordingly differed from the Parisian. The chief studies in Italy were grammar, rhetoric, and law, the latter taught at Rome, Pavia, Ravenna, and Bologna as a department of the arts. Early in the fourteenth century, however, law became a separate branch of study at Bologna, due to the abiding influence of the lawyer Irnerius and the canonist Gratian. Thus practical and legal Bologna became the type of lay and democratic student universities, while speculative and theological Paris and Oxford were models of clerical schools of masters.

3. Bologna University.

At Bologna the foreign students formed themselves into nations on the pattern of the city gilds; but by the middle of the thirteenth century the corporations had become the two great juristic universities of Citramontani and Ultramontani, within which the nations continued to be independent. These two universities (Citramontani and Ultramontani), with their two rectors, existed until the sixteenth century, whereas in offshoots from Bologna reduction to a single university took place at an earlier date. The teachers of law were at first outside the university at Bologna, nor were they organized into a formal board until the second half of the thirteenth century, when it seemed necessary to furnish a corporate counterbalance of teachers to the increased strength of the university students. Since, however, the teachers were chosen by the students, who paid them in cooperation with the city magistracy, they were so far from being independent that the *rector scholarium* was also *rector studii* and subjected even the professors to his jurisdiction. In the early fourteenth century the students of arts (including medicine) formed a third university alongside the other two; and when, in 1360, Innocent VI. founded a *studium generale in theologia*, the masters of theology formed a corporation, their students joining the university of arts.

Parallel with, and in imitation of Paris, the University of Oxford developed with the twelfth century, its peculiarity being that its chancellor, as the representative of the bishop, was anal-

**4. Early
" General "
Schools.**

ogous to the chancellor at Paris, and also exercised the functions of the rector. The chief " general schools " up to the middle of the thirteenth century were Reggio, Modena, Vicenza, Padua, and Vercelli in Italy, and Orléans and Angers in France, all primarily legal schools, the Church itself being a great legal institution. Cambridge, like its parent Oxford, possessed all four faculties. Medical schools were developed at Salerno and Montpellier, the latter also adding in the thirteenth century faculties of arts and law. Another group of universities was designedly founded, on the model of Paris or Bologna, by the pope or the secular prince, or both together; in this class belonged the institutions at Palencia, Salamanca, and Lisbon-Coimbra. These universities, which were national rather than international, numbered thirteen at the close of the Middle Ages.

Italy took the lead in the establishment of universities, but with the exception of Naples (founded with four faculties by Frederick II. in 1224) and Rome (established for theology and law by Innocent IV. in 1224–45), all owed their origin to the economic and political needs of the municipalities. They were devoted first to law and then to medicine, and during this period numbered twenty. In France Toulouse was the first university to be founded on the model of Paris (1229), and its establishment by the pope led to the theory that no university could be founded without the sanction of the pope or of his secular coregent, the head of the Holy Roman Empire. Toulouse was followed in the fourteenth century by Avignon, Cahors, Grénoble, and Orange, and by eight others in the succeeding century. The history of German universities begins with the foundation of the university of Prague by Charles IV. in 1348, followed by those of Vienna (1365), Heidelberg (1386), Cologne (1388), and Erfurt (1392). In 1402 Bishop John of Egloffstein founded the University of Würzburg, but it did not outlive him, being permanently reestablished by Prince-bishop Julius in 1582; and in 1409 the landgraves of Thuringia founded the University of Leipsic, while Rostock was established in 1419. Outside the bounds of Germany Prague and Vienna inspired the kings of Poland and Hun-

gary to found the less successful universities of Cracow, Fünfkirchen, and Ofen-Pest, while the Netherlands received their first university in Louvain in 1425. A second period of founding universities in Germany began in the fifteenth century, inspired by the solicitude of princes anxious to render their power supreme through the introduction of Roman law rather than by love of learning. To this category belong Greifswald (1456), Freiburg (1457), Basel (1460), Ingolstadt and Treves (1472), and Tübingen and Mainz (1477). The last medieval universities founded in Germany were those of Wittenberg (1502), and Frankfort-on-the-Oder (1506). Outside Germany, universities were founded at Upsala in 1477 and at Copenhagen in 1478, at St. Andrews in 1413, Glasgow in 1450, and Aberdeen in 1494.

The German universities were governed by the masters of the four faculties, each faculty being headed by a dean, and the entire university by a rector who was originally

**5. Organ-
ization.**

elected by all the masters and scholars, but later by the " governing masters " alone. The offices rotated semiannually. Only the fourteenth-century universities had " nations," which included masters as well as scholars; but the " nations " disappeared in the fifteenth century, though still retaining a formal existence at Leipsic until 1830. The universities were impossible without generous foundations, their income often being derived from the incorporation of a collegiate church; the theologians and jurists were generally ecclesiastical prebendaries. The staff of teachers was not large; two to four theologians, three to six jurists, two physicians, and twenty to thirty teachers of the arts. Lectures and residence alike were had in the " colleges," or university buildings, whenever possible; and besides the salaried, or " governing," masters, there were unsalaried teachers, some of them seeking the experience required for further promotion, others waiting for a salaried appointment.

Public lectures were delivered by the salaried masters, while in the colleges and halls the salaried (public) and unsalaried (private) teachers combined for private instruction, this being either the training of the younger scholars for the lectures, or the repetition of lectures previously de-

**6. Instruc-
tion and
Degrees.**

livered publicly. Theological lectures were based on the " Sentences " of Peter the Lombard, juristic on the *Corpus juris*, medical on Hippocrates, Galen, and Avicenna, and arts on Aristotle. The lectures were supplemented by public and private disputations. These were required weekly from the faculty of arts, while the teachers in the higher faculties were also bound to dispute in turn. Public inaugural disputations were required from the candidates for degrees. The whole course of instruction was shaped to give proficiency in teaching, and hence arose the degrees of " master " and " doctor," the former preferred in France and the latter in Italy. " Master " was also synonymous with the later " professor." The German universities accepted both titles, though " master " was finally restricted to the faculty of arts. After the humanistic period the degree of M.A. became connected with that of Ph.D., and vanished in the eighteenth century. Originally the degrees of " master " and " doctor " could be gained only after possession of the lower degrees of " bachelor " and " licentiate." The latter, originally denoting merely the interval before receiving permission to assume the insignia of a doctor, developed, by the seventeenth century, into a special degree, since many remained licentiates to save the fees necessary for promotion to the doctorate. In the faculty of arts the licentiate was never popular, and in the eighteenth century the bachelor's degree also disappeared from most German universities, being replaced by the *testimonium maturitatis* from the gymnasium. Promotion to a degree was preceded by a public disputation in which the candidate was required to show his learning before the assembled university, while the doctor's degree was conferred with imposing ceremony. Possession of the doctor's hat conferred the privilege of teaching in any university, but this soon degenerated into an empty title which merely gave certain prerogatives in ecclesiastical and civil life, the degree later still even being sold, though such *doctores bullati* were never recognized by the universities. In virtue of their corporation rights, universities were empowered to choose their own teachers, to make and execute their own laws both in civil and in criminal matters, and to administer their estates. The teachers were exempt from civil duties and taxes, and as doctors ranked as nobles, this probably being due to the jurists after they had come to control the administration of the State by the introduction of Roman law.

Except in the oldest universities, where thousands of students flocked, the most of the German universities were obliged to be content **7. Students.** with a few hundred scholars. The first students were chiefly clergy, nor was it until near the end of the Middle Ages, when juristic activity had fairly begun, that civilians sought university education. The faculty of arts was naturally the largest, and, while at first the theological faculty seems to have outnumbered the juristic, these conditions were reversed from the fifteenth century on. The medical faculty was relatively unimportant in Germany until the nineteenth century. The philosophical faculty is now the university proper, the other faculties being merely technical schools. No special preparation was required for matriculation in the Middle Ages; students began their university careers, with most unequal training, at the age of fifteen, or even younger, and their entire life was rigidly monastic. They heard two or three lectures daily, followed by private repetitions, exercises, and disputations. The lectures in the higher faculties were delivered free by the salaried professors, and it was only in the faculty of arts that, up to the beginning of the sixteenth century, special fees were required for individual lectures and exercises. Charges for tuition in the modern sense were unknown.

The scholastic organization of the medieval universities was shaken by humanism and destroyed by the Reformation, the result being reconstruction, on the Protestant side by Melanchthon and on the

Roman Catholic by the Jesuits. The universities of Wittenberg, Erfurt, Tübingen, Heidelberg, Basel, **8. Post-** Leipsic, Frankfort, Greifswald, Rostock, Copenhagen, and Upsala became **Reformation** Protestant; and new institutions were **Founda-** called into being by the Reformation **tions.** and Counter-Reformation: the Protestant foundations of Marburg (1527), Königsberg (1544), Jena (1558), Strasburg (1566; an academy until 1621), Helmstedt (1576), and Altdorf (1578; an academy until 1623); Roman Catholic institutions were Dillingen (1554), Braunsberg (1565), Olmütz (1574), Würzburg (1582), and Graz (1586). Reformed establishments were founded at Herborn in 1580, at Geneva and Lausanne in Switzerland (both in 1536), and at Leyden (1575) and Franeker (1585) in the Netherlands. A fourth university was founded at Edinburgh in 1583, and in 1591 the Roman Catholic University of Dublin was established. In Italy the Jesuits founded at Rome the famous Gregorian University in the Roman College, and the first institution of learning in the Americas was the Roman Catholic University of Lima (1551). In the seventeenth century Giessen was founded in 1607 and Rinteln in 1621 as a Lutheran protest against Marburg, which had become Reformed, while the Roman Catholics established the Benedictine University of Salzburg (1662), the Jesuit academies of Paderborn (1615), Molsheim (1618), Osnabrück (1630; destroyed by the Swedes three years later), and Bamberg (1648), and the national Hungarian University of Tyrnau (1635; transferred to Ofen-Pest in 1777–83; now the University of Budapest). The Swedes founded the Livonian University of Dorpat in 1632 and the Finnish University of Abo (now at Helsingfors) in 1640, while the Dutch Reformed added the universities of Groningen (1614), Utrecht (1636), and Harderwijk (1648). The first North American university was that of Harvard (1636). With the Thirty-Years' War the establishment of denominational universities practically ended, though the Protestants founded Duisburg (1655; Reformed), Kiel (1665), and Lund (1666), and the Roman Catholics Innsbruck (1672).

The organization of the universities remained essentially unchanged. At the same time, humanism gained recognition beside Aristotelianism, and in Protestant institutions scholasticism was supplanted by Lutheran and Melanch- **9. Changes** thonian or by Calvinistic systems of **Due to** theology. The professors in the faculty **Humanism** of arts were now salaried, in great part **and the Ref-** from secularized property of the **ormation.** Church. Each " public professor " was bound to lecture three or four times a week, his work being supplemented by heavy private instruction. The monastic life of the students ceased, though where no preparatory institution was connected with the university, each young scholar was required to choose a tutor to supervise his studies and character, this being the origin of the modern privat-docents. In the second half of the sixteenth century, moreover, the public lectures gave place, in great measure, to private lectures for which fees were required. During this and the following centuries the universities lost their international character, while their entire faculties were obliged to subscribe to the denominational standard of the university to which they might be attached. From political, religious, and economic motives the universities passed under the control of the State, though their corporation rights and their autonomy were unmolested. The Protestant universities aimed to give their students practical training for the ministry, while the Roman Catholic universities left this work to the seminaries and entrusted their faculties with the scholastic defense of the ancient faith and polemics against the Reformation. The Protestant institutions, therefore, were forced to subordinate Biblical studies to dogmatics, the result being an intensification of religious antagonisms and the outbreak of the Thirty-Years' War. With the close of the struggle interest in theological controversy waned. Spener and Francke brought university theology back to the study of the Bible and to practical Christianity; national law received recognition beside Roman; natural science, mathematics, and modern philosophy all became factors of moment. German replaced Latin in the lectures, and German universities became the home of a general literary culture which they had never known before. French influence was also active, to the especial advantage of the jurists, who now became the leading faculty to the detriment of theology.

The innovator of the new state of affairs was Thomasius, who, with Francke, impressed his stamp on the lately founded University of Halle (1693), until this institution yielded its prestige to Göttingen (1734). In this period of transition to the period of the Enlightenment (q.v.) belongs the foundation of the Protestant University of Erlangen (1743), as well as of the last German Jesuit university, Breslau (1702), and the academy of Fulda (1734). In America Yale was now founded at New Haven (1701), while in 1721 the Dominicans established a Roman Catholic university at Havana. With the rationalism of the reign of Frederick the Great the universities ceased to transmit learning, believing themselves called to create it. Unrestricted philosophical theorizing received its first sanction at Halle. The universities were no longer denominational bodies for the benefit of the national church; the non-theological professors were officially dispensed from subscribing to the creeds (at Giessen, for example, on Oct. 31, 1777); and by the end of the eighteenth century Prussian law could claim them as institutions of a creedless State. The movement spread from the Protestant north to the Roman Catholic south. The Jesuits were charged with being behind the times, and, about the middle of the century, the courses of studies were radically revised at Ingolstadt and Vienna. Würzburg, Treves, Mainz, and Erfurt followed their example; only Cologne remained true to the past. The fate of the last-named, while Erfurt, Mainz, and Treves enjoyed a short revival, was to be supplanted by the rationalistically Roman Catholic University of Bonn in 1777. A new Roman Catholic university was founded, along more con-

10. The Eighteenth Century.

servative lines, at Münster in 1773, while Joseph II. established a German university, unauthorized by the pope, at Lemberg in 1781. In France, during this period, the theological faculties were replaced by the episcopal seminaries advocated by the Council of Trent, while the faculties of arts, divorced from theology, became colleges corresponding to the German gymnasia, so that the university properly comprised only the technical schools of medicine and law. The Revolution officially suppressed all universities. In England the old universities preserved their medieval college organization. East of Germany ignorance prevailed, despite the exertions of Peter the Great and his successors. Moscow was indeed founded in 1755, but Dorpat was silent for a hundred years, first reviving early in the nineteenth century. In North America the eighteenth century saw the foundation of Princeton (1746), Pennsylvania (1749), King's College (1754; now Columbia University), and Rhode Island College (1763; now Brown University).

The early nineteenth century was controlled by the effects of the French Revolution. Not only had this storm overthrown all the French universities, but also Treves, Mainz, Bonn, and Cologne. In 1794 Stuttgart was incorporated with Tübingen, and secularization successively destroyed the universities of Fulda (1802), Bamberg (1803), Duisburg (1806), Altdorf and Dillingen (1809), Salzburg, Rinteln, and Helmstedt (1810), Erfurt (1816); and Münster and Paderborn (1818). Frankfort was incorporated with Breslau in 1811 and Wittenberg with Halle in 1815. Ingolstadt was transferred, under rationalistic influences, to Landshut in 1800, and in 1826 became the University of Munich. Prussia, on the other hand, received two new universities: Berlin (1809–10) and Bonn (1818). The latter, like Breslau, has both a Roman Catholic and a Protestant theological faculty. Tübingen likewise received a Roman Catholic theological faculty in 1817. In place of the suppressed episcopal university at Münster the State founded a Roman Catholic academy with theological and philosophical faculties, which has been restored to university rank by the addition of a legal faculty. A like institution was established by the State at Braunsberg, while since the Franco-Prussian War the University of Strasburg has been founded (1872), which, like Breslau, Bonn, and Tübingen, has received a Roman Catholic theological faculty.

11. Nineteenth Century; Germany.

In Austria some universities, as those of Graz and Innsbruck, which were made lyceums under the reforms of Joseph II., have been restored to their former rank; in 1875 the University of Czernowitz was established, while in 1882 the University of Prague split into a German and a Czech section. In 1872 Hungary received her second national university in Klausenburg. In 1832 and 1834 the old schools of Zurich and Bern were made German Swiss universities beside the ancient university of Basel, while in French Switzerland the Calvinistic academies of Geneva and Lausanne were transformed into universities in 1873 and 1891. In France Napoleon I. combined

12. The Continent and England.

all education in the huge organism of the University of France, but since 1896 the third republic has restored individual universities on the German model, the present state universities being those of Aachen, Besançon, Bordeaux, Caen, Clermont-Ferrand, Dijon, Grenoble, Lille, Lyons, Marseilles, Montpellier, Nancy, Paris, Poitiers, Rennes, and Toulouse. In England Durham University was established in 1832, followed in 1836 by the University of London, which was only an examining body until 1903, when it became also a teaching body, a similar course being followed by the University of Wales after 1893. Spain possesses the following universities, all of them several centuries old: Barcelona, Granada, Madrid, Oviedo, Salamanca, Santiago, Seville, Valencia, Valladolid, and Saragossa. Italy has a superfluity of universities in Bologna, Cagliari, Camerino, Catania, Ferrara, Genoa, Macerata, Messina, Modena, Naples, Padua, Palermo, Parma, Pavia, Perugia, Pisa, Rome, Sassari, Sienna, Turin, and Urbino. The University of Christiania was founded in Norway in 1811, while Belgium received the institutions at Ghent in 1816, Liége in 1817, and Brussels in 1834, Holland also establishing a university at Amsterdam in 1876.

During the nineteenth century, indeed, universities were founded throughout the world. Russia gained the institutions at Charkow, Kazan, Warsaw, St. Petersburg, Kief, Odessa, and **13. Other** Tomsk; while on the Balkan penin-**Founda-** sula the University of Athens was es-**tions.** tablished in 1837, the institutions at Jassy, Bucharest, Belgrade, and Sofia following in the second half of the same century. Even Turkey founded a sort of university at Constantinople in 1900. India possesses universities at Bombay and Madras (both founded in 1857), and at Lahore (1882). In the Philippines the Dominican school which had existed for centuries was made the University of Manila in 1857. Japan has possessed a university at Tokyo since 1868 and at Kyoto since 1895; while there are Australian universities at Sydney (1850) and Melbourne (1853). For universities in the United States see below, §§ 14–16. For Canada mention may be made of the universities of Montreal and Toronto. In South America there has been a university at Montevideo since 1849, and the Argentine Republic also possesses one at Buenos Aires. In Africa mention should be made of the French academy at Algiers (1879), the Mohammedan school of al-Azhar at Cairo (1896), and the university of the Cape of Good Hope (1873), though the latter, like the universities in India, is only an examining body.

(E. HORN.)

Underneath the history of the university in America is the development, through the influence of the American college, of a national interest in higher education, in some of its local aspects perhaps less developed and provincial, but always sincere and often self-sacrificing and heroic. The historic beginning of higher education in America is found in the grant in 1636, by the General Court of Massachusetts Bay, of £400 for the establishment of a college; a few years later, the college received a bequest from John Harvard of half his estate be-sides half his excellent library. In these two transactions appears the dual economic foundation upon which have been reared all the institu-**14. Amer-** tions of higher learning in America, **ican Uni-** namely, the voluntary support of the **versities.** State and private benefaction. State **Economic** aid has come in the form of exemption **Founda-** from taxation of property devoted to **tions.** educational purposes; the grant of public lands to educational institutions; appropriations from the general revenues; the levying of special taxes or the application of specified taxes to the support of schools, colleges, and universities. The private benefactions have included individual gifts running from paltry sums to millions of dollars and concerted movements for the raising of endowments and other funds. Perhaps no other phenomenon of the twentieth century will be more significant than the princely gifts to the higher education which have marked its first decade; with these gifts has come the accompanying recognition of the place of the university in the higher life of the American people, a recognition seen both in the share which falls directly to the universities and in the proportion of university officers who have been made trustees in charge of the disbursement of the gifts. The total private benefactions for the year 1907–08, as reported to the United States Commissioner of Education by 464 institutions of higher learning, amounted to $14,820,955, while the gifts for the previous year were greater by more than eight million dollars. The total value of the property of the institutions reporting was $576,899,342, nearly half of which consists of productive endowments.

The universities of America present most diversified forms of organization; they may be roughly divided into three classes according to the basis of control. (1) State universities, which **15. Types of** are controlled ultimately by the state **American** governments, though the direct control **Universities.** is generally vested in a board of regents or trustees, whose membership may be appointive or elective, according to the law of the particular state. The state university, especially in the western states, is a vital part of the public school system, over all of which it is exerting an increasing influence. Typical examples are the universities of Michigan, Illinois, Wisconsin, and California. (2) Quasi-public universities, which are controlled by boards of trustees, generally self-perpetuating, to membership in which, in theory at least, all men of reputable standing are eligible. Of this type are most of the older foundations in the eastern states (e.g., Harvard, Yale, and Princeton universities), where state-controlled universities have never attained to great importance. In many cases, the alumni have some representative share in the control of this type of university. (3) Denominational universities, which by their charters are controlled by organized religious bodies or which place some religious qualification for membership in the legal board of control. In this third group belong the University of Chicago, Brown University, and the Roman Catholic universities, representing three different forms of religious control.

While there have been some noticeable movements in certain institutions of the second group toward a closer relationship with the State, as in the case of Cornell University, a still more noteworthy phenomenon of recent years has been the transfer of colleges and universities from the third to the second of these groups, under the influence of the Carnegie Foundation for the Advancement of Teaching. The question of the ethics and the wisdom of the change has been frequently raised, but the break from the earlier denominational relationship has usually been one of legal form rather than of actual severance of historic traditions. While ultimate control of all university activities remains in the boards which control the property, the faculty, the teaching force of the institution, generally has wide powers in all matters pertaining to education itself and the discipline of the students.

Probably no satisfactory definition can be made which will differentiate between the college and the university in America. The tests of European usage are not available here. The American university need not comprise the four standard faculties of the German university, nor is it made up necessarily of a group of colleges. Probably the most essential requirement of the American university is that it shall afford to those who have had a collegiate training the opportunity for research and advancement in higher learning; in proportion as this opportunity is present does the institution deserve in America the name "university." To Johns Hopkins University is generally given the honor of having first met this essential requirement, while Harvard University, under the lead of Dr. Charles W. Eliot, first adopted the elective system by which, with various local adjustments, the American college has in many cases been able to raise itself to the university standard, thus keeping the development of the American university in most vital relationship with the college. In recent years there has been a noteworthy movement on the part of the American universities to get closer to the people through various forms of social service. In this, the University of Wisconsin has perhaps gained the leadership, through its efficient schemes of university extension, involving the spread of pure culture, the application of the natural sciences, even the application of the social sciences through assistance rendered to the legislative and municipal bodies. In these various ways the universities are developing a life which is making them perhaps at the present time the most representative of all American institutions, combining freedom and responsibility, idealism and practicality.

Comprehensive statistics of the American colleges and universities may be found in the Annual Reports of the Commissioner of Education.

WILLIAM H. ALLISON.

BIBLIOGRAPHY: General works are: H. Rashdall, *Universities of Europe in the Middle Ages*, 2 vols., Oxford, 1895; F. C. von Savigny, *Geschichte des römischen Rechts im Mittelalter*, 7 vols., Heidelberg, 1826–51; J. H. Newman, *Historical Sketches*, vol. i., London, 1873; H. Denifle, *Die Universitäten des Mittelalters*, Berlin, 1885; S. S. Laurie, *Lectures on the Rise of Universities*, London, 1886; E. Emerton, *Mediæval Europe (814–1300)*, pp. 452–453, 465–471, Boston, 1896; J. R. Mott, *Universities and Colleges as Related to the Progress of Christianity*, London, 1897; G. H. Putnam, *Books and their Makers during the Middle Ages*, i. 178 sqq., New York, 1897; idem, *Censorship of the Church of Rome* (consult Index), 2 vols., ib. 1907; O. Thatcher and F. Schwill, *Europe in the Middle Age*, pp. 597–601, ib. 1900; S. G. Williams, *Hist. of Mediæval Education*, Syracuse, 1903; D. C. Munro and G. C. Sellery, *Medieval Civilization*, pp. 145–147, 217–218, 348–357, et passim, New York, 1904; J. B. Mullinger, *The Schools of Charles the Great*, new ed., Cambridge and New York, 1911; J. M. Stone, *Reformation and Renaissance (c. 1377–1610)*, London, 1904; C. F. Thwing, *Universities of the World*, New York, 1911; F. A. Ogg, *Source Book of Mediæval Hist.*, pp. 340–351, New York, 1908; F. P. Graves, *A History of Education before the Middle Ages*, ib. 1909; Schaff, *Christian Church*, v. 1, chap. xi.; Henderson, *Documents*, pp. 262–266.

On the British Empire: R. Lethbridge, *Higher Education in India*, London, 1882; W. R. Roberts, *British Universities*, Manchester, 1892; R. C. Jebb, *The Work of the Universities for the Nation*, Cambridge, 1893; J. F. Willard, *The Royal Authority and the Early English Universities*, Philadelphia, 1902; L. Hutton, *Literary Landmarks of the Scottish Universities*, New York, 1904; J. Kerr, *Scottish Education. School and University from the Earliest Times to 1908*, Edinburgh, 1910; C. Innes, *Fasti Aberdonenses*, Aberdeen, 1854; C. H. Cooper, *Annals of Cambridge*, 4 vols., Cambridge, 1842–52; idem, *Athenæ Cantabrigienses*, 2 vols., London, 1858–61; J. B. Mullinger, *Hist. of the University of Cambridge*, 3 vols., Cambridge, new ed., 1911; idem, a smaller independent work with same title, London, 1888; A. H. Thompson, *Cambridge and its Colleges*, New York, 1899; W. B. S. Taylor, *Hist. of the University of Dublin*, London, 1845; J. W. Stubbs, *Hist. of the University of Dublin*, Dublin, 1890; Sir A. Grant, *Story of the University of Edinburgh*, London, 1884; W. Stewart, *The University of Glasgow*, Glasgow, 1891; E. V. Vaughan, *Origin and Early Development of the English Universities*, Columbia, Mo., 1908; J. Coutts, *A History of the University of Glasgow. From its Foundation in 1451 to 1909*, London, 1910; A. a Wood, *Athenæ Oxonienses*, ed. P. Bliss, 4 vols., ib. 1813–20; H. C. M. Lyte, *Hist. of the University of Oxford*, Oxford, 1886; G. C. Brodrick, *Hist. of the University of Oxford*, London, 1887; A. Clark, *The Colleges of Oxford*, ib. 1893.

For the United States: A. Ten Brook, *American State Universities*, Cincinnati, 1875; P. de Coubertin, *Universités transatlantiques*, Paris, 1890; A. Zimmerman, *Die Universitäten in den Vereinigten Staaten Amerikas*, Freiburg, 1896; J. L. Chamberlain and others, *Universities and their Sons*, 5 vols., Boston, 1899 (Harvard, New York University, and University of Pennsylvania); E. S. A. Robson, *Report of a Visit to American Educational Institutions*, London, 1905; J. Corbin, *Which College for the Boy? Leading Types in American Education*, Boston, 1908; E. E. Slosson, *Great American Universities*, London, 1910; J. H. Reynolds and D. Y. Thomas, *Hist. of the University of Arkansas*, Fayetteville, Ark., 1910; W. C. Jones, *Illustrated Hist. of the University of California*, Berkeley, 1902; J. H. Van Amringe, *Historical Sketch of Columbia College*, New York, 1876; A. D. White, *Scenery of Ithaca*, New York, 1866 (on Cornell); J. G. Schurmann, *A Generation of Cornell, 1868–1898*, New York, 1898; W. T. Hewett, *Cornell University*, 4 vols., Ithaca, 1905; B. P. Smith, *Hist. of Dartmouth College*, Boston, 1878; F. Chase, *Hist. of Dartmouth College*, Cambridge, Mass., 1891; S. A. Eliot, *A Sketch of the Hist. of Harvard College*, Boston, 1878; F. O. Vaille and H. A. Clark, *The Harvard Book*, 2 vols., ib. 1879; S. B. Harding, *Indiana University*, Bloomington, Ind., 1905; J. W. Andrews, *Historical Sketch of Marietta College*, Cincinnati, 1876; E. M. Farrand, *Hist. of the University of Michigan*, Ann Arbor, 1885; B. A. Hinsdale, *Hist. of the University of Michigan*, ib. 1907; A. H. Wilde, *Northwestern University*, 4 vols., New York, 1906; H. Garst, *Otterbein University*, Dayton, O., 1908; T. H. Montgomery, *Hist. of the University of Pennsylvania*, Philadelphia, 1887; J. Maclean, *Hist. of the College of New Jersey*, Philadelphia, 1877; J. F. Hageman, *Hist. of Princeton and its Institutions*, 2 vols., Philadelphia, 1879; K. P. Battle, *Hist. of the University of North Carolina*, Raleigh, N. C., 1907; M. Laborde, *Hist. of the South Carolina College*, Charleston, 1874; A. Van V. Raymond, *Union University*, 3 vols., New York, 1907; G. R. Fairbanks, *Hist. of the University of the South*, Jacksonville, Fla., 1906; T. Jefferson and J. C. Cubell,

Early Hist. of the University of Virginia, Richmond, 1856; M. M. Fisher, Hist. of Westminster College . . . to 1903, ed. J. J. Price, Columbia, Mo., 1903; A. L. Chapin, Historical Sketches of the Colleges of Wisconsin, Madison, 1876; F. B. Dexter, Sketch of the Hist. of Yale University, New York, 1887; H. A. Brann, History of the American College of the Roman Catholic Church of the U. S., ib. 1910.

For Germany consult: A. Tholuck, Das akademische Leben des 17. Jahrhunderts, 2 parts, Halle, 1853–54; P. Schaff, Germany, its Universities, Theology, and Religion, Philadelphia, 1857; F. Zarncke, Die deutschen Universitäten im Mittelalter, Leipsic, 1857; O. Dolch, Geschichte des deutschen Studententums, ib. 1858; K. von Raumer, Geschichte der Pädagogik, vol. iv., 4 parts, 4th ed., Gütersloh, 1872; M. Arnold, Higher Schools and Universities in Germany, London, 1874; J. M. Heart, German Universities, New York, 1874; J. Conrad, The German Universities, Glasgow, 1885; C. M. Thorden, Under the Shade of German Universities, Upsala, 1883; L. Caron, L'Allemagne universitaire, Amiens, 1886; G. Kaufmann, Geschichte der deutschen Universitäten, 2 vols., Stuttgart, 1888–96; F. Paulsen, Geschichte des gelehrten Unterrichts auf den deutschen Schulen und Universitäten, 2 vols., Leipsic, 1896–97; idem, Die deutschen Universitäten, Berlin, 1902, Eng. transl., German Universities, New York, 1906; W. Lexis, Die Universitäten im deutschen Reich, Berlin, 1904; E. Dreyfus-Brisac L'Université de Bonn, Paris, 1879; J. G. L. Kosegarten, Geschichte der Universität Greifswald, 2 parts, Leipsic, 1857; J. F. Hautz, Geschichte der Universität Heidelberg, 2 vols., Mannheim, 1862–64; E. Winkelmann, Urkundenbuch der Universität Heidelberg, Heidelberg, 1886; J. Probst, Geschichte der Universität in Innsbruck, Innsbruck, 1869; F. Zarncke, Urkundliche Quellen zur Geschichte der Universität Leipzigs, 2 vols., Leipsic, 1857; K. von Prantl, Geschichte der Ludwig-Maximilians-Universität, 2 vols. Munich, 1872; F. K. T. Piderit, Geschichte der hessisch-schaumburgischen Universität Rinteln, Marburg, 1842; O. Krabbe, Die Universität Rostock im xv. und xvi. Jahrhundert, 2 vols., Rostock, 1856; K. Klüpfel, Geschichte und Beschreibung der Universität Tübingen, Tübingen, 1849; F. X. Wegele, Geschichte der Universität Würzburg, 2 vols., Würzburg, 1882.

For France consult: É. Beaussire, L'Université sous la troisième république, Paris, 1884; M. Fournier, Les Statuts et privilèges des universités françaises, 3 vols., Paris, 1890–92; C. Du Boulay, Historia Universitatis Parisiensis, ib. 1665; E. Dubarle, Hist de l'université de Paris, 2 vols., ib. 1844; C. Thurot, De l'organization et l'enseignement dans l'université de Paris, ib. 1850; H. Denifle and A. Chatelain, Chartularium Universitatis Parisiensis, 4 vols., ib. 1889–97; L. Liard, L'Université de Paris, 2 vols., ib. 1909; MGH, Leges, ii. 114, cf. D. C. Munro in University of Pennsylvania Translations and Reprints, ii. no. 3, pp. 2–7 (on the University of Paris); A. Lefranc, Hist. du Collège de France, Paris 1892; L. Legrand, L'Université de Douai, Douay, 1888.

On other countries: F von Krones, Geschichte der . . . Universität in Graz, Graz, 1886; W. W. Tomek, Geschichte der Prager Universität, Prague, 1849; R. Kink, Geschichte der . . . Universität zu Wien, 2 vols., Vienna, 1854; J. von Aschlbach Geschichte der Wiener Universität, 3 vols., ib. 1889; R. A. Renvall, Finlands Universitet, Helsingfors, 1891; J. Kirkpatrick, The University of Bologna, London, 1888; V. de la Fuente, Historia de las Universidades . . . en España, 2 vols., Madrid, 1884–85; G. Reynier, La Vie universitaire dans l'ancienne Espagne, ib. 1902; W. Vischer, Geschichte der Universität Basel, Basel, 1860; H. Mayer, Geschichte der Universität Freiburg, Bonn, 1892; C. Borgeaud, Histoire de l'université de Genève. L'Académie de Calvin dans l'université de Napoléon 1798–1814, Geneva, 1909.

UPHAM, FRANCIS WILLIAM: Layman; b. at Rochester, Stafford County, N. H., Sept. 10, 1817; d. in New York Oct. 17, 1895. He was graduated from Bowdoin College, Brunswick, Me., 1837; admitted to the bar of Massachusetts, 1844; was professor of mental and moral philosophy and lecturer on history in Rutgers Female College, New York, 1867–70. He was the author of The Debate between the Church and Science, or the Ancient Hebraic Idea of the Six Days of Creation; with an Essay on the Literary Character of Tayler Lewis (published anonymously, Andover, 1860); The Wise Men: who they were, and how they came to Jerusalem (New York, 1869); The Star of our Lord, or Jesus Christ King of all Worlds, both of Time and Space; with Thoughts on Inspiration, and the Astronomic Doubt as to Christianity (1873); Thoughts on the Holy Gospels: how they came to be in Manner and Form as they are (1881); and First Words from God (1894).

UPHAM, THOMAS COGSWELL: Congregationalist; b. at Deerfield, N. H., Jan. 30, 1799; d. in New York Apr. 2, 1872. He was graduated from Dartmouth College (1818) and from Andover Theological Seminary (1821); taught Hebrew in Andover from 1821–23; was pastor at Rochester, N. H., for a year; professor of mental and moral philosophy in Bowdoin College, Brunswick, Me., 1824–67; retired to Kennebunkport, Me., 1867, and lived without charge till his death. He was a voluminous writer, and did good service in his day, and deserves to be remembered as one of the earliest advocates of international peace by peace tribunals, an idea represented in The Manual of Peace, Embracing I. Evils and Remedies of War, II. Suggestions on the Law of Nations, III. Considerations of a Congress of Nations (New York, 1836; part III. was reprinted by the American Peace Society, Boston, 1840). Another useful service was in translating Jahn's Biblical Archæology (Andover, 1823). He did much in philosophy, his work on the Will (Portland, 1834) and its text-book on Mental Philosophy (1839) being noteworthy. His interest in Madame Guyon led him to write her life and to bring out a translation of her Method of Prayer. Other books were his biography of Madame Catherine Adorna (4th ed., Boston, 1856); and Letters Written from Europe, Egypt and Palestine (Brunswick, 1855).

UR OF THE CHALDEES. See BABYLONIA, IV., § 3.

URBAN: The name of eight popes.

Urban I.: Pope 222–230. He succeeded Calixtus I., but nothing is known concerning his pontificate. The Liber pontificalis places his death on May 19 and the martyrology of Jerome on May 25. He seems to have been interred in the cemetery of Calixtus, where an inscription has been found which probably marked his grave; yet the Liber pontificalis buries him in the cemetery of Pretextatus.

(A. HAUCK.)

BIBLIOGRAPHY: Liber pontificalis, ed. Mommsen in MGH, Gest. pont. Rom., i (1898), 22–23; Bower, Popes, i. 22; Platina, Popes, i. 31–43; DCB, iv. 1062–64; ASB, May, vi. 11–14; K. J. Neumann, Der römische Staat und die allgemeine Kirche, i. 314–316, Leipsic, 1890.

Urban II. (Odo de Lagny): Pope 1088–99. He was born of knightly descent at Chatillon-sur-Marne and early adopted a clerical career, receiving deep impressions from Bruno of Cologne (q.v.). After being archdeacon of Reims, he entered the monastery of Cluny, where he rose to be prior, but was called to Italy by Gregory VII. and created cardinal bishop of Ostia in 1078, and was elected to the papal throne (Mar. 12, 1088). Though he declared himself a follower of Gregory VII. in all things, he was far less drastic, more politic, and so eventually more successful. At first, however, the followers of the antipope Clement III. (see GUIBERT OF RAVENNA) being more numerous than his own, he was obliged to withdraw from Rome (1089). He held a synod at Melfi, southern Italy, on Sept. 10, 1089, which condemned simony, lay investiture, and the marriage of the clergy. He returned to Rome, but was unable to hold the city; from 1090 to 1093 he was an exile, but meanwhile was not idle. He held synods and devoted special attention to affairs in Germany. For a time it seemed as though peace with the Emperor Henry IV. might be restored, but the imperial refusal to abandon Clement, the antipope, and thus to end the schism frustrated such hopes. Urban strengthened his position with both his Italian and his German allies by promoting a marriage between the younger Guelf of Bavaria and the Margravine Matilda, his strongest supporter in Italy (1089), by assisting Conrad in rebellion against his father (1093), and by availing himself of the Empress Adelheid's treason toward her husband (1094). The result of all this was the fall of Henry and the consolidation of Urban's power.

In the summer of 1094 Urban left Rome and triumphantly traversed central and northern Italy, holding a great synod at Piacenza (Mar. 1–7, 1095), which condemned simony and the marriage of priests, denied the validity of the ordinations by Clement and his adherents, and renewed the anathema against them. He received an embassy from the Emperor Alexius, imploring western aid against the Moslems. Urban echoed the embassy's appeal, and the result was the beginning of the crusades, the first of which was proclaimed at a synod held by Urban at Clermont, France (Nov. 18–28, 1095; see CRUSADES, § 1). The " peace of God " (see TRUCE OF GOD) was declared to be universally binding, and the regulations for the prevention of simony and lay investiture were renewed and made more stringent. But most important was the enthusiasm awakened by Urban for the crusades, whereby the pope became the real head of the western world. In the spring of 1096 Urban held synods at Tours and Nîmes, and then returned to Italy, where the prestige of Henry and Clement was broken. Toward the end of the year Urban resumed residence in Rome, and in Jan., 1097, held a synod in the Lateran, and on Oct. 3, 1098, one at Bari, which was of general importance for its decisions concerning the procession of the Holy Ghost. A second Roman synod was held in St. Peter's on Apr. 24–30, 1099, and shortly afterward, on July 29, 1099, Urban died. (A. HAUCK.)

BIBLIOGRAPHY: The *Epistolæ et privilegia* are in *MPL*, vol. cli.; Jaffé, *Regesta*, pp. 657 sqq.; C. Grünhagen, *Vita Urbani II.*, Halle, 1848; A. de Brimont, *Un pape au moyen âge, Urbain II.*, Paris, 1862; J. M. Watterich, *Romanorum pontificum . . . vitæ*, i. 571 sqq., Leipsic, 1862; A. von Reumont, *Geschichte der Stadt Rom*, vol. ii., Berlin, 1868; M. F. Stern, *Zur Biographie des Papstes Urban II.*, Berlin, 1883; G. Meyer von Knonau, *Jahrbuch des deutschen Reichs unter Heinrich IV. und V.*, Leipsic, 1890 sqq.; J. Langen, *Geschichte der römischen Kirchen*, vol. iv., Bonn, 1893; L. Bernard, *Le Bienheureux Urbain II.*, Paris, 1896; F. Gregorovius, *Hist. of City of Rome*, iv. 269 sqq., London, 1896; G. Richter, *Annalen des deutschen Reichs im Zeitalter der Ottonen*, Halle, 1898; Mann, *Popes*, vii. 245–346; Bower, *Popes*, ii. 413–426; Platina, *Popes*, ii. 13–18; Milman, *Latin Christianity*, iii. 500–523, iv. 26–29; T. Ruinart, *Vita . . . Urbani II.*, in *MPL*, cli. 9–266; Hauck, *KD*, vol. iii.; Hefele, *Conciliengeschichte*, vol. v.; and the literature under CRUSADES.

Urban III. (Uberto Crevelli): Pope 1185–87. Born at Milan and created cardinal by Lucius III., he became archbishop of Milan in 1185, and pope Nov. 25 of the same year. The struggle with Emperor Frederick I. held over from the previous pontificate. Urban repeated his predecessor's demands and retained the see of Milan. Thereupon Frederick appropriated the estates of deceased bishops and the revenues of dioceses during a *sedis vacantia* (see SEDIS VACANS); Urban refused to crown Frederick's son, Henry VI., sought to weaken the allegiance of the German bishops, supported Cremona in its revolt, and, when Frederick reduced the city, consecrated Folmar archbishop of Treves in defiance of the emperor. Later he cited Frederick to appear at Verona, and threatened him with excommunication, but died at Ferrara on Oct. 19, 1187, before he could carry out his intention. (A. HAUCK.)

BIBLIOGRAPHY: The *Epistolæ et privilegia* are in *MPL*, vol. ccii. Consult: Jaffé, *Regesta*, ii. 854; J. M. Watterich, *Romanorum pontificum . . . vitæ*, ii. 663 sqq., Leipsic, 1862; A. von Reumont, *Geschichte der Stadt Rom*, vol. ii., Berlin, 1868; H. Prutz, *Kaiser Friedrich I.*, vol. iii., Danzig, 1873; J. Langen, *Geschichte der römischen Kirche*, iv. 564 sqq., Bonn, 1893; W. von Giesebrecht, *Geschichte der deutschen Kaiserzeit*, vi. 114 sqq., Brunswick, 1895; F. Gregorovius, *Hist. of the City of Rome*, iv. 612–614, London, 1896; Bower, *Popes*, ii. 527–528; Platina, *Popes*, ii. 60–62; Milman, *Latin Christianity*, iv. 440–443; Hauck, *KD*, iv. 304 sqq.

Urban IV. (Jacques Pantaleon): Pope 1261–64. He was educated at Laon and Paris, was canon at Laon, canon and archdeacon at Liége, papal nuncio in Silesia, Poland, Prussia, and Pomerania (1247), archdeacon of Laon (1249), and in 1253 bishop of Verdun. Two years later Alexander IV. appointed him patriarch of Jerusalem, and on Sept. 4, 1261, he succeeded his patron on the papal throne. His first care was the restoration of papal supremacy in Rome and its vicinity. In Germany he sought to continue the confusion that already existed, being determined on the destruction of the Hohenstaufen line. In 1263 the crown of Naples and Sicily was offered to Charles, duke of Anjou. Before Charles entered Italy, however, Urban died at Perugia, Oct. 2, 1264. The sole ecclesiastical events of his pontificate were the general introduction of the festival of Corpus Christi (q.v.), and the negotiations for union with the Greek Church. (A. HAUCK.)

BIBLIOGRAPHY: His " Registers " were edited by G. Guiraud, 2 vols., Paris, 1901; cf. *MGH, Epist.*, iii (1883), 474 sqq. Consult: F. von Raumer, *Geschichte der Hohenstaufen und ihrer Zeit*, iv. 422 sqq., Leipsic, 1841; C. de Cherrier, *Hist. de la lutte des papes . . . de la maison de Souabe*, iii. 113 sqq., Paris, 1858; J. B. Magnan, *Vie du pape Urbain IV.*, Paris, 1863; E. Georges, *Hist. du pape Urbain IV.*, Paris, 1865; A. von Reumont, *Geschichte der Stadt Rom*, vol. ii., Berlin, 1867; F. Schirrmacher, *Die letzten Hohenstaufen*, Göttingen, 1871; O. Posse, *Analecta Vaticana*, pp. 15 sqq., 128 sqq., Innsbruck, 1878; F. Tenckhoff, *Der Kampf der Hohenstaufen um die Mark Ancona*, Paderborn, 1893; F. Gregorovius, *Hist. of the City of Rome*, v. 343 sqq., London, 1897; K. Hampe, *Urban IV. und Manfred*, Heidelberg, 1905; Bower, *Popes*, ii. 571–574; Platina, *Popes*, ii. 94–97; Milman, *Latin Christianity*, vi. 80–91.

Urban V.: Pope 1362–70. He was born at Grisac (in the neighborhood of Mende), southern France, entered the Benedictine order, becoming abbot of St. Germanus at Auxerre and of St. Victor at Marseilles. He was repeatedly employed as papal legate by Clement VI. and Innocent VI., and was enthroned pope at Avignon on Oct. 28, 1362. He was one of the last popes to interest himself in the crusades, but his attention was practically absorbed by more urgent matters nearer home. In upper Italy Bernabo Visconti was developing his power, and when he refused to obey the summons of the new pope, he was placed under the ban and made the object of an unsuccessful crusade (Mar. 3, 1363). The pope deemed it advisable to return to Italy, and, despite the protests of the French cardinals and the French court, Urban left Avignon on Apr. 30, 1367, and landed in Italy near Corneto on June 4, entering Rome on Oct. 16. Italy, however, remained in disorder; Perugia rebelled (1369) and was reduced only by force; even the visits of Joanna of Naples and of Charles IV. to Rome and the conversion of the Greek Emperor John Palæologus to the Roman Church could not hide the fact that the object of the pope's return had not been attained. Urban therefore resolved to go back to Avignon. Despite the warning of St. Bridget of Sweden that he would die if he returned to Avignon, and against the pleas of the Romans, by Sept. 24, 1370, Urban was again at Avignon, where, on Dec. 19 of the same year, he died. While Urban protested repeatedly against various ecclesiastical abuses, he lacked the strength necessary for the conditions that confronted him. He made important architectural improvements on the Lateran Hill in Rome, in the churches of SS. Peter and Paul, and in the papal palace at Avignon, besides founding a college at Montpellier for students of medicine.   (A. HAUCK.)

BIBLIOGRAPHY: For original documents consult the Turin ed. of the *Bullarium Romanum*, iv. 519 sqq., 1859; A. Theiner, *Codex diplomaticus*, ii. 4038 sqq., Rome, 1862; and *Lettres des papes d'Avignon*, vol. v., Paris, 1906. The *Vita* by Aymeric with other documents is in E. Baluze, *Vitæ paparum Avenionensium*, i. 363–424, Paris, 1693; and in Muratori, *Scriptores*, iii. 2, pp. 610–642. Consult further: Creighton, *Papacy*, i. 55–56, 115, 355; Pastor, *Popes*, i. 54, 95–99, 126; J. B. Magnan, *Hist. d'Urbain V. et de son siècle*, Paris, 1862; A. von Reumont, *Geschichte der Stadt Rom*, ii. 937, Berlin, 1867; M. Prou, *Relations politiques du pape Urbain V. avec les rois de France*, Paris, 1888; M. Souchon, *Die Papstwahlen von Bonifaz VIII. bis Urban VI.*, pp. 66 sqq., Brunswick, 1888; Louise Guiraud, *Les Fondations du pape Urbain V. à Montpellier*, 3 vols., Paris, 1889–91; E. Werunsky, *Geschichte König Karls IV.*, iii. 266 sqq., Innsbruck, 1892; *Württembergische Geschichtsquellen*, ii. 448 sqq., Stuttgart, 1895; C. Locke, *The Age of the Great Western Schism*, pp. 26, 72–75, 299, New York, 1896; J. H. Albanis, *Actes anciens et documents concernant . . . Urbain V.*, vol. i., Paris, 1897; J. P. Kirsch, *Die Rückkehr der Päpste Urban V. und Gregor XI.*, Paderborn, 1898; Bower, *Popes*, iii. 109–116; Platina, *Popes*, ii. 160–162; Milman, *Latin Christianity*, vii. 209–218.

Urban VI. (Bartolomeo Prignano): Pope 1378–1389.

He was born at Naples about 1318, studied canon law, became archbishop of Averenza, and of Bari in 1377; and was enthroned as pope Apr. 9, 1378. A man of the utmost personal integrity and a firm opponent of all abuses, Urban yet had the unfortunate faculty of antagonizing all with whom he came in contact. He soon alienated the support of the college of cardinals, and the French members formed a conspiracy against him, asserting that the cardinals had been forced by the populace to elect Urban, and that the election was, therefore, invalid. His opponents went to Fondi and elected Cardinal Robert of Geneva pope on Sept. 20, 1378, under the name of Clement VII. Clement was supported by all the cardinals except four Italians, as well as by Joanna of Naples, by France, and, eventually, by Scotland, Savoy, Castile, Aragon, Navarre, and Lorraine. Urban created a large number of new cardinals, and was supported by Catharine of Sienna (q.v.), Catharine, the daughter of Saint Bridget of Sweden (q.v.), Charles IV., England, the northern and eastern lands, and a great part of Germany.

Urban being master of Rome, Clement hastened to Naples, but so unfavorable was his reception that he determined to go to Avignon, and on June 10, 1379, landed at Marseilles. Meanwhile Joanna sought to make terms with Urban, but the pope declared her deprived of her kingdom, and crowned the heir of Naples, Charles of Durazzo, king of Jerusalem and Sicily. But then, suspecting that some of his cardinals were conspiring with Charles for his deposition, he put the latter under the ban and Naples under an interdict. Charles, in his turn, besieged the pope in Naples; but Urban was finally set free and reached Genoa, where he remained until Dec., 1386. Thence he went to Lucca, and from there to Perugia, but, after an unsuccessful attempt to restore the papal power in Naples, was forced to return to Rome in Oct., 1388. There he remained until his death on Oct. 15, 1389, his only acts of moment being to make the thirty-third year the year of jubilee and to introduce the feast of the Visitation of the Blessed Virgin Mary.

(A. HAUCK.)

BIBLIOGRAPHY: Sources are: The Turin ed. of the *Bullarium Romanum*, iv. 580–601; *Theodorici de Nyem de schismate*, ed. G. Erler, Leipsic, 1890; and the *Vita* in Baluze, *Vitæ paparum Avenionensium*, Paris, 1693. Consult: Creighton, *Papacy*, i. 64–67, 69 sqq., 363–365; Pastor, *Popes*, i. 118–145 et passim; A. von Reumont, *Geschichte der Stadt Rom*, ii. 1015, Berlin, 1867; Lindner, in *ZKG*, iii (1879), 409–428, 525–546; G. Erler, *Dietrich von Nieheim*, Leipsic, 1887; M. Souchon, *Die Papstwahlen von Bonifaz VII. bis Urban VI.*, pp. 81 sqq., Brunswick, 1888; L. Gayet, *Le Grand Schisme d'occident*, vol. i., Paris, 1889; R. Jahr, *Die Wahl Urbans VI.*, Halle, 1892; Sauerland, in *Historisches Jahrbuch der Görres-Gesellschaft*, xiv (1893), 820–832; C. Locke, *The Age of the Great Western Schism*, pp. 85–102, New York, 1896; N. Valois, *La France et le grand schisme*, vol. i., Paris, 1896; F. P. Bliemetzrieder, *Das Generalkonzil*, pp. 1 sqq., Paderborn, 1904; Hefele, *Conciliengeschichte*, vi. 727–807; Bower, *Popes*, iii. 124–142; Platina, *Popes*, ii. 166–176; Milman, *Latin Christianity*, vii. 233–263; *KL*, xii. 446–450.

Urban VII. (Giovanni Baptista Castagna): Pope 1590.

He was born at Rome in 1521, was elected pope Sept. 15, 1590, but died on the twelfth day following.   K. BENRATH.

BIBLIOGRAPHY: L. Arrighi, *Urbani VII. vita*, Bonona, 1614; A. Chacon (Ciaconius), *Vitæ et res gestæ pontificum Romanorum*, iv. 201 sqq., Rome, 1677; Ranke, *Popes*, ii. 32 sqq.; Bower, *Popes*, iii. 325; *KL*, xii. 450–451.

Urban VIII. (Maffeo Barberini): Pope 1623–44.

He was born at Florence in 1568, and was repeatedly employed by Clement VIII. and Paul V. on diplomatic missions to the French court. In 1605 he was created cardinal, and succeeded to the papal chair at the age of fifty-five. He had received a humanistic training, showed constant predilection for literature, and even left some poems. He gave two saints to the Society of Jesus, Ignatius of Loyola and Francis Xavier, and canonized Philip of Neri. The time of his pontificate is wholly covered by the Thirty-Years' War (q.v.); and toward this his policy was naturally directed. According to Gregorovius (*Urban VIII.*, p. 7, Stuttgart, 1879), he " waived the Roman Catholic principle in the case of that war," and turned his attention solely to the question of political domination. So as to limit the power of the emperor, when the house of Gonzaga became extinct, he favored the accession of Mantua to the French line of Nevers, and this transfer was confirmed in 1630. In the great war itself, his favor for the opponents of the house of Austria was undeniable, though this was consonant with the sharpest antipathy toward the Protestants (cf. his brief of June 28, 1631, in which he exults over the destruction of Magdeburg by Tilly, and his rejoicing over the death of Gustavus Adolphus).

Urban VIII. was the last pope who was able to expand the Papal States (q.v.), which he did by the sequestration of Urbino as a vacated tenure. He also erected fortifications at threatened points, as at the north boundary of the legation of Bologna, where he built the fortress Castelfranco, named Fortezza Urbano; fortified Castle Sant' Angelo at Rome; and completed and secured the port of Civita Vecchia. He was also the last pope who used nepotism on a large scale. If he did not make sovereigns of the Barberini, he made them the richest landed proprietors in the Papal States, and this position they attempted to improve by an unsuccessful war on the duke of Parma. It is significant of this pope that he celebrated the memory of Countess Matilda of Tuscany, who laid the foundation for the temporal sovereignty. He had her ashes removed from S. Benedetto near Mantua, and reared for her a magnificent monument in St. Peter's, Rome. K. Benrath.

Bibliography: A. Nicoletti, *Vita di Papa Urbano VIII.* (8 vols. of MS. in the Barberini Library, Rome; cf. on it Ranke, *Popes*, iii. 400–407); A. Chacon (Ciaconius), *Vitæ et res gestæ pontificum Romanorum*, vol. iii., Rome, 1677; A. von Reumont, *Beiträge zur italienischen Geschichte*, v. 117–171, Berlin, 1857; idem, *Geschichte der Stadt Rom*, iii. 2, pp. 611–622, ib. 1870; J. Hergenröther, *Katholische Kirche und christlicher Staat*, pp. 712 sqq., Freiburg, 1872; F. Gregorovius, *Urban VIII. im Widerstreit zu Spanien und dem Kaiser*, Stuttgart, 1879; M. Brosch, *Geschichte des Kirchenstaats*, vol. i., Gotha, 1880; Ehses, in *Historisches Jahrbuch der Görres-Gesellschaft*, xi (1895), 336–341; O. Klopp, *Der dreissigjährige Krieg*, iii. 2, pp. 659–674, Paderborn, 1896; Ranke, *Popes*, ii. 263–271, 281 sqq., et passim; Bower, *Popes*, iii. 329–330; *KL*, xii. 451–452.

URIEL: An archangel, mentioned only in apocryphal and pseudepigraphical literature, chiefly in II Esdras and Enoch. He rules over the (angelic) host and over Tartarus (Enoch xx. 2), and accordingly is the divine guide for Enoch through the under-world. In this capacity Uriel tells Enoch where the fallen angels will have their abodes in hell, both for a period of 10,000 years and then for all eternity (xviii. 11–xix. 3), where the wicked of mankind will dwell in hell, and where the righteous will have their homes in heaven (xxvii. 2–4), besides revealing to him various other divine mysteries (xxxiii. 3–4). As an angel of the under-world, he,

together with Michael, Gabriel, and Raphael, will bring from Tartarus the souls of the dead for judgment at the Last Day, Uriel's division comprising especially the Titans, the giants who perished in the flood, and those who have died by drowning, who have been burned to death, or who have been devoured by birds, beasts, and creeping things (*Sibylline Oracles*, ii. 215 sqq.). According to the *Life of Adam and Eve*, xlviii., Uriel and Michael are commanded by the Lord to wrap the bodies of Adam and Abel in linen and to bury them in Paradise, this forming the model for burial to be followed by Seth and his mother. It is likewise probably as an angel of the under-world that he is sent to warn Noah of the impending deluge (Enoch x. 1–3).

Uriel also appears as an angel giving warning of the future in II Esdras, where he tells the signs of the times to come, although with much reluctance, since man's understanding is unable to comprehend the judgments of God, nor can Esdras himself perform such relatively simple tasks as " weigh me the weight of the fire, or measure me the blast of the wind, or call me again the day that is past " (II Esdras iv.–v.). Nevertheless, by divine command Uriel again appears to Esdras later and explains to him the meaning of a vision (II Esdras x. 28 sqq.). According to fragments of the lost *Prayer of Joseph*, Uriel was the angel who wrestled with Jacob, Uriel declaring that he had descended to earth and taken up his abode among men, who called him Jacob, and Jacob's reply being that he himself was " Israel, the archangel," below whom Uriel was eighth in rank (J. A. Fabricius, *Codex pseudepigraphus Veteris Testamenti*, 2d ed., i. 766, Hamburg, 1722); and the same book is said to have represented Jacob as conversing both with Uriel and with Raphael (ib. p. 768).

The name Uriel denotes " Fire of God " (cf. also the Hebr. proper names Uri, Uriah, Urijah, and Palmyrene *Nurbel*, " Fire of Bel " or " Bel is Fire "), and from this fact his connection with Gehenna, and consequently his aspect as an angel of the under-world, becomes obvious. In later Jewish mysticism he was believed to be the source of the heat of the day in winter and to be the angel of Sunday. His name is found in Greek magic papyri, and it was taught by a French rabbi of the thirteenth century that if Uriel's name is repeated ten times in one breath in the morning, the day will be lucky (cf. further, L. Blau, in *JE*, xii. 383).

The name of Uriel was also borne by a Kohathite chieftain (I Chron. vi. 24, xv. 5, 11) and by a man from Gibeah who was the grandfather of Abijah (II Chron. xiii. 2).

URIM, yūrim, **AND THUMMIM,** thŭm'im: Media employed by the Hebrews in obtaining divine oracles. Concerning the nature and method of employing them there is much doubt; even from the time of Josephus and Philo an
The Basal abundance of conjecture concerning
Scriptural them is in evidence, but no satisfac-
Passages. tory solution. Two sets of data appear, those furnished by P and those by other writers. Until the nineteenth century P was the source generally employed to elucidate the

problem, and Ex. xxviii. 30, " Thou shalt put in the breastplate of judgment the Urim and the Thummim; and they shall be upon Aaron's heart, when he goeth in before Jehovah; and Aaron shall bear the judgment of the children of Israel upon his heart before Jehovah continually " (Am. R. V.), was the basal passage. The words " put in " might in that verse be replaced by " put on or upon," according to the Septuagint; but this and all other interpretations which identify the Urim and Thummim with the precious stones of the breastplate are excluded by the context of Ex. xxviii. 15 sqq.; cf. especially Lev. viii. 8. In both these passages the objects are introduced as something at hand and well known, not as new objects prepared for the purpose. In the parallel, Ex. xxxix. 20 sqq., the objects are not mentioned. From the fundamental passage their function seems purely symbolical—Aaron bears the " judgment " of the children of Israel upon his heart; this is not diminished by the practical purpose involved in the passage Num. xxvii. 21. In any case use of the objects for obtaining oracles is indicated. Outside P, mention is made of these objects in Deut. xxxiii. 8; Ezra ii. 63 = Neh. vii. 65; the original text of I Sam. xiv. 41, and xxviii. 6 (Urim alone). In the passage from Deuteronomy it was formerly the custom to refer " thy holy one " to Aaron on the basis of Ex. xxviii. 30. Against this construction is to be noted: the oracle is directed to Levi, restricting it to Aaron is pure eisegesis; and in the context of the oracle regarding Levi it is the Levites as a whole and their functions which the oracle has in mind, so that the carrying of the Urim and Thummim belongs to the priestly stock as such, without limitation to the high priest. But of the nature and use of the objects this passage gives no further knowledge. Out of I Sam. xxviii. 6 is gleaned that by the Urim direct answer to a question asked of God might be had, as also by dreams or through the prophets. I Sam. xiv. 41, in which the Septuagint has preserved the correct text, to be rendered: " O Yahweh, God of Israel! Why hast thou not answered thy servant this day? If to me or to my son Jonathan falls the blame, give Urim; if to the people, give Thummim." To this reading the Vulgate gives testimony [cf. also S. R. Driver, *Notes on the Hebrew Text of the Books of Samuel*, p. 89, Oxford, 1890]. Granting the correctness of the Septuagint reading, this passage shows that by the use of these objects an alternative was presented, that the issuing of one of them indicated an affirmative, of the other a negative; if neither came out, that indicated divine unwillingness to answer. The context (verses 36 sqq.) implies the presence of a priest, though the passage does not show that the management was exclusively in priestly hands.

When it is noted that in the reports concerning the throwing of the lot the matter is brought into connection with the priests and the ephod, it seems at least probable that in these cases reference is to the use of Urim and Thummim (cf. I Sam. xxiii. 6, 9, xxx. 7 sqq.; note that in xiv. 18 " ephod " is to be read for " ark "; Driver, ut sup., p. 83). But in what way Urim and Thummim were brought into connection with the Ephod (q.v.) absolutely

nothing is known; the earlier narrators are silent concerning these matters because they could assume knowledge on the part of their readers, the later writers because the things had been forgotten. It does not militate against the foregoing exposition that P does not put the Urim and Thummim in relation with images and introduces the ephod as an article of priestly dress. The objects seem to have been used without the ephod and without priestly accessory by David (II Sam. ii. 1, v. 19, 23) and by Samuel (I Sam. x. 20 sqq.; cf. the method in I Sam. xiv. 41–42; Josh. vii. 16); possibly Hos. iv. 12 and Mic. iii. 11 assume the use of Urim and Thummim. The answer seems sometimes to have been a simple affirmative, as often in the cases already cited; sometimes with additional directions (Judges xx. 27; I Sam. xxx. 7 sqq.); sometimes negative with further statement (11 Sam. v. 23). Where names appear in the answer, the case may have been put as an alternative (Josh. vii. 16 sqq.; Judges i. 1, xx. 18; I Sam. x. 20 sqq.; II Sam. ii. 1). The latest mention appears in Ezra ii. 63 = Neh. vii. 65, in which the expectation is expressed of a priestly possessor of the objects. In the fifth century B.C. the management of the objects was no longer known, while the synagogue reckoned them among the five things which the second temple did not possess, and the Talmud declares that with the preexilic prophets the use of the Urim and Thummim ceased. In P, therefore, Urim and Thummim are objects which are found in a pocket attached to the high-priestly ephod or cloak and employed by the high priest in obtaining expressions of the divine will. The occasional references make them the means of casting the lot and getting answers in affirmative or negative form. The ephod, employed in casting the lot, is here not a cloak, but an image overlaid with metal or put on with a cloak. Often a priest is the assumed keeper, but others appear to exercise the same function (Saul, David); and the privilege of consulting the oracle was not merely in public interests, but also in private (cf. Judges xviii. 5–6; I Sam. xxii. 10, xxiii. 11–12, xxx. 7–8).

It appears, then, that either Ex. xxviii. 30 is the original and only legitimate account of the Urim and Thummim—in which case the other reports and the practises named are gross misunderstandings of the real situation—or the very old narratives, such as Judges xvii.–xviii. and I Sam. xiv. 23, etc., tell what was a general custom untrammeled by written law. In the latter case the situation in P is a step in evolution in which the attempt is made to rescue the lot from superstitious or idolatrous usage. Then these objects became representative of Israel's God and the handling of them was restricted to the high priest. But Ex. xxviii. 30 is to be regarded as idealistic in its representations. Investigations regarding the meaning of the names have not resulted very satisfactorily. When it is supposed that both words are abstract plurals, not much progress is made. If from I Sam. xiv. 41 it be gathered that Urim means " revelation (of guilt)," Thummim would mean " revelation of innocence." Other meanings suggested are " illumination and truth," " brightness and righteousness," but they appear rather as mechanical reproductions of the Hebrew than as illuminative renderings.

The Septuagint in its translation of the fundamental passage shows that the correct tradition of the meaning was already lost, and this impression
           is strengthened by Philo, Josephus,
History of and the Talmud. Philo makes the
Interpreta- breastplate to contain two virtues,
tion.   " interpretation and truth " (*De vita Mosis*, iii. 11). Josephus (*Ant.*, III., viii. 9), while not mentioning Urim and Thummim, says that through the precious stones of the high-priest's breastplate God revealed the coming of victory for his hosts; on account of this the Greeks had named that breastplate the " oracle." Josephus' conception, that through the shining of these stones the divine oracle was given, reappears in various forms in the Jewish traditions, including the connection of the quadriliteral name of God or of other secret names which inspired the priest in the delivery of the message. New attempts to explain the objects were made by referring to Diodorus Siculus (I., xlviii. 75) and Ælian (*Varia hist.*, xiv. 34), who report that Egyptian priests, who acted as judges, employed an image of truth cut in halves. To connect this image with Urim and Thummim became very popular; and later the image was made that of Tme, goddess of justice, while later still two images were thought of—those of Ra and Tme. Knobel would even derive Urim and Thummim from the Egyptian, making them to be Hebraized loan words. But this line of explanation is rightly rejected. Buxtorf and Spencer would make Urim to be a little image which the high-priest held to his ear, into which the answer was supposed to be whispered. The usual Protestant explanation is that the objects were purely symbolical, while the priest depended for the answer upon internal illumination. The connection of the Urim and Thummim with the lot led Michaelis to think of three little stones, one of which signified " yes," another " no," and the third no answer at all. This view has remained the prevailing one, but with various modifications. It rests upon the terminology connected with the " throwing " of the lot which " came out " or " fell." But interpreters hesitate as to whether "Urim and Thummim" designates the oracle in general, or the means for casting the lot, or a polished and a rough stone. One view makes them partly polished, partly rough dice, thrown by the priest and interpreted by him in accordance with a code. Others think of two stones, one inscribed " yes " and the other " no." It may be that the correct interpretation of Ezek. xxi. 21–22 gives light, in which it appears that arrows were shaken to and fro before the sacred image, as the Urim and Thummim were shaken before the ephod; and it is not excluded that on one of the lots thus thrown the name " Jerusalem " was inscribed (verse 22). Similar staves, of different colors and inscribed, are described as existing in the Kaaba, and as being used for the purpose of casting lots and influencing decisions. The latest phase of interpretation refers these objects to a Babylonian origin. The Urim

and Thummim are then in the midst of the twelve stones (connected with the zodiac) in the relations of opposites, yes and no, life and death, light and darkness. They are carried on the breast as were the Babylonian tables of fate. But it is unthinkable to derive a usage in the time of David and Samuel from Babylonian practise, and neither David nor Samuel seems to have had in mind either the zodiac or the opposites named. If any connection with Babylon is to be assumed, the analogy holds only so far as the manner in which the objects were carried—on the breast. [The articles EPHOD, and LOTS, HEBREW USE OF, should be read in connection with the above discussion.]

                          (E. KAUTZSCH†.)

BIBLIOGRAPHY: A. F. Kirkpatrick, in his commentary on I Sam., pp. 217–218, London, 1880; Dosker, in *Presbyterian and Reformed Review*, 1892, pp. 717–736; Caldemeyer, in *Neue Jahrbücher für deutsche Theologie*, iii (1893). 107 sqq.; Wellhausen, *Heidentum*, pp. 132 sqq., ed. of 1897; T. W. Davies, *Magic, Divination, Demonology*, p. 75, London, 1898; R. Smend, *Lehrbuch der alttestamentlichen Religionsgeschichte*, pp. 319, 414, Freiburg, 1899; P. Haupt, in *JBL*, xix (1900), 58–59, 70–73; W. Muss-Arnolt, in *American Journal of Semitic Languages*, xvi (1900), 193 sqq.; T. C. Foote, in *JBL*, xxi (1902), 27 sqq.; K. Marti, *Geschichte der israelitischen Religion*, p. 45, Strasburg, 1903; B. Stade, *Biblische Theologie des A. T.*, p. 129, Tübingen, 1905; G. Wildeboer, *TSK*, 1905, part 3, pp. 195 sqq.; Benzinger, *Archäologie*, pp. 347 sqq.; Nowack, *Hebräische Archäologie*, ii. 93–94, 119–120; *DB*, iv. 838–841; *EB*, iv. 5235–37; *JE*, xii. 384–385. The commentaries on the passages cited, especially the excursus in Kalisch's commentary on Exodus, London, 1855; and the literature under EPHOD.

URLSPERGER, ürl'-spär″ger, **JOHANN AUGUST:** German Lutheran and founder of the Deutsche Christentumsgesellschaft (see CHRISTENTUMSGESELLSCHAFT, DIE DEUTSCHE); b. at Augsburg Nov. 25, 1728; d. at Hamburg Dec. 1, 1806. He was educated at the universities of Tübingen (1747–50) and Halle (1751–54); traveled for a year, became assistant to his father, Samuel Urlsperger (q.v.), at Augsburg, and rose to be first pastor there, retiring in 1776 because of illness. In spite of the pressure of pastoral duties, he devoted himself all his life to the demonstration that comprehension of the Trinity is the key to the comprehension of the entire Christian religion. In the course of his studies and sermons he became convinced, in 1767, that Col. ii. 2–3 contained the key of all knowledge, and between 1769 and 1777 he published seven large treatises on the being of God, in which, without any tendency to Sabellianism, he sought to escape the Athanasian confusion of the Trinity of the divine essence with the Trinity of revelation. Though his sole object in setting forth his doctrines of the Trinity was to reestablish the old dogma and to defend it against frivolous attacks of the neological school, Urlsperger was sharply criticized, only to be completely vindicated on appeal to the University of Tübingen. In his teaching he distinguished sharply between the Trinity of essence and the Trinity of revelation. Such concepts as procession appertain to the latter, not to the former; and in like manner, although, absolutely speaking, there can be in the triune nature of God no first and no last person, nor any which can be considered the origin of deity, there is, in the Trinity of revelation, a distinct subordination of the Son and the Holy

Ghost to the Father. The truth that the one God is triune in his very essence, without necessarily being Father, Son, and Holy Ghost, is "the mystery of God." The procession of God from himself in revelation is construed by Urlsperger as the transit from the infinite to the finite, the Son blending the two. With the exaltation of Christ the purpose of the economic Trinity was fulfilled and ceased to be. The Son, subjecting himself to the Father, ceases to be the Son, though remaining, as before his procession, a divine person. And the Holy Ghost, also proceeding from the Father to be with the Son, is the power which effected the procession of the divine Son by birth.

Feeling himself isolated in theological position, Urlsperger sought to get in closer touch with the few who entertained similar views with himself. With this end in view, and also to organize a society for the defense of Christianity along the lines of the English Society for Promoting Christian Knowledge and the Swedish De Fide et Christianismo, he undertook, in Aug., 1779, the tour of sixteen months which resulted in the foundation of the Deutsche Christentumsgesellschaft. Remaining in Holland for a time on his way home, Urlsperger reached Augsburg in Nov., 1780, where he received word of the foundation of the first society at Basel. The English branch, on the other hand, soon succumbed, and even the Basel branch, with its affiliations, quickly turned to works of practical piety rather than to a theoretical defense of Lutheran principles. Though such a step was diametrically opposed to his original idea, even if closely akin to the plans of his early days as a theological candidate at Frankfort, Urlsperger accepted the changes with faith and hope, never losing confidence in the success of the society.   (H. ANSTEIN.)

BIBLIOGRAPHY: Gradmann, *Das gelehrte Schwaben,* pp. 694–704, Nuremberg, 1802; J. G. Meusel, *Das gelehrte Teutschland,* x. 759–761, Lemgo, 1803; *ADB,* xxxix. 355–361.

URLSPERGER, SAMUEL: German Lutheran; father of the preceding; b. at Kirchheim-unter-Teck (22 m. e. of Tübingen) Aug. 31, 1685; d. at Augsburg Apr. 19, 1772. He was educated at Tübingen, and after traveling extensively and holding several other pastoral positions, he became court chaplain and consistorial councilor at Stuttgart in 1714. In this capacity, though lacking the strength of character to protest openly against the moral conditions prevailing at court, he was active in behalf of the new missions in Malabar. In Nov., 1717, he was converted to Pietism by Francke and incited to rebuke the duke, who punished him by securing his suspension till 1720; in 1723 he became senior pastor of St. Ann's in Augsburg. For forty-two years Urlsperger retained his post, forming devotional societies within his church and taking an active part in philanthropic work. The influence of Urlsperger was destined to spread beyond Augsburg. In 1731 the archbishop of Salzburg expelled all Protestants from his domain (see SALZBURG, EVANGELICALS OF), and when the emigrants began to pass through Augsburg, Urlsperger aided them with money as well as by the influence of his sermons and pamphlets, and also appealed for financial assistance for them to England, and large sums

of money passed through his hands. He had agents in many German cities to supervise and provide for the needs of the emigrants, and brought his influence to bear at the courts of Stuttgart, Hanover, and Mecklenburg, and especially of Wernigerode and Copenhagen. His duties were further augmented when he was appointed confidential agent for Oglethorpe's projected colonization of the Salzburg refugees in Pennsylvania. Urlsperger provided for the minutest details of the transportation, and gave special attention to securing proper religious instruction for the emigrants. Thus, under his supervision, Ebenezer, as he named the colony, became a center of Protestant faith and German industry, and developed into an important factor in the religious life of the new world. On the other hand, he came in sharp conflict with Count Zinzendorf (q.v.), deeming the antichurchly Pietism of Herrnhut a dangerous foe. Urlsperger's declining years were cheered by the deep affection in which he was held and by the devotion of his son, Johann August Urlsperger (q.v.). In 1764 he retired from active life. He was the author of several hymns, and of *Ausführliche Nachrichten von den Saltzburgischen Emigranten die sich in Amerika niedergelassen haben* (3 parts, Halle, 1738–52) and its continuation, *Amerikanisches Ackerwerk Gottes* (1766).

(BERNHARD KOCH.)

BIBLIOGRAPHY: A. Stein, *Samuel Urlsperger,* Halle, 1899; J. A. Urlsperger, *Wohlverdientes Ehrengedächtnis des . . . Samuel Urlsperger,* Augsburg, 1873; J. G. Meusel, *Das gelehrte Teutschland,* xiv. 213–215, Lemgo, 1815; E. E. Koch, *Geschichte des Kirchenlieds,* ii. 166–173, 6 vols., Stuttgart, 1866–72; L. Renner, *Lebensbilder aus der Pietistenzeit,* pp. 332 sqq., Bremen, 1886; *ADB,* s.v.

URSA'CIUS: Bishop of Singidunum (Belgrade). The date and place of his birth and death are unknown. His significance comes from the fact that with Valens, bishop of Mursa, he was a leader of the anti-Athanasian party in the fourth century. Both Ursacius and Valens, in all probability, imbibed their Arian views from Arius himself; they cherished especial animosity against Athanasius, against whom they brought false and reckless charges of theft, sacrilege, and murder. When it was convenient, they altered their declared opinions, at one time to the extent of professing orthodoxy; but for the most part they led the homoian party. They yet managed to retain the favor of the Emperor Constantius. See ARIANISM.

BIBLIOGRAPHY: Hefele, *Conciliengeschichte,* vol. i., Eng. transl., vol. ii., and Fr. transl., vol. i., consult Index in each case under "Ursacius" and "Valens"; *DCB,* iv. 1067; and the literature under ARIANISM, especially Gwatkin.

URSINUS, ūr-sîn'us: Antipope to Damasus (q.v.). On the death of Liberius (Sept. 24, 366), two of his deacons, Ursinus and Damasus, were elected to succeed him, the former apparently being enthroned Sept. 24 and the latter Oct. 1, 366. Ursinus seized the Basilica Julii across the Tiber, and the efforts of Damasus to dislodge him led to such tumults that the prefects interfered and exiled Ursinus with two of his deacons. Seven presbyters of his party, however, continued to hold services in the Basilica Liberii, whereupon there was a second scene of bloodshed on Oct. 26. The faction of Ursinus now begged the emperor to convene a synod to decide the matter, and when Valentinian deemed peace restored, he permitted Ursinus to return to Rome (Sept. 15, 367). On Nov. 16, however, the turbulent situation made it necessary to banish Ursinus again with his clergy, whereupon his adherents worshiped in the cemeteries without priests. On Jan. 12, 368, the emperor permitted the clergy of Ursinus to reside anywhere outside of Rome, but a few months later he was obliged to forbid them to approach within twenty miles of the city. Every effort was made, however, to avoid all unnecessary severity. In 378 a Roman synod thanked the emperor for recognizing the authority of Damasus, but at the same time expressed apprehension of the clergy of Ursinus, particularly of a converted but relapsed Jew named Isaac. In his reply the emperor declared that Ursinus had long been confined in Cologne and that his entreaties for release had been ignored, while all disturbers of the peace were forbidden to assemble within a hundred miles of Rome. Nevertheless, in 381 the Synod of Aquileia again complained of Ursinus, and even after the death of Damasus in Dec., 384, the banished antipope was still an object of apprehension. The two rivals, Damasus and Ursinus, seem to have been equally orthodox, the cause of the schism probably being ambition and its attendant passions. Ursinus died after 385.

Gennadius has the following: " Ursinus the monk wrote against those who say that heretics should be rebaptized. . . . He considers that after the simple confession of the Holy Trinity and of Christ, the imposition of the hands of the Catholic priest is sufficient for salvation " (De vir. ill., xxvii., Eng. transl. in NPNF, 2 ser., iii. 391). This Ursinus is doubtless the antipope, and the polemic mentioned by Gennadius is probably the pseudo-Cyprianic De rebaptismate, which modern scholarship places in the third century. Whatever the authorship of the work in question, it is known that during the time of Ursinus a certain deacon named Hilarius demanded the rebaptism of all who had been baptized by Arians, and it is probable that Gennadius was rightly informed when he stated that Ursinus polemized against such tenets.

(G. A. Jülicher.)

Bibliography: Besides the literature under Damasus I. (q.v.), consult: Liber pontificalis, ed. L. Duchesne, i. 212 sqq., Paris, 1886, and Mommsen, MGH, Gest. pont. Rom., i (1898), 37; Collectio Avellana, 1–13, ed. Günther in CSEL, xxxv. 1; Rufinus, Hist. eccl., xi. 1; Ammianus Marcellinus, " Roman Hist.," XXVII., iii. 11–13, ix. 9, Eng. transl. by C. D. Yonge, pp. 441, 457, London, 1887; DCB, iv. 1068–70.

URSINUS, ZACHARIAS: German Reformed; b. at Breslau July 18, 1534; d. at Neustadt-on-Hardt (21 m. s.s.w. of Worms) Mar. 6, 1583. He received his first training in the Elisabethschule at
Breslau, and was matriculated at Wittenberg Apr. 30, 1550, where a municipal allowance and some support by well-to-do patrons, including Johann Krafft (q.v.), afforded him his means of subsistence. He studied here until 1557, and became closely associated with Melanchthon, the vindictive attacks to which the latter was exposed filling him with aversion for the quarrelsome disposition of many theologians. This antipathy

Education and Early Career.

was increased when, in Sept., 1557, just as he was beginning an extensive academic journey, he witnessed the shameful contentions between the Protestants present at the religious conference in Worms. From Worms Ursinus went, by way of Strasburg, Basel, and Lausanne, to Geneva, where Calvin received him kindly, and he then remained for some time in Paris to study Hebrew under Jean Mercier. On his return Ursinus visited Zurich, after which he returned to Wittenberg, where, in Sept., 1558, he received a call from the Breslau Council to teach in the Elisabethschule. Here he gave open expression to his theological convictions, which ranged him, as he had discerned on his journey, on Calvin's side in regard to the doctrine of the Lord's Supper; and being attacked as a " sacramentarian," he made a clear exposition of his tenets in his Theses complectentes . . . summam veræ doctrinæ de sacramentis (Breslau, 1559). The work was prohibited in Breslau, and Ursinus was dismissed. Provided with traveling expenses by Krafft, he started for Zurich toward the end of June, 1560, by way of Wittenberg, Heidelberg, and Basel, reaching his destination Oct. 3.

In the following year, when Elector Friedrich III., the Pious (q.v.), was seeking to obtain a capable Reformed theologian for the directorship of the Heidelberg Collegium Sapientiæ, which had been transformed into a sort of theological seminary, Peter Martyr Vermigli (q.v.) recommended Ursinus, who, after considerable wavering, accepted the call, taking office Oct. 13, 1561. Here, besides the guidance of the institution, he had to supply the chair of dogmatics from Aug., 1562, to 1568; and in addition to all this he was obliged, beginning with 1563, to deliver a catechetical sermon every Sunday and to collaborate in preparing the new Palatine liturgy. His part in the drafting of the Heidelberg Catechism and his preliminary works for this purpose (the Summa theologiæ and the Catechismus minor) have already been indicated in Heidelberg Catechism, § 2. It was Ursinus who had to conduct the philosophic vindication of the Catechism against the vehement attacks of Lutheran theologians, this constraining him, much against his inclination, to engage in ever new theological feuds. It was Ursinus, in like manner, who was obliged to undertake the advocacy of the Palatinate party in connection with the embittered literary disputes at the Maulbronn colloquy (see Maulbronn). In 1566, he sought to confute, in his Augsburger Konfession . . . mit ihren eigenen Worten in Fragstück gestellt, and in his Articul, in denen die evangelischen Kirchen im Handel des Abendmahls einig oder spänig sind, the assertion that the Palatines had fallen away from the Augsburg Confession, and were, therefore, to be excluded from the religious treaty of peace. It was with reluctance that Ursinus had become a contestant in this dispute, and he longed for the time when he could retire from the arena. His official position alone claimed his powers beyond rightful bounds, and, owing to the frequent lack of an assistant, he was often compelled to take sole charge of the seventy pupils. In Feb., 1568, he was relieved of his dogmatic lectures by the call of Zanchi (q.v.),

At Heidelberg.

but the overpressure still continued, the result being impaired health and increasing melancholy. In Aug., 1571, he was called to a theological professorship at Lausanne, but could not accept because the elector would not release him. Before long there arose new heated contentions within the Palatinate church itself, and Ursinus, who took a very pessimistic view of the prevalent ecclesiastical and moral conditions in the Palatinate, deemed it absolutely necessary that a church discipline should be introduced there after the pattern of the one ruling in Calvinistic churches abroad. He boldly promulgated this conviction in his *Monita Ursini*, which he submitted to the elector May 26, 1568, but while Olevianus (q.v.) and Zanchi concurred with him, other influential men, especially Thomas Erastus (q.v.), spoke decidedly against the project. Within a short time Ursinus withdrew from the strife, hopeless of practical results from the inauguration of the church discipline under Palatinate conditions. Prompted, however, by the attitude of Pastor Adam Neuser of Heidelberg, and of Inspector Johann Silvanus of Ladenburg, who belonged to the most zealous opponents of the church discipline, and who not only combated the doctrine of the Trinity, but also sought alliance with the sultan of Turkey, Elector Friedrich nevertheless procured the introduction of the discipline, on July 13, 1570, and of the presbyteries. The report of the Heidelberg theologians, leading to the execution of Neuser Dec. 23, 1572, bears the signature of Ursinus, as well; and when, in 1573, Jakob Andreä (q.v.) rejected the Heidelberg theologians on the ground that their teaching led to Islam, they defended themselves in their *Bekanntnuss . . . von dem einigen Gott in dreyen Personen*, of which, no doubt, Ursinus was one of the chief authors.

After the death of Friedrich III., Ursinus had to leave Heidelberg. On Oct. 3, 1577, the *Collegium Sapientiæ* was dissolved, since none of the sixty-three pupils would accept the Lutheran Smaller Catechism; and a week later Ursinus was dismissed. He found a new sphere of labor, however, at Neustadt-on-Hardt, together with Daniel Toussain (q.v.), Zanchi, and others, in the *Collegium Casimirianum*, a school founded by Palsgrave

The
Closing
Years. Johann Casimir, Friedrich's younger son. He began his functions on May 23, 1578, with lectures on Isaiah, and here, in 1581, he wrote his last fairly considerable work, *De Libro Concordiæ Admonitio Christiana*, which he later revised and expanded in German, the work being intended to vindicate the Reformed doctrinal concept at the signing of the Formula of Concord (q.v.). The bodily powers of Ursinus were already well-nigh completely broken when he entered upon his duties at Neustadt, and at the close of 1582 his sufferings reached an acute stage, which soon terminated his life.   J. NEY.

BIBLIOGRAPHY: M. Adam, *Vitæ Germanorum theologorum*, pp. 529–542, Heidelberg, 1620; K. Sudhoff, *K. Olevianus und Z. Ursinus*, Elberfeld, 1857; J. F. A. Gillet, *Crato von Crafftheim und seine Freunde*, 2 vols., Frankfort, 1860; M. Göbel, *Geschichte des christlichen Lebens in der rheinisch-westphälischen . . . Kirche*, i. 393 sqq., Coblenz, 1862.

URSULA AND THE ELEVEN THOUSAND VIRGINS: The center of a noteworthy medieval cycle of legend in the Roman Catholic Church. In the developed form of the legend St. Ursula was the daughter of Deonotus or Diognetus, a Christian king in Britain, and received her name as the antagonist of the bear, i.e., the devil (cf. I Sam. xvii. 34). Wooed by a heathen prince, she consented to marriage on condition that he become a Christian, and that he allow her three years for pilgrimage with her ten maidens. In eleven triremes, each with a thousand virgins, she went to the harbor of Tila on the coast of Gaul, then up the Rhine to Basel, where she left the fleet and completed the pilgrimage to Rome by land. Returning by the same route, Ursula and her virgins reached Cologne, where they were all massacred by Huns under their King Ezzel. Ursula refused to become the wife of Ezzel, and was killed with an arrow which became her constant attribute in Christian art. Immediately after the massacre, the Huns were routed by a celestial host of 11,000, and then the citizens of Cologne buried the slain virgins on the bank of the Rhine.

The earliest mention of the legend of Ursula and the 11,000 virgins is contained in the martyrology of Wandalbert of Prüm, written at Cologne about 848 (ed. E. Dümmler, in *MGH, Poet. Lat. ævi Car.*, ii. (1884), 569 sqq. The legend is, therefore, not older than the ninth century. The tradition takes its rise from the late fourth- or early fifth-century inscription of Clematius (ed. F. X. Kraus, *Die christlichen Inschriften der Rheinlande*, No. 294, 2 vols., Freiburg, 1890–94). According to this, Clematius, a man of senatorial rank, received a series of visions in which heavenly virgins admonished him in regard to their martyrdom, of which he had been ignorant. Clematius then restored the ruined basilica on his estates that commemorated these martyred virgins, warning the citizens of Cologne that no bodies except those of the virgins who there had suffered martyrdom were to be buried in the basilica. This belief in the martyrdom of an indefinite number of unnamed maiden martyrs, who had suffered at an unknown time and in unknown fashion, forms the kernel of the legend of St. Ursula. Thus, as in the additions to the martyrologies of Bede (*ASB*, Mar., ii. 25) and Ado (*MPL*, cxxiii. 431), arose the number of 11,000, probably from a combination of the " thousands " with the eleven names. [*Ursula et XI M* (" Ursula and eleven M[artyrs]") was read "Ursula and eleven thousand (M being mistaken for *millia*, thousands ").] The account of the virgin martyrs of Cologne was blended in the tenth century with the Cyrmo-Breton legend of the migration of women from Britain to Armorica during the reign of the Emperor Maximus, as narrated by Geoffrey of Monmouth (*Historia regum Britanniæ*, v. 15–16), thus giving the voyage of the virgins and their massacre. In the twelfth century the legend became history, being found in a number of chronicles. The two completely developed recensions of the legend are the *Historia sanctæ Ursulæ et sociarum ejus* (*Analecta Bollandiana*, iii. 7 sqq.) and the *Passio sanctæ Ursulæ et sanctarum undecim millium virginum* (*ASB*, Oct., ix. 157 sqq.). The day of St. Ursula and her virgins is Oct. 21.   (A. HAUCK.)

BIBLIOGRAPHY: The *Passio* and various other early forms of the legends, with commentary, ed. V. de Buck, are in *ASB*, Oct., ix. 75–246, and this material was issued separately as *De S. Ursula et undecim millibus sociarum*, Brussels, 1858 (replies to Schade, below); other materials were ed. by J. Klinkenberg, in *Jahrbücher des Vereins von Altertumsfreunden in Rheinlande*, lxxxviii. 79–95, lxxxix. 105–134, xciii. 130–179, Bonn, 1890–92. Consult further: L. Reischert, *Lebensgeschichte und Märtyrertod der heiligen Ursula*, Cologne, 1837; O. Schade, *Die Sage von der heiligen Ursula*, Hanover, 1854 (began the modern critical investigation of the legend); P. Heber, *Die vorkarolingischen christlichen Glaubensboten am Rhein*, Frankfort, 1858; E. M. J. Heinen, *Leben, Fahrt, und Märtyrtod der heiligen Ursula*, Cologne, 1858; J. H. Kessel, *St. Ursula und ihre Gesellschaft*, ib. 1863 (also replies to Schade); J. B. Dutron, *Le Légende de S. Ursula*, Paris, 1866; *Legend of St. Ursula and her Companions*, London, 1869; G. Beetemé, *S. Ursula et ses onze mille vierges*, Brussels, 1867; G. Floss, *Annalen des historischen Vereins für den Niederrhein*, xxvi. 177–196, Cologne, 1874; Rettberg, *KD*, i. 111–123; Friedrich, *KD*, i. 141–166; *DNB*, lviii. 53–55.

URSULINES, ŭr′siu-lains: A Roman Catholic female order for the instruction and education of girls, established at Brescia in Italy in 1535 in honor of St. Ursula (q.v.) by Angela Merici (q.v.). Her rule is tertiary in type, and provides for the care of the sick and the instruction of the young, as well as for personal development and sanctification. The members of the new order resided with parents or kinsfolk, the discipline regarding fasts and meditations was not strict, nor was the vow of celibacy required, though the three monastic vows were recommended. A " mother " was to be chosen for life, eight " matrons " were to preside over the eight districts of Brescia, eight teachers were to be subordinate to the matrons, and eight supervisors to the teachers. In the course of time the Ursulines became a formal order living according to the rule of St. Augustine, the first step in this direction being the bull of confirmation of Paul III. (June 9, 1544). The spread of the Ursulines in Italy was due especially to the patronage of Cardinal Borromeo, who, in 1581, secured a reconfirmation of the order from Gregory XIII. In 1574 the Ursulines entered southern France, beginning monastic life in 1594. Thence in 1608 they extended to the Parisian suburb of St. Jacques, where a second large nunnery was built for them in 1611, the rule of which, drawn by Jesuits, served as the model for all regular Ursulines. It required a fourth vow of instruction of young girls. The habit was black with a leathern girdle, a black veil lined with white linen and a long veil of thin black material, and, in church, a black sleeveless mantle; and the discipline was mild. The order spread to Switzerland, Germany, Austria, and Hungary. In the second half of the eighteenth century convents were founded at Pereira in Portugal and Cork in Ireland, and in 1670 there was a Greek convent at Naxos. Meanwhile the order had entered America—Quebec (1639), New Orleans (1727), and Brazil (1751). At the time of their greatest expansion, early in the eighteenth century, the Ursulines had 20 independent congregations with 350 nunneries and between 15,000 and 20,000 nuns. There were also tertiary Ursulines in Italy and Switzerland without solemn vows, but still more under the influence of the Jesuits than the regulars.

The Revolution destroyed all the Ursuline convents in France, though in 1806 Napoleon restored

them as an educational society. A new series of congregations soon arose, among them the Sœurs de St. Roche, with their mother-house at Felletin, and the Ursulines of Jesus with 400 sisters and over fifty daughter-houses. The Bavarian convents were secularized, though those at Landshut, Straubing, and Würzburg were revived. In Prussia the most of the nunneries were destroyed by the Seven-Years' War, the Napoleonic wars, and by secularization. During the Kulturkampf the Ursulines were driven from Prussia, but were readmitted in 1887. There are now 36 Ursuline convents in Germany and 28 in Austro-Hungary, where they are the strongest female congregation. The 134 Ursuline convents in France were suppressed by the Associations Law of 1904. The order has two nunneries in Switzerland, 24 in Belgium, 15 in Holland, 8 in Great Britain, 2 in Spain, 3 in Portugal, and 17 in Italy, 24 in North America, 5 in South America, 3 in Asia and Java, 2 in Africa, and one in Australia. The total number of sisters is about 4,500.

(G. GRÜTZMACHER.)

BIBLIOGRAPHY: Besides the literature under MERICI, ANGELA, consult: (Paula de Pomereu), *Chroniques de l'ordre des Ursulines*, 3 vols., Paris, 1673 sqq.; *Journal des illustres religieuses de l'ordre de St. Ursule*, 5 vols., ib. 1684; M. Hamel, *L'Année spirituelle historique . . . des . . . Ursulines*, ib. 1689, ed. Clermont-Farrand, 1891; C. St. Foix, *Annales de l'ordre de S. Ursule*, ed. Clermont-Ferrand, 5 vols., ib. 1858; idem, *Vie des premières Ursulines de France*, ed. the same, 2 vols., ib. 1856; *Die ersten Schwestern der Ursulinerinnen*, Paderborn, 1897; *Handbuch der Klosterfrauen aus der Gesellschaft der heiligen Ursula*, 2d ed., Breslau, 1904; Helyot, *Ordres monastiques*, iv. 150 sqq.; Heimbucher, *Orden und Kongregationen*, ii. 273–287.

URUGUAY: South American republic; bounded on the north by Brazil, on the east by Brazil and the Atlantic, on the south by the Atlantic and the Rio de la Plata, on the west by the Argentine Republic; area, including the islands, 72,151 square miles; population in 1907 estimated at 950,000. As a result of the war of independence between what is now the Argentine Republic and Spain, what is now Uruguay, then known as the Banda Oriental, came into possession of Brazil; during 1825–28 the inhabitants fought for independence, which they finally won and the republic was organized in 1830. Ethnically the people are mestizos, Indians, and settlers from Europe, Brazil, and the Argentine Republic. The population is almost entirely Roman Catholic, which is the state religion, though there is toleration for other faiths. The country forms a Roman Catholic diocese, erected July 15, 1878, with Montevideo, the capital, as see city; it has as suffragan bishoprics Melo and Salto, and there are 40 parishes with 18 subordinate parishes, served by 130 priests. The Protestants number about 5,500. Among these are Swiss Germans, who have two organized churches, one in Montevideo and the other in Nueva Helvetia, each of the communities having a school, and combining in the Evangelical La Plata Synod under the Berlin Superior Church Council. The Anglican church has about 1,800 adherents. The Methodists are also in the country, being derived from the United States. There is a church of the Waldensian settlers, using the French language. Education is well cared for, being free and compulsory, with nearly 900 schools, and there is a university at the capital, with faculties in law, medicine, and mathematics.

(WILHELM GÖTZ†.)

BIBLIOGRAPHY: F. Bauza, *Historia de la Dominacion española en el Uruguay*, Montevideo, 1880; R. P. Lomba, *La Republica Oriental del Uruguay*, Montevideo, 1884; E. J. M. Clemens, *La Plata Countries*, Philadelphia, 1886; H. Rumbold, *The Great Silver River*, London, 1888; F. Vincent, *Round and About South America*, New York, 1890; *Uruguay; its Geography, History, Industries*, Liverpool, 1897; A. H. Keane, in Stanford's *Compendium of Geography and Travel*, London, 1901; T. C. Dawson, *The South American Republics*, New York, 1903; P. F. Martin, *Through Five Republics*, London, 1905.

USHER, ROLAND GREENE: Protestant Episcopal layman and historian; b. at Lynn, Mass., May 3, 1880. He received his education at the Grafton High-school and at Harvard University (B.A., 1901; M.A., 1902; Ph.D., 1905); was Rogers Fellow from Harvard, 1902–04, studying in Europe; assistant in history at Harvard, 1904–07; instructor in history at Washington University, St. Louis, 1907–10, and assistant professor there after 1910. Ecclesiastically he places himself with the Broadchurch party of his denomination. He has issued *The Presbyterian Movement in the Reign of Queen Elizabeth (1582–89). Edited with Introductions and Notes for the Royal Historical Society*, 3d series, vol. viii. (Camden, 1905); and *The Reconstruction of the English Church* (2 vols., New York and London, 1910).

USSHER, JAMES: Archbishop of Armagh; b. in Dublin Jan. 4, 1581; d. at Reigate (22 m. s. of London), Surrey, Mar. 21, 1656. His father was clerk of the Irish court of chancery; his uncle, Henry Ussher (archbishop of Armagh 1595–1613), and his maternal grandfather, James Stanyhurst, were founders of Trinity College, Dublin, and their young relative became one of its earliest scholars (1594). His father wished him to be a lawyer, but the son preferred divinity, and was free to follow his inclination after the father's death in 1598. He was graduated B.A. probably in July, 1597, became fellow 1599, M.A. Feb., 1601, and the same year was made catechist and first proctor of his college, and preacher at Christ Church, and was ordained deacon and priest in December. In 1605 he became chancellor of St. Patrick's Cathedral and rector of Finglas, County Dublin, and was graduated B.D. and appointed professor of divinity in 1607. From c. 1611 to 1620, when he exchanged it for Trim, he also held the rectory of Assey, County Meath. He proceeded D.D. in 1614 (incorporated D.D. at Oxford, 1626), and was chosen vice-chancellor of Trinity College in 1615 and again in 1617, and vice-provost in 1616. He visited England to buy books for the college library in 1602, and again in 1606, and thereafter triennially, spending a month each in Oxford, Cambridge, and London. He became well and favorably known to the foremost scholars and statesmen of England. In 1615 Ussher drafted the 104 articles of the Irish Church (see IRISH ARTICLES), which are anti-Romanist and strongly tinged with Calvinism. In 1621 he resigned his professorship to take up the work of a poor, unremunerative, and badly organized dio-

Career Previous to Being Archbishop.

cese, James I. having nominated him bishop of Meath and Clonmacnoise. He attempted to win the Roman Catholics by his sermons, and possibly by more energetic measures; at any rate, the Roman Catholic Archbishop Hampton interposed a remonstrance. From Dec., 1623, till early in 1626 Ussher was in England, working on his book on the antiquities of the British Church and much of the time suffering from ill-health. He was appointed archbishop of Armagh in Mar., 1625.

His views and tendencies appear in the fact that his name stands first in a list of twelve Irish bishops who signed a protest against toleration of popery in 1626, and also in his desire, expressed in 1627, for the removal of grievances felt by the non-conforming Puritans. As vice-chancellor, he continued to have much to do with the affairs of Trinity College. In 1628 he began a correspondence with William Laud (q.v.), which lasted till 1640; although they differed in theology, the two men had much in common, and their relations were cordial. Moreover, Ussher's acts always showed him alive to the duty of allegiance to constituted authority. In June, 1634, an old dispute between Armagh and Dublin for the primacy of Ireland was settled in favor of the former by Lord Strafford. The Irish convocation met the next month and adopted the Anglican articles without repealing the Irish articles. Ussher thereafter required subscription to both sets, and this course was followed till the Restoration. He opposed the adoption of the English canons as inconsistent with the independence of a national church, and the outcome was the adoption of 100 canons drawn up by John Bramhall, bishop of Derry, and " methodized " by Ussher. They make no concession to Puritan scruples.

Views and Tendencies.

In 1640 Ussher went to England and never returned to Ireland. He lived in Oxford and London, as a guest at St. Donat's Castle, Glamorganshire, Wales, and lastly with an old friend, Elizabeth Mordaunt, dowager countess of Peterborough, at her houses in London and Reigate. The Irish rebellion of 1641 well-nigh impoverished him, and the troubles in England brought him distress of mind. He contemplated retiring to the continent, but declined the offer of a chair at Leyden (1641) and another (after the execution of Charles I.) of a pension in France with religious freedom, made through Richelieu by the queen regent. He preached often and boldly. Soon after the opening of the Long Parliament (Nov., 1640) he drafted a modified scheme of episcopacy as an effort to compose the religious differences (first correctly printed at London in 1656, after Ussher's death, as *The Reduction of Episcopacy unto the Form of Synodical Government Received in the Ancient Church*), which was accepted by the Puritans, and which was used by Charles I. in 1648 and by Charles II. in his " Declaration " in Oct., 1660. He attended Strafford to the block, having previously advised the king to go cautiously in assenting to the condemnation of the earl. In 1642 Charles granted him the bishopric of Carlisle *in commendam*, and in 1643 parliament gave him a pension of £400 annually,

Life in England.

although the first payment was not made till 1647. He was invited to sit in the Westminster Assembly and responded by preaching against its legality. Again in 1647 he was offered a seat in the assembly, but he never attended. None the less the influence of his writings is apparent in the assembly's work. As the crisis drew near between king and parliament, Ussher fearlessly denounced the attitude of the latter and proclaimed the doctrine of divine right. Cromwell sought his advice and promised, without according, pecuniary relief. At Ussher's death he made a treasury grant of £200 toward the expenses of an elaborate public funeral in Westminster Abbey.

Ussher's contemporaries rightly held him too mild for a good administrator, but all parties found in him something with which they could agree— the Puritan his Calvinistic theology, the churchman his reverence for antiquity, the royalist his steadfastness for the king. All respected his goodness and sincerity, felt the charm of his personal gifts, and marveled at his learning (characterized by Selden as " miraculous "). He wrote much (the list of first editions of his books in the *DNB* has 27 numbers) on topics suggested by the controversies of his time, but with a thorough and exact use of original sources which still makes much of his work of first-rate value—notably his contributions to the history of the creed and to the Ignatian problem, and in the field of early British and Irish church history. His chronology was taken from the margin of the Authorized Version and is still printed in English Bibles. His complete *Works*, with life, were published at Dublin in 17 volumes, 1847–64 (vols. i.–xiv. ed. Charles Richard Elrington, vols. xv.–xvii. ed. James Henthorn Todd, index by William Reeves). There are many editions of separate works by both English and foreign editors, the more important being *A Discourse of the Religion Anciently Professed by the Irish* (Dublin, 1623; enlarged London, 1631); *An Answer to a Jesuit in Ireland* (Dublin, 1625); *Gotteschalci et Predestinatianæ Controversiæ Historia* (1631), in which he published for the first time Gottschalk's " Confessions," which he had obtained from Venice; *Veterum Epistolarum Hibernicarum Sylloge* (1632); *Britannicarum Ecclesiarum Antiquitates* (1639; enlarged London, 1677); *Polycarpi et Ignatii Epistolæ* (Oxford, 1644); *Appendix Ignatiana* (1647); *De Romanæ Ecclesiæ Symbolo Apostolico Diatriba* (1647); *Annalium Pars Prior* (1650), and *Pars Posterior* (1654), which in 1659 were combined into the *Annales Veteris Testamenti;* an English translation, with additions, was published at London in 1658 as the *Annals of the World to the Beginning of the Emperor Vespasian's Reign.*

Charac- ter and Writings.

USSING, us'sing, HENRY BRAEM: Danish preacher and theologian, son of the philologist and archeologist Johan Louis Ussing; b. at Copenhagen July 2, 1855. He was graduated from the Metropolitan school of that city (1873), and from the University of Copenhagen (candidate in theology, 1877), continuing his studies in Germany, France, Italy, and England. In 1882 he was appointed pastor at Veilby; in 1883 at Hvidovre and Valby, sub-

urbs of Copenhagen, his present charge. In 1883 he published an apologetic work, *Den kristelige Vished,* which gained for him the university degree of Lic. theol., and the resultant right of delivering lectures at the University of Copenhagen, of which right he has made much and valuable use. He is an able preacher and a thorough scholar, who has made, especially through periodicals, valuable contributions to practical theology. The Scandinavian students know him as one of their most faithful directors at their conventions, and in Sunday-school circles his name is highly cherished. He was a delegate at the centennial celebration of the Sunday-school in London, 1880. Since 1891 he has been coeditor of *Indre Missions Börneblad.* His *Vor Gudstjeneste* (1888) and *Tanker til Overvejelse om Menighedsliv og Kirkeliv* (1890) show the Scriptural conception of liturgy and a firm grasp of the problems of congregational life. The literary work, however, which especially has brought him fame is *Evangeliets Sejrsgang ud over Jorden* (1902). The best collection of his sermons is *Troens gode Strid* (1904; on the epistles of the old church year).

JOHN O. EVJEN.

BIBLIOGRAPHY: C. F. Bricka, *Dansk biographisk Lexikon,* xviii. 120–121, 19 vols., Copenhagen, 1887–1905.

USTERI, üs'te-rî, LEONHARD: Swiss Protestant; b. at Zurich Oct. 22, 1799; d. at Bern Sept. 18, 1833. He was educated in his native city and at the University of Berlin (1820–23), coming in the latter institution under the special influence of Schleiermacher. Returning to Zurich he published his *Commentatio critica in qua evangelium Joannis genuinum esse . . . ostenditur* (Zurich, 1823), and began a private course for his young friends on the Pauline epistles, these lectures forming the basis of his most important work, the *Entwickelung des paulinischen Lehrbegriffes mit Hinsicht auf die übrigen Schriften des Neuen Testamentes* (1824). The work is, however, antiquated, even in its basal concept of the derivation of the Pauline system from the antagonism between Christianity and the pre-Christian period; and it is, moreover, less a development than a presentation of individual Pauline doctrines in accordance with a scheme previously adopted. At the same time the author rightly recognized two points since claimed by others: Paul's search for righteousness, after his conversion, solely in the grace of God and in fellowship with Christ; and the gradual extension of the apostle's purview and activity from the knowledge of Christ as the Redeemer and the Son of God. The work merited its fame, and served to prepare the way for a renewed and deepened knowledge of the great apostle to the gentiles.

Just as the *Entwickelung* was leaving the press, its author accepted a call to Bern as professor of classics and Hebrew, as well as director, at the gymnasium. Here he spent the remainder of his life, also teaching for a time at the university as privatdocent. In addition to his official duties, he found time to prepare an edition of Wolf's lectures on the first four books of the Iliad (2 vols., Bern, 1830) and of Plutarch's *Consolatio ad Apollonium* (1830), and to write a *Commentar über den Brief Pauli an die Galater* (1833), which, though not entirely satisfactory, was to be the first of a series which should embrace all the Pauline writings; but this plan was cut short by death. [He also translated into modern literary German and arranged under appropriate heads extracts from Zwingli's writings, *M. Huldreich Zwingli's sämmtliche Schriften im Auszuge* (2 vols., Zurich, 1819).] His theory of myth as applied to the Gospels makes him the immediate predecessor of Strauss. He held the Reformation to be essentially a revival of the scientific spirit, and regarded the essence of the primitive Church as enthusiasm for truth and brotherly love.   (E. GÜDERT.)

USUARDUS: French Benedictine; flourished in the ninth century; d. at St. Germain-des-Prés, Paris, Jan. 13, probably 875. In 858 he was one of two monks deputed by his order and by Charles the Bald to bring from Valencia the relics of St. Vincent, but on their way they learned that these relics had meanwhile been obtained by the bishop of Saragossa, and they accordingly changed their route to Cordova, where they were enabled to secure the bodies of Saints George and Aurelius, as well as the head of St. Natalia. In Oct., 858, Usuardus and his companion were again on French soil, only to find that, during their absence, a Norman inroad had driven the monks from St. Germain-des-Prés to Emant, in the diocese of Sens, whence they were unable to return until 863. The success of Usuardus in obtaining relics of the saints, together with his knowledge of church history, led Charles to commission him to draw up a martyrology, and it is to this work, which is based, with considerable personal control and investigation of his sources, on the martyrologies of Ado, Bede (as revised by Florus), and the pseudo-Jerome, that his lasting fame is due. Usuardus' martyrology, which was completed about 875, quickly secured great popularity, and was followed in the majority of the churches and monasteries of France, Italy, England, and Spain, naturally with the addition of various saints specially honored in each specific district. Still greater tribute was shown it when, in 1580, Gregory XIII. directed that this martyrology be revised and improved, the result being the issue, in 1583, of the *Martyrologium Romanum*, the foundation of the present Roman martyrology. The first edition of the martyrology of Usuardus appeared at Lübeck in 1475, and was repeatedly republished until superseded by the critical edition of J. B. Sollier (Antwerp, 1714; often reprinted, and also accessible in *ASB*, June, vi.–vii., and in *MPL*, cxxiii.–cxxiv.).

BIBLIOGRAPHY: J. C. F. Bähr, *Geschichte der römischen Literatur im karolingischen Zeitalter*, p. 501, Carlsruhe, 1840; A. Ebert, *Allgemeine Geschichte der Literatur des Mittelalters*, ii. 355, 386, Leipsic, 1880; A. Longnon, in *Notices et documents publiés pour le Société de l'hist. de France*, pp. 19 sqq., Paris, 1884; *Historisch-politische Blätter*, cxvi (1895), 489 sqq., cxvii (1896), 177 sqq.; Ceillier, *Auteurs sacrés*, xii. 611–612; *KL*, xii. 512–513.

USURY (INTEREST).

I. Among the Hebrews: By usury is generally meant the employment of another's need to exact from him in return for some service (usually a loan) a disproportionately large remuneration, and the word suggests something morally blameworthy.

1. Biblical Enactments. In the Bible the word covers the meanings attaching to the words " interest " and " tribute." The Hebrew words are *neshekh, marbith, tarbith*, and the Greek is *tokos*. The laws of the Pentateuch, which so frequently have a philanthropic character, declare that aid to a fellow countryman who is in need is a duty of love (Deut. xv. 17 sqq.). Hence it is forbidden to an Israelite to take from a fellow Israelite interest of any kind in return for a loan (Ex. xxii. 25–27; Lev. xxv. 35–37; Deut. xxiii. 20), whether of money or food; but from one who is not an Israelite it is permitted by the Deuteronomic law to take interest (xxiii. 20; cf. xv. 6, xxviii. 12). The distinction is not difficult to understand. In the first place, from gentiles there could be no expectation of receiving material help without payment for the service, since these did not display disinterestedness toward their own people. In Egypt loaning for interest seems to have been introduced by Bocchoris of the twenty-fourth dynasty (718–712 B.C.), and the rate was 30 per cent for loans of money and 33⅓ per cent for grain. But the Asiatics who traded in Egypt exacted interest from the natives at a much earlier date. In the earliest time the Romans demanded only the return of what was lent (Nonius Marcellus, v. 70). In the second place the position of commerce among the gentiles was essentially different from what it was or was intended to be among the Hebrews, the latter not being wholly devoted to it as were, e.g., the Phenicians (see PHENICIA, PHENICIANS). Among the Babylonians as early as 2,000 B.C. the customary rate of interest was for money 20 per cent, for grain 25 or 33⅓ per cent, and the same rate appears in the New-Babylonian contracts. In the Old Testament the subject is considered in relation to need, and not in connection with commercial transactions. But the legal requirements were carried out in practise only in part. The taking of usury is very often condemned (Prov. xxviii.·8; Ezek. xviii. 13, xxii. 12; Ps. cix. 11); compare the praise of abstention from the practise (Ezek. xviii. 8, 17; Ps. xv. 5, xxxvii. 26). Oppression of the poor is frequently bewailed (Ecclus. xiii. 22–23), especially that arising from insistence upon rights conferred by making a loan (Ezek. xviii. 12; Amos ii. 8; Job xxii. 6, xxiv. 3; cf. Ex. xxii. 26; Deut. xxiv. 6, 10–13). But there is no mention of the rate per cent for loans; for according to Geiger, Guthe, and others, Neh. v. 11 is to be read " and the debt of the money, and of the corn . . ." instead of " the hundredth of the money. . . ." While this rate of interest (one per cent) for a month is from the modern standpoint conceivable, it would be low for that period in

history; yet it was wide-spread in Greece, as well as the monthly reckoning, and was customary in the Roman Empire after the year of the city 704, though Justinian set the rate at 6 per cent for money and 12 for grain. No punishment is mentioned for taking usury, either in Bible or Talmud.

The Talmud also forbids the taking of interest between Hebrews. An exception is found in *Baba Meẓi'a* 75a, where Rab Jehuda affirms that to the wise (those who know the law) it is permitted to borrow and pay interest, since that class knows that

2. Talmudic and Later Usage. usury is forbidden and so make a "present" [in place of interest]. The same rabbi, following Rab Jehuda, declared that it is permitted a man to lend for interest his children and house-folk in order to let them feel the impression of payment of interest. But, the passage goes on, this is wrong, since they may become accustomed to the practise. In the Mishna (*Baba Meẓi'a* 5–6) between Israelites and gentiles the taking of interest is plainly permitted, though in the following Talmudic discussion the privilege is strongly limited; and it appears from the tract *Makkoth*, 24a, that an ideal held forth is to take no interest from gentiles, where in remarking upon Ps. xv. 1, 5, it is added " who takes no usury from a gentile." But the views of later times were various, and apologetic expressions defending the practise are not wanting. It may be mentioned that the prohibition against taking usury from a gentile is reckoned by Maimonides as no. 198 among the commandments, and in the enumeration of the commands this prohibition is no: 613. Some say, again, that one must be guided by his feelings in the matter; others, that it is commendable that no one take interest. In the *Shulḥan arukh*, *Yore de'a*, clix. 1, is the following: " The Torah permits to loan to a gentile for usury. The wise have forbidden it except so far as it is necessary for maintenance of life or in the case of a wise man or so far as concerns a gain forbidden only by rabbis. But now it is permitted." Biblical law forbids taking usury from Israelites; the wise have also forbidden bargaining for gain or taking it for loans of money or wares. Even yet pious Jews regard the taking of interest from Jews as forbidden, even when the debtor is rich, and though the gain is regarded as a present (L. Stern, *Die Vorschriften der Thora, welche Israel in der Zerstreuung zu beobachten hat*, p. 215, 4th ed., Frankfort, 1904). In the training which commerce and intercourse have in the present brought about, complete observance of the prohibition is not possible; and various ways have been devised in order to keep the letter of the law, as when a sort of partnership is agreed upon. An example of the formula employed in such a case is given in B. H. Auerbach, *Lehrbuch der israelitischen Religion*, p. 108 (2d ed., Giessen, 1853). The same authority lays down the maxim that from a gentile the Jew is to receive only a moderate rate of interest, such as is permitted by either the law or the custom of the land; a rate disproportionate to the value as judged by the use to be made of the loan is thievery and sinful. But such regulations have not prevented loud outcries

concerning Jewish usury, though in many cases these had no basis in fact, since orthodox Jews regard this as heinous sin.   (H. L. STRACK.)

II. In the Christian Church: The term usury, being originally equivalent to " fruit," " growth," " increase," and being applied to personal profit or gain, was also used to express the profits derived from money loans. The term, therefore, tallies with the Greek *tokos* (from *tekō*, " to bear," " to bring forth."

In ancient times interest was paid monthly and grew to vast amounts, insomuch that when paid by the poor, who were practically constrained to accept loans, the operation proved highly oppressive. The New Testament, while not expressly forbidding the receipt of interest, yet commends gratuitous lending, in token of neighborly love (Luke vi. 34, 35). In the early days of the Church, the taking of interest was reproved, as by Tertullian, Cyprian, Ambrose, Basil the Great, Gregory of Nyssa, Chrysostom, and others. It was only from the enemy, one who may also be slain in war, that interest could be taken rightfully. But as a general rule the practise was prohibited for all Christians, without distinction of persons (canon 20 of the Synod of Elvira, 310 A.D.). But as the fruition of interest was permitted by civil law, church legislation was confired to regulations forbidding the clergy to enjoy the same, under pain of dismissal (Synod of Arles, 314; Council of Nice, 325, canon xvii.). And in the year 325, again, when Constantine decreed anew that in the case of profits an interest so great as one-half of the loaned amount might be drawn, and in the case of capital, the hundredth part, that is, one per cent a month, or 12 per cent yearly (Theodosian Code, chap. 1., *de usuris*, iv. 33), that ecclesiastical prohibition had reference only to the clergy (Council of Laodicea, 372 A.D., canon 4; Third Synod of Carthage, 397 A.D., canon 16). But this nowise prevented the teachers of the Church from enjoining upon all Christians the duty of lending without interest, as did Augustine and Jerome. Their example was also followed by Pope Leo I., in a brief of the year 447 to the bishops of Campania, Picenum, Tuscany, and all Italian provinces. Nevertheless, the synodical prohibitions continued to be directed only against the clergy (as at the Second Synod of Arles, 443 A.D., canon 14, and that of Tarragona, 516 A.D., canons 2, 3). The Greek Church, however, so far deferred to temporal legislation, which still permitted the taking of interest though under certain restraints, as to relax even the universal interdiction governing the clergy. For in the East they prohibited only the matter of promising interest on loans, whereas they allowed the exaction of interest when the refunding of borrowed capital was immoderately delayed. This was the import of a ruling by Photius (*Nomocanon*, tit. IX., xxviii., in conjunction with Justinian's *Novellæ*, CXXXI., xii.) whereby, for pious ends of the Church, legates were allowed to draw interest arrearages. This construction was also favored by later commentators (cf. Balsamon's commentary on the passage cited from Photius). In the Frankish realm, the interdiction

1. Early Ecclesiastical Legislation.

at first affected only the clergy, though it soon became extended to cover laymen as well. In agreement with this are the decretals of the later popes and the synodical rulings.

The leading idea in all cases is that in both the Old Testament and the New the taking of interest is generally forbidden, as being " avarice and wickedness." Thus Alexander III. declares at the Third Lateran Council, 1179, in canon 25: " Wherefore none may be dispensed in favor of drawing interest." He had previously ruled that the profits derived from the pledged article must be deducted from the loaned capital itself; only the actual object in pawn must be returned to the owner, excepting the case of a church benefice, which might then be acquired from the hands of a layman and so recovered to the Church. As a general thing it was provided that when interest accrued, it should be assigned to the debtors or to their he·rs; but if no such claimants existed, it should go to the poor, and that this should be done alike by the creditor himself and by his heirs. The oath rendered by a debtor, pledging him not to reclaim interest, by no means annulled the obligation about refunding the same; and this held where the payment of interest was voluntary, and not expressly stipulated. The church penalties threatened against receivers of interest are suspension for the clergy and excommunication for laymen, together with the usual consequences of refusal of church burial and exclusion from judicial hearings. Procedure against usurers was to be instituted not only on grounds of a formal accusation, but also as a direct official duty. Against Jews who had taken interest of Christians every means of procedure was to be set afoot. Antecedent rulings were augmented by Gregory X. at the Council of Lyons, 1274, canons 26, 27. He forbade the harboring of foreign usurers, even the leasing to them of habitations. Usurers were to be expelled from the land within three months, under pain of suspension in case of prelates, excommunication in the case of other persons, interdict for colleges and corporate bodies, and in the event of resistance at large, interdict upon the given country. Notorious usurers, besides incurring the penalties earlier stated, were also to be debarred as testamentary witnesses, and their own wills were to be invalid. At the Council of Vienne, 1311, Clement V. decreed in addition that those municipal statutes which allowed the taking of interest and embodied regulations accordingly were to be null and void; whereas authorities who should draw up such measures or give sentence in accordance with them were to be liable to the ban. For the purpose of providing proof against usurers, these were to be held answerable for submitting their account books. Finally the pope declared, " If any lapse into the error of obstinately and presumptuously affirming that it is no sin to practise usury, we decree that he be punished quite as a heretic."

This ruling essentially terminates the canonical construction of the matter, and even stamps the same with a certain dogmatic sanction. This attitude is supported not only by the medieval doctrine of the unfruitfulness of money (an economic theory treating money simply as medium of exchange or measure of value), but also by the interpretation which the schoolmen gave to the related passages of Holy Scripture (Alexander of Hales, pars III., quæst. 86, art. 2; Thomas Aquinas, II., 2, quæst. 87, art. 1 ad 2, quæst. 105, art. 3 ad 3). The objection borrowed from the context in Matt. xxv. and Luke xix. is met from the said standpoint. The matter of lending under direct promise of interest has in all times been reproved from the point of view of canon law. Benedict XIV. simply repeated as much in consonance with the earlier law, in his brief *Vix pervenit* of Nov. 1, 1745, while the Curia still maintains that position.

The high rate of interest prevalent in the Middle Ages rendered life exceedingly burdensome to the poor, if they needed a loan; so that the canonical regulations against taking interest at all were highly acceptable to the common people. It is assumed that no usury exists where the object at issue is an ecclesiastical benefice or tenure, such as is not supposed to rest in lay hands, in the nature of the case. The same is true in respect to the purchase of a fixed annuity or ground-rent, something essentially distinct from an interest-bearing loan in that the buyer (and creditor) could not lay claim to the principal, whereas the rate of interest itself was moderate. The same applies in the case of deferred interest charges, in so far as the " interest " here in question represented proper compensation. Finally, there was no usury involved in moderate interest paid to loan-houses (*Montes pietatis*, q.v.), to the benefit of the poor (Lateran Council of 1517, sess. X.; Tridentine Council, sess. XXII., c. 8 de reform.). Moreover, practical requirements were met by other exceptions, and the canon law was either evaded or else modified with manifold qualifications. In the same direction, even the popes allowed usury in the case of the Jews. But, on the other hand, the notion of usury became extended to every line of trade in which a positive profit was the object in view; particularly was this true of exchange business. The canonical prohibition of usury continued to be supported, in the main, by subsequent civil legislation.

The Reformers, in turn, in agreement with the primitive Church, rejected the taking of interest. Luther pronounced against it in his sermons on usury, 1519 and 1524, and in 1540 issued an admonition to pastors to preach against that practise. To his mind, the notion of usury and of interest are one and the same. But Luther extends the notion of usury to the purchase of ground-rents, though on this point he was not always consistent. For instance, when Jacob Strauss, Evangelical pastor at Eisenach (1523), denounced all interest as void of obligation, Luther and Melanchthon declared, in a formal opinion requested of them, that usury was a great evil and contradictory to love; but that yet not every one should be allowed to withdraw at will from an assumed obligation, or to refuse payment save under forcible compulsion —a course upheld by Strauss. Whether they would

2. Completion and Basis of Ecclesiastical Theory.

3. General Results.

4. Views of the Reformers.

exact usury or accept it should be left free to the creditors' conscience; only the rate ought not to exceed four or five florins to the hundred; and the interest, again, ought not to be redeemable. Not that the question at large was thus by any means resolved, for many minds were still in doubt and unrest over the admissibility of interest in the shape of rent and income (cf. *Instruktion und Befehlch darauff die Visitatores im Kurfürstenthum Sachsen abgefertigt seyn*, 1527; E. Sehling, *Die evangelischen Kirchenordnungen*, i. 142 sqq., Leipsic, 1902). Melanchthon also was not consistent in the matter of judicially defining the admissibility of taking interest, nor did he always adhere to the view that was first held regarding the absolute reprehensibleness of the said practise. Calvin, however, adopted a different standpoint. He gave utterance to his views on various occasions (as in Sermon no. 134, in *CR*, xxviii. 121), and also delivered a special reply to a formal inquiry addressed to him, wherein he allowed the taking of interest in seven contingencies (*CR*, x. 245 sqq.). Calvin's views have since then been reflected by other Evangelical theologians, regarding the propriety of taking interest; as by Wilhelm Amasius in his work *De conscientia et ejus jure vel casibus;* by Spener, in his *Theologische Bedenken*, ii. 227 sqq. (4 vols., Halle, 1700–02); and in modern times by F. V. Reinhard, *System der christlichen Moral*, iii. 27 sqq. (5 vols., Wittenberg, 1788–1815); C. F. von Ammon, *Handbuch der christlichen Sittenlehre*, iii. 194 sqq. (3 vols., 2d ed., Erlangen, 1838); R. Rothe, *Theologische Ethik*, iii. § 1, p. 233 (Wittenberg, 1871). Indeed, even Roman Catholic authors reflect similar views (cf. B. Phillips, *Lehrbuch des Kirchenrechts*, p. 637, Regensburg, 1862: " Forasmuch as the interest prohibitions in the canon law presuppose wholly different social conditions from those of the later age, they have ceased to be valid ").

The force of these reasons was the less to be withstood when supported by the rulings of the Roman law, the authority of which gained wider and wider recognition. There thus grew up a custom contradictory to the canon law; transferring 5. Modern the usual 5-per-cent rate of interest Practise. common to rents and incomes to loans, with direct pledge of interest; and also occasionally raising the rate to 6 per cent. Dating from the latter third of the sixteenth century, this custom was also legalized in the several German sovereignties and also by the terms of the final decree of the imperial diet of 1654. Thenceforward the notion of " usury " in the sense of " avarice and wickedness " is no longer applied to the drawing of interest in general, but denotes illegal interest, especially that in excess of the legal rate. This alone is viewed as a properly penal transaction; whereas the likewise frequently interdicted practise of drawing interest on interest, or arrears of interest exceeding the principal itself, is accounted, under the civil law, as something merely impracticable. In the broad sense, usury also includes the purely artificial enhancement of the price of commodities in the general market. This practise moved the Reformers to open protest, Luther among them. The contemporary German imperial law has a more circumscribed conception of usury. The same, or a similar practise, according to the laws of May 24, 1880, and June 19, 1893, occurs only where one takes advantage of the straitened circumstances, thoughtlessness, or inexperience of another, in the case of a loan, or postponement in settling an account due on demand, or some other legal transaction with reciprocal bearings, all tending to the economic ends of borrowing and lending, i.e., where the creditor contrives to extort and secure for himself or some intermediate third party such pecuniary profits as not only transcend the usual interest rate, but also reach glaring disproportion in comparison with the service rendered. Usury of this kind is requited with penal severity, and the transactions involved are null and void by terms of the civil code, § 138, division 2.

The judicial estimation of usury from the standpoints of Church and State has been divergent. And though the Evangelical church has rejected the inflexible attitude of the Church of Rome in this matter, still, the Evangelical church can not assent to the repeal of all usury laws. At all events, it may not desist from counseling the members of its communion respecting the duty laid upon them in the words of the Lord (Luke vi. 34, 35).

E. SEHLING.

BIBLIOGRAPHY: For the Biblical side consult: J. D. Michaelis, *Syntagma commentationum*, ii. 1 sqq., Göttingen, 1769; idem, *Mosaisches Recht*, ii. 87 sqq., 6 vols., 2d ed., Frankfort, 1771–75, Eng. transl., *Commentaries on the Laws of Moses*, 4 vols., London, 1814; J. L. Saalschütz, *Das mosaische Recht*, pp. 183–184, 277–278, 856–857, Berlin, 1853; M. Duschak, *Das mosaisch-talmudische Strafrecht*, pp. 46–50, Vienna, 1869; H. Ewald *Antiquities of Israel*, pp. 181–185, Boston, 1876; J. M. Rabbinowicz *Legislation civile du Thalmud*, iii. pp. xxi.–xxxiii., Paris, 1878; A. Bertholet, *Die Stellung der Israeliten und Juden zu den Fremden*, Freiburg, 1896; J. Hejel, *Das alttestamentliche Zinsverbot im Lichte der ethnologischen Jurisprudenz*, ib. 1907; Benzinger, *Archäologie*, pp. 292–293; *DB*, i. 579–580; *EB*, iii. 2727–28, 3791–93; *JE*, xii. 388–391.

On the relation of the Church to usury consult: Bingham, *Origines*, VI., ii. 6, XVI., xii. 13; W. Endemann, *Die nationalökonomischen Grundsätze der kanonistischen Lehre*, Jena, 1863; idem, *Studien in der romanisch-kanonistischen Wirtschafts- und Rechtslehre*, 2 vols., Berlin, 1879–1883; M. Neumann, *Geschichte des Wuchers in Deutschland*, Halle, 1865; F. X. Funk, *Geschichte des kirchlichen Zinsverbotes*, Tübingen, 1876; W. Cunningham, *Christian Opinion on Usury*, London, 1884; R. F. Crawford, *Letters on Usury*, ib. 1889; L. Goldschmidt, *Universalgeschichte des Handelsrechts*, i. 137 sqq., Stuttgart, 1891; W. Blissard, *The Ethic of Usury and Interest*, London, 1892; L. Caro, *Der Wucher*, Leipsic, 1893; E. W. Mason, *Forgotten Teaching and Neglected Discipline of the Church as to Usury*, Leicester, 1900; F. Schneider, in *Festgabe für Heinrich Finke*, Münster, 1904; F. Schaub, *Der Kampf gegen den Zinswucher*, Freiburg, 1905; *DCA*, ii. 2006–08.

UTENHEIM, ü'ten-haim, **CHRISTOPH VON:** Bishop of Basel; b. of a noble Alsatian family probably about 1450; d. at Delsberg (or Delémont, 29 m. n. of Bern) Mar. 16, 1527. In 1473 he was rector of the newly founded University of Basel, where, though a nominalist, he became closely associated with a circle of humanists and realists, and the same year provost of St. Thomas's in Strasburg. In 1494 Jacques d'Amboise, abbot of Cluny, made him vicar-general of the Cluniac monks in Alemannia, with special charge of the monastery of St. Alban's until an administrator should be appointed. In 1499 he was chosen auxiliary bishop of Basel, and in 1502 became full diocesan. Utenheim called Wimpfeling (q.v.) to Basel to prepare synodal statutes, these being rather a collection and revision of existing statutes than an independent work. Wimpfeling gladly accepted the task, and the synod assembled on Oct. 23, 1503, when the clergy were commanded to observe the statutes. The bishop himself delivered a short address, referring to the scandal caused among the people by the unspiritual conduct of the clergy, urging them to a better life, and ascribing the corruption of the Church primarily to the omission of synods and the neglect of statutes, amelioration being expected from semiannual synods after the ancient fashion as renewed by the Council of Basel. The statutes show that this effort was only one of many to elevate spiritual life by regulating the minutest details of the life of the clergy. The spirit of the reforms attempted in the statutes is indicated in the books recommended to the clergy for reading: the writings of Johann Gerson, especially his *De arte audiendi confessiones*, and the *Resolutorium dubiorum missæ* of Johannes de Lapide.

The attempted reform was unsuccessful. The holding of regular synods failed; the clergy did not wish to be reformed; and while in the Alsatian portion of the diocese they received the support of the nobility, the gradual loss of the political power in the Swiss portion rendered the bishop's ecclesiastical control but slight. The canons secured exemption from episcopal authority and immediate control by the pope and their dean. In the statutes an endeavor was made to check pilgrimages to places which Utenheim believed had received sanctity from false visions, but this prescript was misconstrued and the papal commissary of indulgences to Germany nullified the efforts. In his endeavor to secure capable men to aid in the administration of his diocese, Utenheim called not only Wimpfeling, but Wolfgang Capito (q.v.), who in 1515 became preacher at the cathedral as well as teacher in the theological faculty. In 1515–16, through the influence of Capito, Œcolampadius (q.v.) was also attached to the cathedral staff. All this, however, by no means proved any sympathy on the part of Utenheim with the Protestant Reformation, though the bishop of Basel was an ardent humanist. It is thus readily explicable that Christoph von Utenheim, with his desire for reforms within the Church, eagerly read and heartily approved the earliest writings of Luther, but that when the logical consequences of the German Reformer's course became manifest, he turned away decisively, and that the events which transformed ecclesiastical conditions in Basel took place without his aid and against his will. A stronger nature than the scholarly bishop's would have proved too weak to stem the tide, and in 1519, weighed down by age and sickness, Utenheim received a coadjutor in Niklaus of Diesbach. The city council now made a determined effort to renounce its allegiance to the bishop, but in 1522 it showed itself willing to meet with him when certain humanists gave a blasphemous dinner on Palm Sunday. Not only were the offenders threatened with dire punishment if they repeated their scandal, but the priests were forbidden to introduce new doctrines into their preaching of the Gospel. The secular priest of St. Alban's, Wilhelm Reublin (q.v.), who had inveighed against the hierarchy and the institutions of the Church, and had carried a Bible instead of relics at the procession of Corpus Christi, was expelled from the city by requirement of the bishop despite all protests. While still evidently inclined toward reforms, Utenheim repeatedly emphasized his conviction that changes were to be introduced gradually and in accordance with the voice of the Church herself. In Basel accordingly he sought to check the new movements which were shattering the foundations of the Church, and when, in 1522, Œcolampadius returned to the city and preached the tenets of Luther, Utenheim forbade the clergy and the members of the university to hear him. To the last he was desirous of reform, though only of such as should proceed from the bishops and leave the basis of the ancient Church unimpaired. The view, frequently expressed, that Utenheim was an Evangelical, as contrasted with a Roman Catholic, bishop has no foundation. In Feb., 1527, he wrote from Pruntrut, where his predecessors had mostly resided, to the chapter, requesting them to relieve him of his duties, but before a new bishop could be chosen, he had passed away.   (EBERHARD VISCHER.)

BIBLIOGRAPHY: J. J. Herzog, *Beiträge zur Geschichte Basels*, pp. 33 sqq., Basel, 1839; *Basler Chroniken*, ed. W. Vischer and A. Stern, Leipsic, 1872 sqq.; K. Pellican, *Chronikon*, ed. B. Riggenbach, Basel, 1877; C. Schmidt, *Hist. littéraire de l'Alsace*, Paris, 1879; J. Knepper, *Jakob Wimpfeling*, Freiburg, 1902; R. Wackernagel, in *Basler Zeitschrift für Geschichte und Alterthumskunde*, ii (1903), 171 sqq.

UTILITARIANISM.

I. Definition.
II. History.
    Cumberland, Berkeley, and Hume (§ 1).
    Bentham, Mill, and Spencer (§ 2).
III. Doctrines of Utilitarianism.
IV. Criticism.

I. **Definition:** Utilitarianism may be considered from two different points of view, viz., from abstract ethical theory, or from a practical relation to social and political institutions. In England, where utilitarianism has had its worthiest exponents, it is usually viewed from the practical side, and is tersely defined in the well-known formula, " The greatest happiness to the greatest number." On the continent and in America, where utilitarianism is known chiefly as one among numerous ethical theories, it is considered to be synonymous with hedonism, and is defined as the doctrine that actions derive their moral character from their consequences; or, that actions are right when they promote happiness, wrong when they produce misery. The ethical value of an action depends on, and is derived from, its utility. An action may, however, be useful to the individual alone; or, to society. This distinction in the extent of utility leads to another. The individual generally considers those actions useful which produce pleasure, which is egoistic hedonism. But if he looks upon his actions not so much from the point of view of single pleasures as from that of happiness, he finds that the latter is closely connected with the happiness of his fellow men; and if he acts with a view to promoting happiness in general, he is an altruistic hedonist, or, properly speaking, a utilitarian.

II. History: Utilitarianism is historically and theoretically connected with the classical Cyrenaic and Epicurean schools of philosophy. The doctrine of these schools was, however, chiefly egoistic hedonism. As a doctrine of altruistic hedonism, utilitarianism is said to have had its origin with the Italian publicist Cesare Marchese de Beccaria Bonesana (1735–94). This doctrine has, however, generally been connected with English philosophy, since England has not only produced the earliest and best exponents of this system, but also the strongest advocates of the practical bearings of this theory.

Richard Cumberland (1631–1718) was the first philosopher to propound a system of utilitarianism.

1. Cumberland, Berkeley, and Hume. The keywords to his doctrine are the statements that feelings are by nature both egoistic and altruistic; and that man is fitted for society by the latter. Rationality emphasizes the altruistic feelings in this respect in two ways: first, by enabling one to recognize his own good as indissolubly connected with that of society and thus leading to objectively moral conduct from ultimately egoistic motives; second, by enabling one to recognize and desire the good in and for itself. " Good " is defined by Cumberland as that which perfects both mind and body. Cumberland is, however, somewhat ambiguous concerning the things which have a tendency in that direction, and speaks more frequently of happiness as the good. Happiness is pleasure depending (1) upon the unimpeded normal activities of mind and body; (2) upon a tranquil frame of mind, which is conditioned sometimes by external circumstances, sometimes by the feeling that one has acted consistently, and again by the consciousness that one has acted for the common weal; and (3) upon the knowledge that others are happy. George Berkeley (1685–1753) is the father of " theological utilitarianism." This term indicates the attempt to reconcile ultimately selfish motives of action with morality. If self-interest is the ruling principle of human nature, it must be shown that the interest of the individual demands moral action. But this can not always be proved to be the case, particularly if supernatural sanction be disregarded, since no man is able to predict the consequences of his actions. Divine omniscience alone can do that and formulate rules of action which will tend toward the well-being of all men and all nations, and, therefore, toward the well-being of the individual. Supernatural sanctions are thus necessary to produce moral actions. David Hume (1711–76) boldly argued that men never actually continue to approve of any quality in human nature which does not at least appear to be either useful or agreeable. A moral distinction is possible only on the ground of utility and pleasure, or uselessness and pain. Usefulness and agreeableness must, however, be extended to others than self; and the consideration of others must become a sentiment of humanity which may be reasonably regarded as the ultimate cause of all moral phenomena. It may happen that by acting in accordance with this sentiment, the individual becomes the loser; but mental tranquillity and consciousness of integrity—so necessary for happiness—will nevertheless be cultivated and cherished by every true man. Hume freed utilitarianism from the dogma that the motive of the agent is always, in the last analysis, egoistic, and defended the altruistic tendencies of human nature.

Jeremy Bentham (1748–1832) emphasized the pleasurable aspect of actions as motives, but chiefly those which give pleasure to the doer.

2. Bentham, Mill, and Spencer. He distinguished thirteen kinds of pleasures with their corresponding pains, viz.: sense, wealth and privation, skill and awkwardness, amity and enmity, reputation and disgrace, power, piety, benevolence and malevolence, memory, imagination, expectation, and association. Only two of these classes—benevolence and malevolence—have reference to fellow men; all others concern only the individual. John Stuart Mill (1806–73) rounded out the system of utilitarianism, freed it from its narrowness, and made it acceptable to statesmen and theologians. By his insistence upon the " acquired character " of moral feelings he emphasized their social nature as no one had done before, and thus gave this system of ethics an importance in English life which hardly any other philosophy has enjoyed. This great influence is due to his claim that disinterested public spirit should be the prominent motive in the performance of all socially useful work, and that, e.g., even hygienic precepts should be inculcated not chiefly on grounds of prudence, but because " by squandering our health we disable ourselves from rendering services to our fellow creatures." Herbert Spencer (1820–1903) introduced the principle of slow racial development into the concepts of utilitarianism. It had always proved insuperably difficult for utilitarians to show how the abstract principle of general happiness could arise from that of personal happiness, since experience demonstrates that actions for the general welfare frequently conflict with personal interests and happiness. Spencer tried to show that this transformation is next to impossible in the individual, but that it is probable in the race by slow and gradual accretions which the individual inherits as he does other traits favorable in the struggle for existence. The habit of acting with a view to other people's happiness is an advantage to any race or nation; and it is, therefore, probable that with growing intelligence the principles of benevolence were developed and eventually inherited by the individual, who practises them as naturally as he does those of personal interest.

III. Doctrines of Utilitarianism: The connection between utilitarianism and hedonism is close, and many defenders of the former have had difficulty in disentangling their system from the latter; some of them have more or less openly espoused hedonism, and have attempted to free it only from its grosser implications. An outline of Bentham's system in its most complete form (*Principles of Morals and Legislation*, London, 1789) makes this clear. He starts with the hedonistic and utilitarian proposition that the desire for pleasure and the fear of pain are the only motives which can influence the human will, and that the attainment of the greatest possible happiness is, therefore, the supreme interest of every individual. Society consists, however, of individuals, and it must be animated by the same desire for happiness; this takes the form of the attainment of the greatest possible happiness for all its component members. This happiness to one and to all can, however, be gaged only by the consequences resulting from actions as the experience of the individual and of the race has registered them. Experience shows pleasurable actions to be useful on the whole, painful actions to be useless, except as warning signals. The principle of utility or of the greatest happiness is, consequently, the only test of morality, since the latter means usefulness in the broadest sense. The moral character of an action is to be ascertained by a calculation of the pleasures and pains involved in the elements which constitute it. Pleasure and pain may be greater or less according to intensity, duration, certainty or uncertainty, nearness or remoteness, strength of expectation, fecundity, purity, and extent, i.e., number of persons affected. Pleasure and pain have different sources or sanctions—physical, political, moral, and also religious, since God himself wills his children to be happy. The moral faculty, with which ethics is alone concerned, is constituted by good-will or benevolence, the love of amity, the love of reputation, and the dictates of religion and of prudence. Ethical systems not in agreement with utilitarianism may be divided into two classes, those of asceticism which disapprove of actions in proportion as they tend to augment happiness, and approve of them as they tend to diminish it; and those of sympathy. John Stuart Mill is the best representative of the newer utilitarianism. He maintains in his *Utilitarianism* (1863) that the criterion of morality, the foundation of morality, and the chief good are identical. From this basis he argues that the steadiness and consistency of the moral beliefs of mankind are mainly due to the tacit influence of utilitarianism, because this doctrine sets before men as chief aim the greatest happiness not of the individual, but of the race. But utilitarianism rests on a distinction of pleasures into kinds—high and low, noble and ignoble. If men make this distinction, they are led to recognize the power to sacrifice their own greatest happiness for that of their fellow men, because actions of this kind may be more useful to the race. In every-day life man does not, as a rule, calculate the consequences of his actions, because conscientious feeling has invested utility with obligatory force—sufficient in the main to lead to right action. Justice is a form of utility, and means originally the animal desire to repel a hurt or to retaliate; but becomes widened so as to include all persons by the human capacity for enlarged sympathy and the conception of intelligent self-interest.

James Mill (1773–1836) contributed a few other elements. Useful actions are of four kinds—acts of prudence, fortitude, justice, and benevolence; the first two include acts primarily useful to us, secondarily to others; the last two, those which are primarily useful to others, and secondarily to ourselves. The moral feelings are a complex growth, of which the ultimate constituents are pleasurable and painful sensations, e.g., disinterestedness is a real fact which has developed by association from personal interest and has eventually been detached from its original roots.

IV. Criticism: Utilitarianism as a theory of life is inadequate (1) from the point of its motive, (2) from that of its fundamental principle. Morality is based on the conception of duty. Utilitarians regard pleasure and self-interest as the original roots of morality. But duty can never be developed from these roots. It is easy to show that virtue is useful; but impossible to prove virtue a derivative of utility. When utilitarians approach this crucial point, they appeal either to the will of God (John Austin), or to the authority of the law (Alexander Bain), or to conscientious feeling (John Stuart Mill). The theory fails, thus, both in regard to sufficiency of motive and of logical consistency. The fundamental principle of utilitarianism is the calculability of actions. Man is to act with a view to the pleasurable or painful effects of his acts, both to himself and to others. That might be a good rule to follow were man omniscient. Since he is limited in his foresight, he must act in many cases according to law and precept—either divine or human. But the moment he does so, he abandons the utilitarian principle, and obeys some rule either of man or of God. The principle " The greatest happiness to the greatest number," if taken as guide, does not afford basis for computation of pleasure and pain, since one can not know what will give pleasure or pain to others. Pains and pleasures differ not only with different individuals, but with different classes and stages of civilization. It was the impossibility of making fixed standards of variable pains and pleasures that caused Herbert Spencer to say: " Hence if the method of egoistic hedonism is unsatisfactory, far more unsatisfactory for the same kindred reasons is the method of universalistic hedonism, or utilitarianism" (*Principles of Ethics*, i. 155, London and New York, 1910).   RUDOLPH M. BINDER.

BIBLIOGRAPHY: E. Albee, *Hist. of English Utilitarianism*, London, 1902; F. E. Beneke, *Grundlinien des natürlichen Systems der praktischen Philosophie*, 3 vols., Berlin, 1837–1840; A. Bain, *The Emotions and the Will*, London, 1859; W. E. H. Lecky, *Hist. of European Morals*, 2d ed., 2 vols., ib. 1869; J. Grote, *Examination of Utilitarian Philosophy*, Cambridge, 1870; H. Bleckley, *A Colloquy on the Utilitarian Theory of Morals*, London, 1873; J. S. Blackie, *Four Phases of Morals*, Edinburgh, 1874; A. Comte, *Positive Philosophy*, 2 vols., 2d ed., ib. 1875; L. Stephen, *Science of Ethics*, ib. 1882; idem, *The English Utilitarians*, 3 vols., ib. 1900; T. H. Green, *Prolegomena to Ethics*, Oxford, 1883; G. P. Best, *Morality and Utility*, London, 1887; H. Calderwood, *Handbook of Moral Philosophy*, 14th ed., ib. 1888; H. Sidgwick, *Method of Ethics*, 4th ed., ib. 1890; idem, *Outlines of the Hist. of Ethics*, 3d ed., ib. 1892; G. von Gizycki, *Introduction to the Study of Ethics*, ib. 1891; G. F. James, *T. H. Green und der Utilitarismus*, Halle, 1894; S. Chapman, *The Æsthetic Element in Morality and its Place in a Utilitarian Theory of Morals*, New York, 1895; A. Germain, *Du beau moral formel*, Paris, 1895; W. Wundt, *Ethical Systems*, New York, 1897; F. Paulsen, *A System of Ethics*, ib. 1899; J. S. Mill, *Utilitarianism, Liberty, and Representative Government*, latest issue, London, 1910.

UTRAQUISTS. See HUSS, JOHN, HUSSITES, II., §§ 3–7.

UYTENBOGAERT, ai''ten-bō'gärt, JAN (HANS):
Influential leader of the Dutch Remonstrants (q.v.);
b. at Utrecht Feb. 11, 1557; d. at The Hague Sept.
4, 1644. He came of Roman Catholic ancestry,
and his early education he received at home
and at the school of St. Jerome in his native city;
he then turned to the study of law, entering the
office of a notary, and a remarkable future seemed
insured by 1578, when he was offended by the conditions attached to an offer, it being demanded that
he cease attendance upon the sermons of the evan-
gelically inclined Huibert Duifhuis. He thereupon
broke with the Roman Catholic Church. He was
a short time at Arnheim in the service of a
secretary of Count John of Nassau, and then
returned to Utrecht with the intention of becoming a pastor. Here the strife between Duifhuis
and his partizans and the Calvinists (called Consistorials) had already broken out. In 1580 Uytenbogaert was sent at the city's expense to
Geneva to study theology and came into connection
with Beza; but his sympathies were not in that
direction, rather they inclined to Arminius. On his
return to Utrecht in 1584 he found the strife between the adherents of Duifhuis and the Consistorials
still sharper, the upper classes siding with the
former. But the Consistorials called him to a pastorate in which he did not feel at home, as the conditions did not favor the expression of his own sentiments. In the course of the controversy between
the parties, the magistrates decided to retire honorably all the preachers of both parties and install
others in their places, and so Uytenbogaert was,
in 1590, out of position.

At the invitation of Prince Maurice he went to
The Hague in 1591, where he was soon installed
over the Walloon congregation, and there his preaching was attended by the prince and the nobility.
He gained the high favor of the prince and of Louise
de Coligny, and undertook the education of the
young Prince Frederik Hendrik, as well as the
labors of court preacher. The appointments were
to the taste of Oldenbarneveld, who expected to
make use of the great influence which Uytenbogaert
had already gained. The latter undertook the education of Oldenbarneveld's two daughters, and in
ecclesiastical matters was the adviser of the grand
pensionary, but the friendship and cooperation of
Uytenbogaert and Oldenbarneveld eventually cost
the former his influence with the ecclesiastics. Yet
for a long time he was the recognized head of an
ecclesiastical party, and to him was attributed practically everything that was done, while his counsel
was constantly sought. Yet as the head of his party
he was no dogmatician, and in his pastoral work he
emphasized piety and the renewing of the life; but
he emphasized freedom of thought and speech, in
which his opponents thought they saw the overthrow of the Church and of the republic. His influence was used time and again for peace, as in the
case of Arminius (q.v.) in 1591, but in several of
these cases he was accused of attempting to subject the Church to the State. On the death of Arminius Uytenbogaert became the head of the Arminians, now compacted into a party, to whom was
to be given the name Remonstrants. Forty of these

as pastors met at the invitation of Oldenbarneveld
and under the leadership of Uytenbogaert, Jan. 14,
1610, the result of which meeting was the famous
" Remonstrance " (see REMONSTRANTS) to the
States of Holland. At the same time came Uytenbogaert's first writing, Tractaet van 't Ampt ende
Authoriteyt eener Hoogher Christelicker Overheydt in
Kerckelicke Saecken (The Hague, 1610), which called
forth a series of answers and focused the strife
which the conferences of 1611 and 1613 could not
abate. The Calvinists began to institute their own
services, the favor of Prince Maurice was lost to
Uytenbogaert, and he at last declared he would no
longer go to hear the latter's preaching. In 1617
the States decided for a synod, against the wish of
the Remonstrants. Uytenbogaert lost courage, in
Mar., 1618, asked to be relieved of his charge, and
when, Aug. 29, 1618, Oldenbarneveld, Grotius, and
Hogerbeets were arrested, Uytenbogaert fled to
Rotterdam and thence to Antwerp. On May 24,
1619, he was publicly banned from the republic and
his goods confiscated, the reason assigned being
that he had introduced new views, contrary to those
of the accepted Reformed doctrine. In October he
sent a document to Prince Maurice in his own defense, Schriftelijcke Verantwoordinghe . . . of de
openbaere Klock inluydinghe Edicte . . . (1619),
and continued from afar to direct the affairs of the
Remonstrants. In Oct., 1621, he removed to Rouen.
When Maurice died, Apr. 23, 1625, and was followed as stadholder by Uytenbogaert's pupil Frederik Hendrik, affairs looked more favorable for the
Remonstrants, and Uytenbogaert returned, reaching Rotterdam unheralded Sept. 26, 1626. But
Frederik would not espouse openly the cause of the
Remonstrants, though he granted his protection to
his old teacher. Uytenbogaert began to preach
quietly at The Hague, and regained possession of
his own house. For the rest of his life he worked
for his cause by his writings and by personal effort.

Although Uytenbogaert's literary activity began
late in his life, the results were fruitful. A list of his
works is given in the appendix to the third edition of his autobiography (see bibliography, below);
most of them were polemics, drawn from him by
the stress of the times. Yet two of his productions,
historical in nature, are of permanent value. The
first is his autobiography, brought down to May
13, 1638. It was not intended for the public eye,
and was edited by Rijckewaert. It is apologetic in
character, and gives valuable information concerning the persons and events of his times. The second work was suggested by another which he issued
anonymously under the title Oorspronck ende Voort-
ganck der Nederlantsche Kerckelijcke verschillen tot
op het Nationale Synodus van Dordrecht (1623), and
aimed to be a history of the Church, especially in
the Netherlands. It was called De Kerkelicke Historie, vervetende verscheyden ghedenckwaerdige saken,
in de Christenheyt voor-gevallen, appeared in 1646,
and covered the period 400–1619. The work is
excellent in character, uses various sources, and
is not uncritical. While the tone is moderate, the
great fault is that in fact it is a defense of the
Remonstrants.

Uytenbogaert was one of the great men of his

times. While he was not a notable scholar, he was a man of learning and earnest in his pursuit of knowledge. He had a talent for organization, the sense of practicality, and a ready eloquence. His diplomatic ability was such that, had his sphere been that of politics, he would have won eminence as a statesman. His piety was earnest, and he died in peace with his conscience. (S. D. VAN VEEN.)

BIBLIOGRAPHY: Sources are: The autobiography, *Johannis Wtenbogaerts Leven*, n.p., 1645, 3d ed., 1647; and his *Brieven en onuitgegeven Stukken*, ed. H. C. Rogge, Utrecht, 1868–75. Consult: H. C. Rogge, *Johannes Wtenbogaert en zijn Tijd*, 3 parts, Amsterdam, 1874–76; idem, in *Godgeleerde Bijdragen*, vol. xxii.; idem, in *Jaarboeken van wetens. Theologie*, new series, vol. i.; J. M. Schröckh, *Christliche Kirchengeschichte seit der Reformation*, v. 226–276, 35 parts, Leipsic, 1772–1803; J. L. Motley, *John of Barneveld*, 2 vols., New York, 1874 (often reprinted); and the literature under ARMINIUS, JAKOBUS; EPISCOPIUS, SIMON; and REMONSTRANTS.

UZZIAH, uz-zai'a (**AZARIAH**): Ninth king of Judah, son and successor of Amaziah (q.v.). His dates, according to the old chronology, are 808–756; according to Kamphausen, 777–736; according to K. Marti (*EB*, i. 797–798), 789–740. His name appears in various forms in the Hebrew: 'Uzziyyahu (II Kings xv. 32, 34; II Chron. xxvi. 1 sqq., xxvii. 2; Isa. i. 1, vi. 1, vii. 1), 'Uzziyyah (II Kings xv. 13, 30; Hos. i. 1; Amos i. 1; Zech. xiv. 5), '*Azaryah* (II Kings xiv. 21, xv. 1, 7, 17, 23, 27; I Chron. iii. 12), and '*Azaryahu* (II Kings xv. 6, 8); the meaning is " Yahweh is my strength " or " Yahweh hath helped." There is no satisfactory explanation of the employment of the two names; the Septuagint does not follow strictly the forms in the Hebrew. Both names have parallels in form and meaning in Assyrian and Phenician.

The narrative in II Kings xiv. 21–22, xv. 1–7 makes Uzziah succeed to the throne at the age of sixteen, assigns to him a reign of fifty-two years, gives him a good character, even though the high places were not removed, states that he restored the possession of Elath (on the eastern arm of the Red Sea) to Judah and so implies the reconquest of Edom, and that he became a leper, on account of which his son Jotham acted as regent. II Chron. xxvi. agrees with Kings so far as this narrative goes, but adds: (1) that Uzziah warred successfully against the Philistines, Arabians, and Meunim, and that the Ammonites became tributary; (2) that he strengthened the fortifications of Jerusalem; (3) developed a strong military establishment; (4) engaged extensively in pastoral, agricultural, and viticultural pursuits; and (5) that, puffed up with pride in his achievements, he became vain and entered the Temple to burn incense, (according to the Chronicler) an exclusively priestly prerogative, and that, in spite of priestly remonstrance, he persisted in his purpose and was stricken on the spot with leprosy. While the Chronicler's explanation of the cause of the leprosy may be regarded as a late midrashic legend, the details regarding Uzziah's military measures receive incidental and weighty corroboration (cf. J. F. McCurdy, in *The Expositor*, Nov., 1891). The success of the Assyrians in their assaults on the Syrian powers would naturally result in such measures of defense as stronger fortifications and increase in munitions and forces, and in the creation of such engines of war as are attributed to Uzziah. Moreover, the control of Philistine territory shown by Hezekiah only a few years later must have dated from this reign (cf. II Kings xviii. 13 sqq.). The Taylor cylinder of Sennacherib speaks of Arabians as forming part of the garrison of Jerusalem during Sennacherib's attempts against the city, which is explained by Uzziah's conquest over a part of the Arabian territory, going well with his command of the region south to Elath. The prosperity of Judah which appears even during the weak reign of Ahaz must be traced to this reign; and the power of Judah at the beginning of the Sennecharib campaigns is explicable on these grounds. Uzziah's force of character and foresight and wisdom doubtless prolonged the life of the southern kingdom, and his achievements thus make him one of the most important kings of Judah.

The passage in the annals of the great Tiglath-Pileser (most accessible in Eng. transl. in *DB*, iv. 844; see ASSYRIA, VI., 3, § 9, cf. VI., 2, § 1) which refers to " Azariah of Yaudi " is now by most scholars held not to refer to the subject of this sketch but to a king Azariah of a territory called Yaudi (the writing of which might easily be read as the Assyrian equivalent of " Judah ") not far from Alexandretta Bay in northwestern Syria. The places named in connection with the confederation against the Assyrians of which the document speaks are regarded as too remote from Judah to permit Azariah of Judah to take the leadership in such a confederation (cf., however, J. F. McCurdy, *History, Prophecy, and the Monuments*, i. 413–415, New York, 1894). A matter of some interest is the occurrence in Uzziah's reign of an earthquake which was so severe as to serve as a sort of date of reckoning (Amos i. 1; Zech. xiv. 5).

GEO. W. GILMORE.

BIBLIOGRAPHY: Besides the pertinent sections in the literature under AHAB; and ISRAEL, HISTORY OF, consult: E. Schrader, *Keilinschrijten und Geschichtsforschung*, Giessen, 1878; H. Winckler, *Alttestamentliche Forschungen*, i. 1–23, Leipsic, 1893; J. F. McCurdy, in *Expositor*, Nov., 1891, pp. 388 sqq.; idem, *History, Prophecy, and the Monuments*, i. 348–351, 413–415, New York, 1894; T. K. Cheyne, *Introduction to the Book of Isaiah*, pp. 4, 16 sqq., London, 1895; C. F. Kent, *Student's O. T.*, ii. 282 sqq., New York, 1905; Schrader, *KAT*, i. 54 sqq., 262; *DB*, iv. 843–845; *EB*, iv. 5240–44; *JE*, xii. 393–394.

V

VADIANUS. See WATT, JOACHIM VON.

VAGANTES, va-gan'tîz or gan'tês (*Clerici vagantes*, or *vagi*): A term applied in early canon law to those clergy who led a wandering life either because they had no benefice or because they had deserted the church to which they had been attached. As early as the fifth and sixth centuries measures were taken against them, as when the Council of Chalcedon forbade ordination without appointment to a specific church, or when the Council of Valencia (524?) threatened the vagantes with excommunication, a penalty extended by the Synod of Arles (524) to those who should give them shelter. Nevertheless, the vagantes still flourished, and frequently aided bishops and other clergy in the discharge of their duties or became chaplains in the castles of the knights, thus making their profession a trade and interfering with the orderly conditions and ministrations of the regular clergy. In 789 Charlemagne renewed the Chalcedon injunctions, and also forbade the entertainment of any clergy who could not produce letters from their bishops. But even these measures failed, and in the ninth century several synods (e.g., Mainz, 847, and Pavia, 845–850) sought to check the vagantes, and their efforts to take possession of benefices already conferred on others, while such prelates as Agobard of Lyons, in his *De privilegio et jure sacerdotii*, also opposed them. In the twelfth century Gerhoh of Reichersberg (q.v.) again complained of them in his *Liber de simonia*, but matters became far worse in the following century, when the Synods of Mainz (1261), Aschaffenburg (1292), Treves (1310), and St. Pölten (1284) declared against the vagantes, while in Bavaria they were expressly excluded from the king's peaces of 1244, 1281, and 1300.

A peculiar type of vagantes arose in France in the twelfth century, later spreading to England and Germany. These were the roving minstrels, mostly dissolute students or wandering clergy, first called *clerici vagantes* or *ribaldi* (" rascals "), and later, after the early thirteenth century, chiefly known as *goliardi* or *goliardenses*, terms apparently meaning " sons of Goliath," i.e., " sons of giants." They were masters of poetic form, but many councils of the thirteenth and fourteenth centuries sought to restrict the goliards and their excesses. These measures seem practically to have suppressed the goliards in France by the end of the thirteenth century; but in Germany they survived until late in the fifteenth century under various names. Hugo of Trimberg devoted a special chapter of his *Renner* to the *ribaldi* and other vagantes, while in England Chaucer alluded to them in no complimentary terms. (A. HAUCK.)

BIBLIOGRAPHY: Bingham, *Origines*, VI., iv. 5, VII., ii. 12, XVI., xii. 19; G. J. Planck, *Geschichte der christlich-kirchlichen Gesellschaftsverfassung*, i. 375, ii. 100 sqq., 5 vols., Hanover, 1803–09; W. Giesebrecht, in *Allgemeine Monatsschrift für Wissenschaft und Literatur*, 1853, pp. 10–43, 344–381; J. Grimm, *Kleinere Schriften*, iii. 1 sqq., Berlin, 1866; O. Hubatsch, *Die lateinischen Vagantenlieder des Mittelalters*, Görlitz, 1870; J. von Pflugk-Harttung, *Diplomatisch-historische Forschungen*, pp. 50 sqq., Gotha, 1879; W. Meyer, in *Festschrift der Göttinger Gesellschaft der Wissenschaften*, Göttingen, 1901; Neander, *Christian Church*, vol. iii. passim.

VALDES, vāl-des', **JUAN** and **ALFONSO DE.**

Alfonso on the Sack of Rome (§ 1).
Juan's " Mercury and Sharon "; Alfonso (§ 2).
Juan's Relations with Rome, and with Giulia Gonzaga (§ 3).
Later Writings (§ 4).
Theological Views (§ 5).

The Hispano-Italian reformers, Juan and Alfonso de Valdés, were born as twins at Cuenca (84 m. s.e. of Madrid), Castile, about the end of the fifteenth century, Juan dying at Naples in the summer of 1541, and Alfonso at Vienna early in Oct., 1532. Alfonso, in 1520, accompanied the young King Charles to his coronation at **1. Alfonso** Aachen, and then went to Worms, **on the Sack** where he witnessed the burning of **of Rome.** Luther's writings, which he, unlike the majority, considered but the beginning of the tragedy of the Reformation. A few years later he was imperial secretary to the high chancellor, Mercurino Arborio da Gattinara, and when the Spanish monks raged against Erasmus, Alfonso warmly defended the Basel scholar. In May, 1527, Rome was stormed and sacked by an imperial army, though without imperial sanction, and the pope himself was made prisoner. Alfonso voiced the sentiment of the court in a dialogue on the catastrophe between Lactantius, a cavalier of the emperor, and an archdeacon just come from Rome to Valladolid. Lactantius, through whom Alfonso expresses his own views, declares that the pope, as a disturber of the peace and as faithless to his word, brought the sack of Rome upon himself. He advocates the surrender of the papal temporal power and asserts that, since the exposure of ecclesiastical corruption by Erasmus and the sedition incited by Luther had alike failed to reform the papacy, God had turned to other means of conversion and had found them in the sack of Rome. The archdeacon himself concludes the dialogue with the hope that the emperor would now take the reformation of the Church in hand. The papal nuncio, Count Baldassare Castiglione, and Alfonso's fellow secretary, Juan Aleman, both sought to have this " ultra-Lutheran " document condemned to the flames, but the archiepiscopal grand inquisitor declared that the dialogue contained nothing heretical.

Meanwhile, probably in Dec., 1528, Juan had written his dialogue " Mercury and Sharon," a piece full of biting satire on false Christians. At the same time, Spain is declared more happy than Germany, where Lutheranism had given birth to many other sects. The justice of the punishment of Rome is maintained, and the absolute need of reform is stressed. Both the " Mercury " and the " Lactantius " were printed anonymously, probably in 1529, repeated editions following; modern editions are by Usóz i Rio in *Reformistas antiguos españoles*, vol. iv. (Madrid, 1850), and by E. Böhmer in his *Romanische Studien*, parts vi., xix. (Halle, 1871–81).

In the year of Castiglione's death, Al-
2. Juan's fonso accompanied the emperor to
"Mercury Italy and Germany. At Bologna he
and attended the coronation of Charles by
Sharon"; Clement VII., and there received
Alfonso. papal favors. At this period, while
a follower of Erasmus, he by no
means understood the attitude of Luther, and his
position with regard to the Reformation was that
of the politician. He constantly acted as a tactful
mediator between the emperor, the papal legate, and
Melanchthon, taking care that the emperor should
be well informed of Protestant doctrines, but deeming the Augsburg Confession too bitter for its opponents to accept it. In Oct., 1531, he wrote from
Brussels the imperial congratulations to the Swiss
Roman Catholics for their victory over the Zwinglians at Kappel. In 1532 he was one of the agents
in securing the imperial sanction of the Protestant
rights of possession until the next council of the
Church on condition of securing their aid against
the Turks. Early in October of the same year, however, Alfonso died at Vienna.

Juan de Valdés remained in Spain when his
brother Alfonso left it with the emperor. In 1531–
1532, however, he was in and near
3. Juan's Rome, where he was made Cameriere
Relations di spada e cappa at the papal court.
with Rome The pope and the emperor at Bologna
and with concluded an alliance on Feb. 24, 1533.
Giulia The pope promised to hasten the deci-
Gonzaga. sion concerning the marriage of the
emperor's aunt with Henry VIII. of
England, who had repudiated her. This decision,
rendered Mar. 23, 1534, was in favor of the queen,
whom Juan had defended in his "Mercury," and
the pope, desiring to prove his amicable intentions,
gave Juan a place at his court, though himself assailed in Valdés's dialogue. Juan's duties were
merely nominal, but he remained at Rome until
the pope's death (Sept. 25, 1534), when he went in
the service of Cardinal Ercole Gonzaga to Naples,
where he passed the remainder of his life. There,
in the latter part of 1534, he wrote, at the earnest
request of friends, his one non-religious work, the
Dialogo de la lengua (Madrid, 1737; latest ed., E.
Böhmer, in *Romanische Studien*, vi. 339–420). At
Naples Juan de Valdés became the spiritual guide
of one of the most distinguished and beautiful
women in Italy, Giulia Gonzaga, widow of Vespa-
siano Colonna, duke of Trajetto. Equally distressed
by personal sorrow and by spiritual unrest, she
poured out her heart to Juan one day in Lent, 1536,
when he was escorting her home from a sermon by
Bernardino Ochino (q.v.). For her consolation he
wrote the *Alfabeto christiano* (Eng. transl. with the
same title, by B. B. Wiffen, London, 1861), in which
he maintained that Christian perfection consists in
loving God above all things and one's neighbor as
oneself. Such perfection is not the exclusive possession of monks and nuns, but is common to all in
proportion to their faith and love of God. In 1534 Giulia seems to have retired to the Franciscan nunnery
of Santa Chiara, though she did not take the vows.

Apparently before the end of 1536 Valdés sent
Giulia his translation of the Psalter from the Hebrew, with an introduction addressed
4. Later to her, and probably his exegesis of
Writings. the Psalms (*El Salterio traduzido*, ed.
E. Böhmer, Bonn, 1880; the commen-
tary on Ps. i.–xli.—all that are known—ed. in *Rivista cristiana*, Madrid, 1882–84; Eng. transl. by J.
Betts, London, 1894). In the following year he sent
her his commentary on Romans and First Corinthians (Geneva, 1556–57; Madrid, 1856 [*Reformistas
antiguos españoles*, x.–xi.]; Eng. transl., London,
1883). He likewise translated and explained the
remaining Pauline epistles, except Hebrews, but
all traces of these writings have been lost. From
the epistles Valdés turned to the Gospels, and in
1540 he seems to have completed his *El Evangelio
segun San Mateo*, which he sent Giulia together
with a general introduction (Madrid, 1880; Eng.
transl., London, 1882). Concerning his further
work on the Gospels nothing is known. In addition
to his exegetical activity, Juan de Valdés wrote
more briefly on a variety of individual problems
of religion, his *Considerazioni* (110 in number,
published in Italian translation at Basel in 1550; ed.
E. Böhmer Halle, 1860; Eng transl., *The Hundred
and Ten Considerations of . . . J. Valdesso*, Oxford,
1638; thirty-nine were edited in the original Spanish
by E. Böhmer, in his *Trataditos de Juan de Valdés*,
Bonn, 1880). This latter work also contains all the
minor Spanish writings of Valdés: seven letters
(collections of at least thirty letters and of thirty-
three responses to questions are known to have
existed, though only one response, in Italian, has
survived), and his *De la Penitencia cristiana, de la
fe cristiana, y del bivir cristiano*. In addition to the
response already noted, there is extant, in Italian
only, the *Modo che si dee tenere ne l'insegnare e pre-
dicare il principio della religione cristiana* (Rome,
1545; ed. E. Böhmer in his *Sul Principio della
dottrina christiana: cinque trattatelli*, Halle, 1870;
reprinted, Rome, 1872), this collection also containing, besides the Italian version of the *De la Penitencia*, the *Della giustificazione, Della medesima giustificazione, Che la vita eterna è dono de Dio per Gesú
Cristo*, and *Se al cristiano conviene dubitare ch'egli
sia in grazia di Dio* (Eng. transl., in *The Spanish Reformers. Three Opuscules*, London, 1882),
Seventeen Opuscules, the introductions to the Psalms,
Romans, I Corinthians, and the Gospels, the seven
didactic letters, " consideration " cix., and the five
" tractates."

The basal principles of the Gospel were summarized from the Bible by Valdés in his *Instrucion
cristiana para los niños* (ed. E. Böhmer, Bonn, 1883).
Children should know, he there main-
5. Theolog- tains, that God is their Father through
ical Views. human birth and Christian regeneration, and that Christ, in whom the
sins of all the world were punished, is the Lord who
redeems them from sin, death, and hell. After his
ascension Christ sent the Holy Ghost, through
whom God began to fulfil what he had promised
Abraham. The union of all those who receive the
Gospel and are baptized in the name of the Trinity
is the Church, and the characteristic of the Chris-

tian is love. The Christian life should be constant prayer (though only for what is promised in the Bible), fasting, and feasting—a Christian Sabbath; and only those will be saved who have so accepted the Gospel that it becomes efficacious in their lives and who have taken refuge in baptism as Noah did in the ark. In his doctrine of the Trinity Valdés is perfectly orthodox, also holding that Christ is the Son of God through generation, while the Christian is the son of God through regeneration. Of confession he speaks at length in the *Alfabeto*, declaring that the sinner receives forgiveness not because he confesses, but because he believes in Christ. In commenting on I Cor. xi. Valdés sharply assailed the abuses then existing in the celebration of the mass, yet in the *Alfabeto* he maintained that the utmost spiritual benefit should be gained from the adoration of the Blessed Sacrament, and advocated the hearing of mass whenever possible. He professed the greatest faith in the Scriptures and in their divine inspiration, yet looked beyond the letter to the spirit from which the letter proceeded, finding his faith freed from the letter by the very inconsistencies in certain details which it seemed to him to have. In his treatise on penance, faith, and life, Juan set forth his views on preaching and on church discipline. Those of evil life and those who adhere to vain ceremonies and superstitious observances should be excommunicated after three warnings. Then there would be a Church very like that of apostolic times and almost a pattern of eternal life. He abstained from all criticism of the Roman Catholic Church. There was, however, at the time a strong tendency toward Evangelical principles in Italy. A general council was in prospect, and among the adherents of Valdés were papal theologians, bishops, and archbishops, while his personal circle included Vermigli, Ochino, and Carnesecchi (qq.v.). It was not till a number of years later that his books were forbidden.

(K. BENRATH.)

BIBLIOGRAPHY: E. Boehmer affixed *Cenni biografici sui fratelli . . . Valdés* to the ed. of the *Considerazioni* of Halle, 1860, added a sketch also to the Germ. transl. of the same, ib. 1870, appearing in English as the *Lives of Spanish Reformers*, London, 1874. A *Life* is also prefixed to the Eng. transl. of the Commentary on Romans, London, 1883. Further works on the subject are B. Wiffen, *Life and Writings of Juan de Valdés*, London, 1869; E. Stern, *Alfonse et Juan de Valdés*, Strasburg, 1869; W. Möller, in *TSK*, 1866, 1871; M. Carrasco, *A. et J. de Valdés*, Geneva, 1880; W. Schlatter, *Die Brüder A. und J. de Valdés*, Basel, 1901; J. Heep, *Juan de Valdes, seine Religion, sein Werden, seine Bedeutung*, Leipsic, 1909.

VALENS, vā'lens: Roman emperor 364–378; b. about 328; d. in the battle of Adrianople Aug. 9, 378. He was the son of Gratian, a soldier who had won his way from a low to a high station in military circles, and was the brother and colleague of Valentinianus I. (q.v.). Both brothers had been brought up in the čamp; as officers they had in the time of Julian made manly confession of Christian faith (Socrates, *Hist. eccl.*, iv. 1; Sozomen, *Hist. eccl.*, vi. 1; both in Eng. transl. in *NPNF*, 1 ser., vol. ii.). Valentinian was called by the soldiers to the throne to succeed Jovian, and soon called as coruler Valens, to whom was assigned the East. Conditions were difficult at the time. The Goths

on the Danube were awaiting the moment to assail the empire. While preparing for this emergency, Valens was confronted by the rebellion and usurpation of the throne by Procopius, who was at length overthrown and executed, and his partizans severely punished.

Valens was soon drawn into ecclesiastical affairs. The general trend had improved the conditions for adherents of Nicene orthodoxy, and the two parties of Homoousians and Homoiousians were drawing together in union against Arianism, under the leadership of such men as Athanasius, Basil the Great, Eusebius of Emesa, and Gregory Nazianzen (qq.v.). Valens was on the other side, though whether this was his early choice or was due to the influence of his consort Albia Dominica and of Bishop Eudoxius is not known. At any rate, Eudoxius was in high favor. Valens in an edict of 365 renewed the deposition by Constantius of the bishops who returned under Julian; among those affected adversely were Athanasius and Meletius of Antioch (qq.v.). There resulted new attacks upon orthodox leaders and churches, but little real harm came of them, as systematic direction was lacking, personal and local relations seeming to dominate. The Pretorian prefect Domitius Modestus was recognized as the enemy of the orthodox (Basil, *MPG*, xxxvi. 557). But Valens had no well-settled ecclesiastical policy, and practical and political cares crowded fast upon him. Ecclesiastical persecution took the form of deposition, banishment, and confiscation of goods; that matters went so far as the infliction of capital punishment is improbable, and such stories as the deliberate burning of a ship with thirty clerics on board seem unlikely. Yet the actions of Valens called up anticipations of evil and evoked courageous opposition though even here exaggeration appears in the tradition (Socrates, iv. 26; Sozomen, vi. 16; Theodoret, iv. 19). The Novatians were involved in the danger because of their agreement in Christology with the Nicene party, but they escaped because of the influence of a certain Marcian, formerly a soldier of the palace and then instructor of the emperor's daughter. An edict of 370 or 373 has been mistakenly interpreted as an attack upon the monks, but certainly had to do with political matters pure and simple. The relation of the emperor to orthodoxy seemed the more unpleasant because his toleration of paganism was apparently open. Theodoret (*Hist. eccl.*, iv. 24) implies that the edict of Valens during his stay at Antioch in the winter of 373–374, giving general toleration, was responsible for an outburst of paganism. But in view of the fact that the population of Antioch was nearly entirely Christian, this information must be mistaken; yet the two rulers handled Hellenism with great care and were repressive only on special occasions. The reason for this was not religious indifference, but the certainty that the old religion was in its last stages.

Meanwhile the Gothic danger had grown, and in the defeat and death of the emperor in the battle of Adrianople the orthodox saw the judgment of God. Yet Valens had performed his royal duties with great conscientiousness and constant regard for the right as he saw it. He was earnest in seeking the welfare of the populace and in maintaining order, and his life was one of fidelity to the morality of Christianity and the Church. He was hampered by lack of education. But the Church saw in him only an anti-Christian persecutor, and has left a tradition of him which is far from the truth.

(VICTOR SCHULTZE.)

BIBLIOGRAPHY: Besides the sources named in the text in the ecclesiastical histories by Sozomen, Socrates, and Theodoret, a valuable source is Ammianus Marcellinus' "Roman History," xxvi. 4 sqq., Eng. transl. in *Bohn's Classical Library*, London, 1887. Consult further: L. S. Le Nain de Tillemont, *Hist. des empereurs*, vol. v., 6 vols., Paris, 1720–38; H. F. Clinton, *Fasti Romani. The civil and literary Chronology of Rome and Constantinople*, i. 476, ii. 119, Oxford, 1845–50; J. V. A. de Broglie, *L'Église et l'empire romain, au iv. siècle*, 6 vols., Paris, 1856–66; Gibbon, *Decline and Fall*, chap. xxv.; H. Richter, *Das weströmische Reich*, Berlin, 1865; H. Schiller, *Geschichte der römischen Kaiserzeit*, ii. 348 sqq., Gotha, 1887; V. Schultze, *Geschichte des Unterganges des griechisch-römischen Heidentums*, i. 186 sqq., Jena, 1887; Schaff, *Christian Church*, iii. 60–61, 638; Neander, *Christian Church*, vol. iii. passim; W. Smith, *Dictionary of Greek and Roman Biography and Mythology*, iii. 1202–05, London, 1890; and in general the works on the history, secular and ecclesiastical, of the period.

VALENS OF MURSA. See URSACIUS.

VALENTINE, val'en-tain: The name of several saints honored as martyrs in the early Church and in the Middle Ages.

1. Near Rome, on the Via Flaminia, is the cemetery of St. Valentine, a Roman priest, whose name is found under Feb. 14 in medieval martyrologies. He was confused, if not originally identical, with Valentine, bishop of Spoleto, or with Valentine, bishop of Terni, though the Bern manuscript of the *Martyrologium Hieronymianum* places the latter under Apr. 14, and does not designate him bishop. The acts of both the priest and the bishop Valentine are late and untrustworthy.

2. The oldest Carthaginian martyrology records a Valentine under Nov. 13, but of this martyr, who was apparently an African, nothing more is known, except that the Bern manuscript already mentioned places him under Feb. 14.

3. There is mention of another Bishop Valentine, who labored in Rhætia in the first half of the fifth century. According to Eugipius (*Vita Severini*, xli.), he was abbot and bishop of the Rhætians and died on Jan. 6 of an unknown year. Churches were dedicated to him in Noricum, and his grave was at Mais, near Meran in Rhætia. In 768 his remains were brought to Passau. The "Acts" of this saint, which date from about the beginning of the eleventh century, describe him as coming from the east to the vicinity of Passau, where he long labored as a missionary bishop. Since his sermons here made scant impression, he besought Leo I. to translate him to some other sphere of activity. The pope twice refused, but at length permitted Valentine to retire to the Tyrolese Alps, where he died shortly afterward. Such is the gist of a lead tablet which, claimed for the fifth century, can scarcely be older than the twelfth. (A. HAUCK.)

BIBLIOGRAPHY: On 1 *ASB*, Feb., ii. 753–754, cf. ib. Jan., i. 368, and 369–372; A. Roschmann, *Glaubwürdige Nachrichten von . . . Valentin*, Ulm, 1746; K. Schanz-

hofer, *Valentins . . . Reisen, Aufenthalt und Grabstätte in Mais*, Botzen, 1794; *Valentin, der . . . erster Bischof von Passau*, Mainz, 1889; Rettberg, *KD*, i. 220–221, ii. 133, Hauck, *KD*, i. 360.

VALENTINE, MILTON: Lutheran; b. near Uniontown, Md., Jan. 1, 1825; d. at Gettysburg, Pa., Feb. 7, 1906. He was educated at Pennsylvania College, Gettysburg, Pa. (A.B., 1850), where he was a tutor (1850–52); he was ordained to the ministry (1852); pastoral supply at Winchester, Va. (1852–53); missionary at Alleghany, Pa. (1853–54); pastor at Greensburg, Pa. (1854–55); principal of Emmaus Institute, Middletown, Pa. (1855–59); pastor of St. Matthew's Lutheran Church at Reading, Pa. (1859–66), professor of ecclesiastical history and church polity in the theological seminary at Gettysburg, Pa. (1866–1868); president of Pennsylvania College (1868–1884); professor of systematic theology and chairman of the faculty of the Lutheran theological seminary at Gettysburg (1884–1903). He was associate editor of *The Lutheran Quarterly* in 1871–76, 1880–85, and also after 1898. He was the author of *Natural Theology, or Rational Theism* (New York, 1885); *Theoretical Ethics* (Chicago, 1897); and *Christian Truth and Life* (Philadelphia, 1898).

VALENTINIAN, val"en-tin'i-an: The name of three Roman emperors.

1. Valentinian I.: Emperor 365–375. For his parentage see VALENS. He was born at Cibalæ (probably near the modern town of Mikanovci in Lower Pannonia, Hungary) in 321; d. of a stroke of apoplexy at Bregetio (probably near Pressburg, 34 m. e.s.e. of Vienna) Nov. 17, 375. He was chosen emperor by the army after the sudden death of Jovian (see JOVIANUS, FLAVIUS CLAUDIUS). He combined with the sturdy qualities of a forceful soldier the superiority of a clever strategist, and was devoted to the welfare of his kingdom. To civil office he carried over military strictness, exacting strict obedience. While he had a certain harshness of disposition, he sought the company of the cultured and himself made essays in poetry. His life was conducted according to the ethical norms of Christianity. In contrast with his predecessors he was predisposed against the interference of the State in religious and ecclesiastical disputes, entering into these only when his duty as chief officer of state was clear or when peace and order were assailed (Ambrose, *Epist.*, i. 21, in *MPL*, xvi. 1004). This was the case in the double choice of bishops after the death of Liberius and in the rescripts which made ecclesiastical jurisdiction independent of civil. Just as he refrained from influencing his brother's course by taking sides with the adherents of Nicene orthodoxy, so he did not enter actively the lists against Arianism—indeed, his second consort Justina was an Arian. His edict forbidding the Montanists to set aside baptism was relatively mild (Theodosian Code, XVI., vi. 1), but the measures against the Manicheans (see MANI, MANICHEANS) were severe (Theodosian Code, XVI., v. 3). His guiding principle was tolerance of all religions. The reason for this was not religious indifference, but a quite modern view of the relation of the State to religion. Yet this did not stand in the way of supporting by authority measures which increased the influence of the actual religion and church of the State, Christianity; thus collection of taxes on Sunday was abolished (ib. XI., vii. 1), and actors who were baptized on their supposed death-bed and then recovered were freed from the claims of their wretched caste (ib. XV., vii. 1). The emperor in a decree of amnesty at an Easter festival expressed his Christian feelings (ib. IX., xxxviii. 3). But on the other hand, he restrained the rich from taking clerical orders to escape civil duties (XVI., ii. 21, XVII., xviii. 19), and was inexorable in denouncing and punishing the faults of the clergy and monks (ib. XVI., ii. 20–21), especially in an edict of July 30, 370, followed by directions to bishops and nuns, of which Jerome remarks, " I do not complain of the law, but I grieve that we merit it " (*Epist.*, lii. 6). He often expressed himself with tolerance toward heathenism at the beginning of his reign. To the (heathen) priesthood their old rights were confirmed, and the haruspices were not really assailed; only nocturnal magic and sacrificial rites were strongly forbidden, but on the ground of the peril to political institutions. The altar of Victory remained in the court where Julian had restored it. But these favors to Hellenism were rooted in the facts that the course of the restoration of heathenism had shown that this religion had no future and that it was undesirable to set any fraction of the population in a position of unrest and opposition. As to the family relations of Valentinian it may be said that he divorced his first consort Valeria Severa, who bore him Gratian, because she abused her imperial position, and married Justina, who bore him Justinian II. He was buried in the Church of the Apostles at Constantinople.

2. **Valentinian II.:** Emperor 375–383. This emperor was the son of Valentinian I. and his second consort Justina. After the death of his father he was proclaimed by the soldiers in the camp, though he was but four years old and his elder brother Gratian was the legitimate heir. In fact Gratian was till his death the real ruler, as is shown by his calling Theodosius (q.v.) to the coregency and by the fact that the laws for the Western Empire until 383 issued from him. After Gratian's death Theodosius yielded to Valentinian the lands of his brother, but kept in his own hands decisions of all weighty matters. Under his mother's influence Valentinian took the Arians under his protection. Auxentius was the Arian bishop of Milan, against whom Ambrose (see AMBROSE, SAINT, OF MILAN) at once took up the fight. An edict of Jan. 23, 386, insured toleration for the [Arian] adherents of the Synod of Ariminum (Theodosian Code, XVI., i. 4), and other enactments were intended for the benefit of the Arians. But Theodosius succeeded in halting this policy and indeed changing it to a contrary tenor (ib. XVI., v. 15). Paganism made an attempt under Valentinian to win back the rights lost under Gratian, this taking place under the leadership of Symmachus and Prætextatus at Rome, and the matter of the restoration of the altar of Victory was again in the foreground; but this and

XII.—9

a later attempt in 392 were resultless. Valentinian was murdered in his twentieth year at Vienne at the instigation of Arbogast; he died unbaptized, and his body was brought to Milan, where Ambrose delivered the oration (extant in *MPL*, xvi. 1557 sqq.). This was one of rhetorical and somewhat exuberant praise, showing that Ambrose had won great influence over the emperor, whose youth and inexperience made necessary the guidance of others; he was therefore not really responsible for the administration. He was, moreover, not strong in physique, and arduous labor was irksome.

3. **Valentinian III.:** Emperor 425–455. Under Flavius Honorius (q.v.) the Western Empire declined rapidly. Germans and Huns flowed over the boundaries and elected their usurpers. In this situation the clever and resolute Galla Placidia, daughter of the great Theodosius (q.v.), became influential. She had been married to the general and (later) coregent Constantius, to whom she bore, in 419, Flavius Placidius Valentinianus. In 425, after the death of Honorius, this son obtained the crown through the help of Theodosius II., though until her death in 450 his mother as guardian carried on the business of State. His reign is notable for the decree of June 6, 445, which states: " Let that be a law to all—whatever the authority of the Roman see has sanctioned or shall sanction " (Mirbt, *Quellen*, p. 65). The contest with Manicheism was continued, though the conflict with heathenism was practically won. Valentinian was murdered in 455, and with him ended the western branch of the Theodosian family.   (VICTOR SCHULTZE.)

BIBLIOGRAPHY: The sources are the same as for Valens (q.v.). Consult: L. S. Le Nain de Tillemont, *Hist. des empereurs*, vol. v., 6 vols., Paris, 1720–38 (not to be overlooked); H. F. Clinton, *Fasti Romani. The civil and literary Chronology of Rome and Constantinople*, 2 vols., Oxford, 1845–50 (important; summarizes legislation); J. V. A. de Broglie, *L'Église et l'empire romain au iv. siècle*, 6 vols., Paris, 1856–66; H. Richter, *Das weströmische Reich*, Berlin, 1865; E. von Wietersheim, *Geschichte der Völkerwanderung*, vol. ii., Leipsic, 1881; M. Rade, *Damasus, Bischof von Rom*, Freiburg, 1882; T. Förster, *Ambrosius, Bischof von Mailand*, Halle, 1884; H. Schiller, *Geschichte der römischen Kaiserzeit*, vol. ii., Gotha, 1887; V. Schultze, *Geschichte des Unterganges des griechisch-römischen Heidentums*, vol. i., Jena, 1887; G. Rauschen, *Jahrbücher der christlichen Kirche unter dem Kaiser Theodosius dem Grossen*, Freiburg, 1897; S. Dill, *Roman Society in the Last Century of the Western Empire*, London, 1898; Mirbt, *Quellen*, pp. 62 sqq. (for the citation of passages from the edicts which concern Christianity); W. Smith, *Dictionary of Greek and Roman Biography and Mythology*, iii. 1207–14, London, 1890 (good and full for the secular and civil sides of these reigns); Neander, *Christian Church*, vol. ii., passim; *DCB*, iv. 1073–75. For the legislation of these emperors an important work is J. Gothofredus, *Codex Theodosianus cum perpetuis commentariis*, vol. vi., Leipsic, 1743.

VALENTINUS, vȧl″en-tai-nŭs: Pope 827, between the pontificates of Eugene II. and Gregory IV. The *Liber pontificalis* gives as the length of his reign only fourteen days, and affirms that he was a Roman by birth, and was ordered deacon by Paschalis, who later raised him to the archdeaconate.

      (A. HAUCK.)

BIBLIOGRAPHY: *Liber pontificalis*, ed. L. Duchesne, vol. ii., Paris, 1892; Mann, *Popes*, ii. 183–186; Bower, *Popes*, ii. 208; Platina, *Popes*, i. 213–214.

VALENTINUS AND HIS SCHOOL.

I. Valentinus: The events of the life of Valentinus, the most important of the Gnostic teachers, are little known. According to an ancient document cited by Irenæus and preserved by **1. Life and Works.** Eusebius (*Hist. eccl.*, IV., xi. 1), he came to Rome during the pontificate of Hyginus; developed his chief activity under Pius; and remained at Rome until the pontificate of Anicetus, thus placing his sojourn at Rome about 136–165. Tertullian (*Adversus Valentinos*, iv.; cf. *De præscriptione*, xxx.) makes him the victim of disappointed ambition for the throne of St. Peter, a *martyrius* (confessor) being preferred to him. The only predecessor of Anicetus who was a confessor was Telesphorus, but during his pontificate Valentinus was not at Rome, and Tertullian's statement remains of little value. Clement of Alexandria (*Strom.*, VII., xvii. 106–107) essentially accords with Irenæus, placing the activity of Basilides (q.v.), Valentinus, and Marcion (q.v.) in the period of 120–160. Epiphanius (*Hist. eccl.*, xxxi.) adds that he had heard that the home of Valentinus was in the Phrebonite coastland of Egypt; and that he had been educated in Alexandria, whence he had gone to Rome to disseminate his teachings. Thence he had gone to Cyprus, where he had lapsed from the faith. The last part of this statement is contradicted by the more probable report of Tertullian and Irenæus that this took place already at Rome. Statements of the opponents of Valentinus imply that he wrote only occasional treatises. The only work evidently dogmatic as shown by its title was " On the Three Natures," a fragment of which may be that preserved by Photius (*Bibliotheca*, ccxxx.). All the other known writings of Valentinus were of a practical character; sermons, hymns, and letters. Fragments of the sermons are preserved by Clement of Alexandria (see below), who has also transmitted fragments of three letters (see below). Tertullian ranked his psalms with those of David (*De carne Christi*, xvii., xx.), a few of which are cited by Hippolytus (*Philosophumena*, VI., xxxvii. 290). Perhaps the newly recovered *Odes of Solomon* (see SOLOMON, ODES OF) are Valentinian.

The teachings of Valentinus are known only as represented by his opponents where they are scarcely distinguished from those of his pupils. Evidently his doctrines sprang from the soil **2. Doctrines.** of Hellenistic syncretism, and their ultimate basis was Platonic dualism, which separated the divine world of ideas from the material world of phenomena. In the intermediate abyss stands man partaking of both and the problem is how to bridge the chasm so as to attain the higher goal and be released from the material. The cosmos is the imperfect image of the eon, the ideal prototype, and the creator of the cosmos is the demiurge, who is termed God and Father, and is an image of the true God. According

to a citation from a reputed sermon (Clement of Alexandria, *Strom.*, IV., xiii., Eng. transl., *ANF*, ii. 425–426) Valentinus held that Wisdom was the " artist " who ordered matter, but it is more probable that the artist who sought to imitate the lineaments of the face of God, and covered the defects of his work with the name, was really the demiurge. It is not improbable that Clement made this citation from a writing elaborated by the Valentinians, as shown by internal resemblance, possibly a commentary on Gen. i. 27, where the extract from Valentinus' sermon also appeared. Valentinus in the fragment of his sermon simply represents that the world is a picture of the invisible God, though imperfect. Yet, the mere picture bears the name of the invisible God, reflecting honor, and inducing faith in mankind. In a fragment of one of the letters of Valentinus (*Strom.*, II., viii. 36), he says that as idols, though made by human hands, are objects of awe to man because divinity is believed to dwell within them, so created man is feared by the angels as containing the seed of the higher nature implanted in him by the creator and divinely proclaimed to exist there. The angels accordingly fear man as the dwelling-place of the preexistent " man " (God); and to escape their terror, they corrupt the work of the Creator by seducing it to sin. Here again Clement seems to have drawn from a Valentinian interpretation of Prov. i. 7, containing a citation from the letter of Valentinus. Doubtless this Valentinian interpretation or writing is one with the other mentioned above, which cited from the sermon of Valentinus. In another fragment of a sermon of Valentinus (*Strom.*, IV., xiii. 89), man is represented from the first a child of immortality, taking death upon him that he might destroy death so that it should no more have power over him, but that, himself being undestroyed, he might rule over creation and all that is transitory. The origin of sin and evil in man is set forth in the longest of the fragments (*Strom.*, II., xx. 114), in which he compares the human heart with an inn, wherein disorderly guests break holes in the walls, and they defile it with offal, because it is not their property; so the demons (the passions) invade the heart until the " good Father " drives them out, and the heart is sanctified and gleams with light. A fragment of a letter to Agathopus (*Strom.*, III., vi. 59) is concerned with Jesus, who lived ascetically, and wholly consumed his food without corruption within his body, apparently thus gaining his divinity. A brief fragment of a homily " On Friends " (*Strom.*, VI., vi. 52), important for a knowledge of Valentinus' theory of the Church, alludes apparently to a spiritual community, not to an external organization. Valentinus, according to Hippolytus (*Philosophumena*, vi. 42), ascribed the source of his teachings to a vision in which he saw a new-born child, who, in answer to his question, declared himself to be the Logos, and whose " tragic narrative " formed the fountain of his doctrine. From these fragments no coherent presentation of the system of Valentinus can be constructed, and they are rendered the more difficult since they have been set in a new context and overladen with the exegesis of the later Valentinian school; nor is it even known whether they are especially characteristic of the heresiarch's teachings.

II. The Valentinians: The description of Valentinianism as given by Irenæus (*Hær.*, I., xi. 1; Eng. transl., *ANF*, i. 332) can scarcely represent the teachings of its founder, corresponding in no points with his authenticated statements. Accordng to this, the system was a genealogy of eons. At the head was a dyad, " the Ineffable "
1. According and " Silence," from whom emanated
to Irenæus. a second dyad, " the Father " and " Truth." From this tetrad proceeded " Logos " and " Life," and, again, " Man " and " Church." These four pairs form the first octad. Ten " powers " emanate from the Logos and " Life," and twelve from " Man " and " Church." This mysticism is clearly a play on the number thirty, the number of the days in the Egyptian month. One of the twelve emanations fell and separated, and from her proceeded the further work of creation. She separated by a first boundary the abyss, or highest ground of the universe, where dwells the unbegotten Father, from the pleroma, where are the begotten eons. A second boundary separates the " Mother " from the pleroma. Christ was no emanation of the eons, but was born of the mother, remembering the pleroma, by a shadow, but since he was male, he cast the shadow from him and returned to the pleroma. " Mother," deprived of her spiritual potency, remained with the shadow, and now brought forth " Demiurge," or the " Almighty," and with him " Left-Hand Archon." Jesus is regarded sometimes as an emanation of *Thelētos*, he " who was separated from their mother and united to the rest " (cf. *ANF*, i. 332); sometimes of Christ; and sometimes of the syzygy, " Man " and " Church." The Holy Ghost is an emanation of " Truth " (Epiphanius reads " Church "), and his work is the proving and fertilizing of the eons whom he enters unperceived, so that they bring forth fruits of truth. This description is closely paralleled by one found in a letter of unknown origin, reported by Epiphanius (*Hær.*, xxxi. 5–6).

Far different is the account of Valentinianism given by Hippolytus (*Philosophumena*, vi. 29 sqq.), who repeatedly alludes to the doctrinal divergencies of individual teachers of the school. At the head he places the " monad," or " father,"
2. According non-sexual, inconceivable, the ulti-
to Hip-   mate cause of all being. Originally
polytus.   self-sufficient and alone, but not loving solitude, and having the power of generation, this " monad " was led to create an object of affection. Thus emanated " Mind " and " Truth," a dyad which became the source of the eons in the pleroma. From this dyad emanated " Logos " and " Life," and from these " Man " and " Church." " Mind " and " Truth " produced the perfect number ten, in ten eons; and in imitation

of the first dyad the second caused the emanation of twelve eons. Thus there were, in all, twenty-eight eons, the number of the days in the lunar month, a fact pointing to the Oriental origin of this form of the system. The twelfth and last of the eons of the second line was the female, " Wisdom," who, seeking to imitate the mode of emanation employed by the Father, produced an abortion in the shape of formless matter. This produced horror and alarm among the eons or the pleroma, and the Father, in pity, sent them to aid. " Mind " and " Truth " emanated Christ and the Holy Ghost, and this new syzygy separated the abortion of Wisdom from the eons, thus removing the cause of alarm. The Father likewise emanated an eon, " Cross," which marks the limit of the eons (also called " Boundary " or " Participator "), beyond whom is the octad, and " Wisdom " outside the pleroma, whom Christ made a perfect eon. The thirty eons now determined on an emanation of a common progeny of the pleroma to present to the Father, and the result was Jesus. Lower Wisdom wistfully longed for her authors, Christ and the Holy Ghost. The eons found Jesus to be compassionate, who entered into a syzygy with lower " Wisdom," and relieved her of her sufferings by converting these into hypostases. From fear, the " psychic being," came the demiurge; from sorrow came matter; from the disorder of ignorance the demons; and from need sprang repentance and the ascent of the soul. The soul belongs to the middle sphere, under the ogdoad, the heavenly Jerusalem, and above matter. The souls come from the demiurge, who gave them bodies of demonic matter, even as he created the world. The law and the prophets likewise came from him. All the psychic have a veil upon their hearts which blinds them to the higher world of spirits; and when this veil was to be removed, the historic Jesus was born of the Virgin by the lower wisdom entering and the demiurge overshadowing her. He cures the sufferings of souls, just as Christ healed those of lower wisdom. A similar description is given by Clement of Alexandria (" Extracts from Theodotus," xxix.–xlii.). The Valentinian school later fell into an Oriental and an Italian branch; to the former belonged Axionicus and Bardesanes (q.v.), and to the latter Ptolemy and Heracleon. The Occidental division was so wide-spread in Italy and southern Gaul that Irenæus first planned his *Adversus Hæreses* against the Valentinians alone. The Oriental Valentinians were found especially in Egypt and Syria. By the second half of the fourth century the sect seems to have been restricted to Egypt, Manicheism elsewhere absorbing its remnants.

Of the chief followers of Valentinus, Irenæus mentions Secundus (*Hær.*, I., xi. 2). Philastrius (*Hær.*, xl.) ascribes to him a docetic Christology which his source, the *Syntagma* of Hippolytus, had assigned to the Valentinians. According to Irenæus, Secundus divided the first ogdoad into
3. Secundus; a male and a female tetrad, the former
Ptolemy. being light and the latter darkness; and he did not reckon the fallen power among the thirty eons but among their fruits, doubtless the higher wisdom. Ptolemy, whose career is

utterly unknown, was still alive when Irenæus wrote against the Gnostics (c. 180). The only extant fragment of his writings, except for his valuable epistle to Flora (Epiphanius, *Hær.*, xxxiii. 5 sqq.), is a citation from an exegetical work in Irenæus (I., viii. 5; Eng. transl., *ANF*, i. 328–329). The epistle to Flora is a reply to a question concerning the origin of the Old-Testament law; and is distinguished for its calm, clear method of proof on a religious basis, as well as a simple theology instead of the abstruse series of eons. While the Church taught that the law came from God the Father and others maintained it to be the work of the devil, Ptolemy held it to be partly from God, partly from Moses, and partly from the Jewish elders. The portion derived from God was subdivided into (1) the pure legislation unmixed with evil and fulfilled by the Savior; (2) the law mixed with evil, as the law of retaliation, destroyed by the Savior; and (3) the typical or symbolical, as the laws on the Sabbath, circumcision, feasts, and fasts, whose literal meaning the Savior abrogated in favor of a spiritual signification. The lawgiver can not be the perfect highest God, nor the devil; but the demiurge. The ultimate reality is the unbegotten unchangeable good principle, essentially immortality and light; simple, absolute, the perfect God, whom the Savior called his Father. Of the two potencies produced by him, the demiurge is also God, but neither good nor evil, but merely just (hating evil). His righteousness is not perfect, yet he is the image of the perfect God. He created the world in which he exercises his providence, and he gave the law, so far as it was not the work of man. The second potency is the devil, who also is " God," but not to be identified with the demiurge. He is the adversary who creates destruction; his sphere is unrighteousness; his nature darkness and destruction, material and multiform. The problem how the supreme God, capable by his nature to produce only what is like himself, could have created such imperfect beings is left unanswered, partly on account of a breach in the text. Possibly this was conceived as a procession of eons, by self-depotentiation (Harnack). As to soteriology, redemption is given in the Savior, who alone knows the " Father of all." His function was to reveal the Father to man, and through this alone has he enabled man to grasp the mystery of the universe. The Christological formula, " of the same substance with the Father," which triumphed at Nicæa, owes its origin to the Gnostic Ptolemy. Irenæus, discussing this school at great length (*Hær.*, I., i.–viii.; Eng. transl., *ANF*, i. 316–339), used certain " memoirs," whether by Ptolemy or by one of his pupils is unclear. In the upper world, or pleroma, rule thirty eons. At their head is the source of all being (" Primal Beginning," " Primal Father," " Abyss "), in whom " Consciousness " (also called " Grace " and " Silence ") is immanent. Like a seed he places in " Silence " the concept of causing a beginning of the universe to appear, whereupon she bears " Mind " (or the " Only Begotten," " Father," " Beginning of All "), together with " Truth." These four—" Abyss " and " Silence," " Mind " and " Truth "—form the first tetrad, the source of the universe. The " Only Be-

gotten " emanates as the beginning of the pleroma " Logos " and " Life," and they, in their turn, " Man " and " Church." This is the first ogdoad, which may also be regarded as a tetrad since the pairs may be combined as androgynous. Ten further eons, or five syzygies, emanated from " Logos " and " Life," and twelve from " Man " and " Church," the last being " Wisdom." The first emanation, the " Only Begotten," alone was able to comprehend the " Primal Father," who was to impart this to the other eons; but " Wisdom," seized by a passionate desire to comprehend the " Father," would have been absorbed by his sweetness had she not been checked by " Boundary," which watches over all outside the indescribable magnitude of God. To prevent a repetition of this, " Only Begotten " emanated another syzygy, Christ and the Holy Ghost, who complete the number of the eons. In thankfulness for the instruction given them by this syzygy, the eons resolved to collect their best, and thus arose Jesus (" Savior," "Christ," " Logos," " The All").

The drama of the fall opens with " Thought " (*'Enthymēsis*), which, as the determination to penetrate the depths of the Father, parted

4. The Fall and Redemption According to Ptolemy. from " Wisdom " and is now hypostatized. This is also called *'Achamōth* (Hebr. abstract plural, *hokhmoth*, " wisdom "), and had sunk with the " passion " she had evoked in " Wisdom," from the pleroma into the " void," without form or figure, like an untimely birth. Christ took pity on her and gave her a substantial, although not an intellectual form. She, retaining an " odor of immortality," still longs for the pleroma and the light of " Logos," which she strains to reach, only to be checked by " Boundary," throwing her into passion, fear, and ignorance. Nevertheless, from her desire toward her creator originate the orderly arrangement of the world, and the souls; while from the aggregate of passions came the substance of matter. From the soul-material *'Achamōth* forms the demiurge, who, in virtue of *'enthymēsis*, creates likenesses of the eons. Thus arise seven heavens or angels, over whom is the demiurge, and above him *'Achamōth*, thus affording a copy of the heavenly ogdoad. From the sorrow of *'Achamōth*, moreover, comes evil which becomes the devil, or " world-ruler," and his evil angels, the demons. Man comes from the demiurge, being formed first of matter and then receiving his psychic element from the creator, finally acquiring his " fleshly mantle." Unknown to the demiurge, *'Achamōth* placed the pneumatic seed in man, so that he constitutes a trichotomy, as follows: matter, which is transitory; the psychic, endowed with free will; and the pneumatic, the salt and light of the world. No longer combined in one person, these three natures result in three classes of men: the pneumatics, who are worthy of perfection and may share in the pleroma; the psychic or animal, who are mentally swayed between the good and the evil, and if they incline toward the former will attain to the intermediate place; and the material, who perish. Only the psychic need redemption, which is fulfilled by Christ. According to some, he had received his material and psychic side from the demiurge, and his pneumatic elements from *'Achamōth;* and at his baptism the Savior, descending from the pleroma, entered him so that he became a copy of the original tetrad. The Church, primarily an organization of psychics, is ruled by the demiurge, hence in it there is no perfect gnosis. Perfection will come when all pneumatic mankind shall possess perfect knowledge of God and *'Achamōth,* who, accompanied by the pneumatics as angels of light, shall then enter the pleroma as the bride of the Savior. The demiurge will then go to the intermediate place hitherto occupied by *'Achamōth,* where the psychics will find rest, while the material world will be destroyed by fire.

The Valentinian of whose writings larger fragments have been preserved (through Origen) than of any of his fellows is Heracleon, of whose life and fortunes almost nothing is known, although Clement of Alexandria terms him the most distinguished of the Valentinian school (*Strom.,* IV., ix.

5. Hera- 71). He evidently flourished about
cleon.   200, possibly at Rome, as is apparent from certain Latinisms in his works; and Hippolytus makes him the leader of the Italian Valentinians. Origen had " notes " by him in which passages of the Gospel of John were briefly explained. According to Heracleon, God, as a pure and invisible spirit, can be honored only spiritually. His counterpart is the material, destructive, demonic principle that has only desires, not will. Between the two spheres is the soul, which is not immortal, but is capable of salvation. It comes from the demiurge, and is distinct from the pneumatic seed. The " pneumatics," essentially akin to God, are the " elect," led by the Logos to the highest wisdom, and destined to salvation. The psychics can perceive only through the senses, and may be convinced only by miracle, and can attain no more than right faith; and material men, or hylics, have lost their relation with God. The " Savior," the image of the pleromatic Christ, originated all the cosmos (not the eons). He proceeded from the " majesty " and became incarnate, his superiority being proclaimed by John the Baptist, the representative of the demiurge. He advanced from the uttermost ends of hylic world, where he neither wrought nor spoke, to the psychic realm, where, through the power of the Holy Ghost, he banished evil and put it to flight by the cross. The demiurge is a subordinate prince ruling over the comparatively small domain of the middle, or psychic, realm. To this comes the Savior, who forgives those who live in ignorance and sin contrary to their true nature, while those who will not thus be led to fellowship with God fall under the judgment of the demiurge, or executioner. The souls form syzygies, each with its reaping angel, the end in view being the union of all " pneumatic natures " with the " pneumatic Church," which constitutes a syzygy with the Savior. Judaism, like the world, was the work of the demiurge, as was the law, which results in death as annihilation for sin. The fragments of Heracleon are especially important as showing how small a factor the speculation concerning eons practically was, though such was tacitly

presupposed. What is vital to Ptolemy and Heracleon is the ascent of the soul to the pleroma, and it is clear that their interest was primarily ethical and religious.

Marcus was apparently a contemporary of Irenæus (I., xiii. 5; *ANF,* i. 335), and developed his activity in Asia Minor; though his pupils came to the West and spread his teachings as far as Gaul. Irenæus used writings of Marcus, without mentioning their titles, and Clement of Alexandria seems to

          have known and utilized some (*Strom.,*
6. **Marcus.** VI., xvi. 140–141). Irenæus likewise expressly states that the sect had a number of apocryphal writings, which they fabricated themselves (I., xx. 1). Close similarity of the system of Marcus to that of the school will save a detailed analysis. Neopythagorean influence and the widely prevalent juggling with numbers and letters are prominent. More important are excerpts from the liturgy of Marcus, which give a glimpse into the sacramental doctrines of the sect (I., xxi.). According to them, baptism by water had only psychic power, the perfect capability of entering the pleroma requiring " redemption," a fact too intangible to be described. Many of the sect were accustomed to construct a bridal chamber in which the mystic marriage of the soul took place. Others performed baptism with such phrases as: " In the name of the unknowable Father of all, in Truth the mother of all, in him who descended on Jesus, in the union, redemption, and communion of the powers," or the Aramaic: " in the name of 'Achamōth, be immersed "; again: " The name hid from all divinity and dominion and truth, which Jesus the Nazarene put on in the zones of light, Christ the lord of him who liveth through the Holy Ghost, to angelic redemption." After suitable responses, anointing with oil of balsam followed. Sometimes the immersion was omitted, and the candidate, with similar invocations, was simply anointed with water and oil together. Others still rejected all sacramental forms, holding it to be impious to attempt to represent the ineffable and inconceivable. The gnosis was perfect salvation, which was restricted to the pneumatic man, and there was also a salvation of the dead. With proper invocations, the head of the deceased was anointed with water and oil, or simply with oil of balsam; so that the inner man, unseen by the demons, might arise and the soul pass to the demiurge. One elaborate mystical formula made progress possible through the realm of angels, and another through the realm of the demiurge; while another prayer was addressed to the higher wisdom, who withdrew the pneumatic man from the judge (the demiurge). The celebration of the Eucharist resolved itself into a magical jugglery. According to Irenæus, who may have given a one-sided, colored effect, when the mystagogue pronounced the prayer of thanksgiving over the chalice of mixed wine, and extended the epiclesis, the ordinary wine changed to red. This was represented to mean that the " higher Grace " had dropped some of her blood into the chalice that the communicants should rejoice to partake of her. Again, Marcus gave the chalice to the assisting prophetess, who made the prayer of thanksgiving.

He himself took a larger cup, in which he poured the contents of the smaller. He then invoked Grace, whereupon the cup overflowed through the influx of Grace. Marcus felt himself to be a prophet and believed himself to be able to communicate his powers to others, the ritual being given by Irenæus (I., xiii. 3); and he likewise solicited the services of women of position and wealth as prophetesses, with high-sounding declamations. Despite the fantastic speculations of Marcus, his religious earnestness is unmistakable, and his prayers show that his central thought was to raise the inner man to the pleroma, not by mystic plunging into depths possible only to the pneumatic, but by turning away from the material and evil world.

The history of the Valentinian Colorbasus is wrapped in obscurity. In referring to him, Epiphanius (Hær., xxxv.) merely repeats comments of Irenæus on the school of Marcus without mentioning to what branch of the school his remarks apply; and Theodoret (Hæreticarum fabularum, i. 12) gives

7. Color-
basus.

an excerpt from the results of Epiphanius. Philaster (Hær., xliii.) contents himself with saying that Colorbasus " likewise declared that the life and generation of all men consist in letters and in the number of the elements and of the seven stars." The source of all information on Colorbasus is apparently the problematical Hær., I., xiv. 1, of Irenæus, according to which Marcus declared himself to be " the matrix and receptacle of the Silence of Colorbasus." This may have been a technical expression of the school which is not mentioned elsewhere. Attempts have been made to explain it as representing the Hebr. kol 'arba', or " all four " (Heumann); or, ḳol 'arba', or " voice of four " (F. C. Baur), in allusion to the higher tetrad, without, however, any further support. That Colorbasus was the name of a historic personage is an unquestioned possibility; for the name Kolorbasios occurs elsewhere (A. Hilgenfeld).

With all its variations Valentinian Gnosticism is in great part founded on Platonism as understood by later generations. The infinite Spirit, to whose realm the spirit in man has an inalienable right, draws the spirits of men back to him, since their longing for the higher world has never been quenched, and their struggle for escape from the terrestrial as from a prison has never

8. Sources
and
Estimation.

ceased. The Eros of Plato finds its counterpart in the " Wisdom," or 'Achamōth, of Valentinus, while the eons are, in the last analysis, simply the Platonic ideas. Pythagoreanism is present in the symbolism of numbers and antitheses; while Stoicism is represented in certain technical terms, as well as in the functions assigned to " seed " and " passion," and in the concept of the cosmic conflagration. The religious side of the system was no less syncretistic than the philosophical, though as to its scope present results are inconclusive, and the sources have scarcely been touched. The pagan syncretism of the Semitic East, though not yet sounded, the Egyptian religion, the popular faiths of Greece and Rome, all contributed, yet at least some of the Valentinian leaders successfully withstood the bewildering maze, and sought to lead the pagans, confused by countless religious teachings, to God by a simpler and safer way through the person of Christ. The authorities to whom they appealed were the words of Jesus and his apostles. Marcus asserted the possession of prophetic gifts and of special inward illumination by the higher Wisdom revealing the supernal mysteries, but both pagans and early Christians did the same. An impartial verdict is impossible from merely the hostile orthodox writings; but, at all events, these Gnostics sought only to be Christian teachers, preachers, and prophets. The Church, however, judged differently, and it was soon forgotten that the Gnostics had assisted to render the reception of Christianity possible in the cultured world. Its dualism threatened to substitute ditheism for monotheism; and its obliteration of all history, which became but a type and symbol, a mere casual factor in the eternal, spiritual drama of emanation and redemption, endangered the firm foundations of the Christian faith. The battle of the Church against Gnosticism was justified, yet the movement proved to involve propitious germs that later unfolded in the Church. How far Valentinus furnished a prototype for the organization of the Church is not fully disclosed by the dearth of information, but the distinction of pneumatics and psychics reechoed far in a dual ecclesiastical ethics. The most pronounced influence of his school was through scientific and edifying literature, such as apocryphal gospels and apostolic adventure in romantic form for the man of average culture, odes for the more educated, sermons for edification, exegetic and systematic treatises for the theologian, an array with which the Church at the time had nothing in comparison. To what degree ecclesiastical literature that first deserved the name of scientific was influenced by Valentinus and his school is best seen in Clement of Alexandria and Origen (qq.v.). Not only did Clement's polemics purely or impurely absorb of the character whom he attacked, but he borrowed of him illustrations, analogies, and courses of thought for his own occasions. The commentaries of Origen were doubtless composed in part to replace Gnostic exegesis (cf. John), and even his sermons may have been more or less inspired by antipathy to the " soul-destroying " homilies of the Valentinians. Even the hymn of Clement may not have been uninfluenced by Valentinian poesy. Thus the Church reshaped the weapons of its enemies to defeat them; but the memory of the Valentinians was retained so long, that after the last remnants had long vanished, they still formed the subject of legislation (Codex Theodosianus, X., v. 65, § 2).   (ERWIN PREUSCHEN.)

BIBLIOGRAPHY: Consult the literature under GNOSTICISM, particularly the works of Matter, Neander, Baur, Mansel, Hilgenfeld, King, and Anz; also: G. Heinrici, Die valentinische Gnosis und die heilige Schrift, Breslau, 1871 (best); DCB, iv. 1076–99 (indispensable); W. Möller, Geschichte der Kosmologie in der griechischen Kirche, pp. 407–442, Halle, 1860; K. Kessler, Ueber Gnosis und altbabylonische Religion, in the Verhandlungen of the 5th International Congress of Orientalists, ii. 1, pp. 288–305, Berlin, 1882; T. Zahn, Geschichte des neutestamentlichen Kanons, i. 718–763, ii. 953–961, Leipsic, 1888–89; A. Hilgenfeld, in ZWT, 1880, pp. 280–300, 1883, pp. 355–384, 1890, 1–63;

A. E. Brooke, in *TS*, i. 4 (1891); C. Schmidt, in *TU*, viii. 1 (1892); Harnack, *Dogma*, passim, consult Index; idem, *Litteratur*, i. 174–184, ii. 1, pp. 291–296; idem, in *SBA*, 1898, pp. 516–520; F. Torm, *Valentinianismens Historie og Lære*, Copenhagen, 1901; E. C. H. Peithmann, *Die Valentinianer*, 2 parts, Bitterfeld, 1903; E. de Faye, *Introduction à l'étude du gnosticisme*, pp. 81 sqq., Paris, 1903; E. H. Schmitt, *Gnosis*, Leipsic, 1903; Bardenhewer, *Geschichte*, pp. 331–337; idem, *Patrologie*, pp. 68–69, Eng. transl., St. Louis, 1908; P. Wendland, *Die hellenistisch-römische Kultur in ihren Beziehungen zu Judentum und Christentum*, pp. 161 sqq., Tübingen, 1907; C. Barth, *Die Interpretation des Neuen Testaments in der valentinianischen Gnosis*, in *TU*, xxxvii. 3 (1911); Ceillier, *Auteurs sacrés*, i. 497 sqq., ii. 540, iv. 171, 510; Schaff, *Christian Church*, ii. 472–482; Neander, *Christian Church*, i. 417–434 et passim; and, in general, works on the church history of the time.

VALERIAN, va-lī'ri-an, **PUBLIUS LICINIUS:** Roman emperor 253–260. Valerian came of distinguished family, and was trained in both military and civil functions. He came to the purple during the bloody times which closed the usurpation of Æmilian, being made emperor in Rhætia by the army in 253. He attempted to meet the difficult situation at home and the warlike conditions on the borders, but his age (sixty years) did not permit the employment of the necessary energy. The result was insecurity and hesitation in the face of foreign influences.

[Valerian had been nominated censor by Decius, who wished to revive this important office in the empire, and the choice was ratified by the Roman senate. But Valerian declined a position which carried with it really imperial power on the ground that the functions belonged to the emperor (Gibbon, *Decline and Fall*, i. 247–248).] In the matter of Christianity Valerian had occupied such a position under Decius that Christian tradition rightly saw in him the instigator of the Decian persecution (see DECIUS, CAIUS MESSIUS QUINTUS TRAJANUS). But he broke away from that policy and gave to Christians unwonted signs of favor; at his court Christians were so numerous that the court seemed like " a church of God " (Dionysius, in Eusebius, *Hist. eccl.*, VII., x. 3; *NPNF*, 2 ser., i. 298). This situation resembles that in the reign of Diocletian, and the development was similar; in both cases an antichristian party gained the ear of the emperor. The antichristian leader was the General Marcus Fulvius Macrianus, a man of great military reputation, and a leader in the Egyptian mysteries, which explains his attitude. His political reasons are in doubt; he may have aimed at the purple, and perhaps attempted to carry out his plans by causing political unrest. At any rate, he induced the emperor to issue a rescript in 257 which forbade the Christians to hold assemblies and to use the cemeteries, also sending the clergy into banishment. Macrianus was evidently aiming at the Christian organization; the heads— the clergy—were to be removed while the rank and file were not to meet. How the emperor was won over by the heathen party is not known; but the terms of the edict, comparatively mild, reveals the emperor's earlier good-will for the Christians.

In 258 a new rescript was issued: bishops, presbyters, and deacons were at once to be executed; Christians of senatorial or equestrian rank were to be degraded and their property confiscated, and, if still contumacious, were to suffer death; women were threatened with confiscation of property and banishment; the Christians of the court were to be put in chains at forced servitude on the imperial domains. As a result the two great Christian communities at Rome and Carthage lost their leaders. Bishop Sixtus of Rome fled to the catacombs, but was captured and executed (see SIXTUS II.); and Cyprian also lost his life the same year. Rome also suffered loss in the death of Saint Laurence (q.v.). The Spanish church lost Bishop Fructuosus of Tarragona (q.v.), and both his deacons. In the part of the empire under Gallienus the persecution spread and was thought of as general. As a matter of fact, persecution broke out only in limited foci of action, and there did not destroy Christianity; for a united and general persecution there was neither time nor strength. Perhaps Valerian did not stand forcefully behind the rescript. Yet none of the persecutions of the Christians has raised so many unanswered questions as this.

Valerian fell into the hands of the Persian king, by whom he was held a prisoner till his death. The two sons of Macrianus attempted to seize the throne, but he and they soon fell. Gallienus caused the persecutions to cease. (VICTOR SCHULTZE.)

BIBLIOGRAPHY: Sources are: Eusebius, *Hist. eccl.*, VII., x.–xi., Eng. transl. in *NPNF*, 2 ser., i. 298–302; and the *Acta proconsularia*, in Cyprian, *Opera*, ed. Hartel, ii. 839, in *CSEL*. Consult: L. S. Le Nain de Tillemont, *Hist. des empereurs*, vol. iii., 6 vols., Paris, 1720–38; H. Schiller, *Geschichte der römischen Kaiserzeit*, i. 2, pp. 811 sqq., Gotha, 1883; W. Smith, *Dictionary of Greek and Roman Biography and Mythology*, iii. 1216–17, London, 1890; P. J. Healy, *The Valerian Persecution*, ib. 1905; Gibbon, *Decline and Fall*, chaps. x., xvi.; Schaff, *Christian Church*, ii. 62; Neander, *Christian Church*, i. 136–140 et passim; *DCB*, iv. 1100–02; the literature under CYPRIAN; SIXTUS II.; and PERSECUTIONS OF CHRISTIANS.

VALERIAN, SAINT: Bishop of Cemelium (near the modern Nice), southeastern Gaul, and homilist; d. about 460. He seems to have been a kinsman of Eucherius of Lyons, but the only details known of his episcopate are that he attended the Councils of Riez (439) and Vaison (452), protested with eighteen other Gallic bishops against Leo the Great in behalf of the primacy of Arles (see ARLES, ARCHBISHOPRIC OF), and opposed the claims of Theodore of Fréjus. He was, therefore, an adherent of Hilary of Arles and of Faustus. Valerian is chiefly important, however, for his homilies. Up to 1612 the only one known was the *De bono disciplinæ*, formerly ascribed to Augustine, but proved to be Valerian's by Melchior Goldast, who edited the homily (Geneva, 1601). In a Corbey manuscript J. Sirmond found nineteen other homilies which he ascribed to Valerian (*Sancti Valeriani episcopi Cemeliensis homiliæ viginti; item epistola ad monachos, de virtutibus et ordine doctrinæ apostolicæ*, Paris, 1612). These homilies are adorned with all the artifices of the Gallic school of rhetoric, including alliteration; the author is at his best in descriptions, and his style is modeled on that of Seneca. The homilies are also important historically as supplementing Salvianus (q.v.). In theology Valerian avoids dogmatic controversy, and in his doctrine of grace he follows Faustus of Riez (q.v.), his point of view scarcely differing from that of Cæsarius of Arles (q.v.). He is primarily a moralist, his chief thought being the advancement of discipline, of work for its own sake with respect to God, Christ, and the martyrs. The rapid decline of his see city is one of the chief causes which consigned many of the homilies of Valerian to an unmerited oblivion, or ascribed them to others, such as Petrus Chrysologus or Eucherius.   (F. ARNOLD.)

BIBLIOGRAPHY: L. Duchesne, *Fastes episcopaux de l'ancienne Gaule*, i. 290, 296, Paris, 1907; *Histoire littéraire de la France*, ii. 328–329; Tillemont, *Mémoires*, xv. 125; N. Schack, *De Valeriano seculi quinti homileta Christiano*, Copenhagen, 1814; T. Raynaud, in *MPL*, lii. 757–836; *Gallia Christiana*, iii. 1268, Paris, 1876; A. Malnory, *S. Césaire évêque d'Arles*, pp. 43, 70, 251, Paris, 1894; Ceillier, *Auteurs sacrés*, x. 154–159, viii. 444, 605; *DCB*, iv. 1103; *KL*, xii. 558–560.

VALESIUS, va-lī'shi-Us, **HENRICUS (HENRI DE VALOIS):** French historian and scholar; b. at Paris Sept. 10, 1603; d. there May 7, 1676. Educated at the Jesuit school in Verdun and at the Collège Clermont in Paris, he went, in 1622, to Bourges to study law, which he abandoned in 1630 to devote himself to scholarship. The first results were his editio princeps of the tenth-century compend " On Virtue and Vice " (*Polybii, Diodori Siculi, Nicolai Damasceni . . . excerpta ex collectaneis Constantini Augusti Porphyrogenetæ*, Paris, 1634), and his edition of Ammianus Marcellinus (1636). His life-work, however, was a critical edition of the Greek church historians, comprising the writings of Eusebius, Socrates, Sozomen, Theodoret, and Evagrius, with excerpts from Philostorgius and Theodorus Lector (3 vols., Paris, 1659–73; ed. W. Reading, Cambridge, 1720 and often). His minor writings were edited by P. Burman the younger under the title *H. Valesii emendationum libri quinque et de critica libri duo* (Amsterdam, 1740), which also contains his orations and a biography by his brother Hadrian.   (G. LAUBMANN†.)

BIBLIOGRAPHY: H. Valesius, *De vita Henrici Valesii*, Paris, 1677; *KL*, xii. 560–563.

VALETON, JOZUA JAN PHILIPPUS: The name of two Dutch Reformed Old-Testament scholars.

1. Jan Valeton the Elder: b. at The Hague Aug. 28, 1814; d. at Utrecht Feb. 8, 1906. He was educated at the University of Leyden (1832–39), and was then pastor at Waalsch until 1844, when, after the publication of his doctor's dissertation, *Taalibii Syntagma Dictorum Brevium et Acutorum* (Leyden, 1884), he was appointed professor of Old Testament at the University of Groningen. In 1876 he left Groningen to accept a similar position at Leyden, where he was the colleague of Abraham Kuenen (q.v.), and there he remained until advancing years forced him to retire from active life. His theological position may be described as that of a liberal conservative. In addition to a number of contributions to theological periodicals, he was the author of *Schets der hebreeisch spraakkunst* (1850).

2. Jan Valeton the Younger: Son of the preceding; b. at Groningen Oct. 14, 1848. He was educated at the universities of Utrecht and Geneva, after which he was pastor successively at Verit, Gelderland (1872–75), and at Bloemendaal, near Haarlem (1875–77). In 1877 he was called to his present position of professor of Hebrew and Old Testament at Utrecht. He has twice been president of the Association (or Synod) of the Province

of Utrecht (1892, 1903), and was the prime mover in the establishment of a college for training future missionaries; he has also exhibited keen interest in the Students' Christian Movement connected with the Dutch universities, and has delivered many addresses at their gatherings. He is also a member of the Literary Association of the Netherlands and of the Royal Academy of Sciences. Like his father, he is theologically a liberal conservative. He accepts the chief position of the Reuss-Graf-Kuenen-Wellhausen School of Old-Testament criticism, but is an uncompromising defender of the divinity of Christ and of his literal resurrection, though his reasons are rather the needs of the Christian life than the evidence of documents and the like.

Besides many contributions to Dutch and German theological periodicals, and in addition to a large number of addresses, etc., he has written *Viertal voorlezingen over propheten des Ouden Verbonds* (Utrecht, 1886, 2d enlarged ed., 1908; dealing with Isaiah, Jeremiah, Ezekiel, and the " Deutero-Isaiah "); *Amos en Hosea, een hoofstuk uit de geschiedenis van Israel's godsdienst* (Nijmegen, 1894; German transl. by F. K. Echternacht, Giessen, 1898); *Christus en het Oude Testament* (1895); *Vergängliches und Ewiges im Alten Testament* (Berlin, 1895); *De Psalmen* (3 parts, Nijmegen, 1902–05); *Het Oude Testament en de critik* (1906); *Het Oude Testament in het licht van wetenschappelijk onderzoeg* (1907); *Oud-testamentische voordrachten* (1909 sqq.); and the section on the Israeliten in P. D. Chantepie de la Saussaye's *Lehrbuch der Religionsgeschichte* (3d ed., Tübingen, 1905).   T. WITTON DAVIES.

VALLA, väl'lä, **LAURENTIUS (LORENZO):** Italian humanist and critic; b. at Rome 1405; d. there Aug. 1, 1457. His father was a consistorial advocate in Rome, and an uncle provided Lorenzo with a humanistic training before he turned to theology. He was consecrated as priest in 1431. His first writing, *De voluptate ac de vero bono*, was not printed until 1483. Meanwhile there appeared *Quæstiones dialecticæ; De libero arbitrio; and De elegantiis Latini sermonis*, a declaration of war against the usual didactics and Latinity of his time. In 1435 or 1436, Valla entered the service of King Alfonso V. of Aragon; and while under his patronage he composed, about 1440, the celebrated *Declamatio de falso credita et ementita Constantini donatione*, which showed the so-called " Donation of Constantine " (q.v.) to be a forgery. By 1442, when he accompanied Alfonso to Naples, rumors were already abroad that his views were in opposition to the Church. But the king still protected him against the Inquisition, so that the judicial proceedings against him were suspended (cf. Valla's *Opera*, pp. 195, 356). At Naples Valla composed *Collatio Novi Testamenti*, though this was not published until sixty years later (ed. Erasmus, *Annotationes in N. T.*, Paris, 1505), being " the first fruit of the newly awakened philological studies in behalf of exegesis " (cf. Mancini, *Vita*, pp. 238 sqq.).

An attempt of Valla's to return to Rome in 1444 miscarried through the fanaticism of the priests, and his *Apologia*, addressed to Eugenius IV., failed to secure favor. It was not until 1447, under Nicholas V., a friend to humanists, to whom Valla dedicated the first part of a Latin translation of the Iliad, that he obtained an appointment at Rome. But at once strife broke out between him and the resident humanists, which, so far as Poggio was concerned, did not cease even with the death of Valla. But the latter's didactic industry and literary productiveness, his perspicacious philological and historical criticism (cf. his *Declamatio*), his efforts to free science from the fetters of scholastic tradition, are great and lasting merits. Certainly Valla ranks as a precursor of modern intellectual freedom, even though the ascription, *præcursor Lutheri*, rather malignly applied to him by Bellarmine, fits him only in limited measure. His writings, besides those already named, are abundant; and several of them, such as the *Elegantiæ* and the *Declamatio*, have undergone repeated editions. Luther's opinion of him was " The like of whom neither Italy nor the whole Church produced in many centuries " (*Responsio ad Lovan. theol.*, *Briefwechsel*, iv. 189).

Mancini, a recent biographer, thus measures him:

" It was his misfortune to clash with Poggio who persecuted him without rest or surcease even beyond his grave. He thus had against him Poggio's followers, and all who wrote in sympathy with the Curia. What availed it that he cultivated Christian principles and served the truth? A father of modern criticism, he exercised the thorny office, not for the sake of bending it to his personal interests, but to elevate humanity. In the process he did not always observe the right measure in his own defense; he answered with insult where he might have silenced the adversary by compelling force and sharpness of demonstration. Hence, brilliant embodiment of the Italian intellect though he was, he did not find the recognition that was his due, in his own time; though now there is justly conceded him a place among the great ones whose achievements have richly furthered human culture."   K. BENRATH.

BIBLIOGRAPHY: Two incomplete editions of the writings of Valla were published, Basel, 1540 (1543) and Venice, 1592; Ulrich von Hutten issued the *Donatio Constantini* in 1519; J. Vahlen edited the *Tria Opuscula*, Vienna, 1869. Accounts of the life have been given by J. Vahlen, Vienna, 1864, Berlin, 1870; J. Clausen, Copenhagen, 1861; C. G. Zampt, in *Zeitschrift für Geschichtswissenschaft*, iv. 397 sqq.; G. Mancini, Florence, 1891; M. von Wolff, Leipsic, 1893; L. V. Schwahn, Berlin, 1896. Consult further: G. Tiraboschi, *Storia della Letteratura italiana*, vi. 3, 11 vols., Modena, 1772–95; D. G. Monrad, *Die erste Controverse über das Glaubensbekenntnis*, Gotha, 1881; A. Gaspary, *Geschichte der italienischen Litteratur*, vol. ii., Strasburg, 1884; L. Amabile, *Inquisizione di Napoli*, i. 73 sqq., Castello, 1892; G. Voigt, *Die Wiederbelebung des klassischen Altertums*, i. 460 sqq., 3d ed., Berlin, 1893; Pastor, *Popes*, vols. iv.–v. passim; Creighton, *Papacy*, iii. 170–173.

VALLOMBROSA, ORDER OF. See GUALBERTO, GIOVANNI.

VALTELLINA, vȧl"tel-lï'na, REFORMATION AND COUNTER-REFORMATION IN: Valtellina, or the upper valley of the Adda in Northern Italy, early became a coveted possession. In 774 Charlemagne gave it to the monastery of St. Denis at Paris, but before long it was the bone of contention between the bishops of Como and of Chur, whose dioceses here met. The former prelate already had estates in Valtellina, and in 1006 received from Henry II. half of the county; accordingly, in 1190, he laid claim to the temporal sovereignty, and fifteen years later subdued Bormio.

Earlier External History.

In 1336, however, Bormio again came into the possession of Chur, but in 1350 was taken by the Visconti and remained part of Milan until 1512. In 1404, the fugitive Mastino Visconti presented Valtellina to the diocese of Chur. In the struggles for the duchy of Milan the allies expelled the French from Valtellina in 1512, and remained there as conquerors until 1797, except for a short time after the " Valtellina massacre " (see below). Ecclesiastically Valtellina remained dependent on the bishop of Como, who was originally under the jurisdiction of the archbishop of Aquileia, and later under that of the archbishop of Milan. The bishop of Chur (placed under the archbishop of Mainz in 843), therefore, had little power in Valtellina, though for a time after 1530 he was given an annual compensation for his loss of jurisdiction.

Valtellina received the " new doctrine " of the Reformation from the south, so that it remained free from the Teutonizing influences of the Reformation proceeding from Zurich. In Grisons, of which Valtellina then formed part, the religious and social reform was accomplished under the influence of the Ilanz Articles of 1524 and 1526 (see KOMANDER, JOHANN), and at Davos in 1526 the diet granted religious freedom to all, with the exception of the Anabaptists. Italian Protestants, driven from their country by the commencement of the Counter-Reformation, took advantage of this toleration and settled in large numbers in the valley of the Adda and elsewhere, many availing themselves of their asylum to wage war on the Roman Catholic Church. After 1523, in like manner, a number of Waldenses and other Protestants fled from Milan to Valtellina, only to be expelled by the allies at the request of the inhabitants. Reformation and Counter-Reformation followed fast in Valtellina. In the second decade of the sixteenth century there were officials with Protestant tendencies there, though the great Protestant movement did not take place until after the issuing of the bull *Licet ab initio* in 1542. The stream of fugitives into the Rhætian valleys included many restless spirits who disturbed both religious and political conditions. In 1529 an Italian preacher was brought from Valtellina to Ilanz for examination of his teachings, and in 1544 two Calabrian monks, Francesco and Hieronimo, were expelled from the Engadine for Anabaptist doctrines. Chiavenna was the home of the Neapolitan Camillo Renato, an antitrinitarian antipedobaptist, and of Laelius Socinus (q.v.), until a church order made it impossible for adherents of heterodox doctrines to remain. A certain Tiziano was banished for antitrinitarianism and antipedobaptism, despite his retractions, and the ex-monk Franciscus Niger of Bassano was not free from suspicion, though he was in close harmony with the position of the Zurich reformers. [Niger was also an antitrinitarian antipedobaptist. A. H. N.] On the other hand, there were among the fugitive Italians many of unquestioned standing in the eyes of the leaders of the Rhætian Reformation. At first the Italian refugees in Valtellina were permitted only to reside there, not to preach. In 1538, however, the latter privilege was granted them, and in

The Reformation.

1544 additional favor was shown Protestant teachers and preachers, though it was still necessary to guard against erroneous doctrines. The Grisons, who were chiefly Protestant, supported the Reformation in Valtellina for political reasons. The result was religious antagonism, the Roman Catholics of Valtellina, both those who had remained true to the ancient faith and those who had been won back by the Jesuits, uniting with the other Roman Catholics of Switzerland, and these in their turn with Austria and Milan. Political and religious antitheses between Valtellina and the Grisons continually became intensified. Valtellina, which had welcomed the Grisons in 1512, was now oppressed by them, and the religious rights of the Roman Catholics were grievously curtailed. In 1551 it was rumored that Austria and Spain planned to invade the region, but Maurice of Saxony came to the aid of the Protestants, who, four months after the treaty of Passau, received a new edict of toleration despite the protests of the pope and of Spain. In the following year, to check the recrudescence of disturbing doctrines, the synod adopted the *Confessio Rhætica*, which was accepted by the Italians in 1553. The pope, aided by Austria and Spain, now sought to induce the Grisons to consent to the introduction of the Inquisition into Valtellina, and when this effort failed, the Capuchins were sent, while officials of the Inquisition were ever on the watch along the Milan border. In 1557 the edict of equal toleration for Protestants and Roman Catholics in Valtellina was renewed after the Jesuits had already firmly established themselves in the district toward the end of the fifth decade.

The most powerful factor in the crushing of Protestantism in this district, however, was the great archbishop of Milan, Cardinal Carlo Borromeo (q.v.), while the external dangers confronting the adherents of the new tenets were complicated by internal doctrinal disputes. In 1564 Philip II. made an unsuccessful demand of the Grisons for the surrender of Protestant heretics, and in 1579 Borromeo established at Milan the Collegium Helveticum, largely to provide priests for Valtellina, whereupon the Grisons renewed their exclusion of foreign priests. Another powerful agency in the reorganization of the Roman Catholic Church here was found in the resumption of ecclesiastical visitations, interrupted since 1532. Two visitations were made by Giovanni Francesco Bonhomini in 1578 and by Borromeo himself in 1580. Nine years later Feliciano Ninguarda, bishop of Como, made a more extensive visitation, since, as a native of Valtellina, the Grisons were unable to forbid him to exercise pastoral activity in the Adda valley. In 1639, moreover, the chapter of Milan conferred upon the bishop of Como plenipotentiary powers for ecclesiastical visitations and for the execution of papal bulls. Closely associated with the Reformation and Counter-Reformation here were the fortunes of the school established by the Grisons for the education of both Protestants and Roman Catholics (apparently the first school of this character) at Sondrio, though Milanese opposition forced its transference to Chur in 1585.

The Counter-Reformation.

In 1584 an armed foray from Milan was planned for the destruction of the Valtellina Protestants and their school, but it was betrayed and failed. In 1621, however, the Spaniards invaded the region, killed 600 Protestants (the so-called " Valtellina massacre "), and with one blow ended the school and the domination of the Swiss Grisons. For nineteen years the latter strove in vain to recover their subjects, but in 1639 Valtellina passed under the control of the chapter of Milan, which forbade all exercise of the Reformed religion. Every effort, even with the help of England and Prussia, to secure mitigation was in vain. Temporary relief was given by the edict of toleration of Joseph II., but in 1796 Napoleon entered Milan, and in the following year made Valtellina part of the Cisalpine republic, since which time its fortunes have been those of upper Italy.   (C. CAMENISCH.)

BIBLIOGRAPHY: Sources are: *Eidgenössische Abschiede*, vols. iv.–v., ed. J. Strickler, Brugg, 1873 sqq.; the *Relazione* of Giacomo and Girolamo Soranzo, included in N. Barozzi and G. Berchet, *Relazioni degli stati europei*, Venice, 1856 sqq.; E. Roth, *Mery de Vic et Padavino*, in *Quellen zur Schweizergeschichte*, vol. v., Basel, 1881; the *Historia Rætica*, in the same, vol. ix., ib. 1890; Wirz, *Akten der römischen Curie*, in the same, vol. xvi., ib. 1895; as well as Bullinger's correspondence in vols. xviii.–xxv. of the same; *Nuntiaturberichte aus der Schweiz*, ed. F. Steffens and H. Reinhardt, vol. i., Solothurn, 1906; G. Alberti, *Antichità di Bormio*, and F. F. Ninguarda, *Atti della visita pastorale diocesana*, in " Publications of the Como Historical Society," Como, 1890 sqq.; Paolo Sarpi, *Breve Relatione di Valtellina*, in Appendix, vol. ii. of his *Opere*, Verona, 1758, and in U. Martinelli, *La Campagna del marchese di Cœuvres*, *Città di Castello;* also Sarpi's *Hist. of the Council of Trent*, London, 1676. Consult also: the literature under BORROMEO, CARLO (biographies of him contain much from the sources); KOMANDER, JOHANN; and the works on the REFORMATION in Switzerland; C. Camenisch, *Carlo Borromeo und die Gegenreformation im Veltlin*, Chur, 1901; P. A. Lavizari, *Memorie della Valtellina*, Coira, 1716; C. Cantu, *Rivoluzione della Valtellina*, Como, 1831; idem, *Il sacro macello di Valtellina*, Milan, 1885; G. Romegialli, *Storia della Valtellina*, Sondrio, 1834; B. Anhorn, *Wiedergeburt der evangelischen Kirche in den 3 Bünden*, Chur, 1860; E. Haffter and Georg Tenatsch, *Beiträge zur Geschichte der Bündner Wirren*, Davos, 1894; J. G. Mayer, *Das Konzil von Trient und die Gegenreformation in der Schweiz*, Stans, 1901–03; J. Dierauer, *Geschichte der schweizerischen Eidgenossenschaft*, vol. iii., Gotha, 1907; Schaff, *Christian Church*, vii. 146, 157, 160.

VAMVAS, vām′vās, NEOPHYTOS: Greek Orthodox; b. in Chios in the latter part of the eighteenth century; d. at Athens 1855. He was first a monk, apparently in Patmos, and later returned to Chios for further study, completing his education at Paris. In 1813 he was appointed teacher at the gymnasium of his native island, and during the Greek war for independence was secretary to Prince Demetrius Ypsilanti. He was then a teacher at the Ionic Academy in Corfu (1828–33) and at Syra (1833–37), and from 1837 until his death was professor at the University of Athens. A representative of liberalism in Church and State, Vamvas became known to the West by being involved in the struggle of the British and Foreign Bible Society in Greece. This society determined, in the second decade of the nineteenth century, to translate the Old Testament without the Apocrypha from Hebrew into Romaic, and Vamvas was engaged to assist in the work as a Greek scholar. In 1833 the Greek Church became independent, and the eleventh paragraph of its statutes required the synod to protect pure doctrine and guard against proselytizing. Under these circumstances, a storm of protest arose against a translation which not only undermined the authority of the Septuagint, but also lacked the Apocrypha, especially as there was an earnest desire to educate the people to use the Old Testament in the Septuagint and the New Testament in the original Greek instead of a Romaic version. So sharp became the controversy that in Apr., 1835, the government forbade the use of the new translations in schools and churches, thus restoring the authority of the Septuagint. The orthodox party was not satisfied, however, and Vamvas was denounced as the chief translator for the English. He replied in a " Brief Answer " (Athens, 1836), defending the translation and his work on it on both religious and scientific grounds, and referring pointedly to abuses existing in the Greek Church, particularly in the ignorance of the clergy. He was now obliged to defend his alleged attacks on the Septuagint before the synod, which condemned both his " Brief Answer " and his pamphlet " On the Modern Greek Church " (Athens, 1839), and sought in vain to have the government proceed against him. Though the entire affair ended disastrously for the Bible Society, Vamvas was instrumental in arousing a more active study of the Bible among his countrymen.

Vamvas was likewise active in other departments of theology. Besides a work on the inspiration of the Scriptures, he wrote a " Handbook of the Rhetoric of the Sacred Pulpit " (Athens, 1851), but became most famous for his " Elements of Ethics " (1818), a rationalistic philosophy of religion and system of ethics. The great ethical principles he held to be God and the human conscience, and he divided duties into those toward God, toward self, and toward man. The proof of the existence of God forms the introduction to the duties toward the Deity, and the demonstration of the immortality of the soul that of the duties toward self; while the theory of human society forms the preface to the duties toward man.   (PHILIPP MEYER.)

BIBLIOGRAPHY: J. Wenger, *Beiträge zur Kenntnis des gegenwärtigen Geistes . . . der griechischen Kirche*, Berlin, 1839; R. Nicolai, *Geschichte der neugriechischen Litteratur*, p. 128, Leipsic, 1876; A. D. Kyriakos, *Geschichte der orientalischen Kirche, 1453-1898*, ib. 1902.

VAN BUREN, JAMES HEARTT: Protestant Episcopal missionary bishop of Porto Rico; b. at Watertown, N. Y., July 7, 1850. He was educated at Yale (A.B., 1873) and at Berkeley Divinity School, Middletown, Conn. (graduated 1876). He was ordained to the priesthood in 1876, and was rector of St. Peter's, Milford, Conn. (1876-78), Trinity, Seymour, Conn. (1878-80), St. Paul's, Englewood, N. J. (1880-84), St. Paul's, Newburyport, Mass. (1884-90), and St. Stephen's, Lynn, Mass. (1890-1901). In 1902 he was consecrated bishop of the missionary district of Porto Rico. He has written *Latin Hymns in English Verse* (Boston, 1904).

VAN DYCK, van daik, **CORNELIUS VAN ALEN:** Reformed Dutch medical missionary; b. at Kinderhook, N. Y., Aug. 13, 1818; d. at Beirut Aug.

13, 1895. He was educated at Kinderhook Academy, and in medicine at Jefferson Medical College, Philadelphia (1839); appointed missionary of the A. B. C. F. M. for Syria, 1839; sailed from Boston for Beirut Jan., 1840; was ordained by Syrian Mission in council, Jan. 14, 1846; principal of Missionary Seminary, 1848-52; then missionary in the Sidon field till 1857; translator of the Bible into Arabic from 1857, and manager of the Mission Press, 1857-80; physician to St. John's Hospital, and professor of pathology in the Syrian Protestant College, Beirut, till 1882; after that, physician to St. George's Hospital. He was " broad Calvinistic " in his theology. He taught Hebrew in Union Theological Seminary, New York City, while superintending the printing of his translation of the Arabic Bible at the American Bible Society, 1866-67. He translated into Arabic the *Westminster Assembly's Shorter Catechism* (Beirut, 1843); *Schönberg-Cotta Family* (1885); and was the author in Arabic of various text-books in mathematics, astronomy, and medicine. He was noted for his mastery of the Arabic language and literature.

VAN DYKE, HENRY JACKSON: Presbyterian; b. at Germantown, Pa., Nov. 10, 1852. He was educated at Princeton College (A.B., 1873) and at Princeton Theological Seminary (graduated 1877). In 1878 he studied at the University of Berlin, and upon his return to the United States held pastorates at the United Congregational Church, Newport, R. I. (1879-82), and the Brick Presbyterian Church, New York City (1883-1900); became professor of English literature in Princeton University, 1900. His writings include: *The Reality of Religion* (New York, 1884); *The Story of the Psalms* (1887); *Sermons to Young Men* (1893); *The Christ Child in Art* (1894); *The Other Wise Man* (1896); *The Gospel for an Age of Doubt* (1896); *The First Christmas Tree* (1897); *The Builders, and other Poems* (1897); *The Lost Word* (1898); *The Gospel for a World of Sin* (1899); *The Toiling of Felix, and other Poems* (1900); *The Poetry of the Psalms* (1900); *The Friendly Year* (1900); *The Ruling Passion* (1901); *The Open Door* (Philadelphia, 1903); *Music, and other Poems* (New York, 1904); *The School of Life* (1905); *Essays in Application* (1905); *The Spirit of Christmas* (1905); *Days off, and Other Digressions* (1907); *The Music-Lover* (1907); *Counsels by the Way* (1908); *House of Rimmon* (1908); *Out of Doors in the Holy Land* (1908); *White Bees and Other Poems* (1909); *Spirit of America* (1910); and *Complete Poems* (1911).

VAN HORNE, DAVID: Reformed (German); b. at Glen, Montgomery Co., N. Y., Dec. 11, 1837. He was graduated from Union College, 1864; and at the New Brunswick Theological Seminary, N. J., 1867; was pastor of Reformed Church (Dutch), Greenwich, N. J., 1868; of Reformed Church (German), Dayton, O., 1868-75; of First Reformed Church (German), Philadelphia, 1875-88; professor of systematic theology in and president of the Heidelberg Theological Seminary, Tiffin, O., 1888-1907; since 1907 he holds the same position in the New Central Theological Seminary, Dayton, O. His theological position is conservative. His publications embrace an edition of the Heidelberg Catechism (Philadelphia, 1881, 9th ed., Cleveland, 1908); *History of the Reformed Church in Philadelphia* (Philadelphia, 1876); *Tent and Saddle Life in the Holy Land* (1885); *The Church and the Future Life* (Cleveland, 1904).

VAN KIRK, HIRAM: Disciple of Christ; b. at Washington Court House, O., Feb. 13, 1868. He was educated at Hiram College, Hiram, O. (A.B., 1892), Yale Divinity School (B.D., 1895), and the University of Chicago (Ph.D., 1900), where he was fellow (1898–1900). He was pastor of the Jefferson Street Church of Christ, Buffalo (1890–91), Central Christian Church, Nevada, Mo. (1896–97), and Christian Church, Jefferson City, Mo. (1897–1898); instructor in the Disciples' Divinity House, Chicago (1898–1900), and since 1900 dean and professor of Biblical theology in Berkeley Bible Seminary, Berkeley, Cal. He has also lectured on oriental history in the University of California since 1902, and was secretary of the Board of Education of the American Christian Missionary Society in 1898–1900. In theology he is " a moderate in his doctrinal positions and active in the practical administration of his denomination." He has written *The Rise of the Current Reformation; or, a Study in the History of Theology of the Disciples of Christ* (St. Louis, 1906).

VAN MANEN, vän-mä′nen, **WILLEM CHRISTIAN:** Dutch theologian; b. at Noordeloos, near Gorkum (22 m. e.s.e. of Rotterdam), Holland, Aug. 8, 1842; d. at Leyden July 12, 1905. He received his early education in the schools at Benschop and at Ijselen; entered the University of Utrecht in 1859, studying especially under Opzoomer and Doedes (D.D., 1865, for his dissertation: *Onderzoek haar de echtheid van Paulus' eersten brief aan de Thessalonicensen*); was pastor of the Dutch Reformed Church at Abbenbroek (1865–70), at Winkel (1870–75), and at Zierksee (1875–84), showing himself a good preacher and taking a prominent part in the ecclesiastical and theological controversies of the time. In Oct., 1884, he became professor of theology in connection with the Dutch Reformed Church at the University of Groningen, and entered upon his office by delivering an inaugural address on Dec. 11, 1884, his subject being *Het persoonlijk karakter der leerstellige godgeleerdheid* (" The personal character of a professorship of theology "); the next year he became professor of old (not early) Christian literature and New-Testament exegesis at Leyden, and inaugurated his work in this his last earthly home by an address on *De leerstoel der Oud-christelijke letter-kunde* (" The Chair of Old Christian Literature "). The very title of the chair indicates the point of view to which Van Manen had brought himself. He had now for some time argued against the prevalent habit of distinguishing between the canonical writings of the New Testament and early Christian literature. He embraced the whole down to about 180 A.D. under one category, " Old Christian Literature," preferring " old " to " early " owing to the previous use of the latter in a different sense.

Van Manen was not a popular preacher, yet he was always listened to with respect and even admiration by thoughtful hearers. His sermons were clear, but too closely reasoned and too full of matter to make it easy for the common man to follow them. That fondness for controversy which never left him showed itself even in his student days when (i.e., in 1864) he joined issue with one of his teachers—Van Ooztersee—on the question of the genuineness of II Thessalonians. In later years he had controversies with Jacobus Cramer, A. Kuyper, and many others. Though at first he vigorously assailed the advanced views of Loman and other members of the Groningen school on the books of the New Testament, he afterward adopted these views, carrying them to a farther point than his predecessors Loman, Steck, and others. He wrote largely for religious magazines—*Vaterländsche letteroefeningen, Gottesdienstig album, Theologische Tijdschrift;* of this last he was editor from 1890 to the time of his death.

In 1903, at the very zenith of his power and influence, probably owing to his excessive industry and zeal, he was suddenly laid low by a paralytic seizure, from which he never sufficiently recovered to attempt any further work, literary or academic, though his name remained among the editors of the *Theologische Tijdschrift* to the end of 1905. After a lingering illness in which the once strong mind gave way more and more, he died, greatly regretted by colleagues and by a large number of scholars in all lands. Even those who rejected his opinions admired his industry, courtesy, kindness, and transparent honesty. He had a tall, imposing figure, and was broad of shoulder, his large head being covered with a goodly quantity of curly hair.

His principal works were the following: (1) *Handleiding voor de Oud-christelijke Letterkunde* (1890; the substance of this work is given by the author himself in the article " Old Christian Literature " in *EB*, vol. iv.; there is a brief analysis also in the *Hibbert Journal,* i. 193). Van Manen denies in this work that the so-called " Epistles " of the New Testament are letters proper: they are rather dogmatic and practical treatises by unknown authors, one of them coming from the pen of the Apostle Paul. (2) *Paulus.* This, his greatest work, is divided into three parts: (a) *De Handelingen der Apostelen* (1890; on the Acts); (b) *De Brief aan de Romanen* (1891; on Romans); (c) *De Brieven aan de Korinthiers* (1896; on I and II Corinthians). Of this work, which discusses more fully most of the problems dealt with in the former work, an analysis is given by Thomas Whittaker in his *Origins of Christianity* (pp. 67 sqq., 2d ed., London, 1909). Especially worthy of notice are his articles " Paul," " Philippians," and " Romans," in *EB*, and those in *The Expository Times,* vol. ix., defending himself against Samuel Davidson. Though few theologians accept the rationalistic conclusions to which Van Manen came, Prof. T. K. Cheyne, of Oxford, speaks of him as " the man whom future readers of the Bible will bless for having set Gospels and Epistles in intelligible time relations." It is significant that in May, 1904, the Rationalistic Press Association in London elected him an " Honorary Associate."   T. Witton Davies.

BIBLIOGRAPHY: *ThT*, 1905, p. 385 (obituary); E. U. Meyboom, in *ThT*, 1906, pp. 193–252 (on Van Manen's life and literary works); R. Steck, in *Protestantische Monatsschrift*, ix (1905), October; Pijper, "Die hollandsche Bibel-Kritik" in *Protestantische Monatsschrift*, vols. x.–xi.; *TJB*, 1906.

VAN PELT, JOHN ROBERT: Methodist Episcopal; b. near Todd's Point, Shelby County, Ky., Nov. 10, 1862. He received his education at Illinois Wesleyan University, Bloomington, Ill. (B.A., 1882; M.A., 1885), Boston University (S.T.B., 1887; Ph.D., 1893), Garrett Biblical Institute, Evanston, Ill., and the University of Halle; he entered the ministry of the Methodist Episcopal Church in 1887, serving in Illinois till 1891, when he became professor of systematic theology in the Iliff School of Theology, Denver, Col.; in 1901 he returned to the pastorate, and served in Illinois and Pennsylvania till in 1909 he went to his present position of professor of philosophy and Biblical literature in Cornell College, Mount Vernon, Ia. He is a member of the committee for preparing a Sunday-school hymnal for the use of his denomination. His theological position is that of a moderate conservative; he holds to the supreme authority of the Christian revelation in the Bible, but concedes full liberty to the processes of criticism. He has been largely influenced by Kähler in his theological thinking.

VAN TIL. See TIL, SALOMON VAN.

VANCE, SELBY FRAME: Presbyterian; b. at Oneida, Knox Co., Ill., Nov. 17, 1864. He was educated at Lake Forest University (B.A., 1885), Princeton Theological Seminary (1888–90), McCormick Theological Seminary (1891), and Berlin University (1893–95); and, after holding a pastorate at Girard, Kan. (1891–93), was professor of Greek in Parsons College (1895–1900) and of English Bible in Wooster University (1900–05). Since 1905 he has been professor of church history in Lane Theological Seminary.

VANDALS: A people of Teutonic stock, distinguished in secular history for their great migrations from the northeast of Europe to the south and then to the extreme southwest of the Roman world, and in church history for their extreme tenacity to Arianism. In the time of Pliny the elder and Tacitus the Vandals were settled between the Elbe and the Vistula, but by the period of the great Marcomannic war (166–181) they had reached the territory represented by the modern Silesia. A century later Aurelian found it necessary to protect the middle Danube against them; but about 330, hard pressed by their northern neighbors, they received protection from Constantine the Great in Pannonia, though forced to recognize Roman sovereignty. About 407 the Vandals, together with the Caucasian Alans and a Swabian tribe, left Pannonia, and, after ravaging Gaul, sought new homes in Spain, where they settled first in the north, in Galicia (409–423), and then in the south, in Bætica, the modern Andalusia (423–429). Their Arian Christianity they received from the Emperor Valens.

In 429 Genseric, Vandal king since 427, landed with some 80,000 followers, of whom 50,000 were warriors, on the coast of northern Africa. The Vandal kingdom properly dates, however, from Oct. 19, 439, when, utterly disregarding the terms of the peace made at Hippo Regius on Feb. 11, 435, Genseric stormed and sacked Carthage, which he made his capital. From 440 until 475 he harried the Mediterranean coasts almost annually, and in June, 455, pillaged Rome itself. He ruled northern Africa from Mauretania to Cyrene, and also Corsica, Sardinia, the Balearic Isles, Iviza, Formentera, and part of Sicily.

The African Vandal kingdom, unprecedentedly isolated in the extreme south of the ancient world, suffered more than any other Teutonic Arian domain on the Mediterranean from a twofold internal antithesis, national and religious. In his new home Genseric found two ruling estates, the ecclesiastical nobility, or bishops, and the secular nobles, or *possessores*. Both were systematically crushed as main supports of Catholic power, but when, in token of allegiance, the Vandal king demanded Arian rebaptism and disciplined loyal Catholics, the persecution was political rather than religious. When, on the other hand, he came into better relation with the two divisions of the Roman Empire, he was lenient toward his orthodox subjects, and at one time the African Bishop Victor of Cartenna could present him with an impassioned refutation of Arianism without ill consequences. On Jan. 25, 477, the aged Vandal king died at peace with all his foes. Except for his religious persecutions, Genseric was a ruler of a high degree of statesmanship, and his personal integrity and purity were irreproachable. The taint of immorality alleged against him by Sidonius Apollinaris (*Panegyricus*, v. 327 sqq.) is refuted by the activity of his life, for until about 474 he led almost all his expeditions in person. He was equally ready to recognize nobility in others; while among his acts of toleration to his orthodox subjects may be mentioned his permission, at the request of Valentinian III., for the Catholics of Carthage to elect Deogratias as their bishop after their community had been desolate for years (Oct. 24, 454).

Genseric was succeeded by his unworthy son, Huneric (477–484), who at first spared the Catholics out of fear of Byzantium, and even permitted them to choose Eugenius bishop of Carthage in 481, only to persecute the orthodox with ever-increasing barbarity after 482. Guntamund (484–496) spared the Catholics, and his successor, Thrasamund (496–523), contented himself with banishing the most important bishops. Hilderic (523–530), the son of Huneric and the West Roman Princess Eudocia, granted absolute religious freedom. Catholic synods were again held on African soil at Junca (523), Sufes (524), and Carthage itself (525). Hilderic's policy, however, allying him with Byzantium, then ruled by Justinian, and estranging him from his natural allies, the Ostrogoths, led to his fall. His aged cousin, Gelimer (or Geilamir), a fervent Arian, had him dethroned and put to death. In 533–534, Gelimer himself succumbed to Belisarius at Decimum and Tricameron, and North Africa with the islands became, under the name of the Exarchate of Carthage, a Byzantine province until it fell a prey to Islam in 709. The last Vandal king, a romantic character, received rich estates in Galicia, where he was prevented from accepting patrician rank, the highest honor that Byzantium could bestow, only by his refusal to abandon the Arian faith.

From the neighboring Moorish tribes Genseric received his so-called testament or law of succession, whereby the son did not regularly follow the father, the heir to the throne in each case being the eldest descendant in direct line from Genseric himself. The aim, as in the corresponding rule of the Osmanli Turks, was to prevent degeneration of the ruling stock, but among both peoples it proved unsuccessful. (FRANZ GÖRRES.)

BIBLIOGRAPHY: Sources are: Victor of Vita, *Hist. persecutionis Africanæ provinciæ*, ed. M. Petschenig, in *CSCE*, vol. vii., and in *MGH*, *Auct. ant.*, iii (1879), 1–58, Germ. transl. by A. Mally, Vienna, 1884; Procopius, *De bello Vandalico*, in *Opera*, ed. J. Haury, i. 307 sqq., Leipsic, 1905, Germ. transl. by D. Coste, ib. 1885; Prosper Tiron, *Epitoma chronica*, ed. T. Mommsen, in *MGH*, *Auct. ant.*, ix (1892); Victor Tonnennensis, *Chronicon*, ed. T. Mommsen, in *MGH*, *Auct. ant.*, xi (1893). Consult further: F. Papencordt, *Geschichte der vandalischen Herrschaft in Afrika*, Berlin, 1837; F. Dahn, *Die Könige der Germanen*, vol. i., Munich, 1881; idem, *Germanisch-romanische Urgeschichte*, i. 147–222, 2d ed., Berlin, 1899; Stadler von Wolffersgrün, *Die Vandalen*, Bozen, 1883–84; F. Wrede, *Ueber die Sprache der Wandalen*, Strasburg, 1886; W. Pötzsch, *Victor von Vita*, Döbeln, 1887; L. Schmidt, *Aelteste Geschichte der Wandalen*, Leipsic, 1888; idem, *Geschichte der Wandalen*, ib. 1901; A. Ebert, *Geschichte der Literatur des Mittelalters*, i. 455 sqq., 2d ed., Leipsic, 1889; G. Boissier, *Études d'hist. religieuse*, in *Revue des deux mondes*, ix (1890), 145–172; T. Hodgkin, *Italy and her Invaders*, vols. ii.–iii., Oxford, 1892; A. Schwarze, *Entwicklung der afrikanischen Kirche*, pp. 153–183, Göttingen, 1892; F. Görres, in *ZWT*, xxxvi. 1 (1893), 494–511; idem, in *Historisches Jahrbuch*, 1911, ii. 323–332; F. Ferrère, *De Victoris Vitensis libro*, Paris, 1898; F. Martroye, *L'Occident à l'époque byzantine*. *Goths et Vandales*, Paris, 1904.

VANE, SIR HENRY, JR.: Statesman and religious enthusiast; b. at Hadlow (18 m. s.e. of London) 1613; beheaded on Tower Hill, London, June 14, 1662. His father, of the same name, was a privy councilor of Charles I. About the age of fifteen the son was converted to Puritanism, and when, shortly after, he became a gentleman commoner of Magdalen Hall, Oxford, he refused to take the oath of supremacy and allegiance. After leaving the university he traveled on the continent, returning to England in 1632. As the son of a courtier and the possessor of great talents, he was naturally equipped for places of preferment, but his hostility to the doctrines and ceremonies of the Church of England was unconquerable. To enjoy greater freedom of worship he emigrated to New England in 1635, and was enthusiastically received at Boston in consideration of his high birth and the sacrifices he was making for the sake of conscience. He became governor of Massachusetts Bay Colony the following year, but failed of reelection because of the religious disputes in which he became involved. Among other things he lent the protection of his position to Mrs. Anne Hutchinson (see ANTINOMIANISM AND ANTINOMIAN CONTROVERSIES, II., 2) in the controversy she occasioned by her energetic preaching concerning the " covenant of grace " and the " covenant of works." Apart from being an upholder of freedom of religious opinion, he naturally sympathized with the mystical teaching that the Holy Spirit dwells in a justified person and that the revelation of the Spirit in the soul of a believer is su-

perior to the ministry of the Word. Vane's interference in ecclesiastical affairs increased the discord, and the agitation which was fraught with real danger to the infant colony cost him his popularity. In Aug., 1637, he sailed for England to play a considerable part in the events that resulted in the overthrow of the monarchy.

In Jan., 1639, through his father's influence, Vane was made joint-treasurer of the navy with Sir W. Russell. He was also elected a member of parliament and soon forged to the front as a leader of the anti-court party. He procured the condemnation of Strafford and carried up the impeachment of Laud from the commons, and on the breaking out of the Civil War was a zealous supporter of Parliament. He attended the Westminster Assembly of Divines (q.v.) and pleaded passionately for full liberty of conscience for all religions. When the English parliament became apprehensive of the security of its position by reason of the progress of the royal arms, Vane was one of the commissioners it dispatched in 1643 to Edinburgh for a closer union with the Scottish nation; and it was due to his force of persuasion that there was then framed the Solemn League and Covenant (see COVENANTERS, § 4). The covenant made ample provision for the preservation of Presbyterianism in Scotland. As far, however, as the establishment of religion in England and Ireland was concerned, the language of the document through an artifice of Vane's was so worded as to bear an interpretation to accord with the sentiments of the Independents. These were willing at first to take shelter under Presbyterianism, but as the victory of the parliamentary forces became assured, they appeared a distinct party. They held to the immediate operation of the Holy Spirit, rejecting any distinction between the laity and clergy they abolished all ceremonies and denying the right of interposition of the magistrate in religious concerns. Vane vainly attempted to bring about a compromise with the royalists. His opposition to a state church was unrelenting, and by it he lost his influence with the Presbyterians, who wished to have their system of doctrines enforced upon the nation and were able to defeat his attempts at compromise in parliament in 1646. Vane was also distrusted by the Levellers (q.v.) because, although no one strove more zealously to vindicate the privileges of parliament against the encroachments of the crown, he did not consider it essential to freedom to overthrow the monarchy and constitution. He became a member of the council of state in 1649, but refused to take the oath approving of the king's execution, swearing only to be faithful to the new government. He directed the navy and took an active part in colonial and foreign affairs. Cromwell and Vane had been on terms of intimate friendship, but a permanent breach between them was caused when Cromwell forcibly dissolved the Long Parliament in 1653. Vane then withdrew from active participation in public affairs and in seclusion indulged those theological reveries which in their extravagance and pious fanaticism contrast strikingly with his ability in matters of finance and civil polity. His religious writings are free from political allusions and never betray the personality of the author. *The retired Man's Meditations, or the Mystery and Power of Godliness* (1655) voices in its last chapter a belief in the coming of a real theocracy on earth, in which Christ will reign for a thousand years as a temporal sovereign and the saints will have the power of the keys. After this millennium Satan will again be let loose to war against human nature; at the end of the struggle, after the saints have been transported to the heavenly mansions, there will take place the final judgment. In 1656 Vane attacked the Commonwealth in *His Question Propounded and Resolved* as favoring the selfish interests of the army, and in consequence was imprisoned in the Isle of Wight for four months. After Cromwell's death Vane served again in parliament. At the Restoration Vane was excluded from the Act of Indemnity and imprisoned in the Tower. He was brought to trial in 1662 and condemned to death, his undaunted behavior on that occasion being represented to the king as a studied vindication of rebellion. Besides political and religious works other than those mentioned above, Vane also published a number of his speeches. His theory of civil government is set forth in a treatise, *The People's Case Stated* (printed in *Trial of Sir H. Vane*, 1662); and though his doctrine is democratic he does not go as far as writers like Milton, who claim that the best form of government is necessarily a republic. Contrasted with the clearness of his political works is the almost unintelligible character of his religious writings. His followers were called " Seekers " (q.v.) because, besides being averse to forms and fixed opinions, they were waiting for some " new and clearer manifestation."

BIBLIOGRAPHY: The earliest life (of comparatively little worth) was by G. Sikes, London, 1662. Later ones are by C. W. Upham, in J. Sparks, *American Biography*, 1 ser., vol. iv., Boston, 1834; J. Forster, London, 1840; and J. K. Hosmer, Boston, 1888. Consult further: A. à Wood, *Athenæ Oxonienses*, ed. P. Bliss, iii. 578, 4 vols., London, 1813–20; C. Dalton, *Hist. of the Family of Wray*, ii. 93–137, ib. 1881; W. A. Shaw, *Hist. of the English Church . . . 1640–60*, passim, 2 vols., ib. 1900; W. Walker, *Ten New England Leaders*, pp. 77–78, New York, 1901; *DNB*, lviii. 116–129.

VANNUTELLI, văn″nu-tel′lî, SERAFINO: Cardinal; b. at Genazzano (24 m. e.s.e. of Rome), Italy, Nov. 26, 1834. After the completion of his studies in the Collegium Capranica, Rome, he became a beneficiary of St. Peter's and professor of theology in the Vatican Seminary. He was sent to Mexico as auditor of the papal nuncio, and later accompanied the same prelate to South America and to Munich. In 1869 he was consecrated titular archbishop of Nicæa and sent as apostolic delegate to Peru and Ecuador, whence he was recalled, in 1875, to become papal nuncio at Brussels. Five years later he went in a similar capacity to Vienna, and in 1887 was created cardinal priest of Santa Sabina, which was exchanged for San Gerolamo degli Schiavori in 1889. He was appointed secretary of memorials in 1892, and later of briefs and the Index; was then at the head of the Congregation of Bishops and Regulars; and was made, in 1899, grand penitentiary and grand secretary of the Holy Office. In 1893 he was elevated to be cardinal bishop of Frascati, but in 1903, on the death

of Cardinal Parocchi, was translated to the suburbicarian see of Porto and Santa Rufina.

VANNUTELLI, VINCENZO: Cardinal, brother of the preceding; b. at Genazzano (24 m. e.s.e. of Rome), Italy, Dec. 5, 1836. He was educated at the Collegium Capranica and the Gregorian University, Rome, and, after being ordained to the priesthood in 1861, was a professor in the Vatican Seminary. After diplomatic service in Holland and Belgium from 1863 to 1869 he was appointed apostolic prothonotary and under-secretary of state; later (1878) auditor of the Sacra Rota Romana, in 1880 was preconized titular archbishop of Sardes and was sent to Constantinople as apostolic delegate and patriarch-vicar, and in 1883 went to Moscow as envoy extraordinary at the coronation of the czar. After another official visit to Russia, he was appointed nuncio in Lisbon, where he concluded the concordat between the Vatican and Portugal, and also reorganized the Roman Catholic hierarchy in the East. In 1890 he was created cardinal priest of San Silvestro in Capite, and in 1900 was elevated to be cardinal bishop of Palestrina. He was for a long time prefect of the Propaganda, and since 1902 has been prefect of the Congregation of the Council, while he is also archpriest of the Liberian patriarchal church of Santa Maria Maggiore.

VARAGINE, JACOBUS DE. See JACOBUS DE VARAGINE.

VASZARY, va-sā′rî, CLAUDIUS FRANZ: Cardinal; b. at Keszthely (96 m. s. of Pressburg), Hungary, Feb. 12, 1832. He entered the Benedictine order in 1847 at Martinsberg, where he received his education, and in 1855 was ordained to the priesthood; was professor of history at the gymnasium of Gran (1861–69); was rector of the similar institution at Raab (1869–85); became archabbot of Martinsberg (1885), with a seat in the Austrian Upper House; was consecrated prince-archbishop of Gran and primate of Hungary (1891); and was created cardinal-priest of Santi Silvestro e Martino di Monti (1893).

BIBLIOGRAPHY: *Der Papst, die Regierung und die Verwaltung der heiligen Kirche in Rom*, pp. 185, 187–188, Munich, 1904.

VATABLUS, vā′ta-blŭs, FRANCISCUS (FRANÇOIS WATEBLED, GASTEBLED, OUATEBLÉ): French Hebraist and theologian; b. at Gamaches (85 m. n.w. of Paris), Picardy; d. at Paris Mar. 16, 1547. He was for a time pastor at Bramet in Valois, after which Francis I. appointed him professor of Hebrew at the Collège de France, later making him also abbot of Bellozane. He died in the Roman Catholic faith. During his lifetime Vatablus published nothing, his Latin translation of Aristotle's *Meteorologica* appearing at Lyons in 1548 and his version of the *Parva Naturalia* being appended by G. Duval to his edition of Aristotle (Paris, 1619). From the lecture-notes of the numerous scholars of Vatablus, Robert Stephens drew the material for the notes which he added to his edition of the Bible of Paris, 1545, though it would seem that to the annotations of Vatablus he added others from various sources. The notes of Vatablus on the Psalms, incorporated in the *Liber Psalmorum Davidis* printed by Stephens in 1557, were reedited, with the notes of Hugo Grotius, by G. J. L. Vogel in his *Francisci Vatabli annotationes in Psalmos* (Halle, 1767). The Sorbonne sharply assailed the Stephens edition of 1545 as heretical and inclining toward Lutheranism; while the Salamanca theologians, on the contrary, esteemed the work so highly that they issued a revision of it in their Latin Bible of 1584.

H. L. STRACK.

BIBLIOGRAPHY: A. Calmet, *Bibliothèque sacrée*, iv. 1 sqq., Paris, 1730; C. G. Jöcher, *Allgemeines Gelehrten-Lexikon*, iv. 1466, 10 parts, Leipsic, 1750–1819; *Biographie universelle*, lxvii. 569 sqq.; Lichtenberger, *ESR*, xii. 307.

VATICAN.

The name Vatican is applied both to the palace of the pope at Rome, and to the papal administration in its official relations with temporal powers. The term is derived from the situation of the palace on the Vatican Hill (on the right bank of the Tiber), which, even as late as the time of Aurelian, formed no part of the city of Rome. During the classical period it was notoriously insalubrious (Tacitus, *Hist.*, ii. 93), and even its wine was regarded as poisonous. Nevertheless, Caligula commenced the building of a circus there, and Nero

1. Outline History. completed it. Here occurred the martyrdom of many early Christians, and here, according to tradition, St. Peter himself suffered crucifixion; to this is due the selection of the Vatican as the residence of the successors of St. Peter. The earliest traces of the Vatican palace thus far known were comprised in an *episcopia* erected by Symmachus (498–514), and successive pontiffs added to the structures until Nicholas III. (1277–80), who was the founder of the Vatican in its historic form. It had been a residence of the popes since the pontificate of Leo IV. (847–855), who enclosed it with strong walls; and after the exile at Avignon (1308–78), during which the older palace of the Lateran had been burned, the Vatican became the chief papal palace. Pope after pope added to the buildings, or substituted new for old, until the result was marvelous. To Nicholas V. (1447–55) is due the foundation of the famous Vatican Library; Sixtus IV. (1471–84) built the renowned Sistine Chapel, with Michelangelo's frescoes of the Prophets and the Last Judgment; Julius II. (1503–13) commenced the celebrated Vatican Museum; Leo X. (1513–21) employed the services of Raffael, and Paul III. (1534–49) and Julius III. (1550–55) of Michelangelo. The real palace of the popes was built by Sixtus V. (1585–90), though it was not completed until the pontificate of Clement VIII. (1592–1605); and among other noteworthy popes to whom important parts of the present Vatican are due were Urban VIII. (1623–44), Pius VI. (1775–99), and Pius VII. (1800–23). The most ancient portion, however, is not in the Vatican

itself, but in the old crypt of St. Peter's, where are portions of the basilica erected by Constantine the Great, as well as the oldest monument of all, the tomb of St. Peter, constructed by popes Linus and Anacletus (67–86).

The Vatican palace itself is a congeries of buildings measuring, according to the usual estimates, some 1,151 feet long by 767 broad (though these figures are probably under the true dimensions), and covering an area of 13½ acres. The number of apartments is enormous, and must be at least 1,000, though some estimates run as high as 12,500. Within the palace precincts are twenty courtyards, of which the most important are the Cortile di San Damaso, at the main entrance to the

2. Papal and other Official Apartments. Vatican, and the Cortile della Sentinella, architecturally one of the most impressively medieval portions of the entire Vatican. Besides some 200 minor stairways, there are eight grand flights, the most noteworthy being the Scala Pia (forming the main approach to the palace) and the Scala Regia, or state stairway, commenced by Urban VIII. (1623–44) and completed in the pontificate of Alexander VII. (1655–67). The actual apartments of the pope are on the east side of the Cortile de San Damaso, and are only some twenty-two in number. This portion of the palace includes the pope's library, study, bedroom, private reception room, and chapel, the Hall of the Grooms (Sala dei Palafrenieri), the Sala Clementina (where a detachment of the famous Swiss Guards is stationed), the Sala dei Bussolanti (a sort of cloak-room for those admitted to a papal audience), the Anticamera d'Onore (where, on the papal throne, the pontiff receives important bodies of visitors and hears the Lenten and Advent sermons), and the Anticamera Segreta (which only privy councilors and cardinals may enter). On the west of the same court are the Borgia Apartments, forming the official residence of the cardinal secretary of state, and comprising the Sala dei Pontifici, the Sala dei Misteri, the Camera della Vita dei Santi, and the Camera delle Arti e Scienze (where the cardinal secretary holds his audiences). These rooms, which were built at the command of Alexander VI. (1492–1503) and adorned with exquisite frescoes by Pinturicchio (notably the Annunciation, Resurrection, and Disputation of St. Catharine), have beyond them the study of the cardinal secretary (the Sala dello Credo, so called from the frescoes of the twelve apostles, each holding a scroll bearing his portion of the Apostles' Creed), and above them are four rooms frescoed mainly by Raffael, while to their right is the exquisite chapel of Nicholas V., which contains the masterpieces of Fra Angelico, executed by him between 1450 and 1455. Running left from the Borgia Apartments are the Sala del Papagello, where the pope is vested before pontificating at St. Peter's, and the Sala dei Paramenti, the robing-room of the cardinals before great functions; while, still to the left, and separated from the Borgia Apartments by the Cortile del Papagello, are the Sala Ducale and the Sala Regia, from the latter of which access is gained to the famous Sistine Chapel, as well as to the Capella Paolina, with two fine frescoes by Michelangelo—

Crucifixion of St. Peter and Conversion of St. Paul —and serving as the parish church for the 2,000 or more persons lodged in the Vatican. Through the Sala Ducale and Sala Regia the pope and cardinals pass to St. Peter's, a staircase behind the Sistine Chapel leading from the palace to the church, while off the Sala Regia (so named because the pope there received ambassadors from foreign princes) opens a gallery containing the Leonine Chapel, with windows opening on the right into St. Peter's and on the left into the piazza of the same church. Here the newly chosen pontiff gives his first papal blessing not only to the faithful, but to all the world; and in this same chapel (hence called also Capella della Beatificazione) are announced beatifications and canonizations.

To the right of the group of buildings thus far considered, and enclosing the Cortile Belvedere as far as the magnificent Sala Sistina (the great hall of the famous Vatican library), are the gallery of inscriptions on the one hand, and the Sala delle Nozze Aldobrandini (with a fine collection of Roman frescoes), the Hall of Papyri (mostly from Ravenna, from the sixth to the eighth centuries), the terra-cotta room, the Christian Museum (with valuable relics from the catacombs), the Hall of Aristides, the Hall of the Obelisk, and the Hall of the Bonaventura. The Sala Sistina, cutting off the Cortile del Belvedere to the right, and with the Hall of Manuscripts at one end, opposite the entrance, is the great repository of the famous collection of manuscripts; and on the floor beneath, in the Leonine Library, is the papal collection of printed books. This world-renowned library owes its inception mainly to Nicholas V. (1447–55), while Sixtus V. (1585–90) gave it a permanent endowment, after Sixtus VI. (1471–84) had already still further increased its store of treasures. In the course of its history the library, the manuscripts alone of which number over 35,000, has absorbed many other collections, among them the Palatine library (presented by Maximilian of Bavaria in 1621), the Bibliotheca Ottoboniana (added in 1746, and including the collection which had been bequeathed to the Ottoboni collection in 1690 by the convert Queen Christina of Sweden, who thus restored to the Roman Church the treasures taken by her father, Gustavus Adolphus), the library of Cardinal Mai (given by Pius IX. in 1856), and the Barberini library (purchased by Leo XIII. in 1902). Beyond these accessory libraries, which have rooms of their own, is the Museum of Pagan Antiquities (Museo Profano), established by Pius VI. (1775–99) to counterbalance the Christian Museum, already mentioned, which was established by Benedict XIV. (1740–58). The entire opposite wing, separated from the rooms just enumerated by the Giardino della Pigna (the *pigna*, or bronze cone from the atrium of Old St. Peter's, occupying a position at its extreme right), is devoted to the Museo Chiaramonti, which consists of a magnificent collection of sculpture gathered by Pius VII. (1800–23), who also gave the Vatican not only the Gallery of Inscriptions (Galleria Lapidaria) and the Braccio Nuovo, forming the left boundary of the Giardino

3. Libraries and Museums.

XII.—10

della Pigna and containing another rich collection of sculpture, but also the Egyptian Museum, at the extreme right of the same Giardino, above which is the valuable collection of the Etruscan Museum. In this same portion of the Vatican are located, among others, the Gallery of Statues, the Cabinet of Masks, the Hall of Busts, and the Galleries of Tapestries, Candelabras, and Maps.

In addition mention should be made of the archives (now in a room facing the Vatican gardens), of the Vatican press (occupying a position between the Sala Sistina and the Braccio Nuovo), of the workshops of mosaics and tapestries, and of the treasury of the Sistine Chapel, situated just behind that chapel, and filled with interesting personal mementos of pontiffs, the collection still valuable, even though Napoleon, one of the many who have tried to carry off the richest treasures of the popes, robbed it of all its gems and gold. One part properly within the Vatican precincts no longer belongs to the pope—the mint, which was seized by the Italian kingdom. And allusion should also be made to the gardens of the Vatican, only a few acres in area, and somewhat frigidly classic, although the effect is relieved by the fine Casino of Pius IV. (also called the Casino Borromeo), built by Pirro Ligorio in 1560.

4. Minor Portions and Gardens.

Within the precincts of the Vatican is the famous Church of St. Peter (officially known as the Basilica di San Pietro in Vaticano), the largest church in the world. The ground plan is that of a Latin cross, $613\frac{1}{2}$ feet long and $446\frac{1}{2}$ feet wide, with a nave $152\frac{1}{2}$ feet high and $87\frac{1}{2}$ feet wide, while the height to the top of the cross on the dome is 448 feet. The style of architecture is pseudo-Roman, and the effect of the interior is unfortunately marred by strong contrasts of light and shadow, and the true proportions are somewhat dwarfed; but notwithstanding these defects the church remains one of the noblest in Christendom. The approach is through the Piazza di San Pietro, enclosed by neoclassic colonnades, and with a famous Egyptian obelisk in the center; still the best view of the church is not obtained here, but from the Vatican gardens. In its present form the Church of St. Peter owes its origin chiefly to Nicholas V., but the first pope really to start the new structure was Julius II., his architect being Bramante, who was succeeded by Raffael; he was followed, in 1546, by Michelangelo, who was in charge until his death in 1564. The cupola was completed about 1590, and the church was dedicated in 1626, after Carlo Maderna had made the final changes involved in transforming the ground plan from a Greek to a Latin cross soon after 1605, his work being marred by the unfortunate front on the Piazza di San Pietro. The interior of the church contains, besides the high altar, with a fine bronze baldachino ninety-five feet high, a large number of altars, shrines, tombs, statues, fonts, etc.

5. Church of St. Peter.

Beneath the present church are the remains of old St. Peter's—the old and new crypts (Grotte Vecchie and Grotte Nuove). The former contains, as already noted, portions of the basilica erected by

Constantine the Great, with its five aisles, and having a large forecourt and baptistery, the former containing the famous Cantharus, or fountain of lustration, the pine-cone core and peacocks of which are now in the Giardino della Pigna, as noted above, and the basilica, containing the chair of St. Peter, added by Damasus I. in 366. Adrian I. (772-795) richly embellished the basilica, as did Leo IV. (847-855); but the humanistic Nicholas V. and Julius II. deemed the old basilica's usefulness outworn, and through the influence of the Florentine architect Alberti and the active plans of Bramante the present church was begun. Among the most sacred relics of St. Peter's are the Volto Santo (the napkin with which Christ wiped his face on the way to Calvary); the lance of St. Longinus, with which his side was pierced; a piece of the True Cross; the head of St. Andrew; and the great bronze doors of the main entrance, which come from the old basilica. Noteworthy, too, are the Colonna Santa (said to be the very column of the temple of Jerusalem against which Christ leaned while disputing with the doctors; in the Capella della Pietá), the chair of St. Peter and the tomb of Innocent VIII., and the tombs of Sixtus IV., Paul II., and Matilda of Tuscany (in the Chapel of the Holy Sacrament, where the body of a dead pope lies in state until burial), and the tomb of Gregory the Great (in the Capella Clementina). It is, however, in the Grotte Vecchie that the most tombs are to be found: the Holy Roman Emperor Otto II., Christina of Sweden (the convert daughter of Gustavus Adolphus, who gave her throne for her faith), the English pretenders James III., Charles III., and Henry IX. (Cardinal York), and the popes Gregory V. (996-999), Adrian IV. (1154-59; the one English pontiff), Boniface VIII. (1294-1303), and the great builders of the present Vatican—Nicholas V. (1447-55) and Paul II. (1464-71). In the Grotte Nuove, which are far later than the Grotte Vecchie, and which, indeed, were constructed to support the dome of the present church, are to be found not only the chapels of S. Maria Prægnantium and Santa Maria della Bocciata, as well as the Shrine of the Holy Lance, the tomb of Junius Bassus, and the frescoes of the old basilica and those of Mina da Fiesole for the mausoleum of Paul II., but the crowning gem of all—the very tomb of St. Peter. This lies almost below the high altar, and, though now concealed from view, was seen by Clement VIII. in 1602 or 1603. He was, however, unable to have it permanently revealed, owing to the Roman belief that he who touched this sacred tomb would be struck dead; but, with singular appropriateness, Clement himself now lies buried in the chapel of the tomb.

Outside the Vatican gates a few places are still reckoned in the papal domains, such as the Palace of the Holy Office, the Armory, Castello Gandolfo, a few palaces and churches in Rome, and a villa in the Alban Hills. But to all intents and purposes, the pope is a prisoner in the Vatican, for though he would unquestionably be personally safe, should he go without its walls, the construction which would be placed upon such an act, in view of the secular power which in 1870 seized his domains, is thought incompatible with the position of the Roman Church. Though the king of Italy is de facto ruler of Italy, the pope regards himself (and is regarded by the faithful) as the de jure potentate. There are, therefore, in Rome two courts, the Quirinal, or royal, and the Vatican, or papal. Those countries which maintain an official connection between the State and the Roman Church accordingly accredit ambassadors to the Vatican as well as to the Quirinal; and delicate questions have arisen in connection with the visits of foreign potentates to Rome in view of the presence of two ruling powers in the same capital; while still more distressing contretemps have come about through the ignorance of those with a quasi-official position regarding the true status of the pope as the head of Christendom and as a temporal sovereign.

The Vatican naturally possesses its own police and military. The police force consists of about 120 carabinieri (the force being collectively known as the Gendarmeria Pontificia); and the military of the Palatine, Swiss, and Noble Guards. The Palatines are practically a militia, recruited from the bourgeoisie and tradesmen, founded by Pius IX., and numbering some 400. Better known are the Swiss and Noble Guards. The Swiss Guards are about 120 in number and form the real military force of the Vatican, mounting guard at the great bronze doors of St. Peter's, in the Cortile della Sentinella, and in the antechamber of the pope's private apartments. They were first organized some four centuries ago. The Noble Guards, formed by Pius VII., are recruited from the Roman nobility that remained faithful to the pope after the erection of the temporal kingdom of Italy, and now consist of fifteen officers and forty-eight privates. Originally they were the pope's bodyguard, attending him in his carriage, accompanying him on his journeys, and being present at functions of state.

For the governmental side of the Vatican see CURIA, and for the relations between the Vatican and the Quirinal, see ITALY, I., § 2.

6. The Crypt of St. Peter's.

7. Vatican and Quirinal.

8. The Vatican Guards.

BIBLIOGRAPHY: D. Sladen, The Secrets of the Vatican, new ed., Philadelphia, 1911; L. De Sanctis, Rome Christian and Papal, New York, 1856; P. M. Letarouilly, Le Vatican et la basilique de Saint-Pierre de Rome, 2 vols., Paris, 1882; E. Muentz and A. L. Frothingham, Il Tesoro della Basilica di S. Pietro in Vaticano, Rome, 1883; F. Wey, Rome, its Monuments, Arts, and Antiquities, London, 1887; H. Lemaire, Basilique de Saint-Pierre, Paris, 1888; P. Batiffol, La Vaticane, de Paul III. à Paul V., Paris, 1890; R. Lanciani, Pagan and Christian Rome, Boston, 1892; F. Gregorovius, Hist. of the City of Rome, London, 1894 sqq.; G. Goyau, A. Pérate, and P. Fabre, Le Vatican, Paris, 1895, new ed., 2 vols., ib. 1901; A. S. Barnes, St. Peter in Rome; and his Tomb on the Vatican Hill, London, 1900; D. A. Mortier, Hist. de la basilique vaticane, Tours, 1900; C. E. Clement, The Eternal City, 2 vols., London, 1901; E. M. Philipps, The Frescoes in the Sixtine Chapel, London, 1901; E. Steinmann, Die sixtinische Kapelle, 2 vols., Munich, 1901-05; P. J. Chandlery, Pilgrim Walks in Rome, New York, 1903; Mary K. Potter, The Art of the Vatican, London, 1903; Der Papst, die Regierung und die Verwaltung der heiligen Kirche in Rom, Munich, 1904; J. P. Kirsch and V. Luksch, Illustrierte Geschichte der katholischen Kirche, pp. 482 sqq., Munich, 1905; A. J. C. Hare, Walks in Rome, new ed., London, 1905; J. A. F. Orbaan, Sixtine Rome, London and New York, 1911; KL, xii. 600-607.

VATICAN COUNCIL.

I. Antecedent History: The first adducible proof that Pius IX. intended to call an ecumenical council appeared Dec. 6, 1864, at a session of the cardinals of the Congregation of Rites. He then
1. Prelimi- directed them, and soon extended this
nary Can- order to include all the cardinals resi-
vass and dent in Rome, to present their views
Committees. on that project, in the form of written opinions; and early in Mar., 1865, a committee of cardinals was appointed to examine these opinions. The majority of the cardinals agreed that a council was necessary, though there was not entire concord as to the matters to be treated. After that, the convening of a council was no longer an open question. So during April and May, and by advice of the college of cardinals, the prefect of the Propaganda, Cardinal Caterini, addressed to thirty-six bishops of various nations a formal request *sub arctissima secreti lege*, to set forth in explicit terms the matters which seemed to them most worthy of consideration before the council, with regard to their diocesan interests. Pius IX. had himself outlined the list of these confidential advisers; he also made the first public announcement of the prospective council, on June 26, 1867, in his address to such princes of the church as had assembled in Rome for the jubilee festival. The preparation of the council devolved upon an extraordinary congregation of the college of cardinals, briefly known as the " Central Committee." Its members included Cardinals Patrizi, Reisach, Panebianco, Bizarro, Caterini, and, later, Barnabo, Bilio, Capalli, de Luca. Their preliminary labors in 1865 were occupied with enlisting distinguished theologians and canonists as expert advisers of the council. These invitations were guided by the propositions advanced by the nuncios and by the various bishops. Only the ultramontane trend received such marked preference herein, at the outset, that when the resultant selections became known, they were sharply contested. Besides the central committee there were accessory committees appointed: (1) on dogmatics, (2) on church discipline, (3) on religious orders, (4) on oriental churches and missions, (5) on ecclesiastical polity, and (6) on ceremonies. The labors of these committees were subject to the central committee's revision. There were ninety-six advisers actively engaged. The question as to who should be invited to the council at large occasioned prolonged inquiries and incidental scruples. Objection was raised against inviting the Roman Catholic princes. The bull *Æterni patris*, subscribed by Pius IX. and the cardinals present in Rome, was

published on June 29, 1868; and convened the council to meet at Rome on Dec. 8, 1869. As the council was to be ecumenical, the bishops of the churches of oriental rites were also invited; and in a subsequent bull, all Protestants and others outside the Roman Catholic pale were summoned, on occasion of the council, to rejoin the Roman Catholic Church. Howbeit, the orientals declined the summons, without exception, and on the Protestant side the invitation was disregarded. The papal invitation found some accordant response within the Anglican church; yet here, too, there was counterbalancing opposition. Thus the Curia's hope of inducing the schismatic orient and the world of Protestant heresy to some recognition of the Curia's contemplated measures came to naught.

The reception accorded to the impending council in Roman Catholic circles was not everywhere alike and underwent great fluctuations. Little could be
deduced from the terms of convocation
2. Recep- respecting the problems to be solved,
tion of because the sweeping phraseology em-
Proposal; braced the entire sphere of Christen-
Topics dom's interests. Yet this very lati-
Suggested. tude allowed the Curia complete
freedom of action. Moreover, because no ecumenical council had assembled in the past three centuries, the present design took on the mists and halo of the extraordinary. Features of this kind at once insured popular favor for the plan of a council, and evoked approval on every side. Nevertheless, an increasingly powerful reaction set in among liberal Roman Catholics, when once the illusions began to dissolve which at first had enshrouded the motives for convening the council. What especially illumined the horizon in advance, was a now famous article in the *Civiltà Cattolica*, a review conducted by Jesuits. This article appeared in the form of correspondence by way of France, under date of Feb. 6, 1869, and purported to reflect the views of many Roman Catholics in France that the council would be brief, seeing that its majority stood unanimous. There were named as topics of procedure: confirmation of the Syllabus (q.v.), promulgation of the infallibility of the pope, and dogmatization of the doctrine as to the bodily assumption of Mary. The impression produced by this article was enhanced by the fact that Archbishop Dechamps of Mechlin was warmly praised in a papal brief, dated June 26, 1869, for his pamphlet on *L'Infaillibilité et le concile général* (Malines, 1869), wherein he requested that doctrine's formal definition. Thenceforth the conviction gained wider currency

that in quarters of chief control there was a determined purpose to have proclaimed the doctrine of papal infallibility. No success attended the attempts at smoothing the agitation over; but rather an opposition took shape whose extent and vigor had been hardly anticipated. A mighty intellectual and social agitation was then pervading Roman Catholic Europe; and for many months the religious question occupied the central position of public interests.

In Germany, the commotion started when Döllinger's articles on the council and the *Civiltà* appeared (in *Augsburger allgemeine Zeitung*, Mar. 10–15, 1869), which kindled men's minds in **3. Opinions** every quarter. Associations were then **in Religious** formed for repelling Ultramontanist **Quarters.** efforts. Rhenish laymen assembled at Coblenz, and forwarded an address to the bishop of Treves, wherein exception was taken to the views espoused in the article of the *Civiltà*, and the demand was put forth that the impending council leave no doubt on the point that the church had parted company with the wish of reinstating the theocratic civil forms of the Middle Ages; that the training of the clergy should not run counter to the whole trend of the times; that a more comprehensive, vital, and systematic plan of associating the laity in Christian and social affairs be inaugurated in the parish congregations; and, lastly, that the *Index librorum prohibitorum* should be repealed. On the other hand, the general convention of Roman Catholic associations in Germany adopted a resolution at Düsseldorf, Sept. 8, in which the utmost confidence was expressed toward the council. When the German episcopate met in council at Fulda, on Sept. 1, 1869, this body issued a common pastoral letter, which was intended to exercise a quieting effect: the council, so it ran, could announce no new doctrine not contained in Holy Scripture and apostolic tradition; whereas the suspicion that freedom of deliberation might be prejudiced at the session was as unfounded as the supposition that the pope was the instrument of a faction or party was insulting. But besides this letter, which was intended for full publicity, quite another message, couched in a different tone, was addressed to the pope by resolution of the same body. For the news that the impending council was to be approached from various quarters in behalf of a proposition covering the pope's infallibility was shown to have evoked great excitement, and this, too, among men of proved loyalty to the Church. It was urged, moreover, that the like apprehensions were shared by the writers themselves. Which document, subscribed by fourteen bishops (only a few held aloof), met with a very unfavorable reception at the hands of Pius IX. In France there broke forth a vehement conflict. The work of Bishop Maret, dean of the Roman Catholic faculty of Paris, against infallibility (*Du concile général et de la paix religieuse*, 2 vols., Paris, 1869), and the writings of Bishop Dupanloup of Orléans, leavened by the same spirit, attracted manifold replies, including those from Archbishop Manning of Westminster and Archbishop Dechamps of Mechlin. Count Montalembert arrayed himself with the opposers. In Austria-

Hungary, as contrasted with Germany, and not without significance touching the mental status of the clergy in those countries, there prevailed a general unconcern. In Italy, Count Ricciardi exerted himself toward opposing the Vatican Council with an "ecumenical council of freethinkers," which actually convened at Naples, in Dec., 1869, but was a feeble affair. Hence, even before the council assembled, the most momentous of the topics afterward presented for its definitive resolutions was already the theme of radical controversy; while the prospects for a smooth acceptance of the projected dogma kept shrinking month by month.

The impending council did not fail to occupy the attention of civil governments in Europe. On Apr. 9, 1869, the Bavarian cabinet president, Prince Chlodwig of Hohenlohe-Schillingsfürst, addressed to Bavaria's diplomatic representatives a circular dispatch, drafted by Döllinger, requesting them to **4. Attitude** inform themselves with reference to **of the** the intentions of the governments **European** whereto they were accredited, as touch **States.** ing the council. And they were to put the question, whether it were not expedient to adopt, in advance, a common or identical course of procedure whereby the holy see could be advised of their contemplated bearing in relation to the ecumenical council? However, Hohenlohe's suggestion found but little response; and the answers, at best, were either negative or evasive. The ill-success of his proposal was attributed by Hohenlohe himself, in the main, to the Austrian government and its repellent attitude, since Austria both rejected his proposals and denied the imminence of any danger, save that emotional tension was to be feared in increasing degree, should there be an appearance of restricting the freedom of the Roman Catholic Church. Prussia deemed preventive measures not in season, and simply declared herself to be ready to safeguard the rights of the State, in the event of contingent resolutions that should encroach upon the civil prerogative or jurisdiction. The position of France in relation to the Curia, since France was the power that was able to determine the further continuance of the States of the Church, was different from that of other governments. But while the attitude of France was an uncertain factor under the influence of the French negotiations with Austria and Italy, still France decided in favor of prolonging the occupation; and even declared, in a note of instruction to the French envoy Banneville at Rome, dated Sept. 19, 1869, for the prospective definition of the doctrine involved when the pope spoke *ex cathedra*, with express recommendation, however, that the utmost wisdom be applied in drafting the terms thereof. Opposition to the Curia's policy was not to have been expected from England, Spain, and Portugal. So the various governments forbore to exert any pressure upon Rome in the direction advised by Hohenlohe; and except Russia, which forbade Russian prelates the journey to Rome, they laid no obstacles in the way of attending the council.

II. Proceedings of the Council. —1. From the Opening until Mar. 6, 1870: The Curia had observed silence in regard to the council's tasks. That the promulgation of infallibility had been long in preparation in that quarter and that the attainment of this goal was the chief object of the entire council, have been demonstrated by Friedrich (see bibliography). This is a point especially to be noted, since Granderath, in his opposing work, affirms the contrary with great certitude, and since a correct understanding of the course of the convention depends on the detail that the Vatican Council be conceived as the product of ultramontanist growth in the nineteenth century. From the beginning of the council, the question of infallibility stood central in point of general interest, and acted in a segregative way, as touching party tactics. That the majority was resolved to vote in the affirmative is above reasonable doubt; although there was some uncertainty as to whether the opposition would prove aggressive, and to what extent, if considerable. In fact, it was stronger than had been expected, and prevented the council sessions from running that expeditious course which had been so confidently predicted by the *Civiltà's* article.

The prelates who had already reached Rome were convened in a preliminary synodical assembly in the Sistine Chapel, Dec. 2, 1869. Pius IX. then delivered an address, the names of the officers were announced, and these officers were
1. Rules of Procedure. sworn in. In the next place, copies of the order of business were distributed, with the heading *Multiplices inter,* dated Nov. 27, 1869. As presidents were named Cardinals de Reisach, de Lucca, Bizarri, Bilio, and Capalli. By this order of business, which he issued without action by the council in the premises, Pius IX. insured for himself a determining influence over the convention. The most important rulings were as follows: In § 2 the pope claimed it as his exclusive right to define the objects of the council's proceedings. The synodical delegates are permitted, of course, to make motions, yet with extreme limitation, since the pope was to decide whether they should be laid before the council; § 3 obligates the members of the council to silence in regard to the proceedings; §§ 7 and 8 touched upon the synodical delegates' assemblings, the congregations general, and the public sessions. In the congregations general, whose directors were named by the pope, the drafts of decrees laid before the council were to be debated and voted upon, but only in a provisory way. At the public sessions, deliberations were no longer in order, but only the final votes. The result of these was certified by the pope, in personal attendance, and was to be proclaimed as his decision, " the holy council approving." The votes were to be phrased *placet* or *non placet.* In the event of no working agreement, the contested proviso, together with the proffered objections thereto, were to be referred to standing committees, and these were to be elected by the council on written ballot. § 9 forbade the attending ecclesiastics to quit the council before its termination, except by permission. For council chamber, and this alike for the congregations general and the public sessions, they made use of the right transept of St. Peter's Church, this being shut off by a lofty wooden partition. From

the very first day, however, this area proved unfit on account of its defective acoustics.

The first public session took place Wednesday Dec. 8, 1869, with the opening on a festival. Undue
2. First and Second Sessions. precipitation set the second public session for Thursday Jan. 6, 1870. To what extent the question of infallibility dominated the council quite from the start appeared from the election of the various committees. The chief promoters of the quorum actively in favor of the definition at issue met in private conferences, and then agreed on the plan that no one be elected of whom it were known that he opposed the definition of papal infallibility. In the next place, lists of the proposed candidates were prepared and lithographed. And all these propositions found acceptance with the council. The ratified order of business provoked some contradiction directly after the work of the council began; but all motions presented before the pope in favor of changing that fixed routine were set aside. The council's debates began only with the fourth congregation general, Dec. 28, and turned on the " schedule of faith." The discussion assumed an unexpectedly prolonged course, for the topic was criticized in many quarters. The premature appointment of the second public session for Jan. 6 occasioned the leaders of the ouncil no small embarrassment. In fact, such a thing as passing upon the " schedule " in the way of a conciliar decree was then and there impossible. So, too, the hope had to be abandoned of seeing the question of infallibility accepted by the council at this session, as though by acclamation and independent of discussion, since Archbishop Darboy of Paris notified Cardinal de Luca, Dec. 27, that in the event of such abruptness, 100 bishops would straightway leave Rome. Accordingly, the second public session, Jan. 6, 1870, had to be occupied by taking the synodical delegates' formal deposition in support of the Council of Trent. The insignificance of this second session is to be explained by the fact that it nowise marks a critical juncture in the council's history. The proceedings extended till Jan. 10. The project under consideration appears to have found unqualified approval with not one of the thirty-five speakers; but rather there prevailed great dissension respecting the degree of requisite amendment in the case. The result of the proceedings in six congregations general was, on Jan. 10, to refer the issue, along with its proffered objections, to the deputation on faith.

In the following weeks (till Feb. 22) the council deliberated in nineteen congregations general (numbered 11–29) concerning schedules of discipline and questions of church life. And though these proceedings form simply an episode in the
3. Prolonged and Resultless Debates. history of the council and led to no practical end, still they afford some insight into the bishops' frames of mind. It appears that many of the synodical delegates entertained a broad conception of the necessity of reforms; while critical utterances were heard to this intent, and in no subdued tone, such as were hardly anticipated by the Curia. During the discussion of the " schedule concerning bish-

ops, synods, and vicars general," the objection was raised that the proposition touched only upon the duties of bishops, but not on the necessary reform of the college of cardinals and the Curia. The demand was also made, that the papal office be made accessible to others than Italians. In like manner, it was proposed to internationalize the Roman congregations and to decentralize the ecclesiastical administration. There was, furthermore, criticism of the manner of treating impediments to marriage, dispensations, and taxes. When the matter of provincial synods came up, some remarkable conditions were debated before the Curia. There was even a demand expressed in the direction of national synods, and of regularly recurrent ecumenical councils. After these " schedules " had been discussed by thirty-seven speakers, they were referred, at the sixteenth congregation general, Jan. 25, to the deputation on discipline for revision. From Jan. 25 to Feb. 8, thirty-eight speakers discussed the " schedule concerning the life and character of the clergy," including such details as the spiritual exercises, the common life of the priests, celibacy, defects in the Breviary, and the propriety of clerical beards. The proposition was referred to the deputation on discipline. From Feb. 10 to 22 (general congregations 24–29), the council was occupied with the schedule " concerning a small catechism," the pope having expressed his intention of having a small catechism prepared, in order to abate the diversity of instruction regarding the elements of the faith. This catechism was then to be translated into the various national tongues, while the bishops retained the liberty of dispensing catechetical instruction independently thereof. However, while the idea of unifying such instruction had strong indorsement, it also encountered vehement opposition, quite variously prompted. This schedule was also referred to the deputation on discipline.

A noteworthy landmark in the history of the council is supplied by the publication, during the twenty-ninth congregation general, on Feb. 22, of the papal decree dated Feb. 20; **4. New Rules of Procedure.** which must be designated a new order of business. The most important of its rulings, which comprised fourteen heads, were the following. Strictures on a " schedule " shall henceforth no longer be made orally, but in writing; and this, too, within a period of time to be determined by the presidents when the given schedule is proposed (§ 1). Such strictures are to be accompanied with suggested amendments (§ 3), and shall be tendered before the secretary of the council, who refers them to the competent deputations (§ 4). Coupled with a summary report on the previously tendered strictures, the schedule, as amended by the committee or deputation in charge, goes to the council for oral discussion (§ 5). Speakers digressing from the question in debate shall be called to order by the presidents (§ 10). In case the subject of debate be exhausted, then the presidents, on written motion of ten synodical delegates, may put the question before the congregation general, as to whether the discussion shall still be protracted; and the majority decides (§ 11). Majority vote also decides the matter of adopting a proposition (§ 13).

The voting is done orally, by *placet* or *non placet*, though a conditional *placet* is also admissible, the given condition being in writing (§ 14). What prompted this change in the order of business was the tedious routine of the council's proceedings, which in the course of three months had brought not a single schedule to formal conclusion. That this new order of business was adapted to expedite the transaction of business proper is evident; yet the advance was only contingent in that the council might have to pay for the abridgment of its proceedings by disadvantages of another kind. Protests were lodged against the altered order of business under the leadership of Archbishop Darboy of Paris, by fifty bishops on Mar. 1, by twenty-two other bishops, led by Cardinal Schwarzenberg, on Mar. 4, and by fourteen bishops, predominantly German, on Mar. 2. However, these protests accomplished nothing, not even a written acknowledgment. Yet the object of altering the order of business was not simply the better dispatch of the council's labors; it especially hinged on the point of carrying the definition of infallibility through the channels of parliamentary resolution, after it was seen that the measure could not be adopted by acclamation.

A fortnight after the council opened, there were conferences in progress on the part of a small coterie of those favoring the definition, touching their manner of procedure. Petitions for mo- **5. Aline- ment on Infallibility.** tion of the definition were subscribed by about 480 bishops. Not until the news of these arrangements transpired did the opponents of definition actively unite. Their deliberations began Jan. 8, and in five counter-addresses, which were subscribed by 136 bishops, the pope was besought to make no proposition to the council on the subject of infallibility. But the committee on motions resolved to commend to the pope the acceptance of definition. Through these memorials for and against the question of definition, the presence of two parties at the council had become altogether patent. What occasioned great surprise was the relative status of the two alinements, broadly surveyed. The process of " ultramontanizing " the Roman Catholic Church had advanced quite too far, and the Ultramontane trend of the council was much too pronounced for any doubt as to the issue of a dogmatic decision on the subject of infallibility. The sensation was the strength of the minority, the impressive gravity of whose opposition stood all the more enhanced by the dignity of not a few personalities on the minority side, as by the partizan grouping along lines of nationality. Among the German bishops there were thirteen opposers of the definition, whereas only four of the German bishops advocated the definition; among the Austro-Hungarian bishops the majority were on the opposing side; in the case of the French bishops, one-third of them sided with the opposition. Several of the bishops from the United States opposed it. Among those members who disclosed special zeal in favoring infallibility, Archbishop Manning of Westminster, and Bishop Senestréy of Regensburg stood forth with prominence. Their strength was in the firm assertion of the necessity of defining the given doctrine; while the strength of the minority was their theological erudition and intelligence. That was no accident which arrayed the Spanish bishops, without exception, on the side of the majority, and three-fourths of the German episcopate on the minority side; this relative attitude was conditioned by the level of the theological training of the clergy in both countries.

It was a serious obstacle to the minority, that the pope took aggressive and open stand against that minority's formulated position. How-**6. Minority's Difficulties; Controversies Aroused.** beit, the decision of the contest depended upon the question whether or not the minority possessed the inherent strength and sufficient confidence in its cause to assert and carry its will. It was precisely this internal compactness which the minority lacked. All that held their imposing array together was the sheer denial of the question of defining the infallibility of the pope on grounds of expediency, not the disavowal of the doctrine itself, though many of the minority had espoused this extraneous position. Accordingly, the minority's platform was one of negation simply. But the sphere of its action was thereby seriously restricted, and it lacked the momentum that produces positive results. It could collectively utilize merely a sectional extract of all that cogent material which scientific scholarship was elaborating in support of the conflict against the doctrine itself. The opposition must needs collapse forthwith when situations occurred wherein considerations of expediency and questions of tact and fitness lost their value, or even contradicted its very existence. Lastly, the minority was handicapped by the lack of a commanding leader.

The drafting and circulation of the memorials with reference to the matter of infallibility was accompanied by extensive discussions in a periodical way, proceeding from members of both parties at the council. Much attention was aroused in France by the controversy on the Honorius question (see HONORIUS I.) between Auguste Joseph Alphonse Gratry, French acamedician and sometime oratorian, and Archbishop Dechamps, and by the pamphlet *Ce qui se passe au concile*, against which the council deemed it necessary to protest, the more because the article showed expert knowledge of the situation. Still stronger was the agitation in Germany, where the scientific training of the clergy was too advanced for a surrender to the new dogma without resistance. On Jan. 19 Döllinger published his signed article on infallibility in the *Augsburger allgemeine Zeitung*, and this evoked wide comment.

On Jan. 21 there had been distributed among the synodical members the schedule entitled *Schema constitutionis dogmaticæ de ecclesia Christi*. This **7. Church and State; Infallibility.** stated, that the Church is the mystical body of Christ (chap. 1); that in this alone can the Christian religion be duly practised (chap. 2); that the Church is the one perfect society (chap. 3); that corporate bodies detached from the Church can not be designated as part or parcel of the Church (chap. 5);

that only through the Church, and consequently in the Church, can salvation be obtained (chaps. 6, 7); that the Church is imperishable and indefectible (chaps. 9, 10); that the Church possesses a peculiar power and authority (*potestas*, chap. 10); that in this body Christ has instituted the primacy of the bishop of Rome (chap. 11), which involves the possession of temporal sovereignty (chap. 12); in case of disharmony between Church and State, the State is to blame (chap. 13). The civil rulers, too, are bound to the law of God, and the decision as to how this is to be administered appertains to the supreme teaching function of the Church (chap. 14). The closing chapter claims for the Church the province of instructing the young, freedom in the sphere of training the clergy, and exemption of the clergy from military service, unrestricted franchise for the religious orders, etc. Under the head of canons may be read (No. XX.): " If any one says that the supreme rule of conscience in respect to public and social affairs is vested in the law of the body politic, or in the public opinion of men, or that the judgments of the Church do not reach over the said affairs (by which judgments the Church pronounces concerning what is lawful, or illicit and unlawful), or that something is lawful to be done by force of the civil justice which is unlawful by the divine justice or law of the Church, let him be anathema." When, in spite of the injunction to secrecy, this proviso came to be known by the press of all Europe, the civil governments were admonished to be vigilant, and were urged to defend the civil organism, now menaced by the doctrines of a vanished era. On Feb. 10, the Austrian Count Beust notified the Austrian ambassador to advise the cardinal secretary that the publication of any such ruling, prejudicial to due respect for the law of the land, was forbidden in Austria and would be visited with legal penalties. In a dispatch of Feb. 20, communicated to the other powers, Count Daru, French minister of foreign affairs, repelled the schedule's express encroachments upon the civil jurisdiction, and demanded that before the council proceeded to draft resolutions upon questions relating to civil statecraft, the holy see should give the French government opportunity to convey to the council the French conception herein. Antonelli, however, answered coldly, and nothing was ultimately achieved by these protests, since more active measures were not initiated. The change in the French ministry on Apr. 18, by which Ollivier became minister of foreign affairs, obviated all danger of direct coercion upon the council from a French quarter. And the same political considerations which decided Napoleon III. in favor of great reserve, were of controlling weight with Bismarck, while England also maintained her policy of reserve and self-restraint. In the council's proceedings, the grand stroke fell on Mar. 6, when a supplementary article to chap. 11 of the schedule *De ecclesia* was addressed to the members of the council. This appendix bore the heading, *Romanum pontificem in rebus fidei et morum definiendis errare non posse*, " The Roman pontiff can not err in defining matters of faith and morals." The time of the Curia's evasive policy was past, and the council faced a clear situation.

2. Third Session, Sunday Apr. 24, 1870: Before the congregations general had resumed their sessions, attempts were made by the majority to accelerate the opening of the proceedings. The minority demanded that this difficult matter be not presented under the order of the day until it was carefully examined by the members of the council. The pope himself was approached, first in an audience, next in a memorial dated Apr. 22, with the outcome that the desired proceedings were not further postponed.

The congregations general from Mar. 18 to Apr. 19 were occupied with deliberations over the revised schedule *De doctrina catholica.* Within the main committee on this business, a subcommittee of three members had been appointed, who, in turn, delegated the substance of their labor to Bishop Martin of Paderborn, and he utilized the aid and support of Professor Kleutgen. The entire deputation's transactions eventually reachéd the result that only the first part of the schedule, that under the head *De fide catholica,* was referred to the congregation general; whereas the second part of the schedule did not come up for action at all. In the general debate beginning on Mar. 18, and inaugurated by the report of Archbishop Simon of Gran, the projected revision met both approval and censure. Among the speeches delivered in course of the special debate, the one by Bishop Strossmayer, on Mar. 22, created a tempest. The designation of Protestantism as a " pest," in the discussion then forward, is believed to have provoked a very vigorous retort by way of Berlin. That strong influences were brought to bear, indeed, against such definition and sentence of Protestantism is evident from the circumstance that the offending passage was altered by the deputation on faith, so as to modify the sense advocated by Strossmayer. So the revised text no longer derived naturalism from Protestantism, etc.; while the term *pestis* was replaced by *impietas.* After these alterations, the preliminary part of the schedule gained formal adoption. At the forty-fifth congregation general, on Apr. 12, the entire schedule came up for action, and was adopted by a vote of 575, while eighty-three voted *placet juxta modum;* not until Apr. 23 did the minority decide, and this chiefly owing to the efforts of Cardinals Rauscher and Schwarzenberg, in favor of voting *placet.* At the public third session, which occurred on Apr. 24, with an attendance of 667 ecclesiastics, the *Constitutio de fide catholica* was unanimously adopted; the ratification of the same was at once " confirmed " by the pope.

3. Fourth Session, Monday July 18, 1870: Worthy of note here are the attempts of some bishops of the minority to enlighten, along literary lines, their fellow synodical delegates in regard to the momentous difficulties opposing their definition. But owing to censorship of the press, these writers were obliged to produce their articles away from Rome. Cardinal Rauscher thus wrote *Observationes quædam de infallibilitatis ecclesiæ subjecto;* from Bishop Hefele there appeared *Causa Honorii papæ;* Cardinal Schwarzenberg prompted the tract composed by his counselor (Prof. S. Mayer, of Prague): *De summi pontificis infallibilitate;* while Bishop

Ketteler distributed his *Quæstio,* which on arriving in Rome was seized by the post-office, and liberated only after vigorous effort. The impression produced by these writings was not inconsiderable in its way; although it had no decisive effect upon the council.

So far back as at the congregation general of Apr. 29, the proposal of a " schedule dealing with the bishop of Rome " was formally announced. Among **1. The Program.** the majority this step was hailed with joy, though seventy-one members lodged vigorous but vain protest on the ground that the doctrine of infallibility was treated irrespective of prior determination of the doctrine of the church on that subject. The statements which the members were to tender by Mar. 25 concerning the schedule *De ecclesia* had already largely been turned in; and on Apr. 27 proceedings were begun in regard to the draft of the new schedule, which proceedings were completed on May 8. The new schedule, together with the report of the deputation on faith, was referred to the synodical delegates on May 9. The title of this ran: *Constitutio dogmatica prima de ecclesia Christi;* and the document comprised four chapters, besides introduction: (1) " On the institution in the blessed Peter of the apostolic primacy "; (2) " On the perpetuity of Peter's primacy in the bishops of Rome "; (3) " On the force and reason of the Roman bishop's primacy "; (4) " On the Roman bishop's infallibility." There were three collateral canons. This new schedule was based on chap. 11 of the former *schema de ecclesia Christi,* and the supplementary chapter of Mar. 6.

On May 13, the general debate began at the fiftieth congregation general, being inaugurated by the report of Bishop Pius of Poitiers. This debate **2. Debate on Infalli-bility.** occupied fourteen congregations general, and occasioned sixty-four speeches. On general theoretical grounds in favor of formulating a dogma, it is held not only to be necessary that such doctrine be contained in the divine revelation, but that the weal of the Church requires its definition; accordingly the question of opportuneness or seasonable expediency persistently came forward in the debate. Bishops on the minority side denied the expediency outright, while the majority attempted to demonstrate the necessity of the dogma, and, above all, to justify the same by reference to conditions at the time. That whole countries yearned for the institution of the definition was asserted widely, and its expediency was postulated largely on the defection from the non-Catholic churches of such men as Cardinal Manning in England, Archbishop Schæpann of Utrecht, Holland, Archbishop Maddalena of Corfu, of the schismatic Greeks. But neither side could work conviction on the opposing side; the debate might have lasted months longer without effect. So, on June 3, a motion was adopted for closing the debate, though forty enrolled speakers were thus deprived of the floor, a fact which evoked a futile protest presented by eighty-one synodical delegates. The special debate, beginning on June 6, turned on the introduction, while discussion over the first and second chapters, ut sup., was soon dispatched, and these portions were adopted with but slight alterations. Greater difficulties came to light over the third chapter, wherein the nature and the meaning of the primacy were defined. In this case the statement that the pope enjoys " the full power of feeding, ruling, and governing the universal Church " provoked the demand for some supplementary statement as to limitations. There were also differences of opinion regarding the propositions embraced in the measure projected declaring the pope to be the supreme judge in the sense that an appeal to an ecumenical council from his ultimatum was thereby precluded; because the recognition of this clause involved a direct rider to the issue of infallibility. Finally, some scruples were aroused on the point that the pope's power of jurisdiction was designated as *episcopalis, ordinaria et immediata*. Subsequently, when the deputation on faith turned in its report, on July 5, over the proffered forms of amendment, still further sharp disputes occurred over the third canon, which had been modified and revised in a manner not provided by the original motion. Chap. 3, together with the appertaining canon, was formally adopted on June 11.

It was with blunted force that the council took up on June 15 the special debate on chap. 4. The **3. Close of the Contest.** address of the Dominican, Cardinal Guidi, archbishop of Bologna, attracted peculiar attention. The speaker did not contest the pope's infallibility, save that he attributed this purely to the decisions of the pope, not to his person. He also asserted that the pope is bound by the antecedently tendered counsel of the bishops, who testify to the tradition of the Church. Cardinal Guidi was directly summoned to the Vatican, where Pius received him austerely, and quashed the appeal to the tradition of the Church with his now famous retort: " I am tradition." Early in July the conviction permeated the council that what could be said for and against the proposition had already been said. The tale of speakers foregoing their turn to debate increased from day to day, so that on July 4 the synodical debate could be closed; by this time fifty-seven had spoken on the pending topic, chap. 4, and sixty-one had refrained from debating. The great contest now rapidly reached its end; chap. 4 was adopted on July 13, whereupon the entire schedule was brought to vote. The result caused great surprise, not because the schedule was adopted, since this was foregone, but for the reasons that of the 601 ecclesiastics in attendance, only 451 voted *placet* (i.e., yes), whereas 88 voted *non placet*, and 62 in the form *placet juxta modum* (i.e., yes, with a qualification). Eighty who were in Rome or in the neighborhood did not vote at all.

In view of the impending decision, the opponents of the definition made a last attempt to influence the result. In his memorial *La Dernière Heure du concile*, Archbishop Darboy addressed an appeal to **4. Final Efforts of Minority.** the members of synod; but his theses aroused such intense emotion among the majority and the leaders of the council, and were to them so irksome, that it was deemed necessary to protest against his pamphlet. On the evening of July 15 a delegation

of six bishops of the minority (Simon, Ginoulhiac, Darboy, Scherr, Ketteler, and Rivet) was received by Pius IX. What they requested fell far short of the desires hitherto expressed by the minority, for they now restricted their petition to the two points that the passage on " plenitude of power," in chap. 3, be stricken out, and that in chap. 4 the statement about papal infallibility be supplemented, so as to read that the pope shall support his position upon the witness of the Church. Ketteler prostrated himself before the pope, and besought him, " O that the father of the Catholic world might grant peace to the Church and the episcopate by some small concessions, and so restore that unity now lost." While Pius made no definite admissions, his demeanor produced new hopes. That these were fallacious appeared by the very next day. For the result was to intensify the sharp edge of the decree in its final shape by rendering the definitions absolute of themselves, and not contingent upon the consensus of the Church, which amended form was adopted by the eighty-sixth congregation general, on July 16, without parliamentary deliberation.

With the appointment of the fourth public session for July 18, when the final vote should occur, the contest over infallibility entered upon its last stage. **5. Vote on Infallibility.** The minority was really in a desperate quandary. Firm party organization it neither commanded nor could procure. Indeed, a compact front was now the less possible, seeing that after proclamation of the dogma the base of reckoning had assumed the shape of an immediate, imminent, and instant fact. For in the present contingency, the exercise of that ordinary right of stoutly adhering to the form of voting was opposed by considerations of pious loyalty toward the person of the pope, who had left no doubt on the point that he attached the utmost weight to the adoption of the pending dogma. In circumstances of this kind, there was no other becoming exit for the minority than that of absenting themselves from the session, and this policy was commended and facilitated by the Curia itself. For while up to this point the synodical delegates had been forbidden to quit Rome, on July 16 the members of the council were granted a general leave of absence. Whereupon, on July 17, fifty-five bishops of the minority forwarded a note to the pope, in which they reaffirmed their vote of July 13, and stated that in deference to him they intended to stay away from the session. The danger that any considerable number of bishops would not submit to the forthcoming dogma was accordingly set aside before taking shape at all. At the public session on July 18, 535 ecclesiastics were present, and all voted *placet* save Bishop Riccio of Cajazzo and Bishop Fitzgerald of Little Rock. The pope then announced the definition, and proclaimed the confirmation of the decrees. At the same session, the two opposing bishops tendered their submission.

4. Prorogation of the Council: Three further congregations general assembled after the fourth session; but no important matters engaged the attention of the council, attendance on which dwindled from about 1,050 to 104. Active interest in behalf of the ecclesiastical concourse was now sealed in the past. On July 26 the synodical delegates received copies of the *Schema super apostolicis missionibus,* on which no action was taken. The revised *Schema de sede episcopali vacante* was the subject of a brief debate on Aug. 23, and was adopted Sept. 1. Then followed the repeal of the States of the Church, and this furnished an adequate occasion for dissolving the merely vegetating convention, to say nothing of dealing a blow against the Italian government. In the bull *Postquam Dei munere,* dated Oct. 20, Pius IX. declared that in consequence of the " sacrilegious invasion " of the city of Rome conditions had set in which implied the lack of the necessary freedom, security, and quiet for the council's deliberations. For this reason, as also with due regard to the fact that the state of affairs produced by the great convulsions abroad in Europe required the presence of the bishops in their dioceses, he ordered the prorogation of the council. On the other hand, the Italian government took issue with the assertion that the new régime in Rome prejudiced the council's freedom.

III. **Decrees of the Council.—1. Drafts and Motions:** The committees charged with preparing the measures to be laid before the council elaborated a great number of preliminary drafts of decrees on doctrine and discipline. A first set of these outlined the dogmatic schedules, a second group dealt with discipline, a third with the monastic orders, a fourth with oriental rites and with missions. Not a few bishops availed themselves of their right to propose motions with reference to the subjects to be treated by the council. Yet none of these motions came up for action, although, for that matter, the same was true of most of the drafted measures emanating from the Curia. Still again, of the few propositions which underwent complete advisory action before the assembled convention, only two took the shape of decrees.

2. **Substance and Import of the Council's Resolutions:** The two most momentous decisions of July 18 read as follows (chap. 3, at the close): " Now therefore, if any one say that the Roman pontiff has only the function and office of inspection or direction, but not the full and supreme power of jurisdiction over the Church universal; not merely in things pertaining to faith and morals, but also in those which pertain to the discipline and government of the Church as diffused throughout the world; or that he has only the chiefer parts, the more potent attributes thereof, yet not, indeed, the entire plenitude of this supreme power; or that such his authority is not ordinary and immediate, whether alike over all and sundry churches, or over all and sundry the pastors and faithful; let him be anathema." Chap. 4 concludes: " The sacred council thus approving, we teach, and so define as a dogma divinely revealed: that the Roman pontiff, when he speaks *ex cathedra;* that is, when in the discharge of his office as pastor and teacher of all Christians, and in virtue of his supreme apostolic authority, he defines a doctrine on faith or morals, to be observed by the entire ecumenical Church; thereby using the divine assistance to him vouchsafed by promise to blessed Peter;

1. **The Decrees.**

he then brings to bear that potential infallibility wherewith the divine redeemer desired and willed that his Church be instructed in such definition of doctrine on faith or morals; and therefore the like definitions by the Roman pontiff are absolute, or unalterable in themselves, as by intrinsic force, and not by consension of the Church. Now, therefore, if any were to presume (which may God avert) to contradict our definition; let him be anathema" (Latin text in Mirbt, *Quellen,* 3d ed., pp. 367–368).

The former of these definitions deals with the relation of the episcopal authority to the papal. Even during the Middle Ages the bishops had been obliged to surrender many rights to the papacy, although the Council of Trent (Sessio XXIII., chap. 4; in Schaff, *Creeds,* ii. 189; Mirbt, *Quellen,* 3d ed., pp. 246–247) still attributed to them the rule of God's Church. Indeed, the Vatican itself now denies that the proclamation of the Roman bishop's ordinary and immediate power of jurisdiction over the entire Church infringes the episcopal power. Be this as it may, from the proceedings of the council it altogether clearly transpires that all attempts to formulate some direct expression of the independency of the episcopate were quashed and thwarted. Inasmuch as the pope is here accredited with an episcopate the scope of which is universal, thus allowing him to act in every diocese at all times (wherein he assumes the right of the bishop in ordinary), the status of the diocesan bishop is reduced in power; and this the more because in the pope he has not only a collateral bishop, but also one who by his very position as occupant of the primacy, represents the source of all those vested rights which accrue to a bishop in virtue of episcopal function.

2. **The Pope as Bishop.**

The second definition postulates the inerrancy of the pope's doctrinal decisions, and accordingly claims for them a binding force and lasting validity with reference to every Roman Catholic Christian. The context of the passage defining infallibility implies that Peter's successors have no new commission in the way of disclosing a new doctrine, but rather are charged, under the assistance of the Holy Ghost, sacredly to preserve and faithfully to expound the revelation, or deposit of faith, as transmitted through the apostles. There is this further proviso involved, that the decision at issue must have proceeded *ex cathedra,* that is, in exercise of the pope's function as pastor and teacher of all Christians; it must contain some doctrine on faith or morals; and is defined as a doctrine to be observed by the entire ecumenical Church. But it is to be noted that marks are not given by which it can be certainly discerned, in a concrete instance, whether the inerring decision is present. The postulations in discussion are in only a very limited measure restrictions upon papal authority; for whether a decision belongs to the deposit of faith, falls to the province of faith or of morals, is *ex cathedra,* and what range of operation it shall enjoy all depend exclusively upon the pope's own construction. Nevertheless, the pope is bound to this extent, that, by the proclamation of his infallibility, all papal doctrinal decisions of past cen-

3. **Logic of Infallibility.**

turies are brought under the head of infallible pronouncements, and hence can not be reversed. This rubric then especially comprises those decisions whose debated resistance is menaced with the anathema, acknowledgment of which was required in proof of faith; or even, as in the case of the bull *Unam Sanctam* (q.v.) of Boniface VIII., directly set up as a condition of salvation. These doctrinal decisions among themselves, when judged from the platform of the dogma of infallibility, are presumed to possess an indispensable inner harmony. It is significant, in this connection, that the labor of collecting such papal decisions as are to be " judged " infallible has been essayed in a private way only, but on the part of the pope himself (the sole competent authority, according to the dogma) no similar attempt has been made, nor is it likely to be. There consequently prevails and is likely to prevail much obscurity over the infallible character of papal decisions, whether pronounced since or before the Vatican Council. Indeed, the papacy itself is concerned in the maintenance of this very status. For, on the one hand, the very vagueness of construction of decisions, where such vagueness occurs, tends to cast the halo of inerrancy over all papal decisions on subjects of faith or morals, insuring for them the respect that infallibility warrants; while, on the other hand, liberty is retained for subsequently waiving an enacted decision, if necessary, as not of *ex cathedra* force. There thus ensues the peculiar situation, that some of the papal decisions on faith and morals have a directly binding validity for Roman Catholic Christians, yet, not being issued in exercise of the supreme doctrinal office, they can not claim infallibility; while certain other papal decisions on faith and morals have the prestige of infallibility because they were devised on the basis of the doctrinal office purely. Since, furthermore, the pope, as a mere individual, is not exempt from lapsing into error, the case may occur wherein he, erring as a private individual in matters of faith itself, aims to exercise the supreme doctrinal office under the very influence of his error. But notwithstanding his individual fallibility, he can not succumb to error in his pontifical teaching. The doctrine of the pope's infallibility discloses a prospect of quite complicated speculations, all of which can be avoided, however, through the belief that veritable popes have not erred and can not err.

An important consequence of the erection of the dogma of papal infallibility is a fundamental alteration in the status of ecumenical councils. The demand urged at Constance (1414–18), that the general council be viewed as the exponent of the Church, did not win, the conclusion being that this validity inhered in the council as convening in union with the pope. The Vatican Council affirmed that ecumenical councils were employed by the Fathers for preparing definitions, but were not the sole medium to this intent. This verdict finds its foundation altogether in the fact that, under the conciliar definition of the new dogma, the quality of infallibility is ascribed to the pope alone. Accordingly, the ecumenical council has come to be superfluous in the matter of defining decrees of the faith; it has

4. The Pope and Councils.

lost its constitutive significance, and has become an advisory organ of the Church, one that in future may be drawn into requisition, but need not be called at all. So it no longer possesses any independent importance; but it has value to give brilliant and striking expression to the ecumenical character of Roman Catholicism, to attest before all nations the superior might of the papacy, or to assume a delegated responsibility for grave practical decisions and assist in bearing the brunt thereof.

3. Adoption of the Resolutions: It was only with reference to the bishops of the council's minority that there could be any question as to whether the recognition of the new dogma would meet with obstruction. At Rome they had boldly uttered their scruples, had freely criticized the order of business, and had not suffered themselves to be intimidated by the incident that the presidents of committees interrupted their addresses. The most serious menace to the free action of the council, however, arose from abroad through Ultramontanist agitations. Archbishop Darboy and Archbishop Schwarzenberg quite sharply complained over the intemperate animosity of the Ultramontanist press against the minority bishops. It lay far from the minority's purpose to wield a radical opposition. Indeed, their very weakness inhered in the fact that they themselves blunted the sharpness of their resistance by halting half-way. Alike from the platform of Holy Scripture, by appeal to the history of the Church, and with logical demonstration, they charged on their opponents with no feeble spirit. Every critical review of the Vatican dogma must avail itself of the minority's writings and speeches on the subject, which are a mine of erudite knowledge. Yet their deductions are wanting in full carrying-power, because in their fundamental conception of the essence of the Church and of the Roman primacy they were at one with the majority. Hence the contest against the infallibility of the pope could be waged only with halved force. Then the battle was all the more difficult because Ultramontanism, and that enhanced esteem for the pope which rose to the height of a papal cult, had made great progress. Furthermore, when Pius IX., in the year 1854, defined the doctrine of the Immaculate Conception of Mary, this already presupposed that he had the inherent right to establish a precept of faith. This being admitted, there arose at once a prejudice in favor of the Vatican's transactions thereafter. For assent to the course of action which the pope here initially pursued was admissible only under the condition that he had acted as a trustworthy organ of the inerrantly pronouncing Church in the sphere of faith and the issues thereof. But if this attribute were tacitly conceded to him in a specific instance, it was difficult to contest its immanency with him as a general principle. And, in fact, the greater proportion of the minority bishops shrank from any real quarrel with the doctrine of infallibility; they were willing to let it pass for a scholastic opinion, they objected merely to its dogmatization. So the opposition here at stake was greatly restricted in its practical force or scope of action. Indeed, the Curia correctly discounted the potential resistance. The protesting episcopate firmly withstood all attempts at intimidation; but bowed before the threatening alternative, submission or schism. The Roman Catholic Church experienced one of her most brilliant triumphs, and lost not a single bishop. Thanks to the ultimate assent of the minority bishops to the Vatican dogma, the great crisis which had been evoked was overcome. The accident, nevertheless, was not to be forestalled, that the demurrer to the Vatican's "new Catholicism" led to the formation of the Old Catholic Church (see OLD CATHOLICS).

IV. Concluding Remarks: The Council of the Vatican marks the beginning of a new period in the history of the Roman Catholic Church. The power of the papacy became enhanced, and the process of centralizing the ecclesiastical administration at Rome has made still further progress. It was a peculiarly happy dispensation for the papacy, that immediately after the council's decrees were passed, the Italian unification movement put an end to the Papal States (q.v.), for thus it came about that Pope Pius IX. could enjoy the privileges of the martyrs, while for his successors the "Roman question" proved an agitation cause of the first rank, and an inexhaustible source of pious demonstrations, while above all the papacy was released from a task notoriously beyond its proper capacity. But now the Roman Catholic Church, as ruled by the infallible pope, has gained in point of solidity, unity, and compactness; the process of thoroughly Romanizing the inner life of the Church was lightened; and the same is true in the application of discipline. In short, the Roman Catholic commonwealth has been fundamentally strengthened. To all this be it added, that hitherto the papacy has wisely avoided stamping its decisions in particular concrete cases as of *ex cathedra* scope. On the political side purely, the council at first produced no further effect than that Austria, on July 30, 1870, "served notice" on the concordat of 1855 (see CONCORDATS, etc., VI., 2, § 6). Later came the outbreak of the Prussian *Kulturkampf,* or ministerial conflict over issues between State and Church (see ULTRAMONTANISM). Finally, Roman Catholic France has in 1906 accomplished the separation of Church and State (see FRANCE, I., §§ 5–6).

The definition of the dogma of the universal episcopate, as a corollary to the infallibility of the bishop of Rome, has fairly closed the history of the growth and institution of the Vatican dogma. Since then, these doctrines belong to the sphere of revealed truths of the faith, and will never be revoked by the Roman Catholic Church; on the contrary, they will gain increasing appreciation. Nevertheless, it may be said of this dogma that its official reception alone does not afford it the full warrant of becoming respected and effectual for all times to the extent desired by the voting council. The history of dogma furnishes not a few examples of permutation and fluctuation, even downright depreciation, in the value of particular dogmas, though the fact of a virtual neglect of their inner substance does not necessarily result in their formal repeal or alteration.

CARL MIRBT.

BIBLIOGRAPHY: Use as sources: *Collectio Lacensis,* vol. vii., Freiburg, 1890; Janus, *Der Papst und das Concil,* Leipsic, 1869, Eng. transl., *The Pope and the Council,*

London, 1869; J. Friedrich, *Documenta ad illustrandum Concilium Vaticanum,* Nördlingen, 1871; idem, *Tagebuch während des vatikanischen Konzils,* ib. 1871; E. Friedberg, *Sammlung der Aktenstücke zum ersten vatikanischen Konzil,* Tübingen, 1872; C. Martin, *Omnium Concilii Vaticani . . . documentorum collectio,* Paderborn, 1873; *Vatican Council, Decrees of,* ed. with Introduction by V. J. McNabb, London, 1907; Pomponio Leto, *Otto mesi a Roma durante il Concilio Vaticano,* Florence, 1873; T. Granderath, *Constitutiones dogmaticæ . . . Concilii Vaticani,* Freiburg, 1892; Mirbt, *Quellen,* 3d ed., pp. 358–367; Quirinus, *Römische Briefe vom Concil,* Munich, 1870, Eng. transl., *Letters from Rome on the Council,* London, 1870; L. Veuillot, *Rome pendant le concile,* 2 vols., Paris, 1872.

For the history and significance of the council consult: J. Friedrich, *Geschichte des vaticanischen Konzils,* 3 vols., Bonn, 1877–87 (most comprehensive); T. Granderath, *Geschichte des vatikanischen Konzils,* 3 vols., Freiburg, 1903–06 (employed the complete records of the council; cf. C. Mirbt, in *Historische Zeitschrift,* ci., 1908, pp. 529–600); F. Bungener, *Rome and the Council in the 19th Century,* Edinburgh, 1870; J. Fessler, *Das vaticanische Concilium, dessen äussere Bedeutung und innerer Verlauf,* Vienna, 1871; J. F. von Schulte, *Die Macht der römischen Päpste,* 2d ed., Prague, 1871; idem, *Die Stellung der Concilien, Päpste, und Bischöfe und die päpstliche Constitution vom 18. Juli, 1870,* ib. 1871; T. Fromman, *Geschichte und Kritik des vaticanischen Concils,* Gotha, 1872; J. Langen, *Das vaticanische Dogma von dem Universal-Episkopat,* 4 parts, Bonn, 1876; H. E. Manning, *True Story of the Vatican Council,* London, 1877; idem, *Vatican Council and its Definitions,* ib. 1887; É. Ollivier, *L'Église et l'état au concile du Vatican,* 2 vols., Paris, 1879; E. Cecconi, *Hist. du concile du Vatican,* 4 vols., Paris, 1887; J. J. I. von Döllinger, *Briefe und Erklärungen über die vaticanischen Decrete, 1869–87,* 2 parts, Munich, 1890, Eng. transl., *Declarations and Letters on the Vatican Decrees, 1869–87,* Edinburgh, 1891; and his other writings (see the article); J. M. L. Monsabré, *Conférences de Notre Dame. Concile et jubilé,* Paris, 1890; H. Sauvé, *Le Pape et le concile du Vatican,* Laval, 1890; T. Mozley, *Letters from Rome on the Occasion of the Œcumenical Council, 1869–70,* 2 vols., London, 1891; F. Nippold, *Handbuch der neuesten Kirchengeschichte,* vol. ii., Elberfeld, 1893; J. M. A. Vacant, *Études sur les constitutions du concile du Vatican,* 2 vols., Paris, 1895; K. Sell, *Die Entwickelung der katholischen Kirche im 19. Jahrhundert,* Leipsic, 1898; W. Arthur, *The Pope, the Kings, and the People. Hist. . . . of the Vatican Council,* London, 1903; A. Machuca Diez, *Los sacrosanctos ecuménicos Concilios de Trento y Vaticano,* Madrid, 1903; C. S. Isaacson, *The Story of the Later Popes,* pp. 265–277, London, 1906; F. Nielsen, *Hist. of Papacy in 19th Century,* ii. 290–374, London, 1906; G. Bartoli, *The Primitive Church and the Primacy of Rome,* pp. 266 sqq., New York (1910); *Cambridge Modern History,* 92 sqq., 147 sqq., New York, 1910; Nippold, *Papacy,* chap. xi.; the literature under INFALLIBILITY, especially the works of Friedrich, Maret, Hefele, Döllinger, and Gladstone; also the literature under ULTRAMONTANISM; and PIUS IX.

VAUDOIS. See WALDENSES.

VAUGHAN, vøn, BERNARD: English Jesuit; b. at Courtfield, Herefordshire, Aug. 20, 1847. He was educated at Stonyhurst, and in 1868 entered the novitiate of the Society of Jesus, being ordained to the priesthood in 1876. After twenty years as rector of the Church of the Holy Name, Manchester, he went, in 1900, to London, where he has since been attached to the staff of the Church of the Immaculate Conception. He is widely known not only for his vigorous work in the East End slums of London, but also as a preacher who unflinchingly assails vice even among the most powerful classes of society. He was cathedral preacher at the Eucharistic Congress in Montreal in 1910, and among his many published sermons and addresses may be mentioned *Ten Lectures in Free Trade Hall: Reply to the Bishop of Manchester on "Roman Claims"* (Manchester, 1896); *Sins of Society* (London, 1906); *So-*

ciety, Sin, and the Saviour (1907); *Socialism: is it Liberty or Tyranny?* (1909); and *Life Lessons from Blessed Joan of Arc* (1910).

VAUGHAN, CHARLES JOHN: Church of England; b. at Leicester Aug. 6, 1816; d. at Llandaff (28 m. w. of Bristol) Oct. 15, 1897. He was educated at Rugby under Dr. Thomas Arnold (q.v.), where he was a classmate of Arthur Penrhyn Stanley (q.v.), and at Trinity College, Cambridge (B.A., 1838; fellow, 1839; M.A., 1841; D.D., 1845); was ordained in 1841, and became almost at once vicar of St. Martin's, Leicester; became head master at Harrow, 1844, into which school he infused new life and vigor, holding this position till 1859; after declining the bishopric of Rochester in 1860, he became vicar of Doncaster. There he assumed, in addition to his pastoral labors, the task of fitting university graduates for the ministry, and this was the work which is regarded as most distinctive of the man. Over 450 students thus passed through his hands, receiving the impress of his deeply religious spirit. He became master of the Temple in 1869, and in 1879 also dean of Llandaff, dividing his time between the two offices. He was a leader in the foundation of University College at Cardiff (1883–84), being made president in 1894, when he resigned his mastership in the Temple.

Vaughan was a voluminous writer, editor, and commentator of books of the New Testament, and sermonizer. He issued by way of texts and commentaries Romans (Greek text and notes, London, 1859, 5th ed., 1880); Philippians (1862; 4th ed., 1882); Revelation (2 vols., 1863; 5th ed., 1 vol., 1882); Philippians (1885); and Hebrews (1890); wrote *Memorials of Harrow Sundays* (1859; 5th ed., 1880); *Notes for Lectures on Confirmation* (1859; 9th ed., 1876); *Epiphany, Lent, and Easter* (sermons; 1860); *Lessons of Life and Godliness* (sermons; 1862); *Words from the Gospels* (1863); *The Church of the First Days* (3 vols., 1864–65); and *The Young Life Equipping itself for God's Service* (1872); besides a very considerable number of volumes of sermons not named above, and works of more general interest, such as *The School of Life* (1885).

VAUGHAN, HERBERT: Cardinal archbishop of Westminster; b. at Gloucester Apr. 15, 1832; d. at St. Joseph's College, Mill Hill (8 m. n.w. of London), Middlesex, June 19, 1903. He was of the Vaughans of Courtfield (an estate in Herefordshire, 5 m. s. of Ross), a very old family, always stanchly Roman Catholic. His mother, a convert from evangelicalism before marriage, was excessively devout and daily asked in prayer that all her children might be priests and nuns—and, in fact, her five daughters all entered convents, while of her eight sons six became priests (three bishops). Herbert (the oldest child) studied at the Jesuit College, Stonyhurst, Lancashire (1841–47); with the Benedictines at Downside, near Bath (twelve months); at a Jesuit college at Brugelette, Belgium (three years), and at the Accademia dei Nobili Ecclesiastici, Rome (from 1851). His health was poor, and he was ordained priest (at Lucca, Oct. 28, 1854) eighteen months in advance of the regular time because

it was believed he could not live to reach the canonical age. After some months of travel, he returned to England (autumn, 1855) as vice-president of St. Edmund's College, Ware (near Hertford), at that time the chief Roman Catholic school and theological seminary of the south of England. Avowedly a disciple of Dr. Manning (later cardinal), and one of six who joined him in introducing the Oblates of St. Charles in England, he became involved in controversies of the time, which made his position at St. Edmund's delicate and ultimately forced his retirement (autumn, 1861). Another period of ill-health followed, during which he was animated by fervent zeal for the cause of foreign missions. The very characteristic outcome was a tour of the Americas (California via the Isthmus of Panama, and Peru, Chili, and Brazil via Cape Horn, Dec., 1863–July, 1864, to beg (literally) for funds to establish a missionary college in England. He came home with £11,000 cash, and founded St. Joseph's College at Mill Hill, opened Mar. 1, 1866, with one student and one professor (Vaughan). He acted as rector of St. Joseph's until 1872, when he was made bishop of Salford (Manchester). His interest in St. Joseph's, however, never abated; he continued its practical head long after he became bishop, served as superior-general of its missionaries, and chose to go there to die. The first graduates (four in number) were sent to the negroes of the United States, Vaughan accompanying them to Baltimore (Nov., 1871), and then making a tour of the southern states to study conditions there. He established feeding-colleges in Lancashire, Holland, and the Tyrol, and lived to see his missionaries—who go forth as priests, vowed never to leave their field of labor, even for a temporary visit home—at work not only in the United States, but also in the Philippines, Uganda, Madras, New Zealand, Borneo, Labuan, the Kongo basin, Kashmir, and Kafiristan. In 1892 he succeeded Manning as archbishop of Westminster (enthroned May 8; invested Aug. 16), and was made cardinal at Rome Jan. 19, 1893.

Cardinal Vaughan is classed as an Ultramontane. He was accounted hard, narrow, and intolerant. Undoubtedly he was a man of strong convictions and pushed theories to their logical conclusions with a rare consistency. He was impetuous to a fault. His virtues—devotion to duty, sparing neither self nor others, energy, resolution, and administrative ability—were such as to emphasize his limitations. It may be doubted if his place in life was that for which he was best fitted either by natural gifts or training. The characterization of him as an " ecclesiastical Cecil Rhodes " is not inapt. He would have been preeminent as an empire-builder or leader in the commercial world. He lacked the broad sympathies, the adaptability, the scholarship, and all the finer intellectual powers and graces so desirable in a prelate. Yet he organized his Manchester diocese to an exemplary efficiency, and in fourteen years reduced its debt by £65,000. He built the cathedral of Westminster in the short space of a decade. His determination was proven early in his Manchester incumbency by a successful contest with the Jesuits, who attempted to work in his diocese independent of his jurisdiction. A little later, when

Cardinal Manning and the bishops undertook to have the relations between the regular and secular clergy in England definitely defined, it was Vaughan who presented the cause of the latter at Rome, and, again, his force and tenacity prevailed after a contest which lasted for months. He was deeply interested in educational work, founded many parochial schools (and strove with no small measure of success to get public money for their support), and established St. Bede's College at Manchester (an excellent Roman Catholic commercial school) —motived throughout by the desire to prevent children of Roman Catholic parents from falling under Protestant influence. Similarly, in rescue and reformatory work—which he pursued with most commendable zeal and efficiency—it was ever the fear lest some of his communion might be swerved from their faith through service rendered by Protestants which spurred him to his greatest exertions. During the years 1894–97 he was forced to take note of a movement looking to the reunion of the Anglican Church with Rome, and it has been said that the condemnation of Anglican orders by the bull *Apostolicæ curæ*, which was the result and end of the movement, was chiefly due to his efforts. He certainly approved of the condemnation, and did all in his power to promote patient investigation of the question at Rome—as he also exerted himself to inform his brethren that the English High-churchmen were but a faction of the English Church. On the larger question involved he could have but one opinion—to settle anything by compromise was foreign to his nature. He was very successful as a writer of popular manuals of devotion and instruction, and wrote much for the *Tablet* (the leading Roman Catholic newspaper of England, of which he was proprietor from 1868), and the *Dublin Review* (which he controlled from 1878), but only on topics closely connected with the sphere of his duties. He prepared an elaborate essay on the education and training of the clergy as an introduction to the *Life of the Blessed John Baptist de Rossi* by E. Mougeot (London, 1883), and an unfinished treatise on the same subject appeared after his death under the title *The Young Priest* (London and St. Louis, 1904), while he also wrote *The Year of Preparation for the Vatican Council* (2 parts, London, 1869–70); *Peter-Tide; or, St. Peter's Month* (1880); *On the Holy Sacrifice of the Mass* (1884); *The Reunion of Christendom* (1896); and *Vindication of the Bull "Apostolicæ Curæ"* (1898).

BIBLIOGRAPHY: J. G. Snead-Cox, *The Life of Herbert Cardinal Vaughan*, 2 vols., London, 1910.

VAUGHAN, ROBERT: Congregationalist; b. in England near the border of Wales Oct. 14, 1795; d. at Torquay (29 m. e. of Plymouth) June 15, 1868. He early displayed a marked taste for history, but prepared for the ministry under the guidance of William Thorpe, pastor at Castle Green, Bristol; he was ordained to the charge of the congregation in Angel Street, Worcester, 1819; thence went to the charge of the church at Hornton Street, Kensington. He commenced a literary activity during this period, issuing his *Life and Opinions of John de Wycliffe, Illustrated principally from his Manuscripts* (2 vols., London, 1828), and *Memorials of the Stuart Dynasty*

(2 vols., 1831). In 1834 he took the chair of history in London University, and the same year delivered the Congregational lecture on *Causes of the Corruption of Christianity* (1835). His next works were *The Protectorate of Oliver Cromwell and the State of Europe during the Early Part of the Reign of Louis XIV.* (2 vols., 1838), and *The History of England under the House of Stuart* (1840). He next assumed the labors of president and professor of theology in the Lancashire Independent College, in 1843, entering upon his duties with the inaugural lecture on *Protestant Nonconformity in its Relation to Learning and Piety* (1843). He was the founder in 1845 of *The British Quarterly*, and for twenty years its editor, publishing some of his essays contributed to it in the work *Essays on History, Philosophy, and Theology* (2 vols., 1849). For the Wyclif Society he edited *Tracts and Treatises of John de Wycliffe . . . with . . . Memoir* (1845), and issued also *John de Wycliffe, D.D.: a Monograph* (1853). He resigned his presidency of Lancashire College in 1857, acted as minister to a congregation at Uxbridge, Middlesex, and then retired to devote himself to literary work. He accepted in 1867 a call to a church at Torquay, but his death speedily brought an end to his activities.

The works named above by no means exhaust his literary productions, and mention may be made here of his *Thoughts on the Past and Present State of Religious Parties in England* (1838); *Congregationalism; or the Polity of Independent Churches, viewed in Relation to the State and Tendencies of Modern Society* (1842); *The Modern Pulpit Viewed in its Relation to the State of Society* (1842); *The Credulities of Scepticism* (1856); and *English Nonconformity* (1862).

BIBLIOGRAPHY: *Robert Vaughan, a Memorial*, London, 1869; J. Waddington, *Congregational History*, iv. 318 sqq., v. 8 sqq., ib. 1878–80; J. Stoughton, *Religion in England during the First Half of the Present Century*, ii. 278, ib. 1884; W. Urwick, *Nonconformity in Worcester*, pp. 120 sqq., 205, ib. 1897.

VEDANTA: A school of Indian philosophy. See INDIA, I., 1, § 2.

VEDANTA SOCIETY. See MISCELLANEOUS RELIGIOUS BODIES, 23.

VEDAS. See BRAHMANISM I., §§ 2–4.

VEDDER, HENRY CLAY: Baptist; b. at De Ruyter, N. Y., Feb. 26, 1853. He was educated at the University of Rochester (A.B., 1873) and at the Rochester Theological Seminary (graduated, 1876); was a member of the editorial staff of *The Examiner* (1876–92); also editor of the *Baptist Quarterly Review* (1885–92); editor in chief of *The Examiner* (1892–94); and since 1894 has been professor of church history in Crozer Theological Seminary, Chester, Pa. He has written *Baptists and Liberty of Conscience* (Cincinnati, 1885); *A Short History of the Baptists* (Philadelphia, 1891); *The Dawn of Christianity* (Philadelphia, 1894); *Talks with Baptist Young People* (1895); *American Writers of To-day* (New York, 1894; new ed., 1910); *A History of the Baptists of the Middle States* (Philadelphia, 1898); *The Baptists* (New York, 1903); *Balthasar Hübmaier, the Leader of the Anabaptists* (1905); *Short History of the Baptists* (Philadelphia,

1907); *Christian Epoch Makers: Story of the great Missionary Eras* (1908); and *Church History Handbooks* (4 vols., 1909–10).

VEESENMEYER, fê′zen-mai″er, **GEORG:** German Lutheran; b. at Ulm Nov. 20, 1760; d. there Apr. 6, 1832. He was educated in his native city, where he early manifested his interest in the history of the Reformation period, and at the University of Altdorf (1786–89), where he became an instructor in 1790. In October of 1791 he returned to Ulm as a candidate for a gymnasial position, which he gained the next year, and in Feb., 1793, was made professor of rhetoric, which position he held, occasionally assisting as a preacher, until his retirement from active life in 1826, after which he still served his city as municipal librarian. In the theological controversies of his time Veesenmeyer took no part. His mind was essentially that of the historian and of the patient investigator of the less-known facts and characters of the period of the Reformation. The writings of Veesenmeyer, though extremely numerous, are mostly of brief compass. Many of them are concerned with the local history of Ulm, and others deal with classical problems. Omitting the latter, his writings of chief theological interest are as follows:

Particula annalium manuscriptorum inedita (a portion of Melanchthon's annals on the Peasants' War; Altdorf, 1788); *De vicissitudinibus doctrinæ de sancta cæna in ecclesia Ulmensi* (1789); *De recto et vario historiæ reformationis sacrorum usu* (1790); *Beiträge zur Geschichte der Litteratur und Reformation* (Ulm, 1792); *Versuch einer Geschichte der Beichte in der ulmischen Kirche* (1792); *Nachricht von Hans Jacob Wehe, erstem evangelischen Pfarrer in Leipheim* (1794); *Nachricht von Conrad Sams, des ersten ordentlich berufenen Ulmischen Reformators, Leben, Verdiensten und Schriften* (1795); *Collectaneen von Melanchthons Verhältnissen, in welchen er mit den Ulmern stand* (1797); *Von dem ehemaligen Aufenthalte der Juden in Ulm* (1797); *De Ulmensibus Erasmi amicis* (1797–98); *Nachricht von Ulrich Krafts Leben* (1802); *Versuch einer Geschichte des ulmischen Katechismus* (3 parts, 1803–05); *Versuch einer Geschichte des ehemaligen Dominikanerklosters in Ulm* (1803); *Nachricht von Lorenz Walter Küchel* (1800); *De Johanne Boemo Aubano* (1806); *Versuch von Annalen des ehemaligen Franziskanerklosters in Ulm* (1807); *De schola Latina Ulmana ante et sub Reformationis sacrorum tempus* (1817); *Litterarische Nachricht von Luthers Schriften, die Empfehlung des Schulwesens betreffend* (Stuttgart, 1819); *Litterargeschichte der Briefsammlungen und einiger Schriften von Dr. Martin Luther* (Berlin, 1821); *Sammlung von Aufsätzen zur Erläuterung der Kirchenlitteratur-, Münz- und Sittengeschichte besonders des sechzehnten Jahrhunderts* (Ulm, 1827); *Litterarisch-bibliographische Nachrichten von einigen evangelischen katechetischen Schriften und Katechismen vor und nach Luthers Katechismen* (1830); and *Kleine Beiträge zur Geschichte des Reichstags zu Augsburg 1530 und der Augsburgischen Konfession* (Nuremberg, 1830).

(T. KOLDE.)

VEGHE, fê′gê **(TEN LOE), JOHANNES:** Brother of the Common Life; b. at Münster in the first half of the fifteenth century; d. there Sept. 24, 1504. He received his early education in his native city—whether from the Brethren of the Common Life is uncertain, but he entered their house in Münster in 1451. Later he studied at the university of Cologne. Macharius Welinck, rector of the Münster brother-house, sent him to Rostock to organize the brethren in that city, where they had a settlement from 1462. Veghe is mentioned as rector *pro tempore* in Rostock under date of Jan. 13, 1470, but was back in Münster in Sept., 1471, and in 1475 he became sixth rector of the Münster house. Under

his rule the Münster community prospered, and the union with the affiliated houses in other cities was regulated and strengthened. In 1481, finding the duties of his position with the many journeys made necessary by visitations and colloquies too arduous for his strength, Veghe resigned and was made confessor and rector of the sister-house at Niesink near Münster. Münster in Veghe's time was a center of humanism not only for Westphalia, but for all Germany. Under the scholarly bishops, Henry of Schwarzburg (1454–94) and Conrad of Rietberg (1497–1502), and under the efforts of Provost Rudolf of Langen (b. 1438; d. 1518) in behalf of education it became the home of a number of noteworthy men all permeated with the spirit and learning of the Renaissance. Veghe occupied a prominent position in this circle and the references to him in their writings show the esteem in which he was held. His uprightness and comprehensive learning are especially praised (cf. Franz Jostes, *Johannes Veghe*, pp. xxvi.–xxvii., Halle, 1883). The numerous citations in his sermons testify to the extent and breadth of his study, covering the classics, Church Fathers, and mystics.

Veghe's writings, which have been the subject of painstaking study in recent years, include two religious poems (published by B. Hölscher in his *Niederdeutsche geistliche Lieder*, pp. 132–133, Berlin, 1854, and by Jostes, ut sup., p. 392) and a collection of twenty-four sermons (published by Jostes, ut sup.) made by the sisters in Niesink, before whom they were delivered apparently in the year 1492. These last are rather long, and do not follow the scholastic model of a theme developed artistically; instead they are free addresses springing spontaneously from religious experience, with earnest exhortation intermixed. This was indeed the chosen manner of the Brethren of the Common Life, whence they preferred to call their discourses " collations " rather than " sermons." Veghe takes his subject usually from the Gospel for the day and proceeds in a style which is popular without overstepping the bounds of good taste. He makes skilful use of Bible stories, introduces incidents from saints' lives less often, and deals sparingly in other stories and anecdote. He draws illustrations from familiar things of nature and experience, his comparisons are apt and striking, and at times he displays a genial humor. The Church he regards from the point of view introduced among the Brethren by Gerhard Groote and familiar from the *Imitatio Christi* of Thomas à Kempis. Veghe's sermons are truly Scriptural; yet the Roman doctrine of the Church is very evident in their contents. He speaks of the merit of one's own works in the current fashion; concerning indulgences he says that no indulgence can be won for departed souls; but faith which is counted for righteousness is nowhere emphasized. If indulgences are futile, still mercy, which is the greatest and most meritorious of works, with prayer, penitence, alms, and the mass can help the miserable souls in purgatory. Without the grace of God man can not be saved; but the grace of God is insufficient without man's individual accomplishment. For other writings by Veghe (the " Vineyard of the Soul," " Consolation of Mary," " Spiritual

Hunt," and " Flower-garden ") consult Jostes in the *Historische Jahrbücher* for 1885, Krause in the *Rostocker Zeitung* for 1885, L. Schulze in *ZKG* for 1890, and A. Böhmer, in *Aus dem geistigen Leben und Schaffen in Westfalen*, pp. 111 sqq. (Münster, 1906).   (L. Schulze.)

Bibliography: To the literature named in the text add H. Triloff, *Die Traktate und Predigten Veghes*, Halle, 1904.

VEHICLES, HEBREW: War-chariots (see War) were known by the Hebrews long before they used them, these vehicles being employed by the Egyptians (Ex. xiv. 6 sqq.) and the Canaanites (Josh. xi. 4; Judges i. 19); they were constructed in whole or part of iron (Josh. xi. 9). After the time of Saul, trade in horses and vehicles sprang up between Israel and the Hittites and Syrians, though the most of the trade seems to have been with Egypt (I Kings x. 28; II Chron. i. 16), a horse costing 150 shekels and a chariot 600. The import of these things was opposed by the prophets (Isa. xxx. 2, 16; Ezek. xvii. 15) as evidence of greater trust in man than in God (Hos. i. 7), so that in Messianic times they were not to be used (Zech. ix. 10). In post-exilic times the war-chariot was used by Syria (Dan. xi. 40). During peace the use of war-chariots was a prerogative of the great (Gen. xli. 43; II Sam. xv. 1; I Kings i. 5). Probably the horses of the sun (II Kings xxiii. 11) belonged to chariots.

Vehicles for riding and transport of goods differed greatly from chariots of war. In spite of the fact that in very early times routes for commerce traversed Palestine, the region was not suited for vehicles, though clumsy carts or wagons with two or four wheels were probably in use from an early time, with wheels either solid or with six or eight spokes, and drawn by oxen (Num. vii. 3; I Sam. vi. 7, 10) by a yoke attached to the pole. Probably the wagons of Num. vii. 3 were vehicles with removable body (cf. the description of the bases of brass in the Temple, I Kings vii. 27–37). The threshing-wagon of Amos ii. 13, cf. Isa. xxviii. 27, may have been an instrument with rollers underneath (cf. the illustration in Benzinger, *Archäologie*, p. 142). The carriage for personal use had either two or four wheels, and sometimes contained seats.   (R. Zehnpfund.)

Bibliography: A. Jeremias, *Das Alte Testament im Lichte des alten Orients*, p. 206, Leipsic, 1906, Eng. transl., *The Old Testament in the Light of the Ancient East*, 2 vols., London and New York, 1911; F. Sengstake, in *Globus*, lx., no. 5; *DB*, i. 357, 372; *EB*, i. 724–731; *JE*, iii. 666–667.

VENABLES, GEORGE: Church of England; b. at Hampton Gay (6 m. n. of Oxford) Apr. 23, 1821; d. at Burgh Castle (17 m. e. of Norwich) Dec. 30, 1906. He was educated at St. Edmund Hall, Oxford, and was ordered deacon in 1850 and ordained priest 1852. He was curate of Nether Warton and Deddington, Oxfordshire (1850–53), and Broadwater, Sussex (1853–54); and vicar of St. Paul's, Chatham, Kent (1854–58), Friezland, Yorkshire (1858–69); St. Matthew's, Leicester (1869–74), and Great Yarmouth (1874–86). After 1888 he was rector of Burgh Castle, Suffolk. He was also chaplain of Shoreham Union in 1853–54, rural dean of Flegg in 1878–86, select preacher at Cambridge in 1883, and honorary canon of Norwich after 1881.

Among his numerous writings special mention may be made of his *How did they get there?* or, *The Non-Conforming Ministers of 1662* (London, 1862); *Our Church and our Country; or, From A.D. 62 to A.D. 1862* (1862); *Counsel for Communicants* (1865); *The Churchman's Manual* (1871); *Unity and Uniformity* (1892); *Considerations on the Epistle to the Ephesians* (1893); *Thoughts at the Eventide concerning the Church of the Anglican Communion* (1898); *Up* (1902); *The True and Visible Unity of the Church* (1903); *My Church* (1905); and *Who and What am I?* (1906).

VENANTIUS FORTUNATUS. See Fortunatus.

VENATORIUS, vī''nā-tō′rī-us **(GECHAUF, JAEGER), THOMAS:** German Protestant and humanist; b. at Nuremberg about 1488; d. there Feb. 4, 1551. He seems to have received his humanistic training in Italy, probably at Padua; in 1522 he was called as preacher to the Neues Spital at Nuremberg, and from 1533 until his death was preacher at St. James's in the same city, except during the summer of 1544, when he introduced the Reformation at Rothenburg-on-the-Tauber. Venatorius was, primarily, a humanist, the last among the clergy of Nuremberg. Even his *Catechismus minor, hoc est de instituenda juventute in fide Christiana* (Nuremberg, 1535) is essentially humanistic in spirit, and he edited the *Plutus* of Aristophanes (Nuremberg, 1531) and the first edition of the works of Archimedes (Basel, 1544).

The first independent theological production of Venatorius was his *Axiomata quædam rerum Christianarum* (Nuremberg, 1526), a compend of Evangelical doctrines in which special stress is laid on the permanent signification of baptism, while the Reformed theory of the Lord's Supper is energetically rejected. In 1527 he wrote his *Pro baptismo et fide parvulorum* against the Anabaptists, and in 1527 a purely devotional work, *Ein kurz Unterricht den sterbenden Menschen ganz tröstlich*. Venatorius is best known, however, for his *De virtute Christiana libri tres* (Nuremberg, 1529), through which he became the real founder of Protestant ethics. With a careful avoidance of savage polemics, Venatorius discussed the theory of the sacraments in his *Kurtze vnterrichtung von beyden sacramenten, dem Tauff vnd Nachtmal Christi* (Nuremberg, 1530); and in Sept., 1530, he published his *Ermanung zum Creutz in der zeyt der verfolgung*, apparently with allusion to the prospective decision of the Diet of Augsburg. A series of exegetical lectures seems to have been the basis of *In divi Pauli apostoli priorem ad Timotheum epistolam distributiones viginti* (Basel, 1533), which is dogmatic rather than exegetical in nature. His one polemic work is the *De sola fide justificante nos in oculis Dei, ad Johannem Hanerum epistola apologetica* (Nuremberg, 1534), in which he defended the Lutheran point of view.   (T. Kolde.)

Bibliography: J. C. E. Schwartz, in *TSK*, 1850, pp. 79 sqq.; T. Kolde, in *Beiträge zur bayerischen Kirchengeschichte*, xiii. 97 sqq., 157 sqq., Erlangen, 1905.

VENEMA, vê-nê′mä, **HERMANNUS (HARM):** Dutch Reformed; b. at Wildervank (14 m. s.e. of Groningen), Holland, 1697; d. at Leeuwarden May 25, 1787. He was educated at Groningen (1711–14) and Franeker (1714–18), and in 1719 became pastor at Dronrijp near Franeker. On the death of the younger Vitringa Venema was appointed to succeed him at Franeker, and this position he held until his retirement in 1774. Venema was especially distinguished as an Old-Testament exegete, his chief work being his *Commentarius in Psalmos* (6 vols., Leeuwarden, 1762–66); while among his writings on the prophets special mention may be made of his *Dissertationes ad vaticinia Danielis emblematica* (1745); his commentary on Jeremiah (2 vols., 1765); *Sermones vice commentarii ad librum prophetiarum Zachariæ* (1787); his commentary on Malachi (1788); and his lectures on Ezekiel (ed. J. K. Verschuir, 1790). Of importance also for the period was his *Institutiones historiæ ecclesiasticæ Veteris ac Novi Testamenti* (7 vols., Leyden, 1777–1783), in which he showed himself an impartial student of original sources.

Venema was independent in theology, constructing his system on the two bases of reason and the Bible. There is an Eng. transl. of his *Inedited Institutes of Theology* (Edinburgh, 1850). He was deemed the leader of the tolerants, and was the only Dutch professor to defend the Mennonite Jan Stinstra when the latter was charged with Socinianism. Venema was himself suspected of heretical tendencies, and was obliged to defend his orthodoxy in his *Korte verdediging van syne eere en leere* (Leeuwarden, 1735) and *Justa cum viro clarissimo Antonio Driessenio expostulatio* (Franeker, 1736); and the charges being renewed, he was again forced to write in his own defense *Exercitationes de Christi vera divinitate* (Leeuwarden, 1755), by which he secured immunity from further attack.

(S. D. VAN VEEN.)

BIBLIOGRAPHY: The *Elogium* by J. H. Verschuir was published at Franeker, 1787, in Dutch transl. by J. Bakker, as *Lofrede op Herman Venema*, Amsterdam, 1801. Consult: B. Glasius, *Godgeleerd Nederland*, iii. 489–496, Bois-le-Duc, 1851–56; C. Sepp, *J. Stinstra en zijn tijd*, Amsterdam, 1865; W. B. S. Boeles, *Frieslands Hoogeschool en het Rijks Athenæum te Franeker*, ii. 399–407, Leeuwarden, 1889.

VENEZUELA: South American republic; bounded on the north by the Caribbean Sea, on the east by the Atlantic and British Guiana, on the south by Brazil and Colombia, and on the west by Colombia; its area is estimated at 363,728 square miles; its population (1908) is estimated at 2,661,569. It became independent of Spain in 1823, but remained a part of the united republic which then embraced also Colombia and Ecuador. As a separate country it began its existence in 1829, though only to pass through a period of internal unrest and civil wars. In 1864 it became the United States of Venezuela. The population is very largely of a mixed race, the pure whites forming only about 10 per cent, negroes numbering 120,000 (slavery was abolished in 1833), and there are 325,000 Indians, 270,000 of whom are civilized. Nearly all are of the Roman Catholic faith, which is the state religion, with toleration for other forms. The organization of the Roman Catholic Church came relatively late, though in 1637 Caracas was the seat of a bishopric for the whole land, and in 1803 it was made the metropolitan city; it now has five suffragan sees, viz.:

Barquisimeto (erected 1847, received a bishop 1868); Calabozo (erected 1863, received a bishop 1881); Sto. Guayana (erected 1791); Merida (erected 1777), and Zulia. There are 428 parishes. The Anglican communion is represented, as is the Presbyterian, with two congregations, the Methodists with one, the Reformed Church of the Netherlands with one, and the German Lutheran with one. Education is free and compulsory, with 2,000 public schools, 59 high schools and colleges, five teachers' seminaries, two universities, and three lesser-developed high schools. Yet most of the population can neither read nor write. [A concordat was negotiated between Pius IX. and the president of Venezuela July 26, 1862.] (WILHELM GÖTZ†.)

BIBLIOGRAPHY: R. M. Baralt and R. Díaz, *Resumen de la Historia de Venezuela*, 3 vols., Curaçao, 1887; W. Sievers, *Venezuela*, Hamburg, 1888; F. Tejera, *Manual de Historia de Venezuela*, Caracas, 1895; W. E. Curtis, *Venezuela*, London, 1896; T. C. Dawson, *The South American Republics*, part 2, New York, 1904; J. Humbert, *Les Origines vénézuéliennes*, Bordeaux, 1905; W. L. Scruggs, *The Colombian and Venezuelan Republics*, Boston, 1905.

VENI, CREATOR SPIRITUS: An early hymn of disputed authorship. George Fabricius (1564) assigns it to Ambrose; Thomasius and Daniel, to Charlemagne; the *Encyclopædia Britannica* (11th ed., xiv. 185–186), to Charles the Bald; and Mone, Wackernagel, and March, to Gregory the Great. It is first mentioned in the *ASM* in an account of the removal of the relics of St. Marculfus, 898 A.D. The Anglican Church retains it in the offices for ordering of priests and consecrating of bishops; the Roman Church, additionally, in the consecration of the pope and coronation of a king. It is found, generally, in the German breviaries and missals of the thirteenth to the fourteenth century. Its true author is doubtless Rabanus Maurus (q.v.), pupil of Alcuin, bishop of Mayence, and poet-laureate of the time of Charlemagne. The arguments in behalf of this view are: (1) The hymn can be attributable only to a scholar, a theologian, and a poet. (2) Its latest date is restricted by the considerations just offered, and its earliest date depends on the doctrinal point of the procession of the Holy Spirit from both the Father and the Son. This was affirmed (by adding *Filioque* to the Creed) by the Council of Toledo, 589, and reaffirmed by the Synod of Aquisgranum (Aachen), 809 A.D. (3) The word "*paracletos*" in the hymn is scanned differently from Prudentius and Adam of St. Victor, who in the usual manner make the penultimate syllable short. This would tend to establish the author as a person who pronounced Greek by quantity rather than by accent, and certainly shows him to have understood that language. (4) The hymn (divested of its modern stanza, *Da gaudiorum*, etc., and of Hincmar of Reims' doxology, *Sit laus*, etc.) was found by Christopher Brower (1559–1617) in " an approved and very ancient manuscript." Brower was a Jesuit and the antiquarian and rector of the college at Fulda, and he published the poems of Rabanus Maurus as an appendix to those of Fortunatus (Cologne, 1617). Wackernagel (i. 75) admits that this assignment deserves " some notice," though he prefers the Gregorian authorship. (5) But this hymn does not appear among the eight which are included in the works of Gregory the Great and does appear in those of Rabanus Maurus (*MPL*, cxii., 1657). (6) Charlemagne was not scholar enough to have composed it without Alcuin's help (Wackernagel, i. 75). (7) The hymn is really a paraphrase of Rabanus Maurus' own chapter on the Holy Spirit (*MPL*, cxi., 25); and in his hymn *Æterne rerum conditor, et clarus*, etc., Rabanus Maurus scans " paracletos " as in the *Veni, Creator*. The best-known English translations are " Come, Holy Ghost, all quickening fire," by John Cosin (1627), and " Come, O Creator Spirit blest," by Edward Caswall (1849).

SAMUEL W. DUFFIELD†.

BIBLIOGRAPHY: S. W. Duffield, *Latin Hymn-Writers and their Hymns*, chap. xii., New York, 1889; Julian, *Hymnology*, pp. 1206–11; H. A. Daniel, *Thesaurus hymnologicus*, i. 213, iv. 124, 5 vols., Leipsic, 1841–56; R. C. Trench, *Sacred Latin Poetry*, pp. 184–186, London, 1864; P. Wackernagel, *Das deutsche Kirchenlied*, i. 75, Leipsic, 1864; *Seven Great Hymns of the Mediæval Church*, pp. 134–139, New York, 1868; D. T. Morgan, *Hymns of the Latin Church*, pp. 153–154, 263–264 (London), 1871 (Eng. transl. and Latin text); N. Smith, *Hymns historically Famous*, pp. 15–17, Chicago, 1901; D. J. Donahoe, *Early Christian Hymns*, pp. 107–108, New York, 1908 (Eng. transl.).

VENI, SANCTE SPIRITUS: A sequence of uncertain authorship. It is part of a manuscript of the eleventh century in the British Museum, and is also in another manuscript of about 1100. Durand and the earlier writers ascribed it variously to Robert II. and to Hermannus Contractus. English translations are by J. D. Chambers (1852), and by Ray Palmer, " Come, Holy Ghost in love " (1858).

VENIAMINOF, vê″nî-ãm′inõf, IVAN: Bishop of Alaska, archbishop of Kamchatka, and metropolitan of Moscow with the name of Innocent. See EASTERN CHURCH, IV.

VENN, HENRY: Church of England; b. at Barnes (a suburb of southwest London) Mar. 2, 1724–25; d. at Yelling (12 m. w.n.w. of Cambridge) June 24, 1797. He entered St. John's College, Cambridge, 1742, but changed to Jesus College (B.A., 1745–46; M.A. and fellow, 1749); was ordered deacon, 1747, and ordained priest, 1749; held several minor curacies; became curate of Clapham, 1754; vicar of Huddersfield, Yorkshire, 1759, whence he removed, in 1771, to become vicar of Yelling. Henry Venn stands alongside of the foremost workers in the Christian ministry in England in the eighteenth century. He was upon intimate terms with Whitefield and Lady Huntingdon, and his sympathies were broad and Evangelical. At Huddersfield he leavened the irreligious mass of the working population with Gospel truth, and was among the first to carry the Gospel with success to the manufacturing classes. He was an indefatigable preacher, delivering often eight or ten sermons a week. His most popular work was *The Complete Duty of Man* (London, 1763 and often). He wrote also *Mistakes in Religion* (1774, etc.), a collection of essays on the prophecy of Zacharias (Luke i. 68–79); and many sermons, including one on the death of Whitefield (1770).

BIBLIOGRAPHY: John and Henry Venn, *The Life and a Selection from the Letters of . . . Henry Venn*, London, 1834, new ed., 1870; J. Telford, *A Sect that Moved the World*, ib. 1907; *DNB*, lviii. 207–208.

VERBECK, vär-bek′ (originally VERBEEK), GUIDO HERMAN FRIDOLIN: Missionary in Japan; b. at Zeist (5 m. e. of Utrecht), Holland, Jan. 23, 1830; d. at Tokyo, Japan, Mar. 10, 1898. He was the fifth of the eight children in a well-to-do household, was educated at the Moravian school in Zeist, graduated from it in 1848, and studied then at the Polytechnic Institute in Utrecht and became an engineer. For a short while he worked in the foundry at Zeist. In 1852 he emigrated to America, had a brief experience of foundry and engineering work, but after a serious illness turned definitely to the foreign missionary service, entered Auburn Theological Seminary in 1856, and graduated with the class of 1859. He was ordained by the presbytery of Cayuga Mar. 22, 1859, received as a member of the Reformed (Dutch) classis of Cayuga the next day; married Apr. 18, 1859, and sailed from New York May 7, 1859. He went out as a missionary of the Reformed Dutch church to Japan, and entered the harbor of Nagasaki on Nov. 7, 1859. In his student days he had mastered German, French, and English, and to these he quickly added Japanese, and that not in any halting fashion, but so completely that he spoke it better than most natives. He identified himself with the Japanese, and as he had come before the opening of the country to Western influences he witnessed those changes which have brought Japan into the family of progressive nations, and was himself an important agent in rendering the transition easy and radical. His first work was Bible distribution, as he was not allowed to preach to the Japanese; indeed it was death to a Japanese to become a Christian. In 1860 he was principal of a school for foreign languages and sciences in Nagasaki, attended by samurai, whom he influenced religiously as well as intellectually, and thus he formed the men who a little later were to play a prominent part in new Japan. The school became famous, and gave him personally such a reputation that in 1869 he was summoned by the government to Tokyo to help it solve its educational problems. When the Imperial University at Tokyo was established he naturally was made the head of it. From 1863–78 he was attached to the Japanese senate. Under the pressure of his multifarious and heavy work, teaching, preaching both in Japanese and English, translating books on law and political economy, on international law, and other topics, consulting with government officials, dealing with foreigners and natives, living in short a full life although never robust, he broke down in 1878 and came to America for recuperation. He returned the next year and resumed work. He taught in the union theological seminary in Tokyo and in the school for nobles, and took part in Bible translation. He could not be restrained; there was so much that he could do that he was perpetually working beyond his strength. On May 16, 1889, he had a slight attack of paralysis on his right side. He kept on and died in the harness.

He was commonly spoken of as " Verbeck of Japan," and thus his devotion to that people was set forth, but also the curious fact that having left Holland a minor and having failed to obtain naturalization in the United States while a resident of that country, he could not be naturalized there later, whereas in Japan there was no way in which a foreigner could be naturalized. Consequently he was in a sense a man without a country. In 1891 he applied to the Japanese government to be made a citizen, and in reply the government in view of his services took him and his family under its protection and gave him the right to travel freely throughout the empire in the same manner as the subjects of the same, and to sojourn and reside in any locality.

Verbeck with Samuel Robbins Brown (q.v.) and James Curtis Hepburn (q.v.) formed the triumvirate who are held in grateful memory by the Japanese people. They spent their lives in the service of that people, and brought to them the knowledge of Western science and above all of Christianity.

BIBLIOGRAPHY: W. E. Griffis, *Verbeck of Japan*, New York, 1900; C. C. Creegan, *Pioneer Missionaries of the Church*, pp. 90–101, ib. 1903; R. E. Speer, *Servants of the King*, pp. 75–87, ib. 1909.

VERBESSERUNGSPUNKTE, fär-bes′er-rungz-punk′te: Certain requirements introduced into Hesse by the Landgrave Maurice in 1605 for the amendment of religious conditions and the cessation of sectarian strife, and summarized as follows: (1) dangerous and unedifying controversies on the person of Christ must end, and ubiquity must be held to mean concretely that Christ is

The Articles. everywhere, not abstractly that the humanity of Christ is everywhere; (2) the Decalogue must be taught according to the words of Christ, and the images surviving from Roman Catholicism must be removed; and (3) in the Lord's Supper the bread must be broken after institution. On the death of Landgrave Philip in 1567, Hesse was divided among his four sons, but by his will ecclesiastical organization and doctrine were to remain unchanged. At first this was observed, but in 1575, at the instance of his wife, a Württemberg princess, Louis, who had received Upper Hesse and Marburg as his inheritance, called Ægidius Hunnius (q.v.) to a professorial chair; and at the general convention at Treysa (1577) it became evident that a new, ultra-Lutheran tendency was gaining ground. It was here decided, however, that, until final decision, the use of the new phrases concerning the doctrine of the two natures of Christ should be discontinued; that their personal union was to be discussed only in the concrete; that the dogma of the *Communicatio Idiomatum* (q.v.) should not be set forth; and that all polemics should be prohibited. The general synod held at Marburg in 1578, however, deferred decision, and with the last general synod (1582) ecclesiastical harmony had become impossible. Louis and his brother William, landgrave of Hesse-Cassel, adhered to views diametrically opposed, the latter inclining more and more to Reformed tenets and appointing many of the Philippists expelled from Saxony to high positions in the church. Under Maurice, successor of William in 1592, things took a new turn. Heartily weary of fruitless dogmatic controversies and desirous of a new reform, especially with regard to added emphasis on soteriological and practical preaching, the

new landgrave, a man highly endowed, energetic, eloquent, and well trained even in theology, was led to reactionary measures which caused him to seek to banish Lutheranism. Since the general synods had ceased (1582), important church affairs had been referred to the chancery and thus to the sovereign. The authority of the superintendents, moreover, had lately been considerably reduced, and in 1599 Maurice established at Cassel a consistory combined with the chancery to examine, install, and supervise pastors, this being replaced, in 1610, by an independent consistory at Marburg. Until the death of Louis in 1604, Maurice could proceed but slowly, hindered by the attachment of the ignorant populace to the images and the defense of the patronage on the part of the nobles, though in the mean time he sought to place his sympathizers in places of high ecclesiastical authority. When, however, his uncle Louis died and Maurice received the Marburg half of Upper Hesse, he sought first to reform this stronghold of Lutheranism, and, ordering controversies to cease, forbade (June 16, 1605) the teaching of the doctrine of Ubiquity (q.v.). When the Marburg theologians protested, he not only admonished them to obey the conclusions of the convention at Treysa and succeeding general synods, but also issued for strict observance the *Verbesserungspunkte* already noted.

The theologians, readily perceiving that these articles were but the entering wedge of a much more comprehensive reformation, again protested, but in vain. After fruitless efforts to win over their four leaders, Johann Winckelmann, Balthasar Mentzer, Heinrich Leuchter, and Konrad Dietrich,

Enforcement in Cassel. the landgrave deposed them. Open riot was the result, and the citizens were awed into submission only by force of arms. After an eloquent appeal from Maurice, all pictures were removed from the churches by his order, and early in August the Lord's Supper was administered according to Reformed usage. In Dec., 1605, with a view to more sweeping measures, Maurice convened the superintendents and provincial governors at Cassel. This convention proposed, (1) the issuance of a mandate authorizing superintendents and civil officials to introduce the *Verbesserungspunkte;* (2) the admission to the Lord's Supper of those also who did not accept the Hessian teaching; (3) the introduction of a new liturgy and a new catechism based on the Lutheran; and (4) the establishment of a consistory in Marburg to consolidate the reforms. Notwithstanding all this, opposition only increased, nor did even the deposition of ten clergy in Upper Hesse act as a deterrent. On Jan. 16, 1607, therefore, the landgrave convened diocesan synods at Cassel, Eschwege, Marburg, and St. Goar, where there was a strong sentiment in favor of the *Verbesserungspunkte*, and, on Apr. 12, a general synod at Cassel. This busied itself with the reform and the harmonizing of worship and doctrine, resolving upon the universal introduction of the catechism ordered in 1605, and now revised (*Kinderlehre für christliche Schulen und Kirchen in Hessen*, 1607). It also ordered a hymnal, and a creed of six articles was adopted which officially published adhesion to the Reformed Church (*Christliches und richtiges Glaubensbekenntnis*, Cassel, 1607). Immediately after the synod Maurice proceeded to enforce its enactments, but was met with repeated opposition in the refractory districts, specially at Schmalkald, where it lasted ten years, and the images could only be removed by the military. To secure the fruits of the Reformation Maurice in the following years gave much attention to education; and his representation at the Synod of Dort (1618) led to the introduction of the Heidelberg Catechism.

Political and military struggles went hand in hand with this religious strife, and led in many parts, especially in Upper Hesse, to a Lutheran reaction. Louis of Darmstadt, the co-
Reaction. heir of Upper Hesse, laid claim to the entire principality on the ground that Maurice had violated the religious provisions of the will of Philip. He allied himself more closely to the Lutheran estates and the emperor and fought on their side in the Thirty-Years' War. He invited the professors expelled from Marburg to Darmstadt, and, to offset Marburg, he founded, in 1605, a gymnasium at Giessen, and in 1607 a Lutheran university, while in 1607 he also required all the clergy to be bound by the unaltered Augsburg Confession and the Schmalkald Articles. In 1623 the inherited domain of Maurice was declared by imperial judgment to be forfeit, and the electors of Cologne and Saxony, aided by the troops of Tilly, carried the sentence into effect. The Reformed professors and pastors were deposed, and two years later the Lutheran university was transferred from Giessen to Marburg. In 1627, Maurice, broken by his reverses, abdicated in favor of his son, William V., and the latter, in the same year, was forced to cede to Louis George II., the successor of Louis V., Upper Hesse, Schmalkald, and Katzenelnbogen, where the Reformed preachers were suppressed and Lutheranism was introduced. After the defeat following the death of Gustavus Adolphus, Lower Hesse was placed under the administration of George II., while William died a fugitive. The widow regent, however, Amelia Elizabeth, defeated George in several battles, and by the treaty of Apr. 14, 1646, confirmed by the peace of Osnabrück, Hesse-Cassel resumed possession of the Marburg half of Upper Hesse, Schmalkald, and Katzenelnbogen. This peace guaranteed the *status quo* in religious matters, the districts named remaining Lutheran. A Lutheran university was established at Giessen in 1650, and a similar Reformed institution at Marburg in 1653. On Dec. 27, 1657, Landgrave William VI. issued for entire Hesse-Cassel a church order which was essentially Reformed, though with all possible consideration for his Lutheran subjects; but in Upper Hesse this order enjoyed less general usage than the Darmstadt church order of 1562.

(CARL MIRBT.)

BIBLIOGRAPHY: C. von Rommel, *Geschichte von Hessen*, vols. vi.–vii., Cassel, 1837–39; H. Heppe, *Die Einführung der Verbesserungspunkte in Hessen*, ib. 1849; idem, *Kirchengeschichte beider Hessen*, 2 vols., Marburg, 1876; A. F. C. Vilmar, *Geschichte des Confessionsstandes der evangelischen Kirche in Hessen*, pp. 164 sqq., 2d ed., Frankfort, 1868; E. Hofsommer, *Die kirchlichen Verbesserungspunkte des Landgrafen Moritz . . . von Hessen*, Marburg, 1910.

VERCELLONE, vär″chel-lō′nê, CARLO: Italian Biblical scholar; b. at Biella (55 m. w. of Milan) Jan. 10, 1814; d. in Rome Jan. 19, 1869. He entered the order of the Barnabites at Genoa in 1829; studied philosophy at Turin and theology at Rome; taught at Alexandria, Turin, Perugia, and Parma; became president of the College of the Barnabites at Rome in 1847, and held that position till his death. He devoted himself to the textual criticism of the Vulgate, and his fame rests upon his *Variæ lectiones Vulgatæ Latinæ editionis Bibliorum* (2 vols., Rome, 1860–64), epoch-making in the study of the Vulgate, the prolegomena being especially valuable; his edition (the best) of the simple Clementine Vulgate, 1861, and, with Cozza, his edition of the Codex Vaticanus (5 vols., 1868–81).

BIBLIOGRAPHY: A sketch of the life and works, by G. M. Sergio, appeared Rome, 1869; another is in the facsimile edition of the Codex Vaticanus, vi., pp. xiv.–xv.; cf. *KL*, xii. 678–680.

VERDEN, BISHOPRIC OF: An ancient Saxon diocese, doubtless established in the eighth century. It would seem that the region about Verden was given to the monastery of Amorbach as a mission field, and that Charlemagne conferred the rank of bishop on the abbot of the monastery (i.e., " St. Patto," probably the same as Bishop Pacificus; d. June 2, 788) as the head of the mission. The original see city of the diocese is as uncertain as the date of the creation of the bishopric. Saxon sources later than the thirteenth century describe the diocese as founded at Bardowiek and transferred to Verden in 814, but these documents are too late to be authoritative. The same holds true of the assertion of the Saxon chronicle that the original see city was Kuhfeld in Salzwedel. It seems most probable, therefore, that the diocese was established at Verden from the very first.

To the diocese of Verden belonged the districts of Mosidi, Bardengau, Drevani, and Osterwalde. They were inhabited partly by Wends, among whom paganism survived up to the thirteenth century, while among the Germanic population it apparently vanished in the course of the ninth.

(A. HAUCK.)

BIBLIOGRAPHY: G. G. Leibniz, *Script. rer. Brunsvicensium*, ii. 211 sqq., 3 vols., Hanover, 1707–11; C. G. Pfannkuche, *Aeltere Geschichte des vormaligen Bisthums Verden*, 2 vols., Hamburg, 1830; F. Wichmann, *Untersuchungen zur älteren Geschichte des Bistums Verden*, Göttingen, 1904; Hauck, *KD*, ii. 390–391. Lists of the bishops are in *MGH, Script.*, xiii (1881), 343; Gams, *Series episcoporum*, pp. 320–321; Hauck-Herzog, *RE*, xx. 499–500.

VERGERIO, vār-jär-î′ō, PIETRO PAOLO: Reformer; b. at Capodistria (8 m. s. of Trieste), Austria, in 1498; d. at Tübingen Oct. 4, 1565. He studied jurisprudence in Padua, where he delivered lectures in 1522; he also practised law in Verona, Padua, and Venice. In 1526 he married Diana Contarini, whose early death was at least a partial cause of his entering upon an ecclesiastical career. Here his advancement was so rapid that as early as 1533 he was papal nuncio to King Ferdinand in Germany; and he was there again in 1535 on business connected with the council. The nuncio's eagerness in the cause of the council brought him into a personal encounter with Luther at Wittenberg, which he himself reports (cf. H. Lämmer,

Analecta Romana, pp. 128 sqq., Schaffhausen, 1861; W. Friedensburg, in *Nuntiaturberichte*, i., 539 sqq., Gotha, 1898). Although Vergerio achieved little in the way of his appointed task, which was to induce the Protestants to send delegates to the council, Paul III. twice dispatched him across the Alps; and meanwhile rewarded him, first with the bishopric of Modrusz in Croatia, next with Capodistria. In the year 1540, Vergerio again entered active diplomatic service; he was at Worms at the religious conference as commissioner for King Francis I. (cf. *Ad oratores principum . . .* in F. Hubert, *Vergerio's publizistische Thätigkeit*, Bibliography, no. 9, Göttingen, 1893). It was in memory of the council that he dedicated the tract *De unitate et pace ecclesiæ*. Like Cardinal Contarini (q.v.), beside whom he also appeared at Regensburg in 1541 (see REGENSBURG, CONFERENCE OF), he was charged with having conceded too much to the Protestants. He then resolved to return to Capodistria and pursue thoroughgoing studies. Vergerio had yet no thought of withdrawing from the Roman Catholic Church, nor did he overstep the line of reformatory attempts within that church, such as were espoused by Contarini and others (cf. K. Benrath, *Geschichte der Reformation in Venedig*, p. 47, Halle, 1887). But suspicion was awakened; so that Dec. 13, 1544, a denunciation of Vergerio was lodged with the Venetian Inquisition; and although after due examination Vergerio was released, Cardinal Cervini took advantage of the fact that Vergerio was not yet formally absolved to prevent his participation in the council, for which he had labored so many years. Vergerio had to return from Riva, and began a publicistic activity which turned more and more against the Roman Catholic Church. In connection with the *Historia* of Francesco Spiera (q.v.) of Dec. 7, 1549, Vergerio directed a sharp reply to the suffragan bishop of Padua; and instead of responding to a second summons, by the Nuncio Della Casa, to appear before the tribunal in Venice, on May 1, 1549, he left Italy forever. The experiences at Spiera's sick-bed had brought Vergerio to inward decision. The twelve treatises which he produced at Basel in 1550 supply information regarding his dogmatic position. Meanwhile the second trial had been conducted in Venice, and was confirmed at Rome, July 3, 1549. Vergerio was convicted of heresy in thirty-four points, deposed from his episcopal dignity, and made subject to arrest. At that time, however, he was in the Swiss Grisons, and became active in a brisk round of polemics (cf. Hubert, ut sup.). His themes were the papacy, its origin and policy; the jubilees; saint and relic worship, and the like. Vergerio continued in the Grisons till 1553, when he heeded a call from Duke Christopher of Württemberg to write and travel in behalf of Evangelical doctrine. While he never again set foot in Italy, in 1556 he made his way to Poland, and incidentally conferred with Duke Albrecht of Prussia. He was in Poland in 1559 with the twofold object of meeting the moves of the Nuncio Lipomano, and of working counter to Johannes à Lasco (q.v.). In vain he sought permission to take part in the religious conference at Poissy in 1560, and he was not allowed to appear

at the Council of Trent as the duke's delegate. During all these years he continued his polemical authorship, and worked toward the publication of his *Opera*, though but the first volume appeared (1563). "A just appreciation of the man is difficult. That Rome saw in him only the apostate is a matter of course. But the Protestants, in turn, had to complain of his vanity, his excessive pragmatism. Open honest simplicity is not to be sought in Vergerio. Yet it is to his merit that he accomplished the transition to which his conscience and outward conditions impelled him, whereas most of his countrymen at the last moment faced about " (Kausler and Schott, in *Vergerios Briefwechsel mit Herzog Christoph*, Tübingen, 1875).   K. BENRATH.

BIBLIOGRAPHY: A review of the writings of Vergerio will be found in Niceron, *Hommes illustres*, xxxviii. 69 sqq.; Weller, in *Serapeum*, vols. xix (1858), and xxvi (1866), and F. Hubert, *Die publizistische Thätigkeit Vergerios*, pp. 259 sqq., Göttingen, 1893. Some of his tracts were reprinted in *Biblioteca della Riforma*, Florence, 1883. Eighty of his letters to Bullinger are in *Quellen zur Schweizergeschichte*, vol. xxiii., Basel, 1902, forty-three to Duke Albrecht are in Sixt (see below), those to Duke Christoph are in Kausler and Schott's work named in the text. A number unprinted are in various libraries and other repositories in Venice, Mantua, Zurich, and Munich. Consult: J. Sleidanus, *De statu religionis et reipublicæ*, in the ed. of his *Opera*, Frankfort, 1786; Bayle, *Dictionary*, v. 451–461 (useful for its quotation of sources); C. A. Salig, *Hist. der augsburgischen Confession*, ii. 1148–1200, Halle, 1730; F. Meyer, *Die evangelische Gemeinde in Locarno*, 2 vols., Zurich, 1836; C. H. Sixt, *P. P. Vergerio*, 2d ed., Brunswick, 1871; C. Cantu, *Gli Eretici d'Italia*, parts i.–iii., Turin, 1865–66; idem, *Italiani illustri*, vol. ii., Milan, 1875; A. Dittrich, *Regesten und Briefe des Cardinals G. Contarini*, Braunsberg, 1881; L. A. Ferrai, *Il Processo di Pier Paolo Vergerio*, in *Archivio storico italiano*, xv (1885), 201 sqq., xvi (1886), 25 sqq.; P. Stancovich, *Biografia degli uomini*, 2d ed., Capodistria, 1888; E. Comba, *I Nostri Protestanti*, ii. 395–476, Florence, 1897; *Cambridge Modern History*, ii. 233, 394–395, 588, New York, 1904; Schaff, *Christian Church*, vol. vii. passim; the works of Friedensburg (i. 1533 sqq.) and Benrath named in the text; the introduction to the *Quellen zur Schweizergeschichte*, vol. xxiii., ut sup.; *KL*, xii. 769–776.

VERMIGLI, ver-mî′lyî, **PIETRO MARTIRE:** Italian Reformer; b. at Florence Sept. 8, 1500; d. at Zurich Dec. 12, 1562. He entered the Augustinian cloister near Fiesole at the age of sixteen, and studied afterward in Padua and Bologna; after 1525 he was frequently employed as Lenten preacher and lecturer. Early in his career he became prior of the great convent of S. Pietro ad Aram, in Naples, where he joined the devout circle that gathered about Juan de Valdés (q.v.), to which band came, in 1538, Bernardino Ochino (q.v.). Both Vermigli and Ochino at first taught and preached without coming into open conflict with the traditional system; yet their tone, like that of Valdés, was already Evangelical. In 1541 Vermigli became visitator in his order, and in 1542 was dispatched to Lucca as prior of San Frediano. There he introduced strict discipline, while in behalf of better equipment of the novices he summoned such capable teachers as Celio Secondo Curione (q.v.); at the same time he issued his first Evangelical tract, *Una semplice dichiarazione sopra i dodici articoli della fede cristiana* (reissued in *Biblioteca della Riforma italiana*, vol. i., Florence, 1883), for which he was summoned before the chapter of his order in Genoa. He preferred to quit his native land that he might be able to live in his faith. He went to Basel and then to Strasburg, where he assumed the professorship of Hebrew, and addressed a statement to his fellow believers in Lucca (*De fuga in persecutione*). He taught for four years in Strasburg, till 1547, then at Oxford; but after the accession of Mary Tudor to the throne, he accepted an invitation to return to Strasburg. Meanwhile his wife had died at Oxford.

When news of this reached Strasburg, Vermigli was involved in conflict over the doctrine of the Lord's Supper with Westphal (q.v.). Moreover, he had already left Strasburg for Zurich, where he lived, beside Ochino, as the most highly esteemed member of the Italian congregation. Vermigli further took part in the dogmatic conflicts of the age in a pronouncement on Stancaro's doctrine as to the merit of Christ, and against Bibliander's lax doctrine of free will (1560). He also controverted the doctrine of Ubiquity (q.v.), much in favor with Lutherans, in his *Dialogus de utraque natura in Christo*. He took prominent part in the conference at Poissy, 1561, and brought with him to Zurich a note of acknowledgment from Catherine de' Medici.

K. BENRATH.

BIBLIOGRAPHY: Works, other than those named in the text, worth noting are his *Tractatio de sacra Eucharistia* and *Disputatio de eodem sacramento*, London, 1549, Eng. transl., *A Discourse or Traictise of Petur Martyr Vermill*, 1562; and his commentaries on Romans, 1561, and on several books of the Old Testament. A worthy memorial is the ed. of Vermigli's *Loci communes* by Masson, London, 1576, and elsewhere often, Eng. transl., *The Common Places . . . of Peter Martyr*, London, 1583. Consult further: N. Taillepied, *Hist. des vies . . . de . . . Pierre Martyr*, Douay, 1580 (Roman Catholic); the *Oratio* by Simler, Zurich, 1562; F. C. Schlosser, *Leben des . . . P. M. Vermigli*, Heidelberg, 1807; C. Schmidt, *Peter Martyr Vermigli*, Elberfeld, 1858; *Cambridge Modern History*, ii. 302, 390 sqq., 477, 502–503, 508, New York, 1904; *KL*, xii. 789–793.

VERNON, AMBROSE WHITE: Congregationalist; b. in New York City Oct. 13, 1870. He was educated at Princeton (B.A., 1891), Union Theological Seminary (1894), and the universities of Berlin, Halle, and Göttingen (1894–96). He was pastor of the First Congregational churches at Hiawatha, Kan. (1896–99), and East Orange, N. J. (1899–1904); pastor of Church of Christ, Dartmouth College, N. H.; professor of Biblical literature in the same college (1904–07); and professor of practical theology in Yale Divinity School (1907–09). Since 1909 he has been pastor of Harvard Church, Brookline, Mass. He has written *The Religious Value of the Old Testament* (New York, 1907), and has edited the series *Modern Religious Problems* (1909), *Songs for the Chapel* (in collaboration with C. H. Morse, 1909), and *Hymns of the Kingdom of God* (in collaboration with H. S. Coffin, 1910).

VERONA, PETER OF. See PETER MARTYR.

VERONICA, ve-ren'i-ca or ver''ro-ni'ca: The traditional name of a pious woman of Jerusalem, who, according to the legend in its most common form, when Christ passed by her on his way to Golgotha, took off her head-cloth, and handed it to him in order that he might wipe the blood and sweat from his face; and, when he returned the cloth, his features had become impressed upon it (see JESUS CHRIST, PICTURES AND IMAGES OF, III.,

1, § 2). A modification of the legend identifies Veronica (or rather Berenice, according to Johannes of Malala, in *Chronographia*, x. 306–308; in *CSHB*) with the woman " diseased with an issue of blood " (Matt. ix. 20–22). Another represents her as sprung from royal blood, a grand-daughter of Herod the Great, evidently confounding her with Berenice, the niece of Herodias. The manner in which the portrait was brought to Rome is generally represented as follows: the Emperor Tiberius was sick; and, having heard of the wondrous cures wrought by the portrait, he sent for Veronica. She obeyed the call, and went to Rome, and, as soon as the emperor had touched the cloth, he was cured. Veronica remained in Rome, and, when she died, bequeathed the relic to Clement, the successor of Peter. In the beginning of the eighth century, Pope John VII. asserted that the Church of St. Maria Maggiore was in possession of the miraculous portrait; but it was shown only to kings and princes, and only under special conditions. Both Milan, however, and Jaen in Spain, claim to have the genuine head-cloth of Veronica. It is worth noticing that in the thirteenth century (Gervasius of Tilburg, *Otia imperialia*, xxv.; Matthew of Paris, on the year 1216), it was not the possessor of the cloth, but the cloth itself which was called " Veronica," this being based on the word-play *vera icon*, " the true picture." Most probably the legend is a growth; first came the story, which is even likely— Christ may well have received this kindness from a pitying bystander; then the legend that the cloth had upon it the " true picture " of Christ's face; then the name of this became the name of the person giving it.

BIBLIOGRAPHY: *ASB*, Feb., i. 449–457; W. Grimm, *Die Sage vom Ursprung der Christusbilder*, Berlin, 1843; Tillemont, *Mémoires*, i. 471–472; K. Pearson, *Die Fronica, ein Beitrag zur Geschichte der Christusbilder im Mittelalter*, Strasburg, 1887; J. Palme, *Die deutschen Veronicalegenden des 12. Jahrhunderts*, Prague, 1892; E. von Dobschütz, in *TU*, iii (1899); idem, *Christusbilder*, Leipsic, 1899; idem and L. Cust, in *Burlington Magazine*, Sept., 1904; W. Weale, in *Dietsche Warande*, new series, iii. 600–616; C. G. N. de Booys, in *Tijdschrift voor Nederlandsche Taalen Letterkunde*, vol. xx., 1901; *DCB*, iv. 1107–08.

VESPASIAN, ves-pê'zhi-an, **TITUS FLAVIUS:** Roman emperor 69–79. He was born in a little Sabine village of noble family on his mother's side 9 A.D.; d. there June 23, 79. In the confusion and turmoil which followed the death of Nero, Vespasian was proclaimed emperor by the army in Egypt July 1, 69. His officers subdued Italy for him, then in the possession of Vitellius, when he left Titus in charge of the forces and went to the capital. Although he held high civil offices, his genius lay in the direction of military affairs. Serious in nature, he gave himself to the unreserved performance of his duties. Possessed of a good education, he was a man of order and discipline, and gave the impression of an upright, painstaking, and benevolent man, though tainted with sensuality. He married Flavia Domatilla, who bore him Titus, Domitian, and Flavia Domatilla. His attitude toward the Christians is unknown; the statement that he was not pleased at slaughter and lamented even just punishment (Suetonius, " Vespasian," chap. xv.) has been construed to mean that he continued to assail Christianity. Possibly in the attack on the Davidic house (Eusebius, *Hist. eccl.*, III., xii.; *NPNF*, i. 146) some Christians suffered, but the motive was purely political, and no sure records of martyrs exist. His reign was significant in Jewish history, the capture of Jerusalem taking place then through the operations of Titus. The Christians had earlier left the city (Eusebius, *Hist. eccl.*, III., v. 3; *NPNF*, i. 138) and settled at Pella.   (VICTOR SCHULTZE.)

BIBLIOGRAPHY: Sources are the " Lives " of Suetonius (good ed. by M. Nisard, with Fr. transl., Paris, 1883); Dion Cassius, *Hist.*, chap. lxvi.; Eusebius, *Hist. eccl.*, III., v., xii., Eng. transl. in *NPNF*, 1 ser., vol. i.; Epiphanius, *Hær.*, xxxix. 7. Consult in general the works on the history of the period, including those on the Apostolic Age; L. S. Le Nain de Tillemont, *Hist. des empereurs*, ii. 1 sqq., 6 vols., Paris, 1700–38; H. Schiller, *Geschichte der römischen Kaiserzeit*, i. 2, pp. 499 sqq., Gotha, 1883; W. M. Ramsay, *Church in the Roman Empire*, pp. 256–258 et passim, London, 1893; W. Smith, *Dictionary of Greek and Roman Biography and Mythology*, iv. 1246–48, ib. 1890 (good for the secular side); *DCB*, iv. 1116–1117; and the works under PERSECUTIONS OF THE CHRISTIANS.

VESPERS: The principal evening service of the Breviary (q.v.). In signification it was held to correspond to the evening sacrifice of the Old Testament, and also to commemorate the descent from the cross, the interrelation of the canonical hours being given in the mnemonic verses:

" Matins bindeth Christ, who purgeth our evil away;
Prime sees him spat upon, and terce condemns him to death;
Sext him doth crucify, nones pierceth his side;
Vespers takes him from the cross, at compline he rests in
  the tomb."

And a third mystic meaning is given vespers by the fact that it is recited about the hour of the day when the Last Supper was celebrated.

Vespers was the first canonical hour to be added to the original three, terce, sext, and nones (Dan. vi. 10; Acts ii. 15, iii. 1, x. 9), which alone were known to Clement of Alexandria, Tertullian, and Cyprian, while vespers and matins were known by the time of Chrysostom. By the time of Jerome there were six hours, three in the day and three in the night. In the course of the fifth century compline, originally recited about nine in the evening, was added, thus making the complete number of seven canonical hours, which later became eight when the first hour was divided into matins (about 3 A.M.) and prime (about 6 A.M.), as is found in the rules of Benedict of Nursia, Columban, Isidore, and the majority of monastic writers of the sixth and seventh centuries. From that time vespers was recited about 6 P.M., which is the present usage in the Roman Catholic Church. Until compline became a distinct hour, twelve psalms were usually sung at vespers, but later this number was reduced to seven, four being sung at vespers and three at compline. Benedict required also the reading of a chapter of the Bible, a responsory, the hymn of St. Ambrose with the versicles, the Magnificat, Kyrie eleison, Lord's Prayer, and collects.

Many of the older Lutheran liturgies retained matins and vespers, but these all proved unsuccessful. In the nineteenth century, however, many successful efforts were made for the restoration of vespers on Sundays and festivals. [In the Anglican Church the ancient hours of vespers and compline are combined in the service for daily evening prayer (cf. J. H. Blunt, *Annotated Book of Common Prayer*, pp. 17–18, 178, New York, 1903).] See BREVIARY; CANONICAL HOURS.   (O. ZÖCKLER†.)

BIBLIOGRAPHY: Besides the works of Bäumer and Batiffol named under BREVIARY, consult: H. M. Sengelmann, *Vesperglocke*, Leipsic, 1855; I. Hengstenberg, *Ueber Vespergottesdienste*, Berlin, 1861; *Evangelische Kirchenzeitung*, 1860, pp. 349 sqq., 487 sqq.; M. Herold, *Vesperale oder die Nachmittage unsrer Feste und ihre gottesdienstliche Bereicherung*, Nördlingen, 1875; K. von Liliencron, *Litterarisch-musikalische Geschichte der evangelischen Gottesdienste*, pp. 1523–1700, Sleswick, 1893; *KL*, xii. 869–871.

VESSELS, SACRED.

The Chalice or Cup (§ 1).
The Paten (§ 2).
The Pyx or Ciborium and Monstrance (§ 3).
Spoons; the Holy Spear; the Colum (§ 4).
Sacred Vessels in the Wider Sense (§ 5).

The expression sacred vessels (*vasa sacra*) denotes those used in the Lord's Supper, or, in wider sense, all the vessels and utensils of the church service. First in order comes the chalice or cup (Lat. *calix;* Gk. *potērion*), which was used from the very beginning. No examples from early Christian times are extant, but it is known that **1. The** there were various forms, the chief **Chalice** being the bulging two-handled *can-* **or Cup.** *tharus*, beside which the simple cup and bowl were also used (cf. V. Schultze, *Archäologie der altchristlichen Kunst*, pp. 125–126, Munich, 1895). Precious and ordinary metals, clay, and glass are mentioned as material. In course of the two art eras of the Middle Ages, a uniform style was developed. The Romanesque chalice has a conical circular base upon which rises, interrupted by a bulging knob (*nodus*), a short stem, supporting a hemispherical bowl (*cuppa*). Base, shaft, and cup are ornamented freely. Noteworthy German examples are the " Bernward " chalice in St. Gotthard's Church at Hildesheim (twelfth century), with Old- and New-Testament scenes; a chalice in the Church of the Holy Apostles at Cologne, with fine filigree work and figures of the apostles; above all the chalice of the abbey at Wilten, in Tyrol, the surfaces of which are entirely overlaid with engraved and beaten designs and adornments (cf. H. Otte, *Kunstarchäologie des deutschen Mittelalters*, i. 215 sqq., Leipsic, 1883). The Gothic in its aspiration toward elegance and vertical construction supersedes the hemisphere by a coniform cup, designs the base after foliage patterns, usually with six leaves, employs a polygonal stem, and ornaments the same with diagonally arranged bosses (*rotuli*). The engraver's art is restricted. The Renaissance increases the height of the chalice, makes the bowl wider, and applies its decoration richly. The baroque and rococo styles carry this tendency to extremes. The Lutheran Church retained the traditional forms, or favored their further development; whereas the Reformed churches undertook to restore the chalice to " apostolic " simplicity, even allowing the wooden cup. The Greek Church, so far as is known, has generally adhered to the plain forms of about 800. The medieval Church of the West, so long as it retained communion in both kinds, distinguished between " ministerial chalices " (*calices ministeriales*) for the

use of the laity (*ministerialis* = " of lower condition
or status ") for more convenient handling, often
provided with two handles (*calices ansati*), and
priestly chalices for the daily observance of the
mass. The wine was usually consecrated in the
latter cup, and then poured into the larger cup, already partly filled with unconsecrated wine. Only
on extraordinary occasions, as at episcopal masses
(whence the designation " pontifical chalice "), were
vessels used which had come to the Church by way
of costly gifts. For the use of the newly baptized,
moreover, they had so-called " baptismal chalices "
(*calices baptismales*). Precaution against spilling
the consecrated wine, elicited, from about the ninth
century, the use of the suction tube (*fistula, pipa*)
of precious metal or glass; it had a handle attachment and was offered to the communicants by the
deacon. On occasion of festival masses the pope
still uses the same, and in some instances the practise was retained for some time in the churches of
the Reformation. To satisfy ecclesiastical uses the
chalice had to be consecrated, and when so set apart
it was marked with an engraved cross. In the matter of the material, various church ordinances came
into existence, the object of which above everything else was to exclude unworthy materials (wood,
lead), or brittle stuff (earthenware, glass; cf. Hefele,
Conciliengeschichte, iii. 639, iv. 554, 756, v. 688, vi.
491). Silver and gold ranked as excellent materials.
Inscriptions, such as dedications, Old- and New-Testament quotations, religious and dogmatic statements, were often employed, preferably about the
base. The practise in primitive Christian worship
of having the wine supplied by members of the
congregation required larger jars (*scyphi, amœ*) to
receive the same, which appear to have resembled
in form the ancient mixing jars (V. Schultze, ut
sup., p. 126). Even after this custom died out, it
remained necessary, so long as the laity received
full communion, to keep the wine in readiness in
larger vessels of clay, stone, or metal, which the
subsequent legendary accretion often resolved into
waterpots of the marriage in Cana. Upon exclusion of the cup from the laity, these vessels naturally
decreased in size, and merged into the eucharistic
vials (*ampullœ*). Even at an early period, art appropriated these objects, creating specimens costly
both in material (silver, gold, sardonyx, agate)
and workmanship (enamel, chasing). The duplication of the vessels finds its reason in the prescribed mixing of the wine with water; hence it
happens, toward the close of the Middle Ages, that
eucharistic vials are found distinguished by the
letters V (*vinum*, " wine ") and A (*aqua*, " water ").

The vessel which serves to receive the consecrated bread during the communion is the paten
(Lat. *patena*, Gk. *patanē*, " plate "). The use of
ordinary bread at the earlier, or more
2. The   ancient, celebration of the eucharist,
Paten.   implies that this was a real platter, of
considerable size and weight. So it
remained in the early Middle Ages, as the wafer was
much larger down to the twelfth or thirteenth century than in later times. The material of the paten
was probably at first terra-cotta or glass; but in the
era following Constantine heavy gold and silver

patens are heard of in the treasure of Roman bishops and in other connections. In the cathedral
treasury at Halberstadt there is a magnificent gilded
silver paten, sixteen inches in diameter, with richly
decorated figures and other ornamentation, brought
by Bishop Conrad to Halberstadt from Byzantium
in 1215. Noteworthy specimens of German origin
are also extant, such as the one in St. Gotthard's
Church at Hildesheim, with a filigree setting of
pearls and precious stones. Most of these elaborate
specimens are associated with ministerial chalices.
In the Gothic period the paten becomes smaller and
less ornamental. It has also very little depth in
this period. The rim not infrequently contains
inscriptions relating to the communion. In the
Greek Church, for protection of the consecrated
bread when it is veiled, two metal strips (*asteriskoi*),
put together in the form of a cross and provided
with bent feet, are placed over the paten (Gk. *dis-
kos;* cf. design in D. Sokolow, *Darstellung des Gottesdienstes der orthodox-katholischen Kirche des Morgenlandes*, p. 11, Berlin, 1893).

For holding the consecrated as well as the unconsecrated bread, whether in church or on occasion
of the administration of communion abroad, vessels
of various forms and sizes were used under the general designation of *pyxis, capsa, arca;* also *ciborium*
and *suspensio*, from their place beneath the altar
canopy (*ciborium*). The simplest form is that of
the cylindrical wafer caskets, with flat
3. The   or arching cover, of metal or ivory,
Pyx or   some few of which have come down
Ciborium   from Christian antiquity (cf. Victor
and   Schultze, ut sup., pp. 274 sqq.). In
Monstrance. the second half of the Middle Ages
the pyx was much elaborated; resting
upon a cup-like base, it copied the structural plan
of a tower (*turris, turriculum*). In the later Middle
Ages this development reached its culmination in
the stone or metal tabernacle erected at the north
end of the choir, on the wafer side of the altar, being
sometimes executed with admirable artistic skill;
its structural pattern was the Gothic tower (superior examples of this kind in the Ulm Cathedral;
in the Church of St. Lawrence in Nuremberg, by
Adam Kraft; and elsewhere). This development
was anticipated in the eucharistic shrines of earlier
ages. The consecrated element was enclosed in a
compartment of lattice-work.

During that stage of its development when processions and public display of the Host became
prominent, the festival of Corpus Christi led to the
construction and use of a vessel that should at once
augustly and visibly present the blessed sacrament
to the eye. Thus the monstrance came into being
(*monstrantia, ostensorium, custodia, tabernaculum*).
There was, however, no need of a new invention,
and the makers confined themselves to copying the
transparent reliquaries and *ciboria*, which were already at hand, being occasioned by quite a similar
purpose. For the base the Gothic chalice was imitated in the diversity of its standard forms. Its
knob (*nodus*) likewise recurs, but with a greater
tendency toward sumptuous elaboration. Upon
the like support there mounts an artistic super-
structure, designed like the transept of a church

having three to five naves. The free plane surfaces are of both simpler and richer disposition. To crown all, there are one or more turrets (hence the designation *turricula*). The effect of richness is enhanced by settings of pearls and precious stones.

The Greek liturgy prescribes the presentation of the elements mingled in the chalice, for which pur-

**4. Spoons;
the Holy
Spear; the
Colum.**
pose there was in use, from quite early times, a metal spoon (*labis, labida*), the handle of which ends in a cross. Western Church inventories and donation records of the same time frequently mention spoons (*cochlearia*), which may have served partly for mixing water and wine, partly in administering to the poor, being still in use for that purpose in Spain. To the Greek rites exclusively belongs the sacred spear (*hē hagia lonchē*), with which the bread is divided in the process of preparation. The Western liturgy no longer provides occasion for the *colum* (*colum vinarium, colatorium*—a strainer with a long handle, used as the wine was poured), which was widely employed in the first half of the Middle Ages, before the withdrawal of the cup from the laity.

Of sacred vessels in the more comprehensive sense the following may be briefly mentioned: vessels for

**5. Sacred
Vessels in
the Wider
Sense.**
the sacred oil (*oleum catechumenorum, infirmorum; chrisma*) of various designs; stationary censers with double covers, and the swinging thurible with chains, occasionally of beautiful artistic finish; the sprinkling-utensils used by the priest at mass, which freely affect animal forms, as the bear, griffin, or bird, together·with their appertaining basins; lastly, holy-water vessels (*vasa lustralia*), in the form of simple or decorated little metal pails. The entire category of these lesser and greater articles, comprehended under the designation of sacred utensils, is instructive alike in relation to the history of worship and to that of ecclesiastical art. As the order of divine service became renovated according to the Evangelical conception in the sixteenth century, most of these objects naturally fell out of use; also in the Roman Church the subsequent development ran partly in other channels.   VICTOR SCHULTZE.

BIBLIOGRAPHY: Bingham, *Origines*, II., xix. 17, xx. 4, VI., vi. 13, VIII., vi. sqq.; the articles on the several vessels in the dictionaries, as in *DCA;* and the literature under SYMBOLISM; and WORSHIP.

VESTMENTS AND INSIGNIA, ECCLESIASTICAL.

I. Introduction: The clerical vestments and adornments in Roman Catholic use are almost entirely of ancient and secular origin. Until recent years their historical foundation was sought in the Old-Testament worship; but now research has discovered a different origin; yet this fact has not entirely abrogated the symbolism which attaches to ecclesiastical garments and insignia. The Church before the age of Constantine knew no distinction between secular and religious dress, although it may be understood that the latter was dignified

and rich; this is proved by representations in the catacombs. But the growth of the authority of the clergy, within and without the Church, the increasing esteem for the liturgy and its progressive development, and, not least, the continuous specialization of official dress, all combined to favor the use of richer and more varied materials and the marking of differences of rank among the clergy like that which obtained among secular officials; still, there was no question of a class distinction. The ecclesiastical garb first became peculiar in a strict sense when, under the influence of the migration of the Germanic tribes, the costumes as well as the forms of the ancient world passed away and the more convenient medieval dress was substituted, while the Church—and for a longer or shorter period, the upper classes and the higher officials also—clung to Roman or Greek fashions. Under the influence of the discovery by the liturgists of a supposed connection of the liturgical costume with that of Old-Testament worship, and then through the effect of custom and of the fashions of the beginning of the Middle Ages, a development was initiated, which did not indeed do away with the traditional usage, but transformed it more or less. Nevertheless, the history of ecclesiastical vestments in the Middle Ages shows no sharp divisions. The Renaissance and rococo periods, on the other hand, strongly asserted their peculiar taste. In the Greek Church the movement was much less marked. The Evangelical churches broke with the mode of dress which expressed the priestly and hierarchic character of the clergy, and found a modest substitute. Monuments are in this investigation a safer guide than literary sources. Yet a positive chronology can not, in many cases, be fixed for the historical evolution, and this is explained by the fact that this evolution did not everywhere follow along the same lines.

II. In the Roman Catholic Church.—1. Ordinary Vestments: A starting-point is found in the vestments worn by the priest at the celebration of the mass. The assumption of the separate garments takes place according to ecclesiastical rules in a fixed order, which this discussion follows: (1) The **Amice** (*amictus, humerale*, more rarely *superhumerale*) is an oblong linen cloth (at least thirty-two inches long and twenty-four wide), which is first placed upon the head and then brought down and drawn about the neck where it is fastened with cords. Originally it served as a head-covering for the priest; at present only a few orders wear it over the head on the way to and from the altar. The existence of the amice can be proved only since the end of the eighth century, and it is probably referable to some ancient priestly ceremonies. Its reference to the ephod of the Old Testament (q.v.) is purely arbitrary, as is the symbolical interpretation [faith] of liturgical writers; the attempt to explain it as a neck-cloth to protect the garment which rests upon it from perspiration is unsatisfactory. As long as the amice was worn upon the head or even projected above the other garments, embroidery or other ornamentation might be shown on it; but it gradually became hidden beneath the other vestments, so that at present only a cross is required;

this is kissed by the priest when he assumes the vestment. (2) The **Alb** is identical with the light tunic of antiquity, more precisely with the white tunic with sleeves (*tunica manicata*) which came down to the feet (*tunica talaris, poderis,* Gk. *podērēs, chitōn*). Even into the Carolingian period this was ordinarily worn by the clergy as a part of the ordinary dress. The exclusion of the tunic from daily use raised the alb to the dignity of a specific liturgical garment. Apart from its cut and color, its origin is recalled by the strips of purple or of cloth of gold which were sewed on (*clavi, lorum;* hence the names *albæ monolores, dilores, trilores*), with other ornamental pieces of colored stuffs (*paraturæ, paruræ*), in the form of a square or an oblong; as there were five of these, a connection was found with the five wounds of Christ (cf. the designations *plagæ, plagulæ*). In addition, further ornamentation, even complete pictures, came to be applied. After the sixteenth century a strong reaction set in; laces and edgings came into use. Recently linen lace is required and linen is also prescribed for the garment itself. The alb is worn by the clerics ranking not lower than subdeacon. [The symbolism is purity and innocence.] (3) The **Cincture** (*cingulum, cinctorium, balteus*) is required by the form of the alb. Linen is preferred, although wool and silk are not excluded. In the Middle Ages the cincture was often a splendid decoration of the higher clergy, and was richly ornamented with gold, silver, and precious stones. (4) The **Maniple** (*mappula, manipulus, fanon*) is a narrow strip of material similar to the stole (see below), worn over the left forearm or upper arm; formerly, the ends hung down freely, now, however, they are sewed together. The material was originally linen, but at present it is the same as that of the chasuble (see below). The rich ornamentation of the maniple usual in the Middle Ages, when it was longer, has now almost disappeared. Not more than three crosses are required, while one satisfies the rubric. It is worn by bishops, priests, deacons, and subdeacons, and, as a rule, only during the office of the mass. The origin of this vestment, the liturgical use of which can be proven from the eighth or ninth century, is not certain. It is commonly regarded as having been originally a handkerchief; recently an attempt has been made to connect it with the arm-bands worn by the assistants at the heathen sacrifices. [The symbolism is strength, endurance.] (5) The **Stole** (*orarium*) is a long narrow strip of fabric, which, hanging from the neck, falls down right and left over the breast. During the celebration of mass, the bands are crossed in front, the bishop alone wears them hanging parallel; the deacon, who may wear the stole at greater functions, may only bear it on the left shoulder. The material is usually the same as that of the chasuble. The ornament tion was generally confined to embroidered Latin crosses; in the episcopal stoles, however, it was often very elaborate. The little bells which are sometimes found on the lower edge are based on Ex. xxviii. 33 sqq. The name *stola*, which was introduced only at a later period and does not apply to the article, obscures its origin, since this name designated an article of female apparel. The parallel *orarium-sudarium* shows clearly that the stole comes from the handkerchief which was worn around the neck or the arm in ancient times. [The symbolism is patience.] (6) The **Chasuble,** the special priestly vestment for the mass, was at first a long sleeveless mantle provided with an opening in the center to admit the head. It was originally worn in ancient times by people of the lower orders, but it gradually found entrance into other circles and so reached the monks and the clergy. The historical development of the alb raised this article, about the beginning of the Middle Ages, to the rank of an exclusively liturgical garment for the priesthood, after it had been used for a time in other than clerical circles. This dedication to liturgical purposes necessitated some modifications; for instance, the mantle was shortened, and it was provided with drawing-strings and slits at the sides. During and after the Renaissance the chasuble was deformed into the present tasteless, stiff, bass-viol form, so that both parts, loosely connected, lay on the breast and the back. In the earlier Middle Ages wool was almost exclusively the material. The influence of Gothic art led to the more frequent use of silk and this became the rule in the fifteenth century. In the beginning white was in general use, but gradually a gradation of colors for various times and festivals was established (see SYMBOLISM, ECCLESIASTICAL, II., § 7). The ornamentation was confined in older times to a band edging the head-opening and running down on breast and back. Additions were the furcated cross, leaf patterns, armorial bearings, figures, and scenes. Hand in hand with this went the costly decoration with gold, silver, and jewels. The chasuble now in common use is distinguished by a Latin cross on both sides. Common fabrics—linen, cotton, or especially coarse woolen stuffs—are now forbidden. [The symbolism is charity.] (7) The **Cope (Pluvial)** was in antiquity an open mantle with a hood, *cappa,* and came in from secular use. It seems to have been especially worn by the canons in the choir (*cappa choralis*); it recommended itself for processions also as a protection against inclement weather (*cappa pluvialis, pallium pluviale,* whence the designation pluviale). It found its way into liturgic use and became obligatory for special services, e.g., vespers (vesper-mantle). It also developed into an episcopal robe of state (*cappa pontificalis*) with elaborate ornamentation. The cope resembles the chasuble, but is open in front and is held together on the breast by a clasp. Toward the Middle Ages the hood gradually disappeared and was finally transformed into a small piece of cloth with decoration (*clipeus*), which hung down the back. On the other hand, a train was later added to the episcopal cope. (8) The **Dalmatic** was introduced from Dalmatia, and resembled the tunic, though it was more elaborate; it was much favored by the higher classes. When it passed out of general use, toward the beginning of the Middle Ages, the Church retained it as a vestment for deacons and bishops especially, to whom its use was eventually confined. The sleeves and skirt were shortened and the sides were more and more cut out. On the other hand, the strips which were sewed on (*clavi*) and the color (white) remained. The episcopal dalmatic especially was often the object of costly art-workmanship. The Tunicle (*tunicella*), which is assigned to the subdeacon, differs but little [if at all] from the dalmatic. (9) The Surplice or Cotta, a convenient garment for liturgical purposes, permissible to all the clergy, was created from the alb (which became restricted to use at mass) by shortening and simplification. The designation *superpelliceum* comes from the old custom, especially common in monastic circles, of wearing a linen garment over the fur coats necessitated by the long services. The material is linen. Alongside of the comfortable, wide-armed surplice there exists as a variety the close-fitting Rochet (*rochetum*, from *roccus*, " coat "), a privilege of the higher clergy, although it was worn in many regions by the common clergy also. Lay ministrants (sacristans, choir-boys) are also permitted the use of the surplice. The decoration was generally modest and usually confined to an embroidered hem. From the Renaissance period laces were used. [The symbolism is like that of the chasuble.] (10) The Biretta (*birretum*) used to protect the head, which was rendered especially sensitive by the tonsure, was small and soft at first, and was made larger only after the fifteenth century, when it was given its present stiff, four-cornered shape.

2. **Special Vestments and Insignia:** The pontifical robes of the bishops include the above-mentioned vestments. The higher orders have vestments and insignia as follows: (11) The episcopal shoes and stockings. At the beginning of the Middle Ages the shoes (*sandalia, calceamenta*) belonged to the general liturgical attire; from the tenth or eleventh century, these and the stockings combined with them (*caligæ*)—of linen, later of silk—are a prerogative of the bishops. The usual color is violet. (12) The gloves (*chirotecæ, manica*) are not proved to have been in use before the twelfth century; until the fourteenth century they were of white or red silk, after this the liturgical colors appear. The rim was gradually enlarged to resemble a gauntlet. The oldest and most characteristic ornament is the *circulus aureus* on the upper part of the palm, a gold-embroidered or metal disk, with a figure (lamb, cross, etc.) and precious stones. From the sixteenth century, the woven glove came into use and the shape was developed mainly after the model of the dress glove. (13) The Ring (*annulus episcopalis*) can be proven to have been among the episcopal insignia from an early period. At the mass, the bishop wears it over the pontifical glove on the fourth finger of the right hand. Other clerical dignitaries who are privileged to wear a ring must lay it aside on this occasion. According to rule, this ring should consist of a simple gold circlet with a single stone, but numerous rich and elaborate specimens are found. (14) The Rational (*rationale;* cf. Ex. xxviii. 30) is a light shoulder-cloth of various form which is made up of several strips of material, ornamented with hollow plates on the shoulders or on the breast, or on shoulder and breast, and is awarded by the pope to individual bishops as a special distinction. It is worn immediately over the chasuble and only at the pontifical mass. It can not be determined whether it is patterned after an ancient garment; it is, however, certain that the breast-plate of the high-priest and the Ephod (q.v.) were factors in its evolution. (15) The Pectoral Cross (*crux pectoralis*), which arose from the custom of wearing a cross upon the breast, which according to common opinion acquired a peculiar prophylactic power by means of a relic, was restricted in the Middle Ages to the bishops, who employed this cross, even apart from ecclesiastical ceremonies, as one of the insignia of their dignity. The material is gold. (16) The Miter (*mitra, mitrē, infula*) is the liturgical head-covering of the bishops, including the pope. It is not possible to prove its existence with certainty before the tenth century. The form has passed through many variations. At first it was a round cap fitting the head closely with a brow band and ribbons falling down on the back of the neck. The miter soon developed into a biretta with edges turned up sharply; it then received a tall peaked termination and finally assumed an oval form. An ornamental band, decorated in special cases with precious metals and stones, surrounds the lower rim, a second vertical one divides the breadth. The fabric is also embroidered with designs and figures. The material is silk; only at councils are linen miters prescribed for the bishops, in order to distinguish them from the cardinals. (17) The Crozier (*pedum, pastorale, virga*) had its origin in the conception of the pastoral office of the bishops in connection with the idea of domination. This emblem is unknown to Christian antiquity, only at the beginning of the Middle Ages are traces of its use encountered. At first it seems to have been a staff with a straight handle, but at an early period alongside of this appeared the crook bent like a chamois-horn. In the course of the Romanic period, this takes on a bolder curve and is combined with designs and figures; the termination of a snake's or dragon's head was much favored. As material, ivory was used; in the Gothic period, gilded copper was substituted for the staff and precious metal for the crook. At the same time, Gothic art applies its architectural symbolism and gives the preference to figure-decoration, to scenes from the life of Mary and from the legends of the saints. Fine goldsmith-work now appears. The Renaissance and the rococo periods retain the fundamental form, but the characteristic taste of these periods was asserted in many essential details. The small linen cloth which is attached to the staff just below the crook (*pannisellus, sudarium*) was probably intended originally for a handkerchief; later it disappeared from the episcopal staff and remained on the abbot's staff, as a distinguishing mark (abbots, as also abbesses, bore the crozier). This emblem, however, is only permitted to the bishop within his diocese. Bishops' and abbots' croziers, from the Middle Ages, have been preserved in great numbers, even from early Romanic times, when the custom existed of laying them in the graves of their owners. (18) The Pallium (q.v.) consists of a white woolen band about three inches wide, interwoven with six black silk crosses; it encircles the shoulders, one band falling upon the breast and the other upon the back. Gold pins fasten it to the vestment beneath. It is

worn regularly only by the pope, primates, patri-archs, and archbishops over the chasuble, although certain specially privileged bishops also wore it. The pallia are made by nuns in S. Agnese near Rome, and are supposed to obtain a special conse-cration by being deposited in the grave of St. Peter. [(19) The **Manteletta** or **Chimere** is an episcopal garment which bishops wear when out of their own jurisdiction, in order to cover the rochet, which is one symbol of episcopal authority.] The dignitaries named above also enjoy the privilege of having a cross borne before them (*crux archiepiscopalis*), the crucifix side being turned toward them. (20) The **Mozetta** is a vestment which is the usual state dress of a bishop when not performing sacred functions. It is a short cape or cloak, open in front but sus-ceptible of being buttoned over the breast, and has a small hood behind. It may be worn by the pope, by cardinals, bishops, abbots, and others to whom it is permitted by custom or papal privilege, as by canons in England. It is worn over the rochet, but when the prelate is out of his jurisdiction, he either wears it over the manteletta or not at all. By car-dinals this vestment and the rochet are worn only in the churches from which they take their titles, except at Rome during a papal vacancy or at con-claves. The pope has five of these vestments. From the first vespers of the Ascension during the hot season he wears one of red satin except on vigils or penitential occasions, when the material is of red serge or camlet. The rest of the year the material is of red velvet, except on penitential occasions, when the material is of red woolen cloth; but from Holy Saturday till the second Saturday after Easter the mozetta is of white damask. The cardinals have four mozettas, of red or purple silk, violet silk, rose-colored silk, and violet serge. The cardinals are distinguished by purple garments and by a flat broad-brimmed hat from which hang, on the sides, bands with tassels. The proper costume of the pope is the episcopal, although it is in part more richly made and differs in some respects. For instance, instead of the crozier, he bears a tall cross with two or three arms. (21) A special distinction is, how-ever, the **Tiara** (*regnum, triregnum*). This is the princely emblem of the pope and is, therefore, worn when his princely authority is to be manifested; in liturgical and ecclesiastical functions he wears in-stead the episcopal miter. The tiara does not ap-pear before the eleventh century, and then at first only in the form of a peaked hat edged with em-broidery; later it becomes taller and assumes a conical form. Although the tiara has a certain similarity to the miter, it is distinguished from the latter by having only one point. The difference is still more marked at the coronation. Even into the thirteenth century, a single circlet (*regnum*) sur-rounds the tiara, but under Boniface VIII. (1294–1308), a second was added, and finally a papal in-ventory of 1315 names three. It is possible that even in the time of Boniface VIII. the triple crown had appeared; in any case, this evolution was not far removed from his pontificate. (22) Lastly, brief allusion may be made to the liturgical **comb**, which the priest used for arranging his hair before the celebration of mass. This is also given to the bishop

at his consecration as his personal property, and is therefore often found in bishops' graves; the ma-terial is ivory, often richly carved. Christian an-tiquity knows nothing of this article.

III. In the Greek Church: The history of litur-gical and clerical vestments in Greek Christianity records but little change. The results already at-tained by the end of Christian antiquity were but little enriched. This fact corresponds with the con-servative character of the Greek Church. Never-theless, it appears that in the course of the Middle Ages slight Latin influences were active. Besides this, the relationship or correspondence between the two churches can be explained from the com-mon origin of clerical vestments.

The liturgical vestments of the priest are com-posed of the following articles: the **Sticharion**, a long, white, flowing garment of heavy gold-embroid-ered silk, which corresponds to the alb or the dal-matic of the Latins; the **Zone**, a girdle for drawing in the sticharion, more richly decorated than in the West; the **Epimanikia**, gauntlets, which serve the purpose of fastening the sticharion at the wrists; the **Peritrachelion (Epitrachelion)**, a silken band, ornamented with golden crosses or in some other way, which encircles the neck, its fringed ends hang-ing down to the feet; it is the stole of the Latins and like the latter of antique origin; for the epi-trachelion of the deacon, the Hellenized Latin word *orarium* was employed; the **Phelonion**, the mass-vestment properly so called, had the same origin as the chasuble, but here the earliest form has re-mained. With a simple opening for the head, it hangs in folds about the body. It is commonly made of silk, is richly embroidered with crosses, and is subject to the liturgical change of color. The **Hypogonation**, a sack of a square form with a cross or a sacred image as ornament, worn at the left side, is only an honorary distinction, and does not belong to the ecclesiastical costume. The liturgical vestments of the bishops were the same; but pe-culiar to them are the **Omophorion**, the Greek pal-lium, quite similar to the Latin, and the angular, stiff sack, hypogonation, worn on the right. The origin of the latter, which the bishops received at consecration, is doubtful. The bishop's breast is decorated with a valuable cross and with a me-dallion bearing a sacred image (*panagia*). His office is indicated by the staff (*rhabdos*), whose crook is turned upward. Further, one of the insignia of the bishop is the miter, a low cap resembling a crown, covered with artistic embroidery, precious stones, and gold ornaments; above it rises a cross. The metropolitans and the patriarchs wear instead of the phelonion the **Sakkos**, a richly embroidered, close-fitting garment with wide sleeves. The non-liturgical dress of the priests and bishops consists of a long, black coat of many folds and a cylindrical hat, which is lower in the case of the lesser clergy. The bishops up to the patriarchs inclusive wear besides this a large mantle (*mandyas*), open in front and fastened by clasps; the hem is adorned with cross-stripes and the corners with pieces of colored cloth sewn on. The patriarch has also the right to two crosses; his hood-like head-covering recalls the monastic class from which he comes. Over this he wears a broad flat hat, on the upper surface of which a light blue cross is seen (cf. the rather limited collection of representations in D. Sokolow, *Darstellung des Gottesdienstes der orthodoxen katholischen Kirche des Morgenlandes*, p. 25, Berlin, 1893).

The Armenian church shows great variety and magnificence in her ecclesiastical vestments. Still the common characteristics appear everywhere. The Coptic church has simpler forms (A. J. Butler, *The Ancient Coptic Churches of Egypt*, 2 vols., Oxford, 1884). For the Nestorian Church in Syria cf. R. Percy Badger, *The Nestorians and their Rituals* (London, 1852).

IV. In Protestant Churches: The Reformation, with the exclusion of the hierarchy and the rejection of special acts of worship, was forced to abolish a part of the liturgical vestments and official insignia. While there was no need of a complete break with the past, this step was taken by enthusiasts whenever they were able to accomplish it, and the Reformed Church also pursued the same way more or less radically. In 1523 Zwingli, in his *Auslegung und Grund der Schlussreden,** gave it as his judgment that cowl, cross, surplice, tonsure are not " neither good nor bad," but only "bad," so he abolished them as soon as possible. Luther, on the other hand, saw in these externals things indifferent in themselves, and not only in his time but long after, the mass-vestment was still used. The Interim (q.v.) gave the usage new support and procured for it a wider spread. However, the general trend of development was in another direction, and in fact it took up the gown worn by the middle classes, a full mantle covering the whole body, which varied in material, color, and cut according to rank and fashion. Luther preached for the first time in the black gown of the scholars on the afternoon of Oct. 9, 1524. In the altar picture by Lucas Cranach in the Stadtkirche at Wittenberg he is represented wearing it in the pulpit. Calvin and Zwingli also performed their functions wearing the gown. With the gown went the biretta, which had driven out the hat in the dress of the burghers and appears in a great variety of forms. The clergy wear it as a rule in the form of a rich low cap, which gained a hold on the head by means of a stiff lower projection and was sometimes also provided with an upturned brim. In the seventeenth century the Spanish costume began to influence the gown and led to its complete change. The mantle is transformed into a simple, long coat, buttoned up in front. The large ruff was introduced and has maintained itself up to this day in some parts of Germany. The broad coat collars were reduced in secular as well as clerical usage to two linen strips resting on the breast and called *beffchen* (from the Low German *beffe*, diminutive *beffken*), which have been preserved to the present time. In the eighteenth century, the cloak of the French abbés found its way into German use. The head is covered by a small, round cap. Although there is a certain general agreement in the vestments of Germany and Switzerland, considerable differences also show themselves. However, since the surplice of to-day was prescribed in Prussia by a royal ordinance of Jan. 1, 1811, in which way the gown came to life again, unity was much favored, and it is again as complete as in the sixteenth century. At the same time the stiff biretta, resembling a hat, reappeared. The surplice still survives as a relic of the Middle Ages in some Evangelical churches of Germany. On the other hand, in the Danish, Norwegian, and Swedish churches, it is a permanent part of the liturgical dress. The Anglican church has kept in closer touch with the past (see RITUALISM).

VICTOR SCHULTZE.

BIBLIOGRAPHY: Notable patristic contributions to the subject are: Isidore of Seville, *Officiorum libri II.*, and *Etymologiarum . . . libri xx.;* Walafrid Strabo, *De ecclesiasticarum rerum exordiis et incrementis;* Amalarius of Metz, *De ecclesiasticis officiis;* Rabanus Maurus, *De sacris ordinibus, sacramentis divinis et vestimentis sacerdotalibus;* Pseudo-Alcuin, *De divinis officiis,* in *MPL*, ci. 1174 sqq.; Ivo of Chartres, *Sermo de significatione indumentorum sacerdotalium,* in *MPL*, clxi. 519 sqq.; Hugo of St. Victor, *Sermo de vestibus sacris,* in *MPL*, clxxvii. 927 sqq.; Honorius of Autun, *Gemma animæ,* in *MPL*, clxxii. 543 sqq.; and Innocent III., *De sacro altaris mysterio,* in *MPL*, ccxvii. 780 sqq. Consult further: E. von Muralt, *Lexidion der morgenländischen Kirche,* Leipsic, 1838; J. M. Neale, *Hist. of the Holy Eastern Church,* London, 1850; F. Bock, *Geschichte der liturgischen Gewänder des Mittelalters,* 3 vols., Bonn, 1859–71; A. W. Pugin, *Glossary of Ecclesiastical Ornament and Costume,* London, 1859; H. Weiss, *Kostümkunde,* Stuttgart, 1859 sqq.; K. J. Hefele, *Beiträge zur Kirchengeschichte, Archäologie und Liturgie,* vol. ii., Tübingen, 1864; A. Dolby, *Church Vestments, their Origin, Use, and Ornament,* London, 1868; W. B. Marriott, *Vestiarium Christianum: The original and gradual Development of the Dress of the Holy Ministry in the Church,* ib. 1868; R. Garrucci, *Storia della arte cristiana,* Prato, 1873 sqq.; J. A. Martigny, *Dictionnaire des antiquités chrétiennes,* part iii., new ed., Paris, 1877; J. von Hefner-Alteneck, *Trachten, Kunstwerke und Gerätschaften vom frühen Mittelalter,* 2d ed., Frankfort, 1880 sqq.; A. Kretschmar and C. Rohrbach, *Die Trachten der Völker,* 2d ed., Leipsic, 1880–82; M. H. Bloxam, *Principles of Gothic Ecclesiastical Architecture,* vol. iii., London, 1882; C. Rohault de Fleury, *La Messe. Études archéologiques,* 8 vols., Paris, 1883 sqq. (indispensable, especially vols. vii.–viii.); A. P. Stanley, *Christian Institutions,* chap. viii., London, 1884; V. Thalhofer, *Handbuch der katholischen Liturgik,* i. 856 sqq., Freiburg, 1887; A. Riegl, *Die ägyptischen Textilfunde,* Vienna, 1889; R. Forrer, *Die Gräber- und Textilfunde in Achmim-Panopolis,* Strasburg, 1891; idem, *Römische und byzantische Seiden-Textilien aus . . . Achmim-Panopolis,* ib. 1891; W. Lockhart, *The Chasuble: its Form and Size,* London, 1891; L. Clugnet, *Dictionnaire grec-français des noms liturgiques . . . dans l'église grecque,* Paris, 1895; O. J. Reichel, *English Liturgical Vestments in 13th Century,* London, 1895; J. K. Boyle, *Ecclesiastical Vestments: their Origin and Significance,* ib. 1896; R. A. S. Macalister, *Ecclesiastical Vestments, their Development and History,* ib. 1896; J. Braun, *Die liturgische Gewandung im Occident und Orient,* Freiburg, 1901; G. S. Tyack, *Historic Dress of the Clergy,* London, 1897; W. Durand, *The Sacred Vestments,* an English rendering of the Third Book of the *Rationale divinorum officiorum,* with notes by T. H. Passmore, ib. 1899; J. M. B. Clauss, *Rabat und Chorrock,* Strasburg, 1904; L. Duchesne, *Christian Worship,* passim, London, 1904; F. Procter and W. H. Frere, *New Hist. of the Book of Common Prayer,* ib. 1905; M. MacColl, *The Royal Commission and the Ornaments Rubric,* ib. 1906; J. H. Blunt, *Annotated Book of Common Prayer,* pp. 67–80, new issue, New York, 1908; P. Dearmer, *The Ornaments of the Minister,* London, 1908; H. Wilson, *Why and Wherefore,* Milwaukee, 1909 (deals with ornaments, vestments, and ritual); Mann, *Popes,* i. 413–419 (on the pallium).

VESTRY: A term originally applied to that portion of a church (usually a special room or even a

* *Auslegung des 26. Artikels* (ed. Egli and Finsler, II., 251): " *so sind Kutten, Krütz, hembder, platten nit nun weder gut noch böss sunder sy sind allein bös.*"

separate building) where the sacred vestments and the like were kept, and where the clergy robed for divine services. Since, however, meetings were often held there by those of the parishioners concerned with the business of the parish, the word came to be applied to the body entrusted with the temporal affairs of the parish, even when meeting in some place which had no connection with the church property. The laws governing the duties and rights of vestries differ much in England and America, on account of the far closer relation between Church and State in England, though it is only in connection with the Anglican communion that the vestry, properly speaking, exists.

In England a distinction is drawn between general and special vestries, the former including all rated for poor relief, even though not living within the parish bounds, while the special vestry is a smaller body chosen from the general vestry, and corresponds to the American connotation of the term. The duties of the English vestry are to elect church-wardens, to nominate proper persons for appointment as overseers of the poor, to adminster the parish property, and frequently to levy taxes for and superintend the performance of paving and lighting the parish, and they are also empowered, in case an old burying-ground be deemed inadequate or dangerous to health, to make provision for the acquisition of a new one.

In the United States the constituency and duties of the vestry vary considerably; in some dioceses it is not even required that vestrymen be communicants. In general the vestry consists of the incumbent of the parish as presiding officer, two wardens, and a number of vestrymen. Their duties are concerned almost exclusively with the administration of the finances of the parish, and the rector (or other incumbent, as vicar, priest-in-charge, and the like) can make no disbursements or enter into any contracts involving the parish finances without their approval. They are bound to pay the incumbent the salary agreed upon, and it is out of their power to remove an incumbent after he has been duly accepted. On the other hand, the choice of a new incumbent, when the rectorate has fallen vacant, is practically under the control of the vestry, subject to the approval of the bishop of the diocese, who, either in person or through a bishop or priest appointed by him, is the actual institutor of the new incumbent. At the institution of a new incumbent, according to the American Office of Institution, the two wardens (or two vestrymen appointed by them) stand on the right and left of the altar, the senior warden holding the keys of the church, which, after the reading of the bishop's letter of institution, he gives to the new incumbent with the words: " In the name and behalf of——— Parish [or Church] I do receive and acknowledge you, the Rev. A. B., as Priest and Rector of the same; and in token thereof, give into your hands the keys of this Church."

In case an incumbent fails to meet with the approval of the vestry and parish, complaint is to be lodged with the bishop of the diocese; but if the vestry can not themselves remove their incumbent, neither can he resign his charge without their con-

sent. During the absence of the incumbent the vestry have power to engage substitutes, and they are also empowered to elect the parish delegates to the diocesan conventions, while legally they are responsible for all the finances of the parish and for its debts, and must at any time show their minutes and other records and accounts to the bishop or any other person authorized to see them.

Bibliography: Bingham, Origines, VIII., vii. 7; S. Wilberforce, Hist. of the Protestant Episcopal Church, London, 1856; M. Hoffmann, Ritual Law of the Church, London, 1872; H. M. Baum, Rights and Duties of . . . Vestrymen in the American Church, Philadelphia, 1879; B. H. Paddock, in Journal of the General Convention, 1883, Appendix x.; DCA, ii. 2013–14.

VETTER, fet'ter, PAUL: German Roman Catholic; b. at Oberdettingen (a village near Biberach, 23 m. s.s.w. of Ulm), Württemberg, July 14, 1850; d. at Tübingen Sept. 21, 1906. He was educated at the University of Tübingen (Ph.D., 1872), and, after being lecturer at the Wilhelmstift in Tübingen and parish priest at Weiler, near Rothenburg, was in charge of the courses in Old-Testament exegesis in the Roman Catholic faculty of the University of Tübingen (1890–93), being professor of the same subject there after 1893. He wrote Chosroæ Magni explicatio precum missæ e lingua Armeniaca in Latinam versa (Freiburg, 1880); Der apokryphe dritte Korintherbrief (Tübingen, 1894); and Metrik des Buches Job (Freiburg, 1897).

VEUSTER, vū-stê', JOSEPH DE (better known as FATHER DAMIEN): Roman Catholic; b. at Tremeloo (16 m. n.e. of Brussels), Belgium; d. on the island of Molokai, Hawaii, Apr. 5, 1888. He became a novice of the order of the Fathers of the Sacred Heart of Jesus and Mary in 1858 and was admitted in 1860. In 1863 he was sent as its missionary to Hawaii and was there ordained a priest in 1864. He served on the islands of Hawaii and Molokai, and when the government segregated the lepers on the latter island he chose to live in the leper settlement, and acted not only as priest but as nurse, and in these services displayed both courage and devotion. He began this life in 1873 and remained immune to the disease until 1888, when he contracted it and soon died of it.

Bibliography: Auguste Pamphile de Veuster, Life and Letters of Father Damien, the Apostle of the Lepers. Edited with Introduction by his Brother, Father Pamphile, London, 1889; E. Clifford, Father Damien, 1889; Frances E. Cooke, The Story of Father Damien, 1889; Eugène Hubert, Hommage national au Père Damien, Le Père Damien, l'apôtre belge des lépreux de Molokai, Louvain, 1889; Pauline Craven (Mme. A. Craven), Le Père Damien, Paris, 1890, 5th ed., 1899; R. Butaye, Leven van Pader Damiaan, Brugge, 1890; H. H. Lauscher, Pater Damiaan. Naar het Fransch vertaald, met notas des Vertalers, Diest, 1890; R. L. Stevenson, Father Damien, an open Letter to the Rev. Dr. Hyde of Honolulu, Sydney, 1890, London, 1890; Pater Damien, der Held von Molokai, Freiburg, 1891, 2d ed., 1899; H. F., Pater Damiaan, de Apostel der Melaatschen, Ghent, 1895; C. W. Stoddard, Father Damien, the Martyr of Molokai, San Francisco 1901; Père Tauvel, Father Damien, translated from the French, London, new ed., 1904; Miss M. Quinlan, Damien of Molokai, London, 1909.

VIATICUM: Holy Communion administered to those in immediate danger of death, the term meaning literally " provision for a journey," and translating the Greek ephodion. In early times it was used for spiritual provision for the two great journeys of life and death—baptism and the last communion, the word being employed in the former sense by Basil the Great (*Hom.*, xiii.) and Gregory Nazianzen (*Oratio*, xl. 11). Before long, however, the word became restricted to the last communion. Thus the thirteenth canon of the first Council of Nicæa (325) states that " concerning the departing, the ancient canonical law is still to be maintained, to wit, that, if any man be at the point of death, he must not be deprived of the last and most indispensable Viaticum. But, if any one should be restored to health again who has received the communion when his life was despaired of, let him remain among those who communicate in prayers only. But in general, and in the case of any dying person whatsoever asking to receive the Eucharist, let the bishop, after examination made, give it him." The viaticum is repeatedly mentioned in later synods (e.g., the alleged canons of the Synod of Carthage of 398, 76–77; Orange [441], canon 3; Vaison [442], canon 2; Agde [506], canon 15; Gerunda [517], canon 9; and Toledo [675], canon 11). The earlier mode of administration was evidently under both kinds, and intinction was also permissible; or, if the condition of the sick or injured man required it, either the bread or the wine might alone be given. In other words, the method of administration was and is, so far as may be, similar to the modes of communicating those in perfect health.

The ordinary requirement of fasting communion is dispensed with in the reception of the viaticum, which is now given before the sacrament of extreme unction (q.v.), although in the Middle Ages the reverse order was observed. Like extreme unction, it may be given more than once, and if there is recovery, the recipient is required to attend mass as before. The minister is the parish priest or some one deputed by him, though in case of sudden accident the nearest priest is to administer it. In earlier times this was not the case, for during persecutions it was given even by laymen (Eusebius, *Hist. eccl.*, iv. 44), and Leo IV. (847–855) expressly forbade priests to send it by laymen or women (Mansi, *Concilia*, xiv. 891), while the Synod of Ansa (994) permitted none but priests to give it.

The elements administered in the viaticum are those customarily reserved after mass (see RESERVATION OF THE SACRAMENT). They are borne by the priest, wearing a purple stole, to the place where the sick or injured man may be, and, if possible, his confession is heard, with the ordinary absolution. There are also several versicles and responses, with a number of brief prayers; but the special form of the rite is the sentence, " Receive, *brother*, the Viaticum of the Body of our Lord Jesus Christ; may He preserve thee from the wicked enemy, and bring thee unto life everlasting. Amen."

In the Anglican Church the viaticum, though unmentioned under that name, is practically implied by the offices for the Visitation of the Sick (q.v.) and communion of the sick (see LORD'S SUPPER, V., § 2), and about it has really centered in great part the long struggle within that communion regarding reservation of the Sacrament (q.v.). Unlike the

Roman use, however, the regular order for the celebration of the Eucharist is followed in general, with such deviations only as are appropriate to the special conditions which would naturally prevail in the communion of the sick. There is also in the Anglican offices, from the First Prayer-Book to the modern English and American uses, a special rubric providing that if, for any valid reason, the sick man be unable to be communicated physically, he does, if possessing true penitence and faith, receive the elements, " profitably to his soul's health, although he do not receive the Sacrament with his mouth."

BIBLIOGRAPHY: Bingham, *Origines*, XV., iv. 9; most Roman Catholic manuals of devotion contain the viaticum office, e.g., *Manual of Prayers*, pp. 476–481, Baltimore, 1888; F. Procter and W. H. Frere, *New History of the Book of Common Prayer*, pp. 626–629, London, 1910.

VICAR: An official representative or substitute, especially in ecclesiastical affairs. According to the teaching of the Roman Catholic Church, as Christ appointed Peter his representative (Matt. xvi. 18–19), this power of representation passed to the bishops of Rome for all time, so that very early this bishop was " vicar of St. Peter " (or, " of the apostolic see "), " vicar of Christ," or " vicegerent of God on earth." As " the successor of Blessed Peter, prince of the apostles, and vicar of Jesus Christ," the pope also has vicars—all patriarchs, primates, archbishops, and bishops (qq.v.); and, in a narrower sense, the Curia (q.v.), papal legates and nuncios (see LEGATES AND NUNCIOS, PAPAL), and the like. These vicars, in turn, have their own substitutes. Thus archbishops and bishops have, in their sacerdotal capacity, vicars in suffragans (see WEIHBISCHOF) and Coadjutors (q.v.); and in their jurisdictional capacity Vicars-general (q.v.) and vicars forane [the latter corresponding to the Anglican rural deans], as well as collegiate bodies and canons (see CHAPTER, § 3), while in case of vacancy of a see (see SEDES VACANS) the cathedral chapter administers it, though within a week it must choose a definite temporary head. Rectors of parishes likewise have vicars or curates, and may also have, if need be, perpetual or temporary vicars assigned them. The vicar's powers of representing his rector are, however, limited in many respects.

[In the Anglican Church the vicar is an incumbent of a parish, the tithes of which belong to a religious house or chapter, or to a layman, the vicar receiving only the smaller tithes or a fixed salary, so that in some cases he is termed a vicar-stipendiary. An archbishop or bishop may be assisted in the discharge of his non-episcopal functions by a vicar-general, this office being represented in the American church by a rural dean (see DEAN) or archdeacon (q.v.). Also, the chapels of a parish church are served by vicars, a rector presiding over the parent church, the best instance in the United States being Trinity Church, New York City.]

In the Lutheran Church the consistory and superintendents (qq.v.) are the vicars of church administration. Pastors also have vicars, appointed either at the pastor's desire or by the governing officials, and either temporarily or permanently, as circumstances require. The term is likewise applied loosely to any representative or assistant of a pastor; while permanent vicars are placed in charge of self-supporting communities which peculiar conditions prevent from attaining parochial rank.   (E. Sehling.)

Bibliography: A. J. Binterim, *Denkwürdigkeiten*, i. 2, pp. 415 sqq., Mainz, 1825; *DCA*, ii. 2015–16.

VICAR-GENERAL: In the Roman Catholic system, the representative of the bishop in the exercise of his jurisdiction. Such representatives have been appointed since the thirteenth century, at first apparently in connection with the efforts of the bishops to break down the independent power of the Archdeacon (q.v.). The appointment of a vicar-general is at the discretion of the bishop, though in case of incapacity to conduct the affairs of the diocese he may be required by the pope to appoint one, or one may be appointed for him by the Congregation of Bishops and Regulars at Rome. Qualifications for the office are the possession of orders, or at least of the tonsure, the age of at least twenty-five years, knowledge of canon law (with a degree, if possible), legitimate birth and unmarried condition. He represents the bishop in his ordinary jurisdiction; but in certain specially important matters needs a definite authorization. From him, as the representative of the bishop, appeal lies not to the bishop, but to higher tribunals. His office is vacated by death or resignation, by the loss of jurisdiction on the part of the appointing bishop, or by the latter's revocation of his appointment. While in theory this last is perfectly free to the bishop, yet if he does it without any cause whatever, the vicar-general has recourse to the Congregation of Bishops and Regulars, which may compel his restoration.

(P. Hinschius†.)

Bibliography: P. Hinschius, *Kirchenrecht*, ii. 205, Berlin, 1871; E. Friedberg, *Lehrbuch des . . . Kirchenrechts*, p. 169, Leipsic, 1895.

VICELIN, vî′′cê-lin′: Apostle to the Wagrian Wends; b. at Hameln-on-the-Weser (26 m. s.w. of Hanover) toward the end of the eleventh century; d. at Oldenburg (32 m. n. of Lübeck) Dec. 12, 1154. He studied at Paderborn, where he became the assistant of Master Hartmann at the monastery school; later he was made head of the school at Bremen, where he distinguished himself for severity and ability. He then seems to have resided in France for a time (probably between 1123 and 1126), after which he was ordained priest and returned to his canonry at Bremen, and there found his life-mission when Archbishop Adalbero bade him preach the Gospel to the Wends.

The situation in the northern Slavic region belonging to the province of Hamburg seemed not unfavorable to such an enterprise, for, about 1093, after the reign of the pagan Kruto, Henry, son of the murdered Prince Gottschalk, had succeeded in regaining his father's dominions, ruling for thirty years from Wagria to Hither Pomerania. Between him and the neighboring Christian princes, especially the dukes of Saxony, friendly relations prevailed, but though himself a Christian, he did not imitate the missionary zeal of his father, whose fate he seems to have feared for himself. Notwithstanding this passive attitude of Henry, Adalbero felt that the time had come for the reestablishment

of missions to the Wends, among whom peace at last reigned, and he accordingly sent into the Wendish lands Vicelin and the canons Ludolf of Verden and Rudolf of Hildesheim. They received a friendly reception from Henry, who assigned them the church, apparently in ruins, at Old Lübeck; but hardly had they returned home to organize their labors, when the sudden death of the Wendish ruler (1127) destroyed their plans. Henceforth the life of Vicelin was a struggle against overwhelming odds. A slight consolation came when, shortly afterward, the archbishop appointed Vicelin parish priest at Wipenthorp, the modern Neumünster, near the Wagrian boundary, where he found need of missionary labors among his own flock, who, though nominally Christians, were pagan in belief and practise. Other priests soon gathered about him, and from their number he sent Ludolf and Volcward to Lübeck under the rule of Zwentipolch, the eldest son of Henry, who was distinctly friendly to Christianity. At Lübeck the missionaries were gladly welcomed by the little group of German merchants there, but in 1128 the men of Rügen destroyed the city, and the two priests barely escaped to Wipenthorp. In the struggles which the fall of Henry's line involved, the plans of Vicelin were hopeless, in spite of the warm friendship of the Danish Cnut Lavard, regent of the Wends.

In 1134 Vicelin interested the emperor in Wendish missions, and at his request the castle of Sigeberch was built in the western Wagrian district to form a center for the mission and to protect Holstein against Wendish inroads. The pagan Prince Pribislaw, who had seized the Wagrian and Obotritian districts after the murder of Lavard by his own kinsmen, was required to care for the church at Lübeck; but just as prospects again seemed favorable, they were blighted by the sudden death of Lothar. Pribislaw seized Sigeberch and burned the monastery at its foot, while the monks fled to Neumünster. At the same time Pribislaw's capital, Lübeck, was destroyed by his enemy Race, and the Christians were expelled, thus leaving Wagria destitute of all Christian influence.

Meanwhile Neumünster had flourished, and in 1141 Vicelin became provost of the Augustinian monastery. About this time, too, the cherished dream of his life again seemed hopeful. Henry of Badewide, made count of Holstein by Albert the Bear, now proceeded against the hordes of Pribislaw; the Wendish lands were utterly devastated by furious Holsteiners in 1138–39. Only in the extreme north did a few Wends survive. Wagria and Polabia were thus opened to German colonization; the Christianity that there found entrance formed a center for the missionary plans of Vicelin, still further strengthened by the building of a German Lübeck; and the friendly relations between Count Adolf of Schauenburg and Niklot, despite the latter's aversion to Christianity, guaranteed peace in Wendish Mecklenburg. These prospects, however, were blasted by the senseless crusade against the Wends in 1147, which rendered futile all hopes of peaceable conversion to Christianity (see Wends, Conversion of). Still Vicelin did not despair, and in his zeal even accepted episcopal dignity, only to

become involved in the investiture strife between
his archbishop, Hartwig of Stade, and his secular
lord, Henry the Lion of Saxony. On Sept. 25, 1149,
Vicelin was consecrated bishop of Oldenburg without conference between Hartwig and Henry. Henry,
however, declared that the investiture of bishops in
Wendish territory belonged to him as suzerain, and
ordered Adolf of Schauenburg to exact a tithe from
the new bishop. At first Vicelin hesitated to obey
these illegal demands, but eventually yielded, and in
1150 received investiture from Henry at Lüneburg.
Henry now gave him Bosau as an episcopal estate;
but, on the other hand, Vicelin had incurred the
implacable enmity of Hartwig, and as Oldenburg
remained inaccessible for him, he began to build his
palace at Bosau.

On the death of Conrad III. (1152), Hartwig renewed his protests against the claims of Henry the
Lion before the new king, Frederick Barbarossa. In
1152 Vicelin was required by the archbishop to accompany him to the diet at Merseburg, and there
receive investiture from the king. But the bishop
was crushed by age and infirmity, and declined to
obey, fearing a new outbreak of the controversy.
He returned to his diocese, where he was stricken
with hemiplegia in the summer of 1152, though he
lingered on until the end of 1154.

(E. Schäfer.)

Bibliography: Sources for a life are the Presbyter Helmold's *Chronica Slavorum*, ed. J. M. Lappenberg in *MGH,
Script.*, xxi. (1869), 1–99; the material brought together
by J. Langebek in *Script. rer. Danicarum*, iv. 433–445;
C. Schirren, in *Zeitschrift der Gesellschaft . . . für schleswig — . . . lauenburgische Geschichte*, viii (1878), 302–
318; and N. Beeck, in *Quellensammlung für schleswig —
. . . lauenburgische Geschichte*, iv (1875), 127–204. Consult further: W. von Bippen, *Kritische Untersuchung
über die Versus de vita Vicelini*, Lübeck, 1868; C. Schirren,
Beiträge zur Kritik älterer holsteinischer Geschichtsquellen,
pp. 1–9, 241 sqq., Leipsic, 1876; H. Höhlbaum, in *Forschungen zur deutschen Geschichte*, xvii (1877), 211–229;
R. Haupt, *Die Vizelinskirchen*, pp. 114–122, Kiel, 1884;
A Böhmer, *Vicelin. Ein Beitrag zur Kritik Helmolds*,
Wismar, 1887; G. F. Maclear, *Apostles of Mediæval
Europe*, pp. 240–250, London, 1888; L. Nottrott, *Aus
der Wendenmission*, Halle, 1897.

VICTOR: The name of three popes and two antipopes.

Victor I.: Pope 189–199. According to Jerome,
he was a Latin by birth. The outward condition
of the church in Rome, when Victor became its
head, was most prosperous; internal affairs, however, were less peaceful. The presbyter Florinus
was rousing excitement with writings that smacked
of Valentinianism, and Victor was obliged to expel
him from the Church. At about the same time the
presbyter Blastus declared that Easter (q.v., I., 3,
II., § 3) was to be celebrated on the fourteenth of
Nisan, and since he could cite the precedent of several churches in Asia Minor, he caused a schism in
Rome. The Italian bishops, convened at Rome by
Victor for the first Roman synod of which anything
is known, decided in favor of the Roman usage; but
Victor could not check the schism until he had won
over the churches in Asia Minor, which, accordingly
he threatened with excommunication, and also addressed a circular letter to all Catholic churches
asking their opinions in the matter. These supported Victor's position, but the churches of Asia
Minor refused to submit and were excommunicated.
Many of the bishops, however, disapproved this
course, and Irenæus of Lyons sought, probably unsuccessfully, to induce the bishops of Gaul to take
joint action against the pope, and thus to compel
him to revoke his anathema. But the hegemony of
the pope was now, for the first time, publicly
demonstrated, and by this victory the movement
headed by Blastus was also crushed.

Additional problems soon arose. Theodotus of
Byzantium sought to gain adherents to his Christology, and although Victor excommunicated him
for denying the divinity of Christ, his followers
formed a sort of community and even attempted to
make a bishop of their own. It is debated whether
Victor was the pope who, according to Tertullian
(*Adv. Praxeam*, i.), was ready to accept Montanistic
doctrines and was dissuaded only by Praxeas of
Asia Minor, who persuaded him to adopt his own
Christological ideas. It is equally problematical
whether Victor is to be identified with the Victorinus
who, according to the pseudo-Tertullian (*Hær.*,
viii.), sought to propagate the heresy of Praxeas
at Rome. The only fact certain is that modalism
was not officially taught at Rome during Victor's
pontificate.

According to Jerome, Victor wrote several works,
including one on the date of Easter, but he may not
be credited with the pseudo-Cyprian *Adv. aleatores*.
It is possible that he was the author of the Mura-
torian fragment. (H. Böhmer.)

Bibliography: Eusebius, *Hist. eccl.*, V., xxii.–xxviii.; *Catalogus Liberianus*, in Harnack, *Litteratur*, i. 146; *Liber
pontificalis*, ed. Mommsen in *MGH, Gest. pont. Rom.*, i
(1898), 18, and ed. L. Duchesne, vol. i., Paris, 1886; *ASB*,
July, vi. 534–542; J. Langen, *Geschichte der römischen
Kirche*, i. 179, 182 sqq., Bonn, 1881; A. Harnack, in *TU*,
v. 1 (1889), 110 sqq.; idem, *Litteratur*, i. 595–596, ii. 2,
pp. 370–381; idem, *Dogma*, vols. ii.–iii. passim; K. J.
Neumann, *Der römische Staat und die allgemeine Kirche*,
i. 205, Leipsic, 1890; F. Gregorovius, *Hist. of the City of
Rome*, i. 398, 424, 487, London, 1894; A. Schöne, *Die
Weltchronik des Eusebius in ihrer Bearbeitung durch Hier-
onymus*, pp. 181–201, Berlin, 1900; Schaff, *Christian
Church*, ii. 216–218; Neander, *Christian Church*, vol. i.
passim; Ceillier, *Auteurs sacrés*, i. 531–544, vi. 83–84;
Bower, *Popes*, i. 17–19; Platina, *Popes*, i. 35–36; Mil-
man, *Latin Christianity*, i. 64, 70.

Victor II. (Gebhard): Pope 1055–57. He was
according to tradition a scion of the ancient line
of the counts of Dollenstein and Hirschberg. In
1042 he was consecrated bishop of Eichstädt, and
for ten years his influence was dominant at the
German court. In 1053 he administered the duchy
of Bavaria for the minor Henry IV., and defended
the rights of the Empire against the deposed Duke
Conrad, Bishop Gebhard of Regensburg, and the
rebellious counts of Scheyern. In Sept., 1054, Henry
III. designated him pope at the diet of Mainz, but
Gebhard accepted, at the diet of Regensburg, in
Mar., 1055, only on condition that he retain his
German bishopric and his position as a prince of
the Empire, and that the emperor restore to the
Curia certain dioceses and castles to replete the
papal finances, which the Norman expeditions of
Leo IX. had seriously impaired.

On Apr. 13, 1055, Gebhard was enthroned. His
pontificate was marked by withdrawal from the
policy of secular expansion, and by a strengthening

in Italy of the political power of the German emperor. At Whitsuntide, 1055, he held a great reform synod at Florence, at which the emperor seems to have presided, and he reprimanded the monks of Monte Cassino for choosing an abbot without consulting Henry. The Romans were naturally opposed to a pope who thus favored the imperial aims, and in Sept., 1056, Victor returned to Germany. On Oct. 5 he was at the emperor's death-bed, and at Aachen enthroned the new King Henry IV., besides settling the Lotharingian troubles at the diet of Cologne in December and the conditions in Bavaria at the diet of Regensburg in Jan., 1057. In the following month he returned to Italy; early in the summer he was engaged in adjusting ecclesiastical affairs in Tuscany, but on July 28, 1057, he died at Arezzo.   (H. Böhmer.)

Bibliography: *Liber Pontificalis*, ed. L. Duchesne, vol. ii., Paris, 1892; Jaffé, *Regesta*, i. 549–553; the *Vita* by Boso is in J. M. Watterich, *Romanorum pontificum . . . vitæ*, i. 185–187, Leipsic, 1862; Mann, *Popes*, vi. 183–206; C. A. C. von Höfler, *Die deutschen Päpste*, ii. 208–268, Regensburg, 1839; R. Baxmann, *Die Politik der Päpste*, ii. 252–262, Elberfeld, 1869; M. Lefflad, *Regesten der Bischöfe von Eichstädt*, part 1, Eichstädt, 1871; J. Sax, *Die Bischöfe und Reichsfürsten von Eichstädt*, i. 39–43, Landshut, 1884; J. Langen, *Geschichte der römischen Kirche*, vol. iii., Bonn, 1892; F. Gregorovius, *Hist. of the City of Rome*, iv. 94–99, London, 1896; *ADB*, xxxix. 670–674; Hauck, *KD*, vol. iii. passim; Ceillier, *Auteurs sacrés*, xiii. 239–241, 298; Bower, *Popes*, ii. 361–363; Platina, *Popes*, i. 276; Milman, *Latin Christianity*, iii. 275–290; Schaff, *Christian Church*, v. 1, p. 15.

Victor III. (Daufari, Desiderius): Pope May 9–Dec. 16, 1087. A descendant of the ancient ducal house of Benevento, he was born in 1026 or 1027, and even as a boy showed a determined inclination for monastic life. In 1047 he was forced to marry, but on his wedding day fled to the hermitage of Santari, whence he was brought back by compulsion. In the following year he again fled, and was finally allowed to take the cowl at St. Sofia near Benevento under the name of Desiderius. But St. Sofia was too lax for him, and in 1051–52 he went to Tremite San Nicolo in the Adriatic, whence, early in 1053, he retired to the hermits of Majella in the Abruzzi. In May of the same year, however, Leo IX. recalled him to the south, and for nearly eight months he was a companion of the captive pope at Benevento, where Desiderius became a sympathizer with the ideals of the reform party. In Apr.–May, 1055, he was in Florence to advise with Victor II. concerning the fate of Benevento. He accompanied the pope to the Roman marches, but in December he seized the opportunity once more to retire. Late in 1056 or early in 1057, he was provost of the Benedictine abbey at Capua, a daughter-house of Monte Cassino. On Nov. 30, 1057, Stephen IX. appointed him abbot of Monte Cassino. At Stephen's death, Apr. 10, 1058, he hastened to Campania, where, on Apr. 19, he took possession of his abbey, Monte Cassino. This he speedily restored, morally, strategically, as well as architecturally, while through his zeal for learning a little school grew up in the monastery. His activity extended to other monasteries as well, so that he reformed the daughter-houses of San Liberatore in the Abruzzi and St. Benedict in Capua, established two new houses in Capua and near Fondi, as papal vicar for monasteries in southern Italy reformed the abbeys of Subiaco, Tremite, and others, and made an attempt to reestablish monasticism in Sardinia.

The success of Desiderius was due in no small measure to his ecclesiastical and political activity in behalf of the Curia. As early as Mar. 6, 1059, Nicolas II. had created him cardinal of S. Cæcilia in Trastevere, and in this capacity he attended the Lateran synod of the same year. In June he entertained the pope at Monte Cassino, and accompanied him to Melfi in July. There he induced the Normans Richard of Capua and Robert of Guiscard to accept their territories as fiefs from the pope, so that henceforth he was considered indispensable to the Curia. Desiderius worked for peace among the Norman princes, and associated with those who had been placed under the ban, nor was it until 1078 that he effected an alliance between the Curia and Robert Guiscard. He renewed his policy, however, with Henry IV. in 1082, and even went to Rome to endeavor to negotiate peace for him with the pope; but when he failed, he sided with Gregory, whom, after Henry's victory, he sheltered in Monte Cassino, being one of the faithful few at the pope's death-bed at Salerno (May 25, 1085).

At the preliminary conferences concerning a new pope the name of Desiderius was prominent, but he sought no such dignity and succeeded in deferring the election until the end of May, 1086. He was then finally elected, but four days later, together with the cardinals, was driven from Rome by the imperial prefect of the city. In his flight he laid aside his pontifical robes and returned as abbot to Monte Cassino. In Mar., 1087, as apostolic vicar he convened the Gregorian cardinals to a new election at Capua. Here again the majority declared for him, although a small minority, headed by Hugo, archbishop of Lyons, demanded that he justify his association with Henry IV. In disgust Desiderius left the assembly, but on the following day (Mar. 21, 1087) he appeared in pontifical regalia, dreading to give the papacy to the ultra-Gregorians even more than to become Gregory's successor. To avoid the schism which threatened his pontificate, he sought to win over the Gregorians, confirming the ban on Henry and strictly renewing the prohibition of lay investiture at a synod at Benevento in Aug., 1087. At the same time, he renounced Gregory's dreams of temporal power and sought only to retain Rome. But Rome was in the hands of the antipope, and it was only after Gisulf of Salerno and Jordan of Capua had stormed the city that he could be enthroned as Victor III. (May 9). Almost immediately the antipope renewed his attacks, and on June 20 was again in possession of St. Peter's. Had not Victor retained the abbey of Monte Cassino, he, like Gregory, would have died in exile, for on Sept. 16, 1087, he passed away.

Brief as was the pontificate of Victor III., it was epoch-making in two respects: as inaugurating the break with the temporal policy of Gregory VII.; and as showing the power of the pope to rouse the Christians to war against Islam by his simple word; for shortly before his death he urged a crusade against the Moors of northern Africa which was successfully carried out within the year. Victor was the author of three books of dialogues on the miracles of St. Benedict, a poetic epitaph on Abbot Apollinaris, and information concerning two miracles of Leo IX., all written in a clear and simple style (ed. *ASM*, IV., ii. 425 sqq.; *MPL*, cxlix).

(H. BÖHMER.)

BIBLIOGRAPHY: The early *Vita* from the *Chronicon Casinense*, book iii., with commentary, is in *ASB*, Sept., v. 373–435, and in *MPL*, cxlix. 918–962, cf. *ASM*, vi. 2, pp. 583–625. Other sources are Aimé de Mont-Cassin, *L'Ystoire de li Normant*, iii. 49, ed. O. Delarc, Rouen, 1892; Peter the Deacon, ed. Muratori, in *Scriptores*, vi. 32 sqq. Consult further: Jaffé, *Regesta*, i. 655–656; Mann, *Popes*, vii. 218–244; L. Tosti, *Storia della Badia di Monte Cassino*, vol. i., Naples, 1841; J. M. Watterich, *Romanorum pontificum . . . vitæ*, i. 310 sqq., Leipsic, 1862; F. Hirsch, in *Forschungen zur deutschen Geschichte*, vii. 1–103, Göttingen, 1867; A. Caravita, *I codici e le arti a Monte Cassino*, parts i.–iii., Monte Cassino, 1869–71; J. Langen, *Geschichte der römischen Kirche*, iii. 162 sqq., Bonn, 1892; L. von Heinemann, *Geschichte der Normannen in Unteritalien*, i. 172 sqq., Leipsic, 1894; F. Gregorovius, *Hist. of the City of Rome*, iv. 564–572, London, 1896; Ceillier, *Auteurs sacrés*, ix. 241, 300–301, 317–318, xiii. 415–418; Bower, *Popes*, ii. 410–413; Platina, *Popes*, ii. 12–13; Milman, *Christian Church*, iii. 501–508; Hauck, *KD*, vol. iii. passim; Schaff, *Christian Church*, v. 1, pp. 65, 70.

Victor IV.: Two antipopes: Gregory Conti (1138) and Octavian (1159–64). The former of these was elected in the middle of Mar., 1138, by the Roman Pierleoni to succeed Anacletus II., but on May 29 of the same year, at the instance of Bernard of Clairvaux, he submitted to Innocent II. and resigned his claims. Octavian, the scion of one of the most powerful Roman families and cardinal of St. Cæcilia, was elected to the papal throne Sept. 9, 1159, by four or five cardinals, the clergy of St. Peter's, and the Roman people. Although he relied largely on the support of Emperor Frederick I., the latter remained neutral until the Council of Pavia in Feb., 1160, when he declared for Victor. But all imperial efforts to gain recognition of Victor in England, France, and even in Germany were fruitless; and after the summer of 1163 Alexander III. sought to gain Germany for himself. During the negotiations Victor died at Lucca Apr. 20, 1164.

(H. BÖHMER.)

BIBLIOGRAPHY: Jaffé, *Regesta*, i. 919, ii. 418–426; Moritz Meyer, *Die Wahl Alexander III. und Victor IV., 1159*, Göttingen, 1871; J. Langen, *Geschichte der römischen Kirche*, iii. 439 sqq., Bonn, 1892; Bower, *Popes*, ii. 470, 503–511; Platina, *Popes*, ii. 39–42, 50 sqq.; Milman, *Latin Christianity*, iv. 289; Schaff, *Christian Church*, v. 1, p. 111; Hauck, *KD*, vol. iv. passim; and the literature under INNOCENT II. and ALEXANDER III.

VICTOR OF ANTIOCH: Presbyter and exegete of the middle of the sixth century. The numerous scholia ascribed to him and scattered through the entire catena to Jeremiah show that the author of that catena must have excerpted from the complete commentary on the prophet by Victor (ed. M. Ghislerius in his commentary on Jeremiah, 3 vols., Lyons, 1623). His commentary on Mark (ed. P. Possinus, Rome, 1673; F. C. Matthäi, Moscow, 1775; J. A. Cramer, *Catenæ Græcorum patrum*, i. 259–447, Oxford, 1840) exists in three recensions, all of which may be traced to a single source. Victor states in the prologue to this work that he endeavored to collect interpretations of the best expounders, and his commentary on Jeremiah contains verbal repetitions from Chrysostom, Jerome, and the scholia of Severus and Olympiodorus. His exegetical method is that of the Antiochian school, primarily grammatical and historical, so that his tendency is practical and ethical, although allegory is not absolutely excluded. (N. BONWETSCH.)

BIBLIOGRAPHY: M. Faulhaber, *Die Propheten-Catenen nach römischen Handschriften*, pp. 107 sqq., 133, Freiburg, 1899; H. von Soden, *Die Schriften des N. Ts. in ihrer erreichbaren ältesten Textgestalt*, i. 574 sqq., 826 sqq., 888 sqq., Berlin, 1902.

VICTOR OF CAPUA: Bishop of Capua and harmonist of the Gospels; d. Apr. 2, 554. The only detail known concerning his life is that he was consecrated bishop Feb. 24, 541. On July 27, 1480, his bones were found beneath the high altar of the church of the monastery of Mons Virginis. Of his writings only scanty fragments survive. Bede, in his *De ratione temporum*, xlix., cites from his *De pascha*, directed against the *Cursus paschalis* of Victorius. This must have been written early in 550 to prove that in that year Easter should be celebrated on Apr. 24, not Apr. 17. A number of scholia apparently translated by Victor from a Greek catena, and concerned with Polycarp, Origen, Diodorus of Tarsus, Severianus of Gabala, and a certain Geronticum, have been edited by J. B. Pitra (*Spicilegium Solesmense*, i. 265 sqq., Paris, 1852) from a Paris manuscript which also contains fragments from a work *Reticulus seu de arce Noe* (ib., pp. 287 sqq.). The *Capitula de resurrectione Domini*, apparently extant in the ninth century, is now lost. A catena on the four Gospels which F. Feuardent (*Irenæi quinque libri*, pp. 240–241, Paris, 1639) found in an ancient Verdun manuscript under the name of Victor of Capua is probably identical with the work from which Pitra edited his scholia, which in the Paris manuscript bears the name of Johannes Diaconus.

Far more important than these writings were Victor's endeavors to prepare a Latin harmony of the Gospels. The oldest manuscript of this work is preserved at Fulda, ordered from Victor himself and completed at Capua before Apr. 12, 546. This manuscript (ed. E. Ranke, *Codex Fuldensis*, Marburg, 1868) contains a harmony of the Gospels, the Pauline epistles, including Hebrews, Acts, the canonical epistles, and the Apocalypse. Of these the first is the most important, since through it the West gained its first knowledge of Tatian's *Diatessaron* (see HARMONY OF THE GOSPELS, I., §§ 1–4). It is clear, moreover, that the anonymous harmony which Victor says, in his preface, that he found by chance, and which proved to be by Tatian, must have been in Greek, and that Victor translated or revised it. His work consisted essentially in reproducing the Greek original through the Latin translation of Jerome, a task demanding great patience as well as a thorough knowledge of the Bible. But though he termed his work a translation, he actually divided the Vulgate Gospels into portions which he then rearranged according to the model before him. His work was most valuable, and the Germans first learned the Gospel in their own tongue from the Old High German translation of the harmony of Victor. (ERWIN PREUSCHEN.)

BIBLIOGRAPHY: *ASB*, Oct., viii. 81–83; F. Ughelli, *Italia sacra*, vi. 306–307, Venice, 1720; J. B. Pitra, *Spicilegium Solesmense*, pp. l.–liv., 265–277, 296–301, Paris, 1852; J. L. Jacobi, in *Zeitschrift für christliche Wissenschaft und christliches Leben*, pp. 246 sqq., Berlin, 1854; T. Zahn, in *Patrum apostolicorum opera*, ii., pp. xlvii. sqq., ib. 1876; idem, *Forschungen zur Geschichte des neutestamentlichen Kanons*, i. 1 sqq.. Erlangen, 1881; idem, *Geschichte des neutestamentlichen Kanons*, ii. 535 sqq., Leipsic, 1891; F. Piper, in *ZKG*, i (1877), 239–240; *DCB*, iv. 1123–26.

VICTOR OF CARTENNA: Christian author of the fifth century. The only source of information is Gennadius (*De vir. ill.*, lxxvii.), supplemented by the *Notitia provinciarum et civitatum Africæ* (ed. M. Petschenig, in *CSEL*, vii.). According to these, he was bishop of Cartenna in Mauretania Cæsarea and was the author of a defense of orthodoxy against Arianism, a book on public penance, a "Consolation" to a certain Basil, and a collection of sermons. About 484 he seems to have been succeeded as bishop by Lucidus. Unfortunately all his writings have perished, and the attempts to ascribe to him the *De pœnitentia publicani* sometimes included in earlier editions of Ambrose of Milan are valueless. The *De pœnitentia* has with more probability been ascribed to Victor of Tunnenna (q.v.); while the "Consolation" included in the works of Basil the Great is clearly not by Victor, since it contains absolutely no allusion to Basil. (FRANZ GÖRRES.)

BIBLIOGRAPHY: Gennadius, *De vir. ill.*, lxxviii., Eng. transl. in *NPNF*, 2d ser., iii. 398; F. Görres, in *ZWT*, 1906, pp. 484–494; Tillemont, *Mémoires*, xvi. 611–612; F. Papencordt, *Geschichte der vandalischen Herrschaft in Africa*, passim, Berlin, 1837; *DCB*, iv. 1122; *SBA*, 1861, pp. 529–530; Ceillier, *Auteurs sacrés*, iv. 493, v. 512, x. 468–469.

VICTOR OF TUNNENNA: Bishop of Tunnenna (Tonnonna, Tonnenna, Tunna) in the province of Africa Proconsularis, and historian; d. probably at Byzantium after 565. The details of his life are known only from the fragment of his chronicle (*MPL*, lxviii.; *MGH, Auct. ant.*, xi. 1 (1894), pp. 184–206). According to this, he was exiled, after many persecutions, to Alexandria in 555, whence he was taken, in 564, to Byzantium. He closes his history with the accession of Justin II. in 565, after which nothing is known concerning him. He was a determined opponent of the theology of Justinian and an advocate of the three chapters (see THREE CHAPTER CONTROVERSY). His work, which was a continuation of the chronicles of Jerome and Prosper of Aquitaine, began with the creation, but only the portion from 444 to 565 (567) has survived. With all its historical, chronological, and theological limitations, his work is the only supplement to Jerome and Prosper which possesses human interest. Certain other works have been ascribed to this Victor, and there is a slender manuscript support for his authorship of the pseudo-Ambrosian *De pœnitentia publicani* (*MPL*, xvii. 1059–94), earlier assigned to Victor of Cartenna (q.v.).

(G. A. JÜLICHER.)

BIBLIOGRAPHY: F. Papencordt, *Geschichte der vandalischen Herrschaft in Afrika*, pp. 359–365, Berlin, 1837; Holder-Egger, in *NA*, i (1876), 289 sqq.; T. Hodgkin, *Invaders of Italy*, vol. iii. passim, 4 vols., London, 1880–85; A. Ebert, *Geschichte der christlich-lateinischen Literatur*, i. 586, Leipsic, 1889; G. von Dzialowski, *Isidor und Ildefons als Literarhistoriker*, pp. 62–64, Münster, 1898; Ceillier, *Auteurs sacrés*, v. 512, x. 469, xi. 302; *DCB*, iv. 1126; *KL*, xii. 909–911.

VICTOR OF VITA: Bishop of Vita (apparently his native city) in the African province of Byzacena, probably from before 477 to after 484. Information concerning him is drawn almost exclusively from his one extant work, the *Historia persecutionis Africanæ provinciæ* (*MPL*, lviii.; ed. C. Halm, in *MGH, Auct. Ant.*, iii. 1, 1879; and M. Petschenig, in *CSEL*, vol. vii.), an account of the sufferings of the Catholics under the Vandal kings Geiserich and Hunnerich. The history seems to have been written during the lifetime of Hunnerich and published after his death, between 485 and 489. It is in three books, the first devoted to the reign of Geiserich and the latter two to the eight years of Hunnerich. The vocabulary is meager, the style mediocre, and the theological ability only average; but the work is generally trustworthy, and, at least in the reign of Hunnerich, the author was an eye-witness of what he described. The work is, therefore, valuable for its material concerning the political, religious, social, and liturgical conditions of Vandal Africa about 480.

Appended to the history both in the manuscripts and the editions is a *Passio septem monachorum*, dating from 483 or 484 and ascribed to Victor, though certainly not by him. His work receives a valuable supplement in the *Notitia provinciarum et civitatum Africæ* (ed. Halm and Petschenig, ut sup.), a list of all the Catholic bishops of the seven Vandal provinces of Africa officiating in 484 and bidden to attend a religious colloquy at Carthage on Feb. 1 of that year. Victor of Vita is noted there as "not coming." (G. A. JÜLICHER.)

BIBLIOGRAPHY: *ASB*, Aug., iv. 628–632; M. Petschenig, in the *Sitzungsberichte* of the Vienna Academy, philosophical-historical class, xcvi (1880), 637–732 (the best introduction); J. Liron, *Dissertation sur Victor de Vite*, Paris, 1708; F. Papencordt, *Geschichte der vandalischen Herrschaft in Afrika*, pp. 366–370, Berlin, 1837; F. X. Kraus, *Realencyklopädie der christlichen Altertümer*, i. 259–262, 279, Freiburg, 1880; A. Auler, in *Historische Untersuchungen A. Schäfer gewidmet*, pp. 253–275, Bonn, 1882; W. Pötzsch, *Victor von Vita und die Kirchenverfolgung im Vandalenreiche*, Döbeln, 1887; A. Ebert, *Geschichte der Literatur des Mittelalters*, i. 454–458, 2d ed., Leipsic, 1889; W. S. Teuffel, *Geschichte der römischen Literatur*, § 470, Leipsic, 1890; P. Ferrère, *De Victoris Vitensis libro*, Paris, 1898; A. Schönfelder, *De Victore Vitensi*, Breslau, 1899; Ceillier, *Auteurs sacrés*, x. 448–464 (contains an excellent bibliography); *MPL*, lviii. 395–434; *DCB*, iv. 1122–23; *KL*, xii. 911–913.

VICTOR, CLAUDIUS MARIUS: Christian poet of the fifth century. According to Gennadius (*De vir. ill.*, xli.), he was a rhetorician of Marseilles and died between 425 and 450. The work which has been transmitted under his name is a Biblical epic, entitled *Alethia*, a free paraphrase of Genesis in hexameters, not without poetic beauty. Originally comprising, in all probability, twelve books, only three are extant, going to the destruction of Sodom. The sole edition of value is by K. Schenkl (*CSEL*, xvi.). The earlier editor J. Gagneius (Lyons, 1536) added as a fourth book the "epigram" of an otherwise unknown Paulinus (ed. also K. Schenkl, ut sup.), a poetic penitential sermon apparently written about 408, lamenting that in Gaul, after the ravages of the Vandals and Alans, the care of souls was considered less important than the restoration of vineyards and houses. (R. SCHMID.)

BIBLIOGRAPHY: A. Bourgoin, *De Claudio Mario Victore*, Paris, 1883; S. Gamber, *Le Livre de la Genèse dans la poesie latine du v. siècle*, Marseilles, 1884; A. Ebert, *Geschichte der Literatur des Mittelalters*, i. 320–321, 369 sqq., Leipsic, 1889; W. S. Teuffel, *Geschichte der römischen Literatur*, pp. 1186–87, Leipsic, 1890; M. Manitius, *Geschichte der christlich-lateinischen Poesie*, pp. 164 sqq., 180 sqq., Stuttgart, 1891; H. Maurer, *De exemplis quæ C. Maurius Victor in Alethia secutus sit*, Marburg, 1896; Bardenhewer, *Patrologie*, pp. 394–395, Eng. transl., St. Louis, 1908; *KL*, xii. 909; *DCB*, iv. 1121–22.

VICTORINUS, vic''to-rai'nŭs, **OF PETTAU:** Bishop of Poetovio (the modern Pettau, 128 m. s. of Vienna) and the earliest exegete of the Latin Church; probably born in Pannonia; martyred 304 (according to the martyrologies, on Dec. 2). According to Jerome (*De vir. ill.*, lxxiv.), he was better acquainted with Greek than with Latin, and besides many other works wrote commentaries on Gen., Ex., Lev., Isa., Ezek., Hab., Eccles., Cant., and Rev., as well as " against all heresies." Jerome states also (ib. xviii.) that Victorinus was a chiliast, and in the eleventh book of his commentary on Ezekiel he declares that the bishop of Pettau was an adherent, in his " frequent expositions," of Jewish fables (*MPL*, xxv. 339).

In his commentaries Victorinus knew and employed such works as those of Papias, Origen, Irenæus, and Hippolytus. Stylistically his writings were awkward and overladen with Hellenisms. Besides the nine commentaries listed by Jerome in the *De vir. ill.*, the same author twice mentions a commentary of Victorinus on Matthew, in which he held that the " brothers of the Lord " were such " by nearness, not by nature " (*MPL*, xxiii. 201, xxvi. 220). Of his exegetical writings the commentary on the Apocalypse alone has survived; for the treatise *De fabrica mundi* (ed. M. J. Routh, *Reliquiæ sacræ*, iii. 451–461, Oxford, 1846) is not part of the commentary on Genesis, but an independent work on the week of creation, the " queen of all weeks." Here the number seven is prominent; the true sabbath is the seventh millennium when Christ shall reign with his elect. The original text of the commentary on the Apocalypse, as represented in the Vatican manuscript *Codex Ottobonianus Lat.* 3288 A, was completely revised by Jerome, the latter text being represented by the *editio princeps* (Paris, 1543; reprinted in the *Maxima bibliotheca veterum patrum*, iii. 414–421, Lyons, 1777). Here the chiliasm of Victorinus is expurgated, his harsh Latin is smoothed down, and many minor theological corrections are made. The material substituted by Jerome for the expunged passages was taken largely from the commentary of the Donatist Ticonius on the Apocalypse.

The next stage in the evolution of the text of Victorinus was the addition, frequently in mechanical fashion and with many repetitions, of a fuller, though still incomplete, text of the Apocalypse. Other additions were also made, such as the replacement of 666 as the mystic designation of the future name of Antichrist by specific names. This recension, though still unedited, is found in a series of manuscripts and was used by the Spanish presbyter Beatus of Libana in compiling his commentary on the Apocalypse (ed. H. Florez, Madrid, 1770). The final step is represented by the eleventh- or twelfth-

century manuscript ccxlvii. of the library of Monte Cassino (ed. in the *Florilegium Casinense*, pp. 1–12, appended to the *Bibliotheca Casinensis*, vol. v., Monte Cassino, 1894), this recension also forming the basis of the extremely rare *editio princeps* (Bologna, 1558), reprinted in *MPL*, v. 317–344. The editor of this recension constructed a mixed text from the other recensions, removed various sources of confusion, and even departed from the original form of the commentary to bring it into harmony with the running text of the Apocalypse, besides making many additions, some of which imply an African origin.

The commentary on the Apocalypse and the *De fabrica mundi* are the only works that can certainly be ascribed to Victorinus of Pettau. The *Adv. omnes hæreses*, assigned to him by Jerome and by Optatus of Mileve (*De schismate Donatistarum*, i. 9) is by some identified with a treatise of the same title appended to the *De præscriptione* of Tertullian; but the style deviates widely from the genuine writings of Victorinus, and a passage of the Apocalypse (ii. 6) common to the two has a divergent wording. The antimarcionistic character ascribed to the *Adv. omnes hæreses* of Victorinus by Optatus is not borne out by this pseudo-Tertullian work, but rather by the pseudo-Tertullian poem *Adversus Marcionem libri quinque*. A number of passages in this poem correspond so closely with passages in the commentary on the Apocalypse that the two would almost seem to be by the same author, and it is still a problem whether the assumption that the common source of both is the Greek commentary of Hippolytus on the Apocalypse suffices to explain the resemblance between the two works. It is at least clear that the poem is not by Commodian, as is sometimes maintained. The attempt has also been made to ascribe to Victorinus the *Anonymi chiliastæ in Matthæum cxxiv fragmenta* (ed. G. Mercati, *Studi e testi*, xi. 23–45, Rome, 1903), but it is now recognized that the author of this fragment stands in close relation to the so-called Ambrosiaster. An equally fruitless effort has been made to ascribe to this Victor the following treatises also contained in *Codex Ottobonianus* A: a treatise on Gen. i. 5 (cf. *MPL*, viii. 1009–14); *Ad Justinum Manichæum contra duo principia Manichæorum* (cf. *MPL*, viii. 999–1010); and *De physicis* (cf. *MPL*, viii. 1295–1310). Both style and matter, however, are totally different from those of Victorinus of Pettau. The first two may belong to Caius Marius Victorinus (q.v.). Whether the *De physicis* is to be attributed to him is doubtful; at all events, it was not written by Victorinus of Pettau. (J. HAUSSLEITER.)

BIBLIOGRAPHY: The critical ed. of the *Opera* is in *CSEL*, vol. xxxix.; Eng. transl. of the " Creation " and " Commentary on the Apocalypse " in *ANF*, vii. 341–360. Consult: Jerome, *De vir. ill.*, lxxiv., Eng. transl. in *NPNF*, 2 ser., iii. 377; *ASB*, Nov., i. 432–443; J. de Launoy, *Opera*, ii. 1, pp. 634–649, Geneva, 1731; F. Chamard, *S. Victorin, évêque et martyr*, Poitiers, 1876; Harnack, *Litteratur*, i. 731–735, ii. 2, pp. 426–432; idem, in *ZWT*, xix (1876), 114; idem, *Dogma*, ii. 237, 296, 358, iii. 78, v. 29; J. Haussleiter, in *ZKW*, vii (1886), 239–257; idem, *Der Aufbau der altchristlichen Litteratur*, pp. 35–37, Berlin, 1898; idem, in *Festreden der Universität Greifswald*, no. 9, Greifswald, 1901; F. Kattenbusch, *Das apostolische Symbol*. pp. 212–215, Leipsic, 1894; J. R. Harris, in *The Expositor*, 1895, pp. 448–455; L. Atzberger, *Geschichte der christlichen Eschatologie innerhalb der vornicänischen Zeit*, pp. 566–573, Freiburg, 1896; W. Macholz, *Spuren binitarischer Denkweise im Abendlande seit Tertullian*, Jena, 1902; M. Schanz, in *I. von Müller's Handbuch der klassischen Altertumswissenschaft*, 2d ed., viii. 437–439, Munich, 1905; W. Bousset, *Die Offenbarung Johannis*, pp. 53–55, Göttingen, 1906; Bardenhewer, *Patrologie*, pp. 156, 198–199, Eng. transl., St. Louis, 1908; idem, *Geschichte*, ii. 593–598; Schaff, *Christian Church*, ii. 861–864; *DCB*, iv. 1128–29; *KL*, xii. 925–926.

VICTORINUS, CAIUS MARIUS: Philosopher, rhetorician, grammarian, and theologian; b. in Africa; d. probably at Rome about 363. At Rome he gained distinction as a representative of Neo-Platonic scholasticism and as the commentator and translator of Aristotelian and Neo-Platonic writings. Some time previous to 357, he became an open convert to Christianity and an ardent defender of Nicene orthodoxy in his *De generatione verbi divini*, directed against the Arian Candidus, and in the four books *Adv. Arium*, written in 357–358. When he wrote his commentaries on the Pauline epistles (probably more than the three which have been preserved) is uncertain. The edict of Julian forbidding Christians to teach obliged Victorinus to resign his professorship of rhetoric, and as he seems to have become a convert when an aged man, he probably died shortly afterward. Victorinus was the author of many other philosophical and theological treatises, all of which have perished except those already mentioned (ed., with some doubtful works, *MPL*, viii.).

Even as a Christian Victorinus remained essentially a philosopher, almost undisguisedly developing the entire system of Plotinus in his dogmatics and by its aid seeking speculative support for the Nicene doctrines. His theological writings exercised no lasting influence; the commentaries contained dangerous expressions, and his trinitarian doctrine was too speculative and inaccurate dogmatically to win followers. (R. Schmid.)

Bibliography: Augustine, *Confessions*, viii. 2–5; R. Schmid, *Marius Victorinus und seine Beziehungen zu Augustin*, Kiel, 1895; J. de Launoy, *Opera*, ii. 1, pp. 645–646, 10 vols., Geneva, 1731–32; J. E. B. Mayor, *Clue to Latin Literature*, pp. 172–173, London, 1875; H. Usener, *Anecdoton Holderi*, pp. 59–66, Bonn, 1877; G. Koffmane, *De Mario Victorino*, Breslau, 1880; G. Geiger, *Caius Marius Victorinus Afer*, 2 parts, Metten, 1888–89; A. Ebert, *Geschichte der Literatur des Mittelalters*, i. 124–125, 315–316, Leipsic, 1889; W. S. Teuffel, *Geschichte der römischen Literatur*, pp. 1031–35, Leipsic, 1890; Harnack, *Dogma*, v. 29, 33 sqq., 279–280; idem, in *Zeitschrift für Theologie und Kirche*, 1891; M. Manitius, *Geschichte der christlich-lateinischen Poesie*, pp. 113 sqq., Stuttgart, 1891; M. Schanz, in *I. von Müller's Handbuch der klassischen Altertumswissenschaft*, viii. 137 sqq., Munich, 1904; Bardenhewer, *Patrologie*, pp. 366–367, 417, Eng. transl., St. Louis, 1908; *DCB*, iv. 1129–38; *KL*, xii. 926–927.

VICTRICIUS, vic-trî'shi-us: Bishop of Rouen; d. before 409. He is said to have been a soldier and to have escaped execution as a deserter by miracle after he became a Christian. He went as missionary to the Morini and Nervii and became bishop about 393. He wrote a book, *De laude sanctorum* (in *MPL*, xx. 437–458), in the first chapter of which he states that at the call of his fellow bishops he went to Britain " to make peace " and accomplished his mission, " if not as he ought, yet as best he could." Nothing more is known of the incident, and Victricius' account is highly rhetorical. It is

interesting as an illustration of the relations between the old British and the Gallic churches and in comparison with the mission of Germanus of Auxerre (q.v.) some thirty years later.

Bibliography: *ASB*, Aug., ii. 193–197; *Acta sanctorum Belgii*, i. 374–436, 6 vols., Brussels, 1783–94; A. Le Flaguais, in *Mémoires des antiquaires de Normandie*, vol. xxii., p. xxiv.; *Histoire littéraire de la France*, ii. 752–754; *MPL*, xx. 437–438; *DNB*, iv. 1140.

VIENNA, CONCORDAT OF. See Concordats and Delimiting Bulls, VI., 2, § 6.

VIENNA, PEACE OF: Treaty concluded in behalf of Hungary June 23, 1606. Under Emperor Rudolph II. (1576–1608), the greater part of Hungary had accepted the Reformation. But from the time of the importation of the Jesuits by the archbishop of Colocza, George Draskovich, in 1578, these proceeded to operate against Protestantism. Persecutions opened in 1603 under Count Belgiojoso of Kaschau, imperial commander in upper Hungary. When, therefore, the diet at Presburg in 1604 drafted a complaint in twenty-one articles, charging violation of the religious freedom, and forwarded a copy of these resolutions to the emperor in Prague, Rudolph answered, under the instigation of his bishops and the Jesuits, in the form of a twenty-second article, which summarily rejected the grievances of the estates, renewed all mandates of the Roman Catholic religion, and threatened the penalties prescribed for heresies by the Roman canon law, against the future bearers of religious grievances before the national diet. The Protestant persecutions were resumed with fresh zeal, notably under General Basta, to which opposition was first offered by the Reformed magnate, Stephen Botskai, at the head of the Protestants in Transylvania. The disturbance spread to Hungary, and made such inroads that the Archduke Matthias was constrained to conclude the Peace of Vienna, repealing art. 22 of 1604, and guaranteeing complete religious freedom. Nevertheless, this by no means terminated the persecutions in Hungary in those times. (E. Sehling.)

Bibliography: *Geschichte der evangelischen Kirche in Ungarn*, pp. 145 sqq., Berlin, 1854; *Die Lage der Protestanten in der oesterreichischen Monarchie*, 1855; *Jahrbuch der Gesellschaft für die Geschichte des Protestantismus in Oesterreich*, iv (1883), 96 sqq.; *Cambridge Modern History*, iii. 720–721, New York, 1905.

VIENNE, vî″en': The second oldest seat of Christianity in Gaul (10 m. s. of Lyons), the ecclesiastical metropolis of Gaul after 445, and the place of several synods. [Vienne and Lyons were closely associated in the persecution under Marcus Aurelius (177 A.D.), when the aged Bishop Pothinus and one of its deacons, Sanctus, suffered martyrdom. When Irenæus succeeded Pothinus, he probably ministered to the church at Vienne as well as to that at Lyons (cf. the letter of the brethren at Vienne and Lyons to brethren in Asia and Phrygia, giving an account of the persecution, in Eusebius, *Hist. eccl.*, V., ii., Eng. transl. in *NPNF*, 2 ser., i. 212–218). A. H. N.] The first bishop of whom anything definite is known was Verus, who attended the Synod of Arles. The first synod of Vienne, said to have been held about 474 and to have sanctioned the rogations of Bishop Mamertus, seems never, to have taken place. Another synod in 870 confirmed the privileges conferred on a monastery, and the third, in 892, placed all laymen under the ban who infringed on the rights of the Church or injured the clergy. In 907 a synod settled a dispute between two abbots over monastic revenues, and another in 1060 prepared resolutions against simony, the marriage of priests, etc. Archbishop Guido (later Calixtus II.) in 1112 convened a synod which declared against lay investiture, and seven years later Gelasius II. is said to have held the seventh synod of Vienne, though the historicity of this is disputed. Another, held by Archbishop Petrus in 1124, sought to protect the possessions of the Church, though it is more probable that this synod existed only in the declared intention of Calixtus II. to hold it. The election of a bishop of Valence was the occasion for the convening of a synod in 1141, and. in 1164 Rainald of Cologne convened the Burgundian bishops at Vienne in an unsuccessful effort to induce them to recognize the imperial Antipope Paschalis III. On Jan. 14, 1200, the cardinal legate Petrus held a synod to execute the ban on Philip Augustus of France, and a provincial synod was convened in 1289 of which no details are known.

The only assemblage of real importance at Vienne was the fifteenth ecumenical council convened by Clement V. in 1311. The bull of invitation to this council, *Regnans in cœlis*, was dated Aug. 12, 1308, but circumstances compelled deferment until Oct. 16, 1311. The subjects proposed for its consideration were three: a verdict on the Templars (q.v.), who were accused of grievous crimes; the aid to be given the Holy Land; and the reform of church discipline. How many prelates assembled is uncertain, though the number 114, besides abbots and procurators, given by William of Nangis, seems probable. A series of conferences concerning the Templars prolonged proceedings until Mar., 1312; and the order was declared suppressed at the second session of the council (Apr. 3). It was apparently at the same session that Clement declared his predecessor, Boniface VIII., to be a lawful pope, innocent of the accusations alleged against him. The third session (May 6) closed the council, at which the pope seems to have given the tithes for six years to the kings of France, England, and Navarre for the purpose of a crusade. The synod likewise went deeply into the problem of reform, the results being the decrees issued or prepared by the council, incorporated in the so-called Clementines, and published by John XXII. A final synod was held at Vienne in 1557. It was concerned chiefly with matters of discipline.

(A. HAUCK.)

BIBLIOGRAPHY: KL, xii. 932–946; B. de Richebourg (Charvet), *Hist. de l'église de Vienne*, Lyons, 1761; D. de Maupertuy, *Hist. de sainte-église de Vienne*, Lyons, 1708; F. Z. Collombet, *Hist. de la sainte-église de Vienne*, 4 vols., Lyons, 1847–48; *Gallia Christiana*, xvi. 1 sqq., Paris, 1865; S. Champier, *Du royaume des Allobroges, avec l'antiquité do Vienne*, Lyons, 1884; K. Schotmüller, *Der Untergang des Templerordens*, 2 vols., Berlin, 1887; W. Gundlach, *Der Streit der Bisthümer Arles und Vienne um den Primatus Galliarum*, Hanover, 1890; idem, in *NA*, xx (1895), 263 sqq.; *La philosophie du concile de Vienne*, Paris, 1890; H. Bazin, *Vienne et Lyon gallo-romains*, Paris, 1891; P. Fournier, *Les Royaumes d'Arles et de Vienne, 1138–1378*, Paris, 1891; L. Duchesne, *Fastes épiscopaux de l'ancienne Gaule*, i. 145 sqq., Paris, 1894;

M. Heber, *Gutachten und Reformvorschläge für das Vienner Generalkonzil 1311–12*, Leipsic, 1896; Lichtenberger, *ESR*, xii. 368–370. The reports of the synods are in Mansi, *Concilia*, xxv. 367 sqq., and Hefele, *Conciliengeschichte*, passim.

VIGILANTIUS, vij"i-lan'shi-us: Presbyter of Aquitaine; b. at Calagurris (probably the modern Martres, 142 m. s.s.e. of Bordeaux), doubtless before 370; d. after 406. He seems to have been possessed of some property, and had already been ordained to the priesthood when, with a letter of introduction from Paulinus Nolanus, he visited Jerome at Bethlehem some years previous to 404. According to the letter of Jerome to Paulinus (*Epist.*, lviii.), he had received Vigilantius with all kindness, but for some reason his guest had secretly left him. On his way back to Gaul, and while in Italy, Vigilantius either addressed a letter to Jerome or submitted some treatise for his approval which his former host construed as an allegation that he was infected with the heresies of Origen, whereupon Jerome replied to Vigilantius in a letter of extreme bitterness (*Epist.*, lxi.). In 406, after Vigilantius had returned to Aquitaine, two neighboring priests, Riparius and Desiderius, who felt their parishes infected by his proximity, wrote to Jerome asking him to prepare a refutation of his former guest. At the same time they sent, by a certain monk Sisinnius, the writings of Vigilantius. These Jerome had never seen before, although by 404 he had received from Riparius a summary of the views of Vigilantius. Sisinnius reached Bethlehem late in the autumn of 406 and intended to remain until the following Epiphany, but suddenly felt it to be his duty to leave for Gaul by way of Egypt sooner than he had expected. Jerome was accordingly obliged to dictate his *Apologia adversus Vigilantium* in a single night.

This *Apologia* forms almost the sole source for knowledge concerning Vigilantius. He had raised his voice against the prevailing cult of martyrs, or saints, the homage paid their graves, the prayers addressed to their relics, the building of and pilgrimage to churches erected especially in honor of them, the burning of candles to them, the holding of vigils at their tombs, and the singing of halleluiahs to them, since he deemed all this a concession to paganism. Vigils (q.v.) brought with them the danger of immorality; and the singing of halleluiahs should be restricted to Eastertide, that the populace might not forget the difference between the Redeemer and his redeemed saints. He inveighed against indiscriminate charity and against giving all to monks in pagan lands while the poor at home were left to starve. He had scant sympathy with monastic life, as being destructive to the care of souls, and he seems to have opposed the enforced celibacy of the clergy.

By charging Jerome with Origenistic heresy Vigilantius roused the implacable anger of his quondam host, especially as all question of the latter's orthodoxy had apparently been removed by the personal meeting of Jerome and Vigilantius. Jerome retorted with a counter-charge of yielding to heresy (*Epist.*, lxi. 1, Eng. transl. in *NPNF*, 2 ser., vi. 131), and as early as his *Apologia adversus libros*

Rufini (probably early in 402) he was obliged to defend himself for having declared that Vigilantius had been contaminated by his associates in Alexandria. This charge Jerome repeated in 404, implying that Rufinus and his Egyptian friends had been the cause of Vigilantius' heresy. As a matter of fact, however, Vigilantius had learned to know and admire Origen at least as early as his journey through Egypt and Palestine, and he had not attacked Jerome because of abhorrence of anything savoring of Origenistic teachings, but had contradicted him as an independent and perhaps self-opinionated person, identifying—in the fashion of the Origenistic Controversy (q.v.)—the errors of his opponent with those of the great and dangerous Origen.

Little is known of Vigilantius except for the statements of Jerome. Gennadius, however, states that Vigilantius was a presbyter in the diocese of Barcelona, which would imply that after 406 he was transferred to Spain. Paulinus of Nola, writing to Severus, probably about 395, mentions (*Epist.*, v.) a fellow countryman named Vigilantius whom he had sent to Campania with a letter. [It seems probable that Vigilantius was a protégé of Sulpicius Severus, and that as a messenger of the latter he first came into relations with Paulinus of Nola. A. H. N.] It has been held that this was another Vigilantius, a baptized slave; but the term *puer* seems to refer merely to the relative youth of Vigilantius at the time, as compared with the age of Paulinus; and between this letter and the journey of Vigilantius to Palestine with a letter of introduction to Jerome sufficient time may well have elapsed for his ordination to the priesthood. The general education of Vigilantius seems to have been good, though his theological training was less perfect. Certain incautious expressions, as dubbing those who venerated relics " idolaters," betray the impetuous Gascon; his polemics were, however, not personal or partizan, but were inspired by his belief that religion was imperiled.

While, during his lifetime, Vigilantius was protected by his sympathizers, his permanent achievements were scanty. In his *De dogmatibus ecclesiasticis* (xl., lxxiii.) Gennadius states that only the followers of Vigilantius and Eunomius rejected the veneration of relics and the building 'of and pilgrimage to churches in honor of the martyrs. Later the name of Vigilantius vanishes altogether, even by the time of Isidore of Seville. His motives were not dogmatic; he perceived and assailed a series of what he deemed abuses in the religious life of the Church of his time, considering these to be superstitions that formed the chief barrier to the victorious progress of Christianity. He assailed neither monasticism nor the merit arising from almsgiving nor celibacy in themselves, but only as leading by excess of emphasis to the opposite extreme. He feared that the veneration of martyrs would lead to depreciation of Christ, though some of his arguments, such as the inability of the dead to intercede successfully for the living, seem to have been afterthoughts. His arguments were without effect; he underestimated the religious needs of the multitudes, and was not himself high enough above their level to achieve even temporary success with the great mass of Catholic Christians.

(G. A. JÜLICHER.)

BIBLIOGRAPHY: Jerome, *Epist.*, liii., lviii., lxi., cix., Eng. transl. in *NPNF*, 2d ser., vi. 96 sqq., 119 sqq., 131 sqq., 212 sqq.; idem, " Against Vigilantius," Eng. transl. in *NPNF*, ut sup., pp. 417–423; Gennadius, *De vir. ill.*, xxxvi.; W. S. Gilly, *Vigilantius and his Times*, London, 1844 (thorough); Tillemont, *Mémoires*, xii. 191–196, 266–269, 287–289; *Histoire littéraire de la France*, ii. 57 sqq.; C. W. F. Walch, *Historie der Ketzereien*, iii. 673–704, Leipsic, 1766; Lindner, *De Joviniano et Vigilantio purioris doctrinæ iv. et v. sæculo antesignanis*, Leipsic, 1839; W. Schmidt, *Vigilantius, sein Verhältnis zum heiligen Hieronymus*, Münster, 1860; P. F. Lucius, *Die Anfänge des Heiligenkults*, pp. 327–329, Tübingen, 1904; Bayle, *Dictionary*, v. 470–474; Ceillier, *Auteurs sacrés*, vii. 606–607; *KL*, xii. 953–956; *DCB*, iv. 1141–43.

VIGILIUS, vi-jil′i-ʊs: Pope 537–555. He came of a Roman patrician family, and was a deacon during the pontificate of Boniface II. Vigilius seems to have been an opponent of Gothic rule and to have worked against it after being appointed apocrisiary of the Curia at Constantinople. On the death of Agapetus (Apr. 22, 536), Vigilius promised Empress Theodora that, if he were elected pope, he would oppose the Council of Chalcedon and intercede for the deposed patriarchs Anthimus, Severus, and Theodosius (see MONOPHYSITES). When he arrived in Rome, however, he found Silverius (q.v.), the candidate of Theodahat, already enthroned, but the intruder was removed with the aid of Belisarius, to whom Vigilius had been recommended by Theodora, and on Mar. 29, 537, Vigilius ascended the papal throne. How far Vigilius fulfilled his promise to the empress is uncertain. A letter addressed to him to the patriarchs already mentioned is preserved by Liberatus (*MPL*, lxviii. 1041) and Victor of Tunnenna (q.v.), in which, while strictly enjoining silence upon them, he expresses his sympathy with them, saying: " We do not confess two natures of Christ, but one Christ composed of two natures." But according to the *Liber pontificalis* he wrote Theodora flatly refusing to make peace with heretics. The latter communication is obviously apocryphal, and the authenticity of the former letter is more than doubtful. Several years passed before Vigilius became involved with the government at Constantinople concerning dogmatic problems. On Sept. 17, 540, at the insistance of Justinian, the pope found himself obliged, in two letters to the emperor and the Patriarch Menas (*Litteris clementiæ* and *Licet universa*), to subscribe to the Chalcedonian creed and to anathematize the monophysite patriarchs. Little besides this is known of the early years of his pontificate. The deacon Arator, in his *Epistola ad Vigilium* (*MPL*, lxviii. 73 sqq.), praises him for his activity during the siege of Rome; and an inscription, probably contemporary, states that he restored the graves of the martyrs Alexander, Vitalis, and Martialis. On Mar. 6, 538, he directed Cæsarius of Arles (q.v.) to inform Theudebert, king of Austrasia, of penance to be done because of his marital affairs; on June 29, 538, he issued certain instructions to Profuturus, bishop of Braga; on Oct. 18, 543, he informed Auxanius, the successor of Cæsarius at

(marginal heading) **Early Pontificate.**

Arles, that he could not send him the pallium without first informing the emperor; on May 22, 545, he conferred the pallium on Auxanius, and on Aug. 23, 546, on Auxanius' successor, Aurelian.

By 546 Vigilius was no longer in Rome, for in the mean time the "Three-chapters Controversy" (q.v.) had broken out. His situation was grave from the first, and became still more critical

Three-Chapters Controversy. when Justinian commanded him to appear in person at Constantinople. In 544 or 545 Vigilius accordingly left Rome, never to return; whether he was detained by force, as the *Liber pontificalis* states, is uncertain; and, after a sojourn of some length in Sicily, he reached Constantinople, by way of Illyria and Greece, late in 546 or early in 547, Pelagius (q.v.) remaining in Rome as his representative. In the mean time he had bitterly reproached Menas for subscribing to the edict and had approved the course of Stephanus in breaking off religious fellowship with him, an example followed by many of the clergy and laity, as well as by the African Church. Though he was officially received by Justinian with the highest respect, the gravity of the situation soon became evident. The first step made by the pope is problematical. Theophanes implies that soon after his arrival he condemned the three chapters, but this is highly improbable, since he renewed religious fellowship with Menas, the two being reconciled at the instance of Theodora on June 29. In the mean time, however, Justinian had even threatened to imprison the pope. To this period probably belong the two letters in which Vigilius promised the emperor and empress to condemn the three chapters, these letters to be kept secret for the time being, but later coming to light at a critical moment. The emphasis laid on the rights of the Curia in these documents was plainly intended to create the impression that the pope was the arbitrator in the matter, but as a matter of fact he had tied his own hands. Nevertheless, he convened seventy bishops, and in three sessions debated whether the edict concerning the three chapters was contradictory to the Council of Chalcedon. When, however, Facundus, the most eloquent and learned of the faction under condemnation, desired to speak, Vigilius adjourned the session and required each of those who took part to submit a written opinion. These opinions, under monophysite influence, were rendered in the desired terms, and Vigilius had them presented to the emperor immediately. The pope now took a decisive step, and on Easter Even, 548, sent Menas his *Judicatum*, in which he unreservedly condemned the three chapters and as unreservedly accepted the Chalcedonian creed. The publication of this document by his nephew and deacon Rusticus roused a tumult of opposition throughout the West. This opposition seems to have produced an impression at court, for otherwise Justinian would scarcely have returned his *Judicatum* to Vigilius or have thought of referring the entire matter to a great synod. On Aug. 15, 550, however, he exacted from the pope an oath to proceed in the condemnation of the three chapters, though in conference with the emperor Vigilius secured a promise that no

further action should be taken until the synod had been convened. In the summer of 551 Justinian unexpectedly anticipated the decision of the synod and in a new edict renewed the condemnation of the three chapters.

Vigilius now assumed the offensive instead of the defensive, probably under the influence of Pelagius, who about this time arrived from Rome. The pope

Vacillating Course. correctly saw his chief enemy in Theodorus Ascidas, whom he excommunicated in the middle of July. But Vigilius no longer felt safe, and fled from the Domus Placidia, the residence of the apocrisiary, to the basilica of St. Peter at Hormisda, where, on Aug. 17, he pronounced Theodorus deposed and his adherents, including Menas, excommunicated, though these sentences were to remain secret until their effect upon Justinian and those condemned should be ascertained. The attempt to tear him from sanctuary failed, but on assurance of safety from Justinian the pope returned to the Domus Placidia, only to leave it again on the night of Dec. 23 and take refuge in the chapel of St. Euphemia at Chalcedon. Even there he was exposed to peril, probably in consequence of the publication of his ban on Theodorus and his open letter of Feb. 5, in which he complained of the treatment he had received in Constantinople. His excommunicated opponents, however, now laid before the pope a defense of their tenets with a corresponding creed; and after the death of Menas the new Patriarch Eutychius sent Vigilius a courteous notification of his accession (Jan. 6, 553). Hereupon the pope declared himself ready for a synod, though he desired that it be held in Italy or Sicily. The emperor finally informed the pope that he must either attend the synod or have it opened without his presence. Vigilius remained true to his refusal to appear, declaring that he would give his opinion in writing. On May 5, 553, the synod convened, and on May 14 Vigilius completed his *Constitutum de tribus capitulis*, in which he rejected all community of spirit with the followers of Theodore of Mopsuestia and yet declined to condemn the three chapters. The document was to be presented to Justinian on May 25, but he refused to receive it, and his commissary laid before the synod the secret letters mentioned above, in which Vigilius had promised to condemn the three chapters. At the same time the command was given to strike the pope's name from the diptychs, and the final decision of the synod in its eighth session (June 2) was in harmony with the imperial wish concerning the three chapters. Whether Vigilius was condemned to banishment is uncertain, but at all events he could scarcely return to Italy, where Justinian's power was at its zenith. Nevertheless, efforts seem to have been made at Rome to secure his return, and the result was the complete recantation of Vigilius. He announced his change of position in a letter to the Patriarch Eutychius on Dec. 8, 553, and explained it at length on Feb. 26, 554, in his *Constitutum Vigilii pro damnatione trium capitulorum*. By his recantation he gained return to Rome, formal sanction being given by Justinian on Aug. 13, 554; but he died at Syracuse, on his way home, June 7, 555, being buried in the church of San Marcello on the Via Salaria.

Vigilius was no uncompromising adherent of what he deemed right; and though it is true that the justice of the condemnation of the three chapters is a moot question, that the dogmatic verdict can not be rendered simply from the attitude of the Africans and their sympathizers, and that ecclesiastical polity had some reason to sacrifice Theodore for Chalcedon, all this does not justify his instability. And while his policy was, in its last analysis, the essentially papal principle of refusing to allow the State to dictate to the Church, he lacked ability to attain his ends by other than surreptitious means. When, under the influence of Pelagius, he demanded a free council on western soil and declined to attend the synod at Constantinople, he was on the right path, dangerous as this might prove when opposed to the policy of an emperor like Justinian; but his past was against him, and his recantation might have been expected.

His Character.

(G. KRÜGER.)

BIBLIOGRAPHY: Original documents are in *MPL*, lxix. 15–178; *CSEL*, xxxv. 230–320, 348 sqq.; Jaffé, *Regesta*, i. 117–124; *MGH*, *Epist.*, iii (1891), 57–68, and *Auct. ant.*, xi (1893), 200 sqq. Consult further: *Liber pontificalis*, ed. L. Duchesne, i. 296–302, Paris, 1886; J. Basnage, *Hist. de l'église*, i. 517–547, Rotterdam, 1699; J. Punkes, *Papst Vigilius*, Munich, 1864; L. Duchesne, *Vigile et Pélage*, in *Revue des questions historiques*, xxxvi (1884), 369–381; B. Constant, in Pitra's *Analecta novissima*, i (1885), 370–461; J. Langen, *Geschichte der römischen Kirche*, i. 341–382, Bonn, 1885; *Revue des questions historiques*, xxxvii (1885), 540–578, 579–593; A. Knecht, *Die Religionspolitik Justinians I.*, Würzburg, 1896; L. M. Hartmann, *Geschichte Italiens im Mittelalter*, i. 382–394, Leipsic, 1897; H. Grisar, *Geschichte Roms und der Päpste im Mittelalter*, i. 502–507, 574–580, Freiburg, 1900; Bower, *Popes*, i. 345–370; Platina, *Popes*, i. 128–130; Milman, *Latin Christianity*, i. 462–470; Hefele, *Conciliengeschichte*, vols. ii.–iii. passim, Eng. transl., vol. iv. passim, Fr. transl., vols. ii.–iii. passim; *DCB*, iv. 1144–51 (full, names sources); *KL*, xii. 956–959; and the literature under THREE-CHAPTERS CONTROVERSY.

VIGILIUS OF THAPSUS: Bishop of Thapsus (the modern Dimas or Ras Dimas, 90 m. s.e. of Tunis); flourished in the latter part of the fifth century. He is to be identified with the " Vigilius Tapsitanus," who with others was cited by Hunerich to appear at Carthage on Feb. 1, 484, to give an account of his faith; and probably also with the " Vigilius Tapsensis," who, according to the testimony of manuscripts, wrote three books against Eutychianism. No other details of his life are known with certainty, but it seems probable that after the disastrous termination of the visit to Carthage he was banished; at least, he must have been deposed like all the other Catholic bishops. According to Theodulf of Orléans (*De Spiritu Sancto*, *MPL*, cv. 273), and Æneas of Paris (*Adv. Græcos*, *MPL*, cxxi. 717), Vigilius composed his works against Eutyches at Constantinople. More might be stated concerning the episcopal career of Vigilius could he be identified with the Vigilius to whom Celsus addressed his *De Judaica incredulitate* (Cyprian, ed. G. Hartel, Vienna, 1871, III., iii. 119–132). He would then seem to have been a monk suddenly raised to the episcopate to end the controversies concerning the choice of a bishop at a time of persecution when bishops stood in imminent peril of death. This identification, however, is uncertain, and his own writings contain nothing concerning the events of his life.

Perceiving the spread of Eutychianism in the East, Vigilius wrote at the exhortation of his " holy brethren " the *Libri quinque contra Eutychetem* (*MPL*, lxii. 95–154) formerly ascribed to Vigilius of Trent (q.v.). In his refutation of Eutyches he proceeds from the Catholic principle of the mean between the extreme and mutually antagonistic views of heretics. The date of the work is uncertain, but should probably be set not long after the Council of Chalcedon. In the fifth book Vigilius alludes to his polemics against Sabellius, Photinus, and Arius. This work, in three books, and entitled by the first editor of Vigilius (F. Chifflet, *Victoris Vitensis et Vigilii Tapsensis provinciæ Bizacenæ episcoporum opera*, Dijon, 1664) *Contra Arianos*, etc., *dialogus* (*MPL*, lxii. 179–238), is in the form of a debate between Athanasius (Vigilius himself), Arius, Sabellius, and Photinus before the judge Probus (God). Sabellius and Photinus advance arguments which prove mutually destructive, so that only Athanasius and Arius remain, the victory being awarded the former by the judge. From this work an extract was made, apparently in the Carolingian period, in which only Arius and Athanasius debate, an introduction being provided on the basis of the " Church History " of Rufinus (*MPL*, lxii. 155–180). It is also very probable that the *Liber contra Felicianum et Arianum de unitate Trinitatis ad Optatum* (*MPL*, lxii. 333–352) was written by Vigilius.

Vigilius of Thapsus was the author of a number of other works now lost. In his *Dialogus* (ii. 45) he mentions a polemic " against Maribadus," probably the deacon Marivadus, who enjoyed the special favor of Hunerich. Chifflet wrongly identified this lost work with the *Idacii Clari Hispani contra Varimadum Arianum Liber et difficillimorum quorumque locorum de Trinitate declaratio* (*MPL*, lxii. 351–434), first edited by J. Sichardt in his *Antidotum* (Basel, 1528). Vigilius also replied to the attack of the Arian bishop Palladius on Ambrose (*Dialogus*, ii. 50). This work has likewise vanished. Chifflet wrongly ascribed to Vigilius the *De Trinitate libri duodecim* (*MPL*, lxii. 237–334), but of these only books i.–viii. belong together, ix.–xii. being by another author, while even the first eight books represent a revised and enlarged second edition of the books i.–vii. It is generally conceded that both these recensions were written in Spain, not Africa or Italy, at the end of the fourth or the beginning of the fifth century. In all probability books i.–vii. of the *De Trinitate* were written by Gregory of Elvira (q.v.), the author of the pseudo-Ambrosian *De fide* (*MPL*, lxii. 449–468), whose seven books *De Trinitate*, written before 383, had been suspected of Sabellianism, and who had accordingly composed the *De fide* and revised his seven books, besides adding an eighth. The *Libellus fidei*, the ninth book of the *De Trinitate*, must be by the same author. Books x.–xii. of the *De Trinitate* have not yet been sufficiently studied. The concluding portions of the first and second parts are repeated word for word in the *De rationc fidei* and the *De Spiritu Sancto* of Nicetas of Remesiana (ed. A. E. Burn, Cambridge, 1905); and the twelfth book has been ascribed by the Benedictines to Athanasius. This last is a collection of Scriptural passages demonstrating the divinity of the Holy Ghost, and it is now generally held that it can not be a translation from the Greek. It shows affinities, however, with the pseudo(?)-Athanasian *De incarnatione Dei Verbi et contra Arianos* (*MPL*, xxvi. 981–1028).

Several other works have been ascribed to this Vigilius: *Solutiones objectionum Arianorum* (*MPL*, lxii. 469–472); *Collatio beati Augustini cum Pascentio Ariano* (*MPL*, xxxiii. 1156–62); *Altercatio ecclesiæ et synagogæ* (*MPL*, xlii. 1131–40); *Liber contra Fulgentium Donatistam* (*MPL*, xliii. 763–774; this certainly of African origin); *Conflictus Catholici et Serapionis de Deo trino et uno* (*MPL*, liii. 239–322; usually attributed to Arnobius); and a number of others, one of which, the *De conflictu virtutum et vitiorum* (*MPL*, xl. 1091–1106), was certainly written by Ambrosius Autpertus, while the rest admit of no final decision. In his *Institutio divinarum litterarum* (ix.; *MPL*, lxx. 1122), Cassiodorus mentions an African Bishop Vigilius as the author of an excellent treatise on the thousand years of the Apocalypse, but it is uncertain whether this author was Vigilius of Thapsus.

(GERHARD FICKER.)

BIBLIOGRAPHY: S. A. Morcelli, *Africa Christiana*, i. 307, iii. 216, 235, Brixen, 1816–17; F. Kattenbusch, *Das apostolische Symbol*, passim, Leipsic, 1894; G. Ficker, *Studien zu Vigilius von Thapsus*, Leipsic, 1897; Bardenhewer, *Patrologie*, 3d ed., p. 537, Eng. transl., St. Louis, 1908; J. Quitt, in J. Strzygowski, *Byzantinische Denkmäler*, iii. 83–100, 111–112, Vienna, 1903; H. Leclercq, *L'Afrique chrétienne*, ii. 203, Paris, 1904; M. Schanz, *Geschichte der römischen Litteratur*, i. 280, 348–349, Munich, 1904; Ceillier, *Auteurs sacrés*, x. 472–485; *DCB*, iv. 1143–44; *KL*, xii. 959–962.

VIGILIUS OF TRENT: Bishop of that see; d. at Trent June 26, 400. The actuality of his existence and that of his circle is of great importance in the history of the Christianizing and Catholicizing of the Rhætian Alps district. His predecessor Abundantius, the first known bishop of the place, took part in a synod at Aquileia (q.v.) in 381 which was directed against the Arians. Vigilius arrived at Trent about that time with his mother Maxentia and his brothers Claudianus (Confessor; *ASB*, Mar. i. 427) and Majorianus (Martyr; *ASB*, Mar., ii. 398); and though he was but twenty years old he was consecrated bishop, and received the insignia from Ambrose of Milan with the letter of induction (*Epist.*, xxix., in *MPL*, xvi. 982). He built the churches of Gervasius and Protasius at Trent, and carried on energetic missions in his diocese and in those of Verona and Brixen. Great excitement attended the martyrdom of the three missionaries who hailed from Cappadocia, Sisinnius, Martyrius, and Alexander, of whom Vigilius speaks in two letters, one to Simplician of Milan, successor of Ambrose, and the other to Chrysostom at Constantinople. Because of these letters he appears in the work of Gennadius (*De vir. ill.*, xxxviii., Eng. transl. in *NPNF*, 2 ser., iii. 392). Vigilius himself suffered a martyr's death. The dogmatic writings ascribed to him are not his, but be-

ong to Vigilius of Thapsus (q.v.), with whom he was confused.   (F. ARNOLD.)

BIBLIOGRAPHY: *ASB*, June, v. 165–168, cf. the material collected in *ASB*, May vii. 143 sqq., under the names of Sisinnius and Alexander; J. G. Sulzer, *Die Wiederauffindung der Urne des glorreichen Märtyrers Vigilius Bischofs . . . von Trient*, Trent, 1863; Tillemont, *Mémoires*, x. 542–552; Benedict, Count of Giovanelli, in *Beiträge zur Geschichte von Tirol und Vorarlberg*, iv. 1–152, Innsbruck, 1828; *KL*, xii. 962–964.

VIGILS: Services, originally consisting of hymns, prayers, lessons, and processions, held on the eve of high festivals, for which they form the preparation. Religious meetings were held at night even in the primitive Church, but the only night in the church year which then was wholly passed in fasting and vigil was Easter eve. Somewhat later the eve of Whitsunday was observed with special solemnity. In the fifth and sixth centuries the vigil of Easter was deemed the most appropriate time for baptism, the Eucharist, and ordination, and next in honor were the vigils of Whitsunday and Christmas. After the twelfth century special vigils preceded the feasts of the Virgin. After the fourth century vigils were celebrated with magnificence, and occasionally were marred by conduct which rendered it necessary in places to debar women from them. By the end of the same century vigils in honor of individual martyrs seem also to have been fully developed. In the Middle Ages vigils proper were celebrated only in the monasteries, the celebration of the vigils in the churches being either included in matins or vespers or transformed into fasts. In the Roman Catholic Church the vigil is now celebrated chiefly on the morning before the festival, except at Christmas and Easter Eve. Nominal vigils occur at Epiphany, Ascension, Whitsunday, the Annunciation, and the Purification of the Blessed Virgin, St. John's Day, All Saints', St. Laurence's Day, and the days of the apostles Matthew, Peter, Jude, James, Simon, Thomas, and Andrew. Services among Protestants which correspond in some degree to vigils are the Moravian observances at Good Friday and Easter, and the very common " watch-meetings " lasting until midnight on the last night of the year.

[The Anglican Church has the following vigils, on which abstinence is enjoined: the evens of the Nativity, Purification, Annunciation, Easter, Ascension, and Pentecost, and the days of Saints Matthias, John the Baptist, Peter, James, Bartholomew, Matthew, Simon and Jude, Andrew, Thomas, and All Saints. If any of these feasts falls on Monday, the vigil is held on Saturday. The celebration of the midnight Eucharist at Christmas, frequent in the Anglican communion, is not a vigil.]

(O. ZÖCKLER†.)

BIBLIOGRAPHY: Bingham, *Origines*, VII., x. 1, XIII., ix. 4, XVI. xi. 17, XX., vii. 9; J. C. W. Augusti, *Denkwürdigkeiten*, i. 131, vii. 170 sqq., viii. 138–139, ix. 413, x. 319, 12 vols., Leipsic, 1717–31; S. Bäumer, *Geschichte des Breviers*, passim, Freiburg, 1895; O. Zöckler, *Askese und Mönchtum*, i. 168–169, 2d ed., Frankfort, 1897; K. A. H. Kellner, *Heortologie*, Freiburg, 1901; *DCA*, ii. 2017.

VILATTE, JOSEPH RENÉ (ARCHBISHOP MAR TIMOTHEUS): Old Catholic; b. in Paris Jan. 24, 1854. After service in the Franco-Prussian War, Villatte passed two years in Canada as teacher and lay assistant to a French mission-priest, followed by one year in the House of the Christian Brothers at Naumur, Belgium, and a second devoted to private preparation for the priesthood, before entering the Seminary of St. Laurence, Montreal, Canada. Several anti-Roman lectures of ex-Father Chiniquy, heard in the interval between the third and fourth years, caused spiritual conflict from doctrinal doubts. Unable to continue consistently his seminary studies, an invitation of the president of The Presbyterian College, Montreal, was accepted, and two years' study there convinced him both of papal additions to the primitive Catholic faith, and of defective Protestant interpretation of its traditional teachings. Unwilling, however, to leave the Roman Church, he now entered the monastery of the clerics of St. Viator at Bourbonnais, Ill., but after six months' stay, continuing inner conflicts impelled him to seek counsel from Chiniquy, who advised him to begin mission-work among the French and Belgians of Green Bay, Wis., and send a statement of his doctrinal difficulties to Père Hyacinthe of Paris (see LOYSON, CHARLES JEAN MARIE AUGUSTIN HYACINTHE). The latter replied urging a personal conference regarding Roman Catholic reform in America, and a proposed ordination as priest by Bishop Eduard Herzog (q.v.) of Bern. Circumstances forced Vilatte, however, to follow Hyacinthe's alternative advice to consult with the Episcopal Bishop Brown of Wisconsin, who wished to ordain him in the Protestant Episcopal Church, but Vilatte, adhering to the original counsel of Hyacinthe, later left America for Bern, and was ordained to the priesthood by the Old Catholic Bishop Herzog in 1885.

Vilatte's missionary activity among the French and Belgians in Wisconsin soon won many adherents, including several ex-Roman priests as assistants. Reports of his successful movement in America led the Old Catholic priests and bishops of Holland to submit a proposal, which was accepted, to attach the clergy and missions to their hierarchy instead of remaining in *quasi*-connection with the Episcopal diocese of Fond du Lac. The successor of Bishop Brown, hoping to avert the prospective separation, addressed Archbishop Heykamp of Utrecht, asserting the orthodoxy of Anglican teaching and the validity of its episcopal succession, and concluded with the proposal that Vilatte be consecrated abbot-bishop with monastic jurisdiction only, instead of with the anticipated diocesan authority of a Catholic bishop. The bishops of Holland still insisting, as a necessary condition of conferring the episcopate, on the cessation of all ecclesiastical relations with the Episcopalians, the required separation was formally effected. But the promised consecration was withheld, and soon after the Russian Bishop Vladimir of Alaska, approving the confession of faith and the official acts of Vilatte in seeking to obtain a bishop for the Old Catholics of America, intervened and referred their status to the Holy Synod for determination.

While awaiting its decision, Vilatte also consulted with Archbishop Alvarez of Ceylon who, as the leader of a large number of Portuguese Roman Catholics, had received archiepiscopal consecration from the legate of the Patriarch of Antioch, assisted by two Syrian metropolitans. Alvarez, likewise approving Vilatte's confession of faith and official acts, offered to come to America and consecrate him bishop; but after a number of months' waiting without a decision from the Holy Synod on his status, Vilatte left America for Ceylon to receive the offered episcopate. After a careful consideration of his ecclesiastical position, the Patriarch of Antioch authorized his elevation to the hierarchy, and his consecration as archbishop of the archdiocese of America, which was conferred in May, 1892.

Soon after Vilatte's return to America, Polish Roman Catholic priests in Detroit, Cleveland, Chicago, and other cities placed themselves and their parishes under his jurisdiction, and new missions were begun in other places for which Vilatte ordained priests as needed. The steadily increasing growth of this movement gave hope for the organization of a coherent Polish Catholic Church in America. After successive annual conferences of the priests and delegates from their parishes, the proposal to elect a Polish suffragan bishop was approved, and in 1897 Father Kaminski of Buffalo was chosen. Father Kozlowski of Chicago, the disappointed candidate, unwilling to acquiesce in the result, called in that city a second convention of his partizans, which elected him as rival bishop, but when he sought confirmation, Vilatte was consistently compelled to refuse him recognition. Failing after repeated attempts to secure the promise of consecration, Kozlowski left America for Europe, and was later consecrated rival bishop by Herzog of Bern. Factional strife among the Polish priests soon destroyed all prospect of an organized Polish Catholic Church, and Vilatte, becoming finally convinced that deliberate defiance of the canonical authority of their Roman ordinaries, rather than Catholic reform, was the impelling motive of the movement, advised them either to accept fully and freely the Old Catholic principles, or to return to the Roman Church. The evident unwillingness to accept required doctrinal reforms left Vilatte no alternative but to withdraw his approval of their movement; and in 1898 he consecrated Father Kaminski of Buffalo as suffragan bishop for those priests and parishes which accepted them. Soon after this, Vilatte left America for Paris to consult with advisers regarding his future course, interrupting his journey to ordain to the priesthood Father Ignatius (see LYNE, JOSEPH LEYCESTER) and another monk of Llanthony, Wales. Being advised in Paris to visit Rome, after a retreat at the Benedictine monastery at Ligugé, Vilatte personally offered his acceptance of the plea of the pope to Eastern prelates for union with the Holy See; but after the solemn recognition of his episcopal character by the Holy Office, followed by months of waiting for a decision on his status, and a required retreat in the Trappist monastery of Mt. Mellary, Ireland, later developments compelled him to recall his acceptance on his return to Rome.

His presence in Paris impelled Paolo Miraglia, the leader of Roman Catholic reform in northern Italy, to write to him regarding the movement and concerning consecration to the episcopate. After careful consideration, the request was granted, and on

May 3, 1900, Miraglia was consecrated in Piacenza bishop regionarius for Italy. Returning to America, Chicago was chosen in 1902 as the permanent archiepiscopal seat, and a mission begun by Father Kanski. In 1903 Vilatte was urged by several Anglican clerical adherents to come to England to assist their proposed Catholic reform. The new movement seemed to promise success, and after being assured of the acceptance of the required principles by their designated leader, a married ex-Anglican cleric, he was first successively ordained *de novo* subdeacon, deacon, and priest, and then solemnly consecrated as a Catholic bishop. This third episcopal consecration conferred by Vilatte is especially noteworthy because the bishop-elect was not, like the two preceding priests, a celibate. The precedent of Vilatte was followed by Archbishop Gul of Utrecht in consecrating several years later Arnold H. Mathew of England, who had married after his ordination in the Roman Church. In 1906, after the abolition of the concordat concluded with the Roman Church by the Emperor Napoleon, Vilatte was summoned to Paris by a league of French laymen, directed by Mon. Henri de Houx, members of different parishes in various cities, who were desirous of detaching themselves from the Roman Church, and accepting the associations law. He remained during a part of 1907, assisting their preliminary movement for the eventual organization of an independent French Catholic Church.

In 1909, after the death of Father Ignatius of Llanthony, the two senior surviving Anglican monks requested him to ordain them in succession to their departed abbot. Their petition for the priesthood being approved, the ceremony was performed in Winnipeg, Canada, where Vilatte was then staying during a visitation of his mission-stations in that part of America. During the last two years, Vilatte has been preparing for the establishment of a second center of missionary activity and the building of a monastery for the training of celibate clergy in the South for which land is to be selected and settled by immigrants both from America and Europe, for whose spiritual and secular welfare the brothers are already active.

ERNEST C. MARGRANDER.

VILLEGAGNON, vîl″gä″nyōn′, **NICOLAS DURAND DE:** Founder of a French Protestant colony in Brazil; b. in Provence about 1510; d. at Beauvais (near Nemours, 45 m. s.s.w. of Paris) Jan. 15, 1571. He early entered the order of the Knights of Malta, and served in the African expedition of Charles V., which he chronicled in his *Caroli Quinti imperatoris expeditio in Africam ad Arginam* (Paris, 1542). In 1548 he escorted Mary Stuart from Scotland to France, and in 1554 Henry II. appointed him vice-admiral of Brittany. He won the approval of Coligny for a plan of founding a French colony in South America as a refuge for the Protestants, and gained the cooperation of the king by pointing out that the power and glory of France would be promoted by colonization in those lands side by side with the Spaniards and Portuguese. Receiving two ships and a subvention of 10,000 livres, he secured many followers from the Reformed, since he promised

that religious worship in the new colonies should be conducted according to the usage of Geneva; and he was also joined by a number of soldiers and adventurers. Sailing from Havre, Villegagnon reached the bay of Rio de Janeiro in Nov., 1555. He built a fort on an island in the bay, but provisions ran low and the soldiers and workmen were hard to control. Desiring to offset them by the more tractable Calvinists, Villegagnon sent letters to Coligny and Calvin, asking for more pious Protestants and also for preachers. Pierre Richer and Guillaume Chartier were commissioned the first Protestant missionaries in America, and they were joined by eleven others. At Paris the company, headed by Philippe de Corguilleray, Sieur du Pont, was increased by many more colonists, including a certain Cointa of the Sorbonne. In Nov., 1556, they embarked at Honfleur, under the command of Villegagnon's nephew, Bois le Conte, and in Mar., 1557, the three ships arrived, with nearly 300 colonists. But disputes arose over the Lord's Supper, Cointa and Villegagnon making requirements contrary to Genevan usage, branding Geneva as evil, and finally withdrawing from participation in religious services. A delegation headed by Chartier left for Geneva (June, 1557) to obtain the final decision of Calvin, the administration of the Lord's Supper meanwhile being discontinued. Then Villegagnon, relieved of the presence of the energetic Chartier, attempted to impose the doctrine of transubstantiation, and finally forbade all religious services. At this juncture, while the Protestants were holding secret meetings, a neutral ship arrived, and a number of colonists declared their intention of leaving. These Villegagnon drove from the island, confiscating all their possessions; and finally they set sail in a neutral Breton ship on Jan. 4, 1558. The ship proved unseaworthy, and five of the colonists in a small boat reached a French village on the coast, where Villegagnon happened to be. He received them on condition that they would hold no converse on religion, but later ordered them brought before him, and as they persisted in their religious beliefs, he had them executed as heretics (Feb. 10, 1558). In the mean time, the ship carrying the other colonists, after many disasters, on May 26, 1558, made the Breton harbor of Blavet, where many of the survivers died or were made seriously ill by being fed too generously after semi-starvation. The remainder pushed on a few days later, and scattered at Nantes, the most of them returning to their families. Shortly afterward the Brazilian colony broke up entirely; Villegagnon returned to France; the Portuguese destroyed the fort, put to death as heretics those who remained, and carried the French guns in triumph to Lisbon. Villegagnon finally retired to the estates of the Knights of Malta at Beauvais, where he died loathed by Protestants and suspected by the Roman Catholics. The colony is noteworthy as the first missionary enterprise of the Protestant Church, and as the first attempt of Calvinism to plant a colony in the New World.

(EUGEN LACHENMANN.)

BIBLIOGRAPHY: A list of the works of Villegagnon may be found in the *British Museum Catalogue*, under "Durand de Villegagnon," and in Hauck-Herzog, *RE*, xx. 646.

Consult J. de Léry, *Hist. d'un voyage faict dans le terre du Brésil*, Geneva, 1577, extracts from this in English are in S. Purchas' *Pilgrimes* (numberless reprints and editions); J. Crespin, *Hist. des martyrs*, new ed. by D. Benoit, 3 vols., Toulouse, 1885–89; F. Bourquelot, *Mémoires de Claude Haton*, Paris, 1857; M. T.. Alves Noguoira, *Der Mönchsritter N. D. de Villegaignon*, Leipsic, 1887; A. Heulhard, *Villegagnon, roi d'Amérique*, Paris, 1897; T. E. V. Smith, in *Papers of the American Society of Church History*, iii (1891), 185–206; Lichtenberger, *ESR*, xii. 385–387; and literature under BRAZIL respecting the early history.

VILMAR, fil'mär, **AUGUST FRIEDRICH CHRISTIAN:** German Lutheran; b. at Solz (near Rotenburg, 78 m. n.e. of Frankfort) Nov. 21, 1800; d. at Marburg July 30, 1868. In 1818–20 he studied theology at Marburg, only to learn

Religious Struggles. doubt from rationalism, and doubt to pass to unbelief. In Dec., 1823, he was appointed rector of the municipal school at Rotenburg, where he remained until 1827, when he went to Hersfeld as fourth teacher and collaborator at the gymnasium, being promoted third teacher in 1829. During these years he renounced rationalism, and for a year or two professed the opinion that the world is the feeling of God. He made further progress through reading first the Church Fathers, especially Tertullian and Irenæus, and then Tholuck's *Lehre von der Sünde*, and arrived at unwavering faith in Christ by his fortieth year, realizing that all he sought was to be found in the Lutheran Church, a process begun by the careful study of the Augsburg Confession and its Apology.

In 1831 Vilmar was elected from Hersfeld to the newly created diet of the electorate of Hesse, and in December of the same year he was appointed a member of the ministerial committees for religion and instruction. From Oct., 1832, to the end of Apr., 1833, he was assistant reporter in the ministry of the interior and nominal second

Services to Education. teacher at the gymnasium of Hanau; he was director of the gymnasium at Marburg, 1833–50, being a member of the committee on gymnasial affairs 1836–50; in 1850 he was transferred to the ministry of the interior as consistorial councilor, and from 1851 to 1855 also discharged the duties of the aged superintendent Ernst; in 1855 he became professor of theology at the University of Marburg. In the reports drawn up by Vilmar in the name of his committees for the Hessian Diet in 1831–32 he appealed effectually for the elevation of the national university, for the foundation of new professorships, and for the better equipment of institutions of learning. He also transformed the condition of the public schools, and may truly be termed the reformer of the gymnasia of Hesse. His views on gymnasial instruction are set forth in his twenty-four *Schulreden über Fragen der Zeit* (Marburg, 1846). During this period he published works dealing with Germanic linguistics, among them being *Deutsche Altertümer in Heliand* (1845); *Vorlesungen über die Geschichte der deutschen National-Literatur* (1845); *Geschichte der deutschen National-Literatur* (Marburg, 1846); *Handbüchlein für Freunde des deutschen Volksliedes* (1866); *Ueber Goethes Tasso* (Frankfort, 1869); *Lebensbilder deutscher Dichter* (ed. K. W. Piderit, Mar-

burg, 1869), and *Luther, Melanchthon, Zwingli* (Frankfort, 1869). Of far greater importance, in the present connection, were his services in the reformation of religious instruction in the gymnasia. Deeming that the gymnasium was designed to train up Christian leaders of the nation, and that religious instruction should assume a distinctively churchly character, Vilmar set forth his views in a series of contributions to Hengstenberg's *Evangelische Kirchenzeitung* in 1841 (ed. J. Haussleiter, under the title *Ueber den evangelischen Religionsunterricht in den Gymnasien*, Marburg, 1888). He also prepared for use in the gymnasia a *Kleines evangelisches Gesangbuch* (Marburg, 1838); taking part also in the struggle on behalf of the old hymnals, as well as in the preparation of the *Deutsches evangelisches Kirchengesangbuch* (Stuttgart, 1855).

The Church, Vilmar believed, was about to enter upon a new era, when there would be full recognition of the absolute unity of the visible and the invisible church, and of the communion of saints with one body on earth, foreshadowing the church of the Apocalypse, the New Jerusalem. With such a conviction, Vilmar found before him two tasks: The

Services to the Church. first of these concerned the creed of the church of Hesse, Vilmar maintaining that its future depended on its absolute fidelity to the confessions of the Church from the Apostles' Creed to the unaltered Augsburg Confession. To prove that the creed of the so-called Reformed church of Lower Hesse was this unaltered Augsburg Confession cost Vilmar immense toil. The second task was Vilmar's decided advocacy of the freedom of the Church from the State. In 1839 Vilmar took part in the Hessian confessional controversy, in which the attempt was made to discard the Augsburg Confession. Against such an endeavor Vilmar wrote his *Verhältnis der evangelischen Kirche in Kurhessen zu ihren neuesten Gegnern* (Marburg, 1839). In like spirit, after the faculty of Marburg had required the use of the Heidelberg Catechism in the schools and had designated the doctrines set forth in the Hessian Catechism as " Reformed " (1855), Vilmar sought to prove, especially in his *Geschichte des Konfessionsstandes der evangelischen Kirche in Hessen* (Marburg, 1860), that the church of Lower Hesse was termed " Reformed " not because of the doctrines prevailing in it, but because of the form of worship introduced by the Landgrave Maurice in the *Verbesserungspunkte* (q.v.) in 1605, although after the middle of the seventeenth century the theology of Hesse-Cassel had adopted the strict predestination of the Reformed. In *Die Gegenwart und die Zukunft der niederhessischen Kirche* (1867) he urged that the struggle against impending union be begun with the strongest emphasis on Lutheranism; and the failure to follow this counsel of Vilmar proved a fatal error in the conflict between the Hessian churches.

In 1848–50 Vilmar exercised a profound influence on political affairs. Essentially a conservative and devoted to his sovereign, he not only supported his elector manfully, but also made the *Hessischer Volksfreund*, which he founded in 1848 and edited alone until the middle of 1851, a center for all the loyalists of the land. A number of his contributions to this periodical were reprinted by Vilmar himself under the title *Zur neuesten* **His** *Kulturgeschichte Deutschlands* (3 parts, **Patriotism.** Frankfort, 1858–67).

Vilmar has rightly been characterized as preeminently acquainted with his native land and as a fervent admirer and protector of the relics of her past. His researches into Hessian history are embodied in his *Hessisches Historienbüchlein* (1842) and *Hessische Chronik* (1855), and he was also the author of the admirable *Idiotikon von Kurhessen* (1868). But dearer to him than all else was his church, of which he was acting superintendent, as already noted, from 1851 to 1855. His power as a preacher may still be seen in his *Predigten und geistliche Reden* (1876), while his visitation of churches in the discharge of his duties gave rise to many official communications of importance.

On the death of Superintendent Ernst, Vilmar was elected his successor. The election was subject, however, to the approval of the sovereign, and this the last prince elector of Hesse **Work for** refused. Vilmar, though elected super- **Students** intendent, was now appointed pro- **and Pastors.** fessor of theology at Marburg (Oct. 27, 1855). Unwillingly he entered upon an office which he would have welcomed a quarter of a century before. Yet he became the most influential professor in the university. His program was set forth in *Die Theologie der Thatsachen wider die Theologie der Rhetorik* (1856), and four times, in the spirit of practical religion there propounded, he conducted his theological pupils through a three-years' course which covered the entire Bible. This course of lectures was edited by his pupil C. Müller under the title *Collegium Biblicum* (6 vols., Gütersloh, 1879–83); and most of his other lectures were also edited posthumously: K. W. Piderit preparing the *Die Augsburgische Konfession* (Marburg, 1870), *Lehre vom geistlichen Amt* (1870), *Christliche Kirchenzucht* (1872), *Pastoraltheologie* (Gütersloh, 1872), and *Dogmatik* (2 vols., 1874), and C. C. Israel those on *Theologische Moral* (2 vols., 1871). Vilmar lectured also on homiletics, hymnology, and the literary history of the theology of the Reformation period. Besides his professorial activity, Vilmar was the soul of the conferences of the Lutheran pastors of both Hesses, which were held alternately at Marburg and Friedberg from 1857 to 1866. He further aided the aims of these conferences by editing the *Pastoraltheologische Blätter* (12 vols., Stuttgart, 1861–66), to which he contributed a series of articles edited by C. Müller under the title *Kirche und Welt* (2 vols., Gütersloh, 1872). But despite the companionship of his pupils, Vilmar felt more and more isolated and alone at Marburg, nor could he overcome his grief at the events of 1866. His melancholy continually increased, and a few months after the death of his second wife, he was found dead in bed from a repeated stroke of apoplexy. (J. HAUSSLEITER.)

BIBLIOGRAPHY: An autobiographical sketch is presented in O. Gerland's *Hessische Gelehrten-* . . . *Geschichte*, i. 119–140, Cassel, 1863, and further original matter in the form of correspondence is in E. Stengel, *Private und amtliche Beziehungen der Brüder Grimm*, 2 vols., Marburg, 1886.

Consult further: J. H. Leimbach, *A. F. C. Vilmar*, Hanover, 1875; R. F. Grau, *Vilmar und Von Hofmann, Erinnerungen*, Gütersloh, 1879; E. R. Grebe, *A. F. C. Vilmar*, Cassel, 1900; idem, *A. F. C. Vilmar als Oberhirte der Diöcese Cassel*, Marburg, 1904; *ADB*, xxxix. 715–722.

VINCENT OF BEAUVAIS: French Dominican and polyhistor of the thirteenth century; b. probably about 1190; d. apparently in 1264. Of his life almost nothing is known. He was a monk in the Dominican monastery of Beauvais, and probably studied in Paris, where he was attached to the Jacobin monastery. Possibly he was identical with the Dominican subprior Vincent of Beauvais who is mentioned in 1246. For a time he resided in the Cistercian monastery of Royaumont, where he was reader to the king; here possibly he was employed to supervise the education of the king's children, as is suggested by the fact that he wrote a work *De institutione filiorum regiorum sive nobilium;* and with this is probably connected his consolation to Louis on the death of his eldest son in 1260.

Vincent was a prolific author. In 1481 five of his writings were published at Basel in one volume: *Tractatus de gratia dei* or *Liber gratiæ* in four books on the eternal and temporal generation of Christ, his life, passion, resurrection, ascension, the sending of the Holy Ghost, and the blinding of the Jews; *Liber de laudibus Virginis gloriosæ*, patristic excerpts on the Virgin; *De sancto Johanne evangelista; De eruditione seu modo instruendorum filiorum regalium;* and *Consolatio pro morte amici*, or, more correctly, *Epistola consolatoria ad Ludovicum Francorum regem super morte filii ejus*. Several works are extant only in manuscript.

The chief work of Vincent was his *Speculum triplex* (Strasburg, 1473; Nuremberg, 1483–86; Venice, 1484, 1493–94, 1591; Douai, 1624). It consists of three parts, the "natural, doctrinal, and historical mirror," to which the spurious "moral mirror" was added as a fourth part long after the author's death. The *Speculum* is the most comprehensive of all medieval encyclopedic works, and its author was perhaps the best-read scholar previous to the invention of printing. In his prologue Vincent declares that, despite the active pursuit of learning, especially in his own order, "sacred history" had been neglected; and that he would endeavor to remedy this deficiency by collecting everything worthy of remembrance. The prevailing point of view, therefore, is historical, not systematic. The chief source is the Bible (supplemented by the Apocrypha), to which are added papal decretals, the canons of general councils, and the works of recognized doctors of the Church. For secular matters use is made of such works as the chronicles of Eusebius, Jerome, Prosper, and Sigibert, the histories of Pompeius Trogus, Orosius, Suetonius, Rufinus, and Cassiodorus, the acts of martyrs, and the records of saints and monks. Philosophers and poets are likewise considered, as well as the writings of scientists and physicians from Aristotle, Pliny, and Hippocrates to Avicenna, Razi, and Constantinus Africanus.

The first part, or *Speculum naturale*, in thirty-two books, is based on the scheme of the six days of creation. It treats of all that Vincent had read

concerning angels and demons, light, and color (i.–
ii.), astronomy and astrology, space, time, motion,
air, echo, rain, lightning, and clouds (iii.–iv.), the
sea, tides, healing springs, minerals, plants, and
gardens (v.–xiv.), birds and fishes (xvi.–xvii.), rep-
tiles, mammals, and the anatomy, physiology, and
psychology of man (xviii.–xxviii.), sin (xxix.), generation (xxxi.), and the geography of the three divisions of the world with their importance for the
history of man (xxxii.). History itself is divided,
in Augustinian fashion, not only into sections " before the law," " under the law," and " under grace,"
but also into six ages, corresponding to the six days
of creation, and to six ages of man according to his
varying attitude toward the divine law, these being
infancy (from Adam to Noah), boyhood (to Abraham), adolescence (to David), youth (to the exile),
manhood (to Christ), and old age (to the Last Day),
the seventh age being the eternal rest of the saints.
The second part, the *Speculum doctrinale*, in seventeen books, forms an encyclopedia of science. After
an introduction (i. 3), the origin and division of
sciences are discussed, and a vocabulary of unusual
terms is appended (i. 10 sqq.). Then follow the
elements of grammar (ii.) and a compend of logic,
rhetoric, and poetry (iii.). Passing to " practical
learning," Vincent takes up virtues and religion
(iv.), social life (v. 38), " economics " (marriage,
education, friends, house, agriculture, etc.; vi.),
then political science (vii.), jurisprudence (viii.),
and crimes (ix.–x.); the mechanical arts (xi.), medicine (xii.–xiii.), special diseases (xiv.); " natural
philosophy " (the elements, minerals, trees, zool-
ogy, etc.; xv.) and mathematics, music, geometry,
astronomy, and metaphysics (xvi.). The concluding book treats of theological science. The third
portion, or *Speculum historiale*, is introduced by a
brief presentation of the doctrine of God, the heavenly hierarchy, matter, creation, man, the fall, sin,
the fourteen articles of faith, the three theological
and the four cardinal virtues, and the seven gifts
of the Holy Ghost. Early history is summarized
from the Bible (i.). The second book extends from
Moses to the period of the kings, including the account of Hercules, the Trojan war, Lycurgus, Romulus, the seven wise men, etc.; and the third treats
of Æsop's Fables, the fall of Babylon, Hippias,
Pythagoras, Heraclitus, Ezra, Nehemiah, Socrates,
Plato, Aristotle, etc. Books iv.–vi. recount the
history of Philip, Alexander, and the Diodochi to
Augustus and Herod. The seventh book begins
with Tiberius, and is devoted especially to the birth
of Christ; and the eighth develops the essence of
Christianity and the seven sacraments. The ninth
book contains accounts of Nero, Simon Magus, and
the Roman primate Clement, legends of the apostles, and histories of the martyrs, etc. The tenth
book is a record of the emperors from Vespasian to
Commodus, the destruction of Jerusalem, John,
Pliny, and the Church Fathers. The eleventh book
extends to Origen and Tertullian; the twelfth book
contains the history of the Diocletian persecution,
and the thirteenth and fourteenth the record of the
period of Constantine, with the Church Fathers of
the fourth century. The fifteenth and sixteenth
books tell of India (according to the legend of Bar-

laam and Josaphat, q.v.), Persia, Rome, France,
England, the Vandals, Ostrogoths, and Huns; while
books xvii.–xxiv. are devoted to the period from
Theodosius to the Carolingians, with thorough discussion of the principal ecclesiastical authors. Books
xxv.–xxx. recount the events from the reign of
Henry II. to the author's own time. The thirty-
first book contains an account of the council held at
Lyons in 1245, the sending of Dominicans to the
Tatars in 1245, and the crusade of St. Louis with
his captivity in Damietta until 1250. The last date
given is 1253, but the *Speculum* was completed in
thirty books in 1244, the thirty-first being added
nine years later.

The method of Vincent was to take his data from
some chronology, as that of Eusebius, and to fill in
with material drawn from biographies or similar
historical sources. There are few attempts at analysis or interpretation, the *Speculum* being rather a
gigantic chronicle or work of reference. His purpose was to gather together all the learning of his
time, and its gigantic and all-embracing scope is
characterististic of the endeavor of religious erudition to establish the supremacy of the Church on
every side, even learning being made a means of
grace, and knowledge serving to promote piety.

(R. Seeberg.)

Bibliography: *Histoire littéraire de la France*, xviii. 449–
515; J. Quétif and J. Echard, *Scriptores ordinis prædica-
torum*, i. 212–240, 300 sqq., Paris, 1719; A. Touron, *Hist.
des hommes illustres de l'ordre de S. Dominique*, i. 186,
Paris, 1743; J. F. Eckhardt, *Nachricht von seltenen Büchern der Bibliothek zu Eisenach*, pp. 31–83, Eisenach, 1775;
F. Schlosser, *Vincenz von Beauvais*, 2 vols., Frankfort,
1819; J. B. Bourgeat, *Études sur Vincent de Beauvais*,
Paris, 1856; E. Boutaric, *Examen des sources du speculum
. . . de Vincent de Beauvais*, Paris, 1863; idem, *Vincent de Beauvais et la connaissance de l'antiquité classique
au xiii. siècle*, ib. 1875; A. Stöckl, *Geschichte der Philosophie des Mittelalters*, ii. 345 sqq., Mainz, 1865; T. Des-
barraux-Bernard, *Étude bibliographique sur Vincent de
Beauvais*, Paris, 1872; W. Gass, in *ZKG*, i (1876), 365–
396, ii (1877), 332–365, 510–536; H. Brosien, in *NA*, iv
(1879), 437–439, 463, 500; B. Hauréau, *Hist. de la philosophie scolastique*, ii. 1, pp. 186 sqq., Paris, 1880; idem,
Notices et extraits, v. 110–113, ib. 1892; L. Kellner, *Skizzen und Bilder aus der Erziehungsgeschichte*, i. 184 sqq.,
Ussen, 1880; R. Friedrich, *Vicentius von Beauvais als
Pädagog*, Leipsic, 1883; C. Giambelli, *Di Vincenzo Bello-
vacense*, Rome, 1886; M. de Wulf, *Hist. de la philosophie
médiévale*, pp. 381–382, Louvain, 1900, 2d ed., 1905; *KL.*
xii. 973–978; Lichtenberger, *ESR*, xii. 397; *Biographie
universelle*, xlix. 119 sqq.

VINCENT OF LÉRINS:

Presbyter of Lérins (5
m. s. of Cannes); flourished about the middle of
the fifth century. According to Gennadius (*De vir.
ill.*, lxv.), he was deeply versed in the Bible and in
dogmatic theology, wrote against heretics, and died
during the reign of Theodosius II. and Valentinian
III. Eucherius, in his *Instructiones* (*CSEL*, xxxi.
66), describes him as " preeminent in eloquence and
learning " and as one of the instructors of his son.
Gennadius was acquainted with only a single work
by Vincent, written under the pseudonym of Pere-
grinus (" pilgrim "), the *Adversum hæreticos*,
commonly known as the *Commonitorium* or *Commonitoria* (eds. are by J. Sicard, Basel, 1528, poorly
reprinted by J. Coster, Antwerp, 1560, and
Leyden, 1572; S. Baluze, Paris, 1663, 1684, and
Augsburg, 1757, this last taken into *MPL*, l. 637
sqq.; Klüpfel, Vienna, 1809; Pusey, Oxford, 1838;

Hurter, Innsbruck, 1880; with Eng. transl., Huddersfield, 1880, and London, 1885; G. A. Jülicher, Freiburg, 1895). His work was apparently written some three years after the Council of Ephesus, i.e., about 434. According to his own statements, he composed it simply to aid his weak memory, not for publication; but nevertheless he found it advisable to lay the book before a wider circle, despite its stylistic faults.

One point in the transmission of the *Commonitorium*, however, remains uncertain. According to chap. xxviii., Vincent, after exhausting the theme of the first *Commonitorium*, desired to begin anew the demonstration of the " rule of the faith of the Church " from the history of a council (the Council of Ephesus). Instead of this, chap. xxix. marks the end of the second book, and the remainder of the work is devoted to a brief recapitulation of what was said in both books. This was the condition in which Gennadius found the *Commonitorium*, which he explained by saying that the main portion of the second book had been stolen from the author in its rough draft, whereupon Vincent had briefly summarized the contents of this second book, had appended a new chapter to the first part, and let the whole appear as one book. In the work of Vincent himself there is no trace of such a reason for his recapitulation, and the statement of Gennadius is at best a hypothesis to explain the absence of the second book. The explanation seems to be that Vincent had both books completed before writing the concluding sections, but foresaw that the length of the second book and the mass of documents cited in it would lead many readers to skip it. He had accordingly made a mere excerpt of the second book, since for the first book he might count on close attention. The first book was then transcribed entire, but only the excerpts of the second book were copied.

The importance of the *Commonitorium* rests on the development of a single thought contained in the unmutilated first book. The purpose was to establish principles whereby the right could be distinguished in the struggle between orthodoxy and heresy, to combine in right relation the two great principles of the authority of the Scriptures and the tradition of the Church Catholic, and to secure certainty for the correct determination of both. The Catholic should never be uncertain as to what the Bible and tradition actually prescribe. But while the Bible contains only truth and all things necessary for salvation, it is evidently open to misinterpretation, as is shown by heretical and false exegesis of every kind. The fundamentals of Catholic dogma, therefore, can be decided only in accordance with the authority of the interpretation of the Church; and in a famous sentence he declares that only that is truly and properly Catholic " which is believed everywhere, always, and by all." These three elements decide in favor of the genuine teachings of the Church against every form of heresy. If a new heresy arises, the good Catholic should hold to the universal teaching of the Church as opposed to a single deviating view. If the universal character be lacking because of apostasy in many parts of the Church at

XII.—13

the same time, then appeal must be made to ancient teachings in the Church, in which case the heresy in question will usually be found to be opposed to the entire ancient Church. If, however, similar errors were represented in early times by a single theologian or by a portion of the Church, then the final appeal must be taken to the prevailing majority of teachers in churches in early times. Vincent was firmly convinced that the Church Catholic had been, from the very first, the possessor of truth, and of the whole truth necessary for salvation; and heretics without exception are innovators seeking to destroy a portion of the inheritance of the Church. In matters of faith he held that the surest decisions must ever be sought in the writings of the ancients.

Vincent did not write his *Commonitorium* because of a purely academic interest in the establishment of a canon of Catholic faith, but tacitly to assail the Augustinian doctrine of Predestination (q.v.). Although Augustine is never mentioned by name, and while Pelagius and Julian of Eclanum are rejected with horror, the language employed is essentially Semipelagian, and the entire work is filled with allusions to Augustine and his system of polemics. He would not, indeed, rob that great master of his fame. Nevertheless, he was keenly aware of the dangers of Augustine's teachings, and therefore called upon all Christendom to bethink themselves before it should be too late, giving them a canon disastrous to the new-fangled doctrine of predestination, for whose support no ancient Father of the Church could be cited.

Thus Vincent devised his canon and wrote his book to aid in the controversy then raging among the Gallic theologians concerning free will or grace. There is little doubt that he belonged to the majority who emphasized the necessity both of the human will and of divine grace as opposed to the strictly Augustinian Prosper of Aquitaine. In a brief treatise by Prosper *Pro Augustini doctrina responsiones ad capitula objectionum Vincentianarum* (*MPL*, xlv. 1843–50, li. 177–182) are contained sixteen theses evidently composed by a Semipelagian in criticism of the doctrine of predestination. Since Prosper combated these theses as set up by Vincent, they can scarcely have been posited by any other Vincent than the monk of Lerins. They seem to have been promulgated before their author wrote the pseudonymous *Commonitorium*. It is not impossible that Vincent did not intend them to be made public, but that Prosper in some way gained possession of a copy of them.

It has also been suggested that Vincent, if not the author of the *Capitula calumniantium Gallorum*, closely akin to the *Objectiones Vincentianæ* and answered by Prosper in another work (*MPL*, xlv. 1835–44, li. 155 sqq.), at least inspired and influenced them. Such a hypothesis, however, even if granted, adds little to the information given by the *Commonitorium* alone, that Vincent was one of the Gallic clergy who, in the fifth century, were decidedly opposed to the innovations of Augustine. He can scarcely have restricted himself to the half-hidden allusions in his *Commonitorium* to what he considered a deadly heresy, but none of his possible anti-Augustinian polemics has survived, and even Gennadius did not know of their existence.

(G. A. JÜLICHER.)

BIBLIOGRAPHY: Gennadius, De vir. ill., lxv., Eng. transl. in NPNF, 2d ser., iii. 396; F. X. Elpelt, Des heiligen Vincent von Lerin Ermahnungsbuch, Leben und Lehren, Breslau, 1840; Hefele, in Beiträge zur Kirchengeschichte, Archäologie und Liturgik, i (1864), 145–174; Poitel, De utroque Commonitorio Lerinensi, Nancy, 1895; H. Koch, in TQS, 1899, pp. 396 sqq.; idem, Vincenz von Lerin und Gennadius, in TU, 3d ser., 1, part 2, 1907; Vincenti Lerinensis Commonitoria, in Florilegium patristicum, ed. G. Rauschen, Bonn, 1906; F. Brunetière and P. de Labriolle, Vincent of Lerins, Paris, 1906; KL, xii. 985–989; DCB, iv. 1154–58; Schaff, Christian Church, iii. 344, 613–614, 862–863; Neander, Christian Church, vol. ii. passim; the literature under SEMIPELAGIANISM, and the works on the church history of his period.

VINCENT OF SARAGOSSA, SAINT: Spanish saint and martyr of the early fourth century. According to tradition, he was born of a noble family at Osca (the modern Huesca, 180 m. n.e. of Madrid), was deacon of Bishop Valerius of Saragossa, and on the outbreak of the Diocletian persecution was taken with his bishop to Valencia to defend the faith before Datian, where he spoke with such eloquence that while the bishop was merely banished, he was exposed to the most horrible tortures, thrown into a dark hole, and made to lie on sharp stones and pointed sherds, whereupon angels turned his couch of pain to a soft bed. He then began to preach to the multitudes attracted by the miracle, and even Datian, declaring himself conquered, commanded that Vincent be taken from his place of torture. When, nevertheless, he died, the rage of Datian broke forth afresh. He ordered the corpse to be thrown to wild beasts, when angels and even ravens protected it. The body was then sunk into the sea in a sack filled with stones, but it emerged and was borne by the winds to a haven, where the faithful buried it, later reverencing the relics by founding a chapel. This legend (contained in its fullest form in ASB, Jan., ii. 394–397; in briefer recension, Analecta Bollandiana, i. 263–270; and in entirely different form, MPG, cxiv. 735–756) is at least as old as the fourth century, as is shown by the four sermons of Augustine in honor of Vincent (Sermones, cclxxiv.–cclxxvii.; MPL, xxxviii. 1252–68) and the references of Prudentius in the fifth hymn of his Peristephanon (MPL, lx. 378–411) and Paulinus of Nola (xix. 153).

At an early period the veneration of the saint spread from Spain and Africa to France. Gregory of Tours states that the Frankish kings Childebert and Chlotar were driven to raise the siege of Saragossa by a sight of the tunic of Vincent (MGH, Script. rer. Merov., I., ii. 133), and the anonymous author of the Liber historiæ Francorum (ib. pp. 283–284), writing about 727, records that to the princes the garment was given by the bishop of the city. The relic was honored in the church of St. Vincent built at Paris by Childebert, the later church of St. Germain des Près. The Aquitanian monastery of Castres claimed to possess the body of Vincentius after 864. On the other hand, Stephen, the precentor of Lisbon, declared that the body was brought from Valencia to Lisbon in 1175 (ASB, Jan., ii. 408–413; Analecta Bollandiana, i. 270–278); and the Epistola Hermanni abbatis Sancti Martini Tornacen-

sis de corpore Sancti Vincenti diaconi (Analecta Bollandiana, ii. 243–246) shows that it was venerated in Valencia as late as 1145. Portions of the saint's remains were also reverenced elsewhere, his head at Le Mans, one arm at Vitry-le-François, and the other at Bari in Apulia, etc. Basilicas of St. Vincent are mentioned by Venantius Fortunatus, and the French cathedrals of Châlons-sur-Sâone, Macon, Viviers, and St. Malo were named in his honor. Rome has three churches named after him.

Vincent is honored as the patron saint of stolen goods, as well as in perils at sea; while wine-growers deem sunshine on his day (Jan. 22) a good omen. His attribute is a gridiron with pointed nails (the latter. distinguishing him from St. Lawrence), and sometimes also the raven protecting his corpse.

(G. KRÜGER.)

BIBLIOGRAPHY: Tillemont, Mémoires, v. 215–231, 673–677; P. B. Gams, Kirchengeschichte Spaniens, i. 376–382, Regensburg, 1862; J. E. Stadler and J. N. Ginal, Heiligenlexikon, v. 705–708, Augsburg, 1882; P. Allard, La Persecution de Diocletien, i. 40, 237, 244, 249–250, Paris, 1890; H. Leclercq, L'Espagne chrétienne, pp. 82–85, Paris, 1906; KL, xii. 999–1001; DCB, iv. 1152.

VINCENT DE PAUL, SAINT: Founder of the Roman Catholic orders of the Lazarists and the Sisters of Mercy (qq.v.); b. at Ranquines (a village near Dax, 125 m. w. of Toulouse), Gascony, Apr. 24, 1576; d. at Paris Sept. 27, 1660. He received his early training from the Franciscans at Dax, and then studied in Toulouse 1597–1600. In 1605, while on a voyage to Narbonne, he was captured by corsairs and taken to Tunis, where he fell into the hands of a French renegade whom he succeeded in restoring to the Church, who also brought him back to France. Vincent then went to Rome, and there won the favor of Cardinal d'Orsat, who employed him on a mission to Henry IV. He thus came to Paris early in 1609, and became chaplain to Margaret of Valois. Here, while aiding a troubled theologian to escape from doubt, Vincent himself became involved in a skepticism from which he was freed only by vowing to devote his entire life to the poor.

In 1612 Vincent was made parish priest at Clichy, and in the following year became chaplain and tutor to the family of Philip Emanuel, count of Gondy, finding wide scope for activity among the peasantry of the estate. In 1617, his pupils no longer requiring his care, Vincent became parish priest at the wretched town of Chatillon-les-Dombes, where he founded the first confrérie du charité for the personal aid of the poor by women. Meanwhile the Count and Countess de Gondy induced Vincent to return to their house in 1618. He now founded a number of sisterhoods like that at Chatillon, and gave special attention to the galley slaves, for whom he established a hospital. In 1619 King Louis XIII. appointed him royal almoner of the galleys of France. At Macon in Burgundy, in 1623, he found an enormous number of beggars, for whom, with the aid of the civil and religious authorities, he established an organization which did away with mendicancy.

In 1624 Vincent formed the beginnings of his body of mission priests for the care of the poor. He received as the mother-house of his order the

Collège des bons enfants. His order soon gained powerful aid in the gift of 45,000 livres from the Count de Gondy (1625), the royal approval bestowed by Louis XIII. (1627), and the papal sanction of Urban VIII. (1631); and in 1631 he received from the canons of St. Victor the house of St. Lazarus in Paris, which became the center of activity. At first the priests were sent chiefly to the country districts, but Vincent did not forget the cities, and some of his priests were detailed to visit the soldiers, the blind, the sick, the poor, and the laborers. In 1635 he established a seminary for his order, based on Jesuit lines. Especially admirable were the exertions of the order during the terrible campaign in Lotharingia, where, within ten years, Vincent was able to send no less than 400,000 thalers. He extended his activity to the shepherds of the Roman Campagna, as well as to the provinces of France, to Tunis, Algiers, Ireland, Genoa, Madagascar, Poland, Corsica, Piedmont, etc. He was also spiritual councilor of state, and in 1634 he established a sisterhood of matrons for the care of the sick in the Hotel Dieu of Paris, and in 1657 founded for the poor of Paris a great hospital which later became the Salpetrière. During the closing years of his life he was an invalid, but he bore his sufferings with the humility and fortitude that characterized his entire life. He was beatified by Benedict XIII. in 1723, and canonized in 1737. By a breve of May 12, 1885, Leo XIII. declared him the patron of all Roman Catholic charitable organizations in any way connected with him throughout the world. (EUGEN LACHENMANN.)

BIBLIOGRAPHY: The " Letters " were issued in 2 vols., Paris, 1882. His life has been a frequent theme for biographers, accounts being written by: L. Abelly, Paris, 1664 and often elsewhere, Germ. transl., Regensburg, 1859 (Abelly's *Vertus de S. Vincent de Paul* was issued in a new ed., Paris, 1897); D. Acami, Venice, 1753; P. Collet, new ed., 4 vols., Paris, 1818; M. Orsini, Paris, 1852; H. Bedford, London, 1856; M. U. Maynard, 4 vols., Paris, 1860; F. A. P. Dupanloup, Paris, 1863; G. Rouquette, *St. Vincent de Paul et son siècle*, Lyons, 1864; J. B. H. R. Capcfique, *St. Vincent de Paul et les sœurs de charité*, Paris, 1865; T. S. Preston, New York, 1866; A. J. Ansart, *The Spirit of St. Vincent de Paul*, New York, 1867; C. A. Jones, London, 1873; R. F. Wilson, Edinburgh, 1873; E. Alcan, 2 vols., Paris, 1879; R. de Chantelauze, *St. Vincent de Paul et les Gondi*, Paris, 1882; Cavallier, *St. Vincent de Paul et sa mission sociale*, Montpellier, 1885; J. Morel, Tours, 1888, reissue, 1908; H. Debout, Paris, 1889; J. B. Jeannin, Paris, 1890; H. Simard, Lyons, 1894; J. B. Boudignon, 3d ed., Paris, 1897; E. Bougaud, 3d ed., 2 vols., Paris, 1898, Eng. transl., London and New York, 1908; E. de Broglie, 5th ed., Paris, 1899, Eng. transl. of an earlier ed., London, 1898.

VINCENT FERRER (VINCENTE FERRER), SAINT: Spanish Dominican preacher and leader of the flagellants; b. at Valencia Jan. 23, 1350; d. at Vannes (84 m. n.w. of Nantes) Apr. 5, 1419. He entered the Dominican order Dec. 5, 1374, and in

Life as a Monk. his monastery quickly won recognition by asceticism and application to the study of philosophy and theology. Except for a visit to Toulouse in 1377, he remained in the cloister at Valencia until 1380, when he went to the universities of Barcelona and Lerida, studying at each two years. A fruit of his studies there was his (unpublished) *Tractatus de moderno ecclesiæ schismate*, which was occasioned

by the schism of 1378. In this treatise he took the side of Clement VII., who had been elected at Fondi, and declared Urban VI., who had been chosen at Rome, an apostate and an enemy of the Church. In 1384 Vincent returned to Valencia, where he taught and preached until 1391. Such was his distinction in these duties that he served as councilor to John I. of Aragon and confessor to his queen, Yolanda, until 1395, when he was summoned to Avignoñ by Benedict XIII. as grand penitentiary and magister sacri palatii, but returned to his monastery at Valencia 1398. His distress at the continuance of the schism was intense, and seems to have been instrumental in leading him to adopt a roving prophetic and apostolic life. This is shown by his apocalyptic treatise *De eversione Europæ*, in which he laments bitterly over the decay of ecclesiastical discipline, order, and morality, and prophesies the speedy coming of Antichrist. While it is not proved that Benedict endeavored to dissuade Vincent from his resolve and offered him various bishoprics and even a cardinalate, it is true that he appointed him apostolic preacher with the title of *legatus a latere* and gave him full power to loose and bind on his journey.

In 1399 Vincent began the travels which were to occupy the remainder of his life, and within a short time he was accompanied by multitudes who came

Activity as an Itinerant Preacher. to form a regular itinerant community with their own usages and rules. Their first requirement was the self-castigation in which their leader surpassed them all, which they performed by scourging themselves on their bared shoulders with thick knotted cords to the accompaniment of such cries as, " God have mercy! " (see FLAGELLATION, FLAGELLANTS). Vincent was accustomed to preach in almost every place which he visited, frequently delivering two and three sermons in a single day, which were transmitted by his hearers, for Vincent himself never committed them to writing. These addresses were ethical rather than dogmatic, although the preacher adhered closely to orthodox Roman Catholicism. He was one of the most successful missionaries to the Jews of his time, particularly in Valencia, Toledo, and Valladolid. The scene of his activity was the Spanish peninsula, northern Italy, and France. Various miracles are recounted in his honor by his earliest biographer and fellow Dominican Pietro Razzano, who wrote about a generation after Vincent's death.

Vincent frequently took part in the affairs of his time, both ecclesiastical and secular. In 1412 he exercised a decided influence for Catalonia, Aragon, and Valencia in the election of a king held in the

His Closing Years. Catalonian castle of Daspe. Four years later he was invited to attend the Council of Constance, but declined. In the later years of his life he withdrew from association with the flagellants, although his activity as a preacher suffered no diminution, and in Feb., 1418, he is said to have had some 70,000 auditors in Nantes. The closing months of his life were spent in Brittany. Until the Revolution the anniversary of his burial in the cathedral of Vannes was celebrated on Sept. 6, but since that time it has been held on the first Sunday of September. Vincent was canonized by Calixtus III. on June 29, 1455, although the bull of canonization was first published by Pius II. on Oct. 1, 1458. His chief works, in addition to those already mentioned, are his *Tractatus de vita spirituali* (Magdeburg, 1493); *De fine mundi et tempore Antichristi* (Venice [?], 1475); and his sermons, delivered in the Spanish dialect of Valencia, and repeatedly translated into Latin (first at Lyons, 1490).

(O. ZÖCKLER†.)

BIBLIOGRAPHY: Besides the account by Razzano in *ASB*, April, i. 475–529, lives have been written by V. J. Antist, Valencia, 1578; F. Diago, Barcelona, 1600; V. Gomez, Valencia, 1618; B. Guyard, Paris, 1634; F. Gavalda, Valencia, 1668; M. Marchese, Naples, 1669; L. Coelho, Lisbon, 1713; S. T. Miguel, Valencia, 1713, new ed., Madrid, 1856; G. M. F. Ferrarini, Milan, 1732; A. Teoli, Naples, 1738, new ed., Rome, 1826; A. Valdecebro, Madrid, 1740; P. Fuesi, Oedenburg, 1749; L. Heller, Berlin, 1830; L. Donin, Vienna, 1844; anonymous, Bologna, 1850; M. A. Bayle, Paris, 1855; A. Ferrante, Turin, 1876; and M. S. Hogan, London and New York, 1911. Consult further: P. Fages, *Hist. de S. Vincent Ferrer*, 2 vols., Paris, 1894; A. Pradel, *St. Vincent Ferrer, . . . his Life, Spiritual Teaching, and Practical Devotion*, London, 1875; O. Zöckler, *Zur Würdigung des römischen Mirakelglaubens*, in *Beweis des Glaubens*, 1897, pp. 257–269; J. Rohr, in *Historisches Jahrbuch der Görresgesellschaft*, 1898, i. 32 sqq.; *KL*, xii. 978–983.

VINCENT, BOYD: Protestant Episcopal bishop of southern Ohio; b. at Erie, Pa., May 18, 1845. He was graduated from Yale (A.B., 1867) and Berkeley Divinity School, Middletown, Conn.(1871); was curate of St. Paul's, Erie (1871–72); rector of Cross and Crown Church, in the same city (1872–1874), and of Calvary Church, Pittsburg, Pa. (1874–89); became bishop coadjutor of southern Ohio (1889); and on the retirement of Bishop T. A. Jaggar (1904) became diocesan of the see. He has written *God and Prayer: A Discourse on the Reasonableness of Prayer* (New York, 1897).

BIBLIOGRAPHY: W. S. Perry, *The Episcopate in America*, p. 311, New York, 1895.

VINCENT, van"sän', JACQUES LOUIS SAMUEL: French Protestant; b. at Nîmes Sept. 8, 1787; d. near there July 10, 1837. After studying at Uzès and Montpellier, he pursued a theological training at Geneva (1806–09), and in 1809 was chosen assistant pastor in his native city, where he remained until physical infirmity compelled him to retire to his suburban estate. His greatest services were the reestablishment and promotion of theological studies in the Reformed church in France. Napoleon I. had indeed given the church a care-free existence by including it in the concordat of 1801 (see CONCORDATS, etc., VI., 1), but its theological status was at low ebb, and the seminary at Lausanne was a school for martyrs, not scholars. Vincent was one of the first to perceive the need of remedying the deficiencies, and to the preparation of a French theological literature for French Protestantism he devoted a large portion of his activity. Feeling especially attracted by English moral philosophy he translated, in 1817, Paley's work on that subject, and two years later reproduced the thoughts of Chalmers under the title *Preuves et autorité de la révélation chrétienne*. The problem of authority afforded him the material for his first independent book, in which he crossed

swords with the Abbé de Lamennais, showing in his *Observations sur l'unité religieuse* (Paris, 1820) that while Ultramontanism (q.v.) absorbs the individual in the mass, Protestantism should preserve and increase the freedom and responsibility of each separate person. To the reply of De Lamennais Vincent answered in his *Observations sur la voie d'autorité appliquée à la religion* (1821), by which he attracted the attention of the cultured circles of France and inspired his coreligionists to assume the defensive.

Vincent now sought to acquaint French Protestantism with German theology, writing at first for F. Monod's *Archives du christianisme*, and then editing the *Mélanges de religion, de morale et de critique sacrée* (10 vols., 1820–24), for which he wrote nearly all the articles. In 1829 he published a sketch of the theory of Protestantism in his *Vues sur le protestantisme en France*. Originally conservative in his dogmatic views, Vincent was led by German theology to a position akin to that of Schleiermacher and to a warm sympathy for living piety irrespective of ecclesiastical or dogmatic guise.

In 1830, after the publication of his *Vues*, Vincent was the leading man in the Reformed Church of France. He declined calls to Montauban and to Strasburg, but after the revolution of 1830 was elected president of the consistory of Nîmes, a position from which his republicanism had caused the ministry to exclude him two years before. In the latter years of his life he retired more and more from public duties, though in 1831–33 he lectured on the modern literature of Spain and Italy. Besides the works already mentioned, he was the author of *Méditations religieuses* (Paris, 1829), and in his memory the Liberals founded at Nîmes in 1892 the École Samuel Vincent for the promotion of the preparatory studies of candidates for the ministry.

(EUGEN LACHENMANN.)

BIBLIOGRAPHY: The posthumous editions of Vincent's *Vues* and his *Méditations* usually contain sketches of his life. Consult further: A. Michel, *Samuel Vincent, son temps et ses opinions*, Strasburg, 1864; J. Corbière, *Samuel Vincent, sa conception religieuse et chrétienne*, Geneva, 1873; M. Blanc, *Samuel Vincent*, Montauban, 1890; L. Maury, *Le Réveil religieux à Genève et en France*, 2 vols., Paris, 1892; G. Filhol, *La Pensée religieuse de Samuel Vincent*, Montauban, 1899; Lichtenberger, *ESR*, xii. 393–397.

VINCENT, JOHN HEYL: Methodist Episcopal bishop; b. at Tuscaloosa, Ala., Feb. 23, 1832. He was educated at the academies at Lewisburg and Milton, Pa., and at the age of eighteen began to preach. After teaching school at Catasaqua, Pa., in 1850, and being a circuit preacher in Luzerne County, Pa., in 1851, he was assistant in the city mission at Newark, N. J., in 1852. In 1853 he joined the Newark Conference and received his theological training at the Wesleyan Institute at Newark, N. J., being pastor at that city in 1852–53, and at Franklin in 1853–54 and Irvington in 1855–56 (both near Newark). He was ordained deacon in 1855 and elder two years later, and in 1857 was transferred to the Rock River Conference, Ill., holding pastorates in that state at Joliet (1857–58), Mount Morris (1858–59), Galena (1859–61), Rockford (1862–64), and Trinity Church, Chicago (1864–65). In 1866–1867 he was Sunday-school agent of his denomination, founding the *Northwest Sunday School Quarterly* in 1864; was corresponding secretary of the Sunday School Union and editor of the Methodist Episcopal Sunday-school publications (1868–88), and in 1874 was one of the founders of the Chautauqua Assembly, while in 1878 he established the Chautauqua Literary and Scientific Circle, of which he became chancellor. In 1888 he was elected bishop and in 1900 was placed in charge of the European work of his denomination with residence at Zurich, but in 1904 retired from active life. He has written *Sunday School Institutes and Normal Classes* (New York, 1866); *The Church School and its Officers* (1868); *The Chautauqua Movement* (1886); *The Home Book for the Mothers of our Land* (in collaboration with Josephine Pollard; 1886); *Better Not: Discussion of Certain Social Customs* (1888); *The Church School and the Sunday School Normal Guide* (1889); *Studies in Young Life* (1890); *Our Own Church* (1890); *To Old Bethlehem* (Meadville, Pa., 1890); *The Modern Sunday School* (New York, 1900); and *Family Worship for Every Day in the Year* (1905).

VINCENT, MARVIN RICHARDSON: Presbyterian; b. at Poughkeepsie, N. Y., Sept. 11, 1834. He was educated at Columbia (A.B., 1854), and after being an instructor in the Grammar School of Columbia College (1854–58), was professor of Latin in Troy (N. Y.) University (1858–60). He then entered the Methodist Episcopal ministry, but in 1863 became a Presbyterian; was pastor of the First Presbyterian Church, Troy, N. Y. (1863–73), and of the Church of the Covenant, New York, City (1873–83). Since 1883 he has been professor of New-Testament exegesis and criticism in Union Theological Seminary, New York. Aside from sermons and discourses he has written *The Minister's Handbook* (1882); *In the Shadow of the Pyrenees* (1883); *Word-Studies in the New Testament* (3 vols., 1887–90); *Students' New Testament Handbook* (1893); *The Age of Hildebrand* (1896); *Critical Commentary on Philippians and Philemon* (1897); *History of the Textual Criticim of the New Testament* (1899); and *The Gospel of Luke* in the *Temple Bible* (London, 1902). He likewise translated J. A. Bengel's *Gnomon of the New Testament* (in collaboration with C. T. Lewis; Philadelphia, 1862) and the *Inferno* of Dante (New York, 1904).

VINE, CULTIVATION OF THE. See WINE, HEBREW.

VINEGAR BIBLE. See BIBLE VERSIONS, B, IV., § 9.

VINES, RICHARD: Westminster divine; b. at Blaston, in Leicester County, England, about 1600; d. Feb. 4, 1655–56. He was educated in Magdalen College, Cambridge; became teacher of a school at Hinckly in Warwickshire after finishing his course at the university, and afterward rector of Weddington. He was appointed a member of the Westminster Assembly of Divines in 1643 from Warwickshire, and was very influential in matters of church government and the sacraments. He was chairman of the committee of accommodation with the Independents. He often preached before Parlia-

ment. During the session of the Westminster Assembly he was, in 1643, made minister of the parish of Clements Danes, near Essexhouse; but, this proving too large for him, he removed to the rectory of Walton in Hertfordshire, and soon after became pastor of Lawrence Jewry, London. In 1644 he was also appointed master of Pembroke Hall, Cambridge, and held the position until 1649, when he was turned out for refusing the "engagement" [of allegiance to the existing government]. In 1653 he was appointed by parliament one of the committee of divines to draw up the fundamentals as a basis of toleration. He died on Sabbath evening, from bleeding at the nose, which was brought on by excessive labor in preaching and administering the Lord's Supper. During his life a number of sermons were published, e.g., *Impostures of Seducing Teachers Discovered*, Commons Sermons, Nov. 30, 1642; *Author, Nature, and Danger of Heresy*, Commons Sermon, Apr. 23, 1644. After his death a number of posthumous works were published by his friends, e.g., *Treatise of the Right Institution, Administration, and Receiving of the Sacrament of the Lord's Supper* (4to, pp. 376, London, 1657); *God's Drawing and Man's Coming to Christ* (4to, pp. 335, 1662). His funeral sermon was preached by Thomas Jacombe, entitled *Enoch's Walk and Change*, and published 1656, with introductory remarks by Simeon Ashe and Edmund Calamy, followed by poetic epitaphs from William Spurstone, Matthew Newcommen, Matthew Poole, and others, all speaking of him in the warmest terms. He is represented as "a man of extraordinary ability, a smart disputant, well studied, a perfect master of the Greek, a real orator; his ministry solid, pithy, quick, and searching, having a clear head. He could dive deep into a knotty controversy, and was not afraid of men. He was a man of gracious, tender spirit." Fuller says of him, "He was most charitably moderate to such as dissented from him, though most constant to his own principles." C. A. BRIGGS.

BIBLIOGRAPHY: Thomas Fuller, *Church Hist. of Great Britain*, xi. 215, London, 1656; idem, *Hist. of the Worthies of England*, p. 134, ib. 1662; Samuel Clarke, *Lives of Sundry Eminent Persons*, i. 48–49, 2 parts, ib. 1683; J. Reid, *Memoirs of the Westminster Divines*, pp. 191 sqq., Paisley, 1811–15; *DNB*, lviii. 369–370, where reference to scattering notices is given.

VINET, vî″nê′, ALEXANDRE RODOLFE: Swiss theologian; b. at Ouchy (2 m. s. of Lausanne) June 17, 1797; d. at Clarens (14 m. s.e. of Lausanne) May 4, 1847. He was educated at the gymnasium and academy of Lausanne,
Early Life. where his patriotic *Le Réveil des Vaudois*, long a popular song, was written when he was seventeen. In 1817 he was appointed instructor in French at the gymnasium and normal school at Basel, and in 1819, after passing his theological examination at Lausanne, was ordained to the Reformed ministry. At this period he was filled with religious doubts, and his faith was essentially one of authority and custom. In Basel, however, he came in contact with very different tendencies, though the pietism which he found there was long his antipathy because of its narrowness and because it seemed to reduce the facts of revelation to mere symbols. The revival in Vaud,

originating with English Methodists, at first exercised little influence on Vinet; but all these factors were at work within him, and during an almost fatal illness in 1823, his entire point of view was changed, and he resolved to devote his life to Christ in thanksgiving for redemption.

The year 1823–24 marked the beginning of Vinet's literary activity as well as of his new religious life, and in his first contribution to the journal of the

Career at Basel. Paris society for Christian morals he advanced the view that ethics can not be divorced from dogma. A specific turn was given his energies by the law which, on May 20, 1824, officially sanctioned intolerance in the canton of Vaud, and in his pamphlet *Du respect des opinions* he set forth the kernel of all the theories he was subsequently to advance on religious liberty. In 1826 he was enabled to give wider currency to his views by winning the Lambrecht prize of 2,000 francs offered by the Paris society for Christian morals with his *Mémoire en faveur de la liberté des cultes*, thus establishing a reputation with the leading French Protestants as a thinker and author. In the following years the opposition to which dissenters were exposed in Vaud led Vinet to write much on freedom and conscience, his attitude even causing him to be involved in a suit, resulting in a nominal fine and suspension from all ecclesiastical functions in his canton for a year. The liberal revolution in Vaud in Dec., 1830, gave his energies a fresh impulse, though he was unable to secure the proclamation of religious liberty, to say nothing of the separation of Church and State. Meanwhile Vinet had been appointed associate professor at Basel. His critical essays first appeared in the Protestant *Le Semeur* of Paris, a number of them being reprinted under the title of *Essais de philosophie morale et de morale religieuse* (Paris, 1837). During this period, moreover, it was customary for the professor of literature at Basel to preach frequently in the French church, and in this capacity Vinet won the highest praise. His sermons, carefully revised and characterized at once by classic form and by a union of warmth and culture, were issued under the title of *Discours sur quelques sujets religieux* (Paris, 1831; Eng. transl. of parts of this work and of his *Nouveaux discours, Christian Philosophy*, London, 1846), their themes being dogmatic and apologetic. In the uprising that led to the separation of the city of Basel from its territory, Vinet was made a member of the committee to inform the general public of the condition of affairs in Basel, and was entrusted with a diplomatic mission to Lausanne. In return for these services, a new chair of French literature and rhetoric was founded for him in the university.

In 1837 he accepted a call to the Academy of Lausanne as professor of theology; and during this

Life at Lausanne. period of his life passed through a crisis which resulted in an ever-increasing opposition to the theology of the *Réveil*, with its intellectualism and antinomianism. This change of position found full expression in his *Nouveaux discours sur quelques sujets religieux* (Paris, 1841). Soon after settling in Lausanne, Vinet, as a member of the committee

on church reorganization, found opportunity for practical activity in behalf of his ideals, especially for voluntary admission of members to the Church and for the inclusion of laymen in ecclesiastical government. He advocated the retention of the Helvetic Confession, but the laws governing the Church, adopted in 1839, were so repugnant that he resigned, a year later, from the clergy of Vaud. These experiences seem to have confirmed Vinet in his insistence on the separation of Church and State, and in his *Essai sur la manifestation des convictions religieuses et sur la séparation de l'église et de l'état* (Paris, 1842; Eng. transl., *Essay on the Profession of Personal Religious Conviction, . . .* London, 1843) he wrote a classic on this theme. Nevertheless, he remained a simple member of the national Church; nor was he induced even by his position as professor of practical theology to make a propaganda for his theories. In 1845 the situation changed, and the February revolution in Vaud resulted in intense opposition to Protestantism in every form. When, therefore, the government, instead of heeding Vinet's demand for liberty of worship in the reorganization, repressed such liberty still more, he resigned his theological professorship in 1846. A consequence of this revolution was the Free Church in Vaud, though it would be incorrect to regard Vinet as its founder, even though he were the author of the concept of the freedom and dignity which were its due. Vinet approved the course of the 150 clergy who left the national church rather than obey the State in its attempt to make them recommend the new constitution to their congregations, and accorded them his warmest sympathy; he also set forth the principle unconsciously adopted by them, that the freedom of the Church can be won only by complete separation from the State, in his anonymous *Considérations présentées à Messrs. les démissionaires*. His activity as a publicist in articles for the periodical and daily press and in pamphlets now increased, the ripest of his productions of this type being his *Du socialisme considéré dans son principe* (Geneva, 1846). Vinet naturally joined the Free Church which was soon founded, often preaching for its congregations and acting as a member of the committee on organization. He devoted much thought to the preparation of a confession of faith in which he sought to avoid all theological subtleties and polemics. He continued his activity to the last months of his life, delivering private lectures on practical and exegetical subjects.

Whether appearing as the apostle of the separation of Church and State, as the critic and historian of French literature, or as the Christian thinker, Vinet was, first and foremost, an apologist, ever seeking to reconcile the modern spirit with the Gospel. Holding, as he did, that the high-

Significance as a Writer. est element in man is conscience, and that this is the seat of reason, the instrument of religious feeling, compulsion in matters of religion would naturally be violence to conscience. While, moreover, the individual is, in a sense, higher than the social organism, which is made for man, "society forms a field for the activity of the individual, affords scope for the exercise of his virtues, and sets up a barrier to his selfishness. Thus man becomes master of himself in proportion as he devotes himself to his fellows, is the more free the more social he is, receives more as he demands less, and is more himself the less he belongs to himself." Thus the individual and society grow in unison, attaining mutual perfection in the fulfilment and the service of duty. Applying this doctrine of individualism to the Church, Vinet became an advocate of the separation of Church and State, the step urged in the only two of his works which do not bear the mark of collected essays. Here he maintained that religion is an affair between God and man alone, while the State should have sole control of social morals, which comprize security of person and property and public decency. In 1831 Vinet was still a true son of the national Church, but by the time of the publication of his *Essai sur la manifestation*, etc., ut sup. (1842), his attitude had changed. The tenets set forth in his first essay of 1826 are here carried still further, with special attack upon the theory that the State is the entire man. Vinet maintained, on the contrary, that the State is based on identical traits common to all, while the foundation of the Church is human individuality of conscience. Individuality being thus considered a part of the inmost essence of Christianity, Vinet deemed the union of Church and State as heresy, and allowed validity only to a church independent of the State. A theological system he never evolved, though from him proceeded great ideas destined to bring forth fruit both for theology and for the Church. Thus he became a sort of second Pascal, and there is, therefore, little cause for surprise that Vinet's posthumous *Études sur Blaise Pascal* (Paris, 1848; Eng. transl., *Studies on Pascal*, Edinburgh, 1859) should be the best study yet written on that philosopher. In his apologetics he laid stress on the way in which the Gospel perfectly answers the needs of the heart. He was firmly convinced, moreover, that the most efficacious apologetic is psychological. But the psychological method of apologetics was the weakness, as well as the strength, of Vinet; for though history does not make faith, the neglect of historical factors leads to the peril of subjectivity and ultimately to rationalism. Vinet has even been termed a rationalist, but, in spite of occasional phrases in his letters and in his conversation, he was no skeptic. Had his attitude toward the Bible been clearer, the charge of rationalism might more easily be refuted. Lack of precision is characteristic of his apologetics and of his theology in general, but the reality which he ascribes, in all his writings, to the fall and to original sin, as well as to the great facts of salvation and the miracles, is alone sufficient to prevent rationalists or modern " liberals " from claiming him as one of their number. The entire character of his works demonstrates with equal clearness that he presupposed as absolutely necessary the facts of revelation. Christianity was for him primarily a history and a fact, which it must have been to gain currency.

The sole works of Vinet on practical theology were posthumous. His *Théologie pastorale* (Paris, 1850; Eng. transl., Edinburgh, 1852) is especially valuable for its rich utilization of French Roman Catholic literature. Here he denies any priestly character to the clergy, terms preaching a work of love and a mystery, and regards religious instruction as an act of worship. In his *Homilétique ou théorie de la prédication* (Paris, 1853; Eng. transl., *Homiletics*, Edinburgh and New York, 1853, new ed. 1880; often republished, since it was long a text-book in theological seminaries in the United States of America), he shows himself relatively indifferent to his text, deciding upon the themes of his sermons before choosing their texts. Both theoretically and practically he regarded almost exclusively the synthetic sermon, and sharply reproved any neglect of artistic embellishment. In citations he especially affected German writers on the theory of homiletics and the French preachers, whose works he had studied exhaustively. The results of these latter studies are embodied in his third work on practical theology, *Histoire de la prédication parmi les Réformés de France au dix-septième siècle* (Paris, 1860), a publication of great value. The strength of Vinet's own sermons lies in their masterly control of the psychological method; their weakness in their neglect of Biblical foundation. Of Vinet's five homiletic volumes only one was based on sermons actually delivered by him, the remainder containing, for the most part, apologetic or ethical studies in rhetorical form, presented to a relatively small circle of students. The inner life of Vinet is clearly mirrored in his poems, a large number of which have justly been incorporated in French Protestant hymnals. In addition to the works already mentioned, Vinet was the author of the following: *Chrestomathie française, ou choix de morceaux tirés des meilleurs écrivains français* (3 vols., Basel, 1829–30); *Études évangéliques* (Paris, 1847; Eng. transl., *Gospel Studies*, Glasgow, 1849); *Méditations évangéliques* (1849; Eng. transl., *Evangelical Meditations*, Edinburgh, 1858); *Études sur la littérature française au dix-neuvième siècle* (3 vols., 1849–51); *Nouvelles études évangéliques* (1851); *Histoire de la littérature française au dix-huitième siècle* (2 vols., 1853; Eng. transl., *Hist. of French Literature in the 18th Century*, Edinburgh, 1854); *Liberté religieuse et questions ecclésiastiques* (1854); *L'Éducation, la famille et la société* (1855); *Moralistes des seizième et dix-septième siècles* (1859); *Poètes du siècle de Louis XIV.* (1861); *Mélanges* (1869); and *Lettres* (2 vols., Lausanne, 1880). (Arnold Rüegg†.)

Bibliography: Biographical sketches are by E. Scherer, Paris, 1853; E. Rambert, 3d ed., 2 vols., Lausanne, 1876; Laura M. Lane, New York, 1890; E. de Pressensé, Paris, 1890, cf. his *Contemporary Portraits*, London, 1879; H. Lecoultre, Paris, 1892. On Vinet's activities and thought consult: F. J. Stahl, *Kirchenverfassung nach Lehre und Recht der Protestanten*, pp. 279 sqq., Erlangen, 1840; F. Chavannes, *A. Vinet, notice et mémoires*, Paris, 1847; idem, *A. Vinet . . . comme apologiste et moraliste chrétien*, Leyden, 1883; J. F. Astié, *Esprit d'A. Vinet*, 2 vols., Lausanne, 1861; idem, *Le Vinet de la légende et celui de l'hist.*, ib. 1882; A. F. Langlois, *A. Vinet considéré comme prédicateur*, Strasburg, 1864; J. Widmer, *A. Vinet envisagé comme apologiste*, Lausanne, 1875; J. Cramer, *A. Vinet, moralist et apologiste chrétien*, Lausanne, 1884; L. Molines, *Études sur A. Vinet*, Paris, 1890; J. B. Roy, *L'Individu et la société d'après les . . . ouvrages d'A. Vinet*, Lausanne, 1893; V. Rivet, *Étude sur les origines de la pensée religieuse de Vinet*, Paris, 1896; E. Combe, *Vinet inter-*

prète du N. T., Paris, 1897; A. Rüegg, *A. Vinet, Gedanken und Betrachtungen*, Heilbronn, 1897; A. Schumann, *Vinet, sein Leben, seine Gedankenwelt, seine Bedeutung*, Leipsic, 1907.

VINSON, JOHN: Elder and founder of the Church of the Living God (see LIVING GOD, CHURCH OF THE); born on his father's farm in Madison Co., Ind., July 9, 1851. He was educated at the normal school at Alexandria, and was subsequently a teacher in the public schools of his state, completing his education by private reading. He was converted in 1885, and began his public ministry as an exhorter, later receiving ordination and serving as pastor and evangelist in different parts of Indiana. His further work is bound up in that of his denomination.

VINTON, ALEXANDER HAMILTON: Protestant Episcopal bishop; b. in Brooklyn Mar. 30, 1852; d. at Springfield, Mass., Jan. 19, 1911. He was educated at St. Stephen's College, Annandale, N. Y. (A.B., 1873), General Theological Seminary (graduated, 1876), and the University of Leipsic. He was ordained priest in 1877; was curate of the Church of the Holy Communion, Norwood, N. J. (1878–79), and the Holy Comforter Memorial, Philadelphia (1879–84); rector of All Saints', Worcester, Mass. (1884–1902). In 1902 he was consecrated first bishop of the diocese of Western Massachusetts.

VIRET, vĭ″rê′, PIERRE: Swiss Reformer; b. at Orbe (15 m. n. of Lausanne), Switzerland, May 4, 1511; d. at Orthez (90 m. s. of Bordeaux), France, Apr. 4, 1571. He began to study at Paris for the priesthood, but renounced the Roman Catholic faith and returned to his native town. He was ordained by Farel in 1531, and preached in Orbe and elsewhere. In 1533 he went to Geneva as assistant to Farel, and after the introduction of the Reformation in that city to Neufchâtel, and thence to Lausanne, where his work led to the definite introduction of the Reformation. After the fall of the party hostile to the Reformation at Geneva, Viret labored there until the return of Calvin in 1541. At Lausanne, besides preaching, he lectured on the New Testament in the seminary founded by the citizens of Bern in 1537.

Viret began his literary activity with the *Epistre consolatoire* (Geneva, 1541). He made several journeys in the interests of the Reformation, and in 1549 he received a close friend in Beza (q.v.), who was then appointed professor at Lausanne. To this period belong some of his chief works: *Du devoir et du besoing qu'ont les hommes a s'enquérir de la volonté de Dieu par sa parolle* (Geneva, 1551; against the newly opened Council of Trent); two treatises on clerical duties and the Lord's Supper: *De vero verbi Dei, sacramentorum et ecclesiæ ministerio* (1553), and *De origine, continuatione, auctoritate atque præstantia ministerii verbi Dei et sacramentorum*, etc. (1554); the historical *Des Actes des vrais successeurs de Jésus-Christ et de ses apostres et des apostats de l'église papale*, etc. (1544); and two letters to Frenchmen condemned by the Inquisition, one at Lyons and the other at Chambery. Viret was involved in many troubles with the government of Bern, and it was only in 1549 that he was confirmed in his position

after clearing himself of the charge of holding Butzer's eucharistic doctrines. Matters were brought to a climax by Viret's refusal to celebrate the Lord's Supper without excluding all those who were recognized as unworthy to communicate, and in 1559 he and his colleague Jacques Valier were suspended. Viret was then appointed preacher at Geneva, and during this period wrote *Du vray ministère de la vraye église de Jésus Christ, et de vrais sacremens d'icelle, et des faus sacremens de l'église de l'Antichrist* (Geneva, 1560); *Familière et ample instruction en la doctrine chrestienne, et principalement touchant la divine providence et prédestination* (1559); and *La Metamorphose chrestienne* (1561). In 1561 he was called to Nîmes, but in the following year the French Reformed were obliged to surrender their church to the Roman Catholics, and Viret retired to Montpellier. Thence he was called to Lyons, and on Aug. 19, 1563, he presided over the fourth French national synod as head of the consistory of Lyons. He carried on many controversies with monks and Italian antitrinitarians, and developed an extensive literary activity, publishing no less than nine works between 1563 and 1565, among them his chief work, *Instruction chrestienne en la doctrine de la loy et de l'évangile, . . .* (3 vols., Geneva, 1564), containing a system of morals and politics. In 1565 he was obliged to leave Lyons, whereupon he went to Orange, and after 1566 presided over the academy established by Jeanne d'Albret (q.v.) at Orthez. In the war of 1569 he was taken prisoner by the Roman Catholics, but was soon released.

Viret was highly esteemed by his contemporaries for his preaching. He left also an instructive and interesting body of correspondence, covering the period 1532–67.   (C. SCHNETZLER.)

BIBLIOGRAPHY: T. Beza, *Icones*, Geneva, 1580; J. Scott, *Calvin and the Swiss Reformation*, pp. 312–317 et passim, London, 1833; C. Chenevière, *Farel, Froment, Viret*, Geneva, 1835; A. Sayous, *Études littéraires sur les écrivains français de la réformation*, i. 181–241, Paris, 1841; E. and É. Haag, *La France protestante*, vol. ix., Paris, 1859; C. Schmidt, *Leben und ausgewählte Schriften der Väter . . . der reformierten Kirche*, ix. 39–71, Elberfeld, 1861; J. Cart, *Pierre Viret*, Lausanne, 1864; P. Godet, *P. Viret*, Lausanne, 1892; *Cambridge Modern History*, ii. 293, 368, New York, 1904; C. Schnetzler and J. Barnaud, *Notice bibliographique sur P. Viret*, Lausanne, 1905; *Pierre Vinet d'après lui-même. Extraits de ses œuvres*, Lausanne, 1911; T. Barnaud, *P. Viret, sa vie et son œuvre*, St. Amans, 1911; H. Vuilleumier, *Notre Pierre Viret*, Lausanne, 1911; Schaff, *Christian Church*, vii. 250–252; Lichtenberger, *ESR*, xii. 402–408.

VIRGIL, ver′jil: Bishop of Salzburg; b. in Ireland, probably in the first or second decade of the eighth century; d. at Salzburg Nov. 27, 784. After having risen to be abbot of the monastery of Aghaboe (in the modern County Queens), he joined the court of Pippin in 743, who sent him to Odilo, duke of Bavaria, in 745. Between 746 and 748 he was appointed bishop of Salzburg, but having scruples about receiving consecration, he administered only the temporal affairs of the diocese. Virgil's relations with his archbishop, the famous Boniface, soon became strained. Boniface directed Virgil and his colleague Sidonius, later bishop of Passau, to rebaptize all who had been baptized by a Bavarian priest because the latter had been ungrammatical in the use of the baptismal formula. Virgil and Sidonius, considering this unjustifiable, appealed to Pope Zacharias, who decided against Boniface. Two years later (748) Boniface in his turn lodged complaints against Virgil and Sidonius with the pope, though Virgil was the special object of attack, being charged with intrigue against Boniface and also with holding to the spherical form of the earth. It is uncertain whether he was ever brought to trial, and he certainly was never condemned. On June 15, 767, Virgil received consecration, and was thereafter insistent in maintaining his episcopal rights and dignity. Besides founding many other churches in his see, Virgil built one in honor of St. Rupert at Salzburg, in which he himself was buried. Virgil was active also in the conversion of the Alpine Wends, for whom he appointed a bishop *in partibus*, named Modestus. By his compatriots Virgil was called the " geometer," and he was interested in history, inspiring Aribo of Freising to write the *Vita Corbiniani*, himself composing the *Monumenta necrologia monasterii S. Petri Salisburgensis* (ed. S. Herzberg-Fränkel, in *MGH, Nec.*, vol. ii., 1890). In 1233 he was canonized by Gregory IX.   (A. HAUCK.)

BIBLIOGRAPHY: Consult the literature under SALZBURG, ARCHDIOCESE OF; the *Vita* in *MGH, Script.*, xi (1854), 86–95, and in *ASM*, III., ii. 309–318; Rettberg, *KD*, ii. 223 sqq.; Hauck, *KD*, i. 568–569; F. J. Buss, *Winfrid-Bonifacius*, ed. R. Ritter von Scherer, pp. 293 sqq., Graz, 1880; *KL*, xii. 1002–05.

VIRGIN BIRTH.

The doctrine that Christ was born of the Virgin Mary through the operation of the Holy Ghost received its first authoritatively formulated statement in the earliest Roman Creed, not later than 150 A.D., and probably earlier (in its earliest form dated by Harnack about 140, by Zahn about 120, and by Kattenbusch about 100; cf. APOSTLES' CREED). So far as its Scriptural basis is concerned, this rests exclusively on the narratives in Matthew and Luke, and a consideration of it involves an inquiry concerning (1) the nature and origin of the narratives as they appear in those gospels; (2) their relation to the rest of the New Testament; (3) the position of early church writers; (4) supernatural birth stories in comparative religion; (5) and dogmatic bearings of the subject.

The traditional doctrine of the Church is found in the great confessions, e.g., in the Apostles' Creed, " I believe . . . in Jesus Christ, . . . who was con-
1. Historical ceived by the Holy Ghost, born of the
Outline of Virgin Mary "; and in the Nicene
Attitude Creed, " who . . . was incarnate by
Toward the the Holy Ghost of the Virgin Mary."
Doctrine. This remained for nearly 1,500 years
the common, well-nigh undisputed
tradition of the Church, even among the Arians and the Socinians (cf. the *Racovian Catechism*). In the latter part of the eighteenth century an assault on the doctrine was made by Thomas Paine (*Age of Reason*) and by Voltaire (*Examen important de milord Bolingbroke*, ch. x.), and most of the Deists and Rationalists (see DEISM and RATIONALISM AND SUPERNATURALISM) declared for the natural explanation of Jesus' birth. In the nineteenth century Schleiermacher, while affirming the natural paternity of Joseph, accounted for the archetypal nature of Jesus' consciousness through a creative divine deed in his birth, by means of which the original idea of man became realized. Paulus and Strauss sought a natural explanation for the event; De Wette treated the stories as myths—poetic symbols of religious ideas; and according to Renan Joseph was Jesus' father. In the last half of the nineteenth century the traditional view was elaborated by F. K. L. Steinmeyer, *Die Geschichte der Geburt des Herrn und seiner ersten Schritte mit Bezug auf die neueste Kritik*, Berlin, 1873; F. L. Godet in his *Commentary on Luke*, Eng. transl., 2 vols., Edinburgh, 1875; B. Weiss in his *Life of Jesus*, Eng. transl., 3 vols., Edinburgh, 1884; C. Gore, *Incarnation of the Son of God*, London, 1891, and *Dissertations on Subjects connected with the Incarnation*, 1896. Representing the critical position are C. L. A. Sydow, *Die wunderbare Geburt Jesu*, Berlin, 1873; H. Usener, *Religionsgeschichtliche Untersuchungen*, i., Bonn, 1889; P. Lobstein, *The Virgin Birth of Christ*, Eng. transl., London, 1903; Hillmann, *Die Kindheitsgeschichte Jesu nach Lukas*, *JPT*, 1891; H. J. Holtzmann, *Lehrbuch der neutestamentlichen Theologie*, 2 vols., Freiburg, 1897; and P. Rohrbach, *Geboren von der Jungfrau*, Berlin, 1898. The discussion became acute, however, when C. Schrempf of Württemberg in 1892 declined to assent to the Apostles' Creed, especially to this article. This became the immediate occasion of a vigorous and heated discussion in Germany, echoes of which were heard across the channel and in America. Of the works *pro* and *con*, only a few are mentioned. For the doctrine appeared A. H. Cremer, *Zum Kampf um das Apostolicum*, 7th ed., Berlin, 1893; Th. Zahn, *Das apostolische Symbolum*, Leipsic, 1893; G. Wohlenberg, *Empfangen vom heiligen Geist*, ge-

boren von der Jungfrau Maria, 1893; and J. Haus-
leiter, *Zur Vorgeschichte des apostolischen Glaubensbekenntnisses*, Munich, 1893. In opposition were
A. Harnack, *Das Apostolicum*, Leipsic, 1892; W.
Herrmann, *Worum handelt es um das Apostolikum?*
Magdeburg, 1893; and F. H. Kattenbusch, *Das
apostolische Symbol*, Leipsic, 1894 (3d ed., 1900).

Aside from the particular discussions referred to,
two or three conditions of present-day thought have
made necessary a reopening of the question of the
virgin birth, with presuppositions different from
those which were possible to earlier scholarship.
There is, first, the scientific spirit with its evolutionary view of the world, its deeper
2. Modern study of biology and the processes of
Demand for life, and its conviction that all events
Reopening are related to one another by a law of
the Dis- uniform and concomitant variation.
cussion. Secondly, the historical spirit subjects all alleged facts to far more searching scrutiny than was hitherto possible, as a result
of which many events previously supposed to have
been supernaturally caused are brought within the
range of human historical explanation; and the
hope is expressed that all will ultimately be drawn
into the same category. In addition, many special
disciplines have focused attention on this subject,
such as New-Testament criticism and comparative
religion. Two other impressive facts have secured
recognition in recent times, and these have profoundly influenced Christian thinking. One is, that
this doctrine formed no part of the original preaching or message of Christ or his apostles; the other,
that nowhere else in the New Testament, outside of
the early chapters of Matthew and Luke, is there
any use of this doctrine, or direct or even indirect
reference to it. These omissions in themselves constitute no valid objection to the fact of the virgin
birth; this fact must stand or fall according as it
is authenticated by the narratives in which it is em-
bedded. On the ground that the Scriptures as a
whole and in every part are inerrant and infallible,
a question might indeed arise, but it would be
concerned, not with the virgin birth as a fact, but
with the exposition and defense of the nature and
basis of the alleged inerrancy. With this position,
however, this article is not concerned.

Since, then, this article of the Creed rests on the
narratives in Matthew and Luke, attention must
first be directed to them. It may be laid down as
a safe proposition that these narratives are an integral part of the First and Third Gospels (cf. J.
Weiss, " There were never forms of Matthew and
Luke without the Infancy narratives," *Theologische Rundschau*, 1903, p. 208). In every one of the
early complete manuscripts of the Gospels the chapters containing these narratives are
3. Infancy present. The oldest uncials, such as
Narratives the Sinaitic, the Vatican, Codex Eph-
Integral in raemi, and Codex Bezæ, include these
the Gospels. chapters; the Alexandrian, mutilated
in the first part of Matthew, has Luke
i. and ii. The same is true of the versions—the Latin
in Tertullian's time, the Syriac, Peshito, Curetonian,
Egyptian (Coptic), and the one discovered at Mt.
Sinai in 1892, and also Tatian's *Diatesseron* (with

the exception of the genealogies). The Gospel of
the Ebionites, depending upon the Gospel of the
Hebrews, which in turn depended upon our Matthew, omitted the first two chapters (cf. B. F. Westcott, *Introduction to the Gospels*, p. 465, London,
1895), and the Gnostic Marcion began his Gospel
according to Luke with the third chapter. From
certain characteristics of style this argument is confirmed, for in Matthew a comparison of i. 22, ii. 5–
6, 15, 17, 23, with his frequent reference to fulfilment of Old-Testament prophecy betrays the same
use of the Scripture throughout (cf. F. C. Burkitt,
Evangelion da-Mepharreshe, pp. 258–259, Cambridge, 1904). In Luke also the author's peculiar
Greek style, which is everywhere evident in this
Gospel and in the Acts, shines through in the first
two chapters (cf. A. Plummer, *Commentary on
Luke*, New York, 1896; A. Harnack, *Lukas der
Arzt*, p. 73, Leipsic, 1906, and Appendix ii.).

A further question arises, however, whether every
part of the narrative is equally attested or integrally
related to the whole, and at two points this question becomes critical. In Matt. i. 16 the Sinaitico-
Syriac version reads, " Joseph, to
4. The whom Mary the Virgin was betrothed,
Evidence in begat Jesus, who is called Christ."
Matthew. Concerning the verse in Matthew several suppositions are possible. One is,
that the Codex Sinaiticus gives the original form of
the genealogy, in which the natural paternity of
Joseph is affirmed in the same formula as that of
the others mentioned hitherto. This would harmonize with all the remaining references of the Gospel which allege the fatherhood of Joseph as the
husband of Mary (cf. i. 19–20, 24, xiii. 55), and it
agrees with the common belief of the time, i.e., until
apparently between 60 and 70, that Jesus was the
son of Joseph. If the genealogy was originally
prepared for Jewish Christians, it represented what
they had already believed concerning the parentage of Jesus, and, moreover, it establishes the only
relation of Jesus with David which this Gospel
claims. The verse itself (i. 16), as it appears with
variant readings in some cursives (e.g., 346 of the
Ferrar group), in seven Latin codexes previous to
Jerome, and in the Curetonian Syriac, shows that
it has been the subject of considerable difficulty and
disturbance to the copyists. It is possible that it
was due to a very obvious error of a copyist, or it
may have had an Ebionite source (cf. *Academy*,
1894–95, passim). A contradiction appears on the
face of the Sinaitico-Syriac version, for in the same
verse this says that Joseph begat Jesus and that
Mary is called the Virgin. H. B. Swete suggests
that the virginity of Mary may not have been asserted in the original text; and he intimates that,
if it was asserted, the contradiction would be no
greater than is contained in Luke, who relates the
birth of Jesus from the Virgin, and yet names Joseph
as the father and Joseph and Mary as the parents
of Jesus (Luke ii. 33, 41; see Swete, *The Apostles'
Creed*, pp. 52–53, Cambridge, 1898). The genealogy of Matthew may have ended originally with
Joseph, and its connection with Jesus may have
been carried forward by the Evangelist (cf. C. Gore,
Dissertations, pp. 292 sqq.; also *The Academy*, 1894–

1895; Burkitt, *op. cit.*, pp. 260 sqq.; V. Bartlett, *DB*, iii. 203). In any event, until Syriac specialists have pursued the subject much further, or until other versions are discovered which agree with the Sinaitico-Syriac text, judgment must be suspended as to the exact form of the original genealogy.

With reference to the narrative in Luke, the testimony of the manuscripts is even more decisive in favor of the virgin birth than it is in Matthew, since no manuscript can be cited which radically conflicts with the Gospel as we now have it. The suggestion is, however, made to eliminate i. 34–35, which contains the only direct evidence for the virgin birth in Luke (cf. Harnack, *ZNW*, 1901, pp. 53 sqq.; Usener, "Nativity," in *EB*). Reasons assigned for this elision are—(1) the verses do not harmonize with the context, e.g., verse 36 is naturally connected with verse 33; "Son of the Highest" (i. 32) is Messianic, whereas in verse 35 "Son of God" signifies true origination; the Sinaitico-Syriac appears in ii. 5 to prefer the reading, "with Mary his wife"; Joseph seems to be treated as the husband of Mary, and thus as the father of Jesus. (2) The verses do not agree with the Davidic descent of Jesus—"as was supposed" (iii. 23), or with Mary's conduct—her incredulity as to the possible birth of a son to one already betrothed (i. 34), and with her words in ii. 48. On the other hand, Gunkel maintains that verses 34–35 are translations of a Hebrew original: "Behold thou art conceiving now" (cf. *Zum religionsgeschichtlichen Verständnis des Neuen Testaments*, p. 68, Göttingen, 1903). If, as Briggs suggests, the conception and the theophany coincide, the announcement has begun already to be realized in the womb of the Virgin, which vacates any question of Joseph's part later in the transaction (*The Messiah of the Gospels*, p. 50, New York, 1894). It is further urged that an extraordinary conception by Mary simply parallel to that by Elizabeth is implied in verse 36. The genealogy is also appealed to; as the creation of the first Adam is referred to the immediate action of God, so the second Adam owes his existence to the power of the Holy Spirit—a consideration which confirms "Son of God" in i. 35. Finally, the wholly subordinate position of Joseph throughout the narrative in Luke is alleged as due to the miraculous birth, as set forth in this Gospel.

5. The Evidence in Luke.

With reference to the genealogies, Matt. i. 1–17 and Luke iii. 23–38, it is evident that they are entirely independent of each other. If Matthew's Gospel was composed first, say, in 70–75, and Luke's in 78–93 (Harnack), Luke might have been expected to contain traces of Matthew's treatment, but nothing of the kind is to be alleged. Two names only in the two genealogies as far back as David are the same; the number of generations is different. Matthew traces the ancestral course back in three groups from Joseph through David to Abraham; Luke in an unbroken series carries the line past David and Abraham to Adam, the son of God. The special point of agreement between the genealogies lies in their affirmation that both Joseph and Jesus were de-

6. The Genealogies in Matthew and Luke.

scendants from David (cf. Matt. i. 20, ix. 27, xii. 23, xv. 22; Luke i. 27, 32, 69, ii. 4, iii. 23). The line of each from David down is a different one; for Matthew, through Solomon, for Luke, through Nathan, a fact to which Celsus called attention (cf. Origen, *Contra Celsum*, ii. 32), but both naturally lead to Jesus through Joseph; except on such an interpretation, they are wholly lacking in point. The New Testament offers no proof that Mary was of the lineage of David, although this might be involved in such passages as Acts ii. 30, Rom. i. 3–4, and Heb. vii. 14, if we were sure that the respective authors were cognizant of the virgin birth. The Davidic descent of Mary was affirmed by tradition (Justin, *Dialogus*, xxiii. 45, 100; Irenæus, III., xxi. 5; *ANF*, i. 452–453; cf. also the *Protevangelium of James*, x., and *The Gospel of the Nativity of Mary*), and it has also been defended by modern writers, as Godet, Bernard Weiss, and Edersheim. Mary may have been of the house of David, but so far all attempts to bring her into the genealogies have proved ineffectual. It has been alleged that she was a kinswoman of Joseph, which is, of course, possible, but of which there is no evidence. All of this goes to confirm the supposition that the genealogies—two chosen from perhaps several in existence—originated in a circle which still believed that Joseph was the father of Jesus, and that the evangelists either found these genealogies in their present form, or so modified them in their reference to Jesus that the paternal relation of Joseph became putative—Joseph has by marriage taken the place of a father—and hence not inconsistent with the supernatural conception of Jesus. In the case of Matthew, at least, there is no good ground for surmising that he constructed the genealogy (but cf. R. H. Grützmacher, *The Virgin Birth*, p. 48, New York, 1907), which traced the family-tree of Joseph to David, only to abandon the irresistible conclusion that Joseph was the natural father of Jesus. The same position would be valid as against the conjecture that Matthew's genealogy was compiled by our Lord's relatives, unless, indeed, this is conceived as taking place while they still believed that Jesus was the natural son of Joseph. From what source arose the tradition that Jesus was supernaturally conceived does not appear in the genealogies themselves.

Concerning the relation of the nativity stories to Joseph and Mary, it has been customary to associate Matthew with Joseph and Luke with Mary, as the respective source of each. The main reason for connecting Matthew with Joseph is found in i. 18 sqq. and ii. 19 sqq. The particular difficulty which besets this position arises from the probable time of Joseph's death, and the keeping alive of the tradition originating from him in a circle wholly unknown to the apostles for more than fifty years. That he was not alive during Jesus' ministry is commonly accepted (cf. Mark iii. 31, vi. 3; John xix. 27; Acts i. 14), but how long his death took place after Jesus' appearance as a child in the temple (Luke ii. 45 sqq.) and before Jesus' baptism (Luke iii. 21–22) there is no means of ascertaining. That the testimony of Joseph to the circumstances of Jesus' birth might be needed may well be imagined; but that he gave such a document to Mary as a protection of her good name, that she passed this on to the family of Joseph, and that from them it came **7. The Accounts in Relation to Joseph and Mary.** into the hand of the First Evangelist to be worked over by him according to his purpose is an interesting conjecture, but is nothing more (cf. C. Gore, ut sup., pp. 28–29). If this were true, it is inconceivable that both Peter and Paul, in their contact with the chief persons of the church at Jerusalem, heard nothing of it. An indication that the nativity story of Matthew was employed by catechists appears perhaps in the division of the sections and the length of these to aid the memory of pupils (cf. A. Wright, *Commentary on the Fourth Gospel*, p. 113, New York, 1890). That Mary is the center of interest in Luke's narrative of the infancy is true (cf. i. 27, 36, 40–44, 56–57, ii. 48, 50–51), and this has led to the surmise that the final source of the story was a woman. It is characteristic of Luke, as compared with the other synoptists and with John, to introduce and emphasize the place and ministry of women in relation to the Gospel (cf. vii. 37 sqq., viii. 2–3, x. 38, xxiii. 27, 29, 55), and the same feature marks the Acts. This fact might of itself be enough to account for the large part that Mary plays in the infancy narrative. Out of the traditional material at his disposal, the author was especially attracted to that portion which centered in Elizabeth and Mary, and he has preserved this interest in the record. Nowhere else in the entire Gospel is there disclosed a more delicate reserve or a rarer literary skill than in the handling of the details of this story. The particular content and form of the narrative have, however, led to the opinion that it is to be traced to a woman. W. M. Ramsay identifies her with Mary (Orr, *Virgin Birth of Christ*, pp. 244, 246, New York, 1907), while W. Sanday deems it more likely that Joanna, Chuza's wife (Luke viii. 3), was the intermediary (ib. p. 246; cf. J. Adderley, *Critical Questions*, p. 139, 2d ed., London, 1906). If Mary was still living when Luke visited Palestine in 57 or 58, she may herself have communicated the account to him, or some intimate of hers may have been the immediate source (cf. W. M. Ramsay, *Was Christ Born in Bethlehem?* p. 88, London, 1898), or Luke may have become aware of the story from the church in Jerusalem of which James was then head, and where Mary resided with John (H. B. Swete, ut sup., p. 50). But there is absolutely nothing elsewhere in the New Testament to warrant such conjectures. If, as Harnack thinks likely, Luke came in contact with Mary as well as with James in his visit to Jerusalem (*Lukas der Arzt*, p. 3), it is unaccountable that in his infancy story no place is left for the journey to Egypt (cf. Luke ii. 39).

A further question is closely connected with that just raised, whether Luke availed himself of a written or of an oral source. The almost universal judgment has been that he used a document or documents of Aramaic or Hebrew origin, perhaps about 80 A.D. or earlier, the general view advocated by Weiss, Godet, Ryle, and James (*Psalms of Solomon*, London, 1891), Sanday (*Book by Book*, London, 1892), and Gore (ut sup., p. 14). In support

of this position, reference is made to various features—the Hebraic diction as compared with classic Greek, the archaic quality, the coloring **8. Problem of Oral or Written Sources.** of Jewish national hopes, Judeo-Christian sentiment, similarity to the Psalms of Solomon (70–40 B.C.), use of "Spirit" as prophetic impulse or impersonal power of God, the theophany to Mary corresponding to Old-Testament divine manifestations, and the naive simplicity of the story in contrast with the prologue and the remainder of the Gospel. It is thus maintained that these stories —of the infancy of John and of Jesus—appear to be more primitive than anything else in the New Testament, except parts of the book of Revelation. They arose in a Jewish circle and were first circulated in a restricted Jewish-Christian community in the sixties; their background was far removed from Greek influences, which, passing away in that early period, never recurred. Sanday assigns the forties as the more probable date of their appearance (in Orr, ut sup., pp. 440 sqq.); G. H. Box proposes " as early as the middle of the first century " (*DCG*, art. " Virgin Birth "); and J. Weiss, who allows to them no historical value, places them ten years later (*Schriften des Neuen Testaments*, p. 383, Göttingen, 1906). The last seems the earliest possible date for the story becoming public; and the fact that Paul, although a close companion of Luke, was to the last ignorant of it goes to show that Luke was himself not cognizant of it earlier than the sixties. Another surmise is that there was no written story of the infancy of which Luke availed himself, but only a number of Hebrew (not Aramaic) poems concerning events associated with the infancy, from which the Evangelist selected such as suited his purpose (Matt. i. 20–21 is to be included in this grouping). These poems were the works of several Christian poets who attributed to the angels, and to the various fathers and mothers, the songs which they themselves had composed. The Evangelist is to be credited with the prose-setting to the poems, and also as vouching for their essential trustworthiness (Briggs, ut sup., pp. 41 sqq.), and it has been further conjectured that these hymns were composed and used for liturgical purposes in Palestine. On the other hand, the view is presented that an independently written infancy narrative falling utterly into oblivion is most improbable; and it is also highly improbable that Mary wrote any such document or gave publicity to that which was so intimate and precious to herself, or, indeed, that any one else gave it written form. Ramsay holds it more likely that Luke came into possession of the story by oral communication either from Mary herself or from some one, probably a woman, whose intimacy with Mary furnished the key to the secrets there disclosed, in which case the information is equal to first-hand authority (cf. ut sup., chap. iv.). On this hypothesis differences of style in various sections of the first two chapters are accounted for by the deliberate literary aim of the writer, and in part also by the different form in which the material came to him.

That there are legendary elements in the nativity stories has been alleged. The angelic appearances to

Joseph (Matt. i. 20, ii. 13, 19), to Zachariah (Luke i. 11 sqq.)., to Mary (Luke i. 26 sqq.), and to the shepherds (Luke ii. 8 sqq.) are here in point. There is, indeed, an absence of the crass supernaturalism of the Apocryphal Gospels of the Infancy; there is the same reserve in respect to the **9. The** miraculous which characterizes the **Angelic Ap-** highest moments of the Old-Testament **pearances.** prophetic idealism. But the reference to Gabriel (Luke i. 26) shows that the writer has drawn upon Jewish angelology for the intermediaries between God and the chief actors. To those who believe in angels and in the possibility of their appearance to human beings these accounts present no difficulties. The authors of the Gospels accepted without question the belief of the period, that messengers from God in the guise of angels actually appeared to men and conversed with them in the language with which they were familiar, as one person talks with another. It may, however, without disturbing the credibility of the story as a whole, be possible to interpret these experiences as real divine communications of a purely inward character, yet by the imagination translated into outward form according to subjective notions of the period (cf. Gore, ut sup., pp. 21 sqq.). This view is at bottom only a particular application of Briggs' suggestion given above. The inward reflection, due to divine revelation, is the essential thing; its outer form is a matter of comparative indifference. This, however, is free modern interpretation, not ancient belief.

With reference to the Magi and Herod's slaughter of children in Bethlehem, there is no improbability in the historical supposition of these, irrespective of other records, as containing a basis of fact. Astrologers of the East, whether from Arabia, Persia, Babylonia, or even Egypt, in their reading of the stars may have believed that they saw signs which pointed to the coming of a Jewish Messiah, and may have journeyed to Jerusalem to verify their prognostications. The Jewish Scriptures were widely circulated among cultivated Jews everywhere, and in the ferment of theosophical speculation, of political unrest, and of religious mysteries and dreams of a world-deliverer, symptoms of deep, unsatisfied longing, the spirit of truest **10. The** sincerity and of most brilliant hope, **Magi and** centered in the prophetic promise of **Herod.** the Jewish people. This spirit had widely penetrated and powerfully moved many inquiring minds, and the Magi may have been among those thus influenced. But, allowing for a basis of fact here, has this basis been built upon by legend? Since the first century, this has certainly been the case. According to Ignatius (Eph. x.; about 110 A.D.), the star gives light to sun, moon, and stars, which circle around it as a choir. The Magi (in reliance upon Ps. lxviii. 31–32, lxxii. 10; Isa. xlix. 7, lx. 1 sqq.) have been designated as kings, limited to three, on account of their threefold gifts, and even their names have been given as Caspar, Melchior, and Balthazar. The presents also have had to do service: gold as to a king; frankincense as to a God. Several features of the story may have been suggested by the Old

Testament. Num. xxiv. 17 shows that the Jews believed in a Star of the Messiah. In the East stars were everywhere associated with the birth of great men—Mithridates, Cæsar, Augustus (cf. Suetonius, *Augustus*, xciv. sqq.; W. Soltau, *The Birth of Jesus Christ*, p. 38, London, 1903). It was a universal custom to come into the presence of princes with presents (Gen. xliii. 11; I Kings x. 2), and the Jews expected that the greatest of those outside of Israel would offer both themselves and their gifts to the Messiah (Isa. xlix. 7, lx. 1–10; Rev. xxi. 24). What part these and other familiar and intensely active religious ideas played in the final form of the narrative it is impossible to say. Soltau believes that he has come upon the real source of the story in the journey of Tiridates, a Parthian king, in the year 66 A.D., accompanied by Magi to offer homage to Nero (ut sup., pp. 39–41, 72–73). As to Herod's part in the story, the indiscriminate slaughter of twenty children would be quite in accord with his known character and deeds. It is, however, significant that Josephus, who reports other acts of cruelty, does not mention this (cf. *Ant.*, xv. 7–8, xvi. 11, xvii. 2); and it is hard to understand why one with the distrustful, jealous, and bloodthirsty spirit of Herod should risk defeat either by suffering strangers to ascertain for him a fact which he deemed to be the most serious menace to his ambition, or by delaying to put into execution an effective plan for thwarting Jewish expectation (see INNO- CENTS, FEAST OF THE HOLY). The journey into Egypt, which in Matthew is indissolubly bound up with this event, is simply unhistorical, if Luke's narrative is trustworthy: Jesus had long since arrived in Nazareth when the visit of the Magi to Bethlehem and the slaughter of the infants are alleged to have taken place (cf. Luke ii. 39). In the story of the Magi and Herod some ideal truths are clearly evident: the world-wide significance of the Messiah as the satisfaction of the desire of all nations, typified also in John xii. 20 sqq.; the inevitable conflict between the Messiah and Jewish and other wicked powers of the world; the safety of the Christian cause; and the ultimate confusion and defeat of hostile forces.

If the theory of legend were altogether excluded from the nativity stories, one would have to accept the contradictory supposition, that the narratives are wholly historical. A third hypothesis is conceivable, that a husk of legend contains a kernel of fact. In this latter case, the legendary **11. Fact** aspect may be assigned to Greek and **Contained** other foreign influences or to the Jew- **in Legend.** ish spirit. If it is a mark of legend that events occurred, not in the way they are described, but with other accompaniments than those which time has associated with them, then there is no reasonable doubt that the nativity stories contain legendary accretions. This legendary material has been found, not in Greek or other outside influences, but in the circle of Jewish ideas. In addition to considerations already proposed in this paragraph, attention may be directed to the birth-stories of great men in the Old Testament, as Isaac (Gen. xvii. 15 sqq., xviii. 9 sqq.), Samson (Judges xiii.), and Samuel (I Sam. i.). The point is not that the women involved were virgins, but, in the case of the first, the utter natural impossibility alleged, and in the case of the last two the improbability that they should give birth to a child. The New Testament contains a story like that of Samuel in the birth of John (Luke i. 5–25). In none of these instances is the conception wholly miraculous, in the sense that natural fatherhood is excluded. Yet it is miraculous in this, that it took place contrary to the customary course of nature; second causes are not excluded, but are simply ignored as efficient, and the power and word of God are alone accounted mighty. Associated with the providence and power of God, and, indeed, as due to this, are the singular prerogative, virtue, holiness, and mission of the " child of promise." Lobstein, who furnishes this line of suggestion, sees in the birth of Jesus a further instance of the same kind as those just referred to, only the unique greatness of Jesus involves that he be even physically an immediate creation of divine power (cf. Lobstein, ut sup., pp. 66 sqq.).

The relation of Isa. vii. 14 to the question of the virgin birth has given rise to two exactly opposite conclusions: On the one hand, it is claimed that the belief that Jesus was born of a virgin sprang from this passage (cf. K. T. Keim, *History of Jesus of Nazara*, i. 82 sqq., London, 1873; Harnack, *Dogma*, i. 100; Lobstein, ut sup., pp. 73 sqq.). On the other hand, Orr holds that Matthew already

12. Relation knew of Jesus' birth from a virgin, and **of Isa.** rightly discovered in this passage its **vii. 14.** Messianic import (J. Orr, ut sup., pp. 131 sqq.; cf. W. J. Beecher, *Prophets and Promise*, p. 334, note, New York, 1905; L. M. Sweet, *The Birth and Infancy of Christ*, p. 70, Philadelphia, 1906). The crucial word in the verse under consideration is 'almah, which by both parties is accepted as meaning " a young woman of marriageable age." There is another Hebrew word, bethula, which signifies " virgin " in the strict sense. The first question, then, is whether 'almah (LXX., parthenos) is to be translated " virgin," as in the R. V., or, according to the margin, " maiden." In the other passages where the word occurs, the R. V. renders the word in Gen. xxiv. 43; Ex. ii. 8; Prov. xxx. 19 by " maid " or " maidens"; Ps. lxviii. 25 by " damsels "; Cant. i. 3 and vi. 8 by " virgins " (marg., " maidens "). The primary idea of the word is only that the young woman has reached a marriageable age—she may or may not be a *virgo intacta* (cf. Cant. vi. 8). In Isa. vii. 14 the meaning of the prophet is perfectly clear. Ahaz, king of Judah, had demanded a sign from the prophet as to the outcome of the attacks of Israel and Syria, and had received this as an answer: " The Lord shall give you a sign; behold a young woman shall conceive and bear a son, and shall call his name ' God with us! ' " The point of the prophetic words lies, not in their emphasis upon virginity nor in the foretelling of a miraculous birth from a virgin, but in the nearness of a definite event which would synchronize with delivery from danger by God's power and presence, symbolized by the name of the coming child. Moreover, in the whole scope of Jewish literature outside of the Scriptures, whether apocryphal or apocalyptic, there is no trace of an

exposition of this passage as signifying " virgin," or of an expectation that the Messiah was to be miraculously conceived (cf. V. H. Stanton, *Jewish and Christian Messiah*, p. 377, London, 1887). Jews contemporary with Justin, Tertullian, and Jerome interpreted 'almah in Isa. vii. 14 as a young woman (cf. Justin, *Dialogus*, xliii., lxvi.–lxvii.; Tertullian, *Adv. Judæos*, ix., *Adv. Marcionem*, iii. 13; Jerome, *Adv. Helvidium*, v. 2). The medieval passages cited by F. P. Badham in the *Academy*, June 8, 1895 (pp. 485–487), are without critical support. We have, therefore, to look to the Septuagint as the source from which Matthew derived his idea of the " Virgin," which he appears to have done with deliberate intent. The opinion of Lobstein is that the new faith in Christ was led to an imaginative interpretation of the beginning of the person of Christ which should correspond to its experience of his divine character, and in this procedure hit upon this passage from the Septuagint, which offered to religious feeling its precise formula. On the other hand, Orr and those in agreement with him maintain that in reporting the virgin birth Matthew, following his custom of seeking in the Old Testament for either predictions or illustrations of what he narrates, deliberately selected this passage, and was justified in finding a fulfilment of the prophet's word, not alone to Ahaz, but in a far distant period when the child " Immanuel " should be finally established upon the throne of David. In the first case, faith and prophecy have given rise to a symbolic myth; in the second, the narrative of a fact seeks its parallel or its divine intimation in a word of prophecy.

According to Lobstein, the idea of the person of Christ as the Son of God underwent a development in the early Christian community (see Son of God). The first stage was the ethical or theo-

13. Devel- cratic sonship which is the common **opment of** presentation of the Synoptic Gospels. **Sonship** The term " Son " is equivalent to " Son **Idea.** of God," and that in the Messianic sense (cf. Mark iii. 11, v. 7, xiii. 32, xiv. 61; Matt. xi. 27, xvii. 25–26). This was followed by another step, due to Rabbinic or Alexandrian speculation, seen in Paul's doctrine of a celestial being who was manifested in Christ on earth; in the Apocalypse, where an Alexandrian influence is evident; and, finally, in John, where the Logos idea culminates in one in whom is gathered up the meaning of humanity and the world; this is the metaphysical Sonship. Midway between the earliest and the latest conception arose that of the first two chapters of Matthew and the nativity stories in Luke—a real divine paternity for Jesus, even that of physical generation (cf. Luke i. 35, with Matt. i. 20; Lobstein, ut sup., pp. 58 sqq.). Bornemann designates the three stages differently: (1) supernatural birth; (2) preexistence (Paul); and (3) Logos doctrine (John; cf. his *Unterricht im Christentum*, p. 92, Berlin, 1891). This, of course, presupposes that the story of the virgin birth is a myth; and, on the ground that it arose early, it would have to come to an understanding with the question of sufficient time for the myth to develop.

The attitude of the inner circle of the disciples is of interest. They apparently regarded Jesus as the son of Joseph and Mary (Matt. xiii. 55; Mark vi. 3; Luke iv. 22; John i. 45, vi. 42)—a judgment which is based on the common tradition preserved in all the Gospels. However, it would perhaps be truer to say that they had formed no opinion on the subject, since it had never presented it-

14. Attitude of the Disciples. self to them as a problem. There may be a wide difference between an attitude and a mature judgment. A given attitude may represent only a traditional and unreflective aspect of feeling or action; a mature judgment is the result of critical inquiry, and rests on reasons more or less explicit and well founded. No one would claim that Jesus' followers had in this respect any other attitude toward him in relation to Joseph and Mary than they had toward his brothers. Even Peter, in his great confession at Cæsarea Philippi (Acts x. 34 sqq.), neither affirmed nor denied anything concerning the natural sonship of Jesus as related to Joseph and Mary.

Concerning the virgin birth the remainder of the New Testament is silent. Mark, the oldest Gospel, makes no allusion to it, and apparently knows nothing of it. This silence is, however, explained on the hypothesis that the infancy narrative lay outside the scope of his design, which was to report the common apostolic testimony from the beginning of the Baptist's ministry to the ascension (Swete, ut sup., p. 48; Orr, ut sup., pp. 106 sqq.), so that it is implied that Mark had knowledge of the fact, although the aim of his writing precluded any report of it. That his home was in Jerusalem, that the

15. No References in Mark or Paul. church met in his mother's house (Acts xii. 12), and that he often saw Jesus' mother contain no presumptions value on this subject. Paul is our earliest witness to the tendency of the early Church to arrive at an explanation of the deeper origin of the person of Christ. In his conception are two elements which he has made no attempt to coordinate or fathom. First, of the concrete person of Jesus he affirms all the moral qualities which constitute true and perfect humanity. Secondly, he alleges that a superhuman, preearthly being became incarnate, who thus lived and died under the identical conditions in which human life is passed (II Cor. viii. 9; Phil. ii. 5 sqq.). If he had reflected upon the way in which this celestial being " took upon himself the form of a servant," he has left no trace of it (cf. Rom. i. 3–4; I Cor. viii. 6, xv. 45, 47; II Cor. viii. 9); and the claim is made that it was not necessary for Paul to be aware of the mode of Jesus' birth, since his knowledge embraced only a portion of the Gospel (but cf. R. J. Cooke, *The Incarnation and Recent Criticism*, New York, 1907). Yet it is inferred that there is an allusion to the virgin birth in Gal. iv. 4, on the ground that Paul mentions only a law in general, while instead of mother or the name of the mother, he uses the term " woman," and refers Jesus' true humanity exclusively to " female descent " (Grützmacher, ut sup., pp. 30–31). That Paul speaks of Christ as the " heavenly man," and asserts his perfect sinlessness, is alleged as further

evidence in the same direction (Swete, ut sup., pp. 54–55; cf. Orr, ut sup., p. 116). On the contrary, birth from a woman and under the law signifies that Christ was real man, subject to the conditions of flesh and the discipline of law (cf. Job xiv. 1; Matt. xi. 11; see also Lightfoot, *Galatians, ad loc.*, London, 1865; Lobstein, ut sup., pp. 52–53). Rom. viii. 3 does not necessarily exclude the paternal agency in the generation of Jesus. For Paul the peculiar character of Jesus depended wholly upon the inner nature of his being, and, as far as can be seen, not at all upon an exceptional mode of his entrance into human conditions. There is, indeed, little or nothing in the language of the Apostle inconsistent with the virgin birth of Jesus, but the argument from silence is of no value. The fact that he does not contradict it, but that his association with Luke appears to presuppose some knowledge of the fact, rests upon an assumption that Luke was himself cognizant of the story during the lifetime of the Apostle—an assumption unsupported by evidence.

The Gospel of John is also silent as to the virgin birth. In his prologue John is occupied with two ideas: first, the essential, eternal divine nature of the being who became incarnate, secondly the true humanity of the Word in the earthly life. Several reasons are alleged to show that John, who is thus supposed to be the author of the Fourth Gospel, was not ignorant of the virgin birth: (1) he wrote at a time when this was generally be-

16. Silence of the Rest of the New Testament. lieved in the Christian community; (2) he must have been acquainted with the other Gospels containing the nativity stories, and must have silently accepted, perhaps presupposed, them; (3) in his residence at Ephesus he was a contemporary and antagonist of Cerinthus, who taught that Jesus was the natural son of Joseph and Mary; (4) Mary, whom Jesus entrusted to the care of John, probably lived in his house until her death (Orr, ut sup., p. 109); (5) in his Gospel John accords Mary special prominence, probably due to his knowledge of her supreme privilege (Swete, ut sup., p. 48); (6) John vii. 42 is an undoubted proof that John knew of Jesus' birth at Bethlehem (Sanday, ut sup., p. 97); (7) John i. 13 is also adduced in support of the virgin birth, especially if an exceedingly ancient reading is followed: " who was born not by mixing the blood of a man and a woman, and not by the will of a man "—a type of the new birth of believers (T. Zahn, in Orr, ut sup., pp. 271–273; cf. p. 111); (8) " Only begotten " (*monogenous*) in John i. 14 refers not to the eternal generation of the Son, but to his human birth (Allen, *Interpreter*, Oct., 1905, p. 52). The seventh point is not warranted by textual criticism, and the sixth may be allowed without involving any conclusions concerning the mode of the birth. The remaining points presuppose that John wrote the Gospel. In any case, no dogmatic use is made of the nativity story either for the person of Christ or for the contents of Christian belief. The same affirmation must be made as to the remainder of the New-Testament writings. Neither the Acts nor the Epistle to the Hebrews, nor the Epistles of James, Peter, and John, nor the

Revelation draws any conclusions from the miraculous conception, nor contains any, even remote, reference to it.

The infancy narratives have been traced to prejudice in favor of virginity. Attention is drawn to preference of celibacy to marriage in the Apocryphal books, in Paul's epistles (I Cor. vii.),

17. Ascetic and in Revelation (xiv. 4), and also Influence. among the Essenes, and in Philo—a spirit which early became influential in the Church (cf. W. Baldensperger, *Das Selbstbewusstsein Jesu*, p. 117, Strasburg, 1888, for legend concerning the virginity of Moses' mother). It is to be admitted that there are ascetic elements in the Gospel of Luke which have apparently colored some of the words of Jesus in comparison with Matthew and Mark (yet see Matt. xix. 10–12), but in Luke celibacy is not exalted as the supreme ideal, and certainly not with reference to the family in which Jesus was brought up.

The history of the doctrine of the virgin birth can not here be fully sketched, but only indicated for two centuries after its appearance. With the exception of the Ebionites and certain of the Gnostics, by the middle of the second century, and probably by the close of the first, this belief was nearly universal (cf. Harnack, *Das apostolische Glaubensbekenntniss*, p. 24, Berlin, 1896). Jewish Ebionites (cf. the *Gospel of the Ebionites*, a corruption of the Gospel to the Hebrews)—the only ones in the Christian Church who rejected the first two

18. Views chapters of Matthew—held that Jesus **of Ebionites,** was naturally born of Joseph and Mary, **Ignatius,** and became Messiah in virtue of his **Aristides,** legal piety. Yet among Jewish Chris- **and Justin.** tians this rejection was not universal, for the Nazarenes acknowledged the virgin birth of the Messiah, and the remainder of the old Ebionites seem later to have shared this view (A. Hering, *ZKT*, v. 67). Others, such as Valentinus, Basilides, and the Docetæ described by Hippolytus, *Hær.*, vi. 35, vii. 26, viii. 9 (*ANF*, vol. v.) based their acceptance of the virgin birth on the Gospel of Luke. The first mention of this belief is in Ignatius, though Polycarp (a contemporary of Ignatius), Hermes, and Barnabas are silent concerning it. Ignatius says that Jesus was " truly born of a Virgin," one of the three mysteries of renown wrought in the silence of God, but now proclaimed to the world (*Ad Smyrnæos*, i.; *Ad Ephesios*, xix., cf. also vii.; xviii.; *Ad Trallianos*, ix.; all in *ANF*, vol. i., cf. also Lightfoot, *The Apostolic Fathers, S. Ignatius and S. Polycarp*, i. 315–414, London, 1885). In the newly recovered *Apology* of Aristides (126–140 A.D., ed. J. Rendell Harris in *TS*, i.; cf. Harnack, *Litteratur*, i. 96), we read of Jesus Christ that, " born of a Virgin, . . . he took flesh " (ii.), and Harris adds that early in the second century " the virginity of Mary was a part of the formulated Christian belief " (ib. p. 25). With Justin Martyr the virgin birth is a subject of frequent reference (cf. *Apol.*, i. 32, 46, 63; *Dialogus*, xxiii., xlv., c., cv., cxiii., cxxvii., in *ANF*, vol. i.). It was a second presentment of God to be born of a virgin; *hagion pneuma* is not the Holy Spirit, but the Logos. He connects this with the crea-

tion story of Gen. i. 26, and with the theophanies of the Old Dispensation; he associates this birth with salvation, destruction of the serpent, and deliverance from death to believers. The legend of Perseus and other sons of Jupiter (*Apol.*, i. 21–22; *Dialogus*, lxvi.) were referred to the deceiving power of demons, who fabricated the stories to match the virgin birth of the prophets (*Dialogus*, lxx.). The conception is to be explained by no intercourse of the virgin with any one, whether human or divine, but to the Spirit and Power of God, i.e., his Word. He relies on prophecy, especially Isa. vii. 14, liii. 8 (cf. *Dialogus*, xlii., lxvi., lxxi., lxxxiv.); he repels the suggestion that Hezekiah is referred to in this passage, maintains that *parthenos* can mean only a virgin, which forbids the notion of paternal generation, claims that other portions of the prediction were fulfilled in Herod and the Magi with their gifts (ib. lxvii.–lxviii.), and parallels this unique story by the creation of Eve and of all living beings at first. For those who could not accept the virgin birth, Justin urges that at least they see in Christ the Messiah (ib. xlviii.).

Melito, bishop of Sardis, in his discourse on " The Cross," iii., and on " Faith," iv.–v., attempts to reconcile the birth stories of Matthew and Luke with the prologue of John; Jesus, who preexisted, was carried in the womb of the virgin. Irenæus held that the messiahship of Jesus was proved, not

19. Melito, by his power and exaltation, but by **Irenæus,** his birth (*Hær.*, I., xxx. 12; in *ANF*, **Gnostics,** vol. i.); and relied on Gal. iv. 4, which **and** he refers to the divine agency as **Tertullian.** causing birth from a Virgin (ib. III., xvi. 3; cf. xxii. 1), and on John i. 13 as denying human agency in Jesus' birth (ib. III., xix. 2). Prophecy was also appealed to (Dan. ii. 34; Isa. xxviii. 16)—Joseph had no part, but only God, in Jesus' birth. Adam was formed by the Word of God, and it was fitting that the Word, who recapitulated Adam, himself should be formed as man by God (ib. xxi. 10). He declares that the entire Church (Gaul, Germany, Spain, Egypt, Libya, and the East) has received from the apostles " the faith in God . . . in Jesus Christ . . . the birth from a virgin " (ib. iii. 4). At this time the Church encountered the storm of Gnostic speculations regarding the person of Christ which also involved his birth (see GNOSTICISM, § 6). Some, such as the adherents of Carpocrates and Cerinthus and the early Ophites, rejected the virgin birth altogether (ib. i. 25–26; cf. Hippolytus, *Hær.*, v. 26, vii. 32–33, *ANF*, vol. v.). According to Cerinthus, at the baptism Christ as a dove descended upon him (ib. I., xxvi. 1–2; see CERINTHUS); others alleged that his body was of celestial substance, taking nothing from Mary as he passed through her (ib. III., xxii. 2; cf. V., xix. 2, and see VALENTINUS), or that he was the son of the Demiurge upon whom the dispensational Jesus descended (cf. ib. I., xxvii. 1), or that he was a transfigured man, but neither truly born nor truly incarnate (cf. BASILIDES), to all of which Irenæus opposed the teaching of the Fourth Gospel in John i. 14 (cf. ib. III., xi. 3).

Tertullian continued the polemic against the Gnostics, much of the argument centering in a defense of the true body of Jesus as derived by human birth from Mary, yet without human paternity (cf. *Adv. Valentinum*, xxvii., *Adv. Praxeam*, i.; for Eng. transl. of Tertullian's writings cf. *ANF*, vols. iii.–iv.). Matt. i. 16; John i. 14; and Gal. iv. 4, are used to repel the Gnostic charge that Jesus was begotten in but not of Mary (*De carne Christi*, xx.). He appeals to prophecy, Isa. vii. 14 (*Adv. Judæos*, ix.; *De carne Christi*, xvi.; *Adv. Marcionem*, iv. 10, iii. 12); Isa. xi. 1–2 (cf. *Adv. Judæos*, ix.; *De carne Christi*, xxi.; *Adv. Marcionem*, iii. 20); Isa. liii. (*Adv. Judæos*, xiii.); Ps. cx. 3 (LXX.), and xxii. 9–10. In his use of the New Testament he relies first on Mark and John, and then on Matthew and Luke (*Adv. Marcionem*, iv. 2). The story of Eve is analogous to the birth from Mary (*De carne Christi*, xvii.; cf. xvi.)—a new order of birth, the divine Word entering the earthly body, even as at first the earthly part of Adam was quickened by the breath of God. He bases an argument on the veracity of Jesus, who claimed to be the Son of Man, and, since God was his Father, human fatherhood was precluded (*Adv. Marcionem*, iv. 10). This is connected with the doctrine that " a god is born of a god " (*Ad Nationes*, ii. 3; cf. *Apol.*, xxi.; *De carne Christi*, v. 18). Luke ii. 23, " every male that openeth the womb shall be called holy to the Lord," referring to Jesus, could only signify that, since he opened the womb, his mother was a virgin (ib. xxiii.). Tertullian knew of no salvation to one who denied the virgin birth of Jesus (*Adv. Marcionem*, iv. 36). He attempts no analysis of the human nature, which is thus derived from his mother apart from a human father.

Clement of Alexandria taught unequivocally the virgin birth—the only virgin mother (*Pædagogus*, i. 6)—and appears inclined to the notion of a miraculous birth as well as a miraculous conception (*Strom.*, vii. 16; Eng. transl. in *ANF*, vol. ii.). He uses as prophecy Isa. ix. 6, where, by reference to Deut. xxii. 23–24, he concludes that the Hebrew word *'almah* signifies " virgin." In his commentary on Matt. (x. 23) he speaks of

20. Clement of Alexandria, Origen, and Hippolytus. the body which Jesus received from the Virgin by divine conception and birth, a fact confirmed by the babe leaping in Elizabeth's womb. His virgin birth showed him to be more than a man (commentary on John, i.

34), and he also seems to attribute credibility to the Gospels of Peter and James, which allege that the brethren of Jesus were sons of Joseph by a former wife, in order to preserve the honor of Mary in virginity to the end, i.e., that she might not know intercourse with man after the Holy Ghost came upon her. Jesus was thus the first fruit of virginity (commentary on Matt., x. 17, 23). This doctrine of the perpetual virginity of Mary was advanced a further stage by Origen, whose principal discussion of the virgin birth appears in reply to Celsus, who had assailed this doctrine. First, he refutes the charge of Celsus that Jesus was an illegitimate son of Mary and a soldier named Panthera, and that as a result of this infidelity Mary, being

driven out by Joseph, wandered into Egypt and there brought up her son to learn the art of miracle-working (*Adv. Celsum*, i. 28, 32; Eng. transl. in *ANF*, vol. iv.; cf. Pseudo-Matt., xix.–xxiv.). Secondly, he finds an analogy of the virgin birth of Jesus in that of animals, especially the female vulture, which preserves succession of its race without sexual intercourse (ib. i. 37). Thirdly, he argues that the Greeks themselves hold to the origination of the human species as such from the spermatic elements in the earth (ib. i. 37). Fourthly, he appeals to the legend that Plato was the son of Apollo before Ariston had had marital relations with his mother, as explained by the fact that persons of transcendent wisdom and power were naturally referred to a divine paternity (ib. i. 37). Finally, when Celsus scouts the notion of a virgin birth, comparing it to the incredible myths of Danae, Melanippe, Auge, and Antiope, Origen replies that this is the language of a buffoon (ib. i. 37). Origen, moreover, suggested that birth from a virgin would correspond with the burial of Jesus in a new tomb (ib. i. 39). Hippolytus maintained the perfect purity and perpetual virginity of Mary (*Adv. Veronem*), and his theory of the incarnation alleged that God, by undefiled conception in the Virgin, incorporated with himself a rational soul and sensible body, who thus became perfect God and perfect man. His reliance on Scripture was inconsiderable, and though in the Old Testament he used Ps. cix. or cx.; Prov. xxx. 29; Dan. iii. 26, and vii. 14, he made no allusion to Isaiah. As a result of this brief historical survey, it is evident that by the middle of the third century the virgin birth had become a settled and undisputed article of faith in the Church.

Over against the theory of the virgin birth as a trustworthy historical event is a hypothesis which for the past seventy-five years, since Strauss, has attracted to itself an increasing number of advocates—the mythical or legendary view. Several conditions have been favorable to the development of this idea, among which are—(1) the modern

21. Legendary or Mythical Theory. view of the world, which finds no place for miracles in the traditional sense; (2) the significance of Christ, sought not in any physical basis or metaphysical substratum of his being, but in the moral and spiritual character of

his personality; (3) the history of all people, and especially comparative religion, showing that myth and legend have sprung up in connection with the beginning of every great religion, and (4) historical and textual criticism, laying bare not only different strata of composition in the writings of the New Testament, but also the presence of material which, if not foreign to, is at least derived from other than the essential Gospel sources.

The legendary theory seeks in one or more of several directions for its material and justification. (1) In prophecy and the Old Testament, i.e., in a purely Jewish circle. It has been shown that Harnack and others find the source of the doctrine that Christ was born of a virgin in the prophecy of Isa. vii. 13 sqq. (see § 12), and it is maintained that the constraining motive for this interpretation lay in the impulse to match the story of his wonderful life and resurrection with an account of his birth not less wonderful. The counterpart

22. Arguments from the Old Testament. of the birth-story of Samson and Samuel is that of John; and inasmuch as Jesus, both in his work and his consciousness, was greater than John, his conception must be referred to a more immediate and marvelous divine agency. That the passage in Isaiah had not before received the interpretation which the narrator gives to it is held to be no objection to the legendary theory; for neither the Evangelist nor other early Christians were bound by rules of scientific exegesis. If, contrary to all precedent, *parthenos* (*'almah*) may have been interpreted as " virgin " as foretelling an actual virgin birth, then it is not impossible that some Christian thinker, seeing an explanation of the divine character of Christ, hit upon this passage, and found in it a suggestion which at once gave rise to a new idea of the origin of his earthly existence. Two classes of objection are urged against this position. On the one hand, the peculiar character of the nativity stories renders it improbable that such a legend arose on Jewish soil; (1) there is an utter absence of foreign elements—oriental thought or Greek pantheism; the story is intensely Jewish; (2) Jewish monotheism is in the highest degree transcendental, involving the separateness and total unlikeness of God and man; (3) asceticism, i.e., marriage and virginity, is foreign to the Jewish religion, and is not found either in the Gospels or the infancy stories; (4) since prophecy was so applied only after the event, it could not have been the cause of the belief; (5) " Son of God " had only an ethical or official (Messianic) reference in the First and Third Gospels, and could not, therefore, be defined by metaphysical or physical qualities (cf. C. J. H. Ropes, " Born of the Virgin Mary," *Andover Review*, Nov., 1893). These objections are not, however, wholly convincing, for while the coloring is intensely Jewish, the event itself is absolutely unique in Jewish history. The legend may contain foreign elements which lie unnoticed, but far back and deep down in the past of Israel's religious contact with other peoples. Moreover, God's creative activity in forming man may be again called into play for the miraculous generation of the man from heaven. It is also objected that more time is required for the formation of legend than the documents of the New Testament appear to warrant. This is met by the reply, first, that there is, beyond contradiction, mythical material in the story in its existing form, without doubt much older than the manuscripts of the First and Third Gospels, and that it is arbitrary to draw the line short of the central event itself, if the evidence looks that way. Secondly, the formation of myths is a relative affair, depending upon enthusiasm, poetic imagination, and other conditions, the presence or absence of which, and the degree of their activity, will hasten or retard legendary growth. Finally, in the absence of compelling proof for the data as to the time at which the nativity stories originated—and expert judgment may be cited for both an early and a late origin—it is inept to declare that, if a myth

were in process of formation in any important section of the Church, Paul must have heard of it. For the same difficulty arises concerning his ignorance of the birth-story as a fact. A mystery of a similar kind concerns the origination and extension of the baptismal formula in Matt. xxviii. 19-20. That Paul and Luke, and apparently Peter, never heard of this is demonstrable; and yet it takes its place in Matthew's Gospel as authoritative, having its alleged source in Jesus' last words. If authentic it must have been preserved, and if not authentic it must have arisen, in some group of disciples removed from the great centers of Christian tradition. In any event, the particular place where the nativity story enters the consciousness of the Christian community, whether true or legendary, is inevitably a matter of conjecture. Among Christians at least, whether Jewish or gentile, the virgin birth, once it was announced, never became a subject of doubt or inner apologetic, but only of more convincing faith in their Redeemer. Matthew's account appears to have an apologetic interest; but among Christians, it was in the highest degree honoring to Mary as blessed among women; Joseph was singled out for his devout faith, unquestioning obedience, and tender care for Mary; and it gave to Jesus a beginning which corresponded with his earthly glory and his exaltation to the right hand of God.

(2) In the stories of classical antiquity parallels are sought which religious faith has only to paraphrase in reference to Christ. In an early narrative of the Buddha we read: " the knowledge of his

23. Arguments from Classical Antiquity. birth was made known by rejoicing deities to a hermit named Asita, who thereon repaired to Suddhana's palace, saw the child in his glory surrounded by deities, etc., and announced to the Sakyans that the child was to be a Buddha " (Coppleston, *Buddhism*, p. 34, London, 1892). The journey of the Armenian king, Tiridates, accompanied by Magi, to Rome to initiate Nero into the mysteries of the Mithras-meal, with bended knee and lifted hands calling him Lord and worshiping him even as Mithras, finds its parallel in the Matthew story (cf. Pliny, *Hist. nat.*, xxx. 6; Dio Cassius, xxxii. 1 sqq., xliii. 1-2, 5, 7). The birth of Amenophis III. of Egypt is described on the walls of the temple of Luxor as from a virgin and the god of Thebes, i.e., Ammon-Ra (cf. A. H. Sayce, *Religions of Ancient Egypt and Babylonia*, p. 45, Edinburgh, 1902). Asshurbanipal is described as one whom the gods Asshur and Sin formed in the midst of his mother (cf. *Records of the Past*, 1st series, i. 57; cf. Nebuchadrezzar: " When the god of gods made me, Marduk, he prepared well my birth in the mother," i.e., mother's womb, ib. v. 113; see Cheyne, *Bible Problems*, pp. 235-236, London, 1904). The story of King Sargon of Agade, about 2,800 B.C., relates of himself that he was of a vestal mother (Cheyne, ut sup., p. 86; Grützmacher, ut sup., pp. 57-58). Among the Greeks Speusippus related how Plato owed his birth to a union of his mother Perictione and the phantasm of Apollo (cf. Diogenes Laertius, *De Vitis Philosophorum*; also Jerome, *Adv. Jovinianum*, i. 42). Alexander was desirous that he be known, not as the natural son of Philip, but as the son of Zeus, as announced in the temple of Jupiter-Ammon, begotten by a serpent cohabiting with his mother Olympias (Soltau, ut sup., p. 46; Jane E. Harrison, *Prolegomena to the Study of Greek Religion*, 2d ed., Cambridge, 1908). Pythagoras is reported as a son of Apollo; Apollonius of Tyana as a son of Zeus (Usener, ut sup., i. 70 sqq.). Others who were alleged to have been born in this way were Æsculapius, Dionysus, Hercules, and Hermes; while one may also refer to the fabled Antiope, Auge, Danae, and Melanippe. These births are assigned to intercourse with a god who assumed various forms—an ox, a bird, a serpent, a lover, or a god who appeared in a shower of gold (Tertullian, *Apol.*, xxi.). The Church Fathers were not unwilling to use these legends in their apologetic, and even found them of value in recommending strange and miraculous things to their hearers (cf. Justin Martyr, *Dialogus*, lxvii., lxx.; *Apol.*, i. 21, 22, 54, 64; Origen, *Contra Celsum*, i. 37; Tertullian, *Apol.*, xii. 15). Turning to Roman antiquity, there is found the tradition of Romulus and Remus descended from a vestal virgin, having the god Mars for their father. The Emperor Augustus gave out that he was the son of Apollo, since his mother, Atia, having fallen asleep in the temple of Apollo, was visited by the god in the form of a serpent, and her son, born in the tenth month, was held to be son of Apollo (Suetonius, *Augustus*, xciv.). A similar story appears concerning Scipio Africanus (Gellius, *Noct. Att.*, vi.). In respect to these instances it is to be noted that the mother is not always claimed as a virgin; in some cases she is already a mother of other children for whom no supernatural conception is alleged. Yet it is equally to be noted (a) that a divine paternity is affirmed—a god has taken the place of the human father; and (b) the generative act on the part of the god was always physical, sometimes the fabled deed of an animal, often phantastic, and always impossible. The wide-spread belief of divine paternity is, however, more significant than even the form of the conception.

(3) The legendary theory of the virgin birth seeks in ancient, international redemptive ideas a source of the Christian belief. Harnack has declared that Christian tradition is "free from heathen myths, so far as these had not already been received by wide circles of Jews" (cf. *Dogma*, i. 100, note); and he holds that this does not apply to the virgin birth. The theory in question believes that this

                  statement is true, and, in opposition
24. Arguments from Ancient Messianic Longings. to Harnack, claims that it does not apply to the virgin birth. It assumes a primitive mythological tradition of a world-wide Redeemer, which had become international, to be traced ultimately to a Babylonian source. It assumes among the Jews an intense Messianism long before the Christian era, which was far more absorbing and definite than is ordinarily supposed, of which Dan. vii. 13 sqq. is a symptom, itself the outcome of development. It also assumes that certain Jewish Christians had borrowed this story, which had thus originated outside of Judaism, but

had become current in Jewish-Christian circles, and, transforming it in the interest of Judæo-Christian Messianism, had applied it to Christ's virgin birth. The myth in question appears in its Judæo-Christian dress in Rev. xii. 1 sqq.—the woman arrayed with the sun, etc. Of its earlier form, in case there was such a myth, no clear trace has been found. H. Gunkel has investigated the passage and shown its dependence upon the Babylonian myth of Ishtar, the queen of heaven, and her son, the sun-god who conquered the monster Tiamat—primeval chaos (cf. his *Schöpfung und Chaos in Urzeit und Endzeit*, pp. 379–398, Göttingen, 1895, and his *Zum religionsgeschichtlichen Verständnis des Neuen Testaments*, ib., 1903), and T. K. Cheyne has arrived at the conclusion that the myth enshrined in the book of Revelation was the source of the birth story in Matthew. To the writers of Matthew i. 18–23, however, the woman became a humble Jewish maiden; the son no longer the destroyer of the chaos-monster, or ruling all nations with a rod of iron, but the Savior of his people; his capital not Babylon but Jerusalem; the dragon with devouring jaws, Herod plotting the death of innocent children; the mother's flight changed from flight into the wilderness into the holy family's flight into Egypt (ut sup., pp. 71 sqq.). Parallel to this story is the North Arabian myth of Dusares, "the only begotten of the Lord," worshiped at Petra and Elusa, his mother being the virgin (*parthenos*)—one independent of the marriage tie (see NABATÆANS, II., § 3). It has affinity also with an Egyptian myth—Hathor or Isis, mother of the gods, and of the young sun-god, Horus; the dragon represented by Typhon. Other affinities are suggested: Persian or Zoroastrian, where Saoshyant, the Savior, is born of a virgin who had not had intercourse with a man (cf. *Dinkart*, VII., viii. 55 sqq., ix. 18 sqq., x. 15 sqq. [*SBE*, xlvii. 105 sqq.]). The Greek affinity is discovered in the myth of the pregnant Leto pursued by the dragon Pytho, to whom a prophecy had come that Leto's son would destroy him; she, however, under the protection of favoring gods, gave birth to Apollo, who four days afterward slew the dragon (cf. Cheyne, ut sup., pp. 198–205).

(4) The legendary theory seeks still deeper in folk-lore for the source of its suggestion, where one discovers a fusion of religious, social, and physiological elements. It is now recognized that "stories of supernatural birth may be said to have a currency as wide as the world" (E. S. Hartland, *Stories of Primitive Paternity*, i. 1, London, 1909; cf. J. E. Carpenter, *The Bible in the Nineteenth Century*, p. 490, London, 1903). The heroes of all nations have had an extraordinary entrance upon earthly life,

                  from which masculine agency is essen-
25. Arguments from Folk-lore. tially excluded. Conception is attributed to every cause but the actual one. It is referred to the forces of nature, such as the sun, wind, rain, wells, fires; to contact with magical substances, such as amulets, images, vestments, and stones; to vegetable substances, such as mandrake, or to animal substances, such as absorption of a portion of a

dead man. Among many peoples the belief is general that a previously existing soul, whether human, animal, or vegetable, spontaneously, without union of the sexes, enters the body of a woman and causes pregnancy, whence a new being reappears in a new form. Such beliefs or theories can be explained in part only on the ground of wide-spread ignorance of the invariable physiological conditions of reproduction. As the cause of death, so also the cause of birth remained hidden. The relation of the mother to the offspring is constant and unequivocal, while that of the father, owing to economic or religious conditions, is often indifferent and not well understood. Even where knowledge of the laws of reproduction have become more extended and better established, tradition still maintains its hold in popular myths concerning the birth-stories of great men in primitive times (cf. Hartland, ut sup., and his *Legend of Perseus*, 3 vols., London, 1894–96). Nowhere, perhaps, has comparative religion discovered a more impressive instance of virgin birth than in the Eleusinian Mysteries. The supreme moment of the solemn celebration of these rites was marked by the marriage of the sacred mother and the birth of the sacred child. The mother was Brimo, a maiden, a goddess of the underworld, the Thessalian Kore or Demeter, the goddess of the fruits of the cultivated earth. At night, in deep darkness, and in perfect chastity, the mimetic marriage was enacted by the hierophant and the chief priestess of Demeter. Immediately afterward the hierophant came forth into a blaze of torches, and with a loud voice cried to the initiates that the great and unspeakable mystery was accomplished: "Holy Brimo has borne a sacred child, Brimos," "the mighty has borne the mighty, and holy is the generation that is spiritual, heavenly, from above, and mighty is he who is so engendered" (*Philosophumena*, p. 170, Paris, 1860; cf. Harrison, ut sup., pp. 525, 548 sqq.; Tertullian, *Ad Nationes*, ii. 7). Since the begetting and the birth were both symbolical, the mystic rite was performed without physical contamination, the "mother" remaining a maiden still. Thus at the very heart and culmination of the ceremonies at this sacred shrine in ancient Greece, centuries before its appearance in the Septuagint, the dogma had been created, "A virgin shall conceive and shall bear a son."

The legendary theory has a vast background and makes an impressive showing. The point is not so much that birth from a virgin is alleged—this is seldom the case—as that the conception is supernatural. That the stories are sometimes gross signifies that they are an integral part of the religions in which they are found; a spiritual religion would transform the supernatural agency into forms of action worthy of a spiritual being. The most vigorous advocates of this theory do not, however, claim that they have more than presumptive evidence for their view; the historical connection between the universal myth of supernatural birth and the stories of the New Testament has not yet been traced.

It remains to consider the dogmatic bearings of

26. Criticism of the Legendary Theory.

the virgin birth. To the tenet of the Lutheran church of Germany, "that the Son of God 'conceived by the Holy Ghost, born of the Virgin Mary' is the foundation of Christianity," Harnack replies: "It is a dangerous but fallacious dilemma that the idea of the God-man stands or falls with the virgin birth" (*Das apostolische Glaubensbekenntniss*, p. 39), and he adds, "If this were the case, ill would fare Mark, ill Paul, ill John, ill Christianity." Ropes (ut sup., p. 695) declares that "Good Christian men may take opposite sides of this question, without giving up that which is vital and cardinal to the faith." It formed no part of the preaching or message of the apostles, and no doctrinal use is made of it in the New Testament. On the supposition that the writers of the New Testament outside of the First and Third Gospel knew of the virgin birth, they never availed themselves of it in the formulation of any doctrine. Other theories of the person of Christ were both suggested, and were more or less constitutive in the earliest Christian teaching (see SON OF GOD). The divine element in Christ has been explained as an endowment conferred at his baptism. Paul, John, and the author of the Epistle to the Hebrews make very significant use of both the fact and the nature of the preexistent element in Christ's person. It has been contended that between preexistence and the nativity account in Matthew and Luke there is an irreconcilable contradiction, since both of these Gospels speak as if, by the action of the Spirit of God, a new individual in all respects came into being (cf. A. Réville, *Histoire du dogme de la divinité de Jésus-Christ*, p. 30, Paris, 1869; Orr, ut sup., pp. 208 sqq.). It is true that the Kenosis theories (see CHRISTOLOGY, KENOSIS) have been proposed, and with elaborate and ingenious refinement have been made to serve as mediators between the Pauline and Johannean conscious preexistence, on the one hand, and on the other, the narratives of the infancy and the development of Jesus; but instead of elucidating, they have made still more perplexing the profound mystery of the person of Christ, and are falling into disfavor.

27. Is the Dogma Essential to Christianity?

The dogmatic use of the virgin birth involves two considerations—sinlessness and incarnation. Its bearing on sinlessness rests on two postulates, that contamination derived from Adam's sin through natural generation is inevitable, and that there was in Jesus Christ a divine, preexistent element which is not in us; hence his human nature differed from ours, and, accordingly, he was not affected by Adam's sin. In the position that sinlessness depended upon the virgin birth, there is assumed the Augustinian doctrine of the fall of man, and also the invariable hereditary taint of sin transmitted through ordinary processes of human birth. Of this basis of sinlessness the New Testament knows nothing. Paul finds the secret of Jesus' character in the peculiar nature of his person in relation to preexistence (cf. Phil. ii. 5 sqq.; Rom. viii. 3, ix. 5; Gal. iv. 4; II Cor. viii. 9). For John the Logos doctrine offered the key to the supreme grace and truth of Christ. In the ear-

28. Dogmatic Bearing on Sinlessness.

lier preaching, the clue to the perfect fulfilment of
both the royal and the prophetic hopes of Israel in
a person of divine excellence is found in the divine
designation of Jesus as the Messiah. Schleiermacher
suggested that the exclusion of Joseph from participation in the conception of Jesus does not relieve the difficulty (*Der christliche Glaube*, § 97, 7th
ed., Gotha, 1889; cf. Strauss, *Das Leben Jesu*, i.
153–154, Tübingen, 1835), for Mary was likewise
subject to original sin, and must have contributed
of her sinful principle to Jesus. Moreover, Schultz
has shown that the Scriptures represent woman as
weaker and more susceptible to temptation than is
man (*Die Lehre von der Gottheit Jesu*, p. 593, Gotha,
1881). To avoid this general conclusion, different
positions have been taken: (1) that in the conception Mary was wholly passive; hence no sinful impulse was communicated from her to the new life;
(2) Jesus was born not of (*ek*) but through (*dia*)
Mary, a docetic position of certain Gnostics (cf.
Tertullian, *Adv. Valentinum*, xxvii., *ANF*, vol. iii.);
(3) by the dogma of the Immaculate Conception
(q.v.), Mary, although born of a human father and
mother, was herself miraculously preserved from
both hereditary and actual sinfulness. Yet from
the common Protestant point of view it is objected
that the assumptions underlying these positions
are invalid; the laws of natural generation are
themselves ordained by God, and, accordingly,
are not sinful. Even if the conception was as alleged, still during the period of gestation her influence was normal with the unborn child (Lobstein, ut sup., pp. 84 sqq.). Calvin maintained
that Jesus was perfectly immaculate, not because
man had no part in his conception, but because
he was sanctified by the Spirit so that his generation was as pure and holy as it would have been
before Adam's fall (*Institutes*, II., xiii. 3–4)

A further dogmatic use of the virgin birth grounds
the incarnation on it. While one can not *a priori*
affirm that such a birth was a necessary form of
divine action, nor that the doctrine of the incarnation is historically traced to such a birth, yet this
would seem the more congruous to the event (cf.
W. N. Clarke, *Outline of Christian Theology*, pp.
289 sqq., New York, 1898). The affirmation is
further made that, given an eternal preexisting
being who is born without changing
29. Dog- or taking a new personality, but mere-
matic Bear- ly by assuming a new nature and en-
ing on tering new conditions of experience,
Incarnation. this can not be thought of as occurring
by the ordinary process of generation,
since this involves the beginning of a new personality. Denial of the virgin birth, therefore, is tan-
tamount to the reduction of Jesus to the rank of a
purely human personality, however intimate his
relation with God (cf. Gore, *Dissertations*, pp. 64–
65). In addition it is maintained that the spiritual
miracle in the person of Christ requires a corresponding physical miracle, and since this goes down
to the ultimate ground of Mary's nature, a second
miracle of the same sort with reference to Joseph
would be unnecessary; while the mode of the event
symbolizes the unique character of the person (Orr,
ut sup., pp. 223 sqq.). On the other hand, many of

those who deny the virgin birth deny not only the
virgin life (cf. A. B. Bruce, *Apologetics*, p. 410, New
York, 1892), but also the traditional theory of the
incarnation; the latter, however, not because of
denial of the virgin birth. The Nicene Creed connected the incarnation with the virgin birth, but
this was for the sake, not of basing the incarnation
on the birth of Christ, but of showing its reality,
i.e., the reality of his human nature as against
Gnostic interpretations and tendencies (cf. A. C.
McGiffert, *Apostles' Creed*, New York, 1902). That
view of the incarnation which seeks the proof of
Christ's divinity in his ethical and spiritual revelation of God naturally lays less stress upon the virgin birth than upon the character of his consciousness and the impression he makes upon men.

It has been urged that in the doctrine of the virgin
birth the divinity of Christ is lowered from a spiritual to a natural basis, his full humanity sacrificed,
and an illusory wall reared between the natural and
supernatural (cf. Lobstein, ut sup., pp. 106 sqq.).
Those who hold that the idea of the virgin birth is
an amalgamation of Jewish Messianism and Hellenistic Logos doctrine, or who maintain that the most
exalted Christology owes nothing to this tradition,
have no dogmatic interest in this question (cf. *Biblical World*, x. 1 sqq.). One may ignore the inquiry
into origins, or may declare this to be a secret hidden in the personality of Jesus (cf. A. Ritschl,
Rechtfertigung und Versöhnung, iii. 426, Bonn, 1874;
A. Harnack, *What is Christianity?* 3d ed., London,
1904).

The conclusions may be thus summarized: (1) The
first and third Gospels are our sole authority for the
virgin birth of Jesus. (2) The stories as they appear
in these Gospels are independent of each other and
are from different sources, but whether
30. Sum- they were written or oral, and whether
mary. Matthew's account is dependent on
Joseph and Luke's on Mary, does not
appear. (3) The writings of Paul and John contain
no indisputable reference to these stories—they
neither presuppose, nor contradict, nor draw conclusions from them; they do, however, involve a
superhuman and pre-earthly being who became incarnate in Jesus. (4) With unimportant exceptions
the entire early Church in the interest of Jesus' real
humanity and divine nature acknowledged the virgin birth. (5) The connection proposed between
the story of the virgin birth and stories of supernatural births in the Old Testament, in classic antiquity, in the wide-spread hope of a world Redeemer,
and in folk-lore, has not been established. (6) The
doctrine has important bearings on the incarnation
and sinlessness of Jesus, but it is not essential either
to these or to Christian experience. (7) The story
itself, in comparison with all other stories of supernatural births, is one of unique and incomparable
beauty, befitting the creative entrance of Jesus into
our earthly lot, to live the life of God under human
conditions; he who knows the mystery of the beginnings of life, and remembers with what meaning
this story has been invested by men of deepest insight through the Christian centuries, will not tear
it from the Gospels, but will with the holy Catholic
Church confess, " I believe in . . . Jesus Christ,

. . . who was conceived by the Holy Ghost, born of the Virgin Mary." C. A. BECKWITH.

BIBLIOGRAPHY: The following may be added to the very abundant literature noted in the text: A. Hoben, *The Virgin Birth*, Chicago, 1903; B. W. Randolph, *The Virgin-Birth of Our Lord*, London, 1903; *The Virgin-Birth one of the Principal Foundations of the Christian Faith . . . by a Bibliophile* (Edinburgh), 1905; *Doctrina patrum de incarnatione Verbi. Ein griechisches Florilegium aus . . . 7. und 8. Jahrhunderten*, Münster, 1907; E. R. Hendrix, *The Religion of the Incarnation*, New York, 1907; R. J. Knowling, *Our Lord's Virgin Birth and the Criticism of To-day*, 3d ed., London, 1907; G. Krüger, *Das Dogma von der Dreieinigkeit und Gottmenschheit*, Tübingen, 1905; F. Weston, *The One Christ, an Inquiry into the Manner of the Incarnation*, London, 1907; T. J. Thorburn, *A Critical Examination of the Evidences for the Doctrine of the Virgin Birth*, ib. 1908; E. Petersen, *Die wunderbare Geburt des Heilandes*, Tübingen, 1909; G. S. Streatfield, *The Incarnation*, New York, 1910; J. J. Lanier, *The Church Universal*, ib. 1911; D. Völter, *Die evangelische Erzählung von der Geburt und Kindheit Jesu* (1911).

VIRTUE: An ethical concept almost synonymous with morality, denoting, in its original Greek sense, every excellence which affords worth to a person or a thing and secures recognition, thus incidentally signifying honor and reputation. In the discourses of Socrates the term is yet in its plastic state, but appears at the same time in its ethical application, and this coincides with the usage of the Sophists. After Plato, and especially Aristotle, virtue came to denote that quality of man whereby he is adapted for true moral action. The more popular parenetic or descriptive ethics became, as in the early Middle Ages, a mere enumeration of virtues and vices; and in the period of the Enlightenment the concepts of morality and virtue so coincided that even an individual act might be termed virtue, and Kant distinguished the moral as virtue in distinction from the legal. Schleiermacher, therefore, seeking to delimit virtue from the good and duty, defined it as " the power of reason in nature morally united with it, and in the human individual in particular." In like manner R. Rothe distinguished virtue as the productive power from the good as the moral product, and from duty as the form of the moral process. More generally accepted is the definition of C. F. Schmid, that the good is the character of the will of the human subject. Underlying all these definitions is the view that man in his activities can but acquire a fixed character determinative of conduct, and such a character is either true or perverted, virtue or baseness; and they presuppose the concept of the good or morally true as already given. Aristotle presumes to derive the nature of the ethical itself from virtue; namely, by the Hellenic concept of the mean between extremes. The formal distinction of virtue from the subethical or brutal and the super-ethical, or heroic, as well as his "heap" of virtues, amidst which, only, he sought the class-concept, were the more urgent upon him as empiricist. The other followers of Socrates assumed with their leader that virtue was one, an idea which Plato systematized. Following his anthropological trichotomy he differentiates virtue into " wisdom, courage, and temperance." Justice, bringing these into the equilibrium of the good, completes the character, and determines the social relationship of the

(Margin labels: History of Concept.)

individual. Through Ambrose the four receive the permanent appellative of " cardinal "; and Augustine demonstrated from them the " love of God," so that the " brief and true definition of virtue " sounds, " order is of love." Love, however, practically is unfolded in faith, hope, and charity, later the theological virtues. Thus the sevenfold character of the virtues became traditional, making way for the seven spiritual gifts paralleled by the seven deadly sins. Scholasticism inheriting this scheme continued to lay emphasis on the unity of virtue, and to see in love the basal Christian virtue, and through Thomas Aquinas the scheme has descended canonically to the present. Venatorius, however, substituted faith for love. Melanchthon, developing " civil justice " on a scheme of justice, truth, and moderation, led, by reference to the Decalogue, to the postulation of the precedence of the concept of duty, a scheme commonly accepted by Protestantism, especially by Wolff. This chaos was opposed by Schleiermacher with a reconstruction of the Platonic tetrad of virtues: inner virtue is wisdom in cognition, and love in action; in terms of time, cognition is prudence, and action is perseverance. The Socratic doctrine of the unity of virtue is closely connected with the identification of virtue and understanding. This intellectualistic determinism was completed by Stoicism, which not only derived the primary virtues from the mere moral concept, but maintained that virtue was present *a priori* without the necessity of a gradual approach. The empiricist Aristotle, without overlooking the " determinism of consequence," emphasizes caprice while he recognizes that perfection is to be attained only by practise. Orthodox Semipelagianism had the aid of the " infused grace," following Aristotle in the doctrine of virtue. The antithesis persisted later. C. Wolff triumphantly favored the intellectual determinism, while Rousseau rings the appeal, " back to nature." Such underlying presumptions give rise, here and there dignified by Kant's sternness of duty, to the enthusiasm for the self-sufficient striving of virtue, antagonized, as they are, by the Biblical Evangelical theology.

In fact this concept of virtue has no Biblical connection, except in the Hellenistic portions of the Apocrypha (Wisdom iv. 1, v. 13, viii. 7; IV Macc.). In I Pet. ii. 9 and Phil. iv. 8 the term *aretē* (Gk. " virtue ") denotes the laudable in general; in II Pet. i. 3 it implies a manifestation of divine power; and only in II Pet. i. 5 does it refer to any specific virtue. If Schleiermacher did not employ the concept of virtue in his system of theological ethics, neither did he construct this as a system of duty. Herein he followed the example of G. Calixtus and of the Pietists, who set forth the process of origin and the demonstration of the Christian life, thus affording a substructure for the theory of duty. Here is the point of departure taken up by the ancient Church in dependence upon available scientific forms, and here the doctrine of virtue may be developed in thoroughly Christian style. Social ethics must not crowd out the presuppositions, training, and development of

(Margin labels: In the Bible; Practise of Virtue.)

Christian character; the scientific treatment of virtue will then afford a satisfactory presentation of its unity and origin. At the same time the ground is won also for asceticism and the consideration of the means to virtue. The latter has been defined as " all that has an advantageous influence for the actual exercise and accomplishment of acts in accord with duty." It may include everything, then, within the ethical horizon, even temptation and offenses as tests, and involve the help of God, moral motives, fate, nature, vocation, and every personal relation. Means they become so far as they are used for a special purpose, the practise of virtue or morality, i.e., ascetics. With such was concerned the ancient Church in dependence upon the applied ethics of the Stoics. Ascetics has been defined by Rothe as conduct designed simply to gain personal virtue, without regard to any other end whatsoever lying outside the acting subject. Against the admission of such a view to scientific ethics it is objected that every moral act must have reference to society as well as to the individual; and that duty comprehends life as a whole, and no moment in its course can be conceived as involving merely mediate obligation. But certainly duty demands at every moment the performance of what is most expedient to the purpose. One is bound therefore to the exercise of the means of virtue, if it be fitting. That social relations are to take the place of these modes of activity can be claimed only if the training and purification of personal character are overlooked, in which also one discharges some of his social indebtedness. In character-culture pedagogy and asceticism are materially identified, for self-culture follows training as maturity supersedes immaturity, and what argues for the means of pedagogy argues for the means of asceticism as well. Finally, self-culture has to rid itself of the unethical false culture. Reactionary efforts and preventives are indeed indispensable; but they become superfluous in an ideal self-unfolding. Christian ethics in its intense rebound from immoral corruption, leading to a total disentanglement from a sin-ridden world, swung to the untrue pole of social seclusion and futile performances. On the contrary, only modes of conduct are valid for means to virtue which are justified and required for Christians in general, and their special place is to be perceived in that they afford an advantage to conduct in the building of character and alienation of evil, not otherwise to be gained. Moderation is requisite of itself; it must be raised to abstinence if an evil is to be conquered. The difficulty is that the pedagogy from without the individual possesses no knowledge of the situation within, while the individual himself is not sufficiently master safely to treat himself. Hence Christian asceticism presupposes sanctification, which God affords continually, and in this the means to virtue and grace are provided (Titus ii. 11–12). In the last analysis religious and ethical means to virtue are brought to the same plane; religion and ethics are not exclusive circles, but among ethical means to virtue the most important are the religious. The means to virtue may, accordingly, be more strictly defined as moral modes of conduct with special reference to the development of personal character,

and with particular regard to the imperfections of the individual, different in each one. Since, however, individuals are not absolutely different, the means to virtue may be reduced to categories, though this can properly be done only in connection with the theory of character-culture, or virtue, as a whole, and in this sense ascetics becomes a necessary part of ethics. An enumeration of the means to virtue seems unnecessary; since a classification is self-suggestive, according to the various aspects of the development of character. Protestant ascetics is essentially different from Roman Catholic. The latter makes the individual means laws imposed by the Church, and forcing them from their vital moral relations considers the acts meritorious in themselves, thus transforming them from means. Finally, it develops classes to the abuse of the individual as well as society on the whole, based on the distinction between the legitimate secular and the perfect spiritual life (see CONSILIA EVANGELICA). On the other hand, Protestants variously represent a point of view by which they regard Christian ethics as the fruit of the inner law so that discipline and means to virtue are ignored as such.

(M. KÄHLER.)

BIBLIOGRAPHY: Consult the literature under ETHICS.

VISHNU. See HINDUISM.

VISIGOTHS. See GOTHS, § 6.

VISITATIO LIMINUM SANCTORUM APOSTOLORUM: The visiting of the church of SS. Peter and Paul at Rome, and also of the Curia, in compliance with either a vow or the law of the Roman Catholic Church. Such visitations in consequence of vows were frequent in the Middle Ages; but the popes were compelled to limit such visits, and in 1478 Sixtus IV. issued a special papal reservation on the subject. The papal reservation is no longer set forth in the quinquennial faculties.

The most important form of the visitation is that required by law for the exercise of the necessary supervision over the Church. By a Roman synod of 743 all bishops residing near Rome were required to visit the pope each year about the middle of May, while those whose sees were distant were enjoined to write annually concerning the condition of their dioceses. After 1079 this duty was made incumbent on all metropolitans by Gregory VII., and was soon extended to all bishops, though intervals of varying length were accorded in proportion to the distance of their dioceses from Rome.

In the bull Romanus pontifex (Dec. 20, 1584) Sixtus V. enacted that the bishops of Italy and the neighboring islands, Dalmatia, and Greece should visit every three years; those of Germany, France, Spain, Portugal, Belgium, Bohemia, Hungary, England, Scotland, and Ireland every four years; those of the remainder of Europe, northern Africa, and the islands east of the American continent every five years; and those of all other lands every ten years. This was confirmed by Benedict XIV. in his constitution Quod sancta (Nov. 23, 1740), and he extended the requirement to all possessing quasi-episcopal jurisdiction. It is generally held that titular bishops are also bound to make the visitation.

The visitation should be performed in person at

the designated intervals; but if this is impossible, the prelate concerned may be represented by a special, properly qualified plenipotentiary. The visitation comprises three parts, attested by the *Congregatio super statu ecclesiarum:* the visit to the " church of the apostles " (the church occupied by the pope and the Curia; normally St. Peter's, Rome), and an oral and written statement of the affairs of the diocese of the bishop concerned.

(E. FRIEDBERG†.)

BIBLIOGRAPHY: J. H. Bangen, *Die römische Kurie*, pp. 177 sqq., Münster, 1854; A. Lucidi, *De visitatione liminum*, Rome, 1878; P. Melcher, *De canonica diœcesi visitatione*, Cologne, 1893; Sägmüller, in *TQS*, lxxxviii (1900), 69, 91; *KL*, xii. 1011–13.

VISITATION, ORDER OF THE: A Roman Catholic order founded by St. Francis of Sales (q.v.) and named in honor of the visitation of the Virgin (Luke i. 39 sqq.). While, however, Francis termed himself the father of the order, he designated as their mother their real founder, Jeanne Frémiot Françoise de Chantal, with whom he was bound by a sort of spiritual union. According to the biographers of both, Francis saw in a dream her who was to aid him in establishing a female religious order, later recognizing the lady of his vision in Mme. de Chantal. She, in her turn, though having no dream, received a manifestation of the bishop who was destined to be her spiritual guide and friend. While preaching at Dijon in the Lent of 1604, the attention of Francis was attracted, in his very first sermon, to a lady who listened to him with especial devoutness. At the close of his sermon he learned that she was the Baroness de Chantal, daughter of Frémiot, the Burgundian president of parliament, sister of the archbishop of Bourges, a widow of some years' standing, and then residing, not altogether happily, on the estate of her father-in-law with her four small children. She was profoundly dissatisfied with her confessor, and immediately recognized in Francis her true spiritual guide. The pair met at her father's house, but not till later did she reveal her sufferings to Francis, and afterward she made a full confession. Among other things, she spoke of her desire to pass the remainder of her life in the Holy Land, to which Francis at first gave no response, and she also begged him to take her under his spiritual guidance. After several days he consented to become her spiritual guide, though cautioning her against haste and against the danger of the intrusion of any earthly element in their relations. He then left Dijon with the promise to write to her frequently. The bond thus formed became ever closer, though at first Mme. de Chantal bitterly reproached herself for her course, especially fearing that she had transgressed the laws of the Church by placing herself under the guidance of the bishop, though the latter pointed out that St. Theresa also had had a special spiritual mentor in addition to her confessor. But she long remained in doubt, her faith wavered, it was difficult for her to subject her unbelief to the Church, and her meditations seemed fruitless. In this feeling of vague unrest there seems to have been an unconscious element of personal affection for Francis of Sales. He became to her something more than

a priest and a confessor, and though she could give this indefinable quality no specific name, she felt it estranged her from the Church. But she did not cease from pious meditations and works of asceticism, nor did she abandon the thought of retiring from the world. Francis, with whom she often discussed the subject, no longer kept her wavering between hope and fear. After the middle of 1605 he repeatedly implied that her spiritual regeneration was nearing perfection, and he urged her more and more to contemplate as her final step complete self-renunciation and perfect submission to God. Though as late as Aug., 1606, he had not decided whether she should become a nun, in a personal interview he received her vow of celibacy and obedience, and approved her determination to bring up her daughters in convents.

The first definite intimations of the purpose of Francis to establish a community of female religious under the direction of himself and Mme. de Chantal date from 1607. He planned to locate the community at Annecy, the seat of the bishop of Geneva since the Reformation, so that his association with Mme. de Chantal should become still closer, though the ostensible reason was that there she might be nearer her married daughter, the baroness of Thorens. In the spring of 1610 Mme. de Chantal, abandoning her father and her children, went to Annecy, where, in the night before the dedication of the house of the new order, she seemed to see her father and children invoking divine wrath upon her, her distress being increased by the fear that she had led astray the mind of Francis. After three hours of agony, however, she conquered her temptation, and henceforth the mystic bond between the bishop and his spiritual child became even more strong. Mme. de Chantal was no less devoted to Francis than he to her, giving him constant proofs of her solicitude both for his body and his soul. On the other hand, her affection for her children so diminished that, when her son was about to visit her in Annecy, Francis was obliged to admonish her to give him cordial greeting. She died at Moulin Dec. 13, 1641, was beatified by Benedict XIV. in 1751, and canonized by Clement XIII. in 1767.

The order of the nuns of the Visitation was established in the summer of 1610, when, on Trinity Sunday, Mme. de Chantal and two others received their habit from the hands of Francis of Sales. The order had no solemn vows, no monastic seclusion, and no habit, except a black veil and black clothing. Though Mme. de Chantal had exercised extreme asceticism, this was not made incumbent on the order, and only the recitation of the shorter office of the Virgin was required of the sisters. Retreats were always permitted to women not belonging to the order; and in imitation of the Virgin's visit to St. Elizabeth the nuns were obliged to visit the poor and the sick. In conformity with the usage of the earlier Church, all the houses of the order were to be subject to their diocesan, and every year the sisters interchanged their rosaries, breviaries, crucifixes, etc. The congregation, as it was at first called, increased rapidly, but Francis soon found himself obliged to impose a more rigorous rule of Augustinian type, in which form the order was officially recognized by Paul V. in 1618, and confirmed by Urban VIII. in 1626. The order had no special head, but was placed under the control of the diocesan. A simple black habit with a long black veil and a black head-band was required, and conventual seclusion was introduced, thus rendering it no longer possible to visit the poor and sick. On the other hand, there was no intensification of asceticism. At the death of Francis the order had thirteen houses, to which Mme. de Chantal added eighty-seven. The order reached its greatest prosperity in the eighteenth century, when it had about 200 houses; and about the middle of the nineteenth century it had approximately 100 houses with 3,000 nuns in France, Italy, Switzerland, Austria, Poland, Syria, and North America. At the end of the nineteenth century it had 164 convents with about 7,000 nuns: eight in Germany, four in Austria, two in Switzerland, and one in Spain. Other convents are to be found in Italy, Portugal, England, Syria, and North America, but by far the greater number were in France. In consequence of the change in the character of the order in 1618, the chief activity of the nuns of the Visitation became the education of girls, especially of higher Roman Catholic society. During the Jansenistic troubles nuns of this order were sent to Port Royal to take the place of the expelled Cistercian nuns.

(EUGEN LACHENMANN.)

The order was introduced into America at Georgetown, D. C., in 1799. There were in 1911 twenty-one houses or academies, with 795 sisters or postulants, 27 professed religious, and 1,935 pupils.

BIBLIOGRAPHY: On the foundress consult her *Lettres inédites*, ed. C. Barthélemy, 2 vols., Paris, 1860; the *Acta beatificationis et canonizationis*, Rome, 1732; *Sainte J. F. Frémyot de Chantal, sa vie et ses œuvres*, 8 vols., Paris, 1874–79; H. de Maupas du Tour, *La Vie de . . . mère J. F. F. de Chantal*, Paris, 1644; E. Bougaud, *Hist. de Ste. Chantal et des origines de la Visitation*, 13th ed., Paris, 1899. Other accounts are by: G. Beaufils, Annecy, 1751; C. A. Saccarelli, 2 vols., Augsburg, 1752; W. H. Coombes, 2 vols., London, 1830; G. Hettenkofer, Augsburg, 1836; F. M. de Chaugy, 3 vols., Vienna, 1844; E. M. de Barthélemy, Paris, 1860; Emily Bowles, London, 1872; Cecilia A. Jones, London, 1874.

On the order consult: Helyot, *Ordres monastiques*, iv. 309 sqq.; the Annecy ed. of the works of St. Francis of Sales, especially vol. vi.; the *Constitutiones*, Paris, 1622, 1645, etc.; C. Menetrier, *Projet de l'hist. de l'ordre de la visitation*, Annecy, 1701; L. Clarus, *Leben der besten Mütter . . . des Ordens von der Heimsuchung Mariens*, 2 vols., Regensburg, 1861; H. Heppe, *Geschichte der quietistischen Mystik in der katholischen Kirche*, pp. 43–58, Berlin, 1875; *St. Jane Frances Frémyot de Chantal. Her Exhortations* . . . , Clifton, 1888; Heimbucher, *Orden und Kongregationen*, ii. 288–295; *KL*, x. 1558–61.

VISITATION OF THE SICK: One of the occasional offices in the Book of Common Prayer. Its Scriptural basis is found in James v. 14–15 (cf. also Mark vi. 13), and its necessity, even though the ministrations of the clergy were not explicitly requested, is insisted upon by the canons of many councils, while in the English Church canon lxvii. is devoted to the clerical obligation to visit the sick.

The office as found in the Book of Common Prayer is derived chiefly from the corresponding office in the Sarum Use, and possesses peculiar interest historically in its retention of more than one old usage which Puritanism strove in vain to dislodge. For a correct understanding of the office (which now differs considerably in the American Book from the English) from the Sarum Use to the present time, it seems best to take as the standard of discussion the office as contained in the First Prayer Book of Edward VI. (1549). Omitting the requirement of the Sarum Use, that on the way to the house of the sick the seven penitential Psalms with their antiphon should be recited, the priest, after saying, "Peace be in this house, and to all that dwell in it," recites Ps. cxliii. (omitted in all later Books; the sprinkling with holy water, required by the Sarum Use, is also omitted, even in the First Book) with the anthem "Remember not Lord our iniquities," etc., followed by the *Kyrie*, the Lord's Prayer, and several versicles and responses. Then come two of the nine collects of the Sarum Use, followed by the exhortation of the sick "after this fourme, or other lyke," with provision for curtailment if the person visited be very ill. The articles of the Apostles' Creed are next rehearsed, and the sick man is examined as to his forgiveness of all his enemies and his discharge of all debts, and is admonished of his duty to make his will and to be charitable to the poor, the special wording of these portions being left to the discretion of the priest.

Opening Part of the Office.

Then follows one of the most vital survivals of the old Use, against which Protestant objection has been most strenuously made. The rubric in the first Edwardine Prayer Book reads: "Here shall the sicke person make a speciall confession, yf he fele his conscience troubled with any weightie matter. After which confession, the priest shall absolue hym after this forme, and the same forme of absolucion shalbe used in all pryuate confessions"—the form being "Our Lord Jesus Christ, who hath lefte power to his Churche to absolue all sinners, which truely repent and beleue in hym: of his great mercy forgeue thee thyne offences: and by his autoritie committed to me, I absolue thee frō all thy synnes, in the name," etc. This declaratory absolution, which is also employed in the various unofficial uses for private confession in the Anglican communion, was retained even in the strongly Protestantized second Edwardine Prayer Book (1552) and was included in the proposed Scotch Book of 1619. On the rise of the Commonwealth the Puritans in 1640 (and again at the Savoy Conference of 1661) sought to change this to "I pronounce thee absolved," but they were unsuccessful, and the ancient form, found in the Uses of Sarum and York, is still retained in the English Book, although the "Sealed Book" of 1661 added to the rubric "if he humbly and heartily desire it" (the form retained in the present English Book). In the strongly Protestantized Irish Book (1877) confession is optional, which is true only in a qualified sense of the English Books ("here shall the sick person be moved to make a special confession," etc.), and the form of absolution is the imprecatory one of the Communion Office. The same form was chosen in the ill-starred "Proposed

The Absolution.

Book " of the American Church (1786), but three years later that communion took the step of expunging from the office any allusion to both confession and absolution, which have thus far been unrestored in the United States.

The declaratory absolution is followed by a prayer of absolution, derived from the York and Sarum Uses, and also found in the Gelasian Sacramentary, but the two following collects in the older uses were omitted in all English Books and their derivatives.

Old Office for Unction, and Concluding Portions. In the Sarum Use the visitation office here ends, and that of unction begins. The opening Psalm of that office (lxxi., for which the American Book substitutes Ps. cxxx.) is still retained, followed by another noteworthy survival —the sole instance of the Antiphon (q.v.) in the Anglican ritual: " O Saueour of the world saue us, which by thy crosse and precious bloud hast redemed us, helpe us we beseche the, O God " (used also in various unofficial special offices for the Passion Service on Good Friday). After another collect, expanded from one in the Gregorian Sacramentary for the visitation of the sick, the First Prayer Book has the rubric: " If the sicke person desyre to be annoynted, then shal the priest annoynte him upon the forehead or breast only, makyng the signe of the crosse, saying thus " (followed by a prayer of noteworthy beauty, omitted in all later books). This unction, which, despite the Scriptural warrant of James v. 14, was offensive to Puritanism, disappeared in the second Edwardine Book, and has never been restored. With the recitation of Ps. xiii. the first Edwardine office closes, the second Book ending abruptly just before unction; but in 1661 the Aaronic blessing was added, together with four occasional prayers (for a sick child, etc.), to which the American Book adds three more, one of which is also included in the Irish Book.

The office for the visitation of the sick is immediately followed in all Books by that for the Communion of the Sick (q.v.), with which is inseparably connected the various questions regarding the very ancient practise of Reservation of the Sacrament (q.v.), at least so far as communion of the sick is concerned, a use which even the Calvinistic Thirty-nine Articles did not forbid (cf. Art. xxv.).

As regards the practical use of this office, it is to be observed that it is a formal rite to be employed but once for a person in severe illness; it does not form part of ordinary visits to the sick-room. " It is a solemn recognition of the person over whom it is used as one who is in the fellowship of the Church, and for whom the Church, by its authorized Minister, offers prayer to God; and it is also a solemn recognition of the fact that the sicknesses and infirmities incident to human nature are a consequence of sin, a part of that heritage of death which came upon us through the Fall " (Blunt, p. 460). It is to be used, moreover, only over those who have had the training of the church, particularly as its employment is prefatory to the reception of the Eucharist. To dissenters the visitation office would, in all probability, be unintelligible and even terrifying, unless they were resolved to be reconciled with the church and to accept her last consolations. These latter remarks would apply with doubled force to those who have led irreligious or wicked lives, in which cases the office is applicable only after much instruction and much progress toward true penitence. Otherwise, the sick man might view " the comforts of the Office more prominently than would be advisable for those who do not fully appreciate the necessity of repentance toward the attainment of pardon and true peace " (Blunt, ut sup.). Through a false and un-Christian fear of solemn preparation for death the use of the visitation office is well-nigh abandoned. This is most regrettable. There is no implication of death in the office; indeed, the American Book has a " Thanksgiving for the beginning of a Recovery " (similarly the Irish Book). And even if such implication of approaching death be seen, the true churchman will have no fear of death, though he may well dread it without the final blessing and absolution of the church and the last solemn rite of the Eucharist.

Practical Use of the Office.

BIBLIOGRAPHY: J. H. Blunt, *Annotated Book of Common Prayer*, revised ed., pp. 460–471, London, 1903; F. Procter and W. H. Frere, *New History of the Book of Common Prayer*, 26th ed., pp. 622–626 (with abundant references to older literature and copious bibliography), London, 1910.

VISITATION OF THE VIRGIN MARY, FEAST OF THE. See MARY, MOTHER OF JESUS CHRIST, III.

VITALIAN, vai-tê′li-an: Pope 657–672. He was born at Segni, and on July 30, 657, was enthroned as the successor of Eugenius I. He announced his accession to the Emperor Constans II., thus signalizing the resumption of friendly ecclesiastical relations between Rome and Constantinople; the emperor in return confirmed the privileges of the Roman church. Vitalian was unsuccessful, on the other hand, in his attempt to assert jurisdiction over Maurus, bishop of Ravenna, whom he cited to appear at Rome, only to meet with refusal. Vitalian thereupon deposed Maurus, who in his turn pronounced the ban on the pope. Vitalian seems to have been influential in England, where Theodorus, archbishop of Canterbury, actively promoted the interests of Rome and sought to secure uniformity with the Roman Church. Vitalian died Jan. 27, 672.   (A. HAUCK.)

BIBLIOGRAPHY: The letters are in *MPL*, lxxxvii. 999 sqq. Consult *Liber pontificalis*, ed. T. Mommsen in *MGH, Gest. pont. Rom.*, i (1898), 186–189; Bede, *Hist. eccl.*, iv. 1; Jaffé, *Regesta*, i. 235–237; Agnellus, *Vitæ pontificum Ravennatum*, chaps. 110 sqq., Modena, 1708, also in *MGH, Script. rer. Langob.* (1878), pp. 349 sqq.; Mann, *Popes*, ii. 1–17; J. Langen, *Geschichte der römischen Kirche*, ii. 539, Bonn, 1885; Bower, *Popes*, i. 459–466; Platina, *Popes*, i. 156–158; Milman, *Latin Christianity*, ii. 281–282; *KL*, xii. 1015–18; *DCB*, iv. 1161–63.

VITALIS, ORDERICUS. See ORDERICUS VITALIS.

VITICULTURE. See WINE, HEBREW.

VITRINGA, vî-trin′Hā, **CAMPEGIUS:** Dutch Reformed, Old-Testament scholar; b. at Leeuwarden, Frisia, May 16, 1659; d. at Franeker Mar. 31, 1722. He was educated at the universities of Franeker (1675–78) and Leyden (1678–79), and in 1681 became professor of oriental languages at the former university. Two years later he succeeded his teacher Marck in the theological faculty, and in 1693 the professorship of church history was also added to his duties; at considerable financial sacrifice he remained at Franeker until his death, declining repeated invitations to Utrecht. Theologically he was a child of his communion, ardently devoted to the doctrine of absolute predestination, and his views of the Scriptures and their inspiration were in accord with post-Reformation orthodoxy. In textual criticism, on the other hand, his attitude was more free. His importance as an exegete lies especially in the care and accuracy with which he applied the entire exegetical apparatus to determine the true meaning of his text, with due regard also for its historical background.

The chief work of Vitringa, and that on which his fame rests, was his commentary on Isaiah (2 vols., Leeuwarden, 1714–20), which forms the basis for the commentaries of J. E. Leigh (6 vols., Brunswick, 1726–34), J. J. Rambach (ed. E. F. Neubauer, Züllichau, 1741), and A. F. Büsching (2 vols., Halle, 1749–51). Vitringa planned a similar work on Zechariah, but did not live to complete it, though the prolegomena and the commentary as far as Zech. iv. 6 were edited by H. Venema (Leeuwarden, 1734). The same scholar edited also Vitringa's posthumous *Commentarius ad canticum Mosis Deut. xxxii.* (Haarlem, 1734). On the New Testament Vitringa wrote *Anakrisis Apocalypsios Joannis apostoli.* (Franeker, 1705), in which prophecy is applied to polemics against the Roman Catholic Church. His Latin lectures on the interpretation of the parables were edited in Dutch, with his cooperation, by J. d'Outrein under the title *Verklaaringe van de evangelische parabolen,* etc. (Amsterdam, 1715); in this work the personages of the parables are made to apply to historical figures. Lectures by him formed the basis of the Dutch exegesis of Galatians and Titus (Franeker, 1728) and of the first eight chapters of Romans (1729). His *Observationum sacrarum libri sex* (Franeker, 1683–1708) were chiefly exegetical in character, and based on public disputations.

In the department of Biblical history and archeology Vitringa wrote his *Archisynagogus observationibus novis illustratus* (Franeker, 1685), in which he sought to trace the names and functions of the officers in the primitive Church to the Jewish synagogue. He thus became involved in a controversy with Rhenferd, in the course of which he composed his *De decem viris otiosis* (Franeker, 1687). Another controversy gave rise to his *Anleidinge tot het rechte verstand van den tempel, die de prophet Ezechiel gezien en beschreeven heeft* (2 vols., Franeker, 1687), in which he maintained that Ezekiel's temple corresponded exactly to Solomon's, and was perfectly copied by Zerubbabel and Herod; while to the criticisms of the younger Cocceius he replied in his *t'Rechte verstand van den tempel Ezechiels verdeedigt en bevestigt* (Haarlem, 1693). The chief work of Vitringa, next to his commentary on Isaiah, was his *De synagoga vetere libri tres* (Franeker, 1694; Eng. transl., *The Synagogue and the Church,* London, 1842), in which he amply atoned for the deficiencies of his earlier *Archisynagogus.* He also

wrote *Hypotyposis historiæ et chronologiæ sacræ* (Leeuwarden, 1698; enlarged ed., Franeker, 1708); and *Geographia sacra,* the latter unskilfully edited by D. G. Werner (Jena, 1723).

Vitringa wrote also on Biblical theology, dogmatics, and polemics. Here belongs his *Doctrina Christianæ religionis per aphorismos summatim descripta* (Franeker, 1690), to which, after the fourth edition (1702), was appended his *Hypotyposis theologiæ elencticæ graviores exhibens controversias quæ super Christianæ religionis doctrina ecclesiæ reformatæ cum diversis ejusdem sectis intercedunt.* Against Roell, who defended a sort of tritheism, Vitringa wrote his *Geloove der kercke angaande de geboorte des Sons ende de tydelicke Dood der geloovige* (Franeker, 1695); and he was also the author of *Typus doctrinæ propheticæ in quo de prophetis et prophetiis agitur hujusque scientiæ præcepta traduntur* (appended to the *Hypotyposis historiæ et chronologiæ sacræ* after 1708); *Typus theologiæ practicæ sive de vita spirituali ejusque affectionibus* (Franeker, 1716; setting forth the right imitation of Christ); and the Dutch "Meditations on the Miracles of Jesus Christ" (Franeker, 1725), in which the fulfilment of the types and prophecies contained in the miracles of Christ is sought in the history of the Church. In the domain of practical theology his principal work was *Animadversiones ad methodum homiliarum ecclesiasticarum rite instituendarum* (Leeuwarden, 1721).

Two of Vitringa's sons also lived to write on theology. **Horatius,** though dying at the age of nineteen (Oct. 8, 1704), was the author of *Animadversiones ad Johannem Vorstium de Hebraismis Novi Testamenti* (ed. L. Bos, in his *Observationes miscellaneæ,* Franeker, 1707); and **Campegius** (b. at Franeker Mar. 23, 1693; d. there Jan. 11, 1723; professor of theology at Franeker after 1715) wrote an *Epitome theologiæ naturalis* and *Dissertationes sacræ,* both of which were edited after their author's death by H. Venema (Franeker, 1731).

(E. KAUTZSCH†.)

BIBLIOGRAPHY: The funeral oration by A. Schultens, printed in the Basel edition of the commentary on Isaiah, and the brief *Vita* by T. de Hase, printed in the Jena ed. of the *Observationes sacræ,* formed the material included in Niceron, *Mémoires,* xxxv. 30 sqq. Other editions of the commentary on Isaiah contain the results of the working over of this material, with corrections. Consult also L. Diestel, *Geschichte des A. T. in der christlichen Kirche,* pp. 436 sqq., Jena, 1869.

VITUS, SAINT: See HELPERS IN NEED.

VIVEKANANDA, vî″ve-ka-nān′da, **SWAMI:** Vedantist; b. at Calcutta Jan. 21, 1863; d. at Belur (near Calcutta) July 4, 1902. He was educated at the university of his native city, where he also studied law, and, after teaching for a short time in a private college in Calcutta, renounced the world to become a teacher of the Vedanta. In 1893 he left India for the United States as a delegate to the Parliament of Religions at the World's Fair at Chicago, and in the following year he founded the Vedanta Society in New York City. He lectured before this organization and its branches until 1900, when he returned to India to supervise the education of the monks in the monastery of Belur, training them as teachers of the Vedanta. He issued *Karma*

Yoga (New York, 1896); Vedanta Philosophy (addresses at Harvard; 1896); Raja Yoga (London, 1896); From Colombo to Almora (Madras, 1897); My Master (biography of Ramakrishna; New York, 1901); Jnana Yoga (1902); besides the posthumous volume of selections from his speeches and writings (Madras, 1905); Inspired Talks, Recorded by a Disciple (New York, 1909); The Science and Philosophy of Religion; a comparative Study of Sankhya Vedanta and other Systems (1909); and The East and the West (Madras, 1909). A memorial edition of his Complete Works is in course of publication (London, 1907 sqq.).

BIBLIOGRAPHY: A Short Account of the Life and Teachings of the Swami Vivekananda (Dacca, 1904); Mary E. Noble (" Sister Vivedita "), The Master as I saw him; being Passages from the Life of the Swami Vivekananda, New York, 1910.

VIVÉS Y TUTO, vi'ves-î-tū'tō, JOSÉ CALASANTIO: Cardinal; b. at San André da Llevaneras (a village in the diocese of Barcelona), Spain, Feb. 15, 1854. At the age of fifteen he entered the Capuchin order in Guatemala, and for many years labored in North and South America, as well as in France and Spain. In 1896 he became definitor-general of the Capuchins, and in 1899 was created cardinal-deacon of San Adriano al Foro. He is prefect of the Congregation for the Affairs of Religious.

VOCATION. See CALLING.

VOELTER, fel'ter, DANIEL ERHARD JOHANNES: German theologian; b. at Usslingen (7 m. e.s.e. of Stuttgart), Württemberg, Sept. 14, 1855. He was educated at the universities of Tübingen, Göttingen, and Berlin (Ph.D., Tübingen, 1882), and was connected with the University of Tübingen as lecturer in the theological seminary (1880–84) and as privat-docent (1884–85); since 1886 he has been professor of the New Testament at the Evangelical Lutheran Seminary and the University of Amsterdam. He has written Die Entstehung der Apokalypse (Freiburg, 1882); Der Ursprung des Donatismus (1883); Die Ignatianischen Briefe (Tübingen, 1892); Das Problem der Apokalypse (Freiburg, 1893); Petrusevangelium oder Aegypterevangelium ? (Tübingen, 1893); Die Visionen des Hermas (1900); Der Ursprung des Mönchtums (1900); Aegypten und die Bibel (Leyden, 1903); Die Offenbarung Johannis neu untersucht und erläutert (Strasburg, 1904); Die apostolischen Väter, i.–ii. (Leyden, 1904–10); Paulus und seine Briefe (Strasburg, 1905); Der erste Petrusbrief, seine Entstehung und Stellung in der Geschichte des Urchristentums (1906); Mater Dolorosa und der Lieblingsjünger des Johannesevangelium (1907); Das messianische Bewusstsein Jesu (1907); Die Entstehung des Glaubens an die Auferstehung Jesu (Strasburg, 1910); and Die evangelische Erzählung von der Geburt und Kindheit Jesu (1911).

VOETIUS, vō-î'shi-us, GISBERTUS (GIJSBERT VOET): Dutch Reformed; b. at Heusden (25 m. s. of Utrecht) Mar. 3, 1589; d. at Utrecht Nov. 1, 1676. He was educated at the University of Leyden (1604–11), and in 1611 was made pastor of the village of Vlijmen; in 1617 he accepted the position of minister in his native town, where he preached eight times a week, devoted himself to the study of Arabic, and was privat-docent in various branches of theology, logic, physics, metaphysics, and oriental languages. In 1618 he was a delegate to the Synod of Dort, where he exercised a strong influence against the Remonstrants. For a time he preached also at Gouda against the Arminianism which had there taken root, and when, in 1630, the Roman Catholic stronghold of Bois-le-Duc was wrested from the Spanish, he eagerly devoted himself to promoting the Reformed cause there. In 1634 he accepted the professorship of theology and oriental languages at the newly founded academy of Utrecht, where he passed the remainder of his life. In 1637 he served also as pastor of the Utrecht congregation. He had already written, while still at Heusden, his Proeve van de cracht der godtsalicheyt (Amsterdam, 1628) against Daniel Tilenus, formerly professor of theology at Sedan. In all his teaching he laid no less stress on orthodoxy of belief than on uprightness of life. His vast learning excited admiration, and his zeal for knowledge was insatiable. He lectured on theology, Hebrew, Arabic, and Syriac, and urged his students to hold meetings for personal devotion. Throughout his life he was a bitter and uncompromising foe of Arminianism; as professor at Utrecht he continued his attacks in his lectures and disputations, as well as in his Thersites heautontimorumenos (Utrecht, 1635) and Catechisatie over den catechismus der Remonstranten (1641). His exegesis was designed simply to give a philological demonstration of the truth of the accepted doctrine of his church rather than the religious and Christian truths taught in the Bible. He was inferior as an exegete, and his dogmatics bore an essentially scholastic character. These traits appear strongly in his Selectæ disputationes theologicæ (5 vols, Utrecht, 1648–69; selected disputations ed. A. Kuyper, Amsterdam, 1887). The least deviation from rigid Calvinism was inadmissible in his opinion, and his tendency was, accordingly, prevailingly polemic. He was as Calvinistic in his theory of the relations of Church and State as in his theology, and constantly opposed all forms of patronage, maintaining that the Church should be entirely independent of the State, views set forth in his Politica ecclesiastica (3 vols., Amsterdam, 1663–76; selected treatises ed. F. L. Rutgers and P. J. Hoedemaker [2 parts, Amsterdam, 1885–86]). A bitter enemy of the Roman Catholic Church, as evinced in his Desperata causa papatus (Amsterdam, 1635), written against the Louvain Professor Cornelius Jansenius, bishop of Ypern after 1636, Voetius became involved in a long controversy with Maresius over a question of toleration (cf. his Specimen assertionum partim ambiguarum aut lubricarum, partim periculosarum [Utrecht, 1642]). Both antagonists, however, united against a common foe, Johannes Cocceius (q.v.). The more liberal tendencies of Cocceius, combined with an exegesis of greater independence and a relative depreciation of practical Christianity, aroused the wrath of Voetius. The resulting controversy racked the Dutch Reformed Church till long after the death of the two protagonists, when a truce was patched up between the factions, so that at Amsterdam, for example, a system of rotation was adopted whereby an adherent of Voetius should first be made pastor, then a follower of Cocceius.

A controversy of exceptional bitterness was waged by Voetius against the Cartesian philosophy, which he deemed incompatible with Reformed theology. He had kept silent while Henricus Renerius, professor of philosophy at Utrecht from 1637 to 1639, had adopted the Cartesian method in all his lectures; but his wrath became public when a like course was pursued by Renerius' successor, Henricus Regius (De Roy). Voetius was able to compel Regius to cease lecturing on philosophy, and secured a majority vote from the Utrecht faculty forbidding the use of the new system of philosophy in instruction. He himself polemized against Descartes, and had Martinus Schoock, professor of logic and physics at Groningen, prepare an attack entitled *Admiranda methodus novæ philosophiæ Renati des Cartes* (Utrecht, 1643). Descartes replied in the *Epistola ad celeberrimum virum Gisbertum Voetium* (Amsterdam, 1643), whereupon Voetius continued his attacks, at the same time denying connection with the polemic ostensibly written by Schoock. He was even able to have Descartes condemned by the magistracy of Utrecht as a slanderer and circulator of libelous writings. When, however, the matter was taken up officially by the academic senate at Groningen, Schoock revealed Voetius' complicity in the *Admiranda methodus*. Utrecht was ordered to make amends to the philosopher, and the printing, publishing, and selling of all writings for or against Descartes were forbidden on June 2, 1645, though Voetius still continued his attacks on this " fanatic and fantastic philosophy." Less explicable was the struggle with Jean de Labadie (q.v.), which occupied the closing decades of Voetius' life. He had originally been the friend of Labadie, and had been instrumental in securing his call from Geneva to Middelburg in Zealand, besides encouraging his efforts to inject new life into the dry orthodoxy of the Dutch Reformed. When, however, the activity of Labadie assumed a separatistic tendency, Voetius became his opponent. A disputation *De ecclesiarum separatarum unione et syncretismo* (Amsterdam, 1669), defended under his auspices, dealt a severe blow to Labadie, and the breach widened continually.

Unlike Cocceius, Voetius founded no school in the strict sense of the term. His true importance lay in the practical nature of his theology and in his encyclopedic theological learning. In addition to the works already mentioned, his chief productions were: *Exercitia pietatis* (Gorinchem, 1644); the anonymous *Erpenii bibliotheca Arabica cum augmenta* (Utrecht, 1667); *Diatribe de theologia* (1668); and especially his *Exercitia et bibliotheca studiosi theologiæ* (1644), the last an outline of a four-years' course in theology of impracticable difficulty. A portion of his correspondence has also been edited by A. C. Duker under the title *Eenige onuitgegeven brieven van en aan Voetius* (The Hague, 1893). (S. D. VAN VEEN.)

BIBLIOGRAPHY: The funeral orations by C. Gentman and A. Essenius were published at Utrecht, 1677. Consult: C. Burman, *Trajectum Eruditum*, pp. 396–397, Utrecht, 1738; A. Ijpeij (Ypey), *Geschiedenis van de kristlijke Kerk in de achstiende Euw*, viii. 122 sqq., 12 parts, Utrecht, 1797–1811; M. Goebel, *Geschichte des christlichen Lebens in der rheinisch-westphalischen . . . Kirche*, vol. ii., 3 vols., Coblenz, 1849–60; A. C. Duker, *Schoolgezag en eigen Onderzoek*, Leyden, 1861; idem, *Gisbertus Voetius*, 2 vols., ib. 1897–1907, new ed., 1910; G. H. Lamers, in *Stemmen voor Waarheid in Vrede*, 1879, i. 607–624.

VOGEL, fō′gel, KARL ALBRECHT VON: German Lutheran; b. at Dresden Mar. 10, 1822; d. at Vienna Sept. 11, 1890. Completing his education at Leipsic in 1844, he taught for two years at Dresden, and then studied for a semester at Berlin, after which he returned to Dresden, teaching there for another two years, besides being tutor to Prince Theodore of Thurn and Taxis; he studied again at Jena in 1848, and a final year at Berlin, becoming in 1850 privat-docent at Jena. Four years later appeared his chief work, *Ratherius von Verona und das zehnte Jahrhundert* (2 vols., Jena, 1854), which gained him in 1856 the appointment of associate professor, when he lectured on church history and on the New Testament; in 1861 he became professor of New-Testament exegesis in the Protestant theological faculty at Vienna, where, however, relations were less satisfactory than he had hoped. As a delegate of the faculty he was present at the jubilee of the University of Bonn in 1868, and in 1871 and 1877 he attended the general synods, and was otherwise active in church work. In 1871 he was dean of his faculty, and in his closing years (1887–90) was president of the board of examiners for Protestant theological candidates.

Vogel found his chief delight in works of practical piety. For a time he was interested in the thankless task of Jewish missions in Vienna, and after 1883 was active in conducting a Sunday-school founded by his wife at their home. He was also chairman for a time of the Lower Austrian section of the Gustavus Adolphus association, and established the women's branch of this organization, introducing deaconesses into the Austrian capital. Besides the work already mentioned, and a collection of sermons (Weimar, 1859), mention may be made of his *Peter Damiani* (Gotha, 1856); *Der Kaiser Diokletian* (1857); and *Beiträge zur Herstellung der alten lateinischen Bibelübersetzung* (1868).

(GEORG LOESCHE.)

BIBLIOGRAPHY: J. Günther, *Lebensskizzen der Professoren der Universität Jena*, p. 46, Jena, 1858; the funeral oration by A. Formey, Vienna, 1890; *Evangelische Kirchenzeitung für Oesterreich*, 1890, pp. 312–313; *ADB*, xl. 94.

VOGTHERR, fōt′har, GEORG: German Reformer; b. at Hall (35 m. n.e. of Stuttgart) Mar. 11, 1487; d. at Feuchtwangen (26 m. e. of Hall) Jan. 18, 1539. In 1517 he became vicar at the collegiate church in Feuchtwangen, where he was the only one of the staff who dared to remain when the Peasants' War raged in the vicinity of the city in 1525. In the following year he was deprived of his benefices for his maintenance of Protestant teachings, and was forced to support himself by manual labor and as a notary. When, in 1528, Margrave George the Pious introduced Protestantism in his principalities of Brandenburg, Ansbach, and Brandenburg-Kulmbach, Vogtherr was appointed to the collegiate staff in Feuchtwangen, where he became municipal pastor and superintendent in 1535.

(F. VOGTHERR.)

BIBLIOGRAPHY: C. F. Jacobi, *Geschichte der Stadt und des . . . Stifts Feuchtwangen*, Nuremberg, 1833; A. Steichele, *Das Bistum Augsburg*, iii. 381 sqq., Augsburg, 1872; K. Schornbaum, *Stellung des Markgrafen Kasimir von Brandenburg zur reformatorischen Bewegung*, passim, Nuremberg, 1900; F. Vogtherr, *Geschichte der Familie Vogtherr*, pp. 23–43, Ansbach, 1908.

VOGTHERR, HEINRICH: Younger brother of the preceding and one of the first artists to devote his talents to the Reformation; b. at Hall (35 m. n.e. of Stuttgart) in 1490; d. at Vienna in 1556. By 1522 he was an artist at Wimpfen on the Neckar, where he published, under the pseudonym of Henricus Satrapitanus Pictor, two devotional Protestant tracts in 1523 and a pamphlet in 1524. In 1525 he removed to Strasburg, and by 1527 had written five hymns which enjoyed wide and continued popularity (reprinted by P. Wackernagel, *Geschichte des deutschen Kirchenliedes*, iii. 504–509, Leipsic, 1870). After 1527 he devoted himself to art, especially religious and ecclesiastical woodcuts. To him are doubtless to be ascribed the pictures in J. B. Levit's edition of the New Testament (Strasburg, 1527) and in Luther's version of the Old Testament published at Strasburg and Durlach in 1529–32. His " Redeemer " and the woodcut " Temptation of the feeble-minded " have also been preserved. His most important production was his purely secular *Kunstbüchlein*, written in collaboration with his son of the same name (1538). Vogtherr in 1539 resumed his poetic activity with a *Christliches Lossbuch nach ordnung eines Alfabets*. Being not only an artist and poet, but also a skilful oculist, Vogtherr was called to the court of Charles V. at Vienna in 1550 as court painter and court oculist. These positions he retained until his death.

(F. VOGTHERR.)

BIBLIOGRAPHY: G. H. A. Rittelmeyer, *Die evangelischen Kirchenliederdichter des Elsasses*, pp. 26–27, Jena, 1855; K. Goedeke, *Grundriss zur Geschichte der deutschen Dichtung*, ii. 157, 173, 369, 1161, Dresden, 1862; J. D. Passavant, *Le Peintre-Graveur*, iii. 285–286, 344 sqq., Leipsic, 1862; P. Wackernagel, *Das deutsche Kirchenlied*, iii. 556 sqq., 5 vols., Leipsic, 1864–77; F. Vogtherr, *Geschichte der Familie Vogtherr*, pp. 60–82, Ansbach, 1908; *ADB*, xl. 192–193.

VOIGT, ANDREW GEORGE: Lutheran; b. at Philadelphia Jan. 22, 1859. He studied at the University of Pennsylvania (B.A., 1880), the Lutheran Theological Seminary, Mt. Airy, 1880–82, and the University of Erlangen, 1882–83; was pastor at Mt. Holly, N. J., 1883–85, and at Wilmington, N. C., 1898–1903; professor of theology in Newberry College, S. C., 1885–89 and 1891–98, and at Thiel College, Pa., 1889–91, and professor of theology and dean at the Lutheran Theological Seminary, Mt. Pleasant, S. C., since 1903. He became president of the United Synod of the Evangelical Lutheran Church in 1906. He has contributed the commentary on Ephesians to *The Lutheran Commentary* (New York, 1896), and has written *Why We are Lutherans* (1896).

VOIGT, HEINRICH CARL GISBERT AUGUST: German Protestant; b. at Stade (23 m. w. of Hamburg), Prussia, June 29, 1860. He was educated at the universities of Königsberg, Leipsic, and Berlin (1878–81), and held various pastorates (1883–94); became privat-docent at Berlin, 1892; associate professor of church history at Königsberg (1894);

the same at Kiel (1899); and at Halle (1901). Among his writings are: *Eine verschollene Urkunde des antimontanistischen Kampfes: die Berichte des Epiphanius über die Kataphryger und Quintillianer untersucht* (Leipsic, 1891); *Adalbert von Prag* (Berlin, 1898); *Der Verfasser der römischen Vita des heiligen Adalbert* (Prague, 1904); *Die ältesten Berichte über die Auferstehung Jesu Christi* (Stuttgart, 1906); *Brun von Querfurt* (1907); *Die christliche Kirche des Mittelalters an der deutschen Seeküste* (1907); and *Die Geschichte Jesu und die Astrologie* (1911). He was also editor of the *Altpreussische Monatsschrift* (1901–08).

VOIGT, HEINRICH JOHANN MATTHIAS: German Protestant; b. at Oldenburg Aug. 2, 1821; d. at Charlottenburg (a suburb of Berlin) June 19, 1892. He studied at Halle, Berlin, and Göttingen; became rector in Delmenhorst, then pastor at Stade, 1855; and in 1864 ordinary professor of theology at Königsberg. He was the author of *Die Lehre des Athanasius von Alexandrien* (Bremen, 1861); and *Fundamentaldogmatik*, Gotha, 1874.

VOLCK, fölk, JOHANN CHRISTOPH WILHELM: German Lutheran; b. at Nuremberg Nov. 18, 1835; d. at Rostock May 29, 1904. He was educated at the universities of Erlangen (Ph.D., 1859) and Leipsic, and in 1860 became privat-docent in the theological faculty of the former institution. In 1862 he was called as associate professor to Dorpat, where he was promoted to a full professorship in the following year. He remained there thirty-six years, exercising an important influence on Livonian Lutheranism not only as a teacher but also by practical work, by his membership in the synods, and by establishing a German gymnasium, as well as by striving to prevent the Russification of the university. Lecturing on Semitic philology as well as on theology, Volck continued the course laid down in his doctor's dissertation, *Calendarium Syriacum auctore Cazwinio* (Leipsic, 1859), by an edition of Ibn Mālik's *Lāmiyat al-af'āl* (2 vols., 1864–66). In theology he had already written *Mosis canticum cygneum denuo illustratum* (Nördlingen, 1861), and *Vindiciæ Danielicæ* (Dorpat, 1866), in which he maintained that Daniel was prior to Zechariah; he now wrote his first large work, *Der Chiliasmus seiner neuesten Bekämpfung gegenüber* (Dorpat, 1869). To this same period belongs his *De summa carminis Jobi sententia* (1869); a vigorous defense of Deut. xxxiii. in his *Der Segen Moses* (Erlangen, 1873); *Ueber die Bedeutung der semitischen Philologie für die alttestamentliche Exegese* (Dorpat, 1874); *Zur Erinnerung an J. C. K. v. Hofmann* (Erlangen, 1878); *Ueber den Charakter semitischen Völker und ihre Stellung in der Welt- und Kulturgeschichte* (Dorpat, 1884); *De nonnullis locis Veteris Testamenti ad sacrificia spectantibus* (1884); *Inwieweit ist der Bibel Irrtumslosigkeit zuzuschreiben?* (1885); *Die Bibel als Canon* (1885); and *Zur Lehre von der heiligen Schrift* (1885). The study on the inerrancy of the Bible, though thoroughly orthodox, produced great excitement in the Baltic Church, and was important for the development of the position of the Livonian Lutherans. Volck collaborated with B. Oettli in preparing the poetic hagiographa for O.

Zöckler's *Kurzgefasster Kommentar* (Munich, 1889); supervised the eighth, ninth, and tenth editions of Gesenius' lexicon of the Old Testament (Leipsic, 1878–86); edited J. C. K. von Hofmann's *Die heilige Schrift Neuen Testaments* (3 parts, Nördlingen, 1881–86) and the theological correspondence of F. Delitzsch and Von Hofmann (Leipsic, 1893). During his later years at Dorpat he also wrote *Was lernen wir aus der Geschichte der Auslegung der heiligen Schrift?* (Dorpat, 1894); *Heilige Schrift und Kritik* (Erlangen, 1897); and *Die Urgeschichte nach Gen. 1–11* (Barmen, 1897).

In 1898, in accordance with the university statutes, Volck was retired. He accepted an honorary professorship at Greifswald, but was called to Rostock in 1900, where he labored until his death. To this final period belong his *Alttestamentliche Heilsgeschichte* (Gütersloh, 1902); *Zum Kampf um Bibel und Babel* (Rostock, 1903); and the posthumous *Lebens- und Zeitfragen im Lichte der Bibel* (ed. Hunzinger, Wismar, 1906).

The theological position of Volck remained essentially the same throughout his life. He was antagonistic to the Wellhausen school while in sympathy with honest and unprejudiced historical criticism of the Old Testament. He regarded the Bible as an organic whole from beginning to end, held together by the bond of the divine outworking of the plan of salvation, and attested by its influence on the history of the Church and on the personal religious life of the faithful. (J. Köberle†.)

Bibliography: *Zum Gedächtnis an Prof. Dr. Wilhelm Volck*, Leipsic, 1904.

VOLF, völf, PETER RUDOLF: Danish clergyman; b. at Naur (162 m. n.w. of Copenhagen) Aug. 25, 1838. He was graduated from the gymnasium in Odense, 1857, and from the University of Copenhagen, 1864. As a student he was attracted to Semitic philology and was awarded, in 1861, an " Accessit " for a prize essay in this branch. It was also in his student days that he perceived the necessity of energetic missionary work in the large, partly dechristianized cities. The keynote in his scientific career became Old-Testament research; in his practical work, home missions. In 1859 he traveled in England, and in the year following published a translation from the works of the Scotch Free Church theologian Thomas Guthrie (q.v.): *Hovedstaden, dens Synder og Sorger*. After teaching some years in the Danish School for Missions, he was chaplain in Ballerup-Maalev, 1867–70; and in Farum-Värlöse, 1870–74. But his greatest labors are connected with the Church of St. Stephen in Copenhagen, whose pastor he was, 1874–99. He gained the confidence of the poor and was instrumental in calling forth many congregational activities, up to that time little known in Copenhagen—the parish mission, Princess Thyras Asylum, the Martha Society, and the " Carmel " hall for home missions. He was member of the board for home missions, 1878–99, and for a long time its president.

During these years of practical activity he was not, however, forgetful of theology proper. In 1875 he was made Lic. theol., having presented his thesis on the " Integrity of the Book of Zechariah." He subsequently lectured for some semesters at the Uni-

versity of Copenhagen, and was member of the censor committee on examination of candidates for the theological degree. In 1888 he was given by the University of Rostock the degree of Th.D. for the dissertation *Die 70. Wochen Daniels*. He wrote a learned commentary on Zechariah, and popular expositions of Isaiah, Hosea, and Joel (1902). He is author also of *Indre Missions Historie* (1870); and of biographies of Johann Heinrich Wichern and Johann Albrecht Bengel (1904). His attitude to civil marriage and marriage of the divorced, both much-discussed questions in State churches, as well as his conception of a church are made known in his *Ægtesskabsskilsmisse og fraskiltes Vielse* (1885); *Tör Kirken önske borgerlig Ægteforening* (1902); and *Folkekirken, dens Begreb, Opgave og Forfatning i korte Hovedtræk* (1901). Since 1899 he has been provost in Storehedinge. John O. Evjen.

Bibliography: C. F. Bricka, *Dansk biographisk Lexikon*, xix. 154–155, 19 vols., Copenhagen, 1887–1905.

VOLIVA, WILBUR GLENN: Christian Catholic Apostolic; b. near Newtown, Fountain Co., Ind., Mar. 10, 1870. He was educated at Hiram College, Hiram, O., at Union Christian College, Merom, Ind. (B.D., 1897), and later studied theology privately at Stanfordville, N. Y. (1893–94). He was ordained to the ministry in the Christian Connection (New Light) denomination in 1889, and held pastorates at Linden, Ind. (1889–92), and Urbana, Ill. (1892–93), after which he was supply in Albany, N. Y. (1893–1894), and York Harbor, Me. (1894–95). He united with the Christian (Campbellite) Church in 1895, and was pastor of the Christian church at Washington Court House, O., in 1897–99, but in the latter year joined the Christian Catholic Apostolic Church in Zion, and was elder in charge of North Side Zion Tabernacle, Chicago (1899–1900), whence he was transferred to Cincinnati (1900–01). In 1901–06 he was overseer of the work of his denomination in Australia, but in the latter year returned to Zion City, Ill., as assistant to J. A. Dowie (q.v.), on whose death, in 1907, he became general overseer of the Christian Catholic Apostolic Church.

VOLNEY, CONSTANTIN-FRANCOIS CHASSEBŒUF, COMTE DE: French historian; b. at Craon (168 m. s.w. of Paris) Feb. 3, 1757; d. at Paris Apr. 25, 1820. After several years' traveling in the East he wrote his *Voyage en Egypte et en Syrie* (2 vols., Paris, 1787; Eng. transl., *Travels through Syria and Egypt in 1783, 1784, and 1785*, 2 vols., London, 1787, also 1788, and New York, 1798), which earned a great reputation for him; and in 1794 he was made professor of history in the normal school of Paris. As a man of the Revolution, he became a senator in 1794, but was accused of royalism and imprisoned under Robespierre, whom he opposed. His life was saved by the ending of the Revolution. Later, as an adversary of Napoleon, he was made a peer of France in 1814. In literature he is known also as the author of a number of antichristian or antireligious writings: *Les Ruines* (Paris, 1791, often reprinted, and translated into several foreign languages; into English, *The Ruins: or, a Survey of the Revolutions of Empires*, London, 1795, and often,

New York, 1796), a work which called forth many replies; *La Loi naturelle* (1793; Eng. transl., *The Law of Nature, or Principles of Morality Deduced from the Physical Constitution of Mankind and the Universe,* Philadelphia and London, 1796); and *Histoire de Samuel, inventeur du sacre des rois* (4th ed., 1822). His *Œuvres complètes* in 8 vols. appeared Paris, 1821, and *Œuvres choisies* in 6 vols., in 1827.

BIBLIOGRAPHY: *Brief Sketch of the Life of C. F. Volney,* London, 1840; Lichtenberger, *ESR,* xii. 419–420.

VOLTAIRE, vōl"tar', **FRANÇOIS MARIE AROUET DE:** French writer and deist; b. in Paris Nov. 21, 1694; d. there May 30, 1778. He was educated by the Jesuits in Collège Louis-le-Grand in Paris, where he learnt " nothing but Latin and nonsense." His father intended him for the law, but his natural talent, no less than the levity of his disposition, drew him with irresistible

Earlier Life. force into literary life—the theater, the pamphlet, the salons, where the efforts were short, and the triumphs rapid. He had wit, taste, a wonderful talent for turning everything into verse, and a still more wonderful talent for dropping innuendoes, malicious or lewd, according to circumstances. He wrote small poems, satirical or complimentary, and said smart things at the supper-tables of dukes and abbés. In 1713 he obtained a diplomatic position as secretary to the French ambassador to Holland. But at The Hague he was most ridiculously taken in by a lady of semi-standing—a certain Madame du Noyer, whose daughter he fell in love with and tried to allure into an elopement. He was discharged, and sent back to Paris; and Madame du Noyer repaid herself for her troubles by publishing his love-letters. In 1714 he competed for the prize of the academy, but failed to obtain it. In 1716 some vicious lampoons on the regent and the Duchess of Berri were generally ascribed to him, and brought him to the Bastile, where, in the study of Homer and Vergil, and the preparation of his first tragedy, *Œdipe,* he spent eleven months. Soon after his release, the tragedy was brought on the stage with great success; and the success was followed up with still greater energy. The *Henriade,* a large epic on Henry IV., which he had begun in the Bastile, he printed, though he had not succeeded in obtaining the approbation of the royal censor, and it at once made his fame and his fortune. But Voltaire's ambition was always a little ahead of his powers: *Artémise* failed completely; *Mariamne,* partially. The Chevalier de Rohan, in order to avenge himself for some insolent repartee, had him beaten in the street by his footmen. Voltaire challenged him; but later was put in the Bastile, and released only on the condition that he immediately leave for England.

From 1726 to 1729 he resided in London; and acquaintance with English character and institutions, English literature and philosophy, exercised a profound influence on him. It so-

Maturity. bered his temper a little; it gave him a taste for science and its methods of research; and it developed his sense of the social value of truth. He was much struck by Newton's great discovery as expounded to him by Dr. Samuel Clark in 1726; and by the effect on the English

mind of Newton's death the following year. Later by his *Élémens de la philosophie de Newton* (1738), and *La métaphysique de Newton* (1740), he contributed much to make the views of Newton accepted, not only in France, but on the continent in general. From Locke he derived his whole psychology; from the English Deists (see DEISM), he learned how to attack the traditional, supernaturalistic, dogmatic claims of the prevailing beliefs, and he used the weapons of the Deistic writers in his onslaught upon the credulity and abuses of the Roman Catholic Church; from English history and institutions he gained his social and political ideas. There is a direct and demonstrable connection between the revolution of 1789 and his *Letters Concerning the English Nation* (London, 1733, Fr. eds. later), one of the brightest and most characteristic of his polemical writings. He also made a painstaking study of Shakespeare and Milton and the other great English writers. On his return to France in 1729, he soon found out that Paris was still unsafe for him. In 1734 his *Lettres* were publicly burnt by order of the parliament as subversive to the State, the Church, and public morality. From that time until 1749 he made his home chiefly at Cirey, in the house of Madame du Châtelet, a lady for whose mathematical and philosophical talent he felt great respect. Whatever may be said of their personal relations in other respects, she stimulated and held him up to his highest capacity for literary production. During this period he wrote some of his best tragedies—*Zaïre, Alzire, Mahomet, Mérope;* completed *Charles XII.* and began *Siècle de Louis XIV.;* and sent out a score or more of polemical pamphlets, witty, malicious, indecent to an incredible degree, and an astonishing number of letters to all the most prominent persons in Europe. At the middle of the eighteenth century he stood as the greatest literary celebrity which the European civilization had ever produced, far exceeding Erasmus both in fame and power. And when, in 1750, he set out for Berlin, on the invitation of Frederick II., it was not a pensioner threading his way to the table of his patron, but the king of the pen coming to visit the king of the sword. Voltaire and Frederick admired each other. But Voltaire admired in Frederick only the general, and Frederick wanted to be admired as a poet; while, in Voltaire, Frederick admired only the poet, and Voltaire wanted to be admired as a statesman. Ludicrous conflicts arose, almost from the hour of their first meeting; and soon the conflicts grew into a continuous warfare. At last in 1752 the climax was reached when, under an assumed name, Voltaire held up to ridicule the president of the Berlin Academy. In March of the following year he was permitted to leave the city only to be arrested, by command of the irate king, at Frankfort, where he underwent irritating humiliations, which indeed he had provoked, for which also he took ample vengeance in a scurrilous lampoon on Frederick's private life. Thus ended the strange friendship which on account of the idiosyncrasies of the two concerned contained all the elements of a comic tragedy.

The last part of his life Voltaire spent at Ferney, an estate he bought in the county of Gex (1758), conveniently situated near the Swiss frontier; and during this period some of the best features of his personal character came to light. **Later Life.** There were forty-six miserable peasants at Ferney when he bought the estate; when he died, there were 1,200 well-to-do inhabitants engaged in watch-making, silk-weaving, and other industries, and it was he who built their houses, bought their tools, and sold their productions. His defense of Jean Calas the Huguenot (see Rabaut, Paul) and protection of Sirven show a humanity and courage wholly admirable, while his unwearied endeavors to rehabilitate the names and fortunes of these and of La Barre and Count Lally add only luster to his reputation for justice and fair play. But his writings— and among them are some of his most prominent works: *Essai sur les Mœurs et l'Esprit des Nations, Dictionnaire Philosophique*—show that his polemical passion had become intensified almost to the bursting-point, that his whole mental energy had concentrated itself around the famous motto, *Écrasez l'infâme* (" crush the infamous one "), with which he ended every letter he sent to his friends. *L'infâme* meant, originally, the Roman Catholic Church, then any church which has the support of the State for the enforcement of its doctrine and discipline, and finally it came to mean all religion, so far as it claims a supernatural origin. On this point his hatred is insatiable. It pervades all his writing, from *Candide* and *Le Diner du comte de Boulinvilliers* to *La Pucelle* and *L'Orpheline de la Chine;* and in his minor pamphlets, newspaper articles, letters, it drags him not only below his dignity, but beneath decency. This was not the estimate of his own time. When he went to Paris in 1778, he was received with such enthusiasm and such ovations as the world had hardly ever seen before. But the excitement thereby produced was too much for his strength; he fell ill, took too big a dose of opium, and died in delirium.

Voltaire made his mark in literature as a poet. His *Zaïre, Mahomet,* and *Mérope* were considered the very acme of tragic art. To the public for which Voltaire wrote, tragic art was only a maze of intricate conventional rules; but he mastered those rules so completely that his audience sat enchanted, transported, and gazed upon his tragedies as upon clouds of " woven wind " floating in the sunshine. Of more solid worth are his historical works. His true merit lies in his respect for facts, for which he may very well have been indebted to Newton and Locke. For history as an organic movement with inner laws of development he had no more conception than others of his age. In part owing to him, history has since his day taken its place as essential to all liberal education. As to his philosophy, strictly speaking Voltaire was no philosopher at all. The higher methods of extracting truth he had never learned, and he was by natural disposition incapable of that sustained effort of thought without which systematic views can not be formed. Nevertheless, he is the true representative of the " Age of Reason "; and the great boast of that age was just its philosophy. Voltaire was

His Poetry and Philosophy.

not an atheist. He could sneer as heartily at the atheists as at the fanatics. His deism was partly a reaction against the corruption, cruelty, bigotry, and superstition of both Roman Catholics and Protestants in his day. As a Deist he started from the three well-known premises of Deism: God, the world, and between them no relation which can be represented under the form of divine revelation or special providence. But to Voltaire God is, because he is a necessity of thought: " if he were not, we would have to invent him." Of a personal relation between himself and God there was no trace; and, what is still worse, he did not understand that such a relation could truly exist. Of his general conception of God he often spoke with an undercurrent of cold indifference, illuminated now and then with sparks of cynicism, which, to men of strongly marked religious disposition, has made his works an abomination. His method was to attack not so much the principles as the alleged facts of Christianity, or to show the irreconcilability of one Christian notion with other necessary beliefs. He understood nothing of the deeper truths of the Gospel or the lives of its adherents. His criticism, so far as it related to the ultimate nature of Christianity, was literary, superficial, negative, and transitory. The immortality of the soul had no vital place in his thought. The world, on the contrary, was a very serious affair to Voltaire, and a thing he understood.

As a critic, he stands in the very front rank. His instinct of truth was sharp and vivid. With that instinct he combined a never equaled power of illuminating statement. In the service of his vanity, envy, and malice, and used to cover up deliberate falsehoods and lies, his wit is often shocking. But the directness, clearness, and precision of his statement of a fact or an idea has still more often made truth irresistible; and without entering into the details of his activity, his victories, and his defeats, it may be generally said that his criticism developed in modern literature a sense for that which is simple, natural, and clear. See Deism, II., § 1.

C. A. Beckwith.

Bibliography: The " Works " have been repeatedly published—30 vols., Geneva, 1768–77; 70 vols., Kehl and Paris, 1785–89; 54 vols., ib. 1800; 52 vols., with Condorcet's *Vie de Voltaire,* ib. 1877–85; they appeared in Eng. transl., 25 vols., London, 1761–65; and a splendid edition, with *Life* by Morley, was issued in 42 vols., London and New York, 1901. For full list of works by and on Voltaire consult: G. Benegesco, *Voltaire: bibliographie,* 4 vols., Paris, 1882–90. On his life and works consult: L. M. Chaudon, *Historical and Critical Memoirs of the Life and Writings of M. de Voltaire,* London, 1786; M. J. A. N. Caritat, Marquis de Condorcet, *Vie de Voltaire,* Kehl, 1789, Paris, 1822, 1895, Eng. transl., 2 vols., London, 1790; E. M. G. Lepan, *Vie politique, littéraire et morale de Voltaire,* Paris, 1817, 2d ed., 1819; Henry, Lord Brougham, *Lives of Men of Letters,* vol. iv., London, 1845; J. M. Quérard, *Ferney-Voltaire,* Paris, 1848; J. Janin, *Le Roi Voltaire,* 3d ed., Paris, 1861; M. U. Maynard, *Voltaire, sa vie et ses œuvres,* 2 vols., Paris, 1867; B. H. C. K. van der Wyck, *Voltaire,* Amsterdam, 1868; J. Morley, *Voltaire,* London, 1872, new ed., 1886; H. Beaune, *Voltaire au collège, sa famille, ses études, ses premiers amis,* Paris, 1873; E. B. Humley, *Voltaire,* Edinburgh, 1877; R. d'Argental, *Histoire complète de la vie de Voltaire,* Neuchâtel, 1878; E. Noel, *Voltaire, sa vie et ses œuvres,* Paris, 1878; G. Norga, *Voltaire, sa vie, ses œuvres,* Paris, 1878; E. de Pompery, *La Vie de Voltaire,* Paris, 1878; J. Parton, *Life of Voltaire,* 2 vols., London, 1881; G. Renard, *Vie de Voltaire,* Paris, 1883; R. Kreiten, *Voltaire,* 2d ed.,

Freiburg, 1885; V. Mahrenholtz, *Voltaire's Leben und Werke*, part 2, Oppeln, 1885; E. Champion, *Voltaire*, Paris, 1893; F. Espinasse, *Life of Voltaire*, London, 1892; E. Faguet, *Voltaire*, Paris, 1895; S. G. Tallentyre, *Life of Voltaire*, 2 vols., London, 1903, new ed., New York, 1910; J. C. Collins, *Voltaire, Montesquieu and Rousseau in England*, London, 1909.
  On his philosophy, etc., consult: E. Bersot, *La Philosophie de Voltaire*, Paris, 1848; L. L. Bungener, *Voltaire et son temps*, 2 vols., Paris, 1850, 2d ed., 1851, Eng. transl., Edinburgh, 1854; J. B. Meyer, *Voltaire und Rousseau, in ihrer socialen Bedeutung*, Berlin, 1856; A. Anot, *Études sur Voltaire*, Paris, 1864; J. Barni, *Histoire des idées morales*, pp. 211–349, Paris, 1865; D. F. Strauss, *Voltaire: sechs Vorträge*, 5th ed., Bonn, 1878, Fr. transl., Paris, 1876; H. Martin, *Voltaire et Rousseau et la philosophie du dix-huitième siècle*, Paris, 1878; Moussinot, *Voltaire et l'Église*, Neuchâtel, 1878; J. Stephen, *Horæ sabbaticæ*, 2d series, pp. 211–279, London, 1892; R. Urbach, *Voltaire's Verhältniss zu Newton und Locke*, Halle, 1900; P. Sakmann, *Voltaire's Geistesart und Gedankenwelt*, Stuttgart, 1909.

VOLUNTARY MISSIONARY SOCIETY IN AMERICA. See MISCELLANEOUS RELIGIOUS BODIES, 21.

VOLUNTARYISM: The conviction or the system which holds that churches should be supported, not by the State or other secular authority, but by the voluntary contributions of church attendants themselves. This system practically involves entire separation of Church and State, since the State, ceasing to grant endowments to the Church, to pay salaries to the clergy, and to subvention any project for distinctly religious purposes, thereby forfeits whatever claim it might allege to control or influence the Church, as by patronage, interference with liturgy, and the like. Voluntaryism thus represents the religious counterpart of civil Secularization (q.v.), but while voluntaryism may plead religious reluctance to contribute to the support of institutions which the contributor conscientiously disapproves, it would not be easy to find ethical justification for secularization in the manner in which it is usually carried out.

The principles of voluntaryism are to be seen in action wherever the Church and State are separate (cf. CHURCH AND STATE). It has become a vital interest practically only in England, where dissenters have long voiced their unwillingness to pay for the support of the established Church of England. Their objections are doubtless conscientious, and, at the other extreme, it is felt by many High-churchmen that voluntaryism would be far better for the spiritual welfare and growth of the Church of England than the present system, which presents such unedifying spectacles as appointments to high ecclesiastical position—and even to the episcopate—often from considerations that seem distinctly political, especially as those making such appointments may be dissenters, Roman Catholics, or even non-Christians; and this would also obviate such abuses as the trial of distinctly ecclesiastical cases (e.g., those involving alleged ritualism or refusal of communion to one who, in defiance of the law of the church, has gone through the form of marriage with his deceased wife's sister) by so-called ecclesiastical courts composed of laymen.

The term voluntaryism (better, " voluntarism ") is also sometimes applied, in scholastic philosophy, to that theory of the will which, derived from

Augustine (q.v.) and taught by such scholastics as Anselm of Canterbury, Bonaventura, Duns Scotus, and Henry of Ghent (qq.v.), teaches, with Anselm, that the sovereign will of God rules the world, while the nature of the will is freedom, and maintains in general the primacy of the will and its independence of thought (see SCHOLASTICISM, II., § 2, III., 3, §§ 1–2, 4, § 1; DUNS SCOTUS, § 4).

VOLUNTEERS OF AMERICA: A philanthropic, social, and Christian movement. It was inaugurated in Mar., 1896, in response to a number of requests on the part of American citizens, and was subsequently incorporated Nov. 6, 1896, under the " Membership Act " of the state of New York. It is organized in military style, having as its model the United States army, but, in conjunction with military discipline and methods of work, it possesses a thoroughly democratic form of government. Its constitution and by-laws are framed by a grand field council, which represents the minor councils of officers throughout the country annually. Though only fifteen years old, the Volunteers have representatives and branches of their benevolences and cause in almost all the principal centers of the United States. They have about forty principal homes and institutions of benevolence, many of which are Volunteer property, and are open for poor and deserving people in different sections of the country. During the year 1911, 41,905 beds have been provided for all classes of women in the Volunteer women's homes, and 7,332 persons have been received under the care of, and permanently aided by, the organization. The Volunteer commissioned workers called upon and aided in their visitation 26,308 families. This work was done primarily in the poorer sections of the large cities. In the different permanent philanthropic homes and institutions 398,304 lodgings have been given, while 413,-648 free meals were provided, and 230,622 meals were distributed to persons who paid for them, many doing so by work. In their latest undertaking, the Volunteer Hospital, located at No. 93 Gold Street, New York City, there have been 1,280 ambulance calls, 358 major operations, 7,001 days' treatment given to patients in the surgical and medical wards, 13,943 new cases treated, 19,684 old cases treated, and a total during the year of 33,627 cases of all kinds surgically and medically treated in the institution. The Volunteer Prisoners' League has embraced upward of 75,000 members since its inauguration. It has leagues in about twenty-five state prisons, and over 70 per cent of those having left the prisons are through the " Hope Halls " living reformed and honest lives. Through the fresh-air branch of the work many thousands of mothers and children have been taken from crowded cities to a change in the open air amid hills and rivers, lakes and dales. Through the regimental reports from Volunteer centers, it is calculated that 837,130 persons were gathered at the indoor services, while 2,108,534 persons were listeners in open-air stands. Through these services 4,534 persons were led to testify that they would live a new life.

In addition to the Volunteer reading-rooms, thousands of copies of Christian books are circulated in the state prisons, jails, hospitals, soldiers' and children's homes. The Volunteers also conduct sewing-classes, do hospital-nursing, have temporary financial relief departments, and provide Thanksgiving and Christmas dinners. The headquarters is at No. 34 West Twenty-eighth Street, New York City.

VORST, vōrst, KONRAD (CONRADUS VORSTIUS): Dutch Arminian; b. at Cologne July 19, 1569; d. at Tönning (47 m. e. of Kiel) Sept. 29, 1622. He studied at Düsseldorf (1583–87), and then entered the college of St. Lawrence in Cologne; he next studied for two years to prepare for a mercantile life, but in 1589 again altered his intention and studied at the University of Herborn until 1593, when he went to Heidelberg and there received the theological doctorate in 1594; in 1595 he went to Basel and Geneva, where his disputations *De sacramentis* (Basel, 1595) and *De causis salutis* (1595) gained him the offer of a position as teacher; instead, he went to Steinfurt. There his *De prædestinatione* (Steinfurt, 1597); *De sancta Trinitate* (1597); and *De persona et officio Christi* (1597) had brought upon him the suspicion of Socinianism, but in 1599 he successfully defended his orthodoxy before the theological faculty of Heidelberg. He rose to such honor in Steinfurt that in 1605 he received the additional appointments of preacher and assessor to the consistory. After the death of Arminius, he accepted, in 1610, a call to Leyden, where the Remonstrants hoped to find in him one of their chief supporters. He reprinted in 1610 his *Disputationes decem de natura et attributis Dei* (Steinfurt, 1602) as *Tractatus theologicus de Deo sive de natura et attributis Dei*, and in the same year published his *Anti-Bellarminus* (1610). His statements in the *Tractatus* on God, the divine attributes, predestination, and Christ led the contra-Remonstrants to accuse him of Socinianism and gross heterodoxy. The Heidelberg theologians condemned the book, whereupon Vorst replied in his *Protestatio epistolica contra theologorum Heidelbergensium* (The Hague, 1610). His opponents won over James I. of England, who caused Vorst's book to be burned in London, Oxford, and Cambridge, and informed the States-General, through his Ambassador Rudolph Winwood, that he would consider them his enemies if they tolerated the presence of such a heretic. Vorst wrote in reply his *Christiana ac modesta responsio ad articulos quosdam nuper ex Anglia transmissos* (Leyden, 1611), but the States-General were obliged to dismiss him, though continuing his salary, whereupon he settled as an exile in Gouda, about May, 1612. In the previous year he had seriously injured himself by reediting Socinus' *De auctoritate sanctæ scripturæ*, though he later claimed to have been ignorant of the authorship of the work.

Attacks on Vorst continued without intermission and Vorst pleaded his cause with bitter intensity in a series of polemics, especially *Catalogus errorum sive hallucinationum D. Sibr. Lubberti* (Steinfurt, 1611); *Prodromus plenioris responsi suo tempore secuturi ad declarationem Sibrandi Lubberti et ministrorum Leovardensium iteratam cautionem* (Leyden, 1612); *Responsum plenius ad scripta quædam eristica* (1612); and *Parænesis ad Sibrandum Lubbertum* (Gouda, 1613). Finally, in 1619, he was condemned as a heretic by the Synod of Dort and banished. He accordingly fled from Gouda and remained in hiding, chiefly in or near Utrecht, until 1622, when refuge was afforded him by the duke of Holstein. Shortly before his death he is reported to have drawn up a confession of faith in which he openly professed Socinianism.

Vorst was the author of over forty works, and after his death his Dutch friends published his commentary on the Pauline epistles (Amsterdam, 1631). His son **Willem Hendrijk** (d. Oct. 1, 1652), who was deeply versed in Rabbinical literature, was Remonstrant preacher at Leyden after 1642, and was also suspected of Socinianism. Another son, **Guernerus,** was also a Remonstrant preacher at Doccum in 1632, but was banished for five years in 1634. In the following year he returned, only to be arrested and rebanished, after which he was a preacher at Hoorn (1641), Leyden (1653), and Rotterdam (1658), where he became pastor emeritus in 1680 (d. Mar., 1682). He edited his father's *Doodsteek der calvinistische prædestinatie.* Descendants of Vorst were preachers in Dutch Remonstrant churches as late as 1716.   (S. D. VAN VEEN.)

BIBLIOGRAPHY: The oration of M. Walther was published at Fredirickstein, 1624. Consult: B. Glasius, *Godgeleerd Nederland,* iii. 550–557, 's Hertogenbosch, 1856; A. Schweizer, in *Theologische Jahrbücher,* 1856–57; C. Sepp, *Het godgeleerd Onderwijs in Nederland,* i. 181–214, Leyden, 1873; H. C. Rogge, in *De Gids,* 1873, vol. ii.; J. Reitsma, *Honderd Jaren uit de geschiedenis der Hervorming en der Hervormde Kerk in Friesland,* pp. 342–362, Leeuwarden, 1876; Bayle, *Dictionary,* v. 507–514.

VOSS, GERARD JAN: Dutch humanist and theologian; b. near Heidelberg in the spring of 1577; d. at Amsterdam Mar. 17, 1649. He was educated at the universities of Dort and Leyden (1595–98), where he wrote his first work, *Oratio panegyrica de felici expeditione exercitus fœderatæ Belgicæ, ductu principis Mauritii* (Leyden, 1597). In 1599 he began to lecture at Leyden on Aristotle, but within the year was called to Dort as rector of the Latin school; in 1615 he became regent of the college of the States-General at Leyden, and seven years later professor at the university of the same city, while from 1632 until his death he was professor at the University of Amsterdam. At Dort he published, in 1606, his six books of *Institutiones oratoriæ.* At Leyden he abstained from the controversies between the Arminians and their adversaries, the Gomarists, thus drawing a storm of indignation upon himself, so that, in 1619, the curators of the university decided that both Voss and his assistant, Kaspar Barlæus, should be removed from their positions. Voss' *Theses theologicæ de variis doctrinæ Christianæ capitibus* (Leyden, 1615) and *Historiæ de controversiis quas Pelagius ejusque reliquiæ moverunt libri septem* (Amsterdam, 1618) were regarded as containing views out of harmony with those of the contra-Remonstrants, especially as Voss was known to be in sympathy with some points in the five articles of the Remonstrants. By resigning Voss escaped suspension, and the curators appointed him, in 1622, professor of oratory and chronology, transferring him to the chair of Greek three years later. In 1632 Voss accepted a call to the new university of Amsterdam, his inaugural address, *De historiæ utilitate,* following the lines laid down in his *De historicis*

Græcis libri quatuor (Leyden, 1624) and *De historicis Latinis libri tres* (1627). A complete edition of the works of Voss was published at Amsterdam in 1695–1701. As a grammarian he won distinction by his *Ludolphi Lithocomi syntaxis Latina ex recensione Vossii* (1618), which remained for more than two centuries the standard Latin grammar in Holland. In historical theology he treated the history of dogma, his chief works here being *Dissertationes tres de tribus symbolis, apostolico, Athanasiano et Constantinopolitano* (Amsterdam, 1642) and *Libri quatuor de theologia gentili et physiologia Christiana, sive de origine et progressu idololatriæ deque naturæ mirandis quibus homo adducitur ad Deum* (1642); *De baptismo disputationes viginti* (Amsterdam, 1648). His *Tractatus theologici* appeared posthumously (1701). His letters were edited by P. Colomies under the title *Vossii et clarorum virorum ad eum epistolæ* (Augsburg, 1691). His " Works " were collected in 6 vols., Amsterdam, 1695–1701.

Of the eight children of Voss who reached maturity, **Matthaeus** (b. about 1610; d. Jan. 20, 1646) was historian of the States-General of Holland and Zeeland; **Dionysius** (b. Mar. 11, 1612; d. Oct. 24, 1633) declined, in 1632, a professorship of history and rhetoric at Dorpat, and in the following year was appointed historiographer to the king of Sweden; and **Gerard** (b. 1619; d. Mar. 27, 1640) edited an excellent critical edition of Velleius Paterculus. The only son to survive his father was **Isaac** (b. 1618; d. Feb. 21, 1689), who was at first librarian at Amsterdam, and in 1648 became Greek tutor and librarian to Queen Christina of Sweden. In 1670 he went permanently to England, where he died as canon of Windsor. (S. D. VAN VEEN.)

BIBLIOGRAPHY: C. E. Jöcher, *Allgemeines Gelehrtenlexikon,* iv. 1716 sqq., Leipsic, 1751; H. Tollius, *Oratio de G. J. Vossio,* Amsterdam, 1778; J. G. de Crane, *De Vossiorum Juniorumque familia,* Franeker, 1820; M. Siegenbeek, *Geschiedenis der Leidsche Hoogeschool,* i. 108, ii. 110, Leyden, 1829–32; *Illustris Amstelodami Athenæi Memorabilia,* ed. D. J. van Lennep, pp. 79 sqq., Amsterdam, 1832; *KL,* xii. 1122–24.

VOSSIUS, vesh-i'us, GERHARD: Roman Catholic provost of Tongern, papal prothonotary; b. about the middle of the sixteenth century; d. at Liége Mar. 25, 1609. He was enabled to make researches in the libraries of Italy which resulted in the accumulation of materials on patristics. As a result he acquired great reputation by his edition and Latin translation of the sermons of Chrysostom (Rome, 1580); an edition of part of Theodoret's Works (1585); his editions of the *Gesta et monumenta Gregorii IX.* (1586); of the works of Gregory Thaumaturgus (Mainz, 1604), and Ephraem Syrus (Rome, 1589–98), of St. Bernard's *De consideratione* (with commentary; 1594), and other patristic works. Of his personal life nothing further is known.

BIBLIOGRAPHY: J. F. Foppeus, *Bibliotheca Belgica,* i. 362, Brussels, 1739; *KL,* xii. 1122.

VOTAW, CLYDE WEBER: Congregationalist; b. at Wheaton, Ill., Feb. 6, 1864. He was educated at Amherst College (A.B., 1888), Yale Divinity School (graduated, 1891), and the University of Chicago (Ph.D., 1896); he was reader and tutor in Biblical literature in the University of Chicago (1892–96), instructor in New-Testament literature (1896–1900); assistant professor of Biblical Greek (1900–06), becoming associate professor of New-Testament literature (1906). In 1905–07 he was also acting professor of New-Testament interpretation in Chicago Theological Seminary. He is associate editor of *The Biblical World,* and has written *Inductive Studies in the Founding of the Christian Church* (Hartford, Conn., 1892); *The Use of the Infinitive in Biblical Greek* (Chicago, 1896); *Inductive Studies in the Primitive Era of Christianity* (Chicago, 1898); *The Apostolic Age* (New York, 1905); and *Best Books for Old and New Testament Study* (with J. E. McFadyen; 1909).

VOWS.

I. In the Old Testament.	Ethics of the Vow (§ 3).
II. In the Church.	Roman Catholic Doctrine (§ 4).
Basal Ideas (§ 1).	
New-Testament Indications (§ 2).	Evangelical Views (§ 5).

I. In the Old Testament: The Hebrew word for " vow," *nadar,* is probably connected with the word *nazar,* " dedicate "; for a vow of abstinence the word is *'issar.* The vow, common to the Hebrew and other religions, takes in the Old Testament two forms: (1) a gift to God for a wish granted, a danger escaped, or a difficult undertaking accomplished; or (2) a promise to abstain, until some purpose is accomplished or for some definite time, from some enjoyment or pleasure. This abstinence may be conceived as a self-applied stimulus, or it may be a voluntary sacrifice made to conciliate the deity's good will. The first form is the most common in the Old Testament. Instances are: Jacob (Gen. xxviii. 20 sqq.), Jephthah (Judges xi. 30 sqq.), Hannah (I Sam. i. 11), Absalom (II Sam. xv. 8), cf. also Ps. lxvi. 13; Job xxii. 27. For a vow of abstinence [imposed by another, the taboo] cf. I Sam. xiv. 24; Ps. cxxxii. 3 sqq. The latter has close parallels in Arabic custom and in the Koran. A vow of this sort is implicit in II Sam. xi. 9 sqq. Finally, here belongs the Naziritie vow of abstinence from drink and from trimming of the hair, again paralleled in Arabic custom and in that of other peoples.

The positive vow, as the cases show, may involve very varied issues and circumstances. The most common form is a definite offering promised for a definite benefit. In the case of Jephthah (q.v.) it was a human sacrifice [probably so in intent] for a victory over the enemy; usually it was some other object or service. The severest form of the vow was the ban (see LAW, HEBREW, CIVIL, AND CRIMINAL). Often, particularly in the Psalms, the vow of sacrifice is descriptive of the thanks of the pious for answer to prayer.

It was a natural consequence, as vows were made in the service of religion, that they should come under religious regulation, as in the Pentateuch (Lev. xxii. 17 sqq.; Num. xv. 1 sqq.; cf. Ezek. xlvi. 12; especially Lev. xxvii. and Num. xxx.). Provision was made for the redemption of the vowed object in case its use were forbidden by legislation, and that according to a definite tariff. Such cases arose from vow of house or field which in the jubilee year would ordinarily return to the original owner or his heir, and of unclean beasts or of persons. Num. xxx. provides for the nullifying, or the sanctioning by silence, by the father or husband of daughter's vow or wife's.

The making of a vow is regarded in religious law as not an absolute religious duty (cf. Deut. xxiii. 22 sqq.). But the caution is often repeated that once made it must be kept. For the making of vows that can not be performed a penalty is provided in Lev. v. 4 sqq., but cf. Eccles. v. 4 sqq. The New Testament did not reach a high ethical standard in the matter (but cf. Matt. xv. 5), since it did not consider the cases in which the paying of a vow conflicted with higher duties. Yet the case of Jephthah might have induced such consideration.

(F. Buhl.)

II. In the Church: Connected with the idea of a personal God with whom his creatures have personal relations is the conception of services and gifts which they may offer to him, and thus also of

1. Basal Ideas. religious acts by which they pledge certain services expressly to him. This is the most general notion of a religious vow (cf. the short definition of Thomas Aquinas, " A promise made to God "). In a narrower sense, the word conveys the idea of the promise of something which the promiser does not strictly owe to God, or which he is not already bound to give or perform. The impulse to make such a promise may come from the desire to show gratitude and devotion to God by offering him something of special value; or it may be thought of as a means of advancing in communion with God and in the achievement of perfection; or without such definitely religious motives, it may be offered as giving some sort of a right to receive a desired favor in exchange.

While the Old Testament (see I, above) presents vows as, under certain conditions, a natural part of a religious life, it tells nothing that is necessarily decisive for Christian ethics; nor does the New Testament contain any positive teaching on the

2. New-Testament Indications. subject. From the mouth of Christ there is only a sharp word for those who vow to the temple service that with which they should have supported their parents (Matt. xv. 4; Mark vii. 10). The epistles are silent as to vows. In Acts (xxi. 23–26) it is stated that Paul on one occasion took part in the fulfilment of a vow made by certain brethren of Hebrew birth; but the circumstances do not make it a commendation of vows as such to other Christians, since what Paul did came from loving care for the brethren, not out of any conviction of the intrinsic value of a vow. The reference to a vow in Acts xviii. 18 is obscure. In any case it was not a real Naziritic vow such as the old covenant provided for (see Nazirites), since this could be performed only at Jerusalem, but merely a private vow. It is possible, if the person in question was Paul and not, as the order of the words would suggest, Aquila, that he felt the need, amid the severe conflicts which beset him in Corinth, of devoting himself the more to God by an outward expression analogous to that of the Nazirites; but no more than this purely symbolic meaning can be deduced from it. Acts v. 1–4 can not be cited in this connection, as nothing is said of Ananias having made his offering in the form of a vow.

Views on the subject in general must therefore be formed from the universal principles of Christian ethics as contained in the New Testament and attested by the Christian conscience. The idea of a gift which the pious soul feels compelled to consecrate to God is of the very essence of Christianity. But this gift is nothing less than that of the whole person, will, and life (cf., e.g., Rom. vi. 11, 13, vii. 4; Gal. ii. 20; II Cor. v. 16). This self-dedication to God takes place at baptism, together with the reception of divine grace and the entry upon a new life. The promise made then (and at confirmation) may fairly be called a vow in the usual meaning of the word; but nothing is promised which is not already obligatory. It is justified as the formal expression of the internal impulse called forth by the appeal of redemption (I John iv. 19; Rom. viii. 14 sqq.).

The concrete individual development of the moral life leads to the conception of various special objects of solemn promise, and to that of special vows.

3. Ethics of the Vow. Two kinds of duties and promises may be distinguished: (1) the general ethical duties imposed by the community and accepted by the individual, and (2) special acts or manners of ethical conduct which the individual takes upon himself, either to make progress in the spiritual life or to express a particular sense of obligation toward God. The first class of duties are imposed both by Church and State, as well as by voluntary associations, and solemn promises are required from their members. But these (e.g., the marriage vow) hardly come within the definition, being made rather to the community than to God (see Oath). As to the second class, an examination on approved ethical principles will show that a Christian may, of his own free impulse, undertake to promise to God certain special acts or manners of life which are not of universal obligation, either divine or human. In such a course the logical limits of freedom and obligation must be preserved in their due proportion; and it is true of such promises that they are implicitly involved in the general or baptismal vow to love and serve God with all one's heart. It must be remembered also that all action is conditioned by a variety of subjective and objective circumstances which may alter from time to time. What seems now a positive duty may some day be superseded by a more pressing one, and man must then be free to follow the higher call. There may be cases in which a vow to remain unmarried should be taken by an Evangelical Christian; but if he is to make it unconditionally, he must be absolutely sure that he will never be placed in a position in which it would be better for him to be married. An unconditional vow of the sort may amount to tempting God, with no promise of a blessing in return; and the same may be said of the pledge required by total-abstinence societies. If the formal expression of the resolve becomes a burden on the conscience, it exposes the soul to an additional danger; in that case such special and formal vows will be required only seldom and under extraordinary circumstances in the life of Evangelical Christians. In most cases their place will better be taken by an earnest laying before God of the impulses of devotion, with a prayer to be kept firm in purpose. Any civil compulsion to the observance of vows should of course be excluded; in cases where one's relation to an association or to another person is confirmed in the form of a vow addressed to God, the principles which govern all contracts will naturally be enforced, while the obligation as taken in the sight of God will be left to the conscience of the individual.

* The view of Roman Catholics on this whole matter is entirely different. They distinguish from the duties to which the ordinary Christian is bound another and higher class of duties, imposed not by divine command but by an " Evangelical counsel " whose non-observance is in itself no sin, but the following of which brings a special reward and greater perfection. These counsels cover especially voluntary poverty, obedience, and celibacy, and are connected with the doctrine of works of Supererogation (q.v.). Roman Catholic theologians divide vows into personal and real, the latter concerning property, and they give to the former the higher place. Again, a vow may be for life or for a definite time. It may be solemn (publicly pronounced before the church and accepted by it, as in the case of monastic vows and of the tacit vow of celibacy made at ordination to the sub-diaconate), or simple. Older Roman Catholic theologians used to attempt to demonstrate the existence of a precedent for vows in the practise of the apostles and of the mother church at Jerusalem, especially in its community of goods. It is possible to trace back Christian vows in the sense of voluntary promises as far as the doctrine of works of supererogation can be traced; and this can not be ignored in the " Shepherd " of Hermas. The resolve, amounting to a vow, of life-long celibacy occurs first among women (as early as the Apostolic Constitutions, iii. 2 and iv.; Ignatius, *Ad Polycarpum*, v.). The history of further development is that of monasticism in general. To the doctrine of works of supererogation, on which this system of vows rests, organized Christianity adhered, and so undertook to regulate and enforce the making and observance of vows, finally drawing even simple or private vows within its jurisdiction. By present Roman Catholic practise dispensations from vows can be granted by the pope alone in five cases, in others by the bishop. The Church will not permit vows which prejudice the rights of a third person, or those made by minors without the consent of their parents. It attempts to compel observance of vows by force, especially in the case of the monastic vow, and employs the aid of the secular power when possible.

The medieval view of vows, represented most thoroughly by Thomas Aquinas, was combated even before the Reformation by Johann Pupper von Goch (q.v.) in *De libertate Christiana* (probably 1473) and *Dialogus*, maintaining that God has given but one law and proposed but one sort of perfection to all Christians. Luther took his stand on the all-embracing character of the baptismal vow, to which other vows were derogatory. Carlstadt was the first to advocate the release of monks from their vows; but Luther ended by going to the root

4. Roman Catholic Doctrine.

5. Evangelical Views.

of the matter and declaring monastic vows not merely invalid but sinful and idolatrous (cf., e.g., his *De votis monasticis*, 1522). Special vows, in the sense given in the earlier part of this article, he was willing to tolerate, though he thought little of them. The Augsburg Confession and Apology and the Schmalkald Articles (qq.v.) declared against monastic vows quite in his spirit. While Calvin placed the baptismal vow above all, and asserted Christian liberty against the Romanist conception of vows, he yet insisted on the utility of voluntary special vows, by which a Christian might at times reenforce the weakness of his will or express in a signal manner his gratitude to God. Some Lutheran theologians, such as Chemnitz and J. Gerhard, have leaned to this view much more than Luther himself; but through all their diversity in detail, modern ethical and religious teachers on the Protestant side have adhered more or less to the general line of argument briefly sketched in the beginning of this article.

(J. Köstlin†.)

BIBLIOGRAPHY: On 1 consult: J. L. Saalschütz, *Das mosaische Recht*, i. 358 sqq., Berlin, 1846; A. Edersheim, *Jesus the Messiah*, ii. 17–21, New York, 1896; Smith, *Rel. of Sem*, 2d ed., pp. 481–485; Nowack, *Archäologie*, ii. 168–169, 263–266; Benzinger, *Archäologie*, pp. 387–388 et passim; *DB*, iv. 872–873; *EB*, iv. 5252–55; *JE*, xii. 451–452; *DCG*, ii. 810–811; *KL*, v. 246–249; the talmudic tracts *Nedarim*, *Arakin*, and *Shekalin*, iv. 6–8. On 2 consult: Bingham, *Origines*, VII., iii. 7–8, iv. 2, XVI., vii. 9; Schönen, in *TQS*, 1874, pp. 195 sqq., 447 sqq.; F. Daab, *Die Zulässigkeit der Gelübde*, Gütersloh, 1896; *Virgines Christi. Die Gelübde der gottgeweihten Jungfrauen in den ersten drei Jahrhunderten*, in *TU*, xxxi. 2, 1907; and literature under the articles to which reference is made in the text.

VOYSEY, CHARLES: English theist; b. in London Mar. 18, 1828. He was educated at St. Edmund Hall, Oxford (B.A., 1851), and was Church of England curate at Hessle, Yorkshire (1851–58), incumbent of Craighton, St. Andrews, Jamaica (1858–60), and curate of Great Yarmouth (1860–1861), and of St. Mark's, Whitechapel (1861–63). He had already manifested a change of theological position, however, and in 1863 was ejected from the curacy of St. Mark's for denying the doctrine of eternal punishment. In the following year, after being for a few months curate of Victoria Dock Church, North Woolwich, he became curate of Healaugh, Yorkshire, where he remained seven years (1864–71). Here again his unorthodox views involved him in difficulties, and in 1871, after a legal contest of two years, in which the case was brought before the judicial committee of the privy council, he was deprived of his living for his sermon entitled *Is every Statement of the Bible about our Heavenly Father strictly True?* (preached in 1865). He then founded the Theistic Church in London, of which he is still the head. He has written *The Sling and the Stone* (collections of his weekly sermons; 10 vols., London, 1872–93); *The Mystery of Pain, Death, and Sin* (1878); *Lectures on the Bible, and the Theistic Faith and its Foundations* (1881); *Theism, or, the Religion of Common Sense* (1894); *Theism as a Science of Natural Theology and Natural Religion* (1895); *Testimony of the Four Gospels concerning Jesus Christ* (1896); and *Religion for all Mankind* (1903).

VULGATE. See BIBLE VERSIONS, A, II., 2.

W

WACE, HENRY: Church of England; b. in London Dec. 10, 1836. He was educated at Brasenose College, Oxford (B.A., 1860); was ordered deacon (1861) and ordained priest (1862); was curate of St. Luke's, Berwick Street, London (1861–63), and of St. James', Westminster (1863–69), and lecturer of Grosvenor Chapel (1870–72); chaplain (1872–80) and preacher (1880–96) of Lincoln's Inn, London; rector of St. Michael's, Cornhill (1896–1903), and since 1903 has been dean of Canterbury. He was Boyle Lecturer (1874–75), professor of ecclesiastical history in King's College, London (1875–83), and principal of the same institution (1883–96); select preacher at Cambridge in 1878, 1890, and 1901, and at Oxford in 1880–82, Bampton Lecturer at the latter university in 1879, examining chaplain to the archbishop of Canterbury in 1883–1903, honorary chaplain to the queen in 1884–89, and chaplain-in-ordinary in 1889–1901, and honorary chaplain to the king in 1901–03, prebendary of Consumpta-per-Mare in St. Paul's Cathedral in 1881–1903, rural dean of the East City in 1900–03, and dean of Canterbury since 1903. Besides editing *A Dictionary of Christian Biography, Literature, Sects, and Doctrines, from the time of the Apostles to the Age of Charlemagne* (in collaboration with Sir William Smith; 4 vols., London, 1880–86; in part rewritten, revised, and reissued in one volume as *A Dictionary of Christian Biography and Literature to the End of the Sixth Century,* London and Boston, 1911, in collaboration with W. C. Piercy); *The First Principles of the Reformation; or, The Primary Works of Luther* (in collaboration with C. A. Buchheim; 1884); *The Speaker's Commentary on the Apocrypha* (2 vols., 1886); and the second series of *Nicene and Post-Nicene Fathers* (in collaboration with P. Schaff; 14 vols., New York, 1890–1900), he has written *Christianity and Morality* (Boyle lectures; London, 1876); *The Foundations of Faith* (Bampton lectures; 1880); *The Gospel and its Witnesses* (1883); *The Students' Manual of the Evidences of Christianity* (1886); *Some Central Points of Our Lord's Ministry* (1890); *Christianity and Agnosticism; Reviews of some recent Attacks on the Christian Faith* (1895); *The Sacrifice of Christ* (1898); *Confession and Absolution* (1902); *Criticism Criticised* (1902); *The Bible and Modern Investigation* (1903); *Appeal to the First Six Centuries* (1905); *Principles of the Reformation* (1910); and *Prophecy, Jewish and Christian* (1911).

WACKERNAGEL, vãc″ker-nā″gel, **KARL EDUARD PHILIPP:** Hymnologist and educator; b. in Berlin June 28, 1800; d. at Dresden June 20, 1877. He studied at Berlin and Breslau, devoting himself especially to mineralogy and crystallography. He also entered upon his hymnological studies. He became involved in the political troubles of the time, and had to leave Breslau for Halle and Halle for Nuremberg (in 1823), where he taught in a private school until it was closed for lack of support. In 1829 he obtained his doctor's degree and was called to Berlin as teacher in the Technical School.

In 1839 he went to Stetten in Württemberg as teacher, in 1845 to Wiesbaden as professor in the Realgymnasium, and in 1849 to Elberfeld as director of the Realschule. In 1861 he resigned and lived thenceforth in retirement in Dresden, occupied with literary work and hymnological studies, so far as his strength permitted. He was one of the prominent founders of the German Evangelical Church Diet (see CHURCH DIET). Wackernagel's work and achievements in the domain of pedagogy, as well as in mathematics and the natural sciences, especially crystallography, were important. As an advocate of a Christian national education he opposed the rationalistic pedagogy, and published a series of "German Reading Books," which were much used, and a significant treatise, *Ueber den Unterricht in der deutschen Muttersprache* (Stuttgart, 1843), in support of his views. In like manner he held that in the field of the sciences everything is "spiritually ordered," and he had no sympathy with the empirical point of view which notes only sensuous phenomena. From his youth a deep interest in the poetry and song of the people led him to comprehensive studies in German history and literature. His religious bent forbade his passing over the pearls of German folk-songs—the hymns. In this field no one before him had made so far-reaching, thorough, and methodic investigation, and no one had brought greater natural gifts to the undertaking. The first ripe fruit of his labors was *Das deutsche Kirchenlied von Martin Luther bis auf Nicolaus Herman und Ambrosius Blaurer* (Stuttgart, 1841), a collection of 850 hymns from the oldest and best texts, and a treatise on the sources whence they were derived. In the preface a history of hymnology is attempted on broad lines, and the principles on which it should be studied and written are discussed. Further study brought so much new material to light that Wackernagel determined on a complete recasting of his work. After thirteen years' preparation he published *Bibliographie zur Geschichte des deutschen Kirchenliedes im 16. Jahrhundert* (Frankfort, 1855), in which he described 1,148 song-books and sheets (against 187 in the first edition; the number was augmented by 620 more in a supplement in 1877). The second part, under the title *Das Kirchenlied von der ältesten Zeit bis zu Anfang des 17. Jahrhunderts, mit Berücksichtigung der deutschen kirchlichen Liederdichtung im weiteren Sinne und der lateinischen von Hilarius bis Georg Fabricius und Wolfgang Ammonius,* followed in five volumes (Leipsic, 1864–77). It presents 6,783 hymns. Wackernagel also published *Die Lieder Paul Gerhards* (Stuttgart, 1843); a new edition of Luther's hymns (1848); *Johann Hermanns geistliche Lieder* (1856); *Gesangbuch für Kirche, Schule, und Haus* (1860); and *Beiträge zur niederländischen Hymnologie* (Frankfort, 1867).

(L. SCHULZE.)

BIBLIOGRAPHY: L. Schulze, *Philipp Wackernagel nach seinem Leben und Wirken,* Leipsic, 1879; R. Wackernagel, *Wilhelm Wackernagel. Jugendjahre 1806–33,* Basel, 1885; *ADB,* vol. xl.

WADDING, LUKE: English Franciscan, historian of the Franciscan order; b. at Waterford (63 m. e.n.e. of Cork), Ireland, Oct. 16, 1588; d. at Rome Nov. 18, 1657. He studied theology in Lisbon and Coimbra, Portugal; became a Franciscan 1607; was ordained priest in 1613; went in 1617 to Salamanca, where he became president of the Irish College; went to Rome, 1618, as chaplain to the Spanish ambassador, and remained there the rest of his life. In 1625 he founded there the College of St. Isidore for Irish students of the Franciscan order. From 1630 to 1634 he was procurator of his order at Rome, and from 1645 to 1648 vice-commissary. He was an ardent advocate of the Irish cause in the war of 1641, and sent officers and arms to Ireland. He was one of the councilors in the settlement of the Jansenist controversy, and pronounced an opinion in favor of these doctrines; but, on the appearance of the bull of Innocent X. (*Cum occasione*, 1653), he retracted. His works include *Legatio Philippi III. et IV., regum Hispaniæ, ad Paulum V., Gregorium XV., et Urbanum VIII. pro definienda controversia immaculatæ conceptionis B. Mariæ Virginis*, Louvain, 1624 (a history of the controversy to decide which the bishop of Cartagena went to Rome as an ambassador, which was consequently the occasion of Wadding's Roman residence); *Apologeticus de prætenso monachatu Augustiniano S. Francisci* (Madrid, 1625); especially noteworthy is his work on the *Annales ordinis Minorum* (8 vols., Lyons and Rome, 1625–54; later ed., 16 vols., vol. xvii., Index, Rome, 1731–36)—this is the great history of the Franciscan order; Wadding brought it down to 1540; it has been continued by De Luca to 1553 (vol. xviii., 1740), by Ancona to 1564 (vol. xix., 1745), by Asculano to 1754 (vol. xx., 1794), by De Cerreto to 1584 (vol. xxi., 1844)—*Scriptores ordinis Minorum*, 1650, new edition with Sbaraglia's corrections, 1806 (a bibliography of the order); *Immaculatæ conceptionis Virginis Mariæ opusculum* (1655); *Vita Clementis VIII.* (later edition, 1723). He also edited the " Sermons " of Anthony of Padua (1624), the *Opuscula* of Francis of Assisi (Lyons, 1637), the works of Duns Scotus, with a " Life " (12 vols., 1639), and superintended the publication of the posthumous Hebrew Concordance of Marius de Calasio (4 vols., Rome, 1621), to which he contributed an essay upon the Hebrew language.

BIBLIOGRAPHY: A " Life " was written by his nephew, F. Harold, prefixed to the *Annales*, and separately issued at Rome, 1731; and by J. A. O'Shea, Dublin, 1885. Consult further: C. Anderson, *Historical Sketches of the Native Irish*, London, 1830; C. P. Meehan, *Rise and Fall of the Irish Franciscan Monasteries*, London, 1877; KL, xii. 1141–44.

WAEIJEN, wê"ai'yen, JOHANNES VAN DER: Dutch Reformed theologian; b. at Amsterdam July 13, 1639; d. at Franeker Nov. 4, 1701. He was educated at the universities of Utrecht and Leyden (1655–59), and took courses at Heidelberg, Geneva, and Basel. In 1662 he became preacher at Spaarndam, whence he was called to Leeuwarden in 1665. In 1672 he served as an army-chaplain, but later in the same year was called as pastor to Middelburg. Hitherto he had been generally regarded as an advocate of Voetius (q.v.), whom he sought to recon-

cile with Maresius by his *Epistola ad amicum de reconciliatione D. G. Voetii et D. S. Maresii* (1669). At the same time he showed himself to be no Cocceian by his polemical treatise against Welzogen, *Pro vera et genuina Reformatorum sententia præsertim in negotio de interprete Scriptura* (Amsterdam, 1669); and he also opposed the Cartesian philosophy and the Labadists, the latter in his *Ernstige betuiginge van J. van der Waeijen en H. Witsius aan de afdwalende kinderen der kerke tegen de gronden van Labadie* (1670). In Middelburg, however, his position was radically changed, as was shown by his anonymous *Het lijden van Christus in Gethsémané* (Middelburg, 1674), and his *Over Ps. XVIII. 24* (1675). The latter treatise involved him in a controversy with A. Hulsius, to whom he replied in his *Disputatio van Hulsius over Ps. XVIII. beantwoord door J. v. d. Waeijen* (1675). His zealous advocacy of Cartesian and Cocceian tenets led to his suspension from office on Dec. 11, 1676, at the instance of the stadholder William III. Waeijen was then settled at Amsterdam, but in 1677 was appointed professor of Hebrew at Franeker, receiving at the same time a professorship in theology, though there was no vacancy in the latter faculty. He entered upon office with an oration *De ecclesiæ ex utraque Babylone exitu et eorum inter se convenientia* (Franeker, 1678), and shortly afterward was appointed aulic councilor. In 1680 he resigned his professorship in Hebrew to devote himself entirely to teaching theology, and in the same year was appointed university preacher.

Regarded as the head of the Frisian Cocceians and exercising a very considerable influence, Waeijen had also to be a prolific writer. Among his dogmatic works were his *Summa theologiæ Christianæ, pars prior* (Franeker, 1689); *Varia sacra* (1693; also containing exegetic studies); and *Theologiæ Christianæ enchiridion* (1700). Of his exegetic investigations only the *Disputatio continens analysin epistolæ ad Galatas* (Franeker, 1681) can be mentioned. Waeijen also served three terms as Rector magnificus of Franeker, and his abilities as an orator may be judged from his three addresses in this capacity: *De incremento cognitionis expectando tempore novissimo* (Franeker, 1686); *De semihorio silentii* (1688); and *De numero septenario* (1696). His homiletic capacity is shown by his posthumous *Methodus concionandi* (Franeker, 1704). In his polemics, however, Waeijen was more caustic and magniloquent than convincing. To this category belong his attacks on F. Spanheim the younger, *Epistola apologetica ad Philalethium Eliezerum (Willem Anslaer) adversus nuperas Frid. Spanhemii litteras* (Franeker, 1683); B. Bekker, *De betooverde wereeld van Balthazar Bekker onderzogt en weederlegt* (1693); on P. van Hattem, *Brief ter wederlegginge van sekere brief bij Pontiaan van Hattem met een voorrede, daar in eenige gedachten noopens de so genaamde Hebrëen* (1696); on J. Clericus, *Dissertatio de logo, vocabulo non ex Platone primum repetito et in religionem illato* (1698); on P. à Limborch, *Limborgianæ responsionis discussio* (1699); and on J. Spencer, *Johannis Spenceri dissertatio de hirco Âzazel excussa, principe, de Hebræorum ritibus maximam partem ex Ægypto arces-*

sendis, errore, breviter quoque confutato (in his *Varia sacra*, pp. 265–622). (S. D. VAN VEEN.)

BIBLIOGRAPHY: The funeral oration by A. Schulting was printed at Franeker, 1702. Consult: E. L. Brimoet, *Athenarum Frisicarum libri duo*, pp. 557–577, Leeuwarden, 1758; B. Glasius, *Godgeleerd Nederland*, iii. 570–576, 's Hertogenbusch, 1856; C. Sepp, *Het godgeleerd Onderweis in Nederland gedurende de 16. en 17. Eeuw*, Leyden, 1873–74; W. B. S. Boeles, *Frieslands Hoogeschool en het Rijks Athenæum e Franeker*, ii. 266–274, Leeuwarden, 1889.

WAGENMANN, vāh′en-mān, JULIUS AUGUST: German Lutheran; b. at Berneck (50 m. n.n.e. of Erlangen) Nov. 23, 1823; d. at Tübingen Aug. 27, 1890. Educated at the seminary of Blaubeuren (1837–41), and at Tübingen (1841–45), he served as vicar for a short time, then was lecturer at Blaubeuren (1846–49) and Tübingen (1849–51) on Württemberg church history and other departments of theology. In 1852 he became assistant pastor in Göppingen and first assistant 1857; in 1861 he accepted a professorship of church history at Göttingen. He was, however, too diverse in his interests to concentrate himself on any one field of investigation, nor was he the author of any independent work of magnitude. On the other hand, he was a prolific writer for theological periodicals and encyclopedias. Thus he contributed extensively to the *Jahrbücher für deutsche Theologie*, of which he was editor for many years, while for the first edition of the Herzog *RE* he wrote sixty-seven articles, and for the second 144 (including revisions); he also contributed extensively to the *ADB*.

Wagenmann took an active interest in the practical affairs of his church and his university. As a professor he frequently preached, while after 1873 he was a member of the central committee of the Gustav-Adolf-Verein (q.v.). In 1878 he received appointment as consistorial councilor.

(N. BONWETSCH.)

BIBLIOGRAPHY: *Schwäbischer Merkur*, Oct. 11, 1890; *ADB*, xl. 477 sqq.

WAGENSEIL, vāh′en-sail, JOHANN CHRISTOPH: Apologist; b. at Nuremberg Nov. 26, 1633; d. at Altdorf (11 m. s.w. of Nuremberg) Oct. 9, 1705. He was made professor at Altdorf—first of history (1667), next of Oriental languages (1674), and finally of ecclesiastical law (1697). He wrote the famous works, *Sota, hoc est liber Mischnicus de uxore adulterii suspecta* (Altdorf, 1674; a translation, with notes, of the Mishna tractate upon the treatment of a wife suspected of adultery), and *Tela Ignea Satanæ, sive, arcana et horribiles Judæorum adversus Christum Deum et Christianum religionem libri* (Altdorf, 1681; a translation and refutation, in Latin, of certain antichristian Jewish writings).

WAGER OF BATTLE, DUEL.

I. Wager of Battle.
  The Appeal to Deity (§ 1).
  The Nations Using It (§ 2).
Progress toward its Abolishment (§ 3).
II. The Duel.
  History (§ 1).
Attitude of the Churches; Difficulties (§ 2).
  Ethics of the Duel (§ 3).

I. Wager of Battle: The wager of battle is a form of Ordeal (q.v.), the usual means of which is the single combat, though occasionally the combat is multiplex. The character of the ordeal as an appeal to the deity for decision in a disputed case is fully carried out, as is illustrated by the meeting between Menelaus and Paris (*Iliad*, iii. 276–323).

1. The Appeal to Deity. In this there were sacrifice to Zeus, formal and punctilious arrangement of the field and placing of the combatants, appeal to the lot for precedence, and prayer to the god to decide by sending the guilty to Hades. That the case as described by the poet was not regarded as isolated but as conducted in accordance with the custom of the times, is clear from the fact that the marshals appear to act after a well-known method of procedure. So wherever trial by battle is employed, this same characteristic of appeal to deity is discovered. When the nations using it adopted Christianity, the combat remained, but under appeal to a different arbiter. Each party to the battle asserted the justice of his cause by oath on the Gospels, or on an approved relic; defeat was *ipso facto* evidence of perjury, to punishment for which it exposed the loser, and he was disqualified thereafter for giving evidence or serving in court.

The area for which this custom is demonstrable is that of the western Aryan peoples, with the possible exception of the Romans. Thus that the Celts had it is shown by the *Senchus Mor* and by a canon (no. 8) attributed to St. Patrick (extracts from the *Senchus* are given in Haddan and Stubbs, *Councils*, II., ii. 339 sqq.; the canon is in the same collection, p. 329). Among the Teutons particularly the wager was at home. The holmgang (so named because it was usually fought on a holm or small island) was with the northern Teutons a recognized method of settling a dispute or acquiring a right, and the victor sacrificed an ox at the conclusion.

2. The Nations Using it. When the laws of the Teutons were collected into codes, the judicial combat was conspicuously present, as in the Gundobaldic, Bavarian, Lombardic, Frankish, and other early collections, but not in the Anglo-Saxon and Anglo-Danish. The Slavic peoples constantly settled disputes by this means. It was so thoroughly implanted in the Lombardic legal practise that even Liutprand was unable to make headway against it. It was sanctioned by Charlemagne (with reservations against it in certain cases); Louis-le-Débonnaire permitted it between an ecclesiastic and a layman, and Emperor Guy restored the privilege complete as between ecclesiastics; Otho the Great defended and enforced its use, and sent champions (see below) to enforce his claims in his dispute with Pope John XII., and in 971 ordered the confiscation of the estates of those who refused to employ it; champions became a part of the suite of ambassadors in order the better to enforce the claims of rival powers; Otho II. in 983 substituted it for the sacramental oath; Henry II. allowed it, as an appeal, to murderers; the Guelph line of monarchs is reputed to be founded on the confiscation of the duchy of Bavaria because its duke refused the combat, and his title was thereupon bestowed upon Welf, son of Cunigunda; Henry the Lion of Bavaria lost his possessions because of default in the wager of battle; to the dukes of Austria was granted (1156) and confirmed (1245) the right of representation in the judicial duel; trials for crimes were often settled by the arbitrament of the sword, even the judges who pronounced decision being subject to challenge from the party against whom the case was decided, unless the guilt was clear, a forcible reversion of justice being thus accomplished. As in the case of other ordeals, the wager of battle was employed by the Church. A notable instance of this is the dispute between Hildebrand and the church in Castile, when the pope attempted to replace the Mozarabic liturgy by the Roman; a double ordeal is asserted for this occasion, the combat and the ordeal of fire, and the Spaniards were victorious. It became common even for high ecclesiastics to trust their cause to the lists.

But while civil and ecclesiastical powers so largely had recourse to this means, a more advanced sentiment attempted to curb the combat and eventually to abolish it. Not the least incitement to these efforts was the abuse which arose from the employment of champions. This employment arose in the attempt to make more equal the chances of contestants, to prevent the powerful from overriding the weak. Substitutes were permitted

3. Progress toward its Abolishment. for the aged, the infirm, minors, cripples, women, ecclesiastical institutions, and ecclesiastics after they had been debarred. Gradually this office became a profession, in many cases adopted by desperadoes who assumed no greater risks in the combat than they were wont to undergo in their ordinary life. Agobard (q.v.) opposed the judicial combat in his *Liber adversus legem Gundobardi* and *Liber contra judicium Dei;* Atto of Vercelli (see ATTO, 3) declared it inapplicable to the clergy and indecisive for laymen; in 1080 a synod at Lillebonne required the sanction of a bishop to be given a churchman who would engage; Ivo of Chartres (q.v.; d. 1116) rebuked a bishop for ordering the combat in his court; Pope Innocent II. forbade clerics to enter the lists (1140); Clement III. repeated the prohibition; Celestin III. (1191–98) deposed a priest for the offense, and Innocent III. (1215) confirmed this position; Innocent IV. interfered in 1245 to save the chapter of Notre Dame from being forced to engage. The judicial combat was first formally forbidden in Iceland in 1011, in Denmark in 1074. Restrictions and final abolishment may be traced as follows: by Henry IV. at Pisa, 1081; by Bishop Godfrey at Amiens, 1105; by Baldwin VII. at Ypres, 1116; by Centulla I. at Lourdes, 1138; by Philip Augustus at Tournay, 1187; by Alphonse de Poitiers at Riom, 1270; by Charles IV. at Worms, 1335; while the Council of Trent (session XXV., *De reform.*, xix.) prohibited all potentates from allowing it. In spite of this gathering denunciation and prohibition, how persistent the practise was may be seen from the fact that in 1518 Henry II. of Navarre ordered recourse to it, at Pau; in 1538 Francis I. granted the appeal to arms and the default of the defendant resulted in his being sentenced to death; in Béarn it remained in the code till 1789; Julius had, in 1505, to forbid trial by battle in Italy; in Russia it was not abrogated till 1649;

in 1567 Bothwell offered to justify by the combat his murder of Darnley (J. Knox, *Hist. of Reformation in Scotland*, ed. Laing, ii. 560, Edinburgh, 1895). In Germany throughout the Middle Ages the matter was complicated by questions of birth and standing, though in case of homicide the combat was obligatory; a Jew might not decline the challenge of a Christian, though it is not clear that he might offer the challenge. Among the bills considered by the English Government when restricting the powers of the province of Massachusetts Bay was one which in 1774 contained a clause that took away the " appeal of death," and this article had to be eliminated before final passage was granted, since it was regarded as a step toward denying the same privilege to Englishmen. This right was not abolished in England till 1819.   GEO. W. GILMORE.

II. The Duel: A duel which took place in Germany in 1896 between two men of rank (Von Kotze and Von Schrader) called out a number of investigations and a large interest in the

1. History. origin and development of the duel, and also strenuous opposition to the institution as well as defense of it. Von Bülow attempted to show that its origin was not Germanic, but Spanish and French, that it was derived neither from the wager of battle nor from the tournament. If, however, the duel be defined as a combat between two persons in defense of the honor due their position, in which is involved definite disregard of public justice, then it is difficult to show that it is un-Germanic. While it can not go back to the wager of battle as its direct source, yet in the general disposition to assume the power to right a wrong, to take vengeance, or even to show one's prowess on the foe, even a sort of noble courage in the case of a wrong—in all this the wager of battle of the Middle Ages was the predecessor of the duel. The wager of battle, however, embraced all classes and was not hemmed in by an exclusiveness which characterizes the duel. The disappearance of the former proved the occasion of the latter, but the motives were entirely different; in the wager of battle men sought their rights, while defense of the honor of position is the essence of the duel. The latter institution began to be common about 1500, especially in Spain, Italy, and France, whence it spread elsewhere, and the Romance languages became the vehicle in the sixteenth century of a literature on the duel. In the same century, also, the monarchs began to issue edicts against this practise, which were continued in the two following centuries. But a complete end of the practise was not brought about by these means. In Great Britain a duel between two officers in 1843 caused the authorities to incorporate strong regulations against the practise with trial as for murder in case of fatal issue of the combat. An organization against dueling was formed which included in its membership a large number of the nobility, and of high officers in the army and navy, and in that country the duel has become practically extinct as a barbarous custom. In Germany since the time of Frederick the Great attempts have been made to supersede the duel by a court of honor. William I. on May 2, 1874, and William II. on Jan. 1, 1897, issued regulations to this end, the court of honor being invoked first to avert the combat and then, if that is not reached, to have the conditions under observation of one of the court. Anti-dueling associations have been formed looking to the entire abolition of the custom.

The Roman Catholic Church has taken strong position against the duel (Council of Trent, sess. XXV., chap. xix.); Benedict XIV. refused churchly burial to those even who showed signs of repentance outside the meeting-place, and the ban falls upon the attending physician; even stu-

2. Attitude dents' duels are included under the of the censure. The Evangelical church has Churches; never through its organs approved the Difficulties. duel. During the Reformation period the duel was not so much in evidence as to evoke a pronouncement from Luther. Among the Reformed the matter of Christian burial was not brought to a test, and the care of the surviving duelist came within the reach of the cure of souls. It is strange that while much was said in the Protestant churches of suicide, so little was said of the duel. But the event of 1896, already referred to, evoked some strong expressions of condemnation as traversing human law and the divine order. The difficulties were the greater in that men of serious lives defended the duel as a means of righting wrongs and defending assaults on honor. For the duel is a serious meeting with weapons. The seriousness rests not upon the character of the weapons, however, but in the hostility of the meeting. The jurists discriminate between two species of duel, that in defense of honor and that the purpose of which is punishment. In the first case a man of honor feels that his honor has been assailed, and challenges the assailant in order to wipe out the offense; in turn the challenged is in the position where he must defend his own honor, which would be lost by refusal to accept the challenge. The event is one which in its issue is entirely sundered from the ethical qualities of the participants. In the second species of duel the purpose of the challenger is to punish the challenged for some unbearable breach which may not be passed over; he is placed in the position of a man whose honor might be impugned if he did not adopt this means. Yet the means is inconclusive in its result; there is no guaranty that the guilty will receive the punishment, while the challenger assumes the position of judge and avenger; yet according to the code both the challenger and the challenged from the very process itself are recognized as protecting their honor. This last is the sole sense and significance of the practise. Thus far the two species of duels are identical; the thing at issue is the honor of the participants, which is reckoned with reference to standing in a certain circle and so with reference to ability to give " satisfaction."

A conclusive decision concerning the duel takes into account the value of that derived from position which underlies the entire existence of 3. Ethics of the duel. The sixth commandment is the Duel. not final, for self-defense, war, capital punishment, and exposure to danger are constant; nor is the monopoly claimed for public justice decisive, since the demand for one's rights ever seeks and finds new forms not comprehended

under public law; no more decisive is the fact that in the duel the innocent often suffers and the guilty goes free, for this occurs in public administration of justice; and the Christian idea of honor does not come into the account, since it is conceivable that love for one's neighbor may involve one legitimately in the duel. Abstract and applied ethics are different things. The Christianity of the individual is bound up with a nature in which are ingrown native instincts and prejudices, while the individual moves in an environment in which values are fixed by custom. Hence it results that he has to take account of an honor of position as well as of that honor which is his as a Christian. Each class has something of this, and sometimes with opposite results. A pastor is by a duel made unfit for his office, an army officer may not refuse a duel on pain of losing his position and the honor due to it; yet both have as Christians the same honor. The same conduct can not be exacted of these two men in their diverse associations. For the officer in the army honor of position is a vital thing. If the conditions of life are wrong, the task is to change them; if honor of position is unwarranted, it is to be set aside, and the way is to be prepared for abolishing the duel. Christianity has to deal with analogous conditions, such as the compulsory oath, religious education, baptism, and the like; in the mission field polygamy has to be tolerated. The reason for these things is the imperfection of the state of society. So with society in Germany, where class distinctions are sanctioned at least tacitly by the Church, out of which distinctions grows the duel. Indeed, the latter is rather a symptom. To abolish dueling there is necessary a revulsion of public sentiment, which must work against what is at present an exceedingly strongly entrenched feeling. Even those who maintain the code of honor must work for the alleviation of the duel, for the removal of false positions and the improvement of the code. In the duel, in its very operation, the moral vagabond assumes the position of the morally upright, the innocent stands on the same plane as the guilty. Could this alleged equality, but real inequality, be abolished, the conception of the honor of position would be purified and a way opened for a conservative estimate of the duel which would lead to its inclusion within the strict path of Christian duty.   (M. RADE.)

BIBLIOGRAPHY: Lists of literature on the subject are: Hauck-Herzog, *RE*, xxi. 759-760 (giving titles of books, mainly in German, issued during the controversy in Germany, 1896 sqq., concerning the duel, decided in favor of the practise by public opinion and the emperor); C. A. Thimm, *Bibliography of Fencing and Duelling*, London, 1896; G. E. Levi and J. Gelli, *Bibliografia del Duello*, Milan, 1903. An excellent review of the history of the wager of battle is H. C. Lea, *Superstition and Force*, pp. 93-216, Philadelphia, 1878. Literature which deals with the subject will be found under ORDEAL. Consult further: Thatcher and McNeal, *Source Book*, pp. 388-400; J. Milligan. *Hist. of Duelling*, 2 vols., London, 1841; A. Steinmetz, *The Romance of Duelling*, 2 vols., London, 1868; C. de Massi, *The Hist. of Duelling*, London, 1880; B. C. Truman, *The Field of Honour*, New York, 1884; J. Gelli, *Il Duello nella storia della giurisprudenza*, Florence, 1886; A. von Oppenheim, *Das Wesen des Duello*, Vienna, 1887; C. Thuemmel. *Der gerichtliche Zweikampf und das heutige Duell*, Hamburg, 1887; J. Cockburn, *Hist. of Duels*, 2 vols., Edinburgh, 1888; G. Neilson, *Trial by Combat*, Glasgow, 1890; G.

Letainturier-Fradin, *Le Duel à travers les âges*, Paris, 1892; Vidal de Saint-Urbain, *Le Duel sous l'ancien régime et de nos jours*, Dijon, 1892; C. de Smedt, *Le Duel judiciaire et l'église*, Paris, 1895; A. Wiesinger, *Das Duell vor dem Richterstuhle der Religion*, Graz, 1895; H. Pierquin, *La Juridiction du point d'honneur sous l'ancien régime*, Paris, 1904; H. Fehr, *Der Zweikampf*, Berlin, 1908; C. L. Brace, *Gesta Christi*, chap. xiv., new issue, London and New York, 1911.

WAGNER, vāн'ner, CARL JULIUS IMMANUEL: German Evangelical; b. at Greifenberg (125 m. n.w. of Berlin) Oct. 5, 1847. He served as field chaplain during the Franco-Prussian war; taught in private families and in secondary schools, 1871–73, passing meanwhile his theological examinations; was assistant preacher for the German Reformed congregation in Budapest, 1873–76; pastor of the German Evangelical Church at Sydenham, London, 1876–90; traveling preacher for the Innere Mission, 1890–93; pastor at Pritzerbe (Havel), 1894–1904; and since 1904 has been in charge of the Westdeutscher Verein für Israel. He is the author of *Charles Haddon Spurgeon. Lebensbild* (Berlin, 1893); *Was sagt Christus von den Juden? Ein Beitrag zur Lösung der Judenfrage* (1893); *Volkserholungen im Lichte des Evangeliums* (Darmstadt, 1893); *Die Sittlichkeit auf dem Lande* (Leipsic, 1895); *Zur Frage der Sittlichkeit unter der Landbevölkerung* (1897); *Auf zum Kampf wider die ländliche Unzucht* (Hanover, 1898); *Angelikas Weihnachten* (Darmstadt, 1904); and *Jean Baptist Harth* (Leipsic, 1904).

BIBLIOGRAPHY: A. F. Sanborn, in *Review of Reviews*, xxx (1904), 329–331; G. King, in *Outlook*, 1907, pp. 198–204.

WAGNER, CHARLES: French Protestant; b. at Wibersviller (20 m. n.e. of Nancy), district of Château Salins, Lorraine, Germany, Jan. 3, 1852. His father was the pastor of the village Lutheran church. Two years afterward he became pastor at Tiefenbach, some sixty miles eastward, and there Charles Wagner got his elementary education. From 1866 to 1869 he studied in Paris and took the degree of B.A. He then went to Strasburg for theological study, but ended his studies at Göttingen in 1875. He served for a year at Barr, at the foot of Mount St. Odile in the Central Vosges Mountains. Up to this time his associations had been with Lutherans and the German language. But in 1876 he left Germany and began ministerial service in connection with the liberal wing of the French Protestant Church. He was first pastor at Remiremont, 50 m. s.e. of Nancy. In 1882 he went to Paris. Beginning in a modest way, he won prominence and fame. Besides his strictly pastoral and preaching duties, he interested himself in the uplift of the working classes. With Paul Desjardins he founded "The Union for Moral Action," and cooperated in the university extension courses. He is the author of the following books: *Justice* (Paris, 1889; crowned by the French Academy); *Jeunesse* (1892); *Vaillance* (1893); *La Vie simple* (1895; crowned by the French Academy); *Le Long du chemin* (1896); *L'Evangile et la vie* (1897); *Auprès du foyer* (1898); *Sois un homme* (1899); *L'Ame des choses* (1900); *L'Ami* (1902); *Histoire et farciboles* (1904); *Pour les petits et les grands* (1907); *Par la loi vers la liberté* (1908). The following are the titles of the English translations of his works, arranged chronologically;

places of publication, London and New York: *Youth* (1893); *Courage* (1894); *The Simple Life* (1903); *The Better Way* (1905); *By the Fireside* (1904); *The Voice of Nature* (1904); *The Busy Life* (1904); *My Appeal to America* (1905); *The Gospel·of Life* (1905); *On Life's Threshold* (1905); *Justice* (1905); *The Upright Life* (1905); *Towards the Heights* (1906); *Wayside Talks* (1906); *Home of the Soul* (1909).

WAHABEES, wa-hā'bĭz: Adherents of a reforming sect of Mohammedans. The name is derived from that of the founder, Mohammed ibn Abd al-Wahab (b. in 1691 at Horemeleh, a town in the Nejd, Central Arabia; d. in 1787). In his early days he traveled extensively, perhaps as far as India; and, comparing Mohammedan life, practise, and theology with his reading of the Koran, he concluded that the essence of the faith was no longer held, its primitive faith no more maintained, and that most Mohammedans were idolaters. He therefore determined to attempt a reform which should do away with the accretions of creed and custom, and restore the religion to its primitive purity and simplicity. He began his preaching when he was about forty, polemizing against appeal to Mohammedan walis or saints, pilgrimages to the shrines, and paying honor there by prayers to or through the saints by dedicatory offerings. He emphasized abstinence from liquors and particularly from tobacco. With this went hatred of the Turks, the natural effect of which was that political consequences attended the results of the religious aspirations as the movement ultimately spread over nearly the whole of Arabia, excepting only its extreme borders, and even surging over into the Euphrates valley.

Interested in the movement was Ibn Saoud, who became patron of the founder of the sect and lent his arms to second the religious propaganda. He reaped his reward in the founding of a kingdom which for a time covered central Arabia. His son, who succeeded in 1765, assumed the titles of imam and sultan. The progress of conquest went side by side with the preaching for half a century. By 1804 Mecca and Medinah were in the hands of the Wahabees, and pilgrimages to those places were permitted only to adherents of the sect. This was a direct challenge to the Sublime Porte, and, besides, aroused the animosity of the entire Mohammedan world. As a consequence the Turkish Government entrusted the curbing of Wahabee power to the Egyptian Mehemet Ali. Piratical operations on the part of some Wahabees brought about also intervention by the British government in the region of the Persian Gulf in 1810 and 1819. The campaigns covered eleven years, and not till 1818 was the political power of the Wahabees disintegrated. The remoteness of the Nejd, the focus of Wahabee feeling, permitted about 1840 a renascence of Wahabee politicalism, though on a much smaller scale. This region is still devoted to Wahabism, remaining nominally Turkish, but practically independent, and ruled by two powerful shcikhs.

The essential contentions of the Wahabees, apart from those mentioned above as contained in the preaching of the founder, are rejection, as not bind-

ing, of the decisions in canon law made by the orthodox sects and also of ijma (see MOHAMMED, MOHAM-
MEDANISM, V., § 1) except as embodied in the agreements of the " companions " (of the prophet). The
result is that upon each Mohammedan devolves the
duty and privilege of constructing his own doctrine
from the Koran and from tradition in its strictest
form. As exegetes the Wahabees are extreme liter-
alists. The theological influence of the sect is widely extended, and even in India has been felt as a political complication. But that influence is on the
whole in the direction of purity and makes for the
betterment of Mohammedanism and against its
scholasticism.   GEO. W. GILMORE.

BIBLIOGRAPHY: D. B. Macdonald, *Development of Muslim
Theology, Jurisprudence, and Constitutional Theory,* pp.
60–62, 283–285, New York, 1903; idem, *Aspects of Islam,*
pp. 47, 285, ib. 1911; and the literature under ARABIA;
and MOHAMMED, MOHAMMEDANISM.

WAKE, WILLIAM: Archbishop of Canterbury;
b. at Blandford (16 m. n.e. of Dorchester), Dorset,
Jan. 26, 1656–67; d. at Lambeth Palace, London,
Jan. 24, 1736–37. He was educated at Christ
Church, Oxford (B.A., 1676), and after being ordained, went to Paris in 1682 as chaplain to Viscount
Preston. Here Wake came into close touch with
Gallicanism, for it was in that year that the famous
Declaratio cleri Gallicani (see GALLICANISM, § 2) was
formulated, and it was thus that he gained his lasting interest in the French church, and came to indulge in hopes of its ultimate union with the Anglican church (see UNITY OF THE CHURCHES, A, 1,
§ 5). In 1865 he returned to England with Viscount
Preston, and was later preacher at Gray's Inn (1688–
1696), canon of Christ Church, Oxford (1689–1705),
deputy clerk of the closet and chaplain in ordinary
to William and Mary (1689), rector of St. James's,
Winchester (1693–1706), and canon residentiary and
dean of Exeter (1703–05). On Oct. 21, 1705, he
was consecrated bishop of Lincoln, and in Jan.,
1716, on the death of Thomas Tenison (q.v.), he was
elevated to the archdiocese of Canterbury.

In an age of marked latitudinarianism Wake was
a defender of the true principles of the Anglican
church in her noblest attitude toward those without
her fold. Toward Protestants, on the one hand, he
was courteous and willing even to make certain
modifications in the Prayer Book to remove some
of their honest scruples; and though he opposed
Quaker relief and the repeal of certain clauses in the
Corporation and Test Acts (qq.v.), his motive was
not opposition to those things themselves, but alarm
at a very suspicious alliance with Bolingbroke and
other deists. In like spirit, he was eager for union
with the Gallican church, to form, with the Anglican, independent national churches; but submission
to Rome he would not dream of. It was with union
in mind that he carried on a long correspondence
with Louis Ellies Du Pin (q.v.); it was on the requirement of submission, set forth by Piers de Girar-
din, that the negotiations finally met with wreck.
It is worth noting that from this long correspondence sprang the defense of Anglican orders by Pierre
Francois Le Courayer (q.v.). Wake himself was a
vigorous champion of the historic position of the
Anglican Church, and in a period which cared little

for such things he ardently advocated the value of
patristic studies. As the more important of his
writings the following may be noted: *Exposition of
the Doctrine of the Church of England* (London, 1686),
*Defense of the Exposition of the Doctrine of the Church
of England* (1686), *A Second Defense of the Exposition* (2 parts, 1687–88; all these forming Wake's defense of Anglicanism against Jacques Bénigne Bossuet
[q.v.]), *Genuine Epistles of the Apostolical Fathers,
S. Barnabas, S. Clement, S. Ignatius, S. Polycarp,
the Shepherd of Hermas, and the Martyrdom of St. Ignatius and St. Polycarp* (2 parts, 1693; 5th ed., 1817;
reprinted in Lord Avebury's *Hundred Best Books,*
1893), *The Authority of Christian Princes over their
Ecclesiastical Synods Asserted* (1697), *Principles of
the Christian Religion Explained in a brief Commentary upon the Church Catechism* (1699; 13th ed.,
1812), *State of the Church and Clergy of England in
their Councils, Synods, Convocations, Conventions,
and other their Assemblies, historically deduced from
the Conversion of the Saxons to the present Times*
(1703; a work that is still of value). A number of
his polemics against the Roman Catholic Church
are accessible in E. Gibson's *Preservative against
Popery* (3 vols., London, 1738; new ed., by J. Cumming, 18 vols., 1848–49), *Nature of Idolatry* (ed.
Cumming, vi. 148 sqq.), *Real Presence and Adoration of the Host* (x. 1 sqq.), *Discourse of Purgatory and
of Prayers for the Dead* (xi. 1 sqq., 82 sqq.), and the
Exposition and its defenses (xii. 47 sqq.). His correspondence with Du Pin was edited by " F. G."
under the title *D'un Projet d'union entre les églises
gallicane et anglicane* (Oxford, 1864).

BIBLIOGRAPHY: *DNB,* lviii. 445–446 (with further litera-
ture); J. H. Overton, in *Lincoln Diocesan Magazine,* 1891;
J. H. Lupton, *Archbishop Wake and the Project of Union
(1717–20) between the Gallican and Anglican Churches*
(London, 1896); J. H. Overton and F. Relton, *English
Church from the Accession of George I. to the End of the
Eighteenth Century,* London, 1906, pp. 21–29.

WALA: Abbot of Corbie. See ADALHARD AND
WALA.

WALÆUS, wä-lê′us, **ANTONIUS (ANTOINE DE
WAELE):** Dutch Reformed; b. at Ghent Oct. 3,
1573; d. at Leyden July 9, 1639. He was educated
at the University of Leyden (1596–99); preached
and lectured for a time at Geneva, and toward the
close of 1601 returned to Leyden, where he was
made one of the city preachers; he accepted a call
to Koudekerke near Middelburg in 1602; was made
chaplain to Prince Maurice, 1604; went as preacher
to Middelburg, 1605, where in 1609 he was also appointed professor of dogmatics; he attended the
Synod of Dort (1618–19) as representative of the
States General of Zeeland, where he became a person
of importance, being selected as one of the framers
of the Canons of Dort; in 1619 he was appointed
professor of theology at Leyden; in 1625 he collaborated in issuing the *Synopsis purioris theologiæ,*
and was active in the new translation of the Bible
made under the auspices of the States General.

Walæus was a Contra-Remonstrant and an opponent of Arminianism, but was more irenic in temperament than many of his contemporaries. His
dogmatic position is shown by his *Synopsis, Enchiridion Religionis Reformatæ,* and his unfinished *Loci*

communes theologici. In the controversy on the proper observance of the Sabbath he wrote *Dissertatio de Sabbatho, sive de vero sensu atque usu quarti præcepti* (Leyden, 1628). Thirteen years earlier, he had opposed the views of Uytenbogaert (q.v.) on church government in his *Het ampt der kerckendienaren, midtsgaders de authoriteyt ende opsicht, die een hooghe christelicke overheydt daer over toecompt* (Middelburg, 1615). Walæus rendered valuable service also to Christian ethics by his *Compendium ethicæ Aristotelicæ ad normam veritatis Christianæ revocatum* (Leyden, 1627). He did much for missions in the East Indies by opening, as early as 1622, a seminary in his house to train preachers. His name is still perpetuated by the " Walæus Seminary " in Leyden. His collected works were published after his death (2 vols., Leyden, 1647).   (S. D. VAN VEEN.)

BIBLIOGRAPHY: G. Bates, *Vitæ selectorum aliquot virorum,* London, 1681; C. Sepp, *Het godgeleerd Onderwijs in Nederland gedurende de 16. en 17. Eeuw,* Leyden, 1873–74; J. A. Grothe, in *Berichte van de Utrechtsche Zendingsvereeniging,* vol. xxiii., Utrecht, 1882; J. D. de Lind van Wijngaarden, *Antonius Walæus,* Leyden, 1891.

WALAFRID, vä′lä-frîd (WALAFRIED, WALAHFRID), STRABO: Theologian of the first half of the ninth century; b. in Swabia about 808; d. at Reichenau, an island in Lake Constance, Aug. 18, 849. He was at an early age admitted to the monastery of Reichenau, where he made great progress in his studies; later (826–829) he studied under Rabanus Maurus (q.v.), at Fulda; thence he went to the court of Louis le Débonnaire, becoming chaplain to the Empress Judith and tutor to her son Charles (the Bald). As a partizan of Lothair he received the abbey of Reichenau in 838, but was soon obliged to leave it; he was, however, reinstated in 842.

Walafrid's poems entitle him to rank as one of the classical writers of the Carolingian period. They include epigrams, eulogies, hymns, and two long poems on saints; the larger poem, written when Walafrid was eighteen years of age, describes a vision of the monk Wettin at Reichenau in 824, and is the earliest instance of versified " visions," which later became so popular. While at court Walafrid wrote *De imagine Tetrici,* inspired by the equestrian statue of Theodoric the Great before the palace at Aachen. His epistles, in hexameters or distichs, to princes and prelates are also of interest. His *Liber de cultura hortorum* is a poetical description of the cloister garden. Walafrid revised the biographies of the St. Gall abbots Gallus and Othmar. Special consideration is due to his *De exordiis et incrementis rerum ecclesiasticarum* (written 840–842, printed in Hettorp's *Scriptores,* Cologne, 1568), a compendium of Christian archeology in thirty-two books, still interesting because of its occasional addition of vernacular terms for the objects discussed. He took a middle course between superstitious iconolatry and Greek iconoclasm; his eucharistic doctrine was evidently not the transubstantiation of Paschasius Radbertus (q.v.), his famous contemporary. His chief renown was won by the great exegetic compilation in which he had the major part, the *Glossa ordinaria.* This, for nearly five centuries, served as the main source of Biblical science for the West, and was reissued again and again, usually with the work of Lyra, until the

seventeenth century. In the oldest edition (4 vols., n.p., n.d.) the Latin text of the Bible is surrounded by the glosses, a rich collection of citations from the Church Fathers elucidating the text. Between the lines of the text are brief scholia, written by Anselm of Laon in the twelfth century. Walafrid's own glosses are, in general, apt and scholarly. They include explanations of the names and problems which occasion them, though the majority are devoted to mystical-allegorical exegesis; several glosses, even from the same author, may be given on a single passage. The names of many of the authors cited are given, the most frequent being Jerome, Gregory, Isidore of Seville, and Bede; Ambrose and Chrysostom are quoted more sparingly. Other names predominate in individual books; as Cassiodorus in the Psalms, Origen in Numbers, and " Esicius " (Hesychius) in Leviticus. Many glosses appear without the author's name. These, it has been suggested, were written by Walafrid himself, since his name (" Strabo ") is frequently appended to glosses, especially in the first part of the work; these anonymous glosses have also been ascribed to his teacher Rabanus Maurus.   (A. HAUCK.)

BIBLIOGRAPHY: Walafrid's *Carmina,* ed. E. Dümmler with commentary, etc., are in *MGH, Poet. Lat. ævi Carol.,* ii (1884), 259–473; and the *Opera* are in *MPL,* cxiii. and cxiv. Consult: *Histoire littéraire de la France,* v. 59–76; J. C. F. Bähr, *Geschichte der römischen Literatur im karolingischen Zeitalter,* pp. 100–105, 217–219, 398–401, Carlsruhe, 1840; C. P. Bock, *Die Reiterstatue des Ostgothenkönigs Theodorich . . . zu Aachen,* pp. 1–160, Bonn, 1844; J. König, in *Freiburger Diöcesan-Archiv-Organ . . . der Erzdiöcese Freiburg,* iii (1868), 317–464; A. Ebert, *Allgemeine Geschichte der Litteratur des Mittelalters,* ii. 145–166, Leipsic, 1800; idem, in the *Sitzungsberichte* of the Saxon Academy, 1878, pp. 100 sqq.; *NA,* iv (1879), 270 sqq., xxi (1895), 301 sqq. (by Dümmler); x (1885), 166–169 (by J. Hümer), xxii (1896), 755, xxviii (1903), 507 (by P. von Winterfeld), xxvi (1901), 745 (by M. Manitius); J. von Schlosser in the *Sitzungsberichte* of the Vienna Academy, cxxiii (1891), 167–175; Hauck, *KD,* ii. 654 sqq.; Ceillier, *Auteurs sacrés,* xii. 410–417; Schaff, *Christian Church,* iv. 729–733; *KL,* xii. 1177–80.

WALCH, vālн: A family of German theologians of the eighteenth century.

1. Johann Georg Walch: b. at Jena June 17, 1693; d. there Jan. 13, 1775; was educated at the University of Leipsic (1710–13), and at first devoted himself chiefly to classical studies. In 1718 he was appointed associate professor at Jena for philosophy and antiquities, becoming full professor of oratory in 1719, and professor of poetry in 1721. He took part in the philosophic movements of the time, writing his *Gedanken vom philosophischen Naturell* (1723), and aiding his father-in-law, Buddeus (q.v.) to attack the philosophy of Christian Wolf. In his *Philosophisches Lexikon* (1726) the dawning of rationalism may be discerned, and his acceptance of " natural theology," though with adherence to Lutheran doctrines, is also evident in his *Einleitung in die Philosophie* (Latin ed., 1738) and *Observationes in Novi Testamenti libros, quarum prima pars ea continet loca quæ ex historia philosophiæ illustrantur* (1727).

In 1724 Walch became associate professor of theology, full professor in 1728, senior professor in 1750, and in 1754 ecclesiastical councilor for Saxe-Weimar. He wrote extensively on theology. First editing a compend of Buddeus' *Institutiones dog-*

maticæ (1723), he prepared for his own lectures an *Einleitung in die christliche Moral* (Jena, 1757), and *Einleitung in die dogmatische* and *in die polemische Gottesgelahrheit* (2 vols., 1752–57). Further services in behalf of theological literature are his edition of Bosius' *Introductio in notitiam scriptorum ecclesiasticorum* (1723); the still important *Bibliotheca theologica selecta* (4 vols., 1757–65); and *Bibliotheca patristica litterariis adnotationibus instructa* (1770). He edited the works of Luther (24 vols., Halle, 1740–52) with valuable introductions and the inclusion of many documents of the Reformation period. Mention should also be made of his *Introductio in libros symbolicos ecclesiæ Lutheranæ* (Jena, 1732); and his edition, in German and Latin, of the *Christliches Konkordienbuch* (1750). Inspired by Buddeus, Walch wrote, in 1724, his *Theologische Einleitung in die vornehmsten Religionsstreitigkeiten*, etc., which expanded into five volumes, under the title *Historische und theologische Einleitung in die Religionsstreitigkeiten, welche sonderlich ausser der evangelisch-lutherischen Kirche entstanden* (1733–36). At the same time he began independently his still valuable work, *Historische und theologische Einleitung in die Religionsstreitigkeiten der evangelisch-lutherischen Kirche* (5 vols., 1730–39). He was the author also of *Miscellanea sacra* (Amsterdam, 1744); *Historia ecclesiastica Novi Testamenti variis observationibus illustrata* (Jena, 1744); and *Historia controversiæ Græcorum Latinorumque de processione Spiritus Sancti* (1751). Though in early life inclined toward Pietism, and ever seeking to be just and impartial, he was strongly opposed to the Moravians, whose doctrines were condemned by him in the opinion requested by his sovereign in 1747 (ed. J. P. Fresenius, 1751).

2. Johann Ernst Immanuel: Eldest son of the preceding; b. at Jena Aug. 25, 1725; d. there Dec. 1, 1778. He was educated at the university of his native city, where he became privat-docent in exegesis in 1746, which resulted in his *Einleitung in die Harmonie der Evangelisten* (Jena, 1749). In 1750 he was appointed associate professor and in 1755 full professor of logic and mathematics; in 1759 he became professor of oratory and poetry, in 1768 senior professor of the philosophical faculty, and in 1770 aulic councilor. Walch devoted himself first to philology, though after 1760 his interest in natural science became predominant. He ever retained, however, an active interest in orthodox theology, and in this spirit wrote *Dissertationes in Acta Apostolorum* (3 parts, 1756–66); *Antiquitates nauticæ ex itinere Pauli Romano* (1767); *Antiquitates symbolicæ, quibus symboli apostolici historia illustratur* (1772); the posthumous *Observationes in Matthæum ex Græcis inscriptionibus* (1779); and the following works on persecutions of the Christians: *Marmor Hispaniæ antiquum, vexationis Christianorum Neronianæ insigne documentum* (1750); *Christianorum sub Diocletiano in Hispania persecutio ex antiquis inscriptionibus illustrata* (1751); and *Persequutionis Christianorum Neronianæ in Hispania . . . uberior explanatio* (1753).

3. Christian Wilhelm Franz: Younger brother of the preceding; b. at Jena Dec. 25, 1726; d. at Göttingen Mar. 10, 1784. He was educated at the University of Jena, where, after lecturing on exegesis, philosophy, and history until 1747, he was appointed associate professor of philosophy in 1750. He now accepted a call to Göttingen as full professor of the same subject, but from 1754 until his death was a member of the theological faculty, first as associate (1754–57) and later (1757–84) as full professor. He was able to find time for voluminous works and numerous occasional academic pamphlets; and he was active in the administration of the university. He became the senior professor of his faculty in 1766, and six years later was appointed British consistorial councilor. In his lectures he used many of his own text-books, among them his edition of his father's *Theologiæ dogmaticæ epitome tabulis analyticis expressa* (Jena, 1757); *Compendium historiæ ecclesiasticæ recentissimæ* (1757); *Grundsätze der natürlichen Gottesgelahrheit* (1760); *Grundsätze der Kirchengeschichte des Neuen Testaments* (Göttingen, 1761); and *Breviarium theologiæ symbolicæ ecclesiæ Lutheranæ* (1765). He was a collector of data rather than an original thinker, but his work is still of value, especially in the domain of church history. His theological attitude was, in general, a moderate Lutheranism. His *Geschichte der evangelisch-lutherischen Religion als ein Beweis, dass sie die wahre sei* (Jena, 1753) is little more than the application of a narrow concept of divine providence to the origin and development of the Lutheran Reformation. His accuracy of investigation and his abhorrence of mere hypotheses are better seen in his more noteworthy works on church history, especially the *Entwurf einer vollständigen Historie der Ketzereien, Spaltungen und Religionsstreitigkeiten bis auf die Zeiten der Reformation* (11 parts, Leipsic, 1762–85). He maintained that there is no " necessary truth " in history, but only " chance changes of chance things," and that deductions from historical facts are admissible only when " physical or moral necessities " are present, these principles being urged both in his *Gedanken von der Geschichte der Glaubenslehre* (Göttingen, 1765), and *Kritische Nachricht von den Quellen der Kirchenhistorie* (Leipsic, 1770). He sought to find causes and sources partly in the tendencies, prejudices, and capabilities of persons, and partly in the external circumstances conditioning them; and his final judgment was based on the problem which side represented the truth and on the moral characters of the personages involved. In presenting his conclusions, moreover, he seldom failed to apply a lesson to the conditions of his time. Similar principles underlie Walch's *Entwurf einer vollständigen Historie der römischen Päpste* (1756; Eng. transl., *Compendious Hist. of the Popes*, London, 1759); *Entwurf einer vollständigen Historie der Kirchenversammlungen* (1759); *Bibliotheca symbolica vetus* (Lemgo, 1770); and *Neueste Religions-Geschichte* (in collaboration with others; 9 parts, 1771–83). His polemic against Semler and Lessing, the *Kritische Untersuchung vom Gebrauch der heiligen Schrift in den vier ersten Jahrhunderten* (Leipsic, 1774), is still of value as a collection of material. Besides his important *Monumenta medii ævi ex bibliotheca regia Hannoverana* (2 vols., Göttingen, 1757–64) and *Philologische Bibliothek* (1770 sqq.), Walch also wrote among other works: *Antiquitates pallii philosophici veterum Chris-*

tianorum (Jena, 1746); *Historia canonisationis Caroli Magni* (1750); *Wahrhaftige Geschichte der seligen Frau Katharina von Bora . . . wider Eusebii Engelhards Morgenstern zu Wittenberg* (2 parts, Halle, 1751–54); *Historia Adoptianorum* (Göttingen, 1755); *Historia Protopaschitarum* (1760); *De symboli Athanasiani particulis quibus necessitas fidei catholicæ commendatur* (1774); and *Pseudoparakleton historia* (1781).   (G. Kawerau.)

Bibliography: On 1: A *Jubelgedächtnis* dedicated to him was published Jena, 1768. Consult: J. E. I. Walch, *Leben und Charakter des . . . Johann Georg Walch*, Jena, 1777; J. G. Meusel, *Lexikon verstorbener . . . Schriftsteller*, xiv. 360 sqq., Leipsic, 1815; J. M. H. Döring, *Die gelehrten Theologen Deutschlands*, iv. 630 sqq., Neustadt, 1835; G. Frank, *Die jenaische Theologie in ihrer geschichtlichen Entwickelung*, pp. 71 sqq., Leipsic, 1858; *ADB*, xl. 650 sqq.; *KL*, xii. 1182–83. On 2: *ADB*, xl. 652 sqq. On 3: G. Less, *Dem Andenken des . . . C. W. F. Walch*, Göttingen, 1784; J. N. Pütter, *Versuch einer akademischen Gelehrtengeschichte der Universität*, Göttingen, i. 121 sqq., ii. 28 sqq., Göttingen, |1765; F. C. Baur, *Die Epochen der kirchlichen Geschichtsschreibung*, pp. 145 sqq., Tübingen, 1852; *ADB*, xl. 646 sqq.; *KL*, xii. 1183–85.

WALDECK-PYRMONT, vȧl′dec-pîr′mont: A principality of the German empire consisting of Waldeck—a small state in North Germany lying between Hesse-Nassau and Westphalia—and Pyrmont (about thirty miles to the north), surrounded by Hanover, Lippe, and Brunswick; area 433 square miles, population (1905) 59,127, of whom 56,341 are Evangelical Christians, 1,890 are Roman Catholics, 259 are of various denominations, 629 are Jews, and 8 are not placed as to religious belief. No conversions to Roman Catholicism are reported, but three have joined churches other than the national church. The Old Lutherans, numbering about 520, have several congregations but only two ministers in the principality, and the relations with the state church are friendly. The total number of communicants is 40,984. In type of theology the principality is conservative, holding fast to the old ideals. Philanthropy flourishes in the form of the Sophienheim at Helsen, and a hospital and deaconess' home at Arolsen, the gifts of the late Princess Helene. Religious influence is marked also in connection with education, Luther's Catechism being used.

The church order of the Lutheran type dates from 1556, undergoing revision in 1640 and 1731, and the Reformed religion has never been strong, even the rationalistic movement having little real influence here. Consistorial direction partakes a little of the Episcopal type. Changes were made in 1873 which brought the administration into line with the German states, progressive changes have been made since, and further advance is under discussion. The consistory is in two parts, each consisting of a layman and two clergymen, and there are four superintendents. The synod has sixteen members, two elected by the district synods, and two appointed by the prince, and meets every three years. The district synods meet yearly, and are composed of equal numbers of clergy and laity. The sanction of the prince is required for legal measures.

Under the influence of rationalism the old church

order of service went to pieces. A liturgy was introduced in 1888, but has not met general acceptance. It is hoped that the present confusion will be ended and uniformity brought about by use of the treasures of the past.   (Victor Schultze.)

Bibliography: L. Curtze, *Geschichte der evangelischen Kirchenverfassung in dem Fürstentume Waldeck*, Arolsen, 1850; idem, *Die kirchliche Gesetzgebung des Fürstentums Waldeck*, ib. 1851; E. Friedberg, *Die geltenden Verfassungsgesetze der evangelischen deutschen Landeskirchen*, pp. 828 sqq., Freiburg, 1885; I. Freiensen, *Staat und katholische Kirche in den deutschen Bundesstaaten*, Stuttgart, 1901; V. Schultze, *Waldeckische Reformationsgeschichte*, Leipsic, 1903.

WALDEN, JOHN MORGAN: Methodist Episcopal bishop; b. at Lebanon, O., Feb. 11, 1831. He was educated at Farmers' (now Belmont) College, near Cincinnati, O. (A.B., 1852); was principal of the preparatory department of the same institution (1852–54), and was engaged in editorial work until 1858. Prominent in his advocacy of temperance reform as early as 1847, he was also bitterly opposed to slavery, and in 1857 founded at Quindare, Kan., a paper to promote free state principles, while in the same year he was a member of the Topeka (Kan.) legislature, and in 1858 was elected to the Leavenworth Constitutional Convention. Returning to Ohio in 1858, he entered the Methodist Episcopal ministry, and held pastorates in the Cincinnati conference until 1864, while from 1862 to 1866 he was corresponding secretary of the Western Freedmen's Aid Committee, in which capacity he took an active part in sending teachers to the freedmen in the Mississippi Valley. In 1866–67 he was corresponding secretary of the Freedmen's Aid Society of his denomination, of which he has since been president, and from 1868 to 1884, after being presiding elder of the East Cincinnati district in 1867–68, was agent of the Western Methodist Book Concern, Cincinnati. In 1884 he was elected bishop, and in this capacity has visited the churches and missions of his denomination throughout the United States, Europe, and Asia.

WALDEN, ROGER: Archbishop of Canterbury; b. some time before the middle of the fourteenth century; d. at Much Hadham (7 m. n.e. of Hertford), Hertfordshire, Jan. 6, 1406. Of his early life and training nothing is known, but in 1371 he was incumbent of St. Heliers, Jersey, and was later rector of Fenny Drayton, Leicestershire, and Burton in Kendale, Westmorelandshire. In 1387–95 he was archdeacon of Winchester, but his talents were preeminently secular, and he held also a number of political appointments. He was later secretary to Richard II., in 1395 became treasurer of England and dean of York, and in 1397 was appointed by the pope to the archbishopric of Canterbury, succeeding the banished Thomas Arundel (q.v.). On Arundel's return the pope quashed his appointment, and for a time Walden was confined in the Tower on a charge of conspiracy against Henry IV. He was soon released, however, and in 1405 was formally consecrated archbishop, but lived to enjoy this honor only a few months.

Bibliography: *DNB*, lix. 24–26.

WALDENSES.

I. Early History: Under the name Waldenses—with its variants Valdesii [the modern Vaudois], Vallenses, Leonistæ (of Lyons), Insabbatati, Sabbatati, Xabatati, Ençabots (*sabot*, " shoe "), Sandaliati, Sotularii, and Cotularii—Roman Catholic polemical writers after about 1180 opposed an ascetic body of preachers whose origin they ascribed to a Lyons merchant named Valdes (Peter Waldo), Valdesius, Valdexius, or Gualdensis. While, however, at first only

1. Waldo and the Poor Men. the French members of the organization called their body *Societas Valdesana*, or *Socii Valdesii*, the official name of the society was *Pauperes spiritu* (" Poor in Spirit "); or, later, *Pauperes Christi;* or simply *Pauperes*, with or without the additions *de Lugduno* or *de Lombardia*. The society itself gave practically no information concerning its founder, except that he was a man of reckless determination, and that he died before 1218; and the sole source of knowledge consists, therefore, of Roman Catholic authorities of the twelfth and thirteenth centuries, notably two anonymous writers of Laon and Passau and Stephen of Bourbon. According to the anonymous writer of Laon, Waldo heard, one Sunday in May or April of the famine year (1176), a traveling minstrel singing on the street the last stanzas of the old poem of St. Alexis [who had given away his property and gone on a pilgrimage to the Holy Land, and thereby had won great peace]. He invited him into his house and on the following morning asked a theologian the shortest and best way to God. The answer was that of Christ to the rich young man. Waldo, giving a portion of his property to his wife, sold the remainder, bestowing the greater part of the proceeds on the poor; and later casting the balance upon the street, he begged alms, and soon afterward took a formal vow of poverty. In the following year he was joined by others at Lyons, and gradually the " poor men " began to castigate the sins of both themselves and others. In the spring of 1179 Waldo went to the Lateran Council at Rome, where Alexander III. confirmed his vow of poverty, but forbade him and his companions to preach, unless expressly invited by the priests. This was long observed by the Waldenses, but finally they disobeyed the mandate, only to be involved in ruin for their fault. Stephen of Bourbon, on the other hand, ascribes Waldo's conversion to his curiosity. Hearing of the Gospels, he had two priests translate them for him. In like fashion, he later obtained vernacular versions of many other books of the Bible

XII.—16

and of the sayings of the saints. He now resolved to practise apostolic poverty, sold his property, threw the money in the mire, and began to preach in the streets. He was soon joined by many uncultured men and women, but all being unlettered, they taught many errors. They were accordingly forbidden to preach by Jean aux Blanches-Mains, archbishop of Lyons, but they persisted and were banned and expelled. In 1179 they were cited to appear at Rome, where, proving obstinate, they were declared to be heretics. The anonymous writer of Passau relates that the sudden death at a meeting at Lyons of one of the *majores* so shocked Waldo that he gave his property to the poor; taught them to imitate the voluntary poverty of Christ and the apostles, and forthwith began to translate the Bible into the vernacular. It is clear, moreover, from the account of Walter Map, that the followers of Waldo, when examined in connection with the Lateran Council, displayed utter ignorance of the simplest Christian teachings so that they were at once forbidden to preach. The anonymous writer of Laon, furnishing the most elaborate, immediate, and probable source, followed by Stephen, it may be concluded that the Waldenses originated according to the facts stated by the former; that, turning voluntarily to the Lateran Council (1179), the pope refused them the privilege of preaching; that, continuing, Pope Lucius III., instigated by Archbishop Jean of Lyons, issued against them, from Verona, the bull *Ad abolendam*, Nov. 4, 1184; and that the archbishop expelled them from Lyons toward the end of 1184, or at the beginning of 1185.

Meanwhile the Waldenses had gained a momentous advance elsewhere. In the spring of 1179 the Lombard Humiliati (q.v.) likewise sought at Rome to have their statutes confirmed and to be allowed to preach and hold religious gatherings. They were, however, also refused, and

2. The Lombard Humiliati. the similarity of their aims and fortunes led to a fusion of Waldenses and Humiliati. The latter recognized Waldo as leader, and assumed the name *Pauperes spiritu*, and the customs of apostolic living and preaching abroad, and impressed on their new allies their distinctive custom of uniting those brethren who felt themselves unfitted for preaching and pastoral care into ascetic companies of laborers. A second branch of Waldenses was thus established in Lombardy, their chief center being Milan, where in 1209 they numbered over a hundred. They were also in Cremona (1210), Bergamo, and, at least as missionaries, in a number of towns in northern and northwestern Italy. They were in Strasburg (1211), Bavaria and Austria (1218), and in the diocese of Treves and the region surrounding Mainz (1231). The determined effort to suppress heresy, then made throughout middle and southern Germany, was directed primarily against them. Meanwhile, the French Waldenses had extended their territory, so that it became necessary to take measures against them in Toul (1192), Metz (1199–1200), and Liége (1203). They were also present in Flanders at the beginning of the thirteenth century, but the south remained their chief field of operations. In Languedoc they engaged the attention of the bishops as early as the ninth decade of the twelfth century, and they soon caused commotion in Aragon and Catalonia. Here and in Languedoc they were, in all likelihood, most widely spread, numerous, and influential about the close of the twelfth and the beginning of the thirteenth century. They were drawn chiefly from the laity of the bourgeois and peasant classes, though a few priests and men of culture, and even monks, were to be found among them.

The papal ban (1184) had empowered the authorities of both Church and State to proceed against the Waldenses. In 1194 Alfonso II. of Spain issued an

3. Repression. edict that all who should harbor, give food and drink, or even listen to the Waldenses should be punished by confiscation of property and prosecuted for *lèse majesté*, while any injury might be inflicted on the Insabbatati save death and mutilation. In 1197 Pedro II. renewed this edict, with the added clause that Waldenses should be burned wherever taken, this forming the first public document in which death by burning was prescribed by the State for heresy. How far the mandate was enforced is uncertain, but in Germany about eighty members of the sect were burned at Strasburg in 1211. In their chief missionary centers, France and Italy, they were treated with more leniency. At Milan Archbishop Philip seems to have contented himself with razing their school, and in Pinerolo a vain effort was made to induce the inhabitants to refuse to receive them. In France only some of the bishops at first proceeded against them, and these with such moderate measures as summoning before the courts or burning their translations. Not until the Albigensian war broke out in southern France were bloody persecutions inflicted. Seven were burned at Maurillac in 1214. Throughout this first generation of the sect zealous efforts were made to reclaim them gently, or at least to refute their peculiar tenets; and Bernard of Fontcaud, Alanus ab Insulis, and Eberhard of Bethune then composed their works against the adherents of Waldo. In Languedoc there were attempts to reconcile them with the Church by means of religious colloquies at an unknown place previous to 1191, and at the castle of Pamiers in 1206. At the latter the Waldensian Duran of Huesca agreed to submit, provided he might retain his habit and his mode of life, and the Church was soon able to form from reconciled Waldenses a new brand of poor preachers, the Pauperes Catholici (q.v.), who, it was vainly hoped, would render valuable service in combating the Waldensian heresy.

At a very early date dissensions arose. Waldo vainly demanded the dissolution of the associations of laborers. He permitted the dissolution of marriage in case one wished to join his ranks, while the Lombards were of the opinion that the consent of the wife was necessary. The Lombards, because of his insistence, desired to become independent

4. Lombard Secession. of him, and have a leader of their own. The result was a crisis, which reached its climax about 1210, and a final rupture took place between the two bodies, the Lombards choosing their own leader in the simple and unlettered Giovanni di Ronco. These internal dissensions probably explain why, at this period, the sect made so slight a resistance to Roman Catholic efforts for their conversion, and why it now lost so many of its members, particularly of the more cultured class. This loss, and the considerable success of the Pauperes Catholici made the more moderate spirits in both factions anxious for reunion, and the death of both leaders opened the way. In May, 1218, therefore, six delegates from both sides met at Bergamo. Generous concessions were made to the Lombards, but two points the Waldenses would not yield: Lombard recognition of Waldo and his otherwise unknown colleague Vivet as " blessed "; and the surrender of the distinctively Lombard sacramental doctrine, for which only toleration, not acceptance, had been asked. The Lombards refused to comply on these two points, and negotiations were accordingly broken off, never to be resumed. Both were guilty of narrowness, yet the final cause of the division is to be found in the fact that the Lombards were already an organized community with fixed regulations and self-consciousness when they joined the Waldenses.

II. Ideal, Method, and Government of the Poor Men: That the purpose of Waldo was a return to apostolic poverty, with a general revival of apostolic life based especially on Matt. x., is firmly established. The dearth of direct information concerning his regulations finds, however, a certain degree of compensation in two indirect

1. Character and Rule. sources: the statements regarding the French and Lombard " poor men " in later times; and the authentic data afforded by Innocent III. concerning the Pauperes Catholici, to whom the pope left, so far as possible, their old usages and organization. Inasmuch as all regular intercourse was broken off permanently, it may be considered a rule that all institutions and practises found in later times common to both Waldenses and Lombards date from before the schism. The " society " of the " poor in spirit " was primarily nothing but an ascetic association of men and women who renounced the world, formally vowed to practise apostolic poverty and the apostolic calling, and wore as an outward symbol the apostolic habit. They alone, later called in the Lombard-German group also " masters," " apostles," and even " lords," were members of the " society "; the recent converts and " friends " who remained in the world had no share in their privileges and duties. By the excommunication of the society its character changed long before the schism; and Waldo, who had already claimed recognition as a bishop, and who had asserted the power of consecrating the Eucharist, prepared the way for the transformation of his following into a sect or antichurch, a tendency present already in 1184. Under the pressure of persecution even the "friends" felt themselves sectaries, and became increasingly merged with the main body of Waldenses, although the distinction between the two classes was never forgotten by Roman Catholic writers. The condition for admission to the "society" was, from the first, "conversion," in its monastic sense of renunciation of the worldly state and vocation and personal property, and the dissolution of a previous marriage. Reception into the community seems originally to have followed directly; but even before the schism a period of probation was required of one or two years in the German-Lombard division, and of five or six in the French. This period was devoted especially to committing the New Testament to memory, as well as other books of the Bible; and at its conclusion the neophyte was ceremonially admitted, making at first, probably only among the "brothers and sisters," the following vows: perfect poverty, rigid obedience of the precepts of the Gospel, and the wearing of the apostolic habit. Previous to the schism the vow of celibacy seems also to have been exacted, while later both Lombards and Waldenses admitted only the unmarried. Finally, the novice pledged himself to complete submission to his superiors. The "apostolic habit" apparently consisted at first of a simple woolen cloak. Originally the "poor men" went barefoot, but at least before 1194, they began to wear a sandal, cross-tied and supplied with a small buckle or shield on the instep, whence their nicknames. Considerable significance was attached to the sandal, and to proffer it and put it on came later to be a part of the solemn rite of reception. Thus attired, the "poor men" roamed, two by two, as wandering preachers from city to city, imitating Luke x. 1. They were forbidden to earn their living by their own labors, receiving their food and other necessities from their friends (cf. Matt. x. 10 sqq.; I Cor. ix. 7 sqq.), and at first returning alms given in money. From the very first they attached high value to abstinence, fasting on Mondays, Wednesdays, and Fridays; and they were equally devoted to prayer, though, except for the blessing at meals, they used only the Lord's Prayer (in Biblical strictness). At first they utterly disregarded the canonical hours, but later they prayed seven times daily. At a very early time, moreover, probably under the influence of the Cathari (see NEW MANICHEANS, II.), they refused every form of oath (cf. Matt. v. 34 sqq.), abhorred every falsehood as a mortal sin, and condemned shedding of blood, even in a righteous war or in capital punishment (cf. Matt. v. 21 sqq., vii. 1 sqq.). They held their chief duty to be preaching, though after being excommunicated they began to hear confessions and to celebrate the Lord's Supper, as well as to ordain by prayer and laying on of hands. Yet before the schism they had apparently determined to celebrate the Lord's Supper only once a year, on the evening of Maundy Thursday (q.v.), when it should be celebrated by a bishop. In France it was apparently the custom, from an early time, to partake of fish as well as of unleavened bread and

wine at this celebration, and the power of healing the sick was soon attributed to all these elements.

The preaching of the "poor men" was very simple, normally consisting only of exhortations to repentance and the recitation of long passages from the Bible in the vernacular. From the beginning of the thirteenth century, at latest,

2. Preaching and Scripture. they laid special stress on the prohibition of oaths, falsehood, and the shedding of blood (cf. Matt. v. 21 sqq., vii. 1 sqq.). The heresies alleged by their opponents to exist among them only served to intensify their emphasis upon the preaching of repentance and the assertion of their undertaking against the hierarchy, holding, namely, that, (1) masses, alms, and prayers do not avail the dead; (2) purgatory does not exist; (3) episcopal indulgences are invalid; (4) obedience is due only to those good priests who live the apostolic life; and (5) that "merit is more essential to consecrating, blessing, binding, and loosing than office or ordination." The "poor men" doubted the efficacy of sacraments, especially the Eucharist, administered by unworthy Roman Catholic priests; and they held that prayer is more efficacious in the closet than in the church, besides contesting the peculiar sanctity of the sacred places of the Church. For all their doctrines and distinctive usages they at first gave formal proof by reference to the Bible: e.g., for lay preaching to James iv. 17; Rev. xxii. 17; Mark ix. 38-39; Phil. i. 15; Num. xi. 29; for the admission of women as preachers to Titus ii. 3–4, and the example of Anna (Luke ii. 36–38). While they did not avoid citing Roman Catholic writers occasionally, from the very first they adhered with the extremest rigidity to the minutest and most literal precepts of the Bible. They laid special stress from the beginning on the possession of the Scriptures by the laity in the vernacular. As early as 1179 Waldo seems to have had almost the entire Bible in Provençal, and this was very likely used by his adherents in Catalonia, Aragon, northern France, and Lorraine, and even Lombardy. In Germany, on the other hand, the Bible was translated anew. Many misunderstandings were more than probable; yet, in spite of not always realizing what the text meant, entire books were memorized and orally repeated. Even among the "friends" were some, who, though illiterate, could repeat the words of Christ, the forty Sunday gospels, and even Job and the entire four Gospels.

At first the Waldenses went about publicly in their apostolic habit, preaching in the streets, markets, and even churches. These practises they were able to keep up in Languedoc till late in the thirteenth

3. Missions; Government. century, but elsewhere persecution soon obliged them to lay aside their habit and to prosecute their activity in secret.

They now went disguised as pilgrims, palmers, artizans, or laborers of various kinds, sometimes carrying different costumes with them. Wherever they could find a hearing, they sought to convert some from the world, i.e., to induce them to join them, while their other adherents, or "friends," they urged to hold regular conventicles, and particularly to abstain from oaths and the shedding of blood. In Lombardy the "friends" were at first advised to enter one of the associations of laborers at Milan and elsewhere, and these associations and conventicles, sometimes erecting their own buildings, formed initially the fixed centers of Waldensian missionary activity. To these were added in the German-Lombard section, in the thirteenth century, *studia* or " hospices," in which the " converts " were trained and the preachers entertained. The laborers' associations, special objects of mistrust, apparently disappeared before 1218, but the other two institutions of conventicles and *studia* long lived on. [In the *Rescriptum* (of 1218) of the Poor Men of Lombardy to the Poor Men of Lyons, the former still plead for the toleration of the *Congregationes laborantium* on condition that abuses and vices be abolished. A. H. N.] Until the secession of the Lombards the government of the Waldenses rested in the hands of Waldo, who was regarded as bishop and supervising head. It is evident that after 1184 and before 1210 the society resolved to create anew the three orders of bishops, priests, and deacons. It then recognized Waldo as bishop, and he ordained other " poor men " as presbyters and deacons. The reason for this step was doubtless distrust of the sacramental ministrations of Roman Catholic priests, and these three offices were retained in accordance with the " law of God " in the Bible. Waldo was clearly *præpositus* or *rector* and bishop until the secession, after which the Lombards apparently continued the monarchical system; and till the end of the fifteenth century they had a *summus pontifex*, who, after the second half of the fourteenth century, resided in Apulia or middle Italy. There is mention of several Lombard bishops in Lombardy and Germany about 1266. In France, about 1218, there is no evidence of a monarchical *rector*, only of two " procurators " chosen annually. Toward the end of the thirteenth century, however, a *major minister* chosen for life was to be found in France, together with other bishops, or *majores*, who conferred ordination, but exercised no administrative functions. From all this it is evident that the episcopal dignity conferred by ordination was at first not necessarily joined with the rectorate, which was subject to the election of the assembly and its regulations. Yet it was deemed important that the rector possess also consecration as bishop, which seems always to have been the case in Lombardy. The first exact information concerning the powers and duties of these incumbencies is contained in French sources of the late thirteenth and early fourteenth centuries. The deacon (also called *minor;* in Germany *junior*) was simply the servant of the presbyters, bishops, and rectors; and when the " poor men " went out in pairs, one was usually a presbyter and the other a deacon. Originally the deacon also had the right to preach and hear confession. The presbyter was empowered to preach in the district assigned him by the rector, to hear confession, and to pronounce the blessing at meals. Later he could also confer ordination if no bishop were present. In the Lombard-German Waldenses all consciousness of distinction between the orders of bishop and priest had vanished in the fifteenth century. The bishop, later called *major* or *majoralis* in France, likewise had the right to cele-

brate the Lord's Supper and to confer ordination. The *rector* or *præpositus*, later called *major omnium* or *major minister* in France, had, in addition to his episcopal functions, the prerogative of convening and conducting the assembly which met once or twice annually; and in France he might also preach everywhere and grant absolution. The rite of ordination for all three grades was simply confession of sins (lacking among the Lombard-Germans), the Lord's Prayer, and laying on of hands. In France all " poor men " were at least deacons about 1320. In addition were the " sisters "; but these were never very numerous, and in France, about the beginning of the fourteenth century, it was resolved to admit no more sisters, since they could hold no spiritual office; while in the Lombard-German district they lived in the hospices by the close of the thirteenth century, having given up itinerant preaching. There was likewise a controversy between the Lombards and Waldenses concerning the " ministers," but at Bergamo it was decided that these officials should be chosen by the assembly either from the recent converts or from the " friends," and either for a term or for life. [The question at issue in 1218 between the Poor Men of Lombardy and the Poor Men of Lyons was whether prepositi (or bishops) should be appointed by the former. Waldo, considering his own headship sufficient, had positively refused to allow the appointment of such officials either by the Italians or the French in his own lifetime or even after his death. It was agreed between the parties that prepositi might be appointed for life (eternaliter) or rectors for a time, as might seem more useful or conducive to peace. A. H. N.] These " ministers " were evidently not part of the three spiritual orders of the Waldenses, but were chosen by the assembly to conduct the conventicles of " friends " and the associations of laborers, and to aid the itinerant apostles. It thus becomes clear that before 1218 the attempt was made to organize the " friends " of the Waldenses. *Majores*, bishops, presbyters, and deacons had no fixed residence, but once or twice each year all, or all the older members, of the sect seem to have convened in a *commune*, or assembly, called by the Roman Catholics " council " or " chapter." So long as Waldo was recognized by the Lombards, this assembly was overshadowed by him, but after the schism it became a prominent feature in the administration of the society in Lombardy, as it did in France after the death of Waldo. This assembly decided on the admission of new members; chose presiding officers and " ministers "; determined who should receive ordination to the various grades of its clergy; exercised discipline; considered the general condition of the sect, and received a report from each member concerning the state of the work in his missionary district; and later ruled concerning the use of the alms and funds contributed by the " friends." As the missionary field of the sect grew, it became no longer possible to convene all members, so that from more distant regions three or four delegates were considered sufficient.

III. The Ancient Waldenses: After the schism of the Lombards the old Waldenses were restricted to their early missionary districts in Aragon, Cata-

Ionia, France, and Lorraine. [It is not likely that either party had regard to national or geographical bounds. A. H. N.] In the two regions first named persecutions by Church and State continued, and in the thirteenth century all traces of the Waldenses vanished from Spain, and in the thirteenth century they disappeared from Lorraine and Flanders. In the Franche Comté, Provence, and Languedoc, however, they were so numerous in 1248 that Count John of Burgundy deemed himself able to cope with them only by means of the Inquisition. They were in conflict with the Church in Valentinois and Provence until the second quarter of the fourteenth century; but as late as the first quarter of the same century their great missionary district was Languedoc, where repressive measures failed to diminish their activity or to disperse their " friends," who were sometimes able to form, both there and in Provence, small congregations with cemeteries of their own, as at Montauban, Montcucq, and Gourdon. After the inquisition of Peter Cella (1241–42), however, the " poor men " and their "friends " were gradually dispersed even in Languedoc, so that by the beginning of the fourteenth century they had become a secret organization, and declined in the course of this and the following century. The internal conditions of the sect during its period of decline are revealed fairly well by the protocols of the Inquisition, and by Bernardus Guidonis. The society preserved, so far as possible, its old customs and regulations. As consequences of their conflict with the Church and the Cathari, the Waldenses had abandoned their apostolic habit, and the Church they regarded as the " Church of the wicked " and a " house of lies " because its members were permitted to take oaths and its priests were not bound to apostolic poverty. They denied the right of excommunication and enforcing obedience, and contested the right of Roman Catholic priests to administer the sacraments. They also denied the miracles of the saints, and rejected their invocation, though not the cult of the virgin; and they observed as feasts only Sundays, the days of the virgin, and sometimes the days of the apostles and evangelists. Nevertheless, to escape suspicion, they attended church industriously, sought the favor of priests and monks, and did not hinder the " friends " from confession to Roman Catholic priests. No longer a preaching association with a missionary activity within the Church, the French central affiliation became a sect or anti-church prevented from schism and independence only by the untoward circumstances. Hence the " friends " came to be designated as Waldenses, and only the descendants of parents who were " believers " were eligible for the " poor " class or the *perfecti*. The training imposed for the order of " poor men " consisted successively of five or six years of study, ordination as deacons, and about nine years more of theological study. Entrance was invariably by ordination as deacon, which was regarded as more important than the profession of vows. Women were no longer admitted to this order. The powers and duties of the officers were closely defined with a *major minister* at the head chosen for life. A catechism, apparently transmitted orally from generation to generation, consisting of seven articles on God, seven on man, the Decalogue, and the seven works of mercy, was arranged.

IV. The Lombard-German Branch before the Reformation: The Lombards successfully advanced into Italy, Germany, Bohemia, Poland, and Hungary. In Italy, Milan remained their headquarters and Lombardy their chief missionary district. By 1235, however, the persecution of heresy had begun, on a large scale, though how far the " poor men," who had imitated and borrowed much from the Cathari, despite their opposition to them, were affected is uncertain. At all events, their organization was not destroyed by 1266, when

1. **In Italy.** the assemblies could be held more frequently in Lombardy than anywhere else. Yet by that time the greater amount of money for the support of the clergy came from Germany, thus showing that the German Waldenses were then more numerous and stronger than the Lombard. In the course of the fourteenth century the Lombards seem to have died out in their original center; but as early as the previous century the " poor men " had found asylum in the Alpine valleys of western Piedmont and the neighboring Dauphiny. A tradition of the fifteenth century would have them come from France, crossing the Cottian Alps. However, the resemblance and close connection with the German Lombards, contradicts that tradition. Doubtless the movement entered not by migration but by missionary proselyting among the inhabitants on both declines of the Cottian Alps, who were originally sprung from an East Provençal stock. The dialect of the Waldensian literature supports this view. Precisely when this mission began is uncertain, but the sect was widespread in the valleys on both sides of Mont Génèvre by the beginning of the fourteenth century. By the end of this century Waldenses occupied not only the so-called Waldensian valleys, but they were to be found in the numerous villages in the valleys of Susa and the Sangone, and in the cities of the neighboring plain, Pianezza, Castagnola, Moncalieri, Carmagnola, Chieri. In the course of the same century there were also two southern colonization districts in Calabria and Apulia. The first group of towns were said by Waldensian tradition of the sixteenth and seventeenth centuries to have been founded about 1315 or 1370 at the request of a Calabrian noble, by Waldenses from the Cottian Alps. The accuracy of this tradition is questionable, though the names Borgo d'Oltremontani and Guardia Piemontese, where Waldensian is still spoken, show that these towns owed their origin to the Waldenses. About 1400 some of them are said to have been driven from Provence to Apulia, where they founded the four towns of Monteleone, Faito, Cella, and La Motta Montecorvino, while a century later others were said to have founded the city of Volturara; but it is shown again that Cella and Faito had been in existence in the twelfth century, and had received Provençal colonists in 1345 or 1347, but not Waldenses. However, they were certainly both numerous and influential in Apulia in the fourteenth century, so that about 1380 their *summus pontifex* was residing there, and was still receiving moneys from Piedmont in the middle of the fifteenth century. In their travels

from Calabria and Apulia to the Alpine valleys, the Waldensian apostles evidently made missionary efforts in central Italy, thus explaining the communities found in the fifteenth century in the States of the Church, including Umbria, Tuscany, and Romagna. These communities seem to have been especially numerous in the duchy of Spolato, and small Waldensian conventicles were also to be found in Camerino, Ancona, Perugia, Bologna, Lucca, and Florence. Even Rome contained one, but the conventicles then existing at Genoa and elsewhere in Liguria were apparently survivals of the old Lombard mission. The most remarkable proof of the energy of the Italian Waldenses, however, is, that in the fourteenth and fifteenth centuries they carried their propaganda into the territory of the French " poor men." The occasion was likely the colonizing, by the Barons Bouliers, of a few Waldensian families of Saluzzo on the north bank of the Durance in France, who may have been tracked by the apostles. It is uncertain whether they found remnants of old French communities in their labors in Provence, Valentinois, Vivarais, Venaissin, Auvergne, Limousin, and Bordelais; but at all events they were able to gather a series of conventicles in Auvergne, Valentinois, and near Trévoux, north of Lyons, and even to hold an assembly in Lyons, May 31, 1492.

In Germany occurred the first execution of Waldenses *en masse*, at Strasburg, in 1211 (ut sup.); and in 1231–33 took place there the first general persecution. Nothing was now heard of them for a long time in central Germany, but in upper Germany they soon again attracted attention. They were encountered in Constance in 1243, and in Hall in Swabia in 1248 they dared openly to defend the excommunicated Emperor Frederick II.

2. In Germany, Bohemia, Poland, and Hungary. and to brand Pope Innocent IV. as a heretic. In Bavaria and in Upper and Lower Austria they spread so quickly, despite incessant bloody persecution, that about 1260 the Inquisition found Waldensian schools in forty-two parishes of Upper and Lower Austria; while in 1315 heretics were found in thirty-six places between St. Pölten and Traiskirchen, the " poor men" themselves then estimating the number of their followers in the duchy of Austria at more than 80,000. Meanwhile they had also found their way into Bohemia, Moravia, Silesia, Meissen, Brandenburg, Pomerania, and Poland. By the end of the fourteenth century they were in a series of places in Hungary, and even in Transylvania. Half a century later the sect was first noticed in the duchy of Saxe-Wittenberg and in the district of Magdeburg, and twenty years later in what is now Mecklenburg-Schwerin. In southern Bohemia the Waldenses formed entire villages in the German colonies near Neuhaus, about 1340, and in Moravia they were so numerous that the Church almost despaired of overcoming them. In Brandenburg, Pomerania, and Mecklenburg no less than 443 persons were accused of the Waldensian heresy in 1393–94; and the sect seems to have been a regular concomitant of German colonization in the thirteenth and fourteenth centuries. The Waldenses were equally active in the interior of Germany. In the last decade of the fourteenth century the Inquisition discovered them in many towns beside Erfurt, Mainz, Nuremberg, and Regensburg, and in all Upper and Lower Austria, Salzburg, and Styria. In Swabia, Augsburg was an early center of the sect, and they were found in Ulm, Donauwörth (twenty-six executed in 1393), and other towns. On the Upper Rhine among the notable places which they occupied were Strasburg, Hagenau, and Speyer; and in Switzerland, Basel, Solothurn, St. Gall, Bern, Freiburg, Neuchâtel, Lausanne, Vaud, and others. Records are wanting of their presence only in the Tyrol, in the Rhine valley north of Bingen with its lateral vălleys, Lower Saxony, Frisia, Holstein, and, for a long time, the Netherlands. The Waldensians drew their recruits chiefly from the lower classes. In Upper Germany they were especially influential among the cloth-makers, but only a few of the clergy or of the cultured classes joined their ranks. Among their patrons and adherents, however, were not seldom those of knightly position or high office, so that as diligent artizans and colonists they received open favor in the margravate of Saluzzo, the Montagne du Luberon, Apulia, and Calabria. Among their " friends " were representatives of the higher classes, especially in the cities of Swabia, Franconia, and Bavaria, as well as in Bern and Freiburg in Switzerland.

The Lombard Waldensians developed their organization from an ascetic band of preachers to an antichurch or sect as quickly as their French brethren.

3. Internal Development. As early as 1260 they and their " friends " formed, even in Germany, a loose but practically organized secret church, which considered itself the only Church of Christ, occasionally termed entrance to its number true baptism, and thus implied what it explicitly declared in the fourteenth century, that outside of it there was no salvation. It accordingly declined all the claims, hierarchy, and worship of the Roman Cătholic Church, designating it, as early as about 1240, as the great beast of the Apocalypse, and declaring that it had ceased to be the Church of Christ when Pope Silvester, the first antichrist, received the donation from Constantine. The Waldenses protested against all privileges of rank, clerical prerogatives, the titles of pope and bishop, priestly despotism, all incomes and endowments of churches and monasteries, the division of the land into dioceses and parishes, against councils and synods, the whole system of ecclesiastical courts and penalties and of marriage law, the celibacy of the clergy, and the like. They also rejected, at least after the fourteenth century, monasticism in all its forms; the system of religious instruction; the mystical interpretation of the Scriptures; all ordinations and acts of worship not explicitly directed by the Bible; all church fasts and feasts excepting Sundays and sometimes Christmas, Easter, Ascension, Whitsunday, and the feasts of the apostles; the blessing of all articles such as candles, palms, water, and the use of articles thus blessed; the blessing and dedication of churches, cemeteries, pilgrims, and the like; the churching of women; and pilgrimages, processions, organs, bells, spires, canonical hours, the whole Latin liturgy, and all else appertaining to the externals of worship. More emphatic was their condemnation of the cult of images, relics, saints, and the Virgin, but most productive of offense were their severe strictures upon the sacraments of the Church. Beginning about 1240, with the denial of the efficacy of sacraments administered by evil priests, the radical faction, assuming that all Roman Catholic priests were evil, proceeded to renounce Roman Catholic baptism as unnecessary; infant baptism as worthless; confirmation and extreme unction superfluous; and the Eucharist, ordination, and penance as administered by the Church, futile. The "friends," with the moderates, did not always follow to these extremes, and the Waldenses only very seldom attacked belief in the sacraments itself. This extreme radicalism of the Lombard Waldenses was due, in all probability, to the influence of the Cathari; and the similarity of the two sects occasionally led to their formal confusion, as in the sect of the Piedmontese Martino de Presbytero, which occupies a prominent place in the acts of the Inquisition in 1388. Dogma was not yet the prominent feature in Waldensian preaching, which was mostly content with inculcating abstinence from oaths, falsehood, war, and capital punishment. Masses, prayers, and offerings for the dead were declared futile, and purgatory was denied. Foremost was the admonition of the two ways (Matt. vii. 13–14). In Italy and Germany, for preaching and the instruction of the elders, there were, in addition to the Bible, (1) an anthology entitled, *Verba sanctorum Augustini, Hieronymi, Ambrosii, Gregorii, Chrysostomi, et Isidori* (such a collection was already in the hands of Waldo); (2) *Liber electorum* (probably called also *Liber justorum*); (3) the " Thirty Steps of Augustine," a tractate on the virtues and vices; (4) *Septem articuli fidei*, perhaps identical with the seven articles on God in the French Waldensian catechism (ut sup.); and (5) a " Rule," with data concerning the origin of the sect, apparently transmitted only orally. The German Waldenses of the thirteenth century possessed also vernacular poems, which seem never to have been committed to writing. In the fifteenth century the German Waldenses had interpretations of the Gospels and Pauline epistles in the vernacular, though these were probably from the work of some Roman Catholic author and restricted to the lessons of the Church. The Italian Waldenses evidently possessed a number of books previous to 1368, but after that date had scarcely more than the Bible and the *Liber electorum*. In the sixteenth and seventeenth centuries the Waldenses of the Cottian Alps had a regular *Bibliotheca Waldensis*, but of its contents it is known that a small portion alone dated from the pre-Reformation period. To this portion belonged at least a tractate *Vertucz;* the *Doctor* and *Vergier de consollacion*, both anthologies; *Glosa pater noster*, an exposition of the Lord's Prayer, probably translated from some Roman Catholic author; and *Cantica*, a translation of a Roman Catholic commentary on Canticles in seven books (the first of which is lost), with a few specifically Waldensian additions. This commentary was probably prepared in the Cottian Alps or in Provence toward the end of the fifteenth century, as also the *Penitenca* and *Pecca*. An essentially Waldensian work was the great *Nobla leyçon* (ed. E. Montet, Paris, 1888), a

poem of 479 duodecasyllabic verses, written by an author of some theological training, probably in the Cottian Alps after 1231. It is a missionary sermon in verse after the order of the minstrels, reviewing the contents of the Bible under the threefold head of " the law of nature, the law of Moses, the law of Christ." The other didactic poems were probably likewise of the thirteenth century: namely, *La Barca; Lo Novel Sermon; Lo Novel Confort; Lo Payre Eternal; Lo Despreczi del mont; L'Avangeli de li quatre sementz;* and the corrupt *L'Oraczon*. In Germany, as among the French Waldenses, the Lord's Supper was celebrated in the fourteenth century annually on Maundy Thursday, but in the following century this usage disappeared and the masters were confined mostly to hearing confession. In the Cottian Alps, on the other hand, as well as in Provence, Apulia, Calabria, and middle Italy, the independent celebration of the Lord's Supper lasted longer. In the fifteenth century the Waldenses of the Cottian Alps and middle Italy no longer all received the Eucharist from Roman Catholic priests, but took the bread consecrated by their " barbs " (clericals). But after the great persecution of 1487–1494, it was received only from the priests of the Church, except at clerical ordinations the communion was celebrated in the ancient Waldensian fashion down to the sixteenth century.

Waldensian organization underwent an important change in the fourteenth century, when the German branch separated from the Italian, ceasing to have official relations with the Italian bishops and rector, and regulating its affairs henceforth by its own assemblies, which were held by preference in the large cities at the time of the annual fairs. The Germans did not, however, elect a rector, for in Germany his influence had always been weak and the masters had become accustomed to act on their own responsibility. In all probability there was no general Waldensian assembly in Germany, and no general organization. At the same time there was frequent intercommunication between all the conventicles of Germany, nor were relations with the Lombards entirely broken off. In Italy the strong central organization was maintained until the Reformation period. In the fourteenth century the three orders of clergy were found both in Italy and in Germany, but in the following century they disappeared from both lands. [It seems hardly probable that so radical a change should occur in the polity of so conservative a body within so brief a time. A. H. N.] The only ordination then known was that received at reception into the sect, precedence within the body being determined solely by seniority. At the same time the position of the " juniors " corresponded in a sense to that of the French deacons, and the " seniors " to the French presbyters. In Germany all members of the sect were termed masters, while in Italy they were called " barbs " (East Provençal *barba*, " uncle "). The mode of the life of the Waldenses, who received in Italy a new name at their ordination, was practically that of the early period. The system of training was carefully regulated. In Germany the pupil must study with a master for a year or two. He was then ordained, but must still

4. **Organizations.**

work under the supervision of a master from six to nine years before he could hear confession. In Italy, the chief source of recruits in the fifteenth century being the peasantry, the candidates must first learn to read and commit to memory the Gospels of Matthew and John, as well as several of the New-Testament epistles. This consumed two months of each winter for three or four years, after which the candidate studied and practised manual labor for a year or two in one of the sister houses. He was then ordained, but must still act for years as the assistant of an older "barb." The sisters seem to have been used in missions in Germany as late as the fifteenth century; while in Italy they then lived as virgins in the houses and hospices which sheltered the "barbs" and their pupils. There were also "friends" who, in Germany, raised contributions for the masters, and in Italy also occasionally aided the "barbs" in hearing confession, and in preaching. The masters were well supported by the collections and the small confessional gifts. The Waldenses never ceased to be itinerant preachers; so that in Germany, toward the end of the fourteenth century, they changed their scenes of activity every year or two, and in Italy, as late as 1530, every two or three years. They held an assembly regularly each year. Meetings in Germany and the Cottian Alps occurred almost invariably at night, in a private house or barn, and admission was by a countersign. In Germany, Apulia, Calabria, and other Piedmontese colonies, the Waldenses attended Roman Catholic worship regularly; and only where they were in the majority, as in the Cottian Alps, did they and their "friends," before 1487, dare for years not to confess and commune in the Roman Catholic churches, which they there avoided altogether.

To understand the inner history of the Waldenses in Germany and Italy it must constantly be borne in mind that they were outlawed from 1231, and had to be prepared at every turn for a fresh persecution. After the great persecution in 1231 they seem to have been disturbed only locally, about 1260, in Bavaria and Austria, and perhaps also in Bohemia, Moravia, and the neighboring Hungarian districts. At the beginning of the fourteenth century the persecution started anew in the same districts, spreading, by 1313, to Silesia, and, about 1330, to Poland, Hungary, Brandenburg, Thuringia, and Franconia; but the next general suppression, including also Switzerland, was inspired by Gregory XI. (1370–78). Here such energy was displayed by the inquisitors Petrus Zwicker and Martin of Amberg that these regions long remained unaffected by the Waldenses. It was not until the third decade of the fifteenth century that the surviving associations again dared to make their presence known, being encouraged in such places as the Swiss Freiburg by the long respite, and inspired elsewhere by the Hussite propaganda. In Bohemia, Moravia, and the neighboring Austrian districts they seem to have been incorporated with the Hussites, so impressing their peculiar tenets as to produce a distinct body, the Bohemian Brethren (q.v.). These seem to have sought to attract to themselves all the Waldensians in Austria, Moravia, and Bohemia, though

with imperfect success, for some of the Waldenses even then would not surrender their formal union with the Church. This conservative party seems gradually to have died out. In Swabia and Franconia the Saxon noble, Johann Drändorf (burned 1425), and Peter of Turnau (burned 1426), sought to attach the regular Waldenses to the Hussites; more successful was the Hussite Bishop Friedrich Reiser (burned at Strasburg, 1458), especially at Nuremberg, Würzburg, Schweinfurt, Heilsbronn, Strasburg, Basel, and other parts of southern and central Germany. Yet though many of the Waldenses thus recognized the Hussites as brethren, they did not themselves become Hussites, their adherence consisting merely in deeming Wyclif, Huss, and Jerome of Prague to be Christian teachers, allowing Reiser and the Bohemian Nikolaus Pilgram to ordain priests, from whom they received the communion in both forms. However, they surrendered absolutely none of their own tenets, and Reiser's propaganda accomplished no more than the endeavor of Peter Chelcicky to convert the Hussites to Waldensian doctrines. Nevertheless, the union between the two sects became so close that when, in 1479, a fresh attempt was made to suppress the Waldenses in Uckermark and Neumark, they decided to emigrate to Bohemia and Moravia; some settled in Fulnek and Weisskirchen in Moravia, and others in Landskron in Bohemia. From this time nothing more is heard of German Waldenses, and it can only be conjectured that the sect still lingered on in Egerland and Voigtland. None the less, the influence of the Waldenses lived on, both in the tenets and customs of the Bohemian Brethren, and in the theories of the Anabaptists, for whom they were the forerunners throughout Upper Germany and Austria. In Lombardy the persecutions, which began in 1231, did not achieve their ends until the close of the fourteenth century. In the valleys on the eastern slopes of the Cottian Alps the Inquisition began its work at latest by the end of the thirteenth century, and on the western side by 1289; but real severity first began in 1332. The instigation of Gregory XI. took effect also here. In the French valleys the soul of the movement against the Waldenses was the Minorite Francesco Borelli, who had 169 burned at one time on July 1, 1380; but the Dominicans in the Piedmontese valleys were less zealous, besides being checked by the secular officials. Equally fruitless was the effort of the Spanish Dominican Vincente Ferrer (q.v.) in 1403 to win back the inhabitants of the Vals Louise, Argentière, and Freissinières. In 1412, therefore, the Inquisition resumed its activity in the western valleys, though with little success; but in 1434 it was replaced in Bardonnèche, Oulx, Exilles, and elsewhere by the secular arm, so effectively that the Waldenses emigrated in large numbers. In France, on the contrary, they were protected for a time by Louis XI., who sought to check all exercise of ecclesiastical discipline; but against the chicanery of the incensed archbishop of Embrun and the offended provincial boards of Dauphiny his attempted protection was vain and the accession of Charles VIII. brought with it a fresh persecution transcending in extent and horror all that had hitherto befallen the Waldenses of the Cottian Alps. A crusade was now preached

5. Persecutions.

against them at the direction of Innocent VIII., and under the auspices of the archdeacon Alberto de Cattaneo of Cremona, papal legate for the territories of Charles I. of Savoy, the assault was opened simultaneously in the dioceses of Vienne, Sitten, and elsewhere, and in Piedmont, Dauphiny, and the margravate of Saluzzo. In the Val Angrogna successful resistance was offered and Charles was induced, in 1488 or 1489, to suspend the war in Saluzzo and Piedmont; but in Dauphiny greater success was obtained, where from 1488 the crusading army coerced the Waldenses of the Vals Pragelas, Cluson, Freissinières, Louise, and Argentière. Those who remained loyal either sought refuge in the high valleys of Oulx and Bardonnèche, or returned secretly to their old homes after the storm had subsided, so that in 1495 fresh processes were resumed against them in Val Pragelas, and in 1506 in the Vals Argentière and Freissinières. In Saluzzo the widow of the margrave expelled the Waldenses from the upper valley of the Po in 1509, but they returned three years later and even gained absolution from Leo X. In Dauphiny only the Val Louise was really cleared of the Waldenses. In Piedmont they had proved victorious, and they were not even disturbed in their colonies in Provence, Calabria, Apulia, and middle Italy. In Lombardy they had completely disappeared, and they were practically destroyed in Germany, Switzerland, Hungary, and Poland. The number of Waldensians put to death can not be approximately estimated, but was very high. More numerous than the steadfast were those who recanted under pressure, only to return to their faith. Then they had to be prepared for the worst, for·most sentences of death seemed to have fallen on these. They were also guilty of violence, as in Austria the murder of priests and monks, and in the Cottian Alps of an official of the Inquisition (1374), and more frequently took bloody revenge upon renegade masters and friends who had turned spies and informers for the Inquisition.

V. The Romance Waldenses after the Reformation: After Apr., 1523, Guillaume Farel (q.v.) labored for the Protestant cause for a time at Gap in Dauphiny, and though he was soon expelled, the agitation begun by him quickly reached the Waldenses of the Cottian Alps. Within a few years, by the labors of the " barb " Martin Gonin, a Protestant faction arose, especially among the Waldenses of Provence; and in the summer of 1530 two " barbs," George Morel of Val Freis-

1. Entrance into the Reformed Body. sinières and Pierre Masson of Burgundy, were sent across the Alps to confer with Farel. Morel, who possessed a fair education, also conferred with Berthold Haller in Bern, with Œcolampadius in Basel, and with Butzer and Capito in Strasburg; and on his return was so energetic in behalf of the Protestant cause that Farel and other Protestants of French Switzerland were formally invited to visit his coreligionists at their assembly at Angrogna in 1532. Farel accepted, together with Anton Saunier and Robert Olivétan. Farel dominated the assembly, as is shown by their renunciation of their distinctive doctrines. The doctrine of election and the Zwinglian doctrine of the

Lord's Supper were officially adopted and the only distinctive tenet retained was the prohibition against war. They, accordingly, ceased virtually to be Waldenses, and became merged in the Upper German and Swiss faction of the Protestants. As a result, however, the Waldenses became divided into the Protestant and the old-school factions. In the Cottian Alps the Protestant faction prevailed without serious antagonism, but in Provence the old-school Waldenses did more than protest, for late in 1532 or early in 1533 the two " barbs," Daniel de Valence and Jean de Molines, went to Bohemia for help. The moral support of the Bohemian Brethren they received, but to no purpose; for the assembly of Val San Martino, Aug. 15, 1533, explicitly confirmed the resolutions of Angrogna. The Protestant party now proceeded to carry the Reformation through everywhere in closest harmony with Farel and his followers. The new faith spread most rapidly in the colonies of Provence and Venaissin, where, by 1535, some 10,000 Protestant Waldenses, exhausted by the persecutions of Church and State, were ready to emigrate to Protestant Germany. But in 1545 troops were sent against them by the president of parliament, Jean Maynier, seigneur d'Oppède, which destroyed twenty-two villages and put to death 4,000 Waldenses, only about an equal number escaping to Germany and Geneva. In the Cottian Alps, under Saunier's influence, the Waldenses decided in 1532 to have the Bible printed in French (see BIBLE VERSIONS, B, VI., § 3). In consequence the Waldenses of this district now received French pastors from the Academy of Lausanne, who gradually remodeled their services after those of Geneva; induced them to erect their own churches from 1555, as well as to receive communion in both forms (to the number of 6,000 at Angrogna); and in 1559 drew up at Turin a creed based on the Gallican Confession (q.v.). When, moreover, Piedmont was restored to Duke Emanuel Philibert by the peace of Cateau-Cambresius, Waldensian refusal to receive Roman Catholic priests caused the duke to send troops against them in Nov., 1560. Such was their persistence in petty warfare, however, that by the peace of Cavour (June 5, 1561) the duke was constrained to grant them limited toleration in a series of places in the valleys of Luserna, San Martino, and Perosa. The congregations of these valleys and of Cluson and the margravate of Saluzzo were accordingly able to form an organization modeled after the statutes of Geneva at the synods of Angrogna (1563) and Villar (1564); and on Nov. 11, 1571, they formed a league to resist all infractions of the peace of Cavour. In Calabria and Apulia the Waldenses were less fortunate, and it was not till 1556 that the former appointed their own pastors and administration of the sacrament. For this they were formally extirpated in 1560 by Spanish troops under the auspices of the grand inquisitor Michele Ghislieri (later Pope Pius V.). In eleven days in June, 2,000 persons were put to death, 1,600 were imprisoned, and others were condemned to the galleys. The Apulian Waldenses, who had thus far prudently held themselves in retirement, now fled in larger numbers to Geneva, though the majority, intimidated by the slaughter in Calabria, reentered the Roman Church.

After 1571 there remained of the old Waldensian communities within the bounds of the present kingdom of Italy only those in the margravate of Saluzzo and the so-called Waldensian valleys; and these were no longer Waldensian, but a part of the Calvinistic division of Protestantism.

When Daniel de Valence and Jean de Molines were defeated at the assembly of Val San Martino, on Aug. 15, 1533, they are said, on good authority, to have made away with all ancient Waldensian manuscripts and memoirs that they could secure. In the so-called Waldensian manuscripts, however, there is extant an entire series of treatises doubtless modeled on Czech originals. Here belong the following: *Ayczo es la causa del nostre departiment de la gleysa romana* (based on the " Grounds of Separation " of Luke of Prague, q.v.); *De li sept sacrament, Purgatori, Dejuni, De las invocacions de li sant* (all revisions of chapters of the *Confessio Taboritarum* of 1431); *De la potesta dona a li vicari de Christ* (literal translation of a portion of John Huss's *Tractatus de ecclesia*); *Las Interrogacions menores* (revision of the catechism of the Bohemian Brethren); a fragment of a treatise on anti-Christ; and probably the *Epistola al Lancelau*. All these were apparently translated and adapted by Daniel de Provence and Jean de Molines, who sojourned, on their mission, six months in Bohemia. Five of them are extant only as integral parts of the voluminous *Tresor e lume de fe*, preserved in manuscript at Geneva, Cambridge, and Dublin, and also containing the treatises *Articles de la fe, Li Commandament, Penitenca*, and *De l'oraçon dominical*. The first formulary of the *Articles* is not of Bohemian, but of Waldensian origin, while the remainder of the treatise, like *Li Commandament*, is demonstrably drawn from the *Somme le roy* of the Dominican Laurentius. It is to be concluded that manuscript Cambridge B was the original one, and among those which Daniel and Jean removed; that the prose works in the Waldensian tongue for a very considerable part originated from these two after Aug., 1533; and that the collection and preservation of fragments of the ancient Waldensian literature are quite or wholly due to these two " barbs," especially since, for a long time, the Reformed Waldenses had no interest in the ancient language and its literature.

The history of the Waldensian Reformed of Dauphiny and Provence forms part of the history of the Reformed Church of France; only the development of the Reformed communities in Piedmont, which have retained the name of Waldenses, need here be considered. Outside of the territory covered by the peace of Cavour they were gradually driven from the valleys of De Queryas, Barcelona, Mattias, and Meana, and out of the eight localities in Saluzzo after its annexation to Savoy in 1603. Propaganda failing to render the government pliant, Charles Emanuel II. decided upon force in 1655, only to arouse such commotion in the Protestant world that, at Cromwell's request, Mazarin induced the duke, in August, to grant peace and amnesty. Feeling that the terms of the peace were not observed, the Waldenses rebelled in 1663, and within the year forced the duke solemnly to ratify

2. Literature.

3. The Waldensian Reformed.

the above treaty. Shortly after the revocation of the Edict of Nantes, in 1686, Victor Amadeus II., in agreement with Louis XIV., issued a decree forbidding the Reformed faith in his dominions, requiring all the Reformed preachers and teachers to leave his territories within fourteen days; and empowering the Roman Catholic clergy to baptize and educate all Reformed children in the tenets of that church. The Waldenses again resorted to arms but were defeated. More than 3,000 fell in battle; over 5,000 were taken prisoners; their churches were razed; and their property was confiscated. At the intercession of the Protestant powers, the duke permitted some 2,500, who had been condemned to prison or the galleys, to emigrate, the great majority finding refuge in Germany. Though apparently exterminated in Piedmont, they did not abandon hopes of regaining their old homes, and in the summer of 1689, in the confidence of William III. of Orange, the preacher Henri Arnaud collected 800–900 Waldenses and Huguenots on the shores of Lake Geneva and marched by devious roads to Piedmont. Here in the mountains he waged so stubborn a contest against fifty times his number that the duke broke off his alliance with France and on June 4, 1690, freely permitted all Waldenses and French refugees to return to the valleys, besides releasing all their fellow sectaries who were still in prison or in the galleys. The Waldenses who had fled to Germany now flocked back to Piedmont, but on July 1, 1698, at the instance of Louis XIV., the duke issued a patent forbidding the Reformed in the valleys from having any religious association with French subjects and ordering all French refugees to leave the country within two months. In 1698–1699, therefore, over 2,500 Reformed were forced to emigrate, the majority finding a new home in Germany, especially in Württemberg. The scattered colonies joined in a synod numbering fourteen churches and 4,000 members in 1716. In Piedmont, meanwhile, repressive measures were still enforced despite the protests of Protestant powers, though it was only in the Val Pragelas that real severity was exercised. On June 20, 1730, the duke ordered that all who had been born or baptized in the Roman Catholic Church before 1686, or who had been Roman Catholics after 1696, but had subsequently apostatized, must either become Roman Catholic within six months or leave the country. The latter was preferred by 850, of whom 400 went to Holland, while the remainder were received in French or Waldensian colonies in Germany. During the Napoleonic invasion of 1799 the Waldenses had equal rights with Roman Catholics, and their clergy even received an annual subvention of 13,000 lire. With the return of the house of Savoy, however, conditions changed; and in Jan., 1815, Victor Emanuel I. withdrew the subvention and renewed all previous restrictions, though in the following year he removed some of the most burdensome, and even gave each of the Waldensian clergy an annual stipend of 500 lire. Nevertheless, it was not until the act of emancipation promulgated by Charles Albert on Feb. 17, 1848, that the Waldenses permanently secured all civil rights. The history of the Waldenses, 1526–1848, is the account of a continuous strife with the house of Savoy, and that they were not annihilated was due to their heroic steadfastness as well as to the signal support of the Protestant world. Cromwell rescued them from total destruction in 1655 and instituted a collection which reached the amount of £38,097, he himself contributing £2,000. William of Orange not only assisted their grand return in 1689, but until the French Revolution the crown of Great Britain sustained the preachers and teachers of twelve Waldensian churches. Holland in 1731, for example, collected 308,199 florins, not to mention the amounts of money and asylum given by the German princes. Even in the first half of the nineteenth century the Protestant powers entered into an alliance with Alexander I. of Russia in behalf of the Waldenses. From the sixteenth century they were specially cherished and shielded by sympathetic Protestant Europe; because they were commonly looked upon as the only survivals of the Evangelical primitive Christians of apostolic times, and to protect them was deemed a sacred obligation.

At the outbreak of the great persecution of 1654, there were 14 churches and pastors with 16,000 members. This was reduced in 1699 to 13 churches and 5,000 or 6,000 members; but this membership had increased to 19,710 in 1829. Their organization was essentially that of Geneva. The highest governing body was the synod, and in the interim between synods the government was conducted by a committee called "The Table," consisting of three clericals (with two lay deputies after 1823), led by a moderator. There was no liturgy until 1829, except the various Swiss formularies. The language employed in their services was originally the east Provençal dialect of the Cottian Alps, but after the death of the majority of their pastors from the plague in 1630 and their replacement by French ministers, French was substituted for Waldensian. Schools were to be found in all Waldensian communities as early as 1699, and in the eighteenth century a Latin school was founded at Torre. The period of the Enlightenment was as prejudicial to religious life in the valleys as elsewhere, nor was there a revival of spiritual life among the Waldenses until the third decade of the nineteenth century. With the proclamation of the act of emancipation in 1848 the Waldenses not only received liberty, but aspired to fresh opportunities. At the first synod (Aug. 1–4, 1848), the evangelization of Italy was assumed as an aim, and the resolve was made gradually to replace French by Italian as the language of instruction and worship. In 1855 a Waldensian theological school was founded at Torre Pellice, but was transferred to Florence in 1860. At the synod of 1855 the confession of 1655 was revived and a new constitution was adopted. The Waldensian Church is now an Italian church, and makes a Protestant propaganda not only throughout Italy, but also among Italian emigrants to America. The Waldensian colonies in Germany soon lost all distinctive characteristics. In Württemberg all the Waldensian congregations became incorporated in the national Lutheran Church in 1823, and in only two localities in Württemberg, Pinache-Serres and Neu-Hengstett, does the Waldensian dialect partially linger to the present day.

(H. BÖHMER.)

VI. Present Conditions: The conditions of the Waldenses on the eve of their emancipation in 1848 were most precarious. Although not persecuted openly by sword and fire, they were subjected to many wrongs and indignities. They were excluded from practising any liberal professions, such as those of medicine or law, and the humbler trades alone were open to them. Children under ten were frequently abducted; the universities were closed against students from the valleys; and Waldensian conscripts were kept in the lowest ranks. It was forbidden to open new places of worship; most of the cemeteries were unenclosed. The censorship of books circulating among them was very strict, and the Waldenses were prohibited from settling outside of their own narrow valleys. The act of emancipation, promulgated Feb. 17, 1848, by King Charles Albert, brought this intolerable state of affairs to a close and granted the Waldenses all civil and religious liberties, thus marking the dawn of a new epoch in their history.

1. State of Affairs in 1848.

In their native valleys, the number of the Waldenses has not increased because the poverty of the soil and unbearable economical conditions, as well as new opportunities, have driven thousands to foreign lands, but their social and intellectual conditions are far better than before 1848. They pride themselves on saying that no Waldensian man, woman, or child over six years of age is illiterate, and that no beggar is to be seen in their valleys. Through the interest of General John Charles Beckwith (q.v., Appendix) a school is in every hamlet, and for a higher education the Collegio Valdese in Torre Pellice, founded by William Stephen Gilly, canon of Durham, who paid a first visit to the Waldenses in 1823, and whose *Narrative of an Excursion to the Mountains of Piemont* roused wide-spread interest and gained to the cause Beckwith, who must be regarded as their greatest benefactor. He settled among them in 1843, and, after a most useful career spent in their behalf, died in Torre Pellice July 19, 1862. The Collegio Valdese, where boys and girls are admitted when they are through with the elementary schools, and where they receive instruction for eight years, opens the way to all the university careers. There are now about one hundred students with a staff of eight professors, and the institution is recognized by the Italian government. Torre Pellice is the capital of the Waldensian valleys, not only because the college is there, but also because there is the largest church, and in that city there is held every year, during the first week in September, the General Synod of the Waldensian Church. The house where the synod meets was built in 1889, when the Waldenses celebrated the bicentenary of the " glorious return " of their forefathers to their native valleys, and to its erection King Humbert I. of Italy contributed personally $1,000. There is the synod hall; the library, which has over 40,000 volumes, many of them rare and valuable; the museum of Waldensian history, with interesting relics; the offices of the ruling body of the Church, called La Vénérable table vaudoise; and the offices of the

2. Education in the Piedmont Valleys.

Waldensian historical society, an institution founded in 1889. From the college many young men have gone forth, entering various branches of activity. Lawyers, physicians, professors, business men, and officers in the army and the navy may be found in many cities of Italy who have had their early training and inspiration in that institution.

The valleys are also the center of a great philanthropic activity. There are two general hospitals, one at Pomaretto, in the Val San Martino, and a larger one in Torre Pellice, toward whose erection even Czar Alexander I. contributed. The orphanage for girls in Torre Pellice can accommodate forty-five inmates, and in Luserna San Giovanni is the only home for incurables in Italy. It was founded some twenty years ago, and has accommodations for fifty patients. The condi-

3. Philanthropic Work and Statistics. tion of admission is that the patients have been refused by other hospitals. The institution makes no distinction of nationality or creed, and patients come even from Switzerland or from Sicily. The orphanage for boys in Turin has thirty inmates, the homes for the aged in San Germano and San Giovanni contain some fifty people, and the deaconesses' institute in Turin, the aim of which is to train nurses for hospitals and kindred institutions, has a good number of pupils. All these institutions are partially endowed and supported by the voluntary contributions of the Waldenses. The Waldensian valleys, which form the first of the seven districts into which the whole Waldensian Church is divided, have seventeen churches with nineteen pastors: Prali, Rodoretto, Massello, Perrero-Maniglia, Villasecca, Pomaretto, San Germano, Pramollo, Prarostino, Pinerolo, Toriyo, Luserna San Giovanni, Torre Pellice, Villar Pellice, Bobbio Pellice, Roria, and Angrogna. The latest statistics for the valleys give 19 pastors, 190 teachers, 3,932 children in the Sunday-schools, 12,213 church-members, and 96,400 francs as church contributions. French is spoken as well as Italian by the Waldenses, and two weekly papers are published in Torre Pellice, *L'Echo des vallées* and *L'Avrisatore alpino.* In the Italian Parliament one of the members is a Waldensian.

On account of the knowledge of French which even the less-educated Waldenses possess, it was natural, after the narrow limits of their valleys had been thrown open by the act of 1848, that they should make their way toward France in order to better their economical conditions.

4. Waldensian Emigration to France. Very few settled in the great cities of Italy, but France, being a most resourceful country, attracted them. Thousands of Waldenses are to be found in Marseilles, Toulon, Cannes, Nice, and even in Paris. Many a Waldensian who has been a waiter in fashionable restaurants and hotels in those cities is now at the head of important business firms. In order to keep together and help each other, these "children of the valleys" have organized, in all those cities, societies called Unions vaudoises, which celebrate two dates every year as most important, Feb. 17, commemorating the act of emancipation, and Aug. 16, the departure of their

forefathers, in 1689, from Praugins for their native valleys. In Marseilles the Waldenses attend the French Reformed churches; in Nice, there is a strong Waldensian church with a pastor from the valleys.

It was, however, across the ocean that the Waldenses had to develop the energies of their race and build up strong colonies. In 1859, through the interest of Frederick Henry Pendleton, chaplain of the British embassy in Montevideo, a group of Waldensian families settled in Uruguay and founded Colonia Valdense. They were followed by others, year after year, so that there are now no less than seven regularly organized churches, five in Uruguay and two in Argentina, viz.: Colonia Valdense, Cosmopolita, Artilleros, Belgrano, Lavalle San Salvador, Tarariras-Riachuelo, and Iris. The latest statistics for the seven colonies give 7 pastors, 1,716 church-members, 668 Sunday-school children, and 42,242 francs as church contributions. A college, called Liceo Valdense, has been founded

5. The Waldenses in North and South America. in Colonia Valdense, with forty-two students, and the institution is helped financially by the government of Uruguay. Many groups of Waldenses, amounting altogether to more than 180 families, are scattered throughout Argentina and Uruguay, and are visited periodically by the pastors. A monthly paper in Spanish, *La Union valdense,* is published to keep the people together. In the United States there are three colonies distinctly Waldensian: at Wolf Ridge, near Gainesville, Tex., with some ten families; at Valdese, N. C., founded in 1891, with 42 families and over 200 people; and at Monett, Mo., with 25 families, founded in 1886. Through hard work and perseverance these farmers are now in prosperous circumstances. They have joined the Presbyterian Church, although the services in the churches at Valdese and Monett are still held in French. Groups of Waldensian families are to be found in Chicago, California, and elsewhere, and there are four families at Hawthorne, near Ottawa, Canada. In New York, where there are no less than 350 of them, mostly young men and young women, they have organized Le Groupe vaudois and meet regularly for their services on Sunday afternoons. They have a pastor from their valleys. There are, altogether, no less than 12,000 Waldenses outside of the valleys of Piedmont.

General Beckwith is to be considered the promoter of the missionary work of the Waldenses. Having long been convinced that the Church of the valleys was the divinely predestined instrument for giving the Gospel to Italy, as soon as the political restrictions that had been so long im-

6. Missionary Work in Italy. posed on the Waldenses were removed, he wrote to the "Table," the governing board of the Church, emphatically urging them to undertake active missionary work. The first step taken by the Waldenses in this new field was to erect a beautiful church in Turin in 1853, having secured permission to build through Count Cavour, who was their friend. The clerical party strongly opposed such a grant, and it was for the Waldenses the first victory in the enjoyment of their newly acquired religious liberty. The Waldensian church of Turin has now two pastors and 700 church-members, and contributes yearly 63,000 francs. About the same time a station was begun in Florence under the charge of two pastors, but the grand duke of Tuscany promptly banished those brethren, while seven persons found by the police studying the Bible in a private house were exiled for a year. As soon as Tuscany became part of the united kingdom of Italy, however, the work was resumed, and the Waldensian faculty of theology, which had been instituted in Torre Pellice in 1855, was transferred to Florence in 1860 in the famous palace that belonged formerly to Cardinal Salirati, and which had been secured through the interest of the minister of the Scotch church in Leghorn.

There are now two Waldensian churches in Florence (one of which is self-supporting,) as well as the theological faculty with three professors and some ten students. The curriculum is for three years; then the students usually take a post-graduate course in some foreign university, as at Edinburgh, where they receive a scholarship; at Berlin, where a bursary is provided by the Ho-

7. Waldensian Churches in Italy. henzollern family, or at Geneva. After one or two years as probationers under the care of an elder pastor, the candidates to the ministry are ordained at the age of twenty-five. In Florence, in the same Palazzo Salirati, is the printing-press of the mission work of the Waldenses, known as La Tipografia Claudiana, which publishes a monthly religious magazine, *La Rivista cristiana*, and supplies the churches with religious literature. In fifty years the society has circulated about 102,880 books or tracts, 2,000,000 religious almanacs, and 2,773,-400 Bibles, New Testaments, and portions of the Scriptures. In 1860, when southern Italy and Sicily, under Garibaldi, became part of the united kingdom of Italy, work was begun in Naples, Palermo, and Messina with much success by Rev. Georgio Appia, a Waldensian pastor, who later became minister of a Lutheran church in Paris, and after the war of 1866 was stationed in Milan and Venice. When the Italian troops entered the city of Rome, Sept. 20, 1870, a Waldensian colporteur was with them with copies of the Epistle of St. Paul to the Romans; and on the following Sunday the first Protestant service in Rome in the Italian language was held in a private house by Matteo Prochet (q.v.), president of the Waldensian committee on missions. On Nov. 25, 1883, a beautiful church on the Via Nazionale was dedicated. It can accommodate 500 people, and the congregation is self-supporting. In 1911 a second Waldensian church to accommodate 1,200 people was built in Rome across the Tiber, through the generosity of a wealthy American lady. In Rome are the headquarters of the missionary work of the Waldenses, and there is published the largest Italian Protestant paper, *La Luce* (10,000 copies weekly), which reaches many Italian immigrants in America.

As illiteracy was predominant in southern Italy and Sicily, the work of the Waldensian church in those parts of the country has been especially edu-

cational, and many day schools, evening schools, and Sunday-schools have been established. In Falerna (Catanzaro) such schools provide for 250 children, in Pachino (Sicily) for 200, in Vittoria (Sicily) for 250, in Riesi (Sicily) for 700, in Grotte (Sicily) for 500, in Palermo for 200, etc. The work

8. Educational and Philanthropic Work in Italy. of the Waldensian Church has been developed also along philanthropic lines. Hospitals have been started in Turin, Genoa, Milan, and elsewhere, and orphanages have been instituted in many cities. The Gould Memorial Home for Boys, founded in Rome by Mrs. Bliss Gould, wife of the physician of the American embassy, under the care of the Waldensian Church, can accommodate fifty or sixty boys, the Comandi Home for Boys in Florence has some 150, the Ferretti Home for Girls in Florence has 40 inmates, and the Boyce Memorial Home for Girls in Bordighera has 40 or 50. Moreover, in all the principal cities of Italy, in connection with L'Union internationale des amies de la jeune fille, homes, called Foyers, have been opened to protect and help girls who would otherwise easily become the victims of the white slavers. Along temperance lines the Waldensian Church has started a strong movement in Italy and publishes a monthly paper advocating temperance, *Bene sociale*. The latest statistics for the mission field give 50 pastors, 18 evangelists, 9 teachers' evangelists, 47 teachers, and 12 colporteurs, or a total of 136 workers; $24,000 church contributions, 12,000 church-members, and over 200 churches or stations, including one in Malta, two in Egypt, and one in Abyssinia. The missionary work of the Waldensian Church, in number of churches and stations, is now sixteen times larger than the mother church in the valleys of Piedmont. The churches in the principal cities of Italy are already self-supporting.

On account of the hundreds of thousands of Italian immigrants who come to America every year, some of them belonging to those churches or having been brought up in those schools in southern Italy or Sicily, the influence of the work is felt in this country. There are already 225 Italian Protestant churches in the United States and Canada, connected with various denominations, and having a total membership of no less than 12,000, some 100 of those churches having been started by Protestant

9. Missionary Work Outside Italy. immigrants or having been ministered to by pastors or missionaries from Italy. About 80 pastors, missionaries, Bible women, and colporteurs at work among the Italian immigrants in America were formerly connected with the Waldensian Church. The congregation of Grotte (Sicily) alone has started, through its members, three such churches in the United States. On the other hand, Italian immigrants returning to their native villages and towns in Italy are very often the means of initiating religious movements. Already 16 missionary churches under the care of the Waldenses have been organized in that way and through such agents. The Waldensian Church is not directly engaged in missionary work in heathen countries, although no less than 12 Waldenses, under the Société des missions de Paris are preaching the Gospel in Basutoland and Barotseland, along the Zambesi River (South Africa), and there is one Waldensian missionary in China. Many pastors from the Waldensian valleys work in Switzerland and France, and there are now no less than 300 Christian workers in Italy, France, South Africa, South America, and North America who have been brought up in this church. See AMERICAN WALDENSIAN AID SOCIETY, in Appendix.   ALBERTO CLOT.

BIBLIOGRAPHY: Lists of literature are: A. Muston, *Bibliographie historique et documentaire de l'Israel des Alpes*, Paris, 1851 (valuable though incomplete); J. H. Todd, *The Books of the Vaudois Preserved in Trinity College, Dublin*, London, 1865; W. N. Du Rieu, in *Bulletin de la commission de l'hist. des églises Wallonnes*, iv. 2, The Hague, 1889; *Bulletin de la société d'hist. vaudoise*, xv. 160 sqq. (by J. Jalla), xvi. 48 sqq. (by W. Meille); and Hauck-Herzog, *RE*, xx. 799–806 (valuable, with running comment; an excellent list of fragmentary sources is given).

Among sources for various periods may be named: the " Anonymous of Passau," partly given in P. Despont, *Bibliotheca patrum maxima Lugdunensis*, xxv. 262–277, Leyden, 1677 (other documents also are in xxiv.), and in Preger's *Beiträge zur Geschichte der Waldesier im Mittelalter*, Munich, 1875; David of Augsburg, *Tractatus de inquisitione hæreticorum*, ed. Preger, Munich, 1878; Bernard, in *MPL*, cciv. 793–840; Alanus ab Insulis, in *MPL*, ccx. 377–399; Stephan of Borbone (d. c. 1261), *Tractatus de diversis materiis prædicabilibus*, ed. A. Lecoy de la Marche in *Anecdotis historiques, légendes et apologues*, Paris, 1877; C. Seyssel, *Adversus errores Waldensium*, Paris, 1520 (Roman Catholic); T. Beza, *Hist. eccl. des églises reformées au royaume de France*, Geneva, 1580, new ed. by J. W. Baum and A. E. Cunitz, 3 vols., Paris, 1883–89, also by P. Vesson, 2 vols., Toulouse, 1882–83; G. Miolo, *Hist. breve e vera degl' affari dei Valdesi delle Valli*, 1587, reproduced in *Bulletin de la société d'hist. vaudoise*, xvii. 26 sqq.; S. Lentolo, *Hist. della grandi e crudeli persecutione fatte ai tempe nostri in Provenza, Calabria e Piemonte* (written 1595), ed. T. Gay, Torre, 1906; J. P. Perrin, *Hist. des Albigeois and . . . des Vaudois*, Geneva, 1618–1619 (based on a large collection of first-hand documents, some of which are reproduced; there are several partial Eng. transls., London, 1624, 1655, 1712, and 1865); M. A. Rorenco, *Breve narratione dell' introduttione degli heretici delle Valli*, Turin, 1632; *MGH, Script.*, xxvi (1882), 247–449; P. Gilles, *Hist. eccl. des églises reformées recueillies en quelques vallées de Piemont*, 1664, new ed., 2 vols., Pignerol, 1881; *Waldenser Chronick*, Schaffhausen, 1655; J. Léger, *Hist. générale des églises évangéliques des vallées de Piemont ou Vaudoises*, 2 vols., Leyden, 1669; W. Map, *Liber de nugis curialium, distinctio*, i. 37, ed. T. Wright for Camden Society, pp. 64 sqq., London, 1850, and in *MGH, Script.*, xxvii (1885), 61 sqq.; *La Noble Leçon*, ed. E. Montet, Paris, 1888; *Rescriptum heresiarcharum Lombardie ad Leonistas in Alamannia*, ed. Preger in *AMA, historische Klasse*, xiii. 234 sqq.; J. J. I. von Döllinger, *Beiträge zur Sektengeschichte des Mittelalters*, vol. iii. *Documente*, Munich, 1890; A. L. Herminjard, *Correspondance des réformateurs*, 9 vols., Geneva, 1878–97; statements of Pierre Cella are cited in H. C. Lea, *Inquisition in the Middle Ages*, ii. 579–584, New York, 1906. Treasuries of documents are the *Bulletin de la société de l'hist. des Vaudois*, 27 vols., coming down to 1910, the *Proceedings of the Huguenot Society* and *Rivista Cristiana*, and much of the literature cited under INQUISITION contains citation from documents related to this subject.

On the history the following may be used: E. Comba, *Valdo ed i valdesi avanti la riforma*, Florence, 1880; idem, *Peter Waldo*, London, n. d.; idem, *Hist. des Vaudois d'Italie*, part 1, Turin, 1887, new ed., 1898, Eng. transl., *Hist. of the Waldenses of Italy*, London, 1889; idem, *H. Arnaud*, 1889; idem, *Storia de' Valdesi*, Florence, 1893; idem, in *Bulletin de la société de l'hist. du protestantisme française*, xliii. 7 sqq.; A. Muston, *L'Israel des Alpes, ou hist. des Vaudois*, 4 vols., Paris, 1851 (based on original documents and containing bibliography), Eng. transl., *The Israel of the Alps: A History of the Persecutions of the Waldenses*, London, 1852; *A Collection of the Several Papers sent to the Protector . . . concerning the bloody and*

barbarous *Massacre . . . committed on many Thousand of Reformed . . . dwelling in the Valleys of Piedmont, by the Duke of Savoy's Forces . . . Published by Command of his Highness*, London, 1655; Sir S. Moreland, *The History of the Evangelical Churches of the Valleys of Piemont containing a . . . Description and a Faithfull Account of the Doctrine, Life, and Persecutions . . .* (contains sources), London, 1658; P. Allix, *Some Remarks upon the Ecclesiastical History of the Ancient Churches of Piedmont*, London, 1690; P. Boyer, *Abrégé de l'hist. des Vaudois*, The Hague, 1691; idem, *The History of the Vaudois*, London, 1692; H. Arnaud, *Hist. de la glorieuse rentrée des Vaudois dans leurs vallées*, 1710, new ed., Pignerol, 1880, partly translated in *The Glorious Recovery by the Vaudois of their Valleys, from the Original by Henri Arnaud, their Commander and Pastor, with a Compendious History of that People, previous and subsequent to that Event*, London, 1827; M. Schagen, *Hist. der Cristenen Waldensen*, Haarlem, 1765; T. Newton, *Dissertation on the Prophecies*, vol. ii. 243–249, 251–252, 293–317, Perth, 1790; J. Brez, *Hist. des Vaudois*, 2 vols., Paris, 1796; W. Jones, *The History of the Waldenses*, 2d ed., London, 1816; H. D. Acland, *A Brief Sketch of the History and Present Situation of the Valdenses in Piemont, commonly called Vaudois*, London, 1825; B. Bridge, *A Brief Narrative of a Visit to the Valleys of Piedmont inhabited by the Vaudois*, London, 1825; J. F. Martinet, *Kerkelijke Geschiedenis der Waldensen*, 3d ed., Amsterdam, 1826; J. L. Jackson, *Remarks on the Vaudois of Piemont, during an Excursion in the Summer of 1825*, London, 1826; J. R. Peyran, *An Historical Defence of the Waldenses or Vaudois* [in French]. *With an Introduction and Appendixes by Rev. T. Sims*, London, 1826; T. McCrie, *History of the Progress and Suppression of the Reformation in Italy*, Edinburgh, 1827; G. S. Faber, *Sacred Calendar of Prophecy*, 3 vols., London, 1828; idem, *An Enquiry into the History and Theology of the Ancient Vallenses and Albigenses, as exhibiting, agreeably to the Promises, the Perpetuity of the sincere Church of Christ*, London, 1838; W. S. Gilly, *Narrative of an Excursion to the Mountains of Piemont in 1823, and Researches among the Vaudois, or Waldenses*, London, 1824 (with maps, plates, and copies of ancient manuscripts); idem, *Waldensian Researches during a Second Visit to the Vaudois of Piemont*, London, 1831; idem, *The Valdenses, Valdo, and Vigilantius*, Edinburgh, 1841; W. Dieterici, *Die Waldenser und ihre Verhältnisse zu dem brandenburg-preussischen Staate*, Berlin, 1831; S. R. Maitland, *Facts and Documents Illustrative of the History, Doctrine, and Rites of the Ancient Albigenses and Waldenses*, London, 1832; A. Blair, *History of the Waldenses, with an Introductory Sketch of the History of the Christian Churches in the South of France and North of Italy, till these Churches submitted to the Pope, when the Waldenses continued as formerly independent of the Papal See*, Edinburgh, 1833; P. Jas, *Disputatio . . . de Valdensium secta ab Albigensibus distinguenda*, Leyden, 1834; E. T. Mayerhoff, *Die Waldenser in unseren Tagen*, Berlin, 1834; A. Charvaz, *Recherches historiques sur la véritable origine des Vaudois et sur le caractère de leurs doctrines primitives*, Paris, 1836; W. Beattie, *The Waldenses, or Protestant Valleys of Piedmont*, etc., London, 1838; G. Stanley, *Researches on the Theology and History of the Ancient Vaudois and Albigenses*, London, 1838; W. Sims, *History of Waldenses from the Earliest Period till the Present Time*, 3 vols., Edinburgh, 1839; E. Henderson, *The Vaudois: comprising Observations made on a Tour to the Valleys of Piedmont*, London, 1845; R. Baird, *Sketches of Protestantism in Italy, Past and Present, including a Notice of the Origin, History, and Present State of the Waldenses*, 2d ed., Boston, 1847; C. U. Hahn, *Geschichte der Waldenser*, 2 vols., Stuttgart, 1847; A. Monastier, *Histoire de l'église vaudois depuis son origine, et des Vaudois du Piémont jusqu'à nos jours*, 2 vols., Paris, 1847 (an appendix contains the principal original writings, etc.), Eng. transl., *A History of the Vaudois Church from its Origin, and of the Vaudois of Piedmont to the Present Day*, London, 1848; H. D. Wickham, *An Historical Sketch of the Italian Vaudois, from the First Ages of Christianity to the Present Day*, etc., London, 1847; J. J. Herzog, *De Waldensium origine*, Halle, 1848; idem, in *Revue de théologie et philosophie chrétienne*, 1850; idem, *Die romanischen Waldenser*, Halle, 1857 (reprints documents); F. Bender, *Geschichte der Waldenser*, Ulm, 1850; A. W. Dieckhoff, *Die Waldenser im Mittelalter*, Göttingen, 1851 (epoch-making); E. Baines, *A Visit to the Vaudois of Piedmont*, London, 1855; P. Heber, *Waldo, Kaiser Karls des Grossen geistlicher Rath, und die älteren Waldenser*, Basel, 1858; D. Costello, *Piedmont and Italy*, 2 vols., London, 1859–61; M. Young, *The Life and Times of Aonio Paleario*, 2 vols., London, 1860; P. Melia, *The Origin, Persecutions, and Doctrines of the Waldenses, from Documents, many now the first time collected and edited*, London, 1870; J. P. Meille, *General Beckwith: his Life and Labours among the Waldenses of Piedmont*, London, 1873; J. Goll, *Quellen und Untersuchungen zur Geschichte der böhmischen Brüder*, Prague, 1878–82; Jane L. Willyams, *The Waldensian Church in the Valleys of Piedmont, from the Earliest Period to the Present Time*, new ed., London, 1879; J. N. Worsfold, *Peter Waldo, the Reformer of Lyons*, London, 1880; J. A. Wylie, *History of the Waldenses*, London, 1880; W. Jones, *Hist. of the Waldenses*, new ed., 2 vols., London, 1882; A. Deissmann, *Waldenser in der Grafschaft Schaumburg*, Wiesbaden, 1884; H. Meille, *Recollections of Two Hundred Years ago in the Waldensian Valleys*, Edinburgh, 1886; E. Montet, *Hist. littéraire des Vaudois du Piémont*, Geneva, 1886 (reprints early sources); K. Müller, *Die Waldenser und ihre einzelnen Gruppe bis zum Anfang des 14. Jahrhunderts*, Gotha, 1886; L. Brunel, *Les Vaudois des Alps françaises*, Paris, 1888; D. K. Guthrie, *Lecture on the Waldenses and their Glorious Return*, Edinburgh, 1889; A. Thomson, *Letters Written in Connection with the Bi-Centenary Commemoration of the " Glorious Return " of the Waldenses to their Native Valleys*, Edinburgh, 1889; J. W. Brown, *Italian Campaign*, London, 1890; J. Chevalier, *Mémoire historique sur les hérésies du Dauphiné*, Valence, 1890; H. Haupt, *Waldensertum und Inquisition*, Freiburg, 1890 (reproduces documents); A. Bérard, *Les Vaudois . . . du 4. au 18. siècle*, Paris, 1892; F. Rostan, *The Waldensian Church and her Work of Evangelization in Italy*, Torre Pellice, 1894; T. Gay, *The Waldenses, their Rise, Struggles, Persecutions, and Triumphs*, London, 1895; Sofia V. Bonipiani, *A Short History of the Italian Waldenses who have inhabited the Valleys of the Cottian Alps from Ancient Times to the Present*, New York, 1897; C. Huck, *Dogmenhistorischer Beitrag zur Geschichte der Waldenser*, Freiburg, 1897; W. B. Worsfold, *The Valley of Light: Studies with Pen and Pencil in the Vaudois Valleys of Piedmont*, London, 1899; G. Jalla, *Compendia di storia valdese*, Florence, 1902; J. Gibson, *The Waldenses, their Home and History*, Edinburgh (1903); H. C. Lea, *Inquisition of the Middle Ages*, 3 vols., New York, 1906, and in general works on the Inquisition; T. de Cauzons, *Les Vaudois et l'inquisition*, 2 vols., Paris, 1907; Schaff, *Christian Church*, v. 1, pp. 493–507; *KL*, xii. 1185–95.

On Waldensian literature: F. J. M. Raynouard, *Choix des poésies des troubadours*, ii. 73–102, Paris, 1817; G. von Zezschwitz, *Die Katechismen der Waldenser und böhmischen Brüder*, Erlangen, 1863; H. Haupt, *Die deutsche Bibelübersetzung der mittelalterlichen Waldenser*, Würzburg, 1885; F. Jostes, *Die Waldenser und die vorlutherische deutsche Bibelübersetzung*, Münster, 1885; J. Müller, in *Monumenta Germaniæ pædagogica*, vol. iv., Berlin, 1887.

WALDENSTROEM, văl'den-strŭm, **PAUL PETER:** Swedish theologian and educator; b. at Lulea (106 m. n.e. of Stockholm), Sweden, July 20, 1838. He pursued post-graduate studies at the University of Upsala, 1857–62 (Candidate in Philosophy, 1862; Ph.D., 1863); in 1864 he was ordained and was appointed lector in theology, Greek, and Hebrew at the gymnasium at Umeå. Financially aided by the State, he traveled, in 1867, in Prussia and Württemberg, Germany, for the purpose of studying the German school system. In 1873–74 he studied at the University of Upsala the symbolical books of the Lutheran Church, publishing the results in *De justificatione quid statuant libri symbolici ecclesiæ lutheranæ* (Upsala, 1874). In the spring of 1874 he was appointed lector in theology and Hebrew at the gymnasium in Gefle. He has contributed numerous articles on pedagogy to *Pedagogisk tidsskrift* (1866–73); after the death of Rosenius (q.v.), in 1868, he became the editor of *Pietisten*, in which most of his religious beliefs have found expression; in 1877–80 he was coeditor of *Vittnet*, a monthly periodical; and is the editor of the annual *Calendar Ansgarius*. He is prominent in politics, having been repeatedly elected a representative at the State diet, second chamber.

It is in the ecclesiastical field that he has exerted most of his influence. He is one of the foremost leaders of the Free Church movement in Sweden, and the father of a theological movement the supporters of which, found both in Sweden and in America, are called Waldenströmianere, though they prefer to be known as Missionsvänner. In a sermon, published in *Pietisten*, 1872, he gave impetus to the theological movement with which he is identified by proclaiming his novel idea of the atonement. He holds that the reconciliation through Christ is of us to God, not of God to us: not through grace on account of Christ, but on account of grace through Christ. The subject is God, the Father of Christ; the source is the love of God; the object is the whole world; the mediator is Christ, the only begotten God (Waldenström accepts and defends the reading ὁ μονογενὴς Θεός in John i. 18), the Son of God; the end is the restitution of men to God, not the reconciliation of God to men, which latter teaching, according to Waldenström, finds no support in Scripture.

This sermon called forth a storm of controversy. He then published (1873) *Om försoningens betydelse*, which was combated by theologians but met with the favor of many lay people who were opposed to State religion, the nucleus of his subsequent constituency.

Within the ranks of Evangeliska Fosterlandsstiftelsen (à society for foreign and home missions, founded 1856 as the result of the evangelical work of Carl Olof Rosenius; q.v.), the adherents of Waldenström soon brought matters to a schism. They submitted in 1878 a motion to annul the confessional basis of Fosterlandsstiftelsen by making adherence to the Augsburg Confession no longer obligatory for missionary workers. The motion failed to pass. The Waldenströmians consequently left the Fosterlandsstiftelsen and organized, Aug., 1878, Svenska Missionsförbundet, now consisting of 1,144 congregations with 91,000 members. In 1904, Waldenström became president of Missionsförbundet. Waldenström held his clerical position in the State church till 1882, when he resigned. His conflicts with the church authorities were caused by his manner of accommodating his idea of the Church to circumstances rather than by his doctrine of the atonement. When he once was called to serve a group of " believers " by administering the Lord's Supper, the authorities refused him the use of the church. This furnished him the opportunity of attacking the Church for refusing to believing ministers the opportunity to serve people who for the sake of their conscience could not partake of the Lord's Supper except with believers.

For almost a generation Waldenström has been a leader of the Free Church movement in Sweden. His influence has also been felt in America, where his adherents number about 33,000. He visited America in 1889 and several times subsequently, the last time in 1910, and described his first visit in *Genom Norra Amerikas Förenta Stater* (1890). Two other books, *Nya färder i Amerikas Förenta Stater* (1902), and *Genom Canada, Reseskildringar från 1904* (1905) describe two subsequent tours in America. A visit to the Orient is described in his *Till Oesterland. Skildringar, . . . hösten och vintern, 1894* (Stockholm, 1896).

To the writings already mentioned the following may be added: *Brukspatron Adamsson eller hvar bor du?* (1863, 5th ed., 1891); *Forsök till granskning af M. Luther's lilla katekes med kort utveckling* (1873); *Fader vår eller bön och bönhörelse* (1876); *Predikningar öfver svenska kyrkans nya högmessotexter* (4 vols., 1876–80); *Barndopets historia* (1880, 4th ed., 1883); *En översättelse af Nya testamentet med förklarande anmärkninger* (1883–94); *Guds eviga frälsningsråd* (3 vols., 2d ed., 1891); *Kristi afsked från sina lärjungar* (1894); *Jesu pinas och uppståndelses historia* (1897); *Dop och barndop* (1898); *Frälsning för all verden* (1902); *Låt os behalla vår gamla bibel* (1902); *Bibelns evangelium och de eviga straffen, eller huru staar det skrifvet?* (1904).

There have appeared in English: *Blood of Jesus, What is its Significance?* (Chicago, 1888); *The Reconciliation—who was to be Reconciled, God or Man, or God and Man?* (1888); and *The Lord is Right: Meditations on Psalm xxv.* (1889).

JOHN O. EVJEN.

BIBLIOGRAPHY: M. W. Montgomery: *A Wind from the Holy Spirit in Sweden and Norway*, New York, 1884.

WALDHAUSEN, vält′hau-zen, **KONRAD VON:** Bohemian precursor of Huss (see HUSS, JOHN, HUSSITES), b. at Waldhausen, near Gran (70 m. w. of Vienna), c. 1320; d. at Prague Dec. 8, 1369. Of his early life and education little is known, but he must have entered the Upper Austrian monastery of Augustinian canons at Waldhausen while still a lad. He was ordained to the priesthood about 1343, and in his zeal for learning visited Bologna in 1349, being at Rome in the following year. Returning to Teutonic soil, he labored in various places, especially at Vienna, devoting himself primarily to preaching, for which he had a remarkable talent. At Prague his audiences were so large that he was obliged to deliver his sermons in the market-place instead of in the church of St. Gall; and his activity brought him into close relations with the Austrian court and Bishop Gottfried II. of Passau. The emperor summoned Konrad to Prague, where, at Easter, 1358, he became rector of St. Gall in the Old City. There he unsparingly castigated the immorality, luxury, and greed prevailing in high society, and also incurred the jealousy and antagonism of the mendicant friars whom he accused of simony, unseemly trade in relics, and shameless exploiting of the common people. In their turn they charged him with being a disturber of the peace and a renegade from his order. The Dominican general, Simon of Langres, sought in vain to arbitrate the dispute, but Konrad continued his attacks, and the matter was placed in the hands of the archbishop. The Franciscans now drew up twenty-four charges against Konrad, and in the autumn of 1360 the archbishop nailed the charges to the doors of two monasteries, bidding all who would bring accusation against Konrad to appear

before him. The monks were unable to sustain their charges, and the results of Konrad's preaching became manifest in a marked improvement in the morality of Prague. In 1361 he became rector of St. Thomas', and in the following year invoked the aid of the bishop of Passau. In 1363 he was made parish priest of All Saints' at Leitmeritz, but was still permitted to live in Prague. The Franciscans renewed their attacks, which finally attracted the attention of Konrad's duke, Rudolf IV. of Austria. He visited Prague in May, 1364, and soon satisfied himself of Konrad's integrity. Konrad, however, declined an invitation to return to Vienna in view of his association with the emperor, though he composed a refutation of the twenty-four charges of his opponents. Early in 1365 he was placed over the great Teynkirche in Prague, whence, with the pope's permission, he extended his reforming activity not only over the archdioceses of Bohemia and Salzburg, but also urged the emperor to intervene in the desperate conditions in Italy. His sermons, which have made some consider him a precursor of Huss (though he attacked neither the teaching nor the organization of the Church), have disappeared, those extant being merely some that he delivered before students to serve as sources and inspirations for young priests. (J. LOSERTH.)

BIBLIOGRAPHY: F. Palacky, *Geschichte von Böhmen*, iii. 1, pp. 161–164, 5 vols. Prague, 1836 sqq.; idem, *Die Vorläufer des Husitentums in Böhmen*, pp. 16–17, Prague, 1869; G. V. Lechler, *Johann von Wiclif und die Vorgeschichte der Reformation*, ii. 111 sqq., Leipsic, 1873, Eng. transl., *John Wiclif and his English Precursors*, 2 vols., new ed., London, 1884; E. H. Gillett, *Life and Times of John Huss*, i. 14–19, 25, 72, ii. 628, Philadelphia, 1861.

WALDO, PETER. See WALDENSES.

WALKER, CORNELIUS: Protestant Episcopalian; b. near Richmond, Va., June 12, 1819; d. at Washington, D. C., Jan. 23, 1907. He was educated at Richmond Episcopal High School and the Alexandria Theological Seminary, and was ordered deacon in 1845 and ordained priest in the following year; was minister and rector at Amherst Court House, Va. (1845–47); curate at St. Paul's, Richmond (1847–1848); rector at Winchester, Va. (1848–60), Christ Church, Alexandria, Va. (1860–61), and Emmanuel, Henrico, Va. (1862–66); professor of church history in Virginia Theological Seminary (1866–76); and professor of systematic theology and homiletics in the same institution (1876–98), where he was also dean. In theology he was an old-school evangelical Churchman, and wrote *Biography of Rev. William Duval* (Richmond, 1854); *Biography of Rev. William Sparrow* (Philadelphia, 1877); *Biography of Charles W. Andrews* (1877); *Sorrowing not without Hope* (sermons; New York, 1887); *Outlines of Christian Theology* (1894); and *Lectures on Christian Ethics* (1896).

WALKER, GEORGE LEON: Congregationalist; b. at Rutland, Vt., Apr. 30, 1830; d. at Hartford Mar. 14, 1900. He studied law in Boston, Mass., intending to devote himself to legal practise. Led to prefer the ministry, he studied theology with his father, and at Andover Theological Seminary (1857–1858); was pastor of State Street Church, Portland, Me. (1858–67); First Church, New Haven, Conn. (1868–73): was acting pastor at Brattleboro, Vt.

(1875–78); and pastor of the First Church, Hartford, from 1879, being made emeritus in 1892. He was a corporate member of the American Board of Commissioners for Foreign Missions after 1877, and was on the commission to prepare the Congregational creed (1883). He wrote: *False Ideas of God* (1881; three sermons); *History of the First Church in Hartford, 1633–1883* (Hartford, 1884); *Thomas Hooker, Preacher, Founder, Democrat* (New York, 1891); *Some Aspects of the Religious Life of New England* (1897; Carew lectures); edited *Diary of Rev. Daniel Wadsworth, with Notes* (1894); and issued a large number of individual sermons.

BIBLIOGRAPHY: *Congregational Year Book*, pp. 45–46, Boston, 1901.

WALKER, WILLIAM: Scotch Anglican; b. at Inveramsay (17 m. n.w. of Aberdeen), Aberdeenshire, Nov. 3, 1817. He was educated at King's College, Aberdeen (M.A., University of Aberdeen, 1840), and was ordered deacon in 1832 and ordained priest two years later; was curate of St. Andrew's, Aberdeen (1842–44); rector of Monymusk, Aberdeenshire (1844–1900); and dean of Aberdeen and Orkney united dioceses (1896–1906). He has written *Life of Bishops Jolly and Gleig* (Edinburgh, 1878); *Moses and Deuteronomy* (1880); *Life and Times of the Poet-Priest John Skinner* (Aberdeen, 1882); *The Kings of Israel* (London, 1882); *Life and Times of Bishop John Skinner* (Aberdeen, 1887); *Reminiscences of Three Churchmen* (Primus C. H. Terrot, Bishop M. Russel, and Professor G. Grub; Edinburgh, 1893); and *Epochs of Scottish Church History* (1897).

WALKER, WILLIAM DAVID: Protestant Episcopal, missionary bishop of North Dakota; b. in the city of New York June 29, 1839. He was graduated from Columbia College, New York City (1859), and from the General Theological Seminary (1862); as deacon, he took charge of Calvary Chapel, New York City (1862); was ordained priest (1863); remained in charge of Calvary Chapel until Feb. 1, 1884, when he resigned to enter upon his episcopate, to which he had been consecrated in Dec., 1883. In the exercise of his ministry in Dakota he was the originator of the " cathedral car," by which the services of the church are carried to places where they would not otherwise be rendered.

BIBLIOGRAPHY: W. S. Perry, *The Episcopate in America*, p. 281, New York, 1895.

WALKER, WILLISTON: Congregationalist; b. at Portland, Me., July 1, 1860. He was educated at Amherst College (A.B., 1883), Hartford Theological Seminary (graduated, 1886), and the University of Leipsic (Ph.D., 1888); was associate in history at Bryn Mawr College (1888–89), professor of Germanic and Western church history in Hartford Theological Seminary (1889–1901); since 1901 he has been professor of ecclesiastical history in Yale University. He has written *The Increase of Royal Power under Philip Augustus* (Leipsic, 1888); *The Creeds and Platforms of Congregationalism* (New York, 1893); *A History of the Congregational Churches in the United States* (1894); *The Reformation* (1900); *Ten New England Leaders* (Boston, 1901); *John Calvin* (New York, 1906); and *Greatest Men of the Christian Church* (Chicago, 1908).

XII.—17

WALL, WILLIAM: English divine; b. in the neighborhood of Sevenoaks (20 m. s.e. of London), Kent, Jan. 6, 1646–47; d. at Shoreham (17 m. s.e. of London) Jan. 13, 1727–28. He was educated at Queen's College, Oxford (B.A., 1667; M.A., 1670); became vicar at Shoreham, 1674; and rector of Milton-next-Gravesend, 1708, the same year becoming chaplain to the bishop of Rochester. He is justly famed for his works on infant baptism, which include *The History of Infant Baptism* (2 parts, London, 1705, 3d ed., 1720, new and best ed., combining J. Gale's *Reflections on Mr. Wall's History*, and Wall's *Defence*, by H. Cotton, 4 vols., Oxford, 1836, 2 vols., 1862, reprinted, 1889); *A Conference Between Two Men that had Doubts about Infant Baptism* (London, 1706, frequently reprinted); and his *Defence of the History of Infant Baptism* (London, 1720; usually reprinted with Gale's work and the *History*). He wrote also *Critical Notes* (on the New Testament and the Old, 3 vols., London, 1730–34).

BIBLIOGRAPHY: T. Crosby, *Hist. of the English Baptists*, i. 6, 161, iii. 14, 42, 4 vols., London, 1738–40; *DNB*, lix. 97.

WALLACE, ALEXANDER GILFILLAN: United Presbyterian; b. at Bridgeville, Allegheny County, Pa., Mar. 2, 1829. He graduated from Jefferson College (B.A., 1847) and from Allegheny Theological Seminary; was pastor of the United Presbyterian Church at Bethel, Pa., 1854–68, at New Brighton, 1868–84, and at Sewickley, 1886–88; has been clerk of the United Presbyterian Assembly since 1868, and secretary of the Board of Church Extension of his denomination since 1870; he was also editor of *The Evangelical Repository*, 1886–90, temporary professor in Allegheny Theological Seminary, 1885–87, and was editorial writer, then associate editor, and finally has been senior editor of *The United Presbyterian*, since 1868. He has written *The Scotch and Scotch-Irish in Colonial America* (1909).

WALLACE, WILLIAM: Presbyterian foreign missionary; b. at Santa Fé de Bogotá, United States of Colombia, Apr. 5, 1864. He studied at Washington and Jefferson College (B.A., 1882), Western Theological Seminary, 1884–85, and Union Theological Seminary, New York, 1885–88, having meanwhile taught in private schools, 1881–85; was pastor at St. Peter, Minn., 1888–90; missionary superintendent at Zacatecas, Mexico, 1890–92; became director of the theological seminary at Tlalpam, 1893; was superintendent of missions for Guerrero, Mexico, 1894–95, and for Saltillo, 1895–1907; and has been president of the Presbyterian College and Seminary at Coyoacan since 1907. He is the editor of *El Esforzador*, the organ of the Mexican societies of Christian Endeavor, and stated clerk of the general synod of the Presbyterian Church in Mexico.

WALLOON CHURCH. See HOLLAND, I., 1.

WALPURGIS, väl-pur'gis (**WALDBURGIS, WALPURGA, WALBURGA**): German saint; b. in Sussex, England, early in the eighth century; d. at Heidenheim (32 m. s.s.w. of Nuremberg) before 786. The sister of Willibald, the first bishop of Eichstätt, and of Wunebald, the founder (c. 751), first abbot of the double monastery of Heidenheim, she went to

Germany about 750 and became abbess of the cloister on the death of her brother in 761. Her remains were removed by Bishop Otgar (847–880) to Eichstätt, and by her tomb arose the foundation of St. Walpurgis which Bishop Heribert formed into a nunnery in the eleventh century. In 893 Bishop Erchanbald carried some of her relics to the monastery of Monheim, north of Donauwörth. Several festivals were celebrated in her honor: Aug. 4 as the day of her leaving England; Feb. 25 as the day of her death; and May 1 [the date of an earlier non-Christian festival, marking the commencement of summer; it is on this date that, according to legend, the witches have their annual assemblage].

(A. HAUCK.)

BIBLIOGRAPHY: On the sources consult: T. D. Hardy, *Descriptive Catalogue of Materials Relating to . . . Great Britain and Ireland*, i. 1, p. 486, in *Rolls Series*, no. 26, London, 1862. A number of the earliest sources (*Vita*, *miracula*, etc.) are collected with commentary in *ASB*, Feb., iii. 511–569, part of the same materials being also in *MPL*, cxxix. 867–894, cxl. 1091–1102, and in *MGH*, *Script.* xv (1887), 535–555. Consult further: J. Lespagnol, *Hist. notable de la conversation des Anglais*, Douay, 1614; idem, *Hist. de la vie et des miracles de S. Vaubourg*, Reims, 1612; E. L. Rochholz, *Drei Gaugöttinnen*, Leipsic, 1870; A. Schneider, *Walburga eine Zierde frommer Jungfrauen*, Regensburg, 1880; F. Schanerte, *Die heilige Aebtissin Walburga*, Paderborn, 1892; J. Schlecht, in *Sammelblatt des historischen Vereins Eichstätt*, pp. 111–122, Eichstätt, 1893; *DNB*, lix. 9; Rettberg, *KD*, ii. 359; Hauck, *KD*, i. 537 sqq.

WALSH, JAMES HORNIDGE: Church of Ireland; b. at Calverston, Mullingar (47 m. w.n.w. of Dublin), Ireland, Apr. 13, 1837. He received his education at Trinity College, Dublin (B.A., 1859; M.A., 1864; B.D., 1872; D.D., 1876); was made deacon, 1860, and priest, 1861; was curate of Dundrum, 1860–61, of Adare, Limerick, 1861–64, and of St. Stephen's, Dublin, 1864–66; rector of Chapel Russell, Limerick, 1866–70; of St. Stephen's, Dublin, 1871–1908, serving meanwhile as assistant to Archbishop King's divinity professor, 1877–83, canon of Christ Church, Dublin, 1893–1905, chancellor of Christ Church, Dublin, 1905–08; as prebendary of Croagh in Limerick Cathedral, 1870–1905, and as private and examining chaplain to the bishop of Limerick, 1899–1905. In 1908 he became dean of Christ Church, Dublin.

WALTER OF ST. VICTOR: French theologian of the twelfth century and prior of the monastery of St. Victor. Nothing is known concerning him except that he wrote an impassioned attack on the modernistic theology of his time, his work usually being termed *Contra novas hæreses libri quatuor* (the frequent designation, after a sentence in the introduction, *Contra quatuor labyrinthos Franciæ*, is incorrect). According to internal evidence, he wrote between 1180 and 1190, but of the other works attributed to him only the *Magistri Walteri dialogus quærens quid sentiat Hugo de anima Christi* can seriously be considered. The *Contra hæreses* is instructive for the history of the conflict aroused by the rise of a scientific theology based on dialectic methods. In the Christology of his opponents Walter discerned the Nestorian heresy; in their interpretation of the incarnation they denied the possibility of a change in the Godhead, assuming that the Logos, whose humanity they doubted, had for purposes of revelation assumed the man Jesus like a mantle. Their wavering and unclear theories were offensive to Walter, who held, with the Fathers, to one person and two natures, and maintained that Christ as God was born of the Father and as man of the virgin, and yet was one person.

Walter was in accord with the satisfaction theory of Anselm, but rejected Berengar's Eucharistic doctrine; and he also taught the doctrine of the immaculate conception. Philosophy and dialectics, he held, came from the devil, and his opinion of scientific theology was equally uncomplimentary, his own solution of all problems being authority. Large portions of his chief work are contained in *MPL*, cxcix. 1130 sqq.

(R. SEEBERG.)

BIBLIOGRAPHY: Denifle, in *ALKG*, i. 404–417; A. Planck, in *TSK*, 1844, pp. 823–864; *Histoire littéraire de la France*, xiv. 549 sqq.; H. F. Reuter, *Geschichte der religiösen Aufklärung im Mittelalter*, ii. 15 sqq., Sondershausen, 1877; *KL*, xii. 1206–07.

WALTER, văl′ter, FRANZ XAVER: German Roman Catholic; b. at Amberg (36 m. e. of Nuremberg), Bavaria, Feb. 7, 1870. He was educated at the University of Munich (1888–93; Th.D., 1896), where he became privat-docent in 1899; in 1903 he was called to Strasburg as professor of moral theology, but in the following year returned to Munich in a similar capacity, which position he still holds. He has written *Das Eigentum nach der Lehre des heiligen Thomas von Aquin und des Sozialismus* (Freiburg, 1895); *Sozialpolitik und Moral* (1899); *Die Propheten in ihrem sozialen Beruf und das Wirtschaftsleben ihrer Zeit* (1900); *Sozialismus und moderne Kunst* (1901); *Der Aberglaube mit besonderer Berücksichtigung der Phänomene des Hypnotismus und Spiritismus* (Paderborn, 1904); *Theorie und Praxis in der Moral* (1905); *Kapitalismus, Sozialismus und Christentum* (Munich, 1906); *Primiz, Erntefest und Erstlingsfrucht des Priesters* (1907); *Die sexuelle Erklärung der Jugend* (1908); *Das kirchliche Lehramt und seine Bedeutung für die Kultur und soziale Wohlfahrt der Gegenwart* (1908); and *Der Leib und sein Recht im Christentum* (1910).

WALTER, JOHANNES WILHELM VON: German Protestant; b. at St. Petersburg, Russia, Oct. 26, 1876. He was educated at the universities of Dorpat (1894–99), Leipsic (1899–1900), and Göttingen (1900–01); became privat-docent for historical theology at Göttingen (1901); and extraordinary professor of church history at Breslau, 1909. In theology he belongs to the modern positive school, and has written *Das Leben Roberts von Arbrissel* (Göttingen, 1901); *Die ersten Wanderprediger Frankreichs* (2 vols., Leipsic, 1903–06); *Das Wesen der Religion nach Erasmus und Luther* (1906); *Die Absolutheit des Christentums und die Mission* (1906); *Franz von Assisi und die Nachahmung Christi* (1910); and *Frauenlos und Frauenarbeit in der Geschichte des Christums* (1911); and edited *Erasmus de libero arbitrio* διατριβή (1910). He is also editor of *Die Theologie der Gegenwart* (1907 sqq.)

WALTERS, CHARLES ENSOR: English Methodist; b. at Milborne Port (10 m. s.e. of Ilchester), Somersetshire, Dec. 18, 1872. He was educated at

Wesleyan Theological College, Richmond, Surrey (graduated, 1895); became assistant to H. P. Hughes in the West London Mission, of which he was chosen superintendent on the death of Hughes in 1902. In 1890 he was elected a member of the St. Pancras Borough Council, and from that year until 1892 was chairman of the Public Health Committee, while in 1898 he was made a member of the St. Pancras Vestry and local manager of the London School Board. He is editor of *The Advance*.

WALTHER, väl′ter, CARL FERDINAND WILHELM: German-American Lutheran, founder of the Synod of Missouri (see LUTHERANS, III., 5, § 1); b. at Langenchursdorf (near Waldenburg, 37 m. s.e. of Leipsic) Oct. 25, 1811; d. at St. Louis, Mo., May 7, 1887. He was educated at the University of Leipsic (1829–33); was private tutor at Cahla, Altenburg (1834–36); and pastor at Bräunsdorf for a year (1837–38). His firm orthodoxy and resistance to the rationalism prevailing about him, combined with the hopelessness of his endeavors to reform the moral and spiritual life of his congregation, led him to join the company of emigrants led by a pastor named Stephan. Early in 1839 he reached New Orleans, and by February the party, which numbered about 800, reached Missouri, some settling in St. Louis and the remainder in Perry Co., Mo. But before many months it was found that Stephan was unworthy of confidence, and it was mainly through the efforts of Walther that his wavering comrades regained their courage. In Feb., 1841, he was chosen pastor of the Lutheran congregation at St. Louis, and in Sept., 1844, began to edit the semimonthly *Der Lutheraner*. The next step was the foundation of the Synod of Missouri, and after a preliminary session at Fort Wayne, in 1846, the first convention of the German Evangelical Lutheran Synod of Missouri, Ohio, and Other States was held at Chicago in Apr., 1847. The synod took charge of the educational institution which had been founded at Altenburg, and in 1849 transferred it to St. Louis, Walther becoming the directing professor of the theological seminary, though his old congregation insisted that he should preach thrice annually and exercise a general supervision over it.

Walther now became involved in a controversy with Löhe (q.v.), who was not in sympathy with the democratic organization favored by the head of the Missouri Synod, and in 1851 this body determined to send Walther and Wyneken as delegates to Germany to seek to avoid any possible schism. Löhe was in favor of the plan, and the delegates proceeded to visit all the prominent Lutherans of the mother country, though Walther himself remained chiefly in Erlangen, gathering material for his attack on the High Church principles advocated by Grabau and the Buffalo Synod (see LUTHERANS, III, 5, § 2), the result being *Die Stimme unserer Kirche in der Frage von Kirche und Amt* (Erlangen, 1852). In Oct., 1851, Walther and Löhe met in personal conference, and the former, while recognizing the difficulty of reconciling their views on ordination, was able to express lively hopes of reunion, though this was not destined to be realized. In 1853, to give the Lutherans a trustworthy text of Luther's ver-

sion of the Bible, Walther founded the St. Louis Bible Society, of which he remained president until his death; and in 1855 he established the periodical *Lehre und Wehre*. He was also the leader of the Missourians at the conferences with the Buffalo Synod in 1866 and the Iowa Synod in 1867. In 1868–69 he conducted the conferences with the synods of Ohio, Wisconsin, and Illinois, which led to corporate union between these bodies and the Synod of Missouri, and in 1872 he was chosen president of the synodal conference of all western Lutherans in sympathy with the Missouri position. In addition to his other activities, Walther was a voluminous writer, his chief productions being as follows: *Die rechte Gestalt einer vom Staate unabhängigen evangelisch-lutherischen Ortsgemeinde* (St. Louis, 1863); *Amerikanisch-lutherische Pastoral-Theologie vom Jahr 1872* (1872); a new edition of J. G. Baier's *Compendium theologiæ positivæ* (1879); and the homiletic collections: *Amerikanisch-lutherische Evangelien-Postille* (1871); *Lutherische Brosamen* (1876); *Amerikanisch-lutherische Epistel-Postille* (1882); and the posthumous *Ansprachen und Gebete* (1888) and *Kasual-Predigten und Reden* (1889.)

(ADOLPH SPAETH†.)

BIBLIOGRAPHY: M. Günther, *C. W. F. Walther, Lebensbild*, St. Louis, 1890; C. Hochstetter, *Die Geschichte der Missouri-Synode*, Dresden, 1885; C. W. Ernst, in *The Watchman*, Boston, June 7, 1887; H. E. Jacobs, in *American Church History Series*, vol. iv. passim, New York, 1893; G. I. Fritschel, *Geschichte der lutherischen Kirche in Amerika*, ii. 184 sqq., Gütersloh, 1897; J. Deinzer, *Wilhelm Löhe's Leben*, vol. iii., 3d ed., Gütersloh, 1901.

WALTHER, JOHANN: German Lutheran musician and writer of hymns; b. near Cola, a small Thuringian village, 1496; d. at Torgau (31 m. e.n.e. of Leipsic) perhaps Mar. 25 (at least before Apr. 24), 1570. By 1524 he was at Torgau as bassist to Frederick the Wise, and during the same year he assisted Luther at Wittenberg in adapting the old music to Lutheran requirements, the results, first used in Luther's *Deutsche Messe*, appearing in the *Geystliche gesangk Buchleyn* (Wittenberg, 1524), while Walther himself attended the first German celebration of the Holy Communion, as rearranged by him and Luther, at the Wittenberg Stadtkirche on Oct. 29, 1525. In 1526 Walther was appointed choirmaster by Elector John of Saxony, and eight years later he was also made singing master to the school at Torgau. He went to Dresden in 1548 as choirmaster to Elector Maurice of Saxony, and on Aug. 7, 1554, was pensioned, whereupon he returned to Torgau and there passed the remainder of his life.

Walther's musical settings were for choral, not congregational, singing. In the *Deutsche Messe* his part was the responses of the choir and congregation, while Luther prepared the portions to be sung by the pastor. Walther also made two settings (in 1530 and 1552) for the passion music from Matthew and John. His hymns, ten in number, appeared chiefly in the *Christliches Kinderlied D. Martini Lutheri* (Wittenberg, 1566), and are conveniently collected by P. Wackernagel, *Das deutsche Kirchenlied*, iii. 187–206, nos. 219–229 (5 vols., Leipsic, 1864–77). Two of these have been translated into English: "Herzlich Lieb hab ich dich, mein Gott!" by A. T. Russell as "O God, my Rock, my heart on Thee";

and the far more popular " Herzlich thut mich erfreuen," by Miss Susanna Winkworth as " Now fain my joyous heart would sing," by B. H. Kennedy as " Soon will the heavenly Bridegroom come," by M. Loy as " The Bridegroom soon will call us," and by Miss H. R. Krauth as " Leap forth, my heart, rejoicing," together with one or two less important versions.

BIBLIOGRAPHY: Julian, *Hymnology*, pp. 1231–32; Wackernagel, as noted in the text; and literature under HYMNOLOGY.

WALTHER, RUDOLF. See GUALTHER, RUDOLF.

WALTHER, WILHELM MARKUS: German Evangelical; b. at Cuxhaven (60 m. n.w. of Hamburg) Jan. 7, 1846. He received his education at the universities of Erlangen, Marburg, and Göttingen, 1865–70; was pastor in his native place, 1870–95; and then took his present position of professor of church history and the history of dogma at the University of Rostock. He has given especial attention to the history of the final period of the Middle Ages and of the Reformation. Among his published works are: *Luther vor dem Richterstuhl der Germania* (Hamburg, 1883); *Luther im neuesten römischen Gericht* (4 parts, Halle, 1885–92); *Die Früchte der römischen Beichte* (Brunswick, 1888); *Die Bibelübersetzungen des Mittelalters* (3 parts, 1889–91); *Luthers Bibelübersetzung kein Plagiat* (Leipsic, 1891); *Die Bedeutung der deutschen Reformation für die Gesundheit unseres Volkslebens* (1894); *Melanchthon als Retter des wissenschaftliches Sinnes* (1897); *Ein Merkmal des Schwärmergeistes* (1898); *Das Zeugnis des heiligen Geistes nach Luther und nach moderner Schwärmerei* (1899); *Adolf Harnacks Wesen des Christentums für die christliche Gemeinde geprüft* (1901); *Das Erbe der Reformation in Kampfe der Gegenwart* (3 parts, 1903–09); *Denifles Luther, eine Ausgeburt römischer Moral* (1904); *Für Luther wider Rom. Handbuch der Apologetik Luthers und der Reformation den römischen Anklagen gegenüber* (1906); *Das älteste und das neueste Christusbild* (Wismar, 1906); *Heinrich VIII. von England und Luther* (Leipsic, 1908); *Pauli Christentum, Jesu Evangelium* (1908); *Zur Wertung der deutschen Reformation* (1909); and a number of volumes of sermons. He has also contributed to the Weimar edition of .Luther's works (vols. xix., xxiii.).

WALTON, BRIAN: English Biblical scholar; b. at or near Seymour or Seamer (31 m. n.e. of York), Yorkshire in 1600; d. in London Nov. 29, 1661. He was educated at Cambridge (B.A., 1619–20; M.A., 1623; D.D., 1639); was curate and also schoolmaster in Suffolk; in 1628 became rector of St. Martin's Orgar, London, to which was joined in 1636 the rectorship of Sandon, Essex, at which time he was perhaps chaplain to the king, and prebend of St. Paul's; in 1641 he was dispossessed of both rectories, being prosecuted for " subtile tricks and popish innovations," and in the next year was imprisoned; he fled to Oxford, and there formed the design of the great polyglot (see BIBLES, POLYGLOT, IV.), by which he immortalized himself. After the surrender of Oxford (1646), he went to London with the materials he had collected, and in 1652 published

his prospectus to the polyglot. Subscriptions were placed at ten pounds a set; the six volumes appeared 1654–57. As a help to the student of his polyglot, he published *Introductio ad lectionem linguarum orientalium* (London, 1655; republished Deventer, 1655, 1658). Owen thought that the polyglot, especially the prolegomena, contained things injurious to Christianity. To him he addressed himself in his *Considerator Considered; or a brief View of certain Considerations upon the Biblia Polyglotta, the Prolegomena, and the Appendix* (London, 1660). Walton's polyglot is the first book in England published by subscription. The polyglot was placed on the Index. Walton was at the Restoration made chaplain to the king, and on Dec. 2, 1660, was consecrated, in Westminster Abbey, bishop of Chester.

BIBLIOGRAPHY: H. J. Todd, *Memoirs of the Life and Writings of Brian Walton*, 2 vols., London, 1821 (vol. ii. is a reprint of the *Considerator*); *DNB*, lix. 268–271; F. H. Reusch, *Der Index der verbotenen Bücher*, ii. 124–125, Bonn, 1885.

WALTON'S POLYGLOT. See BIBLES, POLYGLOT; WALTON, BRIAN.

WAMWAS. See VAMVAS.

WANDALBERT, vän'dăl-bert: Ecclesiastical author and monk of Prüm (a monastery 33 m. n.n.w. of Treves); b. in 813; d. at Prüm after 850. His life at the monastery fell under the third abbot, Markward, but prior to that it is practically unknown, though it is possible that he was born in France. His literary activity must have begun when he was young, since his secular poems could hardly have been issued from the cloister, which he entered at least as early as 839. Markward urged him to work over and continue the early " life " of St. Goar (q.v.), out of which arose the *Miracula S. Goaris presbyteri* (with the *Vita* in two books, Mainz, 1489; taken later into *ASM* and *ASB*). Wandalbert's second work was his *Martyrologium* (first printed 1563 with the works of Bede, to whom it was long in part attributed; it is in L. d'Achery, *Spicilegium*, v. 305 sqq., 13 vols., Paris, 1655–77, in 2d ed., ii. 38 sqq., 1723; in *MPL*, cxxi.; and in *MGH*, *Poet. Lat. ævi Car.*, ii (1884), 567 sqq., written in verse and completed about 850. For this he drew largely upon martyrologies, especially that of Bede; but much of it is original. The preface in prose describes the different forms of verse employed by the author. This is followed by six lyrical poems, an invocation to God, beseeching the ability properly to praise the saints, then by an address to the reader admonishing him to emulate the virtues of the saints. Then follow dedications to the Emperor Lothair and his friend Otrich, an outline of the work and a survey of the divisions of the year. Beginning with January, the work contains accounts of one or more saints for each day throughout the year. The Martyrology closes with two hymns to Christ, the *conclusio*, and a hymn in Sapphic measure to all the saints. Connected with this work are poems in hexameter on the months and their signs, and on the various agricultural, pastoral, and horticultural occupations, and a poetic account of creation. These poems, which imitate the ancient classics, exhibit less of poetic genius than of painstaking effort at artistic writing.   (A. HAUCK.)

BIBLIOGRAPHY: C. Oudin, *Commentarius de scriptoribus ecclesiastibus*, ii. 149 sqq., Leipsic, 1722; *Histoire littéraire de la France*, v. 377 sqq.; J. C. F. Bähr, *Geschichte der römischen Litteratur im karolingischen Zeitalter*, pp. 114-115, 229-230, Carlsruhe, 1840; A. Ebert, *Geschichte der Literatur des Mittelalters*, ii. 185-191, Leipsic, 1880; Dümmler, in *NA*, iv (1879), 305 sqq.; Achelis, in the *Abhandlungen* of the Göttingen Academy, new series, iii (1900), no. 3; Rettberg, *KD*, i. 465-482; *KL*, xii. 1211-12.

WANDERING CLERGY. See VAGANTES.

WANDERING JEW: A legendary character doomed to wander over the earth till the return of Christ. The story of the Wandering Jew is not, as has been plausibly supposed, a primitive Christian legend, but a literary product in the guise of a romance. The story first appears in Germany in 1602, in a small pamphlet entitled, *Kurze Beschreibung und Erzählung von einem Jude mit Namen Ahasverus, welcher bei der Kreuzigung Christi selbst persönlich gewesen, auch das Crucifige über Christum hab helfen schreien und um Barrabam bitten*, which pretends to report a conversation that took place at Hamburg in 1542 between the Wandering Jew and Paul von Eitzen, bishop of Sleswick. The Jew tells Von Eitzen that his name is Ahasuerus, that in the time of Christ he was a cobbler in Jerusalem, and that, because he knew no better, he had joined in the cry, " Crucify him "; further, that when Jesus, bearing the Cross, passed by the door of his house and was intending to lean against the wall to rest, he harshly scolded him away, whereupon Jesus gazed at him fixedly and said: " I will stop and rest, but thou shalt go on." Since that time he had had no rest, but had wandered about the world. It is claimed further that Von Eitzen examined him in detail and found him possessed of wonderful knowledge, notably in oriental history. The Jew is then described with reference to his appearance and his humble temperament. Of his adventures it is related merely that he was in Palestine again a century after Christ's crucifixion, finding Jerusalem destroyed, though an appendix mentions that in the year 1575, or shortly before, he was in Spain. The report is subscribed, " *Datum* Sleswick, June 9, 1594." This relation was then frequently reprinted in the seventeenth century. The title and date became altered, but the substance of the narrative continued the same, except for added moral observations and accounts of new apparitions of the Wandering Jew. From the time of the second series of editions the author's name purports to be Chrysostomus Dudulæus Westphalus, unquestionably a pseudonym. From about the beginning of the eighteenth down into the nineteenth century the story appeared in numerous popular editions in which the text became utterly degenerate. For example, the name " Von Eitzen " merged into " Litz." The story was early translated into French, Dutch, etc., with characteristic embellishments.

There can be no doubt as to the fact that the story of the Wandering Jew first became known in the year 1602; and it is probable that it originated then. Some of its features, however, bear marked resemblance to earlier narratives. For example, the story of Cartaphilus, Pilate's doorkeeper, as first related by Roger of Wendover (d. 1237) in his *Flores historiarum*, unquestionably has much in common

with the story of the Wandering Jew, while still other common traits occur in the legends of " deathless John," etc. Yet in its main outline the story of the Wandering Jew is so distinctive that it must be regarded as the independent invention of an individual. Had the author had any inkling of those earlier tales he would have referred to them in some way, as later editors expressly did. The object of the story is undoubtedly apologetic. How the author happened to designate the well-known theologian Paul von Eitzen as the man who saw the Wandering Jew can not be determined.

CARL BERTHEAU†.

BIBLIOGRAPHY: J. G. T. Grässe, *Der Tannhäuser und der ewige Jude*, Dresden, 1861; F. Bässler, *Ueber die Sage vom ewigen Juden*, Berlin, 1870; C. M. Blass, *Der ewige Jude in Deutschland*, Stockerau, 1870; F. Helbig, *Die Sage vom ewigen Juden, ihre poetische Wandlung und Fortbildung*, Berlin, 1874; C. Schöbel, *La Légende du juif-errant*, Paris, 1877; G. Paris, *Le Juif errant*, ib. 1880; M. D. Conway, *The Wandering Jew*, London, 1881; S. Baring-Gould, *Curious Myths of the Middle Ages*, ib. 1884; L. Neubaur, *Die Sage vom ewigen Juden*, Leipsic, 1884; idem, *Neue Mittheilungen über die Sage vom ewigen Juden*, ib. 1893.

WANDERING IN THE WILDERNESS.

The Basal Narratives (§ 1).
Methods of Studying the Narratives (§ 2).
The Four Main Narratives (§ 3).
Sustenance of the People. Other Tribes (§ 4).
Place Names (§ 5).
Chronology and the Route (§ 6).

The accounts of the wandering of the Hebrews in the desert are contained principally in the books of Exodus, Numbers, and Deuteronomy. Ex. xv. 22 tells of the start from the Red Sea, and xix. 1 of the arrival at Sinai; then the narrative of the wandering is interrupted by the collections of laws, except

1. The Basal Narratives. for the golden calf episode in Ex. xxxii.–xxxiii., but is taken up and continued in Num. x. 11–xiv., xvi.–xvii., xx.–xxi.; xxii. 1 states the arrival in the territory of Moab, and Num. xxxiii. contains a statement of the stations of the journey from Rameses in Egypt to the plains of Moab. Further, in Deut. i. 6–ii. 24 is a résumé of the events occurring on the march from Horeb to the Arnon, while x. 6–9 reviews a fragment of the journey and the separation of the Levites. Outside the Pentateuch are only short references to the wandering (Josh. xxiv. 7–8; Judges xi. 16–17; in the prophetical books and the Psalms, particularly Ps. lxxviii.), which, however, in the main depend upon the accounts in the Pentateuch but present some singularities. In its present form the Pentateuch contains about fifteen narratives of events during the wandering, excluding parallels, eleven of which deal with the mutiny of the people against Moses or Yahweh, in eight cases punishment follows, in four cases the murmuring ends in gifts from Yahweh; two accounts of successful war occur (Ex. xvii. 8–16; Num. xxi. 1–3). Deuteronomy views the events of the journey from the point of view of education; Amos regards the period as one of especial favor from Yahweh; Hosea dates rebellion of the people from the entrance into Canaan, as does Jeremiah; Ezekiel sees in the whole history of Israel, including the desert period, only disregard of Yahweh, which view governs the later historians of Israel, and so they account for the destruction of the generation of Moses and Aaron in the wilderness. Some of the accounts suggest that other narratives than those now extant were in the possession of the Hebrews and emphasized Yahweh's providence (so Deut. viii., xxix.; Jer. ii.; Judges v. 11); the account of a holy war appears only in Ex. xvii. 8–16; Num. xxi. 1–3; but this idea influenced mightily the early religion of Israel.

It has long been the custom, and this custom is still followed in part, to employ these sources, as well as accounts in early and late literature of places and names, partly in a harmonistic method, using historical, geographical, and etymological learning, as though the tracing of the journeyings **2. Methods** presented no difficulties of moment, es-**of Study-** pecially since no good maps of the re-**ing the** gion existed. Matters which were by **Narratives.** no means certain were taken as proved (e.g., the situation of Sinai), and without making clear the details of the journeying, by seizing now upon this and now upon that name which sounded like the Biblical name in the narrative, the material was used as if elastic to produce what was hoped to be a satisfying result; the processes of literary and textual criticism not being employed. Indeed, the question was not squarely met whether the conditions for the wandering of so numerous a people with all their possessions really existed. The newer method is to take account of the various threads and sources, to investigate the character of each, to take into consideration investigations into the natural conditions presented by the region, and so to reach conclusions which satisfactorily meet the case.

The account of J involves great difficulties. Moses, according to this narrator, led the people from the Red Sea to the wilderness of Shur, where they were three days without water (Ex. xv. 22); the Marah and Elim episodes are by E (Ex. xv. 23–27). J tells in Ex. xvi. of the gift of manna, in xvii. of the murmuring against Moses at Meribah, and in xxxiii. 1 sqq. of the command to leave Sinai; Num. x. 29–32 deals with the relations with Hobab the **3. The** Midianite as guide, Num. xi. gives the **Four Main** episode of the quails and the journey to **Narratives.** Hazeroth and to Paran (xii. 16). From Kadesh (?) Moses sent out the spies, among them Caleb, who report the land as fruitful but impossible to take into possession (Num. xiii.), so that the people desire to return to Egypt (xiv. 3). The further course of the narrative of J is not clear. Num. xvi. tells of the rebellion of Dathan and Abiram, and xxi. 1–3 of the ban of the city of Hormah. After that comes the capture of the fortified cities east of the Jordan. E is somewhat clearer in his narrative. In Ex. xvii. 8–16 is recounted the victory over Amalek, in chap. xviii. the advice of Jethro to appoint judges; in Ex. xxxiii. 1 sqq. the command to leave Horeb is regarded as punishment for the worship of the golden calf, but the ark shows the way (Num. x. 33–36); Num. xi. 1–3 tells of the fire from Yahweh which destroyed some of the people, and other verses of the chapter deal with the seventy elders; in chap. xi. Miriam's leprosy is accounted for; Num. xiii. 26 tells that from Kadesh Moses sent spies, and Caleb alone entreats the people to trust

Yahweh (xiv. 8–9); in xiv. 25 the people are commanded to return into the wilderness, while the people were defeated in their attempt on Canaan; Num. xx. 1b shows the people again in Kadesh, where Miriam died, after which the people go by way of Edom to the Arnon (Num. xx. 14–21, xxi. 4–9, 12–20). The Deuteronomist (i. 6–ii. 25) gives a short review of the course from Horeb to the Arnon, and (ix. 22) recalls Taberah, Massah, and Kibroth-hattaavah. The indications of the narrative of P are clearer. From Elim " all the congregation " went into the wilderness of Sin (Ex. xvi. 1), and when hunger assailed the people manna and quails were sent them, thence by way of Rephidim they passed to the wilderness of Sinai (Ex. xvii. 1, xix. 1), the separate stations not being named. After the giving of the law, they depart from the wilderness of Sinai, and twelve spies are sent forth, go from the wilderness of Sin, swing northward by way of the entrance to Hamath, and after forty days return to the wilderness of Paran. At their report the assembly expresses its disappointment in an outbreak against Moses and Aaron. The next rebellion is that of Korah against the exclusive priesthood of the Levites, whose right is vindicated by a miracle of destruction and the budding of Aaron's rod (Num. xvi.–xvii.). In the wilderness of Sin the people murmur against the leaders because of lack of water, which is brought them from the rock (Meribah), and thence they proceed to Hor, where Aaron dies (Num. xx.), and to the territory opposite Jericho (Num. xxi.). The omission of the stages of the journey is supplied by Num. xxxiii., which purports to be by Moses (verse 2), and, apart from the starting-point and finish, contains the names of forty places, corresponding to the forty years of the wandering, but twenty-two of these are new and do not appear elsewhere in the Pentateuch. Examination shows that the author of this chapter has used the Pentateuch in practically its present form, hence the chapter is one of the latest in the Pentateuch. It appears to be the work of a Jew of Jerusalem of the end of the fifth pre-Christian century, who used not only the Pentateuch but other sources, involving the journey of others or of himself in that region; and into his account insertions appear to have been made. The wandering according to this chapter appears in four stages: From Rameses to Sinai (3–15); from Sinai to Bene-jaakan (16–30a, 36b–41a, 30a–31); thence south to Ezion-gaber (32–35); and thence north by way of the Wadi 'Arabah to Abel-shittim in Moab (36a, 41b–49). From the dating given above, it follows that among the sources this piece takes not the first but the last place among the data for determining the course of the wandering. The attempt must fail which aims to show that a difference among the narrators reflects itself here; that in the first part of the catalogue of stations the ideas of P and J are followed in that the Hebrews went in a northeasterly direction to Moab, while in the second part the notion of E and D is reproduced, viz., that they went by a circuit which took them first southeastward by Ezion-gaber. The many new place names stand in the way of reconciliation; moreover, of the forty or more names only about one-fourth may with greater or less probability be located, and these do not suffice to guide one on the way the Hebrews took. Moreover, since the number forty is there, not much room probably is left for additions or subtractions (by later editors). The four narratives are not of equal value. That of P is the latest; in this, e.g., Joshua represents the tribe of Ephraim, in E he is the servant of Moses; so Caleb represents Judah, while before the exile he stood out as still an independent tribe. D depends upon JE; while J and E are the earliest sources.

A series of narratives naturally deal with the matter of the sustenance of the people in the desert; it was early recognized that for the assumed two millions this was a difficult problem.

The solution was by miracle—God gave them water, bread, and meat. Yet the natural situation was kept in mind. Water was alleged **4. Suste-** to be given only where it later existed. **nance of** Manna is known, even by modern **the People.** Arabs, as the sweet exudation of the **Other** *Tamarix mannifera*, which when per- **Tribes.** forated by an insect (*coccus manni- parus*) gives forth a sort of gum in drops, which may be collected before the sun causes it to melt (cf. Ex. xvi. 21). These and other narrated facts, as its sweet taste, are in accordance with those observable. On the other hand, some details are rather poetical (Num. xi. 8). Similarly quails are in that region numerous, both as migratory and also as breeding there. Moreover, they do not fly high, especially when fatigued, and may be caught with the hand. An Arab writer of the tenth century speaks of the numbers of quails and says that the flesh often induces illness (cf. Num. xi. 33). In this way the nature of the wilderness and of the life there is accurately reproduced in many particulars in the narratives. Other details have to do with the peoples of other tribes with whom dealing was had. If Num. x. 29–32 originally spoke of Kenites (not Midianites), it leads to the conclusion that the Kenites went with the Hebrews to Canaan (cf. Judges i. 16, iv. 11; I Sam. xv. 6). The war with the Amalekites at Rephidim (Ex. xvii. 8–16) may be put in connection with Massa and Meribah (= Kadesh; cf. verses 2–7); but of the situation of Rephidim apart from this nothing certain is known, nor of the place of the altar of verse 15. The kernel and occasion of Num. xiii.–xiv. is discernible as coming from the history of the Calebite stem as dwelling near Hebron; this narrative explains the connection of the stock with Israel by its obedience to Yahweh. The narrative concerning Hormah and the former name Zephat is etymologically clear, since Hormah is connected with the Hebr. *ḥerem*, " ban "; but the historical content is put in question. In an entirely different class are Ex. xviii.; Num. xi. 14, 16–17, 24b–30, which deal with the selection of laymen as judges and aids in leading the people. Num. xi. places them in a grade lower than Moses, possessing only a part of the divine spirit which rested upon him; Ex. xviii. makes Jethro the teacher of Moses in this matter. Some of the stories are closely connected with the cultus (Ex. xvii. 8–16; Num. xxi. 4–9; cf. II Kings xviii. 4). Other passages deal with etymological explanations of place names (Marah, Ex. xv. 23; Massah and Meribah, Ex.

xvii. 7: Taberah, Num. xi. 1–3; and Hormah, ut sup.). The narratives are partly etiological, partly etymological, and partly popular renarration of historical recollections from various standpoints, some also having their point of departure in pedagogical purpose (so the Korah narrative in its relation to priestly precedence, Num. xvi.). Complicating the discussion is the fact that the subject is the people of Israel as a whole as having the desert experience, though nationality was attained first in Canaan and only little tribes or stocks collected about Moses, with their possessions of flocks lingering where water permitted.

The names of places finding mention in the older narratives and in P are few—chiefly on the Egyptian border and in Edom and Moab. Stretches of territory were often named from adjacent places (e.g., the wilderness of Shur, Ex. xv. 22, from Shur, cf. **5. Place** Gen. xvi. 7, or perhaps from an Egyp- **Names.** tian border fortress Taru). Some explain Elim (Ex. xv. 27) by referring to Phoinikon, a place of worship rich in springs named by Agatharchides (150 B.C.), and putting it into connection with the gods (Elim) of the place, while Marah (Ex. xv. 23) is derived from the name of the Maraniten, a tribe which held possession. A later identification is with 'Ain Hawara in the wadi of that name, and of Elim with the Wadi Gharandel two hours south. The wilderness of Sin (Ex. xvi. 1), which has nothing to do with the deity of that name, is to be located east and northeast of the present Ismailiyeh; according to Ezek. xxx. 15, Sin was the name of a fortress on the northern boundary of Egypt. Of the places in the desert Kadesh is known with certainty (see NEGEB). It figures strongly in all the sources, and it is possible that Massah is the notable spring 'Ain al-Kaderat, not far from Kadesh. The war with the Amalekites and the meeting with Jethro point to Kadesh. It has long been noticed that in the present accounts Kadesh was a station of the Israelites both before and after the giving of the law, and this probably embodies the correct historical tradition; indeed, this place may have been the objective of the march from Egypt, since it must have been known by the nomads for its abundant water supply. It is never reported that water was found at Sinai or Horeb, and a long stay there is not to be supposed. The natural situation implies that Israel stayed long in Kadesh but it is not expressly stated in the older narratives, though it may be read between the lines. The location of the giving of the law might be conjectured for this neighborhood (cf. Judges v. 4), in accordance with the general situation, but this is obscured by the intimations regarding the law as given on Sinai or Horeb. What is in the foreground is the long halt at Kadesh, and this alone offers a reasonable ground upon which to construct the history of this period and of the founding of the religion. Taberah and Kibroth-hattaavah (Num. xi. 3, 34) were possibly not far from Kadesh, as was also Hazeroth (xi. 35), " courts, enclosures." Paran (q.v.), as represented, seems to have been more frequented by the Israelites than Kadesh, but this can hardly be historical. Hormah, to be distinguished from the place of that name in the Negeb (q.v.), is located by Palmer at al-Zebeta, by Robinson at al-Zafa on the border of Edom. The wilderness of Sin lay south of Kadesh, between it and the wilderness of Paran. The latter is made by the narratives the place of the long wandering, and is to be sought west of the Edomitic boundary. Of the period spent there hardly anything is known—there was placed the rebellion of Korah. In the later conceptions of the Hebrews, the double halt of their forefathers at Kadesh was the fast fact. Mount Hor, where Aaron died (Num. xx. 22–29), is, according to the context, to be sought not far from Kadesh, and not in the neighborhood of Petra; Deut. x. 6 sqq. puts his death at Mosera, which may possibly be Jebel Madara, northeast from Kadesh. Oboth (Num. xxi. 10–11, xxxiii. 43) is located by Wetzstein at the watering-places 'Ain al-Webe on the western slope of Wadi 'Arabah south of the Dead Sea; but Num. xxxiii. 43 places it near Phunon (Khirbet Fenan), on the opposite side of the wadi. The location is not certain, but both supposed sites indicate passage through the wadi. Ije-abarim (Num. xxi. 11, xxxiii. 44–45) shows the people already in Moab; it may correspond to Khirbet 'Aij, between Katrabba (Kafrabba) and el-Kerak.

Bound up in the texture of the narrative of P is a chronology which makes frequent mention of forty years. This period as the length of the wandering is surely older than the age of the author of this document, appearing in E and D (Josh. xiv. 7, 10; Deut. viii. 2, 4). In the present text this period is reckoned in various ways; from the march from Kadesh to the end of the desert (Num. xiv. 33, xxxiii. 38); or from the departure from Egypt (Ex. xii. 2 sqq., xvi. 1, xl. 1, 17; Num. x. 11; Deut. i. 3), which would make the period from the leaving of Kadesh thirty-eight years. Sometimes the reckoning is not completed, perhaps because it did not agree with other data (Ex. xix. 1; Num. xx. 1), but perhaps because the reckoning of forty years was a later conception. This conception is worked out into a schematic (i.e., unhistorical) form in Num. xxxiii., making the stations impliedly agree with the number of the years of the wandering. Of the events of these years little is known; the rebellion of Korah, the opening of the springs at Kadesh, and the death of Aaron are all. This lack of material best fits in with the supposition that the forty years were not in the original tradition. As to E and D it is to be noted that the former (Ex. xiii. 17 sqq.) declares that God did not lead the people by the way of the Philistines, but by the way of the Red Sea (q.v.); the other reports of the wandering are given in Deut. i.–ii. The road to the "mountain of the Amorites" (Deut. i. 19) leads out of the desert south of the Negeb, out of the desert of Paran, to the north via Kadesh toward Beersheba and Hebron. The way to the Red Sea (i. 40, ii. 1) led from Kadesh through the desert to Elath. The "way of the plain" (ii. 8) leads (verses 3–4) north through the region of the Edomites. Thence the march was eastward or northeastward after leaving the Wadi 'Arabah to the wilderness of Moab and the brook Zered (verse 13). See ISRAEL, HISTORY OF, I., § 4.   (H. GUTHE.)

6. Chronology and the Route. [marginal]

BIBLIOGRAPHY: E. Naville, in the *Memoirs* of the Egypt Exploration Fund, Nos. 1, 3, for 1883–84; C. Forster, *Israel in the Wilderness*, London, 1865; W. H. Bartlett, *Forty Days in the Desert on the Track of the Israelites*, new ed., London, 1867; E. H. Palmer, *The Desert of the Exodus*, part ii., chaps. 1–5, 2 vols., London, 1871; S. C. Bartlett, *From Egypt to Palestine through Sinai*, New York, 1879; G. Ebers, *Durch Gosen zum Sinai*, Leipsic, 1881; H. C. Trumbull, *Kadesh-Barnea*, New York and London, 1884; M. J. Lagrange, in *Revue biblique*, ix (1900), 66 sqq., 286 sqq., 447 sqq.; C. Steuernagel, *Einwanderung der israelitischen Stämme*, Leipsic, 1901; E. Meyer, *Die Israeliten und ihre Nachbarstämme*, pp. 1 sqq., Halle, 1906; Bönhoff, in *TSK*, 1907, pp. 159 sqq.; A. Musil, *Arabia Petræa* (text), vols. i.–ii., Vienna, 1907–1908; O. A. Toffteen, *Researches in Biblical Archæology*, vol. ii., *The Historic Exodus*, Chicago, 1909; L. Schneller, *Durch die Wüste zum Sinai. In Moses Spuren vom Schilfmeer bis zum Nebo*, Leipsic, 1909; *EB*, iv. 5256–61; *JE*, xii. 520–521; the literature under SINAI, and the commentaries on the Biblical books named in the text.

WAR AND CHRISTIAN SERVICE IN WAR.

I. Theory and Ethics of War.
    Ethics of War (§ 1).
    Patristic and Medieval Views (§ 2).
    Clerics and Military Service (§ 3).
II. Movements and Societies for Mitigation of Horrors of War.
    Origin of Societies for Care of Wounded (§ 1).
    German Societies (§ 2).

I. Theory and Ethics of War: Though war is undoubtedly an evil, it is not unmixed with good, and the view that condemns it unconditionally is one-sided. To base this view on the words of Jesus in the sermon on the mount (Matt. v. 39–44) is to misinterpret the passage. It is true that in the kingdom of heaven there will be no place for war, and that the development of the work of salvation among men points directly to the abolition of war; but the future can not be anticipated. The Christian must bear with patience present evils and tribulations (Rom. xii. 11). Did not Moses say, "The Lord is a man of war" (Ex. xv. 3)? David confidently recommends his martial doings to the Lord (Ps. ix., xviii., lx.). There is no reason for restricting the validity of this view to the time of the old dispensation, for nowhere does the New Testament reject war unconditionally. John the Baptist did not ask of soldiers that they abandon their profession (Luke iii. 14), nor did Jesus ask such a thing of the centurion of Capernaum (Matt. viii. 5–13), or Peter of Cornelius (Acts x.). God has given the sword to rulers that they may punish evil-doers and maintain law and order. It was from this point of view that Luther wrote *Ob Kriegsleute auch in seligem Stande sein können.* He maintained that unnecessary war is a sin, but that necessary war is a duty. The part of the individual Christian in war is a matter of duty to the ruler. It is not for him to decide whether or not the war is justified. This view of the Reformer has not been changed greatly by later Evangelical ethics. The right of intervention, which is now generally recognized, offers a difficult problem; and it is questionable whether, in matters pertaining to the kingdom of God, the sword should be drawn at all (Matt. xxvi. 52). Strategy in war has been recognized from time immemorial, and is justified, in that it serves to shorten the war and diminish loss of life. As regards the care of the

1. Ethics of War. [marginal]

wounded and the life and property of non-combatants, warfare is now conducted on more humane principles than formerly. Even Luther regarded robbing and burning as unavoidable. It can not be too strongly emphasized that the only proper purpose of war is to restore peace and reestablish law and order, and that no more damage should be done to the enemy than is necessary for the accomplishment of this purpose. Recent attempts to secure a world-peace by disarmament are based upon economic considerations rather than upon Christian principles.

The early Christians abhorred war, partly on account of a misinterpretation of the words of Jesus to Peter, "for all they that take the sword shall perish with the sword" (Matt. xxvi. 52); partly because military service brought them **2. Patristic** in contact with many idolatrous rites. **and Medi-** The State seemed to them an expres- **eval Views.** sion of the godlessness of the world and its hostility to Christ. In this spirit Tertullian treated the subject (*De idol.*, xix.; *De corona militis*, xi., both in *ANF*, vol. iii.). Nevertheless, in spite of the reigning aversion, many Christians served in the Roman army (Tertullian, *Apol.*, xlii.; *Ad Scap.*, iv.); and when, under the reign of Constantine, the relation between State and Church became one of intimate friendship and alliance the objections of the Christians to war were gradually silenced. Augustine, who maintained intimate personal and epistolary intercourse with many distinguished statesmen, such as Marcellinus and Bonifacius, considered war a social benefit, and military service an employment of a talent agreeable to God (*Epist.*, ccvii. *ad Bonif.*, and *Epist.*, cxxxviii. *ad Marc.*). In his book against Faustus (XXII., lxxiv.) he exclaims, "What is there bad in war"? Later on, when it became the great task of the Church to convert the Germanic tribes no objections to war were heard. True, its horrors and cruelties were mitigated by the "Truce of God" (q.v.), the sanctity of sacred places (see ASYLUM, RIGHT OF), etc. Indeed, the Church instigated the wars of the Crusades, which were regarded as wars of God. Nor is the attitude which Luther assumed with respect to the Peasants' War and the war against the Turks different in principle from that which the Latin Church originally assumed with respect to the Crusades. In the ancient church the clergy were absolutely forbidden to participate in war; and no one who had served in the army after he had professed Christianity was admitted to holy orders. During the Middle Ages it was not rare to find great generals among the bishops. Such a one was Christian of Mainz. After the decay of the feudal system the clergy were freed from all personal military service.

Now that military service is required of all in Germany, the question of military service by clerics has again become a vital one, and has **3. Clerics** occasioned much discussion. It has **and Mili-** been urged that military duties are in- **tary Service.** consistent with service in the kingdom of God, and that the obligations of the young clergyman to his church should take precedence of secular duties. From the point of view of the Church it is highly objectionable that the work of preparation of the theological student should be unnecessarily interrupted by a period of military service, which may prove both expensive and demoralizing. [For views traversing those of this article see PEACE MOVEMENTS.]

(KARL BURGER†.)

II. Movements and Societies for Mitigation of Horrors of War: Felddiakonie is the German term for voluntary service rendered to combatants in time of war. In its origin it partook of the nature of Christian ministration, but was also influenced largely by the spirit of secular humanitarianism.

The care of the sick and wounded in **1. Origin** war presupposes three essential ele- **of Societies** ments—the existence of a trained and **for Care of** devoted body of voluntary workers, **Wounded.** their harmonious cooperation with the regular military sanitary department, and the recognition of their neutral character by international law. Up to the middle of the nineteenth century the fate of those wounded in battle was pitiful, and even the Crimean War, which witnessed the heroic labors of Florence Nightingale and the first beginnings of organized sanitary activity on the part of volunteers, deprived war of but few of its horrors in the field and the hospital. It was the Lombard War of 1859 that gave the great impulse to the movement. Stirred by the dreadful sights of the battle-field of Solferino Henri Dunant of Geneva began to plead the cause of the wounded soldier, and so eloquently as finally to convince the entire world of the necessity of radical improvement in that sphere. On Aug. 22, 1864, was concluded the Geneva Convention by which the sick and wounded in war together with the staff devoted to their care and all utilities appertaining to the work were declared inviolable under the sign of the Red Cross (q.v.) on a white field. But of more avail than the specific conditions of the Geneva convention itself was the impulse thus given to a great humanitarian movement which speedily came to constitute one of the most wide-spread fields of beneficent human activity. The basis had been laid for the foundation of numerous societies which may be divided into two general categories according as the moving spirit is one of Christian mission work or of secular humanitarianism and patriotism.

Of Protestant associations the Knights of St. John trace back to the time of the crusades. The bailly of Brandenburg in the grand priory of Germany was disbanded in 1812, and revived in 1852 **2. German** as an Evangelical order devoted to the **Societies.** defense of religion and the performance of works of mercy. Both in peace and war it has been active in the care of the sick through the erection and maintenance of hospitals and the knightly protection of sisters engaged in their work of mercy on the battlefield. In 1898 the order counted 770 active and 1,747 affiliated honorary members, and maintained 48 establishments with 2,297 beds, attended exclusively by the members of the sisterhoods. In time of war it can place 1,600 women nurses in the field. Among Roman Catholic orders the first place belongs to the Knights of Malta, divided into two associations, one in Silesia organized in 1864, and one in the Rhenish and Westphalian region founded three years later. Its staff includes about 1,500 sisters of mercy and a smaller number of brethren. The Knights of St. George are a Bavarian order founded in 1729 and reorganized in 1871. Non-religious bodies are the Associations for the Care of the Wounded and Sick in War of which the first was founded in Württemberg in 1863, followed within five years by others in all the principal German states. In 1886 a movement was set on foot for the organization of voluntary associations for the care of the sick under the auspices of Johann Wichern, director of the Rauhes Haus, whose exertions resulted in the establishment of branches throughout Germany and the creation of a body of 2,200 trained nurses with a reserve of almost double that number. The organic law conditioning the existence and character of all these associations is the sanitary ordinance of Jan. 10, 1878. For Red Cross Societies see the article on that subject; see also PEACE MOVEMENTS.   (THEODORE SCHÄFER.)

BIBLIOGRAPHY: The subject is sometimes treated in discussions on ethics, as in R. Rothe, *Ethik*, §§ 1159–62, Wittenberg, 1869, and H. L. Martensen, *Die christliche Ethik*, iii. 280–292, Berlin, 1871, Eng. transl., Edinburgh, 1882. The reverse of this subject with its appropriate bibliography is presented in the article PEACE MOVEMENTS. Consult further: G. W. MacCree, *The Sword and the Olive*, London, 1881; J. F. Bethune-Baker, *Influence of Christianity on War*, Cambridge, 1888; M. Jaehns, *Ueber Krieg, Frieden und Kultur*, Berlin, 1893; A. F. Hamon, *Psychologie du militaire professionnel*, Brussels, 1894; Y. A. Novikov, *La Guerre et ses prétendus bienfaits*, Paris, 1894; M. Anitchkow, *Krieg und Arbeit*, Berlin, 1900, Eng. transl., *War and Labour*, Westminster and New York, 1900; J. J. Green, *War. Is it Consistent with Christianity?* London, 1901; W. Walsh, *The Moral Damage of War*, London, 1902, new ed., Boston, 1909; J. Barr, *Christianity and War*, Glasgow, 1903; K. Blutharsch, *Die Ursache der Völkerkriege und die Grundlage für die Weltfrieden*, Stuttgart, 1905; T. Kattenbusch, *Das sittliche Recht des Krieges*, Giessen, 1906; D. L. Dodge, *War Inconsistent with the Religion of Jesus Christ*, new ed., Boston, 1910.

WAR, HEBREW.

I. The Army.
  Primitive Conditions (§ 1).
  The Standing Army (§ 2).
  The Personnel and Pay (§ 3).

II. Arms and Weapons.
  Offensive and Defensive Armor (§ 1).

  Branches of Service (§ 2).
III. Fortresses.
IV. The Conduct of War.
V. Religious Significance of War.

I. The Army: Not till the royal period did the Hebrews possess a standing army, but from a much earlier time every male adult able to fight was liable to call for field service. Bedouins either on a raid or when attacked expect the help of every member of the tribe. The statement in P (Num. i. 1–2, xxvi. 2) of twenty years as the age when war service may be required may express ancient custom and possibly tells the age at which men became members of the tribe with full rights. The Book of Judges describes conditions from this point of view. In case of an expedition for booty or conquest or of necessity for repelling attack the men capable of bearing arms assembled under a recognized head—the boldest of their number (Judges xi. 1 sqq.); in case the danger was great, messengers were sent to friendly tribes for help. An example of this last was Jabesh-gilead, the elders of which sent for help throughout Israel, when Saul made his stirring appeal and called for the people to come to the war (I Sam. xi. 3 sqq.). In case of victory, each man returned home with his booty. This method did not permit great wars and slaughter or great armies, but resembled the conditions under which at the present Bedouin raids occur. The numbers of men engaged were relatively small; Gideon had 300 men (Judges vii. 16), the Danites numbered 600 (Judges xviii. 11). Larger numbers are mentioned in the Song of Deborah (Judges v. 8, cf. iv. 14). But the methods which had sufficed against the Midianites were not adequate when the enemy was a warlike and relatively great and well-armed people like the Philistines. So Saul recognized the need of a standing army, and after the victory over the Ammonites in view of conflicts with the Philistines he retained 3,000 men under arms (I Sam. xiii. 1 sqq.), though it is not said that this was a permanent force. Yet he had a force as a body-guard, of which David was the leader (I Sam. xxii. 14), the

1. Primitive Conditions.

members of which were noted warriors, selected by Saul from all Israel (I Sam. xiv. 52).

A step momentous in its consequences was the king's assumption of appointment of the leaders, the people's voice being no longer heard in the matter. While at first naturally the heads of the tribes and such men were first chosen by Saul, his own interest led to the placing in responsible positions of those known to be true to him, eventually to members of the royal household, as Jonathan (I Sam. xiii. 1 sqq.), and under David near relations like Joab, Abner, and Amasa. Saul sought to bind David to himself by giving him his daughter Michal. The body-guard had a place in history which was noteworthy. Under David it was 400 strong at Adullam (I Sam. xxii. 2), and a little later numbered 600 (I Sam. xxiii. 13); at the time of the Philistine fight (I Sam. xxviii. 1 sqq.) it must have been a formidable force, as the times then went. This force became David's guard, known as "heroes" and "Cherethites and Pelethites" (I Kings i. 8, 38). The last designation has been taken to show that Philistines were in it; this is not certain, but David had a company of 600 under Ittai of Gath who were trustworthy in critical times (II Sam. xv. 19), and Benaiah was their general (II Sam. xxiii. 23). This body-guard was the kernel of David's army; whether the standing army included more is not known. The Chronicler (I., xxvii. 1 sqq.) divides the whole army into twelve corps of 24,000 each, which served each one month; but the report is untrustworthy. Still, regular organization of the army under David is clear, since Joab's office as general-in-chief was permanent. Considering the number and length of David's wars, it is improbable that the entire force available was always under arms—such a condition was often unnecessary, and economic conditions would not permit it. The numbering of the people by David probably had mili-

2. The Standing Army.

tary purposes behind it. The organization was by thousands, hundreds, and fifties (I Sam. viii. 12, xvii. 18, xviii. 13; II Sam. xviii. 1; II Kings i. 9, xi. 4, 19); such an organization is attributed to Saul's times, but it is doubtful whether this breaking up of the old tribal organization occurred so soon. Regal interests furthered the dissolution of tribal ties, and tribal organization was disregarded in Solomon's divisions (I Kings iv. 7 sqq.), which may have had a military basis. Obligation to bear arms and to pay taxes rested on possession of the soil, so that when Nebuchadrezzar took away " the mighty men of valor " (II Kings xxiv. 14), naturally only " the poorest . . . of the land " remained. In later times among the officers of the army was the " scribe of the host " (Jer. lii. 25).

Limitations to a call to war are placed by Deut. xxiv. 5, xx. 5–8, and certain prescriptions were observed by Judas the Maccabee (I Macc. iii. 55). Which of these prescriptions is the older is difficult to define, and the practicality is both questioned (Wellhausen, *Composition des Hexa-*

3. The *teuch*, p. 182, but cf. p. 359 of the 3d
Personnel ed., 1899) and defended (Schwally,
and Pay. *Semitische Kriegsaltertümer*, i. 74 sqq.).

Since the wars of Israel were wars of Yahweh, ceremonial impurity excluded from service. At the time when these prescriptions were written, customs were still in memory which made them explicable, and some of them can be explained from present knowledge. In Maccabean times there were changes in the military establishment. Judas had, in addition to the groupings already mentioned, one of ten men (I Macc. iii. 55); Simon raised a force paid from his own resources (ib. xiv. 32); Hyrcanus enlisted foreigners (Josephus, *Ant.*, XIII., viii. 4), while Jews increasingly entered the service of foreign kings (both Ptolemies and Seleucidæ; I Macc. x. 36; Josephus, *Ant.*, XII., ii. 5). Under Alexander Jannæus and Alexandra foreign mercenaries held the Jews in check (Josephus, *Ant.*, XIII., xiii. 5); Hyrcanus furnished troops to the Romans (ib. XIV., x. 2); under the Herods, the army was trained in Roman fashion, and Germans were among the forces. In case the need was urgent, the forces were summoned by the trumpet or by the display of signal. Whether the forces carried standards in early times is unknown, but passages in P (Num. i. 52, ii. 2–34) speak of such both for tribes and families, though their character is not determined. Naturally in ancient times the commissariat was not specially governed; each man took what he could, even in his own country (II Sam. xvii. 27)—Jesse sent provisions to his sons through David (I Sam. xvii. 17). Yet Judges xx. 10 (the age of which is not determined) speaks of regular provision for supply of food. Only the standing army and mercenaries received pay, and the warriors' reward consisted in part in their share in the booty (Gen. xiv. 24; Num. xxi. 25 sqq.; Deut. xxi. 11), in which those who remained behind for cause shared (Num. xxxi. 27; Josh. xxii. 8; I Sam. xxx. 24; II Macc. viii. 28, 30).

II. Arms and Weapons: From their nomadic life the Hebrews brought into Canaan the chief weapon of the Bedouins, the lance with wooden

shaft and bronze head. The sling was an early weapon, but the sword became common only after they reached Palestine. There they first met foes whose method of warfare was of a high
1. Offensive standard. Canaanitic weapons were
and Defen- derived from the Hittites on the north,
sive Armor. and the part of their equipment which most terrified the Hebrews was the chariots of iron, to the possession of which is attributed the ability of Canaanites to retain mastery of the plains (Josh. xi. 4; Judges i. 19; I Sam. xiii. 5). The chariots carried three men—driver, warrior, and shield-bearer who protected the others. The Philistines had cavalry also (I Sam. xiii. 5). Infantry were of two kinds, light and heavy armed. The latter had a round helm of bronze, coat of mail, bronze greaves, sword, throwing spear, and lance; the former were bowmen and slingers. This armament the Hebrews adopted from their foes. The Chronicler mentions light-armed Benjaminites, and says that they were ambidextrous with bow and sling (I Chron. viii. 40, xii. 2; II Chron. xiv. 8, xvii. 17; cf. Judges xx. 16). Judahites were heavy armed, carrying spear and shield, as were Gadites and Naphtalites (II Chron. xiv. 8; I Chron. xii. 8, 24, 34). The light-armed had bow or sling and a small shield. The bow was usually of a hard springy wood, though later it was of bronze (Ps. xviii. 34; Job xx. 24); as it was strung by placing one end on the ground and bending the other with the hand, it must have been large; yet another kind was strung by the hands alone. The string was of ox or camel gut. The arrow was of light wood with point of metal, and was carried in a quiver; sometimes the point was poisoned (Jer. li. 11; Isa. xlix. 2; Job vi. 4). Fire arrows were used against city and camp (Isa. l. 11). The sling was also the weapon of the shepherds, and was a strap of leather or such material, broader in the center where the missile, usually a smooth stone, was placed, this being discharged by loosing one end of the sling. The light-armed, at least the bowmen, carried a small shield only half as large as that of the heavy-armed, but the shape of neither is known. From Ezek. xxxix. 9; II Sam. i. 21; and Isa. xxi. 5 it seems clear that the shield was of wood covered with leather or of several layers of leather. Solomon's golden shields were merely for display; Rehoboam furnished instead those covered with bronze (I Kings xiv. 26). Apparently on the march the shields were carried by wagon. The heavy-armed had as weapon of attack the spear (*ḥanith*) used for thrusting, not throwing (I Sam. xvii. 7, xix. 9–10). How this weapon differed from that called *romaḥ* is unknown (II Chron. xi. 12), but the *romaḥ* later became the usual weapon. I Chron. xii. 8, 24, 34 distinguishes the *ḥanith* as the weapon of the Naphtalites, the *romaḥ* as that of Judah and Gad. The weapon called *kidhon* probably differed from both as being a casting spear; Goliath had one besides his *ḥanith* (I Sam. xvii. 6, 45). The sword was of iron, its blade straight and often double-edged, and it was used both to cut and to thrust (I Sam. xiii. 19; Judges iii. 16, 21, xxi. 10). It was carried at the left by a girdle worn over the soldier's coat. The helmet (*ḳobha'* or *ḳobha'*) in early times was worn not

by the man in the ranks but by the king or leader of the host (I Sam. xvii. 5, 38); the Chronicler (II., xxvi. 14) reports first of Uzziah that he equipped the army with helmets, and later it was a common article of defense. Saul and Goliath are reported to have had bronze helmets and coats of mail. Probably these were not wholly of bronze, but of leather covered with the alloy. The form is not known, but the monuments show that of Egyptians and Assyrians. Goliath's coat was of scales of bronze, while Saul's was probably of bronze also, since it was too heavy for David (I Sam. xvii. 38–39). From Assyrian sources it appears that the coat of the common soldier was a thick jacket of felt or leather somewhat strengthened with sheet iron; the charioteers wore the long coat reaching to the knees. In Græco-Roman times the metal coat was more common, in the Syrian armies the common soldiers wore interwoven coats of mail (I Macc. vi. 35). Other weapons of an uncommon sort are mentioned, but do not characterize the armament of the Hebrews (Job xli. 26; Jer. l. 23, li. 20; Prov. xxv. 18; Gen. xlix. 5; Ps. xxxv. 3).

Up till the time of Solomon the Hebrews had only infantry; David's course in the Syrian war when he captured chariots and horses was to disable the

2. Branches of Service. horses (II Sam. viii. 4). But Solomon introduced cavalry and chariots, and is said to have had 12,000 cavalry, 1,400 chariots, and 40,000 chariot horses (I Kings x. 26), which were kept partly in Jerusalem and partly elsewhere (I Kings ix. 19). This marks the beginning of a great standing army over and above the body-guard of the king. Cavalry and chariotry thenceforth were a part of the Hebrew army, although a large part of the land was not suited to their evolutions. For this element of the army the prophets had no liking and frequently denounced reliance upon it (Hos. i. 7, xiv. 3). The chariots were doubtless like those of Philistines and Canaanites, two-wheeled, open behind, and probably carried three persons.

III. Fortresses: When the Hebrews crossed the Jordan, they found the land defended by numerous strong places and fortified cities which, with their high walls, made great impression upon the sons of the desert (Num. xiii. 28; Deut. i. 28), who were not able at once to reduce them. For a time they dwelt in the open, and in time of war fled to woods and caves for refuge (I Sam. xiii. 6). This condition changed in the kingly period, when Canaanitic fortresses fell into their hands, especially Jebus (II Sam. v. 9); they learned also to build their own fortifications, as when David refortified Jebus-Jerusalem, and when Solomon built Hazor and Megiddo on the roads to the north, Gezer, lower Beth-horon, and Balaath toward the west, and Tamar toward the south. Rehoboam erected no less than fifteen border fortresses on the west and south (II Chron. xi. 5 sqq.); Jeroboam fortified Shechem and Penuel in the north (I Kings xii. 25); Baasha attempted to fortify Ramah as an outpost against Judah, but Asa destroyed it and used the material to build Geba and Mizpah (I Kings xv. 16–22). Omri built Samaria on an isolated hill and made it so strong that it was able to hold out for

three years against the Assyrians (II Kings xvii. 5). The Maccabeans and Herods built many fortresses, among which especially worthy of mention are Beth-zur, Jotopata, Herodium (southwest of Bethlehem), Masada, and Machærus. Naturally, these fortresses stood on hills; and it was the custom for each great fortified city to have in or near it also a citadel (so Jerusalem, q.v.; Shechem, Penuel, and Thebez; Judges ix. 46, 51, viii. 9, 17). The primary fortification was an encircling wall, usually of the largest stones obtainable or workable, often not squared, and in ancient times set without mortar; it was so thick that not only the watch but considerable forces could occupy its crown (Neh. xii. 31 sqq.; I Macc. xiii. 45). There were also placed there catapults and other engines of war, beginning from the time of Uzziah (II Chron. xxvi. 15). Massive towers of great stones protected the corners, gate, and other portions of the walls. Battlements protected the defenders. The entrances were not simple openings in the walls, but quite roomy structures with towers and an upper story (II Sam. xviii. 33); the gates were usually double doors of strong wood, probably covered with plates of bronze or iron and fastened with bars of the same metal (Deut. iii. 5; I Kings iv. 13). Commonly a city had but one gate, which was closed at evening (Gen. xxxiv. 20; Josh. ii. 5). Frequently there was a smaller outside wall.

IV. The Conduct of War: A preliminary to war was the consulting of the oracle (Judges i. 1, xx. 27–28; I Sam. xiv. 37) or of the prophet (I Kings xxii. 5 sqq.); there were sacrifices (I Sam. vii. 8 sqq., xiii. 9 sqq.) and consecration, since war was holy (see below). In great conflicts the war palladium, the ark, was present as a matter of course (I Sam. iv. 4 sqq.; II Sam. xi. 11); Deut. xx. 2 prescribes that before the fight the priest address the soldiery and inspire them with courage, and the priestly law requires the presence of the priest with his silver trumpet (Num. x. 9, xxxi. 6). This ordinance was observed by the Maccabees (I Macc. xvi. 8). If possible, the war began in the spring, that return might be had before the winter, when men stayed at home. Of the arrangement of the camp nothing is known; Num. ii. seems to indicate a triangular form, but how nearly this corresponded to actual custom is not clear. Tents are mentioned as being in the camps of Hebrews and Syrians (II Sam. xi. 11; II Kings vii. 7) in connection with protracted sieges of fortresses. The night was divided into three watches (Judges vii. 19); while the main force was away, a camp guard protected the camp. The maintenance of the purity of the camp was strictly enjoined (Deut. xxiii. 10 sqq.). The battle array was either in line or in three parts of center and two wings (I Sam. iv. 2, xvii. 8, 20–21; Judges vii. 16, 20, xx. 20, 30; Isa. viii. 8), with sometimes an ambush at the rear of the enemy (Josh. viii. 13–14). The attack was accompanied by a loud outcry (Josh. vi. 20; I Sam. xvii. 52). The art of war was not highly developed, though stratagem, in the way of surprise or rear attack, was employed, also the turning of the flanks (Josh. ii., vi. 22, viii. 2, 12; Judges vii. 10 sqq., 16 sqq., xx. 36 sqq.; II Sam. v. 23). The fight depended often upon individual bravery, strength, dexterity, and quickness. Occasionally a duel between chosen champions decided the battle (I Sam. xvii.; II Sam. ii. 14 sqq.). Though the Hebrews were behind the Assyrians in cruelty, their treatment of the conquered was harsh. While the latter cut off the heads and hands of the fallen as trophies, the former seem to have done this only in exceptional cases (I Sam. xvii. 5 sqq., xxxi. 9; II Sam. xx. 22); possibly it was an old custom to cut off the foreskins of the fallen foe (I Sam. xviii. 25, 27); not seldom the captive kings or generals were killed (Josh. x. 24 sqq.; Judges vii. 25), though the Hebrew kings bore a reputation for mildness (I Kings xx. 31). Sometimes the entire captive host was slain (Judges vii. 25; Josh. x. 24 sqq.), and severe practises of other kinds are known (Judges i. 6–7; I Sam. xi. 2). As a rule the captives became slaves, yet the usually mild Deuteronomy (xx. 13–14) enjoins the enslaving of women and children only. For examples of other horrors of war cf. II Kings viii. 12, xv. 16; Isa. xiii. 16; Hos. x. 14; Amos i. 13. The land of the enemy was ravaged, the trees cut down, the wells stopped up (Deut. xx. 19; Judges vi. 4; II Kings iii. 19, 25), while cities and villages were burned (Judges ix. 45; I Macc. v. 28). The subjected people were put under ransom of a large sum or under tribute (II Kings xviii. 14; Isa. xxxii. 18), for the payment of which hostages were taken (II Kings xiv. 14). Victory was celebrated with song and dance (Ex. xv.; Judges v.; I Sam. xviii. 6 sqq.). The burial of the fallen was a sacred duty (I Kings xv.); the host mourned fallen leaders (II Sam. iii. 31), whose weapons were buried with them.

V. Religious Significance of War: In common with other Semites, Hebrews regarded war as a sacred thing, a concern of Yahweh (Ex. xvii. 16; Num. xxi. 14; I Sam. xxv. 28); hence in Deborah's song those are cursed who remained away from the battle (Judges v. 23). Israel's foes are also Yahweh's (Judges v. 31; I Sam. xxx. 26). As "Lord of hosts" and "God of the armies of Israel" (I Sam. xvii. 45) Yahweh participated in the battle; and cast stones upon the enemy to assist his people (Josh. x. 11). His presence with the army was believed to be a literal fact, in common with the ordinary belief of the times, and he was represented by the ark, which by the enemy was taken as the presence of God himself (I Sam. iv. 6–7). War was therefore one of the religious institutions of Israel; the warrior was obligated to perform certain cultic duties before battle, being consecrated to God (Josh. iii. 5; Isa. xiii. 3), men spoke of "sanctifying war" (Joel iii. 9, A. V. margin; Jer. vi. 4); and the warrior was to remain ceremonially pure during the war (Smith, *Rel. of Sem.*, p. 455; cf. II Sam. xi. 6 sqq.). From this standpoint has been explained the exemption from warlike duties of those newly married, or who had just built a house; and this, too, explains the fact that the camp is sacred (Deut. xxiii. 10 sqq.). Thus is explained also the custom of the ban; all booty belongs to Yahweh, hence the extreme form of the ban was the killing of all which had life and burning of everything else (Josh. vi. 17; I Sam. vi. 3; cf. Deut. xiii. 16–17). Limitations of the ban are found in Deut. vii. 27 sqq.; while historical

practise or prescription is found in Num. xxxi. 7 sqq., 17–18; Josh. viii. 2, 27–28, xi. 10 sqq.; Judges xxi. 11 sqq. In all probability practise was milder than theory, the desire for booty having its influence. The destruction of a part of the booty signifies consecration of that part to Yahweh, and parallel for the Hebrew custom is found in the Moabite Stone (q.v.), which declares that Mesha devoted 7,000 men to his god Chemosh (lines 3, 11, 12, 16–17).

(I. Benzinger.)

Bibliography: F. Schwally, *Semitische Kriegsaltertümer*, part i., *Der heilige Krieg in Israel*, Leipsic, 1901; J. L. Saalschütz, *Mosaisches Recht*, pp. 258–286, 641 sqq., Berlin, 1846–48; S. Spitzer, *Das Heer- und Wehr-Gesetz der alten Israeliten*, 2d ed., Pressburg, 1879; Benzinger, *Archäologie*, pp. 279–308; Nowack, *Archäologie*, i. 357–375; *DB*, i. 154–156, 346, 703, iv. 892–897; *EB*, i. 312–316, 605–607, ii. 1918, 2013, iii. 4463–65, iv. 5261–70, 5275; *JE*, ii. 120–122, xii. 463–466; and, for comparative purposes, A. Erman, *Life in Ancient Egypt*, pp. 520 sqq., New York, 1894.

WARBURTON, WILLIAM: Church of England bishop of Gloucester; b. at Newark-upon-Trent (17 m. n.e. of Nottingham) Dec. 24, 1698; d. at Gloucester June 7, 1779. His father, an attorney, had him educated for the law, which he probably practised 1719–23; but he had always a passionate liking for theology, and was ordained deacon, 1723, and priest, 1727; he became rector at Greaseley, Nottingham, 1726; was rector at Brant-Broughton, 1728–30; and at Frisby, 1730–56; became chaplain to the Prince of Wales, 1738; preacher to Lincoln's Inn, 1746; chaplain to the king, 1754; prebendary of Durham, 1755; dean of Bristol, 1757; and bishop of Gloucester, 1760. In the retirement of country life during the earlier years of his activity he prosecuted his studies with great diligence, and wrote those works which have perpetuated his memory. The first of these was *The Alliance between Church and State; or the Necessity and Equity of an established Religion, and a Test Law demonstrated, from the Essence and End of civil Society upon the fundamental Principles of the Laws of Nature and Nations* (1736), in which, while taking high ground, as the title indicates, he yet maintains that the State Church should tolerate those who differed from it in doctrine and worship. Soon thereafter came his great work, *The Divine Legation of Moses, Demonstrated on the Principles of a Religious Deist, from the Omission of the Doctrine of a Future State of Rewards and Punishments in the Jewish Dispensation*. Books i.–iii. appeared in vol. i. (1737–38); books iv., v., vi., in vol. ii. (1741); books vii. and viii. never appeared; book ix. was first published in his *Works* (1788; 10th ed. of the entire work, ed. James Nichols, 3 vols., 1846). The treatise was directed against the Deists (see Deism), especially their doctrine of the Old Testament and their stress upon the omission of mention of immortality in the Old Testament. Warburton turns the tables upon them by constructing, out of the very absence of such statements, a proof of the divinity of the Mosaic legislation. The first three books deal with the necessity of the doctrine of a future state of rewards and punishments to civil society from (1) the nature of the thing, (2) the conduct of the ancient lawgivers and founders of civil policy, and (3) the opinions and conduct of the ancient sages and philosophers. The fourth book proves the high antiquity of the arts and empire of Egypt, and that such high antiquity illustrates and confirms the truth of the Mosaic history. The fifth book explains the nature of the Jewish theocracy. In the sixth book Warburton shows from the Old and New Testaments that a future state of rewards and punishments did make part of the Mosaic dispensation. The ninth book treats of the true nature and genius of the Christian religion. The general argument is that because the sacred books of Judaism said nothing respecting a future state of rewards and punishments, it must be divine, since it did really accomplish the punishment of wrong-doers without such a doctrine, and no other legislation has been able to do so without it. This it could do because the foundation and support of the Mosaic legislation was the theocracy which was peculiar to the Jews, and dealt out in this life righteous rewards and punishments upon individual and nation. An extraordinary providence conducted the affairs of this people, and consequently the sending of Moses was divinely ordered. The work is confessedly limited to one line of argument, is defective in exegesis, and does not do justice to the intimations of immortality among the later Jews; yet it is distinguished by freshness and vigor, masterly argumentation, and bold imagination. The excursuses are particularly admirable.

Warburton was a man of untiring energy, wide information, clear insight, and lively imagination. He had a noble, open, guileless heart; yet as a critic he was sharp, and often satirical. His writings, besides those already noted, embrace a commentary upon Pope's *Essay on Man* (1742; by this he won Pope's firm friendship); *Julian* (1750; on the numerous alleged providential interferences which defeated Julian's attempt to rebuild the temple); *The Doctrine of Grace; or the Office and Operations of the Holy Spirit vindicated from the Insults of Infidelity and the Abuses of Fanaticism* (2 vols., 1762; a work directed against the Methodists, which did not advance his reputation). His *Works* were edited with a biographical preface by Bishop Hurd (7 vols., 1788; new ed., 12 vols., 1811; the expense was borne by Warburton's widow). Supplementary to this edition are the *Tracts by Warburton and a Warburtonian* (1789); *Letters* (Kidderminster, 1808; 2d ed., London, 1809); *Selections from the Unpublished Papers of Warburton* (1841).

BIBLIOGRAPHY: The *Life* by Hurd was issued separately, ed. F. Kilvert, London, 1860. There is a life by J. S. Watson, ib. 1863. Consult further: J. Nichols, *Literary Anecdotes of the 18th Century*, v. 529–658, 9 vols., London, 1812–15; idem, *Illustrations of the Literary Hist. of the 18th Century*, ii. 1–654, 8 vols., ib. 1817–58; John Hunt, *Hist. of Religious Thought in England*, iii. 146–151, et passim, ib. 1873; L. Stephen, *Hist. of English Thought in the 18th Century*, passim, New York, 1881; M. Pattison, *Essays and Papers*, ii. 119–176, London, 1889; *DNB*, lix. 301–311.

WARBURTONIAN LECTURE: A lecture course founded by a testamentary bequest of £500 by Bishop William Warburton (q.v.) to prove "the truth of revealed religion in general, and of the Christian in particular, from the completion of the prophecies in the Old and New Testaments, which relate to the Christian Church, and especially to the apostasy of papal Rome." The lecture is to be preached an-

nually, in the chapel of Lincoln's Inn, London, on the first Sunday after Michaelmas Term and the Sunday before and the Sunday after Hilary Term, and no lecturer may continue more than four years. A list of the lectures, so far as they have been published, is as follows:

A number of Warburtonian lecturers have never published the lectures which they delivered. Though not formally issued as a Warburtonian Lecture, the *Propœdia prophetica, a View of the Use and Design of the Old Testament*, by William Rowe Lyall, London, 1840, formed, in its general argument, the substance of the course delivered by him.

BIBLIOGRAPHY: J. Darling, *Cyclopœdia Bibliographica*, cols. 3102–3103, London, 1854; W. T. Lowndes, *Bibliographer's Manual of English Literature*, ed. H. G. Bohn, p. 2834, London, n. d.; private information from Mr. Ernest C. Brown, of the British Museum, and Rev. John Harrington, Chaplain of Lincoln's Inn.

WARD, MARY. See ENGLISH LADIES.

WARD, SETH: Church of England bishop of Salisbury; b. at Aspenden (18 m. n.e. of St. Albans), Hertfordshire, Apr. 5, 1617; d. at Knightsbridge, Salisbury, Jan. 6, 1688–89. He was educated at Sidney-Sussex College, Cambridge (B.A. 1636–37), where he became fellow in 1640 and mathematical lecturer in 1643, but in the following year he was deprived of his fellowship by the Puritans for refusing to subscribe the Solemn League and Covenant. He then resided in London, and at Aspenden, pursuing his mathematical studies and acting as a private tutor, until 1649, when, being willing to take the oath of allegiance to the Commonwealth, he was appointed Savilian professor of astronomy at Oxford, where he enunciated a clever, though unsuccessful, theory of planetary motion, and where he also became involved in a controversy with Thomas Hobbes (q.v.), the results of his astronomical studies being embodied in his *In Ismaelis Bullialdi astronomiæ philolaicæ fundamenta inquisitio brevis* (Oxford, 1653) and *Astronomia geometrica; ubi methodus proponitur qua primariorum planetarum astronomia sive elliptica sive circularis possit geometrice absolvi* (1656), and his points of disagreement with Hobbes being contained in his *Vindiciæ academiarum* (1654) and *In Thomæ Hobbii philosophiam exercitatio epistolica* (1656).

At Oxford Ward resided at Wadham College, and about 1649, on the formation of the Philosophical Society of Oxford, he became a member of that body, while he was later one of the original members of the Royal Society. In 1657 Ward was elected principal of Jesus College, Oxford, but was obliged to give place to an appointee of Cromwell; and two years later he was chosen president of Trinity, but was compelled within a year to resign since he did not possess the statutory qualifications. He now retired to London, where Charles II. appointed him vicar of St. Lawrence Jewry and rector of Uplowman, Devonshire, while in 1662 he was rector of St. Breock, Cornwall. He had been precentor of Exeter since 1656, and in 1660 he was made a prebendary, and dean in the year following. In 1662 he was consecrated bishop of Exeter, and five years later was translated to Salisbury, while in 1671 he was appointed chancellor of the Order of the Garter. In 1672 he declined to become the successor of John Cosin (q.v.) in the see of Durham. Both as dean and as bishop Ward strongly opposed dissenters, suppressing their conventicles and ejecting them and their stalls from his cathedral, although, on the other hand, he was very willing to make certain concessions to win them back to the Church. He restored and beautified the cathedrals and palaces of both his sees, and founded several beneficent institutions, such as a college of matrons at Salisbury (1682) for widows of the Exeter and Salisbury clergy.

The chief theological works of Ward, besides many sermons, were *Certain Disquisitions and Considerations representing to the Conscience the Unlawfullness of the . . . Solemn League and Covenant* (Oxford, 1643; the first edition destroyed by the Puritans, the earliest edition extant being that of 1644), and *Philosophical Essay towards an Eviction of the Being and Attributes of God, the Immortality of the Souls of Men, and the Truth and Authority of Scripture* (1652); and he also edited Samuel Ward's *Dissertatio de baptismatis infantilis vi et efficacia* (London, 1653) and *Opera nonnulla* (1658).

BIBLIOGRAPHY: The primary life is by Walter Pope, London, 1698, on which cf. A. à Wood, *Athenæ Oxoniensis*, ed P. Bliss, i. p. clxx., and iii. 588, 1209, iv. 246, 305, 512, and Fasti, ii. 184, 4 vols., 1813–20, and the same writer's *An Appendix to Pope's Life of Ward*, ib., 1697. On the materials for a life of Ward cf. J. E. B. Mayor, in *Notes and queries*, 2 ser., vii. 269, and for a list of references *DNB*, lix. 336–340.

WARD, WILLIAM GEORGE: English Roman Catholic; b. in London Mar. 21, 1812; d. at Hampstead, London, July 6, 1882. He was educated at Christ Church and Lincoln College, Oxford (B.A., 1834), and was elected fellow of Balliol, where he also acted as lecturer in mathematics and logic. He took orders in the Church of England, and though he was at this time a pronounced latitudinarian, his combination of a severely logical mind with deep personal piety convinced him that there was no middle way between submission to ecclesiastical authority and absolute rationalism. It was at this period that he came under the sway of Tractarianism (q.v.), and he went far beyond the attack of J. H. Newman (q.v.) on the natural meaning of the Thirty-Nine Articles in *Tract Ninety*, Ward's own position being set forth in *A Few Words in Support of No. xc.* and *A Few More Words in Support of No. xc.* (both Oxford, 1841). The result was loss of his lectureships and tutorial position at Balliol, though he was appointed junior bursar in 1841 and senior bursar in the following year. Meanwhile his trend was more and more toward the Roman church, and in 1844 he published at Oxford, in reply to William Palmer, his *Ideal of a Christian Church considered in Comparison with existing Practice*, lauding the Roman communion as an almost perfect embodiment of Christianity, and by his comparisons with non-Roman communions incurring the extreme displeasure of English churchmen of all types. Declining to disavow the book either in whole or in parts specified as contrary to the Thirty-Nine Articles, Ward was formally censured by the vice-chancellor and by the convocation of the University of Oxford and on Feb. 13, 1845, was degraded, a proceeding regarding the legality of which there was much room for doubt. Notwithstanding this doubt, Ward resigned his fellowship and on Sept. 5 of the same year was received into the Roman Catholic Church. In 1846 he removed to Ware, and from 1851 to 1858 was lecturer in moral philosophy in St. Edmund's College, his lectures being designed not only to meet the needs of his students, but also to prepare the way for a systematic monograph *On Nature and Grace*, although only the philosophical introduction was ever published (London, 1860). After residing for three years on one of his estates in the Isle of Wight, he returned to Ware in 1861, and from 1863 to 1878 was editor of *The Dublin Review*, which he transformed from a moribund condition to a powerful organ against all that savored of religious latitudinarianism, lending all his strength to the defense of Ultramontanism (q.v.). In its columns he supported the encyclical *Quanta cura* and the *Syllabus errorum*, and in his abhorrence of all that was not connected with the Roman church, he opposed the scheme of Cardinal Newman for the erection of a Roman Catholic hall at Oxford, while with equal energy he used his influence in behalf of the choice of H. E. Manning (q.v.) as archbishop of Westminster to succeed N. P. S. Wiseman (q.v.). His latter years were passed chiefly on his estate Weston Manor, Freshwater, Isle of Wight.

The chief works of Ward, besides those already noted, were *The Relation of Intellectual Power to Man's True Perfection* (London, 1862), *The Authority of Doctrinal Decisions which are not Definitions of Faith* (1866; essays reprinted from *The Dublin Review*), *De infallibilitatis extensione theses quædam quæstiones* (1869), *Essays on Devotional and Scriptural Subjects* (1879), *Essays on the Church's Doctrinal Authority* (1880; both volumes almost entirely consisting of reprints from *The Dublin Review*), and *Essays on the Philosophy of Theism* (ed. W. Ward, 2 vols., 1884; also reprinted from the same periodical).

BIBLIOGRAPHY: The two books of highest importance are Wilfrid Ward's *William George Ward and the Oxford Movement*, London, 1889, and *William George Ward and the Catholic Revival*, ib., 1893. The literature under TRACTARIANISM should be consulted, especially the works of Browne and Mozley; also that under JOWETT, BENJAMIN; PUSEY, EDWARD BOUVERIE; and STANLEY, ARTHUR PENRHYN.

WARD, WILLIAM HAYES: Congregationalist, orientalist; b. at Abington, Mass., June 25, 1835. He was educated at Phillips Academy, Andover, Mass., and at Amherst College, Mass. (B.A., 1856); studied in Union Theological Seminary, New York City, 1856–57; in the Sheffield Scientific School, New Haven, Conn., 1857; was tutor in Beloit College, Wis., 1857–58; studied at Andover Theological Seminary, Mass., 1858–59 (graduated); was pastor at Oskaloosa and Grasshopper Falls, Kan., 1859–61; teacher in Williston Seminary, Easthampton, Mass., 1861; at Utica, N. Y., 1862–65; professor of Latin, Ripon College, Wis., 1865–67; associate editor New York *Independent*, 1868–70; has been superintending editor since 1870. He was director of the Wolfe expedition to Babylonia, 1884–85. He is the one authority on Assyrian, Babylonian, and Hittite seals. He edited (with Mrs. Lanier) Sidney Lanier's *Poems* (New York, 1884); has written a description of the seals in the J. P. Morgan collection (privately printed, New York, 1909); and *The Seal Cylinders of Western Asia*, published by the Carnegie Institution, Washington, D. C., 1910.

WARDLAW, RALPH: Scotch Congregationalist; b. at Dalkeith (6 m. s.e. of Edinburgh), Scotland, Dec. 22, 1779; d. at Easter-house, near Glasgow, Dec. 17, 1853. He was educated at the grammar-school at Glasgow, and matriculated at the university, 1791; entered the theological school in connection with the Associate Secession Church, beginning his studies at Selkirk in 1795; became a Congregationalist in 1800, joining the independent church in Glasgow; became pastor of the North Albian Street chapel of Glasgow, 1803; a larger chapel on West George Street was built in 1819, and Wardlaw continued to preach there till his death. From 1811 he was professor for many years

of systematic theology in the Glasgow Theological Academy. He was prominent in Scotland as a preacher, but his theological writings made him even more widely known; they embrace, besides his sermons and lectures on the Bible, *Discourses on the Nature and the Extent of the Atonement of Christ* (Glasgow, 1830); *Christian Ethics*, in the Congregational Lecture (London, 1834); *National Church Establishment Examined . . . Lectures . . . in London* (1839); *Memoir of the Rev. John Reid: comprising Incidents of the Bellary Mission from 1830 to 1840* (Glasgow, 1845); *The Headship of Christ, as Affected by National Church Establishments: a Lecture* (1847); *On Miracles* (Edinburgh, 1852); *Systematic Theology . . . ed. J. R. Campbell* (3 vols., 1856–57). J. S. Wardlaw edited his *Posthumous Works* (8 vols., 1861–62).

BIBLIOGRAPHY: W. L. Alexander, *Memoirs of the Life and Writings of R. Wardlaw*, Edinburgh, 1856; *DNB*, lix. 353–354.

WARE, HENRY: One of the founders of Unitarianism in America; b. at Sherburne, Mass., Apr. 1, 1764; d. at Cambridge July 12, 1845. He was graduated from Harvard College (1785); was pastor of the First Church, Hingham, Mass. (1787–1805); was Hollis professor of divinity in Harvard College, 1805–16, and then in the divinity school, which was that year organized, until, in 1840, loss of sight compelled his resignation, though he continued to give instruction in pulpit eloquence till 1842. His significance historically, altogether apart from his own pleasing personality and scholarly attainments, lies in the fact that his election to the chair of divinity evoked a controversy which led to the separation of Unitarians from Congregationalists. His election was opposed on the ground of his "liberal" leanings, but the opposition was unsuccessful. The Rev. Dr. Jedediah Morse then published his *True Reasons on which the Election of a Hollis Professor of Divinity was opposed at the Board of Overseers*, which may be regarded as the commencement of the Unitarian controversy. Ware took no part in this controversy until 1820, when he wrote *Letters to Trinitarians and Calvinists*, occasioned by the Rev. Dr. Leonard Woods's *Letters to Unitarians* (Andover, 1820). This involved him in a controversy with Dr. Woods. Dr. Ware also published *An Inquiry into the Foundation, Evidences, and Truths of Religion* (2 vols., Cambridge, 1842).

BIBLIOGRAPHY: W. B. Sprague, *Annals of the American Unitarian Pulpit*, pp. 199–205, New York, 1865; J. H. Allen, in *American Church History Series*, x. 187 sqq., ib. 1894.

WARE, HENRY, JUN.: Unitarian, son of the preceding; b. at Hingham, Mass., Apr. 21, 1794; d. at Framingham, Mass., Sept. 22, 1843. He was graduated from Harvard College (1812); taught at Phillips Academy, Exeter (1812–14); took postgraduate studies and acted as sublibrarian at Harvard (1814–16); was pastor of the Second Church in Boston (1817–30); and Parkman professor of pulpit eloquence in the divinity school at Cambridge, 1830–42. He edited *The Christian Disciple*, the first Unitarian organ (1819–22); and published *Hints on Extemporaneous Preaching* (1824), *On the Formation of the Christian Character* (1831), and a considerable number of poems and occasional sermons. Four volumes of selections from his writings were issued by C. Robbins (1846–47). He wrote a considerable number of hymns, of which perhaps the best known are, "All nature's works His praise declare," and " Lift your glad voices in triumph on high."

BIBLIOGRAPHY: J. Ware, *Memoirs of Henry Ware, Jun.*, 2 vols., Boston, 1845 (by his brother); W. B. Sprague, *Annals of the American Unitarian Pulpit*, pp. 472–484, New York, 1865; J. H. Allen, in *American Church History Series*, x. 199–207, ib. 1894; Julian, *Hymnology*, p. 1233.

WARFIELD, BENJAMIN BRECKINRIDGE: Presbyterian; b. at Lexington, Ky., Nov. 5, 1851. He was graduated from the College of New Jersey (A.B., 1871) and from Princeton Theological Seminary (1876); studied also at the University of Leipsic (1876–77); was supply at the First Presbyterian Church, Baltimore, Md. (1877–78); professor of New-Testament language and literature in Western Theological Seminary, Allegheny, Pa. (1878–87); and in 1887 was called to his present chair of didactic and polemic theology in Princeton Theological Seminary. In theology he belongs to the conservative school. Besides his work as editor of *The Presbyterian and Reformed Review* from 1890 to 1902, and of St. Augustine's *Anti-Pelagian Writings* (in *NPNF*, 1st series, New York, 1881), he has written *Introduction to the Textual Criticism of the New Testament* (1886); *On the Revision of the Confession of Faith* (1890); *The Gospel of the Incarnation* (1893); *Two Studies in the History of Doctrine* (1897); *The Right of Systematic Theology* (Edinburgh, 1897); *The Significance of the Westminster Standards as a Creed* (New York, 1898); *The Acts and Pastoral Epistles* (Philadelphia, 1902); *The Power of God unto Salvation* (sermons; 1903); and *The Lord of Glory; Study of the Designations of our Lord in the N. T., with especial Reference to his Deity* (New York, 1907).

WARHAM, WILLIAM: Archbishop of Canterbury; b. at Walshanger near Oakley (14 m. n.e. of Winchester) about 1450; d. at St. Stephens, near Canterbury, Aug. 23, 1532. He was educated at Winchester and at New College, Oxford (fellow, 1475; LL.D., 1488); studied particularly civil and canon law, became advocate in the court of arches, then principal of the civil law school at Oxford. He was employed in a series of important missions of state or commerce between 1490 and 1493, when he took orders and became precentor of Wells, then master of the rolls (1494); became rector of Barley, Hertfordshire, 1495, and of Cottenham, near Cambridge, 1500; meanwhile in 1497 he went to Scotland to demand of James IV. the surrender of Perkin Warbeck, and was sent also on several missions to the continent which lasted till 1502; he then became successively keeper of the great seal (1502), bishop of London (1502), lord chancellor and archbishop of Canterbury (1504), and chancellor of the University of Oxford (1506). With the accession of Henry VIII. (1509), at whose coronation he officiated, he suffered no loss of position; but the growth of Wolsey in royal favor was bitter to him, and he resigned the great seal and the chancellorship to Wolsey (1515). He again received the offer of the position after Wolsey's fall, but declined, pleading his age and other reasons.

Warham was possessed of great learning, skill in state-craft, dignity, and honesty. He was, for his age, singularly abstemious, and, although primate, lived in all simplicity. He was the friend of Erasmus and Colet. But he was deaf to the cries for reform, blind to the corruptions of the Church, was an opponent of the Reformation, and considered it an offense to introduce the writings of the Reformers and to translate the Bible into the vernacular. He was subservient to the king, and though appointed counsel to Catherine of Aragon, refused to act, being charged by her with giving as a reason for avoiding the task the Latin motto, *ira principis mors est*, " a prince's wrath brings death."

BIBLIOGRAPHY: Sources are: *Memorials of Henry VII.*, ed. J. Gairdner, London, 1858; *Letters and Papers . . . of . . . Richard III. and Henry VII.*, ed. J. Gairdner, 2 vols., ib. 1861 (nos. 10 and 24 in *Rolls Series*); *State Papers, . . . King Henry VIII.*, 11 vols., London, 1830–52; *Calendar of Letters, . . . State Papers, relating to . . . Spain*, vols. i.–iv., ib. 1862 sqq. Consult: A. à Wood, *Athenæ Oxonienses*, ed. P. Bliss, ii. 738–741, 4 vols., London, 1813–1820; W. F. Hook, *Lives of Archbishops of Canterbury*, new series, vol. i., 12 vols., London, 1860 sqq.; W. Clark, *The Anglican Reformation*, pp. 64–73, New York, 1897; J. H. Overton, *The Church in England*, i. 331–370, London, 1897; J. Gairdner, *English Church in the 16th Century*, passim, London, 1903; *Cambridge Modern History*, ii. 428, 436, 439, New York, 1904; *DNB*, lix. 378–383.

WARNE, FRANCIS WESLEY: Methodist Episcopalian; b. at Erin, Ont., Dec. 30, 1854. After graduation from Albert College, Belleville, Ont., he became, in 1874, a Methodist minister in Canada, where he also did missionary work in 1878–81. He then studied at Garrett Biblical Institute, Evanston, Ill., being graduated in 1887. In 1887 he went to Calcutta, India, as a missionary, and after having been pastor of Thoburn Church in that city, and presiding elder of the Calcutta district, was elected, in 1900, missionary bishop to India.

WARNECK, vär'nec, GUSTAV ADOLF: German Protestant; b. at Naumburg (24 m. s.w. of Halle) Mar. 6, 1834; d. at Halle Dec. 26, 1910. He studied at the University of Halle (1855–58); in 1862 became assistant pastor at Roitzsch; served as archdeacon in Dommitzsch (1863–70); became inspector of missions at Barmen (1870); was pastor of Rothenschirmbach (1875–96), retiring on a pension in 1896, when he became honorary professor of missions in the University of Halle. After 1879 he was president of the Saxon provincial missionary conference founded by him in that year, and from 1885 to 1901 was secretary of the committee of German missions. In theology he was a conservative. Besides editing the *Allgemeine Missionszeitschrift*, which he founded in 1874, he wrote: *Pontius Pilatus, der Richter Jesu Christi* (Gotha, 1867); *Briefe über innere Mission* (Halle, 1871); *Die apostolische und die moderne Mission* (Gütersloh, 1876); *Das Studium der Mission auf der Universität* (1877); *Missionsstunden* (2 parts, 1878–83); *Die gegenseitigen Beziehungen zwischen der modernen Mission und Kultur* (1879; Eng. transl. by T. Smith, *Modern Missions and Culture*, Edinburgh, 1882, new ed., 1888); *Die christliche Mission in der Gegenwart* (Halle, 1879); *Abriss einer Geschichte der protestantischen Missionen von der Reformation bis auf die Gegenwart* (Leipsic, 1882; Eng. transl., by T. Smith, *Outline*

XII.—18

of the History of Protestant Missions, Edinburgh, 1884, new ed., 1901); Protestantische Beleuchtung der römischen Angriffe auf die evangelische Heidenmission (Gütersloh, 1884); Die Mission in der Schule (1887); Der Romanismus im Lichte seiner Heidenmission (Leipsic, 1888); Die Aufgabe der Heidenmission und ihre Trübungen in der Gegenwart (Halle, 1891); Evangelische Missionslehre, ein missionstheoretischer Versuch (3 vols., Gotha, 1892–1903); Das Bürgerrecht der Mission im Organismus der theologischen Wissenschaft (Berlin, 1897); and Die gegenwärtige Lage der deutschen evangelischen Mission (1905).

WARNER, ZEBEDEE: United Brethren in Christ; b. in Pendleton Co., Va., Feb. 28, 1833; d. at Gibbon, Neb., Jan. 10, 1888. Educated at Clarksburg Academy, he entered the ministry of his denomination in 1854, and was presiding elder in 1862–69 and 1880–85, as well as pastor of a church at Parkersburg, W. Va., in 1869–80, and he also taught theology for eight years in the Parkersburg conference. He was a delegate to the general conference seven times, and for two years was president of the eastern Sunday-school assembly of his denomination. He wrote Christian Baptism (Parkersburg, 1864), Rise and Progress of the United Brethren Church (1865), Life and Times of Rev. Jacob Bachtel (Dayton, O., 1867), and The Roman Catholic not a True Christian Church (Parkersburg, 1868).

WARREN, HENRY WHITE: Methodist Episcopal bishop; b. at Williamsburg, Mass., Jan. 4, 1831. He was educated at Wesleyan University, Middletown, Conn. (A.B., 1853), and after teaching classics at Wilbraham (Mass.) Academy (1853–1855), was ordained to the ministry in 1855; he held pastorates at Worcester, Mass. (1855–57), Boston (1857–60), Lynn, Mass. (1861–63), Westfield, Mass. (1863–64), Cambridge, Mass. (1865–67), Charlestown, Mass. (1868–71), Philadelphia (1871–1873, 1877–79), and Brooklyn (1874–76); in 1880 he was elected bishop. In 1862–63 he was a member of the Massachusetts Legislature, and in 1881 was a delegate to the Pan-Methodist Council in London. In theology he is conservative, although " with an open eye for results of recent investigations and inspirations." Besides editing The Study from 1896 to 1900, he has written Sights and Insights: A Book of Observations and Travels (New York, 1874); The Lesser Hymnal (1876); Recreations in Astronomy (1879); The Bible in the World's Education (1892); Among the Forces (1899); and Fifty-two Memory Hymns (1908).

WARREN, WILLIAM FAIRFIELD: Methodist Episcopalian; b. at Williamsburg, Mass., Mar. 13, 1833. He was educated at Wesleyan University, Middletown, Conn. (A.B., 1853), and at the universities of Berlin and Halle (1856–58), traveling extensively in Europe and the East in 1856–58. He held pastorates at Ballardvale, Andover, Mass. (1854–56), Wilbraham, Mass. (1858–60), and Boston (1860–61); was professor of systematic theology in the Missionsanstalt, Bremen, Germany (1861–66); of systematic theology and acting president of Boston Theological Seminary (1866–1871); dean of the School of Theology of Boston

University (1871–73); first president of Boston University (1873–1903); and dean of the School of Theology of the same institution (since 1903). He has also been professor of the comparative history of religions, comparative theology, and the philosophy of religion in Boston University since 1873, this being the first chair of its kind in America. He has repeatedly served his church as delegate to various important conventions. In 1876 he was elected the first president of the Massachusetts Society for the University Education of Women; was a member of the university senate of the Methodist Episcopal Church (1892–1904); and of the Commission on organic law of the same denomination (1896–1900). In 1874 he negotiated reciprocity agreements between Boston University on the one hand, and the National University of Athens and the Royal University of Rome on the other, thus anticipating the similar movement of more recent years. He has written Anfangsgründe der Logik (Bremen, 1863); Allgemeine Einleitung in die systematische Theologie (1865); Paradise Found: The Cradle of the Human Race at the North Pole (Boston, 1885); The Quest of the Perfect Religion (1886); In the Footprints of Arminius (New York, 1888); The Story of Gottlieb (Meadville, Pa., 1890); The Religions of the World and the World-Religion (Boston, 1892); Constitutional Questions before the Methodist Episcopal Church (Cincinnati, 1894); and The Earliest Cosmologies; The Universe as pictured in Thought by the ancient Babylonians, Egyptians, Greeks, Iranians, and Indo-Aryans (New York, 1909).

WASHBURN, GEORGE: Congregationalist; b. at Middleborough, Mass., Mar. 1, 1833. He was graduated from Amherst College (A.B., 1855), and Andover Theological Seminary (1860). He was treasurer of the American Board of Commissioners for Foreign Missions in Turkey (1860–68), with headquarters at Constantinople; professor of philosophy and political economy in Robert College, Constantinople (1869–1903); acting president (1871–77), and president (1877–1903). After a year in the United States he returned to service in Robert College in 1906. Theologically he " accepts the Nicene Creed and believes that the Old and New Testaments contain a revelation from God." His belief " centers in the person of Jesus Christ and in the work of his Spirit," but he does not believe that " the work of the Divine Spirit is limited by any human creed whatsoever." He has had an important part in the religious and political development of the Balkan peninsula, and has written extensively on topics connected with the region for various important reviews and journals. He wrote Fifty Years in Constantinople and Recollections of Robert College (Boston, 1909).

WASHBURN, ROBERT HOOSICK: Methodist Episcopalian; b. at Hoosick Falls, N. Y., Apr. 9, 1869. He was educated at Union College, Schenectady, N. Y. (B.A., 1889), Drew Theological Seminary, and Boston University (S.T.B., 1892), and from 1892 to 1906 held various pastorates in New York and Vermont. Since 1906 he has been professor of Hebrew and church history in Kimball College of Theology, Salem, Ore., and in 1906–07 was also professor of philosophy in Willamette University in the same city. Theologically he is conservative, and besides being long a correspondent of *The Northern Christian Advocate* (Syracuse, N. Y.) has published a number of hymns and poems.

WASHINGTON, BOOKER TALIAFERRO: Afro-American educator; b. near Halesford, Franklin County, Va., 1858 or 1859. He was graduated from Hampton Institute, Hampton, Va., in 1875 and subsequently studied at Wayland Seminary, Washington, D. C. In 1880–81 he was a teacher at Hampton Institute, and since the latter year has been principal of the Tuskegee Normal and Industrial Institute, Tuskegee, Ala. In this position he has shown himself a master in the problem of the education and elevation of the negro race in America. He is a member of the National Municipal League, International Committee on the New Educational Movement, the American Peace Society, the Harmony Club of America, etc., and has written *Future of the American Negro* (Boston, 1899); *Sowing and Reaping* (1900); *Up from Slavery* (New York, 1901; new ed., 1910); *Character Building* (1902); *Story of my Life and Work* (1903); *Working with the Hands* (1904); *Tuskegee and its People* (1905); *Putting the Most into Life* (1906); *Life of Frederick Douglass* (Philadelphia, 1907); *The Negro in Business* (Chicago, 1907); and *The Story of the Negro* (New York, 1909), besides collaborating with W. E. B. Du Bois in *The Negro in the South* (Philadelphia, 1907).

WASSERSCHLEBEN, vās'er-shlê″ben, **FRIEDRICH WILHELM HERMANN:** German statesman and theologian; b. at Liegnitz (40 m. w.n.w. of Breslau) Apr. 22, 1812; d. at Giessen June 28, 1893. He studied at the universities of Breslau and Berlin; began to lecture at Berlin in 1838; became extraordinary professor at Breslau, 1850, and in 1850 ordinary professor at Halle, in both cases in the faculty of law; he removed to Giessen as professor in law in 1852, where he was rector in 1870–71 and chancellor, 1875–84. During life he held a State office, and so avoided unnecessary participation in political affairs, being on the commission which had supervision of the Hessian State Church. As a member of the national synod his voice had weight because of his researches into ecclesiastical law. His literary work commenced early. He published *Beiträge zur Geschichte der vorgratianischen Kirchenrechtsquellen* (Leipsic, 1839); *Reginonis abbatis Prumiensis libri duo de synodalibus causis et disciplinis ecclesiasticis* (1840); two works on Pseudo-Isidore (Breslau, 1841–44); the comprehensive *Die Beichtordnungen der abendländischen Kirche nebst einer rechtsgeschichtlichen Einleitung* (Halle, 1851); issued an edition of the Irish canons (Giessen, 1874); and besides these a host of smaller brochures dealing with various phases of church history and law. He was an advocate of entire freedom of the Church from the State (cf. his *Die Parität der Konfessionen im Staate*, 1871, and his *Bemerkungen zu dem offiziellen Entwurf einer Verfassung der evangelischen Kirche des Grossherzogtums Hessen*, also 1871); while he entered into discussion of the relation of the State to marriage and divorce. Among other works of Wasserschleben, showing the extent of the interests

which absorbed his attention, are: *Das Prinzip der Successionsordnung nach deutschem, insbesondere sächsischem Rechte* (Gotha, 1860); *Das Prinzip der Erbenfolge nach den älteren deutschen und verwandten Rechten* (Leipsic, 1870); and a collection of sources for German law in *Sammlung deutscher Rechtsquellen* (Giessen, 1860 sqq.).　　　　(A. B. SCHMIDT.)

BIBLIOGRAPHY: J. F. von Schulte, *Geschichte der Quellen . . . des canonischen Rechts*, iii. 2 and 3, p. 247; A. Schmidt, in *Ludoviciana*, pp. 71 sqq., Giessen, 1907; *ADB*, xli. 236.

WATER OF JEALOUSY. See ORDEAL, § 7.

WATER, CONSECRATION OF, IN THE GREEK CHURCH: The consecration of water is a custom so early that its beginnings can not be traced. Cyprian (Epist., lxix. [lxx. in Oxford ed.]; *ANF*, v. 376) mentions the requirement that the water of baptism be purified and sanctified by the priest, a requirement enforced by a synod at Carthage in 256; the water then became a miraculous agency. The Apostolic Constitutions (vii. 43; Eng. transl. in *ANF*, vii. 477) preserve a prayer of thanksgiving for the water of baptism, the ceremony corresponding to the thanksgiving preceding the Lord's Supper, though the conception hardly invaded the realm of dogmatics. Yet Ambrose and Augustine, as well as Chrysostom, held that water so blessed was restricted in its use to sacramental purposes. After the ninth century Holy Water (q.v.) became a permanent institution, the consecration of it at first taking place at the usual baptismal seasons at Easter, Whitsuntide, and Epiphany, and then later consecration for the year took place at Easter or Whitsuntide. The Greek Church used Epiphany for this ceremony, in commemoration of the baptism of Christ, and it has long been a tradition that water so treated would never become foul. The practise still continues and is accompanied with great solemnity, while the streams and sources of the water are also the objects of blessings and ceremonies in which processions have their part. The Greek Church observes a " greater " and a " lesser " sanctification of the water. The former takes place at Epiphany, either in the church porch or at the stream, and the liturgy recalls the early ecclesiastical symbolism. Homilies and sermons at this period bear upon the subject, and the mystical doctrines of the church center much on this season. The lesser consecration takes place before a vessel of water and is attended with incensing and touching of the water with a cross. The liturgy invokes the endowment of the water with power to heal soul and body. This corresponds to the employment of holy water in the Church of Rome.

　　　　　　　　　　　　　(PHILIPP MEYER.)

BIBLIOGRAPHY: Bingham, *Origines*, XI., x.; J. Goar, *Euchologion, sive rituale Græcorum*, pp. 353 sqq., 367, Paris, 1647; J. M. Heineccius, *Abbildung der alten und neuen griechischen Kirche*, ii. 244–247, Leipsic, 1711; J. C. W. Augusti, *Denkwürdigkeiten*, ii. 208, Leipsic, 1818; *DCA*, i. 777–779.

WATER SUPPLY IN PALESTINE: With the exception of Galilee or the plain of Jezreel, Palestine is insufficiently supplied with water. Moreover, since the dry season lasts nearly six months, the inhabitants have ever been urgently pressed to husband their natural water supplies. The sources of supply are as follows:

(1) Artificial devices for the better economy of water, for protecting springs from choking or filth, may still be found at many places, especially since the Roman occupation. Thus, the fountain of Ras el-'Ain, near Tyre, is encompassed by a basin of masonry twenty-four and a half feet in height; thereby serving to bring the water to the proper conduit level. Similar contrivances exist in the plain of Gennesaret. The springs which feed Solomon's Pools are provided with reservoir chambers. (2) Wells (*be'er*) were artificial pits, in which either the surface water or that of some underground spring was stored. From the latter came the characteristic term, "wells," or fountains, of "living water" (Gen. xxvi. 19). They were frequently quite deep; thus, Jacob's well, below Mount Gerizim (John iv. 12), shows still a depth of over seventy-three feet. These wells were of more or less adequate masonry, the mouth being covered with stone slabs, while the aperture for drawing was also securely closed (Gen. xxix. 3 sqq.; cf. Ex. xxi. 33). The water was drawn up in a pitcher or bucket with a long rope, and there were troughs for the cattle (Gen. xxx. 38). Such wells were especially provided in the arid pasture country (Gen. xxix. 2 sqq.; II Chron. xxvi. 10); or about appropriate sites for caravans (Gen. xxiv. 62; Num. xxi. 16 sqq.; Deut. x. 6). The best-known among the many wells still preserved are those of Beersheba and Jacob's well. (3) Cisterns (*bôr*) are used for storing rain-water. They are capacious underground cavities. They existed in almost all the old cities: Megiddo, Taanach, Gezer (q.v.); and notably in Jerusalem, where, indeed, every house still has its own cistern. In earlier times, they were hewn out of the rock; later, they were also, sometimes, walled up with masonry. Natural cavities were preferred where available. Particularly renowned are the great cisterns about the square of the Temple, many of which probably date back to the time of Solomon's fortifications. The largest, called the "King's Cistern," is forty-two feet deep and 406 feet in circuit. (4) The "pools" (*berekha*) are uncovered artificial reservoirs. Where it was feasible, they were hewn out of rock. Topographical depressions were utilized, as, in this case, the construction was simpler, and the water more easily collected. Yet again, the pools are formed by dams made by carrying two stout stone walls across the valley, and then excavating the intervening area down to rock bottom. This was the plan of the so-called "Solomon's Pools." The dams were filled with rain-water and with spring water, if such was available. In the case of Solomon's Pools, the water was conveyed in aqueducts from three remote springs. Some idea of the size of the dams may be gained from the dimensions of the nethermost of the three "Solomon's Pools," which is 580 feet long on the lower side, 206 feet broad, and 49 feet in maximum depth. Not a few of Palestine's numerous dams antedate the Israelitish era. (5) Of the aqueducts, the oldest are the tunnel of Siloam, and "Solomon's" conduit (see JERUSALEM, II., V., § 3). The latter work is probably Herodian. To this period, in turn, belong most of the other constructions of the kind yet surviving in ruins. The Romans, and, following their example, the contem-

porary Jewish princes, expended great pains in behalf of adequate water supplies. The conduits, for the most part, were above ground, merely open gutters, which ran along the surface and often made wide détours to avoid depressions. However, the principle of the siphon was also employed with some of the older aqueducts of Jerusalem for spanning a lesser valley, a water-tight carrier being contrived by laying a line of perforated (and cemented) quarry stones across the gap. On the other hand, the Roman conduits, borne by great aqueducts, cleared larger valleys. Hezekiah's tunnel of Siloam is, of course, underground; and, all in all, a plumb level was maintained, the vertical differential between entrance and exit being about one foot.

I. BENZINGER.

BIBLIOGRAPHY: C. Schick, in *ZDPV*, i (1878), 132–176; G. Perrot and C. Chipiez, *Hist. de l'art dans l'antiquité*, vol. iv., Paris, 1887; G. Ebers and H. Guthe, *Palästina in Bild und Wort*, i. 110–126, 150–154, Stuttgart, 1883; Benzinger, *Archäologie*, pp. 207–208.

WATERLAND, DANIEL: English theologian and apologist; b. at Walesby (20 m. s. of Hull) Feb. 14, 1682–83; d. at Twickenham (a western suburb of London) Dec. 23, 1740. He studied at Magdalene College, Cambridge (B.A., 1703; M.A., 1706; B.D., 1714; D.D., 1717); became master of his college (1713), and vice-chancellor of the university (1715); chaplain to George I. (1717); rector of St. Austin and St. Faith, London (1721); chancellor of York (1722); canon of Windsor (1724); archdeacon of Middlesex and vicar of Twickenham, (1730). His significance lies in his defense of trinitarian orthodoxy against Samuel Clarke and Daniel Whitby, and in his check upon the advance of latitudinarianism within the Church of England. He was prolific as an author, his major works including: *Vindication of Christ's Divinity* (Cambridge, 1719; an attack upon Clarke and Whitby, ut sup.), with which is to be placed his *Answer to Dr. Whitby's Reply* (1720); these two works displayed his ability as an apologist, and led to his next work, *Eight Sermons . . . in Defense of the Divinity of our Lord Jesus Christ* (1720; on the Lady Moyer foundation, preached at St. Paul's); *Critical History of the Athanasian Creed* (1723; assigns the symbol to 430–440, and makes St. Hilary of Arles its author); *Importance of the Doctrine of the Holy Trinity Asserted* (London, 1734); and *Review of the Doctrine of the Eucharist as Laid down in Scripture and Antiquity* (Cambridge, 1737). Besides these a considerable number of smaller publications is credited to him. In all of these there appear a learning which is deep and accurate, a style terse and vigorous, and an opposition to mysticism and philosophy which compelled him to have recourse to external evidences for his apologetics. His works were collected in 11 vols., Oxford, 1823–28, reprint in 6 vols., 1843, to which was prefixed a *Life* by Bishop William van Mildert.

BIBLIOGRAPHY: L. Stephen, *English Thought in the 18th Century*, passim, New York, 1881; J. H. Overton, *The Church in England*, ii. 227, London, 1897; J. H. Overton and F. Relton, *The English Church (1714–1800)*, passim, ib. 1906; C. S. Carter, *English Church in the 18th Century*, pp. 31–33, ib. 1910; *DNB*, lix. 446–448.

WATKINS, HENRY WILLIAM: Church of England; b. at Ty-newydel, Monmouthshire, Jan.

14, 1844. He was educated at King's College, London (B.A., University of London, 1868), and was ordered deacon in 1870 and ordained priest in the following year. He was curate of Pluckley, Kent (1870–72); vicar of Much Wenlock (1873–75); after which he was connected with King's College, London, as censor, tutor, and chaplain (1875–78), professor of logic and moral philosophy (1877–79), and professor of logic and metaphysics (1879–80). During this period he was also warden of St. Augustine's College, Canterbury (1878–80), and vicar of St. Gregory the Great, Canterbury (1879–80). He was canon of Durham and archdeacon of Northumberland (1880–82); also curate of All Saints, Newcastle-on-Tyne (1881–82); in 1882 he became archdeacon of Auckland, but resigned this dignity within the year. Since 1882 he has been canon and archdeacon of Durham; also professor of Hebrew in the University of Durham since 1880. He was Bampton lecturer at Oxford in 1890, and has been an honorary fellow of King's College, London, since 1872 and of St. Augustine's College, Canterbury, since 1883, examining chaplain to the bishop of Durham since 1879, and commissary to the bishop of Sydney since 1884. He has written the commentary on the Gospel of St. John for Bishop C. J. Ellicott's *New Testament Commentary for English Readers* (London, 1877; reprinted separately, 1879); *The Church in Northumberland: A Primary Charge* (1882); and *Modern Criticism considered in its Relation to the Fourth Gospel* (Bampton lectures; London, 1891).

WATSON, FREDERICK: Church of England; b. at York Oct. 13, 1844; d. at Cambridge Jan. 1, 1906. He was educated at St. John's College, Cambridge (B.A., 1868; M.A., 1871; B.D., 1884; fellow, 1871–78). He was ordered deacon in 1871 and ordained priest in 1872; was assistant curate at Stow-cum-Quy, 1871–75, and St. Giles', Cambridge, 1875–78; rector of Starston, Norfolk, 1878–1886; vicar of Stow-cum-Quy, 1886–93; after 1893 he was minister of St. Edward's, Cambridge, and being reelected to his fellowship at St. John's, was also lecturer in Hebrew and theology in that college. He was Hulsean lecturer in 1883, and an honorary canon of Ely. He wrote *The Ante-Nicene Apologies* (Cambridge, 1870); *Defenders of the Faith* (1878); *The Law and the Prophets* (Hulsean lectures; 1883); *The Book of Genesis a True History* (London, 1892); and *Inspiration* (1906).

WATSON, JOHN ("IAN MACLAREN"): Presbyterian; b. at Manningtree (9 m. s.w. of Ipswich), Essex, Nov. 3, 1850; d. at Mt. Pleasant, Ia., May 6, 1907. He studied at the universities of Edinburgh (M.A., 1870) and Tübingen, and at New College, Edinburgh; was assistant at Barclay Church, Edinburgh (1874–85); minister of Logiealmond Free Church (1875–77); of St. Matthew's Church, Glasgow (1877–80); and Sexton Park Presbyterian Church, Liverpool (1880–1905). He was Lyman Beecher lecturer at Yale in 1896, and in 1906 again visited the United States, where he was taken ill and died. In theology he was a liberal evangelical. He wrote: *The Upper Room* (London, 1895); *The Mind of the Master* (1896); *The Cure of Souls* (Yale lectures; 1896);

The Potter's Wheel (1897); *Companions of the Sorrowful Way* (1898); *Doctrines of Grace* (1900); *The Life of the Master* (1901); *The Homely Virtues* (1903); and *The Inspiration of our Faith* (1905). He is most widely known, however, for his sketch of Scotch life in the series of studies which was begun with his *Beside the Bonnie Briar Bush* (1894), and these are marked by an intense appreciation of the peculiar qualities which have ever made the Scotch favorite subjects for literary portrayal. Humor and pathos are blended, and he was in the front rank of the successors to Dean Ramsay and Dr. John Brown.
BIBLIOGRAPHY: W. R. Nicoll, "*Ian Maclaren.*" *Life of the Rev. John Watson*, London, 1908–09; Sir E. Russell, in *Hibbert Journal*, July, 1907.

WATSON, RICHARD: The name of two English divines.

1. Bishop of Llandaff: Scientist and apologist; b. at Haversham, Westmoreland (40 m. s. of Carlisle), Aug., 1737; d. at Calgarth Park (37 m. s. of Carlisle) July 4, 1816. He studied at Trinity College, Cambridge (B.A., 1759; fellow, 1760; M.A., 1762; D.D., 1771); became professor of chemistry, 1764, having no prior knowledge of the subject, but fitting himself for the position by assiduous application and achieving a remarkable success both in teaching the subject and by his published contributions; was elected regius professor of divinity, 1771, acknowledging later that his qualifications for that chair were not great; became prebendary at Ely, 1774, and archdeacon there, 1779; rector of Northwold, Norfolk, 1779; of Knaptoft, Leicestershire, 1780; and bishop of Llandaff, 1782. Watson is especially noted for his versatility and power of concentration, for clearness in expounding scientific matters, for ingenuity in working out results, and for his interest in Biblical study as applied by the laity. He issued a number of publications dealing with chemistry, including *Institutionum chemicarum, . . . pars metallurgica* (Cambridge, 1768), which were collected in *Chemical Essays* (5 vols., London, 1781–87). Among his theological works may be noted *Apology for Christianity, . . . Letters . . . to Edward Gibbon* (1776; regarded as the antidote to Gibbon's fifteenth chapter, and frequently reprinted; for the character of this chapter see GIBBON, EDWARD); *A Collection of Theological Tracts* (6 vols., Cambridge, 1785; an assemblage of twenty-four works by many hands, the aim being the furtherance of Biblical study); and *An Apology for the Bible in a Series of Letters Addressed to Thomas Paine* (London, 1796; a work which had a wide popularity both in England and in America). He also gathered sermons and other writings, charges, etc., in his *Miscellaneous Tracts on Religious, Political and Agricultural Subjects* (2 vols., 1815). He contributed material for his life in his *Anecdotes of the Life of Richard Watson*, edited by his son (1817). He was a supporter of Wilberforce in the latter's crusade against slavery, and was interested in the extension of churches in London. He was a man of great breadth of thought and charity of action.

2. English Methodist: b. at Barton upon Humber (32 m. s.e. of York), England, Feb. 22, 1781; d. at London Jan. 8, 1833. He was educated at Lincoln Grammar School; apprenticed to a joiner at Lincoln in 1795; preached his first sermon 1796, and removed to Newark as assistant to Thomas Cooper, Wesleyan preacher; was received on trial at the conference of 1796, and into full connection as a traveling minister in 1801, having been stationed at Ashby-de-la-Zouche, Castle Donington, and Derby. Resenting a charge of Arianism, he withdrew from the Wesleyan connection, and joined the Methodist New Connection in 1803, being fully admitted to its ministry in 1807. He became assistant secretary of its conference in 1805, and secretary in 1807; he was first at Stockport, then from 1806 at Liverpool, where he engaged in literary work for Thomas Kaye. Resigning his ministry in 1807, he returned to the Wesleyan body, being reinstated, 1812. In 1808 he was engaged as editor of the Liverpool *Courier* by Kaye. In 1812 he was stationed at Wakefield, and at Hull 1814–16. In the Wesleyan movement of 1813 for foreign missions, and in particular for the evangelization of India, Watson drew up a plan of a general missionary society, which was accepted. Removed to London in 1816, and made one of the two general secretaries to the Wesleyan missions, he was resident missionary secretary in London, 1821–27, and again, 1832–1833. After holding an appointment at Manchester, 1827–29, he returned to London. At the request in 1820 of the conference he produced his *Observations on Mr. Southey's Life of Wesley* (London, 1820), and later his own *Life of Rev. John Wesley* (1831). Active in the antislavery movement, he was not, however, for immediate emancipation. He was a strong upholder of the connectional discipline, and desired to maintain friendly relations with the established church. In the pulpit his power lay in appeals on great occasions; he had a commanding and deliberate delivery, and was noted as a platform speaker. His works embrace an exposition of St. Matthew and St. Mark (1831); *A Defense of the Wesleyan Methodist Missions in the West Indies* (London, 1817); *Theological Institutes* (3d ed., 3 vols., 1829); *Conversations for the Young* (1830); *A Biblical and Theological Dictionary* (1831); his *Works*, with *Memoirs* by T. Jackson, appeared (12 vols., 1834–37); and his *Sermons and Outlines* (1865).

BIBLIOGRAPHY: On 1: Besides the *Anecdotes*, ut sup., consult: J. Hunt, *Hist. of Religious Thought in England*, iii. 351, London, 1873; L. Stephen, *English Thought in the 18th Century*, passim, New York, 1881; J. H. Overton and F. Relton, *English Church (1714–1800)*, pp. 259–262 et passim, London, 1906; C. S. Carter, *English Church in 18th Century*, passim, London, 1910; *DNB*, lx. 24–27. On 2: Besides the *Memoirs* by T. Jackson, ut sup., consult: J. Bunting, *Memorials of the Late Richard Watson*, London, 1833; W. Willan, in *Sermons and Outlines by Richard Watson*, ib. 1865; *DNB*, lx. 27–29.

WATSON, THOMAS: Non-conformist divine; d. at Barnston (28 m. n.e. of London) 1686 (buried there July 28). He was educated at Emanuel College, Cambridge, and in 1646 was appointed to preach at St. Stephen's, Walbrook. He showed strong Presbyterian views during the civil war, with, however, an attachment for the king; because of his share in Love's plot to recall Charles II., he was imprisoned in 1651, but was released and reinstated vicar of St. Stephen's, 1652. He acquired fame as a preacher, but in 1662 was ejected at the Restoration; he continued, however, to exercise his ministry privately. In 1672 after the declaration of indulgence he obtained a license for Crosby Hall, where he preached for several years, till his retirement to Barnston upon the failure of his health. Watson was a man of learning, and acquired fame by his quaint devotional and expository writings. Of his many works may be mentioned, Αὐταρκεια, *or the Art of Divine Contentment* (London, 1653); *The Saints' Delight* (1657); *Jerusalem's Glory* (1661); *The Divine Cordial* (1663); *The Godly Man's Picture* (1666); *The Holy Eucharist* (1668); *Heaven Taken by Storm* (1669); and *A Body of Practical Divinity*, . . . *One Hundred Seventy Six Sermons on the Lesser Catechism* (1692).

BIBLIOGRAPHY: E. Calamy, *Nonconformist's Memorial*, ed. S. Palmer, i. 188–191, London, 1775; Walter Wilson, *Hist. and Antiquities of Dissenting Churches in London*, i. 331–334, London, 1810; A. à Wood, *Athenæ Oxonienses*, ed. P. Bliss, iii. 982, 1001, 1235, 4 vols., London, 1813–20; W. A. Shaw, *English Church . . . under the Commonwealth, 1640–60*, ii. 104–107, London, 1900; *DNB*, lx. 37–38.

WATT, vet (VADIAN), JOACHIM VON: Reformer of St. Gall; b. at St. Gall Dec. 28, 1484; d. there Apr. 6, 1551. As a humanist Watt was known by the name of Vadianus. He studied at the University of Vienna, where he took his degree in 1508, and in 1517 became teacher of rhetoric and poetics there. In 1518 Watt left Vienna to become city physician of St. Gall. Following the medical profession he was also a member of the legislative council of his native town. Watt's ideas of reform emanated, much like the principles of his friend Zwingli, from Humanism, striving for a simple personal faith, instead of the traditional dogmatism of the church. He was an ardent admirer of Erasmus, whom he first met at Basel in 1522, while Zwingli in Zurich, with whom he had corresponded from 1511, exercised a leading influence over him. In 1520 he opened correspondence with Luther, and distributed his writings among friends. Watt next founded a "Biblical school" at St. Gall. His lectures in this school resulted in the publication of his religious-humanistic work *Epitome trium terræ partium Asiæ, Africæ et Europæ* (Zurich, 1534). Meanwhile the Reformation movement had seized the city. Overstrained enthusiasm for communistic chiliasm made some reservation advisable, particularly in consequence of the wish of the conservatives to avoid a rupture with the abbey of St. Gall. This sentiment controlled the smaller, or executive, council, while at the same time an Anabaptist idea of the kingdom of heaven continued to grow and excite many people, influenced in part by Kessler's Bible lectures. This more conservative party gained the support of the larger or legislative council, where Watt held the leadership, and opposed the radical element. A motion proposed to the joint session, to suspend public explanation of the Bible outside of the churches, made the radicals more determined in their effort for the recognition of their ideal of freedom. Provoked at their ill success and the preferment which Kessler had received at the hands of the council, they became outspoken Anabaptists. They secured the personal aid of Grebel and Blaurock, and, led by Uoliman, gained control of the radical element of the St. Gall populace. Uoliman was called before the council to justify the separatistic administration of the sacraments, but it was determined to reach a decision by a final debate, in which the cause of the Anabaptists was defeated, according to the opinion of the dominant element. Watt, to whom Zwingli had sent his treatise, *Vom Tauf, Wiedertauf und Kindertauf*, in 1524, was the center of this controversy and contributed a comprehensive work against the Anabaptists, which has been lost.

Watt now reorganized the church of St. Gall by measures which included the submission of the clergy to the city council. When Watt finally was elected chief magistrate of the city in 1526, the victory of the St. Gall Reformation seemed assured. The success of the disputation of Bern (1528), in which Watt was moderator, gave occasion for the enforcement of the Reformation in the country region subject to the abbey. Wearied by the disputes growing out of the question of disposal of this abbey, Watt gradually became less prominent in controversial issues. He now devoted his interests to the study of the history of his native city and the abbey to which the city owed its existence. After the battle of Kappel, in which Zwingli fell, 1531, Watt witnessed the restoration of Roman Catholicism in the abbey, and political derangement in the city. He continued his work for the welfare of the church for twenty years. To bring about an agreement concerning the views of the Eucharist, he wrote his *Aphorismorum de consideratione eucharistiæ libri VI* (Zurich, 1535). In his writings *Pro veritate carnis triumphantis Christi* and *Epistola ad Zuiccium*, together with the *Antilogia ad Gasparis Schwenkfeldii argumenta conscripta* (1540), directed against Schwenkfeld, he again defended the Swiss Christology. But the study of the historical past was of more interest to him than theological analysis. His *Grosse Chronik der Aebte des Klosters St. Gallen* (3 vols., St. Gall, 1575–79), a historical justification of the Reformation, may be considered one of the most important controversial works on the history of the Swiss and the German reformation.

(H. HERMELINK.)

BIBLIOGRAPHY: The German historical writings by Watt were edited by E. Götzinger, 3 vols., St. Gall, 1875–79; the *Farrago* is in M. Goldast, *Rerum Alamannicarum scriptores*, iii. 1–80, ed. H. C. Senkenberg, Frankfort, 1730. His letters were collected by E. Arbenz, for the *Historischer Verein* of St. Gall, *Mitteilungen*, vols. xxiv.–xxv., xxvii.–xxix. Other sources are Johann Kessler's *Vita*, revised at St. Gall, 1865, and his *Sabbata*, ed. E. Götzinger, for the St. Gall *Verein*, 1866–68, and in a new ed., St. Gall, 1901. Consult: T. Pressel, *Joachim Vadian*, Elberfeld, 1861; R. Stähelin, in *Beiträge zur vaterländischen Geschichte*, xi. 191–262, Basel, 1882; E. Arbenz, in *Neujahrsblätter des historischen Vereins*, St. Gall, 1886, 1895, 1905; E. Egli, *Die St. Gallen Täufer*, Zurich, 1887; K. Dändliker, *Geschichte der Schweiz*, ii. 424 sqq., Zurich, 1894; idem, *Short Hist. of Switzerland*, pp. 137, 154, 156, London, 1899; E. Götzinger, in *Schriften des Vereins für Reformationsgeschichte*, l (1895); W. D. McCrackan, *Rise of the Swiss Republic*, pp. 93, 264, 2d ed., New York, 1901; S. M. Jackson, *Huldreich Zwingli*, passim, 2d ed., New York, 1903.

WATTS, ISAAC: Founder of English hymnody; b. at Southampton, England, July 17, 1674; d. at Stoke Newington (4 m. n.e. of Charing Cross, London) Nov. 25, 1748. He obtained an excellent education at Southampton grammar-school, then, joining the dissenters, he studied at an academy at Stoke Newington, where he acquired his accuracy of thought and habit of laborious analysis; leaving the academy in 1694, he spent two years at home, beginning his hymn-writing. He was private tutor, 1696–1701; became assistant pastor in the chapel at Mark Lane, 1699, and sole pastor, 1702; because of frequent attacks of illness, Samuel Price had assisted him from 1703 and was chosen copastor 1713; his illness increased with time, but the congregation refused to part with one who had become so famous and beloved. Watts was one of the most popular writers of his time; the *Horæ Lyricæ* (London, 1706) won him fame as a poet, but it was his hymns that so distinguished him. His poetry by giving utterance to the spiritual emotions made hymn-singing an earnest devotional power; the success of his hymns was tremendous, the two staple volumes were the *Hymns* (1707) and the *Psalms of David* (1719). The various pieces numbered about 600, of which quite a number are still in general use. His best pieces rank among the finest hymns in English. Watts was also the founder of children's hymnology, writing the *Divine Songs* (1715). For an estimate of his place in hymnody, see HYMNOLOGY, IX., § 3. He was opposed in 1719 to the imposition of the doctrine of the Trinity on independent ministers. He held a theory which he hoped might close the breach between Arianism and the faith of the Church; he maintained that the human soul of Christ, created before the world, had been united to the divine principle in the Godhead known as the Sophia or Logos, and that the personality of the Holy Ghost was figurative rather than literal. He held liberal views on education, and his learning and piety attracted a great many. His works, outside his hymns, embrace *The Knowledge of the Heavens and the Earth Made Easy* (London, 1726); *An Essay towards the Encouragement of Charity Schools* (1728); *Reliquiæ Juveniles* (1734); *Philosophical Essays* (3d ed., 2 pts., 1742). His *Works* appeared ed. D. Jennings and P. Doddridge (6 vols., London, 1753; with *Memoirs* by G. Burder, 6 vols., 1810–11; 9 vols., Leeds, 1810–11); and *Posthumous Works* (2 vols., London, 1779).

BIBLIOGRAPHY: Lives have been written by T. Gibbons, London, 1780; S. Johnson, London, 1785, 2d ed., 1791; T. Milner, London, 1834; E. Paxton Hood, London, 1875. Consult further: Walter Wilson, *Hist. and Antiquities of the Dissenting Churches*, 4 vols., London, 1808–14; R. E. A. Willmott, *Lives of the Sacred Poets*, London, 1838; F. Saunders, *Evenings with the Sacred Poets*, London, 1870; S. W. Duffield, *English Hymns*, pp. 61–64, New York, 1886; N. Smith, *Hymns historically Famous*, pp. 49–55, Chicago, 1901; Julian, *Hymnology*, pp. 349–350, 920, 1236–1241; *DNB*, lx. 67–70.

WAYLAND, FRANCIS: Baptist preacher and educator; b. in New York Mar. 11, 1796; d. at Providence, R. I., Sept. 30, 1865. He was graduated from Union College in 1813; studied medicine for three years; uniting with the Baptist church, he studied at Andover Theological Seminary, 1816–17; was tutor in Union College, 1817–21; pastor of the First Baptist Church in Boston, 1821–26; professor in Union College in 1826; president of Brown University, 1827–55; pastor of the First Baptist Church in Providence, 1855–57; and subsequently devoted himself to religious and humane work. He is widely remembered as a college officer. The text-books which he prepared for the use of his own classes came into general use. In the reorganization, brought about by him, of the courses of study in Brown University in 1850, he did much to reform the general system of college education. By his lectures on psychology, political economy, and ethics, and by his personality he exerted great influence on his pupils; he delivered weekly chapel sermons, and gathered the students together for Bible instruction. He was one of the founders and the first president of the American Institute of Instruction, for many years presiding over and taking an active part in its deliberations. He did much to secure the founding of free public libraries.

Eminent as an educator, Wayland stands hardly less distinguished as a preacher. He was admired for his broad and deep thought, and grace of expression. Some of his discourses, as, for example, his sermon on *The Moral Dignity of the Missionary Enterprise*, are prominent in[the annals of the American pulpit. In all his course of public service he never ceased to be an earnest and effective preacher of the Gospel.

Besides sermons, addresses, and discourses his works embrace *Elements of Moral Science* (New York, 1835); *Elements of Political Economy* (1837); *Limits of Human Responsibility* (Boston, 1838); *Domestic Slavery Considered as a Scriptural Institution, in a Correspondence* (1845); *Memoir of the Life and Labors of the Rev. Adoniram Judson* (2 vols., 1853); *Elements of Intellectual Philosophy* (1854); *Notes on the Principles and Practices of the Baptist Churches* (1857); *Letters on the Ministry of the Gospel* (1863); and the *Memoir of the Christian Labors . . . of Thomas Chalmers* (1864).

BIBLIOGRAPHY: The funeral sermon by G. I. Chace was published, Providence, 1866; and his *Life and Labors*, by his sons F. and H. L. Wayland, 2 vols., New York, 1869.

WAYLAND, HEMAN LINCOLN: Baptist; b. at Providence, R. I., Apr. 23, 1830; d. at Wernersville, Pa., Nov. 7, 1898. He was graduated from Brown University 1849; studied at Newton Theological Institution, Mass., 1849–50; taught in the academy at Townshend, Vt., 1850–51; was resident graduate at Brown University, 1851–52; tutor at University of Rochester, N. Y., 1852–54; pastor of the Third Baptist Church, Worcester, Mass., 1854–1861; chaplain of the Seventh Connecticut Volunteers, 1861–64; missionary to the colored people at Nashville, Tenn., 1864–65; professor of rhetoric and logic in Kalamazoo College, Mich., 1865–70; president of Franklin College, Ind., 1870–72; and editor of *The National Baptist*, Philadelphia, from 1872. He was the author, in collaboration with his brother, of *A Memoir of the Life and Labors of Francis Wayland* (2 vols., New York, 1867); and independently of *Charles H. Spurgeon: his Faith and Works* (Philadelphia, 1892).

WAZO, wa'zō: Bishop of Liége; b. near Lobbes (a village near Charleroi, 32 m. s. of Brussels) or near Namur (34 m. s. of Brussels) between 980 and 990; d. at Liége July 8, 1048. His importance issues from his efforts in the cause of education, his relations to Emperor Henry III. of Germany, and his views on the connection between the world and the Church and on the treatment of heretics. In every

situation and practical emergency, he proved himself a man capable of independent thought and decisive action. He received his elementary instruction in the cloister schools at Lobbes and Liége; taught in the latter and became its head in 1008, greatly extending its fame and influence; in 1017 he became dean of the cathedral chapter, retaining the directorship of the school until, probably, c. 1030, his resignation being due to differences between himself and other authorities over discipline and administration. He incurred the enmity of the peasants, and did not enjoy the protection of Bishop Reginard himself. The relaxation of strictness in the canonical life under his episcopate reacted untowardly upon the school. From these unfavorable conditions, Wazo fled to his friend, Abbot Poppo of Stablo, who procured him a call to the royal chapel of Conrad II. (1030). Here he soon won good standing in part by a brilliant victory in a debate with the emperor's Jewish physician respecting a passage in the Old Testament. After the death of Provost Johannes, he was himself elected provost and archdeacon, with Bishop Reginard's assent (1033); and in 1042 he was elected bishop, in which office he justified the confidence felt in his ability. During the insurrection of Duke Godfrey of Lorraine, Wazo stood faithful to the king in various crises which successively arose in the affairs of the kingdom. Yet his course did not win entire approval. At the Diet of Aix-la-Chapelle, 1046, during the consideration of the case of Archbishop Widgar of Ravenna (who had been invested by the king two years previously, but had neglected to undergo episcopal consecration), Bishop Wazo contested the competency of that assembly to pronounce in the case of an Italian bishop; and when the king reminded him of the duty of obedience, he defined his position in the pointed terms, " Obedience we owe to the pope, to you—fidelity." With this the other bishops agreed. Shortly afterward, when Wazo protested against an indiscreet transaction at a convention, and so made appeal to the fact of his anointing with holy oil, Henry III. rebuffed him with the retort, " So am I anointed with holy oil, and I thereby obtained the authority to rule." Then Wazo answered the emperor, " Quite a different thing is that boasted anointing of yours; for while by it you are endowed with the power to slay, we, so help us God, receive the power to make alive." It was Wazo, finally, who contested the legality of the deposition of Gregory VI. at Sutri in 1046, and the induction of Clement II., this protest occurring after the latter's death (Oct., 1047), and resting on the fundamental argument, " Certainly neither divine nor human laws allow this; we have alike the words and the writings of the holy Fathers, everywhere prescribing that the supreme pontiff is judicially amenable to none save God alone." Hence in Wazo the great reform party, which acquired controlling influence over the Church in the second third of the eleventh century, was beginning to embody in its schedule of operations certain definite maxims of ecclesiastical polity.

An incident moving him to evince good judgment and conscientious dealing was furnished by the question of Bishop Roger II. of Châlons, who, being

alarmed by the sudden outcropping of Neo-Mani-
chean heresies in his diocese, asked Wazo whether
they were to be combated by the edge of the secular sword or not. Wazo answered in a somewhat
extended written opinion, counseling moderation
and leniency. In the matter of his diocesan administration, it is worthy of note that, during the dire
famine of the year 1043, Wazo had a supply of grain
bought up and judiciously distributed, not only to
the utterly destitute, but also to the " prouder "
poor. In like manner he tided the peasants over
their straits, lest they should be constrained to sell
their cattle. Moreover, he gave constant attention
to the cathedral school's affairs. He won warm
praise from Anselm; while the epitaph transmitted
by a writer of the thirteenth century lavished upon
him this lofty tribute, " Sooner doom will crack
than another Wazo arise." CARL MIRBT.

BIBLIOGRAPHY: Anselm, Gesta episcoporum Leodiensium,
ed. Köpke, in MGH, Script., vii (1846), 189–234; H.
Bresslau, Jahrbücher des deutschen Reichs unter Konrad
II., Leipsic, 1879–84; E. Steindorff, Jahrbücher des
deutschen Reichs unter Heinrich III., 2 vols., ib. 1874–81;
A. Bittner, Wazo und die Schulen von Lüttich, Breslau,
1879; U. Chevalier, Répertoire des sources historiques du
moyen âge, bio-bibliographie, p. 2332, Paris, 1887; E.
Voigt, Egberts von Lüttich Fecunda ratis, pp. xxix. sqq.,
Halle, 1889; E. Sackur, Die Cluniacenser, ii. 294 sqq., 304
sqq., ib. 1894; KL, xii. 1229–30.

WEAVER, JONATHAN: Bishop of the United
Brethren in Christ; b. in Carroll County, O., Feb.
23, 1824; d. at Dayton, O., Feb. 6, 1901. He was
educated in common schools and Hagerston Academy, O.; began preaching when twenty-one; was
pastor, 1847–52; presiding elder, 1852–57; general
agent for Otterbein University, 1857–65; and bishop
after 1865, becoming bishop emeritus in 1893. He
is recognized as one of the strong figures of his church,
and assisted in carrying it through a crisis which
threatened disruption. He was the author of Discourses on the Resurrection (Dayton, O., 1871); Ministerial Salary (1873); Divine Providence (1873);
The Doctrine of Universal Restoration carefully Examined (1878); Practical Comment on the Confession
of Faith of the Church of the United Brethren in Christ
(1894); Heaven; or, that better Country (1899); and
Christian Theology (1900); and edited Christian
Doctrine. A comprehensive View of doctrinal and
practical Theology, by thirty-seven different Writers
(1889).

BIBLIOGRAPHY: H. A. Thompson, Biography of Jonathan
Weaver, Dayton, 1902.

WEBB, ALLAN BECHER: Church of England;
b. at Calcutta Oct. 6, 1839; d. at Salisbury June
12, 1907. He was educated at Corpus Christi College, Oxford (B.A., 1862; fellow of University College, 1863–67); was ordered deacon in 1863, and
ordained priest in 1864; was curate of St. Peter's-
in-the-East, Oxford (1863–64); vice-principal of
Cuddesdon (1864–67); rector of Avon Dassett,
Warwickshire (1867–70); was consecrated bishop
of Bloemfontein (1870), and was translated to the
diocese of Grahamstown (1883); he was assistant
bishop of Moray and Brechin (1898–1900), as
well as provost of Inverness Cathedral, and since
1901 has been dean of Salisbury. He has written
Presence and Office of the Holy Spirit (London,
1881); Sisterhood Life and Woman's Work (1883);

The Minister of the True Tabernacle: Thoughts
and Suggestions for the Eve of Ordination (1888);
The Priesthood of the Laity in the Body of Christ
(1889); Life of Service before the Throne (1897);
Unveiling of the Eternal Word (1898); With Christ in
Paradise (1898).

WEBB, ROBERT ALEXANDER: Presbyterian;
b. at Oxford, Miss., Sept. 20, 1856. He was educated at Southwestern Presbyterian University,
Clarksville, Tenn. (A.B., 1877), and at the Columbia
(S. C.) Theological Seminary (graduated, 1880).
After holding pastorates in his denomination at
Bethel, S. C. (1882–87), Davidson, N. C. (1887–88),
and Westminster Church, Charleston, S. C. (1888–
1892), he became professor of systematic theology in
Southwestern Presbyterian University (1892), and
of apologetics and systematic theology (1908).

WEBB, THOMAS: Methodist pioneer, layman;
b. in England about 1724; d. at Portland, England,
Dec. 20, 1796. He was a man of wealth and position, and an officer in the British army; he was
present at the storming of the French fort of Louis-
burg, Nova Scotia, in 1758, was one of the survivors
of Braddock's defeat in 1755, and was present at
the scaling of the Heights of Abraham at Quebec in
1759. He was converted under the preaching of
John Wesley at Bristol in 1765, united with the
Methodists, and soon after became a local preacher;
about 1766 he was in charge of the barracks at Albany, when an attempt was being made to found
Methodism in New York; he visited the city, became exceedingly active and acceptable as a preacher, and aided financially and in other ways in securing the site for the John Street Church; visited
Philadelphia and organized there a Methodist
church, in 1769 contributing to the purchase of St.
George's Church in that city. In the interest of religion and Methodism he visited Long Island, New
Jersey, Delaware, and Maryland. In 1772 he went
to England in order to secure ministers for the denomination, returning the next year with three men
for work in America. On his return to England he
settled at Portland, but continued active as an open-
air preacher, and was also known for his philanthropic efforts in behalf of French prisoners of war
and for the soldiers and sailors stationed at Portsmouth. His activities were commended by John
Wesley, though Charles had a less favorable opinion
of his work.

BIBLIOGRAPHY: C. Atmore, Methodist Memorial, Bristol,
1801–02; A. Stevens, Hist. of the Religious Movement . . .
Called Methodism, i. 427, iii. 99, New York, 1858–61;
idem, Hist. of the Methodist Episcopal Church, vol. iv.,
passim, ib. 1864; W. B. Sprague, Annals of the American
Pulpit, vii. 5–7, ib. 1861; J. Porter, Comprehensive Hist.
of Methodism, pp. 247–250, 261, Cincinnati, 1876; J. M.
Buckley, in American Church History Series, v. 103–107
et passim, New York, 1896.

WEBB, WILLIAM WALTER: Protestant Episcopal bishop of Milwaukee; b. at Germantown, Pa.,
Nov. 20, 1857. He was educated at the University
of Pennsylvania (1877–79), Trinity College, Hartford, Conn. (A.B., 1882), and Berkeley Divinity
School, Middletown, Conn. (graduated, 1885).
After being curate of Trinity Church, Middletown
(1885–86), and of the Church of the Evangelists,
Philadelphia (1886–89), he was rector of St. Eliza-

beth's, Philadelphia (1889–92); professor of dogmatic and moral theology in Nashotah House, Nashotah, Wis. (1892–97), and president (1897–1906); was consecrated bishop coadjutor of Milwaukee (1906), succeeding to the full administration of the diocese within the year. He was also canon of All Saints' Cathedral, Milwaukee (1892–1906), and president of the Standing Committee of the diocese of Milwaukee (1896–1906). In theology he is a High-churchman of the Anglo-Catholic school, and has written *Guide to Seminarians* (New York, 1889), and *The Cure of Souls* (Milwaukee, 1892, 2d ed., 1910).

WEBB-PEPLOE, HANMER WILLIAM: Church of England; b. at Weobley (47 m. s.w. of Birmingham) Oct. 1, 1837. He received his education at Marlborough College (1848–51), Cheltenham College (1851–56), and Pembroke College, Cambridge (B.A., 1859; M.A., 1878); was ordained deacon 1863 and priest the same year; was curate of Weobley, 1863–66; chaplain of Weobley Union, 1863–76; vicar of Kings Pyon cum Birley, 1866–76; and of St. Paul's, Onslow Square, 1876 sqq.; and has been prebendary of St. Paul's Cathedral since 1893. Among his other services are those he has rendered as Cambridge University select preacher, 1896; president of the Barbican Mission to the Jews, and of the London Clerical and Lay Union; chairman of the Council of the National Church League; vice-president of the Church Missionary Society, Protestant Reformation Society, Missions to Seamen, and the Spanish and Portuguese Church Aid Society; and chairman of the Waldensian Church Mission. He is "a stanch upholder of the Protestant and Evangelical position of the Church of England as bequeathed to us from the Reformation; a strong believer in the absolute inspiration of every part of the Bible . . ., and an earnest upholder of the divinity of Jesus Christ and of his birth by the Holy Ghost, and of the atonement made by him for the sin of the world." He has written: *I Follow after* (London, 1894); *All One; Sermons* (1896); *Life of Privilege* (1896); *Victorious Life* (1896); *Calls to Holiness* (1900); *Within and Without* (1900); *Titles of Jehovah* (1901); *Four Remarkable Letters of St. Paul's* (1903); *He Cometh* (1905); *Consider him; or, Sketches of the Four Gospels* (1906); and *The Beautiful Name* (1910).

WEBER, vê'ber, LUDWIG: Lutheran pastor; b. at Schwelm (28 m. n.e. of Cologne) Apr. 2, 1846. He received his education at the gymnasium in Marienwerder and at the universities of Bonn, Berlin, and Erlangen; was pastor at Iserlohn, 1871–73; at Dellwig, 1873–81; and at Gladbach from 1881 to the present. He describes himself as a "positive Biblical Lutheran." He is the author of *Der lebendige Gott in seiner Schöpfung* (Bonn, 1886); *Behandlung der socialen Frage auf evangelischer Seite* (1888); *Ansprachen für evangelische Arbeiter-, Bürger-, und Volksvereine* (Hattingen, 1890; greatly enlarged, Gütersloh, 1891, and often republished); *Christus ist unser Friede* (Göttingen, 1892); *Geschichte der sittlich reliögisen und sozialen Entwickelung Deutschlands in den letzten 35 Jahren* (Gütersloh, 1895); *Friede sei mit diesem Hause. Predigt- und Andachtsbuch*

(Dresden, 1899–1900); *Die religiöse Entwickelung der Menschheit im Spiegel der Weltlitteratur* (Gütersloh, 1901); *Soziales Handbuch* (Hamburg, 1907); *Alkohol und soziale Verhältnisse* (1908); and a long series of occasional lectures published in various collections.

WEBER, SIMON: German Roman Catholic; b. at Bohlingen (a village near Radolfzell, 17 m. n.w. of Constance), Baden, Jan. 1, 1866. He was educated at the University of Freiburg, St. Peter's seminary for priests, Rome, the College of St. Thomas Aquinas, Rome, and the Academy of St. Apollinaris, Rome (D.D., Rome, 1894); was vicar of Offenburg, Baden (1891–94); curate at Wollmatingen, Baden (1894–96); privat-docent at the University of Freiburg (1896–98); became associate professor of apologetics in 1898, and of the New Testament in 1908. Besides preparing the fifth edition of C. H. Vosen's *Das Christentum und die Einsprüche seiner Gegner* (Freiburg, 1905), he has written *Jesus taufte, Untersuchung zu Joh. iii. 22* (Offenburg, 1895); *Evangelium und Arbeit, Erwägungen über die wirtschaftliche Segungen der Lehre Jesu* (Freiburg, 1898); *Der Gottesbeweis aus der Bewegung bei Thomas von Aquin* (1902); *Die katholische Kirche in Armenien, ihre Begründung und Entwicklung vor der Trennung* (1903); *Christliche Apologetik in Grundzügen* (1907); and *Die katholische Kirche die wahre Kirche Christi* (1907).

WEBER, VALENTIN: German evangelical; b. at Aschaffenburg (22 m. s.e. of Frankfort) Apr. 1, 1858. He received his education at the University of Würzburg, 1877–81; served as chaplain, 1881–86; was prefect at the Julianum of Würzburg, 1886–88; traveled for the next two years, and then was prefect in Aufsees-Seminar at Bamberg; became gymnasial professor at Straubing, 1891; and took up the duties of his present position as professor of New-Testament exegesis at the University of Würzburg, 1896. He is the author of *Kritische Geschichte der Exegese des 9. Kapitels . . . des Römerbriefes bis auf Chrysostomus und Augustinus* (Würzburg, 1889); *Die Addressaten des Galaterbriefes. Beweis der rein-südgalatischen Theorie* (Ravensburg, 1900); *Die Abfassung des Galaterbriefs vor dem Apostelkonzil. Grundlegende Untersuchungen zur Geschichte des Urchristentums und des Lebens Pauli* (1900); and a commentary on the epistle to the Galatians (1901).

WEDDING CUSTOMS. See Marriage, I., § 11.

WEED, EDWIN GARDNER: Protestant Episcopal bishop of Florida; b. at Savannah, Ga., July 23, 1847. He was educated at the University of Georgia and the University of Berlin, after which he was graduated from the General Theological Seminary in 1870. He was ordered deacon in the same year and was advanced to the priesthood in 1871; was rector of the Church of the Good Shepherd, Summerville, Ga., until 1886, when he was consecrated bishop of Florida.

BIBLIOGRAPHY: W. S. Perry, *The Episcopate in America*, p. 295, New York, 1895.

WEEK: Properly a period of seven days in which each day has its definite place; in a wider sense the week is a subdivision of the month which may not contain exactly seven days. The week in its proper sense is now in general use among Christian peoples, but in antiquity was found only among the Hebrews, and about the Christian era among the astrologers of the East. The Hebrew week was based upon the Sabbath of Yahweh (see SABBATH); the astrological week depended upon the conception that each day in turn was controlled by the "seven planets," the sun, moon, Mars, Mercury, Jupiter, Venus, Saturn. In the first Christian centuries these two conceptions were combined in such a way that Saturn's day coincided with the Sabbath. The seven-day week was not found among other ancient peoples than the Hebrews, but smaller divisions of time based on a division of the month were the Greek and Egyptian, by which the month fell into three parts, and the Indian, into two. The Avesta calendar divided the month into two parts of fourteen and sixteen days each, possibly these subdivided into two periods of seven and eight days each. The Chinese had a sixty-day period. The Mexicans divided the year into eighteen months of twenty days each, and the Romans had a sort of eight-day period, the eighth being market-day. Yet even the Babylonians did not have a seven-day week, though the seventh, fourteenth, twenty-first, and twenty-eighth days were "evil days," when fresh bread, fresh roasted meats, fresh clothing, and the like were unlawful for "the shepherd of the great people" (the king?). But of a week proper there was no knowledge, as is shown by the incommensurability of the week and the month. In Cappadocian tablets appears a week of five days, and in Babylonian tablets there are traces of an astronomical division of the month into six and the year into seventy-two five-day periods.

While, then, a regularly ordered week of seven days was in antiquity limited to the Hebrews, the employment of seven-day periods was much wider, owing to the setting of special mystical value upon the number seven. Thus the continuation of festivities in Babylonia for seven days is an instance; and such a period is of frequent mention in the Old Testament for the Hebrews (e.g., Gen. vii. 4, l. 10; Ex. vii. 25; Josh. vi. 4, 15, etc.). Among the Persians and in ancient India the seven-day duration was common for celebrations; the same is true of the ancient Germans, where it was very usual, while seven-day and seven-year periods were known to the early Greeks. But the Hebrew week does not range itself with these. It is not probable that the seven-day period of Babylonia is to be traced to a quartering of the month first, and then to a relationship with seven. A favorite method of explaining the seven-day period is by referring it to the seven planets; but the reckoning of just seven planets is less common than the high estimation placed upon the number seven. In Babylonia the reckoning of seven planets can not be proved for a high antiquity; and a connection of the Hebrew week with the planets is untenable. Nor can the holiness of the number seven be connected with the Pleiades. Yet that the valuation of this number was heightened by the number of planets known and of the Pleiades is clear. The basis of the value placed on sevens must have a more general ground. This is found in the number itself and its qualities

—it is a number in itself representing a comprehensible magnitude not too large yet large enough for common life relationships. Four, five, six, are too small, too common, to carry the idea of mystical holiness; eight (twice four) and ten (twice five) are too common and too obviously transparent; nine approaches the value placed on seven as the square of a sacred number; eleven is too large. But seven is a prime number, its magnitude easily comprehensible yet large enough to be useful. A heightening of the value may have come about through the coincidence of the seven-day periods of the moon, and through observation of like periods in sickness, to say nothing of the planets and the Pleiades. With the planetary week the Hebrew week had originally no connection; indeed, an early age for the relation of the week to the number of planets is not yet proved and does not appear in the cuneiform tablets, certainly not in the order now followed of sun, moon, Mars, Mercury, Jupiter, Venus, Saturn. But other principles of arrangement are discoverable, for instance, that of assumed distance from the earth. The planets were also connected with certain hours of the day in turn. While Dio Cassius attributed the conception that the planets ruled the days to the Egyptians, in reality it came from Babylonia, the motherland of astrology. Rising there in the century before Christ, it spread into the Roman Empire. In the cuneiform tablets nothing has yet been found of the regularly alternating governing of the days by the planets, nor of the arrangement of the planets according to their distance from the earth. The Babylonian arrangement is often moon, sun, Jupiter, Venus, Saturn, Mercury, and Mars; earlier still, moon, sun, Mercury, Venus, Mars, Jupiter, and Saturn. The planet-week arose then among the astrologers of Hellenistic times.

The Jews designated other days than the Sabbath by numbers (cf. Matt. xxviii. 1; Acts xx. 7), and outside of the Sabbath only the sixth day as the day of preparation received a special designation, the Greek equivalent being *prosabbaton* (in the title of Ps. xcii. and Mark xv. 42), alongside of which stood the term *paraskeuē*, and this appears in a rescript of Augustus releasing the Jews from the necessity of appearing before the court on that day. The Christians, who took over the Jewish week, gave to the first day, on which they assembled to break bread, the name "the Lord's day" (*Hē kyriakē hēmera;* e.g., Ignatius, *Ad Magnesios,* ix.; Didache, xiv. 1); but in general they designated the days by numbers, using the Jewish terms as above for the sixth and seventh days. The names given to the days from the planets, which came into common use in the first pre-Christian century, were avoided by the Christians; Justin (*I Apol.,* lxvii.) and Tertullian employed them only in order to make their meaning clear to the non-Christians whom they addressed. Not till after the middle of the third century did the ordinary designation become common among Christians, and then for two centuries more only in the West and in Egypt. But the astrological conception of control of the days or of planetary influence upon them found entrance also, the idea being not that heathen deities were powerful, but that manticism was possible by this means. Still the official language of the Church avoided the names derived from the planets, except that *dies solis* (" day of the sun ") was used, and the use of numerals was constant. In ordinary life, however, even Christians employed the common designation derived from the names of the planets. (W. LOTZ.)

BIBLIOGRAPHY: C. L. Ideler, *Handbuch der . . . Chronologie*, i. 279 sqq., Berlin, 1825; E. Schrader, in *TSK*, 1874, pp. 343–353; E. Mayer, in *ZDMG*, xxxvii (1883), 453–455; F. Hommel, *Aufsätze und Abhandlungen*, pp. 373 sqq., Leipsic, 1892 sqq.; H. Winckler, *Altorientalische Forschungen*, ii. 91 sqq., 354 sqq., iii. 179 sqq., Leipsic, 1898–1902; idem, *Religionsgeschichtlicher und alter Orient*, pp. 58 sqq., ib. 1906; P. Jensen, in *Zeitschrift für deutsche Wortforschung*, i (1900), 150–160; G. Schiaparelli, *Die Astronomie im Alten Testament*, pp. 114–121, Giessen, 1904, Eng. transl., London, 1905; J. Meinhold, *Sabbat und Woche im A. T.*, Göttingen, 1905; F. K. Ginzel, *Handbuch der . . . Chronologie*, i. 94, Leipsic, 1906; A. Jeremias, *Das A. T. im Lichte des alten Orients*, pp. 182–188, Leipsic, 1906, Eng. transl., 2 vols., London, 1911; J. Hehn, *Siebenzahl und Sabbat bei den Babyloniern und im A. T.*, Leipsic, 1907; Schrader, *KAT*, pp. 620 sqq.; Benzinger, *Archäologie*, passim (consult Index under " Woche," " Wochenfest "); and literature under MOON; SABBATH; and YEAR.

WEEKS, FEAST OF. See PENTECOST, I.

WEGSCHEIDER, vêh′shai-der, **JULIUS AUGUST LUDWIG:** German rationalistic theologian; b. at Küblingen (20 m. e. of Brunswick) Sept. 17, 1771; d. at Halle Jan. 27, 1849. He received his preliminary education in the Helmstedt Pädagogium and at the Carolinum in Brunswick; was tutor in the family of a Hamburg merchant (1795–1805), and during this period studied Kant, to whom were devoted his first writings, *Ethices Stoicorum recentiorum fundamenta cum ethicis principiis, quæ critica rationis practicæ secundum Kantium exhibet, comparata* (Hamburg, 1797;) and *Versuch, die Hauptsätze der philosophischen Religionslehre in Predigten darzustellen* (1797). Wegscheider was principally attracted by Kant's rational analysis of religion and morals, and wrote on this subject *Ueber die von der neuesten Philosophie geforderte Trennung der Moral von der Religion* (1804). In 1805 Wegscheider became privat-docent at the University of Göttingen; in 1806 professor of theology and philosophy in Rinteln, and in 1810, after the suppression of this university, professor of theology in Halle. Here he was influential and popular as a teacher almost until his death.

Of Wegscheider's works on New-Testament subjects, the *Versuch einer vollständigen Einleitung in das Evangelium des Johannes* (1806) defends the authenticity of the Fourth Gospel; as does his *Der I. Brief des Apostel Paulus an den Timotheus* (1810) that of Timothy. His principal work, however, is *Institutiones theologiæ Christianæ dogmaticæ, addita dogmatum singulorum historia et censura* (1815), the standard dogmatic work of rationalism. The volume is not distinguished by originality of thought, and is based on the *Lineamenta institutionum fidei Christianæ* of Wegscheider's teacher Henke, and upon Ammon's *Summa theologiæ Christianæ*. Its value consists in its clear presentation of rationalistic dogmatics and in the consequent yet moderate assertion of rationalistic premises. Wegscheider judges the traditional material of Christian dogma-

tics by the standard of reason, rejecting everything as untrue that does not stand this test. He held that there were several types of doctrine contained in the Bible, suited to different periods, and that one of these, of more simple and sane character, is good for all time. To him the most important part of dogmatics is that relating to the concept of God. No single proof of God's existence is sufficient to enforce belief; but taken together they do away with all doubt, so that nothing more absurd than atheism can be conceived. A supernatural revelation was impossible, there could only be a mediate one. Jesus is the supreme messenger of God, founder of his kingdom, and a sublime example for mankind. But his resurrection is to be taken simply as a resuscitation from a trance (though this idea is cautiously insinuated); the Biblical authors wrote " not without inspiration," but they often accommodated themselves to the prejudices of their time and even shared them. The conceptions to be rejected by the " more liberal doctrine " of the present are miracles, angels, devils, original sin, and a sensuous eschatology. Wegscheider was uninfluenced by idealism, and rejected the ideas of God advanced by Fichte, Hegel, and Schelling. He was accused of heresy but acquitted. After Tholuck's work began at Halle in 1826, Wegscheider's popularity waned. In his later years he was interested in the Friends of Light (see FREE CONGREGATIONS IN GERMANY).

(HEINRICH HOFFMANN.)

BIBLIOGRAPHY: W. Steiger, *Kritik des Rationalismus in Wegscheiders Dogmatik*, Berlin, 1830; W. Gass, *Geschichte der protestantischen Dogmatik*, iv. 458 sqq., Berlin, 1867; G. Frank, *Geschichte der protestantischen Theologie*, iii. 337–338, Leipsic, 1875; K. von Hase, *Gesammelte Werke*, viii. 66 sqq., 337 sqq., ib. 1892; W. Schrader, *Geschichte der Friedrichs-Universität zu Halle*, ii. 24, 127 sqq., 165 sqq., Berlin, 1894; J. F. Hurst, *Hist. of Rationalism*, rev. ed., New York, 1902; *ADB*, vol. xli. Some of the literature under RATIONALISM will also furnish information.

WEIDNER, REVERE FRANKLIN: Lutheran; b. at Center Valley, Pa., Nov. 22, 1851. He was graduated from Muhlenberg College, Allentown, Pa. (A.B., 1869), and the Lutheran Theological Seminary, Philadelphia (1873); was Lutheran pastor at Phillipsburg, Pa. (1873–78), and also professor of English, logic, and history in Muhlenberg College (1875–77); pastor in Philadelphia (1878–82); professor of dogmatics and exegesis at Augustana Theological Seminary (Swedish Lutheran), Rock Island, Ill. (1882–91); professor of dogmatic theology in Rock Island and Chicago (1891–94); and since 1891 president and professor of dogmatic theology in the Evangelical Lutheran Theological Seminary, Chicago. In theology he describes himself as an " Evangelical Lutheran, strictly confessional and very conservative." He has written *Luther's Small Catechism* (Philadelphia, 1880); *Commentary on the Gospel of Mark* (1881); *Theological Encyclopaedia and Methodology* (3 vols., Chicago, 1885–91, new ed., 1911); *Biblical Theology of the Old Testament* (1886); *Introduction to Dogmatic Theology* (1888); *Introductory New Testament Greek Method* (New York, 1889); *Studies in the Book* (5 vols., Chicago, 1890–1903); *Biblical Theology of the New Testament* (2 vols., 1891); *Christian Ethics* (1891); *Examination Questions in Church History and Christian Archæology* (1893);

Annotations on the General Epistles (New York, 1897); *Annotations on Revelation* (1898); *Theologia: or, The Doctrine of God* (Chicago, 1903); *Ecclesiologia: or, The Doctrine of the Church* (1903); and *The Doctrine of the Ministry* (1907).

WEIGEL, vai'gel, VALENTIN.

Life (§ 1).
Writings (§ 2).
Doctrine of Space and Time (§ 3).
Theory of Knowledge (§ 4).
Doctrine of God (§ 5).
Relations with Christianity (§ 6).

Valentin Weigel, the German mystic and pantheist, was born at Naundorf (near Grossenhain, 50 m. e. of Leipsic) in 1533, and died at Zschopau (51 m. s.e. of Leipsic) June 10, 1588. He studied at Leipsic and also at Wittenberg in 1564,

1. Life. where he appears to have given instruction to students. In 1567 he was called as pastor to the town of Zschopau, and, while engaged in the visitations incidental to his superintendency, often officiated as adjunct pastor in several parishes. In this work he acquired an enviable repute by his preaching, cure of souls, administration, and care of the poor. Though he was charged in 1572 with holding impure doctrine, he cleared himself promptly and successfully, and subscribed the Formula of Concord without hesitation. It transpired only after his death that he was wholly at variance with the doctrine of his church, an attitude which developed during his pastoral office, the logical consequences of which he strenuously denied.

The first impressions of Weigel's writings appeared at Halle, 1609–14; additional writings and new editions were issued at " Neustadt," 1618 (Neustadt

2. Writings. may be either Magdeburg or Halle), and again at the close of the seventeenth century at Amsterdam and Frankfort. It is possible that Weigel's writings have undergone alterations in even their manuscript stage, and that particular portions among the printed works ascribed to him may have been derived from other hands. The following writings may be pronounced genuine: (1) *Gnothe Seauton* (Neustadt, 1615; only the first part; the second and third parts are spurious); (2) *Ein schön Gebetbüchlein* (1613); (3) *Ein nützliches Tractätlein vom Ort der Welt* (1613); (4) *Der Güldene Griff* (Halle, 1613); (5) *Dialogus de Christianismo* (Neustadt, 1616; his most important and best work). The following are not genuine: *Studium universale*, hitherto much in vogue for knowledge of Weigel's theories; *Von der Gelassenheit* (contains a slightly altered edition of a writing by Carlstadt; cf. Wernle in *ZKG*, 1903, p. 319); the so-called *Theologia Weigelii*. On the other hand, a work cited with notable frequency, *Kirchen- oder Hauspostil/ Uber die Sontags und fürnembsten Fest/ Evangelien durchs gantze Jahr* (1609), probably embodies genuine sermons of Weigel's. Notwithstanding these uncertainties of authorship, the number of the genuine and printed writings of Weigel's is ample enough to afford a truthful picture of his views in all principal questions. In accord with his maxim of deriving everything from the " inner light," and his contempt for all books, Weigel

effaced, almost beyond recovery, the historical sources and points of contact for his reflections. Moreover, he possessed the faculty of largely recasting what he acquired, imparting to the same an air of originality. What dependency he acknowledges is toward ancient and medieval writings— Plato, Dionysius the Areopagite, Thomas à Kempis, Tauler, Eckart, and *Theologia Germanica* (q.v.); the last is by far the most frequently cited. With reference to the Reformers and the earliest confessional documents his pronouncements are generally quite unfriendly. Osiander, Schwenckfeld, Münzer, and others, he declines to know and likewise disclaims all affinity with them; but he adverts to S. Frank's *Weltbuch*. While he frequently cites Paracelsus, it is mostly upon astronomical and astrological speculations, medicine, and natural philosophy (cf. e.g., *Libell. disput.*, p. 26).

Weigel cultivated both philosophy and theology, and placed the two in very intimate connection. His fundamental trend in philosophy might be styled subjective idealism, treating his subjects with a lucidity far in advance of his time.

3. Doctrine of Space and Time. His real significance for the history of philosophy has not yet been fully realized. He examined the problems of space and time, and furnished a subjectively idealistic solution. He treats of space in *Vom Ort der Welt*, chap. x. (Hall, Saxony, 1613); and his conclusion is comprehended in the proposition: " for outside the world is no place, with finite dimensions, . . . hence it is certain that the world stands at no local site; the world itself is a place and concept of all places and bounded things. Therefore it is only according to their contained bounds within the world that places are indicated, but never outside the world." The theological deduction drawn is that " neither heaven nor hell is a bounding physical place," but that " every one bears hell about in himself among the damned; likewise every one bears heaven about in himself among the saints " (chap. xiv.). In the same way, the local conception of Christ's descending into hell and his ascension to heaven must logically lapse (chap. xvi.). Weigel also contests, though not quite so decidedly and clearly, the reality of the time idea; for although the point is not certainly resolvable, how far genuine Weigelian thoughts exist in the treatise devoted to this question, *Scholasterium Christianum*, still the negative opinion appears implied.

His most incisive speculation dealt repeatedly with the question of the practical entity of knowledge, and emphasized the subjective root thereof.

4. Theory of Knowledge. For " the natural discernment passing from the eye to the object is active, and not passive; and therefore all judgment is exercised in the act of discerning or knowing, and rests not in the thing discerned " (*Kurtzer Bericht vom Wege und Weise all Dinge zu erkennen*, B iii. 2 v.). " All knowledge emanates from the knower " (ib. B 1 v.). Everything inheres latently in man, in his personality and subjectivity. " Hence man is also everything himself; what he can and knows, to know and control his art, is his ' spirit ' (*Geist*), or spiritual, intellectual faculty; and this ' spirit ' or faculty is man himself " (*Gnothe Seauton*, p. 39). Therefore there is but one discerning principle and one corresponding task, viz., to know oneself. As main support for his theory, he adduces the proper distinction of knowledge: "for if discernment emanated and issued from the object, and not from the seeing eye, then there must also follow similar and equivalent perceptiveness or discernment from an object itself: be the matter of eyes howsoever it would " (p. 28). From this natural knowledge and its conscious, practical entity, Weigel distinguishes a " supernatural " knowledge by the fact that man's part in the inception and outcome is aroused by means of the object. Only here, in turn, the process rests in the subject's productivity: save that this now becomes identified with the indwelling Spirit of God. Consequently, Weigel affiliates with those men who define the principle of religious knowledge and spiritual potency as the inward natural possession of every man; and he advocates the theory of the inner word, or of the spirit in its naturalistic form. Weigel deduces all the negative consequences of this view, such as rejection of the word of Scripture, mediating office, or channels of grace, the preaching office, external church fellowship, learned theological study with all its pains, but most of all, the conditioning of religious notions and piety about a defined historical point of departure, like that in Christianity. In place of this, he elaborated a pantheistic and gnostic theosophy on vast lines, merely assimilating his vocabulary to Christian terminology. His main outlines are as follows:

God and the All are coincident in the present. Not every existence of God before the world is to be necessarily denied, but God comes to himself, to

5. Doctrine personal and active being, primarily
of God. in and with the world. "Absolutely alone and for himself, apart from all creatures, God is and continues impersonal, detached from time and place, void of energy, will, and feeling; and so he is neither Father, nor Son, nor Holy Ghost. God is eternity itself, apart from time; he hovers and abides in himself about all places; neither works nor wills nor desires, save that in, with, and through the creature he becomes personally effectual, volitional, desirous; he acquires emotion, or suffers the attributes of persons and feeling to be assigned to him " (from the manuscript: *Von der Seligmachenden erkentnus Gottes*). This immanency of God is differentiated only as the matter is one of good or of evil, of the outward world or of men, the kingdom of nature or that of grace. While ideas of chaos, or the negation of the cosmic order, as also the assumption of an eternity, or of a gradual emanation of the world through intermediate stages, do not appear sharply and consistently developed, evil is regarded as a necessary concomitant phenomenon of the creature state of being. The essence of sin is qualified, in one passage, as a " non-existent "; and again, as the independent will of the creature. Therefore the goal and purpose of the " redemption " is also to complement and complete the nonexistent with the divine perfect existence, and to induct and restore the individual will back to the will of God (*Vom Ort der Welt*, chap. xvii.). More-

over, from the beginning God has implanted in man the requisite powers to this intent, so that the " redemption " simply fulfils itself in that process whereby the inner principle in man which is akin to God gains the ascendency over the creature element which is averse toward God. The necessary antecedent condition, and the best means of advancing the advent of this interior process of redemption is resignation, the suppression of the individual will— a virtue which he extols and recommends in the usual formulas of medieval mysticism.

Nevertheless, this simple and consistent rational structure grows involved and confused by its assimilation to the central Christian ideas, the more so

6. Relations because these are stripped, as far as
with Chris- possible, of their historic origin and
tianity. external content. The divine principle in man, as imparted to every one by nature, becomes identified with Christ, especially where fruitfully developed. Christ is an inward, natural factor, without historical import. Only Weigel allows the virtual existence of an external historic Christ, which, however, has no redemptive significance. The formulas of the doctrine of the dual nature were so reconstrued by Weigel that he distinguishes a double " body " of Christ, according to his composite origin; though this, in Weigel's view, virtually covers the total phenomenon of Christ. " The one only Christ has two bodies; the divine body from the Holy Ghost, and the other body from the Virgin Mary, which is visible and mortal " (*Postille*, i. 214 sqq., cf. p. 38). Christ has his true flesh and blood " not from the earth, but from heaven; not from Adam, but from the Holy Ghost " (*Dialogus*, p. 12). Thus Weigel is enabled to emphasize the presence of the " body and blood of Christ " in the Communion. What concerns him is the inner presence of the eternal divine principle of Christ. The same parallel applies to his application of the several concepts of spirit, regeneration, and faith; these all are but new, somewhat modified or qualified formulas for the same topical consideration; that is, for the inner evolutionary process of the divine element and its victory over the creature element. Thus in the moral domain he advocates the fundamental tenets of enthusiasts (*Dialogus*, p. 76). All problems of a concrete phase in individual and social ethics are resolved on quietistic lines with rigorous consistency. He pronounces against all lawsuits, penalties, wars, trade, receiving of interest, and the like.

Weigel was not a renewer of Reformation ideas. With these, in fact, he had nothing to do; his few conceptions which are concordant with the Reformation explain themselves by their parallel relations in a mystical vein. Just as little does he belong to the line of adherents to historical Christianity, since of this he retained merely the husks. He belongs rather to the perpetual chain of thinkers along gnosticizing, mystic, and pantheistic lines; he also paved the way toward the modern elaboration and recasting of lines of thought in the direction of monistic idealism, and in terms of critical reasoning. Though his own times opposed him, his significance was not yet realized. Real opposition to him began about the end of the sixteenth century.

Apparently he left no compacted school, though his opponents charged him with having that purpose. At any rate, "Weigelianism" soon united with the most heterogeneous anti-ecclesiastical and "enthusiastic" trends of both older and younger date, as with the admirers of J. Böhme, and also with the movement comprehended under the term "Rosicrucian" (see ROSICRUCIANS).

R. H. GRÜTZMACHER.

BIBLIOGRAPHY: A. C. Rotth, *Nöthiger Unterricht von prophetischen Weissagungen*, Leipsic, 1694; *Vitam fata et scripta V. Weigelii ex genuinis monumentis comprobata . . . submittit . . . J. G. Reichelius*, Wittenberg, 1721; G. Arnold, *Kirchen- und Ketzerhistorie*, vol. xvii., chap. xv., Frankfort, 1729; J. G. Walch, *Religionsstreitigkeiten*, vols. iv.–v., Jena, 1736; J. O. Opel, *V. Weigel, ein Beitrag zur Litteratur- und Kulturgeschichte Deutschlands im 17. Jahrhundert*, Leipsic, 1864; A. Israel, *M. V. Weigels Leben und Schriften*, Zschopau, 1888; R. H. Grützmacher, *Wort und Geist*, § 19, Leipsic, 1902; *ADB*, vol. xli.

WEIGHTS AND MEASURES, HEBREW.

I. Measures of Length: As in modern systems of measures, so in the ancient, measures of length furnished the basis. The original units of measurement were taken by man from his own body—fingerbreadth, hand-breadth, span, arm, foot, and step, and these are found among all peoples.

1. Basis and Development of Systems. But such measures are only relative, since the bases are not of the same absolute length in different individuals. There was therefore need for an artificial normalization in order to obtain from these relative measures an absolute, secure, and generally applicable measure. This normalization has naturally worked out in different ways among different peoples, so far as they have not borrowed one from another. And yet this process of borrowing has been very extensive. The various systems of weights, measures, and coinage known to us as used in the ancient world appear to go back to the same fundamental system. But whether this fundamental system was of Babylonian or of Egyptian parentage is a question which has of late years once more come to the front; though it must not be forgotten that Egyptian culture was not uninfluenced by the Babylonian. The conclusion must be that the basis for the system of weights and measures used in Hither Asia was given in Babylonia; but again this does not exclude modification of this or that particular measure so as to agree more closely with Egyptian than with Babylonian norms. The system of Hebrew weights and measures can not be considered as a thing apart and by itself; it must be studied in connection with the varied systems in use in Asia.

As instruments of measurement there are mentioned in the Old Testament the measuring reed or rod (Hebr. *keneh ḥammiddah*, also *shebeṭ*, Gk. *ḳalamos*, *kanōn*, Lat. *pertica mensoria*, Assyr. *kanu*; Ezek. xl. 3, 5, xlii. 16 sqq.; Jer. x. 16, li. 19; Rev. xi. 1), and the line (Hebr. *ḳaw*, *pethil pishtim*, *ḥebhel middah*, Septuagint *metron*, *schoinion*, *spartion*; II Kings xxi. 13; Ezek. xl. 3, xlvii. 3; **2. Basal Hebrew Measure.** II Sam. viii. 2). Of the relative size of these two instruments of measurement nothing is known, though they were doubtless related to some basal unit. There is a tradition that in the Second Temple, as at Athens and in Rome, there was deposited a measure which was the norm and an ell (cubit) in length.

In fact, among Hebrews, as in Asia generally, the cubit was the unit of length, and was designated *'ammah*. Whether this term originally meant the fore-arm is not certain; the term is found in the Siloam Inscription (q.v.), and corresponds to the Assyrian *ammatu*. The New-Testament term for the same is *pēchos* (Matt. vi. 27; Luke xii. 25; Rev. xxi. 17). This unit was employed as the basal measure in building-operations (as in the Tabernacle, the Temple, and the "house of the forest of Lebanon"; Ex. xxvi. 15 sqq.; I Kings vi. 2 sqq., vii. 2 sqq.), in the making of furniture and furnishings (I Kings vii. 23 sqq.), was applied to such materials as curtains (Ex. xxvi. 1 sqq.), and to ground measures (Ezek. xlviii. 1 sqq.); it is indeed designated the most general measure (Deut. iii. 11, "the cubit of a man," i.e., the common cubit), and upon it other units were based (Ezek. xl. 5, "a measuring reed of six cubits long by the cubit and a handbreadth," i.e., a handbreadth longer than the common cubit; the reed here is six cubits). The cubit divides into spans (Hebr. *zereth*, Ex. xxviii. 16; I Sam. xvii. 4; Ezek. xliii. 13), and this into handbreadths (Hebr. *ṭephaḥ*, I Kings vii. 26, or *ṭophaḥ*, Ex. xxv. 25, xxxvii. 12; LXX. *palaistē*); while the smallest measure is the fingerbreadth (Hebr. *'ebẓa'*, Gk. *daktylos*, Jer. lii. 21). In an ascending scale, it will be remembered, is to be placed the reed as above, which was equivalent to six cubits (Ezek. xli. 8). Mention is made once (Judges iii. 16) of a unit of measure called the *gomedh* (Judges iii. 16, "cubit"), the relation of which to the ordinary cubit is not at all defined, the Septuagint equating it with the span, the Syriac and Arabic versions with the cubit. Concerning the varied relations of the cubit to other measures (apart from the reed) nothing exact is given in the Old Testament; but there are available the rabinic statements, and, what is of still greater importance, the analogy of the entire orient, so that it is with comparative certainty ascertained that the cubit contained six handbreadths or twenty-four fingerbreadths. The following table therefore results, showing a duodecimal basis:

Reed	1	..	..	..
Cubit...............	6	1	..	..
Span	12	2	1	..
Handbreadth	36	6	3	1
Fingerbreadth	144	24	12	4

There are met in the Old Testament two different

cubits. To be sure, from the expression " cubit of a man " (ut sup.; Deut. iii. 11) one is not to expect a distinction such as between a " holy "

3. Ezekiel's and a " secular " cubit, for there is no
Two Cubits. foundation in Scripture for acceptance of the fact of a " holy " cubit, the expression " cubit of a man " having no other meaning than " common cubit " (cf. for a parallel expression, Isa. viii. 1, " man's pen "). Yet it is seen with great definiteness from Ezekiel that in his time there was in use a cubit other than that employed in an earlier period. He speaks in xl. 5, xliii. 13 of the cubit employed in measuring his temple as being a handbreadth greater than that which was in common use and was known to his readers. Apparently the exact length of his cubit is defined either because it had wholly fallen out of use or was less commonly known. The whole passage leads to the conclusion that Ezekiel's use of the longer cubit implies that this was the measure after which Solomon's Temple was constructed. Similarly the Chronicler (II Chron. iii. 3) knew that the Temple was built " by cubits after the first (i.e., old) measure." Therefore there had been an earlier and greater cubit which was superseded by the later and lesser. Unfortunately nothing is known of when and how this supersession took place, when the lesser came into recognition alongside of the larger and when it came into universal use. It has been held that the small cubit was already very early in existence, reference being made to the Siloam inscription. According to this the Siloam tunnel is 1,200 cubits long, and Conder gives the measurement as 537.60 meters; this would give for the cubit a length of .448 meter [= 17.6 inches], and this is a close approximation to the Egyptian cubit of .450 meter. However, 1,200 is a round number, and whoever knows the Siloam tunnel will regard neither the one nor the other measurement as giving so exact a result that a conclusion may be reached upon the question whether the cubit meant was the greater or the lesser. A full reserve is therefore becoming with reference to the absolute length of the older unit. And it does not follow that the lesser cubit of Ezekiel could not have been employed in the earlier period. The one indication apparently in possession is that the cubit of Ezekiel's time was divided into six handbreadths, the old cubit being one handbreadth larger, giving the proportion of 6 : 7; really, however, this is not absolutely certain, for the statement of Ezekiel may be taken to mean that the later cubit was a handbreadth smaller than the earlier, giving the relation of 5 : 6. And indeed the rabbis speak of a cubit applied to furnishings of the Temple which was five handbreadths in length and of one applied to the structure which was six in length.

These questions have interest because of the fact that for the definition of the absolute length of the Hebrew cubit recourse has to be had entirely to comparison with the Egyptian or the Babylonian cubit. No aid comes from the Old Testament. Just as from the Siloam tunnel no exact result is obtained, so fails the attempt by taking into account the brazen laver (which held 2,000 baths) to deduce the length of the cubit. No better results follow from the rabbinic assertion that the legal cubit had according to tradition the length of 144 barleycorns laid side by side. On the other hand, the size of the Babylonian and the

4. The Egyptian cubit is known. The first is
Cubit, settled by the discovery at Telloh in
Hebrew, South Babylonia (see BABYLONIA, IV.,
Egyptian, § 6) of a statue of King Gudea (see
Babylonian. BABYLONIA, VI., 3, § 3) which carries upon its knees a measure which occurs sixteen times upon the statue. This measure appears as a little unit of the length of 16.5–16.6 millimeters [the equivalent of .65845 of an inch], and this unit is doubtless the fingerbreadth which is so often mentioned in antiquity. Since in the Babylonian system the duodecimal method rules, there would be a measure sixty times the length of the unit just given, which would be 990–996 millimeters ([or 38.9 inches]; it will be noticed that there is a margin of variation or error of six millimeters). The measurement thus given is in agreement with other data; the Babylonian brick had a measurement of 330 millimeters on one side of its square surface. In all systems of the orient that are known the foot is two-thirds of the cubit; hence from the brick there could be inferred a cubit of about 495 millimeters [19.45 inches], and this is exactly half of the 990 millimeters given above (or 38.9 inches). But the Babylonians had two systems, one of which was twice the other in proportions (as appears also in the table from Senkereh, where two sets of measures are given in which this relationship exists). While the Babylonian system is sexagesimal, it is important to note, in connection with the question of the relationship of the Hebrew system to the Babylonian, that there are indications of this kind of subdivision in the Hebrew measures; the reed, Babylonian and Hebrew, is of six cubits, as opposed to the Egyptian. Taking the foot of two-thirds of a cubit into consideration, if Herodotus is right in his statement of a " royal " and a " common " cubit, the division of the cubit into twenty-four fingerbreadths follows, each of 20.6 millimeters in length. According to Herodotus, the " royal " cubit was longer by three fingerbreadths than the " common " cubit, and the foot held to this cubit the relation of 3 : 5, and this is the measure constantly met in Babylonian structures, and its length is at least 550 millimeters (21.6 inches). A cubit from Ushak in Phrygia measures 555 millimeters, and this does not greatly differ from the result of deduction from the figures of Herodotus which would make the royal cubit 556.4–557 millimeters. The Egyptian cubit does not differ much from the Babylonian royal cubit, and in Egypt also there appears a double system—a large " royal " cubit and the " common " one—the latter of six handbreadths or twenty-four fingerbreadths (= 450 millimeters [17.685 inches]), the former of seven handbreadths or twenty-eight fingerbreadths (525 millimeters [or 20.6325 inches]). At first glance one might be disposed to identify the Egyptian and the Hebrew cubit; in both the relation of the large to the small cubit is the same, as are the subdivisions. But, on the other hand, the Babylonian and the Hebrew reed correspond, while the Egyptians have a " fathom " which contains only four cubits; also, the traces of the duo-

decimal system exist in the Babylonian measures. It is therefore well as yet to be reserved in regard to the relation of the Hebrew to the Egyptian set of measures. It is of considerable significance that in the fifteenth century B.C. Babylonian culture was dominant in western Asia; on the other hand, while the Hebrew may be derived ultimately from the Babylonian, the supposition is not excluded that commerce with Egypt introduced modifications.

It is possible, then, to equate the Hebrew cubit with that of Gudea (of 495 millimeters, ut sup.; for Gudea see BABYLONIA, VI., 3, § 3), and after such a standard the Phenician owners of vessels seem to have reckoned the tonnage of their ships (their measurements reduce to a solid standard of 121.2, and the basis of a cubit of 495 millimeters gives as a result a solid standard of 121.28, and this can hardly be accidental). The larger cubit would correspond to a smaller of 424–425 millimeters, but this is not in evidence at all elsewhere. If it could be assumed that Ezekiel's expression is inexact and that the small cubit is five-sixths of the larger, the latter would then be 412.5 millimeters long (the size of the early Italian cubit, which was derived from the Babylonian). But this does not furnish satisfactory proof. In modern times standards in different places do not exactly correspond, even with the advantages of scientific methods; still less can exact correspondence be supposed for antiquity. Moreover, the " royal " cubit may have been precisely defined, yet not followed with exactness in the provinces, and in the course of time the standards may have varied considerably.

In ascending scale the Hebrews have above the cubit only the reed, which in name and proportions (six cubits) agrees with the Babylonian reed. All further designations for measures **5. Larger** of distance indicate not measures in **Measures** the strict sense of closely defined **of Length.** length, but simple approximations like our term " hour's journey " (cf. the expressions in Gen. xxxv. 16, xlviii. 7, which the Septuagint renders by *hippodromos*, " post-station," and the Syriac by *parasang;* owing to this last the expression has been taken to be equivalent to parasang, the Persian measure, = 5.67 kilometers [or nearly three and a half miles]; others take it as = 6.3 kilometers). Similarly the expression " a day's journey " which occurs so often in the Bible has no definite limits. The ordinary journey of a caravan means travel during about six to eight hours; Herodotus reckoned the day's march of Persians at 150 to 200 stadia, representing continuous travel for eight to ten hours, and of Romans at 160 stadia. The case is different with respect to the " Sabbath day's journey " (Acts i. 12; the expression does not occur in the Old Testament, though the rabbis had the expression *tehum hasshabbath*). From the prohibition to gather manna on the Sabbath or to go forth from the camp (Ex. xvi. 26 sqq.) and from the delimitation of the Levitical cities (Num. xxxv. 5) the rabbis concluded that 2,000 cubits was the utmost distance allowed for travel on the Sabbath. There was a tradition that the distance of the Tabernacle from the limits of the camp was 2,000 cubits. In the case of cities the starting-point of

measurement for the Sabbath day's journey was the outer wall; within, even were the city as large as Nineveh, it was permissible to travel without limitation. There were also casuistic methods of circumventing the rabbinic limitation to 2,000 cubits and extending it to 4,000, though the purpose for which this extension could be sought was defined within certain bounds. Similarly, a Jew who on the Sabbath was caught on a journey at a distance from a dwelling might travel more than 2,000 cubits to the nearest travelers' shelter. It seems not unlikely that this distance of 2,000 cubits corresponds to an early measurement or unit of distance; there was an Egyptian unit of 1,000 double steps, and the Talmud mentions a tradition that the Sabbath day's journey was 2,000 steps, while in the same collection pace and cubit are practical equivalents. With the inrush of Greek civilization after the time of Alexander the Great the stadion became a part of the oriental system (cf. II Macc. xi. 5, xii. 9; John vi. 19, xi. 18; Rev. xiv. 20); the Olympic stadion measured 192.27 meters [= 629.7 feet], the Attic stadion, 177.6 or 197.3 meters, according to the length given to the Attic foot. The Romans introduced their mile, with a length of 1,478.7 meters [= approximately 1,600 yards].

II. Measures of Surface: As a surface measure there appears in the Bible only the yoke (Hebr. *zemedh*), a piece of land which a man might plow in a day with a yoke of oxen. It has been compared with the Egyptian measure which Herodotus (*Hist.*, ii. 168) calls *aroura*, measuring 100 royal cubits square. But this and other comparisons with the Babylonian measures of surface are pure conjectures. A similar system of measuring land obtains among the modern fellaheen of Egypt and Palestine.

III. Measures of Capacity: While the measures for liquids (water, wine, and oil) and those for such things as meal and grain were not the same among the Hebrews, they belonged to the **1. Dry and** same system. The smallest unit, the **Liquid** multiple of which made up other meas- **Measure.** ures, was in Hebrew the *log* (Septuagint, *kotylē;* Lev. xiv. 10, 12, etc.), equivalent in volume, according to the rabbis, to six medium-sized hen's eggs. In the one passage in the Old Testament where this occurs, it is as a measure for liquids, but this does not exclude its use as a dry measure. The next measure in size mentioned in the Old Testament is the cab (Hebr. *kab;* Septuagint *kabos*), named in II Kings vi 25. Later data imply that this was used as a dry measure (Photius calls it a " measure for grain," and Hesychius one " for grain and wine "). According to Josephus, paraphrasing the passage, the cab equaled 4 log, which agrees with the Talmud when it makes a cab equal one-sixth of a seah and one-third of a hin. The latter collection divides the cab into halves, fourths, and eighths, and this in connection with II Kings vi. 25 suggests that the designation " log " was seldom in use. The omer (or homer) (Hebr. *'omer*, Septuagint *gomer;* Ex. xvi. 16) seems to have been a measure for grain, and a gloss to the passage cited makes it equal the tenth of an ephah; it is then the equivalent of the *'issaron* (Septuagint *dekaton*, Josephus, *assarōn;* Ex. xxix. 40), designated usually as " a tenth " or as the " tenth of an ephah." Josephus gives the omer as equivalent to seven Attic cotylæ (*Ant.*, III., vi. 6). The corresponding measure for liquids appears as the tenth of a bath (see below, and cf. Ezek. xlv. 14), but no proper name is given for it. For liquids the most common measure is the hin, corresponding to the ephah for dry measure. Consequently the parts or fractions are often mentioned (one-half, one-third, one-fourth, one-sixth; Ex. xxix. 40; Num. xv. 4; Ezek. iv. 11). Josephus (*Ant.*, III., viii. 3) and Jerome (on Ezek. iv. 11) define the hin as equal to two Attic *choas,* that is, to a sixth of a *metrētēs* [that is about one and one-half gallons]; this gives the equation 1 hin = 12 log = one-half seah = one-sixth bath, and the Talmud often defines the hin in this way. The corresponding dry measure is designated in Ezekiel (xlv. 13) as one-sixth of an ephah, and no proper name for this dry measure is known. The seah (Gen. xviii. 6 [A. V., " measure "]; Josephus, *Ant.*, IX., iv. 5, *saton;* Septuagint, *metron*) seems to have been a dry measure, though the Talmud knows of it as also used for liquids. From the translation by the Sep-

sages the kor appears as a dry measure. Josephus regards the kor as the equivalent of ten *medimne.* The table of measures of capacity given herewith results from the preceding discussion.

From the last series one might easily receive the impression that here is not a pure sexagesimal system, but a crossing with the decimal system. Especially does the series 1 homer = 10 **2. The Basis** ephahs = 100 omers have this appear-**Sexagesimal.** ance. But an examination of the series shows that the ephah or bath, the middle factor of the series, is in the Babylonian series purely sexagesimal, consisting of seventy-two units (the mina), and exactly so the kor consists of 720 minas, its position in the sexagesimal system making it not ten times the ephah but twelve times the *maris,* a unit which fell out of the Hebrew system; consequently the presence of what looks like the decimal system is quite fortuitous. The only remnant of the decimal system left is the issaron, ut sup.; the measures indicated by asterisks in the table below and their relations show that the issaron was not an original part of the system and is mentioned in P only, though Ezekiel has the divi-

4 log =	1 cab					
*7½ log =	*1¾ cab =	*1 omer				
12 log =	3 cab =	*1¾ omer =	1 hin			
24 log =	6 cab =	*3⅓ omer =	2 hin =	1 seah		
72 log =	18 cab =	10 omer =	6 hin =	3 seah =	1 ephah	
[360 log =	90 cab =	50 omer =	30 hin =	15 seah =	5 ephah =	1 lethekh]
720 log =	180 cab =	100 omer =	60 hin =	30 seah =	10 ephah =	2 lethekh = 1 homer

tuagint of ephah by " three measures " and of " third " in Ps. lxxx. 5 by the same word, it appears that the seah was equivalent to one-third ephah or 24 log. The dry measure most in use was the ephah, and it receives correspondingly frequent mention (Ex. xvi. 36; Lev. v. 11, etc.). The passages in the Bible indicate that in early times as in late it was in common use. Fractions of it which appear in the Old Testament are the third (Ps. lxxx. 5; disguised in the A. V. by the translation " measure ") and the sixth (Ezek. xlv. 13). The liquid measure corresponding to the ephah was the bath (e.g., I Kings vii. 36; Septuagint *batos,* or *metrētēs;* Josephus, *Ant.*, VIII., ii. 9, *bados*), and Josephus makes this equivalent to the Attic *metrētēs* (about nine gallons), while Ezekiel equates bath and ephah. A tenth is mentioned in Ezek. xlv. 14, corresponding to the tenth of an ephah, ut sup. A *lethekh* appears in Hos. iii. 2 (the only place where it is mentioned) as a dry measure (for barley), and is the equivalent of half a homer according to tradition (e.g., Septuagint *hēmikoros;* Vulg. *corus dimidius*); but it is doubtful whether a unit of this capacity existed; the Vatican manuscript has instead " bottle of wine," which better suits the context. The largest measure is the homer (Lev. xxvii. 16; Isa. v. 10); Ezekiel (xlv. 11) makes it the equivalent of ten baths and also of ten ephahs, a conclusion from which is that the homer served both for liquids and for such things as seed, as was the case with the Assyrian *imir.* According to Ezek. xlv. 14, the kor and the homer were identical measures; and in a number of pas-

sion of the bath into tenths. In Ezekiel in the same connection there is met the division of the bath into sixths, but the early division of the ephah-bath was into thirds. The bath (for liquids) does not appear to have been divided into tenths; P speaks of the hin and its parts, which are not derived from the decimal system. In dry measure, conversely, the sexagesimal seah and cab disappear and in P are displaced by the tenth of an ephah; this is probably to be placed alongside of the introduction of certain coin-values and weights in the later period. For the original system both the issaron and the lethekh are to be stricken out. A distinction of the dry measure from liquid measure results in the tables on page 291, which exhibit purely sexagesimal features. To these the modern equivalents are added.

As an assistance toward finding the absolute value of the capacity of these measures Thenius (in *TSK*, 1846, pp. 72 sqq., 297 sqq.) started with the assertion of the rabbis already noted that the vol-**3. Absolute** ume for the log was equivalent to that **Values.** of six eggs, from which he deduced that the modern equivalent of the log is .2945 liter and of the bath 20.1215 liters. But it is evident that such data afford no sure conclusion, and neither for cubit nor bath are secure data available. With regard to the origins of the Hebrew system, it is to be remembered that not merely the relative proportions of the different measures but the fundamental measure remained the same in the adoption of the system by the Hebrews. The Egyptian system can not be brought into connection here, for its standards proceed in regular geometrical ratio—1, 10, 20, 40, (80), 160 hin. The Babylonian system rests upon a sexagesimal basis; even though no direct inscriptional data confirm this, all that is known of Persian, Phenician, and Syrian-Hebrew measures of capacity is consonant with the supposition that all these systems are one in their main features with the Babylonian, the source of them all. A means of calculation is afforded by the fact that in quite early times the Babylonians defined their measures of capacity by the weight of water or wine.

lation to spices (Ex. xxx. 23), food (Ezek. iv. 10), and Absalom's hair (II Sam. xiv. 26); always the mention is of the shekel or its multiple [or parts].

1. The Shekel. As an instrument of weighing the balance is named (Hebr. *mo'zenayim*, Lev. xix. 36; Job vi. 2; Prov. xi. 1, etc.) also the Hebr. *peles*, or *ḳaneh* (Prov. xvi., 11; Isa. xlvi. 6). The weights were usually of stone (Lev. xix. 36; Deut. xxxv. 13, etc.), which lost less by abrasion and rust than metals, though lead is named in Zech. v. 7. The standard of reference was

DRY MEASURE.

```
  log   = .506 liter [=   .4 quart|
 4 log =    1 cab  =                2.024 liters [=  1.8  quarts]
24 log =    6 cab  = 1 seah=12.148 liters [= 11    quarts]
72 log =   18 cab  = 3 seah = 1    ephah =  36.44 liters [=   3  pecks]
720 log = 180 cab  = 30 seah =10   ephah =  1      homer  = 364.4 liters [= 7½ bushels]
```

LIQUID MEASURE.

```
  log   =   .506 liter [=   .4 quart]
 4 log =    1     cab  =  2.024 liters [= 2.13  quarts]
12 log =    3     cab  = 1     hin  =   6.074 liters [=  6.78 quarts]
72 log =   18     cab  = 6     hin  = 1      bath = 36.44 liters [= [10.1 gallons]
720 log = 180     cab  = 60    hin  = 10     bath = 1    kor  = 364.4 liters [= 101.4 gallons]
```

Thus the unit of the system was a measure (the Persian maris) which would contain water the equivalent in weight of a royal talent (which we would fix at 30.3 kilograms [=66.78 lbs.] were it not that the temperature of water in the East is higher than the temperature assumed in reckoning the standard liter; an approximate reckoning, taking this into account, places the value at 30.37 liters). Only approximate and theoretical conclusions may be looked for in this field. The maris was probably divided into six parts, resulting in the following table.

It is not necessary to look very far in order to see that the incorporation of the decimal system here (5 and 10 hin, 10 bath) is only apparent, and that the sexagesimal system rules; the basis is seen in

the shekel, and in II Sam. xiv. 26 the royal shekel is named; by this is meant not a special standard differing from that in common use, but the implication is rather that of a normalized standard. The priestly codex speaks of a " shekel of the sanctuary " (Ex. xxx. 13, 24, and often). The shekel is divided into halves (*beḳa'*; Gen. xxiv. 22) and fourths (I Sam. ix. 8), which are met as pieces of silver money belonging in the system of weights, since in those times a system of money [coins] had not been worked out as distinct from the system of weights. On the other hand, the " third part of a shekel " of Neh. x. 32 is rather a value than a definite weight in common use, and it is to be regarded as in connection with the introduction of a system of money. In Ezekiel (xlv. 12) there is mention of a gera (" grain ") or

```
  4 mina =    1 kapithe
 12 mina =    3 kapithe = 1 hin
 24 mina =    6 kapithe = 2 hin  = 1 saton
 60 mina =   15 kapithe = 5 hin  = 2½ sata  = 1 maris
 72 mina =   18 kapithe = 6 hin  = 3  sata  = 1⅕ maris = 1 bath
120 mina =   30 kapithe = 10 hin = 5  sata  = 2 maris  = 1⅔ bath = 1 metretes
720 mina =  180 kapithe = 60 hin = 30 sata  = 12 maris = 10 bath = 6 metretes =1 kor
```

the relations of the mina. The identity with the Hebrew system is clear, except that in the latter the measures of 160 and 120 log are missing; comparison shows that one may equate the Hebrew log with the Babylonian mina. The other possibility would be to equate the log with the sextarius, which would make the homer equal to 393.95 liters; but the very complete agreement of the Hebrew and the Babylonian systems render departure from the position taken above unnecessary.

IV. Weights: In this department also the data given by the Old Testament are scanty. Apart from connection with the noble metals, which were weighed out in payments, definition of weights is seldom found. Incidental mention is found in re-

the twentieth of a shekel as a money standard, belonging therefore to a mintage system; wherever it appears elsewhere, it is as part of a system by which payment is made on the basis of the shekel (not the silver shekel; cf. on these matters Benzinger, *Archäologie*, pp. 196 sqq.). As multiples of the shekel are named the mina (maneh) and the talent. It is interesting to note respecting the mina that before the time of Ezekiel it is not mentioned (I Kings x. 17, the *minim* of the Hebrew text is to be changed to *me'oth*, " three hundred " [shekels]), as shown by the figures in Judges viii. 26; I Sam. xvii. 5, 7; II Sam. xxi. 16, xiv. 26; II Chron. iii. 9, where the weights are given in shekels, not in minas. So in later times when the mention is of minas, the discussion is of money, not of weight pure and simple (Ezek. xlv. 12; Ezra ii. 69). It may be concluded that in the earlier period the reckoning of weights by the mina was not the usual one. Of the relation of the mina to the shekel only late data are afforded; in Ex. xxxviii. 25 the free-will offerings for the sanctuary of 603,550 individuals at half a shekel each amounted to 100 talents and 1,775 shekels, according to which the talent equaled 3,000 shekels, that is, a talent is 60 minas and a mina is 50 shekels. This is the reckoning prescribed by Ezekiel (xlv. 12), where the connection with the apparently new division of the shekel into twenty gera and the mina into 50 shekels makes the impression that Ezekiel is recommending either a new or a not-general method of reckoning for universal recognition; and this suspicion is confirmed by the history of the development of the Babylonian system of weights.

The talent (Hebrew *kikkar*, " round," Septuagint and New Testament, *talanton*) is spoken of in con-

heavy talent is reckoned as equivalent to 60,600 grams [or 133.56 lbs.], and the light or small talent at half that; the heavy mina at 1,010 grams [or about 2.214 lbs.], and the light mina at half that; and the heavy shekel at 982.4 grams [or a little less than 2 lbs.]. A reckoning is given by Lehmann (*Zeitschrift für Ethnologie*, 1889, p. 372) which makes the large mina from ten to twenty-two grams heavier. Alongside of the " royal " standard, then, was current a lighter " common " standard. From the three weights which are known as coming from about 2000 B.C. Lehmann reckons the value of the light mina at 491.2 grams, and of the heavy at 982.4 grams. The smaller corresponds exactly to the Roman pound, according to the ordinary reckoning the equivalent of 327.45 grams. It was this smaller mina which passed over to the people of Hither Asia and therefore to the Hebrews. Confirmation of the equivalents stated here is the remark of Josephus (*Ant.*, XIV., vii. 1) that the gold mina

1 shekel	= 16.37 grams	[= .5778 oz.]
60 shekels = 1	mina	=982.4 grams [= 2.165 lbs.]
3,600 shekels = 60	minas=1 talent=	58.944 kilograms [=129.9479 lbs.]

LATER AVOIRDUPOIS AND GOLD TABLE.

1 shekel	= 16.37 grams	[= .5778 oz.]
50 shekels = 1	mina	=818.60 grams [= 1.804 lbs.]
3,000 shekels = 60	minas=1 talent=	49.11 kilograms [= 108.29 lbs.]

JEWISH SILVER.

1 shekel	= 14.55 grams	[= .5136 oz.]
50 shekels = 1	mina	=727.5 grams [= 1.6 lbs.]
3,000 shekels = 60	minas=1 talent=	43.659 kilograms [= 96 lbs.]

PERSIAN SILVER.

1 shekel	= 5.61–5.73 grams	[= .178 oz.]
100 shekels = 1	mina	=561–573 grams [= 1.135 lbs.]
6,000 shekels = 60	minas=1 talent=	34.380 kilograms [= 68.1 lbs.]

nection with gold (Ex. xxv. 39 and often), silver (Ex. xxxviii. 25, and often), copper, " brass " (Ex. xxxviii. 29), and iron (I Chron. xxix.

2. The Talent; Absolute Values.

7, where all four metals are mentioned). The data in the Old Testament are too scanty to afford a secure basis for calculating either the relative or the absolute magnitude of Hebrew weights; recourse must again be had to the Babylonian system, which unquestionably was at the basis of the Hebrew system. In the sixteenth century B.C., long before the settlement of the Hebrews in Palestine, all Syria and Palestine used the Babylonian weights, the tribute to the Egyptian overlord being so reckoned. In the inscription at Karnak there is evident the transference from Babylonian to Egyptian systems, with the former as the basis. Originally in the Babylonian system of weights the sexagesimal order prevailed, and a talent was 3,600 shekels or 60 minas. The weights, found by Layard, in the shape of a lion and a duck (cf. Benzinger, *Archäologie*, p. 195) show that, as in measures of length, two systems obtained, one of them double that of the other. The weights found in the excavations are usually inscribed as so many minas " of the king." The

weighed two (Roman) pounds, the shekel therefore (one-fiftieth of a mina) was 16.37 grams, and consequently the mina of avoirdupois (of sixty shekels) would from this datum equal 982. 2 grams, almost that given above. The Hebrew shekel may therefore be set down as 16.37 grams, the avoirdupois mina (if such was in use) at 982.2 grams, and the talent as 58.944 kilograms [ut sup., where equivalents in ounces and pounds are given].

But in the course of time this system underwent change. While the talent of sixty minas remained, there is found in use among Greeks, Persians, and

3. Changes Introduced.

Hebrews the division of the mina into fifty shekels; but while the shekel retained its value, the mina and the talent were correspondingly reduced. This alteration seems to have come from a mintage system, in which reckoning was based upon the shekel. Since this was found more convenient in use, 3,000 being an easier number to reckon than 3,600, the same division passed over into the system of weights, and there came into use an avoirdupois talent of 3,000 shekels. There is here the beginning of that strife between the decimal and the sexagesimal system which has waged ever since.

Support for the former came from Egypt, mediated by the Phenicians. The influence of the decimal system is seen in the priest code, and first near the time of the exile this method made its way among the Israelites. Inasmuch as the shekel always remained the same, it is not with the change just spoken of that the priest code has to do when it speaks of the " shekel of the sanctuary." It has been suspected by some that a standard shekel was kept in the Temple. This is possible, but in any case there is not involved a " common " weight which was according to the rabbis only half as large, of which there is no other indication. Yet it is known that the silver shekel of the coinage was smaller, weighing only 14.55 grams. Since in all cases where the adjunct " of the sanctuary " is given the discussion concerns payment to the sanctuary, it would be self-evident, if nothing more were said, that the expression " shekel," without reference to the shekel of mintage, would not be understood as referring to the shekel of avoirdupois. According to the preceding, the result will be the two tables for Hebrew weights, as given on page 292.

In both systems the small mina (which was not in use by the Hebrews) was half as large.

For use in commerce as currency, if the same system applied to gold and silver, great difficulty arose on account of the ratio of value (1 : 13) which was constant in antiquity. This ratio was one which was unusable as reduced to weight. Convenience, therefore, required another basis in the reckoning of values in silver and gold, a basis which would produce an easy subdivision with reference to the gold unit and on the other hand would fit well into the system of weights. So for gold there was in use the later proportion as given in the last table. The result was twofold. There came into being a silver shekel which was a tenth of the value of the gold shekel; but among Phenicians the silver shekel was one-fifteenth of the value of the gold shekel. This gives a weight for the Babylonian shekel (one-sixtieth of the small common mina) of 10.91 grams and for the Jews of 14.55 grams (since they had not the small mina); the silver shekel of the Maccabees varies between 14.50 and 14.65 grams. The tables for Jewish and Persian silver above will afford comparison with the tables of weights.

(I. Benzinger.)

Bibliography: R. Hussey, *Essay on the Ancient Weights and Money, and the Roman and Greek Liquid Measures, with an Appendix on the Roman and Greek Foot,* Oxford, 1836; A. Böckh, *Metrologische Untersuchungen über Gewichte, Münzfüsse und Masse des Altertums,* Berlin, 1838; E. Bertheau, *Zur Geschichte der Israeliten,* Dissertation 2, Göttingen, 1842; O. Thenius, in *TSK,* 1846, parts 1–2; L. Fenner von Fennerberg, *Untersuchungen über die Längen-, Feld,- und Wegmasse des Alterthums,* Berlin, 1859; V. V. Queipo, *Essai sur les systèmes métriques et monetaires des anciens peuples,* 3 vols., Paris, 1859; L. Herzfeld, *Metrologische Voruntersuchungen zu einer Geschichte des israelitischen Handels,* 2 parts, Leipsic, 1863–1865; idem, *Handelsgeschichte der Juden des Alterthums,* pp. 171 sqq., Brunswick, 1879; J. Brandis, *Münz-, Mass-, und Gewichtwesen in Vorderasien,* Berlin, 1864; F. Hultsch, *Metrologicorum scriptorum reliquiæ,* 2 vols., Berlin, 1864–1866; idem, *Griechische und römische Metrologie,* 2d ed., ib. 1882; idem, in the *Abhandlungen* of the Royal Saxon Academy of Sciences, iv (1899); B. Zuckermann, *Das jüdische Masssystem und seine Beziehungen zum griechischen und römischen,* Breslau, 1867; J. Oppert, *L'Étalon des mesures assyriennes,* Paris, 1875; C. R. Lepsius, in the *Abhandlungen* of the Berlin Academy, 1882, nos. 39, 45; idem, *Längenmasse der Alten,* Berlin, 1884; C. Rodenbach, *Metrologie. La Coudée, étalon linéaire des Egyptiens,* Brussels, 1883; M. C. Soutzo, *Étalons pondéraux primitifs,* Paris, 1884; idem, *Recherches sur les origines de quelques poids antiques,* ib. 1895; L. Borchardt, in *SBA,* 1888, pp. 129–137; C. F. Lehmann, in the *Verhandlungen* of the Berlin Anthropological Society, 1889, pp. 245–328, 1891, pp. 515 sqq., 1893, pp. 25 sqq., 1898, pp. 216 sqq., 420 sqq.; idem, in the *Actes* of the Eighth Congress of Orientalists, Leyden, 1889, sect. 1 B, pp. 165 sqq.; idem, in the *Verhandlungen* of the Berlin Physical Society, Berlin, 1889; H. Nissen, in *Handbuch der klassischen Altertumswissenschaft,* i (1892), 833–890; F. L. Griffith, in *PSBA,* xiv (1892), 403–450; W. Ridgeway, *Origin of Metallic Currency and Weight-Standards,* Cambridge, 1892; PEF, *Quarterly Statements,* 1892, pp. 289–290, 1897–99, passim; Mauss, in *Revue archéologique,* 1892–93; C. F. Howard, *Tables of Hebrew Weights and Measures,* Melbourne, 1896; R. Klimpert, *Lexikon der Münzen, Masse, Gewichte . . . aller Länder,* Berlin, 1896; U. Wilcken, *Griechische Ostraka,* i. 438–480, Leipsic, 1899; Clermont-Ganneau, in *Recueil d'archéologie orientale,* iv. 1–2 (1900), 18 sqq.; A. E. Weigall, in *PSBA,* xxiii (1901), 378–395; C. H. W. Johns, *Assyrian Deeds and Documents,* vol. ii., chap. iii., London, 1901; W. Shaw-Caldecott, *Biblical Archæology,* ib. 1902; Sir C. Warren, *The Ancient Cubit and our Weights and Measures,* ib. 1903; J. A. Decourdemanche, *Traité des poids et mesures des peuples anciens et des Arabes,* Paris, 1910; Schrader, *KAT,* pp. 337–342; Benzinger, *Archäologie,* pp. 188–204; Nowack, *Archäologie,* pp. 208–209; *DB,* iv, 901–913; *EB,* iv. 5292–99; *JE,* xii. 483–490; Vigouroux, *Dictionnaire,* fasc. xxvi. 1042–1045, xxxii. 482–488; and the literature under Money of the Bible.

WEIHBISCHOF: A suffragan, or assistant bishop, differing from a Coadjutor (q.v.) in having no power of independent jurisdiction. Such suffragans first arose in the seventh century, when, the oriental bishops being driven from their dioceses by the Saracens, the thirty-seventh canon of the Trullan Council of 692, supplementing the older canons (*Constitutiones apostolicæ,* canon xxxviii.; Council of Antioch [341] canon xviii.), safeguarded the rights of these prelates. Later, in the ninth and tenth centuries, their services were utilized in Spain by allowing them to assist in episcopal functions, in other regions, and new bishops were also consecrated for the dioceses which were in the power of the unbelievers (Mansi, *Concilia,* xviii. 183, 219; cf. Bishop, Titular). After the abrogation of the institution of the Chorepiscopus (q.v.), authority was accorded these bishops to discharge the duties of assistants in matters exclusively episcopal, thus doing away with the difficulty of securing such assistants or representatives, this difficulty arising from the eighth canon of the Nicene Council of 325, which allowed but one bishop to be consecrated for each diocese. The number of these exiled bishops increased, more especially in the fourteenth century, when the Latin dioceses founded in the orient after the Crusades had fallen into the hands of unbelievers, though bishops continued to be consecrated for these dioceses rather as a matter of principle than from any hope of soon regaining possession of the sees. Clement V., on account of the abuses which grew out of these conditions, made the nomination and consecration of such bishops directly dependent from the papal chair.

At first the auxiliary position of the suffragan bishops was only temporary, and they often changed the dioceses wherein they discharged their duties. Yet as early as the thirteenth century, the suffragans sought to obtain fuller powers, and they were successful in their efforts toward the end of the fifteenth century, when they were consecrated either for a long term or for life, with the assurance of a stated revenue.

These *episcopi titulares* (the title officially given them by Leo XIII. in 1881), formerly called *episcopi in partibus infidelium* (and also *nullatenses, annulares*), are bishops consecrated for a diocese formerly Roman Catholic, though at the time in the hands of unbelievers (though not of Protestants). They are appointed solely by the pope, and perform the same ceremonies and fulfil the same duties as do the regular bishops, and, since the Roman Curia holds strictly to the tradition that these suffragans really possess a diocese, they receive with their nomination a dispensation from residence in these dioceses. They have a seat and a vote in the general council, and are subject, like all other bishops, to the pope, and not to the diocesans in whose sees they reside.

The titular bishops are composed of the following classes: (1) Those who assist the diocesan bishops in the performance of episcopal functions (hence called *vicarii in pontificalibus, episcopi auxiliares,* or *episcopi suffraganei*). The suffragan can not, however, discharge episcopal functions merely by the direct nomination of the pope, for he must also be specifically commissioned by his diocesan both for special cases and for general assistance. By revocation on the part of the bishop of the diocese, or by the latter's resignation or death, the prerogatives of the suffragan cease, but not his stipend, which can be revoked only by the pope or the Congregation of the Council. If, however, the new bishop desires to retain the suffragan as an assistant, he is obliged to remain. (2) The Greek bishops residing in Rome, San Benedetto di Ullano, and Palermo, who ordain Greek Uniate priests throughout Italy. (3) The principal army prelates, when the army is exempt from ordinary episcopal jurisdiction, as is the case in Austria. (4) The apostolic vicars in the missionary fields. (5) Lastly, the apostolic nuncios and some of the Roman prelates are usually appointed titular bishops or archbishops; and this promotion is also accorded to other ecclesiastics as an honorary distinction. Since titular bishops can draw no incomes from their sees, they are often permitted by papal indult to retain benefices ordinarily incompatible with episcopal consecration.

The Hungarian titular bishops differ from the others in that they are priests, and receive the title of bishop only from the king. In England the position of the suffragans was regulated by Henry VIII. in 1534, but none were nominated after 1592 until 1870, when a suffragan was appointed. Since then the institution has been revived. [In the American branch of the Anglican communion there is, at the present time, considerable agitation in favor of the creation of suffragan bishops as distinct from the bishops coadjutor, and such have been created. See PROTESTANT EPISCOPALIANS, II., 1.]

(A. HAUCK.)

BIBLIOGRAPHY: L. Thomassin, *Vetus et nova ecclesiæ disciplina,* I., i., chaps. 27–28, Paris, 1728; A. H. Andreucci, *De episcopo titulari seu in partibus infidelium,* Rome, 1732; P. Hinschius, *Kirchenrecht,* ii. 171 sqq., Berlin, 1871; *Archiv für katholisches Kirchenrecht,* xlvi. 201 sqq., li. 146.

WEINEL, vaiʹnel, **HEINRICH:** German Protestant; b. at Vonhausen (a village near Büdingen, 27 m. n.e. of Frankfort), Hesse, Apr. 29, 1874. He was educated at the universities of Giessen and Berlin (Ph.D., Giessen, 1898) and at the seminary for preachers at Friedberg, Hesse. He became privat-docent in the University of Berlin in 1899, in the following year went to Bonn as privat-docent and inspector of the Evangelical theological foundation there. In 1904 he became extraordinary professor of New-Testament exegesis at the University of Jena, and ordinary professor in 1907. Besides editing the collection known as *Lebensfragen, Schriften und Reden* (Tübingen, 1904 sqq.), he has written *Die Wirkungen des Geistes und der Geister im nachapostolischen Zeitalter bis auf Irenäus* (Freiburg, 1899); *Die Nichtkirchlichen und die freie Theologie* (Tübingen, 1903); *Jesus im neunzehnten Jahrhundert* (1903); *Die Gleichnisse Jesu* (Leipsic, 1904); *Paulus, der Mensch und sein Werk: Die Entstehung der Kirche, des Christentums und des Dogmas* (Tübingen, 1904; Eng. transl. by G. A. Bienemann, *St. Paul, the Man and his Work,* London, 1906); *Die urchristliche und die heutige Mission* (1907); *Die Stellung des Urchristentum zum Staat* (1908); *Ibsen, Björnson, Nietzsche, Individualismus und Christentum* (1908); *Ist das liberale Jesubild widerlegt?* (1910); and *Biblische Theologie des Neuen Testaments* (1911).

WEINGARTEN, vainʹgärʺten, **HERMANN:** Church historian; b. at Berlin Mar. 12, 1834; d. at Pöpelwitz Sanitarium, near Breslau, Apr. 25, 1892. His determination to be a theologian, settled when he was but twelve years of age, was in part a result of influences arising in the family of his mother, her father being interested in the Berlin controversy concerning hymn-books, and her uncle being the missionary to the Hottentots, Leonhard Ebner, at whose house Hermann met many returned missionaries. Hermann received his early education in Berlin, then went in 1853 to Jena and Berlin for his theological studies, at the latter place taking his licentiate in 1857. The same year he received permission to teach in the theological faculty of Jena, and in 1858 became teacher at the Joachimsthal Gymnasium, giving instruction in religion, Hebrew, German, French, and geography, and making a reputation as an excellent teacher; this post he combined with work as privat-docent at Berlin, and then became teacher at a Realschule in Berlin, going in 1873 as ordinary professor to Marburg, though he had in 1872 become subject to a nervous complaint from which he never recovered; in 1876 he was called to Breslau, where he labored till in 1886 he was stricken with paralysis, which practically ended his life-work.

His literary work began with his " programs " issued while he was at Berlin in 1861 and 1864. He was the author of *Pascal als Apologet des Christenthums* (Leipsic, 1863); *Das Wunder der Erscheinung Christi* (1867), a criticism of Strauss' *Leben Jesu für deutsche Volk,* which can hardly become antiquated, so full is it of historical knowledge; *Die Revolutionskirchen Englands* (1868), in which a beginning was made of using in Germany the work of Carlyle; and especially of the *Zeittafellen und Ueberblicke zur*

Kirchengeschichte (Berlin, 1870; 6th ed. completely recast and brought down to date by Carl Franklin Arnold, Leipsic, 1905—[the standard work of its kind in German]). His later works will not have the permanence of his earlier productions, nor do they merit it, for instance, his *Ursprung des Mönchthums im nachconstantinischen Zeitalter* (Gotha, 1877) being superseded by the studies of Bornemann, Harnack, Grützmacher, and others. He was the editor also of Richard Rothe's *Vorlesungen über Kirchengeschichte.* His lectures would probably richly repay printing, his knowledge of English and French, his sententious diction, and his clearness of treatment giving him eminence as a writer and lecturer.

(F. ARNOLD.)

WEISMANN, CHRISTIAN EBERHARD: German Lutheran; b. at Hirschau (20 m. w. of Stuttgart), Württemberg, Sept. 2, 1677; d. at Tübingen May 26, 1747. He was educated at Tübingen, and was then deacon at Calw (1701–04), court chaplain at Stuttgart (1704–07), and teacher of church history and philosophy in the gymnasium of the same city (1707–21), until in 1721 he was called to Tübingen as professor of theology, being also provost of St. George's after 1729. He had a marked tendency toward pietism, and an equal hostility toward the Collegialism (q.v.) of C. M. Pfaff (q.v.) and the philosophy of G. W. Leibnitz and Christian Wolff (qq.v.). He was a distinguished preacher, and the author of some hymns much admired at the time. His principal works were *Introductio in memorabilia ecclesiastica historiæ sacræ Novi Testamenti, maxime vero sæculorum primorum et novissimorum* (2 vols., Stuttgart, 1718–1719); *Orationes academicæ de causis cur tot eximia Dei dona, nostra maxime ætate, ut plurimum sine fructu pereant* (Tübingen, 1729); and *Institutiones theologicæ exegetico-dogmaticæ* (1739).

BIBLIOGRAPHY: J. Brucker, *Bildersaal heutigen Tages lebender Schriftsteller,* Augsburg, 1741; K. Klüpfel, *Geschichte der Universität Tübingen,* pp. 150 sqq., Tübingen 1849; C. Weizsäcker, *Festprogramm zur 4. Säkularfeier der Universität Tübingen,* ib. 1877.

WEISS, vais, **ADAM:** German Reformer; b. at Crailsheim (48 m. n.e. of Stuttgart) about 1490; d. there Sept. 25, 1534. He came of a distinguished family, and was named after a relative who was canon at Ansbach; he was educated at Mainz, and taught there 1512–21; he was enthusiastic in defense of Humanism, and combined with this in his teaching work lectures on Genesis and on the " Sentences " of Peter Lombard. At the end of 1521 he was called to the pastorate of Crailsheim, which work he undertook in an Evangelical spirit, introducing a new church order. He was in correspondence with Zwingli, whose advice he sought, and soon won influence in the margravate of Brandenburg; and though he was not the clerical superior, he was regarded as the real leader in his district. While the Reformation was making headway in the region, the wife of the Margrave Casimir was strongly Roman Catholic, so that there was a reactionary tendency against which progress was to be made. Weiss worked in accord with Johann Rurer of Ansbach; and though the latter was compelled to leave his work and flee, so strongly was the tide flowing

against reform, Weiss determined to stay at his post, where he was enabled to continue his work.

After the death of Casimir, Sept. 21, 1527, Weiss stimulated the new ruler, Georg, to order a thoroughgoing carrying out of the Reformation, and was directed to perfect measures to that end, in company with Johann Schopper of Heilsbronn and Andreas Althamer (q.v.) of Ansbach. The next year he made attempts at a documentary foundation upon which to build the work of the Reformation and contributed the preliminary formulation to one of the earliest confessional statements of the period. Weiss acted as superintendent. In 1529 he accompanied the Margrave Georg to the Diet of Speyer as chaplain and councilor, and his work there was so appreciated that the margrave took him, with Brenz, Rurer, and others, to the Diet of Augsburg in 1530, where his advice was sought on the weightiest matters; he also preached there and won the regard even of the most influential Roman Catholic theologians.

In carrying out Reformation principles, Weiss was influential beyond the boundaries of the margravate of Brandenburg-Ansbach. He supported Johann Brenz of Hall (q.v.) from 1523 onward, and Hall itself sent for his advice in regard to important matters. He was in close relations also with Erhard Schnepf, Theobald Billican, Kaspar Löner (qq.v.), and with Leonhard Culmann, the poet and teacher of Nuremberg; in September of 1524 Johannes Poliander (q.v.) sought his friendship and intimacy. Carlstadt tried to win him over, in 1525, but failed. Weiss's early tendency was rather in the direction of Zwinglian teaching, but in the matter of the Lord's Supper he took wholly the side of Luther, whom he highly honored. Indeed, he regarded Luther's writings as a great treasury, while Luther wrote to the margrave, May 21, 1527, extolling the worth of Weiss and Rurer. Weiss was a prophet honored in his own country, and one of his abiding labors was the foundation of the church library.

(G. BOSSERT.)

BIBLIOGRAPHY: G. Veesenmeyer, *Kleine Beiträge zur Geschichte des Reichstags zu Augsburg,* 1530, pp. 116 sqq., Nuremberg, 1830; *Acta in Comitiis Augustanis quædam,* in K. E. Förstemann, *Urkundenbuch zur Geschichte des Reichstags in Augsburg,* Halle, 1833–35; J. Hartmann and C. Jäger, *Johann Brenz,* 2 vols., Hamburg, 1840–42; G. Bossert, in *Schwäbischer Merkur,* 1879, no. 153; *Theologische Studien aus Württemberg,* 1880, pp. 190 sqq., 1882, pp. 183, 314 sqq., 1883, pp. 30 sqq., 1885, pp. 1 sqq.; H. Westermeyer, *Die brandenburgisch-nürnbergische Kirchenvisitation . . . 1528–33,* Erlangen, 1894; *Beiträge zur bayerischen Kirchengeschichte,* v. 226 sqq., vii. 32 sqq., 241 sqq., Erlangen, 1898–1900; K. Schornbaum, *Die Stellung des Markgrafen Kasimir von Brandenburg zur reformatorischen Bewegung . . . 1524–27,* Nuremberg, 1900; idem, *Zur Politik des Markgrafen Georg von Brandenburg . . . 1528–32,* Munich, 1906; T. Kolde, *Andreas Althamer,* Erlangen, 1895; *ADB,* xli. 554.

WEISS, CARL PHILIPP BERNHARD: German Protestant; b. at Königsberg June 20, 1827. He was educated at the universities of Königsberg, Halle, and Berlin (1844–48); became privat-docent at the university of his native city (1852); associate professor (1857); and was divisional pastor there (1861–63); was professor of New-Testament exegesis at Kiel (1863–77), being also a member of the Kiel consistory (1874–77); since 1877 he has been professor of New-Testament exegesis at the University of Berlin, being also member of the Berlin consistory (1879–80); supreme consistorial councilor and councilor to the department of public worship (1880–1899); president of the Central Committee for the Inner Mission of the German Evangelical Church (1887–96); vice-president since 1896. Besides editing the New Testament in Greek (11 parts, Leipsic, 1902; small edition, 3 vols., 1902–05) and German (2 vols., 1904), as well as preparing the sixth to the ninth editions of H. A. W. Meyer's commentary on Mark and Luke (Göttingen, 1878–1901), the sixth to the ninth editions of John (1880–1902), the sixth to the ninth editions of Romans (1881–99), the seventh to the ninth editions of Matthew (1883–1897), the fifth to the seventh editions of the pastoral epistles (1885–1902), the fifth and sixth editions of Hebrews (1888–97), and the fifth and sixth editions of the Johannine epistles (1888–1900), he has written *Der petrinische Lehrbegriff* (Berlin, 1855); *Der Philipperbrief* (1859); *Der johanneische Lehrbegriff* (1862); *Lehrbuch der biblischen Theologie des Neuen Testaments* (1868; Eng. transl., *Biblical Theology of the New Testament*, 2 vols., Edinburgh, 1882–1883); *Das Markus-Evangelium und seine synoptischen Parallelen* (1872); *Das Matthäus-Evangelium und seine Lukas-Parallelen* (Halle, 1876); *Das Leben Jesu* (2 vols., Berlin, 1882; Eng. transl., 3 vols., Edinburgh, 1883–84); *Lehrbuch der Einleitung in das Neue Testament* (1886; Eng. transl., *Introduction to the New Testament*, 2 vols., London, 1889); *Die Johannesapokalypse* (Leipsic, 1891); *Die katholischen Briefe* (1892); *Die Apostelgeschichte* (1893); *Das Neue Testament, textkritische Untersuchung und Textherstellung* (3 vols., 1894–1900); *Die paulinischen Briefe im berichtigten Text* (1896); *Der Codex D in der Apostelgeschichte* (1897); *Die vier Evangelien im berichtigten Text* (1900); *Die Religion des Neuen Testaments* (Stuttgart, 1903; Eng. transl., New York, 1905); *Die Geschichtlichkeit des Markus-Evangeliums* (Gross-Lichterfeld, 1905); *Die Quellen des Lukas-Evangeliums* (Stuttgart, 1907); *Die Quellen der synoptischen Ueberlieferung* (Leipsic, 1908); *Morgenandachten über evangelische Texte* (1909); *Abendandachten über apostolische Texte* (1910); *Der Hebräerbrief in zeitgeschichtlicher Beleuchtung* (Leipsic, 1910).

BIBLIOGRAPHY: C. A. Briggs, *Study of Holy Scripture*, passim, New York, 1899; H. S. Nash, *Hist. of the Higher Criticism of the N. T.*, ib. 1900.

WEISS, JOHANNES: German Protestant; b. at Kiel Dec. 13, 1863. He was educated at the universities of Marburg, Berlin, Göttingen, and Breslau (1882–88); became privat-docent at Göttingen (1888), and associate professor of New-Testament exegesis (1890); professor of the same subject in the University of Marburg (1895–1908); since 1908 he has held the same position at Heidelberg. Besides editing *Die Schriften des Neuen Testaments neu übersetzt und für die Gegenwart erklärt* (2 vols., Göttingen, 1906), he has written *Der Barnabasbrief* (Berlin, 1888); *Die Predigt Jesu vom Reiche Gottes* (Göttingen, 1893); *Kommentar zum Lukas-Evangelium* (1893); *Die Nachfolge Christi und die Predigt der Gegenwart* (1895); *Beiträge zur paulinische Rhetorik* (1897); *Ueber die Absicht und den literarischen Char-*

akter der *Apostelgeschichte* (1897); *Die Idee des Reichs Gottes in der Theologie* (Giessen, 1900); *Die christliche Freiheit und die Verkündigung des Apostels Paulus* (Göttingen, 1902); *Das älteste Evangelium* (1903); *Die Offenbarung des Johannes* (1904); *Die Aufgaben der neutestamentlichen Wissenschaft* (1908); *Christus, die Anfänge des Dogmas* (1909); *Paulus und Jesus* (Berlin, 1909; Eng. transl., London, 1909, New York, 1910); *Jesus im Glauben des Urchristentums* (1910); *Jesus von Nazareth, Mythus oder Geschichte?* (1910); and the volume on Corinthians in the *Kritisch-exegetischer Kommentar über das Neue Testament* (Göttingen, 1910).

WEISS, NATHANAEL EMILE: French Reformed; b. at La Croix-aux-Mines, near Saint-Dié (45 m. s.e. of Nancy), Mar. 27, 1845. He studied at the Protestant Gymnasium of Strasburg (B.D., 1867); was tutor to the sons of Count de Maupeau (1867–69); pastor of the Reformed *Église de la Glacière*, Paris (1869–71); missionary agent to the Paris Sunday-school Society (1871–75); pastor at Boulogne-sur-Seine (1875–85). Since 1885 he has been librarian of the Sunday-school Society, Paris, and is also secretary of the Society for the History of French Protestantism. He has been a member of the consistory of the Reformed Church in Paris since 1879, and is an " advocate of what is called ' new theology.' " He puts his strength into the *Bulletin* of the Society for the History of French Protestantism, and is the acknowledged authority in this department of research. He has written *Duplessis-Mornay comme théologien et comme caractère politique* (Strasburg, 1867); *Le Naufrage de la Ville du Havre et du Loch Earn* (Paris, 1874); *La Sortie de France de Claude Brousson* (Orléans, 1885); and *La Chambre ardente* (Paris, 1889).

WEISS, PANTALEON. See CANDIDUS.

WEIZSAECKER, vaits′sek″ker, **KARL HEINRICH VON:** German theologian; b. at Oehringen (35 m. n.n.w. of Stuttgart) Dec. 11, 1822; d. at Tübingen Aug. 13, 1899. He received his education at the seminary at Schöntal and at the University of Tübingen; became privat-docent at Tübingen, 1847; minister at Billingsbach, 1848; preacher to the court at Stuttgart, 1851; assistant in the Kultusministerium, 1856; associate in the consistory, 1859; professor at Tübingen as successor of Baur in church history, 1861; and chancellor of the university, 1890. As early as 1856 he began contributions to theology in his joint efforts in founding and editing *Jahrbücher für deutsche Theologie*, an activity which he extended later by contributions to such journals as the *Theologische Studien und Kritiken* and the *Theologische Litteraturzeitung*. He was the author of *Zur Kritik des Barnabas-Briefes aus dem Codex Sinaiticus* (Tübingen, 1863); *Untersuchungen über die evangelische Geschichte* (Gotha, 1864), a work which placed Weizsäcker in the front rank of writers on early Christianity; and *Die christliche Kirche im apostolische Zeitalter* (Freiburg, 1886, 3d ed., 1902; Eng. transl., *The Apostolic Age*, 2 vols., London, 1894–95), which was preceded by a series of special studies that prepared the way and appeared in various journals. In this work he turned the tide of criticism by insisting that in the Fourth Gospel careful distinction must be made between the historical and the philosophical elements, there being original apostolic reminiscences as fundamental as in the Synoptic Gospels; only in the development of these reminiscences they had become interwoven with a sublime philosophy. The hypothesis of the evolution of Christianity from a Pauline-Petrine opposition was undermined and positions determined for a new advance in historical investigation. But the new position taken by Weizsäcker was the union of a historico-personal and a mystical-idealistic element in the Fourth Gospel. He ever regarded himself as related in spirit and method to Baur, a thankful student of that master, and in this respect his *Untersuchungen* named above bears out his claims.

While Weizsäcker's scholarship is to be recognized, his practical ability should also receive acknowledgment. As pastor among peasants, in official service in the consistory and elsewhere, as professor coming into contact with students, as rector and chancellor of the university, he displayed ever a keen sense of the fitness of things and great wisdom in directing his course of action. He was no doctrinaire, but had an eye to the practical in life, with a humor and a fund of anecdote with which he brightened the intercourse into which he was thrown.

(H. HOLTZMANN†.)

BIBLIOGRAPHY: A. Hegler, *Zur Erinnerung an K. Weizsäcker*, Tübingen, 1900; G. Grützmacher, in *Historische Vierteljahrschrift*, 1899, pp. 566–568; E. Grafe, *Die christliche Welt*, 1899, pp. 749–753; R. Günther, in *Monatsschrift für Pastoraltheologie*, 1907, pp. 10–32, 64–73.

WELLAND, THOMAS JAMES: Anglican bishop of Down, Connor, and Dromore, Ireland; b. in Dublin Mar. 31, 1830; d. at Belfast July 29, 1907. He was educated at Trinity College, Dublin (B.A., 1854), and was ordered deacon in 1854 and ordained priest in the following year; was curate of Carlow (1854–56); perpetual curate of Painstown, County Carlow (1856–58); assistant chaplain of Mariner's Church, Kingstown, County Dublin (1858–62); clerical secretary of the Jews' Society (1862–66); assistant chaplain of Christ Church, Leeson Street, Dublin (1866–70); incumbent of St. Thomas, Belfast, and chaplain of Malone Protestant Reformatory (1870–92), and in 1892 was consecrated bishop of the united dioceses of Down, Connor, and Dromore.

WELLDON, JAMES EDWARD COWELL: Church of England; b. at Tunbridge (16 m. s.w. of Rochester), Kent, Apr. 25, 1854. He was educated at King's College, Cambridge (B.A., 1877), and, after residing abroad for some years, was ordered deacon in 1883 and ordained priest in 1885. He was elected a fellow of his college in 1878; was master of Dulwich College, 1883–85; headmaster of Harrow School, 1885–98; select preacher at Cambridge in 1885, 1888, and 1893, and at Oxford in 1886–87; honorary chaplain to the queen, 1888–92, and chaplain in ordinary, 1892–98; and Hulsean lecturer at Cambridge in 1897. In 1898 he was consecrated bishop of Calcutta and metropolitan of India, but in 1901 resigned his see and was canon of Westminster 1901–06, and since 1906 dean of Manchester. Besides translating Aristotle's *Poli-*

tics (London, 1883); *Rhetoric* (1886); and *Nicomachean Ethics* (1892), he has written *Sermons Preached to Harrow Boys* (3 series, London, 1887–1903); *The Spiritual Life, and Other Sermons* (1888); *The Future and the Past* (1888); *Gerald Eversley's Friendship* (1895); *The Hope of Immortality* (1898; 3d ed., 1905); *The Revelation of the Holy Spirit* (1902); *The School of Faith* (1904); *Be Strong. Lessons for Young Lives* (1907); and *The Gospel in a Great City* (1910).

WELLER, REGINALD HEBER, JR.: Protestant Episcopal bishop coadjutor of Fond du Lac; b. at Jefferson City, Mo., Nov. 6, 1857. He was educated at the University of the South, Sewanee, Tenn. (1875–77), and at Nashotah House (graduated 1884). He was ordered deacon in 1880 and priested in 1884, and was rector of Christ Church, Eau Claire, Wis. (1884–88), St. Matthias, Waukesha, Wis. (1888–1890), and the Church of the Intercession, Stevens Point, Wis. (1890–1900). In 1900 he was consecrated bishop coadjutor of Fond du Lac, Wis.

WELLHAUSEN, JULIUS: German Protestant; b. at Hameln (25 m. s.w. of Hanover) May 17, 1844. He studied at Göttingen (Ph.D., 1870); became privat-docent there (1870) in the theological faculty; professor in the same faculty at Greifswald (1872); associate professor of Semitics at Halle (1882) in the philosophical faculty; full professor of the same subject at Marburg (1885) and at Göttingen (1892). He is best known for his elaboration of the theory that the Pentateuch is post-exilic, and is, consequently, distinctly Jewish, rather than Hebraic or Israelitic. He has written *De gentibus et familiis Judæis quæ I Chron. ii. 4 enumerantur* (Göttingen, 1870), *Der Text der Bücher Samuels untersucht* (1871), *Pharisäer und Saduzäer* (Greifswald, 1874), *Geschichte Israels* (Berlin, 1878; 2d–6th eds., under the title *Prolegomena zur Geschichte Israels*, 1883–1905; Eng. tr. by J. S. Smith and C. A. Menzies, Edinburgh, 1885, 3d ed., 1891), *Muhammad in Medina* (1882), *Skizzen und Vorarbeiten* (6 vols., 1884–92), *Abriss der Geschichte Israels und Judas; Lieder der Hudhailiten* (1884), *Composition des Hexateuchs* (1885; 3d ed., 1899), *Reste arabischen Heidentums* (1887; 2d ed., 1897), *Medina vor dem Islam; Muhammads Gemeindeordnungen von Medina; seine Schreiben und die Gesandtschaften an ihn* (1887), and *Die kleinen Propheten übersetzt mit Noten* (1892; 3d ed., 1898); *Israelitische und jüdische Geschichte* (1894; 6th ed., 1907); *Der arabische Josippus* (1897); *Die religiös-politischen Oppositionsparteien im alten Islam* (1901); *Das arabische Reich und sein Sturz* (1902); *Das Evangelium Marci übersetzt* (1903; 2d ed., 1909); *Matthæi* (1904); *Lucæ* (1904), *Johannis* (1908); and *Einleitung in die drei ersten Evangelien* (1905); and he also prepared the sixth edition of F. Bleek's *Einleitung in das Alte Testament* (Berlin, 1893), and *Psalms* for the *Polychrome Bible* (New York, 1895).

WELLS, AMOS RUSSEL: Congregationalist-Presbyterian layman; b. at Glens Falls, N. Y., Dec. 23, 1862. He received his education in the public schools of Yellow Springs, Ohio, and Antioch College (B.A., 1883); was professor of Greek in his alma mater, 1883–92, and in 1892 assumed his present position of editorial secretary for the United Society of Christian Endeavor. Has also been managing editor, since 1892, of *The Christian Endeavor World*, and is associate editor of Peloubet's *Notes on the International Sunday-School Lessons*. His position theologically is that of a conservative Calvinist. He is a prolific writer, having produced about fifty volumes or booklets, classified into stories, essays, devotional works, poems, books for young people's societies, on the Bible, and on the Sunday-school. Of these mention may be made (1) of the essay *Sermons in Stones* (New York, 1899); *How to Work, How to Play, How to Study* (3 vols., Boston, 1900); *Into All the World* (1903); *Studies in the Art of Illustration* (New York, 1903); *Help for the Tempted* (Boston, 1903); and *That They All may be One* (New York, 1905). (2) Among devotional works mention may be made of *When thou hast Shut thy Door* (New York, 1895); and *The Cheer Book* (1901). For young people's societies there are *The Junior Manual* (Boston, 1895); and *Prayer Meeting Methods* (1896). For the Sunday-school there are *Sunday-School Problems* (1895); *Sunday-School Success* (New York, 1897); *Three Years with the Children* (1900); *Introduction to Bible Study* (Philadelphia, 1909); and *Why we believe the Bible* (1910).

WELLS, LEMUEL HENRY: Protestant Episcopal bishop of Spokane; b. at Yonkers, N. Y., Dec. 3, 1841. He began his college education at Trinity, Hartford, but left in 1861 to enter the Union Army, in which he served three years as second and first lieutenant. He was graduated from Hobart College (1867), and Berkeley Divinity School, Middletown, Conn. (1869). He was ordered deacon in the same year and priested in 1871. Spending the year 1871–72 in study in Europe, he was curate at Trinity Church, New Haven (1872–73), and rector at Walla Walla, Wash. (1873–82). He then resided in the eastern part of the United States for a year and a half, but in 1884 became rector of St. Luke's, Tacoma, Wash., where he remained until 1889. In the latter year he accepted the rectorate of Trinity Church in the same city, and in 1892 was consecrated first missionary bishop of Spokane.

BIBLIOGRAPHY: W. S. Perry, *Episcopate in America*, p. 343, New York, 1895.

WELSH CALVINISTIC METHODISTS. See PRESBYTERIANS, IV., VIII., 8.

WELTZ, velts, JUSTINIAN, FREIHERR VON: Austrian pioneer advocate of Protestant missions to the heathen and missionary; b. at Chemnitz (38 m. s.w. of Dresden) 1621; d. in Surinam (Dutch Guiana) in 1688. Little is known of his life. He wrote at the age of twenty the tractate *De tyrannorum ingenio et arcanis artibus*, discussing the duties of rulers and subjects. In 1663 appeared, *Vom Einsiedlerleben, wie es nach Gottes Wort und der alten heiligen Einsiedlerleben anzustellen sei*, a work inspired with lofty religious and moral earnestness; and his *Kurzer Bericht, wie ein neue Gesellschaft unter den rechtgläubigen Christen Augsburgischer Konfession aufgerichtet werden könne* (1663). His three principal works are: *Eine christliche und treuherzige Vermahnung an alle rechtgläubigen*

Christen der Augsburgischen Konfession, etc.; *Einladungstrieb zum herannahenden grossen Abendmahl und Vorschlag zu einer christlichen Jesus Gesellschaft;* and *Wiederholte treuherzige und ernthafte Vermahnung, die Bekehrung ungläubiger Völker vorzunehmen*, etc. (all 1864).

These three works were written to prove the necessity of missions, to dispose of the objections of opponents, and to give practical suggestions for the realization of his ideas. He presented the first and second of these works to the Corpus Evangelicorum at Regensburg, but failed to secure any results. He wrote his third work and went to Holland. At Zwolle he had himself solemnly ordained apostle to the heathens by the Lutheran preacher, Breckling, and went out into the field, where he found a lonely grave. His ideas found no appreciative reception until Spener took them up.   (G. WARNECK†.)

BIBLIOGRAPHY: W. Grössel, *Der Missionsweckruf des Baron J. von Weltz in . . . Wiedergabe des Originaldrucks vom Jahre 1664*, Leipsic, 1890; idem, *Justinian von Weltz, der Vorkämpfer der lutherischen Mission*, ib. 1891; G. Warneck, *Abriss einer Geschichte der protestantischen Missionen*, pp. 30 sqq., 41 sqq., 8th ed., Berlin, 1905.

WENCESLAUS, ven'ces-laus, SAINT: Sponsor for Christianity among the Czechs; d. Sept. 28, 935 (or 929). The Czechs compose the branch of the Slavic family which penetrated farthest west. At the beginning of the Middle Ages, however, they were separated from central Germany by a more advanced Slavic line of Wends. The Bohemians came in contact with Christian territory only in the south, at the Bavarian frontier. This circumstance accounts for the fact that the Czechs came relatively late into contact with Christianity. According to the oldest narrative, fourteen Bohemian lords received baptism on Jan. 13, 845, from Louis the Fat. But the Frankish power was shattered in the East in the second half of the ninth century and the Czechs entered into relation with their eastern neighbors. The religious consequence was that Methodius (see CYRIL AND METHODIUS) or his pupils extended their activity into Bohemia. In 895 Spitignew I. once more recognized the suzerainty of Germany, and Bohemia became part of the bishopric of Regensburg. But the people remained heathen, while the nobles were divided between heathenism and Christianity. Upon the death of Spitignew and Wratislaw, Dragomir, wife of Wratislaw, assumed control of the government and opposed German Christianizing influence. The power was wrested from her and given to her eldest son Wenceslaus. The legends portray him as a devout Christian, who invited priests into the country, built churches, and cared for all ecclesiastical concerns. But he was not able to convert the Czechs or to suppress the opposition which was headed by his younger and abler brother Boleslaw, by whom he was murdered (Sept. 28, 935?) at the entrance to the church at Bunzlau, whither he had gone as his brother's guest. Boleslaw was chosen count and the Czechs lapsed from Christianity, nothing resulting from an interference by Henry I. In 950 Boleslaw again recognized the suzerainty of the empire, and later Wenzel's body was transferred to the Veitskirche which he had built in Prague.

Since then his fame increased not only because of his services but because of his misfortunes, so that among the Czechs he is to-day, next to St. Nepomuk (see JOHN OF NEPOMUK), the best beloved of the saints. (A. HAUCK.)

BIBLIOGRAPHY: Sources in the shape of the early *Vita* by Bishop Gumpoldus Mantuanus (967), *Passio*, and other *Vitæ* are collected in *MGH, Script.*, iv (1841), 211–223, xv. 1 (1887), 572; *MPL*, cxxxv. 923–42; in *Fontes rerum Bohemicarum*, ed. F. J. Zoubek, i. 125–190, Prague, 1873; and with commentary in *ASB*, Sept., vii. 770–844. Further sources are: F. Miklosich and I. Fiedler, *Slavische Bibliothek*, ii. 270-281, Vienna, 1857; *Abhandlungen der philosophisch-historischen Gessellschaft in Breslau*, i (1858), 203–240. Consult: Dobrowsky, *Wenzel und Boleslaw*, Prague, 1819; F. Palacky, *Geschichte von Böhmen*, i. 195–210, Prague, 1836; E. H. Gillett, *Life and Times of John Huss*, passim (consult Index under " Wenzel "), Philadelphia, 1861; A. Frind, *Kirchengeschichte Böhmens*, i. 16–19, 40–41, Prague, 1862; H. Friedjung, *Kaiser Karl IV. und sein Antheil am geistigen Leben seiner Zeit*, pp. 150–161, Vienna, 1876; W. Vondrák, *Zur Würdigung der altslovenischen Wenzelslegende*, ib. 1892; J. Lippert, *Sozialgeschichte Böhmens in vorhussitischer Zeit*, 2 vols., Prague, 1896–98; H. G. Voigt, *Adalbert von Prague*, pp. 8 sqq., Berlin, 1898; idem, *Die von . . . Christian verfasste Biographie des heiligen Wenzel*, Prague, 1907; A. Bachmann, *Geschichte Böhmens*, i. 121 sqq., Gotha, 1899; H. B. Workman, *Dawn of the Reformation*, vol. ii. passim (consult Index under " Wenzel "), London, 1902; J. Pekár, *Die Wenzels- und Ludmilla-Legenden*, Prague, 1905; Hauck, *KD*, iii. 184 sqq.; Bretholz, in *NA*, xxix. 480 sqq.

WENDELIN, ven'de-lin, **MARKUS FRIEDRICH:** German Reformed theologian; b. at Sandhausen near Heidelberg in 1584; d. at Zerbst (66 m. s.w. of Berlin) Aug. 7, 1652. He received his education at Heidelberg, following Ramus in his philosophy and Pareus in his theology; in 1609 he served as private tutor in Geneva, and, after being in Dessau in 1610, was called in 1612 as rector of the Gymnasium illustre at Zerbst, a position which he retained till his death. The period of the Thirty Years' War was not one in which such an institution could be expected to flourish, but it was maintained at a high level by the new rector, who produced a number of works pedagogical in character. Theological in content were his *De prædestinatione* (Frankfort, 1621); *Christianæ theologiæ libri ii* (Hanover, 1634), later translated into Dutch and Hungarian; *Compendium Christianæ theologiæ* (1634); *Systema majus* (1656), a kind of model Reformed dogmatics which called forth replies from Christoph Franck and Johann Gerhard; though this was preceded by his *Exercitationes theologicæ vindices* (1652). There was also a posthumous *Collatio doctrinæ Christianæ Reformatorum et Lutheranorum* (1660). Wendelin's significance rests in the fact that he was the first to set forth in systematic form on German soil the Reformed system of teaching, on the basis of Scripture and in an objective-synthetic method. This involved the setting forth of a *communio apotelesmatum* as opposed to the *Communicatio idiomatum* (q.v.). (E. F. KARL MÜLLER.)

BIBLIOGRAPHY: J. C. Beckmann, *Hist. des Fürstenthums Anhalt*, vii. 366 sqq., Wittenberg, 1710; F. Kindscher, *Geschichte des . . . Gesamtgymnasiums zu Zerbst*, 2 parts, Zerbst, 1871; W. Gass, *Geschichte der protestantischen Dogmatik*, i. 416 sqq., Berlin, 1854.

WENDS, CONVERSION OF THE: The history of Christian missionary work among the Wends is closely bound up with German political history, and has to do with the period from the close of the eighth to the beginning of the thirteenth century. The power of resistance of these tribes to the influence of the Germans is an essential element in the history. The southern Wends on the Thuringian borders of the German empire offered but little resistance to the advance of the Germans, but the northern Wends of Brandenburg and Mecklenburg carried on their struggle for liberty for centuries until the surviving remnants were subdued. The progress of Christian missions in the south and north was correspondingly different; in the one case there was a gradual but steady advance, in the other notable achievements followed by complete reverses, until the survivors were compelled to submit to Christianization. Three regions in which the movement was carried out show striking diversities in the course of events: Mecklenburg-Brandenburg, the Sorb district, and Pomerania-Poland. The history in the first is by far the most dramatic.

Charlemagne did not concern himself with the conversion of the Wends. But under Ansgar (q.v.), Wendish children were redeemed from slave-dealers in order to educate them as missionaries to their people. Despite the baptism of an Obotrite prince, Sclaomir (821), no further results were obtained, and the Wends withdrew from their alliance with the empire. Under Otto I. an attempt was made to advance from Hamburg on the west and Magdeburg on the east, under which had been placed the bishoprics of Havelberg and Brandenburg, founded in 938. For the western Wends a separate bishopric was founded at Aldenburg (Oldenburg in Holstein) in 968. Conditions were more favorable in Oldenburg, the land of the Obotrites, because the district was under a unified government. Havelberg and Brandenburg had to do with the fierce Leutizi. The defeat of Otto II. at Crotone undid all the work. The weakness of the empire being shown, the Wends in 983 destroyed all traces of Christianity from Brandenburg to Oldenburg, and the three bishoprics were practically destroyed. Matters did not improve under the first Saxon king, Heinrich II. The series of bishops in Oldenburg remained nominally unbroken, and the Obotrite princes Uto and Ratibor consented to be baptized, but the people were unaffected. A hermit named Gunther tried in 1017 to work among the Leutizi, but soon returned to Bohemia.

This unproductive period was followed by the remarkable episode in which Gottschalk (q.v., 2) figured. He was the son of Uto, and undertook the systematic Christianization of the people, with the help of the Saxon counts and especially of Archbishop Adalbert of Hamburg-Bremen (q.v.). His success was only superficial. Upon the archbishop's losing the imperial favor and entering into the dissensions of the Saxons, the Wends arose, caused a massacre of Christians at Lenz in which Gottschalk fell (1066), and destroyed all traces of Christianity. Of the three bishoprics, Oldenburg, Mecklenburg, and Ratzeburg, the names alone remained. A contributing cause of this calamity was largely the prince's own tactlessness in supporting missionaries who were foreigners and refused to learn the language of the people, so that the prince himself had to be their interpreter. One result of the uprising was that the peaceful conversion of the Wends ceased to be thought of; annihilation was now the word. The conditions were not bettered when, in 1067, Bishop Burchard of Halberstadt destroyed the chief sanctuary of the Leutizi and rode the sacred steed of Radigast into Halberstadt. Missionary activity was resumed when Kruto, the successor of Gottschalk, was slain by Heinrich, son of Gottschalk, who with Saxon assistance seized the rule. Heinrich proceded more cautiously than his father, though he was a Christian and had a church at Altlübeck, the only one in Mecklenburg. Constant wars with external foes prevented him from carrying out his plans. His assassination in 1127 caused missionary work again to cease. Under the powerful Niklot, the Mecklenburg country again relapsed into heathenism. The Wends found piracy, which they learned from the Danes, a more attractive occupation than agriculture or cattle-raising. This again showed that what was required for the safety of the kingdom was either thoroughgoing conversion of the Wends or their annihilation. This was the watchword in the Saxon crusade of 1147. Count Adolf of Holstein-Schauenburg and Heinrich of Badewide succeeded in tearing Wagrien and Polabien (East Holstein and Lauenburg) from the Wends, and the former was completely devastated and cleared of its Wendish population. German settlers took their place, to whose spiritual welfare the aged Vicelin devoted his last days.

When Bernard of Clairvaux was preaching a crusade to the Holy Land, the Saxons replied that they had heathens enough at home. Bernard thereupon began to preach with enthusiasm the crusade against the Wends. Niklot had been living in peace with the German princes. Adolf of Holstein being reminded of the alliance between him and Niklot, excused himself, whereupon Niklot attacked and captured Lübeck. The campaign thus inauspiciously begun by the crusaders ended in disaster. The German nobles were finally content to make a sorry peace with Niklot, upon his agreeing to let his people be baptized if they wished. Henry the Lion saw more profit to himself in the Wends as heathens, for so he received the tribute that would have gone to the Church. Upon his receiving the right of investiture for Wendland, he changed his policy, and appointed the Provost Evermod to Ratzeburg, Gerold to Oldenburg, Berno to Mecklenburg (1155). Berno became the Boniface of the Mecklenburg Wend country. He had, indeed, little success before Niklot's heroic death in 1160. Niklot's son Pribislaw was baptized and the Christianizing of the country proceeded rapidly. This was, however, due to the practical extinction of the original Wendish population. German colonists had taken their place. The Mecklenburgian Wends had defied conversion for four hundred years and had gone down without having as a people embraced Christianity.

The Sorbs on the southern borders of the German empire had quite a different history. As early as 782 a war of the Sorbs is referred to as an " uprising," showing their prior subjection to the empire. They lived together with Germans in the valleys of Thuringia and were regarded as Christians in the time of Charlemagne. Advances across the Saale were begun by Count Otto of Saxony and energetically continued by his son Heinrich I. The Daleminzians, the eastern neighbors of the Sorbs, were subdued in 928. Emperor Otto I. undertook the first missionary work among these southern Wends. Meissen, Zeitz, and Merseburg were made suffragan bishoprics of Magdeburg on Wendish soil. The first bishops, Burkhard, Hugo, and Boso, were consecrated by Archbishop Adalbert in 968. These southern Wends clung tenaciously to their national language and religion, but the progress of Christianity was favored by the immigration of Germans. At the end of the century, there were a number of churches, the oldest being at Zeitz and Bosan. In the twelfth century the episcopal cities had become German and had churches, so also had a number of the fortified towns, but the mass of the population clung to heathenism although their sanctuaries and public idol worship had been done away with. The gradual diminution of the Wendish population and the increasing immigration of Germans finally brought about the assimilation of the remaining Wends, which was completed in some parts of the country only at the close of the fourteenth century.

In Poland, Count Miseco accepted Christianity in the tenth century. A Polish bishopric was founded in 968 (Posen, under Magdeburg), although the Polish population for a long time remained more heathen than Christian. Otto III. established the archbishopric of Gnesen, while Boleslaw Chrabry, the conqueror of the Pomeranians, established the bishopric of Kolberg, with a German bishop, Reinbern. After his death Pomerania relapsed, for a time was under Danish rule, and after the middle of the eleventh century became an independent heathen kingdom. In 1119 it again fell into the hands of the Poles. Even at that time Prince Wratislaw, his wife, and some of the nobles were Christians, as were a part of the population in the Pomeranian cities. In 1120 heathenism was disintegrating, which explains its sudden overthrow when Boleslaw III. conquered the Pomeranians and made the acceptance of Christianity one of the conditions of peace. (E. SCHÄFER.)

BIBLIOGRAPHY: Sources are: Thietmar of Merseburg, Chronicon, ed. J. M. Lappenberg in MGH, Script., iii. (1839), 733–871, and in Script. rer. Germ., Hanover, 1889, also in MPL, cxxxix. 1183–1422; Adam of Bremen, Gesta Hammaburgensis ecclesiæ pontificum, ed. J. M. Lappenberg in MGH, Script., vii (1846), 267–389, and in Script. rer. Germ., 2d ed., Hanover, 1876; Helmold, Chronica Slavorum, in MGH, Script., xxi (1869), 11–99, in Germ. transl. by J. C. Laurent, 2d ed. by W. Wattenbach, Leipsic, 1888; Arnoldus Lubecensis, Chronica Slavorum, in MGH, Script., xxi (1869), 115–250, and ed. J. M. Lappenberg, in Script. rer. Germ., Hanover, 1868; F. Wigger, Mecklenburgische Annalen bis . . . 1066, Schwerin, 1860; Mecklenburgisches Urkundenbuch, vol. i., Schwerin, 1863. Consult: L. Giesebrecht, Wendische Geschichten, 3 vols., Berlin, 1843; Wendisches Volksthum in Sage, Brauch, und Sitte, Berlin, 1882; L. Nottrott, Aus der Wendenmission, Halle, 1897–98; Hauck, KD, iii. 69–149, 623–658, iv. 554–625; E. Kreusch, Kirchengeschichte der Wendenlande, Paderborn, 1902; and the articles ANSGAR; GOTTSCHALK, 2; OTTO OF BAMBERG; and VICELIN, with the literature under them.

WENDT, vent, **HANS HINRICH:** German Protestant; b. at Hamburg June 18, 1853. He was

educated at the universities of Tübingen (Ph.D.,
1875) and Göttingen (lic. theol., 1877); became
privat-docent of New-Testament exegesis at the latter university (1877), and associate professor (1881);
was professor at Kiel (1883–85); professor of systematic theology at Heidelberg (1887–93); and since
1893 has been professor of the same subject at Jena.
Besides preparing the fifth to the eighth editions of
H. A. W. Meyer's commentary on Acts (Göttingen,
1880–99), he has written *Die Begriffe Fleisch und
Geist im biblischen Sprachgebrauch* (Gotha, 1878);
*Die christliche Lehre von der menschlichen Vollkom-
menheit* (Göttingen, 1882); *Die Lehre Jesu* (2 vols.,
1886–1890; Eng. transl. by F. Wilson, 1892); *Die
Norm des echten Christentums* (Leipsic, 1893); *Der
Erfahrungsbeweis für die Wahrheit des Christentums*
(Göttingen, 1897); *Das Johannesevangelium* (1900;
Eng. transl. by E. Lummis, Edinburgh, 1902);
The Idea and Reality of Revelation (London, 1904);
System der christlichen Lehre (Göttingen, 1906); and
Die Schichten im vierten Evangelium (1911).

Bibliography: C. A. Briggs, *Study of Holy Scripture*, pp.
498, 589, New York, 1899; H. S. Nash, *Hist. of the Higher
Criticism of the N. T.*, ib., 1900.

WENRICH OF TREVES: Schoolman and controversialist of the eleventh century. He is celebrated for his part in the struggle between Gregory
VII. and Henry IV., in which, at the instigation and
under the name of Bishop Dietrich of Verdun, he
wrote a brief but pungent tract, published probably
in 1081, in the shape of an open letter to the pope,
whose policies he criticized with clever acuteness
(found in *MGH, Lib. de lite*, i., 1890, pp. 284–299;
with introduction, pp. 280–284). The tract made
no ordinary stir, and moved Manegold of Lauterbach (q.v.) to issue his less able countertract, *Liber
ad Gebehardum* (in *MGH, Lib. de lite*, i. 308–430,
1890). Wenrich contested the justice, force, and
validity of the ban of 1080 against the German king,
and asserted that such unwarranted ecxommunica-
tion segregates not the banned member, but his unjust judge. He also vigorously protested against
the celibacy laws of Gregory VII. and warmly advocated royal investiture. He also charged Gregory
VII. with complicity in setting up the rival kingdom
in Germany, asserting that Gregory did violence to
the papal dignity and used force in attaining his
ends.　　　　　　　　　　　　　　　　Carl Mirbt.

Bibliography: Besides the introduction in *MGH, Lib. de
lite*, i (1890), 280–284, consult: C. Mirbt, *Die Publizistik
im Zeitalter Gregors VII.*, passim, Leipsic, 1894; idem,
Die Wahl Gregors VII., Marburg, 1782; G. Meyer von
Knonau, *Jahrbücher des deutschen Reichs unter Heinrich
IV. und V.*, iii. 406–415, Leipsic, 1900; G. Koch, *Manegold von Lauterbach und die Lehre von der Volkssouveräni-
tät*, Berlin, 1902; and the literature under Gregory VII.

**WERDENHAGEN, vär'den-ha''-gen, JOHANN
ANGELIUS VON:** German layman and mystic; b.
at Helmstedt (102 m. s.w. of Berlin) Aug. 1, 1581;
d. at Ratzeburg (31 m. n.e. of Hamburg) Dec. 26,
1652. He studied under the humanists of the university of his native town, to whom he was one of
the first to apply the term *Rationistæ* because of
their undue valuation and use of the reasoning
faculty. In 1618, moreover, he defended Daniel
Hoffmann, whom the humanists expelled from
Helmstedt on account of his attacks on philosophy.

On the other hand, he assailed the Lutheran theologians, whether of the moderate school of Helmstedt,
or of the stricter Lutheran school of electoral
Saxony. He was a private lecturer at Helmstedt
(1601–06); then, except for a brief interval as associate rector at Salzwedel, served as traveling companion to people of rank (1606–10), visiting various
universities; was employed as diplomatic agent by
the court of Brunswick (1612–16); became professor of ethics at Helmstedt (1616), but soon had to
surrender this office because of participation in the
controversies over Daniel Hoffmann. Thereafter,
when he was a syndic of the city of Magdeburg, he
fell into strife with the resident Lutheran canons,
and lost his position in 1626. From that time till
1628, he was employed on various missions in behalf of the administrator. After sojourning several
years at Leyden and The Hague, where he completed
and published his chief writings, he entered in 1632
the service of Archbishop Johann Friedrich of
Bremen, and later, that of the city of Magdeburg
and of Duke August of Brunswick and Lüneburg.
He spent his closing years, 1637–52, at Lübeck,
acting as envoy for Emperor Ferdinand III. to the
Hanseatic towns.

All his writings, even those which deal mainly
with historical and philosophical problems, dwell
upon the moral conditions of his times. He insists
on the incompatibility of the Thirty Years' War
with the precepts of Christ, and demands a better
system of education. In Leyden he wrote under
the pseudonym Angelus Marianus a brief tract:
"Open Gateway of the Heart to the True Kingdom
of Christ" (1632), which arraigns the Lutheran
clergy for the injury done to the Church through
their scholastic and polemical theology. In 1648
he wrote against the Jesuits and in favor of peace,
and declared that Emperor Ferdinand III. trusted
him more than he trusted them.　　　Carl Mirbt.

Bibliography: J. Möller, *Introductio ad hist. ducatuum
Slesvicensis et Holsatici*, ii. 510 sqq., Leipsic, 1699; idem,
Cimbria litterata, ii. 966–970, Copenhagen, 1744; G. Arnold,
Kirchen- und Ketzerhistorie, iii. 88 sqq., iv. 468 sqq., 647
sqq., Frankfort, 1700; E. L. T. Henke, *Georg Calixtus und
seine Zeit*, i. 247 sqq., Halle, 1853; E. Schlee, *Der Streit
des Daniel Hoffmann über das Verhältnis der Philosophie
zur Theologie*, pp. 46 sqq., Marburg, 1862; *ADB*, xli. 759
sqq.

WERENFELS, vär'en-fels, PETER: Swiss pastor; b. at Liestal (4 m. s.w. of Basel) May 20, 1627;
d. at Basel May 23, 1703. He studied at Basel, became court preacher to Count Friedrich Kasimir of
Ortenburg, near Passau, and for half a year conducted the Reformed church service at Strasburg. From
1655 till his death he labored at Basel, being pastor
at the cathedral, and antistes and archdean of the
Basel church. A theological professorship was connected with the office of antistes, and a result of this
activity was a volume of *Disputationes theologicæ*.
But his repute does not rest upon his achievements
as a scholar or teacher. Two volumes of sermons,
David's Pest-Artzney and *Dominicalia*, and numerous single addresses exhibit his homiletic ability.
Werenfels was severely blamed for his attitude in
the fight of a portion of the citizens of Basel against
the oligarchy and its abuses. He had at first expressed sympathy with them, but changed his views

when he saw that the movement was becoming revolutionary. When the government executed three of the ringleaders he preached a sermon admonishing his hearers not to become involved in affairs not their own. He was a protector of Huguenot refugees and of Waldenses. (EBERHARD VISCHER.)

BIBLIOGRAPHY: The one satisfactory account of Werenfels's life is by A. von Salis, in the Beiträge zur vaterlandischen Geschichte, published by the Historical and Antiquarian Society of Basel, new series, v. 1 sqq., Basel, 1901.

WERENFELS, SAMUEL: Swiss theologian: b. at Basel Mar. 1, 1657; d. there June 1, 1740. After finishing his theological and philosophical studies at Basel, he visited the universities at Zurich, Bern, Lausanne, and Geneva. On his return he held, for a short time, the professorship of logic, and in 1685 became professor of Greek at Basel. The next year he undertook an extensive journey through Germany, Belgium, and Holland, one of his companions being Gilbert Burnet (q.v.). In 1687 he was appointed professor of rhetoric, and in 1696 became a member of the theological faculty, occupying successively according to the Basel custom the chairs of dogmatics and polemics, Old Testament, and New Testament. He was thus in a manner compelled to manifest a many-sided activity.

In his De logomachiis eruditorum (Amsterdam, 1688) Werenfels shows how often controversies that divide even Christians are at bottom mere verbal disputes arising from moral deficiencies, especially from pride. He proposed to do away with such disputes by making a universal lexicon of all terms and concepts. In the Oratio de vero et falso theologorum zelo he admonishes those who fight professedly for purity of doctrine but in reality for their own system to show their zeal where the fruits of faith are wanting and Christian love has grown cold. He considers it the duty of the polemist not to combat antiquated heresies and to warm up dead issues, but to overthrow the prevalent enemies of true Christian living. His epigram on the misuse of the Bible is well known: " This is the book in which each both seeks and finds his own dogmas." He had a high conception of his duties as a theological professor, as shown in his address, De scopo doctoris in academia sacras litteras docentis. He believed that it was more important to care for the piety of candidates for the ministry than for their scholarship. It was his belief that a professor of practical theology is as necessary as a professor of practical medicine. He represented a theology that put doctrinal quibbles in the background and laid emphasis upon the pure doctrine which demands a Christian life of purity and love. He stood for the necessity of a special revelation of God, and defended the Biblical miracles as confirmations of the words of the divine evangelists. In his Cogitationes generales de ratione uniendi ecclesias protestantes, quæ vulgo Lutheranarum et Reformatorum nominibus distingui solent, he sought a way of reconciling the two branches of the Protestant Church.

Werenfels's writings went through many editions, as did the sermons he preached in French, which were received with great applause, and were translated into German and Dutch. During the last twenty years of his life he lived in retirement in order to devote his whole time to the care of his soul's welfare, though his solicitude for students did not cease.

It is all the more surprising, on this account, that he thought proper to issue from his retirement and take part in the proceedings against Johann Jakob Wetstein (q.v.) for heresy, especially as he had himself in 1720 expressed the opinion that fallible man ought not to decide upon the regularity of another's faith. He expressed regret afterward at having become involved in the affair.

His Sylloge dissertationum theologicarum appeared first Basel, 1609; a further collection of his works is Opuscula theologica, philologica, et philosophia (Basel, 1718, new ed., 3 vols., 1782).

(EBERHARD VISCHER.)

BIBLIOGRAPHY: Letters by Werenfels are in E. de Budé, Lettres inédites . . . à J. A. Turrettini, vol. iii., Paris and Geneva, 1887, and in Museum Helveticum, part viii., Zurich, 1748. Consult: K. R. Hagenbach, Die theologische Schule Basels und ihre Lehrer, Basel, 1860; A. Schweizer, Die protestantischen Centraldogmen, ii. 776 sqq., Zurich, 1856; L. Junot, in Le chrétien évangélique, xi (1868), 274 sqq.

WERKMEISTER, värk'mai''ster, BENEDIKT MARIA VON (LEONHARD): German Roman Catholic reformer; b. at Füssen (57 m. s.w. of Munich) Oct. 22, 1745; d. at Steinbach (near Stuttgart) July 16, 1823. After preliminary education, by 1764 he had decided to become a monk, and that year entered upon his novitiate; but becoming interested in secular literature, especially in the works of Frederick the Great and Pope's Essay on Man, doubts entered his mind. Nevertheless, his first inclination triumphed and in 1765 he entered the order, assuming the name of the prelate Benedikt Maria. He continued his studies in theology and canon law at Neresheim and Benediktbeuren; was ordained priest in 1769; became master of novices and instructor of philosophy at Neresheim in 1770; held a similar position at the episcopal lyceum of Freising, 1772–74; and then returned to Neresheim as secretary to the abbot, keeper of the archives, librarian, and master of novices. Two works belong to this period in which the reforming tendencies of Werkmeister find expression: Unmassgeblicher Vorschlag zur Reformation des niederen katholischen Klerus nebst Materialien zur Reformation des höheren (" Munich," 1782); and Ueber die christliche Toleranz (" Frankfort and Leipsic," 1784). Both works appeared anonymously through the mediation of Protestants.

In 1784 Werkmeister became court chaplain to Karl Eugen, count of Württemberg. The count was filled with enthusiasm for reform and his wishes coincided with those of his chaplain. Soon after Werkmeister's assumption of his office he issued a modified liturgy, Gesangbuch nebst angehängtem öffentlichem Gebete zum Gebrauch der herzoglich württemburgischen Hofkapelle (1784), the hymns in which were borrowed from Protestant sources. This passed through several editions. The Latin vesper service was next altered to resemble the Protestant afternoon service. Werkmeister introduced the use of German in prayers, readings from the New Testament, and sermons. Gradually he worked into use the German mass and communion service. Only

the *canon missæ* was said in Latin. Werkmeister's
reforms were generally approved, but they were
subject to an attack in the Mainz *Monatschrift von
geistlichen Sachen* (1786, pp. 699 sqq.). Werkmeister replied anonymously with *Ueber die deutschen Mess- und Abendmahlsanstalten in der katholischen Hofkapelle zu Stuttgart* (1787). Further
criticisms were answered in the *Beiträge zur Verbesserung der katholischen Liturgie in Deutschland*
(Ulm, 1789). The influence of the spirit of the
Enlightenment (q.v.) on Werkmeister is further
shown by a collection of sermons, *Predigten in den
Jahren 1784–91* (3 vols., 1812–15). His interest in
catechetics appears in *Ueber den neuen katholischen
Katechismus bei Gelegenheit einer Mainzischen Preis-
aufgabe* (Frankfort, 1789); while his fundamental
religious views appeared in *Thomas Freykirch, oder
freimütige Untersuchungen über die Unfehlbarkeit der
katholischen Kirche* (1792), in which he denied the
infallibility of that church. His reforms seemed
destined to be widely accepted. But the successor
of Karl, Count Ludwig Eugen, who had disapproved of Werkmeister's activity in his brother's
second marriage, did away with the liturgical reforms and retired Werkmeister on a meager pension.
Meanwhile Werkmeister had become secularized;
nevertheless, Abbot Michael Dobler gave him
asylum in Neresheim. But in 1795 he was recalled
by Count Friedrich Eugen, Karl's second brother.
The reforms were restored, except the German mass.
The services of the court chapel became public in
1806, and Werkmeister obtained the parish of
Steinach. In 1807, he was appointed member of
the church council; in 1816, chief councilor for
schools; and in 1817, leading ecclesiastical councilor.
                                              (R. Günther).

Bibliography: I. von Longner, *Beiträge zur Geschichte der
  oberrheinischen Kirchenprovinz*, pp. 291 sqq., Tübingen,
  1863; H. Brück, *Die rationalistischen Bestrebungen im
  katholischen Deutschland*, pp. 21 sqq., Mainz, 1865; J. B.
  Sägmüller, *Die kirchlichen Aufklärung am Hofe des Her-
  zogs Karl Eugen von Württemberg*, Freiburg, 1906; *KL*,
  xii. 1331–32.

WERNER, ver'ner, JOHANNES: German Protestant; b. at Ohrdruf (9 m. s. of Gotha) Sept. 30,
1864. He was educated at the universities of Heidelberg, Berlin, Jena (Ph.D., 1887), and Marburg
(lic. theol., 1889); became privat-docent for church
history and systematic theology at Marburg (1889),
and professor of church history in 1894. Since 1900
he has resided in Leipsic as a private scholar. In
theology he is " liberal." Besides being a collaborator on the *Theologische Rundschau* since 1898 and on
the *Theologischer Jahresbericht* since 1901, he has
written *Hegels Offenbarungsbegriff* (Leipsic, 1887);
Der Paulinismus des Irenæus (1889); *Dogmengeschichtliche Tabellen* (Gotha, 1893; 3d ed., 1903);
and a new edition of K. von Hase's *Hutterus Redivivus* (Leipsic, 1907). Since 1908 he has been one of
the editors of *Die Religion in Geschichte und Gegenwart*.

WERNER, KARL: Roman Catholic; b. at Haf-
nerbach, Lower Austria, Mar. 8, 1821; d. at Vienna
Apr. 4, 1888. He was a student at Melk, Krems,
St. Pölten, and at the priests' institute in Vienna,
1842–45, when he gained his doctorate from Vienna

University. He was professor of moral theology
in the Episcopal Seminary at St. Pölten, 1847–70,
and of New-Testament theology in the University
of Vienna, 1871–81; and was ministerial and consistorial councilor at Vienna, 1880–88. His works
embrace *System der christlichen Ethik* (3 vols.,
Regensburg, 1852); *Grundlinien der Philosophie*
(1855); *Der heilige Thomas von Aquino* (3 vols.,
1858–59); *Franz Suarez und die Scholastik der letzten
Jahrhunderte* (2 vols., 1861); *Geschichte der apolo-
getischen und polemischen Literatur der christlichen
Theologie* (5 vols., Schaffhausen, 1861–67); *Gerbert
von Aurillac* (Vienna, 1878); *Giambattista Vico als
Philosoph und gelehrter Forscher* (1879); *Beda der
Ehrwürdige* (new ed., 1881); *Die Scholastik des
späteren Mittelalters* (7 vols., 1881–87); *Die italien-
ische Philosophie des XIX. Jahrhunderts* (5 vols.,
1884–86).

Bibliography: J. Kopallik, in *Wiener Diöcesanblatt*, 1897,
  pp. 145 sqq.; *KL*, xii. 1332–34.

WERNLE, värn'le, PAUL: Swiss Protestant;
b. in Zurich May 1, 1872. He was educated at the
universities of Göttingen, Berlin, and Basel (lic.
theol., 1896); became privat-docent for exegesis at
Basel (1896), associate professor (1901), and professor of modern church history (1905). He is an
advocate of " free theological science and Christo-
centric religion," and has written *Der Christ und die
Sünde bei Paulus* (Tübingen, 1897); *Paulus als
Heidenmissionar* (1899); *Die synoptische Frage*
(1899); *Die Anfänge unserer Religion* (1901; Eng.
transl. by G. A. Bienemann, *The Beginnings of
Christianity*, 2 vols., London, 1903–04); *Die
Reichsgotteshoffnung in der ältesten christlichen Doku-
menten und bei Jesus* (1903); *Was haben wir heute an
Paulus?* (Basel, 1903); *Die Renaissance des Christentums im sechzehnten Jahrhundert* (Tübingen,
1904); *Einführung in das theologische Studium*
(1908, 2d. ed., 1911), *Johann Hinrich Wichern* (Basel,
1908); and *Renaissance und Reformation* (1911).

WERNSDORF, värns'dorf, ERNST FRIEDRICH:
German theologian, second son of Gottlieb Wernsdorf (q.v.); b. at Wittenberg Dec. 18, 1718; d. there
May 7, 1782. He studied at the University of Leipsic (M.A., 1742; D.D., 1756); was appointed professor of Christian archeology there (1752); and in
1756 he went to Wittenberg as professor of theology.
His writings dealt with matters of Biblical, antiquarian, and Reformation history. His name has
come into new prominence as once the owner of a
manuscript of Luther's *Tischreden*, the document
mentioned so early as 1769 by J. T. Lingke. It
was doubtless through Wernsdorf's widow, who
long survived her husband, that this manuscript
came into the possession of Politz, with whose collection of books it subsequently found its way to the
city library of Leipsic.   Georg Müller.

Bibliography: J. G. Meusel, *Lexicon der . . . teutschen
  Schriftsteller* xv. 35–37, Leipsic, 1816; M. Hoffmann,
  Pförtner Stammbuch 1543–1893, p. 222, Berlin, 1893; E.
  Kroker, *Luthers Tischreden in der Mathesischen Samm-
  lung*, pp. 17 sqq., Leipsic, 1903; *ADB*, xlii. 96–98.

WERNSDORF, GOTTLIEB: German theologian; b. at Schönewalde (48 m. s. of Berlin) Feb.
25, 1668; d. at Wittenberg July 1, 1729. He studied

at Wittenberg (M.A., 1689; D.D., 1700); lectured with success on logic, ethics, and history in the philosophical faculty of that university; was transferred, in 1698, as professor extraordinary in the theological faculty, his thesis treating *De auctoritate librorum symbolicorum;* became regular professor in 1706; in 1710 was appointed provost at the residential church, and, shortly thereafter, general superintendent at Wittenberg. He became, notably in his later years, universally revered among his theological pupils, being affectionately known as " Father Wernsdorf." While his lectures were not always distinguished by depth, they were marked by clearness, excellence of form, and especially by great earnestness in the admonitory portions.

His *Disputationes academicæ* were published by Christian Heinrich Zeibich (2 vols., 1736). Special mention may be made of his *De primordiis emendatæ per Lutherum religionis* (new ed., 1735), and of his most extensive production, *Gründliche Reformationshistorie* (Wittenberg, 1717), which comes down to the Diet of Augsburg, 1530.

Consistently with his theological position, he belonged to the advocates of the more lenient orthodoxy. His anti-Calvinistic arguments appear in the *Demonstratio quod juxta Calvini doctrinam Reformati nec sint nec jure haberi possint socii Augustanæ Confessionis.* He took part in the contemporary controversies with Pietists and Mystics, as with the leading philosophers of the time. If, on the one hand, he opposed the one-sided emphasis of emotion in religion, on the other hand he strongly emphasized the element of inspiration, which he held to be mediately operative even in the symbolical books of Lutheranism.   GEORG MÜLLER.

BIBLIOGRAPHY: C. Coler, *De Wernsdorfii in rem sacram et literariam meritis,* Leipsic, 1719; J. A. Gleich, *Annales ecclesiastici,* i. 369, ii. passim, Dresden, 1730; A. Tholuck, *Der Geist der lutherischen Theologen Wittenbergs,* pp. 259 sqq., Hamburg, 1852; *ADB,* xlii. 96–98.

WERNZ, FRANZ XAVER: General of the Jesuit order; b. at Rottweil (30 m. s.w. of Tübingen) Dec. 4, 1842. On the completion of his education he became, in 1862, a teacher at the school of Stella Matutina in Feldkirch-im-Breisgau, whence he was later transferred to the seminary at Ditton Hall, Lancashire, as instructor in canon law. In 1883 he was appointed to the faculty of the Collegium Romanum, Rome, of which he was made rector in 1894, being at the same time a professor at the Gregorian University. He was chosen general of the Society of Jesus Apr. 18, 1906. He has written *Jus decretalium ad usum prælectionum* (4 vols., Rome, 1898–1904; 2d ed., 1905 sqq.).

WERTHEIM BIBLE. See BIBLES, ANNOTATED, AND BIBLE SUMMARIES, I., § 4.

WESEL, vê′zel, **JOHN OF:** Reformer before the Reformation; b. at Ober-Wesel (26 m. w.n.w. of Mainz) in the early part of the fifteenth century; d. at Mainz after 1479. His family name is variously written Ruchrath or Richrath [Ruchard, Ruchrad, Rucherath], and the family itself was native to the immediate region where John was born. He first appears in history as matriculating at the University of Erfurt (1441–42), where he took his bachelor's degree in 1442, the master's in 1445,

became licentiate in 1456 and the same year doctor of theology. He was rector of the university in 1456–57, and at the end of 1457 was vice-rector for a time. In his work on the councils Luther declares that John ruled the university with his books, and these Luther himself used in preparing for his master's degree. Bartholomæus Arnoldi of Usingen reports in a work first printed in 1499 that John's reputation still lived at Erfurt; he apologizes also for differing in opinion from John, whose statements, he declares, do not always square with the truth, professes to give an example of this from John's commentary on the Aristotelian physics, and adds a cryptic remark to the effect that everything is not to be told to the public at large, though they may be clear to the learned. This can not be pressed so far as to mean that Arnoldi charged John with teachings contrary to those of the Church. Indeed, Johann von Lutter, many years a colleague of Wesel at Erfurt, reports that Wesel often said from his chair that he would maintain nothing which was dissonant from the teaching of the Roman Church or the doctrines of its approved doctors (N. Paulus, *Der Augustiner Bartholomäus Arnoldi von Usingen,* pp. 8 sqq., Strasburg, 1893). Yet Wesel may have given utterance to somewhat bold expressions regarding the early Fathers of the Church. Toward the end of 1460 Wesel was canon at Worms; and early in 1461 he became professor at Basel, though only after protracted negotiations. Here, too, his stay was brief, for in 1463 he was preacher at the cathedral at Worms. But his sermons caused offense, now by pedantic and confusing speculation, now by bold attacks upon the Church, its sacraments, teachings, and tendencies. Bishop Reinhard was compelled to depose him, after warning him at Heidelberg in the presence of the theologians. Yet Diether von Isenberg, archbishop of Mainz, called him as pastor to the cathedral. Here, too, he aroused suspicions by relations with a Bohemian adventurer who had been accustomed to meet him at Worms and had followed him to Mainz, to whom he gave a little treatise for his companions in Bohemia. This came by a circuitous route into the hands of the archbishop, and, after it had been submitted to the professors of the university, brought punishment upon the Hussite and upon Wesel. The latter was put upon his defense before a board of theologians from Cologne and Heidelberg; he was then an old man of eighty, but it was reported that his answers before the inquisitors were indifferent, confused, suspicious, and evasive. On Sunday, Feb. 21, 1479, he recanted in the cathedral, his writings were burned, and he was himself condemned to lifelong repentance in the Augustinian monastery at Mainz, where soon afterward he died.

During the trial Wesel designated as his own four tracts: (1) *Super modo obligationis legum humanarum ad quendam Nicolaum de Bohemia;* (2) *De potestate ecclesiastica;* (3) *De indulgentiis;* and (4) *De jejuniis.* Of these only one can now be positively identified; the *Disputatio adversus indulgentias* is extant in a manuscript, in the royal library at Berlin, bearing the date 1478, and has been printed both by C. W. F. Walch in *Monumenta medii ævi,* i. 1, pp. 111–156

(Göttingen, 1757) and by H. von der Hardt about twenty years earlier in *Septem coronamenta supra septem columnas academiæ regiæ Georgiæ Augustæ, quæ Goetingæ est*, pp. 13–23. The central part is contained in the disputation-theses (chaps. 3–10), which belong probably to the year 1475. The second document acknowledged by Wesel has been sought in the *Opusculum de auctoritate, officio et potestate pastorum ecclesiasticorum*, which was published without place or date (possibly Zwolle, 1522). But this is in style fundamentally different from the work on indulgences, professes to be by a layman, and can not be by Wesel. From the period of Wesel's teaching at Erfurt there has come down in manuscript *Quæstiones de libris physicorum Aristotelis*, the manuscript being at Erfurt, and a commentary on the "Sentences" of Peter Lombard, this being at Berlin. From his period at Basel there is a lecture on logic and a commentary on *Aristotelis libros de omnia*, the manuscripts having been copied in 1462–1463 and being found in the Munich library. In the library of the University of Würzburg there is a copy of an exchange of polemical writings between Wesel and John of Lutter, debating the question whether the pope is the vicar of Christ and whether pope or council have authority in case of deadly sin; in both cases Wesel took the negative.

As a source for the teaching of Wesel only the *Disputatio adversus indulgentias* can be used. His answers during his examination would be pertinent, if only they were clear and consistent. Wesel stood with the general teaching of the Church of the Middle Ages and with Augustine and Thomas Aquinas in his doctrines of sin, grace, forgiveness of sins, and penance. In connection with the sacrament of penance Wesel was a Scotist and nominalist, holding that the priest can not *principaliter et effective* forgive sin, but only through divine assistance, and the priestly forgiving of sin is only a sacramental ministry to the penitent sinner. The one who alone forgives sin is God, who has called the priest to take part therein; the gift of grace in the sacrament of penance is the remission of guilt and punishment in hell, remission of divine punishment is not an accompaniment. Indulgences are a pious imposture upon the faithful; yet so far as pilgrimages and alms and the like good works are done in love to God, they are in themselves useful and contribute to the obtaining of eternal life. Remission is serviceable only in remitting ecclesiastical penalties. Wesel taught of the Church that it is the aggregate of the faithful joined together in love, known to God alone; it is the bride of Christ, is ruled by the Holy Spirit, and in matters essential to salvation can not err. As to Scripture he held that it alone is to be trusted, and neither Fathers nor general councils. To the test of agreement with Scripture all ecclesiastical dogmas and ceremonies are to be submitted. Contrary to Scripture are the Roman Church's teachings respecting indulgences, original sin, transubstantiation, the *filioque*, feasts and fasts, long prayers, ceremonies of the mass, holy oil, consecrated water, and the like. A sentence at the end of the *Paradoxa* sums up the man: "I despise pope, Church, and councils; I love Christ. Let the word of Christ dwell in you richly." (OTTO CLEMEN.)

XII.—20

BIBLIOGRAPHY: C. Ullmann, *Reformers Before the Reformation*, i. 277–374, Edinburgh, 1874, cf. his *Johann Wessel, ein Vorgänger Luthers*, Hamburg, 1834 (comprehensive, includes in the treatment the entire environment, and discusses the principal personages with whom Wesel was connected); N. Serrarius, in *Moguntiarum rerum scriptores*, ed. G. C. Joannis, i. 107 sqq., Frankfort, 1722 (for selection of "heretical" declarations of Wesel); G. Schadé, *Essai sur Jean de Wesel*, Strasburg, 1856; J. C. L. Gieseler, *Text-Book on Church History*, ed. H. B. Smith, iii. 461–465, New York, 1868 (quotes extensively from documents); N. Paulus, in *Der Katholik*, 1898, i. 44–57; idem, in *Zeitschrift für katholische Theologie*, xxiv (1900), 646–656, xxvii (1903), 601–602; J. Falk, *Bibelstudien, Bibelhandschriften und Bibeldrucke zu Mainz*, pp. 60 sqq., Mainz, 1901; F. Kropatschek, *Das Schriftprinzip der lutherischen Kirche*, i. 407 sqq., Leipsic, 1904; O. Clemen, in *Historische Vierteljahrschrift*, iii. 521–523; *Deutsche Zeitschrift für Geschichtswissenschaft*, new series, ii. 143–173 (by O. Clemen), 344–348 (by J. Haussleiter); Schaff, *Christian Church*, v. 2, pp. 681–682; Harnack, *Dogma*, vi. 170, 199, 222, 262, 268–269, vii. 16; *ADB*, xxix. 439–444; *KL*, vi. 1786–89.

For accounts of the trial consult: C. Du Plessis d'Argentré, *Collectio de novis erroribus*, vol. i., Paris, 1728 (contains the *Paradoxa*—a collection of "heretical" sentences abstracted from Wesel's writings, *Examen magistrale*—an account of the trial, and the author's survey, by one of the Heidelberg representatives); this is found also in Æneas Sylvius' *Commentariorum de concilio Basileæ libri duo*, n.p., n.d.; Ortuinus Gratius, *Fasciculus rerum expetendarum et fugiendarum*, pp. clxiii. sqq., Cologne, 1535.

WESLEY, CHARLES: One of the founders of Methodism; b. at Epworth (23 m. n.w. of Lincoln) Dec. 18, 1708, O. S. (Dec. 29, N. S.); d. in London Mar. 29, 1788. He was the son of Samuel Wesley, Sr., and brother of Charles Wesley (qq.v.). In childhood he declined an offer of adoption by a wealthy namesake in Ireland; and the person taken in his stead became an earl, and grandfather to the duke of Wellington. He was educated at Westminster School, London, under his brother Samuel, 1716; at St. Peter's College, Westminster, London, 1721; and at Christ Church, Oxford, 1726, where, with his brother John and one or two others, he received the nickname of "Methodist" in consequence of the method they employed in prayer and daily life. In 1735 he was ordained, and went with John Wesley to Georgia, returning 1736. May 21, 1738, he "experienced the witness of adoption," and at once joined his brother's evangelistic work, traveling much, and preaching with great zeal and success. He never held ecclesiastical preferment, and bore his share of the persecutions which beset the early Methodists. Apr. 8, 1749, he married Sarah Gwynne: by her he had eight children, two of whom became eminent musicians. John Wesley's expression, "his least praise was his talent for poetry," is unmeaning: whatever his other gifts and graces, it is because he was "the poet of Methodism" and one of the most gifted and voluminous of English hymn-writers that his fame and influence live. *The Poetical Works of John and Charles Wesley*, as reprinted by the Wesleyan Conference (London, 1868–72), fill thirteen volumes, or near 6,000 pages. Of the original publications, the earlier ones bore the names of both brothers, but most were the work of Charles alone. While in the books of joint authorship it is not always possible to distinguish with absolute certainty between the two, it is generally agreed that John wrote only the translations (almost wholly from the German, some forty in all) and a very few originals. Their style is the same, save for a little more severity and dignity on John's part. Their first volume (or perhaps John's alone, for it bears no name), possibly also the first English *Collection of Psalms and Hymns*, appeared at Charleston, S. C., 1737 (cf. C. Evans, *American Bibliography*, vol. ii., no. 4207, Chicago, 1904; there is a copy in the Public Library, New York). A single copy was found in London, 1879, and reprinted 1882. The original contains some pieces by John, but apparently none by Charles, who perhaps had not then begun to write. Another small *Collection* was published in London, 1738; and in 1739 began the long series of original works in verse. The more extensive of these were *Hymns and Sacred Poems* (1739, 1740, 1742; three separate books); the same (2 vols., 1749); *Hymns on God's Everlasting Love* (1741); *On the Lord's Supper* (1745); *For those that Seek and those that have Redemption* (1747); *Funeral Hymns* (1746–59); *Short Hymns on Select Passages of Holy Scripture* (2 vols., 1762; 2,348 pieces); *Hymns for Children* (1763); *For Families* (1767); *On the Trinity* (1767). Besides these there are some twenty tracts, minor in size, but containing some of Charles Wesley's most effective lyrics, and a few elegies and epistles. The work of publication went on, though less vigorously in later years, till 1785, and that of composition till his death, at which he left in manuscript a quantity of verse, chiefly on Bible texts, equal to one-third of that printed in his lifetime. His huge fecundity hindered his fame; had he written less, he might be read more; but he had not the gift of condensing. His thoughts, or at least his feelings, flowed more readily in verse than in prose; he wrote on horseback, in a stage-coach, almost in "the article of death." His fifty-six *Hymns for Christian Friends*, some of them continuously and widely used, were dedicated to Miss Gwynne; and his last verse, taken down by her "when he could scarcely articulate," preserves something of the old fire. Nearly every occasion and condition of external life are provided for in the vast range of his productions, which have more "variety of matter and manner" than critics have commonly supposed; and, as to feelings and experiences, "he has celebrated them with an affluence of diction and a splendor of coloring never surpassed and rarely equaled." Temperament and belief alike inclined him to subjective themes, and, guiding his unique lyrical talent, made him preeminently "the poet of Methodism." To the wonderful growth and success of that system his hymns were no less essential than his brother's government. They are the main element in most Wesleyan collections, both English and American. In the newest official hymnal of the Methodist Episcopal Church and the Methodist Episcopal Church, South, no fewer than 121 of the 748 hymns are Charles Wesley's. The most widely used, in America at least, are "Oh for a thousand tongues to sing," "Jesus, lover of my soul," and "Love divine all loves excelling." Probably no school or system in any age or land has owned so mighty an implement in the way of sacred song, and no other hymn-writer has succeeded in voicing so felicitously the varied states of religious feeling. His productions are still esteemed as among the most choice and helpful devotional literature, and many of them seem to be wholly unaffected by the marked changes in religious thought and in the emphasis placed upon various doctrines. Non-Methodists long suspected and shunned this poetry, and still need to exercise discrimination in making selections from it. Its author was given not only to extravagances of expression (which were sometimes pared down by his brother's severer taste), but to unrestrained and often violent emotion. Withal he is too fluent, too rhetorical; his mannerism at times involves a lack of simplicity; his "fatal facility of strong words" is a fault both literary and religious. Yet his intensely sincere and fervent piety, his intellectual strength and acuteness, his unmistakably high culture, and the matchless spontaneity of his eloquence, place him easily near the head of British sacred lyrists. No collection is complete—probably for a century none has been formed—without his hymns; and they are now perhaps more generally and widely used than of old. He is entitled to rank not merely as a hymn-writer, but among Christian poets. Many of his pieces which are not adapted to public worship, and very little known, possess much literary and human interest; his autobiographic and polemic verses, e.g., are probably unequaled. He can not be adequately judged by his fragmentary appearances in the hymnals, not even by John Wesley's *Collection for the Use of the People called Methodists* (1780; supplement 1830); though that presents a considerable fraction of his writings, with much less abridgment and alteration than any other, and has nearly all the qualities claimed by its editor in his vigorous and memorable preface.

[A somewhat higher estimate than the above of the poetry and hymns of Charles Wesley is furnished by Canon Overton (Julian, *Hymnology*, p. 1258): "As a hymn-writer Charles Wesley was unique. He is said to have written . . . 6,500 hymns, and though . . . in so vast a number some are of unequal merit, it is . . . marvelous how many there are which rise to the highest degree of excellence. His feelings on every occasion of importance . . . found their best expression in a hymn. . . . Nor must we forget his hymns for little children, a branch of sacred poetry in which the mantle of Dr. Watts seems to have fallen upon him. . . . The saying that a really good hymn is as rare an appearance as that of a comet is falsified by the work of Charles Wesley."]

(FREDERIC M. BIRD†.) Revised by H. K. CARROLL.

BIBLIOGRAPHY: Besides the preface to John Wesley's *Collection for the Use of the People Called Methodists*, ut sup, and *The Early Journal of 1736–39*, London, 1910, consult: T. Jackson, *Life of Rev. Charles Wesley*, 2 vols., London and New York, 1842 (the authoritative work); D. Creamer, *Methodist Hymnology*, New York, 1848; C. Adams, *Memorials of Charles Wesley*, ib. 1859; F. A. Archibald, *Methodism and Literature*, Cincinnati, 1883; S. W. Duffield, *English Hymns*, pp. 346–351, New York, 1887; J. Telford, *Life of Rev. Charles Wesley*, enlarged ed., London, 1900; N. Smith, *Hymns historically Famous*, pp. 69–83, Chicago, 1901; Julian, *Hymnology*, pp. 726–729, 1255–66; the literature dealing with the early history of METHODISTS, and that under WESLEY, JOHN; and R. Green, *The Works of John and Charles Wesley. A Bibliography containing an exact Account of all the Publications issued by the Wesley Brothers . . . in chronological Order*, London, 1896.

WESLEY, JOHN.

John Wesley, the father of the doctrinal and practical system of Methodism, was born at Epworth (23 m. n.w. of Lincoln) June 28, 1703, and died in London Mar. 2, 1791. The Wesleys were of ancient
1. **Youth.** Saxon lineage, the family history being traced backward to the time of Athelstan the Saxon, when Guy Wesley, or Wellesley, was created a thane or member of parliament. John Wesley was the son of Samuel Wesley (q.v.), a graduate of Oxford, and a minister of the Church of England, who had married in 1689 Susannah, the twenty-fifth child of Dr. Samuel Annesley, and herself became the mother of nineteen children; in 1696 he was appointed rector of Epworth, where John, the fifteenth child, was born. He was christened John Benjamin, but he never used the second name. An incident of his childhood was his rescue, at the age of six, from the burning rectory. The manner of his escape made a deep impression on his mind; and he spoke of himself as a " brand plucked from the burning," and as a child of Providence. The early education of all the children was given by Mrs. Wesley, a woman of remarkable intelligence and deep piety, apt in teaching, and wise and firm in governing. In 1713 John was admitted to the Charterhouse School, London, where he lived the studious, methodical, and (for a while) religious life in which he had been trained at home. In 1720 he entered Christ Church College, Oxford (M.A., 1727), was ordained deacon in 1725 and elected fellow of Lincoln College in the following year. He served his father as curate two years, and then returned to Oxford to fulfil his functions as fellow.

The year of his return to Oxford (1729) marks the beginning of the rise of Methodism. The famous " holy club " was formed; and its members, including John and Charles Wesley, were derisively called " Methodists," because of their methodical habits.
2. **In Oxford and Georgia.** John had enjoyed during his early years a deep religious experience. He went, says one of his best biographers, Tyerman, to Charterhouse a saint; but he became negligent of his religious duties, and left a sinner. In the year of his ordination he read Thomas à Kempis and Jeremy Taylor, and began to grope after those religious truths which underlay the great revival of the eighteenth century. The reading of Law's *Christian Perfection* and *Serious Call* gave him, he said, a sublimer view of the law of God; and he resolved to keep it, inwardly and outwardly, as sacredly as possible, believing that in this obedience he should find salvation. He pursued a rigidly methodical and abstemious life; studied the Scriptures, and performed his religious duties with great diligence; deprived himself that he might have alms to give; and gave his heart, mind, and soul to the effort to live a godly life. When, in 1735, a clergyman " inured to contempt of the ornaments and conveniences of life, to bodily austerities, and to serious thoughts," was wanted

by Governor Oglethorpe to go to Georgia, Wesley responded, and remained in the colony two years, returning to England in 1738, feeling that his mission, which was to convert the Indians and deepen and regulate the religious life of the colonists, had been a failure. His High-church notions, his strict enforcement of the regulations of the church, especially concerning the administration of the holy communion, were not agreeable to the colonists; and he left Georgia with several indictments pending against him (largely due to malice) for alleged violation of church law.

As Wesley's spiritual state is the key to his whole career, an account of his conversion in the year of his return from Georgia may not be omitted. For
3. **Conversion; Open-air Preaching.** ten years he had fought against sin, striven to fulfil the law of the Gospel, endeavored to manifest his righteousness; but he had not, he wrote, obtained freedom from sin, nor the witness of the Spirit, because he sought it, not by faith, but " by the works of the law." He had learned from the Moravians that true faith was inseparably connected with dominion over sin and constant peace proceeding from a sense of forgiveness, and that saving faith is given in a moment. This saving faith he obtained May 24, 1737–38, at a Moravian meeting in Aldersgate Street, London, while listening to the reading of Luther's preface to the Epistle to the Romans, in which explanation of faith and the doctrine of justification by faith is given. " I felt," he wrote, " my heart strangely warmed. I felt I did trust in Christ, Christ alone, for salvation; and an assurance was given me that he had taken away my sins." Two or three weeks later he preached a remarkable sermon, enforcing the doctrine of present personal salvation by faith, which was followed by another, on God's grace " free in all, and free for all." He never ceased in his whole subsequent career to preach this doctrine and that of the witness of the Spirit. He allied himself with the Moravian society in Fetter Lane, and in 1738 went to Herrnhut, the Moravian headquarters in Germany, to learn more of a people to whom he felt deeply indebted. On his return to England he drew up rules for the bands into which the Fetter Lane Society was divided, and published a collection of hymns for them. He met frequently with this and other religious societies in London, but did not preach often in 1738, because most of the parish churches were closed to him. His friend, George Whitefield (q.v.), the great evangelist, upon his return from America, was likewise excluded from the churches of Bristol; and, going to the neighboring village of Kingswood, he there preached in the open air, Feb., 1739, to a company of miners. This was a bold step, and Wesley hesitated to accept Whitefield's earnest request to follow him in this innovation. But he overcame his scru-

ples, and in April preached his first sermon in the open air, near Bristol. He said he could hardly reconcile himself to field-preaching, and would have thought, " till very lately," such a method of saving souls as " almost a sin." These open-air services were very successful; and he never again hesitated to preach in any place where an assembly could be got together, more than once using his father's tombstone at Epworth as a pulpit. He spent upward of fifty years in field-preaching—standing in churches when he was invited, taking his stand in the fields, in halls, cottages, and chapels, when the churches would not receive him. Late in 1739 a rupture with the Moravians in London occurred. Wesley had helped them organize in May, 1738, the Fetter Lane Society; and the converts of the preaching of himself, his brother, and White-field, had become members of their bands. But finding, as he said, that they had fallen into heresies, especially quietism, a separatioh took place; and so, at the close of 1739, Wesley was led to form his followers into a separate society. " Thus," he wrote, " without any previous plan, began the Methodist Society in England." Similar societies were soon formed in Bristol and Kingswood, and wherever Wesley and his coadjutors made converts.

From 1739 onward Wesley and the Methodists were persecuted by clergymen and magistrates, attacked in sermon, tract, and book,

4. Persecutions; Lay Preaching. mobbed by the populace, often in controversy, always at work among the neglected and needy, and ever increasing. They were denounced as promulgators of strange doctrines, fomenters of religious disturbances; as blind fanatics, leading the people astray, claiming miraculous gifts, inveighing against the clergy of the Church of England, and endeavoring to reestablish popery. Wesley was frequently mobbed, and great violence was done both to the persons and property of Methodists. Seeing, however, that the church failed in its duty to call sinners to repentance, that its clergymen were worldly minded, and that souls were perishing in their sins, he regarded himself as commissioned of God to warn men to flee from the wrath to come; and no opposition, or persecution, or obstacles were permitted by him to prevail against the divine urgency and authority of his commission. The prejudices of his High-church training, his strict notions of the methods and proprieties of public worship, his views of the apostolic succession and the prerogatives of the priest, even his most cherished convictions, were not allowed to stand in the way in which Providence seemed to lead. Unwilling that ungodly men should perish in their sins and unable to reach them from the pulpits of the Church, he began field-preaching. Seeing that he and the few clergymen cooperating with him could not do the work that needed to be done, he was led, as early as 1739, to approve tacitly, soon after openly, of lay preaching; and men who were not episcopally ordained were permitted to preach and do pastoral work. Thus one of the great features of Methodism, to which it has largely owed its success, was adopted by Wesley in answer to a necessity.

As his societies must have houses to worship in, he began in 1739 to provide chapels, first in Bristol, and then in London and elsewhere. The

5. Chapels and Organizations. Bristol chapel was at first in the hands of trustees; but as a large debt was contracted, and Wesley's friends urged him to keep its pulpit under his own control, the deed was cancelled, and the trust became vested in himself. Following this precedent, all Methodist chapels were committed in trust to him until by a " deed of declaration " (see METHODISTS, I., 1, § 6) all his interests in them were transferred to a body of preachers called the " Legal Hundred." When disorderly persons began to manifest themselves among the members of the societies, he adopted the plan of giving tickets to members, with their names written thereon by his own hand. These were renewed every three months. Those who proved to be unworthy did not receive new tickets, and thus dropped out of the society without disturbance. The tickets were regarded as commendatory letters. When the debt on a chapel became burdensome, it was proposed that one in every twelve of the members should collect offerings for it regularly from the eleven allotted to him. Out of this, under Wesley's care, grew, in 1742, the Methodist class-meeting system (see METHODISTS, I., 1, § 3). In order more effectually to keep the disorderly out of the societies, he established a probationary system, and resolved to visit each society once in three months. Thus arose the quarterly visitation, or conference. As the societies increased, he could not continue his practise of oral instruction; so he drew up in 1743 a set of " General Rules " for the " United Societies," which were the nucleus of the Methodist *Discipline*, and are still preserved intact and observed by most Methodist bodies. As the number of preachers and preaching-places increased, it was desirable that doctrinal matters should be discussed, difficulties considered, and that an understanding should be had as to the distribution of fields; so the two Wesleys, with four other clergymen and four lay preachers, met for consultation in London in 1744. This was the first Methodist conference (see METHODISTS, I., 1, § 5). Two years later, in order that the preachers might work more systematically, and the societies receive their services more regularly, Wesley appointed his " helpers " to definitive circuits, each of which included at least thirty appointments a month. Believing that their usefulness and efficiency were promoted by being changed from one circuit to another every year or two, he established the itinerancy, and ever insisted that his preachers should submit to its rules. When, in 1788, some persons objected to the frequent changes, he wrote, " For fifty years God has been pleased to bless the itinerant plan, the last year most of all. It must not be altered till I am removed, and I hope it will remain till our Lord comes to reign on earth."

As his societies multiplied, and all these elements of an ecclesiastical system were, one after another, adopted, the breach between Wesley and the Church of England gradually widened. The question of separation from that church, urged, on the one side, by some of his preachers and societies, and most strenuously opposed on the other by his brother

Charles and others, was constantly before him, but was not settled. In 1745 he wrote that he and

6. Ordination of Ministers. his coadjutors would make any concession which their conscience would permit, in order to live in harmony with the clergy; but they could not give up the doctrine of an inward and present salvation by faith alone, nor cease to preach in private houses and the open air, nor dissolve the societies, nor suppress lay preaching. Further than this, however, he refused then to go. "We dare not," he said, "administer baptism or the Lord's Supper without a commission from a bishop in the apostolic succession." But the next year he read Lord King on the Primitive Church, and was convinced by it that apostolic succession was a figment, and that he [Wesley] was "a scriptural *episcopos* as much as any man in England." Some years later Stillingfleet's *Irenicon* led him to renounce the opinion that Christ or his apostles prescribed any form of church government, and to declare ordination valid when performed by a presbyter. It was not until about forty years after this that he ordained by the imposition of hands; but he considered his appointment of his preachers an act of ordination. The conference of 1746 declared that the reason more solemnity in receiving new laborers was not employed was because it savored of stateliness and of haste. "We desire barely to follow Providence as it gradually opens." When, however, he deemed that Providence had opened the way, and the bishop of London had definitely declined to ordain a minister for the American Methodists who were without the ordinances, he ordained by imposition of hands preachers for Scotland and England and America, with power to administer the sacraments. He consecrated, also, by laying on of hands, Dr. Thomas Coke (q.v.), a presbyter of the Church of England, to be superintendent or bishop in America, and a preacher, Alexander Mather, to the same office in England. He designed that both Coke and Mather should ordain others. This act alarmed his brother Charles, who besought him to stop and consider before he had "quite broken down the bridge," and not embitter his [Charles'] last moments on earth, nor "leave an indelible blot on our memory." Wesley declared, in reply, that he had not separated from the church, nor did he intend to, but he must and would save as many souls as he could while alive, "without being careful about what may possibly be when I die." Thus, though he rejoiced that the Methodists in America were freed from entanglements with both Church and State, he counseled his English followers to remain in the established church; and he himself died in that communion.

Wesley was a strong controversialist. The most notable of his controversies was that on Calvinism. His father was of the Arminian school in the church;

7. Advocacy of Arminianism. but John settled the question for himself while in college, and expressed himself strongly against the doctrines of election and reprobation. Whitefield inclined to Calvinism. In his first tour in America, he embraced the views of the New England school of Calvinism; and when Wesley

preached a sermon on *Free Grace*, attacking predestination as blasphemous, as representing "God as worse than the devil," Whitefield besought him (1739) not to repeat or publish the discourse. He deprecated a dispute or discussion. "Let us," he said, "offer salvation freely to all," but be silent about election. Wesley's sermon was published, and among the many replies to it was one by Whitefield. Separation followed in 1741. Wesley wrote of it, that those who held universal redemption did not desire separation, but "those who held particular redemption would not hear of any accommodation." Whitefield, Harris, Cennick, and others, became the founders of Calvinistic Methodism (see PRESBYTERIANS, IV., VIII., 8). Whitefield and Wesley, however, were soon again on very friendly terms, and their friendship remained thenceforth unbroken, though they traveled different paths. Occasional publications appeared on Calvinistic doctrines, by Wesley and others; but in 1770 the controversy broke out anew with violence and bitterness. Toplady, Berridge, Rowland, Richard Hill, and others were engaged on the one side, and Wesley and Fletcher chiefly on the other side. Toplady was editor of *The Gospel Magazine*, which was filled with the controversy. Wesley in 1778 began the publication of *The Arminian Magazine*, not, he said, to convince Calvinists, but to preserve Methodists; not to notice opponents, but to teach the truth that "God willeth all men to be saved." A "lasting peace" he thought could be secured in no other way.

The doctrines which Wesley revived, restated, and emphasized in his sermons and writings, are

8. Doctrines. present personal salvation by faith, the witness of the Spirit, and sanctification. The second he defined thus: "the testimony of the Spirit is an inward impression on the soul of believers, whereby the spirit of God directly testifies to their spirit that they are the children of God." Sanctification he spoke of (1790) as the "grand *depositum* which God has lodged with the people called 'Methodists'; and, for the sake of propagating this chiefly, he appears to have raised them up." He taught that sanctification was obtainable instantaneously by faith, between justification and death. It was not "sinless perfection" that he contended for; but he believed that those who are "perfect in love" feel no sin, feel nothing but love. He was very anxious that this doctrine should be constantly preached for the system of Wesleyan Arminianism, the foundations of which were laid by Wesley and Fletcher (see ARMINIUS, JACOBUS, AND ARMINIANISM).

Wesley was the busiest man in England. He traveled almost constantly, generally on horseback,

9. Personality and Activities. preaching twice or thrice a day. He formed societies, opened chapels, examined and commissioned preachers, administered discipline, raised funds for schools, chapels, and charities, prescribed for the sick, superintended schools and orphanages, prepared commentaries and a vast amount of other religious literature, replied to attacks on Methodism, conducted controversies, and carried on a prodigious correspondence. He is believed to have traveled in the course of his itinerant ministry more than 250,000 miles, and to have preached more than 40,000 times. The number of works he wrote, translated, or edited, exceeds 200. The list includes sermons, commentaries, hymns, a Christian library of fifty volumes, and other religious literature—grammars, dictionaries, and other textbooks, as well as political tracts. He is said to have received not less than £20,000 for his publications, but he used little of it for himself. His charities were limited only by his means. He died poor. He rose at four in the morning, lived simply and methodically, and was never idle, unless by compulsion. In person he was rather under the medium height, well proportioned, strong, with a bright eye, a clear complexion, and a saintly, intellectual face. He married very unhappily, at the age of forty-eight, a widow, and had no children. He died, after a short illness in which he had great spiritual peace and joy, leaving as the result of his life-work 135,000 members, and 541 itinerant preachers, owning the name " Methodist."

Wesley's mind was of a logical cast. His conceptions were clear, his perceptions quick. His thought clothed itself easily and naturally in pure, terse, vigorous language. His logical acuteness, self-control, and scholarly acquirements made him a strong controversialist. He wrote with a ready pen. His written sermons are characterized by spiritual earnestness and by simplicity. They are doctrinal, but not dogmatic; expository, argumentative, practical. His *Notes on the New Testament* (1755) are luminous and suggestive. Both the *Sermons* (of which there are about 140) and the *Notes* are in the Methodist course of study, and are doctrinal standards (see METHODISTS, V., §§ 1–2). He was a fluent, impressive, persuasive, powerful preacher, producing striking effects. He preached generally extemporaneously and briefly, though occasionally at great length, using manuscript only for special occasions. As an organizer, an ecclesiastical general, and a statesman he was eminent. He knew well how to marshal and control men, how to achieve purposes. He had in his hands the powers of a despot; yet he so used them as not only not to provoke rebellion, but to inspire love. His mission was to spread " Scriptural holiness "; his means and plans were such as Providence indicated. The course thus marked out for him he pursued with a determination, a fidelity, from which nothing could swerve him. Wesley's prose *Works* were first collected by himself (32 vols., Bristol, 1771–74, frequently reprinted in editions varying greatly in the number of volumes). His chief prose works are a standard publication in seven octavo volumes of the Methodist Book Concern, New York. The *Poetical Works* of John and Charles, ed. G. Osborn, appeared 13 vols., London, 1868–72. Besides his *Sermons* and *Notes* already referred to, are his *Journals* (originally published in twenty parts, London, 1740–89; new ed. by N. Curnock, is to contain notes from unpublished diaries, 6 vols., vols. i.–ii., London and New York, 1909–11, which are of great interest; *The Doctrine of Original Sin* (Bristol, 1757; in reply to Dr. John Taylor of Norwich); an *Appeal*

10. Literary Work.

to Men of Reason and Religion (originally published in three parts; 2d ed., Bristol, 1743), an elaborate defense of Methodism, describing with great vigor the evils of the times in society and the church; a *Plain Account of Christian Perfection* (1766).

H. K. CARROLL.

BIBLIOGRAPHY: A considerable amount of pertinent literature will be found under METHODISTS, especially that dealing with the early history of the movement. For a bibliography of the works of John and Charles, consult the work of R. Green named under WESLEY, CHARLES; also note the same author's *Books against John Wesley*, London, 1902. The best biography of John is that by Luke Tyerman, 3 vols., London, 1870, often reissued (full, impartial); the earliest, aside from mere pamphlets, is by J. Hampson, 3 vols, ib. 1791. Others are: T. Coke and H. Moore, London, 1792 (popular); J. Whitehead, 2 vols., ib. 1793–96 (deficient); R. Southey, 2 vols., ib. 1820, ed. Curry, New York, 1847 (inadequate and misleading); Adam Clarke, *The Wesley Family*, London, 1823; H. Moore, 2 vols., ib. 1824 (faithful, trustworthy); R. Watson, ib. 1831 (clear and compact, intended for general readers); W. Jones, ib. 1833 (from the Calvinistic point of view); T. Jackson, ib. 1839 (unsatisfactory); I. Taylor, *Wesley and Methodism*, ib. 1851 (may be disregarded); R. Bickersteth, ib. 1856 (acceptable, from the Anglican point of view); M. Lelièvre, Paris, 1868, 3d ed., 1891, Eng. transl., London, 1871 (reliable, but lacking in breadth); Julia Wedgwood, London, 1870 (Unitarian); R. D. Urlin, ib. 1870; G. J. Stevenson, *Memorials of the Wesley Family*, ib. 1876 (excellent in abundance of materials); J. H. Rigg, *The Churchmanship of John Wesley*, ib. 1879 and 1887; F. Bevan, ib. 1891; J. Telford, ib. 1899; G. H. Pike. ib. 1903; F. Banfield, ib. 1900; R. Green, new ed., ib. 1905; *John Wesley, the Methodist*, New York, 1903 (useful and condensed); W. H. Fitchett, *Wesley and his Century*, London, 1906 (discriminating, luminous); E. Miller, ib. 1906; C. T. Winchester, New York, 1906 (impartial and judicial). Excellent sketches will be found in W. Walker, *Greatest Men of the Christian Church*, Chicago, 1908; H. M. Butler, *Ten Great and Good Men*, New York, 1909; L. P. Powell, *Heavenly Heretics*, ib. 1909; A. Leger, *L'Angleterre religieuse et les origines du Méthodisme* . . . *Le Jeunesse de Wesley*, Paris, 1910; *DNB*, lx. 303–314; and his work is estimated in *Cambridge Modern History*, vi. 81 sqq., 1909.

WESLEY, SAMUEL, SR.: Father of John and Charles Wesley; b. at Winterbourne-Whitchurch (28 m. w. of Southampton) Nov. (baptized Dec. 17), 1662; d. at Epworth (23 m. n.w. of Lincoln) Apr. 22, 1735. His early education was received among the dissenters; but in 1683 he renounced non-conformity, and entered Exeter College, Oxford (B.A., 1688). He was ordained deacon that year, and priest Feb. 24, 1689–90, and held various preferments, including a chaplaincy on a man-of-war, and the rectory of South Ormsby, Lincolnshire (1690), until Queen Mary gave him the living of Epworth in Lincolnshire (1695), in return for the compliment of his dedication to her of his *Life of our Blessed Lord and Savior, Jesus Christ, an Heroic Poem* (1693; ed. T. Coke, 2 vols., 1809). He was a man of learning, benevolence, devotional habits, and liberal sentiments. He wrote largely, and by this means eked out his salary, which was insufficient to support his large family. He had nineteen children, of whom, however, nine died in infancy. Of his poetical works mention may be made of: *The History of the New Testament Attempted in Verse*, 1701; *The History of the Old Testament in Verse*, 1704. His learned Latin Commentary on the Book of Job, *Dissertationes in librum Jobi*, in which he was, however, aided by others, appeared posthumously (1736). Other prose works are: *The Pious Communicant rightly Prepared*

(1700); and the posthumous *Letter to a Curate* (1735; an excellent statement of clerical duties). His hymn, "Behold the Saviour of Mankind," written in 1709, has been widely used.   H. K. CARROLL.

BIBLIOGRAPHY: L. Tyerman, *Life and Times of the Rev. Samuel Wesley*, London, 1866 (a painstaking study; includes letters, and others are given in the same author's life of John Wesley); A. à Wood, *Athenæ Oxonienses*, ed. P. Bliss, iv. 503, and *Fasti*, ii. 403, 4 vols., ib. 1813–20; J. Dove, *Biographical Hist. of the Wesley Family*, ib. 1833; W. Beal, *Fathers of the Wesley Family*, 2d ed., ib. 1862; G. J. Stevenson, *Memorials of the Wesley Family*, ib. 1876; S. W. Duffield, *English Hymns*, pp. 64–65, New York, 1886; Julian, *Hymnology*, pp. 1255–56; and the literature under the articles on Charles, John, and Susannah Wesley.

WESLEY, SAMUEL JR.: Eldest son of Samuel Wesley, Sr.; b. in London Feb. 10, 1690; d. at Tiverton (55 m. s.w. of Bristol) Nov. 6, 1739. He was educated at Westminster and Christ Church College, Oxford (B.A., 1715; M.A., 1718); became head usher at Westminster School, 1713, and was ordained soon after; became head master of the Free School at Tiverton, 1733. He was a man of considerable learning, great talent, high character, and decidedly philanthropic in disposition and action. As an old-fashioned churchman, he had no sympathy with the "new faith" of his brothers, but he contributed generously for their education. His *Poems on Several Occasions* (1736; reprinted, with additions and *Life*, 1862) have much merit, and include one or two of our best epigrams, besides hymns to the Trinity, for Sunday, Good Friday, and Easter, and on the death of a young lady. These are of a high order, and show much of Charles Wesley's splendor of diction; they have been largely used in church hymn-books.

F. M. BIRD†.   Revised by H. K. CARROLL.

BIBLIOGRAPHY: Besides the *Life* in the *Poems* (ut sup.), and the literature under the articles on the other Wesleys, consult: Julian, *Hymnology*, pp. 1256–57.

WESLEY, SUSANNAH: Mother of John and Charles Wesley; b. in London Jan. 20, 1669; d. there July 23, 1742. Her father, Samuel Annesley, was a prominent non-conformist divine, but she renounced non-conformity in her thirteenth year, and joined the Church of England. In 1689 she married Samuel Wesley (q.v.), and bore him nineteen children, of whom nine, however, died in infancy. She was a remarkable woman. Tyerman gives this account of her home discipline: "When the child was one year old, he was taught to fear the rod, and, if he cried at all, to cry in softened tones. The children were limited to three meals a day. Eating and drinking between meals was strictly prohibited. All the children were washed and put to bed by eight o'clock, and on no account was a servant to sit by a child till it fell asleep. The children were taught the Lord's Prayer as soon as they could speak, and repeated it every morning and every night. They were on no account allowed to call each other by their proper name without the addition of brother or sister, as the case might be. Six hours a day were spent at school, the parents being the teachers. They were not taught to read till five years old, and then only a single day was allowed wherein to learn the letters of the alphabet, great and small. Psalms were sung every morning, when school was opened, and also every night, when the duties of the day were ended. In addition to this, at the commencement and close of every day, each of the elder children took one of the younger, and read the psalms appointed for the day, and a chapter in the Bible, after which they severally went to their private devotions" (*Life of Wesley*, i. 17–18). It would be unjust to infer from this statement that Mrs. Wesley was a martinet. She was methodical in her ways, but she was a woman of lovely character, a tender mother, quick in perception, wise in judgment, and ever ready to extend the hand of helpfulness. She was very influential with her son John and her impress was made on early Methodism.

H. K. CARROLL.

BIBLIOGRAPHY: J. Kirk, *The Mother of the Wesleys*, London, 1872; Eliza Clarke, *Susanna Wesley*, ib. new ed., 1896; M. R. Brailsford, *Susannah Wesley, the Mother of Methodism*, ib. 1910.

WESLEYAN METHODIST ASSOCIATION. See METHODISTS, I., 6.

WESLEYAN METHODIST CONNECTION OR CHURCH OF AMERICA. See METHODISTS, IV., 4.

WESLEYAN METHODISTS. See METHODISTS, I.

WESSEL, ves'sel, JOHANN (WESSEL HARMENSS GANSFORT or GOESEVOYRDT).

Life (§ 1).   Christology (§ 4).   Penance, Confession, Absolution (§.7).
Writings (§ 2).   Doctrine of Justification (§ 5).   Indulgences and Purgatory (§ 8).
Basal Religious Principles (§ 3).   Doctrine of the Church (§ 6).

Johann Wessel, or, better, Wessel Harmenss Gansfort or Goesevoyrdt, the pre-Lutheran Reformer and one of the Brethren of the Common Life, was born at Groningen, Holland, about 1419, and died there Oct. 4, 1489. While his name is a matter of some doubt, it is most probable that his baptismal name was Wessel, that he assumed
1. Life. the name of Johannes while living with the Brethren at Zwolle, that the name Harmenss comes from the local custom of carrying the father's name (in this case Harmen) with the addition meaning "son," that he Latinized his name Wessel as Basilius, while Gansfort is the name of a Westphalian village. Wessel's preparatory studies were carried on at Zwolle, and he matriculated at Cologne in Oct., 1449. His early days at Zwolle had an abiding influence upon him, though that influence was not controlling; his predilections for the logical and the philosophical were strong, so that while the reverential tendencies of Zwolle affected him, the narrowness of conception there current repelled him. How far Wessel was influenced by the teachers at Cologne is not determinable, though his realism seems to have come through the Thomistic traditions fostered there. He seems to have found his way to Bernard, Augustine, and Plato, and then to have been influenced by Humanism (q.v.). He learned Hebrew and Greek. His interests were very wide, and he journeyed to Heidelberg and Paris to take part in the dispute between nominalism and realism, in the course of which he abjured realism for nominalism, a fact which may be of significance

for his later life, since nominalists were the antipapal party. It appears possible that he lived at Paris for sixteen years, without other definite purpose than to teach and learn. His humanistic interests and his acquaintance with Cardinal Bessarion led him to Rome, where he was found about 1470. Thence he returned to Paris, where he influenced such men as Reuchlin and Agricola, and where he won the title of *magister contradictionum* by his questioning spirit. A more restful place was sought by him in Basel, and he declined an invitation from the bishop of Utrecht to go to that place. By Apr., 1479, he was back in his own home. He lived part of the time at the Clarissa cloister at Groningen, and part of the time with the Brethren at Agnetenberg near Zwolle.

He frequently visited the flourishing abbey of Adewert, and found a friend and protector in Bishop David of Utrecht. He was surrounded by a circle of admiring friends and pupils and enjoyed friendly intercourse with such older men as the abbot of Adewert, Heinrich von Rees, the philologist Rudolf van Langen, and Paulus Pelantius. He taught a religiously deepened and theologically directed Humanism. After a period of gloomy doubting that threatened to rob him of his entire faith, he was able before his death to say, " I know nobody but Jesus crucified." He was buried in the church of the cloister at Groningen, where a memorial stone was laid in 1637, replaced by another between 1730 and 1742.

The extant literary productions of Wessel date from the last decade of his life. They are chiefly short treatises in the form of apho-
2. Writings. risms arranged under special theological topics. His intercourse with the " religious " at Groningen and Zwolle led him to compose two books as guides in practical religion, neither of them published, however, before his death. The one dealt with prayer, the other was the *Scala meditationis*. After his death Cornelius Hoen (Honius) of The Hague industriously collected Wessel's manuscripts. What he found was sent to Luther and Zwingli, so that a collection of the tractlike treatises appeared with the title *Farrago uberrima* (Wittenberg, 1522 and 1523). The fact that few of Wessel's productions have come down may be explained by the remark of the book-dealer Adam Petri, that the mendicant monks acted with fiery zeal against Wessel's papers.

Wessel's basic religious principles are essentially those of Augustine, through whom he reached the Platonic conclusion that God is Abso-
3. Basal lute Being; he is the necessary exist-
Religious ence, as opposed to the finite and in-
Principles. cidental. The end of man is to raise himself to this stage of absolute being by complete self-surrender and self-denial. But such elevation above everything earthly is impossible without divine mediation. God has sent down the fulness of his being through the son, the virgin, and the angels, who act as intermediaries. Nature is the ordinary expression of the will of God, while miracle is the will of the same God expressed in what is unusual. As far as his relations to his immediate physical environments are concerned, man

is left to his own counsel, wherein his personality is recognized in its specific value as against absolute being. Man is essentially in the image of God, bearing the trinitarian characteristics of mind or memory, intelligence, and will. The original state of man was less perfect than that of the angels, since he was on a lower stage. Hence the image of God required purification and perfection through the angels. The mind is to be purified by wise knowledge of God, intelligence is to be illumined by the sublime glorification of God, and the will is to be perfected through the blessed enjoyment of God. The Father works on the mind, the Word on the intelligence, and the Holy Spirit on the will. Evidently such a foundation, mingling together arbitrarily the metaphysical with the ethical, must have its effect upon the doctrine of sin. Sin is defined as an abiding below the ideal, remaining behind the goal of accomplishment. Distinction is made between sins of commission and omission, and the guilt which results from breach of the law which requires man to be perfect as God is perfect. Before the fall there were venal faults in a failure to attain the perfection required; in the fall there was additional the contempt of divine revelation. Wessel knew of a fall not only in the world of man but in that of angels: the former left an abiding degeneration; the latter had also its effects on man because of the intimate relations which existed between men and angels, the latter being mediaries, as stated above. The fallen angels also worked upon man, awakening self-love, in which original sin essentially consists. While man is not in a position alone to reach perfection, the conditions are always at hand for attainment of this, and Father, Son, and Holy Spirit cooperate to this end.

In Wessel's Christology the idea of completeness is put in the foreground as against the idea of redemption and reconciliation. Since
4. Chris- the creature from the beginning is in
tology. need of reconciliation with the absolute God, the incarnation was determined upon and prepared. That apart from the fall the Word would have become flesh is affirmed. Why God became man is answered by the statements that it was in order that the community of the triumphant Church might not be deprived of its head, that the building of the holy temple might have its corner stone, that all creation might have its mediator, and that the whole army and people of God might have its king. The fall from life in God could be remedied and a return effected only through the flesh raised above every creature [through the incarnation]. The human in Christ was only the shell which the divine rulership and completeness was to fill. Wessel, in following out such a train of thought as the foregoing, was not satisfied with merely theoretical consequences. The individual character of the incarnation lay in the fact that in the whole life and particularly in the death of Christ existed the exposition of the content of the eternal Word. Thus the human side was at the fore in Wessel's Christology. The significance of the priesthood of Christ was also emphasized, and in this the self-emptying of the Word had its part in that as the sacrificial lamb the sufferings of Christ and his death were an

equivalent which wrought satisfaction. There is not possible another victim for sin that is past, for when sin is remitted sin ceases; and when that takes place, righteousness begins. Wessel's doctrine of the saving value of Christ's death should not be confused with the theories of Anselm and Luther, although there are similarities of expression. The saving value of Christ's death consists in the absolute devotion of love which makes an immediate impression not only on sinners but upon all the imperfect, awakens love in them, draws them unto itself, and equips them with the Spirit, which in turn becomes a means of the full knowledge of God.

There can be no doubt that Wessel derived the salvation of the individual from a divine and absolute act of grace. As Christ was the

5. Doctrine first predestined one, so were all the
of Justifica- members of the congregation of Christ
tion. predestined. Wessel follows the tradition of Augustine and of other theologians before the Reformation. Faith is a gift of God, inclining the mind to accept the truth of the Gospel, and faith directs itself to the crucified Christ. Wessel's conception of justification is the same as Augustine's, viz., an imparting of God's righteousness. Penitence is essentially contriteness of heart, a readiness to surrender self to the guidance of the divine revelation. It is a step in the process of the establishment of righteousness, and at a higher stage it becomes the right valuation of sin. In so far as penitence is pain, it is sorrow accompanying love because of inability to comprehend divine love in its full extent. The mystic love, which from the beginning operates in faith, can find satisfaction only in an ascetic liberation from the world. Victory over the world does not for Wessel mean the moral conquest and transformation of the world and of one's own life, but rather mystic indifference to the world as compared with knowledge and contemplation of God. In this regard Wessel lacked the true Reformation spirit. His significance for the Reformation of the sixteenth century lies chiefly in his criticism upon ecclesiastical life.

In the medieval view the Church was a kind of sanitarium able with its treasures of grace to provide for men eternal salvation. This

6. Doctrine view Wessel rejected, and regarded the
of the Church as a *communio* to which all
Church. belonged who were united to Christ in one faith, one hope, and one love. He did not stress, as did Augustine and his followers in the Middle Ages, the fact of predestination; he substituted for " the predestined " the phrase " the saints." The external unity of the Church under one pope was not essential but incidental. In expressing this opinion Wessel shook the cornerstone of the medieval ecclesiastical structure. Regarding the external form of the Church as a matter of indifference, Wessel saw no necessity for transforming it and thus his position remained essentially negative. Wessel denied to the Church all authority in matters of faith and all capacity to impart salvation with certainty. Neither the pope nor the Church is infallible. Many popes " committed pestilential errors." That Christians should submit blindly to the mandates of ecclesiastics is " irra-

tional " and " full of blasphemy." Councils are not infallible organs of the Spirit, and their findings are subject to the judgment of the laity. Wessel anticipated the Reformation in that he based his position on the authority of Scripture, though he conceded a certain authority to the Church even when it did not fall in with the Spirit as operative in the Word. Alongside of the inner priesthood there is an external, sacramental priesthood. He grants the rights of papal jurisdiction and of legislation relating to the outer peace and safety of the Church; but this has the nature of a contract. A transgression of the common rights by the ecclesiastical authority might as in the case of civil superiors be met with deposition. Wessel refused any especial efficacy to the priesthood. The claim that salvation was dependent upon the sacraments and that the priests imparted the sacraments, was disposed of by discounting the value of the latter. That Wessel did not expressly dispute the seven sacraments was because he saw no particular significance in them. He did not regard baptism as having power to cleanse from sin, or participation in the communion as a means of receiving the Spirit. In the mass neither the " intention " of the celebrant nor the " judgment " of him for whom the mass was celebrated had any worth; everything depends upon the soul within, on love and internal character and longing, on spiritual hunger and thirst.

Wessel sharply criticized the medieval doctrine of Penance (q.v.). He was not able to see how there could be punishment after forgiveness;

7. Penance, imputation [of sin] comes to expression
Confession, only in punishment, and when impu-
Absolution. tation ceases, there can be no punishment. If God remits eternal punishment, why should he not remit the temporal also? It would be the greatest obstacle to piety if the pious had to carry constantly with them the thought of their own baseness. Corporal " contrition, affliction, chastisement, mortification," involved no more than a contrite body, not a contrite heart. The only real " satisfaction " (in the theological sense) is conversion. No duty can be imposed upon the converted other than that he sin no more, and that he love God with a pure affection. Similarly, confession is the consequence and not the condition of justification; it signifies hatred of sin. Indeed, it is better to praise God than to confess one's sins. Absolution is not within the power of the father confessor; it depends upon the inner disposition, which is unknown to the priest in the confessional. Absolution is an accompaniment, not the essence, of justification. It comes with the awakening of love. God alone can act upon the inner soul of man. Human efficacy, whether of priest or holy person, is excluded. The reception of the believer into the community of the saints is but the recognition of an already accomplished divine act. The activity of the priest in the sacrament is therefore merely ministerial. Penitence remains a purely ecclesiastical institution, and as such is not rejected by Wessel, but it is accompanied by abuses that must be opposed.

The most serious abuse associated with the Church's doctrine of penance was that of indulgences. Wessel attacked this error from many sides. The pope had not the power to separate sin from punishment, the person from his acts.

8. Indulgences and Purgatory. There is to be no such distinction made between temporal and eternal punishments as was often made the basis of an argument in favor of the indulgence. Indulgences, moreover, introduce contradiction into the necessary connection of sin and punishment. Besides this, the pope can not step in between man and God, nor has he power over the merits of Christ nor over the efficacy of the saints' intercession. Wessel declined also the current doctrine of purgatorial fire. He believed in the necessity of a continuous development of Christian life after death, and would not hear of rendering satisfaction for sins in purgatory. While the soul may in the future be purified of dross still clinging to it from its earthly existence, such a process must be spiritual and enjoyable rather than one producing misery. Entrance into " purgatory " must accordingly be one step in a process of betterment, it must lead to a state of being superior to the first state of Adam, since the possibility of temptation is excluded. If there be " pain " in purgatory, that pain is sorrow rather than suffering—sorrow caused by the sense of unworthiness. It is the purifying pain of love of Christ.

While Wessel has been perhaps too enthusiastically praised by Ullmann (see bibliography) as a " Reformer before the Reformation," it is equally a mistake to consider him an orthodox churchman. That he foreshadowed the German Reformation is evinced by his teachings as set forth above. Yet in many respects Wessel's face was turned backward toward Augustine and Bernard.

(S. D. van Veen.)

BIBLIOGRAPHY: The only edition of the *Opera* was published at Groningen, 1614, reprint, Amsterdam, 1617. The earliest " Life " was by A. Hardenberg (A. Rizæus) and was prefixed to the *Opera*, ut sup. Consult further: H. von der Hardt, *Memoria Chrysoloræ, Byzantini*, Helmstadt, 1718; J. Wessel, *G. H. Goetzi . . . commentationem . . . de Joanne Wesselo . . . tuebitur*, Lübeck, 1719; J. M. Schroeckh, *Christliche Kirchengeschichte*, xxxiii. 278–295, 45 vols., Leipsic, 1768–1812; W. Muurling, *Commentatio . . . de Wesseli Gansfortii cum vita*, Utrecht, 1831; idem, *Oratio de Wesseli . . . principiis atque virtutibus*, Groningen, 1840; B. Bähring, *Leben Johann Wessels*, 2d ed., Bielefeld, 1852; O. Jaeger, *J. Wycliffe und seine Bedeutung für die Reformation*, Halle, 1854; J. Friedrich, *Johann Wessel*, Regensburg, 1862; J. J. Doedes, in *TSK*, 1870; P. Hoffstede de Groot, *Johann Wessel Ganzevoort*, Groningen, 1871; C. Ullmann, *Reformers before the Reformation*, ii. 263–615 (a critical account of the literature, pp. 610–615, which the earnest student should not overlook), Edinburgh, 1877, cf. his *Johann Wessel, ein Vorgänger Luthers*, Hamburg, 1834; S. Kettlewell, *Thomas à Kempis, and the Brothers of Common Life*, 2 vols., London, 1882, 2d ed., abridged, chap. xiv., ib. 1885; Bayle, *Dictionary*, v. 543–547.

WESSENBERG, ves'sen-bärg, IGNAZ HEINRICH KARL VON: Liberal Roman Catholic; b. at Dresden Nov. 4, 1774; d. at Constance Aug. 6, 1860. He began his education in the Institut St. Salvator at Augsburg, then changed to Dillingen (where Johann Michael Sailer, q.v., was teaching), and then to the University of Würzburg, where he became acquainted with Karl Theodor von Dalberg, who was greatly to influence his life; he next attended the University of Vienna, spending the most of his energies, however, in the library and in making the acquaintance of a circle of men highly placed in political position. In 1798 he went to Constance, where he had a prebend in the cathedral, pursuing, meanwhile, his studies in history and canon law. Here a poetical letter, *Ueber den Verfall der Sitten in Deutschland* (Zurich, 1799), indicated the general bent of his thought. He held a high ecclesiastical position next in Augsburg; by this time Dalberg was bishop of Constance, and he invited Wessenberg to his diocese as vicar-general. In this position he worked so effectively that he soon gained papal approval in a special brief. He sought to make conditions there higher and more ethical, worked for the foundation of seminaries for the priesthood, inaugurated ministerial conferences, attempted to improve the sermon and catechetical exercises, and aroused by these measures great hostility and caused complaint to Rome. On the death of Dalberg he was nominated as administrator of the diocese, but the false assertion that he denied the deity of Christ and other complaints caused the Curia to reject the nomination. At Rome the pope refused him audience, and his general reception was unfavorable. In 1827 he laid down his office and retired to private life at Constance, though he served in the Baden house of representatives and was honored by high and low.

Two leading ideas controlled Wessenberg's life: he desired to see a national German Catholic Church and the revival of councils, and these purposes gained for him the enmity of the Curia. He regarded the Gallican Church with its four articles of 1682 as an excellent model; and toward a church of this pattern in Germany he labored at the congress at Vienna in 1814, using his influence and his pen— *Die deutsche Kirche, ein Vorschlag zu ihrer neuen Begründung und Einrichtung* (1815)—but in vain. In his ecclesiastical and theological thinking he was midway between Sailer and Benedikt Maria Werkmeister (q.v.), excelling both in political insight and energy. He was especially anxious to see a return to the conditions of primitive Christianity. In his major work, *Die grossen Kirchenversammlungen des 15. und 16. Jahrhunderts* (4 vols., 1840), in spite of the mass of materials which he had read, there fail the notes of solid learning and scientific method. His brochures on practical theology display little depth of acuteness. So his *Gott und die Welt, oder das Verhältnis der Dinge zueinander und zu Gott* (2 vols., 1857) does not transcend the limits of a popularly philosophical presentation. He also was known as a poet (*Sämtliche Dichtungen*, 7 vols., Stuttgart and Tübingen, 1834–54). Other works were: *Betrachtungen über die Verhältnisse der katholischen Kirche in Umfange des deutschen Bundes* (1816); *Die christlichen Bilder* (1826–27); and *Ueber Schwärmerei* (1832). Where he shines is as a Christian character, to which were added the graces of a noble culture. These worked out into a liberal, patriotic, and broad Catholicism, which was, however, denied its fruition through the entrance into his region of a Jesuitical and Romanizing Catholicism.

(K. Benrath.)

BIBLIOGRAPHY: Sketches of the life have been issued by J. Beck, Freiburg, 1862; Kreuz. St. Gall, 1863; Friedrich, in F. von Weech, *Badische Biographien*, vol. ii., Darmstadt, 1875; and in *ADB*, xlii. 147–157. Consult further: *Das Leben I. H. von Wessenbergs, ehemaligen Bisthumsverwesers in Constanz*, Freiburg, 1860; O. Mejer, *Zur Geschichte der römisch-deutschen Frage*, vol. i. passim, ii. 1, pp. 54–86, iii. 271 sqq., Rostock, 1871–74; E. Friedberg, *Der Staat und die Bischofswahlen in Deutschland*, 2 vols., Leipsic, 1874; J. Friedrich, *Geschichte des vatikanischen Konzils*, i. 179 sqq., Bonn, 1877; F. Nippold, *Handbuch der neuesten Kirchengeschichte*, i. 523–531, ii. 543–546, Berlin, 1901.

WESSOBRUNN, ves'sō-brun, **PRAYER:** A poem, followed by a prose prayer, found at the end of the second part of a manuscript collection, entitled *De poeta*, derived from the cloister of Wessobrunn, south of Munich. It is probably of Bavarian origin, and was to all appearances composed in the eighth century. Possibly dependent upon Ps. lxxxix. 2, it pictures in nine alliterative lines the original chaos when only God and his angels existed. The first five lines have been incorrectly supposed to represent heathen cosmological conceptions, but there is no valid reason for disputing the unity and Christian origin of the entire poem. (E. STEINMEYER.)

BIBLIOGRAPHY: The text is in K. Müllenhoff and W. Scherer, *Denkmäler deutscher Poesie und Prosa*, vol. i., 3d ed., Berlin, 1892 (there are also to be found titles of earlier literature on the subject). Consult further: J. N. Kelle, *Geschichte der deutschen Litteratur*, i. 74 sqq., Berlin, 1892; R. Kögel, *Geschichte der deutschen Litteratur*, i. I, pp. 269 sqq. et passim, Strasburg, 1894.

WEST INDIES.

The West Indies constitute an archipelago extending in an eastward curve from North to South America, and separating the Caribbean Sea from the Atlantic Ocean and the Gulf of Mexico. The principal groups from north to south are: (1) The Bahamas, consisting of some thirteen low islands with many keys and reefs; area, 5,450 sq. m.; population, 53,735; Nassau is the capital and chief port.

1. Geography. (2) The Greater Antilles, which include Cuba, the largest of the West Indies, with an area of 44,164 sq. m.; population, 1,820,239, most of whom are white; Havana is the capital, and the commercial center of all the islands. Haiti, the next island, has a total area of 28,250 sq. m., and is divided into the two Republics of Haiti; area, 10,205 sq. m.; population, 960,000, nine-tenths of whom are negroes—and Santo Domingo; area, 18,045 sq. m.; population, 610,000, a mixed race descended from the aborigines and their Spanish conquerors. West of Haiti lies Jamaica, which, including its dependent islands, has an area of 4,424 sq. m., and a population of 716,394, a mixture of whites, blacks, and half-breeds; Kingston is the capital and leading city. (3) The Lesser Antilles, properly including two groups: the Caribbean and Venezuelan, or Windward and Leeward, Islands, of which the largest and best-known are the French island of Martinique, the British island of Barbadoes, and, in the extreme south, Trinidad.

The islands were discovered in 1492 and succeeding years by Columbus in his voyages to the New World. The Spanish first settled at Haiti, and later at Cuba, Porto Rico, and Jamaica, treating the natives with such cruelty that by the middle of the eighteenth century they were practically exterminated, and negro slaves were imported to work on the plantations. During the seventeenth century the Spanish were followed by the

2. History and Population. French, English, and Dutch, who settled in the Bahamas and the Caribbean Islands. Little by little the islands were wrested from their first conquerors, and the opening of the twentieth century sees Cuba an independent republic, under the protection of the United States; Haiti and Santo Domingo, independent republics; Porto Rico, a part of the United States; the Bahamas and Jamaica, crown colonies of Great Britain; and the remaining islands divided among Great Britain, France, Denmark, Holland, Sweden, and Venezuela. Among the population, the larger portion of whom are illiterate, only a remnant of the original inhabitants remain. It is estimated that fully 60 per cent of the entire population are mulattoes; in Cuba and Porto Rico the white race predominates, but in the other islands the colored race is in the majority, and in all there is a sprinkling of Chinese and Hindus. In Cuba, Porto Rico, and Santo Domingo, Spanish is the prevailing language; in Haiti it is French; in the British islands a Negro-English patois is spoken; the southern islands use a conglomerate of Dutch and Spanish, and in all fragments of aboriginal dialects are to be found; Roman Catholicism is the dominant religion.

In the journal of his first voyage Columbus states that, " In all those islands there is no difference of physiognomy, of manners, or of language, but they all clearly understand each other—a circumstance very propitious for the realization of what I conceive to be the principal wish of our Most Serene King, namely, the conversion of these people to the Holy Faith of Christ." In his will he desired his heirs " to spare no pains to put in this island of Española four good professors of theology . . . to convert to our Holy Faith the inhabitants of the Indies." Side by side with the passion for conquest in material things was that of spiritual conquest in the minds of these early Spanish explorers, and conversion, by any means, was the order. Conquest was first; lands were seized, and natives were enslaved; after that came the proselytizing. One of the first missionaries was Bartolomé de Las Casas (q.v.), who came to Cuba in 1502 and began a heroic struggle, not only with the heathenism of the islanders, but with the rapacity of their conquerors, and in this he had many associates of the Dominican order, though their efforts were of little avail to stem the tide. After the death of Las Casas, who was rightly called the " Apostle to the West Indies," conditions rapidly became worse. Still, some efforts were made to improve the condition of the natives, and in 1556 the Jesuits established a mission at Havana, which was continued for six years, though with indifferent success; and at last they, too, were driven out by the determined opposition of the planters. During these and ensuing years the history of the West Indies is a dark record of slavery, piracy, and cruelty. The Church and the State were one, and the former had to bear the blame for both. No faith but Roman Catholicism was allowed, and the inquisition was introduced to extirpate heresy. The native population rapidly disappeared, and Africans, Chinese, and Hindus were either captured or lured into slavery to take their place. Nor was the pall lifted with the coming of the other Christian nations. England made penal colonies of her islands, and in the early days of her occupation " Barbadoed " became a significant term in London, for men and women, as well as boys and girls, were kidnaped and shipped to the islands; and all, Spanish, French, Dutch, and English, vied with each other in lust of land, slaves, and gold.

3. The Spanish Period.

The English conquest of 1661 was followed by the entrance of the Church of England in 1662, but in its early history in the West Indies it did no missionary work, the clergymen devoting themselves wholly to the English residents in the islands. In 1703 the Society for the Propagation of the Gospel began to render aid with books and money, but the first organized Protestant missionary effort in the islands was that of the Unity of the Brethren, or Moravians, in 1732. The Wesleyan Methodist Missionary Society of England followed in 1786; the Baptist Missionary Society of England and the Church Missionary Society in 1814; the Society for the Propagation of the Gospel in 1818; the Scottish Missionary Society in 1824; the United Presbyterian Church of Scotland and the London Missionary Society in 1835; the American Missionary Association in 1847; the Protestant Episcopal Church in 1865; and the Southern Baptist Convention in 1886; while during all these years the Roman Catholic orders, including the Dominicans and Jesuits, have been more or less actively working.

4. Non-Roman Missions.

The first Moravian missionaries to the West Indies were two artizans, Leonard Dober, a potter, and David Nitschmann (q.v.), a carpenter, who, while with Zinzendorf at Herrnhut, had met a negro slave, named Anthony, from St. Thomas, and had been profoundly impressed with the great need of the natives in that island for the Gospel. Amid great difficulties they made their way to the West Indies in 1732, ready themselves to become slaves, if need be, in their enthusiasm to help the oppressed. They were followed the next year by twenty-nine others, many of whom succumbed to the climate, while the planters opposed them on every hand. Nevertheless, a few slaves were baptized, and through one of them a great awakening spread over the entire island of St. Thomas. The planters became more

5. Moravians.

bitter in their opposition, punishing slaves who attended service and increasingly persecuting the missionaries, till, when Zinzendorf visited the island in 1739, he found several of them in prison, under a charge of being dangerous agitators. He secured their release, but laws were passed forbidding work among the slaves, and the banishment of the missionaries was attempted. Yet some few of the planters became friendly, and by their changed attitude greatly helped the work. In 1733 St. Croix was occupied, and subsequently became the principal station of the Moravians in the Danish Islands; the work was pushed as rapidly as possible to other islands, and St. John was occupied in 1741, Jamaica in 1754, Antigua in 1756, Barbadoes in 1767, St. Kitts in 1777, and Tobago in 1787. In the centenary jubilee of 1832, a total of 37,000 persons who had received baptism was reported. The West Indies Mission of the Moravians, with its 40,000 Christians, is becoming an independent Church province. It receives little outside financial support, schools have native teachers, and many of the churches possess native pastors, but the supervision of the work is still in the hands of the European missionaries.

There were in 1911 59 churches, with 16,363 communicants; 51 stations; 39 substations; 50 missionaries; and 854 native helpers.

After the Moravians, the English Wesleyans were the next to enter the field. A Mr. Gilbert, Speaker of the House of Assembly at Antigua, while on a visit in England, heard Wesley preach and was converted. He returned to Antigua in 1760, and at once began work among his slaves, some 200 of whom were converted. After his death the work was continued by two slave women until the arrival of John Baxter, a Christian shipwright, who continued the work alone for eight years, laboring in the dockyards for his support. About 2,000 slaves had become Christians, when, in 1786, Thomas Coke (q.v.), on his way to Nova Scotia with three missionaries, was driven by storm to Antigua, where he remained about six weeks, visiting several islands and locating missionaries in the new stations. The planters opposed the Wesleyans as bitterly as they did the Moravians, and in 1792 a law was passed prohibiting all but rectors of parishes to preach without a license, which no one who had not resided for twelve months on the island could receive; for the first infringement of this law, the punishment was fine or imprisonment; for the second, corporal punishment and banishment; if banished, the penalty for return was death. This law was in force but a short time when it was abrogated by the king, as contrary to the British Constitution, and in 1794 the missionaries again resumed work, the negroes responding joyously. By 1813 over 11,000 Christians were found in the Wesleyan missions alone. In 1820 the entire West Indies field was divided into four districts: Antigua, St. Vincent, Jamaica, and the Bahamas, and the work everywhere progressed rapidly, though not without opposition. The influx of immigrants had an unfavorable effect, those from Africa especially tending to demoralize the people by their heathen proclivities,

6. English Wesleyans.

while new difficulties were experienced through the necessity of learning the languages of the Hindu coolies, this problem being met in part by the coming in 1852 of a missionary who understood the Tamil language, to work specially among them. The emancipation of all slaves in the British Islands in 1834, which was completed in 1838, was followed by a similar proclamation in the Danish possessions in 1848, and many important changes followed. Education now flourished, the governments made grants in aid of land to the missions, and for a time it seemed as if the work of evangelization was to be speedily accomplished. But with their freedom the former slaves deteriorated, and many returned to heathen practises, while the terrible Obi superstition held not a few in its grip, and the lack of moral fiber added to the difficulties of building up a Christian civilization. By the middle of the nineteenth century (1850), the Wesleyan Methodist Mission had 4 circuits with 52 stations and about 400 preaching-places; 79 missionaries and assistants; 146 native helpers; 48,589 church-members; and 259 Sunday- and day-schools, with 18,247 scholars. In spite of opposition from the planters, and notwithstanding the superstition of the natives, the work increased from decade to decade, and, with the exception of the Bahamas District, the West Indies are now an independent church province, being no longer classed as a mission field.

The Baptist Missionary Society of England began work in Jamaica in 1813, building on the foundations laid by a negro from Virginia, who had labored in Kingston since 1783. After his death the work was continued by one of his followers, and he applied to the Baptist Missionary Society
7. English for aid. By the advice of William Wil-
Baptists. berforce (q.v.), missionaries were sent out in 1813; chapels were built and schools established; more missionaries were sent out; and by 1831 there were 14 English missionaries in charge of 24 churches and 10,000 communicants. This year the slaves rebelled against their masters, and missionaries were charged with having instigated the insurrection. They were arrested and their lives were threatened, but when brought to trial they were acquitted. Many of their chapels and schools had been destroyed, however, and two of their number, Knibb and Burchell, were sent to England, not only to ask for assistance, but to enter a vigorous protest against the traffic in slaves. Their mission was successful, the government indemnified the mission for the property which had been destroyed, and the abolition of the slave-trade in their possessions immediately followed. The work was resumed and greatly prospered, so that in 1842 the Jamaica Baptist Missionary Union was formed, including 132 almost entirely self-supporting churches. Other stations were occupied, missionaries were sent to Trinidad, the Turk Islands, Santo Domingo, and the Bahamas, and here also the people contributed largely to their own support. The society gradually discontinued its workers, so that by 1900 of the ten English missionaries on the field, all but two were independent of its aid. At this time there were 286 stations and substations, some 600 native helpers, 186 churches, and 38,341 communicants.

The Church Missionary Society of England entered the field in 1814, beginning work on Antigua, and opening stations on Jamaica in
8. Church 1826, and on Trinidad in 1836. When,
of England. however, the Colonial State Church was organized in 1839, the C. M. S. withdrew from the field. Early in the eighteenth century, General Christopher Codrington bequeathed two estates to the Society for the Propagation of the Gospel, to provide instruction for the negroes in the Barbadoes and other Caribbean Islands, with the stipulation that an institution be maintained where the "students shall be obliged to study and practice Phisick and Chirurgery as well as Divinity, that by the apparent usefulness of the former to all mankind they may do good to men's souls while taking care of their bodies." The college was formally opened in 1745, and the S. P. G. still administers the trust by which it is supported. In 1818 the society sent missionaries to the Barbadoes, and gradually extended its work to the other islands, but it also withdrew from the field in 1839, only continuing its trust of Codrington College.

The Scottish Missionary Society began a work at Jamaica in 1824, which was rapidly pushed to other islands. In 1835 the first missionaries of the United Presbyterian Church of Scotland were sent out, and Trinidad was occupied; while in the following year the two societies united in forming the Jamaica Presbytery. Three new stations were occupied 1837–40, and the work greatly prospered, until, in 1847, the Scottish Society gave the
9. Scotch work over entirely to the United Pres-
Presby- byterian Church. During the next
terians and decade the ill-health of the mission-
English aries and an epidemic of cholera among
Congrega- the people caused a time of deep dis-
tionalists. tress and slow progress, but in 1861 a revival brought renewed interest and a great accession to the membership of the church. A seminary was established, with a department for training a native ministry which sends out capable colored pastors. Since 1900 the work has been carried on by the Committee of the United Free Church of Scotland, and at that time there were 60 churches in Jamaica and Trinidad, with a membership of 21,500, while the work was largely self-supporting. In 1835 the desire of the emancipated slaves for teachers led the London Missionary Society to send missionaries to Jamaica, in connection with their mission in British Guiana. In 1839 the West India Missionary Committee, consisting of residents of New England and New York, was formed to receive and forward contributions for the support of these missionaries; in 1843 the Jamaica Congregational Association was organized as a local missionary agency, though in 1847 the work passed into the care of the American Missionary Association. By 1867 the churches became self-supporting, and in 1876 the Congregational Association of Jamaica assumed full control.

In 1861 James Theodore Holly (q.v.) obtained permission from the Missionary Committee of the Protestant Episcopal Church to go to Haiti with a missionary colony; and he there established a work which, in 1865, was taken under the control of the American Church Missionary Society. The missionaries were greatly hampered by war and pestilence, but nevertheless were so 10. Protes- successful that in less than a decade tant Epis- the Church in Haiti was recognized by copalians. the General Convention, and Holly was consecrated its first bishop. In 1883 the work practically became independent, though receiving some financial aid as one of the churches in communion with the Protestant Episcopal Church. In 1911 there were 11 priests, 2 deacons, 13 lay readers, 21 missions, 753 communicants, 189 day-school pupils, 358 Sunday-school pupils, contributions $2,076.

After the Cuban rebellion of 1880, Captain Diaz of the insurrectos fled to New York to escape the Spanish forces. While there he was converted, and, after some time spent in study, returned to Cuba to preach the gospel to his fellow countrymen. He persevered amid great persecution, but 11. Amer- in 1885 the Southern Baptist Conven- ican Bap- tion went to his assistance, he was or- tists and dained, and the following year the other first Protestant church was organized Protestant in Havana. During the next two years Organiza- over 1,000 people were baptized; nine tions. native pastors were at work; and day- and Sunday-schools were established. Other churches were organized in various parts of the island, and seventeen preaching-stations were maintained. Over 800 persons applied for baptism in one year, but most of them were totally ignorant as to the meaning of the rite. Over 2,000 children were in the Sunday-school in Havana alone, and from 150 to 200 in each of the other churches. The work of Diaz is conspicuous in that it was the only organized Protestant work in Cuba previous to the Spanish-American War. Other organizations working in the remaining islands of the group to a greater or less extent were the Danske Evangelisk-Lutherske Statskirke (1665); the African Methodist Episcopal Church (1824); the United Methodist Free Churches of England (1838); the Presbyterian Church of Canada (1869); the American Baptist Missionary Union (1870); the Methodist Episcopal Church, South, the American Board of Commissioners for Foreign Missions, and the Presbyterian Church in the U. S. A. (1872); the Methodist Episcopal Church (1873); the Presbyterian Church in the U. S. (1874); the Christian Woman's Board of Missions (1876); the American Friends Board of Foreign Missions (1883); the Seventh Day Adventists (1890); the Christian and Missionary Alliance (1891); and the National Baptist Convention (1893).

Up to the time of the Spanish-American War (1898–99), Protestant missionary operations in the West Indies had been confined largely to the Bermudas, Haiti, Jamaica, and the Lesser Antilles; Cuba and Porto Rico being Spanish possessions which missionaries were forbidden to 12. General enter. As a result of the labors of Present various organizations, the Bermudas Conditions. and the Lesser Antilles may be considered Christianized, though many of the people are weak and ignorant, and there is much room for future development on every line. Haiti

and Santo Domingo are outwardly Roman Catholic, but underneath the form of religion is a current of superstition, and African fetishism still holds many in its thrall. Jamaica is perhaps the most thoroughly Christian of any island in the group, owing to the dominance of England and the natural possibilities of the island. While none of these islands are now properly considered as mission fields, there is large opportunity for building up the weak church-members into strong Christian communities, and this is the present work which is engaging the missionary organizations of the various churches.

During the years that the missionaries were slowly working a transformation in these islands, Cuba and Porto Rico were debarred from all progress by the policy of Spain, even the priesthood being against civic reform and freedom of religious worship. The political rulers were in the islands solely for gain, and the religious leaders as a class were ignorant, avaricious, and indifferent to their holy office. Cathedrals were built, and there was a form of religion; all ecclesiastical functions were 13. Cuba. punctiliously performed; but practically nothing was done, during the four centuries of Spanish dominion, for the betterment of the people. In 1790 there were but two schools, outside Havana, in the entire island of Cuba, as the archbishop refused to sanction more on the ground that popular education was unnecessary. In Porto Rico there was a system of education in the cities, but there were few schools of any kind in the rural districts, and fully 87 per cent of the people could neither read nor write. The people rose repeatedly against their conquerors, only to be the more oppressed. Promises of reforms and freedom were made only to be broken, and at last the long history of misgovernment culminated in the revolution of 1895, when a four-years' struggle ensued. The conflict was terminated only by the intervention of the United States, which sent an army to Cuba, the result being the withdrawal of Spain from the group, and ultimately the annexation of Porto Rico to the United States and the formation of the Republic of Cuba under the protection of the United States. In 1900 the Constitution of this new republic guaranteed that " All religious beliefs, as well as the practise of all forms of religion, are free, without further restriction than that demanded by respect for Christian morality and public order." As soon as this clause became effective the field was occupied by various American missionary organizations. The Southern Baptist Convention had been working in Cuba since 1886, but the missionaries were forced from the field by the war, and at its close they found themselves with one nominal church, of " forty scattered and unfindable members." Work was reopened with new vigor, and so prospered that it is said that over one-third of all the Protestants on the island belong to this one church. There are (1911) 2 missionaries, 26 pastors and helpers, 2 stations, 41 substations, and 18 churches, with 1,078 communicants. Other societies which have entered Cuba since 1898 are the Methodist Episcopal Church, South; the American Baptist Home Missionary Society; the Congregational

Home Missionary Society; the Presbyterian Church in the U. S. A.; the Foreign Christian Missionary Society; the Presbyterian Church, South; the Protestant Episcopal Church; the Seventh Day Adventists; and the Universalist Church.

In Porto Rico the Protestant Episcopal Church was already in the field, with a small chapel for the English-speaking residents, and they at once extended their work to reach the other races also. Other organizations are the American Missionary Association; the American Baptist Home Missionary Society; the Presbyterian Church in the U. S.A.; the United Brethren; the General

14. Porto Rico. Council of the Evangelical Lutheran Church; the Methodist Episcopal Church; the Christian Woman's Board of Missions; the Seventh Day Adventists; and the Christian and Missionary Alliance. As the work developed, some plan of cooperation became necessary, and in 1902 representatives of the various missionary organizations met at Cienfuegos in Cuba to consider the question of comity. The Episcopal Church had already made the island a missionary diocese with a resident bishop, but the other communions decided that cities of 6,000 or more inhabitants should be open to all, while the rest of the island was divided among them, each denomination to care for a certain district, so that there should be no overlapping or friction, and give the best result. This division of the field had already been made in Porto Rico, and in both islands there was the most cordial cooperation among the various religious bodies at work. Centuries of Roman Catholic teaching made the task of the Protestant missionaries most difficult. The work was begun vigorously, however, largely along evangelistic lines, though educational and theological institutions for the training of leaders for the churches were at once planned. The multiplication of schools under government and independent auspices; the establishment of hospitals and dispensaries; and, above all, the services of the Christian minister, freely given, not only in solemnizing marriages and in the other sacraments of the Church, but in all lines of Christian activities, are slowly solving the problems of these islands. One happy result of the work of the Protestant missionaries has been to arouse the Roman Catholics to greater activity and new methods, and the once dormant though dominant church is establishing schools and colleges, and doing its share in the uplift of the people.

Bahama Islands: 7 societies; 37 missionaries; 266 helpers and pastors; 10 stations; 134 substations; 2 churches; 19,182 communicants; contributions, $4,622.

Cuba: 16 societies; 142 missionaries; 137 helpers and pastors; 50 stations; 176 substations; 118 churches; 9,173 communicants; contributions, $22,485.

15. Statistical Summary. Porto Rico: 15 societies; 167 missionaries; 200 helpers and pastors; 52 stations; 274 substations; 120 churches, and 9,692 communicants; contributions, $3,777.

Haiti and Santo Domingo: 9 societies; 17 missionaries; 139 helpers and pastors; 21 stations; 41

substations; 4 churches; 2,706 communicants; contributions, $1,635.

Jamaica: 18 societies; 257 missionaries; 1,852 helpers and pastors; 277 stations; 426 substations; 384 churches; 138,333 communicants; contributions, $174,057.

Lesser Antilles: 14 societies; 186 missionaries; 977 helpers and pastors; 54 stations; 189 substations; 104 churches; 80,787 communicants; contributions, $79,193.

Total for the group: 806 missionaries; 3,571 helpers and pastors; 464 stations; 1,240 substations; 732 churches; 259,873 communicants; contributions, $285,769.

THEODORA CROSBY BLISS.

BIBLIOGRAPHY: Works of a general nature are: J. de Acosta, *Natural and Moral Hist. of the West Indies*, London, 1880; C. H. Eden, *The West Indies*, ib. 1881; W. Moister, *The West Indies, Enslaved and Free*, ib. 1883; J. A. Froude, *The English in the West Indies*, ib. 1888; C. E. Taylor, *Leaflets from the Danish West Indies*, ib. 1888; A. M. Kollewijn, *Geschiedenis van Nederlandsch West-Indië*, Amersfoot, 1887; O. T. Bulkeley, *The Lesser Antilles*, London, 1889; C. W. Eves, *The West Indies*, ib. 1889; H. V. F. Bronkhurst, *Geography of the West India Islands*, Demerara, 1890; L. Hearn, *Two Years in the French West Indies*, London, 1890; C. P. Lucas, *Historical Geography of the British Colonies*, vol. ii., *The West Indies*, Oxford, 1894; J. Rodway, *The West Indies*, New York, 1896; L. Peytrand, *L'Esclavage aux Antilles françaises avant 1789*, Paris, 1897; R. T. Hill, *Cuba and Porto Rico, with the other Islands of the West Indies*, New York, 1898; L. Lloréns Torres, *América. Estudios históricos y filológicos*, Madrid, 1898; A. K. Fiske, *The West Indies: a Hist. of the Islands of the West Indian Archipelago*, New York, 1899; M. Halstead, *Hist. of American Expansion and the Story of our new Possessions*, ib. 1899; M. A. Hamm, *Porto Rico and the West Indies*, London, 1899; C. S. Walton, *The Civil Law in Spain and Spanish-America including Puerto Rico*, Washington, D. C., 1900; *A List of Books on the Danish West Indies*, Congress Library, Washington, D. C., 1901; J. de Dampierre, *Essai sur les sources de l'histoire des Antilles françaises, 1492–1664*, Paris, 1904; F. Dodsworth, *The Book of the West Indies*, London, 1904; H. H. van Kol, *Naar de Antillen en Venezuela*, Leyden, 1904; F. A. Ober, *Our West Indian Neighbors*, New York, 1904; idem, *Guide to the West Indies*, ib. 1908; G. Weggener, *Reisen im Westindischen Mittelmeer*, Berlin, 1904; J. Henderson, *The West Indies*, London, 1905, new ed., New York, 1909.

On separate parts of the West Indies: J. H. Stark, *Hist. and Guide to the Bahama Islands*, Boston, 1891; G. Lester, *In Sunny Isles: Chapters treating chiefly of the Bahama Islands*, London, 1897; *The Bahama Islands*, ed. G. B. Shattuck, New York, 1905; N. D. Davis, *Cavaliers and Roundheads in Barbadoes*, ib 1888; J. Y. Edghill, *About Barbados*, London, 1890; J. H. Stark, *Hist. and Guide to Barbados*, Boston, 1893; A. Bachiller y Morales, *Cuba: Monografia historica*, Havana, 1883; F. Vidal y Careta, *Estudio de las razas humanas que han ido poblando sucesivamente la Isla de Cuba*, Madrid, 1897; I. E. Canini, *Four Centuries of Spanish Rule in Cuba*, Chicago, 1898; R. Davey, *Cuba, Past and Present*, London, 1898; F. Matthews, *The New-born Cuba*, New York, 1899; E. Aubert, *Les nouvelles Ameriques. Cuba, etc.*, Paris, 1901; H. Gannett, *A Gazetteer of Cuba*, Washington, D. C., 1902; H. H. S. Aimes, *Hist. of Slavery in Cuba, 1511–1868*, New York, 1907; I. A. Wright, *Cuba*, ib. 1910; Sir S. St. John, *Hayti or the Black Republic*, London, 1889; E. M. Bacon and E. M. Aaron, *The New Jamaica*, New York, 1890; F. Cundall, *Bibliotheca Jamaicensis*, ib. 1895; J. H. Stark, *Jamaica Guide*, Boston, 1898; B. P. Burry, *Jamaica as it is, 1903*, London, 1903; F. Dodsworth, *The Book of Jamaica*, Kingston, 1904; W. J. Gardner, *Hist. of Jamaica*, new ed., New York, 1909; A. D. Hall, *Porto Rico*, New York, 1898; A. G. Robinson, *Porto Rico of To-day*, ib. 1899; R. A. van Middeldyk, *The History of Puerto Rico*, ib. 1903; S. Brau, *Historia de Puerto Rico*, 1904; L. S. Rowe, *The United States and Porto Rico*, ib. 1904; S. Hazard, *Santo Domingo, Past and Present*, London, 1873; D.

Hort, *Trinidad, Historical and Statistical*, ib. 1865; J. A. de Suze, *Geography of Trinidad and Tobago*, Trinidad, 1894. Specifically on the religious side are: H. B. Foster, *Wesleyan-Methodism in Jamaica*, London, 1881; W. Carlile, *Thirty-eight Years' Mission Life in Jamaica*, ib. 1884; E. Nuttall, *The Churchman's Manual*, Jamaica, 1893; J. B. Ellis, *Hist. of the Church of England in Jamaica*, Kingston, 1891; A. Caldecott, *The Church in the West Indies*, London, 1898. Consult also the more general literature under MISSIONS.

WEST, SAMUEL: The name of two American Unitarian ministers.

1. Of New Bedford, Mass.; b. at Yarmouth, Cape Cod, Mass., Mar. 3, 1730 (O. S.); d. at Tiverton, Newport Co., R. I., Sept. 24, 1807. After a youth spent on his father's farm, he entered Harvard College (B.A., 1754), and after graduation spent several years in further study, much of his time being devoted to science, while in later years he developed a very marked interest in alchemy. In 1761 he was ordained to the ministry of the Congregational church at New Bedford, Mass., which he continued to serve, though at times much crippled financially, until age and impairment of mental powers forced him to retire in 1803. During the Revolution he served as a chaplain in the American forces at Boston, and took an active part as a member of the conventions for framing the constitution of Massachusetts and for adopting the constitution of the United States, his personal influence over his former classmate, Governor Hancock, largely securing the adhesion of his state to the American Constitution. Besides his addiction to alchemy, West devoted much time to the study of expected fulfilments of prophecy, and these traits, together with an almost incredible absent-mindedness, give a curious picture to the present day. Although he published a number of sermons, West is chiefly memorable for a polemic against Jonathan Edwards' doctrine of predestination, entitled *Essays on Liberty and Necessity* (2 parts, 1793–95).

2. Of Boston; b. at Martha's Vineyard, Mass., Nov. 19, 1738 (O. S.); d. at Boston, Mass., Apr. 10, 1808. After a youth of privation, he entered Harvard College (B.A., 1761), and on graduation was chosen chaplain to the garrison at Port Pownal, Penobscot, Me., where he spent a year. After acting as an occasional supply at Cambridge, where he had returned for further study, he was ordained in 1764 to the ministry of the church at Needham, Mass., where he remained, despite some friction owing to the delay of his congregation in paying him his salary, until 1789, when he assumed charge of the Hollis Street Church, Boston, where he labored regularly until 1801, after which increasing infirmity of age compelled him gradually to withdraw from active life. Brought up as a Calvinistic Trinitarian, West broke with Calvinism at an early period; his precise views on the Trinity are uncertain, but he was ranked as an opponent of the conservative school. His only publications were a number of sermons.

BIBLIOGRAPHY: W. B. Sprague, *Annals of the American Unitarian Pulpit*, New York, 1865, pp. 37–55; a biographical sketch of West of Boston by T. Thacher is also appended to the funeral sermon delivered by J. Lathrop, Boston, 1808.

WEST, STEPHEN: b. in Tolland, Conn., Nov. 2, 1735; d. at Stockbridge, Mass., May 15, 1819.

He was graduated from Yale College, 1755; pursued his theological studies with Rev. Timothy Woodbridge of Hatfield, Mass.; was called in 1757 to be the military chaplain at Hoosac Fort; in 1758 he was invited, by the commissioners for Indian affairs in Boston, to succeed Jonathan Edwards in the Indian mission at Stockbridge, and was ordained pastor of the church at Stockbridge in 1759; here until 1775 he preached to the Indians in the morning and in the afternoon to the white settlers; after that year he confined his labors to the latter. Early in this pastorate he adopted the views of Jonathan Edwards; he then preached a series of sermons, which were afterward published in the form of an *Essay on Moral Agency* (New Haven, 1772, 2d ed., 1794). He next published his *Essay on the Scripture Doctrine of the Atonement* (1785; 2d ed., with appendix, 1815). After he had passed his eightieth year he issued his *Evidence of the Divinity of the Lord Jesus Christ, Collected from the Scriptures* (1816). He attracted to himself many theological pupils, who resided in his house, and uniformly spoke of him in terms of the highest admiration. At least five of them became eminent as preachers and writers; among them may be noted Samuel Spring (q.v.), of Newburyport, and John Thornton Kirkland, president of Harvard College.

West was not only a man of great diligence in study, but was also noted for practical insight and activity. It was partly in recognition of this that in 1793, when Williams College was incorporated, Dr. West was named as one of the trustees, and at the first meeting of the board was elected vice-president of the institution. He was one of Samuel Spring's chief counselors in forming the Creed and Associate Statutes of Andover Theological Seminary. He was also a pioneer in the organization and operation of various missionary and charitable institutions.

BIBLIOGRAPHY: W. B. Sprague, *Annals of the American Pulpit*, i. 548–556, New York, 1859; W. Walker, in *American Church History Series*, vol. iii. passim, ib. 1894; F. H. Foster, *New England Theology*, pp. 204 sqq., Chicago, 1907.

WESTCOTT, BROOKE FOSS: Church of England, bishop of Durham; b. near Birmingham Jan. 12, 1825; d. at The Castle, Bishop Auckland (9 m. s.s.e. of Durham), July 27, 1901. He was educated at Trinity College, Cambridge (B.A., 1848; fellow, 1849; M.A., 1851; B.D., 1864; D.D., 1870); was ordained deacon and priest (1851); assistant master at Harrow School (1852–69); examining chaplain to the bishop of Peterborough (1868–83); canon residentiary (1869–83); rector of Somersham with Pidley and Colne, Hunts (1870–82); honorary chaplain to the queen (1875–79); select preacher at Oxford (1877–80); in 1870 became regius professor of divinity, Cambridge; in 1879, chaplain in ordinary to the queen; in 1882, fellow of King's College, Cambridge; in 1883, examining chaplain to the archbishop of Canterbury; in 1884, canon of Westminster; and in 1890, bishop of Durham. During 1881–83 he served as a member of the royal commission on ecclesiastical courts; and was also a member of the New Testament Revision Company (1870–81). He is one of the brightest examples of English scholarship and industry, and is as remarkable for the fine quality of his work as for the number of volumes which he produced. He will probably be longest remembered for his joint production with Fenton John Anthony Hort (q.v.) of *The New Testament in the Original Greek* (2 vols., 1881). But the range of his studies was far wider than this, covering the New Testament canon, contributions on philosophy, and exegetical work of the highest rank. He was hardly less noted as a preacher than as a scholar. He was in demand as a speaker on topics of national, industrial, and social interest, and in 1892 almost alone succeeded in securing settlement of a dispute between coal-miners and employers which threatened to wreck the industries and works of transportation in the United Kingdom. He was a valued contributor to William Smith's *Dictionary of the Bible* (1863) and to the same editor's and Dean Henry Wace's *Dictionary of Christian Biography* (1877–87). His independent publications, some of which passed through numerous editions, comprise:

Elements of Gospel Harmony (Cambridge, 1851; Norrisian essay); A General Survey of the History of the Canon of the New Testament during the First Four Centuries (London, 1855); Characteristics of the Gospel Miracles (1859); Introduction to the Study of the Gospels (1860); The Bible in the Church (1864); The Gospel of the Resurrection (1866); A General View of the History of the English Bible (1868); Christian Life Manifold and One (sermons; 1872); Some Points in the Religious Office of the Universities (1873); The Revelation of the Risen Lord (London, 1882); The Gospel according to St. John (1882); The Historic Faith (lectures on the Apostles' Creed (1883); Epistles of St. John, Greek Text, Notes, and Essays (1883); Revelation of the Father: Titles of the Lord (1884); Christus Consummator: Some Aspects of the Work and Person of Christ in Relation to Modern Thought (sermons; 1886); Social Aspects of Christianity (1887); Victory of the Cross: Sermons in Holy Week (1888); Epistle to the Hebrews: Greek Text, with Notes (1889); Gifts for the Ministry: From Strength to Strength· Three Sermons (1890); Gospel of Life: a Study of Christian Doctrine (1892); Bishop Lightfoot (1894); The Incarnation and Common Life (1894, 2d ed., 1908); Christian Aspects of Life (1897); Some Lessons of the Revised Version of the New Testament (1897); Lessons from Work (1901); and the posthumous Words of Faith and Hope (1902); Christian Social Union Addresses (1903); Peterborough Sermons (1904); Village Sermons (1906); and The Two Empires; the Church and the World (1909).

BIBLIOGRAPHY: A. Westcott, *Life and Letters of Brooke Foss Westcott*, 2 vols., London, 1903, abridged ed., 1905; Mrs. H. Porter, *Secret of a great Influence: Notes on Bishop Westcott's Teaching*, ib. 1905; J. Clayton, *Bishop Westcott*, in *Leaders of the Church, 1880–1900*, ib. 1907; H. S. Holland, *Brooke Foss Westcott*, ib. 1910.

WESTEN, ves'ten, **THOMAS:** Apostle to the Norwegian Finns; b. in Trondhjem, Norway, Sept. 13, 1682; d. there Apr. 9, 1727. The people to whom he went live in the region, partly in Norway, north of 64 degrees north latitude; their present number is given as about 30,000, of whom 21,000 are in Norway; but earlier they must have been more numerous. By the Norwegians they are called Finns, which name they prefer; but the Swedes call them Lapps, with sinister suggestion. Their speech shows them related to the inhabitants of Finland. Christianity had earlier been imposed upon them, but heathenism had remained their preferred practise. The character of the ministrations had not been such as to win them to a regard for Christian beliefs. But before the time of Westen something had been done for the Finns by the Danish-Norwegian church. When Erich Bredahl,

XII.—21

bishop of Trondhjem, had been driven from his diocese in 1658, he became vicar of Trondenäs, whence he undertook several journeys to the Finns; some he won to Christianity; in 1703 the schoolmaster Isaac Olsen went to East Finnmark, where the provost Paus recognized his worth and made him teacher at Waranger, where he labored faithfully for fourteen years in all sorts of perils and dangers. Under Frederick IV. of Denmark and Norway in 1707 a commission was given to Paul H. Resen to investigate the condition of schools and churches in the north; the direction following this to the bishop of Trondhjem to better conditions was disregarded in fact. In 1714 the king directed a mission to the Finns to be undertaken, entrusting the task to the Collegium de promovendo cursu Evangelii, and the choice of an agent fell on Westen.

Preliminary training in the school of poverty and hardship had rendered Westen fit for the work. He had studied medicine at his father's command, but after his father's death (just as he was taking his degree) he studied theology under great privations; Frederick IV. appointed him a librarian without pay, 1707, and in 1710 he became pastor at Weö in Romsdalen; then in 1716 the Collegium made him vicar and chief of the mission to the Finns, and the same year he undertook his first journey among his people, while Bishop Krog of Trondhjem attempted to nullify his work. Westen settled missionaries, provided for houses of worship, gathered data, and laid the foundations for further work. On his return he founded a seminary for children of the Finns, at his own cost, and this had much to do with later success. Bishop Krog's hostility pursued him, but the king and the collegium supported him, so that new helpers came to his assistance in the persons of Arvid Bistok, Elias Heltberg, Martin Lund, and Erasmus Rachlew. With these in 1718 he began a new tour among the Finns, leaving his helpers settled in various places to do steady work, himself preaching, teaching, overcoming opposition wantonly placed in his way, and gaining the hearts of his people, who came to call him " the good man." The reports of Westen's labors caused a desire to hear from him in person, and he was called to Copenhagen, where to the king he related what was being done and what was necessary. He gained new helpers, and in 1722 began his third great missionary circuit. He found a thirst for knowledge and for the Gospel awakened, and established new schools, while the assistants gained the complete confidence of their people, who gave up their idolatry. On this journey Westen entered virgin territory, going among those who had sworn to kill him and his companions, and gained them for the Gospel.

From that time till his death Westen was permitted to see the fruits of his labors in the upbuilding of his people's faith. His travels and hardships had so undermined his health that he was unable to take long journeys, but he continued to make short visits to the nearer points, while his literary activities were continually employed in furthering the interests for which he had worked, though his story of the missions was not published and seems to have been lost. The opposition to which he was exposed by Bishop Krog increased and aggravated the illness resulting from his labors; in his closing days he suffered also from temporal needs, having devoted so completely his income to his work that when he died a subscription was necessary for the expenses of his funeral. (J. BELSHEIM†.)

BIBLIOGRAPHY: H. Hammond, *Den nordiske Missions Historie*, Copenhagen, 1787; *Christoterpe*, 1833, pp. 299 sqq.; G. Plitt, *Kurze Geschichte der lutherischen Mission*, pp. 133 sqq., Erlangen, 1871.

WESTMINSTER ASSEMBLY: A synod of Calvinistic divines held in London 1645–52. This synod was the culminating act in the struggle between the Anglican and Puritan parties in the Church of England which had been in progress for more than a century, from the days of William Tyndale, and had been warmly fought during the reign of Elizabeth. It occupies the first place among the synods of the Reformed Church for the distinction of the men who composed it, the character of the documents it sent forth, and the size of the constituency which accepts these documents. It was never accepted, however, on the continent, where the canons and decrees of the Synod of Dort proved to be the most widely accepted Reformed symbols.

In spite of the attempts of Elizabeth to crush all Puritan dissent, Puritanism continued to be a strong force till the end of her reign. Under Elizabeth's successor, James I., 1603–25, and his **Summons** son Charles I., 1625–49, the repressive **and Object.** policy was continued and a certain galling element introduced especially through the *Book of Sports* (q.v.), and under the régime of Archbishop Laud. To the difference which divided the two parties in matters of ritual and church government was added a wide difference in the matter of doctrine. The theology of both was strongly Calvinistic down to the close of Elizabeth's reign, as is shown by the Lambeth Articles (q.v.), which were issued in 1595 with the signatures of the archbishops of Canterbury and York and of other Anglican prelates. Arminianism began to infiltrate from Holland into England under James, and was adopted by Laud as a policy to be carried out in determining the appointment of bishops and other clergy. [The so-called Arminianism of Laud and other High-churchmen was rather the semi-Pelagianism of the Roman Catholic Church. A. H. N.] Through the insane measures of Laud Scotch Presbyterians were to be brought into close alliance with the English Puritans. Following in the line of James II.'s measures to crush out Presbyterianism and abolish permanently the General Assembly, Laud sought to force episcopacy and the ritual of the Anglican Church upon Scotland, and in 1633 made offensive display of the Anglican ritual at Holyrood House, Edinburgh. Laud's *Book of Canons* and a new liturgy based upon the Book of Common Prayer were to be made obligatory and courts of high commission were set up in every diocese to see that they were observed. The attempt to introduce the new order in Edinburgh, July 23, 1637, produced an uproar (see GEDDES, JENNY), and the resistance of the people embodied itself in the National Covenant, Feb. 28, 1638, which bound the people to defend their ecclesiastical liberties against papal corruptions (see COVENANTERS, § 3).

The crisis in England was brought about by the summons of the long parliament in 1640, which Charles, because of his financial straits, was forced to convene. This parliament, although its leaders were Anglicans, was strongly Puritan in spirit. Petitions poured in upon it to institute ecclesiastical changes, including the " Root and Branch Petition " with 15,000 signatures asking that episcopacy be done away " with all its dependencies, roots and branches." In 1641 the house of commons ordered images, altars, crucifixes, and relics of idolatry removed from the church buildings. At the invitation of London ministers, a delegation from the Scotch Assembly led by Alexander Henderson (q.v.) visited London to set up a presbytery. In 1642 parliament abolished episcopacy and the liturgy. The parliamentary and royalist armies were in the field. It was in the midst of this political and ecclesiastical commotion that the Westminster Assembly was called. The " Grand Remonstrance " had been sent up to parliament demanding such a religious assembly to discuss and arrange matters ecclesiastical within the realm. Two bills convening the synod were suppressed by Charles. The third resulted in the gathering which held its first meeting July 1, 1643. The object of the assembly was declared to be " to settle the government and liturgy of the Church of England and for the vindicating and clearing of the doctrine of the said church from false aspersions and vituperations as should be agreeable to the Word of God and most apt to procure and preserve the peace of the church at home and bring it unto near accord with the Church of Scotland and other Reformed churches abroad."

The membership was fixed by parliament at 121 clergymen and 30 laymen, 20 laymen being chosen from the house of commons and 10 from the house of lords. The clergymen were taken two from each county, and two each from Oxford, **Member-** Cambridge, and the Channel Islands, **ship, Place** one from each county of Wales, and **of Meeting,** four from London. To this number **and** was added the delegation sent by the **Parties.** Scotch Assembly. Among the eminent English divines who had no seat in the assembly were Richard Baxter and John Owen (qq.v.). Three delegates are said to have been invited from New England, John Cotton of Boston, Thomas Hooker of Hartford, and John Davenport of New Haven (qq.v.). The first meeting was held in Westminster Abbey, Dr. Twisse preaching the sermon (not extant) from John xiv. 18. Assembling at first in the chapel of Henry VII., the body adjourned to the Jerusalem· Chamber (q.v.) in the deanery of Westminster, where it continued to sit.

In matters of doctrine, all the members were Calvinists, although they were divided between infralapsarianism and supralapsarianism. The *Minutes* of the assembly show that moderate Calvinism was represented by a body of eminent and weighty men. The leading difference was upon the subject of church government. There were five groups, representing four different types of opinion as follows: (1) The Episcopalians, made up of four prelates, including Archbishop Ussher (q.v.), and five doctors of divinity. Only one bishop was seen in the assembly and one doctor of divinity, Dr. Daniel Featley (q.v.), who, however, was expelled for offending against the assembly's law forbidding the divulgence of its proceedings. The prelates had been forbidden by Charles to attend. (2) The Erastians, including the great scholars, John Lightfoot and John Selden (qq.v.), who, with Erastus of Heidelberg, regarded the State as the final seat of authority in ecclesiastical matters. (3) The Independents, few in number but powerful in debate, including Philip Nye and Thomas Goodwin (q.v.), later Cromwell's chaplain, both of them returned from exile in Holland. This group, called " the five dissenting brethren," fought Presbyterianism with great tenacity and acumen. They withdrew after the Presbyterian polity was adopted. (4) The Presbyterians, who were preponderant from the beginning and gained in strength. In their number were William Twisse (q.v.), the prolocutor of the body; Herbert Palmer (q.v.), popularly regarded as the chief author of the Shorter Catechism; Stephen Marshall (q.v.), a great preacher and the chief go-between for the assembly and parliament; and Joseph Caryl (q.v.), the author of the voluminous commentary on Job. (5) The Scotch commissioners, including the élite of the Scotch clergy, appointed by the assembly, namely, Alexander Henderson (q.v.), rector of Edinburgh University; Robert Baillie (q.v.), the Boswell of the assembly, principal of Glasgow University; Samuel Rutherford (q.v.), professor at St. Andrew's; and George Gillespie (q.v.), parish minister in Edinburgh. Rev. Robert Douglas, the fifth clerical delegate, did not attend. The two lay delegates were Lord Maitland and Sir Archibald Johnstone. Of the latter, his nephew, Bishop Burnet, said that he often prayed in his family two hours at a stretch. The Scotch were the most vigorous element in the assembly. They acted in agreement and demanded a place on each of the committees, a demand that was granted. They had a great advantage from the start. Parliament in its struggle with Charles had turned to Scotland for help. To the parliamentary delegation was added a delegation from the assembly which called upon the Scotch to take part in its proceedings. In accepting the invitation, the Scotch made their own terms which were embodied in the Solemn League and Covenant. This famous document, drawn up by Alexander Henderson, stated as its object to defend the Reformed religion in Scotland in doctrine, worship, discipline, and government, and " to secure a reformation of religion in England and Ireland according to the Word of God and the practise of the best Reformed churches," and to bring the two countries " into the nearest conjunction and uniformity in religion, confession of faith, form of church government, directories of worship, and catechizing." The aim of the Scotch was to establish Presbyterianism in England and in its work the assembly followed the program laid down in the five particulars of the Solemn League.

The members were chosen by parliament, as were also the prolocutor and the two clerks. The assembly met every week-day except Saturday, and " commonly " sat from nine in the morning till one

or two in the afternoon. A table stood in the middle of the room at which were seated the prolocutor and the clerks. Benches ran down the room on each side, the Scotch sitting in a body on the moderator's right. The members of parliament sat on chairs near the fire. Usually sixty were present. No one was admitted to the sittings without an order from parliament. The rules provided that no question should be brought to a vote the day it was proposed, and that speakers should make their statements good from Scripture. There was freedom of debate and the speakers spoke as long as seemed to them good. Baillie declares that they " harangue long and learnedly." The body was divided into three committees, to one of which each member belonged, and through these committees the business was brought before the main body. Fast-days were frequently appointed on which religious services were conducted during the day without pause. Baillie speaks of such a day (May 17, 1644, the devotions lasting from nine to five) as the sweetest day he had experienced in England. Up to Feb. 22, 1648, the assembly held 1,163 sessions. The body then seems to have closed its appointed work, but continued an irregular existence as a board of triers for examining ministers until 1652, when it seems to have expired of inanition. Fuller says " it dwindled by degrees and vanished with the parliament."

Mode of Procedure.

The assembly produced five disciplinary and doctrinal statements. At the direction of parliament, it first set itself to revise the Thirty-nine Articles of Religion (q.v.). When it reached Article XVI. it was ordered by the same body to turn aside and devote itself to the preparation of a statement on church government which the Scotch regarded as the key to the situation. The result was the " Propositions concerning Church Government and Ordination of Ministers," which was sent to parliament in completed form Nov. 8, 1644. Parliament took many liberties with the document and sent it back to the assembly for amendment. It was not finished till 1648. By order of parliament the Confession of Faith was taken up in Aug., 1644, and presented to the commons Dec. 4, 1646. The assembly was instructed to add the Scripture proofs and the document was completed Apr. 29, 1647. The Scotch assembly approved it in 1647 and the Scotch parliament in 1649. The English parliament adopted it with some changes 1648. The " Directory for the Public Worship of God " was completed at the close of 1644 and approved by the English parliament for England and Wales Jan. 3, 1645, and a month later by the Scotch general assembly. It gave prescriptions for the conduct of public worship and other clerical functions and set aside the prescribed liturgical forms of the Book of Common Prayer. The two Westminster Catechisms, called the Larger and Shorter Catechisms, were prepared simultaneously with the Confession of Faith. It was at first proposed to prepare but a single one, but the assembly, yielding to the feeling expressed by Rutherford, that it is hard " to dress up meat and milk in the same dish," prepared two. The impression still

Its Work.

prevails that the assembly succeeded in putting much strong meat into both documents.

At the suggestion of parliament the assembly also adopted Rous' version of the psalms, a version which was produced by Sir Francis Rous, himself a member of the house of commons (see HYMNOLOGY, IX., § 2).

(1) Parliament nominated the members, proposed the business of the assembly, revised its work, provided the rules by which it was to conduct business, and appointed its officers. (2) The work of the assembly failed in the land which gave
Things to it birth. Under Cromwell, Independ
be Noted. ency ruled, and, in 1660, episcopacy
was reestablished as the law of England and the Book of Common Prayer and the Thirty-nine Articles of Religion were again enforced. Puritanism produced Milton and the *Pilgrim's Progress*, but it has never since been an organized force till the last half-century. The Presbyterian Church of England has no historical kinship to the Westminster Assembly and is of recent organization. (3) The four outstanding principles emphasized by the assembly are the authority of the Scriptures, which is set forth in a noble form of statement, the sovereignty of God, the rights of conscience, and the sole jurisdiction of the Church within its own domain. The statement of the last two principles easily includes more than the framers intended. When the assembly insisted that " God alone is the Lord of the conscience," it did not mean to issue a brief of religious toleration. The Puritan churches of America were far from any such idea, and Baillie declared " that such a thing as tolerating all and any religion was so prodigious an impiety that this religious parliament can not but abhor the very naming of it." The assembly's assertion of the jurisdiction of the Church over its own affairs did not involve for the men of that day the idea of the separation of Church and State.

The Westminster symbols still remain the canonical books of the Presbyterian churches throughout the world (the word " Presbyterian " being taken in a narrower sense than the expression " Reformed Churches "), but not without important modifications not only in the text of the Confession of Faith, but also in the practical usages in worship and church government, The text of the Catechisms remains,

but the Larger Catechism is now seldom committed to memory and little read. The Westminster symbolical books are the compact historical expression of the Puritan impulse of Great Britain, which was Calvinistic in doctrine and anti-episcopal in government.   DAVID S. SCHAFF.

BIBLIOGRAPHY: Sources: The official manuscript records of the Westminster Assembly were long supposed to have perished in the London fire of 1666, but were discovered in London in the library of Dr. Williams in three folio volumes, and were edited in part by A. F. Mitchell and B. Struthers as *Minutes of the Sessions of the Westminster Assembly of Divines*, Edinburgh, 1874. This volume contains the doctrinal debates; the minutes containing the debates on church government and discipline are not yet published. J. Lightfoot, *Journal of the Proceedings of the Assembly of Divines (July 1, 1643–Dec. 31, 1644)*, in his *Works*, ed. Pitman, vol. xiii., London, 1824; G. Gillespie, *Notes of the Debates and Proceedings of the Assembly of Divines and Other Commissioners at Westminster (Feb. 2, 1644–Jan. 3, 1645)*, in *Presbyterian Armoury*, ed. D. Meek, vol. ii., Edinburgh, 1844; the *Journals of the house of lords and house of commons*, 1643–49; R. Baillie, *Letters and Journals*, ed. *from the Author's Manuscripts by D. Laing*, vols. ii.–iii., Edinburgh, 1841–42; A. F. Mitchell and J. Christie, *Records of the Commissions of the General Assemblies of the Church of Scotland 1646–49*, 2 vols., ib. 1892.

Consult further: J. Reid, *Memoirs of the Westminster Divines*, 2 vols., Paisley, 1811–15; W. M. Hetherington, *History of the Westminster Assembly of Divines*, Edinburgh, 1843, 5th ed., revised by R. Williamson; 1890; C. A. Briggs, in *Presbyterian Review*, 1880, pp. 127–164; A. F. Mitchell, *The Westminster Assembly, its History and Standards*, London, 1883, new ed., Philadelphia, 1897; W. W. Henry, *The Westminster Assembly*, New York, 1897; *Memorial Volume of the Westminster Assembly, 1647–1897*, ib. 1897; *Addresses at the Celebration of the 250th Anniversary of the Westminster Assembly*, ib. 1898; Schaff, *Creeds*, i. 725–811; B. B. Warfield, in *Presbyterian and Reformed Review*, 1901, pp. 226 sqq.; W. Beveridge, *Short Hist. of the Westminster Assembly*, Edinburgh and New York, 1904; idem, *Makers of the Scottish Church*, ib. 1908. Note also *Cambridge Modern History*, iv. 356–363, 897, New York, 1906. The subject is illumined by accounts in T. Fuller, *Church Hist. of Britain*, century xviii., book xi., London, 1655 and often; D. Neal, *Hist. of the Puritans*, ed. J. Toulmin, 5 vols., Bath, 1793–97; J. B. Marsden, *Hist. of the Early Puritans*, and *Hist. of the Later Puritans*, 2 vols., London, 1850–52; A. P. Stanley, *Memorials of Westminster Abbey*, ib. 1868; T. McCrie, *Annals of English Presbytery*, ib. 1872; J. Stoughton, *Hist. of Religion in England*, vol. i., new ed., London, 1881; T. Leishman, *The Westminster Directory*, Edinburgh, 1901; W. H. Hutton, *The English Church (1625–1714)*, pp. 124 sqq., ib. 1903. The largest collection of works relating to the Assembly, including sermons by its members before parliament, is in Union Theological Seminary, New York City.

WESTMINSTER STANDARDS.

The Westminster Standards—i.e., the Westminster Confession of Faith and the Westminster Catechisms—are the doctrinal formulas prepared by the Westminster Assembly of Divines (1643–49), and have been adopted by the churches of English, Scotch, and Scotch-Irish origin which follow the Presbyterian system.

I. The Westminster Confession: In its original form, as it left the assembly and was presented to parliament, the Westminster Confession consisted of thirty-three chapters. On giving up the attempt to revise the Thirty-nine Articles (q.v.), the assembly, at the injunction of parliament (Aug. 20, 1644),

appointed a committee to " prepare a joint Confession of Faith," the committee including such men as Thomas Gataker, Joshua Hoyle, William Gouge (qq.v.), and the Scotch commissioners in a body. Its progress was delayed by a contention between parliament and the assembly over the right of office-bearers to withhold the communion from those who seemed to them to be ignorant or scandalous, and on July 22, 1646, an order was sent to the assembly " desiring that it hasten the perfecting of the Confession of Faith and the Catechism because of the great use they might be for the suppressing of errors and heresies and for informing the ignorance of the people." Nineteen heads were completed and sent to the house of commons Oct. 9, 1646, of which 500 copies were or-

1. Origin of the Confession. dered printed by the house. On Dec. 4, 1646, the whole work was finished and sent to the commons, and three days later to the lords, the assembly being authorized to have 600 copies printed. On Apr. 29, 1647, the house of commons ordered Scripture proofs added, and 600 copies of these .were ordered struck off. Finally, in 1648, the Confession was approved by parliament with the exception of chapters xxx. and xxxi., and parts of chapters xx. and xxiv., these portions bearing on church censures, synods, marriage and divorce, and liberty of conscience. Thus amended, the document was printed in London under the title *Articles of Christian Religion approved and passed by both Houses of Parliament after advice had with the Assembly of Divines.* In spite of the action of parliament, the Confession has been uniformly printed in Great Britain as well as in America in the form in which it left the assembly, and in this form it was adopted by the Scotch assembly in 1647, and by the Scotch estates of parliament in 1649, the latter ordering that it and the two catechisms be published and printed.

The Confession opens with a definition of the Bible as the only rule of faith and practise, and with the proofs by which it attests its authority, and closes with a chapter on the last judgment. It is the clearest, strongest, most logical, and most careful symbolical statement of the Calvinistic scheme of Christian doctrine, and represents the rigorous philosophical type of creedal statement as compared with the Heidelberg Catechism and Bullinger's Second Helvetic Confession, or with the Thirty-nine Articles, while, on the other hand, it

2. Description and Sources. is not so rigid as the Canons of the Synod of Dort. It proceeds from the idea of God's sovereignty and his decrees, and does not by distinct treatment give sufficient prominence to the fatherhood and love of God. Its definitions, starting with the divine foreknowledge and election, may easily be interpreted to nullify the free offer of the Gospel to all men and to deny the readiness of God to redeem all sinners willing to repent. These objections have been met by the Declaratory Statements of the Scotch Churches and the Revision of the American Presbyterian Church (North).

For a long time it was the received opinion that the Westminster Confession bore the stamp of Dutch Theology and of Turretini (q.v.). Even the younger McCrie (*Annals of English Presbytery,* London, 1872, p. 177) took this position, but Mitchell (*Westminster Assembly,* Philadelphia, 1897, pp. 370 sqq.), Schaff (*Creeds,* i. 762 sqq.), and Briggs (*Presbyterian Review,* Jan., 1880) have shown this view to be untenable. The Confession is based upon a thorough study of the Scriptures, the Continental Reformed theology, the earlier English and Scotch confessions, and more particularly upon the Irish Articles of Archbishop Ussher (q.v.), several sections, such as those on the Scriptures, the Trinity, the decrees, the Lord's Supper, and the civil

magistrate, being drawn largely from the Irish statement, as well as such expressions as " the man of sin," applied to the pope. It must be also remembered that a large number of English catechisms, strongly doctrinal, had proceeded from Presbyterian and Puritan sources, and that William Twisse (q.v.), Gataker, and other members of the Westminster assembly were trained theological disputants and writers. As for subscription to the Confession, it remains a matter of doubt whether the English section of the Westminster divines intended anything more than that the document should be a norm of teaching. On the other hand, the Scotch insisted upon subscription, a course adopted by American Presbyterianism, though in a relaxed form.

In England, where parliament formally established Presbyterianism in 1647, the Confession was modified under the Protectorate, and was set aside when episcopacy, with the Thirty-nine Articles and the Book of Common Prayer, were restored under Charles II., in 1660. In Scotland the parliament of 1690 again " ratified and established the Confession of Faith as the public and avowed confession of this Church," and in the Act of Union of the two kingdoms in 1706–07 the Confession was declared " forever confirmed in the Church of Scotland," even as " the Presbyterian government " was declared to be " the only government of the Church within the realm of Scotland." The Scotch assem-

3. History in England and Scotland. blies of 1690, 1699, 1700, 1704, etc., required all ministers and probationers of the Gospel having license to preach, and all ruling elders, to subscribe to the Confession without amendment; and this remained law in the churches of Scotland till 1879, when the United Presbyterian Church of Scotland took the initiative in adopting an explanatory statement, or Declaratory Act, intended to " set forth more fully and clearly " some doctrines of Holy Scripture in regard to whose statement in the Confession a demand had been made that they be freed from certain real or apparent inconsistencies with the Scriptural scheme. The act included seven clauses emphasizing (1) God's love to all mankind and the free offer of salvation to men without distinction; (2) that the doctrine of decrees is to be held in connection with the statement that God desires that all men should come to repentance, and that " he has provided a salvation sufficient for all, adapted to all, and offered to all in the Gospel "; (3) that the doctrine of native inability does not imply that men in the state of nature are not responsible to God's law and to the Gospel; (4) that it is not to be held that God may not extend his grace to persons outside the pale of the preached Word, or that all who die in infancy may not be saved; (5) that all intolerant and persecuting principles of action within the Church or by magistrates are disavowed, and that any statement in the standards teaching such principles need not be approved; (6) that the Church is to preach the Gospel to every creature; and (7) that liberty of opinion is to be allowed in matters which are not of the substance of the faith, such as the interpretation of the six creative days. The United Presbyterian Church was followed by the Free Church in 1892, which passed a Declaratory Act that was substantially the same. In 1894, to remove objections made by the Highlanders, the Free-church assembly passed a supplementary act by which it was left open to office-bearers to take the Confession either with the Declaratory Act or in its original and unmodified form. The Church of Scotland, in 1889 and 1890, also modified the rigor of subscription by going back to the formularies of subscription enjoined prior to that imposed by the General Assembly of 1711; and on the union of the Free and United Presbyterian Churches into the United Free Church in 1900, the Declaratory Acts of both uniting bodies were approved. The English Presbyterian Church, through its synod in 1890, adopted twenty-four *Articles of the Faith*, this result being reached after the attempt to prepare a Declaratory Statement had been abandoned. To the *Articles of the Faith* was subsequently added an " Appendix " of six chapters, taking up matters which do " not enter into the substance of the faith," these being questions of polity, worship, and administration. In 1892 the Synod decided that acceptance of the Westminster standards by office-bearers should be modified by reference to the twenty-four *Articles of the Faith*, the aim in the preparation of which was, while retaining the essential features of Calvinistic doctrine, to lay the emphasis on the love of God in his Gospel.

In America Congregational Churches, through the Cambridge Synod and Platform of 1648, declared that the synod " had perused and considered with much gladness of heart and thankfulness to God the Confession of Faith published of late by the Reverend Assembly in England, and do judge it to be very holy, orthodox, and judicious in all matters of faith, and do therefore freely and fully consent thereunto, for the substance thereof," with the exception of matters of church " government and discipline " as set forth later on in the platform itself. In general these changes were in accord with the amendments made by the Savoy Declaration to the disciplinary sections of the Con-

4. History fession. The American Presbyterian in America. Churches early adopted the Confession and the Westminster Catechisms. The Synod of Philadelphia, in its Adopting Act of Sept. 19, 1729, formally approved these standards by demanding the acceptance of them, either by subscription or by verbal declaration, " as being, in all essential and necessary articles, good forms of sound words and systems of Christian doctrine, and do also adopt the said Confession and Catechisms as the confession of our faith." In case a candidate had scruples about articles that the synod might regard as unessential, they were not to be a bar to his acceptance, and the same friendship and brotherly love were to be extended to such persons as if they had expressed no differences. This action was the result of a compromise between the Presbyterians of New England antecedents led by Jonathan Dickinson (q.v.), and those of Scotch-Irish antecedents, the latter demanding strict subscription. In 1736, the synod, returning to the subject, affirmed the acceptance of " the good old doctrines contained in the Confession without the least varia-

tion or alteration," except in chapters xx. and xxiii., which bear on the authority of the civil magistrate, since the new American Constitution here required some modifications; and the General Assembly, at its first session in 1789, approved a revision of articles xx., xxiii., and xxxi., and a small amendment in the Larger Catechism, while it also prefixed to the Form of Government a preamble in which the rights of conscience in religious matters were pronounced universal and inalienable, and declared that all religious constitutions should have equal protection from the law. The assembly laid upon ministers the duty " of adopting the confession as containing the system of doctrine taught in the Scriptures, and their approval of the government and discipline of the Presbyterian Church in these United States." The reunion of the two branches of the Presbyterian Church, the Old School and the New School, in 1869 was upon the basis of the Confession and other standards of the Church as interpreted in their historic sense. The Cumberland Presbyterian Church modified the Confession and Catechisms in 1814, especially in the statement of the decree of predestination, and again subjected them to revision in 1883. The incorporation of a large part of the Cumberland body in the Presbyterian Church of the United States of America in 1906 was on the basis of the acceptance of the Confession as then authoritatively held by the mother body. A movement toward revision of the Confession failed in 1889–93, but a second movement was successful, resulting in the Revision of 1903, by which chapters xxxiv. and xxxv. on the Holy Spirit, and the Love of God and Missions were added, as well as a Declaratory Statement of 250 words which modifies chapter iii. concerning the decrees of God, and declares that " Christ's propitiation was for the sins of the whole world," and that God is ready to bestow saving grace on all who seek it. With reference to chapter x. it also declares that all infants dying in infancy are included in the election of grace. Changes were likewise introduced with regard to the nature of the works of the unregenerate (chap. xvi. 7), in regard to oaths (xxii. 3), and in the wording of chapter xxv. in regard to Christ's sole headship over the Church. Here the epithet applied to the pope—" that man of sin "—was struck out. In 1887, the clause (chap. xxiv. 4) forbidding marriage with a deceased wife's sister had been struck out. The Presbyterian Church of the United States, commonly called the Southern Presbyterian Church, is now engaged in making a small number of changes.

II. The Westminster Catechisms: The Westminster Catechisms are two in number: a large Catechism for ministers, to be explained from the pulpit according to the custom then prevailing in the Reformed churches on the Continent; and a short Catechism, for the instruction of children. Both were presented to parliament for examination and approval in the autumn of 1647, and were printed under the title *The Humble Advice of the Assembly of Divines now by authority of Parliament sitting at Westminster, concerning a Larger (Shorter) Catechism*, etc. Parliament approved the books, with slight exceptions, Sept. 15, 1648; the Scotch Kirk adopted them in July, 1648, and again (after a temporary repeal under Charles II.) in 1690. In its acts approving the Catechism, the

1. History and Character. Scotch Assembly declared the Larger (July 2, 1648) to be "a directory for catechizing such as have made some proficiency in the knowledge of the grounds of religion," and the Shorter (July 28, 1648) "to be a directory for catechizing such as are of weaker capacity," both being adopted as "being agreeable to the Word of God, and in nothing contrary to the received doctrine, worship, discipline, and government of this kirk." Anthony Tuckney (q.v.) had the chief share in framing the Larger Catechism, and Wallis, the mathematician, in giving the Shorter Catechism its severely logical finish. Both Catechisms contain an exposition of the Ten Commandments and the Lord's Prayer, and an independent statement of the Christian system of doctrine after the Calvinistic type. The Apostles' Creed is not, as in other Catechisms, made the basis of the doctrinal expositions, but is appended "because it is a brief sum of the Christian faith, agreeable to the word of God, and anciently received in the churches of Christ."

The Shorter Catechism has often been regarded as the ripest product of Puritan experience and theological thought. It closed the period of greatest catechetical fertility in England, when Puritan divines for a quarter of a century had been issuing catechetical manuals, as many as twelve or perhaps fourteen such divines, including Samuel Rutherford and Herbert Palmer (qq.v.), having sat in the Westminster Assembly. Of some of **2. The Shorter Catechism.** these catechisms there are direct traces that use was made, the most influential perhaps being the *Chief Grounds of Christian Religion set down by the way of Catechizing* by Ezekiel Rogers, written before 1638, the date when the author emigrated to America. Back of this series of catechisms were John Craig's (q.v.) Scotch Catechism, and, more especially, Calvin's Catechism, whose first question determined the content of the first question and answer of the Shorter Catechism. The Shorter Catechism is, with Luther's Small Catechism and the Heidelberg Catechism, the most extensively used catechism in Protestant Christendom. It exceeds all other catechisms by the terse brevity and precision of the questions and answers, and differs from most by the following peculiarities: (1) it embodies the question in the answer, so as to make this a complete proposition or statement; (2) it substitutes a new and logical order of topics for the old historic order of the Apostles' Creed; (3) it deals in dogmas rather than facts, and addresses the intellect rather than the heart; (4) it puts the questions in an impersonal form, instead of addressing the learner directly; (5) and to this may be added the theological and metaphysical character of the answers. No ecclesiastical attempt has been made to revise the Westminster Shorter Catechism. In 1908 the General Assembly of the Presbyterian Church (North) appointed a committee to prepare a catechism "to be used for home instruction and in the Sabbath-schools, and to be simpler in lan-

guage than the Shorter Catechism," but it was distinctly stipulated that it should not be "one of the standards of the Church."

PHILIP SCHAFF†.　　D. S. SCHAFF.

BIBLIOGRAPHY: As sources consult: A. F. Mitchell and J. Struthers, *Minutes of the Sessions of the Westminster Assembly of Divines . . . (Nov., 1644 to March, 1649)*, London, 1874; J. Lightfoot, *Journal of the Proceedings of the Assembly of Divines, from January 1, 1643, to December 31, 1644*, in *Whole Works*, ed. J. R. Pitman, vol. xiii. 1–344, ib. 1825; G. Gillespie, *Notes of Debates and Proceedings of the Assembly of Divines and other Commissioners at Westminster, from Feb. 1644 to Jan. 1645*, Edinburgh, 1846, cf. idem, *Aaron's Rod Blossoming*, London, 1646, Edinburgh, 1843; *Journals of the house of lords and the house of commons from 1643 to 1649*; *State Calendars* (James I., Charles I., Commonwealth, Charles II.), London, 1857 sqq.; W. Camden, *The Annals . . . of King James I., viz. from the Year 1603 to . . . 1623*, in W. Kennet, *The Complete History of England*, ii., ib. 1706; *Acts and Proceedings of the General Assemblies of the Kirk of Scotland . . . 1560–1618*, ed. T. Thomson, 3 vols., Edinburgh, 1839–45; B. Whitelocke, *Memorials of the English Affairs . . . from the Beginning of the Reign of Charles the First to Charles the Second*, London, 1732; E. Sawyer, *Memorials of Affairs of State . . . Collected (chiefly) from the . . . Papers of . . . Sir R. Winwood*, 3 vols., fol., ib. 1725; W. Laud, *Diary*, in vol. i. of *Remains*, ib. 1695, also in *Library of Anglo-Catholic Theology*, iii., 7 vols., Oxford, 1847–60; Mrs. L. Hutchinson, *Memoirs of Colonel Hutchinson, with . . . a Summary Review of Public Affairs*, 7th ed., London, 1848; J. Rushworth, *Historical Collections . . . from 1616 to 1648*, 8 vols. fol., ib. 1721; E. Cardwell, *Documentary Annals of the Reformed Church of England . . . from the Year 1546, to the Year 1716*, 2 vols., Oxford, 1839; R. Baillie, *Letters and Journals*, ed. D. Laing, 3 vols., Edinburgh, 1841–43; A. F. Mitchell and J. Christie, *Records of the Commissions of the General Assemblies of the Church of Scotland*, 2 vols., ib. 1892–96 (covers the years 1646 to 1649); A. Peterkin, *Records of the Kirk of Scotland, containing the Acts and Proceedings of the General Assemblies . . . with Notes*, etc., ib. 1838.

On the history consult: T. Fuller, *The Church History of Britain, from the Birth of Christ until the Year 1648*, London, 1655, new ed., vols. v.–vi., Oxford, 1845; R. Baxter, *Narrative of his Life and Times*, published as *Reliquiæ Baxterianæ*, 1 vol. fol., London, 1696, an abridgment appearing later, ib. 1702, 2 vols., ib. 1713, and also found in his *Practical Works*, 23 vols., ib. 1830; E. Hyde (Clarendon), *The History of the Rebellion*, 3 vols. fol., Oxford, 1702–04, new ed., 7 vols., ib. 1849; D. Neal, *History of the Puritans, or Protestant Nonconformists, from . . . 1517 to . . . 1688*, 4 vols., London, 1732–38, new ed., 2 vols., New York, 1858; J. Reid, *Memoirs of the Lives and Writings of those Eminent Divines who Convened in the Famous Assembly at Westminster*, 2 vols., Paisley, 1811–15; W. M. Engles, *A History of the Westminster Assembly of Divines, Embracing an Account of its Principal Transactions and Biographical Sketches of its most Conspicuous Members*, Philadelphia, 1841; T. Carlyle, *Life and Letters of Cromwell*, 2 vols., London and New York, 1845; H. Hallam, *Constitutional History of England*, chap. vii.–xi., 5th ed., 2 vols., London, 1846; J. B. Marsden, *The History of the Early Puritans, from the Reformation to . . . 1642*, ib. 1850; idem, *The History of the Later Puritans, from . . . the Civil War in 1642 to . . . 1662*, ib. 1852; J. Stoughton, *Spiritual Heroes; or, Sketches of the Puritans*, chap. vi., pp. 120 sqq., ib. 1850; idem, *Church and State Two Hundred Years Ago. A History of Ecclesiastical Affairs in England from 1660 to 1663*, ib. 1862; idem, *Ecclesiastical History of England*, 5 vols., ib. 1867–75; S. Hopkins, *The Puritans during the Reigns of Edward VI. and Queen Elizabeth*, 3 vols., Boston, 1859–1861; J. Tulloch, *English Puritanism and its Leaders: Cromwell, Milton, Baxter, Bunyan*, London, 1861; A. F. Mitchell, *The Westminster Confession of Faith: a Contribution to the Study of its Historical Relations and to the Defence of its Teaching*, 3d ed., Edinburgh, 1867, cf. his introduction to *Minutes . . . of the Westminster Assembly*, ut sup.; idem, *The Westminster Assembly, its History and Standards*, London, 1883, 2d ed., Philadelphia, 1897; idem, *Catechisms of the Second Reformation: The Shorter*

Catechism of the Westminster Assembly and its Puritan
Precursors; Rutherford's and other Scottish Catechisms of
the Same Epoch, with Historical Introduction and Biographical Notices, London, 1886; A. T. Innes, The
Law of Creeds in Scotland, ib. 1867; D. Masson, The
Life of John Milton: Narrated in Connection with the Political, Ecclesiastical, and Literary History of his Times,
vol. ii (1871), Bks. III.–IV., vol. iii (1873), Bks. I.–III.,
6 vols., ib. 1859–80; T. M'Crie, Annals of English Presbytery from the Earliest Period to the Present Time, ib. 1872;
J. B. Bittinger, The Reformation of Our Standards, in the
Presbyterian Quarterly and Princeton Review, July, 1876,
pp. 387 sqq.; W. M. Hetherington, History of the Westminster Assembly of Divines, 4th ed., Edinburgh, 1878;
C. A. Briggs, Documentary History of the Westminster
Assembly, in Presbyterian Review, 1880, pp. 127–164; T.
Leishman in R. H. Story, The Church of Scotland, Past
and Present, v. 307–426, London, 1890–91; idem, The
Westminster Directory with an Introduction and Notes, ib.
1901; C. G. McCrie, The Public Worship of Presbyterian
Scotland, § 4, 170–240, ib. 1892; idem, The Confessions of
the Church of Scotland: their Evolution in History, Edinburgh, 1907; W. Carruthers, The Shorter Catechism of the
Westminster Divines . . . with Historical Account and
Bibliography, London, 1897; J. H. Overton, The Church
in England, ii. 107–110, ib. 1897; W. H. Roberts, West-
minster Standards and the Formation of the American Re-
public, Philadelphia, 1898; W. Lloyd, The Story of Prot-
estant Dissent and English Presbyterians, London, 1899;
W. A. Shaw, A History of the English Church during the
Civil Wars and under the Commonwealth, 2 vols., ib. 1900;
F. Procter and W. H. Frere, A New History of the Book
of Common Prayer, chap. vi., 158–162, ib. 1901; B. B.
Warfield, in The Presbyterian and Reformed Review, 1901
(Apr., Oct.), 1902 (Jan., Apr., July, Oct.); W. Beveridge,
A Short History of the Westminster Assembly, Edinburgh,
1904; P. Schaff, Creeds of Christendom, i. 701–816 (the
editions and translations of the Confession are noted pp.
753–754), iii. 598–704 (text of Confession and Shorter
Catechism).
    For exposition or doctrinal discussion consult: W.
Parker, The Late Assembly of Divines' Confession of Faith
Examined . . . Wherein many of their Excesses and De-
fects, of their Confusions and Disorders, of their Errors and
Contradictions, are presented, London, 1651; D. Dickson, Truth's Victory over Error; or, an Abridgment of the
Chief Controversies in Religion, etc., Edinburgh, 1684,
Glasgow, 1725 (a catechetical exposition of the West-
minster Confession); idem, A Brief Sum of Christian Doctrine contained in Holy Scripture, and holden forth in the
Confession of Faith and Catechisms of the Westminster Assembly, etc., Edinburgh, 1693. Other notable discussions
of the Confession are by R. Shaw, ib. 1845; two by A. A.
Hodge, Philadelphia, 1869, New York, 1888; J. Macpherson, Edinburgh, 1881; F. Makower, Verfassung der
Kirche in England, Berlin, 1894; Von Rudloff, in ZHT
(1850), 238–296; J. Stark, The Westminster Confession of
Faith critically Compared with the Holy Scripture and
found Wanting, London, 1863; J. T. Goodsir, The Westminster Confession of Faith Examined on the Basis of the
other Protestant Confessions, ib. 1868; W. Marshall, The
Principles of the Westminster Standards Persecuting, Edinburgh, 1873; B. B. Warfield, Significance of the Westminster Standards as a Creed, New York, 1898; E. D.
Morris, Theology of the Westminster Symbols, Columbus,
O., 1901; J. Donaldson, The Westminster Confession of
Faith and the Thirty-Nine Articles of the Church of England, London, 1905.

WESTON, HENRY GRIGGS: Baptist; b. at
Lynn, Mass., Sept. 11, 1820; d. at Crozer Theological Seminary, Upland, Pa., Feb. 6, 1909. He received his education at Brown University (B.A.,
1840), and Newton Theological Institute (1840–
1842); was pastor at Washington and Richland,
Ill., 1843–46; at Peoria, Ill., 1846–59; and of the
Oliver Street Church, New York City, 1859–68;
and was president of Crozer Theological Seminary
after 1868. He edited The Baptist Quarterly, 1869–
1877, and wrote Outline of Systematic Theology; and
of Ecclesiology (Philadelphia, 1895; in collaboration

with E. H. Johnson); and Matthew: Genesis of the
New Testament (New York, 1900).

WESTON, JOHN BURNS: Christian; b. at
Madison, Me., July 6, 1821. He was educated at
Antioch College, Yellow Springs, O. (A.B., 1857),
after having entered the ministry of his denomination immediately upon his graduation from Bloomfield Academy, Bloomfield, Me., in 1843. He
was pastor in West Newberry, Mass. (1843–47);
in 1847–48 was managing editor of The Herald of
Gospel Liberty (then called The Christian Herald);
first head of the preparatory department and later
professor of Greek in Antioch College (1857–81), of
which he was acting president (1862–65); since
1882 he has been president and professor of Biblical
literature and theology, psychology, and ethics in
Christian Biblical Institute, Stanfordville, N. Y.,
removed in 1906 to Defiance, O. While at Antioch
College, he was also associate editor of The Herald
of Gospel Liberty. He has been a member of the
Versions Committee of the American Bible Society
since 1897. In theology he is in sympathy with
general Evangelical liberal theology, and " prefers
especially to state views in Biblical rather than
creedal or traditionally theological terms." He has
written Address on the Life and Character of Horace
Mann (New York, 1886) and Principles or Principle
—Which? (Dayton, O., 1894).

WESTPHAL, vest'fāl, **JOACHIM:** The name of
two Lutheran theologians.

1. Joachim Westphal of Hamburg: Polemical
theologian; b. at Hamburg 1510 or at the beginning of 1511; d. there Jan. 16, 1574. He was educated in the school of St. Nicolai in his native city,
then in Lüneburg, and entered the University of
Wittenberg, where he became the pupil of Melanchthon and Luther. In 1532, on the recommendation of Melanchthon, he was appointed teacher
at the Johanneum in his native city. In 1534 he returned to the University of Wittenberg, and in the
following year removed with the university to Jena.
After his return to Wittenberg in 1537 he lectured
on philology. In 1541 he became preacher of the
church of St. Catharine in Hamburg; then acting
superintendent in 1562, and was elected superintendent in 1571.
    He is best known for his participation in the theo-
logical controversies of his time. He took part in
that on the descent into hell, also in the discussion
concerning the Leipsic Interim. (see INTERIM) and
in that over the Adiaphora (q.v.). More important
was that over the Lord's Supper. In 1552 he published Farrago confusanearum el inter se dissidentium
opinionum de cœna Domini, ex Sacramentariorum
libris congesta, a warning against those who deny the
presence of Christ in the Lord's Supper. He points
out to the adherents of Luther the alarming progress
which the sacramentarians had made and tries to
prove the falsity of their doctrine by its diversity.
In 1553 he issued Recta fides de cœna Domini, an
exegetical discussion of I Cor. xi. and the words of
institution; in 1555 Collectanea sententiarum D.
Aurelii Augustini de cœna Domini and Fides Cyrilli
episcopi Alexandriæ de præsentia corporis et sanguinis

Christi. Calvin answered in Jan., 1555, with his *Defensio sanæ et orthodoxæ doctrinæ de sacramentis.* Thus there was opened a controversy which involved on the side of the Reformed Lasco, Bullinger, Ochino, Valerandus Polanus, Beza, and Bibliander; on the side of the Lutherans Timann, Paul von Eitzen, Schnepff, E. Alberus, Gallus, Flacius, Judex, Brenz, and Andreä. Westphal replied to Calvin in *Adversus cuiusdam sacramentarii falsam criminationem iusta defensio, in qua et eucharistiæ causa agitur* (1555), to which Calvin answered in *Secunda defensio piæ et orthodoxæ de sacramentis fidei* (1556), which was an attempt to draw to his side the Philippists of Saxony and Lower Germany. Other works of Westphal occasioned by this controversy are: *Epistola Joachimi Westphali, qua breviter respondet ad convicia J. Calvini* (1556); *Confessio fidei de eucharistiæ sacramento, in qua ministri ecclesiarum Saxoniæ . . . astruunt corporis et sanguinis D. n. J. Christi præsentiam in cœna sancta, et de libro Calvini ipsis dedicato respondent* (Magdeburg, 1557); *Justa defensio adversus insignia mendacia J. a Lasco, quæ in epistola ad Poloniæ regem contra Saxonicas ecclesias sparsit* (1557); *Apologetica scripta Johannis Westphali, quibus et sanam doctrinam de eucharistia defendit et fœdissimas calumnias sacramentariorum*

diluit (1558); *Confutatio aliquot enormium mendaciorum Johannis Calvini* (1558); *De cœna Domini confessio Johannis Westphali* (1558); *Apologia confessionis de Cœna Domini* (1558).

2. Joachim Westphal of Eisleben: A contemporary of Joachim Westphal of Hamburg, with whom he is often confused, and belonging also to the Gnesio-Lutheran party. He was ordained preacher at Nausitz near Artern in 1553, then served as diaconus in Sangerhausen and finally as preacher in Gerbstedt in the county of Mansfeld, where he died in 1569. He wrote *Faulteufel, wider das Laster des Müssiggangs* (1563); *Wider den Hoffahrtsteufel* (1565); *Willkomm Christi* (1568); *Geistliche Ehe Christi und seiner Kirche, seiner Braut* (1568).

(G. KAWERAU.)

BIBLIOGRAPHY: Sources are the *Briefsammlung,* ed. C. H. W. Sillem, Hamburg, 1903; the letters of Melanchthon and Calvin in *CR*, vols. vii.–ix., xliii., cf. the prolegomena to vol. xxxvii., pp. ix. sqq.; and the *Oratio* of J. Methodius, Hamburg, 1575. Consult further: J. A. Fabricius, *Memoriæ Hamburgenses,* ii. 931 sqq., ib. 1710; A. Greve, *Memoria J. Westphali,* ib. 1749; J. Moller, *Cimbria literata,* iii. 641 sqq., 8 vols., Hamburg, 1710–46; K. Mönckeberg, *Joachim Westphal und Johann Calvin,* ib. 1865; Kruske, *Johannes a Lasco und der Sakramentsstreit,* Leipsic, 1901; H. Dalton, *Miscellaneen,* pp. 302 sqq., Berlin, 1905; *ADB,* xlii. 198 sqq.

WESTPHALIA, PEACE OF.

The Peace of Westphalia is the treaty concluded in 1648, in the then Westphalian cities of Münster and Osnabrück, which terminated the Thirty-Years' War (q.v.). The immediate cause for the war was the state of religious affairs in Bohemia.

1. The Bohemian Succession. Taking advantage of the discord between Emperor Rudolph II. and his brother Matthias, the Evangelical leaders there had secured from the former a letter-patent, July 9, 1609, in which they were assured the free exercise of religion according to their submitted confession, and specially the right to build new churches and schools in the royal towns and dominions. After the emperor had been forced to cede the possession of Bohemia to his brother, Matthias solemnly confirmed the liberties of the estates, together with the imperial patent. But the question whether new churches and schools were also lawfully to be erected in the ecclesiastical jurisdictions soon stirred up strife; and when the imperial commissioners decided against the Evangelical party, the anxiety sprang up that the emperor was designing to revoke the patent. An insurrection arose; the imperial counselors, Martinitz and Slawata, were thrown from the window of the castle chamber at Prague (May 23, 1618); and the insurgents organized a national government of their own, expelled the Jesuits, communicated with the Protestant estates in the other Austrian lands, and, aided by the Union, even attacked Austria. This Union was a defensive alliance, formed, in 1608, of the Evangelical estates of Electoral Palatinate, Palatinate-Neuburg, Brandenburg-Ansbach and Bayreuth, Württemberg, Baden-Durlach, Electoral

Brandenburg, Hesse-Cassel, Strasburg, Nuremberg, and Ulm. Upon the death of Emperor Matthias (1619), Ferdinand II. became his successor. The Bohemians elected Elector Palatine Frederick V. as their king. To the support of Ferdinand rallied the Holy League of Roman Catholic estates organized by Duke Maximilian of Bavaria in 1609. Under his leadership Frederick was defeated at the battle at Prague Oct. 29 (Nov. 8), 1620, unaided by the Union, which had preferred to maintain peace with its fellow estates; and the greater part of Bohemia and Moravia were won back. After Frederick's flight and his sentence under the ban (1621), the Palatinate was gradually subdued by the imperial armies. Upon the investiture of Maximilian with the Electorate Palatine (1623), the court of Mansfeld and Christian of Brunswick undertook the war in northwestern Germany in behalf of the Palatinate, thus drawing the lower Saxon estates into the conflict. These chose King Christian IV. of Denmark (1625) for their joint commander. He allied himself with England and Holland, but in view of the successful results attending the armies of the League and the empire under Tilly and Wallenstein in 1629, he concluded the treaty of Lübeck with the emperor.

The Counter-Reformation went hand in hand with the military results. Specially from the time of their victory at Lutter (1626), the adherents of the League began to voice their demands for the enforced restitution of the ecclesiastical properties (see RESERVATION, ECCLESIASTICAL), which the Evangelicals had seized, as was alleged, contrary to the religious Peace of Augsburg (q.v.); and this was to be effected by a general imperial decree instead of legislation by the diet or due process of law. Incipient

2. The Counter-Reformation. scruples against strengthening the power accruing to the members of the League at the expense of the imperial strength were gradually overcome, partly by the presumption that some of the properties might possibly be applied to strengthen the imperial family prestige, and partly by the persuasive representations of such a measure offered by the imperial confessor, Lämmermann, and the papal nuncio, Caraffa, as a new and imposing advance on the side of the Counter-Reformation. Ferdinand II. issued the edict of restitution Mar. 6, 1629. Besides the provisions for the restoration of the spiritual possessions, it abrogated the declaration of Ferdinand I. at the religious peace of 1555, securing to Protestant subjects in the ecclesiastical provinces religious peace, and proclaimed, in general, that the religious peace was to apply only to the Roman Catholics and the adherents of the unaltered Augsburg Confession, and that every other sect was prohibited in the empire.

To prevent Gustavus Adolphus of Sweden, who in 1630 had occupied the estuaries of the Oder, from forming an alliance with the Protestant estates, the execution of the edict was suspended, and a diet appointed to meet at Frankfort, Feb.,

3. Gustavus Adolphus; the Peace of Prague. 1631, to negotiate a mutual understanding. But the emperor revoked some of his concessions; rebuffed the League of Leipsic, concluded by Elector Johann Georg of Saxony, 1631, with various Evangelical estates for the peace of Germany; and even suffered Tilly to invade Saxony (1631), after the destruction of Magdeburg. The result was an alliance of the elector of Saxony and the remaining Protestant princes with Gustavus Adolphus. After the victorious battle at Breitenfeld Sept. 7 (17), 1631, the Swedish troops roamed over Germany; but in 1632 Gustavus Adolphus was forced by Wallenstein to vacate Bavaria, and after his fall at Lützen (Nov. 6, 1632), the allies dispersed. When, in 1634, the main army of the Swedes was defeated at Nördlingen, the elector of Saxony abandoned the alliance with the Swedes, and concluded with Ferdinand II. the Peace of Prague, May 20 (30), 1635. By the terms of this treaty, all mediate foundations, cloisters, and estates which had been confiscated by the Protestants prior to the Passau treaty of 1552 were to remain in their hands; but the immediate endowments and all possessions confiscated after the said treaty were to be left for a term of forty years, and, if before the expiration of that term no other adjustment should be made, then they were to remain permanently in the status in which they were Nov. 27, 1627. Full amnesty was pledged between the emperor and the Roman Catholic estates on the one hand, and electoral Saxony and the states adhering to the Augsburg Confession on the other, from the year 1630, Bohemia, the Palatinate, and some princes, lords, and counts excepted. According to the imperial patent of June 12, 1635, this peace was to be extended over all Germany; but the restriction of the amnesty, the declaration of war by France against Spain and Austria, and the new advantages gained by the Swedes prevented the cessation of hostilities. In 1640, Ferdinand III. summoned another diet at Regensburg which (1641) made no essential progress beyond the Treaty of Prague. Preliminaries were signed at Hamburg Dec. 15 (25), 1641, providing that negotiations were to be conducted at Münster and Osnabrück. The emperor and the imperial deputation hesitated to sign the protocol until 1644, so that negotiations were not opened until Apr., 1645. At Osnabrück affairs were negotiated between the emperor's delegates, the imperial estates, and Sweden; at Münster, between the emperor, France, and the other foreign powers. The negotiations at Osnabrück were concluded with the peace instrument of Aug. 8, 1648; at Münster, in that of Sept. 17, the same year. The joint subscription occurred at Münster Oct. 14 (24). Simultaneously Spain and the German empire negotiated at Münster for peace with the United Netherlands and with France. While the negotiations with France led to no result, a treaty was concluded with the United Netherlands, on Jan. 20 (30), 1648, by which the independence of the Netherlands and their detachment from Germany were formally conceded. The independence of the Swiss Federation, as defined by the Peace of Basel, Sept. 22, 1499, was reconfirmed. In both treaties, only the emperor and the crowns of France and Sweden are named as contracting parties, each with its constituents, since the imperial estates disclaimed having waged war against the empire. Those provisions pertaining to church affairs only are subject of detail here.

For war indemnities and restitution of strongholds in the hands of foreign powers, the awards were as follows: (1) Sweden obtained all coastwise Pomerania and Rügen, together with a portion of interior Pomerania, the town of Wismar, belonging hitherto to Mecklenburg, and the church foundations of

4. Territorial Awards. Bremen and Verden, as temporal duchies, and all these as hereditary imperial tenures, with seat and vote at imperial and district assemblies. (2) France was vested, without the privilege of investiture or imperial estate, with the sovereignty over the bishoprics and cities of Metz, Toul, and Verdun, which had been occupied from 1552, yet under guaranty of the three bishoprics to the archbishop of Treves. It received, further, the sovereignty over Pignerol, the town of Breisach, the landgraviate of Upper and Lower Alsace, the district of Suntgau, and the government of ten imperial towns in Alsace. On the other hand, the other imperial estates in Alsace, in particular also the bishops of Basel and Strasburg, were expressly secured in their immediate relation to the empire, and their former freedom. The Roman Catholic religion was to be preserved in the ceded possessions and all religious innovations during the war removed. (3) Hesse-Cassel was indemnified with the secularized abbey of Hersfeld. Estates which lost territory by these cessions or had to forego their claims had to be recompensed, which involved further changes in the ecclesiastical apportionment, affecting specially Brandenburg, Mecklenburg, Brunswick, and Lüneburg.

The amnesty granted under the Peace of Prague in 1635 was now declared to be universal in principle. It was further ordered that, so

5. Amnesty and Restitution. far as possible, all spiritual and temporal matters should be restored to their former status. Accordingly the state of affairs as existing in 1618 should have been resumed; but against the overtures to this effect on the part of Sweden, France, and those imperial estates which had formed an alliance with them, the emperor and the Roman Catholic party insisted on regarding the year 1630 as the limit; nor would they relent until certain exceptions from this date were stipulated and the appointment of certain regulative times, respectively, for specific prospective restitutions was conceded. For instance, Bavaria would have had to restore to the descendants of Frederick V. the Electoral Palatinate, thus taking away from the Roman Catholics the balance of power in the electoral college; it would also have raised a claim of 13,000,000 thaler in favor of Bavaria against Austria for war indemnity. By the limit of 1618, Baden-Durlach lost the Upper Mark. Most unfavorably did the terms of settlement affect the Protestants in the hereditary lands of Austria. The efforts of Sweden in their behalf, to make the amnesty apply on the basis of 1618, remained fruitless. Exceptions were accorded only to the dukes of Brieg, Liegnitz, Münsterberg and Oels, and the city of Breslau. To the other Silesian duchies was conceded merely the erection of three new Evangelical churches, the so-called " peace churches " near Schweidnitz, Jauer, and Glogau. Besides, the inhabitants of the Silesian domains and the nobles of Lower Austria were not subject, on account of their adherence to the Augsburg Confession, to confiscation of possessions or to banishment, and they were to be permitted to attend the Evangelical worship outside their territory in neighboring places. In the event of a voluntary emigration, they were allowed freely to visit their unsold real estate for supervision and attention to cultivation.

The peace negotiations also vitally turned on the point of eliminating the confusions and grievances which had grown out of the previous relations of the religious parties, or of forestalling a recurrence of the same. The imperial and the Swedish envoys negotiated the Evangelical grievances

6. Grievances and Religious Relations. in general; pertaining to the relations of the Lutheran and the Reformed, Sweden conducted the transactions for the former; and for the latter, Brandenburg, seconded by the Dutch and the Swiss. (1) The religious Peace of Augsburg and the Passau treaty were confirmed anew. (2) The peace instrument of Osnabrück expressly recognized the parity of the Reformed with the Roman Catholics and the adherents of the Augsburg Confession. However, the proviso in § 17 of the religious peace was reaffirmed, that no other religions than those mentioned were to be tolerated. (3) The legal equality of the two religious parties in the empire was expressly declared; and in application of this principle, it was ordered that a quota of members from both confessions should be chosen for the regular imperial deputations and for the imperial courts of justice. In matters affecting religion, or in a division of opinion between the Roman Catholic and the Protestant estates, the usual parliamentary vote by majority was to make way for an amicable adjustment among the estates of both religious parties. The terms thus stated, especially the principle of equal legal status for both religious parties, was to become practically applicable in accordance with the constitution and laws of the realm, and the consistent provisions of the treaty itself. Their execution was dependent on various actual antecedent conditions, subsisting in the diversity of relations between Roman Catholics and Protestants, and, within the latter, between Lutherans and Reformed. This led to the adoption of measures intended to regulate their mutual relations with reference to the standard principles first adopted. (1) With reference to ecclesiastical properties and institutions, Jan. 1, 1624, was agreed upon as the regulative day. The religious party having possession on that date were permanently to retain it, and all possessions of that date of which it was later deprived were to be restored. The advantages obtained through this measure by the Protestants were inconsiderable. Similar arrangements were made regarding the mediate foundations and cloisters. (2) On the " right of reformation," the religious Peace of Augsburg had sanctioned the right of temporal estates of the realm both to go over to the Evangelical religion and to allow the same to their subjects. This right had not been conceded to the subjects individually; but, at that time, the principle was recognized that the territorial lord was to decide on the religious confession of his domain inclusive of that of his subjects. Now the following extensions were added: (a) Evangelical subjects under Roman Catholic, and Roman Catholic subjects under Evangelical sovereignty were to be left free to exercise what manner of religion they had practised until some time in 1624, and in this they were to be left unmolested in the future.

From this it followed that Evangelical subjects in a Roman Catholic territory or Roman Catholics in an Evangelical territory who had exercised religion neither publicly nor privately in 1624, now remained amenable to the *jus reformandi;* and the same pertained to any who, after the publication of the treaty of peace, would be converts to any other religion than that of the territorial sovereign. In both instances the latter had the alternative right of tolerance or enforcing emigration. In the former instance, the subjects were to be allowed freedom of conscience, the right of household worship, and of attending worship abroad, as well as legal equality with the adherents of the authorized confessions. If, on the contrary, the territorial sovereign should command, or the subjects voluntarily choose, emigration, then all molestation was forbidden, and a five years' respite (or three years in case of a change of religion after the publication of the terms of peace) for emigration was conceded; neither should the testimonials of position and character be denied nor unusual reversions be demanded or emigration taxes be imposed. (b) With reference to the relation between Lutherans and Reformed, the status at the time of the Peace of Westphalia subject to the treaties and privileges in power was to be prescriptive. In the future, if a territorial sovereign changed from the Evangelical state religion to another Evangelical confession, or succeeded to an Evangelical state having a different confession from his own, he was to have the right only to institute his court worship, and irrevocably to grant possible churches of his faith free religious exercise; but all this without altering the existing church order, and without disturbing the previous religious practise, church estates, and institutions. The congregations of the Evangelical state religion were to retain the appointment of their church and school officers, who should be subject to examination and ordination at the hands of a church board, subject to the approval of the sovereign, without obstruction. (3) The diocesan right and the spiritual jurisdiction of Roman Catholic officials, in cases of dispute among Protestants and between Protestants and Roman Catholics, were suspended, excepting (a) where Roman Catholics had been in obvious possession of the ecclesiastical jurisdiction in 1624, this might continue to be exercised in collecting revenues, tithes, and pensions; and (b) where the Protestant subjects of Roman Catholic estates in 1624 had acknowledged the ecclesiastical jurisdiction, the same should continue, without prejudice to confessional freedom and liberty of conscience. On the other hand, in the case of Roman Catholic subjects of Evangelical estates, the ecclesiastical jurisdiction of the Roman Catholic bishops was to continue intact, according to the peaceable exercise of it in 1624, provided, however, that the Roman Catholics in the given territory maintained public exercise of religion in the year stated. The spiritual jurisdiction over Evangelicals in Evangelical territories received no mention; it was presumed to be a privilege of the territorial government.

The interest of the foreign powers in securing for the estates of the realm the largest possible status independent of the emperor coincided with the similar aspirations of the estates, and the difference in religion did not so separate the estates as to induce them to work at cross purposes in this

7. Political common object. The original abso-
Readjust- lute sovereignty of the emperor had
ments; long ceased to be unquestioned, and
Execution. the rights acquired by the estates in
the course of time no longer submitted to be defined as mere feudal investitures. Yet a distinct definition was not then attempted; under the adopted term *jus territorialis* the treaty expressly assured this right to the estates of the realm. In particular they were guaranteed the right of voting on all parliamentary deliberations concerning the affairs of the realm, and in concluding alliances with one another and with foreign powers for their self-preservation and security, reserving the rights of the emperor, the empire, and the peace of the land. The foregoing rights were also accredited in detail to the imperial cities. Likewise, the immediate imperial knighthood in point of religion was placed on a par with the estates of the realm. The peace was declared to be a permanent, universal law of the em-

pire; so that it was ordered to be embodied in the next imperial decree, as also in the imperial " election capitulation," and every objection to and contradiction of it was nullified. Violation of the treaty was made subject to the penalty for breach of the peace. If any one was to suffer injury through the violation of another, and this should not be repaired within three years, whether amicably or legally, he was authorized to resort to arms and lay claim to the help of all parties to the treaty. The formal exchange of ratifications did not take place till Feb. 8, 1649; and the terms of execution were agreed upon by a joint deputation of the three electoral colleges at Nuremberg, June 16, 1650. The inclusion in the decree followed, Regensburg, 1654, and in the " election capitulations," as late as Francis II., pledging the maintenance of the treaty. Already at Münster, the papal legate, Cardinal Fabius Chigi, had protested against the treaty, Oct. 14 and 26, 1648; and Nov. 26 Pope Innocent X. promulgated the bull, *Zelo domus dei*, in which the measures of the treaty were declared null and void, because adopted without the approval of the papal see. This protestation, however, had no practical consequences. On the contrary, the treaty was repeatedly confirmed on subsequent occasions, although its execution was delayed by controversies on individual points. Its provisions on the relations of the religious parties were not abrogated by the dissolution of the empire in 1806; but rather, in view of parity and tolerance, they were enlarged and amplified by the national legislation.   E. SEHLING.

BIBLIOGRAPHY: Sources are: J. G. von Meiern, *Acta pacis publica, oder westphälische Friedenshandlungen und Geschichte,* 6 vols., Hanover, 1734–36, with *Register,* Göttingen, 1740; idem, *Acta pacis executionis publica, oder nürnbergische Friedens-Executions-Handlungen,* 2 parts, ib. 1736; idem, *Acta comitialia Ratisbonensia publica de 1653 et 1654,* 2 parts, Leipsic, 1738; the documents reproduced in *Instrumenta pacis Cæs. Suec. et Cæs. Gallic.,* with preface by Meiern, Göttingen, 1738, and *Die Urkunden der Friedensschlüsse zu Münster und Osnabrück,* Zurich, 1848. Consult: *Cambridge Modern History,* iv. 395–433, and very notable bibliography, pp. 865–869, New York, 1906; J. S. Pütter, *Geist des westphälischen Friedens,* Göttingen, 1795; G. H. Bougeant, *Hist. du traité de Westphalie,* 2 vols., Paris, 1744; R. K. Freiherr von Senkenberg, *Darstellung des westphälischen Friedens,* Frankfort, 1804; K. L. von Woltmann, *Geschichte des westphälischen Friedens,* 2 vols., Berlin, 1808; M. Bernard, *Four Lectures on Subjects Connected with Diplomacy,* lecture 1, London, 1868; G. Bardot, *Quomodo explanandum sit instrumenti pacis Monaster. cap. 86,* Lyons, 1899.

WETTE, dê vet′te, **WILHELM MARTIN LEBERECHT DE:** German exegete and theologian; b. at Ulla (3 m. w. of Weimar) Jan. 12, 1780; d. at Basel June 16, 1849. He entered Jena in 1799, and obtained the doctorate in 1805, becoming privat-docent the same year. His earliest publica-
Life at   tions, a critical dissertation upon
Jena and   Deuteronomy (Jena, 1805, republished
Heidel-   in his *Opuscula theologica,* Berlin, 1830),
berg.   and his *Beiträge zur Einleitung in das Alte Testament* 1806–07) proved his originality and independence. He was called to Heidelberg as extraordinary professor in exegesis, 1807, and became ordinary professor in theology, 1809. While there he made, at first in conjunction with Augusti, but later alone, a translation of the entire Bible (Hei-

delberg, 1809–14, 4th ed., 1858), and wrote his Commentary on the Psalms (1811, 5th ed., ed. G. Baur, 1856), which is so exclusively critical that he felt it necessary to add an appendix " On the Devotional Use of the Psalms " (1837). He denies the Davidic origin of many psalms, and also that the historical Christ is prophesied anywhere in the collection, referring the so-called Messianic incidents and allusions to nearer historical events.

In 1810 he was called to the newly founded university at Berlin, where he came into touch with Schleiermacher, and the two labored for that " better day " in theology when the demands of faith and science should alike be met. In 1815 De Wette published his *Commentatio de morte Jesu Christi expiatoria* (Berlin), in 1814 his *Lehrbuch der hebräisch-jüdischen Archäologie* (4th **At Berlin.** ed. by Räbiger, 1864), in 1817 *Historisch-kritisch Einleitung in . . . das Alte Testament* (seven editions during his lifetime; 8th ed. by E. Schrader, Berlin, 1869, Eng. transl. by T. Parker, 2 vols., Boston, 1843; *A Critical and Historical Introduction to the Canonical Scriptures of the Old Testament*, 2d ed. 1850); in 1826 his *Einleitung in das Neue Testament* (6th ed., 1860, Eng. transl., by F. Frothingham, 1858).

His entrance into the sphere of dogmatic theology was made in the volume on the death of Christ. He followed this up by *Lehrbuch der christlichen Dogmatik* (2 vols., Berlin, 1813–16, 3d ed., 1831–40), *Ueber Religion und Theologie* (1815, 2d ed. 1821), and *Christliche Sittenlehre* (3 vols., 1819–23; Eng. transl., *Human Life; or, Practical Ethics*, by S. Osgood, 2 vols., Boston, 1838, reprint, 1856). This period was made bright with the friendship of Schleiermacher, Lücke, F. W. Krummacher, and Spitta. But he was opposed by Marheineke, who had followed him to Berlin and had lectured against him. De Wette's reply was in the anonymous *Die neue Kirche und Glauben in Bunde* (1815). The last work composed by him in Berlin was *Kritischer Versuch über die Schriften des Lukas* (1817).

Taking a great interest in public affairs, he wrote a letter to the mother of an Erlangen student, Karl Ludwig Sand (who murdered August **Dismissal** von Kotzebue), in which, while ex-**from Ber-** pressing deep abhorrence at the crime, **lin, Call to** he still cleared Sand's motives of sus-**Basel.** picion on the ground that the deed was prompted by pure patriotism. For this bold defense he was summarily dismissed from the university by the king (Oct. 2, 1819). He betook himself to Weimar, and there employed his enforced leisure in preparing the first complete edition of Luther's *Briefe* (1825–28, 5 vols., supplemental volume by Seidemann, 1856), by which, had he done nothing else, he would have proved himself a scholar. In 1822 he issued his first romance, *Theodor, oder des Zweiflers Weihe* (1822, 2d ed., 1828; Eng. transl. by J. F. Clarke, *Theodore, or the Skeptic's Conversion*, 2 vols., Boston, 1849), to which Tholuck replied in *Die wahre Weihe des Zweiflers* (Hamburg, 1823); and his second, *Heinrich Melchthal*, in 1829, 2 vols. In 1822, quite unexpectedly, he was called to Basel,

where he passed the rest of his days. He did excellent service in advancing the university, and won the hearts of many who had bitterly opposed his coming. There he composed his *Vorlesungen über die Sittenlehre* (Berlin, 1823–24, 2 vols.), and *Ueber die Religion, ihr Wesen, ihre Erscheinungsformen und ihren Einfluss auf das Leben* (1827). He also preached to a highly appreciative audience, and published five collections of sermons (Basel, 1825–29). Another series was published after his death (1849). In 1846 he issued the first part of his unfinished *Biblische Geschichte*, and in 1836 he began, and in 1848 he finished, his *Kurzgefasstes exegetisches Handbuch zum Neuen Testament* (3 vols., Leipsic), a work marked by brevity and precision and accurate scholarship.

The numerous works already mentioned make up only a partial list of De Wette's writings. Re-**Varied Ac-** views, criticisms, essays, encyclope-**tivities.** dia and newspaper articles, sermons, addresses, pamphlets, works upon art (Berlin, 1846), even a drama *Die Entsagung* (Berlin, 1823), and poems, came from his gifted pen. He was fond of society, and hospitably inclined; and, although deemed a rationalist and " heretic," he took a leading part in philanthropic movements. He founded (1825) a society in Basel to help the Greeks in their struggle against Turkish tyranny, to send missionaries to Greece, and to educate their children, and adopted a little Greek boy into his own family. He also founded the Basel branch of the Gustav-Adolf-Verein (q. v.).

The theism of the Kantian criticism forms the basis of De Wette's doctrinal system; but he leans visibly toward Jacobi's theory of religion as feeling. He makes a sharp distinction between knowledge and faith. The former has to do only with finite things; while the infinite must be grasped by faith under the form of feeling. The infinite is revealed by the finite in a symbolical manner. **His Phi-** The whole historical revelation is a **losophy and** symbol in which eternal and super-**Theology.** sensuous ideas have found their expression. The miracle is a cross to the understanding, but as a symbol it shows its meaning. The dogma is inaccessible to the understanding, but opens itself to the intuition; for intuition is the only means of conception when the object is a symbol. All religious conception is consequently esthetic, and this esthetic elevation above the merely intelligible is to De Wette the only tenable form of supernaturalism. De Wette closely connected dogma with ethics, made ethical considerations decisive in judging other systems, and held fast to the personality of Christ. (G. FRANK†.)

BIBLIOGRAPHY: K. R. Hagenbach, *Leichenrede*, Basel, 1849; idem, *Akademische Gedächtnissrede*, Leipsic, 1850; D. Schenkel, *W. M. L. 'de Wette und die Bedeutung seiner Theologie für unsere Zeit*, Schaffhausen, 1849; F. Lücke, *W. M. L. de Wette*, Hamburg, 1850; A. Wiegand, *W. M. L. de Wette*, Erfurt, 1879; R. Stähelin, *W. M. L. de Wette nach seiner theologischen Wirksamkeit und Bedeutung*, Basel, 1880.

WETTSTEIN, wet′stain or vet′stain (**WETSTENIUS, WETSTEIN**), **JOHANN JAKOB:** New-Testament scholar; b. at Basel Mar. 5, 1693 (old style);

d. at Amsterdam Mar. 9, 1754. In 1706 he began to study philosophy at Basel; then, in 1709, he changed to the study of theology. At the suggestion of Johann Ludwig Frey, he began work on the criticism of the New-Testament text. In 1714 he undertook a journey by way of Zürich, Bern, Geneva, and Lyons to Paris and thence, in Aug., 1715, to England, searching for manuscripts of the New Testament. In Cambridge he made the acquaintance of Richard Bentley, who aided him in his researches and secured for him a position as field-chaplain in a regiment of Swiss soldiers on service in England; in 1716 Wettstein removed to Holland, where his regiment had gone in the mean time, and in 1717 was called back to Basel as assistant preacher. After three years he became diaconus at St. Leonhard and thus colleague and successor of his father, who shortly before had become preacher in the same church. He soon became exceedingly popular as a preacher. During this period he continued his studies and resolved to publish a critical edition of the Greek New Testament. During his preparatory work on this edition the report gained currency that he intended to use the work to assail the doctrine of the divinity of Christ, and in 1730 he was in consequence dismissed from his office. Wettstein then went to Amsterdam, where Johann Heinrich Wettstein, a brother of his uncle, had founded a bookseller's shop. Here he published [anonymously] a separate edition of the *Prolegomena*, which he had intended to add to his edition of the Greek New Testament, under the title, *Prolegomena ad Novi Testamenti græci editionem accuratissimam, e vetustissimis codd. mss. denuo procurandam, in quibus agitur de codd. mss. Novi Testamenti, scriptoribus græcis, qui Novo Testamento usi sunt, versionibus veteribus, editionibus prioribus et claris interpretibus; et proponuntur animadversiones et cautiones ad examen variarum lectionum Novi Testamenti necessariæ* (Amsterdam, 1730). In 1731 Wettstein was offered the position of professor of philosophy at the college of Remonstrants in Amsterdam under the condition that he should clear himself of the suspicion of holding heterodox views. He therefore went back in the same year to Basel, where his case was again investigated with the result that the government on Mar. 22, 1732, rejected its former judgment, admitting Wettstein " to the office of preaching and the administration of all spiritual functions." But his foes still pressed their case against him, and he returned to Amsterdam, where he was allowed to teach Hebrew and philosophy, but only under the conditions of not expressing Socinian views, not publishing his New Testament, of submitting such works as he desired to publish to the supervision of the Remonstrants, and of printing no apology for his cause. Wettstein submitted to these conditions. Nevertheless, his edition of the New Testament appeared in two volumes at Amsterdam, 1751-52, under the title, *Novum Testamentum græcum editionis receptæ cum lectionibus variantibus codicum mss., editionum aliarum, versionum et patrum necnon commentario pleniore ex scriptoribus veteribus hebræis, græcis et latinis historiam et vim verborum illustrante opera et studio Joannis Jacobi Wetstenii.* It is in very beautiful, but not always correct, print.

The text chosen was [for reasons of expediency] essentially the same as that of the Elzevir edition of 1624 or 1633. The readings preferred by Wettstein stand between the text and the list of variant readings. The principal value of the edition lies in the extensive prolegomena and in the commentary which in consequence of its comparisons from classical and Jewish literature is still a rich treasury. At the same time they reveal Wettstein's inclination to rationalistic explanations so that Tregelles justly said of them, " While some parts are useful, others are such as only excite surprise at their appearance on the same page as the text of the New Testament " (*Account of the Printed Text*, p. 76, London, 1854). Wettstein himself compared more than a hundred manuscripts, others compared others for him.   (CARL BERTHEAU†.)

BIBLIOGRAPHY: The funeral sermon by J. Krightout was printed at Amsterdam, 1754. Consult: J. G. de Chauffepié, *Nouveau Dictionnaire*, iv. 688 sqq., Amsterdam, 1756; *Athenæ Rauricæ*, pp. 379 sqq., Basel, 1778; J. D. Michaelis, *Einleitung in die göttlichen Schriften des neuen Bundes*, i. 805 sqq., Göttingen, 1788; K. R. Hagenbach, *Die theologische Schule Basels und ihre Lehrer*, p. 65, Basel, 1860; S. P. Tregelles, *Account of the Printed Text of the Greek N. T.*, pp. 73 sqq., London, 1854; E. G. E. Reuss, *Geschichte der heiligen Schriften des Neuen Testaments*, ii. 145, 5th ed., Brunswick, 1874; C. R. Gregory, *Prolegomena*, iii. 1, 243 sqq., Leipsic, 1884; idem, *Canon and Text of the N. T.*, pp. 447-448, New York, 1907; P. Schaff, *Companion to the Greek Testament and the English Version*, pp. 82, 247-249, ib. 1883; G. Salmon, *Introduction to . . . N. T.*, pp. 488-544, London, 1892; F. H. Scrivener, *Plain Introduction to the Criticism of the N. T.*, pp. 213-216 et passim, ib. 1894; *ADB*, xlii. 251.

WETZER, vet′zer, HEINRICH JOSEPH: Joint editor, with Welte, of the great Roman Catholic theological encyclopedia; b. at Anzefahr, Hessia, Mar. 19, 1801; d. in Freiburg (40 m. s. of Strasburg), Germany, Nov. 5, 1853. He studied theology at Marburg, also attending lectures on oriental philology, 1820-23, at Tübingen, and at Freiburg, 1824, where he obtained his doctorate; and, 1824-1825, he studied under De Sacy at Paris, where he discovered in the royal library a manuscript of the history of the Coptic Christians in Egypt, which he later translated and published. He became extraordinary professor of oriental philology in Freiburg University, 1828, and ordinary, 1830. He joined Van Ess in his translation of the Old Testament, Sulzbach, 1840. In 1846 he began the issue of the *Kirchenlexikon* (see this work, vol. i., p. xv.), with which his name and that of the coeditor, Benedikt Welte, are indissolubly connected. Wetzer put all his time, strength, and learning at the disposal of the work. The encyclopedia was authoritative, fair-minded, and impartial to a singular degree. He was the author of *Restitutio veræ chronologiæ rerum ex controversiis Arianis inde ab anno 325 usque ad annum 350 exhortarum contra chronologiam hodie receptam exhibita* (Frankfort, 1827).

BIBLIOGRAPHY: *KL*, xii. 1418-1421.

WEYERMUELLER, vai′er-mül″er, FRIEDRICH: German Lutheran hymnist; b. at Niederbronn (26 m. n.w. of Strasburg) Sept. 21, 1810; d. there May 24, 1877. He received his education at the school of his native town and at the hands of the pastor, gaining an excellent knowledge of German poetry. He began early to compose, and from 1838 dedicated his talent to the service of God and his Church, though some of his poems were polemical and had reference to the controversies of the middle of the nineteenth century. In 1852 he became an associate of the consistory of Niederbronn, and his efforts greatly aided the cause of Lutheranism, he being a strong and strict follower of that type of religious activity and thought. His poems reflected this tendency, and were often aimed against Baptists, liberals, and the like. Those which were adapted to worship found entrance over a wide range of church hymnals.   (A. LIENHARD.)

BIBLIOGRAPHY: W. Horning, *Lebensbild von F. T. Horning*, pp. 326–341, 4th ed., Strasburg, 1885; *Evangelisch-lutherischer Friedensbote*, 1877, nos. 52–54.

WEYMOUTH, RICHARD FRANCIS: English Baptist layman and New-Testament translator; b. at Plymouth Dock (now Devonport, 2 m. w.n.w. of Plymouth), Devonshire, Oct. 26, 1822; d. at Brentwood (17 m. e.n.e. of London), Essex, Dec. 27, 1902. He was educated at University College, London (B.A., 1845; D.Lit., 1868), and after spending two years in France he was an assistant master in a private school at Leatherhead, Surrey, later founding a successful school for boys at Plymouth. In 1869 he was chosen head master of a non-conformist school for boys at Mill Hill, London, where he remained until 1886, then retiring from active life to devote himself to his translation of the New Testament into idiomatic modern English, his residence being successively at Acton (until 1891) and at Brentwood (until his death). He was an active member of the Philological Society, and to its journal and other technical periodicals he contributed a number of studies on philological and theological subjects. Besides an edition of Grosseteste's *Castell off Loue* for this society (London, 1864) and a translation of Cynewulf's *Elene* (1888), as well as a work *On Early English Pronunciation with Special Reference to Chaucer* (1874), he is especially noteworthy for his *Resultant Greek Testament* (1886), exhibiting the text on which the majority of modern editors are agreed, and containing the variant readings of the more important of these editors. He will be remembered, above all, for his *New Testament in Modern Speech* (1903). This work he had practically completed in the rough draft before his death, but failing health compelled him to entrust the final revision and correction to E. Hampden-Cook (q.v.).

WEXELSEN, WILHELM ANDREAS: Norwegian Lutheran clergyman, educator, and statesman; b. at Kläbu (a village near Trondhjem) June 5, 1849; d. at Trondhjem July 19, 1909. He was educated at the Cathedral School in Trondhjem (B.A., 1867) and the University of Christiania (cand. theol., 1872), and was then curate in Sparbu (1873–76) and Trondhjem (1876–77) and pastor in Kolvereid (1877–84) and Overhalden (1884–91). His efficiency as an administrator of municipal affairs led to his election to the Norwegian Storthing in 1882, and in 1891 he was appointed councilor of state and chief of the department for ecclesiastical affairs and public instruction. In 1892–93 he was connected with the Stockholm division of the council, and in 1896–97 was director of schools

in Trondhjem, being the same city's representative to the Storthing in 1896, while in 1898–1903 he was again chief of the department for ecclesiastical affairs and public instruction, succeeding Jakob Sverdrup (q.v.). From 1905 until his death he was bishop of the see of Trondhjem.

Wexelsen rendered important services to the public school system of Norway, doing much to foster the growth of the national spirit, and, through legislation, to ameliorate the conditions under which the teachers and clergy were obliged to work; and he also advocated noteworthy measures for the relief of the poor and for modifying the laws relating to marriage.   JOHN O. EVJEN.

WHATELY, RICHARD: Archbishop of Dublin; b. in London Feb. 1, 1787; d. in Dublin Oct. 1, 1863. He matriculated at Oriel College, Oxford, in 1805, was graduated B.A. in 1808, and took orders in due course. He was fellow of Oriel from 1811 till his marriage in 1821, and then held the living of Halesworth, Suffolk, till 1825, when he returned to Oxford as principal of St. Alban's Hall. In 1829 he was appointed Drummond professor of political economy at Oxford, but resigned two years later to become archbishop of Dublin. He was consecrated Oct. 23, 1831, and enthroned the same day.

Life and Character.

As a child Whately was delicate and precocious, exhibiting phenomenal powers of arithmetical computation. Attendance at a school near Bristol from the age of ten strengthened his body and gave him wider intellectual interests than he had found previously in his father's library and garden, so that he entered Oxford with nothing strikingly abnormal about him. He made a few friends at Oxford, but only a few, and set conventions at scorn to a degree that made him notorious. So he went through life singularly independent and self-contained, rough and brusk in manner, outspoken, rashly regardless of popular opinions or prejudices. His biting wit spared neither friend nor foe, and his great powers of argumentation were exercised with more assiduity than judgment. He was master of a lucid expression, and as a thinker and scholar was acute and versatile, though not profound, and hampered by striking limitations. It is said he read a few favorite authors—Aristotle, Thucydides, Bacon, Shakespeare, Butler, Warburton, Adam Smith, Crabbe, Scott—and no others. For nature, music, and art, as well as for historic antiquity, he had no sense whatever. Consequently he found only fatigue in travel, and avoided it as far as possible. He never learned German, and read French with difficulty.

Yet, if he thus exemplified English insularity, it should be added that he represented the type in no unworthy manner. As duties came to him he performed them well. At Oxford he proved himself a good teacher, knowing how to discover and develop the dormant capacities of his pupils, and in a short time he raised St. Alban's Hall from very low estate and made it a chosen home of reading men. He was a faithful parish priest. As archbishop he was scrupulously conscientious in the performance of his ordinary duties, and he grappled courageously and with fair success with the extraordinary difficulties of his position. Personally unpopular, not liked as a preacher, harassed by political considerations and racial differences, he yet won his way **Career as** by his impartial and kindly spirit to-**Archbishop.** ward the Roman Catholics by vigorous efforts continued for twenty years in behalf of popular education and the higher education at Trinity College, of which he was *ex officio* visitor, by his services in stemming the tide toward Rome, and by his interest in and self-sacrificing labor for all that tended to make Ireland better in body and soul. As primate of Ireland he sat in the house of lords and made many speeches noticeable for their independence, advocating a revision of the liturgy and the Authorized Version of the Bible, the abrogation of the prohibition to marry a deceased wife's sister, and the emancipation of Jews and Roman Catholics. His study of political economy led him to oppose the extension of the English system of outdoor relief to Ireland, even in the time of the potato famine, in which extremity he worked manfully to alleviate distress. He favored a gradual rather than a sudden emancipation of slaves, and in advocating the abolition of all legal punishment except such as was unmistakably deterrent in character, he showed himself in advance even of the early twentieth century. His efforts in this direction contributed much to the abolition of transportation.

His theology, always more or less under suspicion of heterodoxy, has been characterized as rational supernaturalism. He started with the assumption of a special revelation which makes known what reason can not discover, and it is then the function of reason to interpret revelation. The incarnation was a fact and an extraordinary act of revelation to make divinity more intelligible and to give a pattern of human perfection. The death of Christ was sacrificial, but was not necessary, **Theology** though it is the only ground of our **and** salvation. The kingdom of Christ is **Writings.** a society, whose members may at the same time belong to other societies. Thus the problem of Church and State is solved. Christ has himself given the plan for the society's government, but the execution of the plan lies with the society. The essentials of Christianity are of universal importance; the minor matters are only relatively important. There is no such thing as apostolic succession in the sense of its securing the transmission of the Holy Spirit and the efficacy of the sacraments; the true apostolic succession is the maintenance of apostolic principles. He was strongly opposed to Calvinism, and in his writings ever quietly fought against tractarianism. The Sabbath, he taught, was done away with by the abrogation of the Mosaic law, for Christ himself broke the Sabbath and left it to the Church to fix the day and its observance, precisely as in the case of other festivals.

Whately wrote much, but nothing of permanent value, and little that outlived himself. His first book was *Historic Doubts Relative to Napoleon Buonaparte* (London, 1819), in which he aimed to reduce to absurdity Hume's doctrine concerning miracles. It is witty and brilliant rather than sound, and is not free from suspicion of unfairness, since Hume had expressly put outside of his general principles

cases in which greater improbability is involved in skepticism than in belief. For once Whately had popular prejudice on his side, and the book went through more than twelve editions during his lifetime, being reprinted as late as 1886 in Henry Morley's *Universal Library* (vol. xliii., London, 1886). *The Use and Abuse of Party Feeling in Matters of Religion* (Oxford, 1822) was the Bampton lectures for 1822. The *Elements of Logic* (London, 1826), and *Elements of Rhetoric* (1828), originally written as articles for the *Encyclopædia Metropolitana*, were for a time much used as text-books (9th ed. of the *Logic*, 1850; 7th ed. of the *Rhetoric*, 1840). Neither work can be called original or epoch-making, but both were admirably arranged and expressed, and the *Logic* revived the study of the discipline at Oxford. The Oxford lectures on political economy were published at London in 1831. Other noteworthy books were *The Errors of Romanism Traced to their Origin in Human Nature* (1830; 5th ed., 1856; abridged edition by his daughter, E. J. Whately, London, 1878) and an edition of Bacon's *Essays* with notes (1856).

BIBLIOGRAPHY: Miss E. J. Whately, *Life and Correspondence of Richard Whately*, 2 vols, London, 1866, new ed., 1875; W. J. Fitzpatrick, *Memoirs of Richard Whately*, 2 vols., ib. 1864; E. W. Whately, *Personal and Family Glimpses of Remarkable People*, ib. 1889; J. H. Overton, *The Church in England*, ii. 311–312, ib. 1897; E. Stock, *The English Church in the 19th Century*, ib. 1910; *DNB*, lx. 423–429, where reference is made to scattering notices.

WHEDON, DANIEL DENISON: Methodist Episcopal; b. at Onondaga, N. Y., Mar. 20, 1808; d. at Atlantic Highlands, N. J., June 8, 1885. He was graduated from Hamilton College, Clinton, N. Y., 1828; studied law at Rochester and Rome, N. Y.; became a teacher in Oneida (N. Y.) Conference Seminary; a tutor in Hamilton College, 1831; professor of ancient languages and literature in Wesleyan University, Middletown, Conn., 1833; Methodist pastor, 1843; professor of rhetoric, logic, and history in the University of Michigan, Ann Arbor, 1845; again entered the pastorate at Jamaica, L. I., N. Y., 1855; was elected editor of *The Methodist Quarterly Review*, 1856, and reelected quadrennially until May, 1884, when his health, which had long been feeble, forbade his continuing in the position. He was a man of learning, literary ability, and great industry. He was the author of *Public Addresses, Collegiate and Popular* (Boston, 1856); *The Freedom of the Will, as a Basis of Human Responsibility, Elucidated and Maintained in its Issue with the Necessitarian Theories of Hobbes, Edwards, the Princeton Essayists, and other Leading Advocates* (1864); *Commentary on the New Testament* (5 vols., 1860–75); *Essays, Reviews and Discourses, with a Biographical Sketch* (1887); *Statements Theological and Critical* (1887); and edited the first seven volumes of a *Commentary on the Old Testament* (9 vols., 1880–1907).

BIBLIOGRAPHY: Besides the sketch in *Essays, Reviews, and Discourses*, ut sup., consult J. M. Buckley, in *American Church History Series*, v. 386, 496, 500, New York, 1896.

WHERRY, ELWOOD MORRIS: Presbyterian missionary to India; b. at South Bend, Pa., Mar. 26, 1843. He studied at Jefferson (now Washington and Jefferson) College (B.A., 1862; M.A., 1875), and Princeton Theological Seminary (graduated,

1867), having meanwhile engaged in teaching, 1862–1864; was ordained an evangelist and went to India in 1867, being stationed at Rawal Pindi, 1868–69, and at Lodiana, 1869–83; was professor in the theological seminary at Saharanpur, 1883–88; returned to America and was district secretary of the American Tract Society in Chicago, 1889–98, for two years managing the bookstore of the society; in 1898 he resumed his work in Lodiana. He is the founder of the *Nur Afshan* "Light Disseminator" (1872), a weekly paper in the Hindu language, of which he was editor for twenty-one years. He also edited, in his capacity of secretary of the World's Congress of Missions at Chicago, 1893: *Missions at Home and Abroad: Papers and Addresses presented at the World's Congress of Missions* . . . (New York, 1895), as well as *Woman in Missions: Papers and Addresses Presented at the Woman's Congress of Missions . . . 1893* (1894). He is the author of *The Comprehensive Commentary on the Qurán* (4 vols., London, 1882–86); *Zainab the Panjabi* (1893); *Islam, or, the Religion of the Turk* (1894); *The Moslem Controversy* (1905), and a number of lesser works on related subjects. He has also translated a number of works in English on religious subjects into the native languages of North India.

WHICHCOTE (WHITCHCOTE, WHICHCOT), BENJAMIN: One of the leaders among the Cambridge Platonists (q.v.); b. at Stoke (11 m. n.e. of Shrewsbury), Shropshire, May 4, 1609; d. at Cambridge May, 1683. He was admitted a pensioner of Emmanuel College, Cambridge, in 1626 (B.A., 1629; M.A. and fellow, 1633), and was ordained in 1636. He was appointed Sunday afternoon lecturer at Trinity College, a post which he held for twenty years, and through the work done there was best known to his contemporaries. In 1643 he was preferred to the college living of North Cadbury in Somersetshire, but in the following year was recalled to Cambridge as provost of King's. The date of this appointment may be said to mark the rise of the new movement, of a type distinct from either the Puritan or the High-church, and one which gave alarm to the Puritan leaders. There was all the more cause for this alarm in that Whichcote spoke not for himself alone, but represented, as he molded, the thought of a younger and more progressive generation. In fact, it was as a teacher that he showed his power. Though Smith and Cudworth and More looked back to him as their intellectual master, he never appeared as an author in his lifetime. In 1649 he resigned the living of North Cadbury, and was presented to that of Milton in Cambridgeshire, which he retained till his death. At the Restoration he was ejected from his headship, but adhered to the church when the Act of Uniformity (see UNIFORMITY, ACT OF) was passed, held the cure of St. Anne's, Blackfriars, from 1662 until the church was burned in the great fire of 1666, and that of St. Lawrence, Jewry, from 1668. Four volumes of his sermons were published at Aberdeen in 1751, and his *Moral and Religious Aphorisms*, London, 1753. Throughout these his conceptions of human nature, of religion, and of the Church are seen to be in distinct contrast to the modes of thought prevailing

when he first formulated them; a broader and more philosophical spirit is evident in them. "God hath set up two lights to enlighten us in our way: the light of reason, which is the light of his creation; and the light of Scripture, which is after-revelation from him. Let us make use of these two lights; and suffer neither to be put out." In this one phrase he takes a higher range of thought than had been reached by any earlier English Protestant theologian, with possibly the single exception of Hooker. His Platonic temper is shown in the way in which he took up the idea of religion in its full breadth, moral and philosophical, and brought it into affinity with all the powers of humanity, showing that Christianity was unique, not in rejecting and casting aside, but in interpreting and completing what is otherwise good in man. It is in this realization of the unity of all the moral forces which govern civilization, this expansion and elevation of the whole conception of religion and of the moral rights of human nature, that Whichcote's great service to his age lay.

BIBLIOGRAPHY: The funeral sermon by Archbishop Tillotson was published London, 1683. Consult further: the literature under CAMBRIDGE PLATONISTS, especially the works of J. Tulloch and E. T. Campagnac; B. F. Westcott, in A. Barry, *Masters of Theology*, London, 1877; E. George, *Seventeenth Century Men of Latitude*, New York, 1908; *DNB*, lxi. 1–3.

WHIPPLE, HENRY BENJAMIN: Protestant Episcopal bishop; b. at Adams, Jefferson County, N. Y., Feb. 15, 1822; d. at Faribault, Minn., Sept. 16, 1901. He was educated at private schools, but, prevented by ill-health from entering college, engaged in business and in politics for several years; took a theological course under W. D. Williams; became deacon, 1849; priest, 1850; was rector of Zion Church, Rome, N. Y., 1850–57; of the Church of the Holy Communion, Chicago, Ill., 1857–59; and became bishop, 1859. He was a founder of Seabury Divinity School, of St. Mary's Hall, and Shattuck Military School, at Faribault, Minn. He devoted a great deal of time and energy to the Indians, and was an authority on all Indian problems, often being called in to the aid of the government. He was the author of *Five Sermons* (New York, 1890); and *Lights and Shadows of a Long Episcopate* (1899, new ed., 1902).

BIBLIOGRAPHY: Besides the autobiographic *Lights and Shadows*, ut sup., consult: W. S. Perry, *The Episcopate in America*, p. 145, New York, 1895.

WHISTON, WILLIAM: Mathematician and Arian theologian; best known to-day as the translator of Josephus; b. at Norton (16 m. w. of Leicester), Leicestershire, Dec. 9, 1667; d. at Lyndon (20 m. e. of Leicester), Rutland, Aug. 22, 1752. He was educated by his father (a clergyman who had been converted from Presbyterianism), at a school at Tamworth and at Clare Hall, Cambridge (B.A., 1690). He was ordained deacon in 1693, and then gave private lessons at Cambridge; but because of ill-health he exchanged teaching for the position of chaplain to John Moore, bishop of Norwich, and later (1698) received from Moore the vicarage of Lowestoft-cum-Kissingland, Suffolk, where he proved himself faithful and energetic in the performance of clerical duties. In 1701 he was appointed deputy to Newton's Lucasian professorship at Cambridge, and in 1703 succeeded Newton

Early   as professor and gave up his living. As
Life and   professor, Whiston lectured on mathe-
Cambridge   matics and natural philosophy, besides
Career.   engaging in scientific experimentation and being one of the first to popularize the theories of Newton. He advocated various reforms, both academic and general, perhaps with more zeal than judgment; and, making theological as well as scientific investigations, he became convinced that Arianism was the dominant faith of the first two centuries and that the Apostolic Constitutions (see APOSTOLIC CONSTITUTIONS AND CANONS) was " the most sacred of the canonical books of the New Testament." This view he expounded in an essay (1708) which the Cambridge vice-chancellor refused to license, though it was printed later in his *Primitive Christianity Revived.* Remonstrances of friends only served to prove the depth of Whiston's conviction—or his stubbornness —and in Oct., 1710, he was deprived of his professorship. Proceedings for his prosecution, instigated by convocation, dragged along for four or five years, but were finally dropped after the death of Queen Anne.

Thenceforth Whiston lived in London. He had a small property and received many gifts from friends and public personages, which, he states, " with eclipses, comets, and lectures," provided him " such a competency as greatly contented him." His lectures were on various topics, e.g., meteors, eclipses, earthquakes, and the like (in which he generally saw the fulfilment of prophecy), the tabernacle of Moses and the temple at Jerusalem (illustrated by

models), and the return of the Jews to
Life in   Palestine (which he believed to be im-
London.   minent). He was one of the first (perhaps the first) to present scientific experiments before popular audiences in London. He tried unsuccessfully to win a reward offered by parliament for the discovery of a means of determining longitude. A fund of £500 raised for him by subscription about 1740 he used for making a survey of the coasts. In 1715 he organized a society for promoting " primitive Christianity," which for two years held weekly meetings in his house in London and numbered among its members John Gale (a Baptist), Arthur Onslow, Thomas Emlyn (Unitarian), Thomas Rundle (afterward bishop of Derry), and Thomas Chubb (q.v.). Until 1747 he maintained communion with the Church of England, but then he joined the Baptists so that he might no longer hear the Athanasian Creed repeated. Among certain " new discoveries " of his later years were that anointing the sick with oil is a Christian duty, that the Tatars are the lost tribes, and that the millennium would begin in 1766.

In spite of his vagaries, Whiston was well liked by a large circle, including such men as Samuel Clarke, the philosopher, and Bishop Benjamin Hoadly (qq.v.; both of whom privately shared some of his views), as well as Addison and Steele, whom he knew well. His integrity and simpleminded honesty won respect, and so consistent was his practise of these virtues that a somewhat blunt manner of commending them to others was generally received with good-nature. The chief of his many publications (for a list of fifty-two titles, " omitting a few occasional papers," cf. *DNB,* lxi. 13–14) was his *Primitive Christianity Revived* (4

vols., London, 1711), which contains the Epistles of Ignatius, the Apostolic Constitutions, and dissertations, a fifth volume, containing
Writings.   the " Recognitions " of Clement, being added in 1712. His first book, *A New Theory of the Earth* (1696; 5th ed., with appendix, 1736), was the result of studies in the Cartesian philosophy and Newton's *Principia,* confirming the narrative of Genesis on Newtonian grounds and explaining the deluge by collision with a comet. The *Accomplishment of Scripture Prophecies* (1708) was the Boyle lectures for 1707 (cf. *The Literal Accomplishment of Scripture Prophecies,* 1724, an answer to Collins' *Grounds and Reasons*). The *Genuine Works of Flavius Josephus, the Jewish Historian, in English,* with dissertations, appeared in 1737. That this has been reprinted innumerable times (as late as 1906, ed. D. S. Margoliouth) and is still the standard English translation of Josephus is due to other causes than the merits of the translator, for Whiston's scholarship was defective for the task even in his time, and the advance of knowledge since the early eighteenth century, as well as the better text now available, make a new translation much to be desired. Other of Whiston's more noteworthy works are: *A Short View of the Chronology of the Old Testament and the Harmony of the Four Evangelists* (London, 1702); *An Essay on the Revelation of St. John* (1706); *Prælectiones physico-mathematicæ sive philosophia clarissimi Newtoni mathematica illustrata* (1710; English, 1716); *Athanasius Convicted of Forgery* (1712); *An Argument to Prove that All Persons Solemnly though Irregularly Set Apart for the Ministry Are Real Clergymen* (1714); *The True Origin of the Sabellian and Athanasian Doctrine of the Trinity* (1720); *A Chronological Table Containing the Hebrew, Phœnician, Egyptian, and Chaldæan Antiquities* (1721); *Athanasian Forgeries, Impositions, and Interpellations* (by a " Lover of Truth," 1736); *The Primitive New Testament,* a translation of the Gospels and Acts from the *Codex Bezæ,* of the Pauline epistles from the Clermont manuscripts, and of the catholic epistles from the *Codex Alexandrinus* (1745); and *Memoirs of William Whiston, Written by Himself* (1749; 2d ed., 1753).

BIBLIOGRAPHY: Besides the autobiographic *Memoirs,* ut sup., consult: J. Nichols, *Literary Anecdotes of the 18th Century,* i. 494–506, London, 1812; L. Stephen, *Hist. of English Thought in the 18th Century,* 2 vols., New York, 1881; J. H. Overton and F. Relton, *The English Church (1714–1800),* London, 1906; *DNB,* lxi. 10–14.

WHITAKER, OZI WILLIAM: Protestant Episcopalian bishop of Pennsylvania; b. at New Salem, Mass., May 10, 1830; d. at Philadelphia Feb. 9, 1911. He was graduated from Middlebury College, Vt. (A.B., 1856), and from the General Theological Seminary, New York City (1863). He went as a missionary to Nevada and was rector of St. John's, Gold Hill (1863–65); of St. Paul's, Englewood, N. J. (1865–67); and of St. Paul's, Virginia

City (1867-69). In 1869 he was consecrated missionary bishop of Nevada, serving until he became bishop coadjutor of Pennsylvania in 1886. A year later (1887), on the death of Bishop Stephens, he became bishop of the diocese.

BIBLIOGRAPHY: W. S. Perry, The Episcopate in America, p. 201, New York, 1895.

WHITAKER, WILLIAM: Church of England; b. at Holme (19 m. n. of Manchester), England, 1548; d. at Cambridge Dec. 4, 1595. He studied at St. Paul's school in London, and at Cambridge (B.A., 1568; M.A., 1571; minor fellow, 1569; major fellow, 1571; B.D., Oxford, 1578); became canon of Norwich Cathedral, 1578; regius professor of divinity, 1580; chancellor of St. Paul's, London, 1580; master of St. John's College, 1586; and canon of Canterbury, 1595. He was a man of great learning, stanch in his Protestantism and Calvinism. Most of his works were polemical, among which may be mentioned *Disputatio de sacra scriptura* (Cambridge, 1588; Eng. transl., *A Disputation on Holy Scripture against the Papists, especially Bellarmine and Stapleton*, ed. for Parker Society, 1849); *Responsionis ad decem illas rationes, quibus fretuo E. Campianus certamen ecclesiæ Anglicanæ ministrio obtulit in causa fidei* . . . (London, 1583; Eng. transl., *An Answere to the Ten Reasons of Edward Campian, the Jesuit*, 1606). His *Opera* were collected and published in 2 vols., Geneva, 1610. See LAMBETH ARTICLES.

BIBLIOGRAPHY: A *Vita* by A. Ashton with other biographic material is in the *Opera*, ut sup., i. 698-716; there is also *An Account of the Life and Death* . . . in Whitaker's *Cygnæa Cantio*, London, 1772. Consult further: The *Life* by Gataker in Fuller's *Abel Redivivus*, pp. 401-408, London, 1651; R. Churton, *Life of A. Nowell*, pp. 325-334, Oxford, 1809; C. H. and T. Cooper, *Athenæ Cantabrigienses*, vol. ii., London, 1861; T. Baker, *Hist. of the College of St. John*, . . . *Cambridge*, ed. J. E. B. Mayor, 2 vols., Cambridge, 1869; W. H. Frere, *The English Church (1558-1625)*, pp. 282-283, 342, London, 1904; *DNB*, lxi. 21-23.

WHITBY, SYNOD OF: An assembly convened by Oswy, king of Northumbria, in the spring of 664 to settle the differences between the Irish and Roman ecclesiastics in his realm concerning the date of Easter, the shape of the tonsure, and the like (see CELTIC CHURCH IN BRITAIN AND IRELAND). Oswy's marriage with Eansfled, daughter of the king of Kent, had brought the dispute to a crisis, as the king adhered to the Celtic usages brought to North England from Iona, while the southern princess, coming from the region of Canterbury, followed Roman custom and brought with her to the north a Catholic chaplain. The assembly met at Hilda's convent at Streanæshalch (Whitby, on the coast of Yorkshire, 40 m. n.n.e. of York). Oswy presided, and among those present were Alchfrid, king of Deira, Oswy's son; Agilbert, bishop of the West Saxons (a native of Gaul); Wilfrid, afterward bishop of York; Colman, bishop of Lindisfarne; Cedd, bishop of the East Saxons; and Hilda. Wilfrid spoke for the Roman party and Colman for the British. The latter claimed to follow St. John and Columba, whereupon Wilfrid asserted the supremacy of St. Peter and quoted Matt. xvi. 18, thereby convincing the king. In consequence of his defeat Colman and the Irish monks, with about thirty of the Angles, left Northumbria. His successor, Tuda, died in a short time of the plague and Wilfrid was then chosen bishop and the see was removed to York.

BIBLIOGRAPHY: Bede, *Hist. eccl.*, iii. 25, in Plummer's ed., i. 183-189, ii. 189-192; Haddan and Stubbs, *Councils*, iii. 100-105; W. Bright, *Early English Church History*, pp. 222-232, 3d ed., Oxford, 1897; J. H. Overton, *The Church in·England*, i. 59-63, 73 et passim, London, 1897; W. Hunt, *The English Church (597-1066)*, pp. 109-115, 128, ib. 1899.

WHITBY, DANIEL: Controversial writer and commentator; b. at Rushden (14 m. n.e. of Northampton), Northamptonshire, Mar. 24, 1638; d. at Salisbury Mar. 24, 1725. He entered Oxford as a commoner of Trinity College in 1653 (B.A., 1657) and was elected fellow in 1664. Four years later he was appointed chaplain to Seth Ward, bishop of Salisbury, who almost immediately made him prebendary of Yatesbury and Husborn-Tarrant, and in 1669 perpetual curate of St. Thomas' and rector of St. Edmund's, Salisbury. He was installed precentor at Salisbury in 1672, and in 1696 was given the prebend of Taunton-Regis. His first book was *Romish Doctrines not from the Beginning* (London, 1664), and it was followed during the next twenty-five years by ten or a dozen similar works against the Roman Catholic Church. At first his writings were well received, but in 1682, in *The Protestant Reconciler Humbly Pleading for Condescension to Dissenting Brethren in Things Immaterial*, he expressed opinions concerning "things immaterial," which were accounted too liberal by the High-church party, and the University of Oxford ordered the book to be burned in the quadrangle, while Bishop Ward compelled the author to retract. A " second part " was then issued urging dissenters to conform. Whitby also wrote on Christian evidences, against Calvinism, on the Fathers, and on the Trinity. On the topic last named, he began with the orthodox doctrine (cf. *Tractatus de vera Christi deitate adversus Arii et Socini hæreses* [Oxford, 1691]), but his view changed, and his *Last Thoughts* (published posthumously by his direction, ed. A. A. Sykes, London, 1727; reprinted by the Unitarian Association, 1841) reveals him as a convinced Unitarian. His *magnum opus* was a *Paraphrase and Commentary on the New Testament* (2 vols., London, 1703), the fruit of fifteen years' labor, which, combined with the work of Simon Patrick (q.v.), Richard Arnold, William Lowth (q.v.), and Moses Lowman in the popular *Critical Commentary on the Old and New Testaments and Apocrypha* (London, 1809), has had a longer life than it deserved (reprinted 1857). He is described as small and very thin physically, affable in manner, sincerely pious and unselfish, and possessed of a remarkable memory, which, with his other faculties (except eyesight), he retained unimpaired to the end of his life. On the day before his death he preached extemporaneously in church. He spent his life in his study, indulging in but one relaxation (tobacco), and was a child in all business matters.

BIBLIOGRAPHY: *A Short Account of the Life*, etc., was prefixed by Sykes to the *Last Thoughts*, ut sup. Consult: A. à Wood, *Athenæ Oxonienses*, ed. P. Bliss, iv. 671, and *Fasti*, ii. 198, 223, 332-333, 4 vols., London, 1813-20; *DNB*, lxi. 28-30.

WHITE, HENRY JULIAN: Church of England; b. in London Aug. 27, 1859. He received his education at Christ Church, Oxford (B.A., 1882; M.A., 1885); was made deacon, 1885, and priest, 1886; was curate of Oxted, Surrey, 1885–86; missioner of St. Andrew's, Sarum, 1886–95; chaplain and theological lecturer of Merton College, Oxford, 1895–1905; and became professor of New-Testament exegesis in King's College, London, 1905. He also filled the offices of domestic chaplain to the bishop of Salisbury, 1887; fellow of Merton College and examining chaplain to the bishop of Oxford, 1897–1905; and examiner in theology at Oxford, 1903–05. He has collaborated with J. Wordsworth, bishop of Salisbury, and W. Sanday in the production of *Old Latin Biblical Texts* (Oxford, 1883 sqq.); of *Novum Testamentum Latine* (1889 sqq.; the critical edition of the Vulgate); contributed "The Codex Amatianus and its Birthplace" to *Studia Biblia et Ecclesiastica* (1890); has issued also *Acta Apostolorum* (1890), and *Merton College* in *College Monographs* (1906).

WHITE, JOHN HAZEN: Protestant Episcopal bishop of Michigan City; b. at Cincinnati Mar. 10, 1849. He was graduated from Kenyon College, (A.B., 1872) and from Berkeley Divinity School (1875). He was ordered deacon (1875), and priest (1876); he was curate at St. Andrew's, Meriden, Conn. (1875–77); curate at St. John's, Waterbury, Conn. (1877–78), as well as vice-rector and instructor of Latin in St. Margaret's School, in the same city; he then held the rectorship at the following churches: Grace Church, Old Saybrook, Conn. (1878–81); Christ Church, Joliet, Ill. (1881–89); St. John's, St. Paul's, Minn. (1889–91); was warden of the Seabury Divinity School (1891–95), and in 1895 was consecrated bishop of Indiana. When the diocese was divided in 1899, he took the northern portion of the former see, with the title of bishop of Michigan City.

BIBLIOGRAPAY: W. S. Perry, *The Episcopate in America*, p. 367, New York, 1895.

WHITE, NEWPORT JOHN DAVIS: Church of England; b. at Dublin Feb. 16, 1860. He received his education at Rathmines School and Trinity College, Dublin (B.A., 1883; M.A., B.D., 1887; D.D., 1904); he was made deacon in 1885, and priest in 1886; was curate of Bowdon, Cheshire, 1885–87, and of St. John's, Birkenhead, 1888–90; private teacher of divinity in Trinity College, Dublin, 1890–1897; assistant lecturer in divinity and Hebrew in the same institution, 1897–1907; librarian of Archbishop Marsh's Library, Dublin, 1898; professor of Biblical Greek in Trinity College, Dublin, since 1906; and deputy for the regius professor of divinity, Dublin University, 1907. He has also been canon of St. Patrick's Cathedral, Dublin, since 1906. He has edited *The Latin Writings of St. Patrick* (in the *Proceedings* of the Royal Irish Academy, Dublin, 1905); and G. Salmon's *Human Element in the Gospels. A Commentary of the Synoptic Narrative* (London, 1907); contributed to *The Psalms of Israel: Lectures delivered in St. Patrick's Cathedral, Dublin, 1903* (1904); *Elias Bouhéreau of La Rochelle* (in *Proceedings* of the Royal Irish Academy, 1908); and

the commentary on the Pastoral Epistles in the *Expositor's Greek Testament* (1909); together with articles in Hastings, *DB* and *DCG*.

WHITE, THOMAS: English Roman Catholic, controversial writer under various pseudonyms (Thomas Anglus, Albius, Bianchi, Blacklow, Candidus); b. probably at Hutton (20 m. e.n.e. of London), Essex, 1593; d. in London July 6, 1676. He studied at the English College at St. Omer, at Valladolid (entered 1609), and at Douai; was ordained priest at Arras 1617, taught at Douai at different times (vice-president in 1650), was president of the English college at Lisbon 1633, and also lived in Paris and Rome. His last years were spent in England in literary work. He wrote much upon philosophical and theological questions, and developed a system of his own and applied it to religious doctrines, especially freedom, grace, and predestination, with an independence that brought him into conflict with those of his own faith; his works were put upon the index. At the same time he saw no way to solve the difficulties of Scripture except by permanent authority, and hence fell into controversy with Protestants. He ultimately submitted unreservedly to the Roman Catholic Church. He edited William Rushworth's *Dialogues or the Judgment of Common Sense in the Choice of Religion* (Paris, 1654), adding a dialogue of his own, and published *An Apology for Rushworth's Dialogues* (2 parts, 1654), wherein his views are best set forth. Other works include *Institutiones peripateticæ* (Lyons, 1646), and *Institutiones sacræ* (1652), from which twenty-two propositions were censured by the University of Douai in 1660; *De medio animarum statu* (Paris, 1653; Eng., 1659); *The Grounds of Obedience and Government* (London, 1655), in which, it was charged, he tried to flatter Cromwell to gain his favor for the Roman Catholics; *Institutiones ethicæ sive stateræ morum* (2 vols., 1660).

BIBLIOGRAPHY: [P. Talbot], *Blackloanæ hæresis hist. et confutatio*, Ghent, 1675; C. Plowden, *Remarks on a Book Entitled "Memoirs of Gregorio Panzani,"* pp. 255–273, London, 1794; C. Dodd, *Church Hist. of England*, iii. 285, 350–356, 5 vols., London, 1839–43; F. H. Reusch, *Der Index der verbotenen Bücher*, ii. 384, 411, Bonn, 1885; J. Gillow, *Biographical Dictionary of English Catholics*, v. 578–581, London, n.d.; Bayle, *Dictionary*, i. 338–340; *DNB*, lxi. 79–81; *KL*, i. 853–854.

WHITE, WILBERT WEBSTER: United Presbyterian; b. at Ashland, O., Jan. 16, 1863. He studied at the University of Wooster (B.A., 1881; M.A., 1884), Xenia Theological Seminary (graduated 1885), and Yale University (Ph.D., 1891); was pastor at Peotone, Ill., 1885–86; professor of Hebrew and Old-Testament literature in the Xenia Theological Seminary, 1890–95; taught in the Moody Bible Institute, Chicago, 1895–97; engaged in Bible work in India and England, 1897–1900; and became president of the Bible Teachers' Training School, New York City, 1900. He has written *Inductive Studies in the Twelve Minor Prophets* (Chicago, 1894); *Thirty Studies in the Gospel by John* (New York, 1895); *Thirty Studies in Jeremiah* (1895); *Thirty Studies in the Revelation of Jesus Christ to John* (1898); *Studies in Old Testament Characters* (1900); and *Thirty Studies in the Gospel by Matthew* (1903).

WHITE, WILLIAM: Protestant Episcopal bishop; b. in Philadelphia, Pa., Apr. 4, 1748; d. there July 17, 1836. He was educated in the schools and College of Philadelphia, graduating in 1765; soon began his theological studies, completed in 1770, when he sailed for England to receive orders; was ordered deacon in the Chapel Royal, Westminster, 1770, and ordained priest 1772; became assistant minister of Christ Church and St. Peter's, Philadelphia, 1772, and soon after rector of the united parishes of Christ, St. Peter's, and St. James'. Upon the outbreak of the Revolution he sided with the colonies, and was chaplain to the Continental Congress, 1787–1801. He was active during the war in trying to sustain the life of the church, and later in obtaining the episcopate essential to reorganization. In 1785 he was chosen president of the general convention in Philadelphia, and in 1786 its first bishop, being consecrated in the chapel of Lambeth Palace, England, 1787. He exercised the episcopal office until his death, being in orders more than sixty-five years, standing at the head of the American Church nearly half a century, and consecrating about twenty-six bishops. He was a man of large and comprehensive views, and of wisdom in his administration. His works embrace *Comparative View of the Controversy between the Calvinists and the Arminians* (2 vols., Philadelphia, 1817); and *Memoirs of the Protestant Episcopal Church in the United States of America* (1820; 2d ed., with continuation, New York, 1835).

BIBLIOGRAPHY: W. B. Sprague, *Annals of the American Pulpit*, v. 280–292, New York, 1859; W. S. Perry, *Hist. of the American Episcopal Church*, 2 vols., Boston, 1885; idem, *Episcopate in America*, pp. xxii. sqq., 5–7, New York, 1895; C. C. Tiffany, in *American Church History Series*, vii. 217, 289 et passim, 564 sqq., New York, 1895; S. D. McConnell, *Hist. of the American Episcopal Church*, 7th ed., New York, 1897; and in general the literature under PROTESTANT EPISCOPALIANS dealing with the early history of that church.

WHITEFIELD, GEORGE: Calvinistic Methodist; b. in Gloucester, England, Dec. 27, 1714; d. in Newburyport, Mass., Sept. 30, 1770. He was the son of an innkeeper. At the age of twelve he was placed in the school of St. Mary de Crypt at Gloucester, and in 1732, after a year's intermission of his studies so that he might be drawer of liquor in the inn (kept by his mother since his father's death in 1716), he entered Pembroke College, Oxford. The religious impressions which he had felt on different occasions had been deepened while he was at school the second time, and at Oxford he fell in with the Wesleys, joined the " Holy Club," and observed its rules rigorously, being the first of the Oxford "Methodists" to profess conversion (1735). His health being impaired, he left Oxford for a year, returning in Mar., 1736, and was ordained deacon in the following June, taking his B.A. in the same year. He now spent much time among the prisoners in Oxford, preached in London and elsewhere, and speedily rose to great prominence as a pulpit orator. At the age of twenty-four he had been requested by the Wesleys to come to them in Georgia, and he finally resolved to go, though he did not sail until the beginning of 1738. He spent several months in Georgia, preaching with great acceptance, but in the same year returned to England to be ordained priest. Here he found many London churches closed to him because he was considered erratic and fanatical, but he preached in such as would receive him, and also visited and worked among the Moravians and other religious societies in London. Early in 1739 he held a conference with the Wesleys and other Oxford Methodists, and in February went to Bristol. Being excluded from the churches, he preached in the open air, and induced Wesley to take a similar step, thus establishing an innovation which gave opportunity to the Methodist movement. At Kingswood, near Bristol, he laid the foundations of the Kingswood School, which became so important to Methodism.

Whitefield now began his career as an itinerant evangelist. He visited Wales, and gave an impulse to the revival movement already begun by Howel Harris (q.v.); and he next traveled through Scotland, and then went through England, attracting extraordinary attention everywhere. But his arraignment of the clergy as " blind guides " roused many to oppose him, and this hostile feeling preceded him to America, where some of the Anglican churches refused him their pulpits, though other churches were open to him. He preached in Philadelphia and New York, and on his way to Georgia; while during a visit to New England the revival which had begun in Northampton in 1736 was renewed. (See REVIVALS, III., 1.) Whitefield paid seven visits to America, the results of his evangelistic tours being shared by Congregationalists, Presbyterians, and Baptists from Massachusetts to Georgia; and when he was not in America he was addressing immense audiences in England, Scotland, and Wales.

He early became Calvinistic in his views, and his association with Calvinistic divines in America deepened them. He complained to Wesley because he attacked the doctrine of election, and there was a sharp controversy between them which led to a temporary alienation, though the unwillingness of either to offend the other soon brought about a reconciliation, and the two were henceforth firm friends despite the fact that their paths were different. Whitefield was nominally the head of the Calvinistic Methodists, but he left to others the work of organization. His time was divided between Great Britain and America, and he preached among all denominations. He continued in active service until the end, preaching for two hours at Exeter, Mass., the day before his death, while it was his regular custom to preach every day in the week, often three and four times daily.

[The *Works* of Whitefield were edited in seven volumes by J. Gillies (London, 1771–72), but this edition contains only selected sermons, letters, and tracts, with a few pieces which had not yet been published. It does not, indeed, include some of the writings of most interest in connection with Whitefield's life, such as his *Journal of a Voyage from London to Savannah in Georgia* (London, 1738; six other *Journals* of kindred content were published between 1738 and 1741; it is interesting to note that several of the *Journals*, as well as some of the following books, were reprinted, not only in Boston, but also by Benjamin Franklin in Philadelphia); *A Short Account of God's Dealings with . . . G.W. . . . from his Infancy to the Time of his Entering into Holy Orders* (1740); *The Full Account*, etc. (1747) and *A Further Account*, etc. (1747); *The Christian History; or, A General Account of the Progress of the Gospel in England, Wales, Scotland, and America, so far as Mr. W., his Fellow-Labourers, and Assistants are Concerned* (1747); and *The Two First Parts of his Life, with his Journals, Revised, Corrected, and Abridged* (1756). The *Journals, Short Account*, and *Further Account* were reissued at London, 1905. Whitefield also compiled a *Collection of Hymns for Social Worship*, which by 1790 had run through thirty-three editions (revised by M. Wilks, London, 1798, and again by J. Campbell, London, 1837), but it is doubtful whether any of the hymns ascribed to him are really original, while his alterations of the hymns of the Wesleys were such as to cause John Wesley to speak of them in somewhat biting terms. He preached his sermons over and over again. Much of his success depended upon his dramatic delivery, for the sermons which have come down seem somewhat tame and not to rise above the commonplace.] H. K. CARROLL.

BIBLIOGRAPHY: The principal sources are his own *Journals, Short Account, Full Account, Further Account*, etc. The fullest and most nearly exhaustive life is that by L. Tyerman, 2 vols., London, 1876–77; a good one for general use is J. P. Gladstone's *Life and Travels of George Whitefield*, ib. 1871; cf. his *George Whitefield, . . . Field Preacher*, ib. 1901; excellent in its original form is J. Gillies, *Memoirs of . . . G. Whitefield*, ib. 1772, often re-edited and republished. Consult further: R. Philip, *Life and Times of . . . G. Whitefield*, London, 1832; D. Newell, *Life of Rev. G. Whitefield*, New York, 1846; J. Stoughton, *The Pen, the Palm, and the Pulpit*, London, 1858; D. A. Harsha, *Life of Rev. G. Whitefield*, Albany, 1866; J. C. Ryle, *Christian Leaders of the Last Century*, London, 1868; J. B. Wakeley, *Anecdotes of Rev. G. Whitefield*, ib. 1879, new ed., 1900; J. Macaulay, *Whitefield Anecdotes*, ib. 1886; *Cambridge Modern History*, vi. 82 sqq., New York, 1909; *DNB*, lxi. 85–92; and the literature under METHODISTS dealing with the history of that movement. See also under REVIVALS, and the literature on the Wesleys.

WHITEHEAD, CORTLANDT: Protestant Episcopal bishop of Pittsburg; b. in New York City Oct. 30, 1842. He was graduated from Yale College (A.B., 1863) and the Philadelphia Divinity School (1867); was ordered deacon (1867), and ordained priest (1868); he served as missionary at Blackhawk, Central City, and Georgetown (1867–1870); was rector of the Church of the Nativity at Bethlehem, Pa. (1870–82), and in 1882 he was consecrated bishop of Pittsburg. He has edited Bishop A. C. Coxe's *Thoughts on the Services* (New York, 1899).

WHITEHOUSE, OWEN CHARLES: English Congregationalist; b. at Palamkotta (5 m. s.e. of Tinnevelli), Tinnevelli, Madras Presidency, India, Nov. 15, 1849. He was educated at University College, London (B.A., University of London, 1870), Cheshunt College, Herts (1872–74), and the University of Bonn (1876–77); was professor of classics and Hebrew in Cheshunt College, Herts (1877–95); principal and professor of Biblical exegesis and theology there (1895–1905). Since 1905, when Cheshunt College was removed to Cambridge, he has been its senior theological tutor. He was a member of the board of theological studies and of oriental languages in London University in 1901–1906, and examiner on Hebrew in the same institution in 1903–07. " In Old-Testament criticism he accepts the main conclusions of Kuenen and Wellhausen as definitely established, but adopts an attitude of reserve toward more recent theories of Cheyne, Marti, and others; in dogmatic theology he regards with sympathy the views of Ritschl and Hermann; in New-Testament criticism he agrees in the main with Harnack, although adopting a somewhat conservative attitude, regarding with disfavor the conclusions of Schmiedel and Van Manen." Besides contributing the commentary on Isaiah to *The Century Bible* (1902) and on Ezekiel to *The Temple Bible* (1905), he has translated E. Schrader's *Cuneiform Inscriptions and the Old Testament* (London, 1889) and has written *Primer of Hebrew Antiquities* (1895).

WHITFIELD, EDWARD ELIHU: Plymouth Brother; b. at Newcastle-upon-Tyne Nov. 5, 1848. He was educated at Oriel College, Oxford (B.A., 1874), and the University of Heidelberg, and after being a private tutor at Oxford, was modern language master at Sir Joseph Williamson's School, Rochester (1889–99), lecturer in the School of Commerce at University College, Liverpool (1899–1901), and modern language master at Rutlish School, Merton, Surrey (1901–04) and King Edward VII.'s School, King's Lynn, Norfolk (1904–05). In 1905 he retired from active life. Besides editing J. N. Darby's English version of the Old Testament (4 parts, London, 1883–89) and W. Kelly's expositions of Mark and John (2 vols., 1907–08), he has written *Outlines of Old Testament Study, Historical and Critical* (1883).

WHITGIFT, JOHN: Archbishop of Canterbury; b. at Great Grimsby (30 m. n.e. of Lincoln), England, in 1530 (1533?); d. at Lambeth (2 m. s. of Charing Cross, London) Feb. 29, 1604. He studied at Queen's College and at Pembroke Hall, Cambridge (B.A., 1553–54; M.A., 1557; B.D., 1563); was fellow of Peterhouse, Cambridge, 1555–67; took holy orders, 1560; was rector of Teversham, Cambridgeshire, 1560–72; became chaplain to the bishop of Ely, 1560; was Lady Margaret professor of divinity, 1563–67; master of Pembroke Hall, 1567; master of Trinity College, 1567–77; regius professor of divinity, 1567–69; became prebendary of Ely, 1568; dean of Lincoln, 1571; prebendary of Nassington in the church of Lincoln, and rector of Laceby, Lincolnshire, 1572; bishop of Worcester, 1577; and in 1583 was raised to the primacy. He headed the prelatical party, and for years carried on a controversy with Thomas Cartwright, the great champion of Puritanism. When raised to the primacy, Whitgift was in position to carry out repressive measures against the Puritan party. Agreeing to identify himself absolutely with the cause of uniformity, he obtained a free hand from Elizabeth. In the stifling of Puritanism and in the administration of a coercive policy he was determined. In 1583 he drew up a series of stringent articles which, among other things, required, for the exercise of ecclesiastical functions, a pledge of fidelity to the

Book of Common Prayer, and of acceptance of the Thirty-nine Articles. In 1584 he drew up his interrogations, to be administered to any of the clergy whom the amended court of high commission saw fit to question. Although this evoked strong protest and remonstrance, Whitgift refused to show greater moderation, and followed up his policy with the Star-chamber decree of 1586, prohibiting any manuscript from being set up in type until it had been read and licensed by the archbishop or the bishop of London. He was the object, later, of a series of attacks printed secretly by the Puritans. In 1595 he drew up the Lambeth Articles (q.v.), which adopted unqualifyingly the Calvinist views of predestination and election. These were the result of a request, from the Calvinist leaders of Cambridge, for him to pronounce authoritatively in their favor at Cambridge. He won the favor of James VI. of Scotland (James I. of England) and the confidence of the officers of State. Whitgift's character stood high in the esteem of his contemporaries; he was not self-indulgent, despite the pomp of his palace at Lambeth, and he was said to be pious and earnest in his labors. But the animosities aroused by his policy of coercion lived long after him, causing his better qualities to be overlooked. His *Works* appeared, edited for the Parker Society by John Ayre (3 vols., Cambridge, 1851–54).

BIBLIOGRAPHY: Illustrative documents are reproduced in Gee and Hardy, *Documents*, pp. 481 sqq. Consult: J. Strype, *Life and Acts of John Whitgift*, 2 parts, Oxford, 1718, new ed., 1822; G. Paule, *Life . . . of John Whitgift*, London, 1612; *Life of John Whitgift*, added to D. W. Garrow, *Hist. and Antiquities of Croyden*, Croyden, 1818; W. Maskell, *Hist. of the Marprelate Controversy*, London, 1845; C. Wordsworth, *Ecclesiastical Biography*, 4 vols., London, 1853; W. F. Hook, *Lives of the Archbishops of Canterbury*, vol. v., 12 vols., London, 1860–76; C. H. and T. Cooper, *Athenæ Cantabrigienses*, vol. ii., London, 1861; E. Arber, *Introductory Sketch to the Martin Marprelate Controversy*, London, 1879; W. Clark, *The Anglican Reformation*, New York, 1879; J. H. Overton, *The Church in England*, i. 467, 472–475 et passim, vol. ii. passim, London, 1897; W. H. Frere, *The English Church (1558–1625)*, London, 1904; *Cambridge Modern History*, ii. 161, 592, 597, New York, 1904; *DNB*, lxi. 129–137.

WHITMAN, MARCUS: Congregational missionary and pioneer; b. at Rushville, N. Y., Sept. 4, 1802; d. at Waiilatpu, Ore., Nov. 29, 1847. He was educated privately and then studied medicine at Pittsfield, Mass., after which he practised as a physician in Canada for four years, removing in 1828 to Wheeler, N. Y. In 1835 he went, with a missionary named Samuel Parker, to study American Indian conditions west of the Mississippi and the Rocky Mountains, with a view to introducing Christianity among them; and so favorable were the prospects among Flathead and Nez Perces tribes in what is now Wyoming that Whitman returned to New York to organize a mission, while Parker continued his way in search of sites for missionary stations. Early in 1836 Whitman and his companions set out, reaching Walla Walla in September, and making his first center at Waiilatpu, near that post. In 1842 he was transferred by the American Board of Commissioners for Foreign Missions to a missionary station near Fort Colville, but he almost immediately started on a return journey to the east, wishing to obtain helpers in view of the rapid immigration into Oregon and of the Roman Catholic missionary activity among the Indians. He gained the retention of the posts at Waiilatpu and Clearwater, but had not enough time to secure the assistants he desired. During his return journey he acted as guide and physician to a large emigrant caravan, and on reaching Waiilatpu he resumed his missionary labors. In 1847, however, an epidemic of measles among the Cayuse caused so large a number of fatalities that Whitman and the other missionaries were believed to be using black magic against them; and the Indians accordingly attacked the mission and killed him and fifteen others.

Apart from his importance as a missionary, Whitman was the man who, above all others, roused popular interest in Oregon and thus largely promoted its settlement. On the other hand, there appears to be little evidence for the common belief that he discovered a plot of the Hudson Bay Company to obtain Oregon for England by colonizing it from Canada, and that his trip of 1842 was to secure American immigrants to forestall such action. Equally fictitious is the story that, when reaching Washington to expose this plot, he found the United States about to exchange Oregon for the fisheries of Newfoundland, and that his representations prevented this exchange and thus secured the retention of the territory.

BIBLIOGRAPHY: W. Barrows, *Oregon; the Struggle for Possession*, Boston, 1884; J. G. Craighead, *The Story of Marcus Whitman*, Philadelphia, 1895; O. W. Nixon, *How Marcus Whitman saved Oregon*, Chicago, 1895; idem, *Whitman's Ride through Savage Lands*, ib. 1905; W. A. Mowry, *Marcus Whitman and the Early Days of Oregon*, New York, 1901; W. I. Marshall, *History vs. the " Whitman saved Oregon " Story*, privately printed, Chicago, 1904; C. W. Smith, *A Contribution toward a Bibliography of Marcus Whitman*, Seattle, 1908; M. Eolls, *Marcus Whitman; Pathfinder and Patriot*, ib. 1909.

WHITON, JAMES MORRIS: Congregationalist; b. at Boston, Mass., Apr. 11, 1833. He was educated at Yale College (A.B., 1853), and, after being rector of Hopkins Grammar School, New Haven, Conn. (1854–64), was pastor of the First Congregational Church, Lynn, Mass. (1865–69), and of the North Congregational Church in the same city (1869–75); principal of Williston Seminary, Easthampton, Mass. (1876–78); pastor of the First Congregational Church, Newark, N. J. (1879–85), and of Trinity Congregational Church, New York City (1886–91); acting professor of ethics in the Meadville Theological School (1893–94), and acting pastor of the Congregational Church at Haworth, N. J. (1898–1901). He has been a member of the editorial staff of *The Outlook* since 1897. He has been chairman of the Executive Committee of the New York State Conference of Religions since 1899. In theology he is a " conservative-liberal " with a " monistic basis." He is the author of *Latin Lessons* (Boston, 1860); *Greek Lessons* (New York, 1861); *Select Orations of Lysias* (Boston, 1875); *Is Eternal Punishment Endless?* (New York, 1876; maintaining that endless punishment is not decisively revealed in the New Testament, thus raising a question as to his further fellowship in the Congregational body, which was decided in his favor by a council at Newark, N. J., in 1879); *Six Weeks' Preparation for Reading Cæsar* (Boston, 1877); *Essay on the Gospel according to Matthew* (1880);

Beyond the Shadow, or the Gospel of the Resurrection (New York, 1881); *The Evolution of Revelation* (1885); *Three Months' Preparation for Reading Xenophon* (in collaboration with his daughter, 1885); *The Divine Satisfaction* (1886); *Turning Points of Thought and Conduct* (1887); *The Law of Liberty* (1888); *New Points to Old Texts* (1889); *What of Samuel?* (1890); *Gloria Patri, or Talks on the Trinity* (1892); *Reconsiderations and Reenforcements* (1896); *Miracles and Supernatural Religion* (1903); and *Interludes, Ethical, Social and Theological* (1910).

WHITSITT, WILLIAM HETH: Baptist; b. near Nashville, Tenn., Nov. 25, 1841; d. at Richmond Jan. 20, 1911. He was educated at Union University (1857–60), dropping his studies during the Civil War to become private, later chaplain, in the Confederate Army (1861–65). He then studied at the University of Virginia (1866–67), later taking a course at the Southern Baptist Seminary (1867–1869), as well as at Leipsic (1869–70) and at Berlin (1870–71); he was pastor at the Mill Creek Church, Nashville, Tenn. (1865–66), and for part of the year 1872 was pastor of the Baptist church at Albany, Ga., when he received an appointment as professor of Biblical introduction and ecclesiastical history in the Southern Baptist Theological Seminary, of which he was president from 1895 to 1899. About 1880 he saw for the first time materials which led him to believe that among English antipedobaptists immersion was not in use till 1641. Publication of statements embodying these materials educed assaults upon him as not supporting his denomination, and these were intensified by the publication of his *Question in Baptist History* (Louisville, 1896). Feeling it best for the institution over which he had presided that he should retire, he did so and for two years held no office. The publication of his articles and his book occasioned a sharp controversy respecting the right and duty of a historian in a denominational school to exercise an untrammeled freedom in the expression of conclusions as to historical facts. After 1901 he was professor of philosophy in Richmond College, Va. Besides being an associate editor of *Johnson's Universal Cyclopædia* (1894), he wrote *History of the Rise of Infant Baptism* (Louisville, Ky., 1878); *History of Communion Among Baptists* (1880); *Origin of the Disciples of Christ* (New York, 1888); *Life and Times of Judge Caleb Wallace* (Louisville, 1888); *Annals of a Scotch-Irish Family—the Whitsitts of Nashville, Tenn.* (1904); and *Genealogy of Jefferson Davis* (1908).

WHITSUNDAY. See Pentecost, II.

WHITTINGHAM, WILLIAM. See Sternhold, Thomas.

WHYTE, ALEXANDER: Free Church of Scotland; b. at Kirriemuir (14 m. n. of Dundee), Forfarshire, Jan. 13, 1837. He was educated at the University of Aberdeen (M.A., 1862) and at New College, Edinburgh (1862–66); was assistant minister of Free St. John's, Glasgow (1866–70); then assistant minister, and, later (1873), minister of Free St. George's, Edinburgh; and, in 1909, became professor of New-Testament literature and

principal of New College, Edinburgh. He has written *Commentary on the Shorter Catechism* (Edinburgh, 1882); *Bunyan Characters* (4 series, 1893–1908); *Samuel Rutherford and some of his Correspondents* (1894); *Jacob Behmen: An Appreciation* (1894); *Lancelot Andrewes and his Private Devotions* (1895); *Four Temperaments* (London, 1895, reissue, 1910); *Bible Characters* (6 vols., Edinburgh, 1896–1902); *Santa Teresa: An Appreciation* (1897, reissue, 1910); *Father John of the Greek Church* (1898); *Sir Thomas Browne: An Appreciation* (1898); *Characters and Characteristics of William Law* (1898); *Newman: An Appreciation* (1901); *Bishop Butler: An Appreciation* (1903); *The Apostle Paul* (1903); *Walk, Conversation, Character of Jesus Christ Our Lord* (1905); and *Thomas Shepard, Pilgrim Father and Founder of Harvard* (1909).

WIBEL, vi'bel, **JOHANN CHRISTIAN:** German theologian; b. at Ernsbach near Oehringen (35 m. n.n.e. of Stuttgart) May 3, 1711; d. at Langenburg (48 m. n.e. of Stuttgart) May 10, 1772. He prepared for the university at Oehringen, and studied at Jena under Buddeus and Johann Georg Walch (qq.v.), 1728–32, especially busying himself with church history; he became chaplain at Wilhermsdorf near Nuremberg in 1732, where he began to write history; in 1746 he was called as teacher and assistant preacher to the gymnasium at Oehringen, where he undertook extensive researches in the archives; he went as court preacher to Langenburg in 1749, where he remained, exercising a wholesome and extended influence. His literary activity began as early as 1733 with a collection of poems on the Order of Salvation (q.v.). In Wilhermsdorf he became interested in the Jews, planned a new edition of the *Masorah parva* and collected material for a *Codex diplomaticus* on the history of the Jews, and came into connection with Johann Heinrich Callenberg (q.v.). His later work resulted in the production of his chief writing, *Hohenlohische Kirchen- und Reformationshistorie* (4 vols., Ansbach, 1752–55), an impartial and worthy compilation which, with the adjunct *Codex diplomaticus*, contained much original material and is indispensable as a source. On his religious side Wibel was an orthodox Lutheran and somewhat pietistic, and his activities were worthy and far-reaching.

(G. Bossert.)

Bibliography: E. F. Neubauer, *Nachricht von den jetztlebenden . . . Theologen in . . . Deutschland*, pp. 10, 20 sqq., Züllichau, 1743; *ADB*, xlii. 300–301.

WIBALD OF STABLO: Statesman and abbot of Corvey (q.v.); b. near the abbey of Corvey in 1098; d. at Butellia in Macedonia July 19, 1158. He received his education in various cloister schools, including that of Corvey; took vows in the abbey of Waussor after being head of the school there; in 1118 he went to the abbey of Stablo-Malmedy (25 m. s. of Aix-la-Chapelle), and in 1130 became its head; he undertook the reformation of the abbey with success; under Lothair (1125–37) he was called to the court and employed in diplomatic missions between king and pope; in 1137 he accompanied the king to Italy, and was chosen abbot of Monte Cassino, but was soon compelled to retire. His influence increased under Conrad III., and his advice was sought on all important matters. After 1146 he purposed to devote himself to his cloister, but in October of the same year was made abbot of Corvey. When Conrad entered upon a crusade, he had his son Heinrich made king and placed him under the tutelage of Wibald. His appointment to Corvey caused opposition there, and even an attempt to murder him. In 1149 he was again sent to Rome, this time with Arnold of Wied; and he was also engaged deeply in the imperial controversies of the time, being part of the time in the field with the army, and often engaged in diplomatic missions to Rome. After the death of Conrad in 1152, Wibald became adviser to Frederick Barbarossa, whom he accompanied in the Italian expedition. He was by him sent on a mission to Constantinople, 1154–55, and a second time in 1157–58; it was on his return from this second mission that he met sudden death, though whether by poison is not made out. In 1159 his remains were taken to Corvey.

His principal and most praiseworthy activities were exercised as the mediator between the Church and the Empire, and his death was followed by adversity to both.

BIBLIOGRAPHY: A part of a collection of letters is preserved and published in the *Bibliotheca rerum Germanorum*, i. 76 sqq., Berlin, 1864. Consult: J. Janssen, *Wibald von Stablo und Corvey*, Münster, 1854; *ADB*, xlii. 298 sqq.

WIBERT OF RAVENNA. See GUIBERT.

WICHERN, vî′cärn, **JOHANN HINRICH:** Founder of the Innere Mission (q.v.); b. at Hamburg Apr. 21, 1808; d. there Apr. 7, 1881. He studied at the gymnasium in his native city and at Göttingen and Berlin. In Berlin he became acquainted with the philanthropists Baron von Kottwitz and Dr. Julius, the latter a physician who advocated prison reform. After his return to Hamburg Wichern immediately plunged into Sunday-school work, which had been founded upon the English model by Pastor Rautenberg. In this way he gained the deepest insight into the desolate condition of the poor, and became convinced that the most abandoned children could be helped only by the erection of an asylum. With this his life-work may be said to have begun. His ideal of such an asylum was to have it resemble a village with small houses in which every child should be recognized and educated according to his individuality; it should harbor a family in different groups, the members of which shared life and work as sisters and brothers, each group being guided by an assistant. A respected syndic of Hamburg, Sieveking, offered him a small house with garden and field, the so-called Rauhe Haus in Horn, a suburb of Hamburg. Hither Wichern removed in 1833 with his mother and his sister Therese, taking into the establishment twelve most unpromising boys. In the day time they were instructed in practical employments, such as tailoring, cleaning, and gardening, and in the evening Wichern taught them reading, writing, arithmetic, singing, and Biblical history. In the course of time one family house was erected after another; girls were also received in special houses. Still more important than his work in behalf of children was his epoch-making education of helpers not only for the education of children, but also for service among the

people in newly opened fields of labor. From year to year the Rauhe Haus became more widely known, more frequently visited, and imitated as a model, and its founder was asked to supply workers. As his personal connections and correspondence became more extended, he edited after 1844 *Die Fliegenden Blätter aus dem Rauhen Hause.* It became the organ of that entire charitable work in the different German Evangelical state churches which received the collective name of Innere Mission (q.v.) in distinction from the mission to the heathen. A famine caused by failures of crops and destructive floods in Upper Silesia in 1848 induced Wichern to extend his charitable activity to that region. With eleven brethren he superintended the care of the sick and especially gathered together destitute children. The lasting fruit of his efforts there was the orphans' home at Warschowitz. Long before the revolution of 1848 Wichern had pointed out the dangers which threatened to arise from the dissatisfaction of the masses and the need of the work of home missions, but had preached to deaf ears. Only after the catastrophe was it possible for him to bring the associations serving the different purposes of home missions into an organic connection. He took the most prominent part in the first German Evangelical church diet (Sept. 21–23, 1848), which powerfully aroused the spirit of repentance and faith and awakened hundreds of brave Evangelicals to new efforts in the renewal of Christian life among the people. In 1852 King Frederic William IV. granted the brethren of the Rauhe Haus the privilege of acting as overseers in the Prussian prison service; and in the following year the Prussian government commissioned Wichern to visit the prisons throughout the monarchy, to investigate their conditions, and to suggest means of correcting existing defects. In this connection he was appointed councilor in the ministry of the interior and a supreme church councilor. In Berlin Wichern founded in 1858 a second institution, the Evangelisches Johannisstift, its work to be along the same general lines as those of the Rauhe Haus.

Among his most noted writings were *Die Innere Mission der deutschen evangelischen Kirche* (Hamburg, 1849); *Die Behandlung der Verbrecher und entlassenen Sträflinge* (1853); *Der Dienst der Frauen in der Kirche* (1858). His *Gesammelte Schriften* appeared in 6 vols., Hamburg, 1901–08.

(H. RAHLENBECK.)

BIBLIOGRAPHY: Biographies have been written by F. Oldenberg, 2 vols., Hamburg, 1882–87; O. Schnizer, Calw, 1904; E. Knodt, Herborn, 1908; and H. Petrich, Hamburg, 1908. Consult also the literature under INNERE MISSION; Schäfer, in *Monatsschrift für Innere Mission*, 1882, pp. 443 sqq., 1894, pp. 489 sqq., 1898, pp. 313 sqq.; P. Schaff, *Germany; its Universities, Theology, and Religion*, chap. xxxviii., Philadelphia, 1857; M. Hennig, *J. H. Wicherns Lebenswerk in seiner Bedeutung für das deutsche Volk*, Hamburg, 1908.

WICKED BIBLE. See BIBLE VERSIONS, B, IV., § 9.

WICKEDNESS: A term which has varied connotations in dogmatics according to its general or individual application. In the former sense it implies the destruction caused by sin in its active aspect (Gen. vi. 5; Ps. xciv. 23; Isa. xiii. 11; Jer. ii.

19) and merits condemnation and death (Jer. xviii. 8; xxxv. 17; Ezek. xviii. 26; xxxiii. 13). Wickedness is essentially the active aspect of sin, and connotes a false tendency of the reason and the will which is persistent and determined in its course (Jer. ix. 3; Rom. i. 29). It is the self-centered pride in which the natural man identifies himself with his sinful impulses (Jer. viii. 6; I Cor. v. 8), and despite its reprehensibility and condemnation (Ps. xciv. 23; Isa. xiii. 11), it is ineradicable (Jer. vi. 7; viii. 6, ix. 3; Nah. iii. 19). Naturally the term " wickedness " can be applied in this sense to individuals, since the sinfulness of each man may be regarded either as particular or general, according as preeminence is given to personal responsibility or to the universal corruption of sin (Wisd. of Sol., ii. 21; I Pet. ii. 1).

As applied to the individual, wickedness connotes unholy delight in the intentional infliction of injury on others (Esther viii. 3; Ps. liv. 5), as well as pride at success in working harm (Matt. xxii. 18; Eph. iv. 31; Col. iii. 8). Ferocity, cruelty, revenge, and calumny are forms in which wickedness is manifested, while destructiveness and malice often receive modifications from it.

The ancient classification of sins as those of ignorance, weakness, and malice, current since St. Augustine, finds its justification in the general concept of wickedness, though it is inadequate. Johann Gerhard divided sins into involuntary, or those committed from ignorance and weakness, and voluntary, or those done with malice prepense. From the point of view of ethical religion, a distinction may be drawn between sins of ignorance and those committed knowingly, the latter being divisible into sins of weakness and of malice, and it is also permissible to distinguish between conscious and unconscious sins as well as between those which are voluntary and such as are involuntary.

(L. Lemme.)

WICKHAM, EDWARD CHARLES: Church of England; b. at Hammersmith (7 m. w. of St. Paul's, London) Dec. 7, 1834. He received his education at Winchester College, and at New College, Oxford (B.A., 1856; M.A., 1859; D.D., 1894); was made deacon in 1857, and priest in 1859; fellow and tutor of New College, 1859–73; Whitehall preacher, 1872–1873; headmaster of Wellington College, 1873–93; dean of Lincoln since 1894; honorary fellow of New College, 1894 to the present time; and select preacher at Oxford, 1866–67, 1883–85, 1896–97, and 1901–03. He has devoted much time to the study of Horace, his labors resulting in *Horace, Works with Commentary and Notes* (2 vols., London, 1874 sqq.), *Opera* (1901), and *Horace for English Readers. Translation* (1903). He is the author also of *Wellington College Sermons* (1887); *Notes and Questions on the Catechism* (1892, latest ed., 1899); *Notes on the Prayer Book* (1895, latest ed., 1902); and *Questions to Hebrews* (1910).

WICKSTEED, PHILIP HENRY: English Unitarian; b. at Leeds, Yorkshire, Oct. 25, 1844. He was educated at University College and at Manchester New College, London (A.B., University of London, 1864), and in 1867 entered the ministry; he held pastorates at Taunton (1867–70), Dukin-

field, near Manchester (1870–74), and Portland Street Chapel, London (1874–87). In 1897 he retired from the ministry, but since 1887 has been a lecturer in the University Extension movement. He has written *Dante* (six sermons; London, 1879); *Alphabet of Economic Science, i.* (1888); *Hendrik Ibsen* (lectures; 1891); *The Religion of Time and the Religion of Eternity* (1899); *Dante and Giovanni del Virgilio* (in collaboration with E. G. Gardner; 1901); *Studies in Theology* (in collaboration with E. Carpenter; 1903); and *The Common Sense of Political Economy* (1910).

WIDOWS IN THE EARLY CHURCH. See Deaconess, I.–II.

WIDUKIND, wid′ū-kind: Monk of Corvey, historian of the Saxons; d. after 973. Of his life it is known only that he was of Saxon origin, that about 940 he entered the famous Saxon Benedictine monastery of Corvey, and that he wrote there his Saxon history. Before he undertook this work, he worked over existing lives of saints, partly in rime, partly in prose, among them *Passio Theclæ virginis* and *Vita Pauli primi eremitæ*, but these compilations are lost. Widukind began his *Rerum gestarum Saxonicarum libri tres* after 962, and dedicated it to the abbess of Quedlinburg Machthild (Matilda), the youthful daughter of Emperor Otto I. The first book begins with the origin of the Saxons, tells of their landing in the country called after them " Saxon-land," their battles with the Thuringians as allies of the Franks, and the conquest of the country. Although the author used some sources as, for instance, Bede's " Church History," he followed almost entirely the popular accounts which he learned from epic songs. His account is fragmentary rather than continuous and detailed. The first book closes with the death of Henry I., king of the Franks and Saxons (936). The second and third book treat the history of the reign of King Otto I. (936–973). For the earlier period, including the history of Henry I., the work has only secondary value; for the time of Otto I. it is of the greatest importance, but the author knows only the events that happened in Saxony and in the immediate neighborhood of the Saxons. Though a monk, he was little interested in the church and ecclesiastical affairs, which he hardly mentions. Perhaps the chief value of the book is that it portrays vividly the views of a sound and sturdy Low Saxon of the middle of the tenth century.

(O. Holder-Egger†.)

Bibliography: The editions of Widukind's work to be noted are M. Frecht, Basel, 1532 (valuable because it prints a lost manuscript); G. Waitz, in *MGH, Script.*, iii (1839), 408–467; and K. A. Kehr, in *Script. rer. Germ.*, 1904 (contains literature on Widukind). Consult: A. Gloel, in *Forschungen zur deutschen Geschichte*, iv. 197–240, Göttingen, 1864; R. Köpke, *Widukind von Korvei*, Berlin, 1867; O. Grund, in *Forschungen zur deutschen Geschichte*, xi (1871), 563–592; J. Raase, *Widukind von Korvei*, Rostock, 1880; C. Bruckner, *Studien zur Geschichte der sächsischen Kaiser*, Basel, 1889; A. Ebert, *Geschichte der Literatur des Mittelalters im Abendlande*, iii. 428–434, Leipsic, 1889; 1889; B. Simson, in *NA*, xv (1890), 565–575; Wattenbach, *DGQ*, i (1904), 363–368; M. Herrmann, *Die Latinität Widukinds von Korvei*, Greifswald, 1907.

WIED, HERMAN VON. See Herman of Wied.

WIEGAND, vî'gant, FRIEDRICH LUDWIG LEONHARD: German Protestant; b. at Hanau (12 m. e. of Frankfort) Oct. 14, 1860. He was educated at the universities of Marburg, Leipsic (Ph.D., 1886), Erlangen, and Göttingen (1879–83); was a member of the faculty of the Lutheran missionary seminary in Leipsic, 1883–87; in 1891 he became privat-docent for church history and Christian archeology at the University of Erlangen, and associate professor in 1899; in 1902 he was called in a similar capacity to Marburg, and since 1907 has been professor of church history at Greifswald. He has written Der Erzengel Michael in der bildenden Kunst (Stuttgart, 1886); De ecclesiæ notione quid Wiclif docuerit (Leipsic, 1891); Eine Wanderung durch die römischen Katakomben (Erlangen, 1893); Das Homilarium Karls des Grossen auf seine ursprüngliche Gestalt hin untersucht (Leipsic, 1897); Erzbischof Odilbert von Mailand über die Taufe (1899); Die Stellung des apostolischen Symbols im kirchlichen Leben des Mittelalters, i. (1899); Agobert von Lyon und die Judenfrage (Erlangen, 1901); Mathurin Veyssière La Croze als Verfasser der ersten deutschen Missionsgeschichte (Gütersloh, 1902); Philipp der Grossmütige als evangelischer Christ (Marburg, 1904); and Das apostolische Symbol im Mittelalter, eine Skizze (Giessen, 1904); and is the editor of Kirchliche Bewegungen der Gegenwart.

WIENER, HAROLD MARCUS: English Jew; b. in London Oct. 28, 1875. He was educated at Gonville and Caius College, Cambridge (B.A., 1897), and in 1901 was called to the bar by the Honorable Society of Lincoln's Inn. He " defends the Mosaic authenticity of the Pentateuchal legislation and attacks the documentary and evolutionary theories of the origin of the Pentateuch." Besides many briefer contributions to Murray's Illustrated Bible Dictionary (London, 1908) and to theological periodicals, among which his " Legislations of Israel and Babylonia " (in the Journal of the Transactions of the Victoria Institute, xli.) deserves special mention, he has written Studies in Biblical Law (London, (1904), Essays in Pentateuchal Criticism (Oberlin, 1909), and The Origin of the Pentateuch (1910).

WIESELER, vî'sel-er, KARL: German Lutheran theologian; b. at Altenzelle, near Celle in Hanover, Feb. 28, 1813; d. at Greifswald Mar. 11, 1883. In 1826 he entered the gymnasium at Salzwedel, in 1831 the University of Göttingen, where in 1836 he became repetent, in 1839 licentiate of theology, lecturing on Old- and New-Testament exegesis, and 1843 associate professor; in 1851 he became professor of Old- and New-Testament exegesis at Kiel; and in 1863 professor of the New Testament at Greifswald. In 1870 he assumed the position also of consistorial councilor at Stettin. Beginning his publications with a prize essay published at Göttingen, 1835, he next wrote Auslegung und Kritik der apokalyptischen Literatur des A. und N. T. (1839). His first principal work is Chronologische Synopsis der vier Evangelien; ein Beitrag zur Apologie der Evangelien und evangelischen Geschichte vom Standpunkte der Voraussetzungslosigkeit (Hamburg, 1843; Eng. transl., Chronology of the Four Gospels, London, 1864). Other works which followed are: Chrono-

logie des apostolischen Zeitalters (Hamburg, 1848); Kommentar über den Brief Pauli an die Galater (1859); Untersuchung über den Hebräerbrief, namentlich seinen Verfasser und seine Leser (2 parts, Kiel, 1860–61); Beiträge zur richtigen Würdigung der Evangelien und der evangelischen Geschichte (Gotha, 1869); Geschichte des Bekenntnisstandes der lutherischen Kirche Pommerns bis zur Einführung der Union (Stettin, 1870); Ueber Römer vii. 7–25 (Greifswald, 1875); Die Christenverfolgungen der Cäsaren bis zum 3. Jahrhundert (1878); and Zur Geschichte der neutestamentlichen Schrift und des Urchristentums (Leipsic, 1880). (O. Zöckler†.)

WIFE-HATER BIBLE. See Bible Versions, B, IV., § 9.

WIGAND, vî'gant, JOHANN: Lutheran theologian; b. at Mansfeld (60 m. s.e. of Brunswick) 1523; d. at Liebemühl (63 m. s.e. of Danzig) Oct. 21, 1587. He studied theology at the University of Wittenberg, where he heard Luther, Melanchthon, and Cruciger. In 1541 he became teacher in the school of St. Lawrence in Nuremberg, but in 1544 returned to Wittenberg in order to complete his studies. In 1546 he became preacher in Mansfeld, and in 1553 at St. Ulrich in Magdeburg, where he was also town superintendent, and took an active part in the theological controversies of the time. With his younger colleague Judex he became one of the most zealous companions of Flacius in his struggle against adiaphorism (see Adiaphora), Majorism (see Major, Georg; Majoristic Controversy), and Synergism (q.v.). In 1560 he went as professor of theology to Jena, where, with Flacius, Judex, and Musæus, he assisted in upholding Lutheran orthodoxy. In August of the same year he was active as one of the recorders in the colloquy between Flacius and Strigel. Though not in entire accord with Flacius, on Nov. 25, 1561, both he and Flacius were deposed because of their antagonism to the Philippists (q.v.). Wigand returned to Magdeburg until, in 1562, John Albrecht and Ulrich of Mecklenburg called him as superintendent to Wismar, but he was recalled by Duke Johannes Wilhelm to Jena in 1568. He again became involved with Flacius in the controversy on hereditary sin and rupture between Flacius and the theologians of Jena followed. Meanwhile Wigand enjoyed the favor of the duke, at whose request he undertook a church and school visitation in Thuringia and accompanied him in 1570 to the Diet of Speyer, but on the death of the duke in 1573, Wigand and Hesshusen were deposed by Elector Augustus. They went to Brunswick, where they were received by Duke Julius and Martin Chemnitz, and Wigand became professor of theology at the University of Königsberg. In 1575 he was elected and consecrated bishop of Pomesania. But a controversy soon broke out between Hesshusen and Wigand because of Hesshusen's statement that Christ is omnipotent, omniscient, etc., not only concretely, but also that the humanity possesses the same attributes. Hesshusen was deposed on May 5, 1577, and Wigand was entrusted with the administration of his bishopric so that he administered two bishoprics until his death. In Prussia not until 1581 were the followers of Hesshusen and those of Wigand reconciled. Wigand had an important part in the compilation of the Magdeburg Centuries. At first he assisted Flacius in his great work and then continued it at Wismar in Mecklenburg together with Judex, Andreas Corvinus, Thomas Holzhüter, and Andreas Schoppen, completing it from the seventh to the sixteenth century. Of his numerous other works may be mentioned: *Catechismi majoris Sidonii refutatio* (Magdeburg, 1550); *Argumenta sacramentariorum refutata* (1557); *Syntagma seu corpus doctrinæ ex Novo Testamento* (1558; in collaboration with Judex); *De adiaphoristicis corruptelis* (1559); *Censura de Victorini declaratione sive potius occultatione errorum* (1562); *De libero arbitrio* (1562); *Errores Majoris* (1563); *Syntagma seu corpus doctrinæ ex Veteri Testamento collectum* (1564); *Argumenta de necessitate bonorum operum refutata* (1565); *De communicatione idiomatum* (1568); *Von der Erbsünde* (1571); *Septem spectra Manichæorum* (1571); *De dicto Joannis: peccatum est anomia* (1574); *Analysis exegeseos sacramentariæ sparsæ in sede Lutheri* (1574); *In Evangelium Johannis explicationes* (1575); *De Servetianismo* (1575); *De sacramentarismo* (1584); *De Osiandrismo* (1586); *De Schwenckfeldismo* (1586 and 1587); *De Manichæismo renovato* (1587). Most of these have now only a historical interest.

(G. KAWERAU.)

BIBLIOGRAPHY: His autobiography was printed in the *Fortgesetzte Sammlung*, 1738, pp. 601–620. The funeral sermon by C. Schlüsselburg was issued, Frankfort, 1591. Other material sources are Schlüsselburg's *Epistolæ clarissimorum theologorum*, 1624; J. Westphal's *Briefsammlung*, ed. C. H. W. Sillem, Hamburg, 1903. Consult: M. Adam, *Vitæ Germanorum theologorum*, pp. 60 sqq., Heidelberg, 1620; C. A. Salig, *Historie der augsburgischen Confession*, i. 639 sqq., iii. 279 sqq., Halle, 1733–35; J. G. Walch, *Religionsstreitigkeiten der evangelisch-lutherischen Kirche*, i. 57 sqq., iv. 100 sqq., Jena, 1733 sqq.; J. G. Planck, *Geschichte des protestantischen Lehrbegriffs*, iv. 195 sqq., 5 vols., Hanover, 1803–09; J. W. Schulte, *Beiträge zur Entstehungsgeschichte der Magdeb. Centurien*, Neisse, 1877; F. X. von Wegele, *Geschichte der deutschen Historiographie*, pp. 328 sqq., Munich, 1885; *ADB*, xlii. 452 sqq.; and the literature under MAGDEBURG CENTURIES.

WIGBERT: First abbot of Fritzlar (32 m. n.e. of Marburg); d. about 746. What little is known of Wigbert's life is largely derived from the account by Servatus Lupus of Ferrières, who compiled his biography at the desire of Abbot Bun of Hersfeld, but seems to have possessed only meager information as he furnishes hardly more than the outlines of the life of his hero. [Wigbert received his education in England at the monasteries of Winbrun and Glaston.] Boniface induced Wigbert to come from England to Germany and entrusted him with the charge of the abbey of Fritzlar, and at a later time transferred him to Ordruff, whence he returned to Fritzlar after a few years to spend the rest of his days. During an invasion of the Saxons his corpse was taken to Buraburg and some years afterward Lullus of Mainz (q.v.) transported it to Hersfeld. Besides these few facts, the biography contains only the usual valueless eulogies of the saint, and a number of miraculous stories. The letters of Boniface contain hardly any more information than the biography, there being mentioned a number of persons named Wigbert, who can not always be differentiated.

(A. HAUCK.)

BIBLIOGRAPHY: The *Vita* is by Servatus Lupus (q.v. for editions of the "works"), reproduced in *ASB*, Aug. iii. 133–137, *ASM*, iii. 1, pp. 671–682, *MGH, Script.*, xv. 1 (1887), 37–43, and *MPL*, cxix. 679–694 (other material, pp. 694–700). The *Miracula* are in *MGH, Script.*, iv (1841), 224–228. Consult: F. Schauerté, *Der heilige Wigbert*, Paderborn, 1895; J. C. F. Bähr, *Geschichte der römischen Literatur im karolingischen Zeitalter*, pp. 228, 456–461, Carlsruhe, 1840; F. Sprotte, *Biographie des . . . Servatus Lupus*, pp. 161 sqq., Regensburg, 1880; A. Ebert, *Geschichte der Literatur des Mittelalters*, ii. 206, Leipsic, 1880; Rettberg, *KD*, i. 593–594; Hauck, *KD*, i. 489–490.

WIGGLESWORTH, MICHAEL: New England divine; b. probably in Yorkshire, England, Oct. 28, 1631; d. at Malden, Mass., June 10, 1705. He was brought to New England, 1638; was graduated from Harvard, 1651; was tutor there, 1652–54; studied theology, and supplied the pulpit of Charleston for the winter of 1653–54; began to preach at Malden in 1655, and was pastor there, 1657–1705. He was kept from officiating personally in the pulpit for about twenty years because of ill-health; during this time he studied medicine and became a skilful physician. In 1686 he resumed his pulpit labors, but continued to practise as a physician. He was the author of *The Day of Doom. A Poem* (Cambridge, 1662, and often; printed again, New York, 1867; contains the famous (unsuccessful) "Reprobate Infants' Plea" against being eternally punished; *A Poem on the Sanctification of Afflictions* (1669); and *Meat out of the Eater* (1670).

BIBLIOGRAPHY: W. B. Sprague, *Annals of the American Pulpit*, i. 143–146, New York, 1859.

WIGRAM, GEORGE VICESIMUS: Plymouth Brother; b. at Walthamstow (5 m. n.e. of London) in 1805; d. in London Jan. 1, 1879. He was the twentieth child of Sir Robert Wigram, one of whose sons became vice-chancellor in the old court of chancery, and another bishop of Rochester. George in 1826 entered at Queen's College, Oxford, with the view of taking orders. As an undergraduate he came in contact with James Harris and Benjamin Wills Newton, both of Exeter College; the three were in 1830 associated with J. N. Darby (q.v.) in the formation of a company of Christians at Plymouth, who separated from the organized churches for "testimony" to the unity of the Church, and to its direction by the Holy Spirit alone, without official rule, while awaiting the Second Advent (see PLYMOUTH BRETHREN). Between 1830 and 1838 Wigram was active in initiation of like "gatherings" at London; also in superintendence of the preparation of Bible Concordances, produced at his expense: The *Englishman's Greek and English Concordance to the New Testament* appeared in 1839, and *The Englishman's Hebrew and Chaldee Concordance* in 1863.

In the years 1845–50 Wigram was prominently concerned in an upheaval which affected Bristol in particular. For several years thenceforth he conducted a periodical entitled *The Present Testimony*. In 1856 he produced a hymnal under the title of *Hymns for the Little Flock*. In 1866, at another critical juncture, he gave his support to Darby when the leader's doctrine introduced further dissension. Wigram will rank as a devotional writer.   E. E. WHITFIELD.

BIBLIOGRAPHY: E. D[ennett], *Memorials of the Ministry of G. V. W.*, 2d ed., London, 1881.

WILBERFORCE, ERNEST ROLAND: Church of England, bishop of Chichester; b. at Brightstone, Newport, Isle of Wight, Jan. 22, 1840; d. at Bembridge (9 m. e. of Newport), Isle of Wight, Sept. 9, 1907. He was educated at Exeter College, Oxford (B.A., 1864); was ordered deacon (1864) and ordained priest (1865); was curate of Cuddesdon (1864–66), and of Lea, Lincolnshire (1866); rector of Middleton-Stony, Oxfordshire (1866–69); vicar of Seaforth, Lancastershire (1873–78); canon of Winchester and warden of the Wilberforce Missionary College, Winchester (1878–82). He was chaplain to his father while bishop of Oxford (1864–69), domestic chaplain to the same prelate while bishop of Winchester (1869–73), and sub-almoner to the queen (1871–82). In 1882 he was consecrated bishop of Newcastle, whence he was translated, in 1895, to the see of Chichester.

WILBERFORCE, SAMUEL: Church of England, bishop of Winchester, father of Ernest Roland Wilberforce (q. v.); b. at Clapham, London, Sept. 7, 1805; killed by a fall from his horse at Abinger (30 m. s.w. of London), Surrey, July 19, 1873. He was a son of the philanthropist William Wilberforce (q.v.), studied at Oriel College, Oxford (B.A., 1826; M.A., 1829; D.D., 1845), and took deacon's orders in 1828. After serving for a year and a half as curate-in-charge of Checkendon, Oxfordshire, he became rector of Brightstone, Isle of Wight, in Jan., 1840. In 1839 he was appointed archdeacon of Surrey, and in 1840 was collated canon of Winchester. At the close of 1840 he resigned Brightstone and accepted the living of Alverstoke, Hampshire. He was appointed chaplain to the prince consort in 1841, sub-almoner to the queen in 1843, dean of Westminster in Mar., 1845, and bishop of Oxford the following October. Within a few months he had completely reorganized his diocese and overcome the unusual difficulties offered by the Oxford movement. He was an indefatigable preacher and a tireless worker in devising and carrying out plans to render the Church more efficient. He established a theological college at Cuddesdon and a training-college for schoolmasters at Culham; was for a time chaplain to the house of lords, and lord high almoner to the queen, 1847–69. He signed the remonstrance against the appointment of Renn Dickson Hampden (q.v.) to the see of Hereford, drew up the address of the bishops calling on John Colenso (q.v.) to resign his bishopric, started the agitation against *Essays and Reviews*, and secured a synodical condemnation of the volume. It was in connection with the famous controversy that he won the nickname of " Soapy Sam " (see ESSAYS AND REVIEWS). Soon after his elevation to the episcopate he became recognized as a power in the house of lords, where he took a prominent part in discussions on social and ecclesiastical matters. It was he who brought about the revival of Convocation (q.v.). In 1869 he was translated to the see of Winchester. By a resolution offered in the upper house of the convocation of Canterbury Feb. 10, 1870, he started the movement for the revision of the Authorized Version, and until his death he presided over the revision of the New Testament.

Though a leader of the High-church party he strongly opposed ritualistic innovations savoring of Romanism. In collaboration with his brother, Robert I. Wilberforce, he wrote. *The Life of William Wilberforce* (5 vols., London, 1838; abridged, 1 vol., 1868), and edited *The Correspondence of William Wilberforce* (2 vols., 1840). Other works are: *Sermons Preached before the University of Oxford* (3 vols., 1839–71); *Agathos, and other Sunday Stories* (1840); *The Rocky Island, and other Parables* (1840); *History of the Protestant Episcopal Church in America* (New York, 1844); *Heroes of Hebrew History* (London, 1870); *Speeches on Missions* (ed. H. Rowley, 1874); and *Sermons Preached on Various Occasions* (ed. J. R. Woodford, 1877).

BIBLIOGRAPHY: The *Life* was written by A. R. Ashwell, vol. i., and R. G. Wilberforce (his son), vols. ii.–iii., London, 1879, revised from the preceding by R. G. Wilberforce, 1888, who also wrote the account in *Leaders of the Church, 1800–1900*, ib. 1907. Consult also the *Reminiscences* of Thomas Mozley, London, 1882; J. B. Mozley's *Letters*, ib. 1885; J. W. Burgon, *Lives of Twelve Good Men*, 2 vols., ib. 1888; H. P. Liddon's *Life of E. B. Pusey*, 4 vols., ib. 1893–97; Mary C. Church, *Life and Letters of Dean Church*, ib. 1894; J. H. Overton, *The Church in England*, vol. ii. passim, ib. 1897; F. W. Cornish, *The English Church in the 19th Century*, 2 parts, passim, ib. 1910; E. Stock, *English Church in the 19th Century*, passim, ib. 1910; *DNB*, lxi. 204–208.

WILBERFORCE, WILLIAM: Statesman and philanthropist, father of the preceding, and leader of England in the abolition of the slave-trade; b. at Hull Aug. 24, 1759; d. at London July 29, 1833. He was of an old and wealthy Yorkshire family, and his father and grandfather were prominent citizens of Hull. He was a delicate child, lost his father at the early age of ten, and then went to live with an uncle, whose wife was deeply imbued with piety of the Whitefieldian type. Fearing that the boy would be made a Methodist, his mother removed him from the aunt's influence after two years, but his religious nature had already received a permanent impress, and the tendency thus induced was strengthened later by association with Isaac Milner (q.v.), who had been one of his first teachers at the Hull grammar-school and was always an intimate friend. For fifty years Wilberforce was accounted the lay leader of the evangelical branch of the English Church. He entered St. John's College, Cambridge, in 1776. Being rich, witty, and fond of society,. courted by his fellows and clever enough to pass examinations with slight effort, he mingled in the world of fashion and made study a secondary thing. On reaching his majority he left college, renounced the mercantile career and large business interests which were his by inheritance from father and grandfather, and determined to enter public life. He was elected to parliament from Hull (after the expenditure of £8,000) in 1780, and thenceforth sat continuously in the house of commons till 1825, when failing strength and illness induced his retirement.

When Wilberforce entered parliament the ministry of Lord North had been in power for ten years, serving virtually as a mere cloak for the direction of public affairs by the king (George III.). Rebellion had been instigated in the American colonies, then combated stubbornly and inefficiently; the country had been involved in war with Holland and France; public expenditures had risen alarmingly. On the other hand, certain of the laws against the Roman Catholics had been repealed, and Clive had founded the English dominion in India, while Warren Hastings was following brilliantly in his footsteps. Though professedly opposed to the North ministry, at first Wilberforce voted with it on certain secondary measures. In 1782 the younger Pitt came into power, and thenceforth, with but brief intervals, stood at the head of affairs till his death in 1806. Pitt and Wilberforce were contemporaries at Cambridge, they became friendly during the parliamentary election of 1780, and soon after they became close and intimate friends. In general Wilberforce supported heartily the liberal and reformatory policy of the minister, especially during the prerevolutionary period. Yet he was never a blind partizan, and at times worked and voted against his friend—notably, he opposed English participation in the war with France in 1793 and succeeding years, and in 1805 supported the impeachment of Lord Melville for financial irregularities as treasurer of the navy. Measures which interested him personally in his earlier parliamentary career concerned reforms in the criminal law and the conduct of elections.

After the session of 1786 Wilberforce retired to the country to meditate and form plans. One outcome was a society for the reformation of manners, known popularly as the " Proclamation Society " from a royal proclamation against vice which the founder secured in June, 1787. The society instituted proceedings against blasphemous and indecent publications, and Wilberforce was long active in its affairs. At this time, furthermore, he enlisted against slavery. It is true that his interest had been aroused earlier; and the agitation against the slave-trade, started by Quakers and others, had already made progress. But the greatest advance yet attained was made when, in 1787, Wilberforce came forward as the parliamentary leader of the cause. Probably no other man in England was so fit for the post. In the struggle which followed and lasted for twenty years he was ably seconded by Pitt, Burke, and Fox. One measure after another aiming at the abolition of the slave-trade (of which England had enjoyed a monopoly since the Peace of Utrecht in 1713) failed to become law because of the opposition of the planters, the West India merchants, and many good people (including the king) who looked upon slavery as a natural and Scriptural institution, not to be lightly interfered with. The questions forced to the front by the French Revolution, with the slave insurrection in St. Domingo in 1791, interposed obstacles during the nineties. But in 1802 a parliament was elected which reflected new conditions and an aroused public opinion. A bill abolishing the slave-trade was passed by both houses of parliament in Feb., 1806, and received the royal assent on Mar. 25 of the same year. The " African Institution " was then founded to see to the enforcement of the law and work for the suppression of the slave-trade in other countries. Through it, by further measures in parliament, by personal appeals and exertions and the expenditure of money,

Wilberforce continued to work for the negro race. He had been one of the founders of the colony of Sierra Leone in 1791. In 1823 he issued an *Appeal to the Religion, Justice, and Humanity of the Inhabitants of the British Empire on Behalf of the Negro Slaves in the West Indies,* which was followed by the formation of the Anti-slavery Society. Three days before his death he had the satisfaction of learning that slavery was abolished in British dominion.

He supported Catholic emancipation and spoke in its favor in parliament in 1813. In the renewal of the charter of the East India Company in the same year, he saw an opportunity to " introduce Christian light into India "; the foundation of the bishopric of Calcutta was the result. In 1815 he spoke for the corn bill. Among the societies which he helped to found, support, and direct were one for " Bettering the Condition of the Poor " (1796), the Church Missionary Society (1798), and the Bible Society (1803). In 1798 he granted an annuity of £400 to Hannah More (whom he had known since 1787) as a help in her good works. He was a conspicuous member of the " Clapham Sect " of Evangelicals. He was ever generous (and not always wise) in the dispensation of charity, and by his gifts and lavish hospitality even impaired his fortune. The position which he won and retained, however, in the hearts and minds of his countrymen was compensation. Personally attractive and winning, broad and quick in sympathy, kindly and simple in life, free from the grossness which disfigured so many public men of his time, he lived respected by friends and foes alike, and at his death was buried in Westminster Abbey. It has been said that he was regarded as " the authorized interpreter of the national conscience." Besides the *Appeal* already mentioned, he published a few speeches and addresses, a book on the slave-trade (1806), and *A Practical View of the Prevailing Religious System of Professed Christians in the Higher and Middle Classes of this Country Contrasted with Real Christianity* (1797). Seventy-five hundred copies of the work last mentioned were sold in six months, and there were fifteen editions in England by 1824 and twenty-five in America. It was translated into French, Italian, Spanish, Dutch, and German. His *Family Prayers* were edited by his son Robert in 1834; his *Correspondence* by R. I. and S. Wilberforce (2 vols., 1840), and his *Private Papers* by A. M. Wilberforce (1897).

BIBLIOGRAPHY: Besides the *Correspondence* and *Private Papers* noted above, the principal source is the *Life* by his sons Robert Isaac and Samuel, 5 vols., London, 1838. Consult further: J. J. Gurney, *Familiar Sketch of Wilberforce,* London, 1838; *Memoirs of the Life of Sir Samuel Romilly,* passim, especially iii. 1–178, 3 vols., ib. 1840; C. Buxton, *Memoirs of Sir Thomas Fowell Buxton,* pp. 117–136 et passim, ib. 1848; H. M. Wheeler, *The Slaves' Champion,* ib. 1860; J. C. Colquhoun, *William Wilberforce, his Friends and Times,* ib. 1867; Sir J. Stephen, *Essays in Ecclesiastical Biography,* ib. 1867; F. Piper, *Lives of the Leaders of our Church Universal,* ed. H. M. Maccracken, pp. 525–533, Philadelphia, 1879; J. Stoughton, *William Wilberforce,* London, 1880 (a good summary); P. Bayne, *Six Christian Biographies,* ib. 1887; C. D. Michael, *The Slave and his Champions,* ib. 1891; J. Telford, *A Sect that moved the World,* ib. 1907; H. M. Butler, *Ten Great and Good Men,* New York, 1909; and much of the literature on slavery.

WILBUR, JOHN: A noted minister of the Society of Friends; b. at Hopkinton, R. I., July 17, 1774; d. there May 1, 1856. He came into prominence in 1838, by opposing Joseph J. Gurney (q.v.), an English minister, who, he claimed, was exalting the letter of the Bible as against the inward light. His own Meeting sustained him, but the New England Yearly Meeting was opposed to him and, to depose him from the ministry, joined his Monthly Meeting to another which had a majority against him. In this manner he was disowned by Friends; but a considerable number of his sympathizers separated from the main body and formed a separate Yearly Meeting which still exists. A number of Meetings in different parts of the United States which held similar views became separated from the larger bodies of Friends about the same time, and have been designated by the name " Wilburite " (see FRIENDS, SOCIETY OF, I., § 7). John Wilbur published certain polemical pamphlets during his life, and his *Journal and Correspondence* appeared after his death (Providence, 1859).

BIBLIOGRAPHY: F. S. Turner, *The Quakers*, pp. 247, 300, 302, London, 1889; *American Church History Series*, xii. 264–272, New York, 1894.

WILDEBOER, vil'de-bōr, GERRIT: Dutch Protestant, Old-Testament scholar; b. at Amsterdam Sept. 9, 1855; d. at Leyden Sept. 4, 1911. He was educated at the University of Leyden (D. D., 1880); was pastor of the Dutch Reformed Church at Heiloo, near Alkmaar (1881–84); became professor of Old-Testament exegesis, literature, and religion at the University of Groningen (1884), where he was rector (1897–98); went to Leyden in a similar capacity (1907). In theology he was " historico-critical, believing in God's particular revelation given to Israel." He wrote *De waarde der syrische Evangeliën van Cureton* (Leyden, 1880); *De profeet Micha en zijne beteekenis voor het verstand der profetie onder Israel* (1884); *De profetie onder Israel in hare grondbeteekenis voor christendom en theologie* (1884); *Het ontstaan van den kanon des Ouden Verbonds* (Groningen, 1889; 4th ed., 1908; Eng. transl. by B. W. Bacon, *The Origin of the Canon of the Old Testament*, London, 1895); *De letterkunde des Ouden Verbonds naar de tijdsorde van haar ontstaan* (1893, 3d. ed., 1903); *Karakter en beginselen van het historisch-kritisch onderzoek des Ouden Verbonds* (Utrecht, 1897); the volumes on Proverbs, Ecclesiastes, and Esther in K. Marti's *Kurzer Handkommentar zum Alten Testament* (Freiburg, 1897–1908); and *Jahvedienst en Volksreligie* (Groningen, 1898).

WILDENSPUCH, vil'den-spūн, CRUCIFIXION, THE: An event which took place in the hamlet of Wildenspuch (about 6 m. s. of Schaffhausen), canton of Zurich, Switzerland, Mar. 15, 1823. The deed is partially explicable from the religious ferment caused quite widely in Europe by several series of events, such as the Napoleonic wars, the German wars for freedom, the lingering effects of the French Revolution, the famine years of 1816–1817, and the celebration of the Reformation, which in the region named took place in 1819. A sort of revival, attended by violent physical convulsions and other like phenomena, involved the district and

induced singular experiences and led to singular beliefs in numbers of cases.

In the hamlet of Wildenspuch, consisting of about twenty houses, lived a well-to-do family named Peter engaged in agriculture, in which there were one son and five daughters, one of the latter married to a shoemaker and farmer named Johannes Moser, of the neighboring village of Oerlingen. The youngest daughter was Margareta, born in 1794, unusually gifted mentally and spiritually, and from an early age very precocious. She became the favorite of the family and neighborhood, and was expected to develop into something extraordinary. She, however, developed chronic phthisis, and seemed destined to an early death. But one day at noon during her illness, while in her father's vineyard, she had a vision of an angel who showed her a herb in a place about an hour distant from her home which was to cure her. She found the herb, distilled from it a tea which she drank, and found herself restored. In thankfulness she dedicated herself to God, became associated with pious persons, attended with her brother-in-law Moser the assemblies of the Herrnhut Brethren, began to preach, and conceived that she had battles with the devil and evil spirits. She came into connection with Barbara Juliana von Kruedener (q.v.), being accompanied by her brother-in-law and her sisters Elizabeth and Susanna, and she came to have the opinion that the events of the period presaged the imminent end of the world.

A new influence upon her at this time was the personality and opinions of Jakob Ganz, a man of lowly birth and moderate equipment, vicar of Embrach in the canton of Zurich, and a preacher of revival type. He had developed the theory that in order to attain blessedness no real change was necessary in man's life, but that there was needed simply a development of the good in man which had been latent but not lost. His watchword was: Not Christ for us, but Christ in us. The Church was Antichrist since Christ had not arisen in it. In each Christian Christ must fight Satan, suffer, die, and rise again. Under this influence Margareta deserted the association of the Brethren and preached at home. In a vision she found herself before the throne of God, saw there the Father and the Spirit surrounded by angels, patriarchs, Elijah, and the apostles; but the Son was not there, and God told her that the Son was to live, suffer, die, and abide in her; she also looked into hell, where she saw thousands of poor souls whom she was to save. Through Ganz a certain melancholic shoemaker named Morf, a married man and a father, was summoned to receive in his house Margareta and her sister Elizabeth, where they remained inactive for a year and a half, while to Morf was revealed that with Margareta he was to enjoy a spiritual love and was to be transported to heaven. The two sisters returned home Jan. 11, 1823, after Margareta had given birth the night before to a daughter by Morf —as Margareta stated, altogether unexpectedly to her, therefore by God's doing. She declared that she must prepare for the great event which was to happen, and therefore undertook no more visits and remained at home inactive. On Mar. 13, she assembled her relations to fight against the devil for the salvation of many lost souls. From morning till night they beat the walls and the floor of the house, crying out epithets against the devil; the next day the same was done, until the house was weakened, parts of partitions fell, and the police interfered. The next day Margareta declared that to complete the victory blood must flow, obtained from her sister a statement of willingness to die, and then smote her sister to death. She told the maid that on the third day she would raise her sister from the dead. The final revelation was to the effect that Margareta must herself die, and she commanded the maid to strike her, which was done with a knife on neck and forehead; Margareta had the blood received in a basin with the words: Now will souls be saved and Satan be overpowered. She then commanded the maid to crucify her, and, when the latter demurred, asked whether she was unwilling to do God's work in order to prevent souls from remaining unsaved. She threw herself on the bed while the maid drove nails through feet, hands, elbows, and breast, Margareta giving no sign of suffering and promising to rise on the third day. The end came when a knife was driven through her head. Until the following Tuesday all awaited the predicted resurrection, when the father reported the death, and all concerned were taken into custody. The authorities made a thorough investigation, punished the participants with terms of imprisonment ranging from six months to sixteen years, and had the house torn down with the command that the spot remain uninhabited.

This strange occurrence has been widely debated and attributed to various causes, including vainglory, spiritual pride, and the like. But the case is better understood as that of a weak and hysterical girl with an extraordinarily active mind, which the religious excitability of the times aroused to unusual conceptions; the effect of the mingling of her own experiences with the doctrine of Ganz, together with the effect of her preaching and the leadership yielded to her by the circle which heard her sufficiently explain the processes by which Margareta Peter was led to her astounding course. It is to be added that the participants in the events received their sentences and punishment in the sense of a martyrdom.

(CARL PESTALOZZI†.)

BIBLIOGRAPHY: J. L. Meyer, *Schwärmerische Grevelscenen . . . in Wildenspuch*, 2d ed., Zurich, 1824; C. E. Jarcke, in J. E. Hitzig's *Annalen der . . . Criminalrechtspflege*, Berlin, 1830, also in Jarcke's *Vermischte Schriften*, vol. ii., Munich, 1839; J. F. von Meyer, in *Blätter für höhere Wahrheit*, v (1824), 282 sqq., vi (1825), 377 sqq.; *Evangelische Kirchenzeitung*, viii (1831), nos. 20–23; and J. Scherr's novel, *Die Gekreuzigte . . . von Wildisbuch*, St. Gall, 1860.

WILFRID (WILFRITH), SAINT: Bishop of York; b. 634; d. at Oundle (70 m. n.n.w. of London), Northamptonshire, Oct. 3 (or 12; cf. Plummer's *Bede*, ii. 328), 709. He was the son of a Northumbrian thane, and was educated at Lindisfarne, where he won esteem by his diligence and manly qualities; after spending a year at Canterbury, he accompanied Benedict Biscop to Rome in 653. He was at Lyons, 655–658, and received the Roman tonsure there from Archbishop Aunemund. Returning to Northumbria about 660, Alchfrid, king of Deira (son of Oswy, king of Northumbria), made him head of the monastery at Ripon in 661. He was ordained priest in 663. In 664 he spoke for the Roman party at the Synod of Whitby (q.v) against Colman and the Celtic party, and prevailed. Alchfrid then secured Wilfrid's election as bishop, with his see at York, where there had been no bishop since the departure of Paulinus (q.v.) in 663. He went to Gaul to be consecrated late in 664 or early in 665, and when he returned, in 666, finding that Oswy had installed Ceadda (q.v.) in his place, retired to Ripon. He performed episcopal functions in Mercia and Kent. In 669 Theodore, archbishop of Canterbury (see THEODORE OF TARSUS), instated him in his bishopric. By upholding Etheldred, queen of Northumbria, in her desire to become a nun, he gained the ill-will of King Egfrid (see ETHELDRED, SAINT). In 678 Egfrid and Theodore undertook to divide his bishopric without consulting him. Wilfrid resisted, and made the first appeal by an Englishman to Rome. On his way thither he spent the winter (678–679) in Frisia, where he preached to the heathen and baptized many. At Rome he attended the synod held in March, 680, against the Monothelite heresy. His appeal was successful; but, when he came back to England, Egfrid put him in prison for nine months, then forced him to flee to Mercia, Wessex, and finally to Sussex (681), the one English kingdom whose people were still heathen. He converted them, after he had relieved their need in a severe famine by teaching them to fish. Later he introduced the Gospel in the Isle of Wight, thus completing the christianization of the English. Meanwhile his rights and claims were wholly ignored in Northumbria. In 686 he was reconciled with Theodore and returned to York. But he quarreled again with the king in 691 and went to Etheldred of Mercia, who made him bishop of Leicester. Again he pleaded his cause at Rome in 704, making the journey thither on foot, notwithstanding his seventy years. He returned to England in 705, and was restored to the bishopric of Hexham and the monastery of Ripon.

Wilfrid's energy in introducing the civilization of the continent caused opposition among the rude Angles and Saxons, while his appeals to Rome aroused political animosities. He was wealthy and lived magnificently, as befitted his station, and thus he incurred envy. His life was troubled, and he has been called haughty and worldly; but there is abundant evidence that his character was lovable. He is described as a singularly attractive youth, and he made warm friends everywhere in his travels; at home his monks and clergy stood by him devotedly, while his missionary zeal, proven in Frisia and South England, is noteworthy. His services to his country and church were great, and he is justly classed among the foremost of English churchmen. He perceived that what was most needful was to introduce the arts and learning; and to this end he labored at the cost of much personal suffering. He had constantly in his retinue masons, glaziers, and other artizans, whom he employed in building churches and monasteries. He gave his cathedral church at York a new roof covered with lead, put glass in its windows, plastered its walls, and ornamented the altar. He built a basilica at Ripon with columns and porches, and a grand church at Hexham. For the former he provided a copy of the Gospels in letters of gold on purple vellum, and placed it in a richly adorned case. He made the church service more seemly and dignified, and reestablished, if he did not introduce, the Benedictine rule in the English monasteries.

BIBLIOGRAPHY: A series of lives of Wilfrid are collected with comment in *The Historians of the Church of York and its Archbishops*, vol. i., pp. xxxi.-xlv., 1–509, ed. J. Raine in *Rolls Series*, no. 73, London, 1879 (these include the life by his friend and disciple, Eddius Stephanus, and the one by Eadmer, q.v., who died 1124, as well as a number of lesser productions); cf. the discussion of Eddius' work by B. W. Wells, in *The English Historical Review*, vi (1891), 535–550. Some facts not given in Eddius are to be found in Bede, *Hist. eccl.*, v. 19 (use Plummer's ed. of Bede, Oxford, 1896, and consult the notes). Consult *Fasti Eboracenses*, ed. W. H. Dixon and J. Raine, i. 55–83, London, 1863; T. Wright, *Biographia Britannica literaria*, i. 164–184, 229, 432–434, London, 1842; F. W. Faber, *Lives of the English Saints: Wilfrid, Bishop of York*, ib. 1844; H. Soames, *Anglo-Saxon Church*, pp. 68–88, 3d. ed., ib. 1856; C. F. de T. Montalembert, *Les Moines d'occident*, iv. 137–390, 5 vols., P ris, 1860–67, Eng. transl., 7 vols., London, 1861–79; W. F. Hook, *Lives of the Archbishops of Canterbury*, vol. i., chap. 4, London, 1860; K. Obser, *Wilfrid der ältere*, Heidelberg, 1884; W. Bright, *Early English Church History*, passim, Oxford, 1897 (important); G. F. Browne, *Theodore and Wilfrith*, London, 1897; A. Streeter, *St. Wilfrid, Archbishop of Canterbury*, ib. 1897; W. Hunt, *The English Church* . . (597–1066), passim, ib. 1899 (also of importance); *DNB*, lxi. 238–242 (gives a discriminating bibliography); *DCB*, iv. 1179–85 (valuable); Milman, *Latin Christianity*, book iv., chaps. 3–4.

WILKINS, GEORGE: Church of Ireland; b. at Dublin July 27, 1858. He was educated at Trinity College, Dublin (B.A., 1880; M.A., 1884), and was ordered deacon in 1891 and ordained priest in 1894; he was made a fellow of his college in 1891, junior dean in 1892, and tutor and junior proctor in 1893. Since 1900 he has been professor of Hebrew in the University of Dublin, where he was classical lecturer and examiner in 1892, divinity lecturer in 1893, and university preacher in 1895. He has written *The Growth of the Homeric Poems* (London, 1885); has contributed the volume on Deuteronomy to *The Temple Bible* (1902); and has edited part of the book of Genesis (chaps. i.-iv., xii.-xv.) in unpointed Hebrew (1909).

WILKINSON, GEORGE HOWARD: Primus of the Scottish Episcopal Church, and bishop of St. Andrews, Dunkeld, and Dunblane; b. at Oswald House, Durham, England, May 12, 1833; d. at Edinburgh Dec. 11, 1907. He was educated at Oriel College, Oxford (B.A., 1855), and was ordered deacon in 1857 and ordained priest in 1858. He was curate of Kensington (1857–59), perpetual curate of Seaham Harbour (1859–63), of Auckland, Durham (1863–67), and of St. Peter's, Great Windmill Street, Westminster (1867–70), and vicar of St. Peter's, Pimlico (1870–83); honorary canon of St. Petroc in Truro Cathedral (1878–83), select preacher at Oxford (1879–81), and proctor of the diocese of London (1880–83). In 1883 he was consecrated bishop of Truro, whence he was translated, in 1893, to the diocese of St. Andrews, Dunkeld, and Dunblane. In 1904 he was chosen primus of the Episcopal Church in Scotland. Among his publications special mention may be made of his *Instructions in the Devotional Life* (London, 1871); *Instructions in the Way of Salvation* (1872); *Lent Lectures* (1873); *Hindrances and Helps to the Deepening of the Spiritual Life among Clergy and People* (1880); *Holy Week and Easter* (1880); "*The Chastening of the Lord*" (1883); *The Communion of Saints: A Help to the Higher Life of Communicants* (1883); *Some Laws in God's Spiritual Kingdom* (1886); *The Heavenly Vision* (1909); and *Invisible Glory, Selected Sermons* (1909).

BIBLIOGRAPHY: A. J. Mason, *Memoir of George Howard Wilkinson*, 2 vols., London and New York, 1909.

WILKINSON, THOMAS EDWARD: Anglican bishop for Northern and Central Europe; b. at Bury St. Edmunds, Suffolk, Dec. 26, 1837. He was educated at Jesus College, Cambridge (B.A., 1859); was ordered deacon in 1861 and ordained priest in 1862; was curate at Cavendish, Suffolk (1861–64), and Rickinghall, Suffolk (1864–70); was consecrated bishop of Zululand in the latter year. He traveled extensively in South Africa, and in 1874 visited the Transvaal, his tour resulting in the creation of a new African diocese. He resigned his see of Zululand in 1876; was rector of Caerhayes, Cornwall (1878–82), was chosen in 1886 to be bishop-coadjutor of London for North and Central Europe, his jurisdiction extending over Norway, Sweden, Denmark, Holland, Belgium, France, Switzerland, Germany, Austria, and Russia. He has also been rector of St. Catherine Coleman, London, since 1886. In addition to preparing a Zulu translation of selections from *Hymns Ancient and Modern* (Natal, 1874), he has written *A Suffolk Boy in East Africa* (London, 1875); *A Lady's Life in Zululand and the Transvaal* (the journal of his late wife; 1876); *Does England wish her Boys and Girls to grow up Atheists and Anarchists?* (1894); *Emigration the true Solution of the Social Question* (1894); *Saat, the Slave Boy of Khartoum* (1898); and *Twenty Years of Continental Work and Travel* (1906).

WILKINSON, WILLIAM CLEAVER: Baptist; b. at Westford, Vt., Oct. 19, 1833. He was educated at the University of Rochester (A.B., 1857) and Rochester Theological Seminary, from which he was graduated in 1859; in the same year he was ordained to the ministry; was pastor of the Second Baptist Church, New Haven, Conn. (1859–61); acting professor of modern languages in the University of Rochester (1863–64); pastor of Mount Auburn Baptist Church, Cincinnati (1865–66), but was compelled by failing health to retire from the ministry, and opened a school at Tarrytown, N. Y.; he was professor of homiletics and pastoral theology in Rochester Theological Seminary (1872–81). He was then engaged in literary work until 1892, when he was appointed to his present position of professor of poetry and criticism in the University of Chicago. He was prominent in the Chautauqua movement, being one of the counselors of the Chautauqua Literary and Scientific Circle and dean of the department of literature and art in the Chautauqua School of Theology. He lectured at Crozer Theological Seminary and Drew Theological Seminary in 1903, and at Baylor University in the following year. Among his writings, which include numerous text-books for Chautauqua courses, special mention may be made of *The Dance of Modern Society* (New York, 1868); *A Free Lance in the Field of Life and Letters* (1874); *The Baptist Principle* (Philadelphia, 1881); *Edwin Arnold as Poetizer and Paganizer* (New York, 1885); *The Epic of Saul* (1889); *The Epic of* *Paul* (1897); *The Epic of Moses* (1905); and *Modern Masters of Pulpit Discourse* (1905); *Good of Life and Other Little Essays* (1910); and *Daniel Webster; a Vindication, and other historical Essays* (1911). His poems have been collected in five volumes (New York, 1909).

WILL, FREEDOM OF THE.

I. Biblical.
II. Historical.
    Classical Antiquity (§ 1).
    Greek Patristics (§ 2).
    Latin Patristics; Pelagian Controversy (§ 3).
    Medieval Catholicism (§ 4).
    The Reformation Period (§ 5).
    Modern Philosophy (§ 6).
    The Nineteenth Century (§ 7).
III. Analysis of the Problem.
    The Nature of Freedom (§ 1).
    The Avoidability of Sin (§ 2).
    Omniscience and Freedom (§ 3).
IV. Supplement.

I. Biblical: The Old Testament as a Biblical theological basis is favorable to the assumption of the freedom of the human will. The will of God always appeals to the autonomy of man. Nothing happens without the divine will (Job vii. 17–21; Isa. xlv. 17–21; Jer. x. 23, xxxi. 18); . on the other hand, the autonomous decision of the human will, whether in relation to enticing sin (Gen. iv. 7) or to grace (Jer. xxix. 13–14), is asserted more frequently and positively. The law makes its appeal to free choice (Deut. xxx. 15 sqq.); the relation of man and God adapts itself to the free inclination of the human heart (Ps. xviii. 26–29). In view of this parallelism striking antitheses and paradoxical symbolisms are inevitable (Ex. xxxiv. 6–7; Hos. xiii.; cf. Deut. xxx., xxxi.; Jer. xviii.). The tradition of the Mosaic idea of hereditary guilt gives way to that of personal accountability (Jer. xxxi.; Ezek. xviii.). A distinction between hereditary guilt and original sin would not resolve the contradiction: because (1) it would exceed the simple Old-Testament representation; (2) the same figures applied to ordinary human weaknesses are also referred to man's proneness to sin; (3) a development of the idea of freedom appears in prophecy (Isa. xxix., xlv.; Jer. xviii.). Western thought first laid open the logical alternative between these two trains of religious and ethical thought series, which lie in the Old Testament in embryo: Is the good such because God wills it or *vice versa?* (Plato.) Must man will the good because God works within him to do so? (Augustine.) Or, is the willing of man good because of voluntary adaptation to the divine will? (Duns Scotus.) This dilemma gave rise to a theological antinomy and became the principal point of controversy between the Roman Catholics and the Protestants; and the cleavage was present already between the free-will Sadducees, the deterministic Essenes, and the Pharisees holding to a general dependence upon divine omnipotence, with free choice to the individual. The synoptical discourses of Jesus emphasize sometimes the moral freedom of the individual (Matt. vii. 24, xii. 27, 37, xix. 14, xxiii. 37); at other times the causal connection of character with education, heredity, or divine descent (Matt. xii. 34, xv. 13, xviii. 7, xxiii. 32). Paul, too, emphasizes the idea of freedom. Although everything good, especially forgiveness, is a gift of God and sanctification the work of God, yet there is the direct appeal (Rom. vi. 12); damnation is just (iii. 7–8), and every one is accountable (II Cor. v. 10). To the contrary is the fact of experience that conduct does not result from perception of the good and corresponding willing (Rom. vii. 20; Gal. v. 17); much less may the natural man sold under sin (Rom. vii. 14) be called free (vii. 23, viii. 7). Grace has broken the bond of sin (vi. 18), but the new state is another servitude (vi. 19), and God performed the act of transformation (iii. 21 sqq.; Eph. ii. 8). The descent of sin according to the law may be traced back to the progenitor of the race (Rom. v. 12 sqq.), and the growth of sin falls into unison with the purpose of grace (v. 20–21). Formal freedom may seem implied at least for the reason (vii. 16); but free deliberation is expressly denied the arbitrament (iii. 19, ix. 20; II Cor. x. 5); and beside the duality of "mind" and "flesh," is pictured the monism of the absolute dependence on God (Rom. xi. 32). The contrast is yet sharper in the Johannine writings. The knowledge of truth and the reception of eternal life depend on the will of the individual (John v. 40, vii. 17; cf. viii. 45–46). I John betrays a strong undertone sounding an appeal to faithfulness and brotherly love, and casually calls for the duty of self-sacrifice (iii. 16). On the other hand, the Christian state of grace appears so exclusively the work of divine omnipotence that the believer is designated as the offspring of God, as the product of a divine "seed," even incapable of sinning (iii. 9, iv. 4–5). The Gospel, too, teaches this dualism (viii. 34, 44, 47). God wills the salvation of all men (II Pet. iii. 9), and voluntary surrender to corruption results in the inevitable doom (ii. 9). On the other side, unbelievers are appointed to stumble (I Pet. ii. 8). The New-Testament doctrine teaches freedom as well as constraint. There is no theoretical contradiction, since there is no thematic discussion, but a multiplicity of particular expressions bear upon the various sides of the problem in the vivid, Oriental symbolical fashion. The individual is now God's planting, offspring, elect, and now self-determining: partly fundamentally one with God, and partly distinct and different. Dualism applies now to the antithesis of God and man, now of God and Satan, and again of good and evil. The only difference between the Old and New Testaments is that in the latter the duty of moral volition and the sense of natural impotence have been intensified (Mark xiii. 37; I Cor. xvi. 13; Gal. v.; Rom. vii.).

II. Historical: The Old Hellenic theory of the will was predominantly deterministic, partly in the metaphysical, religious sense of fate (Heraclitus, the Pythagoreans, and the Eleatics), and partly in the psychological, ethical sense that the will is governed by the degree of understanding (the Socratic school).

Epicurus, in spite of his atomic philosophy and his doctrine of blind fortuity, advocated the sense of
1. Classical Antiquity. freedom, perhaps as a postulate of happiness; and Aristotle consented to the preponderance of free moral practise to mere understanding. The doctrine of the Sophists that man is the measure of all things favored freedom. The Stoics emphasized the independence of man from external influences, but at the same time held to the fixedness of the basic character. The problem how to reconcile freedom and necessity they tried to solve by the use of the Socratic conception of providence and by moral education for voluntary submission to the cosmic purpose. The Neoplatonists distinguished between the servitude of the sensuous life with its imagined freedom and the contemplative transport of the soul to participation in the divine life. Plato taught that virtue uncoerced was free to every one. Whoever chooses it, chooses life, to which he then is attached of necessity; and not God but the individual is responsible for an evil destiny. This became the basis for the predeterminism of Origen. Interesting were the distinctions of Aristotle: (1) between the free and the necessary; (2) the indifferent mean, not perceived as necessity and not taking place by design; (3) the free act under involuntary circumstances; (4) the purpose ripening from rational premeditation; (5) the future subject to decision in contrast with the past as apparently the result of necessity; and (6) in double contrast with necessity the contingent and the free volitional, both involving alternative possibilities. An ascending series is thus formed as follows: (1) necessity to nature, (2) partial freedom, (3) entire freedom but with unripe judgment, and (4) deliberate design with ripened judgment. Enlightened freedom is a goal, only to be reached by practise, and every man is responsible for his own acts. Plato and Aristotle coined the terminology for the future. From the time of Boethius the Christian influence prevails in speculative philosophy. Only the personal God is free; man's reason thinks in terms of temporal change and the human will is complicated with temporal change.

According to the Greek Fathers freedom of will formed the central characteristic of the divine image in man. But between this divine gift of the good and human independence there is only a formal difference: on the one hand, the incipient freedom of choice is to be considered a gift of God by creation, and the goal or complete conscious conformity
2. Greek Patristics. with the divine will, as a purposive human object; on the other hand, the beginning in moral development seems more a matter of human freedom, and the providential consequence more a matter of divine concern. The human subject, exercising the primal gift of God in choosing the good, happens to choose, at the same time, in conformity with the will of the giver, God. According to Chrysostom (q.v.), choice and decision belong to man, the fulfilment to God. According to Clement of Alexandria (q.v.) Adam was only "adapted for virtue," not "perfect"; without free consent there is no salvation; self-determination is the nature of the soul. Cyril of Jerusalem (q.v.) remarks that grace needs a willing-

ness to believe as the stylus requires the hand that writes. Gregory Nazianzen (q.v.) comments on Rom. ix. 16, stating that "not merely human willing" was of more importance than "willing and running." The Antiochians (see ANTIOCH, SCHOOL OF) taught that faith and faithfulness were wholly matters of self-resolution, in spite of the grace of providence. Gregory of Nyssa strongly emphasizes objective purpose as independent volition. Origen's predeterminism, the doctrine of the pretemporal fall, only offers a peculiar expression to the conviction of individual self-determination. The typical representative of extreme indeterminism was Isaac of Antioch (c. 450). According to him the whole struggle of life rests upon freedom; even regeneration is the personal act of man. Man in his freedom ranks higher than the angels and is more free than Satan who lacks the power of execution, although his will is capable of taking up every concept of evil. On the contrary man, by moral dietetics, may intensify his moral power to a godlike perfection. However, this virtue of moral independence, by which man resembles God, is not by nature but grace. The Greek position transmits itself to the Pelagian controversy, except that it blunts the assertion of freedom by emphasis on grace. The analogy of the physician and the free acceptance of his remedies by Origen and Clement returns in Semi-Pelagianism (q.v.).

In the West other motives enter with the Biblical, corresponding to the stern sense of Roman law, the Stoic basic necessity, and the Platonic-Manichean dualism with the consequence of the
3. Latin Patristics; Pelagian Controversy. doctrine of the hereditary corruption of man, of the exclusiveness of grace, and the necessity of a vicarious atonement. The line of thought becomes more soteriological than anthropological. Tertullian (q.v.) admits, beside the omnipotent freedom of God, limited human freedom; but holds that human volition, in so far as it is good, is the work of God. Cyprian (q.v.) accedes that grace is received in proportion to the "capacity of faith" offered by man, but presupposes everything, even the latter, as determined in God's will. Ambrose perceived that the idea of freedom lies in the conception of obedience as well as in that of transgression, but emphasized that the efficient work of redemption demands the initiative of God. The first scientific discussion of the problem of the will within the history of the development of the Christian dogma was occasioned by the Pelagian controversy (see PELAGIUS, PELAGIAN CONTROVERSIES). Pelagius and Celestius were offended by Augustine's formula of prayer: "Give what thou commandest and command what thou wilt"; because of the apparent elimination of all human freedom. The Council at Ephesus (431) consented to the rejection of the Pelagian doctrine according to which man also after the fall retained the capacity to choose the good, since man has kept some commandments while Adam kept none; and without the freedom of good or evil there can be no imputation of guilt. Conscience, it maintained, shows a certain sanctity of the nature made by God, from which issues responsibility. Sin is not nature, for man shall do the good; therefore he can: but it is a

"contingency," which consequently may disappear according as the will decides. Man has a free will, which Pelagius estimated merely as a divine gift, not an ideal factor of the good. In the judgment of Pelagianism, in its first stage, the excess of Augustine should be borne in mind which served as an irritant and was the product of three unsound motives; namely, survivals of Platonism and Stoicism, Manicheistic views, and the overmastering interest of the Church upon his mind. While Pelagius dwells upon the logical side of formal freedom, Augustine naturally takes the religious side of real freedom (power to do good), without, however, keeping clear of the other. Semi-Pelagianism distinguished between the acts, more or less free, of the inclination toward the good; one person seizes with conscious longing the grace not yet effective in him, another is suddenly overtaken and possessed by prevenient grace without his own action. Each is free to resist grace; and no one is (according to Augustine) morally dead, no one (according to Pelagius) morally sound, but all are morally diseased, and as the diseased must turn to the physician, the sinner must, of his own free will, offer himself to grace.

Medieval theology on the whole did not materially advance beyond the patristic state of the problem. According to Bernard of Clairvaux (q.v.), free will remains also after the fall, wretched, to be sure, but intact. Only with volition itself its freedom would cease. "Remove grace, and you have nothing whereby to be saved; remove
4. Medieval free will and you have nothing that
Catholicism. could be saved." Anselm (q.v.) rejects the judgment that the depraved are free only to do evil (Augustine), but censures also the presumption that the freedom to do good was as unbiased as that to do evil. True freedom is a divinely given power to preserve divinely given virtue. Prevenient grace gives the power, subsequent grace aids the will to keep it; but also this will is a gift. Thomas Aquinas (q.v.), in an anti-Pelagian manner, declares, that not only the perfection, but the very beginning of virtue is the work of God. Duns Scotus (q.v.) reverts decidedly to the Pelagian mode of thought. As God the type is free, so also man, his image; it was the purpose of the Creator that man as will should be absolutely free; that the deed only, not the volition, should be subject to external necessity. Willing is the original essence, he teaches, like Schelling and Schopenhauer; to go back further to a causality beyond will, would be absurd. Albert the Great (see ALBERTUS MAGNUS) held that by grace virtue is established in the believer, but the decision whether to follow virtue or its opposite, belongs to the hegemony of the will. The greatest opponent of the nominalistic doctrine of freedom by Duns was the wholly deterministic Thomas Bradwardine (q.v.), seconded by Albert of Halberstadt. The mystics produced the dual consequences, the logical result of such a determinism; namely, that sin is willed of God and therefore not really sin; and that the will of man and the will of God merge into a mystic unity. A revolutionizing influence on the doctrine was the secular philosophy since Descartes, especially of Spinoza, Leibnitz, and Kant. In spite of its new points of view, the pre-

Kantian philosophy does not get beyond the older forms of conceptual construction and analysis of problems. The contentions of Luther
5. The Ref- and Erasmus (q.v.), the synergistic
ormation controversies (see SYNERGISM), and the
Period. variance between Luther and Melanchthon, did not move the problem, inasmuch as the interest was soteriological. Vital for Luther was it, in throwing all weight upon trust in divine grace, to emphasize the impotence of the natural will. Salvation depends wholly upon the will of God. Although this pronouncement of the death of free will prevailed even until the adoption of the Formula of Concord (q.v.), yet the open problem revived from time to time, and in reaction against the hyper-Lutherans, Matthias Flacius and Nikolaus von Amsdorf (qq.v.), the orthodox Lutherans put forth the doctrine of the "foreknowledge of faith," mediating between the demands of faith and the moral consciousness, which if not proof against logical metaphysical objections was yet psychologically true. God predestinated for salvation those whose faith he foresaw. All salvation is of God, but faith conditions its appropriation, and in faith the submission of the will is more essential than the knowledge of grace and of being passively apprehended by it. The Socinians (see SOCINUS, FAUSTUS, SOCINIANS) presented such a combination of omniscience and human freedom, that God seemed like a wise pedagogue not willing to scrutinize free human activity too closely. According to Calvin, omnipotence is absolute. Adam had to succumb to the "hidden decree"; he was free only from external constraint. Also in evil men God effects to will and to do according to his pleasure, and it is inherent in this universal purpose that the large majority should perish to glorify his justice. In order not to make God the author of evil, the Augsburg Confession (q.v.) removed the cause of sins into the "will of evil men, which, if God will not aid, turns from God." The question, why God, by not aiding the will, permits the victory of the evil propensities, remained unanswered. A certain freedom to do good was, however, submitted by postulating "civil justice" over against "spiritual justice." The synergistic controversy gave rise to the opinion that the will might contribute a minimum to salvation. In the later editions of his *Loci* Melanchthon had declared that three causes cooperate in conversion; the Word, the Holy Spirit, and human will, in so far as it does not resist, but assent. The Formula of Concord concluded with a mediating position, that will has a certain "locomotive power" such as going to church to hear the Gospel, but in the reception of grace it is absolutely inactive, since in consequence of universal sinfulness there is left "not even a spark of spiritual powers," so that man from himself and by himself can not even take the offered grace. The only thing that he can do is reject grace.

René Descartes (q.v.) declared that nothing is so evident as the certainty that human thought and action rest upon free will, and that freedom belongs to the nature of the will, since will is nothing else but freedom of choice. This freedom means the non-determination by external [secondary] causes; from the view-point of God, everything must be dependent upon him. Human reason is influenced by will; its judgments are muffled acts of will. Error of reason must be ascribed to the vol-

6. Modern untary affirmation of ideas which are
Philosophy. as yet problematical. The capacity to affirm or deny, however, is merely categorical; the will amenable to reasons is higher. The former, or merely unbiased vacillation between motives, is really lack of freedom since it rests upon deficient power of judgment. Clear insight into the practical enables weaker subjects to independence from passions. Nicolas Malebranche (q.v.) called will the natural inclination of the mind toward the good; it is always without compulsion, spontaneous, but not always capable of indifferently taking the alternative. Impression and motive, receptivity and spontaneity, are respectively identified. Spinoza (q.v.) represented absolute determinism; free will is a delusion due to a failure to comprehend the absolute cause. Leibnitz (q.v.) defines freedom as self-determination in accordance with understanding, the product of which is inclination, not necessity. Free will is to be compared to the magnetic needle obeying its own inherent laws. A freedom of neutrality would not be free will but wilfulness. To apply the law of causation to the will would be to insert in volitional subjectivity a retrogressive infinity. The English and French empiricism of the seventeenth and eighteenth centuries culminated in absolute materialism, most pronounced in the *De la nature* (1744) of J. B. R. Robinet. David Hume, theoretically concerned with a destructive criticism of the idea of causation, acknowledged an antipathy against the judgment that human willing is determined. On the other hand, conduct can not be the necessary resultant of the ego, since the unity of the ego is only concluded from a series of reciprocal functions. The solution is resolved in skepticism: if accidental, then conduct is irrational; if causally determined, then it is not one's own but another's, a thesis which is untenable. Joseph Priestley (q.v.), following David Hartley, represented the physiological determinism, deriving all psychical phenomena from physiological neural antecedents; yet inconsistently he maintained the immortality of the soul. According to Kant, causal necessity issues *a priori* from pure reason, which legislates upon nature. In his practical philosophy, he proceeds to demonstrate that what was before considered freedom, the capability on the part of the empirical ego of alternative choice, was only an apparent freedom. Empirically, as sensual beings belonging to the world of phenomena, men are determined in their future actions the same as everything that is causally determined, because the empirical ego belongs not to the world of reality but of phenomena, which is subject to the *a priori* law of causation. This is predicated of the transcendental ego or soul noumenon, which also affords in practical ethical deductions, by synthetic judgment, the categorical imperative "thou shalt." With this also freedom is absolutely given; "thou canst, for thou shalt." Logically the conscience or moral law is primarily given; but ethically and metaphysically this freedom is the first implication, since by a "practical syllogism" it is deduced as the adequate ground of the moral impera-

tive. Since the time of Kant there is therefore no longer any contradiction between identification with the causal complexity of nature and the consciousness of ethical, religious freedom; and the value and instructiveness of later treatments depend upon their attitude positively or negatively toward Kant's system.

In the philosophical development of the idea of freedom after Kant four different types may be distinguished: (1) According to F. W. J. Schelling (q.v.); *Ueber das Wesen der menschlichen Freiheit*, 1809; 1834), freedom of the will proceeds from the separable coexistence of light and darkness, i.e., from the possibility of good and evil, in distinction from the inseparable divine identity.

7. The From it results the contradiction be-
Nineteenth tween necessity and freedom, as well as
Century. their unity, which is the subordination of the finite to the infinite, and which will resolve the despair of the practical reason by personal recourse in the divine, or the incarnation of God. (2) J. F. Herbart strictly distinguishes between the metaphysical "fiction" of freedom which he denies, and the idea of "inner freedom." Schleiermacher's position approximates that of Herbart, making the will a mode of thought, and freedom independence over against causality as collectivity, without the subordination of effect to cause. (3) The Hegelian school maintained that freedom is implied in the rational will. But more important than formal free will is moral freedom, which, according to the degree of its development and perfection, is determined by the truth of its content; and in its last stage, where it, as the absolute rational knowledge of the absolute rational purpose, is identical with the will of God; where will and its object, volition and duty are one, freedom and necessity are no longer distinct. (4) Arthur Schopenhauer taught that "necessity is the kingdom of nature, freedom the kingdom of grace." Grace comes immediately from outside and has not the least in common with the law of cause and effect. The empirical man can do what he would, but he can not will what he would; he can not change himself; he is determined. Only by the total, radical negation of the will to live, salvation may be attained. This negation, however, does not result from philosophical reflection, but, momentarily, upon an intuitive technical vision; permanently, only upon the miracle of the rupture of the intellect from its root in the will, by means of a transcendental process of supermundane passivity. Refined by Eduard von Hartmann (q.v.) and his adherents, and subjected to thorough criticism by others, Schopenhauer's doctrine has remained the most remarkable type after the time of Hegel. Positivistic naturalism and materialistic historiography have found a psychological counterpart in the deterministic mechanization of the life of the will and the denial of will itself. More recently individual apologists, ushering in a new appreciation of the Fichtian egoism (Liebmann), have revived belief in the freedom of the will, with an unsurpassed intensity; while the school of the consciousness theory and the psychomonism, directly or indirectly, reassert the verity of the sense of freedom. Liebmann teaches that the man is free

who is not diverted by other motives to act contrary to valid maxims, which reminds of Goethe's dictum: "Freedom is the possibility to perform the rational under all circumstances." Such freedom may be proved only individually, by the voice of conscience, repentance, and the sense of responsibility. A. Bolliger teaches that the rational will is a potency transcending time; it is accordingly a reflection and image of the divine freedom. The free act consists in the original act of the representative power of the subject in representing a consequent and antecedent in their causal relation. C. E. Luthardt teaches a formal freedom, consisting in the capability of alternative choice and a real material freedom of the power to execute. Real experience of necessity comes first with the consciousness of sin. All persons begin morally determined in a respective degree and real freedom results with the self-determination of man according to his divinely patterned nature.

III. Analysis of the Problem: The theological interest has as its object how to reconcile with religious faith in the omniscience and omnipotence of divine providence the moral duty to shun evil and the conscious capability to fulfil moral obligation. Cosmic necessity, or divine omnipotence, is apparently in conflict with individual responsibility. God being good and not coercing the ego to sin; therefore man must be free. God being perfectly good, omniscient, and almighty, the origin of sin becomes inexplicable, but if placed in free human will, the omnipotence and omniscience are jeopardized. The plan of salvation presupposes the moral reality and possibility of sinning and at the same time contradicts with the possibility also its reality. If everything depends upon human responsibility, man is too weak to bear the responsibility for the coming of the kingdom of God. If everything depends upon the sole effect of prevenient grace, man's most positive feeling and most sacred certainty, that he is free and that naught is good in the world but to will the good, is delusion. Above all, the sense of guilt would be self-deception. Not only would the origin of evil be an insoluble riddle, but evil itself would be an illusion. While bias lay with the opposite tendency from Augustine to Schopenhauer, the interest of modern psychology, introduced by the methods of Kant and Fichte, swings the balance in favor of the defense of the internal validity of the consciousness of freedom.

In all human action there is an incalculable and incontrollable element that awakens the impression that the action was exempt from the law of cause and effect. This impression is created by the belief in freedom, which is merely negative; but more important is the comparison of different representations of possibilities of conduct in the consciousness of the agent. This capacity of choice subsisting in the sense of spiritual ability and accompanied by the representation of the alternative possibility, is called formal freedom or decision. The moral character is sensible of the impulse to do good by inner necessity, especially when numerous and strong external inducements urge it to the contrary. The more the character is ordered morally,

1. The Nature of Freedom.

i.e., the more the individually necessary is in accord with the universal objective good, the more urgent the bidding of the conscience to pursue the law of the good. The precept "I can" completes and lifts itself with, "I will what I shall." This power to perform the morally necessary that has been willed is called real freedom. The moral will feels free even if it is capable only of the good; i.e., if the alternative possibility is merely hypothetical. The apparent limitation to the necessary good is amply compensated for by the consciousness of mastery. Exemption from, or superiority over, the law of causality, at first but seeming, is now positive reality; the mightiest and most irresistible of all causes is the wholly ethicized will in its constancy. Time may be discounted by a pledge for the future absolutely certain of fulfilment. This consciousness of freedom is a reality of psychological experience which can not be encroached upon by any metaphysical law of causality, which itself is a mere product of the nominative understanding. From this law it only follows that also the human will is part of the universe; man did not create himself; over him rules eternal necessity. But, on the contrary, of everything that is, this part of the universe is the freest. Only the world-ruling and world-creating power has greater freedom than human will, which is not only most efficient, but feels most free when harmoniously obedient to the divine will. As long, therefore, as in consequence of natural imperfection and, still more, in consequence of the proportionate growth of sin and its gross effects, the standpoint of that perfect and conscious self-adaptation to God's universal will and his plan of salvation is not attained by all, nobody has a right to take to account the wisdom and omnipotence of God, for defects which proceed from sin. Sin should and could be avoided; otherwise the consciousness of God would disappear to make way for a debased sense of causal, legal necessity. Its avoidableness follows immediately from the moral consciousness and the ethically qualified faith in God; and its unconditioned presupposition is the elementary consciousness of freedom. In explaining the morally evil, there must be no crossing beyond the boundaries of the conception of the freedom of the will. This derivation, however, suffices, making the idea of the freedom of the will of the utmost significance for dogmatic theology. The question of the origin of sin is no easier of explanation in the time of Adam than now, but is more important within the later ethical, psychological field. The old Evangelical resort of referring it to self-love is scarcely tenable, for Christ places this as the measure of love of neighbor, and it is the basic function of the neutral will, developing later into ethical bloom even to love of God. Will in its freedom is itself the possibility of sin; what is still necessary to its realization lies outside of the sphere of that which can be explained by cause and effect. For actual facts of the will the law of sufficient reason applying to things never suffices, because the innermost value of the personality of one can not be observed by another, not even by self. The best explanation of sin proves to be the psychologically true description after the actual fact. Fundamentally the problem of solution is an individual one in the history of each person, and a universal generalization is impracticable.

The orthodox anti-Pelagian doctrine regards man not only in need of salvation, but also the saved one as being so addicted to original sin that it is permanently inherent throughout the whole life. This doctrine is objectively sustained by the observance of the actual transmission and progress-

2. The Avoidability of Sin. ive propagation of sinful propensities and tendencies and subjectively by the consciousness of the servitude of sin and the exclusive effectiveness of grace. The doctrine is supplemented by the faith confirmed in experience that God is able to utilize also the evil for his purposes. A correlate of this faith is the ineradicable peculiarity of mind to think under the category of cause and effect. It apparently follows that the individual sin is neither avoidable nor condemnable. On the contrary, Kant taught a "causality by freedom" which must be thought as quite different from mechanical causality. The will of man, as self-conscious, self-determining being, is determined by no external power. The Church, too, teaches that God from the beginning gave man freedom and returned it to those who are saved in Christ; and that the servant of sin, and still more the believer, chooses what line of conduct he will follow, so as to attain to respectable character, at least in civil virtues. This doctrine is supplemented by the ideal of a high degree of sterling solidity and godlike-eminence, to be emulated by identification with lofty virtues (cf. Schleiermacher's "perseverance," and Calvin's "gift of perseverance"). The deterministic theology answers that the man in sin "was able if he willed," but he "could not will to be able." This objection may be answered that the divine law is addressed to this very ability, and its truth can be maintained only by the presupposition of the real possibility that man can fulfil the will of God. Only thus can individual responsibility stand. Therefore every past sin, because condemnable, might have been altogether avoided; and every future sin must be judged as condemnable because it is avoidable. Sins not avoidable are at most the "unconscious faults," which, however, do not escape aggregate condemnation. It may next be asked whether specific sinful acts apparently having their setting in the complexity of life were unavoidable, and to what limit the sinful state, which gave rise to specific sins, is condemnable; or more properly whether the antithesis between the avoidable and unavoidable, between responsibility and causal influence, is religious and ethical, psychological and metaphysical, or only philological, esthetic, and pedagogical. The problem affects the theory of "natural selection," and is pertinent to the consequences of the theory of heredity, but is vital to penology and pedagogy, and is determinative in palliation and criticism. From an analysis of social ethics, the fundamental characteristic of freedom, i.e., avoidableness of individual conduct, must be defended on two grounds; because it is a moral duty to respect the independent decision of the will in a fellow man as a particular good, which is preempted from the causal mechanism of nature, and because it is impossible to prove the unavoidableness by the practical calculation of future actions. Experience attests the comparison of different representations of the possibility of an action of which the one executed was in no way accompanied by the consciousness of singularity.

The reconciliation of omniscience and freedom is vital to theology; namely, the fact of being eternally known of God, or how in the creation of the individual he appoints its conditions of development, preforms its character, and imparts a potential self-determination which may divert to hostile conduct and in the aggregate with others challenge his universal plan. The fundamental harmony in the divine will of grace and the aspiration to redemption do not provide a solution; in part, because such aspiration is the work of grace—in part, because grace has a preference, amidst natural differences, for the most fitted for improvement. There thus results a reciprocation between divine determination, which at the same time produces the differences of the tend-

3. Omniscience and Freedom. encies of will and penetrates them in their attitude by omniscience (Isa. xliii. 1, xlv. 3–4), and responsible human self-activity. If this free attitude itself were a work of omnipotence, the value of human personality might be considered problematical. On the threshold of free personality determining omnipotence voluntarily resigns; but not omniscience, the all-effective justice and wisdom. Of extreme theories, the doctrine of predestination annihilates human freedom; the doctrine of total depravity, also of the spiritual nature, deprives the pedagogical effect of providence of its starting-point. On the other hand, the theories which favor the idea of freedom, at the expense of omniscience, also err; like that of the Socinians, R. Rothe, and C. F. Callisen, who maintained that God foresees the various conditions and circumstances subject to which man must act, and he adapts his counsels to man's various possible transactions. J. A. L. Wegscheider (q.v.) proposed that the human spirit rising above the order of things is led to secure its freedom by colliding with the limits of nature divinely appointed. Heinrich Lang (q.v.) maintained that, God being the immanent ground of all being, to be determined by him means to be determined by one's own being, thus representing pantheism of personality. Johann Gerhard (q.v.) correctly says: "God is not the author of the evil tendency of will, but he orders it in harmony with his universal purpose." The fewness of the elect able to perceive this theodicy might bring the plan of providence into question; but the Biblical basis of faith in the final victory of the kingdom of God, or the realization of the universal plan of redemption, is indisputable. While the thought of predestination is repugnant to the feeling of freedom, faith, on the contrary, in the fact of being eternally known by God is not at all disturbing, if only beforehand the truth of the microcosmic feeling of independence is securely implied. As regards the total organism of humanity, providential determination is unassailable. Empirical statistics rises only to a generalization revealing that order prevails in freedom, law amidst free choice, and reason in the causal; it imposes no law of nature or teleological law of reason inevitably upon the individual will. The problem defies solution. Ethics as well as logic evades a psychological deduction, for it is not possible by observation and experiment to dismember the free subject, in order to ascertain what is the active unanalyzable principle in every act of ethical volition or attentive cognition, becoming the more mysterious the more intensively the reflecting subject is itself made the object of inspection. An intellectual perception is precluded. In the free self-disclosure of the soul the individual ego, in and with its freest special existence, knows itself absolutely conditioned by the universal supreme Ego; and no less the fascination of the consciousness of freedom will always remain precisely for the pious heart.   (G. Runze.)

IV. Supplement: The problem of freedom is complicated by two other interests: (1) theological, derived from early Christian thought, involving the reconciliation of omniscience and omnipotence with moral acts; and (2) moral, arising from the conflict of ethical presuppositions with psychology and scientific notions of mechanical causation. For two centuries and a half (1600–1850) in England and America the discussion continued along lines traced above in continental thought. Indeterminism was advocated by S. Clarke (q.v.) in *A Collection of Papers which passed between Dr. Clarke and Mr. Leibnitz* (London, 1717), by T. Reid, who claimed that free will was proved by universal consciousness of active power and of accountability (*Essays on the Active Powers of Man*, 1788), and this general position has been characteristic of Socinian and Arminian writers since that date. The most recent upholder of free will in the interest of a pluralistic universe asserts that "free will means nothing but real novelty;" so pluralism accepts the notion of free will " (W. James, *Some Problems of Philosophy*, New York, 1911; cf. idem, *The Will to Believe*, " The Dilemma of Determinism," pp. 145 sqq., ib. 1897).

Until the last third of the nineteenth century deterministic theories of the will were influenced by Locke, who provided the mold in which the theological considerations of Calvinism as related to the will were run. According to him, the will is always moved by the greatest present uneasiness. Jonathan Edwards held that although the will is guided by the last dictate of the understanding, yet this dictate depends upon the prevailing inclinations, these upon the moral necessity of habits and dispositions, while habits and dispositions in turn are caused by the providential disposing of the sovereign will of God (*Works*, vol. ii., New York, 1830; cf. W. G. T. Shedd, *Calvinism, Pure and Mixed*, ib. 1893). This doctrine received its first serious modification at the hand of N. W. Taylor (q.v.), who sought to guard both divine foreordination and ability to obey God by the formula that moral action is characterized by " certainty with power to the contrary." The sinner can, if he will, and " he can if he won't! " (cf. G. P. Fisher, *Discussions in History and Theology*, p. 313, ib. 1880).

Determinism has received support from a materialistic basis of the mind (cf. J. Priestley, *A Free Discussion of the Doctrine of Materialism*, Birmingham, 1782; H. Maudsley, *Body and Will*, New York, 1884; A. Bain, *Mind and Body*, ib. 1887).

Two other forms of determinism have received wide attention, the first of which has been associated with T. H. Green: one is free in his choices so far as his action is determined by nothing but himself. The man himself and his circumstances being what they are at a stated juncture, the determination of the will is already given—a different determination would require a different man. Choice expresses one's character, interest, attention, motive; action has its roots in character (*Works*, ii. 318 sqq., London, 1893; cf. J. S. Mackenzie, *Manual of Ethics*, p. 94, New York, 1901). The second of these views, in the interest of monistic personal idealism, maintains that every individual will is free so far as its life is unique, in some respect underivable from all other wills, or so far as it is a self and not mere temporal phenomenon and different from the Absolute. It is conceived as an act of attention, occurring only at the moment, never before, never afterward, individual, yet incapable of complete causal explanation (J. Royce, *The World and the Individual*, ii. 337 sqq., New York, 1901; M. W. Calkins, *Persistent Problems of Philosophy*, ib. 1911).   C. A. Beckwith.

Bibliography: Among the works on the history of the doctrine may be named: F. Keller, *Spinoza und Leibniz über Willensfreiheit*, Erlangen, 1847; C. E. Luthardt, *Die Lehre vom freien Willen . . . in ihrer geschichtlichen Entwickelung*, Leipsic, 1863; O. Liebmann, *Ueber den individuellen Beweis für die Freiheit des Willens*, Stuttgart, 1866; H. T. Buckle, *Hist. of Civilization*, new ed., 3 vols., London, 1869; T. Wildauer, *Die Psychologie des Willens bei Sokrates, Platon und Aristoteles*, 2 parts, Innsbruck, 1877–79; W. Gass, *Geschichte der christlichen Ethik*, 3 vols., Berlin, 1881–87; L. Bräutigam, *Leibniz und Herbart, über Willensfreiheit*, Heidelberg, 1882; H. Sidgwick, *Outlines of the History of Ethics*, London, 1886, 2d ed., 1888; J. Martineau, *Types of Ethical Theory*, pt. 2, bk. I., ch. i., §§ 1, 5, 3d ed., Oxford, 1891; idem, *Study of Religion*, bk. III., ch. ii., 2 vols., ib., 1888; H. Alexander, *Theories of Will in the History of Philosophy*, New York, 1898; M. Krieg, *Der Wille und die Freiheit in der neuern Philosophie*, Freiburg, 1898; K. Dunkmann, *Das Problem der Freiheit in der gegenwärtigen Philosophie*, Halle, 1899; J. A. Froehlich, *Freiheit und Notwendigkeit als Element einer einheitlichen Weltanschauung*, Leipsic, 1908; J. Verweyen, *Das Problem der Willensfreiheit in der Scholastik*, Heidelberg, 1909; K. Zickendraht, *Der Streit zwischen Erasmus und Luther über die Willensfreiheit*, Leipsic, 1909.

Works of epochal importance are: The *Ethica* of Aristotle (see the article for editions and translations); Augustine's *De gratia et libero arbitrio*, Eng. transl. in *NPNF*, 1 ser., v. 443 sqq.; Isaac of Antioch, *Prædestinatus;* B. Spinoza, *Die Ethica*, e.g., Leipsic, 1875; D. Hume, *Treatise on Human Nature*, 3 vols., London, 1739–40, ed. Selby-Bigge, Oxford, 1888; J. Edwards, *A Careful and Strict Enquiry into the Modern Prevailing Notions of the Freedom of the Will*, Boston, 1754, new ed., London, 1856 (discussed by J. Dana, *An Examination of Pres. Edwards' Inquiry on Freedom of the Will*, New Haven, 1773; J. Day, *An Examination of Pres. Edwards' Inquiry into the Freedom of the Will*, New Haven, 1821; T. T. Crybace, *An Essay on Moral Freedom*, etc., Edinburgh, 1829; H. P. Tappan, *A Treatise on the Will containing a Review of Edward's " Inquiry, &c.,"* New York, 1839, Glasgow, 1857; A. T. Bledsoe, *An Examination of President Edwards' Inquiry into the Freedom of the Will*, Philadelphia, 1845; W. B. Greene, *Remarks in Refutation of the Treatise of J. Edwards on the Freedom of the Will*, West Brookfield, Mass., 1848; J. G. Stewart, *Freedom of the Will Vindicated; or, Pres. Edwards' Necessarian Theory Refuted*, Glasgow, 1876); G. W. Leibnitz, *Nouveaux essais*, book II., ch. xxi., in *Œuvres philosophiques*, Amsterdam, 1765; J. Priestley, *The Doctrine of Philosophical Necessity*, London, 1777; I. Kant, *Kritik der reinen Vernunft*, Riga, 1781; J. F. Herbart, *Freiheit des menschlichen Willens*, Göttingen 1836; A. Schopenhauer *Die beiden Grund-*

probleme der Ethik, pt. 1, *Ueber die Freiheit der menschlichen Freiheit*, 4th ed., Frankfort, 1891; R. Cudworth, *A Treatise on Freewill*, ed. J. Allen, London, 1838; F. W. J. von Schelling, *Ueber das Wesen der menschlichen Freiheit*, in his *Werke*, Stuttgart, 1856–61; A. Bolliger, *Die Willensfreiheit*, Berlin, 1903.

Discussions from a philosophical or more strictly theological standpoint are: L. Creuzer, *Skeptische Betrachtungen über die Freiheit des Willens*, Giessen, 1793; J. P. Romang, *Willensfreiheit und Determinismus*, Bern, 1835; H. C. W. Sigwart, *Das Problem von der Freiheit und der Unfreiheit des menschlichen Wollens*, Tübingen, 1839; W. Cairns, *Treatise on Moral Freedom*, London, 1844; J. P. Espy, *The Human Will*, Cincinnati, 1860; D. D. Whedon, *The Freedom of the Will*, New York, 1864; T. Hughes, *The Human Will*, London, 1867; P. P. Alexander, *Freedom or Moral Causation*, Edinburgh, 1868, rev. ed., 1875; A. de Gasparin, *La Liberté morale*, 2 vols., Paris, 1868; P. Dupuy, *Du libre arbitre*, Paris, 1870; J. C. Fischer, *Ueber die Freiheit des menschlichen Willens*, 2d ed., Leipsic, 1871; F. W. Otto, *Die Freiheit des Menschen, ihr Wesen und ihre Schränke*, Gütersloh, 1872; F. Körner, *Instinkt und freier Wille*, Leipsic, 1875; W. B. Carpenter, *Principles of Mental Physiology*, §§ 333–339, London, 1876; R. Schellwien, *Der Wille, die Lebensgrundmacht*, Berlin, 1879; L. A. Wiese, *Die Bildung des Willens*, 4th ed., Berlin, 1879; P. Le Blois, *Étude sur la volonté et libre arbitre*, Paris, 1881; G. Renard, *L'Homme est-il libre?* 4th ed., Paris, 1881; L. Michel, *Libre arbitre et liberté*, Paris, 1882; G. H. Schneider, *Der menschliche Wille vom Standpunkte der neueren Entwickelungstheorien*, Berlin, 1882; J. H. Witte, *Ueber die Freiheit des Willens, das sittliche Leben und seine Gesetze*, Bonn, 1882; P. Janet, *La Morale*, Bk. III., ch. vi.–vii., Paris, 1874, Eng. transl., New York, 1883; H. Maudsley, *Body and Will*, London, 1883; A. Fouillée, *La Liberté et le déterminisme*, 2d ed., Paris, 1884; W. G. Ward, *Philosophy of Theism*, 2 vols., London, 1884; G. Friedrich, *Die Krankheiten des Willens*, Munich, 1885, 2d ed., 1886; L. Dieffenbach, *Der menschliche Wille und seine Grundlagen*, Darmstadt, 1886; W. Meyer, *Die Wahlfreiheit des Willens in ihrer Nichtigkeit dargelegt*, Gotha, 1886; G. L. Fonsegrive, *Essai sur le libre arbitre: sa théorie et son histoire*, Paris, 1887, 2d ed., 1896; A. Bain, *Emotions and the Will*, ch. ii., 4th ed., New York, 1887; idem, *Mental and Moral Science*, bk. IV., ch. ii., 3d ed., Aberdeen, 1892; C. F. Heman, *Zur Geschichte der Lehre von der Freiheit des menschlichen Willens*, Leipsic, 1887; O. K. Notowich, *La Liberté de la volonté*, Paris, 1888; N. Kurt, *Willensfreiheit*, Leipsic, 1890; idem, *Die Willensprobleme*, Weimar, 1902; C. Berger, *Das Problem der Willensfreiheit*, Leipsic, 1891; J. Dewey, *Outlines of a Critical Theory of Ethics*, pt. 1, ch. iii., Ann Arbor, 1891; H. C. Hiller, *Against Dogma and Free-Will*, London, 1892; C. Gutberlet, *Die Willensfreiheit und ihre Gegner*, Fulda, 1893; C. Klein, *Die Freiheitslehre des Origenes*, Strasburg, 1894; F. J. Mach, *Die Willensfreiheit des Menschen*, Paderborn, 1894; G. B. Milesi, *La negazione del libero arbitrio*, Milan, 1894; B. Wille, *Philosophie der Befreiung durch das reine Mittel*, Berlin, 1894; W. Baumm, *Die Willensfreiheit*, Kreuzburg, 1895; H. Gayraud, *Saint Thomas et le prédéterminisme*, Paris, 1895; G. Cimbali, *La volontà umana*, 2d ed., Rome, 1897; W. James, *The Will to Believe*, New York, 1897; A. Lovell, *Volo; or the Will*, London, 1897; P. Moriaud, *La Question de la liberté et la conduite humaine*, Paris, 1897; E. W. Scripture, *Thinking, Feeling, Doing*, London, 1897; E. Naville, *Le libre arbitre*, Paris, 1890, 2d ed., 1898; C. Biuso, *Del libero arbitrio*, Florence, 1899; L. Noël, *La Conscience du libre arbitre*, Paris, 1899; J. Rehmke, *Trieb und Wille im menschlichen Handeln*, Langensalza, 1899; D. J. Snider, *The Will and its World*, St. Louis, 1899; T. Gollwitzer, *Plotins Lehre von der Willensfreiheit*, Kempten, 1900; J. Royce, *The World and the Individual*, New York, 1900–01; M. Wentscher, *Das Problem der Willensfreiheit bei Lotze*, Halle, 1901; P. Lapie, *Logique de la volonté*, Paris, 1902; F. Paulhan, *La Volonté*, Paris, 1902; A. Seitz, *Willensfreiheit und moderner psychologischer Determinismus*, Cologne, 1902; A. Marucci, *La Volontà secondo i progressi della biologia e della filosofia*, Rome, 1903; K. Fahrion, *Das Problem der Willensfreiheit*, Heidelberg, 1904; G. Graue, *Selbstbewusstsein und Willensfreiheit*, Berlin, 1904; O. Pfister, *Die Willensfreiheit*, ib., 1904; G. Torres, *Willensfreiheit und wahre Freiheit*, Munich, 1904; W. Windelband, *Ueber Willensfreiheit*, Tübingen,

1904; K. Joël, *Der freie Wille. Eine Entwicklung in Gesprächen*, Munich, 1908; L. Pochhammer, *Zum Problem der Willensfreiheit*, Stuttgart, 1908; R. Beschoren, *Das Problem der Willensfreiheit in theoretischer und praktischer Beziehung*, Hanover, 1910; E. Pfennigsdorf, *Der religiöse Wille. Ein Beitrag zur Psychologie und Praxis der Religion*, Leipsic, 1910; E. Wentscher, *Der Wille. Versuch einer psychologischen Analyse*, Leipsic, 1910; A. Messer, *Das Problem der Willensfreiheit*, Göttingen, 1911; C. Surbled, *La Volonté*, Paris, 1911; the article on PREDESTINATION and the literature under it, as also the articles and bibliographies there referred to; and the works of Windelband, Erdmann, and Ueberweg-Heinze on the history of philosophy.

WILLEHAD: Bishop of Bremen; b. in Northumberland, probably in the third decade of the eighth century; d. at Blexen (about 60 m. w. of Hamburg) Nov. 8, 789. Of Anglo-Saxon descent [and educated at York under Alcuin], after having been consecrated presbyter he left his native country c. 770 to preach the Gospel to the Frisians. He began his missionary activity at Dokkum, the place where Boniface was slain on June 5, 754, where the population was already half Christian. He preferred to break new ground, however; but on entering the county of Hugmerke in East Frisia, his sermons so aroused the rage of the people that he hardly escaped death. In 780 Charlemagne entrusted him with the promulgation of Christianity and the organization of the Church in the extensive territory of Wigmodia on the Lower Weser where the diocese of Bremen later originated. Willehad was successful, but an insurrection of Widukind, duke of the Saxons, in 782, halted his progress. Willehad escaped to Frisia, but several of his assistants and friends were killed, while the converts were forced to relinquish the Christian faith. Then Willehad, together with St. Liudger (q.v.), who until that time had labored in Dokkum, undertook a journey to Rome. After his return to Germany, Willehad settled at Echternach near Treves, where he lived the life of a monk, occupied with literary works. After the baptism of Widukind in 785 Willehad resumed his missionary activity at the Lower Weser. On July 13, 787, he was consecrated bishop, and Bremen became the seat of the bishopric. During his life Willehad was credited with doing miracles, and after his death his remains were believed still to be efficacious in that direction.

(A. HAUCK.)

BIBLIOGRAPHY: The *Vita et miracula* by Ansgar was first published, ed. P. Cæsar, at Cologne, 1642, is abbreviated in *ASM*, iii. 2, pp. 404–418, and in *MPL*, cxviii. 1013–32, better in *MGH., Script.*, ii (1829), 378–390 (Germ. transl., *Lebensbeschreibungen des heiligen . . . Willehads*, Leipsic, 1888); cf. *MGH. Script.* vii (1846), 267 sqq. Consult: A. Tappehorn, *Das Leben des heiligen Willehad*, Dülmen, 1901; W. Wright, *Biographia Britannia*, i. 345–349, London, 1842; G. H. Klippel, *Lebensbeschreibung des Erzbischofs Ansgar*, Bremen, 1845; G. Dehio, *Geschichte des Erzbisthums Hamburg-Bremen*, i. 51, 52, 55 sqq., vol. iii., Berlin, 1877; A. Ebert, *Geschichte der Literatur des Mittelalters*, ii. 340–341, Leipsic, 1880; W. von Bippen, *Aus Bremens Vorzeit*, pp. 1–14, Bremen, 1885; J. F. Wolf, *Sanct Willehad*, Breslau, 1889; Rettberg, *KD*, ii. 450–455, 537; Hauck, *KD*, ii. 350 sqq.

WILLIAM OF CHAMPEAUX: Schoolman and bishop of Châlons; b. at Champeaux (near Melun, 26 m. s.e. of Paris) 1070; d. 1121. He enjoyed the instruction of the philosopher Manegold, of Ansellus of Laon, and of Roscellin; became teacher of dialectics and rhetoric at Notre Dame in Paris; enjoyed the esteem of Louis VI., and became archdeacon of the diocese of Paris. Abelard (q.v., I., § 1) was for a time his pupil, but later caused him no little annoyance. He attacked one of the main theses of William and forced him to give it up and attack it even himself. By this William, if the account of Abelard is to be credited, lost his reputation among the schoolmen so that almost all his pupils left him and he retired altogether from his activity as teacher. He then joined the communion of the regulars of St. Victor who beside their principal seat in Marseilles possessed a small settlement in Paris. Here William resumed his activity as teacher, swayed by the requests of students, and lectured especially on theology from 1110 to 1113. In 1113 he was elected bishop of Châlons.

It was to the first period of his life that the few literary remains of this author belong. It is probable that the *De origine animæ* and *Dialogus . . . cuiusdam Christiani et Judæi de fide Catholica* (*MPL*, clxiii. 1039–1040, 1043–1045) are not his. Forty-seven fragments of his are collected in Lefèvre (see bibliography). These deal with theological questions only, so that nothing is given of the philosophical views connected with William's name, for which Abelard is the authority. William, according to Abelard, had asserted that the same thing in its entirety could be essentially in different individuals, there being no diversity in essence but variety only in the multitude of accidents; but Abelard had objected that if the whole humanity were in Socrates and in the same way also in Plato, it would be impossible for Socrates to be in Rome and Plato in Greece. From William's change of opinion it is evident that he had not the ability to discuss difficult questions in a thorough and convincing manner. The same appears in the theological fragments. Here, too, he avoids the discussion of difficult questions and appeals to faith or to the superior knowledge of God. Yet some ability must be granted him in order to explain the demands of his pupils that he continue his work as a teacher.   (S. M. DEUTSCH†.)

BIBLIOGRAPHY: *Hist. littéraire de la France*, x. 307–316; G. A. Patru, *Wilhelmi Campallensis de natura et de origine rerum placita*, Paris, 1847; C. Prantl, *Geschichte der Logik im Abendland*, ii. 128–131, Leipsic 1861; E. Michaud, *Guillaume de Champeaux et les écoles de Paris*, 2d ed., Paris, 1868; B. Hauréau, *Hist. de la philosophie scolastique*, i. 320–344, ib., 1872; G. Lefèvre, in *Travaux et mémoires de l'université de Lille*, 1898; A. Sabatier, in *Revue chrétienne*, xv. 721 sqq.; Lichtenberger, *ESR*, v. 786–788; *KL*, xii. 1599.

WILLIAM OF CONCHES: Philosopher of the twelfth century; b. at Conches (64 m. w. of Paris) toward the end of the eleventh century; d. at Paris about 1154. He taught at Chartres in the school of Bernhard Sylvester, where one of his pupils was John of Salisbury (q.v.), who calls him a grammarian. His works, however, show that he was interested especially in questions of natural philosophy. He was not a theologian. He held to the older Platonic views of the universe, applying these to the problems of natural philosophy. William of Thierry denounced him before St. Bernhard for holding certain heresies—the assumption of a world soul, the Sabellian doctrine of the Trinity, the doctrine of demons, and the creation of Eve. William thereupon wrote his *Dragmaticon*, clothing his earlier views in the dress of a dialogue.

The school of Chartres pursued a tendency other than Abelard's; it was not concerned with the dialectical reconciliation of reason and faith, but with the increase of human knowledge and the perception of verity. Bernhard Sylvester's *De mundi universitate* breathes the same spirit, and William of Conches followed this path. Philosophy, according to him, comprehends everything. Like Plato, he tries to understand the universe from God down to man by way of pure knowledge, following not the Church Fathers but the philosophers and physicists. Like Abelard, he submits to the authority of Scripture, but finds no contradiction with Scripture, if one expounds what the Bible affirms. According to his system, the basis of the world is God as creative power, wisdom, and will. The saints apply these three terms to three persons, designating power as God the Father, wisdom as God the Son, and will as the Holy Spirit. The divine power would have sufficed to deliver man from the power of Satan, but God willed that his wisdom should become man, since in this way the divinity was concealed from the devil, and he laid hands on it, thus forfeiting his power over man. In connection with the universe the wisdom and power of God are revealed, but its origin and continuance William explains as purely natural processes. The corporeal world is composed of the elements which are in all things, but according to the preponderance of certain elements there originates matter or the elementary bodies, earth, water, air, and fire. The fiery bodies of the stars moved and warmed the air and through it the water. From the heated water proceeded the birds and fishes. Land originated from the absorption of humidity by the heat. From the heated mud of the earth proceeded the animals and man. The bodies of the universe are in constant movement, the firmament, i.e., the sky with its fixed stars, moving in the opposite direction of the planets, since otherwise the movement of the latter would be too violent. The earth is a sphere, since otherwise the time of the day would be the same everywhere and the same stars ought to be visible everywhere. The relation of the earth to the sun causes the change in seasons. Man consists of body and soul. The soul is the purely spiritual capacity of discerning and reasoning which is peculiar to man. From this spiritual soul are to be distinguished the natural powers, the spiritual and animal powers which move up and down in the arteries and nerves. The proper seat of the spiritual power is the heart, while the animal power is located in the brain. In general, William follows the *Timæus* of Plato, but he amplifies and modifies the views of Plato according to the learned tradition of the early Middle Ages, and makes use also of the works of Constantine the African.

The following works of William are extant: *Quatuor libri de elementis philosophiæ* or *De philosophia mundi* (printed in Bede's *Opera*, ii. 311–343, Basel, 1563; in the *Maxima bibliotheca patrum*, xx. 995–1020, as the work of Honorius Augustodunensis; and as the work of William of Hirschau under the title, *Philosophicarum et astronomicarum institutionum Guilielmi Hirsgauiensis olim abbatis*, Basel, 1531); *Dragmaticon philosophiæ*, printed with the title, *Dialogus de substantiis physicis confectus a Wilhelmo*

Aneponymo philosopho (Strasburg, 1567); glossary on the *Timæus* of Plato, preserved in manuscript; a commentary on the *De consolatione philosophiæ* of Boëtius, preserved only in manuscript. The authenticity of other works attributed to William is not beyond question. (R. SEEBERG.)

BIBLIOGRAPHY: *Hist. littéraire de la France*, vol. xii.; A. Charma, *Guillaume de Conches*, Paris, 1857; B. Hauréau, *Singularités historiques et littéraires*, ib. 1861; C. Prantl, *Geschichte der Logik im Abendland*, ii. 127 sqq., Leipsic, 1861; C. Werner, *Die Kosmologie . . . des Mittelalters mit . . . Beziehung auf Wilhelm von Conches*, in the *Sitzungsberichte* of the Vienna Academy, philosophical-historical class, lxxv (1873), 309–403; H. Reuter, *Geschichte der Aufklärung im Mittelalter*, ii. 6 sqq., Berlin, 1877; O. Zöckler, *Geschichte der Beziehungen zwischen Theologie und Naturwissenschaft*, i. 411–412, Gütersloh, 1877; R. L. Poole, *Illustrations of the Hist. of Medieval Thought*, pp. 124 sqq., London, 1884; *DNB*, lxi. 355–356; *KL*, xii. 1599–1602.

WILLIAM OF HIRSCHAU. See HIRSCHAU.

WILLIAM OF MALMESBURY: English historian; b. in the south or the west of England about 1090; d. at Malmesbury (38 m. n.w. of Salisbury) after 1142. He was brought up from childhood in Malmesbury Abbey, became a monk there, also librarian and precentor, and in all probability spent his whole life in that abbey except for a possible brief period during which he may have lived at Glastonbury. He became interested at an early age in the study of history; the perusal of the story of other nations made him dissatisfied with what was accessible on his own, and so he was led to the composition of the works on the history of England which have made his name famous. His principal works are *Gesta regum Anglorum*, with its sequel *Historia novella*, and *Gesta pontificum Anglorum*. The first writing of the first and third of these was finished by 1125, but between 1135 and 1140 he twice revised the first. The *Gesta regum Anglorum* begins at the beginning of English history, and in the revised form comes down to 1127–28. The materials have value from two points of view—as a "step forward in the working out of historiography," and in the "illustrations of character and of the foreign relations" of the period. Much of anecdote is interspersed, showing the writer's power as a narrator, but not adding to the historical worth of his work. The *Historia novella* continues the work just characterized, bringing it down to 1142, and holds a high place as a source for the history of the reign of Stephen. The *Gesta pontificum Anglorum* is also of high importance, being a basis for the early ecclesiastical history of England. Other works are: *Vita S. Dunstani; Vita S. Wulfstani; De antiquitate Glanstoniensis ecclesiæ*; and collections of historical and legal material still extant in manuscript.

BIBLIOGRAPHY: The two editions of the *Gesta regum Anglorum* and *Historia novella* which are of importance are by W. Stubbs, in the *Rolls Series*, 2 vols., London, 1887–1889, and by T. D. Hardy, for the *English Historical Society*, 2 vols., London, 1840; the prefaces and prolegomena to both these editions are of value for the life, and that of Stubbs for the inclusion of minor works or of selections from minor works of William. English translations of the *Gesta* are by J. Sharpe, *The History of the Kings of England* . . . , London, 1815; J. A. Giles, in *Bohn's Antiquarian Library*, ib. 1847; and by J. Stevenson, *Church Historians of England*, vol. iii., part 1, ib. 1854. Of the *Gesta pontificum* the best ed. is that by N. E. S. A. Hamilton in the *Rolls Series*, London, 1870, based on the author's autograph. The *Vita S. Dunstani*, ed. W. Stubbs, is in *Memorials of St. Dunstan, Rolls Series*, London, 1874. For the life and estimate of the works the reader is referred first of all to the prefaces of the editions named above. Consult further: W. de Gray Birch, *Life and Writings of William of Malmesbury*, London, 1874; T. Wright, *Biographia Britannica literaria*, ii. 134–142, ib. 1846; Kate Norgate, *England under the Angevin Kings*, i. 183–193, ib. 1887; *DNB*, lxi. 351–354; Gross, *Sources*, consult Index; Potthast, *Wegweiser*, pp. 557–558; Lichtenberger, *ESR*, v. 788–789; *KL*, xii. 1611–12.

WILLIAM OF NEWBURGH: English historian; b. at Bridlington (37 m. n.e. of York) between Dec. 26, 1135, and Dec. 25, 1136; d. at Newburgh (near Coxwold, 16 m. n. of York) after May, 1198. He was educated as an Augustinian oblate at Newburgh, where he ultimately became canon and spent his life. He was the author of a commentary on the Song of Solomon (preserved in manuscript at Cambridge), three sermons (ed. with the following by T. Hearne, Oxford, 1719), and especially of *Historia rerum Anglicarum* (ed. T. Hearne, 3 vols., Oxford, 1719; H. C. Hamilton, for the English Historical Society, 2 vols., London, 1856; and R. Howlett, in *Chronicles of the Reigns of Stephen, Henry II., and Richard I.*, i. 1–408, ii. 409–583, in *Rolls Series*, 2 vols., London, 1884–85; Eng. transl. by J. Stevenson, in *Church Historians of England*, vol. iv., part 2, 297–672, London, 1856). The latter work, which has established William's fame as the first critical historian of Europe, was begun probably in 1196. It depends for its material upon Simeon of Durham, Henry of Huntingdon, and other earlier chroniclers, but displays excellence of judgment, good taste, and force and elegance of style. The period covered is 1066–1198. While the work is not exact either in dates or in statements of fact, it is noteworthy as being philosophical, and especially as so leading in criticism as to warrant Freeman's calling the author the "father of historical criticism." This last characteristic is exemplified by the criticism of Geoffry of Monmouth. (H. BÖHMER.)

BIBLIOGRAPHY: Consult the prolegomena or prefaces to the editions named above, particularly that of Howlett; T. Wright, *Biographia Britannica literaria*, ii. 407–410, London, 1846; *DNB*, lxi. 360–363 (excellent); Gross, *Sources*, p. 298; Potthast, *Wegweiser*, p. 559; *KL*, xii. 1613–14.

WILLIAM OF NORWICH: According to tradition, the victim of a ritual murder committed by Jews; b. probably at Haveringland (9 m. n. of Norwich), Norfolk, Feb. 2, 1132 or 1133; murdered in Norwich Mar., 1144. When eight years old, he was apprenticed to a skinner at Norwich who came in frequent commercial relations with local Jews. According to tradition, the child was enticed away Mar. 20, 1144 (the Monday in Holy Week) by a man alleging himself to be the cook of the archdeacon of Norwich, was seen to enter the house of a Jew, and was there murdered, the body being kept in the house, despite the fact that it was Passover tide, until Good Friday, when it was hung by stealth on a tree near the city. The corpse was found on Easter Eve, and was buried the following Monday without religious rites. On Tuesday it was identified, and a priest of the city accused the Jews of the murder. The belief of both clergy and laity was long divided on the question, but ultimately, through the influence of William Turbe, who became bishop of Norwich in 1146, the fact of the child's martyrdom became an established belief. His body was translated to the monastery cemetery, and finally to the cathedral, where it ultimately had a special altar, forming a center of pilgrimage until the middle of the fifteenth century.

·The traditions connected with William of Norwich, considerably amplified in course of time, are particularly interesting as being, whatever their true basis may be, the earliest known instance of the blood accusation against the Jews for ritual murder.
BIBLIOGRAPHY: The one authority is Thomas of Monmouth, *The Life and Miracles of St. William of Norwich*, ed. with transl. by A. Jessopp and M. R. James, Cambridge, 1896 (compiled by a monk of Norwich, 1172–73; it is valuable otherwise for the light it throws on English religious life n those times). Consult also J. Jacobs, *Jews of Angevin England*, pp. 19–21, 256–258, London, 1893; *DNB*, lxi. 354–355; *JE*, xii. 524.

WILLIAM OF OCCAM. See OCCAM (OCKHAM), WILLIAM OF.

WILLIAM OF SAINT AMOUR: Professor at the Sorbonne, opponent of the mendicant orders; b. possibly at St. Amour (200 m. s.e. of Paris) about the middle of the thirteenth century; d. at Paris about 1272. About 1250 he was teacher of theology at the University of Paris, which he defended against the encroachments of the Dominicans and Franciscans. The university was then at the height of its fame, numbered thousands of students, and was a power in the state. It was therefore coveted by the monks who were aided by the pope; but the university, the existence of which was threatened, issued an energetic appeal to all bishops. Innocent IV. was convinced that he ought to interfere, and in a bull of 1254 guarded the privileges of the secular clergy and the bishops. He died, however, fourteen days afterward, and the friars avenged themselves by representing this sudden death as a judgment of God. They were protected by Alexander IV., the successor of Innocent, and also by King Louis IX.; but the university was in no way willing to give up the struggle, finding a brilliant protagonist in William of St. Amour. With caustic satire he opened his campaign against the "pappelards," as he called the monks. His wit and humorous style won him the favor of the public; the bishops, whose privileges were also in danger, secretly took his side. In 1256 William wrote his witty and biting *Tractatus brevis de periculis novissimorum temporum, Opera Const.* (Paris, 1632), in which he applied the utterances of Christ against the Pharisees to the monks, the effects of which lasted for 300 years. But he had powerful opponents in the Dominican Thomas Aquinas and the Franciscan Bonaventura (qq.v.). His cause was tried before the pope in Anagni; the mendicant friars gained a complete victory, and William's writing was burned. The opposition of the university was broken for a long time. Only after the death of Alexander IV., in 1263, was William allowed to return to Paris and resume his lectures. Besides the work mentioned above he wrote *Liber de Antichristo et ejusdem ministris.* (C. PFENDER).

BIBLIOGRAPHY: *Hist. littéraire de la France*, xix. 197 sqq., xxi. 468 sqq.; C. E. Du Boulay, *Historia universitatis Parisiensis*, vol. iii., Paris, 1666; Le Nain de Tillemont, *Vie de St. Louis*, vi. 143 sqq., ib. 1851; Corneille St. Marc, *Étude sur Guillaume de S. Amour*, Lons-le-Saunier, 1865;

H. Denifle, *Chartularium universitatis Parisiensis*, vol. i., Paris, 1889; Neander, *Christian Church*, iv. 282–288 et passim; Lichtenberger, *ESR*, v. 786–788; *KL*, xii. 1580–1586. The reader may also consult the *Opusculum contra impugnantes dei cultum et religionem* of Thomas Aquinas, and Bonaventura's *Libellus apologeticus in eos qui ordini fratrum minorum advertantur*, and his *De paupertate Christi.*

WILLIAM II. OF TYRE: Archbishop of that city; b. in Jerusalem c. 1128; d. at Tyre between Oct. 17 and 21, 1186. His earlier education was received in Jerusalem; but when he was thirty years of age or older he studied in France (probably) and very likely in Paris, then the seat of learning in the West (see WILLIAM OF ST. AMOUR). After his return to the Holy Land in 1163 he became leading cleric in the cathedral at Tyre, and in 1167 was archdeacon. In 1168 he went on a diplomatic mission for King Amalric to the Emperor Manuel, and the next year was in Rome. On his return he had charge of the education of Amalric's son and heir, who succeeded his father in 1173, and the next year made William his chancellor, while in 1175 William became archbishop of Tyre, thus being in charge of the weightiest matters in Church and State. In 1179 he attended the Lateran Council and was then engaged in diplomatic matters with the emperor, returning home in 1180. His importance ceased with the accession of Baldwin IV. in 1185.

William himself reports that he wrote an account of the Lateran Council which he attended, also a *Historia* or *Gesta orientalium principum* dealing with the times after Mohammed till 1184; both these are lost. His great work is a *Historia rerum in partibus transmarinis gestarum* in twenty-three books (editions published at Basel, 1564, 1583; in Bongar, *Gesta Dei per Francos*, i. 625–1046, Hanover, 1611; and in *Recueil des historiens des croisades, Historiens occidentaux*, vol. i., Paris, 1844), but of the last book he finished only the first chapter, coming down to 1184; indeed he had not completed all of the preceding books. The work begins with the conquest of Syria by Omar, but passes in eleven chapters of the first books to the events which brought about the first crusade. The first fifteen books rest upon Latin sources which the author does not name; the other books have considerable value as a source. The work gained great repute, and was widely diffused through an early French translation, of which various continuations were made, partly anonymous and partly under the name of Ernoul, and of others. A part circulated also in Latin translation.

(O. HOLDER-EGGER†.)

BIBLIOGRAPHY: *Hist. littéraire de la France*, xiv. 587–596; J. F. Michaud, *Bibliothèque des croisades*, ii. 555–582, Paris, 1829; B. Kugler, *Geschichte des zweitens Kreuzzuges*, pp. 21 sqq., Stuttgart, 1866; H. Hagenemayer, *Peter der Eremite*, pp. 4–7, 10, et passim, Leipsic, 1879; H. von Sybel, *Geschichte des ersten Kreuzzuges*, pp. 108 sqq., Leipsic, 1881; H. Prutz, *Kulturgeschichte der Kreuzzüge*, pp. 458–469, Berlin, 1883; idem, in *NA*, viii (1883), 91–132; R. Röhricht, *Geschichte des königsreichs Jerusalem*, Innsbruck, 1898. Cf. the extended bibliography in Potthast, *Wegweiser*, pp. 560–562.

WILLIAM OF WYKEHAM (WICKWANE, WYCKEHAM): Bishop of Winchester; b. at Wykeham (13 m. s.e. of Winchester), England, in the summer of 1324; d. at South Waltham Sept. 24, 1404. He was educated at Winchester; and in 1356 was surveyor of King Edward III.'s works at Windsor, and was rewarded for his merit by the gift of the rectory of Pulham, Norfolk, 1357, by a prebendary's stall at Lichfield, 1359, and by the deanery of St. Martin-le-Grand, 1360. He was ordained acolyte, 1361, and priest, 1362, and held a great number of prebends 1361-62. Resigning Pulham in 1361, he exchanged the canonry of Lichfield for that at Southwell. In 1364 he was made keeper of the privy seal; secretary to the king, 1365; bishop of Winchester, 1367; and was chancellor, 1367-71. In 1369 he began the work which developed into New College at Oxford, completed, 1386; and in 1378 was engaged in founding St. Mary College of Winchester, completed 1394. In 1376 he was accused of malfeasance in office, and deprived of the temporalities of his see. But his rectitude was subsequently established, and Richard II. restored him to his offices and dignities, 1379, and he was again chancellor, 1389-1391, but from 1391 kept aloof from politics. He rebuilt Winchester Cathedral, 1395-1405. He was the author of *W. de Wycumba libri duo de vita R. Betun episcopi Herefordensis*, with *Vita* by T. Chaundler, published in H. Wharton's *Anglia Sacra* (London, 1691).

BIBLIOGRAPHY: Lives have been written by R. Lowth, London, 1758, 3d ed., Oxford, 1777; J. Chandler, ib. 1842; and G. H. Moberly, 2d ed., London, 1893. Consult further: M. E. C. Walcott, *William of Wykeham and his Colleges*, London, 1852; *The Three Chancellors: . . . Lives of William of Wykeham . . . and Sir T. More*, London, 1860; S. R. Gardiner, *Student's History of England*, pp. 260-262, London, 1895; J. H. Overton, *The Church in England*, i. 287-292, 315, London, 1897; W. W. Capes, *English Church in the 14th and 15th Centuries*, pp. 93 sqq., ib., 1900; W. A. Spooner, in *Typical English Churchmen*, ib., 1909; *DNB*, lxi. 178-179; W. L. Fox, *William of Wykeham, the Complete Life and Pilgrimage*, 2 parts, London, 1909.

WILLIAMITES: The name of two orders.

1. Benedictine Hermits of Monte Vergine (a high mountain near Avellino upon which in 1123 William of Vercelli in Piedmont—d. 1142—erected a convent). The order was confirmed by Pope Alexander III. under the Benedictine rule, spread in numerous monasteries and convents over Italy, and was reformed by Peter Leonardi at the request of Pope Clement VIII. It has now only the parent convent on Monte Vergine.

2. The Followers of Saint William of Maleval (d. Feb. 10, 1157). He was a hermit who in 1153 settled on the island of Lupocavio near Pisa, and in 1155 in the territory of Siena, in the bishopric of Grosseto in a stony valley later called Malavalle. There he found an associate in a certain Albert, who became his biographer. The congregation that formed about him followed his rule and spread over Italy, France, Germany, and Flanders. In 1229 Gregory IX. moderated the severity of the rule, giving the order the rule of Benedict, and Innocent IV. enlarged their privileges. In 1256 Pope Alexander IV. attempted to incorporate the order within the mendicant Augustinians and to prescribe for them the rule of Augustine, but they opposed this measure and preserved their independence. The order was divided into the three provinces of Tuscany, Germany, and Flanders. In 1435 the council of Basel confirmed their privileges. In the course of time most of the monasteries went over into other orders

until they entirely disappeared during the eighteenth century. (G. GRÜTZMACHER.)

BIBLIOGRAPHY: On 1 consult: G. Jordano, *Chroniche di Monte Vergine*, Naples, 1581; T. Costo, *Istoria dell' origine del s. luogi di Montevergine*, Venice, 1691; Hélyot, *Ordres monastiques*, vi. 122 sqq.; *KL*, xii. 1626 sqq. On 2 consult: *ASB*, Feb., ii. 433-472, cf. *Analecta Bollandiana*, i (1882), 525-527; *ASB*, ut sup., contains selections from the *Vita* by Albert, which was published at Siena, 1770; Hélyot, *Ordres monastiques*, vi. 142 sqq.; Heimbucher, *Orden und Kongregationen*, ii. 180-181.

WILLIAMS, ARTHUR LLEWELLYN: Protestant Episcopal bishop of Nebraska; b. at Owen Sound, Ont., Jan. 30, 1856. He received a high-school education, and in 1888 was graduated from the Western Theological Seminary, Chicago. He was ordered deacon in the same year and priested in 1889. After being a missionary in White River Valley, Col., in 1888-89, he became rector of St. Paul's, Denver, Col., in 1891, and was rector of Christ Church, Woodlawn Park, Chicago, 1892-1899. In 1899 he was consecrated bishop coadjutor of Nebraska, becoming bishop in 1908.

WILLIAMS, CHANNING MOORE: Protestant Episcopal missionary bishop of Yeddo, Japan (retired); b. at Richmond, Va., July 18, 1829; d. at Richmond, Va., Dec. 2, 1910. He was educated at William and Mary College (A.B., 1853) and at the Theological Seminary of Virginia (graduated 1855). He was ordered deacon in 1853 and priested in 1857, in which year he was appointed missionary in China, where he served until 1866. In the latter year he was consecrated missionary bishop of Yeddo, which bishopric he held until 1889, when he retired. He continued, however, his missionary labors under his successor.

BIBLIOGRAPHY: W. S. Perry, *The Episcopate in America*, p. 171, New York, 1895.

WILLIAMS, CHARLES DAVID: Protestant Episcopal bishop of Michigan; b. at Bellevue, O., July 30, 1860. He was educated at Kenyon College, Gambier, O. (A.B., 1880), and Bexly Hall, the theological seminary of the same institution (graduated 1883). He was a tutor in Kenyon College (1881-1884), and also curate of Trinity, Columbus, O. (1883-84); rector of the Church of the Resurrection, Fernbank, O., and of the Church of the Atonement, Riverside, Cincinnati (1884-89), and of St. Paul's, Steubenville, O. (1889-93); dean of Trinity Cathedral, Cleveland, O. (1893-1906); and in 1906 was consecrated bishop of Michigan. He was president of the Cleveland Public Library Board in 1902-06, and of Hiram House (a social settlement), Cleveland, in 1894. In theology he is a Broad-churchman. He has written *A Valid Christianity for To-Day* (New Orleans, 1905, new ed., 1909).

WILLIAMS, DANIEL: English Presbyterian; b. in Wales, at (or near) Wrexham (25 m. s. of Liverpool), about 1643; d. at Hoxton Jan. 26, 1716. He began to preach 1663; became chaplain to the Countess of Meath, 1664; preached to an independent congregation at Drogheda, 1664-67; was pastor of Wood Street congregation, Dublin, 1667-87; of Hand Alley, Bishopsgate, London, 1688 till his death. He held the Pinners' Hall lectureship, 1691-1694. He acquired a large estate, a great part of which he devoted to charitable uses. By will he founded the Red Cross Street Library, originally embracing his own library and that of William Bates. He was the author of *Gospel Truth Stated and Vindicated* (2d ed., London, 1692); *Man Made Righteous by Christ's Obedience . . . Sermons* (1694); *The Ministerial Office. 3 parts* (1708); *The Vanity of Childhood and Youth . . . Sermons* (3rd ed., 1729); *Select Sermons and Tracts* (2 vols., 1832); and there appeared, with an account of his life, his *Practical Discourses* (5 vols., 1738–50).

BIBLIOGRAPHY: The funeral sermon by John Evans was printed London, 1716. Besides the Life prefixed to the *Practical Discourses*, ut sup., consult: *True Copy of the Last Will and Testament of Daniel Williams*, London, 1717; reprint with additions, 1804; D. Defoe, *Memoirs of the Life of . . . Daniel Williams*, ib. 1718; *Papers Relating to Daniel Williams*, ib. 1816; *DNB*, lxi. 385–388.

WILLIAMS, DAVID: English deist; b. at Watford, Glamorganshire, Wales, 1738; d. in London June 29, 1816. He was educated at Carmarthen Academy (1753–57), and in 1758 was ordained to a dissenting congregation at Frome, Somerset, though three years later his lax theological views compelled him to leave Frome for the Mint meeting-house in Exeter, where he was reordained, while from about 1769 to 1773 he was in charge of a dwindling congregation in Highgate, Middlesex. In 1773 he removed to Chelsea, and there opened a school which was conducted successfully for two or three years, when his wife's death so unnerved him that he abruptly abandoned his teaching. In Apr., 1776, he opened a chapel, where he conducted services on the basis of his *Liturgy on the Universal Principles of Religion and Morality* (London, 1776), in the compilation of which he had been assisted by Benjamin Franklin. He continued these services, with at least one change of location, until about 1780, the year in which he first formed the idea of founding a " Literary Fund " for the aid of unrecognized men of genius, this project not being incorporated until after Williams' death (1818), though it ultimately became the Royal Literary Fund (1842). After the failure of his services, Williams supported himself chiefly by private teaching, until, in 1792, he was invited to write a history of Monmouthshire, the result, his *History of Monmouthshire* (London, 1796), being still the standard on its subject. In 1792 and in 1802 he paid brief visits to France, being made a French citizen on his first trip. In his closing years his finances ran very low, and after 1811 he resided in the house of the Literary Fund, which had been able to commence its benefactions in 1790.

The principal writings of Williams were *The Philosopher, in Three Conversations* (London, 1771); *Essays on Public Worship, Patriotism, and Projects of Reformation* (1773); *Sermons, Chiefly upon Religious Hypocrisy* (1774); *Treatise on Education* (1774); *Letter to the Body of Protestant Dissenters* (1777); *Lectures on the Universal Principles and Duties of Religion and Morality* (2 vols., 1779); *Nature and Extent of Intellectual Liberty* (1779); *Letters on Political Liberty* (1782); *Letters Concerning Education* (1785); *Lectures on Political Principles* (1789); *Lectures on Education* (3 vols., 1789); *Claims of Literature* (1802); and *Egeria; or, Elementary Studies on the Progress of Nations in Political Economy, Legislation, and Government* (1803).

BIBLIOGRAPHY: *DNB*, lxi. 390–393.

WILLIAMS, SIR GEORGE: Founder of the Young Men's Christian Association; b. at Dulverton (45 m. s.w. of Bath), Somersetshire, Oct. 11, 1821; d. at Torquay Nov. 6, 1905. As youthful apprentice in a business house at Bridgewater he was the subject of the religious impressions which molded his subsequent career. In 1841 he removed to London, entering the drapery house of Hitchcock and Rogers; married Helen Hitchcock, and upon the death of her father in 1863 became head of the establishment. Immediately upon his arrival in London his keen interest in the well-being of his fellow employees began. Through his personal efforts and leadership there was formed within the establishment a society to help forward foreign mission work. But the work of his life commenced in June, 1844, when he led in forming the Young Men's Christian Association (q.v.). Originally planned to benefit young men engaged in the drapery and other trades, this institution developed rapidly. Branch associations were formed in different parts of London, Britain, and Ireland, and later in Australia, India, and South Africa, and by his personal initiative also in Paris, Switzerland, and other parts of Europe, and the work took root also in the United States and Canada. In 1855 he had a leading part in the first world's conference which met in Paris. In the extension of the organization he was actively interested, wisely distributing his gifts where the associations had most need of help from abroad. In 1880 he was the first to give a contribution of £5,000 toward the purchase of Exeter Hall as the headquarters of the English work. In 1882 he led in forming the National Union of English Associations, over which he presided to the end of his life. In 1885, upon the death of the Earl of Shaftesbury, who for thirty years had filled the office, he was unanimously elected president.

In 1894 the London Association jubilee was celebrated by a world's conference of 2,000 delegates from all the continents, accompanied by a series of religious demonstrations without parallel in the history of London Christian organizations. The corporation of the city of London then conferred upon Williams the honorary freedom of the city because " coming to the city as a young man he had for fifty years made it his principal business unselfishly and efficiently to promote the best welfare of the young men of the city," and following this Queen Victoria bestowed upon him the honor of knighthood.

Sir George also maintained a relation of strong and generous leadership to the work of the British and Foreign Bible Society, the London City Mission, the Church Missionary Society, the Band of Hope Union, and many kindred organizations—in a large number of which he filled the office of president, evincing in a remarkable degree the possession of great public spirit, of broad Christian sympathy, and of the highest and truest philanthropy.

RICHARD C. MORSE.

BIBLIOGRAPHY: J. E. H. Williams, *Life of Sir George Williams*, London and New York, 1906; and literature under YOUNG MEN'S CHRISTIAN ASSOCIATION.

WILLIAMS, GERSHOM MOTT: Protestant Episcopal bishop of Marquette, Mich.; b. at Fort Hamilton, New York Harbor, Feb. 11, 1857. He studied at Cornell (1875–77), and was admitted to the Michigan bar in 1879. In the following year, however, he was ordered deacon, and, after being curate of St. John's, Detroit (1880–82), he was rector of the Church of the Messiah, Hamtramck (now part of Detroit), Mich. (1882–84), and of St. George's, Detroit (1885–89), also being in charge of St. Matthew's church for colored people in the same city (1880–85); he was dean of All Saints' Cathedral, Milwaukee, Wis. (1889–96), as well as archdeacon of northern Michigan (1891–96), and rector of St. Paul's, Marquette, Mich. (1891–93). In 1896 he was consecrated first bishop of the diocese of Marquette. He is the author of *The Church of Sweden and the Anglican Communion* (Milwaukee, 1910).

WILLIAMS, GRIFFITH: Church of England bishop of Ossory; b. at Treveilian (a hamlet near Carnarvon), Wales, 1589 or 1590; d. at Kilkenny (62 m. s.w. of Dublin), Ireland, Mar. 29, 1672. He was educated at Christ Church, Oxford, and Jesus College, Cambridge (B.A., 1605–06). After ordination he served as a curate at Hanwell, Middlesex, became rector of Foxcott, Buckinghamshire, in 1608, which he resigned for St. Bennet Sherehog, London, in 1611–12, and was also lecturer in St. Peter's, Cheapside, and in St. Paul's Cathedral for a number of years. A High-churchman, he incurred the hatred of the Puritans, and in 1616 the bishop of London was compelled by them to suspend Williams for his *Resolution of Pilate*, just then published. He then spent a short time in Cambridge, and, returning to London, gained the friendship of the extreme Puritan, Archbishop George Abbot (q.v.), and through Abbot's chancellor obtained the rectory of Llanllechid, Carnarvonshire. Here, however, he came in conflict with his strongly Puritan diocesan, who, when Williams refused to resign his living for another, preferred charges against him, only to be reprimanded by Abbot, who licensed Williams to preach in several dioceses of the province of Canterbury. Four years later Williams returned to London, and after a year as chaplain to the earl of Montgomery, became, in 1626, rector of Trefdraeth, Anglesey, while in 1628 he was appointed a prebendary in Westminster, and in 1634 was instituted dean of Bangor. In 1641 he was consecrated bishop of Ossory, but within a month was driven back to England by the outbreak of the Irish rebellion. In England he was arrested by the Parliamentarians, but succeeded in obtaining a safe-conduct and joined King Charles as chaplain. He incurred fresh hostility from the enemies of the king by publishing his *Vindiciæ regum, or, The Grand Rebellion* (Oxford, 1643), which the Parliamentarians ordered to be publicly burned; and he followed this, within the year, by his *Discovery of Mysteries, or, The Plots and Practices of a prevalent Faction in this present Parliament to overthrow the established Religion . . . and to subvert the fundamentall Lawes of this famous Kingdome.* In revenge the Parliamentarians drove his family from their temporary home at Apethorpe, Northamptonshire, and confiscated his property,

but undauntedly he issued against them a third work, *Jura majestatis; The Rights of Kings both in Church and State . . . and the Wickedness of the Faction of this pretended Parliament at Westminster* (Oxford, 1644).

After another narrow escape from arrest while in London on the king's business, Williams contrived to make his way again to Ireland, but was back in England in 1645, when he vainly urged the Royalists to make firm stand against the Parliamentarian general, Thomas Mytton, in Anglesey. He later succeeded in returning to Ireland, where he was appointed rector of Rathfarnham, County Dublin, in 1647. Before the year was out, he had been driven out by the surrender of Dublin to the Parliamentarians, and after much hardship he managed to reach Llanllechid again, where he lived in abject poverty, refusing to accept either a rich living or a pension in return for submission to the Parliamentarian party. In 1651 his loyalty to the king again nearly cost him at least his liberty, but with the Restoration in 1660, when he was the first in Ireland to pray publicly for the king, his position naturally became secure, and he was now able to publish his Ὁ Ἀντίχριστος, *the Great Antichrist revealed* (London, 1660), in which he proved that Antichrist was the Westminster Assembly (q.v.).

Returning to his diocese, which was in sorry condition as a result of the war, he set about repairing the damage and restoring the cathedral which the Parliamentarians had injured, and it was at this same time that he published a *quasi*-autobiography, *The Persecution and Oppression of John Bale, Bishop of Ossory, . . . and of Griffith Williams* (London, 1664). Besides his bishopric, he held for several years the prebendary of Mayne, in his own see.

In addition to the works already mentioned and many sermons, etc., Williams wrote: *The Delights of the Saints* (London, 1622), *Seven Golden Candlesticks, holding the Seven Greatest Lights of Christian Religion* (1627), *The True Church, shewed to all Men that Desire to be Members of the same* (1629), *The Right Way to the best Religion* (1636), and, perhaps, *An Examination of such Particulars in the Solemne League and Covenant as concern the Law; proving it to be destructive of the Lawes of England, both Ancient and Moderne* (Oxford, 1644).

BIBLIOGRAPHY: A. à Wood, *Athenæ Oxonienses*, ed. P. Bliss, iii. 952–956, 4 vols., London, 1813–20; *DNB*, lxi. 401–403; and his own works.

WILLIAMS, HELEN MARIA: English Unitarian; b. in London 1762; d. in Paris Dec. 15, 1827, where she lived from 1788, becoming naturalized in 1817. She gained reputation by her letters from France (published in several volumes from 1790 to 1819) and other political writings, which, written in ardent sympathy with the idea of the French Revolution, are prejudiced and inaccurate; and by her translations (including *Paul and Virginia*, 1795, and Humboldt's travels, 7 vols., 1814–1829). She wrote the hymn "While thee I seek, protecting power" (published in *Poems*, 2 vols., 1786; with addition, 1 vol., 1823). She was aunt of Athanase Laurent Charles Coquerel (q.v.).

BIBLIOGRAPHY: S. W. Duffield, *English Hymns*, pp. 610–612, New York, 1886; *DNB*, lxi. 404–405; S. A. Allibone,

Critical Dictionary of English Literature, iii. 2739, Philadelphia, 1891; Julian, *Hymnology*, pp. 1281–82.

WILLIAMS, HUGH: Welsh Presbyterian; b. at Menai Bridge (6 m. n. of Carnarvon), Carnarvonshire, Sept. 17, 1843. He was educated at Calvinistic Methodist College, Bala, Wales, and the University of London (B.A., 1870; M.A., 1871), and, after being master of the grammar-school at Menai Bridge (1871–73), was ordained to the ministry in 1873; was appointed professor of Greek at Bala College (1874–91), and when the college was made a theological institution (1891) his appointment was changed to his present chair of church history. In theology he " welcomes the progress and expansion due to all modern research " and " retains in the main a position of faithful adherence " to the standards of his church. He has prepared a Welsh " Commentary on the Epistle to the Galatians " (Carnarvon, 1892) and " Handbook on the Sacraments of the Church " (Bala, 1894) and edited Gildas's *De excidio Britanniæ* (London, 1901).

WILLIAMS, ISAAC: Church of England, poet and harmonist; b. at Cwmcynfelyn, near Aberystwith (40 m. n.n.e. of Carmarthen), Wales, Dec. 12, 1802; d. at Stinchcombe (12 m. s.w. of Gloucester) May 1, 1865. He studied with Polehampton of Eton and King's College, and at Harrow, and then at Trinity College, Oxford (B.A., 1826; M.A., 1831; fellow, 1831; and B.D., 1839); was ordained deacon, 1829, and became curate of Windrush-cum-Sherborne; was ordained priest, 1832, and became tutor at Trinity College, Oxford; philosophy lecturer, 1832, and dean of the college, 1833; was rhetoric lecturer, 1834–40; and vice-president, 1840–42. Soon after his settlement at Trinity College he became curate to John H. Newman at St. Mary's, Oxford, and later had charge of the church at Littlemore. He was curate to Thomas Keble at Bisley, 1842–48; and at Stinchcombe, near Dursley, 1848–65. He was associated with Newman and Keble in *Lyra Apostolica* and *Tracts for the Times*, writing Tracts 80, 86, and 87. His literary industry was great, and his works embrace commentaries on the Psalms, the Gospels, and the Apocalypse; *The Cathedral, or the Catholic and the Apostolic Church of England. In Verse* (Oxford, 1838); *A Harmony of the Four Evangelists* (London, 1850); *A Short Memoir of R. A. Suckling, with Correspondence and Sermons* (1852); and many sermons, individual and in series. He was also a writer of hymns, but none of them had great currency.

BIBLIOGRAPHY: His *Autobiography*, ed. Sir G. Provost, appeared London, 1892. Consult also: S. W. Duffield, *English Hymns*, pp. 329–330, New York, 1886; R. W. Church, *The Oxford Movement*, pp. 57–69, London, 1891; W. R. W. Stephens, *Life of Edward Freeman*, i. 43–50, ib. 1895; *DNB*, lxi. 408–411; Julian, *Hymnology*, pp. 1282–1284.

WILLIAMS, JOHN: Name of two important workers in the religious field.

1. " The apostle of Polynesia," missionary; b. in London June 29, 1796; d. at Erromanga, New Hebrides Islands, Nov. 20, 1839. After a commercial education he was apprenticed to be an ironmonger, but in 1816 was led to give himself to missionary labor, and was sent by the London Mis-

sionary Society to the Society Islands, 1816. First at Papetoai, then at Huahine, in 1818 he settled in the Island of Raiatea, the largest of the Leeward group. From there as a center he carried on his work of educating and developing the natives not only in religion but in industry and economic living. In 1821 he bought a schooner and used her as a missionary ship; with her he discovered the Island of Rarotonga in 1823, where he later translated parts of the Bible and other books into the native language.

Williams was in England, 1838–44, where the fame of his adventures made him a center of interest. He left England with sixteen other missionaries, in a newly equipped ship and some funds for the continuance of his work, all the result of his labor and energy. On reaching the Pacific he made a tour of the Society Islands and then of the New Hebrides, a new field for him, where he was killed by natives. His work was eminently successful and extensive, and his adventures truly unique, and both displayed his practical sagacity and his initiative. He was the author of *A Narrative of Missionary Enterprises in the South Sea Islands, with Remarks upon the natural History of the Islands, Origin, Languages, Tradition, and Usages of the Inhabitants* (London, 1837), one of the most important works on the subject.

2. Protestant Episcopal, bishop of Connecticut; b. at Deerfield, Mass., Aug. 30, 1817; d. at Middletown, Conn., Feb. 7, 1899. He studied in Harvard College, Cambridge, Mass., 1831–33, and was graduated from Trinity College, Hartford, Conn., 1835; was tutor in the college, 1837–40; ordained, 1838; assistant in Christ Church, Middletown, Conn., 1841–42; rector of St. George's, Schenectady, N. Y., 1842–48; president of Trinity College and professor of history and literature, 1848–53; assistant bishop of Connecticut, 1851–65; and bishop from 1865. From 1854 he was dean, and principal instructor in doctrinal theology, history of the Reformation, and in the prayer-book, at Middletown. He also continued to lecture in history at Trinity College, of which he became vice-chancellor, 1851, and chancellor, 1865. He was appointed first lecturer at the General Theological Seminary, New York, 1881; and the same year delivered the Bedell lectures at the seminary and college in Gambier, O. He was a student of ecclesiastical history, an eloquent speaker, and later became presiding bishop of the Protestant Episcopal Church. His works embrace *Ancient Hymns of Holy Church* (Hartford, 1845); *Thoughts on the Gospel Miracles* (New York, 1848); Paddock lectures on *The English Reformation* (1881); Bedell lectures on *The World's Witness to Jesus Christ* (1882); and he edited an American edition of Bishop Harold Browne's *Exposition of the Thirty-nine Articles* (1870).

BIBLIOGRAPHY: On 1, besides Williams' *Missionary Enterprises in the South Sea*, new ed., Philadelphia, 1889, consult: the biographies by J. Campbell, *The Martyr of Erromanga*, London, 1843; E. Prout, ib., 4th ed., 1847; W. F. Besser, Berlin, 1847; also A. Buzacott, *Mission Life in the Islands of the Pacific*, London, 1866; R. Lovett, *Story of the London Missionary Society*, vol. i., ib. 1899; *DNB*, lxi. 423–425.
  On 2 consult: W. S. Perry, *The Episcopate in America*, p. 117, New York, 1895.

WILLIAMS, ROGER: Separatist Anglo-American theologian, advocate of liberty of conscience, and founder of Rhode Island; b. probably in London about 1600 (the date is uncertain; Knowles gives 1599; Waters, 1599–1602; Guild, Dec. 21, 1602; Straus, 1607); d. at Providence, R. I., 1684.

Early Life; Removal to America.

Under the patronage of Sir Edward Coke, the famous jurist, he was educated at Sutton's Hospital and at the University of Cambridge (B.A., 1627).

He seems to have had a gift for languages, and early acquired familiarity with Latin, Greek, Dutch, and French, and, during his early years in New England, mastered the language of the natives to a remarkable degree. At an earlier date he gave John Milton lessons in Dutch in exchange for lessons in Hebrew. Some time before the end of 1630 he adopted separatist views and reached the conviction that he could not labor in England under Laud's rigorous administration. He turned aside from offers of preferment in the university and in the Church, and resolved to seek in New England the liberty of conscience denied him at home. Arriving at Boston (Feb., 1631), he was almost immediately invited to supply the place of the pastor, who was returning to England. But he had found that it was " an unseparated church " and he " durst not officiate to " it. He was prompted to give utterance to his conviction, formed no doubt before he left England, that the magistrate may not punish any sort of " breach of the first table," such as idolatry, Sabbath-breaking, false worship, and blasphemy; and that every individual should be free to follow his own convictions in religious matters. The Salem church, which through intercourse with the Plymouth colonists had imbibed separatist sentiments, invited Williams to become its teacher; but his settlement was prevented by a remonstrance addressed to Governor Endicott by six of the Boston leaders. The Plymouth colony received him gladly as teacher or associate pastor. Here he remained about two years, and, according to Governor Bradford, " his teaching was well approved." While there he spent much time among the Indians, his " soul's desire " being " to do the natives good." " God was pleased to give me a painful, patient spirit, to lodge with them in their filthy, smoky holes . . . to gain their tongue." Toward the close of his ministry at Plymouth, according to Brewster, he began to " vent . . . divers of his own singular opinions " and to " seek to impose them upon others."

Meeting with opposition, Williams removed to Salem (summer of 1633) and became unofficial assistant to Pastor Skelton. In Aug., 1634 (Skelton having died), he became acting pastor and entered almost immediately upon controversies with the Massachusetts authorities that in a few months were to lead to his banishment. He was formally set apart as pastor of the church about May, 1635, in the midst of the controversies and against the remonstrance of the Massachusetts authorities. An outline of the issues raised by Williams and uncompromisingly pressed includes the following: (1) He regarded the Church

Life at Salem; Distinctive Views.

of England as apostate, and any kind of fellowship with it as grievous sin. He accordingly renounced communion not only with this church but with all who would not join with him in repudiating it. (2) He denounced the charter of the Massachusetts Company because it falsely represented the king of England as a Christian, and assumed that he had the right to give to his own subjects the land of the native Indians. He disapproved of " the unchristian oaths swallowed down " by the colonists " at their coming forth from Old England, especially in the superstitious Laud's time and domineering." He drew up a letter addressed to the king expressing his dissatisfaction with the charter and sought to secure for it the endorsement of prominent colonists. In this letter he is said to have charged King James I. with blasphemy for calling Europe " Christendom " and to have applied to the reigning king some of the most opprobrious epithets in the Apocalypse. (3) Equally disquieting was Williams' opposition to the " citizens' oath," which magistrates sought to force upon the colonists in order to be assured of their loyalty. Williams maintained that it was Christ's sole prerogative to have his office established by oath, and that unregenerate men ought not in any case to be invited to perform any religious act. In opposing the oath Williams gained so much popular support that the measure had to be abandoned. (4) In a dispute between the Massachusetts Bay court and the Salem colony regarding the possession of a piece of land (Marblehead) claimed by the latter, the court offered to accede to the claims of Salem on condition that the Salem church make amends for its insolent conduct in installing Williams as pastor in defiance of the court and ministers. This demand involved the removal of the pastor. Williams regarded this proposal as an outrageous attempt at bribery and had the Salem church send to the other Massachusetts churches a denunciation of the proceeding and demand that the churches exclude the magistrates from membership. This act was sharply resented by magistrates and churches, and such pressure was brought to bear upon the Salem church as led a majority to consent to the removal of their pastor. He never entered the chapel again, but held religious services in his own house with his faithful adherents.

Banishment; Settlement at Providence.

The decree of banishment (Oct. 19, 1635, carried into effect Jan., 1636) was grounded on his aggressive and uncompromising hostility to the charter and the theocracy, and was the immediate result of the controversy about the Marblehead land. His radical tenets, involving complete separation of Church and State and absolute voluntaryism in matters of religion, and his refusal to have communion with any who gave countenance or support to the existing order, made his banishment seem necessary to the theocratic leaders of Massachusetts. He had scarcely recovered from a severe illness contracted during his trial, when it was intimated to him that the authorities were arranging to send him back to England to be dealt with by the Laudian government. Accompanied or followed by a few devoted adherents, he plunged into the wilderness and made his way to his Indian friends, who gave him such entertainment as they could. " I was sorely tossed for one fourteen weeks, in a bitter winter season, not knowing what bread or bed did mean." In June he arrived at the present site of Providence and, having secured land from the natives, he admitted to equal rights with himself twelve " loving friends and neighbors " (several had come to him from Massachusetts since the opening of spring). It was provided that " such others as the major part of us shall admit into the same fellowship of vote with us " from time to time should become members of their commonwealth. Obedience to the majority was promised by all, but " only in civil things." In 1640 another agreement was signed by thirty-nine freemen, in which they express their determination " still to hold forth liberty of conscience." In 1643 Williams was sent to England by his fellow citizens to secure a charter for the colony. The Puritans were then in power, and through the good offices of Sir Henry Vane a thoroughly democratic charter was readily obtained. In 1647 a somewhat similar but larger colony having been planted on Rhode Island by William Coddington, John Clarke, and others, Providence was united with the Rhode Island towns under a single government, and liberty of conscience was again proclaimed. Disagreement having arisen between Providence and Warwick on the mainland and the towns on the island and between the followers of Clarke on the island and those of Coddington, Coddington had gone to England and in 1651 had secured from the council of state a commission to rule the islands of Rhode Island and Conanicut. This arrangement left Providence and Warwick to themselves. Coddington's scheme was strongly disapproved by Williams and Clarke and their followers, especially as it seemed to involve a federation of Coddington's domain with Massachusetts and Connecticut and a consequent imperiling of liberty of conscience not only on the islands but also in Providence and Warwick, which would be left unprotected. Many of the opponents of Coddington were by this time Baptists. Later in the same year Williams and Clarke went to England on behalf of their friends to secure from Cromwell's government the annulling of Coddington's charter and the recognition of the colony as a republic dependent only on England. This they succeeded in accomplishing, and Williams soon returned to Providence. To the end of his life he continued to take a deep interest in public affairs.

In 1638 several Massachusetts Christians who had been led to adopt antipedobaptist views and found themselves subject to persecution removed to Providence. Most of these had probably been
Relations   under Williams' influence while he was
with the   in Massachusetts, and some of them
Baptists.   may have been influenced by English antipedobaptists before they left England. Williams himself probably knew of the Arminian antipedobaptist party of which John Smyth, Thomas Helwys, and John Murton were founders (1609) and of the rich literature in advocacy of liberty of conscience produced by this party after its return to England (see BAPTISTS, I.,

1, §§ 1–9). He could hardly have failed to learn something of the Calvinistic antipedobaptist party that arose in London in 1633, a short time after his departure, led by Spilsbury, Eaton, and others. It is not likely that Williams adopted antipedobaptist views before his banishment from Massachusette, for antipedobaptism was not laid to his account by his opponents. Winthrop attributes Williams' " Anabaptist " views to the influence of Mrs. Scott, a sister of Anne Hutchinson, the Antinomian (see ANTINOMIANISM AND ANTINOMIAN CONTROVERSIES, II., 2). It is probable that Ezekiel Holliman came to Providence as an antipedobaptist and joined with Mrs. Scott in impressing upon Williams the importance of believers' baptism. About Mar., 1639, Williams was baptized by Holliman and immediately proceeded to baptize Holliman and eleven others. Thus was constituted the first Baptist church in America, which still survives. Williams remained with the little church only a few months. He became convinced that the ordinances having been lost in the apostasy could not be validly restored without a special divine commission. He assumed the attitude of a " Seeker " or " Comeouter," always deeply religious and active in the propagation of Christian truth, yet not feeling satisfied that any body of Christians had all of the marks of the true Church. He continued on the most friendly terms with the Baptists, being in agreement with them in their rejection of infant baptism as in most other matters. Williams' religious and ecclesiastical attitude is well expressed in the following sentences (1643): " The two first principles and foundations of true religion, or worship of the true God in Christ, are repentance from dead works and faith toward God, before the doctrines of baptism or washing and the laying on of hands, which continue the ordinances and practises of worship; the want of which I conceive is the bane of millions of souls in England and all other nations professing to be Christian nations, who are brought by public authority to baptism and fellowship with God in ordinances of worship, before the saving work of repentance and a true turning to God."

Williams' career as an author began with A Key into the Language of America (London, 1643), written during his first voyage to England. His next publication was Mr. Cotton's Letter lately Printed, Examined and Answered (London, 1644; reprinted, with Cotton's letter, which it answered, in Publications of the Narragansett Club, vol. ii.). Soon after Williams' banishment he had written to John Cotton of Boston, bitterly complaining of the treatment he had received from the Massachusetts authorities. Cotton had written a long letter in reply, in which he sought to win him from the error of his way and at the same time to justify his banishment. Cotton expressed the opinion in this letter that if Williams had perished in the wilderness his blood would have been upon his own head. Williams examines minutely Cotton's argument, elaborately states his own position, and defends his attitude toward the Massachusetts authorities. The Bloudy Tenent of Persecution, for Cause of Conscience soon followed (London, 1644). This is his most famous work, and was the ablest statement and defense of the principle of absolute liberty of conscience that had appeared in any language. It is in the form of a dialogue between Truth and Peace, and well illustrates the vigor of his style. During the same year appeared in London an anonymous pamphlet which has been commonly ascribed to Williams, entitled: *Queries of Highest Consideration Proposed to Mr. Tho. Goodwin, Mr. Phillip Nye, Mr. Wil. Bridges, Mr. Jer. Burroughs, Mr. Sidr. Simpson, all Independents,* etc. These Independents were members of the Westminster Assembly and their *Apologetical Narration,* in which they plead for toleration, fell very far short of Williams' doctrine of liberty of conscience. In 1652, during his second visit to England, Williams published *The Bloody Tenent yet more Bloody: by Mr. Cotton's Endeavor to wash it white in the Blood of the Lamb; of whose precious Blood, spilt in the Blood of his Servants; and of the Blood of Millions spilt in former and later Wars for Conscience sake, that most Bloody Tenent of Persecution for cause of Conscience, upon a second Tryal is found more apparently and more notoriously guilty,* etc. (London, 1652). This work traverses anew much of the ground covered by the *Bloudy Tenent;* but it has the advantage of being written in answer to Cotton's elaborate defense of New England persecution, *A Reply to Mr. Williams his Examination* (*Publications of the Narragansett Club,* vol. ii.). Other works by Williams are *The Hireling Ministry None of Christ's* (London, 1652); *Experiments of Spiritual Life and Health, and their Preservatives* (London, 1652; reprinted, Providence, 1863), and *George Fox Digged out of his Burrowes* (Boston, 1676). A volume of his letters is included in the Narragansett Club edition of Williams' *Works* (7 vols., Providence, 1866–74), and a volume was edited by J. R. Bartlett (1882).   A. H. NEWMAN.

BIBLIOGRAPHY: Besides the Narragansett ed. of the *Works* noted above (which contains also John Cotton's writings against liberty of conscience), *The Bloudy Tenent* was reprinted, with introduction by E. B. Underhill, by the Hanserd Knollys Society, London, 1848; *A Key into the Language,* etc., is in *Collections of the Massachusetts Historical Society,* vols. iv.–v., and in *Collections of the Rhode Island Historical Society,* vol. i.; *Experiments of Spiritual Life and Health, and their Preservatives* was reprinted in facsimile, Providence, 1863; and his *Christenings Make not Christians* was published at the same place, no. 14 of *Rhode Island Historical Tracts,* 1881.
    On his life and work consult: O. S. Straus, *Roger Williams, the Pioneer of Religious Liberty,* New York, 1894; J. D. Knowles, *Memoir of Roger Williams,* Boston, 1834; W. Gammell, *Life of Roger Williams,* Boston, 1845; J. Durfee, *Works,* ed. by his son, pp. 1–178, Providence, 1849; R. Elton, *Life of Roger Williams,* Providence, 1853; S. G. Arnold, *Hist. of the State of Rhode Island,* vol. i., New York, 1859; D. C. Eddy, *Roger Williams and the Baptists,* Boston, 1861; W. E. H. Lecky, *Hist. of the Rise of the Spirit of Rationalism in Europe,* ii. 70–84, London, 1865; R. A. Guild, *Biographical Introduction to the Writings of Roger Williams,* Providence, 1866; C. Deane, *Roger Williams and the Massachusetts Charter,* Cambridge, Mass., 1873; H. M. Dexter, *As to Roger Williams and his " Banishment " from the Massachusetts Plantation,* Boston, 1876; T. M. Merriman, *The Pilgrims, Puritans, and Roger Williams Vindicated,* Boston, 1892; A. H. Newman, *American Church History Series,* ii. passim, New York, 1894; W. H. Whitsitt, *A Question in Baptist History,* Louisville, 1896; H. M. King, *The Baptism of Roger Williams,* Providence, 1897; E. J. Carpenter, *A Study of Roger Williams,* New York, 1909; *DNB,* lxi. 445–450; and works on the history of New England, especially of Rhode Island.

WILLIAMS, ROWLAND: English Broad-church theologian; b. at Halkyn (12 m. e.s.e. of St. Asaph), Wales, Aug. 16, 1817; d. at Broad Chalke (7 m. w.s.w. of Salisbury), Wiltshire, Jan. 18, 1870. He studied at Eton and at King's College, Cambridge (B.A., 1841; M.A., 1844; B.D., 1851; D.D., 1857), where he was fellow 1839–59, and classical tutor 1842–50. During 1843–46 he was instrumental in averting the proposed amalgamation of the sees of St. Asaph and Bangor, publishing in the press a number of remonstrances against the measure. In 1848 he won the Muir prize for a preliminary essay on the comparative merits of Christianity and Hinduism. From 1850 until 1862 he was vice-principal and professor of Hebrew at the theological college of St. David's, Lampeter, Wales. Despite the most uncompromising opposition on account of his liberal views regarding the interpretation of Scripture, his administration of the college was aggressive and successful. In Dec., 1854, he was appointed select preacher at Cambridge, though his sermons there were quickly interrupted by his father's death. In 1858 he accepted the living of Broad Chalke, whither he removed in 1862. In 1860 he contributed *Bunsen's Biblical Researches* to the famous *Essays and Reviews,* which resulted in his trial for heterodoxy before the Court of Arches (see ESSAYS AND REVIEWS). His principal works were, *Rational Godliness* (London, 1855), sermons preached at Cambridge and at St. David's College; *Christianity and Hinduism Compared* (1856), his greatest work; *The Hebrew Prophets Translated . . . with Introduction and Notes* (2 parts, 1866–71); *Broad Chalke Sermon-Essays* (1867); *Owen Glendower: a Dramatic Biography . . . and Other Poems* (1870); and *Psalms and Litanies* (1872).

BIBLIOGRAPHY: His *Life and Letters* was published by his widow, 2 vols., London, 1874. Consult: John Owen, in *Contemporary Review,* Apr., 1870; C. K. Paul, *Biographical Sketches,* London, 1883; *DNB,* lxi. 450–453; literature under ESSAYS AND REVIEWS. The *Judgment* of S. Lushington in the Court of Arches was published, London, 1862.

WILLIAMS, SAMUEL WELLS: Congregational layman and sinologue; b. at Utica, N. Y., Sept. 22, 1812; d. at New Haven, Conn., Feb. 16, 1884. In 1831 he entered Rensselaer Polytechnic Institute at Troy, N. Y.; went to Canton, China, in 1833 as a printer for the American Board of Commissioners for Foreign Missions; there he was editor, contributor to, and printer of *The Chinese Repository,* 1838–51; removed to Macao, 1835, to complete the printing of Medhurst's *Hokkeën Dictionary,* 1835; visited Japan, 1837, and translated into Japanese Genesis and Matthew; began to print Bridgman's *Chinese Christomathy,* to which he contributed one-half, 1837–38; he was away from China, 1844–48, spending three years in America, where he was instrumental in raising funds for a full font of Chinese type; was interpreter to Commodore Perry's Japan expeditions, 1853–54; became secretary and interpreter of the U. S. Legation, Peking, 1855; assisted Minister Reed in negotiating the treaty with China, 1858. He made two more visits to America, and in 1877 he returned to become professor of the Chinese language and literature at Yale University. He had been chargé d'affaires nine times during his term as secretary and interpreter in China. His great work was *A Syllabic Dictionary of the Chinese Language* (Shanghai, 1874); it was a quarto volume of 1,336 pages, containing 12,527 characters, and their pronunciation in four dialects. He was the author also of *Easy Lessons in Chinese* (Macao, 1842); *English and Chinese Vocabulary* (1843); *Chinese Topography* (1844); *A Chinese Commercial Guide* (1844); *The Middle Kingdom: a Survey of the Geography, Government, Education, Social Life . . . of China and its Inhabitants* (2 vols., New York, 1848; new ed. rev., 2 vols., 1883; a standard work); *Tonic Dictionary of the Chinese Language* (Canton, 1856); and, in collaboration with F. K. Dobbins, *False Gods; or the Idol Worship of the World* (Philadelphia, 1881).

BIBLIOGRAPHY: F. W. Williams (his son), *Life and Letters of S. Wells Williams*, New York, 1888.

WILLIAMS, WILLIAM: Welsh Calvinistic Methodist and hymn-writer; b. at Cefn-y-Coed (a hamlet near Llandovery), Carmarthenshire, Wales, 1717; d. at Pant y Celyn (near the same city) Jan. 11, 1791. His father was a Calvinist, who intended his son for the medical profession, but the young man, chancing to hear Howel Harris (q.v.) preach, determined to devote his life to religion. He was ordained to the deaconate in 1740 and appointed curate of the Established parishes of Llan Wrtyd and Llan Ddewi Aber Gwesin, but his interest became centered in Methodism, and in three years, without having been priested, he ceased to hold any position in the Church of England, though he still alleged himself one of her clergy. From 1749 his home was at Pant y Celyn, though he preached regularly at several small stations and devoted some weeks each year to evangelistic tours in Wales. Williams wrote some 800 hymns, both in English and in Welsh, and was one of the greatest hymn-writers that his country has ever produced. Among the more noteworthy of his collections, hymns from which still form the staple of Welsh hymnals, may be mentioned *Aleluia* (Carmarthen, 1744; complete ed., Bristol, 1758), *Golwg ar Deyrnas Crist* (" A Prospect of Christ's Kingdom," a long religious poem, Bristol, 1756; 6th ed., Newcastle Emlyn, 1845), *Hosanna to the Son of David* (Bristol, 1759), *Caniadau y rhai sydd ar y môr o wydr* (" Songs of those who are on the Sea of Glass," Carmarthen, 1762; repeatedly reprinted), *Aleluia Drachefn* (1785[?]; a collection of three former hymnals), *Gloria in Excelsis* (Llandovery and Carmarthen, 1771–72; Eng. ed., Carmarthen, 1772), and *Rhai Hymnau Newyddion* (3 parts, Brecon, 1871–87). Of his hymns by far the best known are his " Guide me, O Thou great Jehovah " and " O'er those gloomy hills of darkness," while some others still in use are " Jesus, my Saviour is enough," " My God, my God, Who art my all," " Beneath Thy Cross I lay me down," and " Jesus, lead us with Thy power."

Among the other writings of Williams the more noteworthy are *Pantheologia* (a Welsh dialogue history of the religions of the world; Carmarthen and Brecon, 1762–74), " Life and Death of Theomemphus " (a Welsh allegorical poem in dialogue, somewhat analogous to *Pilgrim's Progress;* Carmarthen, 1774; 7th ed., Newcastle Emlyn, 1845), *Crocodil Afon yr Aipht* (Carmarthen, 1767), *Hanes Bywyd a*

Marwolaeth y Tri Wyr o Sodom (1768; 3d ed., Swansea, 1852; dialogues on envy and the use of riches respectively), *Aurora Borealis* (Brecon, 1774; 3d ed., Ruthin, 1832; a Welsh letter on the revivals in the north of Wales), *Templum Experientiæ Apertum* (Brecon, 1777; a Welsh essay in dialogue on " experience " meetings), and *Ductor Nuptiarum* (1777; a like essay on the marriage of believers).

A complete edition of Williams' hymns was edited by his son John at Carmarthen in 1811; and editions of his collected writings have been prepared by J. R. Jones (Glasgow, 1867) and by N. C. Jones (Holywell and Newport, 1887–91).

BIBLIOGRAPHY: E. Morgan, *Ministerial Record; . . . Account of the Progress of Religion under . . . the Rev. W. Williams*, London, 1847; S. W. Duffield, *English Hymns*, pp. 197–199, New York, 1886; *DNB*, lxi. 462–464; Julian, *Hymnology*, pp. 1284–1285, 1251.

WILLIAMS, WILLIAM R: Baptist; b. in New York Oct. 14, 1804; d. there Apr. 1, 1885. He was graduated from Columbia College, New York, 1822; studied law for three years in the office of Peter A. Jay, whose partner he became; but because of religious convictions he abandoned law and turned to theology. He was ordained and installed as pastor of the Amity Baptist Church in 1832, where he remained till his death. He was a man of great learning and famous for his eloquence. He was the author of *Miscellanies* (New York, 1850); *Religious Progress: Discourses on the Development of Christian Character* (Boston, 1850); *Discourses and Essays* (New York, 1850); *Lectures on the Lord's Prayer* (Boston, 1851); *God's Rescues; or, the Lost Sheep, the Lost Coin, and the Lost Son* (New York, 1871); *Lectures on Baptist History* (Philadelphia, 1877); and *Eras and Characters of History* (New York, 1882).

WILLIBALD: First bishop of Eichstädt; b. in England 700; d. at Eichstädt probably July 7, 787. He came of a noble Anglo-Saxon family, to which Boniface was related. Later accounts call his father Richard and erroneously give him the title of king. In consequence of a sickness when Willibald was three years old, his parents vowed that if he recovered he should enter a monastery. In accordance with this vow, he was sent in his sixth year to the Abbot Egwald of Waltham for his education. There he renounced not only worldly position but also his native land in his desire to carry out fully his idea of complete monastic devotion. In this he persuaded his father, after considerable pleading, and a brother Wunebald (Winebald), who was a year younger, to accompany him; and the three, with a considerable retinue, left England in 720 and traveled through France, visiting the tombs of the saints, and went to Italy, where the father died and was buried at Lucca. The brothers went on to Rome, where they stayed two years, keeping monastic discipline, although suffering from fever much of the time. After Easter of 722 the brothers separated, and Willibald undertook a pilgrimage to the Holy Land by way of Naples, Reggio, Syracuse, Cos, Samos, Ephesus, Asia Minor, and Damascus to Jerusalem, he and two companions arriving there in 724. From 727 to 729 he was in Constantinople, whence he went by way of Sicily to Monte Cassino, where he stayed till Easter of 739. Meanwhile Wunebald stayed in Rome till 727, when he returned home and persuaded another brother to go with him to Rome, where they lived as monks till 739, when Boniface persuaded Wunebald to go to Germany, receive priestly orders, and take up work in Thuringia.

When Willibald returned to Rome in 739, Gregory III. persuaded him to follow his brother to Germany, whither he went in 740, first to Count Odilo of Bavaria and then to Suitgar of Nordgau, who had recently made over to Boniface the region about Eichstädt, where in 740 Willibald was raised to the priesthood, and the next year was made bishop, beginning his episcopal activities by the erection of a monastery. He is known to have taken part in synods in 742 and 762. Of Willibald's work as a bishop his biography says little. Wunebald's biography tells of Willibald's part in founding the monastery at Heidenheim. The former labored in Thuringia at least till 741, and after that as a wandering preacher in Bavaria, and then assisted his brother at Heidenheim. He died on a journey to Monte Cassino Dec. 19, 761, having been abbot at Heidenheim more than ten years, over the nuns of which his surviving sister Walpurgis presided. Willibald outlived all the pupils and associates of Boniface, and the reports which place his death in 777 or 781 are to be rejected in favor of that given above. (A. HAUCK.)

BIBLIOGRAPHY: For information about sources cf. T. H. Hardy, *Descriptive Catalogue of Materials*, i. 2, p. 490, nos. 1049, 1050, in *Rolls Series*, no. 26, London, 1862. The earliest lives with commentary are in *ASB*, July, ii. 483–519, and excerpts are in *MGH, Script.*, xv. 1 (1887), 86–106, cf. T. Meyrick, *Life of St. Walburge with the Itinerary of St. Willibald*, pp. 39–76, London, 1873. Consult further: T. Wright, *Biographia Britannica*, i. 335–345, London, 1842; *The Family of St. Richard, the Saxon St. Richard, King; St. Willibald, Bishop*, London, 1844; H. Hahn, *Die Reise des heiligen Willibald*, Berlin, 1856; W. A. Neumann, in *TQ*, 1874, pp. 524–526; Rettberg, *KD*, ii. 348; Hauck, *KD*, i. 534; *DNB*, lxii. 12–13; *KL*, xii. 1669.

WILLIBRORD (WILBRORD): Apostle of Frisia and archbishop of Utrecht; b. in Northumberland, England, in 658; d. in the monastery at Echternach (19 m. n.e. of Luxemburg) Nov. 6, 739. His father, Wilgils, had built a chapel dedicated to St. Andrew at the mouth of the Humber, where he dwelt as a hermit; later royal gifts and donations from the nobles made possible the foundation of a fine monastery, over which later Alcuin presided. He imbued his son Willibrord with the monastic spirit, and sent him to the monastery at Ripon for his education, where he early received the tonsure. He went in 678 to Ireland to prosecute his studies under St. Egbert (q.v.), this being the year when Wilfrid of York (q.v.) was deposed and exiled by King Egfrid. After twelve years of this life he desired higher service in the shape of preaching to the heathen, and Egbert sent him to Frisia. The Frisians were the northern neighbors of the Franks, inhabiting a narrow strip of land between the Weser and the Sinkfal, an arm of the Schelde, as well as the adjacent islands. At this period the southern part of Friesland belonged to the Frankish kingdom. Attempts to introduce Christianity had been made under Lothair II. and Dagobert I. (i.e., c. 620–639),

while a mission had been undertaken also from Cologne, to the bishop of which the charge had been committed. St. Eligius (q.v.) had also worked here. Results had not been large. When the Franks grew weak, the Frisians relapsed into paganism. Wilfrid (q.v.) had gained the favor of the Frisians during a winter's hunting, and had preached and baptized. His friend Egbert had also been interested in the land and had sent laborers. But the new prince, Radbod, who succeeded Wilfrid's friend Aldgild, was unfriendly to Christianity as leading to the subjection of his people to the Franks. In 689 Radbod was compelled to see the southern part of his land fall under Frankish control, in which part a door for the Gospel seemed to Willibrord to open. Willibrord sought the protection and aid of Pippin, whose own desires were in that direction, but wished to work only under an understanding with the Frankish majordomos and with Rome. He therefore visited Rome to obtain full power, a blessing, and relics to put in the churches he hoped to found. The success of Willibrord and his companions was so great that in 692–693 it seemed fitting to select a bishop from their number to govern the territory, and the choice fell on Suidbert. But Pippin's consent had not been gained, and Suidbert could not take possession of the office. After some delay, while the companions took no further step, Pippin took the matter in his own hands, designated Willibrord for the office and sent him to Rome to receive consecration. By Bede and Alcuin and in two *diplomata* of Charles Martel, Willibrord is called archbishop; he received consecration Nov. 22, 695, and Pippin designated Wiltaburg (Utrecht) as his seat.

During the next few years the introduction of Christianity went on rapidly, while churches and monasteries arose and were richly endowed by Pippin. Yet among the free Friesians Willibrord had no success, though he labored among them and Radbod was friendly to Willibrord himself. Willibrord carried his mission to the Danes, but with no results. But he brought back thirty Danish lads in order to instruct them and send them back as missionaries. On his return to Friesland he endeavored to secure the welfare of the churches, founded the monastery of Echternach in the diocese of Treves (706) and that of Süstern in the diocese of Mastricht (714). After the death of Pippin (714) Radbod saw his chance to gain his territory back, and took the field against Charles Martel, and recovered his dominions. The priests were hunted out, the churches destroyed, and the entire work of Willibrord seemed lost, while he abode at Echternach. But in the new war which broke out in 718 Charles was victorious, Radbod died the next year, and his successor, the younger Aldgild, made peace, the consequence of which was a free road for the Gospel. Willibrord returned to Utrecht and completed the Christianization of the country so far as it was in Frankish hands, with the full assistance of Charles. The further steps that were taken are not traceable. It is known, however, that for three years Willibrord had an assistant in Boniface.

(A. HAUCK.)

BIBLIOGRAPHY: Sources are: Bede, *Hist. eccl.*, iii. 13, v. 10–11, 19—note especially Plummer's ed., with notes,

Oxford, 1896; the earliest extant life, by Alcuin, based on a lost work by an Irish monk, in *ASM*, iii. 1, pp. 603–629, and partly in *MGH, Poet. Lat. ævi Carol.*, i (1881), 207–220; other early matter in *ASM*, ut sup., pp. 629–630; *MPL*, clvii. 405–412; *MGH, Script.*, xxiii (1874), 23 sqq. Consult further: A. Le Mire, *Cort Verhael van het Leven van den H. Willibrordus*, Antwerp, 1613; T. Wright, *Biographia Britannica*, i. 250–262, London, 1842; A. Dederich, *Beiträge zur römisch-deutschen Geschichte am Niederrhein*, appendix, Emmerich, 1850; P. Heber, *Die vorkarolingischen christlichen Glaubensboten am Rhein und deren Zeit*, pp. 193–212, Frankfort, 1858; A. Thym, *Der heilige Willibrord*, Münster, 1863; J. Engling, *Apostolat des heiligen Willibrord im Lande der Luxemburger*, Luxemburg, 1863; W. Moll, *Kerkgeschiedenis van Nederland*, pp. 95–118, Utrecht, 1864; J. Müllendorff, *Leben des heiligen Clemens Willibrord*, Weimar, 1868; J. B. Krier, *La Procession dansante . . . au tombeau de St. Willibrord*, Luxemburg, 1870; *Life of St. Willibrord*, London, 1877; J. B. Stamminger, *Franconia sancta*, pp. 145 sqq., Würzburg, 1881; G. F. Maclear, *Apostles of Mediæval Europe*, London, 1888; Poncelet, in *Analecta Bollandiana*, xxii (1903), 419 sqq., xxvi (1907), 73 sqq.; Friedrich, *KD*, vol. ii., pt. 1; Rettberg, *KD*, ii. 517 sqq.; Hauck, *KD*, i. 433 sqq.; Levison, in *NA*, xxxiii (1908), 1 sqq.; *DNB*, lxii. 13–15; *KL*, xii. 1669–71.

WILLIGIS, wil'lĭ-gis: Archbishop of Mainz 975–1011; d. at Mainz Feb. 23, 1011. He was one of the great ecclesiastical princes of the Middle Ages. Of his origin all that is known is that he came of a poor family, and that he received a good education under Wolcold, later bishop of Meissen, who recommended him to Otto I. Otto II. made him archbishop of Mainz and chancellor of Germany, positions which he long held, and in them rendered great services to his royal masters. He was able to strengthen the position of the archdiocese over which he presided so as to take rank after the pope over all the prelates in Germany and France, while his cathedral acquired vast wealth through imperial gifts in Bingen and the vicinity. St. Martin's at Mainz was built by him, also St. Stephen's, and he extended St. Victor's; he built also the church at Brunnen in Nassau and rebuilt the monastery of Bleidenstadt, founded the Benedictine monastery of Jechaburg, restored that of Disibodenburg and endowed it richly, and to a great number of institutions either secured great gifts or extended their privileges, in which activity he did not limit himself to his own diocese. That he was a disciplinarian is shown by the case of Gozmar, a cantor in the institution of St. Peter at Aschaffenburg, who in a contention with a teacher of the institution killed a boy, while his opponent was besieged in a tower by Gozmar's adherents. Willigis tried Gozmar before a synod at Mainz and condemned him to solitary confinement at Neustadt, and regulated the appointments of church and school.

Of general importance was Willigis' contest over the monastery of Gandersheim, a very important foundation in Lower Saxony, founded by Liudolf, grandfather of Otto the Great, lying on the border of the dioceses of Mainz and Hildesheim. Its original site was Brunhausen, which was in the diocese of Hildesheim, while Gandersheim belonged to Mainz, which claimed it when Sophia, the daughter of Otto II., became abbess. Through pride Sophia wished to be consecrated by an archbishop and asked Willigis to perform the ceremony. But Osdag of Hildesheim claimed the prerogative, and the Empress Theophano commanded the two prelates

to unite in the function. The contest between the dioceses was carried on by Osdag's successor, Bernward, and the presence of Willigis at a synod over which Bernward presided was construed by Hildesheim as granting the latter's claims to Gandersheim. In 1000, when the new building was to be dedicated, Sophia invited Willigis to officiate; he invited Bernward to assist and appointed Sept. 14–21 as the time. Bernward appeared on Sept. 14 and was prevented from officiating alone by Sophia, and the protest entered by Bernward was allowed by Willigis when he came on the 20th, so that the consecration did not take place. He called a synod for Nov. 28 to settle the affair, at which Bernward was not present, having carried his protest to Rome and left his case with Bishop Eckhard of Sleswick, whom Willigis did not recognize as a member of the synod. Eckhard and his adherents then left the assemblage, while the rest acknowledged Willigis' claim to Gandersheim. But a synod called by Pope Sylvester II. annulled this action and confirmed the claims of Hildesheim to Gandersheim, warning Willigis to take care in his actions. A further synod under Cardinal Friedrich as papal legate was set for June 21, which a tumult of the popular supporters disturbed at its first session, while at the second judgment was pronounced on Willigis, who had absented himself, the legate appointing a further synod for Christmas. A synod called by Willigis at Frankfort Aug. 15, 1001, was resultless through the absence of Bernward, and another synod was held at Todi in the presence of Otto III., was postponed to a later date, and then indefinitely, since pope and king both died early the next year. At first Henry IV. recognized the rights of Mainz, and Willigis consecrated Sophia as abbess Aug. 10, 1002. The consecration of the church was postponed till Christmas of 1006, and the contest rested till Bernward's successor, Godehard, reopened it.

The bishopric of Mersëburg had been founded by Otto the Great, but under the second bishop Giseler had been dissolved to enable the ambitious prelate to go to Magdeburg, a proceeding frowned upon by Gregory V. At a synod the restoration of the see was resolved upon, and Giseler was offered the choice between Magdeburg and Merseburg, with his deposition in view. The archbishop was meanwhile on guard to maintain his rights. The death of Giseler in 1004 cleared the way, Henry's court chaplain Tagino was appointed to Magdeburg, and his consent to the restoration of Merseburg opened the road for the consecration of a bishop for the diocese in 1004.

The erection of the bishopric of Bamberg was possible only in case the bishops of Würzburg and Eichstätt would give up part of their dioceses. The negotiations were successfully carried through by Willigis in two synods held in 1007, and Willigis consecrated Eberhard, Henry's chancellor, bishop at Frankfort.   (A. HAUCK.)

BIBLIOGRAPHY: The earlier lives are collected and edited by F. Falk in *Der Katholik*, 1869, i. 224–230, 1873, ii. 729–731, and *Theologische Litteraturblatt*, 1869, no. 22, p. 819 (cf. *Der Katholik*, 1869, i. 219–231, 1871, i. 499 sqq., 1881, ii. 273–290, 383–405); and by G. Waitz, in *MGH, Script.*, xvi. 2 (1887), 729–731, 746–748. Consult: H. Boehmer, *Willigis von Mainz*, Leipsic, 1895; Feller, in Buder's *Sammlung ungedruckter Schriften und Urkunden*, pp. 473 sqq., ib. 1735; R. Wilmans, *Jahrbücher des deutschen Reichs unter Otto III.*, Berlin, 1840; C. Euler, *Erzbischof Willigis von Mainz*, Naumburg, 1860; S. Hirsch, *Jahrbücher des deutschen Reichs unter Heinrich II.*, vols. i.–ii., Berlin, 1862–64; F. Gehle, *De S. Bernwardi . . . vita et rebus gestis*, Bonn, 1866; C. Will, in *Der Katholik*, 1873, ii. 715–734; idem, *Regesten zur Geschichte der Mainzer Erzbischöfe*, i. pp. xxxvii.–xliii., 117–144, Innsbruck, 1877; W. Giesebrecht, *Geschichte der deutschen Kaiserzeit*, vols. i.–ii., Brunswick, 1874; Hauck, *KD*, vol. iii.

WILLIRAM (WILTRAM, WALTRAM): German Benedictine and translator of the Song of Solomon; b. in the region of Worms; d. at Ebersberg (18 m. e.s.e. of Munich) Jan. 5, 1085. After studying for a time at Paris, he was attached to the cathedral at Bamberg, but later retired to Fulda, which he left in 1048 to become abbot of Ebersberg. His efforts to raise the tone of his monastery seem not to have been unopposed, and he frequently lamented the neglect of study as compared with the zeal for learning at Fulda. Williram is remembered for his Old High German paraphrase of the Song of Solomon, for which he availed himself entirely of patristic exegesis, adding nothing of his own. His method of interpretation was allegoristic, the Song referring to the love of Christ for the Church. His work was in three columns, the first containing a paraphrase of the Vulgate (which occupied the middle column) in Latin leonine hexameters, and the third being devoted to his exegesis in vernacular prose. The popularity of his production is evident from the fact that within a century it was translated into Dutch, while between 1147 and 1196 it was revised for use in another monastery, either by Rilindis and Herrat, abbesses of Hohenburg in Alsace, for nuns, or by some monk for a male order. The first edition of Williram's work was by Menrad Molther (Hagenau, 1528), and among more recent editions may be mentioned those of H. Hoffmann (on the basis of the Breslau and Leyden manuscripts; Breslau, 1827), J. Haupt (*Das Hohe Lied, ubersetzt von Willeram, erklärt von Rilindis und Herrat, Aebtissinen zu Hohenburg im Elsass*, Vienna, 1864), and J. Seemüller (Strasburg, 1878).

Bibliography: H. R. S. Riechau, *Williram, Abt zu Ebersberg in Oberbaiern*, Magdeburg, 1877; J. Seemüller, *Die Handschriften und Quellen von Willirams deutscher Paraphrase des Hohen Liedes*, Strasburg, 1877; F. Junghans, *Die Mischprosa Willirams*, Berlin, 1893; Hayner, " Das St. Trudperter [Hohenburger] Hohe Lied," in H. Paul and W. Braune, *Beiträge zur Geschichte der deutschen Sprache und Literatur*, iii (1876), 491 sqq.

WILLSON, DAVID BURT: Reformed Presbyterian; b. in Philadelphia, Pa., Sept. 27, 1842. He was educated at the University of Pennsylvania (A.B., 1860), Jefferson Medical College, Philadelphia (graduated, 1863), the Reformed Presbyterian Theological Seminary, Pittsburg, Pa (1865–69), and the Law School of the University of Pennsylvania (1869–70). From 1862 to 1865 he was in the medical service of the Union Army, and in 1866–68, while pursuing his theological studies, was a teacher at the Newell Institute, Pittsburg, Pa.; was pastor in Pittsburg, Pa. (1870–75), and was appointed professor of Biblical literature in the seminary of his denomination in the same city (1875), which position he still holds. He edited the monthly *Reformed Presbyterian and Covenanter* (1874–95), and is an associate editor of *The Christian Nation* (New York).

WILSNACK: A town 67 miles n.w. of Berlin, at present unimportant, but from 1383 to 1552 one of the most noted places of pilgrimage in Germany, in the contest over which the varied tendencies of the theology of the fifteenth century came to light, while ecclesiastical, territorial, and financial interests clashed violently. In a strife between a certain Von Bülow and the bishop of Havelberg the town and church of Wilsnack were reduced to ashes. The story goes that three sacred wafers were rescued from the ruins singed only on the edges, and in the middle of each was what looked like a drop of blood; that when these were taken to the neighboring church of Gross-Lüben a new wonder appeared, the wafers becoming luminous and fiery yet not being destroyed. The wonder drew pilgrims, and Bishop Dietrich II. (1370–85) conducted an investigation; new miracles resolved every doubt, and the pilgrimage grew greater. The bishop began the erection of a new and stately church, for which Pope Urban VI. granted the customary bull, but without mentioning the " blood-wonder "; in the episcopal permission, however, the archbishop of Magdeburg duly exploited it. Bishop Johann Wöpelitz of Havelberg secured for himself the rights of the place, obtained from Boniface IX. in 1395 a bull to incorporate the new church with the obligation to maintain a perpetual vicar there. He took a third of the income from the offerings of pilgrims and the sale of leaden models of the blood-bearing wafers. The pilgrimage became extensive and from all quarters; the place grew into a city. But opposition began to be heard, especially from Prague, and an investigation showed priestly contrivance. A synod at Prague of 1405 forbade pilgrimage to the place, and Huss wrote on the subject his *De omni sanguine Christi glorificato*. In 1412 a synod at Magdeburg took up the matter, proposed to the bishop of Havelberg a series of questions which elicited a fundamental report charging fraud on the clergy, withholding credence from the discoverer of the miracle, and asserting that there was neither blood nor anything like it. Evasion was attempted at Havelberg by asserting that it was the sacrament and not the blood which was honored, but left the pilgrims to venerate the miracle; a fourth newly consecrated wafer was added to the three. The literary polemic continued, and was carried forward by Heinrich Tocke, professor of theology in Erfurt, a man of reformatory spirit; but his representations had no effect upon the Council of Basel, to which he accompanied the archbishop; but his plea was effective with the bishop of Havelberg so far that the latter forbade his clergy to spread questionable tales of miracles performed. An inspection of the wafers showed that they were practically consumed, only the form being left, with no signs of blood. Yet his zeal for reform broke against the varied interests involved; the archbishop turned the battle against the pilgrimage to the advantage of his diocese; the bishop of Havelberg enlisted in the aid of his financial interest in the affair the political interests of the local lord of the manor, whose ecclesiastical patronage was of value. In 1445 the new archbishop of Magdeburg, Count Friedrich von Beichlingen, took the position of Tocke, while Frederick

II. took into his service in defense of the Wilsnack miracle Matthias Döring, the Franciscan provincial. The bishop of Havelberg evaded the attempts of the archbishop to treat with him personally, and the matter went to Rome for a decision at a time when the recognition of Frederick was needed for Pope Eugene IV., with the result of a guarded and evasive pronouncement to the effect that it was the sacrament which was honored, and not the bloody wafers. An attack had been made upon Tocke by Döring charging the former with being a Hussite; the Erfurt theologians disallowed this, but it became the question before a provincial synod. Frederick complained to the archbishop of Magdeburg against Tocke and others, and then secured the renewal of the bull of Eugene IV. by Nicholas V. (1447), protecting the rights of Havelberg, the bishop of which now offered passive resistance to the archbishop. At a synod in 1451 the papal legate (Nicholas of Cusa) forbade the exhibition of alleged bloody wafers and of the leaden models, thus discouraging the pilgrimage. In turn the Havelbergers secured the excommunication of the archbishop, while bands plundered his territory. In 1453 Nicholas issued a bull relieving both sides from the censures to which they were subject, forbade them to occasion new strife, and awarded the archbishop damages for the brigandage committed; the result was on the whole favorable to Havelberg, the archbishop being obstructed in his opposition to the Havelbergers, while the latter were in a manner protected.

The literary assault continued, the Carthusian Jacob of Jueterbog and the Augustinian Johann von Dorsten of Erfurt leading. The object of attack now was not the priestly trickery, but the mania for pilgrimage, which was likened to a plague. When the Reformation began, Wilsnack was still most popular as a goal of pilgrimage. No effective steps were taken till 1548, the ecclesiastical and civil powers being faithful to Rome. In that year Joachim Ellefeld, an Evangelical preacher, was installed, but enjoined by the chapter to leave ceremonial untouched. But Johann Agricola urged Ellefeld to cast out the idolatry, and he entered the church and burned the wafers. In indignation the chapter had Ellefeld imprisoned. But it happened that the latter had not burned the freshly consecrated host, and he was set free by the elector on Nov. 11, 1552. The church from that time was Evangelical, though pilgrims from distant regions continued to visit the church for some decades. The bloody host of Wilsnack, however, furnished a pattern which other places employed.   (G. KAWERAU.)

BIBLIOGRAPHY: Dat ys dy Erfindunge und Wunderwerke des hilligen Sakramentes tho der Wilsnagk, Magdeburg, 1509, reprinted in P. Heitz und W. L. Schreiber, Drucke und Holzschnitte . . . , pp. 8–11, Strasburg, 1904; Historia inventionis et ostensionis vivifici sacramenti in Wilsnagk, Lübeck, 1520; M. Ludecus, Hist. von der Erfindung . . . des vermeinten heiligen Bluts zur Wilsnagk, Wittenberg, 1586; E. Breest, in Märkische Forschungen, xvi (1881), 133 sqq.; idem, in Magbeburger Geschichtsblätter, 1883, 43 sqq., 97 sqq.; idem, in Blätter für Handel, Gewerbe, etc., 1882, pp. 167 sqq.; Wattenbach, in SBA, 1882, pp. 603 sqq.; B. Hennig, in Forschungen zur brandenb. und preussischen Geschichte, xix (1906), 391 sqq.; KL, v. 1729–1734.

WILSON, DANIEL: Bishop of Calcutta; b. in Spitalfields, London, July 2, 1778; d. in Calcutta Jan. 2, 1858. He was educated at St. Edmund Hall, Oxford (B.A., 1802; M.A., 1804; D.D., 1832); was ordained, and became curate of Richard Cecil at Chobham and Bisley in Surrey, where he developed into a strong Evangelical preacher; was tutor or vice-principal of St. Edmund Hall, Oxford, and minister of Worton, Oxfordshire, 1807–12; assistant curate at St. John's Chapel, Bedford Row, Bloomsbury, 1808–12; sole minister there, 1812–1824; and vicar of St. Mary's, Islington, 1824–32, when he was consecrated bishop of Calcutta, and metropolitan of India. He founded an English church at Rangoon, Ceylon, 1855, and the cathedral church, St. Paul's, consecrated at Calcutta, 1847. He was an indefatigable worker, and as bishop was noted for fidelity and firmness. He was the author of numerous sermons published separately and in collections, and of *The Evidences of Christianity,* . . . *a Course of Lectures* (2 vols., London, 1828–30); and of *Bishop Wilson's Journal Letters, addressed to his Family the first Nine Years of his Indian Episcopacy* (1863; ed. his son Daniel).

BIBLIOGRAPHY: Besides the Journal Letters, ut sup., consult the Life by J. Bateman, 2 vols., London, 1860; E. Stock, Hist. of the Church Missionary Society, passim, ib. 1899.

WILSON, HENRY BRISTOW: Church of England; b. in London June 10, 1803; d. there Aug. 10, 1888. He studied at the Merchant Taylors' School, London, and at St. John's College, Oxford (B.A., 1825; M.A., 1829; B.D., 1834), and was fellow of St. John's 1825–50, tutor 1833–35, and Rawlinson professor of Anglo-Saxon 1839–44. He opposed the Oxford movement, and in Mar., 1841, joined A. C. Campbell, T. T. Churton, and John Griffiths in the memorable protest against Newman's *Tract XC.* In 1850 he was presented to the college living of Great Staughton, Huntingdonshire, which he retained till his death. He is memorable as the projector and editor of the volume of *Essays and Reviews* (q.v.) which started a great controversy in 1860 and subjected him to a trial for heresy. He published *The Communion of Saints* (Oxford, 1851), Bampton lectures for 1851; *A Letter . . . on University and College Reform* (London, 1854); *Schemes of Christian Comprehension* (in *Oxford Essays,* 1857); *The National Church* (in *Essays and Reviews,* 1860); *A Brief Examination of Prevalent Opinions on the Inspiration of the Old and New Testaments* (1861); and *Three Sermons* (1861).

BIBLIOGRAPHY: Life and Letters of Rowland Williams, by Mrs. Williams, vol. i., London, 1874; G. C. Brodrick and W. H. Fremantle, Judgments of the Judicial Committee of the Privy Council, pp. 247–290, ib. 1865; R. E. Prothero, Life and Correspondence of Dean Stanley, ii. 30–44, 157–158, ib. 1893; E. Abbott and L. Campbell, Life and Letters of Benjamin Jowett, passim, ib. 1897; H. P. Liddon, Life of Edward Bouverie Pusey, ii. 167, iv. 38–68, ib. 1897; DNB, lxii. 97; literature under ESSAYS AND REVIEWS.

WILSON, JOHN: The name of two divines.

1. Puritan; b. at Windsor (21 m. w. by s. of London), Berkshire, 1588; d. in Boston, Mass., Aug. 7, 1667. He was educated at Eton and Cambridge, graduating from the university about 1606, after which he not only studied law for three years, but also took orders in the Church of England. He preached at Mortlake, Henley, Bumstead, Stoke,

Clare, and Candish, and was for several years rector of Sudbury, Sussex. He was, however, a Puritan rather than a churchman, and on Apr. 8, 1630, he sailed for Massachusetts with John Winthrop (q.v.). Landing at Salem, he soon removed to Charlestown, where within a few months he organized what was to become the First Church in Boston. He was ordained its teacher by his own communicants, but in 1631–32 he was in England, where he was ordained pastor. He was again in England in 1634–35, and soon after he had returned to America the Antinomian Controversy (see ANTINOMIANISM AND ANTINOMIAN CONTROVERSIES, II., 2) invaded his congregation. With Winthrop Wilson became one of the principal opponents of the movement and of its leader, Anne Hutchinson; but before it was settled Wilson was appointed chaplain to the expedition against the Pequots. Later he was a companion of John Eliot (q.v.) in his labors for the conversion of the Indians. His two colleagues, both of whom he outlived, were John Cotton and John Norton (qq.v.).

The principal writings of Wilson were *Some Helps to Faith* (London, 1625); *A Song of Deliverance for the Lasting Remembrance of God's Wonderful Works* (1626; new ed., Boston, 1680); *The Day Breaking, if not the Sun Rising, of the Gospel with the Indians in New England* (1647; new ed., New York, 1865); and *A Seasonable Watch-Word unto Christians against the Dreams and Dreamers of this Generation* (Cambridge, Mass., 1677; the last sermon of Wilson, preached Nov. 16, 1665).

BIBLIOGRAPHY: W. B. Sprague, *Annals of the American Pulpit*, i. 12–15, New York, 1859; A. W. MacClure, *Lives of the Chief Fathers of New England*, ii., Boston, 1870.

2. Presbyterian missionary to India and educator; b. at Lauder (18 m. s.e. of Edinburgh) Dec. 11, 1804; d. at Bombay, India, . Dec. 1, 1875. From early childhood he knew what personal religion was. During his college course at the University of Edinburgh, through tutoring some Anglo-Indian boys his mind was turned toward India. He was a diligent student of natural science as well as of languages, and besides taking his theological course he further qualified himself before going out by attending medical classes. He sailed in the service of the Scottish Missionary Society, but shortly afterward the Church of Scotland awoke to missionary enterprise and took over the society's work. Wilson became head of the mission college in Bombay, and in that city, where he is still remembered as perhaps the greatest of her citizens, he spent his long, laborious, and influential life. He rapidly acquired a wide and profound acquaintance with Indian languages and literature, knowledge which he turned to use in multifarious controversial writings and public disputations in the cause of Christianity and in research into the obscure field of Indian antiquities. While on cordial terms with Dr. Duff, he laid greater stress on work among the common people, on their own ground, in the vernacular. His first wife, who went out with him, did much in her brief six years for the cause of female education. In 1843, like all the Church of Scotland missionaries, he adhered to the Free Church. He visited the Holy Land, publish-

ing in 1845 *Lands of the Bible*, and stirring up interest in Syrian missions. In 1846, on a visit home, he married again, and for the next twenty years his wife evinced unusual interest and attained great success in mission work among Indian women of all ranks. He himself became vice-chancellor of Bombay University, a position of vast educational importance, and president of the Bombay branch of the Royal Asiatic Society. His relations with the governor, Sir William Elphinstone, were close and intimate. In 1870 he was called to the moderator's chair of the Free Church General Assembly, taking his place among the leaders on the progressive side and afterward returning to end his days in Bombay.

BIBLIOGRAPHY: Wilson was the author of *An Exposure of the Hindu Religion*, and *A Second Exposure* (Bombay, 1832–34); *Memoirs of Mrs. Wilson* (Edinburgh, 1838); *Lands of the Bible Visited and Described* (2 vols., 1847); *History of the Suppression of Infanticide in Western India* (Bombay, 1855); *India Three Thousand Years Ago* (1858); and *Indian Caste*, ed. P. Peterson (2 vols., 1877). For his life consult: G. Smith, *Life of John Wilson*, London, 1878; R. Hunter, *Hist. of Free Church Missions in India and Africa*, ib. 1873; G. Smith, *Life of Alexander Duff*, ib. 1881; J. Marrat, *Two Standard Bearers in the East*, ib. 1882; *DNB*, lxii. 113–115.

WILSON, JOHN A: United Presbyterian; b. at Pleasantville, Pa., Oct. 4, 1839. He was graduated from Westminster College, Pa. (A.B., 1864), and, after studying law and practising for two years, from Alleghany Theological Seminary (1872); he then held pastorates at Beaver, Pa. (1872–76), St. Louis (1876–86), and Wooster, O. (1886–93), and since 1893 has been professor of church history and pastoral theology at Alleghany Theological Seminary, Pittsburg.

WILSON, JOHN LEIGHTON: Presbyterian, Southern Church; b. in Sumter County, S. C., Mar. 25, 1809; d. near Mayesville, S. C., July 13, 1886. He was graduated from Union College, Schenectady, N. Y., 1829, and from Columbia Theological Seminary, S. C., 1833; was foreign missionary in Western Africa, 1834–53; secretary of Foreign Missions for the Presbyterian Church, New York, 1853–61; for the Southern Presbyterian Church, Columbia, S. C., 1861–85, and secretary emeritus, 1885–86. He was instrumental in breaking up the slave-trade in Africa. He made a grammar and dictionary of the Grebo and Mpongwe languages, and translated parts of the Bible. He edited *The Foreign Record*, New York, 1853–61, and *The Missionary*, Baltimore, 1861–85. He wrote *Western Africa: Its History, Condition, and Prospects* (New York, 1857).

WILSON, JOSEPH DAWSON: Reformed Episcopalian; b. in New York City July 9, 1840. He was educated at the College of the City of New York (then called the Free Academy), St. Stephen's College, Annandale, N. Y. (B.A., 1863), and the General Theological Seminary (graduated, 1866); was ordained to the priesthood of the Protestant Episcopal Church; he was curate of St. Luke's, New York City (1866–67), and rector of Calvary, Pittsburg, Pa. (1867–74). He then left the Protestant Episcopal Church for Reformed Episcopalianism, and was rector of Christ Church, Peoria, Ill. (1874–1879); St. John's, Chicago (1879–95); acting rec-

tor of the Church of Our Lord, Victoria, B. C. (1895–
1901); and since 1901 has been professor of history
and apologetics at the Reformed Episcopal Theological Seminary, Philadelphia. In theology he is a
moderate Calvinist and a conservative, and has written *Words from the Cross* (sermons, Chicago, 1881)
and *Did Daniel Write Daniel?* (New York, 1906).

WILSON, LUTHER BARTON: Methodist Epis-
copal bishop; b. at Baltimore, Md., Nov. 14, 1856.
He was educated at Dickinson College (A.B., 1875)
and at the School of Medicine of the University of
Maryland (M.D., 1877). In 1878 he entered the
Baltimore Annual Conference of his denomination
and held pastorates at Hancock, Woodberry, and
Baltimore, Md., and at Washington, D. C. He was
presiding elder of the Washington District of the
Baltimore Conference in 1894–1900 and of the West
Baltimore District in 1903–04, and was elected
bishop in 1904.

WILSON, MARGARET: One of the two "martyrs of the Solway"; b. at Glenvernock (65 m.
s.s.w. of Glasgow), Scotland, 1667; drowned near
Wigtown (75 m. s. of Glasgow) May 11, 1685. For
refusing to conform to episcopacy, she, together
with her younger sister Agnes, and Margaret Mac-
Lachlan, a woman of sixty-three, was tried at the
Wigtown assize and condemned to death by drowning in the Bladenoch. The younger sister was bailed
out, but on May 11, 1685, the two other women
were tied to stakes within the flood-mark of the
water of the Bladenoch and were drowned by the
incoming tide. The incident furnished the subject
of Millais' picture, "The Martyr of the Solway"
(1871), now in Liverpool. An obelisk to the memory of the martyrs was erected on Windy Hill, Wigtown, in 1861, and there is another well-known
monument at Stirling. See COVENANTERS, § 6.

BIBLIOGRAPHY: A. Stewart, *History Vindicated in the Case
of the Wigtown Martyrs*, Edinburgh, 1869; R. Wodrow,
Hist. of the Sufferings of the Church of Scotland, ib. 1829–
1830; J. Anderson, *Ladies of the Covenant*, Glasgow, 1850,
New York, 1880; W. M. Hetherington, *Hist. of the Church
of Scotland*, pp. 281–282, New York, 1881; *DNB*, lxii.
118–119; and literature under COVENANTERS.

WILSON, THOMAS: Church of England, bishop
of Sodor and Man; b. at Burton (10 m. s. of Liverpool), England, Dec. 20, 1663; d. on the Isle of
Man Mar. 7, 1755. He was graduated from Trinity College, Dublin (B.A., 1686; M.A., 1696); was
ordained deacon, 1686; became curate in the
chapelry of Newchurch Kenyon, Lancashire, 1687;
was ordained priest, 1689, and remained in charge
of Newchurch till 1692, when he was appointed
chaplain to the Earl of Derby, who, in 1697, appointed him bishop of Sodor and Man, and he
was consecrated, 1698. He accomplished two
great reforms in his diocese: the first, of 1703, relating to the tenures of landed property, which
had been very uncertain; and the second, accomplished by his *Ecclesiastical Constitutions*, to the
rules and discipline of the church there. He had
remarkable qualities as an administrator, and was,
from his position, compelled to take a great share
in secular affairs. He wrote comparatively little.
In 1707 he issued at London his *Principles and
Duties of Christianity*, commonly called the
"Manx Catechism," in English and Manx; this

was the first book ever printed in Manx. In
1735 he showed his interest in the missionary aspects of General Oglethorpe's Georgia plantation
scheme, by writing his *Essay towards an Instruction
for the Indians, Explaining the most Essential Doctrines of Christianity . . . with Directions and Prayers*. The *Essay*, which was translated into French
and Italian, and met with great favor, was published
in 1740 at London. In 1749 he accepted from the
Unity of the Brethren (q.v.) the office of honorary
president of the reformed section of the Moravian
Church. His age at the time debarred him from
active service, but he was glad of the opportunity
of publicly testifying to his interest in that people.
His life was marked by rare unselfishness and devotion to duty. His works embrace devotional writings of extended private and public use, numerous
sermons, and *Short and Plain Instructions for the
Better Understanding of the Lord's Supper* (2d ed.,
London, 1736; and often); *Parochialia, or Instructions to the Clergy* (Bath, 1821); and *The Holy Bible,
with Notes, by Thomas Wilson . . . and various
Renderings, by . . . C. Cruttwell* (3 vols., London,
1785); His *Works* were first published in a collected edition, with his *Life*, by C. Cruttwell (2 vols.,
Bath, 1781; 4th ed., 4 vols., 1796–97; and best ed.,
with his *Life* by J. Keble, 7 vols., Oxford, 1847–63).

BIBLIOGRAPHY: Besides the accounts of the life in the col-
lected *Works*, ut sup., there are biographies by H. Stowell,
London, 1819; R. B. Hone, in *Lives of Eminent Chris-
tians*, vol. i., ib. 1833; W. H. Teale, in *Lives of Eminent
Divines*, ib. 1846. Consult further: J. Rosse, *Hist. of
Wesleyan Methodism in the Isle of Man*, Douglas, 1849;
M. Arnold, *Culture and Anarchy*, preface, London, 1869;
J. H. Overton and F. Relton, *The English Church (1714–
1800)*, pp. 125–136 et passim, ib. 1906; *DNB*, lxii. 139–142.

WIMPFELING, vimp'fê-ling **(WIMPHELING),
JAKOB:** Humanistic theologian; b. at Schlettstadt (29 m. s.w. of Strasburg) July 25, 1450; d.
there Nov. 17, 1528. He entered in 1464 the University of Freiburg, and in 1468 removed to the
University of Erfurt; in the following year he went
to Heidelberg where he became master of philosophy in 1471. In 1483 he was called as cathedral
preacher to Speyer, where he remained fourteen
years, though the pulpit work was done by others
because of the vocal weakness of Wimpfeling; but
as prebendary he wrote and worked in the interest
of the church of Speyer and its clergy. His efforts
were aimed at a better discipline of the clergy, a
more frequent convocation of synods, and a devoted
adoration of Mary. After 1487 he seems to have
possessed the parish in Sulz near Molsheim as an
inheritance from a paternal uncle. He refused prebends in the chapter of St. Thomas in Strasburg
and at the cathedral in Mainz as hindrances to
study in science and to contemplation. In 1498 he
became professor of rhetoric and poetics at the University of Heidelberg, and in 1501 his friend Geiler
von Kaisersberg induced him to remove to Strasburg, where he, Sebastian Brant, and Geiler were
active in the interest of church and school and exercised a decisive influence upon the spiritual life
of Strasburg which lasted until the days of Butzer,
Capito, and Sturm. In 1503 Wimpfeling followed
his friend Bishop Christoph von Utenheim to Basel,
and soon went to the University of Freiburg, whence
he had to remove because of his invectives against

the monks, while a flood of literature poured forth in poetry and prose. Wimpfeling was accused at Rome and cited before the pope; but the popular voice was in his favor, and the two bishops of Strasburg and Basel defended him. Between 1508 and 1512 Wimpfeling frequently changed his home, and in 1513 Christoph von Utenheim, bishop of Basel, requested him " to assume the leadership of a newly reformed convent," the locality of which is not known. In 1515 he left this office and removed to Schlettstadt, where he spent the last years of his life. As in Strasburg, so here he gathered a circle of disciples and admirers who about 1518 seem to have organized in a literary society which fell to pieces before Luther's movement.

Wimpfeling planned great things, but accomplished little. He was overshadowed by Erasmus and left no generally diffused influence; in his narrower circle he unintentionally prepared the way for the Reformation. His numerous works are concerned with politics, philology, theology, history, and poetry. Worthy of special mention are his pedagogical treatises *Isidoneus germanicus* (1496) and *Adolescentia*, which are distinguished by sound thoughts on education. In his *Germania* (1501) he showed himself an enthusiastic German patriot; in the first part he attempted to prove that the left border of the Rhine never belonged to Gaul. In *Epitome rerum Germanicarum* (1505) Wimpfeling presented a concise history of the Germans.

(H. HERMELINK.)

BIBLIOGRAPHY: The autobiographic *Expurgatio* is reproduced in J. A. Riegger's *Amoenitatis litterariæ Friburgenses*, Ulm, 1775. Consult further: J. Knepper, in *Erläuterungen . . . zu Janssens Geschichte*, vol. iii., parts 2–4, Freiburg, 1902; *Zeitschrift für Geschichte des Oberrheins*, 1903, pp. 46 sqq., 1906, pp. 40 sqq., 262 sqq., 1907, pp. 478 sqq.; also C. Schmidt, *Hist. littéraire de l'Alsace*, Paris, 1879; and J. Janssen, *Hist. of the German People*, iii. 1–8, St. Louis, 1900; *KL*, xii. 1675–82 (gives titles of the earlier biographies, which are reviewed ably in Knepper's work referred to above).

WIMPINA, vim-pî'na **(KOCH), KONRAD:** Catholic theologian; b. at Buchen (29 m. e.n.e. of Heidelberg) about 1465; d. at Amorbach (44 m. s.s.e. of Frankfort) May 17, 1531. The family name was Koch, but Konrad called himself Wimpina, probably because his family originally had their home in the neighboring Wimpfen-on-the-Neckar. In 1479 he entered the University of Leipsic, became a Thomist in philosophy; in 1491 he was received into the council of the philosophical faculty; in 1494 was rector, and the same year dean of his faculty, at a later time vice-chancellor for three years. After 1486 he devoted himself also to the study of theology, and in 1495 became subdeacon. In 1500 he became involved with his former teacher and friend Polich in a passionate dispute concerning Humanism and Scholasticism, or, as the opponents formulated it, over the question whether the art of poetry is the source of theology. In assigning a very low place to poetry, Wimpina aroused the Humanists against himself, while Polich became one of their stanchest defenders. In 1505 Joachim I. and his brother Albrecht called Wimpina to the newly established University of Frankfort as its first rector. In 1518 he became involved in a dispute with Luther concerning indulgences, and into this dispute Tetzel was drawn, participating on Jan. 20, 1518, in Frankfort in a disputation concerning theses which had been formulated by Wimpina in opposition to Luther. Wimpina thus appears as one of the earliest literary opponents of Luther, and he devoted the following years to an intensive refutation of the doctrine of Luther, at first only in disputations, then, in 1528, he published his great work of refutation *Anacephalæosis*, a production of intense intellectual labor. It represents Lutheranism as the rallying-point of the sects and heresies of all times. All heresy, Wimpina states, is directed fundamentally against the Church as a divine foundation. Wyclif is the father of the doctrine of the Hussites, and that is the source of the Lutheran heresy. By a necessity of nature the pope, Wimpina argues, stands above the emperor and possesses not only doctrinal power, but also executive and disciplinary power. Wimpina went to the Diet of Augsburg as the theologian of Joachim I. When at the beginning of the diet without the knowledge of Luther the Articles of Schwabach (see SCHWABACH ARTICLES) had been printed and communicated to Joachim, Wimpina together with his Brandenburg colleagues Mensing, Redorfer, and Elgersma published as refutation *Christlicher Unterricht gegen die Bekanntnus M. Luthers*. He was also one of the circle of theologians to whom was entrusted the confutation of the Augsburg Confession, but Wimpina's part was evidently small. After the diet he accompanied his elector to Cologne. Then he returned to his native state and lived thereafter in the Benedictine monastery of Amorbach. Besides his great work *Anacephalæosis* (1528) he published *Præcepta coaugmentandæ Rethoricæ orationis*, or *Ars epistolandi* (c. 1486); *Almæ universitatis studii Lipzensis et urbis Liptzg descriptio* (1488, newly edited by C. F. Eberhard, Leipsic, 1802); *Tractatus de erroribus philosophorum* (1493); *Congestio textus novæ proprietatum logicalium cum commentatione* (1498); *Apologeticus in sacræ theologiæ defensionem* (1500); *De D. Annæ trinubio* (1518); *De signis et insomniis* (1529); *Farrago miscellaneorum* (1531; contains his Leipsic writings); his anti-Luther writings are in *Sectarum, errorum . . . librorum partes tres* (Frankfort, 1528).

(G. KAWERAU.)

BIBLIOGRAPHY: J. C. Beckmann, *Notitia Universitatis Francofurtanæ*, Frankfort, 1707; J. Gropp, *Ætas mille annorum . . . monasterii . . . in Amorbach*, Frankfort, 1736; G. Bauch, in *Zeitschrift des Vereins für Geschichte und Alterthum Schlesiens*, xxx (1896), 133 sqq.; idem in *Neues Archiv für sächsische Gesellschaft*, xviii (1897), 293 sqq.; idem, *Geschichte des Leipziger Frühhumanismus*, Leipsic, 1899; idem, *Die Anfänge der Universität Frankfurt*, Freiburg, 1903; E. Friedländer, *Matrikel der Universität Frankfurt*, pp. 1–2, 48, Leipsic, 1887; N. Müller, in *TSK*, 1893, pp. 83 sqq., 1894, pp. 389 sqq.; G. Erler, *Die Matrikel der Universität Leipzig*, Leipsic, 1895–97; N. Paulus, in *Der Katholik*, 1900, ii. 281 sqq.; idem, *Die deutschen Dominikaner im Kampfe gegen Luther*, pp. 134 sqq., Freiburg, 1903; J. Negwer, *Konrad Wimpina*, Breslau, 1907–1909; *ADB*, xliii. 330 sqq.; *KL*, xii. 1682–85.

WINCHESTER, CALEB THOMAS: Methodist Episcopal layman; b. at Montville, Conn., Jan. 18, 1847. He was educated at Wesleyan University, Middletown, Conn. (A.B., 1869), with which he has been connected ever since, being librarian (1869–1879), associate professor of English (1872–78), and full professor of the same subject since 1878. He was a member of the joint committee of the Methodist Episcopal Church, and the Methodist Episcopal Church, South, to prepare the hymnal, which was published in 1905. He has written *The Life of John Wesley* (New York, 1906); and *A Group of English Essayists* (1910).

WINCHESTER, ELHANAN: Universalist; b. in Brookline, Mass., Sept. 30, 1751; d. in Hartford, Conn., Apr. 18, 1797. In 1769 he began to preach, and was ordained pastor of an open-communion church at Rehoboth, Mass., 1771; about a year later he became a close-communionist, and was excommunicated; residing in Charleston, S. C., 1774–1780, he then became pastor in Philadelphia of the First Baptist Church, and founded with a majority of his congregation a Universalist church there in 1781. From 1787 to 1794 he preached Restorationism in England. His works embrace a *Collection of Psalms, Hymns and Poems* (Boston, 1772); *A New Book of Poems, on Several Occasions* (1773); *The Universal Restoration* (London, 1788, and often); *A Course of Lectures on the Prophecies that Remain to be Fulfilled* (4 vols., 1789–90); and *Progress and Empire of Christ* (1793).

BIBLIOGRAPHY: Sketches of the *Life* are by W. Vidler, London, 1797; and E. M. Stone, Boston, 1836. Consult further R. Eddy, in *American Church History Series*, x. 408–413 et passim, New York, 1894; and the literature under UNIVERSALISTS.

WINCKLER, vink'ler, HUGO: German Protestant, orientalist; b. at Gräfenhainichen (12 m. s.w. of Wittenberg) July 4, 1863. He was educated at the University of Berlin, where he became privatdocent for Semitic philology in the philosophical faculty, and since 1904 has been professor of the same subject. Besides editing *Mitteilungen der vorderasiatischen Gesellschaft*, *Das alte Orient*, and *Ex Oriente Lux*, he has written: *Die Keilschrifttexte Sargons* (2 vols., Leipsic, 1889); *Untersuchungen zur altorientalischen Geschichte* (1889); *Der Thontafelfund von Tell el-Amarna* (1889); *Geschichte Babyloniens und Assyriens* (1892); *Alttestamentliche Untersuchungen* (1892); *Sammlung von Keilschrifttexten* (3 parts; 1893–95); *Altorientalische Forschungen* (21 parts, 1893–1906); *Geschichte Israels* (2 vols., 1895–1900); *Die Thontafeln von Tell-el-Amarna* (Berlin, 1896); *Kritische Schriften* (6 vols., 1901–08); *Die Gesetze Hammurabis* (Leipsic, 1904); *Kritische Schriften* (Berlin, 1906); *Die babylonische Geisteskultur in ihren Beziehungen zur Kulturentwicklung der Menschheit* (1907); *Die Panbabylonisten* (Leipsic, 1907); *Die im Sommer '06 in Klein-Asien ausgeführten Ausgrabungen* (1907); and edited with H. Zimmern the 3d ed. of E. Schrader's *Keilinschriften und das A. T.* (Berlin, 1903).

WINCKLER, JOHANN: German Lutheran and defender of Philipp Jakob Spener (q.v.); b. at Gölzern, near Grimma (17 m. s.e. of Leipsic) July 13, 1642; d. at Hamburg Apr. 5, 1705. His parents, who were poor peasants, self-sacrificingly had him educated at the school in Grimma and at St. Thomas' in Leipsic, and at the University of Leipsic; but his poverty interrupted his university studies, and he became private tutor in Grimma, then in 1664 mas-

ter in Jena, and he delivered private lectures at Leipsic. He was with a son of Duke Philipp Ludwig of Holstein-Sonderburg at Tübingen, 1668–71, when began that acquaintance with Philipp Jakob Spener which had a decisive influence upon his life. In 1671 he was called to his first ministerial office in Homburg vor der Höhe; in the following year he became superintendent in Braubach, and in 1676 court preacher in Darmstadt, in 1678 pastor in Mannheim, and in 1679 superintendent in Wertheim. In 1684 he was appointed chief preacher of St. Michael's in Hamburg, where he remained until his death. According to the unanimous testimony of his contemporaries Winckler had few equals as preacher, though his printed sermons make difficult reading because of the inserted excursuses. In several works he appears as a decided representative of the principles of Spener; but while defending in a bitter controversy at Hamburg Spener's private conventicles, Winckler was not a blind follower, and maintained an independent position. He rendered great services to the cause of education, and several schools were on his initiative enlarged or newly founded. About 1688 he conceived the plan of a Bible society and himself took an active part in it by editing several editions of the Bible. Among his works mention may be made of: *Bedenken über Kriegsmanns Symphonesis oder Büchlein von einzelnen Zusammenkünften der Christen* (Hanau, 1679); *Antwort auf Dilfelds Gründliche Erörterung der Frage von den Privatzusammenkünften* (1681); *Sendschreiben an D. Hannekenium* (Hamburg, 1690); *Schriftmässiges und wohlgemeintes Bedenken* (1693).

(CARL BERTHEAU†.)

BIBLIOGRAPHY: J. A. Fabricius, *Memoriæ Hamburgenses*, iii. 351, Hamburg, 1711; J. Moller, *Cimbria literata*, ii. 990 sqq., Sleswick, 1687; J. Geffcken, *Johann Winckler und die hamburgische Kirche in seiner Zeit*, Hamburg, 1861; K. J. W. Wolters, in *Gesammelte Vorträge*, ed. T. Schrader, pp. 143–216, ib. 1892; *ADB*, xliii. 365–373.

WINDESHEIM (WINDESEM), MONASTERY OF: A celebrated establishment situated at Windesheim (4 m. s. of Zwolle), the mother-house of a number of reformed cloisters of regular canons which flourished in the beginning and middle of the fifteenth century. Its history affords a glimpse into the reforming movement which in Holland, Germany, England, France, Bohemia, and even in Italy was a promise of the real Reformation. It stands in the closest relations with the Brethren of the Common Life (see COMMON LIFE, BRETHREN OF THE), an organization which embodied in itself the impulses received from Geert Groote (q.v.). Jan Busch (q.v.), the author of the *Chronicon Windeshemense*, relates that Groote stated as his wish and counsel to his pupil and follower Florens Radewijns and his associates that they should seek to obtain in the founding of a monastery a center for the brethren and sisters who felt attracted by his (Groote's) personality. He also recommended the order of regular canons as that most suitable for their purposes. This choice is explicable from two standpoints. The times were not ripe for an association not founded on the rules and patterns then in existence. The Evangelical spirit was not then strong enough to stand on its own feet, the Church furnished still the legal spirit and forms. Further, the Carthusian rules would take the brethren out of the world, the Cistercian rules were too severe. The basis was to be simply the three vows of celibacy, poverty, and obedience; and the regular canons worked in Groote's own lines of preaching and the saving of souls.

A beginning was made when Berthold ten Hove (Have), a citizen of Zwolle in Salland, donated his patrimony " de hof to Windesem," for the future cloister. Hendrik van Wilsem, formerly assessor at Kampen, gave a piece of land. Other donations came in, and in 1386 it was decided to erect the monastery, in which Floris van Wevelinkhoven, the worthy bishop of Utrecht, showed interest. The six associates in the work were the two named above as making donations, Hendrik Klingebijl, Werner Keynkamp, Johannes van Kempen (Kempis), brother of the celebrated Thomas à Kempis (q.v.), and Hendrik de Wilde, all of them coming from the Brethren of the Common Life. Buildings for the purpose did not exist and must therefore be erected. The structures were begun in Mar., 1387, and the church was consecrated and the brethren were hooded on Nov. 17, of the same year. The vow of obedience was specifically made not to the bishop (of Utrecht) but to the superior who was to be chosen. At first Klingebijl, with the title of rector, assumed the direction; a year later Keynkamp became the leader with the title of prior. After about three years he resigned the position to Johannes Goswini Vos, who stamped his influence upon the order and gave it its unique significance.

Equally remarkable are the growth in wealth and the number of monasteries affiliated with Windesheim, while nunneries were founded which were governed by the same spirit. Among these may be named Marienborn near Arnhem (1392), Nieuwlicht near Hoorn in West Frisia (1392), while Eemstein was in close relations. These four combined in 1394 and formed a chapter, with Windesheim at the head and its prior the prior-superior of the order, and a yearly assemblage, approved by Boniface IX., May 16, 1395. By 1402 seven institutions were affiliated, by 1423 there were twenty-nine, twenty-four for men and five for women. In 1464 the chronicler speaks of an *octogenarius numerus*, twenty-eight under the priorate of Johannes Vos (cf. Acquoy, iii. 1-232, for the list). The congregation won its first triumph at the Synod of Costnitz, where Prior Vos gained recognition as well as the favor of Martin V. by his defense of the Brethren of the Common Life against the attack of the Dominican Grabow. A second was that of the year 1435 in bringing about a reformation of the Augustinian cloisters in Germany. Epochal was the visit of Nicholas of Cusa (see Cusa) in celebrating his jubilee (1451). The cardinal's legation had as its purpose the initiation of a new religious-ethical life in Germany, especially in relation to the religious orders. Cusa appointed Jan Busch and Dr. Paulus, of the monastery of St. Mauritius at Halle, to visit the regular monasteries of Saxony, Thuringia, and Meissen, and to reform them in accordance with the statutes of the Windesheim congregation. The movement spread to the cloisters of other orders and beyond the limits of the region where it was initiated. A further result was the increase of institutions affiliated with Windesheim. But the Reformation brought to an end the significance of this monastery, though it lived on till the end of the sixteenth century, while the last prior-general, Constantinus Belling of Grauhoff near Goslar, died Jan. 17, 1807, and the last monastery (Frenswegen near Nordhorn) closed in 1809.

A point of importance is the connection with the Brethren of the Common Life, out of which Windesheim proceeded, with the spirit of which association it was in intimate sympathy. The distinction between the institutions of the Brethren and of Windesheim was that the latter's reform was in the direction of the modern " devotion," the former rejected monastic rules and vows in order to a renewal of life in the common association of its members. The manner of living of the Brethren was often a door by which men entered the regular orders. On the other hand, the extension of the Windesheim congregation affected the Brethren by stimulating their zeal. Yet the Windesheim purpose was by no means indulgence in ascetic practises to an unhealthy degree. While personal freedom in this direction was not disallowed, it is significant that the members did not recount the miracles of their associates. Yet there was a growing tendency to emphasize asceticism, a characteristic which comes out in Busch's account of such externals as the habit, method of singing, and the like to the exclusion of more important matters. A still further point of connection between the two orders is that the Windesheim people busied themselves in the making of books for their common use (not usually for commercial purposes). These activities were concerned with a correct text of the Bible, and with correct copies of the Fathers, especially of Augustine's writings; some of the members were celebrated for their work in this direction. But while the Brethren developed an independent literary purpose, in the monasteries an increasingly ascetic purpose robbed the results of much of their value, though they still rendered great service to following generations. Handicrafts, however, and to the extent of mercantile significance, were not unknown among them. The schools which they here and there conducted were of limited value because of their ecclesiastical character.

The reform of Windesheim did not contemplate a break with Rome; its direction was controlled by the forms and ideals of the Church of the Middle Ages; it would befriend ethical purposes and control asceticism within sufferable bounds. So far as these failed in producing real reform, it was shown that the Church was awaiting and expecting mightier reformers. The Windesheim congregation forbade the possession and the reading of Lutheran books, and till its end remained true to the Roman Catholic Church. (S. D. van Veen.)

Bibliography: Besides the literature under Busch, Jan, and Common Life, Brethren of the, especially the works named there of Busch, Delprat, and Acquoy, consult: J. C. van Slee, *De Kloostervereeniging te Windesheim*, Leyden, 1874; J. H. Hofman, in *Archief voor de Geschiedenis van het Aartsbisdom Utrecht*, vols. ii., v.; K. Grube, *Die litterarische Thätigkeit der Windesheimer Congregation*, in *Der Katholik*, 1881; W. Becker, in *De Katholiek*, 1884; D. J. M. Wüstenhoff, in *Archief voor Nederlandsche Kerkgeschiedenis*, v (1895), 326-335; *KL*, xii. 1686-1694.

WINE, HEBREW.

Names (§ 1).   Making of Wine (§ 3).   Use of Wine (§ 5).
Cultivation of the Vine (§ 2).   Dried Grapes (§ 4).   Artificial Wines (§ 6).

The usual designation for fermented grape juice is *yayin*, a loan-word in the Hebrew, corresponding to Greek *oinos* and Latin *vinum; tirosh* is used to denote the newly extracted grape juice

1. **Names** (Lat. *mustum;* cf. Mic. vi. 15) and also the juice yet contained in the cluster (Isa. lxv. 8). There is, however, no special emphasis herein upon the distinction " not yet fermented," since in the orient fermentation begins very quickly after the pressing, and even the *tirosh* is accredited with intoxicating effects (Hos. iv. 11; cf. Deut. xii. 17, xviii. 4). Less frequent terms are *hemer* (Deut. xxxii. 14), *aram, hemra* (Ezra vi. 9, etc.). Poetical forms are *'asis, sobhe*, etc. On the other hand, *mesekh* and *mimsakh* denote mixed wine (see below); while *shekhar* comprehensively applies to all intoxicating drinks (cf. *shikari*, in the Amarna Tablets).

Both by climate and by the character of its soil Palestine is adapted to vine-growing. Indeed the vine has been cultivated there from

2. **Cultiva-** high antiquity (Gen. xiv. 18, xix. 32
tion of the sqq., xxxvii. 25). In the Old Testa-
Vine. ment, vineyards and the vine invariably betoken the fruitfulness of the promised land (Deut. vi. 11, viii. 8, xi. 14, etc.). And the vine is nearly everywhere grown, both on the hills and in the plains, and in the valley of the Jordan (I Kings xxi. 1; Cant. i. 14, viii. 11; Hos. xiv. 7; Isa. v. 1; Jer. xxxi. 5; Josephus, *War*, III., x. 8). Eastward of the Jordan the Moabites, Ammonites, Amorites, and the inhabitants of Auranitis had vineyards in early times (Num. xxi. 22, xxxii. 24; Judges xi. 33; Isa. xvi. 8). In the later Jewish period the vine appears as an emblem on coins. For the messianic times, in turn, the prophet announces that the mountains shall flow with new wine (Amos ix. 13; Joel iii. 18, etc.). After the Moslem conquest the culture of the vine was somewhat retarded, but it is once again assuming importance. The vine largely runs wild in the ridges of central and northern Syria, and in Palestine the wild vine was known, bearing sourly astringent grapes (Isa. v. 2; Jer. ii. 21). The species now in cultivation bear mostly white oblong fruit. Clusters from twelve to fifteen inches long and weighing from two to three pounds are no rarity. While the species of vines planted in antiquity can not be positively identified, generally they appear to have been the black and purplish sorts whose juice is described as red "blood of the grape" and also typifies the blood, as in the Eucharist (Gen. xlix. 11; Deut. xxxii. 14; Isa. lxiii. 2 sqq.; I Macc. vi. 34; Matt. xxvi. 27 sqq.; Rev. xiv. 19 sqq., etc.). The vine termed *sorek* appears to have been a noble variety (Isa. v. 2, xvi. 8; Jer. ii. 21), according to Kimchi a grape with small, seedless, white fruit. The Israelites borrowed viticulture from the Canaanites. Like the cultivation of figs and olives (see FRUIT-TREES IN THE OLD TESTAMENT), it is everywhere the token of a higher civilization; hence the Greeks manifest much discernment in referring the intellectual and material culture of their country to the introduc-tion of vine- and olive-growing. Conversely, as among the Rechabites, antagonism to viticulture found expression in the particular fact that they abstained as a matter of principle from the enjoyment of wine. The cultivation of the vine requires much labor (Isa. v. 1 sqq.); and whoever plants a vineyard is to be sure that the field remain even for decades in the family possession, because only then is the cultivation remunerative. The preparation of the land exacted much toil. Along hillsides, the land had to be reclaimed by wearisome terrace cultivation, and the soil secured from erosion. Then the ground was to be cleared of stones, the plot surrounded with a wall or hedge (Ex. xxii. 5; Ps. lxxx. 14; Jer. xii. 10; Cant. ii. 15, etc.), and stone watch-towers, together with a booth or hut, had to be built for the vintners at the ripening season (Isa. i. 8, v. 1 sqq.). Lastly, a wine-press had to be hewn out in the rock (see below). Equally wearisome was the work of maintenance (Prov. xxiv. 30 sqq.); twice or thrice a year the vineyard needed to be plowed or hoed, that the soil might stay constantly mellow (Isa. v. 2, 6, vii. 25); weeds were to be removed, and large stones picked out again and again. The vines were carefully pruned, and rank shoots cut away (Lev. xxv. 3 sqq.; Isa. ii. 4). The plants were either allowed to trail along the ground (Isa. xvi. 8; Ezek. xvii. 6), or trained up to stakes or trees (Isa. vii. 23; Ps. lxxx. 11), whence the phrase "dwelling beneath the vine" (I Kings iv. 25; Mic. iv. 4).

The time when grapes ripen varies with local conditions; in the district of Tiberias and in the valley of the Jordan, some kinds are ripe in June; in the coast plain, the vintage season

3. **Making** occurs about the middle of August; in
of Wine. the mountainous country, during September. This was ever a joyful season (Isa. xvi. 10; Jer. xxv. 30). Then it was that the Canaanites celebrated their great harvest festival (Judges ix. 27), the Israelites their Feast of Tabernacles; and both these feasts, besides their special features, bear the stamp of a harvest thanksgiving (cf. I Sam. i. 1–18; the threatened curses in Deut. xxviii. 30, 51; Amos v. 21). The wine-press (*gath*) was hewn from the rock in the vineyard itself. It consisted of two round or angular basins. The upper one was as much as thirteen feet wide, but only from seven to twelve inches deep. In this the grapes were trodden or pressed with stones (cf. Isa. xvi. 10; Jer. xxv. 30). The second, rather lower basin, was of smaller area, but about three feet in depth. This was the receiving basin (*yekebh;* Num. xviii. 27; Deut. xv. 14). Sometimes there was still a third basin, receiving the flow of partially clarified new wine from the vat (for drawings of existing wine-presses cf. *ZDPV*, vol. x., plates 5 and 7). From the vats the wine was dipped into leather bottles or earthen jars (Josh. ix. 13; Jer. xiii. 12). There it was allowed to ferment, and this process began within from six to twelve hours after the pressing. Next the wine remained settling for some time on the lees (Isa. xxv. 6; Jer. xlviii. 11; Zeph.

i. 12); and afterward it was transferred to other vessels. Before drinking, it had still to be strained through a cloth for purification (Isa. xxv. 6; Matt. xxiii. 24).

Besides the wine, the dried grapes were and still are much esteemed (Num. vi. 3). The so-called raisin cakes (*zimmuḳim*) of the Old Testament are not a product of the baker's art, but **4. Dried** dried grapes pressed in the form of a **Grapes.** cake (I Sam. xxv. 18, xxx. 12; I Chron. xii. 40); with these may be compared the modern apricot cakes of Damascus, thin cakes of the crushed and sun-dried mass of apricots, that can be rolled like flexible leather. The other word for raisin cakes, *ashishah*, probably denotes baked cakes of dough, containing raisins (II Sam. vi. 19; I Chron. xvi. 3).

The use of wine was quite general; it belonged to the list of indispensable provisions (Judges xix. 19; I Sam. xvi. 20, xxv. 18). It rejoices the heart of man, even of God (Judges ix. 13; Ps. **5. Use of** civ. 15; Ecclus. xxxi. 27, 28). Hence **Wine.** it was not to be lacking as a drink offering on God's table. The vice of drunkenness was not unknown to the ancient Israelites, as is shown by the often quite caustic descriptions of the prophets (Isa. xix. 14, xxviii. 7 sqq.). Only the Rechabites and Nazirites drank no wine, and it was forbidden the priests during the time of ministration (Lev. x. 8 sqq.). It was drunk undiluted; addition of water was deemed a deterioration (Isa. i. 22). It was only in later times, under the influence of Greek and Roman manners, that the usage of mixing it with water came into vogue (II Macc. xv. 39). Yet the addition of spices was favored (Ps. lxxv. 8; Cant. viii. 2; Isa. lxv. 11), such as myrrh, honey, frankincense (cf. III Macc. v. 2), oil of roses, wormwood, pepper, etc. Wine mingled with myrrh was employed as a narcotic (Mark xv. 23); while as a milder sort of intoxicant it was a favorite beverage of women among the Greeks and Romans. The use of such spiced wine in the sanctuary service was not allowed.

Artificial wines (*shekhar*, see below; cf. Deut. xxix. 6; Judges xiii. 4 sqq.; I Sam. i. 15), which were drunk among the ancient Israel- **6. Artificial** ites, are not to be defined with much **Wines.** certainty apart from the general meaning of the word *shekhar*, "intoxicating drinks." Even Jerome was not sure what drinks were indicated by the term. In Cant. viii. 2, a drink from pomegranates is mentioned along with spiced wine. The rabbis use the term to designate Egyptian beer (*zythos*), brewed of barley, saffron, and salt, and also the Median barley liquor. They also mention cider and mead. Owing to the active commerce with Egypt, possibly *zythos* was known even in ancient times; at all events, this is true of palm wine, which was pressed from the pulp of ripe dates, and so drunk throughout the early orient. Artificial wine was forbidden in the sanctuary service.

From wine and *shekhar*, vinegar (*ḥomez*) was prepared; and this was also forbidden to the Nazirites (Num. vi. 3), though else enjoyed, when diluted with water, as a refreshing and thirst-quenching drink, at least by the humbler people (Ruth ii. 14;

Mark xv. 36; on the other hand, cf. Ps. lxix. 21). The same was true among the Romans, where *essica* was the usual beverage of slaves and soldiers, just as it still nowadays is in the East.

I. Benzinger.

Bibliography: A. Henderson, *Hist. of Ancient and Modern Wines*. London, 1824; A. M. Wilson, *The Wines of the Bible*, ib. 1877; C. H. Fowler, *The Wine of the Bible*, New York, 1878; H. B. Tristram, *Natural Hist. of the Bible*, 5th ed., London, 1880; Anderlind, in *ZDPV*, xi (1888), 160 sqq.; Benzinger, *Archäologie*, pp. 71–72, 143 et passim; G. M. Mackie, *Bible Manners and Customs*, Edinburgh, 1898; V. Hehn, *Kulturpflanzen und Haustiere*, 7th ed., Berlin, 1902; W. Ebstein, *Die Medizin im Neuen Testament und im Talmud*, i. 36, 167, ii. 250, Stuttgart, 1903; *DB*, ii. 33–34; iv. 868–870; *EB*, iv. 5306–22; *JE*, xii. 532–535.

WINEBRENNER, JOHN, WINEBRENNERIANS. See Church (Churches) of God, I.

WINER, vī'ner, JOHANN GEORG BENEDIKT: Orientalist and New-Testament grammarian; b. at Leipsic Apr. 13, 1789; d. there May 12, 1858. He was educated at the gymnasium and the university of his native city, zealously studying not only theology but classical philology and oriental languages. In 1817 he became privat-docent at the University of Leipsic, and in 1819 extraordinary professor of theology; in 1823 professor at Erlangen; but returned in 1832 to Leipsic, where he remained until his death, being also a canon of Meissen after 1845. His literary activity was directed mainly to the interpretation of single books or passages of the Bible, to Biblical linguistics, and to historical studies. He published a commentary on the Epistle to the Galatians (1821; 4th ed., 1859), with dissertations on questions of Biblical history and antiquities. His *Biblisches Realwörterbuch* (1820; 2d ed., revised and enlarged, 2 vols., 1833–38; 3d ed., considerably enlarged, 1847) is a comprehensive handbook of Biblical subjects arranged alphabetically, a work of extraordinary industry and a thesaurus of historical, geographical, archeological, and scientific knowledge. Of still greater importance were Winer's various labors in the linguistic sphere. He published a *Grammatik des biblischen und targumischen Chaldäismus* (1824; 2d ed., 1842; Eng. transl., *A Grammar of the Chaldee Language*, Andover, 1845), and to supplement it a *Chaldäisches Lesebuch* (1825). His masterwork in Biblical science is his *Grammatik des neutestamentlichen Sprachidioms als sichere Grundlage der neutestamentlichen Exegese bearbeitet* (1822; frequent Eng. transls., *Grammar of the Idioms of the New Testament*, Andover, 1825, Edinburgh, 1859, 1877), [which remained the standard work for nearly three-quarters of a century, but has been superseded largely through the discoveries of the last two decades (see Hellenistic Greek)]. It was a path-breaking achievement, and in producing it Winer rendered immortal services by doing away with vague presuppositions respecting the Hebraizing character of the language of the New Testament and by thus leaving less reason for arbitrariness in interpretation. He showed the laws of linguistics applying in the New-Testament language, employing the same principles that Gottfried Hermann had developed for classical Greek. While apparently merely a scientific work, there was at its basis a truly moral and religious motive—a conscientious earnestness in seeking the truth, and a pious reverence for Holy Scripture. Winer published also *Beitrag zur Verbesserung der neutestamentlichen Lexikographie* (1823), and gathered materials for a dictionary of the New Testament, but died before its elaboration. Worthy of mention, though in another department, is his *Comparative Darstellung des Lehrbegriffs der verschiedenen Kirchenparteien* (1824; Eng. transl., *Comparative View of the Doctrines and Confessions of Christendom*, Edinburgh, 1873; new ed., 1887); while notice should not be omitted of his *Handbuch der theologischen Literatur* (1821; 2 vols., 1838–40, and supplement, 1842), giving not merely titles of books but brief notices of the authors.

(G. LECHLER†.)

WINFRID (WYNFRITH). See BONIFACE, SAINT.

WINKELER, vin′ke-ler: A designation of the Waldensians (q.v.) and then of the Waldensian itinerant preachers, employed especially in Strasburg and perhaps also in neighboring regions. It is transmitted through a document discovered about 1840 in old church archives in Strasburg. The document contains the records of a Waldensian trial held about 1400 and bears the superscription *Secta hereticorum*, beside which has been written by a later hand " Die Winkeler." At first it was thought that they formed a separate sect whose views agreed with those of the Waldenses; but since the discovery of further sources it has been proved that they are identical with the Waldenses. The term may have been a nickname. Thirty-two adherents of the Waldensian preachers in Strasburg were captured and banished about 1400 on charges of heresy. But there remained in Strasburg a Waldensian congregation to which at a later time belonged Friedrich Reiser (b. 1401 in Deutach near Donauwörth, and because of that named Tunawer or Danuvius), one of the best-known Waldensian preachers of those days, whose aim was to unite Hussites and Waldensians. In 1458 Reiser together with many male and female adherents was burned (among whom was Anna or Barbara Weiler) under the Strasburg inquisitor Johannes Wegrauf.   (FERDINAND COHRS.)

BIBLIOGRAPHY: T. W. Röhrich, in *ZHT*, x (1840), 118 sqq.; idem, *Mittheilungen aus der Geschichte der evangelischen Kirche des Alsass*, i. 38 sqq., Strasburg, 1855; K. Schmidt, in *ZHT*, 3, x (1840), 31 sqq.; G. F. Ochsenbein, *Aus dem schweizerischen Volksleben des 15. Jahrhunderts*, Bern, 1881; H. Haupt, *Die religiösen Sekten in Franken vor der Reformation*, Würzburg, 1882; idem, *Waldensertum und Inquisition im südöstlichen Deutschland*, Freiburg, 1890; idem, in *Historisches Taschenbuch* for 1888; L. Keller, *Die Reformation und die ältere Reformparteien*, Leipsic, 1885; idem, *Johann von Staupitz und die Anfänge der Reformation*, ib. 1888; K. Müller, *Die Waldenser und ihre einzelnen Gruppen*, Gotha, 1886; W. Böhm, *Friedrich Reisers Reformation des Kaisers Sigmund*, ib. 1876; and the literature under WALDENSES.

WINSLOW, MIRON (MYRON): Congregational missionary; b. at Williston, Vt., Dec. 11, 1789; d. at the Cape of Good Hope Oct. 22, 1864. He was graduated from Middlebury College, 1815, and from Andover Theological Seminary, 1818. In June, 1819, he sailed as missionary to Ceylon, where he established a mission, laboring for seventeen years at Jaffna and Oodoville, where he founded a seminary; he established the mission at Madras, 1836, and

spent the rest of his life there, establishing a native college and a number of vernacular schools. He became president of the Madras College about 1840. He was the author of *Sketch of the Missions* (Andover, 1819); *Memoir of Harriet Wadsworth Winslow, of the Ceylon Mission* (New York, 1835; republished in London, France, and Turkey); *Hints on Missions to India* (1856); and *A Comprehensive Tamil and English Dictionary, of High and Low Tamil* (Madras, 1862). The *Dictionary*, his great work, on which he spent three hours a day for over twenty years, was based partly upon manuscript materials left by Joseph Knight, and consisted of 68,000 words and definitions. He was assisted in this by native scholars. Winslow also translated the Bible into Tamil (Madras, 1855).

WINSLOW, WILLIAM COPLEY: Protestant Episcopalian; b. at Boston, Mass., Jan. 13, 1840. He was graduated from Hamilton College (A.B., 1862) and the General Theological Seminary, New York City (1865). He was ordained to the priesthood in 1867; was rector of St. George's, Lee, Mass. (1867–70); chaplain of St. Luke's Home, Boston (1878–82), having temporary charge of various parishes, particularly at Weymouth, Mass., and Taunton, Mass., in the interim. In 1883 he established the Free Church Association in Boston, and likewise founded the American branch of the Egypt Exploration Fund (q.v.), of which he was the chief official until 1902, securing large funds for its use and being the pioneer in America in creating a popular interest in explorations in Egypt. He also took an active part in the establishment of the Greco-Roman branch of the Egypt Exploration Fund, and was one of the chief distributors of the antiquities thus discovered among the various American institutions which had contributed to the society's support. Theologically he describes himself as " of evangelical belief; thoroughly progressive in all forms of educational and religious work; a believer in all that is essential to faith in the Old Testament." In 1860–62 he was editor of *The University Quarterly;* in 1862–63, assistant editor of *The New York World*, and in 1864–65 of *The Christian Times*. He is the associate editor of *The American Antiquarian* and of *The American Historical Register*. He has of late done much to raise funds for the Egyptian Research Account (q.v.).

WINTHROP, JOHN: Puritan governor of Massachusetts; b. at Edwardston (15 m. s.e. of Bury St. Edmunds), Suffolk, Jan. 22, 1588; d. in Boston, Mass., Mar. 26, 1649. In the latter part of 1602 he entered Trinity College, Cambridge, but his university career came to an abrupt close in Apr., 1605, when he married. Although reared as a member of the Church of England, Winthrop early manifested marked sympathies with Puritanism, while the death of his first wife in 1615, followed by the death of his second in the year following, heightened a tendency, already present, to gloomy introspection. During this time he evidently thought of taking orders, but a third marriage, in Apr., 1618, changed in great measure the morbid trend of his thoughts, and, following his father's advice, he devoted himself to his duties as justice of the peace and lord of Groton manor, and was probably admitted to the Inner Temple in Nov., 1628.

But to one of Winthrop's type of mind the England of Charles I. was not pleasant, and by May, 1629, he was considering the advisability of leaving his native country. Late in August he had formally agreed to sail, and on Oct. 20 he was chosen to be governor of the colony Massachusetts for the year following. With his expedition he sailed from Southampton in Mar., 1630, and, after landing at Salem, soon was led to choose Charlestown as a residence, only to leave it before long for the present site of Boston. Winthrop was repeatedly elected governor of the colony, annually until 1634, and then in 1637–40, in 1642–44, and from 1646 until his death, having also been chosen one of the two councilors of the colony for life in 1636. In 1635 he defended the banishment of Roger Williams (q.v.), and in return was accused of excess of leniency in his administration of justice. He humbly acknowledged the justice of the charge and promised to endeavor to be less remiss in future. Of more importance for the colony was his opposition to the Antinomian Controversy (see ANTINOMIANISM AND ANTINOMIAN CONTROVERSIES, II., 2) headed by Anne Hutchinson and defended by Sir Henry Vane (q.v.). The result was Vane's supersession by Winthrop in the gubernatorial election of 1637, followed by the banishment of Anne Hutchinson and the punishment of a large number of her adherents. The only other event of special interest was his arraignment in 1645 on a charge of exercising arbitrary authority, of which he was acquitted. In the following year certain persons in the colony presented to the court a petition setting forth that they were forbidden the civil privileges of Englishmen on the ground that they were not church-members; but the authority of Winthrop was such that the remonstrants were imprisoned and heavily fined.

Winthrop wrote *Journal of the Transactions and Occurrences in the Settlement of Massachusetts and the other New England Colonies from the Year 1630 to 1644* (Hartford, 1790), the complete journal being later edited by J. Savage, *The History of New England from 1630 to 1649* (2 vols., 1825–26; new ed., by J. K. Hosmer, New York, 1908), and *Model of Christian Charity* (ed. in *Collections of the Massachusetts Historical Society*, 3d series, vol. vii., Boston, 1838). His letters to his third wife have been edited by J. H. Twichell under the title *Some old Puritan Love-Letters* (London, 1893).

BIBLIOGRAPHY: R. C. Winthrop, *Life and Letters of John Winthrop*, 2 vols., Boston, 1864–67; *DNB*, lxii. 226–231.

WIRZ, JAKOB. See NAZARENES.

WISDOM.

I. The Term: The Hebrew word for wisdom, *ḥokmah*, as is shown by a comparison with the Arabic, has the fundamental meaning of "fasten" or "hold fast." The Septuagint, with few exceptions, translates *sophia*. In secular Greek *sophia* means, on the one hand, capability, skill, experience, and, on the other, a profound insight into the significance and the tasks of life. In the Bible, wisdom is, firstly, an attribute of God, more especially a divine organ of revelation; and, secondly, a quality of man. Theoretically, human wisdom is cognition, in a religious and ethical sense it is conduct based on the fear of God and tending to shape life to satisfactory results; it may also signify practical skill and proficiency. Divine wisdom is regarded as the original principle of all divine activity and rule, and from it are derived the concepts of teleology and divine providence.

II. Wisdom in the Old Testament: In the historical and prophetical books wisdom is generally understood to be that talent and knowledge which surpass the average intellectual endowment. He is wise who is clever in artistic work, who is his own counselor, who is able to judge things rightly as well as to comprehend their essence (cf. Gen. xli. 8; Ex. xxviii. 3, xxxi. 6, xxxv. 25, 35; Deut. i. 13, 15; Judges v. 29; I Kings v. 12). To recognize this quality of the divine being many religious experiences were necessary, and also a conception of wisdom based on faith; only gradually could the divine wisdom have revealed itself to the prophets. They understood it to be a quality in accordance with which God establishes and realizes his aims. According to Isa. xxxi. 2, God alone is wise, and in xi. 2 it is said that the spirit of wisdom will rest upon the Messiah. In Isa. iii. 3 wisdom signifies artistic capacity in handiwork and in xxix. 14 it denotes political skill and prudence. In Deutero-Isaiah human intelligence is pronounced to be nothing as compared with the infinite wisdom (xl. 28). Jeremiah says that creation is the work of God's might and wisdom (x. 12).

In the "Wisdom literature," principally composed by those belonging to the class of "wise men," the concept of wisdom became much more prominent. This class arose after the cessation of prophecy and was of the greatest importance for the development of Judaism. These wise men had found that the religious doctrines contradicted the experiences of daily life, and they felt the necessity of investigating the source of this contradiction. They made no boast of divine inspiration, but strove through reflection to solve the problem of the world and of life. Like the priests, they started with the assumption that the law is the way which leads to God. Practical ethics was their principal field, and the results of their reflections were usually formulated in maxims, parables, and fables. In the Book of Job (q.v.), the religious and philosophical problem of how to reconcile the sufferings of the pious with the justice of God occupies a prominent place. Wisdom is impenetrable; no one knows where to find it; only God knows it and possesses it. In xxviii. 12, when the dialogue reaches its culmination, wisdom is described in highly poetic language. The writer also speaks of human wisdom and looks upon it as the essence of all morality and prudence. Naturally, it can be attained only through the fear of God (v. 13, xxviii. 28), even though it be transmitted by tradition (xv. 18). The Psalms do not often allude to wisdom. In creation and the order of nature, the divine wisdom appears (civ. 24, cxxxvi. 5). God communicates wisdom to men (li. 6, cv. 22); the fear of the Lord is the beginning of wisdom (cxi. 10). Proverbs being a composite book (see PROVERBS OF SOLOMON), wisdom is variously defined. In the earliest portions (x. 1–xxii. 16, xxii. 17–xxiv. 22, xxxiii., xxxiv.), wisdom is treated only as a quality, the abstract conception is not prominent; in the latest collection (i.–ix.), however, the origin of wisdom is considered and to it great importance assigned. As elsewhere justice, so here wisdom is the highest ethical conception. Wisdom and piety are closely related (i. 29, ii. 5, xiv. 16), but not identical; man can attain piety by his own efforts, but not wisdom. In its essence human wisdom is only an emanation of the divine (ii. 6). In the latter are combined God's omniscience, omnipotence, and goodness, and he reveals himself thereby. Wisdom is a creation of God, it stood by his side at the creation of the world, and is ever active in human life (viii. 22–31). In Ecclesiastes (q.v.) a philosophical writer puts his teachings into the mouth of Solomon, the prototype of the seekers after wisdom. All through his book, wisdom is spoken of as the practical art of how to live rightly. The author is persuaded that all striving after wisdom is vanity; that it is vain to seek to discover the eternal in the ever-changing aspects of life. Nevertheless, the writer gives in eloquent words the result of his search for wisdom: resignation, the fear of God, and an assurance of an eternal living God and of his judgment (ii. 13, v. ii. 11–12, ix. 13).

In the polemic and apologetic diatribe against paganism called the Wisdom of Solomon (see APOCRYPHA, IV., 13), all moral and religious convictions are referred to wisdom. For the author wisdom is the chief emanation from the absolute being of God, a radiation of his eternal light (vii. 22–29). It appears as a half-celestial, half-terrestrial being, a mediatress between God and man. The whole book gives the impression that wisdom is definitely distinguished from God and independent of him, and effects are attributed to it which elsewhere in the Old Testament are referred to God (vii. 27, ix. 4, x. 10). Spirit and wisdom are identical for the author; both manifest the divine power and activity in the physical as well as in the moral world (cf. i. 4, 5, 7, ix. 17), but wisdom and the word (logos) are nowhere identical. In xvi. 12, the word is the will of God; in xviii. 15, it is a poetical personification of the divine will and action. In Ecclesiasticus (see APOCRYPHA, IV., 12) wisdom is identical with ancestral faith and is the criterion

3. In Apocryphal Wisdom Literature.

of moral action and the essence of life. The fundamental conception is the same as in the above-mentioned books. Israel is the abiding-place of true wisdom and the law is pronounced to be the principle of wisdom and its imparter (cf. xxiv. 16, i. 16, xlii. 21). It is uncertain whether the author hypostatized wisdom, although this has often been assumed from chap. xxiv. Here wisdom appears as the first of all spirits and boasts that she was created from the beginning (verse 3), an independent entity, creating and ordering the world. However, all this is probably only a poetic personification just as God's activity is frequently represented by personifying his various powers. Certain of the ideas of Jesus ben Sirach regarding wisdom are again encountered in the Book of Baruch. The author distinguishes wisdom from God and personifies it poetically. He writes that wisdom lived with God, was bestowed upon Israel, and dwelt among mankind (iii. 32–37). The peoples of the earth did not find wisdom, Israel alone attained it through the Law.

III. Wisdom in the New Testament: In order to understand the conception of wisdom in the New Testament, study is necessary of the form which it assumed among the Jews of the first century before and after Christ. Among the rabbis wisdom was confined to the Law, and the scribes were called wise men simply because they expounded it (cf. F. Weber, *Jüdische Theologie auf Grund des Talmud*, pp. 95–98, 125–126, Leipsic, 1897). The Book of Enoch (see PSEUDEPIGRAPHA, III.) is typical in this respect. The author endeavors to offer an exclusively Biblical system of world-philosophy and wisdom. God is the possessor of wisdom which dwells in heaven and is bestowed upon the just in the time of the Messiah. The Messiah is the incarnation of wisdom who reveals all the mysteries of justice (xxxviii. 3, xlvi. 3; cf. A. Dillmann, *Das Buch Henoch*, Leipsic, 1853). The concept of wisdom occupies a more important place in the Hellenistic writings. Here wisdom bridges the chasm between the hidden God and the world and is identical with the concept of religion. Moses is not only a founder of religion, he is also a teacher of wisdom. Wisdom leads to virtue (so Philo, the epistle of Aristeas, IV Maccabees, and Josephus).

1. The Current Conception.

In the Synoptic Gospels the word (*sophia*) appears six times in Luke, but once in Mark, and three times in Matthew. It is variously used: (1) Without any religious connection whatever and only in the sense of intellectual capability (cf. Matt. xii. 42; Luke xi. 31, xxi. 15). In Matt. xi. 25, xxiii. 34, the learned in the Law are called wise men (cf. Luke x. 21). (2) In the religious sense of an understanding of the will and ways of God, as well as the capacity to give testimony thereto (cf. Matt. xiii. 54; Mark vi. 2; Luke ii. 40). (3) In Matt. xi. 19 and Luke vii. 34–35, Jesus appears as the divine representative of wisdom. The idea is that God's wisdom manifests and justifies itself in Christ's life, and those who order their lives accordingly will recognize the truth of this wisdom (" wisdom is justified of all her children "). (4) The wis-

2. In Gospels and Acts.

dom of God is mentioned in Luke xi. 49. Here Luke probably reproduces a Jewish-Christian tradition; the form in Matt. xxiii. 34 is not the original one. The phrase "Therefore also said the wisdom of God" is somewhat obscure. Some think that Luke refers to Jesus, who designates himself as the wisdom of God; while others believe that the decree of the divine wisdom is meant. It is, however, evident that Jesus here cites some lost Jewish prophetic apocalyptic writing in which the wisdom of God was the speaker, or which was entitled "The wisdom of God." It is singular that this concept of wisdom is lacking in the Gospel of John, although from the range of the writer's thought one would expect to find it there. This has been explained by supposing that the Gospel was composed at a time when the Gnostic heresies were rife and that, as the Gnostics employed the word *sophia* in a dualistic sense, the author of the Gospel avoided its use (cf. J. Grill, *Untersuchungen über die Entstehung des vierten Evangeliums*, i. 199–200, Tübingen, 1902). This view, however, lays undue stress on the employment of the word in Gnostic speculations. The idea of the word (*logos*) is not identical with that of wisdom (*sophia*); indeed nowhere in early Christian writings are *sophia* and *logos* confounded with each other as they are in Philo. In the Acts, *sophia* is sometimes religious knowledge and discourse, an emanation of the Holy Ghost (cf. vi. 3, 10); at other times prudence in the practical conduct of life (cf. vii. 10, 22).

Paul speaks of wisdom in his principal epistles, especially in I Corinthians. Circumstances forced him to do this; since it had been doubted whether he could preach wisdom, he showed that it was not unfamiliar to him. Paul conceives wisdom as a force which manifested itself in Christ;

3. In the Epistles. in him all the treasures of God's wisdom were included (cf. I Cor. i. 21, 24).

God, the only wise one, did not save the world by human wisdom because the world did not recognize the divine wisdom in the natural revelation. Through Christ as well as through the Holy Spirit, the knowledge of God, of his divine plan of salvation and of heavenly things, was made possible (I Cor. ii. 9 sqq.). Paul in this epistle emphasizes the fact that the divine wisdom is not to be presented to believers shortly after their conversion (iii. 1, 2; "babes in Christ"). Such wisdom is only for the perfect (ii. 6–7); this does not signify a condition of absolute perfection, only attainable for a few, but rather a relative and normal excellence. The exposition in Ephesians of the relation of wisdom to the Church is characteristic. The Church is organically connected with Christ; in it God's purpose for the world begins to be realized, and through it the divine wisdom is manifested more and more clearly. Even the angels learn through the Church a better understanding of wisdom (Eph. iii. 10). In the Catholic Epistles the concept of wisdom appears only in James. *Sophia* is a gift (i. 5), the primary ethical virtue, the foundation of moral life. In wisdom the faithful possess the new principle of life through which law and freedom are revealed. And revelation teaches that wisdom gives the key to all apocalyptic problems.

IV. Summary: Wisdom is the epitome of God's perfection. Because of his wisdom, which is inseparable from love, God knows and works all things. Wisdom, however, is also objective for God; it is the world-thought, produced, created, and ordered by God, and it serves for the realization of his decrees. The true reason for the existence of the world, which had been rendered doubtful through sin, was revealed and explained by the salvation of Christ. Through his son, God has given expression to his thoughts and incarnated the divine wisdom. Only in the New Testament is the idea of wisdom especially referred to the scheme of salvation and to its realization in history. Human wisdom is a reflex of the divine. Through the spirit alone is man disposed to recognize this divine wisdom. Knowledge consists in the conformity of the human mind with the divine wisdom and the works it has created. This refers to the revelation of God, both in nature and history. God is knowable only in so far as he reveals himself; only revelation can give the knowledge of God. (G. HOENNICKE.)

BIBLIOGRAPHY: W. T. Davison, *Wisdom Literature of the O. T.*, London, 1894; C. F. Kent, *The Wise Men of Ancient Israel and their Proverbs*, Boston, 1895; J. F. Bruch, *Weisheitslehrer der Hebräer*, Strasburg, 1851; G. Oehler, *Grundzüge der alttestamentlichen Weisheit*, Tübingen, 1854; M. Nicolas, *Des doctrines religieuses des Juifs*, Paris, 1860; C. Siegfried, *Philo von Alexandria*, Jena, 1872; F. Klasen, *Die alttestamentliche Weisheit und der Logos der jüdisch-alexandrinischen Religionsphilosophie*, Freiburg, 1878; H. Blois, *La Poesie gnomique chez les Hebreux et les Grecs*, Toulouse, 1886; idem, *Origines de la philosophie Judéo-Alexandrine*, Paris, 1889; T. K. Cheyne, *Job and Solomon, or the Wisdom of the O. T.*, London, 1887; idem, *Jewish Religious Life after the Exile*, New York, 1898; J. F. Genung, *The Epic of the Inner Life*, Boston, 1891; W. von Baudissin, *Die alttestamentliche Spruchdichtung*, Berlin, 1893; A. Aall, *Geschichte der Logooidee*, Leipsic, 1896; M. D. Conway, *Solomon and Solomonic Literature*, London, 1899; R. G. Moulton, *Literary Study of the Bible*, Boston, 1899; M Friedländer, *Griechische Philosophie im A. T.*, Berlin, 1904; E. Sellin, *Die Spuren griechischer Philosophie im A. T.*, Leipsic, 1905; H. Meinhold, *Die Weisheit Israels in Spruch, Sage und Dichtung*, Leipsic, 1908; DB, iv. 924–928; EB, iv. 5322–36; JE, xii. 537–538. The reader is also referred to the introductions to the commentaries on the several books which embody the Hebrew "wisdom," including the apocryphal books, also to the works on O. T. theology.

WISDOM OF SOLOMON. See APOCRYPHA, A, IV., 13.

WISE, ISAAC MAYER: American Reformed rabbi; b. at Steingrub, Bohemia, Mar. 20, 1819; d. at Cincinnati, O., Mar. 26, 1900. He received his education at Prague, and from 1843 to 1845 was rabbi at Radnitz, Bohemia. In the following year he emigrated to the United States, and was soon appointed rabbi of Congregation Beth-El at Albany, N. Y., and when, in 1850, a split occurred in this congregation, Wise was chosen to be the head of the new Congregation Anshe Emeth. Here he remained until 1854, when he accepted the position which he was to occupy for the remainder of his life, the rabbinate of Congregation Bene Yeshurun, Cincinnati.

Wise took a foremost place among the Reformed Jews of America almost from his first arrival in America, beginning with his work in the Congregation Beth-El. As early as 1847 he sought to end the lack of uniform services in the American Jewish congregations by his *Minhag America*, though it was not until 1855 that his efforts were successful. The *Minhag* which then appeared was practically all prepared by Wise, who himself withdrew it on the issuance of the *Union Prayer Book* in 1894. In 1848 he began the agitation which, in 1873, resulted in the organization of the Union of American Hebrew Congregations; and to him is also due, after the short-lived Zion Collegiate Association (1855), the foundation, in 1875, of the Hebrew Union College (see Theological Seminaries, VI., 1), of which he was president until his death; while he was likewise the ultimate inspirer of the Central Conference of American Rabbis, over which he presided from its inception in 1889 until his death.

Besides editing the *American Israelite* and *Deborah*, and in addition to a number of novels in German and English (first appearing as serials in the two periodicals just mentioned), and even a couple of German plays, Wise wrote *History of the Israelitish Nation from Abraham to the Present Time* (Albany, 1854), *Essence of Judaism* (Cincinnati, 1861), *Origin of Christianity, and a Commentary on the Acts of the Apostles* (1868), *Judaism, its Doctrines and Duties* (1872), *The Martyrdom of Jesus of Nazareth* (1874), *The Cosmic God* (1876), *History of the Hebrews' Second Commonwealth* (1880), *Judaism and Christianity, their Agreements and Disagreements* (1883), *Defense of Judaism vs. Proselytizing Christianity* (1889), and *Pronaos to Holy Writ* (1891).

WISE, JOHN: Congregationalist; baptized at Roxbury, Mass., Aug. 15, 1652; d. at Essex, Mass., Apr. 8, 1725. He was graduated from Harvard, 1673; studied theology, and in 1683 became pastor of Chebacco parish in Ipswich, now Essex, and so continued the rest of his life. In 1688 he was imprisoned in Boston jail, fined, and deprived of his ministerial office by Governor Andros because he had led the citizens of Ipswich in refusing to pay certain taxes which they declared had been arbitrarily imposed. The town paid his fine, and the next year sent him to Boston as its representative at the convention to reorganize the colonial government. In 1710 he issued a satirical pamphlet, *The Churches Quarrel Espoused* (Boston, 3d ed., 1717), vigorously attacking " The Proposals of 1705," advocated by the Mathers and approved by many Massachusetts and Connecticut ministers, to give associations of ministers authority over individual churches. In 1717 he issued another pamphlet to the same intent, *A Vindication of the Government of New England Churches*. These tracts made a profound impression and powerfully contributed to block the scheme. " They are certainly," says Walker, " the most able exposition of the democratic principles which modern Congregationalism has come to claim as its own that the eighteenth century produced " (*Creeds and Platforms of Congregationalism*, p. 492). The two pamphlets were reprinted with an introduction by J. S. Clark (Boston, 1860); and a portion of the second as *Old South Leaflet No. 165* (Boston, 1908), with the title, *The Law of Nature in Government*.

Bibliography: W. B. Sprague, *Annals of the American Pulpit*, i. 188–189, New York, 1859; A. E. Dunning, *Congregationalists in America*, pp. 197, 207, 218–219, 270, ib.

1894; W. Walker, *Creeds and Platforms of Congregationalism*, pp. 470, 490–494, ib. 1893; idem, in *American Church History Series*, iii. 209–212, 307, ib. 1894; F. F. Waters, *Ipswich in the Massachusetts Bay Colony*, Ipswich, 1905.

WISEMAN, NICHOLAS PATRICK STEPHEN: First Roman archbishop of Westminster, and cardinal; b. at Seville Aug. 2, 1802; d. at London Feb. 15, 1865. His father, an Irish merchant who had settled in Spain, died in 1804, when the family returned to Ireland. The future cardinal studied at St. Cuthbert's College, Ushaw (near Durham), England, 1810–18, and then at the English College, Rome; and though he states that at St. Cuthbert's he was " dull and stupid, and never said a clever or witty thing," he was a diligent and good student, and in Rome his career was brilliant in scholarship. He received minor orders before leaving England, became doctor in divinity in Rome, 1824, and was ordained priest Mar., 1825. He assisted the Abbate Molza in the compilation of a Syriac grammar and lexicon and pursued independent studies in oriental languages, became vice-rector of the English College, Nov., 1827, was nominated professor supernumerary of Hebrew and Syro-Chaldaic in the archigymnasium of the Sapienza, Oct., 1828, and became rector of the English College the same year. In 1840 Pope Gregory XVI. appointed him coadjutor to Dr. Walsh, vicar-apostolic in England, and he was consecrated bishop of Melipotamus *in partibus*, and made president of St. Mary's College, Oscott (in Staffordshire, 4 m. n. of Birmingham). In 1847 he visited Rome, returning to England the next year as the pope's diplomatic envoy to Lord Palmerston. In 1849 he succeeded Walsh as vicar-apostolic. On Sept. 29, 1850, Pius IX. issued an apostolic letter announcing the restoration of the hierarchy in England, and by a brief at the same time he elevated Wiseman (who had been summoned to Rome) to the archbishopric of Westminster. He was created cardinal the next day with the title of St. Pudentiana. The news was not acceptable in England, and feeling ran so high that in 1851 parliament forbade Roman Catholics to assume the title of bishop in the country, but the law remained inoperative and was repealed in 1872. Wiseman possessed undoubted scholarly and intellectual abilities (his linguistic attainments were remarkable), and he was gifted with a suave manner and, in general, with good judgment. By the end of his fourteen years' archiepiscopate he had in large measure lived down the prejudices and passion of its beginning, as he also ultimately overcame opposition which at times developed on the part of his bishops and others of his own communion. He won a high reputation as a preacher early in his career in Rome, and later, in England, he was much in demand as a speaker on literary, artistic, and social questions.

Besides sermons, pastoral letters, addresses, etc., he published: *Horæ Syriacæ, seu commentationes et anecdota res vel litteras Syriacas spectantia* (Rome, 1828); *On the Connection between Science and Revealed Religion* (2 vols., London, 1836), twelve lectures, dealing chiefly with geology, originally delivered in the drawing-room of Cardinal Thomas Weld in Rome during Lent, 1835; *Twelve Lectures on the Principal Doctrines and Practices of the Roman Cath-*

olic Church (1836), first delivered in the chapel of the Sardinian embassy in London; *Eight Lectures on the Body and Blood of Our Lord in the Blessed Eucharist* (1836); *Four Lectures on the Offices and Ceremonies of Holy Week as Performed in the Papal Chapel* (1837); *High Church Claims* (1841), articles from *The Dublin Review* relating to the Oxford movement (at its height at the time; Wiseman's writings had much influence in its development; John Henry Newman and Richard Hurrell Froude [qq.v.] had been in consultation with him in Rome as early as 1833, and from that time he devoted himself to the restoration of the Roman Catholic Church in England), and a public letter to Newman after the appearance of *Tract XC.; Three Lectures on the Catholic Hierarchy Delivered in St. George's, Southwark* (1851), explanatory of his new position as archbishop of Westminster; *Essays on Various Subjects* (3 vols., 1853; new ed. with biographical introduction by J. Murphy, 1888), chiefly from *The Dublin Review; Fabiola, or the Church of the Catacombs* (1854), a story of the third century, widely translated, and a Roman Catholic classic; *Recollections of the Last Four Popes* (1858); *The Hidden Gem* (1858), a two-act drama; a volume of sermons, lectures, and addresses delivered on a public tour through Ireland in 1858 (1859); and *Sermons on Our Lord Jesus Christ* (Dublin, 1864). With Daniel O'Connell and Michael Joseph Quin he founded *The Dublin Review* in May, 1836.

BIBLIOGRAPHY: W. Ward, *Life and Times of Cardinal Wiseman*, 2 vols., London, 1897; G. White, *Memoir of . . . Cardinal Wiseman*, ib. 1865; W. P. Ward, *Ten Personal Studies*, New York, 1908; *DNB*, lxi. 243–246; E. Stock, *English Church in the 19th Century*, pp. 35–36, 42, London, 1910; F. W. Cornish, *English Church in the 19th Century* i. 274, 337–342, ib. 1910.

WISHART, GEORGE: Name of two Scotch notables.

1. Scotch Reformer; b. 1513 (?); burned at the stake at St. Andrews Mar. 1, 1546. He belonged to the family of Wishart of Pittarrow (near Montrose), but little or nothing is known with certainty as to his early history. In 1538, while master of the grammar-school in Montrose, he was summoned by John Hepburn, bishop of Brechin, for teaching his scholars the Greek New Testament (Greek being at this period almost unknown in Scotland), and to save his life was obliged to flee to England. In 1539 he again got into trouble in Bristol for preaching—according to the contemporary testimony of the *Mayor of Bristol's Calendar* (*Camden Society Publications*, new ser., v., p. 55, London, 1872)—that there is no imputation of the " merit " of Christ to men. His teaching was pronounced to be heretical by Thomas Cranmer (q.v.) and other prelates, and he made a public recantation at Canterbury. He seems to have lived abroad, chiefly in Germany and Switzerland, from 1539 to 1542. In 1543 he was again in England and a member of Corpus Christi College, Cambridge. The next year, probably, he ventured back to his native country and began to preach what he regarded as the fundamental doctrines of Christianity in Montrose, Dundee, Ayrshire, Leith, and elsewhere. East Lothian was the scene of his last labors, and the crowning result of his evangelistic work was the conversion of John Knox, who at the time was still a Roman priest but already prepossessed in favor of the new doctrines, and was tutor to the families of two of the landed gentry of that county.

Early in Jan., 1546, after preaching in Haddington, Wishart, at the instigation of Cardinal David Beaton (q.v.), was apprehended at Ormiston House by the Earl of Bothwell, who, after promising to protect him from violence, surrendered him to the regent, Arran, and to the cardinal. The latter imprisoned him in his castle at St. Andrews. On Feb. 28 Wishart was tried and convicted, and the next day was illegally burned without the sanction of the regent. He died with unflinching courage and with the prayer to his Lord to " forgive them that have condemned me to death this day ignorantly." His alleged prophecy that " he who feedeth his eyes with my torments [Beaton] shall, within few days, be hanged out at the same window to be seen with as much ignominy as he now leaneth there in pride " is not contained in the earliest account of the martyrdom (1547), in Knox's *History*, or in the first edition of Foxe's *Acts*. The earliest reference occurs in a reprint of Foxe's work (1570), which has a marginal note " Mr. George Wishart prophesieth of the death of the cardinal." George Buchanan (*Rerum Scoticarum historia*, p. 178, Edinburgh, 1582) expands this alleged prophecy into a saying similar to the traditional utterance, which first occurs in David Buchanan's edition of Knox's *History* (1644), p. 171. The tradition of the prophecy grew, presumably, out of Wishart's warning to the prelates that if they would not convert themselves from their wicked error there should hastily come upon them the wrath of God (Knox, *History*, ut sup., p. 170). The unauthenticity of Wishart's alleged prophecy of Beaton's death " within few days " removes one foundation of the charge that he was implicated in the assassination of the cardinal—a charge first made by Thomas Dempster in the seventeenth century (*Hist. eccl. gentis Scotorum*, Bannatyne Club ed., ii. 599, Edinburgh, 1829). Other alleged grounds are mere conjectures, and the cardinal can have had no suspicion of Wishart's complicity or he would have brought it forward to secure the regent's sanction of the execution. No contemporary writer suggests such complicity, and it is hardly compatible with Wishart's prayer for the forgiveness of his judges.

2. Bishop of Edinburgh; b. in East Lothian 1599; d. in Edinburgh July 25 (?), 1671. He belonged to the Wisharts of Logie in Forfarshire, and was educated, at least in part, at the University of Edinburgh for the Scottish Church during the period when Presbyterianism was being superseded by episcopacy, to which, both from family connections and personal predilections, he was inclined. He was minister of Monifieth, Forfarshire, 1625–26, whence he was translated to the second charge of St. Andrews. When the general assembly of 1638 renounced episcopacy, deposed the bishops, and imposed the Covenant (see HENDERSON, ALEXANDER), Wishart, who would not sign the covenant, withdrew to England and was deposed in 1639 for desertion of his parish. As compensation he was appointed to two lectureships in Newcastle churches, but, when the town was captured by General Leslie in 1644, his house was plundered and he was sent a captive to Edinburgh. In 1645, having been sent to the Marquis of Montrose, then everywhere victorious, with other royalist prisoners to plead for royal clemency, he appears to have joined the family of Montrose as chaplain. He continued with him to the close of the campaign, and then accompanied him abroad. After the fall of Montrose (1650), he received protection and favor from Elizabeth, queen of Bohemia, sister of Charles I. At the Restoration he returned to England, obtained the rectory of Newcastle, and in 1662 was promoted to the bishopric of Edinburgh.

Wishart's character is very differently represented by the Presbyterians and the Episcopalians. Robert Wodrow says he was notoriously profane, a drunkard, and the author of " lascivious poems " which " gave scandal to all the world." Bishop Keith calls him " a person of great religion," and says that, when the unfortunate rising at Pentland failed, he interested himself to obtain mercy for the captive insurgents; and, " having been a prisoner himself, he was always careful at each dinner to send away the first mess to the prisoners." The " lascivious poems " referred to by Wodrow, have never been discovered. The bishop was an elegant Latinist and a man of general literary ability. His chief writing was a Latin history of a campaign in Scot-

land under Montrose (composed at the Hague; Amsterdam [?], 1647). He also left in manuscript a second part completing the life of his patron. The work has often been translated and reprinted (text, transl., and notes, by A. D. Murdoch and H. F. M. Simpson, London, 1893).

W. Lee†. Revised by Henry Cowan.

Bibliography: On 1 consult: John Knox, Works, ed. D Laing, vol. i. passim, Edinburgh, 1864; T. McCrie, Life of John Knox, Edinburgh, 1841; P. Lorimer, Scottish Reformation, pp. 90–155, London, 1860; D. Hay Fleming, Martyrs and Confessors of St. Andrews, 1887; DNB, lxii. 248–251. For and against Wishart's complicity in the assassination of Cardinal Beaton, consult: P. F. Tytler, Hist. of Scotland, vol. v., chap. v., Edinburgh, 1834; Weir, in North British Review, 1868; J. H. Burton, Hist. of Scotland, vol. iii., chap. xxxvi., London, 1873; C. Rogers, Life of George Wishart, pp. 82–87, Edinburgh, 1876; J. Cunningham, Church Hist. of Scotland, vol. i., chap. viii., ib. 1882; W. Cramond, The Truth about George Wishart, 1898; A. F. Mitchell, The Scottish Reformation, p. 69, ib. 1900; P. H. Brown, Hist. of Scotland, ii. 20–25, Cambridge, 1902; H. Cowan, John Knox, New York, 1905. On 2 consult his Memoirs of James, Marquis of Montrose, 1639–50, transl. and ed. A. D. Murdoch and H F M. Simpson, London, 1893; R. Wodrow, Sufferings of the Church of Scotland, vol. i., ib. 1721; R. Keith, Catalogue of the Bishops of . . . Scotland, ib. 1755; DNB, lxii. 251–253.

WISLICENUS, GUSTAV ADOLF. See Free Congregations, §§ 1–2.

WISZOWATY, ANDREAS. See Socinus, Faustus, Socinians, I., § 2.

WITCHCRAFT AND WITCH TRIALS.

I. General History: In primitive belief the witch is a person who by supernatural means injures the possessions of her neighbors or of the inhabitants of a district, directing her destructive activity particularly against the corn and wine and cattle and what nourishes the cattle. Witchcraft is in general the accomplishment of some purpose through the help of supernatural means, particularly through subordinated spirits with which alliance is made. It involves belief in such spirits and in the possibility of entering into association with them and in a practical philosophy of magic (see Magic). But these dealings may upon such grounds as the injury done to others be regarded as punishable offenses, especially under the control of a religion of revelation. But the better ground for interdiction of these practises lies in the essential impiety and idolatry which witchcraft involves. On this ground witchcraft was forbidden by the Mosaic law (Deut. xviii. 10 sqq.), and also by the early Christian Church either on the ground of the emptiness of the practise or of its positive godlessness and commerce with the devil. A less strenuous opposition was begun in the early Middle Ages, as, for example, at the Synod of Reisbach (799 A.D.), where rules of penance were made for women convicted of witchcraft, but capital pun-

1. Official Deliverances Prior to the Reformation.

ishment was prohibited (Hefele, Conciliengeschichte, iii. 730). John of Damascus occupied a similar standpoint in his writing " Concerning Dragons and Witches " (MPG, xciv. 1599–1604), in treating of the superstitions among Jews and Saracens; and to the same purport may be cited Agobard of Lyon (d. 840 A.D.) and John of Salisbury (d. 1180 A.D.), all holding witchcraft to be a delusion. At the beginning of the thirteenth century at the erection of the Inquisition the use of magic and heresy were regarded as two sides of the same offense and as the desertion of God for the service of evil spirits. Yet this very action of the Inquisition diffused and strengthened the superstition. Gregory IX., drawing his information from Conrad of Marburg, in a bull of the year 1231 invoked the use of civil punishment against heretical associations at the meetings of which the devil appeared as a toad or a ghost or a black cat. Dominican theologians were, however, the principal diffusers of belief in these meetings with the devil and of the superstitions of incubi and succubi, going back to Augustine, " City of God," xv. 23. The Dominican inquisitor Nicolas Eymericus wrote in 1376 his Directorium inquisitorium, setting forth the use of magic as heretical, and stigmatizing those who used it as infideles, superstitiosi, apostatæ, and subject to the Inquisition. Innocent VIII. in his bull of 1484 renewed the provisions which brought witches under the judgment of the Inquisition, and enlarged the powers of the inquisitors upon the basis of the close relationship between witchcraft and heresy (the text of the bull is in G. Roskoff, *Geschichte des Teufels*, Leipsic, 1869, ii. 222–225). Supplementing these directions there was put forth under the Dominican inquisitors Jacob Sprenger and Heinrich Krämer a great work directing the process of inquiry into witchcraft, viz., the celebrated *Malleus maleficarum* (Cologne, 1489, and very frequently thereafter), the title of which notes as a peculiarity that the practise of leaguing with the devil was charged principally upon women. The first book shows the proof of the occurrence of the offense and its detestability according to Deut. xviii. and Lev. xix.–xx., and cites Augustine, St. Thomas, and experience. The second book continues along the line of experience and directs in the methods of detecting, dismissing, and curing the evils. The third book introduces the matter of trials and punishments. While the ordinary tribunals are competent, the union of heresy and witchcraft makes the inquisitors' duty plain, and there is no need to wait for an accuser; the witnesses need not be named; a counsel for defense was not necessary, indeed if such a one were too zealous he might be suspected of complicity in the offense; instruments of torture are suggested. The authority most quoted by this book is the *Formicarius* of Johann Nider (d. 1438), dependent upon Wisd. Sol., vi. 6.

Thus a few centuries before the Reformation, in part under direct stimulus from the popes, there was a great increase of belief in witches and of prosecution of those charged with the offense.

2. Official Responsibility and Private Discussion. Modern apologies for the bull of Innocent VIII. miss the mark altogether in view of the chain of deliverances from the papal chair, including those of Alexander VI., Julius II., Leo X., and Hadrian VI. That the sponsors for the Reformation made no point of opposing specifically the attack upon witchcraft even in the countries evangelized rests upon the general background of conception of such possibilities as existed in the minds of the ministry during the last two centuries prior to the Reformation. The Elector August of Saxony included in his criminal code of 1572 as a capital offense " that anyone should forget his Christian faith and make an agreement with the devil." Wächter speaks of the epidemic of witchcraft which broke out in Germany at the end of the fifteenth century, and resulted in the prosecution of thousands of unfortunates; and when the spread of the epidemic into France, Italy, Spain, the Netherlands, and England is taken into account, the victims coming not only out of the Catholic but out of the Protestant Church, the estimate of many thousands is not beyond bounds. Not the least guilty part of the process was the secularizing of the trials, i.e., the turning of the trials over to the civil power, which took place in Protestant countries at the end of the sixteenth century. The earlier dependence upon " Italian habit and teaching " continued, and the conception was fostered by the makers of the confessions as a part of orthodox belief, while among the masses of the people the superstition had the strongest hold. Among the Roman Catholic theorists who sought to justify the experiences of the witch trials by philosophical principles were Jean Bodin (*Magorum dæmonomania*, Basel, 1579), Peter Binsfeld, the suffragan bishop of Treves, the Jesuit Martin del Rio of Antwerp (*Disquisitiones magicæ*, Louvain, 1599), and Georg Stengel of Ingolstadt (d. 1651, *De judiciis*). On the Protestant side the subject was discussed by the Heidelberg physician Thomas Erastus (*Repetitio disputationis de lamiis seu strigibus*, Basel, 1578); James I. of England (*Dæmonologie*, Edinburgh, 1597), and especially Benedict Carpzov (*Practicæ novæ . . . rerum criminalium*, Leipsic, 1635).

In recent times Protestants and Roman Catholics have joined in showing the unreality at the basis of this series of conceptions. It is due to the work of **3. Individual Opposition.** a Bonn professor of medicine, C. Binz, that a series of Protestant opposers of witch trials have become known as in past centuries exerting their powers in this direction. Thus the Lutheran Johann Weier (d. 1588) wrote the oldest Latin treatise against the practise of trying witches (*De præstigiis dæmonum*, Frankfort, 1566), and he had several doughty followers during the sixteenth century. Similarly the German Protestant John Ewich, physician at Bremen (1584), Johann Georg Gödelmann, professor of law at Rostock, and Augustin Lerchheimer, professor at Heidelberg (*Christlich Bedencken und Erinnerung von Zauberei*, Heidelberg, 1585, new ed., Strasburg, 1888), as well as the English Reginald Scot (d. 1599; *The Discovery of Witchcraft*, London, 1584, reprint, 1886), energetically opposed the burning of witches. The Arminian preacher J. Greve, of Arnheim in Holland (*Tribunal reformatum*, 1622), was another forerunner of the Jesuits Tanner and Spee. Tanner's *Theologia scholastica* appeared in 4 vols., Ingolstadt, 1626, and Spee's book was five years later, both protesting against the prosecution of the witches. The same cause was espoused at the end of the seventeenth century by Balthasar Bekker (*De Betoverde Wereld*, Leeuwarden, 1691), and at the beginning of the eighteenth by Christian Thomasius (*Theses de crimine magiæ*, Halle, 1701).

The century of the *Aufklärung* was not quite free from official execution of witches on German or German-Swiss territory. In Würzburg in 1749 occurred the burning of the nun Marie Renate Singer, in Memmingen in 1775 the be-
4. Superstition Abolished; Survivals. heading of Anna Maria Schwägelin and in 1782 that of the serving-maid Anna Göldi at Glarus. Since then the dreadful epidemic seems to have died out, at least from European lands. But in Roman Catholic Middle and South America prosecution for witchcraft has survived almost to the present. Execution by burning for the alleged crime was visited upon a woman at Camargo in Mexico in 1860, upon a woman and her son in San Juan de Jacobo in the Mexican state of Sinaloa in 1874, and upon a woman, after frequent castigation, in the market-place of a city of Peru in 1888. That this should be the case under Roman Catholic domination is not surprising when it is recalled that a

basis is laid for it in the Thomistic theology, which is practically the officially recognized and normative system of the Roman Catholic Church.

(O. Zöckler†.)

II. In Great Britain and the American Colonies: The belief in witchcraft was one of the earliest delusions entertained by man under the primitive dualism which events in the sphere of nature made to appear so much a matter of course

1. Legal (see Comparative Religion, VI., 1, Provisions a, §§ 4–5). That legislation under the against earlier civilizations should take cogWitchcraft. nizance of it was equally a matter of course. Thus Hammurabi (see Hammurabi and His Code, II., § 2; cf. *DB*, extra vol., p. 599) began his codified legislation with two sections dealing with the subject, and the Brahman and Zoroastrian legislation has much to say on it. Under Christianity the basis of the synodical, papal, and scholastic pronouncements described in the preceding discussion was found in the Mosaic and prophetic denunciations (e.g., Ex. xxii. 18; Deut. xviii. 10–11; Micah v. 12). The Biblical interdiction together with the remnants of heathen superstition aided in perpetuating the belief; and this accounts for the fact that the educated, especially the clergy, were so prominent in the actual outbreaks which occurred like epidemics. In Western Europe the seventeenth century may be described as the era of the witchcraft delusions, exemplified by the execution of seventy persons in Sweden in 1670, while 1,000 are reported to have been executed in a single province in Italy in one year. This epidemic period was anticipated by sporadic prosecutions of witches in the previous century. In England, Scotland, and the North American colonies the actual prosecutions were based on legal provisions which were provided from time to time, beginning in the sixteenth century. In England witchcraft, defined as a compact made by man or woman with Satan, was made a felony in 1541 under King Henry VIII. (33 Henry VIII., chap. 8), and this act was extended under Elizabeth in 1562. The volume of James I. referred to above was partly the occasion of the new act of parliament in the first year of his reign (1603; 1 James I., chap. 12) exactly defining the crime. A well-known legal authority (M. Dalton, *The Countrey Justice*, London, 1618, latest ed., 1746) had a chapter on witchcraft aiming to define exactly the marks on the body of a witch. In Scotland the first act on the subject was dated 1563, amended 1649, under which the clergy were often the instruments of justice and presbyteries frequently the petitioners for the same. The repeal of the laws in England and Scotland in 1735 evoked many and persistent protests from high and low. Massachusetts in 1641 made witchcraft a capital offense; Connecticut followed in December, 1642; and in 1655 New Haven Colony based a similar law explicitly upon Ex. xxii. 18; Lev. xx. 27; and Deut. xviii. 10–11.

One of the noteworthy features of the witchcraft prosecutions of the sixteenth and seventeenth centuries, due in part to the Biblical basis, is the eminence of those in Church, State, science, and society, who supported by voice and act the idea itself and the civil procedure against witches. Thus

Cranmer, in 1549 (*Articles of Visitation*), enjoined the clergy to make inquiries concerning the practise of witchcraft. Bishop Jewel in a ser-

2. Classes mon before Queen Elizabeth in 1558 Affected lamented the multiplication of witches. by Richard Baxter's *Certainty of the* the Belief. *Worlds of Spirits* (London, 1691) places him on record to the same effect. Cotton Mather in New England, who served on a commission to advise the special court which tried the cases and suggested caution in accepting certain lines of evidence offered (though on grounds which emphasize the extravagance of the superstition), approved after six executions at Salem the evidence and the convictions which resulted so fatally (*Discourse on the Wonders of the Invisible World*, Boston, 1693). The offense was understood as cognizable in courts of justice by great English jurists like Sir Edward Coke and Sir Matthew Hale, while Lord Bacon and Sir Henry More gave utterance to their belief in the reality of compacts made between human beings and Satan. William Penn is reported to have sat as justice at the trial of two Swedish women accused of witchcraft, and they escaped only through a technicality in the proceedings. Physicians diagnosed cases as due to witchcraft. The pronouncement of Dr. Griggs, the Salem village physician in the case of the " afflicted " children of that place, is responsible in large part for the prosecutions which made it notorious, in which, between Mar. and Sept., 1692, nineteen were hanged and one was pressed to death. While among the people the opinions of the educated were reflected with a thousand weird and fantastic enlargements.

Under the Scotch statutes in Aberdeen in 1597 twenty-four persons were burned at the stake for this offense. At Prestonpans (?) Isobel Grierson met the same fate in 1607, a part of 3. Prose- the evidence being that she had apcutions in peared in the form of a cat to work Great her evil deeds. In 1617 twenty-seven Britain. persons were executed in Aberdeen or the vicinity; in 1622 Margaret Wallace suffered death, her accuser being the minister at Garmunnock; and an intimate of hers, Alexander Hunter or Hatteraic, shortly after suffered death; Alice Nisbet was executed at Hilton in 1632. In the same vicinity the year 1643 saw several executions, some of them by mobs, one by the awful penalty of pressing to death. Ninety women are reported to have been hanged in Scotland in 1645, and 120 in 1661. Possibly the last execution for this cause in that country was that of Little Dean at Dornoch in 1722. In England the authority of King James I. gave increased currency to the belief in witches. In 1645–47 the infamous witch-finder, Matthew Hopkins, ran his horrible course, and in that time in Suffolk and Essex 200 witches were tried and most of them executed (J. Howell, *Familiar Letters*, 1645, 10th ed., Aberdeen, 1753). In 1664 two women were tried in Suffolk before Sir Matthew Hale, who then affirmed the certainty of the fact of witchcraft.

When in the mother country there was manifested among all classes so lively a sense of the supposedly supernatural, reenforced by official prosecution and executions, it is not surprizing that the infection should have found lodgment in the colonies where contact with Indian su-

4. Early Prosecutions in the Colonies. perstition was so close. The legal provisions already cited are an index of public official opinion. The first victim in the colonies, so far as extant testimony goes, was Alse Young (not Mary Johnson) in Windsor, Conn. (in all probability the case referred to by J. Winthrop, *History of New England*, ed. J. Savage, ii. 374, Boston, 1853). Margaret (or Martha) Jones, against whom suspicion was raised in part by her skill in the use of healing herbs, was hanged in Boston in 1648; and Ann Hibbins, widow of a reputable merchant of the same city, was executed June 19, 1656. Mrs. Bassett suffered the death penalty at Stratford, Conn., in 1651, Mrs. Knapp at Fairfield in the same colony in 1653 (this was a particularly malignant case); Nathaniel and Rebecca Greensmith were hanged at Hartford in Jan., 1662, the wife after a " confession " in which she implicated her husband. The most important case, however, not in itself but because it was in great part the inciting cause of the Salem outbreak, was that of Mrs. Glover, executed in Boston Nov. 16, 1688, for bewitching the four children, aged, respectively, thirteen, eleven, seven, and five, of a Boston mason named Goodwin. The account of the antics of these children, and of part of the legal proceedings which followed, given by Cotton Mather (*Memorable Providences Relating to Witchcraft and Possession*, Boston, 1689) illustrates the hold which this belief had among the intelligent, as well as the credulity which could induce belief in impossible happenings. These children, according to Mather, barked like dogs and purred or mewed like cats; they fell into strange contortions; one of them cried out that she was being strangled, or that a chain bound her leg, or that she was in an oven, while the physical manifestations of choking, lameness, or perspiration were evident to bear out the statements. " Yea, they would *fly* like *Geese;* and be carried with an incredible *Swiftness* thro' the *air*, having but just their *Toes* now and then upon the ground, their *Arms* waved like the Wings of a *Bird* "—so reports Mr. Mather! One of the children manifested an unnatural precocity and pertness in her intercourse with Mr. Mather, who undertook to exorcise her, playing upon his antipathies with astounding cunning. The children accused Mrs. Glover, a woman of violent temper, and the result was her conviction and execution. Between 1646 and 1688 twelve persons were executed for this offense in New England (W. F. Poole, in J. Winsor's *Memorial Hist. of Boston*, ii. 133, Boston, 1881), and this is only a small proportion of prosecutions some of which resulted in acquittal, though in all cases a stigma was attached which probably remained for life.

The Goodwin case was naturally much discussed, and application of the laws of psychology suggests its relationship to the Salem episode. This subtle influence was enforced by the explicit statements of men in high esteem to the effect that Satan was making, in the situation so favorable to him in New England because of the newness and wildness of the country, a strenuous assault on mankind. The manifestations around which the Salem persecutions centered began in the home of

5. The Salem Episode; Early Stage. the Rev. Samuel Parris, minister of the village since 1689. He had in his family his daughter Elizabeth (nine years of age; she was early removed to another place), his niece Abigail Williams (eleven years), and a slave called Tituba. With these there used to meet in the afternoons of the winter of 1691–92 a circle composed as follows: Ann Putnam (twelve), Mary Walcott, Mercy Lewis, and Elizabeth Hubbard (seventeen), Elizabeth Booth and Susannah Sheldon (eighteen), Mary Warren and Sarah Churchill (twenty), all unmarried, and Mrs. Putnam, Mrs. Pope, and a woman named Wenham, all of middle age. The object of the meeting was the practise of palmistry, fortune-telling, magic, and spiritualism. Before the winter was over these persons began to display before others certain curious actions, crawling under chairs, assuming queer postures, making strange outcries, falling into fits, and writhing as though in great agony. The village physician already named, Dr. Griggs, being called in diagnosed the case as one of witchcraft. It seems at least credible that this gave the circle its cue. The news spread concerning the doings, witnesses increased in numbers, and the excitement mounted. The exhibitions were no longer confined to the houses of the minister and the families to which the members of the circle belonged, but took place in public, even in the church, the services of which were interrupted by the " afflicted " with outcry or assertion of the occurrence of something unseen by the congregation. Under the assumption that Satan was at work, the children went unrebuked, and their impudence grew. Some members who seem to have retained their sense of the fitness of things were incensed and stayed away from church, thereby becoming marked characters and some of them figuring in the subsequent prosecutions as defendants. Mr. Parris called in for consultation the neighboring ministers, who witnessed some of the performances and accepted Dr. Griggs' diagnosis. The little world was now aflame, and the question naturally arose, who was accountable for the behavior of the circle. Questioning educed the statement from the girls that the witches were Sarah Good, Sarah Osburn, and Tituba. The magistrates entered upon their duties, the accused were examined, the assumption of guilt being at the basis of the examination. Tituba " confessed," while the others strenuously maintained their innocence. During these and the following trials the girls appeared to suffer whenever the accused looked toward them. Soon new culprits were sought, Martha Corey was accused, and in her examination and all her subsequent acts was manifested as a woman of unusual ability and strong common sense. Her husband was put on the stand and adduced some trivial circumstances which were interpreted as substantiating the charge, but were clearly the result of the current ferment. So it went, and person after person was accused until it seemed that no station, calling, or character was exempt from peril of accusation.

The attention of students has been called to the fact that those first charged with active agency in the Satanic persecution of the girls were persons of little standing in the community, or even of disrepute; that the next stage was accusa-

6. The Later Stages and End. tion of those who for property or other reasons were *personæ non gratæ* either in the community or to the girls. Then the accusers became bolder; those who under other circumstances could not have been thought of were charged with this guilt, and of especial significance is the fact that those who opposed or denounced the proceedings were noted and pursued with vindictiveness by the band of girls. Particularly noteworthy in this last relation was the case of John Proctor, whose entire family, including his wife's relations, were brought into the scope of the proceedings and suffered great personal and property damage. Among those who were assailed by these terrible experiences were Dorcas Good, a child between four and five years of age, Rev. Samuel Willard of the Old South Church, Boston, John Alden, and finally Mrs. Hale, the wife of the minister of the First Church of Beverly. The virtues of the last-named were so eminent and her services so distinguished that the accusers at last overreached themselves, people came to their senses, and the delusion was dispelled. While arrests continued in 1693, in January of which year fifty indictments were found though only three convictions resulted, yet Chief Justice William Stoughton maintained to the last his position respecting the evidence to be admitted and his prejudice against all who were accused. In April of the same year the governor by proclamation set free all who were imprisoned on this charge, and in 1711 there was issued a legislative reversal of attainder in favor of those who had suffered, or their surviving relatives, and compensation to them or the survivors was ordered to the amount of £578 12s. Thus ended the Salem delusion. That sporadic cases of prosecution and even of execution elsewhere should occur was natural. In July, 1706, at Princess Anne Court House, Va., Grace Sherwood suffered the ordeal by water and was committed to jail in fetters, though the final disposition of the case is not recorded. In 1712 in South Carolina a vigilance committee is reported to have seized and "roasted" several witches (whether to death is not clear), and a jury refused to award damages to the sufferers or their representatives. And in Illinois, under the jurisdiction of Virginia, as late as 1790, negro slaves, male and female, were done to death under legal prosecution by burning, hanging, or shooting.

The dire results of the outbreak appear only partially in the executions. Hundreds were put under arrest and confined in fetters, some died in prison, others were laid under suspicion with all the natural consequences thereof in communities which under the superstition developed a cruel fa-

7 Financial and Moral Effects. naticism. Even where conviction was not reached, the victims were often mulcted in heavy costs for the trial which had issued in their release. Some broke prison and fled from the places where they had by hardship won a home from the forest and had to begin again in fresh surroundings. Others, though not convicted, were banished, or suffered under the unjust avoidance of their neighbors. The families of the victims suffered under the legal attainder which rested on them for eighteen years. These are but the most obvious of the consequences to the victims and their families. Others were those which came to the community in the demoralization caused by the excitement of passions and the yielding to the opportunity for revenge. This does not overlook the deception of the group of girls and women to whose action the Salem outbreak was due, as they played on the sympathies, superstitions, and animosities of the neighborhood. While all classes, and especially the learned in law, medicine, and theology, were caught in the epidemic, obloquy rests in large measure upon the ministers who were so active in the affair. Much has been written both in accusation and defense of this class. Yet after two centuries the verdict, in view of the almost preponderating influence wielded in society by the clergy, must be that had they been free from superstition the outbreak could not have occurred, even with the physicians pronouncing in favor of witchcraft. Their prepossessions supporting the possibilities of compact between a physical Satan and men and women cast the deciding vote, and in this relation the influence of Cotton Mather was not the least. On the other hand, many of the clergy, from the first, labored mightily against the proceedings, mitigated the severity where possible, and finally aided in bringing about recovery from the delusion.

The attendant circumstances present many problems to the psychologist. The first set of questions focuses upon the circle of girls and women who were

8 Psychological Problems. regarded as bewitched. Many elements of trouble were present; the knowledge concerning the Goodwin children was doubtless a primary stimulus; there was the intent to study occult phenomena which was the purpose of the meetings; also the presence of the possibly half-witted Tituba with her Indian-negro proclivities acting on the minds of the others, which were gardens evidently tilled for that kind of growth; not to be forgotten is the impressionability of the members of the circle, who were clearly open to suggestion and self-suggestion, and were probably nervous in temperament; the wonder that they excited awakened, stimulated, and ministered to a desire for notice which grew as it fed; and this developed into a craving for publicity and an astonishing boldness, together with a precocious cunning and a progressive callousness and vindictiveness which at the last overreached itself; finally, there was the predisposition of the community to accept at its face value every claim and assertion made by the "afflicted." The second set of problems is raised by the last condition noted. How could the ideas of justice of all classes, the common sense of the ordinary man and woman, the medical knowledge of the physician, the legal perception of the magistrate, and the acumen of the minister be so obscured as to permit the orgy of prosecution to continue for a year? The credulity evinced, the silliness of the beliefs publicly owned, seem at this date almost impossible. This lack of restraining sensibility was so pronounced that would-be defenders of the accused were for the time almost completely silenced, held back by fear and soon by the fact that defense of the accused involved danger of the charge of complicity in the alleged witchcraft. Previous good records and useful lives went for nothing in the frenzy which paralyzed humane impulses. The feature of the Salem episode ,which is most noticeable is the epidemic of spiritual insanity. The third set of problems is presented by the "confessions" of the victims. In some cases doubtless a morbid desire for notoriety, for which the opportunity so unique for creating a sensation furnished the occasion, was the moving cause. Moreover, the leading questions asked by the prosecutors and judges indicate a superstitious sub-current in the life of the day which in the minds of the weakly could easily stimulate the unhealthy imagination of the accused. In some instances it may well be that sensitive victims, shrinking from the badgering incident to the trials, and worn out by their tortures and the terrible situation in which they found themselves, confessed in order that an end might be put to their sufferings, and then concocted the story of their dealings with Satan, adding the details which the suggestive questioning indicated in order to bear out the "confession." But when all is said, there is much in the story which calls for further study. Few occurrences present more, or more difficult, problems than the Salem witchcraft delusion.

GEO. W. GILMORE.

BIBLIOGRAPHY: On the general subject consult: E. D. Hauber, *Bibliotheca, acta et scripta magica*, 3 vols., Lemgo, 1738–41; G. K. Hörst, *Dämonomagie, oder Geschichte des Glaubens an Zauberei und dämonische Wunder*, 2 vols., Frankfort, 1818; idem, *Zauberbibliothek*, 6 vols., Mainz, 1821–26; idem, *Deuteroskopie*, 2 vols., Frankfort, 1830; J. E. D. Esquirol, *Des maladies mentales*, 2 vols., Paris, 1838; W. von Waldbrühl, *Naturforschung und Hexenglaube*, Berlin, 1863; G. Roskoff, *Geschichte des Teufels*, ii. 206–364, Leipsic, 1869; J. Buchmann, *Unfreie und freie Kirche in ihren Beziehungen zur Sklaverei . . . und zum Dämonismus*, Breslau, 1873; G. Diefenbach, *Hexenwahn vor und nach der Glaubensspaltung*, Frankfort, 1886; P. Pitres and E. Regis, *Les Obsessions et les impulsions*, Paris, 1902; O. M. Hueffer, *The Book of Witches*, New York, 1909.

On prosecutions for witchcraft in the Middle Ages and in Europe generally consult: L. Scheltema, *Geschiedenis der Heksenprocessen*, Haarlem, 1828; F. Fischer, *Die Basler Hexenprozesse*, Basel, 1840; C. G. von Wächter, *Die gerichtlichen Verfolgungen der Hexen und Zauberer in Deutschland*, Tübingen, 1845; L. Kopp, *Die Hexenprozesse und ihre Gegner in Tyrol*, Innsbruck, 1874; F. Nippold, *Die gegenwärtige Wiederbelebung des Hexenglaubens*, Berlin, 1875; W. G. Soldan, *Geschichte der Hexenprozesse*, ed. H. Heppe, Stuttgart, 1880; G. Längin, *Religion und Hexenprozesse*, Leipsic, 1888 (against the polemic of Diefenbach above); W. H. D. Adams, *Witch, Warlock and Magician*, London, 1889; A. D. White, *A Hist. of the Warfare of Science with Theology*, 2 vols., New York, 1896 (several chapters deal with the subject); S. Riezler, *Hexenprozesse in Bayern*, Stuttgart, 1896; J. Hansen, *Zauberwahn, Inquisition und Hexenprozess im Mittelalter*, Munich, 1900; idem, *Quellen und Untersuchungen zur Geschichte des Hexenwahns und der Hexenverfolgung im Mittelalter*, Berlin, 1901; H. C. Lea, *History of the Inquisition*, vol. ii., New York, 1900, cf. idem, *Superstition and Force*, Philadelphia, 1878 (consult Index); N. Paulus, *Hexenwahn und Hexenprozess . . . im 16. Jahrhundert*, Freiburg, 1910.

For England and Scotland consult: T. Wright, *Narratives of Sorcery and Magic*, London, 1851; C. K. Sharpe, *Account of the Belief in Witchcraft in Scotland*, ib. 1884 (gives an excellent list of early books on witchcraft); J. Ashton, *The Devil in Britain and America*, ib. 1896 (con-

tains a bibliography); J. G. Campbell, *Witchcraft and Second Sight in Scotland*, New York, 1902; *Witches. Original Documents and Reprints from the original Sources of European History*, vol. iii., Philadelphia, 1902.

For the American colonies consult, besides the works of Cotton Mather: (Governor) Thomas Hutchinson, *Hist. of Massachsetts Bay*, vols. i. and ii., Boston, 1764–67, vol. iii., London, 1728 (of high value, using documents no longer extant); S. P. Fowler, *Account of Samuel Parris and of his Connection with the Witchcraft Delusion of 1692*, Salem, 1857; *Records of Salem Witchcraft, faithfully Copied from the Original Documents*, Roxbury, 1864; C. W. Upham, *Hist. of Salem Witchcraft*, 2 vols., Boston, 1867 (the standard work, somewhat extreme against Cotton Mather); S. G. Drake, *Annals of Witchcraft in New England and . . . the United States*, Albany, 1869, cf. his *Witchcraft Delusion in New England*, 3 vols., ib. 1866; J. H. Trumbull, *True Blue Laws of Connecticut and the False Blue Laws Invented by the Rev Samuel Peters*, New York, 1876; G. M. Beard, *The Psychology of the Salem Witchcraft*, ib. 1882; G. H. Moore, *Notes on the Hist. of Witchcraft in Massachusetts, . . . in Worcester, . . . in Cambridge, Supplementary Notes . . . , and Final Notes on Witchcraft in Masachusetts*, 5 vols., Worcester, Cambridge, and New York, 1883–85; F. W. Palfrey, *Compendious Hist. of New England*, iv. 96–127, Boston, 1884; W. S. Nevins, *Witchcraft in Salem Village in 1622*, ib. 1892; E. H. Byington, *The Puritan in England and New England*, pp. 335–381, ib. 1900; J. M. Taylor, *The Witchcraft Delusion in Colonial Connecticut, 1647–97*, New York, 1908 (cites from public documents both published and in manuscript, and gives excellent bibliographical suggestions); Amelia MaGummere, *Witchcraft and Quakerism*, Philadelphia, 1909; M. V. B. Perley, *A Short Hist. of the Salem Village Witchcraft Trials*, Salem, Mass., 1911.

WITHERSPOON, JOHN: Presbyterian divine and signer of the Declaration of Independence; b. in the parish of Yester (11 m. e. of Edinburgh), Scotland, Feb. 5, 1722; d. near Princeton, N. J., Nov. 15, 1794. Through his mother he counted descent from John Knox. He was graduated from the University of Edinburgh (1742); licensed in the Church of Scotland (1743) and settled at Beith (1744) and at Paisley (1757). By this time his publications had shown that he possessed equal power as a theologian, guardian of morals, and satirist, displaying consecutive thinking, deep perception, ready wit, and earnestness of purpose. Hence he received calls to positions of prominence, and accepted the invitation to the presidency of the College of New Jersey, 1768. In his new position he was eminently useful. He introduced a number of improvements, particularly the lecture-system, previously unknown in American colleges (himself lecturing upon rhetoric, moral philosophy, and divinity), the study of French and Hebrew, the latter of which he taught, philosophical instruments, among them the first orrery made by Rittenhouse, and additions to the library, to which he made noteworthy gifts. He attracted, by his reputation and ability as a teacher, a large number of students. He was pastor of the church at Princeton during his presidency, a New Jersey representative to the Continental Congress, 1776–1782 (with the exception of 1780, when he declined the election), in which body he wrote several important state papers, and exerted his influence in favor of independence. During the war the college was suspended. In 1790 he became totally blind. He was a versatile man and a voluminous writer. His *Works* were edited by Rev. Dr. Green (4 vols., Philadelphia, 1803; Edinburgh, 1804–05, in 9 vols., 1815). They include *Ecclesiastical Characteristics, or the Arcana of Church Policy, being an Attempt to open up* *the Mystery of Moderation* (Edinburgh, 1753, 5th ed., 1763; a satire upon the moderate party in the Church of Scotland, published anonymously, but acknowledged by Witherspoon as his own in his *Serious Apology*, 1763); *Essay on the Connection between the Doctrine of Justification by the Imputed Righteousness of Christ and Holiness of Life* (Glasgow, 1756; one of the ablest Calvinistic expositions of that doctrine in any language); *A Serious Enquiry into the Nature and Effects of the Stage* (1757; new ed. by W. Moffat, Edinburgh, 1876; occasioned by the performance of the Rev. John Home's drama, *Douglas*); *A Practical Treatise on Regeneration* (1764); *The History of a Corporation of Servants Discovered a Few Years Ago in the Interior Parts of South America* (Glasgow, 1765; a clever satire upon abuses in the Church of Scotland). He was the author also of several volumes of sermons, besides works dealing with matters of civil government.

BIBLIOGRAPHY: Besides the *Life* prefixed to the *Works* (ut sup.), consult: D. W. Woods, *John Witherspoon*, New York, 1906 (by his great grandson, who used rare public documents); E. H. Gillett, *Hist. of the Presbyterian Church*, 2 vols., Philadelphia, 1864; R. Chambers, *Biographical Dictionary of Eminent Scotsmen*, new ed. by T. Thomson, Edinburgh, 1856; W. B. Sprague, *Annals of the American Pulpit*, iii. 288–300, New York, 1858; J. Sanderson, *Biography of the Signers to the Declaration of Independence*, pp. 296–314, Philadelphia, 1865; J. Maclean, *Hist. of the College of New Jersey*, 2 vols., Philadelphia, 1877; *Princeton Book*; *Hist., Organization, and present Condition of the College of New Jersey*, Boston, 1880; C. A. Briggs, *American Presbyterianism*, New York, 1885; M. C. Tyler, *Literary Hist. of the American Revolution*, ii. 319–330, New York, 1897; I. W. Riley, *American Philosophy, the Early Schools*, pp. 483–497, New York, 1907; C. Evans, *American Bibliography*, vol. v., nos. 15224, 16173, Chicago, 1909; *DNB*, lxii. 271–274.

WITSCHEL, vit′shel, **JOHANN HEINRICH WILHELM:** German pastor, author of devotional literature; b. at Henfenfeld (17 m. e.n.e. of Nuremberg) May 9, 1769; d. at Kattenhochstädt near Weissenburg (30 m. s.w. of Nuremberg) Apr. 24, 1847. After preparatory studies at Gräfenberg and Nuremberg he attended the University of Altdorf (1788–93); in 1794 was appointed noon preacher at the Dominican Church in Nuremberg; removed to the parish of Igensdorf in Nuremberg, 1801; succeeded his father as preacher in Gräfenberg in 1810, becoming dean in 1815 and school-inspector of the district; in 1819 he assumed charge of the parish of Kattenhochstädt, where after 1820 he conducted for thirteen years an institution for the higher education of school-teachers. He was the author of several collections of poems that corresponded to the taste of the time. He was the representative of an amiable and respectable rationalism, as is evident from his principal work, *Morgen- und Abendopfer in Gesängen* (Sulzbach, 1803). This contains a series of devotional exercises in rime, for morning and evening, arranged according to weeks and seasons, and became a very popular book of devotion in spite of its rationalism. It is still used in all parts of Germany, among both Protestants and Catholics, and the demand remains so large that it is constantly reprinted. Other works are *Pantheon für Damen* (1799); and *Moralische Blätter* (1801).

(T. KOLDE.)

BIBLIOGRAPHY: The *Morgen- und Abendopfer* after the 11th ed. contains a biography.

WITSIUS, HERMANNUS (HERMANN WITS): Dutch theologian; b. at Enkhuizen (30 m. n.e. of Amsterdam) Feb. 12, 1636; d. at Leyden Oct. 22, 1708. After a very thorough training, especially in the classics, in 1651 he entered the University of Utrecht, and in 1654 removed to the University of Groningen; in 1656 he passed his theological examination at Utrecht, and in 1657 was installed preacher of Westwoud, not far from his native place; in 1661 he removed to Wormer, in 1666 to Goes, and in 1668 to Leeuwarden. In all these pastorates he proved to be an excellent preacher, a distinguished catechist, and a faithful pastor. In 1675 he accepted a call as professor and preacher to Franeker; in 1680 he undertook like duties at Utrecht; in 1698 he became professor at Leyden, remaining till illness caused his retirement in 1707. While in his theology Witsius aimed at a reconciliation between orthodoxy and federalism, he was first of all a Biblical theologian, his principal field being systematic theology. His chief work is entitled, *De œconomia fœderum Dei cum hominibus* (Leeuwarden, 1677; often reprinted, e.g., Basel, 1739; it appeared in Dutch transl, also in Engl. transl., *The Œconomy of the Covenants between God and Man*, 3 vols., Edinburgh, 1771–72). He was induced to publish this work by his grief at the controversies between Voetians and Cocceians. Although himself a member of the federalistic school, he was in no way blind to the value of the scholastically established dogmatic system of the Church. Besides his principal work he published, *Exercitationes sacræ in symbolum, quod Apostolorum dicitur* (Franeker, 1681; Dutch transl., Delft, 1700; Eng. transl., *Sacred Dissertations on what is commonly called the Apostles Creed*, 2 vols., Edinburgh, 1823); *Ægyptiaca: sive, de Ægyptiacorum sacrorum cum Hebraicis collatione* (Franeker, 1683; frequent eds.); *Exercitationum academicarum, maxima ex parte historico-critico-theologicarum duodecas* (Utrecht, 1694); *Animadversiones irenicæ ad controversias, quæ sub infaustis antinomorum et neonomorum nominibus in Britannia nunc agitantur* (1696); *Meletemata Leidensia* (Leyden, 1703); *Disquisitio critico-theologica de Paulo Tarsensi, cive Romano* (1704). Of minor works there have appeared in Eng. transl. *A Treatise on Christian Faith* (London, 1761); *On the Character of a True Theologian* (Edinburgh, 1877); and *The Question: Was Moses the Author of the Pentateuch Answered in the Affirmative* (1877). (S. D. VAN VEEN.)

BIBLIOGRAPHY: The funeral oration by J. a Marck, Leyden, 1708; Witsius, *Schediasma theologia practica*, Groningen, 1729, contains a biography by H. C. van Bijler; B. Glasius, *Godgeleerd Nederland*, iii. 611–617, 's Hertogenbosch, 1856; W. B S. Boeles, *Frieslands Hoogeschool en het Rijes Athenæum te Franeker*, ii. 256–261, Leeuwarden, 1889; C. Sepp, *Het godgeleerd Onderwijs in Nederland gedurende de 16. en 17. Eeuw*, Leyden, 1874.

WITTENBERG, CONCORD OF.

Efforts of Butzer (§ 1). Meeting at Cassel (§ 3).
Butzer's Formula (§ 2). Conference at Wittenberg (§ 4).
Result of the Conference (§ 5).

The Concord of Wittenberg was an attempt of the sixteenth century toward an agreement on the Lord's Supper between the Saxons and representatives of Upper Germany and Switzerland. The preliminary history, until the fall of 1529, is that of the

Marburg Conference (see MARBURG, CONFERENCE OF). This rather deepened the prejudices and brought to light the diversity of point of view than paved the way for agreement. The **1. Efforts** diet of Schmalkald toward the end of **of Butzer.** 1529 led to a complete rupture with South Germany. A renewed attempt at reconciliation at the diet at Nuremberg (1530) failed on account of the attitude of the council of that city, and an agreement was no longer deemed possible. Each estate approached the Augsburg diet (see AUGSBURG CONFESSION AND ITS APOLOGY) armed for its own justification; and, as it has proved, the Saxon plan contemplated at the outset a special confession in the narrowest sense. The elector and his theologians had in mind to present their domestic church affairs and their loyalty in the most favorable light, and, in the specific renunciation of the Zwinglian teaching, to make their open appeal to the emperor as the protector of pure doctrine and religious peace. Although under the stress of circumstances and the influence of Philip of Hesse, supported by Hesse, Lüneburg, Brandenburg, Anhalt, Nuremberg, and Reutlingen, Melanchthon's preamble to the "Saxon Apology" was laid aside and the severest strictures against the "sacramentarians" were mitigated, yet the aversion to Zwingli and the South Germans remained unchanged. Melanchthon took every opportunity in public and private letters to warn against the so-called heresy, and their presumed connivance against the emperor enhanced the anxiety not to be taken in the same category as the South Germans and Zwingli. On the contrary the Strasburg delegates to the Diet of Augsburg had been ordered to emphasize that the difference on the doctrine of the Lord's Supper should be no reason for a separation among the Evangelicals. Feeling the need of the aid of their own preachers, they secured the presence of Martin Butzer and Wolfgang Capito (qq.v.), a consequence of which was the Tetrapolitan Confession (q.v.). Butzer now made the harmonizing of the parties his life purpose. A conference sought with Melanchthon was refused. Johann Brenz (q.v.) first acceded to a disputation with the Strasburg contingent, which insisted that the variance was only one of words. Butzer tried to make the same clear in a conference with the Saxon Chancellor Brück, and further in two letters, which were passed on to Melanchthon, who finally acceded to a correspondence (July 25), with the result that he rejected the Strasburg overture with the charge that they made a "pretense" by affirming the real presence and then qualifying it with the addition, "by the contemplation of faith." Successful elsewhere, Butzer ultimately (after Aug. 22) brought it to a conference with Melanchthon. The result was that Butzer considered himself agreed with Melanchthon and wrote to that effect, while the latter advised him to transmit his views in the form of articles to Luther, and he himself informed Luther that "Butzer desires to accede to our opinion," and that he held that the body of Christ is really present in the bread by ordination. To the propositions transmitted to Luther, the latter replied to Melanchthon (Sept. 11) from Coburg that he would

not reply to Butzer. Not more encouraging were the reports of Capito who had been sent with compromise propositions to Basel and Zurich. Undaunted, the Strasburg company resolved to send Butzer to Luther, by whom he was cordially received at Coburg (Sept. 25). But Luther refused to be convinced that he and his associates had always taught as Butzer now explained his doctrine, and he could not induce Luther to a joint signature to articles to be proposed, as all depended upon the interpretation. Luther, however, was inspired with hope, and Butzer, departing after two days, much encouraged, proceeded by way of Nuremberg, where he had a friendly consultation with Melanchthon and Andreas Osiander, to the towns of Upper Germany on behalf of the concord. Here his amiable approach and eloquence overcame all hesitation. Even Zwingli's assent was yielded, upon urging, to the formula: "The real body of Christ is truly offered." Returning home, greatly elated, by way of Basel, where he met with the heartiest accord of Œcolampadius, he undertook to draft a formula satisfactory to both parties. Thus there originated a document of concord in the form of a letter to Duke Ernst of Lüneburg, which stated, after reaffirm- **2. Butzer's** ing that the strife was one of words, **Formula.** that the true body and the true blood of Christ are truly present in the Lord's Supper, offered with the words of the Lord and the sacrament, and that upon the minister devolved nothing but the outer service of word and token, the inner blessing and the bread of heaven being given of God alone, and being therefore alone vital. Zwingli, meantime, had become suspicious, and personally objected to the formula on the ground that simple people would conceive the expression, "true body of Christ," always "as if they ate the body, chewing it with the teeth, as Luther also taught." He, however, would not object to the transmission of the document to Duke Ernst, reserving, however, in case of alleged recall, the privilege of reference to the statement made. Depending on this, and in view of the endorsement of his letter put forth by the council at Strasburg (Dec. 31, 1530), while a somewhat altered copy of the confession was forwarded to the elector of Saxony, Butzer not only assumed to depend on the support of the Swiss but also undertook their defense. Luther, who received the formula from the elector (Jan. 21, 1531), excluded the Swiss from his reply to Butzer and the South Germans, expressed his gratification at so much agreement, but marveled at the hesitation to admit the eating of the body also by unbelievers, a point on which he stated that he must remain steadfast. He would, however, await further divine guidance, without presuming a full and sound concord. Though no concord, yet a certain truce was thus accomplished, one result of which was the admission of the adherents of the Tetrapolitana to the Schmalkald League. An attempt during the early months of the League at a union with the Swiss failed. The Wittenberg party, however, expected more of Strasburg, which on account of the Swiss internal turmoil and from political reasons began to gravitate more northward. In the towns of Upper Germany the work of conciliation at the hands of the tireless Butzer was making notable progress, save as it was somewhat neutralized by the severe judgment of Luther on Zwingli's death. This catastrophe in Switzerland left Butzer a freer hand, and his influence, as of the foremost South German theologian and churchman, after the death of Œcolampadius, was materially increasing. A forward step was the subscription of the Augsburg Confession at the Diet of Schweinfurt (1532), on the part of the representatives of Upper Germany. Melanchthon, gradually relinquishing his distrust toward Butzer, was warming more and more toward his project as shown by his communications from Apr., 1531, and his expressed desire for a meeting, Oct., 1533. A fruit of this meeting was Butzer's projection of a new general conference to give formal and public statement to the reconciliation that seemed now to have been practically accomplished. Soon better results were promising by a stronger inclination toward harmony in Switzerland; the agreement of the South German Ambrosius Blaurer (q.v.) at Stuttgart to a formula stating the real presence according to substance; and by the adoption, by the much-contested Augsburg, of the Confession and Apology, through Butzer's exertions.

In view of the exclusion of the "sacramentarians" by the Peace of Kadan, Philip of Hesse invited Butzer and Melanchthon to a consultation Dec. 27, 1534. Butzer obtained the consensus of the South German preachers assembled quietly at Constance (Dec. 15), which, however, to his disappointment, Zurich and other Swiss towns avoided, after handing in a communion confession previously agreed to. Melanchthon's own view as expressed to

3. Meeting at Cassel. Philip, was that the body and blood of Christ were truly not figuratively present with the bread and wine, and the thoughts dictated by reason were to be disregarded, but Luther's instructions were stated in as strict and crass forms as in the *Bekenntniss vom Abendmahl* (1528) itself. He made secure against Butzer's favorite plea of a misunderstanding of words by defining the sharp antithesis as existing between the real body to which he and his colleagues adhered and the bread as a mere sign or token, as he alleged was held by the opponents; and he maintained that to make a compromise was against conscience. Moreover, the proffering, the eating, and the chewing with the teeth of the real body, he affirmed as his absolutely unalterable position. A reconciliation was out of the question. Against Luther's strictures Butzer protested formally; namely: that his plea of mutual misunderstanding was sincere, and that he meant no compromise but to set forth the points held in common by both parties; and for the rest, he extended the discussion skilfully in terms of Luther's larger *Bekenntniss*, acceding that he could even assume Luther's statement of the chewing of the Lord's body. Rather as the profession of the South Germans he announced that the body is essentially and truly received; that bread and wine are only signs (*signa exhibitiva*), with which the body and blood are simultaneously offered and received; and that bread and body are not united by a mixture of substance, but by a "sacramental conjunction."

In the course of time there developed at Wittenberg an earnest desire for peace. Luther came to find himself satisfied with Butzer's views. Melanchthon, himself burning with longing for unity, held consultations with the theologians, and special-

4. Conference at Wittenberg. ly importuned Landgrave Philip, the father of the idea, to spare no endeavor. Rumors of the prospective understanding began to stir Roman Catholic and political circles. The outcome of the Cassel conference as well as the unconditioned statements in the new edition of Luther's larger *Bekenntniss vom Abendmahl* (1535) aroused much soreness among the Swiss. The closer relations which Augsburg, hitherto indecisive, now assumed toward Wittenberg inspired Luther the more in the hope for the speedy consummation of the concord, and he dispatched five letters to South German cities for a voluntary assembly in Hesse or Coburg. Signs of a more conciliatory spirit appeared in Switzerland. At a meeting of theologians at Aarau, where Basel and Zurich were represented, a formula was adopted in favor of the true eating of the body in the "mysterious communion," for the salvation of the soul and the spiritual life. At a diet at Basel, to which Butzer gained admission only after long resistance, an unpublished provisional formula was drawn up not strictly Zwinglian. When at the Diet of Schmalkald (Dec., 1535) Württemberg, Augsburg, Frankfort, and Kempten had been received into the League, the way seemed to have been paved for the successful agreement with the Saxon theologians. The meeting was called for May 14, 1536, at Eisenach. The Swiss, who had decided at Aarau (Apr. 30) not to attend and to stand by their Basel agreement, excused themselves by the brevity of time and long distance. A large representation of South Germans, among whom were Butzer and Capito, arrived at Wittenberg May 21. Meanwhile, Melanchthon was beset with great fear lest the chasm should be widened and sought till the last moment to frustrate the plan. Notice of a republication of Zwingli's *Expositio fidei*, with a eulogistic estimate of the author by H. Bullinger in the introduction, and of the correspondence of Œcolampadius and Zwingli, with a preface by Butzer, caused Luther likewise to despair; so that upon the arrival of the delegates he, more suspicious and inflexible than ever, took the attitude first of demanding proof of their sincere intentions. When Luther met Butzer and Capito next day, in the presence of a number of his own colleagues, and Butzer proposed modes of proceeding and recounted his strong efforts at concord in doctrine and order, Luther replied abruptly and emphatically that until unity was reached on the Sacrament, he would not treat on any other article. He stated further that the introductions (ut sup.) by Butzer and Bullinger had killed his hopes, since with men who taught one way here and another there no agreement was possible or desirable. Luther now demanded of Butzer that he renounce his former doctrine ("We hold that there is nothing in the elements but bread and wine"); and to acknowledge that the body is eaten both by the wicked and the pious. Then Luther would be willing to acknowledge that he had been too harsh in his writings against Zwingli and Œcolampadius. Butzer taken by surprise protested his innocence with respect to those publications, made appeal to his utterances and writings on every occasion in defense of his sincerity, and insisted that he and his associates could not take back that which Luther charged, which they never taught, but recall was limited to such a too gross representation as they might have entertained through misunderstanding of Luther's views. The faith of the churches in the free imperial cities with respect to eating with the mouth was in accord with Luther's teaching ("the true body and blood were set forth by the visible signs of bread and wine"), and as to the impious these were not in question, since any recognized as such were not admissible at all to the communion. Their idea, moreover, was that the godless received only the elements, whereas those gifted with faith in general, but "not that vital faith due to the grace of God," received the body for their judgment. After protracted discussions in which Luther laid stress on the reality of the gift of grace, independent of faith and in dependence upon the institution of Christ, the session adjourned on account of Luther's feebleness. The next day, in the presence of all the representatives, including for the first time Melanchthon, Butzer reported progress, so as to be able to recall what was previously taught amiss, and revised his former profession, but declined the partaking of the body by the ungodly, although conceding the same by the unworthy, and Luther's plea that the presence of the body depended, regardless of belief or unbelief, simply on God's Word and ordinance. After so much progress, and after Luther had 'questioned Butzer's associates seriatim and had satisfied himself of their complete accord, and ascertained that in their home churches they had not tolerated the doctrine of mere bread and wine, and had even punished the same, in some places, as blasphemy, he seemed to think that he ought to be satisfied. He was joined in a private conference by his colleagues who felt likewise; only that the other party should be required to affirm once more that the body was present also for the unworthy. But Luther deemed this unnecessary and, returning, pronounced the brotherly conciliation accomplished. Melanchthon was assigned to draft a formula. Agreement on the other points of difference quickly followed. Butzer represented the scruples of the South Germans against the actual faith of infants held by Luther, but he, unwilling also to discuss such a faith, was content with an affirmation that baptism was essential to salvation, and was the medium of regeneration; and on absolution and private confession Luther's argument prevailed. Melanchthon, still doubting the outcome, presented his formula, May 26; and after Luther had called attention to the fact that such could not be binding until submitted to wider circles as well as to the sovereigns for confirmation, it was read by K. Cruciger, teaching, in substance, that there was a sacramental union of the bread and body; that the real body was taken as set forth by the bread; and that the unworthy, because they abused the sacrament availing in the Church, when they used it without penitence and faith, received it to their judgment. There

was required also assent to the Augsburg Confession and to the Apology. Butzer handed the confession of the Swiss (ut sup.) to Luther who promised to read it. As a seal of the compact Butzer was one of the preachers on the following Sunday, and he and Capito participated in the communion. On Monday the subscription took place, and the delegates departed in the most hopeful frame of mind.

In most of the cities people were indeed astonished at the new articles. In Ulm they openly spoke of a new doctrine; they quickly perceived that Luther had made not the least concession. At Constance, where the agreements on baptism and auricular confession were offensive, a new formula on the Lord's Supper, baptism, and church discipline was planned in rebuttal, but left in abeyance. Strasburg, always the van of the movement, where all subscribed but the former abbot, P. Volzius, had a strained position. Yet by July 22, Frankfort, Worms, Landau, Weissenburg, Esslingen, Augsburg, Memmingen, and Kempten had assented, and Reutlingen followed, Sept. 13, 1536. As to the Swiss, Luther had expressed, before Butzer's departure, his pleasure concerning the confession handed to him; and sent along an amiable missive to the burgomaster of Basel, who in turn was much gratified. Basel and Mühlhausen seemed to be in accord, but after various movements a council at Basel (Nov. 14, 1536), unable to decide between the Roman and the Lutheran doctrines, declined the presence in substance. At the Diet of Schmalkald (Feb., 1537) Butzer was to confer with Luther in regard to the declaration (Jan. 12, 1537) by seven Swiss cities, including Zurich, Bern, and Basel; but this was prevented by Luther's illness, and only the fact that the official approval of Luther's articles at the diet was not called for averted a most probable breach with the South Germans. Meanwhile, a letter of Butzer to Luther (Jan. 19, 1537) in disparagement of the Swiss declaration, enabled the former's enemies to make his efforts also unpopular. Johann Zwick of Constance, who seems to have received intimation of Luther's teaching in the Schmalkald Articles of the eating of the ungodly, now made an appeal for opposition to the union and was joined by Bullinger against Butzer's movement. At a synod at Bern, during the middle of 1537, in the presence of Calvin and P. Viret, Butzer achieved a brilliant vindication, but met with the impatient inquiry concerning the delayed answer of Luther. Finally, Luther, in answer to Butzer who had urged an official reply (Dec. 3, 1539), showed that the Swiss formula was not at all satisfactory; but in his reply to the Swiss (Dec. 1), without touching the dogmatic discussion except to dispose of a misunderstanding on some point on the Lord's Supper, he again professed his adherence to the idea of concord, expressed his joy over their honest efforts and the progress made, presumed that the steps toward concord had not been completed but only opened, and recommended forbearance and good will until further progress. This answer produced great satisfaction in Switzerland. Bullinger was of the mind to suspend further procedure except that of promoting peace by writing, speech, and preach-

5. Result of the Conference.

ing. But hopes were disappointed. At a synod at Zurich (May 4, 1538), in which the note was loudly voiced that the agreement should only be assumed as valid after Luther had formally recalled his written attacks against Zwingli, a reply to Luther was resolved upon, in which the Swiss asserted the partaking of the body through a believing spirit; presumed that no difference longer existed; and begged the privilege, under present circumstances, of presenting such instruction to the people as would be most intelligible to them. But before its receipt, Luther, in an answer to Bullinger, assumed the harmony to be an assured thing, and the missive of the Swiss he acknowledged briefly by referring them, regarding his scruples, to Butzer as mediator. Thus, the movement resolved itself for years into polite correspondence; of an ultimate concord, by the action of a general convention, there was no more mention; and Butzer, who had made another attempt at Wittenberg (1538), seemed to have lost his former interest. The only fruit was a temporary truce of friendliness with the cities of upper Germany. Luther's comparison of Zwingli with Nestorius (*Concilien und Kirchen*, 1539) caused deep resentment in Switzerland. His restrictions upon the Swiss and their orthodoxy became ever severer until by a letter (Aug. 31, 1543) he broke off all relations with them, offering to pray and teach against them until his end.   (T. KOLDE.)

BIBLIOGRAPHY: The sources are the official reports in Butzer's *Scripta Anglicana*, pp. 648 sqq., Basel, 1577, and in Walch's ed. of Luther's *Werke*, xvii. 2543; the matter in Tentzel, *Supplementum hist. Gothanæ*, pp. 114 sqq., Jena, 1716; Wolfgang Musculus' reports in his *Itinerarium*, given in T. Kolde, *Analecta Lutherana*, pp. 216 sqq., Gotha, 1883. Consult: J. C. G. Neudecker, *Urkunden aus der Reformationszeit*, Cassel, 1836; idem, *Merkwürdige Aktenstücke aus der Zeit der Reformation*, 2 parts, Nuremberg, 1838; idem, *Neue Beiträge zur Geschichte der Reformation*, Leipsic, 1841; T. Keim, *Die Reformation der Reichstadt Ulm*, Stuttgart, 1851; idem, *Schwäbische Reformationsgeschichte*, Tübingen, 1855; C. Pestalozzi, *Heinrich Bullinger*, Elberfeld, 1858; J. W. Baum, *Capito und Butzer*, ib. 1860; G. Uhlhorn, *Urbanus Rhegius*, ib., 1861; F. W. Hassencamp, *Hessische Reformationsgeschichte*, vol. i., Frankfort, 1864; M. Lenz, *Briefwechsel Landgraf Philipps mit Bucer*, 3 vols., Leipsic, 1880–91; G. Kawerau, *Der Briefwechsel des Justus Jonas*, Halle, 1884 sqq.; H. E. Jacobs, *The Book of Concord*, ii. 253–259, Philadelphia, 1893; idem, *Martin Luther*, pp. 316 sqq., New York, 1898; W. Germann, *Johann Forster*, Meiningen, 1894; J. W. Richard, *Philip Melanchthon*, pp. 254–255, New York, 1898; E. Egli, *Analecta reformatoria*, Zurich, 1899 sqq.; K. Wolfart, *Die Augsburger Reformation in . . . 1533–1534*, Leipsic, 1901; F. Roth, *Augsburgs Reformationsgeschichte*, 3 vols., Munich, 1901–07; *Cambridge Modern History*, ii. 234, 339, New York, 1904; K. Schornbaum, *Zur Politik des Markgrafen Georg von Brandenburg*, Munich, 1906; T. Kolde, *Die älteste Redaktion der Augsburger Konfession*, Gütersloh, 1906; idem, *Historische Einleitung in die symbolischen Bücher der evang.-lutherischen Kirche*, ib. 1907; the letters and lives of Luther (see under article on him), and the literature on the later stages of the German Reformation.

WITZEL, vit'sel, **GEORG:** German Roman Catholic theologian; b. at Vacha-on-the-Werra (30 m. s.w. of Gotha) 1501; d. at Mainz Feb. 16, 1573. He studied at the University of Erfurt 1516–18, then interrupted his studies and became parish schoolmaster in Vacha; after that he continued work at the University of Wittenberg for twenty-eight weeks under Luther, Carlstadt, and Melanchthon. In the same year he was consecrated priest and served as vicar and also a part of the time as town-clerk in his native city until his twenty-fourth year. In 1523 he petitioned the abbot of Fulda for permission to marry, and in the silence of the abbot married without dispensation the daughter of a citizen in Eisenach. In 1524 he lost his clerical position. In Eisenach he became acquainted with Jakob Strauss (q.v.), in conjunction with whom he preached sermons against princes and bishops, against Roman abuses, picturing also the heavy burdens of the peasantry. Strauss made him preacher of Wenigen-Lupnitz, where he zealously began his work when the excitement among the peasants had already reached an alarming height. However much he may have been influenced by the social ideas of Strauss, his later assurance is to be received that he tried to subdue the rebellious spirit. In consequence of the Peasants' War he lost his position and was in great need until at the recommendation of Luther he became preacher at the small town of Niemegk. His leisure at that place he employed in comprehensive studies, especially of the Church Fathers, while the works of Erasmus influenced his views of the Church. What had led him to the Evangelical cause had not been assent to Luther's doctrine of justification or personal longing for certainty of faith, but a desire for the purification of the Church from abuses in worship and discipline, partly also in doctrine, but principally in life. Seeing in Lutheranism disagreement between doctrine and life, he at a later time returned to the Roman Catholic Church. Lutherans mistakenly accused Witzel of the Antitrinitarianism of Campanus, so that in Mar., 1530, he was arrested and imprisoned in the castle of Belzig. His innocence was soon proved and he returned, sick, to Niemegk, greatly disappointed and dissatisfied with Luther and his associates. In 1531 he left Niemegk, and began his open contest with the "Lutheran sect." Two years he spent in Vacha, trying in vain to find a new position, his marriage naturally proving an obstacle. But he was at this time diligently engaged in literary work. In 1533 Count Hoyer of Mansfeld called him as minister to St. Andrew's in Eisleben, where he as preacher and pastor of a small number of Roman Catholics experienced five years of bitter struggle with Johann Agricola, Güttel, Cordatus, Coelius, Kymaeus, Balthasar Raidt, and especially with Jonas. He also tried to put into practise his program of a renewal of the Roman Catholic Church in accordance with the principles of the primitive Church. On Aug. 30, 1538, he was still in Eisleben, when he accepted a call from Duke George to Dresden or Leipsic, where he attempted to reconcile the two religious parties by leading them back to the doctrine and custom of the apostolic and early Church. Duke George laid no obstacles in his way, but under Duke Henry, his successor, Witzel was compelled to flee into the mountains of Bohemia. Thence he went to Berlin to Joachim II., who at first seemed to be inclined to adopt the Catholicism of Witzel, whom soon the sentiment of the country compelled to introduce the Reformation. Berlin was therefore no longer open to Witzel, who began to lead a migratory life, trying to find a receptive soil for his ideas in Lusatia, Silesia, Bamberg, and in 1540 in Würzburg. In 1541 he found a place of refuge with Abbot John of Fulda, who by concessions attempted to stem the tide of Evangelical ideas, and with his successor Philip Schenck of Schweinsberg. Bishop Nausea of Vienna recommended him to Ferdinand, with whom he thenceforth remained in connection. He was present at the religious discussions in Regensburg. In the Schmalkald War he fled from Fulda to Würzburg, but returned again. In 1553 he removed to Mainz, where he passed the remainder of his life. His most prominent works are *Methodus concordiæ ecclesiasticæ* (written 1532, printed 1537), and *Via regia* (1564). In the former work he demanded the convocation of a council, at which both parties should be heard; the basis of agreement was to be the doctrine of the apostles as found in Holy Scripture and the earlier Church Fathers; in all questions of the salvation of the soul Holy Scripture is sufficient, but the right of the Church to make valid and binding ordinances in other questions is to be acknowledged; the institution of the mass was to be reformed, especially its performance for money; communion in both kinds should be restored and compulsory clerical celibacy abolished; the number of monasteries was to be reduced; those that were allowed to remain were to be reformed. In *Via regia*, the program essentially agrees with that of 1532; only criticism deals more relentlessly with Roman Catholic conditions. Reconciliation is not possible without a thorough reform of that church. In the system which came to rule in the Counter-Reformation he saw the burial of his own plans of church reform after the Erasmian pattern.

(G. KAWERAU.)

BIBLIOGRAPHY: C. L. Callidius, *Germaniæ scriptorum catalogus*, Mainz, 1582; G. T. Strobel, *Beiträge zur Literatur . . . des 16. Jahrhunderts*, ii. 2, Nuremberg, 1787; F. W. P. von Ammon, *Gallerie der denkwürdigsten Personen*, pp. 1 sqq., Erlangen, 1833; J. Neander, *Commentatio de Georgio Vicelio*, Berlin, 1839; J. J. I von Döllinger, *Die Reformation*, i. 21 sqq., Regensburg, 1848; W. Kampschulte, *De Georgio Vicelio eiusque studiis et scriptis*, Bonn, 1856; G. Schmidt, *Georg Witzel, ein Altkatholik des 16. Jahrhunderts*, Vienna, 1876; A. Räss, *Die Konvertiten*, i. 122 sqq., Freiburg, 1866; C. Schlottmann, *Erasmus redivivus*, pp. 342 sqq., Halle, 1883; *Archiv für Reformationsgeschichte*, vi (1909), 234 sqq.; *ADB*, xliii. 657 sqq.; *KL*, xii. 1726 sqq.

WOBBERMIN, vob'er-min, **ERNST GUSTAV GEORG:** German Protestant; b. at Stettin Oct. 27, 1869. He was educated at the universities of Halle (1888–90) and Berlin (1890–94; Ph.D., 1894; lic. theol., 1895), and, after spending the year 1896–1897 in travel in Greece, became privat-docent for systematic theology and the philosophy of religion at Berlin, and in 1907 went to Breslau as professor of the philosophy of religion. He has written *Religionsgeschichtliche Studien zur Frage der Beeinflussung des Urchristentums durch das antike Mysterienwesen* (Berlin, 1896); *Theologie und Metaphysik* (1901); *Der christliche Gottesglaube in seinem Verhältnis zur gegenwärtigen Philosophie* (1902); *Aufgabe und Bedeutung der Religionspsychologie* (1910); *Monismus und Monotheismus* (1911); and translated into German W. James, *Varieties of Religious Experience* (Leipsic, 1907).

WODROW, ROBERT: Historian of the Scottish Church; b. at Glasgow 1679; d. at Eastwood

XII.—26

(3 m. s.w. of Glasgow) Mar. 21, 1734. He was graduated in arts at Glasgow, studied theology there, and served as university librarian from 1697 till 1701. Then he became tutor in the family of a relative, Sir John Maxwell of Pollock. He was licensed by the presbytery of Paisley in Jan., 1703, and in October was ordained minister of Eastwood, where he remained till his death, notwithstanding repeated calls to other spheres. Wodrow early gave all his spare time to the collection of materials for Scottish church history; but he also discharged the duties of his profession with zeal and fidelity, and took a deep interest in science and literature. After the accession of George I. he was active in the unsuccessful attempt to repeal the patronage act passed in the reign of Queen Anne, but he advocated loyal compliance with that act so long as it remained the law of the land. As a historian he is trustworthy on the whole, though not altogether free from prejudice and credulity. His published works include *The History of the Sufferings of the Church of Scotland from the Restoration to the Revolution* (2 vols., Edinburgh, 1721–22; 2 ed., 4 vols., Glasgow, 1829–1830); *Collections upon the Lives of the Reformers and most Eminent Ministers of the Church of Scotland* (published by the Maitland Club, 2 vols., Glasgow, 1834–45); *Analecta; or Materials for a History of Remarkable Providences, mostly relating to Scotch Ministers and Christians* (for the Maitland Club, 4 vols., 1842–43); *Life of Alexander Seaton* (1829); *Life of Robert Bruce* (1843); *Selections from Wodrow's Biographical Collections; Divines of the Northeast of Scotland* (for the New Spalding Club, Aberdeen, 1890). In 1841 the Wodrow Society was established at Edinburgh to publish works of "early writers of the reformed church of Scotland"; it was dissolved in 1847 after publishing twelve works.

W. LEE]. Revised by HENRY COWAN.

BIBLIOGRAPHY: Biographical material is found in the prefatory Notice prefixed to the *Analecta*, Glasgow, 1843; in the *Correspondence*, ed. McCrie, 1842–43; a *Memoir* by R. Burns in the *Sufferings of the Church of Scotland*, ib. 1829; in R. Lippe's "Introduction" to the *Selections*; and in Wodrow's *Life of James Wodrow*, ed. Campbell, Edinburgh, 1828. Consult also *DNB*, lxii. 280–281.

WOELLNER, vül'ner, **JOHANN CHRISTOPH:** Prussian minister of public worship; b. at Döberitz (9 m. w. of Berlin) May 19, 1732; d. on his estate near Beskow (41 m. s.e. of Berlin) Sept. 10, 1800. He received his preliminary education at Spandau and studied theology at Halle; was tutor in a private family, 1753–55; pastor at Gross-Behnitz, 1755–59; turned next to agriculture in the same place; in 1766 his marriage met with opposition and caused the anger of the king and the prevention of advancement under that reign, though he became canon at Halberstadt, 1768; he engaged in the study of political economy, became interested in freemasonry, and finally in the Rosicrucians (q.v.), entering their order and promoting heartily their cause. In this connection he founded a lodge, a member of which the crown prince, Frederick William, became, thus coming under the influence of the founder, an event which led up to the affairs for which Wöllner is remembered. To the prince Wöllner delivered a series of lectures dealing with the science of government, presenting to him subsequently the manuscripts of the lectures, including one which outlined the edict to be mentioned hereafter. Its significance lay in its suggestions of measures to be taken toward the suppression of the Aufklärung (see ENLIGHTENMENT) and of the accompanying rationalism. Thus Wöllner gained a quite complete ascendancy over the mind and actions of the crown prince, the results of which appeared after the latter came to the throne as Frederick William II. in 1757. Not till 1786, however, did Wöllner gain a title, when he became chief of the board of public works; two years later he became privy councilor and was put in charge of the department of public worship. Meanwhile there had been issued in 1786 a royal edict regarding the "constitutional status of religion in the German states," the authorship of which Wöllner later acknowledged. The edict begins with the king's declaration of the duty of the ruler to maintain the Christian religion in Prussian territories; establishes as the chief confessions the Reformed, Lutheran, and Roman Catholic, but affirms the continuance of that customary tolerance according to which no constraint of conscience shall be permitted, this, however, on the condition that the citizen keep his views to himself without attempting to propagate them or to shake the faith of others; Moravians, Mennonites, and the Bohemian Brethren are "publicly tolerated," as are the Jews; but conventicles prejudicial to the nation and State are forbidden, also proselyting; the Lutheran and Reformed Churches are to retain their liturgies intact, though verbal changes are permitted; the "unbridled liberty" assumed by some of the Protestant clergy in respect to the doctrinal tone of their statements is denounced [aiming at the Enlightenment], and the duty of the Christian ruler is asserted to be that of maintaining the high dignity and original purity of the Christian religion; the clergy and the teaching force are, therefore, forbidden to diffuse these errors; the conscience of these men are, indeed, not to be bound, but they must cease from teaching things contrary to religion on pain of dismissal with the possibility of further punishment; the chiefs of the departments of instruction and worship are to see that the incumbents of the teaching and the spiritual offices be men whose convictions accord with the tenor of the edict.

The promulgation of the edict, though it was not without precedent, both because of the suddenness after half a century of silence, and because the ecclesiastical and teaching authorities had not been consulted, caused great astonishment. The injunction against free discussion of one's opinions was regarded as usurpation. A storm of protest was evoked and a large literature, mostly denunciatory of the edict; it was regarded as particularly strange that Johann Salomo Semler (q.v.) of Halle sided with the pronunciamento. The members of the supreme council at Berlin protested against the edict, but in vain. Administrative measures for the enforcement of the policy thus declared were taken, and legal action was instituted against some of the more radical criticisms of the edict. Wöllner sought the introduction of a new catechism, attempted to have a new text-book on dogmatics prepared at Halle to be used in all the Prussian universities, and established a central committee on the examination of candidates for the ministry, while, later, subordinate committees for the provinces were appointed. Minute directions were issued with regard to details, which the ministry were expected to follow. The success of these measures was, however, small. The University of Halle finally declined to furnish the desired text-book, and the *Epitome religionis Christianæ* of Samuel Friedrich Nathanael Morus (q.v.), of Leipsic, was chosen as basis for lectures in dogmatics. Repressive action was taken in some quarters, as against August Hermann Niemeyer (q.v.) of Halle. Attempts which were almost resultless were made to "reform" the faculty at Halle, while the attempted dogmatic reform was just as futile. On the accession of Frederick William III. (1797) the measures went out of force, and the attempt of Wöllner to revive them brought about his retirement in disfavor and without a pension.

(C. MIRBT.)

BIBLIOGRAPHY: Articles in *ZHT* as follows: 1859, i. 3 sqq., 1862, iii. 412 sqq.; in *Zeitschrift für preussische Geschichte und Landeskunde*, ii (1865), 577–604, 746–774, iii. (1866), 65–95. Also M. Philippson, *Geschichte des preussischen Staatswesens*, 2 vols., Leipsic, 1880–82; C. Mirbt, in *Christliche Welt*, 1888, pp. 269 sqq.; C. Varrentrapp, *Johannes Schulze, und das höhere preussische Unterrichtswesen in seiner Zeit*, pp. 226–232, Leipsic, 1889; K. Rieker, *Die rechtliche Stellung der evangelischen Kirche Deutschlands*, pp. 311 sqq., ib. 1893; E. Förster, *Die Entstehung der preussischen Landeskirche unter . . . Friedrich Wilhelms III.*, i. 38 sqq., 95 sqq., Tübingen, 1905; *ADB*, xliv. 148–158.

WOLFENBUETTEL FRAGMENTS: The name given to a German deistic work published but not written by Lessing (q.v.) in the last quarter of the eighteenth century. As early as 1771, and against the advice of Nicolai and Mendelssohn, Lessing sought a publisher for the work; but the royal censor, though not openly opposing, refused to authorize the publication, and Lessing gave up the project for the time being. In connection with his duties as librarian at Wolfenbüttel he proposed to issue a series of contributions on history and literature drawn from the treasures of the library, and for this he was relieved of liability to hindrance from the censor. In the third of this series he published (1774) the first of these fragments as *Von Duldung der Deïsten: Fragment eines Ungenannten*, for which adroit preparation had been made in the preceding number. The fourth issue (1777) was devoted to more from the "unknown," together with comments of Lessing upon the contents of the rest. There were here five fragments which dealt with assaults of the pulpit upon reason, the impossibility of a revelation which could be satisfactorily relied upon by all men, the passage of the Red Sea by the Israelites, that the purpose of the New-Testament writings was not the revelation of a new religion, and on the history of the resurrection. While the first publication had aroused little interest, these five fragments aroused great feeling. In 1778 a further issue discussed the purpose of Jesus and the disciples. Hereupon Lessing was forbidden to publish anything more upon religious matters without official sanction, though he refused to obey. Other editions were issued after his death (4th ed., 1835), and parts not issued by him appeared 1787. The authorship did not remain hidden, though Lessing tried to lay a false scent by suggesting the name of Johann Lorenz Schmidt, the editor of the Wertheim Bible (see BIBLES, ANNOTATED, I., § 4). The author was Herrmann Samuel Reimarus, as is confirmed by his own son, Johann Albert Heinrich Reimarus, who gave to the Hamburg city library the complete work from which the fragments were taken (a letter from the younger Reimarus is published in the *Leipziger Litteraturzeitung*, 1827, no. 55, in which the authorship is asserted).

Hermann Samuel Reimarus was born at Hamburg Dec. 22, 1694, and died there Mar. 1, 1768. He came of a family of ministers, though his father was a teacher, but one of rare talents, and was himself the oldest son. In his preparatory course he was under such instructors as Johann Christian Wolff; he studied at the universities of Jena and Wittenberg, at the latter of which he taught in the philosophical faculty. In 1723 he became rector of the city school at Wismar, and in 1717 professor of oriental languages in the gymnasium of Hamburg, where he remained in spite of a call to Göttingen to succeed Gesner. Reimarus was held in high honor in his native city, and his house was the gatheringplace of choice spirits. He employed the leisure which his duties left him in the study of one branch of learning after another. His official position entailed upon him the duty of preparing memorials of deceased persons. Outside of these he left but three larger works, which appeared in the earlier portion of his life. These were: *Die vornehmsten Wahrheiten der naturlichen Religion* (Hamburg, 1754); *Die Vernunftlehre, als eine Anweisung zum richtigen Gebrauch der Vernunft in der Erkenntnis der Wahrheit* (1756); and *Allgemeine Betrachtungen über die Triebe der Tiere* (1760). These appeared in several editions after the death of Reimarus and were translated into Dutch. The philosophical standpoint of Reimarus was essentially that of Wolff, though more radical; the being of God, the divine plan in the world, the annihilation of doubt of the divine providence, the immortality of the soul, the advantages of religion were proved by reason, and so far his attitude was apologetic. He was awake to the fact that in his time many little works had appeared which assailed not only Christianity but all religion and ethics, and his aim was to oppose these and to set forth by the claims of reason the truths of natural religion as well as of Christianity. Hence he named the great work which he left behind "Apology or Defense for the Rational Worshiper of God." In this he subjected the entire Biblical history to the tests of analytical criticism; according to the deistic standpoint of Reimarus, miracle is impossible, so that if the prophets and Jesus and the apostles pretended to work miracles, they were impostors. Such "impurities" he found to be conceivable in the Bible, since it contained much that was at variance with virtue as tested by the laws of nature and of peoples. A psychological explanation of this attitude of Reimarus appears when it is recalled that he was a man highly honored by his contemporaries, and that he held fast to the observances of the

Church, even though he regarded both Judaism and Christianity to have been founded by processes which involved imposture. He recognized that his book would cause unrest, and so did not print it, preferring that it remain concealed, being available for the use of such friends of his as were possessed of discretion. Some parts he had frequently worked over, and had revised the whole shortly before his death; this revised autograph is still extant.

While Lessing went to Hamburg in Apr., 1767, and Reimarus did not die until March of the next year, there is no evidence that the two met; but soon after the death of Reimarus, Lessing became acquainted with the son and daughter of Reimarus. According to a letter of Lessing to the son (in *Lessing's Briefe, Nachträge und Berichtigungen*, p. 17, no. 183a, Berlin, 1886), the latter was aware of Lessing's possession of parts of the elder Reimarus' work. These parts were in the author's handwriting, but not in their final shape, though the main thought was in no way different. Permission to publish excerpts was obtained by Lessing only on condition that the name of the author be not divulged. The complete work was carefully guarded by the family and shown to but few—"the community" of friends of Reimarus. In 1779 Lessing was allowed to copy from the final draft the chapters which related to the passage of the Red Sea, in which the results with reference to the numbers differed from what had been published. In 1779 the publisher Ettinger of Gotha was ready to publish the whole work, but the family decisively negatived the proposition, fearing a loss of the good reputation which it enjoyed and the effect upon the health of the mother of the family. The intention to republish portions (*Zeitschrift für historische Theologie*, 1850–52) failed through lack of interest in the work on the part of the public. (CARL BERTHEAU†.)

BIBLIOGRAPHY: An ed. of the "Fragments" as issued by Lessing appeared Berlin, 1895. There is an Eng. transl. of part, *Fragments from Reimarus*, ed. C. Voysey, London, 1879 (cf. J. Sawyer, *A Criticism of . . . C. Voysey's* "*Fragments from Reimarus*," ib. 1880). Consult: the literature under GOEZE, JOHAN MELCHIOR; and LESSING, GOTTHOLD EPHRAIM; D. F. Strauss, *Hermann Samuel Reimarus und seine Schutzschrift für die vernünftigen Verehrer Gottes*, Leipsic, 1862; J. A. H. Reimari . . . *de vita sua commentarius. Additæ sunt de vita H. S. Reimari narrationes J. G. Büschii et C. A. Klotzii*, Hamburg, 1815; C. Mönckeberg, *Hermann Samuel Reimarus und Johann Christian Edelmann*, ib. 1867; K. Fischer, *Geschichte der neueren Philosophie*, ii. 759–772, Heidelberg, 1867; K. C. Scherer, *Das Tier in die Philosophie der H. S. Reimarus*, Würzburg, 1898; B. Brandl, *Die Ueberlieferung der* "*Schutzschrift*" *des H. S. Reimarus*, Pilsen, 1907.

WOLFF, völf, CHRISTIAN, AND THE WOLFFIAN SCHOOL: German philosopher; b. at Breslau Jan. 24, 1679; d. at Halle May 9, 1754. He was educated at the gymnasium in Breslau and the University of Jena, where he was greatly attracted to the study of mathematics by the certainty of its method, which seemed to him typical for science. Without entirely giving up the thought of a theological career, he took his master's degree in Leipsic, then studied philosophy at Jena, and in 1703 established himself as privat-docent of philosophy at Leipsic. In 1707 he accepted a call to Halle where he lectured on mathematics, after 1709 also on physics, then on other branches of philosophy. His success as a teacher was extraordinary and was soon supplemented by the impression made by his writings. His fame extended over Europe. At home king and government heaped honors upon him, and scholars gathered about him; but in Halle itself the Pietists and Christian Thomasius (q.v.) were hostile. After some friction the address *De Sinarum philosophia practica* (Frankfort, 1726; Eng. transl., *The Real Happiness of a People under a Philosophical King Demonstrated*, London, 1750), which Wolff delivered in 1721, led to a complete rupture. His enemies found in it a glorification of the morality of Confucius and inferred that Wolff taught the dispensability of Christian revelation for human happiness. The Pietists won the ear of the king who on Nov. 8, 1723, ordered the deposition of Wolff and ordered him to leave the realm within forty-eight hours. From 1723 to 1740 Wolff was professor in Marburg. It was the most brilliant and the happiest period of his life. He continually gained philosophical adherents and new students and earned rich honors. In the mean time conditions in Prussia became better. Provost Reinbeck in Berlin was active in his behalf; the king changed his opinion, ordered candidates to study his works, and would have liked to recall Wolff to Prussia as early as 1733, but he died during the negotiations. Frederic II., who in 1736 had designated Wolff as the greatest philosopher of his time, carried out his father's plan, and since Wolff declined a position in the academy at Berlin, he was called as privy councilor and vice-chancellor to Halle where he arrived in 1740, was received with unusual honors, and was active until his death.

Of his numerous treatises and books those of especial importance for theology, many of which reached numerous editions, are: *Methodus demonstrandi veritatem religionis Christianæ* (1707); *Vernünftige Gedanken von den Kraften des*
Works. *menschlichen Verstandes und ihrem richtigen Gebrauche in Erkenntnis der Wahrheit* (1712; Eng. transl., *Logic, or Rational Thoughts on the Powers of the Human Understanding*, London, 1770); *Ratio prælectionum Wolfianarum in Mathesin et philosophiam universam* (1718); *Vernünftige Gedanken von Gott, der Welt und der Seele des Menschen* (1719; his great theological work); *Vernünftige Gedanken von der Menschen Thun und Lassen zu Beförderung ihrer Glückseligkeit* (1720); *Vernünftige Gedanken von dem gesellschaftlichen Leben der Menschen und insonderheit dem gemeinen Wesen zur Beförderung der Glückseligkeit des menschlichen Geschlechts* (1721); *Vernünftige Gedanken von den Wirkungen der Natur* (3 parts, 1723–25); *Vernünftige Gedanken von den Absichten der natürlichen Dinge* (1724); *Philosophia rationalis sive Logica* (1728); *Philosophia prima sive ontologia* (1729); *Cosmologia generalis* (1731); *Psychologia empirica* (1732); *Psychologia rationalis* (1734); *Theologia naturalis* (2 parts, 1736–37), *Philosophia practica universalis* (1738). G. F. Hagen edited his *Gesammelte kleine philosophische Schriften* (6 parts, Halle, 1736–40).

Wolff was not a great creative spirit, but rather the philosopher in whom the scientific efforts of the time combined and in their connection influenced the future. By the application of the mathematical-syllogistic method he tried to give to all sciences the same formal certainty and thus to make possible a universal system of human science.

Philosophy. Philosophy is for him the science of the conceivable or the possible, which appears as the essence of reality. Upon the relation of the higher (rational) and the lower (sensual) faculty of the soul is built the distinction between rational and empirical knowledge. The objective order of the sciences is based upon psychology, upon the distinction between knowledge and desire. On the one side stands theoretical, on the other side practical philosophy. In the system of Wolff logic leads as a sort of propædeutic. Then follow the rational theoretical sciences, metaphysics, ontology; then in the order of the three main objects (world, soul, and God), cosmology, rational psychology, natural theology. The rational practical sciences begin with general practical philosophy and natural law, and then consider man in Aristotelian fashion successively as individual being (ethics), citizen (politics), and member of the family (economy). The empirical sciences are empirical-theoretical science (empirical psychology, teleology, empirical theology, dogmatic physics) and empirical-practical science (technology, experimental physics). Esthetics is not taken into the system. The most characteristic feature of Wolff's theology is the emphasis upon natural religion. While he strictly separated this from the knowledge given by revelation and refrained from encroachments upon the dogmatic sphere, he based upon natural religion the general religious truths which seemed to be assailed by naturalism, brought it to the front in the spiritual struggle, and focused about it the religious and theological interest which hitherto had been directed to revelation. In the proof of the existence of the deity he stressed the cosmological argument, and employed also the ontological. However much the philosophy of Wolff tended to depreciate miracles and revelation, he himself fully acknowledged both in so far as they fulfil definite conditions in the system. Since God does nothing superfluous, revelation can comprehend only necessary, otherwise unknowable things, mysteries; it may not contain any inner contradictions, nor may it contradict the attributes of God, reason, or experience. Miracles are changes which by the nature of the bodies concerned are not impossible, though they lack the natural cause. In psychology Wolff taught that souls are simple· created substance, originating at creation, and existing without consciousness until the latter was induced through birth. He held that the bodily and spiritual processes are independent of each other; their agreement does not rest upon perpetual miracle, as the occasionalists teach, but upon preestablished harmony. The intellectual faculty takes precedence over the will. In practical philosophy Wolff separated ethics from religion and based it upon reason. His system is, therefore, rationalistic throughout.

The success of the philosophy of Wolff is a proof that it victoriously comprehended and satisfied the longing of his time. To this contributed his talent for popularizing and teaching. It gave to the German "Enlightenment" its scientific independence. The disciples of Wolff not only repeated the principles of their master, but applied them more exactly to special departments of science. In His Philosophy and Theology Victorious. jurisprudence, in philology, and even in medicine there arose scholars who tried to give their science a greater stability by employing the "scientific" method of Wolff. Representatives of German culture, like Gottsched, transmitted his influence to larger circles of educated people. Among the disciples of Wolff must be mentioned especially Alexander Gottlieb Baumgarten (d. 1762), who supplemented the system at an important point and anticipated its further development. Like Leibnitz, Wolff had separated the lower sensual and the higher intellectual knowledge, but in his logic he represented only the latter. Baumgarten treated in his Æsthetica the doctrine of sensual knowledge as esthetics. The philosophy of Wolff was of course not without its opponents, especially among the theologians, among the orthodox as well as among the Pietists. The orthodox, it is true, also combined theology and philosophy in an intellectualistic way, but so that philosophy served theology; philosophy in its independence seemed to them not only against the rule of theology, but also against religion and revelation. The Pietists, on the other hand, were offended by the intellectualism of the followers of Wolff as well as of the orthodox. The spokesman of Pietistic polemics was Joachim Lange (q.v.), the principal defender of orthodoxy was Valentin Ernst Löscher (q.v.); but the opponents of Wolff were either representatives of a vanishing period of thought or precursors of a later culture that possessed no influence, and Wolff gained the victory. The theologians of his school developed the thoughts of their master by applying his method to the Bible and revelation. In conformity with the later orthodoxy they conceded to natural theology an increasing influence in the dogmatic system. Owing to the expansion of intellectualism, the independent position of revelation still asserted by Wolff proved impossible; it was gradually supplanted by the rationalistic element. The history of the Wolffian school of theology became the history of the dissolution of the orthodox system; it was in every respect a theology of transition. Far more positive is its practical importance for Church and Christianity as it secured for undogmatic piety, which had arisen since the stagnation of orthodoxy and the influence of Pietism, a solid background of ideas and conceptions. Protestant apologetics owed to it a good deal of its first bloom. It provided for the transition from Pietism as well as from orthodoxy to the period of "Enlightenment" without the sacrifice of the universal character of Christianity. (H. STEPHAN.)

BIBLIOGRAPHY: On the life consult: F. C. Baumeister, *Vita, fata et scripta Wolfii*, Leipsic, 1739; J. C. Gottsched, *Historische Lobschrift auf Christian Freiherr von Wolff*, Halle, 1755; F. W. Kluge, *Christian von Wolff, der Philosoph*, Breslau, 1831; *Briefwechsel zwischen Leibniz und Christian Wolff*, ed. C J. Gerhardt, Halle, 1860; B. Erdmann, *M. Knutzen und seine Zeit*, Leipsic, 1876; J. Cæsar, *Christian Wolff in Marburg*, Marburg, 1879; *ADB*, xliv. 12–28.

On his philosophy and theology consult: J. F. Buddeus, *Bedenken über die wolffische Philosophie*, Freiburg, 1724;

L. P. Thümmig, *Institutiones philosophiæ Wolffianæ*, 2 vols., Leipsic, 1725–26; I. G. Canz, *Philosophiæ Leibnitzianæ et Wolfianæ usus in theologia*, ib. 1728–34; K. G. Ludovici, *Ausführlicher Entwurf einer vollständigen Historie der wolffischen Philosophie*, 3 vols., ib. 1736–38; idem, *Sammlung und Auszüge der sämmtlichen Streitschriften wegen der wolfischen Philosophie*, 2 parts, ib. 1737; idem, *Neueste Merkwürdigkeiten der leibnitz-wolffischen Philosophie*, ib. 1738; G. V. Hartmann, *Anleitung zur Historie der leibnitz-wolffischen Philosophie*, Hof, Bavaria, 1737; J. J. Koethen, *Principia quædam metaphysicæ Wolfianæ*, Cologne, 1737; J. G. Darjes, *Anmerkungen über einige Lehrsätze der wolffischen Metaphysik*, Leipsic, 1748; J. M. Schröckh, *Christliche Kirchengeschichte seit der Reformation*, vi. 100 sqq., viii. 26 sqq. (the whole series, 45 vols.), ib. 1768–1812; J. C. Schwab, *Vergleichung des kantischen Moralprincips mit dem leibnitzisch-wolffischen*, Berlin, 1800; W. Gass, *Geschichte der protestantischen Dogmatik*, ii. 160 sqq., 4 vols., ib. 1854–67; G. W. Frank, *Geschichte der protestantischen Theologie*, ii. 384 sqq., 4 vols., Leipsic, 1862–1905; E. Zeller, *Geschichte der deutschen Philosophie seit Leibniz*, Munich, 1873; R. Frank, *Die wolff'sche Strafrechtsphilosophie*, Göttingen, 1887; G. Kraus, *Christian Wolff als Botaniker*, Halle, 1892; W. Arnsperger, *Christian Wolff's Verhältnis zu Leibniz*, Weimar, 1897; O. Willareth, *Die Lehre vom Uebel bei Leibniz und seiner Schule*, Strasburg, 1898; K. Fischer, *Geschichte der neueren Philosophie*, iii. 627–638, Heidelberg, 1902; J. Reinhard, *Die Prinzipienlehre der lutherischen Dogmatik 1700–50*, Leipsic, 1906; E. Weber, *Die philosophische Scholastik des deutschen Protestantismus im Zeitalter der Orthodozie*, ib. 1907; H. Pichler, *Ueber Christian Wolffs Ontologie*, ib. 1900; the works on the history of philosophy by W. Windelband, New York, 1893; J. E. Erdmann, 3 vols., London, 1892–98; Ueberweg-Heinze, 9th ed., Berlin, 1905.

WOLFF, JOSEPH: Missionary and traveler; b. of Jewish parentage, at Weilersbach, near Bamberg, Germany, 1795; d. at Isle Brewers (35 m. s.w. of Bristol), England, May 2, 1862. His father was a rabbi, and he was sent to a Protestant lyceum at Stuttgart, and later to Bamberg. He left home, and was converted to Christianity, being baptized in 1812, when he took the Christian name of Joseph, his single name, Wolff, becoming his surname. In 1814 he attended theological lectures at Vienna and studied oriental languages, and was at Tübingen 1815–16, in the same pursuit. He went to Rome in 1816, where he was a pupil in the Collegium Romanum and the Collegio di Propaganda, but was expelled from the city in 1818 for attacking the doctrine of infallibility and the teaching of the professors. He entered the monastery of the Redemptionists at Val Sainte, but in 1819 went to England, and joined the Church of England. He studied for two years oriental languages at Cambridge; went out as missionary to the Jews, 1821–1826, traveling extensively in the East; again, 1828–34, he was traveling in search of the ten lost tribes, going through Palestine, Turkey, Egypt, Central Asia, and India; his third journey of 1836–1838 took him to Abyssinia, Yemen, and Bombay, and then to the United States. He was ordained deacon, 1837, and priest, 1838, when he became rector at Linthwaite, and later at High Hoyland, Yorkshire. In 1843 he made a daring journey to Bokhara, to learn the fate of two British officers, and barely escaped death himself; on returning, 1845, he became vicar of Isle Brewers in Somerset, where he remained till his death. He has been justly styled "a comet in the missionary heaven." His journeys were essentially missionary in their character, and full of peril and adventure. His was a singular personality that fascinated by its vitality and nervous energy. Of his journeys he left recitals in the *Journal of his Missionary Labours, 1827–38* (London, 1839); *Narrative of a Mission to Bokhara in the Years 1843–45* (2 vols., 1845, and often); and *Travels and Adventures of Rev. Joseph Wolff* (2 vols., 1861).

BIBLIOGRAPHY: Mme. L. Roehrich, *S. Gobat, Bishop of Jerusalem, his Life and Work*, pp. 177–180, London, 1884; George Smith, *Life of John Wilson*, pp. 251–252, ib. 1878; *DNB*, lxii. 306–307; and his own *Travels and Adventures*, and *Journal*, ut sup.

WOLFGANG OF REGENSBURG: Bishop of that city 972–994. He was born in the beginning of the century of a family in good circumstances; d. at Pupping (near Linz, 98 m. w. of Vienna) Oct. 31, 994. He was educated in the monastery of Reichenau in company with a scion of a noble Frankish family named Heinrich, brother of Poppo, bishop of Würzburg 941–962, with whom later at Würzburg he studied under an Italian scholar Stephen. In 956 he was appointed master of the cathedral school at Treves, where Heinrich had become archbishop; but on the death of Heinrich in 964 he entered the Benedictine order at Einsiedeln, where under Abbot Gregory he gave instruction. Bishop Ulrich of Augsburg made him a priest and sent him on a missionary journey to Hungary, and his activities, though not very successful, resulted in his choice for the bishopric of Regensburg. He took the field at the head of his feudal forces with Otto II. against Paris (978), and had part in other warlike and political activities. But his closest interest was in his episcopal duties, occupying himself in visitations, and furnishing to the clergy of his diocese an excellent example in the performance of duty. He looked after the instruction of the younger clergy, and gave them the model for simple and effective preaching. Connected with his duty as bishop was that as abbot of St. Emmeram, but he thought the two positions incompatible, and broke away from the latter position, placing Ramuold of Treves in the abbacy. He also did his best to improve the two nunneries in Regensburg, which were then in a low condition; the results were not satisfactory to him, and he founded a third with the name of St. Paul's. With the help of Heinrich the Quarrelsome he afterward improved the condition of the older institutions. It was largely due to him that the bishopric of Prague was established, which was a leading cause of the rise of national feeling in Bohemia. After his death his body was carried to Regensburg for burial, and it was not long before there were reports of miracles at his tomb. He left a reputation as a true and diligent shepherd of his flock, furthering the cause of piety among them by elevating the condition of the clergy. (A. HAUCK.)

BIBLIOGRAPHY: The early material is collected by H. Delehaye, *Acta S. Wolfgangi, episcopi Ratisbonensis*, Brussels, 1894. For parts of this matter cf. *ASB*, Nov., ii. 527–586; *ASM*, v. 812–833; *MPL*, cxlvi. 395–422; and *MGH, Script.*, iv (1841), 525–566. Consult further: S. Rebiser, *Leben und Wunderthaten des heiligen Bischofs Wolfgangi in seiner Einsiedeley*, Passau, 1655; F. X. Sulzbeck, *Leben des heiligen Wolfgang, Bischofs und Hauptpatrons des Bisthums Regensburg*, Regensburg, 1844; F. Janner, *Geschichte der Bischöfe von Regensburg*, i. 350–419, ib. 1883; J. Schindler, *Der heilige Wolfgang in seinem Leben und Wirken*, Prague, 1885; W. Schratz, in *Studien und Mittheilungen aus dem Benedictiner- und dem Cistercienser-Orden*, x (1889), 627–643; K. Kolbe, *Die Ver-*

dienste des Bischofs Wolfgang . . . um das Bildungswesen Süddeutschlands, Breslau, 1893; Kornmüller, in *Kirchenmusikalische Jahrbücher*, 1894, pp. 6–22; J. B. Mehler, *Der heilige Wolfgang, Bischof von Regensburg. Historische Festschrift zum 900-jährigen Gedächtnisse seines Todes (31. Oct., 1894). In Verbindung mit zahlreichen Historikern*, Regensburg, 1894. Some excellent magazine articles are indicated in Richardson, *Encyclopaedia*, p. 1151.

WOLFGANG, COUNT PALATINE: Palsgrave and duke of Zweibrücken and Neuburg, and ardent supporter of the Reformation; b. at Zweibrücken (50 m. w. of Speyer) Sept. 26, 1526; d. at Nessun (near Limoges), France, June 11, 1569. He was the only son of Louis II. of Zweibrücken (d. 1532), and after receiving his first training, at the instance of his Reformed uncle, Rupert, who was regent during Wolfgang's minority, under Kaspar Glaser, he was sent, in 1541, for further instruction first to the electoral court at Treves, and later to that of the Palatinate. In the latter part of 1543 he assumed personal control of his duchy, and during the Schmalkald War, though he was a firm Protestant, he remained neutral. On the close of Until the hostilities the emperor, despite WolfAbrogation gang's protests, commanded him to of the introduce the Augsburg Interim (see Augsburg INTERIM, 2), which the duke accordInterim. ingly did Aug. 22, 1548, declaring that he would obey so far as he conscientiously could. But the clergy declared that the Interim contained much that they could not do with a good conscience, and Wolfgang reported to the emperor that, while he had fulfilled the requirements as to fasts and feasts, the attitude of his clergy rendered him unable to carry out the other injunctions of the Interim. The emperor then referred him to the bishops, but as they were unwilling to send him any but Roman Catholic clergy, while he would receive only those who, according to the terms of the Interim, would administer communion under both kinds, the Interim was only partially enforced. A renewal of the imperial demands led Wolfgang, on April 19, 1549, again to insist that the fasts and feasts be observed as secular ordinances, but at the same time he informed the emperor that his clergy, without exception, refused to carry out the Interim, and that the bishops had sent him no clergy who were ready to do so. He therefore begged the emperor himself to adjust the matter. In Sept., 1549, and in March, 1550, the bishops performed their visitations in the district of Zweibrücken, but since Wolfgang refused to allow the clergy any concessions beyond the Interim, ecclesiastical affairs seem, even then, to have gone on as before.

As soon as the Treaty of Passau (cf. AUGSBURG, RELIGIOUS PEACE OF) rendered it possible, Wolfgang directed the visitation held in the Meisenheim district in July, 1553, the results showing that the pastors were discharging their functions in Protestant fashion. In the Upper Palatinate, of which he was regent from 1551 to 1557, he directed that the liturgy issued by the Palsgrave Otto Henry be followed, and in Zweibrücken he replaced the liturgy of 1533 on June 1, 1557, by one which was akin to the Lutheran liturgies of Württemberg and Mecklenburg. To insure the acceptance of the new liturgy a visitation was made in July and Aug., 1553, and it was also desired that there should be a school in every village of considerable size and a Latin school in every four cities; while in Hornbach

Liturgical and Educational Measures. an institution for higher instruction was opened Jan. 16, 1559, under the care of Immanuel Tremellius (q.v.), and in the principality of Neuburg on the Danube, devised to Wolfgang by the Elector Otto Henry, a similar institution was opened at Lauingen in 1561.

In 1559 Wolfgang interposed in favor of the Protestants at Treves, and in 1561 he pleaded, with other Protestant princes, at the Diet of Naumburg, for his French coreligionists before Charles IX. At the same time he soon manifested increasing antipathy to Calvinism, and to prevent it from entering his domains he directed the rigid Lutheran Johann Marbach (q.v.) to make a new visitation in 1564, while in the year following he appointed Tilemann Hesshusen (q.v.) his chaplain. At the Diet of Augsburg he even sought, though without success, to induce the

Assistance to the Huguenots. Protestant princes to refuse to recognize the Elector Frederick III.; and with the restlessness that characterized him at this time, he entered into negotiations with the adventurer Wilhelm of Grumbach and made a military treaty with Philip II. of Spain. The year 1568 saw a new change of position, doubtless caused in part by the deeds of Alva in the Netherlands, for Wolfgang now canceled his Spanish alliance and entered into close relations with the Elector Frederick. The duke had never forgotten that peril to the foreign Reformed meant danger to German Protestants, and as early as 1563 he had raised troops to assist the French Huguenots, nor did he disband them until after the news of the peace of Amboise. When, therefore, Condé and Coligny again sought help for the French Protestants from the Protestant princes of Germany, Wolfgang bound himself, on Sept. 18, 1568, to assist them at his own expense. With a small force of 8,440 infantry and 8,750 cavalry he set forth, though the French king had already sent against him, under the duke of Aumale, a force at least equal to his own. On Feb. 20, 1569, he broke camp from Bergzabern, crossed the Saône on Mar. 28, and continued his march despite the news of the Huguenot defeat near Jarnac (March 13) and the death of Condé. On Apr. 23 he crossed from Burgundy into France, and on June 9 gained a battle on the Vienne. Here only a three-days' march separated him from the Huguenot forces, and Coligny was already advancing, with a few cavalry, to meet him. On June 11 the two forces met at Nessun, but illness and exertion had completely exhausted Wolfgang, and a few hours later he died. His body was temporarily interred at Angoulême, whence it was taken, two years later, by sea via La Rochelle and Lübeck to Germany, where it was finally buried in the church at Meisenheim Sept. 23, 1571.

The assistance rendered by Wolfgang of Zweibrücken materially strengthened the position of the French Protestants, and without it they would scarcely have gained the terms secured them by the treaty of St. Germain (Aug. 1, 1570), so that it was with good reason that the Huguenot leaders wrote

his sons, June 8, 1571, that, next to God, they owed to Wolfgang their lives, estates, honor, and religious freedom. The family laws of the present house of Wittelsbach, which traces

Character and Influence. its lineage to Wolfgang, are strongly influenced by his famous will of Aug. 18, 1568; and the sincerity of his character, the purity of his family life, the insight and rectitude evinced in the government of his little territory, and his extraordinary prowess insure him a place of honorable memory among all Protestants.

JULIUS NEY.

BIBLIOGRAPHY: K. Menzel, *Wolfgang von Zweibrücken,* Munich, 1893 (the earlier literature is fully given); J. Ney, *Pfalzgraf Wolfgang,* Leipsic, 1912.

WOLLEB, vŏl′lêb, **JOHANNES:** Reformed dogmatician; b. at Basel Nov. 30, 1586; d. there Nov. 24, 1629. He studied philosophy and theology at Basel, was ordained at the age of twenty, in 1607 became diaconus in Basel and in 1611 preacher at St. Elisabeth's. In 1618 he became the successor of Johann Jakob Grynæus as preacher at the cathedral and in the same year professor of Old-Testament theology. Besides dissertations and theses, he published only one theological work, his *Compendium theologiæ Christianæ* (Basel, 1626), which by its masterly brevity, conciseness, clear arrangement, and perspicuity caused a considerable sensation. In Basel as well as at several other Reformed universities it was made the basis of lectures on dogmatics and ethics. It appeared in several editions, and Alexander Ross translated it into English (*Abridgement of Christian Divinitie,* London, 1650). After his death, in 1657, there appeared in print a number of *Trost und Leichenreden.* The theological importance assigned to Wolleb by Ebrard in his *Christliche Dogmatik,* has been questioned by Gass in his *Geschichte der protestantischen Dogmatik* (i. 396 sqq., Berlin, 1854). The latter emphasizes the "purity and sharpness of dogmatic thinking," but denies that there could be ascribed to Wolleb any epoch-making importance, and in this judgment he is supported by Hagenbach and Alexander Schweizer. (W. HADORN.)

BIBLIOGRAPHY: H. J. Leu, *Allgemeines helvetisches . . . Lexicon,* xix. 552 sqq., 20 vols., Zurich, 1747–65

WOLLIN, BISHOPRIC OF. See KAMMIN, BISHOPRIC OF.

WOLSEY, THOMAS.

His Rise and Dignities (§ 1).
His Policies and Statesmanship (§ 2).
His Fall (§ 3).
His Faults and their Extenuation (§ 4).

Thomas Wolsey, cardinal, papal legate, and chancellor of England, was born, according to tradition, at Ipswich, Mar., 1471 (more probably Mar., 1475, or late in 1474), and died at Leicester Abbey (¾ m. n. of Leicester) Nov. 29, 1530. That he was a

1. His Rise and Dignities. "butcher's boy" was probably the slander of an enemy, for his father seems to have been a grazier and woolmerchant, and certainly possessed land and other property at Ipswich, while he also had relatives who were well-to-do. The future cardinal studied at Magdalen College, Oxford, and received his first degree at the age of fifteen, win-

ning the name of the " boy bachelor." He became
fellow of Magdalen, then master of a grammar-school
attached to the college, and was its bursar, 1498–
1500. He was ordained priest Mar. 10, 1498, and
in 1500 Thomas Grey, marquis of Dorset (whose
sons attended the Magdalen grammar-school), gave
him the living of Limington in Somerset. About
1501 he became chaplain to Henry Deane, archbishop of Canterbury, and after Deane's death
(Feb., 1503) he was chaplain to Sir Richard
Nanfan, deputy lieutenant of Calais. Nanfan was
an old man and turned over to Wolsey the
more arduous duties of his post; he commended
him to the king (Henry VII.), and about 1507
Wolsey entered the royal service as chaplain.
In 1509 he became dean and prebendary of
Lincoln and royal almoner (the latter by appointment of Henry VIII., who succeeded to the throne
in April), and the next year he was appointed prebendary of Hereford; in 1511 canon of Windsor
and registrar of the Knights of the Garter; in 1512,
dean of Hereford; in 1513, prebendary and dean of
York and precentor of London; in 1514 bishop of
Lincoln and archbishop of York; and in 1515
cardinal (the red hat was placed on his head with
magnificent ceremonial in Westminster Abbey Nov.
18, John Colet preaching the sermon; his title was
S. Cæcilia trans Tiberim), and (Dec. 14) lord chancellor. In 1518 he became *legatus a latere* and bishop
of Bath and Wells (*in commendam*); in 1521 abbot of
St. Albans; in 1523 bishop of Durham (resigning
Bath and Wells); and in 1529 bishop of Winchester
(*in commendam;* soon after this appointment he resigned Durham). In addition to these dignities in
England, he was made bishop of Tournai after the
English captured the town in 1513, and in 1520, at
the instigation of Charles V., was made bishop of
Badajoz (he never actually obtained possession of
Tournai, and surrendered his claims to it in 1518 for
a pension of 12,000 livres; Badajoz was worth 5,000
ducats; an annual pension of 2,000 ducats was
added from the bishopric of Palencia). His princely revenues from all these appointments were augmented by various livings in England, and as early
as 1501 he obtained a dispensation to hold two incompatible benefices with Limington. In 1506 he
was instituted to the parish church of Redgrave,
Suffolk, and a papal bull permitted him to hold the
vicarage of Lydd, Kent, and two other benefices
with Limington. In 1509 or 1510 he was granted
the parsonage of St. Bride's, Fleet Street, London,
and from Nov., 1510, until he became bishop he held
the parish church of Torrington, Devonshire. He
resigned Limington before July 2, 1509.

Wolsey's first diplomatic employment was a mission to Scotland in 1508, and later in the same year
he was sent to the Emperor Maximilian in Flanders,
acquitting himself with such dispatch that he was
back in England on the evening of the third day
after his departure. His signature as privy councilor first appears in the latter part of 1511, after
which his hand soon became the guiding one in
English public affairs, and till 1530 his history was
the history of England. It is a dreary recital of
diplomatic intrigue and sixteenth century statecraft,
belonging to secular, not religious, history. His

paramount aim was to exalt his country abroad—and
herein he succeeded; he found England a third-rate
power; he made her the arbiter of
Europe. Secondarily, he contemplated
at home a judicious scheme of social,
economic, and ecclesiastical reform,
which he failed to carry out; changes
were made later by others, who used
methods they had learned from Wolsey, though they
worked with a spirit and a motive far different from
his. Of all his misfortunes, none was greater than
this, for it led men of his time, and long after, to
judge him by merely apparent results of his policies;
and the evil was aggravated because these results
were more or less closely bound up with matters of
religion and ethics. Since the publication of the
state papers of Henry VIII. and other authoritative documents in the latter half of the nineteenth
century, the enlightened judgment of an age more
free from religious prejudice and personal animosities has increasingly recognized that Wolsey was a
statesman rather than an ecclesiastic; that he comprehended the problems and conditions of his time
as probably no other did; that his aims were wise
and good; that he made skilful use of indifferent
opportunities and instruments; that he was unsparing in labor, tenacious of purpose, fertile in expedient, ever undismayed and ready to begin anew
when a particular plan failed; above all, that he
fired the English imagination, roused the national
spirit, and, more than any other, created the English greatness of the later time. Bishop Creighton,
his latest Anglican biographer, pronounces him the
greatest political genius and most devoted patriot
that England has ever produced. The Roman
Catholic Ethelred Taunton acclaims him as the
greatest statesman of all Europe, the master mind
of his age, and thinks that, had he been made pope,
he might have averted the schism of the sixteenth
century.*

**2. His
Policies
and States-
manship.**

What he might have attempted at Rome is indicated by his plan of ecclesiastical reform for England. He aimed to bring the English Church into
accord with national needs by restricting its
excessive privileges; by limiting the jurisdiction of
its vexatious courts; by reducing the number of its
unnecessary officials; by reorganizing on a more
efficient basis its antiquated episcopal system; and
by applying some of its superabundant revenues to
the social welfare, particularly by diversion of some
of its wealth from the maintenance of idle and ignorant monks to the education of a body of learned
clergy. This comprehensive and judicious plan

---

* He was three times a candidate, or quasi-candidate, for
the papacy—in 1521–22, when Adrian VI. succeeded Leo
X.; in 1523, when Clement VII. succeeded Adrian VI.; and
in 1529, when Clement VII. fell ill and it was believed he
would die. On the two former occasions Wolsey seems
neither to have expected nor desired to be elected; it was
Henry who was eager that his cardinal and minister should
be chosen, and Wolsey's own attitude can not justly be
characterized as more than one of willingness to gratify the
king by accepting the honor in case the choice should fall
upon him. Certainly he did not shape his previous policy
with any such end in view. In 1529 the case was different;
election then would have meant triumphant escape from the
difficulties crowding hard upon him at home. But Clement
recovered, and Wolsey was not to be saved in this way.

failed, partly because Wolsey made his domestic policy secondary to foreign affairs, more because he thought to carry reforms through by power rather than by persuasion, and strove unwisely to gather and wield all power in his own hands. It may well be doubted whether mistakes would not have frustrated his good intentions, had he occupied the chair of St. Peter. He was a churchman and theologian of the old school, deeply versed in Thomas Aquinas. His studies did not lead in the direction of the new learning, and he had not its spirit, though his practical sense and experience made him friendly to some of its representatives and ideals. He was ready to spend himself to confer benefits on those beneath him, but he would have all reforms made in due order, propriety, and dignity, and would have repressed democratic aspirations. On his deathbed he admonished Henry to " have a vigilant eye to suppress the hellish Lutherans "—having in mind, as the full text of his message shows, the social and political disorders bound up with the Reformation on the continent.

Wolsey was never popular with the old nobility, whom he thrust aside, while he fell into disfavor with men of lesser rank when they had to pay the cost of his (and the king's) policies. He was secure only so long as he had the royal support; and this he lost when he failed

3. His Fall. to obtain the divorce for Henry from Catharine of Aragon. The divorce became a pressing matter in 1527, but Wolsey did not approve of the new marriage, however willing he may have been to be rid of Catharine, who was an obstacle to his plans. On other occasions, when his judgment differed from the king's—as when Henry chose to be a candidate for the imperial crown in 1519, and desired war with France in 1521–25—he had temporized and striven, successfully, to minimize the harm from following the less judicious course. The matter of the divorce, however, was too hard for him, and as it dragged along his enemies obtained the king's ear, finding a potent ally in the ambitious and frivolous Anne Boleyn. Wolsey gave up the great seal on Nov. 19, 1529, and three days later he acknowledged a *Præmunire* (q.v.) and turned his property over to the king. He was ordered to repair to a house belonging to his bishopric of Winchester at Esher (in Surrey, 15 m. s.w. of London), where he lived for three months, in great distress of mind, ill, and suffering pecuniary straits. In Feb., 1530, he resigned (unwillingly) Winchester and St. Albans, but was granted a general pardon and had the possessions of his archbishopric restored to him. It does not appear that Henry was ever, even to the last, of his own volition unfriendly to Wolsey, and probably the real situation was that the king (one of the ablest of English sovereigns, and an apt scholar) felt that he had learned the moves and stratagems of statecraft, and could now play the game as well as the minister. He was content to be rid of the cardinal in public affairs, and purposed to relegate him to the ecclesiastical sphere—incidentally appropriating his wealth, especially as by this course he hoped to keep Wolsey in reserve, should need of him yet arise. Wolsey's foes bent their energies to prevent a meeting between him and the king, and when

Henry permitted him, for his health, to move to Richmond (nearer the court), they ordered him threateningly to go to his archbishopric. He proceeded northward by slow stages, apparently hoping things would yet turn in his favor, and reached Cawood (10 m. s. of York) in the early fall. He avoided ostentation, busied himself with ecclesiastical duties, and won the hearts of many who had previously been prejudiced against him, although he was continually subjected to much petty persecution. He arranged to be instituted, quietly, on Nov. 7, but three days before that date he was arrested, charged with high treason. He seems to have hoped for some amelioration of his affairs through the intervention of Francis I., and attempted to open negotiations with the French envoy; really his offense was not great, but this indiscretion was enough to equip his enemies with a trumped-up charge against him, though his keepers were lenient and traveled slowly toward London because of his weakness. He was very despondent and asserted constantly that he was being led to execution. Death, however, saved him from this possible fate. Midway between York and London, at Leicester Abbey, his strength failed completely, and here, tended by the kindly ministrations of his brother monks (he had joined the abbey some years before), he breathed his last. He was buried in the abbey.

Wolsey was ambitious; proud, perhaps arrogant; lavish, even extravagant, in both public and private expenditure.* He applied church revenues shamelessly to personal ends as well as to the devious scheming of diplomacy, and he followed all the tortuous ways of his profession, prevaricating, bribing, and choosing the means to his ends with the recklessness and cynicism of a very practical politician. He accepted bribes. His private life is said to have been impure. He was subservient to the king, even cringing when he feared to lose his master's favor. He appears weak and pitiable in adversity. On the other hand, he was no mere self-seeker. He was not ruthless, vindictive, or blood-thirsty.† He must have been lovable, for in his fall his servants stood by him

4. His Faults and their Extenuation.

---

* He accompanied Henry to France in 1513 (not yet even a bishop) with a retinue double those of Bishops Fox and Ruthall. His household in London numbered 800 persons (cf. Cavendish, chap. v., *Of the Orders and Offices of his House and Chapel;* cf. also chap. vii., *Of the Manner of his Going to Westminster Hall;* chap. viii., *Of the Cardinal's Magnificence in his House,* an account of an entertainment for the king and court, utilized—in many lines *verbatim*—in Shakespeare's *Henry VIII.*, I., iv.; chap. xiii., *Of the French King's Redemption out of Captivity and of the Cardinal's Ambassage into France;* chap. xiv., *Of the French Ambassador's Entertainment and Dispatch*. The Field of the Cloth of Gold, the most magnificent of medieval pageants (1520), was entirely under Wolsey's direction, and in all the glittering throng none was more splendid than Wolsey; none also was busier with weighty matters of state amid all the show. He took a ninety-nine years' lease of Hampton Court from the Knights of St. John in 1515, adorned and extended the palace in succeeding years to suit his taste, and made it his favorite retreat, though in 1525 he presented it to the king as " too magnificent for a subject."

† It is worth noting that no one brought before his legatine court on a charge of heresy was burned; and in political matters and toward personal enemies he showed a like self-restraint and toleration.

nobly, and he made friends of all with whom he came personally in contact; when he was led from Cawood the crowd ran after him crying: " God save your Grace! The foul evil take them that have taken you from us!" His subserviency to his royal master was grounded in a conviction that Henry's sovereignty was the only guaranty against civil strife; furthermore, that the royal power was the only power in England strong enough to work necessary reforms. Herein public opinion strenuously endorsed Wolsey's. Likewise, his magnificent life accorded with the spirit of his time; the subventions he received from France and Spain were questioned by no one; his apparent misuse of church offices and revenues was sanctioned by time-honored custom. And he has better extenuation than the specious and commonplace plea that " his faults were those of his time." The ostentatious display in which he lived and with which he clothed all his enterprises was a part of his great aspirations and plans, and was, moreover, an effective means toward the ends he was striving for. It impressed foreign potentates, and pleased and animated men at home; probably nothing contributed more to Wolsey's greatest and permanent achievement—the awakening and invigorating of the English spirit—than the magnificent life of the English cardinal. " Bribes " may be too harsh a word to apply to his pensions, annuities, and subsidies; they were given and accepted openly, and they never caused him to waver in his duty to England. A churchman of the highest rank, he served the State and used the Church's money for the public good, because in the early sixteenth century churchmen alone had the education, experience in affairs, and general training requisite for public duties, and the Church possessed by far the larger share of the national wealth—a greater share, moreover, than it needed for the work it was doing. A conspicuous example is his diversion of abundant wealth to grand educational foundations. As early as 1518 he sought and obtained exceptional powers in the visitation of monasteries. Making use of these powers, augmented by later bulls, he suppressed a number of religious houses and applied their revenues to the foundation of Christ Church College at Oxford (1525) and a school at Ipswich (1528), the latter intended to be the first of a series of institutions scattered over England to meet local needs. Thus he would have corrected a fault in the English educational system, which, after his fall, remained unrelieved until the century just ended. No incident of his fall occasioned him deeper grief than the news that his two colleges were to be suppressed. The Oxford institution was ultimately saved (partly in response to Wolsey's earnest entreaties), but its name was changed from Cardinal College to King's (it is now Christ Church) and its plan was much curtailed. Another trait, less patent but more noteworthy, linking Wolsey with the opening twentieth century, is his steadfast belief that the greatness and prosperity of his land and of all lands are truly promoted by peace, not by war. He worked constantly, devotedly, untiringly for peace, winning the title of *cardinalis pacificus*, and he stands forth, in the long line of English statesmen,

as the great peace minister—than whom no other is more fit to be taken as patron by those who would now substitute arbitration and reason for pillage and bloodshed in the settlement of international disputes.

BIBLIOGRAPHY: Among the sources may be mentioned in the Rolls Series: *Letters and Papers of . . . Richard III. and Henry VII.*, 2 vols., 1861–63; *Calendars of Letters and Papers, Henry VIII.*, vols. i.–vi., 1862 sqq.; *Calendar of Letters between England and Spain*, vols. ii.–v., 1868 sqq.; *Venice, State Papers and Manuscripts*, vols. ii.–v., 1864 sqq.; and J. S. Brewer, *Reign of Henry VIII.*, ed. Gairdner, 2 vols., 1884. Besides these, reference should be made to all original publications dealing with the reign of Henry VIII., as well as to the works on the history, secular and ecclesiastical, dealing with that period. The so-called life by George (not William) Cavendish contains the reminiscences of a faithful servant, written late in life (in the reign of Mary). Cavendish remained with Wolsey to the end, was present at his deathbed, and personally carried the news of his death to Henry VIII. The book is gossipy, deficient in dates and other data for reconstructing Wolsey's life, and has value chiefly for the picture it gives (very favorable) of Wolsey the man by one who knew him long and intimately. A copy of the first edition (*The Negotiations of Thomas Wolsey, the Great Cardinall of England, Containing his Life and Death, etc.*, London, 1641), bound in red levant morocco, gilt edges, brought $50 at the Hoe sale (1910). The work has frequently been reproduced and in cheap form, as in *Morley's Universal Library*, London, 1885, recent ed., ib., 1908. The best life of Wolsey is Mandell Creighton's *Cardinal Wolsey* in *Twelve English Statesmen Series*, London, 1888 (written with abundant knowledge of English and continental history and shrewd discrimination, treats of Wolsey as a statesman, but is rather hard reading). Of importance is E. L. Taunton's *Thomas Wolsey, Legate and Reformer*, London, 1901 (a eulogy of Wolsey as churchman, thus supplementing Creighton; it is rather loosely written, and is not to be implicitly trusted in dates, citations, and, perhaps, conclusions, though it has interest and value as the work of a liberal Roman Catholic; cf. his article in *American Catholic Quarterly Review*, xxv (1900), 289–329); F. A. Gasquet, *Henry VIII. and the English Monasteries*, chap. ii., London, 1888, rev. ed., 1899 (unfavorable to Wolsey). The drama, *Henry VIII.*, attributed to Shakespeare (really written by him and Fletcher and containing more of Fletcher than Shakespeare), is not history, but has value in that it doubtless presents Wolsey as men of his time and immediately succeeding generations saw him; the eulogy (IV., ii. 48–68) is inadequate, but just as far as it goes. Other works which may be consulted to advantage are: T. Storer, *Life and Death of Thomas Wolsey*, London, 1599, reprint, Oxford, 1826; R. Fiddes, *Life of Cardinal Wolsey*, ib. 1724; J. Grove, *Hist. of the Life and Times of Cardinal Wolsey*, 4 vols., ib. 1742–44; C. Wordsworth, *Ecclesiastical Biography*, 4 vols., ib. 1853; W. Busch, *Drei Jahre englischer Vermittlungspolitik, 1518–21*, Bonn, 1884; idem, *Cardinal Wolsey und die englische kaiserliche Allianz, 1522–25*, ib. 1884; idem, in *Historisches Taschenbuch*, vols. viii.–ix.; *Cambridge Modern History*, ii. 42–45, 416–435, New York, 1904; *DNB*, lxii. 325–343.

WOLTERS, völt'ers, ALBRECHT JULIUS KONSTANTIN: German theologian; b. at Emmerich-on-the-Rhine (60 m. w. of Münster) Aug. 22, 1822; d. at Bonn Mar. 29, 1877. He began his education in the gymnasium of his native town, and the relics of early Christian art of various kinds accessible there gave him a taste for archeological studies. He attended the University of Bonn, where he came under the influence of Friedrich Bleek and Karl Immanuel Nitzsch (qq.v.); then went to Berlin and pursued theological and philosophical studies under Marheineke, Vatke, Hengstenberg, and others, developing his talent for languages; he closed his studies by returning to Bonn. His first work was done as private tutor at Naples, during three years of which activity he acquired a mastery of the Italian; returning to Germany he took a position as unordained assistant at Krefeld, then held a teachership for a brief time at a girls' school at Cologne, after which he became pastor at Wesel (1851); in 1857 he went to Bonn to do the work of a pastor, and showed a comprehensive activity in preaching, organization, leadership and the cure of souls, adding to his other duties the religious instruction of the upper classes in the gymnasium; after 1862 he was a standing representative at the provincial synod, and in 1869 he became superintendent of the district of Mülheim. In 1874 he assumed a new line of duty as professor of practical theology at Halle, lecturing also on various New-Testament epistles, on church order, and on the history of Christian art; here he served also as head of the governing body of the deaconess institution, while other activities, such as the Gustav-Adolf-Verein, drew upon his strength. Besides three volumes of sermons (Krefeld, 1851, Bonn, 1860–74), he issued *Ernst Moritz Arndt, ein Zeuge für den evangelischen Glauben* (Elberfeld, 1860); *Ueber die Prinzipien der rheinisch-westphälischen Kirchenordnung* (Bonn, 1862); *Der Heidelberger Katechismus . . . nebst der Geschichte seines Textes* (1864); *Konrad von Heresbach und der clev. Hof zu seiner Zeit* (Elberfeld, 1867); *Reformationsgeschichte der Stadt Wesel* (Bonn, 1868); *Ein Blatt aus der Geschichte des truchsess'schen Krieges* (1872); *Der Abgott zu Halle* (1877); and the posthumous *Nachgelassene Gedichte* (1879).

(K. H. PAHNCKE.)

BIBLIOGRAPHY : W. Beyschlag, *Erinnerungen an Albrecht Wolters*, Halle, 1880; and the address at the interment, by Pastor Krabb, in *Kirchlicher Anzeiger für die evangelischen Gemeinden in Bonn und Umgegend*, 1878, no. 15.

WOLTERSDORF, vōlt'ers-dorf, **ERNST GOTTLIEB:** German poet, educator, preacher, and author; b. at Friedrichsfelde, a suburb of Berlin, May 31, 1725; d. at Bunzlau (65 m. w.n.w. of Breslau) Dec. 17, 1761. He received his preparatory training at Berlin, entered the University of Halle in 1742; was compelled by illness to break off his studies and to travel in 1744; became tutor and vicar in the family of Pastor Stilke in Zerrenthin near Prenzlau; in 1746 was called to Drehna to preach and to instruct young Count Seyfried, when he gave of his time for the instruction of the school-children; he was called as second pastor to Bunzlau in 1748, and there he was active in a revival during which the numbers attending his services compelled him to preach in the open air, while his excellent service and his devotion to his work won over the faction which had opposed his selection; in 1754 he became interested in an orphan asylum, entered the directorate, with which he became even more closely identified in 1758, declining a call to a professorship that he might continue his work. Under his able direction during the short time remaining to him the importance and usefulness of the institution increased greatly. Of his poems he issued volumes in 1750–51 under the title *Evangelische Psalmen* (new ed. by R. Schneider, Dresden, 1849), and a complete collection appeared after his death (Berlin, 1767). They have become precious possessions of the church, though they are for the most part too long for use in hymnals. A collection of his sermons appeared at Bunzlau, 1771. (A. FREYBE†.)

BIBLIOGRAPHY: There is a biography by R. Schneider in his edition of the *Evangelische Psalmen* noted in the text; one by R. Besser, Bielefeld, 1854; also one by A. Brüssau-Vielguth, in *Bilder aus der Geschichte des evangelischen Kirchenliedes*, no. 36.

WOLZOGEN, JOHANN LUDWIG VON. See SOCINUS, FAUSTUS, SOCINIANS, I., § 2.

WOMEN, ROMAN CATHOLIC CONGREGATIONS OF: Communities of women, usually monastic in character, organized for religious or philanthropic purposes. The female branches of such orders as the Benedictines, Franciscans, and Dominicans, as well as such famous orders and congregations as the Brigittines, Sisters of Mercy, and Ursulines, are dealt with under the articles devoted to those subjects. But a list may here be given of the smaller and more or less local female congregations of the Roman Catholic Church, the order adopted being chronological.

The **Oblates of the Tower of Specchi** (Oblate di Tor de' Specchi) were established in 1425 during the pontificate of Martin V. by Franzcesca Romana of Trastevere for the care of the sick. The members of this order have been distinguished by their self-sacrificing devotion, down to the present century. The **Conceptionists**, or Order of the Conception of Mary, were founded at Toledo in 1484 by Beatrix de Silva, and were confirmed by Innocent VIII., 1589. A similar society, that of the **Immaculate Conception of the Holy Virgin**, was established in connection with Pierre Fourier's Lorraine congregation of Our Lady at Nancy. The **Dimesses** were founded in 1584 by Dianira Valmarana, a widow of Verona, for the instruction of girls and the care of the sick under the sanction of Cardinal-bishop Augustin Valier. The **Daughters of the Purification of Mary** were established in 1590 at Arona near Milan, principally for the instruction of women.

The **Daughters of Our Lady of Bordeaux** (Filles de Notre Dame de Bordeaux) were founded in 1607 by Jeanne Lestonac, marquise of Montferrat, and were confirmed by Paul V. The congregation is devoted chiefly to the instruction of Roman Catholic girls, and possessed in 1898 more than thirty houses in France and some twenty in Spain, Italy, and America. The **Sisters of Christian Teaching of Nancy** (Vatelottes) were established in 1615 by the Lorraine priest Vatel for the care of the sick and the instruction of girls, and have about 900 sisters and 200 houses. The **Daughters of Mount Calvary** (Brignolines, Suore Brignole) were established at Genoa in 1619 by Virginia Centurione for the care of the sick and young children. The **Nuns of the Incarnate Word** (Religieuses du Verbe incarné) were founded at Lyons in 1625 by Jeanne Marie Chezard for the adoration of the sacrament. They are divided into three classes, the first of which maintains the original purpose of the congregation; the second supports boarding-schools for girls; and the third nurses the sick. The **Daughters of the Holy Cross,** founded at Roye in Picardy in 1625, has been divided since 1668 into a congregation of religious with simple

Foundations before 1600.

Foundations of the Seventeenth Century.

vows and a mother house at Paris, and a secular congregation devoted to the instruction of girls, particularly in the rural districts. In the beginning of the nineteenth century the congregation was again divided into seven independent bodies, including the Ladies of the Cross (Religieuses de la croix) with a mother house at St. Quentin; the Sisters of the Cross (Sœurs de la croix) with a mother house at Lavaux; and the Daughters of the Cross (Filles de la croix) with a mother house at St. Brieuc. The **Sisters of the Mercy of Jesus** (Sœurs hospitalières de la misericorde de Jésus) were founded at Dieppe in 1630 for the care of the sick and aged. The **Penitents of Our Lady of Refuge** were established at Nancy in 1631 by Marie Elisabeth de la Croix for the reformation of fallen women, were confirmed three years later by Urban VIII., and are under Augustinian rule with certain Jesuit modifications. The **Nuns of Our Lady of Mercy** were founded at Aix in 1633 by the Oratorian Antoine Yvan to imitate the life of the Virgin by pious seclusion and to give a Christian education to poor girls. The **Hospital-Nuns of St. Joseph of Bordeaux** were established in 1638 by Marie Delpech de l'Estang for the education of orphan girls, later taking the names of Congregation of Jesus, Mary, and Joseph, or Congregation of the Created Trinity, and also being called Sisters of Joseph. The **Sisters of Refuge** (or Nuns of St. Michael) were an order of penitents established at Caen in 1644 (1641) by Jean Eudes, but later removed to Paris, where the great monastery or magdaleneum became their chief center, in addition to which they had twenty-three other houses. The **Nuns of Our Lady of Grace** (or Sisters of St. Thomas of Villanova) were established at Lamballe in Brittany in 1660 by the Augustinian Angelus le Proust, and originally cared for the sick, although they now also give instruction to the young in their institutions, which number more than a hundred. The **Sisters of the Christ-Child** were founded at Reims by Abbé Roland in 1674 for the instruction of girls, forming the model for similar congregations at Soissons, Neuchâtel, and Claveizolles, as well as in England, where they are called the Sisters of the Holy Child Jesus, and in Japan. The **Nuns of St. Maurus and Providence** were founded at Paris in 1681 by the Minimite Nicholas Barre, who united them with the Sisters of the Christian and Loving Child Jesus, whom he had established three years previously. They enjoyed the special favor of Louis XIV., who gave them a school at St. Cyr, and they possessed in 1898 forty houses in France and the French colonies. The **Nuns of St. Joseph of the Good Shepherd** were established at Clermont in 1666 by Canon Laborieux for the care of fallen women, which was the aim also of the **Daughters of the Good Shepherd,** established at Paris about 1690 by Marie de Combe. These were the predecessors of the **Nuns of the Good Shepherd,** who were an offshoot of the Sisters of Refuge already mentioned. The congregation possesses about 115 houses, including thirteen in Germany and fifty-one in America.

The **Daughters of Wisdom** were established at St. Laurent in 1719 by Marie Louise Trichet, and con-

trol nearly 200 houses, most of which are in France, and devote themselves to various forms of philanthropy, including the instruction of deaf-mutes. The **Daughters of the Good Saviour** were founded at Caen by Anne Leroy in 1720, and aim to relieve all forms of suffering, including deaf-mutes and the insane. The **Presentation Nuns** were founded at Cork in 1756 by Nano Nagle for the gratuitous instruction of poor children, and have twenty-nine branches in Ireland and India. In 1797 they formed the model of the Sœurs de Presentation (White Ladies, Dames Blanches), established by Marie Rivier, and transplanted to Canada in 1853. The **Sisters of Providence** were established at Metz in 1762, and are still active in educational work and the care of the sick. Similar congregations were later formed at Strasburg, Rappoltsweiler, and other cities, as well as at Evreux in Normandy in 1775. The **Ladies of the Holy Sacrament** (or of St. Justus) were founded at Macon in 1773 for the education of girls and the care of the sick, and later served as a model for another congregation of the same name established at Romances in 1823.

The **Ladies of the Most Holy Heart of Jesus** (Dames de sacré cœur) were founded in 1800 by Madelaine Sophie Barat (see SACRED HEART OF JESUS, DEVOTION TO). The **Sisters of the Cross of St. Andrew** were established at Puy in 1806 by Elisabeth Béchier and André Hubert Fournet for the education of children and the care of the sick, and has about 2,500 sisters in about 380 houses, the most of which are in France. The **Sisters of the Perpetual Adoration** (Adoratrices perpetuæ) were founded at Rome in 1807 by Caterina Sordini (later known as a Franciscan Tertiary by her name in religion, Maria Magdalena de Incarnatione) for the perpetual adoration of the sacrament and the expiation of wrongs done to it. It possesses houses in Rome, Naples, Turin, and Innsbruck.

The **Sisters of St. Sophia** were established at Metz in 1807 for the education of girls, but were incorporated in 1824 with the Dames de Sacre Cœur. The **Sisters of St. Christina** were also established at Metz in 1807 by Madame Tailleur, and gave gratuitous instruction in seventy schools in the dioceses of Metz, Châlons, Verdun, and Reims. The **Daughters of Jesus** were founded at Verona in 1809 by Pietro Liomardi for the education of girls, and formed the model for four French congregations with the same name and object. The **Ladies of Good Succor** (Dames du bon secours) were established at Aurignac in 1810 by Abbé Desentis and the widowed Baroness de Benque for the care of the sick and the poor. They number over 4,000 in 160 houses in France. The **Sisters of Loreto** (Loretines, Ladies of Loreto) include three congregations established about the same time; one at Loreto, Ky., in 1812 for the education of girls; the second at Bordeaux in 1821 for the protection of servants without positions; and the third at Dublin in 1822 on the model of the English Ladies (q.v.).

The **Sisters of Joseph** comprise a number of con-

Marginal notes:

Foundations of the Eighteenth Century.

Foundations of the Nineteenth Century.

gregations established for various purposes. One was founded at Chambrey in Savoy in 1808 for the elementary instruction of children; and a second was founded at Lyons in 1821 to provide for the welfare of female prisoners. The **Ladies of the Holy Trinity** (Sœurs or Dames de la Sainte Trinité) were founded at Valence in 1824 for the instruction of the poor, the training of orphans, and hospital work, and became active in thirteen dioceses of France, in addition to some twenty houses in Algeria. The **Sisters of Our Lady of Good Succor** (Sœurs de Notre Dame du bon secours) were established at Paris in 1827 by Madame de Montal for the education of girls, and spread thence to other cities of France. A similar congregation was established under the name of **Sœurs de Marie Auxiliatrice** in Paris and Castelnaudary in 1854 by Abbé de Soubiran for elementary education, the care of the sick, and the control of homes for working girls.

The **Ladies of the Holy Union** (Dames de la sainte union) were founded by the priest Debrabant in 1838 with their mother house at Douai for educational purposes. The congregation had over 500 sisters in northern France and Belgium, while an older congregation of the same name had its mother house at Fontenay-le-Comte. The **Sisters of Our Lady of Salette** were established at Grenoble in 1852, in cooperation with the Missioners of Our Lady of Salette, and, though having but four convents with about sixty sisters, controlled a number of asylums for orphans and the insane. The **Society of Mary the Restorer** (Société de Marie-Réparatrice) was established at Paris in 1855 by the Baroness Emelie d'Hooghvorst for the perpetual adoration of the sacrament, the equipment of poor churches, and religious instruction. The mother house is in Rome, but the congregation is represented in almost all the Roman Catholic countries of Europe, and in Palestine, India, Reunion, Mauritius, and elsewhere.

The **Daughters of Divine Love** were founded at Vienna in 1868 by Franziska Lechner to obtain positions for working girls, to train orphans for housework, and to provide homes for aged women. The sisters number more than 400 and possess some thirty institutions. The **Missionary Sisters of Our Lady of Missions of Africa** (or White Sisters) were founded in 1868 by Cardinal Lavigerie (q.v.) of Algiers as the female branch of his Société des Missionaires de Notre-Dame des Missions d'Afrique. Originally restricted to the care of orphans and hospitals and other works of charity in Algiers, they have engaged since 1894 in missionary activity in central Africa, although in small numbers. The **Indian Sisters of Our Lady of the Seven Dolors** were founded in 1876 for giving Roman Catholic instruction in the missionary schools of India. The **Indian Sisters of St. Anne** were established in Trichinopoli in 1877 for the care of orphans, the control of hospitals, the providing of homes for widows, and similar objects. The **Sisters of St. Anne in Canada** are in charge of hospitals in Montreal, Vancouver, Three Rivers, and other Canadian districts.

See also AMBROSIANS; ANGELICALS; BRIDGET, SAINT, OF SWEDEN; CHARITY, SISTERS OF; ENGLISH LADIES; MERCY, SISTERS OF; SACRED HEART OF JESUS; URSULINES; VISITANTINES; etc.

(O. ZÖCKLER†.)

BIBLIOGRAPHY: Helyot, *Ordres monastiques;* Heimbucher, *Orden und Kongregationen;* Currier, *Religious Orders;* T. D. Fosbroke, *British Monasticism,* 2 vols., London, 1802, 3d ed., 1843; M. R. A. Henrion, *Hist. générale des missions catholiques,* 2 vols., Paris, 1846–47; L. Badiche, *Dictionnaire des ordres religieux,* 4 vols., ib. 1858; O'D. T. Hill, *English Monasticism,* London, 1867; C. E. Stephen, *The Service of the Poor,* ib. 1871; E. Keller, *Les Congregations religieuses en France, leurs œuvres et leurs services,* Paris, 1880; M. du Camp, *La Charité privée à Paris,* ib. 1886; G. Uhlhorn, *Die christliche Liebesthätigkeit,* iii. 414–448, Stuttgart, 1890; F. C. Woodhouse, *Monasticism, Ancient and Modern,* London, 1896; Lina Eckenstein, *Woman under Monasticism,* Cambridge, 1896 (a valuable contribution; deals mainly with English and German nunneries); Theodosia Benson, in *RDM,* Apr., 1898; the *Official Catholic Directory,* pp. 805–835 Milwaukee, 1911; the literature under MONASTICISM.

WOMEN'S WORK IN THE CHURCH.

I. In the Early Church: By the greetings in the epistles of the New Testament it is seen that women were in some way in the apostolic age serving the Christian community. Many followed

1. In the Apostolic Period. the example of those women who ministered to Christ and shared their wealth with him. Others, like Mary and Martha, Mary the mother of Mark, Lydia, Priscilla, Nympha, probably Damaris, and some of the "honorable women" of Berea, made their homes the center of the little community in each city and the place where the love-feast could take place. In such homes the messengers of the Gospel found safe entertainment. Paul experienced this hospitality, which contributed much to the extension of Christianity. From the earliest times certain women seem to have been singled out for special duties by special fitness. Phœbe (see DEACONESS) appears to have been one of these. Legend (Acts of Paul and Thekla) gives to Paul a woman missionary assistant, and it is certain that there were women teachers to the end of the second century, and women missionaries much later. In the apostolic period women instructed new converts (Acts xviii. 26), they also spoke in meetings. The daughters of Philip (Acts xxi. 8–9) were not the only prophetesses. Christianity was in the outset charismatic, and women shared in these gifts. Paul regulated the public speaking of women (I Cor. xi. 5). Early Christian art gives examples of women speaking, with their veils fastened back from their faces by the ornament usually worn for the purpose. The context shows the prohibition of I Cor. xiv. 34 to refer not to prophesying but to interrupting a discourse by questions. "In the gospel" (Phil. iv. 3) can mean nothing else than "In the preaching of the Gospel." Toward the end of the first century (I Tim. ii. 12) women were, on the score of seemliness, forbidden to speak in public. What had been proper in the small, familiar meetings of the early days ceased to be so when religious services took on a more public character, especially in the East, where reputable women lived in comparative seclusion. This rule did not extend to newly evangelized districts, as is proved by the fact that the Acts of Paul and Thekla were considered authentic through the second century.

Throughout the East women continued to teach those of their own sex as a matter of necessity, apostles and men missionaries being ex-
2. In the cluded from women's apartments. The **Sub-Apos-** spread of Christianity in the East is **tolic Age.** unthinkable without this service. The method of administering baptism made the assistance of women in this rite indispensable. As numbers grew and special buildings were provided for religious services, where women sat apart from men, the service of women in the administration of the communion was equally indispensable. The whole question of woman's work was one not of doctrine nor of office, but of good manners and actual need. In general, woman's service was naturally along womanly lines, hospitality, care of the poor, the sick, prisoners and orphans, the oversight and instruction of women and children, and the last offices to the dead. In this period of first love there was need neither of organization nor of institutions. Every Christian was a worker, and every Christian home an asylum for travelers and the poor. Persecution, when it arose, created new duties in which, as well as in martyrdom, women had their full share. Their share in service and suffering is a stronger testimony to the position of women in the early Church than any special office.

Special offices, however, came into existence at a very early time. Official widows (see DEACONESS, II., § 1) appear at the close of the apostolic age. Later sources shed light upon the directions in I Tim. v. 3–10. In the early days, when families were divided religiously, believing **3. Widows.** widows must often have been thrown upon the community for support. These, being presumably free from family cares, were by years and experience peculiarly competent for womanly service. Official widows were to be at least sixty years old, and must have borne children (I Tim. v. 9, 10) that they might have experience and sympathy. Their especial duties were prayer and fasting (the widow was the "intercessor of the church"; cf. Apostolic Constitutions, iii. 5); but it was her part also to care for other widows and for the poor in general, especially for orphans and for those who were imprisoned for conscience' sake, to have oversight of the female part of the community, being virtually the presbyter of the women, and to be "keeper of the door" in service time. Widows spoke at marriages, instructed the women, and prepared them for baptism, in which service they assisted, and held a position of such honor that they were designated the "altar of God." Widows are named in the second century with bishops, presbyters, and deacons as church functionaries. Married women and even young girls came to be included in this order. Ignatius (*Ad Smyrnæos*, xiii.) speaks of "virgins who were also called widows." The Testament of our Lord (end of fourth century) mentions in the following order the viduate, deaconesses, female presbyters, virgins, putting widows before deaconesses. The Apostolic Constitutions (q.v.) says, on the contrary, that widows must always obey the deaconesses, and prescribes the duties of each. The probably still earlier Didascalia, in the appendix of which is given the ritual for the consecration of widows and deaconesses, shows that by the third century many official duties were taken from the widow and conferred upon the deaconess, precisely in order that the former might keep to her original duty of prayer and fasting (I Tim. v. 5). Yet even in this century she still claimed the right to baptize, and a fifth-century synod at Carthage says that since widows assist in the baptism of women they must, therefore, be qualified to teach. The Testament of Our Lord names among the widow's duties to pray at certain hours in the church and at home, to discipline the women, punish the refractory, warn the backward, teach the unlearned, visit the sick, and help in the baptism of women "because she is herself anointed." She is also to take the communion to sick women.

Among the functions sooner or later withdrawn from woman was that of presbyteress, which was for a time a distinct office. There was also a canoness, whose duty was chiefly to serve in the choir at funerals and other ceremonies. The **4. Other** heretical sects, especially the Monta- **Offices.** nists, had also female bishops and prophetesses, and it was in part because of the excesses of the latter that the orders above named were comparatively short-lived in the orthodox church. The growing concern for purity of doctrine doubtless counted for something in the increasing distrust of women as teachers; to this contributed the development of clericalism which began early in the third century, and the exaltation of the sacerdotal function of the clergy; the rise of monasticism completed the work. By the end of the fourth century the teaching office in the Church had ceased to be vested in women. While it may be disputed that Christianity emancipated woman, it certainly opened for the first time an honorable career to respectable unmarried women, for whom until that time there had been neither place nor dignity. Before the close of the first century appears the institution of the popular order of virgins, women who dedicated themselves to a single life and took a special place of honor as the Brides of Christ. They seem to have put themselves at the call of the bishop for any helpful service, were not cloistered, but lived at home and thence exercised their official functions. At first they claimed the right to teach. At a later day Tertullian forbade it, and this prohibition contributed much to the popularity of the monastic life. If the "consecrated virgin" might not be a leader in the Christian community, she had no part in it. The result was that virgins formed themselves into communities, first in the East and afterward in the West. The communities of virgins were naturally preceded by the female anchorite. It was only after the peace of the Church under Constantine that monastic orders became possible, and one of his daughters founded the first woman's cloister. All that had preceded led to the merging of the institution of virgins, and to some extent of that of widows, in the orders of the nun. " Heresy, hierarchy, monasticism " were the three factors which checked the development of woman's service in the community in the fourth and fifth centuries.

In the fourth century, which marks the zenith of female activity in the early Church, the importance of services performed by women not of any order is emphasized by Chrysostom and others. At this time the development of hospitals and hospices appears to have displaced those earlier activities from which women had been gradually shut out. Helena (q.v.), the mother of the Emperor Constantine, built the first hospices for strangers and pilgrims. A group of noble Roman matrons did much to promote Christianity by founding hospitals and convents and forwarding education. Jerome in his various writings especially mentions fifteen, among others Paula, a distinguished Hebrew scholar who assisted him in the translation of the Bible. The first hospital in Rome was founded by Fabiola, whom Jerome calls " the praise of Christians, the wonder of the Gentiles, the mourning of the poor, and the consolation of the monks."

The influence of Christian women upon husbands, sons, and grandsons was very marked. Nearly all the distinguished names of the ancient Church are accompanied by that of mother or sister. Macrina (q.v., 2) helped to rear in the love of God her three brothers, " the eloquent Basil, the judicious Gregory of Nyssa, and the charitable Peter of Sebaste " (qq.v.). Noma, the mother of Gregory Nazianzen, converted her heathen husband and brought her distinguished son under Christian influences. Arethusa, mother of Chrysostom, devoted her life to the education of her children, and kept her son from becoming a hermit. The influence of Monnica (q.v.) upon Augustine (q.v.) is well known. Ambrose (q.v.) was brought up and educated by his sister Marcellina. Pulcheria (q.v.), the granddaughter of Theodosius the Great, superintended the education of her brother Theodosius II., with whom she reigned as Augusta. Benedict (see BENEDICT OF NURSIA) owed much to his sister Scholastica. The part of women in the adoption of Christianity by pagan nations was large. It was due to the Christian teachings of Chlotildis that her husband Clovis was ready to accept Christianity after a victory in battle won by prayer. Her granddaughter Bertha prepared her husband, Ethelbert, king of Kent (see AUGUSTINE, SAINT, OF CANTERBURY), to embrace the Christian faith when it was preached in Britain by Augustine. Ludmilla of Bohemia trained her grandson Wenceslas in such piety that, after making Christianity the religion of Bohemia, he became a martyr and saint. Dambrowka of Bohemia persuaded her husband Micislaus of Poland to embrace Christian-

5. Influence of Women.

ity. The office of missionary was never forbidden to women, and with the right of the woman missionary to teach went of necessity her right to baptize. Gradually, however, this right was withdrawn. But the missionary service of women continued through the entire period of the conversion of Europe, where women rendered large service. Bridget (see BRIDGET, SAINT, OF KILDARE) worked with Patrick in the evangelization of Ireland. Anglo-Saxon nuns were especially active in this service. The monastery at Whitby was a school of missionaries, female and male. In the eighth century Boniface (see BONIFACE, SAINT) called his cousin Lioba from her convent in Dorset to help him evangelize the heathen of northern Europe. Walburga and Barthgytha, Anglo-Saxons nuns, assisted in evangelizing Germany.

II. In the Middle Ages: The rise of Monasticism (q.v.) in the fifth century changed in a large degree, though for a long time it did not diminish, the activities of women in the Church. Nursing the sick and ministering to the poor were their special duties, and also teaching, especially in the foundations of Benedictines (see BENEDICT OF NURSIA). The monastery as originally conceived was not a place of limited opportunity, but rather a religious settlement extending its influence over a wide area. During the turbulent centuries after the break-up of the empire, it offered to women the only place where they could work fruitfully, and develop and cultivate intellectual tastes. It afforded them also the only opportunity for social life. The monotony of castle and burg life for women was great. The men went to camp and court, the women were at home alone. Convent life was varied and interesting, including as it did the presence of a large number of royal princesses. Up to the tenth century a large number of " double " monasteries (of men and women) were ruled by women. The need of physical protection in those troubled times made this arrangement nearly imperative. Bede speaks of a double monastery in Rome in the seventh century; there were many in Gaul and Britain, and later in Belgium and Germany, but they were most popular in Ireland. The custom was not unknown in the East, but in the nature of things was not favored there. The custom died out in the ninth century (though revived at Port Royal in the seventeenth). The Benedictine settlement at Fontevrault, including monks and nuns to the number of 3,000 souls, was ruled for 600 years by a line of thirty-two abbesses of remarkable administrative ability. In the sixth century the Princess Radegonde, in her double monastery of the Holy Cross at Poitiers, nursed lepers, fostered literature and the arts, and often made peace in the quarrels of rulers of her time. In the same century Florentine of Spain became the superior of forty monasteries and " by her knowledge, her virtues, and even by her sacred songs " ranks high among nuns. Bertile of Chelles in this century drew large audiences of men and women to her lectures on the Scriptures. The abbey of Whitby in Yorkshire, a double institution, founded by Hilda (q.v.), a woman of " rare capacity for the government of souls and for the consolidation of monastic institutions," was re-

1. As Rulers of Monastic Institutions.

sorted to for education by kings and princes as well as by the "old cowherd Caedmon" (q.v.), who under Hilda's tuition became the father of English poetry. Her successor Elfleda, like all cloistered Anglo-Saxon princesses, took a passionate interest in the affairs of her race and country, and did much to mitigate the jealousies of kings and bishops. Abbesses administered the communion in their convents up to the ninth century, and in England in the tenth century four abbesses sat in Parliament as peers. The authority of such persons was enormous. As feudal lords they had the right of ban, sent their contingents of armed knights to the field, gave judgment in courts, and in Germany (as in England) were summoned to the imperial diet. Certain German abbesses had even the right to mint coin.

During all these centuries when the business of men was war, and princes were not disgraced by total illiteracy, women-ruled institutions became centers not only of philanthropy but of intellectual life, training the sons and daughters of kings and nobles for public life, and contributing much to the progress of learning. In the tenth century the Saxon monastery at Gandersheim was especially distinguished for the brilliant learning and the dramatic productions of the nun Roswitha (q.v.). In the eleventh century women of exalted position, whether cloistered or otherwise, felt the stirrings of that national consciousness which was marked by the struggle between pope and emperor. In this struggle more than one woman took an active part, notably Matilda, Countess of Tuscany (q.v.), who, at her castle at Canossa, more than indirectly contributed to that "peace of the Church" during which letters were revived and the progress of science fostered.

During this and the following centuries religious houses had fallen into great disorder, especially through luxury. Not until the twelfth century did nuns become entirely cloistered; up to this time they had enjoyed great freedom of action, and only by degrees had a conventual costume become obligatory. Both these changes were in the direction of reform. The sisterhood of the Poor Clares (see CLARE, SAINT, AND THE POOR CLARES) had great influence in correcting the evils of monastic life. The sisters also nursed the sick, especially lepers. A contemporary of the founder of the order was Saint Elizabeth of Thuringia (q.v.), whose service to the Church was far larger than the charities for which she is famous in legend. The hospitals which she founded were of lasting social importance, and her friendship for the Franciscans was hardly less so. The work of founding hospitals took a new impulse during this period, chiefly as a result of the changes in monastic life. Many notable women left the convent to create voluntary associations for charity and philanthropy, forming the "active" or "secular orders," within the Church but bound by no vows, devoted to prayer, the service of the poor, the sick, orphans, widows, and weaker brethren and sisters. Conspicuous among these were the Tertiaries of St. Francis (see FRANCIS, SAINT, OF ASSISI) and St.

2. In Philanthropy and Literature.

Dominic (see DOMINIC, SAINT), the Sisters of the Common Life (see COMMON LIFE, BRETHREN OF THE, § 5), and the Beguines of Flanders (see BEGHARDS, BEGUINES). This last order was a protest against formalism and useless repression, and an assertion of the right of spontaneous self-expression in work. In the thirteenth century a wave of mysticism swept over the Church, in which women had a large part. Much mystic literature, some of it held to be divinely inspired, was contributed by nuns. The convent of Helfta near Eisleben was a center of this activity, and in this convent four women, the Abbess Gertrude, her sister Saint Matilda of Hackeborn, the beguine Matilda of Magdeburg, and Gertrud the Great (qq.v.) were conspicuous. Their writings were characterized by great elevation, impassioned fervor, intense realism, and high inspiration. The beguine Matilda (who joined the convent later) was one of the earliest writers in German. Her work, "The Flowing Light of Divinity," in seven books has been republished (ed. G. Morel, Regensburg, 1869, and selected passages in Germ. transl. by S. Simon, Berlin, 1907). It is a serious inquiry into the nature of the soul and its relation to God, and it paved the way for more rational views than had prevailed in the earlier mysticism. Matilda of Hackeborn's "Book of Special Grace" (best ed., by the Benedictines of Solesmes, *Revelationes Gertrudis ac Mathildianæ*, ii. 1–421, Paris, 1877), a series of visions and revelations, often translated and frequently reprinted, was notable in that class of literature which had its culmination in Dante.

The abuses which unquestionably sullied monastic life in the centuries preceding the Reformation were in large part attributable to concentration of interest upon the care of the individual soul—the effort to attain personal sanctity by prayer, fasting, and later by discipline. Moral disorders ultimately resulted from this ideal. Education was maintained, but its scope was narrowed, its chief purpose being to fit the young for cloistered life. Still, intellectual pursuits were cherished in some German nunneries even into the fifteenth century. But a growing indifference to the intellectual occupations of women and the education of girls was evident, and the Humanists of the period, in their far-reaching plans for an improved system of education, left girls entirely out of account. The development of Universities (q.v.) (in which the existence of women was ignored) resulted in a serious lowering of the educational standard of the convent. The separation of the sexes and the stricter confinement of women, in the interests of morality, cut off the nuns from secular learning and from those public interests in which they had formerly been active. Thus the high ideals with which woman's service had been claimed and rendered in the early days became entirely obscured. Later monasticism was unable to make the lavished treasures of woman's love and self-sacrifice useful to the world, and woman lost her practical place in the service of the Church.

The decline of monasticism was inevitable so soon as the idea that virginity was in itself pleasing

3. Decline in Culture.

to God ceased to be in the foreground of moral consciousness. The persuasion that the vocation of women was the home was in part the effect and in part the cause of the decline in female education. This idea agreed with the views of Protestant Reformers, and prepared the way for the dissolution of nunneries. To this important revolution the growing change in social ideas, the decline of the system of association not only in religious but in artizan and commercial life, with the development of individualistic tendencies, contributed quite as much as the disorders of the monasteries and their failure to serve the public need.

Before the Reformation women had been conspicuous in attempts to reform or to preserve the purity of the Church. Toward the close of the sixth century Theodolinda, queen of the Lombards, extirpated the Arian heresy from her realm. In the eleventh century Margaret, patroness of Scotland, wife of Malcolm Conmore, instituted important reforms in the church of that country. St. Catharine of Sienna (q.v.) in the fourteenth century was not only hospital nurse, prophetess, preacher, and reformer of society, but did much to reform ecclesiastical abuses. In the sixteenth century St. Theresa (q.v.) wrought a remarkable reformation in the Carmelite monasteries and convents of Spain. It was largely due to her reforming work within the Roman Catholic Church that the progress of Protestantism was arrested in Spain. In the seventeenth century Angélique Arnauld's attempt at Port Royal to reform abuses in the monastic system, though rejected by the Roman Church, and without ultimate success, gives her a high place among women. The dissolution of religious houses had led to the formation of the great hospitals in the sixteenth and seventeenth centuries. They were preceded by many small confraternities for the care of the sick. Such were found in nearly every village in Germany; they were always religious—lay hospitals did not exist until long after this. In them, as in the earlier monasteries, men and women worked together, though they communicated only for the needs of the service. The Sisters of Charity of St. Vincent de Paul (q.v.) more nearly resemble a modern church society than any previous form of benevolent activity in the Church. Under the direction of St. Francis de Sales (q.v.), his friend Mme. de Chantal founded the first Order of Visiting Nurses and herself acted in that capacity. Rosa Gavona, a Sardinian needlewoman, built up a society of young and unprotected needlewomen, which spread into many towns. The members take no vows, but support not only themselves, but the sick and infirm of their order. Marie Agnesi of Milan, rich and noble, a celebrated mathematician and theologian, and the recipient of many public honors, founded a hospital in her own house. With the reforms which were the reflex influence of Protestantism upon the Roman Catholic Church, new associations of women came into being, not so free as the early hospital and other associations, yet not strictly cloistered. See MAGDALENE, ORDERS OF ST. MARY.

III. **Under Protestantism:** The development of the sense of individuality which was the special

contribution of Protestantism did not restore woman to her early position of usefulness in the Reformation churches. Unlike Romanism, the Reformed Church found no sphere for the activities of uneducated women, and the lowered educational standards and opportunities conspired with the growing conviction that woman's sphere is properly domestic to close against her for two hundred years the door of activity. Yet there were noble exceptions. Katherine Zell of Strasburg stood with her husband for toleration, Argula von Grumbach held her own as a controversialist, and by a letter which she wrote to Luther turned his thought to matrimony. Luther's brave wife, Katherine von Bora, was an important factor in his reforming work. In France Queen Marguerite of Navarre (q.v.), the friend of Calvin, her sister, Renée of France (q.v.), her daughter, Jeanne d'Albret (q.v.), mother of Henri IV., were nursing mothers of Protestantism. Charlotte de Laval persuaded her husband, Admiral Coligny, to take up the sword for the Protestant faith. In England Queen Catherine Parr, Lady Jane Grey, Elizabeth herself, served the Protestant cause. Anne Clifford, countess of Pembroke (1590–1676), rebuilt churches, pensioned distressed clergymen, admitting dissenting ministers to the bounty, repaired and restored almshouses, and built a hospital for poor women. Jane Welsh, daughter of John Knox and ancestress of Mrs. Carlyle, stood nobly for the Protestant faith. The rise of Quakerism made women prominent. Judge Fell's widow, Margaret, the wife of George Fox, William Penn's first wife, Gulielma Springett, Mary Dyer the martyr, and many others preached the doctrine of the "inward light." Friendly patrons were Lady Claypole, also connected with the Cambridge Platonists (q.v.), and Elizabeth, abbess of Herford, who welcomed Penn, and who was attached to the Labbadist party of Holland (see LABADIE, JEAN DE, LABADISTS). The great ornament of that party was Anna Maria van Schurman, accounted the most learned and accomplished woman of her age. The cause of religion in the eighteenth century owes a great debt to Susannah Wesley (q.v.), the mother of the Wesleys, and to Lady Huntingdon (see HUNTINGDON, SELINA HASTINGS), the foster mother of ministers during the evangelical revival, in which Miss Anne Steele, the hymn-writer, had a part. Margaret Baxter, who shared her husband's prison in the common jail, was a woman of large charities, as was Lady Rachel Russell. Hannah More (q.v.) carried on a large work of free education of the poor. With her pen and influence she rendered important aid to Wilberforce in his crusade against slavery, and also instituted an important temperance work among country clergy and farmers. The mystic Jane Lead (q.v.) was the English founder of the Philadelphian Society for the dissemination of the ideas of Jakob Boehme and her own revealings. From one branch of this society came Ann Lee, founder of Shakerism in America. Jemima Wilkinson in this century founded the White Quakers. The Pietist movement in Germany shows the prophetess Eleanora von Merlau, and Frau Peterson, who shared her husband's literary toil in defense of

The marginal keywords in the left column read: **4. Women in Reform.** The keywords in the right column read: **1. Early Examples of Service.**

inward religion and universal salvation. Amalie Sieveking, a wealthy woman, broke new ground in dealing with the poor. She was the first exponent of the modern doctrine, " not alms but a friend," founding the society of " the Friends of the Poor " for systematic visiting in homes to relieve distress in all ways except by money. Beata Sturmin, " the Tabitha of Württemberg," and a woman of great devotion, exerted an unusual influence. Dorothea Trudel, a Swiss woman, began the " Faith Cure movement." But in spiritual power no woman of the eighteenth century can compare with Sarah Pierrepont, the wife of Jonathan Edwards and mother of a long line of notables in American church history.

The divisions of Protestantism prevented that large cooperation in good work which the requirements and the growing social consciousness of the nineteenth century rendered necessary,

2. Later Philanthropic Work. and therefore many of the noblest organizations founded or participated in by Protestant women of the past hundred years have been distinctly outside of the Church. The prison reforms of Elizabeth Fry (q.v.), the army and hospital reforms of Florence Nightingale, the German Frauenverein founded by three women in 1813 to care for the wounded in the field whether friend or foe (now with auxiliaries all over the German empire), the Sanitary Commission of the American Civil War, the States Charities Aid Association, the Young Women's Christian Association (see YOUNG PEOPLE'S SOCIETIES), the Women's Christian Temperance Union, the Needlework Gild, the Society for the Prevention of Cruelty to Children, the Consumers' League, the National Association of Mothers, Working Girls' Clubs, all of them religious services and all due to woman's initiative, belong in this category. To the individual initiative of Protestant women is due much religious work of far-reaching importance, yet not in any sense " in the Church." About 1863, Mrs. Daniell, an officer's widow, made at Aldershot, England, the first attempt to teach soldiers the blessings of religion. The work of Miss Sarah Robinson among soldiers resulted in the founding of the Soldiers' Institute, in 1874, and of an important work in the troop ships. Miss Marsh carried on effective work among navvies, and especially among the workmen on the Crystal Palace, in Sydenham. Josephine E. Butler founded first in England and then on the continent the most efficient and far-sighted work for outcast women ever instituted. Agnes Weston, the sailors' friend, has founded sailors' rests and homes all over the world. She also founded the Royal Naval Temperance Society. Countess Schimmelman carries on a large work for sailors. In the later field of Christian benevolence the names of Dora Pattison, Octavia Hill, and Ellice Hopkins are conspicuous among many. The work of Mrs. Nassau Senior, first female inspector of workhouses in England, is truly a religious service. Mrs. Senior has done more for servants than any one else in our time. Mrs. MacPherson in 1870 instituted the work of sending friendless children to the colonies. The direct services of women to the Church have, how-

ever, not been few. Baroness Burdett-Coutts founded and endowed the three colonial bishoprics of Natal, British Columbia, and Adelaide, and opened many schools. Catherine Booth (q.v.) opened a great door of opportunity through which women of small education have been admitted to work side by side with women of fine attainments. When she died, the number of women officers of the Salvation Army exceeded 5,000, and of Halleluiah lassies the number was in the tens of thousands. Mrs. Ballington Booth, a woman of rare eloquence, is one of the founders of the Volunteers of America (q.v.) and the founder of the Prison Gate Mission of America. Mrs. Meredith, of England, who was the first to advocate cottage homes for children, was, with Mrs. Pennefether, the moving spirit of the Mildmay mission.

In the Church of England and later in churches in the United States the movement toward denominational sisterhoods (see DEACONESS) and associations of women and girls is rapidly growing. The

3. Sisterhoods, Education, Missions. Wesleyan Methodists have an order of Sisters of the Poor. The Church of England has twenty-nine sisterhoods devoted to helping girls, church work, etc. The Order of St. Margaret's, London, has founded a colored sisterhood in Baltimore. Mrs. Hugh Price Hughes of London has introduced some varieties of the sisterhood idea. Mary Aikenhead introduced into Ireland the Sisters of Charity, Catherine Elizabeth McAuley (q.v.) the Sisters of Mercy (see MERCY, SISTERS OF). From the Sisterhood of All Saints, founded in England about 1857, came Helen Bowden, Sister Helen, who founded Bellevue Hospital Training School for Nurses. The Girls' Friendly Society, founded in 1875 in England by Mrs. M. G. Townsend, to bring together Christian ladies and working girls, was introduced into this country by Mrs. Owen Thomas. The Girls' Letter Gild, to bring cultured Christian women into correspondence with working girls, founded in England in 1889, was introduced into America in 1892 by Miss F. Wadleigh. Movements analagous to these of the Anglican communion are now taking form in other denominations. The order of The King's Daughters, founded in 1886 by Mrs. Margaret Bottome (see YOUNG PEOPLE'S SOCIETIES, IV.) has spread into all countries where Protestant churches are found. The rise of Sunday-schools (q.v.) opened a wide field for women's service in the Church, a field of increasing usefulness now that ·the importance of special training for this work is being recognized. It is hardly more than a century since the right and the necessity of the higher education for women—unquestioned in the early Church, and the secret of much of its usefulness—became recognized by modern civilization. In no sense due to the Church, yet to Christian women it is due that that right has again been won. The name of Mary Lyon stands first among these women, and by her side must stand the names of Emma Willard and Alice Freeman Palmer. Elizabeth Blackwell and Alice Jex Blake opened the doors of the medical profession to women, with all that this involves of blessing upon the mission field. The rise of modern missions had already opened to women a sphere of growing importance. The names of Harriet Newell, of Ann Hasseltine Judson, Emily Chubbock Judson, Fidelia Fiske, Eliza Everett, of the English Anne and Alice Mackenzie, and of A. L. O. E. (i.e., A Lady of England), Miss Charlotte Tucker (aunt of the Salvation Army officer, Booth-Tucker), whose pen did much to interest England in the evangelization of India, mark the first half of the century. In 1834 a little company of Englishwomen formed the Society for Promoting Female Education in the East. Fidelia Fiske introduced girls' schools into Persia; Sarah L. Huntington, the first wife of Dr. Eli Smith, first taught Syrian women to read. In 1860 Mrs. Bowen Thompson founded the British Syrian Schools. In 1862 Lady Kinnaird organized the India Female Normal School and Instruction Society, out of which sprang the Church of England Zenana Missionary Society, and the Zenana Bible and Medical Mission. Pandita Ramabai (q.v.) of India has done a remarkable work for Hindu widows. Mrs. Anna Satthianadhan in 1863 began zenana work in Madras. Her daughter-in-law, Mrs. S. (Krupabai) Satthianadhan, has rendered effective missionary service with her pen. Up to 1880 the idea of unmarried women in the mission field was coldly received notwithstanding some brilliant examples of such service, but in 1894 there were about 1,000 more women than men in mission work. Geraldine Guinness (Mrs. Howard Taylor, of the China Inland Mission) has done much to arouse missionary interest and consecration among the women of England and America.

The initiative in woman's medical missions was taken by Mrs. Sarah J. Hale of Philadelphia about 1838, but a long struggle was involved to complete the movement. The first woman medical missionary was Dr. Swain, who went to India in 1870; the names of Dr. Mary Niles in China, Dr. Mary Patrick in Turkey, Dr. Mary P. Eddy in Syria, are conspicuous.

In 1860 Mrs. Anna Mason of Assam, coming home on furlough, inspired Mrs. Caroline Doremus with the thought of organizing women for mission work. In 1861 Mrs. Doremus formed the Woman's Union Missionary Society. Denominational women's missionary societies came later. The contributions of all these in twenty-eight years aggregated $13,500,000. For Home Missions (q.v.) in the United States between 1876 and 1893 seventeen women's societies were formed. The names of Sue MacBeth and Alice Fletcher among Indians, of Joanna Moore among negroes, and of Emilia Brewer among the poor whites of the South may be mentioned among hundreds of heroic workers.

The rapid development of the principles of church federation permitting concerted action between women of all denominations will surely result in bringing back to strengthen the Church many of those feminine activities which are truly Christian, though by the necessities of the case not now in the Church.   LOUISE SEYMOUR HOUGHTON.

BIBLIOGRAPHY: Besides the literature under DEACONESS, consult: H. Grégoire, De l'influence du christianisme sur la condition des femmes, Paris, 1821; J. Kavanagh, Women of Christianity, Exemplary for Piety and Charity, new ed., London, 1859; W. Landels, Woman's Sphere and Work Considered in the Light of Scripture, 7th ed., ib. 1866; C. E. Stephen, The Service of the Poor, ib. 1871; W. Welsh, Women Helpers in the Church, their Sayings and Doings, Philadelphia, 1872; H. C. G. Moule, Public Ministry of Women, London, 1892; Baroness Burdett-Coutts, Woman's Mission, New York, 1893; W. de L. Love, St. Paul and Woman, ib. 1894; Lina Eckenstein, Woman under Monasticism, Cambridge, 1896; E. Modersohn, Die Frauen des Alten Testaments . . . des Neuen Testaments, 2 vols., Mülheim, 1903–06; E. F. von der Goltz, Der Dienst der Frau in der christlichen Kirche, Potsdam, 1905; J. Donaldson, Woman; her Position and Influence in Ancient Greece and Rome, and among the Early Christians, London, 1907; H. Merz, Christliche Frauenbilder, 6th ed., Stuttgart, 1907; L. Stöcker, Die Frau in der alten Kirche, Tübingen, 1907; F. Wilke, Das Frauenideal und die Schätzung des Weibes im Alten Testament, Leipsic, 1907; F. Harrison, Realities and Ideals· Social, Political, Literary and Artistic, New York, 1908; M. Löhr, Die Stellung des Weibes zu Jahwe-Religion und Kult, Leipsic 1908; A. D. Sertillanges, Feminisme et Christianisme, Paris, 1908; J. Apolant, Stellung und Mitarbeit der Frau in der Gemeinde, Leipsic, 1910; S. Coit, Woman in Church and State, London, 1910; J. W. von Walter, Frauenlos und Frauenarbeit in der Geschichte des Christentums, Leipsic, 1911; C. L. Brace, Gesta Christi, chap. xi., new issue, London and New York, 1911; G. Bäumer, Die Frau und das geistige Leben, Leipsic, 1911.

WOOD, NATHAN EUSEBIUS: Baptist; b. at Forrestville, N. Y., June 6, 1849. He was graduated from Chicago University (A.B., 1872) and the Baptist Union Theological Seminary, Chicago (1875); was pastor of Centennial Baptist Church, Chicago (1875–77); principal of Wayland Academy, Beaver Dam, Wis. (1877–83); held pastorates at Memorial Baptist Church, Chicago (1883–86); Strong Place Baptist Church, Brooklyn (1886–92); Brookline, Mass. (1892–94), and the First Baptist Church, Boston (1894–99); and was president of Newton Theological Institution, Newton Center, Mass. (1899–1908). He is president of the Northern Baptist Education Society, chairman of the executive committee of the American Baptist Missionary Union, and a member of the executive board of the American Baptist Home Missionary Society and of the American Baptist Education Society. In theology he is moderately conservative, and has edited J. R. Boise's Exegetical Notes on the Greek Epistles of the Apostle Paul (New York, 1896), and has written History of the First Baptist Church of Boston, Mass. (Philadelphia, 1899).

WOODCOCK, CHARLES EDWARD: Protestant Episcopal bishop of Kentucky; b. at New Britain, Conn., June 12, 1854. He was educated by private tutors and was graduated from Berkeley Divinity School, Middletown, Conn. (1882). He was curate of Grace Church, Baltimore (1882–84); rector of the Church of the Ascension, New Haven, Conn. (1884–88); Christ Church, Ansonia, Conn. (1888–1900); and St. John's, Detroit, Mich. (1900–1905). In 1905 he was consecrated bishop of Kentucky.

WOODROW, JAMES: Presbyterian; b. at Carlisle, England, May 30, 1828; d. at Columbia, S. C., Jan. 17, 1907. He was educated at Jefferson College, Cannonsburg, Pa. (A.B., 1849), Lawrence Scientific School, Harvard (1853), and the University of Heidelberg (Ph.D., 1856), after which he spent an additional year of study in Europe. He was professor of natural science in Oglethorpe University, Milledgeville, Ga., in 1853–61, and in 1861 was appointed professor of natural science in connection with revelation in the Presbyterian Theological Seminary at Columbia, S. C. In 1884 he was deposed from his position on account of the views which he advocated regarding evolution, but the action was not sustained by the controlling synods, and in the following year he was officially informed by the board, which had been remodeled in the mean time, that he had not been removed, but was still in office, whereupon he resumed his duties as chairman of the faculty and professor. He was chief of the laboratory of the medical department of the Confederate Army at Columbia, S. C., in 1863–65, and was also professor of natural science in South Carolina College, Columbia, S. C., in 1869–72 and again in 1880–97, while from 1891 to 1897, when he retired, he was president of the same institution. He was editor and proprietor of the quarterly *Southern Presbyterian Review* (1861–1885) and of the weekly *Southern' Presbyterian* (1865–93).

WOODS, HENRY GEORGE: Church of England; b. at Wood End, Northamptonshire, June 16, 1842. He was educated at Corpus Christi College, Oxford (B.A., 1865), and was connected with Trinity College, Oxford, as fellow (1865–87), tutor (1866–80), bursar (1865–87), and president (1887–1897), besides being senior proctor of the university in 1877–78. Since 1898 he has been honorary fellow of Trinity. He was ordered deacon in 1866 and ordained priest in the following year. In 1900–04 he was rector of Little Gaddesden, Herts, and chaplain and librarian to Earl Brownlow, Ashridge, and since 1904 has been master of the Temple, London. In theology he is a moderate Broad churchman, and has prepared an annotated edition of the first two books of Herodotus (2 vols., London, 1873).

WOODS, LEONARD: American Congregationalist; b. at Princeton, Mass., June 19, 1774; d. at Andover, Mass., Aug. 24, 1854. He was graduated from Harvard College, 1796; taught for a while, and studied theology at Somers, Conn.; was ordained 1798, and was pastor at Newbury, Mass., 1798–1808, when he became professor of theology at Andover Seminary, and was made professor emeritus, 1846. He then devoted himself to a *History of Andover Seminary*, which was published (Boston, 1885), and to preparing his lectures for the press. He was one of the founders of the American Tract Society, the American Education Society, American Temperance Society, and the American Board of Commissioners for Foreign Missions. He was a champion of orthodox Calvinism against the assaults of Ware, Buckminster, and Channing. His writings embrace *Letters to Unitarians* (Andover, 1820); *Reply to Dr. Ware's Letters to Trinitarians and Calvinists* (1821); *Remarks on Dr. Ware's Answer* (1822); *Lectures on the Inspiration of the Scriptures* (1829); *Lectures on Infant Baptism* (1829); *Lectures on Church Government* (New York, 1844); *Lectures on Swedenborgianism* (1846); *Theology of the Puritans* (Boston, 1851). He published a collective edition of his works (5 vols., Andover, 1849–50; 2d ed., Boston, 1851).

BIBLIOGRAPHY: W. B. Sprague, *Annals of the American Pulpit*, ii. 438–444, New York, 1859; A. E. Dunning, *Congregationalists in America*, passim, ib. 1894; W. Walker, in *American Church History Series*, iii. 351 sqq., ib. 1894; idem, *Ten New England Leaders*, pp. 360–405, ib. 1901; F. H. Foster, *New England Theology*, passim, Chicago, 1907.

WOODS, LEONARD, JR.: Congregationalist and educator; b. in Newbury, Mass., Nov. 24, 1807; d. in Boston Dec. 24, 1878. He was graduated from Union College, 1827, and from Andover Seminary, 1830; was resident graduate scholar at Andover for a year; was ordained, 1833; editor of *The New York Literary and Theological Review*, 1834–37; professor of sacred literature in Bangor Theological Seminary, 1836–39; and president of Bowdoin College, Me., 1839–66. In 1867 he visited Europe, under a commission to secure materials for a documentary history of Maine. He had the assistance of J. G. Kohl of Bremen, and the result of his work was the procuring of the Hakluyt manuscript of the *Westerne Planting*, and the publication of the *Discovery of Maine* (Portland, 1868). His only independent theological publication was his translation of George C. Knapp's *Lectures on Christian Theology* (2 vols., New York and Andover, 1831–33). He was famous for oratory, and even more remarkable for his conversational gifts.

BIBLIOGRAPHY: The *Memorial Discourse* by C. C. Everett is in *Collections of the Maine Historical Society*, vol. viii., Portland, Me., 1881; and Professor Park's *Memorial Sermon* was published at Andover, 1879.

WOOLSEY, THEODORE DWIGHT: American Congregationalist; b. in New York Oct. 31, 1801; d. in New Haven, Conn., July 1, 1889. He was graduated from Yale College, 1820; studied law for a year in Philadelphia, and theology at Princeton Theological Seminary, N. J., 1821–23; was a tutor at Yale College, 1823–25; was licensed to preach, 1825; and studied the Greek language and literature in Germany, France, and Italy, 1827–30. Returning to the United States, he was professor of Greek at Yale, 1831–46, when he was chosen president; in 1871 he resigned and withdrew from public life. He was an authority on international law, and was also a member of the American Company of Revision of the New Testament, and its chairman, 1871–81. He had extended literary interests, but his works pertaining to theology were *Religion of the Present and of the Future: Sermons preached chiefly at Yale College* (New York, 1871); *Helpful Thoughts for Young Men* (Boston, 1874); and *Communism and Socialism in their History and Theory: A Sketch* (New York, 1880); his chief work was the standard *Introduction to the Study of International Law, designed as an Aid in Teaching and in Historical Studies* (Boston, 1860); and *Essays on Divorce and Divorce Legislation, with Special Reference to the United States* (New York, 1869).

BIBLIOGRAPHY: An excellent appreciation by J. Cooper is found in the *Bibliotheca Sacra*, lvi (1899), 607–638.

WOOLSTON, THOMAS. See DEISM, I., § 5.

WORCESTER, ELWOOD: Protestant Episcopalian; b. at Massilon, O., May 16, 1862. He was graduated from Columbia University (B.A., 1886), the General Theological Seminary (1887), and the University of Leipsic (Ph.D., 1889); was ordered deacon in 1890 and priested in the following year; was assistant at St. Ann's, Brooklyn (1888–90), chaplain and professor of philosophy at Lehigh University (1890–96), acting rector of St. John's, Dresden, Germany (1894–95), and rector of St. Stephen's, Philadelphia (1896–1904), since 1904 of Emmanuel Church, Boston, where he has introduced the so-called " Emmanuel Movement," for the cure of ailments physical or mental wherein the influence of mind is a factor. He has written *Genesis in the Light of Modern Knowledge* (New York, 1898); *Religion and Medicine* (1908); *The Living Word* (1908); and *The Christian Religion as a Healing Power* (1909; in collaboration with S. McComb).

WORCESTER, JOHN: Church of the New Jerusalem; b. in Boston Feb. 13, 1834; d. at Newtonville, Mass., May 2, 1900. He became pastor of the New Church Society at Newtonville, Mass., 1869; instructor in theology in the New Church Theological School, Boston, 1878, and its president, 1881. His works embrace *A Year's Lessons from the Psalms* (Boston, 1869); *Correspondences of the Bible: the Animals* (1875; new ed., extended, 3 vols., 1884–89); and *Lectures upon the Doctrines of the New Church* (1886).

WORCESTER, NOAH: Unitarian; b. at Hollis, N. H., Nov. 25, 1758; d. at Brighton (now part of Cambridge), Mass., Oct. 31, 1837. After serving for some time in the Continental army (1775–77), being present at the battles of Bunker Hill and Bennington, he taught for four years (1778–82) at Plymouth, N. H., and then settled at Thornton, N. H., where he was town clerk, justice of the peace, and member of the legislature. In 1786, just after having published at Newburyport his *Letter to the Rev. John Murray Concerning the Origin of Evil*, he was licensed as a Congregational minister, and in the following year was ordained to the church at Thornton, where he remained until 1802. From this year until 1810 he was missionary for the newly established New Hampshire Missionary Society, and as its first chosen evangelist traveled throughout the wildest portions of the state. In 1810–13 he was supply for his brother's church at Salisbury, N. H., but his *Bible News, or Sacred Truths Relating to the Living God, his only Son, and Holy Spirit* (Concord, 1810) was censured by the Hopkinsians as anti-Trinitarian, though he sought to defend his position in his *Impartial Review of the Testimonies in Favor of the Divinity of the Son of God* (1810). Two years later he issued at Boston his *Respectful Address to the Trinitarian Clergy*, which so attracted the Unitarian party headed by W. E. Channing (q.v.) that Worcester was invited to become the editor of the newly founded *Christian Disciple* (later *The Christian Examiner*). He accordingly removed to Brighton, where the remainder of his life was passed, editing *The Christian Disciple* in 1813–18 and the quarterly *Friend of Peace* in 1819–29. As a result of his *Solemn Review of the Custom of War*, published under the pseudonym of " Philo Pacificus " (Cambridge, 1814), he was able, in 1815, to establish the Massachusetts Peace Society, of which he was secretary until 1828.

In addition to the works already mentioned, Worcester wrote *Familiar Dialogue between Cephas and Bereas* (Worcester, 1792); *Solemn Reasons for Declining to Accept the Baptist Theory and Practice* (Charlestown, 1809); *The Atoning Sacrifice a Display of Love, not of Wrath* (Cambridge, 1829); *The Causes and Evils of Contentions among Christians* (Boston, 1831); and *Last Thoughts on Important Subjects* (Cambridge, 1833); besides many sermons, tracts, and contributions to *The Theological Magazine* and other religious publications.

BIBLIOGRAPHY: H. Ware, Jr., *Memoirs of Noah Worcester*, Boston, 1844; W. B. Sprague, *Annals of the American Unitarian Pulpit*, pp.191–199, New York, 1865.

WORCESTER, SAMUEL: Trinitarian Congregationalist; b. in Hollis, N. H., Nov. 1, 1770; d. at Brainerd, Tenn., June 7, 1821. He was graduated from Dartmouth College, 1795; licensed to preach, 1796; was pastor of the Congregational church at Fitchburg, Mass., 1797–1802; and was pastor of the Tabernacle church in Salem, Mass., 1803–21. He was a man of clear mind, firm will, and steadfast Christian principles. In 1821, for the sake of his health, he made a visit to the South, to the missionary stations among the Cherokee and Choctaw Indians, where he died.

Dr. Worcester was distinguished by the vast amount of labor which he performed in connection with the foreign missionary enterprise. Either he or Dr. Samuel Spring, or both together, originated the idea of forming the American Board of Commissioners for Foreign Missions, and were intimately associated with it. The detailed plan of the board was doubtless formed mainly by Dr. Worcester. He wrote the first ten, which are in some respects most important, annual reports of this society.

As an author he was noted for his logical acumen, and vigorous, pointed style. Besides his sermons, reviews, and essays, he published three controversial *Letters to Rev. Dr. William E. Channing* (Boston, 1815).

BIBLIOGRAPHY: S. M. Worcester (his son), *Life and Labors of Rev. Samuel Worcester*, 2 vols., Boston, 1852; W. B. Sprague, *Annals of the American Pulpit*, ii. 398–407, New York, 1859; W. Walker, in *American Church History Series*, vol. iii. passim, ib. 1894; idem, *Ten New England Leaders*, pp. 388–389, ib. 1901.

WORD OF GOD.

Use of the Term (§ 1).   Inspiration (§ 4).
The Gospel (§ 2).   Word and Spirit (§ 5).
Preaching (§ 3).   Law and Gospel (§ 6).

The term word of God refers, in the immediate sense, not to the Bible, but to the word in general, in so far as it is a means of grace or of religious influence. The Christian religion is the spiritual communion of man and God or the personal intercourse of God and man. Words are the sole means for transmitting ideas or impulses of will from person to person.

1. Use of the Term.

Inasmuch as sensuous beings can communicate only through a sense medium, the audible, articulate word may lend itself also to the soul life in communication with other spirits. The soul may also employ the medium of visions, and transmit its effects by symbols and illustrations; but these rather represent moods and feelings and require words for their definite formulation, like the sacraments. Likewise an intercourse between God and man presupposes a word of God employed in some way by him. In the Old Testament the lawgiver reports the word of God and the prophet imparts what the word of Yahweh has revealed. Christ commissions his disciples to preach the word, guided by the Holy Spirit (Matt. x. 7, 20, xxviii. 20; John vi. 63); the increase of Christianity is a growth of the word (Acts vi. 7, xii. 24, xix. 20). Christ's word must dwell richly among Christians (Col. iii. 16); "faith cometh by hearing, and hearing by the word of God" (Rom. x. 17; cf. Gal. iii. 2 sqq.). In the ancient Church salvation is offered and preserved through the word; but gradually the sacraments, as independent factors of salvation, take their place alongside; and ultimately they become the real means of grace in the Roman Catholic Church for which the word was efficacious only in a preparatory and concomitant sense. The scholastics indulged in elaborate developments of the sacraments as instruments of grace with only incidental references to the significance of the word of God. The Reformation from the first laid its emphasis on the word as the essential medium of the divine operation in man. Hence the chief function of the Church was the preaching of the Gospel, followed by the Scriptural use of the sacraments. By word of God was meant primarily not the language of the Bible, but the orally proclaimed Biblical truth.

The word of God as a means of grace is, therefore, the published Gospel of Christ, through which the divine revelation enters the human heart. This word begets faith, and reciprocally faith works the word of God, so that the **2. The Gospel.** Church is essentially edified and sustained, and the word, as means of grace, becomes the expression of its life. This argues that in every period the word has a particular form and a common content; which applies equally to the periods of historical development and the contemporary life of the Christian community. This assertion is true, however, only of the essence of the Gospel. The traditional generally prevails, yet every successive age impresses its own peculiar interest; for the Gospel must adapt itself in every case to the interpretation of the individual period or person. This extreme adaptability and plasticity, even while involving the danger of misinterpretation, yet renders the teachings of the Gospel available and permanent through all ages and to all men under all conditions. It is indeed possible that misinterpretation may be carried to such a degree that, as among the Gnostics, the word can no longer produce Christian faith, so that it ceases to be the word of God; and it is equally possible that an unbeliever or a hypocrite may preach the word (cf. Phil. i. 18). In the latter case attention and faith may be aroused, so that the preaching of such individuals (who may even momentarily be moved by a certain impulse or excitement in their preaching) is really thinkable as the divine word, unless their true character be perceived, and the efficacy of their preaching be thus impaired. The word of God must not be considered as restricted to formal preaching; it includes all discussion in private intercourse, attesting the divine truth among teachers, pupils, and friends, such as is essential to the Christian life.

That the preaching of the Gospel is the word of God may either be proved empirically and then historically, or its self-attestation by the inherent power of God may be accepted. Christ had taught his disciples that their preaching was **3. Preach-** to be of the Spirit of God (Matt. x. 20), **ing.** and Paul attributed to the Gospel the divine efficacy which had been lacking in the Law (Rom. i. 16); the word of God is "the sword of the Spirit" (Eph. vi. 17). Paul's preaching was "in demonstration of the Spirit and of power," so that the faith wrought thereby depended not on the wisdom of men, but the power of God (I Cor. ii. 4–5). The Christian accordingly speaks "as the oracles of God" (I Pet. iv. 11), and the word penetrates into man's inmost depths (Heb. iv. 12), being the seed whereby God forms man into a new creature (Jas. i. 18; I Pet. i. 23–25). It is evident, therefore, that the Holy Spirit is active with his almighty power in the human word. This was the position assumed by the Reformation. God speaks through preaching and works upon the human heart. The medium of preaching is a complex of ideas, appealing to the practical human reason, which this may either reject or disregard as contrary to the natural sense, but nevertheless they obtain their control not by a perception of their correctness and utility, but by the experience of their overmastering power. The complex of ideas proves to be the expression of the single, personal will of God for the redemption of man. This personal presence is described in Scripture as the Spirit of God. Christ is the Spirit of God (II Cor. iii. 17) in the sense of substituting the single personal will as the object of the joint activity of the Church for the pervading spiritual energy. Spoken to arouse attention and understanding, the word, subject to the personal impression and adaptability of the hearer, is the organ of the activities of the Holy Spirit.

The Spirit, then, issues from the word to man; but the word, though constant in essence, in form, and substance, is subject to historical limitations. Particular persons delivered it in specially Hebraic types of thought. These words produce spiritual results; hence, they **4. Inspira-** must have originated from the Spirit **tion.** through their early proclaimers. The same holds true of the human words of Jesus as well as of his earlier witnesses, and those of the relevant witnesses of Israel. This responsive operation of divine revelation upon the human soul may well be termed Inspiration (q.v.). Whatever be the basis of this inspiration, whether an actual fact, an event in history, a vision, or some experience of the soul, it is always some incitation from without, which man must understand and render intelligible by means of words. In the case of the apostles each gave expression to his experience from his own personal point of view. Consequently, the real subject of inspiration is the understanding issuing from the experience of the revelation together with the competence and the interest to express it intelligibly (I Cor. ii. 12); and, likewise, not the natural science of the historical facts or even of the laws of the natural process is inspired, but only the realizations and judgments. This rules out all verbal inspiration. Inspiration transpired in the gifts of knowledge, wisdom, prophecy, and the "discernment of spirits" (I Cor. xii. 8–10). The coherent complex of ideas and judgments in which inspiration has obtained expression constitutes revelation in the objective sense; while the sum of the divine acts introduced as real facts and events into history constitutes the same as revealing activity. Revelation (q.v.) is disclosed in accordance with the gradual historical development of the human spirit; not that revelation and such historical development are identical, but that the spirit appropriates revelation after its order in progressive development. This revelation is preserved historically in the sources of the revelation period. The Bible is the historical report of this period and contains essentially the inspired complex of ideas with an interpretation of its given history and related facts. The Holy Spirit has brought to pass a revelation and led to its interpretation, which is the word of God attested to faith by its internal power. The word of God is primarily so called because by this form of human speech the divine Spirit is perceived as operative upon the human heart. Religious experience accordingly forms the test of the true word. On the other hand, the word of God is such by virtue of divine revelation and inspiration. The process whereby the spirit becomes word is "immediate revelation"; that whereby word becomes spirit is "mediate revelation." In both cases the actual content of revelation is the same, for what the prophets and apostles experienced and put in words is experienced and received by man to-day in so far as their words communicate the same to him with divine power. Subjectively, the word is adjudged to be the word of God because the Spirit is operative in it; objectively the word is seen to bring the Spirit because it is of the Spirit. Both aspects find their confirmation in the New Testament. Christ spoke the words of God because he had received the Spirit in immeasurable degree (John iii. 34); and his revelation follows from his relation to the Father (Matt. xi. 27). The words of Paul were taught by the Spirit (I Cor. ii. 10, 13); the Gospel which he preached, however, came from Christ himself (cf. I Tim. vi. 3). The "words of faith" and "commands of doctrine" (Barnabas xvi. 9; cf. I Tim. iv. 6, v. 17), "the faith which was once delivered unto the saints" (Jude 3) and "sound doctrine" (I Tim. i. 10; II Tim. iv. 3) were the chief themes of Gospel preaching, which, however, was held to be derived, in all essentials, from the risen Christ (Matt. xxviii. 18 sqq.; Luke xxiv. 44 sqq.). The recognized relation between the preached word and the word of primitive Christianity necessarily implies that the latter was the source of the former, but the word as preached can never be a mere reproduction of the word as contained in the Bible, being the interpretation given by each period to the Bible. Wherefore the Church properly requires that the Scripture must always remain as the norm of preaching. This does not imply, however, an excessive literalness, but only a general conformity of spirit with spirit. While the Bible also serves the individual for edification, he understands it in the light of the preached word which is itself made more vivid. The employment of the Bible as the critical norm of prevailing views in the Church is a matter only for the joint effort of the Church and free theological science.

The problem of the connection of word and spirit next arises. The distinction between word and spirit appears first in Augustine, who taught, in contrast with the audible word, the inner word, which is the Spirit, working in the hearts of the elect, producing faith. Medieval theology, preoccupied by a similar distinction in the sacraments, lost sight of the problem. Luther, in reference to Ps. xxxviii. 2, recalled the position of Augustine; so that, according to him, the Spirit works only in and through the word, though his view was never worked out theoretically. The Reformed theologians, after the manner of Augustine, tended more toward a separation of the two. Martin Butzer antagonized Luther's position as Thomism; and Calvin, who gave the normative view to Reformed theology, held that God converts by the Spirit, without omitting the instrument of his word. The word incites toward regeneration, but the Spirit illumines, moves, and renews the heart. "God works in a twofold way upon his elect, by the Spirit within, and by the word without." The universal calling is by the latter; the special calling of the elect is by the illumination of the former. A third form of the relation of word and Spirit is the "inner word" of the mystics in its twofold form: (1) the Spirit operates without any relation to the outer word; and (2) in the depths of the soul the Spirit dwells as the light of reason or conscience. The Rahtmann controversy (see RAHTMANN, HERMANN) led to a clearer outline. Rahtmann taught that the Scriptures constituted a testimony of God's will and acts, which God inspired in the apostles and prophets. They, containing the image of God's being and will, were a guide toward the attainment of an aim, without, however, affording the power to reach it, which was to be furnished by the Spirit. The orthodox reply was to the effect that the Spirit was immanent in Scripture; potentially the Spirit was always in the word, actually only when rightly employed. Upon closer inspection both views contain genuine elements; for though the Spirit must be understood as ever potentially present, this is not to be taken in an abstract sense but as the will of redemption. The word is God's word not only as to its objective content but also in the impact of man on man within the Christian body. The Spirit is objectively present in the complex of ideas of revelation as well as in its particular interpretation and application, and neither excludes the other.

5. Word and Spirit.

Thus far the word of God has been considered as identical with the Gospel. From an early period, however, it has been customary to divide the word into the Law, which commands, and the Gospel, which promises and fulfils. The two may be easily confounded with the division of the Old and New Testaments; but the former also contains Gospel, while the latter holds commandments likewise; in fact the Gospel has been termed the "new law" from the time of the Fathers. Following the Reformers the law as offering the commandments to sinful man and inducing him to repentance, and the Gospel inspiring faith and affording, as its content, pardon and the works of the Spirit, have been sharply distinguished. The Law and the Gospel stand in the relation of two stages of religious development, apparently making every individual experience the counterpart of the religious development as a whole. However, the same word may work on the same individual both as Law and Gospel; the cross of Christ may judge as well as forgive. A correct distinction within the limits of the Christian faith can be drawn only from the individual experience produced by the preaching of the word. Unable to be conscious of the word as a vital power, the natural or unbelieving man receives it as a new outlook on the universe or a new morality, assuming it as addressed to the practical reason for ethical realization. What he infers from the word is the obligation of a faith of assent and obedience to the new law, but he is unable to exercise the faith and love required. Thus the word may be said to confront him with his sin, the word of God proclaimed being assumed as authority. Hence the conjunction of the law with certain natural moral tendencies may subject man to a double bondage. More important is it that the nascent Christian should gain a sense of the presence of the Spirit through the word; and as the power of the Spirit gains greater and greater ascendency, the word ceases to be a merely external authority and becomes a living, inwardly experienced, and truly believed authority. The loving Father is actually realized in the word, and its whole content is found to be but a component of the single will of God. Man receives a new life in the fellowship into which God inducts him. In this double boon of the inner gift and the forgiveness of God man experiences the divine grace, brought to the soul by the word as Gospel. Such experience is the fulfilment of the moral and religious needs of the soul. The word redeems and thereby approves itself as the word of God. It is wholly correct that the regenerate Christian requires also the discipline of the law; for the Christian good experienced in its power becomes a norm for all his conduct. In this sense the word remains moral law, though only as inward authority spiritually recognized. Not according to an outward order but a necessity determining the inner psychological motives, the Christian experiences in the Gospel not only the vivifying motive power of the divine Spirit, but obtains also the norm of his moral activity. The personal efficient divine presence in man is capable of stimulating a large scope of thoughts, resolutions, and volutions, but whether in the learned intellectual processes or the moral law of Christianity, this internal possession will fall short of accomplishment except as it becomes the fixed efficient norm against opposing thoughts and tendencies. See also REVELATION.   (R. SEEBERG.)

6. Law and its Gospel.

BIBLIOGRAPHY. The literature of this subject is comprised in that in and under the articles on BIBLE, BIBLICAL CRITICISM, BIBLICAL INTRODUCTION, BIBLICAL THEOLOGY, INSPIRATION, and REVELATION. The subject is discussed in all the principal systems of systematic divinity (see DOGMA, DOGMATICS). Reference may be made here to J. Müller, *Dogmatische Abhandlungen*, pp. 127–277, Bremen, 1870; R. Grützmacher, *Wort und Geist*, Leipsic, 1902; and R. Seeberg, *Offenbarung und Inspiration*, Gross Lichterfelde, 1908.

WORDSWORTH, CHARLES Bishop of St. Andrew's, Dunkeld, and Dunblane, Episcopal Church in Scotland, second son of Christopher Wordsworth (q.v., no. 1); b. at Lambeth (2 m. s. of Charing Cross, London) Aug. 22, 1806; d. at St. Andrew's (9 m. s.e. of Dundee), Scotland, Dec. 5, 1892. He was a student of Sevenoaks school, and at Harrow, and then of Christ Church College, Oxford (B.A., 1830); took the prize for Latin verse, 1827, and for the Latin essay, 1831; was ordained deacon 1834, priest 1840; was a private tutor for several years, and had under his instruction both Mr. Gladstone and Cardinal Manning; was second master of Winchester College, 1835–46; warden of Trinity College, Glenalmond, Perthshire, 1847–1854; and in 1853 was consecrated bishop. He had a strong faculty for teaching. As bishop he endeavored to prevent the capture of the Scottish Episcopal church by a narrow party, to make manifest to Scotsmen the value of Episcopacy and Episcopal ordinances, and to concede somewhat to Presbyterians, whereby they might be conciliated. He was a stanch upholder of the synodal system and of the duty of establishment of religion. The diocese developed considerably during his episcopate. He was a member of the New Testament Company of Bible Revisers, and was a fellow at Winchester, 1866–71. He published a Greek grammar (London, 1839), and his theological works, outside of a number of volumes of, and individual, sermons, embrace, *Catechetical Questions* (1844); *What is National Humiliation without National Repentance* (Glasgow, 1855); *On Shakespeare's Knowledge and Use of the Bible* (London, 1864); *Outlines of the Christian Ministry* (1872); *Three Conclusive Proofs that the Use of the Eastward Position in the Celebration of the Holy Eucharist is contrary to the . . . Intention of our Reformed Church* (1876); *Some Remarks on the Essay by Dr. Lightfoot . . . on the Christian Ministry* (1879); *Annals of my Early Life* (1891); *Primary Witness to the Truth of the Gospel. A Series of Discourses* (1892); and *Annals of my Life*, ed. W. Earl Hodgson (1893).

BIBLIOGRAPHY: Besides his own *Annals* (ut sup., 2 vols.), consult: John Wordsworth, *Episcopate of Charles Wordsworth*, London, 1899; *DNB*, lxiii. 1–7.

WORDSWORTH, CHRISTOPHER: Name of three Anglican scholars.

1. Biographer, younger brother of the poet William Wordsworth; b. at Cockermouth (23 m. s.w. of Carlisle) June 9, 1774; d. at Buxted (39 m. s.s.e. of London) Feb. 2, 1846. He was graduated at Trinity College, Cambridge (B.A., 1796; fellow, 1798; M.A., 1799; D.D., 1810); became rector of Ashby with Oby and Thinne (1804); domestic chaplain to the archbishop of Canterbury (1805); rector of Woodchurch, Kent (1806), of Bocking, Essex (1808), St. Mary's, Lambeth, and Sundridge, Kent (1816); chaplain of the House of Commons (1817); and rector of Buxted-with-Uckfield, Sussex (1820); he was master of Trinity College from 1820 till 1841, when he retired to Buxted. He is best remembered for his *Ecclesiastical Biography; or, Lives of Eminent Men connected with the History of Religion in England from the Commencement of the Reformation to the Revolution* (London, 1810, 6 vols.; 4th ed., 1853, 4 vols.), and for his *Who Wrote ΕΙΚΩΝ ΒΑΣΙΛΙΚΗ?* (1824), a defense of King Charles' claim to be the author of *Eikon Basilike*. He was also the author of two volumes of *Sermons* (1814), and edited *Christian Institutes: a Series of Discourses and Tracts selected from the Writings of the most eminent Divines of the English Church* (4 vols., 1836).

2. Youngest son of the preceding, bishop of Lincoln, and commentator; b. at Bocking (38 m. n.e. of London) Oct. 30, 1807; d. at Lincoln Mar. 21, 1885. He was educated at Winchester and at Trinity College, Cambridge (B.A., 1830; M.A., 1833; D.D., 1839); traveled in Greece (1832–33); was ordained deacon (1833), priest (1835); fellow of Trinity College, Cambridge (1830–36); public orator (1836); head master of Harrow School (1836–1844); canon of Westminster (1844–69); Hulsean lecturer, Cambridge (1847–48); vicar of Stanford-in-the-Vale, Berkshire, and rural dean (1850–69); archdeacon of Westminster (1865–69); consecrated bishop of Lincoln (1869). In the administration of his diocese he was noted for independence and extreme courage in carrying out his convictions; he caused a violent conflict with the Wesleyan Methodists by inviting them to "return" to the Church of England; was reversed in the privy council in his decision not to permit "Reverend" on the gravestone of a Wesleyan in a churchyard; and was besides pronouncedly anti-Roman. He took part in the Old Catholic Congress held at Cologne, Sept., 1872. He was the author of *Athens and Attica: Journal of a Residence there* (London, 1836); *Inscriptiones Pompeianæ: Ancient Writings copied from the Walls of the City of Pompeii* (1837); *Greece: Pictorial, Descriptive, and Historical* (1839; 8th ed., 1883); *Theophilus Anglicanus; or, Instructions concerning the Church and the Anglican Branch of it* (1843; 9th ed., 1865); *Discourses on Public Education* (1844); *Diary in France* (1845); *Letters to M. Goudon on the Destructive Character of the Church of Rome both in Religion and Polity* (1847); *Sequel to the Previou Letters* (1848); *Scripture Inspiration; or, On the Canon of Holy Scripture* (Hulsean lectures for 1847 1848); *On the Apocalypse; or, Book of Revelation* (Hulsean lecture for 1848; 1849); *Harmony of the Apocalypse* (1849); *The Apocalypse in Greek* (1849); *Memoirs of William Wordsworth* (2 vols., 1851); *S. Hippolytus and the Church of Rome in the Third Century, from the newly discovered "Philosophumena"* (1853; new ed., 1880); *The Greek New Testament, with Prefaces, Introductions, and Notes* (4 parts, 1856–60; 2d ed., 1872); occasional sermons preached in Westminster Abbey (1850–68); *On the Inspiration of the Bible* (1861); *The Holy Year; or, Original Hymns for Sundays and Holy Days* (1862); *The Old Testament in the Authorized Version, with Notes and Introductions* (6 vols., 1864–71; 2d ed., 1868–72); *Union with Rome: An Essay* (1867); *History of the Church of Ireland* (eight sermons; 1869); *Twelve Addresses at the Visitation of the Diocese and Cathedral of Lincoln* (1873); *On the Sale of Church Patronage; Irenicum Wesleyanum* (1876); *Diocesan Addresses at Visitation*

(1876); *Ethica et Spiritualia* (1877); *The Newtonian System: Its Analogy to Christianity* (1877); *Letters to Sir George Prevost, on Sisterhoods and Vows* (1878); *Ten Addresses at the Triennial Visitation* (1879); *Translations of the Pastoral Letters of Lambeth Conferences into Greek and Latin, Made by Desire of the Presiding Archbishops* (1868 and 1878); *A Church History to the Council of Chalcedon, A.D. 481* (4 vols., 1881–83; new ed., 1906); *Discourse on Scottish Church History* (1884); *Public Appeals in Behalf of Christian Liberty* (2 vols., 1886).

3. Historian; b. at Westminster, London, Mar. 26, 1848. He was educated at Trinity College, Cambridge (B.A., 1870), and was ordered deacon in 1871 and ordained priest in the following year; was fellow of Peterhouse, Cambridge (1870–78), where he was tutor (1872–74 and 1875–77); was curate of Alvechurch (1874–75), and of St. Giles, Cambridge (1875–77); rector of Glaston, Rutlandshire (1877–1889), Steeple with Tyneham, Dorsetshire (1889–1897), East Holme, Isle of Purbeck, Dorsetshire (1890–97), and since 1897 of St. Peter with St. Paul, Marlborough. He has also been prebendary of Liddington in Lincoln Cathedral since 1886, surrogate of the diocese of Salisbury since 1898, and rural dean of Marlborough Portion and examining chaplain to the bishop of Worcester since 1905. He has written or edited *Social Life at the English Universities in the Eighteenth Century* (Cambridge, 1874); *Scholæ Academicæ: Some Account of the Studies at the English Universities in the Eighteenth Century* (1877); *Breviarium ad Usum Sarum* (in collaboration with F. Procter; 3 vols., 1879–86); *Pontificale Ecclesiæ Sancti Andreæ* (Edinburgh, 1885); *Lincoln Cathedral Statutes* (3 vols., London, 1892–97); *Coronation of King Charles I.* (1892); *Tracts of Clement Maydeston* (1894); *Notes on Mediæval Services in England* (1898); *Ceremonies and Processions of the Cathedral Church of Salisbury* (1901); *Old Service-Books of the English Church* (in collaboration with H. Littlehales; 1904); and *Precedence of English Bishops and the Provincial Chapters* (1906).

BIBLIOGRAPHY: On 1: Charles Wordsworth, *Annals of my Early Life*, London, 1891; E. Churton, *Memoir of Joshua Watson*, Oxford, 1861; *DNB*, lxiii. 7–8. On 2: J. H. Overton and Elizabeth Wordsworth, *Christopher Wordsworth, Bishop of Lincoln*, London, 1888; J. H. Overton, *The Church in England*, ii. 399, 401, 415, ib. 1897; F. W. Cornish, *English Church in the 19th Century*, passim, ib. 1910; E. Stock, *English Church in the 19th Century*, passim, ib. 1910; *DNB*, lxiii. 9–10.

WORDSWORTH, JOHN: Church of England, bishop of Salisbury; b. at Harrow-on-the-Hill (11 m. n.w. of London), Middlesex, Sept. 21, 1843; d. in London Aug. 16, 1911. He was educated at New College, Oxford (B.A., 1863; M.A., 1868), and was ordered deacon in 1867 and ordained priest two years later; was assistant master of Wellington College (1866–67); was elected fellow of Brasenose College (1867), was tutor (1868–83); also prebendary of Langford Ecclesia in Lincoln Cathedral (1870–83), as well as chaplain of Brasenose College and examining chaplain to the bishop of Lincoln (his father); select preacher at Oxford (1875–77 and 1888–90), Grinfeld Lecturer on the Septuagint (1876–78), university preacher at Whitehall (1879), and Bampton Lecturer (1881); Oriel professor of the interpretation of Holy Scripture in Oxford University (1883–85), at the same time being fellow of Oriel College and canon of Rochester; in 1885 he was consecrated bishop of Salisbury. In 1872 he attended the Old Catholic Congress at Cologne, and from 1878 to 1883 spent much time in Italy, France, and Spain, collating manuscripts for an edition of the Vulgate New Testament. He did much to secure the practical settlement of the status of readers in the Anglican Church, and it was he who prepared the Latin draft of the *Responsio Archiepiscoporum Angliæ* (published in 1897) in reply to the papal bull of Sept. 13, 1896, denying the validity of Anglican orders. He wrote *Keble College and the Present University Crisis* (London, 1869); *Lectures Introductory to a Study of Latin Literature* (Oxford, 1870); *Fragments and Specimens of Early Latin* (1874); *University Sermons on Gospel Subjects* (1878); *The One Religion, Truth, Holiness, and Peace, Desired by the Nations and Revealed by Jesus Christ* (Bampton lectures; 1881); *Old Latin Biblical Texts* (in collaboration with W. Sanday and H. J. White; 2 vols., 1883–86); *Novum Testamentum Latine ad codicum manuscriptorum fidem* (in collaboration with H. J. White; 5 parts, comprising the Gospels and Acts, 1889–1905); *The Holy Communion* (London, 1891); *De validitate ordinum Anglicanorum* (Salisbury, 1894); *Trois lettres sur la position de l'église anglicane* (1894); *The Church of England and the Eastern Patriarchs* (Oxford, 1892); *On the Rite of Consecration of Churches* (with the Sarum form; London, 1899); *The Episcopate of Charles Wordsworth, Bishop of St. Andrews* (1899); *Bishop Sarapion's Prayer Book* (1899; rev. ed., 1910); *The Ministry of Grace* (1891; new ed., 1903); *The Baptismal Confession and the Creed* (London, 1904); *The Law of the Church and Marriage with a Deceased Wife's Sister* (1908); *The Invocation of Saints and the 22d Article* (1908); *Ordination Problems* (1909); and *Unity and Fellowship* (1910).

WORDSWORTH, WILLIAM: Poet-philosopher; b. at Cockermouth (24 m. s.w. of Carlisle), England, Apr. 7, 1770; d. at Rydal Mount (31 m. s. of Carlisle) Apr. 23, 1850. He was second son of John Wordsworth, attorney-at-law, and law agent for Sir James Lowther, afterward Earl of Lonsdale. His mother died in 1778, his father in 1783. He graduated from St. John's College, Cambridge, in 1791. He traveled extensively, making frequent visits to France, Switzerland, Italy, Germany, Holland, and Belgium, as well as Scotland and Wales, but made his home at Grasmere, 1799–1813, whither he brought his bride in 1802—and at Rydal Mount, 1813–50. By severe simplicity of life, by frugal husbanding of slender resources derived from legacies, later from additional income from a governmental office requiring but little personal attention (1813–43), recipient of a government annuity of £300 for literary distinction (1843–50), he was enabled to devote himself unremittingly to the vocation of poet to which he had early consecrated himself. At the Oxford Commemoration in 1839 the degree of LL.D. was conferred upon him. On the death of Southey in 1843 he became poet laureate. Near him dwelling in the Lake District there were at different periods Southey, Coleridge, Thomas

Arnold, De Quincy, and Prof. John Wilson (Christopher North). His sister Dorothy, a woman of rare insight and beauty of spirit, was his constant companion until her death. With the single exception of the "Ode composed on an evening of extraordinary splendor and beauty" (1818), all of his most memorable work was done between 1798 and 1808. He became the most illustrious representative of the Romantic movement in English poetry of the eighteenth and the first half of the nineteenth century. This was an extension of the wave of Romanticism (q.v.) in Germany and France, in which the spirit, revolting from the reign of reason in the Enlightenment and of classical form in literature, set out to vindicate the right and glory of feeling, imagination, art, and the spontaneous revelations of mystical consciousness. In Great Britain this phenomenon was rather an atmosphere, a reactionary attitude, characterized by a self-unconscious creative freedom, a new sense of the meaning of nature and of the mind of man in relation to nature, in which there was added to the feeling of beauty that of strangeness and mystery (cf. W. Pater, *Appreciations*, pp. 243 ff., London, 1889; W. L. Phelps, *The Beginnings of the English Romantic Movement*, Boston, 1893; A. Symons, *The Romantic Movement in English Poetry*, New York, 1909). In Wordsworth reappeared all the signs which have marked the mystics of all ages, from whatever angle they have approached reality—reliance on instinct, trust in emotion, confidence in the "inner light," and surrender to all the deepest impulses quickened by self-renunciation and silence. His relation to the mystics is evinced (1) in his austerity of life, his aloofness from the world, his purposed and unbroken freedom from distraction; (2) in his uninterrupted meditation on nature and human life, through concentration and absorption of attention attaining the rational vision of truth in which feeling becomes a direct source of illumination; (3) in the "beatific vision" which crowns his self-purification and all the intellectual and emotional stages of his experience (cf. *The Excursion*, bk. I., 197–218). Not Plotinus nor Bernard of Clairvaux was more truly detached from the cares and contaminations of the world, nor were these men surrounded by friends and conditions better suited to self-discipline, contemplation, and ecstasy. Like all mystics his attitude toward the world was pantheistic. He found divinity in all natural objects and in the mind of man. Man and nature formed a unity in which the mood of each—what was fairest and most interesting in each—was reflected in the other. Ecstasy was born of quietness and silence, and poetry, the spontaneous expression of concentrated and highly wrought feeling, originated from "emotion recollected in tranquillity." (Cf. Wordsworth's *Works*, "Preface to 'Lyrical Ballads,'" "Expostulation and Reply," "The Prelude," bk. II., "Lines composed a few miles above Tintern Abbey.") See MYSTICISM.   C. A. BECKWITH.

BIBLIOGRAPHY: Much of the literature under RELIGION AND LITERATURE deals with the subject, notably Brooke's *Theology in the English Poets*. Consult: C. Wordsworth, *Memoirs of William Wordsworth*, 2 vols., London, 1851 (by his nephew); A. S. Patterson, *Poets and Preachers of the Nineteenth Century*, Glasgow, 1862; S. T. Coleridge,

Biographia Literaria, London, 1866; H. Lonsdale, *The Worthies of Cumberland*, 6 vols., ib. 1867–75; D. Masson, *Wordsworth, Shelley, Keats, and Other Essays*, new ed., ib. 1881; A. J. Symington, *William Wordsworth*, ib. 1881; F. W. H. Myers, *Wordsworth*, ib. 1888, new ed., 1909 (admirable); J. M. utherland, *William Wordsworth*, ib. 1888; W. Knight, *Life of Wordsworth*, 3 vols., in his ed. of the *Works*, vols. ix.–xi., Edinburgh, 1889 (authoritative); *Wordsworthiana*, ed. W. Knight, London, 1889 (selection of papers read before the Wordsworth Society; of high value); T. De Quincy, *Recollections of the Lake Poets*, in *Works*, vols. i.–iii., ib. 1889–90; Elizabeth Wordsworth, *William Wordsworth*, ib. 1891; M. Gothein, *William Wordsworth; sein Leben, seine Werke, seine Zeitgenossen*, 2 vols., Halle, 1893; E. Legouis, *La Jeunesse de Wordsworth*, Paris, 1896, Eng. transl., London, 1898 (careful and interesting); W. R. Inge, *Christian Mysticism*, pp. 305 sqq., ib. 1899; W. Raleigh, *Wordsworth*, ib. 1903; F. W. Robertson, *Influence of Poetry*. *Wordsworth*, ib. 1906; D. W. Rannie, *Wordsworth and his Circle*, ib. 1907; S. F. Gingerich, *Wordsworth: a Study in Memory and Mysticism*, Elkhart, Ind., 1908; *DNB*, lxiii. 12–27.

WORK AND SADDLE ANIMALS, HEBREW:

This article deals with certain animals used for draft and riding and in those relations; for further information concerning them see Ass; Camel; Horse; Mule; Pastoral Life, Hebrew. Of neat cattle the bull was used for field work, hence the large proportion of the male in the herd (Gen. xxxii. 15); oxen in pairs drew the plow (I Sam. xi. 7), the harrow (Job. xxxix. 10), and the threshing-sled (II Sam. xxiv. 22); they were employed also to tread out the grain (Deut. xxv. 4). The ox was a valued possession; whoever took a widow's ox as a pledge was an oppressor (Prov. xiv. 4; Job xxiv. 3). A goad was and is still used in driving the animal (Judges iii. 31; I Sam. xiii. 21). Ox and ass were not to be yoked together (Deut. xxii. 10); neat cattle were used before the cart (I Sam. vi. 7) and as beasts of burden (I Chron. xii. 40).

For the ass there were many names: *hamor; 'athon*, " she ass "; *'ayir*, Gk. *onos, pōlos*, " young ass "; *pere'*, " wild ass." Before the introduction of the horse the ass and neat cattle were the agriculturist's only work animals. In early times ass and ox were doubtless yoked together; the prohibition of Deut. xxii. 10 arose from the sentiment against any commingling of unlike. In plowing heavy land the ass was not in use; it was used, however, to turn millstones. Its principal value was for riding by rich and poor, with or without saddle or bridle, while the driver traveled on foot (II Kings iv. 24). Women especially rode it, also children (Ex. iv. 20), and the feeble (II Chron. xxviii. 15); even a corpse might be carried on it (I Kings xiii. 29); the young asses served children as riding animals (Judges x. 4). Only in very early times was it used in war, except as a pack animal (II Kings vii. 7, 10; but cf. Isa. xxi. 7), being especially employed in times of peace (Zech. ix. 9). In patriarchal times it was a pack animal (Gen. xlii. 26 and often), and in New-Testament times ox and ass were of animals the most common possessions (Luke xiii. 15, xiv. 5).

By *peredh* the Hebrews denoted the offspring of the ass and the mare. This animal was used for riding, being too costly for use in early times for ordinary pack purposes; as a saddle animal it was used by kings and princes (I Kings i. 23, xviii. 5). It seems to have come from the Armenian highlands by way of Phenicia (Ezek. xxvii. 1 4).

The single-humped camel is the variety of which some mention is made in Scripture, used generally by the caravans, therefore seldom by Hebrews (cf. I Chron. xii. 40; Isa. xxx. 6); but the returning exiles employed it (Ezra ii. 67). Its burden was about three hundredweight, and was distributed on both sides of the hump in a sort of saddle; the beast knelt while the load was adjusted. Freight camels move slowly, and last for from twelve to fifteen hours; the riding camel can surpass in endurance the best horse. Different forms of saddle are used for men and women, the latter being upholstered and with high knobs, surmounted by a pannier. The rider often dismounted with the aid of a pole carried by the driver. The animal might be adorned with rings and chains upon the neck (Judges viii. 21, 26). It was useful also in war, and was employed by Arabs, Bactrians, and Africans as a sort of cavalry. Camel's milk is mentioned (Gen. xxxii. 15), but its flesh was forbidden to Hebrews (Lev. xi. 4), although the heathen used it in sacrifice; its hair was woven into a rough cloth, used also for tent covering (Matt. iii. 4; Jer. xlix. 29).

For the horse there are several designations in Hebrew: *sus* is the general name; *parash* is a saddle horse; the exact sense of *rekhebh* is doubtful; *kal* means " the runner," and is applied to the horse (Isa. xxx. 16), while *'abbir*, " the strong," is so applied Judges v. 22. The New-Testament term is *hippos*, often in Revelation. The horse was introduced into Palestine after the time of Solomon; when David overcame Hadadezer of Zoba and took as booty horses and chariots, he knew only to destroy the chariots and hock the horses—except sufficient for 100 chariots (II Sam. viii. 4). Solomon is said to have had 1,400 chariots and 12,000 horsemen (I Kings x. 26). It is usually held that the probable market of the horse for the Hebrews was Egypt, in which it had long been prized, while Egyptian influence was stronger at the time than that of Assyria. Israel appears to have been the latest of the people of Hither Asia to introduce the horse for the army, especially for the use of cavalry; at first reserved for the use of the king (I Kings i. 5), the horse was used by the nobles in the time of Jeremiah. The reference in I Kings x. 28 is probably to be read *Muzri* instead of *Mizraim*, " Egypt " (see Assyria, VI., 2, § 1). Accordingly Winckler holds that Cilicia and Cappadocia were the marts where the Israelites obtained their horses; while *Muzri* in Arabia may be the reference in such passages as Isa. xxxi. 1. The much-debated passage I Kings x. 28, cf. verse 26, is probably the starting-point of much legendary matter regarding Solomon's relation to the establishment of the horse as a possession among the Hebrews. The arrival of the horse from Cappadocia among the Babylonians is demonstrable for the period 1420–1100, and among the Egyptians after the eighteenth dynasty. The breed of the horses derived by Solomon from Asia can no longer be determined. Tradition attributes the derivation of the celebrated breed of Arab horses from those brought back by the exiles (Ezra ii. 66), which were supposedly from Solomon's brood. Riding never appears among the Hebrews as a pastime, and such passages as Job xxxix. 19–25 show the sentiment with which the animal was regarded. In war the Israelitic leader rode not on horseback but in a chariot (see VEHICLES, HEBREW); but this was not the case with Assyrians and Chaldeans. Cyrus first made riding an accomplishment of the noble (cf. Esther vi. 8 sqq.; Eccles. x. 6–7); indeed, even in later times this remained an accomplishment foreign to the Jew. The Bible knows horses of all colors (Zech. vi. 2–3; Rev. vi. 2 sqq.). Shoeing of the animal was unknown, hence hardness of hoof was a valuable quality (Isa. v. 28); and this explains partly their employment only on the plains. In the earlier times stirrups were unknown, and in a still earlier period the saddle was not used. Decorations for the horse, the bridle, and the plume for the head appear in the Scriptures, and are pictured on Assyrian reliefs. In poetical imagery the horse figures frequently; in Rev. xix. 11, 14, Christ rides as victor a white horse. (R. ZEHNPFUND.)

BIBLIOGRAPHY: The literature on the subject is already principaily given under ASS, CAMEL, HORSE, and MULE. Consult further: A. Zeller, *Das Pferd, der Esel und der Hund in der heiligen Schrift*, Plauen, 1890; J. Wimmer, *Palästinas Boden mit seiner Pflanzen- und Tierwelt*, Cologne, 1902; Nehring, *Die geographische Verbreitung der Säugetiere in Palästina und Syrien*, in *Globus*, vol. lxxxi.; W. R. Arnold in *JAOS*, vol. xxvi.; *DB*, i. 173, 344, 629, ii. 416, iii. 456.

WORKMAN, HERBERT BROOK: Wesleyan Methodist; b. at Peckham, London, Nov. 2, 1862. He received his education at Kingswood School, Bath, 1873–80, Owen's College, Manchester, 1880–1883, Didsbury Wesleyan Theological College, Manchester, and London University, 1883 sqq. (B.A., 1884; M.A., 1885; D. Lit., 1907). He served in various charges in the regular pastorate of his denomination, 1885–1903, when he became principal of the Westminster Training College for Schoolmasters. He was Fernley lecturer in 1906; has been member of the Board of Studies of the faculty of theology, London University, since 1906; and was elected to the Legal Hundred (see METHODISTS, I., 1, § 6). As a Wesleyan Methodist he believes " that many of the old truths need restatement in new forms." He is the author of *What is the Gottenberg System?* (London, 1895); *The Church of the West in the Middle Ages* (2 vols., 1898–1900); *The Dawn of the Reformation* (2 vols., 1902); *Persecution in the Early Church* (1906); *Influence of the Christian Church upon the Civilization of the Middle Ages* (in Garvie's *Christ and Civilization;* 1910); and *History of Christian Thought up to the Reformation* (1910); and has edited *The Letters of John Hus* (1904); and assisted in editing *The New History of Methodism* (2 vols., 1909).

WORKS, GOOD. See GOOD WORKS.

WORLD, THE.

The expression " heaven and earth," borrowed by the New Testament from the Old (Gen. i. 1; Isa. i. 2; Ps. lxxiii. 25), is a popular and imperfect combining of the two main parts of the universe. Properly there are three divisions (Ex. xx. 4, 11; Ps. lxix. 34; Acts iv. 24), namely, heaven, earth, and sea (cf. Phil. ii. 10). This corresponds to the tripartite universe of ancient Babylonia (cf. P. Jensen, *Die Kosmologie der Babylonier*, Strasburg, 1890; Benzinger, *Archäologie*, pp. 159 sqq.).

In ancient Israel, indeed, not only was the word for world lacking, but also the conception of a creation of the world by Yahweh; at least it is not certain that the Babylonian myth of creation was assimilated before the prophetic period. During this period, however, and certainly in exilic and postexilic times, as a parallel to the consequent development of monotheism, appears the conception of a universe dependent upon Yahweh as its creator and preserver, even though the expression " heaven and earth " is still retained (*hakkol*, in Eccles. xi. 5, is a sort of substitute for " world "). This appears more clearly in Deutero-Isaiah, who never wearies of proclaiming the majesty of the almighty Creator. In the story of creation (Gen. i.), in spite of the dual expression, " heaven and earth " (" earth, air, and sea," i. 28), creation is clearly conceived as standing before the almighty Creator, the work of his will and of his word. Disregarding the influence of Babylonian and Persian ideas upon this monotheism and the

1. Old-Testament Conception.

conception of creation and world, it is evident that the conception of a universe owed its origin not to cosmological speculations, but to religious development and especially to the conception of God held by the Hebrew prophets. The attainment of the belief in a single almighty Lord and ruler of the world, is a result of the historical experience of Israel, especially during the exile and after the return therefrom. The religion of Israel differs from that of the heathen world in this, that it has its roots not in the life of nature, but in the history of Israel. Originally the historical horizon was restricted, and hence the universality of Yahweh was scarcely realized. The prophets, however, passed these narrow bounds, and when an Amos could announce that Yahweh would use the Assyrians to chastise Israel for its violation of his commandments, the particularistic view of Yahweh's rule, according to which he always favored his people, gave way to the conception of a world of nations and the idea of a moral government of this world by God. This appears when Yahweh is called " judge of all the earth," that is, of all peoples (Gen. xviii. 25), and lord of all the earth (Josh. iii. 11); he is everywhere to be feared (Ps. xxii. 28, xxxiii. 8, etc.); his salvation shall be everywhere revealed (Jer. xvi. 19). This train of thought gives birth to new words and phrases, such as " all the nations of the earth " (Gen. xviii. 18; Deut. xxviii. 1) particularly in contradistinction and in opposition to Israel; " the ends of the earth " (Isa. xli. 5); above all to the poetic word *tebel*, which is originally a synonym of *'erez*, signifying the earth as a whole, but is frequently used in the sense of *oikoumenē*, e.g., "all the inhabitants of the world" (Isa. xviii. 3; Ps. xxxiii. 8). Another view of the world is shown in Dan. ii. 37–39, which contains a specimen of the hyperbolical style of expression, common in oriental courts. Although the etymology and content of the word *'olam-aiōn* is imperfectly known, there is no doubt that it expressed originally a conception of time, not the world itself in the sense of a qualitatively defined organism (cf. IV Esdras iv. 27–32).

In Greek mythology the conception of a universe is also lacking; the whole being paraphrased by the statement of its parts, as in Homer's description of the shield of Achilles, where are named earth, heaven, and sea (cf. E. H. Berger, **2. Greek** *Mythische Kosmographie der Griechen,* **and** Suppl. III. to Roscher's *Lexikon,* Leip- **Apocryphal** sic, 1904). The word *Kosmos* is said **Conception.** to have been first used by Pythagoras to designate the universe (Plutarch, *De placitis philosophorum*). This Hellenic conception of the Kosmos was first introduced into Biblical literature by the author of the Wisdom of Solomon. The word as used here combines Old-Testament and Hellenic conceptions; sometimes *ho kosmos* alternates with *ta panta,* "the whole." The whole universe (*hē sustasis kosmou*) is made from formless matter by God, through his word, his wisdom being with him (ix. 1, 9, xi. 17); hence the eternal spirit of God is in all things (xii. 1). As the world is permeated by the divine wisdom, it is the foundation of man's cognition of the order of the world (vii. 17–23); from the grandeur and beauty of creation, man learns by comparison to know the creator (xiii. 5). The kosmos also signifies man, since Adam is called the first-formed father of the world (x. 1); a multitude of wise men is termed the salvation of the world, while the family of Noah is "the hope of the world" (vi. 26, xiv. 6). However, the entirety of things in nature and the history of nations is also expressed by the words *kosmos* and *aiōn* (v. 16–17, xvi. 17, xiii. 9, xiv. 6).

In the New Testament, the formula "heaven and earth" continues to be used; the creator being God, the father of Jesus Christ (Matt. v. 18, vi. 10, xi. 25; Mark xiii. 31; Luke x. 21; Eph. **3. General** iii. 15; Col. i. 16, 20; II Pet. iii. 7, 13; **New-** Rev. xxi. 1). Paul uses *ta panta* for **Testament** both divisions of creation (Rom. ix. **Conception.** 5; I Cor. viii. 6; Eph. i. 10; Phil. iii. 21; Col. i. 16, 20). In the Acts of the Apostles, to heaven and earth are added the sea and all that it contains (iv. 24, xiv. 15), and God is addressed as the creator of the kosmos and the lord of heaven and earth; this is the same as if he were called the lord of the world. Particular stress has been laid upon the use of the phrase, "the whole world," by Jesus. It is not indeed improbable that Jesus, in common with strictly monotheistic Judaism, possessed a conception of the world as a unity, in accord with his conception of God. When, in Matt. xi. 25, he praises God as the lord of heaven and earth, this signifies, in spite of the antiquity of the phrase, the same as lord of the world. Whether "world" had for Jesus precisely the significance of "kosmos" remains uncertain, since he spoke in Aramaic and it is not known what Aramaic words are represented by *kosmos* and *aiōn.* Dalman believes that in Mark viii. 36, *kol 'olmah* is the Aramaic equivalent for *holon ton kosmon;* the conception of the whole world as a possession is met elsewhere in Jewish writings.

Paul uses *kosmos* with several shades of meaning: (1) As the universe: "from the creation of the world" (Rom. i. 20; Eph. i. 4); cf. **4. Pauline** also the phrase *ta stoicheia tou kosmou* **Usage.** ("elements, rudiments, of the world," Gal. iv. 3; Col. ii. 8, 20). In general he prefers the term *ta panta.* (2) In accord with the Stoic idea of a "system of gods and men," he separates the concept of the world into angels and men (cf. I Cor. vi. 1, 2). (3) It sometimes signifies *oikoumenē,* the "inhabited earth," when he is thinking of his missionary field. (4) In II Cor. i. 12 it seems to mean life; related to this is the phrase cited by Dalman as rabbinical, *ek tou kosmou exerchesthai,* "to go out of the world" (I Cor. v. 10). (5) Kosmos often signifies for Paul the human race, for example, in Rom. iii. 19, v. 12–13. (6) From this is evolved the peculiarly Christian significance, especially emphasized in the Johannine writings, according to which the "world" as an essence is far removed from and even opposed to God. Its standards and values are rejected by Christians (II Cor. vii. 10). (7) The word *kosmos* can also be used to express earthly possession (cf. Mark viii. 36). For Christian "the world" is only "this world," the fashion of which passeth away (I Cor. vii. 31). The Christian has nothing in common with it, for, by Christ's death, he is crucified for the world (Gal. vi. 14).

The Johannine writings must be treated separately. Here the word *kosmos,* besides being used in a similar way to that of the Pauline epistles, is employed in a thoroughly Jewish manner, **5. Johannine** e.g., in John vii. 4, xii. 19, where it **Usage.** denotes the people. Even more clearly than for Paul, the kosmos is for John not only the whole of creation, but more especially mankind as the object of salvation (i. 29, iii. 16, 17; I John ii. 2), of enlightenment (John viii. 12), and judgment (iii. 17). "This world" is conceived in a thoroughly Jewish and Pauline spirit; it is ruled by the devil (xii. 31) and passes away with all its pleasures (I John ii. 17), for the world is essentially opposition to God (I John ii. 15); it "lieth in wickedness" (I John v. 19) and can neither know nor believe in God and his Son, and must therefore hate those who are "not of the world" (John xvii. 14). Christians must overcome the world (I John v. 4) as Jesus has overcome it (John xvi. 33).

The most important characteristic of the conception "the world" in the New Testament is that, as a whole, it is subordinated to the recognition of the salvation of Christ and his foundation of the kingdom of God among mankind. Hence arises a religious conception of the world which is folly for the partizans of Hellenic philosophy but God-given wisdom for Christian believers (I Cor. i. 21–24). For Paul, God the Father is the creator of the world and the goal of the Christian community; Christ is, in salvation, the mediator for the world and the community. The statement is to be explained by Christ's words when he bases his rulership of the world on the fact that God alone knows him. He who is known and revealed by God alone stands for this very reason nearer to God than to the world; hence, in spite of his existence in the world, he is raised above it and has power over it. To God the Father, the Son of God, and the world he rules Paul adds a fourth quantity: the community which has been created in Christ from eternity. Hellenic philosophy always recognizes the morally cultured man as merely a part of the kosmos; Christianity, however, looks upon the man who is reconciled to God in Christ, who also works for the kingdom of God, as of greater value than the world. This view is a corollary of the knowledge that God is the Father of Jesus Christ and our Father. Although only a part of the universe is known to him, the Christian believes that the unity of the world is guaranteed by general laws and by a supreme law above all these.

The use of this Biblical train of thought has always been checked in dogmatic theology by a Neoplatonic rationalism which holds medieval scholasticism higher than all the results of Scriptural exegesis. The scholastics before and after
6. Dogmatic the Reformation have always ap-
Conception. proached the conception of God by looking away from the determination, limitation, and order of the world, and predicate as God the undetermined and unlimited Being. By attributing to this abstraction power and goodness, qualities which do not pertain to it, this God who is a negation of the world is looked upon as the creator of the world. A variant of this conception is the more recent one of the absolute, which, without relation to anything, therefore without relation to the world, has the quality of being in, by, and for itself. As the world is not made the basis of this absolute (cf. Rom. i. 19, 20), it does not express the concept of an almighty God. Indeed, the thinker who suppresses the world in order to look upon God as the absolute, must begin by suppressing himself, since as a thinking being he is a part of the world. The right understanding of the doctrine of God, however, is the recognition that Christ is the ground of our knowledge of God and of his relation to the world. He must therefore be conceived as Paul conceived him, as the aim of the world for which it was created.

The religious explanation of the world assumes that all things redound to the benefit of those who are chosen and loved by God. The
7. Religious theological amplification of this thought
Conception. does not have to deal with the investigation of each particular event; for the decrees and ways of God are usually unsearchable (Rom. xi. 33). The theological conception is that the whole world, the entire circle of the inter-

action of the forces of nature and man's free will, are under the control of God, who directs all this for the salvation and bliss of his children among mankind, so that all experiences of ill also serve God's purposes. In theological ethics, the world is used to signify earthly goods, in so far as they are temptations to sin. Therefore, the Church catholic teaches that Christian perfection is to be sought by withdrawal from all the relations of life in common. This end could only be attained in the life of the hermit, not even in that of the cloister, since any community offers occasion for vexation and anger. Hence the rules given by Paul (Gal. vi. 14; Rom. xii. 2) can be understood to mean only that each individual Christian is peculiarly tempted by certain special worldly relations, and Christianity, therefore, requires that its followers should avoid those things which possess this quality for them. In general, however, the use of all worldly goods is permitted to the Christian since they give him an opportunity to prove the mastery of the world by the self-control he exhibits.

(L. DIESTEL†; A. RITSCHL†.   Revised by J. WEISS.)

BIBLIOGRAPHY: For the Biblical side reference is to be made to the works named in and under BIBLICAL THEOLOGY, and to the commentaries on the passages cited. For the modern philosophic conceptions consult: L. Frobenius, Die Weltanschauung der Naturvölker, Weimar, 1898; W. Lutoslawski, Ueber die Grundvoraussetzungen und Consequenzen der individualistischen Weltanschauung, Helsingfors, 1898; W. Bender, Die Entstehung der Weltanschauungen im griechischen Altertum, Stuttgart, 1899; G. Mohr, Christliche Weltanschauung auf biblischen Grunde, Ulm, 1899; P. Paulsen, Die Gewissheit der christlichen Weltanschauung im modernen Geistleben, Stuttgart, 1900; R. Steiner, Welt- und Lebensanschauungen im 19. Jahrhundert, 2 vols., Berlin, 1900–01; K. A. von Hase, Die psychologische Begründung der religiösen Weltanschauung im XIX. Jahrhundert, ib. 1901; O. Hellberg, Die Welt unserer Begriffe, Halle, 1901; G. Meisel-Hess, In der modernen Weltanschauung, Leipsic, 1901; R. Eucken, Die Lebensanschauungen der grossen Denker, 4th ed., ib. 1902; A. Rüscher, Göttliche Notwendigkeits-Weltanschauung, Teleologie, mechanische Naturansicht und Gottesidee, Zurich, 1902; A. Kalthoff, Religiöse Weltanschauung, Leipsic, 1903; J. Baumann, Dichterische und wissenschaftliche Weltansicht, Gotha, 1904; idem, Welt- und Lebensansicht in ihren realwissenschaftlichen und philosophischen Grundzügen, ib. 1906; R. Otto, Naturalistische und religiöse Weltansicht, Tübingen, 1904; L. Ragaz, Du sollst. Grundzüge einer sittlichen Weltanschauung, 2d ed., Freiburg, 1904; H. Winckler, Die Weltanschauung des alten Orients, Leipsic, 1904; H. Gomperz, Weltanschauungslehre, vol. i., Methodologie, ib. 1905; J. Reiner, Aus der modernen Weltanschauung, Hanover, 1905; H. Bavinck, Christliche Weltanschauung, Heidelberg, 1907; J. Behrens, Die natürliche Welteinheit. Bausteine zu einer idealistischen Weltanschauung, Wismar, 1907; L. Busse, Die Weltanschauungen der grossen Philosophen der Neuzeit, 3d ed., Leipsic, 1907; E. Dennert, Die Weltanschauung des modernen Naturforschers, Stuttgart, 1907; C. Wenzig, Die Weltanschauungen der Gegenwart im Gegensatz und Ausgleich. Einführung in der Grundprobleme und Grundbegriffe der Philosophie, Leipsic, 1907; S. Arrhenius, The Life of the Universe, London, 1909; A. Heussner, Die philosophischen Weltanschauungen und ihre Hauptvertreter, Göttingen, 1910; P. W. Van Peyma, The Why of the Will: the Unity of the Universe, Boston, 1910; B. Kern, Weltanschauungen und Welterkenntnis, Berlin, 1911.

WORMS.

I. The City and Bishopric: [Worms, one of the oldest and most interesting cities in Germany, also long one of the most important, lies in the plain of the Wonne on the left bank of the Rhine, twenty-five miles south of Mainz. It has about 42,000 inhabitants, of whom two-thirds are Protestants, about one-third Roman Catholic, and 2,500 are Jews. Its name in the Roman period was Borbetomagus, in a Celtic district, and it was the seat of the Vangiones, a small tribe settled there by Julius Cæsar, where arose the civitas Vangionum. In the fifth century it came under the Burgundians, and there the legends of Gunther and Brunhilde, Siegfried and Kriemhild, and later of Eginhard and Emma are laid. It was the see city of an ancient bishopric, was often the residence of the Frankish kings and of Charlemagne and his successors, gave its name to a famous concordat, and was the scene of the diet where Luther made his famous defense and declaration before Charles V. (see LUTHER, MARTIN, § 9), and of two important conferences. It is noted also for its Romanesque cathedral, of red sandstone, dating from the twelfth to the fourteenth century, and for the great monument to Luther, designed by Rietschel (see SCULPTURE, CHRISTIAN USE OF, III., § 3).] The circumstances of the founding of the bishopric are unknown; even when Christianity entered the region is uncertain, since it is not known whether the reference of Irenæus (Hær., I., x. 2) to churches in the German provinces refers to this place. The first secure trace is the statement of Orosius (Hist., VII., xxxii. 13) that in the beginning of the fifth century the Burgundians received Christianity, and that the left bank of the Rhine was in general organized ecclesiastically (cf. Socrates, Hist. eccl., VII., xxx.). But there is no report of a bishopric, and no list of bishops for this period. For 200 years nothing more is heard, meanwhile the Franks took possession of the land, the Burgundians having withdrawn; the city thus became German instead of Roman. The Christian community survived the change, and at the synod held at Paris in 614 a Bishop Berhtulfus of Uarnacium appeared; in 696 Rupert of Salzburg was bishop, after which follows a gap of a century in knowledge of the see. From the end of the eighth century the bishops' names are known. The diocese itself was located on both sides of the Rhine. The bishopric was suppressed in 1801.

(A. HAUCK.)

II. The Concordat: [For the terms of this agreement see CONCORDATS AND DELIMITING BULLS, I. Its significance rests in the fact that it ended the dispute between pope and emperor regarding Investiture (q.v.) in an agreement between Calixtus II. and Henry V. The terms of the concordat were read before a multitude in a meadow near the city.

III. The Diet: This important gathering, before which Luther was summoned to appear, closed the first period of the Reformation, showing to the world that the movement started by Luther was something greater than that started by Huss, and likely to take quite another turn. Luther arrived on Tuesday, Apr. 16, 1521, in the forenoon, and was lodged in the house of the Knights of St. John. The next day at six o'clock in the afternoon, he appeared before the diet, assembled in the episcopal palace. For the proceedings and result see LUTHER, MARTIN, § 9.]

IV. Religious Conferences. — 1. Conference of 1540–41: The Hagenau Conference (q.v.) having proved ineffective, a new one was called for Oct. 28 of the same year (1540). Paul III. decided to have

1. The Occasion and Preliminaries. as his representative a man not a cardinal, and appointed Tommaso Campeggi, bishop of Feltre. His instructions emphasized the grace of the pope in accepting a conference of this kind, which he so abhorred, and directed that the authority of the Curia be guarded and all proposals be reserved for papal decision. Morone, the nuncio, also appeared, his purpose being to obstruct the conference as much as possible. Pietro Paolo Vergerio (q.v.) came ostensibly as the French representative, really in the secret service of the pope to encourage the return of Protestants to the Church. Melanchthon set on foot on Oct. 22 in Gotha a protest against the claim of the pope to precedence and to the ultimate decision in such a conference. His own instructions were definite to refuse recognition of the papal supremacy, and warned of the danger of cleavage in Protestant ranks in case certain positions should not be maintained. The Protestants were to stand by the Schmalkald conclusions. The members of the conference arrived promptly, but the emperor's representative delayed his arrival till Nov. 22. Roman Catholics of note deputed were Nausea, Cochlæus, Pflug, Pelargus, Gropper, Eck, and Mensing, while for the Evangelicals appeared Jakob Sturm, Butzer, Capito, Calvin, W. Link, Osiander, Schnepf, Brenz, and Amsdorf. Representatives of Mainz, Bavaria, Pfalz, and Strasburg were to officiate as presidents. The Evangelicals used the delay in cementing a united front. On Nov. 25 Granvella opened the conference. To the Evangelicals it was suggested that they submit in writing what they proposed to hold, to which they replied by submitting the Augsburg Confession and Apology.

The real beginning of the conference was continually postponed, and on Dec. 8 Campeggi appeared and spoke of the zeal of the pope for a healing of the religious divisions, and to this

2. Progress and Close. assent was given without mention of the pope. The Evangelicals opposed the delivery of the summaries of action to the emperor alone, and demanded that each side receive an original set of documents, though they finally agreed to accept certified copies. The Roman Catholic party was not in agreement as to the measures to be adopted. It seemed as though the conference was going to pieces upon the question of the form of interchange of proposals. Granvella had from the beginning no confidence in a public conference, and endeavored to get some individuals from the Protestant side to consent to more private proceedings and so to enable a compromise to be reached. On Jan. 2, 1541, the proposition was put forward that each of the eleven participants should speak together with the chief speaker for each side, the notaries to take down the chief points; on this the Evangelicals were not at one, Melanchthon and Butzer seeking to mediate, the effect of Granvella's astute policy being seen in this attitude, the result being the anger of Osiander, who saw that some secret understanding was obtained. The Protestants desired that each of the participants should have free speech. Granvella sought from the emperor authority to close the conference, but on Jan. 14 the conference began with Eck as the Roman Catholic speaker. He excused the delay on the ground that the Confession (of 1540) laid before them differed from that of 1530 and that comparison had required time, to which Melanchthon replied that they were essentially the same. Eck practically passed article 1, and began debate on article 2 dealing with original sin, upon which he and Melanchthon disputed till the 17th, when Granvella called both, together with Mensing and Butzer, to a meeting, where the four agreed upon a formula which the Evangelicals could accept. Meanwhile, on the day before Granvella had received orders from the emperor to close the conference, and on Jan. 18, when further proceedings were to be carried on, the president declared that the emperor had ordered, since no progress had been made, that the matters be deferred to the coming diet, and the conference was abruptly broken off.

2. Conference of 1557: By the Augsburg Religious Peace (q.v.) of 1555 the states of the Augsburg Confession had won as a permanent right freedom to exercise their religion. But the hope of a religious union and ecclesiastical agreement in matters of teaching and ceremonies had not been given up. The discussion of the equalization of the religious parties was referred at the time to the then future diet appointed for Mar. 1, 1556. The difficulty of the Evangelical princes was that since Luther's death their churches had become disunited through various controversies, and there was no recognized leader; Melanchthon's authority was challenged by a part even of his own scholars, while Brenz was suspected by one whole group. At the Augsburg Diet Christoph of Württemberg had desired a meeting of Evangelical princes; Philip of Hesse had wanted a meeting of their counselors and theologians; the Ernestine dukes sought to bring both about. But the theologians (Amsdorf, Stolz, Aurifaber, Schnepff, and Strigel) disapproved and wanted a decision against false doctrines. The Regensburg Diet proposed a committee of eight. The Roman Catholics preferred a council, the Protestants a religious conference; Ferdinand saw that a council was impossible at the time and declared for a conference, which he appointed to meet at Worms Aug. 24, 1557. Each side was to have six debaters, six associates, six "auditors," and two notaries. The presidency fell ultimately to Julius von Pflug (q.v.), bishop of Naumburg; the Protestant principals were Melanch-

thon, Brenz, Schnepf, Professor Macchabäus of Copenhagen (later, Runge of Greifswald), Karg, and Pistorius; the Roman Catholic representatives were Pflug, Helding, Gropper, P. Canisius, Delfius of Strasburg, and Professor Rithoven of Louvain.

Attempts had been made in vain to heal the breach between Melanchthon and Flacius (qq.v.), and in view of the coming conference it was resolved to have the Evangelical states come together at Worms Aug. 1 in order to make a new **2. The Flacian Breach.** attempt to heal the breach. A preliminary meeting of the princes under Duke Christoph was held at Frankfort in June, but Elector August was absent by the advice of Melanchthon; agreement was reached that they unanimously maintained the Augsburg Confession. Flacius insisted upon a condemnation of all errant teaching, brought definite charges against some of the Protestant principals, and declared a pronouncement against all corruptions of doctrine to be absolutely necessary. Melanchthon and his associates arrived at Worms Aug. 28, and the Ernestine theologians soon saw that they were practically isolated, nearly all "adoring Philip as a divinity." The Evangelicals met together Sept. 5, and Monner and Schnepff brought up their proposal for the condemnation of all corruptions of the last ten years, with especial reference to Melanchthon; in reply, it was pointed out that common action against the common foe was necessary, even if to accomplish this other representatives had to be secured. A new attempt was made on Sept. 9, but with the result that the Flacians threatened to make open statement of their position.

On Sept. 11 the conference began, and at once arose the inevitable discussion concerning the order of procedure; Melanchthon's proposal for oral methods was rejected in favor of Helding's that written documents be handed in. Instead of the Augsburg Confession a statement by **3. The Conference Futile.** Canisius, in twenty-three articles, of the chief points in dispute was to be the basis of discussion. At the fifth session, Sept. 16, Canisius referred to the split among the Evangelicals, which the Flacians seized upon to emphasize their position. On Sept. 20, Canisius again read a document referring to Osiander and Major (see MAJOR, GEORG; OSIANDER, ANDREAS), and the Flacians again pointed out the logic of their position and affirmed that they were compelled to justify themselves, and to the threat to replace them replied that they would appeal to the president. Peace could not be obtained, though strenuous efforts were made to heal the breach and to get the Evangelicals to present a united front. All was useless, for on Sept. 27 the representatives of Johann Friedrich gave to the Roman Catholic assessors their protestation, and on Oct. 1 the notification that they were about to depart, and then left Worms on the same day. The conference had in fact been interrupted since Sept. 20; the Roman Catholic part would gladly have closed the matter at once, but the Evangelicals hoped to find a way, by continuing, to relieve the sad impression of this conflict in their own camp. The conference was resumed Oct. 6, but at once there arose a dispute as to whether the Flacian declaration was official or private. A new question then arose as to whether the remaining Protestant disputants were competent as adherents of the Augsburg Confession and had rightly excluded the Flacians; further, would the Flacians recognize the conference? So objection after objection arose, and the Evangelicals did not succeed in bringing under discussion the doctrines at issue. Postponements ensued to obtain word from Ferdinand, which came at last instructing the reinstatement of the Weimar theologians in their rights as participants; over the interpretation of this message new strife arose. Finally, on Nov. 28, the Roman Catholics having declared that they could not treat with a divided party, the whole matter was referred to the next diet, each party asserting its innocence of the causes leading to this result.

If the Regensburg Conference (q.v.) revealed the strength of the Protestant party, that at Worms had shown its weakness. The split had become a spectacle for the opponents and made these latter see the turn in the tide for their cause. Canisius thought that the princes of the Roman party would no longer oppose a general council, while the Counter-Reformation was already on its way. For further developments on the Protestant side see FRANKFORT RECESS. (G. KAWERAU.)

BIBLIOGRAPHY: On the city and bishopric consult: J. F. Schannat, *Historia episcopatus Wormatiensis*, Frankfort, 1734; W. Wagner, *Die vormaligen geistlichen Stifte im Grossherzogthum Hessen*, 2 vols., Darmstadt, 1873–78; H. Boos, *Quellen zur Geschichte der Stadt Worms*, 3 vols., Berlin, 1886–93; idem, *Geschichte der rheinischen Städtekultur*, vols. i.–iv., ib. 1897–1901; A. Köster, *Die Wormser Annalen*, Leipsic, 1887; F. Soldan, *Die Zerstörung der Stadt Worms im Jahre 1689*, Worms, 1889; idem, *Beiträge zur Geschichte der Stadt Worms*, ib. 1896; F. X. Kraus, *Die christlichen Inschriften der Rheinlande*, nos. 22–29, Freiburg, 1890; H. Haupt, *Beiträge zur Reformationsgeschichte der Reichsstadt Worms*, Giessen, 1897; C. Koehne, *Die Wormser Stadtrechtsreformation vom Jahre 1499*, Berlin, 1897; O. Beckmann *Führer durch Worms*, Stuttgart, 1902; Rettberg *KD*, i. 633; Hauck, *KD*, 4 vols.; *KL*, xii. 1759–68. On the concordat, besides the literature in iii. 218 of this work consult: G. Wolfram, *Friedrich I. und das Wormser Concordat*, Marburg, 1883.

On the diet the following are available: J. Friedrich, *Der Reichstag in Worms, 1521*, Munich, 1870; K. Jansen, *Aleander am Reichstage zu Worms 1521*, Kiel, 1883; T. Kolde, *Luther und der Reichstag zu Worms*, Gotha, 1883; F. Soldan, *Der Reichstag zu Worms, 1521*, Worms, 1883; W. Oncken, *Martin Luther in Worms*, Giessen, 1884; *Cambridge Modern History*, ii. 139 sqq., 146 sqq., 158, 166, 170 sqq., New York, 1904.

On the conferences consult: Melanchthon, *Colloquium Wormaciense*, Wittenberg, 1542; *CR*, iii. 1121 sqq., iv. 1–91; *ZHT*, 1872, pp. 36 sqq.; J. P. Roeder, *De colloquio Wormatiensi*, Nuremberg, 1744; H. Laemmer, *Monumenta Vaticana*, pp. 300–342, Freiburg, 1861; R. Moses, *Die Religionsverhandlungen zu Hagenau und Worms, 1540 und 1541*, Jena, 1889; J. W. Richard, *Philip Melanchthon*, chap. xxiii., New York, 1898; J. Janssen, *Hist. of the German People*, vi. 107–113, vii. 34–45, St. Louis, 1903–1905; *Cambridge Modern History*, ii. 239, New York, 1904; W. Friedensburg, in *ZKG*, xxi. 112 sqq.; the literature under BUTZER; ECK; and MELANCHTHON.

WORSHIP.

Worship may be defined as the acknowledgment by some formal act of mind or body, or both, of God's supreme dominion, or (among pagans) of the exalted power of some divine or semi-divine being. In older English the word was used in a less limited sense, denoting honor or reverence in general. Traces of this usage are seen in the formula of the marriage-service in the English Prayer-book, where the bridegroom says to the bride, " With my body I thee worship, and with all my worldly goods I thee endow," as well as in the current application of the title " his Worship " and the epithet " worshipful " to the mayors of English towns; while to this day, among Roman Catholics, it would be possible to hear the expression " the worship of the saints " used without offense, although, as will be seen, nothing is clearer to them than the distinction between the supreme honor due to God alone and the subordinate or relative honor paid to even the highest and holiest of his creatures.

1. Definition.

The conception instinctively suggested to Christian people by the word in its narrower sense is inevitably stamped by the definition of the Founder of their religion, " God is a Spirit: and they that worship him must worship him in spirit and in truth " (John iv. 24); but an encyclopedic treatment of the subject must go back for many centuries beyond the Christian era, and patiently seek to penetrate the obscurity which veils the mental processes of primitive and uncivilized man. The modern study of comparative religion, also, has brought to light the profound significance of many rites of savage tribes which until recent years were contemptuously dismissed as mere barbarism or child's play, unworthy of the attention of serious thinkers. In them is often found the answer to many questions, which would otherwise have seemed insoluble, as to the manner in which primitive man regarded the supernatural and his relation to it. " It is ritual," says L. R. Farnell (*Cults of the Greek States*, i. 9, Oxford, 1896), " that is chiefly the conservative part of religion. And in ritual the older and cruder ideas are often held as in petrifaction, so that the study of it is often as it were the study of unconscious matter, in so far as it deals with facts of worship of which the worshiper does not know the meaning, and which frequently are out of accord with the highest

2. Necessity of Study of Primitive Religions.

religious consciousness of the community." So important is worship that one eminent German scholar (Otto Gruppe, quoted by Otto Schrader) has declared ritual to be the source of religion; but if this is going too far and putting the cart before the horse, at least the study of its development is one of the most interesting and instructive chapters in the history of the human mind.

When approach is made to what is logically the first step in the consideration of the subject—the origin to be assigned, according to the best results of comparative religion and anthropological science, to what is understood by worship, a wide divergence of views comes to light. This is not to be wondered at, if the fact is taken into consideration that Comparative Religion (q.v.) itself, the discipline which attempts to answer such questions by the inductive method, is of very recent growth, dating practically from the last third of the nineteenth century. For many ages it was considered that these methods were wholly inapplicable to the study of a question whose solution seemed to be already included within the province of revelation. Even so independent a thinker as Hobbes expressly excluded " the doctrine of God's worship " from philosophy, " as being not to be known by natural reason, but by the authority of the Church; and as being the object of faith and not of knowledge " (*Elements of Philosophy*, I., viii., London, 1656). The first stimulus came from the discovery and study of the sacred books of the East, followed by the deciphering of the Assyro-Babylonian and Egyptian texts; but the past forty years have been so fruitful of results for the scientific study of religion that a large body of data bearing on the subject of this article is now accessible, even though the conclusions to be drawn from them are not as yet by any means matters of general agreement. Working along these lines, one must start with some knowledge of the manner in which the idea of God may be supposed, apart from any case of an immediate revelation, to have grown up in the mind of primitive and utterly uncivilized man. It may be taken for granted that some more or less definite idea of the existence of a supernatural being or beings is to be found in all branches of the human race; writers who approach the question from such diverse points of view, as E. B. Tylor, T. Waitz, J. L. A. de Quatrefages, Max Müller, G. Gerland, and C. P. Tiele, are agreed upon so much. One principal ground of controversy seems to be whether fear or veneration is the predominant sentiment in the attempt to enter into communion with these superhuman beings. Some observers are inclined to attach by far the greater importance to the motive of fear. Thus E. A. Westermarck says (*Origin and Development of the Moral Ideas*, ii. 612, London, 1908): " In early religion the most common motive [for sacrifice] is undoubtedly a desire to avert evils; and we have reason to believe that such a desire was the first source of religious worship." And even in modern times Sir M. Monier-Williams (*Brahmanism and Hinduism*, p. 230, 4th ed., London, 1891) asserts that " no one who has

3. Widely Divergent Theories of Comparative Religion.

4. The Theory of Fear.

ever been brought into contact with the Hindus in their own country can doubt that the worship of at least 90 per cent of the people of India in the present day is a worship of fear." This view has been stated in various forms, the most often quoted of the earlier ones being the saying of Statius in the first century, *Primus in orbe timor fecit deos*— "First in the world fear created gods," which, says Hobbes in the seventeenth, " spoken of the gods (that is to say, of the many gods of the Gentiles) is very true "; and Renan in the nineteenth was equally convinced that religion began by endeavors to propitiate the hostile powers by which man found himself surrounded.

Tiele, on the other hand, in his sober and thoughtful *Gifford Lectures* (*Elements of the Science of Religion*, Edinburgh, 1897–99), says deliberately that prolonged research and reflection have more and more convinced him of the inaccuracy of this view, and that he would far rather indorse the words of Robertson Smith (*Rel. of Sem.*, p. 55): " From the earliest times religion, as distinct from magic and sorcery, addresses itself to kindred and friendly beings, who may indeed be angry with their people for a time, but are always placable except to the enemies of their worshipers or to renegade members of the community. It is not with a vague fear of unknown powers, but with a loving reverence for known gods who are knit to their worshipers by strong bonds of kinship, that religion in the only true sense of the word begins." His distinction between religion in the proper sense and magic is one which deserves attention; but even those who, with F. B. Jevons, maintain that " it is in love and not in fear that religion in any true sense of the word has its origin " (*Introduction to the History of Religion*, p. 109, 4th ed., London, 1908) admit that " it is none the less true that fear—not of irrational dangers, but of deserved punishment—is essential to the moral and religious education of man; it is ' the fear of the Lord ' that is ' the beginning of wisdom.' "

5. The Theory of Love.

Another much-controverted point is the order in which the various aspects of worship emerged. Many hold, following Robertson Smith, that the idea of communion with the supernatural being or beings is antecedent in time to the gift sacrifice. Tylor, on the other hand (*Primitive Culture*, ii. ch. xviii., 4th ed., London, 1903), believes that the gift sacrifice is the most primitive form, basing this conclusion on the analogy of man's dealings with his fellow men, and assuming that he treated his god as he would a chief (according to the usual ancient custom, illustrated in Gen. xxxii. 20; xliii. 11). He thus places as the stages in the development first the gift, second the idea of homage, and third that of abnegation or expiation.

6. Rival Theories of Order of Development.

The fact is that, in this as in all other questions which concern the history of worship, it is necessary to base a judgment upon a wide and patient investigation of data from different ages and different parts of the world. There has been too frequent a tendency to lay down *a priori* conclusions as certain, with the same finality as Hobbes (*Leviathan*, I., xii.): "For the worship which naturally men exhibit to powers invisible, it can be no other but such

7. **Caution** expressions of their reverence as they
Requisite in would use toward men; gifts, petitions,
Constructing thanks, submission of body, considerate
Theories. addresses, sober behavior, premeditated
words, swearing (that is, assuring one
another of their promises) by invoking them. Beyond that reason suggesteth nothing; but leaves them either to rest there, or for further ceremonies to rely on those they believe to be wiser than themselves." Too often, again, a whole theory has been constructed upon observations relating to a single group of phenomena, and then boldly given forth as accounting for the origin and significance of worship in general, if not of religion itself. Thus, those who maintain that the origin of primitive religious worship was fear may be supposed to have neglected such records as the answer made to the early Spanish missionaries in America, questioning the Indians on their belief as to the origin of their gods; the usual reply was that they had come from the air or heaven, to dwell among them and do them good. Other investigators of aboriginal beliefs in the same continent have dwelt, and even with astonishment, on the prevalence of the worship of malicious spirits rather than good, led to their conclusion by the somewhat serious failure to take into account the totem-god in a land where totemism flourished to a degree unequaled elsewhere except in Australia. Again, among the Aryan races, which to this day are the most thoroughly known, the simple household worship, in no sense public, did not attract the attention of the poets, whose verses are filled with the more picturesque marvels of mythological legend. Very little testimony concerning this system of worship has made its way into literature; what is known about it has been largely recovered by a patient piecing together of information recovered from an illuminating interpretation of a sentence here and a paragraph there.

It is not, however, a rash speculation to see in the history of primitive man first a recognition of the existence of superhuman powers controlling his destinies, or at least intervening in them

8. **Probable** at times; then a tendency to see in
Origin of these powers a personal will analogous
Worship. to that of which he was conscious in himself; and finally a casting about for means of entering into relations with them to his own advantage. His sentiment of a certain kinship with the supernatural powers, combined with his conviction of entire dependence upon them, impelled him to seek communion with them, and to reestablish such communion when he thought it had been broken off through his own fault. From this impulse, according to Tiele, spring all those religious observances which are usually embraced in the term worship.

The content of this term, however, was very much smaller in prehistoric times. Holding strongly to the idea of blood-kinship; extending it beyond the visible family to include the deceased members with whom communion is still desired; then seeking, under totemism, for alliance with another tribe,

some mysterious supernatural clan—a prehistoric race develops but slowly a definite idea of worship offered "to" some one. According to

9. **The** Jevons, worship in its rudimentary
Earliest stage meant the sprinkling upon the
Forms of altar of the blood of the totem-animal,
Worship. with the sole purpose of renewing the blood-covenant and procuring the presence and aid of the totem-god. On this theory, the idea of offering a sacrifice "to" a god could be developed only in a later stage of totemism, when the stone had come to be identified with the god, and the god was no longer in the animal. The idea of worship, further, implies the existence, for the worshiper, not merely of a supernatural being as such, but of a supernatural being who "has stated relations with a community" (Robertson Smith, ut sup., p. 119).

In the nature-religions—those which have grown up by a gradual process of evolution, not derived from the authority of a conscious and definite founder—the organization of the worship continues to coincide with that of social life, this social life being, according to the stage of development, that of the clan, the family, or the nation. In the head of the family are combined the temporal rule

10. **Worship** and the religious leadership; and the
and the same prerogatives are conceded to the
Kingship. heads of a larger family, the early kings. In Egypt the king and his sons held as of right the highest sacerdotal dignities, while the other priests were merely their deputies in religious as well as in civil and even military affairs. The same thing is found in the Babylonian and Assyrian systems; the kings attached great importance to their sacerdotal titles, and they conducted all religious observances without the assistance of any other priests. Long after historical memory of this state of things had faded in Greece and Rome, its record was preserved in the attribution of the title *archon basileus* (king) to the official who conducted the public worship, and that of *rex* to the patrician who, in the Roman republic, presided over the ancient *sacra*. Then and later the title of *pontifex maximus*, or high-priest, still borne by the pope, was conferred upon the head of the state; nor may it be unduly fanciful to see a reminiscence of this early feeling in the concession to the later heads of the Holy Roman Empire of the right to assist as subdeacons, wearing the dalmatic, in the solemn mass celebrated by the pope—although it would more probably be consciously referred to the analogy in Jewish history of the similar anointing of prophets, priests, and kings. There is, then, much evidence to show that in the older forms of society the two offices were one, and only gradually became differentiated, owing in great measure to the practical difficulties arising from the strict taboo which surrounded these sacred personages. The evolution, however, of a separate priestly class, and the way in which its rights and duties developed, belongs less to this place than to the article PRIEST (q.v.)

Among strictly communal rites of worship, a time comes when disasters and distresses impress the tribe with the idea that they have offended their divine protector, and they seek to propitiate him by what are called piacular sacrifices. The development of this sentiment on a large scale may more fitly be treated later, when the discussion comes to the gradual loosening of the bonds of

11. Relation the predominantly tribal or national **of Fetishism** cult. The mention of it here will afford **to Worship.** an opportunity to speak of what is somewhat loosely known as Fetishism (q.v.). The term calls up all the associations which are vaguely present to the minds of average people when they sing the words " The heathen in his blindness Bows down to wood and stone "; and indeed the objects supposed to be endued with supernatural power are often, to our minds, of a very inadequate and even ridiculous nature. But, as far as the mind of the African savage, for example, can be studied, it seems tolerably clear that the original source of these strange proceedings is nothing more than the desire to secure the countenance or protection of some mighty spirit, possibly one not already preoccupied with the tribal affairs, who chooses to take up his abode in or render himself accessible through some such object as a prominent rock or a curiously carved piece of wood. There is no longer likelihood of falling into the error, once so prevalent, of supposing that the African savage worships an inanimate object, knowing it to be inanimate. As Pfleiderer puts the matter generally, " what is really worshiped in the object anywhere is not itself but a transcendental x within and beyond it." Fetishism, in the sense of the worship which finds its way, frequently from the individual, to dimly conceived supernatural beings by and through such means of approach, leads to the next branch of the subject.

As the clan dissolved, or else increased so that its members were at too great a distance from the official seat of worship, guardian spirits or family gods were chosen for the smaller groups or for individuals, the rites of their worship being modeled on those already familiar to the race. Among the

12. Ancestor Semites, the *Teraphim* (q.v.) were fam-
Worship. ily gods, as the *lares* were among the Romans; while the Greeks had their *theoi patrōioi*. The tendency here indicated connected itself very easily and naturally with the respect paid to deceased members of the family; and the ceremonies at first usual as mere signs of grief developed, as they grew conventional, into rites of worship. It was the danger of this development which caused the special prohibition of them to the Hebrews (Lev. xix. 28). It comes up first in the period of settled agricultural life, when the family begins to be an institution. " The worship of ancestors," says E. Clodd (*Myths and Dreams*, p. 113, 2d ed., London, 1891), " is not primal. The comparatively late recognition of kinship by savages, among whom some rude form of religion existed, tells against it as the earliest mode of worship." Herbert Spencer and Grant Allen attempted to account for the origin of religion by the worship of ghosts; but there are countless phenomena which can not be traced back to it—and it can be proved that wherever ancestor-worship exists, as in China, it exists side by side with the public worship of the community. The two have

their sources in the same feeling, quite as the Latin word *pietas* was applied indifferently to reverence for the gods and to filial obedience; and, just as sacrifice survived the materialistic ideas often attached to it in the early stages and became a symbol of humility and reverence, so, according to the belief of many races, the disembodied spirits, like the gods, desire to be worshiped not only because they depend on human care for their sustenance or comfort, but because it is an act of homage. The one never develops into the other.

Tree-worship, and more especially plant-worship, belong again to the agricultural stage. In the animistic philosophy of the savage, in his blind search through the universe for manifestations

13. Worship of the supernatural, he came to believe, **of Trees and** in many widely separated lands, that **Plants.** trees and plants possessed supernatural powers; and, in accordance with the earlier totem-principle, he attempted to establish relations with any species which he believed to be of especial importance for his own life. Jevons dwells at some length on the history of plant-worship, attributing to it great importance for the history not only of religion but also of civilization, " for it was through plant-worship that cereals and food-plants came to be cultivated, and it was in consequence of their cultivation that the act of worship received a remarkable extension " (ut sup., p. 210).

So far from the religious impulse having originated, as Grant Allen contends, in " the worship of death," it would be far truer, if either must be said, to find its source in the thought of the potency and the preciousness of life. This feeling expressed itself in a great variety of different

14. Worship forms. One, to which too much im-
of Life-giv- portance has apparently been attached **ing Forces.** by some modern investigators, is the symbolic worship known as phallicism. Phallic worship, as a separate and organized cult, is extremely rare, in spite of the temptation to use it as a cloak for unbridled excesses. It is found, to be sure, as a phase of some other cult, among many savage tribes in America and Asia (and, as has been recently pointed out, in Japan); but where it attained its greatest development, among the Semitic and Dravidian races, in Greece under Semitic influences, or connected among the Aztecs with the higher forms of nature-worship, it put on sooner or later a symbolic meaning as typifying the mysterious force which renews the earth in spring and provides for the continuance of the wonderful thing which is called life. All over the world, with rites bearing at least a superficial similarity, the deities or spirits of vegetation, on whom man was thought to depend for the food which sustained his life, were worshiped with ceremonies of which there are curious survivals, no longer understood, in the spring and harvest customs of European countries. Likewise, in the pastoral and agricultural stage, men were impressed with the need of winning the favor of the great forces of nature—streams and fountains, clouds, the sky, the sun and moon. Communion was sought, where possible, by placing the offerings of the worshiper in contact with the di-

vine power, as by throwing them into water; in the case of the sun, the old principle of classification suggested fire as akin to his substance.

Certainly the most wide-spread, as well as the most important, of primitive religious rites are those which set forth the public worship of the tribe or clan. Robertson Smith is inclined to regard communal worship as the only worship in very early times. " In antiquity," he says, " all religion was the affair of the community rather than of the individual " (op. cit., p. 236). Here, however, Daniel G. Brinton strongly disagrees with
15. Communal Worship. him, attributing to his special researches among the Semitic peoples the general theory, which " is contradicted by nearly every primitive religion known to me "; and of course it is obvious that in so far as one's notions are unconsciously colored by records such as those of the Greek poets one will lean toward the former view—little definite record is likely to be left of the worship of the individual or of the small private group of the family in the earliest stages of its growth. Again, there is often an unconscious tendency to depend on official explanations, which are, in many cases, far later than the primitive rites for which they undertake to account, and are the work of men who were ashamed of some feature of the rite, or who were unwilling to confess themselves unable to give an authentic explanation of it. It is necessary to bear in mind that often they may give only a partial or factitious view of their subject, while quite another may be the true one, or may have been held at the same time by large numbers of people. Thus, for example, the animal-worship of Egypt was explained in several different ways. The official or priestly interpretation varied. It was said that the gods had concealed themselves in the forms of beasts during the revolutionary wars of Set against Horus; or that the adoration was directed not to the animal but to the qualities which it personified; or that the beast-gods were memorials of badges (representing animals) borne by the various tribal companies in the forces of Osiris. Apollonius of Tyana is quoted as holding that the beasts were symbols of deity, not deities; and Porphyry (*De abstinentia*, iv. 9) asserts definitely that " under the semblance of animals the Egyptians worship the universal power which the gods have revealed in the various forms of living nature." But these are theories constructed by learned men long after the origin of the rites; and it is obvious that there is a grave disadvantage in having no record of what the simple peasantry thought of customs in which recent scholars have been inclined to see " a consecration and elaborate survival of totemism." In view of the natural inclination to concentrate the attention on public acts, it is not surprising that Pfleiderer defines religious cult as " an utterance or manifestation of the religious consciousness by means of the representative observances of the community, whereby its aspiration for communion with the divine attains actual consummation." Yet, however true the second part of his definition may be, it must not be forgotten that the religious rites practised by the individual in perfect solitude and by the father in the midst of his immediate family are to be included in any comprehensive definition.

Also, in a period as a rule far later than the primitive (speaking generally, about the sixth century B.C.), the historian of worship is obliged to take into account the gradual formation of small associations which aimed at supplementing the public worship, or at superseding it. This tendency is found even in religions which are swayed by animism. Thus among the North American Indians
16. Associational Cults. it led to the formation of small bands to which no one was admitted without having first undergone severe tests of self-control and perseverance; their members were regarded as elevated above the rest of the tribe and in closer relation with the spirits. Among the Hebrews, at the time of the Captivity, when the old national religion seemed to have broken down, we find in the strange sacrifices of " unclean creatures " —swine, dogs, mice, and other vermin—what may be considered as the recrudescence of a cult of the most primitive totem type; though it is distinguished from the old in that it is practised now by men who desert the religion of their birth, as a means of initiation into a new brotherhood. These obscure rites, says Robertson Smith, " have a vastly greater importance than has been commonly recognized; they mark the first appearance in Semitic history of the tendency to found religious societies on voluntary association and mystic initiation, instead of natural kinship and nationality " (ut sup., p. 339). Sects of this kind are found growing out of other higher religions, such as those of China, India, and Persia; and in a similar class may be placed the Hanifites of Arabia, the Eleusinian mysteries, the Pythagoreans, Orphics, and Neoplatonists (see NEOPLATONISM) in Greece, and the Essenes (q.v.) in Israel, with their partly Persian and partly Greek affinities; while not a few of the heretical associations of the Middle Ages—Cathari (see NEW MANICHEANS, II.), Fraticelli, Friends of God (qq.v.), and the like—stand in exactly the same relation to the accepted cult. In the older stages of civilization, too, there is a special incentive to the formation of such voluntary associations in the fact that as a general rule women as well as children were not admitted to the tribal worship, and would thus be likely to welcome anything in which they would have more latitude (see, further, TRIBAL AND CULTIC MYSTERIES).

But the tendency which in ancient times led people to draw together in such societies has its roots far deeper in human psychology than in a mere wish to have the distinction of belonging to something not open to the great body of the community and of possessing secrets unknown to them. As a general rule, the official or tribal worship was
17. Joyous Character of Primitive Worship. of a cheerful nature. " Worship the gods with a joyous worship," says Cicero; and this precept was widely obeyed. A superficial survey of Greek religion would give the impression that by far the larger part of it was like that which Robertson Smith describes as the type of worship prevalent among the earlier Hebrews, and characteristic of their Semitic neighbors in general: " universal

hilarity prevailed, men ate, drank, and were merry together, rejoicing before their god." The same attitude of mind was seen among the Germanic tribes; Grimm says (*Teutonic Mythology*, Eng. transl., i. 42, London, 1879) that the religious rites of the ancient Germans were, as a rule, cheerful, and those which were of this nature were the earliest and the commonest. This, of course, was natural if the first of public rites was one of joyousness, an invitation to the god to be present and partake of a repast spread for him by his worshipers. Purely religious banquets, festal commemorations, and thanksgivings would thus make up a large part of early rites among those religions in which " the habitual temper of the worshipers is one of joyous confidence in their god, untroubled by any habitual sense of human guilt, and resting on the firm conviction that they and the deity they adore are good friends, who understand each other perfectly and are united by bonds not easily broken." This temper of mind may be put down to the ease with which in the childhood of the race, as in that of the individual, troublesome thoughts are cast off; but it could never have spread as widely or lasted as long if it had not been for the view that religion was in large measure the affair of the community, and the conviction that the benefits expected from the gods were of a public character. In widely separated regions, the mourner was " unclean," excluded from the worship of the tribe; as Robertson Smith puts it, " the very occasions of life in which spiritual things are nearest to the Christian, and the comfort of religion is most fervently sought, were in the ancient world the times when a man was forbidden to approach the seat of God's presence."

It is not, then, surprising to find in a large number of the later cults of the private or non-official kind, whose history, precisely because they were non-official and more or less secret, has filled far less space than the other in literary records, an effort to propitiate or to drive away supernatural beings conceived, not as the friends of the worshipers, but as hostile, or in some way dangerous. Skilled and scientific investigation of these cults is even more recent than study of the general subject; but such thorough and painstaking work as that done for one group of them by Miss Jane Harrison in her *Prolegomena to the Study of Greek Religion* (2d ed., Cambridge, 1908), and the amount of new light thrown by it on a subject which was supposed to be pretty thoroughly known fifty years ago, show conclusively the need of much more research along these lines. In her opening chapter she admits that one factor, and a prominent one, in the Greek religion of the fifth century B.C. was the idea of service (*therapeia*), in which there was no element of fear; if man did his part in the friendly transaction, the gods would do theirs But the whole tenor of her book, with its wealth of piled-up instances and its acute analysis, goes to show that side by side with the worship of the kindly Olympian deities there existed a whole mass of cult-forms which expressed awe and reverence of spirits or beings of the under-world. Plutarch protests eloquently against the religion of fear; but

18. Propitiatory and Apotropaic Worship.

Miss Harrison has supplied sufficient evidence to warrant the conclusion that what he regards as superstition (*deisidaimonia*, in its later and unfavorable sense) was, in the sixth and even in the fifth century B.C., the real religion of the great mass of the Greek people. The formula of this religion is not, like the other, *do ut des* (" I give that you may give "), but *do ut abeas* (" I give that you may go, and keep, away "). The evidence consists not only in direct statements such as that of the orator Isocrates (436–338 B.C.), which is worth quoting for its direct completeness: " Those of the gods who are the source to us of good things have the title of Olympians, those whose department is that of calamities and punishments have harsher titles; to the first class both private persons and states erect altars and temples, the second is not worshiped either with prayers or burnt-sacrifices, but in their case we perform ceremonies of riddance " (*Oratio*, v. 117). His contemporàry Plato, in the *Laws* (717 A), arranges the objects of divine worship in a regular sequence; first, the Olympian gods, together with " those who keep the city "; second, the underworld gods, whose share are things of unlucky omen; third, the *dæmons*, whose worship is characterized as " orgiastic "; fourth, the heroes; and fifth, the ancestral gods—concluding the list with living parents, to whom much honor should be offered. The classification evidenced by ritual is, however, much less minute; the only recognized distinction is that burnt-offerings are the meed of the Olympians, while " devoted " offerings (*enagismoi*) belong to the chthonic or underworld gods.

In Greece there was, moreover, a long series of ritual acts intended to propitiate or avert the presence of these latter—the Anthesteria, or spring festival of the revocation and aversion of ghosts; the Thargelia, an early summer festival of first-fruits (singularly cognate with the Australian *intichiuma* for the removal of taboo on the harvest-store); the women's festivals—Thesmophoria, Arrhephoria, Skirophoria, Stenia, and Haloa—leading up to the Eleusinian mysteries, which have acquired a greater fame (owing to their adoption by Athens and their later affiliation to the mysteries of Dionysus), but which originally may have been nothing more than the Haloa, or harvest-festival, of Eleusis. Their development, as shown by Jevons, acquires its significance first from the fact that, by an exception wholly alien to the spirit of the antique religions and strictly confined to an exceptional case, the State threw open to all Greeks, men and women, bond and free, the national worship of a national god, and adopted initiation by purification (*myēsis*) as the qualification for admission to a cult hitherto confined to citizens. The opening of the Eleusinian sanctuary to the Athenians coincided with a wave of religious revivalism, which (spreading from Semitic territory in the sixth century B.C.) infused into men's minds the idea of a definite possibility of happiness in a future life, conditioned on a closer communion with the gods than was attainable on the gift-theory of sacrifice. Purification is the keynote of the worship in the mysteries; by the word mystery is meant a rite in which certain very sacred

19. The Greek Mysteries.

things are exhibited, which can not be safely seen by the worshiper until he has passed through the prescribed purifications. There followed the introduction to these mysteries of the cult of Iacchus, and his identification with Dionysus; the dramatic performances held in his honor (the fact of the close association between the genesis of the drama, both in Greece and in western Europe—to say nothing of the curious parallel in the recently gained knowledge of Australian tribes—and religious worship can only be alluded to in passing); the spread of the idea, so pregnant with results as a preparation for Christianity, that this communion, with its hopes of future bliss, was open to all who chose to avail themselves of the grace offered; and the conception of a religious community bound together, not by physical or political ties, but by spiritual fellowship and participation in a common worship.

Edward Caird, treating rather in the abstract the evolution of religion, without much detail, reaches the same point in the development by a somewhat different road. Tracing the growth of the human mind from the almost purely objective view of phenomena which it takes in
20. Influ- its most ignorant form, he says that
ence of Sub- " in so far as God is conceived as mere-
jectivity on ly an object, the worshiper must feel
Worship. toward him as a slave, who obeys without any consciousness of anything that lifts him into unity with the power to which he submits "; while later he remarks that the gradual growth of self-consciousness, subjectiveness (which of course is an indispensable preliminary to a sense of guilt and need of purification), changes all this. " The later Judaism breaks away in the prophets and psalmists from the forms of national worship, and becomes an inner religion of the individual heart—thus preparing the way for the universalism of Christianity " (*Evolution of Religion*, i. 190–193, London, 1893).

There is no need to give here an extended treatment of Christian worship, which is abundantly illustrated in all its details in other articles (see especially LITURGY; MASS; etc.); nor is there any need to explain, still less to apologize for, the reappearance in it of many principles familiar to students of the earlier history of the religious ideas of the race, although to some unreflecting minds the conclusions of advanced modern an-
21. Justifi- thropology have seemed upsetting.
cation of There is really nothing to wonder at in
Christian the adoption and consecration of cult-
Analogies principles familiar to earlier genera-
with Ju- tions; the wonder would have been if
dæo-Ethnic Christianity, intended to take root in
Cults. a soil impregnated with the germs of old beliefs, had utterly ignored the centuries of preparation, and had brought a message in no wise recalling what had so long been sacred to the world. In dealing with what primitive Christian worship borrowed from the Jewish rites, it is important to distinguish between the Temple service, which had little direct influence, and that of the synagogue, which in its four main features— reading of the Scriptures, chants, homilies, and prayers—was continued in morphological complete-

ness by the first Christian congregations. In regard to the principal rite which was not taken over from the synagogue, the Lord's Supper, it is hardly necessary to dwell on the radical divergence between the modern Protestant and Roman Catholic views of its purpose and nature—the former holding it to be a mere symbolic commemoration of a past historic event, while the latter regards it as not merely the representation in figure but the re-presentation in actual reality of the sacrifice of Christ, and the feeding of priest and worshipers with the body and blood of their God (see, for the contrasting views, LORD'S SUPPER, IV., §§ 1–3; MASS). It falls within the scope of the present treatment to point out that from the whole pagan world—although some of the Jews, unmindful of the primitive traditions of their forefathers, said skeptically, " how can this man give us his flesh to eat? "—the doctrine of John vi. in its literal sense would have evoked a responsive memory of their most ancient religious traditions. In like manner baptism, as the means of initiation into a voluntary and extranational religious brotherhood, was a ceremony familiar to the adherents of the mysteries among the Mediterranean peoples. Some of them had already regarded their lustrations as not merely a washing away of old sins, but as a spiritual regeneration; and in the rites of Isis baptism with water was supposed to raise the mortal to participation in the divine nature. (For various parallels among savage tribes, showing the prevalence in primitive societies of the idea of death and rebirth at initiation, see J. G. Frazer, *Golden Bough*, iii. 424–446, London, 1900; E. Crawley, *The Tree of Life*, p. 57, ib., 1905.)

Worship, reaching its culmination in the Eucharist, became from the first a recognized part of Christian duty. The celebration of the Lord's Day was from the first in universal custom, as it has long been by strict and positive law throughout the Catholic Church, marked by participation in this rite, including, besides the central
22. Eucha- mystic offering, the presentation of
ristic Wor- bread and wine by the congregation
ship; Latria (a reminder of primitive cereal obla-
and Dulia. tions, preserved in the Roman rite as late as the ninth century), and, tacitly at least, the self-oblation of the worshipers as " a living sacrifice, holy, acceptable unto God," their " reasonable service " (Rom. xii. 1). An interesting feature of the liturgical researches of Duchesne (*Christian Worship*, p. 161, Eng. transl., 2d ed., London, 1904) is the distinction in the early *Ordines Romani* between the " stational," or public, and the less solemn, or private, masses. To the great liturgical assemblies known under the former title, all the clergy and people of the entire local church were convoked; and whether in one of the great basilicas or in a simple presbyteral church, whether the pope or an ordinary priest was the celebrant, the ceremonies were of an elaborate type; and the entire function was thus a reproduction in essence of the ancient communal sacrifices offered by and in presence of the whole tribe. In this place it may be well to speak of the distinction (alluded to at the beginning of this article) between various forms

of veneration understood in Roman Catholic theology. It is emphatically laid down that worship in the stricter sense of the word, or what is called technically *latria*, is and can be offered to none, under any circumstances, but to God alone; and the supreme and perfect form of such worship, the only adequate worship, is the eucharistic sacrifice, in which Christ is conceived to be both priest and victim. The derived or lower reverence paid to the saints is known as *Dulia* (q.v.), with *hyperdulia*, attributed to the Blessed Virgin Mary, as its highest possible form.

In closing, it may be well to say a few words on the ethical aspect of worship, and its results upon the man who offers it. It has been pointed out by Caird that religions of the objective type are not wholly without ethical influence upon their followers. "Even in a very primitive form of such religion, the gods are regarded as the forefathers of the race of their worshipers; and their worship is therefore bound up with the natural piety which unites the individual to his kinsmen. So also in Greece and Rome civic patriotism was consecrated by a religion which combined the worship of the gods with the service of the state. And it may fairly be said that, throughout all the ancient world, the principle of nationality and the worship of a national god were bound up together." This, however, is very far from being all that follows from it as the subjective consciousness develops. Rites of purification were at first conceived in a half-conscious and non-moral spirit; but they did not remain on this low ground. As the religious consciousness broadened and deepened, men saw more and more clearly what must be in their hearts as they brought their gifts to the altar. Among the Chinese, worship was regarded as one aspect of an exercise in good manners and in human dignity through offerings and through observance of rules and respectful conduct toward the great forefathers and divinities; and this moral conception was a special feature of Chinese worship. Prayer, a very prominent and well-nigh universal element in primitive religions, whether it appears as thanksgiving by praise, or as petition for assistance and protection, or, again, as penitence for neglect of duty, can not be sincerely offered without affecting him who makes it. It has been justly remarked by L. W. E. Rauwenhoff that all worship is of a twofold character. Man approaches his God, and God approaches man. This reciprocal relation is suggested to Augustine by the Latin word for worship; *cultus* designates not only the adoration of the Deity, but the tilling of a field or the care of the body (*Serm.*, ccxiii. 9). The transition is abrupt to a sage of a very different temper from the African bishop; but Emerson teaches the same lesson of result: "The happiest man is he who learns from nature the lesson of worship." The student of the history of worship must journey far, through obscure and perplexing paths; but at least he sees that worship, in its origin and essence, is "a striving after union with God, and the worshiper's periodical escape from the turmoil of everyday life, with its petty cares and great sorrows, its strife and

discord, its complete immersion in the material, in order that he may for a while breathe a higher and purer atmosphere." A. I. DU P. COLEMAN.

BIBLIOGRAPHY: On worship in non-Christian religions consult: Lord Avebury, *Origin of Civilization*, London, 1870; C. F. Keary, *Outlines of Primitive Beliefs among the Indo-European Races*, New York, 1882; A. Kuenen, *Natural Religions and Universal Religions*, London, 1882; A. Réville, *Religions des peuples non-civilisés*, 2 vols., Paris, 1883; C. P. Tiele, *Babylonisch-Assyrische Geschichte*, Gotha, 1886; idem, *Elements of the Science of Religion*, 2 vols., London, 1897–99; O. Speeman, *Die gottesdienstlichen Gebräuche der Griechen und Römer*, Leipsic, 1888; E. Clodd, *Myths and Dreams*, 2d ed., London, 1891; C. Caird, *The Evolution of Religion*, ib. 1893; Smith, *Rel. of Sem.*, 2d ed., Edinburgh, 1894; F. Granger, *The Worship of the Romans*, London, 1895; L. R. Farnell, *The Cults of the Greek States*, 5 vols., Oxford, 1896 sqq.; A. Wiedemann, *Religion of the Ancient Egyptians*, New York, 1897; D. G. Brinton, *Religions of Primitive Peoples*, ib. 1899; A. Lang, *Myth, Ritual, and Religion*, 2 vols., 2d ed., London, 1899; idem, *Magic and Religion*, ib. 1901; B. Spencer and F. J. Gillen, *The Native Tribes of Western Australia*, ib. 1899; idem, *Northern Tribes of Central Australia*, ib. 1904; J. G. Frazer, *The Golden Bough*, 3d ed., ib., 1906 sqq.; P. Gardner, *An Historic View of the New Testament*, ib. 1901; E. B. Tylor, *Primitive Culture*, 2 vols., 4th ed., ib. 1903; P. Le Page Renouf, *The Religion of the Ancient Egyptians*, new ed., ib. 1904; W. Mannhardt, *Baumkultus der Germanen*, new ed., Berlin, 1904; idem, *Wald- und Feldkulte*, 2d ed., ib. 1905; R. H. Nassau, *Fetishism in West Africa*, New York, 1904; E. Crawley, *The Tree of Life*, London, 1905; P. D. Chantepie de la Saussaye, *Lehrbuch der Religionsgeschichte*, 3d ed., Tübingen, 1905; W. Karsten, *Origin of Worship*, Wasa, 1905; R. E. Dennett, *At the Back of the Black Man's Mind*, London, 1906; Jane E. Harrison, *Prolegomena to the Study of Greek Religion*, 2d ed., Cambridge, 1908; F. B. Jevons, *Introduction to the History of Religion*, 4th ed., London, 1908; E. Westermarck, *Origin and Development of the Moral Ideas*, 2 vols., ib. 1908; S. Reinach, *Cultes, mythes, et religions*, 3 vols., 2d ed., Paris, 1908; idem, *Orpheus, a General Hist. of Religions*, New York, 1909; A. Le Roy, *La Religion des primitifs*, Paris, 1909; R. R. Marett, *The Threshold of Religion*, London, 1909; F. Cumont, *Oriental Religions in Roman Paganism*, Chicago, 1911; M. Jastrow, Jr., *Aspects of Religious Belief and Practice in Babylonia and Assyria*, New York, 1911.

For Christian worship use: Bingham, *Origines* (above all usable for the details and history); E. Martène, *De antiquis ecclesiæ ritibus*, 2d ed., 4 vols., Antwerp, 1736–1738; M. A. Nickel, *Die heiligen Zeiten und Feste der katholischen Kirche*, 6 vols., Mainz, 1836; H. Alt, *Der christlichen Cultus nach seinen verschiedenen Entwickelungsformen und seinen einzelnen Theilen historisch dargestellt*, Berlin, 1843, 2d ed., 2 vols., 1851–60; J. G. Müller, *Geschichte der christlichen Feste*, Berlin, 1843; K. L. Weitzel, *Die christlichen Passafeier der drei ersten Jahrhunderten*, Pforzheim, 1848; G. Huyssen, *Die Feste der christlichen Kirche*, 2 vols., Iserlohn, 1850–59; H. Abeken, *Der Gottesdienst der alten Kirche*, Berlin, 1853; T. Harnack, *christliche Gemeindegottesdienst im apostolischen und altkatholischen Zeitalter*, Erlangen, 1854; F. Probst, *Lehre und Gebet in den ersten christlichen Jahrhunderten*, Tübingen, 1871; H. Otte, *Glockenkunde*, 2d ed., Leipsic, 1884; H. A. Köstlin, *Geschichte des christlichen Gottesdienstes*, Freiburg, 1887; O. Gisler, *Gottesdienst der katholischen Kirche*, Einsiedeln, 1888; P. Kleinert, *Zur christlichen Kultus-und Kulturgeschichte*, Berlin, 1889; E. Doumergue, *Essai sur l'histoire du culte réformé principalement au XVI. et XIX. siècle*, Paris, 1890; M. A. Goldstein, *Gebet und Glaube*. *Beitrag zur Erklärung des Gottesdienstes*, Budapest, 1890; K. Moser, *Der Gottesdienst in Kirche, Schule, und Haus*, 4th ed., Innsbruck, 1891; E. Meuss, *Die Gottesdienstlichen Handlungen in der evangelischen Kirche*, Gotha, 1892; D. Sokolow, *Darstellung des Gottesdienstes der orthodox-katholischen Kirche des Morgenlandes*, Berlin, 1893; G. R. Crooks and J. F. Hurst, *Theological Encyclopædia and Methodology*, pp. 527–547, new ed., New York, 1894; C. C. Hall and others, *Christian Worship*, New York, 1897; F. Lemme, *Wegweiser in den evangelischen Gottesdienst*, 3 parts, Breslau, 1897; J. Keating, *The Agape and the Eucharist in the Early*

Church, London, 1901; H. Kellner, *Heortologie oder das Kirchenjahr und die heiligen Feste in ihrer geschichtlichen Entwickelung*, Freiburg, 1901; L. Ruland, *Geschichte der kirchlichen Leichenfeier*, Regensburg, 1901; O. J. Mehl, *Die schönen Gottesdienste*, Hamburg, 1902; P. Drews, *Studien zur Geschichte des Gottesdienstes*, 4 parts, Tübingen, 1902–10; A. J. Maclean, *Recent Discoveries Illustrating Early Christian Life and Worship*, London, 1904; W. H. Dolbeer, *The Benediction*, Philadelphia, 1908; G. A. J. Ross, *The Value of Worship*, New York, 1909; L. Duchesne, *Christian Worship: its Origin and Evolution*, 3d Eng. ed., London, 1910; the literature under COMMON PRAYER, BOOK OF; FEASTS AND FESTIVALS; LITURGICS; PRACTICAL THEOLOGY; SUNDAY; also under the articles on the ethnic religions much will be found apart from those works specifically noted above.

WORTHINGTON, GEORGE: Protestant Episcopal bishop; b. at Lenox, Mass., Oct. 14, 1840; d. at Mentone Jan. 7, 1908. He was graduated from Hobart College, Geneva, N. Y., 1860, and from the General Theological Seminary, New York, 1863; was ordered deacon, 1863, and ordained priest, 1864; became assistant at St. Paul's Church, Troy, N. Y., 1863; rector of Christ Church, Ballston Spa, N. Y., 1865; was rector of St. John's Church, Detroit, Mich., 1868–85; and was bishop of Nebraska from 1885. His administration was marked by a great development in the affairs of the see.

BIBLIOGRAPHY: W. S. Perry, *The Episcopate in America*, p. 291, New York, 1895.

WORTHINGTON, JOHN: An English clergyman, known as a member of the school of "Cambridge Platonists" (q.v.), into whose inner life his *Diary and Correspondence* (ed. Crossley, for the Chetham Society, Manchester, 1847) gives valuable glimpses. He was b. at Manchester, Feb., 1618; d. in London, Nov. 30, 1671; was educated at Emmanuel College, Cambridge (B.A., 1635; M.A., 1639; fellow, 1641), where he had Benjamin Whichcote for his tutor and Nathanael Culverwel (qq.v.) for his friend; became a clergyman in 1646. Besides several parochial preferments, he was master of Jesus College, Cambridge, from 1650 to 1660, when he was displaced to make room for the restoration of a former master who had been ejected by the Puritans. He spent his remaining years between London and Lincolnshire, where he held the living of Ingoldsby, of which More was the patron, and a prebend in Lincoln cathedral. His original work consists mainly of a volume of *Discourses* (London, 1725), and a smaller volume of *Miscellanies* (1704); but he also edited with great care the works of Joseph Mead, from whom the Cambridge movement may in a sense be said to take its rise, and the *Select Discourses* of John Smith, one of its most important members.

BIBLIOGRAPHY: Besides the literature under CAMBRIDGE PLATONISTS, and under the articles on the members of that school, consult Worthington's *Diary and Correspondence*, ut sup.; Simon Patrick's *Autobiography*, Oxford, 1839; J. Tulloch, *Rational Theology and Christian Philosophy*, ii. 426–433, Edinburgh, 1874; *DNB*, lxiii. 40–42.

WORTMAN, DENIS: Dutch Reformed; b. at East Fishkill, N. Y., Apr. 30, 1835. He was graduated from Amherst (B.A., 1857) and the Reformed Church Seminary, New Brunswick, N. J. (1860). He held pastorates at Brooklyn, N. Y. (1860–63), Philadelphia (1863–65), Schenectady, N. Y. (1865–1871); Fort Plain, N. Y. (1880–83), and Saugerties (1883–1901). He was debarred from regular pas-

toral work in 1871–76 by ill-health, and for the next four years acted as supply to various churches. Since 1901 he has been secretary of the Ministerial Relief Fund of the Reformed Church in America. In theology he holds "to the Reformed faith, with modifications as suggested by scientific learning and broader sympathies." He has written the two poems *Reliques of the Christ* (New York, 1888), and *The Divine Processional* (1903). Several of his hymns are in current use.

WRATH OF GOD: The Hebrew language is rich in terms for "anger," these picturing either the inward fire of wrath, or its outward manifestations in terms of animated physical life, specially breathing (*'anaph*), then overflowing rage, and consuming fire (Deut. xxxii. 19 sqq). The anger of God is kindled (Isa. v. 25), and he comes "to render his anger with fury, and his rebuke with flames of fire" (Isa. lxvi. 15); his indignation is poured out (Zeph. iii. 8); and his wrath produces the tempest described in Ps. xviii. 7 sqq. Jeremiah and Ezekiel may be described as *par excellence* the prophets of wrath. Nor is this wrath a mere figure of speech; it is real anger, manifested not only in its effects, but in the divine motive toward his creation. It is the divine counterpart of human anger, and one tacitly accepted by the New Testament from the Old. The traditional view holds that the first sin and the divine anger are correlates, so that man is now a "child of wrath," while God has withdrawn far from him. Drop by drop man must drink the cup of divine wrath to the dregs, until finally the angry divine majesty snaps the thread of the life of man who selfishly withdraws in sin from the service of God (cf. Gen. ii., iii. with Ps. xc.). Since anger is possible only when one associates with another, and since, after Yahweh had chosen Israel, such intercommunication was possible only with his own people, and no longer with the Gentiles, whom he left "to walk in their own ways" (Acts xiv. 16), therefore the wrath of God is generally spoken of in the Old Testament only in connection with human interference in Yahweh's personal relations with Israel. The very basis of the entire dispensation whereby Yahweh restricted his presence to Israel and left the Gentiles to their own devices was his wrath, which led him to deliver to death the race which had proved recreant to him (Gen. iii., vi., xi.); and this divine wrath, separating sinful man from life, is typified in the cherubim and the flaming sword at the gates of Eden (Gen. iii. 24). All this makes clear the relation of the wrath of God to his holiness. When man becomes sensible of the separation between himself and God, he must seek to repair the breach, and since repentance is the object of all divine judgments, God then restrains his wrath, so that mention is made, throughout all periods of the Old-Testament revelation, of the mercy and long-suffering of Yahweh. And yet, the rendering of love is not unlimited by the claims of wrath, and the holiness of God must still set up a barrier against the sin of man, so that all who draw near unworthily encounter divine wrath which is, in the most literal sense, a devouring flame (cf. Deut. iv. 33; Lev. x. 1–3). But despite his sin, man

(Marginal label:) Old Testament.

may draw near to God, approaching by means of prayer and intercession. This was true not only of such men of God as Abraham and Moses, but also of the priests, though even the latter must bring gifts and sacrifices. Sin must be "covered" from the sight of a wrathful God, and the killing of the sacrificial victim symbolizes the punishment of death which Yahweh's representative must exact. When death or sickness or other distresses approach, the righteous cry: "Rebuke me not in thine anger, neither chasten me in thy hot displeasure" (Ps. vi. 1, xxxviii. 1); but even when the faithful experience the wrath of God, this is but transitory, vividly contrasting with the divine grace which endures forever (Ps. xxx. 5; Isa. liv. 7–8, lx. 10). Intermediate between these passages are those which represent the people of God, just and unjust, as one, in which the wrath of God is salvation to the faithful remnant and to the others a consuming fire (Isa. xxvi. 20; Mic. vii. 9). Here the wrath of God can not be assumed as merely instrumental or feigned, concealing the real motive of love. The entire earthly relation between God and man, and especially between Yahweh and Israel, is entirely preparatory and transitional, and the sharp antithesis between wrath and grace is reached only at the end. "Days of wrath" come in the present world to individuals and communities (Prov. xi. 4); and for Israel it is the day of the destruction of Jerusalem (Ezek. vii. 19). The "after time" brings the day of the Lord and his wrath against the apostate, and especially against the Gentiles opposed to him and Israel (cf. Deut. xxxii. 35–36; Isa. lxi. 2, lxiii. 4); and from the time of Joel this judgment gradually widens into the judgment of the world, and the day of the Lord is resolved into a final judgment issuing into an eternal dualism of grace and wrath (Isa. lxv.-lxvi.).

The wrath of God is as prominent in the New Testament as in the Old. Christ is described as angry (Mark iii. 5), especially at the cleansing of the temple (Matt. xxi. 12–13), while **The New** such parables as those of the talents **Testament.** and of the sheep and the goats imply a similar feeling. The wrath of God described in the New Testament is essentially eschatological. John the Baptist speaks of flight from "the wrath to come" (Matt. iii. 7); from which Christ gives deliverance (1 Thess. i. 10). Paul mentions a series of sins that provoke the divine wrath (Eph. v. 3–6; Col. iii. 5–6); and to him wrath is the antithesis of justification, being the imputation and punishment of guilt (Rom. v. 9). In other passages it may be uncertain whether the wrath mentioned is in character eschatological, or general, embracing a combination of the two with alternative emphasis (John iii. 36; Rom. i. 18, iii. 5, iv. 15, ix. 22, xii. 19; Eph. ii. 3, v. 6; I Thess. ii. 16). It seems most probable, however, that these passages do not exclusively refer to the eschatological idea, but also allude to the wrath of God as essentially present in this world. This view also justifies the orthodox idea of the Atonement (q.v.), that through Christ the divine wrath, which doomed a sinful world to the judgment of death, was averted, and in its place, mercy, justice, and life were brought

to mankind (practically to those who believe). By its implications the New Testament seems to justify the doctrine that Christ bore the wrath of God for man (cf. Gal. iii. 13; II Cor. v. 21). If to the Pauline utterances concerning the relation of the death of Christ to mankind and to death, the wages of sin, there be added the synoptic statements regarding the death of Christ, who must suffer according to the Scriptures, and give his life a ransom for many (Matt. xx. 28; cf. Isa. liii.; Zech. xi.), then it becomes clear that the apostolic Church was convinced that Christ had turned away the divine wrath. To this must be added the fourth Word from the Cross, the agony in the garden, and the numerous references of Paul and other New-Testament writers to sacrifice and to prophecy (especially Isa. liii.) with reference to Christ, all of which imply that the judgment of divine wrath for a sinful world was actually borne, in concentrated form, by Christ. The fact that there is no specific mention of the wrath of God in connection with the work of Christ is doubtless due to the lack of anthropomorphism in the New Testament, where the wrath of God, except in its eschatological sense, is used only to denote the cause of the condemnation of fallen man. This does not imply that the wrath of God is not real, or that it is a mere figure of speech for the concept of righteous recompense; but the Old-Testament relation of Yahweh to Israel no longer existed, and the Old-Testament covenantal concept was at an end. There could be, therefore, no such allusions to divine wrath as in the Old Testament, except in eschatological passages like Rev. xvi. 19, xix. 15; and since a wrong connotation might be given to the Old-Testament concept, the phrase "wrath of God" seems to have been intentionally omitted in the New-Testament passages concerning the atonement.

In opposition to the Epicurean and Stoic concepts of God, Lactantius (q.v.) postulated not merely the possibility but the necessity of the "wrath in God"; not alone because of the divine personality, of which man's nature was a pattern, but also because of the divine love, **Dogma.** since "he who hates not, loves not" (De ira Dei, iv., vii.; Eng. transl., ANF, vii. 260–263), besides laying stress on the practical perils lurking in the denial of so restraining a doctrine. It is true that a living, personal God is unimaginable without emotions and will, the former taking cognizance of pleasure and displeasure, and the latter acting and reacting. Thus wrath becomes an attribute of God, with whom it forms the constant protector of the divine self-complacency against all disturbing elements. A wrathless association of God with others than himself is unthinkable, without sacrificing his personality. A "natural side" to the divine being (F. Delitzsch), or a "dark background" or abyss (J. Boehme), to ground the possibility of God's wrath, are futile conjectures; it can come in view only in God's intercourse with others, or revelation. The Fathers, biased by a philosophy which abhorred anthropomorphic aspects of deity, and clinging to the idea of an impassible God, were strangely at one with the rationalistic deists, who deny the divine wrath;

but their belief in the true revelation of God and its record in the Bible forestalled the consequences of the divorce between God and man on the part of the latter.

The relation of the divine wrath to the holiness of God depends largely on the problem whether wrath is an emotion with God as with man. This is rightly affirmed by Lactantius, when he defines anger as "an emotion of the mind arousing itself for the restraining of faults" (De ira, xvii.), a definition followed by many later theologians. The relation of God's wrath to his holiness may be thus stated. In the conditions of life created by the divine holiness God participates personally with his feeling and self-complacency. Any disturbance of these conditions of life involves an alteration of the motive life and self-complacency of God who reveals himself to and dwells among men; and thus necessarily not only brings about an instantaneous reaction, but results in a personal defensive attitude, a personal antagonism and the withdrawal of self from the disturbing factor, and the removal of the latter from self. It is not altogether correct to consider wrath as the energy of divine justice in its punitive aspect, for the latter appertains to the divine will, while wrath is primarily a part of emotion and self-sensibility. Justice is concerned with the preservation of divine order; wrath with the protection of God's personal interest. To avert the questionable aspects of personal emotion and passion, many theologians would seek for anger a close coordination with love. Just as an earthly father, in punishing a naughty child, becomes really angry and exercises the right of stern chastisement, while contemplating at the same time loving intention and hope, rendered, however, only on condition of improvement, so God is at the same time truly wrathful against the sinful, but full of love toward them when they repent. In so far as the experience of this wrath tends to produce repentance, it is, of course, a means to the end of love. To man's conduct toward God corresponds God's conduct toward man. Partial separation and partial alienation of man from God entails the dual dispensation of love and wrath. To these alternating preponderances of God's rendering to the individual corresponds also God's attitude toward the obdurate as a class and inversely toward the believers.

By sin man not only violates the divinely appointed order, which consequently reacts against him, but he also invades the sphere of God's life and so conflicts, as person against person, with the divine self-consciousness as to draw upon himself the movement which negates both him and the relation to God. The power of life becomes a power of death and destruction. The first negation of sin by God followed the first emission of wrath that placed the sinful world universally under the permanent sway of the powers of death and destruction (Gen. iii.). This the New Testa-
Sin and ment frequently designates as "wrath
Atonement. of God," and it warrants the Church in referring God's anger to original sin. There are climaxes of this revelation of wrath, partly against all mankind because of "ungodliness and unrighteousness" (Rom. i. 18), and principally

within the sphere of the special covenant, because of personal fellowship between God and man. A distinction must be drawn between an objective wrath, which, pregnant with destruction, lowers over a sinful world, breaking with fury from time to time, and a personal wrath manifested by God toward and apperceived by individuals. The latter is felt in proportion to the tenderness of conscience, and thus is found especially among believers. Among these the sense of divine wrath may become excited to a morbid experience confounding truth and error, as in the case of many mystics. In the atonement, he who places himself under the wrath of God over the sinful world, in order to withdraw it from others, must do this by the free ethical assumption of the judgment of penalty pending over the world. On the other hand, only he is qualified to do this who is the organic head of the race. The coalescence of the two produces the ethical mystical view, presented here as the Biblical. In this substitute is realized that toward which humanity aspired symbolically by their sacrifices, and for which God set up a type in the Old Testament, not only in the sacrifices and prophecies but on the whole in the entire institution in which he accepted propitiation, whether through persons, acts, intercessions, or suffering. As before Christ the time of wrath was indeed the time of "forbearance" (Rom. iii. 25–26), so, inversely, in Christ, the revealer of grace and truth, the wrath and curse over sin come first to light in the full sense; and there is ushered in the crisis continuing throughout the centuries dividing the human race into "vessels of wrath" and "vessels of mercy," until the last day of wrath (see DAY OF THE LORD) shall bring the ultimate decision. To those who persist to the end in self-estrangement from God, it can mean only interminable separation from him and the divine life.

(ARNOLD RÜEGG†.)

BIBLIOGRAPHY: For discussions of the Biblical idea the reader is referred to the works named in and under BIBLICAL THEOLOGY. From the dogmatic standpoint the literature is to be found in the works specified in and under DOGMA, DOGMATICS; and under SIN. Consult further: Lactantius, De ira Dei, Eng. transl. in ANF, vii. 259–280; A. Ritschl, De ira Dei, Bonn, 1859 (cf. L. Haug, Darstellung und Beurtheilung der Ritschl'schen Theologie, Ludwigsburg, 1885—combats Ritschl); idem, Rechtfertigung und Versöhnung, ii. 119–156, 3 vols., Bonn, 1870–74; F. Weber, Vom Zorne Gottes, Erlangen, 1862; C. von Orelli, in ZKW, 1884, pp. 22–33; W. G. T. Shedd, Doctrine of Endless Punishment, New York, 1886; J. Ninck, Jesus als Charakter, pp. 27–40, Berlin, 1906; M. Pohlenz, Vom Zorne Gottes. Ein Studie über den Einfluss der griechischen Philosophie auf das alte Christentum, Göttingen, 1909.

WRATISLAW, ALBERT HENRY: Church of England, Slavonic scholar; b. at Rugby (28 m. s.e. of Birmingham), England, Nov. 5, 1821; d. at Southsea, a suburb of Portsmouth, Nov. 3, 1892. He studied at Rugby School, and at Trinity, later at Christ College, Cambridge (B.A., 1844; M.A., 1847; and fellow, 1844–53); became a tutor in his college; in 1849 visited Bohemia, studying the Czech language in Prague; was head master of Felstead School, 1850–55; of Bury St. Edmunds Grammar School, 1855–79; and held the college living of Manorbier in Pembrokeshire, 1877–89, when he retired to Southsea. From 1850 to 1870 Wratislaw was deeply engaged in scholastic work, and in 1877 he delivered lectures at the Taylorian Institution in Oxford, which were published as *The Native Literature of Bohemia in the Fourteenth Century* (London, 1878). He translated from the Bohemian the *Adventures of Baron W. Wratislaw of Mitrowitz* (London, 1862), and a number of poems issued as *Lyra Czecho-Slovanska* (1849). His theological works embrace *Barabbas the Scapegoat, and other Sermons and Dissertations* (London, 1859); *Historical and Statistical Sketch of the Slavonic Protestants, in the north of the Austrian Empire* (1861); *Notes and Dissertations, principally on Difficulties in the Scriptures of the New Covenant* (1863); *How Saints are made at Rome in Modern Days* (1866); *Intercourse and Intercommunion among Christians. Rome and England. Two Essays* (1866); *Life, Legend, and Canonization of St. John Nepomucen* (1873); and *John Hus. The Commencement of Resistance to Papal Authority on the Part of the Inferior Clergy* (1882).

BIBLIOGRAPHY: *DNB*, lxiii. 68–69.

WREDE, vrĕ'de, **WILLIAM:** German New-Testament scholar; b. at Bücken (25 m. s.s.e. of Bremen) May 10, 1859; d. at Breslau Nov. 23, 1906. He received his education at the gymnasium at Celle, the universities of Leipsic and Göttingen, and the theological seminary at Loccum; became inspector of the theological foundation at Göttingen, 1884; took a pastorate at Langenholzen, 1887; returned to Göttingen to teach, 1889; became extraordinary professor for the New Testament at Breslau, 1893, and professor, 1895. His principal works are *Untersuchungen zum ersten Clemensbriefe* (Göttingen, 1891); *Ueber Aufgabe und Methode der . . . neutestamentlichen Theologie* (1897); *Das Messiasgeheimnis in den Evangelien* (1901); *Charakter und Tendenz des Johannesevangeliums* (1903); *Paulus* (Tübingen, 1905; Eng. transl., *Paul*, London, 1907); and the posthumous *Vorträge und Reden* (1907); and *Die Entstehung der Schriften des Neuen Testaments* (1907; Eng. transl., *The Origin of the New Testament*, New York, 1910).

The two works for which Wrede is best known, the *Messiasgeheimnis* and the *Paulus*, illustrate well both the excellences and the defects of their author as well as his services to theological science. Even in his first work on the First Epistle of Clement, he revealed himself as not only a learned, careful, and keen-sighted scholar, but also as an independent and thoughtful critic. Anew he proved the value of that letter as a source of knowledge not only for the Roman community but for the general tendencies and needs of the postapostolic generation. His interest was not in the details, but in the general relations both to the preceding and the following literature and events. So in his treatment of New-Testament theology he bound together religion and theology. His *Paulus* deals with a side of what he regarded as within the province of New-Testament theology. In all this work he consciously limited himself to certain lines of investigation, not because he had no interest in what lay beyond, but because in this chosen field he found problems that required answers which he felt he must find before he advanced to the wider field, in answering, which, too, he felt that he was preparing himself for advance.

In his researches he did not permit himself to be fettered by tradition, no matter what its source. While he honored profoundly his teachers, he subjected himself to none of them; he neither belonged to a "school" nor did he build one. As a teacher he evinced these same qualities, took his work earnestly, and stimulated his pupils to thoroughgoing patience and industry in their labors.

His *Paulus* is rather a work of art than a popular book, though it belongs to a popular series. It does not concern itself with detail, but is a polished treatment of the essential life and work of the apostle, comparing that life with the life of Jesus. In that it does not furnish a purely historical decision it reflects Wrede's subjective standpoint. The author regards Paul as the second founder of Christianity, the builder of ecclesiastical orthodoxy, who changed, by his doctrine of the incarnation, death, and resurrection of Christ, the religion of Jesus. Not that he charges Paul with a fault here, but rather regrets that it was Paul who did what had to be done. As a check upon the unwholesome and panegyrical exposition of the life of Paul, Wrede's work was valuable; but Wrede does not present the entire Paul to his readers, it is a profile picture which he paints. Similarly in his treatment of the Gospel of John, only one side is presented, not a consideration of the entire problem. A one-sidedness of another kind comes to light in the *Messiasgeheimnis*. To bring up earnestly the question whether, according to the consensus of the New Testament, Jesus conceived of himself as Messiah was a great service and as a stimulus has borne good fruit. Since his work investigation concerning the self-consciousness of Jesus has taken a new start. The error of Wrede lies in the fact that he overestimated the conclusiveness and deliberateness with which the evangelists individually assumed one or another of the view-points possible in their time. He worked too much in logical categories, asked too often why and how; he handled Mark and Paul as though they were men of our times.

In spite of these defects his short period of work, shortened even beyond the actual time by calamity and illness, was uncommonly fruitful. His plow went deep, and he scattered his seed beyond his own furrow.   (G. A. JÜLICHER.)

WRIGHT, CHARLES HENRY HAMILTON: Church of England; b. at Dublin Mar. 9, 1836; d. in London Mar. 22, 1909. He was educated at Trinity College, Dublin (B.A., 1857; M.A., 1859), and was ordered deacon in 1859 and ordained priest in the following year. He was curate of Middleton-Tyas, Yorkshire, in 1859–63, chaplain of the English church at Dresden in 1863–68, chaplain of Holy Trinity, Boulogne-sur-Mer, in 1868–73, incumbent of St. Mary's, Dublin, in 1874–85, and of Bethesda Church in the same city in 1885–91, and vicar of St. John's, Liverpool, in 1891–98. After 1898 he was clerical superintendent of the Protestant Reformation Society. He was also Bampton Lecturer at Oxford in 1878, Donellan Lecturer at Trinity College, Dublin, in 1880–81, and Grinfeld Lecturer on the Septuagint at Oxford in 1893–97, besides being examiner in Hebrew at different times to the universities of Oxford, London, Manchester, and Wales. In theology he described himself as "evangelical and conservative, but quite willing to adopt opinions based on real evidence and not on mere conjectures or hypotheses of scholars however eminent." He wrote or edited *A Grammar of the Modern Irish Language* (Dublin, 1855); *The Book of Genesis in Hebrew* (London, 1859); *The Book of Ruth in Hebrew* (1864); *Bunyan's Allegorical and Select Poetical Works* (1866); *The Fatherhood of God, and its Relation to the Person and Work of Christ, and the Operations of the Holy Spirit* (Edinburgh, 1867); *Zechariah and his Prophecies Considered in Relation to Modern Criticism* (Bampton lectures; London, 1879); *The Book of Koheleth, commonly called Ecclesiastes, Considered in Relation to Modern Criticism and to the Doctrines of Modern Pessimism* ((Donellan lectures; 1883); *Biblical Essays* (Edinburgh, 1886); *The Writings of St. Patrick, the Apostle of Ireland* (London, 1887); *Introduction to the Old Testament* (1890); *The Bible Readers' Manual; or, Aids to Biblical Study* (1895); *The Service of the Mass in the Greek and Roman Churches* (1898); *Roman Catholicism: or, The Doctrines of the Church of Rome briefly examined in the Light of Scripture* (1896; 4th ed., 1909); *The Intermediate State and Prayers for the Dead examined in the Light of Scripture and Ancient Jewish and Christian Literature* (1900); *The Statutory Prayer Book* (in collaboration with J. J. Tomlinson; 1902); *A Protestant Dictionary* (edited in collaboration with C. Neil; 1904); *The Book of Isaiah, and other Historical Essays* (1905); *Daniel and his Prophecies* (1906); *Daniel and its Critics* (1906); and *Light from Egyptian Papyri on Jewish Hist. before Christ* (1908).

WRIGHT, GEORGE FREDERICK: Congregationalist; b. at Whitehall, N. Y., Jan. 22, 1838. He was graduated from Oberlin College, Oberlin, O. (A.B., 1859), and Oberlin Theological Seminary (1862), after serving for five months as a private in the Union Army in 1861; held pastorates at Bakersfield, Vt. (1862–72), and Andover, Mass. (1872–1881); after which he was professor of New-Testament language and literature in Oberlin Theological Seminary (1881–92). Since 1892 he has been professor of the harmony of science and revelation in the same institution. He was also an assistant in the Pennsylvania Geological Survey in 1881–82, and in the United States Geological Survey in 1884–92. Since 1884 he has been editor of the *Bibliotheca Sacra*, and in addition to briefer contributions, many of them devoted to establishing the harmony of geological discoveries with the accounts of the Bible, has written *Logic of Christian Evidences* (Andover, 1880); *Studies in Science and Religion* (1882); *An Inquiry concerning the Relation of Death to Probation* (Boston, 1882); *The Divine Authority of the Bible* (1884); *The Glacial Boundary in Ohio, Indiana, and Kentucky* (Cleveland, O., 1884); *The Ice Age in North America, and its Bearings upon the Antiquity of Man* (New York, 1889; 5th ed., 1911); *Charles Grandison Finney* (Boston, 1891); *Man and the Glacial Period* (New York, 1892); *Greenland Icefields and Life in the North Atlantic* (1896); *Scientific Aspects of Christian Evidences* (1898); *Asiatic Russia* (1902); and *Scientific Confirmations of Old Testament History* (Oberlin, O., 1907).

WRIGHT, THEODORE FRANCIS: Swedenborgian; b. at Dorchester (now a part of Boston), Mass., Aug. 3, 1845; d. at sea near Alexandria, Egypt, Nov. 13, 1907. He was graduated from Harvard (A.B., 1866) and the New Church Theological School (then at Waltham, Mass., 1868); in 1864–65 he served in the Union Army as first lieutenant of the 108th Colored Volunteers; after the completion of his studies was pastor of the Church of the New Jerusalem at Bridgewater, Mass. (1868–1889); and after 1889 was dean of the New Church Theological School at Cambridge, Mass., where he was professor of history after 1884. He was also honorary American secretary of the Palestine Exploration Fund after 1890. In addition to editing *The New Church Review* after 1893, he wrote *The Realities of Heaven* (New York, 1880); *Life Eternal* (Boston, 1885); *The Human and its Relation to the Divine* (Philadelphia, 1892); and *Psalms from Swedenborg's Latin Translations* (Germantown, Pa., 1900).

WRIGHT, THOMAS: Church of England layman; b. at Olney (51 m. n.w. of London), Bucks, May 16, 1859. He was educated at Buxton College, Forest Gate, London; since 1882 he has been principal of Cowper School, Olney. Besides being a trustee and the secretary of the Cowper Museum, formed by the gift of the poet Cowper's house to the town of Olney in 1900, he is the founder and secretary of the Cowper Society (founded in 1900) and of the John Payne Society (founded in 1905). Theologically he belongs to the Evangelical school of the Church of England. Besides being editor of all works published by the Cowper and John Payne societies, he has edited the letters of Cowper (4 vols., London, 1904); and has written: *The Town of Cowper* (London, 1886); *The Chalice of Carden* (1889); *The Blue Firedrake* (1892); *The Mystery of St. Dunstan's* (1892); *The Life of William Cowper* (1892); *The Life of Daniel Defoe* (1894); *The Acid Sisters* (poems; 1897); *Hind Head* (1898); *Ianthe* (1900); *The Ivory Coffer* (poems; 1903); *The Life of Edward Fitzgerald* (2 vols., 1904); *The Life of Sir Richard Burton* (2 vols., 1906); *The Life of Walter Pater* (2 vols., 1907); *The Life of Colonel Fred Burnaby* (1908); *The Life of William Huntington* (1909); and *Joseph Hart. Being personal Memoirs . . . from unpublished Materials* (1910).

WRIGHT, WILLIAM: Orientalist; b. at Mallye or Mallai, on the Nepal frontier, India, Jan. 17, 1830; d. at Cambridge, England, May 22, 1889. He early developed a fondness for oriental languages; studied at St. Andrews, from which he was graduated; then at Halle, devoting his main efforts to Syriac, but acquiring all the Semitic languages together with Sanskrit; and lastly at Leyden; was professor of Arabic at University College, London, 1855–56; and at Trinity College, Dublin, 1856–61, lecturing there on Hindustani; for the opportunity of original work, he held a post in the department of manuscripts at the British Museum, 1861–70; and was professor of Arabic at Cambridge, 1870–89, where he also became a fellow. As a member of the Old-Testament revision committee he had a field for the exercise of his extensive scholarship. His cooperative activity yielded such fruits as the oriental series of the Palæographical Society, drawn up under his editorship, and contributions to the lexical works of Payne Smith in Syriac, of Dozy in Arabic, and of Neubauer in Hebrew. He was an eminent teacher. He edited the book of Jonah in four Semitic versions (1857); *Fragments of the Curetonian Gospels* (1872); *Fragments of the Homilies of Cyril of Alexandria on the Gospel of S. Luke* (1874); translated and edited Caspari's *Grammar of the Arabic Language* (2 vols., London, 1859–62); collected and edited *Opuscula*

Arabica (Leyden, 1859); and with English translation and notes *Contributions to the Apocryphal Literature of the New Testament* (London, 1865); edited and translated *Apocryphal Acts of the Apostles* (2 vols., 1871); edited with English translation and notes *The Chronicle of Joshua the Stylite* (1882); and wrote *Lectures on the Comparative Grammar of the Semitic Languages* (Cambridge, 1890); and *A Short History of Syriac Literature* (London, 1894).

BIBLIOGRAPHY: R. L. Bensly, in *Journal of the Royal Asiatic Society*, 1889, pp. 708 sqq.; *DNB*, lxiii. 138–139.

WRITING AND THE ART OF WRITING, HEBREW.

I. The Biblical Statements.
  Statements Implying Early Use of Writing (§ 1).
  The Materials Employed (§ 2).
II. Information from Other Sources.
III. The North Semitic and Early Hebrew Script.

North Semitic Script (§ 1).
Development of the Alphabet (§ 2).
IV. Aramaic Varieties of Writing and the Hebrew Square Character
  The Older Forms (§ 1).

Development of the Square Characters (§ 2).
Sacredness of the Square Character (§ 3).
Documentary Testimony to Hebrew Script (§ 4).
Printed Documents (§ 5).

I. The Biblical Statements: For an acquaintance of the Hebrews with the art of writing in the period before Moses there are no direct testimonies. Though on the signet of Judah (Gen. xxxviii. 18) was engraved probably some pictorial representation, the account in Gen. xxiii. of the transaction before witnesses between Abraham and Ephron can only by employing the argument from silence be used against the idea of the possession by the Hebrews of the knowledge of writing. The old name of the city of Debir was Kirjath-sepher (Josh. xv. 15–16; Judges i. 11–12; Septuagint, *Kariassophar*, Egyptian *Bait tupar* [the rendering of this is disputed: it has been interpreted "Book-town," and the claim founded thereupon that writing was widely diffused in Palestine and that books were numerous; the Septuagint suggests rather the rendering "town of the scribe," and this conveys a directly opposite meaning]). The "officers" of the Hebrews in Egypt (Ex. v. 6) are called in Hebrew *shotarim;* in Assyrian and Arabic the root of this word has the meaning "to write," and the corresponding noun in Aramaic carries the meaning "document." But does this involve anything regarding the employment of this art among the Hebrews of that period? At any rate, if writing was diffused as an art among the Hebrews of the time of Moses, it can not be reckoned a new invention. Moses wrote matter that was legal (Ex. xxiv. 4, 7 [in the E record], xxxiv. 27; Deut. xxxi. 9, 24), and historical (Ex. xvii. 24 [E]; Numbers xxxiii. 2 [P]); the Song of Moses (Deut. xxxi. 22; cf. also Num. xvii. 2). The priests wrote (Num. v. 23 [P]) the imprecation in the water of Ordeal (q.v., § 7); and according to Deuteronomy (vi. 9, xi. 20, xxiv. 1, 3) others wrote. The engraving of names and other words on stone and metal is mentioned (Ex. xxviii. 9, 36 [P]). Joshua is recorded as having written the law of Moses (Josh. viii. 32), as having the land of Canaan described in a book for purposes of allotment (xviii. 6, 8, 9), and himself as writing certain matters in the book of the law of God at the assembly of the people at Shechem (xxiv. 26). In the period of the Judges the ability to use writing must have been common, for a youth caught by chance was able to give in writing to

Gideon the names of seventy-seven of the princes and elders of the city (Judges viii. 14, margin). According to I Sam. x. 25 Samuel wrote down the "law of the kingdom." Poems like those in Num. xxi. and Judges v. were certainly set down in writing at an early period; in Num. xxi. 14 are some lines of a poem cited from "the book of the wars of the Lord"; citations are made from "the book of Jasher" in Josh. x. 13; II Sam. i. 18, 19; and I Kings viii. 53 (according to the Septuagint—cf. J. C. Matthes in *ZATW*, 1903, p. 121, who would read in all three passages "book of the ode" instead of "book of Jasher," the difference being in the transposition of two letters). Consequently the assertion of T. T. Hartmann, W. Vatke, and P. von Bohlen is not defensible that not until shortly before Solomon, or even later, was the art of writing an accomplishment of the Hebrews. From the regal period there are numerous testimonies to the application of writing both in public and in private life; such are the letter concerning Uriah (II Sam. xi. 14), the letters of Jezebel concerning Naboth (I Kings xxi. 8, 11); the letters of commendation for Naaman to the king of Israel (II Kings v. 5 sqq.); the roll of Isaiah in Isa. viii. 1 sqq.; the letter from the Assyrian to Hezekiah (Isa. xxxvii. 14), and of Merodach-baladan to the same (Isa. xxxix. 1); that from Huram of Tyre to Solomon (II Chron. ii. 11); witness of the purchase of a piece of land (Jer. xxxii. 10); and the recording of accusations (Job xiii. 26, xxxi. 35). Not altogether clear is the activity of the royal officers called scribes, as under David (II Sam. viii. 17), Solomon (I Kings iv. 3), Hezekiah (II Kings xviii. 18, 37, xix. 2), and Josiah (II Kings xxii. 3); apparently their duty was to keep the archives and prepare the correspondence of the king; while according to II Kings xii. 11 the scribe had the oversight of the money applied to the restoration of the temple. From Isa. x. 19 it appears that in the time of that prophet a child could write.

The material upon which men generally wrote was probably papyrus (II John 12). To be sure, this is not affirmed in the Old Testament; but just as little testimony exists to the employment (assumed by many) of dressed skins. Certainly the Septuagint is right in so translating *chartion* and *chartēs* in Jer. xxxvi. (Septuagint xliii.), for it has been correctly remarked by Schlottmann that the king would hardly have cast whole pieces of leather upon the open firebox of the orient; and so **2. The** far as Num. v. 23 is concerned, one can **Materials** easily wash fresh ink from papyrus. **Employed.** Papyrus (q.v.) still grows in Palestine at various places, as in the marshes on the coast, at Lake Huleh, at the Sea of Tiberias, and lower down on the Jordan to the Dead Sea (cf. L. Fonck, *Streifzüge durch die biblische Flora*, pp. 36 sqq., Freiburg, 1900). Import of papyrus from Egypt to Phenicia is authenticated for the eleventh century B.C. Nevertheless, the use of rolls of leather was so common in antiquity, that its use among the Israelites can well be assumed. The later discovery of parchment (Eumenes II. of Pergamon, 197–158 B.C.) has bearing only on the New Testament (II Tim. iv. 13). The books were in the form of rolls (Jer. xxxvi.; Ezek. ii. 9, iii. 1 sqq.; Ps. xl. 7; Zech. v. 1 sqq.). The writing-instrument was a stylus (Hebr. *'eṭ*; Ps. xlv. 1; Jer. viii. 8; *kalamos*, III John 13) which was brought to a point by the use of the scribe's knife (Jer. xxxvi. 23) and was dipped in ink (Hebr. *dyp*, Jer. xxxvi. 18; Gk. *melan*, II Cor. iii. 3; II John 12; III John 13). The ink-horn was called *ḳeseth hassopher* (Ezek. ix. 2, 3, 11). The writer's equipment was carried in his girdle (Ezek. ix.). For engraving upon metal or stone there was in use the iron stylus (*'eṭ barzel*, Jer. xvii.1; Job xix. 24); the term used in Isa. viii. 1 is *ḥereṭ*, from a root meaning to incise or engrave.

II. Information from Other Sources: The discoveries in the winter of 1887–88 at Tell el-Amarna (see AMARNA TABLETS) and the more recent discoveries at Taanach have in surprising fashion shown that in Palestine about 1400 B.C., there were in use the Babylonian script and the Babylonian language, this being employed not only on the part of Egyptians and official Palestinians in reports and petitions to the pharaohs Amenophis III. and IV., but also in communications from the upper-class Palestinians to the people of the land. It is concluded from these facts that in that period a script better suited to Canaanitic needs was either not yet available or was not widely diffused (H. Winckler in *Keilinschriftliche Bibliothek*, vol. v., Berlin, 1896; also in Schrader, *KAT;* E. Sellin, *Tel Ta'annek*, Vienna, 1904). It is unknown at which point of contact of Babylonia with Palestine the use of the Babylonian script became common. If the theory of J. Halévy (*Revue sémitique*, 1904, pp. 240–248) becomes established, this being that the Habiri of the Amarna Tablets were descendants of Casshite military colonies, it will be necessary to think of the seventeenth or the sixteenth century before Christ as the period. That the Israelites after the conquest of Canaan in any great measure made use of the cuneiform writing has no support in actual evidence. With this would fall the supposition of some Englishmen and of H. Winckler that the Decalogue was first written in the cuneiform script. So far as it is possible to trace back the course of events, the Israelites seem to have used the same form of writing as that discovered in June, 1880, in the Siloam Inscription (q.v.), which apparently belongs to the time of Hezekiah. This is the form

which appears on the seal found in 1904 at Tell el-Mutasilim (Megiddo), which reads: "(seal) of Shema', servant of Jeroboam" (i.e., of Jeroboam II.) —cf. E. Kautzsch, in *Mittheilungen und Nachrichten des deutschen Palästina-Vereins*, 1904, pp. 1–14.

III. The North Semitic and Early Hebrew Script: The writing just mentioned is essentially that of the Moabite Stone (q.v.), the Sendjirli inscription, and the inscriptions of Phenicia. These are called North Semitic in distinction from **1. North** the South Semitic, which include the **Semitic** Sabean, Minæan, Safaite, and proto- **Script.** Arabic. The South Semitic, toward the deciphering of which J. Halévy has contributed a great deal, is derived from the North Semitic (cf. the convincing discussions of M. Lidzbarski in his *Ephemeris für semitische Epigraphik*, i. 109–123, Giessen, 1901). And yet some of these forms of writing show an older type of writing, standing nearer the Old Canaanitic than does the Sabean (cf. F. Prætorius, in *ZDMG*, 1902, 676–680, 1904, pp. 715–726). With respect to the age of the North Semitic all that can be said is that comparison with the Greek alphabet, which depends upon it, shows that this most significant of all inventions was made some considerable period before the end of the second century B.C., possibly several centuries before that end. This script is found in use by a West Semitic (Aramaic, possibly Canaanitic) people which stood in close contact with Egypt. For the close connection with the Egyptian Emmanuel de Rougé was the first sponsor, alleging the writing from right to left, the principle of acrophony (i.e., each letter formed after the figure of some thing the name of which began with the sound of that letter), and the writing of the consonants only. This would make the writing of the Old Canaanitic script common with that of the Old Egyptians. But comparison with both the hieroglyphic and the hieratic writing seems to make derivation from the Egyptian an untenable supposition. Also to be rejected are the hypotheses which derive the North Semitic script from the Babylonian-Assyrian cuneiform writing (Deecke, in *ZDMG*, 1877, pp. 102 sqq.; F. Delitzsch, *Entstehung des ältesten Schriftsystems oder der Ursprung der Keilschriftzeichen*, pp. 221–231, Leipsic, 1896). Delitzsch, to be sure, does not derive the Canaanitic writing from the cuneiform of the period of the invention, but from the much older pictorial forms known only to the learned of that time.

The names of the letters are in great part taken from the names of the things which were used to figure forth the oldest forms. Thus *Ayin* means "eye," and *Resh* means "head." In Codex Vaticanus of the Septuagint (in the Lamentations of Jeremiah) the names of the Greek forms are given as Aleph, Bēth, Gimel, Daleth, Ē, Ouau, Zain, Hēth, Tēth, Iōth, Chaph, Lamed, Mēm, Noun, Samch, Ain, Phē, Tiadē, Kōph, Rēchs, Chsen, Thau. The Greek-Latin Psalter in Verona has in Psalm cxix. a few variant forms, viz., Zai, Labd, Nun, Samech, Sade, Res, Sen.

With respect to the history of the North Semitic alphabet it may be said that some of the letters arose through differentiation from others (M. A. Levy,

Phönizische Studien, i. 49 sqq., Leipsic, 1856; J. Halévy, *Mélanges d'épigraphie et d'archéologie orientale*, p. 179, Paris, 1874). It may be
2. Develop- taken as certain that ḥ developed
ment of the from h, s (samekh) from z, ṭ from t.
Alphabet. It is improbable that ẓ developed from
s if it be true that the meaning assigned to the name of the former is correct. It is also held in some quarters that z and ḳ developed later. This would leave sixteen letters which the Greeks, according to the statements of their grammarians, first received from the Phenicians, viz., a, b, g, d, e, i, k, l, m, n, o, p, r, s, t, u. But the remark is in place here that there is no proof that the North Semitic alphabet ever had less than twenty-two letters, to which may be added that the letters which appear in the South Semitic alphabet and not in the North Semitic might easily be represented from the existing letters by means of diacritical signs (D. H. Müller, *Epigraphische Denkmäler aus Arabien*, p. 19, Vienna, 1889; F. Prætorius, in *ZDMG*, 1904, 720 sqq.). The arrangement of the letters in the alphabet is witnessed by the alphabetical arrangement in certain poetical pieces, Ps. cxi., cxii., cxix.; Prov. xxxi. 10 sqq.; Lam. i., as well as by the numerical equivalents assigned to them (Aleph to Tēth [Alpha to Theta]=1–9, Yodh to Pe [Iota to Pi] = 10–80, etc.). Variations which appear in the numerical equivalents are easily explicable, while the variations in Arabic and Ethiopic are secondary. The oldest known document in North Semitic is the Moabite Stone (q.v.), and belongs to the ninth century B.C. (cf. II Kings iii. 4 sqq.); it contains essentially the same forms of writing as appear on early Hebrew seals and gems after the eighth century (M. A. Levy, *Siegel und Gemmen mit aramäischen, phönizischen, althebräischen . . . Inschriften*, Breslau, 1869; G. A. Cooke, *Text-Book of North-Semitic Inscriptions*, p. 362, London, 1903). The eight fragments found in Limassol and Cyprus mentioned in G. A. Cooke (ut sup., pp. 52–54) and Lidzbarski (*Nordsemitische Epigraphik*, p. 419) are probably of the eighth century. Of other Phenician inscriptions that of Yehawmilk, king of Byblos, belongs to the fifth or fourth century B.C., and that of Tabnith, priest of Ashtoreth and king of the Sidonians, belongs about 300 B.C.

IV. Aramaic Varieties of Writing and the Hebrew Square Character: From the common North Semitic script there issued not only the South Semitic writing and the Greek alphabet, but also the Aramaic character. The most important changes which took place here are the opening of the closed tops of the letters and a rounding off of many angular
forms. But the oldest of the forms
1. The now under consideration differ either
Older Forms. not at all or very slightly from those
previously considered, as is shown by the early Aramaic seals and the three Sendjirli inscriptions. Of the latter, which were discovered in 1888–91 at Sendjirli in North Syria, only one is pure Aramaic—the inscription of Barrekhubh, which dates from the period of Tiglath-Pileser III.; both the others (the Panammu inscription, dedicated to Panammu by his son Barrekhubh, and the rather

older Hadad inscription) are in the dialect spoken in the region. To the seventh or the sixth century belong the inscriptions discovered in 1891 in Nerab, southeast of Aleppo. There is a fifth-century inscription of the priest Zalm-Shezeb from Teimaa, Arabia. In Egypt were composed the stele of Zakkara, of the fourth year of Xerxes (482 B.C.), now in Berlin, and that of Taba, of the fifth or fourth pre-Christian century, now in Carpentras. There are besides numerous Aramaic papyri written in Egypt during the Persian period, of which especial note may be taken of one of the year 411–410, published by Euting in *Mémoires . . . de l'académie* (Paris, 1903; cf. G. A. Cooke, *Text-Book*, ut sup., pp. 206–213). There are others acquired for England by A. H. Sayce and published by Cowley [cf. also A. H. Sayce, *Aramaic Papyri Discovered at Assouan*, London, 1906]. There are also coins from Tarsus of the fourth century, while from Ptolemaic and Roman times there are numerous inscribed bits of papyri and potsherds. The same development is observable in the lands east of the Jordan and in Palestine. The inscription of Araḳ al–Emir (half-way between Rabbath Ammon and Jericho), dating probably from the first third of the second century B.C., has the early form of Ayin, the letters Resh and Beth are open at the top, the Yodh has lost a stroke, and He is practically a square letter. The inscription of the priestly family, the Beni Ḥzyr (cf. I Chron. xxiv. 15) at the "tomb of Jacob" in the valley of the Kedron, of the first century B.C. (earlier according to E. Meyer, *Entstehung des Judenthums*, p. 143, Halle, 1896), has in four of the six letters the later form. The dated Palmyrene inscriptions range from 9 B.C. to 271 A.D., and the rounded and free forms give the impression of ornament. Entitled to mention here because of its extent and content is the Palmyrene and Greek tariff of imposts and taxes of the year 137 A.D. (cf. S. Reckendorf, in *ZDMG*, 1888; Lidzbarski, in *Nordsemitische Epigraphik*, pp. 463–473; and Cooke, ut sup., pp. 313–340). The Nabatæans (q.v.), though Arabs, used the Aramaic script and language (cf. J. Euting, *Nabatäische Inschriften aus Arabien*, Berlin, 1885, and *Sinaitische Inschriften*, ib. 1891). The Nabatæan script was the parent of the Arabic.

The Hebrew "square character" arose from the Aramaic type of writing in part through distinct calligraphic effort. In Palestine, as already seen,
the types existed beside each other in
2. Develop- actual use. General acquaintance with
ment of the type due to Aramaic development
the Square receives testimony from the time of
Characters. Jesus by his words in Matt. v. 18,
where the early Canaanitic form of the Yodh can not be in mind. On the other side, it must be accepted that the Canaanitic script remained fully known in the second Christian century, for the coins of Bar Kokba (q.v.) have their inscriptions in this writing. Bar Kokba, who appealed to the national feeling of the Jews, would certainly not have had recourse to a forgotten script in order to make an appeal to patriotism, especially when that script was essentially the same as what was used by the hated Samaritans. Testimony to the employment of the old form in the second century appears in the

Mishna tract *Yadayim*, iv. 5, where the statement is that the Aramaic in Ezra and Daniel is sacred; but Aramaic which is written in Hebrew speech (script) and Hebrew which is written in Hebrew, and what is written [*de novo*] in Hebrew is not sacred. The Hebrew text (of the Old Testament) is sacred only when it is written in the square character with ink on the skins of beasts. Origen also gives testimony to the continuance in use of the old character in his remark on Ps. ii. 2 (in Montfaucon, *Hexaplorum Origenis quæ supersunt*, i. 86, Paris, 1713; in the Benedictine edition, ii. 39; and in Lommatzsch's edition, xi. 396, 25 vols., Berlin, 1831–48), also in his *Prologus galeatus* (q.v.), where he says that the name of God is in some Greek manuscripts "up to this day" written in the old characters. Fragments of the translation of Aquila from I Kings xx.; II Kings xxiii.; and several of the Psalms are known in which the name of deity (the tetragrammaton *Yhwh*) is written in the early character, but evidently copied mechanically by a scribe who did not understand it (cf. F. C. Burkitt, *Fragments of the Books of Kings according to the Translation of Aquila*, Cambridge, 1897; and C. Taylor, *Hebrew-Greek Cairo Genizah Palimpsests*, ib., 1900). But this is the last trace of the use of the old forms of letters. The fact, so far as it is obtainable, seems to be that after the quelling of the revolt of Bar Kokba the ancient script went out of use among the people, and ceased altogether to exist as a means of writing after the fourth Christian century.

So that some centuries before Christ the Aramaic forms began to make their way into Palestine, and by the end of the second century the Old Hebrew script was discarded by the Jews. The explanation of this complete disappearance may possibly lie in an early conception that the Aramaic was sacred and the old Hebrew secular. The passage already cited above from the Mishna and other passages indicate that Biblical codices were regarded as sacred only when they were written in the square character with ink upon leather, and were not sacred if in the old Hebrew forms. But why was this script considered to be sacred? Testimony from the second century is important in this matter, it being to the effect that Ezra brought the square character from Assyria (Palestinian Talmud, *Megilla*, i. 71b, lines 56 sqq.; Babylonian Talmud, *Sanhedrin*, 21b), to which there may be added the statement of Epiphanius (*De XII gemmis*, § 63) to the effect that Ezra did this to distinguish the Israelites from the other peoples, while Jerome, in the *Prologus galeatus*, says that "it is certain that Ezra found in use characters others than those now in use." To be sure, this tradition is not historical, since the Aramaic forms came in with the Aramaic language; but it is highly probable that after Ezra's time that form of writing was used in making copies of the law. The opposition to the Samaritans was such as to facilitate the introduction of a style of writing different from theirs. From various expressions in the Talmud (e.g., *Sabbath*, 103–104) it appears that the square character had long before reached its full development, while the forms as seen in the manuscripts and in print are

3. Sacredness of the Square Character.

essentially the same (A. Berliner, *Beiträge zur hebräischen Grammatik*, pp. 15–26, Berlin, 1879). This stability is explained by the unique estimate placed upon the law which was written in these characters. Yet, without prejudice to the uniformity just asserted, from the peculiarities evident in the Biblical codices it is often possible to decide from which region a manuscript came and in some cases to tell those which are by the same scribe (it is easy to discriminate, for instance, between Spanish and German Biblical manuscripts). To a far lesser degree can one safely assert the age of a codex.

Early witnesses to the nature of the Hebrew script in early times are (a) inscriptions. There are the sarcophagus of Queen Ẓaddah (Queen Helena of Adiabene?); the words *thm gzr* found in five places near Gezer to indicate the Sabbath limits; two small inscriptions on sarcophagi from the period before 135 A.D. (in Lidzbarski, *Nordsemitische Epigraphik*, ut sup., table 43); there are inscriptions on three stone sarcophagi found in 1905 on the site of the Syrian orphan asylum at Jerusalem, on one of the smaller sides appear *Papias* in Greek and Hebrew, *Ḥanyn* and *'byh*, before each of which is prefixed the adjective *Hbsny*, written defectively and meaning "who belonged to Beth Shean" (i.e., Scythopolis), indicating that they are of a period prior to the fall of Jerusalem, since it is hardly likely that after that event people would remove from Beth Shean to settle at Jerusalem. The script on these last is very like that given in Lidzbarski (*Nordsemitische Epigraphik*, table xliii., no. 6); the Yodh is the smallest letter, and parts have so fallen away that it is not unlike the Resh of the early writing. The inscription over the door of the synagogue at Kefr Bir'im was written in the third Christian century (also in Lidzbarski, ut sup). To the same period belong the synagogue inscriptions found in Palmyra containing the Shema' (cf. P. Berger, *Hist. de l'écriture dans l'antiquité*, 2d ed., p. 259, Paris, 1892); Jewish catacomb inscriptions from Rome and Venosa should be dated in the third to the sixth centuries according to Ascoli, while ten dated inscriptions from Venosa, Lavello, and Brindisi are of the period 810–846 A.D. (G. J. Ascoli, *Iscrizione inedite o mal note greghe, latine ebraiche, di antichi sepolchri giudaiche del Napolitano*, Turin, 1880).

4. Documentary Testimony to Hebrew Script.

There does not come into account here the epitaph found in Aden (given in *The Palæographical Society*, *Facsimiles of Ancient Manuscripts, Oriental Series*, ed. W. Wright, London, 1875–83, part i., p. 29), for to the apparent date 29 of the Seleucid must be prefixed the numerals making it read 1029 (=717 A.D.); nor very many " finds " of the year 1874 at Chufut-Kale in the Crimea by A. Firkovitch, published by Firkovitch in Hebrew at Vilna, 1872 [cf. for the story *JE*, v. 393–394].

The *Oriental Series* of the Palæographical Society (ut sup.) contain facsimiles of many Hebrew manuscripts: i. 13, a page from a Hebrew dictionary by Menahem ben Saruk of the year 1091; i. 14, the same from the year 1189; i. 15, from Rashi's commentary on the Talmud, of the year 1190; ii. 30 has a sheet from a work by Moses ben Shem Tob of the year 1363–64; iii. 40–41, and iv. 54 contain facsimiles of Biblical manuscripts; iv. 55, a sheet from Al-Ḥarizi, year 1282; iv. 56, one from the Babylonian Talmud of the year 1288–89; v. 68 has a selection from Isaac ben Joseph, of 1401; vii. 79, a piece copied by

5. Printed Documents.

Eleazar of Worms from Elias Levita, 1515. S. Landauer, *Katalog der hebräischen Handschriften der königlichen Bibliothek, Strassburg*, Strasburg, 1881; A. Neubauer has published *Catalogue of the Hebrew Manuscripts in the Bodleian Library* (Oxford, 1886); C. D. Ginsburg, *A Series of Fifteen Facsimiles from Manuscript Pages of the Hebrew Bible with a Letterpress Description* (London, 1897); idem, *18 Facsimiles of Manuscripts of the Hebrew Bible* (1898); G. Margoliouth, *Catalogue of the Hebrew and Samaritan Manuscripts in the British Museum* (London, 1899); cf. his *Descriptive List of Hebrew and Samaritan Manuscripts* (1893). Other material is furnished in H. Strack's *Prophetarum posteriorum codex Babylonicus Petropolitanus* (St. Petersburg and Leipsic, 1876); R. Hoerning, *British Museum Karaite Manuscripts. Description and Collation of six Karaite Manuscripts of Portions of the Hebrew Bible in Arabic Characters* (London, 1889); *Facsimiles of the Fragments hitherto Recovered of the Book of Ecclesiasticus in Hebrew* (London, 1901); M. Steinschneider, *Catalogus codicum Hebræorum bibliothecæ Lugduno-Batavæ* (Leyden, 1858); idem, *Die Handschriftenverzeichnisse der königlichen Bibliothek zu Berlin*, vol. ii., *Verzeichnis der hebräischen Handschriften* (Berlin, 1878); idem, *Die hebräischen Handschriften der königlichen Hof- und Staatsbibliothek in München* (Munich, 1875, 2d ed., 1895); D. A. Chwolson, *Corpus inscriptionum Hebraicarum* (St. Petersburg, 1882) contains numerous reproductions of Hebrew manuscripts; B. Stade gives as appendices to his *Geschichte des Volkes Israel*, vol. i. (Berlin, 1887), a number of examples of codices; W. Wickes, *Treatise on the Accentuation of the Twenty-one so-called Prose Books of the Old Testament* (Oxford, 1887) furnishes a facsimile of a noted Biblical manuscript by Moses ben Asher; A. Neubauer, *Studia Biblica et ecclesiastica*, vol. iii., gives a number of examples; and *Facsimiles of Biblical Manuscripts in the British Museum*, ed. F. G. Kenyon (London, 1900). A number of important examples of Hebrew writing are furnished in *JQR*, as follows: 1899, pp. 533, 643; 1902, pp. 44–45, 51; 1903, pp. 177 sqq., 392, 678 sqq.; 1904, 1 sqq., 560; 1905, 123 sqq., 428, 609 sqq.

(H. L. Strack.)

Bibliography: In general on the invention and early use of writing consult: J. L. Hug, *Die Erfindung der Buchstabenschrift, ihr Zustand und frühester Gebrauch im Alterthume*, Ulm, 1801; U. F. Kopp, *Bilder und Schriften der Vorzeit*, 2 vols., Mannheim, 1819–21; J. Olshausen, *Ueber den Ursprung des Alphabets*, in *Kieler philologischen Studien*, 1841, pp. 4 sqq.; H. Steinthal, *Die Entwicklung der Schrift*, Berlin, 1852; H. Brugsch, *Ueber Bildung und Entwicklung der Schrift*, ib. 1868; H. Wuttke, *Geschichte der Schrift*, vol. i., Leipsic, 1872; idem, *Abbildungen zur Geschichte der Schrift*, part 1, ib. 1873; A. J. Evans, *On the Alphabet and its Origin*, London, 1872; idem, in *American Antiquary and Orient*, 1903, pp. 183–184; idem, in *Biblia*, xvi (1903), 263–272; E. von Drival, *De l'origine de l'écriture*, 3d ed., Paris, 1879; J. C. C. Clarke, *The Semitic Alphabet*, Chicago, 1884; A. Maury, *La Invencion de la Escritura*, Madrid, 1891; P. Berger, *Hist. de l'écriture dans l'antiquité*, Paris, 1892; A. É. J. B. Terrier de Lacouperie, *Beginnings of Writing in Central and Eastern Asia*, London, 1894; S. A. Fries, in *ZDPV*, 1899, pp. 263–272; I. Taylor, *The History of the Alphabet*, 2 vols., London, 1899. More special inquiries are set forth in: F. Delitzsch, *Der Ursprung der Keilschriftzeichen. Lösung der Frage nach der Entstehung des ältesten Schriftsystems*, Leipsic, 1896; idem, in *Berichte der königlichen sächsischen Gesellschaft der Wissenschaften*, July 13, 1896, pp. 167–198; H. Zimmern, in *ZDMG*, 1896, pp. 667–670; F. Thureau-Dangin, *Récherches sur l'origine de l'écriture cunéiforme*, vol. i., Paris, 1899; I. M. Price, in *American Journal of Semitic Languages*, xv (1898–92), 145–156. On the Phenician alphabet cf. E. de Rougé, *Mémoire sur l'origine égyptienne de l'alphabet phénicien, publié par J. de Rougé*, Paris, 1874; F. Lenormant, *Essai sur la propagation de l'alphabet phénicien dans l'ancien monde*, 2 vols., ib., 2d ed., 1875. On the Greek: A. Kirchhoff, *Studien zur Geschichte des griechischen Alphabets*, 4th ed., Gütersloh, 1887. On the Hebrew: G. Bickell, *Outlines of Hebrew Grammar*, Leipsic, 1876; the Paleographical Society's *Publications*, ut sup., vii. 87 sqq., London, 1882; and Chwolson, *Corpus*, ut inf.

On Semitic epigraphy: *Revue sémitique d'épigraphie et d'hist. ancienne*, ed. J. Halévy, Paris, 1890 sqq.; M. Lidzbarski, *Handbuch der nordsemitischen Epigraphik nebst ausgewählten Inschriften*, Weimar, 1898; idem, *Ephemeris*

für semitische Epigraphik, vol. i., Giessen, 1902; *Répertoire d'épigraphie sémitique*, ed. C. Clermont-Ganneau, Paris, 1900 sqq.; *Répertoire d'épigraphie sémitique publié par la commission du Corpus inscriptionum Semiticarum*, ib. 1904 sqq.; G. A. Cooke, *A Text-Book of North Semitic Inscriptions*, Oxford, 1903, cf. *JQR*, 1904, 258–259; note also D. von Muralt, *Beiträge zur hebräischen Paläographie*, in *TSK*, 1874.

With especial relation to Hebrew writing and the Bible it is to be noted that many of the works named in and under Biblical Introduction (cf. ii. 99 of this work) contain matter of interest and value. Consult further: W. Gesenius, *Geschichte der hebräischen Sprache und Schrift*, pp. 137 sqq., Leipsic, 1815; J. G. Eichhorn, *Einleitung in das A. T.*, vols., i. ii., §§ 63–78, 342–377, 4th ed., Göttingen, 1823; H. Hupfeld, in *TSK*, 1830, parts 2–4, 1837, part 3; idem, *Ausführliche hebräische Grammatik*, pp. 7 sqq.; B. Stade, *Lehrbuch der hebräischen Grammatik*, i. 22–44, Leipsic, 1879; G. Hoffmann, in *ZATW*, 1881, pp. 334–338; G. E. Merrill, *Story of the Manuscripts of the Bible*, Boston, 1881; D. Chwolson, *Corpus inscriptionarum Hebraicarum*, St. Petersburg, 1882; S. B. Driver, *Notes on the Hebrew Text of the Books of Samuel*, pp. ix., xxix., Oxford, 1890; A. Neubauer, in *Studia Biblica et ecclesiastica*, iii. 1–36, Oxford, 1891; L. Blau, *Zur Einführung in die heilige Schrift*, pp. 48–80, Strasburg, 1894; idem, in *Gedenkbuch zur Erinnerung an David Kaufmann*, pp. 44–57, Breslau, 1900; W. A. Copinger, *The Bible and its Transmission*, London, 1897; C. D. Ginsburg, *Introduction to the Massoretico-Critical Edition of the Hebrew Bible*, ib. 1897; F. G. Kenyon, *Our Bible and the Ancient Manuscripts*, ib. 1898; T. H. Weir, *Short Hist. of the Hebrew Text of the O. T.*, ib. 1899; E. N. Adler, *About Hebrew Manuscripts*, ib. 1905; *JE*, i. 439–454. Further illustrative matter is to be found in L. Löw, *Graphische Requisiten und Erzeugnisse bei den Juden*, 2 vols., Leipsic, 1870–71; T. Birt, *Das antike Buchwesen in seinem Verhältniss zur Litteratur*, Berlin, 1882; M. Steinschneider, *Vorlesungen über die Kunde hebräischer Handschriften, deren Sammlungen und Verzeichnisse*, Leipsic, 1897; K. Dziatzko, *Untersuchungen über ausgewählte Kapitel des antiken Buchwesens*, ib. 1900; L. Blau, *Studien zum althebräischen Buchwesen und zur biblischen Litteraturgeschichte*, Strasburg, 1902; idem, *Ueber den Einfluss des althebräischen Buchwesens auf die Originale und auf die ältesten Handschriften der Septuaginta, des Neuen Testaments und der Hexapla*, in *Festschrift für A. Berliner*, Frankfort, 1903.

For the coins and their inscriptions see under Money. On the Sendjirli inscriptions consult: *Ausgrabungen in Sendschirli ausgeführt*, Berlin, 1893; D. H. Müller, in *Wiener Zeitschrift für die Kunde des Morgenlandes*, 1893, pp. 33–70, 113–140, and 1896, 193, 197; J. Halévy, in *Revue sémitique*, 1893, pp. 138–167, 217–258, 319–336, 1894, pp. 25–60, 394–395, 1896, pp. 185–187, 1897, pp. 84–91; Lidzbarski, *Nordsemitische Epigraphik*, ut sup., pp. 440 sqq.; and Cooke, ut sup., 159–185; E. Sachau, in *SBA*, Oct. 22, 1856, p. 1051.

WUENSCHE, KARL AUGUST: German orientalist; b. at Hainewalde near Zittau (47 m. s.e. of Dresden) Aug. 22, 1838. His life has been singular in its uniformity and quietness; he was Oberlehrer in the girls' high school at Dresden from 1869 till his retirement in 1905. His literary activity has been very great, as is attested by the following (incomplete) list of works: Commentary on Hosea (Leipsic, 1868); *Die Leiden der Messias in ihrer Uebereinstimmung mit der Lehre des Alten Testaments und der Aussprüchender Rabbinen* (1870); *Jesus in seiner Stellung zu den Frauen, mit Hinblick auf die Bedeutung derselben im Mosaismus, im talmudischen Judenthum, und Christenthum* (1872); *Die Weissagungen des Propheten Joel* (1874); *Der lebensfreudige Jesus der synoptischen Evangelien im Gegensatze zum leidenden Messias der Kirche* (1876); *Neue Beiträge zur Erläuterung der Evangelien aus Talmud und Midrasch* (Göttingen, 1878); *Der Jerusalemische Talmud in seinen haggadischen Bestandtheilen . . .*

in's Deutsch übertragen (Zurich, 1880); *Die Räthsel-weisheit bei den Hebräern, mit Hinblick auf andere alten Völker* (Leipsic, 1883); an annotated translation of the Talmud into German (1886 sqq., this being outside *Bibliotheca Rabbinica*, a collection of Midrashim translated into German, 1880 sqq.); *Die jüdische Litteratur seit Abschluss des Kanons* (1891 sqq.; in collaboration with J. Winter); *Midrasch Tehillim oder haggadische Erklärung der Psalmen* (Treves, 1893); *Die Freude in den Schriften des Alten Bundes* (Leipsic, 1896); *Die Naturbildersprache des Alten Testaments* (1897); *Die Pflanzenfabel in der Weltlitteratur* (Vienna, 1905); *Die Sagen von Lebensbaum und Lebenswasser* (1905); *Der Sagenkreis von geprellten Teufel* (1905); *Die Schönheit der Bibel* (Leipsic, 1906); *Die Bildersprache des Alten Testaments* (1906); *Monumenta judaica* (1906 sqq.); *Schöpfung und Sündenfall des ersten Menschenpaares nach jüdischer und moslemischer Sage* (1906); *Aus Israels Lehrhallen. Kleine Midraschim zur späteren legendarischen Literatur des Alten Testaments* (5 vols., 1907–10); *Mechilta; Midrasch zu Exodus* (1909; in collaboration with J. Winter and L. Blau); and *Der Kuss in Bibel, Talmud und Midrasch* (Breslau, 1911).

WUERTTEMBERG, vür'tem-berH: Constitutional monarchy, the third in size of the German states; bounded on the east and northeast by Bavaria, on the west, northwest, and southwest by Baden, on the south by Baden and Switzerland; the area is 7,528 square miles; and the population (1905) is 2,302,179. Of the population 1,580,361 are reckoned to the Evangelical State Church; 695,808 to the Roman Catholic Church, 12,053 are Jews, 10,726 belong to various sects or to no church, 380 are members of churches of other lands. In the State Church there are 1,187 congregations with 1,158 charges, or one charge to every 1,368 Evangelical adherents; and there are 716,564 communicants. In the old duchy of Württemberg the Evangelical church was connected by the closest bonds with the State. Duke Ulrich (1498–1550) introduced the Reformation with the aid of Erhard Schnepff and Ambrosius Blaurer (qq.v.); organization was effected by his son Christoph (1550–68) with the aid of Johann Brenz (q.v.), at which time the fundamental ecclesiastical law was settled, including the matter of the schools, while the Augsburg Confession and the Württemberg Confession of 1551 were made the doctrinal standards. Church government was arranged under a collegium consisting of a consistory and a church council, the former taking charge of the matters of inner control, the latter of the church economics, while four (later, six) superintendents acted with the collegium. The pastors led the local churches with the aid of local officers, ecclesiastical and civil. Under Johann Valentin Andreä (q.v.) further developments in government were carried through. When in 1733 Duke Karl Alexander went over to the Roman Catholic Church, provision was made that whenever the head of the State was a Roman Catholic, control of the Church should pass to the highest governmental authority. The next Protestant ruler was Duke (later King) Friedrich (1797–1816), and in his reign

(1806) the three confessions were put on an equality, for which further regulations were made under Wilhelm I., 1819, but the exigencies of the case made progressive modification necessary. By the act of March 28, 1898, when the ruler belongs to any but an Evangelical confession, control of the Evangelical church passes to a collegium, composed of two Evangelical members of the Geheimrat, the president of the Evangelical consistory, the president of the national synod, and the senior general superintendent. On July 16, 1906, the six Evangelical superintendents lost their seats in the second chamber, but the care of Evangelical interests rests in the first chamber on the president of the consistory, the president of the Evangelical synod, and two superintendents chosen by their colleagues.

The highest authority is vested in the Evangelical consistory, over which the minister for churches and schools has supervisory powers. The consistory is composed of a president and the requisite number of clerical and lay representatives; the chief court preacher and the first preacher at the Stiftskirche are *ex officio* members; extraordinary members are usually two general superintendents; this body has supervision of the interests of the churches. Once a year the general superintendents meet with the consistory as a synod. Forty-nine deans are subordinate to the consistory. The consistory has care of education so far as it is on a confessional basis. The coordination of the synodal and consistorial systems has been long in progress in Württemberg. For a long time contentment was felt with the control by the consistory. In 1851 the laity was introduced into church government through pastors' councils, partly elective; in 1854 came the next step in the establishment of diocesan synods, newly constituted in 1901, consisting of the pastors and chosen elders from the pastors' councils, meeting yearly at the call of the dean. The national synod was created in 1867, first met in 1869, established under new rules in 1888, meeting every sixth year and consisting of twenty-five clergymen and an equal number of laymen elected by the diocesan synods. The Evangelical clergy receive their preparatory education for the most part in the four lower Evangelical theological seminaries of Maulbronn, Schöntal, Blaubeuren, and Urach; for the higher theological studies attendance at the "Stift" in Tübingen is required. Ordination comes with entrance into the first parish as "vicars." Compensation begins with 400 marks per year with increases for length of service and rise in position, and the salaries range from that to 5,000 marks. The form of worship is simple—greeting from the chancel, silent prayer at entrance, pericope, sermon, closing prayer with the Lord's Prayer, blessing; to the old system of pericopes there was added in 1830 a second and in 1894 a third year's reading from Gospels and epistles. At certain celebrations there are sermons, and also every fourth Friday, while the Reformation is celebrated now on the Sunday next following Oct. 30.

Societies make their contribution to the religious life of the kingdom. Among these are (1) societies which recall early Pietistic tendencies such as are represented at Herrnhut, which stress simple edification based upon the Bible; (2) the Societies Michelians (see HAHN, JOHANN MICHAEL), among whom there is a mixture of speculative-theosophical teachings with an ascetic tendency, and withal a somewhat firm organization; (3) the Pregizerians (q.v.), whose influence is not altogether favorable, indeed rather the reverse, to the churches. Among the sects which have entered the kingdom the Methodists take precedence, two bodies being represented, the American Methodist Episcopal and the Evangelical Association; they have their preachers, chapels, regular services, Sunday-schools, and literature. In 1905 they numbered 5,442. Other denominations are Baptists with 1,832 communicants, New Irvingites with 1,375, Mennonites with 277, and Friends of Jerusalem with 244. There are also Adventists, Mormons, and the Salvation Army. In 1905 the total number belonging to various denominations was 10,426.

The Roman Catholic Church has existed in Württemberg only since the beginning of the nineteenth century, the entrance being made through enlargement of the territory, about 500,000 **The Roman** people with 650 pastors being included **Catholic** in what was then entirely Evangelical **Church.** territory. The basis of the present organization of that communion consists of the bulls of Aug. 16, 1821, and April 11, 1827, the document of May 14, 1828, and the royal ordinance of Jan. 30, 1830. A new bishopric, Rottenburg, was erected with Rottenburg-on-the-Neckar as see-city, and the first bishop was enthroned May 20, 1828. The constitution of 1819 gave the bishop, a representative of the chapter, and the ranking dean seats in the chamber of deputies. This arrangement was abrogated in 1906, when a representative of the bishop and an elected dean were given seats in the first chamber. The legal basis is now the law of Jan. 30, 1862, a part of which is the provision that spiritual orders may be introduced only by express permission of the civil government. As yet monks have been refused admission, though several congregations of women are at work. The number of pastorates and other clerical positions among the Roman Catholics is given as 1,008, or one to every 690 Roman Catholics.

(E. WITTICH.)

BIBLIOGRAPHY: *Bibliographie der württembergischen Geschichte*, Stuttgart, 1908; T. Eisenlohr and A. L. Reyscher, *Sammlung der württembergischen Kirchengesetze*, vol. ix., 2 parts, Tübingen, 1834–35; F. A. Hauber, *Recht und Brauch der evangelisch-lutherischen Kirche Württembergs*, Stuttgart, 1854; L. Golther, *Der Staat und die katholische Kirche in Württemberg*, ib. 1874; C. Palmer, *Die Gemeinschaften und Sekten Württembergs*, Tübingen, 1877; O. Schmid-Sonneck, *Die evangelische Diaspora Württembergs nach Entstehung und gegenwärtigen Bestand*, Stuttgart, 1879; K. Helfferich, *Chronik der evangelischen Kirche Württembergs*, ib. 1880; C. H. Klaiber, *Urkundliche Geschichte der reformirten Gemeinden Cannstatt-Stuttgart-Ludwigsburg*, ib. 1884; L. Haug, *Die evangelischen Kirchenstellen in Württemberg*, ib. 1886; W. Claus, *Württembergische Väter*, 2 vols., ib. 1887–88; C. Rothenhäusler, *Der Untergang der katholischen Religion in Altwürttemberg*, Leutkirch, 1887; E. Schneider, *Württembergische Reformationsgeschichte*, Stuttgart, 1887; P. W. Keppler, *Württembergs kirchliche Kunstalterthümer*, Rottenburg, 1888; S. von Steinheil, *Gesetze und Verfügungen über die Kirchengemeinden . . . in der . . . Landeskirche Württembergs*, Stuttgart, 1890; *Württembergische Geschichte*, Calw, 1893; D. Schäfer, *Württembergische Geschichtsquellen*, Stuttgart, 1894 sqq.; G. Bossert, *Das Interim in Württemberg*, Halle, 1895; T. Brecht, *Die Klosterfrage in Württemberg*, Stuttgart, 1895; H. Günther, *Das Restitutionsedikt von 1629 und die katholische Restauration Altwirtembergs*, ib. 1901; M. Erzberger, *Die Säkularization in Württemberg von 1802–10*, ib. 1902; E. Kalb, *Kirchen und Sekten der Gegenwart*, 2d ed., ib. 1907; C. Kolb, *Die Aufklärung in der württembergischen Kirche*, ib. 1908.

WUERTTEMBERG SUMMARIES. See BIBLES, ANNOTATED.

WUERZBURG, vürts′burH, **BISHOPRIC OF:** One of the largest of the sees of central Germany. Originally a part of the Thuringian kingdom, the district about the central course of the Main became Frankish by the victory of Theuderich I. in 531, and the Thuringian forest became the boundary between the Franks and Thuringians. The region was thinly populated and wholly by non-Christians until the Frankish immigration. The bishop of Mainz seems to have claimed jurisdiction over it in the seventh century; under Dagobert (623–634) it was closely connected with his kingdom, but he made it a duchy, and under his successor Sigibert III. it separated from the kingdom. Celtic missionaries worked there so that in the beginning of the eighth century it was partly Christianized, but not organized ecclesiastically, though there were a number of monasteries of Frankish origin. Through the activities of St. Boniface (q.v.) after 719 the remains of heathenism were eradicated and ecclesiastical organization was effected in 741. The first bishop was his pupil Burchard, who had followed him from England, and the see was constituted by Pope Zacharias Apr. 1, 743, since which time it has continued to exist. The land of the Wends was formerly included within the limits of the diocese, but was separated when the bishopric of Bamberg was instituted (q.v.; 1007). (A. HAUCK.)

BIBLIOGRAPHY: Sources are *Monumenta Boica*, vols. xxxvii.–xlv., Munich, 1864 sqq.; the " Annals " and " Chronicles " of Würzburg, in *MGH, Script.*, vols. ii (1829), vi (1844), xvi (1859), xxiv (1879), also the list of bishops in xiii (1881), 337–340; *Wirtembergische Urkundenbuch*, 8 vols., Stuttgart, 1849 sqq.; J. P. von Ludewig, *Geschichtsschreiber von dem Bischofthum Würzburg*, Leipsic, 1713; J. Gropp, *Collectio novissima scriptorum et rerum Wirceburgensium*, 2 vols., Frankfort, 1741–44. Consult further: J. G. von Eckart, *Commentarii de rebus . . . episcoporum Wircebergensium*, 2 vols., Würzburg, 1729; A. Ussermann, *Episcopatus Wirciburgensis*, St. Blasien, 1794; F. Stein, *Geschichte Frankens*, 2 vols., Schweinfurt, 1883–86; J. Hofmann, *Die Heiligen und Seligen des Bisthums Würzburg*, Würzburg, 1889; F. J. B. Stamminger, *Franconia Sacra*, 3 parts, Würzburg, 1889–97; J. Baier, *Geschichte der beiden Karmelitenklöster in Würzburg*, ib. 1902; S. Göbl, *Würzburg*, 5th ed., ib., 1904; A. F. Ludwig, *Weihbischof Zirkel von Würzburg*, 2 vols., Paderborn 1904–06; K. Wild, *Staat und Wirtschaft in den Bistümern Würzburg und Bamberg*, . . . *1729–46*, Heidelberg, 1906; Rettberg, *KD*, ii. 313 sqq.; Hauck, *KD*, vols. i–iv.

WULFRAM: Bishop of Sens near the end of the seventh century. Little is known of him except that his relics were raised in 704, the probability being that he died in 695. Two biographies exist, a shorter one in *ASB*, March, iii. 143 sqq., the other and longer in *ASM*, iii. 1, pp. 340 sqq. It was long thought that the second arose from the first through interpolation, the first containing nothing impossible of belief, apart from the miracles. But Levison (*NA*, xxv. 601 sqq.) has shown that the shorter is but a condensation of the first or an excerpt from it, and that neither is a primary source.

(A. HAUCK.)

BIBLIOGRAPHY: The early material is collected in *ASB*, Mar., iii. 143–165. Consult: *Histoire littéraire de la France*, vii. 512; A. Kluit, *Num S. Wulfrannus . . . regem aqua baptismi initiare potuit*, in his *Hist. critica comitatus Hollandiæ et Zeelandiæ*, i. 2, pp. 1 sqq., Middelburg, 1777; J. Ghesquière, *Acta sanctorum Belgii*, vi. 485 sqq., Brussels, 1794; L. M. Duru, *Bibliothèque historique de l'Yonne*, i. 184–188, Auxerre, 1850; A. Thijm, *Der heilige Willibrord*, pp. 94 sqq., Münster, 1863; G. La Vieille, *Abrégé de la vie . . . de S. Wulfran*, Rouen, 1876; W. Glaister, *Life and Times of St. Wulfram*, London, 1878; A. Molinier, *Les Sources de l'hist. de France*, i. 140–141, Paris, 1901; Legris, in *Analecta Bollandiana*, xvii. 287 sqq.; Levison, in *NA*, xxv. 601 sqq.; Rettberg, *KD*, ii. 514–517; *DCB*, iv. 1195; *KL*, xii. 1810–11.

WULFSTAN: Bishop of Worcester; b. at Long Itchington (a village near Warwick) in or before 1012; d. at Worcester Jan. 18, 1095. Educated in the monastic schools at Evesham and Peterborough, he was ordained between 1033 and 1038, and, preferring the regular to the secular clergy, he was professed in the cathedral monastery, where he ultimately rose to be prior. After considerable reluctance, due to his excessive modesty, Wulfstan was consecrated, Sept. 8, 1062, bishop of Worcester by Aldred, archbishop of York, who had been obliged by the pope to promise to resign the see of Worcester. Despite this, it was some time before Wulfstan could induce Aldred to resign the temporalities of the diocese, and even then the archbishop retained no less than twelve estates properly belonging to the bishopric of Worcester. After the successful issue of the Norman invasion, Wulfstan made his submission to William the Conqueror, and at the council of 1070 again petitioned for the possession of the estates, which were in the royal possession during the vacancy of the archdiocese of York in consequence of Aldred's death. Two years later the request was granted through the influence of Lanfranc (q.v.), although this prelate had at first sought to have Wulfstan deprived of his see because of insufficient education. The bishop of Worcester ultimately became the friend of the new archbishop of York, Thomas, as well, despite the fact that Worcester had been detached from the province of York, probably to the satisfaction of Wulfstan, and had been transferred to its present connection with the province of Canterbury.

Himself ascetic, humble, and devout, Wulfstan insisted on the observance of the same virtues on the part of his monks, and he was equally rigid in the performance of his episcopal duties. He built or restored many churches, some of his work being still preserved in the crypt and other parts of the cathedral of Worcester, and as a preacher and confessor he was highly esteemed. He successfully ended the slave-traffic in Bristol, where even William the Conqueror had failed, and he was beloved by English and Normans alike. He remained loyal to the king throughout, helping to hold Worcester for William Rufus against the rebels in 1088, and in 1085 he assisted the Worcestershire commissioners in taking their survey for Domesday. He was too infirm to attend the consecration of Anselm (q.v.) as archbishop of Canterbury in 1093, but early in the next year he was asked, as the only survivor of the pre-Norman episcopate, to decide a dispute between Anselm and Maurice, bishop of London, his verdict being in the archbishop's favor.

Wulfstan was popularly reckoned a saint from the day of his death, but he was not canonized until 1203, his day being Jan. 19. His shrine in Worcester cathedral was melted in 1216 to furnish money demanded for the convent, and two years later his body was translated to a new shrine when the restored cathedral was dedicated.

BIBLIOGRAPHY: The earliest lives, some of them going back to the period of their subject, are collected most fully in *ASB*, Jan., ii. 238–249, cf. ib., May, vi. 79; some are in *ASM*, vi. 2, pp. 840–865; and one is in *MPL*, clxxix. 1734–72; others are in H. Wharton, *Anglia sacra*, i. 541–542, ii. 241–270, London, 1691. Consult further: W. F. Hook, in the *Archæological Journal*, xx (1863), 1–28; *DNB*, lxiii. 174–176.

WUNDT, WILHELM: German philosopher; b. at Neckerau (now a part of Mannheim, 11 m. n.w. of Heidelberg) Aug. 16, 1832. He obtained his education at the universities of Tübingen, Heidelberg, and Berlin, 1851–56; became privat-docent at Heidelberg in physiology, 1857, and extraordinary professor, 1864; was elected to the legislative chamber of Baden, 1866; became extraordinary professor at Zurich, 1874; and professor of philosophy at Leipsic, 1875, where he was rector, 1889–90. In the realm of psychology his contributions have been notable. Of works which are of interest in theology, or because of their relation to the subject, notice may be taken of his *Vorlesungen über die Menschen- und Thierseele* (2 vols., Leipsic, 1863, 4th ed., 1906; Eng. transls., *Lectures on Human and Animal Psychology*, London, 1894, 1896, and 1901); *Die physikalischen Axiome und ihre Beziehung zum Causalprinzip* (Erlangen, 1866); *Grundzüge der physiologischen Psychologie* (Leipsic, 1873–74, 6th ed., 1910; Eng. transl., *Principles of Physiological Psychology*, London, 1904); *Ueber die Aufgabe der Philosophie in der Gegenwart* (Leipsic, 1874); *Der Spiritismus. Eine sogenannte wissenschaftliche Frage* (1879); *Logik* (2 vols., Stuttgart, 1880–83); *Philosophische Studien* (1883 sqq.); *Ethik. Eine Untersuchung der Thatsachen und Gesetze des sittlichen Lebens* (1886, 2d. ed., 2 vols., 1903; Eng. transl., *Ethics*, 3 vols., London, 1897–1901, and *Ethical Systems*, London, 1897, and 1902; also, *Facts of the Moral Life*, ib., 1902; and *Principles of Morality and Departments of Moral Life*, ib., 1901); *Grundriss der Psychologie* (Leipsic, 1896, 8th ed., 1907; Eng. transl., *Outlines of Psychology*, London, 1902); *Völkerpsychologie* (2 vols., 1904–05, 2d ed., 1910); and *Kleine Schriften*, 2 vols. (1910–1911).

WUNEBALD (WINEBALD). See WILLEBALD.

WURSTER, PAUL: German theologian; b. at Hohenstaufen (26 m. e. of Stuttgart) Dec. 6, 1860. He studied at the seminaries of Schöntal and Urach, and at the University of Tübingen; after a year given to work in philanthropic institutions, he spent some time in travel; he was pastor at Heilbronn, 1888–1903; dean at Blaubeuren, 1903; and professor and director of the preachers' seminary at Friedberg in Hesse, 1903–07. He has written *Gustav*

Werners Leben und Werken (Reutlingen, 1888); *Segen und Wohlthuns* (Heilbronn, 1891); *Die Lehre von der Innern Mission* (Berlin, 1894–95); and *Christliche Glaubens- und Sittenlehre* (Heilbronn, 1896).

WUTTKE, vut′ke, **KARL FRIEDRICH ADOLF:** German Lutheran theologian; b. at Breslau Nov. 10, 1819; d. at Halle Apr. 12, 1870. He received his education in his native city, the principal factors there being August Hahn (q.v.) in theology and Karl Julius Braniss in philosophy; he was for some years a private teacher, and for a year was editor of a conservative magazine; became a lecturer in the University of Breslau, treating logic, psychology, and history of philosophy; was made extraordinary professor of theology at Berlin in 1854, lecturing upon New-Testament exegesis, dogmatics, ethics, and symbolics; in 1861 he was called as professor to Halle, where he spent the rest of his life. He was interested in politics, and served as a member of the house of deputies, coining the somewhat famous epigram: No democrat can be a Christian and no Christian can be a democrat. The works of theo-

logical interest coming from his pen are: *Abhandlung über die Cosmogonie der heidnischen Völker vor der Zeit Jesu und der Apostel* (The Hague, 1850); *Geschichte des Heidenthums in Beziehung auf Religion, Wissen, Kunst, Sittlichkeit und Staatsleben* (Breslau, 1851–1853), a pioneer work in the domain of comparative religion; *Der deutsche Volksaberglaube der Gegenwart* (Hamburg, 1860); and his principal work, *Handbuch der christlichen Sittenlehre* (2 vols., Berlin, 1862; Eng. transl., *Christian Ethics*, 2 vols., New York, 1873), in a field little cultivated by theologians at that time. In his theology Wuttke was a defender of Lutheran orthodoxy, though in his work he was not one-sided either as a Biblical or as a confessional theologian. While he did not take foremost rank as a thinker, he was regarded as one of the most philosophical and learned of the defenders of the Lutheran standards. He was interested and active in support of home and foreign missions, as well as in fortifying and supporting the work of pastors.

(L. Schulze.)

Bibliography: *Evangelische Kirchenzeitung*, 1870, pp. 708 sqq.; the sketch by L. Schulze in Wuttke's *Sittenlehre*, vol. i., pp. iii. sqq., 3d ed., Leipsic, 1874; *ADB*, vol. xliv.

WYCLIF, JOHN.

I. His Life: John Wyclif, the most prominent of the Reformers before the Reformation, was born at Ipreswell (the modern Hipswell; 44 m. n.w. of York), Yorkshire, England, perhaps between 1320 and 1330; d. at Lutterworth (12 m. s. of Leicester) Dec. 31, 1384. His eminence rests not only upon his works, which still have influence, but upon his ecclesiastical activities. Although the Reformers of the sixteenth century knew and valued his life and works, his fame has grown largely in modern times, which have brought his productions into more complete knowledge, these in former times having suffered eclipse and long rested unknown. It is true that many a riddle still proposes itself concerning the course of his life and activities, and that many events occurring during his academical period are still involved in obscurity; but at least enough is known to make secure the rank he takes among the men who foreshadowed the Reformation, together with the reasons for this preeminence.

Wyclif seems to be the best form of the name. The family from which he came was of early Saxon origin, long settled in Yorkshire; it became extinct in the first half of the nineteenth century, remaining true to the Church of Rome until the end. In his day the family was a large one, and covered a considerable territory, and its principal seat was Wycliffe-on-Tees, of which Ipreswell was an outlying hamlet. His birth-year is not noted in contemporary sources, and the data afforded by his writings are so general that no secure conclusions

1. His Family and Youth.

can be based upon them. Yet they seem to indicate that his birth-year is to be reckoned rather before 1320 than after.* His childhood and youth fall in a period when England was winning increasing regard abroad, and when the ecclesiastical-political position of the land was marked by a leadership in influence which did not seem likely to diminish. Wyclif probably received his early training in the neighborhood of his home.

No reports are left to determine when he first went to Oxford, with which he was so closely connected till the end of his life. While it is certain that mere lads were enrolled at the universities of the Middle Ages, such cases were exceptions. The normal curriculum of the universities of the period is well known (see Universities), and consequently the university course of Wyclif is also approximately known. The time when he was at Oxford was about 1345, and then a series of shining names was adding glory to the fame of the university—such as those of Roger Bacon, Robert Grosseteste, Thomas Bradwardine, William of Occam (qq.v.), and Richard Fitzralph (see Appendix). To the writings of Occam Wyclif owed much; his interest in natural science and mathematics was considerable, but he applied himself most diligently to the study of theology and of ecclesiastical law, and also early

2. University Career.

---

* The year 1324 is the one usually given; Rashdall in *DNB*, lxiii. 202-204, reaches a conclusion different from that in the text, and says: " 1324 is too early rather than too late a date."

won recognition in philosophy. Even his opponents acknowledged the keenness of his dialectic. His writings prove him to have been well grounded in Roman law and in that of his own country, as well as in native history—in this last branch he set great store by the *Polychronicon* of Ranulf Higden [ed. in *Rolls Series*, 9 vols., London, 1865–86]. In the university there was no lack of sharp friction both political and scientific. As in other universities of the period, the students were enrolled in "nations"; in Oxford there were two of these—the northern or "Boreales" and southern or "Australes," each of which had its procurator chosen by the corps or nation. Wyclif belonged to the former of these, in which the prevailing tendency was anticurial, while the other was curial in its preferences. Not less sharp was the separation over Nominalism and Realism (see SCHOLASTICISM, IV.). Wyclif was a Realist. In the midst of these controversies the university studies of Wyclif were pursued. A family whose seat was in the neighborhood of Wyclif's home—Bernard Castle— had founded in Oxford the college named after itself—Balliol. To this Wyclif belonged, first as scholar, then as master, and had finally attained to the headship not later than 1360.

When he received from the college the presentation in 1361 of the parish of Fylingham in Lincolnshire, he had to give up the leadership of the college, though he received the courtesy of per-

3. Early Ap- mission to live at Oxford; original tes-
pointments. timony indicates that he had rooms in
the buildings of Queen's College. His university advancement followed the usual course. While as baccalaureate he busied himself with natural science and mathematics, as master he had the right to read in philosophy, and in this he soon gained repute. But of marked significance was his zeal in Bible study, which he pursued after becoming bachelor in theology. His fidelity, truth, and diligence led Simon Islip, archbishop of Canterbury, to place him at the head of Canterbury Hall in December, 1365, in which twelve young men were preparing for the priesthood.* Islip had designed the foundation especially for secular clergy; but when he died in April of 1366, his successor Simon Langham, a man of monastic training, turned the leadership of the college over to a monk. Though Wyclif appealed to Rome, the issue was unfavorable to him. This case would hardly have been thought of again had not contemporaries of Wyclif, such as William Woodford, erroneously seen in it the genesis of his later energetic assaults upon Rome and monasticism. Between 1366 and 1372 he became a doctor of theology; as such he had the right to lecture upon systematic divinity, which right he zealously exercised. But it is an error to trace to these lectures the origin of his *Summa*, which was due to quite other stimuli. In 1368 he gave up his living at Fylingham and took over the rectory of Ludgershall in Buckinghamshire, not far from Oxford, and this was a position which enabled him to retain his connection with the university. Six years later (1374) he received the crown living of Lutterworth in Leicestershire, which he retained till his

---

* Rashdall holds that the Wyclif of Canterbury Hall was not the Reformer.

death. He had already resigned a prebend in Westbury because it was contrary to his convictions to hold command of more positions than those in which he could personally exercise the cure of souls.

At Oxford he developed a comprehensive activity as academic teacher; there he penned his first reformatory writings and also preached with success. But it was not in these fields
4. Bases that Wyclif gained his position in his-
of his Re- tory; this came from his activities in
formatory ecclesiastical politics, in which he en-
Activities. gaged about the middle of the seventies,
when also his reformatory operations began. In 1374 he was among the English delegates at a peace congress at Bruges. It has been the general opinion that he was given this honorable position in consequence of his spirited and naturally patriotic behavior with which in the year 1366 he sought the interests of his country as against the demands of the papacy. It seems as though he had already a distinguished place as a patriot and reformer; and it suggests the answer to the question how he came to his reformatory ideas. There have been many erroneous ideas as to this, particularly with reference to Wyclif's relation to earlier reform movements in the Church. Little can be said in favor of a connection with the Waldenses (q.v.), whose activities hardly reached England. [Even if it were certain that older evangelical parties did not exist in England before the time of Wyclif, he might easily have been influenced by continental evangelicals who abounded, whose views were combated by men the works of whom were known to the English reformers. But it seems incredible that continental parties, who were sorely persecuted in the various countries across the channel from England should not have found their way to a land where the inquisition was not at work. Besides, it is highly probable that the older type of doctrine and practise represented by the Iro-Scottish Christians of the pre-Roman time persisted till the time of Wyclif and reappeared in Lollardism. A.H.N.] Rather the root of the Wyclifite reformatory movement must be traced to his Bible study and especially to the ecclesiastical-political lawmaking of his times and of those immediately preceding him. He was well acquainted with the tendencies of the ecclesiastical politics to which England owed the honorable position which she possessed in the fourteenth century. He had given study to the proceedings of Edward I. (1272–1306), England's most popular king, and had not only attributed to them the basis of parliamentary opposition to papal usurpations, but had found a model therein for methods of procedure in matters connected with the questions of worldly possessions and the Church. Many sentences in his book on the Church recall the institution of the commission of 1274, the activity of which prepared so much pain and sorrow for the English clergy. He considered that the example of Edward I. should be held in mind by the government of his time; but that with keener implements and to higher purposes the aim should be a reformation of the entire ecclesiastical establishment. And similar was his position with reference to the enactments induced by the ecclesiastical politics of Edward III. (1327–76), with which

he was well acquainted, which appear fully reflected in his political tracts. His own tendencies were in complete accord with the laws of Edward I. and his grandson of the same name.

The Reformer's entrance upon the stage of ecclesiastical politics is usually related to the question of feudal tribute to which England had been rendered liable by John Lackland (1200–16), which had remained unpaid for thirty-three years until Urban V. in 1365, it is said, had menacingly demanded it. It is related that the whole country was aroused in one patriotic mass on account of this demand of the pope, and that parliament the next year declared that neither King John nor any other had the right without its agreement to subject England to any foreign power. Should the pope attempt to enforce his claim by arms, he would be met with united resistance. It is further said that Urban recognized the mistake he had made and suffered his claim to fall to the ground. However sure may be the fact of the pope's demand, of such a patriotic uprising there was no talk. The tone of the pope was, in fact, not so threatening, and it was not his intention so to act as to draw England into the maelstrom of politics of western and southern Europe. It was to be expected that sharp words would be heard in England, and this because of the close relations of the papacy with the hereditary foe of England, the French kingdom. It is asserted also that on this occasion Wyclif was prominent, that he served as theological counsel to the government and composed a polemical tract dealing with the tribute, and defended an unnamed monk over against the conduct of the government and parliament. This would place the entrance of Wyclif into politics about 1365–66. But the tract upon which this conclusion is based, which is known only from an incomplete and incorrect reprint by Lewis, takes its occasion from circumstances which arose a century later. Wyclif's earlier activities in this direction were exercised in the narrower circle at Oxford, and his more important participation began with the peace congress at Bruges. There in 1374 negotiations were carried on between France and England respecting peace, while at the same time commissioners from England dealt with papal delegates respecting the doing away with ecclesiastical annoyances. Wyclif was among those who served in these affairs in consequence of a decree dated July 26, 1374. If it be claimed that his appointment in this case was due to his earlier stand against the demands of the papacy, the claim overlooks the fact that the choice of a harsh opponent of the Avignon system would rather have broken up than have furthered the peace negotiations, and, once more, that he was designated purely as a theologian, and so considered himself, since a noted Scripture scholar was required alongside of those learned in civil and canon law. There was no necessity here for a man of renown, still less of a pure advocate of state interests. Illustrative of this is the fact that a predecessor in a like case was John Owtred, a monk, who yet formulated the statement that St. Peter had united in his hands spiritual and temporal power—just the opposite of what Wyclif

5. Beginning of Political Career.

taught. In the days of the mission to Bruges this monk still belonged in the circle of friends of Wyclif. It will therefore be seen that the construction hitherto placed on Wyclif's part in this mission was altogether too exalted, since he took by no means a leading part.

As yet the Reformer could be regarded by papal partizans as trustworthy, for his opposition to the ruling conduct of the Church might have escaped notice. Testimony to this comes from a later but well-informed source that found it difficult to recognize him as a heretic. The controversies in which men engaged at Oxford were rather philosophical than purely theological or ecclesiastical-political, and the method of discussion was academic and scholastic. Walden shows the kind of men with whom Wyclif dealt, though very few writings are preserved which exhibit the method. There may be mentioned the tilt with the Carmelite monk John Kyningham (Cunningham; cf. *Fasciculi Zizaniorum*, p. 3, London, 1858) over theological questions (*utrum Christus esset humanitas*), or ecclesiastical-political ones (*De dominatione civili; De dotatione ecclesiæ*). Wyclif's contest with John Owtred and William Wynham (or Wyrinham) were formerly unknown, as were the earlier ones with his opponent William Wadeford. When it is recalled that it was once the task of Owtred to defend the political interests of England against the demands of Avignon, one would more likely see him in agreement with Wyclif than in opposition. But unanimity of sentiment between them was by no means complete. Owtred believed that he committed a sin who held that the temporal power might deprive a priest, even an unrighteous one, of his temporalities; Wyclif regarded that priest a sinner who incited the pope to excommunicate laymen when these had deprived wicked clergy of their temporalities, and enunciated the dictum that a man in a condition of sin had no claim upon government. Light upon another opponent of Wyclif has appeared only in recent investigations. This was the monk William Wynham of St. Albans, where the anti-Wyclifite trend was considerable. Wyclif complained bitterly of this Benedictine and professor of theology at Oxford as the one who dragged into the street the controversies which had hitherto been confined to the academic arena. But public notice of this was bound to come in any event, since the controversies were related in their fundamentals to the opposition which found expression in parliament against the Curia. Wyclif himself narrates (*Sermones*, iii. 199) how under the deep impression made upon him by his Biblical studies he came to the conclusion that there was a great contrast between what the Church was and what it ought to be, and saw the necessity for reforming it. His reform ideas stress particularly the perniciousness of the temporal rule of the clergy and its incompatibility with the teaching of Christ and the apostles, and they make note of the tendencies which were evident in the measures of the "Good Parliament" (1376–77). A long bill was introduced, with 140 headings, in which were stated the grievances caused by the aggressions of the Curia; all reservations and commissions were to

6. Growth of Anti-Curial Tendencies.

be done away, the exportation of money was forbidden, and the foreign collectors were to be removed.

It was in this period that Wyclif came significantly to the fore. He was found among those to whom the thought of the secularization of the ecclesiastical properties in England was welcome. He had as patron no less a man than John, duke of Lancaster. He was no longer satisfied with his chair as the means of propagating his ideas, and soon after his return from Bruges he began to express them in tracts and larger works—his great work, the *Summa theologiæ*, was written in support of them. In the very first book, concerned with the government of God and the ten commandments, he assailed the temporal rule of the clergy—in temporal things the king is above the pope, and the collection of annates and indulgences is simony. But his entrance into the politics of the day was made in his great work *De civili dominio*. Here were precipitated those ideas by which the good parliament was governed—which involved the renunciation by the Church of temporal dominion. From his formulation the items of the "long bill" appear to have been derived. In this book there were found the strongest outcries against the entire Avignon system with its commissions, its exactions, its squandering of charities by unfit priests, and the like. To change all this is the business of the State. If the clergy misuses ecclesiastical property, it must be taken away; if the king does not do this, he is remiss in his duty. The work contains eighteen strongly stated theses, the point of which was opposition to the governing methods of the rule of the Church and the straightening out of its temporal possessions. [These are conveniently given in *DNB*, lxiii. 208–209.] Wyclif had set these ideas forth before his students at Oxford in the autumn and winter of 1376, after he had become involved in controversy with such men as William Wadeford, William Wynham, and others. While he would at first have preferred to have these matters restricted in discussion to the classroom, he soon wanted them proclaimed from the very roofs and would have temporal and spiritual lords take note of them. While the last made earnest assault upon him and sought to have him put under ecclesiastical censure, he recommended himself to the former by his mighty attacks upon the worldly possessions of the clergy. This period began a stage of unusual literary fruitfulness which ended only with his death.

Wyclif was possessed with the great desire to see each of his ideas actualized—the fundamental was that the Church should be poor, as it was in the days of the apostles. He had not yet broken with the mendicant friars, and from these the duke of Lancaster chose Wyclif's defenders. While the Reformer offered reassurances, in the explanations which he necessarily gave later, that it was not his purpose to incite temporal lords to confiscation of the property of the Church, the real tendencies of the propositions remained unconcealed. This was evident as the result of the same doctrines in Bohemia—that land which was richest

7. Public Declaration of his Ideas.

8. Conflict with the Church Opened.

in ecclesiastical foundations—where in a very brief time the entire church estate was taken over and a most remarkable revolution brought about in the relations of temporal holdings. Since such views existed as the Curia charged upon him and its condemnation implies, they must have been strongly emphasized. It was altogether concordant with the plans of Lancaster to have a personality like that of Wyclif on his side. Especially in London the Reformer's views won support; numerous partizans of the nobility attached themselves to him, and the lower orders gladly heard his sermons. He preached in various churches of the city, and all London rang with his praises. But he found adversaries. The first to oppose his theses were monks of those orders which held possessions, to whom his theories were dangerous. The University of Oxford and the episcopate later came under blame from the Curia, which charged them with so neglecting their duty that the breaking of the evil fiend into the English sheepfold could be noticed in Rome before it was in England. And yet the bishops were not inactive, as though they would prefer to deal with the case at home. Wyclif was summoned before William Courtenay, bishop of London, on Feb. 19, 1377, in order, as one source ironically says, "to explain the wonderful things which had streamed forth from his mouth." What the exact charges were is not known, as the matter did not get so far as a definite examination. Lancaster, the earl marshal Henry Percy, and a number of other friends accompanied Wyclif, and four begging friars were his advocates, who were whole-hearted in a matter which affected the question of the ideal of poverty. A great crowd gathered at the church, and at the entrance of the party animosities began to show, especially in a wrathy exchange of words between the imperious bishop and the Reformer's protectors. Lancaster declared that he would humble the pride of the English clergy and their partizans, even if they had sprung from noble parents (Bishop Courtenay was of high birth [his father was earl of Devonshire])—doubtless hinting at the intent to secularize the possessions of the Church. The assembly broke up and the lords departed with their protégé.*

The greater part of the English clergy regarded this encounter with great irritation, and attacks upon Wyclif now began with vehemence, which found their echo in the second and third books of his work dealing with civil government. These books carry a sharp polemic, which can hardly be a cause of wonder when it is recalled that his opponents charged Wyclif with blasphemy and scandal, pride and heresy. It is concluded from his performances that he had openly advised the secularization of English church property, and the dominant parties shared with him the conviction that the monks could better be held in check if they were relieved from the care of secular affairs. The bitterness occasioned by this advice will be the better understood when it is remembered that at that time the papacy was engaged in its war with the

9. Papal Condemnation.

---

* An excellent account of this wordy dispute between the bishop and the protectors of Wyclif is given in the *Chronicon Angliæ*, the gist of which is quoted in *DNB*, lxiii. 206–207.

Florentines and was in great straits. The demand of the Minorites that the Church should live in poverty as it did in the days of the apostles was not pleasing in such a crisis. It was under these conditions that Gregory XI., who in January, 1377, had gone from Avignon to Rome, sent on May 22 five copies of his bull against Wyclif, despatching one to the archbishop of Canterbury, and the others to the bishop of London, Edward III., the chancellor, and the university; among the enclosures were eighteen theses of his, which were denounced as erroneous and dangerous to Church and State. The position may well be taken that the reformatory activities of Wyclif began here, since all the great works, especially his *Summa theologiæ*, stand in a more or less close connection with the condemnation of his eighteen theses, while the entire literary energies of his later years rest upon this foundation. The aim of his opponents which next appears—to make him out a revolutionary in politics—failed in achievement. Indeed the situation in England resulted rather in damage to them; for on June 21, 1377, Edward III. died, and his inglorious end was a sad contrast to the brilliant days of Crécy and Maupertuis. His successor was Richard II., who was under the influence of Lancaster, the protector of the Reformer. So it resulted that the bull against Wyclif, although dated May 22, 1377, did not become public till Dec. 18. Moreover parliament, which met in October, came into sharp conflict with the Curia. Among the propositions which Wyclif, at the direction of the government, worked out for parliament was one which speaks out with distinctness against the exhaustion of England by the Curia.

When the censure of his theses became known in England, Wyclif sought to gain the favor of the public. He first laid his theses before parliament, and then made them public in a tract, accompanying them, however, with explanations, limitations, and here and there with interpretations. After the session of parliament was over, in accordance with papal directions he was called upon to make answer, and in March, 1378, he appeared at the episcopal palace at Lambeth to defend himself. The preliminaries were not yet finished when a noisy mob gathered with the purpose of delivering him; the queen mother also took up his cause. The bishops, who were of two minds, satisfied themselves with forbidding the Reformer to speak further on the subjects in controversy. At Oxford the vicechancellor, following papal directions, had confined the Reformer for some time in Black Hall, from which Wyclif was released at the threats of his friends; not long after the vice-chancellor was himself confined in the same place because of this indignity to Wyclif. The latter then took up the usage according to which one who remained for forty-four days under excommunication came under the penalties executed by the State, and wrote his *De incarcerandis fidelibus*, in which he demanded that it should be legal for the excommunicated to appeal to the king and his council against the excommunication; in this writing he laid open the entire case and in such a way that it came within the ken of the laity. He wrote his thirty-three conclusions, this

10. Sharpening of the Conflict.

time not merely in Latin but also in English. The masses of the people, a part of the nobility, and his former protector, the duke of Lancaster, rallied to his side. Before any further steps could be taken at Rome in the affair, Gregory XI. died (1378). But Wyclif was already engaged upon one of his most important works, that dealing with the truth of Holy Scripture. Indeed, the sharper the strife became, the more did Wyclif have recourse to Scripture as the basis of all Christian doctrinal opinion, and expressly proved this to be the only norm for Christian faith. To drag this basis from beneath him was the thankless task of his opponents; it was in order to refute them that he wrote the book in which he showed that Holy Scripture contains all truth and, being from God, is the only authority. He did not fail in this book to refer to the conditions under which the condemnation of his eighteen theses was brought about; and the same may be said of his books dealing with the Church, the office of king, and the power of the pope—all completed within the short space of two years (1378–79). Since all the world, he taught, understands by "the Church" the pope and the cardinals (whom one must obey in order to obtain salvation), it is necessary to make clear the distinction between what the Church is and what the common man supposes it to be. The Church is the totality of those who are predestined to blessedness. It includes the Church triumphant in heaven, those who are in purgatory, and the Church militant or men on earth. No one who is eternally lost has part in it. There is but one universal Church, and outside of it there is no salvation. Its head is Christ. No pope may say that he is the head, for he can not say that he is elect or even a member of the Church.

It would be a great mistake to assume that Wyclif's doctrine of the Church—which made so great an impression upon Huss, who adopted it literally and fully—was occasioned by the great schism (1378–1429). In its principles that doctrine was already embodied in his *De civili dominio*. How closely the contents of the book dealing with the Church are connected with the decision respecting the eighteen theses appears in every chapter. The attacks upon Gregory XI. grow ever more unsparing and in places are extreme. His stand with respect to the ideal of poverty became continually firmer, as well as his position with regard to the temporal rule of the clergy. Closely related to this attitude was his book *De officio regis*, the content of which was foreshadowed in his thirty-three conclusions: One should be instructed with reference to the obligations which lie in regard to the kingdom in order that he may know how the two powers, the royal and the ecclesiastical, may support each other in harmony in the body corporate of the Church. The royal power, Wyclif taught, is consecrated through the testimony of Holy Scripture and the Fathers. Christ and the apostles rendered tribute to the emperor. The king is the servant of God. Sinful indeed is he who opposes the power of the king, since this is derived immediately from God. For this reason Paul appealed to Cæsar, and subjects, above all the clergy

11. Statement Regarding Royal Power.

who hold under the king, should pay him dutiful tribute. To this end temporal power offers protection, justice, and in its earliest times gave account for its employment. The honors which attach to temporal power hark back to the king; those which belong to precedence in the priestly office, to the priest. In what does the royal office consist? The king must apply his power with wisdom, his laws are to be in unison with those of God. From God laws derive their authority, including those which royalty has over against the clergy. If one of the clergy neglects his office, he is a traitor to the king who calls him to answer for it. It follows from this that the king has an "evangelical" control. Every one in the service of the Church must have regard to the laws of the State. In confirmation of this fundamental principle the archbishops in England make sworn submission to the king and in view of that receive their temporalities. This is a relation based upon the law. The king is, moreover, to protect his poor vassals against every damage which might happen to their possessions; in case the clergy through their misuse of the temporalities in this respect cause injury, the king must afford protection. When the king turns over temporalities to the clergy, he places them under his jurisdiction, from which later pronouncements of the popes can not release them. If the clergy relies on papal pronouncements, it must be subjected to obedience to the king.

It appears thus that this book, like those that preceded and followed, had to do with the reform of the Church in head and members, in which the temporal arm was to have an influential part. Especially interesting is the teaching which Wyclif addressed to the king on the protection of his theologians, i.e., the theological faculty, whose duty it is to advise king and people in theological concerns. By this was not meant theology in its modern sense, but rather knowledge of the Bible. Since the laws of the land are to be in agreement with Scripture, knowledge of theology is necessary to the strengthening of the kingdom; it is a consequence of this that the king has theologians in his entourage to stand at his side as he exercises power. The position of these is that of the prophets under the old covenant. It is their duty to explain Scripture according to the rule of reason and in conformity with the witness of the saints; also to proclaim the law of the king and to protect his welfare and that of his kingdom.

In all the books and tracts of Wyclif's last six years one may discover an immense and almost unreviewable mass of attacks upon the papacy and the entire hierarchy of his times. Each successive year they focus more and more, and at the last pope and
Antichrist seem to him practically

12. Attitude equivalent conceptions. Yet there are
toward the to be found in his writings passages
Papacy which are moderate in tone in dealing
Constant. with pope and papacy; in fact, Lechler's opinion that in Wyclif's relations with the papacy three steps of development are to be discovered finds confirmation both among German and English scholars. The first step, which carried him to the outbreak of the schism, involves a moderate recognition of the papal primacy; the second, which carried him to 1381, is marked by an

estrangement from the papacy; and the third shows him in sharp contest. However, Wyclif reached no valuation of the papacy before the outbreak of the schism different from his later appraisal. If in his last years in his keen tracts he identified the papacy with antichristianity, the dispensability of this papacy was strong in his mind before the schism. If it be remarked that it was this very man who labored to bring about the recognition of Urban VI. (1378–1389), this fact appears to contradict his former attitude and to demand an explanation. In fact, Wyclif's influence was never greater than at the moment when pope and antipope sent their ambassadors to England in order to gain recognition for themselves. In the presence of the ambassadors he delivered an opinion before parliament that showed, in an important ecclesiastical political question, viz., the matter of the right of asylum in Westminster abbey, a position that was to the liking of the State. How Wyclif came to be active in the interest of Urban is seen in passages in his latest writings, in which he expressed himself in regard to the papacy in a favorable sense. On the other hand he says explicitly that it is not necessary to go either to Rome or to Avignon in order to seek a decision from the pope. Every place is sufficient for the penitent, since the triune God is everywhere. Our pope is Christ. Here Wyclif has broken with the papacy, though only with it as it exists. If one thoroughly examines the situation, it seems clear that he was an opponent of that papacy which had developed since the donation of Constantine. He taught that the Church can continue to exist even though it have no visible leader; but as on earth there is no order unless there be a higher unity, there can be no damage when the Church possesses a leader of the right kind. But what qualities must such a leader possess? How does he appear with his pretensions to temporal power? In a word—to make firm the distinction between what the pope should be, in case one is necessary, and the pope as he appeared in Wyclif's day was the purpose of his book on the power of the pope. The Church militant, Wyclif taught, needs a head; but such a head is not the one whom the cardinals choose but one whom God gives the Church. Such a one is of the elect. The elector [cardinal] can then only make some one a pope if the choice relates to one who is elect [of God]. But that is not always the case. It may be that the elector is himself not predestinated and chooses one who is in the same case—a veritable Antichrist. One must regard as a true pope one who in teaching and life most nearly follows Christ and Peter, whose rule is not of this world.

These are the teachings and fundamentals of Wyclif before the outbreak of the schism; but their expression became sharper in the later period. The point is that he distinguished the true from the false papacy. Since all signs indicated that Urban VI. was a reforming and consequently a "true" pope, the enthusiasm which Wyclif manifested for him is easily understood as it comes to expression in his work on the Church. These views concerning the Church and church government are those which are brought forward also in the last books of his *Summa, "De simonia, de apostasia, de blasphemia."* To be sure, the battle which had been begun over the theses was lost to sight in the significance attaching to the more vehement one that he waged against the monastic orders when he saw the hopes quenched which had gathered around the "reform pope," and when he was withdrawn from the scene as an ecclesiastical politician and occupied himself exclusively with the question of the reform of the Church.

His teachings concerning the danger attaching to the secularizing of the Church must have put Wyclif
13. Attack on Monasticism.
into line with the mendicant orders, since in 1377 Minorites were his defenders. If he took the mendicants at that time to be an order worthy of honor, whose zeal for poverty he praised to the skies, there appear in the last chapters of his *De civili dominio* traces of a rift. Upon his making the statement that "the case of the orders which hold property is that of them all," the mendicant orders turned against him; and from that time Wyclif began against them a fight which grew sharper all the time even till his death. This battle against the imperialized papacy and its supporters the "sects," as he denominated the orders, finds a large space not only in such of his large later works as the *Trialogus, Dialogus, Opus evangelicum*, and in his sermons, but also in a series of sharp tracts and polemical productions in Latin and English (of which those issued in his later years have been collected as "Polemical Writings"). In these he teaches that the Church needs no new sects; sufficient for it now is the religion of Christ which sufficed in the first three centuries of its existence. The monastic orders are bodies which have not the least support in the Bible, which rejoice in vices, cause harm to Church and State, and must be abolished together with their haughty possessions. Such teaching, particularly as it was brought forward in sermons, had one immediate effect—in London and other cities there was produced a serious rising of the people. The monks were deprived of their alms and were bidden in accordance with these doctrines to apply themselves to manual labor. These teachings had more important results upon the orders and their possessions in Bohemia, where the instructions of the "Evangelical master" were followed out to the letter in such a way that the noble foundations and practically the whole of the property of the Church were sacrificed. But the result was not as Wyclif would have had it in England—the property fell not to the State but to the barons of the land. The scope of the conflict in England widened; finally it involved no longer the mendicant monks alone, but took in the entire hierarchy as it was then constituted, the unflagging zeal of Wyclif carrying it along. An element of the contest appears also in Wyclif's doctrine of the Lord's Supper (see below).

To his proposition that the Bible ought to be the common possession of all Christians was due the fact
14. Relation to the English Bible.
that it now was made available for common use in the language of the people. Indeed the national honor seemed to require this, since there were members of the nobility who possessed the Bible in French. Wyclif set himself to the task. While it is not possible exactly to define the part

which he had in the translation—which was on the basis of the Vulgate—there can be no doubt that the inception was due to his initiative, and that the successful carrying out of the project was due to his leadership. From him comes the translation of the New Testament, which was smoother, clearer, and more readable than the rendering of the Old Testament, which was done by his friend Nicholas of Hereford (q.v.). The whole was revised by Wyclif's younger contemporary John Purvey (q.v.) in 1388. Thus the mass of the people came into possession of the Bible; but the cry of his opponents may be heard: "The jewel of the clergy has become the toy of the laity." As a matter of fact, not merely those who bore a proud name, but members of the middle class possessed it, and in spite of the zeal with which the hierarchy sought after heretical books and aimed to destroy it utterly, and in reality did, in course of time, do away with very numerous copies, there still exist about 150 manuscripts, complete or partial, which contain the translation in its revised form. From this one may easily infer how widely diffused it was in the fifteenth century. For this reason the Wyclifites in England were often designated by their opponents as "Bible men." Just as Luther's version had great influence upon the German language, so Wyclif's, by reason of its clarity, beauty, and strength, worked mightily upon the English tongue.

Another task to which Wyclif gave himself was preaching and the care of souls, himself toiling as
15. Activity as a Preacher.
preacher to the people and as their teacher. Inasmuch as it was his desire to do away with the existing hierarchy on the ground that it had no warrant in Scripture, he put in the place of its members the "poor priests" who lived in poverty, were bound by no vows and had received no formal consecration, and preached the Gospel to the people. These priests as itinerant preachers spread abroad among the people the teachings of Wyclif. Two by two they went barefoot, clad in long dark-red robes and carrying a staff in the hand, this latter having symbolic reference to their pastoral calling, and passed from place to place preaching the sovereignty of God. The bull of Gregory XI. impressed upon them the name of Lollards (q.v.), intended as an opprobrious epithet, but it became later a name of honor. Even in his time the "Lollards" had reached wide circles in England and preached "God's law, without which no one could be justified."

In the summer of 1381 Wyclif formulated his doctrine of the Lord's Supper in twelve short sentences, and made it a duty to advocate it everywhere. Then
16. Anti-Wyclif Synod.
the English hierarchy proceeded against him. The chancellor of the University of Oxford had certain of the declarations pronounced heretical. In the auditorium this fact was announced to him, whereupon he declared that neither the chancellor nor any other could change his convictions. He then appealed—not to the pope nor to the ecclesiastical authorities of the land, but—to the king. He published his great confession upon the subject and also a second writing in English in-

tended for the common people. His performances grew in keenness, his following ever became greater. His pronouncements were no longer hedged in by the bounds of the classroom, they spread to the masses. "Every second man that you meet," writes a contemporary, "is a Lollard." In the midst of this commotion, which moved onward in victorious fashion, fell the great peasant uprising (1381), called forth by the misery of the suffering masses under epidemics, failure of harvests, and mistakes of government. Although Wyclif disapproved of the revolt, it was laid to his charge. And yet his friend and protector Lancaster was, among the revolutionaries, the most hated of all, and where Wyclif's influence was the greatest the uprising found the least semblance of support. While in general the aim of the revolt was against the spiritual nobility, this came about because they were of the nobles, not because they were of the Church. So prosecution was directed against Wyclif. His old enemy, Courtenay, now archbishop of Canterbury, called (1382) an ecclesiastical assembly of notables at London. During the consultations an earthquake occurred (May 21); the participants were terrified and wished to break up the assembly, but Courtenay declared the earthquake a favorable sign which meant the purification of the earth from erroneous doctrine. Of the twenty-four propositions, attributed to Wyclif without mentioning his name, ten were declared heretical and fourteen erroneous. The former had reference to the transformation in the sacrament, the latter to matters of church order and institutions. It was forbidden from that time to hold these opinions or to advance them in sermons or in academic discussions. All persons disregarding this order were to be subject to prosecution. To accomplish this latter end the help of the State was necessary; the upper house, frightened by the uprising, was won over, but the commons rejected the bill. The king, however, had a decree issued which permitted the arrest of those in error. The citadel of the reformatory movement was Oxford, where were Wyclif's most active helpers; these were laid under the ban and summoned to recant, and one of them, Nicholas of Hereford, went to Rome to appeal. In similar fashion the poor priests were hindered in their work. Finally the chief blow fell upon himself. On Nov. 18, 1382, a synod was opened at Oxford, before which he was summoned; he appeared, though apparently broken in body in consequence of a stroke of paralysis, but nevertheless strong in conviction and unbent in will. That he recanted is a baseless calumny. He still commanded the favor of the court and of parliament, to which he addressed a memorial. He was neither excommunicated then, nor deprived of his living.

He returned to Lutterworth, and thence sent out tracts—exceedingly pungent—against the monks and Urban VI. since the latter, con-

17. Last Days. trary to the hopes of Wyclif, had not turned out to be a reforming or "true" pope, but had exerted his activities in mischievous conflicts. The crusade in Flanders called forth the Reformer's biting scorn, while his sermons became yet fuller-voiced and dealt with the imperfections of the Church. The literary achievements of his last days, such as the *Trialogus*, stand at the peak of the knowledge of his day. His last work, the *Opus evangelicum*, the last part of which he named in characteristic fashion "Of Antichrist," remained uncompleted. While he was hearing mass in the parish church on Holy Innocents' Day, Dec. 28, 1384, he was again stricken down with apoplexy and died on the last day of the year. His remains found no quiet in the grave, for in his lifetime the great Hussite movement (see HUSS, JOHN, HUSSITES) arose and set afire the entire West of Europe. The Council of Constance took cognizance of Wyclif as well as of Huss and declared the former (on May 4, 1415) a stiff-necked heretic and under the ban of the Church. It was decreed that his books be burned and his remains be exhumed. This last did not happen till twelve years afterward, when at the command of Martin V. they were dug up, burned, and the ashes cast into the Swift which flows through Lutterworth.

Significant though the work of this man was in the last decade of his life, none of his contemporaries left

18. Personality. a complete picture of his person, his life, and his activities. It is most difficult to be certain of his external appearance. While pictures representing him have been found, they are from a later period. Those of the fourteenth century are strongly typical, and yet it can not be said with certainty that they belong to a definite individual. One must therefore be content with certain scattered expressions found in the history of the trial by William Thorpe (1407). It appears that Wyclif was spare of body, indeed of wasted appearance, and not strong physically. He was of unblemished walk in life, says Thorpe, and was regarded affectionately by people of rank, who often consorted with him, took down his sayings, and clung to him. "I indeed clove to none closer than to him, the wisest and most blessed of all men whom I have ever found. From him one could learn in truth what the Church of Christ is and how it should be ruled and led." If one rejects this testimony as that of a partizan, one may yet adduce Henry Knighton, who says of him that in philosophy there was no one of his opponents who was his equal, and in Bohemia, according to John Pribram, "every one cleaves to the declarations of John Wyclif as though he were the fifth Gospel"; while with a certain excessive warmth Huss wished that his soul might be wherever that of Wyclif was found.

One may not say that Wyclif was a comfortable opponent to meet. On this account Thomas Netter of Walden highly esteemed the old Carmelite monk John Kynyngham in that he "so bravely offered himself to the biting speech of the heretic and to words that stung as being without the religion of Christ." But this example of Netter is not well chosen, since the tone of Wyclif toward Kynyngham is that of a junior toward an elder whom one respects, and in similar fashion he handled also other opponents. But when he turned upon them his roughest side, as for example in his sermons or in his polemical writings and tracts, it is not to be denied that he met the attacks with a tone that could not be styled friendly.

II. Wyclif's Doctrines: It was long ago remarked that the philosophical-theological system of Wyclif would be understood in its fulness only when his chief Latin works were published, but that upon the basis of those already known the view was unsound which had long been current to

1. His System a Development.

the effect that from his entrance into public life Wyclif was in possession of a practically completed system of thought. Wyclif's first encounter with the official Church of his time was prompted by his zeal in the interests of the State, his first tracts and greater works of ecclesiastical-political content defended the privileges of the State, and from these sources there developed a strife out of which the next phases, let alone the ultimate purposes, could hardly be determined. One who studies these books in the order of their production with reference to their inner content finds therein a direct development with a strong reformatory tendency. This was not originally doctrinal but had to do with the excrescences of the hierarchical system; and when it later took up matters of dogma, as in the teaching concerning transubstantiation, the purpose in mind was the dissipation of the powers of the hierarchy and return to the original simplicity in the government of the Church. To the question whether there were in Wyclif's academical writings and disputations (none of them are extant) erroneous declarations, one may rather answer with a negative than an affirmative, in spite of the statement of Netter (*His Earliest Heresies*, 2). For it would have been against the diplomatic practise of the time to have sent to the peace congress at Bruges, in which the Curia had an essential part, a participant who had become known at home by heretical teaching. One may quote here the words of a man most intimately acquainted with Wyclif's works, Waddington Shirley:

"As it is in the light of subsequent events that we see the greatness of Wyclif as a reformer, so it is from the later growth of the language that we best learn to appreciate the beauty of his writing. But it was less the reformer, or the master of English prose, than the great schoolman that inspired the respect of his contemporaries; and, next to the deep influence of personal holiness and the attractive greatness of his moral character, it was to his supreme command of the weapons of scholastic discussion that he owed his astonishing influence" (in his ed. of the *Fasciculi zizaniorum*, p. xlvii.).

Wyclif must have earned his great repute as a philosopher even at an early date, since this was willingly or unwillingly conceded by his ecclesiastical opponents. A contemporary historian—for Henry Knighton may be designated as such—says of him that in philosophy he was reputed second to none, and in scholastic discipline incomparable. If this pronouncement seems hardly justified now that Wyclif's writings are in print, it must be borne in mind that not all his philosophical works are extant, and that Knighton had not so much these in thought as the learned disputations. If Wyclif was in philosophy the superior of his contemporaries and if he had no equal in scholastic discipline, he belongs with the series of great scholastic philosophers and theologians in which England in the Middle Ages was so rich—with Alexander of Hales, Roger Bacon, Duns Scotus, William Occam, and Bradwardine

(qq.v.). There was a period in his life when he devoted himself exclusively to scholastic philosophy: "when I was still a logician," he used later to say as he looked back upon that period. The first "heresy" which "he cast forth into the world" rests as much upon philosophical as upon theological grounds. But there will be considered here only how he was related to the early philosophers.

In Plato, the knowledge of whom came to him through Augustine, he thought he saw traces of a knowledge of the Trinity, and he championed the doctrine of ideas as against Aristotle. The latter Wyclif did not highly esteem, and he said once that

2. Basal Positions in Philosophy.

Democritus, Plato, Augustine, and Grosseteste far outranked Aristotle. In Aristotle he missed the provision for the immortality of the soul, and in his ethics the tendency toward the eternal.

He was himself a close follower of Augustine, so much so that, as Netter reports, he was called "John of Augustine" by his pupils. In some of his teachings, as in *De annihilatione*, the influence of Thomas Aquinas is to be detected. So far as his relations to the philosophers of the Middle Ages are concerned, he held to realism as opposed to the nominalism which was newly advanced by Occam, although in questions that had to do with ecclesiastical politics he stood related to Occam and indeed went beyond him. His views therefore are based upon the conviction of the reality of the universal, and he employed realism in order to avoid dogmatic difficulties. The uni-divine existence in the Trinity is the real universal of the three Persons, and in the Eucharist the ever-real presence of Christ justifies the deliverance that complete reality is compatible with the spatial division of the existence. The center of Wyclif's philosophical system is formed by the doctrine of the prior existence in the thought of God of all things and events. This involves the definiteness of things and especially their number, so that neither their infinity, infinite extension, nor infinite divisibility can be assumed. Space consists of a number of points of space determined from eternity, and time of exactly such a number of moments, and the number of these is known only to the divine spirit. Geometrical figures consist of arranged series of points, and enlargement or diminution of these figures rests upon the addition or subtraction of points. Because the existence of these points of space as such, that is, as truly indivisible unities, has its basis in the fact that the points are one with the bodies that fill them; because, therefore, all possible space is coincident with the physical world (as in Wyclif's system, in general, reality and possibility correspond), there can as little be a vacuum as bounding surfaces that are common to different bodies. The assumption of such surfaces impinges, according to Wyclif, upon the contradictory principle as does the conception of a truly continuous transition of one condition into another. Wyclif's doctrine of atoms connects itself, therefore, with the doctrine of the composition of time from real moments, but is distinguished by the denial of interspaces as assumed in other systems. From the identity of space and the physical world on the one side, and the circular motion of the heavens on the other, Wyclif deduces the spherical form of the universe. If the world-structure had edges, the circular movement would be impossible, since the edges could not pass through a space which was non-existent.

It immediately follows that Wyclif's fundamental principle of the preexistence in thought of all reality involves the most serious obstacle to freedom of the will; the philosopher could assist himself only by the formula that the free will of

3. Attitude toward Speculation. man was something predetermined of God. In particulars he demanded a strict dialectical training as the means of distinguishing the true from the false, and he asserted that logic (or the syllogism) furthered the knowledge of catholic verities; ignorance of logic was the reason why men misunderstood Scripture, since men overlooked the connection—the distinction between idea and appearance. In general, it may be said that Wyclif was not merely conscious of the distinction between theology and philosophy, but that his sense of reality led him to pass by scholastic questions as if they were empty shells. He left aside philosophical discussions which seemed to him to have no significance for the religious consciousness and those which pertained purely to scholasticism, and found no enjoyment in the hairsplitting of a degenerate scholastic and in its inanities. He held that we ought not to roam around in the realm of mere possibilities: " we concern ourselves with the verities that are, and leave aside the errors which arise from speculation on matters which are not." It is more wholesome to concern oneself with the study of verities than to be busy with fictions which one can prove neither to be possible nor useful to mankind; for vast is the number of solid and useful truths which yet are concealed from man.

Since it was from dealing with ecclesiastical-political questions that Wyclif turned to reformatory activities, naturally the former have a large part in his reformatory writings. It would be a mistake to suppose, however, that his opposition to the Church was a continuation of that of

4. Doctrine of Scripture. the French under Philip the Fair (1285–1314) or of that of the Germans under Louis the Bavarian (1314–46). While he took his start in affairs of church policy from the English legislation which was passed in the times of Edward I., he declined the connection into which his contemporaries brought it under the lead of Occam. Indeed, he distinctly disavows taking his conclusions from Occam, and avers that he draws them from Scripture, and that they were supported by the Doctors of the Church. So that dependence upon earlier schismatic parties in the Church, which he never mentions in his writings (as though he had never derived anything from them), is counterindicated, and attention is directed to the true sources in Scripture, to which he added the collections of canons of the Church. [Wyclif would have had nothing to gain and everything to lose by professing indebtedness to " heretical " parties or to opponents of the papacy whose efforts had come to naught. His reference to Scripture and orthodox Fathers as authorities is what might in any case have been expected. So far as his polemics are accordant

with those of earlier antagonists of the papacy, it is fair to assume that he was not ignorant of them and was more or less influenced by them. A. H. N.] To these last, although in his later years he rejected them explicitly as being the laws of men, he frequently had recourse. But in those last years fully authoritative was the Bible alone, which, according to his own conviction and that of his disciples, was fully sufficient for the government of this world (*De sufficientia legis Christi*). Out of it he drew his comprehensive averments in support of his reformatory views—not without intense study and many spiritual conflicts. He tells that when he was yet a beginner he was much concerned to comprehend the passages which treated of the activities of the divine Word, until by the grace of God he was enabled to gather the right sense of Scripture, which he then understood. But that was not a light task, for the Word is not to be opened by means of the grammar used by boys; Scripture has its own rules, it contains all verity and has the highest authority; for it is the law of Christ who can not lie, and is, therefore, to be placed above all human writings. The law of Christ is that which all men ought to learn, for the faith rests in it alone. Without knowledge of the Bible there can be peace neither in the life of the Church nor in that of society, and outside of it there is no real and abiding good; it contains all that is necessary for the salvation of men, it alone is infallible, sublime above error and failing, and consequently the one authority for the faith. He then is known as a true Christian who as a priest feeds his flock on the Word of God.

These teachings Wyclif promulgated not only in his great work on the truth of Scripture, but also in numerous other greater and lesser writings. For him the Bible was the fundamental source of Christianity which is binding on all men, who are therefore obligated to know it. From this one can easily see how the next step came about, viz., the furnishing of the Bible to the people in their mother tongue. Also not difficult to understand is the honor title of " Doctor evangelicus " which English and Bohemian Wyclifites gave to their master. Of all the reformers who preceded Luther, Wyclif most emphasized the importance of Scripture: " Even though there were a hundred popes and though every mendicant monk were a cardinal," he taught, " they would be entitled to confidence only in so far as they accorded with the Bible." Therefore in this early period it was Wyclif who recognized and formulated the formal principle of the Reformation—the unique authority of the Bible for the belief and life of the Christian.

Upon this Biblical foundation was reared the structure of Wyclif's doctrinal teachings. But he did not shake himself clear of scholastic methods.

5. Theology and Christology Realistic. His doctrine of God bears on its face the stamp of speculative realism. He rejects the view that the idea of the Godhead is a mere general conception, as well as the conception that a personal God is an individual, since both these rest upon a nominalistic basis. The omnipotence of God is for him not at all unlimited capacity, so that, e.g., God could lie; it is rather a power that is morally regulated, self-determined, and ordered by its own inner laws. The realism of Wyclif comes to light with especial clarity in his doctrine of God the Son as the Logos, who as the essential Word is the summation of all ideas, that is, of all intelligible realities. Such pronouncements as the following result: " Every creature (thing created) that can be known is the word of God in relation to its intelligible being and therefore in relation to its essential being; every being is in fact God himself." Although these and other declarations aim at a monistic doctrine, Wyclif declined to accept pantheism. In this respect he was a follower of Augustine, who in his philosophical discussions was not always able to avoid a pantheistic tinge.

The same tendency is discoverable in his anthropology and his doctrine of the freedom of the human will and of sin. He regarded as especially important the affirmation of the freedom of the will, being conscious that the ethical worth **6. Will,** of an action is conditioned by this. **Evil, Faith,** The complete guarding of the holiness **Salvation.** of Deity is an especial care, and he would not admit at all the imputation of responsibility in God for the existence of evil. He held fast to the conception that in the innermost region of the heart and of the will there is at least a relative autonomy elevated above all compulsion. He also affirmed the view that evil is not a positive existence, but rather a non-existence, not an activity but a defect. These views were inspired by Augustine. He did not hesitate to state these ideas in his sermons, but he carefully guarded against the thought that it was permissible to do evil that good might result. In his doctrine of the person of Christ he held to the ecclesiastical view as it was speculatively constructed by Augustine, Anselm of Canterbury, and others. Above all was emphasized the incomparable exaltation of Jesus Christ as the one mediator between God and man, the living medium between man and man's one Ruler; and this he expressed in manifold methods and with many illustrations, as: " Christ is the Saint of all saints, the one Fountain of salvation." The saints, he taught, attained their dignity through the imitation of Christ. With respect to the festivals of the saints and their cult the " Evangelical Doctor " affirmed that they could be of service only so far as the soul could be through them inflamed with the love of Christ. In that Wyclif clearly and consciously established the truth that salvation was through Christ alone, and with this as a fundamental, he showed himself a real precursor of the Reformation. How far he dealt with the order of salvation and did not oppose the Roman-scholastic doctrine of the merits of the saints may on the other side be recognized from his dissent on the subject of the merit of works and his declaration for the truth of the free grace of God in Christ. He stressed the affirmation that faith is a gift of God which comes by grace to men. And with this corresponded his ethics, in which he valued humility as the root of all virtues, while the germ of Christian virtue is love to God and one's neighbor. Yet he did not possess the Biblical and really Evangelical idea of faith; he still adhered to the scholastic conception according to which faith becomes what it should be only through love, i.e., he ascribed justification in the presence of God to sanctification and good works, and did not deny all merit to the latter. Justification through faith alone was not within his view.

His conception of the Church, as shown above, was different from that usual in his day; it was not **7. Doctrine** the congregation of the bishop of Rome **of the** but the communion of those elected of **Church.** God that formed the Church. Not prelates and priests as such, but all pious members of Christ belong to that Church. Like Augustine, he made a distinction between the " true " and the " pretended " or " mixed " body of Christ—unconverted hypocritical brothers are in but not of the Church, i.e., they do not belong to it. Of no man, not even the pope, can one be sure that he is a member of the Church; one can not recognize him as such except by his ethical fruits. So he applied the ethical measure, and by this he reached his conclusion with respect to the claims of Urban VI. and Gregory XI. to be true popes. His entire teaching respecting a true and a false papacy, a true and a false priesthood, rests upon this principle. Just as the powers of the apostles were equal, so may in the present no pope arrogate to himself the rule of the Church; if Peter possessed any prerogative above the others, it did not relate to jurisdictional powers but to his greater humility. The Church of his own day, he thought, needed no other ministry or priesthood than that of the primitive Church. He would, therefore, make no distinction between priest and bishop; every " elect " may assume the office of priest, even though he have no episcopal ordination—he is a real priest made of God. His most serviceable work is the preaching of the Gospel, more precious than the distribution of the sacrament, and among all works charity is the noblest, best, and most desired. With this all the blessings and consecrations of wax and bread, of palms and candles, of salt and of other things, which have no relation to faith and so are to be rejected, similarly the worship of relics, the cult of the dead, pilgrimages, and worship of images do not compare. For the preacher nothing is more worth while than preaching; the only question is, what shall he preach to the people? Certainly not those comedies and tragedies, those apocryphal events and trifles, with which the preachers tickle the ears of their congregations in order that their purses may be made to ring with money after the sermon; but rather preach the Gospel truth. And this is to be done in a way that fits the capacity of the hearers. The object of the sermon is to induce the imitation of Christ: " because to-day the Word of God is not heard, spiritual death broods over all." Consequently this is to be brought to renewed life, and in the two languages—Latin for the learned and the common speech for the rest of the people. Hence in his Latin sermons Wyclif addressed himself to the learned, the priests, and those who were candidates for priesthood. His earlier sermons which he preached while he was teaching, those out of his earlier Oxford period, miss the reformatory note which rings out in the others; these latter found an echo louder in Bohemia than in England, because in many circles they were regarded as the product of Huss. Simpler in form and content are his English sermons, but they do not lack the pointed turn of address and the warm feeling which stimulate the hearer. Many of his single teachings, such as that on purgatory, did not reach so adequate formulation.

His teaching on the sacraments occupies much space in his writings. If the sacrament is simply the symbol of a holy object, an invisible grace, then seven is an insufficient number to express the sacraments, since of such signs there are many. For example, preaching God's Word is as much a sacrament as any one of the seven which bear that name. While according to this test the number seven is too small, it is too large if the Biblical basis of their ordination be the norm. For the Lord's Supper the Scripture testimony is the strongest; for Extreme Unction (q.v.), the weakest. Among the sacraments the former, rightly administered, has saving power; but there is a further condition for the operation of grace in the sacrament which lies in the repentant attitude and the posture of the soul of the recipient. The operation of salvation does not depend upon the ethical condition of the priest who administers the sacrament—teaching contrary to this is not to be discovered in the writings of Wyclif. Upon the Lord's Supper Wyclif spent much thought as the one which was of all the holiest and most worthy. But he fought his hardest against the Roman-scholastic doctrine of its transformation. The usual opinion has been that Wyclif made his first attack upon transubstantiation in 1381, but the date must be carried back to 1379, while the basis of his teaching is to be found in earlier writings and formulations. It was, however, in 1381 that he first cast aside in sermons and theses, in polemic tracts and philosophical treatises, and finally in a comprehensive work, the ecclesiastical teaching that after the consecration the bread and the wine are changed into Christ's body and blood in such a way that only the appearance (the accidents but not the content) of bread and wine remained. The sacrament of the altar is rather natural bread and wine, but sacramentally it is body and blood. After the consecration the host remains local and substantial bread, but concomitantly in a figurative and sacramental sense it is the body of Christ which believers receive spiritually. Wyclif attempted to make this clear by the use of illustrations. Just as there is a double vision, the physical and the spiritual, so there is a double eating. Hence in the sacrament we do not see with the physical eye the body of the Lord, but by faith as in a mirror and by parable; similarly, as an image is complete at every point of a mirror, so is it with the body of the Lord in the consecrated host—we do not touch or grasp it, we do not masticate it, nor, in general, do we take it corporeally, but spiritually and completely intact. When Wyclif entered upon his campaign against what he called the "novel" doctrine of transubstantiation, it was his express purpose to oppose those "heathenish" views according to which every priest was in a position to "create" the body of Christ, a thought which seemed to him horrible in that there was ascribed to the priest the transcendent power by which a creature gave existence to his creator. Moreover, God was humiliated when men asserted that the Eternal could daily be created, while that holy thing, the sacrament itself, was by this means desecrated. After Wyclif had once broken away from the doctrine of the Church on transubstantiation, he handled the subject with unwearying zeal in his philosophical and popular works, in his greater productions, his small tracts, and especially in his sermons.

Similarly in the case of other sacraments, so far as he did not reject them outright, he did not cease to oppose the arrogated power of the priesthood in whose hands the administration of those sacraments lay. He held that distinction must be made in baptism among the external symbols—there is a baptism with water and one with the power of God; or he distinguished a threefold baptism—by water, by blood (that of the holy martyrs), and by the Spirit; the last alone is unqualifiedly necessary to salvation, the first are so to speak the precedent signs, the necessary antecedents. Baptism by water is not to be superseded, however, for children who receive it are also baptized with the Spirit, since they receive the baptism of grace. Confirmation, according to Wyclif, has no foundation in the Bible; it is an arrogation of the bishops to assume that they have the gift of imparting the Holy Ghost. In it they seek an unwarranted increase of their power, without which they assert the Church can not exist. Similarly, consecration of the priests had as little basis in Scripture. He rejected the teaching that the priests received authority from the laying on of hands by the bishop appropriately to perform the offices of the Church, and that the bishop imparted to the priest the Holy Ghost and impressed upon his soul an inextinguishable quality, as well as the assertion that "as by baptism the believer is distinguished from the unbeliever, so by ordination the priest is distinguished from the layman." The apostolic Church had only two grades of clergy, priests and deacons; bishops and priests were the same. There is no priesthood mediating between God and man, no qualification for office dependent upon ordination by a bishop, and no indelible characteristic imparted by priestly ordination. Since Wyclif recognized only a simple priesthood, all episcopal privileges went by the board; the entire hierarchical gradation into orders from pope down to the lowest grades of the first tonsure he called the invention of an imperialized papacy. Once more, for extreme unction no Scriptural basis could be found. The sacrament of confession, too, was one introduced since the time of Innocent III. (1198–1216), for the sake of gain, supplanting confession to God and that of the apostolic Church in the presence of the congregation. The pronouncement of absolution is an encroachment upon the divine power; and there is as little justification for the imposition of penance, since the priest can not

8. The Eucharist.

9. The Other Sacraments.

know its relation to sin, and for excommunication. Marriage Wyclif regarded as a sacrament, for it is a divine institution and demands divine sanction. Every hindrance to it not prescribed by Scripture he would throw aside, but would permit divorce when urgent reasons demanded it. He did not favor ostentatious nuptial ceremonies, but rather those that befitted the character of the institution.

The basis of the reform of the Church advocated by Wyclif rested upon the fact that he designated the Bible as the one authority for believers, and so teachings, traditions, bulls, symbols, and censures go by the board so far as they do not rest on Scripture. He carefully distinguished Church and State, and relegated the former to control purely in the spiritual realm; upon that principle are abolished the rights of inflicting penalties and granting immunities, temporal offices and positions, temporal power and possessions, as held by the Church. Inasmuch as he would go back to the apostolic Church for church polity, the fall of the hierarchy and abolition of monasticism were involved. In worship the chief element was the preaching of the Gospel.

The Reformer lived and died in the hope that church reform was something that was soon to be realized, "for the truth of the Gospel

10. Wyclif- may perhaps for a time by the hostility
ism after   of Antichrist be obscured in silence,
Wyclif.   but can not be entirely done away."

In fact, in the period immediately succeeding the death of the Reformer, Wyclifism made significant progress in England; under the leadership of such men as Nicholas of Hereford, John Aston, and John Purvey it penetrated all ranks of society, and eleven years after Wyclif's death claimed the cooperation of parliament (1395) in its reforms. But after Thomas Arundel (q.v.) became archbishop of Canterbury, and particularly after the change in dynasty and the House of Lancaster occupied the throne (1399), Church and State united to extirpate Wyclifism. In the earliest years of the new dynasty there issued the notorious statute, *De hæretico comburendo*, which made it a duty to surrender heretical writings and sacrificed public heretics to the flames. This was the first English statute that made heresy a capital offense. In spite of the union of the forces of Church and State, it was a difficult task to reestablish the unity of the faith against the Lollards in England. The adoption of severe measures in England was doubtless stimulated by the transformation of state affairs in Bohemia within the short space of two decades. The measures which were especially pressed were those against the itinerant preachers, then against the University of Oxford, where the Wyclifite traditions remained in strength; in 1408 there issued the "constitutions," the seventh article of which forbade the translation of Biblical texts and books into English; finally, the attack was directed against the advocates of Wyclifism among the nobility, whose most prominent representative was Sir John Oldcastle (q.v.), martyred by burning in 1417. Some of the English followers of Wyclif sought a new home in Bohemia, the most prominent of whom was Peter Payne (q.v.). In general, Wyclifism survived the period of persecution, and in the sixteenth century

put forth new branches which finally met and coalesced with the reform movement which originated in Germany (see LOLLARDS).   (J. LOSERTH.)

BIBLIOGRAPHY: A brief statement of the early editions of such works of Wyclif as were published before the editions now authoritative is made in Hauck-Herzog, *RE*, xii. 225. For a survey of the list of Wyclif's writings use W. W. Shirley, *Catalogue of the Original Works of John Wyclif*, Oxford, 1865 (lists 96 Latin and 65 English writings), and cf. Lechler's *Life* (as below), pp. 483–498, and *DNB*, lxiii. 221–222. Under the auspices of the Wyclif Society a definitive edition of the Latin works of the Reformer is in progress, 34 vols. having appeared up to 1912, London, 1883 sqq. These volumes have marginal analyses, so that it is easy to follow them throughout. Of the other works there are available the *Select English Works of John Wyclif*, ed. T. Arnold, 3 vols., Oxford, 1869–71; *English Works of Wyclif hitherto Unprinted*, ed. F. D. Matthew, London, 1880 (contains also a valuable introduction on the life of Wyclif); *Wyclif's Translation of the Bible*, ed. Forshall and Madden, 4 vols., Oxford, 1850; his *New Testament, with Glossary*, ed. W. W. Skeat, Cambridge, 1879; J. Loserth, *Die ältesten Streitschriften Wiclifs*, in the *Sitzungsberichte* of the Vienna Academy, vol. clx., of the philosoph.-historical class, 1908.

The chief early sources for knowledge of Wyclif, apart from his own writings, are: T. Netter, *Fasciculi zizaniorum Johannis Wyclif . . .* ed. W. W. Shirley, in *Rolls Series*, London, 1858 (a series of important documents, with a very admirable preface); R. Pecock, *The Repressor of Overmuch Blaming of the Clergy*, ed. C. Babington in *Rolls Series*, 2 vols., ib. 1860 (the introduction is valuable); *Chronicon Angliæ*, ed. M. Thompson, ib. 1874; H. Knighton, *Chronicon*, ed. J. R. Lumby, vol. ii., ib. 1895; *Eulogium historiarum sive temporis*, ed. F. S. Haydon in *Rolls Series*, vol. iii., ib. 1863; T. Walsingham, *Historia Anglicana* in *Rolls Series*, 2 vols., ib., 1863–64.

The authoritative biography is still G. V. Lechler, *Johann von Wiclif und die Vorgeschichte der Reformation*, 2 vols., Leipsic, 1873, Eng. transl. by P. Lorimer, *John Wiclif and his English Precursors*, 2 vols., London, 1873, new ed., 1 vol., with summary of vol. ii. by S. G. Green, 1884, reissue 1904. Books of high importance, after that of Lechler, and dealing with the life, are: John Fox, *Book of Martyrs*, London, 1632 and often; J. Lewis, *Life of Wicliffe*, new ed., Oxford, 1820 (valuable for documents cited); R. Vaughan, *Life and Opinions of Wyclif*, 2 vols., London, 1828, superseded by his *John de Wycliffe*, ib. 1853; J. Loserth, *Hus und Wiclif*, Prague, 1884, Eng. transl., *Wiclif and Hus*, London, 1884; idem, in *English Historical Review*, xi (1896), 319–328; A. R. Pennington, *John Wiclif*, London, 1884; R. L. Poole, *Wycliffe and Movements for Reform*, ib. 1889 (cf. his *Illustrations of the Hist. of Medieval Thought*, chap. x., ib. 1884; both of these to be taken well into account); L. Sergeant, *John Wyclif, Last of the Schoolmen and First of the English Reformers*, New York, 1893; G. S. Innis, *Wiclif the Morning Star*, Cincinnati, 1907; W. Walker, *Greatest Men of the Christian Church*, Chicago, 1908; J. N. Figgis, *Typical English Churchmen*, London, 1909.

Other literature dealing with the life, times, doctrines, and influence of the Reformer are: T. James, *Apologie for John Wycliffe*, Oxford, 1608; A. Varillas, *Hist. du Wiclefianisme*, Lyons, 1682, Eng. transl. in *The Pretended Reformers*, London, 1717 (interesting only as being a rather remarkable libel); J. and I. Milne, *Hist. of the Church of Christ*, vol. iv., London, 1847 (treats this subject with great care); O. Jäger, *John Wycliffe und seine Bedeutung für die Reformation*, Halle, 1854; F. Böhringer, *Die Vorreformatoren des 14. und 15. Jahrhunderts*, Stuttgart, 1856; P. Reinhold, *Pictures of Old England*, chap. viii., Cambridge, 1861; J. E. T. Rogers, *Historical Gleanings*, 2 ser., pp. 1–63, London, 1870; M. Burrows, *Wiclif's Place in Hist.*, new ed., ib. 1884; R. Buddensieg, *Johann Wyclif und seine Zeit*, Gotha, 1885 (highly praised); J. Stevenson, *The Truth about John Wyclif*, London, 1885 (condemns the Reformer's doctrines); V. Vattier, *John Wycliffe, sa vie, ses œuvres, sa doctrine*, Paris, 1886 (a study of the principal writings); F. D. Matthew, in *English Historical Review*, 1890, 1895; H. Morley, *English Writers*, vol. v., London, 1890; T. R. Lounsbury, *Studies in Chaucer*, ii. 459–494, New York, 1891; F. Wiegand, *De ecclesiæ notione quid Wiclif docuerit*, Leipsic, 1891; C. Petit-Dutaillis, in *Études d'hist. du moyen âge dediées à Gabriel Monod*, Paris, 1896; J. Loserth, *Studien zur Kirchenpolitik Englands im 14. Jahrhundert*, Vienna, 1897–1907; E. L. Cutts, *Parish Priests in the Middle Ages in England*, London, 1898; E. P. Chantard, in *American Historical Review*, iv (1899), 423–428; W. W. Capes, *English Church in the 14th and 15th Centuries*, pp. 94 sqq., London, 1900; H. Fürstenau, *Johann von Wyclifs Lehren von der Stellung der kirchlichen Gewalt*, Berlin, 1900; G. M. Trevelyan, *England in the Age of Wycliffe*, 3d ed., London, 1900; idem and E. Powell, *The Peasants' Rising and the Lollards*, ib. 1899; F. A. Gasquet, *The Eve of the Reformation*, pp. 185 sqq., new ed., ib. 1901; H. B. Workman, *The Age of Wyclif*, ib. 1901; R. S. Storrs, in *Sermons and Addresses*, Boston, 1902; W. H. Summers, *Lollards of the Chiltern Hills*, London, 1906; C. Bigg, *Wayside Sketches in Eccl. Hist.*, ib. 1906; C. Oman, *Hist. of England 1377–1485*, ib. 1906; J. Gairdner, *Lollardy and the Reformation in England*, vol. i., chap. i., London, 1908; J. Lindsay, *Studies in European Philosophy*, Edinburgh, 1909; W. Wundt, *Kleine Schriften*, vol. i., Leipsic, 1910; J. Loserth, *Wiclifs Sendschreiben, Flugschriften und kleinere Werke kirchenpolitischen Inhalts*, Vienna, 1910; Schaff, *Christian Church*, v. 2, pp. 314–348; *DNB*, lxiii. 202–223; and works on the history of England of the period, also on the church history of the time, and on the history of the English Bible (see this work, vol. ii., p. 141). The literature on John Huss contains much on Wyclif.

WYLIE, JAMES AITKEN: Free Church of Scotland; b. at Kirriemuir (15 m. n. of Dundee), Scotland, Aug. 9, 1808; d. at Edinburgh May 1, 1890. He was educated at Marischall College, Aberdeen, 1822–25, and at St. Andrew's, 1826; entered the Original Secession Divinity Hall, Edinburgh, 1827; was licensed, 1829; was minister of Original Secession Congregation at Dollar, 1831–46; in 1846 became associated with Hugh Miller in the editorship of *The Witness*, Edinburgh, contributing some 800 articles from 1846–64; in. 1852 joined the Free Church of Scotland, and for eight years was editor of *The Free Church Record;* and was lecturer on popery at the Protestant Institute of Scotland, Edinburgh, 1860–90. He wrote the Evangelical Alliance's prize essay on *The Papacy* (Edinburgh, 1851). His works embrace *A Journey over the Region of Fulfilled Prophecy* (Edinburgh, 1845, and often); *The Awakening of Italy and the Crisis of Rome* (London, 1866); *The Road to Rome via Oxford; or, Ritualism identical with Romanism* (1868); *The History of Protestantism . . . Illustrated* (3 vols., 1874–1877); *The Papal Hierarchy: an Exposure of the Tactics of Rome for the Overthrow of the Liberty and Christianity of Great Britain* (1878); *The Jesuits, their Moral Maxims, and Plots against Kings, Nations and Churches. With Dissertation on Ireland*

(1881); and *Disruption Worthies; a Memorial of 1843. With an historical Sketch of the Free Church of Scotland from 1843* . . . (new ed., Edinburgh, 1881).

WYTTENBACH, vit'ten-bāн, THOMAS: Reformer, and teacher of Zwingli; b. at Biel (60 m. s.w. of Zurich), Switzerland, 1472; d. there 1526. He studied at Tübingen, 1496–1504, Konrad Summenhart and Christian Scriver (qq.v.) being among his teachers; went to Basel in 1505, where he lectured on the "Sentences" and also on the Bible, being heard by Zwingli and Leo Jud (qq.v.), both of whom were influenced by him and acknowledged their indebtedness. The former says that Wyttenbach won him to the Church, the latter that Wyttenbach won him for theology and the Bible. In 1507 Wyttenbach was called to the pastorate at Biel, but his office there did not prevent him from obtaining his baccalaureate and doctor's degree at Basel in 1510 and 1515 respectively. In 1515 he was called by the council to Berne, but in 1519 laid down his position of custos and in 1520 his canonry at Berne and devoted himself to his duties at Biel, in several cases defending successfully the rights of his church against assailants. He preached against the abuse of indulgences and the mass, and married in 1524; this was the beginning of the Reformation in Biel. His step caused a division of sentiment, especially as seven other priests followed his example. He was deprived of his charge, but continued to preach, at times in the open air, winning many to his side. But the consequence to him was severe poverty, in spite of the facts that the council favored him and that the decision was made in favor of the unhindered preaching of the Word. The council attempted in vain to secure his restoration to his benefice, but finally obtained for him in 1526 the payment for life of twelve gulden yearly, and if he should die before the end of twelve years, the payment of this sum to his heirs during that period. During the course of that year he died. The only writings left by him were some letters, preserved for the most part in the archives of Biel. These prove him to have been an intrepid man of strong convictions, a sturdy champion of truth and right.
(H. HERMELINK.)

BIBLIOGRAPHY: R. Stähelin, *Huldreich Zwingli*, i. 38 sqq., Basel, 1895; S. M. Jackson, *Huldreich Zwingli*, pp. 58–59, 182, 2d ed., New York, 1903; H. Hermelink, *Die theologische Fakultät in Tübingen*, pp. 169–170, 215, Tübingen, 1906.

X

XAVERIAN BROTHERS: A Roman Catholic teaching congregation, established at Bruges, Belgium, in 1839 by Theodor Jakob Rycken (1797–1871), who was at first interested in the conversion of the American Indians, and visited America for that purpose, but who later turned his attention to the religious education of youth. In 1838, believing that Europe already had an abundance of teaching orders, he went to St. Louis and laid his plans before the bishop of that diocese. These plans were approved, and the favor of the bishop of Bruges, in whose diocese the mother house of the congregation was to be established, was also secured, while the benediction of the pope quickly followed. The constitution and rules were now drawn up, and on the feast of St. Francis Xavier (Dec. 3), 1843, Rycken was invested with the religious habit under the name of the patron saint of the new congregation, the final vows of poverty, celibacy, and obedience being taken by the founder and his associates in 1846. A school was immediately established in Bruges, which has since developed into St. Xavier's College, and in 1848 the congregation was planted in England.

Though the congregation was primarily established for American work, it was not until 1854 that Brother Francis was able to introduce it into the United States, its first house being St. Patrick's school, Louisville, Ky. In 1860 the founder resigned the generality of the congregation, of which Brother John Chrysostom became superior general, at the mother house in Bruges, Brother Isidore being provincial for America, and the other two provinces being Belgium and England. In 1866 the congregation was introduced into the archdiocese of Baltimore, where the major number of its houses are still centered; in 1881 they entered Richmond, Va., and in 1882 Lowell, Mass. The task of the Xaverian Brothers is the Christian training of youth in parochial schools, academies, and colleges, and the superintendence of homes for boys, male orphanages, industrial schools, etc. In 1911 there were in the American province 250 brothers, with 6,889 pupils, and with houses in the archdioceses of Baltimore and Boston, and the dioceses of Louisville, Springfield, Richmond, Wheeling, Manchester, Detroit, Hartford, and Newark; while in England the congregation possesses schools or colleges in the dioceses of Salford and Southwark.

BIBLIOGRAPHY: Currier, *Religious Orders*, pp. 518–524.

XAVIER, FRANCIS. See FRANCIS XAVIER, SAINT.

XENAIA. See PHILOXENUS.

XEROPHAGIA. See MONTANUS, MONTANISM, § 3.

XIMENES, zĭ″me-nes′ **(JIMENEZ), DE CISNEROS, FRANZISCO (GONZALES):** Spanish cardinal and inquisitor; b. at Torrelaguna (28 m. n. of Madrid) in 1436; d. at Roa (95 m. n. of Madrid) Nov. 8, 1517. His life fell in a period of supreme importance for Spain. The little kingdoms were
Life till   unified; the Moors were finally over-
1492.   come or driven out; America was dis-
          covered, and the royal power received great strength. The Roman Catholic Church, which was in closest union with Spanish nationality, shared in these advantages to an enormous degree. In the history of this period Ximenes had great part, and helped to create the new Spain which was distinguished by ecclesiastical and political absolutism; and this he did in no spirit of self-seeking, but as a patriot and loyal son of the Church, doing his duty as he saw it. His family was not the famous Cisneros, but of lower, though noble dignity, receiving its name from the city where its members had earlier lived. His father was a royal collector of contributions for the war against the Moors. He himself, known as Gonzales before he took the cloister name of Franzisco, received his schooling at Alcala and Salamanca, taking the bachelor degree in both branches of law in 1556. During the next six years he was in Rome engaged in law; the death of his father caused his return to Spain. There he was soon called by Mendoza, bishop of Siguenza, to serve as vicar of the diocese, where his administration was a shining success. Against the wishes of his friends he determined to enter as a novice the Franciscan order in the monastery of the Observantists at Toledo. Here, too, his

fame grew as preacher and confessor. Again he left what promised to be new fame, and retired as a solitary to a hut which he built, remaining there three years in prayer and leading the life of an anchorite. His superiors directed him to enter a cloister in Salpeda, where in a short time he was made guardian.

A new direction was given to the life of Ximenes in 1492, when he was chosen confessor to the queen. This carried with it a large influence, since Isabella was wont to consult her confessor on matters both of Church and State. Mendoza, who had become
          cardinal and archbishop of Toledo,
As Con-   persuaded Ximenes to accept, but the
fessor, Arch-latter imposed the condition that he
bishop, Re- should remain in his order and in the
former, and monastery when actual duty did not
Evangelist. hinder; and he was actually chosen
          provincial for Castile two years later. This gave him opportunity to correct the lax practises which prevailed in the institutions, and through the queen he obtained a bull which gave him unlimited power for effecting reform. In 1495 the death of Mendoza left the archbishopric vacant, and the appointment was in the hands of Isabella. The king desired the position for his natural son, but the queen appointed Ximenes. The place was the highest, ecclesiastically, in Spain, with an immense income. But Ximenes was loath to accept, and did so only under express command of the pope. No change was made in his manner of living, while the income was applied to deeds of public and private philanthropy; it required a brief from the pope to have him conduct his household more in accordance with his position. His first care was to reform the secular clergy, and in so doing he aroused intense opposition, which with the queen's help he broke down. Canon Albornoz, whom his colleagues had sent to Rome to lodge complaints against Ximenes before the pope, was seized as he debarked at Ostia and brought back to Spain to suffer imprisonment for twenty-two months. In the reform of the orders, especially his own, he met opposition and caused the withdrawal of over 1,000 monks, who left in order to avoid the new rules. The pope withdrew a hostile bull, and had his nuncio work with Ximenes. The archbishop was equally bent on the conversion of the Moors. This, too, was the purpose of Fray Fernando de Talavera, who had become archbishop of Granada. But the capitulation of 1491 contained a stipulation for freedom in religion; hence Talavera had worked for the conversion of the Moors in friendly methods, learned Arabic so as to be able to address them, and had his clergy do the same. He issued an Arabic lexicon, instruction book, catechism, and selections from the Gospels; and these measures were effectual in bringing many over. But there were fanatics who thought these measures too mild, and among them was Ximenes, who assembled the Arabic scholars and set before them Christian doctrine in impressive form. He also flattered the Arabic love of dress, and presented the people with showy raiment, and many were thus won, so that he is said to have baptized 3,000 in one day. But the opposition of the Moors was aroused, upon which Ximenes used new measures. The learned Zegri he so tortured that

the latter pretended to accept Christianity at the direction of Allah, and a mass of new conversions resulted. He collected large numbers of Arabic works and had them burned in a city square. Finally, choice was offered the Moors either to accept Christianity or to submit to banishment. In sheer love of home many received baptism.

As chancellor of Castile, his activity was characterized by philanthropy. Oppression of the poor and malfeasance in office he attempted to eradicate, and created a new era in that province. Though by the death of the queen in 1504 he lost his supreme protector, yet the veneration in which **As Chan-** the people held him helped him to **cellor and** limit the power to harm which resided **Patron of** in his foes; indeed, he was able to **Learning.** create in Ferdinand a new protector. After Isabella's death Ferdinand sought to have his daughter Johanna recognized as queen of Castile. Political complications arose, and in these Ximenes stood as mediator, winning Ferdinand's favor so that the latter secured for the archbishop the cardinal's hat and made him inquisitor-general of Spain. The next project which occupied Ximenes was the new University of Alaca de Henares (the old Complutum). He had already chosen the site and laid the foundation stone (1498, 1500), and by 1508 the structures, including a hospital, were completed. There were forty-two chairs: six for theology proper, six for ecclesiastical law, four for medicine, one for anatomy, one for surgery, eight for philosophy, one for moral philosophy, one for mathematics, four for Greek and Hebrew, four for rhetoric, and six for " grammar." Rich scholarships were provided, especially in theology. Soon there were 7,000 students. Related to this was Ximenes' plan for the Complutensian Polyglot (see BIBLES, POLYGLOT, I.), and he parceled the work among scholars, including a Greek and a Jew among the workers. The work was completed in 1517. [It was not published till 1520.] The greater praise is due the cardinal for this accomplishment as he was himself not distinguished for scholarship, yet saw the worth of such a piece of work.

Among the projects which Ximenes had at heart was the renewal of the crusades in service for the Church and the kingdom. But he turned this desire in a practical direction, against the Moors of Africa who by piratical raids on the southern coast of Spain were making reprisals for their **As Soldier** experiences in Spain. Since Ferdinand **and** had not funds available, Ximenes **Inquisitor.** equipped from his own income a force and personally led it to the conquest of Oran, thus breaking up the nest of pirates. Another of the noted activities of this prelate-statesman was as grand inquisitor of Castile. But he is not to be held responsible for the introduction of the office into Spain, since he came to court twelve years after this took place. When he assumed the office, he provided for instruction of the converts, Jews and Moors, so that they might avoid falling under suspicion of apostasy; he also limited the powers of the lower officials of the inquisition in order to prevent persecution, and dismissed unworthy occupants of office. He took under his pro-

tection some who under the rules of the inquisition would have been prosecuted, though unjustly, as in the case of Elio Antonio de Nebrija (cf. H. C. Lea, *Inquisition of Spain*, iv. 529, New York, 1907). On the other hand, he strenuously opposed the publication of names of informers and betrayers of the apostates, even in writing, when to Charles, during his minority, there was offered an immense sum provided the process and names of witnesses were made known. Ximenes showed that the lives of the informers could not, under such conditions, be made safe, and that information would consequently cease. While deliberate efforts have been made to minimize the effects, in actual slaughter, of the workings of the inquisition, the number of victims was undoubtedly great, and under Ximenes it was introduced into Oran, the Canary Isles, and America. Throughout all this, the aim of Ximenes was to exalt the power of the Church. Although he could not attend the Lateran Council, he supported the pope by his letters and published the results of the deliberations in his diocese even before the conclusion of the council. He changed the conditions of entrance into the priesthood, substituting for five years' training in philosophy a part of the course in theology. He supported Leo's plan to improve the Julian calendar; but when the indulgence was offered by the pope for the purpose of obtaining funds for building St. Peter's, and was published in Spain, Ximenes spoke openly against it.

The highest pinnacle of Ximenes' greatness came through his appointment by Ferdinand as regent for Castile during the minority and absence of Charles after Ferdinand's death. Though eighty **Last Years.** years of age, he took up his task with youthful energy and great wisdom. With foresight he had Charles' younger brother Ferdinand kept under his eye so that the latter might not be led by a court party to make pretensions upon the regency. But Hadrian of Utrecht claimed to have a document of Ferdinand's appointing him regent, and when this was submitted to Charles, the latter supported Ximenes against the court party. Yet Charles proved ungrateful to Ximenes for the many ways in which the latter had paved the way to his accession, sought to limit the powers of Ximenes, and finally wrote an unworthy letter, though it is asserted that it was kept from him by those who knew how despondent he had already become. His last years were not saved from sadness by the conduct of those whom he had most benefited.   (K. BENRATH.)

BIBLIOGRAPHY: The chief source for the life of Ximenes is the work of Alvaro Gomez de Castro, professor of classical literature in Salamanca, Toledo, and Alcala: *De rebus gestis a Francisco Ximenio Cisnerio*, Alcala, 1569, republished in *Rerum Hispaniæ scriptores aliquot*, Frankfort, 1581, and in A. Schottus, *Hispaniæ illustratæ*, vol. i., Frankfort, 1603. As sources reference may be made to *Cartas de Jimenez*, Madrid, 1874, and *Cartas de los Secretarios de Cisneros*, 2 vols., ib. 1874–75. The best life for general purposes is C. J. Hefele *Der Kardinal Ximenes und die kirchliche Zustände Spaniens am Ende des 15. und Anfang des 16. Jahrhunderts*, Tübingen, 1844 Eng. transl., *Life of Cardinal Ximenez*, London, 1860. Consult further, M. Baudier, *Hist. de l'administration du Cardinal Ximenes*: Paris, 1635, Eng. transl., London, 1671; V. E. Fléchier, *Hist. du Cardinal Ximenes*, Paris, 1693; B. Barrett, *Life of Cardinal Ximenes*, London, 1813; S. A. Dunham, *Hist.*

of Spain and Portugal, 5 vols., ib. 1832 (the best general treatment of the subject); F. X. von Havemann, Francisco Ximenes, Göttingen 1848; W. Irving, Chronicles of the Conquest of Granada (accessible in editions of the Works, e.g., New York, 1902–03); W. H. Prescott, Hist. of the Reign of Ferdinand and Isabella (a classic; constantly republished in cheap form); E. F. A. Rosseeuw-St.-Hilaire, Hist. d'Espagne, vol. vi., Paris, 1852; C. Navarro y Rodrigo, El Cardenal Cisneros, Madrid, 1869; W. Maurenbrecher, Studien und Skizzen, pp. 114 sqq., Leipsic, 1874; W. Ulrich, Ximenes der grosse Kardinal und Reichsverweser

Spaniens, Langensalza, 1883; F. J. Simonet, El Cardenal Ximenez de Cisneros y los manuscritos arábigo-granadinos, Granada, 1885; H. C. Lea, Chapters from the Religious Hist. of Spain, Philadelphia. 1890; idem, Hist. of the Inquisition of Spain, passim, 4 vols., New York, 1906–07; idem, The Inquisition in the Spanish Dependencies, ib. 1908; Huidobro, Hist. del Cardenal Fray Fr. Jiménez de Cisneros, Santander, 1901; Pastor, Popes, vols. v.–viii.

XYSTUS. See SIXTUS (pope).

Y

YAHBALAHA, yā-bāl'ā-hā (**YABHALLAHA**), III.. Nestorian patriarch 1281–1317. The name (=Deusdedit, Theodore) is not uncommon among the Syrians and was borne by the eighteenth and the seventy-seventh patriarchs of Antioch (c. 489 and 1233). The best known of the name, however, is Yahbalaha III., with whom Bar Hebræus closes his church history. He was a Uigurian monk, born near Peking, and died Nov. 13, 1317. He started on a pilgrimage to the Holy Land, but when he came to Bagdad remained there with the Patriarch Denha, who made him metropolitan of China because of his relations with the khan of the Mongols. For the same reason he succeeded Denha as patriarch, though he was poor in Syriac learning. His companion from China, Rabban Sauma, was sent by Khan Argun in 1287–88 to Rome, Paris, and London. The original description of this embassy, ed. P. Bedjan, was published at Paris, 1888 (better ed., 1895), and has been translated by J. B. Chabot (in Revue de l'orient latin, i.–ii., and separately, Paris, 1895). A translation into modern Syriac appeared at Urumiah in the periodical Zahrire de Bahra, Oct., 1885–May, 1886.　　　　　　　　　　　　E. NESTLE.

BIBLIOGRAPHY: I. H. Hall, in Journal of the American Oriental Society, 1886, pp. clxxxi. sqq.; idem, in Proceedings of the American Oriental Society, 1886, pp. cxxv.–cxxix.; Lamy, in Mémoires of the Academie royale de Belgique, 1889, 223–243; R. Duval, in JA, 8th ser., xiii. 313–354; W. Wright, Short Hist. of Syriac Literature, London, 1894; R. Hilgenfeld, Jabalahæ III., Catholici Nestoriani vita ex Slivæ Mossulani libro, Leipsic, 1896; R. Gottheil, in Hebraica, xiii (1897), 222–223, 227–229; R. Duval, Littérature syriaque, Paris, 1899; Supplement à l'hist. du patriarche Mar Jabalaha et du moine Rabban Çauna, Paris, 1900. Older sources are O. Raynaldus, Annales ecclesiastici for year 1304, vol. xiv., vols. xiii.–xxi., Cologne, 1694–1727; J. S. Assemani, Bibliotheca orientalis, iii. 2, pp. 129 sqq., Rome, 1719–28; Gregory Bar Hebræus, Chronicon ecclesiasticum, ii. 471.

YAHWEH, yā'wê.

I. The Pronunciation.
　The Massoretic Form (§ 1).
　The Original Pronunciation (§ 2).
II. Meaning and Derivation.
　The Etymological Meaning (§ 1).
　Other Origins Proposed (§ 2).
　Was Yahweh a Kenite Deity ? (§ 3).
　Was he God of the Leah Tribes ? (§ 4).

The Hebrew YHWH (the tetragrammaton) denotes in the Old Testament the proper name of the God of Israel. Jews regard it as expressing not merely the name but the essence of God.

I. The Pronunciation: In the Massoretic text the usual form would give the pronunciation Yehowah, or Yehowih when the word Adhonai, "my(?) Lord," precedes. The second form shows the vowels

of Elohim, "God": the first form has a close relation to the pronunciation of Adhonai (see JEHOVAH). It is demonstrable, however, **1. The** that the form Yehowah does not re-**Massoretic** produce the original pronunciation. **Form.** Theodoret (c. 450) showed that in his time the Jews did not pronounce the name and already called it the tetragrammaton (cf. F. Field, Hexapla, i. 90, on Ex. vi. 3, London, 1871). Similarly Jerome, Origen, and the translators of the Bible before Origen found the tetragrammaton in their manuscripts, even in the Greek translations, where the name was represented by the capital letters iota and pi, closely resembling the Hebrew yodh and he. Origen seems to have transferred the Hebrew quadriliteral in his column of transliterated Hebrew and a later hand rendered it into the Greek iota and pi, and this transference seems to have been the custom of Aquila, Symmachus, and Theodotion. Philo gives the first sure case of a translation of the name by the Greek Kurios, "Lord." These and other indications suggest that the Jewish custom of not pronouncing the name (Jerome calls it "the ineffable") is very old, and this custom still obtained when the Massoretes affixed the pointing to the text; it is not probable that these scholars intended to imply that they were giving the correct pronunciation. The pronunciation indicated by "Jehovah" (J being pronounced as Y) has been traced as far back as Wessel (d. 1489), who used Johavah and Jehovah, and Petrus Galatinus, confessor of Leo X. (1513–21; see JEHOVAH). Beside the two facts, that the Massoretes would not be likely to disregard the custom regarding the non-pronunciation of the name, and the variation in the pointing given above, a third fact appears in the forms which YHWH takes when following a preposition. In this case the form resulting shows that the pronunciation is based on a fundamental form beginning with an aleph pointed with an a-vowel and not on one beginning with the sound ye. Further, the pointing of the succeeding word often indicates the pronunciation of a word ending not with the consonant he (a mere vowel sign) but with a full consonant, and the abbreviations yahu or yah in many proper names, as well as the form Yah, do not lead back to a pronunciation represented by Yehowah (or Jehovah). Did the form Yahowah anywhere occur, there could be no possible doubt that the two forms actually occurring represent the pronunciation of Elohim and Adhonai in place of the tetragrammaton. But the case is almost as cogent, in view of the treatment of the word with prefixed preposition and of the habit of the Massoretes when a word to be pronounced was written in the margin. And it is demonstrable that not only in the time of the Massoretes, but as early as the time of Jesus, it was the custom to pronounce *Adhonai* where YHWH occurred, a custom then so fast rooted that it must have been much older; indeed, the Septuagint appears to have used *Kurios* and later purists to have substituted the Greek quadriliteral. Moreover, the form *Yehowah* occasions no difficulty in view of the Babylonian Jewish custom of letting shewa represent hateph pathah, while *Yehowih* is probably a later form introduced to avoid a double reading " Adhonai Adhonai," when this form immediately preceded the tetragrammaton. The form was never pronounced *Yehowah* (*Jehovah*).

The earliest testimony as to the original pronunciation of the name comes from the Assyrian pronunciation of the Hebrew in such proper names as Hezekiah, which is so given as to represent *yahu*. From the Old Testament itself the evidence comes

2. The Original Pronunciation. from Ex. iii., and from two classes of proper names, those in which the divine name is the first element and those in which it is the last element. In Ex. iii. it is clear that the narrator connects the name with the verb *hayah*, " to be," or its variant *hawah*. The Hebrew names *Yehonathan* or *Yonathan* (Jonathan) and *Ḥizḳiyahu* or *Ḥiṣḳiyah* (Hezekiah) are fairly representative of names compounded with the divine name, and the Assyrian pronunciation indicates the correctness of the Massoretic pointing given Hezekiah's name. This shows clearly and decisively the pronunciation "yah" for the first syllable. For the final syllable the analogy of verbal forms ending in *weh* and their shortening (by dropping of the final consonant and its vowel) into *u* renders it exceedingly probable that the original pronunciation was " *weh*." This is strengthened by the common process of rendering *yhw* by *yo* when the middle h is dropped (cf. *Yonathan* above). Such a conclusion, giving " Yahweh " as the pronunciation of the name, is confirmed by the testimony of the Fathers and gentile writers, where the forms *Iao*, *Yaho*, *Yaou*, *Yahouai*, and *Yaoue* appear. Especially important is the statement of Theodoret in relation to Ex. vi., when he says: " the Samaritans call it [the tetragrammaton] ' Yabe,' the Jews [call it] ' *Aia* ' " (the latter form representing the *'ehyeh*, " I will be," of Ex. iii. 14). The Samaritan pronunciation doubtless depends upon a living tradition.*

* Note should be taken, however, of the recent very decided trend toward a belief that the original pronunciation was Yahu. This rests partly upon the forms employed in Hebrew compound names, illustrated in the text (which do not necessarily imply that the element *Yahu* or *Yaho* in such names was an abbreviation). The supposition here is that the Hebrew Waw was vocal and not consonantal (as it often becomes in conjugation). Corroboration is found in the preference in Gnostic gems for the form *Iao* or *Iaou*, and similar forms. For examples of these consult the literature under GNOSTICISM, especially the work of King, to which add A. F. Gori, *Thesaurus gemmarum astriferarum*, Florence, 1570; A. Capello, *Prodromus iconicus sculptilium gemmarum*, Venice, 1702; J. M. A. Chabouillet, *Catalogue général . . . des camées et pierres gravés de la bibliothèque impériale*, Paris, 1858; also R. Kittel, *Geschichte des Volkes Israel*, i. 628–629, 2d ed., Leipsic, 1912.—G. W. G.

II. Meaning and Derivation: The form is doubtless derived from the verb *hayah* (*hawah*), " to be or become," as an imperfect either of the simple or causative species, differentiated as a proper name from the imperfect of the verb. But as this verb does not appear to have a causative species, it is better to take it as the simple form. In Ex. iii. 14 the question of Moses is answered by the statement " I AM THAT I AM." If for the first person were substituted the third, the form might

1. The Etymological Meaning. well be *yahweh*, and the idea is not that of being, existence (an abstract thought of late reflection), but of happening, coming to pass; the concept of being, existence, is a secondary derivation from that of coming to pass. In this case the translation is not " I am that I am," nor (Aquila and Theodotion) " I will be what I will be," upon which ideas are based the general Jewish notion of " the Eternal." The idea conveyed is " I, who manifest myself, reveal myself," representing therefore not an abstract something, but a being who corresponds to a concrete need. Out of this flows a rich harvest of suggestion of Yahweh as the one living fact, out of which the form of the oath of Israel is derived—" as Yahweh liveth." God did not intend in the passage to assert his existence, for that was self-evident; the intention was to define himself as regnant in nature and history, revealing himself in life and force, rich in help for his people. The idea of eternity as represented in such passages as Isa. xl. 28, xli. 4, xliii. 13 is not to be imported into the Exodus passage. This rendering is related to that of Ibn Ezra, J. D. Michaelis, and J. Wellhausen, the last of whom renders " I am because I am." The rendering of W. R. Smith, which involves an implied idea that help to Israel is involved and imports " to you " in some such way as " I will be what I will be [to you] " is refuted by Dillmann, who, however, was wrong in making it " I am what I am (inexpressible and inexplicable in essence)," which rendering he later renounced.

It is entirely a different question whether this etymological sense is now binding. Old-Testament usage allows more than a single meaning to a proper name, whether of place or person. It may be that in Exodus there is a definite attempt

2. Other Origins Proposed. to etymologize, and that duty demands an attempt to go behind this. In fact many attempts of this sort have been made, divisible into two classes, those which derive the name from Hebrew origin and those which regard as possible derivation of the name and the deity from non-Israelitic sources. The first group depends in part upon the supposition that the idea of existence is too metaphysical to be found at the very origin of a religion—an objection which does not lie against the rendering adopted above. Thus the meaning " creator " has been suggested (J. LeClerc, Gesenius) from the causative idea of calling into existence. Cognate with this is the supposition that the verbs *hayah* and *hawah*, " live," were fused in thought, with the result of a meaning similar to that just given, " life-giver " or creator. But it may be asked whether in the text *hayah*, " to be or become " is to stand,

and whether a verb *hawah*, " to fall " or another of the same form meaning " to breathe, ask, or demand " is not to be understood. In case Yahweh was a deity known in Israel long before the time of Moses, or was the deity of one of the ancestors of the people or of a non-Israelitic Semitic stock adopted by the whole people in Mosaic times, it would follow that an etymological origin in Hebrew either could receive no guaranty or would be excluded, and a Semitic stem *hawah* should be sought, leading far back into origins in nature religion. Hence Lagarde derived the name from the verb " to (cause to) fall," i.e., she storm-god (*Orientalia*, ii. 27, Göttingen, 1880), with whom practically agree W. R. Smith, Schwally, and Kerber; while Holzinger from the same root derives the meaning " destroyer " and Wellhausen obtains " the breather " or " weather god "—a meaning with which Ewald is in substantial accord. Other attempts have been made, as by Baudissin, Lenormant, and Schrader, to find the sources in Syrian or Babylonian religion, these attempts obtaining their support in the name *Yaubidi*, variant *Ilubidi*, of Hamath, which seems to look back to a deity Yau, or in a component of Babylonian names which appears as *Ya* or *Yawa*, Winckler supposing that the Babylonian deity was spiritualized into the Hebrew divinity, but derived directly from the Canaanites through whom he passed to the Israelites. Even F. Hommel is found as sponsor for the theory of a Babylonian origin (*Expository Times*, 1899, pp. 42 sqq.). But an objection to these proposals is that the ground form of the name does not appear to be *Yahu* but *Yahweh*, while *Yah* in Hebrew seems to be a poetic or liturgic abbreviation; and this is attested by the form on the Moabite Stone where Mesha wrote *Yhwh* and not *Yhw* or *Yh*. The occurrence of the forms in Syrian environment (such as *Yaubidi*, ut sup., or *Azriyahu*, H. Winckler, *Forschungen*, i. 16, Leipsic, 1893) or in Babylonia may be explained as direct loan names from Israel or as names carried by Hebrew captives or in part as not divine names, or even in some cases to be rendered as expansions of the prefix of the imperfect tense. Granted that there was a Sumerian deity Yau, it is highly improbable that he had any relationship to the Hebrew deity. *Yahweh* as a derivation from *Yau* is inexplicable, but to derive *Yahu* from *Yahweh* is easy and natural. Similarly the case alleged by W. M. Müller (*Asien und Europa*, pp. 312–313, Leipsic, 1893) of a place-name *Bait-ya* (Beth-Yah or Beth-el) mentioned in the lists of Thothmes III. might possibly point to an old Canaanitic deity *Ya*, but whether this questionable deity had any relation to Yahweh is very problematical. So that the probabilities reduce to two; the form is native Hebrew or comes from a closely related (Arabic) stem.

From the historical standpoint it is to be remarked that, of the chief narrators of the Pentateuch, E and P refer the introduction of the worship of Yahweh among the Hebrews to Moses, while J in the manner of folk-lore carries this worship back into the earliest times of the race. In other words, Hebrews attributed to Moses the origin of Yahweh worship, and from the song of Deborah it appears that this cult was established before the time of Deb-

orah. And the narratives connect the origins closely with Sinai, in the neighborhood of which the deity revealed himself to Moses; so in Deborah's Song he comes forth from Sinai and later Elijah goes to Sinai. At the time of this revelation, Moses was in connection with the shepherd stock of Midianites, a stock related to the Kenites, who were in turn associated with the later Rechabites, strenuous maintainers of the Yahweh cult. Thus Yahweh appears as an old deity of Sinai, revered in untold antiquity as a weather-god, and as such brought by Moses to Israel, to him revealed through his connection with the Midianite priestly family. In this way the difference of representations in J and E received explanation, since J belongs to Judah, as did the Kenites to whom Yahweh was the long-possessed ancestral deity. This is the view of Tiele, Stade, and Budde. To this it must be said that so essential a part is not assigned in the history to the Kenites; it is the Kenites who came to Israel and not the reverse (Num. x. 29 sqq.), and the conception assigns to the Hebrews no peculiarity, no religion, and no deity, while of a transfer from the Kenites no direct trace appears. If it is true, Moses must have discovered in this weather-god something new and singular entitling him to distinguish between the Kenites and the Israelites and enabling Moses to regard him ethically as the God of heaven and earth. If this ethical idea is lacking, the entire religious development of Israel remains a riddle. Budde lays stress upon the fact that the religion was a matter of election, of choice. But choice is not necessarily a matter of ethics, it may be one of arbitrary dealing. What Yahweh became in course of time he must have been, at least in germ, at the time of choice, the God of the right and the good. Of a change in the conception of God from a mere weather-god to an ethical being the narrative says nothing; there is not a word which corresponds to the hypothesis of a derivation of their deity by Israel from the Kenites.

3. Was Yahweh a Kenite Deity?

There remains the possibility that in the time before Moses a part of the people dwelt near Sinai and that by this part Yahweh was worshiped, and that from it Moses learned of him (so Nowack). It is supposed that the sojourn in Egypt was by the Rachel tribes, while the Leah tribes, to which Moses belonged, remained at Sinai, whence Moses went to summon the tribes in Egypt. But while this method of Nowack's is the only method by which the hypothesis of the Yahweh cult by a portion of the people can be supported, the matter remains pure hypothesis. Tradition knows of no abiding of an Israelitic stock at Sinai, only of a close connection of the Yahweh worship with Sinai. Further, it may be remarked that of the character of a pre-Mosaic Israelitic Sinai-god, Yahweh, nothing further is known except that he must have been other than he is conceived as the Yahweh of Moses. What can be affirmed is that with the person of Moses and the location of Sinai is bound up the revelation of Yahweh, so important for the history of Israel. The way in which

4. Was he the God of the Leah Tribes?

this came to Moses must, from the standpoint of human occurrences, remain an insolvable riddle.

(R. KITTEL.)

BIBLIOGRAPHY: Besides the lexicons, especially Gesenius, *Thesaurus*, the works on O. T. theology, especially Schulze, the works on O. T. introduction, on the history of Israel, and the commentaries on Ex. vi., consult: S. R. Driver, in *Studia Biblica*, i. 1 sqq., Oxford, 1885; A. Köhler, *De pronunciatione . . . Tetragrammaton*, Erlangen, 1867; W, W. von Baudissin, *Studien zur semitischen Religionsgeschichte*, i. 181–254, Leipsic, 1876; E. Nestle, *Die israelitischen Eigennamen*, ib. 1876; Tiele, in *ThT*, xvi (1882), 262 sqq.; A. Kuenen, *Volksreligion und Weltreligion*, pp. 307 sqq., Berlin, 1883; Dietrich, in *ZATW*, iii (1883), iv (1884), 21 sqq.; Wellhausen, *Heidentums*; G. H. Dalman, *Der Gottesname Adonaj*, Berlin, 1889; P. de Lagarde, *Uebersicht über die Nominalbildung*, Göttingen, 1889; Pinches, in *PSBA*, xv (1892), 13 sqq.; G. Margoliouth, in *PSBA*, xviii (1895), 57 sqq.; J. Meinhold, *Wider den Kleinglauben*, vol. i., Freiburg, 1895; W. Nowack, *Die Entstehung der israelitischen Religion*, Strasburg, 1895; M. Jastrow, in *ZA*, x (1896), 222 sqq., *ZATW*, xv (1896), 1 sqq.; J. Robertson, *Early Religion of Israel*, Edinburgh, 1896; F. Hommel, *Altisraelitische Ueberlieferung*, Munich, 1897; G. Kerber, *Die religionsgeschichtliche Bedeutung der hebräischen Eigennamen*, Tübingen, 1897; E. König, in *ZATW*, xvii (1897), 172 sqq., *NKZ*, x (1899), 703 sqq.; B. Stade, *Die Entstehung des Volkes Israel*, Giessen, 1897; B. Steinführer, *Untersuchung über den Namen Jehovah*, Neustrelitz, 1898; K. Budde, *Die Religion des Volkes Israel*, Giessen, 1900; idem, *Religion of Israel to the Exile*, New York, 1899; Smith, *Prophets*; T. Tyler, in *JQR*, July, 1901; H. H. Spoer, in *American Journal of Semitic Languages*, Oct., 1901; G. A. Barton, *Semitic Origins*, chap. vii., New York, 1902; J. A. Montgomery, in *JBL*, xxv. 1 (1906); *Expository Times*, xviii (1907), 525; R. W. Rogers, *Religions of Babylonia and Assyria*, pp. 91 sqq., New York, 1909 (deals with the name as found outside of Israel); P. C. Purves, *The Jehovah Titles of the O. T.*, London, 1910; S. R. Driver, in his commentary on Genesis, Addendum II., ib. 1911; Schrader, *KAT*, pp. 457 et passim; *Expository Times*, Nov. 11, 1911; R. Kittel, *Geschichte des Volkes Israel*, i. 555 sqq., 628–629, Leipsic, 1912; *DB*, ii. 199–200; iv. 845; *EB*, iii. 3320–23; *JE*, vii. 87–88.

YEAR, THE CHURCH. See CHURCH YEAR.

YEAR, THE HEBREW.

Solar and Lunar Bases (§ 1).
Hebrew Months Lunar (§ 2).
Time when the Year Began (§ 3).
Hebrew Names for Months (§ 4).

The regular course of nature, caused by the change in the position of the sun in the heavens, has naturally made the year the division of time most important after the day all over the earth. The word employed by Semites generally to express the idea year shows the dependence of the reckoning upon the sun. While the period itself is common to all peoples, there is no general agreement as to the time when the year begins. Necessity for fixing a time of reckoning occurs only when some matter has to be dated, and from this fact in the de-

1. Solar and Lunar Bases. velopment of culture arose the definition of a starting-point for the year. Among many peoples the course of the moon furnished a means to the yearly reckoning, the month varying between twenty-nine and thirty days in length, and twelve months being reckoned a year (see MOON, § 1). But when this is strictly adhered to, there is a discrepancy of about eleven days between a solar and a lunar year, and such a reckoning brings the beginning of the year backward through all the seasons in the course of thirty-three years, as is the case with the Mohammedans. But adherence to a strict solar year

does not produce agreement of solar and lunar reckoning, so some peoples assigned thirty days to a month and added five days besides to complete the solar year. The Hebrews employed the lunar month, but from time to time intercalated a month, in this matter following the Babylonians, and thus the beginning of the year fluctuated only within narrow limits.

That the Hebrew month was lunar is proved by the term for month, *ḥodhesh*, "newness" (of the moon)," and *yerah*, from *yareah*, "moon," cognate with the Assyrian and Babylonian *arḥu*. Dillmann's hypothesis that the Hebrews derived their use of *yerah* from the Canaanites does not seem well supported, nor does the other supposition that the latter had a sun-month, either by Phenician or by Cypriote inscriptions. Nor are the names of the month as found in the Old Testament or in the inscriptions indicative of months based on solar reckoning. Indeed, no special name was

2. Hebrew Months Lunar. given to the intercalated month, which would be required on the Dillmann hypothesis. And his contention that, since no mention of an intercalated month occurs in I Kings iv. 7, the reckoning there must be on a solar basis, is beside the mark, inasmuch as the narrator there is not concerned with an exact report of time and does not assert that each officer performed his duty in the same month. That the usual length of the month is thirty days is only natural, since that is the apparent length of about half of the lunar months. So in the account of the flood, where lunar months are meant, the period of five months gives 150 days (Gen. vii. 11, viii. 3–4). Similarly, the division of the month into three parts is as natural to a lunar month as to one based on the sun. It is highly probable that the editor of the Book of Kings by his addition of the later designations of the months conveyed intentionally the implication of the identity of the earlier and the later reckoning (I Kings vi., viii., cf. vi. 1, 37). In all probability in civil life the early Hebrews had proper names as well as numbers for the months. That the names of only four occur is due merely to the fact that the occasion for naming the others did not arise (Ex. xiii. 4, etc.; I Kings vi. 1, 37, etc., viii. 2, vi. 38).

No definite and fast assertion is made in the Old Testament of the month with which the New Year began. While the autumn festival is designated as "the end of the year" (Ex. xxiii. 16), the "return of the year" is marked as "the time when kings go forth to battle." Probably the

3. Time when the Year Began. autumn marks simply the end of the season the beginning of which is the sowing of the crops, coincident with the time when the operations of war can be carried on; while the season of the winter rains marked a pause when the staple business life was interrupted. Such designations as these are indeed inexact, though sufficient for the needs of the times. Yet the demands of civil life caused a demand for definite agreement, and in the priestly account of the flood and in Nehemiah the beginning of the year fell in autumn, in earlier times in the spring. In the Books of Kings, Jeremiah, and Ezekiel, the year began with the spring. Wellhausen's hypothesis to the contrary is untenable, and the priestly writings agree with this, except the interpolated passage Ex. xii. 2, and the passage in the account of the flood already referred to. The designation of the autumn as the end of the year flows in part from the resemblance of the following part of the year to the night as the close of active work. The reckoning of the regnal years of the kings is based upon the year which began in the spring, and is parallel to the Babylonian method in which this prevailed. Dillmann concludes from the dating of the battle of Carchemish in the fourth year of Jehoiakim (Jer. xlvi. 2) that the Jewish regnal year began in the autumn. But this is contrary to the general custom as indicated by the usage both of the Books of Kings and of Jeremiah. The synchronism in Jer. xlvi. 2 must therefore be given up. Just as inconclusive is the deduction from II Kings xxii. 3 sqq., xxiii. 22 sqq., that since the finding of the book of the law and the consequent observance of the Passover fell in the eighteenth year of Josiah, that year began in the autumn (cf. the Septuagintal fuller text of II Kings xxii. 3). All indications point to the fact that in early as in late Hebrew times, when enumeration of the months occurred, the reckoning began with the spring month. A change took place toward the end of the regal period due to the fact that the names of the months fell into disuse and the reckoning of the priestly calendar came into civil life. But whether the regnal years of kings from David on were always reckoned from the month Abib is doubtful. Possibly the difficulties of the chronology are in part the result of vacillating usage.

After the exile the Babylonian names for the months gradually came into use, this being determined by Persian control of Hither Asia and the official use by the Persians of these names. In Zech. i. 7, vii. 1, the names of the months may be interpolations; but in the books of Nehemiah and Ezra the names are used as customary, while 4. Hebrew in Esther the numbers are added for the Names for sake of clearness. The Chronicler adMonths. heres to the usage in the law. The names used by the Jews are as follows: *Nisan*, Assyr. *Nisanu* (Neh. ii. 1, etc.); *Iyyar*, Assyr. *Airu* (Targum on II Chron. xxx. 2); *Siwan*, Assyr. *Simanu* (Esth. viii. 9); *Tammuz*, Assyr. *Duzu* (Targum Jerusalem, Gen. viii. 5); *Ab*, Assyr. *Abu* (Targum Jerusalem, Num. xx. 29, etc.); *Elul*, Assyr. *Ululu* (Neh. vi. 15); *Tishri*, Assyr. *Tishritu* (Targum Jerusalem, Lev. xxiii. 24); *Marheshwan*, Assyr. *Arah-shamnu* (Targum Jerusalem, Deut. xi. 14); *Kishlew*, Assyr. *Kislimu* (Neh. i. 1, etc.); *Tebeth*, Assyr. *Tebetu* (Esth. ii. 16); *Shebat*, Assyr. *Shabatu* (Zech. i. 7); *Adar*, Assyr. *Adaru* (Esth. iii. 7, etc.). The beginning of the month was doubtless in both early and later times determined by actual observation of the new moon. The intercalation of a month was in late times determined by the Sanhedrin, but whether that month was called Adar or (with the Babylonians) Elul is not determined. Reckoning by cycles belongs to times in the Christian era.

From Neh. ii. 1 compared with Neh. i. 1 it appears that the regnal years of Persian kings were reckoned from the first of Tishri. Whether a New Year beginning on that date first began to be observed by the Jews in Persian times or originated under the Seleucidæ is not determined, though the later date is the more probable. The seasons among the Jews were two, summer and winter, the dry, hot season and the cool and wet one. A hard and fast division is not made, since sometimes the late rains of spring were reckoned to the summer.   (W. Lotz.)

Bibliography: Besides the works of Ideler and Wieseler cited under Day, consult: L. M. Lewisohn, *Geschichte und System des jüdischen Kalenderwesens*, Leipsic, 1855; A. Schwarz, *Der jüdische Kalender*, Breslau, 1872; H. Grätz, *Hist. of the Jews*, ii. 134, London, 1891; Dillmann, in the *Monatsberichte* of the Vienna Royal Academy, 1881, pp. 914–935; Schürer, *Geschichte*, i. 745–760, Eng. transl., I., ii. 363–398 and the sources there cited; *DB*, iv. 762–766; *EB*, iv. 5363–70.

YEATMAN-BIGGS, HUYSHE WOLCOTT: Church of England, bishop of Worcester; b. at Manston House (18 m. n.e. of Dorchester), Dorset, Feb. 2, 1845. He was educated at Emmanuel College, Cambridge (B.A., 1868), and was ordered deacon in 1869 and ordained priest in 1870; was curate of St. Edmund's, Salisbury (1869–77); vicar of Netherbury, Dorset (1877–79), and of St. Bartholomew's, Sydenham (1879–91); chaplain to the bishop of Salisbury (1875–85), examining chaplain to the bishop of Winchester (1890–91); proctor in convocation for the diocese of Rochester (1891–1905); honorary canon of Rochester (1884–1905); warden of St. Saviour's, Southwark (1894–1905), and subdean in 1898–1905. He was select preacher at Oxford in 1896 and at Cambridge in 1905. In 1891 he was consecrated bishop suffragan of Southwark (diocese of Rochester), and in 1904 was translated to his present see of Worcester. In theology he " holds the English Catholic Church as defined by the Book of Common Prayer to be the Apostolic Church in this land."

YEOMANS, EDWARD DORR: American Presbyterian; b. at North Adams, Mass., Sept. 27, 1829; d. at Orange, N. J., Aug. 26, 1868. He studied at Lafayette College, Pa.; continued academic and theological studies under his father's direction until his licensure in 1847; was stated supply at New Columbia, Pa., 1848–54; pastor at Warrior Run, Pa., 1854–58; at Trenton, N. J., until 1863; at Rochester, N. Y., until 1867, when he was installed over the Central Church, Orange, N. J., and was pastor there at his death. He was the author of the translation of Dr. Schaff's *History of the Apostolic Church* (New York, 1853) and the first two volumes of his *History of the Christian Church* (1858–67), all written originally in German. He also prepared a book of worship and a collection of hymns.

YORKER BRETHREN. See River Brethren.

YOUNG, BRIGHAM. See Mormons, I., §§ 3–4, II., §§ 9, 12, 13.

YOUNG, EDWARD: Church of England, poet; b. at Upham (6 m. s.e. of Winchester), England, 1683 (baptized July 3); d. at Welwyn (18 m. n. of London) Apr. 5, 1765. He was educated at Winchester, and at New College and Corpus Christi College, Oxford (B.C.L., 1714; D.C.L., 1719); became a fellow of All Souls', 1708; took orders, and in 1728 became chaplain to the king; and rector of Welwyn, Hertfordshire, 1730. He was the author of the once widely read *Night Thoughts*, and his satires often compared favorably with those of Pope. His *Works* appeared (5 vols., London, 1774).

BIBLIOGRAPHY: Various editions of Young's *Poems* contain sketches of his life—as that in the *British Poets*, vols. xlix.-li., by Sir H. Croft in S. Johnson's ed., often printed, e.g., London. 1822; by A. Chalmers, in *English Poets*, vol. xiii., ib. 1810; in E. Sandford's ed. of the *Works of the British Poets*, vols. xxv.-xxvi., ib. 1819; and by J. Mitford, in *Aldine Poets*, ib. 1871. Consult further: *Biographia Britannica*, vol. vi., ib. 1766; John Nichols, *Literary Anecdotes of the 18th Century*, 9 vols., ib. 1812–15; J. Barnstorff, *Young's Nachtgedanken und ihr Einfluss auf die deutsche Litteratur*, Bamberg, 1895; *DNB*, lxiii. 368–373.

YOUNG, EGERTON RYERSON: Canadian Methodist Episcopalian; b. at Smith's Falls, Ont., Apr. 7, 1840. He was educated at the Normal School of the Province of Ontario, after having taught for several years, and in 1863 entered the ministry. Four years later he was ordained, and, after being stationed at the First Methodist Episcopal Church, Hamilton, Ont., in 1867–68, was sent as a missionary to Norway House, Northwest Territory. There he worked among the Indians for five years, and in 1873 went in a similar capacity to Beren's River, Northwest Territory, where he remained three years (1873–76). In 1876 he returned to Ontario and was stationed successively at Port Perry (1876–79), Colborne (1879–82), Bowmanville (1882–85), Medford (1885–87), and St. Paul's, Brampton (1887–88). Since 1888 he has been prominent as a lecturer on work among the American Indians, and in this cause has made repeated tours of the world. He has written *By Canoe and Dog-Train among the Cree and Saulteaux Indians* (New York, 1890); *Stories from Indian Wigwams and Northern Camp-Fires* (1893); *Oowikapun: or, How*

the Gospel reached Nelson River Indians (1894); *Three Boys in the Wild North Land* (1896); *On the Indian Trail: Stories of Missionary Work among the Cree and Saulteaux Indians* (1897); *Winter Adventures of Three Boys in the Great Lone Land* (1899); *The Apostle of the North, James Evans* (1899); *My Dogs in the Northland* (1902); *Algonquin Indian Tales* (1903); *Children of the Forest* (1904); *Duck Lake* (1905); *Hector my Dog* (Boston, 1905); and *Battle of the Bears* (1907).

YOUNG, PATRICK: Scotch Biblical scholar; b. at Seaton (18 m. n.e. of Dundee), Scotland, Aug. 29, 1584; d. at Bromfield, Essex, England, Sept. 7, 1652. He was educated at the University of St. Andrews (M.A., 1603); became librarian and secretary to the bishop of Chester, 1603; was incorporated at Oxford, 1605, and, taking holy orders, became a chaplain of All Souls' College; was librarian successively to Prince Henry, James I., and Charles I.; in 1613 held a prebend in Chester Cathedral; became a burgess of Dundee, 1618; prebendary and treasurer of St. Paul's Cathedral, 1621; Latin secretary to Bishop John Williams, 1624; rector of Llanynys, Denbighshire, 1623; and was rector of Hayes, Middlesex, 1623–47. He was an eminent scholar in Greek; and his reputation was such that he was entrusted with the revision of Codex A of the Septuagint. He made contributions to Walton's Polyglot, and edited I Clement, 1633, and I and II Clement, 1637; in 1637 he published a catena of the Greek Fathers on Job, and in 1639 a commentary on Canticles.

BIBLIOGRAPHY: J. Kemke, *Patricius Junius (Patrick Young)*, Leipsic, 1898; Thomas Smith, *Vitæ quorundam eruditissimorum et illustrium virorum*, London, 1707; Hugh Young, *Sir Peter Young of Seaton*, privately printed, 1896; *DNB*, lxiii. 385–386.

YOUNG PEOPLE'S SOCIETIES.

I. Baptist Young People's Union of America: A fraternal organization of young people's societies in Baptist churches, which does not insist upon any one particular constitution or uniformity of name in the local organizations. It was organized in Chicago, Ill., in July, 1891, and was incorporated under the laws of Illinois in September of the same

year. The organization is international in its scope and has auxiliary organizations in all the states of the Union, in all the provinces of Canada, and in Brazil, while its work is followed by many individuals in foreign countries as well. The membership of the union consists of accredited delegates from young people's societies in Baptist churches and from

Baptist churches where no young people's society exists. The union maintains international headquarters in Chicago, Ill., and holds its meetings annually, in such places as may be decided upon from year to year, in what is known as the International Convention of the Baptist Young People's Union of America. The object of the union is declared to be, " The unification of Baptist young people; their increased spirituality; their stimulation in Christian service; their edification in Scripture knowledge; their instruction in Baptist doctrine and history, and their enlistment in missionary activity through existing denominational organizations." For the accomplishment of these ends the union, immediately after its organization, inaugurated a scheme of studies which are known as the Christian Culture Courses. These are three in number and are as follows: the Bible Readers' Course, a system of daily, devotional Bible readings which goes through the Bible every four years; the Sacred Literature Course, a four-years' course of study in church history and Christian doctrine; and the Conquest Missionary Course, a comprehensive and correlated system of missionary study, including all departments of missionary activity in which the denomination is engaged. To meet the increasing needs of the union these courses have been extended into the Junior and Advanced Departments, so that now the Baptist Young People's Union of America is carrying forward nine courses of study in all.

The Junior Union, with the same object as the senior society, was called into existence to serve those of younger age, and is supposed to be made up of those between twelve and sixteen years old. The Advanced Department is for those who, having completed the regular courses, wish to pursue further study in any of the same lines. The courses of study in the Junior and Senior Departments are followed by annual examinations, and diplomas are issued to successful students. While only a small proportion of those taking the studies undergo examination, it is conservatively estimated that not less than 1,500,000 young people have taken one or more of these courses during the past sixteen years.

In the first years of the movement the enthusiasm was phenomenal, and though the interest is not now so vigorous, it is far more satisfactory and significant. The most recent statistics would indicate that there are 600,000 persons connected with the societies of the Union in the United States and Canada.

The organs of the movement are two, *Service*, a monthly illustrated magazine which is the successor of *The Baptist Union*, the original organ; and *Our Juniors*, a monthly sixteen-page paper devoted to the interests of the Junior work. These organs carry the text of the study work and general information of the movement, and are now published by the American Baptist Publication Society in Philadelphia, the denominational publishing-house. The Rev. E. Y. Mullins (q.v.), of Louisville, Ky., is president of the union, and the Rev. George T. Webb is the general secretary.

GEORGE T. WEBB.

II. Brotherhood of Andrew and Philip. See AN-DREW AND PHILIP, BROTHERHOOD OF.

III. Brotherhood of St. Andrew. See PROTESTANT EPISCOPALIANS, II., § 6.

IV. Daughters of the King: An order of women in the Protestant Episcopal Church, having as its object the spread of Christ's kingdom among women and the strengthening of parish life. It had its origin in the senior Bible class for women in the Church of the Holy Sepulchre, New York City, which had chosen as its class name " Daughters of the King." The teacher of the class, Mrs. M. J. Franklin, who also became the founder of the order, called a meeting on Easter Eve, 1885, and, the rector's consent for the formation of an association being obtained, a committee was appointed to select a badge and a motto for the order. The badge chosen was a Greek cross fleury of silver, charged on the horizontal with the words *Magnanimiter crucem sustine*, which became the motto of the order, and at the base of the perpendicular were the initials of the watchword, F. H. S. (" For His Sake "). It was neither intended nor expected that the order would in any way supersede the old-established aid societies, women's gilds, or other parochial activities, since it was organized as a semi-religious order, standing for the ratification of the confirmation vow. Only communicants of the Episcopal Church are eligible to membership. They are admitted with a solemn service before the altar, invested with the cross—the emblem of their faith—and pledged by a vow to prayer and service.

The order works through parochial chapters, and has a central council, composed of fifteen members elected at the triennial convention, these members themselves meeting twice annually. Local assemblies have been formed in nearly every diocese in the United States, and the order is also well established in Canada, England, China, Haiti, the Danish West Indies, Honolulu, and Australia. The order is distinctively churchly in character, loyal to the rector of the parish, and intended to give the best expression to the Christian life. Its aim is quality rather than quantity. There are at present nearly 900 chapters and about 15,000 members on the roll of the order. It supports a Daughter in the foreign field, and its office is in the Church Missions House, New York City. The official organ of the order, *The Royal Cross*, has been issued since 1891, and serves as a medium for the free exchange of views and as a record of chapter work for the spread of Christ's kingdom among women.

SARA D. BLUXOME.

V. Epworth League: The name given to the independent, though closely similar, official organizations for young people in the leading Methodist denominations of America. The Epworth League in the Methodist Episcopal Church is the outgrowth of organized work for young people within the denomination, and, as far as can now be determined, the movement began in Philadelphia prior to 1872 in the Fifty-first Street Methodist Episcopal Church, of which the Rev. T. B. Neely, now a bishop, was then pastor. It spread among the churches of the city, and a union was organized. The general conference at Brooklyn in 1872 was memorialized but took no action; the general conference of 1876 gave official recognition. As the new movement did not fully meet the demand, other organizations sprang up, and some of them became bodies of importance.

Because of the manifest advantages of **1. Origin and Development.** consolidation, representatives of the five principal organizations met at Cleveland, O., May 15, 1889, and merged them into a single society to be called the Epworth League, which received official standing in the church from the general conference of 1892. An official organ, *The Epworth Herald*, was founded, and soon attained the largest circulation of any denominational religious paper for young people.

In the Methodist Episcopal Church, South, unassociated local societies existed for years until a commission appointed by the general conference, in 1890, organized a connectional society for young people similar in plan to that recently formed in the Methodist Episcopal Church, and to this new organization they also gave the name of Epworth League. In the same year the Methodist Church of Canada provided a similar organization with the same name, and these two denominations each gave their organization an official paper called, in both instances, *The Epworth Era*. The movement thus rapidly established in the three great **2. Organization.** Methodist denominations of the continent grew amazingly in numbers and enthusiasm, spreading throughout the Methodist churches and into the mission fields, and became the leading denominational young people's society.

In each denomination the Epworth League is under the oversight of a board, with a general secretary. A representative international committee manages all interdenominational interests, and eight great international conventions have been held. The local chapters are grouped for administration chiefly by districts and conferences following the denominational organization; and the local chapters of the league are, according to the age of the membership, organized as junior, intermediate, and senior, with adaptations to the needs of those served. The distinctive work is done under four departments, among which are distributed the oversight and promotion of the devotional and evangelistic activities, study and training in the Bible, the missionary and cognate movements, Christian citizenship, temperance and other reforms, social service and Christian philanthropy, and the general literary and social activities required by young life. The avowed purpose of the Epworth League is to win, to save, and to train the young people for Jesus Christ, and thereby to create a world-conquering Church. For this purpose it is marshaling the Christian young people and adding their splendid capabilities to the resources of the Church in the winning, saving, and training of their associates. The heart of the work is in its weekly devotional meeting, and it is developing a mighty leavening power through study classes in the Bible missions, evangelism, Christian stewardship, and Christian experience.

The enthusiasm of the early days of the Epworth League has been succeeded by a policy of practical and systematic achievement, and the organization is now accomplishing a service of greater value than ever before, while its future is believed to contain possibilities yet unmeasured. Of late years the intensive forms of work have rapidly increased, and this fact has radically changed the character of the conventions, and has given rise to **3. Results and Statistics.** summer institutes for instruction and training in the Christian life and in practical service. Out of these have come hundreds of volunteers for the ministry, the mission fields, and other forms of service. The Epworth League has profoundly influenced the life of the Methodist churches through the effect of these methods upon the younger ministry, the later missionary recruits, and the young laymen promoted from chapter cabinets to official boards. It is developing a spirit of liberality that promises well for the future Church. From small incomes the young people contribute hundreds of thousands of dollars annually to the official benevolences, in addition to their contributions for local support. In the Methodist Episcopal Church there are now Epworth League secretaries under appointment for India and Mexico, and money has been provided for the publication in the native languages of literature for the systematic religious culture of the young people. The practical ideal of a world-encircling army of trained Christian young people of all nations, united to win the world, is rapidly coming into view. The Epworth League is still increasing in numbers, though approaching the limit fixed by the denominational strength. The statistics given by the Methodist Episcopal Church, South, are: chapters 4,067, members 145,091; by the Methodist Episcopal Church: senior chapters 13,427, members 573,317, junior chapters 6,127, members 235,646—a total of 19,554 chapters and 808,963 members. These numbers are, however, inadequate, for official statistics have been required but recently, and these figures do not include about thirty unreported conferences and missions. Statistics for the Methodist Church of Canada are not at command. The general secretaries and headquarters of the Epworth Leagues for the three leading denominations given above are as follows: for the Methodist Episcopal Church, South, the Rev. F. S. Parker, Nashville, Tenn.; for the Methodist Church of Canada, the Rev. S. T. Bartlett, Toronto, Ont.; and for the Methodist Episcopal Church, the Rev. Edwin M. Randall, Chicago, Ill.

VI. International Order of the King's Daughters and Sons: An interdenominational young people's society, founded Jan. 13, 1886, by Mrs. Margaret Bottome (q.v.). Its real origin was in a New York circle of the type of the Lend-a-Hand Clubs (see VII.), which took the name of " The King's Daughters," and, after its reorganization as a club of ten members, adopted the four mottoes of the older society, with the watchword, " In His Name," and the badge of a silver Maltese cross, bearing the initials " I. H. N." and the date " 1886." This circle soon formed the model for others, the distinction between the King's Daughters and the Lend-a-Hand Clubs lying in the former's firm Trinitarianism and in its declaration that " ours is distinctly a spiritual organization, based on strictly evangelical principles. Our foundation is Jesus Christ, our Lord, in *whose atonement alone* we rely for salvation, and by *whose power*, and in *whose name* and to *whose glory* all our work is done." On the other hand, it neither sought to make minute inquiry into the theological views of its members nor did it endeavor to found a new sect, but advocated close allegiance to the denominations with which its members were already affiliated. In 1887 the society was opened to men and boys, and within a decade it numbered some 400,000 members, its present membership being over 500,000. It is to be found in North and South America, Great Britain, Germany, France, Italy, Greece, Switzerland, Denmark, Turkey, India, China, Japan, Australia, New Zealand, Hawaii, and the West Indies; and it has extended its work to the sick and the prisoner, to the victim of calamity, and to the mission field, as well as to educational institutions of all sorts.

The purpose of the society is to influence " first, the heart, next the home, then the Church, and after that the great outside." The constitution provides for circles and chapters of circles with state secretaries, a general supervision being exercised by a central council, though the greatest latitude is allowed individual circles in aims and methods. The official organ is the weekly *Silver Cross*, published in New York City.

VII. Lend-a-Hand Clubs: An interdenominational society for the promotion of the Christian life of its members and the extension of the kingdom of God. Since the last quarter of the nineteenth century a large number of young people's societies have grown up in churches of different communions, with a desire, on the part of those who formed them, to enter into the missionary and philanthropic work of the world. In many instances these societies are affiliated with one another, so that they keep up a mutual acquaintance by correspondence and by meetings through local organizations and at national congresses. As early as the year 1874 Miss Mary A. Lathbury, then directing the children's department of *The Christian Advocate*, founded the Look-up Legion, based upon what are generally known among the societies as the " four mottoes,"

" Look up and not down,
　Look forward and not backward,
　Look out and not in,
　Lend a hand."

Such societies were formed generally among the older children of Sunday-schools, each with its own officers, under the direction, however, of some older person. The Look-up Legion spread so far that it was divided into several groups, and its membership extended to perhaps 100,000 persons. Each of the members wore a Maltese cross with a rising sun behind it.

The earliest society formed under the " four mottoes " was established by Miss Ella Russell in the city of New York in the year 1871. The boys who formed it were members of a mission-school in which she was a teacher. They took the name of the " Harry Wadsworth Helpers " from the hero of E. E. Hale's (q.v.) story of *Ten Times One is Ten* (Boston, 1870), in which the " four mottoes " first

appeared. Various other Harry Wadsworth Clubs, Ten-Times-One Clubs, Lend-a-Hand Clubs, Lookout Clubs, etc., exist in various parts of the world. The United Society of these clubs, at Boston, receives communications from Japan, from China, from the countries on the east of the Mediterranean, from various island groups of the Pacific, from South America, and from every part of the United States. All these societies, while they attempt to maintain mutual good-fellowship, and while members are pledged to help each other in sympathy and Christian union, have at the same time some duty each in bringing in the kingdom of God. It is understood in their organization that the members must not live for themselves alone, but must bear each other's burdens. The greater part of the clubs are formed among young people, although some clubs are in existence which were formed in 1871, in which the adult members are still personally interested. *The Lend a Hand Record* is a monthly journal, published in Boston, and forming the medium of communication between the members of the different societies.　　　　　　　　EDWARD EVERETT HALE†.

VIII. Luther League of America: The young people's society of the Lutheran Church in America, organized at Pittsburg, Pa., Oct. 30–31, 1895. It unites, in a common cause and for a common purpose, the Lutheran young people's societies in the Lutheran Church, regardless of synodical affiliation or linguistic difference. They acknowledged, as the bond of their union, the Word of God as the only infallible rule of faith and practise, and the unaltered Augsburg Confession as the correct exponent of that Word. The founda-

1. Founda- tion upon which this organization is
tion and built is that of the church itself, and
Purpose. any society, no matter what its name, connected with a Lutheran congregation or institution of learning, is entitled to membership by conforming to and subscribing the constitution of the Luther League of America. It insists that each society cooperating with the League should be connected with either a Lutheran church or Lutheran institution of learning, and that its active members should be composed of communicants of the Lutheran Church, so that it embraces to-day, upon consistent grounds, Young People's Associations, Luther Alliances, Christian Endeavor Societies, King's Sons and King's Daughters, Young Men's and Young Women's Societies, gilds, and kindred organizations. Wherever these societies exist in Lutheran churches, it is presumed, and rightly so, that they are established in the interest and for the upbuilding of the Lutheran Church. The purpose of these leagues is to encourage the formation of young people's societies in the Lutheran congregations, to stimulate the various young people's societies to greater Christian activity, and to foster the spirit of loyalty to the church. It develops clear Christian faith by encouraging Bible study and imparting a knowledge of the Lutheran Church, historical and doctrinal, and of its usages. It trains the church's youth for active service; and it insists that care be exercised in the assignment of work. To the individual member of the league it proposes to quicken a clearer consciousness of

Christian faith, and it seeks to produce in each member fidelity to his own church by promoting his usefulness as one of its workers, and to help each member to be a true witness for Christ and an efficient teacher of the Gospel.

Four classes of members are recognized, active members, associate members, cooperating members, that is, those who for any reason can not accept the duties of full membership, but who are willing to render either financial or other valuable services to the league, and finally, in view of

2. Organization and Principles. the relation of the league to the church, and the pastor and members of the church council, who are *ex-officio* honorary members of the league. The principles of the league are federation, which is the governmental principle, and cooperation, which is the economic principle, seeking to avoid waste in the development and utilization of the energies of the young people of the church. The league presents to the young people of the Lutheran Church the opportunity for self-culture. As an organization it means to aid young people in the Christian life, and it proposes doctrinal intelligence as the highest form of self-culture for the Lutheran youth. The Lutheran Church follows up baptism by catechization and confirmation, and the preparation of Lutheran Christians for the work of Christ and his Church is to know their own work and way of working best of all. The league does not offer the Lutheran young people a system of study entirely colorless of doctrine, but it proposes to give the great truths of the Gospel to its members, as received by the Lutheran Church, by a systematic Bible study.

The Luther League has an organization in almost every state of the union where a Lutheran congregation is to be found. Since its organization as a national body in 1895, its work has extended around the world. At the national convention in Chicago in 1908, the Luther League of Porto Rico and the Luther League of Canada were received into membership. Immediately following the Chicago convention, Rev. Luther M. Kuhns, the general secretary of the Luther League of America, by action of the convention, visited the

3. Extension and Administration. Lutheran missions throughout the world. Steps were taken for the organization of the Luther League in the Lutheran missions in Japan, China, Federated Malay States, and India; and the character of the work of the organization has been brought to the attention of the pastors and Christian workers in Germany. The official organ of the society is *The Luther League Review*, founded and edited by E. F. Eilert, of New York City, and it also publishes *The Luther League Topics* and *Junior Topics*. The organization of the Sullin League consists of the National as the thinking, suggesting, directing head, and the local societies as the active, operating factor. The locals compose the district, and the district organizations the state. Local, district, and state societies are represented in the National conventions by duly elected and accredited delegates. Since the Cincinnati convention of 1900 the President of the Luther League has been Wm. C. Stoever, a Philadelphia layman, and the

other officers are as follows: general secretary, Rev. Luther M. Kuhns, Omaha, Neb.; assistant general secretary, Harry Hodges, Philadelphia, Pa.; treasurer, C. T. A. Anderson, Chicago, Ill.; statistical secretary, Rev. C. K. Hunton, Salem, Va.; literature secretary, Rev. Paul H. Roth, Beloit, Wis.; topic secretary, Rev. George H. Schnur, St. Paul, Minn. Besides these, an executive committee of ten members has entire charge of the work of the league. LUTHER M. KUHNS.

IX. Young Men's, Apprentices', and Working Men's Associations in Germany: The young men's associations in Germany had their origin in the desire of young men to associate with persons of equal position and age, as well as in the anxiety of parents and pastors to protect young men, living away from home, against temptation, an additional factor being the desire of those interested in the welfare of society to keep them from the dan-

1. Origin of Young Men's Associations in Germany. gers of the spirit of the time in its peculiar forms of revolutionary ideas, social democracy, and estrangement from the Church. The oldest of these societies date from the middle of the eighteenth century; and though there were at first only vague ideas of such associations and some sporadic germs, the second stage of their development clearly showed the beginnings of systematic activity and of federation, as well as a realization of the importance of such societies for larger classes, while in the third stage the work has advanced so far, through the enlargements of its unions and their international connections, that it has become an important factor in Christian social life.

The first small associations had an essentially Pietistic character, and the one founded at Basel by Pastor Meyenrock in 1758 is usually considered the earliest. Among the rules of this society we find the injunction to remain faithful to the word of God and to the Apostles' Creed, and to consider it one's right, and even duty, to admonish one's neighbor.

About fifty years later this society was

2. History. dissolved, although it was soon revived, and shortly afterward, in 1817, a similar association grew up in Stuttgart under the leadership of an official named Engelmann, who established it chiefly as a gathering for prayer. Another society, established at Elberfeld in 1816 by Pastor K. A. Döring (1783–1844) for the purpose of fostering zeal for missions, was even more successful. An association very similar to that of Basel was founded in 1834 by F. L. Mallet (q.v.) in Bremen, the rules of which became the basis of the West German associations. From Bremen the cause of these societies received a vigorous impulse and entered larger circles, owing chiefly to the services of a merchant, C. F. Klein, while J. H. Wichern (q.v.) and his activity in the field of home missions also contributed to the general spread of publicity. Thus far the work had been carried on chiefly by laymen, but now theological and other trained workers were employed. About this same time, moreover, federations were formed, as, for example, the Rhenish-Westphalian federation of young men (1848), the East German federation (1856), the

South German (1869), the Saxon (1878), the North German (1880), the federation of Alsace-Lorraine (1884), the Silesian (1887), and the Thuringian (1890). At the head of all was placed, in 1896, a general federation representing all smaller unions under the leadership of Superintendent K. Krummacher in Elberfeld. Since 1855 international conferences have been held triennially, and in 1878 an international committee with two agents was instituted at Geneva. In this way the German associations have been influenced by foreign ones, especially by English and American societies of the same kind.

The principal difference between the Anglo-American and German unions consists in the fact that the former lay the chief stress upon the missionary activity of their members in regard to outsiders, while the latter do not. Another difference is the equal recognition of all denominations on the part of Anglo-American societies, while the German and Scandinavian societies consider themselves as belonging to their respective state churches. Of about 1,800 German young men's associations some 1,400 belong to the federations already mentioned, which have 14 newspapers, 40 buildings of their own, and 25 secretaries and agents. The life of the
3. Methods, Aims, and Results. societies in their inward aspect is developed by devotional exercises, instruction, and entertainment. According to their motto, Ps. cxix. 9, God's word is the basis, center, and rule of the associations. In their headquarters special Bible hours are held, and discussions of the Bible take place even on evenings which are devoted to other purposes. Yet religion is only one phase of the life of these societies, although it is their all-permeating spirit. Education is also a very important factor; there are libraries in the different houses of the societies; courses are given in the branches of the public schools, as well as in book-keeping, drawing, French, and English; exercises in debates and recitations take place; and popular lectures are delivered on history and natural science. Instruction in the strict sense, however, is the weakest point in these associations, since the available funds very rarely enable them to secure teaching forces which can compete with those of better-endowed institutions. The social side shows more satisfactory results; vocal and instrumental music are especially fostered, as are gymnastics, games, and theatricals. It is inevitable that such strenuous activity within the associations must have some influence upon the outside world. Although proselyting is prohibited, sermons and tracts are distributed, aid is given to the teaching forces of Sunday-schools, and destitute young men are cared for even though they may not belong to the association, special assistance being given young men coming to Berlin and other large cities. Since 1891 there has also been a mission for soldiers, and similar missions have been formed for waiters, bakers, and other working men who can not attend church on Sunday. The associations have likewise been active in charitable work by creating employment bureaus, provisions for lodgings, saving-banks, sick funds, and burial funds.

From these young men's associations have been developed the so-called *Jugendvereine*, or apprentices' associations, the Christian associations for young business people, the young men's Christian associations (formed in strict accordance with the American Y. M. C. A.), and the Christian Endeavor societies. The Jugendvereine naturally branched off from the young men's associations in the wider sense, and since young men under seventeen did not
4. Protestant Offshoots from Young Men's Associations. harmonize in all respects with their older companions on account of the difference in age, and since the journeymen (*Gesellen*) clung strictly to their higher rank over against the apprentices, special associations for younger people were formed. The fostering of this special branch of young men found its characteristic expression in Stuttgart, where a building was erected in 1867 with dormitories, dining-rooms, and assembly halls. The Christian associations for young business people owe their existence to the desire of these young men to maintain their interests as a separate class of people. They were founded in 1848, and consist of ten societies, which form a confederation. The young men's Christian associations, modeled on the American institution, were founded in Berlin in 1883 by the German-American Fritz Schlümbach. Here the distinction between the different Protestant denominations is wiped out, and efforts are made to attract outsiders to the associations. These societies have enjoyed aristocratic patronage and are provided with large sums of money; and they have been introduced in a number of German cities, where their stately buildings have gained them many members. Their work is divided among different committees according to the different talents of the individuals, and is directed especially to bakers, soldiers, waiters, gardeners, and street-railway men. The endeavor societies do not differ from the American societies of the same character. Their purpose is to further the religious life of their members by Christian fellowship.

The Roman Catholic associations of working men (*Gesellenvereine*) form the counterpart of the Protestant young men's associations, and were founded by A. Kolping (1813–65), who had himself been an artizan until he succeeded, after great toil and labor, in entering the priesthood. He knew his former associates and their wants, and possessed
5. Roman Catholic Young Men's Associations. a talent for organization. The beginnings of these societies date back to 1845. Their president must be always a priest, who is proposed to the bishop of the diocese in agreement with the general committee of the local union. These associations have been successfully incorporated within the Roman Church, the whole matter being treated from the very first as a diocesan affair. The chief purpose of these associations is the awakening and fostering of the religious life of their members. Cologne is their central seat, and their hospices for working men correspond to the Protestant homes of a similar character. On the evenings of Sundays and holidays there are lectures of an instructive and entertaining nature; in summer outings take

place; and on Christmas a dramatic production of a religious character is presented. The associations lay great stress upon the industrial education of their members, and for this purpose special departments have been instituted for bakers, tailors, carpenters, etc. There is an employment bureau, a sick fund, and a savings-bank, and two dwelling-houses with twenty-three rooms for working men.

(THEODOR SCHÄFER.)

X.· Young Men's Christian Associations: These are interdenominational societies of young men, organized on an evangelical basis to promote the mental, moral, social, and physical welfare of young men. Active, voting membership is confined to church-members, but larger numbers unconnected with churches become associate members for the sake of physical, social, and educational privileges. The work is carried on by the Christian young men themselves, laboring individually in the sphere of their daily calling, and collectively on

1. General Character and Origin.

committees having charge of reading-rooms, libraries, gymnasia, athletic fields, educational classes, lecture-courses, religious meetings, and Bible-classes, for young men exclusively, boarding-houses, dormitories, with which most modern city association buildings are equipped, employment bureaus, visitation of sick young men, etc. The associations also, as opportunity offers, hold interdenominational religious services in shops, in neglected neighborhoods, public institutions, theaters, halls, etc. The parent English-speaking association was organized at London by George Williams (q.v.), June 6, 1844. Societies earlier formed in Germany (see above, IX.) came into affiliation with the English-speaking associations and those of other lands in 1855. By suggestion from London, associations were formed in Montreal Nov. 25, 1851; in Boston Dec. 29, 1851; and in New York June 30, 1852. The first international convention of the associations of the United States and British Provinces met in Buffalo, N. Y., June 7, 1854, and the first world's conference convened in Paris Aug. 19, 1855. Here the following test of membership, since known as the "Paris Basis," was adopted:

"The Young Men's Christian Associations seek to unite those young men, who, regarding Jesus Christ as their God and Savior, according to the Holy Scriptures, desire to be his disciples in their doctrine and in their life, and to associate their efforts for the extension of his kingdom among young men."

In Apr., 1860, the 203 associations of North America had about 25,000 members. At the outbreak of the Civil War, many members entered the armies on both sides, and the associations

2. Rapid Growth in America.

followed them with efforts for their welfare. At the instance of the New York Association, a special convention was called, Nov. 14, 1861, which resulted in the organization of the United States Christian Commission (q.v.); and during the war the associations were largely absorbed in army work. With the close of hostilities, a new season of growth and activity began. In 1866 the executive committee of the convention, which had been located from year to year in different cities, was situated for a term of years in New York City (where the

XII.—31

working quorum has since been continued) and has become known and incorporated as the "International Committee." The convention which met in Detroit June 24, 1868, adopted the following test of active membership, since known as the "Evangelical Test":

"*Resolved*, That as these organizations bear the name of Christian, and profess to be engaged directly in the Savior's service, so it is clearly their duty to maintain the control and management of all their affairs in the hands of those who profess to love, and publicly avow their faith in Jesus, the Redeemer, as divine; and who testify their faith by becoming and remaining members of churches held to be evangelical; and that such persons, and none others, should be allowed to vote, or hold office."

At the Portland convention, July 14, 1869, the word "Evangelical" was thus defined:

"We hold those churches to be evangelical, which, maintaining the Holy Scriptures to be the only infallible rule of faith and practise, do believe in the Lord Jesus Christ (the only-begotten of the Father, King of kings, and Lord of lords, in whom dwelleth all the fulness of the Godhead bodily, and who was made sin for us, though knowing no sin, bearing our sins in his own body on the tree), as the only name under heaven given among men whereby we must be saved from everlasting punishment."

All associations organized in North America since the passage of this resolution, in order to be entitled to representation in the international convention, must limit their active, voting membership to members of Evangelical churches. The formal adoption of this test by the American associations has secured for them the active sympathy of churches and Christian communities. It is only since this time that the associations have received the real estate and 713 buildings which are valued at over $60,000,000, and which give the societies a permanent foothold in the communities where they are located.

While the associations originated in Europe, their expansion has been most marked in North America. The American association agency of supervision, The International Committee, with the state and provincial committees which it has organized, has greatly contributed to this. It was not

3. Special Reasons for this Growth.

till 1878 that the World's Committee, with its headquarters at Geneva, Switzerland, created a similar committee. Four features of the North American associations have given them preeminence: (1) the development of the all-round work, physical, educational, social, and religious; (2) the extension (which is still in progress) of the organization beyond the commercial class of city young men, among whom it originated on both sides of the Atlantic, to students in colleges and schools, railroad employees, miners, lumbermen, factory operatives, mill hands, quarrymen, and other industrial classes, soldiers and sailors, immigrants, young men in country neighborhoods, and, with an increasing emphasis, to boys, or "the young men of to-morrow," in all these groups; (3) the enlistment and training of employed officers with varied qualifications for the leadership of this varied work; and (4) the erection of association buildings specially adapted to the accommodation of the work. Superior emphasis upon the development of all these lines has given such preeminence to the North American associations that they contain one-half the total membership of the world brotherhood, two-thirds of the employed officers, and three-fourths of the property in buildings. When, in 1889, missionaries from all the Christian nations in the foreign mission field desired the establishment of associations on their fields, they sought and obtained from the International Committee American secretaries to plant associations of the American type. There are 8,472 associations in ten countries of America, twenty-two countries of Europe, nine of Asia, and five of Africa and Oceania, with 934,934 members, 1,697 employed general secretaries, and 1,325 buildings worth $68,699,150.

The affiliated associations of North America have organized, through their international committee, thirty-eight state and provincial conventions. Each of these appoints an executive committee on the plan of the international committee, and a so-called "County work" is promoting through county organizations a systematic and helpful work in rural districts. The state and provincial

4. General Organization. committees now employ 127 visiting secretaries, whose efforts are essential in the development of their work. The yearly expenditure of the international committee is $301,037 on its home field in North America and $225,919 on its foreign field. The state and provincial committees expend annually over $389,802, and 1,297 associations reported their annual current expenses as $9,351,113, while 1,794 associations reported an aggregate membership of 536,037; 713 reported the ownership of buildings and other real estate valued at $61,854,110; and 3,351 persons were employed as general secretaries or as agents of the local associations and of the international and state committees. The chief aim of the general secretary is to enlist and train volunteer workers, using his tact to discover the post of duty for which each member is specially fitted to serve on the various working committees, and over 72,938 members were, in 1911, enrolled as volunteers on such committees. Appropriate methods have been wrought out to meet with timely aid the stranger, the unemployed, the destitute, the sick, and the intemperate. The social, literary, and physical department appliances have been made more effective for good, and the various religious meetings have been largely increased in number and usefulness.

The international committee has over 100 employed secretaries on its home field in North America and the Philippines, some of these being occupied with the work of supervision at the office, and others with work on the field. Twelve secretaries supervise the railroad associations organized at 235 railroad-terminal points with 90,000 members,

5. Sub-divisions of Activity. supported by the railroad companies, which contribute $400,000 annually, and by the members, who give $600,000 yearly. Twelve secretaries labor among college students, and 669 student associations have been organized with a membership of 58,696 students, of whom 25,000 are members of Bible classes. An outgrowth of this American student work is the World's Student Christian Federation, organized in 1895, and now having a membership of 150,000

students in 2,200 universities or colleges in thirty-one countries. The student general secretary of the international committee is also the federation's general secretary. Another outgrowth is "the Student Volunteer Movement for Foreign Missions," beginning in 1887, which has enrolled many thousand students as volunteers for the foreign-mission field. Of these over 4,700 have already been sent out as foreign missionaries by the foreign-mission boards of the various churches, the average number sent out being 250. Twenty-five secretaries supervise and extend association work among soldiers and sailors at United States military posts and naval stations in America, the Philippines, and China, and $2,000,000 have already been invested in the buildings which accommodate the work at some of these posts and stations. Five colored secretaries supervise and extend the work of 132 colored associations with 12,000 members. Three secretaries supervise and extend the physical, educational, and religious work of the associations, and twelve are at work among employees in the Panama Canal Zone. In their physical department the associations own and administer 648 gymnasia with 172 athletic fields, manned by 284,842 gymnasium and athletic members under the training of 418 expert physical directors, assisted by a corps of 8,920 gymnasium-class leaders. The educational department of the association contains 61,904 pupils, paying $527,346 in tuition fees. In the religious work the Bible-class attendance in 1,360 associations numbers 101,546 members, and the aggregate annual attendance of the religious meetings in 1,500 associations numbers 6,400,000. Seventeen secretaries give attention to the work in small towns and country neighborhoods among miners, mill operatives, and various industrial classes, and among boys, and they are also specially occupied with the problems of city, state, and provincial organizations, and of the training, transfer, and locating of employed officers, who number 2,954, including physical, educational, religious, social, membership, employment, boys, railroad, and industrial secretaries. Thirteen secretaries, including the general secretary and his two associates, administer the work as a whole, caring for the office and publication and business departments. Training-schools for secretaries, physical directors, and other employed officers have been established in Springfield, Mass., and in Chicago.

The International Committee upon its foreign field—in China, Japan, Korea, India, Ceylon, Syria, and South America, where 365 associations have already been organized—employs 105 secretaries and expends on this field $225,919. The World's Committee, with headquarters at Geneva, Switzerland, has given its principal attention to the associations of continental Europe. It employs eight secretaries with an annual expenditure of $15,000, cooperating with the national committees of Europe

6. Work Outside America. in supervision and extension of association work, and keeping in correspondence and communication with other members of the world's brotherhood. The strongest association groups in Europe are those of Great Britain and Germany; the former with 1,241 associations, 146,871 members, and 119 secretaries, and the latter with 2,310 associations, 127,835 members, and over 169 secretaries. In Great Britain there are 191 association buildings valued at $5,577,600, and in Germany, 154 buildings worth $2,380,000. The general statistics of the remaining foreign field for 1911 may be summarized as follows:

	Associations	Members.	Secretaries.	Buildings.	Value.
In France........	143	5,700	17	13	$290,000
" Holland.......	469	12,019	3	39	....
" Denmark......	312	12,300	14	16	426,500
" Norway.......	514	15,834	18	92	438,000
" Russia	13	2,012	1	2	112,000
" Sweden........	113	10,890	21	13	577,000
" Switzerland....	519	9,820	12	10	290,000
" India-Ceylon-Burma......	158	11,430	61	. 23	576,000
" China-Korea-Hongkong...	89	9,080	79	4	258,200
" Japan.........	72	6,475	12	23	281,500
" South Africa...	8	2,743	11	3	338,000
" Australia, New Zealand, and Tasmania....	19	9,907	40	13	824,000
" South America and Mexico..	14	4,058	28	5	475,000

XI. Young People's Christian Endeavor Union of the Church of the United Brethren in Christ: A young people's society of the Church of the United Brethren in Christ, organized by a called convention of 200 pastors and young people's society workers at Dayton, O., June 4–5, 1890. The organization then effected was called the Young People's Christian Union, and included all young people's societies, of whatever name, connected with United Brethren churches. Previous to the organization a number of Young People's Christian Endeavor Societies, Young People's Christian Associations, and local societies of other names existed, and the Young People's Christian Union included all these. Constitutions for local Christian Union Societies and Christian Endeavor Societies were provided, leaving to each congregation the choice as to form and name. In addition to the general union, each annual conference is organized as a branch union, there being forty of these. General conventions are held biennially, and branch conventions are held annually. The conventions are mass gatherings, but executive business is transacted by delegates properly constituted by the branch unions and by the local societies. For twenty years the direction of the organization was in the hands of an executive council of seven members, including the president and secretary, three of whom were elected by the General Conference, to which the union reported quadrennially. In 1909 the General Conference placed the management of the Christian Endeavor under a board which has oversight of the Sunday-school, brotherhood, and Young People's work. Each local society pays annual dues of one dollar, half of which goes to the treasury of the general union and half to the branch union treasuries. The first Sunday in May is observed as " anniversary day," when offerings are made to missionary enterprises at home and in foreign fields. These offerings have aided in establishing churches in Los Angeles, Chicago, Porto Rico, and Japan, and schools in Freetown and Shenge, Africa, and mission work among foreigners in America. They are now used in promoting Christian Endeavor work.

At the biennial convention held in June, 1908, the name of the general union was changed to Young People's Christian Endeavor Union, and all branch unions and local societies were recommended to adopt the Christian Endeavor name, which was done. In 1893 the general conference of the United Brethren Church formally constituted the Young People's Christian Union as a department of the denomination, and established *The Watchword* as the organ of the department, electing Rev. H. F. Shupe as editor. This paper is a sixteen-page illustrated weekly, with a circulation of 42,000, published by the United Brethren Publishing House, at Dayton, O. The first president was Prof. J. P. Landis, who served twelve years, when Rev. J. G. Huber was elected to succeed him. The organization numbers: Young People's Societies, 1,574, with 63,358 members; Junior Societies, 562, with 22,155 members; total, 2,136 societies, with 85,513 members. These societies pay annually to special missionary objects about $10,000.　　H. F. SHUPE.

XII. Young People's Christian Union of the Universalist Church: A denominational young people's society organized at Lynn, Mass., Oct. 22, 1889, and incorporated under Massachusetts laws on Mar. 10, 1898, its object being to promote the religious and spiritual life of its members, to train the young people of the church in missionary work, and to prepare them for efficient service in the larger work of the church. Since its organization the union has held twenty-three annual conventions, the last one being held at Portland, Me., in July, 1911. The union has built four churches in various parts of the country, and in addition to paying for the buildings it has assisted materially in paying the salaries of pastors of several churches, reducing the contribution from year to year as the members of the individual organizations have been able to increase their income. In its post-office mission department thousands of pieces of Universalist literature bearing upon all phases of Universalism have been distributed through the agency of the United States mail to people in isolated places throughout the country. In its Christian citizenship work the union has endeavored to train its members to grow up as Christian men and women, loyal to the highest ideals of their country, and examples of the best type of manhood and womanhood. The national union comprises sixteen state unions and 225 local unions, while its total membership is about 7,000. The officers consist of a president, secretary, treasurer, and four others who, with the officers, comprise the executive board, which governs the union between conventions. The state unions hold annual conventions, composed of delegates from the local unions. Financially, the union is in a very good condition, its annual report for the past year showing a satisfactory surplus in every department. Its running expenses, including salaries, supplies, etc., are met by an annual per-capita tax levied upon the state unions on the basis of their membership. The expenses of the mission department are met by receipts from convention pledges, which annually amount into the thousands, and from the two-cents-a-week system, in which every member who is able contributes two cents a week to the work of the union. The income from this latter source has shown a remarkable increase in the last few years. The department of social service is commanding much interest among the young people. This employs social addresses, summer camps, antituberculosis campaigns, visiting nurse associations, and other forms of applied Christianity, through individuals and unions.

One of the most important departments of the union is that of the Junior Union, in which all children of the Universalist Church too young to take up the work of the union itself are enrolled. These local unions meet weekly under the care of a superintendent appointed by the senior union, and the meetings are along similar lines to those of their elders, though much more simple in form. State and national superintendents supervise the work of these local organizations and direct their energies. The official organ of the union is *Onward*, a bi-weekly paper of twelve pages, published by the Universalist Publishing House at Boston, and edited by Roger F. Etz, of Boston; and the union maintains permanent headquarters at 359 Boylston Street, Boston, Mass.   ROBERT W. HILL.

XIII. Young People's Society of Christian Endeavor: The Young People's Society of Christian Endeavor is an interdenominational organization founded by Rev. Francis E. Clark (q.v.) on Feb. 2, 1881, in the Williston Congregational Church, Portland, Me., of which he was then pastor. This church was well fitted to be the birthplace of such a society, for it was a young church, filled with young people, and presided over by a young pastor, not out of his twenties, and neither pastor nor people were afraid to try new plans. In fact, they had made a number of experiments before the method which proved successful was

1. **Origin and Primary Characteristics.** adopted, these running largely to debating, musical, or amusement societies, which, though very well in their way, had not enough of the strenuously religious element to attract and permanently hold the enthusiasm of the best young people. This new society, however, was distinctively a religious organization. It did not despise other attractions, but it did recognize the fact that religion is the most interesting thing in the world to old and young, and it put the emphasis upon the word "Christian" in its title. Another word in the title which was underscored in practise was the word "Endeavor." It did not boast overmuch as a society of Christian accomplishment, but more modestly it claimed to be a company of triers, who were willing to make an attempt, even though it might fail. This characteristic of the new society was made evident by the constitution which was adopted at the pastor's house on the evening of organization. By signing their names to that constitution the members promised to try to attend and to take some little part in each weekly meeting, and also to try to do their duty on whatever committee they might be placed. None of them were speechmakers, and none of them were expert in Christian work, but they could try to do their best, and so they became the first society of Christian Endeavor. This pledge to try to do these

things proved to be the strength of the society, as well as of all the tens of thousands formed upon this model in subsequent years, for the constitution then adopted is the same one, in its essential features, as that which now, for three decades, has been adopted in all parts of the world. It has been translated into at least a hundred languages, and has been subscribed by at least 10,000,000 of young people, many of whom are now no longer young, and who have gone on to other forms of Christian work. Most of the failures that have occurred may be ascribed to a lack of adherence to these simple principles of putting religion first, and of making an attempt to speak some word and do some service, however small, in the Master's name and in his strength. In a word, outspoken devotion to Christ, constant service for him, and loyalty to his Church were the characteristics of this first society and of those that succeeded it. As the movement developed in all denominations and in all lands, universal fellowship with all Christians became a prominent and ever-enlarging feature of the organization.

The second society was formed eight months after the first in the North Congregational Church of Newburyport, Mass., under the leadership of the pastor, Rev. Charles Perry Mills, who, until the time of his death, was a warm advocate of this form of work for young people. Then the

2. **Rapid Growth.** societies, some accounts of which had appeared in *The Congregationalist* of Boston and *The Sunday School Times* of Philadelphia, began to multiply, at first slowly, but with rapidly increasing momentum. They broke through boundaries of state and denominational lines, and were taken up with eagerness and enthusiasm by young people in city and country, East and West, and in all walks and conditions of life. The following figures will show the accelerated rate of growth of the movement in the earlier years:

1882,	7	1886,	850	1890,	11,013	1894,	33,720
1883,	56	1887,	2,314	1891,	16,274	1895,	41,229
1884,	156	1888,	4,879	1892,	21,080	1896,	46,125
1885,	253	1889,	7,672	1893,	26,284	1897,	48,000

The society was not long confined to America, and it was scarcely four years old before it was introduced by a missionary, Miss Margaret Leitch, to India by way of Ceylon. About the same time, Rev. George H. Hubbard, a young missionary from Connecticut, started a little society in Fu-chau, China, which soon multiplied itself over and over again, until now 150 societies exist in the Fu-kien province of China alone, and hundreds more throughout that great empire. In 1888 the founder of the society was first invited to go to England to tell about Christian Endeavor, which had already become a movement of some importance in America, at the May meeting of the Sunday School Union in London. There was then one society in Great Britain, in the Hightown Church of Crewe. At first the growth was slow, but soon it gathered force, and now more than 10,000 societies are found in the United Kingdom, numbering something like 500,000 members. In Australia the society took root about the same time as in Great Britain, introduced by a young sailor who belonged to the second society in Newburyport, and the movement has spread into every city and almost every hamlet of the island continent. Into Japan it found its way, into Hawaii, Samoa, and the other islands of the South Seas. Then to Germany (where a strong contingent of 500 societies is now found) it made its way, as well as to Spain, France, Switzerland, Scandinavia, Russia, Bulgaria, Hungary, Turkey, Persia, Egypt, and South Africa; and in all lands the characteristics are very much the same.

But the society was not destined to make progress unchallenged or unhindered, for many opposed it and predicted its early demise. After a few years, its rapid growth alarmed the stricter sectarians, who feared some weakening of denominational loyalty on the part of the young people if they were allowed to mingle too freely with other **3. Unavail-** young people at conventions and union **ing Op-** meetings, though loyalty to their own **position.** denomination was one of the cardinal tenets of Christian Endeavor. The best way, they thought, to head off the new movement was to start another society with substantially the same principles and methods, but purely denominational in name and affiliation. This was done in several instances, the first of these societies being started some eight years after the beginning of the Christian Endeavor movement, but several of these organizations, feeling the impulse of these later days toward a larger fellowship, have come into the ranks of Christian Endeavor. This larger fellowship of Christians has been greatly promoted by the different unions which began to spring up very early in the history of the Christian Endeavor movement. The United Society (or national union of the United States and Canada) was organized in 1885, and now numbers more than 50,000 societies. Local unions and state unions soon followed, and now every state and territory and province, and every city and nearly every considerable town in the United States, has its Christian Endeavor union, which holds yearly, semiannual, or quarterly conventions or conferences, which are great sources of interdenominational Christian fellowship.

When the societies began to grow numerous in other lands, similar unions sprang up there, until now there is scarcely a Christian country in the world that does not have its National Christian Endeavor Union, while in India, China, and Japan these unions are equally flourishing and influential.

The conventions conducted by these **4. Christian** national unions have been interesting, **Endeavor** and in some respects phenomenal **Conven-** features of the religious life of the last **tions.** quarter of a century. In numbers, they are said by well-informed church historians to have surpassed any religious gatherings in the history of the Church. The national convention held in Boston in 1895 brought together 56,425 registered delegates, and several others have approached that number in attendance. Notable conventions of this sort that have attracted the attention of the nation have been held in New York, Washington, San Francisco, Baltimore, Seattle, and other cities. For these conventions, cities make elaborate preparations; parks and railway stations, public buildings, stores, and private residences are elaborately decorated; great tents, holding 10,000 people each, are called into service when more substantial meeting-places are inadequate, and the spiritual life of the community is often profoundly stirred. In Melbourne, Sydney, Adelaide, London, Glasgow, Belfast, and Berlin, in Fu-chau and Ningpo in China, and in Osaka and Kobe in Japan similar national conventions, great in numbers and religious power, have been held, while thousands of smaller conventions, but of a like character, are held every year in different parts of the world. The World's Union of Christian Endeavor was organized in Boston in 1895, and since then has held three great conventions, one in London in 1900, which was attended, it is estimated, by 50,000 delegates; the second in Geneva, Switzerland, in 1906, attended by people speaking thirty different languages and representing forty countries and more than fifty different denominations; and the third in Agra, India, in 1909. These Christian Endeavor unions of all kinds—world's, national, state, district, county, and local—exercise no authority over any local society, but exist simply for fellowship and inspiration. The only authority for any Christian Endeavor society is its own church and pastor.

In many unusual and unexpected places the society has found a place for itself, as on the ships of the United States Navy and on ships of the merchant marine, where many "floating societies" exist. In many prisons societies have been established among the converted prisoners after special evangelistic meetings, and, so far as is known, these **5. Wide** Endeavor prisoners, when once re- **Range of** leased, have never gone back again. **Activity.** In soldiers' barracks, policemen's quarters, fire-engine stations, trolley-car barns, factories, department stores, and large hotels (among the employees) societies have been formed that have done great good. A very interesting development of the Boer War was the formation of societies in the prison camps of St. Helena, Ceylon, and the Bermudas, which resulted in the conversion of hundreds of young Boers, and in sending more than 200 of them into the mission fields of Africa on their release. The society has always striven to cultivate the missionary spirit among its members, and it has contributed thousands of its members and millions of dollars to the mission fields. Good citizenship has for many years been a leading plank in the platform of the society, and temperance, civic purity, national patriotism, and international peace have a large place in its literature and on its program.

The scope and principles of the society have never been stated more succinctly than at the world's convention at Geneva, when the following **6. Scope,** platform of principles was adopted by **Principles,** the representatives of all the great **and** nations and Protestant denominations: **Statistics.** Christian Endeavor is a providential movement, and is promoted by societies composed largely of young people of both sexes found in every land and in every section of the Christian church. Its covenant for active members demands faith in Christ, open acknowledgment of Christ, service for Christ, and loyalty to Christ's church.

Its activities are as wide as the needs of mankind, are directed by the churches of which the societies are an integral part, and are carried on by carefully organized committees, embracing all the members.

Its strength lies in the voluntary obligation of its covenant pledge, and its adaptability to all classes and conditions of men.

Its ideals are spirituality, sanity, enthusiasm, loyalty, fellowship, thorough organization, and consecrated devotion.

Christian Endeavor stands for Spirituality and Catholicity. Its spiritual purpose is guaranteed by the fact that its active and controlling members are active, experimental Christians; its catholicity, by the fact that through other classes of members, and through various activities, all young persons may be brought under its influence and share in its blessings.

Christian Endeavor stands for Loyalty and Fellowship. Its loyalty to the local church and its work is guaranteed by its covenant pledge, which embodies its motto, "For Christ and the Church"; its fellowship is guaranteed by its insistence only on fundamental Christian principles, which has enabled it already to find a home in every Christian land and denomination.

Christian Endeavor stands for Christian Missions and all wise philanthropies at home and abroad, approved by the churches to which the societies belong.

Christian Endeavor stands for Good Citizenship in the broadest sense of the term, and is unalterably opposed to private and corporate greed, to intemperance, impurity, and everything that lowers the standard of manhood and womanhood.

Christian Endeavor stands for Peace and Good Will among men, and is opposed to all unjust war and unjust industrial strife, as contrary to the principles of the Prince of Peace. "Arbitration and Conciliation" are two of its watchwords for the twentieth century, and an "International Christian Brotherhood" and a universal language for intercommunication two of its ideals.

Christian Endeavor stands for Beneficence and generous giving, which it has embodied and made concrete in its "Tenth Legion"* and the "Macedonian Phalanx."†

Christian Endeavor stands for High Intellectual Attainments, which are promoted by its literature, its conventions, its institutes, summer assemblies, schools of methods, reading-courses, and correspondence-schools, and by the study of the Bible demanded by its weekly meetings for the most helpful participation.

Christian Endeavor stands for High Devotional Attainments and for communion with the Unseen, as embodied in the "Comrades of the Quiet Hour,"‡ whose methods have brought help and comfort to so many thousands.

Christian Endeavor stands for Pure Home Life, Honest Business Life, Loyal Church Life, Patriotic National Life, Joyous Social Life, and Brotherhood with all mankind.

The following are the latest statistics at the last enumeration, July 1, 1911:

UNITED STATES.	No. of Societies.
Young People's	31,365
Junior	16,265
Intermediate	2,987
Floating	45
Mothers'	63
Senior	50
Allen C. E. Leagues	1,905
Varick C. E. Leagues	525
United Brethren Societies	761
Total	53,966
Total membership	2,698,300

CANADA.	No. of Societies.
Young People's	2,855
Junior	703
Intermediate	62
Mothers'	1
Parents'	2
Total	3,623
Total membership	181,150

* Consisting of those who give regularly at least one-tenth of their income for distinctively religious work.
† No longer in existence.
‡ Consisting of those who make it a rule to spend at least fifteen minutes each day in quiet communion with God and religious meditation.

FOREIGN.	No. of Societies.
Young People's	17,402
Junior	3,991
Intermediate	57
Mothers'	15
Senior	23
Total	21,488
Total membership	1,074,400
Grand total number of societies	79,077
Grand total membership	3,953,850

Some of the chief journals of the society are The Christian Endeavor World, The Junior Christian Endeavor World, published in Boston; The Christian Endeavour Times, published in London; The Irish Endeavourer, of Portadown; The India Christian Endeavour, of Allahabad; The South African Endeavourer, of Cape Town; Die Jugendhilfe, of Berlin; Esfuerzo Cristiano, of Madrid; The Australian Christian Endeavour Link, of Melbourne; The Roll Call, of Sydney; and fifty or more other papers are published by national, state, or local unions.

The president of the United Society is Rev. Francis E. Clark, the general secretary is William Shaw, the treasurer is Hiram N. Lathrop, and the editorial secretary is Amos R. Wells; while the officers of the World Union are Rev. Francis E. Clark (president), John Willis Baer (secretary), W. Shaw (treasurer and office secretary), and George W. Coleman (auditor).   FRANCIS E. CLARK.

BIBLIOGRAPHY: By F. E. Clark, Young People's Prayer Meetings, New York, 1887; World-Wide Endeavor, Boston, ton, 1895; Training the Church of the Future, New York, 1902; Christian Endeavor Manual, Boston, 1903; Christian Endeavor in All Lands, Philadelphia, 1906; and by A. R. Wells, Social Evenings, Boston, 1895; Junior Manual, ib. 1895; Prayer-Meeting Methods, ib. 1896; Our Unions, ib. 1896; Citizens in Training, ib. 1898; The Missionary Manual, ib. 1899; The Officer's Handbook, ib. 1900; The Young People's Pastor, ib. 1905; Expert Endeavor, ib. 1911.

XIV. Young Women's Christian Association of the United States of America: The organization known as the Young Women's Christian Association of the United States of America, with thousands of members and over 875 local associations, had its beginning in 1858, in a small society formed in New York by Mrs. Marshall O. Roberts, and called at first a Union Prayer Circle. Later in the same year the name was changed to Ladies' Christian Association, its object being " to labor for the temporal, moral, and religious welfare of young self-supporting women," and two years later this society opened a boarding-home for such young women. In 1866 the name of the organization was changed to Ladies' Christian Union, and its charter was secured, and in the same year the Young Women's Christian Association of Boston was organized, modeled more or less after the Young Men's Christian Association (q.v.). In 1872–73 a prayer group in Normal University, Normal, Ill., was formed and organized into a Young Ladies' Christian Association, which later took the name Young Women's Christian Association, and these organizations were duplicated in other city and student centers until the present large organization has been developed. The purpose of the association

1. Origin and Purpose.

in every case has been to develop a well-rounded Christian womanhood in the community where the organization exists. To build up a strong body, to increase healthy, social instincts, to train the mind, and to strengthen the spiritual and moral forces, nothing less than this has been the aim. To accomplish this purpose, methods are employed which differ from each other as widely as do the local surroundings of the various associations, but whatever the methods, the underlying principles are the same in all. These fundamentals are that the individual improves far more when she herself desires it than when some one else is trying to improve her; that cooperation will accomplish much more than isolated effort; and that cooperation is easier to attain when it is possible to have like working with like. Any young woman of good moral character may become a member of the association by the payment of an annual fee (generally $1), though voting and office-holding are in most cases confined to those who are members of Protestant Evangelical churches.

Four general departments exist in a city association: physical, social, educational, and religious work. The physical department requires a gymnasium, where a girl may gain strength and vigor through careful drill exercise, watched over by a competent and trained director. A girl who has stood at a loom or who has been bending over a needle all day needs a general limbering up in the gymnasium before she is ready to go into a study class or a religious meeting and get the best out of it. Swimming-pools and bowling-alleys are provided in many associations. The social department makes provision for a young woman in a strange city, or even for one who in her own city is busy in an office all day long, and has no time

2. City and Student Associations. or opportunity to make friends. For the enlarging of her life, parties and clubs are formed in which she may meet other girls and women, and have a good time in a natural and healthy way. There is also a lunch and rest room where a young woman may buy her whole luncheon, or may bring her sandwiches and buy only a bowl of soup or a cup of tea, and sit at a pleasant table to eat it. In many of these lunch rooms the "cafeteria" system is used—where from a side table the young women gather on a tray the dishes of food they wish and carry it themselves to their table. As this does away with most of the expense of service, lower prices can be charged, and a good luncheon can be supplied at an average cost of eleven or twelve cents. In a room nearby will be found couches where girls may rest after luncheon before returning to work. Under the educational department is grouped the work for the mental or manual training of the young women, and classes as widely differing as Latin, stenography, or domestic science are provided at low rates. It is the aim of this department to provide any class for which there may be a real demand in the community, and some associations recently have been holding a summer school to coach girls who have fallen behind in their high-school work. Although there is an individual department for the religious work of the association, this work in real-

ity threads in and out of all departments, and binds them together, so that no one can come into any part of the association without coming also under its religious influence. A great deal of this is necessarily an invisible and unspoken influence, but it is present none the less. Under the organized religious work come the Bible-study classes, the devotional meetings, the personal service groups, and the missionary and evangelistic meetings. Through these the effort is made to ground a girl in the Christian faith, so that she will have a reason for what she believes, and will have a spiritual strength that will not only enable her to fulfil her duties, but will cause her to be a source of strength and helpfulness to others. The association does not rival the Church in any way, but endeavors to develop a trained and useful membership for the Church. These four departments constituted for many years a city association, but gradually the members began to realize that many young women lived at too great a distance from the association to come to it. Therefore an extension department was formed to carry the benefits of the association into the factories and shops at the noon hour. From this small beginning a large industrial work has grown, with clubs in many factories, while in some cities and mill villages there may be found a full-fledged industrial association managed by the workers themselves. In such associations a large subscription is paid by the factory or mill owners to the association, but the control of the association work and the employment of the secretary are left to the young women employees. In the student centers for women the need was felt of a vitalizing Christian organization that should be under the auspices of the students themselves. From small prayer groups developed the Young Women's Christian Associations which provide for Bible- and mission-study classes and devotional meetings among the students, and which also have charge of such philanthropic enterprises as the young women have time for. From the one prayer group in Normal University in 1873 have grown 667 student associations now affiliated with the national movement.

The work of all associations is directed in general by a board of managers or a cabinet, which is elected from the membership, while standing committees have charge of the different departments. The general secretary and the other department secretaries are the executives of the board of directors. It is the duty of the general secretary to be in touch with all the departments, to make plans for the strengthening and enlarging of the association, to have knowledge of the latest methods employed elsewhere, and herself to originate

3. Organization and Conferences. methods which are particularly adapted to the local surroundings. She is the true executive of the association, one with the board of managers in their councils and plans, and able to guide them though employed by them. One of her chief duties is to harmonize conflicting personalities, so that she must be a woman of tact and resources; she must have great executive ability, and must have, first of all, a deep spiritual nature, for the success of all departments hangs on the religious strength of the association. More and more the secretaryship is being recognized as a legitimate and satisfactory profession for college women, who would make their lives tell in the spiritual uplift of the world. There were for some time in the United States two national organizations of the Young Women's Christian Associations, but in Dec., 1906, 398 delegates from the local associations, formally affiliated with the International Board of Women's and Young Women's Christian Associations and with the American Committee, met in New York and formed The Young Women's Christian Associations of the United States of America. A national board of thirty representative women was elected with Miss Grace H. Dodge as president. The national board has eight departments, viz., field work, secretarial, finance, publication, office, foreign, conventions and conferences, and method. A training-school for secretaries was opened in New York City in Oct., 1908, and the national headquarters are at 125 East Twenty-seventh Street, New York City. Under this national board are formed territorial committees who come in close touch with the local associations and have traveling secretaries, experts in the various departments, to give advice and help wherever it shall be necessary. The relation between the territorial and local associations is purely advisory. To give additional strength to the associations, ten conferences are held in different sections of the country. These are arranged by the national board, and to them come members of the local associations for Bible and mission study, for open conference on plans and methods of work, and for inspirational meetings. Each conference lasts about ten days, the smallest numbering some 200 delegates, the largest 800. The leaders of these conferences are national board and territorial secretaries and committee members, and among the speakers are some of the best-known clergymen and social-betterment workers of the country.

Certain phases of work promoted by the specialists of the national board in suitable communities or in a general way are as follows: the provision for club houses for professional women students; the organizing of associations for Indian students and for those in colored schools; the linking-up of recent college graduates to volunteer work along such religious and philanthropic lines as they may indicate preference for; recognition of the recent " rural awakening " by the formation of county associations; and a system of meeting and protecting young immigrant women and equipping them, by instruction in English and other help, for life in a new country.

Besides the work in the United States the Young Women's Christian Association is strengthened by its international bonds. It is affiliated with the World's Young Women's Christian Association, which has branches on every continent and in almost every country, and with the World's Student Christian Federation. These world's associations have their own conferences, the last being the World's Young Women's Christian Association Conference in Berlin, in 1910; and the World's Student Christian Federation Convention in Constantinople, in 1911.

The following statistics for 1910–11 show something of the growth of this organization in the course of a little over fifty years. Now that

4. International Affiliations and Statistics. it is united under one central board, a still greater increase may be expected. City associations (with 32 branches), 196; extension associations, 12; total membership, 228,757; 147 associations report an average weekly attendance of 6,719 at the religious meetings; 151 report 22,193 enrolled in Bible classes; 57 report 1,434 enrolled in mission-study classes; 109 report equipped in gymnasia, and 152 report 25,133 enrolled in physical training classes; 158 report 36,153 enrolled in educational classes and clubs; 131 report libraries with 109,931 volumes, and 144 report reading-rooms with 2,269 periodicals; 97 report 7,496 enrolled in domestic-science classes, and 134 report 14,079 enrolled in domestic-art classes; 126 report lunch departments serving 5,652,145 meals during the year; 104 report boarding departments with capacity for 4,531; 94 report 27,150 positions secured through the employment bureau; 44 report travelers' aid departments; 80 report buildings owned, and 32 report summer homes; the secretaries, directors, teachers, etc., number 1,106.

The student associations number 667, with an active membership of 54,369 out of 115,703 young women students in the institutions; the general secretaries number 47; the mission-study classes number 1,262, with 14,196 students (reported by 342 associations); the Bible-study classes number 1,485, with 18,957 students (reported by 345 associations); 16 associations have buildings, and 201 have libraries; 253 associations held special evangelistic meetings.

XV. Young Women's Christian Association of Great Britain and Ireland: An organization formed in 1855 in two sections by Lady Kinnaird (then Hon. Mrs. Arthur Kinnaird) in London, with the idea of establishing suitable Christian homes and institutes for young women; and by Miss Robarts in the country, who, believing in the

1. Origin and History. power and influence of women, "banded together a union of women whose work should be cemented by prayer," which was called the Prayer Union. These two sections, the one with its purely spiritual aim, and the other combining to meet both the spiritual and practical needs of young women at that time, grew side by side, until in 1877 both were united under the presidentship of Mrs. Pennefather (of the Prayer Union) and Lady Kinnaird, and called the Young Women's Christian Association; the work had already extended to Scotland and Ireland, thus making the association to consist of four divisions —London, provincial, Scotland, and Ireland. By 1884 it had become evident that the time was ripe for a more united constitution and regular organization in the work, and after much prayer and consultation a united basis and constitution were agreed upon, still adhering strictly to the lines upon which the London and country branches had worked, and in harmony with the motto of the association, " Not by might, nor by power, but by my spirit, saith the Lord of hosts " (Zech. iv. 6). A united central council under the presidentship of the earl of Shaftesbury was formed, the first meeting being held in London Jan. 22, 1885. At this meeting the affiliation of the Young Women's Christian Association with the kindred work carried on by the "Union des amies de la jeune fille" for the benefit of foreign girls in England was agreed to, and the consent of the council was gained for an office to be secured for this purpose. In the mean while branches of the association had been formed in America, India, and the continent of Europe, and in Apr., 1892, the first gathering of an international character was held in London, after careful consultation and with the cooperation of leaders of the American Young Women's Christian Association. Representatives from India, America, France, Norway, and other countries were present, and the result of this meeting was the formation of the World's Young Women's Christian Association in 1894, as a center for all national associations, the first president being Mrs. J. H. Tritton. A general committee was formed, consisting of representatives of every country included in the union, and a constitution was drawn up. International conferences are held quadrennially, these having met in London in 1898, in Geneva in 1902, in Paris in 1906, and in Berlin in 1910. There are now nineteen national associations linked with the World's Young Women's Christian Association, with a membership of 512,000.

Corresponding to the united central council, which was formed to unify the British work of the Young Women's Christian Association, there now exists the British National Young Women's Christian Association, representing the five divisions of London, south of England, north of England, Scotland, and Ireland, and united under the name of British National Council. Nine representatives from each division, together with other members representing various departments of work, form this council, which is the responsible and legislative body of the whole association in Great Britain and Ireland. It appoints standing committees for special duties, e.g., general executive (on which are the representatives of the five divisions), finance, selection, and allocation of workers, editorial, and foreign, while there are also various departmental committees for nurses, teachers, etc. The five divisions are autonomous in their working, though all are linked together under the national council, which formulates the general policy of the association. The local associations work with local committees, and are in direct communication with the office of the division in which they are situated. The work of each division is carried on through its divisional council, to which all questions relating to the general work of the local associations are carried.

2. General Organization.

The membership in the local associations may be either general or special. General membership is divided into prayer union (active) and associate, the former class including those who wish to devote themselves to the service of Christ in daily life, and to work and pray for others; while associate members are all those who wish simply to enjoy the benefits of a Christian association. Special members consist of juniors (girls under fourteen years of age),

teachers, nurses, the gild of helpers (girls of leisure), and the blind, the latter division having a Braille library and a monthly letter to members, also published in Braille. The local association may consist of a home and institute combined, or merely of club-rooms opened in the evenings. The homes, holiday and residential, meet a great need, especially the latter, of which there are thirty-five in London alone, accommodating women in business, teachers, students, etc.; while by means of its holiday homes (country and seaside) many thousands of association members are yearly enabled to enjoy restful and inexpensive holidays, reduced fares being often allowed by the railway companies to Young Women's Christian Association members visiting homes. In several large towns, such as London, Edinburgh, Liverpool, etc., restaurants, noon rest-rooms, and lunch clubs have been opened for the benefit of girls in business, which provide good food at as cheap a rate as possible. In the institutes, besides the advantages to lonely girls of intercourse with others, and of the help and counsel to be had from the association secretary, educational classes are held and lectures on various subjects are given.

3. The Local Associations.

The home organization may be divided into religious, educational, and social service. The religious work is carried on by meetings, Bible study, evangelistic services, etc.; and the educational by classes in institutes, provision being also made for home study and loan libraries. The department of social service is more complex, and includes subdivisions for employment (with registries in different parts of the country, as well as a registry for immigrant girls), emigration (advising emigrant girls and cooperating with the British Women's Emigration Society), thrift, total abstinence, factory work (in affiliation with the Federation of Working Girls' Clubs), and the convalescent and holiday department. The Social Service Council has recently been formed, and may be applied to for advice and information on the subject of factory laws, etc., should members be in difficulty and need help in this way. The foreign department of the association unites not only the foreign missionary work, which is largely supported by the local associations, but also Young Women's Christian Association work in other lands. Besides the large sums of money which are contributed annually by Young Women's Christian Association members to foreign missions, twenty-eight workers are supported by this department, who carry on chiefly Young Women's Christian Association work among English-speaking girls in foreign lands. The number of branches in Great Britain and Ireland is 1,290, and the membership, 102,710. The president is Mrs. J. H. Tritton (previous presidents being Lords Kinnaird and Overtoun), and the general secretary is Miss Thorold.

4. Home, Social Service, and Foreign Departments.

BIBLIOGRAPHY: The most important literature is contained in the manuals of the various organizations, which usually afford not only statistics, but the history of the respective societies. Consult further: T. Chalmers, *Juvenile Revival; or, Philosophy of the Christian Endeavor Movement,* St. Louis, 1895; *Young Men's Christian Associations;*

Handbook of the Hist., Organization, and Methods of Work,
New York, 1892; L. L. Doggett, *Hist. of the Y. M. C. A.,*
vol. i., ib. 1896; R. C. Morse, *Polity of Y. M. C. A.'s,* ib.
1904; W. D. Murray, *Principles and Organization of the
Y. M. C. A.,* ib. 1910; P. Green, *How to deal with Lads; a
Handbook of Church Work,* ib. 1910. A comprehensive
little book, a new edition of which is needed, is L. W.
Bacon and C. A. Northrop, *Young People's Societies,* New
York, 1900.

YOUNG, ROBERT: Lay theologian and orientalist; b. at Edinburgh Sept. 10, 1822; d. there
Oct. 14, 1888. He received his education at private
schools, 1827–38; served an apprenticeship to the
printing business, 1838–45, using his spare time to
study the oriental languages; became a communicant in 1842; joined the Free Church, and became
a Sabbath-school teacher in 1843. In 1847 he took
up printing and bookselling on his own account,
proceeding to publish books that tended to further
the study of the Old Testament and its ancient versions; his first publication was an edition with
translation of Maimonides' 613 precepts. He went
to India as a literary missionary and superintendent
of the mission press at Surat, in 1856, returning in
1861; conducted the " Missionary Institute," 1864–
1874; and visited America in 1867. He was a moderate Calvinist, a simple Presbyterian, and a strict
textual critic and theologian. His important work
was the *Analytical Concordance to the Bible . . .
containing every Word in alphabetical Order, arranged
under its Hebrew or Greek Original* (Edinburgh, 1879);
one may cite also his *Concise Commentary on the
Holy Bible, being a Companion to the new Translation of the Old and New Covenants . . . 2 pt.* (1865);
*Contributions to a New Revision; or, a critical Com-
panion to the New Testament* (1881); and the *Christology of the Targums, or the Doctrine of the Messiah,
as it is unfolded in the ancient Jewish Targums, or
Chaldee Paraphrases of the Holy Scriptures.* Young
was celebrated as an editor and translator of Jewish and Biblical writings in various languages, especially in Hebrew, Samaritan, Aramaic, Syriac,
Arabic, and Gujarati, thus and in other ways contributing to the apparatus for textual criticism. He
was also active in the region of comparative linguistics and in Semitic philology.

BIBLIOGRAPHY: *Banner of Ulster,* Dec. 18, 1855; *DNB,*
lxiii. 390.

YOUNG, SAMUEL EDWARD: Presbyterian;
b. at Deep Cut, Auglaize Co., O., June 6, 1866. He
was educated at Westminster College, Mo. (1883–
1886), and Princeton (1886–88) and Union (1888–
1889) Theological Seminaries. He has been pastor
of Westminster Church, Asbury Park, N. J. (1889–
1894), Central Church, Newark, N. J. (1894–97),
Second Church, Pittsburg, Pa. (1898–1908), and
Bedford Church, Brooklyn, N. Y. (since 1908). He
has been active in ameliorating the conditions of
the life-saving service, and while at Pittsburg organized both a system of summer services in the
city parks and afternoon theater services. He was
vice-chairman of the committee of the General Assembly that organized the Presbyterian Brotherhood of America, and, besides being a member of
the evangelistic committee of the General Assembly,
is a chaplain of the Actors' Church Alliance of
America.

YOUTZ, HERBERT ALDEN: Presbyterian; b.
at Des Moines, Ia., Apr. 28, 1867. He was graduated from Simpson College, Indianola, Ia. (B.A.,
1890), and Boston University, where he took a
degree in 1895 (Ph.D., 1903), also studying at
Berlin and Marburg in 1901–03. He held Congregational pastorates at Quincy, Mass. (1894–96), Mid-
dlefield, Mass. (1896–98), and Plymouth Congregational Church, Providence, R. I. (1898–1901); was
acting professor of theology in the Chicago Theological Seminary (1903–05); professor of the same
subject in the Congregational College of Montreal
(1905–08); and was in 1908 appointed to his present position of professor of systematic theology in
Auburn Theological Seminary, Auburn, N. Y.

YULETIDE: A popular, somewhat poetic designation of the Christmastide. The name of the central festival in Greek is *hēmera genethlios, ta genethlia
Iēsou Christou (tou Sotēros)* (" the birthday of Jesus
Christ [or, of the Savior] "), though Gregory Nazianzen (*Oratio,* xxxviii. [*MPG,* xxxvi. 312–313]) unsuc-
cessfully sought to introduce the name Theophany to distinguish this festival from that of the
Epiphany (q.v.), celebrated separately on Jan. 6. In
Latin, the name is *Natalis (dies), Natalitia, Nativitas
Domini (Jesu Christi),* whence the Italian *Natale*
and the Spanish *Nadal, Natividad.* The French
      Noël may be derived from *natalis,* or
The Name. possibly from *noë,* a cry of rejoicing on
      the occasion of the birth of a prince.
The Anglo-Saxon *géol, yole, yule* is thought to signify the solstice. In Scandinavia, the period from
Christmas to Epiphany is called *Jólafridr, Jóla-
hälgh. Yule* and *Yuletide* are still used in Scotland,
while in England this older designation has been
replaced by Christmas (" Christ mass "), which appears in Dutch as Kerstmisse, Kersmis. The German *Weihnachten* represents the Middle High
German *Wīhen Nahten* (" Holy Nights "). The festival either includes the whole period from Dec. 25
to Jan. 6 (the twelve nights, since the ancient Germans reckoned by nights and not by days), the
Christmas week up to Dec. 31, the four days Dec.
25–28 (the feasts of the Nativity, St. Stephan, St.
John the Evangelist, and Holy Innocents), or,
finally, the Christ day alone. For Jan. 6 as the
feast of the birth and of the baptism of Christ see
EPIPHANY, FEAST OF THE.

The choice of Dec. 25 as the birthday of Christ
must be clearly distinguished from the celebration
of the Christmas festival. Long before there was
any question of a festival of Christ's birth, the date
of his birth had been sought and determined. The
Church of the first two centuries had no thought of
celebrating it as a festival. Origen (*In Lev. hom.,*
viii. 3, *In Matt.* xiv. 6 [*MPG,* xii. 495, xiii. 893–894]),
followed by Jerome (*In Matt.* xiv. 6 [*MPL,* xxvi.
97]), pronounced decisively against the celebration
      of birthdays of saints and martyrs, for
Relation to the days of their death should rather
the Vernal be considered their *natales dies.* Clem-
Equinox. ent of Alexandria (*Strom.,* i. 21 [*MPG,*
      viii. 885–886]) says that from the birth
of the Lord to the death of Commodus (Dec. 31,
192) 194 years, 1 month, and 13 days had passed,

so that Nov. 18, 751 A.U.C., was the birthday of Christ. Probably we should read 23 instead of 13 days, so that the date becomes Nov. 8. In the *De pascha computus*, incorrectly ascribed to Cyprian (dated by Usener in 243 A.D.), the day of the spring equinox (Mar. 25) is reckoned as the first day of creation, and Mar. 28, the day on which the sun and the moon were made, is the birthday of Jesus, in the year 1549 after the Exodus; while the Clementine Homilies set this day on the vernal equinox itself. In his chronography Julius Africanus, in 221, choosing the same day as that of the conception of Jesus, is the first to give Dec. 25, exactly nine months later, as the date of his birth; and Hippolytus, in the fourth book of his commentary on Daniel, gives Dec. 25, 4 B.C., as the day of Christ's birth, and Mar. 25, 29 A.D., as the day of his death. In all these computations the spring equinox plays a part, as the time both of the creation of the world and of the incarnation or conception of Jesus; in the latter case the birthday follows nine months later. Duchesne assumes that Dec. 25 was chosen in the West and Jan. 6 in the East as the day of Christ's birth through a reckoning which gave Mar. 25 (Tertullian, *Adv. Judæos*, viii.; Hippolytus, *Acta Pilati*) or Apr. 6 as the day of his death, and also as the day of his conception, so that nine months later—in one case Dec. 25, in the other, Jan. 6—became the date of his birth, although Duchesne himself admits that a celebration of Apr. 6 as the day of Christ's death appears only in a Montanist sect (Sozomen, *Hist. eccl.*, vii. 18).

It has also been conjectured that the day was selected because of its significance in the Roman calendar, where it bore the name of *dies invicti solis* (" the day of the unconquered sun "), since on this day the sun began to regain its power and overcame the night. This view is supported by Polydore Vergil (*De rerum inventoribus*, v., **Alleged** Lyons, 1558), J. A. Fabricius, D. E. **Relation to** Jablonski, E. F. Wernsdorf, J. A. W. **Sun-cult and** Neander, K. A. Hase, and others; and **Saturnalia.** it is true that, after the introduction of the Christmas festival, the coming of Christ as the Light of the world was often compared with the *dies invicti solis* of the Romans, as by Augustine (*Sermo in nativitatem Domini*, vii., and *in nativitatem Johannis Baptistæ* [*MPL*, xxxviii. 1007, 1302]), Gregory of Nyssa, Maximus of Turin (*Sermo*, iii. and iv. *De nativitate Domini*, *MPL*, lvii. 535, 537), etc. It is, however, unlikely that the birthday of Jesus was first determined by this heathen festival. Nor can Christmas be assumed to owe its origin to the Roman Saturnalia, since they lasted from Dec. 17 to Dec. 19, and even with the later prolongation to seven days, ended on Dec. 23. Still less can the origin be sought in the Germanic solar festival, since the Christmas festival arose long before the Christianizing of the Germans, although some popular usages connected with Christmas may have a Roman or Teutonic source.

The chief question in relation to Christmas is when the birthday festival, originally combined with the baptismal festival on Jan. 6, was first celebrated separately on Dec. 25. Usener has made an exhaustive investigation of this matter, starting with the chronography of Philocalus (354 A.D.), which contains a list of memorial days of the **Date of** Church (*depositio martyrum*), the first **Earliest** entry being: " viii. of the Calends of **Roman** January; Christ born in Bethlehem of **Celebra-** Judea." Usener then adduces an ad**tion in** dress delivered by Pope Liberius (con**December.** secrated May 22, 352) when Marcellina, the sister of Ambrose, took the vow of virginity (Ambrose, *De virginitate*, iii. 1 [*MPL*, xvi. 219–220]). Liberius begins by alluding to the day as the birthday of the Lord, and then proceeds to treat of the miracle at the marriage of Cana and of that of the loaves and fishes. Usener insists that the words must have been spoken on Jan. 6 and not on Dec. 25, because the marriage at Cana and the miracle of the loaves and fishes were always connected with the festival of the Epiphany. Besides, according to an ancient usage of the Church, a vow of virginity could be pronounced only on either Epiphany or Easter, as the two baptismal days, so that the earliest date for this event must have been Jan. 6, 353; and since in the chronography of 354, Dec. 25 is already given as the day of Christ's birth, that day must have been observed for the first time in Rome in 354. This theory of Usener has gained much approval, and P. Lagarde and A. Harnack look upon the proofs as irrefutable. Duchesne, however (*Bulletin critique*, xi. 41 sqq.), regards Usener's argumentation as "more ingenious than correct." No proof is given that Marcellina took the vows before the exile of Liberius (355–358); the report of the discourse was not written down by Ambrose until twenty-four years after its delivery; even if the report is absolutely correct, Ambrose himself declares that Liberius spoke on the " birthday of the Savior," and in 377, when he wrote, this could only be understood as Dec. 25. The most important point, however, is that, in the chronography preceding the *depositio martyrum*, there is a *depositio episcoporum*, i.e., of the last twelve bishops of Rome. The names are not given in chronological order, but according to the days of the calendar year. The last two bishops, however, Marcus (d. Oct. 7, 336) and Julius (d. Apr. 12, 352), are entered after Eutychianus, who died in Dec., 283, and this shows that the chronography was already completed before Oct., 336, the last names being added in 354. Hence the date of Dec. 25, given in the *depositio martyrum*, proves that the Christmas festival must have been observed in Rome at the latest in 335.

Thus all that can be stated positively is that the festival was first celebrated in Rome in the fourth century, and not later than 354. For a long time it yielded to other festivals in importance, and even in 389 Valentinian did not include it among the church days on which legal proceedings were interdicted. How tenaciously many still clung to Jan. 6 as the birthday of Jesus, even after Dec. 25 had become usual in the West, is shown by Maximus of Turin (first half of the fifth century), who says in a sermon for the Epiphany: " On this day the Lord Jesus was either born or baptized; different opinions are held in the world " (*Sermo*, vi; *MPL*, lvii. 545). From Rome, Christmas, as a festival distinct from that of the Epiphany, spread to the East, according to the express testimony of Chrysostom (*Hom. in nativitatem Domini; MPG*, xlix. 353), especially as confirming orthodoxy against Arianism. Gregory Nazianzen first celebrated it in Constantinople in 378, and Chrysostom delivered an eloquent Christmas sermon in Antioch in 388 or 387, in which he says: " It is not yet ten years that this day has been clearly known to us." There can be no doubt that this Christmas celebration by Chrysostom was of peculiar significance, and that the whole population now participated for the first time. In 352, Gregory of Nyssa celebrated Christmas and the Epiphany together in Cappadocia (*MPG*, xlvi. 580, 701), and in Egypt, at the close of the fifth century, according to Cassianus (*Collationes*, x. 2 [*CSEL*, xiii. 286]), the birth and baptism of Jesus were still combined with the Epiphany. Only after the Council of Ephesus, in 431, did Paul of Emesa preach a Christmas sermon in the chief church of Alexandria. The land of Christ's birth, Palestine, long resisted the introduction of this festival, and is blamed for its stubbornness by Jerome (*Commentarium in Ezek.*, i. 3 [*MPL*, xxv. 18]). In a sermon delivered on St. Stephen's Day (Dec. 26), Basil of Seleucia praises Juvenal of Jerusalem for having celebrated Christmas (*MPG*, lxxxv. 469), although, on the other hand, Cosmas Indicopleustes (c. 550) expressly states that in his day both the nativity and the baptism of Christ were celebrated together on Epiphany at Jerusalem, while Dec. 25 was the feast of the family of Jesus (i.e., David, his ancestor, and James, his brother and first bishop of Jerusalem), the precise nature of this festival being somewhat uncertain. The birth and baptism of Christ are still celebrated together on Jan. 6 by the Armenians (F. C. Conybeare, *Rituale Armenorum*, pp. 181, 517–518, London, 1905). [Dr. Enrico Masini, a learned Italian scholar, in his elaborate " Chronography of the Life of Christ," maintains that the true date of the nativity of Jesus was Sunday, Nov. 28, 748, year of Rome. He also gives Mar. 18, 782, year of Rome, as the date of his death.]

The *Missale Romanum* especially distinguishes this festival by assigning to it three masses, the first celebrated *in nocte* (after the *Te Deum* in matins), the second *in aurora* (after lauds and prime), and the third *in die* (after terce). Every priest is not required to say all these masses, although he may do so. The liturgical color of the altar covering and of the chasuble is white until In the Roman Rite. the octave of the Epiphany. At an early date a manger was set up in the church with the appropriate figures. In the church of S. Maria ad præsepe (later called Maria Maggiore), built by Liberius and entirely renovated by Sixtus III. (432–440), there was, in the right transept, a chapel for the sacred manger. This usage led to the manger-plays, with songs and dialogue, first given in the churches and later outside of them (cf. RELIGIOUS DRAMA). Of the popular observances, the Christmas-tree does not owe its origin, as many suppose, to old German custom,

for the first notice of it is in Strasburg, in the seventeenth century. The octave of Christmas is observed on Jan. 1, the feast of the Circumcision, a substitute for the heathen new year's festival (see NEW YEAR'S CELEBRATION; for further details cf. CHRISTMAS).   (GEORG RIETSCHEL.)

BIBLIOGRAPHY: Besides the literature under CHRISTMAS, consult: W. Sandys, *Christmastide, its Hist., Festivities and Carols*, London, 1852; J. W. Wolf, *Beiträge zur deutschen Mythologie*, 2 vols., Göttingen, 1852–57; J. Grimm, *Deutsche Mythologie*, 4th ed., Berlin, 1875, Eng. transl., *Teutonic Mythology*, 3 vols., London, 1880–83; W. Mannhardt, *Der Baumkultus der Germanen und ihrer Nachbarstämne*, Berlin, 1875; J. Sepp, *Die Religion der alten Deutschen und ihr Fortstand in Volkssagen . . . bis zur Gegenwart*, Munich, 1890; J. de Kersaint-Gilly, *Fêtes de Noël en Provence*, Paris, 1900; G. Bilfinger, *Untersuchungen über die Zeitrechnung der alten Germanen*, part II., *Das germanische Julfest*, Stuttgart, 1901; W. F. Dawson, *Christmas: its Origin and Associations*, London, 1902; G. Hager, *Die Weihnachtskrippe*, Munich, 1902; T. A. Janvier, *The Christmas Kalends of Provence*, London, 1902; G. Rietschel, *Weihnachten in Kirche, Kunst und Volksleben*, pp. 13 sqq., Bielefeld, 1902; N. Hervé, *Les Noëls français*, Niort, 1905; M. Höfler, *Weihnachtsgebäcke*, Vienna, 1905.

YVON, î''von', **PIERRE:** Leader of the Labadists; b. at Montauban in the French province of that name (not at either of the cities of that name of the present time) in 1646; d. in 1707. As a child he was with his mother an attendant at the church of Labadie (see LABADIE, JEAN DE, LABADISTS), and after Labadie removed to Geneva, Yvon was sent there to live with him and study under him. After pursuing courses in philosophy and theology, he took part in Labadie's work, followed him to Middelburg in 1668, and thence to Amsterdam, where Yvon became one of the most earnest propagandists of Labadie's ideas. In this interest he also visited Wesel, Duisburg, Mülheim, Düsseldorf, and Cologne, and also worked at The Hague and in Dort and Utrecht with some success. In 1670 he went with the Labadists to Herford. After the death of Labadie in 1674, Yvon became the recognized head of the community, and led them back into the fatherland in 1675, where the measure of success which attended the community for a time was changed into decay and decline after 1688.

Yvon was a man of power and devotedness, more sober than Labadie, better educated in theology, a diligent author, and ever full of zeal for the cause which he had espoused. His writings appeared in Latin, German, Dutch, and French; of these perhaps the best known is his *Kurtzer Bericht von Zustand . . . derjenigen Personen welche Gott . . . zu seinem Dienst vereiniget . . . hat*, 1659, which appeared in French, Amsterdam, 1681, and in Eng. transl., *A Faithful Relation of the State and Last Words . . . of Certain Persons whom God hath taken to Himself out of the Church*, Amsterdam, 1685. (For list of minor writings cf. Hauck-Herzog, *RE*, xxi. 585–586.)   (S. D. VAN VEEN.)

BIBLIOGRAPHY: Consult the literature under LABADIE, JEAN, LABADISTS; *Actes publics tant politiques qu'ecclésiastiques . . . des . . . J. de Labadie et P. Yvon*, Amsterdam, 1669; J. Koelman, *Der Labadisten*, ib. 1684; J. Reitsma, *J. Hesener en Balthasar Cohlerus*, in *De Vrije Fries*, xiii (1877).

YVONETUS, î''von-ê'tūs: Dominican, the supposed author of a thirteenth-century *Tractatus de* *hæresi pauperum de Lugduno.* The tract is found in E. Martène and N. Durand, *Thesaurus novus anecdotorum*, v. 1777 (Paris, 1717). The assumed authorship is stated by Pegna in his edition of the *Directorium inquisitorum* of Eymericus, pp. 229, 279 (Rome, 1587) and by D'Argentré in *Collectio judiciorum*, i. 84, 95 (Paris, 1818), but assailed by F. Pfeiffer in *Zeitschrift für deutsches Alterthum*, 1853,

p. 55, who attributes the work to David of Augsburg (q.v.). Preger has made this sure in his edition of the manuscript extant at Munich in *Abhandlungen der Berliner Akademie*, xiv. 2 (1879), 183 sqq. Two other manuscripts exist, one at Strasburg and one at Stuttgart. See WALDENSES.   (C. SCHMIDT†.)

BIBLIOGRAPHY: K. Müller, *Die Waldenser*, pp. 157 sqq., Gotha, 1886; *KL*, xii. 1844.

Z

ZABARELLA, dzā''bā-rel'lā, **FRANCESCO:** Cardinal, jurisprudent, and diplomatist; b. at Padua in 1360 (not 1339); d. at Constance (?) Sept. 26, 1417. He came of the Paduan patrician family of Sabarini or Sabarelli, began his study of law in Bologna under the canonist John of Lignano, and received his degree of licentiate in 1383. He continued his studies at Florence, where he took his doctorate in 1385, and delivered lectures which were well attended; he took orders and served also as vicar of Bishop Acciajola, and was the logical successor to the bishopric when Acciajola resigned had it not been for the pope's opposition. In 1390 he returned to his own city and labored there for twenty years as teacher and author, in 1398 becoming archpresbyter at the cathedral. After the subjection of Padua to Venice he became prominent in diplomatic ways, and at the Council of Pisa (1409) he was counsel to the Venetian embassy. By John XXIII. he was made bishop of Florence and then cardinal with the title S. Cosma e Damiano. He was henceforth much in the public eye. He treated with King Sigismund with reference to the place and date of assembling of the Council of Florence and took part in the same; after John XXIII. (q.v.) fled from the council, Zabarella remained as his representative, and was deputed to communicate the council's decision. He was active also in the proceedings against Benedict XIII. (q.v.), and took part in those against Huss and Jerome of Prague (qq.v.), in which he sought to secure mild action.

His writings are partly philosophical and philological, as *De felicitate* (written c. 1398, printed Padua, 1655); *De arte metrica;* and *De natura rerum diversarum;* and the theological tract *De corpore Christi.* But the most of his works are on ecclesiastical law: *Lectura super Clementinis* (1471); *Commentaria in libros decretalium* (1502); *Tractatus de unione ecclesiæ; De schismatibus authoritate imperatoris tollendis.* A large number of letters remain in manuscript in the Vienna library; two letters to Zabarella from Coluccio Salutato are in *Fonti per la storia d'Italia*, xvii (1896), 408 sqq., 456 sqq.

(K. BENRATH.)

BIBLIOGRAPHY: Not to be overlooked is the literature on the Council of Constance, particularly the work of Van der Hardt, i. 537 sqq. Consult further: A. Kneer, *Kardinal Zabarella. Ein Beitrag zur Geschichte des grossen abendländischen Schismas*, Münster, 1891; J. P. Tomasini, *Illustrium virorum elogia*, pp. 3–10, Padua, 1630; B. Brudersenius, *De augusta regiaque origine . . . familiæ Zabarella*, ib. 1670; A. Gloria, *Monumenti della univ. di Padova*, ib. 1888; H. Finke, *Acta concilii Constanciensis*, vol. i., Münster, 1896; and the dissertation of Keppler, *Die Politik des Kardinalskollegiums in Konstanz*, ib. 1899;

there is a very full and excellent treatment, from the Roman standpoint, in *KL*, xii. 1845–50; cf. also Creighton, *Papacy*, i. 287, 331 sqq., ii. 40–44, 74, 118.

ZACCARIA, ANTONIO MARIA. See BARNABITES.

ZACHARIÆ, tsā''Hā-rî'ê, **GOTTHILF TRAUGOTT:** Pioneer in Biblical theology; born at Tauchardt in Thuringia Nov. 17, 1729; d. in Kiel Feb. 8, 1777. He studied at Königsberg and Halle (M.A., 1752); became adjunct in the philosophical faculty at Halle, 1753; rector of the Ratsschule in Stettin, 1755; professor of theology at the University of Bützow, 1760; and at Göttingen, 1765; and finally at Kiel, 1775. His significance comes entirely from his *Biblische Theologie oder Untersuchung des biblischen Grundes der vornehmsten theologischen Lehren* (4 parts, Göttingen, 1771–75). The stimulus to the work came from the tendency of the old Enlightenment to trace theology backward to the Bible in its correct meaning. Zachariæ had forerunners in the matter of furnishing a Biblical basis for theology, such as Büsching with his *Epitome theologiæ e solis sacris literis concinnatæ* (1757). But his aim was to prepare the way for a better method of theological teaching by a thorough exegetical examination of the Biblical material out of which dogmatic theology is built. Yet Biblical theology was not for him an independent discipline; nor did he distinguish between different Biblical conceptions. His work dealt with the principal passages used as proofs. He was intent upon the historical sense, and cautioned against eisegesis, recognizing the temporal and local limitations of the parts of Scripture. His theological position was supernaturalistic in that he held firmly to revelation, miracles, original sin, the divine sonship of Christ, and the Trinity. These same characteristics appeared also in his *Doctrinæ Christianæ institutio* (1773). In spite of his conservatism, his piety was of a type which, like that of many supernaturalists of the period of the Enlightenment, was hardly distinguishable from that of the rationalists.

(HEINRICH HOFFMANN.)

BIBLIOGRAPHY: C. G. Perschke, *Züge des gelehrten Charakters Zachariäs*, Bremen, 1777; H. Döring, *Die gelehrten Theologen Deutschlands*, vol. iv., Neustadt, 1835; Schenkel in *TSK*, 1852; F. C. Baur, *Vorlesungen über neutestamentliche Theologie*, pp. 4–6, Leipsic, 1864.

ZACHARIAH, zac''a-rai'a **(ZECHARIAH):** Fourteenth king of Israel, son and successor of Jeroboam II. (q.v.). His date according to the old chronology is 772–771; according to Kamphausen, 741; according to K. Marti (*EB*, i. 797–798), 743. It is possible that he did not succeed immediately to the throne upon his father's death, but that a period of strife for the throne prevented his accession for about ten years. He was the last of the dynasty of Jehu (cf. II Kings x. 30), reigned only six months, and was slain by Shallum (q.v.), who usurped the throne.

BIBLIOGRAPHY: The literature on his period as given under AHAB, and ISRAEL, HISTORY OF; also the articles in the Bible dictionaries.

ZACHARIAS, zac"a-rai'as: Pope 741–752. He was chosen successor of Gregory III., with whom he had maintained close connection. He was reputed to be a learned man, and had rendered into Greek the " Dialogues " of Gregory the Great. He upheld successfully the interests of the Roman see in relation to the Lombards, the Greek Church, Boniface, and the Frankish kingdom, his achievements with the last being momentous for the future history of the Church. In these efforts he was ably assisted by Boniface (q.v.), by whom the reform of the Frankish Church was carried through. Similarly in Germany the interests of the pope were guarded and the organization extended by the organization of bishoprics. Under Boniface the Frankish bishops were led to draw up a confession and send it to Rome, in which was expressed their subordination to Rome. Pepin also came into relations with Rome some time after he ascended the throne. In his dealings with the Lombards Zacharias sacrificed to King Liutprand Duke Thrasimund of Spoleto, the ally of Gregory III., thereby buying back the cities of Ameria, Horta, Polimartium, and Bleda, while a peace for twenty years was arranged with the Roman duchies. Still greater was the pope's influence with King Ratchis. In relation to the Greek Church Zacharias directed to the Emperor Constantine Copronymus a letter on image worship. The two synods held by Zacharias (743 and 745) dealt with the discipline of clergy and monks, church property, marriage, and the renewed condemnation of the heretics Aldebert and Clement, who had already been condemned by Boniface.

(A. HAUCK.)

BIBLIOGRAPHY: The *Epistolæ et decreta* are in *MPL*, vols. lxxxix., xcviii. Consult: *Liber pontificalis*, ed. L. Duchesne, vol. ii., Paris, 1892; Jaffé, *Regesta*, i. 262–263; C. Mann, *Popes*, i. 2, pp. 225–288; H. Hahn, *Jahrbücher des fränkischen Reichs*, pp. 24 sqq., Berlin, 1863; *Papst Zacharias und Pius IX* Eine geschichtliche Parallele, Wiesbaden, 1866; A. von Reumont, *Geschichte der Stadt Rom*, ii. 110–111, Berlin, 1867; R. Baxmann, *Die Politik der Päpste*, i. 218 sqq., Elberfeld, 1869; A. J. Uhrig, *Bedenken gegen die Aechtheit der . . . Sage von der Entthronung des merowingischen Königshauses durch den Papst Zacharias*, Leipsic, 1875; J. Langen, *Geschichte der römischen Kirche*, ii. 628, Bonn, 1885; A. J. Nürnberger, *Der römische Synode von . . . 743*, Mainz, 1898; L. M. Hartmann, *Geschichte Italiens im Mittelalter*, ii. 2, pp. 140 sqq., Gotha, 1903; Hauck, *KD*, vol. i. passim; Bower, *Popes*, ii. 76–90; Platina, *Popes*, i. 186–189; Milman, *Latin Christianity*, ii. 402–416.

ZACHARIAS GERGANOS: Theologian of the Eastern Church of the seventeenth century. What little is known of his life is gathered from the titles and prefaces to his writings. He came of a distinguished family of Ithaca, and probably studied as a monk at Mt. Athos. He intended to study at Rome, but was turned aside to Wittenberg, where he became a protégé of Elector Johann Georg I.,

who furthered the prosecution of his studies. By 1622 he appears to have become metropolitan of Arta.

In the seventeenth century in the Eastern Church three tendencies were discernible. Such men as Dositheus of Jerusalem exalted the orthodox faith. Others, like Leo Allatius, strove for union with Rome. The third class, like Cyril Lucar, favored a protestantizing direction. To this third class belonged Zacharias, who was perhaps the pioneer, and his importance in this respect has been overlooked. His chief work was a " Christian Catechism " (Wittenberg, 1622), a volume of about 300 pages, of which only two copies are known to exist, one in the Barbarini library at Rome and the other at Hamburg. The Athanasian Creed comes first (omitting the *filioque*) after the introduction, then a new title. The catechism is modeled after well-known examples like that of Simeon of Thessalonica, and it is in the Greek of ordinary speech, in eleven books (incorrectly numbered, since the sixth and seventh are both numbered six). The first deals with theology and anthropology, the next six deal with the person and work of Christ, two with the Church, one treats of the sacraments, and the last of eschatology. The Scriptures are given through the Holy Spirit, and teach the mystery of the Trinity and other divine mysteries and the will of God. It is its own interpreter, not the pope, and papal tradition is rejected. The laity are to read the Scriptures, in which is eternal life. God is the first cause; but angels are his intermediaries. Man's body is composed of four elements, the soul is God's creation; man was created immortal without sin; he could sin because he had free will, and sin came through the fall, whence came death. Had man not sinned, Christ would not have become flesh. God is not the author of sin. The Spirit of God works faith in man, who is otherwise unable to believe; faith comes through hearing the Gospel and the illumination of the Spirit. But faith without works is dead; it may be lost, and also regained by repentance and the sacraments. The Christology contains nothing remarkable except that emphasis is laid on the proof of Christ's messiahship through messianic prophecy, miracles, and passion; the crucifixion took place that the predictions of the prophets might be fulfilled. In Christ's death the Logos took part. The Church is the aggregate of holy Christians; Christ, not the pope, is the head. The sacraments are not simply signs, but are effective and necessary. Baptism is by water and the Spirit, not by water alone; rebaptism is rejected, heretic baptism recognized. In the Lord's Supper there are visible and invisible substances. Only two sacraments are explicitly recognized, though in this connection marriage is treated. The eschatology is very concrete. The ideas presented are a commingling of Greek orthodox and Lutheranizing doctrines, Lutheranism coming out particularly in the Christology and in the teaching concerning the sacrament.

Besides this catechism, Zacharias edited the New Testament in modern Greek (Wittenberg, 1622), using the Stephens-Beza text; but the edition did not gain currency.   (PHILIPP MEYER.)

BIBLIOGRAPHY: M. LeQuien, *Oriens Christianus*, ii. 202, Paris, 1740; Fabricius-Harles, *Bibliotheca Græca*, x. 637,

xi. 722, Hamburg, 1807–08; E. Reuss, *Bibliotheca Novi
Testamenti Græci*, p. 100, Brunswick, 1872; E. Legrand,
Bibliographie Hellenique, vol. i. passim and iv. 392, Paris,
1894–95.

ZACHARIAS SCHOLASTICUS (RHETOR):
Bishop of Mitylene and ecclesiastical writer; b. at
Majuma, the port of Gaza; d. probably before 553.
The assumption of this article is that Zacharias
Scholasticus, Zacharias Rhetor, and Zacharias,
brother of Procopius, are one and the same personality. His own writings show that his father's house
was near the monastery of Peter the Iberian, and
that the family was large, that one brother was a
monk and a physician, and that facilities for study
were furnished the sons. Zacharias studied in Alexandria (probably 485–487) at the time when Petrus
Mongus (q.v.) was there as archbishop. He came
into relations with Severus of Antioch at that place,
and a friendship sprang up between them. He was
baptized there, was earnest in performance of religious duties, and took part in the actions of the
Christian students against the idolaters. He regarded the monks with respect, but thought his
brother Stephen too delicate to endure the monastic
life. After a short visit at home, he went to Berytus
in 487 to pursue studies in law, where Leontius, son
of Eudoxius, was one of his teachers, and perhaps
also Diodorus; he also read diligently in the Church
Fathers. He emphasizes the fact that he held aloof
from the bishop of Phenicia, since he held with the
monks in Egypt and Palestine, i.e., was a straight
Monophysite. With all his strong piety Zacharias
did not become a monk, as did so many of his acquaintances, in this matter probably following both
his father's wish and his own disinclination for that
mode of life. In this he seems to have been confirmed by the advice of Peter the Iberian. After
his studies were completed, he returned home, but
soon after, possibly in 492, he was settled in Constantinople as an advocate, and the two names of
Scholasticus (" advocate ") and Rhetor (" plead-
er ") are explained by his vocation there. He seems
soon to have gained an enviable position, though
knowledge of his exact estate is not known because
of ignorance of the significance of terms expressing
functions. He appears at any rate as an assessor
of the emperor's chancellor or *comes patrimonii*, and
is once addressed as " high chancellor." The position
of advocate was a step toward higher state offices.
Among his friends were men of influence, such as
the eunuch Eupraxius and Misael, both marked for
piety and also interested in ecclesiastical affairs.
Zacharias did not neglect ecclesiastical opportunities, and when Severus visited the capital, the two
came into close relationship. A speedy change from
worldly to ecclesiastical position was not unusual at
that time. In 527 Zacharias was still a layman (his
writing against the Manicheans could not have been
composed before that time); in 536 he had taken
part in the synod at Constantinople as bishop of
Mitylene. He attended as a delegate for whom it
was the unpleasant duty to summon the Patriarch
Anthimus to answer before the fathers; he took
part in the discussion and agreed to the condemnation of Anthimus. He heartily favored the Henoticon of Zeno (see HENOTICON), and denounced the
fanatical exclusiveness of the Alexandrians. Of his
later years nothing is known, not even the date of
his death. At the fifth ecumenical council of 553
Mitylene was represented by the Metropolitan
Palladius.

Zacharias was the author of a number of writings:
(1) A church history is contained in Syriac in Cod.
Mus. Brit. Add. 17, 202, ed. in *Anecdota Syriaca*,
J. P. N. Land (3 vols., Leyden, 1870); K. Ahrens
and G. Krüger (Leipsic, 1899; in German with
notes, introduction, and commentary); and F. J.
Hamilton and E. W. Brooks, *The Syriac Chronicle
Known as that of Zachariah of Mitylene* (London,
1899). The " Church History " is only books iii.
to vi. out of a composite work in twelve books,
which was a universal history from creation to the
author's (editor's?) time (568–569), and deals with
the period 450–491, not claiming, however, to continue the " history " of Socrates, Sozomen, or Theodoret. The author's horizon is limited to Alexandria
and Palestine, and contains sources of great value
which Evagrius (q.v.) used. It must have been
written before 515. The general work was used by
Michael the Syrian and Bar Hebræus, who regard it
as the work of Zacharias, whom they designate
bishop of Mitylene. Zacharias wrote also a life of
Severus, patriarch of Antioch (editions are: Syriac
by J. Spanuth, Göttingen, 1893; Syriac and French
by M. A. Kugener, Paris, 1903), which aims to dis-
prove the charges of idolatry made against Severus,
and is an account of the times possessing great value.
He wrote accounts of Peter the Iberian, Theodore
of Antinoe in Egypt, and of the Egyptian ascetic
Isaiah, of which only the last is extant (ed. Land
in *Anecdota Syriaca*, ut sup.; E. W. Brooks, in
CSCO, 3 ser., xxv. 1–16, Paris, 1907). Polemic writings of Zacharias are: *De mundi opificio* (ed. J. F.
Boissonade, Paris, 1836; *MPG*, lxxxv. 1011–1144),
a dialogue between the author and a pupil of the
Alexandrian philosopher Ammonius, in which appear
also Ammonius and a physician, whose arguments
are contested (the *De immortalitate animæ* of Æneas
of Gaza is the model); a treatise against certain writings by a Manichean (editions: Demetrakopulos,
Bibliotheca ecclesiastica, pp. 1–18, Leipsic, 1866;
J. B. Pitra, *Analecta sacra*, v. 67–70, Paris, 1888).
A manuscript in Moscow has a preface, not by the
author, which explains the title. The work was
composed while Zacharias was still a layman and
is to be brought into connection with the edict of
527 concerning the Manicheans. It appears that
the author had written " Seven Chapters " against
the Manicheans before this. What remains in the
manuscripts can be but a fragment.

(G. KRÜGER.)

BIBLIOGRAPHY: W. Cave, *Historia litteraria*, i. 462, 579,
Basel, 1741; K. Seitz, *Die Schule von Gaza*, Heidelberg,
1892; M. A. Kugener, in *Revue de l'orient chrétien*, v (1900),
201–214, 461–480; idem, in *Byzantische Zeitschrift*, ix
(1900), 464–470; H. Grisar, *Hist. of Rome and the Popes
in the Middle Ages*, i. 67, 102, London, 1911.

ZAHN, tsän, JOSEF: Roman Catholic; b. at
Stradtprozelten (near Aschaffenburg, 23 m. e.s.e.
of Frankfort) June 20, 1862. He studied at the
universities of Würzburg and Vienna, 1880–85;
became subregent of the priests' seminary at Würz-

burg, 1889; in 1903 professor of pastoral theology and homiletics at the University of Strasburg; in 1910 regent at Würzburg, and professor of dogmatics there in 1911. He is the author of *Apologetische Grundgedanken bei den Kirchenschriftstellern der drei ersten Jahrhunderten* (1890); cooperated with J. Grimm in *Das Leben Jesu* (2 vols., Regensburg, 1903–06); writing also *Einführung in die christliche Mystik* (Paderborn, 1908); and *Vollkommenheitsideale* (vol. i., 1911).

ZAHN, THEODOR: German Protestant; b. at Mörs (17 m. w. of Essen) Oct. 10, 1838. He was educated at the universities of Basel, Erlangen, and Berlin (1854–58); was teacher in the gymnasium at Neustrelitz (1861–65); became a lecturer at the University of Göttingen (1865), privat-docent (1868), associate professor (1871); professor at Kiel (1877), at Erlangen (1878), and at Leipsic (1888), while in 1892 he returned to Erlangen as professor of pedagogics and New-Testament exegesis, a position which he still retains. His literary activity has been great, commensurate with his responsibility as virtual leader of the conservatives in New-Testament criticism. Among his works may be named: *Die Voraussetzungen rechter Weihnachtsfeier* (Berlin, 1865); *Marcellus von Ancyra* (Gotha, 1867); *Der Hirt des Hermas untersucht* (1868); *Ignatius von Antiochien* (1873); *Konstantin der Grosse und die Kirche* (Hanover, 1876); *Weltverkehr und Kirche während der drei ersten Jahrhunderte* (1877); *Geschichte des Sonntags vornehmlich in der alten Kirche* (1878); *Forschungen zur Geschichte des neutestamentlichen Kanons und der altkirchlichen Literatur* (7 vols., Erlangen, 1881–1903); *Cyprian von Antiochien und die deutschen Fausttage* (1882); *Missionsmethoden im Zeitalter der Apostel* (1886); *Geschichte des neutestamentlichen Kanons* (2 vols., 1889–92); *Einige Bemerkungen zu Adolf Harnacks Prüfung der Geschichte des neutestamentlichen Kanons* (Leipsic, 1889); *Brot und Wein im Abendmahl der alten Kirche* (1892); *Das Evangelium des Petrus* (1893); *Das apostolische Symbol, eine Skizze seiner Geschichte und eine Prüfung seines Inhalts* (1893); *Die bleibende Bedeutung des neutestamentlichen Kanons* (1898); *Einleitung in das Neue Testament* (2 vols., 1897–1900; Eng. transl., *Introduction to the N. T.*, 3 vols., Edinburgh, 1909); *Die Dormitio Sanctæ Virginis und das Haus des Johannes Marcus* (1899); *Brot und Salz aus Gottes Wort in zwanzig Predigten* (1901); *Grundriss der Geschichte des neutestamentlichen Kanons* (1901; 2d ed., 1904). He has also edited, in collaboration with O. von Gebhardt and A. Harnack, the *Patrum apostolicorum opera* (3 vols., Leipsic, 1875–77; 5th ed., 1905; minor ed., 1877), to which he contributed the volume on *Ignatii et Polycarpi epistulæ, martyria, fragmenta* (1876); *Kommentar zum Neuen Testament* (1903 sqq.), for which he prepared the volumes on Matthew (1903), Galatians (1905), and John (1907); he edited also the Acts of John (Erlangen, 1880).

ZANCHI, dzän'kî, GIROLAMO (HIERONYMUS ZANCHIUS): Calvinistic theologian; b. at Alzano (34 m. n.e. of Milan), Italy, Feb. 2, 1516; d. at Heidelberg Nov. 15, 1590. He was the son of the historian Zanchi, entered the Augustinian order of

regular canons, and completed his linguistic, philosophic, and scholastic studies; he then went with his friend, Count Celso Martinengo of Brescia, to become canon of the Lateran congregation at Lucca, where they met Pietro Martire Vermigli (q.v.) and read the Church Fathers, and then the writings of the Reformers, including Luther, Butzer, Melanchthon, Musculus, Bullinger, and Calvin, by which they were convinced of the truth of Reformation doctrines. By Evangelical preaching Zanchi came into notice and was compelled to flee from Italy, and after traveling he received a call to Strasburg, where he became professor of the Old Testament, dealing with exegesis in great detail. Zanchi was at some pains to emphasize his freedom from partizanship and from attachment to any of the reform parties. The seeds of dissension existed in the Calvinistic predilections of Zanchi and the Lutheran position of his colleague Johann Marbach; but for some time strife was avoided by mutual forbearance, and while Vermigli left Strasburg in 1556, Zanchi stayed on. But the Lutheran position was gradually more strongly stressed, especially against the French congregation. In 1561 Zanchi came under suspicion, especially because of an expressed opinion that the difference concerning the Lord's Supper was of little importance and the dispute mere logomachy. Marbach took the opposite ground and the contest became sharp; mediation ensued, a formula was drawn up, dealing with the Lord's Supper and predestination, by mediators who were called in, and Zanchi signed this with reservations. But Zanchi was blamed by Calvin and other Reformed theologians for yielding, spoke out again freely, and in 1563 gave up his position and went as preacher to Chiavenna, where he was much annoyed by restless Italian agitators. A pestilence broke out, and he went to the mountains near Piuri and wrote an account of the strife with Marbach under the title of *Miscellanea* (1566). A second part was issued after his death. In 1568 he went to Heidelberg as professor, where he soon took front rank as a theologian and was appealed to for answers to vexed questions. In 1572 he wrote *De tribus Elohim sive de uno vero Deo æterno, Patre, Filio, et Spiritu Sancto*, an argument for the unity of God. The work bases its conclusions upon the Old and the New Testament and upon analogies in nature, and its exegesis is arbitrary. Related to this is a second work, *De natura Dei sive de divinis attributis* —a kind of religious philosophy, and a third, *De operibus Dei intra spatium sex dierum creatis*, dealing with God as creator and with cosmology. Another work was begun but not finished—*De primi hominis lapsu, de peccato et de lege Dei*. When Ludwig VI. in 1576 succeeded Friedrich III. in the Palatinate, Lutheran reform was pressed and most of the professors had to give up their posts. Zanchi found a post in the newly founded school at Neustadt-on-the-Hardt, declining calls to Leyden and Antwerp, and there continued till he died. In 1577 to him was given the task of assisting Ursinus in the creation of a confession, which was used in the *Harmonia confessionum fidei* of 1581. After the death of Ludwig and the return of the Palatinate to Calvinism, Zanchi had an opportunity to return to

Heidelberg, but decided to stay at Neustadt. He was buried in the University Church at Heidelberg, where he died while on a visit.

Zanchi had a keen intellect, warm feelings, consecutiveness in thought and discussion, tenacity in holding to his convictions combined with friendliness and understanding of others. He ever hoped for a reunited Church. His opinions were highly valued and his counsel was often sought. He was well equipped philosophically and theologically, and his horizon was wider than that of most of his contemporaries. Though he was neither original nor creative, he was one of the most learned among the theologians of the sixteenth century.

(JOHANNES FICKER.)

BIBLIOGRAPHY: A letter by Zanchi to Queen Elizabeth is in W. Ames' *Fresh Suit against Human Ceremonies*, Rotterdam (?), 1633, and his " Confession touching the Supper of the Lord " is in R. Hill, *Pathway to Prayer*, London, 1615. Consult: C. Schmidt, in *TSK*, xxxii (1859), 625–708; M. Adam, *Decades duæ continentes vitas theologorum*, pp. 148–153, Frankfort, 1618; C. A. Salig, *Vollständige Historie der augspurgischen Konfession*, i. 441 sqq., iii. passim, Halle, 1730; D. Gerdes, *Specimen Italiæ reformatæ*, pp. 351–353, Leyden, 1765; G. B. Gallizioli, *Memorie istoriche e letterarie della vita e delle opere di G. Zanchi*, Bergamo, 1785; K. Sudhoff, *C. Olevianus und Z. Ursinus*, pp. 333 sqq., 341 sqq., Elberfeld, 1857; J. F. A. Gillett, *Crato von Crafftheim und seine Freunde*, ii. 130 sqq., 164 sqq., 191 sqq., Frankfort, 1860; F. H. R. von Frank, *Theologie der Concordienformel*, vols., iii.–iv., Erlangen, 1863–1865; H. L. J. Heppe, *Dogmatik des deutschen Protestantismus*, vol. iii., Frankfort, 1866; Paulus, in *Der Katholik*, lxxi. 1 (1891), 201–228; idem, *Die Strassburger Reformatoren und die Gewissensfreiheit*, pp. 83 sqq., Freiburg, 1895; F. W. Cuno, *Daniel Tossanus*, Amsterdam, 1898; H. Preuss, *Der Antichrist am Ausgange des Mittelalters*, Leipsic, 1906; *ADB*, xliv. 679–683; *KL*, xii. 1867–68.

ZAPLETAL, tsäp'letāl, **VINCENZ:** Swiss Roman Catholic; b. at Willimau, Moravia, Jan. 15, 1867. He was educated at the gymnasium of Olmütz, Moravia, after which he studied philosophy and theology at the Dominican Seminary in Vienna, Orientalia at the Biblical academy in Jerusalem (1891–93), and Hebrew and Syriac at the University of Vienna. He made a tour of the peninsula of Sinai and the East Jordan country, and since 1893 has been professor of Old-Testament exegesis at the University of Freiburg, Switzerland. He has written: *Hermeneutica Biblica* (Freiburg, 1897; 2d ed., 1908); *Der Totemismus und die Religion Israels* (1901); *Grammatica linguæ hebraicæ* (Paderborn, 1902); *Der Schöpfungsbericht der Genesis* (Freiburg, 1902); *Alttestamentliches* (1903); *Die Metrik des Buches Kohelet* (1904); *Das Buch Kohelet kritisch und metrisch untersucht* (1905); *Das Deboralied erklärt* (1905); *Der biblische Samson* (1906); a critical edition of the Hebrew text of Ecclesiastes (Halle, 1905); *Die Hohelied* (Freiburg, 1907); *De poesi Hebræorum in Veteri Testamento* (1909); and *L'Exégèse catholique de l. A. T.* (1911).

ZAREPHATH. See PHENICIA, PHENICIANS, I., § 4.

ZEAL: An active state of mind compounded of feeling and will and intent upon an objective purpose. The Hebr. ḳin'ah and the Gk. zēlos imply a fiery consuming element analogous to the motive of zeal. As an equivocal term, " zeal " was originally employed now with a good and now with a bad implication. When roused to a passionate degree, it

becomes wrath; when consuming itself in self-seeking, it becomes jealousy. When, in the Old Testament, jealousy is frequently attributed to God (Ex. xxxiv. 14), the mode of expression is anthropopathic. In no other way could God's personality be presented and emphasized. God's jealousy, like his wrath, is the expression of his righteousness and holiness, no less necessary to his being than love. As a loving God, he must chastise his faithless spouse Israel (Ezek. xvi. 38). God is also jealous for his people against the heathen (Ezek. xxxvi. 5–6, xxxviii. 19). Men who are jealous for God reap the reward of praise, as the Levites (Ex. xxxii. 25–29) and Phinehas (Num. xxv. 11); even though the jealous Elijah is subjected to correction (1 Kings xix. 14).

In the New Testament divine jealousy recedes to the background (cf. I Cor. x. 22; II Cor. xi. 2). The Greek zēlos, zēloun, zēlōtēs, occurring in the New Testament thirty-three times, are used exclusively of men. As God, in the Old Testament, had been jealous for his holiness, his holy ones now show the same zeal, Jesus above all (John ii. 17; II Cor. vii. 11). Yet zeal may bear a perverse motive, as on the part of the Jews (Rom. x. 2). Zeal is therefore capable of ennoblement, and God himself does not despise it. Without earnest prophets and apostles, a living religion is not conceivable: without zeal there is no triumph of the Gospel; without the fiery zeal of perfected Christian personalities, no heroic deeds of the Christian faith. Lukewarmness betokens spiritual death (Rev. iii. 15–16). But zeal has also its perverse side. It must not be the energy of baser motives, lest it become intolerant bigotry and persecuting fanaticism, as in the instance of Saul of Tarsus (Phil. iii. 6).   ARNOLD RÜEGG†.

ZEALOTS: The Biblical term (Hebr. ḳenaim; Gk. zēlōtai) for those who in glowing love and holy anger act against all who would scorn God's honor and revelation. A particular use of the term is shown in I Cor. xiv. 12, where Paul describes the Corinthians as zealous for the divine gifts. In the Old Testament the passion is represented as manifesting itself in behalf of the law or against idolatry (Ex. xx. 5, xxxiv. 14; Deut. iv. 24), while in the New Testament Paul describes himself as formerly a zealot in behalf of the traditions of the fathers (Gal. i. 14), and the Christian community at Jerusalem is also said to have been zealous for the law (Acts xxi. 20). The word is used in exactly the same sense in the Talmud of those who discountenanced contempt of the law (Mishna, *Sanhedrim*, ix. 6). This general sense may have been that in which the surname of the Apostle Simon Zelotes was applied. A narrower application was to that party which would push to the extreme opposition to the Roman overlordship, and Josephus repeatedly employs the word in this sense. He implies (*War*, IV., iii. 9) that the name was one the members of the party assumed. In the Talmud this usage is not found, clearly because, while the Pharisaism of the Talmud assumes the anti-Gentile pose of the zealots, the nationalizing significance was forgotten; yet it reappears in this sense in the very late " Fathers " of Rabbi Nathan, chap. vi.

The origins of the party of zealots are in close connection with Pharisaism (see PHARISEES AND SAD-

DUCEES). The Pharisees had their roots in the Hasideans of the early Maccabean times, and they remained a party of scribes in which religious interests far outweighed all others. But by a transformation they developed away from the Hasideans, attempted to get closer to the life of the people, and to have larger influence upon the Maccabean state. This brought them into connection with politics, which indeed their ideals did not forbid. They could see in heathen control of the Holy Land the working of divine providence, even though this seemed to contradict the choice by God of the Hebrews as his own people while it did not oppose efforts to set aside this heathen control. Their religious motives were often made politically effective by the Pharisees, as when they won over the Maccabean princes, stirred up trouble for Alexander Jannæus when he sided with the Sadducees, actually ruled through Queen Alexandra, protected the weak Hyrcanus, and furnished trouble for Herod the Great. This makes intelligible the report of Josephus that after the introduction of the census into Judæa by Quirinius (q.v.) the Galilean Judas (a man learned in the law), in common with Sadduc the Pharisee, aroused the people against the Romans and thereby furnished the basis for a party which in general was in full agreement with the Pharisees, but inspired with a boundless love for freedom would recognize God alone as lord and king, thereby occasioning the troubles which came later under Gessius Florus and ended in the destruction of Jerusalem (*Ant.*, XVIII., i. 1, 6). The war party which came into control in the time of Gessius Florus was by Josephus called that of the zealots (*War*, IV., iii. 10), whose origin in the Pharisees he recognizes, though the party of Judas is not to be confused with Pharisees, Sadducees, or Essenes (*War*, II., viii. 1). As a Pharisee and friend of the Romans he had an interest, indeed, in transferring responsibility for the war from the Pharisees and emphasizing the distinction between the two parties. Yet one may not with Montet (see bibliography) think of the zealots as a combination half Pharisee and half Sadducee. They emphasized the theocratic ideals of the Pharisees and then pursued these to their extreme consequences. And since the Sadduc mentioned above may well be the pupil of Shammai, it is probable that this heathen-hating school contributed ideas as well as persons to the zealots of the Jewish war. Thus is explained the proverbial regard of the zealots for the Sabbath together with their willingness to fight on that day in accordance with Shammai's principles. Yet one must not identify the school of Shammai with the zealots, who allowed to obtrude more and more the national, social, and material in place of the legal and theocratic.

The insurrection provoked by Judas and Sadduc made so little impression that a decade afterward Gamaliel could speak as is reported in Acts v. 37. But there were consequences which appeared afterward in Judas' own family, since two sons were crucified by the procurator Tiberius Alexander. Abortive attempts were made to carry out their ideas till the times of Gessius Florus, when open insurrection broke out, and then was affixed the name zealots. The historical relationship with the earlier movement is proved by the connection with the insurrection of Menahem the son of Judas, also a man learned in the law (scribe), and some of his relations. While some of the zealots belonged to the business class, this latter was generally in favor of peace. The zealots did not scruple to employ the bandits or sicarii, indeed were themselves in the later Jewish period considered as identical with them. Their fanaticism caused them to be disowned and denounced by the Pharisees (Josephus, *War*, IV., iii. 9). But even in these times their Pharisaic origin is clear, since they never entered into relationship with the Sadducaic priesthood, while something is evident always of the theocratic ideas with which their development began, which were drawn from the Old Testament.

(F. SIEFFERT†.)

BIBLIOGRAPHY: J. Derenbourg, *Essai sur l'hist. et la géographie de la Palestine d'après les thalmuds*, pp. 237 sqq., Paris, 1867; J. Wellhausen, *Die Pharisäer und die Sadducäer*, pp. 22 sqq., 110 sqq., Greifswald, 1874; H. Graetz, *Geschichte der Judäer*, vol. iii. passim, Leipsic, 1888; Schürer, *Geschichte*, i. 486–487, 573–574, 617 sqq., Eng. transl., I., ii. 80–81, 177, 229; Oppenhaim, in *Literaturblatt des Orients*, 1849, cols. 289–292; *JE*, xii. 639–643; *DCG*, ii. 846; the commentaries on Matthew at x. 4, and those on Mark at iii. 18; the histories of Israel which deal with the period of the Jewish War. The Assumption of Moses (see PSEUDEPIGRAPHA, 6) is an embodiment of the ideas of the zealots.

ZECHARIAH, zec″a-rai′ā.

I. The Prophet: The name of the Prophet Zechariah occurs several times in the book called after him (i. 1, 7, vii. 1, 8) and also in Ezra v. 1, vi. 14. Berechiah, the son of Iddo, is mentioned as his father, while he himself is called in Ezra v. 1, vi. 14 " the son of Iddo," these passages evidently giving his genealogy in abridged form. If the Iddo alluded to in Neh. xii. 4, 16 is identical with the father of Zechariah, the prophet was of a priestly family; the statement of Ezra that he was active at the same time as Haggai under Darius Hystaspis agrees with the dates in the first part of the book, which includes the period from Nov., 520, to Dec., 518.

II. The Book.—1. Chapters i.–viii.: The book which bears the name of Zechariah consists of two principal parts: chaps. i.–viii. and chaps. ix.–xiv. These divisions are so sharply defined that each must be treated separately: the first, containing frequent mention of the prophet's name and numerous dates, consists of a short introduction, i. 1–5, and a series of visions, i. 6–vi. 8, with an addition, vi. 9–15, and a discourse regarding the continuance of the fasts, chapters vii.–viii. The introduction, i. 1–5, dated in the eighth month of the second year of Darius's reign, that is, Nov., 520, a few months later than Haggai's first discourse (i. 1), contains a solemn warning not to follow the example of the fathers who would not listen to the prophet's admonitions and therefore had to be forced to believe in the truth of the prophetic sayings by the misfortunes that befell them. Then follows a series of eight

1. Analysis and Contents.

visions, skilfully combined. The date at the beginning, the twenty-fourth of the eleventh month of the year in question (Feb., 519), refers undoubtedly to all the visions. The theme is the approaching deliverance from the oppression under which Israel suffers. Israel's oppressor, the world-power Babylon, is to feel the divine punishment, Israel is to be delivered, Yahweh's temple is to be rebuilt, and Zerubbabel will be installed as a secular and Joshua as a religious ruler, and everything that delays the period of salvation, above all, the people's sin, shall be removed. The visions are in the main easily understood, but there are some obscurities in the details, resulting doubtless from corruption of the text. For instance, in the first vision (i. 8–17), Ewald omits the words " riding upon a red horse," and adds a horse of a fourth color to the three mentioned later on. Part of the fourth vision is also somewhat obscure. It is stated that Joshua and his companions (the other priests) are signs that God's promise will be fulfilled. This promise runs: " I will bring forth my servant the Branch " (cf. Isa. xxiii. 5). As elsewhere in Zechariah and in Haggai, the messianic hope centers about Zerubbabel; hardly any other person can be meant by " the Branch." However, in this case the words " I will bring forth " are rather strange, since Zerubbabel was then in Jerusalem. Previous attempts to solve this problem are not satisfactory and the supposition is forced that the original text, which alluded to Zerubbabel, was later revised in a messianic sense. In the seventh vision v. 6 should read " their sin " instead of " their resemblance "; this sin is represented as a woman, who is borne in a closed ephah-measure by two angels to Babylon. The idea is, therefore, that Israel is to be purified from sin, while the guilt and its consequent punishment shall fall upon Babylon.

What was the connection between these visions and the contemporary political situation in western Asia? Did historical events induce the prophet to

2. Relation to Political Events. expect the fall of Babylon; or was he influenced by the general trend of prophetic thought? In the first years of Darius, there were several revolts, threatening the destruction of the Persian empire. In Babylon, Nidintubal assumed the name of Nebuchadrezzar and sought to reestablish the Babylonian empire. Darius, indeed, succeeded in crushing this usurper (Babylon was taken between Oct., 521, and Feb., 520), but during this campaign most of the other provinces rebelled, especially Media and Persia. While Darius marched against these provinces, Babylon revolted anew, under another Nebuchadrezzar, but in 519 the city was again taken, and by the spring of that year the other revolts had been suppressed. Syria was never involved in these troubles. It might be conjectured that in the book of Zechariah Babylon signifies the Persian empire as heir to the Babylonian, but when there are taken into account the part played by Cyrus in Deutero-Isaiah as the conqueror of Babylon and the dependence of Zechariah and Haggai upon Deutero-Isaiah it appears that the prophets of the time still saw in Babylon the great enemy and found in the new hostilities against that city a fulfilment of the older

prophecies. Hence they did not see in Darius an enemy of Israel, but rather an instrument of divine vengeance who would bring the heathen world into subjection to Israel's God and to his vicegerent Zerubbabel.

The recital of a symbolical action of the prophet (vi. 9) is appended to the visions. Here also the text appears corrupt. The original text probably

3. The Closing Section. stated that the prophet was commanded to receive from four Jews, who had come from Babylon to Jerusalem, gold and silver, and to make thereof a crown for Zerubbabel; for the latter was to complete the Temple and rule as king in perfect concord with the high-priest Joshua. The fact that this promise was not fulfilled led to the changes in the text, so that now Joshua takes the place of Zerubbabel and the crown is to be preserved in the Temple for a future time. The first division of the book closes with a prophetic discourse (vii.–viii.), dated on the fifth day of the ninth month of the fourth year of Darius (i.e., Dec., 518). The Temple was nearly completed (Ezra vi. 15) and the question arose whether the fasts in memory of the downfall of the nation should be continued; as, however, the messianic promise of the previous chapter had not been fulfilled, the people hesitated to abandon their mourning. Zechariah declares that God does not require fasting, but justice and neighborly love, and that precisely the neglect of this command brought destruction upon Israel; he then proceeds to encourage the people in their messianic faith by the assurance of Yahweh's love and of the coming messianic salvation. The present time is the turning-point; a great change will take place; fasting will no longer be necessary, and all their sorrow will be turned to joy.

In these chapters there is a clear picture of Zechariah. He did not express any new prophetic ideas, but only repeated those of his great predecessors; nevertheless, he grasped those ideas in all their purity, and the discourse in chaps. vii.–viii. must be regarded as a typical specimen of prophetic preaching. Although both Haggai and Zechariah were disappointed in the hopes they associated with Zerubbabel, their importance for the postexilic period can not be overestimated, since they reawakened the faith of the people at a time when the latter were discouraged and on the point of abandoning the messianic hope. A new element in angelology appears in this book, namely, the interpreting angel, who explains the visions to the prophet; there is also a tendency to personify the active forces as is shown in the representation of one side of the concept of justice by Satan.

2. Chapters ix.–xiv.: In the second division the reader enters an entirely new world. The name of the prophet and exact dates are lacking, instead there exist only the titles ix. 1 and xii. 1 with the

1. Chapters ix.–xi. peculiar formula: " The burden of the word of the Lord," which appears elsewhere only in the book of Malachi. There are no direct references to the events of the years 520–518 and the whole train of thought is dissimilar. Syria, Phenicia, and Philistia are denounced, ix. 1–8; Zion is to rejoice over its messianic king, who comes as a pious and humble victor to govern the old extent of the land of Israel in undisturbed peace (9–10); the exiled Israelites are to return to their homes (11–12); God arms Judah and Ephraim and allows them to massacre " the sons of Yawan " (the Greeks; 13–15), and the Israelites then enjoy the messianic glory in their land (16–17). God's wrath is directed against the wicked shepherds of Judah to whom he will give leaders " out of him," meaning from Judah; with God's help Judah and Joseph (Ephraim) will conquer their enemies and return to their homes (x. 5, 6) while Egypt and Assyria will be humbled. In xi. 4–17 there is a peculiar narration wherein the prophet himself is made to impersonate the fortunes of his people. He is to become the shepherd of the sacred flock, the buyers and sellers of which think only of their own enrichment while the shepherds neglect their charge. As shepherd he takes two staves, " welfare " and " union " (A.V., " beauty " and " bands ") to protect the people. In the course of a month he removes the three shepherds; but the flock becomes unfriendly and he decides to resign his office. He breaks his staff " welfare," whereby the alliance between the people and the other nations is dissolved. The owners of the flock show their contempt by paying him thirty shekels, the wages of a slave; at God's command he casts this sum into the temple treasury (according to the Aramaic version; A. V., " to the potter in the house of the Lord "). This clearly shows that the insult was noted and that it was to be reckoned against the owners of the flock. Thereupon the prophet breaks his staff " union " so that the brotherhood of Judah and Israel is destroyed; only a third of the flock is spared, but the remnant will be recognized by God as his people (xiii. 7–9).

In xii. 1–xiii. 6 it appears that Jerusalem is now attacked by the whole heathen world, but the heathen nations themselves are destroyed and Jerusalem is not captured. Chap. xiv. describes anew the last battle for Jerusalem, with the singular discrepancy, however, that the city is first taken and plundered before the judgment of God overtakes the heathen. God, surrounded by his angels, appears on the Mount of Olives, which is rent by an earthquake. Now begins the messianic age, which is like a perpetual day without cold or burning heat. The outlines of the land are changed, it becomes an immense plain above which rises Jerusalem alone; ever-flowing streams issue from the city and run toward the east and the west. Those heathen who have survived the dreadful defeat recognize Yahweh's rule and come yearly to Jerusalem for the feast of tabernacles.

For a long time these chapters were believed to be by the same hand as chapters i.–viii.; it was only the citation of Zech. xi. 12–13 in Matt. xxvii. 9–10 as a word of Jeremiah that gave rise to a different view. Joseph Mede, in *Dissertationum ecclesiasticarum triga* (London, 1653), conjectured that chaps. ix.–xi. were by Jeremiah. This hypothesis, although valueless, led to a closer study of the book and at the present time but few critics attribute chaps. ix.–xiv. to Zechariah. Indeed, it seems almost impossible that the

2. Chapters xii.-xiv.

3. Authorship.

same author could have written i.–viii. and ix.–xiv. The marked characteristics of the earlier chapters are lacking in the later, and the political situation, as well as the prophetic quality, is totally unlike. Of these chapters, xii.–xiv. (excepting xiii. 7–9) appear to constitute a typical specimen of the deuteroprophetic literature. A conclusive proof of the late composition of this section is the announcement of the cessation of prophecy (xiii. 2–3), since this indicates a period when the prophets who appeared in public (not purely literary prophets like the author) were degenerate and deceivers; that is, a period when literary study had taken the place of immediate prophetic inspiration. It is, however, unlikely that xii. 1–xiii. 6 is by the same hand as xiv., especially since Jerusalem is said to have been taken in xiv., while the contrary is stated in xii.

Strange to say, the portions ix. 1–ix. 17 and xiii. 7–9 are thought by some critics to constitute one of the earliest prophetic writings (from the period before 722 B.C.), while others place this section in the second century B.C. In x. 6–9 the departure of Ephraim and Judah, and in ix. 11 that of the whole people, is assumed as having already taken place. A still more important point is that in ix. 13, " the sons of Yawan," that is the Greeks, appear as enemies whose destruction marks the beginning of the messianic era. This can signify only that the Greeks were then a world-power and that this verse was written after the appearance of Alexander the Great. It is true that the mention of Egypt and Assyria as the two great world-powers recalls Hosea (cf. viii. 13, ix. 3–6); but this name may just as well signify the Ptolemies and the Seleucidæ (cf. also Isa. xxvii. 13), since in later prophetic writings designations from the older prophets are freely adapted to contemporary conditions. The repeated mention of Ephraim alongside of Judah is more significant, but not decisive; for in x. 6 sqq. it appears that Ephraim must first return from captivity. The conclusion therefore follows that some passages in chaps. ix.–x. belong to the Greek period, while nothing certainly proves that the remainder is of earlier date. Chap. xi., with its continuation xiii. 7–9, offers much greater difficulties. Kuenen and others have rightly asserted that the words " to break the brotherhood between Judah and Israel " are incompatible with a postexilic origin. It can not be denied that the condition of the Ephraimitic kingdom under Pekah, when the Ephraimites in alliance with the Arameans attacked Judah, suits this perfectly. The shepherds killed within a month (verse 8) might then be explained by the murders of Zechariah and Shallum (II Kings xv. 8, 13). However, the designation of an Ephraimitic king as " the man that is my fellow," xiii. 7, would be strange. Two Septuagint manuscripts read Israel instead of Jerusalem in verse 14, and in this case the text would refer to conflicts between the capital and the rest of the country; while these can not be proved, they are quite possible in the Greek period (cf. also xii. 7), so that this chapter might also be referred to that epoch. Any satisfactory result as to chapter xi. is therefore impossible, but this has nothing to do with the date of the other chapters, since it can not

4. Isolated Passages.

be proved that they are by the same writer. Thus it appears probable that Zech. ix.–xiv. is composed of at least four prophetic writings or fragments, of which chapters ix., x., and xii.–xiv. at least belong to a late time; the former probably to the Greek and the latter to either the Persian or the Greek period. (F. BUHL.)

BIBLIOGRAPHY: For questions of introduction recourse is to be had to the works named in and under BIBLICAL INTRODUCTION; also: E. W. Hengstenberg, *Dissertations on the Genuineness of Daniel and the Integrity of Zechariah*, New York, 1858; E. F. J. von Ortenberg, *Die Bestandtheile des Buches Sacharja*, Gotha, 1859; B. Stade, in *ZATW*, i (1881), 1 sqq., ii (1882), 151 sqq., 275 sqq.; C. H. H. Wright, *Zechariah and his Prophecies . . . in Relation to Modern Criticism*, London, 1879 (holds to the unity of the book); W. Stärk, *Untersuchungen über die Composition und Abfassungszeit von Zach 9–14*, Halle, 1891; B. Blake, *How to Read the Prophets*, part 1, New York, 1892; G. K. Grützmacher, *Untersuchung über den Ursprung der in Zach. ix.–xiv. vorliegenden Prophetien*, Heidelberg, 1892; N. J. Rubinkam, *Second Part of . . . Zechariah*, Basel, 1892; W. H. Kosters, *Widerherstellung Israels*, Heidelberg, 1895; T. K. Cheyne, *Jewish Religious Life after the Exile*, New York, 1898; E. Sellin, *Studien zur Entstehungsgeschichte der jüdischen Gemeinde*, ii. 63 sqq., Leipsic, 1900; J. Boehmer, in *NKZ*, 1901, pp. 717 sqq.; A. van Hoonacker, in *Revue biblique*, 1902, pp. 161 sqq.; J. W. Rothstein, *Die Nachtgesichte des Sacharja. Studien zur Sacharjaprophetie und zur jüdischen Geschichte im 1. nachexilischen Jahrhundert*, Leipsic, 1910; Smith, *Prophets; DB*, iv. 967–970; *EB*, iv. 5390–95; *JE*, xii. 645–647.

Commentaries are: J. D. F. Burger, *Études exégétiques et critiques sur le prophète Zacharie*, Strasburg, 1841; J. Calvin, Eng. transl., in *Minor Prophets*, 5 vols., Edinburgh, 1846–49; T. V. Moore, *The Prophets of the Restoration*, New York, 1856; W. Neumann, Stuttgart, 1860; A. Köhler, 2 vols., Erlangen, 1861–63; R. Wardlaw, in *Posthumous Works*, vol. vii., Edinburgh, 1862; L. Reinke, Münster, 1864; H. Cowles, *Minor Prophets*, New York, 1866; E. Henderson, *Book of the Twelve Minor Prophets*, new ed., Andover, 1868; C. F. Keil, Edinburgh, 1868; E. B. Pusey, *The Minor Prophets*, new ed., Oxford, 1877, New York, 1885; C. J. Bredenkamp, Erlangen, 1879; W. J. Deane, in *Pulpit Commentary*, New York, 1880; H. Ewald, *Commentary on the Prophets*, vol. v., London, 1881; E. G. King, *The Yalkut on Zechariah*, Cambridge, 1882; J. van Eaton, *Expository . . . Lectures on . . . Zechariah*, Pittsburg, 1883; W. L. Alexander, *Zechariah, his Visions and Warnings*, London, 1885; T. T. Perowne, in *Cambridge Bible*, New York, 1888; S. Lasserre, Montauban, 1891; C. von Orelli, *The Twelve Minor Prophets*, New York, 1893; G. A. Smith, in *Expositor's Bible*, London, 1896–97; K. Marti, Freiburg, 1892, and Tübingen, 1904.

ZEDEKIAH, zed"e-kai'ā: Nineteenth and last king of Judah (597–586), son of Josiah, successor of Jehoiachin. By the sudden death of Josiah his sons Jehoahaz and then Jehoiakim (qq.v.) came to the throne, the last named, at first a vassal of Egypt and later of Babylonia, revolting from Babylonia and bringing about the interference of the Babylonian king. His successor was his son Jehoiachin (q.v.), who with a number of his subjects was deported to Babylon, while his uncle Zedekiah was made king in his place. In other circumstances Zedekiah might have made a good king, but the situation was too difficult for him to control. He lacked the firmness of will and the courage to restrain the fanatical elements among his people, especially those which counseled attempts at national independence. The diplomacy of Egypt, perhaps intensified by a change of rulers there, and the unrest of the neighboring states induced a tentative revolt from Babylonian vassalage, on account of which Zedekiah was com-

pelled to journey to Babylon, where he seems to have conciliated Nebuchadrezzar. When Hophra came to the throne in Egypt, a false patriotism in Judah brought about revolt in Judah from Babylon in 588, and in 587 Nebuchadrezzar began the siege of Jerusalem. Relief seemed about to come from Hophra, and the siege was raised for a brief time, only to be renewed; the wall was breached, and Zedekiah tried to escape, getting as far as Jericho, when he was captured and taken before Nebuchadrezzar at Riblah; his sons were slain before his eyes, he was then blinded and carried in chains to Babylon, where he died in prison. (R. KITTEL.)

BIBLIOGRAPHY: The literature on the period as given under AHAB; and ISRAEL, HISTORY OF; and the articles in the Bible dictionaries.

ZEISBERGER, DAVID: Moravian missionary to the American Indians; b. at Zauchenthal (a hamlet in Moravia) Apr. 11, 1721; d. at Goshen, O., Nov. 17, 1808. When he was five years old, his parents fled with him to Herrnhut, and in this Moravian center he received his first training. He was then sent, after his father and mother had already emigrated to Georgia, to the Moravian settlement of Herrendyk, Holland, but the discipline was so stern that he ran away to England, where Oglethorpe assisted him to rejoin his parents in Georgia. With his brother Moravians he left Georgia in 1740 and was one of those who built the Pennsylvania towns of Nazareth and Bethlehem. In 1743 he was designated a member of the escort to accompany Count Zinzendorf on his return to Europe, nor was it until just before the ship sailed that his unwillingness to leave America became manifest, and he was permitted to remain. Soon afterward he resolved to devote his life to the evangelization of the American Indians, and from 1745 until 1807 he labored unceasingly in this cause. Studying first Delaware and Onondaga, he later acquired Mohican, Monsey, and Chippewa. His initial work was at Shamokin, Pa., and Onondaga, N. Y. (1745–50), and after a visit to Europe in behalf of his mission, he returned to Onondaga in 1751, but was forced by the outbreak of the French and Indian War to return to Bethlehem, though he was a sachem and keeper of records to the Six Nations and an adopted member of the Monsey tribe. In 1755–62 he was largely employed in work among the Connecticut Indians, and during the war with Pontiac he was in charge of the Moravian Indians, whom he accompanied to Wyalusing, Pa., on the close of hostilities. He established a Monsey mission on the Alleghany River in 1767, and in 1770 commenced the building of the town of Friedenstadt on the Beaver. In 1772 he organized a mission on the Muskingum, in Ohio, and during the American Revolution it was mainly his influence that kept the Delawares from joining the British side. The Wyandottes, in revenge, broke up Zeisberger's mission in 1781, and he and his fellow missionaries were tried at Detroit as American spies, but were acquitted. In the year following nearly a hundred Christian Indians were massacred by settlers at Gnadenhütten, one of the many missions that Zeisberger founded, and he then led the remnant to the Clinton River, Mich., and thence to New Salem,

O. (1787), and to his new settlement of Fairfield, Ont. (1791). In 1789 he was at last able to bring back a part of his Indians to the Tuscarawas Valley, O., where Congress granted them a large tract of land, and there he founded his last settlement, Goshen, where he passed the remainder of his life.

Among all the non-Roman Catholic missionaries to the American Indians Zeisberger deserves a foremost place. Though almost none of the settlements founded by him survived him, and although the immediate results of his work were small, yet his devotion to his cause was unsurpassed and his influence on his wards by no means ended with his death. His works thus far published are *Delaware Indian and English Spelling-Book* (Philadelphia, 1776); *Collection of Hymns for the Christian Indians* (in Delaware; 1803); *Sermons to Children* (in Delaware; 1803); *History of our Lord . . . Jesus Christ* (Delaware harmony of the four Gospels, translated from S. Lieberkühn's harmony; 1821); *Diary, 1781–1798* (transl. E. F. Bliss, 2 vols., Cincinnati, 1885); *Indian Dictionary, English, German, Iroquois* [Onondaga] *and Algonquin* [Delaware] (ed. E. N. Horsford, Cambridge, 1887); *Essay of an Onondaga Grammar* (Philadelphia, 1888); and *History of North American Indians* (ed. A. B. Hulbert and W. N. Schwarze, Columbus, O., 1910). Some of his most important works still remain unedited, e.g., his "German and Onondaga Lexicon" (in 7 vols.) and his "Delaware Grammar," the manuscripts being preserved partly in the library of the American Philosophical Society at Philadelphia and partly in the library of Harvard University.

BIBLIOGRAPHY: C. G. Blumhardt, *Vie de David Zeisberger*, Neuchâtel, 1844; J. J. Heim, *David Zeisberger*, Bielefeld, 1849; E. De Schweinitz, *Life and Times of David Zeisberger*, Philadelphia, 1838, reissue, 1870; H. Römer, *Die Indianer und ihr Freund David Zeisberger*, Gütersloh, 1890; J. Grunewald, *David Zeisberger*, 2d ed., Niesky, 1895; P. Steiner, *David Zeisberger*, Basel, 1905.

ZELL, tsel, MATTHAEUS and KATHARINA: German Reformer and first Evangelical preacher at Strasburg, and his wife. Matthäus was born at Kaisersberg (98 m. s.w. of Stuttgart) Sept. 21, 1477; d. at Strasburg Jan. 9, 1548. He studied at Mainz, Erfurt, and Freiburg (M.A., 1505; Th.B., 1509), and in 1511 began to lecture at Freiburg, where he became rector in 1517. In 1518 he was called as minister to the cathedral at Strasburg. In 1521 he embraced the principles of the Reformation and began to preach in an Evangelical spirit. Against the attacks of priests and monks people and magistracy protected him, while to the bishop's written attacks he replied in *Christlichen Verantwortung* (1523)—the first historical work dealing with the Reformation in Alsace. In Strasburg the Reformation went forward, priests married, and Zell himself took a wife in that year. When a few months later the bishop banned married priests, Zell answered in his *Appellatio sacerdotum maritorum* (1524). He was disinclined to theological dialectic and dogmatic formulation, was not in the strict sense a scholar nor was he a politician, and severe discipline did not accord with his ideas. Through this he was enabled to avoid the strifes into which many of the Reformers fell. His plan of life and his Christianity were simple, he was a friend of and beloved by the people, dealing kindly even with the Anabaptists. His interests covered more than his own city, and his judgments were always in the interests of peace. He was especially interested in Christian education, and issued various writings in dialogue form, collected in *Frag und Antwort* (1536).

His wife, Katharina, outlived him, and was known as the benefactress of the poor, especially of those who were fugitives for the sake of their religion. Indeed, the pastor's house became in miniature what Strasburg was in a larger sense, the refuge of the persecuted. Katharina's activity was not, however, confined to deeds of charity; she had ability both in discourse and with her pen. She was well read in theology. In the early years of her married life (1524) she wrote a reply to the bishop in defense of her husband, and the same year wrote a consolatory tract to the Evangelical women of Kenzingen. In 1534 she issued with a preface an extract from the hymn-book of the Bohemian Brethren, and had this published in parts so that it might be within reach of the very poor. She also issued an explanation of two psalms and of the Lord's Prayer. She carried on a versatile correspondence with such Reformers as Blaurer, Fagius, Butzer, Pellican, and even with Luther. Her charitable labors she continued till her death in 1562.

(JOHANNES FICKER.)

BIBLIOGRAPHY: There are biographies by: M. Adam, *Vitæ Germanorum theologorum*, pp. 189–192, Heidelberg, 1620; F. Unselt, Strasburg, 1854; E. and E. Haag, *La France protestante*, ix. 555–558, Paris, 1859; E. Lehr, Paris, 1861; I. Walther, Strasburg, 1864; A. Erichson, Strasburg, 1878; and in *ADB*, xlv. 17–18. Consult further, besides works on the Reformation: A. Jung, *Beiträge zu der Geschichte der Reformation*, ii. 28 sqq., 159 sqq., 174 sqq., Strasburg, 1830; T. W. Röhrich, *Geschichte der Reformation im Elsass*, Strasburg, 1830–32; idem, *Mittheilungen aus der Geschichte der evangelischen Kirche des Elsasses*, iii. 84–154, ib. 1855; J. W. Baum, *Capito und Butzer*, pp. 195 sqq., Elberfeld, 1860; A. Ernst and J. Adam, *Katechetische Geschichte des Elsasses bis zur Revolution*, pp. 72–96, Strasburg, 1897.

ZELLER, tsel′er, CHRISTIAN HEINRICH: German educator; b. at the village of Entringen (18 m. s.w. of Stuttgart) Mar. 29, 1779; d. at Beuggen (12 m. e. of Basel) May 18, 1860. He received his early education in the institutions of Ludwigsburg, and when eighteen entered the University of Tübingen, his father's desire being that he should study law, though his own heart was already turned to the teaching profession; in 1801 he began to teach privately at Augsburg, showing signs of genius in this direction. He was besought to found a private school at St. Gall in 1803, where he stayed till 1809; he had charge of schools in the district about Zofingen, 1809–20; and in 1820 he was called to the charge of the institution at Beuggen devoted to the care of neglected children, where he spent the rest of his life. Under his care that institution became the model for its class, a pattern exhibition of Christian philanthropic work. In this work he was ably assisted by his wife and later by his sons. In connection with it he developed a literary activity which has had permanent effects. He edited the periodical *Monatsblättern aus Beuggen;* and published *Lehren der Erfahrung für christliche Land- und Armenschullehrer* (Basel, 1827), containing a system of pedagogy which gathered up all that was best in the methods then available; *Göttliche Antworten auf menschliche Fragen* (Basel, 1840); *Ueber Kleinkinderpflege* (1840); *Kurze Seelenlehre, gegründet auf Schrift und Erfahrung* (Calw, 1846). All of these passed through numerous editions. Zeller was also a contributor of worthy hymns to the hymnals, some of them among the best loved of the Church; worthy of mention are: " Gott bei mir an jedem Orte," Eng. transl. by Mrs. Findlater, " My God with me in every place "; and " Treuer Heiland, wir sind hier," Eng. transl., " Savior, here to Thee we come." Among the praises which his personality merited was that given to his simplicity, it being said of him that he " always remained a little one," with the humility of a child.

(C. von Palmer.†)

Bibliography: Lives are by H. Thiersch, 2 vols., Basel, 1876; E. Zeller, Basel, 1899, and Berlin, 1900; and T. Schölly, Basel, 1901. Consult also Julian, *Hymnology*, p. 1300.

ZEND-AVESTA. See Zoroaster, Zoroastrianism.

ZEND FOLK.

[The Zend Folk form a sect, termed by its adherents Mazdaznan, which purports to be founded on the teachings of Zoroastrianism (see Zoroaster, Zoroastrianism)]. They explain their name Mazdaznan from the [alleged] Avestan *Maz-da-znan*, *Maz* being held to mean " great, master," *da* " to think, knowledge," and *znan*, or *yaznan*, as " worshipful, to be worshiped," the consequent meaning of the compound being " master thought " or " thought that masters." Mazdaznan is maintained by its followers to have risen to notice in Europe and America after the return of Anquetil du Perron, in 1762, from Surat, India, where he had made the first translation of the fragmentary writings of the Avesta of the Zarathushtrian religion, with the help of Dastur Darab. About eighty years after the Mohammedan invasion a large number of Zarathushtrian fugitives left Persia and settled in India, where they have since lived peacefully, having guarded the sacredness of their monotheistic faith, which had been brought from Bactria, whence, many centuries before, Mazdaism had been spread throughout Asia by the missionaries of Zarathushtra, who was held to have communed with Mazda on the mountain of the " holy Questions," where the faith which was to bear his name was revealed to him. It is further maintained by the followers of Mazdaznan that the Freemasons (q.v.), who sprang up in England at the beginning of the eighteenth century, drew most liberally from the Zarathushtrian ritual after the return of Anquetil, and they accordingly hold that freemasonry is indebted to the Zarathushtrian, or Parsee, religion for most of its mystic ceremonies, various points of striking resemblance being alleged to exist between the two systems. Among these are ablution, the acacia, the all-seeing eye, the

1. Supposed Source and Relation to Freemasonry.

apron, the cock, the ear of corn, the annual feast, the sacred numbers three, five, and nine, the right hand, the thirty-third degree, the white color, and the six periods.

During the first part of the nineteenth century attempts were made in Germany, France, Russia, and America to introduce Zarathushtrian teachings from England under various names, and even without special names, the result being the establishment of manifold occult schools and new-thought cults. In 1890 Dr. Otoman Zar-Adusht Hanish formed the first Mazdaznan Peace Center in America, giving due credit to the source of his teachings. In 1899 he organized his movement for the more effectual spread of the " message of peace," and established permanent headquarters in Chicago, where there is a magnificent temple of the cult. The Mazdaznan people throughout the country style themselves " associates of God," having formed a " society of collective thought." In Jan., 1902, their first monthly appeared under the title of *Sunworshiper* (now *Mazdaznan*), and at Christmas, 1905, a provisional tribunal was instituted for a term of four years. At Christmas, 1909, the movement was reorganized with a Tribunal of Three, a Celestial Twelve, and a Terrestrial Twelve, which constitute the Supreme Court of the Mazdaznan Association. They consider themselves merely messengers of peace, and their organization simply as a mission of peace to give to every soul, in accordance with the demands of the times, its full due and rightful portion of gratitude. The institution may be termed purely educational, and without obligations. All applications for membership must be voluntary and free from suggestion or influence. The membership is divided into three classes: associates, friends, and fellows.

2. Establishment in America.

Mazdaznan recognizes the Bibles of all races as inspired, and regards the Avesta as the key to all final interpretations. The teaching is monotheistic in principle and pantheistic in application. All great men and women, irrespective of nationality and creed, are regarded as incarnations of the " will of the Lord " and of the " law of holiness," and respect and homage are paid to one and all of them. The sect holds that man takes up where spirit leaves off, and is incarnated " to reclaim the earth, to turn the deserts into a paradise, a paradise most suitable unto God and his associates to dwell therein." It considers the body of man to be the temple of the living God, and, by breathing the formula of " a prayer on the breath," man awakens to his higher consciousness of a living soul, endowed with the attributes of Mazda. Through a systematic method of religious health exercises, fasting, chastisement, and diet, Mazdaznan proposes to eradicate all prenatal influences and error of ancestral relations. Three methods of healing are recognized: the knife, medicine, and prayer, but for their followers they stress " prayer on the breath " (*Vendidad*, vii. 44, xx. 11–12; *Confession*, xv.; *Declaration*, xix.; James v. 15–16).

3. Tenets of Mazdaznan.

The followers of this cult are considered to be admirable culinarists and dietarians, while they also manifest great endurance, many of their leading adherents having lived without food for fifty-four days. They observe the commands of the Vendidad and of Genesis, and consequently hold strictly to vegetarianism (*Vendidad*, v. 19–20); **4. Outward Life and Sacred Texts.** Gen. i. 29–30). In their public life they are very plain, unceremonial, and unpretentious. They accept the leading thought of society as the tone of their message of peace, relying on the voice of *daēna* [" religion "] within, and holding to the " light of illumination " or " the sun of the soul." To be ever mindful of the existing relationship of intelligence to substance and vice versa, they recite scriptures daily (*Vendidad*, xix. 2, 22; *Declaration*, xix.; *Confession*, viii. 10–12). They observe holidays very religiously, the chief ones being the Christmas Gahanbar, which generally lasts ten days, and the Midsummer Peace Conference, for five days. They celebrate Easter, or the Birth of Ainyahita [Anahita], and Autumn, or the Birth of Zarathushtra. The greetings of the followers of Mazdaznan to each other are characteristically oriental, and each season and holiday has its particular greetings and blessings. Besides the scriptures they recognize, as pathfinders setting forth most clearly their scientific, philosophic, and religious views, *The Dialogues of Ainyahita*, *Necklace of Humata, Huhata, Huvarashta, Prayer-Beads, Mazdaznan Declaration, Confession, Statement,* and *Affirmation.* Among their many religious views are the following two affirmations: " I am a Mazdaznan, and I recognize the eternal designs in *humata* (good thought), *huhata* [*hūkhta*] (good word), *huvarashta* [*huvarshta*] (good deed)," and " The will of the Lord is the law of holiness; holiness is the best of all good," or *Yathā ahū vairyō* and *Ashem vohu.* Among themselves the followers of Mazdaznan are divided into four different classes: celibates, companions, minimites, and maximites.

Their belief in *karma*, reincarnation, and transmigration differs materially from that of the other oriental religions, and they claim absolute scientific and evolutionary substantiation. **5. Attitude toward Science.** Salvation and redemption are, to them, natural consequences in the evolutionary process of racial ties, while resurrection is a natural process, and immortality is universal to substance and intelligence. However complex the hypothesis of the speculative side of their philosophy may be, they claim to have ample proofs from the living word of God or nature to bear out their statements.

At their services they burn incense, candles, and sacrifices; and wear costly robes, largely of oriental design, while their religious solemnities are celebrated with the greatest pomp. The order of services, as well as their decorations, change with the seasons and occasions. They hold firmly to inspiration and revelation, and they consider **6. Liturgy and Organization.** the body to be the manifestation of God and all the physical attributes to be the temple of the living God. They do not believe in erecting special edifices for worship, and their temples serve merely for initiation and the imparting of inner teaching to the advanced. The sect has two magnificent temples in America, one in Chicago and the other in Lowell, Mass., fitted with all the splendor of oriental and occidental brilliancy. With Otoman Zar-Adusht Hanish as Elector, a Grand Vizier, and a Khalif, constituting a triumvirate, assisted by the Celestial Twelve and the Terrestrial Twelve with their different orders, they conduct the Mazdaznan commonwealth, each official being unsalaried, since all obligations are considered to be those of honor and duty.

The sect carries on a mission in Germany under Ambassador David Ammann, and also conducts missions in Canada, England, Switzerland, Holland, Africa, and South America. Their active membership in the United States is estimated by them at about 100,000, while they maintain that their following is much more numerous. Because of their belief in the universality of their teachings, they forbid proselytizing.   OTTO YEOUAN SCHMID.

ZENO, zī'nō, **THE ISAURIAN:** Byzantine emperor 474–475 and 476–491. An Isaurian force was long a part of the garrison of Constantinople, and there Zeno rose to power. Aspar, an Ossetian, had under Leo I. reached a high degree of power, and his son Patricius had been betrothed to a daughter of the emperor and been named Cæsar. But Leo became estranged from Aspar and his Germans and in his opposition to them leaned upon the Isaurians and Zeno. Zeno married Ariadne, a daughter of Leo, and the betrothal and appointment of Patricius were recalled, while Zeno became consul. Zeno, however, seemed unsuited for the succession because of doubts concerning his orthodoxy, so his son and Ariadne's, Leo's grandson, was named successor and became emperor under Zeno's regency on the death of Leo in 474; but he died in the same year, and under the influence of the dowager empress Verina and of his wife Zeno was named emperor; a disagreement with the dowager empress, however, in connection with an uprising of the Thracian Goths and of the capital, compelled Zeno to flee in Jan., 475, and Basiliscus, brother of Verina, assumed the crown. The new emperor favored the Monophysites (q.v.) and issued an encyclical to that effect, while Acacius, patriarch of Constantinople, upheld the orthodoxy of Chalcedon. The encyclical called forth two letters from Pope Simplicius to Acacius and Basiliscus. Zeno with his Isaurians was enabled to return to Constantinople, captured Basiliscus, and in 476 resumed the reins of empire. The pope hailed the return of Zeno as a triumph of orthodoxy. The power of the Monophysites compelled Zeno, however, to adopt a mediating course, and he issued his *Henoticon* (q.v.), which attempted a compromise, in which Acacius and Petrus Mongus (qq.v.) had part. The attempt was a failure, and instead of producing peace caused new struggles, and one result was a breach with Rome, begun with the excommunication of Acacius and continuing thirty-five years. Zeno started the East Goths on their way to Italy, while Theodoric as a German king and an imperial officer held Italy as a part of the empire. Justinian's policy was to restore the direct imperial control in

Italy, and so leaned toward a settlement of the schism, which in 519 came to an end.

(K. J. NEUMANN.)

BIBLIOGRAPHY: The sources are discussed by Bury in his ed. of Gibbon's *Decline and Fall*, cf. the historical account in Gibbon's chap. xxxix. Consult: the monograph on Zeno in W. Barth's dissertation, Basel, 1894; the notes in K. Ahrens and G. Krüger's ed. of the "Church History" of Zacharias Rhetor, Leipsic, 1899; Schaff, *Christian Church*, iii. 765; and the literature under the articles named in the text, especially under MONOPHYSITES.

ZENO OF VERONA: Bishop and patron saint of that city. As early as 1692 Jean Mabillon (*Traité des études monastiques*, pp. 503, 554, Brussels, 1692) raised the question whether there was toward the end of the third century a bishop of that name and

Evidence of his Reality. title, and whether the works attributed to him were his. The repeated asking of this question since has gone to the returning of an affirmative answer and to the establishment of the ninety tractates attributed to Zeno as both genuine and worthful. Visitors to that city will recall the memorials to him in the shape of church, square, and portal (cf. K. Baedeker, *Northern Italy*, p. 235, Leipsic, 1906); the earliest part of the church was built in the sixth century, and from an early date Verona has honored this saint in these and other places. The oldest testimony to this fact is an address delivered at the invitation of the clergy of the city on the occasion of the celebration of a festival to him, which is to be dated about the year 412; it may have been by Bishop Petronius of Bologna (d. between 425 and 450). This address calls Zeno not a martyr but "most holy confessor." A second testimony to the existence of Zeno is the story of a miracle said to have occurred at the time of a flooding of the city about the year 588 in which the saint saved his basilica (cf. Paul the Deacon, *Historia Langobardarum*, III., xxiii., Eng. transl., Philadelphia, 1907). Moreover, practically all the churches of Verona profess to possess relics of the patron saint of the city. His celebrity traveled over the Alps to Germany, to Ulm, Reichenhall, and even into Belgium through Bishop Ratherius of Verona (q.v.). This bishop cited frequently the tractates of Zeno, and brought a manuscript to Lobbes containing a rhythmic description of Verona (*De laudibus Veronæ*, dated about 790), which deals with the first eight bishops, of whom the eighth was Zeno. Older than this manuscript, however, is the chief codex of the tractates (Codex Remensis), which Hincmar of Reims (q.v.) presented to the Benedictine library at Reims. It contains the ninety-three tractates (or fragments of them), and is especially interesting because of the marginal glosses which relate to the use of collections of sermons in divine worship, and show further that this manuscript had been used in worship at Verona. To the short tract concerning the three men in the fiery furnace the remark is annexed that it was to be used at the festivals of Firmus and Rusticus (who were honored at Verona about 765). The same tractates are preserved in numerous other manuscripts under the name of Zeno.

The question arises whether these tractates are a unity, or whether, as Tillemont said of the 105 first printed under the name of Zeno, they are a collection from various authors. In the older col-

Unity of the Tractates. lection there were pieces which are to be credited to Cæsarius of Arles, the letter of Bishop Vigilius of Trent to Chrysostom, three tracts by Bishop Potamius of Olisipo (*MPL*, viii. 1411 sqq.), five expositions of psalms by Hilary of Poitiers, and four sermons of Basil of Cæsarea in the Latin translation of Rufinus. Since in the ninety-three tractates there are considerable parts which go back to Lactantius and Hilary of Poitiers, the appearance is presented of a collection; and this is enhanced by the fact that Zeno has been supposed to belong to the third century, not to the fourth. In spite of this, there are very decided indications of the unity of the collection. As in the works of Tertullian, Cyprian, and others, many citations are taken verbally from Seneca, apocryphal writings, and even from Apuleius, but these are worked into the texture. Hilary was very popular (Jerome, *Epist.*, xxxiv. *ad Marcellam*, *MPL*, xxii. 448); but the style of Zeno betrays a far stronger influence of the Asian school and is richer in use of figures and in rhythm. The proof of unity has been well worked out by Weyman, Giuliari, and Bigelmair (see bibliography). Especially indicative of this is the employment of a pre-Hieronymian Bible-text, in which the agreement with the text of Cyprian is particularly noticeable. Even though the unity of the tractates is conceded, it still does not follow that Zeno is the author, for it is a possible supposition that they had been attributed to the patron saint of the place through veneration of him. This hypothesis is hardly tenable, however, if it be granted that Zeno lived in the time of the Emperor Gallienus (260–268); for it is a desperate rather than sane conclusion that the tractates were used by Lactantius and Hilary rather than the reverse. Equally beside the mark is the hypothesis of Baronius that there were in Verona two Zenos, one living in the third and another in the fourth century. And it is not good exegesis to explain polemics against Photinians, Audians, and Arians by a polemic against Origen and Origenists.

Reasons for putting the work back into the third century are: that Christian women appear frequently as marrying heathen husbands; that sacrifices to heathen deities are yet in evidence, which were forbidden after Constantine and Con-

The Evidence Concerning the Date. stantius; that coins are mentioned bearing the heads of the emperors and not the cross; that the Christian churches are small and simple in construction in comparison with the heathen temples; and that the influence of the Jews is one of the objects of attack. In addition to this it is to be remarked that the dogmatic conceptions are those of the third century. It has been brought to notice that in Zeno neither the Greek *homoousios* nor the Latin *consubstantialis* is found, and in their place are older formulas that have their origin in Tertullianistic expressions. This distinguishes the author from Phœbadius (q.v.), who, though as a dogmatician he was inclined to archaisms, yet wrote of the "divinity and consubstantiality of the Son."

It is natural to refer to Hilary and other conservative Westerners; but it does not appear from the tractates of Zeno that the West without dogmatic controversies felt itself to be in possession of Catholic verity. In fact Zeno appears to be even more naive than Hilary himself before his contact with the East. The expression " Catholic verity " is not found, and the word " Catholic " seldom appears in Zeno. The tractates know nothing of a hierarchically governed Church guaranteeing the truth. The highly interesting first tractate does not countenance the suggestion that the faith has come under subjection to a legal formulary; it indeed says that we are not under the law but under grace. The faith is the form of religious possession and is under private control (" the law is something in common, faith is a private matter "). The teaching concerning the Church savors of Novatianism. This institution is indeed founded upon Peter, who has, however, no precedence over the other apostles, but appears as the representative of the rest though in a sense the first of them. There is no discussion as to the position of Rome. While it is noticeable how considerable is the dependence upon Cyprian, it is curious that the bishops receive little attention. If, as the common idea has it, Zeno was African in origin, it is very remarkable that there is not a trace in the tractates of the violent Donatistic controversy. The great question which troubled men there was concerned with the consecration of bishops, but in the tractates the matter of ordination is dealt with entirely without passion. Similarly in the doctrine of the Trinity, as in the doctrine of the Church, the treatises might have been written not only before there was an Arian, but before there was a Donatistic strife, while Novatian ideas seem to be in the air.

These suggestions are so indicative that the disposition is to attribute the unity to a single editor who is responsible for the contact with Hilary by way of interpolations and a working over or else through a common source. Before the middle of the fourth century the candidates for baptism were never. called **The Work of the Editor.** competentes, but in tractate ii. 27, 46, 50 the expression is found. There are indications of change from the original text. In this category there come up for consideration the suggestions involved in the marginal glosses, which show that in the eighth century the tractates were employed liturgically. But liturgical use involves considerable change. Tractate ii. 50 sqq. was used later in the monastery at Verona, " being recited in the presence of the priest before the station," and this suggests a procession. Still stranger is the marginal note on the Reims codex at ii. 42, which directs the tractate to be read by the deacon at the chief monastery when on Easter Sunday the bishop takes his place there and at the kiss of peace " according to custom " distributes apples to the brethren. The original Easter sermon on the four seasons is aptly chosen for this use, but the usage can hardly have been original. Whoever reads the later, formladen, and repetitious tractates (cf. ii. 39–40 with 41 and ii. 47 with the preceding) receives the impression of a liturgical piece which has been lopped out of sermons, probably Zeno's. Again, Tractate I., v. 4 gives the time of the inditing of the Pauline epistles as " nearly 400 years ago or a little more." The number 200 which appears in the second edition of Verona in 1586 has no support in any of the manuscripts, where the number 400 is written out. The Ballerini have taken much pains to prove that the Church Fathers reckon at times very inexactly. But Bigelmair shows that 400 is used as a round number, and sees in the expression the hand of a redactor who was active about 450. That would explain how Jerome in his De viris illustribus passes by Zeno; for at that time no publications of Zeno were in circulation. Bigelmair concludes that Zeno was dead in 370, the year in which the commentary of Hilary on the Psalms was issued. Hilary is used often in the tractates. Bigelmair supposes that the commentary as a whole was issued then, though in its parts it had earlier seen the light; but this is merely a possibility. So that a working in of the Hilary passages is within the bounds of possibility.

But all these difficulties come seriously into consideration if that Zeno, to whom were attributed according to a very early tradition the tractates which are essentially unitary in composition and were used at a very early date at Verona, lived in the third and not in the fourth century. The church of Verona had a double interest in carrying back as far as possible Zeno's dates. Its earliest bishops had Greek names, and tradition made the first bishop one of the seventy disciples. If Zeno was the eighth in sequence, he could not have lived in the fourth century. Gregory the Great (Dialogus, iii. 19) several times calls Zeno a martyr; to be sure it was Bishop Lippomanus in the sixteenth century who first changed the form of veneration offered from that of a confessor to that of a martyr, which then became popular. That Zeno suffered martyrdöm in the fourth century through the Emperor Julian or the Arians is improbable; the report of martyrdom would fit better in the third century. The Reims codex contains a life of Zeno by the notary Coronatus, which must have been written before 807 (when the relics of Zeno were transferred). This tells how the bishop healed Galla the daughter of Emperor Gallienus (260–268) and with the help of the grateful father Christianized Verona. While the fact of such a daughter is not assailable, the " Life " abounds so in impossibilities that it has been pronounced unhistorical; yet to the martyrdom it gives no support, indeed (chap. viii.) it reports: " not much later he passed away in peace." The miracle of healing passed into the later reports, as in the poem De laudibus Veronæ, where it takes the form of saving from an evil spirit. In spite of the improbabilities this account of the life has been influential, and has made its mark on hymns, ritual, and hagiologies. It is not strange that Gallienus is brought into connection with the legend when it is remembered that the city was a colony under Pompey, endowed with citizenship rights by Cæsar, was the birthplace of Catullus, and finally was refortified by Gallienus and called itself Gallieneia after him (F. Ughelli, Italia sacra, v. 655, 10 vols., Venice, 1717–22). Bigelmair derives

Traditions Concerning Zeno's Period.

the first bishop from the East, though the Greek name does not necessitate this. In the time of Gregory the Great (c. 600) Aquileia was the metropolis, earlier the city was under Milan. The correspondence of Ambrose (*Epist.*, v.–vi.) with Bishop Syagrius is that of a metropolitan with his suffragan. The latter had proceeded illegally and injuriously against the consecrated virgin Indicia, to whom Ambrose refers as approved by " Zeno of sacred memory." This is the earliest and surest testimony to the life of Zeno. It has been objected that the reference does not affirm either the episcopal standing of Zeno or his residence at Verona; but this follows from the whole situation. Syagrius had threatened his metropolitan with the results of outraged public opinion. Ambrose replied that such was not the character of the Veronese, and he would moreover make the matter clear through a commission and pacify them; for Syagrius had passed a misjudgment on a virgin consecrated by Zeno of blessed memory, to whom he had thus by implication set himself in opposition. That Zeno belonged in Verona follows from the fact that Indicia lived there, and from the implication that Syagrius knew that fact; of what other Bishop Zeno could this be true? An additional circumstance is alleged, the consecration of a sister Marcellina. Bishops, not presbyters, were obligated to perform such ceremonies according to the rules in force before 390 (L. Duchesne, *Origines du culte chrétien*, p. 408, Paris, 1889, Eng. transl., *Christian Worship, its Origin and Evolution*, p. 423, London, 1904). That is to say, some years before Ambrose wrote the letter, Zeno had officiated at the veiling of a virgin whose testimony was still obtainable.

Still, the exact date is not ascertainable. It does not follow from the words " of blessed memory " that Ambrose was personally unacquainted with Zeno; all that is necessarily involved is that Zeno was an older contemporary of Ambrose. It is known from Athanasius (*MPG*, xxv. 599 B) that in 356 Bishop Lucillus (Lucius) of Verona was still alive; according to the catalogues Zeno was his second successor in the see. Much effort has been expended to determine from this the years of beginning and end of Zeno's episcopate, employing the datum that Zeno was consecrated Dec. 3, and from that determining the year on which that day fell on a Sunday. But that datum is insecure. It is indeed one of the days on which Zeno is commemorated; but Rabanus first names Apr. 12 as the date of martyrdom, elsewhere Dec. 8 is named. *ASB*, April, ii. 69 E derives this date from the *Missale Ambrosianum*, but there Zeno appears as confessor (a good indication of the early date of the tradition). It seems as though Petrus Galesini, apostolic prothonotary, was the first to be so definite as to name Dec. 8 as the day of consecration and Apr. 12 as the natal day. The basis of this entire system of reckoning is so doubtful that it seems unnecessary to note the objections that have been advanced against it. Both the assumed year of beginning and the assumed year of the end (362 and 370) are uncertain. Even the duration of his episcopate (eight or nine years) does not depend upon

Zeno of the Fourth Century.

the liturgical indications of the sermon fragments. The best that can be done is to affirm that some time about 356 Zeno became bishop, and on internal grounds it is improbable that he was active as an author after 381, since there are no traces in his writings of the Council of Constantinople in 381.

It is usual to trace Zeno's origin to Africa. Ordinarily one does not speak of African Latin; but an exception is made when the peculiarities of the " Apuleian style " so abound as they do in Zeno. It follows that he used much other African writers. Tractate 18 of book ii. has as title " On the natal day of S. Arcadius, which occurs on the day before the Ides of January in the city of Cæsarea Mauretania." Duchesne thinks that this tract is only by chance among Zeno's works, but Bigelmair points to its literary relationship with the rest. It purports to be a historical writing, but is so lacking in concrete detail that no local coloring is left to speak for an origin in Madaura. The most of the tractates are fragments of sermons; i. 1 is a letter and may have been written when Fortunatianus was bishop of Aquileia. Until recently it was held that Zeno's writings were the earliest examples of sermons in the Latin language, but that has become questionable. Their literary value consists in the fact that they are high-water mark in the application of the rules of art to the Latin sermon. The author had read widely, observed closely, thought matters out, polished, built up, and reconstructed until he had finished his task. But he was always desirous of having something to say, and back of the discourses was an unusual, worthful, pious, and delightful personality. The sermons have their own peculiarity. II. 44, for example, is perhaps the best description extant from early times of the process of baking bread, and every detail is treated symbolically; similarly ii. 27 deals with viticulture, and ii. 43 with horoscopes. Dogmatically they are important as revealing Western theology before the stress of the Apollinarian controversy. Pauline thoughts predominate (James is never cited), Mary is to the fore, with considerable use of apocryphal material.

(F. ARNOLD.)

Zeno of Verona, Tractate 18.
Conclusions.

BIBLIOGRAPHY: The *Sermones*, ed. P. and H. Ballerini, were issued at Verona, 1739, this edition being repeated in A. Gallandius, *Bibliotheca veterum patrum*, v. 109 sqq., 14 vols., Venice, 1765–81, and in *MPL*, xi. 10 sqq.; a new ed. of Ballerini was issued at Augsburg, 1758, enlarged by two essays by Bonacchi (also included in *MPL*). Note further: Tillemont, *Mémoires*, iv. 1, pp. 24 sqq.; P. Ughelli, *Italia sacra*, v. 679 sqq., Venice, 1720; G. B. C. Giuliari, *S. Zenones sermones*, Verona, 1883, new impression, 1900, cf. the editor's *Vita di S. Zenone*, ib. 1877 (this edition contains on pp. lxxxix.–cviii., cxiii.–cxxxix. a painstaking index to the literature on Zeno up to the year 1881); cf. on Giuliari C. Weyman in *AMA*, 1893, ii. 359 sqq., and note the same author in *AMA*, 1893, ii. 350–361. In addition to the foregoing, consult: I. A. Dorner, *Person Christi*, ii. 754–759, 4 vols., Stuttgart, 1846–56, Eng. transl., *Hist. of the Development of the Doctrine of the Person of Christ*, 5 vols., Edinburgh, 1861–63; F. A. Schütz, *S. Zenonis doctrina Christiana*, Leipsic, 1854; L. Jazdzewski, *Zeno . . . commentatio patrologica*, Regensburg, 1862; L. Duchesne, in *Bulletin critique*, iv (1883), 136–141; Hurter, in *Zeitschrift für katholische Theologie*, viii (1884), 233 sqq.; J. Fessler, *Institutiones patrologiæ*, ed. B. Jungmann, i. 712–715, Innsbruck, 1890; A. Harnack, *Abhandlungen* of the Berlin Academy, 1895 (shows the influence of Tertullian); especially important is A. Bigelmair, *Zeno von Verona*, Münster, 1904; H. Brewer, in *Zeitschrift für katholische Theologie*, xxviii. 1 (1904), 92–115; idem, in *Revue bénédictine*, xxii (1905), 470; H. Januel, *Commentationes philologicæ in Zenonem Veronensem*, program of the gymnasium at Regensburg, 1905–06; *DCB*, iv. 1213.

ZENOS, ANDREAS CONSTANTINIDES: Presbyterian; b. at Constantinople Aug. 13, 1855. He was educated at Robert College, Constantinople (A.B., 1872); was pastor of the Presbyterian church at Brandt, Pa. (1881–83), and in 1883 was appointed professor of Greek at Lake Forest University, where he remained five years. He was then professor of New-Testament exegesis in Hartford Theological Seminary (1888–91), and since 1891 has been connected with McCormick Theological Seminary, Chicago, as professor of church history (1891–1894) and of Biblical theology (since 1894). He collaborated with F. W. Kelsey in an edition of Xenophon's *Anabasis* (Boston, 1889); translated the "Ecclesiastical History" of Socrates for the *Nicene and Post-Nicene Fathers* (New York, 1890); edited, with M. W. Jacobus and E. E. Nourse, *The Standard Bible Dictionary* (New York, 1909); and has written *Elements of Higher Criticism* (New York, 1895); *Compendium of Church History* (Philadelphia, 1896); and *The Teaching of Jesus concerning Christian Conduct* (New York, 1905).

ZEPHANIAH, zef″a-nai′ā: Ninth of the Minor Prophets in the arrangement of the English version. His genealogy is traced (in i. 1) back to the fourth generation to "Hizkiah," probably Hezekiah, king of Judah, although this is not stated in the title. That this was Hezekiah is not **Author and** disproved by the fact that no son of **Contents.** Hezekiah named Amariah is elsewhere spoken of; while the long reign of Manasseh suffices to cover the apparent discrepancy of the known three steps between Hezekiah and Josiah and the four generations named in this passage. Nothing inherently improbable attaches to the supposed Davidic descent of Zephaniah. In chap. i. appear first a threat of judgment against the earth in general, and then against Judah and Jerusalem because of heathenism in worship, the use of foreign customs by princes and nobles, and distrust of or disbelief in Yahweh. In chap. ii. is an exhortation to turn to righteousness, before judgment falls upon the Philistines, Moabites, Ammonites, Cushites (see Cush), and Assyrians. Chap. iii. 1–7 is a lament over Jerusalem, arraigning all classes, 7–13 promises return to purity, 14–20 is a triumphal song in view of deliverance, since Jerusalem's foes are cast out and Yahweh is her king. The prophecy falls, therefore, into two parts: chaps. i.–ii., the menace; chap. iii., the announcement of salvation, verses 1–7 being merely introductory. The unity of the prophecy rests upon the idea of the day of Yahweh (see Day of the Lord); the aspects of this for the heathen and for Israel are discriminated. It is a day of destruction for man and beast, for Israel and the heathen; for special classes of Israelites—the idolaters, the fashionable, merchants, atheists, and sinners; for the foes of Israel. Then the isles are to worship Yahweh, the peoples will serve him, the Cushites will bring gifts, the

diaspora of Israel shall be celebrated in all lands. Thus the picture of the Day of Yahweh is not altogether one, in which it agrees with the twofold aspect of the day in Isaiah. If the prophecy is a unit, the author has used various aspects in a fashion all his own. The pattern, however, was Ezekiel. Thus the prophecies against the heathen are in the middle (cf. Ezek. xxv.–xxxii.; Zeph. ii. 4–15). Ezekiel's order is menace, exhortation, the oracles concerning the heathen, which Zephaniah seems to copy. It seems likely, also, that the text has not remained in its original form, but has received additions.

The activity of Zephaniah is placed in the time of Josiah (i. 1), and shortly before 625 b.c. This is corroborated by the religious and ethical situation in Judah and Jerusalem reflected in the book. The inhabitants are compared with wine settled on the dregs; the city has long remained free **The Date.** from war and other calamities; the star-worship is there, which dates after the time of Assyrian influence (i. 5); religious syncretism was coincident with foreign influence, in which the princes lead and the king does not object. This fits the period of the minority of Josiah, when he had no influence upon the practises of the people. On attaining his majority, he broke with the party friendly to Assyrian control, developed a national policy in religion and politics, and then came his reform (i. 4). Definiteness of time is indicated also by the idea of the Day of Yahweh, which in Zephaniah is motived by the Scythians from the north (i. 10, 13), who are to plunder the inhabitants. The enemy could be none of the neighbors of Judah, did not menace Egypt or Assyria, could hardly be Babylonia, and appeared suddenly—characteristics which depict the Scythians, who come as bringing a sacrifice (i. 7). The moderated expression in ii. 1–3 may be due the passing of the Scythians, which happened c. 625, while Zephaniah's activity shortly preceded this time. But this period is not the situation reflected in iii. 14–20, the atmosphere of which is that of the exile and the spirit that of Isa. xl.–lxvi., the restoration of Israel and return of the exiles; similar in tone is iii. 9–10, a basis for which is found only after Israel had dwelt among the heathen (cf. II Kings v. 1 sqq.); with the foregoing should be placed also ii. 11. Further, the attitude of Moab and Ammon toward Israel reflects the events of 586, while ii. 7a seems a reference to the brilliant Maccabean period (cf. I Macc. xi. 61). The passage iii. 1–7 is general in tone as compared with the concreteness of chap. i., while the expression "meek of the earth" (ii. 3) recalls the epithets applied to the pious of the exile. As secondary elements then may be reckoned ii. 1–3, 7, 8–10, 15, and iii.; the rest may be ascribed to Zephaniah.

From the primary portions as thus distinguished may be seen the conditions in Judah shortly before Josiah's reform, the indications of strife between popular and prophetic piety. There is religious syncretism, influenced by the East, and Yahweh is made to say that he will not share his rulership with Baal and other deities; the judgment is coming, the Scythians are the instruments. Dependence is seen upon Isaiah and Amos in the shaking of the earth and the anger of Yahweh, which involve other

nations and Israel. Precise expression of the purpose of judgment against the nations is lacking, but
　　　　　the sins of Israel are exactly stated and
　The　　afford thus in the original prophecy a
Religious-　victory for the ethical. Zephaniah
Historical　has in mind a righteous Israel, as have
Situation.　Isaiah, Amos, and Hosea, while the
　　　　　recovery of this condition was to be
brought about by the end of the State. In the present text there are alongside of the threats exhortations, which were probably not in the original. These
additions were placed possibly in the time when the
early prophecies were put into form for the use of
the community. These were employed not as historical documents that were dead, but as living witnesses for the present and future. In the working
over, therefore, where exhortation was lacking it
was supplied from the growing treasury of Scripture,
and in accordance with the enlarging national hope
and wish. On this basis there was added to Zephaniah's original prophecies those turns of thought
which seemed to be justified by the historical situation as it was in the time of redaction, when the
territory of Moabites, Ammonites, and Philistines
seemed likely to be added to the national possessions.
For the Lord of the world, Yahweh, the possessions
of his people seemed too small; to it then the possessions of the heathen were to be annexed, or, as
an alternative, the heathen were to be converted to
the Yahweh religion. It is to be noted, that Zephaniah knows of no Messiah; Yahweh himself gives
salvation.　　　　　　　　　　　　(G. BEER.)

BIBLIOGRAPHY: On questions of introduction use the works
noted in and under BIBLICAL INTRODUCTION, and: G. G.
Findlay, The Books of the Prophets in their Historical Succession, vol. ii., London, 1907 (excellent); B. L. Duhm,
Theologie der Propheten, pp. 222–225, Bonn, 1875; Duhl,
in ZATW, 1885, pp. 183 sqq.; F. W. Farrar, The Minor
Prophets, pp. 153–158, London, 1890; Schwally, in
ZATW, 1890, pp. 165 sqq.; A. F. Kirkpatrick, Doctrine
of the Prophets, pp. 253–263, London, 1892; Budde, in
TSK, 1893, pp. 393 sqq.; Bachmann, in TSK, 1894, pp.
641 sqq.; T. K. Cheyne, Critica Biblica, ii. 174–178, London, 1903; Halévy, in Revue sémitique, xii. 193–198, 298–
313; S. Zandstra, Witness of the Vulgate, Peshitta and
Septuagint to the Text of Zephaniah, New York, 1909;
DB, iv. 974–977; EB, iv. 5402–09; JE, xii. 660.
　Commentaries are: G. A. Smith, Book of the Twelve
Prophets, 2 vols., London, 1896–97; A. B. Davidson, in
Cambridge Bible, Cambridge, 1896; F. A. Strauss, Berlin,
1843; H. Cowles, The Minor Prophets, New York, 1866;
E. Henderson, Book of the Twelve Minor Prophets, new ed.,
Andover, 1868; C. F. Keil, Biblical Commentary, vol.
xxv., Edinburgh, 1868; L. Reinke, Münster, 1868; H.
Ewald, in his Commentary on the Prophets of the O. T.,
vol. iii., 5 vols., London, 1875–81; P. Kleinert, in Lange's
Commentary, New York, 1875, 2d ed. of the German,
Bielefeld, 1893; F. Hitzig, 4th ed. by H. Steiner, Leipsic,
1881; J. Wolfendale, in Preacher's Complete Homiletical
Commentary, 20 vols., London, 1885–91, New York, 1892;
I. Knabenbauer, Paris, 1886; C. von Orelli, Munich, 1888;
2d ed., 1896; Eng. transl., New York, 1893; W. Schulz,
Hanover, 1892; J. Wellhausen, Die kleinen Propheten,
2d ed., Berlin, 1893; W. Nowack, Göttingen, 1897, 2d
ed., 1903; J. T. Beck, Gütersloh, 1899; E. B. Pusey,
Minor Prophets, new ed., vol. vii., London, 1907.

ZEPHYRINUS, zef"i-rai'nus: Pope 198 (199)–
217. He succeeded Victor I., and was an opponent
of the school of the Theodotus who was excommunicated by Victor (see MONARCHIANISM). He appears to have been much under the influence of
Calixtus, later the first pope of that name. The
view is now generally accepted that he issued the

edict concerning the readmission of unchaste sinners into the community to which Tertullian refers
(De pudicitia, i.). Hippolytus, his opponent, pictures him as a man of little eminence or learning
(Hær., IX., ii. sqq., Eng. transl., ANF, v. 125 sqq.)
and a favorer of heretics. Zephyrinus was the first
bishop of Rome to be buried in the catacombs, of
which he made Calixtus administrator, to one of
which the latter gave his name. (G. KRÜGER.)

BIBLIOGRAPHY: Sources are Eusebius, Hist. eccl., V., xxviii.,
Eng. transl. in NPNF, 2 ser., i. 246–248; Hippolytus,
Hær., ix.; and Liber pontificalis, ed. L. Duchesne, vol.
i., Paris, 1886, ed. Mommsen, in MGH, Gest. pont. Rom.,
i (1898), 20. Consult further: DCB, iv. 1215–1220 (elaborate); ASB, Aug., v. 783–789; J. J. I. von Döllinger,
Hippolytus und Kallistus, pp. 122 sqq., 220 sqq., Regensburg, 1853; K. Hagemann, Die römische Kirche in den 3
ersten Jahrhunderten, pp. 84 sqq., Freiburg, 1864; R. A.
Lipsius, Chronologie der römischen Bischöfe, pp. 171 sqq.,
Kiel, 1869; idem, Die Quellen der ältesten Ketzergeschichte,
pp. 137 sqq., Leipsic, 1875; K. J. Neumann, Der römische
Staat, i. 308–309, ib. 1890; J. Langen, Geschichte der
römischen Kirche, i. 182–226, Bonn, 1881; Bower, Popes,
i. 19–20; Platina, Popes, i. 36–38; Milman, Latin Christianity, i. 75; Harnack, Litteratur, i. 151 sqq.; Schaff,
Christian Church, ii. 193, 765; Neander, Christian Church,
i. 581, iii. 347; Ceillier, Auteurs sacrés, vi. 84–85.

ZERBOLT, tsär'bôlt, VAN ZUETPHEN, tsüt'fen
(ZUTFEN), GERARD: Member of the Brotherhood of the Common Life; b. in Zütphen (58 m. s.e.
of Amsterdam) in 1367; d. at Windesheim Dec. 4,
1398. He came of a family of some repute, and
was early distinguished by an insatiable thirst for
knowledge. Prior to 1384 he was in Deventer, where
at school he came into connection with Geert Groote
and Florentius Radewyns (qq.v.); under the influence of the latter he left the world and entered the
fellowship of the Brethren in the house of which Florentius was the head. There, engaged in spiritual
exercises, in the copying of books, and in the study
of theology and canon law, he passed nearly all the
rest of his life, secluded as much as possible in his
cell. He was interested both in increasing the
library left by Groote and in having the books read
by the clergy in the neighborhood. He received the
priesthood, and his sermons were gladly heard. He
was noted for his sane view of things, and his counsel was continually sought, his knowledge of law
being extremely useful. Yet his highest pleasure
was in monastic virtues. During an outbreak of
the pestilence Zerbolt and Florentius withdrew to
Amersfoort, and there Zerbolt's talents were available for the brethren's use. On the return from a
mission he was taken ill at Windesheim and died
there. Less widely known than Groote and Florentius, his influence was wide and deep; he represents
the noblest and best of the association with which
he was connected.

His writings show his devotion to the brotherhood.
The charge of heresy brought by the monks because
the association was without vows, rule, or patron,
he repelled in his Super modo vivendi devotorum hominum simul commorantium. He also advocated the
reading of the Scriptures and other religious books
in the vernacular (in his De libris Teutonicalibus,
though the authenticity of this tract is questioned).
In Tractatus de vestibus pretiosis he assailed luxury
in dress, and struck at unworthy ambition in In
quendam inordinate grados ecclesiasticos et prædica-

tionis officium affectantem. His most detailed works are *De spiritualibus ascensionibus* and *De reformatione virium animæ,* ethical treatises which establish his fame. In his works are the evidence of knowledge, piety, and independence of thought. Though a recluse by disposition, he was a man of practical sense; his mysticism was subjected to his understanding and experience, and vision and ecstasy do not appear in him. He was a faithful son of the Church, valuing highly its ordinances and especially the sacraments. As preacher and as author of useful writings Zerbolt served well his generation, and particularly the brotherhood. One of the services he rendered the latter was his influence against its conversion into a monastic order. He was the real head of the community at Deventer by reason of his great learning and spiritual intensity. (S. D. VAN VEEN.)

BIBLIOGRAPHY: The earliest life, by Thomas à Kempis, is in the latter's *Opera,* in the English in his *Founders of the New Devotion,* transl. by J. P. Arthur, pp. 220-225, London, 1905. Consult further: J. Revius, *Daventria illustrata,* pp. 36–60, Leyden, 1651; H. J. van Henssen, *Hist. episcopatuum fœderati Belgii,* vol. ii., ib. 1719; G. H. M. Delprat, *Verhandeling over de Broederschap van G. Groote* pp. 349–352, Arnheim, 1856; W. A. Koning, *Specimen historico-theologicum de Gerardi Zutphaniensis vita,* Utrecht, 1858; C. M. Vos, in *Kerkhistorisch Jaarboekje,* pp. 102–138, Schoonhoven, 1864; C. Ullmann, *Reformers before the Reformation,* ii. 105–114, 164–165, Edinburgh, 1877; G. H. J. W. J. Geesink, *Gerard Zerbolt van Zutfen,* Amsterdam, 1879; F. Jostes, in *Historisches Jahrbuch der Görresgesellschaft,* xi. 1 sqq., 709 sqq.; W. Preger, in the *Abhandlungen* of the Bavarian Academy, XXI., i. 1 sqq.

ZERUBBABEL

ZERUBBABEL, ze-rub′a-bel: Very little is known of the history of Zerubbabel. As Persian governor in the postexilic Jewish community, influenced by the prophets Haggai and Zechariah, he laid the corner-stone of the second Temple in Jerusalem, in the second year of King Darius (520), and in conjunction with the high-priest Joshua promoted energetically its erection (Hag. i. 12, 14; Zech. iv. 9–10, 14, viii. 9; Ezra v. 2). The undertaking was favored by the difficulties of the Persian kingdom at this time and by the messianic hopes centering in Zerubbabel's person. The work was also furthered by the attempted interference of the Satrap Tatnai, who under Samaritan influence tried to arrest its progress, but instead brought about acknowledgment by Darius of the legitimacy of the Jewish claims as based on the privileges which were accorded by Cyrus to the Temple at Jerusalem (Ezra v. 3–6, 14).

The meagerness of the sources raises several questions in connections with Zerubbabel: (1) Was he a native of Israel, or did he belong to the exiled Jews in Babylon? His name ("branch of Babylon") suggests that he was born in Babylon. The messianic expectations centering about him testifies to membership in the family of David. The Chronicler (I., iii. 19) calls him the son of Pedaiah, while Haggai (i. 1, 12, 14, etc.) and Ezra (v. 2) call him the son of Shealtiel. This question is complicated by the difficulty as to the exact condition of the text of Haggai, and the reliability of the genealogical table in the Book of Chronicles. (2) What was the relation between Zerubbabel and Sheshbazzar (Ezra i. 8, cf. ii. 2)? Older authorities identify the two, but it is not likely that a Jew would bear two Baby-

lonian names of the character of these. Besides, although both are mentioned as laying the corner-stone (Ezra v. 16, Sheshbazzar; Zech. iv. 9, Zerubbabel), it is probable that the one belonged to the second year of Cyrus and the other to the second year of Darius. Allowing that they were two different persons, when did Zerubbabel return home? Not much reliance can be placed in the list of Ezra ii., since it is evidently artificial in its construction. Note the number twelve. Probabilities point to the fact that in the year 519 this young member of the house of David, then in his twentieth year, returned to his fatherland. Confirmation (not proof) of this is found in III Esdras v. 1 sqq. (3) What was Zerubbabel's career? The rest of his life, after the completion and consecration of the Temple in 516, lies in obscurity. This is all the more remarkable because the books of Haggai and Zechariah leave the impression that Zerubbabel was about to be elevated to the throne. Possibly there was a rebellion (or attempt to set up an independent kingdom) against the "great king" (of Persia) which ended in a catastrophe. Such an ending to a satrapy was common in the Persian empire. It is likely that Zerubbabel was put to death, and possibly this event is alluded to in Ps. lxxxix. 39–52. Yet the mention in I Chron. iii. 21 of a Hattush belonging to the family of David allows the hypothesis that Zerubbabel was not executed but rather recalled to Babylon. (ERNST SELLIN.)

BIBLIOGRAPHY: Of high value are the later commentaries on the books of Ezra-Nehemiah, Haggai, and Zechariah. Consult further: A. van Hoonacker, *Zorobabel et le second temple,* Ghent, 1891; idem, *Nouvelles études sur la restauration juive après l'exil de Babylone,* ib. 1896; idem, in *Expository Times,* viii (1897), 351 sqq.; W. H. Kosters, *Het Herstel van Israel,* Leyden, 1893 (epoch-making); F. de Saulcy, *Étude chronologique des livres d'Esdras et Néhémie,* Paris, 1868; J. Imbert, *Le Temple reconstruit par Zorobabel,* Louvain, 1888; P. H. Hunter, *After the Exile,* London, 1890; A. Kuenen, *Gesammelte Abhandlungen,* pp. 212 sqq., Freiburg, 1894; A. H. Sayce, *Higher Criticism and the Monuments,* pp. 539 sqq., London, 1894; E. Meyer, *Entstehung des Judentums,* Halle, 1896; T. K. Cheyne, *Jewish Religious Life After the Exile,* New York, 1898, cf. his *Introduction to Isaiah,* pp. xxxiii.–xxxix., London, 1895; C. C. Torrey, *The Composition and Historical Value of Ezra-Nehemiah,* Giessen, 1896; E. Sellin, *Serubbabel,* Leipsic, 1898; idem, *Studien zur Entstehungsgeschichte der jüdischen Gemeinde nach dem babylonischen Exil,* part ii., ib. 1901; J. Nikel, *Die Wiederherstellung des jüdischen Gemeinwesens nach dem babylonischen Exil,* Freiburg, 1900; J. W. Rothstein, *Die Genealogie des Königs Jojachin und seiner Nachkommern in geschichtlicher Beleuchtung,* Berlin, 1902; J. Fischer, *Die chronologischen Fragen in den Büchern Esra-Nehemia,* Freiburg, 1903; *DB,* iv. 978–979; *EB,* iv. 5411–14; *JE,* xii. 662–663; and the works on the history of Israel dealing with the period, cited under AHAB, and ISRAEL, HISTORY OF.

ZEZSCHWITZ, tsetsh′wits, **KARL ADOLF GERHARD VON:** Lutheran theologian; b. at Bautzen (31 m. e.n.e. of Dresden) July 2, 1825; d. at Erlangen July 20, 1886. After elementary instruction at Dresden and Bautzen, he entered in 1846 the University of Leipsic, studying under Winer and Harless; he then became an assistant in the Mission House at Leipsic, and also taught in a girls' school; next he became substitute pastor at Grosszschocher, a village near Leipsic; from there he went to Leipsic as second university preacher in 1856, having developed a rich experience which he was hereafter to utilize in the department of catechetics. In 1857 he became a teacher in the university, and published *Petri apostoli de Christi descensu ad inferos sententia* . . . (Leipsic, 1857), also *Profangräcität und biblischer Sprachgeist* (1859). Besides exegesis, he dealt with catechetics; his work as preacher was acceptable, and he issued two volumes of sermons (1860, 1864). By 1862 he had finished the first volume of his *System der christlich-kirchlichen Katechetik*, completed in 1864. Beginning in 1862 he issued a series of smaller works on catechetics which was not completed till the issue of his *Christenlehre im Zusammenhang* (1885). During 1863–65 he delivered lectures at Frankfort, Darmstadt, and Basel, afterward published as *Innere Mission, Volkserziehung und Prophetenthum* (Frankfort, 1864), and *Apologie des Christenthums nach Geschichte und Lehre* (Leipsic, 1866). In 1865 he received a call as professor to Giessen, and the next year to Erlangen to teach practical theology; in 1867 the position of university preacher came to him; in 1868 he founded the Studienhaus, which became influential in the university, in which he exercised a useful leadership. In 1885 he laid down his position of university preacher, but devoted himself the more earnestly to his work of teaching.

Alongside his works on catechetics stands his chief work, *Das System der praktischen Theologie* (Leipsic, 1878), which found a wide and welcome field of usefulness. Other works are: *Vom römischen Kaiserthum deutscher Nation* (1877); *Das mittelalterliche Drama vom Ende des römischen Kaiserthums* (1878); and *Einleitung in die praktische Theologie* (Nördlingen, 1883). In his ecclesiastical relations Zezschwitz was a faithful Lutheran, opposing Romanism and also the "Union." In his culture he was wide and catholic, and his influence was salutary. (T. FICKER.)

ZIDON (SIDON). See PHENICIA, PHŒNICIANS, I., § 5.

ZIEGENBALG, BARTHOLOMÆUS: The first German Protestant missionary to India; b. at Pulsnitz (16 m. n.e. of Dresden), Saxony, June 14, 1683; d. at Tranquebar (140 m. s. by w. of Madras), India, Feb. 23, 1719. He was educated at Halle, and in 1705 was one of two missionaries selected by the king of Denmark to spread the Gospel in the Danish possessions in India. Landing in Tranquebar in July, 1706, Ziegenbalg and his companion began their labors under the most adverse conditions, being forced to encounter not only the antipathy of the Hindus, but also the ill-concealed hostility of the Danish governor and of the other European residents. Nevertheless, Ziegenbalg contrived to learn Tamil within a year, although when he arrived in India he was utterly unacquainted with the language, and he was soon able to prepare for baptism five slaves of Europeans. In 1707 he made an extensive preaching-tour, and in the following year was enabled by the Dutch magistrate at Negapatam to hold there a friendly conference on religious matters with the Brahmans. Ziegenbalg remained at Tranquebar until 1715, busily engaged in preaching to Hindus, half-breed Portuguese, and slaves, as well as holding a weekly German service, besides his necessary labor of translating the New Testament and a considerable portion of the Old

into Tamil, and writing much in his adopted language. In 1715 ill-health forced him to return to Europe, and he was received with high honors both in Germany and in England. Early in 1719 he went once more to India, but died within a short time.

The Tamil translation of the Bible, in which Ziegenbalg was assisted by B. Schultze and J. E. Gründler, commenced to appear at Tranquebar in 1714, though the work was not finished until 1728; it is especially noteworthy as being the first translation of the Scriptures into any of the languages of India. Ziegenbalg was likewise the author, among other works (many of them in Tamil), of *Grammatica Damulica* (Halle, 1716), the earliest portions of *Der königlichen dänischen Missionarien aus Ost-Indien eingesandte ausführliche Berichte* (95 parts, 1718–1848), which had been preceded by his *Merckwürdige Nachricht aus Ost-Indien* (3d ed., Leipsic, 1709; Eng. transl., *Propagation of the Gospel in the East*, 3 parts, London, 1709–14) and his *Ausführlicher Bericht, wie er . . . das Amt des Evangelii . . . führe* (2d ed., 7 parts, Halle, 1713–14; partial Eng. transl., *Account of the . . . Malabarians*, London, 1717); *Brevis delineatio missionis operis, quod ad propagandam Christi cognitionem . . . inter paganos Orientales et præcipue inter Damulos . . . Tranquebariæ geritur* (in collaboration with J. E. Gründler, Tranquebar, 1717); and *Genealogie der malabarischen Götter* (ed. W. Germann, Madras, 1867).

BIBLIOGRAPHY: J. H. Brauer, *Bartholomäus Ziegenbalg und seine Mitarbeiter in Trankebar*, Altona, 1837; W. Germann, *Ziegenbalg und Plütschau*, Erlangen, 1868; F. Schlegelmilch, *Bartholomäus Ziegenbalg*, Berlin, 1902; A. Gehring, *Bartholomäus Ziegenbalg*, 2d ed., Leipsic, 1907.

ZIEGLER, tsīH'ler, **JAKOB:** Humanist and theologian; b. about 1471; d. at Passau in 1549. Ziegler becomes known in 1491 as coming from Landau to the University of Ingolstadt and taking there his master's degree; in 1504 he dedicated an unprinted description of an astronomical instrument at Cologne to the Abbot Trithemius; soon after he was at Vienna, and after that at the castle of Baron Heinrich Kuna in Moravia, where he wrote a work against the Bohemian Brethren (Leipsic, 1512). A friendship with Caelio Calcagnini and with Bishop Ladislaus Szalkan of Waitzen led to an introduction to Cardinal Hippolytus of Este, through whom he received in 1521 an invitation to Rome from Pope Leo X. to complete there his mathematical and geographical works. Papal protection ceased on the death of Leo, but Ziegler remained there till 1525, working on a harmony of the Gospels. In 1523 he issued a defense of Erasmus against the Spaniard Stunica, *Libellus adversus Jacobi Stunicæ maledicentiam* (Basel, 1523). In 1525–31 he was with Calcagnini at Ferrara, where he gave expression to his opinions of the worldliness of the papal court and the tyranny of the pope in his *Vita Clementis VII.* Most noteworthy is his program for a new constitution of Christendom, *Rei Christianæ infirmitas*. In this he proposed a peace union of German cities and princes, confiscation of ecclesiastical possessions, establishment of a rule of peace after a campaign against the Turks and their Christian allies (Venice and Zapolya), election of two consuls to rule Italy and Rome and two Cæsars for the control of France and Spain, recasting of taxes in favor of the peasants and review of economic conditions, settling of German colonies in Austria and Hungary, care for education and philanthropy, and the political education of the people, with the seat of the empire in a Germanized Rome. After sending his controversial writings to Luther in 1529 he was invited to take a professorship at Wittenberg, but declined on account of his age. He was invited to Strasburg and funds were provided for his journey; he arrived there in 1531 and was given a pension of 100 gulden yearly. But the conditions in Germany seemed unpromising on account of the theological controversies. He disapproved of Butzer's guidance of the synod of 1533 against the Anabaptists and free spirits and the use of the temporal power against them, whereupon he was charged by Butzer with ingratitude, having in a little publication accused the Protestants of erecting a new papacy. From Baden-Baden he justified himself in a published apology. Ziegler thus showed himself one who had broken with the old Church but found no place in the new. After that he approached nearer the position of Roman Catholicism; he received an instructorship under Margrave Karl of Baden, in 1539–40 he was with Philip of Ehingen, went in 1541 to Vienna, where the next year he joined the theological faculty. The threatening situation arising from the Turkish invasion led him to take refuge at the court of the bishop of Passau, where he spent the rest of his life, dedicating to that prelate his exegetical works, which were put on the Index. His chief works were a commentary on Pliny (1531) and a description of the holy land (*Terræ sanctæ . . . doctissima descriptio*, Strasburg, 1536).   (K. Schottenloher.)

Bibliography: K. Schottenloher, *Jacob Ziegler, aus Landau an der Isar*, Münster, 1910; J. G. Schellhorn, *Amœnitates historiæ ecclesiasticæ et literariæ*, ii. 210 sqq., Leipsic, 1740; S. Günther, in *Forschungen zur Kultur- und Litteraturgeschichte Bayerns*, iv. 1–61, v. 116–128, Berlin, 1896–97; T. Kolde, in *Beiträge zur bayerischen Kirchengeschichte*, iii. 53–54, 239 sqq., Erlangen, 1897; G. Eneström, in *Bibliotheca mathematica*, 1896, pp. 53 sqq.; S. Riezler, *Geschichte Baierns*, vi. 406 sqq., 521, Gotha, 1903; P. Kalkoff, in *Archiv für Reformationsgeschichte*, iii (1905), 65 sqq.; *ADB*, xlv. 176 sqq.

ZIGABENUS (ZIGADENUS, ZYGADENUS).
See Euthymius Zigabenus.

ZILLERTHAL, tsil'er-täl″, EVANGELICALS OF:
A body of Protestants whose home was on the Ziller, a river of the Tyrol, which discharges into the Inn about twenty-two miles northeast of Innsbruck. About a century after the great emigration of the Salzburgers (see Salzburg, Evangelicals of), there took place an immigration of the Protestant Zillerthalers into the Riesengebirge. Both movements arose from the same causes and had analogous courses. By gift of King Arnulph in 889, the Zillerthal (valley of the Ziller) belonged to the archbishopric of Salzburg. It was first joined to the Tyrol in 1816, after various changes of fortune, coming finally into the possession of Austria in that year. It was a long time before the inhabitants felt themselves to be Tyroleans. While in the Tyrol between 1585 and 1619 the non-Roman Catholic (largely Baptist) element was completely rooted out, the success of the Salzburg archbishops

with the Lutherans had been much less. In 1532 Luther directed his celebrated letter to Martin Lodinger in Gastein, in 1549 a Salzburg Roman Catholic reform synod sought to suppress Lutheranism, and in 1563 a petition for freedom of religious belief succeeded from Bischofshofen, St. Veit, St. Johann, and Grossarl. Complaints had just been made (1562) about the progress of Lutheranism on the left bank of the Ziller. In 1618 in Hippach in the bishopric of Brixen Lutheran books were confiscated, and in 1617 the same had taken place in other towns; in 1672, 1674, and 1682 great unrest was manifested in several places in the vicinity. The emigration of 800 Protestants of Defereger-Thal seemed likely to disturb Zillerthal; and in 1689 two brothers named Stainer of Mairhofen preached the Evangelical doctrine. Yet when the great movements which convulsed Europe began in 1731, Zillerthal remained quiet, though it was generally known that Roman Catholicism had no hold upon the population. One reason for this was the complicated governmental conditions in Zillerthal; for the valley was cut by enclaves which belonged to the Tyrol, there being six different jurisdictions. Moreover, both the government of the Tyrol and that of Bavaria were averse to oppressive measures. While the " Emigration patent " was published in Zillerthal, it remained a dead letter there. Its republication in 1742 was only an alarm shot to further the surrender of Lutheran books. The time was not ripe for extreme measures, for Charles VII. was just seated on the imperial throne, and the archbishopric was alarmed by a mooted secularization. Later Maria Theresa showed a mailed fist in the catholicizing of this region, going to the extent of using imprisonment in 1758 at St. Jakob. Measures began to hem in the inhabitants, the toleration edict of 1781 brought no relief for this district, and the inhabitants were dealt with as seducers and makers of converts. The Lutherans continued to read their concealed books, including the annotated Luther Bible and Johann Arndt's *Postille*, and hung the scapularies given to their children about the necks of sheep and goats. Their Protestant tendencies were accentuated by visiting North Germans and by commercial travels to foreign parts, especially to Hamburg. But politics played no part in the development.

Thus since the Reformation this religious current made itself continually stronger in Zillerthal. Neither reactionary bureaucratic oppression, mutinous and foreign democrats, nor foreign propaganda affected the Zillerthal movement. In 1816, when the region passed into Austrian control, the inhabitants of the valley begged in vain for the concession of a meeting-place for worship and for recognition as an Evangelical community. The (Roman Catholic) pastor sought in vain by means of Roman Catholic " house-teachers " to win over the " Inclinantes " (as those were called who were of Protestant inclinations). In 1829 a crisis was created by the application of six people of Mairhofen for the six weeks of religious instruction that since 1783 had been prescribed for those who would go over into a tolerated non-Roman Catholic communion in Austria. Such a demand was unheard in the

Tyrol, and it caused debate whether the laws for toleration were applicable there. Especial opposition was manifested to the entrance of an Evangelical pastor in the "land of religious unity." Official pressure against Evangelicals followed. In May, 1834, from the emperor came a refusal of the petition sent up two years earlier for relief from oppression of conscience and for permission to receive an Evangelical pastor, the only relief granted being permission to emigrate to a part of Austria where non-Roman Catholic communities were allowed to exist. Permission to send a delegation, with Johann Fleidl at its head, to the emperor to plead eleven points was refused. The Grand Duke Johann, uncle of the emperor, announced that Evangelical worship could not be permitted in the Tyrol, though emigration was conceded. The "Inclinantes" remained and increased in numbers, and this caused perturbation; attempts followed with increasing stress to drive the Evangelicals from the district. Yet this official action was more humane in its purpose than the fanatical attacks of the Salzburg clergy. On Jan. 12, 1837, an imperial edict required declaration within fourteen days of intention to leave the Roman Catholic Church; after that time all not so indicating intention would be treated as Roman Catholics. Those who declared themselves Protestants were to leave the Tyrol within four months. In spite of the sorrow at leaving their native place, 385 persons, later increased to 437, declared their intention to emigrate. Fleidl went to Berlin and was kindly received by Frederick William III.; the Prussian Upper Consistory sent Court Preacher Strauss to investigate, and he received a very favorable impression; finally (July 13, 1837) permission was given to receive the exiles into Prussia. Only a few betook themselves into the Austrian provinces open to them. The lot of those who remained in the valley became constantly more unendurable, pressure being brought by restrictions concerning marriage, burial, and meeting together. Finally in six wagons the emigrants set forth, most of them going into Silesia, and on Oct. 17, 1737, they arrived in Schmiedeberg. The colony has since that time developed normally and successfully.   (F. ARNOLD.)

BIBLIOGRAPHY: K. Hübner, in the *Mittheilungen* of the Society for Knowledge concerning Salzburg, xlv (1895), 41–79; S. Ruf, *Das Luthertum im Zillerthale, 1617–1794*, in *Tiroler Boten*, 1868, nos. 95–96; M. Beheim-Schwarzbach, *Die Zillerthaler in Schlesien*, Breslau, 1875; G. von Gasteiger, *Die Zillerthaler Protestanten und ihr Ausweisung aus Tirol*, Meran, 1892; G. Hahn, *Die Zillerthaler im Riesengebirge*, Schmiedeberg, 1887; idem, *Aus der Tiroler Schule zu Zillerthal im Riesengebirge in den ersten 50 Jahren ihres Bestehens*, Breslau, 1896; E. Reuss, *Friederike Gräfin von Reden, Ein Lebensbild nach Briefen und Tagebüchern*, ii. 152–235, Berlin, 1888.

ZIMMER, tsim´er, **KARL FRIEDRICH:** German Protestant; b. at Gardelegen (87 m. w. of Berlin) Sept. 22, 1855. He was educated at the universities of Tübingen and Berlin, and in 1880 became privat-docent in the theological faculty at the University of Bonn; three years later he accepted a call to the pastorate of Mahnsfeld (1883), then became associate professor at Königsberg (1884); was director of the seminary for preachers at Herborn (1890–94), and since 1894 has been con-

nected with the *Diakonieverein* of Berlin, of which he has been successively assistant director (1894–1898) and director-in-chief (since 1898). Besides editing, among other works, *Bücherkleinode evangelischer Theologen* (Gotha, 1888); *Handbibliothek für praktische Theologie* (17 vols., 1890–93); *Perthes Handlexikon für evangelische Theologie* (Gotha, 1890); *Perthes theologisches Hilfslexikon* (1894); and the periodicals *Halleluja* (1880–85); *Blätter aus dem evangelischen Diakonieverein* (since 1897); and *Frauendienst* (since 1092), he has written *J. G. Fichtes Religionsphilosophie* (Berlin, 1878); *Der Spruch vom Jonazeichen* (Hildburghausen, 1881); commentaries on Galatians and Acts (1882); *Exegetische Probleme des Hebräer- und Galaterbriefs* (1882); *Concordantiæ supplementariæ omnium vocum Novi Testamenta* (Gotha, 1882); *Die deutschen evangelischen Kirchengesangvereine der Gegenwart* (Quedlinburg, 1882); *Der Verfall des Kantoren- und Organistenamtes in der evangelischen Landeskirche Preussens* (1885); *Königsberger Kirchenliederdichter und Kirchenkomponisten* (Königsberg, 1885); commentary on Romans (Quedlinburg, 1887); *Der Galaterbrief im altlateinischen Text* (Königsberg, 1887); *Das Gebet nach den paulinischen Schriften* (1887); *Kirchenchorbuch für Knaben- [Frauen- oder Männer-] Chor* (2 parts, Quedlinburg, 1888–89); commentary on the epistles to the Thessalonians (Herborn, 1891); *Sünde oder Krankheit?* (Leipsic, 1894); *Die Grundlegungen der praktischen Theologie* (Berlin, 1894); *Der evangelische Diakonie-Verein* (Herborn, 1895); *Das erste Jahrzehnt des evangelischen Diakonievereins* (Berlin, 1904, 3d ed., 1911); *Lebenserziehung* (2 parts, 1909); *Soziale Arbeit der Haustochter* (1910); *Die Haustochter* (1910); and *Brauchen wir noch Töchterpensionate?* (1910).

ZIMMERMANN, tsim´er-mān´´, **PAUL AUGUST BERNHARD VON:** Austrian Protestant; b. at Dresden Sept. 3, 1843. He was educated at the universities of Leipsic (1864–67; Ph.D., 1869) and Berlin (1867–68), after which he was a catechist and pastor of St. Thomas's, Leipsic, until 1874. Since 1875 he has been pastor of the Evangelical Lutheran church in Vienna, and since 1888 has also been privat-docent for the philosophy of religion in the Evangelical theological faculty in the same city. He is a member of the governing board of the Vienna Christlicher Verein junger Männer and the founder and president of the Verein für evangelische Diakonie. In theology his position is positive. He has been editor of *Der evangelische Hausfreund;* and has written, *Platos Lehre von der Unsterblichkeit der Seele* (Leipsic, 1869); *Gottesgrüsse aus Natur und Menschenleben* (1872); *Tropfen ins Meer* (sermons and confirmation addresses; 1875); *Das Rätsel des Lebens und die Ratlosigkeit des Materialismus* (1877); *Toleranz und Intoleranz gegen das Evangelium in Oesterreich* (1881); *Liebe und Leid* (collected addresses; 1885); *Das Evangelium in Oesterreich und Frankreich* (1885); *Vor der Pforte des Heiligtums* (1887); *Vaterunser* (Vienna, 1894); *Für stille Stunden* (meditations; 1896); *Das Evangelium in Wien* (Leipsic, 1903); and *Was wir der Reformation zu verdanken haben, und Hauptpunkte des evangelischen Glaubensbekenntnisses* (7th ed., Heilbronn, 1907).

ZIMMERN, tsim'ūrn, **HEINRICH:** German Protestant; b. at Graben (20 m. s.w. of Heidelberg), Baden, July 14, 1862. He was educated at the universities of Leipsic (Ph.D., 1884) and Erlangen (1884-85); was curate in Baden (1885-87); a member of the staff of the university library at Leipsic (1887-88); privat-docent for Semitics successively at Königsberg (1889-90) and Halle (1890-94); associate professor of Assyriology at Leipsic (1894-1899); associate professor of Semitics at Breslau (1899-1900); and returned in 1901 to Leipsic to become professor of oriental languages. He has written *Beiträge zur Kenntnis der babylonischen Religion* (3 parts, Leipsic, 1896-1901); and *Vergleichende Grammatik der semitischen Sprachen* (Berlin, 1898); and edited the *Leipziger semitistische Studien* (1904 sqq.).

ZIM'RI: Fifth king of Israel, usurper and successor of Elah, whom he slew. The source, I Kings xvi. 9-20, states that he was captain of half the chariots of Elah, that he killed his master while the latter was drinking and afterward exterminated the family; that he reigned only seven days, since the rest of the army, engaged in a campaign against the Philistines, chose Omri, the other army commander, for king and then besieged Tirzah, at that time the capital. When Zimri saw that the position was untenable, he fired the palace and perished in the flames. His deeds seem to have been regarded as unusually heinous even in a kingdom where change of dynasty by assassination was frequent (cf. II Kings ix. 31).

The name appears also as the name of several Israelites: (1) son of Zerah (I Chron. ii. 6; but according to Josh. vii. 1. the name was Zabdi); (2) a Benjamite, descendant of Saul (I Chron. viii. 36, ix. 42). In Jer. xxv. 25 Zimri appears as the name of a region in connection with Elam and Media, but the locality and name have not been satisfactorily identified.   (R. KITTEL.)

BIBLIOGRAPHY: Consult, besides the Bible dictionaries, the literature on the period cited under AHAB; and ISRAEL, HISTORY OF.

ZINZENDORF, tsin'tsen-dorf, **NICOLAUS LUDWIG, COUNT.**

Early Life and Education (§ 1).
Beginnings of Religious Activities (§ 2).
Relations with the Brethren; Theological Development (§ 3).
Activities as Leader of the Brethren (§ 4).
Last Years (§ 5).
Leading Idea; Literary Works (§ 6).

Count Nicolaus Ludwig Zinzendorf, founder of the Unity of the Brethren (q.v.), was born at Dresden May 26, 1700; d. at Herrnhut May 9, 1760. His ancestry on both sides was noble; his father, a

1. Early Life and Education. high Saxon official, died while the son was a small infant; his early boyhood was passed under the care of his maternal grandmother, who was a distinguished representative of Pietism, and this influence became dominant in the formation of the boy's character, since before his ninth year the aim of his life was the attainment of a living communion with Christ. Further education was gained at the Pädagogium at Halle (1710-16), where toward the end of his course he came into closer relations with Francke; the influence of this

period was also an abiding one, and the organization of societies of youth for the betterment of personal life and the diffusion of the Gospel gave promise of what he was later to accomplish. His own predilections were toward theology, but his family desired him to prepare himself for a career in the service of the State; he therefore took up the study of law at Wittenberg (1716-19), which did not prevent him from spending much time on the Bible, Luther's works, and the writings of the Pietists. The years 1719-20 he spent in travel, in Holland coming into connection with prominent representatives of the Reformed theology and with those outside church circles. He came to an understanding of the bond which united all Christians, that which consisted in a relation of personal trust in Christ. In France a new circle of acquaintances was made, including the devout Cardinal Noailles, with whom the tie of their common love for Christ became a strong one. In the choice for personal lifework a career like that of Canstein in the orphan establishment was his preference; but his family was strongly opposed to this, and in deference to their wishes he took up his work as a counselor in Dresden in the late autumn of 1721. With a part of his patrimony he bought the estate of Berthelsdorf and as patron settled there the pastor and poet Johann Andreas Rothe; and in 1722 he married Countess Erdmute Dorothea, sister of his friend Heinrich, count of Reuss-Ebersdorf.

The way to the entrance upon official duties seemed at first to have been closed by Zinzendorf's refusal to subscribe to the Formula of Concord, and

2. Beginnings of Religious Activities. he was looking to service at the Danish court when subscription was waived and in 1721 he took up his duties. But of his work there little is known. His chief interest was in the formation of an ecclesiola like that of Spener's, which found a nucleus on his own estate. With Friedrich von Watteville, Rothe, the pastor at Berthelsdorf, and Melchior Schäffer-Görlitz he formed the "Union of four Brethren" bound to work for the interests of faith in Christ as a "heart-religion." Missions to the Jews and to the heathen were also in mind. In the winter of 1723-24 a building was begun which was intended to serve purposes like those of the Halle Pädagogium, which in 1727 became an orphan asylum. A printing-press was set up in order to further the proposed movement, and a series of tractates and two catechisms were issued. Those who were impressed by rationalism and were outside of church influences were sought through a weekly called *Le Socrate de Dresde* (1725-26), in which a sort of practical philosophy, proving religion to be a universal need, was expounded, reconciling a positive Christian piety with philosophic thought. The meetings at Görlitz and at Dresden raised up opposition, and Zinzendorf sought to show the legitimacy of the assemblages by the Schmalkald Articles.

The Bohemian Brethren (q.v.) had spread from Bohemia and Moravia into Poland. The Bohemians had in 1609 formed a union with the Evangelical church of Bohemia, but in the Counter-Reformation the Bohemian and Moravian branches had become

practically extinct. The Polish branch with a Reformed tinge had maintained itself as a separate
3. Relations organization with the old episcopal
with the consecration, while, in Poland, Moravian and Bohemian refugees had
Brethren; their independent organization which
Theological was, however, finally obliterated. But
Develop- some Moravian communities still ex-
ment. isted in Bohemia and Moravia, and
under the stress of a series of edicts
by Charles VI. (1717–26) a new emigration was
begun which was brought to the notice of Zinzendorf, though he knew nothing of the inner relations
and of the connection with the Bohemian Brethren.
Indeed, only his official relations brought Zinzendorf as yet into connections with them. But interest was awakened as it became clear that the emigrants were resolved not to take on the yoke of a
new church when they had just escaped from the
yoke of Roman Catholic impositions. Meanwhile
by the death of his grandmother (1726) Zinzendorf
saw his way clear to retire from his official position,
which he did in 1728. He concentrated his attention now upon Herrnhut, took advantage of the law
which permitted a newly established village to establish its own rules of living, enabling it to form a community within the church, and thus preventing the
danger of separatism, but possessing the right of
private assembly. The *ecclesiola* became a great
union, but with a legal basis as a part of the parish
of Berthelsdorf. Meanwhile, during the years 1725
and following, Zinzendorf's religious convictions had
been undergoing development into their final form.
At the beginning of that period he was still an adherent of the Halle school, though he had no interest in the Pietistic themes of dispute. His life in
Dresden gave him also a valuable insight into the
" world " with its activities. With the development
in Pietism, after Francke's death, of a party spirit,
Zinzendorf's attitude to it became less cordial.
During the period 1729–34 he found himself in position to oppose the doctrines of Johann Konrad Dippel (q.v.) as set forth in the latter's *Vera demonstratio evangelica*, with the author of which he had
correspondence. This opposition was in spite of fundamental agreement on the part of the two men in
placing stress in the doctrine of the atonement upon
the love of God. Zinzendorf's attitude toward mysticism and separatism became ever more decidedly
opposed. His position toward Herrnhut was meanwhile developing into closeness through their common activities. But this course had important
results upon his own fortunes and made him the object of attack. An opinion gained from the faculty
of Tübingen was favorable to the orthodoxy of the
Bohemian Brethren. But suspicion on the part of
the authorities made itself manifest in investigations by the state authorities, and an order was
issued in 1732 that Zinzendorf sell his goods and
leave Saxony, though the next year this was withdrawn because of a change in the ministry. But the
general attitude seemed to indicate to the Herrnhuters the wisdom of further emigrations, to which
the success of missionary undertakings in North
America seemed to invite. Accordingly, in 1735 the
first company took their departure for Georgia, and

in connection with this appeared the necessity for
ecclesiastical authority based upon ordination, the
Bohemian consecration being imparted by Daniel
Ernst Jablonski (q.v.) to the missionary David
Nitschmann. Zinzendorf wished at that time himself to receive consecration, but Jablonski demurred
because of the sensation such a step would cause.
This episcopal office had no immediate relation to
Herrnhut, and had in view simple leadership for the
colonies and missions abroad. In the mean time the
opponents of Zinzendorf had been busy; on Mar.
20, 1736, a rescript required him to leave Saxony,
while a commission was appointed to investigate
conditions at Herrnhut. The commission, which
proceeded impartially, found little to criticize, and
that practically the Lutheran standards were respected. The result was the announcement of toleration for the community upon express recognition
of the standards.

Zinzendorf went to the Wetterau, a strip of land
between the Taunus and the Vogelsberg, rented the
castle known as the Ronneburg as a residence, and
4. Activities began work among the lower classes
as Leader in the way of Bible translation and
of the teaching. His associates formed
Brethren. " pilgrim unions " for the carrying out
of the general plans. Out of the work
here arose the work among the " Diaspora " in the Baltic provinces which the brethren
later carried on. On a return journey Zinzendorf,
stopped at Berlin, came into close relations with
King Frederick William I. of Prussia, won him over
to advocate Zinzendorf's consecration as bishop,
submitted himself to examination as to his worthiness, and received consecration May 20, 1737, from
Jablonski. While Zinzendorf's aim had been to
maintain the Brethren as a community within the
Lutheran Church, events were forcing the trend
toward the formation of an independent body.
Especially in the mission fields and abroad generally
the work stood out as that of a church alongside of
the other churches. This resulted especially from
Zinzendorf's visit to the West Indies (Dec., 1738, to
June, 1739), which showed him the necessity of this
development. Questions of polity and government
obtruded themselves, whether the episcopal or presbyterial form were the better. In 1741 Zinzendorf,
on the eve of a visit to America, laid down his episcopal office that he might work simply as " Brother
Ludwig," this action being coincident with a synodal
conference at London called to decide the polity of
the Brethren's organization. [In America, 1741–43,
his activities were considerable, centering about
Bethlehem and Germantown in Pennsylvania. He
was especially interested in two lines of work, missions to the Indians and endeavors after church
union, the latter being sought through frequent conferences. But the impression was gained that union
was to be brought about by merging in the Moravian
communion. He acted as pastor of the Lutheran
church in Philadelphia, and assumed the title of
inspector-general of the Lutheran churches then in
America. But the result of his activities seems to
have been rather dissension than a larger unity.
He was required by the mayor of Philadelphia to
give up the records of the Lutheran churches so far

as they were in his possession, and the organization of the Lutherans was taken up by Henry Melchior Mühlenberg (q.v.).] Even among the Brethren dissident views prevailed and in various parts where their establishments were placed different tendencies not in harmony with Zinzendorf's aims revealed themselves. The reconciliation of these more or less divergent lines of development was carried on as far as possible so as to harmonize with the local conditions, with the aim, also, of avoiding sectarian tendencies and of working in harmony with the church of the region. Zinzendorf's doctrinal development proceeded also, and a statement of his belief concerning the Trinity was formulated so as to reconcile it practically with the central " heart theology " of the Brethren. But this statement and the accompanying developments in the communities aroused opposition and a considerable number of adverse brochures were issued, which affected the regard in which the entire Brotherhood was held, " Herrnhuters " becoming a term of reproach. In some parts the alternative was placed before the Brethren of sundering their connection with Zinzendorf or of removing to other regions.

The last years of Zinzendorf from 1749 contain much that is depressing. Until 1755 he was in England, except for the period July, 1750–July, 1751, and during those years he revised his teachings and eliminated much which had been or

5. Last Years. seemed fantastic. The Unity arising from the Herrnhut colony was originally without property, and Zinzendorf had devoted all the income from his own possessions without stint to its uses. He had also made loans to carry on the work in Holland and England, and the result was that he was at the beginning of this last period on the verge of bankruptcy. The only possibility of recovery seemed to be to have the Unity consider the position of Zinzendorf bound up with its own and to have the financial side of affairs put under definite authorities. In this matter the aid of skilful jurists was invoked, the private property of Zinzendorf was separated from the possessions of the organization, and the administration of the latter provided for. This led to a more complete development of the administrative side of the Unity of the Brethren. In 1752 Zinzendorf was saddened by the death of his son Christian Renatus, in whom he had hoped to see his successor in the work to which he himself had given his life. From 1755 Zinzendorf's labors were chiefly in the direction of pastoral visitation of the Unity's communities. In 1756 his wife died, and in 1760, in the midst of his restless activities, he was seized with a fever which soon resulted in his own death.

The one idea which controlled Zinzendorf's life was the thought which obtained possession of him in early boyhood, which he expressed by the word *Herzensreligion*, " Heart religion." The central thought here was a life in communion with God. This resolved itself into a living communion with Christ, since God was revealed to mankind only in him; religion was then an orienting of the life to the person and work of Christ. But the formulation of these thoughts in the direction of instruction led to

expressions which in their concrete illustration were paradoxical and strange. The purpose to which this whole work was to lead was not only the blessedness mediated through Christ but

6. Leading Idea; Literary Works. participation in a common activity for the kingdom of God. The more such unions as were introduced were founded, the more could the Christlife be realized historically. Yet the ideal Zinzendorf ever held was not the creation of a new church; he expected his ideal to be realized within the existing churches, especially within the Lutheran. So he would restore the Bohemian Brethren's organization as a community within the Lutheran Church, retaining the right of private assemblage alongside of the stated public services. But as already noted, external circumstances, particularly the situation in the mission field, led to ecclesiastical and separate organization, though with fidelity to the Augsburg standards, with " Inner Mission " work, foreign missions, and educational missions. Among the writings of Zinzendorf may be named his *Kleine Schrifften* (Frankfort, 1740); *Bedencken und Besondere Sendschreiben in allerhand practischen Materien* (1734); *Theologischer und dahin einschlagender Bedencken* (1741); *Sieben letzte Reden* (Büdingen, 1743); and also the *Sammlung geistlicher und lieblicher Lieder* (Leipsic, 1725). Of English translations mention may be made of *Sixteen Discourses on the Redemption of Man by the Death of Christ* (London, 1740); *Seven Sermons on the Godhead of the Lamb; or, the Divinity of Jesus Christ* (1742); *Extract of Count Zinzendorf's Discourses on the Redemption of Man by the Death of Christ* (Newcastle, 1744); *Maxims, Theological Ideas and Sentences* (1751); and *Hymns Composed for the Use of the Brethren* (1749).   (JOSEF MÜLLER.)

BIBLIOGRAPHY: Accounts of the life of Zinzendorf have been written by A. G. Spangenberg, 8 parts, Barby, 1772–75, Eng. transl., London, 1838; O. A. Woldershausen, Wittenberg, 1749; L. von Schrautenbach, written 1782, ed. by Kölbing, 2d ed., Gnadau, 1871; J. C. Duvernoy, Barby, 1793; G. B. Reichel, Leipsic, 1790; J. G. Müller, Winterthur, 1822; J. W. Verbeek, Gnadau, 1845; Varnhagen von Ense, 2d ed., Berlin, 1846; O. Glaubrecht, Frankfort, 1852; J. F. Schröder, Nordhausen, 1857; F. Pilgram, Leipsic, 1857; F. Bovet, Paris, 1860, Eng. transl., London, 1896; G. Burkhardt, 2d ed., Berlin, 1878; H. Tietzen, Gütersloh, 1888; J. Jüngst-Stettin, *Pietisten*, pp. 57–75, Tübingen, 1906; and W. Walker, in *Greatest Men of the Christian Church*, Chicago, 1908. Consult further: J. Hutton, *An Essay toward Giving Some Just Ideas of the Personal Character of Count Zinzendorff*, London, 1755; J. G. Müller, *Bekenntnisse merkwürdiger Männer*, 2d ed., 6 vols., Winterthur, 1793–1822; É. É. Jacob, *Essai sur Zinzendorf et sur l'église et Herrnhut*, Strasburg, 1852; C. H. C. Plath, *Sieben Zeugen des Herrn*, Berlin, 1867; H. Plitt, *Zinzendorfs Theologie*, 3 vols., Gotha, 1869–74; W. Binnie, in *Evangelical Succession*, Edinburgh, 1882; B. Becker, *Zinzendorf im Verhältnis zu Philosophie und Kirchentum seiner Zeit*, Leipsic, 1886; J. T. Müller, *Zinzendorf als Erneuerer der alten Brüderkirche*, Leipsic, 1900; O. Steinecke, *Zinzendorfs Bildungsreise*, Halle, 1900; idem, *Zinzendorf und der Katholicismus*, ib. 1902; T. Schmidt, *Zinzendorfs soziale Stellung*, Basel, 1900; G. E. von Ratzmer, *Die Jugend Zinzendorfs*, Eisenach, 1904.

ZION (SION). See JERUSALEM, V., §§ 1–3.

ZION UNION APOSTOLIC CHURCH. See METHODISTS, IV., 9.

ZIONISM.

Theodor Herzl and his Predecessors (§ 1).
Inception of the Movement and its Congresses (§ 2).
Zionist Organization (§ 3).
Enforced Changes of Original Purpose (§ 4).
Jewish Colonial Trust and Affiliations (§ 5).
Agricultural Colonies and Educational Work in Palestine (§ 6).
The Territorialist Zionists (§ 7).

Zionism, the modern movement which has for its object the segregation of the Jews in a home of their own, took its rise when Dr. Theodor Herzl, a Viennese journalist, published *Der Judenstaat* (Vienna, 1896). In seeking for the cause of anti-Semitism, which had raged in various portions of continental Europe for some fifteen years previous, Herzl found

1. Theodor Herzl and his Predecessors. it to be the impossibility of the Jews to enter completely into the social life of the peoples among whom they now live without becoming submerged. In order to preserve their identity it was necessary, he argued, for the Jews to have some definite center and home, and to effect this purpose, a " Society of Jews " and a " Jewish Company," similar to the English charter companies, were to be formed. It was immaterial to Herzl, at this time, where this home was to be; he suggested either Argentina or Palestine. He attacked the problem purely from an economic and political point of view; the religious sanctions, so dear to many of his fellow Jews, had not appealed to him at all. This idea of segregating the Jews was not entirely new. Judaism had, at all times, retained the hope of a restoration to the land of promise as a part of its creed; and the hope figures prominently in the prayers recited in all orthodox and conservative congregations. It had, however, remained nothing but a pious wish, and only rarely had attempts been made to translate these hopes into deeds. Propositions of various kinds had been put forward in the sixteenth century, and they were renewed in the eighteenth and in the first half of the nineteenth centuries; notably in America by Warder Cresson, a convert to Judaism, and by Major Mordecai M. Noah. But these plans found no echo in the Jewish masses until the increasing pressure of anti-Semitism in eastern Europe produced a Jewish national sentiment in which they took deep root. In the sixties of the nineteenth century this sentiment had been presaged by such men as David Gordon in Lyck, Hirsch Kalischer in Thorn, and Moses Hess, the associate of Marx and Engels. They gave the impulse to the founding of the Chovevei Zion (" Lovers of Zion ") Societies, the chief object of which was the colonization of Palestine by Jews. Jewish national sentiment was also strengthened by the rise of nationalism all over Europe. The Germans had achieved racial solidarity by the Franco-Prussian war of 1870–71, and they were followed by Rumanians, Serbs, and Bulgarians, while the Jews alone found themselves scattered over the face of the globe without a racial or ideal center. The riots of 1880 and 1881 in Russia warned them that, though they had achieved emancipation in most of the culture-nations, that emancipation had been largely a mere paper one. Not only in Russia, but also in Germany, France, England, and America, societies for colonization in Palestine were founded.

The first of these colonies was started in 1878, and they saw their greatest extension in the eighties and nineties of the nineteenth century.

The Jewish national movement had spread also into Austria; especially among the students at the University of Vienna. Immediately upon the publication of Herzl's pamphlet, the Zion Society of that city promised its adhesion, and Herzl was enabled to send out an invitation for the first international Jewish congress to be held in

2. Inception of the Movement and its Congresses. Munich. It was this call that gave prominence to the inception of the new movement. Herzl had supposed that the Jews in all parts of the world would rally to his assistance, and it is true that large numbers did, especially among the intellectuals. But the opposition to any attempt to put his theories into practise revealed great strength. Many of the orthodox-minded imagined that this was an attempt to " force the hand of Providence," that the religious sanctions were wanting, and that salvation for the Jew—in other words, the final ingathering—could come only with direct divine help. Others, again, feared that they might endanger their recently acquired emancipation; and it was openly said that Zionism would give a fillip to anti-Semitism. The project to hold the first congress in Munich was dropped out of deference to the opposition manifested by the Jews of that city, and the place of meeting was changed to Basel in Switzerland. There, on Aug. 29–31, 1897, 204 delegates assembled and drew up what is known as the " Basel Program," stating that the object of Zionism was " to establish for the Jewish people a publicly and legally assured home in Palestine." Thus, the new movement attached itself to the old hope of a restoration. Since 1897, ten congresses have been held, those of 1898, 1899, 1901, 1903, 1905, and 1911 in Basel. The congress of 1900 sat in London, that of 1907 in The Hague, and that of 1909 in Hamburg.

The Zionist organization is thoroughly democratic, the supreme power residing in the congress, which is made up of representatives chosen by the various groupings of societies. As long as Herzl lived, the general direction rested in his hands, supported by a smaller " Actions-Committee," having its seat in Vienna and being elected by the congress. In addition, there is a larger " Actions-Committee,"

3. Zionist Organization. made up of representatives of the different Zionist federations in which the societies in each country are grouped. This larger committee meets regularly in the year in which no congress is held, or at the call of the smaller committee. Federations of Zionist societies exist in Russia, Germany, England, the United States, Canada, Austria, Galicia, Hungary, Switzerland, the South Slavic lands, Rumania, Belgium, Holland, and South Africa. In addition, societies are to be found in France, Turkey, Bulgaria, Servia, Italy, Scandinavia, Morocco, Egypt, the Argentine Republic, Australia, and China (Shanghai). In 1905 the seat of the smaller " Actions-Committee " was transferred to Cologne, with David Wolfssohn of that city as presiding officer, and the number of members was reduced to three. In 1908 a branch of the central office was opened in Berlin. In 1911 David Wolfssohn resigned; no new president was elected, the smaller "Actions-Committee" being empowered to choose its own presiding officer. The seat of the "Actions-Committee" was removed to Berlin. Comprising, as it does, Jews living in such various lands, it is natural that differences of views on economic and religious questions have found their expression in peculiar groupings. The ultra-orthodox Zionists are represented by the "Mizrachi," who in 1909 formed a federation of their own, the statutes of the organization having been changed so as to permit all who pay 3,000 shekels to band themselves together. On the other hand, the labor members have formed a group of their own, and are known as the "Po'ale-Zion" or "Democratic Fraction."

It was Herzl's idea to obtain from the late Sultan Abdul Hamid a charter which would grant certain rights and privileges to the Jews settled in Palestine, in return for a definite sum and an annual payment. With this end in view, Herzl had several interviews with the sultan, which, however, resulted in no definite proposals being made. Two events have rendered a different orientation of Zionist effort necessary; the death of Herzl (July 3, 1904) and the changed régime in Turkey (1908). The first deprived the movement of a trained diplomat who could lead it through the tortuous ways of political negotiations; the second made impossible the granting of a charter with any extended rights. In view of this, Zionist work has been directed toward developing the natural resources of Palestine, and toward securing for the Jews there a preponderating influence, so as to make of it a real home which the Jews shall seek as an abiding place, and to which they may look as a spiritual center. It had been Herzl's idea that no practical work should be attempted in Palestine before the necessary legal guaranties had been secured, but even Herzl was carried off his feet by the natural impulse of Jewish sentiment; and under the present changed circumstances, every effort is being bent to this practical work, and various institutions have been established to further it.

The practical organization through which the Zionists have worked, and which has taken official part in all the more important negotiations, is the "Jewish Colonial Trust," established in London in 1899. In 1910 this institution had a capital of £446,539. Since 1903 the trust has devoted most of its capital and of its energy toward assisting active work in Palestine. In that year it founded in Jaffa the "Anglo-Palestine Company" as a Jewish banking-house. Branch offices have since then been opened in Jerusalem, Haifa, Beirut, Hebron, Gaza, and Safed. This company has rendered signal service in connection with the loan-associations formed to assist colonists and workmen. In 1908 the "Anglo-Levantine Banking Company" was formed in Constantinople. The shares of both these daughter banks are held by the Jewish Colonial Trust. In 1904 the "Jew-

4. Enforced Changes of Original Purpose.

5. Jewish Colonial Trust and Affiliations.

ish National Fund" was definitely organized; its seat is also in London, and its purpose is to acquire land in Palestine which shall remain the inalienable possession of the Jewish people. The collections, which come from the use of "National Fund Stamps," from free-will offerings, and from payments made to inscribe persons or societies in the "Golden Book," reached in 1910 the sum of $500,-000. Nearly $100,000 is added each year to this fund. It is represented in Palestine by the "Palestine administration," with its seat in Jaffa, which attends to the various undertakings in which the fund is interested and acts as a bureau of information in regard to economic questions connected with Palestine. It is also charged with the supervision of the work being done by various Zionistic societies, e.g., the Society for Planting Olive-trees, the Palestine Land-Development Company (with its model farm at Kinnereth), and the Palestine Industrial Syndicate. The official organ of the Zionist movement is *Die Welt*, published in Cologne 1897–1911, since then in Berlin. In addition, there are some fifty other newspapers and magazines published by Zionists in various languages and in different parts of the Jewish world.

The Jewish agricultural colonies in Palestine, while not founded officially by the Zionist body, are due largely to the efforts of individual Zionists. Financial aid to found them and see them through the first years of their existence was furnished by Baron Edmond de Rothschild of Paris. In 1899 the Rothschild colonies came under the management of the Jewish Colonization Society of London, but since then they have emancipated themselves from this control, and have become self-supporting and self-governing. In 1911 there were some 39 Jewish colonies in Palestine, without counting a number of smaller settlements which do not deserve the name of colonies. Of these 17 are in Judea, 13 in Galilee, 8 in Samaria, and 1 beyond the Jordan on the Sea of Tiberias. These colonies contain about 8,000 inhabitants. Great attention has been paid by the Zionists to the intellectual development of the Jews in Palestine, especially to education. Many of the existing schools are due, it is true, to the initiative of non-Zionist Jewish societies, e.g., the Alliance Israélite Universelle in Paris, the Hilfsverein der deutschen Juden in Berlin, the Chovevei Zion in Odessa, and the Jewish Colonization Society in London. But under the influence of Zionist pressure, a national Jewish character is being given to these schools, especially to those in the colonies, and Hebrew is quickly becoming the common language of instruction, as it is becoming that of intercourse among all the Jews in Palestine. Specific Zionist foundations are the Hebrew high school for boys and the Hebrew high school for girls in Jaffa, the Hebrew high school in Jerusalem, and the Hebrew technical school now in process of building at Haifa. The Bezalel School at Jerusalem deserves special mention—a technical school for the industrial arts, founded in 1905 by Boris Schatz, in which 400 persons are taught carpet-weaving, filigree work in silver, basket-making, and woodwork,

6. Agricultural Colonies and Educational Work in Palestine.

while at the same time they earn their livelihood in the school. To these institutions must be added the Central Jewish Library (Midrash Abrabanel), founded in 1900 by Joseph Chazanowicz of Bielostok (35,000 volumes) and the Agricultural Experiment Station founded in 1910 in the neighborhood of Haifa. These and other similar institutions have the object of making Palestine a center of Jewish activity, to which the Jew will be attracted, not in order to die there, as the pious did in former times, but to live and work.

An offshoot of the Zionist movement is the so-called " Territorial Organization." This grouping is the result of impatience at the failure of the various negotiations entered into by Herzl with the late sultan, and of the wish to relieve more speedily the increasing distress of the Jewish masses **7. The** in eastern Europe than seems possible **Territorial-** in Palestine. In 1902 Herzl himself **ist Zionists.** had opened negotiations with the Anglo-Egyptian government looking to a concession of certain territories in El-Arish, between Palestine and Egypt, but these negotiations failed because that government was unwilling to allow any of the water of the Nile to be diverted from Egypt proper for the irrigation of El-Arish. In 1903 proposals were made, at the initiative of the English government, for establishing a Jewish settlement on the Guas Ngishu Plateau in the East African Protectorate. When these proposals were brought before the Sixth Zionist Congress, they were met by a most determined opposition, both the religious and the national Zionists feeling that the abandonment of Palestine as an objective, if only for a time and for specific reasons, was contrary to the deeper spirit and meaning of the Zionist movement. But the minority did not disarm; and when the seventh congress accepted the adverse report of the commission that had been sent to East Africa, this minority formed itself into the " Jewish Territorial Organization," with Israel Zangwill at its head. Its object is to procure some territory, no matter where, to which those Jews can go who can not or will not remain in the lands in which they live at present, and where they can form a community upon an autonomous basis. This organization has grown rapidly, and has the sympathy of many Jews who do not share the national sentiment of the Zionists. But it has been quite unsuccessful in its search for such a territory—the attempts made to secure a footing in Canada, Australia, Cyrenaica, and Mesopotamia having proved abortive. Its chief practical work has been confined to assisting organized immigration from eastern Europe to Galveston, Texas, and to the southern states of the American union.   RICHARD GOTTHEIL.

BIBLIOGRAPHY: Besides the files of *Die Welt*, the "Protokolls" of the congresses, *Publications of the Federation of American Zionists*, and the present author's article in JE, xii. 666–686, consult: T. Herzl, *Zionistische Schriften*, ed. L. Kellner, Berlin, 1905; B. Walker, *The Future of Palestine*, London, 1881; J. Neil, *Palestine Re-Peopled*, London, 1883; B. Negroni, *Del ritorno degli Ebrei nella Palestina*, Modena, 1891; J. Bahar, *La Question juive Restons*, Paris, 1897; F. Heman, *Das Erwachen der jüdischen Nation*, Basel, 1897; M. Jaffe, *Die nationale Wiedergeburt der Juden*, Berlin, 1897; H. Sachse, *Zionistenkongress und Zionismus eine Gefahr?* Berlin, 1897; B. Elieser, *Die Judenfrage und der socialistische Judenstaat*,

Bern, 1898; D. Farbstein, *Der Zionismus und die Judenfrage*, Bern, 1898; T. Bogianckino, *Del Sionnismo: osservazioni di diritto internazionale*, Bologna, 1899; C. Waldstein, *The Jewish Question and the Missions of the Jews*, London, 1899; D. Baron, *La Question juive et sa solution*, Lyons, 1900; M. S. Nordau, *Der Zionismus*, Brunn, 1902, Eng. transl., London, 1905; idem and G. Gottheil, *Zionism and Anti-Semitism*, New York, 1903; Sapir, *Der Zionismus*, Brünn, 1903; H. Hoppe, *Hervorragende Nichtjuden über den Zionismus*, Königsberg, 1904; A. Sandler, *Anthropologie und Zionismus*, Brünn, 1904; *Die Stimme der Wahrheit*, ed. E. Nossig, Berlin, 1905; C. Joubert, *Aspects of the Jewish Question: Zionism and Anti-Semitism*, New York, 1906; S. Levy, *Zionism and Liberal Judaism*, London, 1911; *Zeitschrift für hebräische Bibliographie*, xii. 52 sqq.

ZO'BAH (ARAM-ZOBAH): An Aramean kingdom or people. The fundamental passage is II Sam. x. 6–15, which relates to the war against the Ammonitic Hanun waged by David, in which Syrians of Beth-rehob, Zobah, and of " king Maacah " were engaged. These peoples were supposed to be neighbors of the Ammonites, and this fits with Beth-rehob, located by Schumacher at Riḥab, twenty-five miles east of 'Ajlun and thirty-one north of Rabbath Ammon, the Ammonite capital. Maacah lay between Hermon on the north and Geshur on the south, and between Bashan on the east and the upper Jordan on the west, north of the Yarmuk. Between these two Zobah is mentioned, and its position is likely to be between them, i.e., in eastern 'Ajlun toward the upper Yarmuk. From the passage in question, no closer definition of the position is possible, and no place of like name has yet been found, since the village Suf, seven miles e. of the village of 'Ajlun and nineteen w. of Rihab, hardly fits the case. To the district doubtless belonged the Hamath-zobah of II Chron. viii. 3, which is to be distinguished from " Hamath the great " of Amos vi. 2 on the Orontes; the former is the city of II Sam. viii. 9–10. Of David's campaign against the Arameans east of the Jordan II Sam. x. 6 sqq. testifies, but of his war far to the north in the valley of the Upper Orontes nothing sure is known. Other passages speak of a king of Zobah—Hadarezer in II Sam. x. 15–19a; I Chron. xix. 16–19, who summoned the Arameans from beyond the Euphrates to the war and had a number of kings under him. Since I Chron. xix. 6 knows of Aram-naharain (i.e., Arameans of the banks of the Euphrates) and Maacah and Zobah being in a confederacy, and Ps. lx., title, speaks of Aram-naharaim and Aram-zobah as opponents of David, a great Aramean kingdom in Syria east of the Orontes used to be assumed. But this is questionable, since David does not appear to have extended his operations beyond Damascus. Assyrian records give no trace of such a kingdom. Moreover, the expression " beyond the river " (II Sam. x. 16) is late and is from the point of view of Assyria, and verses 15–19a belong also to late tradition; the entire chapter, indeed, is redactorial. Verse 17 suggests that the region (immediately) east of the Jordan was the region in question. An Assyrian inscription from the time of Asshurbanipal mentions a Ẓubiti or Zupiti south of Damascus, the site of which is not determined, but which Winckler and Schrader identify with Zobah. The position indicated by the cuneiform inscription would agree with the probable location as suggested by the date given above. See HADADEZER. (H. GUTHE.)

BIBLIOGRAPHY: H. Winckler, *Altorientalische Forschungen*, i. 465–468, Leipsic, 1893; idem, *Geschichte Israels,* i. 138–144, ib. 1895; H. Guthe, *Geschichte des Volkes Israel*, 2d ed., pp. 102–103, 123, Tübingen, 1904; G. Schumacher, in the *Mittheilungen und Nachrichten des deutschen Palästinavereins*, 1900, pp. 71 sqq.; Schrader, *KAT*, pp. 60–61, 97, 135; *DB*, iv. 987; *EB*, iv. 5425–26.

ZOECKLER, tsŭk'ler, **OTTO:** German Lutheran theologian; b. at Grünberg (12 m. e.s.e. of Giessen) May 27, 1833; d. at Greifswald Feb. 9, 1906. His early life was spent at Laubach, only a few miles south of his birthplace; and in 1849 he entered the gymnasium at Marburg, going thence in 1851 to the University of Giessen; under the influence of Anton Lutterbeck and Leopold Schmid he developed the liking which strengthened during his life for treating the harmony of religion and secular science. The result was that his university course yielded larger philosophical than theological acquirements. This was more or less corrected by later study at the universities of Erlangen, Berlin, Halle, and Göttingen. In 1857 he returned to Giessen and began to lecture there, dealing with the New Testament, advancing to church history, and treating also the history of doctrine, encyclopedia, patristics, and history of modern theology. His first book was the *Theologia naturalis, Entwurf einer systematischen Naturtheologie vom offenbarungsgläubigen Standpunkt aus* (vol. i., Frankfurt, 1860), in which his purpose was to give to natural theology its rights as a third discipline beside dogmatics and ethics, the aim being also essentially apologetic. The work was never extended beyond the first volume. A higher warrant than this for advancement in his professional career appeared in his *Kritische Geschichte der Askese* (1863), a work of learning and circumspection, which was completely worked over into the *Askese und Mönchtum*, which appeared in 1897 and revealed intimately the author's personality. After 1863 his literary activity increased greatly, that year witnessed also his advancement to the post of extraordinary professor. The year 1865 saw the issue of his *Hieronymus. Sein Leben und Wirken* (Gotha), and also the founding of *Beweis des Glaubens*, with Zöckler as one of the editors and a chief contributor, later the sole editor.

A new period began in the life of Zöckler with his call to Greifswald in 1866. That university presented at that time only seventeen students in theology in a total of about 400; but the united reputations of Hermann Cremer (q.v.) and Zöckler brought the number up in a few years to about 380. The latter's scholarship was rated very high, as was his authority as a theologian in the realm of natural science. His contributions of Chronicles, Job, Proverbs, Ecclesiastes, the Song, and Daniel to Lange's commentary (5 vols., Bielefeld, 1866–74; Eng. transl., New York, 1870–77) showed that he stood among the positive theologians of his day. In 1869 he began his work as editor on *Allgemeine litterarische Anzeiger für das evangelische Deutschland*. Up to this time his lectures had been confined to the domain of history; but on the death of his colleague Vogt he took in the realm of dogmatics, and a result of this was his *Augsburgische Confession*

(Frankfort, 1870). Apologetics assumed the chief place in his work of the following years, and among the works produced were *Geschichte der Beziehung zwischen Theologie und Naturwissenschaft mit besonderer Rücksicht auf die Schöpfungsgeschichte* (2 vols., 1877–79), *Gotteszeugen im Reiche der Natur, Biographieen und Bekenntnisse aus alter und neuer Zeit* (1881; 4th ed., 1906), and perhaps his richest book, *Das Kreuz Christi* (Gütersloh, 1875; Eng. transl., *The Cross of Christ: Studies in the History of Religion and the inner Life of the Church*, London, 1877), which exhibited the reflections of the sufferings of Christ in art, theology, and mysticism. In 1882 the editorship of the *Evangelische Kirchenzeitung* added a new task, as did that of the *Handbuch der theologischen Wissenschaft* (3 vols., 3d ed., 4 vols., 1889), a considerable part of which came from Zöckler's own pen. In 1886 he began in cooperation with H. L. Strack the issue of *Kurzgefasster Kommentar*, to which he contributed the parts on the Old-Testament Apocrypha and Pseudepigrapha, the Acts of the Apostles, Thessalonians, and Galatians. His last three years of life witnessed the issue of two important works, *Die Tugendlehre des Christentums, geschichtlich dargestellt in der Entwickelung ihrer Lehrformen* (1904), and *Die christliche Apologetik im 19. Jahrhundert. Lebensbilder und Charakteristiken deutscher evangelischer Glaubenszeugen aus der jüngsten Vergangenheit* (1904). He had projected what was intended to be the crown of his labors in apologetics, but death intervened, and only the first volume appeared, under the editorship of Hermann Jordan and Ernst Schlapp, *Geschichte der Apologie des Christentums* (1907). Besides the above-mentioned works he wrote the *Biblische und kirchenhistorische Studien* (1893); and contributed to the second edition of the Herzog *Realencyklopädie für protestantische Theologie*, while of the third edition his articles are a notable feature.

The mere mention of the publications of this scholar reveal the broad and scientific interests which demanded his attention. In the center of these was history; even apologetics he dealt with from this standpoint, and the same is true of his ventures in the dogmatic sphere. Indeed, theology could not bound his activities, and he often went beyond it; an example of this is his *Urgeschichte der Erde und des Menschen* (Gütersloh, 1868). Work was to him the breath of life. Withal he was clear in his exposition, whether given in the professor's chair or through the medium of books. His conclusions were the result of profound consideration. In the life of the church of his day he was a considerable figure, representing the theological faculty in the general synod several times. He was also a supporter of both home and foreign missions. Students found in him an able advocate and friend. He was also with full consciousness an earnest advocate of Lutheranism, while in all his relations he exhibited the marks of a kindly and pious individuality. [His deafness doubtless led to the concentration of his energy upon the printed page. The range of his learning was extraordinary.] (VICTOR SCHULTZE.)

BIBLIOGRAPHY: Otto Zöckler, *Erinnerungsblätter*, Gütersloh, 1906. A careful index of Zöckler's writings are given in an appendix to the *Geschichte der Apologie*, ut sup.

ZOEPFFEL, tsŭp′fel, **RICHARD OTTO:** Theologian; b. at Arensburg (on the island of Osel, Gulf of Riga), Russia, June 14, 1843; d. at Strasburg Jan. 7, 1891. He studied theology at Dorpat, 1862–1868, and history at Göttingen, 1868–70, becoming in 1870 privat-docent at the latter university; he was called to Strasburg as extraordinary professor of church history in 1872, was made ordinary professor in 1877, and rector in 1887. His chief writing was *Die Papstwahlen . . . vom 11. bis 14. Jahrhundert* (Göttingen, 1871); he also issued *Johannes Sturm, Der erste Rektor der Strassburger Akademie* (Strasburg, 1887). Besides these works, he was a contributor to the Herzog *RE*, was collaborator with H. Holtzmann in the *Lexikon für Theologie und Kirchenwesen* (1882), was a contributor to the *Allgemeine deutsche Biographie*, and to various theological journals. In all of these labors his most characteristic trait was tirelessness in reaching fundamental facts, combined with impartiality in setting them forth.   (H. Holtzmann†.)

Bibliography: Erichson, in *Evangelisch protestantische Kirchenbote*, 1891, p. 10; *ADB*, xlv. 431–432.

ZOHAR. See Cabala, § 17.

ZOLLIKOFER, tsol′lĭ-cof″er, **GEORG JOACHIM:** Renowned preacher, poet, and hymnwriter; b. at St. Gall Aug. 5, 1730; d. at Leipsic Jan. 22, 1788. He received his education at the gymnasia of St. Gall and Bremen and the high school of Utrecht; taught for four years in a family of Frankfort; took position in 1754 as minister at Murten, canton Bern, Switzerland, then at Monstein, and later at Isenburg; in 1758 he became pastor of the Reformed congregation at Leipsic, to which he gave the rest of his life. Among his services to the Church may be named in the front rank that to hymnology. He recognized the fact that many of the hymns used were unworthy, and made a contribution in his *Neues Gesangbuch* (1766), in which he incorporated some of his own compositions, including " Dein, Gott, ist Majestät und Macht " and " Willst du der Weisheit Quelle kennen." In the region of devotional works he issued *Anreden und Gebete* (Leipsic, 1777) and *Andachtsübungen und Gebete zum Privatgebrauche* (1785; Eng. transl., *Devotional Exercises and Prayers*, London, 1815). But his place in history is best assured by his sermons (collected edition, 15 vols., 1789–1804; Eng. transl., 10 vols., London, 1803–12; some of these also reproduced in the United States). For his style he has been given a worthy place in the history of German literature by such a critic as Goethe. While his theology was that of the Enlightenment (q.v.), he did not belong to the " storm and stress " movement. He is best described as a rational supernaturalist. His preaching was both textual and thematic, while his treatment was tasteful, clear, lively, warm, rarely glowing.

           (P. Mehlhorn.)

Bibliography: C. Garve, *Ueber den Charakter Zollikofers*, Leipsic, 1788; F. K. G. Hirsching, *Historisch-litterarisches Handbuch*, xvii. 372 sqq., ib. 1815; J. M. H. Döring, *Die deutschen Kanzelredner*, pp. 856 sqq., Neustadt, 1830; C. G. H. Lentz, *Geschichte der christlichen Homiletik*, ii. 327 sqq., Brunswick, 1839; K. H. Sack, *Geschichte der Predigt in der deutsch-evangelischen Kirche*, 2d ed., pp. 185 sqq., Heidelberg, n.d.; R. Rothe, *Geschichte der Predigt*, pp. 435 sqq., Bremen, 1881; P. Weinmeister, *Beiträge zur Geschichte der evangelisch-reformierten Gemeinde zu Leipzig, 1700–1900*, pp. 158 sqq., Leipsic, 1900; *ADB*, xlv. 415 sqq.

ZONARAS, zon′a-ras, **JOHANNES:** Byzantine writer on ecclesiastical law and history; flourished in the last part of the eleventh and the first half of the twelfth century. He filled many offices under the Emperor Alexius Comnenus, among them "commander of the bodyguard " and " head of the chancery." In later life he entered a monastery in the present Niandro. The reason for his becoming a monk is not quite clear; it may have been because of loss of relatives, but more likely because he was involved in intrigues concerning the succession to the throne in 1118.

Of first importance is his great work on eastern ecclesiastical law. The collection of ecclesiastical law on which he commented was completed practically in his own times, but of this collection only parts of secondary importance have come down. According to Zonaras' commentary, it consisted of the Apostolic Canons, the canons of the councils of Nicæa 325, Constantinople 381, Ephesus 431, Chalcedon 451, the Trullan Synod of 692, the Photian synods of 861 and 879, the provincial synods of Carthage under Cyprian, Ancyra 314, Neocæsarea 315, Gangra 340, Antioch 341, Laodicea 343, Sardica 347, Carthage 419, and Constantinople 394. Zonaras also commented upon the Canons of Dionysius of Alexandria, Basilides of Pentapolis, excerpts from the *Peri metanoias* of Peter of Alexandria, and writings of Gregory Thaumaturgus, Athanasius of Alexandria, Basil of Cæsarea, and Gregory of Nyssa. Many manuscripts exist of Zonaras' work, and it was put into vernacular Greek. The first full edition, with the commentaries of Balsamon and Aristenos is by Beveridge, *Synodikon* (Oxford, 1672), but because of its form it is not very useful. It is surpassed by the edition of G. Rhallis and M. Potlis (6 vols., Athens, 1852–59); the commentaries of Zonaras are in vols. ii.–iv. The purpose of Zonaras was not to write for the learned, and his work is consequently clear and simple, though splendid in its diction and written in flowing Greek. The work reveals the historical point of view, and the author uses various methods to make clear his position. He expounds the matter in hand from history or archeology, compares similar or seemingly opposed canons, explains the opposition with clarity, and proceeds from the simple to the more difficult. He has the critical sense, seeks to reconcile or expound opposing declarations, in cases of doubt employs the milder or humanitarian exegesis, and he is on the watch for the ethical. The work was highly prized in the Church, and, alongside of the works of Balsamon and Aristenos, was regarded as a source of ecclesiastical law. For Nicodemus Hagiorites Zonaras is the chief authority.

Besides the commentaries Zonaras issued on the same general subject *Peri tou mē dein, duo disexadelphous tēn autēn agagesthai pros gamon*, and *Logos pros tous tēn physikēn tēs gonēs ekroēn miasma hegoumenous* (earlier ed. in Fabricius-Harles, *Bibliotheca Græca*, xi. 225 sqq.; better in Rhallis and Potlis, ut sup., iv. 592–611). Zonaras worked also as an exegete in the purely theological realm, and aimed to make usable for his period the *Tetrasticha* and *Monosticha* of Gregory Nazianzen. In this he succeeded, but his work was confused and blended with that of Nicetas Paphlago, and the many manuscripts and editions reveal this. A work formerly attributed to Nicetas on this theme is now to be given to Zonaras (cf. Legrand, *Bibliographie Hellenique*, i. 314, Paris, 1885). Zonaras also wrote a commentary on the *Kanones anastasimoi* of the *Octoechos*, now lost except for the introduction (in *Specilegium Romanum*, v. 384–389, Rome, 1841). The *Canon eis tēn hyperagian theotokon* appears to be an independent work (printed in Cotelier, *Monumenta Grœce ecclesiœ*, iii. 465–472, Paris, 1686), a noteworthy poem in nine odes and twenty-nine verses giving a catalogue of heretics from Arius on. It has always given great offense to the Roman Catholics. Zonaras is also the author of the well-known *Epitome historiōn*, one of the most important historical works of the Byzantine period, valuable for secular and ecclesiastical history. It treats of world history from creation till 1118, and is of particular value because of the use it makes of very early and now lost sources. The work was edited by H. Wolf (Basel, 1557), Ducange (Paris, 1686), and Dindorf (in *CSHB*, 6 vols., 1868–76). (PHILIPP MEYER.)

BIBLIOGRAPHY: W. Cave, *Scriptorum ecclesiasticorum historia literaria*, ii. 201 sqq., Oxford, 1743; Fabricius-Harles, *Bibliotheca Grœca*, vii. 465–468, viii. 433, xi. 222–228, Hamburg, 1801–08; E. Dronke, *De Niceta Davide et Zonara interpretibus carmina S. Gregorii Nazianzeni*, Coblenz, 1839; idem, *S. Gregorii Nazianzeni carmina selecta*, Göttingen, 1840; C. W. E. Heimbach, in Ersch and Gruber, *Encyklopädie*, I., lxxxvi. 376 sqq., 461–462; Christ, in *SMA*, 1870, pp. 75–108; A. C. Demetracopulos, *Grœcia orthodoxa*, p. 15, Leipsic, 1872; H. Haupt, *Neue Beiträge zu den Fragmenten des Dio Cassius*, in *Hermes*, xiv (1879), 430–446; P. Sauerbrei, in *Commentationes philologicœ Jenenses*, i (1881), 1–81; T. Büttner-Wobst, in *Commentationes Fleckeisenianæ*, pp. 123–170, Leipsic, 1890; idem, in *Byzantinische Zeitschrift*, 1896, pp. 610–611; U. P. Boissevain, in *Hermes*, xxvi (1891), 440–452; idem, in *Byzantinische Zeitschrift*, 1895, pp. 250–271; M. Heinemann, *Quœstiones Zonareœ*, Dresden, 1895; E. Patzig, in *Byzantinische Zeitschrift*, 1896, pp. 24–53, 1897, pp. 322–356, 1906, pp. 513–514; K. Prachter, in the same, 1897, pp. 509–525; Krumbacher, *Geschichte*, pp. 370–376 et passim (with excellent bibliography); N. Milasch, *Das Kirchenrecht der morgenländischen Kirche*, 2d ed., Vienna, 1905.

ZONE. See VESTMENTS AND INSIGNIA, ECCLESIASTICAL.

ZOROASTER, ZOROASTRIANISM.

I. Introduction: Interest in the religion of Zoroaster is evoked by several historical circumstances, aside from the veil of obscurity and romance which hides the person of the prophet and founder from the eye of the present, so that he seems like a veritable Moses in the mountains of Iran. The lofty monotheism (for Zoroastrianism is this in its issue, whatever one may say of its practical and theoretical dualism, or of the polytheism which it long was to the rank and file of its followers) gives it a place in the history of religion beside Judaism, Christianity, and Mohammedanism. It has also been said of it with considerable truth that it missed only narrowly becoming a world religion. As Charles Martel in 732 and Leo III. in 740 saved western Europe from Mohammedanism, so possibly the battles of Marathon and Salamis averted from eastern Europe, perhaps from the entire West, subjection to the religion of Zoroaster. Before this it had begun to supplant the old faith and polytheism of Babylonia, where also it had come into contact with Judaism. How extensive its influence was upon Judaism, and then upon Christianity, is one of the problems yet under debate; most competent scholars admit a debt on the part of both with respect to angelology and the doctrine of Satan. The indebtedness of Mohammedanism in the realm of eschatology is very considerable, although it must be admitted that the lingering influence of Babylonian religion somewhat obscures the exact degree which is to be conceded here. As the old form of the faith and parent of the institutions and community of the modern Parsees this religion claims attention, for they assert their possession of the pure religion of the Persian prophet. Still further, Zoroastrianism is remarkable for its implied hostility to the Brahman faith of India, whose deities it in part reduced to the rank of demons, choosing (possibly) one of its chief deities as its own and calling him Ahura Mazda. One of the strangest and most difficult features of the faith is the remarkable series of abstractions which received personification as good and evil beings, the former being approached with an adoration that differed little from worship. This religion also furnishes another example of the faiths of the world whose religious books seem to have been the object of persecution and have suffered fatal losses. Once more, for the philologist and the textual critic and exegete no literature offers deeper problems or more exacting tasks than that of Iran. And, finally, the story of the recovery of the ancient books and sources, so far as they exist, is a romance both in its beginnings and in the discussions which have followed.

II. The People: The Zoroastrian religion arose and ran almost its entire course among one of the earliest of the seven branches of the Indo-European family, named "Aryans" in the sacred literature.

They are regarded by ethnologists as forming with the Aryans who entered India from the northwest a section of the family named above, and the language of the Avesta is close in structure and formation to the Sanskrit. The native literature classifies peoples with reference to their attitude toward the Zoroastrian or " Mazdayaznian " faith. Yet, as was the case with Mohammedanism (see MOHAMMED, MOHAMMEDANISM), the religious tie overcame the tribal, though great pride was always manifested in the common origin of the people. The hostility born of difference of race appears often in the scriptures, especially that toward the nomadic Turanians (*Vendidad*, iii. 11; *Yasht*, viii., x.). Prayers for protection from these are frequent. But opponents in faith were fair objects of raids, whatever their race, and the believer asked in his prayers for permission to snatch away from the enemy fields and herds. The foes, however, were not all of alien race; some Iranians rejected the truth and were reckoned among the adversaries. The sacred writings bear witness to their origin in a period of stress, caused in no little degree by the nomadic Turanians. True believers lived a life of hazard, and the faith won its way through persecution and conflict, based upon religious, racial, and economic grounds. The Avesta praises the agriculturist and the herdsman, for both reclaim the waste places, forward productiveness, and advance civilization (*Vendidad*, iii.). To the people physical perfection was a boon sought of deity, health and bodily vigor were highly prized. This lay in the very roots of the religion, since evil of all kinds, including physical defect and disease, were of Angra Mainyu. Width of chest, breadth of hips, high instep, and a clear eye were marks of a good physique. Man craved height of stature, litheness, strength, length of arm, and a goodly measurement around the calves; woman desired symmetry of form, a slender waist, large eyes, a blooming complexion, and well-developed bosom.

III. Sources: The principal sources for a knowledge of the religion of Zoroaster are (1) the literature emanating from the Zoroastrians themselves: (a) the so-called Zend-Avesta; (b) the Old-Persian inscriptions in Behistun, Naks-i-Rustem, and Persepólis; (c) a large number of writings in what is known as Pahlavi (see below, IV., §§ 8-9); (d) translations and fragments in Sanskrit, Persian, and Arabic; and (2) reports of classical writers such as: the " History " of Herodotus; citations from the " Philippics " of Theopompus (flourished c. 340 B.C.) in Plutarch's " Isis and Osiris," xlvi.–xlvii.; those from Hermippus in the writings of the younger Pliny (the loss of the work of Hermippus is irreparable, since there is considerable reason to think that it was an account of Zoroastrianism from the early sources in the then extant sacred books); and mention in Diogenes Laertius, Strabo, Dio Chrysostom, Pausanias, and other classical writers (these are most conveniently collected and with practical completeness in A. V. W. Jackson's *Zoroaster*, New York, 1899); (3) a number of Persian writings, such as Firdusi's *Shah Namah*.

IV. The Literature: Under the Sassanians the literature was very much more extensive than at present. Evidence of the loss of much of the literature consists (1) in the tradition of the Parsees, who assert, e.g., that there were originally

1. Outline thirty Yasts, one for each day in the
History month; (2) in the Pahlavi translations
of the there are references to and citations
Literature. from many lost books; (3) classic Persian and Arabic literature furnishes additional citations and references, as when Pliny speaks of 2,000,000 verses by Zoroaster (*Hist. nat.*, xxx. 1–2), or when Pahlavi books speak of 1,200 chapters or Masudi tells of a copy of sacred writings on 12,000 cowhides; (4) an analysis of Zoroastrian sacred literature in Pahlavi made in the ninth century shows as either extant or at least then within knowledge a very much larger body than has remained to the present. The tradition of twenty-one Nasks is fairly constant (as against the conceptually complete thirty), and the amount of this has been estimated as consisting of 345,700 words, while of the Pahlavi translations and commentaries the estimated extent was 2,094,200 words. The twenty-one Nasks asserted as existent under the Sassanidæ were divided into three groups: the Gatha (" song " or " theological ") group, the legal group, and the mixed group. The names of these Nasks are known (for a list cf. *SBE*, vol. iv., pp. xxxiv.–xxxv.). Of the twenty-one only two remain entire, there are also the most important part of another, considerable sections from four others, and selections or fragments from eight besides. That the remains of a literature so vast are now comparatively scanty (though yet equaling in bulk the Iliad and the Odyssey) is attributed by the Parsees to Alexander's destruction of one of the complete copies, and by losses under the Mohammedan conquest and during the subsequent removal to India of the Parsees. In spite of these losses, however, it may be remarked that the general outlines of the lost writings are given in the Pahlavi literature, notably in the *Dinkart* (ninth century A.D.).

The accounts are mixed up with theories that evince once again claims to an origin for the sacred books of Zoroastrianism similar to that made for his by the devotee of another faith.

2. Native Thus, much as the Koran existed in a
Accounts heavenly exemplar communicated to
of the Mohammed by Gabriel, so the twenty-
Scriptures. one Nasks were created by Ahura Mazda from the twenty-one words of the Ahuna Vairya (one of the most sacred prayers of the faith). The *Dinkart* affirms that the Nasks were brought by Zoroaster to Vishtaspes, the king who was the first royal convert, who had two copies made, each on 12,000 ox-hides, one of which copies was placed in the treasury and the other in the record office. Zoroaster is credited with mental possession of the scriptures, so that a third copy is not in question. Alexander's invasion is charged with the burning of one of these in the treasury, while it is asserted that the other was carried off by the Greeks and translated into their language. The most that can be said for this tradition is that there is likely a historical basis, and that sacred writings were lost at the time mentioned; but the Nask remaining (*Vendidad*) bears marks of a much later origin,

though embodying unquestionably early material. According to the account which is being cited, a Parthian king Valkhash (Vologeses I., a contemporary of Nero) ordered the collection of the fragments still remaining in various quarters. Then in the Sassanian dynasty, so the story runs, Ardashir (226–240 A.D.) commissioned the high-priest Tansar* to collect the fragments and complete an edition of the Avesta, and by a decree made the resulting work canonical. This indicates the reaffirmation or establishment of a certain type of Zoroastrianism as the state religion, with a definite redaction of the scriptures as sacred, possibly in opposition to some other redaction. Ardashir's son and successor, Shahpur I. (241–272 A.D.), is said to have ordered the collection of scattered documents on the sciences and their incorporation in the Avesta. And under Shahpur II. (309–379), after a final revision, the ordeal of fire (molten brass) established the true religion as dominant and inclusive (c. 350 A.D.).

This account, when one reads between the lines with the aid of the Tansar letter and other historical allusions, is luminous. It indicates the Gathas as the kernel of Zoroastrian literature and the most sacred portion. There is also suggested a considerable antiquity for parts of the extant books, with a series of misfortunes to the religion and its literature which the history of Persia bears out (see in part MEDO-PERSIA; SELEUCIDÆ). The area of this religion was full of unrest for a millennium, continuing till the Tatar and Arab invasions, and there was security for neither religion nor people, for sacred writings nor continuous rule. Accordingly the literature suffered, and even in the religion itself there were sects and divisions, as is common in the history of every great faith. Then came the attempts to save the rest and to stamp it as authoritative. Successive canons are indicated, with accretions from foreign sources. After that came the use of a new language (the Pahlavi), in which were written translations of the sacred books, and also studies and commentaries (see below), and these came also to have high value among Zoroastrians. How close a parallel to this history is furnished by the Hebrew religion with its threefold canon (see CANON OF SCRIPTURE) and its Talmud (q.v.) is apparent at once. It will be recalled that a Jewish saying regards Yahweh himself as engaging on the Sabbath in the study of the Talmud.

3. Significance of this Account.

Interest in this literature was for modern times first aroused by Thomas Hyde, author of *Historia religionis veterum Persarum eorumque magorum ubi . . . Zoroastris vita, ejusque et aliorum vaticinia . . . eruuntur . . .* (Oxford, 1700, 2d ed., 1760, with somewhat changed title), in which he appealed to travelers in the East to procure the sacred books of the Parsees. In 1723 a manuscript copy (made 1680–81) of the *Vendidad Sada* (the Vendidad without commentary) was brought by Richard Cobbe

to England and deposited in the Bodleian Library, but was, of course, entirely useless in the state of knowledge then existing. In 1754 the sight of four leaves of this manuscript fired the imagination of Anquetil Duperron, a young French student in the École des langues orientales at Paris, and he determined to secure for France the Zoroastrian books and the honor of attaching to the first translation of them. To achieve this end he enlisted in 1755 with the French East India Company's forces, and finally in 1758 reached Surat and the Parsees. It took him several years to win the confidence of the community, and to obtain their books and such knowledge of them as was then possible to gain, so that not until 1764 could he return to Paris. In 1771 he published *Zend-Avesta, ouvrage de Zoroastre, contenant les idées theologiques, physiques et morales de ce législateur, traduit en françois sur l'original Zend* (3 vols., Paris). A violent controversy at once broke out, the book was pronounced a modern production, and the contents were denounced as impossible from the standpoint of what was known of the religion. William Jones, afterward Sir William, the noted orientalist and pioneer in Sanskrit, led the attack, which continued till the end of the century. Yet it was due to this scholar that the relations of the language of the Avesta to the Sanskrit were first seen. A step forward was taken by Sylvestre de Sacy in 1793 through the decipherment of Sassanian Pahlavi inscriptions, using Duperron's Pahlavi dictionary. Eugene Burnouf made the next advance about 1825–30 by the use of a Sanskrit translation of the *Yasna* and established thoroughly the relationship of the Old Persian and Sanskrit tongues and even began a comparative mythology. While Duperron's translation was found defective and misleading, the decipherment of the Persepolis and Behistun inscriptions made clear the fact of a language closely related to that of the Avesta in use under the Achæmenians. And so, for more than a century investigation has been applied to the elucidation of the Avesta, and still many problems remain unsolved. And in connection with this literature it may still be said that few fields offer so alluring opportunities for original and profitable research as the Zoroastrian sacred books. Especial need exists for the thoroughgoing application of textual and historical criticism.

4. Discovery and Early Study of the Avesta.

The name Zend-Avesta, by which the principal work is generally known in the West, is a mistake in terminology fastened upon it by Hyde and Duperron. Parsees unaffected by European influence call their sacred books " Avesta and Zend," the equivalent of which is very nearly " Avesta with (Pahlavi) translation and commentary." These two words, " Avesta " and " Zend," though coming from different roots, are each almost equivalent to " knowledge," Avesta signifying perhaps knowledge that is revealed (or divine law) and Zend that which is acquired by study of the books and is written in Pahlavi. The combination is due to the fact that in very many cases the Avesta and the commentary accompany each

5. The Name " Zend-Avesta."

---

* A letter from this Tansar, interpolated but easily purified by critical methods, is extant and is given in *JA*, 1894, i. 185–250, 502–555. This is the earliest extant document throwing native light on the history of Zoroastrianism.

other. Of the character of the Avesta it has been well said (E. Rindtorff, *Die Religion des Zarathustra*, p. 4, Weimar, 1897) that one would gain a good idea of it had he a collection culled from the Hebrew literature containing some Psalms, old songs like that of Deborah, laws from the Pentateuch, selections from the prophets, and pieces from Mishnah and Gemara, all welded into one piece.

The Avesta exists in two principal parts: A. The Avesta Proper, which divides into (1) the **Vendidad,** "anti-demon law," a blend of mythology and religious legislation, the " priest-code " of Zoroastrianism. It is divided into twenty-two
6. The chapters or " Fargards." The first two
Avesta. of these are mythological, of which the first enumerates sixteen lands which were created by Ahura Mazda and were therefore perfect, constituting (almost certainly) Iran; the second is a remote parallel to the flood account of Babylonians and Hebrews, though the catastrophe comes not by water but by cold. The remnant of all life is preserved by Yima, under the direction of Ahura, in a sort of paradise (see below, VI., § 5). Fargard III. deals with the earth as a sentient thing, and forbids its desecration by burial of the dead in it. Succeeding Fargards treat of contracts, outrages against the person, defilements and purifications, formulas used at purifications, of the dog (an important feature), of various impurities and sins, of hair and nails, of the cock, and of invocations, with mythological materials interspersed. (2) The **Yasna,** " book of the offering," the chief liturgy of the religion, is in seventy-two chapters, and is purely ritualistic, a collection of litanies, prayers, exhortations, and praises, for the use of the priests at the " sacrifice " or adoration of all the principal beings connected with the faith. These are usually arranged according to the services in which they are used. This book is made up of several parts: (a) chaps. 1–27, usually explained as invocations—a term which, in its largest sense, is not inapt; (b) chaps. 28–34, 43–51, and 53, which constitute the **Gathas,** " songs," and are received as addresses, sermons, and revelations of Zoroaster and his immediate disciples, arranged according to meter in five subdivisions and seventeen sections. These are the kernel of the Avesta and, for students, the most important part, as well as the earliest. The consensus of scholarship is that the bulk is genuine, the work of the prophet. The style is manifestly different, the matter more original and decidedly prophetic in tone, and they remind one of the earlier Surahs of the Koran; (c) chaps. 35–42, 52, 54–72 constitute the later Yasna, and the word invocation, as used above, applies. (3) The **Vispered,** " all the chiefs " (i.e., the spiritual heads of the religion), is a liturgical work in twenty-three (twenty-four or twenty-seven) chapters. It is an appendix to the Yasna, and the use approximates that of litanies. (4) The **Yashts,** " sacrificial psalms " or " songs " (the literal meaning is given as " act of worship "), are twenty-one in number, besides some fragments, and are devoted to the praise of certain spiritual beings. They vary greatly in age and in length, some of them are doubtless composite, and they were composed in honor of the Yazatas (see below, VI.,

§ 4). B. The **Khorda Avesta,** "Little Avesta," consists of short prayers, and is meant for the people as well as the priests as opposed to the Avesta proper, which is for the latter alone. It includes five **Gahs** (invocations for the five divisions of the day); two **Sirozahs,** invocations to the Izeds who are over the days of the month; four **Afrinagans,** or blessings at a meal to which angels or spirits are invited at stated seasons; and five **Nyayis** (Nyaishes), or prayers to the sun, Mithra, the moon, the waters, and to fire, recited at set times.

The language in which the Avesta is written belongs to one of the seven original branches of the Indo-European family. Its closest affiliation is with the Sanskrit, which it resembles
7. Language so closely that translation of the Avesta
and into Sanskrit is comparatively simple,
Alphabet. regard being had to the phonetic laws of the group, and to variations in syntax. But considerable difference exists within the Avesta itself, where scholars recognize two dialects —the Gathic or dialect of the earlier portions, which may owe its peculiarities either to age or to provincial peculiarities; and the younger Avestan, which shows in parts very notable linguistic decay. The alphabet, however, is very much later than the material of the text, and is derived from the Sassanian Pahlavi; the script, moreover, bears marks of this derivation, being read from right to left, which is uncommon in the Indo-European family. Later study of the Avesta has shown that a large part of it is in meter, and this fact, like the same one in Hebrew literature, has helped in the historical criticism of the text and the recognition of the intrusion of later insertions therein. But in this department very much still remains to be done.

Pahlavi, the language in which the principal translations, commentaries, and annotations of the Avesta were originally written, was the language of medieval Persia. The oldest indications of its use go back as far as the third century B.C.
8. The (Levy in *ZDMG*, xxi., 1867, pp. 421–
Pahlavi 463), and its age of ascendency and
Language. principal use covers the period 226–800 A.D., with a literary employment extending perhaps two centuries later. The alphabet is Semitic, and practically half the vocabulary of these early documents is also Semitic (Aramaic), but often with Persian terminations, the rest of the vocabulary being Persian. But when read, it seems, these Semitic words were not pronounced as written, but the Persian words corresponding to the Pahlavi Semitic were uttered (*Malkan malka,* "king of kings," was pronounced " Shahan Shah," just as " i.e.," or " *id est,*" is in English pronounced as though " that is " were written, or " viz." is written and pronounced " namely "). The number of these Semitic logograms is computed at about 400. In the later post-Mohammedan writings instruction was conveyed through the Persian, which came to have a large intermixture of Arabic. The Pahlavi alphabet contains only fourteen (eighteen) symbols; consequently some symbols represent several sounds; moreover, some letters combined with others or doubled are exactly or nearly equivalent in form to some single letters, so that a single sym-

bol may represent as many as seventeen sounds. This at once shows the enormous difficulty and possible ambiguity of the script, paralleled only, perhaps, by the Babylonian-Assyrian cuneiform writing in its several stages. Yet the importance of the Pahlavi for knowledge of the religion can not be overestimated. The earliest manuscripts, apart from a few papyrus fragments of the eighth(?) century, are four which date from the fourteenth century, and contain the Yasna and the Vendidad, with the corresponding Zend or commentary.

The principal Pahlavi texts are: (1) the **Bundahish** (Bundahishn) " original creation," a fragmentary work dealing with cosmogony, mythology, and legend, therefore sometimes compared with the Genesis of the Hebrew Scriptures. It **9. Pahlavi** describes what is evidently assumed **Literature.** in the Avesta, the original condition of the universe, with the omniscient good spirit, Ahura Mazda (Ormuzd) dwelling in light, and the evil spirit, Angra Mainyu (Ahriman), dwelling in darkness and with limited knowledge. The course of creation is described, and there is then given a legendary or mythical geography and history of the earth with all its affairs, coming down to the legendary history of Persia and continuing till the Mohammedan conquest, including genealogies of kings, of Zoroaster, and of other priests, as also the Zoroastrian philosophy of creation. The conclusion of Zend scholars is that the book is an extract from or an epitome of one of the twenty-one Nasks. Its date is subsequent to the Mohammedan conquest in 651, more closely, about 850. There exists a paraphrase in the Gujarati language (edited and published, Mumbai, 1877). (2) The **Dinkart,** " acts of Religion," is a collection dealing with the history, customs, doctrines, literature, legends, and myths of the religion. Its compilation was begun near the beginning of the ninth century, and was finished before the end of the same, but by other hands. Its sources were the Pahlavi translations of the Nasks, not the originals. Six books have been preserved, and these are of great importance. (3) **Dadistan-i Dinik,** " religious decisions," written shortly before 881 by Manuskihar, probably a supreme high-priest of the religion. It is in form a sort of catechism, consisting of ninety-two questions on religion addressed to the author and the answers thereto. Usually connected with this writing are three epistles by the author, inspired partly by the desire to combat certain heretical ritual tendencies in modes of purification. The questions and answers concern matters religious, historical, philosophical, and practical. They bring up the question of the existence of evil, the creation of man, good works and evil and their rewards and punishments and the fate of the soul, the contests between good spirits and evil, and also matters which would be likely to arise in the ordinary experience of the people. The book is therefore a sort of guide to Zoroastrian life, covering thought, word, and deed. Its value is great as showing what an authority in his own day declared to be the duty of the faithful. So far as essential doctrine is concerned, there seems little change as compared with the prescriptions of the Avesta. The ultimate monotheistic issue is as clear

as the dualistic origins. (4) The **Dina-i Mainog-i Khirad,** " opinions of the spirit of wisdom," consists of an introduction followed by a series of questions assumed to be asked by an anonymous magus or wise man and answered by the spirit of wisdom. The author seems to have been a devoted lay Zoroastrian, whose purpose was to summarize the essentials of belief and practise. His interest was not ritualistic, and the work is therefore in some sense distinctive. The date is uncertain, but some time soon after the Arab conquest is possible (c. 650). (5) The **Shikand-Gumanik Vijar,** " doubt-dispelling explanation," is controversial, philosophic, and apologetic, and is particularly concerned with the proof that evil has an independent origin At some length is shown the fundamental agreement with Zoroastrianism in this particular of other religions, such as Mohammedanism, Manicheism, and Christianity, even while they assert a unitary creation. The doctrine of the Trinity is assailed. The author acknowledges his indebtedness to earlier writings, and is diplomatic and courteous in his references to other faiths, particularly to Mohammedanism. The date is to be placed near the end of the ninth century. (6) The **Shayast la-Shayast,** " thou shalt, thou shalt not," prescribes what may and what may not be done by the true believer, and deals with trespasses, impurities, and ceremonies. It is composite, in two parts which are somewhat repetitious, by at least two authors, who discuss means against various sources of ceremonial pollution, correct methods of dress, good works, conduct toward the sun and fire, and minutiæ of correct procedure in a large variety of circumstances. Its age must be high, as it quotes no less than twelve of the Nasks, and it may have been compiled in the seventh century from much older material. Its value is great as presenting the great body of ceremonial customs and prescriptions current in Persia twelve centuries ago. It has been likened to the Leviticus of the Hebrew Bible. (7) The **Arta-i Viraf Namak** and the **Bahman Yasht** are eschatological, and the former is historically useful as giving the Persian view of the devastation caused by the conquest of Alexander and of the revival of the religion under the Sassanidæ. Mention may be made here of some Persian literature, such as the **Zartush Nama,** " book of Zoroaster," of the thirteenth century; the **Sad Dar,** " 100 chapters," an epitome of Zoroastrian doctrines, in three recensions, one prose and two poetical; **Rivayats,** which give traditions; and **Kissa-i-Sanjan,** professing to give an account of the migration of the Zoroastrians to India; as well as the Shah Namah already named.

V. The Prophet: The name Zoroaster, by which the prophet of Iran is known in the West, comes from the common Latin form (and the Greek) *Zoroastres,* though other forms are known in Greek, **1. The** the most observable being *Zathraustes,* **Name.** which approximates closely to the Avestan form. The common Pahlavi form is *Zaratusht,* to which the modern Persian form is very close (see extracts from catechism at the close of this article). The Avestan names are *Zarathushtra, Zarathushtra Spitama, Spitama Zarathushtra,* or *Spitama.* The last is a family name and probably means " descendant of white " (cf. the English " Whiting "; Jackson, ut sup., p. 13). The derivation of *Zarathushtra* is doubtful; *ushtra* means " camel," but no agreement has been reached upon the first element in the name.

The question whether Zoroaster is a historical personage may now be regarded as settled in the affirmative. But that doubts should **2. Zoroaster** have been raised is quite explicable. **Historical.** As M. Haug well puts it (*Essays on the Sacred Language, Writings, and Religion of the Parsis*, ed. Dr. E. West, pp. 295–296, London, 1878):

"The events of his life are almost all enshrouded in darkness, to dispel which will be for ever impossible, should no authentic historical records be discovered in Bactria, his home. The reports regarding him, given by the Greeks and Romans, . . . are as unhistorical and legendary as those found in the majority of the Avesta books themselves. In the Vendidad and the Yashts he is represented . . . as not a historical, but as a dogmatical personality, stripped of nearly everything that is peculiar to human nature, and vested with a supernatural and wholly divine power, standing next to God himself and being elevated above the archangels. . . . He was the concentration of all wisdom and truth, and master and head of the whole creation. The only source whence we may derive some very scanty historical facts is the older Yasna. In this part of the Scriptures only he appears to the eye as a real man, acting a great and prominent part in the history of his country, and even in the history of the whole human race in general."

The counts against a historical Zoroaster are three: (1) his figure is so large and in later development so enveloped in legend; (2) classical writers placed him in a hoary antiquity, and (3) details of his life historically verifiable are so few that doubt of his existence was almost a matter of course. These counts seem now of less value since it has become known that the accumulation of legend about the figure of a religious genius is customary, as witness Lao Tzse and Gautama, and no longer furnish presumption against the historicity of a personality. As to the classical references the following is to be said. Pliny the Elder (*Hist. nat.*, XXX., ii. 1) cites Eudoxus of Cnidus (c. 368 B.C.), Aristotle (350 B.C.), and Hermippus (c. 250 B.C.) for a date 6,000 years before the death of Plato, 5,000 before the Trojan war; he is followed in substance by Plutarch (" Isis and Osiris," xlvi.), a scholion to the Platonic " Alcibiades " (i. 22), Diogenes Laertius (*De vitis philosophorum*, proem. 2), and Suidas the lexicographer. Pliny and Suidas agree upon two Zoroasters, one (significantly) in the seventh to the sixth century. Still further, a set of references connect the prophet with the legendary Ninus and Semiramis, evidently intending a reference to a date about 800 B.C. (found in Ctesias, c. 400 B.C., Cephalion, 120 A.D., preserved in Eusebius, *Chronikon*, i. 43; Theon, 130 A.D., Justin Martyr, 114–165 A.D.; and Arnobius, 290 A.D.). The explanation of this early date is a misunderstanding by these writers of the Zoroastrian apocalyptics, which deal with cycles of 3,000 years (references in Jackson, ut sup., where the passages are collected).

The basis for a historical account of the prophet's life are the Gathas as noted above, the *Bundahish*, xxxiv. 1–9, and the *Arta-i Viraf*, i. 2–5. These sum up the native tradition, though of course other literature reflects it. The *Bundahish*, in the chronol-

ogy of the world period, makes the era of Zoroaster fall at the close of the third tri-millennium, and his ministry (begun at the age of thirty) at the beginning of the final tri-millennium. Historic-**3. His** ally this is placed 272 years before the **Early Life.** conquest by Alexander in 331, which would make Zoroaster's ministry begin in 603 and his birth take place 633 B.C. West and Jackson (see bibliography) settle respectively upon c. 660 and 630 B.C. as the birth-year. This Persian tradition is practically reproduced in the Arab historian and geographer Albiruni (973–1048 A.D.), by Masudi (d. 957), who says that the Magians reckon 258 years between Zoroaster and Alexander (cited in Jackson, ut sup., p. 162), by Tabari (also an Arab; d. 923), and in a series of allusions in Pahlavi and other Persian writings. Very little can with certainty be said of Zoroaster's origin and the course of his life. Legend was very busy surrounding him with glory. Thus the soul of the primeval bull had a vision of his fravashi (ideal image, spiritual counterpart) 3,000 years before the revelation of his religion (*Bundahish*, iv. 4–5), and an ox endowed with speech 300 years before his birth predicted his advent. The question of Zoroaster's native place is one of the vexed questions. Classical allusions (cf. Jackson, ut sup., pp. 186–191) locate it in Bactria (Eastern Iran), in Persia, or in Media; the Persian and (secondary) Arabic literature (Jackson, ut sup., pp. 191–205) is quite generally in favor of Adarbaijan, the modern Azerbaijan, west of the Caspian and including Urumiah. Especially does the native tradition connect the prophet with the River Daryai, one of the tributaries of the Araxes taking its rise in Mt. Savalan and flowing north. This tradition regards Zoroaster's youth as spent in the same region, and his visions as seen there or to the south of the Caspian. His mother was Dughdhova, a virgin, and he was of triple nature, including the " kingly glory," fravashi, and material body; his mother, after conceiving him, became so resplendent that she was thought bewitched and sent away from home, where she married. Nature participated in the rejoicing at his birth, the demons fled in terror, and the child at once burst into exultant laughter. The contest with evil was at once precipitated by the evil spirits and their servants among men; attempts to kill him failed and beasts became his protectors. His education began before the age of seven, and his majority came at fifteen; at twenty he gave up the world and began the life of a wanderer seeking religious truth. What little is said of his life from twenty to thirty years of age (cf. Jackson, ut sup., pp. 34, 231 sqq.) leads to the conclusion that something like the life of an Indian ascetic was not unknown in Iran. The tradition includes retirement to a mountain cave (*Vendidad*, xxii. 19) in a manner which recalls Mohammed's experience; at the age of thirty he received his first vision, followed by others for ten years at intervals until he had seven, out of which he constructed his religion. The facts of religious psychology and the part which Ecstasy (q.v.) played support a construction of his religious development as follows. He early displayed a vigorous mentality, to which his mother and her husband made response in provision for his education. The period between his fifteenth and his twentieth year he passed in ordinary vocations, and this appears to have ended to his dissatisfaction. Then came the period of wandering, meditation, retirement, and the beginning of his visions, these last psychologically the result of his experiences. Evidence of this is found not merely in the visions themselves, but in the series of abstractions which seem to have been taught from the very beginning, including the very remarkable one of "the soul of the kine " (*Yasna*, xxviii.), whether this personifies the people, or the brute creation, which latter, especially the domestic animals, has so large a part in the religion.

The seven visions of Zoroaster began when he was thirty and covered a period of ten years. During this time he was engaged in preaching, but without success. When he was forty, his instruction being complete, tradition affirms that he sustained his final temptation. As Gautama, after **4. Founding of the Religion.** attaining Nirvana, was assailed by Maya, so Zoroaster was assailed by Angra Mainyu and his demons, whom he repelled by the words of the holy benediction (*Vendidad*, xix. 1–10). His preaching had carried him not only to his own people but also among the Turanian nomads, and, according to tradition, to India and China; but he met only rebuff; it is thought that some of the denunciatory passages of the sacred books had their origin in these failures. During these years he made but one convert, his own cousin (*Zatsparam*, xviii. 1). It was two years more before victory came in the conversion of King Vishtaspa, " the Constantine of Zoroastrianism." This raises the difficult problem of the scene of the prophet's ministry (cf. Jackson, ut sup., pp. 205–225), and the solution in no small part depends upon the identification of Vishtaspa. The earlier identification with Hystaspes, father of Darius, has gone by the board. Vishtaspa does not bear the title " king of kings " usually borne by the Persian monarchs. The details of the tradition, whether in classical, native Persian, or Arabic sources, are not decisive, but rather point to this king as a quite petty monarch in eastern Iran (Bactria); at any rate, the probability is not great that Zoroaster's success was won in his own region. Even with the court in his favor, full adoption was not attained, as the native stories speak of a struggle of two years with the " wise men." The narrative has, of course, become befogged with the addition of the miraculous. For instance, the prophet is thrown into prison, and escapes and wins victory over the king by healing the latter's favorite steed, and, so the story goes, became vizier, hence his progress became after a little time quite rapid. The Gathas most plausibly attributed to the prophet or his immediate disciples still indicate times of stress and conflict, as they also reflect moods which might well be the effect of varying success or failure, acceptance or rejection of the religion. The indications are clear (*Yasna*, xlvi. 12) that among the converts Turanians were numbered, while Hindus, Greeks, and Babylonians are also claimed as believers. The religion was strongly and militantly missionary, and the propaganda seems to have been insistent and diffused.

The organization was in this period the care of the founder, especially the establishment of the sacred fire—taken up into the cult—in new places. Among these tradition assigns a chief **5. Final Work and Death of Zoroaster.** place to the *Atur Farnbag*, or fire of the priests, probably to the east of the Caspian; then came the *Atur Gushnash*, or fire of the warriors, located near Lake Urumiah; and the *Atur Burzhin Mitro*, or fire of the laborer. These point to a system of society like that in the early Indian system of caste, and suggest a common Indo-Iranian institution which agrees with other indications of racial and social relationship. Apparently the final stage in the life of Zoroaster was that of the " holy wars." Many indications exist in the Avesta not only of fighting for the religion, but also of a persistent enmity between Iranians and Turanians (e.g., *Yasht*, v. 109, 113–117, ix. 30–31, xix. 87). The religion from its very foundation was not one of forbearance with other beliefs; its pronouncements were those of exclusive claim, and the foe marked for special disfavor was the Turanian, whose flocks and herds were singled out in the sacred books as legitimate booty, while the faithful prays for protection against this enemy (*Vendidad*, iii. 11; *Yasht*, viii. 6, 9, 37, 56). Vishtaspa and Arejat-aspa (Arjasp) are the respective champions in the war of the religion which is most noted, approximately dated 601 B.C. Political causes (refusal of Vishtaspa longer to pay tribute; *Dinkart*, vii. 4, 77) were evidently involved, though later writings (*Shah Namah*, ed. J. Mohl, iv. 289, 294, 7 vols., Paris, 1876–78) emphasize the religious motive. Arjasp refused the faith, and demanded that Vishtaspa renounce it; and in two great battles the latter was victorious. The traditions indicate a militant spirit for Zoroastrianism, not unlike that of Mohammedanism, and crusades with the sword as well as by propaganda are annaled. A second war between the same foes as those named followed after an interval, and the foe gained a temporary success, captured the royal city of Balkh, and slaughtered the priests at worship, when Zoroaster fell at the age of seventy-seven. In a second battle Vishtaspa was defeated, but in a third was finally victorious. The death of the prophet became the center of hostile and favoring legend, even entering into Christian writings (" Clementine Recognitions," iv. 27–29, Eng. transl. in *ANF*, viii. 140–141; " Clementine Homilies," ix. 4–6, Eng. transl., *ANF*, viii. 276; other documents cited in Jackson, ut sup., pp. 126–127).

VI. History of the Religion after Zoroaster: The death of the founder did not mean the extinction of the religion. Early narratives now lost except for abstracts or summaries, as well as later tradition, imply the continuance of crusades for **1. To the Sassanian Empire.** the faith and the conquest by it of the Persian kingdom. Artaxerxes Longimanus (465–424) is credited with the effecting of this last. The religion spread into Armenia, Indo-Scythia, and into Asia Minor. Yet of its history under the Achaemenides (558–331 B.C.) hardly anything is known, and some doubt the fidelity of Persians to this religion in that age. The question is really legitimate—were the

Achaemenides confirmed Zoroastrians? Native tradition emphatically asserts it. The first great disaster to the religion, assuming that under the Achaemenides this faith had become national, was that which befell it under Alexander the Great, and stress is laid particularly upon the loss of the great body of scriptures, when he conquered Darius III. Codomannus in 331 B.C. While the great body of the *Vendidad* bears marks of a considerably later age, and many modern scholars dispute the credibility of the Parsee tradition as to the loss of the literature, there are facts which indicate that at the time given some disaster was received which included in its scope that literature. Few would now hold, however, that the twenty-one Nasks were in existence and were so nearly completely lost. The period which set in with the break-up of the Alexandrian empire, especially the times of the Seleucidæ (q.v.), who at times controlled considerable portions of Persia, was surely not favorable to the religion, and its continuance, or at least its dominance, was confined to the eastern portion of the region. Independent kingdoms arose in Bactria and Parthia, and there the seeds of the later rejuvenescence were preserved. But Greek ideas and colonization had their effect and seriously threatened the existence of Zoroastrianism. A period of revival came under the Arsacidæ (248 B.C.–229 A.D.), though the adherence of this line to Zoroastrianism seems to have been rather formal than deep-seated. Among the royal advisers were the " Magians," whose council existed alongside that of the nobles and had weight in political affairs. But the force of Hellenism was probably felt in the lessened zeal of the dynasty for the Mazdayaznian faith, and it had made inroads into custom and religious belief. Yet the native religion seems to have gathered strength and to have taken on some of the features of a national faith. The Iranian element of the population appears to have gained in importance, rising toward dominance in the region and preparing for the Sassanian fuller revival. To a king Valkhash of the Sassanian dynasty (211–641 A.D.) is ascribed (*Dinkart*, iii.–iv.) the collection of the Avesta fragments, which is itself a suggestive fact. This king may have been the Vologeses I. who was contemporary with Nero.

With the establishment of the Sassanian empire began a new period of splendor and dominion for the Mazdayaznian religion. The founder of this empire, Ardashir (Artaxerxes) I., began his reign in 211–212 A.D., and by 226 A.D. had **2. To the** overthrown the Parthian rule, while **Moham-** his son and successor, Shapur (Sapor) **medan** I., continued the extension of the king- **Conquest.** dom, and meeting the Roman Emperor Valerian (q.v.) defeated him and took him prisoner. But reverses met Shapur in Asia Minor and nearer home, so that the Sassanian power was restricted to eastern and southern Mesopotamia and Iran proper. This had much to do with the area over which Zoroastrianism spread. The new dynasty managed to combine in its ideals national and religious elements. Ardashir seems to have been a devoted Zoroastrian, and again under him the priesthood ranked with the nobility. He is recognized in Persian tradition as the second father of

the Avesta, who assigned the task of collecting the fragments to the high-priest Tansar (Jansar), and the *Vendidad* is by a number of scholars assigned to this period. After Shapur I. Greek influence died out in that region and the Pahlavi came into its own as the vehicle of thought. The detail of cultic ceremonial was worked out—not, of course, that this was a creation of the period, but rather the codification of traditions and customs that in many cases reached far back and bear the stamp of primitive belief. Under Shapur I. Mani (see MANI, MANICHEANS) arose and began his propaganda, and found some favor even at court. Zoroastrian tradition tells of a great debate in which the old religion conquered; it yet had to combat the persistency of Manicheism, which continued to spread, and under Bahram I., successor to Shapur, Mani was executed. In this period also the Iranian faith came into conflict with Christianity, each firmly insistent upon its own exclusive claims. Each therefore became a bulwark against the diffusion of the other; where Christianity penetrated the Persian empire, it was only to become the object of persecution, as under Shapur II. (310–379). Then, some hold, the Avesta was completed, heresy (against Zoroastrianism) was proscribed, and defection from the faith made a capital offense (Sachall, in the *Mittheilungen* of the Seminar for Oriental Languages in Berlin, X., ii., 1907). Still, under later rulers, attacks upon the true faith of Mazdayaznians were made by new sects like the Mazdakites under Kavadh I. (488–531), whose successor Chosroes I. (531–579) restored the old religion in what was supposed to be its early purity. The beginning of the end of Zoroastrianism in this region is seen in the coming of the Turks c. 560. Romans and Parthians had nearly worn each other out in their wars, and the conflict continued in the seventh century. Then a new foe arose in the south, whose attack ranged eastward, and in 641 the Persian kingdom fell to the Arabs in the battle of Nehavend. Zoroastrianism soon was almost extinct in Iran, and the Parsees (see below, VII.) emigrated to India.

VII. The Zoroastrian System: A history of Mazdeism in detail would involve discussion of three stages: the pre-Zoroastrian, the Zoroastrian, and the post-Zoroastrian. In this article **1. Maz-** the last two will be treated together, **deism and** since it is not possible to separate them **Vedism.** with entire certainty in tracing the several doctrines, although it is clear that the principal doctrines and beliefs of the later form are present implicitly in the earlier Zoroastrian teaching. The first of the three stages is revealed in the effects it had upon the notions concerning the spiritual beings, worships, and ideals of the Zoroastrian system, in the features common to it and the Vedic-Brahmanic beliefs. For although there are Zoroastrian conceptions which are common to the Indo-European peoples, the connections with the Aryans of India are particularly intimate. Thus the supreme place occupied by fire is but an exaltation of the function of fire in the Indian religion (Agni); the Soma of India has its correlative in the Haoma of Iran; the investiture with the sacred thread is common to both, though differently explained; the great place held by the cow or bull in both is indicative of relationship; Mithra is possessed by both; Ahura Mazda reminds both of the Asura and of Varuna, and may be a composite; the sevenfold Adityas of Vedism are reproduced in the (dual) sevenfold hierarchy of Persia; the Indian Yama, with changed functions and conceptions, abides in the Mazdean Yima; the horse as a noble sacrifice appears in both; and in Vedism, as always in Zoroastrianism, priestly functions were not originally those of a caste. Both possessed *devas*; the high consideration given in both to sun, moon, stars, Sirius, water, the earth and its vegetable products, are noticeable; and the irrepressible conflict between good and evil appears in both, though in very different ways. These are but salient examples of common features which lead to the conclusion that the pre-Zoroastrian and Vedic systems were twin sisters. Yet it is important to note that the Iranian religion followed a course which seems to imply conscious enmity, or at least opposition, to Vedism which induced a quite diverse emphasis. Thus in India *deva*, " shining one," became continually more honorific; in Iran *dœva* became the name for demons; *Asura* in India, at first equivalent to " supreme spirit," tended to become less honorable and finally was demonic in significance, while its correlative (?) Ahura became the chief or sole deity in Persia; India developed an increasing polytheism by syncretism, while under Zoroaster Mazdeism became in ideal monotheistic, though there are indications that it was difficult for the people to think of the whilom deities as angels or spirits in any other sense than as gods.

Zoroaster found this contrariety already developed, and latent in it the (philosophic) dualism (which under his system concerned practically only the course of this world) by which he explained terrestrial phenomena. This dualistic tendency was intensified by the conflict, already noted, between pastoral or agricultural peoples and nomadic raiders. To his people he introduced as their one god Ahura Mazda—probably in essence not a new deity, but rather with glorified attributes. He taught that the gods of the nomads and raiders were demons banded to destroy the good Ahura's works and those of his followers. Man had been blind and deluded (cf. the Indian *maya*, " delusion "), so Ahura sent his prophet to teach men the right way and to choose the right side in the great battle between good and evil. It is this last which sharply characterizes Zoroastrianism, leading to the ethical dualism which explains it. This comes out in the cosmology and apocalyptics of Mazdeism. The idea of duration and space is fundamental, though its philosophic form may be quite late. Duration takes the form of two periods of infinite time, separated by a world age of 12,000 years blocked out into four sub-periods of 3,000 years each. The first time is infinite in a receding past and comes down to the beginning of the world age. The second infinity of time begins with the complete triumph of good at the end of the world age, and extends into a never-ending future. With this set of time-thoughts correspond the two spatial infinities, that of light (the

2. Cosmology.

dwelling of Ahura) and that of darkness (the home of Angra Mainyu), separated by the visible world which is the arena of human and animal activities and of the conflict between good and evil. According to the *Bundahish*, after Ahura made the creatures which were to minister to his mastery of evil, they remained passive, inactive, and intangible for 3,000 years. Angra Mainyu then accepted the proposal that the conflict should continue for 9,000 years, not knowing that for the first tri-millennium Ahura's will would control, for the second the two wills would intermingle, and that in the final period Angra Mainyu's would be subdued. Being thus shown the issue, he was so confounded that he remained passive for the second period, when Ahura created the six archangels (see below, § 3), to which his opponent answered by creating the six archdemons. Ahura created successively the sky and luminaries, water, earth, animals, and mankind. The Fravashis (see below, VI., § 4) of men had already been created, and to them was promised ultimate perfection and immortality if they should choose Ahura's side. In the struggle beginning with the seventh millennium the primeval man and primeval ox fell; from the earth the primeval man's seed produced a plant that after forty years brought forth or became the first pair. This third millennium is accounted for by a mythical chronology. The period of humanity covers 6,000 years, the prophet beginning his ministry at the middle of this period with his thirtieth year. At the end of the first thousand years of this period the first forerunner of Saoshyant (see below, § 4) appears with the name *Ukhshyaterata*, " who makes piety grow." In the middle of the second millennium of this period was the season of cold caused by a wizard, salvation for a remnant of men and animals being secured by Yima (see below, § 5). At the beginning a second forerunner of the Saoshyant appears, and at the end the Saoshyant closes the world age. The final conflict breaks out, man makes progress to pure spirituality, finally needing no food; and after the resurrection and judgment begins again infinite time, human history and the victory having been consummated.

Corresponding to the two infinities in space and time were the two existences, independent, contrary in nature, both *ab initio* infinite, though only one is to continue his eternity of being. **Ahura Mazda,** " Lord All-knowing " (shortened to Ormuzd) is described in the Ormuzd *Yasht* (Eng. transl. in *SBE*, xxiii. 21–31) as the creator, omniscient, holy, beneficent, eternal in the full sense, bestower of health, happiness, and possessions, essential light. He was apparently unfigured in the religion, represented by no statue or form. Essentially opposed to him was **Angra Mainyu** (or **Ahriman**), " Hostile Spirit," coeval in origin with Ahura, but not eternal in the full sense, since he is to cease to be. He is essentially evil, unconsecrate, limited in knowledge (he did not even know of the existence of Ahura), gross darkness. He could not foresee the future, so could not guard against its issues. Ahura, to assist him in the foreseen conflict, and in the guidance of the world, created the six **Amesha Spentas** (**Amshashpands**), " Immortal Beneficents," with whom

3. The Hierarchies.

he formed the holy heptad, his servitors with the attributes of immortality, invisibility, beneficence. These are the personifications of virtues or abstract qualities, and are perhaps the most remarkable evidences of the founder's thought. Their names are: **Vohu Manah**, " Good Thought "; **Asha Vahishta**, " Best Righteousness "; **Khshathra Vairya**, " Desired Kingdom "; **Spenta Armaiti**, " Holy Harmony "; **Haurvatat**, " Saving Health," and **Ameretat**, " Immortality." The first three are male, the others female. They are assigned to the protection of specific departments or elements in the world: thus the first cares for domestic animals, Khshathra for metals, Asha Vahishta for fire, Armaiti for the earth, Haurvatat for water, Ameretat for vegetation. To each a month was dedicated in special honor, also a holy day and a special flower. Their place in the heavenly hierarchy corresponds in some degree to the Jewish and Christian archangels. Yet the name " Amshashpands " later took in other beings than the six named, such as Sraosha, Atar, Gosurvan (see below; § 4). To offset these Angra Mainyu created six archdemons, **Aka Manah**, " Evil Mind," **Indra, Sauru, Naonhaithya, Tauru,** and **Zairi** (*Vendidad*, x. 9–10; *Yasht*, xix. 96). Then as he had introduced into the good world of animals created by Ahura evil creations such as serpents and vermin, so he created hordes of lesser demons and " drujes," as well as the evils of disease and deformity and death and all sorts of loathsomeness among men. Indeed, during his day, while not omnipotent (even Ahura had not that attribute), he had ability to work all the evils which Zoroaster found in this world. It is to be remarked here, as illustrating one of the limitations of thought in the system in common with like ethical religions, the powers of evil have far less sharpness of definition than the beings who work for good. This speaks well for the minds that created and developed the system.

Besides the Amesha Spentas there were in the religion a number of beings named in the Avesta (and of course in the later writings) as receiving special honor. Theoretically these were not divinities to whom worship was paid, but were beneficent spirits active under the direction of Ahura Mazda. Notable are the Yazatas, abstractions or personifications of natural elements, bodies, or qualities, of whom **Mithra**, celebrated in *Yasht*, x. (see MITHRA, MITHRAISM for later developments), was of Indo-Iranian derivation, originally a solar deity of light, knower of truth and a witness to it, guardian of oaths, and a judge of the dead. **Atar**, or fire, the purest of the elements, was next in importance, if he were second even to Mithra. He was the messenger of Ahura, the holiest spirit against whose defilement in his material form most stringent regulations were drawn. As with Agni in India, the conception varies from material to spiritual, from personal to impersonal. The cult associated with this element gave one of the names to the Zoroastrians by which they were long and widely though erroneously known, " Fire Worshipers." **Anahita**, celebrated in *Yasht*, v., was the spirit of the waters. Her Avesta name is *Ardvi Sura Anahita*, " high, powerful, immaculate being." She

4. Other Celestial Spirits.

was the heavenly spring and source of all terrestrial waters, located on the summit of a mythical mountain in the region of the stars. She was the assistant of many holy heroes before and after the prophet, as well as of himself. Having power to fertilize the earth, she used this power beneficently for the good of animals and mankind, and was the good genius of marriageable girls and parturient women. Her cult came to have a great independent vogue, like that of Mithra, spread widely in Armenia (Pliny v. 83) and through Asia Minor (Strabo xi. 512), where she became fused with the " Great Mother Goddess." Greeks identified her with both Athene and Aphrodite. The " **Star Yazatas** " were also of high importance, these being the fixed stars, not the planets, which were regarded as creations of Angra Mainyu. **Tistriya**, Sirius, celebrated in *Yasht*, viii., was the leader of the stars, who seems to have been the counterpart of Indra, fighting the dragon of drought and precipitating the rains. In later writings (e.g., *Bundahish*, viii.) transfer is made to the cosmology, and this being forms lakes and seas. Other figures not Yazatas are **Sraosha**, " obedience," angel of worship (*Yasht*, xi.; *Yasna*, lvii.), the incarnate word, protector of the poor, mediator between heaven and earth, and a judge and conductor of the dead. **Rashnu Razista**, " genius of truth " (*Yasht*, xii.), was especially concerned with the dead, holding the balance in which their deeds are weighed, and with Mithra and Sraosha forming the triad of judges. **Gosurun** (Gos, Drvaspa) is the soul of the cow or bull, the abstract representative of the animal kingdom, an important figure in the mythology, celebrated in *Yasht*, ix. **Kavaem Hvareno**, " kingly majesty," or " royal glory," was perhaps the abstraction of the principle of divine right of kings; possibly because of this the title of deity appears among the titles of the Sassanidæ. **Ashi Vanguhi** was the personification of piety, the genius of fortune and wealth, health, and intellectual vigor. Other figures celebrated are **Arstat** or truthfulness (*Yasht*, xviii.); **Verethragma** (*Yasht*, xiv.), genius of victory, who appeared to Zoroaster in ten incarnations and bestowed on him various gifts; **Rama Hvastra** (*Yasht*, xv.), **Daena** or **Din** (*Yasht*, xvi.), the personification of the religion; and the Fravashis (*Yasht*, xiii.), corresponding in some degree to the Manes of the Romans, though specialized and philosophized after the peculiar Zoroastrian fashion. The notion was extended in the later thinking, and not only spirits and men have fravashis, but the sky, the earth, and other things. The notion seems to be in part an abstraction including the vigor by which the object it possesses grows and develops. Especially significant is the doctrine of the **Saoshyant**, usually rendered " savior," who is to come, having been foreshadowed by prophets in the line of Zoroaster who were virgin-born. He is to end the battle with evil, preside over the resurrection, and accomplish the rejuvenation of the world. The parallelism with messianism is at once discerned.

Thus the angelology of the system is seen to be highly developed. Equally noticeable is the ethical foundation of the entire hierarchy on which the structure is built. The demonology is less definite, and the evil spirits are far less individualized.

According to *Yasht*, xiii. 149, man is in constitution fivefold: spirit or intellectuality, the knowing power; conscience, a sort of personality which warns of possible wrong, but deserts the incorrigible; vital force, coexistent with the body; soul, perhaps moral choice; and the fravashi, which seems to assume the post-mortem personality. The essential idea of man is that of a being having to choose between Ahura and Angra Mainyu, between good and evil, and this choice determines his future lot. His period of existence is divided into two parts by death, and his place after death is determined by inflexible justice upon the basis of his deeds in the body. Of soteriology, in the Christian sense, there is none in the system; there is no pardon for sin apart from the fact that a convert to the religion is by confessing the faith relieved from the consequence of prior sins of ignorance when he knew not the religion. Yet man is not left, in the developed form of the religion at least, to his own efforts, since guardian angels assist in overcoming temptation and evading the pitfalls set by the demons. An important part in the Zoroastrian anthropology is that embodied in the Yima story. Ahura proposed to make Yima the founder of the new religion, but he declined; so Ahura made him guardian of the world and the creatures of Ahura (*Vendidad*, ii.). This duty he performed, so that the flocks and herds and mankind increased, and twice the area of the inhabited earth had to be enlarged. He was then warned of the approach of a series of cold winters which should wipe out life, and was commanded to create a sort of paradise, two miles square, and bring thither specimens of the different species, eliminating from the humans thus saved the deformed, impotent, lunatic, malicious, evil-minded, leprous, and wicked. This was done, and the 1,900 men and women there lived a life of perfect happiness and repeopled the earth after the magician who had wrought the cold had ceased his work. This story is not to be taken as a direct parallel of the "flood legend," but is a combination of the "golden-age" legend and recollection of the migrations.

The soul after death remains near the body for three days, in pain or joy, according to its deeds. On the fourth day at dawn it takes up its journey to its final home. Its experiences correspond to the individual's actions during life. Have they been righteous, the soul is cheered by delicious experiences on its way, and is met by a beautiful maiden, the impersonation of its good deeds, who guides it to the Chinvat bridge, where Mithra, Sraosha, and Rashnu pass judgment (on the basis of the daily record kept by Vohu Manah and the trying in Rashnu's scales of its good deeds and bad). Then it passes across the Chinvat bridge (*Yasna*, xix. 6, xlvi. 11) to the bridge of the angels; finally, received by Vohu Manah, the soul passes before Ahura and the Amesha Spentas to take up its abode permanently with the righteous (*Vendidad*, xix. 28–34; cf. *Yasht*, xxii., xxiv. 53–64; *Yasna*, xxxi. 14). The hap of the wicked is the reverse of this, the soul being met by an evil-favored hag and dragged by it after the judgment to the depths of darkness. There is, however,

a place called *Hamestagan*, the abiding-place of souls whose good and evil deeds exactly balance. These and the evil dead abide in their places till the last day, when the human denizens of hell are purified and join, with those of Hamestagan, the blessed in the new heaven and new earth. So that universalism is the final creed, and hell is not an eternal torture or retribution (*Dadistan-i Dinik*, xiv. 8, xxxii. 10–16; *Bundahish*, xxx. 1–33; cf. G. C. O. Haas, in *Spiegel Memorial Volume*, Bombay, 1908). On the day of judgment the Saoshyant completes the victory over evil in a final battle (*Yasht*, xix. 89–96), and is to reign for fifty-seven years. By that time man will have become spiritualized, needing neither food nor drink (*Bundahish*, xxx. 3; *Dinkart*, VII., xi. 4). A star is to fall and its heat will melt the terrestrial metals, this molten mass coursing over the earth and becoming the purification of men and making the earth a mountainless plain. The resurrection takes place, all souls gather, and the wicked suffer three days' torture in hell. All souls pass through the molten flood, which to the good is pleasant and to the bad is extremest pain. Then all are united in heaven (*Dadistan-i Dinik*, lxxv. 4), and the new earth is established, itself immortal, it and its inhabitants radiant with light, yet possessing sun, moon, and stars.

The universally present ideal inculcated by the Mazdean religion is summed up in activity as represented in the triple phrase, " good thoughts, good words, good deeds." By the first is meant primarily acceptance of the religion and then regard for the law, practical and ritual, abstention from presumption, covetousness, anger, lust, envy, anxiety, and disobedience to superiors. " Good words " involves the eschewing of slander and of dispute even with the evil-minded and malicious. The ideal of good works is based upon the pastoral and agricultural foundations of Avestan society. Perjury, impurity of body or mind, violence, and untruthfulness are especially denounced, charity and generosity are forcefully enjoined. *Vendidad* iii. pronounces the best situations on earth those where a Zoroastrian is worshiping, and the homestead of a believer with wife, children, flocks, and herds all in good condition, where the fields are under irrigation and the flocks yield most urine (for purification). The fight against demons is in part carried on by agriculture—" Who sows corn sows holiness." Procrastination of labor is forbidden (*Sad Dar*, lxxxi. 10). Asceticism is frowned on, especially is celibacy opposed; the possession of wife and children is commended, the latter being among the chief blessings of mankind, and childlessness a curse (*Yasna*, xi. 3; *SBE*, xxxi. 244–245; Herodotus, ix. 111), while a sacred virginity was considered irreligious. To foster fertility, the sacred fire was maintained in the house (*Shayast*, xii. 3), and the period of gestation was marked at intervals by joyous celebrations. The child at six begins to learn prayers, and some little time after that is invested with the sacred thread. Since labor is a prime duty, fasting is prohibited, because it deprives of proper strength for the active duties of life (*Vendidad*, iii. 33, iv. 48–49). Self-mortification is sinful, and later writings seem to have a polemic directed against Christian and Manichean asceticism. Penalties enjoined for breaches of the law are often useful labors either in the field or for the ritual service. Inhibitions of sexual intercourse where they exist rest in the main upon considerations of essential healthful propriety. Among the punishments prescribed are the killing of snakes or vermin (the creatures of Angra Mainyu), building of bridges over water, and making of ditches for irrigation.

The cult involved a priesthood, called Athravan. The priests were held to a high level of obligation. It is noticeable that the *Vendidad* shows no traces of the self-seeking of the priesthood such as characterizes the Brahmanic writings of India.

8. The Cult. Priestly duties involved service not only at the temples but in the homes of the believers, particularly in the care of the sacred fire, the brewing of haoma, and the chanting of the liturgy. Training for the priesthood began at the age of seven and continued till at least fourteen, and the memorizing of *Yasna* and *Vendidad* seems to have been required. Sacrificial animals named are the horse, cow, lamb, and even the camel (*Vendidad*, xxii. 16–20). Special importance attached to the **Baresma (Barsom)**, originally a bundle of twigs held by the priest while he recited the prayers (*Vendidad*, iii. 1, xix. 63). It is represented now by a bunch of silver rods varying in number from three to thirty-three. The Baresma was employed in the invocation to Ahura, the service for the dead, the offerings to the Yazatas and other spirits, including the Fravashis. Its virtues increase in the later periods of the religion, until by its offering the just are borne to paradise. Great emphasis was laid also upon haoma, a drink supposed to bring the participant into communion with God, and later becoming sacramental. Haoma seems to have been originally a deity of exhilaration, the apotheosized fermented drink (the intoxicating character is evident in *Yasna*, ix.–xi., note x. 13). The chief claim to the spirit thus apotheosized was that he is the " holy one who driveth death afar." Altogether novel is the place of the dog in the religion, so that two Fargards are taken up with the subject (*Vendidad*, xiii.–xiv., cf. viii. 14 sqq., xv. 20–51). Killing of the animal is forbidden. Two " four-eyed " dogs guard the Chinvat bridge (probably dogs with spots over the eyes), and a like animal expels from a corpse the " corpse demon." Since all that Ahura created was pure, healthful, and good, Angra Mainyu's activities producing impurity, disease, and death, the effort of life was to avoid and banish the impure. In ritual, impurity is contact with something tainted by contact with the demons—with death or disease or deformity. All that passes from a man is impure, hence one may not breathe on the fire, nor for ceremonial purposes cleanse in the first instance in water. The dead may not be burned, nor buried unless first encased in wax or kindred substance, but exposed to carrion birds in " towers of silence." Funeral services for the dead are conducted on the three days succeeding the decease, with memorial services on the fourth, tenth, and thirtieth days and the annual anniversary. Priests are the celebrants, while the symbolic elements, fire and water and also

flowers and fruits, are used. Recollections from primitive times appear in the host of charms used, these parts of the Avesta being those that show the early character of part of the religious usages. The principle that underlies the entire code is the primitive one that offenses against the individual are far less dangerous than against the religion—spiritual beings—since these endanger all mankind by arousing the anger of the exalted spirits. Thus the solidarity of the Zoroastrian community is emphasized. To maintain the purity of the community in early times close intermarriage was practised, but in modern times observance of this is less stringent.

VIII. The Parsees: Modern Zoroastrians are known as Parsees (Parsis), and are found principally in India. After the Mohammedan conquest of Persia in 641, the Zoroastrians were in large part under the necessity of leaving the country in order to practise their religion, though scattered communities continued to exist there. The Island of Ormuz in the Persian Gulf was the first refuge, but was inadequate for a permanent home. A series of emigrations led them to Diu on the Gulf of Cambay on the western coast of India about 700. They settled in Guzerat, and in 721 built their fire temple; this was their home till about 1300, when the Moslem invasion of India again drove them away to take refuge in such places somewhat inland as Broach, Surat, and Thana. In the sixteenth century the Portuguese attempted to force their conversion to Christianity, but the advent of the British in India in the early part of the seventeenth century brought relief from pressure. On the occupation in 1668 of Bombay by the British East India Company as its seat of power, the Parsees made that city their headquarters. Many of them took service with the company in a wide variety of capacities. They have ever since displayed a remarkable readiness to adapt themselves to modern conditions, and the Parsee community as a whole is noted for its wealth and culture. Their industrial, educational, and charitable enterprises are of a very high type, and they regard as a disgrace to the community the existence of the few Parsee beggars that remain. Small Parsee communities still exist in Persia, chiefly in Yezd, where perhaps 8,000 Parsees (known as *Iranis* to distinguish them from their Indian brethren) still live. In India there are not far from 100,000 professing this religion, nearly all of whom are in the Bombay presidency. They claim to have preserved the pure faith taught by Zoroaster, and their principal beliefs and practises may be gathered from the following extracts from a Parsee catechism.

In whom do we, of the Zarthosti community, believe?

We believe in only one God, and do not believe in any beside him.

Who is that one God?

The God who created the heavens, the earth, the angels, the stars, the sun, the moon, the fire, the water, or all the four elements, and all things of the two worlds: that God we believe in, him we worship, him we invoke, him we adore.

Do we not believe in any other god?

Whoever believes in any other god but this is an infidel, and shall suffer the punishment of hell.

What is the form of our God?

Our God has neither face nor form, color nor shape, nor fixed place. There is no other like him; he is him-

self singly such a glory that we can not praise or describe him, nor our mind comprehend him.
Is there any such thing that God can not create it?
Yes, there is one thing that God himself even can not create.
What that thing is must be explained to me.
God is the creator of all things; but if he wish to create another like himself, he can not do it. God can not create another like himself.
How many names are there for God?
It is said that there are 1,001 names; but of these 101 are extant.
Why are there so many names of God?
God's names, expressive of his nature, are two— Yazdan ("omnipotence") and Pauk ("holy"). He is also named Hormuzd (the highest of spirits), Dadar (the distributor of justice), Purvurdegar (provider), Purvurtar (protector), by which names we praise him. There are many other names also, descriptive of his good doings.
What is our religion?
Our religion is worship of God.
Whence did we receive our religion?
God's true prophet—the true Zarthost Asphantaman Anosirwan—brought the religion for us from God.
Where should I turn my face when worshiping the holy Hormuzd?
We should worship the holy just Hormuzd with our face toward some of his creations of light and glory and brightness.
Which are those things?
Such as the sun, the moon, the stars, the fire, water, and other such things of glory. To such things we turn our face, and consider them our Kibleh ("the thing opposite"), because God has bestowed upon them a small spark of his pure glory, and they are therefore more exalted in the creation, and fit to be our Kibleh. . . . . . .
What commands has God sent us through his prophet, the exalted Zarthost?
Many are those commands, but I give you the principal, which must always be remembered, by which we must guide ourselves. To know God as one; to know the prophet, the exalted Zarthost, as his true prophet; to believe the religion, and the Avesta brought by him, as true beyond all manner of doubt; to believe in the goodness of God; not to disobey any of the commands of the Mazdiashna religion; to avoid evil deeds; to exert for good deeds; to pray five times in the day; to believe in the reckoning and justice on the fourth morning after death; to hope for heaven and to fear hell; to consider doubtless the day of general destruction and purification (of all suffering souls); to remember always that God has done what he willed, and shall do what he wills; to face some luminous object while worshiping God.

GEO. W. GILMORE.

BIBLIOGRAPHY: For a survey of the literature use E. Wilhelm, Catalogue of Books on Iranian Literature, Bombay, 1901. Many of the books noted below contain lists of books and of discussions, notably those by A. V. W. Jackson. Texts of the Avesta to be noted are: K. F. Geldner, 3 vols., Stuttgart, 1886–96 (best); E. Burnouf, Paris, 1829–43 (Vendidad Sade); H. Brockhaus, Leipsic, 1850 (Vendidad Sade); N. L. Westergaard, Copenhagen, 1852–54; F. Spiegel, 2 vols., Vienna, 1853–58 (Yasna, Vispered, Vendidad); M. Haug, 2 vols., Leipsic, 1858–1860 (five Gathas); C. Bartholomae, Halle, 1879 (Gathas); L. H. Mills, Leipsic, 1892–94 (Gathas); Antia, Bombay, 1901 (Vendidad Sade); M. M. Gandavia, Bombay (Vendidad); M. N. Dhalla, The Nyaishes or Zoroastrian Litanies, New York, 1909. Eng. transls. by J. Darmesteter and L. H. Mills are in SBE, vols. iv., xxiii., xxxi.; Fr. transls. of the whole or parts are by J. Thonnelier, Paris, 1855–62; C. de Harlez, 2d ed., ib. 1881; J. Darmesteter, 3 vols., ib. 1892–93; Germ. transls. are by M. Haug, Leipsic, 1858–60 (five Gathas); F. Spiegel, 3 vols., ib. 1852–63 (reproduced in Eng. transl. by Bleeck, London, 1864); partial transl. in F. Windischmann, Zoroastrische Studien, Vienna, 1868; C. Geldner, Stuttgart, 1884 (three Yashts); C. Bartholomae, Strasburg, 1905 (the Gathas); F. Wolff, ib. 1910. Editions of Pahlavi literature that may be noted are the Dinkart by D. B. Sanjana, 6 vols., Bombay, 1874–91; the Bundahish, by N. L. Westergaard, Copenhagen, 1851; and a series of Yasna texts by L. H. Mills in the Journal of the Royal Asiatic Society, 1902–08; as well as the Bundahish, with transl. and glossary, Leipsic, 1868. Eng. transls. of Pahlavi texts are in SBE, vols. v., xviii., xxiv., xxxvii., xlvii. Note also F. H. Weissbach, Die Keilinschriften der Achämeniden, Leipsic, 1911, since this has value as a source.

On the literature especially to be noted are the introductions to the texts and translations named in the preceding paragraph. Linguistic helps are: F. Justi, Handbuch der Zendsprache, Leipsic, 1864; C. de Harlez, Manuel de l'Avesta, Paris, 1878; idem, Manuel de Pahlevi, ib. 1880; W. Geiger, Handbuch der Awesta-Sprache, Grammatik, Chrestomathie und Glossar, Erlangen, 1879; C. Bartholomae, Handbuch der altiranischen Sprachen, Leipsic, 1883; idem, Altiranisches Wörterbuch, Strasburg, 1905; A. V. W. Jackson, Avesta Grammar, Stuttgart, 1891; L. H. Mills, Dictionary of the Gathic Language, Leipsic, 1902 sqq.; M. Schuyler, Index verborum of the Fragments of the Avesta, New York, 1902; H. Reichelt, Awestisches Elementarbuch, Heidelberg, 1909; idem, Avesta Reader. Text, Notes, Glossary and Index, Strasburg, 1911. For discussions on various phases of the literature consult: M. Haug, Ueber die Pehlevi-Sprache und den Bundahesh, Göttingen, 1854; idem, Essays on the Sacred Language, Writings, and Religion of the Parsees, Bombay, 1862, 3d ed., 1884; idem, Essay on the Pahlavi Language, Stuttgart, 1870; F. Spiegel, Die traditionelle Literatur der Parsen in ihrem Zusammenhange mit den angrenzenden Literaturen, Vienna, 1860; F. Windischmann, Zoroastrische Studien, ed. F. Spiegel, Berlin, 1863; F. Spiegel, Commentar über das Avesta, 2 vols., Vienna, 1864–68; W. D. Whitney, Oriental and Linguistic Studies, chap. vi., New York, 1873–75; K. F. Geldner, Studien zum Avesta, Strasburg, 1882; J. Darmesteter, Études iraniennes, 2 vols., Paris, 1883 (principally linguistic); C. de Harlez, De l'exégèse et de la correction des textes avestiques, Leipsic, 1883; F. Justi, Iranisches Namenbuch, Marburg, 1895; T. Nöldeke, Das altiranische Nationalepos, Strasburg, 1896; K. F. Geldner, Avestalitteratur, in Grundriss der iranischen Philologie, vol. ii., no. 1, pp. 1–53, Stuttgart, 1896 sqq.; E. G. Browne, A Literary Hist. of Persia, pp. 88–110, New York, 1902; D. M. Madan, Discourses on Iranian Literature, Bombay, 1909.

On the general background and history use the Grundriss der iranischen Philologie named above; F. Justi, Geschichte des alten Persiens, Berlin, 1879; T. Nöldeke, Geschichte der Perser . . . zur Zeit der Sassaniden, Leyden, 1879; idem, Aufsätze der persischen Geschichte, Leipsic, 1887; idem, Orientalische Skizzen, Berlin, 1892, Eng. transl., Sketches from Eastern Hist., London, 1892; W. Geiger, Ostiranische Kultur im Altertum, Erlangen, 1882, Eng. transl., Civilization of the Eastern Iranians in Ancient Times, London, 1885; A. von Gutschmid, Geschichte Irans von Alexander . . . bis zum Untergang der Arsaciden, Tübingen, 1888; A. V. W. Jackson, Persia Past and Present, New York, 1906; idem, From Constantinople to the Home of Omar Khayyam, ib. 1911; J. V. Prásek, Geschichte der Meder und Perser bis zur Makedonischen Eroberung, vol. ii., chap. xi., Gotha, 1910, cf. A. V. W. Jackson in American Historical Review, Oct., 1910, pp. 103 sqq.

On the prophet the one book is A. V. W. Jackson, Zoroaster, the Prophet of Iran, New York, 1899, cf. his article in The Biblical World, 1907. Consult further: J. H. C. Kern, in the Verslagen en Mededeelingen of the Amsterdam Academy, 1868, pp. 132–164; W. Geiger and F. Windischmann, Zarathushtra in the Gathas and in the Greek and Roman Classics, ib. 1899; E. Lehmann, Zarathustra, en Bog om Persernes Gamle Tro, 2 vols., Copenhagen, 1899–1902; F. Krippner, Zoroaster, Bitterfeld, 1900; L. H. Whitney, Life and Teachings of Zoroaster, the Great Persian, Chicago, 1905; Dastoor Peshotan Sanjana, Zarathushtra and Zarathushtrianism in the Avesta, Leipsic, 1906; D. Menant, Zoroastre, Paris, 1908; and much of the literature quoted in the next paragraph on the religion.

On the religion the best compend is A. V. W. Jackson, Die iranische Religion, in the Grundriss der iranischen Philologie, ut sup., vol. iii., no 5, cf. his article in the Journal of the American Oriental Society, 1901, pp. 160–184. Consult further: J. G. Rhode, Die heilige Sage und das gesammte Religionssystem der alten Baktrer, Meder und Persen oder des Zendvolks, Frankfort, 1820; C. P. Tiele, De Godsdienst van Zarathustra van haar Ontstaan in Batrie

tot den Val van het Oud-Perzische Rijk, Haarlem, 1864;
W. D. Whitney, *Oriental and Linguistic Studies*, pp. 149–
197, New York, 1873; C. de Harlez, *Les Origenes du Zo-
roastrisme*, Paris, 1879; J. Caird and Others, *Oriental
Religions*, New York, 1882; J. Milne, in *Faiths of the
World*, pp. 91–121, London, 1882; L. C. Casartelli, *La
Philosophie religieuse du Mazdéisme sous les Sassanids*,
Paris, 1884, Eng. transl., *Philosophy of the Mazdayasnian
Religion under the Sassanids*, Bombay, 1889; G. de La-
font, *Le Mazdéisme; l'Avesta*, Paris, 1897; E. Rindtorff,
Die Religion des Zarathushtra, Weimar, 1897; M. Flügel,
Zend-Avesta and Eastern Religions, Baltimore, 1898; A.
S. Geden, *Studies in Comparative Religion*, pp. 129 sqq.,
London, 1898; J. Scheftelowitz, *Altiranische Studien*, in
ZDMG, lvii (1903), 107–172; P. D. Chantepie de la Saus-
saye, *Lehrbuch der Religionsgeschichte*, ii. 162–234, Tü-
bingen, 1905; H. Hinneberg, *Die Kultur der Gegenwart*,
1, *Die orientalischen Religionen*, pp. 77–86, Berlin, 1906;
Dastoor Peshotan Sanjana, ut sup.; R. H. Mistri, *Zoro-
aster and Zoroastrianism*, London, 1907; O. Gramzov,
Kurzer Kommentar zum Zarathustra, Berlin, 1907; H.
Hüsing, *Die iranische Ueberlieferung und das arische Sys-
tem*, Leipsic, 1909; H. Brunhofer, *Arische Urzeit*, Bern, 1910;
Geiger's *Civilization*, ut sup. M. Haug, *Essays*, ut sup.
On various topics, including the eschatology, consult:
F. Windischmann, *Die persische Anahita oder Anaïtis*,
Munich, 1856; M. Wolff, *Muhammedanische Eschatologie*,
Leipsic, 1872; J. Darmesteter, *Ormazd et Ahriman, leurs
origines et leur hist.*, Paris, 1877; D. P. Sanjana, *Position
of Woman in Remote Antiquity as Illustrated in the Avesta*,
Bombay, 1892; J. B. Rüling, *Beiträge zur Eschatologie des
Islam*, Leipsic, 1895; A. V. W. Jackson, in *Biblical World*,
Aug., 1896; N. Söderblom, *Les Fravashis*, Paris, 1899;
idem, *La Vie future d'après le Mazdéisme*, Paris, 1901;
E. W. West, *Notes on Zarathustra's Doctrine Regarding
the Soul*, in the *Journal of the Royal Asiatic Society*, 1899,
pp. 605–611; F. Böklen, *Die Verwandtschaft der jüdisch-
christlichen mit der persischen Eschatologie*, Göttingen,
1902; L. H. Mills, *Zarathushtra, Philo, the Achaemenids
and Israel*, Oxford, 1906; idem, *Avesta Eschatology Compared with the Books of Daniel and Revelations*, Chicago,
1908; Shaporji Aspaniarji, *The Teachings of Zoroaster and the
Philosophy of the Parsee Religion*, New York, 1908; K.
Schirmeisen, *Die arischen Göttergestalten*, Brünn, 1910.
On the Parsees consult: D. F. Karaka, *History of the
Parsis*, London, 1884; D. Menant, *Les Parsis*, Paris,
1898, new ed., 1908; V. Henry, *Le Parsisme*, ib. 1905;
S. A. Kapadia, *The Teachings of Zoroaster and the Phi-
osophy of the Parsi Religion*, London, 1905 (not very
valuable).

ZOSIMUS, zŏs'i-mŭs: Pope 417–418. The *Liber
pontificalis* makes Zosimus a Greek, while Harnack
supposes from his father's name Abram that he was
of Hebrew descent. He succeeded Innocent I., and
is known for his participation in the Pelagian controversy (see PELAGIUS AND PELAGIAN CONTROVERSIES)
and for his attempts at the extension of the power
of the Roman see. The latter came about through
the matter of Appeals to the Pope (q.v.), an issue
raised by his predecessor. Zosimus became involved
through the fact that Bishop Urban of Sicca in
Numidia had deposed a presbyter Apiarius, who appealed to Rome. But a general synod of Africans
forbade this in 418, and the pope sent legates to
deal with the general matter as well as to force
Urban to retract. Zosimus' claims regarding appeals were based on supposed canons of the Nicene
Council, really of that of Sardica. No real progress
was made, and the successors of Zosimus carried the
matter further.

Affairs in the Gallic Church also afforded Zosimus
an opportunity to interfere. Patroclus of Arles
wished to found a new primacy in South Gaul, which
Zosimus approved; the pope also would put in
Patroclus' hands the ordination of certain bishops
of the province, and gave him control of the *For-

matæ* for Gallic clergy going to Rome. Zosimus declared certain ordinations by Proculus of Marseilles
invalid, and also the pronouncements of a synod
of Turin (401) which supported the contention of
Proculus. The latter maintained himself, however,
and Boniface I. allowed Patroclus' claims to fall.

(A. HAUCK.)

BIBLIOGRAPHY: *Liber pontificalis*, ed. Mommsen in *MGH,
Gest. pont. Rom.*, i (1898), 91; Jaffe, *Regesta*, i. 49–51;
J. Langen, *Geschichte der römischen Kirche*, i. 742–763,
Bonn, 1881; L. Duchesne, *Fastes épiscopaux de l'ancienne
Gaule*, i. 93–110, Paris, 1894; Mirbt, *Quellen*, pp. 57–58,
2d ed., 1901; Mansi, *Concilia*, iv. 345–376; Hefele, *Con-
ciliengeschichte*, pp. 357–358, Fr. transl., i. 1, pp. 504–505,
Eng. transl., ii. 128, 456 sqq., 462–464; Ceillier, *Auteurs
sacrés*, vii. 528–540, viii. 533–534, 569, ix. 453, 477, 484,
510, 635; Bower, *Popes*, i. 149–162; Platina, *Popes*, i.
96–99; Milman, *Latin Christianity*, i. 179–195, 265, 267;
KL, xii. 1988–89; *DCB*, iv. 1221–25 (elaborate).

ZSCHOKKE, chŏk'ke, **JOHANN HEINRICH
DANIEL:** German-Swiss novelist, author of *Stunden der Andacht;* b. at Magdeburg Mar. 22, 1771; d.
on his estate called Blumenhalde, opposite the city
of Aarau, Switzerland, June 27, 1848. He was early
left an orphan, and when seventeen left school to
accompany a company of strolling actors and to
serve as playwright; in 1790 he prosecuted his
studies at Frankfort, studying theology there, and
then serving for six months as preacher at Magdeburg and afterward as pastor at St. Catherine's
Church; next he became privat-docent for theology
at Frankfort, meanwhile pursuing a wide range of
reading in history, politics, finance, and forestry.
He had already issued several publications, among
them the drama *Aballino*. His retirement from the
university followed upon his opposition to a ministerial order and his expressed sympathy with the
French Revolution, and he traveled widely, at
length, in 1795, taking up his residence in Switzerland, becoming in 1796 an instructor at Reichenau in
the Grisons. The victory of the Austrian party there
in 1798 compelled the ardent lover of liberty to
leave, and at Aarau he was welcomed and served
his adopted country in literature and also in various civil posts. In his literary works he had distinctly the purpose of contributing to the ethical
and social uplift of the people, coining the maxim:
The education of the people is the people's liberation. He retained his interest in theology and religion, and noted the decadence resulting from the
French Revolution and the Napoleonic régime. In
order to counteract this he published anonymously
from 1808 to 1816 *Stunden der Andacht*, a religious
but rationalistic journal, which had an immense
success, and was brought together and published
as a devotional collection in 1816. It was twice
translated into English, in whole or in part (*Hours
of Meditation and Devotional Reflection*, London,
1843; and *Handbook of Family Devotion*, 1863).
The secret of its authorship was preserved till
1842, when the author, in his autobiographic
Selbstschau, acknowledged its source. The work was
violently assailed by the Roman Catholic clergy,
and such Protestants as Tholuck denied its Christian
character, the latter writing his " Hours of Devotion " to counteract its effects. While theologians
decried it, the popular estimation of it was high;
it met a great need in the world of laymen.

Zschokke's works, consisting of novels, tales, dramas, and historical writings, were collected in 35 vols., Aarau, 1851–54. Some of these were several times translated into English, e.g., *The Bravo of Venice*, London, 1805, 1844, and often; his *Popular History of Switzerland*, or *History of Switzerland*, London, 1833, 1834; *The Goldmaker's Village*, London, 1845; and individual tales in various collections. Some of them went also into most of the continental languages of Europe.

(W. Hadorn.)

Bibliography: Consult, besides the *Selbstschau* noted above, the biographies by O. Hunziker, Zurich, 1884; J. J. Bäbler, Aarau, 1884; in *ADB*, xlv. 449 sqq.; and in *Schweizer Rundschau*, 1891.

ZUETPHEN, GERARD ZERBOLT VAN. See Zerbolt van Zuetphen.

ZUNZ, tsunts, LEOPOLD: Jewish scholar; b. at Detmold (50 m. s.w. of Hanover), Germany, Aug. 10, 1794; d. at Berlin Mar. 18, 1886. He was educated at the University of Berlin; became rabbi to the new synagogue there, 1820; was an editor of the *Spenerschen Zeitung*, 1823–31; provisory director of the new Jewish Congregational School, 1826–1829; preacher in Prague, 1835–39; and director of the Normal Seminary of Berlin, 1840–50. After 1845 he was a member of the board of commissioners for the communal and educational interests of the Jews in Prussia. His life was one of great literary activity, and his works were distinguished by learning, beauty, and clearness of style. Among them may be mentioned *Predigten* (Berlin, 1823); *Die gottesdienstlichen Vorträge der Juden, historisch entwickelt* (1832), his most valuable book; *Namen der Juden* (Leipsic, 1837); *Zur Geschichte und Literatur* (Berlin, 1845); *Die Vorschriften über Eidesleistungen der Juden* (1859); *Die Monatstage des Kalenderjahrs* (1872); his works appeared as *Gesammelten Schriften* (3 vols., 1875–76).

Bibliography: S. Maybaum, *Aus dem Leben von Leopold Zunz*, Berlin, 1894; *JE*, xii. 699–704.

ZURICH CONSENSUS (CONSENSUS TIGURINUS): A creed of the Reformed Church embodying the united views of Calvin and Bullinger on the Lord's Supper, and forming one of the best sources for a knowledge of Reformed theory on this subject. In 1541 Calvin had published his Genevan Catechism, setting forth a view of the Lord's Supper which inclined toward that of Luther rather than that of Zwingli. For a time there seemed to be a prospect of union between the Lutherans and the Reformed, but in 1541 Luther began a series of impassioned attacks on Zwingli and the Reformed, calling their leader a foe of the sacrament and putting him in a class with the Anabaptists. As Zwingli's successor and the recognized head of the German-Swiss Reformed, Bullinger, in 1545, replied to Luther with a defense of Zwingli's character and doctrine, as well as of the Reformed in general, in his *Wahrhafte Bekenntnis der Diener der Kirche zu Zürich . . . insbesondere über das Nachtmahl*. As a result the confession of the Zurich preachers, who had ever felt themselves essentially in sympathy with Zwingli, strongly manifested the original Zwinglian type. This found approval in Bern, where the Lutheranizing tendencies under the in-

fluence of Butzer had been overthrown by Zwinglianism after all attempts at union had proved hopeless. But these proceedings at Bern, which included stern measures against Lutheranizing pastors and the disuse of a catechism which Butzer had helped to revise in 1537, directly affected Calvin and his views of the Lord's Supper, for the Vaud preachers, controlled by Bern since 1536, were placed in a serious position by the contradictions between the catechism of their spiritual lord in Geneva and the Zwinglian catechism prescribed to them by Bern. It thus became necessary for Calvin and Bullinger to enter into negotiations, especially as Calvin was already eager for a union of at least all the Reformed, while Bullinger, however loyal to Zwinglian tradition and however mistrustful of Butzer's tactics, was fully inclined to alliance, provided it admitted of no misinterpretation. In 1547 Calvin spent some days in Zurich, and the two leaders met. After three more visits to Zurich, Calvin, accompanied by Farel, who had also worked in the interests of harmony, met Butzer at Zurich in the latter part of May, 1549. A few days later the twenty-six articles were agreed upon which united Zwinglians and Calvinists in one Reformed body. The basis of the deliberations had been the twenty articles sent by Calvin two months earlier to the Bern synod.

The articles of the Zurich Consensus fall into two divisions: the first nine declaring that the Lord's Supper is not a mere " empty symbol," and the remainder aiming to refute the charge that Calvin's teaching tended toward consubstantiation. The Zwinglian conception of " a testimony and seal of grace " and the spiritual communion with Christ are emphasized, but neither the distinctly Calvinistic tenet of the miraculous influence, through the Holy Ghost, of the vivifying body of Christ on the believing soul nor the Zwinglian theory of the Lord's Supper as a mere commemorative meal receives perspicuous mention. In arts. 10–26 the Roman Catholic and Lutheran doctrines of the Eucharist are denied in favor of the Reformed theories of the Lord's Supper, and the tenet of predestination is pressed to its full logical conclusion as regards the reception of the elements. These articles were submitted to each of the Protestant estates of the Swiss confederation, as well as to certain foreign theologians, and after some hesitation, particularly on the part of Bern and Basel, they were accepted, appearing in their Latin original, with a few emendations by Pierre Viret (q.v.), at Zurich in 1551. German and French translations were issued at the same time. Later editions included an explanation and defense of the Consensus by Calvin, this being rendered necessary by the violent Lutheran attacks upon the document. The Consensus never became a formal confession of the Reformed Church, yet it is noteworthy as the first bond that united the Swiss Reformed among themselves and with their coreligionists abroad, thus giving them the consciousness of being members of the great Reformed body, and avoiding the threatening danger of a second Protestant cleavage into Calvinism and Zwinglianism.

(Paul Christ†.)

Bibliography: The *Consensus* was printed at Zurich, 1549, may also be found conveniently in H. A. Niemeyer, *Col-*

lectio confessionum, pp. 191–217, Leipsic, 1840; and E. F. K. Müller, *Bekenntnisschriften der reformierten Kirche*, ib. 1903. Consult: Schaff, *Creeds*, i. 471–473; A. Ruchat, *Hist. de la réformation en Suisse*, vol. v., 6 vols., Geneva, 1727–28; K. B. Hundeshagen, *Conflicte des Zwinglianismus*, Bern, 1842; J. H. A. Ebrard, *Das Dogma vom heiligen Abendmahl*, ii. 484–524, Frankfort, 1846; C. Pestalozzi, *Bullinger*, pp. 373–387, Elberfeld, 1858; W. Walker, *John Calvin*, pp. 395–397, New York, 1906; and, in general, works on the lives of Bullinger, Calvin, and Farel.

ZWEMER, SAMUEL MARINUS: Reformed; b. at Vriesland, Ottawa Co., Mich., Apr. 12, 1867. He was educated at Hope College, Holland, Mich. (A.B., 1887), and New Brunswick Theological Seminary (1890). From 1891 to 1905 he was a missionary at Busrah, Bahrein, and elsewhere in Arabia, and during this time traveled extensively through the peninsula. He was organizer and chairman of the Mohammedan Missionary Conference at Cairo in 1906, but resided chiefly in the United States, 1905–10, and did much missionary work in the churches of his denomination. In 1910 he returned to his missionary field on the Arabian Gulf. He has written *Arabia, the Cradle of Islam, with an Account of Islam and Mission-Work* (New York, 1900); *Raymond Lull, First Missionary to the Moslems* (1902); *Topsy-Turvy Land: Arabia Pictured for Children* (in collaboration with his wife; 1902); *Islam: A Challenge to Faith* (1908); *Nearer and Farther East: Studies of Moslem Lands and Siam, Burma, and Korea* (in collaboration with A. J. Brown; 1908); *The Unoccupied Mission Fields of Africa and Asia* (1911); *Daylight in the Harem* (1911; in collaboration with Annie Van Sommer); and (in part) *Islam and Missions* (1911). In 1911 he began the publication of the quarterly *The Moslem World*, issued in London, and he has collaborated with Annie Van Sommer in editing *Our Moslem Sisters* (New York, 1907), and with E. M. Wherry and J. L. Barton in editing *Mohammedan World of To-Day* (1907).

ZWICK, tsvik, JOHANNES: Reformer in Constance and South Germany; b. at Constance c. 1496; d. at Bischofszell (8 m. n.w. of St. Gall), Switzerland, Oct. 23, 1542. He received his early education in Constance and Basel, entered the lower ranks of the clergy, went in 1509 to Freiburg to study law under his fellow countryman Zasius; with his younger brother Konrad he journeyed to Bologna in 1518, and in 1520 took his doctorate in both kinds of law at Siena. Both brothers came under the influence of Luther, and while Konrad went to Wittenberg, Johannes went to Basel as teacher of law, though soon regretting that for the sake of law he had neglected theology. In 1522 he sought out Zwingli at Zurich, and then went to Constance to prepare for taking up his ministry, having been made priest in 1518. Though warned by his bishop not to teach anything new, on taking his first charge at Riedlingen he preached Evangelical doctrine. He worked for the general betterment of life, and amid conditions which were especially difficult. He also married. He was present at the great disputation at Zurich Oct. 25–28, 1523. On his return to Riedlingen the attempt was made to arrest him, but the people prevented this. In the spring of 1524 he visited Basel and Strasburg, and on his return the chapter began persecutions

anew. When he married a divorced pair who had not the money to secure a papal dispensation and in a tractate urged other pastors to the same course, the storm broke. For a time he went to Constance, where he was besought to accept a preaching office; meanwhile he was cited to Rome, which mandate he disregarded, and in 1526 by imperial rescript his office was taken from him, and he was declared a heretic. The same year he wrote a tract of exhortation to his old parishioners which had its recognized effect in confirming them in the Gospel. In 1527 Zwick assumed the preaching office in his native city, where with Ambrosius and Thomas Blaurer and his brother Konrad he worked in advancing the Reformation, which was firmly established by May 6 of that year and was practically completed when, in 1531, an order of discipline was introduced. In the work of building up the church Zwick was indefatigable, especially in his labors for youth, issuing writings and catechetical works for their instruction. Not less important were his labors in the cause of hymnology, issuing as early as 1536 a hymn-book for church use, to which he contributed seventeen hymns, among them the well-known " Auf diesen Tag bedenken wir." In collaboration with Pellican in 1535 he issued at Zurich a New Testament in Latin and German. He also edited numerous smaller books of educational, confessional, or historical value. Meanwhile he was an earnest and effective pastor, looking after the schools, the poor, the sick, and the refugees.

His labor was not confined to his native city, but in the neighboring regions of Switzerland and in South Germany he did pioneer and yeoman work. Although he came into close and friendly connection with Luther and Melanchthon, he did not favor the Wittenberg Concord (q.v.), and his influence in 1540 prevented Constance from entering the Swiss Union, there being no apparent reason for withdrawing from the Schmalkald League. In his large-hearted geniality he subjected himself to suspicion by entertaining those who as fugitives appealed to his pity, even though they were opposed by the orthodox. Under his constant labors his health broke down; in 1541 he was near to death, but recovered. In 1542 he went to render service in the plague-stricken Bischofszell, was himself seized by the disease, and died in harness. After his death Blaurer purposed to edit Zwick's works, and began with the sermons preached just before Zwick left for Bischofszell, prefixing a noble preface and the first short sketch of Zwick's life. Subsequent events prevented the carrying out of the plan. Zwick's *Gebete und Lieder für die Jugend* were edited by Spitta (Göttingen, 1901). (G. BOSSERT.)

BIBLIOGRAPHY: T. Keim, in *Jahrbücher für deutsche Theologie*, 1854, pp. 536, 584, 1855, pp. 356–411; T. Kolde, *Analecta Lutherana*, Gotha, 1883; *Briefe und Akten*, in *Mitteilungen zur vaterländischen Geschichte*, vols. xxiv. sqq., St. Gall, 1891 sqq.; F. Cohrs, *Die evangelischen Katechismusversuche vor Luther*, iv. 44–141, 245, Berlin, 1902; *Monatschrift für Gottesdienst und kirchliche Kunst*, 1897, pp. 267, 326–350, 1898, pp. 323–332; and the works on the lives of Bullinger, Butzer, Capito, and Zwingli.

ZWICKAU PROPHETS: A short-lived subsect of the radical Anabaptists (see ANABAPTISTS, II.), taking their name from their origin in the city of Zwickau (60 m. s.w. of Dresden), and receiving their doctrines from Nikolaus Storch, a weaver (d. 1525), and Markus Stübner, who enjoyed the favor and support of Thomas Münzer (q.v.), with whose views, indeed, their own seem to have been practically identical. Storch, the real founder of the sect, apparently derived his tenets from the Bohemian Brethren (q.v.), with a strong coloring from the chiliasm of the Taborites (see HUSS, JOHN, HUSSITES, II., § 4), while the great inspiration of the whole was the young Protestant principle of conforming rigidly to the explicit commands of the Bible. He also claimed to possess prophetic powers, and among the elements of his attempted " return to the Bible " were apparently the separation of a believing husband or wife from the unbelieving partner, rejection of oaths, civil power, and military service, and communism—in other words, the entire movement was a phase of Antinomianism (q.v.). It is further declared that Storch secured the appointment of twelve " apostles " and seventy-two " disciples," in imitation of New-Testament records, and that, as a result of a vision in which Gabriel appeared to him, he believed himself divinely empowered to act as the leader in the establishment of the millennial kingdom upon earth.

While Münzer was in Zwickau, all went well with the " prophets," but his successor, Nicolaus Hausmann (q.v.), was less amenable, and on Dec. 16, 1521, Storch and his followers were accused of repudiating infant baptism. He and one other alone remained obdurate and, ignoring a summons to reappear later for a second examination, he went, together with Stübner and a certain Markus Thomä, to Wittenberg to secure university support. Here he succeeded in half winning Andreas Rudolf Bodenstein von Carlstadt (q.v.), convinced Martin Borrhaus (q.v.), and for an instant swayed even Melanchthon. So serious, indeed, became the situation that Luther, then in hiding in the Wartburg, was forced to leave his retreat and return to Wittenberg, where he arrived Mar. 7, 1522. [Before he left the Wartburg, in answer to Melanchthon's difficulties about infant baptism Luther wrote a letter justifying the practise on the ground of unconscious or subconscious faith exercised by the infant, and defying his opponents to prove that the infant does not exercise saving faith. A. H. N.] He sternly repressed the radicals, though he was unable to supply their demand for Scripture passages explicitly commanding infant baptism, his conclusion being that " what is not against Scripture is in favor of Scripture, and Scripture in favor of it "—an argument ill calculated to satisfy his opponents. Nevertheless, his presence in Wittenberg made it impossible for the Zwickau prophets to remain, and both Carlstadt and Borrhaus, continuing in their radicalism, ultimately found a more congenial home amid Zwinglian surroundings. With the exit of Storch and Münzer from Zwickau, their sectaries soon subsided, and in Apr., 1522, Luther visited the city and delivered four sermons to enormous audiences (estimated by one contemporary at 14,000 and by another at 25,000) on the evils of religious radicalism and fanaticism.

The story of the wild career of Thomas Münzer is well known. Of Stübner nothing is recorded except that, after leaving Wittenberg, he went to Kemberg, a town of Prussian Saxony, where he disappeared from history. Concerning the fortunes of Storch there is more information. After the Wittenberg episode he apparently remained for some time in Thuringia, for Luther seems to have had another interview with him shortly before Sept., 1522. He would also appear to have remained with Carlstadt in Orlamünde, but in 1524 he was in Hof, where he renewed his agitation until he was driven from the place, only to repeat his madness at Glogau in Silesia. Early in 1525 he was apparently cooperating with Münzer in stirring up the Peasants' War, and in the course of this occupation he seems to have come to Munich, where he is said to have died in a hospital. During the closing years of his life it would seem that his radicalism increased, for he is reported to have taught rejection not only of marriage and of infant baptism, and the renunciation of all worldly goods, but also to have inculcated full indulgence of the flesh and the right of deposing and even of killing civil authorities.

BIBLIOGRAPHY: A. H. Newman, History of Anti-Pedobaptism, pp. 62–76, Philadelphia, 1897; G. Tumbült, Die Wiedertäufer, pp. 8–11, Bielefeld, 1899; R. Bachmann, Niclas Storch, der Anfänger der Zwickauer Wiedertäufer, Zwickau, 1880.

ZWINGLI, HULDREICH.

I. Life and Labors.
  Early Life and Education (§ 1).
  Initial Doubts at Einsiedeln of Roman Catholicism (§ 2).
  Leut-Priestship at Zurich and Marriage (§ 3).
  Increasing Alienation from the Roman Church (§ 4).
  The Final Rupture (§ 5).
  Peasant and Anabaptist Disturbances (§ 6).
  The Conference at Baden (§ 7).
  Eucharistic Conference with Luther at Marburg (§ 8).
  Unsuccessful Plans against the Hapsburgs and the Pope (§ 9).
  Diet of Augsburg and Work in Zurich (§ 10).
  Civil War and Death of Zwingli (§ 11).
II. Theological System.
  Theories of Zeller and Sigwart (§ 1).
  Criticism of Sigwart's Theory (§ 2).
  Criticism of Zeller's Theory (§ 3).
  Direct Relation of the Human Soul to God (§ 4).
  Philosophical Elements of Zwingli's Theology (§ 5).
  Rigid Practicality and Exclusion of Speculation (§ 6).
  Centered in Christian Consciousness and Experience of Sanctification (§ 7).

I. Life and Labors: Huldreich Zwingli, the Reformer of German Switzerland as preacher of Evangelical truth, contemporary with, but independent of, Martin Luther, was born at Wildhaus (42 m. e. by s. of Zurich), in the valley of the Toggenburg, Jan. 1, 1484; and died at Cappel (10 m. s. of Zurich) Oct. 11, 1531. His first name shows the variants Ulric, Ulrich, Ulricus, Huldricus, and Huldrych, while his last name, which appears in Latin as Zwinglius and in English as Zwingle, was originally Zwilling (" Twin "). His father, Ulrich Zwingli, was the chief magistrate of the village; his father's brother, Bartholomew, was the village priest.

1. Early Life and Education. His mother's maiden name was Margaretha Meili, and her brother, Johannes (d. 1524), was abbot of the Benedictine abbey of Fischingen (about 25 m. e. by w. of Zurich), while a near relative, probably an uncle, was abbot of Old St. John's, near Wildhaus. Zwingli was the third of his parents' eight sons. In 1487 his uncle Bartholomew moved to Wesen (some 10 m. s. of Wildhaus) on the Walen-see, where he was pastor and dean, and then, or a little later, he took his nephew into his house and sent him to the village school. Being a friend of the New Learning, and noticing the promise of the child, he determined to educate him for the Church, but in agreement with the new ideas; accordingly he sent him to the school of Gregory Buenzli in Klein Basel, in 1494, and in 1498 to that of Heinrich Woelfli (Lupulus) in Bern. There the lad particularly distinguished himself, and made many friends, as he, like Luther, was a born musician and fond of company. These qualities induced the Dominicans to invite him to live in their monastery, but when his father and uncle heard of this, they took him out of the city, lest he should become a monk, and sent him to Vienna. For the next two years he studied there (1500–02), and in 1502 he matriculated at Basel, took his B.A. degree there in 1504, and his M.A. in 1506, teaching meanwhile in the school of St. Martin's Church. In 1506 he became pastor at Glarus, where he remained for ten years.

Being a scholar, Zwingli applied himself to his books and laid deep and wide foundations. He also evinced his capacity as a preacher, and with flaming zeal denounced the evils of the time, the chief of these, to his patriotic mind, being the hiring out of the Swiss to any one else than the pope to fight as mercenaries, an occupation which, in numerous cases, resulted in their moral ruin. Because some of the leading persons in his congrega-

2. Initial tion were carrying on this traffic, his **Doubts at** opposition awoke their animosity and **Einsiedeln** made his position so uncomfortable **of Roman** that he was glad to accept a call to be **Catholicism.** preacher at Einsiedeln, only a few miles from Glarus, the chief place of pilgrimage for Switzerland, South Germany, and Alsace. There he met with great numbers of people, including many prominent men, and thus he clarified his thinking on the burning questions of the day. He had a candid mind, and his faith in traditional orthodoxy had already received several shocks. Thomas Wyttenbach (q.v.) was the first one to question in his hearing the traditional base of the Church's teaching, in 1505–06, and a little later he came upon a service book containing the liturgy as used in Mollis, near Glarus, two hundred years before, and found that it expressly enjoined that the cup was to be administered to a babe after its baptism. Again, when on a campaign in Italy as chaplain of the Glarus contingent in the papal army, he discovered that the Milan liturgy differed in many points from that used elsewhere. Meditation on these points showed him that the Church had really not taught absolutely the same truths from the beginning, nor had observed everywhere the same practises. Like all other Humanists, he read Erasmus, and from him learned that the source of doctrine was the Bible and not the Church. When, therefore, he could read the New Testament in the original in 1516, thanks to Erasmus, he drank truth from the fountain rather than through the more or less troubled stream of tradition. Then, when he met leading men at Einsiedeln, and found

that the corruption of the Church in clergy and theology was a common theme, he ventured to discuss these matters in the pulpit. He also exalted the Bible above the Church as the guide into truth, and Jesus Christ above the Virgin Mary as the intercessor with the Father, and in so doing he acted independently of Luther, for, as a matter of fact, he had not heard of him. Zwingli always pretended to be ignorant of what Luther wrote, and it was his constant boast that he had started the Reformation in Switzerland independently of Luther. It was a drawback to the general cause of the Reformation that these two Reformers did not fraternize. Because Zwingli would not accept Luther's doctrine of the Lord's Supper, Luther declared him to be of a different spirit; and Zwingli found much in Luther's teachings and proceedings that he strongly disapproved.

It is not likely that Zwingli was brought into any trouble by his doctrine at Einsiedeln; rather it was welcome and increased his reputation. So, when the position of *leut*-priest (preacher and pastor) in the Great Minster in Zurich fell vacant in the latter part of 1518, he was suggested for the place. Then was brought to light a fact which has ever since been a humiliation to his friends and a source of triumph to his foes. Like the clergy about him, he believed himself absolved from the obligation of chastity because bound by the vow of **3. Leut-** celibacy. Lapses from sexual purity **priestship at** were too common to be considered ob-**Zurich and** jections in a priest, but the charge **Marriage.** against him was then made that he had seduced a girl of good family, and this was considered a valid reason for rejecting his nomination. He was written to on the subject and his reply is extant. He denied the charge of seduction, but frankly admitted the charge of habitual incontinence, and he does it in a jesting tone which shows that he had no conception that his offense was any other than a trifling one. The chapter of the Great Minster agreed to this view and elected him, and it was, therefore, as a confessedly libidinous man that he came to Zurich, but only the pure in heart can see God; the Gospel had not yet entered his heart. It so happened that in his parish was a beautiful widow, Anna Reinhard (b. 1484), a Zurich innkeeper's daughter, who had married (1504) Hans Meyer von Knonau, scion of a Zurich patrician family, who had died in 1517. Her son, Gerold, was in the Great Minster Latin school when Zwingli came to Zurich and made the acquaintance of the mother. When their intimacy passed the bounds of propriety is unknown, but certain it is that from the spring of 1522 Zwingli and Anna Reinhard were living together in what was euphemistically called a " clerical marriage." Such concubinages, while not put on a level with marriage, were entered into without stigma, as it was assumed that without extraordinary supply of divine grace it was not possible for a priest to live in purity; and since, in fact, very few did, hence it was better for the morals of the community that they should have nominal wives. They were expected to, and probably did, live faithful to these women, and the women to them. When, however, the relations between Zwingli and Anna Reinhard were formed, many Protestant priests had married their mistresses or other women, and it was expected that Zwingli, who was the head of the reformatory movement in Zurich, would show equal courage and set a good example. Why he did not has been explained on the ground of his reluctance to face the monetary and social complications involved in a burgher marrying a patrician's widow; but at last he married her, on Apr. 2, 1524. Between 1526 and 1530 four children were born to him, but there are no direct descendants of his now living.

Zwingli held the *leut*-priestship from 1519 to 1522, and till the end of his life retained the preachership in the Great Minster. His fame spread through all German Switzerland and southern **4. Increas-** Germany. His sermons as printed are **ing Aliena-** long, discursive, and dull, though clear **tion from** and simple in style, but, in the process **the Roman** of the expansion they have under-**Church.** gone, all their liveliness has probably been removed. Having uncommon Biblical and patristic scholarship, a frank, candid, independent, and progressive nature, and a great desire to advance the interests of his country in religious, political, and social matters, he won general approval from the start, not only as a preacher but as a man. When a preacher of indulgences named Bernhardin Samson appeared in the canton (1519), Zwingli successfully opposed him—a course which received the approval of the hierarchy, for the fathers of Trent recognized that there were abuses connected with the proclamation of indulgences (cf. the decree concerning indulgences passed by the Council of Trent Dec. 4, 1563; given in Schaff, *Creeds*, ii. 205–206). When the plague broke out in Zurich in 1520, Zwingli labored so assiduously among his people that, worn out, he fell sick himself and looked into the eyes of death. He used the position won by his devotion and independence to advance reform, but very cautiously and by attacking externals first. Thus he showed that fasting in Lent had no Scriptural support, which teaching was eagerly taken up by those who wanted to have good meals all the year round; next, that tithes had only state and church laws to rest upon, but no Scripture, this teaching being heartily welcomed by those who paid taxes and groaned under them. He had his say in regard to the proper way to treat beggars, who were considered by the good people about him as aids in devotion and pathways to heaven, but whom he denounced as nuisances and would have changed into self-supporting members of the community, and he showed how this might be done. Next came simplification of the breviary and plans for a liturgy in the vernacular and a much-altered service for the administration of the Lord's Supper. Proceeding step by step, with the assent of the Zurich magistracy, he yet alarmed the local hierarchy, who appealed to Constance, where their bishop lived, and the bishop sent to Zurich an investigation committee which sat Apr. 7–9, 1522, but availed nothing against the manifest satisfaction of the citizens with the positions Zwingli had taken. It was evident that the wave of reform had passed from Germany into Switzerland.

After three years of preaching, Zwingli judged that the time was ripe for a bolder step. Consequently he prepared sixty-five theses, not at all like the ninety-five theses of Luther, which were on the single topic of indulgences and were intended primarily for a university audience, while Zwingli's theses were for a popular audience and covered all the points of the " Gospel," as he called it. In accordance with the Swiss plan that before radical measures were taken in a canton there was to be a public debate as to their expediency, presided over by the burgomaster, a meeting was held in the town hall of Zurich on Jan. 29, 1523. All the clergy were invited, and the frankest expression of opinion was courted. As a matter of fact, there was **5. The Final** no real debate, but only a dialogue be-**Rupture.** tween Zwingli and the vicar-general of Constance. The decision of the magistracy was that the doctrines Zwingli had preached were enjoined on all priests in the canton. This was satisfactory so far, but only as an entering wedge. Zwingli kept on applying the " Gospel " to practical matters and began preparations for a second discussion, which was held Oct. 26–28, 1523, this being still less a debate between the Old and the Reform Church parties, since it was almost entirely in the hands of the latter. Of special interest is the part which the radicals among the followers of Zwingli played. They accepted his whole program, but they were for immediate application of its practical teaching, and wished Zwingli to accept some of its logical consequences—both of which courses were hostile to his cautious nature. The decisions of the magistracy after this discussion were, however, radical enough to suit any but a radical, for they removed the images and pictures out of the churches, made the vernacular the language of the religious services, and, still more startlingly, stripped the mass of all its incrustations through the centuries and brought it back, as far as possible, to its first institution. A third disputation was held Jan. 19–20, 1524, but this was a last desperate attempt of the Old Church party to stem the tide of change which Zwingli had set in motion. By the end of 1524 church life in Zurich was quite different in many of its outward manifestations from that in any other Swiss city. The convents for men and women had been abolished, and the music had been silenced in the churches, a strange proceeding for one so fond of music as Zwingli, and defensible only on his theory that the Reformed Church should have no practise which recalled the Old Church as music did. The mass alone stood, and that was so wrapped up with the life of the people that he hesitated to destroy it before the people were fully prepared to accept a substitute. At last the decree went forth that on Thursday of Holy Week, Apr. 13, 1525, in the Great Minster the Lord's Supper would be for the first time observed according to the liturgy Zwingli had composed. On that eventful day men and women sat on opposite sides of the table which extended down the middle aisle, and were served with bread upon wooden platters and wine out of wooden beakers. The contrast to the former custom was shocking to many, yet the new way was accepted. With this radical break with the past the Reformation in Zurich may be said to have been completed.

No sooner had the Reformation been established than internal troubles nearly disrupted the State. First came the peasants with their undoubted grievances, although they did not give the trouble they made in Germany, both because their demands were less radical, and because the authorities, on the advice of Zwingli, were more conciliatory. But **6. Peasant** the other disturbing element, the de-**and Ana-** tested, the dreaded, the misunder-**baptist Dis-** stood and persecuted Anabaptists, **turbances.** were the real trial. They did not orig-inate in Zurich, but the earliest mem-bers of the party in Zurich were members of Zwingli's congregation. He had taught them to ask Scripture proof for doctrines and practises seeking church acceptance, and they accordingly asked him to give such proof for infant baptism. Because he could not, he was at first inclined to grant that logically the practise had no Scriptural support; but when they pressed him to declare himself plainly, they only stirred his anger by so doing. He fell back upon the assumptions of the Old Church, and for a man so radical on all other points he showed a singular reluctance to accept the consistent teaching of his Anabaptist friends. [It was only when it became manifest to him that rejection of infant baptism involved an effort to establish churches of the regenerates, and to effect the unchurching of all who could not make a public confession of an experience of grace and the aboli-tion of secular authority in religious matters, that Zwingli felt compelled to oppose it with all his might. A. H. N.] He sought to silence them by sermon and treatise, and because they would not keep si-lence he became their persecutor. This attitude can be explained only by his acceptance of the propriety of suppressing what is deemed to be erroneous, even at the expense of life, on the claim that it is better that a few should die for their erroneous faith than that they should be allowed to live and propagate their errors. This doctrine was accepted by Protestants and by Roman and Greek Catholics in the sixteenth century, and the first alone have repudiated it. (For the experiences of the Swiss Anabaptists see ANABAPTISTS.)

The years of Zwingli's life from 1524 to 1529 were extremely busy, and were passed almost entirely in Zurich. One occasion for a visit outside of it was very pressing. At Baden, a famous watering-place, only twelve miles northwest of Zurich, there was a disputation between the Old Church representatives and the Zwingli party from May 21 to June 8, 1526 (see BADEN [IM AARGAU], CONFERENCE OF). It was thought to be dangerous for Zwingli to go **7. The** thither because the Old Church party **Conference** meditated his death. But though not **at Baden.** present in person, Zwingli had the closest connection with those from Zurich who spoke for him, and gave them daily instruction. The debates were probably as fair as such debates can be, but things were exactly reversed from what they were in the Zurich debates, for the speakers and the audience were overwhelmingly Roman Catholic. Of course each side claimed the victory. In 1528 Zwingli was in Bern and played the most prominent part in the formal introduction, through magisterial action, of the Reformation into that city.

To this period of Zwingli's life also belongs the debate with Luther over the Lord's Supper, one of the great misfortunes the consequences of which are felt to-day. As Luther said at Marburg, he and Zwingli were not of the same spirit. Zwingli taught that the sacraments were signs and symbols of holy things, but in themselves had no power to cleanse, so that in the Lord's Supper there is a bringing back to memory of the work of grace done by Jesus Christ, who lives before the believer, though there is no participation of grace through the sacrament itself. He had a clear mind upon this point, and the mystical **8. Eucha-** view in any of its phases had no attrac-**ristic Con-** tions for him. Consequently, the **ference with** interchange of reading material **Luther at** between himself and Luther accom-**Marburg.** plished nothing, and only angered Luther. Thus baptism and the Eucha-rist, which were intended by Christ to be unifying practises, produced by their varied interpretation a breach between the Old Church and Protestants and between parties among the Protestants. Among the leaders of the Protestants was Philip the Magnani-mous, landgrave of Hesse (see PHILIP OF HESSE), who desired to see unity among Protestants upon the Eucharist, and to this end arranged a meeting in his castle at Marburg between Zwingli and Lu-ther (see MARBURG, CONFERENCE OF), which had one good result. Luther discovered that he and Zwingli had much in common. Although the terri-tory through which Zwingli had to pass on his way to Marburg was, with the exception of a few miles, friendly to Protestants, yet so panic-stricken were Zwingli and all his friends at the possibility of encountering members of the Old Church on their own ground that the Reformer con-sidered himself to be doing a bold thing in obeying the summons of the landgrave. He left Zurich by stealth, without permission of the government and with a false statement to his wife as to his destina-tion, but nothing happened to him. As it was thought unwise to pit him directly against Luther, he was introduced to Melanchthon, but neverthe-less the debate was between the German and the Swiss chief reformers. Both sides boasted of vic-tory, and the usual interchange of disgraceful epi-thets followed the debate which the landgrave hoped would seal their union.

After his return to Zurich Zwingli prosecuted more vigorously those political schemes which were in-tended to result in a union of all Protestants, and also of states which were not Protestant, against the house of Hapsburg and the pope, in the interest of religious liberty. The time Zwingli gave to these negotiations must have been considerable, for he sought to unite in this " Christian Burgher Rights," as he called his league, bodies as widely scattered as France and the Republic of Venice. What might have come of this scheme if his life had been longer continued it is, of course, impossible to say, but in 1530 he saw the making of the Schmalkald League, which shut off Lutheran membership in the Christian Burgher Rights, and the final refusal of France and Venice to enter. Inside of Switzerland Zwingli's schemes for religious liberty were equally unsuccessful, since the Five Forest Cantons, i.e., the cantons of Uri, Schwyz, Unterwalden, Luzern, and Zug, all adjoining Zurich, refused to allow the preaching of the Reformed faith within their borders. War actually broke out; but at Kappel, ten miles south of Zurich, where the opposing armies were about to come to blows, a hasty and ill-considered peace was patched up. The Forest Cantons refused to ratify the action of their representatives, and so the bill for the war was left unpaid by them, and the gospel preachers were still excluded from their territories. Zwingli saw clearly that such a peace was transitory, but though he wished that the cantons might be forced to keep the promises they had made, he did not desire to have them forced by the cruel measures which the Protestant cantons adopted, namely, by preventing the Forest Cantons from buying necessary things, especially salt, by blocking their entrance into the lower levels where alone these things could be obtained.

9. Unsuccessful Plans against the Hapsburgs and the Pope.

On June 30, 1530, the famous Diet of Augsburg convened. To it Zwingli sent a brief confession of faith and tried, probably unsuccessfully, to get it into the emperor's hands. It was a personal confession, but is one of the most interesting documents of the Reformation. In it he thus expresses himself respecting the Eucharist: " I believe that in the holy Eucharist—i.e., the supper of thanksgiving—the true body of Christ is present by the contemplation of faith; i.e., that they who thank the Lord for the kindness conferred on us in his Son acknowledge that he assumed true flesh, in it truly suffered, truly washed away our sins in his own blood; and thus everything done by Christ becomes present to them by the contemplation of faith. But that the body of Christ in essence and really—i.e., the natural body itself—is either present in the supper or masticated with our mouth or teeth, as the papists and some who long for the flesh-pots of Egypt assert, we not only deny, but firmly maintain is an error opposed to God's Word." Zwingli played a prominent part in Protestantism and made Zurich a prominent place. His educational work was important. He was a born teacher, and when at Glarus had pupils, some of whose letters have been preserved and show how well he had taught them. His little book which was his present to his stepson reveals the wise pedagogue, and so, as soon as his other engagements permitted, he accepted the post of rector of the Carolinum, the school of the Great Minster in Zurich (1525), and did much to improve the curriculum, besides teaching there in the religious department. But not education and instruction alone claimed his attention. He was the great man of Zurich, and was consulted on every topic by everybody from the chief magistrate to the lowliest citizen. His correspondence often compelled him to toil late into the night after

10. Diet of Augsburg and Work in Zurich.

the crowded days, and there came from his pen a stream of treatises, in Latin when he sought the widest public, or in German when he had his own nation more in view. These treatises were sometimes hastily written and are often of little present interest, but most of them are still worthy of reading. They are polemical, as those in exchange with Luther's on the Eucharist; expository of his position on theology in general or upon particular points; practical, giving guidance to the preachers about him how to preach the Gospel; or patriotic, noble utterances against war and the mercenary service. These writings show the broad-mindedness of Zwingli, and give ground for the claim that if he were living to-day he would be in all respects a modern man.

But this life of strenuous endeavor in so many directions was drawing to its close, not through the weakening of its bodily powers, not because under a strain the brain had given way, but because the fratricidal strife which had been temporarily avoided broke out again. On May 15, 1531, the cantons which had accepted the Reformation assembled, and learning that the Forest Cantons, which were strongly Roman Catholic, had flatly refused to keep the treaty which they had signed through their representatives the year before, resolved to bring them to terms by preventing them from crossing their borders, as they would have to do if they would purchase wheat, salt, iron, steel, and other necessary things. It was a cruel measure, as already said, and Zurich resisted it, but was outvoted. As soon as this edict came to execution, it brought the Forest Cantons to warlike preparation, and since Zurich lay directly in their path as they descended from the mountains, they attacked it first. On Oct. 9, 1531, their troops crossed the Zurich border, which was only twelve miles from the city, and the news reached there that evening. Strangely enough, there seems to have been no apprehension that war was so near, and, consequently, there was no adequate preparation for it. It was a mob rather than a little army of the famous Swiss soldiers which rushed out of the city. Their objective was Kappel, and there they were joined the next day, Wednesday, Oct. 11, 1531, by the main army. With it was Zwingli, dressed in armor, it is true, though he was a noncombatant, but he staid in the rear of the battle, and was there because he was the chief pastor of Zurich. It was a foregone conclusion that Zurich would be overthrown. She had only 2,700 men against 8,000 and they were very badly led. Overwhelmed, it took only a short time to be almost annihilated, and the battle of Kappel was a repetition of Flodden Field (Sept. 9, 1513). Five hundred Zurichers were slain, among them representatives of every prominent family in the city. But the greatest of them was Zwingli. Wounded first by a spear, and then struck on the head by a stone, he was put out of his misery by a sword thrust. He lay unrecognized for awhile, but when it became known that the corpse was that of Zwingli, it was treated with every indignity because he was held to be the author of the regulations which had brought on the war, which

11. Civil War, and Death of Zwingli.

was not true, and also as the leader of the Reformation, which was true. The body was given over to the hangman, who quartered it as if it had been that of a traitor, and then burned it, as if that of a heretic. The war ended in a treaty which was, of course, favorable to the Forest Cantons, though not so harsh as might have been expected. But all Zwingli's plans for a league of princes, cantons, and cities against pope and emperor, and all his hopes of providing the Old Church cantons with Reformed Church missionaries were forever ended. Much that he stood for in church practise and in theology did not long outlive him. Music was restored to the churches (1598) and his eucharistic views were superseded among the Reformed by those of Calvin. Yet, as he becomes better known, his clear-headedness, his independence, and his progressiveness will gain him increasing fame, and men will put him beside Luther as a leader of the Protestant host.

II. Theological System: * It has been the subject of some controversy what is to be considered the determinative element of Zwingli's theological system. Is it the religious interest of the Christian in salvation, or, more precisely, his faith in his election, which constitutes the central point in his religious life, as E. Zeller supposes? And, in this case, is it the doctrine of election, not as a theoretical proposition, but as a consequence of the consciousness of election, which forms the ultimate background of his religious convictions, the **1. Theories** foundation and the center of his doc**of Zeller** trine? Or, on the other hand, would **and** Zwingli lay down as the determinative **Sigwart.** standard of all other theological propositions the idea of God, conceived in a deterministic way, the idea of the absolute, all-embracing activity of God, who is the Highest Good, absolute Being, and Essence and Life of all things? In this case is the determinative element of the system a theological (i.e., a philosophical), an objective one, in short, a principle which could be "maintained even without the Scriptures," as C. Sigwart declares? Both of these main suppositions place an undue emphasis upon single elements of the case, although they are characteristic elements, and both theories are, therefore, to be decidedly rejected.

To Sigwart's conception it may be objected that the idea of God, however great the consistency with which it is employed in Zwingli's doctrinal structure, is, nevertheless, not its determinative element at all—at least not after such a manner as to furnish the explanation of every individual element, or of the whole tenor of the system, of its radical and thoroughly practical tendency. Certainly it **2. Criticism** is not correct to estimate Zwingli's **of Sigwart's** idea of God as a speculative and *a* **Theory.** *priori* idea, and to designate Pico della Mirandola (q.v.) as the source of the same (cf. Usteri, *TSK*, 1885, iv. 625 sqq.). For, however surprizing an influence Pico has exercised upon many of Zwingli's theoretical expositions, there is to be found in that writer not

only no doctrine of faith, but, in the definiteness which is so characteristic of Zwingli, not even a doctrine of providence and election. Zwingli himself also explicitly testifies that he was led to the quite peculiar doctrine of election which he teaches by the Scriptures (*Werke*, ed. Schuler and Schulthess, iv. 113, 8 vols., Zurich, 1828–42), that it is, therefore, not the consequence of speculative premises. Besides, it is a frequently recurring proposition of Zwingli's that we are concerned in religious knowledge not with the productions of the natural, blind reason, but with facts of experience wrought by God, with immediate illumination by the Spirit of God (iii. 130, 152, 157, 72; i. 208, 212, and 70, often).

Again, Zeller's development of the doctrinal system of Zwingli from the consciousness of election does not touch its real center. We are rather, if we are seeking the decisive source, to select in a more general way faith and the doctrine of faith. Faith, which is the direct operation of the Spirit of God in man, is itself the real life in God, the real unity with him, the "conclusion of all religion" (iii. 540); it embraces the entire religious relation **3. Criticism** of the man, the definite attitude **of Zeller's** wrought in him by God himself. With **Theory.** this, consequently, is immediately given the unconditioned certainty of salvation; it is salvation made objectively real and "conscious" (ii. 1, pp. 359, 283; i. 269, 277; iii. 230, and often). Accordingly, the conclusion which Zwingli draws can not be this: "I am elect, therefore I must be saved; and without this election, resting upon the eternal purpose of God, my consciousness of salvation would lack its indubitable certainty"; but, on the contrary: "I know that I am in possession of a God-wrought faith and of the salvation which is involved in this: consequently I must be elect." He who believes "is already certain that he is elected of God" (iv. 8); "he who is covered by the shield of faith knows that he is elected of God by the very basis and firmness of his faith" (iv. 122). It is an immediate consequence of this that the consciousness of election, which is, in any case, a derived and never an independent consciousness, is, by its very origin, not so much the chief object of faith as it is the most important (though not, of course, exclusive) contents of faith; and, consequently, it follows that the doctrine of election can not properly serve as the fundamental doctrine in which the original form of the religious consciousness expresses itself. It is only afterward, when the reflective faculty makes the relation an object of consideration (i.e., in the system of doctrine), that election comes to stand above and before faith; or, as Zeller himself says, the doctrine of providence and election is the product of the unconditioned certainty of faith. "It is evident that those who believe know that they have been elected; for those who believe have been elected. Election, therefore, precedes faith" (iv. 123–127, iii. 426). Faith is "the fruit and present pledge of election, so that he who has faith already knows that he has been elected, which aforetime he did not know when he had not yet come to the fulness of faith, even though he was no less elect in the sight

---

* This section on Zwingli's theology is translated by Frank Hugh Foster from Egli's article in Hauck-Herzog *RE*, xxi. 774–815. The references are necessarily to the Schuler and Schulthess edition.

of God before faith was given him as after" (iii. 575).

When Zwingli began the Reformation, his religious consciousness had essentially come to definite results in every direction. He rejected the many forms of intervention between the soul and God with which Roman Catholicism abounds, these broken cisterns in which he found no water, this suspension of the immediate relation of the soul to God, arising from the obscuration of the Christian consciousness of God, and pressed his way on through all obstacles to God, to God himself. In God he is at peace and rest, God is the Sabbath of his soul, God his One and his All, God the incomparable and highest Good, the only exclusive originator and bestower of salvation; his hold on God it is impossible for him to let go, to God, whose instrument he is, he surrenders himself **4. Direct** without condition. God is, therefore, **Relation of** most truly the object of faith, for to **the Human** believe is nothing else than to trust in **Soul to** God alone, to have God; and all the **God.** rest that belongs to the Christian faith —even Christ and redemption through him, even the word of God and the means of grace in the Christian Church not excepted—stands in an auxiliary capacity to the immediate and exclusive relation in which the Christian stands to God. The entire safety of the soul is in intimately trusting in God, and this is the faith that everything has its existence only through God. Salvation can be founded upon God alone, upon the grace of God, the Mediator and Surety of which is Christ, upon the operations of divine grace in man and for man, that is, upon nothing which is human, nothing external, nothing finite. All trust whose center is not God, rests upon unfaith and is idolatry, while the greater the faith in God who controls all things, the greater is God in man, the eternal unchangeable power of all good. So Zwingli expresses himself from the beginning in innumerable passages, whether he is carrying on a polemic against the features of Roman Catholicism by which it made religion an external thing, or is quietly developing the essence of piety. The Christian, reconciled and united with God through Christ, laid hold of and directed by his Spirit, is perfectly conscious of his personal salvation; and, if we ask how he has arrived at this peace in God, which is one almost mystical, and yet one full of impelling power, and if we inquire how he has reached this fundamental trait of his religious life, which also controls his theology, there is no other answer than this: it was the study of the holy Scriptures, especially of the epistles of Paul and of the Gospel of John, or, rather, it was the drawing of God through his Spirit, which, by means of the study of the Scriptures, led him to it.

Zwingli had accepted, in part before and in part in connection with the study of the Scriptures, a number of other elements of culture which belonged both to classic heathenism and to the later science developed in the Christian church. He had busied himself to a considerable degree with the Stoic Seneca, with the deterministic and anti-Pelagian Augustine, and especially with the modern Platonist, Pico. Under their influence, as well as under that of the widely accepted views which accompanied humanism, he had formed a general theory of the universe which it is impossible to define in detail. The conceptions and **5. Philo-** the general views and points of depar- **sophical** ture which he had gained from these **Elements** writers may have already exercised **of Zwingli's** more or less influence upon his concep- **Theology.** tion of the Scriptures and upon the tendency of his religious life. When, then, practical needs gradually led to the demand that he should summarize Christian doctrine in a connected system, as an organic whole, he employed for the dogmatic development and proof of the truths of the Scriptures the scientific principles which had become familiar to him from other sources, combining their various elements after a fashion of his own, as is, of course, always the case in the formation and development of a system. His philosophical conceptions and speculative ideas, so far as they appeared to be applicable, gave the form in which he set forth the substance of his religious consciousness, which had been developed, so far as its specific contents were concerned, under the influence of the Scriptures. If one should object that, according to this, the dogmatic formulation would come to sustain a rather mechanical relation to its religious contents, we should maintain in reply that everywhere in Zwingli the impelling religious interest and the theological exposition are carefully separated, as will be seen as soon as one compares his reformatory and practical writings with his system. Certainly, among the methods of viewing such subjects and the definitions which were familiar to him, he has incorporated in his system precisely those which corresponded most to his ruling convictions. And although he has produced no detailed development of the whole system, and has written no "Institutes of the Christian Religion," he has, nevertheless, set forth the body of Christian doctrine from premises of his own with a logical sequence which is worthy of all recognition. Though he is sometimes indefinite and often incomplete, he has succeeded in sketching the firm outlines of the great principles of theology within which the diverging tendencies of the Reformed Church and its doctrinal development have moved in subsequent times. At the same time, it is not to be doubted that he would have given a very different aspect to the dogmatic formulation of his doctrinal conceptions if he had had, for instance, the more advanced scientific ideas of the present at his disposal. While the religious substance of his doctrine would have essentially varied from that to be found in his present writings in scarcely a single important point, we should have certainly found a more carefully formulated concept of God, an anthropology quite different from his present abstract and dualistic one, a deeper doctrine of sin, a less mechanical Christology and one determined by the doctrine of God and of the essence of man, and, in general, a more satisfactory adjustment of the antitheses between the absolute and the finite causality, between determinism and freedom, between spirit and body.

Zwingli takes his theological standpoint essentially in the concrete reality of Christian experience

(so far as this is reflected in his consciousness, in consequence of his own religious life) and in the real life in and with God, in which he has come to see that the essence of religion lies. He feels an interest in every doctrine in precisely the degree in which
6. Rigid it is the expression of such relations as
Practicality appear to be decisive for the life of
and Exclu- faith that men actually experience.
sion of Everything, on the contrary, which
Speculation. does not touch the immediate present, or touches it only remotely, which does not have to do with the actual relation of God to man and of man to him, which belongs in the region of the merely transcendent, and, consequently, can not be the object of experience, he places, even in doctrine, far in the background. The being of God as such, God in his premundane self-existent being, does not disturb him; the trinitarian definitions of the church doctrine, with the ontological hypostatization of the Father, Son, and Spirit, he cites only in a formal way, and certainly betrays, while he does this, an undeniable tendency to Unitarianism (iii. 179, ii. 1, p. 208); the doctrine of creation, the angels, the miracles, the " state of integrity," the question as to the possibility of the Fall, and that as to the method in which the sinful tendency of our nature is transmitted, the intercession and the royal office of Christ, the beginning of the new life in conversion, the distinguishable elements of the life in the world to come, and the condition after the final judgment do not fix his attention. On the contrary, the decisive weight in the doctrine of God falls upon the active presence of God in his entire creation, upon the self-communication of God to man and mediately, through man, to the world, and, consequently, upon providence as the "present operation of God," the absolute activity of God as the unity of his power, wisdom, and goodness; while in the doctrine of the provision of salvation and the realization of salvation this stress falls upon the impartation and the indwelling of the Spirit of God and the union with God produced thereby, and upon salvation conferred by faith as a present possession. Even the doctrine of the eternal decree of election (in antithesis to which nothing but the stubborn fact drives him to the affirmation of reprobation) is employed in the development of the concrete religious consciousness; it aims at the establishment of faith which is, to be sure, the product of the divine causality, although this faith does not in this world correspond to its ideal in any respect.

If we add to this that religion has for its central point not so much the atonement as liberation from evil, viz., redemption; that the significance of Christ is found less in his merit than in his example, to which we are bound; that the specific principle of redemption is found, not so much in Christ as in the freely ruling and guiding Holy Spirit; that faith appears to be, not so much the organ of receptivity, as itself a spontaneity, a God-filled motive force, and an " effectual power and unwearing activity " which exhibit their result in the fulfilment of the will of God; that the struggle for moral perfection, for a righteousness which is not merely imputed but real, and the active battle which this demands be-

tween the flesh and spirit, controls the religious life, even in the development of doctrine, more, and
7. Centered disproportionately more, than the need
in Christian of the forgiveness of sins and justifica-
Conscious- tion (which are already always assured
ness and in God); that, side by side with the
Experience gospel, the law also has its place as
of Sancti- revelation for the impartation of the re-
fication. deeming grace of God to man; that the deepest motive for repentance is recognized as consisting in the knowledge of the grace of God which the Gospel brings; and that, finally, the ethical standard of Christ is applied alike both to the individual person and to all the organizations which unite to form human society, we may venture to ask whether we may not apply to Zwingli, when we confine ourselves to the essential substance of his doctrine, what has elsewhere been maintained as universally true of the Reformed theology—that it is, in general, that presentation of evangelical truth which describes it from the standpoint of the Christian consciousness, and upon the high level and under the definite forms of the experience of sanctification (M. Schneckenburger, *Vergleichende Darstellung des lutherischen und reformierten Lehrbegriffs*, ed. E. Güder, p. xxxvi. sqq., Stuttgart, 1855).

BIBLIOGRAPHY: The definitive edition of Zwingli's works has been appearing since 1904 under this title: *Huldreich Zwinglis sämtliche Werke unter Mitwirkung des Zwingli-Vereins in Zürich.* Volume i. goes down to the First Zurich Disputation, 1523, and was published in Berlin by C. A. Schwetschke und Sohn. Volume ii. begins with Zwingli's exposition and defense of the forty-nine articles he had drawn up for the first Zurich disputation, which was originally published July 14, 1523, and goes down to Zwingli's " Advice respecting the Mass and the use of Pictures in the Churches," and was published in 1908 in Leipsic by Verlag von M. Heinsius Nachfolger. The editors of both volumes were Emil Egli and Georg Finsler. Egli died Dec. 31, 1908. Walther Köhler, his successor in Zurich University, was called in to take his place upon the edition. It was decided to begin the publication of the Zwingli correspondence as volume vii., so it appeared with this title-page: *Huldreich Zwinglis sämtliche Werke unter Mitwirkung des Zwingli-Vereins in Zürich herausgegeben von Dr. Emil Egli†, Professor an der Universität in Zürich, D. Dr. Georg Finsler, Religionslehrer am Gymnasium in Basel, und D. Dr. Walther Köhler, Professor an der Universität in Zürich,* Band vii., Leipsic, Verlag von M. Heinsius Nachfolger, 1911. Volume iii. was begun in 1911, and so was volume viii., the two are to run in parts alternately. But as it will be several years before this edition is finished the students of Zwingli will frequently have to fall back upon the old edition of Schuler and Schulthess (8 vols., with small supplement, Zurich, bey Friedrich Schulthess, 1828–61). In this edition the Latin works are separated from the German and the arrangement is frequently inconvenient, whereas in the definitive edition there is no such separation and the contents are in chronological order. Great attention has been paid in the new edition to editorial details in the way of special historical and bibliographical introductions, minute study of the text, especially the German text which is furnished with a glossary. Many new letters appear in the correspondence as the result of the labors of Egli, who ransacked every place likely to yield them. Both the Latin and the German treatises are annotated in a manner very superior to that in the Schuler and Schulthess edition.

Georg Finsler, *Zwingli-Bibliographie. Verzeichniss der gedruckten Schriften von und über Ulrich Zwingli*, Zurich, Orell Fussli, 1897, gives an exhaustive list of Zwingli literature down to date, continued in *Zwingliana*, 1902, No. 1—in *Zwingliana* attention is paid to this literature. The biographies based on the sources and the resultants of years of special studies and therefore not soon to be superseded are these: (1) Raget Christoffel: *Huldreich Zwingli. Leben und ausgewählte Schriften*, Elberfeld, 1857, Eng. transl. by John Cochran, *Zwingli; or, the Rise of the Reformation in Switzerland*, Edinburgh, 1858 (an excellent translation; the selections given by Christoffel of Zwingli's writings are, however, entirely omitted); (2) Johann Caspar Moerikofer, *Ulrich Zwingli nach den urkundlichen Quellen*, 2 parts, Leipsic, 1869; (3) Rudolf Staehelin, *Huldreich Zwingli. Sein Leben und Wirken, nach den Quellen dargestellt*, 2 vols., Basel, 1897 (generally accepted as the best). In English there are two works of high grade: (1) Samuel Macauley Jackson, *Huldreich Zwingli, the Reformer of German Switzerland*, New York, 1901 (with bibliographical introduction; 2d ed., revised 1903; like Staehelin Jackson draws directly from the correspondence as his chief source. He spent four years on the book and has enriched it with special contributions from John Martin Vincent on Switzerland before the Reformation and from Frank Hugh Foster on Zwingli's theology). (2) Samuel Simpson, *Life of Ulrich Zwingli, the Swiss Patriot and Reformer*, New York, 1902 (more popular than Jackson's book but scholarly and independent).

For the study of Zwingli's theology at first hand there is nothing approaching *M. Huldreich Zwingli's sämmtliche Schriften im Auszuge*, 2 vols., Zurich, 1819. It is the work of Salomon Voegelin, and presents Zwingli's teachings on all subjects systematically arranged under appropriate heads, by quoting his exact language. The only edition accessible to Voegelin was that of 1581.

When the definitive edition is finished it would be worth while to refer these quotations to it. The only thorough study of Zwingli's theology is by August Baur, *Zwinglis Theologie. Ihr Werden und ihr System*, 2 vols., Halle, 1885–89 (gives far more than its title would indicate).

For the setting of the life of Zwingli see the contemporary history by Heinrich Bullinger, who was Zwingli's successor, *Reformationsgeschichte*, 3 vols., Frauenfeld, 1838–40; Egli's *Actensammlung zur Geschichte der Zürcher Reformation in den Jahren 1519–33*, Zurich, 1879; and Johann Strickler's *Actensammlung zur Schweizerischen Reformationsgeschichte in den Jahren 1521–32, im Anschluss an die gleichzeitigen eidgenossischen Abschiede*, 5 vols., Zurich, 1878–84 (give official records and cover much ground).

Emil Egli left in MS. an unfinished *Schweizerische Reformations-Geschichte*, upon which he had not worked since 1902, and the first volume from 1519–25 was edited and carried through the press by Georg Finsler, Zurich, 1910. For all questions bearing on Zwingli and his times see *Zwingliana. Mittheilungen zur Geschichte Zwinglis und der Reformation. Herausgegeben von der Vereinigung für das Zwinglimuseum in Zürich*, Zurich, 1897 sqq., published semiannually. Many of the German treatises were transferred into modern literary German by R. Christoffel. Jackson in his *Zwingli*, and in his *Selections from Zwingli* (Philadelphia, 1901), edited several German and Latin translations, and has announced for 1912 the first volume of a translation of the Latin works and of the correspondence of Zwingli, together with selections from his German works.

END OF VOL. XII.

APPENDIX

APPENDIX

AMERICAN WALDENSIAN AID SOCIETY:
This organization, having its headquarters at 213 West Seventy-sixth Street, New York City, was incorporated under the laws of the State of New York May, 1906, " To collect funds and apply the same to the aid of the Waldensian Church in Italy and elsewhere, in its evangelistic, institutional, and educational work, . . . and to arouse and maintain interest throughout the United States in the work of said Church and otherwise to aid the said Waldensian Church." It is governed by a board of twenty-four directors, twelve of whom are chosen from New York City and vicinity and twelve from the various sections where branches are located.

The organization has now twenty-five branch societies in the various cities of the United States and Canada, affiliated with it, and twenty-two circles throughout the country, which are aiding in the work and will become legalized branches of the national organization.

The funds raised by the society pay the salaries of many of the Protestant pastors in Italy and aid in the construction of churches and schoolhouses. The primary training of the Italian in the ways and customs of this country has a very beneficial influence on the Italian immigrants coming to our shores. Through the Waldenses about 100 Protestant Italian churches have been founded in America. The American Waldensian Aid Society is helping to support this reflex mission, and a bureau to care for the religious welfare of the incoming and outgoing Italian Protestants is now in contemplation as a department of this organization.

In Great Britain there is a similar organization with like purposes, which publishes as its organ *A Voice from Italy*, a periodical under the editorship of Rev. James Gibson.

BARNUM, HERMAN NORTON: Congregationalist; b. at Auburn, N. Y., Dec. 5, 1826; d. at Harput (60 m. n.n.w. of Diarbekr), Turkish Armenia, May 20, 1910. He was educated at Amherst (B.A., 1852) and Andover Theological Seminary (1855), and after being missionary-at-large in Vermont in 1855–56 and traveling for a year (1857–58) became connected with the American Board of Commissioners for Foreign Missions, with which he remained until his death. His main activity, apart from his general missionary duties, was teaching in Harput Theological Seminary and in Euphrates College, in the same city, and it was due in great measure to his firm attitude during the threatened Turkish massacres of Nov., 1895, that no actual harm came to the Armenians of Harput.

BECKWITH, JOHN CHARLES: English soldier and missionary to the Waldenses (q.v.); b. at Halifax, Nova Scotia, Oct. 2, 1789; d. at his villa, La Torre, in the Piedmont valleys, July 19, 1862. He served in Denmark, Portugal, Spain, France, and the Netherlands, but at Waterloo he lost a leg, and, although promoted lieutenant-colonel, was debarred from active service, retiring in 1820 on half pay. In 1827 he chanced to look into a book on the Waldenses, and became so interested in them that he removed to Italy and took the villa in which he resided for the remainder of his life. His two endeavors were to raise the educational standard of the Waldenses and to revive their uncompromising Protestantism, and to him is due the foundation of no less than 120 schools throughout the valleys of the Piedmont. In recognition of his services Charles Albert of Sardinia created him a knight of St. Maurice and St. Lazarus in 1848, two years after he had been promoted major-general in the English service. His memory is still held in deep respect by the people whose condition he so successfully sought to elevate.

BIBLIOGRAPHY: J. P. Meille, *General Beckwith: His Life and Labours among the Waldenses of Piedmont*, London, 1873; *DNB*, iv. 89–90.

BERGSON, HENRI-LOUIS: French philosopher; b. in Paris Oct. 18, 1859. He was educated at the Lycée Condorcet and the École normale supérieure (Litt.D., 1889), and was professor of philosophy at the lyceums of Angers (1881–83) and of Clermont (1883–88), also conducting courses in the university of the latter city. He was then a professor at the Collège Rollin (1888–89) and the Lycée Henri IV. (1889–97), and a lecturer at the École normale supérieure (1897–1900). Since 1900 he has been professor of modern philosophy at the Collège de France, in 1901 being elected a member of the Académie des sciences morales et politiques. In his teaching he belongs to the idealistic school, and he maintains that life can be accounted for only on the hypothesis of a mysterious superconsciousness. In man alone is consciousness able to overcome the limitations imposed by matter, and this fact not only explains the essential freedom of the human mind, but also gives ground for a scientific basis of belief in immortality. He thus opposes strongly the materialistic philosophy and the crasser forms of the theory of evolution, at the same time avoiding the vagueness of extreme idealism of the older type.

The principal writings of Bergson are *Extraits de Lucrèce* (Paris, 1884); *Essai sur les données immédiates de la conscience* (1889, 2d ed., 1898; Eng. transl. by F. L. Pogson, *Time and Free Will*, London, 1910); *Quid Aristoteles de loco senserit* (1890); *Matière et mémoire* (1896; Eng. transl. by N. M. Paul and W. S. Palmer, *Matter and Memory*, New York, 1911); *Le Rire; Essai sur la signification du comique* (1900; Eng. transl., *Laughter; an Essay on the Meaning of the Comic*, New York, 1911); and

L'Évolution créatrice (1907; Eng. transl. by A. Mitchell, *Creative Evolution*, New York, 1911).

BIBLIOGRAPHY: J. Solomon, *Bergson*, Edinburgh, 1911; W. Durban, " The Philosophy of Henri Bergson," in *Homiletic Review*, lxiii (1912), 20–23.

BOSSERT, GUSTAV: German Lutheran; b. at Täbingen (a village near Rottweil, 30 m. s.w. of Tübingen) Oct. 21, 1841. After being vicar at Dürrmenz, Mühlacker (1864–67), during which time he made a tour of northern Germany, Holland, and Belgium, he taught Hebrew at the gymnasium of Heilbronn and religion in the Ober-Realschule in the same town until 1869. From that year until 1888 he was pastor in Bächlingen, near Langenburg, being also editor of the *Zeitschrift des historischen Vereins für Württemberg-Franken* in 1878–88 and assistant editor of the *Württembergischer Vierteljahrsheft* in 1879–1888. From 1888 until his retirement from active life in 1907 he was pastor in Nabern, and in 1894 he was a delegate to the district synod. Among his writings special mention may be made of his *Württemberg und Janssen* (2 parts, Halle, 1882–85), *Eberhard im Bart* (Stuttgart, 1884), and *Der Interim in Württemberg* (Halle, 1895).

CABROL, FERNAND MICHAEL: Roman Catholic historian and archeologist; b. at Marseilles, France, Dec. 11, 1855. He received his education at the Institut Belzunce, petit séminaire, and grand séminaire, all at Marseilles, and at the abbey of Solesmes (1878); was professor of ecclesiastical history in the theological school at Solesmes, 1879–90; of ecclesiastical literature at the Catholic University of Angers, 1892–95, being also prior during 1890–95; prior of Farnborough, Hampshire, England, 1895–1903; and abbot of Farnborough since 1903. He has been vice-president of the Plainsong and Medieval Music Society since 1901, and in 1908 was president of the French section of the Eucharistic Congress. He is the author of *Bibliographie des Bénédictines de la congrégation de France* (Solesmes, 1889); *Histoire du Cardinal Pitra* (Paris, 1893); *Étude sur la Peregrinatio Silviæ; les églises de Jérusalem; la discipline et la liturgie au iv. siècle* (1893); *Le Livre de la prière antique; étude de liturgie* (1900; 4th ed., 1910); *La Devotion liturgique à la Sainte Vièrge* (1905); *Les Origines liturgiques* (1906); and is editing with H. Leclercq *Monumenta ecclesiæ liturgica* (1900 sqq.) and the important *Dictionnaire d'archéologie chrétienne et de liturgie* (1903 sqq.). Not the least important of his work is contained in such journals as *La Science catholique, Revue du clergé français, Revue des questions historiques, Revue d'archéologie chrétienne et de liturgie,* and *Revue des facultés catholiques,* to which he has made valuable contributions in his chosen line of Christian antiquities and liturgics.

DAVIES, BENJAMIN: Welsh Baptist and Hebrew scholar; b. at Llanboidy (12 m. w. of Carmarthen), Carmarthenshire, Feb. 26, 1814; d. at Frome (a suburb of London) July 19, 1875. He was educated at the Bristol Baptist College, and the universities of Dublin, Glasgow, Halle, and Leipsic (Ph.D., 1838). From 1838 to 1844 he was president of the Baptist College, Montreal, Canada, resigning on account of his open-communion views,

which brought him into conflict with the governors of the college. He was then president of the Baptist College, Regent's Park, London, for two years, but in 1846 he returned to the Baptist College at Montreal as professor of Hebrew, a position which he exchanged in 1852 for the professorship of classics in McGill University, Montreal. During this period he continued his Hebrew studies, winning the reputation of being, with one possible exception, the best Hebraist of his time on the American continent. In 1857 Davies returned to Regent's Park as professor of classic Hebrew and Old-Testament literature, retaining this post until his death. In his early years he was a popular preacher in Welsh and English, but later he lost this popularity; though slow of speech, his knowledge was encyclopedic, and he had in a very rare degree the teacher's instinct and the power of winning the esteem and affection of his pupils.

Much of Davies' literary work was done in collaboration with others and published anonymously. It is known, however, that he wrote the introductions and notes for most of the Old-Testament books in the *Annotated Paragraph Bible* (London, 1850–57), and he edited and greatly improved E. Robinson's *Harmony of the Gospels* (1878), besides editing Vergil, Homer, and other classic authors. But his chief work was in the domain of Hebrew. He translated, enlarged, corrected, and annotated several editions of F. W. H. Gesenius' *Hebrew Grammar* (1846–80), and in 1871 published at London his *Compendious and Complete Hebrew and Chaldee Lexicon to the Old Testament with an English-Hebrew Index, chiefly founded on the Works of Gesenius and Fürst, with Improvements from Dieterich and other Sources,* which, until the publication of the *Oxford Hebrew Lexicon* in 1906, was the most accurate, up-to-date, and valuable in the English language. Though so profound a scholar, Davies was a very simple, devout Christian, and had it not been for his excessive modesty, which led him to prefer to produce anonymously, much other literary work would have been known as his.

T. WITTON DAVIES.

BIBLIOGRAPHY: T. W. Davies in *Nottingham Free Church Record,* May–June, 1898, and *Soren Gomer* (Welsh), May, 1898; *The Baptist,* July 30, 1875; *Baptist Handbook,* 1876.

EDDY, MARY BAKER: * Discoverer and founder of Christian Science (see SCIENCE, CHRISTIAN); b. at Bow, N. H., July 16, 1821; d. at Newton, Mass., Dec. 3, 1910. Her parents were Mark and Abigail Ambrose Baker, and she numbered among her ancestors a member of the Provincial Congress and soldiers in the War of the Revolution. She was educated at an academy at Tilton, N. H., and by private tutors, among whom was her brother, Albert Baker, a graduate of Dartmouth and a member of the New Hampshire legislature. As a young woman, Mrs. Eddy was delicate and markedly individual. During her middle life she was a confirmed invalid, until the healing incident occurred which ushered her to the threshold of Christian Science. In 1843 she married Major

* Statement from the Christian Science Committee on Publication of the First Church, Boston.

George W. Glover, a contractor, of Charleston, S. C., and removed with him to that city, where she was left a widow in June, 1844. She returned to New Hampshire, where her only child, George Washington Glover, was born. In 1853 she married Daniel Patterson, from whom she was divorced in 1873, on the ground of desertion. In her search for health Mrs. Eddy went in 1863 to Portland, Me., to consult P. P. Quimby, a magnetic healer. Mrs. Eddy was temporarily benefited, but later had a relapse. In 1866 she recovered from an accident, which was the immediate cause of her discovery of Christian Science. A fall on the ice resulted in severe internal injuries. In her extremity Mrs. Eddy turned to her Bible and was healed. In 1877 she married Dr. Asa G. Eddy, one of her early students in Christian Science, who died in 1882. The text-book of Christian Science, *Science and Health with Key to the Scriptures*, was published by Mrs. Eddy at Boston in 1875. In 1881 Mrs. Eddy chartered the Massachusetts Metaphysical College in Boston. The charter for the First Christian Science Church was obtained in June, 1879; and in that year Mrs. Eddy was called to become its pastor. Mrs. Eddy founded, and for a long time edited, *The Christian Science Journal*, a monthly magazine. Mrs. Eddy's principal works are: *People's Idea of God* (1886); *Christian Healing* (1886); *Unity of Good* (1887); *Retrospection and Introspection* (1891); *No and Yes* (1891); *Christ and Christmas* (1893); *Pulpit and Press* (1895); *Church Manual* (1895); *Miscellaneous Writings* (1897); *Christian Science versus Pantheism* (1898); and *Message to the Mother Church* (1900–02).   EUGENE R. Cox.

BIBLIOGRAPHY: A. Brisbane, *Mary Baker G. Eddy*, Boston, 1908; Sybil Wilbur, *Life of Mary Baker Eddy*, New York, 1908.

EUCKEN, CHRISTIAN RUDOLF: German Protestant philosopher and the leading exponent of modern German idealism; b. at Aurich (60 m. n.w. of Bremen) Jan 5, 1846. He was educated at the universities of Göttingen and Berlin (1863–67), and after teaching in a gymnasium until 1871 was called to Basel as professor of philosophy, whence he was transferred, in 1874, to his present position as professor of the same subject at Jena. He has written *Die Methode der aristotelischen Forschung in ihrem Zusammenhang mit den philosophischen Grundprincipien des Aristoteles* (Berlin, 1872): *Geschichte und Kritik der Grundbegriffe der Gegenwart* (Leipsic, 1878; 4th ed., *Geistige Strömungen der Gegenwart*, 1909; Eng. transl. by M. S. Phelps, *Fundamental Concepts of Modern Philosophic Thought*, New York, 1880); *Geschichte der philosophischen Terminologie* (1879); *Prolegomena zu Forschungen über die Einheit des Geisteslebens in Bewusstsein und That der Menschheit* (1885); *Beiträge zur Geschichte der neueren Philosophie, vornehmlich der deutschen* (Heidelberg, 1886; 2d ed., *Beiträge zur Einführung in die Geschichte der Philosophie*, Leipsic, 1906); *Einheit des Geisteslebens in Bewusstsein und That der Menschheit* (Leipsic, 1888); *Lebansanschauungen der grossen Denker* (1890; 8th ed., 1909; Eng. transl., W. S. Hough and W. R. B. Gibson, *Problem of Human Life as Viewed by the Great Thinkers*, New York, 1909); *Kampf um einen geistlichen*

Lebensinhalt (1896; 2d ed., 1907); *Wahrheitsgehalt der Religion* (1901; 2d ed., 1905; Eng. transl., *The Truth of Religion*, New York, 1911); *Gesammelte Aussätze zu Philosophie und Lebensanschauung* (1903); *Grundlinien einer neuen Lebensanschauung* (1907); *Hauptprobleme der Religionsphilosophie der Gegenwart* (Berlin, 1907; 3d ed., 1909); *Sinn und Wert des Lebens* (Leipsic, 1908; 3d ed., 1910; Eng. transl., *Meaning and Value of Life*, New York, 1909); and *Einführung in eine Philosophie des Geisteslebens* (1908; Eng. trans., F. L. Pogson, *Life of the Spirit*, New York, 1909).

EVJEN, JOHN OLUF: Lutheran; b. at Ishpeming, Mich., Dec. 13, 1874. He was educated at Augsburg Seminary, Minneapolis, Minn. (B.A., 1895), the theological seminary of the same institution (1898), and the University of Leipsic (Ph.D., 1903), and after being for a short time a pastor at Muskegon and Grand Rapids, Mich., was successively acting professor of church history at the United Church Theological Seminary, St. Paul, Minn. (1903–05), ánd professor of Biblical history in Pennsylvania College, Gettysburg, Pa. (1905–1909). Since 1909 he has been professor of theology in Augsburg Seminary, Minneapolis. He has written *Die Staatsumwälzung in Dänemark im Jahre 1660* (Leipsic, 1904), *Scandinavia and the Book of Concord* (Gettysburg, Pa., 1906), *Et Kapitel fra Symbolforpligtelsens Historie* (Minneapolis, 1911), and *Lutheran Germany and the Book of Concord* (1911).

FELICITAS: The name of two early Christian martyrs and saints.

1. Roman matron; martyred either during the reign of Marcus Aurelius or during that of Antoninus Pius. Her day was Nov. 23 as early as the sixth century, when Gregory the Great delivered an oration in the basilica above her tomb, this tomb being rediscovered in 1884. According to tradition equally old, she suffered martyrdom together with her seven sons, who are represented with her in a seventh-century fresco in her tomb; but there is reason to believe that between the seventh and ninth centuries confusion arose between these seven fellow martyrs of Felicitas and seven other martyrs (Januarius, Felix, Philippus, Silvanus, Alexander, Vitalis, and Martialis), whose day has been kept at least since the time of the *Depositio Martyrum* (middle of the fourth century) on July 10, and who came to be regarded as the sons of Felicitas.

2. Carthaginian slave; martyred with Perpetua (q.v.) Mar. 7, 202 or 203. Throughout the account of her passion she is a secondary figure to Perpetua, the chief detail recorded being that, in answer to her prayers, she was enabled to give premature birth to her child (who was adopted by a Christian woman) two days before the time set for her martyrdom, since otherwise she would not have been allowed to be thrown to the beasts as were Perpetua, Revocatus, Saturus, and Saturninus.

BIBLIOGRAPHY: On 1, the early *Vita* with *Passio, Acta*, and commentary are in *ASB*, July, iii. 5–28. Consult further on 1: B. Aubé, *Hist. des persécutions de l'église jusqu'à la fin des Antonins*, pp. 439–440, Paris, 1875; idem, *Les Actes de SS. Félicité . . . et des leurs compagnons*, p. 90, ib. 1881; J. B. Lightfoot, *Apostolic Fathers*, i. 498–499,

London, 1885; P. Allard, *Hist. des Persécutions*, vol. ii., Paris, 1886; E. Egli, *Altchristliche Studien*, pp. 91–98, Zurich, 1887; J. Führer, *Ein Beitrag zur Lösung der Felicitas-Frage*, Freising, 1890; idem, *Zum Felicitasfrage*, Leipsic, 1894; K. J. Neumann, *Der römische Staat und die allgemeine Kirche*, i. 294, ib. 1890; K. Kunstle, *Hagiographische Studien über die Passio S. Felicitatis*, Paderborn, 1894; Neander, *Christian Church*, i. 123–124; *DCB*, ii. 478.

On 2, *DCB*, ii. 478; Schaff, *Christian Church*, ii. 58.

FITZRALPH, RICHARD: Archbishop of Armagh; b. at Dundalk (45 m. n. by w. of Dublin), County Louth, toward the end of the thirteenth century; d., probably at Avignon, presumably Nov. 16, 1360. He was educated at Oxford, where he became fellow of Balliol, and where, about 1333, he seems to have been commissary (i.e., vice-chancellor), or, more probably, chancellor, of the university. On July 10, 1334, he was collated chancellor of Lincoln Cathedral, and soon afterward seems to have become archdeacon of Chester, while on Apr. 20, 1337, he was installed dean of Lichfield, and on July 8, 1347, was consecrated archbishop of Armagh at Exeter.

Fitzralph made throughout his life repeated visits to Avignon, and sermons are still extant in manuscript preached by him before the pope in 1335, 1338, 1341, 1342, and 1344; nor is it impossible that during this period he actually resided at Avignon for some time. In 1349 he was again in Avignon, in connection with the jubilee commanded by Edward III. for 1350, and it was probably then that the archbishop became involved in the negotiations pending between the pope and the Armenians who desired to be reconciled to the Roman obedience. Fitzralph was present at the negotiations with the Armenian envoys at Avignon, and in his nineteen books entitled *Summa in quæstionibus Armenorum* (of which only the first book, *Summa de erroribus Armenorum*, was printed, ed. J. Sudoris, Paris, 1511) formally refuted the 117 heresies which they were required to abjure before their request could be granted. In the same year he became involved in a controversy far more disquieting to him, when he presented to the pope a remonstrance of the English secular clergy against the regulars. Hitherto he had been the friend of Franciscan and Dominican alike, as well as of the parish clergy, but even after his return to Ireland the opposition of the regulars was still potent, and in 1357 Fitzralph was cited to appear at Avignon. Many of his views he had already set forth in his *De pauperie Salvatoris* (the first four books of which have been edited by R. L. Poole in his edition of Wyclif's *De dominio divino*, London, 1890), and in a sermon before the papal court, Nov. 8, 1357, he still further defended his position in his *Defensio curatorum contra eos qui privilegiatos se dicunt* (Louvain, 1475 [?]; in *Fasciculus rerum expetendarum et fugiendarum*, ed. E. Brown, ii. 466–487, London, 1690; and often), maintaining that monastic mendicancy was incompatible with the teachings of Christ, and holding that the privileges of the regular clergy were inimical to the interests of the secular. The result was indeterminate. The friars were not directly molested, and the archbishop was commanded to keep silent. On the other hand, he evidently lost none of the papal favor, and the English clergy were directed to provide moneys for his support during his residence at Avignon, where he seems to have remained until his death. His preference for Avignon may have been due in part to the fact that the English king was opposed to him because he was considered to presume on the papal approval of him. Accordingly, in Nov., 1349, the king forbade the archiepiscopal cross to be borne before Fitzralph, and in Feb., 1350, the same monarch sought to have Fitzralph's claims to supremacy over the see of Dublin disallowed, while in 1357 the archbishop was forbidden to leave the country without express permission, a prohibition that was, however, almost immediately revoked. At the same time, he enjoyed the affection of his people, for the government was forced to interfere because of riots arising from the attempts to deprive Fitzralph of his rights.

Some ten years after the archbishop's death his remains were said to have been taken to the church of St. Nicholas at Dundalk, and within twenty years it was popularly believed that miracles were performed at his tomb. Nevertheless, the commission appointed by Boniface IV. (between 1400 and 1404) to examine his claims to canonization came to no conclusion. Besides the works already mentioned, Fitzralph was the author of many sermons (e.g., the collection *De laudibus Mariæ Avenioni*) and letters, as well as of the more permanent *Lectura sententiarum, Quæstiones sententiarum, Lectura theologiæ, De statu universalis Ecclesiæ, De peccato ignorantiæ, De vafritiis Judæorum, Dialogus de rebus ad sanctam scripturam pertinentibus*, and *Vita Sancti Manchini abbatis*, most of which are still unedited.

BIBLIOGRAPHY: *DNB*, xix. 194–198 (which should be consulted for the early authorities on which the individual statements are made); J. Prince, *Worthies of Devon*, pp. 294 sqq., Exeter, 1701. Autobiographic material is found in his own writings, especially in the *Defensio curatorum*.

GOOD, JEREMIAH HAAK: Reformed; b. at Rehrersberg, Pa., Nov. 23, 1822; d. at Tiffin, O., Jan. 25, 1888. He was educated at Marshall College, Mercersburg, Pa. (B.A., 1843) and Mercersburg Theological Seminary (1846). After two years as pastor at Lancaster, O., he became, in 1848, editor of *The Western Missionary*, of which he was also the founder, and from 1850 to 1869 was professor of mathematics in Heidelberg College, Tiffin, O. From 1869 until his death he was professor of systematic theology in the Reformed theological seminary in the same city. He was one of the prime movers in the founding of both these institutions. In the liturgical controversy in his denomination he was a leader, together with J. H. A. Bomberger (q.v.), against elaborate services; and he was likewise a member of the committee appointed to harmonize the differences within the Reformed Church, later becoming a member of the liturgical committee which completed the peace. Besides editing *The Reformed Church Hymnal* (Cleveland, O., 1878, and many later editions), he wrote *The Heidelberg Catechism, Newly Arranged* (Tiffin, 1879, and often), *The Children's Catechism* (1881 and often), *Prayer-Book and Aids to Private Devotion* (1881), and *The Church-Member's Handbook* (1882).

GRAF, KARL HEINRICH: German Protestant Old-Testament critic; b. at Mühlhausen (29 m. n.w. of Erfurt), Alsace, Feb. 28, 1815; d. at Meissen (15 m. n.w. of Dresden), Saxony, July 16, 1869. In 1833 he entered the University of Strasburg, where he came under the influence of E. G. E. Reuss (q.v.), in whose classes he received the first suggestions of the theory of the post-exilic origin of much of the legislation commonly ascribed to Moses, so that the fundamental position of the views associated with the names of A. Kuenen and J. Wellhausen (qq.v.) go back, through Graf, to Reuss. In 1836 Graf received the degree of candidate of theology, but at the close of his student life at Strasburg he accepted a post as private tutor in a family residing at Paris. In 1844 he became a teacher in a gymnasium at Leipsic, and also studied Arabic and Persian under H. L. Fleischer at the university of that city. From 1847 until his enforced retirement, on account of ill-health, in 1868 he was teacher of French and Hebrew in the gymnasium at Meissen, and after 1852 titular professor.

Besides translations of Sa'di's *Gulistan* and *Bustan* (Leipsic, 1846; Jena, 1850), an edition of the latter work (Vienna, 1858), and *Afrika* (under the pseudonym "Karl Elsässer," 2 vols., Zwickau, 1855–56), Graf wrote *Der Segen Moses, Deut. 23* (Leipsic, 1857) and *Der Prophet Jeremia erklärt* (1862), the first great commentary on this book. His chief fame, however, is due to his *Die geschichtlichen Bücher des Alten Testaments* (1866), although as a matter of fact it did little more than reproduce, with added proofs and illustrations, what Graf had learned from Reuss. Since this work contains the fundamental position of Old-Testament criticism, it would be fairer and more accurate to link these modern views on the Old Testament with the names of Reuss and Graf, though Wellhausen and especially Kuenen did much to correct, amplify, confirm, and illustrate what the older scholars taught. The work has two principal parts, the first of which is an examination of the historical books of the Old Testament from Genesis to II Kings. The conclusion reached is that the laws in Leviticus and the allied parts of Exodus and Numbers (or the legal section of the Priestly Code) constitute the latest parts of the Pentateuch and belong mostly to a time later than that of Ezra, though portions are ascribed to Ezra himself, and the remainder are but little older. The book of Deuteronomy is made the basis of the investigation, and the kernel of the Deuteronomic legislation is held to have come into being, as W. M. L. de Wette (q.v.) had taught, in the twenty-first year of the reign of Josiah. Graf then endeavors to distinguish (1) parts of the Pentateuch implied by D (e.g., the laws in Ex. xx.–xxiii., xxxiv. 10–27, etc.) and (2) parts of the Pentateuch which imply D and which are, therefore, later. He maintained the older view, current till the time of H. Hupfeld (q.v.), that what is now known as P was included in E and ascribed to a period long before the exile. He acknowledged that the narrative and legal portions of what was known as the *Grundschrift* agreed in general style and matter, but this was attributed to imitation, not to identity of date and origin. Kuenen and Well-

hausen soon showed that Graf's own investigation proved the whole of what is now known as P to be post-Deuteronomic, and, in its present form, post-exilic.   T. WITTON DAVIES.

BIBLIOGRAPHY: K. Budde and H. J. Holzmann, *E. Reuss' Briefwechsel mit Graf*, Giessen, 1904; F. Bleek, *Einleitung in das Alte Testament*, ed. J. Wellhausen, 5th ed., Berlin, 1886, p. 619 sqq.; H. Holzinger, *Einleitung in den Hexateuch*, i. 65 sqq., Freiburg, 1893.

GUETZLAFF, KARL FRIEDRICH AUGUST: German Lutheran missionary to the Chinese; b. at Pyritz (24 m. s.e. of Stettin), Pomerania, July 8, 1803; d. at Hongkong Aug. 9, 1851. He was apprenticed to a saddler in Stettin, but was enabled by the king of Prussia to receive training for a missionary career at the Halle Pädagogium and at Johannes Jänicke's missionary institute in Berlin. He then made a visit to England, where Robert Morrison (q.v.) directed his interest especially to Chinese missions, and accordingly he went, under the auspices of the Dutch missionary society, in 1826, to Batavia, where in two years he became proficient in Chinese. He then severed his connection with the Dutch society, and in 1828 went first to Bangkok and thence to Macao, and there collaborated with W. H. Medhurst (q.v.) in translating the Bible into the Wen-li dialect of Chinese (Hongkong [?], 1854–55), besides editing a Chinese monthly. Between 1831 and 1834 he made three voyages along the coasts of China, Siam, Korea, and the Lu-chu Islands, and in 1835 he was appointed interpreter (later secretary) to the British embassy in China, in which capacity his knowledge of China and Chinese enabled him to render great services to England in the opium war of 1840–42, while later he was made superintendent of trade, an office which he retained until his death. In 1844 he was one of the founders, at Hongkong, of an association to train converted Chinese to become missionaries to their own people, but the time had not yet come for such an institution to be successful. In 1849–51 Gützlaff made a tour of England and Germany in behalf of his mission, but died almost immediately on his return to China.

The principal writings of Gützlaff, besides a Japanese translation of the Gospel of John (Singapore [1830?]), were *Journal of Three Voyages along the Coast of China, in 1831, 1832, and 1833* (London, 1834); *Sketch of Chinese History, Ancient and Modern* (2 vols., 1834); *China Opened; or, A Display of the Topography, History, etc., of the Chinese Empire* (2 vols., 1838); *Verslag van een driejarig verblijf in Siam en van een reize langs de kust van China* (Rotterdam, 1838); *Geschichte des chinesischen Reiches von den ältesten Zeiten bis auf den Frieden von Nanking* (ed. K. F. Neumann, Stuttgart, 1847); *Die Mission in China* (lectures delivered in Berlin; Berlin, 1850); *Bericht seiner Reise von China nach England und durch die verschiedenen Länder Europa's im Interesse der chinesischen Mission* (Cassel, 1851); and *Life of Taou-Kwang, late Emperor of China, with Memoirs of the Court of Peking* (ed. Sir G. T. Staunton, London, 1852); in addition to the *Chinesische Berichte von der Mitte des Jahres 1841 bis zum Schluss des Jahres 1846* (Cassel, 1850), which he published under the pseudonym "Gaihan."

BIBLIOGRAPHY: K. *Gützlaff's Leben und Heimgang*, Berlin, 1851; G. R. Erdbrink, *Gütelaff, de Apostel der Chinezen*, Rotterdam, 1850.

HAMPDEN-COOK, ERNEST: English Congregationalist; b. in London Mar. 11, 1860. He was educated at University College, London (B.A., 1881), Owens College, and Lancashire Independent College, Manchester, and St. John's College, Cambridge (B.A., 1885), and, besides being resident secretary of Mill Hill School, London (1891-96), has held Congregational pastorates at Cricklewood, London (1886-87), Thames Goldfield, New Zealand (1887-89), Broken Hills Silver Mines, New South Wales (1889-90), Dolgelley, Wales (1897-1900), and Sandbach, Cheshire (since 1900). Theologically he is a broad Evangelical and believes in three personal advents of Christ, holding that the second took place in 70 A.D., and that there is a third yet to come, death being meanwhile to the individual the coming of the Lord. Besides editing and partly revising *The New Testament in Modern Speech* (London, 1894; 3d ed., 1909) of R. F. Weymouth (q.v.) and being one of the translators of the Pauline epistles in *The Twentieth Century New Testament* (1900), he has compiled *Register of Mill Hill School, London, from 1807* (1894) and written *The Christ has Come: The Second Advent an Event of the Past* (1894; 3d ed., 1904).

HEINZE, FRANZ FRIEDRICH MAXIMILIAN: German Lutheran, philosopher; b. at Priessnitz (a village near Borna, 16 m. s.s.e. of Leipsic) Dec. 13, 1835; d. at Leipsic Sept. 17, 1909. He was educated at the universities of Leipsic, Tübingen, Erlangen, Halle, and Berlin (1854-60; Ph.D., Berlin, 1860), and after teaching in Schulpforta (1860-1863) and being the instructor of the present grand duke of Oldenburg and his brother, became, in 1872, privat-docent in Leipsic. In 1874 he was called to Basel as professor, but the next year, after a few months at Königsberg, was transferred in a similar capacity to Leipsic, where he passed the remainder of his life. He was prochancellor of the university in 1877-88, dean of the philosophical faculty in 1880-81, and rector of the university in 1883-84. He was one of the contributors to the Hauck-Herzog *RE*, and also wrote *Die Lehre vom Logos in der griechischen Philosophie* (Oldenburg, 1872), *Der Eudämonismus in der griechischen Philosophie, i.* (Leipsic, 1883), and *Vorlesungen Kants über Metaphysik aus drei Semestern* (1894), besides editing the fifth to the tenth editions of F. Ueberweg's *Grundriss der Geschichte der Philosophie* (Berlin, 1876-1907) and being one of the editors of the *Vierteljahrsschrift für wissenschaftliche Philosophie*.

HODGES, GEORGE: Protestant Episcopalian; b. at Rome, N. Y., Oct. 6, 1856. He was educated at Hamilton College (B.A., 1877) and was ordained to the priesthood in 1882. After being successively curate (1881-89) and rector (1889-94) of Calvary Church, Pittsburg, Pa., he became, in 1894, dean of the Episcopal Theological School at Cambridge, Mass., the position which he still holds. He has written *The Episcopal Church* (New York, 1889); *Christianity between Sundays* (1892); *The Heresy of Cain* (1894); *This Present World*

(1896); *Faith and Social Service* (1896); *The Battles of Peace* (1897); *The Path of Life* (1899); *William Penn* (Boston, 1900); *Fountains Abbey* (London, 1904); *The Human Nature of the Saints* (New York, 1904); *The Cross and Passion* (1904); *When the King Came* (Boston, 1904); *Three Hundred Years of the Episcopal Church in America* (Philadelphia, 1906); *The Administration of an Institutional Church* (in collaboration with J. Reichert; New York, 1906); *The Happy Family* (1906); *The Pursuit of Happiness* (1906); *The Year of Grace* (1907); *Holderness: Account of the Beginnings of a New Hampshire Town* (Boston, 1907); *Apprenticeship of Washington* (New York, 1909); *The Garden of Eden* (Boston, 1909); *The Training of Children in Religion* (New York, 1911); and *Everyman's Religion* (1911).

HOEFFDING, HARALD: Danish philosopher; b. at Copenhagen Mar. 11, 1843. He was educated at the university of his native city (cand. theol., 1865; Ph.D., 1870), and, after teaching in schools for several years, became, in 1880, privat-docent for philosophy at the University of Copenhagen, where he has been full professor of the same subject since 1883. Much influenced in his earlier years by S. A. Kierkegaard (q.v.), Höffding later turned to Positivism (q.v.). Among his writings the most noteworthy are *Philosophien i Tydskland efter Hegel* (Copenhagen, 1872), *Den engelske Filosofi i vor Tid* (1874), *Etik* (1876), *Spinozas Liv og Lære* (1877), *Psychologi i Omrids* (1882; Eng. transl. by M. E. Lowndes, *Outlines of Psychology*, London, 1891), *Psychologiske Undersögelser* (1889), *Charles Darwin* (1889), *Sören Kierkegaard som Filosof* (1892), *Kontinuiteten i Kants filosofiske Udviklingsgang* (1893), *Den nyere Filosofis Historie* (1894; Eng. transl. by B. E. Meyer, *History of Modern Philosophy*, 2 vols., London, 1900), *Jean Jacques Rousseau og hans Filosofi* (1896), *Det psykologiske Grundlag for logiske Domme* (1899), *Mindre Arbejder* (1899), and *Philosophische Probleme* (Leipsic, 1903; Eng. transl. by G. M. Fisher, *Problems of Philosophy*, London, 1906), and he is likewise the author of *Philosophy of Religion* (1901; Eng. transl. by B. E. Meyer, London, 1906), *Modern Philosophers* (1903), and *Human Thought* (1910).

ILLINGWORTH, JOHN RICHARDSON: Church of England; b. in London June 26, 1848. He was educated at Christ Church, Oxford (B.A., 1871), and was ordered deacon in 1875 and priested in the following year. From 1872 to 1883 he was fellow of Jesus College, Oxford, and tutor of Keble College in the same university, and since the latter year he has been rector of Longworth, Berkshire, as well as honorary canon of Christ Church, Oxford, since 1905. He was select preacher at Oxford in 1882 and 1891 and at Cambridge in 1884 and 1895, and was Bampton lecturer in 1894. Besides two essays in Charles Gore's *Lux Mundi* (London, 1890), he has written *Sermons Preached in a College Chapel* (London, 1888), *University and Cathedral Sermons* (1893), *Personality, Human and Divine* (Bampton lectures, 1894), *Divine Immanence* (1898), *Reason and Revelation* (1902), *Christian Character* (1904), *The Doctrine of the Trinity* (1907), and *Divine Transcendence and its Reflection in Religious Authority* (1911).

JACKSON, SAMUEL MACAULEY: Editor-in-chief of this Encyclopedia; b. in New York City June 19, 1851. He was graduated from the College of the City of New York (1870) and Union Theological Seminary (1873); was Presbyterian pastor at Norwood, N. J., 1876–80; and has since been engaged in literary work. He is honorary fellow of the Huguenot Society of London, president of the board of trustees of the Christian College of Canton, China, and president elect (1912) of the American Society of Church History.

KALOPOTHAKES, MICHAEL DEMETRIUS: Greek Protestant; b. at Areopolis (27 m. s. of Sparta), Laconia, Dec. 20, 1825; d. at Athens June 29, 1911. He came of a family of considerable distinction, and at the age of ten entered a school which had recently been established at Aeropolis by two American Presbyterian missionaries, G. W. Leyburn and S. Houston, where he formed the habit of daily reading and study of the Bible. He then spent two years (1841–43) in the gymnasium at Athens, and on graduation was for five Early Life years head master of an intermediate and Con- school at Gytheion, in Laconia. After version to five years of study in the medical Protes-   school of the University of Athens tantism. (M.D., 1853), Kalopothakes entered the army as a surgeon. In 1850 he had become a regular attendant at the services conducted by the American missionary Jonas King (q.v.), and when King was condemned judicially for attacking the Greek Church by publishing extracts from the Greek Church Fathers against the worship of the saints and of the Virgin, Kalopothakes, hitherto a member of the Orthodox Church, felt himself unable to remain connected with a communion which could countenance such a course on the part of the government. He accordingly determined to devote himself to the cause of religious liberty in Greece, and, after taking the regular course at Union Theological Seminary, New York City, he was ordained by the East Hanover Presbytery of Virginia in 1857 and returned to Greece to take up his life-work.

Perceiving that the only way of beginning his task would be through the press, to which the Greek constitution allows wide scope, Kalopothakes determined to found a religious paper which should stand for entire liberty of conscience, and be the means of disseminating Protestant doctrines among a far wider circle than could be reached by pulpit-preaching. He accordingly established, in 1858, the weekly (now fortnightly) " Star of the East," which, by reason of its criticisms of Wide Scope the established church, exposed its edi- of his   tor for nearly two decades to the most Activities. virulent attacks from his opponents.

From 1859 until his retirement from active life in 1904 Kalopothakes was also Greek agent for the British and Foreign Bible Society, and for a few years he held a similar position under the American Bible Society until it withdrew from Greece in 1886. In this capacity Kalopothakes traveled widely throughout the country, often in considerable personal danger, but he succeeded in

establishing a system of colporteurs, whom he superintended for forty-five years. This circulation of the Scriptures Kalopothakes regarded as of paramount importance for the regeneration of Greece, yet he also saw the necessity of the dissemination of religious tracts and books to impress upon the people the duty of studying and obeying the Bible. In this work he received invaluable assistance from the Religious Tract Society of London, and besides this phase of his activity he found time to publish not only several volumes of his own sermons and a long series of " Children's Special Service Mission " leaflets, but also translations of such works as Butler's *Analogy*, Bunyan's *Pilgrim's Progress*, and A. A. Hodge's *Outlines of Theology*, while from 1868 to 1894 he was also editor of the illustrated monthly " Child's Paper," of which he had been the founder.

Previous to 1864 Kalopothakes did not preach, his time being too fully occupied by his work in publication. In 1860 he opened the first Sunday-school in Greece, to which even children of Orthodox parents came until, eight weeks later, the school was mobbed, after which only the His Work children of the few Greek Protestants as a Pastor. then in Athens were received. During this period a small group of Protestants formed about him, their meetings being held in King's house until King discontinued his preaching in 1864; while from that year until 1871 they met in Kalopothakes' house, where he and George Constantine, the second Greek to enter the Protestant ministry, preached alternately. Kalopothakes had at first conducted his work independently of any missionary society, although small contributions were given him by the American and Foreign Christian Union and by the Virginian Synod of the Presbyterian Church of the United States. From the outbreak of the American Civil War until 1872 the American and Foreign Missionary Union supported his work, the Southern Presbyterian Church carrying it on from that year until 1886.

It was, however, the desire of Kalopothakes that the Greek Protestant churches should be self-supporting, and in 1886, after four organizations—at Athens, Piræus, Volo, and Janina—had been formed, the Greek Evangelical Synod was constituted, the church at Salonica being added in 1893. Since 1886, therefore, Greek Protestant work has been carried on by this synod, with the aid of friends in England and the United States; and in 1894, Results of that he might be free for the manifold his Labors. activities demanded by the synod, Kalopothakes resigned the pastorate of the Athens church, which he had established in 1870. This work for the synod, together with his labors for the Bible Society and the publication department, occupied him until his death, and in his closing years he could see Greek Protestants possessed of a constitutional guaranty of freedom of worship and speech, this arousing the Orthodox Church to renewed activity to counteract the influences of Protestantism. Kalopothakes likewise had intense sympathy with the poor and suffering. He was connected for years with various philanthropic societies, such as the Parnassos Club for newsboys; he was one of the founders of the Greek Society for the Prevention of Cruelty to Animals; he habitually visited prisoners, to whom he was often permitted to preach; and during the Cretan insurrection of 1866–69 he not only assisted in relieving the Cretan refugees, but he also established in the suburbs of Athens schools for thousands of refugee children.

DEMETRIUS KALOPOTHAKES.

KRUMBACHER, KARL: German scholar of Byzantine and modern Greek literature; b. at Kürnach (a hamlet near Würzburg) Sept. 23, 1856; d. at Munich Dec. 12, 1909. He was educated at the universities of Munich and Leipsic, and from 1879 to 1892 was teacher in a gymnasium in Munich, but in the latter year was appointed associate professor of Byzantine and modern Greek at the University of Munich, being promoted to the full professorship five years later. He is especially noted for his great *Geschichte der byzantinischen Literatur* (Munich, 1890; 2d ed., 1897), and for his founding of the *Byzantinische Zeitschrift* in 1892, supplemented by the *Byzantinisches Archiv* in 1898. He is, indeed, one of the few figures of prominence in the field of Byzantine research that Germany has yet produced. Among his other works the most noteworthy are *Griechische Reise* (Berlin, 1886), *Studien zu den Legenden des heiligen Theodosius* (Munich, 1892), *Mittelgriechische Sprichwörter* (1893), *Das Problem der neugriechischen Schriftsprache* (1903), *Miscellen zu Romanos* (1907), and *Populäre Aufsätze* (Leipsic, 1909).

LAY PREACHING.

Conditions in the Primitive Church (§ 1).
Decay of Lay Preaching until the Middle Ages (§ 2).
Medieval and Pre-Reformation Revival (§ 3).
English Reformation and Commonwealth Periods (§ 4).
The Quakers (§ 5).
John Wesley and the Lay Preachers (§ 6).
The Primitive Methodist Connection (§ 7).
In the Scotch Presbyterian and Anglican Churches (§ 8).
The Salvation Army (§ 9).
In the Foreign Mission Field (§ 10).
In Labor Circles; Other Recent Movements (§ 11).
Beneficial Results to Pastorate Churches (§ 12).

Lay preaching, commonly described in Great Britain as local preaching, is voluntary unpaid pulpit-service, or open-air or cottage evangelism, by men, sometimes women, who are commissioned by their denomination to preach, after undergoing a certain examinational test, but without receiving ordination. There is **1. Condi-** out receiving ordination. There is **tions in the** Old-Testament justification for lay **Primitive** preaching in Moses' wish that " all **Church.** the Lord's people were prophets " (Num. xi. 29), and in the free operation of the prophetic spirit, which sent out such men as Hosea, Micah, and Amos, though they did not belong to the priestly order. The New-Testament justification is in the facts that Christ himself received no ecclesiastical commission, neither did any of his disciples, while Paul claimed to have received his commission not from the hands of men, but direct from Christ himself (Gal. i. 1). Advocates of lay preaching claim that in the apostolic churches there was no distinction between clergy and laity, but that the members of the church were expected to exercise whatever evangelistic or teaching gift they possessed. It must be remembered that the first Christian churches were largely " churches in the house," nor did the idea of a pastorate church arise until the necessity for pastoral oversight became urgent, as the churches increased in membership and perfected their organization. During that primitive period the churches were dependent on the prophetic gift of such members as possessed it, and the clerical order gradually evolved itself to meet the need of continuous specialized oversight, while the development of dogma and the combat with multiplying heresies strengthened the idea of an ordained clergy commissioned to teach what the Church, as a whole, held to be the fundamentals of the faith. The clergy took on increasingly a sacerdotal character, and the dogmatism and the sacerdotalism, together, told against the continuance of lay evangelism. There was always the possibility that the lay preacher, unskilled in theological polemic and with undisciplined enthusiasm, might commit himself to dangerous positions, playing into the hands of the heretical sects and leading the people astray. The " liberty of prophesying " was checked, and by the middle of the second century it is probable that lay evangelism, except in missionary fields, was almost abandoned.

In the middle of the second century, however, the Montanist movement in Asia Minor led to a revival of enthusiastic lay preaching (see MONTANUS, MONTANISM). The Montanists laid the greatest stress on the inspiration, by the Holy Spirit, of believing men and women **2. Decay** without distinction, and without regard **of Lay** to any authorized clerical channels. **Preaching** Montanus associated with himself two **until the** prophetesses, and the enthusiasm of **Middle** the sect generated a host of preach- **Ages.** ers who gave prominence to the concepts of the dignity of the universal Christian calling and the royal priesthood of all Christians. With many extravagances, Montanism was the precursor of Puritanism and non-conformity, especially in the place which non-conformity has given to lay evangelism. With the downfall of the Roman Empire and the adoption of Latin, fast becoming a dead language, as the language in which the Bible was to be read and liturgies to be performed, lay preaching became more and more impossible. The ministry demanded a scholastic training; liturgical practise usurped the place of preaching; and the layman was reduced to the position of a submissive hearer. Yet throughout the Middle Ages the lay preacher sprang up sporadically and had a hearing, for he at least could talk to the people in their own tongue, and whenever there was a movement of spiritual revival there was a reappearance of lay preaching.

The leaders of all the medieval revivals recognized the value of the lay preacher. St. Francis of Assisi's Minorites were laymen, and throughout Europe they traveled, artizans most of them, who earned their living by working at their trades. Francis founded also his order of Tertiaries, or Brothers and Sisters of Penitence, who made their direct appeal to the working classes whence they sprang, finding their flocks in the slums and hovels of overcrowded cities and neglected suburbs (see FRANCIS, SAINT, OF ASSISI, AND THE FRANCISCAN ORDER).

3. Medieval and Pre-Reformation Revival. The same revival of lay preaching took place in Germany for two centuries preceding the Reformation. The Brethren of the Common Life (see COMMON LIFE, BRETHREN OF THE) was founded with the double object of a return to simplicity of Christian living and of evangelism of "the common people"; the Brothers united in communities, and worked at their various trades. They were laymen, trained to preach in the vulgar tongue, and the tenets of the Church, when introduced in their preaching, were practically applied, rather than doctrinally expounded, while their discourses were enlivened by examples and confirmed by the statements of wise and experienced teachers. Collations, which were a sort of edifying private addresses, and possessed still more of a popular character, served among the Brethren as a supplement to preaching. They took place first in the community-houses, in each of which, upon the afternoons of Sundays and saints' days, a collation was given and a passage of Scripture, especially from the Gospels, was read, explained, and practically applied, while occasionally, in order to enliven and improve the discourse, questions were addressed by the speaker to the audience. The Brethren of the Common Life did very much to prepare the Germans for the Reformation, and it was the Reformation which ended their existence by taking over their work. In England Wyclif did not scruple to send out "unauthorized preachers," with Bible-portions in the vulgar tongue, who preached simple, practical Gospel sermons in homely style to homely people. It is probable that some of the "unauthorized" preachers had received priestly orders, although they lacked the bishop's license to preach; some, however, were laymen pure and simple.

The English Reformation did not, as might have been expected, lead to any immediate revival of lay preaching. This was largely due to the heavy hand of the State on the clergy, whose **4. English Reformation and Commonwealth Periods.** preaching was restricted as much as possible lest it might prove too exciting, and to the penal laws against all separation from the State Church. But when the conflict came between the Stuarts and the Puritans, the lay preacher began to assert himself; and the more the State Church sought to repress nonconformist ministers, the more willing were devout dissidents from the State Church to listen to the lay preacher. In a petition to James I. on his accession, the Independents and others held that laymen, "discreet, faithful, and able men, though not in the office of the ministry," might be appointed to preach the Gospel. There was, however, considerable division of opinion in the Puritan ranks on the subject, for the Independents and Presbyterians were engaged in defending the freely chosen minister of a "separated church" as divinely commissioned equally with the minister episcopally ordained, and it was feared that the use of lay preachers might prejudice the controversial claim. Crom-

well supported lay preaching and sharply rebuked the Presbyterians who were the chief Puritan objectors to it. There was a great deficiency of preachers during the time of the Civil War, especially as hostilities had brought university work to a standstill, but the pious soldiers of the Parliamentary armies remedied the deficiency by raising preachers in their own ranks who exercised their gifts in camps and garrisons. Parliament took the matter in hand and required intending preachers to submit to a test of their gifts, " by those who shall be appointed thereto by both Houses of Parliament "; but the soldiers ignored the direction and were loyal to their favorite preachers.

The rise of the Quakers was the first example of a sect dependent entirely on lay evangelism. George Fox (q.v.), like Montanus, held as a primary article of faith that the Holy Spirit inspires men and women irrespective of all human **5. The Quakers.** ordinances, and that the man or woman so inspired is bound to exercise the prophetic gift. Fox and his followers traveled the country over, fearlessly preaching their gospel. Under Cromwell the Quakers were allowed the largest liberty, and Fox organized Quaker lay preaching. In 1663 thirty itinerant preachers were with him and the number was doubled in the following year; a woman preacher belonged to his little band as early as 1650, and he had seventy-three women evangelists at his command before his death. All the Friends, to this day, give equal rights to men and women preachers. The Quaker preachers were great missionaries. They established themselves in New England, and it seemed likely that they would become the dominant spiritual power in several States. The audacity of the Quakers is almost incredible, for George Robinson preached in Jerusalem, and Mary Fisher succeeded in delivering a gospel message to Mohammed IV. in full divan, encompassed with his army, girt with glittering, adoring courtiers.

The cold wave of rationalism almost quenched lay preaching in England, while the tolerance of non-conformity, with the freedom given for the training of ministers and the opening of chapels, made it seem unnecessary. The evangelical revival came, however, and established lay preach- **6. John Wesley and the Lay Preachers.** ing on such a footing as has made it the mainstay of Methodist evangelization ever since. John Wesley himself, as an ordained Anglican clergyman, was at first prejudiced against lay preaching, but he later changed his position and himself undertook the training of lay preachers, for whose instruction many of his books were primarily written. In 1745 he replied to attacks on lay preaching in his *Farther Appeal to Men of Reason and Religion*, reminding critics of the severe examination of lay preachers in practical and experimental theology, calling attention to the fact that the Jewish scribes, who were the ordinary preachers of their time, were laymen, and showing that in Sweden, Germany, Holland, and in almost every Reformed Church of Europe, before any one was ordained he was required to preach publicly for a year or more *ad probandum facultatem*. It is noteworthy that to this day Wesleyan Methodist lay preachers, before being "put on the plan," have to pass an examination in Wesley's *Notes on the New Testament* and his *Fifty-three Standard Sermons*, in addition to examination on the leading doctrines of Christianity, and giving an account of their conversion, their Christian experience, and their vocation. When the Methodist Quarterly Meeting—the circuit governing body, and the unit of the denominational organization—was constituted, the local preachers "on the plan" were made members of it *ex officio*.

The Methodist lay preachers were the means by which Methodism spread so rapidly not only over Great Britain, but also over the United States and throughout the English-speaking world. They were the advance guard of Methodism; cottage meetings and open-air meetings, supplied by lay preachers, prepared the way for chapels, which

7. The Primitive Methodist Connection. were the permanent garrisons of the districts occupied. The "traveling Methodist preacher" might have ten to thirty chapels and mission-stations under his oversight, and, with thirty to fifty lay preachers "on the plan," he arranged quarterly for all the pulpits to be filled, while "mission bands" of lay preachers carried on aggressive evangelistic campaigns in towns and villages as yet unoccupied. The lay preachers were drawn from all classes— university graduates, country gentlemen, business men, artizans, and agricultural laborers being on the same "plan." This promoted fellowship, and saved the Methodist Church from being divided into class cliques to the extent that has happened in some other churches. After the Wesleys had passed away, the connection underwent a cooling-period, for its own success tended toward a satisfied settling down. "Field preaching" lost favor, and the lay preachers were subjected to restrictions that became irksome to the more enthusiastic spirits. In many circuits "field preaching" was classed among irregular exercises which were better left alone. These restrictions were the cause of the origin (1807–11) of the Primitive Methodist Connection (see METHODISTS, I., 4) which, next to the mother Church, has made the greatest use of lay preaching. Two lay preachers on the Tunstall (Staffordshire) plan, Hugh Bourne and William Clowes, organized an "All Day of Prayer," on Mow Cop, a prominent hill. This drew a vast crowd, and there were many conversions, but it had not received official sanction, and Bourne and Clowes were refused their class tickets, which meant exclusion from the "plan." They accordingly formed independent "classes," which united in the Primitive Methodist Connection, which has in 1911 completed its centenary celebration by raising a thanksgiving fund of £300,000. In its early years this church depended almost entirely on lay preachers, men and sometimes women, who revived the evangelistic fervor and audacity of the first Methodists, and invaded every part of the country, establishing themselves in special strength in the colliery and rural districts, and in such fishery-centers as Hull and Grimsby.

Scotland, early in the nineteenth century, saw a very remarkable revival movement in which the principal part was played by Presbyterian laymen.

The movement was led by the brothers James and Robert Haldane (qq.v.). In 1800 the General Assembly prohibited field preaching,

8. In the Scotch Presbyterian and Anglican Churches. whereupon there was a secession by Robert Haldane, who trained 300 young men. These went out stirring up revival feeling everywhere, and the Church of Scotland, the United Free Church, and the United Church alike shared in the raising of the spiritual temperature. Recognizing the value of lay evangelism, the Anglican Church, in the middle of the nineteenth century, instituted lay readers, or laymen who, after examination, receive the bishop's license to preach under strictly prescribed conditions. The commission entitles the holder "to conduct, in any parish to which he may be licensed, services in school and other rooms and in the open air, and also such extra services in consecrated buildings as the incumbent may wish and as the bishop may approve; and, further, to perform occasionally similar duties in any other parish in the diocese at the request of the incumbent." There are now between 2,500 and 3,000 Anglican lay readers, among them being peers, judges, knights, members of parliament, and eminent professional men.

The marvel of the nineteenth century, so far as lay preaching is concerned, was the founding by General William Booth (q.v.) of the Salvation Army (q.v.). Booth was a United Methodist Free Church minister, but he left that church to start an independent "Christian Mission" in East London.

9. The Salvation Army. He conceived the idea of an evangelistic movement with a military organization, and his wife, Catharine Booth (q.v.), rivaled him in organizing-ability and driving-power. The Salvation Army, now working in nearly every country of the world, has something like 16,000 "officers," all evangelists, men and women, and all laics. They receive training from three to nine months, with an extension in special cases, and are then sent out with authority to preach. At first General Booth disliked the idea of women preachers, but his objection was overcome by a friend taking him to hear a woman preacher at a chapel in Fetter Lane, London. The Anglican Church founded the Church Army (q.v.) on the model of the Salvation Army, but it has been clerically directed, and women preachers are not admitted. The Salvation Army has worked in the lowest stratum of society, the "submerged tenth," and its lay preaching has not suffered from the exiguity of its training, as it would have done if it had ministered to more critical classes. It has had countless conversions, and its social salvage operations have won for it the support of many governments.

Lay preaching has been a valuable auxiliary to missionary evangelism. The Wesleyan and Primitive Methodist Missionaries have introduced the circuit system, with its "plan" of local preachers, and when native converts have given evidence of Christian character and spiritual experience, with the gift of speaking, and have undergone an examination in Biblical and theological knowledge, they have been sent out to the mission-stations and have largely increased the area of influence of the mission. In Uganda, the Anglican Church has multiplied lay evangelists, and to that multiplication is due the rapid and complete Christianization of the country. The China Inland Mission, worked mainly by lay missionaries, has made very large use of native lay evangelists, undeterred by the fear which denominational missions have had of making premature use of converts for such responsible work. Within the last few years, however, the London Missionary Society and other societies working in the more civilized provinces of China have begun to make freer use of lay preachers, this becoming easier as the Chinese have taken advantage of modern educational facilities.

10. In the Foreign Mission Field.

In Great Britain the by-products of lay preaching have been exceedingly valuable. In lay preaching men have acquired the art of clear and logical thinking and the gift of powerful and lucid expression. Such men naturally become the spokesmen of the community to which they belong; they are leaders of the local public life, and are elected to town councils, district councils, boards of guardians, and other public bodies, where their lay-preaching experience proves an invaluable advantage. The trade-unionism of England is largely led by lay preachers, who, in the service of the churches, have developed their business capacity and their speaking-power, and have trained themselves to become the forcible mouthpieces and the trusted leaders of their fellow craftsmen. There are at least a score of lay preachers in the British parliament, a dozen of whom belong to the Labor Party, most of them being officials of great trade-unions. It is certain that it is this leadership by religious men, trained in lay preaching, that has saved the British labor movement from the agnostic and materialistic socialism characteristic of the labor movement of the continent of Europe. Lay preaching accounts for the high numerical position taken by the Methodist and the Baptist Churches in the Southern States of America. In the Northern States the lay preacher has never taken the position accorded to him in Great Britain, but the feeling is growing that the creation of bodies of lay preachers in the various churches would enable those churches to maintain their position in villages and country towns, where migration of population has made it difficult to support the pastorate, since with a corps of lay preachers one minister might act as pastor-in-chief of a group of churches within a workable district. During the last ten years the principal non-conformist churches of Great Britain have done much to improve the organization and training of their lay preachers, who are trained in " correspondence classes," papers being set monthly in denominational lay preachers' magazines, while names of accredited Baptist lay preachers are included in the denominational *Year Book.*

11. In Labor Circles; Other Recent Movements.

In Great Britain the lay preachers are being increasingly used by their denominations and by the Free Church Councils to carry on outdoor evangelism during the summer months. It is found that their knowledge of the people among whom they live, and with whom they work in similar conditions, enables them to speak very effectively to casual gatherings of hearers who have dropped out of church attendance, and who often have misconceptions as to what the churches really teach and as to the Bible and the Christian religion. These lay preachers have intimate knowledge of the prejudices that keep people out of churches, and of the many reasons, good or bad, that account for their indifference to religion and their hostility to churches. The lay preacher in the open air is the surest antidote to the agnostic materialist park and street-corner orator. The success of the Brotherhood movement and the Adult Sunday Morning School movement, which have a collective membership of three-quarters of a million, is largely owing to the speaking- and teaching-power of the lay preachers. While it is recognized that the average lay preacher can not be fairly expected to make himself an expert in Biblical and theological scholarship, he has distinct advantages which ordained ministers frankly recognize. When working in collaboration with and under the direction of a minister, the lay preacher enables a pastorate church to establish mission-halls in poor districts and mission-stations in the villages. In the county of Surrey, for example, the Congregational Church at Guildford has established ten village stations supplied by forty lay preachers, while the church in the neighboring county town of Godalming has established six village stations. It is found that the drawing into actual evangelistic service of members of a church has a most beneficial influence on the church-life, for the minister feels that with so many preachers in his congregation he has an appreciative and critical audience and that he must always preach at his best.

12. Beneficial Results to Pastorate Churches.

Statistics of Lay Preachers.

GREAT BRITAIN (1911)

Wesleyan Methodists	19,578
Primitive Methodists	16,241
United Methodist Church	6,239
Baptists	5,692
Congregationalists	5,438
Churches of Christ	580
Wesleyan Reform Union	520
Calvinistic Methodists	344
Disciples of Christ	20
	54,662

UNITED STATES (1908)

Methodist Episcopal Church	14,057
African Methodist Episcopal	15,885
Methodist Episcopal South	4,800
Colored Methodist Episcopal	2,786
African Methodist Episcopal Zion	1,520
Free Methodist	1,299
Methodist Protestant	1,135
African Union Methodist Protestant	750
Other Methodist Churches	665
	42,847

H. JEFFS.

BIBLIOGRAPHY: A. P. Stanley, *Christian Institutions*, London, 1881; C. Ullmann, *Reformers before the Reformation*, 2 vols., Edinburgh, 1874–77; W. G. Townsend, H. B. Workman, and G. Eayrs, *New History of Method-*

ism, London, 1909; H. B. Kendall, *History of the Primitive Methodist Church*, London, 1905; J. Telford, *Lay Preaching in the Christian Church*, London, 1896; S. Horne, *Popular History of the Free Churches*, London, 1903; A. L. Garvie, *Guide to Preaching*, London, 1906; H. Jeffs, *Practical Lay Preaching*, London, 1907; idem, *Modern Minor Prophets*, London, 1909.

LINDBERG, CONRAD EMIL: Lutheran; b. at Jönköping (80 m. e. of Gothenburg), Sweden, June 9, 1852. He was educated at the gymnasium of his native city; Augustana College, Rock Island, Ill.; Augustana Theological Seminary (1872); and Philadelphia Lutheran Theological Seminary (1876). He was pastor successively of Zion Church, Philadelphia (1876–79), and Gustavus Adolphus Lutheran Church, New York (1879–90), being also president of the New York Conference of the Augustana Synod from 1879 to 1889. Since 1890 he has been professor of systematic theology, liturgics, and church polity at Augustana Theological Seminary, Rock Island, and has also been vice-president of the Augustana Synod (1899–1907), and vice-president of Augustana College (1901–10), besides being a member of his synodical mission board since 1899 and a member of the committees on the Swedish and English catechism (1894–1902) and liturgy (1894–99). Theologically he belongs to the conservative wing, and he has written, besides many minor contributions, as to the *Augustana Theological Quarterly* (of which he was chief editor in 1900–02), the following treatises in Swedish: " Exegesis on the First Three Chapters of the Book of Revelation " (Chicago, 1883), " On Baptism " (New York, 1890), " Syllabus in Church Polity " (Rock Island, 1897), and " Dogmatics and History of Dogmas " (1898). In 1901 he was decorated by the king of Sweden with the Royal Order of the North Star.

MONOPHYSITISM AND THE ORIENTAL SEPARATED CHURCHES.

I. The Monophysite Controversies: The incarnation of Christ has given to the historic development of human life an irresistibly transforming impulse, and to human thought an even more irresistibly transforming intuition of the relation of God to man and of man to God. Divinity descends to humanity, that humanity may ascend to divinity. From the beginning of that earthly ministry to man, the first followers saw in the person of Christ the Messianic ideal of humanity (cf. the synoptic gospels), a Godlike man. He was so real to their expectant Jewish minds that his perfect humanity seemingly obscured his hidden divinity, and it was only later, after the resurrection and the ascension, when they saw no longer the once visible presence of the Messiah of Israel, that they began to perceive the reality of his invisible yet truly incarnated divinity (cf. the Johannine gospel), a manlike God, " the Word made flesh." Henceforth the question came continually to the minds of men, was this a man become God, or a God become man, since both conceptions of the relation of divinity and humanity have persisted from the primitive period of human history. The answer of the Evangelists and the Apostles is that Christ the Messiah was truly God and truly man. The Christian Church of that apostolic and subapostolic age was a preaching, proselyting, and expanding missionary ecclesia. Exact theological definition and dogmatic declaration were alike alien to its primitive principles and antagonistic to that first freedom in the faith. But the speculative tendencies of those transitional times

1. Early Views on the Two Natures of Christ.

soon showed that two opposite opinions concerning the person of the Messiah Christ were already active. The one was that of the Jewish Ebionites (q.v.), who, tenacious of the inherited tradition of those first followers, permitted the historic presence of his visible humanity to obscure or occlude his invisible divinity. This erroneous overemphasis of the humanity of the Messiah, which was evoked by a defective perception of his dual nature as true God and true man, was not as evident during the apostolic age as it afterward became, when it persisted in more or less definite denials of his true divinity. The other opinion was that of the Jewish and Gentile Gnostics (see GNOSTICISM), who, seeking to combine the Christian revelation with various Oriental and Greek systems of speculative cosmology, and equally tenacious of acquired dualistic tendencies, permitted their differing theories of the divine Logos to obscure or occlude his visible humanity; and this equally erroneous exaltation of the Logos Christ above the material world in which he had been incarnated led logically to that overemphasis of his invisible divinity, which was likewise evoked by a defective perception of his dual nature as true man and true God, which had been more or less evident from the first in the doubt, or in the docetic denial, of his true humanity (see DOCETISM).

The insidious, persistent influences of these two speculative schools of opposite opinions, neither perceiving the dual aspect of the traditional apostolic teaching that in Christ the Messiah and the incarnate Logos both divinity and humanity must be united in the one person of the Redeemer of man, was to become more and more evident in the Christological controversies of the succeeding centuries. Convincing evidence of the pervading presence, in the subconscious theological thought

2. Controversies between Judaizing and Platonizing Schools.
of the Christian Church, of these differing speculative tendencies concerning the person of the Messiah and Logos became manifest toward the end of the second century, during the controversy caused by the first definite coordination of Christ as God with the indefinite Mosaic monotheism of Old-Testament tradition. The Judaizing school of Christians seemingly taught more or less publicly that the Messiah was a man in whom divinity, or the Spirit of God, had dwelt during his earthly existence. Defending their doctrine from texts of the synoptic Gospels, they tended in their teaching toward the error of Ebionitism during their constant Christological controversy with the opposing Platonizing school of Christians. These latter taught, on the contrary, the preexistence and the eternity of the incarnate Logos. Defending their doctrine from texts of the Johannine Gospel, they tended, in their ditheism—as their Judaizing opponents declared—toward the error of Gnosticism and the docetic denial of the real humanity of Christ. Yet the Messianic teaching of the Judaizers themselves, although apparently truly accepting Christ as the Redeemer of men, continued to cling to that indefinite Mosaic monotheism from whose persistent presence throughout Asia Minor was developed later not only the definite heresy of dynamic Monarchianism (q.v.), which denied the essential divinity of Christ, or asserted it to be a power imparted to his humanity, but also the opposite, though related, heresy of modalistic Monarchianism, known also as that of Sabellius, and of the Patripassians, who admitted the divinity, but denied the personality, of Christ.

During the continuance of these first Christological controversies in the ante-conciliar Church, there were slowly and silently established two ecclesiastical schools of Scripture-study and theological teaching, Antioch and Alexandria (see ANTIOCH, SCHOOL OF; ALEXANDRIA, SCHOOL OF). The school of Antioch, influenced by the Jewish traditions of Syria, was literal, grammatical, and historic in its exegesis; yet this very literalistic interpretation, applied to the synoptic Gospels, tended

3. Struggle between Antiochene and Alexandrine Theology.
constantly toward that characteristic overemphasis of the humanity of Christ which exposed its Christological teaching to the insidious Ebionitic influence persisting in the doctrines of the dynamic and the modalistic Monarchianists. The school of Alexandria, influenced by the Greek traditions of that famous center of philosophical speculation, was free, allegorical, and mystical in its exegesis. Thus its freer interpretation, the opposite in method of the rival school of Antioch, of the Johannine Gospel tended continually toward that characteristic overemphasis of the divinity of the incarnate Logos which exposed its Christological teaching to the influence of Gnostic docetism that denied or ignored the real humanity of Christ. Soon after the middle of the third century, the traditionally opposite tendencies of these

two ecclesiastical schools came into conflict during the doctrinal dissensions caused by the teaching of Paul of Samosata (see MONARCHIANISM, IV., §§ 2–3). He, while bishop of Antioch, was impelled to assert again the characteristic Antiochene overemphasis of the human nature of Christ in terms of a modified dynamic Monarchianism, in opposition to the traditional Alexandrine tendency of overemphasizing the divinity of the Logos, already developing in the words of the later Trinitarian teaching of the councils of the Church. The teaching of Paul was condemned as heretical by several successive synods assembled at Antioch to compare his doctrine with that deduced from the traditional orthodox teaching of the several apostolic sees. What this traditional apostolic teaching of the Christian Church was during this ante-conciliar age is shown by the following " Confession of Faith " of the synod convened at Antioch in 251, the heads of which were Dionysius of Rome and Dionysius of Alexandria (qq.v.), while Gregory Thaumaturgus (q.v.) was also an important figure:

" We believe that our Lord Jesus Christ, who was of God and the Father, who was begotten before the worlds of the Spirit, but in the end of days was born of a virgin in the flesh, is one compound person of heavenly deity and human flesh; and also in this, that he is man, wholly God and wholly man; wholly God and with a body, but not in this, that the flesh is God; and wholly man and with man, and with deity, but not in this, that the Deity is man. So also he is wholly to be worshiped, and with the body, but not in this, that the body is to be worshiped; wholly to be worshiped and with the Deity, but not in this, that the Deity is to be worshiped (apart from the body?); wholly increate and with a body, but not in this, that the body is increate; wholly made and with the Deity; but not in this, that the Deity is made; wholly coessential with God, and with the body, but not in this, that the body is coessential with God; as not in this, that God is coessential with man; though with Deity in the flesh, he is coessential with us. For also when we say that he, being in the Spirit, is a partaker of the nature of God, we say not that he in the Spirit is a partaker of the nature of man. And again, when we declare him in the flesh a partaker of the nature of man, we declare him not in the flesh a partaker of the nature of God. For as in the Spirit, he is not connatural with us, because he is herein coessential with God; so in the flesh he is not connatural with God, because he is a partaker of our nature. Now these things we correct and approve, not the dividing of one person indivisible, but the unconfused peculiar confession of the flesh and of the Deity." (B. H. Cowper, *Syriac Miscellanies*, pp. 40–41, London, 1861.)

This ante-conciliar Christological confession of faith evidently contains within itself the complete cause of the subsequent Chalcedonian controversy which resulted historically in the century-long charge against the primitive national churches of the East that they teach the Eutychian error, are Monophysites (see EUTYCHIANISM; MONOPHYSITES), and, therefore, are heretical in their Christology.

That same insidious Ebionitic influence, whose persistent presence in the differing doctrines of Monarchianism had caused the condemnation of Paul of Samosata, appeared again in the erroneous teaching of Arius (see ARIANISM), denying the eternal divinity of the Logos, which was condemned as heretical by the first ecumenical council of the Church, convened in 325 at Nicæa. Later in the same century, the Alexandrine Apollinaris of Laodicea (q.v.), one of the chief defenders of the Athanasian Logos doctrine accepted by the Council of Nicæa, began to teach the error named from himself, that the humanity assumed by Christ in the incarnation was only a human body with its complementing animal soul, the Logos existing in the place of its missing spirit. This novel teaching was a proof of the tenacious presence, in Alexandrine Christological thought, of that insidious docetic influence from whence had come this definite denial of the real humanity of the Logos, condemned as heretical by the second ecumenical council, convened in 381 at Constantinople. During the controversy caused by the Alexandrine Apollinaris, who overemphasized the divinity of the Logos, the Antiochene Diodorus (q.v.), likewise one of the chief defenders of the conciliar Christology of Nicæa against the Arian schismatics, while opposing, as bishop of Tarsus, Apollinaris' docetic denial of the complete humanity of Christ, and though remaining faithful to the traditional teaching of his own synoptic school, developed a theory of the relation of the seemingly separate coexistence of the divine and the human natures in the one person of Christ which, through the teaching of his pupil, Theodore of Mopsuestia (q.v.), was to reappear in the doctrinal dissensions caused by Nestorius (q.v.) in the succeeding century.

4. Controversies of the Fourth Century.

A conflict between the traditional Christological teachings of the two rival schools was inevitable when the Antiochene Nestorius, soon after his elevation to the patriarchate at Constantinople, defended his Antiochene presbyter Anastasius in public protests against the use of the Alexandrine term *Theotokos* (" Mother of God ") as applied to the incarnation of the Logos in the Virgin Mary. This newer imperial see of Constantinople, established by Constantine the Great, was the object of persistent ecclesiastical plotting by the partizans of the apostolic see of Alexandria, the aggressive opponent of the equally apostolic see of Antioch, and each of these two rival schools of doctrine contested the theological terms used by the other. Thus it was that the bishop of Alexandria entered so eagerly into the strife caused by this Antiochene attack on the use of *Theotokos*. The fanatical Cyril (see CYRIL OF ALEXANDRIA) was very willing to become the accuser of the equally fanatical Nestorius, and each charged the other with defending that evident Christological error which the traditional teaching of his own school was suspected of propagating. It is doubtful whether or not Nestorius had really asserted a double personality in Christ, as the doctrine of his preceptor, Theodore of Mopsuestia (also ascribed to his predecessor, Diodorus of Tarsus [see DIODORUS]), seemed to teach, when he declared that the Logos was not inseparably incarnated in Christ, but had united his divinity with the man Jesus, " the Son of God dwelling in the Son of David "; and that, therefore, the Logos only cooperated with the human Jesus, two persons, a divine and a human, becoming one in will and act. The Antiochenes were consistently compelled to emphasize the humanity of Christ, in opposition to the Alexandrine overemphasis of the divinity of the Logos, evident in the do-

5. Conflict between Nestorius and Cyril of Alexandria.

cetism of the Apollinarian heresy. Cyril, after formulating twelve anathematizing statements of the alleged errors of Nestorius, including " that Immanuel is not really God, and the Virgin not *Theotokos;* that there was a connection (*synapheia*) of two persons; that Christ is a God-bearing man (*theophoros*); that he was a separate individual acted on by the Logos, and called ' God with him '; that his flesh was not truly that of the Logos; and that the Logos did not suffer death in the flesh," sought to compel his subscription to them. The answer of Nestorius was a counter-statement of twelve anathematizing articles of the alleged errors of Cyril. Alexandria, with its traditional emphasis on the divinity of the Logos, denied defiantly the orthodoxy of Antioch, with its traditional emphasis on the humanity of Christ.

The third ecumenical council was convened in 431 at Ephesus to declare and define the true teaching of the Church on this contested question of the relation of the divine and the human natures in the incarnate Logos Christ. Neither Christological school seemingly perceived that its doctrine was dogmatically defective in emphasizing a single aspect of the duality of the person of Christ, nor that their differing characteristic definitions could be combined in one orthodox statement. To the deliberate defiance of this truth by Cyril of Alexandria, who with his partizans controlled the proceedings of this council of Ephesus, can be confidently ascribed all those succeeding schisms and destructive divisions which were later to divide the Christian Church of the East into two antagonistic communions of confederated national churches, unreconciled to this day. The school of Antioch was at this time surprisingly conservative, for the teaching of Theodore of Mopsuestia, developed from that of his predecessor, Diodorus of Tarsus, and defended apparently by his own pupil, Nestorius, had not affected adversely its general orthodoxy, even in the opinion of its opponents. It depended on Alexandria, whether or not their truly complementing teachings were to be combined in a fuller form of the common Christological creed. But Cyril, defiant in his defense of the anathematizing articles rejected by the Antiochene Nestorius, and assured that his partizans predominated in the assembled council, continued in his predetermined course of condemning the errors ascribed to Nestorius and of deposing him from his episcopate, without awaiting the delayed arrival of John of Antioch and his Syrian suffragans, who, therefore, justly rejected, as contrary to the canons, all completed acts of the council. The third council of Ephesus having approved and adopted as its own declaration of dogma the twelve anathematizing articles of Cyril, every attempt thereafter on the part of the Antiochenes to emphasize the humanity of Christ against the Alexandrines was condemned by them as Nestorianism; and, on the contrary, every attempt on the part of the Alexandrines to emphasize the divinity of the Logos against the Antiochenes was denounced by them as Apollinarianism.

6. Condemnation of Nestorius.

Since the Antiochene bishops persisted in their

refusal to approve the anathematizing, anti-Nestorian articles of Alexandrine Cyril, a compromise between them was eventually effected by his subscription of a formula of faith prepared by them for the consideration of the council. This dogmatic declaration defines the Logos as being of one essence (*homoousion*) with the Father as to divinity, and of one essence with man as to humanity, for there was effected, say the Antiochene bishops, " a union of

7. Unavailing Compromise between Antioch and Alexandria.
two natures; whereupon we confess one Christ, one Son, one Lord. And according to the teaching of a union without confusion, we confess the holy Virgin to be *Theotokos*, because God the Son was incarnate and made man, and from his very conception united to himself the temple assumed from her " (Hefele, *Conciliengeschichte*, ii. 228). If this concise Christological creed of 431 be compared with the earlier Antiochene confession of 251, it is evident that, excepting the Athanasian term *homoousion* and the later Alexandrian *Theotokos*, the traditional teaching of the former common faith appears unchanged in the latter. In the first formula, the characteristic Christological confession of the incarnation of Christ the Logos is " one compound person of heavenly deity and human flesh "; in the second is seen " a union of two natures . . . without confusion," etc. The concluding declaration of the first formula, " Now these things we correct and approve, not the dividing of one person indivisible, but the unconfused peculiar confession of the flesh, and of the Deity," has no counterpart in the second, shorter symbol, although its causal connection with the attitude of the Syrians and, through them, of the Armenians, toward the Council of Chalcedon, which was soon to follow, will be shown below. This definite dogmatic declaration of the divine and the human natures in Christ the Logos was what the Antiochene bishops required of the Alexandrine Cyril as a test of his orthodoxy. But the compromise confession accepted by both parties neither conciliated nor satisfied the extremists of those two opposite Christological schools. Cyril had, after defining the natural distinction and necessary difference between the nature of God and the nature of man which before the incarnation are manifestly two natures and are combined in Christ, asserted that they are two only before the incarnation; in their union in the Incarnate Logos they cease to be two and become one. Thus Cyril, in deliberate defiance of the statement subscribed by himself, seemingly taught, as before, the indefinite earlier doctrine of the " one nature of the Word made flesh " of Athanasius (q.v.). According to this traditional Alexandrine teaching, the two natures, distinct before, became one after their union in Christ. The one divine person acted in and through both, but it was a single and, therefore, the divine activity, that of the Logos. This was condemned by the Antiochene school as undeniably docetic in its tendency. The Alexandrine school, in answer to this accusation, charged that the Antiochenes taught the Nestorianism condemned by the Council of Ephesus. This ceaseless Christological controversy could not fail to force

another conciliar conflict between the two rival schools.

In that same imperial city in which the Antiochene presbyter Anastasius, by denouncing, in 428, the Alexandrine term *Theotokos*, had caused the convening of the third ecumenical council in the city of Ephesus, the Alexandrine partizan Eutyches, archimandrite of a monastery near the city, by denouncing, in 448, the alleged Antiochene teaching of Nestorianism, was likewise to become the cause of the convening of the fourth and final council of the united Christian Church in the East. But without warning Eutyches himself was accused of heresy concerning the incarnation of Christ. Cited before the assembled synod of Con-

8. The Eutychian Controversy.
stantinople, he was compelled to confess teaching that the person of Christ was of, or out of, two natures, though not in two natures; that the two natures, distinct before the incarnation, after their union became one; that the human nature of the incarnate Son was changed, since the body of Christ, by union with divinity, became thereby different from that of other men. This docetic denial of the true humanity of Christ, evidently developed directly from the Alexandrine overemphasis of the divinity of the incarnate Logos, was condemned as heretical by this same synod, and its author was deposed from his dignities. Then Eutyches, who had already accused the Antiochenes to Leo (q.v.), bishop of Rome, of teaching tenaciously the Nestorianism condemned by the Council of Ephesus, sought his support, assuming that Leo, like himself, was a partizan of the deceased Cyril of Alexandria. Flavian, bishop of Constantinople (see FLAVIAN OF CONSTANTINOPLE), however, hoping to avert the threatened conciliar conflict, was the one who really secured the support of Leo, who had already sent him his " Tome " concerning the Christological controversy between the two opposite schools of doctrine. Now Dioscurus, the even more fanatical anti-Nestorian successor of Cyril of Alexandria, allying himself with the powerful political and the numerous monastic defenders of Eutyches against Flavian, and defeated in his attacks on the regularity and canonical course of the synod which had both denounced and degraded that aggressive partizan of his predecessor, secured from the emperor the summoning of a pseudo-council, which, assembling in 449 at Ephesus, was dominated by himself. The acts of the synod of Constantinople having been annulled and the teaching of Eutyches pronounced orthodox by the assembled partizans of Dioscurus, the accused archimandrite, Eutyches was restored to his monastery. The predominating power of the Alexandrine party seemed secure until the unexpected death of their imperial protector, Theodosius II., occurred. Then the succeeding rulers confirmed anew the original deposition of Eutyches by the first synod of Constantinople, and later, hoping to harmonize all dissent within the Church, convened, in 451, the fourth ecumenical council at Chalcedon.

After the assembled bishops had deposed and degraded Dioscurus for his part in the repudiated proceedings of the Synod of Ephesus, the Christological controversy between Antioch and Alexandria was debated. Although both the declarations of the Alexandrine Cyril against the alleged heresy of the Antiochene Nestorius and the "Tome" of Leo [I. (q.v.)] against that of Nestorius and Eutyches combined had been accepted by the bishops, who at first asserted that the canon of the Church (canon VII. of the Council of Ephesus) forbade them to add to the existing conciliar creed, they were eventually compelled by the secular rulers to declare the decision of the council on the controverted question in the dogmatic definition called the Creed of Chalcedon (see CHRISTOLOGY, IV., § 2). The "Tome" of Leo, whose doctrinal declarations had undeniably been deduced directly from the several opposite statements submitted to him, first by Nestorius and Cyril, and later by Eutyches and Flavian, had consistently condemned both the crypto-Ebionitism inferred from the alleged Antiochene teaching of Nestorius, and the docetic heresy evident in the Alexandrine teaching of Eutyches. The Council of Chalcedon, in formulating its own creedal statement, not only thereby reaffirmed the truth of the traditional apostolic teaching contained in the Antiochene formula of 251, the Nicæno-Constantinopolitan Creed of 381 (see CONSTANTINOPOLITAN CREED), and, indirectly, the compromise Antiochene confession subscribed by Cyril (431), but it developed these comparatively simple doctrinal statements into a complex dogmatic formula of Christological faith, deduced directly from the "Tome" of Leo, the theological terms of which were clear and comprehensible only to bishops whose language was the Greek of the dominant division of the Church in the East.

II. The Separated Syrian Churches: But there were also the two allied non-Greek divisions, whose participation in the ecumenical councils of the Church was necessarily limited, since their ecclesiastical languages were Syriac and Armenian. The Syrian-speaking bishops throughout the East, because of this diversity of language, were free from the immediate influence of the incessant Christological controversies between the Greek schools of Antioch and of Alexandria. In the dissension evoked by the errors of Eutyches, their history tells freely and fully why the Creed of Chalcedon was rejected, and indirectly explains how the stigma of defending Eutyches and accepting his heresy was unjustly affixed to them by the Chalcedonians or Greek partizans of the fourth ecumenical council, whose dogmatic declaration was repeatedly confirmed or ignored, according as the emperors of the East were swayed by the political and ecclesiastical defenders or opposers of its course and of its canon. After reciting how Flavian and Eusebius had "insisted to the wicked Eutyches that the body of our Lord was a partaker of our nature, he confessed this which before he would not confess. They also urged him to confess that there are two (i.e., separate) natures in Christ. And because he would not confess this, they made this deposition. This cause forced Theodosius to assemble the second synod of

Ephesus. And when that was read before them which was done in the imperial city, they found that Flavian required Eutyches to confess two (i.e., separate) natures; and they made the deposition of Flavian and Eusebius. Eutyches presented a document in which was the creed of Nicæa, and the Godclad fathers anathematized all who had accused him, 'by this which deceived them as men, that wicked matter of ungodly heresy which was in his soul'; for it is written that man sees into the eyes, and the Lord sees into the heart" (Cowper, ut sup., pp. 89–91). The ceaseless controversy between the Greek defenders of the Council of Chalcedon and the anti-Chalcedonians was precisely this question of the two natures in Christ, whether they existed separately after, as Nestorianism seemed to say, or became united in and through his incarnation in the flesh, as taught by all the accepted confessions of the Church. That the anti-Chalcedonians—the Syrians, Copts, and Armenians—rejected consistently this Eutychian error of an absorption of Christ's humanity into his divinity is conclusively proved by the assertion, already cited, that Eutyches' deceptive confession of faith (like the equivocal creed of Arius) had actually deceived his own defender, Dioscurus, and the entire synod of Ephesus. Only because of this were they misled in declaring him orthodox, not heretical. The term "Eutychianism" therefore, must be accepted as synonymous with "Monophysitism," i.e., the docetic denial of the reality of the human nature of Christ. It can have, historically, no other or added meaning; to deny this is to assert that the entire ante-conciliar Church, which had accepted the Antiochene confession of 251, was then and thereafter also Monophysite, and, therefore, heretical in its traditional Christological teaching. The difference between the anti-Chalcedonians and the Chalcedonians was, as they state themselves, whether the disputed dogmatic declaration of this council, in condemning the evident error of Eutychianism, had not inclined instead to the alleged opposite teaching ascribed to Nestorius. The traditional Christological term of the first Antiochene formula is "one compound person of heavenly deity and human flesh"; the definition of the second compromise formula is similar in statement, "a union of two natures, wherefore we confess one Christ." Furthermore, the first formula asserts, finally, "Now these things we correct and approve, not the dividing of one person indivisible, but the unconfused peculiar confession of the flesh and of the Deity." This, then, was the justification of the anti-Chalcedonians for charging the Chalcedonians with teaching, in their dogmatic conciliar declaration, a seeming separation of the two natures, in opposition to the confessions asserting a union of the two natures in Christ.

To a Greek bishop, the Greek terms of the Creed of Chalcedon were clear and convincing. To a Syrian bishop speaking Syriac, with its one word for the two Greek terms *physis* ("nature") and *prosōpon* ("person") or *hypostasis*, these same terms were debatable, unorthodox, and doubtful. Even in orthodox Greek Alexandria, the anti-Chalcedonian partizans of their former patriarch Dioscurus, charging that he had been deposed by that "Nestorianizing council," secured the consecration of the presbyter Timotheus Ælurus (see MONOPHY-SITES, §§ 3–5) as antibishop to his Chalcedonian successor. Throughout Syria, Egypt, and the entire East the charge of Nestorianizing continued to be asserted and reasserted against the council of Chalcedon. A schism between the conciliar and the anti-conciliar partizans was inevitably approaching. Likewise in orthodox Greek Antioch, Peter the Fuller, supported by his political and ecclesiastical partizans, eventually displaced the Chalcedonian occupant of this other apostolic see, and succeeded to his patriarchal authority. During the rule of the

3. Fruitless Attempts at Reconciliation. Chalcedonian Leo, who had succeeded the Emperor Marcian, the Creed of Chalcedon was opposed generally by the monks and their political partizans throughout the East. After his death, the intruding Basiliscus annulled the imperial approval of his two predecessors in confirming the conciliar acceptance of the "Tome" with the creed, but he was soon displaced by the Chalcedonian Zeno (q.v.) whose unsuccessful efforts to reconcile the opposing ecclesiastical parties resulted in the promulgation of the compromise Henoticon (q.v.) in 482, condemning both Nestorianism and Eutyches, but not imposing on the Church the creed of the fourth Council of Chalcedon in addition to the dogmatic declarations of the three councils preceding. As before, during the ceaseless controversy after the compromise Antiochene confession had been accepted by the Alexandrine Cyril, the extremists of both the Chalcedonian and the anti-Chalcedonian parties refused to be reconciled by this substitute neutral statement.

What the Christological teaching of the Syrians was during these troubled times is evident from the doctrine of Philoxenus (q.v.), the anti-Chalcedonian bishop of Hierapolis (c. 500), and from that of the anti-conciliar Severus (q.v.), his contemporary, and

4. Syrian Christology at this Period. anti-Chalcedonian patriarch of Antioch in 513. "Disturbances being caused in Palestine (in 508) by a certain Nephalius, who, from being one of the extreme Monophysite party, had turned Chalcedonian, and, with the assistance of the Patriarch of Jerusalem, was expelling many monks from their monasteries, Severus, seeking to counteract the movement, went to Constantinople, where he wrote a treatise against the charge of Eutychianism, the *Philalethes*, against those who found the Chalcedonian doctrine in Cyril. Here he remained three years until after the ordination of Timothy to the see of Constantinople (511); after which he returned to Majuma and immediately set himself to abolish the Henoticon compromise, whereby all mention of the Council of Chalcedon had been expunged, and to procure the deposition of the patriarchs Flavian of Antioch and Elijah of Jerusalem" (*Sixth Book of the Select Letters of Severus*, ed. E. W. Brooks, Introduction, 2 vols., London, 1902–04). "And at the same time Severus of Antioch became known who wrote several books concerning the question of the one nature of the divine and the human, without mixture and without confusion or corruption;

so that they continue each in its own place, as the nature of man consists of a spiritual nature and of the body, and the nature of the body consists of two natures, the one material and the other of form, without the soul being changed into the body, or the material parts into the form, or the contrary" (E. F. K. Fortescue, *The Armenian Church*, p. 281, London, 1872). Herein is again asserted the traditional Antiochene teaching of "one compound person" of the first formula, with the added dogmatic declaration against the error of Eutyches, "without mixture, confusion, or corruption," the last word against the "aphthartodocetics" (see JULIAN OF HALICARNASSUS). The use throughout of the term "nature," where the Greeks would alternate their two corresponding terms *physis* ("nature") and *prosōpon* ("person") or *hypostasis*, proves that the Creed of Chalcedon is untranslatable into Syriac, as it also is into Armenian and into Coptic.

This Christological creed is found developed more fully in the doctrinal declaration of Philoxenus who, in his treatise on the incarnation, asserts that the nature (i.e., the person) of Christ is composed of divinity and of humanity, without conversion, confusion, or commixture. He teaches that the Son, one of the Trinity, united himself with a human body and a rational soul in the womb of the Virgin. His body had no being before this union. In it he was born, in it he was nourished, in it he suffered and died. Yet the divine nature of the Son did not

5. Christology of Philoxenus. suffer or die, nor was his human nature or his agency or death merely visionary, as the docetic Gnostics asserted, but actual and real. Furthermore, the divine nature was not changed or transformed into the human, or confused or commixed with it; neither was the human nature changed or transmuted into the divine, or commixed or confused with it; but a peculiar cooperation (i.e., *Communicatio idiomatum* [q.v.]) of the two natures was effected, similar to that by means of whose union the body and soul become one human being. For as the soul and body are united in one human nature, so from the union of the divinity and the humanity of Jesus Christ has proceeded a nature (i.e., person) peculiar to himself, not simple but compound; the "one compound person" of the first Antiochene formula, also ascribed to Athanasius in his term "The one nature of the Word made flesh," and continually used by his Alexandrine successor Cyril. The Eutychians or Monophysites were, however, notorious, even before the Council of Chalcedon, for asserting, in addition to their original heresy of the absorption of the humanity of Christ by his divinity, the error that the human nature of Christ existed before his incarnation in the womb of the Virgin.

During the centuries following the final separation of the anti-Chalcedonian Syrians from the Greeks of the Byzantine patriarchates, their traditional teaching concerning the several sections of the fundamental apostolic faith of the Christian Church was like that of the Greeks, formulated in an authoritative and accepted system of dogma. Therefore when the patriarch of the Syrian Jacobite Churc

Peter Ignatius III., in the interest of the Syrians of South India under the secular authority of the English government, presented himself in

6. Modern Syrian Confession of Faith. 1874 to the archbishop of Canterbury and the bishops of the Anglican Church, the traditional imputation to the Syrians of the heresy of Eutyches, or Monophysitism, could not fail to become prominent. This century-long charge was fully controverted by the following sections of the " Creed of our Holy Fathers, the Pillars of our Eastern Syrian Church, St. James of Nisibis, St. Ephraem, St. James the Divine, and others, recognized by all (churches), and also of my unworthy self (the patriarch), as taken from our Lords the Holy Apostles, and divided into twenty-five chapters or articles ":

I. Whosoever shall say that the Son of God is not very God, even as the Father is very God, and that he is not coequal with the Father in essence, sovereignty, and eternity, let him be anathema.

II. Whosoever shall say, that the Son is not begotten of the Father, essentially and eternally, let him be anathema.

III. Whosoever shall say that the Son of God, when he sojourned on earth in the flesh, was not in heaven with the Father, let him be anathema.

IV. Whosoever shall say that in that humanity, he did not sit at the right hand of the Father, and that he shall not come again as he is, to judge both the living and the dead, let him be anathema.

V. Whosoever shall say that Christ underwent change and alteration, and does not confess that his soul underwent no change, and that his body did not see corruption as it is written, let him be anathema.

VI. Whosoever shall say that Christ became perfect man by separation (from the divine essence?), and does not confess of our Lord Jesus Christ that he is one as it is written, let him be anathema.

VII. Whosoever shall say that one (nature) suffered, and that the other (nature) was absent at the time of the Passion, and does not believe that God, the impassible, suffered in the flesh as it is written, let him be anathema.

VIII. Whosoever shall say that Christ was human like all other men, and does not believe of him that he was incarnate and became man by the Holy Ghost and the Virgin Mary, a daughter of David, as it is written, let him be anathema.

IX. Whosoever shall say that the holy Virgin Mary is the mother of Christ, and does not confess that she brought forth the Word of God, who was incarnate, and became man, let him be anathema.

X. Whosoever shall say that the body of Christ is an offspring of the divine essence, and does not confess that he was God before the foundation of the world, who humbled himself and took upon him the form of a servant, as it is written, let him be anathema.

XI. Whosoever shall say that the body of Christ was a phantom or mere image, and does not confess that his was a real body like ours, and that the Virgin Mary brought forth the incarnate Word in a real body, let him be anathema.

XII. Whosoever shall say that when God the Word became united to the body, the divine nature was commingled with the human nature, or that the two natures became commixed and changed so as to give rise to a third nature, and does not confess that the two natures became united in indissoluble union without confusion, mixture, or transmutation, and that they remained two natures in an unalterable unity, let him be anathema.

XIII. Whosoever shall say that the Word of God is created, and not Creator, and does not confess that he is Creator even as is the Father, and that he is coequal with the Father and the Holy Spirit in essence, power, the creation of created things, sovereignty, and eternity, let him be anathema.

XIV. Whosoever shall say that the Holy Spirit is created and not Creator, and that he is of time and not eternal, and does not confess that he is Creator even as is the Father, and as is the Son, and that he is coequal with the Father and the Son in essence, eternity, dominion, power, creation,

majesty, and sovereignty, and that he proceeds from the Father and receives from the Son, and that he is with the Father and the Son, eternal and everlasting, let him be anathema.

XV. Whosoever shall say that the Holy Spirit is not of the essence of the Father, as the Son is of the essence of his Father, and God of God, let him be anathema.

XVI. Whosoever shall say that the Holy Spirit is not omnipotent, omniscient, and omnipresent, as is the Father, and as is the Son, let him be anathema.

XVII. Whosoever shall say that the visible and invisible things of creation were not created by the Father, Son, and Holy Spirit, let him be anathema.

XVIII. Whosoever shall say that the Godhead of the Father, Son, and Holy Spirit is not all of one, and does not confess that the three blessed persons are verily and indeed one in eternity, dominion, sovereignty, and will, let him be anathema.

XIX. Whosoever shall say that the persons of the Father, Son, and Holy Spirit are not verily and indeed coequal in all things, ever-living, having dominion over all things visible and invisible, all-judging, all-recompensing, and giving life to all, let him be anathema.

XX. Whosoever shall say that the Holy Spirit is not to be adored and worshiped by all creatures, equally with the Father and the Son, let him be anathema.

XXI. Whosoever shall say that God the Father is alone God, to the exclusion of the Son, and of the Holy Spirit, and shall teach or believe that worship belongs to the Father alone, excepting them, and does not believe of the three blessed persons, the Father, the Son, and the Holy Spirit, that they are one God, one (object of) adoration, one judge, as the holy catholic and apostolic Church believes, let him be anathema.

XXII. Whosoever shall say that the Trisagion which is said in the liturgy is (addressed) to the three blessed persons, and shall truly so believe, and shall then improperly add to the Trisagion, "Who wast crucified for us," and shall not believe what our Syrian Jacobite Church believes with a firm faith undoubtingly, and which ascribes the Trisagion to the only begotten Son, the Word, who was pleased to be born of the holy Virgin Mary, and become flesh, as it is written, and of his own will and pleasure was crucified out of his great love for us, in token of his overflowing bounty and beneficence to us, let him be anathema. (*Church Times*, September, London, 1874.)

III. The Separated Armenian Churches: Since the Armenian Church existed, for the greater part, in the borderland between the Byzantine and the Persian empires, and was actually under the rule of the latter, it was, both for this reason and because of its differing ecclesiastical language, unable to participate freely and fully in the successive ecumenical councils of the Christian Church convened in the East. Although unrepresented at the third council, that of Ephesus (431), Cyril of Alexandria addressed to the patriarch of the Armenians a statement of the doctrines discussed and the decision of the council condemning as heretical the alleged errors of Nestorius. This letter was entrusted to certain pupils

1. Reasons for Non-representation at Ecumenical Councils. of Mesrob (q.v.), whom he had sent to Constantinople to translate into Armenian the several books written by the fathers of the Greek Church, and was soon after delivered by them to their preceptor. Thereupon Mesrob convened a synod of the Armenian bishops, doctors, and confessors, to whom this letter of Cyril's, containing the acts and the decision of the council, was read. After they had discussed and approved its several statements, they condemned and anathematized anew the heresy ascribed to Nestorius. During the early part of 451, while the fourth council was assembling at Chalcedon, the Armenians were being persecuted persistently by their anti-Christian rulers, who sought to compel them to abandon their traditional faith and teaching, and accept the Zoroastrianism of their Persian oppressors. For this reason it was impossible for the Armenians to send representatives to the council, of whose deliberations and decisions, unlike that of the previous council of Ephesus, they were left in ignorance by the assembled Greek bishops.

But soon after this, the many monastic and other opponents of the council of Chalcedon began to spread themselves farther and farther over Asia, asserting continually that the Greeks had accepted the errors of Nestorius which had been rejected by the preceding council of Ephesus. Later the followers and partizans of Eutyches came to Armenia, seeking to secure Armenian sympathy by defending his teachings and denouncing the Creed of Chalcedon, while, at the same time, the supporters of Nestorius, seeking also to influence the Armenians in his favor, asserted that this council was compelled to accept his teaching even though the Council of Ephesus had condemned him, since only thus 2. Hesita- could they controvert the heresy of tion to Eutyches. During this time, when Accept the these opponents of the Greeks were Creed of seeking to secure the support of the Chalcedon. Armenians, a very defective translation of the letter of Leo to Flavian, concerning the errors of Eutyches, was brought to their attention. The bishops, in examining its teaching concerning the two natures of Christ, one of which was divine and the other human, could not fail to perceive that the phrase " the one and the other " had been translated by a term used only of persons but not of attributes. Thus it was that, although Leo spoke of two natures, the Armenian translation referred instead to two persons. And although the Greek defenders of the Creed of Chalcedon asserted its undoubted orthodoxy, the counter-claims of the defenders of Nestorius and his teaching seemed to be supported by the dubious doctrine of Leo's letter, which had been used in the formulation of this disputed conciliar declaration of the faith. While the Armenian bishops were deliberating year after year whether to reject or to accept this decision of the Council of Chalcedon, a copy of the proclamation of the Greek Emperor Zeno, imposing the acceptance of his Henoticon, which had already been signed by many Byzantine bishops, was brought to their attention. Babken, the patriarch of the Armenians, having examined the Henoticon with its many subscriptions, which, although condemning both the asserted errors of Nestorius and the evident heresy of Eutyches, had passed over without notice the disputed dogmatic declaration of the Council of Chalcedon, approved and accepted it as orthodox, since it undeniably agreed with the teaching of the three first councils of the Church. Then, after these dissensions over this disputed council had continued year after year, the patriarch convened, in 491, a synod of all the Armenian bishops, including the primates and suffragans of the Albanians and the Georgians, to determine finally whether to reject or accept as ecumenical the Council of Chalcedon. After they had again anathematized the errors of

Nestorius and Eutyches, the Henoticon was read, approved, and accepted as orthodox throughout; and since it was known to all that the Greeks themselves were divided on the question of recognizing their own council, they also refused to consider it as an ecumenical council of the Catholic Church (see ARMENIA, III., § 3). Then, when later in that same year the successor of Zeno, the Emperor Anastasius, issued a decree forbidding all further discussion concerning the Council of Chalcedon and its creed, the Armenian bishops were confirmed in their decision to refuse it recognition. And, although doubting the entire orthodoxy of the dogmatic conciliar declaration, in view of the apparent heterodoxy perceived in the translation of the Letter of Leo which they had already examined, they admitted and accepted the teaching of the Creed of Chalcedon in so far as it had reasserted the traditional apostolic teaching of the three first, and undisputed, councils of the Church.

But the expression used in Leo's letter, " the two natures in Christ," continued to confuse the Armenians, since the Syrians, who were also active anti-Chalcedonians, asserted that it had inclined to the error ascribed to Nestorius, and by the term " two natures " it seemingly taught a separation of the two natures in the one Christ. The Armenians, therefore, to contradict the asserted error of the Chalcedonians, adopted as their own the expression of Cyril of Alexandria against Nesto- 3. Armenian rius, " the one nature of the Word Doubts on made flesh "; and in using this term Leo's " one nature in Christ," they taught Letter to and believed it to be equivalent to Flavian. one personality (Armenian, like Syriac, must use its one term, where the Greek can alternate *physis* with *hypostasis* or *prosopon*) resulting from the indivisible union of the two natures. This expression later became the cause of many controversies which continued for centuries between the Armenians and the Greeks, the latter seeking, through the secular authority of the emperors of the East, to secure Armenian acceptance of the disputed Creed of Chalcedon, thus compelling their theologians to write defenses of their orthodox doctrine of the person of Christ to counteract the claims of their Greek opponents that they taught the Monophysite heresy of Eutyches. In these declarations, they state definitely that the formula " two natures in Christ " signifies that " Christ is one," true God and true man, possessing perfectly both the divine and the human natures united in him without confusion and without division; having suffered the passion and death in his humanity, but impassible and immortal in his divinity.

The Armenian Church, as a result of its contact with the Latins during these centuries before and after the final separation, in 1054, of the Greek and Latin churches, unlike the other divisions of the Christian Church in the East, accepts the Apostles' Creed and the Athanasian Creed (i.e., without the Filioque) in addition to the Nicæno-Constantinopolitan, which is imposed on all divisions of the Catholic Church throughout the entire East and the entire West. The teaching of the Armenians on those disputed doctrines connected with the Creed of Chalcedon is seen in the following commentaries on the confession of the Catholic faith found in all copies of their prayer-books used by the clergy and laity:

Wherefore, since we, in common with all other Orthodox Christians, confess the same God and the same Christ, it is most necessary to show what the Armenian Church teaches concerning the chief articles of the Christian faith, namely, of God, one in three persons, of the incarnation, person, office, and merits of Christ, with all other doctrines connected with these. For from this may be seen whether or not the Armenians teach, as they have been charged continually by their opponents, the heresies of the Monophysites and of the Monothelites, who assert that in Christ there is only one nature and only one will.

4. Armenian Confession of Faith.

I. We confess, and with our whole (most perfect) heart believe in, the Father, God (who is) not created, not begotten, but without beginning (who also is begetter of the Son, and breather forth of the Holy Spirit.

II. We believe in the Word (of) God, (who is) not created, (but) begotten, and (who has his) beginning from the Father, before the worlds. Who is neither posterior nor less, but as the Father is Father, so also is the Son (truly) Son.

III. We believe in the Holy Spirit, (who is) not created (and) not of time; not begotten, but breathed forth from the Father, of the same essence with the Father, and of the same glory with the Son.

IV. We believe in the Holy Trinity, one nature, one Godhead—not three Gods but one God—one will, one kingdom, one sovereignty, maker of things visible and invisible.

V. We believe in a holy Church, a remission of sins, and a communion of saints.

VI. We believe (that) one of the three persons, the Word (of) God, begotten of the Father before the worlds, in time came into the Virgin Mary, the mother of God (*Theotokos*), took of her blood, and united it with his Godhead (divinity), dwelt patiently nine months in the womb of that pure Virgin, and was made (or became) perfect man, in spirit (or soul), and mind, and body; one person, one figure (or appearance), and united in one nature. God was made (or became) man, without change, without alteration; conception without seed, and generation without corruption. And as there is no beginning to his Godhead (divinity), so also is there no end to his humanity; for Jesus Christ is the same, yesterday, and to-day, and even forever.

VII. We believe (that) our Lord Jesus Christ, having gone about on the earth, after thirty years, came to baptism; (that) the Father bare witness, "This is my beloved Son," and the Holy Spirit, in the likeness of a dove, came down (above him). (That) he was tempted of Satan and overcame him; preached the salvation of men, labored in the body, hungered and thirsted; and after that, of his own free will, came into (his) passion, was crucified, dead in the body, but alive in his Godhead (divinity). His body was laid in the grave, united with his Godhead (divinity), and in spirit he went down into Hades in his undivided Godhead (divinity), preached to the spirits, spoiled Hell (i.e., Hades) and set free the spirits. After three days, he arose from the dead, and appeared to the disciples.

VIII. We believe (that) our Lord Jesus Christ ascended to heaven in that same body, and sat at the right hand of God (the Father), and that he is to come (again) in the same body, and with the glory of the Father, to judge the living and the dead; that is also the resurrection of all men.

IX. We believe also in the retribution for works (done in the body); to the righteous, life everlasting, and to sinners, everlasting torments.

The Armenian Church teaches constantly that Christ the Savior is God-Man, "perfect God and perfect man." But when, as a consequence of the error of Eutyches, unceasing controversies were evoked throughout the entire East, the Armenian Church introduced into its confession, to controvert his heresy, "in spirit (or soul), and mind, and body," thereby declaring that the human nature of Christ consists of all the essential parts that constitute man, truly and really, and not in appearance only. Furthermore as (the words) "spirit and mind (or intellect)" are understood (by all) to be synonymous in meaning, they therefore explain each other. The word "spirit" (in Armenian) is used for the uncreated spirit, and for the created spirit or soul, while the word "mind" is used for the intellect or conscience,

the whole of which, taken together, perfect, and true man. For as "since our human nature was not alone, but wholly, in spirit (or soul) also did the Word assume it wholly and (with his divinity). This, therefore, Armenian Church in opposition to the linaris, as is later asserted by Nerses is the body without mind, as Apollina the Word dwelt in the body as a stat (Fortescue, ut sup., pp. 256–258). And th in his formula of faith, submitted to the Em Comnenus, declares also that the words figure (or aspect)" were added against the torianism. Wherefore, says he (Fortescue, ut "do we not sever, like Nestorius, the one Ch natures and two parts," quoting the words Názianzen, "he is not one, and another, but mixture (union)"; adding also the declaration of orthodox father, "that it is clear that Christ is nature but not in personality" (cf. *NPNF*, 2 ser. 312).

Thus do the Armenians teach the two gener or births, the one from the Father before the w and the other from the holy Virgin in the fuln time, but they also confess the two natures (as separable, i.e., the *Communicatio idiomatum*) w mention is made either of the one or the oth abstractedly; for they confess that the divine natur of Christ, which is of the essence of the Father, i united in the Word with human nature. Therefore Nerses IV. says, "thou who, when giving proof of thy human nature during that night, wast greatly troubled with fear." And again, when mention is made of the person of the Son of God and of man, in a concrete sense alone, Armenian fathers declare fearlessly that he has one nature (i.e., personality) by reason of the intimate union (of the two natures within himself); wherefore to the confession of faith were added the words, "he is united in one nature." All the ceaseless controversies, during the centuries after the rejection of the Council of Chalcedon by the Armenians, between them and their opponents, the Greek defenders of its dogmatic conciliar declaration, were evoked by the use of this term to define the incarnation of the Word. These words, added to the confession of faith after Cyril of Alexandria had used them in his controversy with Nestorius (i.e., the Alexandrine phrase of Athanasius, "the one nature of the Word made flesh"), as adopted by an orthodox father, were thenceforth defended by the Armenians, even though their adversaries, by citing the words against them, seemingly proved that the Armenian teaching on the incarnation and the person of Christ was heterodox, and Eutychian or Monophysitic. But during this same period when the Armenians began to use this term against the assumed Nestorianizing teaching of the Creed of Chalcedon, Severus, later the anti-Chalcedonian patriarch of Antioch, was likewise using it against those who sought to support the doctrine of Chalcedon by citations from the writings of Cyril. Athanasius declares (*De incarnatione*, vol. ii.): "We confess the Son of God to be God according to the Spirit, and man according to the flesh; not two natures in the one, and only one nature to be worshipped and another not (cf. the

5. Armenian Teaching on the Two Natures.

---

* Fortescue, ut sup. p. 273.

Antiochene formula of faith, above), but one nature made flesh of the Word of God, and adored with his flesh in one and the same worship." And, later, his Alexandrine successor, Cyril, asserts anew this declaration of Athanasius against the error ascribed to Nestorius: "We say that the two natures are united, yet so that, after the union, the division exists no longer. We believe the nature of the Son to be one, when made man, and in the flesh" (*Epist. ad Eulog.*). But since Eutyches had also asserted that the divinity and humanity in Christ resulted only in one nature, the use of these same words, taken from Athanasius and Cyril, although both were orthodox Fathers of the Church, after the dissensions evoked by the disputes concerning the Chalcedonian doctrine, compelled the Armenians, like the Syrian opponents of the Creed of Chalcedon, to defend themselves against the Greek Chalcedonians, who charged both Armenians and Syrians with concealing their Eutychian monophysitic error by adhering to them. Therefore Nerses of Lambron declares definitely (Fortescue, ut sup., p. 277): "We do not say of the Word made flesh that he has one nature, confounding the property of essences, as they (i.e., the Greeks) imagine, but according to an ineffable union of these

6. Armenian two natures in one personality and
Rejection Godhead (in one divine person)."
of Eutych- This same statement was reaffirmed by
ianism. him at the Synod of Tarsus, when, as
a result of the antagonism between the Greeks and the Armenians arising from their refusal to accept the Creed of Chalcedon, they had been denounced to the Latins of the West as Eutychians. Nerses IV., in his declaration of doctrine delivered to the Greek emperor of the East, states solemnly (Fortescue, ut sup., p. 277): "Neither do we, like Eutyches and his followers, gather two (natures) into one by confusion and alteration"; and later he affirms this again by saying: "Thus have they refuted and disproved the mode of confusion held by Eutyches and his followers, and all those who, before and after him, said erroneously that in Christ is only one nature, by declaring that each nature, the divine and the human, continues unchanged, undestroyed in the union of the two." And, finally, he concludes his dissertation on the doctrines taught by the Armenian Church by declaring (Fortescue, ut sup. p. 277): "Wherefore, in accordance with what has been delivered unto us by the orthodox fathers, we do anathematize all those who say that the nature of the Word made flesh is one, by means of confusion and alteration; and that he did not take his human nature and unite it with his Godhead, but that he created for himself a body in the womb of the Virgin; or that he brought it from heaven; or that he appeared man only to the eye and not really (or in truth); and all others who may hold one nature in any such sense." The true teaching concerning the person of Christ as expressed in the phrase "the union of Christ in one nature," according to these doctrinal declarations of the Armenians, is summarized clearly and convincingly by the Patriarch Nerses IV. (Fortescue, ut sup. p. 278): "We believe thus, that God the Word, who was begotten of the Father before all worlds,

who is invisible and impassible, took our nature perfectly from the Virgin and united it with his divine nature, without confusion in an indivisible union; and he continued invisible in his divinity, but visible through his humanity; impalpable and palpable." (See, further, CHRISTOLOGY, MONOPHYSITES.)   ERNEST C. MARGRANDER.

NESTORIUS: J. F. Bethune-Baker's *Nestorius and his Teaching: a Fresh Examination of the Evidence, with Special Reference to the Newly Discovered Apology of Nestorius* (*The Bazaar of Heraclides*; Cambridge, 1908), referred to in the article NESTORIUS, was not much utilized in the preparation of the article. The importance of the newly discovered Syriac work, translations of the more important parts of which Bethune-Baker has incorporated in his book, seems to the editors to justify a supplementary article. It may be remarked that Bethune-Baker, an English Churchman, is deeply interested in the Nestorians of Persia, and is anxious to see every obstacle to the union of the Nestorians with the Anglican church removed. He rejoices in the discovery of Nestorius's account of his own part in the great controversy, written in his Egyptian exile near the close of his life when all hope of personal advantage had vanished, and evidently expressing his inmost convictions respecting the relation of the divine and the human in the person of Christ.

The conclusion has long seemed warranted that Nestorius was a victim of malicious partizanship in which Cyril of Alexandria was the chief actor, and the hatred of the monks aroused by Nestorius's objection to the expression "Mother of God" applied to Mary. The *Bazaar of Heraclides* makes this conclusion certain. His description of the proceedings of the Council of Ephesus (431), while it manifests a bitter feeling against Cyril, must be regarded as essentially correct. "Was it the synod and the emperor who summoned it that heard my cause, if he (Cyril) was ranked among the judges? But why should I say 'ranked among the judges'? He was the whole tribunal; for everything that he said was at once said by all of them as well, and they unhesitatingly agreed with him as the personification of the court. Now if all the judges were assembled, and the accusers were set in their ranks, and the accused also in like manner, all should have had equal liberty of speech. But if he (Cyril) was everything—accuser and emperor and judge—then he did everything, ousting from this authority him who was appointed by the emperor and setting himself in his place, and assembling to himself those whom he wanted, both far and near, and making himself the court. And so I was summoned by Cyril, who assembled the synod, and by Cyril who was its head. Who is judge? Cyril. And who the accuser? Cyril. Who the bishop of Rome? Cyril. Cyril was everything." After giving still further emphasis to the statement that Cyril had managed to equip himself with imperial and papal authority, and had packed the synod to suit himself, he describes the "rabble of idlers and country-folk" assembled by Memnon, bishop of Ephesus, and Cyril, who armed with clubs paraded the streets shouting and yelling against Nestorius and his friends, building fires and burning their writings, and threatening their lives. " Who could refrain from weeping when he remembers the wrongs done at Ephesus! And would God it were against me and against my life they were done, and not in a wrong cause! For then I should have no need of these words on behalf of one who was meet to be punished; but on behalf of our Savior Jesus Christ, the just Judge, for whose sake I have undertaken to endure patiently, that the whole body of Christ may not be accused."

Nestorius was deeply concerned to maintain the true and complete humanity of Christ over against Arian curtailment to mere body and Appollinarian curtailment to body and soul, as well as against monophysite absorption of the humanity by the infinite deity. The following clear statement from the *Bazaar of Heraclides* is significant: " We were discussing whether it was right to understand and to say that the proper things of the flesh and of the reasonable (rational) soul, and the proper things of God the Word, both belong to God the Word by nature; or whether we should say of Christ that the two natures were united in him in a union of one person. And I was saying and maintaining that the union was of the one person of Christ. And I was showing that God the Word certainly became man, and that Christ is God the Word and at the same time man, inasmuch as he became man. And for this reason it was that the Fathers (Nicene), when teaching us who Christ is, about whom there was a dissension, first laid down those things of which Christ consists. But thou (Cyril) because thou wishest that the person of the union should be God the Word in both natures, dost neglect these things as superfluous, and dost neglect to make a beginning from them." He thus charges Cyril with contradicting the Nicene teaching in maintaining that after the union the humanity is no longer distinguishable, but that Christ is God the Word in whom there is no distinction between humanity and deity.

In his private discussions at Ephesus with Theodotus and Acacius, Nestorius was reported to have said that he " would not call a two- or three-months old babe God," and much was made of the seeming irreverence of the statement. According to his own account of the matter in the Syriac version, he did not mean to say that he could not bring himself to call a babe God, but that he objected to calling God a babe (see Bethune-Baker, ut sup., pp. 75-77). In his discussion at Ephesus with Acacius of Melitene Nestorius found that the latter " had fallen into two errors. For first he perversely asked a question which laid upon those who were to answer it the necessity of either denying altogether that the Godhead of the Only-begotten became man, or confessing—what is impious—that the Godhead of the Father and the Holy Spirit also became incarnate with the Word."

When we consider how completely accordant Nestorius's teaching respecting the person of Christ was with that of his predecessors of the Antiochian school and with the Nicene Christology, it seems strange that John of Antioch should have consented to his anathematization and his banishment. Either John misunderstood Nestorius's teaching, or he was weak enough to sacrifice a great and good man with whom he was in substantial agreement for the sake of peace. The latter alternative seems the more probable.

When Nestorius learned of the proceedings of the " Robber Synod " of Ephesus in 449, at which Flavian, patriarch of Constantinople, was almost beaten to death by a howling mob instigated by Dioscurus, patriarch of Alexandria, he felt that history had repeated itself, Dioscurus having gone beyond Cyril not in principle, but only in the degree of the violence for which he was responsible. He rejoiced exceedingly when Leo of Rome, in his letter to Flavian, adopted almost *in toto* the statement of the doctrine of the person of Christ for which he had been anathematized, and for which he was dying in exile. He considered the symbol of Chalcedon and the endorsement by the synod of Leo's letter, the writings of Theodoret, Theodore of Mopsuestia, and Ibas, all of which were in full agreement with his own teaching, as a complete vindication of his orthodoxy, and he was content to die an excommunicated heretic now that the truth had prevailed. He naturally viewed with satisfaction the utter discomfiture of Dioscurus. Nothing was done at Chalcedon or in Rome to relieve the aged theologian of the obloquy that had cost him so much suffering. " The goal of my earnest wish, then, is that God may be blessed on earth as in heaven. But as for Nestorius let him be anathema. . . . And would to God that all men by anathematizing me might attain to a reconciliation with God; for to me there is nothing greater or more precious than this " (Bethune-Baker, ut sup., p. 190). The concluding sentences of the *Bazaar of Heraclides* are full of pathos: " As for me, I have borne the sufferings of my life and all that has befallen me in this world as the suffering of a single day; and I have not changed, lo, all these years. And now, lo, I am already on the point to depart, and daily I pray to God to dismiss me—me, whose eyes have seen his salvation. Rejoice with me, O Desert, thou my friend and mine upbringer and my place of sojourning; and thou, Exile, my mother, who after my death shalt keep my body until the resurrection cometh in the time of God's good pleasure " (Bethune-Baker, ut sup., p. 36).   A. H. NEWMAN.

OBERLIN THEOLOGY: The name given to the theological views of A. Mahan, C. G. Finney, and J. H. Fairchild (qq.v.) between the years 1833 and 1902. The basis for this theology is found in the New England theology (q.v.), with which it is in general agreement on the doctrine of the Scriptures, the Trinity, the atonement, means of grace, and eschatology. Its distinctive features are, (1) its notion of the ground of obligation, which is defined as the good of being in general, or of sentient being (cf. J. H. Fairchild, *Moral Philosophy*, New York, 1869); (2) its theory of " the simplicity of moral action "—the will, self-determining, is at each moment either wholly virtuous or wholly sinful; (3) the idea of sanctification as that of a process which, beginning in an act of will, is characterized either by alternating states of holiness and sin, which finally issue in the supremacy of holiness, or by uninterrupted and increasing holiness. Perfection is possible in this life. This theology as a whole is presented by Finney with acute logical force and lucidity, and by Fairchild with ethical emphasis and practical common sense.

C. A. BECKWITH.

ORTHODOX CATHOLIC CHURCH IN AMERICA.

Rise of the Old Catholic Church (§ 1).
Orthodox Catholic Church and its Statement of Faith (§ 2).
Aims of the Orthodox Catholic Church (§ 3).
Pastoral of Vilatte, Kaminski, and Miraglia (§ 4).
The Utrecht Declaration (§ 5).

The Orthodox Catholic Church of America is a branch of the Orthodox Church of the Latin Rite in the Western patriarchate, which, in addition to its primitive historic divisions of Europe and Africa, includes also, since the discovery of the Western continent, the whole of America. This distinction of rite is both necessary and desirable, because there are now throughout the nations of the Western world Orthodox Catholic churches of the Greek Rite, some of them in communion with each other, and all with their parent national churches in the several Eastern patriarchates.

The gradual growth of the comparatively late order of Jesuits, compelled, as they were, by the trend of the times and by the inevitable antagonism of the established monastic orders of the Latin Church to become the special self-constituted clerical supporters and political defenders of the papal power, introduced into that church a new theological tendency, whose ecclesiastical influence within the Roman Church, weakened as it was by the final loss of Germany, England, and Scandinavia, was to cause later many unforeseen and momentous con-

1. Rise of the Old Catholic Church. sequences. The arbitrary act, in 1653, of Innocent X. in denouncing as heretical the Augustinian doctrines taught by Jansen (see JANSEN, CORNELIUS, JANSENISM), with the renewal of the controversy early in the eighteenth century by the repeated condemnation, in 1713, of the alleged Jansenist errors of Pasquier Quesnel (q.v.), in the bull *Unigenitus* (q.v.) of Clement XI., resulted in the consecration by the French bishop Maria Varlet, titular of Babylon, without awaiting papal confirmation, first of Cornelis Steenoven as archbishop of Utrecht, then of his two successors, and again of a fourth archbishop, Pieter Jan Meindaerts, who, to prevent the future loss of this newly transmitted Latin episcopal succession in the Catholic Church of Holland, established the two suffragan sees of Haarlem and Deventer (see, further, JANSENIST CHURCH IN HOLLAND). The consistently orthodox course of their successors in the episcopate was proved convincingly when they protested solemnly against the pronouncement of Pius IX. on the dogma of the Immaculate Conception (q.v.) of the Virgin Mary, which was only the prelude to the dogmatic declarations of the Vatican Council of 1870 (see VATICAN COUNCIL) on the constitution of the Catholic Church and the primacy and the infallibility of the bishop of Rome. Here again the bish-

ops of the Church of Holland reaffirmed their agreement with the orthodox doctrine of the undivided Catholic Church, East and West, by rejecting solemnly these Vatican decrees. And when, soon after, the excommunicated priests in Germany, faithful to their theological leader, Johann Josef Ignaz von Döllinger (q.v.), were compelled, by the repressive measures of the Roman prelates, to organize separate congregations, the bishops of Holland not only approved this inevitable consequence of their opposition to these ultramontane doctrines of the Roman Church by administering the sacrament of confirmation to their catechumens, but later transferred in turn to them their Latin episcopal succession by consecrating Joseph Hubert Reinkens (q.v.) of Bonn. The union conference of 1874 in Bonn, summoned by Döllinger and attended by Old Catholic prelates, priests, and theologians, by theological representatives from both the Greek and the Russian churches, and by participating members from the Anglican churches of England and America, is historically the first free assembly of both Greek and Latin ecclesiastics since the unsuccessful Roman Council of Ferrara-Florence in 1438. This synod, after free and full discussion of the fundamentals of the orthodox faith of the undivided Catholic Church, East and West, accepted fourteen theses which are the first irenic formulation of those debated dogmas which divide the several reformed communions from each other and from their common ecclesiastical mother, the Latin Church of the West, also from the entire Greek Church of the East (see, further, OLD CATHOLICS).

The extension of the Old Catholic movement from Europe to America through the missionary activity of its pioneer priest, Joseph Réné Vilatte (q.v.), of Wisconsin, and his subsequently authorized consecration, by the Syrian patriarch of Antioch, as archbishop of the Orthodox Church of the Latin Rite in America, has resulted not only in the introduction of the Syrian succession into the Catholic hierarchy of the Western patriarchate, but it is also aiding, slowly and silently, the other ecclesiastical influences which are assisting, year by year, the movement for Catholic reform and Christian union on the basis of the fundamental faith of the undivided Church, through this new ecclesiastical connection with the primitive national orthodox churches of all the East. The Orthodox Catholic church, orthodox because it accepts the universally admitted dogmatic decrees of the seven ecumenical councils of the undivided church, East and West, and Catholic because it possesses a validly consecrated hierarchy in the apostolic Syrian succession, exercising its duly designated canonical authority in the archdiocese of America, and being in communion with the several divisions of the one holy Catholic and apostolic Church of Christ, summarizes its teaching in the following short statement of faith.

I. The only historical and consistent bond of church unity is that of the "faith once for all delivered to the saints," as taught by the united Catholic Church, East and West, during the period of the seven general councils. Orthodox Catholics join in faith, hope, and love with all churches possessing and exercising the apostolic ministry, and accepting the teaching of the holy Scriptures as understood by the fathers, doctors, and confessors of the first eight centuries of the undivided Christian Church throughout the world.

II. A validly ordained ministry in the apostolic succession is not alone sufficient for Christian and Catholic unity. For we must also accept the Apostles', the Nicene, and the Athanasian Creeds without addition (of the *Filioque*) or subtraction from the faith.

III. We also acknowledge and accept the dogmatic decrees of the seven ecumenical councils as the fundamental basis of unity in the Christian faith, and, in addition, all orthodox definitions of the synods of Bethlehem [see JERUSALEM, SYNOD OF] and of Trent, concerning the seven sacraments, as clear and concise statements of the doctrines taught by the Catholic Church throughout the world.

IV. We reject the authority and deny the infallibility of any patriarch who claims, contrary to the canons of the seven ecumenical councils, supreme and sole jurisdiction over the one holy Catholic and apostolic Church of Christ.

V. The monastic life among Orthodox Catholics is a devout life of voluntary sacrifice to God, and of willing service and love toward men. We do not adore the images of Jesus Christ, the Blessed Virgin, and the saints, but venerate them as representing sacred persons.

VI. We believe firmly, according to the inspired teaching of the holy Scriptures, that there is only one Mediator of redemption between God and man, Christ Jesus (I Tim. ii. 5). We believe also that the intercessory prayers of the saints, who are our glorified brethren in the Church Triumphant, are joined with those of us who are in the Church Militant on earth, for we are united in that one communion of saints of the creed.

VII. Finally, we permit no dissent from the orthodox doctrines of our faith, for no one may add to, or take away from, the fundamental faith of the one holy Catholic and apostolic Church of Christ.

The Orthodox Catholic Church, therefore, invites all clergy and Christians in the Western patriarchate who seek to assist and support the movement for Christian union, not only of the separated non-Roman communions organized since the sixteenth, seventeenth, and later centuries, but also of all divisions, Eastern and Western, older or younger, larger or smaller, of the one holy Catholic Church to study seriously that fundamental faith of the undivided Christian Church of the seven ecumenical councils. Only by returning freely and fully to the primitive apostolic principles, and to that traditional orthodox teaching developed carefully and consistently from them, which preserved, for generation after generation, the unity in the faith of the Christian Church during the passing perils of those destructive divisions, can sectarianism, heresy, and schism be restrained, averted, and resisted in the present and the future, as it has been historically in those past ecclesiastical periods. Finally, the archbishop of the Orthodox Catholic Church of America, with his two senior suffragans, has recently reaffirmed the same principles promulgated by the Orthodox Catholic episcopate of Europe in their Utrecht Declaration (for which see below) in the following pastoral addressed to the clergy and Christians throughout the western world:

3. Aims of the Orthodox Catholic Church.

Declaration of faith and ecclesiastical principles solemnly promulgated for the purpose of aiding in the reformation of the Latin Church, and the reorganization of the Roman Curia, according to the spirit of the primitive Christian Church in the Western Patriarchate, of orthodox and glorious memory.

In the name of the Father, the Son, and the Holy Spirit, the eternal, consubstantial, and undivided Trinity.

We, Joseph Réné Archbishop Vilatte, Stephen Bishop Kaminski, and Paul Bishop Miraglia—by the grace of God and the free suffrages of our faithful, through the Apostolic Succession transmitted lawfully, validly, and canonically to us from that venerable Patriarchal See of the East, founded in Antioch by the blessed Apostle Peter himself, which, with its indisputable apostolic authority, rights, and powers, has been continued without interruption unto this day—validly consecrated bishops of the Catholic Church, joined in ecclesiastical union, and canonically assembled in the name of the Lord, in the orthodox Catholic Cathedral of Buffalo, on this the Feast of the Circumcision of Christ commemorated in the year nineteen hundred and ten, do hereby solemnly affirm, repeat, and declare anew, that our Faith and Teaching is the apostolic, orthodox, and catholic doctrine as it has been truly defined, confirmed, and established by the seven ecumenical councils of the undivided Church. Moreover, in the canonical exercise of our apostolic mission and authority, and especially for the strengthening of our faithful, and the perfecting of our ministry in the several divisions of the Western Patriarchate, viz., in America, Europe, and Africa, we accept and declare the general authority of the use of the Latin Rite. For from the Western Ritual books we are able not only to extract and teach truly and faithfully the apostolic and primitive orthodox doctrine of the Church of Christ, but also, by means of their careful explanation and use, to restore it more and more to its former exalted state. Furthermore, we exhort with our whole heart and in boundless charity all those who call themselves Christians, who believe and hope in Christ the Incarnate Son of God and Savior of men, that while preserving and defending all consistent spiritual liberty which is the fruit of righteousness, we may truly become more and more one in faith, hope, and love, offering without ceasing continual prayers and devout petitions to the compassionate and most high God, beseeching him, the eternal Father of us all, to have mercy on those who are commonly called unbelievers, materialists, and rationalists, the members of whom through the grievous circumstances of our times, are increasing more and more, and to illumine the darkness of their doubting restless minds, so that, converted and led by the Holy Spirit, they may be restored to the communion of the Church of Christ.

4. Pastoral of Vilatte, Kaminski, and Miraglia.

Finally, let us both labor for Christian and fraternal unity, and pray ever more fervently to the Triune God imploring the hastening of that coming day which is to bring the long-awaited triumph of the one Holy Catholic and Apostolic Church, that glorious future day when all faithful followers of the Incarnate Son of God shall become united again, one fold and one shepherd, who is the risen and ascended Christ alone.

May the Triune God, the Father, the Son, and the Holy Spirit, through the ceaseless proclamation of the holy and eternal Gospel of Christ, favor and assist us in our work for his Glory in the Church Militant on earth. Amen.

Given in the city of Buffalo on the day, month, and year designated above.

To this document may be appended the Utrecht Declaration, to which allusion has already been made:

We, Johannes Heykamp, Archbishop of Utrecht, Casparus Johannes Rinkel, Bishop of Haarlem, Cornelius Diependaal, Bishop of Deventer, Joseph Hubert Reinkens, Bishop of the Old Catholic Church of Germany, and Eduard Herzog, Bishop of the Christian Catholic Church of Switzerland, assembled on this four and twentieth day of September, eighteen hundred and eighty-nine, at the archiepiscopal residence at Utrecht, having invoked the assistance of the Holy Spirit, address the following Declaration to the Catholic Church: " Having assembled in conference in response to an invitation from the undersigned Archbishop of Utrecht, we have determined henceforward to hold consultation together from time to time on matters of common interest, in conjunction with our assistants, councilors, and theologians. We deem it fitting that, at this our first meeting, we should set forth a brief declaration of the ecclesiastical principles on which we have hitherto exercised our episcopal office, and shall continue to exercise it in the future, as we have already in separate declarations repeatedly taken occasion to state.

5. The Utrecht Declaration.

"I. We hold firmly to the ancient ecclesiastical rule formulated by Vincent of Lerins, 'Id teneamus quod ubique, quod semper, quod ab omnibus creditum est; hoc etenim vere proprieque catholicum.'

"We therefore hold fast to the faith of the Ancient Church as expressed in the Ecumenical Creeds, and in the universally accepted dogmatic decisions of the Ecumenical Councils of the Undivided Church of the first one thousand years.

"II. We reject as opposed to the Faith of the Ancient Church, and destructive of its primitive constitution, the Vatican Decrees of July 18, 1870, concerning the infallibility and the universal episcopate or the ecclesiastical omnipotence of the Pope of Rome. But this does not hinder us from recognizing the historical primacy attributed by various Ecumenical Councils, and Fathers of the early Church, to the Bishop of Rome as *primus inter pares*, with the consent of the entire Church of the first one thousand years.

"III. We reject also as not founded on Holy Scripture, and on the traditions of the first centuries, the declaration of Pius IX. in the year 1854, concerning the Immaculate Conception of Mary.

"IV. So also respecting the other dogmatic decrees issued by the Bishops of Rome in later times, viz., the Bulls 'Unigenitus' and 'Auctorem fidei,' the 'Syllabus of 1864' and the like pronouncements, we reject them so far as they are opposed to the teaching of the early Church, and do not therefore regard them as authoritative. Furthermore, we renew all the solemn protests which, in times past, the Ancient Catholic Church of Holland has made against Rome.

"V. We do not accept the Council of Trent in its decisions concerning discipline; and its doctrinal definitions we accept only in so far as they agree with the teaching of the early Church.

"VI. Since the Holy Eucharist has always formed the central act in the divine service of the Catholic Church, we deem it our duty to declare that we hold firmly, and with all sincerity, the ancient Catholic faith concerning the Sacrament of the Altar, in which we believe that we truly receive the Body and Blood of our Lord Jesus Christ himself, under the forms of bread and wine.

"The celebration of the Eucharist in the Church is not a constant repetition or renewal of that atoning sacrifice which Christ offered once for all upon the Cross, but its sacrificial character consists in this, that it is a perpetual memorial of that sacrifice, and a real representation on Earth of that one offering of Christ for the salvation of redeemed mankind, which, according to Heb. ix. 11–12, is continually presented by Christ in Heaven, where he now appears for us in the presence of God (Heb. ix. 24). While this is truly the nature of the Eucharist in its relation to that one sacrifice of Christ, it is, at the same time, a holy sacrificial feast in which the faithful, receiving the Body and Blood of Christ, have communion one with another (I Cor. x. 17).

"VII. We trust that, through the efforts of theologians, a way may be found, while holding fast to the Faith of the Undivided Church, to reconcile the differences which have arisen since the divisions. We exhort the clergy under our charge, both in their sermons and in other religious instruction, to emphasize chiefly those essential truths of the Christian Faith which the ecclesiastically separated confessions hold in common; in dealing with existing differences, to avoid carefully the offending against truth and love; and both by precept and example to exhort members of our congregations to treat those who differ from them in belief in such a manner that they will truly exhibit the spirit of Jesus Christ who is the Savior of us all.

"VIII. We believe that it is by holding firmly to the teaching of Jesus Christ, while rejecting all errors which through the frailty of men have been mingled with it, and also all ecclesiastical abuses and hierarchical ambitions, that we shall do most to counteract the unbelief and the religious indifference which are the sorest evils of our times.

"Given at Utrecht September 24, 1889."

ERNEST C. MARGRANDER.

PSYCHOTHERAPY AND CHRISTIAN SCIENCE:*

Two systems which, both seeking to cure disease by mental healing, possess, at least superficially, points in common. For the better elucida-

* Statement from the Christian Science standpoint.

tion of the relation between the two, the following should be read in connection with PSYCHOTHERAPY, § 6. It is admitted, and it must so be understood by the reader, that this emendation is from the standpoint of a Christian Science practitioner; and it must also be understood that the theology and the healing of Christian Science are inseparable—in other words, it is the religious activity of the Christian Scientist, regenerating and transforming the mental, moral, and spiritual state of practitioner and patient, that brings physical healing. Christian Science, therefore, is a system which treats a diseased condition successfully, because it makes a whole man (cf. definition and derivation of the word "health" in the *Standard Dictionary*). Briefly, the therapeutics of Christian Science (see SCIENCE, CHRISTIAN, I., 1, § 6) may be said to be set forth in the following passage from *Science and Health with Key to the Scriptures*, p. 138: "Jesus established in the Christian era the precedent for all Christianity, theology, and healing. Christians are under as direct orders now, as they were then, to be Christ-like, to possess the Christ-spirit, to follow the Christ-example, and to heal the sick as well as the sinning. It is easier for Christianity to cast out sickness than sin, for the sick are more willing to part with pain than are sinners to give up the sinful, so-called pleasure of the senses. The Christian can prove this to-day as readily as it was proved centuries ago. Our Master said to every follower: 'Go ye into all the world, and preach the gospel to every creature! . . . Heal the sick! . . . Love thy neighbor as thyself!' It was this theology of Jesus which healed the sick and the sinning. It is his theology in this book and the spiritual meaning of this theology, which heals the sick and causes the wicked to 'forsake his way, and the unrighteous man his thoughts.'" Lack of space prevents amplification of the statement that the theology and the healing of Christian Science are one, but if the earnest inquirer will accept the scriptural accounts of healing as being true, and will conform his mental attitude, reading, and study to the endeavor of proving, and not of disproving, these statements, he will get an insight into the methods by which the healing works of Jesus and others were accomplished, and understand why Mrs. Eddy refers to such works, no matter in what century they are done, as mind-healing. As an aid and incentive to further research the student is directed to the following definitions from the *Standard Dictionary*: "Christian. Relating to or derived from Christ or his doctrines." "Science. Knowledge gained or verified by exact observation and correct thinking, especially as methodically formulated and arranged in a rational system." "Theology. The branch of theological science that treats of God, etc." "Theological Science. The branch of science that treats of God and the relations of God and man." (Cf. also the word "soteriology," appropriated by both materia medica and scholastic theology, but which explains Christian Science as Christ Jesus exemplified its true meaning, i.e., the science of delivering.) No Christian can doubt that the relation of God to man is that of a deliverer from all evil, including the evil of disease; nor can the Christian doubt that Christ Jesus brought to the world just that message. Christian Science is a rational system of exact knowledge, derived from the spiritual meaning of the Bible and the doctrines of Christ Jesus, setting forth the relations of God and man. The understanding of this demonstrable system as methodically formulated by Mrs. Eddy so influences the mental, moral, and spiritual state of man as to heal him and make him " every whit whole " (John vii. 23). This is true and sure healing, and the highest expression of psychotherapy.

HENRY VAN ARSDALE.

RENTOUL, JOHN LAURENCE: Australian Presbyterian; b. at Garvagh (25 m. e. of Londonderry), County Derry, Ireland, July 6, 1846. He was educated at Queen's College, Belfast, Queen's University, Dublin (M.A., 1868), the Assembly College, Belfast, and the University of Leipsic. He was minister successively of St. George's, Southport, Lancashire (1872–79), and of St. George's, St. Kilda, Melbourne (1879–84), and since 1884 has been connected with Ormond College, Melbourne University, first as professor of Hebrew and of Christian philosophy (1884–88) and later as professor of New-Testament Greek and exegesis (since 1888). He is president of the faculty of Ormond College, and was moderator of the General Assembly at Victoria in 1890, and a delegate to the Pan-Presbyterian Council at Toronto two years later. He is founder and president of the Peace, Humanity, and Arbitration Society, and from this point of view has opposed the South African war, defended the Australian aborigines, and sought to further the settlement of labor difficulties by arbitration. In addition to a large number of contributions to periodicals, etc., he has written *Sermons . . . Preached at Southport* (London, 1876); also *The Early Church and the Roman Claims;* and *Prayers for Australian Households.*

SCOTT, ERNEST FINDLAY: Canadian Presbyterian; b. at Tow Law (10 m. w. of Durham), England, March 18, 1868. He was educated at Glasgow University (M.A., 1888), Balliol College, Oxford (B.A., 1892), and the United Presbyterian College, Edinburgh (1894). He was minister of the United Free Church at Prestwick, Scotland, from 1895 to 1908, and was also Robertson Lecturer in Glasgow University in 1906–07, while since 1908 he has been professor of New-Testament literature in Queen's University, Kingston, Ont. In theology he belongs to the liberal school, and has written *The Fourth Gospel, its Purpose and Theology* (Edinburgh, 1906; 2d ed., 1908), *The Apologetic of the New Testament* (London, 1907), *The Historical and Religious Value of the Fourth Gospel* (Boston, 1909), and *The Kingdom and the Messiah* (Edinburgh, 1911).

SOUTH SEA ISLANDS: Niue or Savage Island: This island lies between 18 and 19° south latitude and 170° west longitude. It is about 350 miles s.e. of Samoa, is about 40 miles in circumference, and has a population of about 5,000. It was annexed to New Zealand in 1901. It was called Savage Island by Captain Cook owing to the character of the natives who, he says, rushed upon him like wild boars. Unsuccessful attempts at evangelization were made by the Rev. John Williams and others of the London

Missionary Society, but in 1846 the Rev. William Wyatt Gill and Rev. Henry Nisbet were able to place on the island a native teacher named Peniamina. In 1849 Paulo and his wife, Samoans who had been trained at the Malua Institution, were landed there, and several of the missionaries visited the island. In 1861 the Rev. William George Lawes became the first resident missionary, and after his appointment to New Guinea his brother, Rev. Francis Edwin Lawes, was in sole charge of the mission till 1909. There are now in connection with the London Missionary Society 11 native ordained agents, 16 native preachers, 1,800 church-members, 2,077 adherents, 11 Sunday-schools with 1,312 scholars, and 12 day schools with 1,220 scholars.

ARTHUR N. JOHNSON.

SUPERANNUATION: Disqualification for active service by reason primarily of age, then of physical or mental disability. In Germany there exist institutions known as Emeritenanstalten which have as their object the support of superannuated servants of the Church, the basis being the consideration that those who have devoted their powers to this service have a claim upon the Church for support so long as they live, and that it is a duty of the organization to provide for them. But it is considered nothing less than fair that the minister, so long as he holds a lucrative position, contribute an allotted proportion of his income in view of the possibility of his becoming emeritus. There are in many places also funds which are derived in part at least from the income from a parish during the intervals when by reason of a vacancy there is no salary to be paid or from some portion of it. In different parts of the German Empire different ordinances are in force with reference to the proportion thus to be applied. The Roman Catholics have institutions known as domus emeritorum or Priesterhospitale which serve the purpose of supporting aged or disabled priests, in some cases the buildings of former monastic institutions being applied to this end.

(H. F. JACOBSON†.)

In England and America the support of superannuated ministers is accomplished by the establishment of special funds, partly derived from endowments and partly from collections made annually or more frequently, under the care of boards which form a part of the machinery of the different denominations. Homes are also maintained to which the minister may retire when his service is ended.

THEOLOGICAL SEMINARIES: XIXa. United Brethren in Christ—Bonebrake Theological Seminary: This is the only theological institution under the auspices of the church of the United Brethren in Christ, which now numbers 293,000 members. It is located at Dayton, O., and was opened for work Oct. 11, 1871, under the name of Union Biblical Seminary. In recognition of a gift of Kansas lands by Mr. and Mrs. John M. Bonebrake of Veedersburg, Ind., valued at $50,000 and upward, the board of directors in Jan., 1909, changed the name. The first faculty consisted of Rev. Lewis Davis, D.D., and Rev. George A. Funkhouser, A.M. Rev. J. P. Landis, A.M., then pastor of Summit Street Church, rendered assistance in Hebrew

and homiletics, and in 1880 was elected to the
chair of Hebrew and pastoral theology. The same
year Rev. A. W. Drury, A.M., was called to the
chair of church history, being transferred to the
chair of systematic theology in 1895, upon the death
of John W. Etter, D.D.

The present faculty consists of Rev. J. P. Landis,
Ph.D., D.D., president and professor of Old-Testa-
ment theology and Hebrew exegesis; Rev. G. A.
Funkhouser, D.D., LL.D., Greek exegesis; Rev.
A. W. Drury, D.D., systematic theology; Rev. S.
D. Faust, D.D., church history; Rev. J. G. Huber,
D.D., homiletics and secretary of faculty; Rev. J.
Balmer Showers, B.D., New-Testament exegesis;
Rev. W. A. Weber, B.D., religious pedagogy and
education.

Four courses of study are offered: the regular
course, which is substantially the equivalent of theological courses in the seminaries of our country;
the English course, offered to persons not having a
college diploma, and others who may not wish the
Hebrew; a two-years' missionary course and a two-
years' deaconess course. It will thus appear that
women are admitted, most of whom have prepared
for mission work or as parish deaconesses, though
several have completed the English course and several have taken the regular course, which includes
Hebrew and Greek.

This seminary was one of the very first to introduce studies in Sunday-school lines, and six years
ago the chair of religious pedagogy and education
was constituted. Prominence has also for years
been given to missions. Thirty-eight students have
gone to the foreign field, and a large number into
the home-mission field of the West. While work has
for several years been done in sociology, in 1911 the
work in this department was considerably extended,
and the authorities are looking to the establishment
soon of a chair of sociology and applied Christianity.

Upward of 400 have graduated and as many more
have taken partial courses. The effort is to keep
theological scholarship and practical training as well
balanced as possible. Extensive grounds have been
purchased in the northwestern part of the city for
relocation of the seminary, the expansion of the institution requiring more room and greater facilities.

The general conference of the church elects the
board of directors and a business manager, the present incumbent (1911) being Rev. J. E. Fout, D.D.
J. P. LANDIS.

VOS, GEERHARDUS: Presbyterian; b. at
Heerenveen (32 m. s.w. of Groningen), Holland,
Mar. 14, 1862. He was educated at the gymnasium
at Amsterdam (1881), the theological school of the
Holland Christian Reformed Church, Grand Rapids,
Mich. (1881–83), Princeton Theological Seminary
(1883–85), and the universities of Berlin (1885–86)
and Strasburg (Ph.D., 1888). From 1888 to 1893 he
was a professor in the theological seminary at Grand
Rapids, and since that time has been professor of
Biblical theology in Princeton Theological Seminary.
He has written *The Mosaic Origin of the Pentateuchal Codes* (New York, 1886), *Kämpfe und Streitigkeiten zwischen den Banu Ummajja und den Banu
Hashim* (1888), *De verbondsleer in de gereformeerde
theologie* (1891), and *Teaching of Jesus concerning
the Kingdom of God and the Church* (1903).